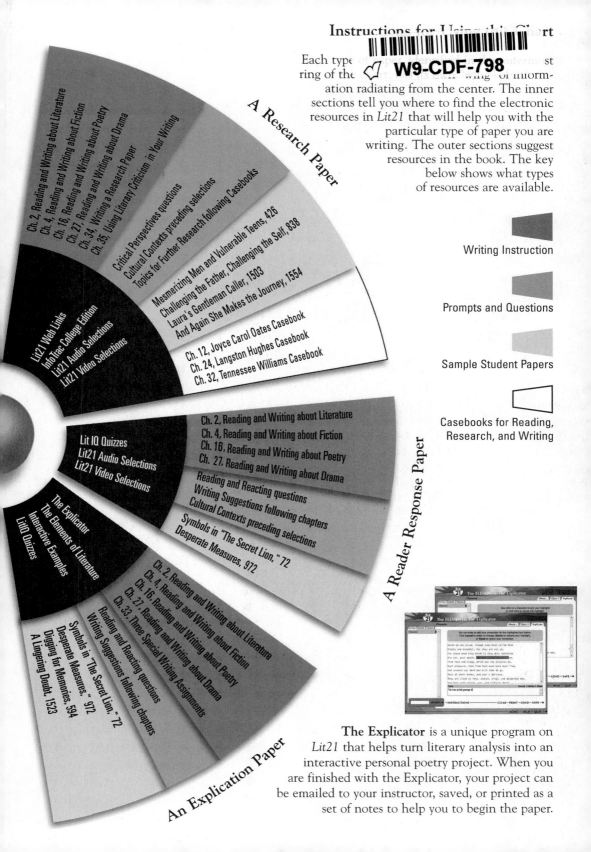

W9-CDF-798

Each type of paper refers to an outermost ring of the chart, with a "slice" of information radiating from the center. The inner sections tell you where to find the electronic resources in *Lit21* that will help you with the particular type of paper you are writing. The outer sections suggest resources in the book. The key below shows what types of resources are available.

Writing Instruction

Prompts and Questions

Sample Student Papers

Casebooks for Reading, Research, and Writing

A Research Paper

Ch. 2, Reading and Writing about Literature
Ch. 4, Reading and Writing about Fiction
Ch. 16, Reading and Writing about Poetry
Ch. 27, Reading and Writing about Drama
Ch. 34, Writing a Research Paper
Ch. 35, Using Literary Criticism in Your Writing

Critical Perspectives questions
Cultural Contexts preceding selections
Topics for Further Research following Casebooks

Mesmerizing Men and Vulnerable Teens, 426
Challenging the Father, Challenging the Self, 838
Laura's Gentleman Caller, 1503
And Again She Makes the Journey, 1554

Lit21 Web Links
InfoTrac College Edition
Lit21 Audio Selections
Lit21 Video Selections

Ch. 12, Joyce Carol Oates Casebook
Ch. 24, Langston Hughes Casebook
Ch. 32, Tennessee Williams Casebook

A Reader Response Paper

Lit IQ Quizzes
Lit21 Audio Selections
Lit21 Video Selections

Ch. 2, Reading and Writing about Literature
Ch. 4, Reading and Writing about Fiction
Ch. 16, Reading and Writing about Poetry
Ch. 27, Reading and Writing about Drama

Reading and Reacting questions
Writing Suggestions following chapters
Cultural Contexts preceding selections

Symbols in "The Secret Lion," 72
Desperate Measures, 972

An Explication Paper

The Explicator
The Elements of Literature
Interactive Examples
LitIQ Quizzes

Ch. 2, Reading and Writing about Literature
Ch. 4, Reading and Writing about Fiction
Ch. 16, Reading and Writing about Poetry
Ch. 27, Reading and Writing about Poetry
Ch. 33, Three Special Writing Assignments

Reading and Reacting questions
Writing Suggestions following chapters

Symbols in "The Secret Lion," 72
Desperate Measures, 594
Digging for Memories, 1523
A Lingering Doubt, 1523

The Explicator is a unique program on *Lit21* that helps turn literary analysis into an interactive personal poetry project. When you are finished with the Explicator, your project can be emailed to your instructor, saved, or printed as a set of notes to help you to begin the paper.

LITERATURE

READING ✹ REACTING ✹ WRITING

Compact Fifth Edition

LAURIE G. KIRSZNER
University of the Sciences in Philadelphia

STEPHEN R. MANDELL
Drexel University

LITERATURE

READING ✸ REACTING ✸ WRITING

Compact Fifth Edition

THOMSON

HEINLE

United States • Australia • Canada • Mexico • Singapore • Spain • United Kingdom

THOMSON
™
HEINLE

LITERATURE: READING, REACTING, WRITING
Compact Fifth Edition
Laurie Kirszner and Stephen Mandell

Publisher: Michael Rosenberg

Senior Editor: Aron Keesbury

Editorial Assistant: Marita Sermolins

Production Editor: Michael Burggren

Marketing Manager: Katrina Byrd

Manufacturing Coordinator:
  Mary Beth Hennebury

Compositor: G&S Typesetters, Inc.

Project Manager: Matrix Productions, Inc.

Photography Manager: Sheri Blaney

Photo Researchers: Jill Engebretson,
  Sarah Evertson

Interior Designer: Garry Harman,
  The ArtWorks

Cover Designer: Brian Salisbury

Printer: Transcontinental

ISBN 0-8837-7101-2

Printed in Canada.
1 2 3 4 5 6 7 8 9 10 08 07 06 05 04 03

For more information contact Heinle Publishers,
25 Thomson Place, Boston, Massachusetts 02210 USA,
or you can visit our Internet site at http://www.heinle.com

For permission to use material from this text or product contact us:

Tel	1-800-730-2214
Fax	1-800-730-2215
Web	www.thomsonrights.com

Brief Contents

Contents

Authors Represented by Multiple Works

Preface

In Alice Walker's short story "Everyday Use" (p. 310), two sisters — one rural and traditional, one urban and modern — compete for possession of two quilts that have been in their family for years. At the end of the story, the narrator's description of the quilts suggests their significance — as a link between the old and the new, between what was and what is:

> One was in the Lone Star pattern. The other was Walk Around the Mountain. In both of them were scraps of dresses that Grandma Dee had worn fifty and more years ago. Bits and pieces of Grandpa Jarrell's Paisley shirts. And one teeny faded blue piece, about the size of a penny matchbox, that was from Great Grandpa Eza's uniform that he wore in the Civil War. (315)

In a sense, *Literature: Reading, Reacting, Writing* is a kind of literary quilt, one that places nontraditional works alongside classics, integrates the familiar with the unfamiliar, and invites students to see well-known works in new contexts. To convey this message, the publisher has commissioned a hand-made quilt by textile artist Greta Vaught for each edition of the book. The quilt designed for this new edition uses contemporary as well as traditional quilting techniques to reflect our own increased focus on contemporary and emerging writers as well as on writers from diverse cultures and backgrounds.

Literature: Reading, Reacting, Writing, Fifth Edition, like the previous editions, is designed to demystify the study of literature and to prepare students to explore the literary works collected here. Our goal in this edition remains what it has been from the start: to expand students' personal literary boundaries. To this end, we have fine-tuned both the reading selections and the pedagogical features that support the study of literature, acting in response to thoughtful comments from our reviewers and from our students. Having class-tested this book in our own literature classrooms, we have learned what kinds of selections and features best help our students to read, think about, understand, and write about literature in ways that make it meaningful to their lives in the twenty-first century.

Some of the elements that students and instructors have found appealing in previous editions of *Literature: Reading, Reacting, Writing* are listed below.

Balanced Selections

The stories, poems, and plays collected here represent a balance of old and new as well as a wide variety of nations and cultures and a wide range of styles.

- **An extensive selection of fiction.** The fiction selection includes not only perennial classics — "The Lottery," "A Rose for Emily," "The Cask of Amontillado" — and stories we introduced to readers in the first edition, such as David Michael Kaplan's "Doe Season" and Charles Baxter's "Gryphon," but also a number of works never previously collected in a college literature anthology, such as Mary Ladd Gavell's "The Swing."

- **A blend of contemporary and classic poetry.** The poetry section balances works by classic poets like Robert Frost, Emily Dickinson, and Langston Hughes with works by more contemporary poets.

- **A varied selection of plays.** The drama section juxtaposes selections retained from previous editions — William Shakespeare's *Hamlet*, August Wilson's *Fences*, Milcha Sanchez-Scott's *The Cuban Swimmer* — with very contemporary plays, such as Margaret Edson's *Wit*.

- **Authors represented by multiple works.** Many writers are represented in the text by more than one work, and a number of these writers have written works in more than one literary genre. A list of all such works follows the book's table of contents, giving students an opportunity to see how a particular writer explores different themes, styles, and genres.

Comprehensive Writing Coverage

To help students see writing about literature as a process of discovering and testing ideas, coverage of writing extends through eight chapters and is reinforced in numerous questions and prompts throughout.

- **A general introduction to the writing process.** Chapter 2, "Reading and Writing about Literature," explains and illustrates the process of planning, drafting, and revising essays about literary works, concluding with an exercise asking students to evaluate and compare two different student papers that examine the same three short stories.

- **Special treatment for writing about each genre.** "Reading and Writing about Fiction" (Chapter 4), "Reading and Writing about Poetry" (Chapter 16), and "Reading and Writing about Drama" (Chapter 27) follow the writing process of students as they write about each genre: Alberto Alvaro Ríos's short story "The Secret Lion" (p. 54); Seamus Heaney's poem "Digging" (p. 560) and Robert Hayden's poem "Those Winter Sundays" (p. 560); and Susan Glaspell's one-act play *Trifles* (p. 983).

- **A new section, "Writing about Literature."** Following the fiction, poetry, and drama sections is a new section titled "Writing about Literature." This section features a new chapter, "Three Special Writing Assignments," as well as three additional chapters: "Writing a Research Paper," "Using Literary Criticism in Your Writing," and "Writing Essay Exams about Literature."

- **Thirteen model student papers.** Because our own experience in the classroom has shown us that students often learn most easily from models, the text includes 13 model student papers written in response to the kind of topics that are frequently assigned in introduction to literature classes. Some of these model papers are source-based, and three are shown in multiple drafts, along with annotations and commentary.

- **Casebooks for Reading, Research, and Writing.** These three casebooks — on Joyce Carol Oates, Langston Hughes, and Tennessee Williams — feature seminal works by each writer, accompanied by literary criticism, biographical essays, and other useful and interesting materials (interviews, photographs, popular magazine articles, and so on); the casebooks also include discussion questions, writing prompts for research papers, and a list of relevant Web sites. Students can use these casebooks to supplement their reading or as source material for a research project. (A model student paper in each casebook shows students how to use sources, including Internet sources, in their writing.) By gathering research materials in a convenient, accessible format, these casebooks offer students a controlled, self-contained introduction to source-based writing as well as all the materials they need to begin a research project.

- **Checklists.** Most chapter introductions end with a checklist designed to help students measure their understanding of concepts introduced in the chapter. These checklists can also guide students as they generate, explore, focus, and organize ideas for writing about works of literature.

- **Writing suggestions with Web activities.** Imaginative suggestions for paper topics are included at the end of each chapter. A Web activity is provided in most sets to spark students' interest and generate engaged writing.

Thorough Contextual Coverage

As we have learned in our classrooms over the years, part of helping students to demystify literature is helping them to demystify the context in which the stories, poems, and plays were written. As in previous editions, we have included contextual and background materials throughout the book in various forms.

- **Cultural context notes.** A cultural context paragraph is included in each author headnote in fiction and drama, providing vital background about the social and historical climate in which the work was written.

- **Literary history appendix.** An appendix, "Literary History: From Aristotle to the Present," gives students a brief historical overview of Western literary criticism.

Other Pedagogical Features

A number of other pedagogical features occur throughout the text to prompt students to think critically about reading and to spark class discussions and energetic, thoughtful writing.

- **Chapter 1, "Understanding Literature."** This introductory chapter presents an overview of some of the most important issues surrounding the study of literature, acquainting students with traditional literary themes as well as with the concept of the literary canon. The chapter also lays the groundwork for students' independent exploration of literary texts by discussing the processes of interpreting and evaluating literary texts, placing special emphasis on how readers' personal experiences affect meaning. Finally, the chapter examines the role of literary criticism and considers how critics' interpretations can help students expand their literary horizons.

- **Reading and Reacting questions.** Reading and Reacting questions, including journal prompts, follow many selections throughout the text. These questions ask students to interpret and evaluate what they have read, sometimes encouraging them to make connections between the literary work being studied and other works in the text.

- **Critical Perspectives.** Most chapters open with a group of quotations by literary critics that provide a thought-provoking yet accessible introduction to a particular element of literature, such as point of view or language. In addition, Critical Perspective questions (included in most sets of Reading and Reacting questions) ask students to respond to analytical, interpretative, or evaluative comments critics have made about the work. This feature encourages students to apply their own critical thinking skills to literary criticism as well as to literature itself.

- **Related Works.** A Related Works list following the Reading and Reacting questions includes works linked (by theme, author, or genre) to the particular work under study. This feature encourages students to see connections between works by different writers, between works in different genres, or between two themes — connections they can explore in class discussion and in writing.

New to the Fifth Edition

The features described above encourage students to appreciate works that represent diverse literary subjects, styles, and perspectives and teach them to develop their own critical abilities by studying and writing about these works. In this edition, we have added new readings and new features designed to provide even more of the support and inspiration our students need to read, react to, and write about literature.

- **Twelve new stories.** Selected primarily for their appeal to today's students, the new stories include absorbing works by Bessie Head, Raymond Carver, Chinua Achebe, Gish Jen, Richard Russo, Andrea Barrett, Toni Cade Bambara, and others.

- **A large number of new poems.** The poetry section has been greatly expanded and now includes many celebrated contemporary voices. Among the many poets new to this edition are Billy Collins, Wislawa Szymborska, Deborah Garrison, Robert Pinsky, Chitra Divakaruni, Sherod Santos, Mona Van Duyn, Martín Espada, Czeslaw Milosz, Elizabeth Alexander, Joy Harjo, Jane Kenyon, Li-Young Lee, and C.K. Williams.

- **Two new plays.** New dramatic works have been selected to introduce students to characters and conflicts they may recognize from their own lives. We have added two plays published or performed for the first time in 2000 or

after: Jane Martin's *Beauty* and Margaret Edson's *Wit*, a recent Pulitzer
Prize–winner.

- **A new chapter, "Three Special Writing Assignments."** The newly revised
  and expanded four-chapter section on writing about literature now includes
  a new Chapter 33, "Three Special Writing Assignments," that showcases
  three student papers: a comparison/contrast of two short stories, an explication of a poem, and an analysis of a character in a play. Each assignment is
  explained and illustrated with an annotated student paper, and numerous
  writing prompts keyed to works in the text are provided for each of the
  three kinds of assignments.

- **Revised chapters on particular writing tasks.** Chapter 34, "Writing a Research Paper," takes students through the process of writing a short paper on
  Eudora Welty's "A Worn Path" (p. 361), explaining and illustrating MLA
  documentation style (including the most up-to-date guidelines and many
  examples of MLA-style citations for electronic sources). This chapter includes two source-based student papers: one, on "A Worn Path," relies on
  conventional print sources; the other, on John Updike's "A&P" (p. 115),
  cites a variety of electronic sources, including an e-mail communication
  and a magazine article accessed through an online database. In addition, each paper cites a filmed interview with the story's author. Chapter 35, "Using Literary Criticism in Your Writing," explains and illustrates
  the key schools of literary criticism and shows how each can be applied
  to a typical student writing assignment inspired by a work in the text. Finally, Chapter 36, "Writing Essay Exams about Literature," guides students
  through the process of planning, shaping, drafting, and revising an essay response to a literature exam question. (An annotated student essay exam is
  included.)

- **Five additional student papers.** In addition to the eight student papers included in the last edition, we include five new papers, for a total of 13. Five
  of these papers are based on research, and three are shown in multiple drafts.
  In addition to the student papers, a sample student answer to an essay exam
  is included, with annotations.

- **New Chapter 3, "Understanding Fiction."** This new chapter briefly traces
  the development of fiction through the modern short story, showcasing two
  contemporary short-short stories: Gary Gildner's "Sleepy Time Gal" and
  Margaret Atwood's "Happy Endings."

- **New Chapter 15, "Discovering Themes in Poetry."** This new chapter expands the previous edition's discussion of poets' thematic options, adding
  four new poems to the discussion of three popular poetic themes (poems
  about parents, poems about love, and poems about war).

- **Lit21: Literature in the Twenty-First Century CD-ROM.** Packaged with
  this book, *Lit21* is a CD-ROM designed to provide students with a unique,
  interactive environment that can supplement the many aspects of the study
  of literature. In addition to 68 stories, poems, and scenes from plays read

aloud on the disk, *Lit21* offers 30 video clips of poetry readings, interviews, and selected scenes. Quizzes for every story, play, and element of literature help students review for class and complement the "brush-up" instruction on the elements of literature. Finally, a unique new program, the Explicator, actually guides students step by step through the process of close literary analysis while helping them prepare notes for an explication paper.

A Full Package of Supplementary Materials

To support students and instructors who use the fifth edition of *Literature: Reading, Reacting, Writing*, the following ancillary materials are available from Heinle:

Instructor's Resource Manual. With discussion and activities for every story, poem, and play in the anthology; a thematic table of contents; semester and quarterly sample syllabi; and articles on the evolution of the literary canon and reader-response theory, this comprehensive instructor's manual provides all the materials necessary to support a variety of teaching styles. In addition, this edition includes brief, entertaining notes called "Do Your Students Know?" that provide interesting, sometimes offbeat contextual information.

The Heinle Original Film Series in Literature. Original adaptations of Raymond Carver's "Cathedral," Eudora Welty's "A Worn Path," and John Updike's "A&P," accompanied by interviews with the authors, are available on a single DVD or separately on VHS.

The Heinle Casebook Series for Reading, Research, and Writing. Previously titled *The Harcourt Brace Casebook Series in Literature*, ten complete casebooks, each providing all the materials students need to jumpstart a literary research project, are available:

In Fiction
William Faulkner's "A Rose for Emily"
Charlotte Perkin's Gilman's "The Yellow Wallpaper"
Flannery O'Connor's "A Good Man is Hard to Find"
John Updike's "A & P"
Eudora Welty's "A Worn Path"

In Poetry
Emily Dickinson, A Collection of Poems
Langston Hughes, A Collection of Poems
Walt Whitman, A Collection of Poems

In Drama
Athol Fugard's *Master Harold and the Boys*
William Shakespeare's *Hamlet*

Additional Videos. Fourteen videos, including adaptations of plays in the fifth edition and films to accompany each casebook in the fiction and drama sections, are available.

Arden Shakespeare. Nine titles from the Arden Shakespeare Series can be packaged with *Literature: Reading, Reacting, Writing,* Fifth Edition, including *Hamlet, King Lear, A Midsummer Night's Dream, The Tempest, Othello,* and *Twelfth Night.*

ACKNOWLEDGMENTS

From start to finish, this text has been a true collaboration for us, not only with each other, but also with our students and colleagues. We have worked hard on this book, and many people at Heinle have worked hard along with us.

We would like to begin by thanking our terrific and talented new senior editor, Aron Keesbury, for his creativity, enthusiasm, and persistence as well as for his belief in the book. For her incredibly efficient day-to-day coordination of people and pages, we thank editorial assistant Marita Sermolins, who is clearly going places (but not, we hope, too soon). And we remain very grateful to Michael Rosenberg, Publisher, for coming back just in time to pick up our project (and our friendship) where we left off.

Also at Heinle, we thank Mike Burggren for guiding the manuscript through production, with skilled help from the team at Matrix Productions: Merrill Peterson, Jaye Caldwell, Kelly Cavill, and Sue Kimber. We owe a special debt to our first-rate copy editor, Pat Herbst, for her creative insights as well as for her thoroughness.

We also very much appreciate the help we got on this project from William Coyle on the Instructor's Resource Manual and the Critical Perspective questions; from Molly Kalkstein on the new casebook material; and from Todd Hearon on the new biographical headnotes and Cultural Contexts.

We would like to thank the following reviewers of the fifth edition: Jane Anderson Jones, Manatee Community College — Venice Campus; Lee Barnes, Community College of Southern Nevada; Robin Calitri, Merced College; Janet Eber, County College of Morris; Charles Fisher, Aims Community College; Maryanne Garbowsky, County College of Morris; Clinton Gardner, Salt Lake City Community College; Diana Gatz, St. Petersburg College; Dawn Marie Hershberger, University of Indianapolis; Isara Kelley Tyson, Manatee Community College; Andrew Kozma, University of Florida; Bernard Morris, Modesto College; David Neff, University of Alabama, — Huntsville; Diana Nystedt, Palo Alto College; Roger Platizky, Austin College; Angela M. Rhoe, Prince George's Community College; Mark Rollins, University of Ohio; Christine Roth, University of Wisconsin; David A. Salomon, Black Hills State University; Ann Spurlock, Mississippi State University; and Pam Sutton, Union University.

We continue to be grateful to those who reviewed the fourth edition: Crystal V. Bacon, Glouchester County College; Gwen Barklay-Toy, North Carolina State University; Eric Birdsall, University of Akron; John Doyle, Quinnipiac College; David Fear, Valencia Community College; Elizabeth Keats Flores, College of

Lake Country; Linda Gruber, Kishwaukee College; Lynn Hildenbrand, Chesa-peake College; Teresa Kennedy, Mary Washington College; Michael Kraus, Mar-ian College of Fond du Lac; Teri Maddox, Jackson State Community College; Ju-dith P. Moray, Moraine Valley Community College; Mary Beth Namm, North Carolina State University; Rodney D. Newton, Central Texas College; Monte Prater, Tulsa Community College — Northeast; Gail Rung, Black Hawk College; Robert M. Temple, Manatee Community College; Maria W. Warren, University of West Florida; Donnie Yeilding, Central Texas College; and Laura Mandell Zaidman, University of South Carolina — Sumter.

We would also like to thank all the reviewers who made valuable contributions to the third edition: Ben Accardi, University of Kansas; Thomas Bailey, Western Michigan University; John Bails, University of Sioux Falls; Leigh Boyd, Temple Junior College; Cathy Cowan, Cabrillo College; Pat Cowart, Frostburg State Uni-versity; Kitty Dean, Nassau Community College; Jo Devine, University of Alaska — Southeast; Jack Doyle, University of South Carolina — Sumter; Lynn Fauth, Oxnard College; David Fear, Valencia Community College; Mary Fleming, Jackson State Community College; Ann Fogg, University of Maine; Wayne Gilbert, Community College of Aurora; Shain Graham, Orange Coast College; Linda Gruber, Kishwaukee College; Chris Hacskaylo, University of Alaska — Ketchikan; Richard Hascal, Contra Costa College; Gwen Hauk, Temple Junior College; Michael Herzog, Gonzaga University; Andrew Kelly, Jackson State Community College; Benna Kime, Jackson State Community College; Army Sparks Kolker, University of Kansas; Michael Kraus, Marian College of Fond du Lac; Heidi Ledett, Ulster County Community College; Teri Maddox, Jackson State Community College; Jeanne Mauzy, Valenica Community College; Fred Milley, Anderson University; Robert Milliken, University of Southern Maine; An-drew Moody, University of Kansas; Paul Perry, Palo Alto Community College; An-gela Rapkin, Manatee Community College; Jean Reynolds, Polk Community Col-lege; Ellen Robbins, Ulster County Community College; Paul Rogauls, Plymouth State College; Neil Sebacher, Valencia Community College; Larry Severeid, College of Eastern Utah; Sharon Small, Des Moines Area Community College; Virginia Streamer, Dundalk Community College; Robert Temple, Manatee Community College; Margie Whelan, Mt. San Antonio College; Mike White, Odessa College; Rebecca Yancey, Jackson State Community College; Donnie Yielding, Central Texas College; and Martha Zamorano, Miami Dade – Kendall Campus.

Reviewers of the second edition were Deborah Barberousse, Horry-Georgetown Technical College; Bob Mayberry, University of Nevada — Las Vegas; Shireen Carroll, University of Miami; Stephen Wright, Seminole Com-munity College; Robert Dees, Orange Coast College; Larry Gray, Southeastern Louisiana University; Nancy Rayl, Cypress College; James Clemmer, Austin Peay State University; Roberta Kramer, Nassau Community College.

Reviewers of the first edition included Anne Agee, Anne Arundel Commu-nity College; Lucien Agosta, California State University — Sacramento; Diana Austin, University of New Brunswick; Judith Bechtel; Northern Kentucky Uni-versity; Laureen Belmont, North Idaho College; Vivian Brown, Laredo Junior

College; Rebecca Butler, Dalton Junior College; Susan Coffey, Central Virginia Community College; Douglas Crowell, Texas Tech University; Shirley Ann Curtis, Polk Community College; Kitty Dean, Nassau Community College; Robert Dees, Orange Coast College; Joyce Dempsey, Arkansas Tech University; Mindy Doyle, Orange County Community College; James Egan, University of Akron; Susan Fenyves, University of North Carolina — Charlotte; Marvin Garrett, University of Cincinnati; Ann Gebhard, State University of New York — Cortland; Emma Givaltney, Arkansas Tech University; Corrinne Hales, California State University — Fresno; Gary Hall, North Harris County College; Iris Hart, Santa Fe Community College; James Helvey, Davidson County Community College; Chris Henson, California State University — Fresno; Gloria Hochstein, University of Wisconsin — Eau Claire; Angela Ingram, Southwest Texas State University; John Iorio, University of South Florida; George Ives, North Idaho College; Lavinia Jennings, University of North Carolina — Chapel Hill; Judy Kidd, North Carolina State University; Leonard Leff, Oklahoma State University; Michael Matthews, Tarrant County Junior College — Northeast; Craig McLuckie, Okanagan College; Candy Meier, Des Moines Area Community College; Judith Michna, DeKalb College — North; Christopher O'Hearn, Los Angeles Harbor College; James O'Neil, Edison Community College; Melissa Pennell, University of Lowell; Sam Phillips, Gaston College; Robbie Pinter, Belmont College; Joseph Sternberg, Harper College; Kathleen Tickner, Brevard Community College; Betty Wells, Central Virginia Community College; Susan Yaeger, Monroe Business Institute.

We would also like to thank our families — Mark, Adam, and Rebecca Kirszner and Demi, David, and Sarah Mandell — for being there when we needed them. And finally, we each thank the person on the other side of the ampersand for making our collaboration work one more time.

CHAPTER 1

UNDERSTANDING LITERATURE

IMAGINATIVE LITERATURE

Imaginative literature begins with a writer's need to convey a personal vision to readers. Consider, for example, how William Wordsworth uses language in these lines from his poem "Composed upon Westminster Bridge, September 3, 1802" (p. 922):

> This City now doth, like a garment, wear
> The beauty of the morning; silent, bare,
> Ships, towers, domes, theatres, and temples lie
> Open unto the fields, and to the sky;
>   All bright and glittering in the smokeless air.

Wordsworth does not try to present a picture of London that is topographically or sociologically accurate. Instead, by comparing the city at dawn to a person wearing a beautiful garment, he creates a striking picture that has its own kind of truth. By using a vivid, original comparison, the poet is able to suggest the oneness of the city, nature, and himself — an idea that is not easily communicated.

Even when writers use factual material — historical documents, newspaper stories, or personal experience, for example — their primary purpose is to present their unique view of experience, one that has significance beyond the moment. (As the poet Ezra Pound said, "Literature is the news that *stays* news.") To convey their views of experience, writers of imaginative literature often manipulate facts — changing dates, creating new characters, and inventing dialogue. For example, when Herman Melville wrote his nineteenth-century novella *Benito Cereno*, he drew many of his facts from an account of an actual slave revolt. In his story, he reproduces court records and plot details from this primary source, but he leaves out incidents, and he adds material of his own. The result is an original work of literature that serves the author's purpose. Wanting to do more than retell the original story, Melville used the factual material as "a skeleton of actual reality" on which he built a story that attacks the institution of slavery and examines the nature of truth.

Imaginative literature is more likely than other types of writing to include words chosen not only because they communicate the writer's ideas, but also because they are memorable. Using vivid imagery and evocative comparisons, writers of imaginative literature often stretch language to its limits. By relying on the multiple connotations of words and images, a work of imaginative literature encourages readers to see the possibilities of language and to move beyond the factual details of an event.

Even though imaginative literature can be divided into types called **genres** — fiction, poetry, and drama — the nature of literary genres varies from culture to culture. In fact, some literary forms that Western readers take for granted are alien to other literary traditions. The sonnet, though fairly common in the West, is not a conventional literary form in Chinese or Arabic poetry. Similarly, the most popular theatrical entertainment in Japan since the mid-seventeenth century, the Kabuki play, has no exact counterpart in the West. (In a Kabuki play, which includes stories, scenes, dances, music, acrobatics, and elaborate costumes and stage settings, all of the actors are men, some of whom play the parts of females. Many Kabuki plays have little plot and seem to be primarily concerned with spectacle. One feature of this form of drama is a walkway that extends from the stage through the audience to the back of the theater.)

Conventions of narrative organization and character development can also vary considerably from culture to culture, especially in literature derived from oral traditions. For example, narrative organization in some Native American stories (and, even more commonly, in some African stories) can be very different from what contemporary Western readers are accustomed to. Events may be arranged spatially instead of chronologically: first a story presents all the events that happened in one place, then it presents everything that happened in another location, and so on. Character development is also much less important in some traditional African and Native American stories than it is in modern short fiction. In fact, a character's name, description, and personality can change dramatically (and without warning) during the course of a story.

Despite such differences, the imaginative literature of all cultures can have similar effects on readers: memorable characters, vivid descriptions, imaginative use of language, and intricately developed plots can fascinate and delight. Literature can take readers where they have never been before and, in so doing, can create a sense of wonder and adventure.

At another level, however, readers can find more than just pleasure or escape in literature. Beyond transporting readers out of their lives and times, literature can enable readers to see their lives and times more clearly. Whether a work of imaginative literature depicts a young girl as she experiences the disillusionment of adulthood for the first time, as in David Michael Kaplan's "Doe Season" (p. 336), or examines the effect of discrimination on a black African who is looking for an apartment, as in Wole Soyinka's "Telephone Conversation" (p. 6), it can help readers to understand their own experiences and the experiences of others. In this sense, literature offers readers increased insight and awareness. As the Chilean poet Pablo Neruda said, works of imaginative literature fulfill "the most ancient rites of our conscience in the awareness of being human and of believing in a common destiny."

CONVENTIONAL THEMES

The **theme** of a work of literature is its central or dominant idea. This idea is seldom stated explicitly. Instead, it is conveyed through the selection and arrangement of details; through the emphasis of certain words, events, or images; and through the actions and reactions of characters.

Although one central theme may dominate a literary work, most works explore a number of different themes or ideas. For example, the central theme of Mark Twain's *Adventures of Huckleberry Finn* might be the idea that an individual's innate sense of right and wrong is superior to society's artificial and sometimes unnatural values. The main character, Huck, gains a growing awareness of this idea by witnessing feuds, duels, and all manner of human folly. As a result, he makes a decision to help his friend Jim escape from slavery despite the fact that society, as well as his own conscience, condemns this action. However, *Huckleberry Finn* also examines other themes. Throughout his novel Twain criticizes many of the ideas that prevailed in the pre–Civil War South, such as the racism and religious hypocrisy that pervaded the towns along the Mississippi.

A literary work can explore any theme, but certain themes have recurred so frequently over the years that they have become **conventions.** One theme frequently explored in literature, a character's loss of innocence, appears in the biblical story of Adam and Eve and later finds its way into such works as Nathaniel Hawthorne's 1835 short story "Young Goodman Brown" (p. 292) and James Joyce's 1914 short story "Araby" (p. 252). Another conventional theme — the conflict between an individual's values and the values of society — is examined in the ancient Greek play *Antigone* by Sophocles. Almost two thousand years later, Norwegian playwright Henrik Ibsen deals with the same theme in *A Doll House* (p. 995).

Other conventional themes examined in literary works include the individual's quest for spiritual enlightenment, the *carpe diem* ("seize the day") theme, the making of the artist, the nostalgia for a vanished past, the disillusionment of adulthood, the pain of love, the struggle of women for equality, the conflict between parents and children, the clash between civilization and the wilderness, the evils of unchecked ambition, the inevitability of fate, the impact of the past on the present, the conflict between human beings and machines, and the tension between the ideal and the actual realms of experience.

Nearly every culture explores similar themes, but writers from different cultures may develop these themes differently. A culture's history, a particular region's geography, or a country's social structure can suggest unique ways of developing conventional themes. In addition, the assumptions, concerns, values, ideals, and beliefs of a particular country or society — or of a particular group within that society — can help to determine the themes writers choose to explore and the manner in which they do so.

In American literature, for instance, familiar themes include the loss of innocence, rites of passage, childhood epiphanies, and the ability (or inability) to form relationships. American writers of color, in addition to exploring these themes, may also express their frustration with racism or celebrate their cultural identities. Even when they explore conventional themes, writers of color in America may choose to do so in the context of their own experience. For example, the theme of loss of innocence may be presented as a first encounter with racial prejudice; a conflict between the individual and society may be presented as a conflict between a minority view and the values of the dominant group; and the theme of failure or aborted relationships may be explored in a work about cultural misunderstandings.

Finally, modern works of literature sometimes treat conventional themes in new ways. For example, in *1984* George Orwell explores the negative consequences of unchecked power by creating a nightmare world in which the government controls and dehumanizes a population. Even though Orwell's novel is set in an imaginary future (it was written in 1948), its theme echoes ideas frequently examined in the plays of both Sophocles and Shakespeare.

THE LITERARY CANON

Originally the term *canon* referred to the authoritative or accepted list of books that made up the Christian Bible. Recently, the term **literary canon** has come to denote a group of works generally agreed upon by writers, teachers, and critics to be worth reading and studying. Over the years, as standards have changed, the definition of "good" literature has also changed, and the literary canon has been modified accordingly. For example, at various times, critics have characterized Shakespeare's plays as mundane, immoral, commonplace, and brilliant. The eighteenth-century critic Samuel Johnson said of Shakespeare that "in his comick scenes he is seldom very successful" and in tragedy "his performance seems constantly to be worse, as his labor is more." Many people find it difficult to believe that a writer whose name today is synonymous with great literature could ever have been judged so harshly. Like all aesthetic works, however, the plays of Shakespeare affect individuals in different periods of history or in different societies in different ways.

Lately, educators and literary scholars have charged that the traditional literary canon, like a restricted club, arbitrarily admits some authors and excludes all others. This fact is borne out, they say, by an examination of the literature curriculum that until recently was standard at many North American universities. This curriculum typically began with Homer, Plato, Dante, and Chaucer, progressed to Shakespeare, Milton, the eighteenth-century novel, the Romantics, and the Victorians, and ended with some of the "classics" of modern British and American literature. Most of the authors of these works are white and male, and their writing for the most part reflects Western values.

Missing from the literature courses in North American universities for many years were South American, African, and Asian writers. Students of American literature were not encouraged to consider the perspectives of women or of Latinos, Native Americans, or other ethnic or racial groups. During the past three decades, however, many universities have expanded the traditional canon by including more works by women, people of color, and writers from a variety of cultures. These additional works, studied alongside those representing the traditional canon, have opened up the curriculum and redefined the standards by which literature is judged.

One example of a literary work that challenges the traditional canon is "All about Suicide" by Luisa Valenzuela, an Argentinean writer. A brief, shocking story, "All about Suicide" is part of a large and growing genre of literature from around the world that purposely violates our standard literary expectations to make its point — in this case, a point about the political realities of Argentina in the 1960s.

LUISA VALENZUELA (1938–   )

All about Suicide (1967)

Translated by Helen Lane

Ismael grabbed the gun and slowly rubbed it across his face. Then he pulled the trigger and there was a shot. Bang. One more person dead in the city. It's getting to be a vice. First he grabbed the revolver that was in a desk drawer, rubbed it gently across his face, put it to his temple, and pulled the trigger. Without saying a word. Bang. Dead.

Let's recapitulate: the office is grand, fit for a minister. The desk is ministerial too, and covered with a glass that must have reflected the scene, the shock. Ismael knew where the gun was, he'd hidden it there himself. So he didn't lose any time, all he had to do was open the right-hand drawer and stick his hand in. Then he got a good hold on it and rubbed it over his face with a certain pleasure before putting it to his temple and pulling the trigger. It was something almost sensual and quite unexpected. He hadn't even had time to think about it. A trivial gesture, and the gun had fired.

There's something missing: Ismael in the bar with a glass in his hand thinking over his future act and its possible consequences.

We must go back farther if we want to get at the truth: Ismael in the cradle crying because his diapers are dirty and nobody is changing him.

Not that far.

Ismael in the first grade fighting with a classmate who'll one day become a minister, his friend, a traitor.

No, Ismael in the ministry without being able to tell what he knew, forced to be silent. Ismael in the bar with the glass (his third) in his hand, and the irrevocable decision: better death.

Ismael pushing the revolving door at the entrance to the building, pushing the swinging door leading to the office section, saying good morning to the guard, opening the door of his office. Once in his office, seven steps to his desk. Terror, the act of opening the drawer, taking out the revolver, and rubbing it across his face, almost a single gesture and very quick. The act of putting it to his temple and pulling the trigger — another act, immediately following the previous one. Bang. Dead. And Ismael coming out of his office (the other man's office, the minister's) almost relieved, even though he can predict what awaits him.

◊   ◊   ◊

The Nigerian poet and playwright Wole Soyinka is another writer whose works are not part of the traditional Western canon. The subject of the following poem may not seem "relevant" to European audiences, and the language ("pillar-box," "omnibus") may not be clear to Americans. Still, as a reading of the poem demonstrates, Soyinka's work makes a compelling plea for individual rights and self-determination — a theme that transcends the boundaries of time and place.

WOLE SOYINKA (1934–   )

Telephone Conversation   (1962)

The price seemed reasonable, location
Indifferent. The landlady swore she lived
Off premises. Nothing remained
But self-confession. "Madam," I warned
"I hate a wasted journey — I am — African."   5
Silence. Silenced transmission of
Pressurized good-breeding. Voice, when it came,
Lip-stick coated, long gold-rolled
Cigarette-holder pipped. Caught I was, foully.
"HOW DARK?" . . . I had not misheard . . .   10
    "ARE YOU LIGHT
OR VERY DARK?" Button B. Button A. Stench
Of rancid breath of public-hide-and-speak.
Red booth. Red pillar-box. Red double-tiered
Omnibus squelching tar. It *was* real! Shamed   15
By ill-mannered silence, surrender
Pushed dumbfoundment to beg simplification.
Considerate she was, varying the emphasis —
"ARE YOU DARK? OR VERY LIGHT?" Revelation came.
"You mean — like plain or milk chocolate?"   20
Her assent was clinical, crushing in its light,
Impersonality. Rapidly, wave-length adjusted,
I chose, "West African sepia"— and as an afterthought,
"Down in my passport." Silence for spectroscopic
Flight of fancy, till truthfulness clanged her accent   25
Hard on the mouthpiece. "WHAT'S THAT?" conceding
"DON'T KNOW WHAT THAT IS." "Like brunette."
"THAT'S DARK, ISN'T IT?" "Not altogether.
Facially, I am brunette, but madam, you should see
The rest of me. Palm of my hand, soles of my feet   30
Are a peroxide blond. Friction, caused —
Foolishly madam — by sitting down, has turned
My bottom raven black — One moment madam!"— sensing

> Her receiver rearing on the thunder clap
> About my ears — "Madam," I pleaded, "Wouldn't you rather   35
> See for yourself?"

Certainly canon revision is not without problems — for example, the possibility of including a work more for political or sociological reasons than for literary merit. Nevertheless, if the debate about the literary canon has accomplished anything, it has revealed that the canon is not fixed and that many works formerly excluded — African-American slave narratives and eighteenth-century women's diaries, for example — have merit and deserve to be read.

INTERPRETING LITERATURE

When you *interpret* a literary work, you explore its possible meanings. One commonly held idea about reading a literary work is that its meaning lies buried somewhere within it, waiting to be unearthed. This reasoning suggests that a clever reader has only to discover the author's intent to find out what a story or poem means, and that the one actual meaning of a work is hidden between the lines, unaffected by a reader's experiences or interpretations. More recently, however, a different model of the reading process — one that takes into consideration the reader as well as the work he or she is interpreting — has emerged.

Many contemporary critics see the reading process as *interactive*. In other words, meaning is created through the reader's interaction with a text. Thus, the meaning of a particular work comes alive in the imagination of an individual reader, and no reader can determine a work's meaning without considering his or her own reaction to the text. Meaning, therefore, is created partly by what is supplied by a work and partly by what is supplied by the reader.

The most obvious meaning a work supplies is factual, the information that enables a reader to follow the plot of a story, the action of a play, or the development of a poem. The work itself will provide factual details about the setting; the characters' names, ages, and appearances; the sequence of events; and the emotions and attitudes of a poem's speaker, a story's narrator, or the characters in a play or story. This factual information cannot be ignored: if a play's stage directions identify its setting as nineteenth-century Norway or the forest of Arden, that is where the play is set.

In addition to facts, a work also conveys the social, political, class, and gender attitudes of the writer. Thus, a work may have an overt feminist or working-class bias or a subtle political agenda; it may confirm or challenge contemporary attitudes; it may communicate a writer's nostalgia for a vanished past or outrage at a corrupt present; it may take an elitist, distant view of characters and events or present a sympathetic perspective. A reader's understanding of these attitudes will contribute to his or her interpretation of the work.

Finally, a work also includes assumptions about literary conventions. A poet, for example, may have definite ideas about whether a poem should be rhymed or unrhymed or about whether a particular subject is appropriate or inappropriate for poetic treatment. Therefore, a knowledge of the literary conventions of a particular period or the preferences of a particular writer can provide a starting point for your interpretation of literature.

As a reader, you also bring to a work your own personal perspectives. Your experiences, your beliefs, your ideas about the issues discussed in the work, and your assumptions about literature color your interpretations. In fact, nearly every literary work has somewhat different meanings to different people, depending on their age, gender, nationality, political and religious beliefs, ethnic background, social and economic class, education, knowledge, and experiences. Depending on your religious beliefs, for instance, you can react to a passage from the Old Testament as literal truth, symbolic truth, or fiction. Depending on your race, where you live, your biases, and the nature of your experience, a story about racial discrimination can strike you as accurate and realistic, exaggerated and unrealistic, or understated and restrained.

In a sense, then, the process of determining meaning is like a conversation, one in which both you and the text have a voice. Sometimes, by clearly dictating the terms of the discussion, the text determines the direction of the conversation; at other times, by using your knowledge and experience to interpret the text, you dominate. Thus, because every reading of a literary work is actually an interpretation, it is a mistake to look for a single "correct" reading.

The 1923 poem "Stopping by Woods on a Snowy Evening" (p. 880), by the American poet Robert Frost, illustrates how a single work can have more than one interpretation. Readers may interpret the poem as being about the inevitability of death; as suggesting that the poet is tired or world weary; or as making a comment about duty and the need to persevere or about the conflicting pulls of life and art. Beyond these possibilities, readers' own associations of snow with quiet and sadness could lead them to define the mood of the poem as sorrowful or melancholy. Information about Robert Frost's life or his ideas about poetry could add to readers' understanding of the poem, and they might even develop ideas about the poem that are quite different from the poet's. In fact, on several occasions, Frost himself gave strikingly different — even contradictory — interpretations of "Stopping by Woods on a Snowy Evening," sometimes insisting that the poem had no hidden meaning and at other times saying that it required a good deal of explication. (Literary critics also disagree about its meaning.) When reading a work of literature, then, keep in mind that the meaning of the text is not fixed. Your best strategy is to open yourself up to the text's many possibilities and explore the full range of your responses.

Although no single reading of a literary work is "correct," some readings are more defensible than others. Like a scientific theory, a literary interpretation must have a basis in fact, and the text supplies the facts against which your interpretation should be judged. For example, after you read Shirley Jackson's "The Lottery" (p. 303), a 1948 short story in which a randomly chosen victim is stoned to death by her neighbors, it would be reasonable for you to conclude that the ceremonial aspects of the lottery suggest a pagan ritual. Your understanding of what a pagan ritual is, combined with your observation that a number of details in the text suggest ancient fertility rites, might lead you to this conclusion. Another possibility is that "The Lottery" provides a commentary on mob psychology. The way characters reinforce one another's violent tendencies lends support to this interpretation. However, the interpretation that the ritual of the lottery is a thinly veiled attack on the death penalty would be difficult to support. Certainly a character in the story is killed, but she is not accused of a crime, nor is she tried or convicted; in fact, the killing is random and seemingly without motivation. Still, although seeing "The Lottery" as a comment on the death penalty may be far-fetched, this interpretation is a reasonable starting point. A second, closer reading of the story will allow you to explore other, more plausible, interpretations.

As you read, do not be afraid to take chances and develop unusual or creative interpretations. A **safe** reading of a work is likely to result in a dull paper that simply states the obvious, but an aggressive or **strong** reading of a work — one that challenges generally held assumptions — can lead to interesting and intellectually challenging conclusions. Even if your reading differs from established critics' interpretations, you should not automatically assume it has no merit. Your own special knowledge of the material discussed in the text — a regional practice, an ethnic custom, an attitude toward gender — may give you a unique perspective from which to view the work. Whatever interpretation you make, be sure that you support it with specific references to the text. If your interpretation is based on your own experiences, explain those experiences and relate them clearly to the work you are discussing. As long as you can make a reasonable case, you have the right (and perhaps the obligation) to present your ideas. By doing so, you may provide your fellow students and your instructor with new insight into the work.

Remember, however, that some interpretations are *not* reasonable. You may contribute ideas based on your own perspectives, but you cannot ignore or contradict evidence in the text to suit your own biases. As you read and reread a text, continue to question and reexamine your judgments. The conversation between you and the text should be a dialogue, not a monologue or a shouting match.

EVALUATING LITERATURE

When you *evaluate* a work of literature, you do more than interpret it; you make a judgment about it. You reach conclusions not simply about whether the work is good or bad, but also about how effectively the work presents itself to you, the reader. To evaluate a work, you *analyze* it, breaking it apart and considering its individual elements. As you evaluate a work of literature, remember that different works are designed to fulfill different needs — entertainment, education, or enlightenment, for example. Before you begin to evaluate a work, be sure you understand its purpose; then, follow these guidelines:

Begin your evaluation by considering how various literary elements function within a work. Fiction may be divided into chapters and use flashbacks and foreshadowing; plays may be divided into scenes and acts and include dialogue and special staging techniques; poems may be arranged in regularly ordered groups of lines and use poetic devices such as rhyme and meter. Understanding the choices writers make about these and other literary elements can help you form judgments about a work. For example, why does Alberto Alvaro Ríos use a first-person narrator (*I* and *we*) in his story "The Secret Lion" (p. 54)? Would the story have been different had it been told in the third person *(they)* by a narrator who was not a character in the story? How does unusual staging contribute to the effect Milcha Sanchez-Scott achieves in his play *The Cuban Swimmer* (p. 1258)? How would a more realistic setting change the play? Naturally, you cannot focus on every aspect of a particular story, poem, or play. But you can and should focus on those aspects that play a major role in determining your responses to a work. For this reason, the unusual stanzaic form in E. E. Cummings's poem "Buffalo Bill's" (p. 864) or the very specific stage directions in Arthur Miller's play *Death of a Salesman* (p. 1178) should be of special interest to you.

As you read, then, you should ask questions. Do the characters in a short story seem real, or do they seem like cardboard cutouts? Are the images in a poem original and thought provoking, or are they clichéd? Are the stage directions of a play sketchy or very detailed? The answers to these questions will help you to shape your evaluation.

As you continue your evaluation, decide whether the literary elements of a work interact to achieve a common goal. Well-crafted literary works are aesthetically pleasing, fitting together in a way that conceals the craft of the writer. Good writers are like master cabinetmakers; their skill disguises the actual work that has gone into the process of creation. Consider the following stanza from the 1862 poem "Echo" by Christina Rossetti:

> Come to me in the silence of the night;
> Come to me in the speaking silence of a dream;
> Come with soft round cheeks and eyes as bright
>   As sunlight on a stream;
>   Come back in tears,
> O memory, hope, love of finished years.

Throughout this stanza Rossetti repeats words ("<u>Come</u> to me . . . / <u>Come</u> with soft . . . / <u>Come</u> back . . .") and initial consonants ("<u>s</u>peaking <u>s</u>ilence"; "<u>s</u>unlight on a <u>s</u>tream") to create an almost hypnotic mood. The rhyme scheme (*night/ bright*, *dream/stream*, and *tears/years*) reinforces the mood by creating a musical undercurrent that extends throughout the poem. Thus, this stanza is effective because its repeated words and sounds work together to create a single lyrical effect.

The chorus in *Oedipus the King* by Sophocles (p. 1271) also illustrates how the elements of a well-crafted work of literature function together. In ancient Greece, plays were performed by masked male actors who played both male and female roles. A chorus of fifteen men remained in a central circle called the *orchestra* and commented on and reacted to the action taking place around them. The chorus expresses the judgment of the community and acts as a moral guide for the audience. Once modern audiences grow accustomed to the presence of the chorus, it becomes an integral part of the play. It neither distracts the audience nor intrudes on the action. In fact, eliminating the chorus would diminish the impact of the play.

Next, consider whether a work reinforces or calls into question your ideas about the world. The 1985 short story "Gryphon" by Charles Baxter (p. 126) may lead readers to question their assumptions. It presents a boy in a rural town whose ailing teacher is temporarily replaced by an eccentric substitute. In her idiosyncratic way, the substitute introduces the boy to a whole new range of intellectual possibilities. Because we, like the children in the story, have learned to expect substitute teachers to be dull and conventional, the story challenges our basic assumptions about substitute teachers and, by extension, about education itself.

Works of popular fiction — those aimed at a mass audience — usually do little more than reassure readers that what they believe is correct. Catering to people's prejudices, or to their desires (for wealth or success, for example), or to their fears, these works serve as escapes from life. Serious fiction, however, often goes against the grain, challenging cherished beliefs and leading readers to reexamine long-held assumptions. For instance, in the 1957 short story "Big Black Good Man" (p. 206) Richard Wright's protagonist, a night porter at a hotel, struggles with his consuming yet irrational fear of a "big black" sailor and with his inability to see beyond the sailor's size and color. Only at the end of the story do many readers see that they, like the night porter, have stereotyped and dehumanized the sailor.

Then, consider whether a work is intellectually challenging. The extended comparison between a draftsperson's compass and two people in love in "A Valediction: Forbidding Mourning" by the seventeenth-century English poet John Donne (p. 687) illustrates how effectively an image can communicate complex ideas to a reader. Compressed into this comparison are ideas about the perfection of love, the pain of enforced separation, and the difference between sexual and spiritual love. As intellectually challenging as the extended comparison is, it is nonetheless accessible to the careful reader. After all, many people have used a compass to draw a circle and, therefore, are able to understand the relationship between the two points of the compass and the two lovers.

A fine line exists, however, between works that are intellectually challenging and those that are simply obscure. An *intellectually challenging* work requires effort from readers to unlock ideas that enrich and expand their understanding of themselves and the world. Although complex, the work gives readers a sense that they have gained something by putting forth the effort to interpret it. An *obscure* work exists solely to display a writer's erudition or intellectual idiosyncrasies. Allusions to other works and events are so numerous and confusing that the work may seem more like a private code than an effort to enlighten readers. Consider this excerpt from "Canto LXXVI" by the twentieth-century American poet Ezra Pound:

Le Paradis n'est pas artificiel
    States of mind are inexplicable to us.
    δακρύων δακρύων δακρύων
L.   P. gli onesti
        J'ai eu pitié des autres
    probablement pas assez, and at moments that suited my own
        convenience
            Le paradis n'est pas artificiel,

> l'enfer non plus.
> Came Eurus as comforter
> and at sunset la pastorella dei suini
> driving the pigs home, benecomata dea
> under the two-winged cloud
> as of less and more than a day

This passage contains lines in French, Greek, and Italian; a reference to Eurus, the ancient Greek personification of the east wind; and the initials L.P. (Loomis Pound?). It demands a lot from readers; the question is whether the reward is worth the effort.

No hard and fast rule exists for determining whether a work is intellectually challenging or simply obscure. Just as a poem has no fixed meaning, it also has no fixed value. Some readers would say that the passage from "Canto LXXVI" is good, even great, poetry. Others would argue that those lines do not yield enough pleasure and insight to justify the work needed to analyze them. As a reader, you must draw your own conclusions and justify them in a clear and reasonable way. Do not assume that because a work is difficult, it is obscure. (Nor should you assume that all difficult works are great literature or that all accessible literature is trivial.) Some of the most beautiful and inspiring literary works demand a great deal of effort. Most readers would agree, however, that the time spent exploring such works yields tremendous rewards.

Finally, consider whether a work gives you pleasure. One of the primary reasons why literature endures is that it gives readers enjoyment. As subjective as this assessment is, it is a starting point for critical judgment. When readers ask themselves what they liked about a work, why they liked it, or what they learned, they begin the process of evaluation. Although this process is largely uncritical, it can lead to an involvement with the work and to a critical response. When you encounter great literature, with all its complexities, you may lose sight of the idea of literature as a source of pleasure. But literature should touch you on a deep emotional or intellectual level, and if it does not — despite its technical perfection — it fails to achieve one of its primary aims.

THE FUNCTION OF LITERARY CRITICISM

Sometimes your personal reactions and knowledge cannot give you enough insight into a literary work. For example, archaic language, references to mythology, historical allusions, and textual inconsistencies can make reading a work difficult. Similarly, an intellectual or philosophical movement such as Darwinism, Marxism, naturalism, structuralism, or feminism may influence a work, and if this is the case, you need some knowledge of the movement before you can interpret the work. In addition, you may not have the background to appreciate the technical or historical dimensions of a work. To increase your understanding, you may choose to read **literary criticism**—books and journal articles written by experts who describe, analyze, interpret, or evaluate a work of literature (see Chapter 35,

"Using Literary Criticism in Your Writing"). Reading literary criticism enables you to expand your knowledge of a particular work and to participate in the public dialogue about literature. In a sense, you become part of a community of scholars who share their ideas and who are connected to one another through their writing.

Literary criticism is written by experts, but this does not mean you must always agree with it. You have to evaluate literary criticism just as you would any new opinion that you encounter. Not all criticism is sound, timely, or responsible (and not all literary criticism is pertinent to your assignment or useful for your purposes). Some critical comments will strike you as plausible; others will seem unfounded or biased. Quite often, two critics will reach strikingly different conclusions about the quality or significance of the same work or writer or will interpret a character, a symbol, or even the entire work quite differently.

The Fiction Casebook that begins on page 384 includes articles in which critics disagree in just this fashion. In "In Fairyland, without a Map: Connie's Exploration Inward in Joyce Carol Oates's 'Where Are You Going, Where Have You Been?'" Gretchen Schulz and R. J. R. Rockwood examine the parallels between a character, Arnold Friend, and a real-life psychopathic killer. They see Arnold in mythological terms and conclude that he is the "exact transpositional counterpart of the real-life Pied Piper of Tucson." In Mike Tierce and John Michael Crafton's "Connie's Tambourine Man: A New Reading of Arnold Friend," however, the authors explicitly reject this suggestion as well as other critical interpretations, concluding instead that "The key question . . . is who is this musical messiah, and the key to the answer is the dedication 'For Bob Dylan.'"

Although critics may disagree, even conflicting ideas can help you reach your own conclusions about a work. It is up to you to sort out the various opinions and decide which have merit and which do not.

CHECKLIST EVALUATING LITERARY CRITICISM

✓ What is the main point of the book or article you are reading?

✓ Does the critic supply enough examples to support his or her conclusions?

✓ Does the critic acknowledge and refute the most obvious arguments against his or her position?

✓ Does the critic ignore any information in the text that might call his or her conclusions into question?

✓ Does the critic present historical information? Biographical information? Literary information? How does this information shed light on the work or works being discussed?

continued on next page

✓   Does the critic hold any beliefs that might interfere with his or her critical judgment?

✓   Does the critic slant the facts, or does he or she approach the text critically and objectively?

✓   Does the critic support conclusions with references to other sources? Does the critic provide documentation and a list of works cited?

✓   Do other critics mention the book or article you are reading? Do they agree or disagree with its conclusions?

With your instructor's help, you might also try to answer these questions:

✓   Does the critic identify with a particular critical school of thought — deconstruction or Marxism, for example? What perspective does this school of thought provide?

✓   Is the critic well known and respected?

✓   Does the critic take into consideration the most important critical books and articles on his or her subject? Are there works that should have been mentioned but were not? Do these omissions cast doubt on the critic's conclusions?

✓   Is the critical work's publication date of any significance?

CHAPTER 2

READING AND WRITING ABOUT LITERATURE

READING LITERATURE

The process of writing about literature starts the moment you begin to read, when you begin interacting with a work and start to discover ideas about it. This **active reading** helps you to interpret what you read and, eventually, to develop your ideas into a clear and logical paper.

Most readers are passive; they expect the text to give them everything they need, and they do not expect to contribute much to the reading process. Active readers, in contrast, participate in the reading process — thinking about what they read, asking questions, and challenging ideas. Active reading is excellent preparation for the discussion and writing you will do in college literature classes. And, because it helps you understand and appreciate the works you read, active reading will continue to be of value long after your formal classroom study of literature has ended.

Three strategies in particular —*previewing, highlighting,* and *annotating*— will help you to become a more effective reader. Remember, though, that reading and responding to what you read is not an orderly process — or even a sequential one. You will most likely find yourself doing more than one thing at a time — annotating at the same time you highlight, for example. For the sake of clarity, however, we discuss each active reading strategy separately.

Previewing

You begin active reading by **previewing** a work to get a general idea of what to look for later, when you read it more carefully.

Start with the work's most obvious physical characteristics. How long is a short story? How many acts and scenes does a play have? Is a poem divided into stanzas? The answers to these and similar questions will help you begin to notice more subtle aspects of the work's form. For example, previewing may reveal that a contemporary short story is presented entirely in a question-and-answer format, that it is organized as diary entries, or that it is divided into sections by headings. Previewing may identify poems that seem to lack formal structure, such as E. E. Cummings's unconventional "l(a" (p. 552); poems written in traditional forms (such as **sonnets**) or in experimental forms, such as the numbered list of questions and answers in Denise Levertov's "What Were They Like?" (p. 573); or **concrete poems,** such as

George Herbert's "Easter Wings" (p. 764). Your awareness of these and other distinctive features at this point may help you gain insight into a work later on.

Perhaps the most physically distinctive element of a work is its title. Not only can the title give you a general idea of what the work is about, as straightforward titles like "Miss Brill" and "The Cask of Amontillado" do, but it can also isolate (and thus call attention to) a word or phrase that emphasizes an important idea. For example, the title of Amy Tan's short story "Two Kinds" (p. 527) refers to two kinds of daughters — Chinese and American — suggesting the two perspectives that create the story's conflict. A title can also be an allusion to another work. Thus, *The Sound and the Fury*, the title of a novel by William Faulkner, alludes to a speech from Shakespeare's *Macbeth* that reinforces the major theme of the novel. Finally, a title can introduce a symbol that will gain meaning in the course of a work — as the quilt does in Alice Walker's "Everyday Use" (p. 310).

Other physical elements — such as paragraphing, capitalization, italics, and punctuation — can also provide clues about how to read a work. In William Faulkner's short story "Barn Burning" (p. 223), for instance, previewing would help you to notice passages in italic type, indicating the protagonist's thoughts, which occasionally interrupt the narrator's story.

Finally, previewing can enable you to see some of the more obvious stylistic and structural features of a work — the point of view used in a story, how many characters a play has and where it is set, or the repetition of certain words or lines in a poem, for example. Such features may or may not be important; at this stage, your goal is to observe, not to analyze or evaluate.

Previewing is a useful strategy not because it provides answers but because it suggests questions to ask later, as you read more closely. For instance, *why* does Faulkner use italics in "Barn Burning," and *why* does Herbert shape his poem like a pair of wings? Elements such as those described above may be noticeable as you preview, but they will gain significance as you read more carefully and review your notes.

Highlighting

When you read a work closely, you will notice additional, sometimes more subtle, elements that you may want to examine further. At this point, you should begin **highlighting** — physically marking the text to identify key details and to note relationships among ideas.

What should you highlight? As you read, ask yourself whether repeated words or phrases form a pattern, as they do in Ernest Hemingway's short story "A Clean, Well-Lighted Place" (p. 267), in which the Spanish word *nada* ("nothing") appears again and again. Because this word appears so frequently, and because it appears at key points in the story, it helps to reinforce the story's pessimistic theme — that all human experience amounts to *nada*, or nothingness. Repeated words and phrases are particularly important in poetry. In Dylan Thomas's "Do not go gentle into that good night" (p. 559), for example, the repetition of two of the poem's nineteen lines four times each enhances the poem's rhythmic, almost monotonous, cadence. As you read, highlight your text to identify such repeated words and phrases. Later, you can consider *why* they are repeated.

During the highlighting stage, also pay particular attention to **images** that occur repeatedly, keeping in mind that such repeated images may form patterns that can help you to interpret the work. When you reread, you can begin to determine what pattern the images form and perhaps decide how this pattern enhances the work's ideas. When highlighting Robert Frost's "Stopping by Woods on a Snowy Evening" (p. 880), for instance, you might identify the related images of silence, cold, and darkness. Later, you can consider their significance.

CHECKLIST **USING HIGHLIGHTING SYMBOLS**

✓ Underline important ideas.

✓ Box or circle words, phrases, or images that you want to think more about.

✓ Put question marks beside confusing passages, unfamiliar references, or words that need to be defined.

✓ Circle related words, ideas, or images and draw lines or arrows to connect them.

✓ Number incidents that occur in sequence.

✓ Set off a key portion of the text with a vertical line in the margin.

✓ Place stars beside particularly important ideas.

The following poem by Maya Angelou has been highlighted by a student preparing to write about it. Notice how the student uses highlighting symbols to help him identify stylistic features, key ideas, and patterns of repetition that he may want to examine later.

MAYA ANGELOU (1928 –   )

My Arkansas (1978)

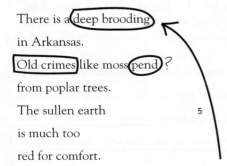

There is a deep brooding
in Arkansas.
Old crimes like moss pend ?
from poplar trees.
The sullen earth   5
is much too
red for comfort.

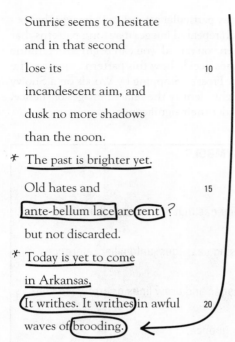

Sunrise seems to hesitate

and in that second

lose its   10

incandescent aim, and

dusk no more shadows

than the noon.

*   The past is brighter yet.

Old hates and   15

~~ante-bellum lace~~ are (rent) ?

but not discarded.

*   Today is yet to come

in Arkansas,

(It writhes. It writhes) in awful   20

waves of (brooding.)

This student identifies repeated words and phases ("brooding"; "It writhes") and places question marks beside the two words ("pend" and "rent") that he plans to look up in a dictionary. He also boxes two phrases — "Old crimes" and "ante-bellum lace" — that he needs to think more about. Finally, he stars what he tentatively identifies as the poem's key ideas. When he rereads the poem, his highlighting will make it easier for him to react to and interpret the writer's ideas.

Annotating

At the same time you highlight a text, you also **annotate** it, recording your reactions as marginal notes. In these notes you may define new words, identify allusions, identify patterns of language or imagery, summarize plot relationships, list a work's possible themes, suggest a character's motivation, examine the possible significance of particular images or symbols, or record questions that occur to you as you read. Ideally, your annotations will help you find ideas to write about.

The following paragraph from John Updike's 1961 short story "A&P" (p. 115) was highlighted and annotated by a student in an introduction to literature course who was writing an essay in response to the question "Why does Sammy quit his job?":

Action isn't the result of thought.

Lengel sighs and begins to look very patient and old and gray. He's been a friend of my parents for years. "Sammy, you don't want to do this to your Mom and Dad," he tells me. It's true, I don't. But it seems to me that once you begin a gesture it's fatal not to go through with it. I *fold

Sammy reacts to the girl's embarrassment.

the apron, "Sammy" stitched in red on the pocket, and put it on the counter, and drop the bow tie on top of it. The bow tie is theirs, if you've ever wondered. "You'll feel this for the rest of your life," Lengel＊ says, and I know that's true, too, but remembering how he made the pretty girl blush makes me so scrunchy inside I punch the No Sale tab and the machine whirs "pee-pul" and the drawer splats out. One advantage to this scene taking place in summer, I can follow this up with a clean exit, there's no fumbling around getting your coat and galoshes, I just saunter into the electric eye in my white shirt that my mother ironed the night before, and the door heaves itself open, and outside the sunshine is skating around on the asphalt.

Romantic cowboy, but his mother irons his shirt. Irony.

＊Need for a clean exit— reinforces immature romantic ideas.

Because the instructor had discussed the story in class and given the class a specific assignment, the student's annotations are quite focused. In addition to highlighting important information, she notes her reactions to the story and tries to interpret Sammy's actions.

Sometimes you annotate a work before you have decided on a topic. In fact, the process of reading and responding to the text can help you to focus on a topic. In the absence of a topic, your annotations are likely to be somewhat unfocused, so you will probably need to repeat the process when your paper's direction is clearer.

WRITING ABOUT LITERATURE

Writing about literature — or about anything else — is an idiosyncratic process during which many activities occur at once: as you write, you think of ideas; as you think of ideas, you clarify the focus of your essay; and as you clarify your focus, you reshape your paragraphs and sentences and refine your word choice. Even though this process sounds chaotic, it has three stages: *planning, drafting,* and *revising and editing.*

Planning an Essay

Considering Your Audience

Sometimes — for example, in a journal entry — you write primarily for yourself. At other times, you write for others. As you write an essay, consider the special requirements of your **audience.** Is your audience your classmates or your instructor? Can you assume your readers are familiar with your paper's topic and with any technical terms you will use, or will they need brief plot summaries or definitions of key terms? If your audience is your instructor, remember that he or she is a representative of a larger academic audience and therefore expects accurate information; standard English; correct grammar, mechanics, and spelling; logical arguments; and a certain degree of stylistic fluency. In addition, your instructor expects you to support your statements with specific information, to express your-self clearly and explicitly, and to document your sources. In short, your instructor wants to see how clearly you think and whether you are able to arrange your ideas into a well-organized, coherent essay.

In addition to being a member of a general academic audience, your instruc-tor is also a member of a particular community of scholars — in this case, those who study literature. By writing about literature, you engage in a dialogue with this community. For this reason, you should adhere to the specific **conventions** — procedures that by habitual use have become accepted practice — its members follow. Many of the conventions that apply specifically to writing about litera-ture — matters of style, format, and the like — are discussed in this book. (The checklist on page 33 addresses some of these conventions.)

Understanding Your Purpose

Sometimes you write with a single **purpose** in mind. At other times, a writing as-signment may suggest more than one purpose. In general terms, you may write for any of the following reasons.

Writing to respond   When you write to *respond*, your goal is to discover and ex-press your reactions to a work. To record your responses, you engage in relatively informal activities, such as brainstorming, listing, and journal writing (see pp. 22–24). As you write, you explore your own ideas, forming and re-forming your impressions of the work.

Writing to interpret   When you write to *interpret*, your aim is to explain a work's possible meanings. To do so, you may summarize, give examples, or compare and contrast the work to other works or to your own experiences. Then, you may go on to analyze the work, studying each of its elements in turn, putting complex state-ments into your own words, defining difficult concepts, or placing ideas in context.

Writing to evaluate   When you write to *evaluate*, your purpose is to assess a work's literary merits. You may consider not only its aesthetic appeal, but also its ability to retain that appeal over time and across national or cultural boundaries. As you write, you use your own critical sense and the opinions of experts to help you make judgments about the work.

Choosing a Topic

When you write an essay about literature, you develop and support an idea about a literary work or works. Before you begin your writing, make certain that you un-derstand your assignment. Do you know how much time you have to complete your essay? Are you expected to rely on your own ideas, or are you able to consult outside sources? Is your essay to focus on a specific work or on a particular element of literature? Do you have to write on an assigned topic, or are you free to choose a topic? About how long should your essay be? Do you understand exactly what the assignment is asking you to do?

Sometimes your assignment limits your options by telling you what you should discuss.

- Write an essay in which you analyze Thomas Hardy's use of irony in his poem "The Man He Killed."
- Discuss Hawthorne's use of allegory in his short story "Young Goodman Brown."
- Write a short essay in which you explain Nora's actions at the end of Ibsen's *A Doll House*.

At other times, your instructor may give you few guidelines other than a paper's length and format. In such situations, where you must choose a topic on your own, you can often find a topic by brainstorming or by writing journal entries. As you engage in these activities, however, keep in mind that you have many options for writing papers about literature. Among them are the following:

- You can explicate a poem or a passage of a play or short story, doing a close reading and analyzing the text.
- You can compare two works of literature. ("Related Works" listed at the end of each set of "Reading and Reacting" questions in this text suggest possible connections.)
- You can compare two characters or discuss some trait those characters share.
- You can trace a common theme — jealousy, revenge, power, coming of age — in several works.
- You can consider how a common subject — war, love, nature — is treated in several works.
- You can examine a single element in one or more works — for instance, plot, point of view, or character development.
- You can focus on a single aspect of that element, such as the use of flashbacks, the effect of a shifting narrative perspective, or the role of a minor character.
- You can apply a critical theory to a work of literature — for instance, apply a feminist perspective to Tillie Olsen's "I Stand Here Ironing" (p. 187).
- You can examine connections between an issue treated in a work of literature — for instance, racism in Ralph Ellison's "Battle Royal" (p. 175) — and that same issue as it is treated in sociological or psychological journals or in the popular press.
- You can examine some aspect of history or biography and consider its impact on a literary work — for instance, the influence of World War I on Wilfred Owen's poems.
- You can explore a problem within a work and propose a possible solution — for example, consider Montresor's actual reason for killing Fortunato in Edgar Allan Poe's "The Cask of Amontillado" (p. 217).

Any of those options may lead you to an interesting topic. Remember, however, that you will have to narrow the scope of your topic so that it fits within the limits of your assignment.

Finding Something to Say

Once you have a topic, you have to find something to say about it. The information you collected when you highlighted and annotated will help you formulate the statement that will be the central idea of your essay and will help you find ideas that can support that statement.

You can use a variety of different strategies to find supporting material.

- You can discuss ideas with others — friends, classmates, instructors, or parents, for example.
- You can ask questions.
- You can do research, either in the library or on the Internet.
- You can *freewrite* — that is, keep writing on your topic for a given period of time without pausing to consider style, structure, or content.

Two additional strategies — *brainstorming and keeping a journal* — are especially helpful.

Brainstorming   When you **brainstorm,** you record ideas — single words, phrases, or sentences (in the form of statements or questions) — as they occur to you, moving as quickly as possible. Your starting point may be a general assignment, a particular work (or works) of literature, a specific topic, or even a **thesis statement.** You can brainstorm at any stage of the writing process (alone or in a group), and you can repeat this activity as often as you like.

The brainstorming notes that follow were made by a student preparing to write a paper on the relationships between children and parents in four poems. She began by brainstorming about each poem and went on to consider thematic relationships among the poems. These notes are her preliminary reactions to one of the four poems she planned to study, Adrienne Rich's "A Woman Mourned by Daughters" (p. 555):

```
Memory: then and now

    Then: leaf, straw, dead insect (= light);

          ignored

    Now: swollen, puffed up, weight (= heavy);

          focus of attention controls their

          movements.
* Kitchen = a "universe"
```

Teaspoons, goblets, etc. = concrete

representations of mother; also =

obligations, responsibilities (like

plants and father)

(weigh on them, keep

them under her spell)

Milestones of past: weddings, being fed as

children "You breathe upon us now"

PARADOX? (Dead, she breathes, has weight,

fills house and sky. Alive, she was a dead

insect, no one paid attention to her.)

Keeping a journal   You can use a journal (a notebook, a small notepad, or a computer file) to help you find ideas — and, later, to help you find a topic or a thesis. In a **journal** you expand your marginal annotations, recording your responses to works you have read, noting questions, exploring emerging ideas, experimenting with possible paper topics, trying to paraphrase or summarize difficult concepts, or speculating about a work's ambiguities. A journal is the place to take chances, to try out ideas that may initially seem frivolous or irrelevant; here you can think on paper (or on a computer screen) until connections become clear or ideas crystallize. You can also use your journal as a convenient place to collect your brainstorming notes and, later, your lists of related ideas.

As he prepared to write a paper analyzing the role of Jim, the "gentleman caller" in Tennessee Williams's play *The Glass Menagerie* (p. 1416), a student explored ideas in the following journal entry:

When he tells Laura that being disappointed is not the
same as being discouraged, and that he's disappointed but
not discouraged, Jim reveals his role as a symbol of the
power of newness and change—a "bulldozer" that will clear
out whatever is in its path, even delicate people like
Laura. But the fact that he is disappointed shows Jim's
human side. He has run into problems since high school, and
these problems have blocked his progress toward a successful
future. Working at the warehouse, Jim needs Tom's
friendship to remind him of what he used to be (and what
he still can be?), and this shows his insecurity. He isn't
as sure of himself as he seems to be.

Although this journal entry represents only the student's preliminary explorations, it can help him to decide on a specific direction for his essay.

Seeing Connections: Listing

After actively reading a work, you should have a good many underlinings and marginal notes. Some of this material will be useful, and some will be irrelevant. **Listing** is the process of reviewing your notes, deciding which ideas are most interesting, and arranging related ideas into lists. Listing enables you to discover patterns: to see repeated images, similar characters, recurring words and phrases, and interrelated themes or ideas. Identifying these patterns can help you to decide which points to make in your paper and what information you will use to support these points.

A student preparing a paper about D. H. Lawrence's short story "The Rocking-Horse Winner" (p. 349) made the following list of related details:

```
Secrets
    Mother can't feel love
    Paul gambles
    Paul gives mother money
    Family lives beyond means
    Paul gets information from horse
Religion
    Gambling becomes like a religion
    They all worship money
    Specific references: "serious as a church"; "It's as if
    he had it from heaven"; "secret, religious voice"
Luck
    Father is unlucky
    Mother is desperate for luck
    Paul is lucky (ironic)
```

This kind of listing can be a helpful preliminary organizing strategy, but remember that the lists you make now do not necessarily reflect the order or emphasis of ideas in your paper. As your thoughts become more focused, you will add, delete, and rearrange material.

Deciding on a Thesis

Whenever you are ready, you should try to express the main idea of your emerging essay in a tentative **thesis statement** — an idea, often expressed in a single sentence, that the rest of your essay supports. This idea should emerge logically out of your highlighting, annotating, brainstorming notes, journal entries, and lists. Eventually, you will write a **thesis-and-support paper:** stating your thesis in your introduction, supporting the thesis in the body paragraphs of your essay, and reinforcing the thesis or summarizing your points in your conclusion.

An effective thesis statement tells readers what your essay will discuss and how you will approach your material. Consequently, it should be precisely worded, making its point clear to your readers, and it should contain no vague words or inexact diction that will make it difficult for readers to follow your discussion.

Although the statement "The use of sound in Tennyson's poem 'The Eagle' is interesting" is accurate, it does not convey a precise idea to your readers because the words *sound* and *interesting* are not specific. A more effective thesis statement would be "Unity in 'The Eagle' is achieved by Tennyson's use of alliteration, assonance, and rhyme throughout the poem." In addition to being specific, your thesis statement should give your readers an accurate sense of the scope and direction of your essay. It should not make promises that you do not intend to fulfill or contain extraneous details that might confuse your readers. If, for example, you are going to write a paper about the dominant image in a poem, your thesis should not imply that you will focus on the poem's setting or tone.

Remember that as you organize your ideas and as you write, you will probably modify and sharpen your tentative thesis. Sometimes you will even begin planning your essay with one thesis in mind and end it with an entirely different idea. If this happens, be sure to revise your support paragraphs so that they are consistent with your changes and so that the points you include support your new thesis. If you find that your thoughts about your topic are changing, don't be concerned; this is how the writing process works.

Preparing an Outline

Once you have decided on a tentative thesis and have some idea of how you will support it, you can begin to plan your essay's structure. Quite often, an outline can help you to shape your essay. Not all writers outline, but many do because it helps them to clarify their ideas and the relationship of these ideas to one another. Realizing, however, that they will discover many new ideas as they write, these writers seldom take the time to prepare a detailed formal outline, preferring instead to make a scratch outline that lists just the major points they plan to discuss.

A **scratch outline** is perhaps the most useful kind of outline for a short paper. An informal list of the main points you will discuss in your essay, a scratch outline is more focused than a simple list of related points because it presents ideas in the order in which they will be introduced. As its name implies, however, a scratch outline lacks the detail and the degree of organization of a more formal outline. The main purpose of a scratch outline is to give you a sense of the shape and order of your paper and thus enable you to begin writing.

A student writing a short essay on Edwin Arlington Robinson's use of irony in his poem "Miniver Cheevy" (p. 906) used this scratch outline as a guide:

```
Speaker's Attitude
    Ironic
    Cynical
    Critical
Use of Diction
    Formal
    Detached
Use of Allusions
    Thebes
    Camelot
```

```
    Priam
    Medici
Use of Repetition
    "Miniver"
    "thought"
    regular rhyme scheme
```

Once this outline was complete, the student was ready to write a first draft.

Drafting an Essay

Your first draft is a preliminary version of your paper, something to react to and revise. Still, before you actually begin drafting your paper, you should review the material you have collected to support your thesis.

First, make sure you have collected enough information to support your thesis. The points you make are only as convincing as the evidence you present to support them. As you were reading and taking notes, you collected examples from the work or works about which you are writing — summaries, paraphrases, or quoted lines of narrative, verse, or dialogue — to back up your statements. How many of these examples you need to use in your draft depends on the breadth of your thesis and how skeptical you believe your audience to be. In general, the more inclusive your thesis, the more material you need to support it. For example, if you were supporting the rather narrow thesis that the speech of a certain character in the second scene of a play was wooden or awkward, only a few examples would be needed. However, if you wanted to support the inclusive thesis that Nora and Torvald Helmer in Henrik Ibsen's *A Doll House* (p. 995) are trapped in their roles, you would need to present a wide range of examples.

Second, see if the work includes any details that contradict your thesis. Before you begin writing, test the validity of your thesis by looking for details that contradict it. For example, if you plan to support the thesis that in *A Doll House* Ibsen makes a strong case for the rights of women, you should look for counterexamples. Can you find subtle hints in the play that suggest women should remain locked in their traditional roles and continue to defer to their fathers and husbands? If so, you will want to modify your thesis accordingly.

Finally, consider whether you need to use outside sources to help you support your thesis. You could, for example, strengthen the thesis that *A Doll House* challenged contemporary attitudes about marriage by including the information that when the play first opened, Ibsen was convinced by an apprehensive theater manager to write an alternative ending. In this new ending, Ibsen had Nora decide, after she stopped briefly to look in at her sleeping children, that she could not leave her family. Sometimes information from another source can even lead you to change your thesis. For example, after reading *A Doll House*, you might have decided that Ibsen's purpose was to make a strong case for the rights of women. In class, however, you might learn that Ibsen repeatedly said that his play was about the rights of all human beings, not just of women. This information could lead you to a thesis that suggests Torvald is just as trapped in his role as Nora is in hers. Naturally, Ibsen's interpretation of his work does not invalidate your first judgment, but it does suggest another conclusion that is worth investigating.

After carefully evaluating the completeness, relevance, and validity of your supporting material, you can begin drafting your essay, using your scratch outline as a guide. Your goal is to get your ideas down on paper, so you should write quickly. Once you have a draft, you will be able to examine the connections among ideas and to evaluate preliminary versions of your paragraphs and sentences. Your focus in this draft should be on the body of your essay; this is not the time to worry about constructing the "perfect" introduction and conclusion. (Many writers, knowing that their ideas will change as they write, postpone writing these paragraphs until a later draft, preferring instead to begin with their tentative thesis.) As you write, remember that your first draft is going to be rough and will probably not be as clear as you would like it to be; still, it will enable you to see the ideas you have outlined begin to take shape.

Revising and Editing an Essay

As soon as you begin to draft your essay, you begin the process of revision. When you **revise,** you literally "re-see" your draft and, in many cases, you go on to re-order and rewrite substantial portions of your essay. Before you are satisfied with your essay, you will probably write several drafts, each more closely focused and more coherent than the previous one.

Strategies for Revision

Two strategies can help you to revise your drafts: *peer review* and *a dialogue with your instructor*.

Peer review is a process in which students assess each other's work-in-progress. This activity may be carried out in informal sessions during which one student comments on another's draft, or it may be a formal process in which a student responds to specific questions on a form supplied by the instructor. In either case, one student's reactions can help another student revise.

A **dialogue with your instructor** — in conference or by e-mail — can give you a sense of how to proceed with your revision. Establishing such an oral or written dialogue can help you learn how to respond critically to your own writing, and your reactions to your instructor's comments on any draft can help you to clarify your essay's goals. (If your instructor is not available, try to schedule a conference with a writing center tutor, if your school offers this service.) Using your own responses as well as those of your classmates and your instructor, you can write drafts that are increasingly more consistent with these goals.

The Revision Process

As you move through successive drafts, the task of revising your essay will be easier if you follow a systematic process. As you read and react to your essay, begin by assessing the effectiveness of the larger elements — thesis and support, for instance — and then move on to examine increasingly smaller elements.

Thesis statement First, reconsider your **thesis statement.** Is it carefully and precisely worded? Does it provide a realistic idea of what your essay will cover? Does it make a point that is worth supporting? The following vague thesis statements are imprecise and unfocused:

Vague: Many important reasons exist to explain why Margot Macomber's shooting of her husband was probably intentional.

Vague: Dickens's characters are a lot like those of Addison and Steele.

To give focus and direction to your essay, a thesis statement must be more pointed and more specific:

Revised: Although Hemingway's text states that Margot Macomber "shot at the buffalo," a careful analysis of her relationship with her husband suggests that in fact she intended to kill him.

Revised: With their extremely familiar, almost caricature-like physical and moral traits, many of Charles Dickens's minor characters reveal that Dickens owes a debt to the "characters" created by the eighteenth-century essayists Joseph Addison and Richard Steele for the newspaper <u>The Spectator</u>.

Support Next, assess the appropriateness of your **supporting ideas,** and consider whether you present enough support for your thesis and whether all the details you include are relevant to that thesis. Make sure you have supported all points with specific, concrete examples from the work or works you are discussing, briefly summarizing key events, quoting dialogue or description, describing characters or settings, or paraphrasing important ideas. Make certain, however, that your own ideas control the essay and that you have not substituted plot summary for analysis and interpretation. Your goal is to draw a conclusion about one or more works and to support that conclusion with pertinent details. If a plot detail supports a point you wish to make, include a *brief* summary of the event or series of events, showing its relevance by explicitly connecting the summary to the point you are making.

In the following excerpt from a paper on a short story by James Joyce, the first sentence summarizes a key event, and the second sentence explains its significance:

At the end of "Counterparts," when Farrington returns home after a day of frustration and abuse at work, his reaction is to strike out at his son Tom. This act shows that `although he and his son are similarly victimized, Farrington is also the counterpart of his tyrannical boss.`

Topic sentences   Now, turn your attention to the **topic sentences** that present the main idea of each body paragraph, making sure that they are clearly worded and communicate the direction of your ideas and the precise relationships of ideas to one another.

Be especially careful to avoid abstractions and vague generalities in topic sentences:

Vague: `One similarity revolves around the dominance of the men by women.` (What exactly is the similarity?)

Revised: `In both stories, a man is dominated by a woman.`

Vague: `There is one reason for the fact that Jay Gatsby remains a mystery.` (What is the reason?)

Revised: `Because` `The Great Gatsby` `is narrated by the outsider Nick Carraway, Jay Gatsby himself remains a mystery.`

When revising topic sentences that are intended to move readers from one point (or section of your paper) to another, be sure the relationship between the ideas they link is clear:

Unclear relationship between ideas: `Now the poem's imagery will be discussed.`

Revised: `Another reason for the poem's effectiveness is its unusual imagery.`

Unclear relationship between ideas: `The sheriff's wife is another interesting character.`

Revised: `Like her friend Mrs. Hale, the sheriff's wife has mixed feelings about what Mrs. Wright has done.`

Introductions and conclusions   When you are satisfied with the body of your essay, you can focus on your paper's *introduction* and *conclusion*.

The **introduction** of an essay about literature should identify the works to be discussed and their authors and indicate the emphasis of the discussion to follow. Depending on your purpose and on your paper's topic, you may want to provide some historical background or biographical information or to briefly discuss the work in relation to other, similar works. Like all introductions, the one you write for an essay about literature should create interest in your topic and include a clear thesis statement.

The following introduction, though acceptable for a first draft, is in need of revision:

> Revenge, which is defined as "the chance to retaliate, get satisfaction, take vengeance, or inflict damage or injury in return for an injury, insult, etc.," is a major component in many of the stories we have read. The stories that will be discussed here deal with a variety of ways to seek revenge. In my essay, I will show some of these differences.

Although the student clearly identifies her paper's topic, she does not identify the works she will discuss or the particular point she will make about revenge. Her tired opening strategy, a dictionary definition, is not likely to create interest in her topic, and her announcement of her intention in the last sentence is awkward and unnecessary. The following revision is much more effective:

> In Edgar Allan Poe's "The Cask of Amontillado," Montresor vows revenge on Fortunato for an unspecified "insult"; in Ring Lardner's "Haircut," Paul, a young retarded man, gets even with a cruel practical joker who has taunted him for years. Both of these stories present characters who seek revenge, and both stories end in murder. However, the murderers' motivations are presented very differently. In "Haircut," the unreliable narrator is unaware of the significance of many events, and his ignorance helps to create sympathy for the murderer. In "The Cask of Amontillado," where the untrustworthy narrator is the murderer himself, Montresor's inability to offer a convincing motive turns the reader against him.

In your **conclusion,** you restate your thesis or sum up your essay's main points; then, you make a graceful exit.

The concluding paragraph that follows is acceptable for a first draft but communicates little information:

> Although the characters of Montresor and Paul were created by different authors at different times, they do have similar motives and goals. However, they are portrayed very differently.

The following revision reinforces the essay's main point, effectively incorporating a brief quotation from "The Cask of Amontillado" (p. 217):

> In fact, then, what is significant is not whether each murderer's act is justified, but rather how each murderer, and each victim, is portrayed by the narrator. Montresor—driven by a thirst to avenge "a thousand injuries" as well as a final insult—is shown to be sadistic and unrepentant; in "Haircut," it is Jim, the victim, whose sadism and lack of remorse are revealed to the reader.

Sentences and words Now, focus on the individual sentences and words of your essay. Begin by evaluating your **transitions,** the words and phrases that link sentences and paragraphs. Be sure that every necessary transitional element has been supplied and that each word or phrase you have selected accurately conveys the exact relationship (sequence, contradiction, and so on) between ideas. When you are satisfied with the clarity and appropriateness of your paper's transitions, consider sentence variety and word choice.

First, be sure you have varied your sentence structure. You will bore your readers if all your sentences begin the same way ("The story. . . ."; "The story. . . ."), or if they are all about the same length. In addition, make sure that all the words you have selected communicate your ideas accurately and that you have not used vague, inexact diction. For example, saying that a character is *bad* is a lot less effective than describing him or her as *ruthless, conniving,* or *malicious.* Finally, eliminate subjective expressions, such as *I think, in my opinion, I believe, it seems to me,* and *I feel.* These phrases weaken your essay by suggesting that its ideas are "only" opinions and have no objective validity.

Using and documenting sources Make certain that all references to sources are integrated smoothly into your sentences and that all information that is not your own is documented appropriately. See "Integrating Sources" (p. 1538) and Avoiding Plagiarism" (p. 1538) in Chapter 34, "Writing a Research Paper."

CHECKLIST USING SOURCES

✓ Acknowledge all sources, including the work or works under discussion, using the documentation style of the Modern Language Association (MLA).

✓ Combine paraphrases, summaries, and quotations with your own interpretations, weaving quotations smoothly into your paper. Introduce the words or ideas of others with a phrase that identifies their source ("According to Richard Wright's biographer, . . ."), and end with appropriate parenthetical documentation.

continued on next page

✓ Use quotations *only* when something vital would be lost if you did not reproduce the author's exact words.

✓ Integrate short quotations (four lines or fewer of prose or three lines or fewer of poetry) smoothly into your paper. (Use a slash — to separate lines of poetry.) Be sure to enclose quotations in quotation marks.

✓ Set off quotations of more than four lines of prose or three lines of poetry by indenting ten spaces (approximately one inch) from the left-hand margin. Double-space, and do not use quotation marks. If you are quoting a single paragraph, do not indent the first line.

✓ Use ellipses — three spaced periods — to indicate that you have omitted material within a quotation. See Chapter 34 for further information.

✓ Use brackets to indicate that you have added words to a quotation: As Earl notes, "[Willie] is a modern-day Everyman" (201). Use brackets to alter a quotation so that it fits grammatically into your sentence: Wilson says that Miller "offer[s] audiences a dark view of the present" (74).

✓ Place commas and periods *inside* quotation marks: According to Robert Coles, the child could "make others smile."

✓ Place punctuation marks other than commas and periods *outside* quotation marks: What does Frost mean when he says "a poem must ride on its own melting"? If the punctuation mark is part of the quoted material, place it *inside* the quotation marks: In "Mending Wall," Frost asks, "*Why* do they make good neighbors?"

✓ When citing part of a short story or novel, supply the page number (143). For a poem, supply line numbers (3–5). For a play, supply act, scene, and line numbers (2.2.17–22) unless your instructor tells you otherwise.

✓ Include a Works Cited list (unless your instructor tells you not to).

Editing

Once you have finished revising, you **edit** — that is, you make certain that your paper's grammar, punctuation, spelling, and mechanics are correct. Always run a spell check — but remember that you still have to proofread carefully for errors that the spell checker will not identify. These include homophones (*brake* incorrectly used instead of *break*), typos that create correctly spelled words (*work* instead of *word*), and proper nouns that may not be in your computer's dictionary. If you use a grammar checker, remember that grammar programs may identify potential problems — long sentences, for example — but may not be able to determine whether a particular long sentence is grammatically correct (let alone stylistically pleasing). Always keep a style handbook as well as a dictionary nearby so that you can double-check any problems a spell checker or grammar checker highlights in your writing.

As you edit, pay particular attention to the mechanical conventions of literary essays, some of which are addressed in the checklist below. When your editing is complete, give your essay a descriptive title. Before you reprint it, be sure that its format conforms to your instructor's requirements.

CHECKLIST **CONVENTIONS OF WRITING ABOUT LITERATURE**

✓ Use present-tense verbs when discussing works of literature: "The character of Mrs. Mallard's husband *is* not developed. . . ."

✓ Use past-tense verbs only when discussing historical events ("Owen's poem conveys the destructiveness of World War I, which at the time the poem *was* written *was* considered to be . . ."); when presenting historical or biographical data ("Her first novel, which *was* published in 1811 when Austen *was* thirty-six, . . ."); or when identifying events that occurred prior to the time of the story's main action ("Miss Emily is a recluse; since her father's death she *has lived* alone except for a servant").

✓ Support all points with specific, concrete examples from the work you are discussing, briefly summarizing key events, quoting dialogue or description, describing characters or setting, or paraphrasing ideas.

✓ Avoid unnecessary plot summary. Your goal is to draw a conclusion about one or more works and to support that conclusion with pertinent details. If a plot detail supports a point you wish to make, a *brief* summary is acceptable. But plot summary is no substitute for analysis.

✓ Use literary terms accurately. For example, be careful not to confuse *narrator* or *speaker* with *author;* feelings or opinions expressed by a narrator or character do not necessarily represent those of the author. You should not say, "In the poem's last stanza, *Frost* expresses his indecision" when you mean that the poem's *speaker* is indecisive.

✓ Underline titles of novels and plays; place titles of short stories and poems within quotation marks.

✓ Refer to authors of literary works by their full names *(Edgar Allan Poe)* in your first reference to them and by their last names *(Poe)* in subsequent references. Never refer to authors by their first names, and never use titles that indicate marital status (*Flannery O'Connor* or *O'Connor*, never *Flannery* or *Miss O'Connor*).

Exercise: Two Student Papers

The following student papers, "Initiation into Adulthood" and "Hard Choices," were written for the same introduction to literature class. Both consider the initiation theme in the same three short stories: James Joyce's "Eveline" (p. 489), John Updike's "A&P" (p. 115), and William Faulkner's "Barn Burning" (p. 223). "Hard Choices" conforms to the conventions of writing about literature discussed in this chapter. "Initiation into Adulthood" does not.

Read the two essays. Then, guided by this chapter's discussion of writing about literature and by the checklists on pages 31–33, identify the features that make "Hard Choices" the more effective essay, and decide where "Initiation into Adulthood" needs further revision. Finally, suggest some possible revisions for "Hard Choices."

Initiation into Adulthood

At an early age, the main focus in a child's life is his parents. But as this child grows, he begins to get his own view of life, which may be, and usually is, different from that of his parents. Sooner or later there will come a time in this child's life when he must stand up for what he truly believes in. At this point in his life, he can no longer be called a child, and he becomes part of the adult world. In literature, many stories—such as James Joyce's "Eveline," John Updike's "A&P," and William Faulkner's "Barn Burning"—focus on this initiation into adulthood.

James Joyce's "Eveline" is a story that describes a major turning point in a woman's life. At home, Eveline's life was very hard. She was responsible for keeping the house together and caring for the younger children left to her after her mother's death. Unfortunately, the only thoughts that ran through her mind were thoughts of escape, of leaving her unhappy life and beginning a new life of her own. The night before she was to secretly leave with Frank on a boat to Buenos Ayres, a street organ playing reminded her of her promise to her dying mother to keep the home together as long as she could. She was now forced to make a decision between life with Frank and her present life, which didn't look wholly undesirable now that she was about to leave. The next night, just as she was about to step on the boat, she realized she could not leave. The making of this decision was in essence Eveline's initiation into adulthood.

Introduction

Thesis statement

Discussion of first story: "Eveline"

Discussion of
second story:
"A&P"

John Updike's "A&P" presented the brief infatuation of a young boy, Sammy, and the consequences that followed. Sammy's home was a small quiet town a few miles from the shore. He worked in the local A&P as a cashier, a job his father had gotten for him. One day, three girls in nothing but bathing suits walked through the front door. Immediately they caught Sammy's eye, especially the leader, the one he nicknamed "Queenie." After prancing through the store, eventually they came to Sammy's checkout with an unusual order. It was not long before they caught the attention of Mr. Lengel, the manager. Unpleasant words were exchanged between the manager and Queenie pertaining to their inappropriate shopping attire. Before the girls left the store, Sammy told Lengel that he quit, hoping they would stop and watch their unsuspected hero. But they kept walking, and Sammy was faced with the decision of whether or not to follow through with his gesture. Knowing that it is "fatal" not to follow through with a gesture once you've started, he removed his apron and bow tie and walked out the door, realizing how hard the world was going to be to him hereafter. The making of this decision, to leave the mundane life of the A&P and enter the harsh world, was in essence Sammy's initiation into adulthood.

Discussion of
third story:
"Barn Burning"

William Faulkner's "Barn Burning" is a story about Sarty Snopes, an innocent young boy who must make a decision between his family and his honor. Because Abner Snopes, Sarty's father, had so little, he

tried to hurt those who had more than he had—often
by burning their barns. These acts forced the Snopes
family to move around quite a bit. The last time
Snopes burned a barn, he did it without warning his
victim, making Sarty realize how cruel and dishonest
his father really was. Because of this realization,
Sarty decided to leave his family. This decision of
Sarty's not to stick to his own blood was his
initiation into adulthood.

"Eveline," "A&P," and "Barn Burning" all deal
with a youth maturing to adulthood in the process of
deciding whether to stay unhappy or to go and seek a
better life. Sammy and Sarty leave their unpleasant
situations because of something done unfairly.
Eveline, on the other hand, decides to stay,
remembering a responsibility to her mother. The
decisions of these characters presented in their
respective stories are focal points in the literary
works and pertain to initiation into adulthood.

Conclusion

Hard Choices

Introduction

Although William Faulkner's "Barn Burning" focuses on a young boy in the American South, John Updike's "A&P" on a teenager in a town north of Boston,
and James Joyce's "Eveline" on a young woman in
Dublin, each of the three stories revolves around a
decision the central character must make. These decisions are not easy ones; in all three cases, family
loyalty competes with a desire for individual free-

Thesis statement

dom. However, the difficult decision-making process
helps each character to mature, and in this sense,
all three works are initiation stories.

Discussion of
first story:
"Barn Burning"

For Sarty Snopes in "Barn Burning," initiation
into adulthood means coming to terms with his
father's concept of revenge. Mr. Snopes believes that
a person should take revenge into his own hands if he
cannot get justice in court. Revenge, for this bitter
man, means burning down barns. Sarty knows that his
father is doing wrong, but Mr. Snopes drills into his
son's mind the idea that "You got to learn to stick
to your own blood or you ain't going to have any
blood to stick to you" (Faulkner 226), and for a long
time Sarty believes him. Naturally, this blood tie
makes Sarty's decision to leave his family extremely
difficult. In the end, though, Sarty decides to reject
his father's values and remain behind when his family
moves.

Discussion of
second story:
"A&P"

In a similar manner, Sammy must choose between
his values and his parents' values (reflected in his
job at the supermarket). While Sammy is working in
the A&P, he notices how "sheep-like" people are. Most

customers have a routine life that they never
consider changing, and Sammy does not want to wind up
like them. When three seemingly carefree girls enter
the store and exhibit nonconformist behavior—such as
going against the flow of people in the aisles, not
having a grocery list, and wearing bathing suits—
Sammy sees them as rebels, and he longs to escape
through them from his humdrum world. In the end, he
chooses to defend the girls and quit the job his
parents helped him to get.

Likewise, Eveline has to decide between a new
life with her boyfriend, Frank, in South America and
her dull, hard life at home with her father. The new
life offers change and freedom, while her life at
home is spent working and keeping house. Still, when
given the chance to leave, she declines because she
has promised her dying mother to keep the house as
long as she could.

All three characters enter adulthood by making
difficult decisions. Sarty realizes that in order to
grow, he must repudiate his father's wrongdoings. He
stands up for his values and rejects his "blood."
Sammy makes the same decision, although with less
extreme consequences: knowing that he will have to
confront his parents, he defends the three girls and
stands up to his boss, rejecting a life of conformity
and security. Unlike the other two, Eveline does not
reject her parents' values. Instead, she decides to
sacrifice her own future by remaining with her father.
She keeps her promise to her mother and places her

Discussion of third
story: "Eveline"

Comparative
analysis of the
three stories

father before herself because she believes that caring for him is her duty.

Further analysis of the three stories

Each of the three characters confronts a challenging future. Sarty must support himself and make a new life. Because he is very young and because he has no one to help him, his future is the most uncertain of the three. Unlike Sammy and Eveline, who still have homes, Sarty has only his judgment and his values to guide him. Sammy's future is less bleak but still unpredictable: he knows that the world will be a harder place for him from now on (Updike 119) because now he is a man of principle. Unlike the other two, Eveline knows exactly what her future holds: work, pain, and boredom. She has no fear or uncertainty—but no hope for a better tomorrow either.

Conclusion

"Barn Burning," "A&P," and "Eveline" are stories of initiation in which the main characters struggle with decisions that help them to grow up. All three consider giving up the known for the unknown, challenging their parents and becoming truly themselves, but only Sarty and Sammy actually do so. Both boys defy their parents and thus trade difficult lives for uncertain ones. Eveline, however, chooses to stay on in her familiar life, choosing the known—however deadening—over the unknown. Still, all three, in confronting hard choices and deciding to do what their values tell them they must do, experience an initiation into adulthood.

FICTION

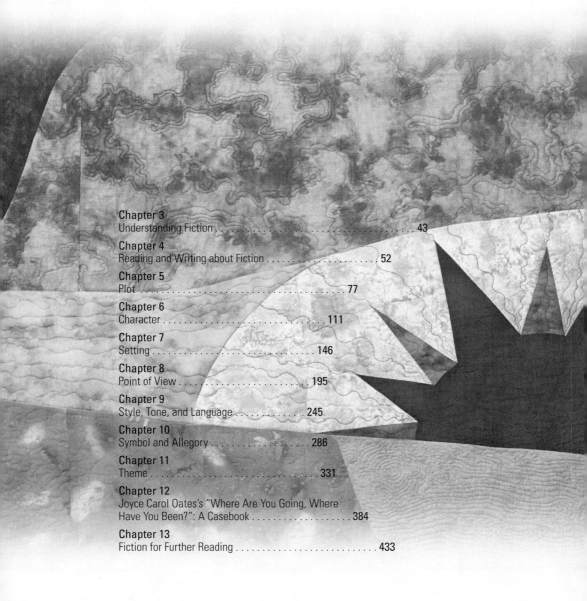

CHAPTER 3

UNDERSTANDING FICTION

DEFINING FICTION

A **narrative** tells a story by presenting events in some logical or orderly way. A work of **fiction** is a narrative that originates in the imagination of the author, not in history or fact. Certainly some fiction — historical or autobiographical fiction, for example — focuses on real people and is grounded in actual events, but the way the characters interact and how the plot unfolds are the author's invention.

Even before they know how to read, most people have learned how narratives are structured. Once children can tell a story, they also know how to exaggerate, how to add or delete details, how to rearrange events, and how to bend facts — in other words, how to fictionalize a narrative to achieve a desired effect. This kind of informal, personal narrative is similar in many ways to the more structured literary narratives included in this anthology.

The earliest examples of narrative fiction are stories and songs that came out of a prehistoric oral tradition. These stories, embellished with each telling, were often quite long, embodying the history, the central myths, and the religious beliefs of the cultures in which they originated. Eventually transcribed, these extended narratives became **epics** — long narrative poems about heroic figures whose actions determine the fate of a nation or an entire race. Homer's *Iliad* and *Odyssey*, the ancient Babylonian *Epic of Gilgamesh*, the Hindu *Bhagavad Gita*, and the Anglo-Saxon *Beowulf* are examples. Many of the tales of the Old Testament also came out of this tradition. The setting of an epic is vast — sometimes worldwide or cosmic, including heaven and hell — and the action commonly involves a battle or a perilous journey. Quite often, divine beings participate in the action and influence the outcome of events, as they do in the Trojan War in the *Iliad* and in the founding of Rome in Virgil's *Aeneid*.

Folktales and **fairy tales** also come out of an oral tradition. These tales, which developed along with other narrative forms, have influenced works as diverse as Chaucer's *The Canterbury Tales* and D. H. Lawrence's "The Rocking-Horse Winner" (p. 349). The folktales and fairy tales that survive (such as "Cinderella" and Aesop's *Fables*) are contemporary versions of old, even ancient, tales that can be traced back centuries through many different cultures. Folktales and fairy tales share several characteristics. First, they feature simple characters who illustrate a quality or trait that can be summed up in a few words. Much of the appeal of "Cinderella," for example, depends on the contrast between the selfish, sadistic stepsisters and poor, gentle, victimized Cinderella. In addition, the folktale or fairy tale has an obvious theme or moral — good triumphing over evil, for instance. The stories move directly to their conclusions, never interrupted by ingenious or unexpected twists of plot. (Love is temporarily thwarted, but the prince eventually finds Cinderella and marries her.) Finally, these tales are anchored not in specific times or places but in "Once upon a time" settings, green worlds of prehistory filled with royalty, talking animals, and magic.

During the Middle Ages, the **romance** supplanted the epic. Written initially in verse but later in prose, the romance replaced the epic's gods, goddesses, and central heroic figures with knights, kings, and damsels in distress. Events were controlled by enchantments rather than by the will of divine beings. *Sir Gawain and the Green Knight* and other tales of King Arthur and the Knights of the Round Table are examples of romances. Eventually, the romance gave way to other types of narratives. Short prose tales, such as those collected in Giovanni Boccaccio's *The Decameron*, originated in fourteenth-century Italy, and the **picaresque,** an episodic, often satirical work about a rogue or rascal (such as Miguel de Cervantes's *Don Quixote*), emerged in seventeenth-century Spain. The **pastoral romance,** a prose tale set in an idealized rural world, and the **character,** a brief satirical sketch illustrating a type of personality, both became popular in Renaissance England.

From these diverse sources emerged the **novel.** The English writer Daniel Defoe is commonly given credit for writing the first novel, in 1719. His *Robinson Crusoe* is an episodic narrative similar to a picaresque but unified by a single setting as well as by a central character. By the nineteenth century, the novel reached a high point in its development, replacing other kinds of extended narratives. Because of its ability to present a wide range of characters in realistic settings and to develop them in depth, the novel appealed to members of the rising middle class, who seemed to have an insatiable desire to see themselves portrayed. Writers such as George Eliot, Charles Dickens, William Thackeray, and Charlotte and Emily Brontë appealed to this desire by creating large fictional worlds populated by many different characters who reflected the complexity — and at times the melodrama — of Victorian society. From these roots, the novel as a literary form continued to develop throughout the twentieth century and into the twenty-first.

THE SHORT STORY

Like the novel, the short story evolved from the various forms of narrative discussed earlier. Because the short story comes from so many different sources from all over the world, it is difficult to determine where it originated. We can say with certainty, however, that in the United States during the nineteenth century a group of writers — in particular Nathaniel Hawthorne and Edgar Allan Poe — took it seriously and exploited its fictional possibilities. Because the short story was embraced so readily and developed so quickly in the United States, it is commonly, although not quite accurately, thought of as an American literary form.

Whereas the novel is an extended piece of narrative fiction, the **short story** is limited in length and scope. These limitations account for the characteristics that distinguish the short story from longer prose forms. Unlike the novelist, the short story writer cannot devote a great deal of space to developing a highly complex plot or a large number of characters. As a result, the short story begins close to or at the height of action and develops only one character in depth. Usually concentrating on a single incident, the writer develops a character by showing his or her responses to events. (This attention to character development, as well as its detailed description of setting, is what distinguishes the short story from earlier short narrative forms, such as folktales and fairy tales.) In many contemporary stories, a character experiences an **epiphany,** a moment of illumination in which something hidden or not understood becomes immediately clear. Examples of epiphany are found in this anthology in James Joyce's "Araby," John Updike's "A&P," and David Michael Kaplan's "Doe Season."

Today, the term *short story* is applied to a wide variety of prose narratives: short stories such as Charles Baxter's "Gryphon" (p. 126), which runs about twelve pages; **short short stories,** such as Luisa Valenzuela's "All about Suicide" (p. 5), which are under five pages in length; and long stories, such as Herman Melville's "Bartleby, the Scrivener," which may more accurately be called short novels or **novellas.**

The two stories that follow, Gary Gildner's "Sleepy Time Gal" (1979) and Margaret Atwood's "Happy Endings" (1982), are in some ways typical of the modern short story and in other ways not typical at all. Although both include the usual components of the short story — a plot, characters, and so on — they also self-consciously play with the conventions of short fiction, testing the limits of the genre. In doing so, these writers, like many others of the last quarter century, reveal their intense preoccupation with the process of creating fiction. At the same time they are writing their stories, they are also observing themselves as writers engaged with their craft.

Gary Gildner's story, with its easy-to-follow narrative and sympathetic characters, is the more conventional of the two.

GARY GILDNER (1938–   ) is an award-winning writer living in Idaho with his wife and daughter. His work includes *Blue Like the Heavens: New and Selected Poems* (1984), *Clackamas* (1991), and *The Swing* (1996), as well as a novel, *The Second Bridge* (1987), and two collections of stories, The *Crush* (1983) and *A Week in South Dakota* (1987). His popular memoir *The Warsaw Sparks* (1990) recounts his experiences as a baseball coach in Warsaw, Poland. A new memoir, *My Grandfather's Book,* was published in 2002.

One of Gildner's most acclaimed collections of poetry, *The Bunker in the Parsley Fields* (1997), won the Iowa Poetry Prize. Most of the poems in this award-winning collection are based on the experiences Gildner and his wife shared while living in Slovakia during 1992–1993, when Czechoslovakia split in two. They lived, like thousands around them, in cramped quarters in a cement flat above an abandoned bunker not far from the Tatra Mountains. Gildner has also received a National Magazine Award for fiction, a William Carlos Williams Award, and a Pushcart Prize.

In his short story "Sleepy Time Gal," Gildner writes of love and loss in a small town during the Depression. The narrator attempts to tell a simple story without intruding, but his perspective, as well as the perspective of others in the story, makes it clear that stories of love and loss are never simple.

Cultural Context   "Sleepy Time Gal" is the actual name of a blues song first published in 1925. The blues is a form of secular folk music with its origins among Southern blacks in the early twentieth century. Its simple but expressive style makes the blues an important influence on popular music in the United States.

Sleepy Time Gal (1979)

In the small town in northern Michigan where my father lived as a young man, he had an Italian friend who worked in a restaurant. I will call his friend Phil. Phil's job in the restaurant was as ordinary as you can imagine — from making coffee in the morning to sweeping up at night. But what was not ordinary about Phil was his piano playing. On Saturday nights my father and Phil and their girlfriends would drive ten or fifteen miles to a roadhouse by a lake where they would drink beer from schooners and dance and Phil would play an old beat-up piano. He could play any song you named, my father said, but the song everyone waited for was the one he wrote, which he would always play at the end before they left to go back to the town. And everyone knew of course that he had written the song for his girl, who was as pretty as she was rich. Her father was the banker in their town, and he was a tough old German, and he didn't like Phil going around with his daughter.

My father, when he told the story, which was not often, would tell it in an off-hand way and emphasize the Depression and not having much, instead of the important parts. I will try to tell it the way he did, if I can.

So they would go to the roadhouse by the lake, and finally Phil would play his song, and everyone would say, Phil, that's a great song, you could make a lot of money from it. But Phil would only shake his head and smile and look at his girl. I have to break in here and say that my father, a gentle but practical man, was not inclined to emphasize the part about Phil looking at his girl. It was my mother who said the girl would rest her head on Phil's shoulder while he played, and that he got the idea for the song from the pretty way she looked when she got sleepy. My mother was not part of the story, but she had heard it when she and my father were younger and therefore had that information. I would like to intrude further and add something about Phil writing the song, maybe show him whistling the tune and going over the words slowly and carefully to get the best ones, while peeling onions or potatoes in the restaurant; but my father is already driving them home from the roadhouse, and saying how patched up his tires were, and how his car's engine was a gingerbread of parts from different makes, and some parts were his own invention as well. And my mother is saying that the old German had made his daughter promise not to get involved with any man until after college, and they couldn't be late. Also my mother likes the sad parts and is eager to get to their last night before the girl goes away to college.

So they all went out to the roadhouse, and it was sad. The women got tears in their eyes when Phil played her song, my mother said. My father said that Phil spent his week's pay on a new shirt and tie, the first tie he ever owned, and people kidded him. Somebody piped up and said, Phil, you ought to take that song down to Bay City — which was like saying New York City to them, only more realistic — and sell it and take the money and go to college too. Which was not meant to be cruel, but that was the result because Phil had never even got to high school. But you can see people were trying to cheer him up, my mother said.

Well, she'd come home for Thanksgiving and Christmas and Easter and they'd all sneak out to the roadhouse and drink beer from schooners and dance and everything would be like always. And of course there were the summers. And everyone knew Phil and the girl would get married after she made good her promise to her father because you could see it in their eyes when he sat at the old beat-up piano and played her song. 5

That last part about their eyes was not, of course, in my father's telling, but I couldn't help putting it in there even though I know it is making some of you impatient. Remember that this happened many years ago in the woods by a lake in northern Michigan, before television. I wish I could put more in, especially about the song and how it felt to Phil to sing it and how the girl felt when hearing it and knowing it was hers, but I've already intruded too much in a simple story that isn't even mine.

Well, here's the kicker part. Probably by now many of you have guessed that one vacation near the end she doesn't come home to see Phil, because she meets some guy at college who is good-looking and as rich as she is and, because her father knew about Phil all along and was pressuring her into forgetting about him, she gives in to this new guy and goes to his hometown during the vacation and falls in love with him. That's how the people in town figured it, because after she graduates they turn up, already married, and right away he takes over the old German's bank — and buys a new Pontiac at the place where my father is the mechanic and pays cash for it. The paying cash always made my father pause and shake his head and mention again that times were tough, but here comes this guy in a spiffy white shirt (with French cuffs, my mother said) and pays the full price in cash.

And this made my father shake his head too: Phil took the song down to Bay City and sold it for twenty-five dollars, the only money he ever got for it. It was the same song we'd just heard on the radio and which reminded my father of the story I just told you. What happened to Phil? Well, he stayed in Bay City and got a job managing a movie theater. My father saw him there after the Depression when he was on his way to Detroit to work for Ford. He stopped and Phil gave him a box of popcorn. The song he wrote for the girl has sold many millions of records, and if I told you the name of it you could probably sing it, or at least whistle the tune. I wonder what the girl thinks when she hears it. Oh yes, my father met Phil's wife too. She worked in the movie theater with him, selling tickets and cleaning the carpet after the show with one of those sweepers you push. She was also big and loud and nothing like the other one, my mother said.

◊   ◊   ◊

While Gildner's narrator is a character in his story, a son who is trying to make sense of the story of his parents' courtship, the narrator of Atwood's story is closer to Atwood herself, trying to make sense of her own creative process.

MARGARET ATWOOD (1939–   ) is one of the most widely read Canadian writers of her generation. Born in Ottawa, Ontario, she was educated at Victoria College in the University of Toronto, at Radcliffe College, and at Harvard University. Her first collection of poems, *The Circle Game,* appeared in 1964. Since then she has produced works in many genres — poetry, short stories, novels, children's books, nonfiction, and scripts for television. Her most recent novel is *The Blind Assassin* (2000); other novels include *Cat's Eye* (1989) and *The Handmaid's Tale* (1985), adapted for the screen and released as a film in 1990. Her poetry collections include *Selected Poems* (1976), *Selected Poems II* (1986), and *Eating Fire: Selected Poems 1965–1995.*

Probably the most conspicuous feature about Atwood's "Happy Endings" is its haywire, unpredictable form: "What happens next?" asks the story's own narrator. Atwood herself admits to being puzzled, at first, by the shape the work took. "When I wrote 'Happy Endings,'" she remembers, "I did not know what sort of creature it was. It was not a poem, a short story, or a prose poem. It was not quite a condensation, a commentary, a questionnaire, and it missed being a parable, a proverb, a paradox. It was a mutation."

Cultural Context The fairy-tale ending — two lovers riding off into the sunset to live happily ever after — has become formulaic, a feature of countless children's stories as well as serious literature. No force has carried it further or produced more unlikely variations than Hollywood; we have even come to call it the "Hollywood ending." Apparently, the demands of customers at the box office keep the "Dream Factory" (as Hollywood has been called) churning out its formula stories of romantic well-being and wish-fulfillment. It is this fairy-tale, or Hollywood, ending that Atwood investigates in the story.

Happy Endings (1983)

John and Mary meet.
What happens next?
If you want a happy ending, try A.

A. John and Mary fall in love and get married. They both have worthwhile and remunerative jobs which they find stimulating and challenging. They buy a charming house. Real estate values go up. Eventually, when they can afford live-in help, they have two children, to whom they are devoted. The children turn out well. John and Mary have a stimulating and challenging sex life and worthwhile friends. They go on fun vacations together. They retire. They both have hobbies which they find stimulating and challenging. Eventually they die. This is the end of the story.

B. Mary falls in love with John but John doesn't fall in love with Mary. He merely ⁵ uses her body for selfish pleasure and ego gratification of a tepid kind. He comes to her apartment twice a week and she cooks him dinner, you'll notice that he doesn't even consider her worth the price of a dinner out, and after he's eaten the dinner he fucks her and after that he falls asleep, while she does the dishes so he won't think she's untidy, having all those dirty dishes lying around, and puts on fresh lipstick so she'll look good when he wakes up, but when he wakes up he doesn't even notice, he puts on his socks and his shorts and his pants and his shirt and his tie and his shoes, the reverse order from the one in which he took them off. He doesn't take off Mary's clothes, she takes them off herself, she acts as if she's dying for it every time, not because she likes sex exactly, she doesn't, but she wants John to think she does because if they do it often enough surely he'll get used to her, he'll come to depend on her and they will get married, but John goes out the door with hardly so much as a good-night and three days later he turns up at six o'clock and they do the whole thing over again.

Mary gets run-down. Crying is bad for your face, everyone knows that and so does Mary but she can't stop. People at work notice. Her friends tell her John is a rat, a pig, a dog, he isn't good enough for her, but she can't believe it. Inside John, she thinks, is another John, who is much nicer. This other John will emerge like a butterfly from a cocoon, a Jack from a box, a pit from a prune, if the first John is only squeezed enough.

One evening John complains about the food. He has never complained about the food before. Mary is hurt.

Her friends tell her they've seen him in a restaurant with another woman, whose name is Madge. It's not even Madge that finally gets to Mary: it's the restaurant. John has never taken Mary to a restaurant. Mary collects all the sleeping pills and aspirins she can find, and takes them and a half a bottle of sherry. You can see what kind of a woman she is by the fact that it's not even whiskey. She leaves a note for John. She hopes he'll discover her and get her to the hospital in time and repent and then they can get married, but this fails to happen and she dies.

John marries Madge and everything continues as in A.

C. John, who is an older man, falls in love with Mary, and Mary, who is only ¹⁰ twenty-two, feels sorry for him because he's worried about his hair falling out. She sleeps with him even though she's not in love with him. She met him at work. She's in love with someone called James, who is twenty-two also and not yet ready to settle down.

John on the contrary settled down long ago: this is what is bothering him. John has a steady, respectable job and is getting ahead in his field, but Mary isn't impressed by him, she's impressed by James, who has a motorcycle and a fabulous record collection. But James is often away on his motorcycle, being free. Freedom isn't the same for girls, so in the meantime Mary spends Thursday evenings with John. Thursdays are the only days John can get away.

John is married to a woman called Madge and they have two children, a charming house which they bought just before the real estate values went up, and hobbies which they find stimulating and challenging, when they have the time. John tells Mary how important she is to him, but of course he can't leave his wife because a commitment is a commitment. He goes on about this more than is necessary and Mary finds it boring, but older men can keep it up longer so on the whole she has a fairly good time.

One day James breezes in on his motorcycle with some top-grade California hybrid and James and Mary get higher than you'd believe possible and they climb into bed. Everything becomes very underwater, but along comes John, who has a key to Mary's apartment. He finds them stoned and entwined. He's hardly in any position to be jealous, considering Madge, but nevertheless he's overcome with despair. Finally he's middle-aged, in two years he'll be bald as an egg and he can't stand it. He purchases a handgun, saying he needs it for target practice — this is the thin part of the plot, but it can be dealt with later — and shoots the two of them and himself.

Madge, after a suitable period of mourning, marries an understanding man called Fred and everything continues as in A, but under different names.

15 D. Fred and Madge have no problems. They get along exceptionally well and are good at working out any little difficulties that may arise. But their charming house is by the seashore and one day a giant tidal wave approaches. Real estate values go down. The rest of the story is about what caused the tidal wave and how they escape from it. They do, though thousands drown, but Fred and Madge are virtuous and lucky. Finally on high ground they clasp each other, wet and dripping and grateful, and continue as in A.

E. Yes, but Fred has a bad heart. The rest of the story is about how kind and understanding they both are until Fred dies. Then Madge devotes herself to charity work until the end of A. If you like, it can be "Madge," "cancer," "guilty and confused," and "bird watching."

F. If you think this is all too bourgeois, make John a revolutionary and Mary a counterespionage agent and see how far that gets you. Remember, this is Canada. You'll still end up with A, though in between you may get a lustful brawling saga of passionate involvement, a chronicle of our times, sort of.

You'll have to face it, the endings are the same however you slice it. Don't be deluded by any other endings, they're all fake, either deliberately fake, with malicious intent to deceive, or just motivated by excessive optimism if not by downright sentimentality.

The only authentic ending is the one provided here:
John and Mary die. John and Mary die. John and Mary die.

20 So much for endings. Beginnings are always more fun. True connoisseurs, however, are known to favor the stretch in between, since it's the hardest to do anything with.

That's about all that can be said for plots, which anyway are just one thing after another, a what and a what and a what.

Now try How and Why.

◇   ◇   ◇

A FINAL NOTE

A short story may be comic or tragic; its subject may be growing up, marriage, crime and punishment, war, sexual awakening, death, or any number of other human concerns. The setting can be an imaginary world, the old West, rural America, the jungles of Uruguay, nineteenth-century Russia, precommunist China, or modern Egypt. The story may have a conventional form, with a definite beginning, middle, and end, or it may be structured as a letter, as a diary entry, or even as a collection of random notes. The narrator of a story may be trustworthy or unreliable, involved in the action or a disinterested observer, sympathetic or deserving of scorn, extremely ignorant or highly insightful, limited in vision or able to see inside the minds of all the characters. As the selections in this anthology show, the possibilities of the short story are infinite.

CHAPTER 4

READING AND WRITING ABOUT FICTION

READING FICTION

As you read more works of short fiction, you will begin paying careful attention to elements such as plot; character; setting; point of view; style, tone, and language; symbol and allegory; and theme. By looking at these elements you will be able to understand and appreciate the story more fully. The following guidelines, designed to help you explore works of fiction, focus on issues that are examined in depth in chapters to come.

- Look at the **plot** of the story. How do the events in the story relate to one another, and how do they relate to the story as a whole? What conflicts occur in the story, and how are these conflicts developed or resolved? Does the story include any noteworthy plot devices, such as flashbacks or foreshadowing? (See Chapter 5.)
- Analyze the **characters** of the story. What are their most striking traits? How do these individuals interact with one another? What motivates them? Are the characters fully developed, or are they stereotypes whose sole purpose is to express a single trait (good, evil, generosity) or to move the plot along? (See Chapter 6.)
- Identify the **setting** of the story. At what time period and in what geographic location does the action of the story occur? How does the setting affect the characters of the story? How does it determine the relationships among the characters? How does the setting affect the plot? Does the setting create a mood for the story? In what way does the setting reinforce the central ideas that the story examines? (See Chapter 7.)
- Examine the narrative **point of view** of the story. What person or persons are telling the story? Is the story told in the first person (using *I* or *we*) or in the third person (using *he, she,* and *they*)? Does the narrator see from various perspectives, or is the story restricted to the perspective of one person? Is the narrator a major character telling his or her own story or a minor character who witnesses events? How much does the narrator know about the events in the story? Does the narrator present an accurate

picture of events? Does the narrator understand the full significance of the story he or she is telling? (See Chapter 8.)

- Analyze the **style, tone,** and **language** of the story. Does the writer make any unusual use of diction or syntax? Does the writer use imaginative figures of speech? Patterns of imagery? What styles or levels of speech are associated with particular characters? What words or phrases are repeated throughout the work? Is the story's style plain or elaborate? Does the narrator's tone reveal his or her attitude toward characters or events? Are there any discrepancies between the narrator's attitude and the attitude of the author? Is the tone of the story playful, humorous, ironic, satirical, serious, somber, solemn, bitter, condescending, formal, or informal — or does the tone suggest some other attitude? (See Chapter 9.)

- Focus on **symbolism** and **allegory.** Does the author use any objects or ideas symbolically? What characters or objects in the story are part of an *allegorical framework?* How does an object establish its symbolic or allegorical significance in the story? Does the same object have different meanings at different places in the story? Are the symbols or *allegorical figures* conventional or unusual? At what points in the story do symbols or allegorical figures appear? (See Chapter 10.)

- Identify the **themes** of the story. What is the central theme? How is this idea or concept expressed in the work? What elements of the story develop the central theme? How do character, plot, setting, point of view, and symbols reinforce the central theme? How does the title of the story contribute to readers' understanding of the central theme? What other themes are explored? (See Chapter 11.)

Active Reading

John Frei, a student in an introduction to literature course, was assigned to write a two- to three-page essay on a topic of his choice, focusing on any short story in this literature anthology, without consulting outside sources. After considering a number of possible choices, John selected Alberto Alvaro Ríos's "The Secret Lion."

ALBERTO ALVARO RÍOS (1952–   ) was born and raised in the border town of Nogales, Arizona, the son of a Mexican father and an English mother. He has published many poems and short stories, including the poetry collections *Teodora Luna's Two Kisses* (1990); *The Warring Poems* (1989); *The Lime Orchard Woman* (1988); and *Whispering to Fool the Wind* (1982), which won the American Academy of Poets Walt Whitman Award; and the short story collections *Pig Cookies and Other Stories* (1995) and *The Iguana Killer: Twelve Stories of the Heart* (1984), from which "The Secret Lion" is drawn. Ríos lives in Chandler, Arizona, and teaches at Arizona State University in Tempe.

Reviewer Mary Logue, writing in the October 1982 *Village Voice Literary Supplement,* says that Ríos's writings "carry the feel of another world. . . . Ríos's tongue is both foreign and familiar," reflecting an upbringing "where one is neither in this country nor the other." In many of his stories, Ríos expresses the seeming "other-ness" of Anglo culture as seen through the eyes of Chicano children: a little boy frightened by the sight of his first snowfall or (as in "The Secret Lion") boys amazed by the otherworldly sight of "heaven." Through Ríos's children, we see our own world with new eyes.

Cultural Context With their rolling hills, freshwater ponds, lush greens, and fastidiously trimmed turf, golf courses are designed to give off an aura of wealth and ease, typically providing recreation for the middle and upper classes. In a dry region — or even in a highly populated city — an irrigated, sculpted golf course may look like an oasis in the desert. The golf course that plays a role in this story is probably (like many others) part of a privately owned, exclusive country club for which membership is required.

The Secret Lion   (1984)

I was twelve and in junior high school and something happened that we didn't have a name for, but it was there nonetheless like a lion, and roaring, roaring that way the biggest things do. Everything changed. Just that. Like the rug, the one that gets pulled — or better, like the tablecloth those magicians pull where the stuff on the table stays the same but the gasp! from the audience makes the staying-the-same part not matter. Like that.

What happened was there were teachers now, not just one teacher, teach-erz, and we felt personally abandoned somehow. When a person had all these teachers now, he didn't get taken care of the same way, even though six was more than one. Arithmetic went out the door when we walked in. And we saw girls now, but they weren't the same girls we used to know because we couldn't talk to them anymore, not the same way we used to, certainly not to Sandy, even though she was my neighbor, too. Not even to her. She just played the piano all the time. And there were words, oh there were words in junior high school, and we wanted to know what they were, and how a person did them — that's what school was supposed to be for. Only, in junior high school, school wasn't school, everything was backward-like. If you went up to a teacher and said the word to try and find out what it meant you got in trouble for saying it. So we didn't. And we figured it must have been that way about other stuff, too, so we never said anything about anything — we weren't stupid.

But my friend Sergio and I, we solved junior high school. We would come home from school on the bus, put our books away, change shoes, and go across the highway to the arroyo. It was the one place we were not supposed to go. So we did. This was, after all, what junior high had at least shown us. It was our river, though, our personal Mississippi, our friend from long back, and it was full of stories and all the branch forts we had built in it when we were still the Vikings of America, with our own symbol, which we had carved everywhere, even in the sand, which let the water take it. That was good, we had decided; whoever was at the end of this river would know about us.

At the very very top of our growing lungs, what we would do down there was shout every dirty word we could think of, in every combination we could come up with, and we would yell about girls, and all the things we wanted to do with them, as loud as we could — we didn't know what we wanted to do with them, just things — and we would yell about teachers, and how we loved some of them, like Miss Crevelone, and how we wanted to dissect some of them, making signs of the cross, like priests, and we would yell this stuff over and over because it felt good, we couldn't explain why, it just felt good and for the first time in our lives there was nobody to tell us we couldn't. So we did.

One Thursday we were walking along shouting this way, and the railroad, the Southern Pacific, which ran above and along the far side of the arroyo, had dropped a grinding ball down there, which was, we found out later, a cannonball thing used in mining. A bunch of them were put in a big vat which turned around and crushed the ore. One had been dropped, or thrown — what do caboose men do when they get bored — but it got down there regardless and as we were walking along yelling about one girl or another, a particular Claudia, we found it, one of these things, looked at it, picked it up, and got very very excited, and held it and passed it back and forth, and we were saying "Guythisis, this is is, geeGuythis...": we had this perception about nature then, that nature is imperfect and that round things are perfect: we said "GuyGodthis is perfect, thisisthis is perfect, it's round, round and heavy, it'sit's the best thing we'veeverseen. Whatisit?" We didn't know. We just knew it was great. We just, whatever, we played with it, held it some more.

And then we had to decide what to do with it. We knew, because of a lot of things, that if we were going to take this and show it to anybody, this discovery, this best thing, was going to be taken away from us. That's the way it works with little kids, like all the polished quartz, the tons of it we had collected piece by piece over the years. Junior high kids too. If we took it home, my mother, we knew, was going to look at it and say "throw that dirty thing in the, get rid of it." Simple like, like that. "But ma it's the best thing I" "Getridofit." Simple.

So we didn't. Take it home. Instead, we came up with the answer. We dug a hole and buried it. And we marked it secretly. Lots of secret signs. And came back the next week to dig it up and, we didn't know, pass it around some more or something, but we didn't find it. We dug up that whole bank, and we never found it again. We tried.

Sergio and I talked about that ball or whatever it was when we couldn't find it. All we used were small words, neat, good. Kid words. What we were really saying, but didn't know the words, was how much that ball was like that place, that whole arroyo: couldn't tell anybody about it, didn't understand what it was, didn't have a name for it. It just felt good. It was just perfect in the way it was that place, that whole going to that place, that whole junior high school lion. It was just iron-heavy, it had no name, it felt good or not, we couldn't take it home to show our mothers, and once we buried it, it was gone forever.

The ball was gone, like the first reasons we had come to that arroyo years earlier, like the first time we had seen the arroyo, it was gone like everything else that had been taken away. This was not our first lesson. We stopped going to the arroyo after not finding the thing, the same way we had stopped going there years earlier and headed for the mountains. Nature seemed to keep pushing us around one way or another, teaching us the same thing every place we ended up. Nature's gang was tough that way, teaching us stuff.

10   When we were young we moved away from town, me and my family. Sergio's was already out there. Out in the wilds. Or at least the new place seemed like the wilds since everything looks bigger the smaller a man is. I was five, I guess, and we had moved three miles north of Nogales where we had lived, three miles north of the Mexican border. We looked across the highway in one direction and there was the arroyo; hills stood up in the other direction. Mountains, for a small man.

When the first summer came the very first place we went to was of course the one place we weren't supposed to go, the arroyo. We went down in there and found water running, summer rain water mostly, and we went swimming. But every third or fourth or fifth day, the sewage treatment plant that was, we found out, upstream, would release whatever it was that it released, and we would never know exactly what day that was, and a person really couldn't tell right off by looking at the water, not every time, not so a person could get out in time. So, we went swimming that summer and some days we had a lot of fun. Some days we didn't. We found a thousand ways to explain what happened on those other days, constructing elaborate stories about the neighborhood dogs, and hadn't she, my mother, miscalculated her step before, too? But she knew something was up because we'd come running into the house those days, wanting to take a shower, even — if this can be imagined — in the middle of the day.

That was the first time we stopped going to the arroyo. It taught us to look the other way. We decided, as the second side of summer came, we wanted to go into the mountains. They were still mountains then. We went running in one summer Thursday morning, my friend Sergio and I, into my mother's kitchen, and said, well, what'zin, what'zin those hills over there — we used her word so she'd understand us — and she said nothingdon'tworryaboutit. So we went out, and we weren't dumb, we thought with our eyes to each other, ohhoshe'stryingtokeepsomethingfromus. We knew adults.

We had read the books, after all; we knew about bridges and castles and wildtreacherousraging alligatormouth rivers. We wanted them. So we were going to go out and get them. We went back that morning into that kitchen and we said, "We're going out there, we're going into the hills, we're going away for three days, don't worry." She said, "All right."

"You know," I said to Sergio, "if we're going to go away for three days, well, we ought to at least pack a lunch."

15   But we were two young boys with no patience for what we thought at the time was mom-stuff: making sa-and-wiches. My mother didn't offer. So we got out little kid knapsacks that my mother had sewn for us, and into them we put the jar of mustard. A loaf of bread. Knivesforksplates, bottles of Coke, a can opener. This was lunch for the two of us. And we were weighed down, humped over to be strong enough to carry this stuff. But we started walking anyway, into the hills. We were going to eat berries and stuff otherwise. "Goodbye." My mom said that.

After the first hill we were dead. But we walked. My mother could still see us. And we kept walking. We walked until we got to where the sun is straight overhead, noon. That place. Where that is doesn't matter; it's time to eat. The truth is we weren't anywhere close to that place. We just agreed that the sun was overhead and that it was time to eat, and by tilting our heads a little we could make that the truth.

"We really ought to start looking for a place to eat."

"Yeah. Let's look for a good place to eat." We went back and forth saying that for fifteen minutes, making it lunchtime because that's what we always said back and forth before lunchtimes at home. "Yeah, I'm hungry all right." I nodded my head. "Yeah, I'm hungry all right too. I'm hungry." He nodded his head. I nodded my head back. After a good deal more nodding, we were ready, just as we came over a little hill. We hadn't found the mountains yet. This was a little hill.

And on the other side of this hill we found heaven.

It was just what we thought it would be.   20

Perfect. Heaven was green, like nothing else in Arizona. And it wasn't a cemetery or like that because we had seen cemeteries and they had gravestones and stuff and this didn't. This was perfect, had trees, lots of trees, had birds, like we had never seen before. It was like "The Wizard of Oz," like when they got to Oz and everything was so green, so emerald, they had to wear those glasses, and we ran just like them, laughing, laughing that way we did that moment, and we went running down to this clearing in it all, hitting each other that good way we did.

We got down there, we kept laughing, we kept hitting each other, we unpacked our stuff, and we started acting "rich." We knew all about how to do that, like blowing on our nails, then rubbing them on our chests for the shine. We made our sandwiches, opened our Cokes, got out the rest of the stuff, the salt and pepper shakers. I found this particular hole and I put my Coke right into it, a perfect fit, and I called it my Coke-holder. I got down next to it on my back, because everyone knows that rich people eat lying down, and I got my sandwich in one hand and put my other arm around the Coke in its holder. When I wanted a drink, I lifted my neck a little, put out my lips, and tipped my Coke a little with the crook of my elbow. Ah.

We were there, lying down, eating our sandwiches, laughing, throwing bread at each other and out for the birds. This was heaven. We were laughing and we couldn't believe it. My mother was keeping something from us, ah ha, but we had found her out. We even found water over at the side of the clearing to wash our plates with — we had brought plates. Sergio started washing his plates when he was done, and I was being rich with my Coke, and this day in summer was right.

When suddenly these two men came, from around a corner of trees and the tallest grass we had ever seen. They had bags on their backs, leather bags, bags and sticks.

We didn't know what clubs were, but I learned later, like I learned about the   25
grinding balls. The two men yelled at us. Most specifically, one wanted me to take my Coke out of my Coke-holder so he could sink his golf ball into it.

Something got taken away from us that moment. Heaven. We grew up a little bit, and couldn't go backward. We learned. No one had ever told us about golf. They had told us about heaven. And it went away. We got golf in exchange.

We went back to the arroyo for the rest of that summer, and tried to have fun the best we could. We learned to be ready for finding the grinding ball. We loved it, and when we buried it we knew what would happen. The truth is, we didn't look so hard for it. We were two boys and twelve summers then, and not stupid. Things get taken away.

We buried it because it was perfect. We didn't tell my mother, but together it was all we talked about, till we forgot. It was the lion.

◊ ◊ ◊

Previewing

Student John Frei began the reading process by previewing his text. A quick glance at the story showed him that it was quite short (under five pages), that it was written in the first person ("I was twelve"), that it included dialogue as well as narrative, and that it had a provocative title.

Previewing "The Secret Lion" prepared John to read it more closely and, eventually, to write about it. In preparation for writing, he read and reread the story, highlighting and annotating it as he went along.

Highlighting and Annotating

As he reread the story, John highlighted words and ideas that he thought might be useful to him, indicated possible connections among ideas, and noted questions and comments as they occurred to him. During this process, he considered the meaning of the term *secret lion*, and he paid close attention to the narrator's voice. The highlighted and annotated passage that follows illustrates his responses to the last five paragraphs of the story:

> When suddenly these two men came, from around a corner of trees and the tallest grass we had ever seen. They had bags on their backs, leather bags, bags and sticks.
>
> *[annotation: pt. of view]* We didn't know what clubs were, but I learned later, like I learned about the grinding balls. The two men yelled at us. Most specifically, one wanted me to take my Coke out of my Coke-holder so he could sink his golf ball into it.
>
> *[annotation: Heaven = innocence]* Something got taken away from us that moment. Heaven. We grew up a little bit, and couldn't go backward. We learned. No one had ever told us *[annotation: Golf = adulthood]* about golf. They had told us about heaven. And it went away. We got golf in exchange.
>
> *[annotation: Things lose their magic + special-ness. Also—]* We went back to the arroyo for the rest of that summer, and tried to have fun the best we could. We learned to be ready for finding the grinding ball. We loved it, and when we buried it we knew what would happen. The truth

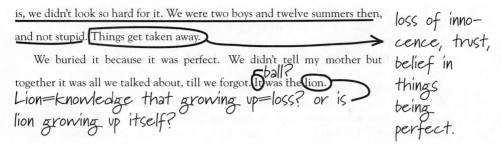

is, we didn't look so hard for it. We were two boys and twelve summers then, ~~loss of inno-~~
and not stupid. Things get taken away. → ~~cence, trust,~~

We buried it because it was perfect. We didn't tell my mother but
together it was all we talked about, till we forgot. It was the lion.

loss of inno-
cence, trust,
belief in
things
being
perfect.

ball?

Lion=knowledge that growing up=loss? or is
lion growing up itself?

John's highlighting and annotations suggested a number of interesting possibilities for his paper. First, he noticed that the story reveals both the narrator's childhood innocence and his adult knowledge. John's highlighting also identified some unusual stylistic features, such as words run together ("Getridofit") and repetition of words like *neat* and *perfect*. Finally, he noticed that four items — the arroyo, the grinding ball, the golf course, and the lion — are mentioned again and again. This emphasis led him to suspect that one or more of these items — particularly the secret lion, prominently mentioned in the story's title — had symbolic significance.

WRITING ABOUT FICTION

Planning an Essay

At this stage, John had not thought of a topic; he knew only that he would be writing a paper on "The Secret Lion." However, his previewing, highlighting, and annotations had revealed some interesting ideas about style and point of view — and, possibly, about symbolism. Now, because his paper was to be no more than three pages long, he needed to select one element on which to concentrate.

Choosing a Topic

John decided to explore possible topics in his journal. Here is his journal entry on the story's style and point of view:

```
Style—Style is informal, with lots of contractions and
slang terms like "neat." Words are run together. Most of
the time, the boys combine words to indicate something
unimportant to them. When they're packing the lunch, they
include "knivesforksplates." They're not interested in
packing the lunch—they just want to get to the "mountains."
Packing lunches is very important to the mother, so she
does the opposite of combining words: she breaks them down
("sa-and-wiches"). Maybe the words running together are
supposed to suggest the days of a child, especially in the
summer, when days just blend together. This style gets
pretty annoying after a while, though—it's too cute.
```

> <u>Point of view</u>—We see the story through the eyes of the
> narrator, who is a character in the story. Sergio is
> developed along with the narrator as part of a "we." It's
> unusual that the characters are not really individuals—they
> function as "we" for most of the story, and nothing is done
> to give them separate voices. We don't see into the minds of
> the boys to any greater extent than what the narrator tells
> us, but the narrator has a double perspective: he takes the
> reader back to childhood, and this helps us understand the
> boys' excitement and disappointment, but he also shows us
> how much more he knows now, so we know that too.

John had no trouble writing paragraphs on style and point of view in his journal, but he ran out of ideas quickly; he knew that he did not have enough material to write a paper about either of these two possible topics. When he started to
write a journal entry about the symbolic significance of certain elements in the
story, however, he found that he had a lot to say. As a result, he chose "Symbols
in 'The Secret Lion'" as his paper's topic. Here is his journal entry on symbolism:

> <u>Symbolism</u>—The arroyo, the grinding ball, the golf
> course, and of course the secret lion all seem to mean
> something beyond their literal meanings as objects and
> places. (Maybe the "mountains" do too.) For one thing,
> they're all repeated over and over again. Also, they all seem
> to be related somehow to magic and perfection and surprise
> and expectation and idealism (and, later, to disillusionment
> and disappointment). If this is a story about growing up,
> these things could be related somehow to that theme.

Finding Something to Say

Brainstorming   Once he decided to write about symbolism, John moved on to
brainstorm about his topic, focusing on what he considered the story's most important — and most obvious — symbol: the secret lion itself.

> (Lion) = "roaring, roaring that way the biggest things do"
>
> EVERYTHING CHANGED   (=secret because it's
>   something they have to find
>   out on their own, not from
>   adults?)
>
> (Tablecloth)-rug (= magic). "Staying-the-same part" is
>   most important—why?

Arroyo: not supposed to go (= rebellion)—Mississippi,
"friend from long back"; freedom. Place that doesn't
change.
Grinding ball—Perfection in imperfect world,
innocence in adult world. "Nature = imperfect," but
"round things = "perfect"—"the best thing." ("That
ball was like that place, that whole arroyo")
   Buried and "gone forever"—"taken away" (like arroyo)
   Mountains: "everything looks bigger the smaller
a man is"; hills = "Mountains for a small man."
(Mother calls them hills)
   Arroyo = polluted with sewage (never know when it's
coming)—went to mts. On other side of hills = golf course
(= heaven) "perfect"

"perfect"
×3

                              *Like Oz—green, emerald
                              *Place to act "rich"
                              *Men with clubs =
                              reality, future—they
                              go back to arroyo
                              (= end of innocence)

"Things get taken away" (heaven, ball—something
buried and lost—arroyo)
"We buried it because it was "perfect." . . . It
was the lion."
Lion = secret place inside us that still craves
childhood (as adults, we learn we have to keep it
buried, like ball). How can a roaring lion be secret?

Seeing Connections

Listing When John looked over his brainstorming notes in search of an organizing scheme for his paper, he saw that he had plenty of information about the
secret lion, the arroyo, the grinding ball, and the golf course. His most obvious

option was to discuss one item at a time, but he knew that he needed to find a common element among the four separate items, a thematic connection that would relate them to one another. When he noticed that each item seemed to have different meanings at different periods of the boys' lives, he realized that his essay could discuss the changes in meaning that occurred as the boys move from childhood to adolescence to adulthood. He experimented with this possibility in the following lists of related details:

```
The secret lion
Beginning: "raging beast" inside of them (6th grade
class) = frustration, puberty
Beginning: "roaring, roaring that way the biggest things do"
Middle: "that whole junior high school lion"
End: Lion = greatness, something important
(also = puberty?)
Also = great discoveries they expect to make in their lives.
End: "It was the lion."

Arroyo
Place that doesn't change (= childhood); constant in their
changing lives. (But it changes too)
Mississippi—horizons
Freedom of childhood
Waste dump

Grinding ball
Perfection (in imperfect world)
Childhood innocence (in adult world)
Undiscovered knowledge?
Secrets of childhood (buried)
Something lost: "Things get taken away"

Golf course
Heaven—knowledge that there is no heaven, that it's a
fraud, like the Wizard of Oz.
Adulthood—men with clubs
Scene of remembered humiliation
End of innocence (realization that it's just a golf course)
```

John's lists confirmed that the meanings of the four items did seem to change as the boys grew up. To the boys, the arroyo, the grinding ball, and the golf course were magical, but when the boys grew up, all three lost their magic and became ordinary. The secret lion, however, seemed more complex than the other three items, and John knew that he would have to develop his ideas further before he could show how the lion's meaning changes and how these changes affect the story as a whole.

Deciding on a Thesis

With his ideas organized into lists that clarified some possible relationships among them, John began to see a central idea for his essay. He expressed this idea in a tentative thesis statement, a sentence that he could use to guide his essay's first draft. (For a full discussion of this stage of the writing process, see "Deciding on a Thesis," p. 24, in Chapter 2.)

Tentative Thesis statement: The meanings of the story's key symbols change as the boys move from childhood to adolescence to adulthood; these changes reveal corresponding changes in the boys' view of the world from idealism to frustration to resignation.

Preparing an Outline

Even though his essay was to be short, John prepared a scratch outline that mapped out an arrangement for his ideas. He decided to discuss the four key symbols one by one, tracing each through the boys' childhood, adolescence, and adulthood. He planned to discuss the lion last because he saw it as the story's most important symbol. Looking back over all his notes, and paying close attention to his tentative thesis statement, John constructed this scratch outline:

Arroyo
    Mississippi
    Rebellion
    Waste dump

Grinding ball
    [Not yet discovered]
    Lost perfection
    "Things get taken away."

Golf course
    Heaven
    Humiliation
    Golf course

Lion
    [Not yet discovered]
    "roaring"; "raging beast"
    Just the lion

Drafting an Essay

Guided by his scratch outline, his tentative thesis statement, and his notes, John wrote the following first draft. Because his notes included many ideas not represented on his scratch outline, and because he discovered new ideas and connections among ideas as he wrote, the draft does not follow the scratch outline exactly.

first draft

Symbols in "The Secret Lion"

"The Secret Lion" is a story that is rich in symbols. It is also a story about change. The meanings of the story's key symbols change as the boys move from childhood to adolescence to adulthood; these changes reveal corresponding changes in the boys' view of the world from idealism to frustration to resignation.

The arroyo, a dry gulch that can fill up with water, is special to the narrator and his friend Sergio when they are boys. Literally, it is a place to play. Symbolically, it is a place to rebel (they're not supposed to be there; they yell forbidden words). It could also symbolize the continuum of discoveries they will make before they are completely grown up. To the young boys, the arroyo symbolizes a retreat from the disappointment of the golf course; it is their second choice. Later, it represented adventure, the uncertainty and unpredictability of adolescence, as illustrated by the fact that they cannot tell just by looking at it from the riverside whether the river was going to be tainted with sewage. When they are children, it is their Mississippi. When they are adolescents, it is a place to hang out and a symbol of adolescent rebellion; as an adult, the narrator looks back at it for what it was: an ordinary river polluted by sewage. The arroyo doesn't change, but the boys' view of it changes as they change.

At first, when they find the grinding ball, it stands for everything that is perfect and fascinating (and therefore forbidden and unattainable) in life. Like a child's life, it is perfect. They knew they couldn't keep it forever, just as they couldn't be children forever, so they buried it. When they tried to look for it again, they couldn't find it. They admit later that they don't look very hard. (People always wish they can find youth again, but they can't.) The ball represents perfection in an imperfect world, childhood innocence in an adult world. They hide it from their mother because they know she won't see it as perfect; she'll make them "getridofit" (55). They hide it because they want to retain the excitement of the undiscovered, but once they've used it and seen it and buried it, it's not new anymore. Even if they'd been able to find it, it would still be lost. To the adult narrator, it's just an ordinary object used in mining.

The golf course, which they wander into at age five, is, for a short period of time, "heaven" (57). It is lush and green and carefully cared for, and it is the opposite of the polluted arroyo. It is also another world, as mysterious as the Land of Oz. With the realization that it is not heaven to the golfers, the boys see what outsiders they really are. They may start "acting 'rich'" (57), but it will be just an act. There are no Coke-holders, no Oz, no heaven. The adolescents see the golf course as a scene of defeat and embarrassment, the setting for the confrontation that sent them back to the arroyo. To the adult, the golf course is just a golf course.

The secret lion is the most complex symbol in the story. In a sense it stands for the innocence of childhood, something we lose when we learn more. The lion symbolizes a great "roaring" disturbance (54). It is a change that unsettles everything for a brief time and then passes, leaving everything changed in irrevocable, indescribable ways. It symbolizes the boys' growing up: they are changed, but still the same people. The "secret lion" is that thing that changes little boys into men. It is secret because no one notices it happening; before it is noticed, the change has occurred, and the little boy is gone forever. It is a lion because it "roars" through the boy like a storm and makes all of the growing-up changes, which can be "the biggest things" (54). In a more specific sense, the lion stands for puberty, reflected in their rage and frustration when they shout profanity. In the beginning of the story, the lion is rage (puberty, adolescence); in the middle, it suggests greatness (passing through adolescence into manhood); at the end, it's just the lion—"It was the lion" (58)—without any symbolic significance.

By the time they bury the ball, they have already learned one lesson, and the force of adulthood is pushing childhood aside. The golf course changes from heaven to shame to golf course; the ball changes from a special, perfect thing to something ordinary; the arroyo changes from grand river to polluted stream. Maybe it is the knowledge that life is not perfect, the knowledge that comes from growing up, that is the secret lion.

First Draft: Commentary

As John reviewed his first draft, he made a number of changes in content, style, and organization. He deleted wordiness and repetition; added more specific references, including quotations, from the story; sharpened transitions and added clearer topic sentences; and reorganized paragraphs to make logical and causal connections more obvious.

Discussions with classmates in a peer review group gave him some additional insights. The students' major criticism was that John's thesis seemed to make a complicated claim he could not support: that the development of all four symbols follows the three stages of the boys' lives. One student pointed out that two of the four symbols (the grinding ball and the secret lion) do not even enter the boys' lives until adolescence and that John's treatment of the story's most prominent symbol — the lion — does not show it to change in any significant way. The group agreed that he should simplify his thesis, focusing on the way the four symbols all reflect the story's theme about the inevitability of change.

John also discussed his draft with his instructor, who helped him with the arrangement of his essay, suggesting that he discuss the golf course first because it is the setting for the event that occurs first in time and because the disillusionment associated with it influences subsequent events. John and his instructor also explored ideas for his introduction and conclusion, deciding to use these paragraphs to stress the common theme that all four symbols convey instead of focusing on the different ways in which each of the four separate symbols changes.

Finally, John's instructor expressed his concern about John's tendency to engage in "symbol hunting." He suggested that rather than focusing on finding equivalents for each of the four items ("the ball represents perfection," "the lion stands for puberty," and so on), John should consider how the use of these symbols opens up the story, how they work together to communicate the story's theme. His instructor pointed out that in looking for neat equivalent values for each symbol, John was oversimplifying very complex, suggestive symbols. And, as John's own draft indicated, the symbols seem to suggest different things at different stages in the boys' lives.

Revising and Editing an Essay

The revisions John decided to make are reflected in his second draft.

second draft

Symbols in "The Secret Lion"

"The Secret Lion" is a story about change. The first paragraph of the story gives a twelve-year-old's view of growing up: everything changes. When the child watches the magician, he is amazed at the "staying-the-same part" (54); adults focus on the tablecloth. As adults, we lose the ability to see the world through innocent eyes. We have the benefit of experience, confident the trick will work as long as the magician pulls the tablecloth in the proper way. The "staying-the-same part" is less important than the technique. In a story full of prominent symbols, the magician's trick does not seem very important, but all the key symbols, like the sleight of hand, are about change. In fact, each of the story's key symbols highlights the theme of the inevitability of change that permeates the lives of the narrator and his friend Sergio.

The golf course is one such symbol. When the boys first see it, it is "heaven" (57). Lush and green and carefully cared for, it is completely different from the dry brown Arizona countryside and the polluted arroyo. In fact, to the boys it is another world, as mysterious as Oz—and just as unreal. Almost at once, the Emerald City becomes black and white again, the "Coke-holders" disappear, and the boys stop "acting 'rich'" (57). Heaven becomes a golf course, and the boys are changed forever.

The arroyo, a dry gulch that can fill up with

water, is another symbol that reinforces the theme of the inevitability of change. It is a special place for the boys—place to rebel, to shout forbidden words, to swim in waters polluted by a sewage treatment plant. Although it represents a retreat from the disillusionment of the golf course, clearly second choice, it is the boys' "personal Mississippi" (54), full of possibilities. Eventually, though, the arroyo too disappoints the boys, and they stop going there. "Nature seemed to keep pushing us around one way or another, teaching us the same thing every place we ended up" (56). The lesson they keep learning is that nothing is permanent.

The grinding ball, round and perfect, seems to suggest permanence and stability. But when the boys find it, they realize at once that they cannot keep it forever, just as they cannot remain children forever. Like a child's life, it is perfect—but temporary. Burying it is their futile attempt to make time stand still, to preserve perfection in an imperfect world, innocence in an adult world, and they have already learned Nature's lesson well enough to know that this is not possible. They do not look very hard for the ball, but even if they'd been able to find it, the perfection and the innocence it represents would still be unattainable.

The secret lion, the most complex symbol, suggests the most profound kind of change: moving from innocence to experience, from childhood to adulthood. When the narrator is twelve, he says, "something happened that we didn't have a name for, but it was there nonetheless like a lion, and roaring, roaring that way the biggest things do. Everything changed" (54). School is different, girls are different, language is different. Innocence was lost. The lion is associated with a great "roaring" disturbance, a change that unsettles everything for a brief time and then passes, leaving everything changed in irrevocable, indescribable ways. The secret lion is the thing that changes little boys into men. It is a lion because it "roars" through the boys like a storm; everything changes.

In an attempt to make things stay the same, to make time stand still, the boys bury the grinding ball "because it was perfect. . . . It was the lion" (58). The grinding ball is "like that place, that whole arroyo" (55): secret and perfect. In other words, the ball and the arroyo and the lion are all tightly connected. By the time the boys bury the ball, they have already learned one sad lesson and are already on their way to adulthood. Heaven is just a golf course; the round, perfect object is only "a cannonball thing used in mining" (55); the arroyo is no Mississippi but only a polluted stream; and childhood does not last forever. "Things get taken away" (58), and this knowledge that things do not last is the secret lion.

Second Draft: Commentary

John felt satisfied with his second draft. His revised thesis statement was clearer and simpler than the one in his first draft; it was also convincingly supported, with clearly worded topic sentences that introduced support paragraphs and connected them to the thesis statement. The second draft was also a good deal less wordy and more focused than the first, notably in the paragraphs about the arroyo and the grinding ball, and the introduction and conclusion were more fully developed. Moreover, he had given up his search for the one true "meaning" of each symbol, focusing instead on the many possibilities of each.

Now, John felt ready to turn his attention to smaller items, such as style, grammar, mechanics, punctuation, and format. For instance, he planned to eliminate contractions, to check all verb tenses carefully, to work quotations into his text more smoothly, to make his thesis statement more precise and his title more interesting, and to revise the language of his introduction and conclusion further. As he made his revisions, he planned to scrutinize this draft carefully, aiming to make his final paper even more concise.

John Frei

Professor Nyysola

English 102

14 April 2002

"The Secret Lion": Everything Changes

Opening paragraph identifies work and author.

Parenthetical documentation identifies source of quotation.

The first paragraph of Alberto Alvaro Ríos's "The Secret Lion" presents a twelve-year-old's view of growing up: everything changes. When the magician pulls a tablecloth out from under a pile of dishes, the child is amazed at the "staying-the-same part" (54); adults focus on the tablecloth. As adults, we have the benefit of experience; we know the trick will work as long as the technique is correct. We gain confidence, but we lose our innocence, and we lose our

Thesis statement

sense of wonder. The price we pay for knowledge is a permanent sense of loss, and this tradeoff is central to "The Secret Lion," a story whose key symbols reinforce its central theme: that change is inevitable and that change is always accompanied by loss.

Topic sentence identifies one key symbol.

The golf course is one symbol that helps to convey this theme. When the boys first see the golf course, it is "heaven" (57). Lush and green and carefully tended, it is the antithesis of the dry, brown Arizona landscape and the polluted arroyo. In fact, to the boys it is another world, as exotic as Oz and ultimately as unreal. Before long, the Emerald City becomes black and white again. They learn that there is no such thing as a "Coke-holder," that their "acting 'rich'" is just an act, and that their heaven is only a golf course (57). As the narrator acknowl-

Frei 2

edges, "Something got taken away from us that moment. Heaven" (57).

The arroyo, a dry gulch that can fill up with water, is another symbol that reflects the idea of the inevitability of change and of the loss that accompanies change. It is a special, Edenlike place for the boys—a place where they can rebel by shouting forbidden words and by swimming in forbidden waters. Although it is a retreat from the disillusionment of the golf course, it is still their "personal Mississippi" (54), full of possibilities. Eventually, though, the arroyo too disappoints the boys, and they stop going there. As the narrator says, "Nature seemed to keep pushing us around one way or another, teaching us the same thing every place we ended up" (56). The lesson they keep learning is that nothing is permanent.

> Topic sentence identifies another key symbol.

The grinding ball, round and perfect, suggests permanence and stability. But when the boys find it, they realize at once that they cannot keep it forever, just as they cannot remain balanced forever between childhood and adulthood. Like a child's life, the ball is perfect—but temporary. Burying it is their desperate attempt to stop time, to preserve perfection in an imperfect world, innocence in an adult world. But the boys are already twelve years old, and they have learned nature's lesson well enough to know that this action will not work. Even if they had been able to find the ball, the perfection

> Topic sentence identifies another key symbol.

Frei 3

and the innocence it suggests to them would still be
unattainable. Perhaps that is why they do not try
very hard to find it.

Topic sentence identifies final (and most important) symbol.

    Like the story's other symbols, the secret lion
itself suggests the most profound kind of change: the
movement from innocence to experience, from childhood
to adulthood, from expectation to disappointment to
resignation. The narrator explains that when he was
twelve, "something happened that we didn't have a
name for, but it was there nonetheless like a lion,
and roaring, roaring that way the biggest things do.
Everything changed" (54). School was different, girls
were different, language was different. Despite its
loud roar, the lion remained paradoxically "secret,"
unnoticed until it passed. Like adolescence, the
secret lion is a roaring disturbance that unsettles
everything for a brief time and then passes, leaving
everything changed.

Conclusion

    In an attempt to make things stay the same, to
make time stand still, the boys bury the grinding
ball "because it was perfect. . . . It was the
lion" (58). The grinding ball is "like that place,
that whole arroyo" (55): secret and perfect. The ball
and the arroyo and the lion are all perfect, but all,
ironically, are temporary. The first paragraph of "The
Secret Lion" tells us "Everything changed" (54); by
the last paragraph we learn what this change means:
"Things get taken away" (58). In other words, change
implies loss. Heaven turns out to be just a golf

course; the round, perfect object only "a cannonball
thing used in mining" (55); the arroyo just a
polluted stream; and childhood just a phase. "Things
get taken away," and this knowledge that things do
not last is the lion, secret yet roaring.

Final Draft: Commentary

As John revised and edited his second draft, he made many changes in word choice and sentence structure. He also changed his title, edited to eliminate errors in mechanics and punctuation, and ran a spell check. In this final draft, he made his thesis statement even more precise than it was in the previous draft, to communicate the idea of the relationship between change and loss that is central to the essay. In addition, he worked all quoted material smoothly into his discussion, taking care to use quotations only when the author's words added something vital to the paper. (Because students in John's class were permitted to write papers only about works in this anthology, his instructor did not require a Works Cited page.) Finally, John checked all his references to page numbers in the story, so readers would be able to return to his source if necessary to check the accuracy and appropriateness of his quotations.

CHAPTER 5

PLOT

It's a truism that there are only two basic plots in fiction: one, somebody takes a trip; two, a stranger comes to town. —**Lee Smith,** *New York Times Book Review*

The beginning of an action always presents us with a situation in which there is some element of instability, some conflict; in the middle of an action there is a period of readjustment of forces in the process of seeking a new kind of stability; in the end of an action, some point of stability is reached, the forces that have been brought into play have been resolved. —**Cleanth Brooks and Robert Penn Warren,** *Understanding Fiction*

The simplest way to tell a story, equally favoured by tribal bards and parents at bedtime, is to begin at the beginning, and go on until you reach the end, or your audience falls asleep. But even in antiquity, storytellers perceived the interesting effects that could be obtained by deviating from chronological order. [. . .] A shift of narrative focus back in time may change our interpretation of something which happened much later in the chronology of the story, but which we have already experienced as readers of the text. This is a familiar device of cinema, the flashback. —**David Lodge,** *The Art of Fiction*

So much for endings. Beginnings are always more fun. True connoisseurs, however, are known to favor the stretch in between, since it's the hardest to do anything with.

That's about all that can be said for plots, which anyway are just one thing after another, a what and a what and a what.

Now try How and Why. —**Margaret Atwood,** *"Happy Endings"*

I like stories that end rather than merely stop, stories that somehow assure me that their stopping point is the best moment for all progress to cease.
—**Richard Ford,** *New York Times Book Review*

Alfred Hitchcock's 1951 film *Strangers on a Train,* based on a suspense novel by Patricia Highsmith, offers an intriguing premise: two men, strangers, each can murder someone the other wishes dead; because they have no apparent connection to their victims, both can escape suspicion. Many people would describe this ingenious scheme as the film's "plot," but in fact it is simply the gimmick around which the complex plot revolves. Certainly a clever twist can be an important ingredient of a story's plot, but plot is more than "what happens"; it is how what happens is presented. **Plot** is the way in which a story's events are arranged; it is shaped by causal connections — historical, social, and personal — by the interaction between characters, and by the juxtaposition of events. In *Strangers on a Train,* as in many well-developed works of fiction, the plot that unfolds is complex: one character directs the events and determines their order while the other character is drawn into the action against his will. The same elements that enrich the plot of the film — unexpected events, conflict, suspense, flashbacks, foreshadowing — can also enrich the plot of a work of short fiction.

CONFLICT

Readers' interest and involvement are heightened by a story's **conflict,** the struggle between opposing forces that emerges as the action develops. This conflict is a clash between the **protagonist,** a story's principal character, and an **antagonist,** someone or something presented in opposition to the protagonist. Sometimes the antagonist is a villain; more often, he or she simply represents a conflicting point of view or advocates a course of action different from the one the protagonist follows. Sometimes the antagonist is not a character at all but a situation (for instance, war or poverty) or an event (a natural disaster, such as a flood or a storm, for example) that challenges the protagonist. In other stories, the protagonist may struggle against a supernatural force, or the conflict may occur within a character's mind. It may, for example, be a struggle between two moral choices, such as whether to stay at home and care for an aging parent or to leave and make a new life.

STAGES OF PLOT

A work's plot explores one or more conflicts, moving from *exposition* through a series of *complications* to a *climax* and, finally, to a *resolution.*

In a story's **exposition,** the writer presents the basic information readers need to understand the events that follow. Typically, the exposition sets the story in motion: it establishes the scene, introduces the major characters, and perhaps suggests the major events or conflicts to come. Sometimes a single sentence can present exposition clearly and economically, giving readers information vital to their understanding of the plot that will unfold. For example, the opening sentence of Amy Tan's "Two Kinds" (p. 527 mother believed you could be anything you wanted to be in America"—establishes an important fact about a central character. Similarly, the opening sentence of Shirley Jackson's "The Lottery" (p. 303)—"The morning of June 27th was clear and sunny, with the fresh warmth of a full-summer day; the flowers were blossoming profusely and the grass was richly green"—introduces the picture-perfect setting that is essential to the story's irony. At other times, as in John Updike's "A&P" (p. 115), a more fully developed exposition section establishes the story's setting, introduces the main characters, and suggests possible conflicts. In some experimental stories, a distinct exposition component may be absent, as it is in Luisa Valenzuela's

"All about Suicide" (p. 5) and Lorrie Moore's "How to Talk to Your Mother (Notes)" (p. 100).

As the plot progresses, the story's conflict unfolds through a series of complications that eventually lead readers to the story's climax. The action may include several crises. A **crisis** is a peak in the story's action, a moment of considerable tension or importance. The **climax** is the point of greatest tension or importance, the scene that presents a story's decisive action or event.

The final stage of plot, the **resolution,** or **denouement** (French for "untying of the knot"), draws the action to a close and accounts for all remaining loose ends. Sometimes this resolution is achieved with the help of a **deus ex machina** (Latin for "a god from a machine"), an intervention of some force or agent previously extraneous to the story — for example, the appearance of a long-lost relative or a fortuitous inheritance, the discovery of a character's true identity, or a last-minute rescue by a character not previously introduced. Usually, however, the resolution is more plausible: all the events lead logically and convincingly (though not necessarily predictably) to the resolution. Sometimes the ending of a story is indefinite — that is, readers are not quite sure what the protagonist will do or what will happen next. This kind of resolution, although it may leave some readers feeling cheated, has its advantages: it mirrors the complexity of life, where closure rarely occurs, and it can draw readers into the action as they try to understand the significance of the story's ending or to decide how conflicts should have been resolved.

ORDER AND SEQUENCE

A writer may present a story's events in strict chronological order, presenting each event in the sequence in which it actually takes place. More often, however, especially in relatively modern fiction, writers do not present events chronologically. Instead, they present incidents out of expected order, or in no apparent order. For example, a writer may choose to begin **in medias res** (Latin for "in the midst of things"), starting with a key event and later going back in time to explain events that preceded it, as Tillie Olsen does in "I Stand Here Ironing" (p. 187). Or, a writer can decide to begin a work of fiction at the end and then move back to reconstruct events that led up to the final outcome, as William Faulkner does in "A Rose for Emily" (p. 91). Many sequences are possible as the writer manipulates events to create interest, suspense, confusion, wonder, or some other effect.

Writers who wish to depart from strict chronological order use *flashbacks* and *foreshadowing*. A **flashback** moves out of sequence to examine an event or situation that occurred before the time in which the story's action takes place. A character can remember an earlier event, or a story's narrator can re-create an earlier situation. For example, in Alberto Alvaro Ríos's "The Secret Lion" (p. 54), the adult narrator looks back at events that occurred when he was twelve years old, and then moves farther back in time to consider related events that occurred when he was five. In Edgar Allan Poe's "The Cask of Amontillado" (p. 217), the entire story is told as a flashback. Flashbacks are valuable because they can substitute for or supplement formal exposition by presenting background vital to readers' understanding of a story's events. One disadvantage of flashbacks is that, because they interrupt the natural flow of events, they may be intrusive or distracting. Such distractions, however, can be an advantage if the writer wishes to reveal events gradually and subtly or to obscure causal links.

Foreshadowing is the introduction early in a story of situations, events, characters, or objects that hint at things to come. A chance remark, a natural occurrence, or a seemingly trivial event is eventually revealed to have great significance. For example, a dark cloud passing across the sky can foreshadow future problems. In this way, foreshadowing allows a writer to hint provocatively at what is to come, so that readers only gradually become aware of a particular detail's role in a story. Thus, foreshadowing helps readers sense what will occur and grow increasingly involved as they see the likelihood (or even the inevitability) of a particular outcome.

In addition to employing conventional techniques like flashbacks and foreshadowing, writers may experiment with sequence by substantially tampering with — or even dispensing with — chronological order. (An example is the scrambled chronology of "A Rose for Emily.") In such instances, the experimental form enhances interest and encourages readers to become involved with the story as they work to untangle or reorder the events and determine their logical and causal connections.

A FINAL NOTE

In popular fiction, plot is likely to dominate the story, as it does, for example, in mystery or adventure stories, which tend to lack fully developed characters, complex themes, and elaborately described settings. In richer, more complicated works of fiction, however, plot is often more complex and less obvious.

CHECKLIST   **WRITING ABOUT PLOT**

✓ What happens in the story?

✓ Where does the story's formal exposition section end? What do readers learn about characters in this section? What do readers learn about setting? What possible conflicts are suggested here?

✓ What is the story's central conflict? What other conflicts are presented? Who is the protagonist? Who (or what) serves as the antagonist?

✓ Identify the story's crisis or crises.

✓ Identify the story's climax.

✓ How is the story's central conflict resolved? Is this resolution plausible? Satisfying?

✓ Which portion of the story constitutes the resolution? Do any problems remain unresolved? Does any uncertainty remain? If so, does this uncertainty strengthen or weaken the story? Would another ending be more effective?

✓ How are the story's events arranged? Are they presented in chronological order? What events are presented out of logical sequence? Does the story use foreshadowing? Flashbacks? Are the causal connections between events clear? Logical? If not, can you explain why?

KATE CHOPIN (1851–1904) must, in a sense, be considered a contemporary writer. Her honest, sexually frank stories (many of them out of print for more than half a century) were rediscovered in the 1960s and 1970s, influencing a new generation of writers. Though she was a popular contributor of stories and sketches to the magazines of her day, Chopin scandalized many critics with her outspoken novel *The Awakening* (1899), in which a woman seeks sexual and emotional fulfillment with a man who is not her husband. The book was removed from the shelves of the public library in St. Louis, where Chopin was born.

Chopin was born Katherine O'Flaherty, the daughter of a wealthy Irish-born merchant and his aristocratic Creole wife. Educated at convent schools, she was married at nineteen to Oscar Chopin, a Louisiana cotton broker, who took her to live first in New Orleans and later on a plantation at Cloutierville, near Natchitoches, in central Louisiana, where it is said she offended members of polite society by drinking beer and crossing her legs — at the knees. Chopin's representations of the Cane River region and its people in two volumes of short stories — *Bayou Folk* (1894) and *A Night in Arcadie* (1897) — are the foundation of her reputation as a local colorist. Resemblances have been noted between these stories and certain works of Guy de Maupassant that Chopin had translated from French to English.

A busy wife and mother, Chopin seems to have begun writing only after she returned to St. Louis following her husband's sudden death in 1883. "The Story of an Hour" depicts a brief event in a woman's life, but in this single hour, Chopin reveals both a lifetime's emotional torment and the momentary joy of freedom.

Cultural Context: Louisiana, where Chopin lived during her marriage, has a different legal system from the rest of the country. Louisiana is the only civil-law state in the United States; the legal systems of all other states are based on common law. The civil code of Louisiana is closely connected with the Napoleonic Code, the French civil code enacted in France in 1804. Under the Napoleonic Code, married women had no control over their property, and men were the only ones allowed to request a divorce. (These laws were in force until 1980.)

The Story of an Hour (1894)

Knowing that Mrs. Mallard was afflicted with a heart trouble, great care was taken to break to her as gently as possible the news of her husband's death.

It was her sister Josephine who told her, in broken sentences, veiled hints that revealed in half concealing. Her husband's friend Richards was there, too, near her. It was he who had been in the newspaper office when intelligence of the railroad disaster was received, with Brently Mallard's name leading the list of "killed." He had only taken the time to assure himself of its truth by a second telegram, and had hastened to forestall any less careful, less tender friend in bearing the sad message.

She did not hear the story as many women have heard the same, with a paralyzed inability to accept its significance. She wept at once, with sudden, wild abandonment, in her sister's arms. When the storm of grief had spent itself she went away to her room alone. She would have no one follow her.

There stood, facing the open window, a comfortable, roomy armchair. Into this she sank, pressed down by a physical exhaustion that haunted her body and seemed to reach into her soul.

5   She could see in the open square before her house the tops of trees that were all aquiver with the new spring life. The delicious breath of rain was in the air. In the street below a peddler was crying his wares. The notes of a distant song which some one was singing reached her faintly, and countless sparrows were twittering in the eaves.

There were patches of blue sky showing here and there through the clouds that had met and piled one above the other in the west facing her window.

She sat with her head thrown back upon the cushion of the chair, quite motionless, except when a sob came up into her throat and shook her, as a child who has cried itself to sleep continues to sob in its dreams.

She was young, with a fair, calm face, whose lines bespoke repression and even a certain strength. But now there was a dull stare in her eyes, whose gaze was fixed away off yonder on one of those patches of blue sky. It was not a glance of reflection, but rather indicated a suspension of intelligent thought.

There was something coming to her and she was waiting for it, fearfully. What was it? She did not know; it was too subtle and elusive to name. But she felt it, creeping out of the sky, reaching toward her through the sounds, the scents, the color that filled the air.

10   Now her bosom rose and fell tumultuously. She was beginning to recognize this thing that was approaching to possess her, and she was striving to beat it back with her will — as powerless as her two white slender hands would have been.

When she abandoned herself a little whispered word escaped her slightly parted lips. She said it over and over under her breath: "Free, free, free!" The vacant stare and the look of terror that had followed it went from her eyes. They stayed keen and bright. Her pulses beat fast, and the coursing blood warmed and relaxed every inch of her body.

She did not stop to ask if it were not a monstrous joy that held her. A clear and exalted perception enabled her to dismiss the suggestion as trivial.

She knew that she would weep again when she saw the kind, tender hands folded in death; the face that had never looked save with love upon her, fixed and gray and dead. But she saw beyond that bitter moment a long procession of years to come that would belong to her absolutely. And she opened and spread her arms out to them in welcome.

There would be no one to live for during those coming years; she would live for herself. There would be no powerful will bending her in that blind persistence with which men and women believe they have a right to impose a private will upon a fellow creature. A kind intention or a cruel intention made the act seem no less a crime as she looked upon it in that brief moment of illumination.

And yet she had loved him — sometimes. Often she had not. What did it   15 matter! What could love, the unsolved mystery, count for in face of this posses-sion of self-assertion which she suddenly recognized as the strongest impulse of her being.

"Free! Body and soul free!" she kept whispering.

Josephine was kneeling before the closed door with her lips to the key-hole, imploring for admission. "Louise, open the door! I beg; open the door — you will make yourself ill. What are you doing, Louise? For heaven's sake open the door."

"Go away. I am not making myself ill." No; she was drinking in a very elixir of life through that open window.

Her fancy was running riot along those days ahead of her. Spring days, and summer days, and all sorts of days that would be her own. She breathed a quick prayer that life might be long. It was only yesterday she had thought with a shud-der that life might be long.

She arose at length and opened the door to her sister's importunities. There as   20 a feverish triumph in her eyes, and she carried herself unwittingly like a goddess of Victory. She clasped her sister's waist, and together they descended the stairs. Richards stood waiting for them at the bottom.

Some one was opening the front door with a latchkey. It was Brently Mallard who entered, a little travel-stained, composedly carrying his grip-sack and um-brella. He had been far from the scene of the accident, and did not even know there had been one. He stood amazed at Josephine's piercing cry; at Richards' quick motion to screen him from the view of his wife.

But Richards was too late.

When the doctors came they said she had died of heart disease — of joy that kills.

Reading and Reacting

1. The story's basic exposition is presented in its first two paragraphs. What additional information about character or setting would you like to know? Why do you suppose the writer does not supply this information?

2. "The Story of an Hour" is a very economical story, with little action or dia-logue. Is this a strength or a weakness? Explain.

3. When "The Story of an Hour" was first published in *Vogue* magazine in 1894, the magazine's editors titled it "The Dream of an Hour." A film ver-sion, echoing the last words of the story, is called *The Joy That Kills*. Which

of the three titles do you believe most accurately represents what happens
in the story? Why?

4. Did Brently Mallard abuse his wife? Did he love her? Did she love him? Exactly why was she so relieved to be rid of him? Can you answer any of these
   questions with certainty?

5. What is the nature of the conflict in this story? Who, or what, do you see as
   Mrs. Mallard's antagonist?

6. What emotions does Mrs. Mallard experience during the hour she spends
   alone in her room? What events do you imagine take place during this same
   period outside her room? Outside her house?

7. Do you find the story's ending satisfying? Believable? Contrived?

8. Was the story's ending unexpected, or were you prepared for it? What elements in the story foreshadow this ending?

9. JOURNAL ENTRY Rewrite the story's ending, substituting a few paragraphs
   of your own for the last three paragraphs.

10. CRITICAL PERSPECTIVE Closely following the publication of *Bayou Folk*,
    Chopin's 1894 short story collection, the *Atlantic Monthly* printed a review
    suggesting that when Chopin "deals with what is familiar to her . . . [s]he
    deals with it as an artist, and the entire ease with which she uses her mate-
    rial is born not less of an instinct for story-telling than of familiarity with
    the stuff out of which she weaves her stories." The reviewer continues to
    praise the the stories.

    > All of the stories are very simple in structure, but the simplicity is that which be-
    > longs to clearness of perception, not to meagreness of imagination. Now and
    > then she strikes a passionate note, and the naturalness and ease with which she
    > does it impress one as characteristic of power awaiting opportunity.

    Although "The Story of an Hour" was not included in the collection, it was
    published the same year. Do you think that the critic's comments about the
    stories in *Bayou Folk* also apply to "The Story of an Hour"? For example, is
    the story's simplicity due to a "clearness of perception"? Are there "passion-
    ate note[s]" in the story that seem to be "characteristic of power awaiting
    opportunity"?

Related Works: "The Yellow Wallpaper" (p. 161), "The Disappearance" (p. 458),
"Women" (p. 763), *A Doll House* (p. 995)

STEPHEN DOBYNS (1941–   ) is a prolific writer in a variety of genres —
poetry, novels, short stories, essays — whose work has been translated into ten
languages. Born in Orange, New Jersey, Dobyns was educated at Wayne State
University; he went on to obtain his MFA from the University of Iowa. Of his ten
books of poetry and twenty novels, the most recent are *Pallbearers Envying the
One Who Rides* and *Boy in the Water* (both 1999). His collection of short stories,
Eating Naked, was published in 2000; his essays appear in *Best Words, Best
Order* (1996). His most recent book is a collection of prose poems, aphorisms, and
definitions entitled *Porcupine Kisses* (2002). The recipient of numerous literary

awards, Dobyns has taught at a variety of places, including the University of Iowa, Boston University, Sarah Lawrence College, and Emerson College.

Cultural Context: On Black Tuesday — October 29, 1929 — the U.S. stock market crashed, triggering the Great Depression, the worst economic collapse in modern history. It is during this period that "Kansas" takes place. With banks failing and businesses closing, more than fifteen million Americans (one-quarter of the workforce) were eventually unemployed. The economic disaster was soon paralleled by an agricultural one: attracted by the promise of rich, plentiful soil, thousands of farm families had moved from the North and East to Kansas as well as to Oklahoma, Texas, New Mexico, and Colorado. Farmers in this region plowed millions of acres of grassland; then, in the summer of 1931, the rains stopped. A drought that lasted eight years caused this area to be called the "Dust Bowl."

Kansas   (1999)

The boy hitchhiking on the back-country Kansas road was nineteen years old. He had been dropped there by a farmer in a Model T Ford who had turned off to the north. Then he waited for three hours. It was July and there were no clouds. The wheat fields were flat and went straight to the horizon. The boy had two plums and he ate them. A blue Plymouth coupe° went by with a man and a woman. They were laughing. The woman had blond hair and it was all loose and blew from the window. They didn't even see the boy. The strands of straw-colored hair seemed to be waving to him. Half an hour later a farmer stopped in a Ford pickup covered with a layer of dust. The boy clambered into the front seat. The farmer took off again without glancing at him. A forty-five revolver lay next to the farmer's buttocks on the seat. Seeing it, the boy felt something electric go off inside of him. The revolver was old and there were rust spots on the barrel. Black electrician's tape was wrapped around the handle.

"You seen a woman and a man go by here in a Plymouth coupe?" asked the farmer. He pronounced it "koo-pay."

The boy said he had.

"How long ago?"

"About thirty minutes."

The farmer had light blue eyes and there was stubble on his chin. Perhaps he   5 was forty, but to the boy he looked old. His skin was leather-colored from the sun. The farmer pressed his foot to the floor and the pickup roared. It was a dirt road and the boy had to hold his hands against the dashboard to keep from being bounced around. It was hot and both windows were open. There was grit in the boy's eyes and on his tongue. He kept glancing sideways at the revolver.

"They friends of yours?" asked the boy.

---

coupe: A two-door car, often one that seats only two people.

The farmer didn't look at him. "That's my wife," he said. "I'm going to put a bullet in her head." He put a hand to the revolver to make sure it was still there. "The man too," he added.

The boy didn't say anything. He was hitchhiking back to summer school from Oklahoma. He was the middle of three boys and the only one who had left home. He had already spent a year at the University of Oklahoma and was spending the summer at Lawrence. And there were other places, farther places. The boy played the piano. He intended to go to those farther places.

"What did they do?" the boy asked at last.

"You just guess," said the farmer.

The pickup was going about fifty miles per hour. The boy was afraid of seeing the dust cloud from the Plymouth up ahead, but there was only straight road. Then he was afraid that the Plymouth might have pulled off someplace. He touched his tongue to his upper lip but it was just one dry thing against another. Getting into the pickup, the boy had had a clear idea of the direction of his life. He meant to go to New York City at the end of summer. He meant to play the piano in Carnegie Hall.° The farmer and his forty-five seemed to stand between him and that future. They formed a wall that the boy was afraid to climb over.

"Do you have to kill them?" the boy asked. He didn't want to talk but he felt unable to remain silent.

The farmer had a red boil on the side of his neck and he kept touching it with two fingers. "When you have something wicked, what do you do?" asked the farmer.

The boy wanted to say he didn't know or he wanted to say he would call the police, but the farmer would have no patience with those answers. And the boy also wanted to say he would forgive the wickedness, but he was afraid of that answer as well. He was afraid of making the farmer angry and so he only shrugged.

"You stomp it out," said the farmer. "That's what you do — you stomp it out."

The boy stared straight ahead, searching for the dust cloud and hoping not to see it. The hot air seemed to bend in front of them. The boy was so frightened of seeing the dust cloud that he was sure he saw it. A little puff of gray getting closer. The pickup went straight down the middle of the road. There was no other traffic. Even if there had been other cars, the boy felt certain that the farmer wouldn't have moved out of the way. The wheat on either side of the road was coated with layers of dust, making it a reddish color, the color of dried blood.

"What about the police?" asked the boy.

"It's my wife," said the farmer. "It's my problem."

The boy never did see the dust cloud. They reached Lawrence and the boy got out as soon as he could. His shirt was stuck to his back and he kept rubbing his palms on his dungarees. He thanked the farmer but the man didn't look at him, he just kept staring straight ahead.

Carnegie Hall: A large, famous performance hall in New York City.

"Don't tell the police," said the farmer. His hand rested lightly on the forty-five beside him on the seat.

"No," said the boy. "I promise." He slammed shut the dusty door of the pickup.

The boy didn't tell the police. For several days he didn't tell anyone at all. He looked at the newspapers twice a day for news of a killing, but he didn't find anything. More than the farmer's gun, he had been frightened by the strength of the farmer's resolve. It had been like a chunk of stone and compared to it the boy had felt as soft as a piece of white bread. The boy never knew what happened. Perhaps nothing had happened.

The summer wound to its conclusion. The boy went to New York. He never did play in Carnegie Hall. His piano playing never got good enough. The war came and went. He wasn't a boy any longer. He was a married man with two sons. The family moved to Michigan. The man was a teacher, then a minister. His own parents died. He told his sons the story about the farmer in the pickup. "What do you think happened?" they asked. Nobody knew. Perhaps the farmer caught up with them; perhaps he didn't. The man's sons went off to college and began their own lives. The man and his wife moved to New Hampshire. They grew old. Sixty years went by between that summer in Kansas and the present. The man entered his last illness. He stayed at home but he couldn't get out of bed. His wife gave him shots of morphine. He began to have dreams even when he was awake. The visiting nurse was always chipper. "Feeling better today?" she would ask. He tried to be polite, but he had no illusions. He went from one shot a day to two, and then three. The doctor said, "Give him as many as he needs." His wife started to ask about the danger of addiction, then she said nothing.

The man hardly knew when he was asleep or awake. He hardly knew if one day had passed or many. He had oxygen. He didn't eat. The space between his eyes and the bedroom wall was always occupied with people of his invention, people of his past. He would lift his hand to wave them away, only to find his hand still lying motionless on the counterpane. Even music distracted him now. Always he was listening for something in the distance. 25

The boy was standing by the side of a dirt road. A Ford pickup stopped beside him and he got in. The farmer lifted a forty-five revolver. "I'm going to shoot my wife in the head."

"No," said the boy, "don't do it!"

The farmer drove fast. He had a red boil on the side of his neck and he kept touching it with two fingers. They found the Plymouth coupe pulled off into a hollow. There were shade trees and a brook. The farmer jammed down the brakes and the pickup slid sideways across the dirt. The man and woman were in the front seat of the Plymouth. Their clothes were half off. They jumped out of the car. The woman had big red breasts. The farmer jumped out with his forty-five. "No!" shouted the boy. The farmer shot the man in the head. His whole head exploded and he fell down in the dust. His head was just a broken thing on the ground. The woman covered her face and tried to cover her breasts as well. The farmer shot her as well. Bits of dust floated on the surface of her blood. "One last for me," said the farmer. He put the barrel of the gun in his mouth. "No, no!" cried the boy.

The boy was standing by the side of a dirt road. A Ford pickup stopped beside him and he got in. "I'm going to shoot my wife," said the farmer. He had a big revolver on the seat beside him.

"You can't," said the boy.

They talked all the way to Lawrence. The farmer was crying. "I've always been good to her," he said. He had a red boil on the side of his neck and he kept touching it.

"Give the gun to the police," said the boy.

"I'm afraid," said the farmer.

"You needn't be," said the boy. "The police won't hurt you."

They drove to the police station. The boy told the desk sergeant what had happened. The sergeant shook his head. He took the revolver away from the farmer. "We'll get her back, sir," he said. "Wife stealing's not permitted around here."

"I could have got in real trouble," said the farmer.

The boy was standing by the side of a dirt road. A pickup stopped beside him and he got in. The farmer said, "I'm going to kill my wife."

The boy was too frightened to say anything. He kept looking at the forty-five revolver. He was sure that he would be shot himself. He regretted not staying in Oklahoma, where he had friends and family. He couldn't imagine why he had moved away. The farmer drove straight to Lawrence. The boy was bounced all over the cab of the pickup but he didn't say anything. He was afraid that something would happen to his hands and he wouldn't be able to play the piano. It seemed to him that playing the piano was the only important thing in the entire world. The farmer had a red boil on the side of his neck and he kept touching it.

When they got to Lawrence, the boy jumped out of the pickup and ran. He saw a policeman and told him what had happened. An hour later he was getting a hamburger at a White Tower restaurant. He heard shooting. He ran out and saw the farmer's dusty pickup. There were police cars with their lights flashing. The boy pushed through the crowd. The farmer was hanging half out of the door of his pickup truck. There was blood all over the front of his workshirt. The forty-five revolver lay on the pavement. The policemen were clapping each other on the back. They had big grins. The boy began cracking his knuckles. They made snapping noises.

The boy was standing by the side of a dirt road. A pickup stopped beside him and he got in. The farmer pointed a forty-five revolver at his head. "Get in here," he said. They drove toward Lawrence.

"I'm going to shoot my wife for wickedness," said the farmer.

"No," said the boy, "you must forgive her."

"I'm going to kill her," said the farmer, "and her fancy man besides."

The boy said, "You can't take the law into your own hands."

The farmer raised his forty-five revolver. "They're as good as dead." He had a red boil on the side of his neck.

The boy was a college student. It was the Depression. He wanted to go to New   45
York and become a classical pianist. He had already been accepted by Juilliard.°
"Justice does not belong to you," said the boy.

"Wickedness must be punished," said the farmer.

They argued all the way to Lawrence. The boy stayed with the farmer. He
could have jumped out of the pickup, but he didn't. The boy kept trying to convince him that he was wrong. The farmer drove to the train station.

The farmer's wife was in the waiting room with the man who had been driving the Plymouth coupe. She was very pretty, with blond hair and milky pink
skin. She screamed when she saw the farmer. Her companion put his arms around
her to protect her.

The boy hurried to stand between the woman and her husband. "Think of
what you are doing," he said. "Think how you are throwing your life away." The
first bullet struck him in the shoulder and whipped him around. He could see the
woman open her mouth in a startled *Oh* of surprise. The second bullet caught him
in the small of his back.

The man's family was with him in New Hampshire when he died: his wife and his   50
two sons, neither of them young anymore. It was early evening in October at the
very height of color. Even after sundown the maple trees seemed bright. The older
son watched his father breathing. He kept twisting and trying to kick his feet. His
face was very thin, his whole body was just a ridge under the middle of the sheet.
He didn't talk anymore. He didn't want anyone to touch him. He seemed to be
focusing his attention. He took a breath and they waited. He exhaled slowly.
They continued to wait. He didn't breathe again. They waited several minutes.
Then his wife removed the oxygen tubes from his nose, doing it quickly, as if
afraid of doing something wrong.

The older son went back into the bedroom with the two men from the funeral
home. They had a collapsible stretcher which they put next to the bed. They unrolled a dark blue body bag. They shifted the dead man onto the stretcher and
wrestled him into the body bag, one at his feet, one at his head. The son stood in
the doorway. The men from the funeral home muttered directions to each other.
They were breathing heavily and their hair was mussed. At last they got him into
the body bag. The son watched closely as the zipper was drawn up and across his
father's face. It was a large silver zipper and the son watched it being pulled across
his father's forehead. All the days after that he kept seeing its glittering progress,
a picture repeating itself in his mind.

Reading and Reacting

1. Paragraph 1 presents the story's exposition. List the specific pieces of information this paragraph presents. How will each detail be important later in

---

Juilliard: A respected school for artists and performers in New York City.

the story? Are any details unnecessary? What important details are *not* introduced in paragraph 1?

2. Summarize the story's plot in three sentences.

3. In paragraph 12, the narrator says, "Getting into the pickup, the boy had had a clear idea of the direction of his life. . . . The farmer and his forty-five seemed to stand between him and that future." What direction do you think the boy imagined his life would take? What direction did it actually take? Were "the farmer and his forty-five" in any way responsible for this change of direction? Explain.

4. How would the story be different without the presence of the revolver lying on the seat?

5. What specific information are readers told in the story's first twenty-five paragraphs about the boy? The farmer? The couple in the blue Plymouth? Why is this information important to the story's plot? What additional information might you want to know? Why?

6. The first twenty-five paragraphs present the story's basic plot; then, this section of the story is followed by three alternate versions of the boy's experience, each beginning with the sentence "The boy was standing by the side of a dirt road." What is the point of these alternate versions? What is the author trying to accomplish?

7. How are the three alternate versions of events similar to and different from the boy's story as it is first presented? Which version is most satisfying? Most logical? Most believable? Explain.

8. At the end of paragraph 25, as the boy (now a man) is dying, he is "listening for something in the distance." What do you suppose he might be listening for? Explain.

9. The red boil on the side of the farmer's neck is mentioned several times. What other physical details are repeated in the story's descriptions of characters and setting? What is the effect of these repetitions? Are any important physical details omitted?

10. What does the last sentence add to the story?

11. JOURNAL ENTRY In paragraph 23, the narrator says, "The boy never knew what happened. Perhaps nothing had happened." What does he mean by this? What do you think really happened to the boy that day?

12. CRITICAL PERSPECTIVE In reviewing *Eating Naked*, the collection in which "Kansas" appeared, Roger Boylan says that Dobyns "almost gleefully imposes life's unpredictability on his characters." Boylan then goes on to give examples of the ways in which Dobyns "imposes life's unpredictability":

> Cancer ends a life in one story; a car crash does so in another. A kidnapping goes ludicrously wrong. People betray each other. Lust overrides good sense. Absurdity rules. Marriages fall apart with depressing regularity — and if yours doesn't seem to be on the rocks, well, can you be sure you know what your better half's up to when you're away?

Do you think "Kansas" fits the pattern Boylan has identified? Is it a story in which "absurdity rules"?

Related Works: "Sleepy Time Gal" (p. 46), "Do not go gentle into that good night" (p. 559), "The Road Not Taken" (p. 880)

WILLIAM FAULKNER (1897–1962), winner of the 1949 Nobel Prize in Literature and the 1955 and 1963 Pulitzer Prizes for fiction, was an unabashedly Southern writer whose work continues to transcend the regional label. His nineteen novels, notably *The Sound and the Fury* (1929), *As I Lay Dying* (1930), *Light in August* (1932), *Absalom, Absalom!* (1936), and *The Reivers* (1962), explore a wide range of human experience — from high comedy to tragedy — as seen in the life of one community, Faulkner's fictional Yoknapatawpha County (modeled on the area around Faulkner's own hometown of Oxford, Mississippi). Faulkner's Yoknapatawpha stories — a fascinating blend of complex Latinate prose and primitive Southern dialect — paint an extraordinary portrait of a community bound together by ties of blood, by a shared belief in moral "verities," and by an old grief (the Civil War). Faulkner's grandfather raised "Billy" on Civil War tales and local legends, including many about the "Old Colonel," the writer's great-grandfather, who was a colorful Confederate officer. But Faulkner was no Margaret Mitchell. Like Mitchell's *Gone with the Wind*, his stories elegize the agrarian virtues of the Old South, but they look unflinchingly at that world's tragic flaw: the "peculiar institution" of slavery.

Local legends and gossip frequently served as the spark for Faulkner's stories. As John B. Cullen, writing in *Old Times in Faulkner Country,* notes, "A Rose for Emily," Faulkner's first nationally published short story, was based on the tale of Oxford's aristocratic "Miss Mary" Neilson, who married Captain Jack Hume, the charming Yankee foreman of a street-paving crew, over her family's shocked protests. According to Cullen, one of Faulkner's neighbors said he created his story "out of fears and rumors" — the dire predictions of what *might* happen if Mary Neilson married her Yankee.

Cultural Context: The Old South has been idealized as a land of prosperous plantations, large white houses, cultured people, and a stable economy based on cotton. Like any utopia, however, this picture is a distortion. It hides many of the unpleasant, even appalling, realities of plantation life — one of which was slavery. Still, long after the Civil War (1861–1865), with much of the South destroyed and beset by economic hardship, the myth persisted among many white Southerners (like Emily and her neighbors) as a kind of nostalgia for a golden age.

A Rose for Emily   (1930)

I

When Miss Emily Grierson died, our whole town went to her funeral: the men through a sort of respectful affection for a fallen monument, the women mostly out of curiosity to see the inside of her house, which no one save an old manservant — a combined gardener and cook — had seen in at least ten years.

It was a big, squarish frame house that had once been white, decorated with cupolas and spires and scrolled balconies in the heavily lightsome style of the seventies, set on what had once been our most select street. But garages and cotton gins had encroached and obliterated even the august names of that neighborhood; only Miss Emily's house was left, lifting its stubborn and coquettish decay above the cotton wagons and the gasoline pumps — an eyesore among eyesores. And now Miss Emily had gone to join the representatives of those august names where they lay in the cedar-bemused cemetery among the ranked and anonymous graves of Union and Confederate soldiers who fell at the battle of Jefferson.

Alive, Miss Emily had been a tradition, a duty, and a care; a sort of hereditary obligation upon the town, dating from that day in 1894 when Colonel Sartoris, the mayor — he who fathered the edict that no Negro woman should appear on the streets without an apron — remitted her taxes, the dispensation dating from the death of her father on into perpetuity. Not that Miss Emily would have accepted charity. Colonel Sartoris invented an involved tale to the effect that Miss Emily's father had loaned money to the town, which the town, as a matter of business, preferred this way of repaying. Only a man of Colonel Sartoris' generation and thought could have invented it, and only a woman could have believed it.

When the next generation, with its more modern ideas, became mayors and aldermen, this arrangement created some little dissatisfaction. On the first of the year they mailed her a tax notice. February came, and there was no reply. They wrote her a formal letter, asking her to call at the sheriff's office at her convenience. A week later the mayor wrote her himself, offering to call or to send his car for her, and received in reply a note on paper of an archaic shape, in a thin, flowing calligraphy in faded ink, to the effect that she no longer went out at all. The tax notice was also enclosed, without comment.

5   They called a special meeting of the Board of Aldermen. A deputation waited upon her, knocked at the door through which no visitor had passed since she ceased giving china-painting lessons eight or ten years earlier. They were admitted by the old Negro into a dim hall from which a stairway mounted into still more shadow. It smelled of dust and disuse — a close, dank smell. The Negro led them into the parlor. It was furnished in heavy, leather-covered furniture. When the Negro opened the blinds of one window, they could see that the leather was cracked; and when they sat down, a faint dust rose sluggishly about their thighs, spinning with slow motes in the single sun-ray. On a tarnished gilt easel before the fireplace stood a crayon portrait of Miss Emily's father.

They rose when she entered — a small, fat woman in black, with a thin gold chain descending to her waist and vanishing into her belt, leaning on an ebony cane with a tarnished gold head. Her skeleton was small and spare; perhaps that was why what would have been merely plumpness in another was obesity in her. She looked bloated, like a body long submerged in motionless water, and of that pallid hue. Her eyes, lost in the fatty ridges of her face, looked like two small pieces of coal pressed into a lump of dough as they moved from one face to another while the visitors stated their errand.

She did not ask them to sit. She just stood in the door and listened quietly until the spokesman came to a stumbling halt. Then they could hear the invisible watch ticking at the end of the gold chain.

Her voice was dry and cold. "I have no taxes in Jefferson. Colonel Sartoris explained it to me. Perhaps one of you can gain access to the city records and satisfy yourselves."

"But we have. We are the city authorities, Miss Emily. Didn't you get a notice from the sheriff, signed by him?"

"I received a paper, yes," Miss Emily said. "Perhaps he considers himself the   10 sheriff . . . I have no taxes in Jefferson."

"But there is nothing on the books to show that, you see. We must go by the —"

"See Colonel Sartoris. I have no taxes in Jefferson."

"But, Miss Emily —"

"See Colonel Sartoris." (Colonel Sartoris had been dead almost ten years.) "I have no taxes in Jefferson. Tobe!" The Negro appeared. "Show these gentlemen out."

II

So she vanquished them, horse and foot, just as she had vanquished their fathers   15 thirty years before about the smell. That was two years after her father's death and a short time after her sweetheart — the one we believed would marry her — had deserted her. After her father's death she went out very little; after her sweetheart went away, people hardly saw her at all. A few of the ladies had the temerity to call, but were not received, and the only sign of life about the place was the Negro man — a young man then — going in and out with a market basket.

"Just as if a man — any man — could keep a kitchen properly," the ladies said; so they were not surprised when the smell developed. It was another link between the gross, teeming world and the high and mighty Griersons.

A neighbor, a woman, complained to the mayor, Judge Stevens, eighty years old.

"But what will you have me do about it, madam?" he said.

"Why, send her word to stop it," the woman said. "Isn't there a law?"

"I'm sure that won't be necessary," Judge Stevens said. "It's probably just a   20 snake or a rat that nigger of hers killed in the yard. I'll speak to him about it."

The next day he received two more complaints, one from a man who came in diffident deprecation. "We really must do something about it, Judge. I'd be the last one in the world to bother Miss Emily, but we've got to do something." That night the Board of Aldermen met — three graybeards and one younger man, a member of the rising generation.

"It's simple enough," he said. "Send her word to have her place cleaned up. Give her a certain time to do it in, and if she don't . . ."

"Dammit, sir," Judge Stevens said, "will you accuse a lady to her face of smelling bad?"

So the next night, after midnight, four men crossed Miss Emily's lawn and slunk about the house like burglars, sniffing along the base of the brickwork and at the cellar openings while one of them performed a regular sowing motion with his hand out of a sack slung from his shoulder. They broke open the cellar door and sprinkled lime there, and in all the outbuildings. As they recrossed the lawn, a window that had been dark was lighted and Miss Emily sat in it, the light behind her, and her upright torso motionless as that of an idol. They crept quietly across the lawn and into the shadow of the locusts that lined the street. After a week or two the smell went away.

25   That was when people had begun to feel really sorry for her. People in our town, remembering how old lady Wyatt, her great-aunt, had gone completely crazy at last, believed that the Griersons held themselves a little too high for what they really were. None of the young men were quite good enough for Miss Emily and such. We had long thought of them as a tableau, Miss Emily a slender figure in white in the background, her father a spraddled silhouette in the foreground, his back to her and clutching a horsewhip, the two of them framed by the back-flung front door. So when she got to be thirty and was still single, we were not pleased exactly, but vindicated; even with insanity in the family she wouldn't have turned down all of her chances if they had really materialized.

When her father died, it got about that the house was all that was left to her; and in a way, people were glad. At last they could pity Miss Emily. Being left alone, and a pauper, she had become humanized. Now she too would know the old thrill and the old despair of a penny more or less.

The day after his death all the ladies prepared to call at the house and offer condolence and aid, as is our custom. Miss Emily met them at the door, dressed as usual and with no trace of grief on her face. She told them that her father was not dead. She did that for three days, with the ministers calling on her, and the doctors, trying to persuade her to let them dispose of the body. Just as they were about to resort to law and force, she broke down, and they buried her father quickly.

We did not say she was crazy then. We believed she had to do that. We remembered all the young men her father had driven away, and we knew that with nothing left, she would have to cling to that which had robbed her, as people will.

III

30   She was sick for a long time. When we saw her again, her hair was cut short, making her look like a girl, with a vague resemblance to those angels in colored church windows — sort of tragic and serene.

The town had just let the contracts for paving the sidewalks, and in the summer after her father's death they began the work. The construction company came with niggers and mules and machinery, and a foreman named Homer Barron, a Yankee — a big, dark, ready man, with a big voice and eyes lighter than his face. The little boys would follow in groups to hear him cuss the niggers, and the niggers singing in time to the rise and fall of picks. Pretty soon he knew everybody in town. Whenever you heard a lot of laughing anywhere about the square, Homer Barron would be in the center of the group. Presently we began to see him and Miss Emily on Sunday afternoons driving in the yellow-wheeled buggy and the matched team of bays from the livery stable.

At first we were glad that Miss Emily would have an interest, because the ladies all said, "Of course a Grierson would not think seriously of a Northerner, a day laborer." But there were still others, older people, who said that even grief could not cause a real lady to forget *noblesse oblige*° — without calling it *noblesse oblige*. They just said, "Poor Emily. Her kinsfolk should come to her." She had some kin in Alabama; but years ago her father had fallen out with them over the estate of old lady Wyatt, the crazy woman, and there was no communication between the two families. They had not even been represented at the funeral.

And as soon as the old people said, "Poor Emily," the whispering began. "Do you suppose it's really so?" they said to one another. "Of course it is. What else could . . ." This behind their hands; rustling of craned silk and satin behind jalousies closed upon the sun of Sunday afternoon as the thin, swift clop-clop-clop of the matched team passed: "Poor Emily."

She carried her head high enough — even when we believed that she was fallen. It was as if she demanded more than ever the recognition of her dignity as the last Grierson; as if it had wanted that touch of earthiness to reaffirm her imperviousness. Like when she bought the rat poison, the arsenic. That was over a year after they had begun to say "Poor Emily," and while the two female cousins were visiting her.

"I want some poison," she said to the druggist. She was over thirty then, still a 35 slight woman, though thinner than usual, with cold, haughty black eyes in a face the flesh of which was strained across the temples and about the eye-sockets as you imagine a lighthouse-keeper's face ought to look. "I want some poison," she said.

"Yes, Miss Emily. What kind? For rats and such? I'd recom —"

"I want the best you have. I don't care what kind."

The druggist named several. "They'll kill anything up to an elephant. But what you want is —"

"Arsenic," Miss Emily said. "Is that a good one?"

"Is . . . arsenic? Yes, ma'am. But what you want —"

"I want arsenic."   40

The druggist looked down at her. She looked back at him, erect, her face like a strained flag. "Why, of course," the druggist said. "If that's what you want. But the law requires you to tell what you are going to use it for."

Miss Emily just stared at him, her head tilted back in order to look him eye for eye, until he looked away and went and got the arsenic and wrapped it up. The Negro delivery boy brought her the package; the druggist didn't come back. When she opened the package at home there was written on the box, under the skull and bones: "For rats."

IV

So the next day we all said, "She will kill herself"; and we said it would be the best thing. When she had first begun to be seen with Homer Barron, we had said, "She will marry him." Then we said, "She will persuade him yet," because Homer him-

---

noblesse oblige: The obligation of those of high birth or rank to behave honorably.

self had remarked — he liked men, and it was known that he drank with the younger men in the Elks' Club — that he was not a marrying man. Later we said, "Poor Emily" behind the jalousies as they passed on Sunday afternoon in the glittering buggy, Miss Emily with her head high and Homer Barron with his hat cocked and a cigar in his teeth, reins and whip in a yellow glove.

Then some of the ladies began to say that it was a disgrace to the town and a bad example to the young people. The men did not want to interfere, but at last the ladies forced the Baptist minister — Miss Emily's people were Episcopal — to call upon her. He would never divulge what happened during that interview, but he refused to go back again. The next Sunday they again drove about the streets, and the following day the minister's wife wrote to Miss Emily's relations in Alabama.

45   So she had blood-kin under her roof again and we sat back to watch developments. At first nothing happened. Then we were sure that they were to be married. We learned that Miss Emily had been to the jeweler's and ordered a man's toilet set in silver, with the letters H. B. on each piece. Two days later we learned that she had bought complete outfit of men's clothing, including a nightshirt, and we said, "They are married." We were really glad. We were glad because the two female cousins were even more Grierson than Miss Emily had ever been.

So we were not surprised when Homer Barron — the streets had been finished some time since — was gone. We were a little disappointed that there was not a public blowing-off, but we believed that he had gone on to prepare for Miss Emily's coming, or to give her a chance to get rid of the cousins. (By that time it was a cabal, and we were all Miss Emily's allies to help circumvent the cousins.) Sure enough, after another week they departed. And, as we had expected all along, within three days Homer Barron was back in town. A neighbor saw the Negro man admit him at the kitchen door at dusk one evening.

And that was the last we saw of Homer Barron. And of Miss Emily for some time. The Negro man went in and out with the market basket, but the front door remained closed. Now and then we would see her at a window for a moment, as the men did that night when they sprinkled the lime, but for almost six months she did not appear on the streets. Then we knew that this was to be expected too; as if that quality of her father which had thwarted her woman's life so many times had been too virulent and too furious to die.

When we next saw Miss Emily, she had grown fat and her hair was turning gray. During the next few years it grew grayer and grayer until it attained an even pepper-and-salt iron-gray, when it ceased turning. Up to the day of her death at seventy-four it was still that vigorous iron-gray, like the hair of an active man.

From that time on her front door remained closed, save for a period of six or seven years, when she was about forty, during which she gave lessons in china-painting. She fitted up a studio in one of the downstairs rooms, where the daughters and granddaughters of Colonel Sartoris' contemporaries were sent to her with the same regularity and in the same spirit that they were sent to church on Sundays with a twenty-five-cent piece for the collection plate. Meanwhile her taxes had been remitted.

50   Then the newer generation became the backbone and the spirit of the town, and the painting pupils grew up and fell away and did not send their children to

her with boxes of color and tedious brushes and pictures cut from the ladies' magazines. The front door closed upon the last one and remained closed for good. When the town got free postal delivery, Miss Emily alone refused to let them fasten the metal numbers above her door and attach a mailbox to it. She would not listen to them.

Daily, monthly, yearly we watched the Negro grow grayer and more stooped, going in and out with the market basket. Each December we sent her a tax notice, which would be returned by the post office a week later, unclaimed. Now and then we would see her in one of the downstairs windows — she had evidently shut up the top floor of the house — like the carven torso of an idol in a niche, looking or not looking at us, we could never tell which. Thus she passed from generation to generation — dear, inescapable, impervious, tranquil, and perverse.

And so she died. Fell ill in the house filled with dust and shadows, with only a doddering Negro man to wait on her. We did not even know she was sick; we had long since given up trying to get any information from the Negro. He talked to no one, probably not even to her, for his voice had grown harsh and rusty, as if from disuse.

She died in one of the downstairs rooms, in a heavy walnut bed with a curtain, her gray head propped on a pillow yellow and moldy with age and lack of sunlight.

V

The Negro met the first of the ladies at the front door and let them in, with their hushed, sibilant voices and their quick, curious glances, and then he disappeared. He walked right through the house and out the back and was not seen again.

The two female cousins came at once. They held the funeral on the second day, with the town coming to look at Miss Emily beneath a mass of bought flowers, with the crayon face of her father musing profoundly above the bier and the ladies sibilant and macabre; and the very old men — some in their brushed Confederate uniforms — on the porch and the lawn, talking of Miss Emily as if she had been a contemporary of theirs, believing that they had danced with her and courted her perhaps, confusing time with its mathematical progression, as the old do, to whom all the past is not a diminishing road but, instead, a huge meadow which no winter ever quite touches, divided from them now by the narrow bottleneck of the most recent decade of years.

Already we knew that there was one room in that region above stairs which no one had seen in forty years, and which would have to be forced. They waited until Miss Emily was decently in the ground before they opened it.

The violence of breaking down the door seemed to fill this room with pervading dust. A thin, acrid pall as of the tomb seemed to lie everywhere upon this room decked and furnished as for a bridal: upon the valance curtains of faded rose color, upon the rose-shaded lights, upon the dressing table, upon the delicate array of crystal and the man's toilet things backed with tarnished silver, silver so tarnished that the monogram was obscured. Among them lay collar and tie, as if they had just been removed, which, lifted, left upon the surface a pale crescent in the dust. Upon a chair hung the suit, carefully folded; beneath it the two mute shoes and the discarded socks.

The man himself lay in the bed.

For a long while we just stood there, looking down at the profound and flesh-less grin. The body had apparently once lain in the attitude of an embrace, but now the long sleep that outlasts love, that conquers even the grimace of love, had cuckolded him. What was left of him, rotted beneath what was left of the night-shirt, had become inextricable from the bed in which he lay; and upon him and upon the pillow beside him lay that even coating of the patient and biding dust.

60   Then we noticed that in the second pillow was the indentation of a head. One of us lifted something from it, and leaning forward, that faint and invisible dust dry and acrid in the nostrils, we saw a long strand of iron-gray hair.

Reading and Reacting

1. Arrange these events in the sequence in which they actually occur: Homer's arrival in town, the aldermen's visit, Emily's purchase of poison, Colonel Sartoris's decision to remit Emily's taxes, the development of the odor around Emily's house, Emily's father's death, the arrival of Emily's relatives, Homer's disappearance. Then, list the events in the sequence in which they are presented in the story. Why do you suppose Faulkner presents these events out of their actual chronological order?

2. Despite the story's confusing sequence, many events are foreshadowed. Give some examples of this technique. How does foreshadowing enrich the story?

3. Where does the exposition end and the movement toward the story's climax begin? Where does the resolution stage begin?

4. Emily is clearly the story's protagonist. In the sense that he opposes her wishes, Homer is the antagonist. What other characters — or what larger forces — are in conflict with Emily?

5. Explain how each of these phrases moves the story's plot along: "So she van-quished them, horse and foot . . .." (par. 15); "After a week or two the smell went away" (par. 24); "And that was the last we saw of Homer Barron" (par. 47); "And so she died" (par. 52); "The man himself lay in the bed" (par. 58).

6. The narrator of the story is an observer, not a participant. Who might this narrator be? How do you suppose the narrator might know so much about Emily? Why do you think the narrator uses *we* instead of *I?*

7. The original version of "A Rose for Emily" included a two-page deathbed scene revealing that Tobe, Emily's servant, has shared her terrible secret all these years, and that Emily has left her house to him. Why do you think Faulkner deleted this scene? Do you think he made the right decision?

8. Some critics have suggested that Miss Emily Grierson is a kind of symbol of the Old South, the last defender of its outdated ideas of chivalry, formal manners, and tradition. Do you think this interpretation is justified? Would you characterize Miss Emily as a champion or a victim of the values her town tries to preserve?

9. JOURNAL ENTRY When asked at a seminar at the University of Virginia about the meaning of the title "A Rose for Emily," Faulkner replied, "Oh, it's simply the poor woman had no life at all. Her father had kept her more or less locked up and then she had a lover who was about to quit her, she had to murder him. It was just 'A Rose for Emily'— that's all." In another interview, asked the same question, he replied, "I pitied her and this was a salute, just as if you were to make a gesture, a salute, to anyone; to a woman you would hand a rose, as you would lift a cup of *sake* to a man." What do you make of Faulkner's responses? Can you offer other possible interpretations of the title's significance?

10. CRITICAL PERSPECTIVE In his essay "William Faulkner: An American Dickens," literary critic Leslie A. Fiedler characterizes Faulkner as "primarily . . . a sentimental writer; not a writer with the occasional vice of sentimentality, but one whose basic mode of experience is sentimental." He continues, "In a writer whose very method is self-indulgence, that sentimentality becomes sometimes downright embarrassing." Fiedler also notes Faulkner's "excesses of maudlin feelings and absurd indulgences in overripe rhetoric."

   Do you think these criticisms apply to "A Rose for Emily"? If so, does the "vice of sentimentality" diminish the story, or do you agree with Fiedler — who calls Faulkner a "supereminently good 'bad' writer"— that the author is able to transcend these excesses?

Related Works: "Miss Brill" (p. 121), "Nice Car, Camille" (p. 609), "Porphyria's Lover" (p. 622), "Richard Cory" (p. 907), *Trifles* (p. 983)

LORRIE MOORE (1957–   ) gives this advice in her story "How to Become a Writer": "First, try to become something, anything, else. A movie star/astronaut. A movie star/missionary. A movie star/kindergarten teacher. President of the World. Fail miserably." Born in Glens Falls, New York, Moore was educated at St. Lawrence University and at Cornell University. Her first book was *Self-Help* (1985), a collection of short stories — including "How to Talk to Your Mother (Notes)"— that rated an enthusiastic front-page review in the *New York Times Book Review.* More recent works include *Anagrams* (1986), *The Forgotten Helper* (1987), *Like Life* (1990), *Who Will Run the Frog Hospital?* (1994), and *Birds of America* (1998). Moore divides her time between New York City and Madison, Wisconsin, where she holds a teaching position at the University of Wisconsin.

About the origins of her writing career, Moore is typically humorous. In a 1985 interview printed in the magazine *Vanity Fair,* she explains, "I signed up for a course called 'The Romance and Reality of Words' in high school and got put in the creative writing class by mistake." Her voice is what *New York Times* reviewer Michiko Kakutani describes as the "wry, crackly" and vulnerable voice of the women in her stories: women who fend off anxiety with irreverent, self-bolstering humor. The stories of *Self-Help* are, according to Moore's comments in *Contemporary Authors,* "second person, mock-imperative narratives . . . what happens when one appropriates the 'how-to' form for a fiction, for an irony, for a 'how-not-to.'"

> **Cultural Context:** Mother-daughter relationships can often be emotionally charged, fraught with tension, miscommunication, and hurt feelings. As Mary Pipher suggests in her bestselling 1994 book, *Reviving Ophelia,* daughters trying to assert their independence often do so by shunning the support of their mothers, which could ultimately help them. This struggle for self-definition and healthy communication may continue long into a daughter's adult life.

How to Talk to Your Mother (Notes) (1985)

1982 Without her, for years now, murmur at the defrosting refrigerator, "What?" "Huh?" "Shush now," as it creaks, aches, groans, until the final ice block drops from the ceiling of the freezer like something vanquished.

Dream, and in your dreams babies with the personalities of dachshunds, fat as Macy balloons, float by the treetops.

The first permanent polyurethane heart is surgically implanted.°

Someone upstairs is playing "You'll Never Walk Alone" on the recorder. Now it's "Oklahoma!" They must have a Rodgers and Hammerstein book.°

5 *1981* On public transportation, mothers with soft, soapy, corduroyed seraphs glance at you, their faces dominoes of compassion. Their seraphs are small and quiet or else restlessly counting bus-seat colors: "Blue-blue-blue, red-red-red, lul-low-lullow-lullow." The mothers see you eyeing their children. They smile sympathetically. They believe you envy them. They believe you are childless. They believe they know why. Look quickly away, out the smudge of the window.

1980 The hum, rush, clack of things in the kitchen. These are some of the sounds that organize your life. The clink of the silverware inside the drawer, piled like bones in a mass grave. Your similes grow grim, grow tired.

Reagan is elected President, though you distributed donuts and brochures for Carter.

Date an Italian. He rubs your stomach and says, "These are marks of stretch, no? Marks of stretch?" and in your dizzy mind you think: Marks of Harpo, Ideas of Marx, Ides of March, Beware.° He plants kisses on the sloping ramp of your neck, and you fall asleep against him, your underpants peeled and rolled around one thigh like a bride's garter.

The first . . . implanted: The Jarvik-7, created by Robert K. Jarvik, was implanted in Barney Clark by Dr. William C. DeVries on December 2, 1982.

Rodgers and Hammerstein: The American songwriting team of composer Richard Rodgers (1902–1979) and lyricist Oscar Hammerstein II (1895–1960) created many modern classics, including "You'll Never Walk Alone" (from *Carousel*) and "Oklahoma!" (from the musical of the same name).

Marks . . . Beware!: The narrator's "free association," prompted by "marks of stretch" (stretch marks) alludes to comedian Arthur 'Harpo' Marx (1893–1964), philosopher Karl Marx (1818–1883), and the warning the soothsayer issues ("Beware the Ides of March") in Shakespeare's *Julius Caesar.*

1979   Once in a while take evening trips past the old unsold house you grew up in, that haunted rural crossroads two hours from where you now live. It is like Halloween: the raked, moonlit lawn, the mammoth, tumid trees, arms and fingers raised into the starless wipe of sky like burns, cracks, map rivers. Their black shadows rock against the side of the east porch. There are dream shadows, other lives here. Turn the corner slowly but continue to stare from the car window. This house is embedded in you deep, something still here you know, you think you know, a voice at the top of those stairs, perhaps, a figure on the porch, an odd apron caught high in the twigs, in the too-warm-for-a-fall-night breeze, something not right, that turret window you can still see from here, from outside, but which can't be reached from within. (The ghostly brag of your childhood: "We have a mystery room. The window shows from the front, but you can't go in, there's no door. A doctor lived there years ago and gave secret operations, and now it's blocked off.") The window sits like a dead eye in the turret.

You see a ghost, something like a spinning statue by a shrub.   10

1978   Bury her in the cold south sideyard of that Halloweenish house. Your brother and his kids are there. Hug. The minister in a tweed sportscoat, the neighborless fields, the crossroads, are all like some stark Kansas. There is praying, then someone shoveling. People walk toward the cars and hug again. Get inside your car with your niece. Wait. Look up through the windshield. In the November sky a wedge of wrens moves south, the lines of their formation, the very sides and vertices mysteriously choreographed, shifting, flowing, crossing like a skater's legs. "They'll descend instinctively upon a tree somewhere," you say, "but not for miles yet." You marvel, watch, until, amoeba-slow, they are dark, faraway stitches in the horizon. You do not start the car. The quiet niece next to you finally speaks: "Aunt Ginnie, are we going to the restaurant with the others?" Look at her. Recognize her: nine in a pile parka. Smile and start the car.

1977   She ages, rocks in your rocker, noiseless as wind. The front strands of her white hair dangle yellow at her eyes from too many cigarettes. She smokes even now, her voice husky with phlegm. Sometimes at dinner in your tiny kitchen she will simply stare, rheumy-eyed, at you, then burst into a fit of coughing that racks her small old man's body like a storm.

Stop eating your baked potato. Ask if she is all right.

She will croak: "Do you remember, Ginnie, your father used to say that one day, with these cigarettes, I was going to have to 'face the mucus'?" At this she chuckles, chokes, gasps again.

Make her stand up.   15

Lean her against you.

Slap her lightly on the curved mound of her back.

Ask her for chrissakes to stop smoking.

She will smile and say: "For chrissakes? Is that any way to talk to your mother?"

At night go in and check on her. She lies there awake, her lips apart, open and   20
drying. Bring her some juice. She murmurs, "Thank you, honey." Her mouth smells, swells like a grave.

1976   The Bicentennial. In the laundromat, you wait for the time on your coins to run out. Through the porthole of the dryer, you watch your bedeviled towels and sheets leap and fall. The radio station piped in from the ceiling plays slow, sad Motown; it encircles you with the desperate hopefulness of a boy at a dance, and it makes you cry. When you get back to your apartment, dump everything on your bed. Your mother is knitting crookedly: red, white, and blue. Kiss her hello. Say: "Sure was warm in that place." She will seem not to hear you.

1975   Attend poetry readings alone at the local library. Find you don't really listen well. Stare at your crossed thighs. Think about your mother. Sometimes you confuse her with the first man you ever loved, who ever loved you, who buried his head in the pills of your sweater and said magnificent things like "Oh god, oh god," who loved you unconditionally, terrifically, like a mother.

The poet loses his nerve for a second, a red flush through his neck and ears, but he regains his composure. When he is finished, people clap. There is wine and cheese.

Leave alone, walk home alone. The downtown streets are corridors of light holding you, holding you, past the church, past the community center. March, like Stella Dallas,° spine straight, through the melodrama of street lamps, phone posts, toward the green house past Borealis Avenue, toward the rear apartment with the tilt and the squash on the stove.

25   Your horoscope says: Be kind, be brief.

You are pregnant again. Decide what you must do.

1974   She will have bouts with a mad sort of senility. She calls you at work. "There's no food here! Help me! I'm starving!" although you just bought forty dollars' worth of groceries yesterday. "Mom, there is too food there!"

When you get home the refrigerator is mostly empty. "Mom, where did you put all the milk and cheese and stuff?" Your mother stares at you from where she is sitting in front of the TV set. She has tears leaking out of her eyes. "There's no food here, Ginnie."

There is a rustling, scratching noise in the dishwasher. You open it up, and the eyes of a small rodent glint back at you. It scrambles out, off to the baseboards behind the refrigerator. Your mother, apparently, has put all the groceries inside the dishwasher. The milk is spilled, a white pool against blue, and things like cheese and bologna and apples have been nibbled at.

30   *1973*   At a party when a woman tells you where she bought some wonderful pair of shoes, say that you believe shopping for clothes is like masturbation — everyone does it, but it isn't very interesting and therefore should be done alone, in an embarrassed fashion, and never be the topic of party conversation. The woman will

---

Stella Dallas: A fictional character introduced in Olive Higgins Prouty's novel *Stella Dallas* (1922); also the main character in a radio show of the same name, which the announcer introduced as a "world famous drama of mother love and sacrifice." *Stella Dallas* was filmed three times, in 1926 (with Belle Bennett), in 1937 (with Barbara Stanwyck), and in 1990 (with Bette Midler).

tighten her lips and eyebrows and say, "Oh, I suppose you have something more fascinating to talk about." Grow clumsy and uneasy. Say, "No," and head for the ginger ale. Tell the person next to you that your insides feel sort of sinking and vinyl like a Claes Oldenburg toilet.° They will say, "Oh?" and point out that the print on your dress is one of paisleys impregnating paisleys. Pour yourself more ginger ale.

1972 Nixon wins by a landslide.

Sometimes your mother calls you by her sister's name. Say, "No, Mom, it's me. Virginia." Learn to repeat things. Learn that you have a way of knowing each other which somehow slips out and beyond the ways you have of not knowing each other at all.

Make apple crisp for the first time.

1971 Go for long walks to get away from her. Walk through wooded areas; there is a life there you have forgotten. The smells and sounds seem sudden, unchanged, exact, the papery crunch of the leaves, the mouldering sachet of the mud. The trees are crooked as backs, the fence posts splintered, trusting and precarious in their solid grasp of arms, the asters spindly, dry, white, havishammed (Havishammed!)° by frost. Find a beautiful reddish stone and bring it home for your mother. Kiss her. Say: "This is for you." She grasps it and smiles. "You were always such a sensitive child," she says.

Say: "Yeah, I know."   35

1970 You are pregnant again. Try to decide what you should do.

Get your hair chopped, short as a boy's.

1969 Mankind leaps upon the moon.

Disposable diapers are first sold in supermarkets.

Have occasional affairs with absurd, silly men who tell you to grow your hair   40
to your waist and who, when you are sad, tickle your ribs to cheer you up. Moonlight through the blinds stripes you like zebras. You laugh. You never marry.

1968 Do not resent her. Think about the situation, for instance, when you take the last trash bag from its box: you must throw out the box by putting it in that very trash bag. What was once contained, now must contain. The container, then, becomes the contained, the enveloped, the held. Find more and more that you like to muse over things like this.

1967 Your mother is sick and comes to live with you. There is no place else for her to go. You feel many different emptinesses.

The first successful heart transplant is performed in South Africa.°

Claes Oldenburg: American artist (1929–   ) noted for his oversized soft sculptures of everyday objects, made from such materials as canvas and vinyl.

Havishammed: Miss Havisham, in Charles Dickens's *Great Expectations,* is an elderly recluse who lives surrounded by the decaying remnants of her aborted wedding, called off years earlier by her fiancé.

The first . . . Africa: By Dr. Christiaan Barnard (1923–2001).

1966   You confuse lovers, mix up who had what scar, what car, what mother.

45 *1965*   Smoke marijuana. Try to figure out what has made your life go wrong. It is like trying to figure out what is stinking up the refrigerator. It could be anything. The lid off the mayonnaise, Uncle Ron's honey wine four years in the left corner. Broccoli yellowing, flowering fast. They are all metaphors. They are all problems. Your horoscope says: Speak gently to a loved one.

1964   Your mother calls long distance and asks whether you are coming home for Thanksgiving, your brother and the baby will be there. Make excuses.

"As a mother gets older," your mother says, "these sorts of holidays become increasingly important."

Say: "I'm sorry, Mom."

1963   Wake up one morning with a man you had thought you'd spend your life with, and realize, a rock in your gut, that you don't even like him. Spend a weepy afternoon in his bathroom, not coming out when he knocks. You can no longer trust your affections. People and places you think you love may be people and places you hate.

50 Kennedy is shot.

Someone invents a temporary artificial heart, for use during operations.

1962   Eat Chinese food for the first time, with a lawyer from California. He will show you how to hold the chopsticks. He will pat your leg. Attack his profession. Ask him whether he feels the law makes large spokes out of the short stakes of men.

1961   Grandma Moses dies.°

You are a zoo of insecurities. You take to putting brandy in your morning coffee and to falling in love too easily. You have an abortion.

55 *1960*   There is money from your father's will and his life insurance. You buy a car and a green velvet dress you don't need. You drive two hours to meet your mother for lunch on Saturdays. She suggests things for you to write about, things she's heard on the radio: a woman with telepathic twins, a woman with no feet.

1959   At the funeral she says: "He had his problems, but he was a generous man," though you know he was tight as a scout knot, couldn't listen to anyone, the only time you remember loving him being that once when he got the punchline of one of your jokes before your mom did and looked up from his science journal and guffawed loud as a giant, the two of you, for one split moment, communing like angels in the middle of that room, in that warm, shared light of mind.

Grandma Moses: (Anna Mary Robertson Moses) (1860–1961)—American artist famous for her "primitive" paintings depicting rural life. Completely self-taught, she did not begin painting seriously until the age of sixty-seven.

Say: "He was okay."

"You shouldn't be bitter," your mother snaps. "He financed you and your brother's college educations." She buttons her coat. "He was also the first man to isolate a particular isotope of helium, I forget the name, but he should have won the Nobel Prize." She dabs at her nose.

Say: "Yeah, Mom."

1958 At your brother's wedding, your father is taken away in an ambulance. A 60 tiny cousin whispers loudly to her mother, "Did Uncle Will have a hard attack?" For seven straight days say things to your mother like: "I'm sure it'll be okay," and "I'll stay here, why don't you go home and get some sleep."

1957 Dance the calypso with boys from a different college. Get looped on New York State burgundy, lose your virginity, and buy one of the first portable electric typewriters.

1956 Tell your mother about all the books you are reading at college. This will please her.

1955 Do a paint-by-numbers of Elvis Presley. Tell your mother you are in love with him. She will shake her head.

1954 Shoplift a cashmere sweater.

1953 Smoke a cigarette with Hillary Swedelson. Tell each other your crushes. 65 Become blood sisters.

1952 When your mother asks you if there are any nice boys in junior high, ask her how on earth would you ever know, having to come in at nine! every night. Her eyebrows will lift like theater curtains. "You poor, abused thing," she will say.

Say, "Don't I know it," and slam the door.

1951 Your mother tells you about menstruation. The following day you promptly menstruate, your body only waiting for permission, for a signal. You wake up in the morning and feel embarrassed.

1949 You learn how to blow gum bubbles and to add negative numbers.

1947 The Dead Sea Scrolls° are discovered. 70
You have seen too many Hollywood musicals. You have seen too many people singing in public places and you assume you can do it, too. Practice. Your teacher

---

Dead Sea Scrolls: Parchment scrolls containing Hebrew and Aramaic scriptural texts, as well as communal writings. Generally dated from 100 B.C. to A.D. 100, they were discovered in a cave near the Dead Sea, between Israel and Jordan.

asks you a question. You warble back: "The answer to number two is twelve." Most of the class laughs at you, though some stare, eyes jewel-still, fascinated. At home your mother asks you to dust your dresser. Work up a vibrato you could drive a truck through. Sing: "Why do I have to do it now?" and tap your way through the dining room. Your mother requests that you calm down and go take a nap. Shout: "You don't care about me! You don't care about me at all!"

1946   Your brother plays "Shoofly Pie" all day long on the Victrola.

Ask your mother if you can go to Ellen's for supper. She will say, "Go ask your father," and you, pulling at your fingers, walk out to the living room and whimper by his chair. He is reading. Tap his arm. "Dad? Daddy? Dad?" He continues reading his science journal. Pull harder on your fingers and run back to the kitchen to tell your mother, who storms into the living room, saying, "Why don't you ever listen to your children when they try to talk to you?" You hear them arguing. Press your face into a kitchen towel, ashamed, the hum of the refrigerator motor, the drip in the sink scaring you.

1945   Your father comes home from his war work. He gives you a piggyback ride around the broad yellow thatch of your yard, the dead window in the turret, dark as a wound, watching you. He gives you wordless pushes on the swing.

75   Your brother has new friends, acts older and distant, even while you wait for the school bus together.

You spend too much time alone. You tell your mother that when you grow up you will bring your babies to Australia to see the kangaroos.

Forty thousand people are killed in Nagasaki.

1944   Dress and cuddle a tiny babydoll you have named "the Sue." Bring her everywhere. Get lost in the Wilson Creek fruit market, and call softly, "Mom, where are you?" Watch other children picking grapes, but never dare yourself. Your eyes are small, dark throats, your hand clutches the Sue.

1943   Ask your mother about babies. Have her read to you only the stories about babies. Ask her if she is going to have a baby. Ask her about the baby that died. Cry into her arm.

80   *1940*   Clutch her hair in your fist. Rub it against your cheek.

1939   As through a helix, as through an ear, it is here you are nearer the dream flashes, the other lives.

There is a tent of legs, a sundering of selves, as you both gasp blindly for breath. Across the bright and cold, she knows it when you try to talk to her, though this is something you never really manage to understand.

Germany invades Poland.

The year's big song is "Three Little Fishies" and someone, somewhere, is playing it.

Reading and Reacting

1. What do you think the word *notes* in the story's title means?

2. Who is the story's protagonist? With whom (or what) is the protagonist in conflict? Explain the nature of this conflict.

3. What does the writer gain by arranging the story's events in reverse chronological order? What, if anything, does she lose?

4. What do the dates and the references to historical events contribute to the story?

5. Despite its unconventional sequence of events, does the story contain any foreshadowing? Explain.

6. A student, encountering this story for the first time, commented, "It's hard to follow because it has no plot." Do you agree with this student's assessment? Does this story include any of the conventional stages of plot (exposition, resolution, and so on)? If so, where? Identify several crises (peaks of tension). Does the story have a climax? Explain.

7. Moore says that in the stories in *Self-Help* she is "telling a how-to that is, of course, a how-not-to." What do you think she means? What does the narrator in this story want to teach her readers?

8. What is the effect of the narrator's use of what Moore calls the "mock imperative" ("Date an Italian.")? What is the effect of her use of the second person (*you*), as in the title and in phrases like "The mothers see you eyeing their children"?

9. JOURNAL ENTRY Although the story's title is "How to Talk to Your Mother (Notes)," the narrator actually does *not* talk to her mother. What do you think she wants to tell her mother? What stops her?

10. CRITICAL PERSPECTIVE When *Self-Help*, the collection in which "How to Talk to Your Mother (Notes)" appeared, was published in 1985, reviews were mixed. For example, *Kirkus Reviews* called the book a "flimsy, strained collection" that relied on "a single gimmick and two limited situations. The gimmick? Stories in the form of self-help/instruction manuals. . . . The situations: a young woman caught in an unhappy no-win romantic relationship; and a young woman's recollections of her unhappy, unstable mother. . . ." The reviewer concluded by characterizing the book as "maudlin/juvenile work overall: boutique fiction at its most cutesy-poo." Other critics disagreed. Jay McInerney, writing in the *New York Times Book Review*, called "How to Talk to Your Mother (Notes)" a "splendid" story and saw the "complex puzzle of maternal love" as "haunting the quests" of many of Moore's narrators. Ray Olson's review in *Booklist*, although it expressed disappointment with the way the distant narrative voice robbed the stories of emotion, nevertheless called the book "absorbing," and the critic commented that it contained "many funny and sharp lines and effects."

How can you account for such different opinions of Moore's work? With which evaluation do you agree?

Related Works: "Everyday Use" (p. 310), "Two Kinds" (p. 527), "Those Winter Sundays" (p. 560), *The Glass Menagerie* (p. 1416)

WRITING SUGGESTIONS: Plot

1. Write a sequel to "The Story of an Hour," telling the story in the voice of Brently Mallard. Use flashbacks to provide information about his view of the Mallards' marriage.

2. Write your own life story, imitating the style and structure of "How to Talk to Your Mother (Notes)." Use reverse chronology, use *you* instead of *I*, and divide your story into sections according to year. Be sure to include mentions of world events, song titles, and the like, as well as recurring themes in your life, to provide continuity and to unify your "notes" into a story.

3. "The Story of an Hour" includes a deus ex machina, an outside force or agent that suddenly appears to change the course of events. Consider the possible effects of a deus ex machina on the other four stories in this chapter. What might this outside force be in each story? How might it change the story's action? How plausible would such a dramatic turn of events be in each case?

4. Like the man in "Kansas," the woman in "The Swing" (p. 139) seems to have created an alternate reality for herself — one she can understand, enjoy, and (she thinks) perhaps control. Consider the reasons these two characters might have for needing to "rewrite" their life stories. Compare and contrast their motivations and the relative success of their efforts.

5. Read the following article from the January 30, 1987, *Philadelphia Inquirer*. After listing some similarities and differences between the events in the article's story and those in "A Rose for Emily," write an essay in which you discuss how the presentation of events differs. Can you draw any conclusions about journalistic and fictional treatments of similar incidents?

DICK POTHIER AND THOMAS J. GIBBONS, JR.

A Woman's Wintry Death Leads
to a Long-Dead Friend

For more than two years, Frances Dawson Hamilton lived with the body of her long-time companion, draping his skeletonized remains with palm fronds and rosary beads.

Yesterday, the 70-year-old woman was found frozen to death in the home in the 4500 block of Higbee Street where she had lived all her life — the last year without heat or hot water. Her body was found by police accompanying a city social worker who came bearing an order to have her taken to a hospital.

Police investigators said the body of Bernard J. Kelly, 84, was found in an upstairs bedroom of the two-story brick home in the Wissinoming section, on the twin bed where he apparently died at least two years ago.

Two beds had been pushed together, and Hamilton apparently had been sleeping beside Kelly's remains since he died of unknown causes, police said.

Kelly's remains were clothed in long johns and socks, investigators said. The body was draped with rosary beads and palm fronds, and on the bed near his body were two boxes of Valentine's Day candy.

"It was basically a funeral — we've seen it before in such cases," said one investigator who was at the scene but declined to be identified.

Neighbors and investigators said Hamilton and Kelly had lived together in the house for at least 15 years. Several neighbors said Hamilton came from an affluent family, was educated in Europe, and lived on a trust fund until a year or so ago.

Last winter, said John Wasniewski, Hamilton's next-door neighbor, the basement of the home was flooded and the heater destroyed. "There was no heat in that house last winter or this winter," he said.

An autopsy will be performed on Hamilton today, but she apparently froze to death sometime since Monday, when a friend spoke to her on the telephone, investigators said.

Over the last two years, neighbors said, Hamilton had become increasingly reclusive and irrational. Just last week, a city social worker summoned by a friend arranged for a Philadelphia Gas Works team to visit the home and try to repair the furnace — but she refused to let them in.

The friend was James Phillips, 44, of Horsham, a salesman for Apex Electric in Souderton.

In October 1985, he said, Hamilton visited the Frankford Avenue electrical shop where he was then working, told him that she had an electrical problem in her house and had no lights, and asked whether he could help.

Phillips said he visited the house, fixed the problem and gave her some light bulbs.

"She was really paranoid," Phillips said. "She believed that all her problems were from people doing things to her. For some reason or other, she took to me."

Phillips said that he began visiting her, taking her shopping and doing some shopping for her. But, he said, he never saw the body on the second floor.

Hamilton told him there was a man up there. "I thought it was a story she was telling to protect herself," Phillips said.

He provided her with electric heaters and also contacted a caseworker with the city's Department of Human Services whom Phillips identified as Albert Zbik.

Between the two of them, he said, "we got her through last winter." Phillips said Zbik helped her obtain food stamps and Social Security assistance.

When the snowstorm hit last week, Phillips became concerned because he knew Hamilton would have trouble getting food. On Saturday, he took her a plate of hot food and bought more food from a local store.

On Monday, she telephoned him. "I didn't like the way she sounded," he said. He called Zbik and told him he felt it was time that they forced her to go to a hospital.

Phillips said Zbik went to her home yesterday, carrying a form authorizing an involuntary admission to a hospital for observation or required medical treatment.

Phillips told police that he was never allowed above the first floor and was often told by Hamilton that "Bernie is not feeling well today."

Neighbors and police investigators said Kelly was last seen alive about two years ago, and appeared to be quite ill at the time.

"As recently as last month, I asked Frances how Bernard was and whether she should get a doctor, and she said it wasn't necessary. She said 'He's sick, but I'm taking care of him — I'm feeding him with an eyedropper,'" Wasniewski said.

"I told her in December that if he was that sick, she should call a doctor, but she'd say she was taking care of him very well," Wasniewski said.

6. WEB ACTIVITY The following Web site contains information about Kate Chopin:

http://falcon.jmu.edu/~ramseyil/chopin.html

From that site, follow the link under "Reviews" to "Southern Women Writers." After reading the article "Southern Literature: Women Writers" by Patricia Evans, write an essay discussing Chopin's role as a Southern woman writer and, in particular, her role in the Southern Renaissance. Use Chopin's story "The Story of an Hour" (p. 82) to illustrate the points you make in your essay.

CHAPTER 6

CHARACTER

New writers think the way to begin a piece of fiction is to invent the most origi-nal plot possible. It is the way I myself was taught in college and too many classes still use that approach. Think up a plot, think up some characters, think up a conflict and suspense, pigeonhole them into the plot. *Voilà,* a story! Baloney. Every real writer I ever knew, and I have known many both in Europe and in this country, starts with people and their emotions and actions and lets them make their own stories. A woman once applied for one of my classes when I was teaching at Columbia University. "I want to be a writer," she told me, "so I can be like God and make people do what I want them to do." I had to tell her it was just the opposite. Characters make the author do what they want him to do. —**Martha Foley,** *Best American Short Stories* (Foreword)

Making false biography, false history, concocting a half-imaginary existence out of the actual drama of my life *is* my life. There has to be some pleasure in this job, and that's it. To go around in disguise. To act a character. To pass one-self off as what one is not. To *pretend.* . . . You don't necessarily, as a writer, have to abandon your biography completely to engage in an act of imperson-ation. It may be more intriguing when you don't. —**Philip Roth,** *Writers at Work,* 7th ed.

Much of what a writer learns he learns simply by imitation. Making up a scene, he asks himself at every step. "Would she really say that?" or "Would he really throw the shoe?" He plays the scene through in his imagination, taking all the parts, being absolutely fair to everyone involved (mimicking each in turn, as Aristotle pointed out, and never sinking to stereotype for even the most minor characters), and when he finishes the scene he understands by sympathetic imitation what each character has done throughout and why the fight, or accident, or whatever, developed as it did. —**John Gardner,** *On Moral Fiction*

A **character** is a fictional representation of a person — usually (but not nec-essarily) a psychologically realistic depiction. **Characterization** is the way writers develop characters and reveal those characters' traits to readers. Writers may por-tray characters through their actions, through their reactions to situations or to other characters, through their physical appearance, through their speech and gestures and expressions, and even through their names.

Generally speaking, characters are developed in two ways. First, readers can be *told* about characters. Third-person narrators can give us information about what characters are doing and thinking, what experiences they have had, what they look like, how they are dressed, and so on. Sometimes they also offer analysis of and judgments about a character's behavior. Similarly, first-person narrators can tell us about themselves or about other characters. Thus, Sammy in John Updike's "A&P" (p. 115) tells us that he lives with his parents and that he disapproves of the supermarket's customers. He also tells us what various characters are wearing and describes their actions, attitudes, and gestures. (For more information about first-person narrators, see Chapter 8, "Point of View.")

Alternatively, a character's personality traits and motivation may be *revealed* through actions, dialogue, or thoughts. For instance, Sammy's vivid fantasies and his disapproval of his customers' lives suggest to readers that he is something of a nonconformist; however, Sammy himself does not actually tell us this information.

ROUND AND FLAT CHARACTERS

In his influential 1927 work *Aspects of the Novel*, English novelist E. M. Forster classifies characters as either **round** (well developed, closely involved in and responsive to the action) or **flat** (barely developed or stereotypical). In an effective story, the major characters are usually complex and fully developed; if they are not, readers do not care what happens to them. In much fiction, readers are encouraged to become involved with the characters, even to identify with them. This empathy is possible only when we know something about the characters — their strengths and weaknesses, their likes and dislikes. We must know at least enough to understand why characters act the way they do. In some cases, of course, a story can be effective even when its central characters are not well developed. Sometimes, in fact, a story's effectiveness is enhanced by an *absence* of character development, as in Shirley Jackson's "The Lottery" (p. 303).

Readers often expect characters to behave as "real people" in their situation might behave. Real people are not perfect, and realistic characters cannot be perfect either. The flaws that are revealed as round characters are developed — greed, gullibility, naïveté, shyness, a quick temper, or a lack of insight or judgment or tolerance or even intelligence — make them believable. In modern fiction, the protagonist is seldom if ever the noble "hero"; more often, he or she is at least partly a victim, someone to whom some unpleasant things happen, and someone who is sometimes ill equipped to cope with events.

Unlike major characters, minor characters are frequently not well developed. Often they are flat, perhaps acting as *foils* for the protagonist. A **foil** is a supporting character whose role in the story is to highlight a major character by presenting a contrast with him or her. For instance, in "A&P," Stokesie, another young checkout clerk, is a foil for Sammy. Because he is a little older than Sammy and shows none of Sammy's imagination, restlessness, or nonconformity, Stokesie suggests what Sammy might become if he were to continue to work at the A&P. Some flat characters are **stock characters,** easily identifiable types who behave so predictably that readers can readily recognize them. The kindly old priest, the tough young bully, the ruthless business executive, and the reckless adventurer are all stock characters. Some flat characters can even be **caricatures,** characterized by a single dominant trait, such as miserliness, or even by one physical trait, such as nearsightedness.

DYNAMIC AND STATIC CHARACTERS

Characters may also be classified as either *dynamic* or *static*. **Dynamic** characters grow and change in the course of a story, developing as they react to events and to other characters. In "A&P," for instance, Sammy's decision to speak out in defense of the girls — as well as the events that lead him to do so — changes him. His view of the world has changed at the end of the story, and as a result his position in the world will change too. A **static** character may face the same challenges a dynamic character might face but will remain essentially unchanged: a static character who was selfish and arrogant will remain selfish and arrogant, regardless of the nature of the story's conflict. In the fairy tale "Cinderella," for example, the title character is as sweet and good-natured at the end of the story — despite her mistreatment by her family — as she is at the beginning. Her situation may have changed, but her character has not.

Whereas round characters tend to be dynamic, flat characters tend to be static. But even a very complex, well-developed major character may be static; sometimes, in fact, the point of a story may hinge on a character's inability to change. A familiar example is the title character in William Faulkner's "A Rose for Emily" (p. 91), who lives a wasted, empty life, at least in part because she is unwilling or unable to accept that the world around her and the people in it have changed.

A story's minor characters are often static; their growth is not usually relevant to the story's development. Moreover, we usually do not learn enough about a minor character's traits, thoughts, actions, or motivation to determine whether the character changes significantly.

MOTIVATION

Because round characters are complex, they are not always easy to understand. They may act differently in similar situations, just as real people do. They wrestle with decisions, resist or succumb to temptation, make mistakes, ask questions, search for answers, hope and dream, rejoice and despair. What is important is not whether we approve of a character's actions but whether those actions are *plausible* — whether the actions make sense in light of what we know about the character. We need to see a character's **motivation** — the reasons behind his or her behavior — or we will not believe or accept that behavior. For instance, given Sammy's age, his dissatisfaction with his job, and his desire to impress the young woman he calls Queenie, the decision he makes at the end of the story is perfectly plausible. Without having established his motivation, Updike could not have expected readers to accept Sammy's actions.

Even when readers get to know a character, they still are not able to predict how a complex, round character will behave in a given situation; only a flat character is predictable. The tension that develops as readers wait to see how a character will act or react, and thus how a story's conflict will be resolved, is what holds readers' interest and keeps them involved as a story's action unfolds.

CHECKLIST   **WRITING ABOUT CHARACTER**

✓ Who is the story's protagonist? Who is the antagonist? Who are the other major characters?

✓ Who are the minor characters? What roles do they play in the story? How would the story be different without them?

✓ What do the major characters look like? Is their physical appearance important?

✓ What are the major characters' most noticeable personality traits?

✓ What are the major characters' likes and dislikes? Their strengths and weaknesses?

✓ What are we told about the major characters' backgrounds and prior experiences? What can we infer?

✓ Are characters developed for the most part through the narrator's comments and descriptions or through the characters' actions and dialogue?

✓ Are the characters round or flat?

✓ Are the characters dynamic or static?

✓ Does the story include any stock characters? Any caricatures? Does any character serve as a foil?

✓ Do the characters act in a way that is consistent with how readers expect them to act?

✓ With which characters are readers likely to be most sympathetic? Least sympathetic?

JOHN UPDIKE (1932–   ) is a prolific writer of novels, short stories, essays, poems, plays, and children's tales. Updike's earliest ambition was to be a cartoonist for *The New Yorker*. He attended Harvard hoping to draw cartoons for *The Lampoon,* studied drawing and fine art at Oxford, and in 1955 went to work for *The New Yorker* — not as a cartoonist, but as a "Talk of the Town" reporter. Updike left *The New Yorker* after three years to write full-time but (over forty years later) is still contributing stories, reviews, and essays to the magazine. Among his novels are *Rabbit, Run* (1960), *The Centaur* (1963), *Rabbit Redux* (1971), *Rabbit Is Rich* (1981), *The Witches of Eastwick* (1985), *Rabbit at Rest* (1990), *Memories of*

the Ford Administration (1992), *Brazil* (1994), *In the Beauty of the Lilies* (1996), and *Toward the End of Time* (1997). His most recent novel is *Seek My Face* (2002). Updike has also published *Collected Poems 1953–1993* (1993) and a collection of essays titled *The Afterlife and Other Stories* (1994). In 1998, Updike received the National Book Foundation Medal for Distinguished Contribution to American Letters.

In early stories such as "A&P" (1961), Updike draws on memories of his childhood and teenage years for the sort of "small" scenes and stories for which he quickly became famous. "There is a great deal to be said about almost anything," Updike comments in an interview in *Contemporary Authors.* "All people can be equally interesting. . . . Now either nobody is a hero or everybody is. I vote for everybody. My subject is the American Protestant small-town middle class. I like middles. It is in middles that extremes clash. . . ."

"What John Updike does for a living," writes John Romano in the *New York Times Book Review,* "is remind us of the human costliness of an everyday situation." In "A&P," there is cost, and a small triumph — and a young man's growing awareness of the "hard" world ahead.

Cultural Context: Throughout the 1950s, many Americans profited from the post–World War II economic boom, enjoying a period of long-awaited material prosperity. Business, especially the corporate world, offered the promise of the good life (usually in the suburbs), with its real and symbolic marks of success — house, car, television, and the latest in home appliances. Attached to this ideal were assumptions concerning the "typical" American lifestyle, the "proper" family (in terms of its size and its rigidly defined gender roles), and codes of "appropriate" behavior, all of which contributed to the nation's conformist mentality.

A&P (1961)

In walks these three girls in nothing but bathing suits. I'm in the third check-out slot, with my back to the door, so I don't see them until they're over by the bread. The one that caught my eye first was the one in the plaid green two-piece. She was a chunky kid, with a good tan and a sweet broad soft-looking can with those two crescents of white just under it, where the sun never seems to hit, at the top of the backs of her legs. I stood there with my hand on a box of HiHo crackers trying to remember if I rang it up or not. I ring it up again and the customer starts giving me hell. She's one of these cash-register-watchers, a witch about fifty with rouge on her cheekbones and no eyebrows, and I know it made her day to trip me up. She'd been watching cash registers for fifty years and probably never seen a mistake before.

By the time I got her feathers smoothed and her goodies into a bag — she gives me a little snort in passing, if she'd been born at the right time they would have burned her over in Salem — by the time I get her on her way the girls had circled around the bread and were coming back, without a push-cart, back my way along the counters, in the aisle between the check-outs and the Special bins.

They didn't even have shoes on. There was this chunky one, with the two-piece — it was bright green and the seams on the bra were still sharp and her belly was still pretty pale so I guessed she just got it (the suit) — there was this one, with one of those chubby berry-faces, the lips all bunched together under her nose, this one, and a tall one, with black hair that hadn't quite frizzed right, and one of these sunburns right across under the eyes, and a chin that was too long — you know, the kind of girl other girls think is very "striking" and "attractive" but never quite makes it, as they very well know, which is why they like her so much — and then the third one, that wasn't quite so tall. She was the queen. She kind of led them, the other two peeking around and making their shoulders round. She didn't look around, not this queen, she just walked straight on slowly, on these long white prima-donna legs. She came down a little hard on her heels, as if she didn't walk in her bare feet that much, putting down her heels and then letting the weight move along to her toes as if she was testing the floor with every step, putting a little deliberate extra action into it. You never know for sure how girls' minds work (do you really think it's a mind in there or just a little buzz like a bee in a glass jar?) but you got the idea she had talked the other two into coming in here with her, and now she was showing them how to do it, walk slow and hold yourself straight.

She had on a kind of dirty-pink — beige maybe, I don't know — bathing suit with a little nubble all over it and, what got me, the straps were down. They were off her shoulders looped loose around the cool tops of her arms, and I guess as a result the suit had slipped a little on her, so all around the top of the cloth there was this shining rim. If it hadn't been there you wouldn't have known there could have been anything whiter than those shoulders. With the straps pushed off, there was nothing between the top of the suit and the top of her head except just *her*, this clean bare plane of the top of her chest down from the shoulder bones like a dented sheet of metal tilted in the light. I mean, it was more than pretty.

She had sort of oaky hair that the sun and salt had bleached, done up in a bun that was unravelling, and a kind of prim face. Walking into the A&P with your straps down, I suppose it's the only kind of face you *can* have. She held her head so high her neck, coming up out of those white shoulders, looked kind of stretched, but I didn't mind. The longer her neck was, the more of her there was.

5　　She must have felt in the corner of her eye me and over my shoulder Stokesie in the second slot watching, but she didn't tip. Not this queen. She kept her eyes moving across the racks, and stopped, and turned so slow it made my stomach rub the inside of my apron, and buzzed to the other two, who kind of huddled against her for relief, and they all three of them went up the cat-and-dog-food-breakfast-cereal-macaroni-rice-raisins-seasonings-spreads-spaghetti-soft-drinks-crackers-and-cookies aisle. From the third slot I look straight up this aisle to the meat counter, and I watched them all the way. The fat one with the tan sort of fumbled with the cookies, but on second thought she put the packages back. The sheep pushing their carts down the aisle — the girls were walking against the usual traffic (not that we have one-way signs or anything) — were pretty hilarious. You could see them, when Queenie's white shoulders dawned on them, kind of jerk, or hop, or hiccup, but their eyes snapped back to their own baskets and on they pushed. I bet you could set off dynamite in an A&P and the people would by and large keep reaching and checking oatmeal off their lists and muttering "Let me see, there was a third thing, began with A, asparagus, no, ah, yes, applesauce!" or whatever it is they do mutter. But there was no doubt, this jiggled them. A few houseslaves in pin curlers even looked around after pushing their carts past to make sure what they had seen was correct.

You know, it's one thing to have a girl in a bathing suit down on the beach, where what with the glare nobody can look at each other much anyway, and another thing in the cool of the A&P, under the fluorescent lights, against all those stacked packages, with her feet paddling along naked over our checkerboard green-and-cream rubber-tile floor.

"Oh Daddy," Stokesie said beside me. "I feel so faint."

"Darling," I said. "Hold me tight." Stokesie's married, with two babies chalked up on his fuselage already, but as far as I can tell that's the only difference. He's twenty-two, and I was nineteen this April.

"Is it done?" he asks, the responsible married man finding his voice. I forgot to say he thinks he's going to be manager some sunny day, maybe in 1990 when it's called the Great Alexandrov and Petrooshki Tea Company or something.

What he meant was, our town is five miles from a beach, with a big summer   10
colony out on the Point, but we're right in the middle of town, and the women generally put on a shirt or shorts or something before they get out of the car into the street. And anyway these are usually women with six children and varicose veins mapping their legs and nobody, including them, could care less. As I say, we're right in the middle of town, and if you stand at our front doors you can see two banks and the Congregational church and the newspaper store and three real-estate offices and about twenty-seven old freeloaders tearing up Central Street because the sewer broke again. It's not as if we're on the Cape; we're north of Boston and there's people in this town haven't seen the ocean for twenty years.

The girls had reached the meat counter and were asking McMahon something. He pointed, they pointed, and they shuffled out of sight behind a pyramid of Diet Delight peaches. All that was left for us to see was old McMahon patting his mouth and looking after them sizing up their joints. Poor kids, I began to feel sorry for them, they couldn't help it.

Now here comes the sad part of the story, at least my family says it's sad but I don't think it's sad myself. The store's pretty empty, it being Thursday afternoon, so there was nothing much to do except lean on the register and wait for the girls to show up again. The whole store was like a pinball machine and I didn't know which tunnel they'd come out of. After a while they come around out of the far aisle, around the light bulbs, records at discount of the Caribbean Six or Tony Martin Sings or some such gunk you wonder they waste the wax on, sixpacks of candy bars, and plastic toys done up in cellophane that fall apart when a kid looks at them anyway. Around they come, Queenie still leading the way, and holding a little gray jar in her hand. Slots Three through Seven are unmanned and I could see her wondering between Stokes and me, but Stokesie with his usual luck draws an old party in baggy gray pants who stumbles up with four giant cans of pineapple juice (what do these bums *do* with all that pineapple juice? I've often asked myself) so the girls come to me. Queenie puts down the jar and I take it into my fingers icy cold. Kingfish Fancy Herring Snacks in Pure Sour Cream: 49. Now her hands are empty, not a ring or a bracelet, bare as God made them, and I wonder where the money's coming from. Still with that prim look she lifts a folded dollar bill out of the hollow at the center of her nubbled pink top. The jar went heavy in my hand. Really, I thought that was so cute.

Then everybody's luck begins to run out. Lengel comes in from haggling with a truck full of cabbages on the lot and is about to scuttle into that door marked MANAGER behind which he hides all day when the girls touch his eye. Lengel's pretty dreary, teaches Sunday school and the rest, but he doesn't miss that much. He comes over and says, "Girls, this isn't the beach."

Queenie blushes, though maybe it's just a brush of sunburn I was noticing for the first time, now that she was so close. "My mother asked me to pick up a jar of herring snacks." Her voice kind of startled me, the way voices do when you see the people first, coming out so flat and dumb yet kind of tony, too, the way it ticked over "pick up" and "snacks." All of a sudden I slid right down her voice into her living room. Her father and the other men were standing around in ice-cream coats and bow ties and the women were in sandals picking up herring snacks on toothpicks off a big plate and they were all holding drinks the color of water with olives and sprigs of mint in them. When my parents have somebody over they get lemonade and if it's a real racy affair Schlitz in tall glasses with "They'll Do It Every Time" cartoons stenciled on.

15 "That's all right," Lengel said. "But this isn't the beach." His repeating this struck me as funny, as if it had just occurred to him, and he had been thinking all these years the A&P was a great big dune and he was the head lifeguard. He didn't like my smiling — as I say he doesn't miss much — but he concentrates on giving the girls that sad Sunday-school-superintendent stare.

Queenie's blush is no sunburn now, and the plump one in plaid, that I liked better from the back — a really sweet can — pipes up, "We weren't doing any shopping. We just came in for the one thing."

"That makes no difference," Lengel tells her, and I could see from the way his eyes went that he hadn't noticed she was wearing a two-piece before. "We want you decently dressed when you come in here."

"We *are* decent," Queenie says suddenly, her lower lip pushing, getting sore now that she remembers her place, a place from which the crowd that runs the A&P must look pretty crummy. Fancy Herring Snacks flashed in her very blue eyes.

"Girls, I don't want to argue with you. After this come in here with your shoulders covered. It's our policy." He turns his back. That's policy for you. Policy is what the kingpins want. What the others want is juvenile delinquency.

20 All this while, the customers had been showing up with their carts but, you know, sheep, seeing a scene, they had all bunched up on Stokesie, who shook open a paper bag as gently as peeling a peach, not wanting to miss a word. I could feel in the silence everybody getting nervous, most of all Lengel, who asks me, "Sammy, have you rung up this purchase?"

I thought and said "No" but it wasn't about that I was thinking. I go through the punches, 4, 9, GROC, TOT—it's more complicated than you think, and after you do it often enough, it begins to make a little song, that you hear words to, in my case "Hello *(bing)* there, you *(gung)* hap-py *pee*-pul *(splat)*!"—the *splat* being the drawer flying out. I uncrease the bill, tenderly as you may imagine, it just hav-ing come from between the two smoothest scoops of vanilla I had ever known were there, and pass a half and a penny into her narrow pink palm, and nestle the herrings in a bag and twist its neck and hand it over, all the time thinking.

The girls, and who'd blame them, are in a hurry to get out, so I say "I quit" to Lengel quick enough for them to hear, hoping they'll stop and watch me, their unsuspected hero. They keep right on going, into the electric eye; the door flies open and they flicker across the lot to their car, Queenie and Plaid and Big Tall Goony-Goony (not that as raw material she was so bad), leaving me with Lengel and a kink in his eyebrow.

"Did you say something, Sammy?"

"I said I quit."

"I thought you did."   25

"You didn't have to embarrass them."

"It was they who were embarrassing us."

I started to say something that came out "Fiddle-de-doo." It's a saying of my grandmother's, and I know she would have been pleased.

"I don't think you know what you're saying," Lengel said.

"I know you don't," I said. "But I do." I pull the bow at the back of my apron   30 and start shrugging it off my shoulders. A couple customers that had been heading for my slot begin to knock against each other, like scared pigs in a chute.

Lengel sighs and begins to look very patient and old and gray. He's been a friend of my parents for years. "Sammy, you don't want to do this to your Mom and Dad," he tells me. It's true, I don't. But it seems to me that once you begin a ges-ture it's fatal not to go through with it. I fold the apron, "Sammy" stitched in red on the pocket, and put it on the counter, and drop the bow tie on top of it. The bow tie is theirs, if you've ever wondered. "You'll feel this for the rest of your life," Lengel says, and I know that's true, too, but remembering how he made that pretty girl blush makes me so scrunchy inside I punch the No Sale tab and the machine whirs "pee-pul" and the drawer splats out. One advantage to this scene taking place in summer, I can follow this up with a clean exit, there's no fumbling around getting your coat and galoshes, I just saunter into the electric eye in my white shirt that my mother ironed the night before, and the door heaves itself open, and outside the sunshine is skating around the asphalt.

I look around for my girls, but they're gone, of course. There wasn't anybody but some young married screaming with her children about some candy they didn't get by the door of a powder-blue Falcon station wagon. Looking back in the big windows, over the bags of peat moss and aluminum lawn furniture stacked on the pavement, I could see Lengel in my place in the slot, checking the sheep through. His face was dark gray and his back stiff, as if he'd just had an injection of iron, and my stomach kind of fell as I felt how hard the world was going to be to me hereafter.

Reading and Reacting

1. Summarize the information Sammy gives readers about his tastes and background. Why is this exposition vital to the story's development?
2. List some of the most obvious physical characteristics of the A&P's customers. How do these characteristics make them foils for Queenie and her friends?
3. What is it about Queenie and her friends that appeals to Sammy?
4. Is Queenie a stock character? Explain.
5. What rules and conventions are customers expected to follow in a supermarket? How does the behavior of Queenie and her friends violate these conventions?
6. Is the supermarket setting vital to the story? Could the story have been set in a car wash? In a fast-food restaurant? In a business office?
7. How accurate are Sammy's judgments about the other characters? How might the characters be portrayed if the story were told by Lengel?
8. Given what you learn about Sammy during the course of the story, what do you see as his *primary* motivation for quitting his job? What other factors motivate him?
9. **JOURNAL ENTRY** Where do you think Sammy will find himself in ten years? Why?
10. **CRITICAL PERSPECTIVE** In her 1976 book *The Necessary Blackness*, critic Mary Allen observes, "Updike's most tender reverence is reserved for women's bodies. The elegant style with which he describes female anatomy often becomes overwrought, as his descriptions do generally. But it always conveys wonder."

    In what passages in "A&P" does Updike (through Sammy) convey this sense of wonder? Do you think today's audience, reading the story more than forty years after Updike wrote it, and more than twenty-five years after Allen's essay was published, would still see such passages as conveying "tender reverence"? Or do you think readers might now see Sammy (and, indeed, Updike) as sexist? How do you see these passages?

Related Works: "Araby" (p. 52), "Boys and Girls" (p. 493), "Ex-Basketball Player" (p. 684), "A Supermarket in California" (p. 704), "The Road Not Taken" (p. 880)

KATHERINE MANSFIELD (1888–1923), one of the pioneers of the modern short story, was born in New Zealand and educated in England. Very much a "modern young woman," she began living on her own in London at the age of nineteen, soon publishing stories and book reviews in many of the most influential literary magazines of the day. One of these she edited with critic John Middleton Murry, whom she married in 1918.

A short story writer of great versatility, Mansfield produced sparkling social comedies for popular consumption as well as more intellectually and technically complex works intended for "perceptive readers." According to one critic, her best works "[w]ith delicate plainness . . . present elusive moments of decision, defeat, and small triumph." Her last two story collections — *Bliss and Other Stories* (1920) and *The Garden Party and Other Stories* (1922) — were met with immediate critical acclaim, but Mansfield's career was cut short in 1923 when she died of complications from tuberculosis at the age of thirty-five.

One notable theme in Mansfield's work is the *dame seule,* the "woman alone," which provides the basis for the poignant "Miss Brill."

Cultural Context: During the nineteenth century, the task of spinning wool was typically given to unmarried women as a way for them to earn their keep in the home. Thus, the term *spinster* came into existence. Over time, the word acquired a negative stereotype, conjuring up the image of a lonely, childless, frumpy, middle-aged woman who longs to be like other "normal" women — wives and mothers. Today, the word *spinster* is rarely used, reflecting the changed perception of unmarried women and the wider lifestyle choices open to them.

Miss Brill (1922)

Although it was so brilliantly fine — the blue sky powdered with gold and great spots of light like white wine splashed over the Jardins Publiques° — Miss Brill was glad that she had decided on her fur. The air was motionless, but when you opened your mouth there was just a faint chill, like a chill from a glass of iced water before you sip, and now and again a leaf came drifting — from nowhere, from the sky. Miss Brill put up her hand and touched her fur. Dear little thing! It was nice to feel it again. She had taken it out of its box that afternoon, shaken out the moth-powder, given it a good brush, and rubbed the life back into the dim little eyes. "What has been happening to me?" said the sad little eyes. Oh, how sweet it was to see them snap at her again from the red eiderdown! . . . But the nose, which was of some black composition, wasn't at all firm. It must have had a knock, somehow. Never mind — a little dab of black sealing-wax when the time came — when it was absolutely necessary. . . . Little rogue! Yes, she really felt like that about it. Little rogue biting its tail just by her left ear. She could have taken it off and laid in on her lap and stroked it. She felt a tingling in her hands and arms, but that came from walking, she supposed. And when she breathed, something light and sad — no, not sad, exactly — something gentle seemed to move in her bosom.

There were a number of people out this afternoon, far more than last Sunday. And the band sounded louder and gayer. That was because the Season had begun. For although the band played all year round on Sundays, out of season it was never the same. It was like some one playing with only the family to listen; it didn't care how it played if there weren't any strangers present. Wasn't the conductor wearing a new coat, too? She was sure it was new. He scraped with his foot and flapped

---

Jardins Publiques: "Public Gardens" (French).

his arms like a rooster about to crow, and the bandsmen sitting in the green rotunda blew out their cheeks and glared at the music. Now there came a little
"flutey" bit — very pretty! — a little chain of bright drops. She was sure it would
be repeated. It was; she lifted her head and smiled.

Only two people shared her "special" seat: a fine old man in a velvet coat, his
hands clasped over a huge carved walking-stick, and a big old woman, sitting upright, with a roll of knitting on her embroidered apron. They did not speak. This
was disappointing, for Miss Brill always looked forward to the conversation. She
had become really quite expert, she thought, at listening as though she didn't listen, at sitting in other people's lives just for a minute while they talked round her.

She glanced, sideways, at the old couple. Perhaps they would go soon. Last
Sunday, too, hadn't been as interesting as usual. An Englishman and his wife, he
wearing a dreadful Panama hat and she button boots. And she'd gone on the whole
time about how she ought to wear spectacles; she knew she needed them; but that
it was no good getting any; they'd be sure to break and they'd never keep on. And
he'd been so patient. He'd suggested everything — gold rims, the kind that curved
round your ears, little pads inside the bridge. No, nothing would please her.
"They'll always be sliding down my nose!" Miss Brill wanted to shake her.

5   The old people sat on the bench, still as statues. Never mind, there was always
the crowd to watch. To and fro, in front of the flower-beds and the band rotunda,
the couples and groups paraded, stopped to talk, to greet, to buy a handful of flowers from the old beggar who had his tray fixed to the railings. Little children ran
among them, swooping and laughing; little boys with big white silk bows under
their chins, little girls, little French dolls, dressed up in velvet and lace. And
sometimes a tiny staggerer came suddenly rocking into the open from under the
trees, stopped, stared, as suddenly sat down "flop," until its small high-stepping
mother, like a young hen, rushed scolding to its rescue. Other people sat on the
benches and green chairs, but they were nearly always the same, Sunday after
Sunday, and — Miss Brill had often noticed — there was something funny about
nearly all of them. They were odd, silent, nearly all old, and from the way they
stared they looked as though they'd just come from dark little rooms or even —
even cupboards!

Behind the rotunda the slender trees with yellow leaves down drooping, and
through them just a line of sea, and beyond the blue sky with gold-veined clouds.

Tum-tum-tum tiddle-um! tiddle-um! tum tiddley-um tum ta! blew the band.

Two young girls in red came by and two young soldiers in blue met them,
and they laughed and paired and went off arm-in-arm. Two peasant women with
funny straw hats passed, gravely, leading beautiful smoke-colored donkeys. A cold,
pale nun hurried by. A beautiful woman came along and dropped her bunch of violets, and a little boy ran after to hand them to her, and she took them and threw
them away as if they'd been poisoned. Dear me! Miss Brill didn't know whether to
admire that or not! And now an ermine toque° and a gentleman in grey met just
in front of her. He was tall, stiff, dignified, and she was wearing the ermine toque

---

toque: Small, close-fitting woman's hat.

she'd bought when her hair was yellow. Now everything, her hair, her face, even her eyes, was the same color as the shabby ermine, and her hand, in its cleaned glove, lifted to dab her lips, was a tiny yellowish paw. Oh, she was so pleased to see him — delighted! She rather thought they were going to meet that afternoon. She described where she'd been — everywhere, here, there, along by the sea. The day was so charming — didn't he agree? And wouldn't he, perhaps? . . . But he shook his head, lighted a cigarette, slowly breathed a great deep puff into her face, and, even while she was still talking and laughing, flicked the match away and walked on. The ermine toque was alone; she smiled more brightly than ever. But even the band seemed to know what she was feeling and played more softly, played tenderly, and the drum beat, "The Brute! The Brute!" over and over. What would she do? What was going to happen now? But as Miss Brill wondered, the ermine toque turned, raised her hand as though she'd seen some one else, much nicer, just over there, and pattered away. And the band changed again and played more quickly, more gaily than ever, and the old couple on Miss Brill's seat got up and marched away, and such a funny old man with long whiskers hobbled along in time to the music and was nearly knocked over by four girls walking abreast.

Oh, how fascinating it was! How she enjoyed it! How she loved sitting here, watching it all! It was like a play. It was exactly like a play. Who could believe the sky at the back wasn't painted? But it wasn't till a little brown dog trotted on solemn and then slowly trotted off, like a little "theatre" dog, a little dog that had been drugged, that Miss Brill discovered what it was that made it so exciting. They were all on the stage. They weren't only the audience, not only looking on; they were acting. Even she had a part and came every Sunday. No doubt somebody would have noticed if she hadn't been there; she was part of the performance after all. How strange she'd never thought of it like that before! And yet it explained why she made such a point of starting from home at just the same time each week — so as not to be late for the performance — and it also explained why she had quite a queer, shy feeling at telling her English pupils how she spent her Sunday afternoons. No wonder! Miss Brill nearly laughed out loud. She was on the stage. She thought of the old invalid gentleman to whom she read the newspaper four afternoons a week while he slept in the garden. She had got quite used to the frail head on the cotton pillow, the hollowed eyes, the open mouth and the high pinched nose. If he'd been dead she mightn't have noticed for weeks; she wouldn't have minded. But suddenly he knew he was having the paper read to him by an actress! "An actress!" The old head lifted; two points of light quivered in the old eyes. "An actress — are ye?" And Miss Brill smoothed the newspaper as though it were the manuscript of her part and said gently: "Yes, I have been an actress for a long time."

The band had been having a rest. Now they started again. And what they 10
played was warm, sunny, yet there was just a faint chill — a something, what was it? — not sadness — no, not sadness — a something that made you want to sing. The tune lifted, lifted, the light shone; and it seemed to Miss Brill that in another moment all of them, all the whole company, would begin singing. The young ones, the laughing ones who were moving together, they would begin, and the men's voices, very resolute and brave, would join them. And then she too, she too,

and the others on the benches — they would come in with a kind of accompaniment — something low, that scarcely rose or fell, something so beautiful — moving. . . . And Miss Brill's eyes filled with tears and she looked smiling at all the other members of the company. Yes, we understand, we understand, she thought — though what they understood she didn't know.

Just at that moment a boy and a girl came and sat down where the old couple had been. They were beautifully dressed; they were in love. The hero and heroine, of course, just arrived from his father's yacht. And still soundlessly singing, still with that trembling smile, Miss Brill prepared to listen.

"No, not now," said the girl. "Not here, I can't."

"But why? Because of that stupid old thing at the end there?" asked the boy. "Why does she come here at all — who wants her? Why doesn't she keep her silly old mug at home?"

"It's her fu-fur which is so funny," giggled the girl. "It's exactly like a fried whiting."°

15   "Ah, be off with you!" said the boy in an angry whisper. Then: "Tell me, my petite chérie —"°

"No, not here," said the girl. "Not yet."

On her way home she usually bought a slice of honeycake at the baker's. It was her Sunday treat. Sometimes there was an almond in her slice, sometimes not. It made a great difference. If there was an almond it was like carrying home a tiny present — a surprise — something that might very well not have been there. She hurried on the almond Sundays and struck the match for the kettle in quite a dashing way.

But to-day she passed the baker's boy, climbed the stairs, went into the little dark room — her room like a cupboard — and sat down on the red eiderdown. She sat there for a long time. The box that the fur came out of was on the bed. She unclasped the necklet quickly; quickly, without looking, laid it inside. But when she put the lid on she thought she heard something crying.

Reading and Reacting

1. What specific details can you infer about Miss Brill's character (and, perhaps, about her life) from this statement: "She had become really quite expert, she thought, at listening as though she didn't listen, at sitting in other people's lives just for a minute while they talked round her" (par. 3)?

2. How do Miss Brill's observations of the people around her give us insight into her own character? Why do you suppose she doesn't interact with any of the people she observes?

3. In paragraph 9, Miss Brill realizes that the scene she observes is "exactly like a play" and that "Even she had a part and came every Sunday." What part does Miss Brill play? Is she a stock character in this play, or is she a three-dimensional character? Does she play a lead role or a supporting role?

---

whiting: Food fish related to the cod.
petite chérie: "Little darling" (French).

4. What do you think Miss Brill means when she says, "I have been an actress for a long time" (par. 9)? What does this comment reveal about how Miss Brill sees herself? Is her view of herself similar to or different from the view the other characters have of her?

5. What role does Miss Brill's fur piece play in the story? In what sense, if any, does it function as a character?

6. What happens in paragraphs 11–16 to break Miss Brill's mood? Why is the scene she observes so upsetting to her?

7. At the end of the story, has Miss Brill changed as a result of what she has overheard, or is she the same person she was at the beginning? Do you think she will return to the park the following Sunday?

8. The story's last paragraph describes Miss Brill's room as being "like a cupboard." Where else has this image appeared in the story? What does its repetition in the conclusion tell us?

9. **JOURNAL ENTRY** Write a character sketch of Miss Brill, inventing a plausible family and personal history that might help to explain the character you see in the story.

10. **CRITICAL PERSPECTIVE** Critic Gillian Boddy, in *Katherine Mansfield: The Woman, The Writer,* offers the following analysis of Mansfield's fiction:

> The story evolves through the characters' minds. The external narrator is almost eliminated. As so often in her work, the reader is dropped into the story and simply confronted by a particular situation. There is no preliminary establishing and identification of time and place. The reader is immediately involved; it is assumed that he or she has any necessary prerequisite knowledge and is, in a sense, part of the story too.

Do you see this absence of conventional exposition as a problem in "Miss Brill"? Do you think the story would be more effective if Mansfield had supplied more preliminary information about setting and character? Or do you believe that what Boddy calls Mansfield's "concentration on a moment or episode" is a satisfactory substitute for the missing exposition, effectively shifting interest from "*what* happens" to "*why* it happens"?

Related Works: "A Clean, Well-Lighted Place" (p. 267), "Rooming houses are old women" (p. 687), "Aunt Jennifer's Tigers" (p. 715), "After great pain, a formal feeling comes —" (p. 866), "Acquainted with the Night" (p. 876), *The Stronger* (p. 947)

CHARLES BAXTER (1947–   ) was born in Minneapolis and educated at Macalester College and at the State University of New York, Buffalo. He is currently a professor of English at the University of Michigan. Baxter is the author of four critically praised collections of short stories: *Harmony of the World* (1984), *Through the Safety Net* (1985), *A Relative Stranger: Stories* (1990), and *Believers: A Novella and Stories* (1997). He is the author of three novels, *First Light* (1987), *Shadow Play* (1993), and *The Feast of Love* (2002), and one book of poetry, *Imaginary Paintings and Other Poems* (1989). Baxter has also written a book of nonfiction, *Burning Down the House* (1997), a collection of essays on fiction.

Baxter's critics often mention the compassion he shows in writing about his fictional characters: a couple who lose their child, a hospital worker who wants to be famous, a tired businessman who really wants to paint. In many of the short stories in *Through the Safety Net* (from which "Gryphon" is taken), unexpected events jar Baxter's characters out of their routines — forcing them to consider different choices, to call on inner strength, or to swim against the tide of "middle America's" conventions.

Cultural Context: Although educational *methods* differ from teacher to teacher, educational *standards* are designed at the statewide and national levels to ensure that students receive the same minimum amount of instruction in a set number of subjects. The standards, which apply to all teachers, dictate what students need to know and which skills they should possess at different grade levels. One disadvantage of such standardized education is that teachers find they have to "teach to the test" instead of designing curricula that stimulate students' creative imaginations.

Gryphon (1985)

On Wednesday afternoon, between the geography lesson on ancient Egypt's hand-operated irrigation system and an art project that involved drawing a model city next to a mountain, our fourth-grade teacher, Mr. Hibler, developed a cough. This cough began with a series of muffled throat clearings and progressed to propulsive noises contained within Mr. Hibler's closed mouth. "Listen to him," Carol Peterson whispered to me. "He's gonna blow up." Mr. Hibler's laughter — dazed and infrequent — sounded a bit like his cough, but as we worked on our model cities we would look up, thinking he was enjoying a joke, and see Mr. Hibler's face turning red, his cheeks puffed out. This was not laughter. Twice he bent over, and his loose tie, like a plumb line, hung down straight from his neck as he exploded himself into a Kleenex. He would excuse himself, then go on coughing. "I'll bet you a dime," Carol Peterson whispered, "we get a substitute tomorrow."

Carol sat at the desk in front of mine and was a bad person — when she thought no one was looking she would blow her nose on notebook paper, then crumble it up and throw it into the wastebasket — but at times of crisis she spoke the truth. I knew I'd lose the dime.

"No deal," I said.

When Mr. Hibler stood us up in formation at the door just prior to the final bell, he was almost incapable of speech. "I'm sorry, boys and girls," he said. "I seem to be coming down with something."

5   "I hope you feel better tomorrow, Mr. Hibler," Bobby Kryzanowicz, the faultless brown-noser said, and I heard Carol Peterson's evil giggle. Then Mr. Hibler opened the door and we walked out to the buses, a clique of us starting noisily to hawk and cough as soon as we thought we were a few feet beyond Mr. Hibler's earshot.

Five Oaks being a rural community, and in Michigan, the supply of substitute teachers was limited to the town's unemployed community college graduates, a pool of about four mothers. These ladies fluttered, provided easeful class days, and

nervously covered material we had mastered weeks earlier. Therefore it was a surprise when a woman we had never seen came into the class the next day, carrying
a purple purse, a checkerboard lunchbox, and a few books. She put the books on
one side of Mr. Hibler's desk and the lunchbox on the other, next to the Voice of
Music phonograph. Three of us in the back of the room were playing with Heever,
the chameleon that lived in the terrarium and on one of the plastic drapes, when
she walked in.

She clapped her hands at us. "Little boys," she said, "why are you bent over together like that?" She didn't wait for us to answer. "Are you tormenting an animal? Put it back. Please sit down at your desks. I want no cabals this time of the
day." We just stared at her. "Boys," she repeated, "I asked you to sit down."

I put the chameleon in his terrarium and felt my way to my desk, never taking
my eyes off the woman. With white and green chalk, she had started to draw a tree
on the left side of the blackboard. She didn't look usual. Furthermore, her tree was
outsized, disproportionate, for some reason.

"This room needs a tree," she said, with one line drawing the suggestion of a
leaf. "A large, leafy, shady, deciduous . . . oak."

Her fine, light hair had been done up in what I would learn years later was   10
called a chignon, and she wore gold-rimmed glasses whose lenses seemed to have
the faintest blue tint. Harold Knardahl, who sat across from me, whispered
"Mars," and I nodded slowly, savoring the imminent weirdness of the day. The substitute drew another branch with an extravagant arm gesture, then turned around
and said, "Good morning. I don't believe I said good morning to all you yet."

Facing us, she was no special age — an adult is an adult — but her face had
two prominent lines, descending vertically from the sides of her mouth to her
chin. I knew where I had seen those lines before: *Pinocchio*. They were marionette
lines. "You may stare at me," she said to us, as a few more kids from the last bus
came into the room, their eyes fixed on her, "for a few more seconds, until the bell
rings. Then I will permit no more staring. Looking I will permit. Staring, no. It is
impolite to stare, and a sign of bad breeding. You cannot make a social effort while
staring."

Harold Knardahl did not glance at me, or nudge, but I heard him whisper
"Mars" again, trying to get more mileage out of his single joke with the kids who
had just come in.

When everyone was seated, the substitute teacher finished her tree, put down
her chalk fastidiously on the phonograph, brushed her hands, and faced us. "Good
morning," she said. "I am Miss Ferenczi, your teacher for the day. I am fairly new
to your community, and I don't believe any of you know me. I will therefore start
by telling you a story about myself."

While we settled back, she launched into her tale. She said her grandfather
had been a Hungarian prince; her mother had been born in some place called
Flanders, had been a pianist, and had played concerts for people Miss Ferenczi referred to as "crowned heads." She gave us a knowing look. "Grieg," she said, "the
Norwegian master, wrote a concerto for piano that was," she paused, "my mother's
triumph at her debut concert in London." Her eyes searched the ceiling. Our eyes
followed. Nothing up there but ceiling tile. "For reasons that I shall not go into,

my family's fortunes took us to Detroit, then north to dreadful Saginaw, and now here I am in Five Oaks, as your substitute teacher, for today, Thursday, October the eleventh. I believe it will be a good day: All the forecasts coincide. We shall start with your reading lesson. Take out your reading book. I believe it is called *Broad Horizons,* or something along those lines."

15   Jeannie Vermeesch raised her hand. Miss Ferenczi nodded at her. "Mr. Hibler always starts the day with the Pledge of Allegiance," Jeannie whined.

"Oh, does he? In that case," Miss Ferenczi said, "you must know it *very* well by now, and we certainly need not spend our time on it. No, no allegiance pledging on the premises today, by my reckoning. Not with so much sunlight coming into the room. A pledge does not suit my mood." She glanced at her watch. "Time *is* flying. Take out *Broad Horizons.*"

She disappointed us by giving us an ordinary lesson, complete with vocabulary word drills, comprehension questions, and recitation. She didn't seem to care for the material, however. She sighed every few minutes and rubbed her glasses with a frilly perfumed handkerchief that she withdrew, magician style, from her left sleeve.

After reading we moved on to arithmetic. It was my favorite time of the morning, when the lazy autumn sunlight dazzled its way through ribbons of clouds past the windows on the east side of the classroom, and crept across the linoleum floor. On the playground the first group of children, the kindergartners, were running on the quack grass just beyond the monkey bars. We were doing multiplication tables. Miss Ferenczi had made John Wazny stand up at his desk in the front row. He was supposed to go through the tables of six. From where I was sitting, I could smell the Vitalis soaked into John's plastered hair. He was doing fine until he came to six times eleven and six times twelve. "Six times eleven," he said, "is sixty-eight. Six times twelve is . . ." He put his fingers to his head, quickly and secretly sniffed his fingertips, and said, "seventy-two." Then he sat down.

"Fine," Miss Ferenczi said. "Well now. That was very good."

20   "Miss Ferenczi!" One of the Eddy twins was waving her hand desperately in the air. "Miss Ferenczi! Miss Ferenczi!"

"Yes?"

"John said that six times eleven is sixty-eight and you said he was right!"

"*Did* I?" She gazed at the class with a jolly look breaking across her marionette's face. "Did I say that? Well, what *is* six times eleven?"

"It's sixty-six!"

25   She nodded. "Yes. So it is. But, and I know some people will not entirely agree with me, at some times it is sixty-eight."

"When? When is it sixty-eight?"

We were all waiting.

"In higher mathematics, which you children do not yet understand, six times eleven can be considered to be sixty-eight." She laughed through her nose. "In higher mathematics numbers are . . . more fluid. The only thing a number does is contain a certain amount of something. Think of water. A cup is not the only way to measure a certain amount of water, is it?" We were staring, shaking our heads.

"You could use saucepans or thimbles. In either case, the water *would be the same*. Perhaps," she started again, "it would be better for you to think that six times eleven is sixty-eight only when I am in the room."

"Why is it sixty-eight," Mark Poole asked, "when you're in the room?"

"Because it's more interesting that way," she said, smiling very rapidly behind   30 her blue-tinted glasses. "Besides, I'm your substitute teacher, am I not?" We all nodded. "Well, then, think of six times eleven equals sixty-eight as a substitute fact."

"A substitute fact?"

"Yes." Then she looked at us carefully. "Do you think," she asked, "that anyone is going to be hurt by a substitute fact?"

We looked back at her.

"Will the plants on the windowsill be hurt?" We glanced at them. There were sensitive plants thriving in a green plastic tray, and several wilted ferns in small clay pots. "Your dogs and cats, or your moms and dads?" She waited. "So," she concluded, "what's the problem?"

"But it's wrong," Janice Weber said, "isn't it?"   35

"What's your name, young lady?"

"Janice Weber."

"And you think it's wrong, Janice?"

"I was just asking."

"Well, all right. You were just asking. I think we've spent enough time on this   40 matter by now, don't you, class? You are free to think what you like. When your teacher, Mr. Hibler, returns, six times eleven will be sixty-six again, you can rest assured. And it will be that for the rest of your lives in Five Oaks. Too bad, eh?" She raised her eyebrows and glinted herself at us. "But for now, it wasn't. So much for that. Let us go to your assigned problems for today, as painstakingly outlined, I see, in Mr. Hibler's lesson plan. Take out a sheet of paper and write your names in the upper left-hand corner."

For the next half hour we did the rest of our arithmetic problems. We handed them in and went on to spelling, my worst subject. Spelling always came before lunch. We were taking spelling dictation and looking at the clock. "Thorough," Miss Ferenczi said. "Boundary." She walked in the aisles between the desks, holding the spelling book open and looking down at our papers. "Balcony." I clutched my pencil. Somehow, the way she said those words, they seemed foreign, Hungarian, mis-voweled and mis-consonanted. I stared down at what I had spelled. *Balconie.* I turned my pencil upside down and erased my mistake. *Balconey.* That looked better, but still incorrect. I cursed the world of spelling and tried erasing it again and saw the paper beginning to wear away. *Balkony.* Suddenly I felt a hand on my shoulder.

"I don't like that word either," Miss Ferenczi whispered, bent over, her mouth near my ear. "It's ugly. My feeling is, if you don't like a word, you don't have to use it." She straightened up, leaving behind a slight odor of Clorets.

At lunchtime we went out to get our trays of sloppy joes, peaches in heavy syrup, coconut cookies, and milk, and brought them back to the classroom, where Miss Ferenczi was sitting at the desk, eating a brown sticky thing she had unwrapped from tightly rubber-banded wax paper. "Miss Ferenczi," I said, raising my hand. "You don't have to eat with us. You can eat with the other teachers. There's a teachers' lounge," I ended up, "next to the principal's office."

"No, thank you," she said. "I prefer it here."

45 "We've got a room monitor," I said. "Mrs. Eddy." I pointed to where Mrs. Eddy, Joyce and Judy's mother, sat silently at the back of the room, doing her knitting.

"That's fine," Miss Ferenczi said. "But I shall continue to eat here, with you children. I prefer it," she repeated.

"How come?" Wayne Razmer asked without raising his hand.

"I talked with the other teachers before class this morning," Miss Ferenczi said, biting into her brown food. "There was a great rattling of the words for the fewness of ideas. I didn't care for their brand of hilarity. I don't like ditto machine jokes."

"Oh," Wayne said.

50 "What's that you're eating?" Maxine Sylvester asked, twitching her nose. "Is it food?"

"It most certainly *is* food. It's a stuffed fig. I had to drive almost down to Detroit to get it. I also bought some smoked sturgeon. And this," she said, lifting some green leaves out of her lunchbox, "is raw spinach, cleaned this morning before I came out here to the Garfield-Murry school."

"Why're you eating raw spinach?" Maxine asked.

"It's good for you," Miss Ferenczi said. "More stimulating than soda pop or smelling salts." I bit into my sloppy joe and stared blankly out the window. An almost invisible moon was faintly silvered in the daytime autumn sky. "As far as food is concerned," Miss Ferenczi was saying, "you have to shuffle the pack. Mix it up. Too many people eat . . . well, never mind."

"Miss Ferenczi," Carol Peterson said, "what are we going to do this afternoon?"

55 "Well," she said, looking down at Mr. Hibler's lesson plan, "I see that your teacher, Mr. Hibler, has you scheduled for a unit on the Egyptians." Carol groaned. "Yessss," Miss Ferenczi continued, "that is what we will do: the Egyptians. A remarkable people. Almost as remarkable as the Americans. But not quite." She lowered her head, did her quick smile, and went back to eating her spinach.

After noon recess we came back into the classroom and saw that Miss Ferenczi had drawn a pyramid on the blackboard, close to her oak tree. Some of us who had been playing baseball were messing around in the back of the room, dropping the bats and the gloves into the playground box, and I think that Ray Schontzeler had just slugged me when I heard Miss Ferenczi's high-pitched voice quavering with emotion. "Boys," she said, "come to order right this minute and take your seats. I do not wish to waste a minute of class time. Take out your geography books." We trudged to our desks and, still sweating, pulled out *Distant Lands and Their People*. "Turn to page forty-two." She waited for thirty seconds, then looked over at Kelly Munger. "Young man," she said, "why are you still fossicking in your desk?"

Kelly looked as if his foot had been stepped on. "Why am I what?"

"Why are you . . . burrowing in your desk like that?"

"I'm lookin' for the book, Miss Ferenczi."

60 Bobby Kryzanowicz, the faultless brown-noser who sat in the first row by choice, softly said, "His name is Kelly Munger. He can't ever find his stuff. He always does that."

"I don't care what his name is, especially after lunch," Miss Ferenczi said. *"Where is your book?"*

"I just found it." Kelly was peering into his desk and with both hands pulled at the book, shoveling along in front of it several pencils and crayons, which fell into his lap and then to the floor.

"I hate a mess," Miss Ferenczi said. "I hate a mess in a desk or a mind. It's . . . unsanitary. You wouldn't want your house at home to look like your desk at school, now, would you?" She didn't wait for an answer. "I should think not. A house at home should be as neat as human hands can make it. What were we talking about? Egypt. Page forty-two. I note from Mr. Hibler's lesson plan that you have been discussing the modes of Egyptian irrigation. Interesting, in my view, but not so interesting as what we are about to cover. The pyramids and Egyptian slave labor. A plus on one side, a minus on the other." We had our books open to page forty-two, where there was a picture of a pyramid, but Miss Ferenczi wasn't looking at the book. Instead, she was staring at some object just outside the window.

"Pyramids," Miss Ferenczi said, still looking past the window. "I want you to think about the pyramids. And what was inside. The bodies of the pharaohs, of course, and their attendant treasures. Scrolls. Perhaps," Miss Ferenczi said, with something gleeful but unsmiling in her face, "these scrolls were novels for the pharaohs, helping them to pass the time in their long voyage through the centuries. But then, I am joking." I was looking at the lines on Miss Ferenczi's face. "Pyramids," Miss Ferenczi went on, "were the repositories of special cosmic powers. The nature of a pyramid is to guide cosmic energy forces into a concentrated point. The Egyptians knew that; we have generally forgotten it. Did you know," she asked, walking to the side of the room so that she was standing by the coat closet, "that George Washington had Egyptian blood, from his grandmother? Certain features of the Constitution of the United States are notable for their Egyptian ideas."

Without glancing down at the book, she began to talk about the movement of souls in Egyptian religion. She said that when people die, their souls return to Earth in the form of carpenter ants or walnut trees, depending on how they behaved —"well or ill"— in life. She said that the Egyptians believed that people act the way they do because of magnetism produced by tidal forces in the solar system, forces produced by the sun and by its "planetary ally," Jupiter. Jupiter, she said, was a planet, as we had been told, but had "certain properties of stars." She was speaking very fast. She said that the Egyptians were great explorers and conquerors. She said that the greatest of all the conquerors, Genghis Khan, had had forty horses and forty young women killed on the site of his grave. We listened. No one tried to stop her. "I myself have been in Egypt," she said, "and have witnessed much dust and many brutalities." She said that an old man in Egypt who worked for a circus had personally shown her an animal in a cage, a monster, half bird and half lion. She said that this monster was called a gryphon and that she had heard about them but never seen them until she traveled to the outskirts of Cairo. She said that Egyptian astronomers had discovered the planet Saturn, but had not seen its rings. She said that the Egyptians were the first to discover that dogs, when they are ill, will not drink from rivers, but wait for rain, and hold their jaws open to catch it.

*　　　*　　　*

"She lies."

We were on the school bus home. I was sitting next to Carl Whiteside, who had bad breath and a huge collection of marbles. We were arguing. Carl thought she was lying. I said she wasn't, probably.

"I didn't believe that stuff about the bird," Carl said, "and what she told us about the pyramids? I didn't believe that either. She didn't know what she was talking about."

"Oh yeah?" I had liked her. She was strange. I thought I could nail him. "If she was lying," I said, "what'd she say that was a lie?"

70   "Six times eleven isn't sixty-eight. It isn't ever. It's sixty-six, I know for a fact."

"She said so. She admitted it. What else did she lie about?"

"I don't know," he said. "Stuff."

"What stuff?"

"Well." He swung his legs back and forth. "You ever see an animal that was half lion and half bird?" He crossed his arms. "It sounded real fakey to me."

75   "It could happen," I said. I had to improvise, to outrage him. "I read in this newspaper my mom bought in the IGA about this scientist, this mad scientist in the Swiss Alps, and he's been putting genes and chromosomes and stuff together in test tubes, and he combined a human being and a hamster." I waited, for effect. "It's called a humster."

"You never." Carl was staring at me, his mouth open, his terrible bad breath making its way toward me. "What newspaper was it?"

"The *National Enquirer*," I said, "that they sell next to the cash registers." When I saw his look of recognition, I knew I had bested him. "And this mad scientist," I said, "his name was, um, Dr. Frankenbush." I realized belatedly that this name was a mistake and waited for Carl to notice its resemblance to the name of the other famous mad master of permutations, but he only sat there.

"A man and a hamster?" He was staring at me, squinting, his mouth opening in distaste. "Jeez. What'd it look like?"

When the bus reached my stop, I took off down our dirt road and ran up through the back yard, kicking the tire swing for good luck. I dropped my books on the back steps so I could hug and kiss our dog, Mr. Selby. Then I hurried inside. I could smell Brussels sprouts cooking, my unfavorite vegetable. My mother was washing other vegetables in the kitchen sink, and my baby brother was hollering in his yellow playpen on the kitchen floor.

80   "Hi, Mom," I said, hopping around the playpen to kiss her, "Guess what?"

"I have no idea."

"We had this substitute today, Miss Ferenczi, and I'd never seen her before, and she had all these stories and ideas and stuff."

"Well. That's good." My mother looked out the window behind the sink, her eyes on the pine woods west of our house. Her face and hairstyle always reminded other people of Betty Crocker, whose picture was framed inside a gigantic spoon on the side of the Bisquick box; to me, though, my mother's face just looked white. "Listen, Tommy," she said, "go upstairs and pick your clothes off the bathroom floor, then go outside to the shed and put the shovel and ax away that your father left outside this morning."

"She said that six times eleven was sometimes sixty-eight!" I said. "And she said she once saw a monster that was half lion and half bird." I waited. "In Egypt, she said."

"Did you hear me?" my mother asked, raising her arm to wipe her forehead with the back of her hand. "You have chores to do." 85

"I know," I said. "I was just telling you about the substitute."

"It's very interesting," my mother said, quickly glancing down at me, "and we can talk about it later when your father gets home. But right now you have some work to do."

"Okay, Mom." I took a cookie out of the jar on the counter and was about to go outside when I had a thought. I ran into the living room, pulled out a dictionary next to the TV stand, and opened it to the G's. *Gryphon:* "variant of griffin." *Griffin:* "a fabulous beast with the head and wings of an eagle and the body of a lion." Fabulous was right. I shouted with triumph and ran outside to put my father's tools back in their place.

Miss Ferenczi was back the next day, slightly altered. She had pulled her hair down and twisted it into pigtails, with red rubber bands holding them tight one inch from the ends. She was wearing a green blouse and pink scarf, making her difficult to look at for a full class day. This time there was no pretense of doing a reading lesson or moving on to arithmetic. As soon as the bell rang, she simply began to talk.

She talked for forty minutes straight. There seemed to be less connection be- 90
tween her ideas, but the ideas themselves were, as the dictionary would say, fabulous. She said she had heard of a huge jewel, in what she called the Antipodes, that was so brilliant that when the light shone into it at a certain angle it would blind whoever was looking at its center. She said that the biggest diamond in the world was cursed and had killed everyone who owned it, and that by a trick of fate it was called the Hope diamond. Diamonds are magic, she said, and this is why women wear them on their fingers, as a sign of the magic of womanhood. Men have strength, Miss Ferenczi said, but no true magic. That is why men fall in love with women but women do not fall in love with men; they just love being loved. George Washington had died because of a mistake he made about a diamond. Washington was not the first *true* President, but she did not say who was. In some places in the world, she said, men and women still live in the trees and eat monkeys for breakfast. Their doctors are magicians. At the bottom of the sea are creatures thin as pancakes which have never been studied by scientists because when you take them up to the air, the fish explode.

There was not a sound in the classroom, except for Miss Ferenczi's voice, and Donna DeShano's coughing. No one even went to the bathroom.

Beethoven, she said, had not been deaf; it was a trick to make himself famous, and it worked. As she talked, Miss Ferenczi's pigtails swung back and forth. There are trees in the world, she said, that eat meat: their leaves are sticky and close up on bugs like hands. She lifted her hands and brought them together, palm to palm. Venus, which most people think is the next closest planet to the sun, is not always closer, and, besides, it is the planet of greatest mystery because of its thick cloud cover. "I know what lies underneath those clouds," Miss Ferenczi said, and waited. After the silence, she said, "Angels. Angels live under those clouds." She said that angels were not invisible to everyone and were in fact smarter than most people. They did not dress in robes as was often claimed but instead wore formal evening clothes, as if they were about to attend a concert. Often angels *do* attend concerts and sit in the aisles where, she said, most people pay no attention to them. She said the most terrible angel had the shape of the Sphinx. "There is no running away from that one," she said. She said that unquenchable fires burn just under the surface of the earth in Ohio, and that the baby Mozart fainted dead away in his cradle when he first heard the sound of a trumpet. She said that some-one named Narzim al Harrardim was the greatest writer who ever lived. She said that planets control behavior, and anyone conceived during a solar eclipse would be born with webbed feet.

"I know you children like to hear these things," she said, "these secrets, and that is why I am telling you all this." We nodded. It was better than doing com-prehension questions for the readings in *Broad Horizons*.

"I will tell you one more story," she said, "and then we will have to do arith-metic." She leaned over, and her voice grew soft. "There is no death," she said. "You must never be afraid. Never. That which is, cannot die. It will change into different earthly and unearthly elements, but I know this as sure as I stand here in front of you, and I swear it: you must not be afraid. I have seen this truth with these eyes. I know it because in a dream God kissed me. Here." And she pointed with her right index finger to the side of her head, below the mouth, where the vertical lines were carved into her skin.

95   Absent-mindedly we all did our arithmetic problems. At recess the class was out on the playground, but no one was playing. We were all standing in small groups, talking about Miss Ferenczi. We didn't know if she was crazy, or what. I looked out beyond the playground, at the rusted cars piled in a small heap behind a clump of sumac, and I wanted to see shapes there, approaching me.

On the way home, Carl sat next to me again. He didn't say much, and I didn't either. At last he turned to me. "You know what she said about the leaves that close up on bugs?"

"Huh?"

"The leaves," Carl insisted. "The meat-eating plants. I know it's true. I saw it on television. The leaves have this icky glue that the plants have got smeared all over them and the insects can't get off 'cause they're stuck. I saw it." He seemed demoralized. "She's tellin' the truth."

"Yeah."

100   "You think she's seen all those angels?"

I shrugged.

"I don't think she has," Carl informed me. "I think she made that part up."

"There's a tree," I suddenly said. I was looking out the window at the farms along County Road H. I knew every barn, every broken windmill, every fence, every anhydrous ammonia tank, by heart. "There's a tree that's . . . that I've seen . . ."

"Don't you try to do it," Carl said. "You'll just sound like a jerk."

I kissed my mother. She was standing in front of the stove. "How was your 105
day?" she asked.

"Fine."

"Did you have Miss Ferenczi again?"

"Yeah."

"Well?"

"She was fine. Mom," I asked, "can I go to my room?" 110

"No," she said, "not until you've gone out to the vegetable garden and picked
me a few tomatoes." She glanced at the sky. "I think it's going to rain. Skedaddle
and do it now. Then you come back inside and watch your brother for a few minutes while I go upstairs. I need to clean up before dinner." She looked down at me.
"You're looking a little pale, Tommy." She touched the back of her hand to my
forehead and I felt her diamond ring against my skin. "Do you feel all right?"

"I'm fine," I said, and went out to pick the tomatoes.

Coughing mutedly, Mr. Hibler was back the next day, slipping lozenges into
his mouth when his back was turned at forty-five minute intervals and asking us
how much of the prepared lesson plan Miss Ferenczi had followed. Edith Atwater
took the responsibility for the class of explaining to Mr. Hibler that the substitute
hadn't always done exactly what he would have done, but we had worked hard
even though she talked a lot. About what? he asked. All kinds of things, Edith
said. I sort of forgot. To our relief, Mr. Hibler seemed not at all interested in what
Miss Ferenczi had said to fill the day. He probably thought it was woman's talk; un-
serious and not suited for school. It was enough that he had a pile of arithmetic
problems from us to correct.

For the next month, the sumac turned a distracting red in the field, and the
sun traveled toward the southern sky, so that its rays reached Mr. Hibler's Halloween display on the bulletin board in the back of the room, fading the scarecrow with a pumpkin head from orange to tan. Every three days I measured how
much farther the sun had moved toward the southern horizon by making small
marks with my black Crayola on the north wall, ant-sized marks only I knew were
there, inching west.

And then in early December, four days after the first permanent snowfall, she 115
appeared again in our classroom. The minute she came in the door, I felt my heart
begin to pound. Once again, she was different: this time, her hair hung straight
down and seemed hardly to have been combed. She hadn't brought her lunchbox
with her, but she was carrying what seemed to be a small box. She greeted all of
us and talked about the weather. Donna DeShano had to remind her to take her
overcoat off.

When the bell to start the day finally rang, Miss Ferenczi looked out at all of
us and said, "Children, I have enjoyed your company in the past, and today I am
going to reward you." She held up the small box. "Do you know what this is?" She
waited. "Of course you don't. It is a tarot pack."

Edith Atwater raised her hand. "What's a tarot pack, Miss Ferenczi?"

"It is used to tell fortunes," she said. "And that is what I shall do this morning.
I shall tell your fortunes, as I have been taught to do."

"What's fortune?" Bobby Kryzanowicz asked.

120   "The future, young man. I shall tell you what your future will be. I can't do your whole future, of course. I shall have to limit myself to the five-card system, the wands, cups, swords, pentacles, and the higher arcanes. Now who wants to be first?"

There was a long silence. Then Carol Peterson raised her hand.

"All right," Miss Ferenczi said. She divided the pack into five smaller packs and walked back to Carol's desk, in front of mine. "Pick one card from each of these packs," she said. I saw that Carol had a four of cups, a six of swords, but I couldn't see the other cards. Miss Ferenczi studied the cards on Carol's desk for a minute. "Not bad," she said. "I do not see much higher education. Probably an early marriage. Many children. There's something bleak and dreary here, but I can't tell what. Perhaps just the tasks of a housewife life. I think you'll do very well, for the most part." She smiled at Carol, a smile with a certain lack of interest. "Who wants to be next?"

Carl Whiteside raised his hand slowly.

"Yes," Miss Ferenczi said, "let's do a boy." She walked over to where Carl sat. After he picked his five cards, she gazed at them for a long time. "Travel," she said. "Much distant travel. You might go into the Army. Not too much romantic interest here. A late marriage, if at all. Squabbles. But the Sun is in your major arcana, here, yes, that's a very good card." She giggled. "Maybe a good life."

125   Next I raised my hand, and she told me my future. She did the same with Bobby Kryzanowicz, Kelly Munger, Edith Atwater, and Kim Foor. Then she came to Wayne Razmer. He picked his five cards, and I could see that the Death card was one of them.

"What's your name?" Miss Ferenczi asked.

"Wayne."

"Well, Wayne," she said, you will undergo a *great* metamorphosis, the greatest, before you become an adult. Your earthly element will leap away, into thin air, you sweet boy. This card, this nine of swords here, tells of suffering and desolation. And this ten of wands, well, that's certainly a heavy load."

"What about this one?" Wayne pointed to the Death card.

130   "That one? That one means you will die soon, my dear." She gathered up the cards. We were all looking at Wayne. "But do not fear," she said. "It's not really death, so much as change." She put the cards on Mr. Hibler's desk. "And now, let's do some arithmetic."

At lunchtime Wayne went to Mr. Faegre, the principal, and told him what Miss Ferenczi had done. During the noon recess, we saw Miss Ferenczi drive out of the parking lot in her green Rambler. I stood under the slide, listening to the other kids coasting down and landing in the little depressive bowl at the bottom. I was kicking stones and tugging at my hair right up to the moment when I saw Wayne come out to the playground. He smiled, the dead fool, and with the fingers of his right hand he was showing everyone how he had told on Miss Ferenczi.

I made my way toward Wayne, pushing myself past two girls from another class. He was watching me with his little pinhead eyes.

"You told," I shouted at him. "She was just kidding."

"She shouldn't have," he shouted back. "We were supposed to be doing arithmetic."

"She just scared you," I said. "You're a chicken. You're a chicken, Wayne. You are. Scared of a little card," I singsonged.   135

Wayne fell at me, his two fists hammering down on my nose. I gave him a good one in the stomach and then I tried for his head. Aiming my fist, I saw that he was crying. I slugged him.

"She was right," I yelled. "She was always right! She told the truth!" Other kids were whooping. "You were just scared, that's all!"

And then large hands pulled at us, and it was my turn to speak to Mr. Faegre.

In the afternoon Miss Ferenczi was gone, and my nose was stuffed with cotton clotted with blood, and my lip had swelled, and our class had been combined with Mrs. Mantei's sixth-grade class for a crowded afternoon science unit on insect life in ditches and swamps. I knew where Mrs. Mantei lived: she had a new house trailer just down the road from us, at the Clearwater Park. She was no mystery. Somehow she and Mr. Bodine, the other fourth-grade teacher, had managed to fit forty-five desks into the room. Kelly Munger asked if Miss Ferenczi had been arrested, and Mrs. Mantei said no, of course not. All that afternoon, until the buses came to pick us up, we learned about field crickets and two-striped grasshoppers, water bugs, cicadas, mosquitoes, flies, and moths. We learned about insects' hard outer shell, the exoskeleton, and the usual parts of the mouth, including the labrum, mandible, maxilla, and glossa. We learned about compound eyes and the four-stage metamorphosis from egg to larva to pupa to adult. We learned something, but not much, about mating. Mrs. Mantei drew, very skillfully, the internal anatomy of the grasshopper on the blackboard. We learned about the dance of the honeybee, directing other bees in the hive to pollen. We found out about which insects were pests to man, and which were not. On lined white pieces of paper we made lists of insects we might actually see, then a list of insects too small to be clearly visible, such as fleas; Mrs. Mantei said that our assignment would be to memorize these lists for the next day, when Mr. Hibler would certainly return and test us on our knowledge.

Reading and Reacting

1. In classical mythology, a gryphon (also spelled *griffin*) is a monster that has the head and wings of an eagle and the body of a lion. Why is this story called "Gryphon"?

2. Describe Miss Ferenczi's physical appearance. Why is her appearance important to the story? How does it change as the story progresses?

3. How is Miss Ferenczi different from other teachers? From other substitute teachers? From other people in general? How is her differentness communicated to her pupils? To the story's readers?

4. What is the significance of the narrator's comment, in paragraph 11, that the lines on Miss Ferenczi's face remind him of Pinocchio?

5. Is Miss Ferenczi a round or a flat character? Explain.

6. In what sense is the narrator's mother a foil for Miss Ferenczi?

7. Why does the narrator defend Miss Ferenczi, first in his argument with Carl Whiteside and later on the playground? What does his attitude toward Miss Ferenczi reveal about his character?

8. Are all of Miss Ferenczi's "substitute facts" lies, or is there some truth in what she says? Is she correct when she says that substitute facts cannot hurt anyone? Could it be argued that much of what is taught in schools today could be viewed as "substitute facts"? Explain.

9. JOURNAL ENTRY Is Miss Ferenczi a good teacher? Why or why not?

10. CRITICAL PERSPECTIVE Writing in the *New York Times Book Review*, critic William Ferguson characterizes *A Relative Stranger*, a more recent collection of Baxter's short stories than the one in which "Gryphon" appeared, as follows:

> The thirteen stories in *A Relative Stranger*, all quietly accomplished, suggest a mysterious yet fundamental marriage of despair and joy. Though in one way or another each story ends in disillusionment, the road that leads to that dismal state is so richly peopled, so finely drawn, that the effect is oddly reassuring.

Do you think this characterization of Baxter's work in *A Relative Stranger* applies to "Gryphon" as well? For example, how are despair and joy joined? Do you find the story reassuring in any way, or does it convey only a sense of disillusionment?

Related Works: "The Secret Lion" (p. 54), "A&P" (p. 115), "A Worn Path" (p. 361), "When I Heard the Learn'd Astronomer" (p. 639), "On First Looking into Chapman's Homer" (p. 740)

MARY LADD GAVELL (1919–1967) was born in Cuero, Texas, and was raised in Driscoll. Her mother, Pauline Amande Schostag, a teacher of German, was one of the early female graduates of the University of Texas; Arlington Ladd, her father, was a farmer. Gavell attended the Texas College of Arts and Industries in Kingsville (now Texas A&M, Kingsville) and graduated in 1940. She went on to conduct a study of regional linguistics at the University of Texas at Austin. During World War II, she lived in Washington, D.C., where she worked for the War Production Board; she returned to Texas, married with two sons, in 1957. In the final decade of her life, Gavell was managing editor of the magazine *Psychiatry: Journal for the Study of Interpersonal Processes.* She wrote her stories, not published during her lifetime, in the time remaining after she attended to professional and familial obligations. After her death (of lung cancer), some of her colleagues at *Psychiatry* published one of her stories, "The Rotifer," as a tribute. The story found its way into *The Best American Short Stories 1968* and was chosen by John Updike for his anthology *The Best American Short Stories of the Century* (1999). Now collected and recently published, her stories may be read in *I Cannot Tell a Lie, Exactly* (2001).

Cultural Context: "Empty nest syndrome" is the name given to a condition that affects parents around the time their children leave home — for college or for the military or to move into their own homes. Many parents report feelings of loss or sadness around this time. Although "empty-nest syndrome" is often said to be a significant cause of depression — and certainly individual parents experience different feelings — recent studies indicate that there is little or no increase in depression among most parents at this stage of life.

The Swing (2001)

As she grew old, she began to dream again. She had not dreamed much in her middle years; or, if she had, the busyness of her days, converging on her the moment she awoke, had pushed her dreams right out of her head, and any fragments that remained were as busy and prosaic as the day itself. She had only the one son, James, but she had also mothered her younger sister after their parents died, and she had done all of the office work during the years when her husband's small engineering firm was getting on its feet. And Julius's health had not been too good, even then; it was she who had mowed the lawn and had helped Jamie to learn to ride his bicycle and pitched balls to him in the backyard until he learned to hit them.

But she was dreaming again now, as she had when she was a child. Oh, not the lovely, foolish dreams of finding oneself alone in a candy store, or the horrible dreams of being pursued through endless corridors without doors by nameless terrors. But as her days grew in quietness and solitude — for James was grown and gone, and Julius was drawing in upon himself, becoming every day more small and chill and dim — color and life and drama were returning to her dreams.

But on that first night when she heard the creak of the swing, she did not think that she was dreaming at all. She had been lying in bed quite awake, she thought, in the little room that used to be Jamie's — for nowadays her reading in bed, and afterward her tossing and turning, disturbed Julius. The swing was not an ordinary one. Julius had put it up, in one of the few flashes of poetry in all his worrisome, hardworking life, when Jamie was only a baby and nowhere near old enough to swing in it. The ladder Julius had was not tall enough, and he had to buy a new one, for the tree was tremendous and the branch on which he proposed to hang the swing arched a full forty feet from the ground, and much thought and consideration and care were given to the chain, and the hooks, and the seat. The swing was suspended from so high, and its arc was so wide, that riding in it was like sailing through the air with the leisurely swoop of a wheeling bird. One seemed to travel from one horizon to the other. And how proud Julius had been of it when Jamie was old enough to swing in it, and the neighborhood children had stood around to admire and be given a turn, for there was no other swing like it.

The swing was hardly ever used now; it was only a treat, once in a while, for a visiting child, and occasionally when she was outside working in her flower border she would sit and rest in it for a moment or two, idling, pushing herself a little with a toe. But the rhythmic creak of the chains was so familiar that she could not mistake it, she thought. Could the wind be strong enough to move it, if it came from the right angle? She finally gave up thinking about it and went to sleep.

5   Nor did she think of it the next day, for they were due for Sunday dinner at James's house. He lived in a suburb on the opposite side of the city —just the right distance away, she often thought, far enough so that aging parents could not meddle and embarrass and interfere, but near enough so that she could see him fairly often. She loved him with all her heart, her dear, her only son. She was enormously proud of him, too; he was a highly paid mathematician in a research foundation, an expert in a field so esoteric that she had given up trying to grasp its point. But secretly she took some credit, for it was she — who had kept the engineering firm's books balanced and done the income tax — who had played little mathematical games with him before he had ever gone to school and had sat cross-legged with him on the floor tossing coins to test the law of probability. Oh, they had had fun together in all sorts of ways; they had done crossword puzzles together, and studied the stars together, and read books together that were over his head and sometimes over hers too. And he had turned out well; he was a scholar, and a success, and a worthy citizen, and he had a pretty wife, a charming home, and two handsome children. She could not have asked for more. He was the light and the warmth of her life, and her heart beat fast on the way to his house.

She drove. She had always enjoyed driving, and nowadays Julius, who used to insist on doing it himself, let her do it without a word. They drove in silence mostly, but her heart was as light as the wind that blew on her face, and she hummed under her breath, for she was on her way to see James. Julius said querulously, "I could have told you you'd get into a lot of traffic this way and you'd do better to go by the river road, but I knew you wouldn't listen," but she was so happy that she forbore to mention that whenever she took the river road he remarked how much longer it was, and only answered, "I expect you're quite right, Julius. We'll come back that way."

They did go home by the river road, and it seemed very long; she was a little depressed, as she often was when she returned from James's house. "I love him with all my heart"— the words walked unbidden into her mind —"but I wish that when I ask him how he is he wouldn't tell me that there is every likelihood that the Basic Research Division will be merged with the Statistics Division." He had kissed her on the cheek, and Anne, his wife, had kissed her on the cheek, and the two children had kissed her on the cheek, and he had slipped a footstool under her feet and had seated his father away from drafts, and they had had a fire in the magnificent stone fireplace the architect had dreamed up and the builder added to the cost, and Anne had served them an excellent dinner, and the children had, on request, told her of suitable A's in English and Boy Scout merit badges. They had asked her how she had been, and she told them, in a burst of confidence, that she had had the ancient piano tuned and had been practicing an hour a day. They looked puzzled. "What are you planning to do with it, Mother?" Anne asked. "Oh, well nothing, really," she said, embarrassed. She said later on that she had been reading books on China for she was so terribly ignorant about it, and they asked politely how her eyes were holding up, and when she said that she was sick of phlox and was going to dig it all up and try iris, James said mildly, "You really shouldn't do all that heavy gardening anymore, Mother." They were loving, they were devoted, and it was the most pleasant of ordinary family Sunday afternoons. James told her that he had another salary increase, and that the paper he had delivered before the Mathematical Research Institute had been, he felt he could say without exaggeration, most well received, and that they were getting a new station wagon. But what, she wondered, did he feel, what did he love and hate, and what upset him or made him happy, and what did he look forward to? Nonsense, she thought, I can't expect him to tell me his secret thoughts. People can't, once they're grown, to their parents. But the terrible fear rose in her that these *were* his secret thoughts, and that was all there was.

That night she heard the swing again, the gentle, regular creak of the chains. What *can* be making that noise, she wondered, for it was a still night, with surely not enough wind to stir the swing. She asked Julius the next day if he ever heard a creaking sound at night, a sound like the swing used to make. Julius peered out from his afghan and said deafly, "Hah?" and she answered irritably, "Oh, never mind." The afghan maddened her. He was always chilly nowadays, and she had knitted the afghan for him for Christmas, working on it in snatches when he was out from under foot for a bit, with a vision of its warming his knees as they sat together in the evenings, companionably watching television, or reading, or chatting. But he sat less and less with her in the evenings; he went to bed very early nowadays, and he had taken to wearing the afghan daytimes around his shoulders like a shawl. She was sorry immediately for her irritation, and she tried to be very thoughtful of him the rest of the day. But he didn't seem to notice; he noticed so little now.

Other things maddened her too. She decided that she should get out more and, heartlessly abandoning Julius, she made a luncheon date with Jessie Carling, who had once been a girl as gay and scatterbrained as a kitten. Jessie spent the entire lunch discussing her digestion and the problem of making the plaids match across the front in a housecoat she was making for herself. A couple of days later, she paid a call on Joyce Simmons, who had trouble with her back and didn't get out much, and Joyce told her in minute detail about her son, dwelling, in full circumstantial detail, on the virtues of him, his wife, and his children. She held her tongue, though it was hard. My trouble, she thought wryly, is that I think my son is so really superior that a kind of noblesse oblige forces me not to mention it.

The next time she heard it was several nights later. She sat up in bed and, half aloud, said, "I'm not dreaming, and it *certainly* is the swing!" She threw on her robe and her slippers and went downstairs, feeling her way in the dark carefully, for though sounds seemed not to reach Julius, lights did wake him. Softly she unlocked the back door and, stepping out into the moonlight, picked her way through the wet grass, holding her nightgown up a little. When she got beyond the thick grove of trees and in sight of the big oak, she saw it, swooping powerfully through the air in its wide arc, and the shock it gave her told her that she had not really believed it. There was a child in the swing, and she paused with a terrible fear clutching at her. Could it be a sleepwalking child from somewhere in the neighborhood? And would it be dangerous to call out to the child, or would it be better to go up and put out a hand to catch the swing gently and stop it? She walked nearer softly and slowly, afraid to startle the child, her heart beating with panicky speed. It seemed to be a little boy and, she noticed, he was dressed in ordinary clothes, not pajamas, as a sleepwalker might be. Nearer she came, still undecided what she should do, shaking with fear and strangeness.

She saw then that it was James. "Jamie?" she cried out questioningly, and immediately shrank back, feeling that she must be making some kind of terrible mistake. But he looked and saw her, and, bright in the moonlight, his face lit up, as it had used to do when he saw her, and he answered gaily, "Mommy!"

She ran to him and stopped the swing — he had slowed down when he saw her — and knelt on the mossy ground and put her arms around him and he put his arms around her and squeezed tight. "I'm so glad to see you!" she cried. "It's been such a long time since I've seen you!"

"I'm glad to see you too," he cried, grinning, and kissed her teasingly behind the ear, for he knew it gave her goose bumps. "You know," he said, "I like this swing. I like to swing better than anything, and I can pretend I'm a pilot flying an airplane, and sometimes I go *r-r-r-r* and that's the engine."

"Well," she said, "it is sort of like flying. Like an airplane, or maybe like a bird. Do you remember, Jamie, when you used to want to be a bird and would wave your arms and try to fly?"

15   "That was when I was a real little kid," he said scornfully.

She suddenly realized that she didn't know how old he was. One tooth was out in front; could that have been when he was six? Or seven? Surely not five? One forgot so much. She couldn't very well ask him; he would think that very odd, for a mother, of all people, should know. She noticed, then, his red checked jacket hanging on the nail on the tree; Julius had given him that jacket for his sixth birthday, she remembered now; he had loved it and had insisted on carrying it with him all the time, even when it was too warm to wear it, and Julius had driven a little nail in the oak tree for him to hang it on while he swung; the nail was still there, old and rusty.

"Mommy, how high does an airplane fly?" he asked.

"Oh, I don't know," she said, "two thousand feet, maybe."

"How much is a foot?"

20   "Oh, about as long as Daddy's foot — I guess that's why they call it that."

"Have people always been the same size?"

"Well, not exactly. They say people are getting a little bigger, and that most people are a little bigger than their great-granddaddies were."

"Well [she saw the trap too late], then if feet used not to be as big, why did they call it a foot?"

"I don't know. Maybe that isn't why they call it a foot. We should look it up in the dictionary."

25   "Does a dictionary tell you *everything*?"

"Not everything. Just about words and what they mean and how they started to mean that."

"But if there's a word for everything, and if a dictionary tells you about every word, then how can it help but tell you about everything?"

"Well," she said, "you've got a good point there. I'll have to think that one over."

Another time he would ask, "Why is it, if the world is turning round all the time, we don't fall off?"

"Gravity. You know what a magnet is. The earth is just like a big magnet."   30

"But where *is* the gravity? If you pick up a handful of dirt, it doesn't have any gravity."

"Well, I don't know. The center of the earth, I guess. Well, I don't really know," she said.

She felt as if the wheels of her mind, rusty from disuse, were beginning to turn again, as if she had not engaged in a real conversation, or thought about anything real, in so long that she was like a swimmer out of practice.

They talked for an hour, and then he said he had to go, with the conscientious keeping track of time he had used to show when it was time to go to school.

"See you later, alligator," he said, and the answer sprang easily to her lips: 35
"After a while, crocodile."

He came every night or two after that, and she lay in bed in happy anticipation, listening for the creak of the swing. She did not go out in her robe again; she hastily dressed herself properly, and put on her shoes, for she had always felt that a mother should look tidy and proper. There by the swing they sat, and they talked about the stars and where the Big Dipper was, and about what you do about a boy who is sort of mean to you at school *all* the time, not just now and then, the way most children are to each other, only they don't especially mean it, and about what you should say in Sunday school when they say the world was made in six days but your mother has explained it differently, and about why the days get shorter in winter and longer in summer.

She bloomed; she sang around the house until even Julius noticed it, and said, disapprovingly, "You seem to be awfully frisky lately." And when Anne phoned apologetically to say that they would have to call off Sunday dinner because James had to attend a committee meeting, she was not only perfectly understanding — as she always tried to be in such instances — but she put down the phone with an utterly light heart, and took up her song where she had left it off.

Then one night, after they had talked for an hour, Jamie said, "I have to go now, and I don't think I can come again, Mommy."

"Okay," she said, and whatever reserve had supplied the cheerful matter-of-factness with which she had once taken him to the hospital to have his appendix out, when he was four, came to her aid and saw to it that there was not a tremor in her voice or a tear in her eye. She kissed him, and then she sat and watched as he walked down the little back lane that had taken him to school, and off to college, and off to a job, and finally off to be married — and he turned, at the bend in the road, and waved to her, as he always used to do.

When he was out of sight, she sat on the soft mossy ground and rested her arms   40
in the swing and buried her face in them and wept. How long she had sat there, she did not know, when a sound made her look up. It was Julius, standing there, frail and stooped, in the moonlight, in his nightshirt with the everlasting afghan hung around his thin old shoulders. She hastily tried to rearrange her attitude, to somehow make it look as if she was doing something quite reasonable, sitting there on the ground with her head pillowed on the swing in the middle of the night. Julius had always felt she was a little foolish and needed a good deal of admonishing, and now he would think she was quite out of her mind and talk very sharply to her.

But his cracked old voice spoke mildly. "He went off and left his jacket," he said.

She looked, and there was the little red jacket hanging on the nail.

Reading and Reacting

1. The story opens with the sentence "As she grew old, she began to dream again." What do you think had made her stop dreaming?
2. How old do you think the woman is? What makes you think so?
3. What do you think the woman's marriage has been like over the years? Given what happens in the story, does it matter?
4. What is it about Julius that annoys his wife? Why do you think he behaves the way he does?
5. How would you characterize the woman's current relationship with her son? What is his attitude toward her? What more does she want from this relationship?
6. Contrast the scene in which the woman talks for the first time to the boy on the swing with the scene in which she visits her adult son's home. How is the interaction between mother and son different? How is the young James different from the adult?
7. Near the end of the story, the woman watches the boy walk away "down the little back lane that had taken him to school, and off to college, and off to a job, and finally off to be married —" (par. 39), and she starts to cry. What do you suppose she realizes?
8. Do the woman's meetings with the boy change her in any way? If so, how?
9. What is so special about the swing? Do you see the swing as a symbol? If so, what do you think it symbolizes?
10. **JOURNAL ENTRY** How do you explain the presence of the child on the swing? The jacket left hanging on the nail? Is the woman dreaming, or is the boy real?
11. **CRITICAL PERSPECTIVE** Author and critic Stacey D'Erasmo, in reviewing *I Cannot Tell a Lie, Exactly*, the collection of short stories in which "The Swing" appears, notes Gavell's "concern with the ambiguities of motherhood: the pain of separateness, of powerlessness, of being unable to protect the ones you love from their history."

    Do you think the mother in "The Swing" experiences these feelings in her relationship with her son? Do you think that she is trying to protect him from something? If so, from what?

Related Works: "Kansas" (p. 85), "The Story of an Hour" (p. 82), "How to Talk to Your Mother (Notes)" (p. 100), "The Rocking-Horse Winner" (p. 349), "The Boy Beheld His Mother's Past" (p. 562), "My Son, My Executioner" (p. 699), "Not Waving but Drowning" (p. 912)

WRITING SUGGESTIONS: Character

1. Focusing on an unconventional character in a conventional setting, "Gryphon" explores the question of what constitutes a good education. Tak-

ing into account your own school experiences as well as those of the students in the story, write an essay in which you discuss what you believe the purpose of education should (and should not) be.

2. In both "A&P," and "Gryphon," the main characters (Sammy and Tommy, respectively) struggle against rules, authority figures, and inflexible social systems. Compare and contrast the struggles in which these two characters are engaged.

3. Write an essay in which you contrast the character of Miss Brill with the character of the woman in "The Swing"— or with Phoenix Jackson in "A Worn Path" (p. 361). Consider how each character interacts with those around her as well as how each seems to see her role or mission in the world.

4. Sammy, Miss Brill, and Miss Ferenczi all use their active imaginations to create scenarios that help get them through the day. None of them is able to sustain the illusion, however. As a result, all three find out how harsh reality can be. What steps could these three characters take to fit more comfortably into the worlds they inhabit? *Should* they take such steps? Are they able to do so?

5. **WEB ACTIVITY** The following Web site consists of an article from the *Austin Chronicle* that discusses Mary Ladd Gavell's book of short stories, *I Cannot Tell a Lie, Exactly*, from which "The Swing" was reprinted.

http://www.austinchronicle.com/issues/dispatch/2001-08-31/books_feature.html

After reading the article, write an essay in which you examine how the circumstances of Gavell's life and the manner and situation in which she wrote (and eventually published) her stories may have influenced the ways that she portrays mother-children and wife-husband relations in "The Swing." Use excerpts from the article as well as quotations from the story as support as you discuss the similarities and differences between Gavell's life and the lives of the characters in the story. Consider how Gavell's writing and revision process —for example, with whom she shared her works, and when — as well as her literary education might have affected her presentation of the characters' feelings and motivations.

CHAPTER 7

SETTING

Many authors find it hard to write about new environments that they did not know in childhood. The voices reheard from childhood have a truer pitch. And the foliage — the trees of childhood — are remembered more exactly. When I work from within a different locale from the South, I have to wonder what time the flowers are in bloom — and what flowers? I hardly let characters speak unless they are Southern. —**Carson McCullers,** *"The Flowering Dream"*

I think that the sense of place is extremely important to most writers. Certainly it is to me. I identify very strongly with places where I have lived, where I have been, where I have invested some part of my being. . . . The earth was here before I was. When I came, I simply identified place by living in it or looking at it. One does create place in the same way that the storyteller creates himself, creates his listener. The writer creates a place. —**N. Scott Momaday,** *Ancestral Voices*

We all know that the weather affects our moods. The [writer] is in the happy position of being able to invent whatever weather is appropriate to the mood he or she wants to evoke.

Weather is therefore frequently a trigger for the effect John Ruskin called the pathetic fallacy, the projection of human emotions onto phenomena in the natural world. "All violent feelings . . . produce in us a falseness in our impressions of external things, which I would generally characterize as the pathetic fallacy," he wrote. As the name implies, Ruskin thought it was a bad thing, a symptom of the decadence of modern (as compared to classical) art and literature, and it is indeed often the occasion of overblown, self-indulgent writing. But used with intelligence and discretion it is a rhetorical device capable of moving and powerful effects, without which fiction would be much the poorer. —**David Lodge,** *The Art of Fiction*

The **setting** of a work of fiction establishes its historical, geographical, and physical location. *Where* a work is set — on a tropical island, in a dungeon, at a crowded party, in a tent in the woods — influences our interpretation of the story's events and characters. *When* a work takes place — during the French Revolution, during the Vietnam War, today, or in the future — is equally important. Setting, however, is more than just the approximate time and place in which the work is set; setting also encompasses a wide variety of physical and cultural elements.

Clearly, setting is more important in some works than in others. In some stories, no particular time or place is specified or even suggested, perhaps because the writer does not consider a specific setting to be important or because the writer wishes the story's events to seem timeless and universal. In Nadine Gordimer's "Once upon a Time," for example, the writer follows the conventions of fairy tales, which are set in unidentified faraway places. In other stories, a writer may provide only minimal information about setting, telling readers little more than where and when the action takes place. Sometimes, however, a particular setting may be vital to the story, perhaps influencing characters' behavior, as it does in Charlotte Perkins Gilman's "The Yellow Wallpaper" (p. 161). In such cases, of course, setting must be fully described.

Sometimes a story's central conflict is between the protagonist and the setting — for example, Alice in Wonderland, a northerner in the South, an unsophisticated American tourist in an old European city, a sane person in a mental hospital, a moral person in a corrupt environment, an immigrant in a new world, or a city dweller in the country. This conflict helps to define the characters as well as drive the plot. (A conflict between events and setting — for example, the intrusion of nuclear war into a typical suburban neighborhood, the intrusion of modern social ideas into an old-fashioned world, or the intrusion of a brutal murder into a peaceful English village — can also enrich a story.)

HISTORICAL SETTING

A particular historical period, and the events associated with it, can be important in a story; therefore, some familiarity with a period can be useful (or even essential) to readers who wish to understand a story fully. Historical context establishes a social, cultural, economic, and political environment. Knowing, for instance, that "The Yellow Wallpaper" was written in the late nineteenth century, when doctors treated women as delicate and dependent creatures, helps to explain the narrator's emotional state. Likewise, it may be important to know that a story is set during a particularly volatile (or static) political era, during a time of permissive (or repressive) attitudes toward sex, during a war, or during a period of economic prosperity or recession. Any one of these factors may determine — or help to explain — characters' actions. Historical events or cultural norms may, for instance, limit or expand a character's options, and our knowledge of history may reveal to us a character's incompatibility with his or her milieu. In F. Scott Fitzgerald's "Bernice Bobs Her Hair," set in the 1920s in a midwestern town, a young girl is goaded into cutting her long hair. To understand the significance of Bernice's act — and to understand the reactions of others to that act — readers must know that during that era only racy "society vampires," not nice girls from good families, bobbed their hair.

Knowing the approximate year or historical period during which a story takes place can explain forces that act on characters, help to account for their behavior, clarify circumstances that influence the story's action, and help to justify a writer's use of plot devices that might otherwise seem improbable. For instance, stories set before the development of modern transportation and communication systems may hinge on plot devices readers would not accept in a modern story. Thus, in "Paul's Case," a 1904 story by Willa Cather, a young man who steals a large sum of money in Pittsburgh is able to spend several days enjoying it before the news of the theft reaches New York, where he has fled. In other stories, we see such outdated plot devices as characters threatened by diseases that have now been eradicated (and subjected to outdated medical or psychiatric treatment). Finally, characters may be constrained by social conventions different from those that operate in our own society.

GEOGRAPHICAL SETTING

In addition to knowing *when* a work takes place, readers need to know *where* it takes place. Knowing whether a story is set in the United States, in Europe, or in a developing nation can help to explain anything from why language and customs are unfamiliar to us to why characters act in ways we find improbable. Even in stories set in our own country, regional differences may account for differences in plot development and characters' motivation. For example, knowing that William Faulkner's "A Rose for Emily" (p. 91) is set in the post–Civil War American South helps to explain why the townspeople are so chivalrously protective of Miss Emily. Similarly, the fact that Bret Harte's "The Outcasts of Poker Flat" (1869) is set in a California mining camp accounts for its varied cast of characters — including a gambler, a prostitute, and a traveling salesman.

The size of the town or city in which a story takes place may also be important. In a small town, for example, a character's problems are more likely to be subject to intense scrutiny by other characters, as they are in stories of small-town life such as those in Sherwood Anderson's *Winesburg, Ohio*. In a large city, characters may be more likely to be isolated and anonymous, like Mrs. Miller in Truman Capote's "Miriam," who is so lonely that she creates an imaginary companion. Characters may also be alienated by their big-city surroundings, as Gregor Samsa is in Franz Kafka's classic novella "The Metamorphosis."

Of course, a story may not have a recognizable geographical setting; its location may not be specified, or it may be set in a fantasy world. Such settings may free writers from the constraints placed on them by familiar environments, allowing them to experiment with situations and characters, unaffected by readers' expectations or associations with familiar settings.

PHYSICAL SETTING

The *time of day* can clearly influence a story's mood as well as its development. The gruesome murder described in Edgar Allan Poe's "The Cask of Amontillado" (p. 217) takes place in an appropriate setting: not just underground but in the darkness of night. Conversely, the horrifying events of Shirley Jackson's "The Lottery" (p. 303) take place in broad daylight, contrasting dramatically with the darkness of the society that permits — and even participates in — such events.

Many stories, of course, move through several time periods as the action unfolds, and changes in time may also be important. For instance, the approach of evening, or of dawn, can signal the end of a crisis in the plot.

Whether a story is set primarily *inside* or *out-of-doors* may also be significant. The characters may be physically constrained by a closed-in setting or liberated by an expansive landscape. Some interior settings may be psychologically limiting. For instance, the narrator in "The Yellow Wallpaper" feels suffocated by her room, whose ugly wallpaper comes to haunt her. In many of Poe's stories, the central character is trapped, physically or psychologically, in a confined, suffocating space. In other stories, an interior setting may serve a symbolic function. For instance, in "A Rose for Emily," the house is for Miss Emily a symbol of the South's past glory as well as a refuge, a fortress, and a hiding place. Similarly, a building or house may represent society, with its rules and norms and limitations. In John Updike's "A&P" (p. 115), for instance, the supermarket establishes social as well as physical limits. This is also the case in Katherine Mansfield's "Her First Ball," where a ballroom serves as the setting for a young girl's initiation into the rules and realities of adult society, as is the case in Stephen Crane's "The Open Boat."

Conversely, an outdoor setting can free a character from social norms of behavior, as it does for Ernest Hemingway's Nick Adams, a war veteran who, in "Big Two-Hearted River," finds order, comfort, and peace only when he is away from civilization. An outdoor setting can also expose characters to physical dangers, such as untamed wilderness, uncharted seas, and frighteningly empty open spaces.

Weather can be another important aspect of setting. A storm can threaten a character's life or just make the character — and readers — *think* danger is present, distracting us from other, more subtle threats. Extreme weather conditions can make characters act irrationally or uncharacteristically, as in Kate Chopin's "The Storm," where a storm provides the complication and determines the characters' actions. In numerous stories set in hostile landscapes, where extremes of heat and cold influence the action, weather may pose a test for characters, as in Jack London's "To Build a Fire," in which the main character struggles unsuccessfully against the brutally cold, hostile environment of the Yukon.

The various physical attributes of setting combine to create a story's **atmosphere** or **mood.** In "The Cask of Amontillado," for example, several factors work together to create the eerie, intense atmosphere appropriate to the story's events: it is nighttime; it is the hectic carnival season; and the catacombs are dark, damp, and filled with the bones of the narrator's ancestors. The atmosphere that is created in a story can reflect a character's mental state. For example, darkness and isolation can reflect a character's depression, whereas an idyllic, peaceful atmosphere can express a character's joy. A story's atmosphere may also *influence* the characters' reactions or state of mind, causing them to react one way in a crowded, busy, hectic atmosphere but to react very differently in a peaceful rural atmosphere. At the same time, the mood or atmosphere that is created often helps to convey a story's central theme — as the ironic contrast between the pleasant atmosphere and the shocking events that unfold communicates the theme of "The Lottery."

CHECKLIST   WRITING ABOUT SETTING

✓ Is the setting specified or unidentified? Is it fully described or only sketched in?

✓ Is the setting just background, or is it a key force in the story?

✓ How does the setting influence the characters? Does it affect (or reflect) their emotional state? Does it help to explain their motivation?

✓ Are any characters in conflict with their environment?

✓ Are any situations set in sharp contrast to the setting?

✓ How does the setting influence the story's plot? Does it cause characters to act?

✓ Does the setting add irony to the story?

✓ In what time period does the story take place? How can you tell? What social, political, or economic characteristics of the historical period might influence the story?

✓ In what geographical location is the story set? Is this location important to the story?

✓ At what time of day is the story set? Is time important to the development of the story?

✓ Is the story set primarily indoors or out-of-doors? What role does this aspect of the setting play in the story?

✓ What role do weather conditions play in the story?

✓ Is the story's general atmosphere dark or bright? Clear or murky? Tumultuous or calm? Gloomy or cheerful?

✓ Does the atmosphere change as the story progresses? Is this change significant?

SHERMAN ALEXIE (1966–   ), a highly praised Native American writer of Spokane and Coeur d'Alene heritage, was born in Spokane, Washington. He attended Pullman State University with plans to become a doctor but changed his mind after attending a poetry workshop; by the time he left school, he had already written over two hundred poems. Since then, his work has appeared in various magazines and journals, and he has published six poetry collections, two novels, and two collections of short stories, one of which, *The Lone Ranger and Tonto Fistfight in Heaven* (1993), was adapted for the screen in the 1997 film *Smoke Signals*. His most recent short story collection, *The Toughest Indian in the World,* earned him a nomination for the 2000 National Magazine Award. In

2001, Alexie was honored with the PEN/Malamud Award, along with fellow short story writer Richard Ford.

Of Native American culture, Alexie has said, "One of the biggest misconceptions about Indians is that we're stoic, but humor is an essential part of our culture." "This Is What It Means to Say Phoenix, Arizona" (from *The Lone Ranger and Tonto Fistfight in Heaven*) demonstrates this unique use of humor to transcend the harsh realities of life on the reservation and of the struggle to adapt to contemporary American life.

Cultural Context: When the American explorers Lewis and Clark first encountered the Coeur d'Alene Indians in 1805, they were wanderers who lived in communal houses. In 1841, a Jesuit priest established the Sacred Heart mission among the Coeur d'Alene, and within ten years, the tribe had adopted many of the traditions introduced by the missionaries. Today, drastically changed by the settlement of the West and a century and a half of treaty disputes, the traditional cultural practices of the Coeur d'Alene and the neighboring Spokane Indians are largely confined to reservations.

This Is What It Means to Say
Phoenix, Arizona (1993)

Just after Victor lost his job at the Bureau of Indian Affairs,° he also found out that his father had died of a heart attack in Phoenix, Arizona. Victor hadn't seen his father in a few years, had only talked to him on the telephone once or twice, but there still was a genetic pain, which was as real and immediate as a broken bone. Victor didn't have any money. Who does have money on a reservation, except the cigarette and fireworks salespeople? His father had a savings account waiting to be claimed, but Victor needed to find a way to get from Spokane to Phoenix. Victor's mother was just as poor as he was, and the rest of his family didn't have any use at all for him. So Victor called the tribal council.

"Listen," Victor said. "My father just died. I need some money to get to Phoenix to make arrangements."

"Now Victor," the council said, "you know we're having a difficult time financially."

"But I thought the council had special funds set aside for stuff like this."

"Now, Victor, we do have some money available for the proper return of tribal members' bodies. But I don't think we have enough to bring your father all the way back from Phoenix." 5

"Well," Victor said. "It ain't going to cost all that much. He had to be cremated. Things were kind of ugly. He died of a heart attack in his trailer and nobody found him for a week. It was really hot, too. You get the picture."

"Now, Victor, we're sorry for your loss and the circumstances. But we can really only afford to give you one hundred dollars."

Bureau of Indian Affairs: The division of the U.S. Department of the Interior that manages Native American matters; operated by government officials, not tribal leaders.

"That's not even enough for a plane ticket."

"Well, you might consider driving down to Phoenix."

10   "I don't have a car. Besides, I was going to drive my father's pickup back up here."

"Now, Victor," the council said, "we're sure there is somebody who could drive you to Phoenix. Or could anybody lend you the rest of the money?"

"You know there ain't nobody around with that kind of money."

"Well, we're sorry, Victor, but that's the best we can do."

Victor accepted the tribal council's offer. What else could he do? So he signed the proper papers, picked up his check, and walked over to the Trading Post to cash it.

15   While Victor stood in line, he watched Thomas Builds-the-Fire standing near the magazine rack talking to himself. Like he always did. Thomas was a storyteller whom nobody wanted to listen to. That's like being a dentist in a town where everybody has false teeth.

Victor and Thomas Builds-the-Fire were the same age, had grown up and played in the dirt together. Ever since Victor could remember, it was Thomas who had always had something to say.

Once, when they were seven years old, when Victor's father still lived with the family, Thomas closed his eyes and told Victor this story: "Your father's heart is weak. He is afraid of his own family. He is afraid of you. Late at night, he sits in the dark. Watches the television until there's nothing but that white noise. Sometimes he feels like he wants to buy a motorcycle and ride away. He wants to run and hide. He doesn't want to be found."

Thomas Builds-the-Fire had known that Victor's father was going to leave, known it before anyone. Now Victor stood in the Trading Post with a one-hundred-dollar check in his hand, wondering if Thomas knew that Victor's father was dead, if he knew what was going to happen next.

Just then, Thomas looked at Victor, smiled, and walked over to him.

20   "Victor, I'm sorry about your father," Thomas said.

"How did you know about it?" Victor asked.

"I heard it on the wind. I heard it from the birds. I felt it in the sunlight. Also, your mother was just in here crying."

"Oh," Victor said and looked around the Trading Post. All the other Indians stared, surprised that Victor was even talking to Thomas. Nobody talked to Thomas anymore because he told the same damn stories over and over again. Victor was embarrassed, but he thought that Thomas might be able to help him. Victor felt a sudden need for tradition.

"I can lend you the money you need," Thomas said suddenly. "But you have to take me with you."

25   "I can't take your money," Victor said. "I mean, I haven't hardly talked to you in years. We're not really friends anymore."

"I didn't say we were friends. I said you had to take me with you."

"Let me think about it."

Victor went home with his one hundred dollars and sat at the kitchen table. He held his head in his hands and thought about Thomas Builds-the-Fire, remembered little details, tears and scars, the bicycle they shared for a summer, so many stories.

*   *   *

Thomas Builds-the-Fire sat on the bicycle, waiting in Victor's yard. He was ten years old and skinny. His hair was dirty because it was the Fourth of July.

"Victor," Thomas yelled. "Hurry up. We're going to miss the fireworks."   30

After a few minutes, Victor ran out of his family's house, vaulted over the porch railing, and landed gracefully on the sidewalk.

Thomas gave him the bike and they headed for the fireworks. It was nearly dark and the fireworks were about to start.

"You know," Thomas said, "it's strange how us Indians celebrate the Fourth of July. It ain't like it was our independence everybody was fighting for."

"You think about things too much," Victor said. "It's just supposed to be fun. Maybe Junior will be there."

"Which Junior? Everybody on this reservation is named Junior."   35

The fireworks were small, hardly more than a few bottle rockets and a fountain. But it was enough for two Indian boys. Years later, they would need much more.

Afterward, sitting in the dark, fighting off mosquitoes, Victor turned to Thomas Builds-the-Fire.

"Hey," Victor said. "Tell me a story."

Thomas closed his eyes and told this story: "There were these two Indian boys who wanted to be warriors. But it was too late to be warriors in the old way. All the horses were gone. So the two Indian boys stole a car and drove to the city. They parked the stolen car in the front of the police station and then hitchhiked back home to the reservation. When they got back, all their friends cheered and their parents' eyes shone with pride. 'You were very brave,' everybody said to the two Indian boys. 'Very brave.'"

"Ya-hey," Victor said. "That's a good one. I wish I could be a warrior."   40

"Me too," Thomas said.

Victor sat at his kitchen table. He counted his one hundred dollars again and again. He knew he needed more to make it to Phoenix and back. He knew he needed Thomas Builds-the-Fire. So he put his money in his wallet and opened the front door to find Thomas on the porch.

"Ya-hey, Victor," Thomas said. "I knew you'd call me."

Thomas walked into the living room and sat down in Victor's favorite chair.

"I've got some money saved up," Thomas said. "It's enough to get us down   45 there, but you have to get us back."

"I've got this hundred dollars," Victor said. "And my dad had a savings account I'm going to claim."

"How much in your dad's account?"

"Enough. A few hundred."

"Sounds good. When we leaving?"

50   When they were fifteen and had long since stopped being friends, Victor and Thomas got into a fistfight. That is, Victor was really drunk and beat Thomas up for no reason at all. All the other Indian boys stood around and watched it happen. Junior was there and so were Lester, Seymour, and a lot of others.

The beating might have gone on until Thomas was dead if Norma Many Horses hadn't come along and stopped it.

"Hey, you boys," Norma yelled and jumped out of her car. "Leave him alone."

If it had been someone else, even another man, the Indian boys would've just ignored the warnings. But Norma was a warrior. She was powerful. She could have picked up any two of the boys and smashed their skulls together. But worse than that, she would have dragged them all over to some tepee and made them listen to some elder tell a dusty old story.

The Indian boys scattered, and Norma walked over to Thomas and picked him up.

55   "Hey, little man, are you O.K.?" she asked.

Thomas gave her a thumbs-up.

"Why they always picking on you?"

Thomas shook his head, closed his eyes, but no stories came to him, no words or music. He just wanted to go home, to lie in his bed and let his dreams tell the stories for him.

Thomas Builds-the-Fire and Victor sat next to each other in the airplane, coach section. A tiny white woman had the window seat. She was busy twisting her body into pretzels. She was flexible.

60   "I have to ask," Thomas said, and Victor closed his eyes in embarrassment.

"Don't," Victor said.

"Excuse me, miss," Thomas asked. "Are you a gymnast or something?"

"There's no something about it," she said. "I was first alternate on the 1980 Olympic team."

"Really?" Thomas asked.

65   "Really."

"I mean, you used to be a world-class athlete?" Thomas asked.

"My husband thinks I still am."

Thomas Builds-the-Fire smiled. She was a mental gymnast too. She pulled her leg straight up against her body so that she could've kissed her kneecap.

"I wish I could do that," Thomas said.

70   Victor was ready to jump out of the plane. Thomas, that crazy Indian storyteller with ratty old braids and broken teeth, was flirting with a beautiful Olympic gymnast. Nobody back home on the reservation would ever believe it.

"Well," the gymnast said. "It's easy. Try it."

Thomas grabbed at his leg and tried to pull it up into the same position as the gymnast's. He couldn't even come close, which made Victor and the gymnast laugh.

"Hey," she asked. "You two are Indian, right?"

"Full-blood," Victor said.

"Not me," Thomas said. "I'm half magician on my mother's side and half clown on my father's." 75

They all laughed.

"What are your names?" she asked.

"Victor and Thomas."

"Mine is Cathy. Pleased to meet you all."

The three of them talked for the duration of the flight. Cathy the gymnast 80 complained about the government, how they screwed the 1980 Olympic team by boycotting the games.

"Sounds like you all got a lot in common with Indians," Thomas said.

Nobody laughed.

After the plane landed in Phoenix and they had all found their way to the terminal, Cathy the gymnast smiled and waved goodbye.

"She was really nice," Thomas said.

"Yeah, but everybody talks to everybody on airplanes," Victor said. 85

"You always used to tell me I think too much," Thomas said. "Now it sounds like you do."

"Maybe I caught it from you."

"Yeah."

Thomas and Victor rode in a taxi to the trailer where Victor's father had died.

"Listen," Victor said as they stopped in front of the trailer. "I never told you I 90 was sorry for beating you up that time."

"Oh, it was nothing. We were just kids and you were drunk."

"Yeah, but I'm still sorry."

"That's all right."

Victor paid for the taxi, and the two of them stood in the hot Phoenix summer. They could smell the trailer.

"This ain't going to be nice," Victor said. "You don't have to go in." 95

"You're going to need help."

Victor walked to the front door and opened it. The stink rolled out and made them both gag. Victor's father had lain in that trailer for a week in hundred-degree temperatures before anyone had found him. And the only reason anyone found him was the smell. They needed dental records to identify him. That's exactly what the coroner said. They needed dental records.

"Oh, man," Victor said. "I don't know if I can do this."

"Well, then don't."

"But there might be something valuable in there." 100

"I thought his money was in the bank."

"It is: I was talking about pictures and letters and stuff like that."

"Oh," Thomas said as he held his breath and followed Victor into the trailer.

When Victor was twelve, he stepped into an underground wasps' nest. His foot was caught in the hole and no matter how hard he struggled, Victor couldn't pull free. He might have died there, stung a thousand times, if Thomas Builds-the-Fire had not come by.

105   "Run," Thomas yelled and pulled Victor's foot from the hole. They ran then, hard as they ever had, faster than Billy Mills, faster than Jim Thorpe, faster than the wasps could fly.

Victor and Thomas ran until they couldn't breathe, ran until it was cold and dark outside, ran until they were lost and it took hours to find their way home. All the way back, Victor counted his stings.

"Seven," Victor said. "My lucky number."

*   *   *

Victor didn't find much to keep in the trailer. Only a photo album and a stereo. Everything else had that smell stuck in it or was useless anyway. "I guess this is all," Victor said. "It ain't much."

"Better than nothing," Thomas said.

110   "Yeah, and I do have the pickup."

"Yeah," Thomas said. "It's in good shape."

"Dad was good about that stuff."

"Yeah, I remember your dad."

"Really?" Victor asked. "What do you remember?"

115   Thomas Builds-the-Fire closed his eyes and told this story: "I remember when I had this dream that told me to go to Spokane, to stand by the falls in the middle of the city and wait for a sign. I knew I had to go there but I didn't have a car. Didn't have a license. I was only thirteen. So I walked all the way, took me all day, and I finally made it to the falls. I stood there for an hour waiting. Then your dad came walking up. 'What the hell are you doing here?' he asked me. I said, 'Waiting for a vision.' Then your father said, 'All you're going to get here is mugged.' So he drove me over to Denny's, bought me dinner, and then drove me home to the reservation. For a long time, I was mad because I thought my dreams had lied to me. But they hadn't. Your dad was my vision. *Take care of each other* is what my dreams were saying. *Take care of each other.*"

Victor was quiet for a long time. He searched his mind for memories of his father, found the good ones, found a few bad ones, added it all up, and smiled.

"My father never told me about finding you in Spokane," Victor said.

"He said he wouldn't tell anybody. Didn't want me to get in trouble. But he said I had to watch out for you as part of the deal."

"Really?"

120   "Really. Your father said you would need the help. He was right."

"That's why you came down here with me, isn't it?" Victor asked.

"I came because of your father."

Victor and Thomas climbed into the pickup, drove over to the bank, and claimed the three hundred dollars in the savings account.

Thomas Builds-the-Fire could fly.

125   Once, he jumped off the roof of the tribal school and flapped his arms like a crazy eagle. And he flew. For a second he hovered, suspended above all the other Indian boys, who were too smart or too scared to jump too.

"He's flying," Junior yelled, and Seymour was busy looking for the trick wires or mirrors. But it was real. As real as the dirt when Thomas lost altitude and crashed to the ground.

He broke his arm in two places.

"He broke his wing, he broke his wing, he broke his wing," all the Indian boys chanted as they ran off, flapping their wings, wishing they could fly too. They hated Thomas for his courage, his brief moment as a bird. Everybody has dreams about flying. Thomas flew.

One of his dreams came true for just a second, just enough to make it real.

*   *   *

Victor's father, his ashes, fit in one wooden box with enough left over to fill a cardboard box.   130

"He always was a big man," Thomas said.

Victor carried part of his father out to the pickup, and Thomas carried the rest. They set him down carefully behind the seats, put a cowboy hat on the wooden box and a Dodgers cap on the cardboard box. That was the way it was supposed to be.

"Ready to head back home?" Victor asked.

"It's going to be a long drive."

"Yeah, take a couple days, maybe."   135

"We can take turns," Thomas said.

"O.K.," Victor said, but they didn't take turns. Victor drove for sixteen hours straight north, made it halfway up Nevada toward home before he finally pulled over.

"Hey, Thomas," Victor said. "You got to drive for a while."

"O.K."

Thomas Builds-the-Fire slid behind the wheel and started off down the road.   140
All through Nevada, Thomas and Victor had been amazed at the lack of animal life, at the absence of water, of movement.

"Where is everything?" Victor had asked more than once.

Now, when Thomas was finally driving, they saw the first animal, maybe the only animal in Nevada. It was a long-eared jackrabbit.

"Look," Victor yelled. "It's alive."

Thomas and Victor were busy congratulating themselves on their discovery when the jackrabbit darted out into the road and under the wheels of the pickup.

"Stop the goddamn car," Victor yelled, and Thomas did stop and backed the   145
pickup to the dead jackrabbit.

"Oh, man, he's dead," Victor said as he looked at the squashed animal.

"Really dead."

"The only thing alive in this whole state and we just killed it."

"I don't know," Thomas said. "I think it was suicide."

Victor looked around the desert, sniffed the air, felt the emptiness and   150
loneliness, and nodded his head.

"Yeah," Victor said. "It had to be suicide."

"I can't believe this," Thomas said. "You drive for a thousand miles and there ain't even any bugs smashed on the windshield. I drive for ten seconds and kill the only living thing in Nevada."

"Yeah," Victor said. "Maybe I should drive."

"Maybe you should."

155   Thomas Builds-the-Fire walked through the corridors of the tribal school by himself. Nobody wanted to be anywhere near him because of all those stories. Story after story.

Thomas closed his eyes and this story came to him: "We are all given one thing by which our lives are measured, one determination. Mine are the stories that can change or not change the world. It doesn't matter which, as long as I continue to tell the stories. My father, he died on Okinawa° in World War II, died fighting for this country, which had tried to kill him for years. My mother, she died giving birth to me, died while I was still inside her. She pushed me out into the world with her last breath. I have no brothers or sisters. I have only my stories, which came to me before I even had the words to speak. I learned a thousand stories before I took my first thousand steps. They are all I have. It's all I can do."

Thomas Builds-the-Fire told his stories to all those who would stop and listen. He kept telling them long after people had stopped listening.

Victor and Thomas made it back to the reservation just as the sun was rising. It was the beginning of a new day on earth, but the same old shit on the reservation.

"Good morning," Thomas said.

160   "Good morning."

The tribe was waking up, ready for work, eating breakfast, reading the newspaper, just like everybody else does. Willene LeBret was out in her garden, wearing a bathrobe. She waved when Thomas and Victor drove by.

"Crazy Indians made it," she said to herself and went back to her roses.

Victor stopped the pickup in front of Thomas Builds-the-Fire's HUD° house. They both yawned, stretched a little, shook dust from their bodies.

"I'm tired," Victor said.

165   "Of everything," Thomas added.

They both searched for words to end the journey. Victor needed to thank Thomas for his help and for the money, and to make the promise to pay it all back.

"Don't worry about the money," Thomas said. "It don't make any difference anyhow."

"Probably not, enit?"

"Nope."

170   Victor knew that Thomas would remain the crazy storyteller who talked to dogs and cars, who listened to the wind and pine trees. Victor knew that he

---

Okinawa: Largest island of the Ryukyus, a chain of Japanese islands in the western Pacific Ocean.
HUD: The U.S. Department of Housing and Urban Development.

couldn't really be friends with Thomas, even after all that had happened. It was cruel but it was real. As real as the ash, as Victor's father, sitting behind the seats.

"I know how it is," Thomas said. "I know you ain't going to treat me any better than you did before. I know your friends would give you too much shit about it."

Victor was ashamed of himself. Whatever happened to the tribal ties, the sense of community? The only real thing he shared with anybody was a bottle and broken dreams. He owed Thomas something, anything.

"Listen," Victor said and handed Thomas the cardboard box that contained half of his father. "I want you to have this."

Thomas took the ashes and smiled, closed his eyes, and told this story: "I'm going to travel to Spokane Falls one last time and toss these ashes into the water. And your father will rise like a salmon, leap over the bridge, over me, and find his way home. It will be beautiful. His teeth will shine like silver, like a rainbow. He will rise, Victor, he will rise."

Victor smiled.   175

"I was planning on doing the same thing with my half," Victor said. "But I didn't imagine my father looking anything like a salmon. I thought it'd be like cleaning the attic or something. Like letting things go after they've stopped having any use."

"Nothing stops, cousin," Thomas said. "Nothing stops."

Thomas Builds-the-Fire got out of the pickup and walked up his driveway. Victor started the pickup and began the drive home.

"Wait," Thomas yelled suddenly from his porch. "I just got to ask one favor."

Victor stopped the pickup, leaned out the window, and shouted back.   180

"What do you want?" he asked.

"Just one time when I'm telling a story somewhere, why don't you stop and listen?" Thomas asked.

"Just once?"

"Just once."

Victor waved his arms to let Thomas know that the deal was good. It was a fair   185
trade. That's all Thomas had ever wanted from his whole life. So Victor drove his father's pickup toward home while Thomas went into his house, closed the door behind him, and heard a new story come to him in the silence afterward.

Reading and Reacting

1. In paragraph 1, readers are told that Victor lives on an Indian reservation. What details elsewhere in the story establish this setting? What associations does this setting have for you? Do you think the story could take place anywhere else?

2. In addition to various locations on the reservation, the story's settings include an airplane, a trailer in Phoenix, and a road through Nevada. What does each of these settings contribute to the story's plot?

3. Is the scene on the plane necessary? Intrusive? Distracting? Farfetched?

4. How would you characterize the story's mood or atmosphere? How do Thomas's stories help to create this mood? How do they help to establish his character? Do you think Alexie should have included more of these stories?

5. Why do you suppose Victor and Thomas cannot be friends when they get back to the reservation? Why can they be friends when they are traveling to Phoenix?

6. Do the flashbacks to the two men's childhood add something vital to the story? What purpose do these flashbacks serve?

7. In Native American culture, the storyteller holds an important position, telling tales that transmit and preserve the tribe's basic beliefs. Do you think Thomas's stories serve such a function? Or is he, as Victor characterizes him near the end of the story, simply "the crazy storyteller who talked to dogs and cars, who listened to the wind and pine trees" (par. 170)?

8. What do you think the story's title means?

9. JOURNAL ENTRY At the end of the story, when Thomas returns home, he hears "a new story come to him in the silence" after he closes the door. What kind of story do you think comes to him at this point? Why do you think so?

10. CRITICAL PERSPECTIVE In the introduction to a collection of Native American literature, Clifford E. Trafzer, the collection's editor, discusses the unique characteristics of Native American writers:

> Due to their grounding in the oral tradition of their people, Native American writers do not follow the literary canon of the dominant society in their approach to short stories. Rather than focusing on one theme or character in a brief time frame, or using one geographical area, they often use multiple themes and characters with few boundaries of time or place. Their stories do not always follow a linear and clear path, and frequently the past and present, real and mythic, and conscious and unconscious are not distinguishable. Multidimensional characters are common, and involved stories usually lack absolute conclusions. Native American writers may also play tricks with language, deliberately misusing grammar, syntax, and spelling — sometimes in defiance of the dominant culture — in order to make English reflect the language of their peoples.

Do you think "This Is What It Means to Say Phoenix, Arizona" has the characteristics Trafzer associates with Native American writers?

Related Works: "Sleepy Time Gal" (p. 46), "How to Write the Great American Indian Novel" (p. 629), *The Glass Menagerie* (p. 1416)

CHARLOTTE PERKINS GILMAN (1860–1935) was a prominent feminist and social thinker at the turn of the century. Her essays, lectures, and nonfiction works — such as *Women and Economics* (1898), *Concerning Children* (1900), and *The Man-Made World* (1911) — are forceful statements of Gilman's opinions on women's need for economic independence and social equality. In the main, Gilman's fiction is a didactic expression of her social views. She is probably best known for three utopian feminist novels: *Moving the Mountain* (1911), *Herland* (1915; unpublished until 1978), and *With Her in Ourland* (1916). Gilman's fictional works are full of humor and satire: In *Herland,* for instance, a male sociologist (wandering in by accident from the outside world) is chagrined to find that the women of "Herland" want him for a friend, not a lover.

Although "The Yellow Wallpaper" (1892) is not typical of Gilman's other fiction, it is considered her artistic masterpiece. The terse, clinical precision of the writing, conveying the tightly wound and distraught mental state of the narrator, is particularly chilling when it is read with a knowledge of Gilman's personal history. In the 1880s, she met and married a young artist, Charles Walter Stetson. Following the birth of their daughter, she grew increasingly depressed and turned to a noted Philadelphia neurologist for help. Following the traditions of the time, he prescribed complete bed rest and mental inactivity—a treatment that, Gilman said later, drove her "so near the borderline of utter mental ruin that I could see over." "The Yellow Wallpaper" is not simply a psychological study. Like most of Gilman's work, it makes a point — this time about the dangers of women's utter dependence on a male interpretation of their needs.

Cultural Context: Until the eighteenth century, mental illness was believed to be caused by demonic possession. Eventually it came to be considered a sickness requiring treatment. Much of modern psychiatry developed from the efforts of Philippe Pinel in France and J. Connolly in England, both of whom advocated a more humane approach to mental illness. By the nineteenth century, research and treatment of mental illness evolved from its origins in spiritual healing, and by the twentieth century, behavior therapies were developed.

CHARLOTTE PERKINS GILMAN

The Yellow Wallpaper   (1892)

It is very seldom that mere ordinary people like John and myself secure ancestral halls for the summer.

A colonial mansion, a hereditary estate, I would say a haunted house, and reach the height of romantic felicity — but that would be asking too much of fate!

Still I will proudly declare that there is something queer about it.

Else, why should it be let so cheaply? And why have stood so long untenanted?

John laughs at me, of course, but one expects that in marriage.   5

John is practical in the extreme. He has no patience with faith, an intense horror of superstition, and he scoffs openly at any talk of things not to be felt and seen and put down in figures.

John is a physician, and *perhaps*—(I would not say it to a living soul, of course, but this is dead paper and a great relief to my mind —) *perhaps* that is one reason I do not get well faster.

You see he does not believe I am sick!

And what can one do?

If a physician of high standing, and one's own husband, assures friends and   10
relatives that there is really nothing the matter with one but temporary nervous depression — a slight hysterical tendency — what is one to do?

My brother is also a physician, and also of high standing, and he says the same thing.

So I take phosphates or phosphites°— whichever it is, and tonics, and journeys, and air, and exercise, and am absolutely forbidden to "work" until I am well again.

Personally, I disagree with their ideas.

Personally, I believe that congenial work, with excitement and change, would do me good.

15   But what is one to do?

I did write for a while in spite of them; but it *does* exhaust me a good deal — having to be so sly about it, or else meet with heavy opposition.

I sometimes fancy that in my condition if I had less opposition and more society and stimulus — but John says the very worst thing I can do is to think about my condition, and I confess it always makes me feel bad.

So I will let it alone and talk about the house.

The most beautiful place! It is quite alone, standing well back from the road, quite three miles from the village. It makes me think of English places that you read about, for there are hedges and walls and gates that lock, and lots of separate little houses for the gardeners and people.

20   There is a *delicious* garden! I never saw such a garden — large and shady, full of box-bordered paths, and lined with long grape-covered arbors with seats under them.

There were greenhouses, too, but they are all broken now.

There was some legal trouble, I believe, something about the heirs and co-heirs; anyhow, the place has been empty for years.

That spoils my ghostliness, I am afraid, but I don't care — there is something strange about the house — I can feel it.

I even said so to John one moonlight evening, but he said what I felt was a *draught*, and shut the window.

25   I get unreasonably angry with John sometimes. I'm sure I never used to be so sensitive. I think it is due to this nervous condition.

But John says if I feel so, I shall neglect proper self-control; so I take pains to control myself — before him, at least, and that makes me very tired.

I don't like our room a bit. I wanted one downstairs that opened on the piazza and had roses all over the window, and such pretty old-fashioned chintz hangings! But John would not hear of it.

He said there was only one window and not room for two beds, and no near room for him if he took another.

He is very careful and loving, and hardly lets me stir without special direction.

30   I have a schedule prescription for each hour in the day; he takes all care from me, and so I feel basely ungrateful not to value it more.

---

phosphates or phosphites: Both terms refer to salts of phosphorous acid. The narrator, however, means "phosphate," a carbonated beverage of water, flavoring, and a small amount of phosphoric acid.

He said we came here solely on my account, that I was to have perfect rest and all the air I could get. "Your exercise depends on your strength, my dear," said he, "and your food somewhat on your appetite; but air you can absorb all the time." So we took the nursery at the top of the house.

It is a big, airy room, the whole floor nearly, with windows that look all ways, and air and sunshine galore. It was nursery first and then playroom and gymnasium, I should judge; for the windows are barred for little children, and there are rings and things in the walls.

The paint and paper look as if a boys' school had used it. It is stripped off — the paper — in great patches all around the head of my bed, about as far as I can reach, and in a great place on the other side of the room low down. I never saw a worse paper in my life.

One of those sprawling flamboyant patterns committing every artistic sin.

It is dull enough to confuse the eye in following, pronounced enough to con- 35
stantly irritate and provoke study, and when you follow the lame uncertain curves for a little distance they suddenly commit suicide — plunge off at outrageous angles, destroy themselves in unheard of contradictions.

The color is repellent, almost revolting; a smouldering unclean yellow, strangely faded by the slow-turning sunlight.

It is a dull yet lurid orange in some places, a sickly sulphur tint in others.

No wonder the children hated it! I should hate it myself if I had to live in this room long.

There comes John, and I must put this away, — he hates to have me write a word.

*   *   *

We have been here two weeks, and I haven't felt like writing before, since that 40
first day.

I am sitting by the window now, up in this atrocious nursery, and there is nothing to hinder my writing as much as I please, save lack of strength.

John is away all day, and even some nights when his cases are serious.

I am glad my case is not serious!

But these nervous troubles are dreadfully depressing.

John does not know how much I really suffer. He knows there is no *reason* to 45
suffer, and that satisfies him.

Of course it is only nervousness. It does weigh on me so not to do my duty in any way!

I meant to be such a help to John, such a real rest and comfort, and here I am a comparative burden already!

Nobody would believe what an effort it is to do what little I am able, — to dress and entertain, and order things.

It is fortunate Mary is so good with the baby. Such a dear baby!

And yet I *cannot* be with him, it makes me so nervous. 50

I suppose John never was nervous in his life. He laughs at me so about this wallpaper!

At first he meant to repaper the room, but afterwards he said that I was letting it get the better of me, and that nothing was worse for a nervous patient than to give way to such fancies.

He said that after the wallpaper was changed it would be the heavy bedstead, and then the barred windows, and then that gate at the head of the stairs, and so on.

"You know the place is doing you good," he said, "and really, dear, I don't care to renovate the house just for a three months' rental."

55 "Then do let us go downstairs," I said, "there are such pretty rooms there."

Then he took me in his arms and called me a blessed little goose, and said he would go down cellar, if I wished, and have it whitewashed into the bargain.

But he is right enough about the beds and windows and things.

It is an airy and comfortable room as any one need wish, and, of course, I would not be so silly as to make him uncomfortable just for a whim.

I'm really getting quite fond of the big room, all but that horrid paper.

60 Out of one window I can see the garden, those mysterious deep-shaded arbors, the riotous old-fashioned flowers, and bushes and gnarly trees.

Out of another I get a lovely view of the bay and a little private wharf belonging to the estate. There is a beautiful shaded lane that runs down there from the house. I always fancy I see people walking in these numerous paths and arbors, but John has cautioned me not to give way to fancy in the least. He says that with my imaginative power and habit of story-making, a nervous weakness like mine is sure to lead to all manner of excited fancies, and that I ought to use my will and good sense to check the tendency. So I try.

I think sometimes that if I were only well enough to write a little it would relieve the press of ideas and rest me.

But I find I get pretty tired when I try.

It is so discouraging not to have any advice and companionship about my work. When I get really well, John says we will ask Cousin Henry and Julia down for a long visit; but he says he would as soon put fireworks in my pillow-case as to let me have those stimulating people about now.

I wish I could get well faster.

65 But I must not think about that. This paper looks to me as if it *knew* what a vicious influence it had!

There is a recurrent spot where the pattern lolls like a broken neck and two bulbous eyes stare at you upside down.

I get positively angry with the impertinence of it and the everlastingness. Up and down and sideways they crawl, and those absurd, unblinking eyes are everywhere. There is one place where two breadths didn't match, and the eyes go all up and down the line, one a little higher than the other.

I never saw so much expression in an inanimate thing before, and we all know how much expression they have! I used to lie awake as a child and get more entertainment and terror out of blank walls and plain furniture than most children could find in a toy-store.

70 I remember what a kindly wink the knobs of our big, old bureau used to have, and there was one chair that always seemed like a strong friend.

I used to feel that if any of the other things looked too fierce I could always hop into that chair and be safe.

The furniture in this room is no worse than inharmonious, however, for we had to bring it all from downstairs. I suppose when this was used as a playroom they had to take the nursery things out, and no wonder! I never saw such ravages as the children have made here.

The wallpaper, as I said before, is torn off in spots, and it sticketh closer than a brother — they must have had perseverance as well as hatred.

Then the floor is scratched and gouged and splintered, the plaster itself is dug out here and there, and this great heavy bed which is all we found in the room, looks as if it had been through the wars.

But I don't mind it a bit — only the paper. 75

There comes John's sister. Such a dear girl as she is, and so careful of me! I must not let her find me writing.

She is a perfect and enthusiastic housekeeper, and hopes for no better profession. I verily believe she thinks it is the writing which made me sick!

But I can write when she is out, and see her a long way off from these windows.

There is one that commands the road, a lovely shaded winding road, and one that just looks off over the country. A lovely country, too, full of great elms and velvet meadows.

This wallpaper has a kind of sub-pattern in a different shade, a particularly ir- 80 ritating one, for you can only see it in certain lights, and not clearly then.

But in the places where it isn't faded and where the sun is just so — I can see a strange, provoking, formless sort of figure, that seems to skulk about behind that silly and conspicuous front design.

There's sister on the stairs!

* * *

Well, the Fourth of July is over! The people are all gone and I am tired out. John thought it might do me good to see a little company, so we just had mother and Nellie and the children down for a week.

Of course I didn't do a thing. Jennie sees to everything now.

But it tired me all the same. 85

John says if I don't pick up faster he shall send me to Weir Mitchell° in the fall.

But I don't want to go there at all. I had a friend who was in his hands once, and she says he is just like John and my brother, only more so!

Besides, it is such an undertaking to go so far.

I don't feel as if it was worth while to turn my hand over for anything, and I'm getting dreadfully fretful and querulous.

I cry at nothing, and cry most of the time. 90

Of course I don't when John is here, or anybody else, but when I am alone.

Weir Mitchell: Silas Weir Mitchell (1829–1914)— a Philadelphia neurologist-psychologist who introduced the "rest cure" for nervous diseases.

And I am alone a good deal just now. John is kept in town very often by serious cases, and Jennie is good and lets me alone when I want her to.

So I walk a little in the garden or down that lovely lane, sit on the porch under the roses, and lie down up here a good deal.

I'm getting really fond of the room in spite of the wallpaper. Perhaps *because* of the wallpaper.

95   It dwells in my mind so!

I lie here on this great immovable bed — it is nailed down, I believe — and follow that pattern about by the hour. It is as good as gymnastics, I assure you. I start, we'll say, at the bottom, down in the corner over there where it has not been touched, and I determine for the thousandth time that I *will* follow that pointless pattern to some sort of a conclusion.

I know a little of the principle of design, and I know this thing was not arranged on any laws of radiation, or alternation, or repetition, or symmetry, or anything else that I ever heard of.

It is repeated, of course, by the breadths, but not otherwise.

Looked at in one way each breadth stands alone, the bloated curves and flourishes — a kind of "debased Romanesque" with *delirium tremens*° go waddling up and down in isolated columns of fatuity.

100   But, on the other hand, they connect diagonally, and the sprawling outlines run off in great slanting waves of optic horror, like a lot of wallowing seaweeds in full chase.

The whole thing goes horizontally, too, at least it seems so, and I exhaust myself in trying to distinguish the order of its going in that direction.

They have used a horizontal breadth for a frieze, and that adds wonderfully to the confusion.

There is one end of the room where it is almost intact, and there, when the crosslights fade and the low sun shines directly upon it, I can almost fancy radiation after all, — the interminable grotesques seems to form around a common center and rush off in headlong plunges of equal distraction.

It makes me tired to follow it. I will take a nap I guess.

105   I don't know why I should write this.

I don't want to.

I don't feel able.

And I know John would think it absurd. But I *must* say what I feel and think in some way — it is such a relief!

But the effort is getting to be greater than the relief.

110   Half the time now I am awfully lazy, and lie down ever so much.

John says I mustn't lose my strength, and has me take cod liver oil and lots of tonics and things, to say nothing of ale and wine and rare meat.

Dear John! He loves me very dearly, and hates to have me sick. I tried to have a real earnest reasonable talk with him the other day, and tell him how I wish he would let me go and make a visit to Cousin Henry and Julia.

---

delirium tremens: Mental confusion caused by alcohol poisoning and characterized by physical tremors and hallucinations.1

But he said I wasn't able to go, nor able to stand it after I got there; and I did not make out a very good case for myself, for I was crying before I had finished.

It is getting to be a great effort for me to think straight. Just this nervous weakness I suppose.

And dear John gathered me up in his arms, and just carried me upstairs and laid me on the bed, and sat by me and read to me till it tired my head.   115

He said I was his darling and his comfort and all he had, and that I must take care of myself for his sake, and keep well.

He says no one but myself can help me out of it, that I must use my will and self-control and not let any silly fancies run away with me.

There's one comfort, the baby is well and happy, and does not have to occupy this nursery with the horrid wallpaper.

If we had not used it, that blessed child would have! What a fortunate escape! Why, I wouldn't have a child of mine, an impressionable little thing, live in such a room for worlds.

I never thought of it before, but it is lucky that John kept me here after all,   120
I can stand it so much easier than a baby, you see.

Of course I never mention it to them any more — I am too wise, — but I keep watch of it all the same.

There are things in that paper that nobody knows but me, or ever will.

Behind that outside pattern the dim shapes get clearer every day.

It is always the same shape, only very numerous.

And it is like a woman stooping down and creeping about behind that pattern.   125
I don't like it a bit. I wonder — I begin to think — I wish John would take me away from here!

It is so hard to talk with John about my case, because he is so wise, and because he loves me so.

But I tried it last night.

It was moonlight. The moon shines in all around just as the sun does.

I hate to see it sometimes, it creeps so slowly, and always comes in by one window or another.

John was asleep and I hated to waken him, so I kept still and watched the   130
moonlight on that undulating wallpaper till I felt creepy.

The faint figure behind seemed to shake the pattern, just as if she wanted to get out.

I got up softly and went to feel and see if the paper *did* move, and when I came back John was awake.

"What is it, little girl?" he said. "Don't go walking about like that — you'll get cold."

I thought it was a good time to talk, so I told him that I really was not gaining here, and that I wished he would take me away.

"Why, darling!" said he, "our lease will be up in three weeks, and I can't see   135
how to leave before.

"The repairs are not done at home, and I cannot possibly leave town just now. Of course if you were in any danger, I could and would, but you really are better, dear, whether you can see it or not. I am a doctor, dear, and I know.

You are gaining flesh and color, your appetite is better, I feel really much easier about you."

"I don't weigh a bit more," said I, "nor as much; and my appetite may be better in the evening when you are here, but it is worse in the morning when you are away!"

"Bless her little heart!" said he with a big hug, "she shall be as sick as she pleases! But now let's improve the shining hours by going to sleep, and talk about it in the morning!"

"And you won't go away?" I asked gloomily.

140   "Why, how can I, dear? It is only three weeks more and then we will take a nice little trip of a few days while Jennie is getting the house ready. Really dear you are better!"

"Better in body perhaps —" I began, and stopped short, for he sat up straight and looked at me with such a stern, reproachful look that I could not say another word.

"My darling," said he, "I beg of you, for my sake and for our child's sake, as well as for your own, that you will never for one instant let that idea enter your mind! There is nothing so dangerous, so fascinating, to a temperament like yours. It is a false and foolish fancy. Can you not trust me as a physician when I tell you so?"

So of course I said no more on that score, and we went to sleep before long. He thought I was asleep first, but I wasn't, and lay there for hours trying to decide whether that front pattern and the back pattern really did move together or separately.

On a pattern like this, by daylight, there is a lack of sequence, a defiance of law, that is a constant irritant to a normal mind.

145   The color is hideous enough, and unreliable enough, and infuriating enough, but the pattern is torturing.

You think you have mastered it, but just as you get well underway in following, it turns back-somersault and there you are. It slaps you in the face, knocks you down, and tramples upon you. It is like a bad dream.

The outside pattern is a florid arabesque, reminding one of a fungus. If you can imagine a toadstool in joints, an interminable string of toadstools, budding and sprouting in endless convolutions — why, that is something like it.

That is, sometimes!

There is one marked peculiarity about this paper, a thing nobody seems to notice but myself, and that is that it changes as the light changes.

150   When the sun shoots in through the east window — I always watch for that first long, straight ray — it changes so quickly that I never can quite believe it.

That is why I watch it always.

By moonlight — the moon shines in all night when there is a moon — I wouldn't know it was the same paper.

At night in any kind of light, in twilight, candlelight, lamplight, and worst of all by moonlight, it becomes bars! The outside pattern I mean, and the woman behind it is as plain as can be.

I didn't realize for a long time what the thing was that showed behind, that dim sub-pattern, but now I am quite sure it is a woman.

By daylight she is subdued, quiet. I fancy it is the pattern that keeps her so still. It is so puzzling. It keeps me quiet by the hour.

I lie down ever so much now. John says it is good for me, and to sleep all I can.

Indeed he started the habit by making me lie down for an hour after each meal.

It is a very bad habit I am convinced, for you see I don't sleep.

And that cultivates deceit, for I don't tell them I'm awake — O no!

The fact is I am getting a little afraid of John.

He seems very queer sometimes, and even Jennie has an inexplicable look.

It strikes me occasionally, just as a scientific hypothesis, — that perhaps it is the paper!

I have watched John when he did not know I was looking, and come into the room suddenly on the most innocent excuses, and I've caught him several times *looking at the paper!* And Jennie too. I caught Jennie with her hand on it once.

She didn't know I was in the room, and when I asked her in a quiet, a very quiet voice, with the most restrained manner possible, what she was doing with the paper — she turned around as if she had been caught stealing, and looked quite angry — asked me why I should frighten her so!

Then she said that the paper stained everything it touched, that she had found yellow smooches on all my clothes and John's, and she wished we would be more careful!

Did not that sound innocent? But I know she was studying that pattern, and I am determined that nobody shall find it out but myself!

Life is very much more exciting now than it used to be. You see I have something more to expect, to look forward to, to watch. I really do eat better, and am more quiet than I was.

John is so pleased to see me improve! He laughed a little the other day, and said I seemed to be flourishing in spite of my wallpaper.

I turned it off with a laugh. I had no intention of telling him it was *because* of the wallpaper — he would make fun of me. He might even want to take me away.

I don't want to leave now until I have found it out. There is a week more, and I think that will be enough.

I'm feeling ever so much better! I don't sleep much at night, for it is so interesting to watch developments; but I sleep a good deal in the daytime.

In the daytime it is tiresome and perplexing.

There are always new shoots on the fungus, and new shades of yellow all over it. I cannot keep count of them, though I have tried conscientiously.

It is the strangest yellow, that wallpaper! It makes me think of all the yellow things I ever saw — not beautiful ones like buttercups, but old foul, bad yellow things.

But there is something else about that paper — the smell! I noticed it the moment we came into the room, but with so much air and sun it was not bad. Now we have had a week of fog and rain, and whether the windows are open or not, the smell is here.

It creeps all over the house.

I find it hovering in the dining-room, skulking in the parlor, hiding in the hall, lying in wait for me on the stairs.

It gets into my hair.

Even when I go to ride, if I turn my head suddenly and surprise it — there is that smell!

180   Such a peculiar odor, too! I have spent hours in trying to analyze it, to find what it smelled like.

It is not bad — at first, and very gentle, but quite the subtlest, most enduring odor I ever met.

In this damp weather it is awful, I wake up in the night and find it hanging over me.

It used to disturb me at first. I thought seriously of burning the house — to reach the smell.

But now I am used to it. The only thing I can think of that it is like is the *color* of the paper! A yellow smell.

185   There is a very funny mark on this wall, low down, near the mop-board. A streak that runs round the room. It goes behind every piece of furniture, except the bed, a long, straight, even *smooch,* as if it had been rubbed over and over.

I wonder how it was done and who did it, and what they did it for. Round and round and round — round and round and round! — it makes me dizzy!

I really have discovered something at last.

Through watching so much at night, when it changes so, I have finally found out.

The front pattern *does* move — and no wonder! The woman behind shakes it!

190   Sometimes I think there are a great many women behind, and sometimes only one, and she crawls around fast, and her crawling shakes it all over.

Then in the very bright spots she keeps still, and in the very shady spots she just takes hold of the bars and shakes them hard.

And she is all the time trying to climb through. But nobody could climb through that pattern — it strangles so; I think that is why it has so many heads.

They get through, and then the pattern strangles them off and turns them upside down, and makes their eyes white!

If those heads were covered or taken off it would not be half so bad.

195   I think that woman gets out in the daytime!

And I'll tell you why — privately — I've seen her!

I can see her out of every one of my windows!

It is the same woman, I know, for she is always creeping, and most women do not creep by daylight.

I see her in that long shaded lane, creeping up and down. I see her in those dark grape arbors, creeping all around the garden.

200   I see her on that long road under the trees, creeping along, and when a carriage comes she hides under the blackberry vines.

I don't blame her a bit. It must be very humiliating to be caught creeping by daylight!

I always lock the door when I creep by daylight. I can't do it at night, for I know John would suspect something at once.

And John is so queer now, that I don't want to irritate him. I wish he would take another room! Besides, I don't want anybody to get that woman out at night but myself.

I often wonder if I could see her out of all the windows at once.

But, turn as fast as I can, I can only see out of one at one time. 205

And though I always see her, she *may* be able to creep faster than I can turn!

I have watched her sometimes away off in the open country, creeping as fast as a cloud shadow in a high wind.

If only that top pattern could be gotten off from the under one! I mean to try it, little by little.

I have found out another funny thing, but I shan't tell it this time! It does not do to trust people too much.

There are only two more days to get this paper off, and I believe John is 210 beginning to notice. I don't like the look in his eyes.

And I heard him ask Jennie a lot of professional questions about me. She had a very good report to give.

She said I slept a good deal in the daytime.

John knows I don't sleep very well at night, for all I'm so quiet!

He asked me all sorts of questions, too, and pretended to be very loving and kind.

As if I couldn't see through him! 215

Still, I don't wonder he acts so, sleeping under this paper for three months.

It only interests me, but I feel sure John and Jennie are secretly affected by it.

*   *   *

Hurrah! This is the last day, but it is enough. John to stay in town over night, and won't be out until this evening.

Jennie wanted to sleep with me — the sly thing! But I told her I should undoubtedly rest better for a night all alone.

That was clever, for really I wasn't alone a bit! As soon as it was moon-light and 220 that poor thing began to crawl and shake the pattern, I got up and ran to help her.

I pulled and she shook, I shook and she pulled, and before morning we had peeled off yards of that paper.

A strip about as high as my head and half around the room.

And then when the sun came and that awful pattern began to laugh at me, I declared I would finish it to-day!

We go away to-morrow, and they are moving all my furniture down again to leave things as they were before.

Jennie looked at the wall in amazement, but I told her merrily that I did it out 225 of pure spite at the vicious thing.

She laughed and said she wouldn't mind doing it herself, but I must not get tired.

How she betrayed herself that time!

But I am here, and no person touches this paper but me, — not *alive!*

She tried to get me out of the room — it was too patent! But I said it was so quiet and empty and clean now that I believed I would lie down again and sleep all I could; and not to wake me even for dinner — I would call when I woke.

230 So now she is gone, and the servants are gone, and the things are gone, and there is nothing left but that great bedstead nailed down, with the canvas mattress we found on it.

We shall sleep downstairs to-night, and take the boat home tomorrow.

I quite enjoy the room, now it is bare again.

How those children did tear about here!

This bedstead is fairly gnawed!

235 But I must get to work.

I have locked the door and thrown the key down into the front path.

I don't want to go out, and I don't want to have anybody come in, till John comes.

I want to astonish him.

I've got a rope up here that even Jennie did not find. If that woman does get out, and tries to get away, I can tie her!

240 But I forgot I could not reach far without anything to stand on!

This bed will *not* move!

I tried to lift and push it until I was lame, and then I got so angry I bit off a little piece at one corner — but it hurt my teeth.

Then I peeled off all the paper I could reach standing on the floor. It sticks horribly and the pattern just enjoys it! All those strangled heads and bulbous eyes and waddling fungus growths just shriek with derision!

I am getting angry enough to do something desperate. To jump out of the window would be admirable exercise, but the bars are too strong even to try.

245 Besides I wouldn't do it. Of course not. I know well enough that a step like that is improper and might be misconstrued.

I don't like to *look* out of the windows even — there are so many of those creeping women, and they creep so fast.

I wonder if they come out of that wall-paper as I did?

But I am securely fastened now by my well-hidden rope — you don't get *me* out in the road there!

I suppose I shall have to get back behind the pattern when it comes night, and that is hard!

250 It is so pleasant to be out in this great room and creep around as I please!

I don't want to go outside. I won't, even if Jennie asks me to.

For outside you have to creep on the ground, and everything is green instead of yellow.

But here I can creep smoothly on the floor, and my shoulder just fits in that long smooch around the wall, so I cannot lose my way.

Why there's John at the door!

255 It is no use, young man, you can't open it!

How he does call and pound!

Now he's crying for an axe.

It would be a shame to break down that beautiful door!

"John dear!" said I in the gentlest voice, "the key is down by the front steps, under a plantain leaf!"

That silenced him for a few moments.   260

Then he said — very quietly indeed, "Open the door, my darling!"

"I can't," said I. "The key is down by the front door under a plantain leaf!"

And then I said it again, several times, very gently and slowly, and said it so often that he had to go and see, and he got it of course, and came in. He stopped short by the door.

"What is the matter?" he cried. "For God's sake, what are you doing!"

I kept on creeping just the same, but I looked at him over my shoulder.   265

"I've got out at last," said I, "in spite of you and Jane. And I've pulled off most of the paper, so you can't put me back!"

Now why should that man have fainted? But he did, and right across my path by the wall, so that I had to creep over him every time!

Reading and Reacting

1. The story's narrator, who has recently had a baby, is suffering from what her husband, a doctor, calls "temporary nervous depression — a slight hysterical tendency" (par. 10). What has probably caused this depression? What factors aggravate it? How much insight does the narrator seem to have into her situation?

2. In your own words, describe the house and grounds, the room, and the wallpaper. What is it about each of these elements that upsets the narrator? Do you believe her descriptions of her setting are accurate? Why or why not? What do you think she sees, and what do you think she imagines?

3. What do the following comments reveal about the relationship between the narrator and her husband?
   - "John laughs at me, of course, but one expects that in marriage" (par. 5).
   - "I must put this away,—he hates to have me write a word" (par. 39).
   - "He laughs at me so about this wallpaper" (par. 51).
   - "Then he took me in his arms and called me a blessed little goose . . ." (par. 56).

4. How does the narrator's mood change as the story progresses? Why does her husband apparently not see the seriousness of her deterioration?

5. How might this story be different if it were told by the husband? By the woman's doctor?

6. How would you expect a woman today to respond if her husband or doctor gave her the advice given the narrator? Could the events described in the story happen today? Explain.

7. Why do you suppose the story has so many short paragraphs?

8. The narrator is the protagonist of this story, and her husband John appears to be the antagonist. What other characters or forces are pitted against the narrator?

9. JOURNAL ENTRY The ending of this story leaves much unanswered. What do you think might happen in the hours or days to follow?

10. CRITICAL PERSPECTIVE "The Yellow Wallpaper" was originally seen by some readers as a ghost story and was anthologized as such. More recently, critics have tended to interpret the story from a feminist perspective, focusing on the way in which the nameless narrator is victimized by the men around her and by the values of the Victorian society they uphold. In the essay "An Unnecessary Maze of Sign-Reading," Mary Jacobus concludes that the overwhelmingly feminist perspective of recent criticism, though certainly valuable and enlightening, has overlooked other promising critical possibilities — for example, "the Gothic and uncanny elements present in the text."

If you were teaching "The Yellow Wallpaper," would you present it as a feminist story or as a chilling gothic ghost story? Do you think interpreting the story as a gothic horror tale precludes a feminist reading, or do you see the two interpretations as compatible?

Related Works: "The Story of an Hour" (p. 82), "The Disappearance" (p. 458), "Barbie Doll" (p. 902), *A Doll House* (p. 995)

RALPH ELLISON (1914–1994) was born in Oklahoma City, Oklahoma. After his father's death when Ellison was three, Ellison's mother took up work as a domestic servant to support herself and her son. Early on, Ellison developed an interest in literature and music. He enrolled as a musician in Tuskegee Institute, in Alabama; then in 1936, he moved to New York City, where he worked with the Federal Writers' Project. While there, Ellison met prominent African American writers Langston Hughes and Richard Wright, who encouraged his literary ambitions. He began to publish stories in journals and became an editor of *Negro Quarterly.* After service in the merchant marine during World War II, Ellison returned to New York and taught literature at New York University for many years.

Ellison's first novel, *Invisible Man* (1952), was an instant success. The book — a semi-autobiographical chronicle of a young black man's search for intellectual identity — won the National Book Award for fiction and was listed in *Book Week* as the most distinguished American novel of the preceding twenty years. Ellison published two collections of essays, *Shadow and Act* (1964) and *Going to the Territories* (1986); his collected essays appeared in 1995. His short story "Battle Royal" was first published in 1948; it went on to become, in a slightly revised form, the opening chapter of *Invisible Man.*

Cultural Context: A "battle royal" is a fight involving numerous combatants (or, more generally, a fierce contest). The expression has its origin in cockfighting, where birds often fight to the death. In 1948, when Ellison's story was published, racial segregation was still prevalent throughout the United States. The military had been integrated after World War II, but in the South, "colored" people could not use the same public water fountains as "whites" and had to ride in the backs of public buses. "Jim Crow" laws in the South were designed to keep blacks from voting and holding local office; these, combined with a dismal, segregated educational system, ensured that black Americans were "separate" but not "equal."

Battle Royal (1952)

It goes a long way back, some twenty years. All my life I had been looking for something, and everywhere I turned someone tried to tell me what it was. I accepted their answers too, though they were often in contradiction and even self-contradictory. I was naïve. I was looking for myself and asking everyone except myself questions which I, and only I, could answer. It took me a long time and much painful boomeranging of my expectations to achieve a realization everyone else appears to have been born with: That I am nobody but myself. But first I had to discover that I am an invisible man!°

And yet I am no freak of nature, nor of history. I was in the cards, other things having been equal (or unequal) eighty-five years ago. I am not ashamed of my grandparents for having been slaves. I am only ashamed of myself for having at one time been ashamed. About eighty-five years ago they were told that they were free, united with others of our country in everything pertaining to the common good, and, in everything social, separate like the fingers of the hand. And they believed it. They exulted in it. They stayed in their place, worked hard, and brought up my father to do the same. But my grandfather is the one. He was an odd old guy, my grandfather, and I am told I take after him. It was he who caused the trouble. On his deathbed he called my father to him and said, "Son, after I'm gone I want you to keep up the good fight. I never told you, but our life is a war and I have been a traitor all my born days, a spy in the enemy's country ever since I give up my gun back in the Reconstruction. Live with your head in the lion's mouth. I want you to overcome 'em with yeses, undermine 'em with grins, agree 'em to death and destruction, let 'em swoller you till they vomit or bust wide open." They thought the old man had gone out of his mind. He had been the meekest of men. The younger children were rushed from the room, the shades drawn and the flame of the lamp turned so low that it sputtered on the wick like the old man's breathing. "Learn it to the younguns," he whispered fiercely; then he died.

But my folks were more alarmed over his last words than over his dying. It was as though he had not died at all, his words caused so much anxiety. I was warned emphatically to forget what he had said and, indeed, this is the first time it has been mentioned outside the family circle. It had a tremendous effect upon me, however. I could never be sure of what he meant. Grandfather had been a quiet old man who never made any trouble, yet on his deathbed he had called himself a traitor and a spy, and he had spoken of his meekness as a dangerous activity. It became a constant puzzle which lay unanswered in the back of my mind. And whenever things went well for me I remembered my grandfather and felt guilty and uncomfortable. It was as though I was carrying out his advice in spite of myself. And to make it worse, everyone loved me for it. I was praised by the most lily-white men of the town. I was considered an example of desirable conduct — just as my grandfather had been. And what puzzled me was that the old man had defined it as *treachery*. When I was praised for my conduct I felt a guilt that in some way I was doing something that was really against the wishes of the white folks, that if they had understood they would have desired me to act just the opposite, that I should have been sulky and mean, and that that really would have been what they wanted, even though they were fooled and thought they wanted me to act as I did. It made me afraid that some day they would look upon me as a traitor and I would be lost. Still I was more afraid to act any other way because they didn't like that at all. The old man's words were like a curse. On my graduation day I delivered an oration in which I showed that humility was the secret, indeed, the very essence of progress. (Not that I believed this — how could I, remembering my grandfather?— I only believed that it worked.) It was a great success. Everyone praised me and I was invited to give the speech at a gathering of the town's leading white citizens. It was a triumph for our whole community.

It was in the main ballroom of the leading hotel. When I got there I discovered that it was on the occasion of a smoker° and I was told that since I was to be there anyway I might as well take part in the battle royal to be fought by some of my schoolmates as part of the entertainment. The battle royal came first.

5   All of the town's big shots were there in their tuxedoes, wolfing down the buffet foods, drinking beer and whiskey and smoking black cigars. It was a large room with a high ceiling. Chairs were arranged in neat rows around three sides of a portable boxing ring. The fourth side was clear, revealing a gleaming space of polished floor. I had some misgivings over the battle royal, by the way. Not from a distaste for fighting, but because I didn't care too much for the other fellows who were to take part. They were tough guys who seemed to have no grandfather's curse worrying their minds. No one could mistake their toughness. And besides, I suspected that fighting a battle royal might detract from the dignity of my speech. In those pre-invisible days I visualized myself as a potential Booker T. Washington.° But the other fellows didn't care too much for me either, and there were nine of them. I felt superior to them in my way, and I didn't like the manner in which we were all crowded together into the servants' elevator. Nor did they like my being there. In fact, as the warmly lighted floors flashed past the elevator we had words over the fact that I, by taking part in the fight, had knocked one of their friends out of a night's work.

We were led out of the elevator through a rococo hall into an anteroom and told to get into our fighting togs. Each of us was issued a pair of boxing gloves and ushered out into the big mirrored hall, which we entered looking cautiously about us and whispering, lest we might accidentally be heard above the noise of the room. It was foggy with cigar smoke. And already the whiskey was taking effect. I was shocked to see some of the most important men of the town quite tipsy. They were all there — bankers, lawyers, judges, doctors, fire chiefs, teachers, merchants. Even one of the more fashionable pastors. Something we could not see was going on up front. A clarinet was vibrating sensuously and the men were standing up and mov-

---

smoker: Informal men-only social gathering.

Booker T. Washington: American educator (1856–1915) born into slavery who gained an education after emancipation and in 1881 organized Tuskegee Institute, a vocational school for African Americans.

ing eagerly forward. We were a small tight group, clustered together, our bare upper bodies touching and shining with anticipatory sweat; while up front the big shots were becoming increasingly excited over something we still could not see. Suddenly I heard the school superintendent, who had told me to come, yell, "Bring up the shines° gentlemen! Bring up the little shines!"

We were rushed up to the front of the ballroom, where it smelled even more strongly of tobacco and whiskey. Then we were pushed into place. I almost wet my pants. A sea of faces, some hostile, some amused, ringed around us, and in the center, facing us, stood a magnificent blonde — stark naked. There was dead silence. I felt a blast of cold air chill me. I tried to back away, but they were behind me and around me. Some of the boys stood with lowered heads, trembling. I felt a wave of irrational guilt and fear. My teeth chattered, my skin turned to goose flesh, my knees knocked. Yet I was strongly attracted and looked in spite of myself. Had the price of looking been blindness, I would have looked. The hair was yellow like that of a circus kewpie doll, the face heavily powdered and rouged, as though to form an abstract mask, the eyes hollow and smeared a cool blue, the color of a baboon's butt. I felt a desire to spit upon her as my eyes brushed slowly over her body. Her breasts were firm and round as the domes of East Indian temples, and I stood so close as to see the fine skin texture and beads of pearly perspiration glistening like dew around the pink and erected buds of her nipples. I wanted at one and the same time to run from the room, to sink through the floor, or go to her and cover her from my eyes and the eyes of the others with my body; to feel the soft thighs, to caress her and destroy her, to love her and murder her, to hide from her, and yet to stroke where below the small American flag tattooed upon her belly her thighs formed a capital V. I had a notion that of all in the room she saw only me with her impersonal eyes.

And then she began to dance, a slow sensuous movement; the smoke of a hundred cigars clinging to her like the thinnest of veils. She seemed like a fair bird-girl girdled in veils calling to me from the angry surface of some gray and threatening sea. I was transported. Then I became aware of the clarinet playing and the big shots yelling at us. Some threatened us if we looked and others if we did not. On my right I saw one boy faint. And now a man grabbed a silver pitcher from a table and stepped close as he dashed ice water upon him and stood him up and forced two of us to support him as his head hung and moans issued from his thick bluish lips. Another boy began to plead to go home. He was the largest of the group, wearing dark red fighting trunks much too small to conceal the erection which projected from him as though in answer to the insinuating low-registered moaning of the clarinet. He tried to hide himself with his boxing gloves.

And all the while the blonde continued dancing, smiling faintly at the big shots who watched her with fascination, and faintly smiling at our fear. I noticed a certain merchant who followed her hungrily, his lips loose and drooling. He was a large man who wore diamond studs in a shirtfront which swelled with the ample

----

shines: A racial slur.

paunch underneath, and each time the blonde swayed her undulating hips he ran his hand through the thin hair of his bald head and, with his arms upheld, his posture clumsy like that of an intoxicated panda, wound his belly in a slow and obscene grind. This creature was completely hypnotized. The music had quickened. As the dancer flung herself about with a detached expression on her face, the men began reaching out to touch her. I could see their beefy fingers sink into her soft flesh. Some of the others tried to stop them and she began to move around the floor in graceful circles, as they gave chase, slipping and sliding over the polished floor. It was mad. Chairs went crashing, drinks were spilt, as they ran laughing and howling after her. They caught her just as she reached a door, raised her from the floor, and tossed her as college boys are tossed at a hazing, and above her red, fixed-smiling lips I saw the terror and disgust in her eyes, almost like my own terror and that which I saw in some of the other boys. As I watched, they tossed her twice and her soft breasts seemed to flatten against the air and her legs flung wildly as she spun. Some of the more sober ones helped her to escape. And I started off the floor, heading for the anteroom with the rest of the boys.

10   Some were still crying and in hysteria. But as we tried to leave we were stopped and ordered to get into the ring. There was nothing to do but what we were told. All ten of us climbed under the ropes and allowed ourselves to be blindfolded with broad bands of white cloth. One of the men seemed to feel a bit sympathetic and tried to cheer us up as we stood with our backs against the ropes. Some of us tried to grin. "See that boy over there?" one of the men said. "I want you to run across at the bell and give it to him right in the belly. If you don't get him, I'm going to get you. I don't like his looks." Each of us was told the same. The blindfolds were put on. Yet even then I had been going over my speech. In my mind each word was as bright as flame. I felt the cloth pressed into place, and frowned so that it would be loosened when I relaxed.

But now I felt a sudden fit of blind terror. I was unused to darkness. It was as though I had suddenly found myself in a dark room filled with poisonous cottonmouths. I could hear the bleary voices yelling insistently for the battle royal to begin.

"Get going in there!"

"Let me at that big nigger!"

I strained to pick up the school superintendent's voice, as though to squeeze some security out of that slightly more familiar sound.

15   "Let me at those black sonsabitches!" someone yelled.

"No, Jackson, no!" another voice yelled. "Here, somebody, help me hold Jack."

"I want to get at that ginger-colored nigger. Tear him limb from limb," the first voice yelled.

I stood against the ropes trembling. For in those days I was what they called ginger-colored, and he sounded as though he might crunch me between his teeth like a crisp ginger cookie.

Quite a struggle was going on. Chairs were being kicked about and I could hear voices grunting as with a terrific effort. I wanted to see, to see more desperately than ever before. But the blindfold was as tight as a thick skin-puckering scab and when I raised my gloved hands to push the layers of white aside a voice yelled, "Oh, no you don't! black bastard! Leave that alone!"

"Ring the bell before Jackson kills him a coon!" someone boomed in the sudden silence. And I heard the bell clang and the sound of the feet scuffling forward. 20

A glove smacked against my head. I pivoted, striking out stiffly as someone went past, and felt the jar ripple along the length of my arm to my shoulder. Then it seemed as though all nine of the boys had turned upon me at once. Blows pounded me from all sides while I struck out as best I could. So many blows landed upon me that I wondered if I were not the only blindfolded fighter in the ring, or if the man called Jackson hadn't succeeded in getting me after all.

Blindfolded, I could no longer control my motions. I had no dignity. I stumbled about like a baby or a drunken man. The smoke had become thicker and with each new blow it seemed to sear and further restrict my lungs. My saliva became like hot bitter glue. A glove connected with my head, filling my mouth with warm blood. It was everywhere. I could not tell if the moisture I felt upon my body was sweat or blood. A blow landed hard against the nape of my neck. I felt myself going over, my head hitting the floor. Streaks of blue light filled the black world behind the blindfold. I lay prone, pretending that I was knocked out, but felt myself seized by hands and yanked to my feet. "Get going, black boy! Mix it up!" My arms were like lead, my head smarting from blows. I managed to feel my way to the ropes and held on, trying to catch my breath. A glove landed in my midsection and I went over again, feeling as though the smoke had become a knife jabbed into my guts. Pushed this way and that by the legs milling around me, I finally pulled erect and discovered that I could see the black, sweat-washed forms weaving in the smoky-blue atmosphere like drunken dancers weaving to the rapid drum-like thuds of blows.

Everyone fought hysterically. It was complete anarchy. Everybody fought everybody else. No group fought together for long. Two, three, four, fought one, then turned to fight each other, were themselves attacked. Blows landed below the belt and in the kidney, with the gloves open as well as closed, and with my eye partly opened now there was not so much terror. I moved carefully, avoiding blows, although not too many to attract attention, fighting from group to group. The boys groped about like blind, cautious crabs crouching to protect their midsections, their heads pulled in short against their shoulders, their arms stretched nervously before them, with their fists testing the smoke-filled air like the knobbed feelers of hypersensitive snails. In one corner I glimpsed a boy violently punching the air and heard him scream in pain as he smashed his hand against a ring post. For a second I saw him bent over holding his hand, then going down as a blow caught his unprotected head. I played one group against the other, slipping in and throwing a punch then stepping out of range while pushing the others into the melee to take the blows blindly aimed at me. The smoke was agonizing and there were no rounds, no bells at three minute intervals to relieve our exhaustion. The room spun round me, a swirl of lights, smoke, sweating bodies surrounded by tense white faces. I bled from both nose and mouth, the blood spattering upon my chest.

The men kept yelling, "Slug him, black boy! Knock his guts out!"

25   "Uppercut him! Kill him! Kill that big boy!"

Taking a fake fall, I saw a boy going down heavily beside me as though we were felled by a single blow, saw a sneaker-clad foot shoot into his groin as the two who had knocked him down stumbled upon him. I rolled out of range, feeling a twinge of nausea.

The harder we fought the more threatening the men became. And yet, I had begun to worry about my speech again. How would it go? Would they recognize my ability? What would they give me?

I was fighting automatically and suddenly I noticed that one after another of the boys was leaving the ring. I was surprised, filled with panic, as though I had been left alone with an unknown danger. Then I understood. The boys had arranged it among themselves. It was the custom for the two men left in the ring to slug it out for the winner's prize. I discovered this too late. When the bell sounded two men in tuxedoes leaped into the ring and removed the blindfold. I found myself facing Tatlock, the biggest of the gang. I felt sick at my stomach. Hardly had the bell stopped ringing in my ears than it clanged again and I saw him moving swiftly toward me. Thinking of nothing else to do I hit him smash on the nose. He kept coming, bringing the rank sharp violence of stale sweat. His face was a black blank of a face, only his eyes alive — with hate of me and aglow with a feverish terror from what had happened to us all. I became anxious. I wanted to deliver my speech and he came at me as though he meant to beat it out of me. I smashed him again and again, taking his blows as they came. Then on a sudden impulse I struck him lightly and as we clinched, I whispered, "Fake like I knocked you out, you can have the prize."

"I'll break your behind," he whispered hoarsely.

30   "For *them?*"

"For *me,* sonofabitch!"

They were yelling for us to break it up and Tatlock spun me half around with a blow, and as a joggled camera sweeps in a reeling scene, I saw the howling red faces crouching tense beneath the cloud of blue-gray smoke. For a moment the world wavered, unraveled, flowed, then my head cleared and Tatlock bounced before me. That fluttering shadow before my eyes was his jabbing left hand. Then falling forward, my head against his damp shoulder, I whispered, "I'll make it five dollars more."

"Go to hell!"

But his muscles relaxed a trifle beneath my pressure and I breathed, "Seven!"

35   "Give it to your ma," he said, ripping me beneath the heart.

And while I still held him I butted him and moved away. I felt myself bombarded with punches. I fought back with hopeless desperation. I wanted to deliver my speech more than anything else in the world, because I felt that only these men could judge truly my ability, and now this stupid clown was ruining my chances. I began fighting carefully now, moving in to punch him and out again with my greater speed. A lucky blow to his chin and I had him going too — until I heard a loud voice yell, "I got my money on the big boy."

Hearing this, I almost dropped my guard. I was confused: Should I try to win against the voice out there? Would not this go against my speech, and was not this a moment for humility, for nonresistance? A blow to my head as I danced about sent my right eye popping like a jack-in-the-box and settled my dilemma. The room went red as I fell. It was a dream fall, my body languid and fastidious as to where to land, until the floor became impatient and smashed up to meet me. A moment later I came to. An hypnotic voice said FIVE emphatically. And I lay there, hazily watching a dark red spot of my own blood shaping itself into a butterfly, glistening and soaking into the soiled gray world of the canvas.

When the voice drawled TEN I was lifted up and dragged to a chair. I sat dazed. My eye pained and swelled with each throb of my pounding heart and I wondered if now I would be allowed to speak. I was wringing wet, my mouth still bleeding. We were grouped along the wall now. The other boys ignored me as they congratulated Tatlock and speculated as to how much they would be paid. One boy whimpered over his smashed hand. Looking up front, I saw attendants in white jackets rolling the portable ring away and placing a small square rug in the vacant space surrounded by chairs. Perhaps, I thought, I will stand on the rug to deliver my speech.

Then the M.C. called to us, "Come on up here boys and get your money."

We ran forward to where the men laughed and talked in their chairs, waiting. 40 Everyone seemed friendly now.

"There it is on the rug," the man said. I saw the rug covered with coins of all dimensions and a few crumpled bills. But what excited me, scattered here and there, were the gold pieces.

"Boys, it's all yours," the man said. "You get all you grab."

"That's right, Sambo,"° a blond man said, winking at me confidentially.

I trembled with excitement, forgetting my pain. I would get the gold and the bills, I thought. I would use both hands. I would throw my body against the boys nearest me to block them from the gold.

"Get down around the rug now," the man commanded, "and don't anyone 45 touch it until I give the signal."

"This ought to be good," I heard.

As told, we got around the square rug on our knees. Slowly the man raised his freckled hand as we followed it upward with our eyes.

I heard, "These niggers look like they're about to pray!"

Then, "Ready," the man said. "Go!"

I lunged for a yellow coin lying on the blue design of the carpet, touching it 50 and sending a surprised shriek to join those rising around me. I tried frantically to remove my hand but could not let go. A hot, violent force tore through my body, shaking me like a wet rat. The rug was electrified. The hair bristled up on my head as I shook myself free. My muscles jumped, my nerves jangled, writhed. But I saw that this was not stopping the other boys. Laughing in fear and embarrassment,

---

Sambo: A racial slur, referring to a character in a children's story.

some were holding back and scooping up the coins knocked off by the painful contortions of the others. The men roared above us as we struggled.

"Pick it up, goddamnit, pick it up!" someone called like a bass-voiced parrot. "Go on, get it!"

I crawled rapidly around the floor, picking up the coins, trying to avoid the coppers and to get greenbacks and the gold. Ignoring the shock by laughing, as I brushed the coins off quickly, I discovered that I could contain the electricity — a contradiction, but it works. Then the men began to push us onto the rug. Laughing embarrassedly, we struggled out of their hands and kept after the coins. We were all wet and slippery and hard to hold. Suddenly I saw a boy lifted into the air, glistening with sweat like a circus seal, and dropped, his wet back landing flush upon the charged rug, heard him yell and saw him literally dance upon his back, his elbows beating a frenzied tattoo upon the floor, his muscles twitching like the flesh of a horse stung by many flies. When he finally rolled off, his face was gray and no one stopped him when he ran from the floor amid booming laughter.

"Get the money," the M.C. called. "That's good hard American cash!"

And we snatched and grabbed, snatched and grabbed. I was careful not to come too close to the rug now, and when I felt the hot whiskey breath descend upon me like a cloud of foul air I reached out and grabbed the leg of a chair. It was occupied and I held on desperately.

55   "Leggo, nigger! Leggo!"

The huge face wavered down to mine as he tried to push me free. But my body was slippery and he was too drunk. It was Mr. Colcord, who owned a chain of movie houses and "entertainment palaces." Each time he grabbed me I slipped out of his hands. It became a real struggle. I feared the rug more than I did the drunk, so I held on, surprising myself for a moment by trying to topple *him* upon the rug. It was such an enormous idea that I found myself actually carrying it out. I tried not to be obvious, yet when I grabbed his leg, trying to tumble him out of the chair, he raised up roaring with laughter, and, looking at me with soberness dead in the eye, kicked me viciously in the chest. The chair leg flew out of my hand. I felt myself going and rolled. It was as though I had rolled through a bed of hot coals. It seemed a whole century would pass before I would roll free, a century in which I was seared through the deepest levels of my body to the fearful breath within me and the breath seared and heated to the point of explosion. It'll all be over in a flash, I thought as I rolled clear. It'll all be over in a flash.

But not yet, the men on the other side were waiting, red faces swollen as though from apoplexy as they bent forward in their chairs. Seeing their fingers coming toward me I rolled away as a fumbled football rolls off the receiver's fingertips, back into the coals. That time I luckily sent the rug sliding out of place and heard the coins ringing against the floor and the boys scuffling to pick them up and the M.C. calling, "All right, boys, that's all. Go get dressed and get your money."

I was limp as a dish rag. My back felt as though it had been beaten with wires.

When we had dressed the M.C. came in and gave us each five dollars, except Tatlock, who got ten for being last in the ring. Then he told us to leave. I was not to get a chance to deliver my speech, I thought. I was going out into the dim alley in despair when I was stopped and told to go back. I returned to the ballroom, where the men were pushing back their chairs and gathering in groups to talk.

The M.C. knocked on a table for quiet. "Gentlemen," he said, "we almost forgot an important part of the program. A most serious part, gentlemen. This boy was brought here to deliver a speech which he made at his graduation yesterday. . . ." 60

"Bravo!"

"I'm told that he is the smartest boy we've got out there in Greenwood. I'm told that he knows more big words than a pocket-sized dictionary."

Much applause and laughter.

"So now, gentlemen, I want you to give him your attention."

There was still laughter as I faced them, my mouth dry, my eye throbbing. I began slowly, but evidently my throat was tense, because they began shouting, "Louder! Louder!" 65

"We of the younger generation extol the wisdom of that great leader and educator," I shouted, "who first spoke these flaming words of wisdom: 'A ship lost at sea for many days suddenly sighted a friendly vessel. From the mast of the unfortunate vessel was seen a signal: "Water, water; we die of thirst!" The answer from the friendly vessel came back: "Cast down your bucket where you are." The captain of the distressed vessel, at last heeding the injunction, cast down his bucket, and it came up full of fresh sparkling water from the mouth of the Amazon River.' And like him I say, and in his words, 'To those of my race who depend upon bettering their condition in a foreign land, or who underestimate the importance of cultivating friendly relations with the Southern white man, who is his next-door neighbor, I would say: "Cast down your bucket where you are" — cast it down in making friends in every manly way of the people of all races by whom we are surrounded. . . .'"

I spoke automatically and with such fervor that I did not realize that the men were still talking and laughing until my dry mouth, filling up with blood from the cut, almost strangled me. I coughed, wanting to stop and go to one of the tall brass, sand filled spittoons to relieve myself, but a few of the men, especially the superintendent, were listening and I was afraid. So I gulped it down, blood, saliva and all, and continued. (What powers of endurance I had during those days! What enthusiasm! What a belief in the rightness of things!) I spoke even louder in spite of the pain. But still they talked and still they laughed, as though deaf with cotton in dirty ears. So I spoke with greater emotional emphasis. I closed my ears and swallowed blood until I was nauseated. The speech seemed a hundred times as long as before, but I could not leave out a single word. All had to be said, each memorized nuance considered, rendered. Nor was that all. Whenever I uttered a word of three or more syllables a group of voices would yell for me to repeat it. I used the phrase "social responsibility" and they yelled:

"What's the word you say, boy?"

"Social responsibility," I said.

"What?"

"Social . . ." 70

"Louder."

"... responsibility."

"More!"

75 "Respon —"

"Repeat!"

"— sibility."

The room filled with the uproar of laughter until, no doubt, distracted by having to gulp down my blood, I made a mistake and yelled a phrase I had often seen denounced in newspaper editorials, heard debated in private.

"Social . . ."

80 "What?" they yelled.

". . . equality —"

The laughter hung smokelike in the sudden stillness. I opened my eyes, puzzled. Sounds of displeasure filled the room. The M.C. rushed forward. They shouted hostile phrases at me. But I did not understand.

A small dry mustached man in the front row blared out, "Say that slowly, son!"

"What sir?"

85 "What you just said!"

"Social responsibility, sir," I said.

"You weren't being smart, were you, boy?" he said, not unkindly.

"No, sir!"

"You sure that about 'equality' was a mistake?"

90 "Oh, yes, sir," I said. "I was swallowing blood."

"Well, you had better speak more slowly so we can understand. We mean to do right by you, but you've got to know your place at all times. All right, now, go on with your speech."

I was afraid. I wanted to leave but I wanted also to speak and I was afraid they'd snatch me down.

"Thank you, sir," I said, beginning where I had left off, and having them ignore me as before.

Yet when I finished there was a thunderous applause. I was surprised to see the superintendent come forth with a package wrapped in white tissue paper, and, gesturing for quiet, address the men.

95 "Gentlemen, you see that I did not overpraise this boy. He makes a good speech and some day he'll lead his people in the proper paths. And I don't have to tell you that that is important in these days and times. This is a good, smart boy, and so to encourage him in the right direction, in the name of the Board of Education I wish to present him a prize in the form of this . . ."

He paused, removing the tissue paper and revealing a gleaming calfskin brief case.

". . . in the form of this first-class article from Shad Whitmore's shop."

"Boy," he said, addressing me, "take this prize and keep it well. Consider it a badge of office. Prize it. Keep developing as you are and some day it will be filled with important papers that will help shape the destiny of your people."

I was so moved that I could hardly express my thanks. A rope of bloody saliva forming a shape like an undiscovered continent drooled upon the leather and I wiped it quickly away. I felt an importance that I had never dreamed.

100 "Open it and see what's inside," I was told.

My fingers a-tremble, I complied, smelling the fresh leather and finding an official-looking document inside. It was a scholarship to the state college for Negroes. My eyes filled with tears and I ran awkwardly off the floor.

I was overjoyed; I did not even mind when I discovered that the gold pieces I had scrambled for were brass pocket tokens advertising a certain make of automobile.

When I reached home everyone was excited. Next day the neighbors came to congratulate me. I even felt safe from grandfather, whose deathbed curse usually spoiled my triumphs. I stood beneath his photograph with my brief case in hand and smiled triumphantly into his stolid black peasant's face. It was a face that fascinated me. The eyes seemed to follow everywhere I went.

That night I dreamed I was at a circus with him and that he refused to laugh at the clowns no matter what they did. Then later he told me to open my brief case and read what was inside and I did, finding an official envelope stamped with the state seal; and inside the envelope I found another and another, endlessly, and I thought I would fall of weariness. "Them's years," he said. "Now open that one." And I did and in it I found an engraved document containing a short message in letters of gold. "Read it," my grandfather said. "Out loud."

"To Whom It May Concern," I intoned. "Keep This Nigger-Boy Running." 105
I awoke with the old man's laughter ringing in my ears.

(It was a dream I was to remember and dream again for many years after. But at the time I had no insight into its meaning. First I had to attend college.)

Reading and Reacting

1. "Battle Royal," published in 1952, takes place in the American South. How does the story's historical and geographical setting make possible the events that occur?

2. In paragraph 2, the narrator presents his grandfather's deathbed statement. Why does the narrator think of his grandfather's words as a "curse" (par. 3)?

3. When the narrator is told he is expected to participate in the "battle royal," he feels that the battle will "detract from the dignity" of the speech he is to give (par. 5). Why, then, does he agree to take part in the fight?

4. In his graduation speech, the narrator tells his audience that "humility [is] the secret, indeed, the very essence of progress" (par. 3). What do you suppose he means? How do you think his grandfather would feel about this statement?

5. Describe the physical setting (the sights, sounds, smells) of the ballroom. What is your emotional reaction to this setting?

6. In paragraphs 7–9, a naked woman enters and dances around the room. Why is she there? How do the men react? How does her presence change the atmosphere in the ballroom?

7. Why is the narrator blindfolded before the fight? What effect does the blindfold have on him as a fighter? As a human being?

8. Throughout the fight, the narrator thinks about his speech, reviewing it in his mind and wondering how it will be received. Why is he so intent on delivering his speech to the men assembled in the ballroom?

9. The superintendent tells the audience that the narrator will someday "lead his people in the proper paths" (par. 95). What "proper path" do you think the superintendent has in mind?

10. When the narrator opens his gift, he tells readers, "I was so moved that I could hardly express my thanks" (par. 99). Do you see this comment as **ironic,** even sarcastic, or do you think he is sincere? Explain.

11. Why do you think the narrator dreams about his grandfather after the fight? What do you think his dream means?

12. **JOURNAL ENTRY** Do you think the "battle royal" was simply a necessary evil, a hurdle the narrator had to leap over in order to win the college scholarship? Does the prize in any way make up for the humiliating ordeal? Do you think the narrator should (or even could) have turned down the scholarship?

13. **CRITICAL PERSPECTIVE** Critic Norman German, writing in the CLA *Journal,* notes that Ellison uses animal imagery in describing many of the characters in "Battle Royal":

> Whether consciously woven into the fabric of his story or not, the animal imagery graphically highlights Ellison's theme that when one sex or race treats another as an object or animal, both become dehumanized or bestial. Early in the story, the invisible man (hereafter, IM) overhears his grandfather tell his father to live with his head in the *lion's* mouth. The lion is the white man, who roars throughout the story. The men *roared* as IM struggled for the coins on the electric rug. When he tries to pull a white man onto the rug, the man raises up *roaring* with laughter and kicks him in the chest. During IM's speech, the men yell for him to repeat the polysyllabic [phrase] "social responsibility" and the room fills with the *uproar* of laughter. Because the white men treat the black men as animals and the naked white woman as a sexual object, ironically the white men reduce themselves to animals.

Do you agree that Ellison's use of animal imagery helps convey his theme more effectively? Can you find other examples of such imagery in "Battle Royal"?

Related Works: "The Secretary Chant" (p. 686), "We Wear the Mask" (p. 871), "If We Must Die" (p. 897), *Fences* (p. 1358)

TILLIE OLSEN (1912 or 1913–   ) is known for her works of fiction about working-class Americans. Her short stories and one novel are inhabited by those she called the "despised people"—coal miners, farm laborers, packinghouse butchers, and housewives. Olsen was born in Nebraska into a working-class family. Though she has been described as a Depression-era dropout, Olsen has observed that she educated herself, with libraries as her college. According to an account in her nonfiction work *Silences* (1978), Olsen at age fifteen was inspired to write about working-class people when she read Rebecca Harding Davis's *Life in the Iron Mills,* a tale of the effects of industrialization on workers, in an 1861 issue of *Atlantic Monthly* bought for ten cents in a junk shop.

Shortly after she left high school, she was jailed for helping to organize packinghouse workers. Motivated by her experiences, she began to write a novel, *Yonnondio.* Under her maiden name, Tillie Lerner, she published two poems, a short story, and part of her novel during the 1930s. After her marriage, she did not publish again for twenty-two years, spending her time raising four children and working at a variety of jobs. The collection of short stories *Tell Me a Riddle* (1961), which includes "I Stand Here Ironing" (originally titled "Help Her to Believe"), was published when she was fifty. Her only other work of fiction is *Yonnondio* (1974), which she pieced together from drafts she wrote in the 1930s and edited for publication in 1974.

Because she believed her own career was "ruined" by the passage of time when she could not write because of other responsibilities, Olsen has focused on encouraging young writers by lecturing or reading her own works to writers' groups and holding writer-in-residency positions or visiting professorships at several major universities. She is also known for her efforts to rediscover long-forgotten works by other working-class women. In 1984, she edited *Mother to Daughter, Daughter to Mother: Mothers on Mothering,* a collection of poems, letters, short fiction, and diary excerpts written by famous and not-so-famous women. Olsen lives in San Francisco.

Cultural Context: During the Great Depression of the 1930s in the United States, jobs were scarce, and many people who had jobs were forced to take pay cuts. Many Americans suffered harsh deprivation and struggled daily for survival in the "prerelief" years before the Social Security Act of 1935 established public assistance, unemployment insurance, and social security.

I Stand Here Ironing (1961)

I stand here ironing, and what you asked me moves tormented back and forth with the iron.

"I wish you would manage the time to come and talk with me about your daughter. I'm sure you can help me understand her. She's a youngster who needs help and whom I'm deeply interested in helping."

"Who needs help." . . . Even if I came, what good would it do? You think because I am her mother I have a key, or that in some way you could use me as a key? She has lived for nineteen years. There is all that life that has happened outside of me, beyond me.

And when is there time to remember, to sift, to weigh, to estimate, to total? I will start and there will be an interruption and I will have to gather it all together again. Or I will become engulfed with all I did or did not do, with what should have been and what cannot be helped.

She was a beautiful baby. The first and only one of our five that was beautiful 5 at birth. You do not guess how new and uneasy her tenancy in her now-loveliness. You did not know her all those years she was thought homely, or see her poring over her baby pictures, making me tell her over and over how beautiful she had been — and would be, I would tell her — and was now, to the seeing eye. But the seeing eyes were few or nonexistent. Including mine.

I nursed her. They feel that's important nowadays. I nursed all the children, but with her, with all the fierce rigidity of first motherhood, I did like the books then said. Though her cries battered me to trembling and my breasts ached with swollenness, I waited till the clock decreed.

Why do I put that first? I do not even know if it matters, or if it explains anything.

She was a beautiful baby. She blew shining bubbles of sound. She loved motion, loved light, loved color and music and textures. She would lie on the floor in her blue overalls patting the surface so hard in ecstasy her hands and feet would blur. She was a miracle to me, but when she was eight months old I had to leave her daytimes with the woman downstairs to whom she was no miracle at all, for I worked or looked for work and for Emily's father, who "could no longer endure" (he wrote in his good-bye note) "sharing want with us."

I was nineteen. It was the pre-relief, pre-WPA° world of the depression. I would start running as soon as I got off the streetcar, running up the stairs, the place smelling sour, and awake or asleep to startle awake, when she saw me she would break into a clogged weeping that could not be comforted, a weeping I can hear yet.

10   After a while I found a job hashing at night so I could be with her days, and it was better. But it came to where I had to bring her to his family and leave her.

It took a long time to raise the money for her fare back. Then she got chicken pox and I had to wait longer. When she finally came, I hardly knew her, walking quick and nervous like her father, looking like her father, thin, and dressed in a shoddy red that yellowed her skin and glared at the pockmarks. All the baby loveliness gone.

She was two. Old enough for nursery school they said, and I did not know then what I know now — the fatigue of the long day, and the lacerations of group life in the kinds of nurseries that are only parking places for children.

Except that it would have made no difference if I had known. It was the only place there was. It was the only way we could be together, the only way I could hold a job.

And even without knowing, I knew. I knew the teacher that was evil because all these years it has curdled into my memory, the little boy hunched in the corner, her rasp, "why aren't you outside, because Alvin hits you? that's no reason, go out, scaredy." I knew Emily hated it even if she did not clutch and implore "don't go Mommy" like the other children, mornings.

15   She always had a reason why we should stay home. Momma, you look sick. Momma, I feel sick. Momma, the teachers aren't there today, they're sick. Momma, we can't go, there was a fire there last night. Momma, it's a holiday today, no school, they told me.

But never a direct protest, never rebellion. I think of our others in their three-, four-year-oldness — the explosions, the tempers, the denunciations, the demands — and I feel suddenly ill. I put the iron down. What in me demanded that goodness in her? And what was the cost, the cost to her of such goodness?

WPA: The Works Progress Administration, created in 1935 as part of President Franklin D. Roosevelt's New Deal program. The purpose of the WPA (renamed the Works Projects Administration in 1939) was to provide jobs for the unemployed during the Great Depression.

The old man living in the back once said in his gentle way: "You should smile at Emily more when you look at her." What *was* in my face when I looked at her? I loved her. There were all the acts of love.

It was only with the others I remembered what he said, and it was the face of joy, and not of care or tightness or worry I turned to them — too late for Emily. She does not smile easily, let alone almost always as her brothers and sisters do. Her face is closed and sombre, but when she wants, how fluid. You must have seen it in her pantomimes, you spoke of her rare gift for comedy on the stage that rouses laughter out of the audience so dear they applaud and applaud and do not want to let her go.

Where does it come from, that comedy? There was none of it in her when she came back to me that second time, after I had had to send her away again. She had a new daddy now to learn to love, and I think perhaps it was a better time.

Except when we left her alone nights, telling ourselves she was old enough.   20

"Can't you go some other time, Mommy, like tomorrow?" she would ask. "Will it be just a little while you'll be gone? Do you promise?"

The time we came back, the front door open, the clock on the floor in the hall. She rigid awake. "It wasn't just a little while. I didn't cry. Three times I called you, just three times, and then I ran downstairs to open the door so you could come faster. The clock talked loud. I threw it away, it scared me what it talked."

She said the clock talked loud again that night I went to the hospital to have Susan. She was delirious with the fever that comes before red measles, but she was fully conscious all the week I was gone and the week after we were home when she could not come near the new baby or me.

She did not get well. She stayed skeleton thin, not wanting to eat, and night after night she had nightmares. She would call for me, and I would rouse from exhaustion to sleepily call back: "You're all right, darling, go to sleep, it's just a dream," and if she still called, in a sterner voice, "now go to sleep, Emily, there's nothing to hurt you." Twice, only twice, when I had to get up for Susan anyhow, I went in to sit with her.

Now when it is too late (as if she would let me hold and comfort her like I do   25
the others) I get up and go to her at once at her moan or restless stirring. "Are you awake, Emily? Can I get you something?" And the answer is always the same: "No, I'm all right, go back to sleep, Mother."

They persuaded me at the clinic to send her away to a convalescent home in the country where "she can have the kind of food and care you can't manage for her, and you'll be free to concentrate on the new baby." They still send children to that place. I see pictures on the society page of sleek young women planning affairs to raise money for it, or dancing at the affairs, or decorating Easter eggs or filling Christmas stockings for the children.

They never have a picture of the children so I do not know if the girls still wear those gigantic red bows and the ravaged looks on the every other Sunday when parents can come to visit "unless otherwise notified"— as we were notified the first six weeks.

Oh it is a handsome place, green lawns and tall trees and fluted flower beds. High up on the balconies of each cottage the children stand, the girls in their red bows and white dresses, the boys in white suits and giant red ties. The parents stand below shrieking up to be heard and the children shriek down to be heard, and between them the invisible wall: "Not to Be Contaminated by Parental Germs or Physical Affection."

There was a tiny girl who always stood hand in hand with Emily. Her parents never came. One visit she was gone. "They moved her to Rose Cottage," Emily shouted in explanation. "They don't like you to love anybody here."

30   She wrote once a week, the labored writing of a seven-year-old. "I am fine. How is the baby. If I write my leter nicly I will have a star. Love." There never was a star. We wrote every other day, letters she could never hold or keep but only hear read — once. "We simply do not have room for children to keep any personal possessions," they patiently explained when we pieced one Sunday's shrieking together to plead how much it would mean to Emily, who loved so to keep things, to be allowed to keep her letters and cards.

Each visit she looked frailer. "She isn't eating," they told us.

(They had runny eggs for breakfast or mush with lumps, Emily said later, I'd hold it in my mouth and not swallow. Nothing ever tasted good, just when they had chicken.)

It took us eight months to get her released home, and only the fact that she gained back so little of her seven lost pounds convinced the social worker.

I used to try to hold and love her after she came back, but her body would stay stiff, and after a while she'd push away. She ate little. Food sickened her, and I think much of life too. Oh she had physical lightness and brightness, twinkling by on skates, bouncing like a ball up and down up and down over the jump rope, skimming over the hill; but these were momentary.

35   She fretted about her appearance, thin and dark and foreign-looking at a time when every little girl was supposed to look or thought she should look a chubby blonde replica of Shirley Temple. The doorbell sometimes rang for her, but no one seemed to come and play in the house or be a best friend. Maybe because we moved so much.

There was a boy she loved painfully through two school semesters. Months later she told me how she had taken pennies from my purse to buy him candy. "Licorice was his favorite and I brought him some every day, but he still liked Jennifer better'n me. Why, Mommy?" The kind of question for which there is no answer.

School was a worry to her. She was not glib or quick in a world where glibness and quickness were easily confused with ability to learn. To her overworked and exasperated teachers she was an overconscientious "slow learner" who kept trying to catch up and was absent entirely too often.

I let her be absent, though sometimes the illness was imaginary. How different from my now-strictness about attendance with the others. I wasn't working. We had a new baby, I was home anyhow. Sometimes, after Susan grew old enough, I would keep her home from school, too, to have them all together.

Mostly Emily had asthma, and her breathing, harsh and labored, would fill the house with a curiously tranquil sound. I would bring the two old dresser mirrors and her boxes of collections to her bed. She would select beads and single earrings, bottle tops and shells, dried flowers and pebbles, old postcards and scraps, all sorts of oddments; then she and Susan would play Kingdom, setting up landscapes and furniture, peopling them with action.

Those were the only times of peaceful companionship between her and Susan. 40 I have edged away from it, that poisonous feeling between them, that terrible balancing of hurts and needs I had to do between the two, and did so badly, those earlier years.

Oh there are conflicts between the others too, each one human, needing, demanding, hurting, taking — but only between Emily and Susan, no, Emily toward Susan that corroding resentment. It seems so obvious on the surface, yet it is not obvious. Susan, the second child, Susan, golden- and curly-haired and chubby, quick and articulate and assured, everything in appearance and manner Emily was not; Susan, not able to resist Emily's precious things, losing or sometimes clumsily breaking them; Susan telling jokes and riddles to company for applause while Emily sat silent (to say to me later: that was *my* riddle, Mother, I told it to Susan); Susan, who for all the five years' difference in age was just a year behind Emily in developing physically.

I am glad for that slow physical development that widened the difference between her and her contemporaries, though she suffered over it. She was too vulnerable for that terrible world of youthful competition, of preening and parading, of constant measuring of yourself against every other, of envy, "If I had that copper hair," "If I had that skin. . . ." She tormented herself enough about not looking like the others, there was enough of the unsureness, the having to be conscious of words before you speak, the constant caring — what are they thinking of me? without having it all magnified by the merciless physical drives.

Ronnie is calling. He is wet and I change him. It is rare there is such a cry now. That time of motherhood is almost behind me when the ear is not one's own but must always be racked and listening for the child cry, the child call. We sit for a while and I hold him, looking out over the city spread in charcoal with its soft aisles of light. "*Shoogily,*" he breathes and curls closer. I carry him back to bed, asleep. *Shoogily.* A funny word, a family word, inherited from Emily, invented by her to say: *comfort.*

In this and other ways she leaves her seal, I say aloud. And startle at my saying it. What do I mean? What did I start to gather together, to try and make coherent? I was at the terrible, growing years. War years. I do not remember them well. I was working, there were four smaller ones now, there was not time for her. She had to help be a mother, and housekeeper, and shopper. She had to set her seal. Mornings of crisis and near hysteria trying to get lunches packed, hair combed, coats and shoes found, everyone to school or Child Care on time, the baby ready for transportation. And always the paper scribbled on by a smaller one, the book looked at by Susan then mislaid, the homework not done. Running out to that huge school where she was one, she was lost, she was a drop; suffering over the unpreparedness, stammering and unsure in her classes.

There was so little time left at night after the kids were bedded down. She 45 would struggle over books, always eating (it was in those years she developed her enormous appetite that is legendary in our family) and I would be ironing, or preparing food for the next day, or writing V-mail° to Bill, or tending the baby. Sometimes, to make me laugh, or out of her despair, she would imitate happenings or types at school.

I think I said once: "Why don't you do something like this in the school amateur show?" One morning she phoned me at work, hardly understandable through the weeping: "Mother, I did it. I won, I won; they gave me first prize; they clapped and clapped and wouldn't let me go."

Now suddenly she was Somebody, and as imprisoned in her difference as she had been in anonymity.

She began to be asked to perform at other high schools, even in colleges, then at city and statewide affairs. The first one we went to, I only recognized her that first moment when thin, shy, she almost drowned herself into the curtains. Then: Was this Emily? The control, the command, the convulsing and deadly clowning, the spell, then the roaring, stamping audience, unwilling to let this rare and precious laughter out of their lives.

Afterwards: You ought to do something about her with a gift like that — but without money or knowing how, what does one do? We have left it all to her, and the gift has as often eddied inside, clogged and clotted, as been used and growing.

50   She is coming. She runs up the stairs two at a time with her light graceful step, and I know she is happy tonight. Whatever it was that occasioned your call did not happen today.

"Aren't you ever going to finish the ironing, Mother? Whistler painted his mother in a rocker. I'd have to paint mine standing over an ironing board." This is one of her communicative nights and she tells me everything and nothing as she fixes herself a plate of food out of the icebox.

She is so lovely. Why did you want me to come in at all? Why were you concerned? She will find her way.

She starts up the stairs to bed. "Don't get me up with the rest in the morning." "But I thought you were having midterms." "Oh, those," she comes back in, kisses me, and says quite lightly, "in a couple of years when we'll all be atom-dead they won't matter a bit."

She has said it before. She *believes* it. But because I have been dredging the past, and all that compounds a human being is so heavy and meaningful in me, I cannot endure it tonight.

55   I will never total it all. I will never come in to say: She was a child seldom smiled at. Her father left me before she was a year old. I had to work her first six years when there was work, or I sent her home and to his relatives. There were years she had care she hated. She was dark and thin and foreign-looking in a world where the prestige went to blondeness and curly hair and dimples, she was slow where glibness was prized. She was a child of anxious, not proud, love. We were poor and could not afford for her the soil of easy growth. I was a young mother, I was a distracted mother. There were other children pushing up, demanding. Her

---

V-mail: Mail sent to or from members of the armed forces during World War II. Letters were reduced onto microfilm and enlarged and printed out at their destination.

younger sister seemed all that she was not. There were years she did not want me to touch her. She kept too much in herself, her life was such she had to keep too much in herself. My wisdom came too late. She has much to her and probably little will come of it. She is a child of her age, of depression, of war, of fear.

Let her be. So all that is in her will not bloom — but in how many does it? There is still enough left to live by. Only help her to know — help make it so there is cause for her to know — that she is more than this dress on the ironing board, helpless before the iron.

Reading and Reacting

1. "I Stand Here Ironing" focuses on incidents that took place in the "pre-relief, pre-WPA world" of the Depression (par. 9). In light of social, political, and economic changes that have occurred since the 1930s, do you think the events the story presents could occur today? Explain.

2. In what sense is the image of a mother at an ironing board appropriate for this story?

3. The narrator is overwhelmed by guilt. What does she believe she has done wrong? What, if anything, do *you* think she has done wrong? Do you think she has been a good mother? Why or why not?

4. Who, or what, do you blame for the narrator's problems? For example, do you blame Emily's father? The Depression? The social institutions and "experts" to which the narrator turns?

5. Do you see the narrator as a victim limited by the times in which she lives? Do you agree with the narrator that Emily is "a child of her age, of depression, of war, of fear" (par. 55)? Or do you believe both women have some control over their own destinies, regardless of the story's historical setting?

6. What do you think the narrator wants for her daughter? Do you think her goals for Emily are realistic ones? Why or why not?

7. Paragraph 28 describes the physical setting of the convalescent home to which Emily was sent. What does this description add to the story? Why do you suppose there is no physical description of the apartment in which Emily lived as a child? How do you picture this apartment?

8. To whom do you think the mother is speaking in this story?

9. **Journal Entry** Put yourself in Emily's position. What do you think she would like to tell her mother?

10. **Critical Perspective** Writing in *The Red Wheelbarrow*, psychologist Robert Coles discusses the complex family relationships depicted in "I Stand Here Ironing" and reaches an optimistic conclusion:

    > But the child did not grow to be a mere victim of the kind so many of us these days are rather eager to recognize — a hopeless tangle of psychopathology. The growing child, even in her troubled moments, revealed herself to be persistent, demanding, and observant. In the complaints we make, in the "symptoms" we develop, we reveal our strengths as well as our weaknesses. The hurt child could summon her intelligence, exercise her will, smile and make others smile.

    Do you agree with Coles's psychological evaluation of Emily? Do you find the story's ending as essentially uplifting as he seems to? Why or why not?

Related Works: "How to Talk to Your Mother (Notes)" (p. 100), "The Swing" (p. 139), "Everyday Use" (p. 310), "Those Winter Sundays" (p. 560), *The Glass Menagerie* (p. 1416)

WRITING SUGGESTIONS: Setting

1. In both "The Yellow Wallpaper" and "I Stand Here Ironing," social constraints determined by the story's historical setting limit a woman's options. Explore the options each woman might reasonably exercise in order to break free of the limits that social institutions impose on her.

2. Write an essay in which you consider how any one of the four stories in this chapter would be different if its historical, geographical, or physical setting were changed to a setting of your choice. In your essay, examine the changes (in plot development as well as in the characters' conflicts, reactions, and motivation) that might be caused by the change in setting.

3. Select a story from another chapter, and write an essay in which you consider how setting affects its plot — for example, how it creates conflict or crisis, how it forces characters to act, or how it determines how the plot is resolved.

4. "Battle Royal" uses rich descriptive language to create a mood that dominates the story. Analyze this use of language in the story. How does language help to create and enrich the story's setting?

5. **WEB ACTIVITY** The following Web site contains information about Tillie Olsen:

http://mockingbird.creighton.edu/NCW/olsen.htm

From the Tillie Olsen Web page, link to "Commentary" and then to "Tell Me a Riddle." One of the reviewers states the following about Olsen:

[She] writes about those people who, because of their class, sex, or race, have been denied the opportunity to express and develop themselves. In a strongly emotional style, she tells of their dreams and failures, of what she calls "the unnatural thwarting of what struggles to come into being but cannot."

Now, link to "Selection" from the Olsen page and read "These Things Shall Be." Then, write an essay discussing how "These Things Shall Be" and "I Stand Here Ironing" are about people who "have been denied the opportunity to express and develop themselves." In your essay, you may want to focus on the mother in "I Stand Here Ironing" and the father in "These Things Shall Be." Consider how both have been denied the opportunity for self-expression because of what others have expected of them.

CHAPTER 8

POINT OF VIEW

In dealing with point-of-view the [writer] must always deal with the individual work: which particular character shall tell this particular story, or part of a story, with what precise degree of reliability, privilege, freedom to comment, and so on. . . . Even if the [writer] has decided on a narrator who will fit one of the critic's classifications — "omniscient," "first-person," "limited omniscient," "objective," . . . and so on — his troubles have just begun. He simply cannot find answers to his immediate, precise, practical problems by referring to statements that the "omniscient is the most flexible method," or "the objective the most rapid or vivid," or whatever. Even the soundest of generalizations at this level will be of little use to him. —**Wayne C. Booth,** *"Distance and Point of View"*

For reasons that should not need explanation here, until very recently, and regardless of the race of the author, the readers of virtually all of American fiction have been positioned as white. I am interested to know what that assumption has meant to the literary imagination. . . . What happens to the writerly imagination of a black author who is at some level *always* conscious of representing one's own race to, or in spite of, a race of readers that understands itself to be "universal" or race-free? In other words, how is "literary whiteness" and "literary blackness" made, and what is the consequence of that construction? —**Toni Morrison,** *Playing in the Dark*

Tied to issues of gender, social stratification, racial oppression, and the need to restore the foundations of our history and culture, the most recurrent theme in our writing is what I call claiming America for Asian Americans. That does not mean disappearing like raindrops in the ocean of white America, fighting to become "normal," losing ourselves in the process. It means inventing a new identity, defining ourselves according to the truth instead of a racial fantasy, so that we can be reconciled with one another in order to celebrate our marginality. —**Elaine H. Kim,** *"Defining Asian American Realities through Literature"*

All stories are told, or narrated, by someone, and one of the first choices writers make is who tells the story. This choice determines the story's **point of view**— the vantage point from which events are presented. The implications of this choice are far-reaching. Consider for a moment the following scenario. Five people witness a crime and are questioned by the police. Their stories agree on certain points: a crime was committed, a body was found, and the crime occurred at noon. But in other ways their stories are different. The man who fled the scene was either tall or of average height; his hair was either dark or light; he either was carrying an object or was empty-handed. The events that led up to the crime and even the description of the crime itself are markedly different, depending on who tells the story. Thus, the perspective from which a story is told determines what details are included in the story and how they are arranged — in short, the plot. In addition, the perspective of the narrator affects the story's style, language, and themes.

The narrator of a work of fiction is not the same as the writer — even when a writer uses the first-person *I*. Writers create narrators to tell their stories. Often the personalities and opinions of narrators are far different from those of the author. The term **persona** — which literally means "mask" — is used for such narrators. By assuming this mask, a writer expands the creative possibilities of a work.

When deciding on a point of view for a work of fiction, a writer can choose to tell the story either in the *first person* or in the *third person*.

FIRST-PERSON NARRATORS

Sometimes the narrator is a character who uses the **first person** (*I* or sometimes *we*) to tell the story. Often this narrator is a major character — Sammy in John Updike's "A&P" (p. 115) and the boy in James Joyce's "Araby" (p. 252), for example — who tells his or her own story and is the focus of that story. Sometimes, however, a first-person narrator tells a story that is primarily about someone else. Such a narrator may be a minor character who plays a relatively small part in the story or simply an observer who reports events experienced or related by others. The narrator of William Faulkner's "A Rose for Emily" (p. 91), for example, is an unidentified witness to the story's events. By using *we* instead of *I*, this narrator speaks on behalf of all the town's residents, expressing their shared views of their neighbor, Emily Grierson:

> We did not say she was crazy then. We believed she had to do that. We remembered all the young men her father had driven away, and we knew that with nothing left, she would have to cling to that which had robbed her, as people will.

Writers gain a number of advantages when they use a first-person narrator. First, they are able to present incidents very convincingly. Readers are more willing to accept a statement like "My sister changed a lot after that day" than they are to accept the impersonal observations of a third-person narrator. The first-person narrator also simplifies a writer's task of selecting details. Only the events and details that the narrator could actually have seen or experienced can be introduced into the story.

Another major advantage of first-person narrators is that their restricted view can create **irony** — a discrepancy between what is said and what readers believe to be true. Irony may be *dramatic*, *situational*, or *verbal*. **Dramatic irony** occurs when a narrator or character perceives less than readers do; **situational irony** occurs when what happens is at odds with what readers are led to expect; **verbal irony** occurs when the narrator says one thing but actually means another.

"Gryphon," by Charles Baxter (p. 126), illustrates all three kinds of irony. Baxter creates *dramatic irony* when he has his main character see less than readers do. For example, at the end of the story, the young boy does not yet realize what readers already know — that he has learned more from Miss Ferenczi's way of teaching than from Mr. Hibler's. The setting of the story — a conventional school — creates *situational irony* because it contrasts with the unexpected events that unfold there. In addition, many of the narrator's comments create *verbal irony* because they mean something different from what they seem to mean. At the end of the story, for example, after the substitute, Miss Ferenczi, has been fired, the narrator relates another teacher's comment that life will now return to "normal" and that their regular teacher will soon return to test them on their "knowledge." This comment is ironic in light of all Miss Ferenczi has done to redefine the narrator's ideas about "normal" education and about "knowledge."

Unreliable Narrators

Sometimes first-person narrators are self-serving, mistaken, confused, unstable, or even mad. These **unreliable narrators,** whether intentionally or unintentionally, misrepresent events and misdirect readers. In Edgar Allan Poe's "The Cask of Amontillado" (p. 217), for example, the narrator, Montresor, tells his story to justify a crime he committed fifty years before. Montresor's version of what happened is not accurate, and perceptive readers know it: his obvious self-deception, his sadistic manipulation of Fortunato, his detached description of the cold-blooded murder, and his lack of remorse lead readers to question his sanity and, therefore, to distrust his version of events. This distrust creates an ironic distance between readers and narrator.

The narrator of Charlotte Perkins Gilman's "The Yellow Wallpaper" (p. 161) is also an unreliable narrator. Suffering from "nervous depression," she unintentionally distorts the facts when she says that the shapes in the wallpaper of her bedroom are changing and moving. Moreover, she does not realize what is wrong with her or why, or how her husband's "good intentions" are hurting her. Readers, however, see the disparity between the narrator's interpretation of events and their own, and this irony enriches their understanding of the story.

Some narrators are unreliable because they are naive. Because they are immature, sheltered, or innocent of evil, these narrators are not aware of the full significance of the events they are relating. Having the benefit of experience, readers interpret events differently from the way these narrators do. When we read a passage by a child narrator — such as the following one from J. D. Salinger's novel *The Catcher in the Rye* — we are aware of the narrator's innocence, and we know his interpretation of events is flawed:

> Anyway, I keep picturing all these little kids playing some game in this big field of rye and all. Thousands of little kids, and nobody's around — nobody big, I mean — except me. And I'm standing on the edge of some crazy cliff. What I have to do, I have to catch everybody if they start to go over the cliff — I mean

> if they're running and they don't look where they're going I have to come out
> from somewhere and catch them. I'd just be the catcher in the rye. . . .

The irony in the preceding passage comes from our knowledge that the naive narrator, Holden Caulfield, cannot stop children from growing up. Ultimately, they all fall off the "crazy cliff" and mature into adults. Although he is not aware of the futility of trying to protect children from the dangers of adulthood, readers know that his efforts are doomed from the start.

A naive narrator's background can also limit his or her ability to understand a situation. The narrator in Sherwood Anderson's short story "I'm a Fool," for example, lies to impress a rich girl he meets at a racetrack. At the end of the story, the boy laments the fact that he lied, believing that if he had told the truth, he could have seen the girl again. The reader knows, however, that the narrator (a laborer at a racetrack) is deceiving himself because the social gap that separates the narrator and the girl could never be bridged.

Keep in mind that there is a difference between an unreliable narrator and a narrator whose perspective is limited. All first-person narrators are, by definition, limited because they present a situation as only one person sees it. "In a Grove," a story by the Japanese author Ryūnosuke Akutagawa, illustrates this idea. In this story, seven characters act as narrators and give different accounts of a murder. Some of the characters seem to be lying or bending the facts to suit their own needs, but others simply have an incomplete or mistaken understanding of the event. No character, of course, has all the information the story's author has.

As a reader focusing on a story's point of view, you should look for discrepancies between a narrator's view of events and your own. Discovering that a story has an unreliable narrator enables you not only to question the truth of the narrative but also to recognize the irony in the narrator's version of events. By doing so, you gain insight into the story and learn something about the writer's purpose.

THIRD-PERSON NARRATORS

Third-person narrators are not characters in the story. These narrators fall into three categories.

Omniscient Narrators

Some third-person narrators are **omniscient** (all-knowing) narrators, moving at will from one character's mind to another. One advantage of omniscient narrators is that they have none of the naïveté, dishonesty, gullibility, or mental instability that can characterize first-person narrators. In addition, because omniscient narrators are not characters in the story, their perception is not limited to what any one character can observe or comprehend. As a result, they can present a more inclusive overview of events and characters than first-person narrators can. Omniscient narrators can also convey their attitude toward their subject matter. For example, the omniscient narrator in Nadine Gordimer's "Once upon a Time" uses sentence structure, word choice, and repetition to express her distaste for the scene she describes:

In a house, in a suburb, in a city, there were a man and his wife who loved each other very much and were living happily ever after. They had a little boy, and they loved him very much. They had a cat and a dog that the little boy loved very much. They had a car and a caravan trailer for holidays, and a swimming-pool which was fenced so that the little boy and his playmates would not fall in and drown. They had a housemaid who was absolutely trustworthy and an itinerant gardener who was highly recommended by the neighbours. For when they began to live happily ever after they were warned, by that wise old witch, the husband's mother, not to take anyone off the street.

Occasionally, omniscient narrators move not only in and out of the minds of the characters but also in and out of a **persona** (representing the voice of the author) that speaks directly to readers. This narrative technique was popular with writers during the eighteenth century, when the novel was a new literary form. It permitted writers to present themselves as masters of artifice, able to know and control all aspects of experience. Few contemporary writers would give themselves the license that Henry Fielding does in the following passage from *Tom Jones*:

And true it was that [Mr. Alworthy] did many of these things; but had he done nothing more I should have left him to have recorded his own merit on some fair freestone over the door of that hospital. Matters of a much more extraordinary kind are to be the subject of this history, or I should grossly misspend my time in writing so voluminous a work; and you my sagacious friend, might with equal profit and pleasure travel through some pages which certain droll authors have been facetiously pleased to call *The History of England*.

A contemporary example of this type of omniscient point of view occurs in Ursula K. LeGuin's "The Ones Who Walk Away from Omelas." This story presents a description of a city that in the narrator's words is "like a city in a fairy tale." As the story proceeds, however, the description of Omelas changes, and the narrator's tone changes as well: "Do you believe? Do you accept the festival, the city, the joy? No? Then let me describe one more thing." By undercutting her own narrative, the narrator underscores the ironic theme of the story, which suggests that it is impossible for human beings to ever achieve an ideal society.

Limited Omniscient Narrators

Third-person narrators can have **limited omniscience,** focusing on only what a single character experiences. In other words, events are limited to one character's perspective, and nothing is revealed that the character does not see, hear, feel, or think. Andy in David Michael Kaplan's "Doe Season" (p. 336) is just such a limited-focus character. Limited omniscient narrators, like all third-person narrators, have certain advantages over first-person narrators. When a writer uses a first-person narrator, the narrator's personality and speech color the story, creating a personal or even an idiosyncratic narrative. Also, the first-person narrator's character flaws or lack of knowledge may limit his or her awareness of the significance of events. Limited omniscient narrators are more flexible: they take readers into a particular character's mind just as a first-person narrator does, but without the first-person narrator's subjectivity, self-deception, or naïveté.

In the following example from Anne Tyler's "Teenage Wasteland" (p. 535), the limited omniscient narrator presents the story from the point of view of a single character, Daisy:

> Daisy and Matt sat silent, shocked. Matt rubbed his forehead with his finger-
> tips. Imagine, Daisy thought, how they must look to Mr. Lanham: an over-
> weight housewife in a cotton dress and a too-tall, too-thin insurance agent in a
> baggy, frayed suit. Failures, both of them — the kind of people who are always
> hurrying to catch up, missing the point of things that everyone else grasps at
> once. She wished she'd worn nylons instead of knee socks.

Here the point of view gives readers the impression that they are standing off to the side watching Daisy and her husband Matt. At the same time we have the advantage of this objective view, however, we are also able to see into the mind of one character.

Objective Narrators

Third-person narrators who tell a story from an **objective** (or *dramatic*) point of view remain entirely outside the characters' minds. With objective narrators, events unfold the way they would in a play or a movie: narrators tell the story only by presenting dialogue and recounting events; they do not reveal the characters' (or their own) thoughts or attitudes. Thus, they allow readers to interpret the actions of the characters without any interference. Ernest Hemingway uses the objective point of view in his short story "A Clean, Well-Lighted Place" (p. 267):

> The waiter took the brandy bottle and another saucer from the counter
> inside the café and marched out to the old man's table. He put down the saucer
> and poured the glass full of brandy.
>   "You should have killed yourself last week," he said to the deaf man. The
> old man motioned with his finger. "A little more," he said. The waiter poured
> on into the glass so that the brandy slopped over and ran down the stem into
> the top saucer of the pile. "Thank you," the old man said. The waiter took
> the bottle back inside the café. He sat down at the table with his colleague
> again.

The story's narrator is distant, seemingly emotionless, and this perspective is consistent with the author's purpose: for Hemingway, the attitude of the narrator reflects the stunned, almost anesthetized condition of people in the post–World War I world.

SELECTING AN APPROPRIATE POINT OF VIEW

Writers of short stories often maintain a consistent point of view, but there is no rule that says they must. Although one point of view may be dominant, writers of fiction frequently introduce additional points of view to achieve complexity and depth. The main criterion writers use when they decide on a point of view is how the distance they maintain from their material will affect their narrative. Consider the following passage from "Doe Season":

Limited Omniscient Point of View

> They were always the same woods, she thought sleepily as they drove through the early morning darkness — deep and immense, covered with yesterday's snowfall, which had frozen overnight. They were the same woods that lay behind her house, *and they stretch all the way to here,* she thought, *for miles and miles, longer than I could walk in a day, or a week even, but they are still the same woods.* The thought made her feel good: it was like thinking of God; it was like thinking of the space between here and the moon; it was like thinking of all the foreign countries from her geography book where even now, Andy knew, people were going to bed, while they — she and her father and Charlie Spoon and Mac, Charlie's eleven-year-old son — were driving deeper into the Pennsylvania countryside, to go hunting.
>
> They had risen long before dawn. Her mother, yawning and not trying to hide her sleepiness, cooked them eggs and French toast. Her father smoked a cigarette and flicked ashes into his saucer while Andy listened, wondering *Why doesn't he come?* and *Won't he ever come?* until at last a car pulled into the graveled drive and honked. "That will be Charlie Spoon," her father said; he always said "Charlie Spoon," even though his real name was Spreun, because Charlie was, in a sense, shaped like a spoon, with a large head and a narrow waist and chest.

In this passage, David Michael Kaplan uses a third-person limited omniscient narrator to tell the story of Andy, a nine-year-old girl who is going hunting with her father for the first time. This point of view has the advantage of allowing the narrator to focus on the thoughts, fears, and reactions of the child while at the same time giving readers information about Andy that she herself is too immature or unsophisticated to know. Rather than simply presenting the thoughts of the child (represented in the story by italics), the third-person narrator makes connections between ideas and displays a level of language and a degree of insight that readers would not accept from Andy as a first-person narrator. In addition, the limited omniscient perspective enables the narrator to maintain some distance. Consider how different the passage would be if it were narrated by nine-year-old Andy.

First-Person Point of View (Child)

> "I like the woods," I thought. "They're big and scary. I wonder if they're the same woods that are behind my house. They go on for miles. They're bigger than I could walk in a day, or a week even." It was neat to think that while we were driving into the woods people were going to bed in other countries.
>
> When I woke up this morning, I couldn't wait to go hunting. My mother was cooking breakfast, but all I could think of was, "When will he come?" and "Won't he ever come?" Finally, I heard a car honk. "That will be Charlie Spoon," my father said. I think he called him "Charlie Spoon" because he thought Charlie was shaped like a big spoon.

As a first-person narrator, nine-year-old Andy must have the voice of a child; moreover, she is restricted to only those observations that a nine-year-old could reasonably make. Because of these limitations, the passage lacks the level of vocabulary, syntax, and insight necessary to develop the central character and the themes of the story. This point of view could succeed only if Andy's words established an ironic contrast between her naive sensibility and the reality of the situation.

Kaplan could have avoided these problems and still gained the advantages of using a first-person narrator by having Andy tell her story as an adult looking back on a childhood experience. (This technique is used by James Joyce in "Araby," p. 252; Charles Baxter in "Gryphon," p. 126; and Alberto Alvaro Ríos in "The Secret Lion," p. 54.)

First-Person Point of View (Adult)

"They are always the same woods," I thought sleepily as we drove through the early morning darkness — deep and immense, covered with yesterday's snowfall, which had frozen overnight. "They're the same woods that lie behind my house, and they stretch all the way to here," I thought. I knew that they stretched for miles and miles, longer than I could walk in a day, or even in a week but that they were still the same woods. Knowing this made me feel good: I thought it was like thinking of God; it was like thinking of the space between that place and the moon; it was like thinking of all the foreign countries from my geography book where even then, I knew, people were going to bed, while we — my father and I and Charlie Spoon and Mac, Charlie's eleven-year-old son — were driving deeper into the Pennsylvania countryside, to go hunting.

We had risen before dawn. My mother, who was yawning and not trying to hide her sleepiness, cooked us eggs and French toast. My father smoked a cigarette and flicked ashes into his saucer while I listened, wondering, "Why doesn't he come?" and "Won't he ever come?" until at last a car pulled into our driveway and honked. "That will be Charlie Spoon," my father said. He always said "Charlie Spoon," even though his real name was Spreun, because Charlie was, in a sense, shaped like a spoon, with a large head and a narrow waist and chest.

Although this passage presents the child's point of view, it does not use a child's voice; the language and scope of the passage are too sophisticated for a child. By using a mature style, the adult narrator is able to consider ideas that a child could not possibly understand, such as the symbolic significance of the woods. By doing so, however, he sacrifices the degree of objectivity that characterizes the narrator of the original story.

Kaplan had other options as well. For example, he could have used an omniscient narrator to tell his story. In this case, the narrator would be free to reveal and comment not only on Andy's thoughts but also on those of her father, and possibly even on the thoughts of her mother and Charlie Spoon. In the following passage, the omniscient narrator interprets the behavior of the characters and tells what each one is thinking.

Omniscient Point of View

They were always the same woods, she thought sleepily as they drove through the early morning darkness — deep and immense, covered with yesterday's snowfall, which had frozen overnight. They were the same woods that lay behind her house, and they stretch all the way to here, she thought, for miles and miles, longer than I could walk in a day, or a week even, but they are still the same woods.

They had risen before dawn. The mother, yawning and not trying to hide her sleepiness, cooked them eggs and French toast. She looked at her husband and her daughter and wondered if she was doing the right thing by allowing them to go hunting together. "After all," she thought, "he's not the most careful person. Will he watch her? Make sure that no harm comes to her?"

The father smoked a cigarette and flicked ashes into his saucer. He was listening to the sounds of the early morning. "I know everything will be all right," he thought. "It's about time Andy went hunting. When I was her age. . . ." Andy listened, wondering Why doesn't he come? and Won't he ever come? until at last a car pulled into the graveled drive and honked. Suddenly the father cocked his head and said, "That will be Charlie Spoon."

Andy thought it was funny that her father called Charlie "Spoon" even though his real name was Spreun, because Charlie was, in a sense, shaped like a spoon, with a large head and a narrow waist and chest.

Certainly this point of view has its advantages; for example, the wide scope of this perspective provides a great deal of information about the characters. However, the use of an omniscient point of view deprives the story of its focus on Andy.

Finally, Kaplan could have used an objective narrator. This point of view would eliminate all interpretation by the narrator and force readers to make judgments solely on the basis of what the characters say and do. Here is an example of the passage from "Doe Season" presented from this point of view.

Objective Point of View

Andy sat sleepily staring into her cereal. She played with the dry flakes of bran as they floated in the surface of the milk.

Andy's mother, yawning, cooked them eggs and French toast. She looked at her husband and her daughter, paused for a second, and then went about what she was doing.

Andy's father smoked a cigarette and flicked ashes into his saucer. He looked out the window and said, "I wonder where Charlie Spoon is?"

Andy squirmed restlessly and repeatedly looked up at the clock that hung above the stove.

The disadvantage of this point of view is that it creates a great deal of distance between the characters and the readers. Instead of gaining the intimate knowledge of Andy that the limited omniscient point of view provides — knowledge even greater than she herself has — readers must infer what she thinks and feels without any help from the narrator.

As the preceding examples illustrate, writers choose the point of view that best enables them to achieve their objectives. If they want to create an intimate, subjective portrait of a character, they employ a first-person narrator. If they want to have a great deal of freedom in telling their story, they use an omniscient narrator. A limited omniscient narrator enables writers to maintain the focus on a single individual while commenting on the action. Finally, the objective point of view allows writers to remove the narrator from the story and present events in a distant, emotionless way.

CHECKLIST **SELECTING AN APPROPRIATE POINT OF VIEW: REVIEW**

First-Person Narrators (use *I* or *WE*)

▶ *Major character telling his or her own story*   "Every morning I lay on the floor in the front parlour watching her door." (James Joyce, "Araby")

▶ *Minor character as witness*   "And so she died. . . . We did not even know she was sick; we had long since given up trying to get information. . . ." (William Faulkner, "A Rose for Emily")

Third-Person Narrators (use *HE, SHE,* and *THEY*)

▶ *Omniscient — able to move at will from character to character and comment about them*   "In a house, in a suburb, in a city, there were a man and his wife who loved each other very much. . . ." (Nadine Gordimer, "Once upon a Time")

▶ *Limited Omniscient — restricts focus to a single character*   "The wagon went on. He did not know where they were going." (William Faulkner, "Barn Burning")

▶ *Objective (Dramatic)— simply reports the dialogue and the actions of characters*   " 'You'll be drunk,' the waiter said. The old man looked at him. The waiter went away." (Ernest Hemingway, "A Clean, Well-Lighted Place")

CHECKLIST **WRITING ABOUT POINT OF VIEW**

✓ What is the dominant point of view from which the story is told?

✓ Is the narrator a character in the story? If so, is he or she a participant in the story's events or just a witness?

✓ Does the story's point of view create irony?

✓ If the story has a first-person narrator, is the narrator reliable or unreliable? Are there any inconsistencies in the narrator's presentation of the story?

> ✓ If the story has a third-person narrator, is he or she omniscient? Does he or she have limited omniscience? Is the narrator objective?
>
> ✓ What are the advantages of the story's point of view? How does the point of view accomplish the author's purpose?
>
> ✓ Does the point of view remain consistent throughout the story, or does it shift?
>
> ✓ How might a different point of view change the story?

RICHARD WRIGHT (1908–1960) was born near Natchez, Mississippi, the son of sharecroppers. He had little formal schooling but as a young man was a voracious reader, especially of naturalistic fiction. Relocating to Chicago in the late 1920s, Wright worked as a postal clerk until 1935, when he joined the Federal Writers' Project, an association that took him to New York City. Deeply troubled by the economic and social oppression of African-Americans, Wright joined the Communist Party in 1932, and his early poems and stories reflect a distinctly Marxist perspective. In 1944, he broke with the party because of its stifling effect on "new ideas, new facts, . . . new hints at ways to live."

Wright began to reach a mainstream audience when a group of four long stories on the theme of racial oppression and violence was judged best manuscript in a contest sponsored by *Story* magazine; these stories were published as *Uncle Tom's Children* in 1938. Two years later, Wright published his most famous work, *Native Son,* an angry and brutal novel exploring the moral devastation wrought by a racist society. The auto-biographical *Black Boy* was published in 1945. In later years, Wright abandoned the United States for Paris in protest against the treatment of blacks in his native country and focused his work on reports about national independence movements in Africa and elsewhere in the third world.

The following story, published in the posthumous collection *Eight Men* (1961), is uncharacteristic of Wright's work in a number of ways — not least of which is that it is told through the eyes of a white protagonist.

Cultural Context: In 1957, the year "Big Black Good Man" was written, President Eisenhower sent paratroopers to Little Rock, Arkansas, to forestall violence over desegregation of the public schools. The crisis began on September 2, when Governor Orval Faubus ordered the Arkansas National Guard to blockade Central High School in Little Rock to prevent the entrance of nine black students. On September 20, NAACP lawyers Thurgood Marshall and Wiley Brandon obtained an injunction from the federal district court that ordered the troops removed. On September 25, the students entered the school, escorted by members of the 101st Airborne Division of the United States Army.

Big Black Good Man (1957)

Through the open window Olaf Jenson could smell the sea and hear the occasional foghorn of a freighter; outside, rain pelted down through an August night, drumming softly upon the pavements of Copenhagen,° inducing drowsiness, bringing dreamy memory, relaxing the tired muscles of his work-wracked body. He sat slumped in a swivel chair with his legs outstretched and his feet propped atop an edge of his desk. An inch of white ash tipped the end of his brown cigar and now and then he inserted the end of the stogie° into his mouth and drew gently upon it, letting wisps of blue smoke eddy from the corners of his wide, thin lips. The watery gray irises behind the thick lenses of his eyeglasses gave him a look of abstraction, of absentmindedness, of an almost genial idiocy. He sighed, reached for his half-empty bottle of beer, and drained it into his glass and downed it with a long slow gulp, then licked his lips. Replacing the cigar, he slapped his right palm against his thigh and said half aloud:

"Well, I'll be sixty tomorrow. I'm not rich, but I'm not poor either . . . Really, I can't complain. Got good health. Traveled all over the world and had my share of girls when I was young . . . And my Karen's a good wife. I own my home. Got no debts. And I love digging in my garden in the spring . . . Grew the biggest carrots of anybody last year. Ain't saved much money, but what the hell . . . Money ain't everything. Got a good job. Night portering ain't too bad." He shook his head and yawned. "Karen and I could of had some children, though. Would of been good company . . . 'Specially for Karen. And I could of taught 'em languages . . . English, French, German, Danish, Dutch, Swedish, Norwegian, and Spanish . . ." He took the cigar out of his mouth and eyed the white ash critically. "Hell of a lot of good language learning did me . . . Never got anything out of it. But those ten years in New York were fun . . . Maybe I could of got rich if I'd stayed in America . . . Maybe. But I'm satisfied. You can't have everything."

Behind him the office door opened and a young man, a medical student occupying room number nine, entered.

"Good evening," the student said.

5   "Good evening," Olaf said, turning.

The student went to the keyboard and took hold of the round, brown knob that anchored his key.

"Rain, rain, rain," the student said.

10   "That's Denmark for you," Olaf smiled at him.

"This dampness keeps me clogged up like a drainpipe," the student complained.

"That's Denmark for you," Olaf repeated with a smile.

"Good night," the student said.

"Good night, son," Olaf sighed, watching the door close.

Copenhagen: The capital of Denmark.

stogie: A cheap cigar.

Well, my tenants are my children, Olaf told himself. Almost all of his children were in their rooms now . . . Only seventy-two and forty-four were missing . . . Seventy-two might've gone to Sweden . . . And forty-four was maybe staying at his girl's place tonight, like he sometimes did . . . He studied the pear-shaped blobs of hard rubber, reddish brown like ripe fruit, that hung from the keyboard, then glanced at his watch. Only room thirty, eighty-one, and one hundred and one were empty . . . And it was almost midnight. In a few moments he could take a nap. Nobody hardly ever came looking for accommodations after midnight, unless a stray freighter came in, bringing thirsty, women-hungry sailors. Olaf chuckled softly. Why in hell was I ever a sailor? The whole time I was at sea I was thinking and dreaming about women. Then why didn't I stay on land where women could be had? Hunh? Sailors are crazy . . .

But he liked sailors. They reminded him of his youth, and there was something so direct, simple, and childlike about them. They always said straight out what they wanted, and what they wanted was almost always women and whisky . . . "Well, there's no harm in that . . . Nothing could be more natural," Olaf sighed, looking thirstily at his empty beer bottle. No; he'd not drink any more tonight; he'd had enough; he'd go to sleep . . .

He was bending forward and loosening his shoelaces when he heard the office   15
door crack open. He lifted his eyes, then sucked in his breath. He did not straighten; he just stared up and around at the huge black thing that filled the doorway. His reflexes refused to function; it was not fear; it was just simple astonishment. He was staring at the biggest, strangest, and blackest man he'd ever seen in all his life.

"Good evening," the black giant said in a voice that filled the small office. "Say, you got a room?"

Olaf sat up slowly, not to answer but to look at this brooding black vision; it towered darkly some six and a half feet into the air, almost touching the ceiling, and its skin was so black that it had a bluish tint. And the sheer bulk of the man! . . . His chest bulged like a barrel; his rocklike and humped shoulders hinted of mountain ridges; the stomach ballooned like a threatening stone; and the legs were like telephone poles . . . The big black cloud of a man now lumbered into the office, bending to get its buffalolike head under the door frame, then advanced slowly upon Olaf, like a stormy sky descending.

"You got a room?" the big black man asked again in a resounding voice.

Olaf now noticed that the ebony giant was well dressed, carried a wonderful new suitcase, and wore black shoes that gleamed despite the raindrops that peppered their toes.

"You're American?" Olaf asked him.   20

"Yeah, man; sure," the black giant answered.

"Sailor?"

"Yeah. American Continental Lines."

Olaf had not answered the black man's question. It was not that the hotel did not admit men of color; Olaf took in all comers — blacks, yellows, whites, and browns . . . To Olaf, men were men, and, in his day, he'd worked and eaten and slept and fought with all kinds of men. But this particular black man . . . Well, he didn't seem human. Too big, too black, too loud, too direct, and probably too violent to boot . . . Olaf's five feet seven inches scarcely reached the black giant's shoulder and his frail body weighed less, perhaps, than one of the man's gigantic legs . . . There was something about the man's intense blackness and ungainly bigness that frightened and insulted Olaf; he felt as though this man had come here expressly to remind him how puny, how tiny, and how weak and how white he was. Olaf knew, while registering his reactions, that he was being irrational and foolish; yet, for the first time in his life, he was emotionally determined to refuse a man a room solely on the basis of the man's size and color . . . Olaf's lips parted as he groped for the right words in which to couch his refusal, but the black giant bent forward and boomed:

25   "I asked you if you got a room. I got to put up somewhere tonight, man."

"Yes, we got a room," Olaf murmured.

And at once he was ashamed and confused. Sheer fear had made him yield. And he seethed against himself for his involuntary weakness. Well, he'd look over his book and pretend that he'd made a mistake; he'd tell this hunk of blackness that there was really no free room in the hotel, and that he was so sorry . . . Then, just as he took out the hotel register to make believe that he was poring over it, a thick roll of American bank notes, crisp and green, was thrust under his nose.

"Keep this for me, will you?" the black giant commanded. "Cause I'm gonna get drunk tonight and I don't wanna lose it."

Olaf stared at the roll; it was huge, in denominations of fifties and hundreds. Olaf's eyes widened.

30   "How much is there?" he asked.

"Two thousand six hundred," the giant said. "Just put it into an envelope and write 'Jim' on it and lock it in your safe, hunh?"

The black mass of man had spoken in a manner that indicated that it was taking it for granted that Olaf would obey. Olaf was licked. Resentment clogged the pores of his wrinkled white skin. His hands trembled as he picked up the money. No; he couldn't refuse this man . . . The impulse to deny him was strong, but each time he was about to act upon it something thwarted him, made him shy off. He clutched about desperately for an idea. Oh yes, he could say that if he planned to stay for only one night, then he could not have the room, for it was against the policy of the hotel to rent rooms for only one night . . .

"How long are you staying? Just tonight?" Olaf asked.

"Naw. I'll be here for five or six days, I reckon," the giant answered offhandedly.

35   "You take room number thirty," Olaf heard himself saying. "It's forty kroner a day."

"That's all right with me," the giant said.

With slow, stiff movements, Olaf put the money in the safe and then turned and stared helplessly up into the living, breathing blackness looming above him. Suddenly he became conscious of the outstretched palm of the black giant; he was silently demanding the key to the room. His eyes downcast, Olaf surrendered the key, marveling at the black man's tremendous hands . . . He could kill me with one blow, Olaf told himself in fear.

Feeling himself beaten, Olaf reached for the suitcase, but the black hand of the giant whisked it out of his grasp.

"That's too heavy for you, big boy; I'll take it," the giant said.

Olaf let him. He thinks I'm nothing . . . He led the way down the corridor, sensing the giant's lumbering presence behind him. Olaf opened the door of number thirty and stood politely to one side, allowing the black giant to enter. At once the room seemed like a doll's house, so dwarfed and filled and tiny it was with a great living blackness . . . Flinging his suitcase upon a chair, the giant turned. The two men looked directly at each other now. Olaf saw that the giant's eyes were tiny and red, buried, it seemed, in muscle and fat. Black cheeks spread, flat and broad, topping the wide and flaring nostrils. The mouth was the biggest that Olaf had ever seen on a human face; the lips were thick, pursed, parted, showing snow-white teeth. The black neck was like a bull's . . . The giant advanced upon Olaf and stood over him.

"I want a bottle of whiskey and a woman," he said. "Can you fix me up?"

"Yes," Olaf whispered, wild with anger and insult.

But what was he angry about? He'd had requests like this every night from all sorts of men and he was used to fulfilling them; he was a night porter in a cheap, water-front Copenhagen hotel that catered to sailors and students. Yes, men needed women, but this man, Olaf felt, ought to have a special sort of woman. He felt a deep and strange reluctance to phone any of the women whom he habitually sent to men. Yet he had promised. Could he lie and say that none was available? No. That sounded too fishy. The black giant sat upon the bed, staring straight before him. Olaf moved about quickly, pulling down the window shades, taking the pink coverlet off the bed, nudging the giant with his elbow to make him move as he did so . . . That's the way to treat 'im . . . Show 'im I ain't scared of 'im . . . But he was still seeking for an excuse to refuse. And he could think of nothing. He felt hypnotized, mentally immobilized. He stood hesitantly at the door.

"You send the whiskey and the woman quick, pal?" the black giant asked, rousing himself from a brooding stare.

"Yes," Olaf grunted, shutting the door.

Goddamn, Olaf sighed. He sat in his office at his desk before the phone. Why did *he* have to come here? . . . I'm not prejudiced . . . No, not at all . . . But . . . He couldn't think any more. God oughtn't make men as big and black as that . . . But what the hell was he worrying about? He'd sent women of all races to men of all colors . . . So why not a woman to the black giant? Oh, only if the man were small, brown, and intelligent-looking . . . Olaf felt trapped.

With a reflex movement of his hand, he picked up the phone and dialed Lena. She was big and strong and always cut him in for fifteen per cent instead of the usual ten per cent. Lena had four small children to feed and clothe. Lena was willing; she was, she said, coming over right now. She didn't give a good goddamn about how big and black the man was . . .

"Why you ask me that?" Lena wanted to know over the phone. "You never asked that before . . ."

"But this one is *big*," Olaf found himself saying.

50   "He's just a man," Lena told him, her voice singing stridently, laughingly over the wire. "You just leave that to me. You don't have to do anything. *I'll* handle 'im."

Lena had a key to the hotel door downstairs, but tonight Olaf stayed awake. He wanted to see her. Why? He didn't know. He stretched out on the sofa in his office, but sleep was far from him. When Lena arrived, he told her again how big and black the man was.

"You told me that over the phone," Lena reminded him.

Olaf said nothing. Lena flounced off on her errand of mercy. Olaf shut the office door, then opened it and left it ajar. But why? He didn't know. He lay upon the sofa and stared at the ceiling. He glanced at his watch; it was almost two o'clock . . . She's staying in there a long time . . . Ah, God, but he could do with a drink . . . Why was he so damned worked up and nervous about a nigger and a white whore? . . . He'd never been so upset in all his life. Before he knew it, he had drifted off to sleep. Then he heard the office door swinging creakingly open on its rusty hinges. Lena stood in it, grim and businesslike, her face scrubbed free of powder and rouge. Olaf scrambled to his feet, adjusting his eyeglasses, blinking.

"How was it?" he asked her in a confidential whisper.

55   Lena's eyes blazed.

"What the hell's that to you?" she snapped. "There's your cut," she said, flinging him his money, tossing it upon the covers of the sofa. "You're sure nosy tonight. You wanna take over my work?"

Olaf's pasty cheeks burned red.

"You go to hell," he said, slamming the door.

"I'll meet you there!" Lena's shouting voice reached him dimly.

60   He was being a fool; there was no doubt about it. But, try as he might, he could not shake off a primitive hate for that black mountain of energy, of muscle, of bone; he envied the easy manner in which it moved with such a creeping and powerful motion; he winced at the booming and commanding voice that came to him when the tiny little eyes were not even looking at him; he shivered at the sight of those vast and clawlike hands that seemed always to hint of death . . .

Olaf kept his counsel. He never spoke to Karen about the sordid doings at the hotel. Such things were not for women like Karen. He knew instinctively that Karen would have been amazed had he told her that he was worried sick about a nigger and a blonde whore . . . No; he couldn't talk to anybody about it, not even the hard-bitten° old bitch who owned the hotel. She was concerned only about money; she didn't give a damn about how big and how black a client was as long as he paid his room rent.

Next evening, when Olaf arrived for duty, there was no sight or sound of the black giant. A little later after one o'clock in the morning he appeared, left his key, and went out wordlessly. A few moments past two the giant returned, took his key from the board, and paused.

"I want that Lena again tonight. And another bottle of whiskey," he said boomingly.

---

hard-bitten: Stubborn, tough.

"I'll call her and see if she's in," Olaf said.

"Do that," the black giant said and was gone.

He thinks he's God, Olaf fumed. He picked up the phone and ordered Lena and a bottle of whiskey, and there was a taste of ashes in his mouth. On the third night came the same request: Lena and whiskey. When the black giant appeared on the fifth night, Olaf was about to make a sarcastic remark to the effect that maybe he ought to marry Lena, but he checked it in time . . . After all, he could kill me with one hand, he told himself.

Olaf was nervous and angry with himself for being nervous. Other black sailors came and asked for girls and Olaf sent them, but with none of the fear and loathing that he sent Lena and a bottle of whiskey to the giant . . . All right, the black giant's stay was almost up. He'd said that he was staying for five or six nights; tomorrow night was the sixth night and that ought to be the end of this nameless terror.

On the sixth night Olaf sat in his swivel chair with his bottle of beer and waited, his teeth on edge, his fingers drumming the desk. But what the hell am I fretting for? . . . The hell with 'im . . . Olaf sat and dozed. Occasionally he'd awaken and listen to the foghorns of freighters sounding as ships came and went in the misty Copenhagen harbor. He was half asleep when he felt a rough hand on his shoulder. He blinked his eyes open. The giant, black and vast and powerful, all but blotted out his vision.

"What I owe you, man?" the giant demanded. "And I want my money."

"Sure," Olaf said, relieved, but filled as always with fear of this living wall of black flesh.

With fumbling hands, he made out the bill and received payment, then gave the giant his roll of money, laying it on the desk so as not to let his hands touch the flesh of the black mountain. Well, his ordeal was over. It was past two o'clock in the morning. Olaf even managed a wry smile and muttered a guttural "Thanks" for the generous tip that the giant tossed him.

Then a strange tension entered the office. The office door was shut and Olaf was alone with the black mass of power, yearning for it to leave. But the black mass of power stood still, immobile, looking down at Olaf. And Olaf could not, for the life of him, guess at what was transpiring in that mysterious black mind. The two of them simply stared at each other for a full two minutes, the giant's tiny little beady eyes blinking slowly as they seemed to measure and search Olaf's face. Olaf's vision dimmed for a second as terror seized him and he could feel a flush of heat overspread his body. Then Olaf sucked in his breath as the devil of blackness commanded:

"Stand up!"

Olaf was paralyzed. Sweat broke on his face. His worst premonitions about this black beast were coming true. This evil blackness was about to attack him, maybe kill him . . . Slowly Olaf shook his head, his terror permitting him to breathe:

"What're you talking about?"

"Stand up, I say!" the black giant bellowed.

As though hypnotized, Olaf tried to rise; then he felt the black paw of the beast helping him roughly to his feet.

They stood an inch apart. Olaf's pasty-white features were glued to the giant's swollen black face. The ebony ensemble of eyes and nose and mouth and cheeks looked down at Olaf, silently; then, with a slow and deliberate movement of his go-rillalike arms, he lifted his mammoth hands to Olaf's throat. Olaf had long known and felt that this dreadful moment was coming; he felt trapped in a nightmare. He could not move. He wanted to scream, but could find no words. His lips refused to open; his tongue felt icy and inert. Then he knew that his end had come when the giant's black fingers slowly, softly encircled his throat while a horrible grin of de-light broke out on the sooty face . . . Olaf lost control of the reflexes of his body and he felt a hot stickiness flooding his underwear . . . He stared without breathing, gaz-ing into the grinning blackness of the face that was bent over him, feeling the black fingers caressing his throat and waiting to feel the sharp, stinging ache and pain of the bones in his neck being snapped, crushed . . . He knew all along that I hated 'im . . . Yes, and now he's going to kill me for it, Olaf told himself with despair.

The black fingers still circled Olaf's neck, not closing, but gently massaging it, as it were, moving to and fro, while the obscene face grinned into his. Olaf could feel the giant's warm breath blowing on his eyelashes and he felt like a chicken about to have its neck wrung and its body tossed to flip and flap dyingly in the dust of the barnyard . . . Then suddenly the black giant withdrew his fingers from Olaf's neck and stepped back a pace, still grinning. Olaf sighed, trembling, his body seeming to shrink; he waited. Shame sheeted him for the hot wetness that was in his trousers. Oh, God, he's teasing me . . . He's showing me how easily he can kill me . . . He swallowed, waiting, his eyes stones of gray.

80   The giant's barrel-like chest gave forth a low, rumbling chuckle of delight.

"You laugh?" Olaf asked whimperingly.

"Sure I laugh," the giant shouted.

"Please don't hurt me," Olaf managed to say.

"I wouldn't hurt you, boy," the giant said in a tone of mockery. "So long."

85   And he was gone. Olaf fell limply into the swivel chair and fought off losing consciousness. Then he wept. He was showing me how easily he could kill me . . . He made me shake with terror and then laughed and left . . . Slowly, Olaf recov-ered, stood, then gave vent to a string of curses:

"Goddamn 'im! My gun's right there in the desk drawer; I should of shot 'im. Jesus, I hope the ship he's on sinks . . . I hope he drowns and the sharks eat 'im . . ."

Later, he thought of going to the police, but sheer shame kept him back; and, anyway, the giant was probably on board his ship by now. And he had to get home and clean himself. Oh, Lord, what could he tell Karen? Yes, he would say that his stomach had been upset . . . He'd change clothes and return to work. He phoned the hotel owner that he was ill and wanted an hour off; the old bitch said that she was coming right over and that poor Olaf could have the evening off.

Olaf went home and lied to Karen. Then he lay awake the rest of the night dreaming of revenge. He saw that freighter on which the giant was sailing; he saw it springing a dangerous leak and saw a torrent of sea water flooding, gushing into all the compartments of the ship until it found the bunk in which the black giant slept. Ah, yes, the foamy, surging waters would surprise that sleeping black bastard of a giant and he would drown, gasping and choking like a trapped rat, his tiny eyes bulging until they glittered red, the bitter water of the sea pounding his lungs until they ached and finally burst . . . The ship would sink slowly to the bottom of

the cold, black, silent depths of the sea and a shark, a *white* one, would glide aimlessly about the shut portholes until it found an open one and it would slither inside and nose about until it found that swollen, rotting, stinking carcass of the
black beast and it would then begin to nibble at the decomposing mass of tarlike
flesh, eating the bones clean . . . Olaf always pictured the giant's bones as being
jet black and shining.

Once or twice, during these fantasies of cannibalistic revenge, Olaf felt a little
guilty about all the many innocent people, women and children, all white and
blonde, who would have to go down into watery graves in order that that white
shark could devour the evil giant's black flesh . . . But, despite feelings of remorse,
the fantasy lived persistently on, and when Olaf found himself alone, it would
crowd and cloud his mind to the exclusion of all else, affording him the only
revenge he knew. To make me suffer just for the pleasure of it, he fumed. Just
to show me how strong he was . . . Olaf learned how to hate, and got pleasure out
of it.

Summer fled on wings of rain. Autumn flooded Denmark with color. Winter   90
made rain and snow fall on Copenhagen. Finally spring came, bringing violets
and roses. Olaf kept to his job. For many months he feared the return of the black
giant. But when a year had passed and the giant had not put in an appearance,
Olaf allowed his revenge fantasy to peter out, indulging in it only when recalling
the shame that the black monster had made him feel.

Then one rainy August night, a year later, Olaf sat drowsing at his desk, his
bottle of beer before him, tilting back in his swivel chair, his feet resting atop a
corner of his desk, his mind mulling over the more pleasant aspects of his life. The
office door cracked open. Olaf glanced boredly up and around. His heart jumped
and skipped a beat. The black nightmare of terror and shame that he had hoped
that he had lost forever was again upon him . . . Resplendently dressed, suitcase
in hand, the black looming mountain filled the doorway. Olaf's thin lips parted
and a silent moan, half a curse, escaped them.

"Hi," the black giant boomed from the doorway.

Olaf could not reply. But a sudden resolve swept him: this time he would even
the score. If this black beast came within so much as three feet of him, he would
snatch his gun out of the drawer and shoot him dead, so help him God . . .

"No rooms tonight," Olaf heard himself announcing in a determined
voice.

The black giant grinned; it was the same infernal grimace of delight and tri   95
umph that he had had when his damnable black fingers had been around his
throat . . .

"Don't want no room tonight," the giant announced.

"Then what are you doing here?" Olaf asked in a loud but tremulous voice.

The giant swept toward Olaf and stood over him; and Olaf could not move,
despite his oath to kill him . . .

"What do you want then?" Olaf demanded once more, ashamed that he could
not lift his voice above a whisper.

The giant still grinned, then tossed what seemed the same suitcase upon Olaf's   100
sofa and bent over it; he zippered it open with a sweep of his clawlike hand and

rummaged in it, drawing forth a flat, gleaming white object done up in glowing cellophane. Olaf watched with lowered lids, wondering what trick was now being played on him. Then, before he could defend himself, the giant had whirled and again long, black, snakelike fingers were encircling Olaf's throat . . . Olaf stiffened, his right hand clawing blindly for the drawer where the gun was kept. But the giant was quick.

"Wait," he bellowed, pushing Olaf back from the desk.

The giant turned quickly to the sofa and, still holding his fingers in a wide circle that seemed a noose for Olaf's neck, he inserted the rounded fingers into the top of the flat, gleaming object. Olaf had the drawer open and his sweaty fingers were now touching the gun, but something made him freeze. The flat, gleaming object was a shirt and the black giant's circled fingers were fitting themselves into its neck . . .

"A perfect fit!" the giant shouted.

Olaf stared, trying to understand. His fingers loosened about the gun. A mixture of a laugh and a curse struggled in him. He watched the giant plunge his hands into the suitcase and pull out other flat, gleaming shirts.

105   "One, two, three, four, five, six," the black giant intoned, his voice crisp and businesslike. "Six nylon shirts. And they're all yours. One shirt for each time Lena came . . . See, Daddy-O?"

The black, cupped hands, filled with billowing nylon whiteness, were extended under Olaf's nose. Olaf eased his damp fingers from his gun and pushed the drawer closed, staring at the shirts and then at the black giant's grinning face.

"Don't you like 'em?" the giant asked.

Olaf began to laugh hysterically, then suddenly he was crying, his eyes so flooded with tears that the pile of dazzling nylon looked like snow in the dead of winter. Was this true? Could he believe it? Maybe this too was a trick? But, no. There were six shirts, all nylon, and the black giant had had Lena six nights.

"What's the matter with you, Daddy-O?" the giant asked. "You blowing your top? Laughing and crying . . ."

110   Olaf swallowed, dabbed his withered fists at his dimmed eyes; then he realized that he had his glasses on. He took them off and dried his eyes and sat up. He sighed, the tension and shame and fear and haunting dread of his fantasy went from him, and he leaned limply back in his chair . . .

"Try one on," the giant ordered.

Olaf fumbled with the buttons of his shirt, let down his suspenders, and pulled the shirt off. He donned a gleaming nylon one and the giant began buttoning it for him.

"Perfect, Daddy-O," the giant said.

His spectacled face framed in sparkling nylon, Olaf sat with trembling lips. So he'd not been trying to kill me after all.

115   "You want Lena, don't you?" he asked the giant in a soft whisper. "But I don't know where she is. She never came back here after you left —"

"I know where Lena is," the giant told him. "We been writing to each other. I'm going to her house. And, Daddy-O, I'm late." The giant zipped the suitcase shut and stood a moment gazing down at Olaf, his tiny little red eyes blinking slowly. Then Olaf realized that there was a compassion in that stare that he had never seen before.

"And I thought you wanted to kill me," Olaf told him. "I was scared of you . . ."

"Me? Kill you?" the giant blinked. "When?"

"That night when you put your fingers around my throat —"

"What?" the giant asked, then roared with laughter. "Daddy-O, you're a funny   120
little man. I wouldn't hurt you. I like you. You a *good* man. You helped me."

Olaf smiled, clutching the pile of nylon shirts in his arms.

"You're a good man too," Olaf murmured. Then loudly, "You're a big black good man."

"Daddy-O, you're crazy," the giant said.

He swept his suitcase from the sofa, spun on his heel, and was at the door in one stride.

"Thanks!" Olaf cried after him.   125

The black giant paused, turned his vast black head, and flashed a grin.

"Daddy-O, drop dead," he said and was gone.

Reading and Reacting

1. Why do you suppose Wright has his third-person narrator see events through Olaf's eyes? How would the story be different if the sailor told it?

2. This story was published in 1957. What attitudes about race does Wright expect his American readers to have? Do these attitudes predispose readers to identify with the sailor or with Olaf? Explain.

3. Why does Olaf dislike the sailor? What does the narrator mean in paragraph 24 when he says that the sailor's "intense blackness and ungainly bigness . . . frightened and insulted Olaf"?

4. In what ways do the sailor's words and actions contribute to Olaf's fears? Do you think Olaf's reactions are reasonable, or do you believe he is overreacting?

5. The sailor's name is Jim, but this name is almost never used in the story. Why not? List some words used to describe Jim. Why are they used? How do they affect your reaction to Jim?

6. Do you think the story's title is ironic? In what other respects is the story ironic?

7. How would "Big Black Good Man" be different if Jim were white? Would there even *be* a story?

8. Why do you think Wright set the story in Copenhagen? Could it have been set in the United States in 1957?

9. What do you think Jim thinks of Olaf? Do you suppose he realizes the effect he has on him? How do you explain his last comment?

10. **JOURNAL ENTRY** What point do you think the story makes about racial prejudice? What do Olaf's reactions to the sailor reveal about the nature of racial prejudice? Do you think Wright seems optimistic or pessimistic about race relations in the United States?

11. CRITICAL PERSPECTIVE In his 1982 article "The Short Stories: *Uncle Tom's Children, Eight Men*," Edward Margolies notes that "Big Black Good Man" was somewhat of a departure for Wright:

> "Big Black Good Man," which first appeared in *Esquire* in 1957, is the last short story Wright published in his lifetime. Possibly it is the last he ever wrote. In any event it represents a more traditional approach to storytelling in that Wright here avoids confining himself exclusively to dialogue. On the other hand, "Big Black Good Man" deviates from the usual Wright short story. For one thing, the narrative, by Wright's standards at least, is practically pointless. Scarcely anything "happens." There is no violence, practically no external narrative action, and no change of milieu.

Do you agree that the story is "practically pointless"? If not, what point do you think the story makes?

Related Works: "The Cask of Amontillado" (p. 217), "Girl" (p. 492), "We Wear the Mask" (p. 871), *The Brute* (p. 1062)

EDGAR ALLAN POE (1809–1849) profoundly influenced many writers all over the world. His tales of psychological terror and the macabre, his hauntingly musical lyric poems, and his writings on the craft of poetry and short story writing affected the development of symbolic fiction, the modern detective story, and the gothic horror tale. In most of Poe's horror tales (as in "The Cask of Amontillado"), readers vicariously "live" the story through the first-person narrator who tells the tale.

Poe was born in 1809, the son of a talented English-born actress who, deserted by her actor husband, died of tuberculosis before her son's third birthday. Although Poe was raised in material comfort by foster parents in Richmond, Virginia, his life was increasingly uncertain: his foster mother loved him, but her husband became antagonistic. He kept the young Poe so short of money at the University of Virginia (and later at West Point) that Poe resorted to gambling to raise money for food and clothing. Finally, debt-ridden, he left school altogether.

Poe found work as a magazine editor, gaining recognition as a perceptive (if sometimes vitriolic) literary critic. In 1836, he married his frail thirteen-year-old cousin, Virginia Clemm. Poe produced many of his most famous stories and poems in the next few years, working feverishly to support his tubercular wife; but although his stories were widely admired, financial success never came. His wife died in 1847. Less than two years after her death, Poe was found barely conscious in a Baltimore street after a mysterious disappearance; three days later, he was dead at age forty.

Cultural Context: Throughout antiquity, catacombs were used to bury the dead. Catacombs, such as those in Poe's story, are subterranean cemeteries composed of passages with side recesses for tombs. The early Christian catacombs of Rome, consisting of approximately forty known chambers located in a rough circle about three miles from the center of the city, are the most extensive of all known catacombs. Funeral feasts were often celebrated in family vaults on the day of burial and on anniversary dates of the deaths of loved ones.

The Cask of Amontillado (1846)

The thousand injuries of Fortunato I had borne as I best could, but when he ventured upon insult I vowed revenge. You, who so well know the nature of my soul, will not suppose, however, that I gave utterance to a threat. *At length* I would be avenged; this was a point definitely settled — but the very definitiveness with which it was resolved precluded the idea of risk. I must not only punish but punish with impunity. A wrong is unredressed when retribution overtakes its redresser. It is equally unredressed when the avenger fails to make himself felt as such to him who has done the wrong.

It must be understood that neither by word nor deed had I given Fortunato cause to doubt my good will. I continued, as was my wont, to smile in his face, and he did not perceive that my smile *now* was at the thought of his immolation.

He had a weak point — this Fortunato — although in other regards he was a man to be respected and even feared. He prided himself on his connoisseurship in wine. Few Italians have the true virtuoso spirit. For the most part their enthusiasm is adopted to suit the time and opportunity, to practise imposture upon the British and Austrian *millionaires*. In painting and gemmary, Fortunato, like his countrymen, was a quack, but in the matter of old wines he was sincere. In this respect I did not differ from him materially; — I was skillful in the Italian vintages myself, and bought largely whenever I could.

It was about dusk, one evening during the supreme madness of the carnival season, that I encountered my friend. He accosted me with excessive warmth, for he had been drinking much. The man wore motley.° He had on a tight-fitting parti-striped dress, and his head was surmounted by the conical cap and bells. I was so pleased to see him that I thought I should never have done wringing his hand.

I said to him —"My dear Fortunato, you are luckily met. How remarkably   5 well you are looking to-day. But I have received a pipe° of what passes for Amontillado,° and I have my doubts."

"How?" said he. "Amontillado? A pipe? Impossible! And in the middle of the carnival!"

"I have my doubts," I replied; "and I was silly enough to pay the full Amontillado price without consulting you in the matter. You were not to be found, and I was fearful of losing a bargain."

"Amontillado!"   10

"I have my doubts."

"Amontillado!"

"And I must satisfy them."

"Amontillado!"

"As you are engaged, I am on my way to Luchresi. If any one has a critical turn it is he. He will tell me —"

"Luchresi cannot tell Amontillado from Sherry."

---

motley: The many-colored attire of a court jester.

pipe: In the United States and England, a cask containing a volume equal to 126 gallons.

Amontillado: A pale, dry sherry; literally, a wine "from Montilla" (Spain).

15 "And yet some fools will have it that his taste is a match for your own."

"Come, let us go."

"Whither?"

"To your vaults."

"My friend, no; I will not impose upon your good nature. I perceive you have an engagement. Luchresi —"

20 "I have no engagement; — come."

"My friend, no. It is not the engagement, but the severe cold with which I perceive you are afflicted. The vaults are insufferably damp. They are encrusted with nitre."°

"Let us go, nevertheless. The cold is merely nothing. Amontillado! You have been imposed upon. And as for Luchresi, he cannot distinguish Sherry from Amontillado."

Thus speaking, Fortunato possessed himself of my arm; and putting on a mask of black silk and drawing a *roquelaire*° closely about my person, I suffered him to hurry me to my palazzo.

There were no attendants at home; they had absconded to make merry in honor of the time. I had told them that I should not return until the morning, and had given them explicit orders not to stir from the house. These orders were sufficient, I well knew, to insure their immediate disappearance, one and all, as soon as my back was turned.

25 I took from their sconces two flambeaux, and giving one to Fortunato, bowed him through several suites of rooms to the archway that led into the vaults. I passed down a long and winding staircase, requesting him to be cautious as he followed. We came at length to the foot of the descent, and stood together upon the damp ground of the catacombs of the Montresors.

The gait of my friend was unsteady, and the bells upon his cap jingled as he strode.

"The pipe," he said.

"It is farther on," said I; "but observe the white web-work which gleams from these cavern walls."

He turned towards me, and looked into my eyes with two filmy orbs that distilled the rheum of intoxication.

30 "Nitre?" he asked at length.

"Nitre," I replied. "How long have you had that cough?"

"Ugh! ugh! ugh! — ugh! ugh! ugh! — ugh! ugh! ugh! — ugh! ugh! ugh! — ugh! ugh! ugh!"

My poor friend found it impossible to reply for many minutes.

"It is nothing," he said at last.

35 "Come," I said, with decision, "we will go back; your health is precious. You are rich, respected, admired, beloved; you are happy, as once I was. You are a man to be missed. For me it is no matter. We will go back; you will be ill, and I cannot be responsible. Besides, there is Luchresi —"

---

nitre: Mineral deposits.

roquelaire: A short cloak.

"Enough," he said; "the cough is a mere nothing; it will not kill me. I shall not die of a cough."

"True — true," I replied; "and, indeed, I had no intention of alarming you unnecessarily — but you should use all proper caution. A draught of this Médoc° will defend us from the damps."

Here I knocked off the neck of a bottle which I drew from a long row of its fellows that lay upon the mould.

"Drink," I said, presenting him the wine.

He raised it to his lips with a leer. He paused and nodded to me familiarly, 40 while his bells jingled.

"I drink," he said, "to the buried that repose around us."

"And I to your long life."

He again took my arm, and we proceeded.

"These vaults," he said, "are extensive."

"The Montresors," I replied, "were a great and numerous family." 45

"I forget your arms."

"A huge human foot d'or, in a field azure; the foot crushes a serpent rampant whose fangs are imbedded in the heel."

"And the motto?"

"Nemo me impune lacessit."°

"Good!" he said. 50

The wine sparkled in his eyes and the bells jingled. My own fancy grew warm with the Médoc. We had passed through long walls of piled skeletons, with casks and puncheons° intermingling, into the inmost recesses of the catacombs. I paused again, and this time I made bold to seize Fortunato by an arm above the elbow.

"The nitre!" I said; "see, it increases. It hangs like moss upon the vaults. We are below the river's bed. The drops of moisture trickle among the bones. Come, we will go back ere it is too late. Your cough —"

"It is nothing," he said; "let us go on. But first, another draught of the Médoc."

I broke and reached him a flagon of De Grâve.° He emptied it at a breath. His eyes flashed with a fierce light. He laughed and threw the bottle upwards with a gesticulation I did not understand.

I looked at him in surprise. He repeated the movement — a grotesque one. 55

"You do not comprehend?" he said.

"Not I," I replied.

"Then you are not of the brotherhood."

"How?"

Médoc: A red wine from the Médoc district, near Bordeaux, France.

Nemo me impune lacessit: "No one insults me with impunity" (Latin); this is the legend on the royal coat of arms of Scotland.

puncheons: Barrel.

De Grâve: Correctly, "Graves," a light wine from the Bordeaux area.

60   "You are not of the masons."°

"Yes, yes," I said; "yes, yes."

"You? Impossible! A mason?"

"A mason," I replied.

"A sign," he said, "a sign."

65   "It is this," I answered, producing from beneath the folds of my *roquelaire* a trowel.

"You jest," he exclaimed, recoiling a few paces. "But let us proceed to the Amontillado."

"Be it so," I said, replacing the tool beneath the cloak and again offering him my arm. He leaned upon it heavily. We continued our route in search of the Amontillado. We passed through a range of low arches, descended, passed on, and descending again, arrived at a deep crypt, in which the foulness of the air caused our flambeaux rather to glow than flame.

At the most remote end of the crypt there appeared another less spacious. Its walls had been lined with human remains, piled to the vault overhead, in the fashion of the great catacombs of Paris. Three sides of this interior crypt were still ornamented in this manner. From the fourth side the bones had been thrown down, and lay promiscuously upon the earth, forming at one point a mound of some size. Within the wall thus exposed by the displacing of the bones, we perceived a still interior crypt or recess, in depth about four feet, in width three, in height six or seven. It seemed to have been constructed for no especial use within itself, but formed merely the interval between two of the colossal supports of the roof of the catacombs, and was backed by one of their circumscribing walls of solid granite.

It was in vain that Fortunato, uplifting his dull torch, endeavored to pry into the depth of the recess. Its termination the feeble light did not enable us to see.

70   "Proceed," I said; "herein is the Amontillado. As for Luchresi —"

"He is an ignoramus," interrupted my friend, as he stepped unsteadily forward, while I followed immediately at his heels. In an instant he had reached the extremity of the niche, and finding his progress arrested by the rock, stood stupidly bewildered. A moment more and I had fettered him to the granite. In its surface were two iron staples, distant from each other about two feet, horizontally. From one of these depended a short chain, from the other a padlock. Throwing the links about his waist, it was but the work of a few seconds to secure it. He was too much astounded to resist. Withdrawing the key I stepped back from the recess.

"Pass your hand," I said, "over the wall; you cannot help feeling the nitre. Indeed, it is *very* damp. Once more let me *implore* you to return. No? Then I must positively leave you. But I must first render you all the little attentions in my power."

"The Amontillado!" ejaculated my friend, not yet recovered from his astonishment.

"True," I replied; "the Amontillado."

75   As I said these words I busied myself among the pile of bones of which I have before spoken. Throwing them aside, I soon uncovered a quantity of building

---

masons: Freemasons (members of a secret fraternity). The trowel is a symbol of their alleged origin as a guild of stonemasons.

stone and mortar. With these materials and with the aid of my trowel, I began vigorously to wall up the entrance of the niche.

I had scarcely laid the first tier of the masonry when I discovered that the intoxication of Fortunato had in a great measure worn off. The earliest indication I had of this was a low moaning cry from the depth of the recess. It was *not* the cry of a drunken man. There was a long and obstinate silence. I laid the second tier, and the third, and the fourth; and then I heard the furious vibrations of the chain. The noise lasted for several minutes, during which, that I might hearken to it with the more satisfaction, I ceased my labors and sat down upon the bones. When at last the clanking subsided, I resumed the trowel, and finished without interruption the fifth, the sixth, and the seventh tier. The wall was now nearly upon a level with my breast. I again paused, and holding the flambeaux over the masonwork, threw a few feeble rays upon the figure within.

A succession of loud and shrill screams, bursting suddenly from the throat of the chained form, seemed to thrust me violently back. For a brief moment I hesitated, I trembled. Unsheathing my rapier, I began to grope with it about the recess; but the thought of an instant reassured me. I placed my hand upon the solid fabric of the catacombs, and felt satisfied. I reapproached the wall; I replied to the yells of him who clamoured. I re-echoed, I aided, I surpassed them in volume and in strength. I did this, and the clamourer grew still.

It was now midnight, and my task was drawing to a close. I had completed the eighth, the ninth and the tenth tier. I had finished a portion of the last and the eleventh; there remained but a single stone to be fitted and plastered in. I struggled with its weight; I placed it partially in its destined position. But now there came from out the niche a low laugh that erected the hairs upon my head. It was succeeded by a sad voice, which I had difficulty in recognizing as that of the noble Fortunato. The voice said —

"Ha! ha! ha! — he! he! he! — a very good joke, indeed — an excellent jest. We will have many a rich laugh about it at the palazzo — he! he! he! — over our wine — he! he! he!"

"The Amontillado!" I said.   80

"He! he! he! — he! he! he! — yes, the Amontillado. But is it not getting late? Will not they be awaiting us at the palazzo, the Lady Fortunato and the rest? Let us be gone."

"Yes," I said, "let us be gone."

"For the love of God, Montresor!"

"Yes," I said, "for the love of God."

But to these words I hearkened in vain for a reply. I grew impatient. I called   85
aloud —

"Fortunato!"

No answer. I called again —

"Fortunato!"

No answer still. I thrust a torch through the remaining aperture and let it fall within. There came forth in return only a jingling of the bells. My heart grew sick; it was the dampness of the catacombs that made it so. I hastened to make an end of my labour. I forced the last stone into its position; I plastered it up. Against the new masonry I re-erected the old rampart of bones. For the half of a century no mortal has disturbed them. *In pace requiescat!*°

Reading and Reacting

1. Montresor cites a "thousand injuries" and an "insult" as his motivation for murdering Fortunato. Given what you learn about the two men during the course of the story, what do you suppose the "injuries" and "insult" might be?

2. Do you find Montresor to be a reliable narrator? If not, what makes you question his version of events?

3. What is Montresor's concept of personal honor? Is it consistent or inconsistent with the values of contemporary American society? How relevant are the story's ideas about revenge and guilt to present-day society? Explain.

4. Does Fortunato ever understand why Montresor hates him? What is Fortunato's attitude toward Montresor?

5. What is the significance of Montresor's family coat of arms and motto? What is the significance of Fortunato's costume?

6. In what ways does Montresor manipulate Fortunato? What weaknesses does Montresor exploit?

7. Why does Montresor wait fifty years to tell his story? How might the story be different if he had told it the morning after the murder?

8. Why does Montresor wait for a reply before he puts the last stone in position? What do you think he wants Fortunato to say?

9. JOURNAL ENTRY Do you think the use of a first-person point of view makes you more sympathetic toward Montresor than you would be if his story were told by a third-person narrator? Why or why not?

10. CRITICAL PERSPECTIVE In his discussion of this story in *Edgar Allan Poe: A Study of the Short Fiction*, Charles E. May says, "We can legitimately hypothesize that the listener is a priest and that Montresor is an old man who is dying and making final confession. . . ."

Do you agree or disagree with May's hypothesis? Do you think that Montresor has atoned for his sin? Who else could be listening to Montresor's story?

Related Works: "A Rose for Emily" (p. 91), "Porphyria's Lover" (p. 622), "The Love Song of J. Alfred Prufrock" (p. 871), *Trifles* (p. 983)

WILLIAM FAULKNER: (1897–1962) "Barn Burning" (1939) marks the first appearance of the Snopes clan in Faulkner's fiction. These crafty and unappealing tenant farmers and traders run roughshod over the aristocratic families of Yoknapatawpha County in three Faulkner novels: *The Hamlet* (1940), *The Town* (1957), and *The Mansion* (1959). According to Ben Wasson in *Count No Count*, Faulkner once told a friend that "somebody said I was a genius writer. The only thing I'd claim genius for is thinking up that name *Snopes*." In Southern literary circles, at least, the name "Snopes" still serves as a short-

---

pace requiescat: "May he rest in peace (Latin)."

hand term for the graceless and greedy (but frequently successful) opportunists of the "New South."

> **Cultural Context:** Tenant farming is a system of agriculture in which landowners contribute their land while tenants contribute labor. One form of tenant farming, known as sharecropping, requires the landowner to furnish all the capital and usually the food, clothing, and shelter to the tenant in return for labor. The sharecropper was lucky to end the year without owing money to the landowner. In "Barn Burning," Abner Snopes is a poor sharecropper who takes out his frustrations against the post–Civil War aristocracy of landowners.

Barn Burning (1939)

The store in which the Justice of the Peace's court was sitting smelled of cheese. The boy, crouched on his nail keg at the back of the crowded room, knew he smelled cheese, and more: from where he sat he could see the ranked shelves close-packed with the solid, squat, dynamic shapes of tin cans whose labels his stomach read, not from the lettering which meant nothing to his mind but from the scarlet devils and the silver curve of fish — this, the cheese which he knew he smelled and the hermetic° meat which his intestines believed he smelled coming in intermittent gusts momentary and brief between the other constant one, the smell and sense just a little of fear because mostly of despair and grief, the old fierce pull of blood. He could not see the table where the Justice sat and before which his father and his father's enemy (*our enemy* he thought in that despair; *ourn! mine and hisn both! He's my father!*) stood, but he could hear them, the two of them that is, because his father had said no word yet:

"But what proof have you, Mr. Harris?"

"I told you. The hog got into my corn. I caught it up and sent it back to him. He had no fence that would hold it. I told him so, warned him. The next time I put the hog in my pen. When he came to get it I gave him enough wire to patch up his pen. The next time I put the hog up and kept it. I rode down to his house and saw the wire I gave him still rolled on to the spool in his yard. I told him he could have the hog when he paid me a dollar pound fee. That evening a nigger came with the dollar and got the hog. He was a strange nigger. He said, 'He say to tell you wood and hay kin burn. I said, 'What?' 'That whut he say to tell you,' the nigger said. 'Wood and hay kin burn.' That night my barn burned. I got the stock out but I lost the barn."

"Where is the nigger? Have you got him?"

"He was a strange nigger, I tell you. I don't know what became of him."   5

"But that's not proof. Don't you see that's not proof?"

"Get that boy up here. He knows." For a moment the boy thought too that the man meant his older brother until Harris said, "Not him. The little one. The boy,"

---

hermetic: Canned.

and, crouching, small for his age, small and wiry like his father, in patched and faded jeans even too small for him, with straight, uncombed, brown hair and eyes gray and wild as storm scud, he saw the men between himself and the table part and become a lane of grim faces, at the end of which he saw the Justice, a shabby, collarless, graying man in spectacles, beckoning him. He felt no floor under his bare feet; he seemed to walk beneath the palpable weight of the grim turning faces. His father, stiff in his black Sunday coat donned not for the trial but for the moving, did not even look at him. *He aims for me to lie,* he thought, again with that frantic grief and despair. *And I will have to do hit.*

"What's your name, boy?" the Justice said.

"Colonel Sartoris Snopes," the boy whispered.

10   "Hey?" the Justice said. "Talk louder. Colonel Sartoris? I reckon anybody named for Colonel Sartoris in this country can't help but tell the truth, can they?" The boy said nothing. *Enemy! Enemy!* he thought; for a moment he could not even see, could not see that the Justice's face was kindly nor discern that his voice was troubled when he spoke to the man named Harris: "Do you want me to question this boy?" But he could hear, and during those subsequent long seconds while there was absolutely no sound in the crowded little room save that of quiet and intent breathing it was as if he had swung outward at the end of a grape vine, over a ravine, and at the top of the swing had been caught in a prolonged instant of mesmerized gravity, weightless in time.

"No!" Harris said violently, explosively. "Damnation! Send him out of here!" Now time, the fluid world, rushed beneath him again, the voices coming to him again through the smell of cheese and sealed meat, the fear and despair and the old grief of blood:

"This case is closed. I can't find against you, Snopes, but I can give you advice. Leave this country and don't come back to it."

His father spoke for the first time, his voice cold and harsh, level, without emphasis: "I aim to. I don't figure to stay in a country among people who . . ." he said something unprintable and vile, addressed to no one.

"That'll do," the Justice said. "Take your wagon and get out of this country before dark. Case dismissed."

15   His father turned, and he followed the stiff black coat, the wiry figure walking a little stiffly from where a Confederate provost's man's° musket ball had taken him in the heel on a stolen horse thirty years ago, followed the two backs now, since his older brother had appeared from somewhere in the crowd, no taller than the father but thicker, chewing tobacco steadily, between the two lines of grim-faced men and out of the store and across the worn gallery and down the sagging steps and among the dogs and half-grown boys in the mild May dust, where as he passed a voice hissed:

"Barn burner!"

Again he could not see, whirling; there was a face in a red haze, moonlike, bigger than the full moon, the owner of it half again his size, he leaping in the red haze toward the face, feeling no blow, feeling no shock when his head struck

---

provost's man's: Military policeman's.

the earth, scrabbling up and leaping again, feeling no blow this time either and tasting no blood, scrabbling up to see the other boy in full flight and himself already leaping into pursuit as his father's hand jerked him back, the harsh, cold voice speaking above him: "Go get in the wagon."

It stood in a grove of locusts and mulberries across the road. His two hulking sisters in their Sunday dresses and his mother and her sister in calico and sunbonnets were already in it, sitting on and among the sorry residue of the dozen and more movings which even the boy could remember — the battered stove, the broken beds and chairs, the clock inlaid with mother-of-pearl, which would not run, stopped at some fourteen minutes past two o'clock of a dead and forgotten day and time, which had been his mother's dowry. She was crying, though when she saw him she drew her sleeve across her face and began to descend from the wagon. "Get back," the father said.

"He's hurt. I got to get some water and wash his . . ."

"Get back in the wagon," his father said. He got in too, over the tail-gate. His 20 father mounted to the seat where the older brother already sat and struck the gaunt mules two savage blows with the peeled willow, but without heat. It was not even sadistic; it was exactly that same quality which in later years would cause his descendants to overrun the engine before putting a motor car into motion, striking and reining back in the same movement. The wagon went on, the store with its quiet crowd of grimly watching men dropped behind; a curve in the road hid it. *Forever* he thought. *Maybe he's done satisfied now, now that he has* . . . stopping himself, not to say it aloud even to himself. His mother's hand touched his shoulder.

"Does hit hurt?" she said.

"Naw," he said. "Hit don't hurt. Lemme be."

"Can't you wipe some of the blood off before hit dries?"

"I'll wash to-night," he said. "Lemme be, I tell you."

The wagon went on. He did not know where they were going. None of them 25 ever did or ever asked, because it was always somewhere, always a house of sorts waiting for them a day or two days or even three days away. Likely his father had already arranged to make a crop on another farm before he . . . Again he had to stop himself. He (the father) always did. There was something about his wolflike independence and even courage when the advantage was at least neutral which impressed strangers, as if they got from his latent ravening ferocity not so much a sense of dependability as a feeling that his ferocious conviction in the rightness of his own actions would be of advantage to all whose interest lay with his.

That night they camped, in a grove of oaks and beeches where a spring ran. The nights were still cool and they had a fire against it, of a rail lifted from a nearby fence and cut into lengths — a small fire, neat, niggard almost, a shrewd fire; such fires were his father's habit and custom always, even in freezing weather. Older, the boy might have remarked this and wondered why not a big one; why should not a man who had not only seen the waste and extravagance of war, but who had in his blood an inherent voracious prodigality with material not his own, have burned everything in sight? Then he might have gone a step farther and thought that that was the reason: that niggard blaze was the living fruit of nights passed during those four years in the woods hiding from all men, blue or gray, with his strings of horses (captured horses, he called them). And older still, he might have divined the true reason: that the element of fire spoke to some deep main-spring of his father's being, as the element of steel or of powder spoke to other men, as the one weapon for the preservation of integrity, else breath were not worth the breathing, and hence to be regarded with respect and used with discretion.

But he did not think this now and he had seen those same niggard blazes all his life. He merely ate his supper beside it and was already half asleep over his iron plate when his father called him, and once more he followed the stiff back, the stiff and ruthless limp, up the slope and on to the starlit road where, turning, he could see his father against the stars but without face or depth — a shape black, flat, and bloodless as though cut from tin in the iron folds of the frockcoat which had not been made for him, the voice harsh like tin and without heat like tin:

"You were fixing to tell them. You would have told him." He didn't answer. His father struck him with the flat of his hand on the side of the head, hard but with-out heat, exactly as he had struck the two mules at the store, exactly as he would strike either of them with any stick in order to kill a horse fly, his voice still with-out fear or anger: "You're getting to be a man. You got to learn. You got to learn to stick to your own blood or you ain't going to have any blood to stick to you. Do you think either of them, any man there this morning, would? Don't you know all they wanted was a chance to get at me because they knew I had them beat? Eh?" Later, twenty years later, he was to tell himself, "If I had said they wanted only truth, justice, he would have hit me again." But now he said nothing. He was not crying. He just stood there. "Answer me," his father said.

"Yes," he whispered. His father turned.

30   "Get on to bed. We'll be there tomorrow."

Tomorrow they were there. In the early afternoon the wagon stopped before a paintless two-room house identical almost with the dozen others it had stopped before even in the boy's ten years, and again, as on the other dozen occasions, his mother and aunt got down and began to unload the wagon, although his two sisters and his father and brother had not moved.

"Likely hit ain't fitten for hawgs," one of the sisters said.

"Nevertheless, fit it will and you'll hog it and like it," his father said. "Get out of them chairs and help your Ma unload."

The two sisters got down, big, bovine, in a flutter of cheap ribbons; one of them drew from the jumbled wagon bed a battered lantern, the other a worn broom. His father handed the reins to the older son and began to climb stiffly over the wheel. "When they get unloaded, take the team to the barn and feed them." Then he said, and at first the boy thought he was still speaking to his brother: "Come with me."

35   "Me?" he said.

"Yes," his father said. "You."

"Abner," his mother said. His father paused and looked back — the harsh level stare beneath the shaggy, graying, irascible brows.

"I reckon I'll have a word with the man that aims to begin tomorrow owning me body and soul for the next eight months."

They went back up the road. A week ago — or before last night, that is — he would have asked where they were going, but not now. His father had struck him before last night but never before had he paused afterward to explain why; it was as if the blow and the following calm, outrageous voice still rang, repercussed, divulging nothing to him save the terrible handicap of being young, the light weight of his few years, just heavy enough to prevent his soaring free of the world as it seemed to be ordered but not heavy enough to keep him footed solid in it, to resist it and try to change the course of its events.

Presently he could see the grove of oaks and cedars and the other flowering 40 trees and shrubs, where the house would be, though not the house yet. They walked beside a fence massed with honeysuckle and Cherokee roses and came to a gate swinging open between two brick pillars, and now, beyond a sweep of drive, he saw the house for the first time and at that instant he forgot his father and the terror and despair both, and even when he remembered his father again (who had not stopped) the terror and despair did not return. Because, for all the twelve movings, they had sojourned until now in a poor country, a land of small farms and fields and houses, and he had never seen a house like this before. *Hit's big as a courthouse* he thought quietly, with a surge of peace and joy whose reason he could not have thought into words, being too young for that: *They are safe from him. People whose lives are a part of this peace and dignity are beyond his touch, he no more to them than a buzzing wasp: capable of stinging for a little moment but that's all; the spell of this peace and dignity rendering even the barns and stable and cribs which belong to it impervious to the puny flames he might contrive* . . . this, the peace and joy, ebbing for an instant as he looked again at the stiff black back, the stiff and implacable limp of the figure which was not dwarfed by the house, for the reason that it had never looked big anywhere and which now, against the serene columned backdrop, had more than ever that impervious quality of something cut ruthlessly from tin, depthless, as though, sidewise to the sun, it would cast no shadow. Watching him, the boy remarked the absolutely undeviating course which his father held and saw the stiff foot come squarely down in a pile of fresh droppings where a horse had stood in the drive and which his father could have avoided by a simple change of stride. But it ebbed only for a moment, though he could not have thought this into words either, walking on in the spell of the house, which he could even want but without envy, without sorrow, certainly never with that ravening and jealous rage which unknown to him walked in the ironlike black coat before him: *Maybe he will feel it too. Maybe it will even change him now from what maybe he couldn't help but be.*

They crossed the portico. Now he could hear his father's stiff foot as it came down on the boards with clocklike finality, a sound out of all proportion to the displacement of the body it bore and which was not dwarfed either by the white door before it, as though it had attained to a sort of vicious and ravening minimum not to be dwarfed by anything — the flat, wide, black hat, the formal coat of broadcloth which had once been black but which had now that friction-glazed greenish cast of the bodies of old house flies, the lifted sleeve which was too large, the lifted hand like a curled claw. The door opened so promptly that the boy knew the Negro must have been watching them all the time, an old man with neat grizzled hair, in a linen jacket, who stood barring the door with his body, saying, "Wipe yo foots, white man, fo you come in here. Major ain't home nohow."

"Get out of my way, nigger," his father said, without heat too, flinging the door back and the Negro also and entering, his hat still on his head. And now the boy saw the prints of the stiff foot on the doorjamb and saw them appear on the pale rug behind the machinelike deliberation of the foot which seemed to bear (or transmit) twice the weight which the body compassed. The Negro was shouting "Miss Lula! Miss Lula!" somewhere behind them, then the boy, deluged as though by a warm wave by a suave turn of carpeted stair and a pendant glitter of chandeliers and a mute gleam of gold frames, heard the swift feet and saw her too, a lady — perhaps he had never seen her like before either — in a gray, smooth gown with lace at the throat and an apron tied at the waist and the sleeves turned back, wiping cake or biscuit dough from her hands with a towel as she came up the hall, looking not at his father at all but at the tracks on the blond rug with an expression of incredulous amazement.

"I tried," the Negro cried, "I tole him to . . ."

"Will you please go away?" she said in a shaking voice. "Major de Spain is not at home. Will you please go away?"

45   His father had not spoken again. He did not speak again. He did not even look at her. He just stood stiff in the center of the rug, in his hat, the shaggy iron-gray brows twitching slightly above the pebble-colored eyes as he appeared to examine the house with brief deliberation. Then with the same deliberation he turned; the boy watched him pivot on the good leg and saw the stiff foot drag round the arc of the turning, leaving a final long and fading smear. His father never looked at it, he never once looked down at the rug. The Negro held the door. It closed behind them, upon the hysteric and indistinguishable woman-wail. His father stopped at the top of the steps and scraped his boot clean on the edge of it. At the gate he stopped again. He stood for a moment, planted stiffly on the stiff foot, looking back at the house. "Pretty and white, ain't it?" he said. "That's sweat. Nigger sweat. Maybe it ain't white enough yet to suit him. Maybe he wants to mix some white sweat with it."

Two hours later the boy was chopping wood behind the house within which his mother and aunt and the two sisters (the mother and aunt, not the two girls, he knew that; even at this distance and muffled by walls the flat loud voices of the two girls emanated an incorrigible idle inertia) were setting up the stove to prepare a meal, when he heard the hooves and saw the linen-clad man on a fine sorrel mare, whom he recognized even before he saw the rolled rug in front of the Negro youth following on a fat bay carriage horse — a suffused, angry face vanishing, still at full gallop, beyond the corner of the house where his father and brother were sitting in the two tilted chairs; and a moment later, almost before he could have put the axe down, he heard the hooves again and watched the sorrel mare go back out of the yard, already galloping again. Then his father began to shout one of the sisters' names, who presently emerged backward from the kitchen door dragging the rolled rug along the ground by one end while the other sister walked behind it.

"If you ain't going to tote, go on and set up the wash pot," the first said.

"You, Sarty!" the second shouted. "Set up the wash pot!" His father appeared at the door, framed against that shabbiness, as he had been against that other bland perfection, impervious to either, the mother's anxious face at his shoulder.

"Go on," the father said. "Pick it up." The two sisters stooped, broad, lethargic; stooping, they presented an incredible expanse of pale cloth and a flutter of tawdry ribbons.

"If I thought enough of a rug to have to git hit all the way from France I   50
wouldn't keep hit where folks coming in would have to tromp on hit," the first said. They raised the rug.

"Abner," the mother said. "Let me do it."

"You go back and git dinner," his father said. "I'll tend to this."

From the woodpile through the rest of the afternoon the boy watched them, the rug spread flat in the dust beside the bubbling wash-pot, the two sisters stooping over it with that profound and lethargic reluctance, while the father stood over them in turn, implacable and grim, driving them though never raising his voice again. He could smell the harsh homemade lye° they were using; he saw his mother come to the door once and look toward them with an expression not anxious now but very like despair; he saw his father turn, and he fell to with the axe and saw from the corner of his eye his father raise from the ground a flattish fragment of field stone and examine it and return to the pot, and this time his mother actually spoke: "Abner. Abner. Please don't. Please, Abner."

Then he was done too. It was dusk; the whippoorwills had already begun. He could smell coffee from the room where they would presently eat the cold food remaining from the mid-afternoon meal, though when he entered the house he realized they were having coffee again probably because there was a fire on the hearth, before which the rug now lay spread over the backs of the two chairs. The tracks of his father's foot were gone. Where they had been were now long, water-cloudy scoriations resembling the sporadic course of a Lilliputian mowing machine.

It still hung there while they ate the cold food and then went to bed, scattered   55
without order or claim up and down the two rooms, his mother in one bed, where his father would later lie, the older brother in the other, himself, the aunt, and the two sisters on pallets on the floor. But his father was not in bed yet. The last thing the boy remembered was the depthless, harsh silhouette of the hat and coat bending over the rug and it seemed to him that he had not even closed his eyes when the silhouette was standing over him, the fire almost dead behind it, the stiff foot prodding him awake. "Catch up the mule," his father said.

When he returned with the mule his father was standing in the black door, the rolled rug over his shoulder. "Ain't you going to ride?" he said.

"No. Give me your foot."

---

lye: A soap made from wood ashes and water, unsuitable for washing fine fabrics.

He bent his knee into his father's hand, the wiry, surprising power flowed smoothly, rising, he rising with it, on to the mule's bare back (they had owned a saddle once; the boy could remember it though not when or where) and with the same effortlessness his father swung the rug up in front of him. Now in the starlight they retraced the afternoon's path, up the dusty road rife with honeysuckle, through the gate and up the black tunnel to the drive to the lightless house, where he sat on the mule and felt the rough warp of the rug drag across his thighs and vanish.

"Don't you want me to help?" he whispered. His father did not answer and now he heard again that stiff foot striking the hollow portico with that wooden and clocklike deliberation, that outrageous overstatement of the weight it carried. The rug, hunched, not flung (the boy could tell that even in the darkness) from his father's shoulder struck the angle of wall and floor with a sound unbelievably loud, thunderous, then the foot again, unhurried and enormous; a light came on in the house and the boy sat, tense, breathing steadily and quietly and just a little fast, though the foot itself did not increase its beat at all, descending the steps now; now the boy could see him.

60   "Don't you want to ride now?" he whispered. "We kin both ride now," the light within the house altering now, flaring up and sinking. *He's coming down the stairs now,* he thought. He had already ridden the mule up beside the horse block; presently his father was up behind him and he doubled the reins over and slashed the mule across the neck, but before the animal could begin to trot the hard, thin arm came round him, the hard, knotted hand jerking the mule back to a walk.

In the first red rays of the sun they were in the lot, putting plow gear on the mules. This time the sorrel mare was in the lot before he heard it at all, the rider collarless and even bareheaded, trembling, speaking in a shaking voice as the woman in the house had done, his father merely looking up once before stooping again to the hame° he was buckling, so that the man on the mare spoke to his stooping back:

"You must realize you have ruined that rug. Wasn't there anybody here, any of your women . . ." he ceased, shaking, the boy watching him, the older brother leaning now in the stable door, chewing, blinking slowly and steadily at nothing apparently. "It cost a hundred dollars. But you never had a hundred dollars. You never will. So I'm going to charge you twenty bushels of corn against your crop. I'll add it in your contract and when you come to the commissary you can sign it. That won't keep Mrs. de Spain quiet but maybe it will teach you to wipe your feet off before you enter her house again."

Then he was gone. The boy looked at his father, who still had not spoken or even looked up again, who was now adjusting the loggerhead in the hame.

"Pap," he said. His father looked at him — the inscrutable face, the shaggy brows beneath which the gray eyes glinted coldly. Suddenly the boy went toward him, fast, stopping as suddenly. "You done the best you could!" he cried.

---

hame: Harness.

"If he wanted hit done different why didn't he wait and tell you how? He won't git no twenty bushels! He won't git none! We'll gether hit and hide hit! I kin watch . . ."

"Did you put the cutter back in that straight stock like I told you?" 65

"No, sir," he said.

"Then go do it."

That was Wednesday. During the rest of that week he worked steadily, at what was within his scope and some which was beyond it, with an industry that did not need to be driven nor even commanded twice; he had this from his mother, with the difference that some at least of what he did he liked to do, such as splitting wood with the half-size axe which his mother and aunt had earned, or saved money somehow, to present him with at Christmas. In company with the two older women (and on one afternoon, even one of the sisters), he built pens for the shoat and the cow which were a part of his father's contract with the landlord, and one afternoon, his father being absent, gone somewhere on one of the mules, he went to the field.

They were running a middle buster now, his brother holding the plow straight while he handled the reins, and walking beside the straining mule, the rich black soil shearing cool and damp against his bare ankles, he thought *Maybe this is the end of it. Maybe even that twenty bushels that seems hard to have to pay for just a rug will be a cheap price for him to stop forever and always from being what he used to be;* thinking, dreaming now, so that his brother had to speak sharply to him to mind the mule: *Maybe he even won't collect the twenty bushels. Maybe it will all add up and balance and vanish — corn, rug, fire; the terror and grief, the being pulled two ways like between two teams of horses — gone, done with for ever and ever.*

Then it was Saturday; he looked up from beneath the mule he was harnessing 70
and saw his father in the black coat and hat. "Not that," his father said. "The wagon gear." And then, two hours later, sitting in the wagon bed behind his father and brother on the seat, the wagon accomplished a final curve, and he saw the weathered paintless store with its tattered tobacco- and patent-medicine posters and the tethered wagons and saddle animals below the gallery. He mounted the gnawed steps behind his father and brother, and there again was the lane of quiet, watching faces for the three of them to walk through. He saw the man in spectacles sitting at the plank table and he did not need to be told this was a Justice of the Peace; he sent one glare of fierce, exultant, partisan defiance at the man in collar and cravat now, whom he had seen but twice before in his life, and that on a galloping horse, who now wore on his face an expression not of rage but of amazed unbelief which the boy could not have known was at the incredible circumstance of being sued by one of his own tenants, and came and stood against his father and cried at the Justice: "He ain't done it! He ain't burnt . . ."

"Go back to the wagon," his father said.

"Burnt?" the Justice said. "Do I understand this rug was burned too?"

"Does anybody here claim it was?" his father said. "Go back to the wagon." But he did not, he merely retreated to the rear of the room, crowded as that other had been, but not to sit down this time, instead, to stand pressing among the motion-less bodies, listening to the voices:

"And you claim twenty bushels of corn is too high for the damage you did to the rug?"

75 "He brought the rug to me and said he wanted the tracks washed out of it. I washed the tracks out and took the rug back to him."

"But you didn't carry the rug back to him in the same condition it was in be-fore you made the tracks on it."

His father did not answer, and now for perhaps half a minute there was no sound at all save that of breathing, the faint, steady suspiration of complete and intent listening.

"You decline to answer that, Mr. Snopes?" Again his father did not answer. "I'm going to find against you, Mr. Snopes. I'm going to find that you were re-sponsible for the injury to Major de Spain's rug and hold you liable for it. But twenty bushels of corn seems a little high for a man in your circumstances to have to pay. Major de Spain claims it cost a hundred dollars. October corn will be worth about fifty cents. I figure that if Major de Spain can stand a ninety-five dollar loss on something he paid cash for, you can stand a five-dollar loss you haven't earned yet. I hold you in damages to Major de Spain to the amount of ten bushels of corn over and above your contract with him, to be paid to him out of your crop at gath-ering time. Court adjourned."

It had taken no time hardly, the morning was but half begun. He thought they would return home and perhaps back to the field, since they were late, far behind all other farmers. But instead his father passed on behind the wagon, merely indicating with his hand for the older brother to follow with it, and crossed the road toward the blacksmith shop opposite, pressing on after his father, over-taking him, speaking, whispering up at the harsh, calm face beneath the weath-ered hat: "He won't git no ten bushels neither. He won't git one. We'll . . ." until his father glanced for an instant down at him, the face absolutely calm, the grizzled eyebrows tangled above the cold eyes, the voice almost pleasant, almost gentle:

80 "You think so? Well, we'll wait till October anyway."

The matter of the wagon — the setting of a spoke or two and the tightening of the tires — did not take long either, the business of the tires accomplished by driving the wagon into the spring branch behind the shop and letting it stand there, the mules nuzzling into the water from time to time, and the boy on the seat with the idle reins, looking up the slope and through the sooty tunnel of the shed where the slow hammer rang and where his father sat on an upended cypress bolt, easily, either talking or listening, still sitting there when the boy brought the dripping wagon up out of the branch and halted it before the door.

"Take them on to the shade and hitch," his father said. He did so and returned. His father and the smith and a third man squatting on his heels inside the door were talking, about crops and animals; the boy, squatting too in the ammoniac dust and hoof-parings and scales of rust, heard his father tell a long and unhurried story out of the time before the birth of the older brother even when he had been a professional horsetrader. And then his father came up beside him where he stood before a tattered last year's circus poster on the other side of the store, gazing rapt and quiet at the scarlet horses, the incredible poisings and convolutions of tulle and tights and the painted leers of comedians, and said, "It's time to eat."

But not at home. Squatting beside his brother against the front wall, he watched his father emerge from the store and produce from a paper sack a segment of cheese and divide it carefully and deliberately into three with his pocket knife and produce crackers from the same sack. They all three squatted on the gallery and ate, slowly, without talking; then in the store again, they drank from a tin dipper tepid water smelling of the cedar bucket and of living beech trees. And still they did not go home. It was a horse lot this time, a tall rail fence upon and along which men stood and sat and out of which one by one horses were led, to be walked and trotted and then cantered back and forth along the road while the slow swapping and buying went on and the sun began to slant westward, they — the three of them — watching and listening, the older brother with his muddy eyes and his steady, inevitable tobacco, the father commenting now and then on certain of the animals, to no one in particular.

It was after sundown when they reached home. They ate supper by lamplight, then, sitting on the doorstep, the boy watched the night fully accomplish, listening to the whippoorwills and the frogs, when he heard his mother's voice: "Abner! No! No! Oh, God. Oh, God. Abner!" and he rose, whirled, and saw the altered light through the door where a candle stub now burned in a bottle neck on the table and his father, still in the hat and coat, at once formal and burlesque as though dressed carefully for some shabby and ceremonial violence, emptying the reservoir of the lamp back into the five-gallon kerosene can from which it had been filled, while the mother tugged at his arm until he shifted the lamp to the other hand and flung her back, not savagely or viciously, just hard, into the wall, her hands flung out against the wall for balance, her mouth open and in her face the same quality of hopeless despair as had been in her voice. Then his father saw him standing in the door.

"Go to the barn and get that can of oil we were oiling the wagon with," he said. The boy did not move. Then he could speak. 85

"What . . ." he cried. "What are you . . ."

"Go get that oil," his father said. "Go."

Then he was moving, running, outside the house, toward the stable: this the old habit, the old blood which he had not been permitted to choose for himself, which had been bequeathed him willy nilly and which had run for so long (and who knew where, battening on what of outrage and savagery and lust) before it came to him. *I could keep on*, he thought. *I could run on and on and never look back, never need to see his face again. Only I can't. I can't*, the rusted can in his hand now, the liquid sploshing in it as he ran back to the house and into it, into the sound of his mother's weeping in the next room, and handed the can to his father.

"Ain't you going to even send a nigger?" he cried. "At least you sent a nigger before!"

This time his father didn't strike him. The hand came even faster than the 90 blow had, the same hand which had set the can on the table with almost excruciating care flashing from the can toward him too quick for him to follow it, gripping him by the back of his shirt and on to tiptoe before he had seen it quit the can, the face stooping at him in breathless and frozen ferocity, the cold, dead voice speaking over him to the older brother who leaned against the table, chewing with that steady, curious, sidewise motion of cows:

"Empty the can into the big one and go on. I'll catch up with you."

"Better tie him to the bedpost," the brother said.

"Do like I told you," the father said. Then the boy was moving, his bunched shirt and the hard, bony hand between his shoulderblades, his toes just touching the floor, across the room and into the other one, past the sisters sitting with spread heavy thighs in the two chairs over the cold hearth, and to where his mother and aunt sat side by side on the bed, the aunt's arms about his mother's shoulders.

"Hold him," the father said. The aunt made a startled movement. "Not you," the father said. "Lennie. Take hold of him. I want to see you do it." His mother took him by the wrist. "You'll hold him better than that. If he gets loose don't you know what he is going to do? He will go up yonder." He jerked his head toward the road. "Maybe I'd better tie him."

95   "I'll hold him," his mother whispered.

"See you do then." Then his father was gone, the stiff foot heavy and measured upon the boards, ceasing at last.

Then he began to struggle. His mother caught him in both arms, he jerking and wrenching at them. He would be stronger in the end, he knew that. But he had no time to wait for it. "Lemme go!" he cried. "I don't want to have to hit you!"

"Let him go!" the aunt said. "If he don't go, before God, I am going up there myself!"

"Don't you see I can't?" his mother cried. "Sarty! Sarty! No! No! Help me, Lizzie!"

100   Then he was free. His aunt grasped at him but it was too late. He whirled, running, his mother stumbled forward on to her knees behind him, crying to the nearest sister: "Catch him, Net! Catch him!" But that was too late too, the sister (the sisters were twins, born at the same time, yet either of them now gave the impression of being, encompassing as much living meat and volume and weight as any other two of the family) not yet having begun to rise from the chair, her head, face, alone merely turned, presenting to him in the flying instant an astonishing expanse of young female features untroubled by any surprise even, wearing only an expression of bovine interest. Then he was out of the room, out of the house, in the mild dust of the starlit road and the heavy rifeness of honeysuckle, the pale ribbon unspooling with terrific slowness under his running feet, reaching the gate at last and turning in, running, his heart and lungs drumming, on up the drive toward the lighted house, the lighted door. He did not knock, he burst in, sobbing for breath, incapable for the moment of speech; he saw the astonished face of the Negro in the linen jacket without knowing when the Negro had appeared.

"De Spain!" he cried, panted. "Where's . . ." then he saw the white man too emerging from a white door down the hall. "Barn!" he cried. "Barn!"

"What?" the white man said. "Barn?"

"Yes!" the boy cried. "Barn!"

"Catch him!" the white man shouted.

But it was too late this time too. The Negro grasped his shirt, but the entire   105
sleeve, rotten with washing, carried away, and he was out that door too and in the
drive again, and had actually never ceased to run even while he was screaming
into the white man's face.

Behind him the white man was shouting, "My horse! Fetch my horse!" and he
thought for an instant of cutting across the park and climbing the fence into the
road, but he did not know the park nor how high the vine-massed fence might be
and he dared not risk it. So he ran on down the drive, blood and breath roaring;
presently he was in the road again though he could not see it. He could not hear
either: the galloping mare was almost upon him before he heard her, and even
then he held his course, as if the very urgency of his wild grief and need must in
a moment more find him wings, waiting until the ultimate instant to hurl himself
aside and into the weed-choked roadside ditch as the horse thundered past and
on, for an instant in furious silhouette against the stars, the tranquil early summer
night sky which, even before the shape of the horse and rider vanished, stained
abruptly and violently upward: a long, swirling roar incredible and soundless,
blotting the stars, and he springing up and into the road again, running again,
knowing it was too late yet still running even after he heard the shot and, an instant later, two shots, pausing now without knowing he had ceased to run, crying
"Pap! Pap!", running again before he knew he had begun to run, stumbling, tripping over something and scrabbling up again without ceasing to run, looking
backward over his shoulder at the glare as he got up, running on among the
invisible trees, panting, sobbing, "Father! Father!".

At midnight he was sitting on the crest of a hill. He did not know it was midnight and he did not know how far he had come. But there was no glare behind
him now and he sat now, his back toward what he had called home for four days
anyhow, his face toward the dark woods which he would enter when breath was
strong again, small, shaking steadily in the chill darkness, hugging himself into
the remainder of his thin, rotten shirt, the grief and despair now no longer terror
and fear but just grief and despair. *Father. My father,* he thought. "He was brave!"
he cried suddenly, aloud but not loud, no more than a whisper: "He was! He was
in the war! He was in Colonel Sartoris' cav'ry!" not knowing that his father had
gone to that war a private in the fine old European sense, wearing no uniform, ad-
mitting the authority of and giving fidelity to no man or army or flag, going to war
as Malbrouck° himself did: for booty — it meant nothing and less than nothing
to him if it were enemy booty or his own.

The slow constellations wheeled on. It would be dawn and then sunup after a
while and he would be hungry. But that would be tomorrow and now he was only
cold, and walking would cure that. His breathing was easier now and he decided
to get up and go on, and then he found that he had been asleep because he knew
it was almost dawn, the night almost over. He could tell that from the whippoorwills. They were everywhere now among the dark trees below him, constant and

---

Malbrouck: A character in a popular eighteenth-century nursery rhyme about a famous warrior.

inflectioned and ceaseless, so that, as the instant for giving over to the day birds drew nearer and nearer, there was no interval at all between them. He got up. He was a little stiff, but walking would cure that too as it would the cold, and soon there would be the sun. He went on down the hill, toward the dark woods within which the liquid silver voices of the birds called unceasing — the rapid and urgent beating of the urgent and quiring heart of the late spring night. He did not look back.

Reading and Reacting

1. Is the third-person narrator of "Barn Burning" omniscient, or is his omniscience limited? Explain.

2. What is the point of view of the italicized passages? What do you learn from them? Do they create irony? How would the story have been different without these passages?

3. "Barn Burning" includes a great deal of dialogue. How would you characterize the level of **diction** of this dialogue? What information about various characters does it provide?

4. What conflicts are presented in "Barn Burning"? Which, if any, are resolved in the story? Are the conflicts avoidable? Explain.

5. Why does Ab Snopes burn barns? Do you think his actions are justified? Explain your reasoning.

6. What role does the Civil War play in "Barn Burning"? What does Abner Snopes's behavior during the war tell readers about his character?

7. In the First and Second books of Samuel in the Old Testament, Abner was a relative of King Saul and commander in chief of his armies. Abner supported King Saul against David and was killed as a result of his own jealousy and rage. What, if any, significance is there in the fact that Faulkner names Ab Snopes, loyal to no man, fighter "for booty, and father of the Snopes clan," after this mighty biblical leader?

8. Why does Sarty Snopes insist that his father was brave? How does your knowledge of events unknown to the boy affect your reactions to his defense of his father?

9. **JOURNAL ENTRY** How would the story be different if it were told from Ab's point of view? From Sarty's? From the point of view of Ab's wife? From the point of view of a member of a community in which the Snopeses have lived?

10. **CRITICAL PERSPECTIVE** Critic Edmond L. Volpe argues in his article "'Barn Burning': A Definition of Evil" that "Barn Burning" is not really about the class conflict between the sharecropping Snopeses and landowners like the de Spains:

> The story is centered upon Sarty's emotional dilemma. His conflict would not have been altered in any way if the person whose barn Ab burns had been a simple poor farmer, rather than an aristocratic plantation owner. . . . Sarty's struggle is against the repressive and divisive force his father represents. The boy's anxiety is created by his awakening sense of his own individuality. Torn between strong emotional attachment to the parent and his growing need to assert

his own identity, Sarty's crisis is psychological and his battle is being waged far below the level of his intellectual and moral awareness.

Do you believe "Barn Burning" is, as Volpe suggests, essentially a coming-of-age story, or do you believe it is about something else — class conflict, for example?

Related Works: "A Worn Path" (p. 361), "Eveline" (p. 489), "Child's Grave, Hale County, Alabama" (p. 770), "The Satisfaction Coal Company" (p. 869), *Fences* (p. 1358)

GISH JEN (1956 –   ) was born Lillian Jen in Scarsdale, New York, the daughter of Chinese immigrants. She attended Harvard University, graduating with a degree in English. While on an archaeological dig in Pennsylvania for the National Science Foundation, Jen chose the name Gish, after silent-screen actress Lillian Gish. Widely published, her work has appeared in *The New Yorker,* the *New Republic,* and the *New York Times,* as well as in a variety of anthologies, including *The Best American Short Stories of the Century.* She has published two books, *Typical American* (1991)—a *New York Times* notable book of the year and a finalist for the National Book Critics' Circle Award—and its sequel, *Mona in the Promised Land* (1996), also a *New York Times* notable book. Her collection of short stories, *Who's Irish?,* was published in 1999. She currently lives in Cambridge, Massachusetts, with her husband, her son Luke, and her daughter, Paloma Jen O'Connor.

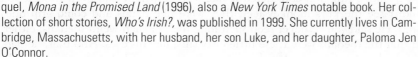

Cultural Context: At the beginning of the twentieth century, Israel Zangwill, a Zionist and well-regarded playwright and novelist, arrived in America from England and wrote a play whose theme continues to exert a powerful hold on the country's imagination. Called *The Melting Pot* (1908), the play pointed to the promise that all immigrants could be transformed into Americans — "melted," regardless of cultural or ethnic differences, into a mixture of democracy, equal opportunity, and civic responsibility. The myth of the melting pot has been challenged as much as it has been championed— not only by historians and sociologists but also by this country's own legislation, as evidenced by the Chinese Exclusion Act of 1882. Given the arrival of a million newcomers per year, the notion of the melting pot is continually being put to the test.

Chin   (1998)

I wasn't his friend, but I wasn't one of the main kids who hounded him up onto the shed roof, either. Sure I'd lob a rock or two, but this was our stage of life back then, someplace between the arm and the fist. Not to chuck nothing would have been against nature, and I never did him one he couldn't duck easy, especially being as fast as he was — basically the fastest kid in the ninth grade, and one of the smartest besides, smarter even than yours truly, the official class underachiever. I tested so high on my IQ that the school psychologists made me take the test over, nobody could believe it. They've been hounding me to apply myself ever since. But Chin was smart, too — not so much in math and science as in stuff like history and English. How's that for irony? And he was a good climber, you had to give him that, the only kid who could scale that shed wall, period. Because that wall didn't have no handholds or footholds. In fact, the naked eye would've pronounced that wall plain concrete; you had to wonder if the kid had some kind of special vision, so that he could look at that wall and see a way up. Maybe where we saw wall, he saw cracks, or maybe there was something he knew in his body about walls; or maybe they didn't have walls in China, besides the Great Wall, that is, so that he knew a wall was only a wall because we thought it was a wall. That might be getting philosophical. But you know, I've seen guys do that in basketball, find the basket in ways you can't account for. You can rewind the tape and watch the replay until your eyeballs pop, but finally you've got to say that obstacles are not always obstacles for these guys. Things melt away for them.

Gus said it was on account of there was monkey feet inside his sneakers that the kid could get up there. That was the day the kid started stockpiling the rocks we threw and raining them back down on us. A fall day, full of the crack and smell of people burning leaves illegally. It was just like the monkeys in the zoo when they get mad at the zookeepers, that's what I said. I saw that on TV once. But Gus blew a smoke ring and considered it like a sunset, then said even though you couldn't see the kid's monkey feet, they were like hands and could grip onto things. He said you've never seen such long toes, or such weird toenails, either, and that the toenails were these little bitty slits, like his eyes. And that, he said, was why he was going to drown me in a douche bag if I threw any more rocks without paying attention. He said I was fucking arming the ape.

We didn't live in the same building, that kid and me. His name was Chin or something, like chin-up we used to say, and his family lived in the garden apartment next door to ours. This was in scenic Yonkers, New York, home of Central Avenue. We were both stuck on the ground floor, where everyone could look right into your kitchen. It was like having people look up your dress, my ma said, and they were smack across the alley from us. So you see, if I'd really wanted to nail him with a rock, I could've done it any time their windows were open if I didn't want to break any glass And I could've done it any time at all if I didn't care about noise and commotion and getting a JD card like the Beyer kid got for climbing the water tower. Of course, they didn't open their windows much, the Chins. My ma said it was because they were Chinese people — you know, like Chinese food, from China, she said, and then she cuffed me for playing dumb and getting her to explain what a Chinese was when they were getting to be a fact of life. Not like in California or Queens, but they were definitely proliferating, along with a lot of other people who could tell you where they came from, if they spoke English. They weren't like us who came from Yonkers and didn't have no special foods, unless you wanted to count fries. Gus never could see why we couldn't count fries. My own hunch, though, guess why, was that they just might be French. Not that I said so. I was more interested in why everybody suddenly had to have a special food. And why was everybody asking what your family was? First time somebody asked me that, I had no idea what they were talking about. But after a while,

I said, Vanilla. I said that because I didn't want to say we were nothing, my family was nothing.

My ma said that the Chins kept their windows shut because they liked their apartment hot, seeing as how it was what they were used to. People keep to what they're used to, she liked to say, though she also liked to say, Wait and see, you know your taste changes. Especially to my big sister she was always saying that, because my sis was getting married for real this time, to this hair dresser who had suddenly started offering her free bang trims anytime. Out of the blue, this was. He was a thinker, this Ray. He had it all figured out, how from doing the bang trim he could get to talking about her beautiful blue eyes. And damned if he wasn't right that a lot of people, including yours truly, had never particularly noticed her eyes, what with the hair hanging in them. A real truth-teller, that Ray was, and sharp as a narc. It was all that practice with women all day long, my ma said. He knows how to make a woman feel like a queen, not like your pa, who knows how to make her feel like shit. She was as excited as my sis, that's the truth, now that this Ray and her Debi were hitting the aisle sure enough. Ray was doing my ma's hair free, too, every other day just about, trying to fine-tune her do for the wedding, and in between she was trying to pitch a couple of last You knows across to Debi while she could. Kind of a cram course.

But my pa said the Chins did that with their windows because somebody put 5 a cherry bomb in their kitchen for fun one day, and it upset them. Maybe they didn't know it was just a cherry bomb. Who knows what they thought it was, but they beat up Chin over it; that much we did know, because we could see everything and hear everything they did over there, especially if we turned the TV down, which we sometimes did for a fight. If only more was in English, we could've understood everything, too. Instead all we caught was that Chin got beat up over the cherry bomb, as if they thought it was owing to him that somebody put the bomb in the window. Go figure.

Chin got beat up a lot — this wasn't the first time. He got beat up on account of he played hooky from school sometimes, and he got beat up on account of he mouthed off to his pa, and he got beat up on account of he once got a C in math, which was why right near the bomb site there was a blackboard in the kitchen. Nights he wasn't getting beaten up, he was parked in front of the blackboard doing equations with his pa, who people said was not satisfied with Chin plain getting the correct answer in algebra, he had to be able to get it two or three ways. Also he got beat up because he liked to find little presents for himself and his sis and his ma. He did this in stores without paying for them, and that pissed the hell out of his pa. On principle, people said, but maybe he just felt left out. I always thought Chin should've known enough to get something for his pa, too.

But really Chin got beat up, my pa said, because Mr. Chin had this weird cheek. He had some kind of infection in some kind of hole, and as a result, the cheek shook and for a long time he wouldn't go to the doctor, seeing as how in China he used to be a doctor himself. Here he was a cab driver — the worst driver in the city, we're talking someone who would sooner puke on the Pope than cut across two lanes of traffic. He had a little plastic sleeve on the passenger-side visor where he displayed his driver's license; that's how much it meant to him that he'd actually gotten one. But in China he'd been a doctor, and as a result, he refused to go to a doctor here until his whole cheek was about gone. Thought he should be able to cure himself with herbs. Now even with the missus out working down at the dry cleaners, they were getting cleaned out themselves, what with the bills. They're going to need that boy for their old age, that's what my pa said. Cabbies don't have no pension plan like firemen and policemen and everybody else. They can't afford for him to go wrong, he's going to have to step up to the plate and hit that ball into the bleachers for them. That's why he gets beat, so he'll grow up to be a doctor who can practice in America. They want that kid to have his M.D. hanging up instead of his driver's license.

That was our general theory of why Chin got the treatment. But this time was maybe different. This time my pa wondered if maybe Chin's pa thought he was in some kind of a gang. He asked me if Chin was or wasn't, and I said no way was he in anything. Nobody hung with Chin, why would anybody hang with the guy everyone wanted to break? Unless you wanted them to try and break you, too. That's when my pa nodded in that captain of the force way you see on TV, and I was glad I told him. It made me feel like I'd forked over valuable information to the guy who ought to know. I felt like I could relax after I'd told him, even though maybe it was Mr. Chin who really should've known. Who knows but maybe my pa should've told Mr. Chin. Though what was he going to do, call him up and say, This is our theory next door? The truth is, I understood my pa. Like maybe I should've told Gus that Chin didn't actually have monkey feet, because I've seen his feet top and bottom through my pa's binoculars, and they were just regular. But let's face it, people don't want to be told much. And what difference did it make that I didn't think his toes were even that long, or that I could see them completely plain because his pa used to make him kneel when he wanted to beat him? What difference does it make what anybody's seen? Sometimes I think I should've kept my eyes on the TV where they belonged, instead of watching stuff I couldn't turn off. Chin's pa used to use a belt mostly, but sometimes he used a metal garden stake, and with every single whack, I used to think how glad I was that it was Chin and not me that had those big welts rising up out of his back skin. They looked like some great special effect, these oozy red caterpillars crawling over some older pinkish ones. Chin never moved or said anything, and that just infuriated his pa more. You could see it so clear, you almost felt sorry for him. Here he had this garden stake and there was nothing he could do. What with his cheek all wrapped up, he had to stop the beating every now and then to readjust his bandage.

My pa used a ruler on me once, just like the one they used at school — Big Bertha, we called it, a solid eighteen inches, and I you flinched, you got hit another three times on the hands. Naturally, Chin never did, as a result of the advanced training he got at home. People said he didn't feel nothing; he was like a horse you had to kick with heel spurs, your plain heel just tickled. But I wasn't used to torture instruments. We didn't believe in that sort of thing in my house. Even that time my pa did get out the ruler, it broke and he had to go back to using his hand. That was bad enough. My pa was a fireman, meaning he was a lot stronger than Chin's pa was ever going to be, which maybe had nothing to do with anything. But my theory was, it was on account of that he knew he

wasn't that strong that Mr. Chin used the garden stake of Chin, and once on the
sister, too.

She wasn't as old as my sister, and she wasn't that pretty, and she wasn't that 10
smart, and you were just glad when you looked at her that you weren't her gym
teacher. She wore these glasses that looked like they were designed to fall off, and
she moseyed down the school halls the way her pa did the highway — keeping all
the way to the right and hesitating dangerously in the intersections. But she had a
beautiful voice and was always doing the solo at school assembly. Some boring
thing — the songs at school were all worse than ever since Mr. Reardon, the math
teacher, had to take over music. He was so musical, people had to show him how
to work those black stands; he didn't know you could adjust them, he thought they
came in sizes. To be fair, he asked three times if he couldn't do study hall instead.
But Chin's sister managed to wring something out of the songs he picked somehow.
Everything she sang sounded like her. It was funny — she never talked, this girl,
and everybody called her quiet, but when she sang, she filled up the whole audito-
rium and you completely forgot she wore these glasses people said were bulletproof.

It wasn't the usual thing that the sister got hit. But one day she threatened to
move out of the house, actually stomped out into the snow, saying that she could
not stand to watch what was going on anymore. Then her pa hauled her back and
beat her, too. At least he left her clothes on and didn't make her kneel. She got to
stand and only fell on the floor, curled up, by choice. But here was the sad thing: It
turned out you could hear her singing voice when she cried; she still sounded like
herself. She didn't look like herself with her glasses off, though, and nobody else did,
either. Chin the unflinching turned so red in the face, he looked as though blood
beads were going to come busting straight out of his pores, and he started pounding
the wall so hard, he put craters in it. His ma told him to stop, but he kept going, until finally she packed a suitcase and put the sister's glasses back on for her. Ma Chin
had to tape the suitcase with duct tape to get it to stay shut. Then Ma Chin and the
sister both put on their coats and headed for the front door. The snowflakes by then
were so giant, you'd think there was a closeout sale on underwear going on up in
heaven. Still the dynamic duo marched out into the neighborhood and up our little
hill without any boots. Right up the middle of the street, they went; I guess there
being two of them bucked up the sister. Ma Chin started out with the suitcase, but
by the time they'd reached the hill, the sister'd wrestled it away from her. Another
unexpected physical feat. It was cold out, and so dark that what with all the snow,
the light from the streetlights appeared to be falling down too, and kind of drifting
around. My pa wondered out loud if he should give our neighbors a friendly lift
someplace. After all, the Chins had no car, and it was a long walk over to the bus
stop. But what would he say? Excuse me, I just happened to be out driving?

He was trying to work this out with my ma, but she had to tell him first how
Ray would know what to say without having to consult nobody and how glad she
was that her Debi wasn't marrying nobody like him. Ray, Ray, Ray! my pa said
finally. Why don't you go fuck him yourself instead of using your daughter? Then
he sat right in the kitchen window, where anybody who bothered to look could see
him, and watched as Ma Chin and the sister stopped and had themselves a little
conference. They were up to their ankles in snow, neither in one streetlight cone

or the next, but smack in between. They jawed for a long time. Then they moved a little farther up the incline and stopped and jawed again, sheltering their glasses from the snow with their hands. They almost looked like lifeguards out there, trying to keep the sun out of their eyes, except that they didn't seem to know that they were supposed to be looking for something. Probably their glasses were all fogged up. Still my pa watched them and watched them while I had a look at Chin and his pa back at the ranch, and saw the most astounding thing of all: They were back at the blackboard, working problems out. Mr. Chin had a cup of tea made, and you couldn't see his face on account of his bandage, but he was gesturing with the eraser and Chin was nodding. How do you figure? I half-wanted to say something to my pa, to point out this useless fact. But my pa was too busy sitting in the window with the lights on, waiting for the Chin women to shout Fire! or something, I guess. He wanted them to behold him there, all lit up, their rescuer. Unfortunately, though, it was snowing out, not burning, and their heads were bent and their eyes were on the ground as they dragged their broken suitcase straight back across our view.

Reading and Reacting

1. This story is told by an adult narrator looking back at his childhood. Why does the narrator tell the story? Why is Chin so important to him?

2. In what way does the point of view of the story limit what readers find out about Chin and his family? How would the story be different if Chin himself told it?

3. The narrator says that his score on his IQ test was so high that the psychologists at school made him retake the test. Why does he volunteer this information? Do you believe him? Is there any evidence in the story to support this statement?

4. Why do the boys throw rocks at Chin? Why does the narrator try to miss Chin when he throws rocks?

5. How are the narrator's family and Chin's family alike? In what ways are they different?

6. What misconceptions about Chin's family do the narrator and his family have? What misconceptions to they have about Chinese people? Why do you think they have these misconceptions?

7. At the beginning of the story, the narrator says that Chin was smart in history and English but not in math and science. In paragraph 6, however, the narrator says that when he was not being beaten, Chin did algebra problems with his father. Why does the narrator make this point? Does it shed light on why Chin's father beats his son and his daughter?

8. At the end of the story, the narrator describes his father watching Chin's sister and mother walking through the snow. What point is the narrator making about his father? About Chin's sister and mother? About his family and the Chin family?

9. **JOURNAL ENTRY** What comment does "Chin" make about Chinese-American culture? What comment does the story make about the larger American culture?

10. **CRITICAL PERSPECTIVE** In an interview with Marilyn Berlin Snell, Gish Jen talks about the ways in which immigrants to the United States attempt to change their environment even as they are being changed by it:

> Any group that comes to America attempts to re-establish the Old World on new soil, which is natural. And yet they are changed by their environment. They are changed by its opportunities as well as by its dangers. And people are changed differently depending on their individual predispositions. The immigrant who longs for economic achievement will be affected by certain opportunities and influences much differently than the immigrant who comes to America to take advantage of one of its universities, for instance. And the women who come to this country see the freedom it offers in different terms still. For instance, they see the opportunity for romantic love. Or they see in their new home the opportunity to study and to excel on their own for perhaps the first time in their lives.

In what ways might Jen's comments apply to the Chin family? In what ways are family members trying to maintain traditions. How are they alert to new opportunities and possibilities?

Related Works: "Gryphon" (p. 126), "Suicide Note" (p. 607), "How to Write the Great American Indian Novel" (p. 629), "What We Heard about the Japanese" (p. 631), "What the Japanese Perhaps Heard" (p. 632), "Daddy" (p. 691), *The Cuban Swimmer* (p. 1258).

WRITING SUGGESTIONS: Point of View

1. How would Poe's "The Cask of Amontillado" be different if it were told by a minor character who observed the events? Rewrite the story from this point of view — or tell the story that precedes the story, explaining the "thousand injuries" and the "insult."

2. Assume that you are the sailor in "Big Black Good Man" and that you are keeping a journal of your travels. Write the journal entries for the time you spent in Copenhagen. Include your impressions of Olaf, Lena, the hotel, and anything else that caught your attention. Make sure you present your version of the key events described in the story — especially Olaf's reaction to you.

3. Both "The Cask of Amontillado" and "Barn Burning" deal with crimes that essentially go unpunished and with the emotions that accompany these crimes. In what sense does each story's use of point of view shape its treatment of the crime in question? For instance, how does point of view determine how much readers know about the motives for the crime, the crime's basic circumstances, and the extent to which the crime is justified?

4. Retell "Chin" entirely from Chin's point of view, giving his impressions of the narrator and explaining why he thinks his classmates torment him. Fill in the gaps in the story by discussing things that the narrator does not know — for example, the nature of Chin's relationship with his father.

5. **WEB ACTIVITY** The following Web site contains information about Richard Wright:

http://www.pbs.org/rwbb/rwtoc.html

Read the "Overview" section, making note of the biographical details and the introduction of themes in Wright's work. Focusing on Wright's experiences with prejudice as he was growing up, write an essay discussing how his story "Big Black Good Man" expresses his "deep interest in the large questions of authority, power, and freedom." Concentrate in particular on the relationship between the white protagonist and the title character in the story as representative of Wright's own struggle against oppression.

CHAPTER 9

STYLE, TONE, AND LANGUAGE

A word is intrinsically powerful. If you believe in the power of words, you can bring about physical change in the universe. This is a notion of language that is ancient and it is valid to me. For example, the words of a charm or a spell are formulaic. They are meant to bring about physical change. The person who utters such a formula believes beyond any shadow of doubt that his utterance is going to have this or that actual effect. Because he believes in it and because words are what they are, it is true. It is true.... Every day we produce magical results with words. —**N. Scott Momaday**, *Ancestral Voices*

INTERVIEWER: You describe seemingly fantastic events in such minute detail that it gives them their own reality. Is this something you have picked up from journalism?

GARCÍA MÁRQUEZ: That's a journalistic trick which you can also apply to literature. For example, if you say that there are elephants flying in the sky, people are not going to believe you. But if you say that there are four hundred and twenty-five elephants in the sky, people will probably believe you.... I remember particularly the story about the character who is surrounded by yellow butterflies.... I discovered that if I didn't say the butterflies were yellow, people would not believe it.... The problem for every writer is credibility. Anybody can write anything so long as it's believed. —**Gabriel García Márquez**, *Writers at Work*, 6th ed.

When a writer starts in very young, his problems apart from his story are those of technique, of words, of rhythms, of story methods, of transition, of characterization, of ways of creating effects. But after years of trial and error most of these things are solved and one gets what is called a style. It is then that a story conceived falls into place neatly and is written down having the indelible personal hallmark of the writer. —**John Steinbeck**, *Letter*

STYLE AND TONE

One of the qualities that gives a work of literature its individual personality is its **style,** the way in which a writer uses language, selecting and arranging words to say what he or she wants to say. Style encompasses elements such as word choice; syntax; sentence length and structure; and the presence, frequency, and prominence of imagery and figures of speech.

Closely related to style is **tone,** the attitude of the narrator or author of a work toward the subject matter, characters, or audience. Word choice and sentence structure help to create a work's tone, which may be intimate or distant, bitter or affectionate, straightforward or cautious, supportive or critical, respectful or condescending. (Tone may also be **ironic;** see Chapter 8, "Point of View," for a discussion of irony.)

THE USES OF LANGUAGE

Language offers almost limitless possibilities to a writer. Creative use of language (such as unusual word choice, word order, or sentence structure) can enrich a story and add to its overall effect. Sometimes, in fact, a writer's use of language can expand a story's possibilities through its very inventiveness. For example, James Joyce's innovative **stream-of-consciousness** style mimics thought, allowing ideas to run into one another as random associations are made so that readers may follow and participate in the thought processes of the narrator. Here is a stream-of-consciousness passage from Joyce's experimental novel *Ulysses:*

> frseeeeeeeefronnnng train somewhere whistling the strength those engines have in them like big giants and the water rolling all over and out of them all sides like the end of Loves old sweet sonnnng the poor men that have to be out all the night from their wives and families in those roasting engines stifling it was today. . . .

Most often, language is used to enhance a story's other elements. It may, for example, help to create an atmosphere that is important to the story's plot or theme, as Kate Chopin's lush, rhythmic sentences help to create the sexually charged atmosphere of "The Storm"—an atmosphere that overpowers the characters and thus drives the plot. Language may also help to delineate character, perhaps by conveying a character's mental state to readers. For instance, the breathless, disjointed style of Edgar Allan Poe's "The Tell-Tale Heart" suggests the narrator's increasing emotional instability: "Was it possible they heard not? Almighty God!— no, no! They heard!— they suspected!— they *knew!*— they were making a mockery of my horror!" In his short story "Big Two-Hearted River," Ernest Hemingway strings sentences together without transitions to create a flat, emotionless prose style that reveals his character's alienation and fragility as he struggles to maintain control: "Now things were done. There had been this to do. Now it was done. It had been a hard trip. He was very tired. That was done. He had made his camp. He was settled. Nothing could touch him."

Use of language that places emphasis on the sounds and rhythm of words and sentences can also enrich a work of fiction. Consider the use of such techniques in the following sentence from James Joyce's "Araby" (p. 252).

> The light from the lamp opposite our door caught the white curve of her neck, lit up her hair that rested there and, falling, lit up the hand upon the railing.

Here the narrator is describing his first conversation with a girl who fascinates him, and the lush, lyrical, almost musical language reflects his enchantment. Note in particular the **alliteration** (light/lamp; caught/curve; hair/hand), the repetition (lit up/lit up), and the rhyme (lit up her *hair*/that rested *there*) and **near rhyme** (falling/railing); these poetic devices connect the words of the sentence into a smooth, rhythmic whole.

Another example of this emphasis on sound may be found in the measured **parallelism** of this sentence from Nathaniel Hawthorne's "The Birthmark" (p. 477):

> He had left his laboratory to the care of an assistant, cleared his fine countenance from the furnace smoke, washed the stain of acids from his fingers, and persuaded a beautiful woman to become his wife.

The style of the preceding sentence, conveying methodical precision and order, reflects the compulsive personality of the character being described.

The following passage from Alberto Alvaro Ríos's story "The Secret Lion" (p. 54) illustrates the power of creative language to enrich a story:

> We had read the books, after all; we knew about bridges and castles and wildtreacherousraging alligatormouth rivers. We wanted them. So we were going to go out and get them. We went back that morning into that kitchen and we said, "We're going out there, we're going into the hills, we're going away for three days, don't worry." She said, "All right."
>
> "You know," I said to Sergio, "if we're going to go away for three days, well, we ought to at least pack a lunch."
>
> But we were two young boys with no patience for what we thought at the time was mom-stuff: making sa-and-wiches. My mother didn't offer. So we got out little kid knapsacks that my mother had sewn for us, and into them we put the jar of mustard. A loaf of bread. Knivesforksplates, bottles of Coke, a can opener. This was lunch for the two of us. And we were weighed down, humped over to be strong enough to carry this stuff. But we started walking anyway, into the hills. We were going to eat berries and stuff otherwise. "Goodbye." My mom said that.

Through language, the adult narrator of the preceding paragraphs recaptures the bravado of the boys in search of "wildtreacherousraging alligatormouth rivers" even as he suggests to readers that the boys are not going far. The story's use of language is original and inventive: words are blended together ("getridofit," "knivesforksplates"), linked to form new language ("mom-stuff"), and drawn out ("sa-and-wiches") to mimic speech. These experiments with language show the narrator's willingness to move back into a child's frame of reference while maintaining the advantage of distance. The adult narrator uses sentence fragments ("A loaf of bread."), colloquialisms ("kid," "mom," "stuff"), and contractions. He also includes conversational elements such as *you know* and *well* in the dialogue, accurately re-creating the childhood scene at the same time he sees its folly and remains aware of the disillusionment that awaits him. Thus, the unique style permits the narrator to bring readers with him into the child's world even as he maintains his adult stance: "But we were two young boys with no patience for what we thought at the time was mom-stuff. . . ."

Although many stylistic options are available to writers, language must be consistent with the writer's purpose and with the effect he or she hopes to create. Just as writers may experiment with point of view or manipulate events to create a complex plot, so they can adjust language to suit a particular narrator or character or convey certain themes. In addition to the creative uses of language described above, writers also frequently experiment with *formal and informal diction*, *imagery*, and *figures of speech*.

FORMAL AND INFORMAL DICTION

The level of diction — how formal or informal a story's language is — can reveal a good deal about those who use the language.

Formal diction is characterized by elaborate, complex sentences; a learned vocabulary; and a serious, objective, detached tone. The speaker avoids contractions, shortened word forms (like *phone*), regional expressions, and slang, and he or she may use *one* or *we* in place of *I*. At its most extreme, formal language may be stiff and stilted, far removed from everyday speech.

Formal diction, whether used by a narrator or by a character, may indicate erudition, a high educational level, a superior social or professional position, or emotional detachment. When one character's language is significantly more formal than others', he or she may seem old-fashioned or stuffy; when language is inappropriately elevated or complex, it may reveal the character to be pompous or ridiculous; when a narrator's language is noticeably more formal than that of the characters, the narrator may seem superior or even condescending. Thus, level of diction conveys information about characters and about the narrator's attitude toward them.

The following passage from "The Birthmark" illustrates formal style:

> In the latter part of the last century there lived a man of science, an eminent proficient in every branch of natural philosophy, who not long before our story opens had made experience of a spiritual affinity more attractive than any chemical one. He had left his laboratory to the care of an assistant, cleared his fine countenance from the furnace smoke, washed the stain of acids from his fingers, and persuaded a beautiful woman to become his wife. In those days when the comparatively recent discovery of electricity and other kindred mysteries of Nature seemed to open paths into the region of miracle, it was not unusual for the love of science to rival the love of woman in its depth and absorbing energy. The higher intellect, the imagination, the spirit, and even the heart might all find their congenial ailment in pursuits which, as some of their ardent votaries believed, would ascend from one step of powerful intelligence to another, until the philosopher should lay his hand on the secret of creative force and perhaps make new worlds for himself.

The long, complex sentences, learned vocabulary ("countenance," "ailment," "votaries"), and absence of colloquialisms suit Hawthorne's purpose well, recreating the formal language of the earlier era in which his story is set. The omniscient narrator, despite his use of the first person in "our story," is aloof and controlled.

Informal diction, consistent with everyday speech, is characterized by slang, contractions, colloquial expressions like *you know* and *I mean*, shortened word forms, incomplete sentences, and a casual, conversational tone. A first-person narrator may use informal style, or characters may speak informally; in either case, informal style tends to narrow the distance between readers and text.

Informal language can range from the straightforward contemporary style of Cal's speech in Anne Tyler's "Teenage Wasteland" ("'I think this kid is hurting. You know?'") to the regionalisms and dialect used in Flannery O'Connor's "A Good Man Is Hard to Find" ("aloose"; "you all"; "britches"). In "Teenage Wasteland" (p. 535), Cal's self-consciously slangy, conversational style tells readers a good deal about his motives and his method of operating; in "A Good Man Is Hard to Find", speech patterns and diction help to identify the region in which the characters live and their social class. In other stories, a character's use of obscenities may suggest his or her crudeness or adolescent bravado, and use of racial or ethnic slurs suggests that a character is insensitive and bigoted.

The following passage from John Updike's "A&P" (p. 115) illustrates informal style:

> She had sort of oaky hair that the sun and salt had bleached, done up in a bun that was unravelling, and a kind of prim face. Walking into the A&P with your straps down, I suppose it's the only kind of face you *can* have. She held her head so high her neck, coming out of those white shoulders, looked kind of stretched, but I didn't mind. The longer her neck was, the more of her there was.

Here, the first-person narrator uses a conversational style, including colloquialisms ("sort of," "I suppose," "kind of"), contractions ("it's," "didn't"), and the imprecise, informal *you* ("Walking into the A&P with *your* straps down . . . ."). The narrator uses neither elaborate syntax nor a learned vocabulary.

IMAGERY

Imagery — words and phrases that describe what is seen, heard, smelled, tasted, or touched — can have a significant impact in a story. A writer may use a pattern of repeated imagery to convey a particular impression about a character or situation or to communicate or reinforce a story's theme. For example, the theme of newly discovered sexuality can be conveyed through repeated use of words and phrases suggesting blooming or ripening.

In T. Coraghessan Boyle's "Greasy Lake" (p. 441), the narrator's vivid description of Greasy Lake itself uses rich visual imagery to evoke a scene:

> Through the center of town, up the strip, past the housing developments and shopping malls, street lights giving way to the thin streaming illumination of the headlights, trees crowding the asphalt in a black unbroken wall: that was the way out to Greasy Lake. The Indians had called it Wakan, a reference to the clarity of its waters. Now it was fetid and murky, the mud banks glittering with broken glass and strewn with beer cans and the charred remains of bonfires. There was a single ravaged island a hundred yards from shore, so stripped of vegetation it looked as if the air force had strafed it. We went up to the lake because everyone went there, because we wanted to snuff the rich scent of possibility on the breeze, watch a girl take off her clothes and plunge into the festering murk, drink beer, smoke pot, howl at the stars, savor the incongruous full-throated roar of rock and roll against the primeval susurrus of frogs and crickets. This was nature.

By characterizing a natural setting with surprising words like "fetid," "murky," and "greasy" and unpleasant images such as the "glittering of broken glass," the "ravaged island," and the "charred remains of bonfires," Boyle creates a picture that is completely at odds with a traditional pastoral view of nature. The incongruous images are nevertheless perfectly consistent with the sordid events that take place at Greasy Lake.

FIGURES OF SPEECH

Figures of speech— such as *similes*, *metaphors*, and *personification*— can enrich a story, subtly revealing information about characters and themes.

By using **metaphors** and **similes**—figures of speech that compare two dissimilar items — writers can indicate a particular attitude toward characters and events. Thus, Flannery O'Connor's many grotesque similes in "A Good Man Is Hard to Find" help to dehumanize her characters; the children's mother, for instance, has a face "as broad and innocent as a cabbage." In Tillie Olsen's "I Stand Here Ironing" (p. 187), an extended metaphor in which a mother compares her daughter to a dress waiting to be ironed expresses the mother's attitude toward her daughter, effectively suggesting to readers the daughter's vulnerability. Similes and metaphors are used throughout in Kate Chopin's "The Storm." In a scene of sexual awakening, Calixta's skin is "like a creamy lily," her passion is "like a white flame," and her mouth is "a fountain of delight"; these figures of speech add a lushness and sensuality to the story.

Personification— a figure of speech, closely related to metaphor, that endows inanimate objects or abstract ideas with life or with human characteristics — is used in "Araby" (p. 252), where houses, "conscious of decent lives within them, gazed at one another with brown imperturbable faces." This use of figurative language expands readers' vision of the story's setting and gives a dreamlike quality to the passage. (Other figures of speech, such as **hyperbole** and **understatement,** can also enrich works of fiction. See Chapter 20, "Figures of Speech," for further information.)

Allusions— references to familiar historical or literary personages or events — may also expand readers' understanding and appreciation of a work. An allusion widens a work's context by bringing it into the context of a related subject or idea. For instance, Wole Soyinka's frequent references to political figures and events in "Future Plans" (p. 778) enable readers who recognize the references to gain a deeper understanding of the speaker's position on various political and social issues. Literary and biblical allusions may be used in much the same way.

A FINAL NOTE

In analyzing the use of language in a work of fiction, you may occasionally encounter obscure allusions, foreign words and phrases, unusual comparisons, and unfamiliar regional expressions — particularly in works treating cultures and historical periods other than your own. Frequently, such language will be clarified by the context, or by explanatory notes in your text. When it is not, you should consult a dictionary, encyclopedia, or other reference work.

CHECKLIST   **WRITING ABOUT STYLE, TONE, AND LANGUAGE**

✓ Does the writer make any unusual creative use of word choice, word order, or sentence structure?

✓ Is the story's tone intimate? Distant? Ironic? How does the tone advance the writer's purpose?

✓ Does the style emphasize the sound and rhythm of language? For example, does the writer use alliteration and assonance? Repetition and parallelism? What do such techniques add to the story?

✓ Is the level of diction generally formal, informal, or somewhere in between?

✓ Is there a difference between the style of the narrator and the style of the characters' speech? If so, what is the effect of this difference?

✓ Do any of the story's characters use regionalisms, colloquial language, or nonstandard speech? If so, what effect does this language have?

✓ What do different characters' levels of diction reveal about them?

✓ What kind of imagery predominates? Where, and why, is imagery used?

✓ Does the story develop a pattern of imagery? How does this pattern of imagery relate to the story's themes?

✓ Does the story use simile and metaphor? Personification? What is the effect of these figures of speech?

✓ Do figures of speech reinforce the story's themes? Reveal information about characters?

✓ Does the story make any historical, literary, or biblical allusions? What do these allusions contribute to the story?

✓ What unfamiliar, obscure, or foreign words, phrases, or images are used in the story? What is the effect of these words or expressions?

JAMES JOYCE (1884–1941) was born in Dublin but lived his entire adult life in self-imposed exile from his native Ireland. Though his parents sent him to schools that trained young men for the priesthood, Joyce saw himself as a religious and artistic rebel and fled to Paris soon after graduation in 1902. Recalled briefly to Dublin by his mother's fatal illness, Joyce returned to the Continent in 1904, taking with him an uneducated Irish country girl named Nora Barnacle, who became his wife in 1931. In dreary quarters in Trieste, Zurich, and Paris, Joyce struggled to support a growing family, sometimes teaching classes in Berlitz language schools.

Though Joyce never again lived in Ireland, he continued to write about Dublin. Publication of *Dubliners* (1914), a collection of short stories that included "Araby," was delayed for seven years because the Irish publisher feared libel suits from local citizens who were thinly disguised as characters in the stories. Joyce's autobiographical *Portrait of the Artist as a Young Man* (1916) tells of a young writer's rejection of family, church, and country. *Ulysses* (1922), the comic tale of eighteen hours in the life of a wandering Dublin advertising salesman, was banned when the U.S. Post Office brought charges of obscenity against the book, and it remained banned in the United States and England for more than a decade. In *Ulysses*, Joyce begins a revolutionary journey away from traditional techniques of plot and characterization to the interior monologues and stream-of-consciousness style that mark his last great novel, *Finnegans Wake* (1939).

Cultural Context: In the years between the Great Famine of the 1840s and World War I, Ireland experienced a severe decline in living standards, and the resulting emigration led to a reduction in population by almost one third. It is against the background of these harsh economic conditions that Joyce juxtaposes a young boy's idealism with the bleakness of his day-to-day life in "Araby."

Araby (1914)

North Richmond Street, being blind,° was a quiet street except at the hour when the Christian Brothers' School set the boys free. An uninhabited house of two storeys stood at the blind end, detached from its neighbours in a square ground. The other houses of the street, conscious of decent lives within them, gazed at one another with brown imperturbable faces.

The former tenant of our house, a priest, had died in the back drawing-room. Air, musty from having been long enclosed, hung in all the rooms, and the waste room behind the kitchen was littered with old useless papers. Among these I found a few paper-covered books, the pages of which were curled and damp: *The Abbot,* by Walter Scott, *The Devout Communicant* and *The Memoirs of Vidocq.*° I liked the last best because its leaves were yellow. The wild garden behind the house contained a central apple-tree and a few straggling bushes under one of which I found the late tenant's rusty bicycle-pump. He had been a very charitable priest; in his will he had left all his money to institutions and the furniture of his house to his sister.

When the short days of winter came dusk fell before we had well eaten our dinners. When we met in the street the houses had grown sombre. The space of sky above us was the colour of ever-changing violet and towards it the lamps of

---

blind: Dead-end.

The Abbot . . . Vidocq: Sir Walter Scott (1771–1832)— an English Romantic novelist; *The Devout Communicant*— a variant title for *Pious Meditations,* written by an eighteenth-century English Franciscan friar, Pacifus Baker; *The Memoirs of Vidocq*— an autobiography of François-Jules Vidocq (1775–1857), a French soldier of fortune turned police agent.

the street lifted their feeble lanterns. The cold air stung us and we played till our bodies glowed. Our shouts echoed in the silent street. The career of our play brought us through the dark muddy lanes behind the houses where we ran the gauntlet of the rough tribes from the cottages, to the back doors of the dark dripping gardens where odours arose from the ashpits, to the dark odorous stables where a coach-man smoothed and combed the horse or shook music from the buckled harness. When we returned to the street light from the kitchen windows had filled the areas. If my uncle was seen turning the corner we hid in the shadow until we had seen him safely housed. Or if Mangan's sister came out on the doorstep to call her brother in to his tea we watched her from our shadow peer up and down the street. We waited to see whether she would remain or go in and, if she remained, we left our shadow and walked up to Mangan's steps resignedly. She was waiting for us, her figure defined by the light from the half-opened door. Her brother always teased her before he obeyed and I stood by the railings looking at her. Her dress swung as she moved her body and the soft rope of her hair tossed from side to side.

Every morning I lay on the floor in the front parlour watching her door. The blind was pulled down to within an inch of the sash so that I could not be seen. When she came out on the doorstep my heart leaped. I ran to the hall, seized my books and followed her. I kept her brown figure always in my eye and, when we came near the point at which our ways diverged, I quickened my pace and passed her. This happened morning after morning. I had never spoken to her, except for a few casual words, and yet her name was like a summons to all my foolish blood.

Her image accompanied me even in places the most hostile to romance. On 5 Saturday evenings when my aunt went marketing I had to go to carry some of the parcels. We walked through the flaring streets, jostled by drunken men and bargaining women, amid the curses of labourers, the shrill litanies of shop-boys who stood on guard by the barrels of pigs' cheeks, the nasal chanting of street-singers, who sang a *come-all-you* about O'Donovan Rossa,° or a ballad about the troubles in our native land. These noises converged in a single sensation of life for me: I imagined that I bore my chalice safely through a throng of foes. Her name sprang to my lips at moments in strange prayers and praises which I myself did not understand. My eyes were often full of tears (I could not tell why) and at times a flood from my heart seemed to pour itself out into my bosom. I thought little of the future. I did not know whether I would ever speak to her or not or, if I spoke to her, how I could tell her of my confused adoration. But my body was like a harp and her words and gestures were like fingers running upon the wires.

One evening I went into the back drawing-room in which the priest had died. It was a dark rainy evening and there was no sound in the house. Through one of the broken panes I heard the rain impinge upon the earth, the fine incessant needles of water playing in the sodden beds. Some distant lamp or lighted window gleamed below me. I was thankful that I could see so little. All my senses

---

O'Donovan Rossa: Any popular song beginning "Come all you gallant Irishmen . . ."; O'Donovan Rossa was an Irish nationalist who was banished in 1870 for advocating violent rebellion against the British.

seemed to desire to veil themselves and, feeling that I was about to slip from them, I pressed the palms of my hands together until they trembled, murmuring: "*O love! O love!*" many times.

At last she spoke to me. When she addressed the first words to me I was so confused that I did not know what to answer. She asked me was I going to *Araby*. I forgot whether I answered yes or no. It would be a splendid bazaar, she said she would love to go.

"And why can't you?" I asked.

While she spoke she turned a silver bracelet round and round her wrist. She could not go, she said, because there would be a retreat that week in her convent.° Her brother and two other boys were fighting for their caps and I was alone at the railings. She held one of the spikes, bowing her head towards me. The light from the lamp opposite our door caught the white curve of her neck, lit up her hair that rested there and, falling, lit up the hand upon the railing. It fell over one side of her dress and caught the white border of a petticoat, just visible as she stood at ease.

10   "It's well for you," she said.

"If I go," I said, "I will bring you something."

What innumerable follies laid waste my waking and sleeping thoughts after that evening! I wished to annihilate the tedious intervening days. I chafed against the work of school. At night in my bedroom and by day in the classroom her image came between me and the page I strove to read. The syllables of the word *Araby* were called to me through the silence in which my soul luxuriated and cast an Eastern enchantment over me. I asked for leave to go to the bazaar on Saturday night. My aunt was surprised and hoped it was not some Freemason° affair. I answered few questions in class. I watched my master's face pass from amiability to sternness; he hoped I was not beginning to idle. I could not call my wandering thoughts together. I had hardly any patience with the serious work of life which, now that it stood between me and my desire, seemed to me child's play, ugly monotonous child's play.

On Saturday morning I reminded my uncle that I wished to go to the bazaar in the evening. He was fussing at the hallstand, looking for the hatbrush, and answered me curtly:

"Yes, boy, I know."

15   As he was in the hall I could not go into the front parlour and lie at the window. I left the house in bad humour and walked slowly towards the school. The air was pitilessly raw and already my heart misgave me.

When I came home to dinner my uncle had not yet been home. Still it was early. I sat staring at the clock for some time and, when its ticking began to irritate me, I left the room. I mounted the staircase and gained the upper part of the house. The high cold empty gloomy rooms liberated me and I went from room to

---

convent: Her convent school.

Freemason: At the time the story takes place, many Catholics in Ireland thought the Masonic Order was a threat to the church.

room singing. From the front window I saw my companions playing below in the street. Their cries reached me weakened and indistinct and, leaning my forehead against the cool glass, I looked over at the dark house where she lived. I may have stood there for an hour, seeing nothing but the brown-clad figure cast by my imagination, touched discreetly by the lamplight at the curved neck, at the hand upon the railings and at the border below the dress.

When I came downstairs again I found Mrs. Mercer sitting at the fire. She was an old garrulous woman, a pawnbroker's widow, who collected used stamps for some pious purpose. I had to endure the gossip of the tea-table. The meal was prolonged beyond an hour and still my uncle did not come. Mrs. Mercer stood up to go: she was sorry she couldn't wait any longer, but it was after eight o'clock and she did not like to be out late, as the night air was bad for her. When she had gone I began to walk up and down the room, clenching my fists. My aunt said:

"I'm afraid you may put off your bazaar for this night of Our Lord."

At nine o'clock I heard my uncle's latchkey in the halldoor. I heard him talking to himself and heard the hallstand rocking when it had received the weight of his overcoat. I could interpret these signs. When he was midway through his dinner I asked him to give me the money to go to the bazaar. He had forgotten.

"The people are in bed and after their first sleep now," he said.   20

I did not smile. My aunt said to him energetically:

"Can't you give him the money and let him go? You've kept him late enough as it is."

My uncle said he was very sorry he had forgotten. He said he believed in the old saying: "All work and no play makes Jack a dull boy." He asked me where I was going and, when I had told him a second time he asked me did I know *The Arab's Farewell to his Steed.*° When I left the kitchen he was about to recite the opening lines of the piece to my aunt.

I held a florin tightly in my hand as I strode down Buckingham Street towards the station. The sight of the streets thronged with buyers and glaring with gas recalled to me the purpose of my journey. I took my seat in a third-class carriage of a deserted train. After an intolerable delay the train moved out of the station slowly. It crept onward among ruinous houses and over the twinkling river. At Westland Row Station a crowd of people pressed to the carriage doors; but the porters moved them back, saying that it was a special train for the bazaar. I remained alone in the bare carriage. In a few minutes the train drew up beside an improvised wooden platform. I passed out on to the road and saw by the lighted dial of a clock that it was ten minutes to ten. In front of me was a large building which displayed the magical name.

I could not find any sixpenny entrance and, fearing that the bazaar would   25
be closed, I passed in quickly through a turnstile, handing a shilling to a weary-looking man. I found myself in a big hall girdled at half its height by a gallery. Nearly all the stalls were closed and the greater part of the hall was in darkness.

The Arab's Farewell of his Steed: A sentimental poem by Caroline Norton (1808–1877) that tells the story of a nomad's heartbreak after selling his much-loved horse.

I recognised a silence like that which pervades a church after a service. I walked into the centre of the bazaar timidly. A few people were gathered about the stalls which were still open. Before a curtain, over which the words *Café Chantant*° were written in coloured lamps, two men were counting money on a salver. I listened to the fall of the coins.

Remembering with difficulty why I had come I went over to one of the stalls and examined porcelain vases and flowered tea-sets. At the door of the stall a young lady was talking and laughing with two young gentlemen. I remarked their English accents and listened vaguely to their conversation.

"O, I never said such a thing!"

"O, but you did!"

"O, but I didn't!"

30   "Didn't she say that?"

"Yes. I heard her."

"O, there's a . . . fib!"

Observing me the young lady came over and asked me did I wish to buy anything. The tone of her voice was not encouraging; she seemed to have spoken to me out of a sense of duty. I looked humbly at the great jars that stood like eastern guards at either side of the dark entrance to the stall and murmured:

"No, thank you."

35   The young lady changed the position of one of the vases and went back to the two young men. They began to talk of the same subject. Once or twice the young lady glanced at me over her shoulder.

I lingered before her stall, though I knew my stay was useless, to make my interest in her wares seem the more real. Then I turned away slowly and walked down the middle of the bazaar. I allowed the two pennies to fall against the sixpence in my pocket. I heard a voice call from one end of the gallery that the light was out. The upper part of the hall was now completely dark.

Gazing up into the darkness I saw myself as a creature driven and derided by vanity; and my eyes burned with anguish and anger.

Reading and Reacting

1. How would you characterize the story's level of diction? Is this level appropriate for a story about a young boy's experiences? Explain.

2. Identify several figures of speech in the story. Where is Joyce most likely to use this kind of language? Why?

3. What words and phrases express the boy's extreme idealism and romantic view of the world? In what way does such language help to communicate the story's major theme?

4. In paragraph 4, the narrator says, "her name was like a summons to all my foolish blood." In the story's last sentence, he sees himself as "a creature driven and derided by vanity." What other expressions does he use to describe his feelings? How would you characterize these feelings?

Café Chantant: A Paris café featuring musical entertainment.

5. How does word choice illustrate the contrast between the narrator's day-to-day life and the exotic promise of the bazaar?

6. What does each of the italicized words suggest: "We walked through the *flaring* streets" (par. 5); "I heard the rain *impinge* upon the earth" (par. 6); "I *chafed* against the work of school" (par. 12); "I found myself in a big hall *girdled* at half its height by a gallery" (par. 25)? What other examples of unusual word choice can you identify in the story?

7. What is it about the events in this story that causes the narrator to remember them years later?

8. Identify words and phrases in the story that are associated with religion. What purpose do these references to religion serve?

9. JOURNAL ENTRY Rewrite a brief passage from this story in the voice of the young boy. Use informal style, simple figures of speech, and vocabulary appropriate for a child.

10. CRITICAL PERSPECTIVE In *Notes on the American Short Story Today*, Richard Kostelanetz discusses the **epiphany**, one of Joyce's most significant contributions to literature:

> In Joyce's pervasively influential theory of the short story we remember, the fiction turned upon an epiphany, a moment of revelation in which, in [critic] Harry Levin's words, "amid the most encumbered circumstances it suddenly happens that the veil is lifted, the . . . mystery laid bare, and the ultimate secret of things made manifest." The epiphany, then, became a technique for jelling the narrative and locking the story's import into place. . . . What made this method revolutionary was the shifting of the focal point of the story from its end . . . to a spot within the body of the text, usually near (but not at) the end.

Where in "Araby" does the story's epiphany occur? Does it do all that Kostelanetz believes an epiphany should do? Or do you think that, at least in the case of "Araby," the epiphany may not be as significant a force as Kostelanetz suggests?

Related Works: "The Secret Lion" (p. 54), "A&P" (p. 115), "Gryphon" (p. 126), "Doe Season" (p. 336), "Shall I compare thee to a summer's day?" (p. 679)

ANDREA BARRETT (1954–   ) was in her thirties when she made the decision to dedicate her life to fiction. Since then, she has authored five novels and two collections of short stories. Her work has been praised for its sensitive and imaginative treatment of science and natural history, and particularly for its fictional portrayal of scientists. Barrett's attraction to science may be traced back to her college career: she received a BS in biology (1976) from Union College in Schenectady, New York. Her novels are *Lucid Stars* (1988), *Secret Harmonies* (1989), *The Middle Kingdom* (1991), *The Forms of Water* (1993), and *The Voyage of the Narwhal* (1998); for her collection of short stories *Ship Fever* (1996), she won the 1996 National Book Award for fiction. She has been the recipient of a National Endowment for the Arts Fellowship (1992), a Guggenheim Fellowship (1997), and a MacArthur Fellowship (2001). Her work has been published in anthologies and in numerous periodicals such as *Salmagundi, Prairie Schooner,* and *The Southern Review.*

Barrett currently lives in Rochester, New York, and teaches part-time in the MFA Program for Writers at Warren Wilson College in Swannanoa, North Carolina. Her most recent book is *Servants of the Map* (2002), a collection of stories.

> **Cultural Context:** According to the 2002 United States census, fifty percent of first marriages in the United States end in divorce. Most of these divorces occur in first marriages between men and women under the age of forty-five. Common reasons for divorce include poor communication, financial problems, lack of commitment to the marriage, a dramatic change in priorities, and infidelity — said to occur in fifty to sixty percent of marriages for both men and women, according to one study. Over half of second marriages also end in divorce.

The Littoral° Zone   (1996)

When they met, fifteen years ago, Jonathan had a job teaching botany at a small college near Albany, and Ruby was teaching invertebrate zoology at a college in the Berkshires. Both of them, along with an ornithologist, an ichthyologist, and an oceanographer, had agreed to spend three weeks of their summer break at a marine biology research station on an island off the New Hampshire coast. They had spouses, children, mortgages, bills; they went, they later told each other, because the pay was too good to refuse. Two-thirds of the way through the course, they agreed that the pay was not enough.

How they reached that first agreement is a story they've repeated to each other again and again and told, separately, to their closest friends. Ruby thinks they had this conversation on the second Friday of the course, after Frank Kenary's slide show on the abyssal fish and before Carol Dagliesh's lecture on the courting behavior of herring gulls. Jonathan maintains that they had it earlier — that Wednesday, maybe, when they were still recovering from Gunnar Erickson's trawling expedition. The days before they became so aware of each other have blurred in their minds, but they agree that their first real conversation took place on the afternoon devoted to the littoral zone.

The tide was all the way out. The students were clumped on the rocky, pitted apron between the water and the ledges, peering into the tidal pools and listing the species they found. Gunnar was in the equipment room, repairing one of the sampling claws. Frank was setting up dissections in the tiny lab; Carol had gone back to the mainland on the supply boat, hoping to replace the camera one of the students had dropped. And so the two of them, Jonathan and Ruby, were left alone for a little while.

They both remember the granite ledge where they sat, and the raucous quarrels of the nesting gulls. They agree that Ruby was scratching furiously at her calves and that Jonathan said, "Take it easy, okay? You'll draw blood."

Littoral: Of or existing on a shore.

Her calves were slim and tan, Jonathan remembers. Covered with blotches 5
and scrapes.

I folded my fingers, Ruby remembers. Then I blushed. My throat felt
sunburned.

Ruby said, "I know, it's so embarrassing. But all this salt on my poison ivy —
God, what I wouldn't give for a bath! They never told me there wouldn't be any
water here. . . ."

Jonathan gestured at the ocean surrounding them and then they started laughing. *Hysteria,* they have told each other since. They were so tired by then, twelve
days into the course, and so dirty and overworked and strained by pretending to
the students that these things didn't matter, that neither of them could understand
that they were also lonely. Their shared laughter felt like pure relief.

"No water?" Jonathan said. "I haven't been dry since we got here. My clothes
are damp, my sneakers are damp, my hair never dries. . . ."

His hair was beautiful, Ruby remembers. Thick, a little too long. Part blond 10
and part brown.

"I know," she said. "But you know what I mean. I didn't realize they'd have to
bring our drinking water over on a boat."

"Or that they'd expect us to wash in the ocean," Jonathan said. Her forearms
were dusted with salt, he remembers. The down along them sparkled in the sun.

"And those cots," Ruby said. "Does yours have a sag in it like a hammock?"

"Like a slingshot," Jonathan said.

For half an hour they sat on their ledge and compared their bubbling patches 15
of poison ivy and the barnacle wounds that scored their hands and feet. Nothing
healed out here, they told each other. Everything got infected. When one of the
students called, "Look what I found!" Jonathan rose and held his hand out to
Ruby. She took it easily and hauled herself up and they walked down to the water together. Jonathan's hand was thick and blunt-fingered, with nails bitten down
so far that the skin around them was raw. Odd, Ruby remembers thinking. Those
bitten stumps attached to such a good-looking man.

They have always agreed that the worst moment, for each of them, was when
they stepped from the boat to the dock on the final day of the course and saw
their families waiting in the parking lot. Jonathan's wife had their four-year-old
daughter balanced on her shoulders. Their two older children were leaning per-
ilously over the guardrails and shrieking at the sight of him. Jessie had turned
nine in Jonathan's absence, and Jonathan can't think of her eager face without
remembering the starfish he brought as his sole, guilty gift.

Ruby's husband had parked their car just a few yards from Jonathan's family. Her
sons were wearing baseball caps, and what Ruby remembers is the way the yellow
linings lit their faces. For a minute she saw the children squealing near her sons as
faceless, inconsequential; Jonathan later told her that her children had been similarly blurred for him. Then Jonathan said, "That's my family, there," and Ruby said,
"That's mine, right next to yours," and all the faces leapt into focus for both of them.

Nothing that was to come — not the days in court, nor the days they moved,
nor the losses of jobs and homes — would ever seem so awful to them as that

moment when they first saw their families standing there, unaware and hopeful. Deceitfully, treacherously, Ruby and Jonathan separated and walked to the people awaiting them. They didn't introduce each other to their spouses. They didn't look at each other — although, they later admitted, they cast covert looks at each other's families. They thought they were invisible, that no one could see what had happened between them. They thought their families would not remember how they had stepped off the boat and stood, for an instant, together.

On that boat, sitting dumb and miserable in the litter of nets and equipment, they had each pretended to be resigned to going home. Each foresaw (or so they later told each other) the hysterical phone calls and the frenzied, secret meetings. Neither foresaw how much the sight of each other's family would hurt. "Sweetie," Jonathan remembers Ruby's husband saying. "You've lost so much weight." Ruby remembers staring over her husband's shoulder and watching Jessie butt her head like a dog under Jonathan's hand.

20   For the first twelve days on the island, Jonathan and Ruby were so busy that they hardly noticed each other. For the next few days, after their conversation on the ledge, they sat near each other during faculty lectures and student presentations. These were held in the library, a ramshackle building separated from the bunkhouse and the dining hall by a stretch of wild roses and poison ivy.

Jonathan had talked about algae in there, holding up samples of *Fucus* and *Hildenbrandtia.*° Ruby had talked about the littoral zone, that space between high and low watermarks where organisms struggled to adapt to the daily rhythm of immersion and exposure. They had drawn on the blackboard in colored chalk while the students, itchy and hot and tired, scratched their arms and legs and feigned attention.

Neither of them, they admitted much later, had focused fully on the other's lecture. "It was *before*," Ruby has said ruefully. "I didn't know that I was going to want to have listened." And Jonathan has laughed and confessed that he was studying the shells and skulls on the walls while Ruby was drawing on the board.

The library was exceedingly hot, they agreed, and the chairs remarkably uncomfortable; the only good spot was the sofa in front of the fireplace. That was the spot they commandeered on the evening after their first conversation, when dinner led to a walk and then the walk led them into the library a few minutes before the scheduled lecture.

Erika Moorhead, Ruby remembers. Talking about the tensile strength of byssus threads.°

25   Walter Schank, Jonathan remembers. Something to do with hydrozoans.°

They both remember feeling comfortable for the first time since their arrival. And for the next few days — three by Ruby's accounting; four by Jonathan's — one of them came early for every lecture and saved a seat on the sofa for the other.

They giggled at Frank Kenary's slides, which he'd arranged like a creepy fashion show: abyssal fish sporting varied blobs of luminescent flesh. When Gunnar

---

Fucus and Hildenbrandtia: Types of seaweed.

byssus threads: Strong threads some shellfish use to fasten themselves to rocks.

hydrozoans: A class of jellyfish.

talked for two hours about subduction zones and the calcium carbonate cycle, they amused themselves exchanging doodles. They can't remember, now, whether Gunnar's endless lecture came before Carol Dagliesh's filmstrip on the herring gulls, or which of the students tipped over the dissecting scope and sent the dish of copepods° to their deaths. But both of them remember those days and nights as being almost purely happy. They swam in that odd, indefinite zone where they were more than friends, not yet lovers, still able to deny to themselves that they were headed where they were headed.

Ruby made the first phone call, a week after they left the island. At eleven o'clock on a Sunday night, she told her husband she'd left something in her office that she needed to prepare the next day's class. She drove to campus, unlocked her door, picked up the phone and called Jonathan at his house. One of his children—Jessie, she thinks—answered the phone. Ruby remembers how, even through the turmoil of her emotions, she'd been shocked at the idea of a child staying up so late.

There was a horrible moment while Jessie went to find her father; another when Jonathan, hearing Ruby's voice, said, "Wait, hang on, I'll just be a minute," and then negotiated Jessie into bed. Ruby waited, dreading his anger, knowing she'd been wrong to call him at home. But Jonathan, when he finally returned, said, "Ruby. You got my letter."

"What letter?" she asked. He wrote to tell me good-bye, she remembers   30
thinking.

"My *letter*," he said. "I wrote you, I have to see you. I can't stand this."

Ruby released the breath she hadn't known she was holding.

"You didn't get it?" he said. "You just called?" It wasn't only me, he remembers thinking. She feels it too.

"I had to hear your voice," she said.

Ruby called, but Jonathan wrote. And so when Jonathan's youngest daughter,   35
Cora, later fell in love and confided in Ruby, and then asked her, "Was it like this with you two? Who started it — you or Dad?" all Ruby could say was, "It happened to both of us."

Sometimes, when Ruby and Jonathan sit on the patio looking out at the hills above Palmyra, they will turn and see their children watching them through the kitchen window. Before the children went off to college, the house bulged with them on weekends and holidays and seemed empty in between; Jonathan's wife had custody of Jessie and Gordon and Cora, and Ruby's husband took her sons, Mickey and Ryan, when he remarried. Now that the children are old enough to come and go as they please, the house is silent almost all the time.

Jessie is twenty-four, and Gordon is twenty-two; Mickey is twenty-one, and Cora and Ryan are both nineteen. When they visit Jonathan and Ruby they spend an unhealthy amount of time talking about their past. In their conversations they seem to split their lives into three epochs: the years when what they think of as

---

copepods: A class of tiny crustaceans that make up plankton.

their real families were whole; the years right after Jonathan and Ruby met, when their parents were coming and going, fighting and making up, separating and divorcing; and the years since Jonathan and Ruby's marriage, when they were forced into a reconstituted family. Which epoch they decide to explore depends on who's visiting and who's getting along with whom.

"But we were happy," Mickey may say to Ruby, if he and Ryan are visiting and Jonathan's children are absent. "We were, we were fine."

"It wasn't like you and Mom ever fought," Cora may say to Jonathan, if Ruby's sons aren't around. "You could have worked it out if you'd tried."

40　　When they are all together, they tend to avoid the first two epochs and to talk about their first strained weekends and holidays together. They've learned to tolerate each other, despite their forced introductions; Cora and Ryan, whose birthdays are less than three months apart, seem especially close. Ruby and Jonathan know that much of what draws their youngest children together is shared speculation about what happened on that island.

They look old to their children, they know. Both of them are nearing fifty. Jonathan has grown quite heavy and has lost much of his hair; Ruby's fine-boned figure has gone gaunt and stringy. They know their children can't imagine them young and strong and wrung by passion. The children can't think — can't stand to think — about what happened on the island, but they can't stop themselves from asking questions.

"Did you have other girlfriends?" Cora asks Jonathan. "Were you so unhappy with Mom?"

"Did you know him before?" Ryan asks Ruby. "Did you go there to be with him?"

"We met there," Jonathan and Ruby say. "We had never seen each other before. We fell in love." That is all they will say, they never give details, they say "yes" or "no" to the easy questions and evade the hard ones. They worry that even the little they offer may be too much.

45　　Jonathan and Ruby tell each other the stories of their talk by the tidal pool, their walks and meals, the sagging sofa, the moment in the parking lot, and the evening Ruby made her call. They tell these to console themselves when their children chide them or when, alone in the house, they sit quietly near each other and struggle to conceal their disappointments.

Of course they have expected some of these. Mickey and Gordon have both had trouble in school, and Jessie has grown much too close to her mother; neither Jonathan nor Ruby has found jobs as good as the ones they lost, and their new home in Palmyra still doesn't feel quite like home. But all they have lost in order to be together would seem bearable had they continued to feel the way they felt on the island.

They're sensible people, and very well-mannered; they remind themselves that they were young then and are middle-aged now, and that their fierce attraction would naturally ebb with time. Neither likes to think about how much of the thrill of their early days together came from the obstacles they had to overcome. Some days, when Ruby pulls into the driveway still thinking about her last class and catches sight of Jonathan out in the garden, she can't believe the heavyset figure pruning shrubs so meticulously is the man for whom she fought such battles. Jonathan, who often wakes very early, sometimes stares at Ruby's sleeping face and thinks how much more gracefully his ex-wife is aging.

They never reproach each other. When the tension builds in the house and the silence becomes overwhelming, one or the other will say, "Do you remember . . . ?" and then launch into one of the myths on which they have founded their lives. But there is one story they never tell each other, because they can't bear to talk about what they have lost. This is the one about the evening that has shaped their life together.

Jonathan's hand on Ruby's back, Ruby's hand on Jonathan's thigh, a shirt unbuttoned, a belt undone. They never mention this moment, or the moments that followed it, because that would mean discussing who seduced whom, and any resolution of that would mean assigning blame. Guilt they can handle; they've been living with guilt for fifteen years. But blame? It would be more than either of them could bear, to know the exact moment when one of them precipitated all that has happened to them. The most either of them has ever said is, "How could we have known?"

But the night in the library is what they both think about, when they lie silently   50
next to each other and listen to the wind. It must be summer for them to think about it; the children must be with their other parents and the rain must be falling on the cedar shingles overhead. A candle must be burning on the mantel above the bed and the maple branches outside their window must be tossing against each other. Then they think of the story they know so well and never say out loud.

There was a huge storm three nights before they left the island, the tail end of a hurricane passing farther out to sea. The cedar trees creaked and swayed in the wind beyond the library windows. The students had staggered off to bed, after the visitor from Woods Hole had finished his lecture on the explorations of the *Alvin* in the Cayman Trough, and Frank and Gunnar and Carol had shrouded themselves in their rain gear and left as well, sheltering the visitor between them. Ruby sat at one end of the long table, preparing bottles of fixative° for their expedition the following morning, and Jonathan lay on the sofa writing notes. The boat was leaving just after dawn and they knew they ought to go to bed.

The wind picked up outside, sweeping the branches against the walls. The windows rattled. Jonathan shivered and said, "Do you suppose we could get a fire going in that old fireplace?"

"I bet we could," said Ruby, which gave both of them the pretext they needed to crouch side by side on the cracked tiles, brushing elbows as they opened the flue and crumpled paper and laid kindling in the form of a grid. The logs Jonathan found near the lobster traps were dry and the fire caught quickly.

Who found the green candle in the drawer below the microscope? Who lit the candle and turned off the lights? And who found the remains of the jug of wine that Frank had brought in honor of the visitor? They sat there side by side, poking at the burning logs and pretending they weren't doing what they were do-

---

fixative: A solution used to preserve fresh tissue so it can be examined under a microscope.

ing. The wind pushed through the window they'd opened a crack, and the tan window shade lifted and then fell back against the frame. The noise was soothing at first; later it seemed irritating.

55   Jonathan, whose fingernails were bitten to the quick, admired the long nail on Ruby's right little finger and then said, half-seriously, how much he'd love to bite a nail like that. When Ruby held her hand to his mouth he took the nail between his teeth and nibbled through the white tip, which days in the water had softened. Ruby slipped her other hand inside his shirt and ran it up his back. Jonathan ran his mouth up her arm and down her neck.

    They started in front of the fire and worked their way across the floor, breaking a glass, knocking the table askew. Ruby rubbed her back raw against the rug and Jonathan scraped his knees, and twice they paused and laughed at their wild excesses. They moved across the floor from east to west and later from west to east, and between those two journeys, during the time when they heaped their clothes and the sofa cushions into a nest in front of the fire, they talked.

    This was not the kind of conversation they'd had during walks and meals since that first time on the rocks: who they were, where they'd come from, how they'd made it here. This was the talk where they instinctively edited out the daily pleasures of their lives on the mainland and spliced together the hard times, the dark times, until they'd constructed versions of themselves that could make sense of what they'd just done.

    For months after this, as they lay in stolen, secret rooms between houses and divorces and jobs and lives, Jonathan would tell Ruby that he swallowed her nail. The nail dissolved in his stomach, he'd say. It passed into his villi° and out to his blood and then flowed to bone and muscle and nerve, where the molecules that had once been part of her became part of him. Ruby, who always seemed to know more acutely than Jonathan that they'd have to leave whatever room this was in an hour or a day, would argue with him.

    "Nails are keratin," she'd tell him. "Like hooves and hair. Like wool. We can't digest wool."

60   "Moths can," Jonathan would tell her. "Moths eat sweaters."

    "Moths have a special enzyme in their saliva," Ruby would say. This was true, she knew it for a fact. She'd been so taken by Jonathan's tale that she'd gone to the library to check out the details and discovered he was wrong.

    But Jonathan didn't care what the biochemists said. He held her against his chest and said, "I have an enzyme for you."

    That night, after the fire burned out, they slept for a couple of hours. Ruby woke first and watched Jonathan sleep for a while. He slept like a child, with his knees bent toward his chest and his hands clasped between his thighs. Ruby picked up the tipped-over chair and swept the fragments of broken glass onto a sheet of paper. Then she woke Jonathan and they tiptoed back to the rooms where they were supposed to be.

---

villi: Tiny, hairlike structures in the intestine that absorb nutrients.

Reading and Reacting

1. In paragraph 21, the term *littoral zone* is defined as "that space between high and low watermarks where organisms [struggle] to adapt to the daily rhythm of immersion and exposure." Given this definition, how is the story's title appropriate?

2. This story contains a good deal of scientific vocabulary. List four or five examples. Is this vocabulary essential to the story? Is it essential that readers know the meanings of these terms? Explain.

3. What is the significance, if any, of the fact that Jonathan and Ruby meet on an island?

4. On the island, Ruby and Jonathan share a language, with a common vocabulary and common allusions. What do they talk about? What don't they talk about? As a married couple, what do Jonathan and Ruby talk about? What don't they talk about?

5. When they first meet, what things do Ruby and Jonathan have in common apart from the fact that both are scientists?

6. What do Ruby and Jonathan gain by marrying? What do they lose? Are they aware of what they have lost? Explain.

7. Although they cannot bear to think about blame, Jonathan and Ruby do feel guilty about the dissolution of their marriages. Do you think they would make the same choices again? Explain.

8. Basically, this is a story about divorce and its effects. Is the fact that Jonathan and Ruby are scientists really important? How would the story be different if they were not?

9. Although this story deals with an emotional subject, its tone is restrained, its language often understated. For example, the narrator tells us that Ruby and Jonathan "struggle to conceal their disappointments" (par. 45) but never shows their sadness or anguish. Find other examples of **understatement** in the story. Do you think the characters' raw emotions should have been revealed? Why or why not?

10. The story's flat, emotionless prose is possible largely because scenes that might require displays of emotion are not described. Give examples of such scenes that could have been included in the story. Do you agree with the writer's decision to omit them?

11. **JOURNAL ENTRY** Consider Jonathan's and Ruby's children, who as young adults spend an "unhealthy amount of time talking about their past" (par. 37). Do you think they could have been spared the pain they have experienced, or was it inevitable given their parents' divorces?

12. **CRITICAL PERSPECTIVE** Critic Erin McGraw points to one moment in "The Littoral Zone" as having a great impact on all that comes after it.

> Ruby and Jonathan meet at a marine biology research station; they return home after three weeks and are met by their respective families on a dock in New Hampshire . . . Ruby and Jonathan go on to share a settled life, and their children come to visit them. But their eventual ease doesn't block out the astonishing pain of this moment on the dock, and whatever pleasure comes in their lives together must always be weighed against the first, wide-spread cost.

Do you agree that this moment on the dock is as important as McGraw says it is?

Related Works: "Dog" (p. 522), "Living in Sin" (p. 643), *A Doll House* (p. 995)

ERNEST HEMINGWAY (1898–1961) grew up in Oak Park, Illinois, and after high school graduation began his writing career as a cub reporter on the *Kansas City Star*. While working as a volunteer ambulance driver in World War I, eighteen-year-old Hemingway was wounded. As Hemingway himself told the story, he was hit by machine-gun fire while carrying an Italian soldier to safety. (Hemingway biographer Michael Reynolds, however, reports that Hemingway was wounded when a mortar shell fell and killed the man next to him.) In 1922, Hemingway and his first wife (he married four times) moved to Paris, where he taught Ezra Pound how to box, let Gertrude Stein mind the baby, and talked literary shop with expatriate writers F. Scott Fitzgerald and James Joyce. He was, said Joyce, "a big, powerful peasant, as strong as a buffalo . . . and ready to live the life he writes about." In fact, this public image of the "man's man"— the war correspondent, the deep-sea fisherman, the hunter on safari—was one Hemingway carefully created for himself.

Success came early, with publication of the short story collection *In Our Time* (1925) and his first and most acclaimed novel, *The Sun Also Rises* (1926), a portrait of a postwar "lost generation" of Americans adrift in Europe. Hemingway's novels make fiction and art out of the reality of his own life. *A Farewell to Arms* (1929) harks back to his war experiences; *For Whom the Bell Tolls* (1940) emerged out of his experiences as a journalist in Spain during the Spanish Civil War. Later in life, he made his home in Key West, Florida, and then in Cuba, where he wrote *The Old Man and the Sea* (1952). Hemingway's heroes embody the writer's own belief that although life may be followed by *nada,* or nothingness, strong individuals can embrace life and live it with dignity and honor. In 1961, plagued by poor health and mental illness — and perhaps by the difficulty of living up to his own image — Hemingway took his own life.

According to novelist and critic Anthony Burgess, Hemingway changed the sound of English prose by struggling to write a "true simple declarative sentence." His spare, unadorned style "sounds easy now, chiefly because Hemingway has shown us how to do it, but it was not easy at a time when 'literature' still meant fine writing in the Victorian sense. . . ." Hemingway was awarded the 1954 Nobel Prize in Literature.

Cultural Context: Ernest Hemingway's granddaughter, Margaux Hemingway, who died in 1996, was the fifth Hemingway to commit suicide. Ernest Hemingway himself committed suicide in 1961, and his father, brother, and sister also died at their own hands.

A Clean, Well-Lighted Place (1933)

It was late and every one had left the café except an old man who sat in the shadow the leaves of the tree made against the electric light. In the day time the street was dusty, but at night the dew settled the dust and the old man liked to sit late because he was deaf and now at night it was quiet and he felt the difference. The two waiters inside the café knew that the old man was a little drunk, and while he was a good client they knew that if he became too drunk he would leave without paying, so they kept watch on him.

"Last week he tried to commit suicide," one waiter said.

"Why?"

"He was in despair."

"What about?"

"Nothing." 5

"How do you know it was nothing?"

"He has plenty of money."

They sat together at a table that was close against the wall near the door of the café and looked at the terrace where the tables were all empty except where the old man sat in the shadow of the leaves of the tree that moved slightly in the wind. A girl and a soldier went by in the street. The street light shone on the brass number on his collar. The girl wore no head covering and hurried beside him.

"The guard will pick him up," one waiter said. 10

"What does it matter if he gets what he's after?"

"He had better get off the street now. The guard will get him. They went by five minutes ago."

The old man sitting in the shadow rapped on his saucer with his glass. The younger waiter went over to him.

"What do you want?"

The old man looked at him. "Another brandy," he said. 15

"You'll be drunk," the waiter said. The old man looked at him. The waiter went away.

"He'll stay all night," he said to his colleague. "I'm sleepy now. I never get into bed before three o'clock. He should have killed himself last week."

The waiter took the brandy bottle and another saucer from the counter inside the café and marched out to the old man's table. He put down the saucer and poured the glass full of brandy.

"You should have killed yourself last week," he said to the deaf man. The old man motioned with his finger. "A little more," he said. The waiter poured on into the glass so that the brandy slopped over and ran down the stem into the top saucer of the pile. "Thank you," the old man said. The waiter took the bottle back inside the café. He sat down at the table with his colleague again.

"He's drunk now," he said. 20

"He's drunk every night."

"What did he want to kill himself for?"

"How should I know."

25 "How did he do it?"

"He hung himself with a rope."

"Who cut him down?"

"His niece."

"Why did they do it?"

"Fear for his soul."

30 "How much money has he got?"

"He's got plenty."

"He must be eighty years old."

"Anyway I should say he was eighty."

"I wish he would go home. I never get to bed before three o'clock. What kind of hour is that to go to bed?"

35 "He stays up because he likes it."

"He's lonely. I'm not lonely. I have a wife waiting in bed for me."

"He had a wife once too."

"A wife would be no good to him now."

"You can't tell. He might be better with a wife."

40 "His niece looks after him. You said she cut him down."

"I know."

"I wouldn't want to be that old. An old man is a nasty thing."

"Not always. This old man is clean. He drinks without spilling. Even now, drunk. Look at him."

"I don't want to look at him. I wish he would go home. He has no regard for those who must work."

45 The old man looked from his glass across the square, then over at the waiters.

"Another brandy," he said, pointing to his glass. The waiter who was in a hurry came over.

"Finished," he said, speaking with that omission of syntax stupid people employ when talking to drunken people or foreigners. "No more tonight. Close now."

"Another," said the old man.

"No. Finished." The waiter wiped the edge of the table with a towel and shook his head.

50 The old man stood up, slowly counted the saucers, took a leather coin purse from his pocket and paid for the drinks, leaving half a peseta tip.

The waiter watched him go down the street, a very old man walking unsteadily but with dignity.

"Why didn't you let him stay and drink?" the unhurried waiter asked. They were putting up the shutters. "It is not half-past two."

"I want to go home to bed."

"What is an hour?"

55 "More to me than to him."

"An hour is the same."

"You talk like an old man yourself. He can buy a bottle and drink at home."

"It's not the same."

"No, it is not," agreed the waiter with a wife. He did not wish to be unjust. He was only in a hurry.

60 "And you? You have no fear of going home before your usual hour?"

"Are you trying to insult me?"

"No, hombre, only to make a joke."

"No," the waiter who was in a hurry said, rising from pulling down the metal shutters. "I have confidence. I am all confidence."

"You have youth, confidence, and a job," the older waiter said. "You have everything."

"And what do you lack?"

"Everything but work."

"You have everything I have."

"No. I have never had confidence and I am not young."

"Come on. Stop talking nonsense and lock up."

"I am of those who like to stay late at the café," the older waiter said. "With all those who do not want to go to bed. With all those who need a light for the night."

"I want to go home and into bed."

"We are of two different kinds," the older waiter said. He was now dressed to go home. "It is not only a question of youth and confidence although those things are very beautiful. Each night I am reluctant to close up because there may be some one who needs the café."

"Hombre, there are bodegas° open all night long."

"You do not understand. This is a clean and pleasant café. It is well lighted. The light is very good and also, now, there are shadows of the leaves."

"Good night," said the younger waiter.

"Good night," the other said. Turning off the electric light he continued the conversation with himself. It is the light of course but it is necessary that the place be clean and pleasant. You do not want music. Certainly you do not want music. Nor can you stand before a bar with dignity although that is all that is provided for these hours. What did he fear? It was not fear or dread. It was a nothing that he knew too well. It was all a nothing and a man was nothing too. It was only that and light was all it needed and a certain cleanness and order. Some lived in it and never felt it but he knew it all was nada y pues nada y nada y pues nada.° Our nada who art in nada, nada be thy name thy kingdom nada thy will be nada in nada as it is in nada. Give us this nada our daily nada and nada us our nada as we nada our nadas and nada us not into nada but deliver us from nada; pues nada. Hail nothing full of nothing, nothing is with thee. He smiled and stood before a bar with a shining steam pressure coffee machine.

"What's yours?" asked the barman.

"Nada."

"Otro loco más°," said the barman and turned away.

"A little cup," said the waiter.

The barman poured it for him.

"The light is very bright and pleasant but the bar is unpolished," the waiter said.

---

bodegas: Small grocery stores, sometimes combined with wineshops.

nada . . . nada: "Nothing and then nothing and nothing and then nothing."

Otro loco más: "Another lunatic."

The barman looked at him but did not answer. It was too late at night for conversation.

"You want another copita°?" the barman asked.

85   "No, thank you," said the waiter and went out. He disliked bars and bodegas. A clean, well-lighted café was a very different thing. Now, without thinking further, he would go home to his room. He would lie in the bed and finally, with daylight, he would go to sleep. After all, he said to himself, it is probably only insomnia. Many must have it.

Reading and Reacting

1. Throughout the story certain words —*nada*, for example — are repeated. Identify as many of these repeated words as you can. What do you think such repetition achieves?

2. The story's dialogue is presented in alternating exchanges of very brief sentences. What is the effect of these clipped exchanges?

3. Characterize the tone of the story.

4. Does the story present the human condition in optimistic or pessimistic terms? In what sense are the story's style and tone well suited to this worldview?

5. The story is set in Spain, yet Hemingway uses only a few Spanish words. Why does he use these words? Would the impact of the prayer be different if it had been spoken in English? Explain.

6. The café is described as "clean" and "pleasant." Why is this description a key element of the story? In what sense, if any, is this description ironic?

7. The story's primary **point of view** is objective. At times, however, a limited omniscient point of view is used. Identify such instances, and try to explain the reason for each shift in point of view.

8. Identify figures of speech used in the story. How does the presence (or absence) of such language help to convey the story's theme?

9. **JOURNAL ENTRY** Rewrite about half a page of the story, supplying logical transitions between sentences. How does your editing change the passage? Do your changes improve the story or take something away?

10. **CRITICAL PERSPECTIVE** In *The Writer's Art of Self-Defense*, Jackson J. Benson states, "Blindness versus awareness is Hemingway's most pervasive theme, and it is borne on a rippling wave of irony into almost everything he writes."

How do the contrasting perspectives of the two waiters in "A Clean, Well-Lighted Place" express this theme? Which one is "blind," and which one is "aware"? How do their words reveal their knowledge or lack of knowledge?

Related Works: "The Swing" (p. 139), "Cathedral" (p. 318), "Dreams of Suicide" (p. 779), "Dover Beach" (p. 847), "The Love Song of J. Alfred Prufrock" (p. 871), "Desert Places" (p. 878), "Not Waving but Drowning" (p. 912)

---

copita: A little cup.

TIM O'BRIEN (1946 –   ) is sometimes described as a writer whose books are on the shortlist of essential fiction about the Vietnam War. His plots focus on danger, violence, courage, endurance, despair, and other topics often associated with war fiction, but O'Brien treats these topics with an emphasis on the contemporary dilemmas faced by those who may be unwilling participants in an unpopular war. O'Brien calls *If I Die in a Combat Zone, Box Me Up and Ship Me Home* (1979) a memoir because it relates his war experiences as a naive young college graduate who suddenly finds himself facing bullets and land mines rather than sitting behind a desk. *Northern Lights* (1975) concentrates on the wilderness survival experiences of two brothers, one of whom has just returned from the Vietnam War. A fantastic daydream of an American soldier, *Going after Cacciato* (1978), which has been compared to Joseph Heller's *Catch 22,* won a National Book Award. *The Things They Carried* (1990) is a quasi-fictional collection of interrelated stories that deal with a single platoon; some stories involve a young soldier named Tim O'Brien and some a forty-three-year-old writer named Tim O'Brien who writes about his memories. *The Vietnam in Me* (1994) emphasizes the destructive effects of war on a soldier, even after he has returned home. *In the Lake of the Woods* (1994) tells a dramatic story of a couple missing in Minnesota. O'Brien's most recent books are *Tomcat in Love* (1998) and *July, July* (2002).

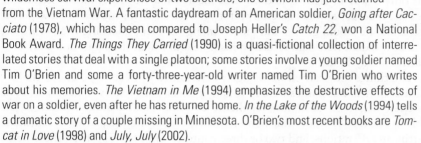

After graduating summa cum laude from Macalester College in 1968, O'Brien was immediately drafted into the United States Army and sent to Vietnam, where he served with the 198th Infantry Brigade. He was promoted to sergeant and awarded a Purple Heart after receiving a shrapnel wound in a battle near My Lai. In 1970, after discharge from the army, he attended Harvard graduate school to study government. He worked as a reporter for the *Washington Post* before pursuing a full-time career as a writer. Currently, O'Brien lives in Cambridge, Massachusetts.

Cultural Context: Although the United States did not become involved until the early 1960s, the Vietnam War actually lasted for twenty years. (The French were involved in Vietnam even earlier.) By the war's end, more than 47,000 Americans had been killed in action, nearly 11,000 had died of other causes, and more than 303,000 had been wounded. Estimates of South Vietnamese army casualties range from 185,000 to 225,000 killed and 500,000 to 570,000 wounded. The North Vietnamese and Viet Cong, the guerrilla force that fought against South Vietnam and the United States, lost about 900,000 troops. In addition, more than 1 million North and South Vietnamese civilians were killed during the war.

The Things They Carried   (1986)

First Lieutenant Jimmy Cross carried letters from a girl named Martha, a junior at Mount Sebastian College in New Jersey. They were not love letters, but Lieutenant Cross was hoping, so he kept them folded in plastic at the bottom of his rucksack. In the late afternoon, after a day's march, he would dig his foxhole, wash his hands under a canteen, unwrap the letters, hold them with the tips of his fingers, and spend the last hour of light pretending. He would imagine romantic camping trips into the White Mountains in New Hampshire. He would sometimes taste the envelope flaps, knowing her tongue had been there. More than anything, he wanted Martha to love him as he loved her, but the letters were mostly chatty, elusive on the matter of love. She was a virgin, he was almost sure. She was an English major at Mount Sebastian, and she wrote beautifully about her professors and roommates and midterm exams, about her respect for Chaucer and her great affection for Virginia Woolf. She often quoted lines of poetry; she never mentioned the war, except to say, Jimmy, take care of yourself. The letters weighed ten ounces. They were signed "Love, Martha," but Lieutenant Cross understood that "Love" was only a way of signing and did not mean what he sometimes pretended it meant. At dusk, he would carefully return the letters to his rucksack. Slowly, a bit distracted, he would get up and move among his men, checking the perimeter, then at full dark he would return to his hole and watch the night and wonder if Martha was a virgin.

The things they carried were largely determined by necessity. Among the necessities or near necessities were P-38 can openers, pocket knives, heat tabs, wrist watches, dog tags, mosquito repellent, chewing gum, candy, cigarettes, salt tablets, packets of Kool-Aid, lighters, matches, sewing kits, Military Payment Certificates, C rations, and two or three canteens of water. Together, these items weighed between fifteen and twenty pounds, depending upon a man's habits or rate of metabolism. Henry Dobbins, who was a big man, carried extra rations; he was especially fond of canned peaches in heavy syrup over pound cake. Dave Jensen, who practiced field hygiene, carried a toothbrush, dental floss, and several hotel-size bars of soap he'd stolen on R&R in Sydney, Australia. Ted Lavender, who was scared, carried tranquilizers until he was shot in the head outside the village of Than Khe in mid-April. By necessity, and because it was SOP, they all carried steel helmets that weighed five pounds including the liner and camouflage cover. They carried the standard fatigue jackets and trousers. Very few carried underwear. On their feet they carried jungle boots — 2.1 pounds — and Dave Jensen carried three pairs of socks and a can of Dr. Scholl's foot powder as a precaution against trench foot. Until he was shot, Ted Lavender carried six or seven ounces of premium dope, which for him was a necessity. Mitchell Sanders, the RTO, carried condoms. Norman Bowker carried a diary. Rat Kiley carried comic books. Kiowa, a devout Baptist, carried an illustrated New Testament that had been presented to him by his father, who taught Sunday school in Oklahoma City, Oklahoma. As a hedge against bad times, however, Kiowa also carried his grandmother's distrust of the white man, his grandfather's old hunting hatchet. Necessity dictated. Because the land was mined and booby-trapped, it was SOP for each man to carry a steel-centered, nylon-covered flak jacket, which weighed 6.7 pounds, but which on hot days seemed much heavier. Because you could die so quickly, each man carried at least one large compress bandage, usually in the helmet band for easy access. Because the nights were cold, and because the monsoons were wet, each carried a green plastic poncho that could be used as a raincoat or ground sheet or makeshift tent. With its quilted liner, the poncho weighed almost two pounds, but it was worth every ounce. In April, for instance, when Ted Lavender was shot, they used his poncho to wrap him up, then to carry him across the paddy, then to lift him into the chopper that took him away.

They were called legs or grunts.

To carry something was to "hump" it, as when Lieutenant Jimmy Cross humped his love for Martha up the hills and through the swamps. In its intransitive form, "to hump" meant "to walk," or "to march," but it implied burdens far beyond the intransitive.

Almost everyone humped photographs. In his wallet, Lieutenant Cross carried two photographs of Martha. The first was a Kodachrome snapshot signed "Love," though he knew better. She stood against a brick wall. Her eyes were gray and neutral, her lips slightly open as she stared straight-on at the camera. At night, sometimes, Lieutenant Cross wondered who had taken the picture, because he knew she had boyfriends, because he loved her so much, and because he could see the shadow of the picture taker spreading out against the brick wall. The second photograph had been clipped from the 1968 Mount Sebastian yearbook. It was an action shot — women's volleyball — and Martha was bent horizontal to the floor, reaching, the palms of her hands in sharp focus, the tongue taut, the expression frank and competitive. There was no visible sweat. She wore white gym shorts. Her legs, he thought, were almost certainly the legs of a virgin, dry and without hair, the left knee cocked and carrying her entire weight, which was just over one hundred pounds. Lieutenant Cross remembered touching that left knee. A dark theater, he remembered, and the movie was *Bonnie and Clyde*, and Martha wore a tweed skirt, and during the final scene, when he touched her knee, she turned and looked at him in a sad, sober way that made him pull his hand back, but he would always remember the feel of the tweed skirt and the knee beneath it and the sound of the gunfire that killed Bonnie and Clyde, how embarrassing it was, how slow and oppressive. He remembered kissing her good night at the dorm door. Right then, he thought, he should've done something brave. He should've carried her up the stairs to her room and tied her to the bed and touched that left knee all night long. He should've risked it. Whenever he looked at the photographs, he thought of new things he should've done.

What they carried was partly a function of rank, partly of field specialty.

As a first lieutenant and platoon leader, Jimmy Cross carried a compass, maps, code books, binoculars, and a .45-caliber pistol that weighed 2.9 pounds fully loaded. He carried a strobe light and the responsibility for the lives of his men.

As an RTO, Mitchell Sanders carried the PRC-25 radio, a killer, twenty-six pounds with its battery.

As a medic, Rat Kiley carried a canvas satchel filled with morphine and plasma and malaria tablets and surgical tape and comic books and all the things a medic must carry, including M&M's for especially bad wounds, for a total weight of nearly twenty pounds.

As a big man, therefore a machine gunner, Henry Dobbins carried the M-60, which weighed twenty-three pounds unloaded, but which was almost always loaded. In addition, Dobbins carried between ten and fifteen pounds of ammunition draped in belts across his chest and shoulders.

As PFCs or Spec 4s, most of them were common grunts and carried the standard M-16 gas-operated assault rifle. The weapon weighed 7.5 pounds unloaded, 8.2 pounds with its full twenty-round magazine. Depending on numerous factors, such as topography and psychology, the riflemen carried anywhere from twelve to twenty magazines, usually in cloth bandoliers, adding on another 8.4 pounds at minimum, fourteen pounds at maximum. When it was available, they also carried M-16 maintenance gear — rods and steel brushes and swabs and tubes of LSA oil — all of which weighed about a pound. Among the grunts, some carried the M-79 grenade launcher, 5.9 pounds unloaded, a reasonably light weapon except for the ammunition, which was heavy. A single round weighed ten ounces. The typical load was twenty-five rounds. But Ted Lavender, who was scared, carried thirty-four rounds when he was shot and killed outside Than Khe, and he went down under an exceptional burden, more than twenty pounds of ammunition, plus the flak jacket and helmet and rations and water and toilet paper and tranquilizers and all the rest, plus the unweighed fear. He was dead weight. There was no twitching or flopping. Kiowa, who saw it happen, said it was like watching a rock fall, or a big sandbag or something — just boom, then down — not like the movies where the dead guy rolls around and does fancy spins and goes ass over teakettle — not like that, Kiowa said, the poor bastard just flat-fuck fell. Boom. Down. Nothing else. It was a bright morning in mid-April. Lieutenant Cross felt the pain. He blamed himself. They stripped off Lavender's canteens and ammo, all the heavy things, and Rat Kiley said the obvious, the guy's dead, and Mitchell Sanders used his radio to report one U.S. KIA and to request a chopper. Then they wrapped Lavender in his poncho. They carried him out to a dry paddy, established security, and sat smoking the dead man's dope until the chopper came. Lieutenant Cross kept to himself. He pictured Martha's smooth young face, thinking he loved her more than anything, more than his men, and now Ted Lavender was dead because he loved her so much and could not stop thinking about her. When the dust-off arrived, they carried Lavender aboard. Afterward they burned Than Khe. They marched until dusk, then dug their holes, and that night Kiowa kept explaining how you had to be there, how fast it was, how the poor guy just dropped like so much concrete. Boom-down, he said. Like cement.

*   *   *

In addition to the three standard weapons — the M-60, M-16, and M-79 — they carried whatever presented itself, or whatever seemed appropriate as a means of killing or staying alive. They carried catch-as-catch-can. At various times, in various situations, they carried M-14s and CAR-15s and Swedish Ks and grease guns and captured AK-47s and Chi-Coms and RPGs and Simonov carbines and black-market Uzis and .38-caliber Smith & Wesson handguns and 66 mm LAWs and shotguns and silencers and blackjacks and bayonets and C-4 plastic explosives. Lee Strunk carried a slingshot; a weapon of last resort, he called it. Mitchell Sanders carried brass knuckles. Kiowa carried his grandfather's feathered hatchet.

Every third or fourth man carried a Claymore antipersonnel mine — 3.5 pounds with its firing device. They all carried fragmentation grenades — fourteen ounces each. They all carried at least one M-18 colored smoke grenade — twenty-four ounces. Some carried CS or tear-gas grenades. Some carried white-phosphorus grenades. They carried all they could bear, and then some, including a silent awe for the terrible power of the things they carried.

In the first week of April, before Lavender died, Lieutenant Jimmy Cross received a good-luck charm from Martha. It was a simple pebble, an ounce at most. Smooth to the touch, it was a milky-white color with flecks of orange and violet, oval-shaped, like a miniature egg. In the accompanying letter, Martha wrote that she had found the pebble on the Jersey shoreline, precisely where the land touched water at high tide, where things came together but also separated. It was this separate-but-together quality, she wrote, that had inspired her to pick up the pebble and to carry it in her breast pocket for several days, where it seemed weightless, and then to send it through the mail, by air, as a token of her truest feelings for him. Lieutenant Cross found this romantic. But he wondered what her truest feelings were, exactly, and what she meant by separate-but-together. He wondered how the tides and waves had come into play on that afternoon along the Jersey shoreline when Martha saw the pebble and bent down to rescue it from geology. He imagined bare feet. Martha was a poet, with the poet's sensibilities, and her feet would be brown and bare, the toenails unpainted, the eyes chilly and somber like the ocean in March, and though it was painful, he wondered who had been with her that afternoon. He imagined a pair of shadows moving along the strip of sand where things came together but also separated. It was phantom jealousy, he knew, but he couldn't help himself. He loved her so much. On the march, through the hot days of early April, he carried the pebble in his mouth, turning it with his tongue, tasting sea salts and moisture. His mind wandered. He had difficulty keeping his attention on the war. On occasion he would yell at his men to spread out the column, to keep their eyes open, but then he would slip away into daydreams, just pretending, walking barefoot along the Jersey shore, with Martha, carrying nothing. He would feel himself rising. Sun and waves and gentle winds, all love and lightness.

What they carried varied by mission.

When a mission took them to the mountains, they carried mosquito netting, machetes, canvas tarps, and extra bug juice.   15

If a mission seemed especially hazardous, or if it involved a place they knew to be bad, they carried everything they could. In certain heavily mined AOs, where the land was dense with Toe Poppers and Bouncing Betties, they took turns humping a twenty-eight-pound mine detector. With its headphones and big sensing plate, the equipment was a stress on the lower back and shoulders, awkward to handle, often useless because of the shrapnel in the earth, but they carried it anyway, partly for safety, partly for the illusion of safety.

On ambush, or other night missions, they carried peculiar little odds and ends. Kiowa always took along his New Testament and a pair of moccasins for silence. Dave Jensen carried night-sight vitamins high in carotin. Lee Strunk carried his slingshot; ammo, he claimed, would never be a problem. Rat Kiley carried brandy and M&M's. Until he was shot, Ted Lavender carried the starlight scope, which weighed 6.3 pounds with its aluminum carrying case. Henry Dobbins carried his girlfriend's panty-hose wrapped around his neck as a comforter. They all carried ghosts. When dark came, they would move out single file across the meadows and paddies to their ambush coordinates, where they would quietly set up the Claymores and lie down and spend the night waiting.

Other missions were more complicated and required special equipment. In mid-April, it was their mission to search out and destroy the elaborate tunnel complexes in the Than Khe area south of Chu Lai. To blow the tunnels, they carried one-pound blocks of pentrite high explosives, four blocks to a man, sixty-eight pounds in all. They carried wiring, detonators, and battery-powered clackers. Dave Jensen carried earplugs. Most often, before blowing the tunnels, they were ordered by higher command to search them, which was considered bad news, but by and large they just shrugged and carried out orders. Because he was a big man, Henry Dobbins was excused from tunnel duty. The others would draw numbers. Before Lavender died there were seventeen men in the platoon, and whoever drew the number seventeen would strip off his gear and crawl in head first with a flashlight and Lieutenant Cross's .45-caliber pistol. The rest of them would fan out as security. They would sit down or kneel, not facing the hole, listening to the ground beneath them, imagining cobwebs and ghosts, whatever was down there — the tunnel walls squeezing in — how the flashlight seemed impossibly heavy in the hand and how it was tunnel vision in the very strictest sense, compression in all ways, even time, and how you had to wiggle in — ass and elbows — a swallowed-up feeling — and how you found yourself worrying about odd things — will your flashlight go dead? Do rats carry rabies? If you screamed, how far would the sound carry? Would your buddies hear it? Would they have the courage to drag you out? In some respects, though not many, the waiting was worse than the tunnel itself. Imagination was a killer.

On April 16, when Lee Strunk drew the number seventeen, he laughed and muttered something and went down quickly. The morning was hot and very still. Not good, Kiowa said. He looked at the tunnel opening, then out across a dry paddy toward the village of Than Khe. Nothing moved. No clouds or birds or people. As they waited, the men smoked and drank Kool-Aid, not talking much, feeling sympathy for Lee Strunk but also feeling the luck of the draw. You win some, you lose some, said Mitchell Sanders, and sometimes you settle for a rain check. It was a tired line and no one laughed.

20   Henry Dobbins ate a tropical chocolate bar. Ted Lavender popped a tranquilizer and went off to pee.

After five minutes, Lieutenant Jimmy Cross moved to the tunnel, leaned down, and examined the darkness. Trouble, he thought — a cave-in maybe. And then suddenly, without willing it, he was thinking about Martha. The stresses and fractures, the quick collapse, the two of them buried alive under all that weight. Dense, crushing love. Kneeling, watching the hole, he tried to concentrate on Lee Strunk and the war, all the dangers, but his love was too much for him, he felt paralyzed, he wanted to sleep inside her lungs and breathe her blood and be smothered. He wanted her to be a virgin and not a virgin, all at once. He wanted to know her. Intimate secrets — why poetry? Why so sad? Why that grayness in her eyes? Why so alone? Not lonely, just alone — riding her bike across campus or sitting off by herself in the cafeteria. Even dancing, she danced alone — and it was the aloneness that filled him with love. He remembered telling her that one evening. How she nodded and looked away. And how, later, when he kissed her, she received the kiss without returning it, her eyes wide open, not afraid, not a virgin's eyes, just flat and uninvolved.

Lieutenant Cross gazed at the tunnel. But he was not there. He was buried with Martha under the white sand at the Jersey shore. They were pressed together, and the pebble in his mouth was her tongue. He was smiling. Vaguely, he was aware of how quiet the day was, the sullen paddies, yet he could not bring himself to worry about matters of security. He was beyond that. He was just a kid at war, in love. He was twenty-two years old. He couldn't help it.

A few moments later Lee Strunk crawled out of the tunnel. He came up grinning, filthy but alive. Lieutenant Cross nodded and closed his eyes while the others clapped Strunk on the back and made jokes about rising from the dead.

Worms, Rat Kiley said. Right out of the grave. Fuckin' zombie.   25

The men laughed. They all felt great relief.

Spook City, said Mitchell Sanders.

Lee Strunk made a funny ghost sound, a kind of moaning, yet very happy, and right then, when Strunk made that high happy moaning sound, when he went *Ahhooooo*, right then Ted Lavender was shot in the head on his way back from peeing. He lay with his mouth open. The teeth were broken. There was a swollen black bruise under his left eye. The cheekbone was gone. Oh shit, Rat Kiley said, the guy's dead. The guy's dead, he kept saying, which seemed profound — the guy's dead. I mean really.

The things they carried were determined to some extent by superstition. Lieutenant Cross carried his good-luck pebble. Dave Jensen carried a rabbit's foot. Norman Bowker, otherwise a very gentle person, carried a thumb that had been presented to him as a gift by Mitchell Sanders. The thumb was dark brown, rubbery to the touch, and weighed four ounces at most. It had been cut from a VC corpse, a boy of fifteen or sixteen. They'd found him at the bottom of an irrigation ditch, badly burned, flies in his mouth and eyes. The boy wore black shorts and sandals. At the time of his death he had been carrying a pouch of rice, a rifle, and three magazines of ammunition.

You want my opinion, Mitchell Sanders said, there's a definite moral here.

He put his hand on the dead boy's wrist. He was quiet for a time, as if count-   30
ing a pulse, then he patted the stomach, almost affectionately, and used Kiowa's hunting hatchet to remove the thumb.

Henry Dobbins asked what the moral was.

Moral?

You know. *Moral.*

Sanders wrapped the thumb in toilet paper and handed it across to Norman Bowker. There was no blood. Smiling, he kicked the boy's head, watched the flies scatter, and said, It's like with that old TV show — Paladin. Have gun, will travel.

35   Henry Dobbins thought about it.
Yeah, well, he finally said. I don't see no moral.
There it *is*, man.
Fuck off.

They carried USO stationery and pencils and pens. They carried Sterno, safety pins, trip flares, signal flares, spools of wire, razor blades, chewing tobacco, liberated joss sticks and statuettes of the smiling Buddha, candles, grease pencils, *The Stars and Stripes*, fingernail clippers, Psy Ops leaflets, bush hats, bolos, and much more. Twice a week, when the resupply choppers came in, they carried hot chow in green Mermite cans and large canvas bags filled with iced beer and soda pop. They carried plastic water containers, each with a two-gallon capacity. Mitchell Sanders carried a set of starched tiger fatigues for special occasions. Henry Dobbins carried Black Flag insecticide. Dave Jensen carried empty sandbags that could be filled at night for added protection. Lee Strunk carried tanning lotion. Some things they carried in common. Taking turns, they carried the big PRC-77 scrambler radio, which weighed thirty pounds with its battery. They shared the weight of memory. They took up what others could no longer bear. Often, they carried each other, the wounded or weak. They carried infections. They carried chess sets, basketballs, Vietnamese-English dictionaries, insignia of rank, Bronze Stars and Purple Hearts, plastic cards imprinted with the Code of Conduct. They carried diseases, among them malaria and dysentery. They carried lice and ringworm and leeches and paddy algae and various rots and molds. They carried the land itself — Vietnam, the place, the soil — a powdery orange-red dust that covered their boots and fatigues and faces. They carried the sky. The whole atmosphere, they carried it, the humidity, the monsoons, the stink of fungus and decay, all of it, they carried gravity. They moved like mules. By daylight they took sniper fire, at night they were mortared, but it was not battle, it was just the endless march, village to village, without purpose, nothing won or lost. They marched for the sake of the march. They plodded along slowly, dumbly, leaning forward against the heat, unthinking, all blood and bone, simple grunts, soldiering with their legs, toiling up the hills and down into the paddies and across the rivers and up again and down, just humping, one step and then the next and then another, but no volition, no will, because it was automatic, it was anatomy, and the war was entirely a matter of posture and carriage, the hump was everything, a kind of inertia, a kind of emptiness, a dullness of desire and intellect and conscience and hope and human sensibility. Their principles were in their feet. Their calculations were biological. They had no sense of strategy or mission. They searched the villages without knowing what to look for, not caring, kicking over jars of rice, frisking children and old men, blowing tunnels, sometimes setting fires and sometimes not, then forming up and moving on to the next village, then other villages, where it would always be the same. They carried their own lives. The pressures were enormous. In the heat of early afternoon, they would remove their helmets and flak jackets, walking bare, which was dangerous but which helped ease the strain. They would often discard things along the route of march. Purely for comfort, they would throw away rations, blow their Claymores and grenades, no matter, because by nightfall the resupply choppers would arrive with more of the same, then a day or two later still more, fresh watermelons and crates of ammunition and sunglasses and woolen sweaters — the resources were stunning — sparklers for the Fourth of July, colored eggs for Easter. It was the great American war chest — the fruits of science, the smokestacks, the canneries, the arsenals at Hartford, the Minnesota forests, the machine shops, the vast fields of corn and wheat — they carried like freight trains; they carried it on their backs and shoulders — and for all the ambiguities of Vietnam, all the mysteries and unknowns, there was at least the single abiding certainty that they would never be at a loss for things to carry.

*   *   *

After the chopper took Lavender away, Lieutenant Jimmy Cross led his men   40
into the village of Than Khe. They burned everything. They shot chickens and dogs, they trashed the village well, they called in artillery and watched the wreckage, then they marched for several hours through the hot afternoon, and then at dusk, while Kiowa explained how Lavender died, Lieutenant Cross found himself trembling.

He tried not to cry. With his entrenching tool, which weighed five pounds, he began digging a hole in the earth.

He felt shame. He hated himself. He had loved Martha more than his men, and as a consequence Lavender was now dead, and this was something he would have to carry like a stone in his stomach for the rest of the war.

All he could do was dig. He used his entrenching tool like an ax, slashing, feeling both love and hate, and then later, when it was full dark, he sat at the bottom of his foxhole and wept. It went on for a long while. In part, he was grieving for Ted Lavender, but mostly it was for Martha, and for himself, because she belonged to another world, which was not quite real, and because she was a junior at Mount Sebastian College in New Jersey, a poet and a virgin and uninvolved, and because he realized she did not love him and never would.

Like cement, Kiowa whispered in the dark. I swear to God — boom-down. Not a word.

I've heard this, said Norman Bowker.   45

A pisser, you know? Still zipping himself up. Zapped while zipping.

All right, fine. That's enough.

Yeah, but you had to see it, the guy just —

I *heard,* man. Cement. So why not shut the fuck *up?*

Kiowa shook his head sadly and glanced over at the hole where Lieutenant   50
Jimmy Cross sat watching the night. The air was thick and wet. A warm, dense fog had settled over the paddies and there was the stillness that precedes rain.

After a time Kiowa sighed.

One thing for sure, he said. The Lieutenant's in some deep hurt. I mean that crying jag — the way he was carrying on — it wasn't fake or anything, it was real heavy-duty hurt. The man cares.

Sure, Norman Bowker said.

Say what you want, the man does care.

55 We all got problems.

Not Lavender.

No, I guess not, Bowker said. Do me a favor, though.

Shut up?

That's a smart Indian. Shut up.

60 Shrugging, Kiowa pulled off his boots. He wanted to say more, just to lighten up his sleep, but instead he opened his New Testament and arranged it beneath his head as a pillow. The fog made things seem hollow and unattached. He tried not to think about Ted Lavender, but then he was thinking how fast it was, no drama, down and dead, and how it was hard to feel anything except surprise. It seemed un-Christian. He wished he could find some great sadness, or even anger, but the emotion wasn't there and he couldn't make it happen. Mostly he felt pleased to be alive. He liked the smell of the New Testament under his cheek, the leather and ink and paper and glue, whatever the chemicals were. He liked hearing the sounds of night. Even his fatigue, it felt fine, the stiff muscles and the prickly awareness of his own body, a floating feeling. He enjoyed not being dead. Lying there, Kiowa admired Lieutenant Jimmy Cross's capacity for grief. He wanted to share the man's pain, he wanted to care as Jimmy Cross cared. And yet when he closed his eyes, all he could think was Boom-down, and all he could feel was the pleasure of having his boots off and the fog curling in around him and the damp soil and the Bible smells and the plush comfort of night.

After a moment Norman Bowker sat up in the dark.

What the hell, he said. You want to talk, *talk*. Tell it to me.

Forget it.

No, man, go on. One thing I hate, it's a silent Indian.

65 For the most part they carried themselves with poise, a kind of dignity. Now and then, however, there were times of panic, when they squealed or wanted to squeal but couldn't, when they twitched and made moaning sounds and covered their heads and said Dear Jesus and flopped around on the earth and fired their weapons blindly and cringed and sobbed and begged for the noise to stop and went wild and made stupid promises to themselves and to God and to their mothers and fathers, hoping not to die. In different ways, it happened to all of them. Afterward, when the firing ended, they would blink and peek up. They would touch their bodies, feeling shame, then quickly hiding it. They would force themselves to stand. As if in slow motion, frame by frame, the world would take on the old logic — absolute silence, then the wind, then sunlight, then voices. It was the burden of being alive. Awkwardly, the men would reassemble themselves, first in private, then in groups, becoming soldiers again. They would repair the leaks in their eyes. They would check for casualties, call in dust-offs, light cigarettes, try to smile, clear their throats and spit and begin cleaning their weapons. After a time someone would shake his head and say, No lie, I almost shit my pants, and someone else would laugh, which meant it was bad, yes, but the guy had obviously not shit his pants, it wasn't that bad, and in any case nobody would ever do such

a thing and then go ahead and talk about it. They would squint into the dense, oppressive sunlight. For a few moments, perhaps, they would fall silent, lighting a joint and tracking its passage from man to man, inhaling, holding in the humiliation. Scary stuff, one of them might say. But then someone else would grin or flick his eyebrows and say, Roger-dodger, almost cut me a new asshole, *almost.*

There were numerous such poses. Some carried themselves with a sort of wistful resignation, others with pride or stiff soldierly discipline or good humor or macho zeal. They were afraid of dying but they were even more afraid to show it.

They found jokes to tell.

They used a hard vocabulary to contain the terrible softness. *Greased,* they'd say. *Offed, lit up,*° *zapped while zipping.*° It wasn't cruelty, just stage presence. They were actors and the war came at them in 3-D. When someone died, it wasn't quite dying, because in a curious way it seemed scripted, and because they had their lines mostly memorized, irony mixed with tragedy, and because they called it by other names, as if to encyst and destroy the reality of death itself. They kicked corpses. They cut off thumbs. They talked grunt lingo. They told stories about Ted Lavender's supply of tranquilizers, how the poor guy didn't feel a thing, how incredibly tranquil he was.

There's a moral here, said Mitchell Sanders.

They were waiting for Lavender's chopper, smoking the dead man's dope.   70

The moral's pretty obvious. Sanders said, and winked. Stay away from drugs. No joke, they'll ruin your day every time.

Cute, said Henry Dobbins.

Mind-blower, get it? Talk about wiggy — nothing left, just blood and brains.

They made themselves laugh.

There it is, they'd say, over and over, as if the repetition itself were an act of   75
poise, a balance between crazy and almost crazy, knowing without going. There it is, which meant be cool, let it ride, because oh yeah, man, you can't change what can't be changed, there it is, there it absolutely and positively and fucking well *is.*

They were tough.

They carried all the emotional baggage of men who might die. Grief, terror, love, longing — these were intangibles, but the intangibles had their own mass and specific gravity, they had tangible weight. They carried shameful memories. They carried the common secret of cowardice barely restrained, the instinct to run or freeze or hide, and in many respects this was the heaviest burden of all, for it could never be put down, it required perfect balance and perfect posture. They carried their reputations. They carried the soldier's greatest fear, which was the fear of blushing. Men killed, and died, because they were embarrassed not to. It was what had brought them to the war in the first place, nothing positive, no dreams of glory or honor, just to avoid the blush of dishonor. They died so as not to die of embarrassment. They crawled into tunnels and walked point and advanced under fire. Each morning, despite the unknowns, they made their legs move. They endured. They kept humping. They did not submit to the obvious al-

---

Offed, lit up: Killed.
zapped while zipping: Killed while urinating.

ternative, which was simply to close the eyes and fall. So easy, really. Go limp and tumble to the ground and let the muscles unwind and not speak and not budge until your buddies picked you up and lifted you into the chopper that would roar and dip its nose and carry you off to the world. A mere matter of falling, yet no one ever fell. It was not courage, exactly; the object was not valor. Rather, they were too frightened to be cowards.

By and large they carried these things inside, maintaining the masks of composure. They sneered at sick call. They spoke bitterly about guys who had found release by shooting off their own toes or fingers. Pussies, they'd say. Candyasses. It was fierce, mocking talk, with only a trace of envy or awe, but even so, the image played itself out behind their eyes.

They imagined the muzzle against flesh. They imagined the quick, sweet pain, then the evacuation to Japan, then a hospital with warm beds and cute geisha nurses.

80   They dreamed of freedom birds.

At night, on guard, staring into the dark, they were carried away by jumbo jets. They felt the rush of takeoff. *Gone!* they yelled. And then velocity, wings and engines, a smiling stewardess — but it was more than a plane, it was a real bird, a big sleek silver bird with feathers and talons and high screeching. They were flying. The weights fell off, there was nothing to bear. They laughed and held on tight, feeling the cold slap of wind and altitude, soaring, thinking *It's over, I'm gone!* — they were naked, they were light and free — it was all lightness, bright and fast and buoyant, light as light, a helium buzz in the brain, a giddy bubbling in the lungs as they were taken up over the clouds and the war, beyond duty, beyond gravity and mortification and global entanglements —*Sin loi!* they yelled, *I'm sorry, motherfuckers, but I'm out of it, I'm goofed, I'm on a space cruise, I'm gone!* — and it was a restful, disencumbered sensation, just riding the light waves, sailing that big silver freedom bird over the mountains and oceans, over America, over the farms and great sleeping cities and cemeteries and highways and the golden arches of McDonald's. It was flight, a kind of fleeing, a kind of falling, falling higher and higher, spinning off the edge of the earth and beyond the sun and through the vast, silent vacuum where there were no burdens and where everything weighed exactly nothing. *Gone!* they screamed, *I'm sorry but I'm gone!* And so at night, not quite dreaming, they gave themselves over to lightness, they were carried, they were purely borne.

On the morning after Ted Lavender died, First Lieutenant Jimmy Cross crouched at the bottom of his foxhole and burned Martha's letters. Then he burned the two photographs. There was a steady rain falling, which made it difficult, but he used heat tabs and Sterno to build a small fire, screening it with his body, holding the photographs over the tight blue flame with the tips of his fingers.

He realized it was only a gesture. Stupid, he thought. Sentimental, too, but mostly just stupid.

Lavender was dead. You couldn't burn the blame.

85   Besides, the letters were in his head. And even now, without photographs, Lieutenant Cross could see Martha playing volleyball in her white gym shorts and yellow T-shirt. He could see her moving in the rain.

When the fire died out, Lieutenant Cross pulled his poncho over his shoulders and ate breakfast from a can.

There was no great mystery, he decided.

In those burned letters Martha had never mentioned the war, except to say, Jimmy, take care of yourself. She wasn't involved. She signed the letters "Love," but it wasn't love, and all the fine lines and technicalities did not matter.

The morning came up wet and blurry. Everything seemed part of everything else, the fog and Martha and the deepening rain.

It was a war, after all.   90

Half smiling, Lieutenant Jimmy Cross took out his maps. He shook his head hard, as if to clear it, then bent forward and began planning the day's march. In ten minutes, or maybe twenty, he would rouse the men and they would pack up and head west, where the maps showed the country to be green and inviting. They would do what they had always done. The rain might add some weight, but otherwise it would be one more day layered upon all the other days.

He was realistic about it. There was that new hardness in his stomach.

No more fantasies, he told himself.

Henceforth, when he thought about Martha, it would be only to think that she belonged elsewhere. He would shut down the daydreams. This was not Mount Sebastian, it was another world, where there were no pretty poems or midterm exams, a place where men died because of carelessness and gross stupidity. Kiowa was right. Boom-down, and you were dead, never partly dead.

Briefly, in the rain, Lieutenant Cross saw Martha's gray eyes gazing back at him.   95

He understood.

It was very sad, he thought. The things men carried inside. The things men did or felt they had to do.

He almost nodded at her, but didn't.

Instead he went back to his maps. He was now determined to perform his duties firmly and without negligence. It wouldn't help Lavender, he knew that, but from this point on he would comport himself as a soldier. He would dispose of his good-luck pebble. Swallow it, maybe, or use Lee Strunk's slingshot, or just drop it along the trail. On the march he would impose strict field discipline. He would be careful to send out flank security, to prevent straggling or bunching up, to keep his troops moving at the proper pace and at the proper interval. He would insist on clean weapons. He would confiscate the remainder of Lavender's dope. Later in the day, perhaps, he would call the men together and speak to them plainly. He would accept the blame for what had happened to Ted Lavender. He would be a man about it. He would look them in the eyes, keeping his chin level, and he would issue the new SOPs in a calm, impersonal tone of voice, an officer's voice, leaving no room for argument or discussion. Commencing immediately, he'd tell them, they would no longer abandon equipment along the route of march. They would police up their acts. They would get their shit together, and keep it together, and maintain it neatly and in good working order.

He would not tolerate laxity. He would show strength, distancing himself.   100

Among the men there would be grumbling, of course, and maybe worse, because their days would seem longer and their loads heavier, but Lieutenant Cross reminded himself that his obligation was not to be loved but to lead. He would

dispense with love; it was not now a factor. And if anyone quarreled or complained, he would simply tighten his lips and arrange his shoulders in the correct
command posture. He might give a curt little nod. Or he might not. He might just
shrug and say Carry on, then they would saddle up and form into a column and
move out toward the villages west of Than Khe.

Reading and Reacting

1. Although the setting and the events described in "The Things They Carried" are dramatic and moving, its tone is often flat and emotionless. How
is this tone created? Why do you think the narrator adopts this kind of tone?

2. Consider the different meanings of the word *carry*, which can refer to burdens abstract or concrete and to things carried physically or emotionally, actively or passively. Give several examples of the different senses in which
O'Brien uses the word. How does his use of the word enhance the story?

3. A striking characteristic of the story's style is its thorough catalogs of the
concrete, tangible "things" the soldiers carry. Why do you suppose such detailed lists are included? What does what each man carries tell you about
him? In a less literal, more abstract sense, what else do these men "carry"?

4. One stylistic technique O'Brien uses is intentional repetition — of phrases
("they carried"); people's names and identifying details (Martha's virginity,
for example); and pieces of equipment. What effect do you think O'Brien
hopes to achieve through such repetition? Is he successful?

5. Interspersed among long paragraphs crammed with detail are short one- or
two-sentence paragraphs. What function do these brief paragraphs serve?

6. What function does Martha serve in the story? Why does Lieutenant Cross
burn her letters?

7. In paragraph 68, the narrator says of the soldiers, "They used a hard vocabulary to contain the terrible softness." What do you think he means by this?
Do you think this "hard vocabulary" is necessary? How does it affect your
reaction to the story?

8. Describing Lieutenant Cross's new sense of purpose in the story's final paragraph, the narrator uses the phrase "Carry on." Do you think this phrase is
linked in any way to the story's other uses of the word *carry*, or do you
believe it is unrelated? Explain.

9. **JOURNAL ENTRY** "The Things They Carried" is a story about war. Do you
think it is an antiwar story? Why or why not?

10. **CRITICAL PERSPECTIVE** In an essay about war memoirs, Clayton W. Lewis
questions O'Brien's decision to present "the nightmare [he] faced in a
Vietnam rice paddy" as fiction. Lewis believes that some of O'Brien's stories
"dissolve into clever artifice" and, therefore, are not as effective as actual
memoirs of the Vietnam experience would be. He concludes that "for all its
brilliance and emotional grounding, [the stories do not] satisfy one's appetite
to hear what happened rendered as it was experienced and remembered."

   Do you think Lewis has a point? Or do you think O'Brien's "artifice" communicates his emotions and experiences more effectively than a straightforward memoir could? Explain your position.

Related Works: "Facing It" (p. 575), "Dulce et Decorum Est" (p. 674)

WRITING SUGGESTIONS: Style, Tone, and Language

1. In "The Things They Carried," Tim O'Brien considers his characters' emotional and psychological burdens as well as the physical "things they carry." Applying O'Brien's criteria to "The Littoral Zone," write an essay in which you consider what Jonathan and Ruby "carry" (and what their children and former spouses "carry"). Or, you may compare the two stories, considering, for example, how O'Brien's war zone is like Barrett's littoral zone, or how the characters in each of these two stories are united by a unique shared vocabulary.

2. Several of the stories in this chapter present characters who are outsiders or misfits in their social milieus. Choose two or three characters, and explain why each is estranged from others and what efforts, if any, each makes to reconcile himself with society. Be sure to show how language helps to convey each character's alienation.

3. In "A Clean, Well-Lighted Place," two waiters discuss an old man, but readers do not really learn what the old man is thinking or feeling. Write a letter (or a suicide note) from the old man to a friend or family member in which you reveal his thoughts about his life and try to account for his despair. Be sure the tone of your letter is consistent with his feelings of sadness.

4. Both "Araby" and "The Things They Carried" deal, at least in part, with infatuation. Compare and contrast the infatuations described in the two stories. How does the language used by the narrators in the two stories communicate the two characters' fascination and subsequent disillusionment?

5. **WEB ACTIVITY** The following Web site contains information about Tim O'Brien:

http://www.illyria.com/tobhp.html

From that Web page, read several excerpts from various O'Brien works. Then link to the O'Brien interview under "Miscellany." Based on what you have discovered about O'Brien from these sites, write an essay discussing how O'Brien's themes in "The Things They Carried" are consistent with the overall themes in his other work. Consider his use of language and tone to express his themes, and consider the perspective he uses in telling his stories.

CHAPTER 10

SYMBOL AND ALLEGORY

> Symbols and metaphors share several qualities, but they are far from being synonymous. Both are figurative expressions that transcend literal language. Both rely heavily on implication and suggestion. Both present the abstract in concrete terms, and both can be interpreted with varying degrees of openness or specificity. They differ, however, in important ways. A symbol expands language by substitution, a metaphor by comparison and interaction. A symbol does not ask a reader to merge two concepts but rather to let one thing suggest another. A symbol derives its meaning through development and consensus, a metaphor through invention and originality. A symbol is strengthened by repetition, but a metaphor is destroyed by it. —**Roland Bartel,** *Metaphors and Symbols*

> Symbols have to spring from the work direct, and stay alive. Symbols for the sake of symbols are counterfeit, and were they all stamped on the page in red they couldn't any more quickly give themselves away. So are symbols failing their purpose when they don't keep to proportion in the book. However alive they are, they should never call for an emphasis greater than the emotional reality they serve, in their moment, to illuminate. —**Eudora Welty,** *"Words into Fiction"*

> The truth is, I do indeed include images in my work, but I don't think of them as symbols, [. . .] To me, symbols are stand-in's for abstract ideas. They belong to the High School of Hidden Meanings: vases symbolize female orifices, broken vases symbolize a loss of virginity and innocence. Heavy stuff. I prefer using images. My writing tends toward the Elementary School of Word Pictures: the accidental shattering of a vase in an empty room changes the emotions of a scene from sanity to uneasiness, perhaps even to dread. The point is, if there are symbols in my work they exist largely by accident or through someone else's interpretive design. —**Amy Tan,** *The Threepenny Review*

SYMBOL

A **symbol** is a person, object, action, place, or event that, in addition to its literal meaning, suggests a more complex meaning or range of meanings. **Universal** or **archetypal symbols,** such as the Old Man, the Mother, or the Grim Reaper, are so much a part of human experience that they suggest the same thing to most people. **Conventional symbols** are also likely to suggest the same thing to most people, provided the people have common cultural and social assumptions (a rose suggests love, a skull and crossbones denotes poison). Such symbols are often used as a kind of shorthand in films, popular literature, and advertising, where they encourage automatic responses.

A conventional symbol such as the stars and stripes of the American flag can evoke powerful feelings of pride and patriotism in a group of people who share a culture, just as the maple leaf and the Union Jack can. Symbols used in works of literature can function in much the same way, enabling writers to convey particular emotions or messages with a high degree of predictability. Thus, spring can be expected to suggest rebirth and promise; autumn, declining years and powers; summer, youth and beauty. Because a writer expects a dark forest to evoke fear, or a rainbow to communicate hope, he or she can be quite confident in using such an image to convey a particular idea or mood (provided the audience shares the writer's frame of reference).

Many symbols, however, suggest different things to different people, and different cultures may react differently to the same symbols. (In the United States, for example, an owl suggests wisdom; in India it suggests the opposite.) Thus, symbols enrich meaning, expanding the possibilities for interpretation and for readers' interaction with the text. Because they are so potentially rich, symbols have the power to open up a work of literature.

Literary Symbols

Both universal and conventional symbols can function as **literary symbols** that take on additional meanings in particular works. For instance, a watch or clock denotes time; as a conventional symbol, it suggests the passing of time; as a literary symbol in a particular work, it might also convey anything from a character's inability to recapture the past to the idea of time running out — or it might suggest more than one of these ideas.

Considering an object's possible symbolic significance can suggest a variety of ways to interpret a text. For instance, William Faulkner focuses attention on an unseen watch in a pivotal scene in "A Rose for Emily" (p. 91). The narrator first describes Emily Grierson as "a small, fat woman in black, with a thin gold chain descending to her waist and vanishing into her belt." Several sentences later, the narrator returns to the watch, noting that Emily's visitors "could hear the invisible watch ticking at the end of the gold chain." Like these visitors, readers are drawn to the unseen watch as it ticks away. Because Emily is portrayed as a woman living in the past, readers can assume that the watch is intended to reinforce the impression that she cannot see that time (the watch) has moved on. The vivid picture of the pale, plump woman in the musty room with the watch invisibly ticking does indeed suggest both that she has been left back in time and that she remains unaware of the progress around her. Thus, the symbol enriches both the depiction of character and the story's theme.

In "Barn Burning" (p. 223), another Faulkner story, the clock is a more complex symbol. The itinerant Snopes family is without financial security and apparently without a future. The clock the mother carries from shack to shack — "The clock inlaid with mother-of-pearl, which would not run, stopped at some fourteen minutes past two o'clock of a dead and forgotten day and time, which had been [Sarty's] mother's dowry" — is their only possession of value. The fact that the clock no longer works seems at first to suggest that time has run out for the family. On another level, the clock stands in pathetic contrast to Major de Spain's grand home, with its gold and glitter and Oriental rugs. Knowing that the clock was part of the mother's dowry, and that a dowry suggests a promise, readers may decide that the broken clock symbolizes lost hope; the fact that the mother still clings to the clock, however, could suggest just the opposite: her refusal to give up.

As you read, you should not try to find the one exact equivalent for each symbol; that kind of search is limiting and not productive. Instead, consider the different meanings a symbol might suggest. Then consider how these various interpretations enrich other elements of the story and the work as a whole.

Recognizing Symbols

When is a clock just a clock, and when is it also a symbol with a meaning or meanings beyond its literal significance? If a character waiting for a friend glances once at his or her watch to verify the time, there is probably nothing symbolic about the watch or about the act of looking at it. If, however, the watch keeps appearing again and again in the story, at key moments; if the narrator devotes a good deal of time to describing it; if it is placed in a conspicuous physical location; if characters keep noticing it and commenting on its presence; if it is lost (or found) at a critical moment; if its function in some way parallels the development of plot or character (for instance, if it stops as a relationship ends or as a character dies); if the story's opening or closing paragraph focuses on the timepiece; or if the story is called "The Watch" — the watch most likely has symbolic significance. In other words, considering how an image is used, how often it is used, and when it appears will help you to determine whether or not it functions as a symbol.

Symbols expand the possible meanings of a story, thereby heightening interest and actively involving readers in the text. In "The Lottery" (p. 303), for example, the mysterious black box has symbolic significance. It is mentioned prominently and repeatedly, and it plays a pivotal role in the story's action. Of course, the black box is important on a purely literal level: it functions as a key component of the lottery. But the box has other associations as well, and it is these associations that suggest what its symbolic significance might be.

The black wooden box is very old, a relic of many past lotteries; the narrator observes that it represents tradition. It is also closed and closely guarded, suggesting mystery and uncertainty. It is shabby, "splintered badly along one side . . . and in places faded or stained," and this state of disrepair could suggest that the ritual it is part of has also deteriorated or that tradition itself has deteriorated. The box is also simple in construction and design, suggesting the primitive (and therefore perhaps outdated) nature of the ritual. Thus, this symbol encourages readers to probe the story for values and ideas, to consider and weigh the suitability of a variety of interpretations. It serves as a "hot spot" that invites questions, and the answers to these questions reinforce and enrich the story's theme.

ALLEGORY

An **allegory** communicates a doctrine, message, or moral principle by making it into a narrative in which the characters personify ideas, concepts, qualities, or other abstractions. Thus, an allegory is a story with two parallel and consistent levels of meaning — one literal and one figurative. The figurative level, which offers some moral or political lesson, is the story's main concern. The allegorical figures are significant only because they represent something beyond their literal meaning in a fixed system.

Whereas a symbol has multiple symbolic associations as well as a literal meaning, an **allegorical figure** — a character, object, place, or event in the allegory — has just one meaning within an **allegorical framework,** the set of ideas that conveys the allegory's message. (At the simplest level, for instance, one character can stand for good and another can stand for evil.) For this reason, allegorical figures do not open up a text to various interpretations the way symbols do. Because the purpose of allegory is to communicate a particular lesson, readers are not encouraged to speculate about the allegory's possible meanings; each element has only one equivalent, which readers must discover if they are to make sense of the story.

Naturally, the better a reader understands the political, religious, and literary assumptions of a writer, the easier it will be to recognize the allegorical significance of his or her work. John Bunyan's *The Pilgrim's Progress,* for example, is a famous seventeenth-century allegory based on the Christian doctrine of salvation. In order to appreciate the complexity of Bunyan's work, you would have to familiarize yourself with this doctrine — possibly by consulting an encyclopedia or a reference work such as *The Oxford Companion to English Literature*.

One type of allegory, called a **beast fable,** is a short tale, usually including a moral, in which animals assume human characteristics. Aesop's fables are the best-known examples of beast fables. More recently, contemporary writers have used beast fables to satirize the political and social conditions of our time. In one such tale, "The Gentlemen of the Jungle" by the Kenyan writer Jomo Kenyatta, an elephant is allowed to put his trunk inside a man's hut during a rainstorm. Not content with keeping his trunk dry, the elephant pushes his entire body inside the hut, displacing the man. When the man protests, the elephant takes the matter to the lion, who appoints a Commission of Enquiry to settle the matter. Eventually, the man is forced not only to abandon his hut to the elephant, but also to build new huts for all the animals on the Commission. Even so, the jealous animals occupy the man's new hut and begin fighting for space; while they are arguing, the man burns down the hut, animals and all. Like the tales told by Aesop, "The Gentlemen of the Jungle" has a moral: "Peace is costly," says the man as he walks away happily, "but it's worth the expense." The following passage from "The Gentlemen of the Jungle" reveals how the allegorical figures work within the framework of the allegory:

The elephant, obeying the command of his master (the lion), got busy with the other ministers to appoint a Commission of Enquiry. The following elders of the jungle were appointed to sit in the Commission: (1) Mr. Rhinoceros; (2) Mr. Buffalo; (3) Mr. Alligator; (4) The Rt. Hon. Mr. Fox to act as chairman; and (5) Mr. Leopard to act as Secretary of the Commission. On seeing the personnel, the man protested and asked if it was not necessary to include in this Commission a member from his side. But he was told that it was impossible, since no one from his side was well enough educated to understand the intricacy of jungle law.

From this excerpt we can see that each character represents a particular idea. For example, the members of the Commission stand for bureaucratic smugness and inequity, and the man stands for the citizens who are victimized by the government. In order to fully understand the allegorical significance of each figure in this story, of course, readers would have to know something about government bureaucracies, colonialism in Africa, and possibly a specific historical event in Kenya.

Some works contain both symbolic elements *and* allegorical elements, as Nathaniel Hawthorne's "Young Goodman Brown" (p. 292) does. The names of the story's two main characters, "Goodman" and "Faith," suggest that they fit within an allegorical system of some sort: Young Goodman Brown represents a good person who, despite his best efforts, strays from the path of righteousness; his wife, Faith, represents the quality he must hold on to in order to avoid temptation. As characters, they have no significance outside of their allegorical functions. Other elements of the story, however, are not so clear-cut. The older man whom Young Goodman Brown meets in the woods carries a staff that has carved on it "the likeness of a great black snake, so curiously wrought, that it might almost be seen to twist and wriggle itself like a living serpent." This staff, carried by a Satanic figure who represents evil and temptation, suggests the snake in the Garden of Eden, an association that neatly fits into the allegorical framework of the story. Alternately, however, the staff could suggest the "slippery," ever-changing nature of sin, the difficulty people have in perceiving sin, or sexuality (which may explain Young Goodman Brown's susceptibility to temptation). This range of possible meanings suggests that the staff functions as a symbol (not an allegorical figure) that enriches Hawthorne's allegory.

Other stories work entirely on a symbolic level and contain no allegorical figures. "The Lottery," despite its moral overtones, is not an allegory because its characters, events, and objects are not arranged to serve one rigid, didactic purpose. In fact, many different interpretations have been suggested for this story. When it was first published in June 1948 in *The New Yorker*, some readers believed it to be a story about an actual custom or ritual. As Shirley Jackson reports in her essay "Biography of a Story," even those who recognized it as fiction speculated about its meaning, seeing it as (among other things) an attack on prejudice, a criticism of society's need for a scapegoat, or a treatise on witchcraft, Christian martyrdom, or village gossip. The fact is that no single allegorical interpretation will account for every major character, object, and event in the story.

CHECKLIST	WRITING ABOUT SYMBOL AND ALLEGORY

✓ Are any universal symbols used in the work? Any conventional symbols? What is their function?

✓ Is any character, place, action, event, or object given unusual prominence or emphasis in the story? If so, does this element seem to have symbolic as well as literal value?

✓ What possible meanings does each symbol suggest?

✓ How do symbols help to depict the story's characters?

✓ How do symbols help to characterize the story's setting?

✓ How do symbols help to advance the story's plot?

✓ Are any of the symbols related? Taken together, do they seem to support a common theme?

✓ Does the story have a moral or didactic purpose? What is the message, idea, or moral principle the story seeks to convey?

✓ What equivalent may be assigned to each allegorical figure in the story?

✓ What is the allegorical framework of the story?

✓ Does the story combine allegorical figures and symbols? How do they work together in the story?

NATHANIEL HAWTHORNE (1804–1864) was born in Salem, Massachusetts, the great-great-grandson of a judge who presided over the infamous Salem witch trials. After his sea captain father was killed on a voyage when Hawthorne was four years old, his childhood was one of genteel poverty. An uncle paid for his education at Bowdoin College in Maine, where Hawthorne's friends included a future president of the United States, Franklin Pierce, who in 1853 appointed him U.S. consul in Liverpool, England. Hawthorne published four novels — *The Scarlet Letter* (1850), *The House of the Seven Gables* (1851), *The Blithedale Romance* (1852), and *The Marble Faun* (1860) — and more than one hundred short stories and sketches.

Hawthorne referred to his own work as *romance*. He used this term to mean not an escape from reality but rather a method of confronting "the depths of our common nature" and "the truth of the heart." His stories probe the dark side of human nature and frequently paint a world that is virtuous on the surface but (as Young Goodman Brown comes to believe) "one stain of guilt, one mighty blood spot" beneath. Hawthorne's stories often emphasize the ambiguity of human experience. For example, the reader is left to wonder whether Goodman Brown actually saw a witch's coven or dreamed a dream.

For Hawthorne, what is important is Brown's recognition that evil may be found every-where. "Young Goodman Brown," as Hawthorne's neighbor and friend Herman Melville once said, is a tale "as deep as Dante."

Cultural Context: During the five months of the Salem witch trials of 1692, nineteen women and men accused of being witches were put to death by hanging. The accusations began when a few young girls claimed they were possessed by the devil and subse-quently accused three Salem women of witchcraft. As the hysteria grew throughout Mas-sachusetts, the list of the accused grew as well. Eventually, 150 people were imprisoned before the governor dismissed the special witchcraft court and released the remaining prisoners. It is in this historical setting that "Young Goodman Brown" takes place.

Young Goodman° Brown   (1835)

Young Goodman Brown came forth at sunset, into the street of Salem village, but put his head back, after crossing the threshold, to exchange a parting kiss with his young wife. And Faith, as the wife was aptly named, thrust her own pretty head into the street, letting the wind play with the pink ribbons of her cap, while she called to Goodman Brown.

"Dearest heart," whispered she, softly and rather sadly, when her lips were close to his ear, "prithee, put off your journey until sunrise, and sleep in your own bed to-night. A lone woman is troubled with such dreams and such thoughts, that she's afeard of herself, sometimes. Pray, tarry with me this night, dear husband, of all nights in the year!"

"My love and my Faith," replied young Goodman Brown, "of all nights in the year, this one night must I tarry away from thee. My journey, as thou callest it, forth and back again, must needs be done 'twixt now and sunrise. What, my sweet, pretty wife, dost thou doubt me already, and we but three months married!"

"Then God bless you!" said Faith with the pink ribbons, "and may you find all well, when you come back."

5   "Amen!" cried Goodman Brown. "Say thy prayers, dear Faith, and go to bed at dusk, and no harm will come to thee."

So they parted; and the young man pursued his way, until, being about to turn the corner by the meeting-house, he looked back and saw the head of Faith still peeping after him, with a melancholy air, in spite of her pink ribbons.

"Poor little Faith!" thought he, for his heart smote him. "What a wretch am I, to leave her on such an errand! She talks of dreams, too. Methought, as she spoke, there was trouble in her face, as if a dream had warned her what work is to be done to-night. But no, no! 't would kill her to think it. Well; she's a blessed angel on earth; and after this one night, I'll cling to her skirts and follow her to Heaven."

With this excellent resolve for the future, Goodman Brown felt himself justified in making more haste on his present evil purpose. He had taken a dreary road, darkened by all the gloomiest trees of the forest, which barely stood aside to

---

Goodman: A form of address, similar to *Mr.,* meaning "husband."

let the narrow path creep through, and closed immediately behind. It was as lonely as could be; and there is this peculiarity in such a solitude, that the traveller knows not who may be concealed by the innumerable trunks and the thick boughs overhead; so that, with lonely footsteps, he may yet be passing through an unseen multitude.

"There may be a devilish Indian behind every tree," said Goodman Brown to himself; and he glanced fearfully behind him, as he added, "What if the devil himself should be at my very elbow!"

His head being turned back, he passed a crook of the road, and looking forward again, beheld the figure of a man, in grave and decent attire, seated at the foot of an old tree. He arose at Goodman Brown's approach, and walked onward, side by side with him.

"You are late, Goodman Brown," said he. "The clock of the Old South° was striking, as I came through Boston; and that is full fifteen minutes agone."

"Faith kept me back awhile," replied the young man, with a tremor in his voice, caused by the sudden appearance of his companion, though not wholly unexpected.

It was now deep dusk in the forest, and deepest in that part of it where these two were journeying. As nearly as could be discerned, the second traveller was about fifty years old, apparently in the same rank of life as Goodman Brown, and bearing a considerable resemblance to him, though perhaps more in expression than features. Still, they might have been taken for father and son. And yet, though the elder person was as simply clad as the younger, and as simple in manner too, he had an indescribable air of one who knew the world, and would not have felt abashed at the governor's dinner-table, or in King William's court,° were it possible that his affairs should call him thither. But the only thing about him that could be fixed upon as remarkable, was his staff, which bore the likeness of a great black snake, so curiously wrought, that it might almost be seen to twist and wriggle itself like a living serpent. This, of course, must have been an ocular deception, assisted by the uncertain light.

"Come, Goodman Brown!" cried his fellow-traveller, "this is a dull pace for the beginning of a journey. Take my staff, if you are so soon weary."

"Friend," said the other, exchanging his slow pace for a full stop, "having kept covenant by meeting thee here, it is my purpose now to return whence I came. I have scruples, touching the matter thou wot'st of."

"Sayest thou so?" replied he of the serpent, smiling apart. "Let us walk on, nevertheless, reasoning as we go, and if I convince thee not, thou shalt turn back. We are but a little way in the forest, yet."

"Too far, too far!" exclaimed the goodman, unconsciously resuming his walk. "My father never went into the woods on such an errand, nor his father before him. We have been a race of honest men and good Christians, since the days of the martyrs. And shall I be the first of the name of Brown that ever took this path and kept —"

Old South: Old South Church in Boston, renowned meeting place for American patriots during the Revolution.
King William: William III, king of England from 1689 to 1702.

"Such company, thou wouldst say," observed the elder person, interrupting his pause. "Well said, Goodman Brown! I have been as well acquainted with your family as with ever a one among the Puritans; and that's no trifle to say. I helped your grandfather, the constable, when he lashed the Quaker woman so smartly through the streets of Salem. And it was I that brought your father a pitch-pine knot, kindled at my own hearth, to set fire to an Indian village, in King Philip's war.° They were my good friends, both; and many a pleasant walk have we had along this path, and returned merrily after midnight. I would fain be friends with you, for their sake."

"If it be as thou sayest," replied Goodman Brown, "I marvel they never spoke of these matters. Or, verily, I marvel not, seeing that the least rumor of the sort would have driven them from New England. We are a people of prayer, and good works to boot, and abide no such wickedness."

20   "Wickedness or not," said the traveller with the twisted staff, "I have a very general acquaintance here in New England. The deacons of many a church have drunk the communion wine with me; the selectmen, of divers towns, make me their chairman; and a majority of the Great and General Court are firm supporters of my interest. The governor and I, too — but these are state secrets."

"Can this be so!" cried Goodman Brown, with a stare of amazement at his undisturbed companion. "Howbeit, I have nothing to do with the governor and council; they have their own ways, and are no rule for a simple husbandman like me. But, were I to go on with thee, how should I meet the eye of that good old man, our minister, at Salem village? Oh, his voice would make me tremble, both Sabbath-day and lecture-day!"°

Thus far, the elder traveller had listened with due gravity, but now burst into a fit of irrepressible mirth, shaking himself so violently, that his snakelike staff actually seemed to wriggle in sympathy.

"Ha, ha, ha!" shouted he, again and again; then composing himself, "Well, go on, Goodman Brown, go on; but, prithee, don't kill me with laughing!"

"Well, then, to end the matter at once," said Goodman Brown, considerably nettled, "there is my wife, Faith. It would break her dear little heart; and I'd rather break my own!"

25   "Nay, if that be the case," answered the other, "e'en go thy ways, Goodman Brown. I would not, for twenty old women like the one hobbling before us, that Faith should come to any harm."

As he spoke, he pointed his staff at a female figure on the path, in whom Goodman Brown recognized a very pious and exemplary dame, who had taught him his catechism in youth, and was still his moral and spiritual adviser, jointly with the minister and Deacon Gookin.

King Philip's war: A war of Indian resistance led by Metacomet of the Wampanoags, known to the English as "King Philip." The war, intended to halt expansion of English settlers in Massachusetts, collapsed after Metacomet's death in August 1676.

lecture-day: The day of the midweek sermon, usually Thursday.

"A marvel, truly, that Goody° Cloyse should be so far in the wilderness, at nightfall!" said he. "But, with your leave, friend, I shall take a cut through the woods, until we have left this Christian woman behind. Being a stranger to you, she might ask whom I was consorting with, and whither I was going."

"Be it so," said his fellow-traveller. "Betake you to the woods, and let me keep the path."

Accordingly, the young man turned aside, but took care to watch his companion, who advanced softly along the road, until he had come within a staff's length of the old dame. She, meanwhile, was making the best of her way, with singular speed for so aged a woman, and mumbling some indistinct words, a prayer, doubtless, as she went. The traveller put forth his staff, and touched her withered neck with what seemed the serpent's tail.

"The devil!" screamed the pious old lady.   30

"Then Goody Cloyse knows her old friend?" observed the traveller, confronting her, and leaning on his writhing stick.

"Ah, forsooth, and is it your worship, indeed?" cried the good dame. "Yea, truly is it, and in the very image of my old gossip, Goodman Brown, the grandfather of the silly fellow that now is. But, would your worship believe it? my broomstick hath strangely disappeared, stolen, as I suspect, by that unhanged witch, Goody Cory, and that, too, when I was all anointed with the juice of smallage and cinque-foil and wolf's bane —"°

"Mingled with fine wheat and the fat of a new-born babe," said the shape of old Goodman Brown.

"Ah, your worship knows the recipe," cried the old lady, cackling aloud. "So, as I was saying, being all ready for the meeting, and no horse to ride on, I made up my mind to foot it; for they tell me there is a nice young man to be taken into communion to-night. But now your good worship will lend me your arm, and we shall be there in a twinkling."

"That can hardly be," answered her friend. "I may not spare you my arm,   35
Goody Cloyse, but here is my staff, if you will."

So saying, he threw it down at her feet, where, perhaps, it assumed life, being one of the rods which its owner had formerly lent to the Egyptian Magi. Of this fact, however, Goodman Brown could not take cognizance. He had cast his eyes in astonishment, and looking down again, beheld neither Goody Cloyse nor the serpentine staff, but his fellow-traveller alone, who waited for him as calmly as if nothing had happened.

"That old woman taught me my catechism!" said the young man; and there was a world of meaning in this simple comment.

They continued to walk onward, while the elder traveller exhorted his companion to make good speed and persevere in the path, discoursing so aptly, that his

---

Goody: A contraction of "Goodwife," a term of politeness used in addressing a woman of humble station. Goody Cloyse, like Goody Cory and Martha Carrier, who appear later in the story, was one of the Salem "witches" sentenced in 1692.

smallage . . . wolf's bane: Plants believed to have magical powers. Smallage is wild celery.

arguments seemed rather to spring up in the bosom of his auditor, than to be suggested by himself. As they went he plucked a branch of maple, to serve for a walking-stick, and began to strip it of the twigs and little boughs, which were wet with evening dew. The moment his fingers touched them, they became strangely withered and dried up, as with a week's sunshine. Thus the pair proceeded, at a good free pace, until suddenly, in a gloomy hollow of the road, Goodman Brown sat himself down on the stump of a tree, and refused to go any farther.

"Friend," said he, stubbornly, "my mind is made up. Not another step will I budge on this errand. What if a wretched old woman do choose to go to the devil, when I thought she was going to Heaven! Is that any reason why I should quit my dear Faith, and go after her?"

40   "You will think better of this by and by," said his acquaintance, composedly. "Sit here and rest yourself awhile; and when you feel like moving again, there is my staff to help you along."

Without more words, he threw his companion the maple stick, and was as speedily out of sight as if he had vanished into the deepening gloom. The young man sat a few moments by the roadside, applauding himself greatly, and thinking with how clear a conscience he should meet the minister, in his morning walk, nor shrink from the eye of good old Deacon Gookin. And what calm sleep would be his, that very night, which was to have been spent so wickedly, but purely and sweetly now, in the arms of Faith! Amidst these pleasant and praiseworthy meditations, Goodman Brown heard the tramp of horses along the road, and deemed it advisable to conceal himself within the verge of the forest, conscious of the guilty purpose that had brought him thither, though now so happily turned from it.

On came the hoof-tramps and the voices of the riders, two grave old voices, conversing soberly as they drew near. These mingled sounds appeared to pass along the road, within a few yards of the young man's hiding-place; but owing, doubtless, to the depth of the gloom, at that particular spot, neither the travellers nor their steeds were visible. Though their figures brushed the small boughs by the wayside, it could not be seen that they intercepted, even for a moment, the faint gleam from the strip of bright sky, athwart which they must have passed. Goodman Brown alternately crouched and stood on tiptoe, pulling aside the branches, and thrusting forth his head as far as he durst, without discerning so much as a shadow. It vexed him the more, because he could have sworn, were such a thing possible, that he recognized the voices of the minister and Deacon Gookin, jogging along quietly, as they were wont to do, when bound to some ordination or ecclesiastical council. While yet within hearing, one of the riders stopped to pluck a switch.

"Of the two, reverend Sir," said the voice like the deacon's, "I had rather miss an ordination dinner than to-night's meeting. They tell me that some of our community are to be here from Falmouth and beyond, and others from Connecticut and Rhode Island; besides several of the Indian powwows, who, after their fashion, know almost as much deviltry as the best of us. Moreover, there is a goodly young woman to be taken into communion."

"Mighty well, Deacon Gookin!" replied the solemn old tones of the minister. "Spur up, or we shall be late. Nothing can be done, you know, until I get on the ground."

The hoofs clattered again, and the voices, talking so strangely in the empty 45 air, passed on through the forest, where no church had ever been gathered, nor solitary Christian prayed. Whither, then, could these holy men be journeying, so deep into the heathen wilderness? Young Goodman Brown caught hold of a tree, for support, being ready to sink down on the ground, faint and over-burthened with the heavy sickness of his heart. He looked up to the sky, doubting whether there really was a Heaven above him. Yet, there was the blue arch, and the stars brightening in it.

"With Heaven above, and Faith below, I will yet stand firm against the devil!" cried Goodman Brown.

While he still gazed upward, into the deep arch of the firmament, and had lifted his hands to pray, a cloud, though no wind was stirring, hurried across the zenith, and hid the brightening stars. The blue sky was still visible, except directly overhead, where this black mass of cloud was sweeping swiftly northward. Aloft in the air, as if from the depths of the cloud, came a confused and doubtful sound of voices. Once, the listener fancied that he could distinguish the accents of townspeople of his own, men and women, both pious and ungodly, many of whom he had met at the communion-table, and had seen others rioting at the tavern. The next moment, so indistinct were the sounds, he doubted whether he had heard aught but the murmur of the old forest, whispering without a wind. Then came a stronger swell of those familiar tones, heard daily in the sunshine, at Salem village, but never, until now, from a cloud at night. There was one voice, of a young woman, uttering lamentations, yet with an uncertain sorrow, and entreating for some favor, which, perhaps, it would grieve her to obtain. And all the unseen multitude, both saints and sinners, seemed to encourage her onward.

"Faith!" shouted Goodman Brown, in a voice of agony and desperation; and the echoes of the forest mocked him, crying — "Faith! Faith!" as if bewildered wretches were seeking her, all through the wilderness.

The cry of grief, rage, and terror was yet piercing the night, when the unhappy husband held his breath for a response. There was a scream, drowned immediately in a louder murmur of voices fading into far-off laughter, as the dark cloud swept away, leaving the clear and silent sky above Goodman Brown. But something fluttered lightly down through the air, and caught on the branch of a tree. The young man seized it and beheld a pink ribbon.

"My Faith is gone!" cried he, after one stupefied moment. "There is no good 50 on earth, and sin is but a name. Come, devil! for to thee is this world given."

And maddened with despair, so that he laughed loud and long, did Goodman Brown grasp his staff and set forth again, at such a rate, that he seemed to fly along the forest path, rather than to walk or run. The road grew wilder and drearier, and more faintly traced, and vanished at length, leaving him in the heart of the dark wilderness, still rushing onward, with the instinct that guides mortal man to evil. The whole forest was peopled with frightful sounds: the creaking of the trees, the howling of wild beasts, and the yell of Indians; while, sometimes, the wind tolled like a distant church bell, and sometimes gave a broad roar around the traveller, as if all Nature was laughing him to scorn. But he was himself the chief horror of the scene, and shrank not from its other horrors.

"Ha! ha! ha!" roared Goodman Brown, when the wind laughed at him. "Let us hear which will laugh loudest! Think not to frighten me with your deviltry! Come witch, come wizard, come Indian powwow, come devil himself! and here comes Goodman Brown. You may as well fear him as he fear you!"

In truth, all through the haunted forest, there could be nothing more frightful than the figure of Goodman Brown. On he flew, among the black pines, brandishing his staff with frenzied gestures, now giving vent to an inspiration of horrid blasphemy, and now shouting forth such laughter, as set all the echoes of the forest laughing like demons around him. The fiend in his own shape is less hideous, than when he rages in the breast of man. Thus sped the demoniac on his course, until, quivering among the trees, he saw a red light before him, as when the felled trunks and branches of a clearing have been set on fire, and throw up their lurid blaze against the sky, at the hour of midnight. He paused, in a lull of the tempest that had driven him onward, and heard the swell of what seemed a hymn, rolling solemnly from a distance, with the weight of many voices. He knew the tune. It was a familiar one in the choir of the village meeting-house. The verse died heavily away, and was lengthened by a chorus, not of human voices, but of all the sounds of the benighted wilderness, pealing in awful harmony together. Goodman Brown cried out; and his cry was lost to his own ear, by its unison with the cry of the desert.

In the interval of silence, he stole forward, until the light glared full upon his eyes. At one extremity of an open space, hemmed in by the dark wall of the forest, arose a rock, bearing some rude, natural resemblance either to an altar or a pulpit, and surrounded by four blazing pines, their tops aflame, their stems untouched, like candles at an evening meeting. The mass of foliage, that had overgrown the summit of the rock, was all on fire, blazing high into the night, and fitfully illuminating the whole field. Each pendent twig and leafy festoon was in a blaze. As the red light arose and fell, a numerous congregation alternately shone forth, then disappeared in shadow, and again grew, as it were, out of the darkness, peopling the heart of the solitary woods at once.

55   "A grave and dark-clad company!" quoth Goodman Brown.

In truth, they were such. Among them, quivering to-and-fro, between gloom and splendor, appeared faces that would be seen, next day, at the council-board of the province, and others which, Sabbath after Sabbath, looked devoutly heavenward, and benignantly over the crowded pews, from the holiest pulpits in the land. Some affirm, that the lady of the governor was there. At least, there were high dames well known to her, and wives of honored husbands, and widows a great multitude, and ancient maidens, all of excellent repute, and fair young girls, who trembled lest their mothers should espy them. Either the sudden gleams of light, flashing over the obscure field, bedazzled Goodman Brown, or he recognized a score of the church members of Salem village, famous for their especial sanctity. Good old Deacon Gookin had arrived, and waited at the skirts of that venerable saint, his reverend pastor. But, irreverently consorting with these grave, reputable, and pious people, these elders of the church, these chaste dames and dewy virgins, there were men of dissolute lives and women of spotted fame, wretches given over to all mean and filthy vice, and suspected even of horrid crimes. It was strange to see, that the good shrank not from the wicked, nor were the sinners abashed by the saints. Scattered, also, among their pale-faced enemies, were the Indian priests, or powwows, who had often scared their native forest with more hideous incantations than any known to English witchcraft.

"But, where is Faith?" thought Goodman Brown; and, as hope came into his heart, he trembled.

Another verse of the hymn arose, a slow and mournful strain, such as the pious love, but joined to words which expressed all that our nature can conceive of sin, and darkly hinted at far more. Unfathomable to mere mortals is the lore of fiends. Verse after verse was sung, and still the chorus of the desert swelled between, like the deepest tone of a mighty organ. And, with the final peal of that dreadful anthem, there came a sound, as if the roaring wind, the rushing streams, the howling beasts, and every other voice of the unconverted wilderness were mingling and according with the voice of guilty man, in homage to the prince of all. The four blazing pines threw up a loftier flame, and obscurely discovered shapes and visages of horror on the smoke-wreaths, above the impious assembly. At the same moment, the fire on the rock shot redly forth, and formed a glowing arch above its base, where now appeared a figure. With reverence be it spoken, the apparition bore no slight similitude, both in garb and manner, to some grave divine of the New England churches.

"Bring forth the converts!" cried a voice, that echoed through the field and rolled into the forest.

At the word, Goodman Brown stepped forth from the shadow of the trees, and approached the congregation, with whom he felt a loathful brotherhood, by the sympathy of all that was wicked in his heart. He could have well-nigh sworn, that the shape of his own dead father beckoned him to advance, looking downward from a smoke-wreath, while a woman, with dim features of despair, threw out her hand to warn him back. Was it his mother? But he had no power to retreat one step, nor to resist, even in thought, when the minister and good old Deacon Gookin seized his arms, and led him to the blazing rock. Thither came also the slender form of a veiled female, led between Goody Cloyse, that pious teacher of the catechism, and Martha Carrier, who had received the devil's promise to be queen of hell. A rampant hag was she! And there stood the proselytes, beneath the canopy of fire. 60

"Welcome, my children," said the dark figure, "to the communion of your race! Ye have found, thus young, your nature and your destiny. My children, look behind you!"

They turned; and flashing forth, as it were, in a sheet of flame, the fiend-worshippers were seen; the smile of welcome gleamed darkly on every visage.

"There," resumed the sable form, "are all whom ye have reverenced from youth. Ye deemed them holier than yourselves, and shrank from your own sin, contrasting it with their lives of righteousness and prayerful aspirations heavenward. Yet, here are they all, in my worshipping assembly! This night it shall be granted you to know their secret deeds; how hoary-bearded elders of the church have whispered wanton words to the young maids of their households; how many a woman, eager for widow's weeds, has given her husband a drink at bedtime, and let him sleep his last sleep in her bosom; how beardless youths have made haste to inherit their father's wealth; and how fair damsels — blush not, sweet ones! — have dug little graves in the garden, and bidden me, the sole guest, to an infant's funeral. By the sympathy of your human hearts for sin, ye shall scent out all the places — whether in church, bedchamber, street, field, or forest — where crime has been committed, and shall exult to behold the whole earth one stain of guilt, one mighty blood-spot. Far more than this! It shall be yours to penetrate, in every bosom, the deep mystery of sin, the fountain of all wicked arts, and which inexhaustibly supplies more evil impulses than human power — than my power, at its utmost! — can make manifest in deeds. And now, my children, look upon each other."

They did so; and, by the blaze of the hell-kindled torches, the wretched man beheld his Faith, and the wife her husband, trembling before that unhallowed altar.

65 　"Lo! there ye stand, my children," said the figure, in a deep and solemn tone, almost sad, with its despairing awfulness, as if his once angelic nature could yet mourn for our miserable race. "Depending upon one another's hearts, ye had still hoped that virtue were not all a dream! Now are ye undeceived! — Evil is the nature of mankind. Evil must be your only happiness. Welcome, again, my children, to the communion of your race!"

"Welcome!" repeated the fiend-worshippers, in one cry of despair and triumph.

And there they stood, the only pair, as it seemed, who were yet hesitating on the verge of wickedness, in this dark world. A basin was hollowed, naturally, in the rock. Did it contain water, reddened by the lurid light? or was it blood? or, perchance, a liquid flame? Herein did the Shape of Evil dip his hand, and prepare to lay the mark of baptism upon their foreheads, that they might be partakers of the mystery of sin, more conscious of the secret guilt of others, both in deed and thought, than they could now be of their own. The husband cast one look at his pale wife, and Faith at him. What polluted wretches would the next glance show them to each other, shuddering alike at what they disclosed and what they saw!

"Faith! Faith!" cried the husband. "Look up to Heaven, and resist the Wicked One!"

Whether Faith obeyed, he knew not. Hardly had he spoken, when he found himself amid calm night and solitude, listening to a roar of the wind, which died heavily away through the forest. He staggered against the rock, and felt it chill and damp, while a hanging twig, that had been all on fire, besprinkled his cheek with the coldest dew.

70 　The next morning, young Goodman Brown came slowly into the street of Salem village staring around him like a bewildered man. The good old minister was taking a walk along the grave-yard, to get an appetite for breakfast and meditate his sermon, and bestowed a blessing, as he passed, on Goodman Brown. He shrank from the venerable saint, as if to avoid an anathema. Old Deacon Gookin was at domestic worship, and the holy words of his prayer were heard through the open window. "What God doth the wizard pray to?" quoth Goodman Brown. Goody Cloyse, that excellent old Christian, stood in the early sunshine, at her own lattice, catechising a little girl, who had brought her a pint of morning's milk. Goodman Brown snatched away the child, as from the grasp of the fiend himself. Turning the corner by the meeting-house, he spied the head of Faith, with the

pink ribbons, gazing anxiously forth, and bursting into such joy at sight of him that she skipt along the street, and almost kissed her husband before the whole village. But Goodman Brown looked sternly and sadly into her face, and passed on without a greeting.

Had Goodman Brown fallen asleep in the forest, and only dreamed a wild dream of a witch-meeting?

Be it so, if you will. But, alas! it was a dream of evil omen for young Goodman Brown. A stern, a sad, a darkly meditative, a distrustful, if not a desperate man did he become, from the night of that fearful dream. On the Sabbath day, when the congregation were singing a holy psalm, he could not listen, because an anthem of sin rushed loudly upon his ear, and drowned all the blessed strain. When the minister spoke from the pulpit, with power and fervid eloquence, and with his hand on the open Bible, of the sacred truths of our religion, and of saint-like lives and triumphant deaths, and of future bliss or misery unutterable, then did Goodman Brown turn pale, dreading lest the roof should thunder down upon the gray blasphemer and his hearers. Often, awaking suddenly at midnight, he shrank from the bosom of Faith, and at morning or eventide, when the family knelt down at prayer, he scowled, and muttered to himself, and gazed sternly at his wife, and turned away. And when he had lived long, and was borne to his grave, a hoary corpse, followed by Faith, an aged woman, and children and grand-children, a goodly procession, besides neighbors not a few, they carved no hopeful verse upon his tombstone; for his dying hour was gloom.

Reading and Reacting

1. Who is the narrator of "Young Goodman Brown"? What advantages does the narrative point of view give the author?
2. What does young Goodman Brown mean when he says "of all nights in the year, this one night must I tarry away from thee" (par. 3)? What is important about *this* night, and why does Goodman Brown believe he must journey " 'twixt now and sunrise"?
3. Is Goodman Brown surprised to encounter the second traveler on the road, or does he seem to expect him? What is the significance of their encounter? What do you make of the fact that the stranger bears a strong resemblance to young Goodman Brown?
4. What sins are the various characters Goodman Brown meets in the woods guilty of committing?
5. "Young Goodman Brown" has two distinct settings: Salem and the woods. What are the differences between these settings? What significance does each setting have in the story?
6. Which figures in the story are allegorical, and which are symbols? On what evidence do you base your conclusions?
7. Why do the people gather in the woods? Why do they attend the ceremony?
8. Explain the change that takes place in young Goodman Brown at the end of the story. Why can he not listen to the singing of holy psalms or to the minister's sermons? What causes him to turn away from Faith and die in gloom?

9. JOURNAL ENTRY At the end of the story, the narrator suggests that Goodman Brown might have fallen asleep and imagined his encounter with the witches. Do you think the events in the story are all a dream?

10 CRITICAL PERSPECTIVE In *The Power of Blackness*, his classic study of nineteenth-century American writers, Harry Levin observes that Hawthorne had doubts about conventional religion. This, Levin believes, is why all efforts to read an enlightening theological message into Hawthorne's works are "doomed to failure."

What comment do you think Hawthorne is making in "Young Goodman Brown" about religious faith?

Related Works: "Where Are You Going, Where Have You Been?" (p. 387), "We Wear the Mask" (p. 871), "La Belle Dame sans Merci: A Ballad" (p. 889)

SHIRLEY JACKSON (1916–1965) is best known for her restrained tales of horror and the supernatural, most notably her novel *The Haunting of Hill House* (1959) and the short story "The Lottery" (1948). Among her other works are two novels dealing with divided personalities — *The Bird's Nest* (1954) and *We Have Always Lived in the Castle* (1962) — and two collections of comic tales about her children and family life, *Life among the Savages* (1953) and *Raising Demons* (1957). A posthumous collection of stories, *Just an Ordinary Day* (1997), was published after the discovery of a box of some of Jackson's unpublished papers in a Vermont barn and her heirs' subsequent search for her other uncollected works.

Jackson was an intense, self-destructive, contradictory personality: a witty hostess to crowds of literary friends; a self-described witch, clairvoyant, and student of magic; a cookie-baking "Mom" who wrote chilling tales between loads of laundry. With her husband, literary critic Stanley Edgar Hyman, she settled in the small town of Bennington, Vermont, but was never accepted by the townspeople. "The Lottery" is set in much the same kind of small, hidebound town. Despite the story's matter-of-fact tone and familiar setting, its publication in *The New Yorker* provoked a torrent of letters from enraged and shocked readers. In her quiet way, Jackson presented the underside of village life and revealed to readers the dark side of human nature. Future writers of gothic tales recognized their great debt to Jackson. Horror master Stephen King dedicated his book *Firestarter* "to Shirley Jackson, who never had to raise her voice."

Cultural Context: "The Lottery" is sometimes seen as a protest against totalitarianism, a form of authoritarian government that permits no individual freedom. In *Eichmann in Jerusalem* (1963), political scientist Hannah Arendt (1906–1975) wrote about totalitarianism as it pertained to Nazi Germany and the Holocaust. Here, she introduced the concept of "the banality of evil," the potential in ordinary people to do evil things. Americans of the post–World War II era saw themselves as "good guys" defending the world against foreign evils. Jackson's story, written scarcely three years after the liberation of Auschwitz, told Americans something they did not want to hear — that the face of human evil could look just like their next-door neighbor.

The Lottery (1948)

The morning of June 27th was clear and sunny, with the fresh warmth of a full-summer day; the flowers were blossoming profusely and the grass was richly green. The people of the village began to gather in the square, between the post office and the bank, around ten o'clock; in some towns there were so many people that the lottery took two days and had to be started on June 26th, but in this village, where there were only about three hundred people, the whole lottery took less than two hours, so it could begin at ten o'clock in the morning and still be through in time to allow the villagers to get home for noon dinner.

The children assembled first, of course. School was recently over for the summer, and the feeling of liberty sat uneasily on most of them; they tended to gather together quietly for a while before they broke into boisterous play, and their talk was still of the classroom and the teacher, of books and reprimands. Bobby Martin had already stuffed his pockets full of stones, and the other boys soon followed his example, selecting the smoothest and roundest stones; Bobby and Harry Jones and Dickie Delacroix — the villagers pronounced this name "Dellacroy" — eventually made a great pile of stones in one corner of the square and guarded it against the raids of the other boys. The girls stood aside, talking among themselves, looking over their shoulders at the boys, and the very small children rolled in the dust or clung to the hands of their older brothers or sisters.

Soon the men began to gather, surveying their own children, speaking of planting and rain, tractors and taxes. They stood together, away from the pile of stones in the corner, and their jokes were quiet and they smiled rather than laughed. The women, wearing faded house dresses and sweaters, came shortly after their menfolk. They greeted one another and exchanged bits of gossip as they went to join their husbands. Soon the women, standing by their husbands, began to call to their children, and the children came reluctantly, having to be called four or five times. Bobby Martin ducked under his mother's grasping hand and ran, laughing, back to the pile of stones. His father spoke up sharply, and Bobby came quickly and took his place between his father and his oldest brother.

The lottery was conducted — as were the square dances, the teen-age club, the Halloween program — by Mr. Summers, who had time and energy to devote to civic activities. He was a round-faced, jovial man and he ran the coal business, and people were sorry for him, because he had no children and his wife was a scold. When he arrived in the square, carrying the black wooden box, there was a murmur of conversation among the villagers, and he waved and called, "Little late today, folks." The postmaster, Mr. Graves, followed him, carrying a three-legged stool, and the stool was put in the center of the square and Mr. Summers set the black box down on it. The villagers kept their distance, leaving a space between themselves and the stool, and when Mr. Summers said, "Some of you fellows want to give me a hand?" there was a hesitation before two men, Mr. Martin and his oldest son, Baxter, came forward to hold the box steady on the stool while Mr. Summers stirred up the papers inside it.

The original paraphernalia for the lottery had been lost long ago, and the black box now resting on the stool had been put into use even before Old Man

Warner, the oldest man in town, was born. Mr. Summers spoke frequently to the villagers about making a new box, but no one liked to upset even as much tradition as was represented by the black box. There was a story that the present box had been made with some pieces of the box that had preceded it, the one that had been constructed when the first people settled down to make a village here. Every year, after the lottery, Mr. Summers began talking again about a new box, but every year the subject was allowed to fade off without anything's being done. The black box grew shabbier each year; by now it was no longer completely black but splintered badly along one side to show the original wood color, and in some places faded or stained.

Mr. Martin and his oldest son, Baxter, held the black box securely on the stool until Mr. Summers had stirred the papers thoroughly with his hand. Because so much of the ritual had been forgotten or discarded, Mr. Summers had been successful in having slips of paper substituted for the chips of wood that had been used for generations. Chips of wood, Mr. Summers had argued, had been all very well when the village was tiny, but now that the population was more than three hundred and likely to keep on growing, it was necessary to use something that would fit more easily into the black box. The night before the lottery, Mr. Summers and Mr. Graves made up the slips of paper and put them in the box, and it was then taken to the safe of Mr. Summers's coal company and locked up until Mr. Summers was ready to take it to the square next morning. The rest of the year, the box was put away, sometimes one place, sometimes another; it had spent one year in Mr. Graves's barn and another year underfoot in the post office, and sometimes it was set on a shelf in the Martin grocery and left there.

There was a great deal of fussing to be done before Mr. Summers declared the lottery open. There were the lists to make up — of heads of families, heads of households in each family, members of each household in each family. There was the proper swearing-in of Mr. Summers by the postmaster, as the official of the lottery; at one time, some people remembered, there had been a recital of some sort, performed by the official of the lottery, a perfunctory, tuneless chant that had been rattled off duly each year; some people believed that the official of the lottery used to stand just so when he said or sang it, others believed that he was supposed to walk among the people, but years and years ago this part of the ritual had been allowed to lapse. There had been, also, a ritual salute, which the official of the lottery had had to use in addressing each person who came up to draw from the box, but this also had changed with time, until now it was felt necessary only for the official to speak to each person approaching. Mr. Summers was very good at all this; in his clean white shirt and blue jeans, with one hand resting carelessly on the black box, he seemed very proper and important as he talked interminably to Mr. Graves and the Martins.

Just as Mr. Summers finally left off talking and turned to the assembled villagers, Mrs. Hutchinson came hurriedly along the path to the square, her sweater thrown over her shoulders, and slid into place in the back of the crowd. "Clean forgot what day it was," she said to Mrs. Delacroix, who stood next to her, and they both laughed softly. "Thought my old man was out back stacking wood," Mrs. Hutchinson went on, "and then I looked out the window and the kids was

gone, and then I remembered it was the twenty-seventh and came a-running."
She dried her hands on her apron, and Mrs. Delacroix said, "You're in time,
though. They're still talking away up there."

Mrs. Hutchinson craned her neck to see through the crowd and found her
husband and children standing near the front. She tapped Mrs. Delacroix on the
arm as a farewell and began to make her way through the crowd. The people separated good-humoredly to let her through; two or three people said, in voices just
loud enough to be heard across the crowd, "Here comes your Missus, Hutchinson,"
and "Bill, she made it after all." Mrs. Hutchinson reached her husband, and Mr.
Summers, who had been waiting, said cheerfully, "Thought we were going to have
to get on without you, Tessie." Mrs. Hutchinson said, grinning, "Wouldn't have
me leave m'dishes in the sink, now, would you, Joe?," and soft laughter ran
through the crowd as the people stirred back into position after Mrs. Hutchinson's
arrival.

"Well, now," Mr. Summers said soberly, "guess we better get started, get this   10
over with, so's we can go back to work. Anybody ain't here?"

"Dunbar," several people said. "Dunbar, Dunbar."

Mr. Summers consulted his list. "Clyde Dunbar," he said. "That's right. He's
broke his leg, hasn't he? Who's drawing for him?"

"Me, I guess," a woman said, and Mr. Summers turned to look at her. "Wife
draws for her husband," Mr. Summers said. "Don't you have a grown boy to do it
for you, Janey?" Although Mr. Summers and everyone else in the village knew the
answer perfectly well, it was the business of the official of the lottery to ask such
questions formally. Mr. Summers waited with an expression of polite interest
while Mrs. Dunbar answered.

"Horace's not but sixteen yet," Mrs. Dunbar said regretfully. "Guess I gotta fill
in for the old man this year."

"Right," Mr. Summers said. He made a note on the list he was holding. Then   15
he asked, "Watson boy drawing this year?"

A tall boy in the crowd raised his hand. "Here," he said. "I'm drawing for
m'mother and me." He blinked his eyes nervously and ducked his head as several
voices in the crowd said things like "Good fellow, Jack," and "Glad to see your
mother's got a man to do it."

"Well," Mr. Summers said, "guess that's everyone. Old Man Warner make it?"

"Here," a voice said, and Mr. Summers nodded.

A sudden hush fell on the crowd as Mr. Summers cleared his throat and looked
at the list. "All ready?" he called. "Now, I'll read the names — heads of families
first — and the men come up and take a paper out of the box. Keep the paper
folded in your hand without looking at it until everyone has had a turn. Everything clear?"

The people had done it so many times that they only half listened to the di-   20
rections; most of them were quiet, wetting their lips, not looking around. Then
Mr. Summers raised one hand high and said, "Adams." A man disengaged himself
from the crowd and came forward. "Hi, Steve," Mr. Summers said, and Mr. Adams
said, "Hi, Joe." They grinned at one another humorlessly and nervously. Then Mr.
Adams reached into the black box and took out a folded paper. He held it firmly

by one corner as he turned and went hastily back to his place in the crowd, where he stood a little apart from his family, not looking down at his hand.

"Allen," Mr. Summers said. "Anderson. . . . Bentham."

"Seems like there's no time at all between lotteries any more," Mrs. Delacroix said to Mrs. Graves in the back row. "Seems like we got through with the last one only last week."

"Time sure goes fast," Mrs. Graves said.

"Clark. . . . Delacroix."

25 "There goes my old man," Mrs. Delacroix said. She held her breath while her husband went forward.

"Dunbar," Mr. Summers said, and Mrs. Dunbar went steadily to the box while one of the women said, "Go on, Janey," and another said, "There she goes."

"We're next," Mrs. Graves said. She watched while Mr. Graves came around from the side of the box, greeted Mr. Summers gravely, and selected a slip of paper from the box. By now, all through the crowd there were men holding the small folded papers in their large hands, turning them over and over nervously. Mrs. Dunbar and her two sons stood together, Mrs. Dunbar holding the slip of paper.

"Harburt. . . . Hutchinson."

"Get up there, Bill," Mrs. Hutchinson said, and the people near her laughed.

30 "Jones."

"They do say," Mr. Adams said to Old Man Warner, who stood next to him, "that over in the north village they're talking of giving up the lottery."

Old Man Warner snorted. "Pack of crazy fools," he said. "Listening to the young folks, nothing's good enough for *them*. Next thing you know, they'll be wanting to go back to living in caves, nobody work any more, live *that* way for a while. Used to be a saying about 'Lottery in June, corn be heavy soon.' First thing you know, we'd all be eating stewed chickweed and acorns. There's *always* been a lottery," he added petulantly. "Bad enough to see young Joe Summers up there joking with everybody."

"Some places have already quit lotteries," Mrs. Adams said.

"Nothing but trouble in *that*," Old Man Warner said stoutly. "Pack of young fools."

35 "Martin." And Bobby Martin watched his father go forward. "Overdyke. . . . Percy."

"I wish they'd hurry," Mrs. Dunbar said to her older son. "I wish they'd hurry."

"They're almost through," her son said.

"You get ready to run tell Dad," Mrs. Dunbar said.

Mr. Summers called his own name and then stepped forward precisely and selected a slip from the box. Then he called, "Warner."

40 "Seventy-seventh year I been in the lottery," Old Man Warner said as he went through the crowd. "Seventy-seventh time."

"Watson." The tall boy came awkwardly through the crowd. Someone said, "Don't be nervous, Jack," and Mr. Summers said, "Take your time, son."

"Zanini."

After that, there was a long pause, a breathless pause, until Mr. Summers, holding his slip of paper in the air, said, "All right, fellows." For a minute, no one moved, and then all the slips of paper were opened. Suddenly, all the women began to speak at once, saying, "Who is it?," "Who's got it?," "Is it the Dunbars?," "Is it the Watsons?" Then the voices began to say, "It's Hutchinson. It's Bill," "Bill Hutchinson's got it."

"Go tell your father," Mrs. Dunbar said to her older son.

People began to look around to see the Hutchinsons. Bill Hutchinson was 45 standing quiet, staring down at the paper in his hand. Suddenly, Tessie Hutchinson shouted to Mr. Summers, "You didn't give him time enough to take any paper he wanted. I saw you. It wasn't fair!"

"Be a good sport, Tessie," Mrs. Delacroix called, and Mrs. Graves said, "All of us took the same chance."

"Shut up, Tessie," Bill Hutchinson said.

"Well, everyone," Mr. Summers said, "that was done pretty fast, and now we've got to be hurrying a little more to get done in time." He consulted his next list. "Bill," he said, "you draw for the Hutchinson family. You got any other households in the Hutchinsons?"

"There's Don and Eva," Mrs. Hutchinson yelled, "Make *them* take their chance!"

"Daughters draw with their husbands' families, Tessie," Mr. Summers said gen- 50 tly. "You know that as well as anyone else."

"It wasn't *fair*," Tessie said.

"I guess not, Joe," Bill Hutchinson said regretfully. "My daughter draws with her husband's family, that's only fair. And I've got no other family except the kids."

"Then, as far as drawing for families is concerned, it's you," Mr. Summers said in explanation, "and as far as drawing for households is concerned, that's you, too. Right?"

"Right," Bill Hutchinson said.

"How many kids, Bill?" Mr. Summers asked formally. 55

"Three," Bill Hutchinson said. "There's Bill, Jr., and Nancy, and little Dave. And Tessie and me."

"All right, then," Mr. Summers said. "Harry, you got their tickets back?"

Mr. Graves nodded and held up the slips of paper. "Put them in the box, then," Mr. Summers directed. "Take Bill's and put it in."

"I think we ought to start over," Mrs. Hutchinson said, as quietly as she could. "I tell you it wasn't *fair*. You didn't give him time enough to choose. *Every*body saw that."

Mr. Graves had selected the five slips and put them in the box, and he dropped 60 all the papers but those onto the ground, where the breeze caught them and lifted them off.

"Listen, everybody," Mrs. Hutchinson was saying to the people around her.

"Ready, Bill?" Mr. Summers asked, and Bill Hutchinson, with one quick glance around at his wife and children, nodded.

"Remember," Mr. Summers said, "take the slips and keep them folded until each person has taken one. Harry, you help little Dave." Mr. Graves took the hand of the little boy, who came willingly with him up to the box. "Take a paper out of the box, Davy," Mr. Summers said. Davy put his hand into the box and laughed.

"Take just *one* paper," Mr. Summers said. "Harry, you hold it for him." Mr. Graves took the child's hand and removed the folded paper from the tight fist and held it while little Dave stood next to him and looked at him wonderingly.

"Nancy next," Mr. Summers said. Nancy was twelve, and her school friends breathed heavily as she went forward, switching her skirt, and took a slip daintily from the box. "Bill, Jr.," Mr. Summers said, and Billy, his face red and his feet over-large, nearly knocked the box over as he got a paper out. "Tessie," Mr. Summers said. She hesitated for a minute, looking around defiantly, and then set her lips and went up to the box. She snatched a paper out and held it behind her.

65   "Bill," Mr. Summers said, and Bill Hutchinson reached into the box and felt around, bringing his hand out at last with the slip of paper in it.

The crowd was quiet. A girl whispered, "I hope it's not Nancy," and the sound of the whisper reached the edges of the crowd.

"It's not the way it used to be," Old Man Warner said clearly. "People ain't the way they used to be."

"All right," Mr. Summers said. "Open the papers. Harry, you open little Dave's."

Mr. Graves opened the slip of paper and there was a general sigh through the crowd as he held it up and everyone could see that it was blank. Nancy and Bill, Jr., opened theirs at the same time, and both beamed and laughed, turning around to the crowd and holding their slips of paper above their heads.

70   "Tessie," Mr. Summers said. There was a pause, and then Mr. Summers looked at Bill Hutchinson, and Bill unfolded his paper and showed it. It was blank.

"It's Tessie," Mr. Summers said, and his voice was hushed. "Show us her paper, Bill."

Bill Hutchinson went over to his wife and forced the slip of paper out of her hand. It had a black spot on it, the black spot Mr. Summers had made the night before with the heavy pencil in the coal-company office. Bill Hutchinson held it up, and there was a stir in the crowd.

"All right, folks," Mr. Summers said. "Let's finish quickly."

Although the villagers had forgotten the ritual and lost the original black box, they still remembered to use stones. The pile of stones the boys had made earlier was ready; there were stones on the ground with the blowing scraps of paper that had come out of the box. Mrs. Delacroix selected a stone so large she had to pick it up with both hands and turned to Mrs. Dunbar. "Come on," she said. "Hurry up."

75   Mrs. Dunbar had small stones in both hands, and she said, gasping for breath, "I can't run at all. You'll have to go ahead and I'll catch up with you."

The children had stones already, and someone gave little Davy Hutchinson a few pebbles.

Tessie Hutchinson was in the center of a cleared space by now, and she held her hands out desperately as the villagers moved in on her. "It isn't fair," she said. A stone hit her on the side of the head.

Old Man Warner was saying, "Come on, come on, everyone." Steve Adams was in the front of the crowd of villagers, with Mrs. Graves beside him.

"It isn't fair, it isn't right," Mrs. Hutchinson screamed, and then they were upon her.

Reading and Reacting

1. What possible significance, beyond their literal meaning, might each of these items have: the village square, Mrs. Hutchinson's apron, Old Man Warner, the slips of paper, the black spot?

2. "The Lottery" takes place in summer, a conventional symbol that has a positive connotation. What does this setting contribute to the story's plot? To its atmosphere?

3. What, if anything, might the names *Graves, Adams, Summers,* and *Delacroix* signify in the context of this story? Do you think these names are intended to have any special significance? Why or why not?

4. What role do the children play in the ritual? How can you explain their presence in the story? Do they have any symbolic role?

5. What symbolic significance might be found in the way the characters are dressed? In their conversation?

6. In what sense is the story's title ironic?

7. Throughout the story, there is a general atmosphere of excitement. What indication is there of nervousness or apprehension?

8. Early in the story, the boys stuff their pockets with stones, foreshadowing the attack in the story's conclusion. What other examples of foreshadowing can you identify?

9. **JOURNAL ENTRY** How can a ritual like the lottery continue to be held year after year? Why does no one move to end it? Can you think of a modern-day counterpart to this lottery — a situation in which people continue to act in ways they know to be wrong rather than challenge the status quo? How can you account for such behavior?

10. **CRITICAL PERSPECTIVE** When "The Lottery" was published in the June 26, 1948, issue of *The New Yorker,* its effect was immediate. The story, as the critic Judy Oppenheimer notes in her book *Private Demons: The Life of Shirley Jackson,* "provoked an unprecedented outpouring of fury, horror, rage, disgust, and intense fascination." As a result, Jackson received hundreds of letters, which contained (among others) the following interpretations of the story:

- The story is an attack on small-town America.
- The story is a parable about the perversion of democracy.
- The story is a criticism of prejudice, particularly anti-Semitism.
- The story has no point at all.

How plausible do you think each of these interpretations is? Which comes closest to your interpretation of the story? Why?

Related Works: "Where Are You Going, Where Have You Been?" (p. 387), "How Did They Kill My Grandmother?" (p. 574), "Patterns" (p. 613)

ALICE WALKER (1944–   ) is an accomplished writer of poetry, fiction, and criticism. Her characters are mainly rural African Americans, often living in her native Georgia, who struggle to survive in hostile environments. Her writing displays a particular sensitivity to the emotions of people who suffer physical or psychological harm in their efforts to assert their own identities.

Walker was the youngest of eight children born to Willie Lee and Minnie Tallulah Grant Walker, sharecroppers who raised cotton. She left the rural South to attend Spelman College in Atlanta (1961–1963) and Sarah Lawrence College in Bronxville, New York (1963–1965).

In 1967, Walker moved to Mississippi, where she was supported in the writing of her first novel, *The Third Life of Grange Copeland* (1970), by a National Endowment for the Arts grant. Her short story "Everyday Use" was included in *Best American Short Stories 1973*. Other novels and short story collections followed, including *In Love and Trouble: Stories of Black Women* (1973), *Meridian* (1976), *You Can't Keep a Good Woman Down* (short stories, 1981), *The Temple of My Familiar* (1989), *Possessing the Secret of Joy* (1993), *The Complete Stories* (short stories, 1994), and *By the Light of My Father's Smile* (1998). Walker's third novel, *The Color Purple* (1982), won the American Book Award and a Pulitzer Prize.

In the third year of her marriage, Walker took back her maiden name because she wanted to honor her great-great-great-grandmother who had walked, carrying her two children, from Virginia to Georgia. Walker's renaming is consistent with one of her goals in writing, which is to further the process of reconnecting people to their ancestors. She has said that "it is fatal to see yourself as separate" and that if people can reaffirm the past, they can "make a different future."

Cultural Context: Quilting attained the status of art in Europe in the fourteenth century. However, quilting reached its fullest development in North America. By the end of the eighteenth century, the American quilt had taken on unique and distinctive features separating it from quilts made in other parts of the world. For African Americans, quilting may have particular significance. Some scholars believe that hidden within the quilting patterns employed by slaves were directions to the Underground Railroad and freedom. Today, quilting reflects a heritage passed down through generations.

Everyday Use   (1973)

For Your Grandma

I will wait for her in the yard that Maggie and I made so clean and wavy yesterday afternoon. A yard like this is more comfortable than most people know. It is not just a yard. It is like an extended living room. When the hard clay is swept clean as a floor and the fine sand around the edges lined with tiny, irregular grooves, anyone can come and sit and look up into the elm tree and wait for the breezes that never come inside the house.

Maggie will be nervous until after her sister goes: she will stand hopelessly in corners, homely and ashamed of the burn scars down her arms and legs, eying her sister with a mixture of envy and awe. She thinks her sister has held life always in the palm of one hand, that "no" is a word the world never learned to say to her.

You've no doubt seen those TV shows where the child who has "made it" is confronted, as a surprise, by her own mother and father, tottering in weakly from backstage. (A pleasant surprise, of course: What would they do if parent and child came on the show only to curse out and insult each other?) On TV mother and child embrace and smile into each other's faces. Sometimes the mother and father weep, the child wraps them in her arms and leans across the table to tell how she would not have made it without their help. I have seen these programs.

Sometimes I dream a dream in which Dee and I are suddenly brought together on a TV program of this sort. Out of a dark and soft-seated limousine I am ushered into a bright room filled with many people. There I meet a smiling, gray, sporty man like Johnny Carson who shakes my hand and tells me what a fine girl I have. Then we are on the stage and Dee is embracing me with tears in her eyes. She pins on my dress a large orchid, even though she has told me once that she thinks orchids are tacky flowers.

In real life I am a large, big-boned woman with rough, man-working hands. 5 In the winter I wear flannel nightgowns to bed and overalls during the day. I can kill and clean a hog as mercilessly as a man. My fat keeps me hot in zero weather. I can work outside all day, breaking ice to get water for washing; I can eat pork liver cooked over the open fire minutes after it comes steaming from the hog. One winter I knocked a bull calf straight in the brain between the eyes with a sledge hammer and had the meat hung up to chill before nightfall. But of course all this does not show on television. I am the way my daughter would want me to be: a hundred pounds lighter, my skin like an uncooked barley pancake. My hair glistens in the hot bright lights. Johnny Carson has much to do to keep up with my quick and witty tongue.

But that is a mistake. I know even before I wake up. Who ever knew a Johnson with a quick tongue? Who can even imagine me looking a strange white man in the eye? It seems to me I have talked to them always with one foot raised in flight, with my head turned in whichever way is farthest from them. Dee, though. She would always look anyone in the eye. Hesitation was no part of her nature.

"How do I look, Mama?" Maggie says, showing just enough of her thin body enveloped in pink skirt and red blouse for me to know she's there, almost hidden by the door.

"Come out into the yard," I say.

Have you ever seen a lame animal, perhaps a dog run over by some careless person rich enough to own a car, sidle up to someone who is ignorant enough to be kind to him? That is the way my Maggie walks. She has been like this, chin on chest, eyes on ground, feet in shuffle, ever since the fire that burned the other house to the ground.

Dee is lighter than Maggie, with nicer hair and a fuller figure. She's a woman 10 now, though sometimes I forget. How long ago was it that the other house burned? Ten, twelve years? Sometimes I can still hear the flames and feel Maggie's arms sticking to me, her hair smoking and her dress falling off her in little black papery flakes. Her eyes seemed stretched open, blazed open by the flames reflected in them. And Dee. I see her standing off under the sweet gum tree she used to dig gum out of; a look of concentration on her face as she watched the last dingy gray board of the house fall in toward the red-hot brick chimney. Why don't you do a dance around the ashes? I'd wanted to ask her. She had hated the house that much.

I used to think she hated Maggie, too. But that was before we raised the money, the church and me, to send her to Augusta to school. She used to read to us without pity; forcing words, lies, other folks' habits, whole lives upon us two, sitting trapped and ignorant underneath her voice. She washed us in a river of make-believe, burned us with a lot of knowledge we didn't necessarily need to know. Pressed us to her with the serious way she read, to shove us away at just the moment, like dimwits, we seemed about to understand.

Dee wanted nice things. A yellow organdy dress to wear to her graduation from high school; black pumps to match a green suit she'd made from an old suit somebody gave me. She was determined to stare down any disaster in her efforts. Her eyelids would not flicker for minutes at a time. Often I fought off the temptation to shake her. At sixteen she had a style of her own, and knew what style was.

I never had an education myself. After second grade the school was closed down. Don't ask me why: in 1927 colored asked fewer questions than they do now. Sometimes Maggie reads to me. She stumbles along good-naturedly but can't see well. She knows she is not bright. Like good looks and money, quickness passed her by. She will marry John Thomas (who has mossy teeth in an earnest face) and then I'll be free to sit here and I guess just sing church songs to myself. Although I never was a good singer. Never could carry a tune. I was always better at a man's job. I used to love to milk till I was hooked in the side in '49. Cows are soothing and slow and don't bother you, unless you try to milk them the wrong way.

I have deliberately turned my back on the house. It is three rooms, just like the one that burned, except the roof is tin; they don't make shingle roofs any more. There are no real windows, just some holes cut in the sides, like the portholes in a ship, but not round and not square, with rawhide holding the shutters up on the outside. This house is in a pasture, too, like the other one. No doubt when Dee sees it she will want to tear it down. She wrote me once that no matter where we "choose" to live, she will manage to come see us. But she will never bring her friends. Maggie and I thought about this and Maggie asked me, "Mama, when did Dee ever *have* any friends?"

15   She had a few. Furtive boys in pink shirts hanging about on washday after school. Nervous girls who never laughed. Impressed with her they worshiped the well-turned phrase, the cute shape, the scalding humor that erupted like bubbles in lye. She read to them.

When she was courting Jimmy T she didn't have much time to pay to us, but turned all her faultfinding power on him. He *flew* to marry a cheap city girl from a family of ignorant flashy people. She hardly had time to recompose herself.

When she comes I will meet — but there they are!

Maggie attempts to make a dash for the house, in her shuffling way, but I stay her with my hand. "Come back here," I say. And she stops and tries to dig a well in the sand with her toe.

It is hard to see them clearly through the strong sun. But even the first glimpse of leg out of the car tells me it is Dee. Her feet were always neat-looking, as if God himself had shaped them with a certain style. From the other side of the car comes a short, stocky man. Hair is all over his head a foot long and hanging from his chin like a kinky mule tail. I hear Maggie suck in her breath. "Uhnnnh," is what it sounds like. Like when you see the wriggling end of a snake just in front of your foot on the road. "Uhnnnh."

Dee next. A dress down to the ground, in this hot weather. A dress so loud it   20
hurts my eyes. There are yellows and oranges enough to throw back the light of the sun. I feel my whole face warming from the heat waves it throws out. Earrings gold, too, and hanging down to her shoulders. Bracelets dangling and making noises when she moves her arm up to shake the folds of the dress out of her armpits. The dress is loose and flows, and as she walks closer, I like it. I hear Maggie go "Uhnnnh" again. It is her sister's hair. It stands straight up like the wool on a sheep. It is black as night and around the edges are two long pigtails that rope about like small lizards disappearing behind her ears.

"Wa-su-zo-Tean-o!"° she says, coming on in that gliding way the dress makes her move. The short stocky fellow with the hair to his navel is all grinning and he follows up with "Asalamalakim,° my mother and sister!" He moves to hug Maggie but she falls back, right up against the back of my chair. I feel her trembling there and when I look up I see the perspiration falling off her chin.

"Don't get up," says Dee. Since I am stout it takes something of a push. You can see me trying to move a second or two before I make it. She turns, showing white heels through her sandals, and goes back to the car. Out she peeks next with a Polaroid. She stoops down quickly and lines up picture after picture of me sitting there in front of the house with Maggie cowering behind me. She never takes a shot without making sure the house is included. When a cow comes nibbling around the edge of the yard she snaps it and me and Maggie *and* the house. Then she puts the Polaroid in the back seat of the car, and comes up and kisses me on the forehead.

Meanwhile Asalamalakim is going through motions with Maggie's hand. Maggie's hand is as limp as a fish, and probably as cold, despite the sweat, and she keeps trying to pull it back. It looks like Asalamalakim wants to shake hands but wants to do it fancy. Or maybe he don't know how people shake hands. Anyhow, he soon gives up on Maggie.

"Well," I say. "Dee."

"No, Mama," she says. "Not 'Dee,' Wangero Leewanika Kemanjo!"   25

"What happened to 'Dee'?" I wanted to know.

Wa-su-zo-Tean-o: A greeting in Swahili; Dee sounds it out one syllable at a time.

Asalamalakim: A greeting in Arabic: "Peace be upon you."

"She's dead," Wangero said. "I couldn't bear it any longer, being named after the people who oppress me."

"You know as well as me you was named after your aunt Dicie," I said. Dicie is my sister. She named Dee. We called her "Big Dee" after Dee was born.

"But who was *she* named after?" asked Wangero.

30   "I guess after Grandma Dee," I said.

"And who was she named after?" asked Wangero.

"Her mother," I said, and saw Wangero was getting tired. "That's about as far back as I can trace it," I said. Though, in fact, I probably could have carried it back beyond the Civil War through the branches.

"Well," said Asalamalakim, "there you are."

"Uhnnnh," I heard Maggie say.

35   "There I was not," I said, "before 'Dicie' cropped up in our family, so why should I try to trace it that far back?"

He just stood there grinning, looking down on me like somebody inspecting a Model A car. Every once in a while he and Wangero sent eye signals over my head.

"How do you pronounce this name?" I asked.

"You don't have to call me by it if you don't want to," said Wangero.

"Why shouldn't I?" I asked. "If that's what you want us to call you, we'll call you."

40   "I know it might sound awkward at first," said Wangero.

"I'll get used to it," I said. "Ream it out again."

Well, soon we got the name out of the way. Asalamalakim had a name twice as long and three times as hard. After I tripped over it two or three times he told me to just call him Hakim-a-barber. I wanted to ask him was he a barber, but I didn't really think he was, so I didn't ask.

"You must belong to those beef-cattle peoples down the road," I said. They said "Asalamalakim" when they met you, too, but they didn't shake hands. Always too busy: feeding the cattle, fixing the fences, putting up salt-lick shelters, throwing down hay. When the white folks poisoned some of the herd the men stayed up all night with rifles in their hands. I walked a mile and a half just to see the sight.

Hakim-a-barber said, "I accept some of their doctrines, but farming and raising cattle is not my style." (They didn't tell me, and I didn't ask, whether Wangero [Dee] had really gone and married him.)

45   We sat down to eat and right away he said he didn't eat collards and pork was unclean. Wangero, though, went on through the chitlins and corn bread, the greens and everything else. She talked a blue streak over the sweet potatoes. Everything delighted her. Even the fact that we still used the benches her daddy made for the table when we couldn't afford to buy chairs.

"Oh, Mama!" she cried. Then turned to Hakim-a-barber. "I never knew how lovely these benches are. You can feel the rump prints," she said, running her hands underneath her and along the bench. Then she gave a sigh and her hand closed over Grandma Dee's butter dish. "That's it!" she said. "I knew there was something I wanted to ask you if I could have." She jumped up from the table and went over in the corner where the churn stood, the milk in it clabber by now. She looked at the churn and looked at it.

"This churn top is what I need," she said. "Didn't Uncle Buddy whittle it out of a tree you all used to have?"

"Yes," I said.

"Uh huh," she said happily. "And I want the dasher, too."

"Uncle Buddy whittle that, too?" asked the barber.   50

Dee (Wangero) looked up at me.

"Aunt Dee's first husband whittled the dash," said Maggie so low you almost couldn't hear her. "His name was Henry, but they called him Stash."

"Maggie's brain is like an elephant's," Wangero said, laughing. "I can use the churn top as a centerpiece for the alcove table," she said, sliding a plate over the churn, "and I'll think of something artistic to do with the dasher."

When she finished wrapping the dasher the handle stuck out. I took it for a moment in my hands. You didn't even have to look close to see where hands pushing the dasher up and down to make butter had left a kind of sink in the wood. In fact, there were a lot of small sinks; you could see where thumb and fingers had sunk into the wood. It was beautiful light yellow wood, from a tree that grew in the yard where Big Dee and Stash had lived.

After dinner Dee (Wangero) went to the trunk at the foot of my bed and   55
started rifling through it. Maggie hung back in the kitchen over the dishpan. Out came Wangero with two quilts. They had been pieced by Grandma Dee and then Big Dee and me had hung them on the quilt frames on the front porch and quilted them. One was in the Lone Star pattern. The other was Walk Around the Mountain. In both of them were scraps of dresses Grandma Dee had worn fifty and more years ago. Bits and pieces of Grandpa Jarrell's Paisley shirts. And one teeny faded blue piece, about the size of a penny matchbox, that was from Great Grandpa Ezra's uniform that he wore in the Civil War.

"Mama," Wangero said sweet as a bird. "Can I have these old quilts?"

I heard something fall in the kitchen, and a minute later the kitchen door slammed.

"Why don't you take one or two of the others?" I asked. "These old things was just done by me and Big Dee from some tops your grandma pieced before she died."

"No," said Wangero. "I don't want those. They are stitched around the borders by machine."

"That'll make them last better," I said.   60

"That's not the point," said Wangero. "These are all pieces of dresses Grandma used to wear. She did all this stitching by hand. Imagine!" She held the quilts securely in her arms, stroking them.

"Some of the pieces, like those lavender ones, come from old clothes her mother handed down to her," I said, moving up to touch the quilts. Dee (Wangero) moved back just enough so that I couldn't reach the quilts. They already belonged to her.

"Imagine!" she breathed again, clutching them closely to her bosom.

"The truth is," I said, "I promised to give them quilts to Maggie, for when she marries John Thomas."

She gasped like a bee had stung her. "Maggie can't appreciate these quilts!" she   65
said. "She'd probably be backward enough to put them to everyday use."

"I reckon she would," I said. "God knows I been saving 'em for long enough with nobody using 'em. I hope she will!" I didn't want to bring up how I had offered Dee (Wangero) a quilt when she went away to college. Then she had told me they were old-fashioned, out of style.

"But, they're *priceless!*" she was saying now, furiously; for she has a temper. "Maggie would put them on the bed and in five years they'd be in rags. Less than that!"

"She can always make some more," I said. "Maggie knows how to quilt."

Dee (Wangero) looked at me with hatred. "You just will not understand. The point is these quilts, *these* quilts!"

70   "Well," I said, stumped. "What would *you* do with them?"

"Hang them," she said. As if that was the only thing you *could* do with quilts.

Maggie by now was standing in the door. I could almost hear the sound her feet made as they scraped over each other.

"She can have them, Mama," she said, like somebody used to never winning anything, or having anything reserved for her. "I can 'member Grandma Dee without the quilts."

I looked at her hard. She had filled her bottom lip with checkerberry snuff and it gave her face a kind of dopey, hangdog look. It was Grandma Dee and Big Dee who taught her how to quilt herself. She stood there with her scarred hands hidden in the folds of her skirt. She looked at her sister with something like fear but she wasn't mad at her. This was Maggie's portion. This was the way she knew God to work.

75   When I looked at her like that something hit me in the top of my head and ran down to the soles of my feet. Just like when I'm in church and the spirit of God touches me and I get happy and shout. I did something I never had done before: hugged Maggie to me, then dragged her on into the room, snatched the quilts out of Miss Wangero's hands and dumped them into Maggie's lap. Maggie just sat there on my bed with her mouth open.

"Take one or two of the others," I said to Dee.

But she turned without a word and went out to Hakim-a-barber.

"You just don't understand," she said, as Maggie and I came out to the car.

"What don't I understand?" I wanted to know.

80   "Your heritage," she said. And then she turned to Maggie, kissed her, and said, "You ought to try to make something of yourself, too, Maggie. It's really a new day for us. But from the way you and Mama still live you'd never know it."

She put on some sunglasses that hid everything above the tip of her nose and her chin.

Maggie smiled; maybe at the sunglasses. But a real smile, not scared. After we watched the car dust settle I asked Maggie to bring me a dip of snuff. And then the two of us sat there just enjoying, until it was time to go in the house and go to bed.

Reading and Reacting

1. In American culture, what does a patchwork quilt symbolize?

2. What is the literal meaning of the two quilts to Maggie and her mother? To Dee? Beyond this literal meaning, what symbolic meaning, if any, do they have to Maggie and her mother? Do the quilts have any symbolic meaning to Dee?

 3. How does the contrast between the two sisters' appearances, personalities, lifestyles, and feelings about the quilts help to convey the story's theme?

 4. What does the name *Wangero* signify to Dee? To her mother and sister? Could the name be considered a symbol? Why or why not?

 5. Why do you think Maggie relinquishes the quilts to her sister?

 6. What is Dee's opinion of her mother and sister? Do you agree with her assessment?

 7. What does the story's title suggest to you? Is it ironic? What other titles would be effective?

 8. What possible meanings, aside from their literal meanings, might each of the following suggest: the family's yard, Maggie's burn scars, the trunk in which the quilts are kept, Dee's Polaroid camera? What symbolic functions, if any, do these items serve in the story?

 9. **JOURNAL ENTRY** What objects have the kind of symbolic value to you that the quilts have to Maggie? What gives these objects this value?

10. **CRITICAL PERSPECTIVE** In her article "The Black Woman Artist as Wayward," critic Barbara Christian characterizes "Everyday Use" as a story in which Alice Walker examines the "creative legacy" of ordinary African-American women. According to Christian, the story "is about the use and misuse of the concept of heritage. The mother of two daughters, one selfish and stylish, the other scarred and caring, passes on to us its true definition."

What definition of *heritage* does the mother attempt to pass on to her children? How is this definition like or unlike Dee's definition?

Related Works: "Two Kinds" (p. 527), "Digging" (p. 560), "The Boy Beheld His Mother's Past" (p. 562), "My Grandmother Would Rock Quietly and Hum" (p. 602), "Aunt Jennifer's Tigers" (p. 715), *Trifles* (p. 983), *Fences* (p. 1358)

RAYMOND CARVER (1938–1988), one of the most influential and widely read writers of our time, fashioned his stories from the stuff of common life uncommonly perceived. He was born in the small logging town of Clatskanie, Oregon, where his father worked in a sawmill. Soon after his birth, the family moved to Yakima, Washington, where Carver grew up. He married at nineteen and fathered two children by the time he was twenty; during this period, he also began to write. He received a degree from Humboldt State University and later from the University of Iowa. His first collection of stories, *Will You Please Be Quiet, Please* (1976), was nominated for a National Book Award. Five more collections of stories followed, including *Cathedral* (1983)— nominated for both a Pulitzer Prize and a National Book Critics Circle Award — and *Where I'm Calling From: New and Selected Stories* (1988). Carver was also the author of five books of poetry. In his last years, before his death of lung cancer, Carver was praised as the best American short story writer since Ernest Hemingway; novelist Robert Stone called him "a hero of perception." He was made an Honorary Doctor of Letters at the University of Hartford and was inducted into the American Academy and Institute of Arts and Letters. At life's end, he married his longtime companion, the poet Tess Gallagher; the two brought Carver's last book of poems to completion together (*A New Path to the Waterfall*). He died at age fifty.

Cultural Context:. Cathedrals, centers of religious authority, civic pomp, and communal worship, began to be built in Europe around the year 1000. They flourished throughout the medieval period as the power of the Catholic Church grew. In time, no city was without a cathedral. The lavish decoration and dazzling design of these structures was meant not only to celebrate God but also to highlight those secular and religious authorities who had financed the construction of the building. Cathedrals — especially those of the Gothic period (roughly 1200 to 1500) — often featured pointed arches, flying buttresses, and high spires designed to lift worshipers' eyes toward heaven.

Cathedral (1983)

This blind man, an old friend of my wife's, he was on his way to spend the night. His wife had died. So he was visiting the dead wife's relatives in Connecticut. He called my wife from his in-laws'. Arrangements were made. He would come by train, a five-hour trip, and my wife would meet him at the station. She hadn't seen him since she worked for him one summer in Seattle ten years ago. But she and the blind man had kept in touch. They made tapes and mailed them back and forth. I wasn't enthusiastic about his visit. He was no one I knew. And his being blind bothered me. My idea of blindness came from the movies. In the movies, the blind moved slowly and never laughed. Sometimes they were led by seeing-eye dogs. A blind man in my house was not something I looked forward to.

That summer in Seattle she had needed a job. She didn't have any money. The man she was going to marry at the end of the summer was in officers' training school. He didn't have any money, either. But she was in love with the guy, and he was in love with her, etc. She'd seen something in the paper: HELP WANTED— *Reading to Blind Man*, and a telephone number. She phoned and went over, was hired on the spot. She'd worked with this blind man all summer. She read stuff to him, case studies, reports, that sort of thing. She helped him organize his little office in the county social-service department. They'd become good friends, my wife and the blind man. How do I know these things? She told me. And she told me something else. On her last day in the office, the blind man asked if he could touch her face. She agreed to this. She told me he touched his fingers to every part of her face, her nose — even her neck! She never forgot it. She even tried to write a poem about it. She was always trying to write a poem. She wrote a poem or two every year, usually after something really important had happened to her.

When we first started going out together, she showed me the poem. In the poem, she recalled his fingers and the way they had moved around over her face. In the poem, she talked about what she had felt at the time, about what went through her mind when the blind man touched her nose and lips. I can remember I didn't think much of the poem. Of course, I didn't tell her that. Maybe I just don't understand poetry. I admit it's not the first thing I reach for when I pick up something to read.

Anyway, this man who'd first enjoyed her favors, the officer-to-be, he'd been her childhood sweetheart. So okay. I'm saying that at the end of the summer she let the blind man run his hands over her face, said goodbye to him, married her childhood etc., who was now a commissioned officer, and she moved away from Seattle. But they'd kept in touch, she and the blind man. She made the first contact after a year or so. She called him up one night from an Air Force base in Alabama. She wanted to talk. They talked. He asked her to send a tape and tell him about her life. She did this. She sent the tape. On the tape, she told the blind man about her husband and about their life together in the military. She told the blind man she loved her husband but she didn't like it where they lived and she didn't like it that he was part of the military-industrial thing. She told the blind man she'd written a poem and he was in it. She told him that she was writing a poem about what it was like to be an Air Force officer's wife. The poem wasn't finished yet. She was still writing it. The blind man made a tape. He sent her the tape. She made a tape. This went on for years. My wife's officer was posted to one base and then another. She sent tapes from Moody AFB, McGuire, McConnell, and finally Travis,° near Sacramento, where one night she got to feeling lonely and cut off from people she kept losing in that moving-around life. She got to feeling she couldn't go it another step. She went in and swallowed all the pills and capsules in the medicine chest and washed them down with a bottle of gin. Then she got into a hot bath and passed out.

But instead of dying, she got sick. She threw up. Her officer — why should he 5 have a name? he was the childhood sweetheart, and what more does he want?— came home from somewhere, found her, and called the ambulance. In time, she put it all on a tape and sent the tape to the blind man. Over the years, she put all kinds of stuff on tapes and sent the tapes off lickety-split. Next to writing a poem every year, I think it was her chief means of recreation. On one tape, she told the blind man she'd decided to live away from her officer for a time. On another tape, she told him about her divorce. She and I began going out, and of course she told her blind man about it. She told him everything, or so it seemed to me. Once she asked me if I'd like to hear the latest tape from the blind man. This was a year ago. I was on the tape, she said. So I said okay, I'd listen to it. I got us drinks and we settled down in the living room. We made ready to listen. First she inserted the tape into the player and adjusted a couple of dials. Then she pushed a lever. The tape squeaked and someone began to talk in this loud voice. She lowered the volume. After a few minutes of harmless chitchat, I heard my own name in the mouth of this stranger, this blind man I didn't even know! And then this: "From all you've said about him, I can only conclude —" But we were interrupted, a knock at the door, something, and we didn't ever get back to the tape. Maybe it was just as well. I'd heard all I wanted to.

Now this same blind man was coming to sleep in my house.

Moody . . . Travis: United States Air Force bases.

"Maybe I could take him bowling," I said to my wife. She was at the draining board doing scalloped potatoes. She put down the knife she was using and turned around.

"If you love me," she said, "you can do this for me. If you don't love me, okay. But if you had a friend, any friend, and the friend came to visit, I'd make him feel comfortable." She wiped her hands with the dish towel.

"I don't have any blind friends," I said.

10   "You don't have *any* friends," she said. "Period. Besides," she said, "goddamn it, his wife's just died! Don't you understand that? The man's lost his wife!"

I didn't answer. She'd told me a little about the blind man's wife. Her name was Beulah. Beulah! That's a name for a colored woman.

"Was his wife a Negro?" I asked.

"Are you crazy?" my wife said. "Have you just flipped or something?" She picked up a potato. I saw it hit the floor, then roll under the stove. "What's wrong with you?" she said. "Are you drunk?"

"I'm just asking," I said.

15   Right then my wife filled me in with more detail than I cared to know. I made a drink and sat at the kitchen table to listen. Pieces of the story began to fall into place.

Beulah had gone to work for the blind man the summer after my wife had stopped working for him. Pretty soon Beulah and the blind man had themselves a church wedding. It was a little wedding — who'd want to go to such a wedding in the first place? — just the two of them, plus the minister and the minister's wife. But it was a church wedding just the same. It was what Beulah had wanted, he'd said. But even then Beulah must have been carrying the cancer in her glands. After they had been inseparable for eight years — my wife's word, *inseparable* — Beulah's health went into a rapid decline. She died in a Seattle hospital room, the blind man sitting beside the bed and holding on to her hand. They'd married, lived and worked together, slept together — had sex, sure — and then the blind man had to bury her. All this without his having ever seen what the goddamned woman looked like. It was beyond my understanding. Hearing this, I felt sorry for the blind man for a little bit. And then I found myself thinking what a pitiful life this woman must have led. Imagine a woman who could never see herself as she was seen in the eyes of her loved one. A woman who could go on day after day and never receive the smallest compliment from her beloved. A woman whose husband could never read the expression on her face, be it misery or something better. Someone who could wear makeup or not — what difference to him? She could, if she wanted, wear green eye-shadow around one eye, a straight pin in her nostril, yellow slacks, and purple shoes, no matter. And then to slip off into death, the blind man's hand on her hand, his blind eyes streaming tears — I'm imagining now — her last thought maybe this: that he never even knew what she looked like, and she on an express to the grave. Robert was left with a small insurance policy and a half of a twenty-peso Mexican coin. The other half of the coin went into the box with her. Pathetic.

So when the time rolled around, my wife went to the depot to pick him up. With nothing to do but wait — sure, I blamed him for that — I was having a drink and watching the TV when I heard the car pull into the drive. I got up from the sofa with my drink and went to the window to have a look.

I saw my wife laughing as she parked the car. I saw her get out of the car and shut the door. She was still wearing a smile. Just amazing. She went around to the other side of the car to where the blind man was already starting to get out. This blind man, feature this, he was wearing a full beard! A beard on a blind man! Too much, I say. The blind man reached into the backseat and dragged out a suitcase. My wife took his arm, shut the car door, and, talking all the way, moved him down the drive and then up the steps to the front porch. I turned off the TV. I finished my drink, rinsed the glass, dried my hands. Then I went to the door.

My wife said, "I want you to meet Robert. Robert, this is my husband. I've told you all about him." She was beaming. She had this blind man by his coat sleeve.

The blind man let go of his suitcase and up came his hand.   20

I took it. He squeezed hard, held my hand, and then he let it go.

"I feel like we've already met," he boomed.

"Likewise," I said. I didn't know what else to say. Then I said, "Welcome. I've heard a lot about you." We began to move then, a little group, from the porch into the living room, my wife guiding him by the arm. The blind man was carrying his suitcase in his other hand. My wife said things like, "To your left here, Robert. That's right. Now watch it, there's a chair. That's it. Sit down right here. This is the sofa. We just bought this sofa two weeks ago."

I started to say something about the old sofa. I'd liked that old sofa. But I didn't say anything. Then I wanted to say something else, small-talk, about the scenic ride along the Hudson.° How going *to* New York, you should sit on the right-hand side of the train, and coming *from* New York, the left-hand side.

"Did you have a good train ride?" I said. "Which side of the train did you sit   25
on, by the way?"

"What a question, which side!" my wife said. "What's it matter which side?" she said.

"I just asked," I said.

"Right side," the blind man said. "I hadn't been on a train in nearly forty years. Not since I was a kid. With my folks. That's been a long time. I'd nearly forgotten the sensation. I have winter in my beard now," he said. "So I've been told, anyway. Do I look distinguished, my dear?" the blind man said to my wife.

"You look distinguished, Robert," she said. "Robert," she said. "Robert, it's just so good to see you."

My wife finally took her eyes off the blind man and looked at me. I had the   30
feeling she didn't like what she saw. I shrugged.

I've never met, or personally known, anyone who was blind. This blind man was late forties, a heavy-set, balding man with stooped shoulders, as if he carried a great weight there. He wore brown slacks, brown shoes, a light-brown shirt, a tie, a sports coat. Spiffy. He also had this full beard. But he didn't use a cane and he didn't wear dark glasses. I'd always thought dark glasses were a must for the

---

Hudson: A river in New York State.

blind. Fact was, I wished he had a pair. At first glance, his eyes looked like anyone else's eyes. But if you looked close, there was something different about them.
Too much white in the iris, for one thing, and the pupils seemed to move around
in the sockets without his knowing it or being able to stop it. Creepy. As I stared
at his face, I saw the left pupil turn in toward his nose while the other made an effort to keep in one place. But it was only an effort, for that eye was on the roam
without his knowing it or wanting it to be.

I said, "Let me get you a drink. What's your pleasure? We have a little of everything. It's one of our pastimes."

"Bub, I'm a Scotch man myself," he said fast enough in this big voice.

"Right," I said. Bub! "Sure you are. I knew it."

He let his fingers touch his suitcase, which was sitting alongside the sofa. He
was taking his bearings. I didn't blame him for that.

"I'll move that up to your room," my wife said.

"No, that's fine," the blind man said loudly. "It can go up when I go up."

"A little water with the Scotch?" I said.

"Very little," he said.

"I knew it," I said.

He said, "Just a tad. The Irish actor, Barry Fitzgerald? I'm like that fellow.
When I drink water, Fitzgerald said, I drink water. When I drink whiskey, I drink
whiskey." My wife laughed. The blind man brought his hand up under his beard.
He lifted his beard slowly and let it drop.

I did the drinks, three big glasses of Scotch with a splash of water in each. Then
we made ourselves comfortable and talked about Robert's travels. First the long
flight from the West Coast to Connecticut, we covered that. Then from Connecticut up here by train. We had another drink concerning that leg of the trip.

I remembered having read somewhere that the blind didn't smoke because, as
speculation had it, they couldn't see the smoke they exhaled. I thought I knew
that much and that much only about blind people. But this blind man smoked his
cigarette down to the nubbin and then lit another one. This blind man filled his
ashtray and my wife emptied it.

When we sat down at the table for dinner, we had another drink. My wife
heaped Robert's plate with cube steak, scalloped potatoes, green beans. I buttered
him up two slices of bread. I said, "Here's bread and butter for you." I swallowed
some of my drink. "Now let us pray," I said, and the blind man lowered his head.
My wife looked at me, her mouth agape. "Pray the phone won't ring and the food
doesn't get cold," I said.

We dug in. We ate everything there was to eat on the table. We ate like there
was no tomorrow. We didn't talk. We ate. We scarfed. We grazed that table. We
were into serious eating. The blind man had right away located his foods, he knew
just where everything was on his plate. I watched with admiration as he used his
knife and fork on the meat. He'd cut two pieces of meat, fork the meat into his
mouth, and then go all out for the scalloped potatoes, the beans next, and then
he'd tear off a hunk of buttered bread and eat that. He'd follow this up with a big
drink of milk. It didn't seem to bother him to use his fingers once in a while, either.

We finished everything, including half a strawberry pie. For a few moments, we
sat as if stunned. Sweat beaded on our faces. Finally, we got up from the table and

left the dirty plates. We didn't look back. We took ourselves into the living room and sank into our places again. Robert and my wife sat on the sofa. I took the big chair. We had us two or three more drinks while they talked about the major things that had come to pass for them in the past ten years. For the most part, I just listened. Now and then I joined in. I didn't want him to think I'd left the room, and I didn't want her to think I was feeling left out. They talked of things that had happened to them — to them! — these past ten years. I waited in vain to hear my name on my wife's sweet lips: "And then my dear husband came into my life"— something like that. But I heard nothing of the sort. More talk of Robert. Robert had done a little of everything, it seemed, a regular blind jack-of-all-trades. But most recently he and his wife had had an Amway distributorship, from which, I gathered, they'd earned their living, such as it was. The blind man was also a ham radio operator.° He talked in his loud voice about conversations he'd had with fellow operators in Guam, in the Philippines, in Alaska, and even in Tahiti. He said he'd have a lot of friends there if he ever wanted to go visit those places. From time to time, he'd turn his blind face toward me, put his hand under his beard, ask me something. How long had I been in my present position? (Three years.) Did I like my work? (I didn't.) Was I going to stay with it? (What were the options?) Finally, when I thought he was beginning to run down, I got up and turned on the TV.

My wife looked at me with irritation. She was heading toward a boil. Then she looked at the blind man and said, "Robert, do you have a TV?"

The blind man said, "My dear, I have two TVs. I have a color set and a black-and-white thing, and old relic. It's funny, but if I turn the TV on, and I'm always turning it on, I turn on the color set. It's funny, don't you think?"

I didn't know what to say to that. I had absolutely nothing to say to that. No opinion. So I watched the news program and tried to listen to what the announcer was saying.

"This is a color TV," the blind man said. "Don't ask me how, but I can tell."   50

"We traded up a while ago," I said.

The blind man had another taste of his drink. He lifted his beard, sniffed it, and let it fall. He leaned forward on the sofa. He positioned his ashtray on the coffee table, then put the lighter to his cigarette. He leaned back on the sofa and crossed his legs at the ankles.

My wife covered her mouth, and then she yawned. She stretched. She said, "I think I'll go upstairs and put on my robe. I think I'll change into something else. Robert, you make yourself comfortable," she said.

"I'm comfortable," the blind man said.

"I want you to feel comfortable in this house," she said.   55

"I am comfortable," the blind man said.

After she'd left the room, he and I listened to the weather report and then to the sports roundup. By that time, she'd been gone so long I didn't know if she was going to come back. I thought she might have gone to bed. I wished she'd come back downstairs. I didn't want to be left alone with a blind man. I asked him if he

---

ham radio operator: A licensed amateur radio operator.

wanted another drink, and he said sure. Then I asked if he wanted to smoke some dope with me. I said I'd just rolled a number. I hadn't, but I planned to do so in about two shakes.

"I'll try some with you," he said.

"Damn right," I said. "That's the stuff."

60   I got our drinks and sat down on the sofa with him. Then I rolled us two fat numbers. I lit one and passed it. I brought it to his fingers. He took it and inhaled.

"Hold it as long as you can," I said. I could tell he didn't know the first thing.

My wife came back downstairs wearing her pink robe and her pink slippers.

"What do I smell?" she said.

"We thought we'd have us some cannabis," I said.

65   My wife gave me a savage look. Then she looked at the blind man and said, "Robert, I didn't know you smoked."

He said, "I do now, my dear. There's a first time for everything. But I don't feel anything yet."

"This stuff is pretty mellow," I said. "This stuff is mild. It's dope you can reason with," I said. "It doesn't mess you up."

"Not much it doesn't, bub," he said, and laughed.

My wife sat on the sofa between the blind man and me. I passed her the number. She took it and toked° and then passed it back to me. "Which way is this going?" she said. Then she said, "I shouldn't be smoking this. I can hardly keep my eyes open as it is. That dinner did me in. I shouldn't have eaten so much."

70   "It was the strawberry pie," the blind man said. "That's what did it," he said, and he laughed his big laugh. Then he shook his head.

"There's more strawberry pie," I said.

"Do you want some more, Robert?" my wife said.

"Maybe in a little while," he said.

We gave our attention to the TV. My wife yawned again. She said, "Your bed is made up when you feel like going to bed, Robert. I know you must have had a long day. When you're ready to go to bed, say so." She pulled his arm. "Robert?"

75   He came to and said, "I've had a real nice time. This beats tapes, doesn't it?"

I said, "Coming at you," and I put the number between his fingers. He inhaled, held the smoke, and then let it go. It was like he'd been doing it since he was nine years old.

"Thanks, bub," he said. "But I think this is all for me. I think I'm beginning to feel it," he said. He held the burning roach out for my wife.

"Same here," she said. "Ditto. Me, too." She took the roach and passed it to me. "I may just sit here for a while between you two guys with my eyes closed. But don't let me bother you, okay? Either one of you. If it bothers you, say so. Otherwise, I may just sit here with my eyes closed until you're ready to go to bed," she said. "Your bed's made up, Robert, when you're ready. It's right next to our room at the top of the stairs. We'll show you up when you're ready. You wake me up now, you guys, if I fall asleep." She said that and then she closed her eyes and went to sleep.

----

toked: Inhaled.

The news program ended. I got up and changed the channel. I sat back down on the sofa. I wished my wife hadn't pooped out. Her head lay across the back of the sofa, her mouth open. She'd turned so that her robe slipped away from her legs, exposing a juicy thigh. I reached to draw her robe back over her, and it was then that I glanced at the blind man. What the hell! I flipped the robe open again.

"You say when you want some strawberry pie," I said.   80

"I will," he said.

I said, "Are you tired? Do you want me to take you up to your bed? Are you ready to hit the hay?"

"Not yet," he said. "No, I'll stay up with you, bub. If that's all right. I'll stay up until you're ready to turn in. We haven't had a chance to talk. Know what I mean? I feel like me and her monopolized the evening." He lifted his beard and he let it fall. He picked up his cigarettes and his lighter.

"That's all right," I said. Then I said, "I'm glad for the company."

And I guess I was. Every night I smoked dope and stayed up as long as I could   85
before I fell asleep. My wife and I hardly ever went to bed at the same time. When I did go to sleep, I had these dreams. Sometimes I'd wake up from one of them, my heart going crazy.

Something about the church and the Middle Ages was on the TV. Not your run-of-the-mill TV fare. I wanted to watch something else. I turned to the other channels. But there was nothing on them, either. So I turned back to the first channel and apologized.

"Bub, it's all right," the blind man said. "It's fine with me. Whatever you want to watch is okay. I'm always learning something. Learning never ends. It won't hurt me to learn something tonight. I got ears," he said.

We didn't say anything for a time. He was leaning forward with his head turned at me, his right ear aimed in the direction of the set. Very disconcerting. Now and then his eyelids drooped and then they snapped open again. Now and then he put his fingers into his beard and tugged, like he was thinking about something he was hearing on the television.

On the screen, a group of men wearing cowls was being set upon and tormented by men dressed in skeleton costumes and men dressed as devils. The men dressed as devils wore devil masks, horns, and long tails. This pageant was part of a procession. The Englishman who was narrating the thing said it took place in Spain once a year. I tried to explain to the blind man what was happening.

"Skeletons," he said. "I know about skeletons," he said, and nodded.   90

The TV showed this one cathedral. Then there was a long, slow look at another one. Finally, the picture switched to the famous one in Paris, with its flying buttresses and its spires reaching up to the clouds. The camera pulled away to show the whole of the cathedral rising above the skyline.

There were times when the Englishman who was telling the thing would shut up, would simply let the camera move around the cathedrals. Or else the camera would tour the countryside, men in fields walking behind oxen. I waited as long as I could. Then I felt I had to say something. I said, "They're showing the outside of this cathedral now. Gargoyles. Little statues carved to look like monsters. Now

I guess they're in Italy. Yeah, they're in Italy. There's paintings on the walls of this one church."

"Are those fresco° paintings, bub?" he asked, and he sipped from his drink.

I reached for my glass. But it was empty. I tried to remember what I could remember. "You're asking me are those frescoes?" I said. "That's a good question. I don't know."

95   The camera moved to a cathedral outside Lisbon.° The differences in the Portuguese cathedral compared with the French and Italian were not that great. But they were there. Mostly the interior stuff. Then something occurred to me, and I said, "Something has occurred to me. Do you have any idea what a cathedral is? What they look like, that is? Do you follow me? If somebody says cathedral to you, do you have any notion what they're talking about? Do you know the difference between that and a Baptist church, say?"

He let the smoke dribble from his mouth. "I know they took hundreds of workers fifty or a hundred years to build," he said. "I just heard the man say that, of course. I know generations of the same families worked on a cathedral. I heard him say that, too. The men who began their life's work on them, they never lived to see the completion of their work. In that wise, bub, they're no different from the rest of us, right?" He laughed. Then his eyelids drooped again. His head nodded. He seemed to be snoozing. Maybe he was imagining himself in Portugal. The TV was showing another cathedral now. This one was in Germany. The Englishman's voice droned on. "Cathedrals," the blind man said. He sat up and rolled his head back and forth. "If you want the truth, bub, that's about all I know. What I just said. What I heard him say. But maybe you could describe one to me? I wish you'd do it. I'd like that. If you want to know, I really don't have a good idea."

I stared hard at the shot of the cathedral on the TV. How could I even begin to describe it? But say my life depended on it. Say my life was being threatened by an insane guy who said I had to do it or else.

I stared some more at the cathedral before the picture flipped off into the countryside. There was no use. I turned to the blind man and said, "To begin with, they're very tall." I was looking around the room for clues. "They reach way up. Up and up. Toward the sky. They're so big, some of them, they have to have these supports. To help hold them up, so to speak. These supports are called buttresses. They remind me of viaducts,° for some reason. But maybe you don't know viaducts, either? Sometimes the cathedrals have devils and such carved into the front. Sometimes lords and ladies. Don't ask me why this is," I said.

He was nodding. The whole upper part of his body seemed to be moving back and forth.

100   "I'm not doing so good, am I?" I said.

He stopped nodding and leaned forward on the edge of the sofa. As he listened to me, he was running his fingers through his beard. I wasn't getting through to

---

Fresco: Painted plaster.

Lisbon: The capital of Portugal.

viaducts: Long, elevated roadways.

him, I could see that. But he waited for me to go on just the same. He nodded, like he was trying to encourage me. I tried to think what else to say. "They're really big," I said. "They're massive. They're built of stone. Marble, too, sometimes. In those olden days, when they built cathedrals, men wanted to be close to God. In those olden days, God was an important part of everyone's life. You could tell this from their cathedral-building. I'm sorry," I said, "but it looks like that's the best I can do for you. I'm just no good at it."

"That's all right, bub," the blind man said. "Hey, listen. I hope you don't mind my asking you. Can I ask you something? Let me ask you a simple question, yes or no. I'm just curious and there's no offense. You're my host. But let me ask if you are in any way religious? You don't mind my asking?"

I shook my head. He couldn't see that, though. A wink is the same as a nod to a blind man. "I guess I don't believe in it. In anything. Sometimes it's hard. You know what I'm saying?"

"Sure, I do," he said.

"Right," I said.

The Englishman was still holding forth. My wife sighed in her sleep. She drew a long breath and went on with her sleeping.

"You'll have to forgive me," I said. "But I can't tell you what a cathedral looks like. It just isn't in me to do it. I can't do any more than I've done."

The blind man sat very still, his head down, as he listened to me.

I said, "The truth is, cathedrals don't mean anything special to me. Nothing. Cathedrals. They're something to look at on late-night TV. That's all they are."

It was then that the blind man cleared his throat. He brought something up. He took a handkerchief from his back pocket. Then he said, "I get it, bub. It's okay. It happens. Don't worry about it," he said. "Hey, listen to me. Will you do me a favor? I got an idea. Why don't you find us some heavy paper? And a pen. We'll do something. We'll draw one together. Get us a pen and some heavy paper. Go on, bub, get the stuff," he said.

So I went upstairs. My legs felt like they didn't have any strength in them. They felt like they did after I'd done some running. In my wife's room, I looked around. I found some ballpoints in a little basket on her table. And then I tried to think where to look for the kind of paper he was talking about.

Downstairs, in the kitchen, I found a shopping bag with onion skins in the bottom of the bag. I emptied the bag and shook it. I brought it into the living room and sat down with it near his legs. I moved some things, smoothed the wrinkles from the bag, spread it out on the coffee table.

The blind man got down from the sofa and sat next to me on the carpet.

He ran his fingers over the paper. He went up and down the sides of the paper. The edges, even the edges. He fingered the corners.

"All right," he said. "All right, let's do her."

He found my hand, the hand with the pen. He closed his hand over my hand. "Go ahead, bub, draw," he said. "Draw. You'll see. I'll follow along with you. It'll be okay. Just begin now like I'm telling you. You'll see. Draw," the blind man said.

So I began. First I drew a box that looked like a house. It could have been the house I lived in. Then I put a roof on it. At either end of the roof, I drew spires. Crazy.

105

110

115

"Swell," he said. "Terrific. You're doing fine," he said. "Never thought anything like this could happen in your lifetime, did you, bub? Well, it's a strange life, we all know that. Go on now. Keep it up."

I put in windows with arches. I drew flying buttresses. I hung great doors. I couldn't stop. The TV station went off the air. I put down the pen and closed and opened my fingers. The blind man felt around over the paper. He moved the tips of his fingers over the paper, all over what I had drawn, and he nodded.

120   "Doing fine," the blind man said.

I took up the pen again, and he found my hand. I kept at it. I'm no artist. But I kept drawing just the same.

My wife opened up her eyes and gazed at us. She sat up on the sofa, her robe hanging open. She said, "What are you doing? Tell me, I want to know."

I didn't answer her.

The blind man said, "We're drawing a cathedral. Me and him are working on it. Press hard," he said to me. "That's right. That's good," he said. "Sure. You got it, bub, I can tell. You didn't think you could. But you can, can't you? You're cooking with gas now. You know what I'm saying? We're going to really have us something here in a minute. How's the old arm?" he said. "Put some people in there now. What's a cathedral without people?"

125   My wife said, "What's going on? Robert, what are you doing? What's going on?"

"It's all right," he said to her. "Close your eyes now," the blind man said to me. I did it. I closed them just like he said.

"Are they closed?" he said. "Don't fudge."

"They're closed," I said.

130   "Keep them that way," he said. He said, "Don't stop now. Draw."

So we kept on with it. His fingers rode my fingers as my hand went over the paper. It was like nothing else in my life up to now.

Then he said, "I think that's it. I think you got it," he said. "Take a look. What do you think?"

But I had my eyes closed. I thought I'd keep them that way for a little longer. I thought it was something I ought to do.

"Well?" he said. "Are you looking?"

135   My eyes were still closed. I was in my house. I knew that. But I didn't feel like I was inside anything.

"It's really something," I said.

Reading and Reacting

1. Who is the narrator? What do we know about him? Why does the impending visit by the blind man disturb him?

2. At several points in the story, the narrator's wife loses patience with him. What causes her displeasure? What do her reactions reveal about the wife? About the narrator?

3. Why did the narrator's wife leave her first husband? What qualities in the narrator might have led his wife to marry him?

4. Why is the narrator's wife so devoted to the blind man? What does she gain from her relationship with him?

5. According to the narrator, his wife never forgot the blind man's running his fingers over her face. Why is this experience so important to her?

6. Toward the end of the story, the blind man asks the narrator to describe a cathedral. Why is the narrator unable to do so? What does his inability to do so reveal about him?

7. Why does the blind man tell the narrator to close his eyes while he is drawing? What does he hope to teach him? What is the narrator able to "see" with his eyes shut that he cannot see with them open?

8. In paragraph 96, the blind man observes that the men who began work on a cathedral never lived to see it completed. In this way, he says, "they're no different from the rest of us." What does the cathedral symbolize to the blind man? What does it come to symbolize to the narrator?

9. What other symbols are present in the story? How do these symbols help develop the central theme of the story?

10. JOURNAL ENTRY The blind man is an old friend of the narrator's wife. Why then does he focus on the narrator? In what way is the narrator's spiritual development the blind man's gift to the narrator's wife?

11. CRITICAL PERSPECTIVE Critic Kirk Nesset, in his discussion of "Cathedral," notes that the narrator becomes more open as the story progresses, and that this coming out is mirrored by rhetoric of the story. Early on in the story, the narrator feels momentarily "sorry for the blind man," his insulated hardness beginning to soften. As the walls of his resentment noticeably crack, he watches with "admiration" as Robert eats, recognizing Robert's handicap to be no impairment to his performance at the dinner table. . . . Like Robert, who is on a journey by train, dropping in on friends and relatives, trying to get over the loss of his wife, the narrator is also on a journey, one signaled by signposts in his language and played out by the events of the story he tells. Do you agree that the narrator becomes more open? If so, can you cite any other instances where the words he chooses reflect this increasing openness?

Related Works: "Gryphon" (p. 126), "Battle Royal" (p. 175), "Doe Season" (p. 336), "When I Heard the Learn'd Astronomer" (p. 639), "The Value of Education" (p. 650), "On First Looking into Chapman's Homer" (p. 740), "Batter My Heart, Three-Personed God" (p. 868), "God's Grandeur" (p. 888), "The Gift" (p. 895)

WRITING SUGGESTIONS: Symbol and Allegory

1. Select a story from this anthology, and discuss its use of symbols.

2. Strangers figure prominently in "Young Goodman Brown" and "Cathedral." Write an essay in which you discuss the possible symbolic significance of strangers in each story. If you like, you can also discuss Arnold Friend in "Where Are You Going, Where Have You Been?" (p. 387).

3. Write an essay in which you discuss the conflicts present in "Young Goodman Brown," showing how the allegorical elements in the story reflect and reinforce these conflicts.

4. If Shirley Jackson had wished to write "The Lottery" as an allegory whose purpose was to expose the evils of Nazi Germany, what revisions would she have had to make to convey the dangers of blind obedience to authority? Consider the story's symbols, the characters (and their names), and the setting.

5. In literary works, characters' prized possessions can function as symbols. In this chapter, for example, the quilt in "Everyday Use" takes on symbolic significance. Write an essay in which you analyze this symbol and discuss how it helps convey the main theme of the story. If you like, read "Dog" in Chapter 13 (p. 522) and include a discussion of that story's symbolism in your essay.

6. **WEB ACTIVITY** The following Web site contains information about Nathaniel Hawthorne:

http://www.cwrl.utexas.edu/~daniel/amlit/goodman/ygbmikosh.html

From that site, read "A View of Young Goodman Brown" by Bert A. Mikosh, and consider what the article says about Puritanism. Then write an essay applying Mikosh's ideas to the theme of good versus evil in "Young Goodman Brown," focusing on the portrait of Puritanism that emerges from the story and on the Puritans' difficulty in dealing with the issue of good versus evil.

CHAPTER 11

THEME

The truth about any subject only comes when all the sides of the story are put together, and all their different meanings make one new meaning. —**Alice Walker,** *Discovering Fiction*

I think a writer's job is to provoke questions. I like to think that if someone's read a book of mine, they've had — I don't know — the literary equivalent of a shower. Something that would start them thinking in a slightly different way perhaps. That's what I think writers are for. —**Doris Lessing,** *Writers at Work,* 9th ed.

A work of art encountered as a work of art is an experience, not a statement or an answer to a question. Art is not only about something; it is something. A work of art is a thing in the world, not just a text or commentary on the world. —**Susan Sontag,** *"On Style"* in *Against Interpretation*

One of the most difficult things is the first paragraph. I have spent many months on a first paragraph, and once I get it, the rest just comes out very easily. In the first paragraph you solve most of the problems with your book. The theme is defined, the style, the tone. At least in my case, the first paragraph is a kind of sample of what the rest of the book is going to be. That's why writing a book of short stories is much more difficult than writing a novel. Every time you write a short story, you have to begin all over again. —**Gabriel García Márquez,** *Writers at Work,* 6th ed.

The concepts of beauty and ugliness are mysterious to me. Many people write about them. In mulling over them, I try to get underneath them and see what they mean, undersand the impact they have on what people do. I also write about love and death. The problem I face as a writer is to make my stories mean something. —**Toni Morrison,** *Discovering Fiction*

The **theme** of a work of literature is its central or dominant idea. *Theme* is not the same as *plot* or *subject,* two terms with which it is sometimes confused. A simple *plot summary* of Tadeusz Borowski's "Silence," a story about survivors of the Holocaust could be, "Prisoners are liberated from a concentration camp, and, despite the warnings of the American officer, they kill a captured German guard." The statement "'Silence' is about freed prisoners and a guard" could define the *subject* of the story. A statement of the *theme* of "Silence," however, has to do more than summarize its plot or identify its subject; it has to convey the values and ideas expressed by the story.

Many effective stories are complex, expressing more than one theme, and "Silence" is no exception. You could say that "Silence" suggests that human beings have a need for vengeance. You could also say the story demonstrates that silence is sometimes the only response possible when a person is confronting unspeakable horrors. Both these themes — and others — are expressed in the story, yet one theme seems to dominate: the idea that under extreme conditions the oppressed can have the same capacity for evil as their oppressors.

When you write about theme, you need to do more than tell what happens in the story. The theme you identify should be a general idea that extends beyond the story and applies to the world outside fiction. Compare these two statements about Edgar Allan Poe's "The Cask of Amontillado" (p. 217):

> Poe's "The Cask of Amontillado" is about a man who has an obsessive desire for revenge.

> Poe's "The Cask of Amontillado" suggests that when the desire for revenge becomes obsessive, it can deprive individuals of all that makes them human.

The first merely tells what the story is about; the second statement identifies the story's theme, a general observation about humanity.

Granted, some short works (fairy tales or fables, for example) have themes that can be summed up as *clichés* — overused phrases or expressions — or as *morals* — lessons dramatized by the work. The fairy tale "Cinderella," for example, expresses the clichéd theme that a virtuous girl who endures misfortune will eventually achieve her just reward; the fable "The Tortoise and the Hare" illustrates the moral "Slow and steady wins the race." Like "The Cask of Amontillado," however, the stories in this anthology have themes that are more complex than clichés or morals.

INTERPRETING THEMES

Contemporary critical theory holds that the theme of a work of fiction is as much the creation of readers as of the writer. Readers' backgrounds, knowledge, values, and beliefs all play a part in determining the theme or themes they will identify in a work. Most readers, for example, will realize that David Michael Kaplan's story "Doe Season" (p. 336) — in which the main character goes hunting, kills her first deer, and is forced to confront suffering and death — expresses a conventional **initiation theme,** revealing growing up to be a disillusioning and painful process. Still, different readers bring different perspectives to the story and, in some cases, see different themes.

During a classroom discussion of "Doe Season," a student familiar with hunting saw more than his classmates did in the story's conventional initiation theme. He knew that in many states there really is a doe season, which lasts approximately three days. Shorter than the ten-day buck season, its purpose is to enable hunters to control the size of the deer herd by killing females. This knowledge enabled the student to conclude that by the end of the story the female child's innocence must inevitably be destroyed, just as the doe must be.

Another student pointed out that the participation of Andy — a female who uses a male name — in hunting, a traditional male rite of passage, leads to her killing the deer and to her subsequent disillusionment. It also leads to her decision to abandon her nickname. By contrasting "Andrea" with "Andy," the story reveals the inner conflict between her "female" nature (illustrated by her compassion) and her desire to emulate the men to whom killing is a sport. This interpretation led the student to conclude that the theme of "Doe Season" is that males and females have very different outlooks on life.

Other students did not accept the negative characterization of the story's male characters that the preceding interpretation implies. They pointed out that the father is a sympathetic figure who is extremely supportive; he encourages and defends his daughter. He takes her hunting because he loves her, not because he wants to initiate her into life or to hurt her. One student mentioned that Andy's reaction (called *buck fever*) when she sees the doe is common in children who kill their first deer. In light of this information, several students thought that far from being about irreconcilable male and female perspectives, "Doe Season" makes a statement about a young girl who is hunting for her own identity and who in the process discovers her own mortality. Her father is therefore the agent who enables her to confront the inevitability of death, a fact she must accept if she is going to take her place in the adult world. In this sense, the theme of the story is the idea that in order to mature, a child must come to terms with the reality of death.

Different readers may see different themes in a story, but any interpretation of a theme must make sense in light of what is actually in the story. Evidence from the work, not just your own feelings or assumptions, must support your interpretation, and a single symbol or one statement by a character is not enough in itself to reveal a story's theme. Therefore, you must identify a cross section of examples from the text to support your interpretation of the story's theme. If you say that the theme of James Joyce's "Araby" (p. 252) is that an innocent idealist is inevitably doomed to disillusionment, you have to find examples from the text to support your statement. You could begin with the title, concluding that the word *Araby* suggests dreams of exotic beauty that the boy tries to find when he goes to the bazaar. You could reinforce your idea about the elusiveness of beauty by pointing out that Mangan's unattainable sister is a symbol of this beauty that the boy wants so desperately to find. Finally, you could show how idealism is ultimately crushed by society: at the end of the story, the boy stands alone in the darkness and realizes that his dreams are childish fantasies. Although other readers may have different responses to "Araby," they should find your interpretation reasonable if you support it with enough examples.

IDENTIFYING THEMES

Every element of a story can shed light on its themes. As you analyze a short story, look for features that reveal and reinforce what you perceive to be the story's most important ideas.

The *title* can often provide insight into the theme or themes of a story. The title of an F. Scott Fitzgerald story, "Babylon Revisited," emphasizes a major idea in the story — that Paris of the 1920s is like Babylon, the ancient city the Bible singles out as the epitome of evil and corruption. The story's protagonist, Charlie Wales, comes to realize that no matter how much money he lost after the stock market crash, he lost more — his wife and his daughter — during the boom, when he was in Paris. Charlie's search through his past — his return to "Babylon" — provides new meaning to his life and offers at least a small bit of hope for the future.

Sometimes a *narrator's or character's statement* can reveal a theme. For example, at the beginning of Alberto Alvaro Ríos's "The Secret Lion" (p. 54), the first-person narrator says, "I was twelve and in junior high school and something happened that we didn't have a name for, but it was there nonetheless like a lion, and roaring, roaring that way the biggest things do. Everything changed." Although the narrator does not directly announce the story's theme, he does suggest that the story will convey the idea that the price children pay for growing up is realizing that everything changes, that nothing stays the way it is.

The *arrangement of events* can suggest a story's theme, as it does in an Ernest Hemingway story, "The Short Happy Life of Francis Macomber." At the beginning of the story, the title character is a coward who is stuck in an unhappy marriage. As the story progresses, he gradually learns the nature of courage and, finally, finds it in himself. At the moment of his triumph, however, Francis is killed; his "happy life" is short indeed. The way the events of the story are presented, through foreshadowing and flashbacks, reveals the connection between Macomber's marriage and his behavior as a hunter, and this connection in turn helps to reveal a possible theme: that sometimes courage can be more important than life itself.

A story's *conflict* can offer clues to its theme. In "Araby," the young boy believes that his society neglects art and beauty and glorifies the mundane. This conflict between the boy's idealism and his world can help readers understand why the boy isolates himself in his room reading books and why he retreats into dreams of idealized love. A major theme of the story — that growing up leads to the loss of youthful idealism — is revealed by this central conflict.

Similarly, the main character in "The Yellow Wallpaper" (p. 161), a woman who has recently had a baby, is in conflict with the nineteenth-century society in which she lives. She is suffering from "temporary nervous depression," what doctors today recognize as postpartum depression. Following the practice of the time, her physician has ordered complete bed rest and has instructed her husband to deprive her of all mental and physical stimulation. This harsh treatment leads the narrator to lose her grasp on reality; eventually, she begins to hallucinate. The central conflict of the story is clearly between the woman and her society, controlled by men. This conflict communicates the theme: that in nineteenth-century America, women are controlled not just by their husbands and the male medical establishment, but also by the society they create.

The *point of view* of a story can also help shed light on theme. For instance, a writer's use of an unreliable first-person narrator can help to communicate the theme of a story. Thus, Montresor's self-serving first-person account of his crime in "The Cask of Amontillado" — along with his attempts to justify these actions — enable readers to understand the dangers of irrational anger and misplaced ideas about honor. The voice of a third-person narrator can also help to convey a story's theme. For example, the detachment of the narrator in Stephen Crane's Civil War novel *The Red Badge of Courage* reinforces the theme of the novel: that bravery, cowardice, war, and even life itself are insignificant when set beside the indifference of the universe.

Quite often a story will give names, places, and objects symbolic significance. These *symbols* can not only enrich the story but also help to convey a central theme. For example, the rocking horse in D. H. Lawrence's "The Rocking-Horse Winner" (p. 349) can be seen as a symbol of the boy's desperate desire to remain a child. Interpreted in this way, it reinforces the theme that innocence cannot survive when it confronts greed and selfishness. Similarly, Hawthorne's "Young Goodman Brown" (p. 292) uses symbols such as the walking stick, the woods, sunset and night, and the vague shadows to develop one of its central themes: that once a person strays from the path of faith, evil is everywhere.

Finally, *changes in a character* can shed light on the theme or themes of the story. The main character in Charles Baxter's "Gryphon" (p. 126), for example, eventually comes to realize that the "lies" Miss Ferenczi tells may be closer to the truth than the "facts" his teachers present, and his changing attitude toward Miss Ferenczi helps to communicate the story's central theme about the nature of truth.

CHECKLIST **WRITING ABOUT THEME**

✓ What is the central theme of the story?

✓ What other themes can you identify?

✓ Does the title of the story suggest a theme?

✓ Does the narrator, or any character, make statements that express or imply a theme?

✓ In what way does the arrangement of events in the story suggest a theme?

✓ In what way does the central conflict of the story suggest a theme?

✓ How does the point of view shed light on the story's central theme?

✓ Do any symbols suggest a theme?

✓ Do any characters in the story change in any significant way? Do their changes convey a particular theme?

✓ Have you clearly identified the story's central theme, rather than just summarized the plot or stated the subject?

✓ Does your statement of the story's central theme make a general observation that has an application beyond the story itself?

DAVID MICHAEL KAPLAN (1946–) is one of a group of American writers who, along with South American writers such as Gabriel García Márquez of Colombia, are called "magic realists." Magic realists work outside of the "hobbits and wizards" borders of traditional fantasy writing, seamlessly interweaving magical elements with detailed, realistically drawn "everyday" settings. These elements, says a reviewer of Kaplan's work, are invoked "to illuminate and underscore heightened moments of reality." The story "Doe Season," which appears in Kaplan's debut short story collection, *Comfort* (1987), was included in *Best American Short Stories 1985.* Kaplan's first novel, *Skating in the Dark,* was published in 1991.

Interestingly, the stories in *Comfort* break from classic "first-time author" tradition by sidestepping the autobiographical, young-man-comes-of-age theme. Instead, these stories are about young girls — or young women — coming to grips with parents (present or absent) and with loss and searching for ways to resolve their ambivalence about becoming women. In "Doe Season," Andy's surreal encounter with the doe may be a dream, but the beauty and horror of their meeting will affect the rest of her life.

Cultural Context: When European settlers came to America, deer roamed freely from coast to coast, and the pioneers hunted deer to put meat on the table. Not until the twentieth century did deer hunting become less a means of survival than a sport. Regardless of its purpose, however, deer hunting has long been viewed as a coming-of-age ritual for young men. Even today, a boy's first hunting trip is symbolic of his first step into adulthood.

Doe Season (1985)

They were always the same woods, she thought sleepily as they drove through the early morning darkness — deep and immense, covered with yesterday's snowfall, which had frozen overnight. They were the same woods that lay behind her house, *and they stretch all the way to here,* she thought, *for miles and miles, longer than I could walk in a day, or a week even, but they are still the same woods.* The thought made her feel good: it was like thinking of God; it was like thinking of the space between here and the moon; it was like thinking of all the foreign countries from her geography book where even now, Andy knew, people were going to bed, while they — she and her father and Charlie Spoon and Mac, Charlie's eleven-year-old son — were driving deeper into the Pennsylvania countryside, to go hunting.

They had risen long before dawn. Her mother, yawning and not trying to hide her sleepiness, cooked them eggs and French toast. Her father smoked a cigarette and flicked ashes into his saucer while Andy listened, wondering *Why doesn't he come?* and *Won't he ever come?* until at last a car pulled into the graveled drive and honked. "That will be Charlie Spoon," her father said; he always said "Charlie Spoon," even though his real name was Spreun, because Charlie was, in a sense, shaped like a spoon, with a large head and a narrow waist and chest.

Andy's mother kissed her and her father and said, "Well, have a good time" and "Be careful." Soon they were outside in the bitter dark, loading gear by the back-porch light, their breath steaming. The woods behind the house were then only a black streak against the wash of night.

Andy dozed in the car and woke to find that it was half light. Mac — also sleeping — had slid against her. She pushed him away and looked out the window. Her breath clouded the glass, and she was cold; the car's heater didn't work right. They were riding over gentle hills, the woods on both sides now — the same woods, she knew, because she had been watching the whole way, even while she slept. They had been in her dreams, and she had never lost sight of them.

Charlie Spoon was driving. "I don't understand why she's coming," he said to   5
her father. "How old is she anyway — eight?"

"Nine," her father replied. "She's small for her age."

"So — nine. What's the difference? She'll just add to the noise and get tired besides."

"No, she won't," her father said. "She can walk me to death. And she'll bring good luck, you'll see. Animals — I don't know how she does it, but they come right up to her. We go walking in the woods, and we'll spot more raccoons and possums and such than I ever see when I'm alone."

Charlie grunted.

"Besides, she's not a bad little shot, even if she doesn't hunt yet. She shoots   10
the .22 real good."

"Popgun," Charlie said, and snorted. "And target shooting ain't deer hunting."

"Well, she's not gonna be shooting anyway, Charlie," her father said. "Don't worry. She'll be no bother."

"I still don't know why she's coming," Charlie said.

"Because she wants to, and I want her to. Just like you and Mac. No difference."

Charlie turned onto a side road and after a mile or so slowed down. "That's it!"   15
he cried. He stopped, backed up, and entered a narrow dirt road almost hidden by trees. Five hundred yards down, the road ran parallel to a fenced-in field. Charlie parked in a cleared area deeply rutted by frozen tractor tracks. The gate was locked. *In the spring,* Andy thought, *there will be cows here, and a dog that chases them,* but now the field was unmarked and bare.

"This is it," Charlie Spoon declared. "Me and Mac was up here just two weeks ago, scouting it out, and there's deer. Mac saw the tracks."

"That's right," Mac said.

"Well, we'll just see about that," her father said, putting on his gloves. He turned to Andy. "How you doing, honeybun?"

"Just fine," she said.

Andy shivered and stamped as they unloaded: first the rifles, which they un-   20
sheathed and checked, sliding the bolts, sighting through scopes, adjusting the slings; then the gear, their food and tents and sleeping bags and stove stored in four backpacks — three big ones for Charlie Spoon and her father and Mac, and a day pack for her.

"That's about your size," Mac said, to tease her.

She reddened and said, "Mac, I can carry a pack big as yours any day." He laughed and pressed his knee against the back of hers, so that her leg buckled. "Cut it out," she said. She wanted to make an iceball and throw it at him, but she knew that her father and Charlie were anxious to get going, and she didn't want to displease them.

Mac slid under the gate, and they handed the packs over to him. Then they slid under and began walking across the field toward the same woods that ran all the way back to her home, where even now her mother was probably rising again to wash their breakfast dishes and make herself a fresh pot of coffee. *She is there, and we are here:* the thought satisfied Andy. There was no place else she would rather be.

Mac came up beside her. "Over there's Canada," he said, nodding toward the woods.

25   "Huh!" she said. "Not likely."

"I don't mean *right* over there. I mean farther up north. You think I'm dumb?" *Dumb as your father,* she thought.

"Look at that," Mac said, pointing to a piece of cow dung lying on a spot scraped bare of snow. "A frozen meadow muffin." He picked it up and sailed it at her. "Catch!"

"Mac!" she yelled. His laugh was as gawky as he was. She walked faster. He seemed different today somehow, bundled in his yellow-and-black-checkered coat, a rifle in hand, his silly floppy hat not quite covering his ears. They all seemed different as she watched them trudge through the snow — Mac and her father and Charlie Spoon — bigger, maybe, as if the cold landscape enlarged rather than diminished them, so that they, the only figures in that landscape, took on size and meaning just by being there. If they weren't there, everything would be quieter, and the woods would be the same as before. *But they are here,* Andy thought, looking behind her at the boot prints in the snow, *and I am too, and so it's all different.*

30   "We'll go down to the cut where we found those deer tracks," Charlie said as they entered the woods. "Maybe we'll get lucky and get a late one coming through."

The woods descended into a gully. The snow was softer and deeper here, so that often Andy sank to her knees. Charlie and Mac worked the top of the gully while she and her father walked along the base some thirty yards behind them. "If they miss the first shot, we'll get the second," her father said, and she nodded as if she had known this all the time. She listened to the crunch of their boots, their breathing, and the drumming of a distant woodpecker. And the crackling. In winter the woods crackled as if everything were straining, ready to snap like dried chicken bones.

We are hunting, Andy thought. The cold air burned her nostrils.

They stopped to make lunch by a rock outcropping that protected them from the wind. Her father heated the bean soup her mother had made for them, and they ate it with bread already stiff from the cold. He and Charlie took a few pulls from a flask of Jim Beam while she scoured the plates with snow and repacked them. Then they all had coffee with sugar and powdered milk, and her father poured her a cup too. "We won't tell your momma," he said, and Mac laughed. Andy held the cup the way her father did, not by the handle but around the rim. The coffee tasted smoky. She felt a little queasy, but she drank it all.

Charlie Spoon picked his teeth with a fingernail. "Now, you might've noticed one thing," he said.

"What's that?" her father asked.

"You might've noticed you don't hear no rifles. That's because there ain't no other hunters here. We've got the whole damn woods to ourselves. Now, I ask you — do I know how to find 'em?"

"We haven't seen deer yet, neither."

"Oh, we will," Charlie said, "but not for a while now." He leaned back against the rock. "Deer're sleeping, resting up for the evening feed."

"I seen a deer behind our house once, and it was afternoon," Andy said.

"Yeah, honey, but that was *before* deer season," Charlie said, grinning. "They know something now. They're smart that way."

"That's right," Mac said.

Andy looked at her father — had she said something stupid?

"Well, Charlie," he said, "if they know so much, how come so many get themselves shot?"

"Them's the ones that don't *believe* what they know," Charlie replied. The men laughed. Andy hesitated, and then laughed with them.

They moved on, as much to keep warm as to find a deer. The wind became even stronger. Blowing through the treetops, it sounded like the ocean, and once Andy thought she could smell salt air. But that was impossible; the ocean was *hundreds* of miles away, farther than Canada even. She and her parents had gone last summer to stay for a week at a motel on the New Jersey shore. That was the first time she'd seen the ocean, and it frightened her. It was huge and empty, yet always moving. Everything lay hidden. If you walked in it, you couldn't see how deep it was or what might be below; if you swam, something could pull you under and you'd never be seen again. Its musky, rank smell made her think of things dying. Her mother had floated beyond the breakers, calling to her to come in, but Andy wouldn't go farther than a few feet into the surf. Her mother swam and splashed with animal-like delight while her father, smiling shyly, held his white arms above the waist-deep water as if afraid to get them wet. Once a comber rolled over and sent them both tossing, and when her mother tried to stand up, the surf receding behind, Andy saw that her mother's swimsuit top had come off, so that her breasts swayed free, her nipples like two dark eyes. Embarrassed, Andy looked around: except for two women under a yellow umbrella farther up, the beach was empty. Her mother stood up unsteadily, regained her footing. Taking what seemed the longest time, she calmly refixed her top. Andy lay on the beach towel and closed her eyes. The sound of the surf made her head ache.

And now it was winter; the sky was already dimming, not just with the absence of light but with a mist that clung to the hunters' faces like cobwebs. They made camp early. Andy was chilled. When she stood still, she kept wiggling her toes to make sure they were there. Her father rubbed her arms and held her to him briefly, and that felt better. She unpacked the food while the others put up the tents.

"How about rounding us up some firewood, Mac?" Charlie asked.

"I'll do it," Andy said. Charlie looked at her thoughtfully and then handed her the canvas carrier.

There wasn't much wood on the ground, so it took her a while to get a good load. She was about a hundred yards from camp, near a cluster of high, lichen-covered boulders, when she saw through a crack in the rock a buck and two does walking gingerly, almost daintily, through the alder trees. She tried to hush her breathing as they passed not more than twenty yards away. There was nothing she could do. If she yelled, they'd be gone; by the time she got back to camp, they'd be gone. The buck stopped, nostrils quivering, tail up and alert. He looked directly at her. Still she didn't move, not one muscle. He was a beautiful buck, the color of late-turned maple leaves. Unafraid, he lowered his tail, and he and his does silently merged into the trees. Andy walked back to camp and dropped the firewood.

50   "I saw three deer," she said. "A buck and two does."

"Where?" Charlie Spoon cried, looking behind her as if they might have followed her into camp.

"In the woods yonder. They're gone now."

"Well, hell!" Charlie banged his coffee cup against his knee.

"Didn't I say she could find animals?" her father said, grinning.

55   "Too late to go after them," Charlie muttered. "It'll be dark in a quarter hour. Damn!"

"Damn," Mac echoed.

"They just walk right up to her," her father said.

"Well, leastwise this proves there's deer here." Charlie began snapping long branches into shorter ones. "You know, I think I'll stick with you," he told Andy, "since you're so good at finding deer and all. How'd that be?"

"Okay, I guess," Andy murmured. She hoped he was kidding; no way did she want to hunt with Charlie Spoon. Still, she was pleased he had said it.

60   Her father and Charlie took one tent, she and Mac the other. When they were in their sleeping bags, Mac said in the darkness, "I bet you really didn't see no deer, did you?"

She sighed. "I did, Mac. Why would I lie?"

"How big was the buck?"

"Four point. I counted."

Mac snorted.

65   "You just believe what you want, Mac," she said testily.

"Too bad it ain't buck season," he said. "Well, I got to go pee."

"So pee."

She heard him turn in his bag. "You ever see it?" he asked.

"It? What's 'it'?"

70   "It. A pecker."

"Sure," she lied.

"Whose? Your father's?"

She was uncomfortable. "No," she said.

"Well, whose then?"

75   "Oh I don't know! Leave me be, why don't you?"

"Didn't see a deer, didn't see a pecker," Mac said teasingly.

She didn't answer right away. Then she said, "My cousin Lewis. I saw his."

"Well, how old's he?"

"One and a half."

"Ha! A baby! A baby's is like a little worm. It ain't a real one at all."   80

If he says he'll show me his, she thought, *I'll kick him. I'll just get out of my bag and kick him.*

"I went hunting with my daddy and Versh and Danny Simmons last year in buck season," Mac said, "and we got ourselves one. And we hog-dressed the thing. You know what that is, don't you?"

"No," she said. She was confused. What was he talking about now?

"That's when you cut him open and take out all his guts, so the meat don't spoil. Makes him lighter to pack out, too."

She tried to imagine what the deer's guts might look like, pulled from the   85 gaping hole. "What do you do with them?" she said. "The guts?"

"Oh, just leave 'em for the bears."

She ran her finger like a knife blade along her belly.

"When we left them on the ground," Mac said, "they smoked. Like they were cooking."

"Huh," she said.

"They cut off the deer's pecker, too, you know."   90

Andy imagined Lewis's pecker and shuddered. "Mac, you're disgusting."

He laughed. "Well, I gotta go pee." She heard him rustle out of his bag. "Broo!" he cried, flapping his arms. "It's cold!"

He makes so much noise, she thought, *just noise and more noise.*

Her father woke them before first light. He warned them to talk softly and said that they were going to the place where Andy had seen the deer, to try to cut them off on their way back from their night feeding. Andy couldn't shake off her sleep. Stuffing her sleeping bag into its sack seemed to take an hour, and tying her boots was the strangest thing she'd ever done. Charlie Spoon made hot chocolate and oatmeal with raisins. Andy closed her eyes and, between beats of her heart, listened to the breathing of the forest. *When I open my eyes, it will be lighter*, she decided. But when she did, it was still just as dark, except for the swaths of their flashlights and the hissing blue flame of the stove. *There has to be just one moment when it all changes from dark to light*, Andy thought. She had missed it yesterday, in the car; today she would watch more closely.

But when she remembered again, it was already first light and they had   95 moved to the rocks by the deer trail and had set up shooting positions — Mac and Charlie Spoon on the up-trail side, she and her father behind them, some six feet up on a ledge. The day became brighter, the sun piercing the tall pines, raking the hunters, yet providing little warmth. Andy now smelled alder and pine and the slightly rotten odor of rock lichen. She rubbed her hand over the stone and considered that it must be very old, had probably been here before the giant pines, *before anyone was in these woods at all*. A chipmunk sniffed on a nearby branch. She aimed an imaginary rifle and pressed the trigger. The chipmunk froze, then scurried away. Her legs were cramping on the narrow ledge. Her father seemed to doze, one hand in his parka, the other cupped lightly around the rifle. She could smell his scent of old wool and leather. His cheeks were speckled with gray-black whiskers, and he worked his jaws slightly, as if chewing a small piece of gum.

Please let us get a deer, she prayed.

A branch snapped on the other side of the rock face. Her father's hand stiffened on the rifle, startling her — *He hasn't been sleeping at all,* she marveled — and then his jaw relaxed, as did the lines around his eyes, and she heard Charlie Spoon call, "Yo, don't shoot, it's us." He and Mac appeared from around the rock. They stopped beneath the ledge. Charlie solemnly crossed his arms.

"I don't believe we're gonna get any deer here," he said drily.

Andy's father lowered his rifle to Charlie and jumped down from the ledge. Then he reached up for Andy. She dropped into his arms and he set her gently on the ground.

100   Mac sidled up to her. "I knew you didn't see no deer," he said.

"Just because they don't come when you want 'em to don't mean she didn't see them," her father said.

Still, she felt bad. Her telling about the deer had caused them to spend the morning there, cold and expectant, with nothing to show for it.

They tramped through the woods for another two hours, not caring much about noise. Mac found some deer tracks, and they argued about how old they were. They split up for a while and then rejoined at an old logging road that deer might use, and followed it. The road crossed a stream, which had mostly frozen over but in a few spots still caught leaves and twigs in an icy swirl. They forded it by jumping from rock to rock. The road narrowed after that, and the woods thickened.

They stopped for lunch, heating up Charlie's wife's corn chowder. Andy's father cut squares of applesauce cake with his hunting knife and handed them to her and Mac, who ate his almost daintily. Andy could faintly taste knife oil on the cake. She was tired. She stretched her leg; the muscle that had cramped on the rock still ached.

105   "Might as well relax," her father said, as if reading her thoughts. "We won't find deer till suppertime."

Charlie Spoon leaned back against his pack and folded his hands across his stomach. "Well, even if we don't get a deer," he said expansively, "it's still great to be out here, breathe some fresh air, clomp around a bit. Get away from the house and the old lady." He winked at Mac, who looked away.

"That's what the woods are all about, anyway," Charlie said. "It's where the women don't want to go." He bowed his head toward Andy. "With your exception, of course, little lady." He helped himself to another piece of applesauce cake.

"She ain't a woman," Mac said.

"Well, she damn well's gonna be," Charlie said. He grinned at her. "Or will you? You're half a boy anyway. You go by a boy's name. What's your real name? Andrea, ain't it?"

110   "That's right," she said. She hoped that if she didn't look at him, Charlie would stop.

"Well, which do you like? Andy or Andrea?"

"Don't matter," she mumbled. "Either."

"She's always been Andy to me," her father said.

Charlie Spoon was still grinning. "So what are you gonna be, Andrea? A boy or a girl?"

"I'm a girl," she said.

"But you want to go hunting and fishing and everything, huh?"

"She can do whatever she likes," her father said.

"Hell, you might as well have just had a boy and be done with it!" Charlie exclaimed.

"That's funny," her father said, and chuckled. "That's just what her momma tells me."

They were looking at her, and she wanted to get away from them all, even from her father, who chose to joke with them.

"I'm going to walk a bit," she said.

She heard them laughing as she walked down the logging trail. She flapped her arms; she whistled. *I don't care how much noise I make*, she thought. Two grouse flew from the underbrush, startling her. A little farther down, the trail ended in a clearing that enlarged into a frozen meadow; beyond it the woods began again. A few moldering posts were all that was left of a fence that had once enclosed the field. The low afternoon sunlight reflected brightly off the snow, so that Andy's eyes hurt. She squinted hard. A gust of wind blew across the field, stinging her face. And then, as if it had been waiting for her, the doe emerged from the trees opposite and stepped cautiously into the field. Andy watched: it stopped and stood quietly for what seemed a long time and then ambled across. It stopped again about seventy yards away and began to browse in a patch of sugar grass uncovered by the wind. Carefully, slowly, never taking her eyes from the doe, Andy walked backward, trying to step into the boot prints she'd already made. When she was far enough back into the woods, she turned and walked faster, her heart racing. *Please let it stay*, she prayed.

"There's doe in the field yonder," she told them.

They got their rifles and hurried down the trail.

"No use," her father said. "We're making too much noise any way you look at it."

"At least we got us the wind in our favor," Charlie Spoon said, breathing heavily.

But the doe was still there, grazing.

"Good Lord," Charlie whispered. He looked at her father. "Well, whose shot?"

"Andy spotted it," her father said in a low voice. "Let her shoot it."

"What!" Charlie's eyes widened.

Andy couldn't believe what her father had just said. She'd only shot tin cans and targets; she'd never even fired her father's .30-.30, and she'd never killed anything.

"I can't," she whispered.

"That's right, she can't," Charlie Spoon insisted. "She's not old enough and she don't have a license even if she was!"

"Well, who's to tell?" her father said in a low voice. "Nobody's going to know but us." He looked at her. "Do you want to shoot it, punkin?"

135   *Why doesn't it hear us?* she wondered. *Why doesn't it run away?* "I don't know," she said.

"Well, I'm sure as hell gonna shoot it," Charlie said. Her father grasped Charlie's rifle barrel and held it. His voice was steady.

"Andy's a good shot. It's her deer. She found it, not you. You'd still be sitting on your ass back in camp." He turned to her again. "Now — do you want to shoot it, Andy? Yes or no."

He was looking at her; they were all looking at her. Suddenly she was angry at the deer, who refused to hear them, who wouldn't run away even when it could. "I'll shoot it," she said. Charlie turned away in disgust.

She lay on the ground and pressed the rifle stock against her shoulder bone. The snow was cold through her parka; she smelled oil and wax and damp earth. She pulled off one glove with her teeth. "It sights just like the .22," her father said gently. "Cartridge's already chambered." As she had done so many times before, she sighted down the scope; now the doe was in the reticle. She moved the barrel until the cross hairs lined up. Her father was breathing beside her.

140   "Aim where the chest and legs meet, or a little above, punkin," he was saying calmly. "That's the killing shot."

But now, seeing it in the scope, Andy was hesitant. Her finger weakened on the trigger. Still, she nodded at what her father said and sighted again, the cross hairs lining up in exactly the same spot — the doe had hardly moved, its brownish-gray body outlined starkly against the blue-backed snow. *It doesn't know,* Andy thought. *It just doesn't know.* And as she looked, deer and snow and faraway trees flattened within the circular frame to become like a picture on a calendar, not real, and she felt calm, as if she had been dreaming everything — the day, the deer, the hunt itself. And she, finger on trigger, was only a part of that dream.

"Shoot!" Charlie hissed.

Through the scope she saw the deer look up, ears high and straining.

Charlie groaned, and just as he did, and just at the moment when Andy knew — *knew* — the doe would bound away, as if she could feel its haunches tensing and gathering power, she pulled the trigger. Later she would think, *I felt the recoil, I smelled the smoke, but I don't remember pulling the trigger.* Through the scope the deer seemed to shrink into itself, and then slowly knelt, hind legs first, head raised as if to cry out. It trembled, still straining to keep its head high, as if that alone would save it; failing, it collapsed, shuddered, and lay still.

145   "Whoee!" Mac cried.

"One shot! One shot!" her father yelled, clapping her on the back. Charlie Spoon was shaking his head and smiling dumbly.

"I told you she was a great little shot!" her father said. "I told you!" Mac danced and clapped his hands. She was dazed, not quite understanding what had happened. And then they were crossing the field toward the fallen doe, she walking dreamlike, the men laughing and joking, released now from the tension of silence and anticipation. Suddenly Mac pointed and cried out, "Look at that!"

The doe was rising, legs unsteady. They stared at it, unable to comprehend, and in that moment the doe regained its feet and looked at them, as if it too were trying to understand. Her father whistled softly. Charlie Spoon unslung his rifle and raised it to his shoulder, but the doe was already bounding away. His hurried shot missed, and the deer disappeared into the woods.

"Damn, damn, damn," he moaned.

"I don't believe it," her father said. "That deer was dead." 150

"Dead, hell!" Charlie yelled. "It was gutshot, that's all. Stunned and gutshot. Clean shot, my ass!"

What have I done? Andy thought.

Her father slung his rifle over his shoulder. "Well, let's go. It can't get too far."

"Hell, I've seen deer run ten miles gutshot," Charlie said. He waved his arms. "We may never find her!"

As they crossed the field, Mac came up to her and said in a low voice, 155 "Gutshoot a deer, you'll go to hell."

"Shut up, Mac," she said, her voice cracking. It was a terrible thing she had done, she knew. She couldn't bear to think of the doe in pain and frightened. *Please let it die*, she prayed.

But though they searched all the last hour of daylight, so that they had to re-cross the field and go up the logging trail in a twilight made even deeper by thick, smoky clouds, they didn't find the doe. They lost its trail almost immediately in the dense stands of alderberry and larch.

"I am cold, and I am tired," Charlie Spoon declared. "And if you ask me, that deer's in another county already."

"No one's asking you, Charlie," her father said.

They had a supper of hard salami and ham, bread, and the rest of the apple- 160 sauce cake. It seemed a bother to heat the coffee, so they had cold chocolate instead. Everyone turned in early.

"We'll find it in the morning, honeybun," her father said, as she went to her tent.

"I don't like to think of it suffering." She was almost in tears.

"It's dead already, punkin. Don't even think about it." He kissed her, his breath sour and his beard rough against her cheek.

Andy was sure she wouldn't get to sleep; the image of the doe falling, falling, then rising again, repeated itself whenever she closed her eyes. Then she heard an owl hoot and realized that it had awakened her, so she must have been asleep after all. She hoped the owl would hush, but instead it hooted louder. She wished her father or Charlie Spoon would wake up and do something about it, but no one moved in the other tent, and suddenly she was afraid that they had all decamped, wanting nothing more to do with her. She whispered, "Mac, Mac," to the sleeping bag where he should be, but no one answered. She tried to find the flashlight she always kept by her side, but couldn't, and she cried in panic, "Mac, are you there?" He mumbled something, and immediately she felt foolish and hoped he wouldn't reply.

When she awoke again, everything had changed. The owl was gone, the woods 165 were still, and she sensed light, blue and pale, light where before there had been none. *The moon must have come out*, she thought. And it was warm, too, warmer than it should have been. She got out of her sleeping bag and took off her parka — it was that warm. Mac was asleep, wheezing like an old man. She unzipped the tent and stepped outside.

The woods were more beautiful than she had ever seen them. The moon made everything ice-rimmed glimmer with a crystallized, immanent light, while underneath that ice the branches of trees were as stark as skeletons. She heard a crunching in the snow, the one sound in all that silence, and there, walking down the logging trail into their camp, was the doe. Its body, like everything around her, was silvered with frost and moonlight. It walked past the tent where her father and Charlie Spoon were sleeping and stopped no more than six feet from her. Andy saw that she had shot it, yes, had shot it cleanly, just where she thought she had, the wound a jagged, bloody hole in the doe's chest.

A heart shot, she thought.

The doe stepped closer, so that Andy, if she wished, could have reached out and touched it. It looked at her as if expecting her to do this, and so she did, running her hand, slowly at first, along the rough, matted fur, then down to the edge of the wound, where she stopped. The doe stood still. Hesitantly, Andy felt the edge of the wound. The torn flesh was sticky and warm. The wound parted under her touch. And then, almost without her knowing it, her fingers were within, probing, yet still the doe didn't move. Andy pressed deeper, through flesh and muscle and sinew, until her whole hand and more was inside the wound and she had found the doe's heart, warm and beating. She cupped it gently in her hand. *Alive,* she marveled. *Alive.*

The heart quickened under her touch, becoming warmer and warmer until it was hot enough to burn. In pain, Andy tried to remove her hand, but the wound closed about it and held her fast. Her hand was burning. She cried out in agony, sure they would all hear and come help, but they didn't. And then her hand pulled free, followed by a steaming rush of blood, more blood than she ever could have imagined — it covered her hand and arm, and she saw to her horror that her hand was steaming. She moaned and fell to her knees and plunged her hand into the snow. The doe looked at her gently and then turned and walked back up the trail.

170   In the morning, when she woke, Andy could still smell the blood, but she felt no pain. She looked at her hand. Even though it appeared unscathed, it felt weak and withered. She couldn't move it freely and was afraid the others would notice. *I will hide it in my jacket pocket,* she decided, *so nobody can see.* She ate the oatmeal that her father cooked and stayed apart from them all. No one spoke to her, and that suited her. A light snow began to fall. It was the last day of their hunting trip. She wanted to be home.

Her father dumped the dregs of his coffee. "Well, let's go look for her," he said.

Again they crossed the field. Andy lagged behind. She averted her eyes from the spot where the doe had fallen, already filling up with snow. Mac and Charlie entered the woods first, followed by her father. Andy remained in the field and considered the smear of gray sky, the nearby flock of crows pecking at unyielding stubble. *I will stay here,* she thought, *and not move for a long while.* But now someone — Mac — was yelling. Her father appeared at the woods' edge and waved for her to come. She ran and pushed through a brake of alderberry and larch. The thick underbrush scratched her face. For a moment she felt lost and looked wildly about. Then, where the brush thinned, she saw them standing quietly in the falling snow. They were staring down at the dead doe. A film covered its upturned eye, and its body was lightly dusted with snow.

"I told you she wouldn't get too far," Andy's father said triumphantly. "We must've just missed her yesterday. Too blind to see."

"We're just damn lucky no animal got to her last night," Charlie muttered.

Her father lifted the doe's foreleg. The wound was blood-clotted, brown, and caked like frozen mud. "Clean shot," he said to Charlie. He grinned. "My little girl." 175

Then he pulled out his knife, the blade gray as the morning. Mac whispered to Andy, "Now watch this," while Charlie Spoon lifted the doe from behind by its forelegs so that its head rested between his knees, its underside exposed. Her father's knife sliced thickly from chest to belly to crotch, and Andy was running from them, back to the field and across, scattering the crows who cawed and circled angrily. And now they were all calling to her — Charlie Spoon and Mac and her father — crying *Andy, Andy* (but that wasn't her name, she would no longer be called that); yet louder than any of them was the wind blowing through the treetops, like the ocean where her mother floated in green water, also calling *Come in, come in*, while all around her roared the mocking of the terrible, now inevitable, sea.

Reading and Reacting

1. The initiation of a child into adulthood is a common literary theme. In this story, hunting is presented as an initiation rite. In what way is hunting an appropriate coming-of-age ritual?

2. Which characters are in conflict in this story? Which ideas are in conflict? How do these conflicts help to communicate the story's initiation theme?

3. In the story's opening paragraph and elsewhere, Andy finds comfort and reassurance in the idea that the woods are "always the same"; later in the story, she remembers the ocean, "huge and empty, yet always moving. Everything lay hidden . . ." (par. 45). How does the contrast between the woods and the ocean suggest the transition she must make from childhood to adulthood?

4. How are the references to blood consistent with the story's initiation theme? Do they suggest another theme as well?

5. Throughout the story, references are made to Andy's ability to inspire the trust of animals. As her father says, "Animals — I don't know how she does it, but they come right up to her" (par. 8). How does his comment foreshadow later events?

6. Why do you think Andy prays that she and the others will get a deer? What makes her change her mind? How does the change in Andy's character help to convey the story's theme?

7. Andy's mother is not an active participant in the story's events. Still, her presence is important to the story. *Why* is it important? How does paragraph 45 reveal the importance of the mother's role?

8. What has Andy learned as a result of her experience? What else do you think she still has to learn?

9. **JOURNAL ENTRY** How would the story be different if Andy were a boy? What would be the same?

10. CRITICAL PERSPECTIVE In a review of *Comfort*, the book in which "Doe Season" appears, Susan Wood makes the following observation:

> The dozen or so stories in David Michael Kaplan's affecting first collection share a common focus on the extraordinary moments of recognition in ordinary lives. He is at his best suggesting how such moments may alter, for better or for worse, our relationships with those to whom we are most deeply bound — children, parents, lovers — in love and guilt.

At what point does "the extraordinary moment of recognition" occur in "Doe Season"? How does this moment alter Andy's relationship with both her parents?

Related Works: "A&P" (p. 115), "The Lesson" (p. 435), "Boys and Girls" (p. 493), "The Lamb" (p. 852), "Traveling through the Dark" (p. 916)

D(AVID) H(ERBERT) LAWRENCE (1885–1930) was born in Nottinghamshire, England, the son of a coal miner and a schoolteacher. Determined to escape the harsh life of a miner, Lawrence taught for several years after graduating from high school. He soon began writing fiction and established himself in London literary circles. He married a German aristocrat, Frieda von Richthofen, in 1912.

During World War I, Lawrence and his wife were suspected of treason because of his pacifism and her connection to German aristocracy. Because Lawrence suffered from tuberculosis, he and his wife left England after the armistice in search of a healthier climate. They traveled in Australia, France, Italy, Mexico, and the United States throughout their lives.

Lawrence is recognized for his impassioned portrayal of our unconscious and instinctive natures. In his novel *Lady Chatterley's Lover* (1928), he attempted to restore explicit sexuality to English fiction, and the book was banned for years in Britain and the United States. His other novels include *Sons and Lovers* (1913), *The Rainbow* (1915), *Women in Love* (1921), and *The Plumed Serpent* (1926). Lawrence was also a gifted poet, essayist, travel writer, and short story writer, and his work and personal magnetism had a strong influence on other writers.

Lawrence's fascination with the struggle between the unconscious and the intellect is revealed in his short story "The Rocking-Horse Winner" (1920). Lawrence sets his story in a house full of secrets and weaves symbolism with elements of the fairy tale and the gothic to produce a tale that is often the subject of literary debate.

Cultural Context: The concepts of superstition and luck as depicted in "The Rocking-Horse Winner" have been influential in almost all cultures throughout history. Many superstitions can be traced to Roman and Anglo-Saxon times, others to Victorian rhymes, and still others to folklore passed down from generation to generation. Even today, many individuals admit to holding irrational beliefs concerning what brings good and bad fortune. For example, baseball players frequently have lucky bats or lucky gloves, and gamblers in casinos often wear lucky hats or shirts.

The Rocking-Horse Winner (1920)

There was a woman who was beautiful, who started with all the advantages, yet she had no luck. She married for love, and the love turned to dust. She had bonny children, yet she felt they had been thrust upon her, and she could not love them. They looked at her coldly, as if they were finding fault with her. And hurriedly she felt she must cover up some fault in herself. Yet what it was that she must cover up she never knew. Nevertheless, when her children were present, she always felt the centre of her heart go hard. This troubled her, and in her manner she was all the more gentle and anxious for her children, as if she loved them very much. Only she herself knew that at the centre of her heart was a hard little place that could not feel love, no, not for anybody. Everybody else said of her: "She is such a good mother. She adores her children." Only she herself, and her children themselves, knew it was not so. They read it in each other's eyes.

There were a boy and two little girls. They lived in a pleasant house, with a garden, and they had discreet servants, and felt themselves superior to anyone in the neighbourhood.

Although they lived in style, they felt always an anxiety in the house. There was never enough money. The mother had a small income, and the father had a small income, but not nearly enough for the social position which they had to keep up. The father went into town to some office. But though he had good prospects, these prospects never materialised. There was always the grinding sense of the shortage of money, though the style was always kept up.

At last the mother said: "I will see if *I* can't make something." But she did not know where to begin. She racked her brains, and tried this thing and the other, but could not find anything successful. The failure made deep lines come into her face. Her children were growing up, they would have to go to school. There must be more money, there must be more money. The father, who was always very handsome and expensive in his tastes, seemed as if he never *would* be able to do anything worth doing. And the mother, who had a great belief in herself, did not succeed any better, and her tastes were just as expensive.

And so the house came to be haunted by the unspoken phrase: *There must be* 5 *more money! There must be more money!* The children could hear it all the time, though nobody said it aloud. They heard it at Christmas, when the expensive and splendid toys filled the nursery. Behind the shining modern rocking-horse, behind the smart doll's house, a voice would start whispering: "There *must* be more money! There *must* be more money!" And the children would stop playing, to listen for a moment. They would look into each other's eyes, to see if they had all heard. And each one saw in the eyes of the other two that they too had heard. "There *must* be more money! There *must* be more money!"

It came whispering from the springs of the still-swaying rocking-horse, and even the horse, bending his wooden, champing head, heard it. The big doll, sitting so pink and smirking in her new pram, could hear it quite plainly, and seemed to be smirking all the more self-consciously because of it. The foolish puppy, too, that took the place of the teddybear, he was looking so extraordinarily foolish for no other reason but that he heard the secret whisper all over the house: "There *must* be more money!"

Yet nobody ever said it aloud. The whisper was everywhere, and therefore no one spoke it. Just as no one ever says: "We are breathing!" in spite of the fact that breath is coming and going all the time.

"Mother," said the boy Paul one day, "why don't we keep a car of our own? Why do we always use uncle's, or else a taxi?"

"Because we're the poor members of the family," said the mother.

10   "But why *are* we, mother?"

"Well — I suppose," she said slowly and bitterly, "it's because your father has no luck."

The boy was silent for some time.

"Is luck money, mother?" he asked, rather timidly.

"No, Paul. Not quite. It's what causes you to have money."

15   "Oh!" said Paul vaguely. "I thought when Uncle Oscar said *filthy lucker,* it meant money."

"*Filthy lucre* does mean money," said the mother. "But it's lucre, not luck."

"Oh!" said the boy. "Then what *is* luck, mother?"

"It's what causes you to have money. If you're lucky you have money. That's why it's better to be born lucky than rich. If you're rich, you may lose your money. But if you're lucky, you will always get more money."

"Oh! Will you? And is father not lucky?"

20   "Very unlucky, I should say," she said bitterly.

The boy watched her with unsure eyes.

"Why?" he asked.

"I don't know. Nobody ever knows why one person is lucky and another unlucky."

"Don't they? Nobody at all? Does *nobody* know?"

25   "Perhaps God. But He never tells."

"He ought to, then. And aren't you lucky either, mother?"

"I can't be, if I married an unlucky husband."

"But by yourself, aren't you?"

"I used to think I was, before I married. Now I think I am very unlucky indeed."

30   "Why?"

"Well — never mind! Perhaps I'm not really," she said.

The child looked at her to see if she meant it. But he saw, by the lines of her mouth, that she was only trying to hide something from him.

"Well, anyhow," he said stoutly, "I'm a lucky person."

"Why?" said his mother, with a sudden laugh.

35   He stared at her. He didn't even know why he had said it.

"God told me," he asserted, brazening it out.

"I hope He did, dear!" she said, again with a laugh, but rather bitter.

"He did, mother!"

"Excellent!" said the mother, using one of her husband's exclamations.

The boy saw she did not believe him; or rather, that she paid no attention to his assertion. This angered him somewhat, and made him want to compel her attention.

He went off by himself, vaguely, in a childish way, seeking for the clue to "luck." Absorbed, taking no heed of other people, he went about with a sort of stealth, seeking inwardly for luck. He wanted luck, he wanted it, he wanted it. When the two girls were playing dolls in the nursery, he would sit on his big rocking-horse, charging madly into space, with a frenzy that made the little girls peer at him uneasily. Wildly the horse careered, the waving dark hair of the boy tossed, his eyes had a strange glare in them. The little girls dared not speak to him.

When he had ridden to the end of his mad little journey, he climbed down and stood in front of his rocking-horse, staring fixedly into its lowered face. Its red mouth was slightly open, its big eye was wide and glassy-bright.

"Now!" he would silently command the snorting steed. "Now, take me to where there is luck! Now take me!"

And he would slash the horse on the neck with the little whip he had asked Uncle Oscar for. He *knew* the horse could take him to where there was luck, if only he forced it. So he would mount again and start on his furious ride, hoping at last to get there. He knew he could get there.

"You'll break your horse, Paul!" said the nurse.

"He's always riding like that! I wish he'd leave off!" said his elder sister Joan.

But he only glared down on them in silence. Nurse gave him up. She could make nothing of him. Anyhow, he was growing beyond her.

One day his mother and his Uncle Oscar came in when he was on one of his furious rides. He did not speak to them.

"Hallo, you young jockey! Riding a winner?" said his uncle.

"Aren't you growing too big for a rocking-horse? You're not a very little boy any longer, you know," said his mother.

But Paul only gave a blue glare from his big, rather close-set eyes. He would speak to nobody when he was in full tilt. His mother watched him with an anxious expression on her face.

At last he suddenly stopped forcing his horse into the mechanical gallop and slid down.

"Well, I got there!" he announced fiercely, his blue eyes still flaring, and his sturdy long legs straddling apart.

"Where did you get to?" asked his mother.

"Where I wanted to go," he flared back at her.

"That's right, son!" said Uncle Oscar. "Don't you stop till you get there. What's the horse's name?"

"He doesn't have a name," said the boy.

"Gets on without all right?" asked the uncle.

"Well, he has different names. He was called Sansovino last week."

"Sansovino, eh? Won the Ascot.° How did you know this name?"

---

the Ascot: The annual horse race at Ascot Heath in England.

"He always talks about horse-races with Bassett," said Joan.

The uncle was delighted to find that his small nephew was posted with all the racing news. Bassett, the young gardener, who had been wounded in the left foot in the war and had got his present job through Oscar Cresswell, whose batman° he had been, was a perfect blade of the "turf." He lived in the racing events, and the small boy lived with him.

Oscar Cresswell got it all from Bassett.

"Master Paul comes and asks me, so I can't do more than tell him, sir," said Bassett, his face terribly serious, as if he were speaking of religious matters.

65 "And does he ever put anything on a horse he fancies?"

"Well — I don't want to give him away — he's a young sport, a fine sport, sir. Would you mind asking him himself? He sort of takes a pleasure in it, and perhaps he'd feel I was giving him away, sir, if you don't mind."

Bassett was serious as a church.

The uncle went back to his nephew and took him off for a ride in the car.

"Say, Paul, old man, do you ever put anything on a horse?" the uncle asked.

70 The boy watched the handsome man closely.

"Why, do you think I oughtn't to?" he parried.

"Not a bit of it! I thought perhaps you might give me a tip for the Lincoln."°

The car sped on into the country, going down to Uncle Oscar's place in Hampshire.

"Honour bright?" said the nephew.

75 "Honour bright, son!" said the uncle.

"Well, then, Daffodil."

"Daffodil! I doubt it, sonny. What about Mirza?"

"I only know the winner," said the boy. "That's Daffodil."

"Daffodil, eh?"

80 There was a pause. Daffodil was an obscure horse comparatively.

"Uncle!"

"Yes, son?"

"You won't let it go any further, will you? I promised Bassett."

"Bassett be damned, old man! What's he got to do with it?"

85 "We're partners. We've been partners from the first. Uncle, he lent me my first five shillings, which I lost. I promised him, honour bright, it was only between me and him; only you gave me that ten-shilling note I started winning with, so I thought you were lucky. You won't let it go any further, will you?"

The boy gazed at his uncle from those big, hot, blue eyes, set rather close together. The uncle stirred and laughed uneasily.

"Right you are, son! I'll keep your tip private. Daffodil, eh? How much are you putting on him?"

"All except twenty pounds," said the boy. "I keep that in reserve."

The uncle thought it a good joke.

---

batman: A British military officer's personal assistant.

the Lincoln: The Lincolnshire Handicap, a horse race.

"You keep twenty pounds in reserve, do you, you young romancer? What are   90
you betting, then?"

"I'm betting three hundred," said the boy gravely. "But it's between you and
me, Uncle Oscar! Honour bright?"

The uncle burst into a roar of laughter.

"It's between you and me all right, you young Nat Gould,"° he said, laughing.
"But where's your three hundred?"

"Bassett keeps it for me. We're partners."

"You are, are you! And what is Bassett putting on Daffodil?"   95

"He won't go quite as high as I do, I expect. Perhaps he'll go a hundred and
fifty."

"What, pennies?" laughed the uncle.

"Pounds," said the child, with a surprised look at his uncle. "Bassett keeps a
bigger reserve than I do."

Between wonder and amusement Uncle Oscar was silent. He pursued the matter no further, but he determined to take his nephew with him to the Lincoln races.

"Now, son," he said, "I'm putting twenty on Mirza, and I'll put five on for you   100
on any horse you fancy. What's your pick?"

"Daffodil, uncle."

"No, not the fiver on Daffodil!"

"I should if it was my own fiver," said the child.

"Good! Good! Right you are! A fiver for me and a fiver for you on Daffodil."

The child had never been to a race-meeting before, and his eyes were blue fire.   105
He pursed his mouth tight and watched. A Frenchman just in front had put his
money on Lancelot. Wild with excitement, he flayed his arms up and down,
yelling *"Lancelot! Lancelot!"* in his French accent.

Daffodil came in first, Lancelot second, Mirza third. The child, flushed and
with eyes blazing, was curiously serene. His uncle brought him four five-pound
notes, four to one.

"What am I to do with these?" he cried, waving them before the boy's eyes.

"I suppose we'll talk to Bassett," said the boy. "I expect I have fifteen hundred
now; and twenty in reserve; and this twenty."

His uncle studied him for some moments.

"Look here, son!" he said. "You're not serious about Bassett and that fifteen   110
hundred, are you?"

"Yes, I am. But it's between you and me, uncle. Honour bright?"

"Honour bright all right, son! But I must talk to Bassett."

"If you'd like to be a partner, uncle, with Bassett and me, we could all be partners. Only, you'd have to promise, honour bright, uncle, not to let it go beyond us
three. Bassett and I are lucky, and you must be lucky, because it was your ten
shillings I started winning with. . . ."

Uncle Oscar took both Bassett and Paul into Richmond Park for an afternoon,
and there they talked.

Nat Gould: Nathaniel Gould (1857–1919), British journalist and writer known for his stories about horse racing.

115   "It's like this, you see, sir," Bassett said. "Master Paul would get me talking about racing events, spinning yarns, you know, sir. And he was always keen on knowing if I'd made or if I'd lost. It's about a year since, now, that I put five shillings on Blush of Dawn for him: and we lost. Then the luck turned, with that ten shillings he had from you: that we put on Singhalese. And since that time, it's been pretty steady, all things considering. What do you say, Master Paul?"

"We're all right when we're sure," said Paul. "It's when we're not quite sure that we go down."

"Oh, but we're careful then," said Bassett.

"But when are you *sure?*" smiled Uncle Oscar.

"It's Master Paul, sir," said Bassett in a secret, religious voice. "It's as if he had it from heaven. Like Daffodil, now, for the Lincoln. That was as sure as eggs."

120   "Did you put anything on Daffodil?" asked Oscar Cresswell.

"Yes, sir. I made my bit."

"And my nephew?"

Bassett was obstinately silent, looking at Paul.

"I made twelve hundred, didn't I, Bassett? I told uncle I was putting three hundred on Daffodil."

125   "That's right," said Bassett, nodding.

"But where's the money?" asked the uncle.

"I keep it safe locked up, sir. Master Paul can have it any minute he likes to ask for it."

"What, fifteen hundred pounds?"

"And twenty! And *forty*, that is, with the twenty he made on the course."

130   "It's amazing!" said the uncle.

"If Master Paul offers you to be partners, sir, I would, if I were you: if you'll excuse me," said Bassett.

Oscar Cresswell thought about it.

"I'll see the money," he said.

They drove home again, and, sure enough, Bassett came round to the garden-house with fifteen hundred pounds in notes. The twenty pounds reserve was left with Joe Glee, in the Turf Commission deposit.

135   "You see, it's all right, uncle, when I'm *sure!* Then we go strong, for all we're worth. Don't we, Bassett?"

"We do that, Master Paul."

"And when are you sure?" said the uncle, laughing.

"Oh, well, sometimes I'm *absolutely* sure, like about Daffodil," said the boy; "and sometimes I have an idea; and sometimes I haven't even an idea, have I, Bassett? Then we're careful, because we mostly go down."

"You do, do you! And when you're sure, like about Daffodil, what makes you sure, sonny?"

140   "Oh, well, I don't know," said the boy uneasily. "I'm sure, you know, uncle; that's all."

"It's as if he had it from heaven, sir," Bassett reiterated.

"I should say so!" said the uncle.

But he became a partner. And when the Leger° was coming on Paul was "sure" about Lively Spark, which was a quite inconsiderable horse. The boy insisted on putting a thousand on the horse, Bassett went for five hundred, and Oscar Cresswell two hundred. Lively Spark came in first, and the betting had been ten to one against him. Paul had made ten thousand.

"You see," he said, "I was absolutely sure of him."

Even Oscar Cresswell had cleared two thousand.   145

"Look here, son," he said, "this sort of thing makes me nervous."

"It needn't, uncle! Perhaps I shan't be sure again for a long time."

"But what are you going to do with your money?" asked the uncle.

"Of course," said the boy, "I started it for mother. She said she had no luck, because father is unlucky, so I thought if *I* was lucky, it might stop whispering."

"What might stop whispering?"   150

"Our house. I *hate* our house for whispering."

"What does it whisper?"

"Why — why"— the boy fidgeted —"why, I don't know. But it's always short of money, you know, uncle."

"I know it, son, I know it."

"You know people send mother writs,° don't you, uncle?"   155

"I'm afraid I do," said the uncle.

"And then the house whispers, like people laughing at you behind your back. It's awful, that is! I thought if I was lucky . . ."

"You might stop it," added the uncle.

The boy watched him with big blue eyes, that had an uncanny cold fire in them, and he said never a word.

"Well, then!" said the uncle. "What are we doing?"   160

"I shouldn't like mother to know I was lucky," said the boy.

"Why not, son?"

"She'd stop me."

"I don't think she would."

"Oh!"— and the boy writhed in an odd way —"I *don't* want her to know,   165
uncle."

"All right, son! We'll manage it without her knowing."

They managed it very easily. Paul, at the other's suggestion, handed over five thousand pounds to his uncle, who deposited it with the family lawyer, who was then to inform Paul's mother that a relative had put five thousand pounds into his hands, which sum was to be paid out a thousand pounds at a time, on the mother's birthday, for the next five years.

"So she'll have a birthday present of a thousand pounds for five successive years," said Uncle Oscar. "I hope it won't make it all the harder for her later."

Paul's mother had her birthday in November. The house had been "whispering" worse than ever lately, and, even in spite of his luck, Paul could not bear up

---

the Leger: The St. Leger Stakes, a horse race.

writs: Letters from creditors requesting payment.

against it. He was very anxious to see the effect of the birthday letter, telling his mother about the thousand pounds.

170   When there were no visitors, Paul now took his meals with his parents, as he was beyond the nursery control. His mother went into town nearly every day. She had discovered that she had an odd knack of sketching furs and dress materials, so she worked secretly in the studio of a friend who was the chief "artist" for the leading drapers. She drew the figures of ladies in furs and ladies in silk and sequins for the newspaper advertisements. This young woman artist earned several thousand pounds a year, but Paul's mother only made several hundreds, and she was again dissatisfied. She so wanted to be first in something, and she did not succeed, even in making sketches for drapery advertisements.

She was down to breakfast on the morning of her birthday. Paul watched her face as she read her letters. He knew the lawyer's letter. As his mother read it, her face hardened and became more expressionless. Then a cold, determined look came on her mouth. She hid the letter under the pile of others, and said not a word about it.

"Didn't you have anything nice in the post for your birthday, mother?" said Paul.

"Quite moderately nice," she said, her voice cold and absent.

She went away to town without saying more.

175   But in the afternoon Uncle Oscar appeared. He said Paul's mother had had a long interview with the lawyer, asking if the whole five thousand could not be advanced at once, as she was in debt.

"What do you think, uncle?" asked the boy.

"I leave it to you, son."

"Oh, let her have it, then! We can get some more with the other," said the boy.

"A bird in the hand is worth two in the bush, laddie!" said Uncle Oscar.

180   "But I'm sure to *know* for the Grand National; or the Lincolnshire; or else the Derby.° I'm sure to know for *one* of them," said Paul.

So Uncle Oscar signed the agreement, and Paul's mother touched the whole five thousand. Then something very curious happened. The voices in the house suddenly went mad, like a chorus of frogs on a spring evening. There was certain new furnishings, and Paul had a tutor. He was *really* going to Eton, his father's school, in the following autumn. There were flowers in the winter, and a blossoming of the luxury Paul's mother had been used to. And yet the voices in the house, behind the sprays of mimosa and almond-blossom, and from under the piles of iridescent cushions, simply trilled and screamed in a sort of ecstasy: "There *must* be more money! Oh-h-h; there *must* be more money. Oh, now, now-w! Now-w-w — there *must* be more money! — more than ever! More than ever!"

It frightened Paul terribly. He studied away at his Latin and Greek with his tutor. But his intense hours were spent with Bassett. The Grand National had gone

---

Grand National . . . Derby: Famous British horse races. The Grand National is run at Aintree; the Derby at Epsom Downs.

by: he had not "known," and had lost a hundred pounds. Summer was at hand. He was in agony for the Lincoln. But even for the Lincoln he didn't "know," and he lost fifty pounds. He became wild-eyed and strange, as if something were going to explode in him.

"Let it alone, son! Don't you bother about it!" urged Uncle Oscar. But it was as if the boy couldn't really hear what his uncle was saying.

"I've got to know for the Derby! I've got to know for the Derby!" the child reiterated, his big blue eyes blazing with a sort of madness.

His mother noticed how overwrought he was.   185

"You'd better go to the seaside. Wouldn't you like to go now to the seaside, instead of waiting? I think you'd better," she said, looking down at him anxiously, her heart curiously heavy because of him.

But the child lifted his uncanny blue eyes.

"I couldn't possibly go before the Derby, mother!" he said. "I couldn't possibly!"

"Why not?" she said, her voice becoming heavy when she was opposed. "Why not? You can still go from the seaside to see the Derby with your Uncle Oscar, if that's what you wish. No need for you to wait here. Besides, I think you care too much about these races. It's a bad sign. My family has been a gambling family, and you won't know till you grow up how much damage it has done. But it has done damage. I shall have to send Bassett away, and ask Uncle Oscar not to talk racing to you, unless you promise to be reasonable about it: go away to the seaside and forget it. You're all nerves!"

"I'll do what you like, mother, so long as you don't send me away till after the   190
Derby," the boy said.

"Send you away from where? Just from this house?"

"Yes," he said, gazing at her.

"Why, you curious child, what makes you care about this house so much, suddenly? I never knew you loved it."

He gazed at her without speaking. He had a secret within a secret, something he had not divulged, even to Bassett or to his Uncle Oscar.

But his mother, after standing undecided and a little bit sullen for some   195
moments, said:

"Very well, then! Don't go to the seaside till after the Derby, if you don't wish it. But promise me you won't let your nerves go to pieces. Promise you won't think so much about horse-racing and *events*, as you call them!"

"Oh no," said the boy casually. "I won't think much about them, mother. You needn't worry. I wouldn't worry, mother, if I were you."

"If you were me and I were you," said his mother, "I wonder what we *should* do!"

"But you know you needn't worry, mother, don't you?" the boy repeated.

"I should be awfully glad to know it," she said wearily.   200

"Oh, well, you *can*, you know. I mean, you *ought* to know you needn't worry," he insisted.

"Ought I? Then I'll see about it," she said.

Paul's secret of secrets was his wooden horse, that which had no name. Since he was emancipated from a nurse and a nursery-governess, he had had his rocking-horse removed to his own bedroom at the top of the house.

"Surely you're too big for a rocking-horse!" his mother had remonstrated.

205   "Well, you see, mother, till I can have a *real* horse, I like to have *some* sort of animal about," had been his quaint answer.

"Do you feel he keeps you company?" she laughed.

"Oh yes! He's very good, he always keeps me company, when I'm there," said Paul.

So the horse, rather shabby, stood in an arrested prance in the boy's bedroom.

The Derby was drawing near, and the boy grew more and more tense. He hardly heard what was spoken to him, he was very frail, and his eyes were really uncanny. His mother had sudden strange seizures of uneasiness about him. Sometimes, for half an hour, she would feel a sudden anxiety about him that was almost anguish. She wanted to rush to him at once, and know he was safe.

210   Two nights before the Derby, she was at a big party in town, when one of her rushes of anxiety about her boy, her firstborn, gripped her heart till she could hardly speak. She fought with the feeling, might and main, for she believed in common sense. But it was too strong. She had to leave the dance and go downstairs to telephone to the country. The children's nursery-governess was terribly surprised and startled at being rung up in the night.

"Are the children all right, Miss Wilmot?"

"Oh yes, they are quite all right."

"Master Paul? Is he all right?"

"He went to bed as right as a trivet. Shall I run up and look at him?"

215   "No," said Paul's mother reluctantly. "No! Don't trouble. It's all right. Don't sit up. We shall be home fairly soon." She did not want her son's privacy intruded upon.

"Very good," said the governess.

It was about one o'clock when Paul's mother and father drove up to their house. All was still. Paul's mother went to her room and slipped off her white fur cloak. She had told her maid not to wait up for her. She heard her husband downstairs, mixing a whisky and soda.

And then, because of the strange anxiety at her heart, she stole upstairs to her son's room. Noiselessly she went along the upper corridor. Was there a faint noise? What was it?

She stood, with arrested muscles, outside his door, listening. There was a strange, heavy, and yet not loud noise. Her heart stood still. It was a soundless noise, yet rushing and powerful. Something huge, in violent, hushed motion. What was it? What in God's name was it? She ought to know. She felt that she knew the noise. She knew what it was.

220   Yet she could not place it. She couldn't say what it was. And on and on it went, like a madness.

Softly, frozen with anxiety and fear, she turned the door-handle.

The room was dark. Yet in the space near the window, she heard and saw something plunging to and fro. She gazed in fear and amazement.

Then suddenly she switched on the light, and saw her son, in his green pyjamas, madly surging on the rocking-horse. The blaze of light suddenly lit him up, as he urged the wooden horse, and lit her up, as she stood, blonde, in her dress of pale green and crystal, in the doorway.

"Paul!" she cried. "Whatever are you doing?"

"It's Malabar!" he screamed in a powerful, strange voice. "It's Malabar!" 225

His eyes blazed at her for one strange and senseless second, as he ceased urging his wooden horse. Then he fell with a crash to the ground, and she, all her tormented motherhood flooding upon her, rushed to gather him up.

But he was unconscious, and unconscious he remained, with some brain-fever. He talked and tossed, and his mother sat stonily by his side.

"Malabar! It's Malabar! Bassett, Bassett, I *know!* It's Malabar!"

So the child cried, trying to get up and urge the rocking-horse that gave him his inspiration.

"What does he mean by Malabar?" asked the heart-frozen mother. 230

"I don't know," said the father stonily.

"What does he mean by Malabar?" she asked her brother Oscar.

"It's one of the horses running for the Derby," was the answer.

And, in spite of himself, Oscar Cresswell spoke to Bassett, and himself put a thousand on Malabar: at fourteen to one.

The third day of the illness was critical: they were waiting for a change. The 235 boy, with his rather long, curly hair, was tossing ceaselessly on the pillow. He neither slept nor regained consciousness, and his eyes were like blue stones. His mother sat, feeling her heart had gone, turned actually into a stone.

In the evening, Oscar Cresswell did not come, but Bassett sent a message, saying could he come up for one moment, just one moment? Paul's mother was very angry at the intrusion, but on second thought she agreed. The boy was the same. Perhaps Bassett might bring him to consciousness.

The gardener, a shortish fellow with a little brown moustache and sharp little brown eyes, tiptoed into the room, touched his imaginary cap to Paul's mother, and stole to the bedside, staring with glittering, smallish eyes at the tossing, dying child.

"Master Paul!" he whispered. "Master Paul! Malabar came in first all right, a clean win. I did as you told me. You've made over seventy thousand pounds, you have; you've got over eighty thousand. Malabar came in all right, Master Paul."

"Malabar! Malabar! Did I say Malabar, mother? Did I say Malabar? Do you think I'm lucky, mother? I knew Malabar, didn't I? Over eighty thousand pounds! I call that lucky, don't you, mother? Over eighty thousand pounds! I knew, didn't I know I knew? Malabar came in all right. If I ride my horse till I'm sure, then I tell you, Bassett, you can go as high as you like. Did you go for all you were worth, Bassett?"

"I went a thousand on it, Master Paul." 240

"I never told you, mother, that if I can ride my horse, and *get there*, then I'm absolutely sure — oh, absolutely! Mother, did I ever tell you? I *am* lucky!"

"No, you never did," said his mother.

But the boy died in the night.

And even as he lay dead, his mother heard her brother's voice saying to her: "My God, Hester, you're eighty-odd thousand to the good, and a poor devil of a son to the bad. But, poor devil, poor devil, he's best gone out of a life where he rides his rocking-horse to find a winner."

Reading and Reacting

1. From what point of view is "The Rocking-Horse Winner" told? How does this point of view help to communicate the story's theme?

2. In what respects is "The Rocking-Horse Winner" like a fairy tale? How is it different?

3. Many fairy tales involve a hero who goes on a journey to search for something of great value. What journey does Paul go on? What does he search for? Is he successful?

4. In paragraph 5, the narrator says that the house is "haunted by the unspoken phrase: '*There must be more money!*'" In what way does the phrase "haunt" the house?

5. How would you characterize Paul's parents? His uncle? Bassett? Are they weak? Evil? What motivates them?

6. Beginning in paragraph 11, Paul's mother attempts to define the word *luck*. According to her definition, does she consider Paul lucky? Do you agree?

7. In what ways does Paul behave like other children? In what ways is he different? How do you account for these differences? How old do you think Paul is? Why is his age significant?

8. The rocking horse is an important literary symbol in the story. What possible meanings might the rocking horse suggest? In what ways does this symbol reinforce the story's theme?

9. What secrets do the various characters keep from one another? Why do they keep them? How do these secrets relate to the story's theme?

10. How does Paul know who the winners will be? Does the rocking horse really tell him? Does he get his information "from heaven" as Bassett suggests (par. 119)? Or does he just guess?

11. JOURNAL ENTRY In your opinion, who or what is responsible for Paul's death?

12. CRITICAL PERSPECTIVE In a letter dated January 17, 1913, Lawrence wrote the following:

> My great religion is a belief in the blood, the flesh, as being wiser than the intellect. We can go wrong in our minds. But what our blood feels and believes and says, is always true. The intellect is only a bit and a bridle. What do I care about knowledge. All I want is to answer to my blood, direct, without fribbling intervention of mind, or moral, or what-not.

How does Lawrence's portrayal of Paul in "The Rocking-Horse Winner" support his belief in "the blood . . . being wiser than the intellect"? How does Lawrence remain true in this story to his metaphor of the intellect as bit and "a bridle"?

Related Works: "Teenage Wasteland" (p. 535), "Gretel in Darkness" (p. 601), "Suicide Note" (p. 607), "Christopher Robin" (p. 761), "The Chimney Sweeper" (p. 852), "Birches" (p. 877)

EUDORA WELTY (1909–2001) was born and raised in Jackson, Mississippi, where she lived in her family's home. After attending the Mississippi College for Women, the University of Wisconsin, and Columbia University (where she studied advertising), she returned to Jackson to pursue her long career as a writer, beginning as a journalist. In 1936, she wrote the first of her many short stories, which are gathered in *Collected Stories* (1980). Welty also authored several novels, including *Delta Wedding* (1946), *Losing Battles* (1970), and the Pulitzer Prize–winning *The Optimist's Daughter* (1972). Her volume of memoirs, *One Writer's Beginnings* (1984), was a best-seller.

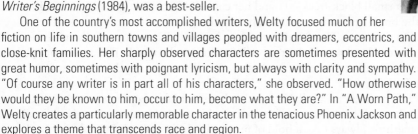

One of the country's most accomplished writers, Welty focused much of her fiction on life in southern towns and villages peopled with dreamers, eccentrics, and close-knit families. Her sharply observed characters are sometimes presented with great humor, sometimes with poignant lyricism, but always with clarity and sympathy. "Of course any writer is in part all of his characters," she observed. "How otherwise would they be known to him, occur to him, become what they are?" In "A Worn Path," Welty creates a particularly memorable character in the tenacious Phoenix Jackson and explores a theme that transcends race and region.

Cultural Context: During the 1930s, the years of the Great Depression, poverty and unemployment were widespread in the United States but weighed especially heavily in isolated rural areas of the Deep South. For the black population living in this poor and undeveloped region, difficult conditions were made worse by the system of segregation then in effect. White and black people were forbidden to mix in schools and theaters, on trains, in restaurants, and elsewhere in public. Blacks were prevented from voting and had little opportunity to receive a good education. Hoping to improve their lot in life, many black families left the South and moved into northern and midwestern cities where there were greater opportunities for education and employment.

A Worn Path   (1940)

It was December — a bright frozen day in the early morning. Far out in the country there was an old Negro woman with her head tied in a red rag, coming along a path through the pinewoods. Her name was Phoenix Jackson. She was very old and small and she walked slowly in the dark pine shadows, moving a little from side to side in her steps, with the balanced heaviness and lightness of a pendulum in a grandfather clock. She carried a thin, small cane made from an umbrella, and with this she kept tapping the frozen earth in front of her. This made a grave and persistent noise in the still air, that seemed meditative like the chirping of a solitary little bird.

She wore a dark striped dress reaching down to her shoe tops, and an equally long apron of bleached sugar sacks, with a full pocket: all neat and tidy, but every time she took a step she might have fallen over her shoelaces, which dragged from her unlaced shoes. She looked straight ahead. Her eyes were blue with age. Her skin had a pattern all its own of numberless branching wrinkles and as though a whole little tree stood in the middle of her forehead, but a golden color ran underneath, and the two knobs of her cheeks were illumined by a yellow burning under the dark. Under the red rag her hair came down on her neck in the frailest of ringlets, still black, and with an odor like copper.

Now and then there was a quivering in the thicket. Old Phoenix said, "Out of my way, all you foxes, owls, beetles, jack rabbits, coons and wild animals! . . . Keep out from under these feet, little bob-whites. . . . Keep the big wild hogs out of my path. Don't let none of those come running my direction. I got a long way." Under her small black-freckled hand her cane, limber as a buggy whip, would switch at the brush as if to rouse up any hiding things.

On she went. The woods were deep and still. The sun made the pine needles almost too bright to look at, up where the wind rocked. The cones dropped as light as feathers. Down in the hollow was the mourning dove — it was not too late for him.

5   The path ran up a hill. "Seem like there is chains about my feet, time I get this far," she said, in the voice of argument old people keep to use with themselves. "Something always take a hold of me on this hill — pleads I should stay."

After she got to the top she turned and gave a full, severe look behind her where she had come. "Up through pines," she said at length. "Now down through oaks."

Her eyes opened their widest, and she started down gently. But before she got to the bottom of the hill a bush caught her dress.

Her fingers were busy and intent, but her skirts were full and long, so that before she could pull them free in one place they were caught in another. It was not possible to allow the dress to tear. "I in the thorny bush," she said. "Thorns, you doing your appointed work. Never want to let folks pass, no sir. Old eyes thought you was a pretty little *green* bush."

Finally, trembling all over, she stood free, and after a moment dared to stoop for her cane.

10   "Sun so high!" she cried, leaning back and looking, while the thick tears went over her eyes. "The time getting all gone here."

At the foot of this hill was a place where a log was laid across the creek.

"Now comes the trial," said Phoenix.

Putting her right foot out, she mounted the log and shut her eyes. Lifting her skirt, leveling her cane fiercely before her, like a festival figure in some parade, she began to march across. Then she opened her eyes and she was safe on the other side.

"I wasn't as old as I thought," she said.

15   But she sat down to rest. She spread her skirts on the bank around her and folded her hands over her knees. Up above her was a tree in a pearly cloud of mistletoe. She did not dare to close her eyes, and when a little boy brought her a plate with a slice of marble-cake on it she spoke to him. "That would be acceptable," she said. But when she went to take it there was just her own hand in the air.

So she left that tree, and had to go through a barbed-wire fence. There she had to creep and crawl, spreading her knees and stretching her fingers like a baby trying to climb the steps. But she talked loudly to herself: she could not let her dress be torn now, so late in the day, and she could not pay for having her arm or her leg sawed off if she got caught fast where she was.

At last she was safe through the fence and risen up out in the clearing. Big dead trees, like black men with one arm, were standing in the purple stalks of the withered cotton field. There sat a buzzard.

"Who you watching?"

In the furrow she made her way along.

"Glad this not the season for bulls," she said, looking sideways, "and the good   20
Lord made his snakes to curl up and sleep in the winter. A pleasure I don't see no two-headed snake coming around that tree, where it come once. It took a while to get by him, back in the summer."

She passed through the old cotton and went into a field of dead corn. It whispered and shook and was taller than her head. "Through the maze now," she said, for there was no path.

Then there was something tall, black, and skinny there, moving before her.

At first she took it for a man. It could have been a man dancing in the field. But she stood still and listened, and it did not make a sound. It was as silent as a ghost.

"Ghost," she said sharply, "who be you the ghost of? For I have heard of nary death close by."

But there was no answer — only the ragged dancing in the wind.   25

She shut her eyes, reached out her hand, and touched a sleeve. She found a coat and inside that an emptiness, cold as ice.

"You scarecrow," she said. Her face lighted. "I ought to be shut up for good," she said with laughter. "My senses is gone. I too old. I the oldest people I ever know. Dance, old scarecrow," she said, "while I dancing with you."

She kicked her foot over the furrow, and with mouth drawn down, shook her head once or twice in a little strutting way. Some husks blew down and whirled in streamers about her skirts.

Then she went on, parting her way from side to side with the cane, through the whispering field. At last she came to the end, to a wagon track where the silver grass blew between the red ruts. The quail were walking around like pullets, seeming all dainty and unseen.

"Walk pretty," she said. "This is the easy place. This the easy going."   30

She followed the track, swaying through the quiet bare fields, through the little strings of trees silver in their dead leaves, past cabins silver from weather, with the doors and windows boarded shut, all like old women under a spell sitting there. "I walking in their sleep," she said, nodding her head vigorously.

In a ravine she went where a spring was silently flowing through a hollow log. Old Phoenix bent and drank. "Sweet-gum makes the water sweet," she said, and drank more. "Nobody know who made this well, for it was here when I was born."

The track crossed a swampy part where the moss hung as white as lace from every limb. "Sleep on, alligators, and blow your bubbles." Then the track went into the road.

Deep, deep the road went down between the high green-colored banks. Overhead the live-oaks met, and it was as dark as a cave.

35   A black dog with a lolling tongue came up out of the weeds by the ditch. She was meditating, and not ready, and when he came at her she only hit him a little with her cane. Over she went in the ditch, like a little puff of milkweed.

Down there, her senses drifted away. A dream visited her, and she reached her hand up, but nothing reached down and gave her a pull. So she lay there and presently went to talking. "Old woman," she said to herself, "that black dog come up out of the weeds to stall you off, and now there he sitting on his fine tail, smiling at you."

A white man finally came along and found her — a hunter, a young man, with his dog on a chain.

"Well, Granny!" he laughed. "What are you doing there?"

"Lying on my back like a June-bug waiting to be turned over, mister," she said, reaching up her hand.

40   He lifted her up, gave her a swing in the air, and set her down. "Anything broken, Granny?"

"No sir, them old dead weeds is springy enough," said Phoenix, when she had got her breath. "I thank you for your trouble."

"Where do you live, Granny?" he asked, while the two dogs were growling at each other.

"Away back yonder, sir, behind the ridge. You can't even see it from here."

"On your way home?"

45   "No sir, I going to town."

"Why, that's too far! That's as far as I walk when I come out myself, and I get something for my trouble." He patted the stuffed bag he carried, and there hung down a little closed claw. It was one of the bob-whites, with its beak hooked bitterly to show it was dead. "Now you go on home, Granny!"

"I bound to go to town, mister," said Phoenix. "The time come around."

He gave another laugh, filling the whole landscape. "I know you old colored people! Wouldn't miss going to town to see Santa Claus!"

But something held old Phoenix very still. The deep lines in her face went into a fierce and different radiation. Without warning, she had seen with her own eyes a flashing nickel fall out of the man's pocket onto the ground.

50   "How old are you, Granny?" he was saying.

"There is no telling, mister," she said, "no telling."

Then she gave a little cry and clapped her hands and said, "Git on away from here, dog! Look! Look at that dog!" She laughed as if in admiration. "He ain't scared of nobody. He a big black dog." She whispered, "Sic him!"

"Watch me get rid of that cur," said the man. "Sic him, Pete! Sic him!"

Phoenix heard the dogs fighting, and heard the man running and throwing sticks. She even heard a gunshot. But she was slowly bending forward by that time, further and further forward, the lid stretched down over her eyes, as if she were doing this in her sleep. Her chin was lowered almost to her knees. The yellow palm of her hand came out from the fold of her apron. Her fingers slid down and along the ground under the piece of money with the grace and care they would have in lifting an egg from under a setting hen. Then she slowly straightened up, she stood erect, and the nickel was in her apron pocket.

A bird flew by. Her lips moved. "God watching me the whole time. I come to stealing."

The man came back, and his own dog panted about them. "Well, I scared him off that time," he said, and then he laughed and lifted his gun and pointed it at Phoenix.

She stood straight and faced him.

"Doesn't the gun scare you?" he said, still pointing it.

"No, sir, I seen plenty go off closer by, in my day, and for less than what I done," she said, holding utterly still.

He smiled, and shouldered the gun. "Well, Granny," he said, "you must be a hundred years old, and scared of nothing. I'd give you a dime if I had any money with me. But you take my advice and stay home, and nothing will happen to you."

"I bound to go on my way, mister," said Phoenix. She inclined her head in the red rag. Then they went in different directions, but she could hear the gun shooting again and again over the hill.

She walked on. The shadows hung from the oak trees to the road like curtains. Then she smelled wood-smoke, and smelled the river, and she saw a steeple and the cabins on their steep steps. Dozens of little black children whirled around her. There ahead was Natchez shining. Bells were ringing. She walked on.

In the paved city it was Christmas time. There were red and green electric lights strung and crisscrossed everywhere, and all turned on in the daytime. Old Phoenix would have been lost if she had not distrusted her eyesight and depended on her feet to know where to take her.

She paused quietly on the sidewalk where people were passing by. A lady came along in the crowd, carrying an armful of red-, green- and silver-wrapped presents; she gave off perfume like the red roses in hot summer, and Phoenix stopped her.

"Please, missy, will you lace up my shoe?" She held up her foot.

"What do you want, Grandma?"

"See my shoe," said Phoenix. "Do all right for out in the country, but wouldn't look right to go in a big building."

"Stand still then, Grandma," said the lady. She put her packages down on the sidewalk beside her and laced and tied both shoes tightly.

"Can't lace 'em with a cane," said Phoenix. "Thank you, missy. I doesn't mind asking a nice lady to tie up my shoe, when I gets out on the street."

Moving slowly and from side to side, she went into the big building, and into a tower of steps, where she walked up and around and around until her feet knew to stop.

She entered a door, and there she saw nailed up on the wall the document that had been stamped with the gold seal and framed in the gold frame, which matched the dream that was hung up in her head.

"Here I be," she said. There was a fixed and ceremonial stiffness over her body.

"A charity case, I suppose," said an attendant who sat at the desk before her.

But Phoenix only looked above her head. There was sweat on her face, the wrinkles in her face shone like a bright net.

"Speak up, Grandma," the woman said. "What's your name? We must have your history, you know. Have you been here before? What seems to be the trouble with you?"

75   Old Phoenix only gave a twitch to her face as if a fly were bothering her.

"Are you deaf?" cried the attendant.

But then the nurse came in.

"Oh, that's just old Aunt Phoenix," she said. "She doesn't come for herself — she has a little grandson. She makes these trips just as regular as clockwork. She lives away back off the Old Natchez Trace." She bent down. "Well, Aunt Phoenix, why don't you just take a seat? We won't keep you standing after your long trip." She pointed.

The old woman sat down, bolt upright in the chair.

80   "Now, how is the boy?" asked the nurse.

Old Phoenix did not speak.

"I said, how is the boy?"

But Phoenix only waited and stared straight ahead, her face very solemn and withdrawn into rigidity.

"Is his throat any better?" asked the nurse. "Aunt Phoenix, don't you hear me? Is your grandson's throat any better since the last time you came for the medicine?"

85   With her hands on her knees, the old woman waited, silent, erect and motionless, just as if she were in armor.

"You mustn't take up our time this way, Aunt Phoenix," the nurse said. "Tell us quickly about your grandson, and get it over. He isn't dead, is he?"

At last there came a flicker and then a flame of comprehension across her face, and she spoke.

"My grandson. It was my memory had left me. There I sat and forgot why I made my long trip."

"Forgot?" The nurse frowned. "After you came so far?"

90   Then Phoenix was like an old woman begging a dignified forgiveness for waking up frightened in the night. "I never did go to school, I was too old at the Surrender,"° she said in a soft voice. "I'm an old woman without an education. It was my memory fail me. My little grandson, he is just the same, and I forgot it in the coming."

"Throat never heals, does it?" said the nurse, speaking in a loud, sure voice to old Phoenix. By now she had a card with something written on it, a little list. "Yes. Swallowed lye. When was it? — January — two-three years ago —"

Phoenix spoke unasked now. "No, missy, he not dead, he just the same. Every little while his throat begin to close up again, and he not able to swallow. He not get his breath. He not able to help himself. So the time come around, and I go on another trip for the soothing medicine."

"All right. The doctor said as long as you came to get it, you could have it," said the nurse. "But it's an obstinate case."

---

the Surrender: The surrender of General Robert E. Lee to General Ulysses S. Grant at the end of the Civil War, April 9, 1865.

"My little grandson, he sit up there in the house all wrapped up, waiting by himself," Phoenix went on. "We is the only two left in the world. He suffer and it don't seem to put him back at all. He got a sweet look. He going to last. He wear a little patch quilt and peep out holding his mouth open like a little bird. I remembers so plain now. I not going to forget him again, no, the whole enduring time. I could tell him from all the others in creation."

"All right." The nurse was trying to hush her now. She brought her a bottle of 95 medicine. "Charity," she said, making a check mark in a book.

Old Phoenix held the bottle close to her eyes, and then carefully put it into her pocket.

"I thank you," she said.

"It's Christmas time, Grandma," said the attendant. "Could I give you a few pennies out of my purse?"

"Five pennies is a nickel," said Phoenix stiffly.

"Here's a nickel," said the attendant. 100

Phoenix rose carefully and held out her hand. She received the nickel and then fished the other nickel out of her pocket and laid it beside the new one. She stared at her palm closely, with her head on one side.

Then she gave a tap with her cane on the floor.

"This is what come to me to do," she said. "I going to the store and buy my child a little windmill they sells, made out of paper. He going to find it hard to believe there such a thing in the world. I'll march myself back where he waiting, holding it straight up in this hand."

She lifted her free hand, gave a little nod, turned around, and walked out of the doctor's office. Then her slow step began on the stairs, going down.

Reading and Reacting

1. How does the first paragraph set the scene for the story? How does it foreshadow the events that will take place later on?
2. Traditionally, a quest is a journey in which a knight overcomes a series of obstacles in order to perform a prescribed feat. In what way is Phoenix's journey like a quest? What obstacles does she face? What feat must she perform?
3. Because Phoenix is so old, she has trouble seeing. What things does she have difficulty seeing? How do her mistakes shed light on her character? How do they contribute to the impact of the story?
4. What is the major theme of this story? What other themes are expressed?
5. A phoenix is a mythical bird that would live for five hundred years, be consumed by fire, and then rise from its own ashes. In what way is the name of this creature appropriate for the main character of this story?
6. Phoenix is not intimidated by the man with the gun and has no difficulty asking a white woman to tie her shoe. In spite of this nobility of character, however, Phoenix has no qualms about stealing a nickel or taking charity from the doctor. How do you account for this apparent contradiction?
7. How do the various people Phoenix encounters react to her? Do they treat her with respect? With disdain? Why do you think they react the way they do?

8. In paragraph 90, Phoenix says that she is an old woman without an education. Does she nevertheless seem to have any knowledge that the other characters lack?

9. **JOURNAL ENTRY** Could "A Worn Path" be an **allegory?** If so, what might each of the characters represent?

10. **CRITICAL PERSPECTIVE** Writing about "A Worn Path," Eudora Welty said that the question she was asked most frequently by both students and teachers is whether Phoenix Jackson's grandson is actually dead. Here she attempts to answer this question:

> I had not meant to mystify readers by withholding any fact; it is not a writer's business to tease. The story is told through Phoenix's mind and she undertakes her errand. As the author at one with the character as I tell it, I must assume that the boy is alive. As the reader, you are free to think as you like, of course; the story invites you to believe that no matter what happens, Phoenix for as long as she is able to walk and can hold to her purpose will make her journey.

Do you think Phoenix's grandson is alive or dead? Why?

Related Works: "Miss Brill" (p. 121), "Araby" (p. 252), "Reapers" (p. 673), "We Wear the Mask" (p. 871), "The Solitary Reaper" (p. 924), *The Cuban Swimmer* (p. 1258)

RICK BASS (1958–) is a novelist, essayist, and short story writer born in Fort Worth, Texas, the son of a geologist. He was raised in Houston and attended Utah State University, where he graduated with a BS in geology in 1979. From 1979 to 1987, Bass worked as a petroleum geologist in Mississippi; in 1987, he moved to Montana and began to devote himself full-time to writing on the environment and endangered wilderness areas. An active environmentalist, Bass has been a member of the Sierra Club, the Montana Wilderness Association, Cabinet Resources Group, Round River Conservation Studies, and the Yaak Valley Forest Council. His articles have appeared widely in magazines such as *Field and Stream, Sports Afield, Gray's Sporting Journal* and *Outdoor Life.* He is the author of six volumes of natural history essays, including *Book of Yaak* (1996), an argument for the salvation of the Montana's Yaak Valley from the forest industry. His first short story collection, *The Watch* (which includes "The Fireman"), won the 1988 PEN/Nelson Algren Award; his first novel, *Where the Sea Used to Be,* appeared in 1998. Most recently, Bass has authored *Brown Dog of the Yaak: Essays on Art and Activism* (1999) and *Colter: The True Story of the Best Dog I Ever Had* (2000). He and his wife, Elizabeth, live in Yaak Valley.

Cultural Context: Communities with populations under 10,000 typically have fire departments composed exclusively of volunteers. Nearly three-quarters of all fire departments in the United States are volunteer fire companies. These men and women provide the first line of defense against fires and are first responders to medical emergencies, spills of hazardous materials, acts of terrorism, natural disasters, and water rescue emergencies.

The Fireman (2001)

They both stand on the other side of the miracle. Their marriage was bad, perhaps even rotting, but then it got better. He — the fireman, Kirby — knows what the reason is: that every time they have an argument, the dispatcher's call sounds, and he must run and disappear into the flames — he is the captain — and while he is gone, his wife, Mary Ann, reorders her priorities, thinks of the children, and worries for him. Her blood cools, as does his. It seems that the dispatcher's call is always saving them. Their marriage settles in and strengthens, afterward, like some healthy, living, supple thing.

She meets him at the door when he returns, kisses him. He is grimy — black, salt-stained, and smoky-smelling. They can't even remember what the argument was about. It's almost like a joke — the fact that they were upset about such a small thing, any small thing. He sheds his bunker gear in the utility room and goes straight to the shower. Later, they sit in the den by the fireplace and he drinks a few beers and tells her about the fire. Sometimes he'll talk about it till dawn. He knows he is lucky — he knows they are both lucky. As long as the city keeps burning, they can avoid becoming weary and numb. Always, he leaves, is drawn away, and then returns, to a second chance.

The children — a girl, four, and a boy, two — sleep soundly. It is not so much a city that they live in but a town — the suburbs on the perimeter of the city — and it could be nameless, so similar is it to so many other places: a city in the center of the southern half of the country, a place where it is warm more often than it is cold, so that the residents are not overly familiar with fires — the way a fire spreads from room to room, the way it takes only one small errant thing in a house to invalidate and erase the whole structure, to bring it all down to ashes and send the building's former occupants — the homeowners, or renters, or leasers — out wandering lost and adrift into the night, poorly dressed and without direction. They talk until dawn. She is his second wife; he is her first husband. Because they are in the suburbs, unincorporated, his is a volunteer department. Kirby's crew has a station with new equipment — all they could ask for — but there are no salaries, and he likes it that way; it keeps things purer. He has a day job as a computer programmer for an engineering firm that designs steel girders and columns used in industrial construction: warehouses, mills, and factories. The job means nothing to him: he slips along through the long hours of it with neither excitement nor despair, his pulse never rising, and when it is over each day he says goodbye to his coworkers and leaves the office without even the faintest echo of his work lingering in his blood. He leaves it all the way behind, or lets it pass through him like some harmless silver laxative.

But after a fire — holding a can of cold beer and sitting there next to the hearth, scrubbed clean, talking to Mary Ann, telling her what it had been like — what the cause had been, and who among his men had performed well, and who had not — his eyes water with pleasure at his knowing how lucky he is to be getting a second chance, with every fire.

5   He would never say anything bad about his first wife, Rhonda — and indeed, perhaps there is nothing bad to say, no fault or failing in which they were not both complicit. It almost doesn't matter; it's almost water under the bridge.

The two children asleep in their rooms; the swing set and jungle gym out in the back yard. The security of love and constancy — the *safety*. Mary Ann teaches the children's choir in church, and is as respected for her work with the children as Kirby is for his work with the fires.

It would seem like a fairy-tale story; a happy marriage, one that turned its deadly familiar course around early into the marriage, that day he signed up to be a volunteer for the fire department six years ago. One of those rare marriages, as rare as a jewel or a forest, that was saved by a combination of inner strength and the grace and luck of fortuitous external circumstances — *the world afire*. Who, given the chance, would not choose to leap across that chasm between a marriage that is heading toward numbness and tiredness and one that is instead strengthened, made more secure daily for its journey into the future?

And yet — even on the other side of the miracle, even on the other side of luck — a thing has been left behind. It's almost a perfect, happy story; it's just this side of it. The one thing behind them — the only thing — is his oldest daughter, his only child from his first marriage, Jenna. She's ten, almost eleven.

There is always excitement and mystery on a fire call. It's as if these things are held in solution, just beneath the skin of the earth, and are then released by the flames; as if the surface of the world, and the way things are, is some errant, artificial crust — almost like a scab — and that there are rivers of blood below, and rivers of fire, rivers of the way things used to be and might someday be again — true but mysterious, and full of power, rather than stale and crusty.

10   It does funny things to people — a fire, and that burning away of the thin crust. Kirby tells Mary Ann about two young men in their thirties — lovers, he thinks — who, bewildered and bereft as their house burned, went out into the front yard and began cooking hamburgers for the firefighters as the building burned down.

He tells her about the man with a house full of antiques that could not be salvaged. The attack crew was fighting the fire hard, deep in the building's interior — the building "fully involved," as they say to one another when the wood becomes flame, air becomes flame, world becomes flame. It is the thing the younger firemen live for — not a smoke alarm, lost kitten, or piddly grass fire but the real thing, a fully involved structure fire — and even the older firemen's hearts are lifted by the sight of one. Even those who have been thinking of retiring (at thirty-seven, Kirby is far and away the oldest man on the force) are made new again by the sight of it, and by the radiant heat, which curls and browns and sometimes even ignites the oak leaves of trees across the street from the fire. The paint of cars that are parked too close to the fire sometimes begins to blaze spontaneously, making it look as if the cars are traveling very fast . . .

Bats, which have been out hunting, begin to return in swarms, dancing above the flames, and begin flying in dark agitated funnels back down into the chimney of the house that's on fire, if it is not a winter fire — if the chimney has been dormant — trying to rescue their flightless young, which are roosting in the chimney, or sometimes the attic, or beneath the eaves. The bats all return to the house as it burns down, but no one ever sees any of them come back out. People stand around on the street, their faces orange in the firelight, and marvel, hypnotized at the sight of it, not understanding what is going on with the bats, or any of it; and drawn too like somnambulists to the scent of those blood rivers, those vapors of new birth that are beginning already to leak back into the world as that skin, that crust, is burned away.

The fires almost always happen at night.

This fire that Kirby is telling Mary Ann about, the one in which the house full of antiques was being lost, was one of the great fires of the year. The men work in teams, as partners, always within sight or one arm's length contact of one another, so that one can help the other if trouble is encountered — if the foundation gives way or a burning beam crashes across the back of one of the two partners, who are not always men; more and more women are volunteering, though none have yet joined Kirby's crew. He welcomes them, since from what he's seen from the multiple-alarm fires he's fought with crews in which there are women firefighters, the women tend to try to outthink rather than outmuscle the fire, which is almost always the best approach.

Kirby's partner now is a young man, Grady, just out of college. Kirby likes to   15 use his intelligence when he fights a fire rather than just hurl himself at it and risk getting sucked too quickly into its born-again maw and becoming trapped — not just perishing in that manner, but possibly causing harm or death to those members of his crew who might then try to save him — and for this reason he likes to pair himself with the youngest, rawest, most adrenaline-rich trainees entrusted to his care, to act as an anchor of caution upon them, to counsel prudence and moderation, even as the world burns down around them.

The fire in the house of antiques — Kirby and Grady had just come out to rest, and to change oxygen tanks. The homeowner had at first been beside himself, shouting and trying to get back into his house, so that the fire marshal had had to restrain him — he had the homeowner bound to a tree with a canvas strap — but now the homeowner was watching the flames almost as if hypnotized. Kirby and Grady were so touched by his change in demeanor, by his coming to his senses — the man wasn't struggling any longer, was instead only leaning slightly away from the tree, like the masthead on a ship's prow, and sagging slightly — that they cut him loose so that he could watch the spectacle of it in freedom, unencumbered.

He made no more moves to rejoin his burning house, only stood there with watery eyes — whether tears of anguish or irritation from the smoke, they could not tell — and, taking pity, Kirby and Grady put on new oxygen tanks, gulped down some water, and though they were supposed to rest, they went back into the burning building and began carrying out those pieces of furniture that had not yet ignited, and sometimes even those that had — burning breakfronts, flaming roll-top desks — and dropped them into the man's back-yard swimming pool for safe-keeping, as the tall trees in the back yard crackled and flamed like giant candles, and floating embers drifted down, scorching whatever they touched; and the neighbors all around them climbed up onto their cedar-shingled roofs in their pajamas and with garden hoses began wetting down their own roofs, trying to keep the conflagration, the spectacle — the phenomenon — from spreading . . .

The business of it has made Kirby neat and precise. He and Grady crouched and lowered the dining room set carefully into the deep end (even as some of the pieces of furniture were still flickering with flame), releasing them to sink slowly, carefully to the bottom, settling in roughly the same manner and arrangement in which they had been positioned back in the burning house.

There is no longer any space or room for excess, unpredictability, or recklessness; these extravagances can no longer be borne, and Kirby wants Grady to see and understand this, and the sooner the better. The fire hoses must always be coiled in the same pattern, so that when unrolled, they can be counted upon; the female nozzle must always be nearest the truck, and the male farthest. The backup generators must always have fresh oil and gas in them and be kept in working order; the spanner wrenches must always hang in the same place.

20

The days go by in long stretches, twenty-three and a half hours at a time, but in that last half-hour, in the moment of fire, when all the old rules melt down and the new world becomes flame, the importance of a moment, of a second, is magnified ten thousandfold — is magnified to almost an eternity, and there is no room for even a single mistake. Time inflates to a density greater than iron. You've got to be able to go through the last half-hour, that wall of flame, on instinct alone, or by force of habit, by rote, by feel.

An interesting phenomenon happens when time catches on fire like this. It happens to even the veteran firefighters. A form of tunnel vision develops — the heart pounding two hundred times a minute, and the pupils contracting so tightly that vision almost vanishes. The field of view becomes reduced to an area about the size of another man's helmet, or face: his partner, either in front of or behind him. If the men ever become separated by sight or sound, they are supposed to freeze instantly and then begin swinging their pikestaff or a free arm in all directions; and if their partner does the same and is within one or even two arm's lengths, their arms will bump one another, and they can continue — they can rejoin the fight, as the walls flame vertical and the ceiling and floors melt and fall away. The firefighters carry motion sensors on their hips, which send out piercing electronic shrieks if the men stop moving for more than thirty seconds. If one of those goes off, it means that a firefighter is down — that he has fallen and injured himself or has passed out from smoke inhalation — and all the firefighters stop what they are doing and turn and converge on the sound, if possible, centering back to it like the bats pouring back down into the chimney.

A person's breathing accelerates inside a burning house — the pulse leaps to over two hundred beats a minute — and the blood heats, as if in a purge. The mind fills with a strange music. Sense of feel and the memory of how things *ought* to be become everything; it seems that even through the ponderous, fire-resistant gloves, the firefighters could read Braille if they had to. As if the essence of all objects exudes a certain clarity, just before igniting.

Everything in its place; the threads, the grain of the canvas weave of the fire hoses, is canted such that it tapers back toward the male nipples; if lost in a house fire, you can crouch on the floor and with your bare hand — or perhaps even through the thickness of your glove, in that hypertactile state —follow the hose back to its source, back outside, to the beginning.

The ears — the lobes of the ear, specifically — are the most temperature-sensitive part of the body. Many times the heat is so intense that the firefighters' suits begin smoking and their helmets begin melting, while deep within, the firefighters are still insulated and protected, but they are taught that if the lobes of their ears begin to feel hot, they are to get out of the building immediately — that they themselves may be about to ignite.

It's intoxicating; it's addictive as hell.   25

The fire does strange things to people. Kirby tells Mary Ann that it's usually the men who melt down first — who seem to lose their reason sooner than the women. That particular fire in which they sank all the man's prize antiques in the swimming pool in order to save them — that man becalmed himself after he was released from the tree (the top of which was flaming, dropping ember-leaves into the yard, and even onto his shoulders, like fiery moths), and he walked around into the back yard and stood next to his pool, with his back turned toward the burning house, and began busying himself with his long-handled dip net, laboriously skimming — or endeavoring to skim — the ashes from the pool's surface.

Another time — a fire in broad daylight — a man walked out of his burning house and went straight out to his greenhouse, which he kept filled with flowering plants and where he held captive twenty or more hummingbirds of various species. He was afraid that the fire would spread to the greenhouse and burn up the birds, so he closed himself in there and began spraying the little birds down with the hose as they flitted and whirled from him, and he kept spraying them, trying to keep their brightly colored wings wet so they would not catch fire.

Kirby tells Mary Ann all of these stories — a new one each time he returns — and they lie together on the couch until dawn. The youngest baby, the boy, has just given up nursing; Kirby and Mary Ann are just beginning to earn back moments of time together —little five- and ten-minute wedges of time — and Mary Ann naps with her head on his freshly showered shoulder, though in close like that, at the skin level, she can still smell the charcoal, can taste it. Kirby has scars across his neck and back, pockmarks where embers have landed and burned through his suit, and she, like the children, likes to touch these; the small, slick feel of them is like smooth stones from a river. Kirby earns several each year, and he says that before it is over, he will look like a Dalmatian. She does not ask him what he means by "when it is all over," and she holds back, reins back like a wild horse to keep from asking the question "When will you stop?" Everyone has fire stories. Mary Ann's is that when she was a child at her grandmother's house, she went into the bathroom and took off her robe, laid it over the plug-in portable electric heater, and sat on the commode; but as she did so, the robe quickly leapt into flame. The peeling old wallpaper caught on fire too — so much flame that she could not get past — and she remembers even now, twenty-five years later, how her father had to come in and lift her up and carry her back out, and how that fire was quickly, easily extinguished.

But that was a long time ago and she has her own life, needs no one to carry her in or out of anywhere. All that has gone away and vanished; her views of fire are not a child's but an adult's. Mary Ann's fire story is tame, it seems, compared to the rest of the world's.

30   She counts the slick, small oval scars on his back: twenty-two of them, like a pox. She knows he is needed. He seems to thrive on it. She remembers both the terror and the euphoria after her father whisked her out of the bathroom, as she looked back at it — at the dancing flames she had birthed. Is there greater power in lighting a fire or in putting one out?

He sleeps contentedly, there on the couch. She will not ask him — not yet. She will hold it in for as long as she can, and watch — some part of her desirous of his stopping, but another part not.

She feels as she imagines the street-side spectators must, or even the victims of the fires themselves, the homeowners and renters: a little hypnotized, a little transfixed; and there is a confusion, as if she could not tell you, or her children — could not be sure — whether she was watching him burn down to the ground or was watching him being born and built up, standing among the flames, like iron being cast from the earth.

She sleeps, her fingers light across his back. She dreams the twenty-two scars are a constellation in the night. She dreams that the more fires he fights, the safer and stronger their lives become.

She wants him to stop. She wants him to go on.

35   They awaken on the couch at dawn to the baby's murmurings from the other room, and soft sleep-breathings of their daughter, the four-year-old. The sun, orange already, rising above the city. Kirby gets up and dresses for work. He could do it in his sleep. It means nothing to him. It is its own form of sleep, and these moments on the couch and in the shells of the flaming buildings are their own form of wakefulness.

Some nights he goes over to Jenna's house — to the house of his ex-wife. No one knows he does this: not Mary Ann, and not his ex-wife, Rhonda, and certainly not Jenna — not unless she knows it in her sleep and in her dreams, which he hopes she does.

He wants to breathe her air; he wants her to breathe his. It is a biological need. He climbs up on the roof and leans over the chimney and listens —*silence*— and inhales, and exhales.

The fires usually come about once a week. The time spent between them is peaceful at first but then increasingly restless, until finally the dispatcher's radio sounds in the night, and Kirby is released. He leaps out of bed — he lives four blocks from the station — kisses Mary Ann, kisses his daughter and son sleeping in their beds, and then is out into the night, hurrying but not running across the lawn. He will be the first one there, or among the first, other than the young firemen who may already be hanging out at the station, watching movies and playing cards, just waiting.

Kirby gets in his car — the chief's car — and cruises the neighborhood slowly, savoring his approach. There's no need to rush and get to the station five or ten seconds sooner, when he'll have to wait another minute or two anyway for the other firemen to arrive.

It takes him only five seconds to slip on his bunker gear, ten seconds to start the truck and get it out of the driveway. There used to be such anxiety, getting to a fire: the tunnel vision beginning to constrict from the very moment he heard the dispatcher's voice. But now he knows how to save it, how to hold it at bay — that powerhousing of the heart, which now does not kick into life, does not come into being, until the moment Kirby comes around the corner and first sees the flames.

In her bed — in their bed — Mary Ann hears and feels the rumble of the big trucks leaving the station; hears and feels in her bones the belch of the air horns, and then the going-away sirens. She listens to the dispatcher's radio — hopefully it will remain silent after the first call, will not crackle again, calling more and more stations to the blaze. Hopefully it will be a small one, and containable.

She lies there, warm and in love with her life — with the blessing of her two children asleep there in her own house, in the other room, safe and asleep — and she tries to imagine the future: tries to picture being sixty years old, seventy, and then eighty. How long — and of that space or distance ahead, what lies within it?

Kirby gets her — Jenna — on Wednesday nights, and on every other weekend. On the weekends, if the weather is good, he sometimes takes her camping and lets the assistant chief cover for him. Kirby and Jenna cook over an open fire; they roast marshmallows. They sleep in sleeping bags in a meadow beneath stars. When he was a child, Kirby used to camp in this meadow with his father and grandfather, and there would be lightning bugs at night, but those are gone now.

On Wednesday nights — Kirby has to have her back at Rhonda's by ten — they cook hamburgers, Jenna's favorite food, on the grill in the back yard. This one constancy — this one thing, small, even tiny, like a sacrament. The diminishment of their lives shames him, especially for her, she for whom the whole world should be widening and opening rather than constricting already.

She plays with the other children, the little children, afterward, all of them keeping one eye on the clock. She is quiet, inordinately so — thrilled just to be in the presence of her father, beneath his huge shadow; she smiles shyly whenever she notices that he is watching her. And how can she not be wondering why it is, when it's time to leave, that the other two children get to stay?

He drives her home cheerfully, steadfastly, refusing to let her see or even sense his despair. He walks her up the sidewalk to Rhonda's like a guest. He does not go inside.

By Saturday — if it is the off-weekend on which he does not have her — he is up on the roof again, trying to catch the scent of her from the chimney; and sometimes he falls asleep up there, in a brief catnap, as if watching over her and standing guard.

A million times he plays it over in his mind. Could I have saved the marriage? Did I give it absolutely every last ounce of effort?

Could I have saved it?

No. Maybe. *No.*

*   *   *

50 It takes a long time to get used to the fires; it takes the young firemen, the beginners, a long time to understand what is required: that they must suit up and walk right on into a burning house.

They make mistakes. They panic, breathe too fast, and use up their oxygen. It takes a long time. It takes a long time before they calm down and meet the fires on their own terms, and the fire's.

In the beginning, they all want to be heroes. Even before they enter their first fire, they will have secretly placed their helmets in the ovens at home to soften them up a bit — to dull and char and melt them slightly, so anxious are they for combat and its validations, its contract with their spirit. Kirby remembers the first house fire he entered. His initial reaction was "You mean I'm going in *that?*" But enter it he did, fighting it from the inside out with huge volumes of water, the water sometimes doing as much damage as the fire, his new shiny suit yellow and clean among the work-darkened suits of the veterans . . .

Kirby tells Mary Ann that after that fire he drove out into the country and set a little grass fire, a little pissant one that was in no danger of spreading, then put on his bunker gear and spent all afternoon walking around in it, dirtying his suit to just the right color of anonymity.

You always make mistakes, in the beginning. You can only hope that they are small or insignificant enough to carry little, if any, price — that they harm no one. Kirby tells Mary Ann that on one of his earliest house fires, he was riding in one of the back seats of the fire engine so that he was facing backward. He was already packed up — bunker gear, air mask, and scuba tank — so that he couldn't hear or see well, and was nervous as hell; and when they got to the house that was on fire — a fully involved, "working" fire — the truck screeched to a stop across the street from it. The captain leapt out and yelled to Kirby that the house across the street was on fire.

55 Kirby could see the flames coming out of the first house, but he took the captain's orders to mean that it was the house across the street from the house on fire that he wanted Kirby to attack — that it too must be burning — and so while the main crew thrust itself into the first burning house, laying out attack lines and hoses and running up the hook-and-ladder, Kirby fastened his own hose to the other side of the truck and went storming across the yard and into the house across the street.

He assumed there was no one in it, but as he turned the knob on the front door and shoved his weight against it, the two women who lived inside opened it so that he fell inside, knocking one of them over and landing on her.

Kirby tells Mary Ann that it was the worst he ever got the tunnel vision; that it was like running along a tightrope; that it was almost like being blind. They are on the couch again, in the hours before dawn; she's laughing. Kirby couldn't see flames anywhere, he tells her — his vision reduced to a space about the size of a pinhead — so he assumed the fire was up in the attic. He was confused as to why his partner was not yet there to help him haul his hose up the stairs. Kirby says that the women were protesting, asking why he was bringing the hose into their house. He did not want to have to take the time to explain to them that the most efficient way to fight a fire is from the inside out. He told them to just be quiet and help him pull. This made them so angry that they pulled extra hard — so hard that Kirby, straining at the top of the stairs now, was bowled over again.

When he opened the attic door, he saw that there were no flames. There was a dusty window in the attic, and out it he could see the flames of the house across the street, really rocking now, going under. Kirby says that he stared at it a moment and then asked the ladies if there was a fire anywhere in their house. They replied angrily that there was not.

He had to roll the hose back up — he left sooty hose- and foot-prints all over the carpet — and by this time the house across the street was so engulfed, and in so great a hurry was Kirby to reach it, that he began to hyperventilate and blacked out there in the living room of the nonburning house.

He got better, of course — learned his craft, his calling better, learned it well in time. No one was hurt. But there is still a clumsiness in his heart, in all of their hearts — the echo and memory of it — that is not that distant. They're all just fuckups, like anyone else, even in their uniforms, even in their fire-resistant gear. You can bet that any of them who come to rescue you or your home have problems that are at least as large as yours. You can count on that. There are no real rescuers.

Kirby tells her about what he thinks was his best moment of grace — his moment of utter, breathtaking, thanks-giving luck. It happened when he was still a lieutenant, leading his men into an apartment fire. Apartments were the worst, because of the confusion; there was always a greater risk of losing an occupant in an apartment fire, simply because there were so many of them. The awe and mystery of making a rescue — the holiness of it, like a birth — is in no way balanced by the despair of finding an occupant who's already died, a smoke or burn victim, and if that victim is a child, the firefighter is never the same and almost always has to retire after that; his or her marriage goes bad, and life is never the same, never has deep joy and wonder to it again . . . The men and women spend all their time and energy fighting the enemy, *fire*—fighting the way it consumes structures, consumes air, consumes darkness — but then when it takes a life, it is as if some threshold has been crossed — it is for the firemen who discover that victim a feeling like falling down an elevator shaft, and there is sometimes guilt too, that the thing they were so passionate about, fighting fire — a thing that could be said to bring them relief, if not pleasure — should have this as one of its costs . . .

They curse stupidity, curse mankind, when they find a victim, and are almost forever after brittle rather than supple . . .

This fire, the apartment fire, had no loss of occupants, no casualties. It was fully involved by the time Kirby got his men into the structure, Christmas Eve, and they were doing room-to-room searches. No one ever knows how many people live in an apartment complex: how many men, women, and children, coming and going. It can never be accounted for. They had to check every room.

Smoke detectors — thank God! — were squawling everywhere, though that only confused the men further — the sound slightly less piercing than but similar to the motion sensors on their hip belts, so that they were constantly looking around in the smoke and heat to be sure that they were all still together, partner with partner.

Part of the crew fought the blazes while the others made searches: horrible searches, for many of the rooms were burning so intensely that if they did still house an occupant, no rescue could be made, and indeed, the casualties would already have occurred . . .

You can jab a hole in the fire hose at your feet if you get trapped by the flames. You can activate your ceased-motion sensor. The water will spew up from the hose, spraying out of the knife hole like an umbrella of steam and moisture — a water shield, which will buy you ten or fifteen more seconds. You crouch low, sucking on your scuba gear, and wait, if you can't get out. They'll come get you if they can.

This fire — the one with no casualties, the one with grace — had all the men stumbling with tunnel vision. There was something different about this fire — they would talk about it afterward — that they could sense as no one else could: that it was almost as if the fire wanted them, had laid a trap for them.

They were all stumbling and clumsy, but still they checked the rooms. Loose electrical wires dangled from the burning walls and from crumbling, flaming ceilings. The power had been shut off, but it was every firefighter's fear that some passerby, well-meaning, would see the breakers thrown and would flip them back on, unthinking.

The hanging, sagging wires trailed over the backs of the men like tentacles as they passed beneath them. The men blew out walls with their pickaxes, ventilated the ceilings with savage maulings from their lances. Trying to sense, *to feel*, amid the confusion, where someone might be — a survivor — if anyone was left.

Kirby and his partner went into the downstairs apartment of a trophy big-game hunter. It was a large apartment — a suite — and on the walls were the stuffed heads of various animals from all over the world. Some of the heads were already ablaze — flaming rhinos, burning gazelles — and as Kirby and his partner entered, boxes of ammunition began to go off: shotgun shells and rifle bullets, whole caseloads of them. Shots were flying in all directions, and Kirby made the decision right then to pull his men from the fire.

In thirty seconds he had them out — still the fusillade continued — and thirty seconds after that the whole second floor collapsed: an inch-and-a-half-thick flooring of solid concrete dropped like a fallen cake down to the first floor, crushing the space where the men had been half a minute earlier, and the building folded in on itself after that and was swallowed by itself, by its fire.

There was a grand piano in the lobby, and somehow it was not entirely obliterated when the ceiling fell, so that a few crooked, clanging tunes issued forth as the rubble shifted, settled, and burned; and still the shots kept firing.

No casualties. They all went home to their families that night.

Grace. One year Rhonda tells Kirby that she is going to Paris with her new fiancé for two weeks and asks if Kirby can keep Jenna for that time. His eyes sting with happiness — with the unexpected grace and blessing of it. Two weeks of clean air, a gift from out of nowhere. A thing that was his and taken away, now brought back. This must be what it feels like to be rescued, he thinks.

Mary Ann thinks often of how hard it is for him — she thinks of it al- 75 most every time she sees him with Jenna, reading to her or helping her with something — and they discuss it often, but even at that, even in Mary Ann's great lovingness, she underestimates it. She thinks she wants to know the full weight of it, but she has no true idea. It transcends words, spills over into his actions; and still she, Mary Ann, cannot know the bottom of it.

Kirby dreams ahead to when Jenna is eighteen; he dreams of reuniting. He continues to take catnaps on the roof by her chimney. The separation from her betrays and belies his training; it is greater than an arm's length distance.

The counselors tell him never to let Jenna see this franticness — this gutted, hollow, gasping feeling. To treat it as casual.

As if wearing blinders, unsure of whether the counselors are right or not, he does as they suggest. He thinks that they are probably right. He knows the horrible dangers of panic.

And in the meantime, the new marriage strengthens, becomes more supple and resilient than ever. Arguments cease to be even arguments anymore, merely pulsings of blood, lung-breaths, differences of opinion, like the sun moving in its arc across the sky, or the stars wheeling into place — the earth spinning, rather, and allowing these things to be scribed into place. It becomes a marriage as strong as a galloping horse, reinforced by the innumerable fires and by the weave of his comings and goings, and by the passion of it. His frantic attempts to keep drawing clean air are good for the body of the marriage.

Kirby and Mary Ann are both sometimes amazed by how fast time is going by. 80 She worries about the fifteen or twenty years she's heard get cut off the back end of all firefighters' lives: all those years of sucking in chemicals — burning rags, burning asbestos, burning formaldehyde — but still she does not ask him to stop.

The cinders continue to fall across his back like meteors: twenty-four scars, twenty-five, twenty-six. She knows she could lose him. But she knows he will be lost for sure without the fires.

She prays in church for his safety. Sometimes she forgets to listen to the service and instead gets lost in her prayers. Her eyes blur upon the votive candles. It's as if she's being led out of a burning building herself: as if she's remaining calm and gentle, as someone — her rescuer, perhaps — has instructed her to do.

She forgets to listen to the service. She finds herself instead holding in her heart the secrets he has told her, the things she knows about fires that no one else around her knows.

The way light bulbs melt and lean or point toward a fire's origin — the gases in incandescent bulbs seeking, sensing that heat, so that you can often use them to tell where a fire started, the direction in which the light bulbs first began to lean.

A baby is getting baptized up at the altar, but Mary Ann is still in some other 85 zone — she's still praying for Kirby's safety, his survival. The water being sprinkled on the baby's head reminds her of the men's water shields, of the umbrella mist of spray that buys them extra time, time on earth.

As he travels through town to and from his day job, he begins to define the space around him by the fires that have visited it and that he has engaged and battled. The individual buildings — some charred husks, others intact — begin to link together in his mind. *I rescued that one, there, and that one*, he thinks. *That one.* The city becomes a tapestry, a weave of that which he has saved and that which he has not, with the rest of the city becoming simply all that which is between points, waiting to burn.

He glides through his work at the office. If he were hollow inside, the work would take a thing from him, would suck something out of him, but he is not hollow, is only asleep, like some cast-iron statue from the century before. Whole days pass without his being able to account for them. Sometimes at night, lying there with Mary Ann, both of them listening for the dispatcher, he cannot recall whether he even went into the office that day or not.

He wonders what she is doing, what she is dreaming of. He rises and goes in to check on his other children — simply to look at them.

When you rescue people from a burning building, the strength of their terror and panic is unimaginable: enough to bend iron bars. The smallest, weakest persons can strangle and overwhelm the burliest. They will always defeat you. There is a drill that the firemen go through on their hook-and-ladder trucks — mock-rescuing someone from a window ledge or the top of a burning building. Kirby picks the strongest fireman to go up on the ladder and then demonstrates how easily he can make the fireman — vulnerable up on that ladder — lose his balance. It's always staged, of course — the fireman is roped to the ladder for safety — but it makes a somber impression on the young recruits watching from below; the big man being pushed backward by one foot, or one hand, and falling backward and dangling, the rescuer suddenly in need of rescuing.

You can see it in their eyes, Kirby tells them, speaking of those who panic. You can see them getting all wall-eyed. The victims-to-be look almost normal, but then their eyes start to cross just a little. It's as if they're generating such strength within, such *torque*, that it's causing their eyes to act weird. So much torque that it seems they'll snap in half — or snap you in half, if you get too close to them.

Kirby counsels distance to the younger firemen. Let the victims climb onto the ladder by themselves when they're like that. Don't let them touch you. They'll break you in half. You can see the torque in their eyes.

Mary Ann knows all this. She knows it will always be this way for him — but she does not draw back. Twenty-seven scars, twenty-eight. He does not snap; he becomes stronger. She'll never know what it's like, and for that, she's glad.

Many nights he runs a fever, for no apparent reason. Some nights it is his radiant heat that awakens her. She wonders what it will be like when he is too old to go out on the fires. She wonders if she and he can survive that: the not going.

There are days when he does not work at his computer. He turns the screen on but then goes over to the window for hours at a time and turns his back on the computer. He's up on the twentieth floor. He watches the flat horizon for smoke. The wind gives a slight sway, a slight tremor to the building.

Sometimes — if he has not been to a fire recently enough — Kirby imag-   95
ines that the soles of his feet are getting hot. He allows himself to consider this
sensation — he does not tune it out.

He stands motionless — still watching the horizon, looking and hoping for
smoke — and feels himself igniting, but makes no movement to still or stop the
flames. He simply burns, and keeps breathing in, detached, as if it is some structure other than his own that is aflame and vanishing; as if he can keep the two
separate — his good life, and the one he left behind.

Reading and Reacting

1. What are advantages of the story's third-person limited omniscient point of
   view? What are the limitations? How would the story be different with a
   first-person narrator?
2. "The Fireman" begins with the statement "They both stand on the other
   side of a miracle." In what sense is this statement true of Kirby and his second wife? How does it apply to Kirby's first wife and child?
3. How does being a firefighter help save Kirby's marriage? In what ways does
   it help him appreciate his family?
4. How is Kirby's full-time job different from his job as a volunteer fireman?
   Other than the excitement, what attracts Kirby to firefighting? How does
   firefighting give Kirby's life meaning?
5. As a fireman, Kirby rescues people who are in danger. Does Kirby see himself as a hero? In what sense is Kirby himself in need of rescue?
6. "The Fireman" alternates between descriptions of Kirby's second wife and
   his firefighting activities and descriptions of his relationship with his daughter, Jenna. How do these two aspects of Kirby's life overlap? How do they
   remain separate?
7. What comment does "The Fireman" make about marriage and family?
   About work? About the human condition?
8. In what way does the story's title express its central theme?
9. At one point in the story, the narrator observes that firefighters are taught
   that if they feel their ear lobes getting hot, they have to leave a burning
   building because they may be about to ignite. At the end of the story, Kirby
   imagines "that the soles of his feet are getting hot." He "feels himself igniting, but makes no movement to still or stop the flames." In what sense is
   Kirby about to ignite? Does he escape his fate? *Can* he escape?
10. **JOURNAL ENTRY** Kirby counsels young firefighters to let panicked victims
    climb onto the ladder on their own (par. 92): "Don't let them touch you,"
    he says. "They'll break you in half." Does Kirby follow this advice when it
    comes to his own life?
11. **CRITICAL PERSPECTIVE** Christopher Merrill, in a review of *The Watch*, the
    volume of short stories containing "The Fireman," discusses some of the
    traits the characters in that volume have in common. In particular, Merrill
    notes that these characters, sometimes for better, sometimes for worse, are
    defined by the commitments they make:

Bass probes the limits of possibility, discovering "nothing will get you into trouble so deep or as sad as faith." His characters are at once damned and redeemed
by their faith — in loyalty, in love, in a simpler way of life, in the belief that at
certain times trouble "was so far away that it seemed it would never return."

Do you feel that the point Merrill is making applies to the character of
Kirby? Does Kirby have faith, for example? If he does, what does he have
faith in, and is he "at once damned and redeemed" by his faith?

Related Works: "Araby" (p. 252), "A Clean, Well-Lighted Place" (p. 267),
"Young Goodman Brown" (p. 292), "The Unknown Citizen" (p. 626), "Volcanoes
be in Sicily" (p. 772), "On the Robbery across the Street" (p. 894)

WRITING SUGGESTIONS: Theme

1. In "Doe Season" a young girl learns a hard lesson. Write an essay in which
   you discuss the lessons that Andy learns and the effects the knowledge she
   gains has on her.
2. "A Worn Path" deals with the importance of patience and persistence.
   Write an essay in which you examine the value of enduring despite difficulties, citing the main character in this story. How is Phoenix successful? How
   do you explain her success?
3. Two of the stories in this chapter deal with characters who take on the role
   of rescuers. In "Doe Season," Andy attempts to save the deer, and in "The
   Fireman," Kirby tries to rescue fire victims. Which of these characters is
   more successful? How do you explain their relative degrees of success? In
   what way do their attempts to save others change their lives?
4. Both "The Rocking-Horse Winner" and "A Worn Path" deal with characters who make journeys. What is the significance of each journey? How do
   the protagonists of these two stories overcome the obstacles they encounter?
   In what sense are these journeys symbolic as well as actual?
5. Like "Doe Season," the following poem focuses on a child's experience with
   hunting. Write an essay in which you contrast its central theme with the
   central theme of "Doe Season."

ROBERT HUFF (1924–1993)

Rainbow *

After the shot the driven feathers rock
In the air and are by sunlight trapped.
Their moment of descent is eloquent.
It is the rainbow echo of a bird

---

* Publication date is not available.

Whose thunder, stopped, puts in my daughter's eyes   5
A question mark. She does not see the rainbow,
And the folding bird-fall was for her too quick.
It is about the stillness of the bird
Her eyes are asking. She is three years old;
Has cut her fingers; found blood tastes of salt;   10
But she has never witnessed quiet blood,
Nor ever seen before the peace of death.
I say: "The feathers — Look!" but she is torn
And wretched and draws back. And I am glad
That I have wounded her, have winged her heart,   15
And that she goes beyond my fathering.

6. **WEB ACTIVITY** The following Web site contains excerpts from D. H. Lawrence's letters:

http://unix.cc.wmich.edu/~cooneys/poems/dhl.letters.html

After reading the excerpt from January 17, 1913, write an essay discussing how Lawrence portrays his belief "in the blood, the flesh . . . being wiser than the intellect." Consider Lawrence's use of Paul, the youthful protagonist of "The Rocking-Horse Winner," to carry out his theme, and explain why Paul's youthful perspective is superior to the rationality of the mature characters.

CHAPTER 12

JOYCE CAROL OATES'S "WHERE ARE YOU GOING, WHERE HAVE YOU BEEN?": A CASEBOOK FOR READING, RESEARCH, AND WRITING

This chapter provides all the materials you will need to begin a research project about a work of fiction. It includes the 1966 short story "Where Are You Going, Where Have You Been?" by Joyce Carol Oates; questions to stimulate discussion and writing; a collection of source materials*; a student paper that shows how one student, Michele Olivari, used the materials in this chapter in her research; and suggestions for further research on Oates.

SOURCE MATERIALS

- Oates, Joyce Carol. "When Characters from the Page Are Made Flesh on the Screen." *New York Times* 23 Mar. 1986, sec. 2:1+. An article by Oates in which she discusses her feelings about the film *Smooth Talk*, based on her story. .... (p. 401)
- Schulz, Gretchen, and R. J. R. Rockwood. From "In Fairyland, without a Map: Connie's Exploration Inward in Joyce Carol Oates's 'Where Are You Going, Where Have You Been?'" *Literature and Psychology* 30 (1980): 155–67. A psychological interpretation of the story. .... (p. 404)
- Tierce, Mike, and John Michael Crafton. From "Connie's Tambourine Man: A New Reading of Arnold Friend." *Studies in Short Fiction* 22 (1985): 219–24. A critical interpretation of the character of Arnold Friend. .... (p. 407)
- Dylan, Bob. "It's All Over Now, Baby Blue." Los Angeles: Warner Bros., 1965. Lyrics from a popular folk song, which, according to Oates, inspired the story. (This and other Dylan songs are discussed in Tierce and Crafton's article.) .... (p. 411)
- Kalpakian, Laura. From a Review of *Where Are You Going, Where Have You Been?: Selected Early Stories*, by Joyce Carol Oates. *The Southern Review* 29.4

---

* Note that some of the critical articles in this Casebook were written before the current MLA documentation style was adopted. See Chapter 34 for current MLA format.

(Autumn 1993): 802–08. A review of Oates's collection that looks at the themes that thread through all of the stories in the book. .... (p. 411)

- Slimp, Stephen. From "Oates's 'Where Are You Going, Where Have You Been?'" *The Explicator* 57.3 (Spring 1999): 179–81. An essay that explores the spiritual side of "Where Are You Going, Where Have You Been?" .... (p. 414)
- Moser, Don. From "The Pied Piper of Tucson." *Life* 4 Mar. 1966: 18–24. An article from *Life* magazine that discusses the real-life character on which Arnold Friend is based. .... (p. 416)
- Anonymous. "The Pied Piper of Hamelin." *Life* 4 Mar. 1966. A version of the fairy tale "The Pied Piper of Hamelin," to which the title "The Pied Piper of Tucson" refers. .... (p. 421)
- Perrault, Charles. "Little Red Riding Hood." From *Little Red Riding Hood: A Casebook*. By Alan Dundes. Madison: U of Wisconsin P, 1989. A fairy tale that explores themes similar to those of the story and other source materials in this Casebook. .... (p. 423)

Each of these sources provides insights (sometimes contradictory ones) into the short story "Where Are You Going, Where Have You Been?" Other kinds of sources can also enrich your understanding of the work — for instance, other stories by Oates, biographical data about the author, or stories by other writers dealing with similar themes. In addition, nonprint sources — such as the film *Smooth Talk* — and Web sites devoted to Oates and her work can offer insight into the story. Several interesting Web sites on Oates are listed below:

- *Academy of Achievement: Joyce Carol Oates.*
  <http://www.achievement.org/autodoc/page/oat0int-1>. An interview with Oates, including some audio and video clips.
- *Celestial Timepiece: A Joyce Carol Oates Home Page.*
  <http://storm.usfca.edu/~southerr/jco.html>. A wealth of resources on Joyce Carol Oates, including news, works, a biography, photos, and discussion groups.
- *Featured Author: Joyce Carol Oates.* <http://www.nytimes.com/books/98/07/05/specials/oates.html>. Articles and reviews from the *New York Times* archives about Joyce Carol Oates, including audio clips.
- *Lit Chat: Joyce Carol Oates: Inhabiting the Mind of a Zombie Killer.*
  <http://www.salon.com/06/departments/litchat.html>. An interview with Oates for the online magazine *Salon*.
- *Biography: Joyce Carol Oates.* <http://www.annonline.com/interviews/981013/biography.html.>. A biography and audio interview.
- *Carolina Navy.* <http://www.carolinanavy.com>. An excellent forum for discussing your questions about Oates and her works. On the left of the homepage, click "Authors," and then select "Joyce Carol Oates" from the list of authors.

Although no analytical or biographical source — not even the author's comments — can give you a magical key that will unlock a story's secrets, such sources can enhance your enjoyment and aid in your understanding of a work; they can also suggest topics that you can explore in writing.

In preparation for writing an essay on a topic of your choice about the story "Where Are You Going, Where Have You Been?" read the story and the accompanying source materials carefully. Then, consider the Reading and Reacting questions that follow the story (p. 399) in light of what you have read, and use your responses to help you find a topic you can develop in a three- to five-page essay. Be sure to document any words or ideas borrowed from the story or from another source, and remember to enclose words that are not your own in quotation marks. (For guidelines on evaluating literary criticism, see page 13; for guidelines on using source materials, see Chapter 34 "Writing a Research Paper.")

A complete student paper, "Mesmerizing Men and Vulnerable Teens: Power Relationships in 'Where Are You Going, Where Have You Been?' and 'Teenage Wasteland,'" based on the source materials in this Casebook, begins on page 426.

JOYCE CAROL OATES (1938–) is one of contemporary America's most prolific novelists and short story writers. Born and raised in rural Erie County, New York, Oates first gained prominence in the 1960s with the publication of *A Garden of Earthly Delights* (1967), *Expensive People* (1968), and *them* (1969), which won the National Book Award. In these and other works, Oates began to explore the multilayered nature of American society, writing about urban slums, decaying rural communities, and exclusive suburbs in a dense and compellingly realistic prose style. In some of her more recent novels, including *Bellefleur* (1980) and *Mysteries of Winterthurn* (1984), Oates reveals her deep fascination with the traditions of nineteenth-century gothic writers Edgar Allan Poe, Fyodor Dostoevski, Mary Shelley, and others. Oates's recent works include *Lock My Door upon Myself* (1990), *The Rise of Life on Earth* (1991), *Black Water* (1992), *Foxfire* (1993), *What I Lived For* (1994), *Haunted* (1994), *Zombie* (1995), *First Love* (1996), *My Heart Laid Bare* (1998), *You Must Remember This* (1998), *I'll Take You There* (2002), and *Middle Age: A Romance* (2002).

Born on June 16, 1938, Joyce Carol Oates grew up in the small hamlet of Millersport, near Lockport, New York, about ten miles east of Niagara Falls and twenty miles north of Buffalo. She is the eldest of three children (her sister, Lynn, who is almost twenty years younger, has been institutionalized with autism since adolescence). Oates attended school in a one-room schoolhouse with other working-class children from the area. Her childhood was hard, yet she writes about it in a loving and respectful tone: "Though frequently denounced and often misunderstood by a somewhat genteel literary community, my writing is, at least in part, an attempt to memorialize my parents' vanished world; my parents' lives. Sometimes directly, sometimes in metaphor." Her childhood town, parents, siblings, relatives, and neighbors all appear in some form in three of Oates's books: *You Must Remember This* (1987) blends Buffalo and Lockport as its backdrop along with the Erie Canal; *Marya: A Life* (1986) contains elements of Oates's mother's childhood as well as her own; and in *Wonderland* (1971), one of Oates's earliest novels, the main character stops off in Millersport and meets her family.

Oates is one of those writers who has always been a writer, and even before she could possibly know the alphabet, she drew and painted words. Once she did learn her letters, she was given a typewriter and learned how to use it, and she was soon churning out book after book. She left her small town to attend Syracuse University on a scholarship and while there won the *Mademoiselle* fiction contest. She earned an MA in English at the University of Wisconsin and while in Madison met and married Raymond J. Smith after a three-month courtship. The newlyweds moved to Detroit in 1962, during a time when social tensions were at the boiling point; Detroit was one of the first American cities to erupt in urban violence in the 1960s: Oates considers her time in Detroit to be significant, shaping her writing as well as her personal beliefs and political views.

In 1968, Oates crossed the Detroit River to teach at the University of Windsor in Ontario, Canada. Although she managed a full-time course load, she embarked on a most-productive period of writing. In less than a decade, she wrote over twenty novels, and her audience grew along with her success. In 1978, she moved to Princeton, New Jersey, to accept a teaching position at Princeton University. Today, Oates continues to teach at Princeton and, with her husband, runs a small press and publishes *The Ontario Review*, a literary magazine.

Oates, wrote *Washington Post* critic Susan Wood, "attempts more than most of our writers . . . to explore the profound issues of evil and innocence, betrayal and revenge and atonement, as they are manifest in contemporary American experience. . . ." Although Oates frequently centers her novels on larger issues and moral questions, she can also focus on the private worlds of her characters, as in *Black Water* (1992).

Critics responding to Oates's work have called it violent, lurid, even depraved. Yet, asks Laura Z. Hobson in a review of Oates's 1981 novel, *Angel of Light,* "Would there be such a hullabaloo about the violence in her books if they had been written by a man? From her earliest books onward, reviewers too often struck an insulting tone of surprise: *What's a nice girl like you doing in a place like this?* [Oates] replies that in these violent times only tales of violence have reality. Well, maybe. But the critics' preoccupation with a single facet of her work ignores everything else: her inventiveness, her insider's knowledge of college life, her evocations of nature . . . her ability to tell a story, to write a spellbinder. . . ."

Oates's work changes as the landscape changes around her. Her earliest novels focused on rural characters who seemingly could have sprung from her hometown, and the dozens of books she wrote while in Detroit and Ontario reveal the often harsh realities of those places and times. The novels she began to write in New Jersey went in an entirely new direction. Published in the 1980s, her series of ambitious gothic novels challenge established literary form and also envision a vastly different American identity and history from that of her earlier books. Her prolific career reveals an ability to experiment with new forms and subject matter, and it is exactly this ability that makes her universally appealing and that makes her books timeless as well as timebound.

Where Are You Going, Where Have You Been? (1966)

For Bob Dylan

Her name was Connie. She was fifteen and she had a quick nervous giggling habit of craning her neck to glance into mirrors, or checking other people's faces to make sure her own was all right. Her mother, who noticed everything and knew everything and who hadn't much reason any longer to look at her own face, always scolded Connie about it. "Stop gawking at yourself, who are you? You think you're so pretty?" she would say. Connie would raise her eye-brows at these familiar complaints and look right through her mother, into a shadowy vision of herself as she was right at that moment: she knew she was pretty and that was everything. Her mother had been pretty once too, if you could believe those old snapshots in the album, but now her looks were gone and that was why she was always after Connie.

"Why don't you keep your room clean like your sister? How've you got your hair fixed — what the hell stinks? Hair spray? You don't see your sister using that junk."

Her sister June was twenty-four and still lived at home. She was a secretary in the high school Connie attended, and if that wasn't bad enough — with her in the same building — she was so plain and chunky and steady that Connie had to hear her praised all the time by her mother and her mother's sisters. June did this, June did that, she saved money and helped clean the house and cooked and Connie couldn't do a thing, her mind was all filled with trashy daydreams. Their father was away at work most of the time and when he came home he wanted supper and he read the newspaper at supper and after supper he went to bed. He didn't bother talking much to them, but around his bent head Connie's mother kept picking at her until Connie wished her mother was dead and she herself was dead and it was all over. "She makes me want to throw up sometimes," she complained to her friends. She had a high, breathless, amused voice which made everything she said sound a little forced, whether it was sincere or not.

There was one good thing: June went places with girl friends of hers, girls who were just as plain and steady as she, and so when Connie wanted to do that her mother had no objections. The father of Connie's best girl friend drove the girls the three miles to town and left them off at a shopping plaza, so that they could walk through the stores or go to a movie, and when he came to pick them up again at eleven he never bothered to ask what they had done.

5   They must have been familiar sights, walking around that shopping plaza in their shorts and flat ballerina slippers that always scuffed the sidewalk, with charm bracelets jingling on their thin wrists; they would lean together to whisper and laugh secretly if someone passed by who amused or interested them. Connie had long dark blond hair that drew anyone's eye to it, and she wore part of it pulled up on her head and puffed out and the rest of it she let fall down her back. She wore a pull-over jersey blouse that looked one way when she was at home and another way when she was away from home. Everything about her had two sides to it, one for home and one for anywhere that was not home: her walk that could be childlike and bobbing, or languid enough to make anyone think she was hearing music in her head, her mouth which was pale and smirking most of the time, but bright and pink on these evenings out, her laugh which was cynical and drawling at home — "Ha, ha, very funny" — but high-pitched and nervous anywhere else, like the jingling of the charms on her bracelet.

Sometimes they did go shopping or to a movie, but sometimes they went across the highway, ducking fast across the busy road, to a drive-in restaurant where older kids hung out. The restaurant was shaped like a big bottle, though squatter than a real bottle, and on its cap was a revolving figure of a grinning boy who held a hamburger aloft. One night in mid-summer they ran across, breathless with daring, and right away someone leaned out a car window and invited them over, but it was just a boy from high school they didn't like. It made them feel good to be able to ignore him. They went up through the maze of parked and cruising cars to the bright-lit, fly-infested restaurant, their faces pleased and expectant as if they were entering a sacred building that loomed out of the night to give them what haven and what blessing they yearned for. They sat at the counter and crossed their legs at the ankles, their thin shoulders rigid with excitement, and listened to the music that made everything so good: the music was always in the background like music at a church service, it was something to depend upon.

A boy named Eddie came in to talk with them. He sat backwards on his stool, turning himself jerkily around in semi-circles and then stopping and turning again, and after a while he asked Connie if she would like something to eat. She said she did and so she tapped her friend's arm on her way out — her friend pulled her face up into a brave droll look — and Connie said she would meet her at eleven, across the way. "I just hate to leave her like that," Connie said earnestly, but the boy said that she wouldn't be alone for long. So they went out to his car and on the way Connie couldn't help but let her eyes wander over the windshields and faces all around her, her face gleaming with a joy that had nothing to do with Eddie or even this place; it might have been the music. She drew her shoulders up and sucked in her breath with the pure pleasure of being alive, and just at that moment she happened to glance at a face just a few feet from hers. It was a boy with shaggy black hair, in a convertible jalopy painted gold. He stared at her and then his lips widened into a grin. Connie slit her eyes at him and turned away, but she couldn't help glancing back and there he was still watching her. He wagged a finger and laughed and said, "Gonna get you, baby," and Connie turned away again without Eddie noticing anything.

She spent three hours with him, at the restaurant where they ate hamburgers and drank Cokes in wax cups that were always sweating, and then down an alley a mile or so away, and when he left her off at five to eleven only the movie house was still open at the plaza. Her girl friend was there, talking with a boy. When Connie came up the two girls smiled at each other and Connie said, "How was the movie?" and the girl said, "*You* should know." They rode off with the girl's father, sleepy and pleased, and Connie couldn't help but look at the darkened shopping plaza with its big empty parking lot and its signs that were faded and ghostly now, and over at the drive-in restaurant where cars were still circling tirelessly. She couldn't hear the music at this distance.

Next morning June asked her how the movie was and Connie said, "So-so."

She and that girl and occasionally another girl went out several times a week   10 that way, and the rest of the time Connie spent around the house — it was summer vacation — getting in her mother's way and thinking, dreaming, about the boys she met. But all the boys fell back and dissolved into a single face that was not even a face, but an idea, a feeling, mixed up with the urgent insistent pounding of the music and the humid night air of July. Connie's mother kept dragging her back to the daylight by finding things for her to do or saying, suddenly, "What's this about the Pettinger girl?"

And Connie would say nervously, "Oh, her. That dope." She always drew thick clear lines between herself and such girls, and her mother was simple and kindly enough to believe her. Her mother was so simple, Connie thought, that it was maybe cruel to fool her so much. Her mother went scuffling around the house in old bedroom slippers and complained over the telephone to one sister about the other, then the other called up and the two of them complained about the third one. If June's name was mentioned her mother's tone was approving, and if Connie's name was mentioned it was disapproving. This did not really mean she disliked Connie and actually Connie thought that her mother preferred her to June because she was prettier, but the two of them kept up a pretense of exasperation, a sense that they were tugging and struggling over something of little value to either of them. Sometimes, over coffee, they were almost friends, but something would come up — some vexation that was like a fly buzzing suddenly around their heads — and their faces went hard with contempt.

One Sunday Connie got up at eleven — none of them bothered with church — and washed her hair so that it could dry all day long, in the sun. Her parents and sister were going to a barbecue at an aunt's house and Connie said no, she wasn't interested, rolling her eyes to let her mother know just what she thought of it. "Stay home alone then," her mother said sharply. Connie sat out back in a lawn chair and watched them drive away, her father quiet and bald, hunched around so that he could back the car out, her mother with a look that was still angry and not at all softened through the windshield, and in the back seat poor old June all dressed up as if she didn't know what a barbecue was, with all the running yelling kids and the flies. Connie sat with her eyes closed in the sun, dreaming and dazed with the warmth about her as if this were a kind of love, the caresses of love, and her mind slipped over onto thoughts of the boy she had been with the night before and how nice he had been, how sweet it always was, not the way someone like June would suppose but sweet, gentle, the way it was in movies and promised in songs; and when she opened her eyes she hardly knew where she was, the back yard ran off into weeds and a fence-line of trees and behind it the sky was perfectly blue and still. The asbestos "ranch house" that was now three years old startled her — it looked small. She shook her head as if to get awake.

It was too hot. She went inside the house and turned on the radio to drown out the quiet. She sat on the edge of her bed, barefoot, and listened for an hour and a half to a program called XYZ Sunday Jamboree, record after record of hard, fast, shrieking songs she sang along with, interspersed by exclamations from "Bobby King": "An' look here you girls at Napoleon's — Son and Charley want you to pay real close attention to this song coming up!"

And Connie paid close attention herself, bathed in a glow of slow-pulsed joy that seemed to rise mysteriously out of the music itself and lay languidly about the airless little room, breathed in and breathed out with each gentle rise and fall of her chest.

15   After a while she heard a car coming up the drive. She sat up at once, startled, because it couldn't be her father so soon. The gravel kept crunching all the way

in from the road — the driveway was long — and Connie ran to the window. It was a car she didn't know. It was an open jalopy, painted a bright gold that caught the sunlight opaquely. Her heart began to pound and her fingers snatched at her hair, checking it, and she whispered "Christ. Christ," wondering how bad she looked. The car came to a stop at the side door and the horn sounded four short taps as if this were a signal Connie knew.

She went into the kitchen and approached the door slowly, then hung out the screen door, her bare toes curling down off the step. There were two boys in the car and now she recognized the driver: he had shaggy, shabby black hair that looked crazy as a wig and he was grinning at her.

"I ain't late, am I?" he said.

"Who the hell do you think you are?" Connie said.

"Toldja I'd be out, didn't I?"

"I don't even know who you are."   20

She spoke sullenly, careful to show no interest or pleasure, and he spoke in a fast bright monotone. Connie looked past him to the other boy, taking her time. He had fair brown hair, with a lock that fell onto his forehead. His sideburns gave him a fierce, embarrassed look, but so far he hadn't even bothered to glance at her. Both boys wore sunglasses. The driver's glasses were metallic and mirrored everything in miniature.

"You wanta come for a ride?" he said.

Connie smirked and let her hair fall loose over one shoulder.

"Don'tcha like my car? New paint job," he said. "Hey."

"What?"   25

"You're cute."

She pretended to fidget, chasing flies away from the door.

"Don'tcha believe me, or what?" he said.

"Look, I don't even know who you are," Connie said in disgust.

"Hey, Ellie's got a radio, see. Mine's broke down." He lifted his friend's arm and   30
showed her the little transistor the boy was holding, and now Connie began to hear the music. It was the same program that was playing inside the house.

"Bobby King?" she said.

"I listen to him all the time. I think he's great."

"He's kind of great," Connie said reluctantly.

"Listen, that guy's *great*. He knows where the action is."

Connie blushed a little, because the glasses made it impossible for her to see   35
just what this boy was looking at. She couldn't decide if she liked him or if he was just a jerk, and so she dawdled in the doorway and wouldn't come down or go back inside. She said, "What's all that stuff painted on your car?"

"Can'tcha read it?" He opened the door very carefully, as if he was afraid it might fall off. He slid out just as carefully, planting his feet firmly on the ground, the tiny metallic world in his glasses slowing down like gelatine hardening and in the midst of it Connie's bright green blouse. "This here is my name, to begin with," he said. ARNOLD FRIEND was written in tarlike black letters on the side, with a drawing of a round grinning face that reminded Connie of a pumpkin, except it wore sunglasses. "I wanta introduce myself, I'm Arnold Friend and that's my real name and I'm gonna be your friend, honey, and inside the car's Ellie Oscar, he's kinda shy." Ellie brought his transistor radio up to his shoulder and balanced it there. "Now these numbers are a secret code, honey," Arnold Friend explained. He read off the numbers 33, 19, 17 and raised his eyebrows at her to see what she thought of that, but she didn't think much of it. The left rear fender had been smashed and around it was written, on the gleaming gold background: DONE BY CRAZY WOMAN DRIVER. Connie had to laugh at that. Arnold Friend was pleased at her laughter and looked up at her. "Around the other side's a lot more — you wanta come and see them?"

"No."

"Why not?"

"Why should I?"

40   "Don'tcha wanta see what's on the car? Don'tcha wanta go for a ride?"

"I don't know."

"Why not?"

"I got things to do."

"Like what?"

45   "Things."

He laughed as if she had said something funny. He slapped his thighs. He was standing in a strange way, leaning back against the car as if he were balancing himself. He wasn't tall, only an inch or so taller than she would be if she came down to him. Connie liked the way he was dressed, which was the way all of them dressed: tight faded jeans stuffed into black, scuffed boots, a belt that pulled his waist in and showed how lean he was, and a white pull-over shirt that was a little soiled and showed the hard small muscles of his arms and shoulders. He looked as if he probably did hard work, lifting and carrying things. Even his neck looked muscular. And his face was a familiar face, somehow: the jaw and chin and cheeks slightly darkened, because he hadn't shaved for a day or two, and the nose long and hawk-like, sniffing as if she were a treat he was going to gobble up and it was all a joke.

"Connie, you ain't telling the truth. This is your day set aside for a ride with me and you know it," he said, still laughing. The way he straightened and recovered from his fit of laughing showed that it had been all fake.

"How do you know what my name is?" she said suspiciously.

"It's Connie."

50   "Maybe and maybe not."

"I know my Connie," he said, wagging his finger. Now she remembered him even better, back at the restaurant, and her cheeks warmed at the thought of how she sucked in her breath just at the moment she passed him — how she must have looked to him. And he had remembered her. "Ellie and I come out here especially for you," he said. "Ellie can sit in back. How about it?"

"Where?"

"Where what?"

"Where're we going?"

55   He looked at her. He took off the sunglasses and she saw how pale the skin around his eyes was, like holes that were not in shadow but instead in light. His

eyes were chips of broken glass that catch the light in an amiable way. He smiled. It was as if the idea of going for a ride somewhere, to some place, was a new idea to him.

"Just for a ride, Connie sweetheart."

"I never said my name was Connie," she said.

"But I know what it is. I know your name and all about you, lots of things," Arnold Friend said. He had not moved yet but stood still leaning back against the side of his jalopy. "I took a special interest in you, such a pretty girl, and found out all about you like I know your parents and sister are gone somewheres and I know where and how long they're going to be gone, and I know who you were with last night, and your best girl friend's name is Betty. Right?"

He spoke in a simple lilting voice, exactly as if he were reciting the words to a song. His smile assured her that everything was fine. In the car Ellie turned up the volume on his radio and did not bother to look around at them.

"Ellie can sit in the back seat," Arnold Friend said. He indicated his friend 60 with a casual jerk of his chin, as if Ellie did not count and she should not bother with him.

"How'd you find out all that stuff?" Connie said.

"Listen: Betty Schultz and Tony Fitch and Jimmy Pettinger and Nancy Pettinger," he said, in a chant. "Raymond Stanley and Bob Hutter —"

"Do you know all those kids?"

"I know everybody."

"Look, you're kidding. You're not from around here." 65

"Sure."

"But — how come we never saw you before?"

"Sure you saw me before," he said. He looked down at his boots, as if he were a little offended. "You just don't remember."

"I guess I'd remember you," Connie said.

"Yeah?" He looked up at this, beaming. He was pleased. He began to mark 70 time with the music from Ellie's radio, tapping his fists lightly together. Connie looked away from his smile to the car, which was painted so bright it almost hurt her eyes to look at it. She looked at that name, ARNOLD FRIEND. And up at the front fender was an expression that was familiar — MAN THE FLYING SAUCERS. It was an expression kids had used the year before, but didn't use this year. She looked at it for a while as if the words meant something to her that she did not yet know.

"What're you thinking about? Huh?" Arnold Friend demanded. "Not worried about your hair blowing around in the car, are you?"

"No."

"Think I maybe can't drive good?"

"How do I know?"

"You're a hard girl to handle. How come?" he said. "Don't you know I'm your 75 friend? Didn't you see me put my sign in the air when you walked by?"

"What sign?"

"My sign." And he drew an X in the air, leaning out toward her. They were maybe ten feet apart. After his hand fell back to his side the X was still in the air, almost visible. Connie let the screen door close and stood perfectly still inside it, listening to the music from her radio and the boy's blend together. She stared at Arnold Friend. He stood there so stiffly relaxed, pretending to be relaxed, with one hand idly on the door handle as if he were keeping himself up that way and had no intention of ever moving again. She recognized most things about him, the tight jeans that showed his thighs and buttocks and the greasy leather boots and the tight shirt, and even that slippery friendly smile of his, that sleepy dreamy smile that all the boys used to get across ideas they didn't want to put into words. She recognized all this and also the singsong way he talked, slightly mocking, kidding, but serious and a little melancholy, and she recognized the way he tapped one fist against the other in homage to the perpetual music behind him. But all these things did not come together.

She said suddenly, "Hey, how old are you?"

His smile faded. She could see then that he wasn't a kid, he was much older — thirty, maybe more. At this knowledge her heart began to pound faster.

80   "That's a crazy thing to ask. Can'tcha see I'm your own age?"

"Like hell you are."

"Or maybe a coupla years older, I'm eighteen."

"Eighteen?" she said doubtfully.

He grinned to reassure her and lines appeared at the corners of his mouth. His teeth were big and white. He grinned so broadly his eyes became slits and she saw how thick the lashes were, thick and black as if painted with a black tarlike material. Then he seemed to become embarrassed, abruptly, and looked over his shoulder at Ellie. "*Him*, he's crazy," he said. "Ain't he a riot, he's a nut, a real character." Ellie was still listening to the music. His sunglasses told nothing about what he was thinking. He wore a bright orange shirt unbuttoned halfway to show his chest, which was a pale, bluish chest and not muscular like Arnold Friend's. His shirt collar was turned up all around and the very tips of the collar pointed out past his chin as if they were protecting him. He was pressing the transistor radio up against his ear and sat there in a kind of daze, right in the sun.

85   "He's kinda strange," Connie said.

"Hey, she says you're kinda strange! Kinda strange!" Arnold Friend cried. He pounded on the car to get Ellie's attention. Ellie turned for the first time and Connie saw with shock that he wasn't a kid either — he had a fair, hairless face, cheeks reddened slightly as if the veins grew too close to the surface of his skin, the face of a forty-year-old baby. Connie felt a wave of dizziness rise in her at this sight and she stared at him as if waiting for something to change the shock of the moment, make it all right again. Ellie's lips kept shaping words, mumbling along with the words blasting in his ear.

"Maybe you two better go away," Connie said faintly.

"What? How come?" Arnold Friend cried. "We come out here to take you for a ride. It's Sunday." He had the voice of the man on the radio now. It was the same voice, Connie thought. "Don'tcha know it's Sunday all day and honey, no matter who you were with last night today you're with Arnold Friend and don't you forget it! — Maybe you better step out here," he said, and this last was in a different voice. It was a little flatter, as if the heat was finally getting to him.

"No. I got things to do."

"Hey." 90

"You two better leave."

"We ain't leaving until you come with us."

"Like hell I am —"

"Connie, don't fool around with me. I mean, I mean, don't fool *around*," he said, shaking his head. He laughed incredulously. He placed his sunglasses on top of his head, carefully, as if he were indeed wearing a wig, and brought the stems down behind his ears. Connie stared at him, another wave of dizziness and fear rising in her so that for a moment he wasn't even in focus but was just a blur, standing there against his gold car, and she had the idea that he had driven up the driveway all right but had come from nowhere before that and belonged nowhere and that everything about him and even about the music that was so familiar to her was only half real.

"If my father comes and sees you —" 95

"He ain't coming. He's at a barbecue."

"How do you know that?"

"Aunt Tillie's. Right now they're — uh — they're drinking. Sitting around," he said vaguely, squinting as if he were staring all the way to town and over to Aunt Tillie's backyard. Then the vision seemed to get clear and he nodded energetically. "Yeah. Sitting around. There's your sister in a blue dress, huh? And high heels, the poor sad bitch — nothing like you sweetheart! And your mother's helping some fat woman with the corn, they're cleaning the corn — husking the corn —"

"What fat woman?" Connie cried.

"How do I know what fat woman. I don't know every goddam fat woman in 100 the world!" Arnold Friend laughed.

"Oh, that's Mrs. Hornby. . . . Who invited her?" Connie said. She felt a little light-headed. Her breath was coming quickly.

"She's too fat. I don't like them fat. I like them the way you are, honey," he said, smiling sleepily at her. They stared at each other for a while, through the screen door. He said softly, "Now what you're going to do is this: you're going to come out that door. You're going to sit up front with me and Ellie's going to sit in the back, the hell with Ellie, right? This isn't Ellie's date. You're my date. I'm your lover, honey."

"What? You're crazy —"

"Yes, I'm your lover. You don't know what that is but you will," he said. "I know that too. I know all about you. But look: it's real nice and you couldn't ask for nobody better than me, or more polite. I always keep my word. I'll tell you how it is, I'm always nice at first, the first time. I'll hold you so tight you won't think you have to try to get away or pretend anything because you'll know you can't. And I'll come inside you where it's all secret and you'll give in to me and you'll love me —"

"Shut up! You're crazy!" Connie said. She backed away from the door. She put 105 her hands against her ears as if she'd heard something terrible, something not meant for her. "People don't talk like that, you're crazy," she muttered. Her heart was almost too big now for her chest and its pumping made sweat break out all over her. She looked out to see Arnold Friend pause and then take a step toward the porch lurching. He almost fell. But, like a clever drunken man, he managed to catch his balance. He wobbled in his high boots and grabbed hold of one of the porch posts.

"Honey?" he said. "You still listening?"

"Get the hell out of here!"

"Be nice, honey. Listen."

"I'm going to call the police —"

110   He wobbled again and out of the side of his mouth came a fast spat curse, an aside not meant for her to hear. But even this "Christ!" sounded forced. Then he began to smile again. She watched this smile come, awkward as if he were smiling from inside a mask. His whole face was a mask, she thought wildly, tanned down onto his throat but then running out as if he had plastered makeup on his face but had forgotten about his throat.

"Honey —? Listen, here's how it is. I always tell the truth and I promise you this: I ain't coming in that house after you."

"You better not! I'm going to call the police if you — if you don't —"

"Honey," he said, talking right through her voice, "honey, I'm not coming in there but you are coming out here. You know why?"

She was panting. The kitchen looked like a place she had never seen before, some room she had run inside but which wasn't good enough, wasn't going to help her. The kitchen window had never had a curtain, after three years, and there were dishes in the sink for her to do — probably — and if you ran your hand across the table you'd probably feel something sticky there.

115   "You listening, honey? Hey?"

"— going to call the police —"

"Soon as you touch the phone I don't need to keep my promise and can come inside. You won't want that."

She rushed forward and tried to lock the door. Her fingers were shaking. "But why lock it," Arnold Friend said gently, talking right into her face. "It's just a screen door. It's just nothing." One of his boots was at a strange angle, as if his foot wasn't in it. It pointed out to the left, bent at the ankle. "I mean, anybody can break through a screen door and glass and wood and iron or anything else if he needs to, anybody at all and specially Arnold Friend. If the place got lit up with a fire honey you'd come running out into my arms, right into my arms and safe at home — like you knew I was your lover and'd stopped fooling around. I don't mind a nice shy girl but I don't like no fooling around." Part of those words were spoken with a slight rhythmic lilt, and Connie somehow recognized them — the echo of a song from last year, about a girl rushing into her boy friend's arms and coming home again —

Connie stood barefoot on the linoleum floor, staring at him. "What do you want?" she whispered.

120   "I want you," he said.

"What?"

"Seen you that night and thought, that's the one, yes sir. I never needed to look any more."

"But my father's coming back. He's coming to get me. I had to wash my hair first —" She spoke in a dry, rapid voice, hardly raising it for him to hear.

"No, your daddy is not coming and yes, you had to wash your hair and you washed it for me. It's nice and shining and all for me, I thank you, sweetheart," he said, with a mock bow, but again he almost lost his balance. He had to bend and adjust his boots. Evidently his feet did not go all the way down; the boots must have been stuffed with something so that he would seem taller. Connie stared out at him and behind him Ellie in the car, who seemed to be looking off toward Connie's right, into nothing. This Ellie said, pulling the words out of the air one after another as if he were just discovering them, "You want me to pull out the phone?"

"Shut your mouth and keep it shut," Arnold Friend said, his face red from   125 bending over or maybe from embarrassment because Connie had seen his boots. "This ain't none of your business."

"What — what are you doing? What do you want?" Connie said. "If I call the police they'll get you, they'll arrest you —"

"Promise was not to come in unless you touch that phone, and I'll keep that promise," he said. He resumed his erect position and tried to force his shoulders back. He sounded like a hero in a movie, declaring something important. He spoke too loudly and it was as if he were speaking to someone behind Connie. "I ain't made plans for coming in that house where I don't belong but just for you to come out to me, the way you should. Don't you know who I am?"

"You're crazy," she whispered. She backed away from the door but did not want to go into another part of the house, as if this would give him permission to come through the door. "What do you. . . . You're crazy, you . . ."

"Huh? What're you saying, honey?"

Her eyes darted everywhere in the kitchen. She could not remember what it   130 was, this room.

"This is how it is, honey: you come out and we'll drive away, have a nice ride. But if you don't come out we're gonna wait till your people come home and then they're all going to get it."

"You want that telephone pulled out?" Ellie said. He held the radio away from his ear and grimaced, as if without the radio the air was too much for him.

"I toldja shut up, Ellie," Arnold Friend said, "you're deaf, get a hearing aid, right? Fix yourself up. This little girl's no trouble and's gonna be nice to me, so Ellie keep to yourself, this ain't your date — right? Don't hem in on me. Don't hog. Don't crush. Don't bird dog. Don't trail me," he said in a rapid meaningless voice, as if he were running through all the expressions he'd learned but was no longer sure which one of them was in style, then rushing on to new ones, making them up with his eyes closed, "Don't crawl under my fence, don't squeeze in my chipmunk hole, don't sniff my glue, suck my popsicle, keep your own greasy fingers on yourself!" He shaded his eyes and peered in at Connie, who was backed against the kitchen table. "Don't mind him honey he's just a creep. He's a dope. Right? I'm the boy for you and like I said you come out here nice like a lady and give me your hand, and nobody else gets hurt, I mean, your nice old bald-headed daddy and your mummy and your sister in her high heels. Because listen: why bring them in this?"

"Leave me alone," Connie whispered.

135 "Hey, you know that old woman down the road, the one with the chickens and stuff — you know her?"

"She's dead!"

"Dead? What? You know her?" Arnold Friend said.

"She's dead —"

"Don't you like her?"

140 "She's dead — she's — she isn't here any more —"

"But don't you like her, I mean, you got something against her? Some grudge or something?" Then his voice dipped as if he were conscious of a rudeness. He touched the sunglasses perched on top of his head as if to make sure they were still there. "Now you be a good girl."

"What are you going to do?"

"Just two things, or maybe three," Arnold Friend said. "But I promise it won't last long and you'll like me that way you get to like people you're close to. You will. It's all over for you here, so come on out. You don't want your people in any trouble, do you?"

She turned and bumped against a chair or something, hurting her leg, but she ran into the back room and picked up the telephone. Something roared in her ear, a tiny roaring, and she was so sick with fear that she could do nothing but listen to it — the telephone was clammy and very heavy and her fingers groped down to the dial but were too weak to touch it. She began to scream into the phone, into the roaring. She cried out, she cried for her mother, she felt her breath start jerking back and forth in her lungs as if it were something Arnold Friend were stabbing her with again and again with no tenderness. A noisy sorrowful wailing rose all about her and she was locked inside it the way she was locked inside the house.

145 After a while she could hear again. She was sitting on the floor with her wet back against the wall.

Arnold Friend was saying from the door, "That's a good girl. Put the phone back."

She kicked the phone away from her.

"No, honey. Pick it up. Put it back right."

She picked it up and put it back. The dial tone stopped.

150 "That's a good girl. Now you come outside."

She was hollow with what had been fear, but what was now just an emptiness. All that screaming had blasted it out of her. She sat, one leg cramped under her, and deep inside her brain was something like a pinpoint of light that kept going and would not let her relax. She thought, I'm not going to see my mother again. She thought, I'm not going to sleep in my bed again. Her bright green blouse was all wet.

Arnold Friend said, in a gentle-loud voice that was like a stage voice, "The place where you came from ain't there any more, and where you had in mind to go is cancelled out. This place you are now — inside your daddy's house — is nothing but a cardboard box I can knock down any time. You know that and always did know it. You hear me?"

She thought, I have got to think. I have to know what to do.

"We'll go out to a nice field, out in the country here where it smells so nice and it's sunny," Arnold Friend said. "I'll have my arms around you so you won't need to try to get away and I'll show you what love is like, what it does. The hell with this house! It looks solid all right," he said. He ran a fingernail down the screen and the noise did not make Connie shiver, as it would have the day before. "Now put your hand on your heart, honey. Feel that? That feels solid too but we know better, be nice to me, be sweet like you can because what else is there for a girl like you but to be sweet and pretty and give in?— and get away before her people come back?"

She felt her pounding heart. Her hand seemed to enclose it. She thought for   155
the first time in her life that it was nothing that was hers, that belonged to her, but just a pounding, living thing inside this body that wasn't really hers either.

"You don't want them to get hurt," Arnold Friend went on. "Now get up, honey. Get up all by yourself."

She stood.

"Now turn this way. That's right. Come over here to me — Ellie, put that away, didn't I tell you? You dope. You miserable creepy dope," Arnold Friend said. His words were not angry but only part of an incantation. The incantation was kindly. "Now come out through the kitchen to me honey and let's see a smile, try it, you're a brave sweet little girl and now they're eating corn and hotdogs cooked to bursting over an outdoor fire, and they don't know one thing about you and never did and honey you're better than them because not a one of them would have done this for you."

Connie felt the linoleum under her feet; it was cool. She brushed her hair back out of her eyes. Arnold Friend let go of the post tentatively and opened his arms for her, his elbows pointing in toward each other and his wrists limp, to show that this was an embarrassed embrace and a little mocking, he didn't want to make her self-conscious.

She put out her hand against the screen. She watched herself push the door   160
slowly open as if she were safe back somewhere in the other doorway, watching this body and this head of long hair moving out into the sunlight where Arnold Friend waited.

"My sweet little blue-eyed girl," he said, in a half-sung sigh that had nothing to do with her brown eyes but was taken up just the same by the vast sunlit reaches of the land behind him and on all sides of him, so much land that Connie had never seen before and did not recognize except to know that she was going to it.

Reading and Reacting

1. How is "Where Are You Going, Where Have You Been?" similar to and different from Anne Tyler's "Teenage Wasteland" (p. 535)?

2. Is Arnold Friend meant to be the devil? An antisocial hoodlum? A rapist and murderer (see the March 4, 1966, *Life* magazine article "The Pied Piper of Tucson" on page 416, or "Killing for Kicks" in the March 14, 1966, issue of *Newsweek*)? Is he actually Bob Dylan (as Tierce and Crafton suggest in

their article on page 407)? Or is he just a misunderstood social misfit who terrifies Connie more because of her innocence than because of his evil?

3. In a note (see p. 404) accompanying the article she coauthored, Gretchen Schulz says that Oates told her the allusions to fairy tales in the story are intentional. What allusions to fairy tales can you identify?

4. Many critical articles see "Where Are You Going, Where Have You Been?" as heavily symbolic, even allegorical, with elements of myth, dream, and fairy tale woven throughout. Do you think such analysis is necessary, or could the story be seen in much simpler terms?

5. Whom do you see as the story's central character, Arnold Friend or Connie? Why?

6. Feminist critics might see this story as a familiar tale of a man who uses flattering seductive language followed by threats of physical violence to coerce a young woman into giving in to him. In what sense is this a story of male power and female powerlessness?

7. Dark undertones aside, in what sense is this story simply about the coming of age of a typical 1960s teenager?

8. What roles do music, sex, the weather, contemporary slang, and physical appearance play in the story? What does each contribute?

9. Why do members of Connie's family play such minor roles in the story? How might expanding their roles change the story?

10. Which aspects of teenage culture have changed in the more than forty years since Oates wrote the story? Which have stayed the same? Given the scope of these changes, is the story dated?

11. Most critics (like Oates herself) see the end of the story as alarmingly negative, suggesting rape and even murder. Do you see it this way?

12. Do you agree with Oates's view, expressed in her article on page 401, that the differences in the endings of the film and the story are justified by the differences between the 1960s and the 1980s?

13. **JOURNAL ENTRY** How is the generation gap — the failure of one generation to understand another's culture, customs, and heroes — central to the story?

14. **CRITICAL PERSPECTIVE** According to *New York Times* book critic Michiko Kakutani, Joyce Carol Oates has several "fictional trademarks":

    > [She has] a penchant for mixing the mundane and Gothic, the ordinary and sensationalistic; a fascination with the dark undercurrents of violence, eroticism and emotional chaos in American life, and a tendency to divide her characters' lives into a Before and After with one "unspeakable turn of destiny."

    In what sense do Kakutani's remarks apply to "Where Are You Going, Where Have You Been?"? Do you see a fascination with "the dark undercurrents of . . . life" in this story? What is the "unspeakable turn of destiny" that divides Connie's life into a "Before and After"?

Related Works: "Kansas" (p. 85), "A&P" (p. 115), "Young Goodman Brown" (p. 292), "The Lottery" (p. 303), "To His Coy Mistress" (p. 696), *Hamlet* (p. 1074)

JOYCE CAROL OATES

When Characters from the Page Are Made Flesh on the Screen

Some years ago in the American Southwest there surfaced a tabloid psychopath known as "The Pied Piper of Tucson." I have forgotten his name but his specialty was the seduction and occasional murder of teen-age girls. He may or may not have had actual accomplices, but his bizarre activities were known among a circle of teen-agers in the Tucson area; for some reason they kept his secrets, deliberately did not inform parents or police. It was this fact, not the fact of the mass murderer himself, that struck me at the time. And this was a pre-Manson time, this was early or mid-1960's.

The "Pied Piper" mimicked teen-agers in their talk, dress and behavior, but he was not a teen-ager — he was a man in his early 30's. Rather short, he stuffed rags in his leather boots to give himself height. (And sometimes walked unsteadily as a consequence: did none among his admiring constituency notice?) He charmed his victims, to the bewilderment of others who fancy themselves free of all lunatic attractions. "The Pied Piper of Tucson": a trashy dream, a tabloid archetype, sheer artifice, comedy, cartoon — surrounded, however improbably, and finally tragically, by real people. You think that, if you look twice, he won't be there. But there he is.

I don't remember any longer where I first read about "The Pied Piper" — very likely in *Life* magazine. I do recall deliberately not reading the full article because I didn't want to be distracted by too much detail. It was not after all the mass murderer himself who intrigued me, but the disturbing fact that a number of teen-agers — from "good" families — aided and abetted his crimes. This is the sort of thing authorities and responsible citizens invariably call "inexplicable" because they can't find explanations for it. *They* would not have fallen under this maniac's spell, after all.

An early draft of my short story "Where Are You Going, Where Have You Been?"—from which the current film "Smooth Talk" has been adapted by Joyce Chopra and Tom Cole — had the rather too explicit title "Death and the Maiden." It was cast in a mode of fiction to which I am still partial — indeed, every third or fourth story of mine is probably in this mode — "realistic allegory," it might be called. It is Hawthornian, romantic, shading into parable. Like the medieval German engraving from which my title was taken the story was minutely detailed yet clearly an allegory of the fatal attractions of death (or the devil). An innocent young girl is seduced by way of her own vanity; she mistakes death for erotic romance of a particularly American/trashy sort.

In subsequent drafts the story changed its tone, its focus, its language, its title. 5
It became "Where Are You Going, Where Have You Been?" Written at a time when the author was intrigued by the music of Bob Dylan, particularly the hauntingly elegiac song "It's All Over Now, Baby Blue," it was dedicated to Bob Dylan.

The charismatic mass murderer drops into the background and his innocent victim, a 15-year-old, moves into the foreground. She becomes the true protagonist of the tale, courting and being courted by her fate, a self-styled 1950's pop figure, alternately absurd and winning.

There is no suggestion in the published story that "Arnold Friend" has seduced and murdered other young girls, or even that he necessarily intends to murder Connie. Is his interest "merely" sexual? (Nor is there anything about the complicity of other teen-agers. I saved that yet more provocative note for a current story, "Testimony.") Connie is shallow, vain, silly, hopeful, doomed — perhaps as I saw, and still see, myself? — but capable nonetheless of an unexpected gesture of heroism at the story's end.

Her smooth-talking seducer, who cannot lie, promises her that her family will be unharmed if she gives herself to him; and so she does. The story ends abruptly at the point of her "crossing over." We don't know the nature of her sacrifice, only that she is generous enough to make it.

In adapting a narrative so spare and thematically foreshortened as "Where Are You Going, Where Have You Been?" film director Joyce Chopra and screenwriter Tom Cole were required to do a good deal of filling in, expanding, inventing. Connie's story becomes lavishly, and lovingly, textured; she is not an allegorical figure so much as a "typical" teen-age girl (if Laura Dern, spectacularly good-looking, can be so defined).

Joyce Chopra, who has done documentary films on contemporary teen-age culture, and, yet more authoritatively, has an adolescent daughter of her own, creates in "Smooth Talk" a believable world for Connie to inhabit. Or worlds: as in the original story there is Connie-at-home, and there is Connie-with-her-friends. Two 15-year-old girls, two finely honed styles, two voices, sometimes but not often overlapping. It is one of the marvelous visual features of the film that we *see* Connie and her friends transform themselves, once they are safely free of parental observation. What freedom, what joy! The girls claim their true identities in the neighborhood shopping mall!

10   "Smooth Talk" is, in a way, as much Connie's mother's story as it is Connie's; its center of gravity, its emotional nexus, is frequently with the mother — played by Mary Kay Place. (Though the mother's sexual jealousy of her daughter is slighted in the film.) Connie's ambiguous relationship with her affable, somewhat mysterious father (played by Levon Helm) is an excellent touch: I had thought, subsequent to the story's publication, that I should have built up the father, suggesting, as subtly as I could, an attraction there paralleling the attraction Connie feels for her seducer Arnold Friend.

Treat Williams impersonates Arnold Friend as Arnold Friend impersonates — is it James Dean? James Dean regarding himself in mirrors, doing James Dean impersonations? Laura Dern is so right as "my" Connie that I may come to think I modeled the fictitious girl on her, in the way that writers frequently delude themselves about notions of causality.

My difficulties with "Smooth Talk" have primarily to do with my chronic hesitation — a justifiable shyness, I'm sure — about seeing/hearing work of mine abstracted from its contexture of language. All writers know that language is their subject; quirky word choices, patterns of rhythm, enigmatic pauses, punctuation marks. Where the quick-scanner sees "quick" writing, the writer conceals nine-tenths of his iceberg.

Of course we all have "real" subjects, and we will fight to the death to defend these subjects, but beneath the tale-telling it is the tale-telling that grips us so very fiercely: "the soul at the *white heat*" in Emily Dickinson's words. Because of this it is always an eerie experience for me, as a writer, to hear "my" dialogue floating back to me from the external world; particularly when it is surrounded, as of course it must be, by "other" dialogue I seem not to recall having written. Perhaps a panic reaction sets in — perhaps I worry that I might be responsible for knowing what "I" meant, in writing things "I" didn't write? Like a student who has handed in work not entirely his own, and dreads interrogation from his teacher?

It is startling too to *see* fictitious characters inhabiting, with such seeming aplomb, roles that until now seemed private, flat on the page. (I don't, like many of my writing colleagues, feel affronted, thinking, "*That* isn't how he/she looks!" I think instead, guiltily, "Is *that* how he/she really looks?")

I have also had a number of plays produced and so characteristically doubtful 15 am I about intruding into my directors' territories that I nearly always abrogate my authority to them. The writer works in a single dimension, the director works in three. I assume that they are professionals to their fingertips; authorities in their medium as I am an authority (if I am) in mine. I would fiercely defend the placement of a semicolon in one of my novels, but I would probably have deferred fairly quickly to Joyce Chopra's decision to reverse the story's ending, turn it upside-down, in a sense, so that the film ends not with death, not with a sleepwalker's crossing-over to her fate, but upon a sense of reconciliation, rejuvenation. Laura Dern's Connie is no longer "my" Connie at the film's conclusion; she is very much alive, assertive, strong-willed — a girl, perhaps, of the mid-1980's, and not of the mid-1960's.

A girl's loss of virginity, bittersweet but not necessarily tragic. Not today. A girl's coming of age that involves her succumbing to, but then rejecting, the "trashy dreams" of her pop teen-age culture. "Where Are You Going, Where Have You Been?" deliberately betrays itself as allegorical in its conclusion: Death and Death's chariot (a funky souped-up convertible) have come for the Maiden. Awakening is, in the story's final lines, moving out into the sunlight where Arnold Friend waits:

> "My sweet little blue-eyed girl," he said, in a half-sung sigh that had nothing to do with (Connie's) brown eyes but was taken up just the same by the vast sunlit reaches of the land behind him and on all sides of him, so much land that Connie had never seen before and did not recognize except to know that she was going to it.

I quite understand that this is an unfilmable conclusion, and "Where Are You Going, Where Have You Been?" is in fact an unfilmable short story. But Joyce Chopra's "Smooth Talk" is an accomplished and sophisticated movie that attempts to do just that.

GRETCHEN SCHULZ AND R. J. R. ROCKWOOD

from In Fairyland, without a Map: Connie's Exploration Inward in Joyce Carol Oates's "Where Are You Going, Where Have You Been?"

Joyce Carol Oates has stated that her prize-winning story *Where Are You Going, Where Have You Been?* (Fall, 1966) came to her "more or less in a piece" after hearing Bob Dylan's song *It's All Over Now, Baby Blue,* and then reading about a "killer in some Southwestern state," and thinking about "the old legends and folk songs of Death and the Maiden."[1] The "killer" that Miss Oates had in mind, the one on whom her character Arnold Friend is modeled, was twenty-three-year-old Charles Schmid of Tucson, Arizona. Schmid had been charged with the murders of three teen-age girls, and was the subject of a lengthy article in the March 4, 1966, issue of *Life* magazine. It is not surprising that this account should have generated mythic musings in Miss Oates — musings that culminated in a short story which has depths as mythic as any of the "old legends and folk songs." The *Life* reporter, Don Moser, himself had found in this raw material such an abundance of the reality which is the stuff of myth, that he entitled his article "The Pied Piper of Tucson."

The article states that Schmid — or "Smitty," as he was called — had sought deliberately "to create an exalted, heroic image of himself." To the teen-agers in Smitty's crowd, who "had little to do but look each other over," their leader was a "folk hero . . . more dramatic, more theatrical, more *interesting* than anyone else in their lives," and seemed to embody the very lyrics of a then popular song: "Hey, c'mon babe, follow me, / I'm the Pied Piper, follow me, / I'm the Pied Piper, / And I'll show you where it's at." With a face which was "his own creation: the hair dyed raven black, the skin darkened to a deep tan with pancake make-up, the lips whitened, the whole effect heightened by a mole he had painted on one cheek," Smitty would cruise "in a golden car," haunting "all the teen-age hangouts," looking for pretty girls, especially ones with long blond hair. Because he was only five-foot-three, Smitty "habitually stuffed three or four inches of old rags and tin cans into the bottoms of his high-topped boots to make himself taller," even though the price he paid for that extra height was an awkward, stumbling walk that made people think he had "wooden feet."[2]

In his transformation into the Arnold Friend of *Where Are You Going, Where Have You Been?*, Smitty underwent the kind of apotheosis° which he had tried, by means of bizarre theatrics, to achieve in actuality, for Arnold is the exact transpersonal° counterpart of the real-life "Pied Piper of Tucson." Thus, although Arnold is a "realistic" figure, drawn from the life of a specific psychopathic killer, that superficial realism is only incidental to the more essential realism of

---

apotheosis: The raising of a human to divine status.

transpersonal: Going beyond the individual or personal.

the mythic characteristics — the archetypal qualities — he shares with the man who was his model. Asked to comment on Arnold, Miss Oates reveals that, to her, the character is *truly* mythological. No longer quite human, he functions as a personified subjective factor: "Arnold Friend," she says, "is a fantastic figure: he is Death, he is the 'elf-[king]' of the ballads, he is the Imagination, he is a Dream, he is a Lover, a Demon, *and all that.*"[3]

If *Where Are You Going, Where Have You Been?* is a "portrait of a psychopathic killer masquerading as a teenager,"[4] it is clear that this portrait is created in the mind of Connie, the teen-age protagonist of the story, and that it exists *there only.* It is thus Connie's inner world that determines how Arnold is, or has to be, at least in her eyes, for her personal problems are so compelling that they effectively rearrange and remodel the world of objective reality. Arnold Friend's own part in the creation of his image — whether he deliberately set about to become the "fantastic" figure he is, or seems to be, as his model, Smitty, did — Miss Oates ignores altogether. She is interested only in Connie, Arnold's young victim, and in how Connie's psychological state shapes her perceptions. We find — as we might expect with a writer who characterizes the mode in which she writes as "psychological realism"[5] — that the "fantastic" or mythological qualities of Arnold Friend (and of all those in the story) are presented as subjective rather than objective facts, aspects of the transpersonal psyche projected outward, products of the unconscious mental processes of a troubled adolescent girl.

Toward Arnold Friend, and what he represents, Connie is ambivalent: she is 5 both fascinated and frightened. She is, after all, at that confusing age when a girl feels, thinks, and acts both like a child, put off by a possible lover, and like a woman, attracted to him. Uncertain how to bridge the chasm between "home" and "anywhere that was not home," she stands — or wavers — at the boundary between childhood and adulthood, hesitant and yet anxious to enter the new world of experience which is opening before her:

> Everything about her had two sides to it, one for home and one for anywhere that was not home: her walk, which could be childlike and bobbing, or languid enough to make anyone think she was hearing music in her head; her mouth, which was pale and smirking most of the time, but bright and pink on these evenings out; her laugh, which was cynical and drawling at home — "Ha, ha, very funny," — but high-pitched and nervous anywhere else, like the jingling of the charms on her bracelet.[6]

That her laugh is "high-pitched and nervous" when she is "anywhere that was not home" betrays the fact that Connie, like all young people, needs help as she begins to move from the past to the future, as she begins the perilous inward journey towards maturity. This journey is an essential part of the adolescent's search for personal identity, and though it is a quest that he must undertake by himself, traditionally it has been the responsibility of culture to help by providing symbolic maps of the territory through which he will travel, territory that lies on the other side of consciousness.

Such models of behavior and maps of the unknown are generally provided by the products of fantasy — myth, legend, and folklore. Folk fairy tales have been especially useful in this way. In his book, *The Uses of Enchantment: The Meaning and*

Importance of Fairy Tales (1976), Bruno Bettelheim argues that children's fairy tales offer "symbolic images" that suggest "happy solutions"[7] to the problems of adolescence. Indeed, Joyce Carol Oates herself has Hugh Petrie, the caricaturist in her novel *The Assassins* (1975), observe that "fairy tales are analogous to life as it is lived in the family."[8] In her fiction both short and long Miss Oates makes frequent use of fairy tale material. Again and again she presents characters and situations which parallel corresponding motifs from the world of folk fantasy. And never is this more true than in the present story — never in all the eight novels and eleven collections of short stories which she has written at last count. Woven into the complex texture of *Where Are You Going, Where Have You Been?* are motifs from such tales as *The Spirit in the Bottle, Snow White, Cinderella, Sleeping Beauty, Rapunzel, Little Red Riding Hood,* and *The Three Little Pigs*.[9] *The Pied Piper of Hamelin,* which ends tragically and so according to Bettelheim does not qualify as a proper fairy tale,[10] serves as the "frame device" that contains all the other tales.

There is a terrible irony here, for although the story is full of fairy tales, Connie, its protagonist, is not. Connie represents an entire generation of young people who have grown up — or tried to — without the help of those bedtime stories which not only entertain the child, but also enable him vicariously to experience and work through problems which he will encounter in adolescence. The only "stories" Connie knows are those of the sexually provocative but superficial lyrics of the popular songs she loves or of the equally insubstantial movies she attends. Such songs and movies provide either no models of behavior for her to imitate, or dangerously inappropriate ones. Connie has thus been led to believe that life and, in particular, love will be "sweet, gentle, the way it was in the movies and promised in songs." She has no idea that life actually can be just as grim as in folk fairy tales. The society that is depicted in *Where Are You Going, Where Have You Been?* has failed to make available to children like Connie maps of the unconscious such as fairy tales provide, because it has failed to recognize that in the unconscious past and future coalesce, and that, psychologically, where the child is going is where he has already been. Since Connie has been left — in the words of yet another of the popular songs — to "wander through that wonderland alone" — it is small wonder, considering her lack of spiritual preparation, that Connie's journey there soon becomes a terrifying schizophrenic separation from reality, with prognosis for recovery extremely poor. . . .

Had she been nurtured on fairy tales instead of popular songs and movies she would not feel at such a loss; she would have "been" to this world before, through the vicarious experience offered by fairy tales, and she would have some sense of how to survive there now. Connie lacks the benefit of such experience, however, and even Arnold Friend appears to realize how that lack has hampered her development. He certainly speaks to the supposed woman as though she were still a child: " 'Now, turn this way. That's right. Come over here to me. . . . and let's see a smile, try it, you're a brave, sweet little girl'." How fatherly he sounds. And how like the Woodcutter. But we know that he is still the Wolf, and that he still intends to "gobble up" this "little girl" as soon as he gets the chance. Connie is not going to live happily ever after. Indeed, it would seem that she is not going to live at all. She simply does not know how. She is stranded in Fairyland, without a map.[11]

Notes

[1] "Interview with Joyce Carol Oates about 'Where Are You Going, Where Have You Been?'" in *Mirrors: An Introduction to Literature,* ed. John R. Knott, Jr., and Christopher R. Keaske, 2nd ed. (San Francisco: Canfield Press, 1975), pp. 18–19.

[2] Don Moser, "The Pied Piper of Tucson," *Life,* 60, no. 9 (March 4, 1966), 18–19, 22–24, 80c–d.

[3] Interview in *Mirrors,* p. 19. For a perceptive analysis of Arnold Friend as a demonic figure, a subject which will not be developed here, see Joyce M. Wegs, "'Don't You Know Who I Am?' The Grotesque in Oates's 'Where Are You Going, Where Have You Been?'," *The Journal of Narrative Technique,* 5 (January 1975), pp. 66–72.

[4] Wegs, p. 69.

[5] Joyce Carol Oates, "Preface," *Where Are You Going, Where Have You Been?: Stories of Young America* (Greenwich, CT: Fawcett Publications, 1974), p. 10.

[6] Joyce Carol Oates, "Where Are You Going, Where Have You Been?," *Where Are You Going, Where Have You Been?: Stories of Young America* (Greenwich, CT: Fawcett Publications, 1974), p. 13. All further references are to this edition of the story and will appear in the text of the essay. The story was originally published in *Epoch,* Fall 1966. It has since been included in *Prize Stories: The O. Henry Awards 1968;* in *The Best American Short Stories of 1967;* and in a collection of Oates' stories, *The Wheel of Love* (New York: Vanguard Press, 1970; Greenwich, CT: Fawcett Publications, 1972). The story is also being anthologized with increasing frequency in collections intended for use in the classroom, such as Donald McQuade and Robert Atwan, *Popular Writing in America: The Interaction of Style and Audience* (New York: Oxford University Press, 1974).

[7] Bruno Bettelheim, *The Uses of Enchantment: The Meaning and Importance of Fairy Tales* (New York: Alfred A. Knopf, 1976), p. 39.

[8] Joyce Carol Oates, *The Assassins* (New York: Vanguard Press, 1975), p. 378.

[9] At the MLA convention in New York, on December 26, 1976, I got a chance to ask Joyce Carol Oates if the many allusions to various fairy tales in "Where Are You Going, Where Have You Been?" were intentional. She replied that they were. (Gretchen Schulz)

[10] Bettelheim, n. 34, p. 316.

[11] Concerning the plight of the Connies of the world, Bettelheim states thus: "unfed by our common fantasy heritage, the folk fairy tale, the child cannot invent stories on his own which help him cope with life's problems. All the stories he can invent are just expressions of his own wishes and anxieties. Relying on his own resources, all the child can imagine are elaborations of where he presently is, since he cannot know where he needs to go, or how to go about getting there" (pp. 121–122).

MIKE TIERCE AND JOHN MICHAEL CRAFTON

from Connie's Tambourine Man:
A New Reading of Arnold Friend

The critical reception of Joyce Carol Oates' "Where Are You Going, Where Have You Been?" reveals a consistent pattern for reducing the text to a manageable, univocal° reading. Generally, this pattern involves two assumptions: Arnold *must*

---

univocal: Having only one meaning.

symbolize Satan and Connie *must* be raped and murdered. No critic has yet questioned Joyce Wegs' assertion that "Arnold is clearly a symbolic Satan."[1] Marie Urbanski argues that Arnold's "feet resemble the devil's cloven hoofs," Joan Winslow calls the story "an encounter with the devil," Tom Quirk maintains the story describes a "demoniac character," and Christina Marsden Gillis refers to "the satanic visitor's incantation."[2] Wegs' assertion that Arnold is "a criminal with plans to rape and probably murder Connie"[3] is also accepted at face value. Gillis assumes that Arnold "leads his victim . . . to a quick and violent sexual assault,"[4] and Quirk refers to "the rape and subsequent murder of Connie."[5] Even though Gretchen Schulz and R. J. R. Rockwood correctly claim that the portrait of Arnold "is created in the mind of Connie . . . and that it exists *there only*," they still persist in having Arnold as a demon and Connie as doomed: "But we know that he is still the Wolf, and that he still intends to 'gobble up' this 'little girl' as soon as he gets the chance. Connie is not going to live happily ever after. Indeed, it would seem that she is not going to live at all."[6]

While all of these critics insist on seeing satanic traces in Arnold, they refuse, on the other hand, to see that these traces are only part of a much more complex, more dynamic symbol. There are indeed diabolic shades to Arnold, but just as Blake and Shelley could see in Milton's Satan[7] a positive, attractive symbol of the poet, the rebellious embodiment of creative energy, so we should also be sensitive to Arnold's multifaceted and creative nature. Within the frame of the story, the fiction of Arnold burns in the day as the embodiment of poetic energy. The story is dedicated to Bob Dylan, the troubadour, the artist. Friend is the artist, the actor, the rhetorician, the teacher, all symbolized by Connie's overheated imagination. We should not assume that Arnold is completely evil because she is afraid of him. Her limited perceptions remind us of Blake's questioner in "The Tyger" who begins to perceive the frightening element of the experiential world but also is rather duped into his fear by his own limitations. Like the figure in Blake, Connie is the framer, the story creator — and the diabolic traces in her fiction frighten her not because they are the manifestations of an outside evil but because they are the symbolic extrapolations of her own psyche.

If the adamant insistence that Arnold Friend is Satan is rejected, then who is this intriguing mysterious visitor? In *Enter Mysterious Stranger: American Cloistral Fiction,* Roy Male asserts that many mysterious intruders throughout American literature "are almost always potential saviors, destroyers, or ambiguous combinations of both, and their initial entrance, however much it may be displaced toward realism, amounts to the entrance of God or the devil on a machine."[8] And if Arnold Friend is *not* satanic, then his arrival could be that of a savior. This possibility moreover is suggested by Connie's whispering "Christ. Christ"[9] when Arnold first arrives in his golden "machine." Not only is "33" part of Arnold's "secret code" of numbers, but his sign, an "X" that seems to hover in the air, is also one of the symbols for Christ. Because music is closely associated with religion — "the music was always in the background, like music at a church service" — it also adds a religious element to Arnold's arrival. The key question then is who is this musical messiah, and the key to the answer is the dedication "For Bob Dylan" — the element of the story so unsatisfactorily accounted for by our predecessors. Not only does the description of Arnold Friend also fit Bob Dylan — a type of rock-and-roll messiah — but three of Dylan's songs (popular when the story was written) are very similar to the story itself.

In the mid-sixties Bob Dylan's followers perceived him to be a messiah. According to his biographer, Dylan was "a rock-and-roll king."[10] It is no wonder then that Arnold speaks with "the voice of the man on the radio," the disc jockey whose name, Bobby King, is a reference to "Bobby" Dylan, the "king" of rock-and-roll. Dylan was more than just a "friend" to his listeners; he was "Christ revisited," "the prophet leading [his followers] into [a new] Consciousness."[11] In fact, "people were making him an idol; . . . thousands of men and women, young and old, felt their lives entwined with his because they saw him as a mystic, a messiah who would lead them to salvation."[12]

That Oates consciously associates Arnold Friend with Bob Dylan is clearly   5
suggested by the similarities of their physical descriptions. Arnold's "shaggy, shabby black hair that looked crazy as a wig," his "long and hawk-like" nose, his unshaven face, his "big and white" teeth, his lashes, "thick and black as if painted with a black tarlike material" and his size ("only an inch or so taller than Connie") are all characteristic of Bob Dylan. Even Arnold's "fast, bright monotone voice" is suggestive of Dylan, especially since he speaks "in a simple lilting voice, exactly as if he were reciting the words to a song."

The reference to "Mister Tambourine Man" implies another connection between the story and Dylan. A few of his song lyrics are very similar to the story itself. Oates herself suggests that part of the story's inspiration was "hearing for some weeks Dylan's song 'It's All Over Now, Baby Blue.'"[13] Such lines as "you must leave now," "something calls for you," "the vagabond who's rapping at your door," and "go start anew" are suggestive of the impending change awaiting Connie. Two other Dylan songs are equally as applicable though. The following lines from "Like a Rolling Stone" — the second most popular song of 1965 (the story was first published in 1966) — are also very similar to Connie's situation at the end of the story:

> You used to be so amused
> At Napoleon in rags and the language that he used
> Go to him now, he calls you, you can't refuse
> When you got nothing, you got nothing to lose
> You're invisible now, you got no secrets to conceal.

But Dylan's "Mr. Tambourine Man" — the number ten song in 1965 — is even more similar. The following stanza establishes the notion of using music to rouse one's imagination into a blissful fantasy world:

> Take me on a trip upon your magic swirlin' ship,
> My senses have been stripped,
> My hands can't feel to grip,
> My toes too numb to step,
> Wait only for my boot heels to be wanderin'.
> I'm ready to go anywhere,
> I'm ready for to fade
> Into my own parade.
> Cast your dancin' spell my way,

I promise to go under it.
Hey, Mister Tambourine Man, play a song for me,
I'm not sleepy and there ain't no place I'm going to.
Hey, Mister Tambourine Man, play a song for me.
In the jingle, jangle morning I'll come followin' you.

Arnold Friend's car — complete with the phrase "MAN THE FLYING SAU-
CERS" — is just such "a magic swirlin' ship." Arnold is the personification of popular music, particularly Bob Dylan's music; and as such, Connie's interaction with
him is a musically induced fantasy, a kind of "magic carpet ride" in "a convertible
jalopy painted gold." Rising out of Connie's radio, Arnold Friend/Bob Dylan is a
magical, musical messiah; he persuades Connie to abandon her father's house. As
a manifestation of her own desires, he frees her from the limitations of a fifteen-
year-old girl, assisting her maturation by stripping her of her childlike vision.

Notes

[1] Joyce M. Wegs, "'Don't You Know Who I Am?' The Grotesque in Oates's 'Where Are You Going,
Where Have You Been?'" in *Critical Essays on Joyce Carol Oates,* ed. Linda W. Wagner (Boston:
G. K. Hall, 1979), p. 90. First printed in *Journal of Narrative Technique,* 5 (1975), pp. 66–72.

[2] Marie Urbanski, "Existential Allegory: Joyce Carol Oates' 'Where Are You Going, Where Have
You Been?'" *Studies in Short Fiction,* 15 (1978), p. 202; Joan Winslow, "The Stranger Within:
Two Stories by Oates and Hawthorne," *Studies in Short Fiction,* 17 (1980), p. 264; Tom Quirk,
"A Source for 'Where Are You Going, Where Have You Been?'" *Studies in Short Fiction,* 18
(1981), p. 416; Christina Marsden Gillis, "'Where Are You Going, Where Have You Been?':
Seduction, Space, and a Fictional Mode," *Studies in Short Fiction,* 18 (1981), p. 70.

[3] Wegs, p. 89.

[4] Gillis, p. 65.

[5] Quirk, p. 416.

[6] Gretchen Schulz and R. J. R. Rockwood, "In Fairyland, without a Map: Connie's Exploration Inward
in Joyce Carol Oates' 'Where Are You Going, Where Have You Been?'" *Literature and Psychology,*
30 (1980), pp. 156, 165, & 166, respectively.

[7] In *Paradise Lost,* Milton clearly intends Satan to be a symbol of archetypal evil. Blake and Shelley,
as true Romantics, saw in their predecessor's portrait of Lucifer a duality that embodied positive
as well as negative traits.

[8] Roy Male, *Enter Mysterious Stranger: American Cloistral Fiction* (Norman: University of Oklahoma
Press, 1979), p. 21.

[9] Joyce Carol Oates, "Where Are You Going, Where Have You Been?" in *The Wheel of Love*
(New York: Vanguard Press, 1970), p. 40. Hereafter cited parenthetically within the text.

[10] Anthony Scaduto, *Bob Dylan* (New York: Grosset and Dunlop. 1971), p. 222.

[11] Scaduto, p. 274.

[12] Scaduto, p. 229.

[13] "Interview with Joyce Carol Oates about 'Where Are You Going, Where Have You Been?'" in
Mirrors: An Introduction to Literature, ed. John R. Knott, Jr., and Christopher R. Keaske, 2nd ed.
(San Francisco: Canfield Press, 1975), pp. 18–19.

BOB DYLAN

It's All Over Now, Baby Blue

You must leave now, take what you need you think will last
But whatever you wish to keep, you better grab it fast
Yonder stands your orphan with his gun
Crying like a fire in the sun.
Look out, the saints are comin' through   5
And it's all over now, baby blue.

The highway is for gamblers, better use your sins
Take what you have gathered from coincidence
The empty-handed painter from your streets
Is drawing crazy patterns on your sheets   10
This sky too is folding under you
And it's all over now, baby blue.

All your seasick sailors they are rowing home
Your empty-handed army men are going home
The lover who has just walked out your door   15
Has taken all his blankets from the floor
The carpet too is moving under you
And it's all over now, baby blue.

Leave your stepping stones behind, something calls for you
Forget the dead you've left, they will not follow you   20
The vagabond who's rapping at your door
Is standing in the clothes that you once wore
Strike another match, go start anew
And it's all over now, baby blue.

LAURA KALPAKIAN

from a review of Where Are You Going, Where Have You Been?: Selected Early Stories

In acknowledging her range, one must celebrate Ms. Oates's bravery. Range requires courage — and always did, though people perpetually insist things are worse now than they were thirty years ago. In any event and for a wide variety of reasons, current American literature seems self-consciously picketed off, writers hunkered over thimble-sized garden plots, No Trespassing signs stuck about tiny terrains of age or race, region, religion, gender, sexual persuasion, politics, each writer farming a tiny furrow: the pen as plow. Joyce Carol Oates, as these early stories [from the collection *Where Are You Going, Where Have You Been?: Selected*

Early Stories] testify, has always declined to be pinned down to her plot, has kicked down the fences. She writes about the rich and poor, urban and rural, black and white, the literate, the tongue-tied, young and old, the primly conventional, the drugged, delinquent, and debilitated. They're all here. Moreover, they're cast out of the comfy old narrative conventions and into structures which demand more from the reader.

Given Ms. Oates's range of structure, character, and voice, we might ask ourselves what unites these pieces. Poured, all of them, into a vial, shaken, what might rise to the top? Drastic acts with drastic consequences, severed connections, doomed love, destructive sex, fear, evil, madness — but not much guilt. Oates's characters all twist about on short tethers, whatever the differences in their worldly circumstances. More often than not a single act or choice or instant plummets these characters not merely into the depths of despair, but into depravity and destruction. In "Upon the Sweeping Flood" (1966), we meet a complacent, well-to-do family man driving home from his father's funeral. Caught in a hurricane, he refuses to obey an order to evacuate and plunges into the maelstrom, thrust finally into the company of two unnamed, abandoned white-trash kids, a boy and a girl. The three survive the night, but in the morning the boy dies at the hands of this man who then lunges toward the girl — he can "already see himself grappling with her in the mud, forcing her down, tearing her ugly clothing from her body" — just as a rescue boat heaves into view. "Save me! Save me!" cries yesterday's prosperous bourgeois and today's murderer.

In the ironically titled "Love and Death" (1972), an equally short distance separates a man (again comfortable, conventional, unloved, and unflappable) from a previously unthinkable fate. Visiting his infirm father, he meets a prostitute he slept with years before, as a young man. Their versions of the past are different; hers is correct. Though he returns to his manicured life, the chance encounter evolves into an obsession, sucking him into abasement and humiliation.

At the conclusion of "In the Warehouse" (1973), the narrator tells us of her tidy married life in "a colonial house on a lane of colonial houses called Meadowbrook Lane." But as a twelve-year-old, she was bullied about by a stronger girl named Ronnie whose toughness sprung from a sort of delinquent passion and unfocused unhappiness. The narrator was completely cowed by Ronnie: "I have never thought about liking Ronnie. I have no choice. She has never given me the privilege of liking or disliking her and if she knew I was thinking such a thought, she would yank my hair out of my head." As the girls prowled the darkened loft of a deserted warehouse, Ronnie urged the narrator up the stairs, ordering, "Do it! Do it!" Atop the loft, the narrator pushed Ronnie, who was impaled on the machinery below and died in a pool of blood. The sleepy narrator then went home, went to bed. Eventually, she "[grew] out of the skinny little body that knocked the clumsy body down — and I have never felt sorry. Never any guilt."

5   The Joyce Carol Oates of these early stories believes that evil lurks everywhere, even in the sunniest lives, the ostensibly to-be-envied lives. The knowledge of this evil defines character for Oates — or, more to the point, the individual's reaction to this knowledge defines character. Oates cares nothing for justice, nor judgment, nor Christian virtue and Christian wickedness. There are only two possible responses to the darkness. One reaction is the murderer's cry, "Save me!

Save me!", the wail of inescapable horror, the wish to be delivered. But there is no deliverance and there is no salvation. The narrator of "In the Warehouse" expresses for Oates the other possible reaction: "Never any guilt." She waits patiently to feel guilt for Ronnie's murder; but guilt, like a missed train, never arrives. In Oates's moral lexicon, the word "retribution" does not exist, nor "punishment," nor even anything so personal as "revenge." Evil is an impersonal, inescapable fact in every life. The central recognition of adulthood — no matter how old or young the character — is the recognition of this evil.

So omnipresent are the evil acts and consequences that Oates's characters seem often to be less created than enslaved by narrative: allegorical figures painted against realistic sunshine. In the title piece, "Where Are You Going, Where Have You Been?" (1970), for instance, there is a struggle between the menacing and cajoling Arnold Friend and the pubescent Connie. In the end Connie is, apparently, raped (in the Afterword Oates calls her "the presumably doomed Connie"). But Connie seems, despite the carefully drawn settings — shopping malls, drive-in restaurants, backyard barbecues — less a character than a cipher. She has no volition, no choices, and therefore it's hard to see her even as a victim. Instead, she suggests in her helplessness the awful inequalities of sex and power and violence. . . .

Emphatically in the stories in this volume, character and landscape serve the narrative rather than vice versa. Moreover, Joyce Carol Oates does not stoop to authorial pleading; she is neither pseudomaternal toward her characters nor pseudo-avuncular toward the reader, and she never importunes us with the unspoken: Please care for these characters. And, though the seasons are always noted and the geographical details of settings are always provided (including the oft-mentioned Detroit and its suburbs, as well as Erie County, New York), landscape in Oates's work seems dreamy, monochromatic, and unrealized — landscape as Tim Burton sometimes uses it in his movies. We may care about these characters or not, as we wish, but we are compelled by vigorous narrative through essentially indifferent landscapes. . . .

In Oates's stories there are no safe relationships, but the most perilous of all possibilities is sex. Sex is always destructive. In "Accomplished Desires" (1970), a two-edged narrative recounts the collision (and collusion) of two women: one a pretty college girl, vacuous but orderly, the other an accomplished woman poet married to a bullying professor. The wife is a prisoner in the upper reaches of her rented home; defeated by her home life, her three children, her inability to write, she drinks and looks out the high window. The smarmy husband not only beds the student but installs her as his secretary and housekeeper and moves her into his home to keep his life in order. According to the husband, this young woman "gets herself pregnant. On purpose." Because sages concerned with the state of modern literature await the professor's lecture at a meeting on the West Coast, the wife drives the student to an appointment with an abortionist. The women strike up a tentative, unspoken alliance (though not against the man, as we might have thought — or hoped). Indeed, the wife bows out of the struggle altogether, almost gracefully: a quiet overdose self-administered in a hotel room. The pretty former student, new wife — now, suddenly, a mother of four —finds herself prisoner in the upper reaches of the rented house, without the consolations of company or poetry or even gin.

Communication — especially sexual communication — is not only baffling and treacherous for Oates's characters; it often seems impossible. My personal favorite in this collection, "Translation" (1977), describes a middle-aged American academic who makes an official visit to an unnamed Central European country and is provided with a translator, Liebert. At a dreary communist cocktail party the American, Oliver, meets a woman whose beauty and fragility strike him to the very heart. He falls in love though he cannot even pronounce her name: "Alisa was as close as he could come to it." Oliver is euphoric, intoxicated, as he spends a memorable evening with her in a cafe (Liebert translating) where they speak of literature, politics, passion, history, and love. Oliver feels himself buoyed, enfolded, welcomed in a country where, in effect, he is a mute. The following day Liebert discreetly suggests that Alisa's roommate could be persuaded to leave overnight if she had train fare, which Oliver provides. But on the morning of the intended assignation, Oliver discovers he has been given a new translator. No explanations offered. No questions answered. This new man — obscene in every way — talks of the weather, smirks lewdly, arranges another cafe date with Alisa that evening. Through the new translator, Alisa inquires after Oliver's life in America, his financial assets, his cars, his wife. She eyeballs his watch. As Oliver leaves the country the next day, desperate for Liebert, he cries, "What shall I do for the rest of my life . . . ?"

10   No doubt the young and gifted writer of these stories found herself facing that same question. The dust-jacket photo for these selected early stories shows Ms. Oates circa 1965, her hair in the "flip" fashionable in that era, shoulders framed by a boat-necked dress. She regards the reader with the serene gaze of a high-school valedictorian. Not at all the look of a woman who willingly, knowingly smashes up the conventions of narrative. She does not look like the author who will unmask the evil of everyday life, who will see allegory in the backyard and real darkness among the metaphoric daisies. But she is.

STEPHEN SLIMP

from Oates's "Where Are You Going, Where Have You Been?"

One of the most arresting features of Joyce Carol Oates's short story "Where Are You Going, Where Have You Been?" is the way in which the story's powerful theme about the spiritual condition of late-twentieth-century American culture is conveyed with an almost palpable intensity. One can visualize the squalid hamburger joint, hear the blaring of Ellie's radio and the touch of Arnold's finger on the screen door. Most amazing, the reader experiences, even with multiple readings, a tightening of the stomach and quickening of the pulse as it slowly becomes clear exactly what Arnold is up to. Just as the sheer physicality of the narrative helps the reader confront the cultural wasteland that Oates believes our society has become, what Connie experiences physically leads her to an increasing awareness of the horrors of human existence and a resulting growth of her spiritual nature.

This interrelation of the physical and spiritual — in a story that Oates herself has described as "realistic allegory," "a mode of fiction to which I am . . . partial"[1] — is illustrated in the author's handling of an old trope common to many languages and many views of reality: the equation of physical breath with spirit. . . . Throughout this story, Oates uses the traditional association of breath and spirit, in a manner appropriate to a story "rich with the imagery of life's deceptions and perils,"[2] to help delineate Connie's progress in her understanding of the evils of the world and the consequent growth of her soul.

As the story opens, Connie is shallow and vapid, believing among other things that the height of human suffering is the annoyance she feels at her mother's chiding. So shallow are her emotions that she responds to her mother's corrections by saying that she would like to die, that is, literally to lose her breath. As the second sentence of the story puts it, "She . . . had a quick nervous giggling habit of craning her neck. . . ." As a shallow laugh, a giggle is a gesture emphatically not drawn from the depths of the soul. A little later, Oates makes the same point more explicitly when she writes of Connie's "high, breathless, amused voice" (388). And on the fateful day at the drive-in restaurant, Oates says of Connie and her friend that "they ran across [the busy road], breathless with daring" (389). At the beginning of the story, Connie's lack of breath symbolizes the lack of spiritual development of one absorbed by trivia.

As the story progresses, however, and as she begins to experience true evil and to grow spiritually as a result, Connie registers a growing capacity for breath. The first intimation of her increased ability to breathe comes, appropriately enough, at the moment she first encounters Arnold Friend:

> Connie couldn't help but let her eyes wander over the windshields and faces all 5
> around her, her face gleaming with a joy that had nothing to do with Eddie
> or even this place; it might have been the music. She drew her shoulders up
> and sucked in her breath with the pure pleasure of being alive, and just at that
> moment she happened to glance at a face a few feet from hers. (389)

The Sunday when Arnold comes to call, Connie is once again described as lacking in breath and air: "And Connie paid close attention [to the music], bathed in a glow of slow-pulsed joy that seemed to rise mysteriously out of the music itself and lay languidly about the airless little room, breathed in and breathed out with each gentle rise and fall of her chest" (390). Oates here emphasizes a room without air, without spirit; what breathing Connie manages is manifestly shallow. But then the pace of the story increases, and Connie gradually gains perspective, understanding, spirit, and breath. When she first recognizes a moment from her past as significant, the moment she first saw Arnold, "she remembered him even better, back at the restaurant, and her cheeks warmed at the thought of how she sucked in her breath just at the moment she passed him" (392). After she begins to recognize the importance of the passage of time, an awareness that comes with her sudden recognition that Arnold Friend and Ellie Oscar are much older than they appear, she begins to feel "a little light-headed. Her breath was coming quickly" (395). At this point Connie has come to experience evil as an unsettling phenomenon; it remains for her to experience the full horror of her encounter with human malice.

Eventually Arnold threatens to enter the house if she attempts to call the police then predicts that Connie will sooner or later come out to him. Connie's panic mounts; "She was panting" (396). The climax of the story comes in a blast of breath, which announces to the reader that Connie has at last developed a soul, has achieved a depth of spirit in the way that most human beings do — through the experience of suffering that brings enlightenment and a proper ordering of one's relationship to the world. When she attempts to use the telephone, Connie finally shows a depth of soul that allows her to cry out from deep within: "She began to scream into the phone. . . . She cried out, she cried for her mother, she felt her breath start jerking back and forth in her lungs as if it were something Arnold Friend were stabbing her with . . ." (398). A few lines further, Oates says that "[Connie] was hollow with what had been fear, but what was now just an emptiness. All that screaming had blasted it out of her" (398). Her screaming, born of her encounter with evil, results in her trying to establish a proper relationship with another human being — in this case, her mother. That her attempt has succeeded is shown when she sacrifices herself by going out, at the end of the story, to meet her fate, thereby sparing her family a violent and deadly encounter. She has shown herself to be a fully breathing human being, one who has, in a moment, developed the spiritual life lacking in her former existence.

Notes

[1] Joyce Carol Oates, *(Woman) Writer: Occasions and Opportunities* (New York: Dutton, 1989) 317.

[2] Walter Sullivan, "The Artificial Demon: Joyce Carol Oates and the Dimensions of the Real," *Joyce Carol Oates: Modern Critical Views*, ed. Harold Bloom (New York: Chelsea, 1987) 8.

DON MOSER

from The Pied Piper of Tucson

Sullen and unshaved, 23 years old and arrested for murder, Charles Schmid did not now look like a hero. But to many of the teen-agers in Tucson, Ariz. he had been someone to admire and emulate. He was different. He was Smitty, with mean, "beautiful" eyes and an interesting way of talking, and if he sometimes did weird things, at least he wasn't dull. He had his own house where he threw good parties, he wore crazy make-up, he was known at all the joints up and down Tucson's Speedway, and girls dyed their hair blond for him. Three of the girls who knew him wound up dead in the desert outside of town. And so last week, in a sun-blessed town where big-city squalor and violence seem far away, Smitty, the cool pied piper, stood trial for murder.

The death of the girls was shocking enough to Tucson, but the city had to face something more. There were indications that Smitty had boasted about the killings to his teen-age followers long before authorities even began to suspect that murder might have been done. Nobody spoke up. As the trial began for the murder of two of the victims — there will be another trial later for the murder of the third — Tucson's parents looked closely at their own children, and at the different young man so many of their children admired.

He Cruised in a Golden Car,
Looking for the Action

> Hey, c'mon babe, follow me,
> I'm the Pied Piper, follow me,
> I'm the Pied Piper,
> And I'll show you where it's at.
>> — Popular song,
>> Tucson, winter 1965

At dusk in Tucson, as the stark, yellow-flared mountains begin to blur against the sky, the golden car slowly cruises Speedway. Smoothly it rolls down the long, divided avenue, past the supermarkets, the gas stations and the motels; past the twist joints, the sprawling drive-in restaurants. The car slows for an intersection, stops, then pulls away again. The exhaust mutters against the pavement as the young man driving takes the machine swiftly, expertly through the gears. A car pulls even with him; the teen-age girls in the front seat laugh, wave and call his name. The young man glances toward the rearview mirror, turned always so that he can look at his own reflection, and he appraises himself.

The face is his own creation: the hair dyed raven black, the skin darkened to a deep tan with pancake make-up, the lips whitened, the whole effect heightened by a mole he has painted on one cheek. But the deep-set blue eyes are all his own. Beautiful eyes, the girls say.

Approaching the Hi-Ho, the teen-agers' nightclub, he backs off on the accelerator, then slowly cruises on past Johnie's Drive-in. There the cars are beginning to orbit and accumulate in the parking lot — neat sharp cars with deep-throated mufflers and Maltese-cross decals on the windows. But it's early yet. Not much going on. The driver shifts up again through the gears, and the golden car slides away along the glitter and gimcrack of Speedway. Smitty keeps looking for the action.

Whether the juries in the two trials decide that Charles Howard Schmid Jr. did or did not brutally murder Alleen Rowe, Gretchen Fritz and Wendy Fritz has from the beginning seemed of almost secondary importance to the people of Tucson. They are not indifferent. But what disturbs them far beyond the question of Smitty's guilt or innocence are the revelations about Tucson itself that have followed on the disclosure of the crimes. Starting with the bizarre circumstances of the killings and on through the ugly fragments of the plot — which in turn hint at other murders as yet undiscovered, at teen-age sex, blackmail, even connections with the Cosa Nostra — they have had to view their city in a new and unpleasant light. The fact is that Charles Schmid — who cannot be dismissed as a freak, an aberrant of no consequence — had for years functioned successfully as a member, even a leader, of the yeastiest stratum of Tucson's teen-age society.

Speedway Boulevard in Tucson (circa 1966) was a hang-out for teenagers with nothing to do, often frequented by murderer Charles Schmid.

5   As a high school student Smitty had been, as classmates remember, an out-sider — but not that far outside. He was small but he was a fine athlete, and in his last year — 1960 — he was a state gymnastics champion. His grades were poor, but he was in no trouble to speak of until his senior year, when he was suspended for stealing tools from a welding class.

But Smitty never really left the school. After his suspension he hung around waiting to pick up kids in a succession of sharp cars which he drove fast and well. He haunted all the teen-age hangouts along Speedway, including the bowling al-leys and the public swimming pool — and he put on spectacular diving exhibitions for girls far younger than he.

At the time of his arrest last November, Charles Schmid was 23 years old. He wore face make-up and dyed his hair. He habitually stuffed three or four inches of old rags and tin cans into the bottoms of his high-topped boots to make himself taller than his five-foot-three and stumbled about so awkwardly while walking that some people thought he had wooden feet. He pursed his lips and let his eye-lids droop in order to emulate his idol, Elvis Presley. He bragged to girls that he knew 100 ways to make love, that he ran dope, that he was a Hell's Angel. He talked about being a rough customer in a fight (he was, though he was rarely in one), and he always carried in his pocket tiny bottles of salt and pepper, which he said he used to blind his opponents. He liked to use highfalutin language and had a favorite saying, "I can manifest my neurotical emotions, emancipate an epicureal instinct, and elaborate on my heterosexual tendencies."

He occasionally shocked even those who thought they knew him well. A friend says he once saw Smitty tie a string to the tail of his pet cat, swing it around his head and beat it bloody against a wall. Then he turned calmly and asked, "You feel compassion — why?"

Yet even while Smitty tried to create an exalted, heroic image of himself, he had worked on a pitiable one. "He thrived on feeling sorry for himself," recalls a friend, "and making others feel sorry for him." At various times Smitty told intimates that he had leukemia and didn't have long to live. He claimed that he was adopted, that his real name was Angel Rodriguez, that his father was a "bean" (local slang for Mexican, an inferior race in Smitty's view), and that his mother was a famous lawyer who would have nothing to do with him.

What made Smitty a hero to Tucson's youth?

Isn't Tucson — out there in the Golden West, in the grand setting where the skies are not cloudy all day — supposed to be a flowering of the American Dream? One envisions teen-agers who drink milk, wear crewcuts, go to bed at half past 9, say "Sir" and "Ma'am," and like to go fishing with Dad. Part of Tucson is like this — but the city is not yet Utopia. It is glass and chrome and well-weathered stucco; it is also gimcrack, ersatz and urban sprawl at its worst. Its suburbs stretch for mile after mile — a level sea of bungalows, broken only by mammoth shopping centers, that ultimately peters out among the cholla and saguaro. The city

Murderer Charles H. Schmid Jr., at the preliminary hearings before the trial.

has grown from 85,000 to 300,000 since World War II. Few who live there were born there, and a lot are just passing through. Its superb climate attracts the old and the infirm, many of whom, as one citizen put it, "have come here to retire from their responsibilities to life." Jobs are hard to find and there is little industry to stabilize employment. ("What do people do in Tucson?" the visitor asks. Answer: "They do each others' laundry.")

As for the youngsters, they must compete with the army of semi-retired who are willing to take on part-time work for the minimum wage. Schools are beautiful but overcrowded; and at those with split sessions, the kids are on the loose from noon on, or from 6 p.m. till noon the next day. When they get into trouble, Tucson teen-agers are capable of getting into trouble in style: a couple of years ago they shocked the city fathers by throwing a series of beer-drinking parties in the desert, attended by scores of kids. The fests were called "boondockers" and if they were no more sinful than any other kids' drinking parties, they were at least on a magnificent scale. One statistic seems relevant: 50 runaways are reported to the Tucson police department each month.

Of an evening kids with nothing to do wind up on Speedway, looking for action. There is the teen-age nightclub ("Pickup Palace," the kids call it). There are the rock 'n' roll beer joints (the owners check ages meticulously, but young girls can enter if they don't drink; besides, anyone can buy a phony I.D. card for $2.50 around the high schools) where they can Jerk, Swim and Frug away the evening to the room-shaking electronic blare of *Hang On Sloopy*, *The Pied Piper* and a number called *The Bo Diddley Rock*. At the drive-in hamburger and pizza stands their cars circle endlessly, mufflers rumbling, as they check each other over.

Here on Speedway you find Richie and Ronny, out of work and bored and with nothing to do. Here you find Debby and Jabron, from the wrong side of the tracks, aimlessly cruising in their battered old car looking for something — anything — to relieve the tedium of their lives, looking for somebody neat. ("Well if the boys look bitchin,' you pull up next to them in your car and you roll down the window and say, 'Hey, how about a dollar for gas?' and if they give you the dollar then maybe you let them take you to Johnie's for a Coke.") Here you find Gretchen, pretty and rich and with problems, bad problems. Of a Saturday night, all of them cruising the long, bright street that seems endlessly in motion with the young. Smitty's people.

15   He had a nice car. He had plenty of money from his parents, who ran a nursing home, and he was always glad to spend it on anyone who'd listen to him. He had a pad of his own where he threw parties and he had impeccable manners. He was always willing to help a friend and he would send flowers to girls who were ill. He was older and more mature than most of his friends. He knew where the action was, and if he wore make-up — well, at least he was *different*.

Some of the older kids — those who worked, who had something else to do — thought Smitty was a creep. But to the youngsters — to the bored and the lonely, to the dropout and the delinquent, to the young girls with beehive hair-dos and tight pants they didn't quite fill out, and to the boys with acne and no jobs — to these people, Smitty was a kind of folk hero. Nutty maybe, but at least more dramatic, more theatrical, more *interesting* than anyone else in their lives: a semi-ludicrous sexy-eyed pied piper who, stumbling along in his rag-stuffed boots led them up and down Speedway. . . .

Out in the respectable Tucson suburbs parents have started to crack down on the youngsters and have declared Speedway hangouts off limits. "I thought my folks were bad before," laments one grounded 16-year-old, "but now they're just impossible."

As for the others — Smitty's people —most don't care very much. Things are duller without Smitty around, but things have always been dull.

"There's nothing to do in this town," says one of his girls, shaking her dyed blond hair. "The only other town I know is Las Vegas and there's nothing to do there either." For her, and for her friends, there's nothing to do in any town.

They are down on Speedway again tonight, cruising, orbiting the drive-ins, stopping by the joints, where the words of *The Bo Diddley Rock* cut through the smoke and the electronic dissonance like some macabre reminder of their fallen hero.

20

> All you women stand in line,
> And I'll love you all in an hour's time. . . .
> I got a cobra snake for a necktie,
> I got a brand-new house on the roadside
> Covered with rattlesnake hide
> I got a brand-new chimney made on top,
> Made out of human skulls.
> Come on baby, take a walk with me,
> And tell me, who do you love?
> Who do you love?
> Who do you love?
> Who do you love?

ANONYMOUS

The Pied Piper Of Hamelin

Once upon a time . . . on the banks of a great river in the north of Germany lay a town called Hamelin. The citizens of Hamelin were honest folk who lived contentedly in their grey stone houses. The years went by, and the town grew very rich. Then one day, an extraordinary thing happened to disturb the peace. Hamelin had always had rats, and a lot too. But they had never been a danger, for the cats had always solved the rat problem in the usual way — by killing them. All at once, however, the rats began to multiply.

In the end, a black sea of rats swarmed over the whole town. First, they attacked the barns and storehouses, then, for lack of anything better, they gnawed the wood, cloth or anything at all. The one thing they didn't eat was metal. The terrified citizens flocked to plead with the town councillors to free them from the plague of rats. But the council had, for a long time, been sitting in the Mayor's room, trying to think of a plan.

"What we need is an army of cats!"

But all the cats were dead.

5   "We'll put down poisoned food then . . ."

But most of the food was already gone and even poison did not stop the rats.

"It just can't be done without help!" said the Mayor sadly.

Just then, while the citizens milled around outside, there was a loud knock at the door. "Who can that be?" the city fathers wondered uneasily, mindful of the angry crowds. They gingerly opened the door. And to their surprise, there stood a tall thin man dressed in brightly coloured clothes, with a long feather in his hat, and waving a gold pipe at them.

"I've freed other towns of beetles and bats," the stranger announced, "and for a thousand florins, I'll rid you of your rats!"

10   "A thousand florins!" exclaimed the Mayor. "We'll give you fifty thousand if you succeed!" At once the stranger hurried away, saying: "It's late now, but at dawn tomorrow, there won't be a rat left in Hamelin!"

The sun was still below the horizon, when the sound of a pipe wafted through the streets of Hamelin. The pied piper slowly made his way through the houses and behind him flocked the rats. Out they scampered from doors, windows and gutters, rats of every size, all after the piper. And as he played, the stranger marched down to the river and straight into the water, up to his middle. Behind him swarmed the rats and every one was drowned and swept away by the current.

By the time the sun was high in the sky, there was not a single rat in the town. There was even greater delight at the town hall, until the piper tried to claim his payment.

"Fifty thousand florins?" exclaimed the councillors, "Never . . ."

"A thousand florins at least!" cried the pied piper angrily. But the Mayor broke in. "The rats are all dead now and they can never come back. So be grateful for fifty florins, or you'll not get even that . . ."

15   His eyes flashing with rage, the pied piper pointed a threatening finger at the Mayor.

"You'll bitterly regret ever breaking your promise," he said, and vanished.

A shiver of fear ran through the councillors, but the Mayor shrugged and said excitedly: "We've saved fifty thousand florins!"

That night, freed from the nightmare of the rats, the citizens of Hamelin slept more soundly than ever. And when the strange sound of piping wafted through the streets at dawn, only the children heard it. Drawn as by magic, they hurried out of their homes. Again, the pied piper paced through the town. This time, it was children of all sizes that flocked at his heels to the sound of his strange piping. The long procession soon left the town and made its way through the wood and across the forest till it reached the foot of a huge mountain. When the piper came to the dark rock, he played his pipe even louder still and a great door creaked open. Beyond lay a cave. In trooped the children behind the pied piper, and when the last child had gone into the darkness, the door creaked shut. A great landslide came down the mountain blocking the entrance to the cave forever. Only one little lame boy escaped this fate. It was he who told the anxious citizens, searching for their children, what had happened. And no matter what people did, the mountain never gave up its victims. Many years were to pass before the merry voices of other children would ring through the streets of Hamelin but the memory of the harsh lesson lingered in everyone's heart and was passed down from father to son through the centuries.

CHARLES PERRAULT

Little Red Riding Hood

Once upon a time there was a little village girl, the prettiest that had ever been seen. Her mother doted on her. Her grandmother was even fonder, and made her a little red hood, which became her so well that everywhere she went by the name of Little Red Riding Hood.

One day her mother, who had just made and baked some cakes, said to her: "Go and see how your grandmother is, for I have been told that she is ill. Take her a cake and this little pot of butter."

Little Red Riding Hood set off at once for the house of her grandmother, who lived in another village. On her way through a wood she met old Father Wolf. He would have very much liked to eat her, but dared not do so on account of some wood-cutters who were in the forest. He asked her where she was going. The poor child, not knowing that it was dangerous to stop and listen to a wolf, said: "I am going to see my grandmother, and am taking her a cake and a pot of butter which my mother has sent to her." "Does she live far away?" asked the Wolf. "Oh, yes," replied Little Red Riding Hood; "it is yonder by the mill which you can see right below there, and it is the first house in the village."

"Well now," said the Wolf, "I think I shall go and see her too. I will go by this path, and you by that path, and we will see who gets there first." The Wolf set off running with all his might by the shorter road, and the little girl continued on her way by the longer road. As she went she amused herself by gathering nuts, running after the butterflies, and making nosegays of the wild flowers which she found.

The Wolf was not long in reaching the grandmother's house. He knocked. 5 Toc Toc. "Who is there?" "It is your granddaughter, Red Riding Hood," said the Wolf, disguising his voice, "and I bring you a cake and a little pot of butter as a present from my mother." The worthy grandmother was in bed, not being very well, and cried out to him: "Pull out the peg and the latch will fall." The Wolf drew out the peg and the door flew open. Then he sprang upon the poor old lady and ate her up in less than no time, for he had been more than three days without food.

After that he shut the door, lay down in the grandmother's bed, and waited for Little Red Riding Hood. Presently she came and knocked. Toc Toc.

"Who is there?"

Now Little Red Riding Hood on hearing the Wolf's gruff voice was at first frightened, but thinking that her grandmother had a bad cold, she replied: "It is your granddaughter, Red Riding Hood, and I bring you a cake and a little pot of butter from my mother."

Softening his voice, the Wolf called out to her: "Pull out the peg and the latch will fall." Little Red Riding Hood drew out the peg and the door flew open. When he saw her enter, the Wolf hid himself in the bed beneath the counterpane. "Put the cake and the little pot of butter on the bin," he said, "and come up on the bed with me."

10   Little Red Riding Hood took off her cloak, but when she climbed up on the bed she was astonished to see how her grandmother looked in her nightgown.

"Grandmother dear!" she exclaimed, "what big arms you have!"

"The better to embrace you, my child!"

"Grandmother dear, what big legs you have!"

"The better to run with, my child!"

15   "Grandmother dear, what big ears you have!"

"The better to hear with, my child!"

"Grandmother dear, what big eyes you have!"

"The better to see with, my child!"

"Grandmother dear, what big teeth you have!"

20   "The better to eat you with!"

With these words the wicked Wolf leapt upon Little Red Riding Hood and gobbled her up.

Moral

From this story one learns that children, especially young lasses, pretty, courteous and well-bred, do very wrong to listen to strangers, and it is not an unheard thing if the Wolf is thereby provided with his dinner. I say Wolf, for all wolves are not of the same sort; there is one kind with an amenable disposition — neither noisy, nor hateful, nor angry, but tame, obliging and gentle, following the young maids in the streets, even into their homes. Alas! Who does not know that these gentle wolves are of all such creatures the most dangerous!

Topics for Further Research

1. In Schulz and Rockwood's essay "In Fairyland, without a Map: Connie's Exploration Inward in Joyce Carol Oates's 'Where Are You Going, Where Have You Been?'" (p. 387), the authors quote Oates on her story's allusions to fairy tales, citing Bruno Bettelheim's views on their importance. After consulting Bettelheim's book *The Uses of Enchantment* (as well as the other sources in this Casebook) and after reading the two fairy tales included here, write an essay in which you consider the importance of fairy tales in the story.

2. In her article "When Characters from the Page Are Made Flesh on the Screen" (p. 401), Oates refers to her use of "realistic allegory" as a mode of fiction that is "Hawthornian . . . shading into parable" (par. 4). Research Hawthorne's views on allegory by reading some of his many essays on the subject, such as "The Custom House." Then, write an essay in which you consider how "Where Are You Going, Where Have You Been?" might be compared to Hawthorne's stories, such as "Young Goodman Brown" (p. 292), in its portrayal of good, evil, and innocence. Try to identify elements in Oates's story that might be considered allegorical in the Hawthornian sense.

3. Oates has been described as a modern realist, and she herself has used the term "psychological realism" to describe her work. Research the history and emergence of literary realism in American literature. What elements of realism as it first appeared in literature at the end of the nineteenth century and the beginning of the twentieth century are found in Oates's work?

4. Critics often see Oates's short stories as gothic. Research the term *gothic* as it applies to works of literature. Then, write a paper in which you make the case for three of her stories, including, "Where Are You Going, Where Have You Been?," as gothic works. You may also wish to discuss gothic stories by other writers — for example, Poe's "The Cask of Amontillado" (p. 217) and Flannery O'Connor's "A Good Man Is Hard to Find."

5. In the excerpt from her book review included in this Casebook (p. 411) critic Laura Kalpakian takes a look at some of the themes of Oates's works as they are represented in the characters she chooses to portray. Do some research to find out what other critics and reviewers have identified as recurring themes in Oates's work. Then, choose one of these themes and write an essay discussing how three of Oates's characters illustrate the theme you have chosen.

STUDENT PAPER

Olivari 1

Michele Olivari

Professor Biemiller

English 102

8 March 2003

Mesmerizing Men and Vulnerable Teens:

Power Relationships in "Where Are You Going,

Where Have You Been?" and "Teenage Wasteland"

Introduction

In both Joyce Carol Oates's "Where Are You Going, Where Have You Been?" (1966) and Anne Tyler's
"Teenage Wasteland" (1984), adolescents are in conflict with their parents. Both stories are set in
"teenage wastelands" in which the protagonists ignore
limits established by authority figures and avoid
making decisions or finding a direction for their
lives. An even more striking similarity between the
two stories is the presence of a hypnotic older
man—one who exerts enormous influence over the teen-
agers, pushing them out of their passive states and
causing them to take action. Ironically, however, the
actions they take, though decisive, have terrifying
consequences.

Background critics'
interpretations
of Arnold Friend

Arnold Friend, the mysterious loner who pursues
Connie in "Where Are You Going, Where Have You
Been?," is characterized by Gretchen Schulz and
R. J. R. Rockwood as the fairy tale wolf who "intends
to 'gobble up' this 'little girl' as soon as he gets
the chance" (406). Many other critics, as Mike Tierce
and John Michael Crafton point out, see Arnold as the
devil; Tierce and Crafton, however, prefer to see
him as a Bob Dylan figure "—a type of rock and roll

Olivari 2

messiah—" (409). Oates herself, in stating that
Arnold is based on a "charismatic mass murderer"
("When Characters" 402), acknowledges both the threat
he poses and his seductive powers. Regardless of
whether Arnold is murderer, devil, wolf, or musical
messiah, it is clear that he is a strong, controlling
personality who has an unnaturally powerful hold over
Connie. In a less dramatic way, Cal, the tutor in
"Teenage Wasteland," has just such a hold over Donny.
Both men, supported by background music, use their
power to mesmerize young people, separating them from
home and family and seducing them into following different—and dangerous—paths. In both stories, it is
the adolescents' tendency to drift without an anchor
that makes them vulnerable to the men.

Both Connie and Donny are passive dreamers,
stuck in numbing adolescence, waiting for something
to happen. Meanwhile, both break the rules set by
their parents. Connie is fifteen, and her mind is
"all filled with trashy daydreams" (388 each). At
night she sneaks out to forbidden hangouts, lying to
her parents about where she is going. As she drifts
through her unstructured summer days, she is
"dazed with the warmth about her" (390) and
caught up in the music she listens to and in
her romantic fantasies. Donny is also stalled,
caught in a cycle of failure and defeat, "noisy,
lazy, and disruptive" (536) and unresponsive

Comparison between Cal and Arnold established

Thesis statement

First parallel between Connie and Donny: passivity

Olivari 3

in school, cutting classes, smoking, and
drinking beer.

Second parallel between Connie and Donny: alienation from parents and society

    Both Connie and Donny are emotionally separated
from their parents. Connie's mother constantly nags
her and compares her unfavorably to her sister June;
her father does not even talk, choosing instead to
read his newspaper and avoid conflict. In "Teenage
Wasteland," Daisy's primary attitude toward her son
Donny is disappointment. When she looks at him, she
sees only "his pathetically poor posture, that slouch
so forlorn that his shoulders [seem] about to meet
his chin" (538). She feels sorry for him, but she is
helpless to rescue him, let alone give him the
emotional support he needs. Like Connie's mother, she
disapproves of her child's behavior. Despite her
efforts to defend and encourage him, she is ashamed
of his failures and upset at how they reflect upon her
as a parent. Both Connie and Donny are unconnected to
people or social institutions, and both are allowed
to remain unconnected by weak, ineffective parents
whom they neither respect nor admire. Both Connie and
Donny, therefore, are vulnerable to the seductive
power of a hypnotic older man.

Arnold's power over Connie

    Arnold Friend, a strange-looking man who acts
like a teenager, has great power over Connie. Initially, she is drawn to him by how he looks and
dresses and by the music they share; later, his
claims to know all about her, to know what she wants
(which she herself does not know), draw her closer to

Olivari 4

him. Although she begins by flirting with him as she
does with other boys, she soon realizes that he is
different. At first "his face [is] a familiar face,
somehow" (392), and "she recognize[s] most things
about him" (394), but her confidence turns to fear
when she realizes that he is older than he appears
(394). By now, though, she is under his spell.
Little by little, things that have been comforting
and familiar—the music, Arnold's clothing and
mannerisms, even Connie's own kitchen—become "only
half real" (394). As Arnold becomes more and more
threatening, Connie becomes more and more helpless;
toward the end of the story, cut off from everything
she has known, she is "hollow with what had been
fear, but what [is] now just an emptiness" (398).
Totally in Arnold's power, she crosses the line into
uncertainty—and, perhaps, death.

Cal Beadle, Donny's tutor, has none of the
frightening mannerisms of Arnold Friend, and he has
no sinister intentions. Nevertheless, he too is a
controlling figure. Like Arnold, Cal is an older man
who dresses and acts as adolescents do and listens
to the music they like. He immediately sides with
Donny, setting himself in opposition to authority
figures and social institutions, such as school and
the family. Never blaming or even criticizing Donny,
Cal suggests that Donny's parents are too controlling
and advises that they "give him more rope" (538).
Cal does not help Donny to function in his world;

Cal's power
over Donny

Olivari 5

he shelters him from it. Still, Donny sides with Cal, adopting his attitudes and expressions: it becomes "Cal this, Cal that, Cal says this, Cal and I did that" (539).

Cal's power over Donny, continued

Eventually, Cal becomes the role model Donny's own parents have failed to provide. Donny comes to depend on Cal, even going straight to Cal's house when he is expelled from school, and Cal comes to enjoy this dependence. But Cal does not necessarily have Donny's best interests at heart. Daisy, who despite her own failures with Donny seems to know him (and Cal) well, sees Cal as predatory and controlling, characterizing his smile as "feverish and avid—a smile of hunger" (542). Although Cal does not cause Donny to leave home, he makes it impossible for him to stay. Once he has convinced Donny that it is acceptable to reject the values established by his parents and teachers, Donny's departure becomes inevitable. Having removed all Donny's anchors, Cal then removes himself from Donny's life, deciding the teenager is "emotionally disturbed" (542) and thus absolving himself of blame. At this point, Donny, "exhausted and defeated" (542), has no real choice but to disappear.

Conclusion

Both Arnold Friend and Cal Beadle—Arnold odd-looking and out-of-date, Cal estranged from his "controlling" wife and surrounded by teenagers—seem to exist outside the adult world and its rules and values. Perhaps as a result, each has a need for

Olivari 6

power, a desire to control. Each selects someone
weaker, less confident, and more confused than
himself, a teenager with strained family
relationships and no focused goals. Clearly, critics'
characterizations of Arnold Friend, and the hypnotic
power those characterizations suggest, apply not just
to Arnold but also to Cal. Even though Cal means
Donny no harm, his casual dismissal of him after he
has separated the boy from all that is familiar to
him pushes Donny from the known and safe to the
unknown and dangerous. It is to this uncertain
world that Connie too is driven: a place she "[does]
not recognize except to know that she [is] going
to it" (399).

Olivari 7

Works Cited

Kirszner, Laurie G., and Stephen R. Mandell, eds.
    <u>Literature: Reading, Reacting, Writing</u>. 5th ed.
    Boston: Heinle, 2004.

Oates, Joyce Carol. "When Characters from the Page
    Are Made Flesh on the Screen." Kirszner and Man-
    dell 401-03.

---. "Where Are You Going, Where Have You Been?"
    Kirszner and Mandell 387-99.

Schulz, Gretchen, and R. J. R. Rockwood. "In Fairy-
    land, without a Map: Connie's Exploration Inward
    in Joyce Carol Oates's 'Where Are You Going,
    Where Have You Been?'" Kirszner and Mandell
    404-07.

Tierce, Mike, and John Michael Crafton. "Connie's
    Tambourine Man: A New Reading of Arnold Friend."
    Kirszner and Mandell 407-10.

Tyler, Anne. "Teenage Wasteland." Kirszner and Man-
    dell 535-543.

CHAPTER 13

FICTION FOR FURTHER READING

CHINUA ACHEBE (1930–)

Dead Man's Path (1953) (1972)

Michael Obi's hopes were fulfilled much earlier than he had expected. He was appointed headmaster of Ndume Central School in January 1949. It had always been an unprogressive school, so the Mission authorities decided to send a young and energetic man to run it. Obi accepted this responsibility with enthusiasm. He had many wonderful ideas and this was an opportunity to put them into practice. He had had sound secondary school education which designated him a "pivotal teacher" in the official records and set him apart from the other headmasters in the mission field. He was outspoken in his condemnation of the narrow views of these older and often less-educated ones.

"We shall make a good job of it, shan't we?" he asked his young wife when they first heard the joyful news of his promotion.

"We shall do our best," she replied. "We shall have such beautiful gardens and everything will be just *modern* and delightful . . ." In their two years of married life she had become completely infected by his passion for "modern methods" and his denigration of "these old and superannuated people in the teaching field who would be better employed as traders in the Onitsha market." She began to see herself already as the admired wife of the young headmaster, the queen of the school.

The wives of the other teachers would envy her position. She would set the fashion in everything . . . Then, suddenly, it occurred to her that there might not be other wives. Wavering between hope and fear, she asked her husband, looking anxiously at him.

"All our colleagues are young and unmarried," he said with enthusiasm which   5
for once she did not share. "Which is a good thing," he continued.

"Why?"

"Why? They will give all their time and energy to the school."

Nancy was downcast. For a few minutes she became skeptical about the new school; but it was only for a few minutes. Her little personal misfortune could not blind her to her husband's happy prospects. She looked at him as he sat folded up in a chair. He was stoop-shouldered and looked frail. But he sometimes surprised people with sudden bursts of physical energy. In his present posture, however, all his bodily strength seemed to have retired behind his deep-set eyes, giving them an extraordinary power of penetration. He was only twenty-six, but looked thirty or more. On the whole, he was not unhandsome.

"A penny for your thoughts, Mike," said Nancy after a while, imitating the woman's magazine she read.

10 "I was thinking what a grand opportunity we've got at last to show these people how a school should be run."

Ndume School was backward in every sense of the word. Mr. Obi put his whole life into the work, and his wife hers too. He had two aims. A high standard of teaching was insisted upon, and the school compound was to be turned into a place of beauty. Nancy's dream-gardens came to life with the coming of the rains, and blossomed. Beautiful hibiscus and allamanda hedges in brilliant red and yellow marked out the carefully tended school compound from the rank neighborhood bushes.

One evening as Obi was admiring his work he was scandalized to see an old woman from the village hobble right across the compound, through a marigold flower-bed and the hedges. On going up there he found faint signs of an almost disused path from the village across the school compound to the bush on the other side.

"It amazes me," said Obi to one of his teachers who had been three years in the school, "that you people allowed the villagers to make use of this footpath. It is simply incredible." He shook his head.

"The path," said the teacher apologetically, "appears to be very important to them. Although it is hardly used, it connects the village shrine with their place of burial."

15 "And what has that got to do with the school"? asked the headmaster.

"Well, I don't know," replied the other with a shrug of the shoulders. "But I remember there was a big row some time ago when we attempted to close it."

"That was some time ago. But it will not be used now," said Obi as he walked away. "What will the Government Education Officer think of this when he comes to inspect the school next week? The villagers might, for all I know, decide to use the schoolroom for pagan ritual during the inspection."

Heavy sticks were planted closely across the path at the two places where it entered and left the school premises. These were further strengthened with barbed wire.

Three days later the village priest of *Ani* called on the headmaster. He was an old man and walked with a slight stoop. He carried a stout walking-stick which he usually tapped on the floor, by way of emphasis, each time he made a new point in his argument.

20 "I have heard," he said after the usual exchange of cordialities, "that our ancestral footpath has recently been closed. . ."

"Yes," replied Mr. Obi. "We cannot allow people to make a highway of our school compound."

"Look here, my son," said the priest bringing down his walking-stick, "this path was here before you were born and before your father was born. The whole life of this village depends on it. Our dead relatives depart by it and our ancestors visit us by it. But most important, it is the path of children coming in to be born . . ."

Mr. Obi listened with a satisfied smile on his face.

"The whole purpose of our school," he said finally, "is to eradicate just such beliefs as that. Dead men do not require footpaths. The whole idea is just fantastic. Our duty is to teach your children to laugh at such ideas."

"What you say may be true," replied the priest, "but we follow the practices of   25 our fathers. If you reopen the path we shall have nothing to quarrel about. What I always say is let the hawk perch and let the eagle perch." He rose to go.

"I am sorry," said the young headmaster. "But the school compound cannot be a thoroughfare. It is against our regulations. I would suggest your constructing another path, skirting our premises. We can even get our boys to help in building it. I don't suppose the ancestors will find the little detour too burdensome."

"I have no more words to say," said the old priest, already outside.

Two days later a young woman in the village died in childbed. A diviner was immediately consulted and he prescribed heavy sacrifices to propitiate ancestors insulted by the fence.

Obi woke up next morning among the ruins of his work. The beautiful hedges were torn up not just near the path but right round the school, the flowers trampled to death and one of the school buildings pulled down . . . That day, the white Supervisor came to inspect the school and wrote a nasty report on the state of the premises but more seriously about the "tribal-war situation developing between the school and the village, arising in part from the misguided zeal of the new headmaster."

◇ ◇ ◇

TONI CADE BAMBARA   (1939–1995)

The Lesson   (1972)

Back in the days when everyone was old and stupid or young and foolish me and Sugar were the only ones just right, this lady moved on our block with nappy hair and proper speech and no makeup. And quite naturally we laughed at her, laughed the way we did at the junk man who went about his business like he was some big-time president and his sorry-ass horse his secretary. And we kinda hated her too, hated the way we did the winos who cluttered up our parks and pissed on our handball walls and stank up our hallways and stairs so you couldn't halfway play hide-and-seek without a goddamn gas mask. Miss Moore was her name. The only woman on the block with no first name. And she was black as hell, cept for her feet, which were fish-white and spooky. And she was always planning these boring-ass things for us to do, us being my cousin, mostly, who lived on the block cause we all moved North the same time and to the same apartment then spread out gradual to breathe. And our parents would yank our heads into some kinda shape and crisp up our clothes so we'd be presentable for travel with Miss Moore, who always looked like she was going to church, though she never did. Which is just one of the things the grownups talked about when they talked behind her back like a dog. But when she came calling with some sachet she'd sewed up or some gingerbread she'd made or some book, why then they'd all be too embarrassed to turn her down and we'd get handed over all spruced up. She'd been to college and said it was only right that she should take responsibility for the young ones' education, and she not even related by marriage or blood. So they'd go for it. Specially Aunt Gretchen. She was the main gofer in the family. You got some ole dumb shit foolishness you want somebody to go for, you send for Aunt Gretchen. She been screwed into the go-along for so long, it's a blood-deep natural thing with her. Which is how she got saddled with me and Sugar and Junior in the first place while our mothers were in a la-de-da apartment up the block having a good ole time.

So this one day Miss Moore rounds us all up at the mailbox and it's puredee hot and she's knockin herself out about arithmetic. And school suppose to let up in summer I heard, but she don't never let up. And the starch in my pinafore scratching the shit outta me and I'm really hating this nappy-head bitch and her goddamn college degree. I'd much rather go to the pool or to the show where it's cool. So me and Sugar leaning on the mailbox being surly, which is a Miss Moore word. And Flyboy checking out what everybody brought for lunch. And Fat Butt already wasting his peanut butter-and-jelly sandwich like the pig he is. And Junebug punchin on Q.T.'s arm for potato chips. And Rosie Giraffe shifting from one hip to the other waiting for somebody to step on her foot or ask her if she from Georgia so she can kick ass, preferably Mercedes'. And Miss Moore asking us do we know what money is, like we a bunch of retards. I mean real money, she say, like it's only poker chips or monopoly papers we lay on the grocer. So right away I'm tired of this and say so. And would much rather snatch Sugar and go to the Sunset and terrorize the West Indian kids and take their hair ribbons and their money too. And Miss Moore files that remark away for next week's lesson on brotherhood, I can tell. And finally I say we oughta get to the subway cause it's cooler and besides we might meet some cute boys. Sugar done swiped her mama's lipstick, so we ready.

So we heading down the street and she's boring us silly about what things cost and what our parents make and how much goes for rent and how money ain't divided up right in this country. And then she gets to the part about we all poor and live in the slums, which I don't feature. And I'm ready to speak on that, but she steps out in the street and hails two cabs just like that. Then she hustles half the crew in with her and hands me a five-dollar bill and tells me to calculate 10 percent tip for the driver. And we're off. Me and Sugar and Junebug and Flyboy hangin out the window and hollering to everybody, putting lipstick on each other cause Flyboy a faggot anyway, and making farts with our sweaty armpits. But I'm mostly trying to figure how to spend this money. But they all fascinated with the meter ticking and Junebug starts laying bets as to how much it'll read when Flyboy can't hold his breath no more. Then Sugar lays bets as to how much it'll be when we get there. So I'm stuck. Don't nobody want to go for my plan, which is to jump out at the next light and run off to the first bar-b-que we can find. Then the driver tells us to get the hell out cause we there already. And the meter reads eighty-five cents. And I'm stalling to figure out the tip and Sugar say give him a dime. And I decide he don't need it bad as I do, so later for him. But then he tries to take off with Junebug foot still in the door so we talk about his mama something ferocious. Then we check out that we on Fifth Avenue and everybody dressed up in stockings. One lady in a fur coat, hot as it is. White folks crazy.

"This is the place," Miss Moore say, presenting it to us in the voice she uses at the museum. "Let's look in the windows before we go in."

"Can we steal?" Sugar asks very serious like she's getting the ground rules   5
squared away before she plays. "I beg your pardon," say Miss Moore, and we fall out. So she leads us around the windows of the toy store and me and Sugar screamin, "This is mine, that's mine, I gotta have that, that was made for me, I was born for that," till Big Butt drowns us out.

"Hey, I'm going to buy that there."

"That there? You don't even know what it is, stupid."

"I do so," he say punchin on Rosie Giraffe. "It's a microscope."

"Whatcha gonna do with a microscope, fool?"

"Look at things."   10

"Like what, Ronald?" ask Miss Moore. And Big Butt ain't got the first notion. So here go Miss Moore gabbing about the thousands of bacteria in a drop of water and the somethinorother in a speck of blood and the million and one living things in the air around us is invisible to the naked eye. And what she say that for? Junebug go to town on that "naked" and we rolling. Then Miss Moore ask what it cost. So we all jam into the window smudgin it up and the price tag say $300. So then she ask how long'd take for Big Butt and Junebug to save up their allowances. "Too long," I say. "Yeh," adds Sugar, "outgrown it by that time." And Miss Moore say no, you never outgrow learning instruments. "Why, even medical students and interns and," blah, blah, blah. And we ready to choke Big Butt for bringing it up in the first damn place.

"This here costs four hundred eighty dollars," say Rosie Giraffe. So we pile up all over her to see what she pointin out. My eyes tell me it's a chunk of glass cracked with something heavy, and different-color inks dripped into the splits, and then the whole thing put into a oven or something. But for $480 it don't make sense.

"That's a paperweight made of semi-precious stones fused together under tremendous pressure," she explains slowly, with her hands doing the mining and all the factory work.

"So what's a paperweight?" asks Rosie Giraffe.

"To weigh paper with, dumbbell," say Flyboy, the wise man from the East.   15

"Not exactly," says Miss Moore, which is what she say when you warm or way off too. "It's to weigh paper down so it won't scatter and make your desk untidy." So right away me and Sugar curtsy to each other and then to Mercedes who is more the tidy type.

"We don't keep paper on top of the desk in my class," say Junebug, figuring Miss Moore crazy or lyin one.

"At home, then," she say "Don't you have a calendar and a pencil case and a blotter and a letter-opener on your desk at home where you do your homework?" And she know damn well what our homes look like cause she nosys around in them every chance she gets.

"I don't even have a desk," say Junebug. "Do we?"

"No. And I don't get no homework neither," says Big Butt.   20

"And I don't even have a home," says Flyboy like he do at school to keep the white folks off his back and sorry for him. Send this poor kid to camp posters, is his specialty.

"I do," says Mercedes. "I have a box of stationery on my desk and a picture of my cat. My godmother bought the stationery and the desk. There's a big rose on each sheet and the envelopes smell like roses."

"Who wants to know about your smelly-ass stationery," say Rosie Giraffe fore I can get my two cents in.

"It's important to have a work area all your own so that . . ."

25   "Will you look at this sailboat, please," say Flyboy, cuttin her off and pointin to the thing like it was his. So once again we tumble all over each other to gaze at this magnificent thing in the toy store which is just big enough to maybe sail two kittens across the pond if you strap them to the posts right. We all start recit-ing the price tag like we in assembly. "Handcrafted sailboat of fiberglass at one thousand one hundred ninety-five dollars."

"Unbelievable," I hear myself say and am really stunned. I read it again for my-self just in case the group recitation put me in a trance. Same thing. For some rea-son this pisses me off. We look at Miss Moore and she lookin at us, waiting for I dunno what.

"Who'd pay all that when you can buy a sailboat set for a quarter at Pop's, a tube of glue for a dime, and a ball of string for eight cents? It must have a motor and a whole lot else besides," I say. "My sailboat cost me about fifty cents."

"But will it take water?" say Mercedes with her smart ass.

"Took mine to Alley Pond Park once," say Flyboy. "String broke. Lost it. Pity."

30   "Sailed mine in Central Park and it keeled over and sank. Had to ask my father for another dollar."

"And you got the strap," laughed Big Butt. "The jerk didn't even have a string on it. My old man wailed on his behind."

Little Q.T. was staring hard at the sailboat and you could see he wanted it bad. But he too little and somebody'd just take it from him. So what the hell. "This boat for kids, Miss Moore?"

"Parents silly to buy something like that just to get all broke up," say Rosie Giraffe.

"That much money it should last forever," I figure.

35   "My father'd buy it for me if I wanted it."

"Your father, my ass," say Rosie Giraffe getting a chance to finally push Mercedes.

"Must be rich people shop here," say Q.T.

"You are a very bright boy," say Flyboy. "What was your first clue?" And he rap him on the head with the back of his knuckles, since Q.T. the only one he could get away with. Though Q.T. liable to come up behind you years later and get his licks in when you half expect it.

"What I want to know is," I says to Miss Moore though I never talk to her, I wouldn't give the bitch the satisfaction, "is how much a real boat costs? I figure a thousand'd get you a yacht any day."

"Why don't you check that out," she says, "and report back to the group?" 40 Which really pains my ass. If you gonna mess up a perfectly good swim day least you could do is have some answers. "Let's go in," she say like she got something up her sleeve. Only she don't lead the way. So me and Sugar turn the corner to where the entrance is, but when we get there I kinda hang back. Not that I'm scared, what's there to be afraid of, just a toy store. But I feel funny, shame. But what I got to be shamed about? Got as much right to go in as anybody. But somehow I can't seem to get hold of the door, so I step away from Sugar to lead. But she hangs back too. And I look at her and she looks at me and this is ridiculous. I mean, damn, I have never ever been shy about doing nothing or going nowhere. But then Mercedes steps up and then Rosie Giraffe and Big Butt crowd in behind and shove, and next thing we all stuffed into the doorway with only Mercedes squeezing past us, smoothing out her jumper and walking right down the aisle. Then the rest of us tumble in like a glued-together jigsaw done all wrong. And people lookin at us. And it's like the time me and Sugar crashed into the Catholic church on a dare. But once we got in there and everything so hushed and holy and the candles and the bowin and the handkerchiefs on all the drooping heads. I just couldn't go through with the plan. Which was for me to run up to the altar and do a tap dance while Sugar played the nose flute and messed around in the holy water. And Sugar kept givin me the elbow. Then later teased me so bad I tied her up in the shower and turned it on and locked her in. And she'd be there till this day if Aunt Gretchen hadn't finally figured I was lyin about the boarder takin a shower.

Same thing in the store. We all walkin on tiptoe and hardly touchin the games and puzzles and things. And I watched Miss Moore who is steady watchin us like she waitin for a sign. Like Mama Drewery watches the sky and sniffs the air and takes note of just how much slant is in the bird formation. Then me and Sugar bump smack into each other, so busy gazing at the toys, 'specially the sailboat. But we don't laugh and go into our fat-lady bump-stomach routine. We just stare at that price tag. Then Sugar run a finger over the whole boat. And I'm jealous and want to hit her. Maybe not her, but I sure want to punch somebody in the mouth.

"Watcha bring us here for, Miss Moore?"

"You sound angry, Sylvia. Are you mad about something?" Givin me one of them grins like she tellin a grown-up joke that never turns out to be funny. And she's lookin very closely at me like maybe she plannin to do my portrait from memory. I'm mad, but I won't give her that satisfaction. So I slouch around the store bein very bored and say, "Let's go."

Me and Sugar at the back of the train watchin the tracks whizzin by large then small then gettin gobbled up in the dark. I'm thinkin about this tricky toy I saw in the store. A clown that somersaults on a bar then does chin-ups just cause you yank lightly at his leg. Cost $35. I could see me askin my mother for a $35 birthday clown. "You wanna who that costs what?" she'd say, cocking her head to the side to get a better view of the hole in my head. Thirty-five dollars could buy new bunk beds for Junior and Gretchen's boy. Thirty-five dollars and the whole household could go visit Granddaddy Nelson in the country. Thirty-five dollars would pay for the rent and the piano bill too. Who are these people that spend that much for performing clowns and $1000 for toy sailboats? What kinda work they do and how they live and how come we ain't in on it? Where we are is who we are, Miss Moore always pointin out. But it don't necessarily have to be that way, she always adds then waits for somebody to say that poor people have to wake up and demand their share of the pie and don't none of us know what kind of pie she talking about in the first damn place. But she ain't so smart cause I still got her four dollars from the taxi and she sure ain't getting it. Messin up my day with this shit. Sugar nudges me in my pocket and winks.

45   Miss Moore lines us up in front of the mailbox where we started from, seem like years ago, and I got a headache for thinkin so hard. And we lean all over each other so we can hold up under the draggy-ass lecture she always finishes us off with at the end before we thank her for borin us to tears. But she just looks at us like she readin tea leaves. Finally she say, "Well, what did you think of F.A.O. Schwarz?"

Rosie Giraffe mumbles, "White folks crazy."

"I'd like to go there again when I get my birthday money," says Mercedes, and we shove her out the pack so she has to lean on the mailbox by herself.

"I'd like a shower. Tiring day," say Flyboy.

Then Sugar surprises me by sayin, "You know, Miss Moore, I don't think all of us here put together eat in a year what that sailboat costs." And Miss Moore lights up like somebody goosed her. "And?" she say, urging Sugar on. Only I'm standin on her foot so she don't continue.

50   "Imagine for a minute what kind of society it is in which some people can spend on a toy what it would cost to feed a family of six or seven. What do you think?"

"I think," say Sugar pushing me off her feet like she never done before, cause I whip her ass in a minute, "that this is not much of a democracy if you ask me. Equal chance to pursue happiness means an equal crack at the dough, don't it?" Miss Moore is beside herself and I am disgusted with Sugar's treachery. So I stand on her foot one more time to see if she'll shove me. She shuts up, and Miss Moore looks at me, sorrowfully I'm thinkin. And somethin weird is goin on, I can feel it in my chest.

"Anybody else learn anything today?" lookin dead at me. I walk away and Sugar has to run to catch up and don't even seem to notice when I shrug her arm off my shoulder.

"Well, we got four dollars anyway," she says.

"Uh hunh."

55   "We could go to Hascombs and get half a chocolate layer and then go to the Sunset and still have plenty of money for potato chips and ice cream sodas."

"Uh hunh."

"Race you to Hascombs," she say.

We start down the block and she gets ahead which is O.K. by me cause I'm going to the West End and then over to the Drive to think this day through. She can run if she want to and even run faster. But ain't nobody gonna beat me at nuthin.

◊   ◊   ◊

T. CORAGHESSAN BOYLE   (1948–   )

Greasy Lake   (1985)

It's about a mile down on the dark side of Route 88.

Bruce Springsteen

There was a time when courtesy and winning ways went out of style, when it was good to be bad, when you cultivated decadence like a taste. We were all danger-ous characters then. We wore torn-up leather jackets, slouched around with toothpicks in our mouths, sniffed glue and ether and what somebody claimed was cocaine. When we wheeled our parents' whining station wagons out into the street we left a patch of rubber half a block long. We drank gin and grape juice, Tango, Thunderbird, and Bali Hai. We were nineteen. We were bad. We read André Gide° and struck elaborate poses to show that we didn't give a shit about anything. At night, we went up to Greasy Lake.

Through the center of town, up the strip, past the housing developments and shopping malls, street lights giving way to the thin streaming illumination of the headlights, trees crowding the asphalt in a black unbroken wall: that was the way out to Greasy Lake. The Indians had called it Wakan, a reference to the clarity of its waters. Now it was fetid and murky, the mud banks glittering with broken glass and strewn with beer cans and the charred remains of bonfires. There was a single ravaged island a hundred yards from shore, so stripped of vegetation it looked as if the air force had strafed it. We went up to the lake because everyone went there, because we wanted to snuff the rich scent of possibility on the breeze, watch a girl take off her clothes and plunge into the festering murk, drink beer, smoke pot, howl at the stars, savor the incongruous full-throated roar of rock and roll against the primeval susurrus° of frogs and crickets. This was nature.

I was there one night, late, in the company of two dangerous characters. Digby wore a gold star in his right ear and allowed his father to pay his tuition at Cornell; Jeff was thinking of quitting school to become a painter/musician/head-shop proprietor. They were both expert in the social graces, quick with a sneer, able to manage a Ford with lousy shocks over a rutted and gutted blacktop road at eighty-five while rolling a joint as compact as a Tootsie Roll Pop stick. They could lounge against a bank of booming speakers and trade "man"s with the best of them or roll out across the dance floor as if their joints worked on bearings. They were slick and quick and they wore their mirror shades at breakfast and dinner, in the shower, in closets and caves. In short, they were bad.

I drove. Digby pounded the dashboard and shouted along with Toots & the Maytals while Jeff hung his head out the window and streaked the side of my mother's Bel Air with vomit. It was early June, the air soft as a hand on your cheek, the third night of summer vacation. The first two nights we'd been out till

---

André Gide: French novelist and critic (1869–1951) whose work — much of it semiautobiographical — examines the conflict between desire and discipline and shows individuals battling conventional morality.

susurrus: A whispering or rustling sound.

dawn, looking for something we never found. On this, the third night, we'd cruised the strip sixty-seven times, been in and out of every bar and club we could think of in a twenty-mile radius, stopped twice for bucket chicken and forty-cent hamburgers, debated going to a party at the house of a girl Jeff's sister knew, and chucked two dozen raw eggs at mailboxes and hitchhikers. It was 2:00 A.M.; the bars were closing. There was nothing to do but take a bottle of lemon-flavored gin up to Greasy Lake.

5   The taillights of a single car winked at us as we swung into the dirt lot with its tufts of weed and washboard corrugations; '57 Chevy, mint, metallic blue. On the far side of the lot, like the exoskeleton of some gaunt chrome insect, a chopper leaned against its kickstand. And that was it for excitement: some junkie half-wit biker and a car freak pumping his girlfriend. Whatever it was we were looking for, we weren't about to find it at Greasy Lake. Not that night.

But then all of a sudden Digby was fighting for the wheel. "Hey, that's Tony Lovett's car! Hey!" he shouted, while I stabbed at the brake pedal and the Bel Air nosed up to the gleaming bumper of the parked Chevy. Digby leaned on the horn, laughing, and instructed me to put my brights on. I flicked on the brights. This was hilarious. A joke. Tony would experience premature withdrawal and expect to be confronted by grim-looking state troopers with flashlights. We hit the horn, strobed the lights, and then jumped out of the car to press our witty faces to Tony's windows; for all we knew we might even catch a glimpse of some little fox's tit, and then we could slap backs with red-faced Tony, roughhouse a little, and go on to new heights of adventure and daring.

The first mistake, the one that opened the whole floodgate, was losing my grip on the keys. In the excitement, leaping from the car with the gin in one hand and a roach clip in the other, I spilled them in the grass — in the dark, rank, mysterious nighttime grass of Greasy Lake. This was a tactical error, as damaging and irreversible in its way as Westmoreland's decision to dig in at Khe Sanh.° I felt it like a jab of intuition, and I stopped there by the open door, peering vaguely into the night that puddled up round my feet.

The second mistake — and this was inextricably bound up with the first — was identifying the car as Tony Lovett's. Even before the very bad character in greasy jeans and engineer boots ripped out of the driver's door, I began to realize that this chrome blue was much lighter than the robin's-egg of Tony's car, and that Tony's car didn't have rear-mounted speakers. Judging from their expressions, Digby and Jeff were privately groping toward the same inevitable and unsettling conclusion as I was.

In any case, there was no reasoning with this bad greasy character — clearly he was a man of action. The first lusty Rockette° kick of his steel-toed boot caught me under the chin, chipped my favorite tooth, and left me sprawled in the

---

Khe Sanh: In late 1967, North Vietnamese and Viet Cong forces mounted a strong attack against American troops at Khe Sanh, thereby causing General William C. Westmoreland, commander of United States forces in Vietnam, to "dig in" to defend an area of relatively little tactical importance.

Rockette: The reference is to the Rockettes, a dancing troupe at New York's Radio City Music Hall noted for precision and cancan-like high kicks.

dirt. Like a fool, I'd gone down on one knee to comb the stiff hacked grass for the keys, my mind making connections in the most dragged-out, testudineous° way, knowing that things had gone wrong, that I was in a lot of trouble, and that the lost ignition key was my grail and my salvation. The three or four succeeding blows were mainly absorbed by my right buttock and the tough piece of bone at the base of my spine.

Meanwhile, Digby vaulted the kissing bumpers and delivered a savage kung-   10
fu blow to the greasy character's collarbone. Digby had just finished a course in martial arts for phys-ed credit and had spent the better part of the past two nights telling us apocryphal tales of Bruce Lee types and of the raw power invested in lightning blows shot from coiled wrists, ankles, and elbows. The greasy character was unimpressed. He merely backed off a step, his face like a Toltec mask, and laid Digby out with a single whistling roundhouse blow . . . but by now Jeff had got into the act, and I was beginning to extricate myself from the dirt, a tinny compound of shock, rage, and impotence wadded in my throat.

Jeff was on the guy's back, biting at his ear. Digby was on the ground, cursing. I went for the tire iron I kept under the driver's seat. I kept it there because bad characters always keep tire irons under the driver's seat, for just such an occasion as this. Never mind that I hadn't been involved in a fight since sixth grade, when a kid with a sleepy eye and two streams of mucus depending from his nostrils hit me in the knee with a Louisville slugger,° never mind that I'd touched the tire iron exactly twice before, to change tires: it was there. And I went for it.

I was terrified. Blood was beating in my ears, my hands were shaking, my heart turning over like a dirtbike in the wrong gear. My antagonist was shirtless, and a single cord of muscle flashed across his chest as he bent forward to peel Jeff from his back like a wet overcoat. "Motherfucker," he spat, over and over, and I was aware in that instant that all four of us — Digby, Jeff, and myself included — were chanting "motherfucker, motherfucker," as if it were a battle cry. (What happened next? the detective asks the murderer from beneath the turned-down brim of his porkpie hat. I don't know, the murderer says, something came over me. Exactly.)

Digby poked the flat of his hand in the bad character's face and I came at him like a kamikaze, mindless, raging, stung with humiliation — the whole thing, from the initial boot in the chin to this murderous primal instant involving no more than sixty hyperventilating, gland-flooding seconds — I came at him and brought the tire iron down across his ear. The effect was instantaneous, astonishing. He was a stunt man and this was Hollywood, he was a big grimacing toothy balloon and I was a man with a straight pin. He collapsed. Wet his pants. Went loose in his boots.

A single second, big as a zeppelin, floated by. We were standing over him in a circle, gritting our teeth, jerking our necks, our limbs and hands and feet twitching with glandular discharges. No one said anything. We just stared down at the guy, the car freak, the lover, the bad greasy character laid low. Digby looked at me; so did Jeff. I was still holding the tire iron, a tuft of hair clinging to the crook like dandelion fluff, like down. Rattled, I dropped it in the dirt, already envisioning

---

testudineous: Slow, like the pace of a tortoise.

Louisville slugger: A popular brand of baseball bat.

the headlines, the pitted faces of the police inquisitors, the gleam of handcuffs, clank of bars, the big black shadows rising from the back of the cell . . . when suddenly a raw torn shriek cut through me like all the juice in all the electric chairs in the country.

15   It was the fox. She was short, barefoot, dressed in panties and a man's shirt. "Animals!" she screamed, running at us with her fists clenched and wisps of blow-dried hair in her face. There was a silver chain round her ankle, and her toenails flashed in the glare of the headlights. I think it was the toenails that did it. Sure, the gin and the cannabis and even the Kentucky Fried may have had a hand in it, but it was the sight of those flaming toes that set us off — the toad emerging from the loaf in *Virgin Spring,*° lipstick smeared on a child: she was already tainted. We were on her like Bergman's deranged brothers — see no evil, hear none, speak none — panting, wheezing, tearing at her clothes, grabbing for flesh. We were bad characters, and we were scared and hot and three steps over the line — anything could have happened.

It didn't.

Before we could pin her to the hood of the car, our eyes masked with lust and greed and the purest primal badness, a pair of headlights swung into the lot. There we were, dirty, bloody, guilty, dissociated from humanity and civilization, the first of the Ur-crimes° behind us, the second in progress, shreds of nylon panty and spandex brassiere dangling from our fingers, our flies open, lips licked — there we were, caught in the spotlight. Nailed.

We bolted. First for the car, and then, realizing we had no way of starting it, for the woods. I thought nothing. I thought escape. The headlights came at me like accusing fingers. I was gone.

Ram-bam-bam, across the parking lot, past the chopper and into the feculent undergrowth at the lake's edge, insects flying up in my face, weeds whipping, frogs and snakes and red-eyed turtles splashing off into the night: I was already ankle-deep in muck and tepid water and still going strong. Behind me, the girl's screams rose in intensity, disconsolate, incriminating, the screams of the Sabine women,° the Christian martyrs, Anne Frank° dragged from the garret. I kept going, pursued by those cries, imagining cops and bloodhounds. The water was up to my knees when I realized what I was doing: I was going to swim for it. Swim the breadth of Greasy Lake and hide myself in the thick clot of woods on the far side. They'd never find me there.

Virgin Spring: A Film by Swedish director Ingmar Bergman.

Ur-crimes: Primitive crimes.

Sabine women: According to legend, members of an ancient Italian tribe abducted by Romans who took them for wives. The "Rape of the Sabine Women" has been depicted by various artists, most notably by seventeenth-century French painter Nicolas Poussin.

Anne Frank: German Jewish girl (1929–1945) whose family hid in an attic in Amsterdam during the Nazi occupation of the Netherlands. Frank, who along with her family was discovered by storm troopers and sent to die at the concentration camp at Belsen, is famous for her diary, which recounts her days in hiding. A new version of the diary containing five missing pages surfaced in 1998.

I was breathing in sobs, in gasps. The water lapped at my waist as I looked out   20
over the moon-burnished ripples, the mats of algae that clung to the surface like
scabs. Digby and Jeff had vanished. I paused. Listened. The girl was quieter now,
screams tapering to sobs, but there were male voices, angry, excited, and the high-
pitched ticking of the second car's engine. I waded deeper, stealthy, hunted, the
ooze sucking at my sneakers. As I was about to take the plunge — at the very instant I dropped my shoulder for the first slashing stroke — I blundered into something. Something unspeakable, obscene, something soft, wet, moss-grown. A
patch of weed? A log? When I reached out to touch it, it gave like a rubber duck,
it gave like flesh.

In one of those nasty little epiphanies for which we are prepared by films and
TV and childhood visits to the funeral home to ponder the shrunken painted
forms of dead grandparents, I understood what it was that bobbed there so inad-
missibly in the dark. Understood, and stumbled back in horror and revulsion, my
mind yanked in six different directions (I was nineteen, a mere child, an infant,
and here in the space of five minutes I'd struck down one greasy character and
blundered into the waterlogged carcass of a second), thinking, The keys, the keys,
why did I have to go and lose the keys? I stumbled back, but the muck took hold
of my feet — a sneaker snagged, balance lost — and suddenly I was pitching face
forward into the buoyant black mass, throwing out my hands in desperation while
simultaneously conjuring the image of reeking frogs and muskrats revolving in
slicks of their own deliquescing° juices. AAAAArrrgh! I shot from the water
like a torpedo, the dead man rotating to expose a mossy beard and eyes cold as the
moon. I must have shouted out, thrashing around in the weeds, because the voices
behind me suddenly became animated.

"What was that?"

"It's them, it's them: they tried to, tried to . . . *rape* me!" Sobs.

A man's voice, flat Midwestern accent. "You sons a bitches, we'll kill you!"

Frogs, crickets.   25

Then another voice, harsh, *r*-less, Lower East Side: "Motherfucker!" I recognized the verbal virtuosity of the bad greasy character in the engineer boots.
Tooth chipped, sneakers gone, coated in mud and slime and worse, crouching
breathless in the weeds waiting to have my ass thoroughly and definitively kicked
and fresh from the hideous stinking embrace of a three-days-dead-corpse, I suddenly felt a rush of joy and vindication: the son of a bitch was alive! Just as
quickly, my bowels turned to ice. "Come on out of there, you pansy mothers!" the
bad greasy character was screaming. He shouted curses till he was out of breath.

The crickets started up again, then the frogs. I held my breath. All at once
there was a sound in the reeds, a swishing, a splash: thunk-a-thunk. They were
throwing rocks. The frogs fell silent. I cradled my head. Swish, swish, thunk-a-
thunk. A wedge of feldspar the size of a cue ball glanced off my knee. I bit my
finger.

---

deliquescing: Melting.

It was then that they turned to the car. I heard a door slam, a curse, and then the sound of the headlights shattering — almost a good-natured sound, celebratory, like corks popping from the necks of bottles. This was succeeded by the dull booming of the fenders, metal on metal, and then the icy crash of the windshield. I inched forward, elbows and knees, my belly pressed to the muck, thinking of guerrillas and commandos and *The Naked and the Dead.*° I parted the weeds and squinted the length of the parking lot.

The second car — it was a Trans-Am — was still running, its high beams washing the scene in a lurid stagy light. Tire iron flailing, the greasy bad character was laying into the side of my mother's Bel Air like an avenging demon, his shadow riding up the trunks of the trees. Whomp. Whomp. Whomp-whomp. The other two guys — blond types, in fraternity jackets — were helping out with tree branches and skull-sized boulders. One of them was gathering up bottles, rocks, muck, candy wrappers, used condoms, pop-tops, and other refuse and pitching it through the window on the driver's side. I could see the fox, a white bulb behind the windshield of the '57 Chevy. "Bobbie," she whined over the thumping, "come *on.*" The greasy character paused a moment, took one good swipe at the left tail-light, and then heaved the tire iron halfway across the lake. Then he fired up the '57 and was gone.

30   Blond head nodded at blond head. One said something to the other, too low for me to catch. They were no doubt thinking that in helping to annihilate my mother's car they'd committed a fairly rash act, and thinking too that there were three bad characters connected with that very car watching them from the woods. Perhaps other possibilities occurred to them as well — police, jail cells, justices of the peace, reparations, lawyers, irate parents, fraternal censure. Whatever they were thinking, they suddenly dropped branches, bottles, and rocks and sprang for their car in unison, as if they'd choreographed it. Five seconds. That's all it took. The engine shrieked, the tires squealed, a cloud of dust rose from the rutted lot and then settled back on darkness.

I don't know how long I lay there, the bad breath of decay all around me, my jacket heavy as a bear, the primordial ooze subtly reconstituting itself to accommodate my upper thighs and testicles. My jaws ached, my knee throbbed, my coccyx° was on fire. I contemplated suicide, wondered if I'd need bridgework, scraped the recesses of my brain for some sort of excuse to give my parents — a tree had fallen on the car, I was blindsided by a bread truck, hit and run, vandals had got to it while we were playing chess at Digby's. Then I thought of the dead man. He was probably the only person on the planet worse off than I was. I thought about him, fog on the lake, insects chirring eerily, and felt the tug of fear, felt the darkness opening up inside me like a set of jaws. Who was he, I wondered, this victim of time and circumstance bobbing sorrowfully in the lake at my back. The owner of the chopper, no doubt, a bad older character come to this.

The Naked and the Dead: A popular and critically successful 1948 novel by Norman Mailer depicting United States Army life during World War II.

coccyx: Tailbone.

Shot during a murky drug deal, drowned while drunkenly frolicking in the lake. Another headline. My car was wrecked; he was dead.

When the eastern half of the sky went from black to cobalt and the trees began to separate themselves from the shadows, I pushed myself up from the mud and stepped out into the open. By now the birds had begun to take over for the crickets, and dew lay slick on the leaves. There was a smell in the air, raw and sweet at the same time, the smell of the sun firing buds and opening blossoms. I contemplated the car. It lay there like a wreck along the highway, like a steel sculpture left over from a vanished civilization. Everything was still. This was nature.

I was circling the car, as dazed and bedraggled as the sole survivor of an air blitz, when Digby and Jeff emerged from the trees behind me. Digby's face was crosshatched with smears of dirt; Jeff's jacket was gone and his shirt was torn across the shoulder. They slouched across the lot, looking sheepish, and silently came up beside me to gape at the ravaged automobile. No one said a word. After a while Jeff swung open the driver's door and began to scoop the broken glass and garbage off the seat. I looked at Digby. He shrugged. "At least they didn't slash the tires," he said.

It was true: the tires were intact. There was no windshield, the headlights were staved in, and the body looked as if it had been sledgehammered for a quarter a shot at the county fair, but the tires were inflated to regulation pressure. The car was drivable. In silence, all three of us bent to scrape the mud and shattered glass from the interior. I said nothing about the biker. When we were finished, I reached in my pocket for the keys, experienced a nasty stab of recollection, cursed myself, and turned to search the grass. I spotted them almost immediately, no more than five feet from the open door, glinting like jewels in the first tapering shaft of sunlight. There was no reason to get philosophical about it: I eased into the seat and turned the engine over.

It was at that precise moment that the silver Mustang with the flame decals 35 rumbled into the lot. All three of us froze; then Digby and Jeff slid into the car and slammed the door. We watched as the Mustang rocked and bobbed across the ruts and finally jerked to a halt beside the forlorn chopper at the far end of the lot. "Let's go," Digby said. I hesitated, the Bel Air wheezing beneath me.

Two girls emerged from the Mustang. Tight jeans, stiletto heels, hair like frozen fur. They bent over the motorcycle, paced back and forth aimlessly, glanced once or twice at us, and then ambled over to where the reeds sprang up in a green fence round the perimeter of the lake. One of them cupped her hands to her mouth. "Al," she called, "Hey, Al!"

"Come on," Digby hissed. "Let's get out of here."

But it was too late. The second girl was picking her way across the lot, unsteady on her heels, looking up at us and then away. She was older — twenty-five or -six — and as she came closer we could see there was something wrong with her: she was stoned or drunk, lurching now and waving her arms for balance. I gripped the steering wheel as if it were the ejection lever of a flaming jet, and Digby spat out my name, twice, terse and impatient.

"Hi," the girl said.

40   We looked at her like zombies, like war veterans, like deaf-and-dumb pencil peddlers.

She smiled, her lips cracked and dry. "Listen," she said, bending from the waist to look in the window, "you guys seen Al?" Her pupils were pinpoints, her eyes glass. She jerked her neck. "That's his bike over there — Al's. You seen him?"

Al. I didn't know what to say. I wanted to get out of the car and retch, I wanted to go home to my parents' house and crawl into bed. Digby poked me in the ribs. "We haven't seen anybody," I said.

The girl seemed to consider this, reaching out a slim veiny arm to brace herself against the car. "No matter," she said, slurring the *t*'s, "he'll turn up." And then, as if she'd just taken stock of the whole scene — the ravaged car and our battered faces, the desolation of the place — she said: "Hey, you guys look like some pretty bad characters — been fightin', huh?" We stared straight ahead, rigid as catatonics. She was fumbling in her pocket and muttering something. Finally she held out a handful of tablets in glassine wrappers: "Hey, you want to party, you want to do some of these with me and Sarah?"

I just looked at her. I thought I was going to cry. Digby broke the silence. "No, thanks," he said, leaning over me. "Some other time."

45   I put the car in gear and it inched forward with a groan, shaking off pellets of glass like an old dog shedding water after a bath, heaving over the ruts on its worn springs, creeping toward the highway. There was a sheen of sun on the lake. I looked back. The girl was still standing there, watching us, her shoulders slumped, hand outstretched.

◇   ◇   ◇

JUNOT DIAZ (1968 –   )

Aguantado (1996)

I

I lived without a father for the first nine years of my life. He was in the States, working, and the only way I knew him was through the photographs my mom kept in a plastic sandwich bag under her bed. Since our zinc roof leaked, almost everything we owned was water-stained: our clothes, Mami's Bible, her makeup, whatever food we had, Abuelo's tools, our cheap wooden furniture. It was only because of that plastic bag that any pictures of my father survived.

When I thought of Papi I thought of one shot specifically. Taken days before the U.S. invasion: 1965. I wasn't even alive then; Mami had been pregnant with my first never-born brother and Abuelo could still see well enough to hold a job. You know the sort of photograph I'm talking about. Scalloped edges, mostly brown in color. On the back my moms's cramped handwriting — the date, his name, even the street, one over from our house. He was dressed in his Guardia uniform, his tan cap at an angle on his shaved head, an unlit Constitución squeezed between his lips. His dark unsmiling eyes were my own.

I did not think of him often. He had left for Nueva York when I was four but since I couldn't remember a single moment with him I excused him from all nine years of my life. On the days I had to imagine him — not often, since Mami didn't much speak of him anymore —he was the soldier in the photo. He was a cloud of cigar smoke, the traces of which could still be found on the uniforms he'd left behind. He was pieces of my friends' fathers, of the domino players on the corner, pieces of Mami and Abuelo. I didn't know him at all. I didn't know that he'd abandoned us. That this waiting for him was all a sham.

We lived south of the Cementerio Nacional in a wood-frame house with three rooms. We were poor. The only way we could have been poorer was to have lived in the campo or to have been Haitian immigrants, and Mami regularly offered these to us as brutal consolation.

At least you're not in the campo. You'd eat rocks then.   5

We didn't eat rocks but we didn't eat meat or beans, either. Almost everything on our plates was boiled: boiled yuca, boiled platano, boiled guineo,° maybe with a piece of cheese or a shred of bacalao.° On the best days the cheese and the platanos were fried. When me and Rafa caught our annual case of worms it was only by skimping on our dinners that Mami could afford to purchase the Verminox. I can't remember how many times I crouched over our latrine, my teeth clenched, watching long gray parasites slide out from between my legs.

At Mauricio Baez, our school, the kids didn't bother us too much, even though we couldn't afford the uniforms or proper mascotas.° The uniforms Mami could do nothing about but with the mascotas she improvised, sewing together sheets of loose paper she had collected from her friends. We each had one pencil and if we lost that pencil, like I did once, we had to stay home from school until Mami could borrow another one for us. Our profesor had us share school books with some of the other kids and these kids wouldn't look at us, tried to hold their breath when we were close to them.

Mami worked at Embajador Chocolate, putting in ten-, twelve-hour shifts for almost no money at all. She woke up every morning at seven and I got up with her because I could never sleep late, and while she drew the water out of our steel drum I brought the soap from the kitchen. There were always leaves and spiders in the water but Mami could draw a clean bucket better than anyone. She was a tiny woman and in the water closet she looked even smaller, her skin dark and her hair surprisingly straight and across her stomach and back the scars from the rocket attack she'd survived in 1965. None of the scars showed when she wore clothes, though if you embraced her you'd feel them hard under your wrist, against the soft part of your palm.

Abuelo was supposed to watch us while Mami was at work but usually he was visiting with his friends or out with his trap. A few years back, when the rat problem in the barrio° had gotten out of hand (Those malditos° were running off with kids, Abuelo told me), he had built himself a trap. A destroyer. He never charged

---

yuca, platano, guineo: Cactus, banana, fig.

bacalao: Cod fish.

mascotas: Mascots.

barrio: Neighborhood.

malditos: Literally, "accursed." A slur.

anyone for using it, something Mami would have done; his only commission was that he be the one to arm the steel bar. I've seen this thing chop off fingers, he explained to the borrowers but in truth he just liked having something to do, a job of some kind. In our house alone Abuelo had killed a dozen rats and in one house on Tunti, forty of these motherfuckers were killed during a two-night massacre. He spent both nights with the Tunti people, resetting the trap and burning the blood and when he came back he was grinning and tired, his white hair everywhere, and my mother had said, You look like you've been out getting ass.

10   Without Abuelo around, me and Rafa did anything we wanted. Mostly Rafa hung out with his friends and I played with our neighbor Wilfredo. Sometimes I climbed trees. There wasn't a tree in the barrio I couldn't climb and on some days I spent entire afternoons in our trees, watching the barrio in motion and when Abuelo was around (and awake) he talked to me about the good old days, when a man could still make a living from his finca,° when the United States wasn't something folks planned on.

Mami came home after sunset, just when the day's worth of drinking was starting to turn some of the neighbors wild. Our barrio was not the safest of places and Mami usually asked one of her co-workers to accompany her home. These men were young, and some of them were unmarried. Mami let them walk her but she never invited them into the house. She barred the door with her arm while she said good-bye, just to show them that nobody was getting in. Mami might have been skinny, a bad thing on the Island, but she was smart and funny and that's hard to find anywhere. Men were drawn to her. From my perch I'd watched more than one of these Porfirio Rubirosas° say, See you tomorrow, and then park his ass across the street just to see if she was playing hard to get. Mami never knew these men were there and after about fifteen minutes of staring expectantly at the front of our house even the loneliest of these fulanos° put their hats on and went home.

We could never get Mami to do anything after work, even cook dinner, if she didn't first sit awhile in her rocking chair. She didn't want to hear nothing about our problems, the scratches we'd put into our knees, who said what. She'd sit on the back patio with her eyes closed and let the bugs bite mountains onto her arms and legs. Sometimes I climbed the guanábana tree and when she'd open her eyes and catch me smiling down on her, she'd close them again and I would drop twigs onto her until she laughed.

II

When times were real flojo,° when the last colored bill flew out Mami's purse, she packed us off to our relatives. She'd use Wilfredo's father's phone and make the calls early in the morning. Lying next to Rafa, I'd listen to her soft unhurried re-

---

finca: Farm.

Rubirosas: The reference to Porfirio Rubirosa (1909–1965), is a famous Dominican diplomat said to be a playboy.

fulanos: Guys, or "so-and-sos."

flojo: Loose.

quests and pray for the day that our relatives would tell her to vete pa'l carajo°
but that never happened in Santo Domingo.

Usually Rafa stayed with our tíos° in Ocoa and I went to tía° Miranda's in
Boca Chica. Sometimes we both went to Ocoa. Neither Boca Chica nor Ocoa
were far but I never wanted to go and it normally took hours of cajoling before I
agreed to climb on the autobus.

How long? I asked Mami truculently.

Not long, she promised me, examining the scabs on the back of my shaved　15
head. A week. Two at the most.

How many days is that?

Ten, twenty.

You'll be fine, Rafa told me, spitting into the gutter.

How do you know? You a brujo°?　　　　　　　　　　　　　　　　　　　20

Yeah, he said, smiling, that's me.

He didn't mind going anywhere; he was at that age when all he wanted was to
be away from the family, meeting people he had not grown up with.

Everybody needs a vacation, Abuelo explained happily. Enjoy yourself. You'll
be down by the water. And just think about all the food you'll eat.

I never wanted to be away from the family. Intuitively, I knew how easily distances could harden and become permanent. On the ride to Boca Chica I was always too depressed to notice the ocean, the young boys fishing and selling cocos
by the side of the road, the surf exploding into the air like a cloud of shredded
silver.

Tía Miranda had a nice block house, with a shingled roof and a tiled floor that　25
her cats had trouble negotiating. She had a set of matching furniture and a television and faucets that worked. All her neighbors were administrators and hombres de negocios° and you had to walk three blocks to find any sort of colmado.°
It was *that* sort of neighborhood. The ocean was never far away and most of the
time I was down by the beach playing with the local kids, turning black in the sun.

Tía wasn't really related to Mami; she was my madrina,° which was why she
took me and my brother in every now and then. No money, though. She never
loaned money to anyone, even to her drunkard of an ex-husband, and Mami must
have known because she never asked. Tía was about fifty and rail-thin and
couldn't put anything in her hair to make it forget itself; her perms never lasted
more than a week before the enthusiasm of her kink returned. She had two kids
of her own, Yennifer and Bienvenido, but she didn't dote on them the way she
doted on me. Her lips were always on me and during meals she watched me like
she was waiting for the poison to take effect.

---

vete pa'l carajo: Go to hell.

tíos: Uncles.

tía: Aunt.

brujo: Wizard, sorcerer.

hombres de negocios: Businessmen.

colmado: A small store or bar.

madrina: Godmother.

I bet this isn't something you've eaten lately, she'd say.

I'd shake my head and Yennifer, who was eighteen and bleached her hair, would say, Leave him alone, Mamá.

Tía also had a penchant for uttering cryptic one-liners about my father, usually after she'd downed a couple of shots of Brugal.

30   *He took too much.*

If only your mother could have noticed his true nature earlier.

He should see how he has left you.

The weeks couldn't pass quickly enough. At night I went down by the water to be alone but that wasn't possible. Not with the tourists making apes out of themselves, and with the tígueres° waiting to rob them.

Las Tres Marías, I pointed out to myself in the sky. They were the only stars I knew.

35   But then one day I'd walk into the house from swimming and Mami and Rafa would be in the living room, holding glasses of sweet lemon-milk.

You're back, I'd say, trying to hide the excitement in my voice.

I hope he behaved himself, Mami would be saying to Tía. Her hair would be cut, her nails painted; she'd have on the same red dress she wore on every one of her outings.

Rafa smiling, slapping me on the shoulder, darker than I'd last seen him. How ya doing, Yunior? You miss me or what?

I'd sit next to him and he'd put his arm around me and we'd listen to Tía telling Mami how well I behaved and all the different things I'd eaten.

III

40 The year Papi came for us, the year I was nine, we expected nothing. There were no signs to speak of. Dominican chocolate was not especially in demand that season and the Puerto Rican owners laid off the majority of the employees for a couple of months. Good for the owners, un desastre° for us. After that, Mami was around the house all the time. Unlike Rafa, who hid his shit well, I was always in trouble. From punching out Wilfredo to chasing somebody's chickens until they passed out from exhaustion. Mami wasn't a hitter; she preferred having me kneel on pebbles with my face against a wall. On the afternoon that the letter arrived, she caught me trying to stab our mango tree with Abuelo's machete. Back to the corner. Abuelo was supposed to make sure I served my ten minutes but he was too busy whittling to bother. He let me up after three minutes and I hid in the bedroom until he said, OK, in a voice that Mami could hear. Then I went to the smokehouse, rubbing my knees, and Mami looked up from peeling platanos.

You better learn, muchacho, or you'll be kneeling the rest of your life.

I watched the rain that had been falling all day. No, I won't, I told her.

You talking back to me?

---

tígueres: Street kids, hoodlums.

un desastre: A disaster.

She whacked me on the nalgas° and I ran outside to look for Wilfredo. I found him under the eaves of his house, the wind throwing pieces of rain onto his dark-dark face. We shook hands elaborately. I called him Muhammad Ali and he called me Sinbad; these were our Northamerican names. We were both in shorts; a disintegrating pair of sandals clung to his toes.

What you got? I asked him.   45

Boats, he said, holding up the paper wedges his father had folded for us. This one's mine.

What does the winner get?

A gold trophy, about this big.

Ok, cabrón, I'm in. Don't let go before me.

OK, he said, stepping to the other side of the gutter. We had a clear run down   50
to the street corner. No cars were parked on our side, except for a drowned Monarch and there was plenty of room between its tires and the curb for us to navigate through.

We completed five runs before I noticed that somebody had parked their battered motorcycle in front of my house.

Who's that? Wilfredo asked me, dropping his soggy boat into the water again.

I don't know, I said.

Go find out.

I was already on my way. The motorcycle driver came out before I could reach   55
out front door. He mounted quickly and was gone in a cloud of exhaust.

Mami and Abuelo were on the back patio, conversating. Abuelo was angry and his cane-cutter's hands were clenched. I hadn't seen Abuelo bravo in a long time, not since his produce truck had been stolen by two of his old employees.

Go outside, Mami told me.

Who was that?

Did I tell you something?

Was that somebody we know?   60

Outside, Mami said, her voice a murder about to happen.

What's wrong? Wilfredo asked me when I rejoined him. His nose was starting to run.

I don't know, I said.

When Rafa showed himself an hour later, swaggering in from a game of pool, I'd already tried to speak to Mami and Abuelo like five times. The last time, Mami had landed a slap on my neck and Wilfredo told me that he could see the imprints of her fingers on my skin. I told it all to Rafa.

That doesn't sound good. He threw out his guttering cigarette. You wait here.   65
He went around the back and I heard his voice and then Mami's. No yelling, no argument.

Come on, he said. She wants us to wait in our room.

Why?

---

nalgas: Backside.

That's what she said. You want me to tell her no?

Not while she's mad.

70   Exactly.

I slapped Wilfredo's hand and walked in the front door with Rafa. What's going on?

She got a letter from Papi.

Really? Is there money?

No.

75   What does it say?

How should I know?

He sat down on his side of the bed and produced a pack of cigarettes. I watched him go through the elaborate ritual of lighting up — the flip of the thin cigarrillo into his lips and then the spark, a single practiced snap of the thumb.

Where'd you get that lighter?

Mi novia° gave it to me.

80   Tell her to give me one.

Here. He tossed it to me. You can have it if you shut up.

Yeah?

See. He reached to take it. You already lost it.

I shut my mouth and he settled back down on the bed.

85   Hey, Sinbad, Wilfredo said, his head appearing in our window. What's going on?

My father wrote us a letter!

Rafa rapped me on the side of my head. This is a *family* affair, Yunior. Don't blab it all over the place.

Wilfredo smiled. I ain't going to tell anybody.

Of course you're not, Rafa said. Because if you do I'll chop your fucking head off.

90   I tried to wait it out. Our room was nothing more than a section of the house that Abuelo had partitioned off with planks of wood. In one corner Mami kept an altar with candles and a cigar in a stone mortar and a glass of water and two toy soldiers we could not touch ever and above the bed hung our mosquito netting, poised to drop on us like a net. I lay back and listened to the rain brushing back and forth across our zinc roof.

Mami served dinner, watched as we ate it, and then ordered us back into our room. I'd never seen her so blank-faced, so stiff, and when I tried to hug her she pushed me away. Back to bed, she said. Back to listening to the rain. I must have fallen asleep because when I woke up Rafa was looking at me pensively and it was dark outside and nobody else in the house was awake.

I read the letter, he told me quietly. He was sitting cross-legged on the bed, his ribs laddering his chest in shadows. Papi says he's coming.

Really?

Don't believe it.

95   Why?

Mi novia: My fiancée.

It ain't the first time he's made that promise, Yunior.
Oh, I said.
Outside Señora Tejada started singing to herself, badly.
Rafa?
Yeah?   100
I didn't know you could read.
I was nine and couldn't even write my own name.
Yeah, he said quietly. Something I picked up. Now go to bed.

IV

Rafa was right. It wasn't the first time. Two years after he left, Papi wrote her saying he was coming for us and like an innocent Mami believed him. After being
alone for two years she was ready to believe anything. She showed everybody his
letter and even spoke to him on the phone. He wasn't an easy man to reach but
on this occasion she got through and he reassured her that yes, he was coming. His
word was his bond. He even spoke to us, something that Rafa vaguely remembers,
a lot of crap about how much he loved us and that we should take care of Mami.

She prepared a party, even lined up to have a goat there for the slaughtering.   105
She bought me and Rafa new clothes and when he didn't show she sent everybody
home, sold the goat back to its owner and then almost lost her mind. I remember
the heaviness of that month, thicker than almost anything. When Abuelo tried
to reach our father at the phone numbers he'd left none of the men who'd lived
with him knew anything about where he had gone.

It didn't help matters that me and Rafa kept asking her when we were leaving
for the States, when Papi was coming. I am told that I wanted to see his picture
almost every day. It's hard for me to imagine myself this way, crazy about Papi.
When she refused to show me the photos I threw myself about like I was on fire.
And, I screamed. Even as a boy my voice carried farther than a man's, turned
heads on the street.

First Mami tried slapping me quiet but that did little. Then she locked me in
my room where my brother told me to cool it but I shook my head and screamed
louder. I was inconsolable. I learned to tear my clothes because this was the one
thing I had whose destruction hurt my mother. She took all my shirts from my
room, left me only with shorts which were hard to damage with bare fingers. I
pulled a nail from our wall and punched a dozen holes in each pair, until Rafa
cuffed me and said, Enough, you little puto.°

Mami spent a lot of time out of the house, at work or down by the Malecón,
where she could watch the waves shred themselves against the rocks, where men
offered cigarettes that she smoked quietly. I don't know how long this went on.
Months, maybe three. Then, one morning in early spring, when the amapolas were
flushed with their flame leaves, I woke up and found Abuelo alone in the house.

She's gone, he said. So cry all you want, malcriado.°

---

puto: Male prostitute.
malcriado: Badly raised.

110   I learned later from Rafa that she was in Ocoa with our tíos.

Mami's time away was never discussed, then or now. When she returned to us, five weeks later, she was thinner and darker and her hands were heavy with calluses. She looked younger, like the girl who had arrived in Santo Domingo fifteen years before, burning to be married. Her friends came and sat and talked and when Papi's name was mentioned her eyes dimmed and when his name left, the darkness of her ojos° returned and she would laugh, a small personal thunder that cleared the air.

She didn't treat me badly on her return but we were no longer as close; she did not call me her Prieto or bring me chocolates from her work. That seemed to suit her fine. And I was young enough to grow out of her rejection. I still had baseball and my brother. I still had trees to climb and lizards to tear apart.

V

The week after the letter came I watched her from my trees. She ironed cheese sandwiches in paper bags for our lunch, boiled platanos for our dinner. Our dirty clothes were pounded clean in the concrete trough on the side of the outhouse. Every time she thought I was scrabbling too high in the branches she called me back to the ground. You ain't Spiderman, you know, she said, rapping the top of my head with her knuckles. On the afternoons that Wilfredo's father came over to play dominos and talk politics, she sat with him and Abuelo and laughed at their campo stories. She seemed more normal to me but I was careful not to provoke her. There was still something volcanic about the way she held herself.

On Saturday a late hurricane passed close to the Capital and the next day folks were talking about how high the waves were down by the Malecón.° Some children had been lost, swept out to sea and Abuelo shook his head when he heard the news. You'd think the sea would be sick of us by now, he said.

115   That Sunday Mami gathered us on the back patio. We're taking a day off, she announced. A day for us as a family.

We don't need a day off, I said and Rafa hit me harder than normal.

Shut up, OK?

I tried to hit him back but Abuelo grabbed us both by the arm. Don't make me have to crack your heads open, he said.

She dressed and put her hair up and even paid for a concho instead of crowding us into an autobus. The driver actually wiped the seats down with a towel while we waited and I said to him, It don't look dirty, and he said, Believe me, muchacho, it is. Mami looked beautiful and many of the men she passed wanted to know where she was heading. We couldn't afford it but she paid for a movie anyway. *The Five Deadly Venoms.* Kung fu movies were the only ones the theaters played in those days. I sat between Mami and Abuelo. Rafa moved to the back, joining a group of boys who were smoking, and arguing with them about some baseball player on Licey.°

---

ojos: Eyes.

Malecón: Sea wall.

Licey: A town in the Dominican Republic.

After the show Mami bought us flavored ices and while we ate them we   120
watched the salamanders crawling around on the sea rocks. The waves were
tremendous and some parts of George Washington were flooded and cars were
churning through the water slowly.

A man in a red guayabera° stopped by us. He lit a cigarette and turned to my
mother, his collar turned up by the wind. So where are you from?

Santiago, she answered.

Rafa snorted.

You must be visiting relatives then.

Yes, she said. My husband's family.   125

He nodded. He was dark-skinned, with light-colored spots about his neck and
hands. His fingers trembled slightly as he worked the cigarette to his lips. I hoped
he'd drop his cigarette, just so I could see what the ocean would do to it. We had
to wait almost a full minute before he said buenos días° and walked away.

What a crazy, Abuelo said.

Rafa lifted up his fist. You should have given me the signal. I would have
kung-fu-punched him in the head.

Your father came at me better than that, Mami said.

Abuelo stared down at the back of his hands, at the long white hairs that   130
covered them. He looked embarrassed.

Your father asked me if I wanted a cigarette and then he gave me the whole
pack to show me that he was a big man.

I held on to the rail. Here?

Oh no, she said. She turned around and looked out over the traffic. That part
of the city isn't here anymore.

VI

Rafa used to think that he'd come in the night, like Jesus, that one morning
we'd find him at our breakfast table, unshaven and smiling. Too real to be believed.
He'll be taller, Rafa predicted. Northamerican food makes people that way. He'd
surprise Mami on her way back from work, pick her up in a German car. Say nothing to the man walking her home. She would not know what to say and neither
would he. They'd drive down to the Malecón and he'd take her to see a movie,
because that's how they met and that's how he'd want to start it again.

I would see him coming from my trees. A man with swinging hands and eyes
like mine. He'd have gold on his fingers, cologne on his neck, a silk shirt, good   135
leather shoes. The whole barrio would come out to greet him.

He'd kiss Mami and Rafa and shake Abuelo's reluctant hand and then he'd see
me behind everyone else. What's wrong with that one? he'd ask and Mami would
say, He doesn't know you. Squatting down so that his pale yellow dress socks
showed, he'd trace the scars on my arms and on my head. Yunior, he'd finally say,
his stubbled face in front of mine, his thumb tracing a circle on my cheek.

◇　◇　◇

---

guayabera: An embroidered shirt.

buenos días: Good day.

CHITRA BANERJEE DIVAKARUNI   (1956–   )

The Disappearance   (1995)

At first when they heard about the disappearance, people didn't believe it.

Why, we saw her just yesterday at the Ram Ratan Indian Grocery, friends said, picking out radishes for pickling. And wasn't she at the Mountain View park with her little boy last week, remember, we waved from our car and she waved back, she was in that blue *salwaar-kameez*, yes, she never did wear American clothes. And the boy waved too, he must be, what, two and a half? Looks just like her with those big black eyes, that dimple. What a shame, they said, it's getting so that you aren't safe anywhere in this country nowadays.

Because that's what everyone suspected, including the husband. Crime. Otherwise, he said to the investigating policeman (he had called the police that very night), how could a young Indian woman wearing a yellow-flowered *kurta* and Nike walking shoes just *disappear*? She'd been out for her evening walk, she took one every day after he got back from the office. Yes, yes, always alone, she said that was her time for herself. (He didn't quite understand that, but he was happy to watch his little boy, play ball with him, perhaps, until she returned to serve them dinner.)

Did you folks have a quarrel, asked the policeman, looking up from his notepad with a frown, and the husband looked directly back into his eyes and said, No, of course we didn't.

5   Later he would think about what the policeman had asked, while he sat in front of his computer in his office, or while he lay in the bed which still seemed to smell of her. (But surely that was his imagination — the linen had been washed already.) He *had* told the truth about them not having a quarrel, hadn't he? (He prided himself on being an honest man, he often told his son how important it was not to lie, see what happened to Pinocchio's nose. And even now when the boy asked him where Mama was, he didn't say she had gone on a trip, as some of his friends' wives had advised him. I don't know, he said. And when the boy's thin face would crumple, want Mama, when she coming back, he held him in his lap awkwardly and tried to stroke his hair, like he had seen his wife do, but he couldn't bring himself to say what the boy needed to hear, *soon-soon*. I don't know, he said over and over.)

They hadn't really had a fight. She wasn't, thank God, the quarrelsome type, like some of his friends' wives. Quiet. That's how she was, at least around him, although sometimes when he came home unexpectedly he would hear her singing to her son, her voice slightly off-key but full and confident. Or laughing as she chased him around the family room, Mama's going to get you, get you, both of them shrieking with delight until they saw him. Hush now, she would tell the boy, settle down, and they would walk over sedately to give him his welcome-home kiss.

He couldn't complain, though. Wasn't that what he had specified when his mother started asking, When are you getting married, I'm getting old, I want to see a grandson before I die.

If you can find me a quiet, pretty girl, he wrote, not brash, like Calcutta girls are nowadays, not with too many western ideas. Someone who would be relieved to have her husband make the major decisions. But she had to be smart, at least a year of college, someone he could introduce to his friends with pride.

He'd flown to Calcutta to view several suitable girls that his mother had picked out. But now, thinking back, he can only remember her. She had sat, head bowed, jasmine plaited into her hair, silk sari draped modestly over her shoulders, just like all the other prospective brides he'd seen. Nervous, he'd thought, yearning to be chosen. But when she'd glanced up there had been a cool, considering look in her eyes. Almost disinterested, almost as though *she* were wondering if he would make a suitable spouse. He had wanted her then, had married her within the week in spite of his mother's protests (had she caught that same look?) that something about the girl just didn't feel *right*.

He was a good husband. No one could deny it. He let her have her way, in-   10
dulged her, even. When the kitchen was remodeled, for example, and she wanted pink and gray tiles even though he preferred white. Or when she wanted to go to Yosemite Park instead of Reno, although he knew he would be dreadfully bored among all those bearshit-filled trails and dried-up waterfalls. Once in a while, of course, he had to put his foot down, like when she wanted to get a job or go back to school or buy American clothes. But he always softened his no's with a remark like, What for, I'm here to take care of you, or, You look so much prettier in your Indian clothes, so much more feminine. He would pull her onto his lap and give her a kiss and a cuddle which usually ended with him taking her to the bedroom.

That was another area where he'd had to be firm. Sex. She was always saying, Please, not tonight, I don't feel up to it. He didn't mind that. She was, after all, a well-bred Indian girl. He didn't expect her to behave like those American women he sometimes watched on X-rated videos, screaming and biting and doing other things he grew hot just thinking about. But her reluctance went beyond womanly modesty. After dinner for instance she would start on the most elaborate household projects, soaping down the floors, changing the liners in cabinets. The night before she disappeared she'd started cleaning windows, taken out the Windex and the rags as soon as she'd put the boy to bed, even though he said, Let's go. Surely he couldn't be blamed for raising his voice at those times (though never so much as to wake his son), or for grabbing her by the elbow and pulling her to the bed, like he did that last night. He was always careful not to hurt her, he prided himself on that. Not even a little slap, not like some of the men he'd known growing up, or even some of his friends now. And he always told himself he'd stop if she really begged him, if she cried. After some time, though, she would quit struggling and let him do what he wanted. But that was nothing new. That could have nothing to do with the disappearance.

Two weeks passed and there was no news of the woman, even though the husband had put a notice in the *San Jose Mercury* as well as a half-page ad in *India West*, which he photocopied and taped to neighborhood lampposts. The ad had a photo of her, a close-up taken in too-bright sunlight where she gazed gravely at something beyond the camera. WOMAN MISSING, read the ad. REWARD $100,000. (How on earth would he come up with that kind of money, asked his friends. The husband confessed that it would be difficult, but he'd manage somehow. His wife was more important to him, after all, than all the money in the world. And to prove it he went to the bank the very same day and brought home a sheaf of forms to fill so that he could take out a second mortgage on the house.) He kept calling the police station, too, but the police weren't much help. They were working on it, they said. They'd checked the local hospitals and morgues, the shelters. They'd even sent her description to other states. But there were no leads. It didn't look very hopeful.

So finally he called India and over a faulty long-distance connection that made his voice echo eerily in his ear told his mother what had happened. My poor boy, she cried, left all alone (the word flickered unpleasantly across his brain, *left, left*), how can you possibly cope with the household and a child as well. And when he admitted that yes, it was very difficult, could she perhaps come and help out for a while if it wasn't too much trouble, she had replied that of course she would come right away and stay as long as he needed her, and what was all this American nonsense about too much trouble, he was her only son, wasn't he. She would contact the wife's family too, she ended, so he wouldn't have to deal with that awkwardness.

Within a week she had closed up the little flat she had lived in since her husband's death, got hold of a special family emergency visa, and was on her way. Almost as though she'd been waiting for something like this to happen, said some of the women spitefully. (These were his wife's friends, though maybe acquaintances would be a more accurate word. His wife had liked to keep to herself, which had been just fine with him. He was glad, he'd told her several times, that she didn't spend hours chattering on the phone like the other Indian wives.)

15   He was angry when this gossip reached him (perhaps because he'd had the same insidious thought for a moment when, at the airport, he noticed how happy his mother looked, her flushed excited face appearing suddenly young). Really, he said to his friends, some people see only what they *want* to see. Didn't *they* think it was a good thing she'd come over? Oh yes, said his friends. Look how well the household was running now, the furniture dusted daily, laundry folded and put into drawers (his mother, a smart woman, had figured out the washing machine in no time at all). She cooked all his favorite dishes, which his wife had never managed to learn quite right, and she took *such* good care of the little boy, walking him to the park each afternoon, bringing him into her bed when he woke up crying at night. (He'd told her once or twice that his wife had never done that, she had this idea about the boy needing to be independent. What nonsense, said his mother.) Lucky man, a couple of his friends added and he silently agreed, although later he thought it was ironic that they would say that about a man whose wife had disappeared.

As the year went on, the husband stopped thinking as much about the wife. It wasn't that he loved her any less, or that the shock of her disappearance was less acute. It was just that it wasn't on his mind all the time. There would be stretches of time — when he was on the phone with an important client, or when he was watching after-dinner TV or driving his son to kiddie gym class — when he would forget that his wife was gone, that he had had a wife at all. And even when he remembered that he had forgotten, he would experience only a slight twinge, similar to what he felt in his teeth when he drank something too cold too fast. The boy, too, didn't ask as often about his mother. He was sleeping through the nights again, he had put on a few pounds (because he was finally being fed right, said the grandmother), and he had started calling her "Ma," just like his father did.

So it seemed quite natural for the husband to, one day, remove the photographs of his wife from the frames that sat on the mantelpiece and replace them with pictures of himself and his little boy that friends had taken on a recent trip to Great America, and also one of the boy on his grandma's lap, holding a red birthday balloon, smiling (she said) exactly like his father used to at that age. He put the old pictures into a manila envelope and slid them to the back of a drawer, intending to show them to his son when he grew up. The next time his mother asked (as she had been doing ever since she got there), shall I put away all those saris and *kameezes*, it'll give you more space in the closet, he said, if you like. When she said, it's now over a year since the tragedy, shouldn't we have a prayer service done at the temple, he said OK. And when she told him, you really should think about getting married again, you're still young, and besides, the boy needs a mother, shall I contact second aunt back home, he remained silent but didn't disagree.

Then one night while cooking cauliflower curry, her specialty, his mother ran out of *hing*, which was, she insisted, essential to the recipe. The Indian grocery was closed, but the husband remembered that sometimes his wife used to keep extra spices on the top shelf. So he climbed on a chair to look. There were no extra spices, but he did find something he had forgotten about, an old tea tin in which he'd asked her to hide her jewelry in case the house ever got burgled. Nothing major was ever kept there. The expensive wedding items were all stored in a vault. Still, the husband thought it would be a good idea to take them into the bank in the morning.

But when he picked up the tin it felt surprisingly light, and when he opened it, there were only empty pink nests of tissue inside.

He stood there holding the tin for a moment, not breathing. Then he reminded himself that his wife had been a careless woman. He'd often had to speak to her about leaving things lying around. The pieces could be anywhere — pushed to the back of her makeup drawer or forgotten under a pile of books in the spare room where she used to spend inordinate amounts of time reading. Nevertheless he was not himself the rest of the evening, so much so that his mother said, What happened, you're awfully quiet, are you all right, your face looks funny. He told her he was fine, just a little pain in the chest area. Yes, he would make an appointment with the doctor tomorrow, no, he wouldn't forget, now could she please leave him alone for a while.

The next day he took the afternoon off from work, but he didn't go to the doctor. He went to the bank. In a small stuffy cubicle that smelled faintly of mold, he opened his safety deposit box to find that all her jewelry was gone. She hadn't taken any of the other valuables.

The edges of the cubicle seemed to fade and darken at the same time, as though the husband had stared at a lightbulb for too long. He ground his fists into his eyes and tried to imagine her on that last morning, putting the boy in his

20

stroller and walking the twenty minutes to the bank (they only had one car, which he took to work; they could have afforded another, but why, he said to his friends, when she didn't even know how to drive). Maybe she had sat in this very cubicle and lifted out the emerald earrings, the pearl choker, the long gold chain. He imagined her wrapping the pieces carefully in plastic bags, the thin, clear kind one got at the grocery for vegetables, then slipping them into her purse. Or did she just throw them in anyhow, the strands of the necklace tangling, the brilliant green stones clicking against each other in the darkness inside the handbag, the boy laughing and clapping his hands at this new game.

At home that night he couldn't eat any dinner, and before he went to bed he did thirty minutes on the dusty exercise bike that sat in the corner of the family room. Have you gone crazy, asked his mother. He didn't answer. When he finally lay down, the tiredness did not put him to sleep as he had hoped. His calves ached from the unaccustomed strain, his head throbbed from the images that would not stop coming, and the bedclothes, when he pulled them up to his neck, smelled again of his wife's hair.

Where was she now? And with whom? Because surely she couldn't manage on her own. He'd always thought her to be like the delicate purple passion-flower vines that they'd put up on trellises along their back fence, and once, early in the marriage, had presented her with a poem he'd written about this. He remembered how, when he held out the sheet to her, she'd stared at him for a long moment and a look he couldn't quite read had flickered in her eyes. Then she'd taken the poem with a small smile. He went over and over all the men she might have known, but they (mostly his Indian friends) were safely married and still at home, every one.

25   The bed felt hot and lumpy. He tossed his feverish body around like a caught animal, punched the pillow, threw the blanket to the floor. Even thought, for a wild moment, of shaking the boy awake and asking him, *Who did your mama see?* And as though he had an inbuilt antenna that picked up his father's agitation, in the next room the boy started crying (which he hadn't done for months), shrill screams that left him breathless. And when his father and grandmother rushed to see what the problem was, he pushed them from him with all the strength in his small arms, saying, Go way, don't want you, want Mama, want Mama.

After the boy had been dosed with gripe water and settled in bed again, the husband sat alone in the family room with a glass of brandy. He wasn't a drinker. He believed that alcohol was for weak men. But somehow he couldn't face the rumpled bed just yet, the pillows wrested onto the floor. The unknown areas of his wife's existence yawning blackly around him like chasms. Should he tell the police, he wondered, would it do any good? What if somehow his friends came to know? *Didn't I tell you, right from the first,* his mother would say. And anyway it was possible she was already dead, killed by a stranger from whom she'd hitched a ride, or by a violent, jealous lover. He felt a small, bitter pleasure at the thought, and then a pang of shame.

Nevertheless he made his way to the dark bedroom (a trifle unsteadily; the drink had made him light-headed) and groped in the bottom drawer beneath his underwear until he felt the course manila envelope with her photos. He drew it out and, without looking at them, tore the pictures into tiny pieces. Then he took them over to the kitchen, where the trash compactor was.

The roar of the compactor seemed to shake the entire house. He stiffened, afraid his mother would wake and ask what was going on, but she didn't. When the machine ground to a halt, he took a long breath. Finished, he thought. Finished. Tomorrow he would contact a lawyer, find out the legal procedure for remarriage. Over dinner he would mention to his mother, casually, that it was OK with him if she wanted to contact second aunt. Only this time he didn't want a college-educated woman. Even good looks weren't that important. A simple girl, maybe from their ancestral village. Someone whose family wasn't well off, who would be suitably appreciative of the comforts he could provide. Someone who would be a real mother to his boy.

He didn't know then that it wasn't finished. That even as he made love to his new wife (a plump, cheerful girl, good-hearted, if slightly unimaginative), or helped his daughters with their homework, or disciplined his increasingly rebellious son, he would wonder about *her*. Was she alive? Was she happy? With a sudden anger that he knew to be irrational, he would try to imagine her body tangled in swaying kelp at the bottom of the ocean where it had been flung. Bloated. Eaten by fish. But all he could conjure up was the intent look on her face when she rocked her son back and forth, singing a children's rhyme in Bengali, *Khoka jabe biye korte, shonge chhasho dhol, my little boy is going to be married, six hundred drummers*. Years later, when he was an old man living in a home for seniors (his second wife dead, his daughters moved away to distant towns, his son not on speaking terms with him), he would continue to be dazzled by that brief unguarded joy in her face, would say to himself, again, how much she must have hated me to choose to give *that* up.

But he had no inkling of any of this yet. So he switched off the trash compactor with a satisfied click, the sense of a job well done and, after taking a shower (long and very hot, the way he liked it, the hard jets of water turning the skin of his chest a dull red), went to bed and fell immediately into a deep, dreamless sleep.

◊   ◊   ◊

LOUISE ERDRICH   (1954 –   )

Fleur   (1986)

The first time she drowned in the cold and glassy waters of Lake Turcot, Fleur Pillager was only a girl. Two men saw the boat tip, saw her struggle in the waves. They rowed over to the place she went down, and jumped in. When they dragged her over the gunwales, she was cold to the touch and stiff, so they slapped her face, shook her by the heels, worked her arms back and forth, and pounded her back until she coughed up lake water. She shivered all over like a dog, then took a breath. But it wasn't long afterward that those two men disappeared. The first wandered off, and the other, Jean Hat, got himself run over by a cart.

It went to show, my grandma said. It figured to her, all right. By saving Fleur Pillager, those two men had lost themselves.

The next time she fell in the lake, Fleur Pillager was twenty years old and no one touched her. She washed onshore, her skin a dull dead gray, but when George

Many Women bent to look closer, he saw her chest move. Then her eyes spun open, sharp black riprock, and she looked at him. "You'll take my place," she hissed. Everybody scattered and left her there, so no one knows how she dragged herself home. Soon after that we noticed Many Women changed, grew afraid, wouldn't leave his house, and would not be forced to go near water. For his caution, he lived until the day that his sons brought him a new tin bathtub. Then the first time he used the tub he slipped, got knocked out, and breathed water while his wife stood in the other room frying breakfast.

Men stayed clear of Fleur Pillager after the second drowning. Even though she was good-looking, nobody dared to court her because it was clear that Misshepeshu, the waterman, the monster, wanted her for himself. He's a devil, that one, love-hungry with desire and maddened for the touch of young girls, the strong and daring especially, the ones like Fleur.

5   Our mothers warn us that we'll think he's handsome, for he appears with green eyes, copper skin, a mouth tender as a child's. But if you fall into his arms, he sprouts horns, fangs, claws, fins. His feet are joined as one and his skin, brass scales, rings to the touch. You're fascinated, cannot move. He casts a shell necklace at your feet, weeps gleaming chips that harden into mica on your breasts. He holds you under. Then he takes the body of a lion or a fat brown worm. He's made of gold. He's made of beach moss. He's a thing of dry foam, a thing of death by drowning, the death a Chippewa cannot survive.

Unless you are Fleur Pillager. We all knew she couldn't swim. After the first time, we thought she'd never go back to Lake Turcot. We thought she'd keep to herself, live quiet, stop killing men off by drowning in the lake. After the first time, we thought she'd keep the good ways. But then, after the second drowning, we knew that we were dealing with something much more serious. She was haywire, out of control. She messed with evil, laughed at the old women's advice, and dressed like a man. She got herself into some half-forgotten medicine, studied ways we shouldn't talk about. Some say she kept the finger of a child in her pocket and a powder of unborn rabbits in a leather thong around her neck. She laid the heart of an owl on her tongue so she could see at night, and went out, hunting, not even in her own body. We know for sure because the next morning, in the snow or dust, we followed the tracks of her bare feet and saw where they changed, where the claws sprang out, the pad broadened and pressed into the dirt. By night we heard her chuffing cough, the bear cough. By day her silence and the wide grin she threw to bring down our guard made us frightened. Some thought that Fleur Pillager should be driven off the reservation, but not a single person who spoke like this had the nerve. And finally, when people were just about to get together and throw her out, she left on her own and didn't come back all summer. That's what this story is about.

During that summer, when she lived a few miles south in Argus, things happened. She almost destroyed that town.

When she got down to Argus in the year of 1920, it was just a small grid of six streets on either side of the railroad depot. There were two elevators, one central, the other a few miles west. Two stores competed for the trade of the three hundred citizens, and three churches quarreled with one another for their souls.

There was a frame building for Lutherans, a heavy brick one for Episcopalians, and a long narrow shingled Catholic church. This last had a tall slender steeple, twice as high as any building or tree.

No doubt, across the low, flat wheat, watching from the road as she came near Argus on foot, Fleur saw that steeple rise, a shadow thin as a needle. Maybe in that raw space it drew her the way a lone tree draws lightning. Maybe, in the end, the Catholics are to blame. For if she hadn't seen that sign of pride, that slim prayer, that marker, maybe she would have kept walking.

But Fleur Pillager turned, and the first place she went once she came into town   10 was to the back door of the priest's residence attached to the landmark church. She didn't go there for a handout, although she got that, but to ask for work. She got that too, or the town got her. It's hard to tell which came out worse, her or the men or the town, although the upshot of it all was that Fleur lived.

The four men who worked at the butcher's had carved up about a thousand carcasses between them, maybe half of that steers and the other half pigs, sheep, and game animals like deer, elk, and bear. That's not even mentioning the chickens, which were beyond counting. Pete Kozka owned the place, and employed Lily Veddar, Tor Grunewald, and my stepfather, Dutch James, who had brought my mother down from the reservation the year before she disappointed him by dying. Dutch took me out of school to take her place. I kept house half the time and worked the other in the butcher shop, sweeping floors, putting sawdust down, running a hambone across the street to a customer's bean pot or a package of sausage to the corner. I was a good one to have around because until they needed me, I was invisible. I blended into the stained brown walls, a skinny, big-nosed girl with staring eyes. Because I could fade into a corner or squeeze beneath a shelf, I knew everything, what the men said when no one was around, and what they did to Fleur.

Kozka's Meats served farmers for a fifty-mile area, both to slaughter, for it had a stock pen and chute, and to cure the meat by smoking it or spicing it in sausage. The storage locker was a marvel, made of many thicknesses of brick, earth insulation, and Minnesota timber, lined inside with sawdust and vast blocks of ice cut from Lake Turcot, hauled down from home each winter by horse and sledge.

A ramshackle board building, part slaughterhouse, part store, was fixed to the low, thick square of the lockers. That's where Fleur worked. Kozka hired her for her strength. She could lift a haunch or carry a pole of sausages without stumbling, and she soon learned cutting from Pete's wife, a string-thin blonde who chain-smoked and handled the razor-sharp knives with nerveless precision, slicing close to her stained fingers. Fleur and Fritzie Kozka worked afternoons, wrapping their cuts in paper, and Fleur hauled the packages to the lockers. The meat was left outside the heavy oak doors that were only opened at 5:00 each afternoon, before the men ate supper.

Sometimes Dutch, Tor, and Lily ate at the lockers, and when they did I stayed too, cleaned floors, restoked the fires in the front smokehouses, while the men sat around the squat cast-iron stove spearing slats of herring onto hardtack bread. They played long games of poker or cribbage on a board made from the planed end of a salt crate. They talked and I listened, although there wasn't much to hear since almost nothing ever happened in Argus. Tor was married, Dutch had lost

my mother, and Lily read circulars. They mainly discussed about the auctions to
come, equipment, or women.

15   Every so often, Pete Kozka came out front to make a whist, leaving Fritzie to
smoke cigarettes and fry raised doughnuts in the back room. He sat and played a
few rounds but kept his thoughts to himself. Fritzie did not tolerate him talking
behind her back, and the one book he read was the New Testament. If he said
something, it concerned weather or a surplus of sheep stomachs, a ham that
smoked green or the markets for corn and wheat. He had a good-luck talisman,
the opal-white lens of a cow's eye. Playing cards, he rubbed it between his fingers.
That soft sound and the slap of cards was about the only conversation.

Fleur finally gave them a subject.

Her cheeks were wide and flat, her hands large, chapped, muscular. Fleur's
shoulders were broad as beams, her hips fishlike, slippery, narrow. An old green
dress clung to her waist, worn thin where she sat. Her braids were thick like the
tails of animals, and swung against her when she moved, deliberately, slowly in
her work, held in and half-tamed, but only half. I could tell, but the others never
saw. They never looked into her sly brown eyes or noticed her teeth, strong and
curved and very white. Her legs were bare, and since she padded around in bead-
work moccasins they never saw that her fifth toes were missing. They never knew
she'd drowned. They were blinded, they were stupid, they only saw her in the
flesh.

And yet it wasn't just that she was a Chippewa, or even that she was a woman,
it wasn't that she was good-looking or even that she was alone that made their
brains hum. It was how she played cards.

Women didn't usually play with men, so the evening that Fleur drew a chair up
to the men's table without being so much as asked, there was a shock of surprise.

20   "What's this," said Lily. He was fat, with a snake's cold pale eyes and precious
skin, smooth and lily-white, which is how he got his name. Lily had a dog, a
stumpy mean little bull of a thing with a belly drum-tight from eating pork rinds.
The dog liked to play cards just like Lily, and straddled his barrel thighs through
games of stud, rum poker, vingt-un.° The dog snapped at Fleur's arm that first
night, but cringed back, its snarl frozen, when she took her place.

"I thought," she said, her voice soft and stroking, "you might deal me in."

There was a space between the heavy bin of spiced flour and the wall where I
just fit. I hunkered down there, kept my eyes open, saw her black hair swing over
the chair, her feet solid on the wood floor. I couldn't see up on the table where the
cards slapped down, so after they were deep in their game I raised myself up in the
shadows, and crouched on a sill of wood.

I watched Fleur's hands stack and ruffle, divide the cards, spill them to each
player in a blur, rake them up and shuffle again. Tor, short and scrappy, shut one
eye and squinted the other at Fleur. Dutch screwed his lips around a wet cigar.

"Gotta see a man," he mumbled, getting up to go out back to the privy. The
others broke, put their cards down, and Fleur sat alone in the lamplight that
glowed in a sheen across the push of her breasts. I watched her closely, then she

---

vingt-un: Twenty-one, a card game.

paid me a beam of notice for the first time. She turned, looked straight at me, and grinned the white wolf grin a Pillager turns on its victims, except that she wasn't after me.

"Pauline there," she said, "how much money you got?"   25

We'd all been paid for the week that day. Eight cents was in my pocket.

"Stake me," she said, holding out her long fingers. I put the coins in her palm and then I melted back to nothing, part of the walls and tables. It was a long time before I understood that the men would not have seen me no matter what I did, how I moved. I wasn't anything like Fleur. My dress hung loose and my back was already curved, an old woman's. Work had roughened me, reading made my eyes sore, caring for my mother before she died had hardened my face. I was not much to look at, so they never saw me.

When the men came back and sat around the table, they had drawn together. They shot each other small glances, stuck their tongues in their cheeks, burst out laughing at odd moments, to rattle Fleur. But she never minded. They played their vingt-un, staying even as Fleur slowly gained. Those pennies I had given her drew nickels and attracted dimes until there was a small pile in front of her.

Then she hooked them with five-card draw, nothing wild. She dealt, discarded, drew, and then she sighed and her cards gave a little shiver. Tor's eye gleamed, and Dutch straightened in his seat.

"I'll pay to see that hand," said Lily Veddar.   30

Fleur showed, and she had nothing there, nothing at all.

Tor's thin smile cracked open, and he threw his hand in too.

"Well, we know one thing," he said, leaning back in his chair, "the squaw can't bluff."

With that I lowered myself into a mound of swept sawdust and slept. I woke up during the night, but none of them had moved yet, so I couldn't either. Still later, the men must have gone out again, or Fritzie come out to break the game, because I was lifted, soothed, cradled in a woman's arms and rocked so quiet that I kept my eyes shut while Fleur rolled me into a closet of grimy ledgers, oiled paper, balls of string, and thick files that fit beneath me like a mattress.

The game went on after work the next evening. I got my eight cents back five   35 times over, and Fleur kept the rest of the dollar she'd won for a stake. This time they didn't play so late, but they played regular, and then kept going at it night after night. They played poker now, or variations, for one week straight, and each time Fleur won exactly one dollar, no more and no less, too consistent for luck.

By this time, Lily and the other men were so lit with suspense that they got Pete to join the game with them. They concentrated, the fat dog sitting tense in Lily Veddar's lap, Tor suspicious, Dutch stroking his huge square brow, Pete steady. It wasn't that Fleur won that hooked them in so, because she lost hands too. It was rather that she never had a freak hand or even anything above a straight. She only took on her low cards, which didn't sit right. By chance, Fleur should have gotten a full or flush by now. The irritating thing was she beat with pairs and never bluffed, because she couldn't, and still she ended up each night with exactly one dollar. Lily couldn't believe, first of all, that a woman could be smart enough to play cards, but even if she was, that she would then be stupid enough to cheat for a dollar a night. By day I watched him turn the problem over, his hard white face dull, small fingers probing at his knuckles, until he finally thought he had Fleur figured out as a bit-time player, caution her game. Raising the stakes would throw her.

More than anything now, he wanted Fleur to come away with something but a dollar. Two bits less or ten more, the sum didn't matter, just so he broke her streak.

Night after night she played, won her dollar, and left to stay in a place that just Fritzie and I knew about. Fleur bathed in the slaughtering tub, then slept in the unused brick smokehouse behind the lockers, a windowless place tarred on the inside with scorched fats. When I brushed against her skin I noticed that she smelled of the walls, rich and woody, slightly burnt. Since that night she put me in the closet I was no longer afraid of her, but followed her close, stayed with her, became her moving shadow that the men never noticed, the shadow that could have saved her.

August, the month that bears fruit, closed around the shop, and Pete and Fritzie left for Minnesota to escape the heat. Night by night, running, Fleur had won thirty dollars, and only Pete's presence had kept Lily at bay. But Pete was gone now, and one payday, with the heat so bad no one could move but Fleur, the men sat and played and waited while she finished work. The cards sweat, limp in their fingers, the table was slick with grease, and even the walls were warm to the touch. The air was motionless. Fleur was in the next room boiling heads.

40   Her green dress, drenched, wrapped her like a transparent sheet. A skin of lakeweed. Black snarls of veining clung to her arms. Her braids were loose, half-unraveled, tied behind her neck in a thick loop. She stood in steam, turning skulls through a vat with a wooden paddle. When scraps boiled to the surface, she bent with a round tin sieve and scooped them out. She'd filled two dishpans.

"Ain't that enough now?" called Lily. "We're waiting." The stump of a dog trembled in his lap, alive with rage. It never smelled me or noticed me above Fleur's smoky skin. The air was heavy in my corner, and pressed me down. Fleur sat with them.

"Now what do you say?" Lily asked the dog. It barked. That was the signal for the real game to start.

"Let's up the ante," said Lily, who had been stalking this night all month. He had a roll of money in his pocket. Fleur had five bills in her dress. The men had each saved their full pay.

"Ante a dollar then," said Fleur, and pitched hers in. She lost, but they let her scrape along, cent by cent. And then she won some. She played unevenly, as if chance was all she had. She reeled them in. The game went on. The dog was stiff now, poised on Lily's knees, a ball of vicious muscle with its yellow eyes slit in concentration. It gave advice, seemed to sniff the lay of Fleur's cards, twitched and nudged. Fleur was up, then down, saved by a scratch. Tor dealt seven cards, three down. The pot grew, round by round, until it held all the money. Nobody folded. Then it all rode on one last card and they went silent. Fleur picked hers up and blew a long breath. The heat lowered like a bell. Her card shook, but she stayed in.

45   Lily smiled and took the dog's head tenderly between his palms.

ERDRICH: FLEUR **469**

"Say, Fatso," he said, crooning the words, "you reckon that girl's bluffing?"

The dog whined and Lily laughed. "Me too," he said, "let's show." He swept his bills and coins into the pot and then they turned their cards over.

Lily looked once, looked again, then he squeezed the dog up like a fist of dough and slammed it on the table.

Fleur threw her arms out and drew the money over, grinning that same wolf grin that she'd used on me, the grin that had them. She jammed the bills in her dress, scooped the coins up in waxed white paper that she tied with string.

"Let's go another round," said Lily, his voice choked with burrs. But Fleur opened her mouth and yawned, then walked out back to gather slops for the one big hog that was waiting in the stock pen to be killed.

The men sat still as rocks, their hands spread on the oiled wood table. Dutch had chewed his cigar to damp shreds, Tor's eye was dull. Lily's gaze was the only one to follow Fleur. I didn't move. I felt them gathering, saw my stepfather's veins, the ones in his forehead that stood out in anger. The dog had rolled off the table and curled in a knot below the counter, where none of the men could touch it.

Lily rose and stepped out back to the closet of ledgers where Pete kept his private stock. He brought back a bottle, uncorked and tipped it between his fingers. The lump in his throat moved, then he passed it on. They drank, quickly felt the whiskey's fire, and planned with their eyes things they couldn't say out loud.

When they left, I followed. I hid out back in the clutter of broken boards and chicken crates beside the stock pen, where they waited. Fleur could not be seen at first, and then the moon broke and showed her, slipping cautiously along the rough board chute with a bucket in her hand. Her hair fell, wild and coarse, to her waist, and her dress was a floating patch in the dark. She made a pig-calling sound, rang the tin pail lightly against the wood, froze suspiciously. But too late. In the sound of the ring Lily moved, fat and nimble, stepped right behind Fleur and put out his creamy hands. At his first touch, she whirled and doused him with the bucket of sour slops. He pushed her against the big fence and the package of coins split, went clinking and jumping, winked against the wood. Fleur rolled over once and vanished in the yard.

The moon fell behind a curtain of ragged clouds, and Lily followed into the dark muck. But he tripped, pitched over the huge flank of the pig, who lay mired to the snout, heavily snoring. I sprang out of the weeds and climbed the side of the pen, stuck like glue. I saw the sow rise to her neat, knobby knees, gain her balance, and sway, curious, as Lily stumbled forward. Fleur had backed into the angle of rough wood just beyond, and when Lily tried to jostle past, the sow tipped up on her hind legs and struck, quick and hard as a snake. She plunged her head into Lily's thick side and snatched a mouthful of his shirt. She lunged again, caught him lower, so that he grunted in pained surprise. He seemed to ponder, breathing deep. Then he launched his huge body in a swimmer's dive.

The sow screamed as his body smacked over hers. She rolled, striking out with her knife-sharp hooves, and Lily gathered himself upon her, took her foot-long face by the ears and scraped her snout and cheeks against the trestles of the pen. He hurled the sow's tight skull against an iron post, but instead of knocking her dead, he merely woke her from her dream.

She reared, shrieked, drew him with her so that they posed standing upright. They bowed jerkily to each other, as if to begin. Then his arms swung and flailed. She sank her black fangs into his shoulder, clasping him, dancing him forward and backward through the pen. Their steps picked up pace, went wild. The two dipped as one, box-stepped, tripped each other. She ran her split foot through his hair. He grabbed her kinked tail. They went down and came up, the same shape and then the same color, until the men couldn't tell one from the other in that light and Fleur was able to launch herself over the gates, swing down, hit gravel.

The men saw, yelled, and chased her at a dead run to the smokehouse. And Lily too, once the sow gave up in disgust and freed him. That is where I should have gone to Fleur, saved her, thrown myself on Dutch. But I went stiff with fear and couldn't unlatch myself from the trestles or move at all. I closed my eyes and put my head in my arms, tried to hide, so there is nothing to describe but what I couldn't block out, Fleur's hoarse breath, so loud it filled me, her cry in the old language, and my name repeated over and over among the words.

The heat was still dense the next morning when I came back to work. Fleur was gone but the men were there, slack-faced, hung over. Lily was paler and softer than ever, as if his flesh had steamed on his bones. They smoked, took pulls off a bottle. It wasn't noon yet. I worked awhile, waiting shop and sharpening steel. But I was sick, I was smothered, I was sweating so hard that my hands slipped on the knives, and I wiped my fingers clean of the greasy touch of the customers' coins. Lily opened his mouth and roared once, not in anger. There was no meaning to the sound. His boxer dog, sprawled limp beside his foot, never lifted its head. Nor did the other men.

They didn't notice when I stepped outside, hoping for a clear breath. And then I forgot them because I knew that we were all balanced, ready to tip, to fly, to be crushed as soon as the weather broke. The sky was so low that I felt the weight of it like a yoke. Clouds hung down, witch teats, a tornado's green-brown cones, and as I watched one flicked out and became a delicate probing thumb. Even as I picked up my heels and ran back inside, the wind blew suddenly, cold, and then came rain.

60   Inside, the men had disappeared already and the whole place was trembling as if a huge hand was pinched at the rafters, shaking it. I ran straight through, screaming for Dutch or for any of them, and then I stopped at the heavy doors of the lockers, where they had surely taken shelter. I stood there a moment. Everything went still. Then I heard a cry building in the wind, faint at first, a whistle and then a shrill scream that tore through the walls and gathered around me, spoke plain so I understood that I should move, put my arms out, and slam down the great iron bar that fit across the hasp and lock.

Outside, the wind was stronger, like a hand held against me. I struggled forward. The bushes tossed, the awnings flapped off storefronts, the rails of porches rattled. The odd cloud became a fat snout that nosed along the earth and sniffled, jabbed, picked at things, sucked them up, blew them apart, rooted around as if it was following a certain scent, then stopped behind me at the butcher shop and bored down like a drill.

I went flying, landed somewhere in a ball. When I opened my eyes and looked, stranger things were happening.

A herd of cattle flew through the air like giant birds, dropping dung, their mouths opened in stunned bellows. A candle, still lighted, blew past, and tables, napkins, garden tools, a whole school of drifting eyeglasses, jackets on hangers, hams, a checkerboard, a lampshade, and at last the sow from behind the lockers, on the run, her hooves a blur, set free, swooping, diving, screaming as everything in Argus fell apart and got turned upside down, smashed, and thoroughly wrecked.

Days passed before the town went looking for the men. They were bachelors, after all, except for Tor, whose wife had suffered a blow to the head that made her forgetful. Everyone was occupied with digging out, in high relief because even though the Catholic steeple had been torn off like a peaked cap and sent across five fields, those huddled in the cellar were unhurt. Walls had fallen, windows were demolished, but the stores were intact and so were the bankers and shop owners who had taken refuge in their safes or beneath their cash registers. It was a fair-minded disaster, no one could be said to have suffered much more than the next, at least not until Fritzie and Pete came home.

Of all the businesses in Argus, Kozka's Meats had suffered worst. The boards 65 of the front building had been split to kindling, piled in a huge pyramid, and the shop equipment was blasted far and wide. Pete paced off the distance the iron bathtub had been flung — a hundred feet. The glass candy case went fifty, and landed without so much as a cracked pane. There were other surprises as well, for the back rooms where Fritzie and Pete lived were undisturbed. Fritzie said the dust still coated her china figures, and upon her kitchen table, in the ashtray, perched the last cigarette she'd put out in haste. She lit it up and finished it, looking through the window. From there, she could see that the old smokehouse Fleur had slept in was crushed to a reddish sand and the stock pens were completely torn apart, the rails stacked helter-skelter. Fritzie asked for Fleur. People shrugged. Then she asked about the others and, suddenly, the town understood that three men were missing.

There was a rally of help, a gathering of shovels and volunteers. We passed boards from hand to hand, stacked them, uncovered what lay beneath the pile of jagged splinters. The lockers, full of the meat that was Pete and Fritzie's invest-ment, slowly came into sight, still intact. When enough room was made for a man to stand on the roof, there were calls, a general urge to hack through and see what lay below. But Fritzie shouted that she wouldn't allow it because the meat would spoil. And so the work continued, board by board, until at last the heavy oak doors of the freezer were revealed and people pressed to the entry. Everyone wanted to be the first, but since it was my stepfather lost, I was let go in when Pete and Fritzie wedged through into the sudden icy air.

Pete scraped a match on his boot, lit the lamp Fritzie held, and then the three of us stood still in its circle. Light glared off the skinned and hanging carcasses, the crates of wrapped sausages, the bright and cloudy blocks of lake ice, pure as win-ter. The cold bit into us, pleasant at first, then numbing. We must have stood there a couple of minutes before we saw the men, or more rightly, the humps of fur, the iced and shaggy hides they wore, the bearskins they had taken down and wrapped around themselves. We stepped closer and tilted the lantern beneath the flaps of fur into their faces. The dog was there, perched among them, heavy as a doorstop. The three had hunched around a barrel where the game was still laid out, and a dead lantern and an empty bottle, too. But they had thrown down their last hands and hunkered tight, clutching one another, knuckles raw from beating at the door they had also attacked with hooks. Frost stars gleamed off their eyelashes and the stubble of their beards. Their faces were set in concentration, mouths open as if to speak some careful thought, some agreement they'd come to in each other's arms.

*   *   *

Power travels in the bloodlines, handed out before birth. It comes down through the hands, which in the Pillagers were strong and knotted, big, spidery, and rough, with sensitive fingertips good at dealing cards. It comes through the eyes, too, belligerent, darkest brown, the eyes of those in the bear clan, impolite as they gaze directly at a person.

In my dreams, I look straight back at Fleur, at the men. I am no longer the watcher on the dark sill, the skinny girl.

70   The blood draws us back, as if it runs through a vein of earth. I've come home and, except for talking to my cousins, live a quiet life. Fleur lives quiet too, down on Lake Turcot with her boat. Some say she's married to the waterman, Misshepeshu, or that she's living in shame with white men or windigos, or that she's killed them all. I'm about the only one here who ever goes to visit her. Last winter, I went to help out in her cabin when she bore the child, whose green eyes and skin the color of an old penny made more talk, as no one could decide if the child was mixed blood or what, fathered in a smokehouse, or by a man with brass scales, or by the lake. The girl is bold, smiling in her sleep, as if she knows what people wonder, as if she hears the old men talk, turning the story over. It comes up different every time and has no ending, no beginning. They get the middle wrong too. They only know that they don't know anything.

◊   ◊   ◊

GABRIEL GARCÍA MÁRQUEZ   (1928 –   )

A Very Old Man with Enormous Wings   (1968)

A Tale for Children

Translated from the Spanish by Gregory Rabassa

On the third day of rain they had killed so many crabs inside the house that Pelayo had to cross his drenched courtyard and throw them into the sea, because the newborn child had a temperature all night and they thought it was due to the stench. The world had been sad since Tuesday. Sea and sky were a single ash-gray thing and the sands of the beach, which on March nights glimmered like powdered light, had become a stew of mud and rotten shellfish. The light was so weak at noon that when Pelayo was coming back to the house after throwing away the crabs, it was hard for him to see what it was that was moving and groaning in the rear of the courtyard. He had to go very close to see that it was an old man, a very old man, lying face down in the mud, who, in spite of his tremendous efforts, couldn't get up, impeded by his enormous wings.

Frightened by that nightmare, Pelayo ran to get Elisenda, his wife, who was putting compresses on the sick child, and he took her to the rear of the courtyard. They both looked at the fallen body with mute stupor. He was dressed like a rag-picker.° There were only a few faded hairs left on his bald skull and very few teeth in his mouth, and his pitiful condition of a drenched great-grandfather had taken away any sense of grandeur he might have had. His huge buzzard wings, dirty and half-plucked, were forever entangled in the mud. They looked at him so long and so closely that Pelayo and Elisenda very soon overcame their surprise and in the end found him familiar. Then they dared speak to him, and he answered in an incomprehensible dialect with a strong sailor's voice. That was how they skipped over the inconvenience of the wings and quite intelligently concluded that he was a lonely castaway from some foreign ship wrecked by the storm. And yet, they called in a neighbor woman who knew everything about life and death to see him, and all she needed was one look to show them their mistake.

"He's an angel," she told them. "He must have been coming for the child, but the poor fellow is so old that the rain knocked him down."

On the following day everyone knew that a flesh-and-blood angel was held captive in Pelayo's house. Against the judgment of the wise neighbor woman, for whom angels in those times were the fugitive survivors of a celestial conspiracy, they did not have the heart to club him to death. Pelayo watched over him all afternoon from the kitchen, armed with his bailiff's club, and before going to bed he dragged him out of the mud and locked him up with the hens in the wire chicken coop. In the middle of the night, when the rain stopped, Pelayo and Elisenda were still killing crabs. A short time afterward the child woke up without a fever and with a desire to eat. Then they felt magnanimous and decided to put the angel on a raft with fresh water and provisions for three days and leave him to his fate on the high seas. But when they went out into the courtyard with the first light of dawn, they found the whole neighborhood in front of the chicken coop having fun with the angel, without the slightest reverence, tossing him things to eat through the openings in the wire as if he weren't a supernatural creature but a circus animal.

Father Gonzaga arrived before seven o'clock, alarmed by the strange news. By 5 that time onlookers less frivolous than those at dawn had already arrived and they were making all kinds of conjectures concerning the captive's future. The simplest among them thought that he should be named mayor of the world. Others of sterner mind felt that he should be promoted to the rank of five-star general in order to win all wars. Some visionaries hoped that he could be put to stud in order to implant on earth a race of winged wise men who could take charge of the universe. But Father Gonzaga, before becoming a priest, had been a robust wood-cutter. Standing by the wire, he reviewed his catechism° in an instant and asked them to open the door so that he could take a close look at that pitiful man who

---

ragpicker: Someone who makes a living collecting rags and other refuse.

catechism: A book that summarizes the doctrines of Roman Catholicism in question-and-answer form.

looked more like a huge decrepit hen among the fascinated chickens. He was ly-ing in a corner drying his open wings in the sunlight among the fruit peels and breakfast leftovers that the early risers had thrown him. Alien to the imperti-nences of the world, he only lifted his antiquarian° eyes and murmured some-thing in his dialect when Father Gonzaga went into the chicken coop and said good morning to him in Latin. The parish priest had his first suspicion of an im-poster when he saw that he did not understand the language of God or know how to greet His ministers. Then he noticed that seen close up he was much too hu-man; he had an unbearable smell of the outdoors, the back side of his wings was strewn with parasites and his main feathers had been mistreated by terrestrial winds, and nothing about him measured up to the proud dignity of angels. Then he came out of the chicken coop and in a brief sermon warned the curious against the risks of being ingenuous. He reminded them that the devil had the bad habit of making use of carnival tricks in order to confuse the unwary. He argued that if wings were not the essential element in determining the difference between a hawk and an airplane, they were even less so in the recognition of angels. Never-theless, he promised to write a letter to his bishop so that the latter would write to his primate so that the latter would write to the Supreme Pontiff° in order to get the final verdict from the highest courts.

His prudence fell on sterile hearts. The news of the captive angel spread with such rapidity that after a few hours the courtyard had the bustle of a marketplace and they had to call in troops with fixed bayonets to disperse the mob that was about to knock the house down. Elisenda, her spine all twisted from sweeping up so much marketplace trash, then got the idea of fencing in the yard and charging five cents admission to see the angel.

The curious came from far away. A traveling carnival arrived with a flying ac-robat who buzzed over the crowd several times, but no one paid any attention to him because his wings were not those of an angel but, rather, those of a sidereal° bat. The most unfortunate invalids on earth came in search of health: a poor woman who since childhood had been counting her heartbeats and had run out of numbers; a Portuguese man who couldn't sleep because the noise of the stars disturbed him; a sleepwalker who got up at night to undo the things he had done while awake; and many others with less serious ailments. In the midst of that ship-wreck disorder that made the earth tremble, Pelayo and Elisenda were happy with fatigue, for in less than a week they had crammed their rooms with money and the line of pilgrims waiting their turn to enter still reached beyond the horizon.

The angel was the only one who took no part in his own act. He spent his time trying to get comfortable in his borrowed nest, befuddled by the hellish heat of the oil lamps and sacramental candles that had been placed along the wire. At first they tried to make him eat some mothballs, which, according to the wisdom of the wise neighbor woman, were the food prescribed for angels. But he turned

---

antiquarian: Ancient.

the Supreme Pontiff: The pope.

sidereal: Relating to the stars.

them down, just as he turned down the papal lunches that the penitents brought him, and they never found out whether it was because he was an angel or because he was an old man that in the end he ate nothing but eggplant mush. His only supernatural virtue seemed to be patience. Especially during the first days, when the hens pecked at him, searching for the stellar parasites that proliferated in his wings, and the cripples pulled out feathers to touch their defective parts with, and even the most merciful threw stones at him, trying to get him to rise so they could see him standing. The only time they succeeded in arousing him was when they burned his side with an iron for branding steers, for he had been motionless for so many hours that they thought he was dead. He awoke with a start, ranting in his hermetic° language and with tears in his eyes, and he flapped his wings a couple of times, which brought on a whirlwind of chicken dung and lunar dust and a gale of panic that did not seem to be of this world. Although many thought that his reaction had been one not of rage but of pain, from then on they were careful not to annoy him, because the majority understood that his passivity was not that of a hero taking his ease but that of a cataclysm in repose.

Father Gonzaga held back the crowd's frivolity with formulas of maid-servant inspiration while awaiting the arrival of a final judgment on the nature of the captive. But the mail from Rome showed no sense of urgency. They spent their time finding out if the prisoner had a navel, if his dialect had any connection with Aramaic,° how many times he could fit on the head of a pin, or whether he wasn't just a Norwegian with wings. Those meager letters might have come and gone until the end of time if a providential event had not put an end to the priest's tribulations.

It so happened that during those days, among so many other carnival attractions, there arrived in town the traveling show of the woman who had been changed into a spider for having disobeyed her parents. The admission to see her was not only less than the admission to see the angel, but people were permitted to ask her all manner of questions about her absurd state and to examine her up and down so that no one would ever doubt the truth of her horror. She was a frightful tarantula the size of a ram and with the head of a sad maiden. What was most heart-rending, however, was not her outlandish shape but the sincere affliction with which she recounted the details of her misfortune. While still practically a child she had sneaked out of her parents' house to go to a dance, and while she was coming back through the woods after having danced all night without permission, a fearful thunderclap rent the sky in two and through the crack came the lightning bolt of brimstone that changed her into a spider. Her only nourishment came from the meatballs that charitable souls chose to toss into her mouth. A spectacle like that, full of so much human truth and with such a fearful lesson, was bound to defeat without even trying that of a haughty angel who scarcely deigned to look at mortals. Besides, the few miracles attributed to the angel showed a certain mental disorder, like the blind man who didn't recover his sight

10

---

hermetic: Occult, magical.

Aramaic: An ancient Middle Eastern language believed to have been the language spoken by Jesus.

but grew three new teeth, or the paralytic who didn't get to walk but almost won the lottery, and the leper whose sores sprouted sunflowers. Those consolation miracles, which were more like mocking fun, had already ruined the angel's reputation when the woman who had been changed into a spider finally crushed him completely. That was how Father Gonzaga was cured forever of his insomnia and Pelayo's courtyard went back to being as empty as during the time it had rained for three days and crabs walked through the bedrooms.

The owners of the house had no reason to lament. With the money they saved they built a two-story mansion with balconies and gardens and high netting so that crabs wouldn't get in during the winter, and with iron bars on the windows so that angels wouldn't get in. Pelayo also set up a rabbit warren close to town and gave up his job as bailiff for good, and Elisenda bought some satin pumps with high heels and many dresses of iridescent silk, the kind worn on Sunday by the most desirable women in those times. The chicken coop was the only thing that didn't receive any attention. If they washed it down with creolin° and burned tears of myrrh° inside it every so often, it was not in homage to the angel but to drive away the dungheap stench that still hung everywhere like a ghost and was turning the new house into an old one. At first, when the child learned to walk, they were careful that he not get too close to the chicken coop. But then they began to lose their fears and got used to the smell, and before the child got his second teeth he'd gone inside the chicken coop to play, where the wires were falling apart. The angel was no less standoffish with him than with other mortals, but he tolerated the most ingenious infamies with the patience of a dog who had no illusions. They both came down with chicken pox at the same time. The doctor who took care of the child couldn't resist the temptation to listen to the angel's heart, and he found so much whistling in the heart and so many sounds in his kidneys that it seemed impossible for him to be alive. What surprised him most, however, was the logic of his wings. They seemed so natural on that completely human organism that he couldn't understand why other men didn't have them too.

When the child began school it had been some time since the sun and rain had caused the collapse of the chicken coop. The angel went dragging himself about here and there like a stray dying man. They would drive him out of the bedroom with a broom and a moment later find him in the kitchen. He seemed to be in so many places at the same time that they grew to think that he'd been duplicated, that he was reproducing himself all through the house, and the exasperated and unhinged Elisenda shouted that it was awful living in that hell full of angels. He could scarcely eat and his antiquarian eyes had also become so foggy that he went about bumping into posts. All he had left were the bare cannulae° of his last feathers. Pelayo threw a blanket over him and extended him the charity of letting him sleep in the shed, and only then did they notice that he had a temperature at night, and was delirious with the tongue twisters of an old Norwegian. That was one of the few

---

creolin: A disinfectant.

myrrh: A type of incense.

cannulae: Quills

times they became alarmed, for they thought he was going to die and not even the wise neighbor woman had been able to tell them what to do with dead angels.

And yet he not only survived his worst winter, but seemed improved with the first sunny days. He remained motionless for several days in the farthest corner of the courtyard, where no one would see him, and at the beginning of December some large, stiff feathers began to grow on his wings, the feathers of a scarecrow, which looked more like another misfortune of decrepitude. But he must have known the reason for those changes, for he was quite careful that no one should notice them, that no one should hear the sea chanteys that he sometimes sang under the stars. One morning Elisenda was cutting some bunches of onions for lunch when a wind that seemed to come from the high seas blew into the kitchen. Then she went to the window and caught the angel in his first attempt at flight. They were so clumsy that his fingernails opened a furrow in the vegetable patch and he was on the point of knocking the shed down with the ungainly flapping that slipped on the light and couldn't get a grip on the air. But he did manage to gain altitude. Elisenda let out a sigh of relief, for herself and for him, when she saw him pass over the last houses, holding himself up in some way with the risky flapping of a senile vulture. She kept watching him even when she was through cutting the onions and she kept on watching until it was no longer possible for her to see him, because then he was no longer an annoyance in her life but an imaginary dot on the horizon of the sea.

◇   ◇   ◇

NATHANIEL HAWTHORNE (1804–1864)

The Birthmark (1843)

In the latter part of the last century there lived a man of science, an eminent proficient in every branch of natural philosophy, who not long before our story opens had made experience of a spiritual affinity more attractive than any chemical one. He had left his laboratory to the care of an assistant, cleared his fine countenance from the furnace smoke, washed the stain of acids from his fingers, and persuaded a beautiful woman to become his wife. In those days when the comparatively recent discovery of electricity and other kindred mysteries of Nature seemed to open paths into the region of miracle, it was not unusual for the love of science to rival the love of woman in its depth and absorbing energy. The higher intellect, the imagination, the spirit, and even the heart might all find their congenial ailment in pursuits which, as some of their ardent votaries believed, would ascend from one step of powerful intelligence to another, until the philosopher should lay his hand on the secret of creative force and perhaps make new worlds for himself. We know not whether Aylmer possessed this degree of faith in man's ultimate control over Nature. He had devoted himself, however, too unreservedly to scientific studies ever to be weaned from them by any second passion. His love for his young wife might prove the stronger of the two; but it could only be by intertwining itself with his love of science, and uniting the strength of the latter to his own.

Such a union accordingly took place, and was attended with truly remarkable consequences and a deeply impressive moral. One day, very soon after their marriage, Aylmer sat gazing at his wife with a trouble in his countenance that grew stronger until he spoke.

"Georgiana," said he, "has it ever occurred to you that the mark upon your cheek might be removed?"

"No, indeed," said she, smiling; but perceiving the seriousness of his manner, she blushed deeply. "To tell you the truth it has been so often called a charm that I was simple enough to imagine it might be so."

5   "Ah, upon another face perhaps it might," replied her husband; "but never on yours. No, dearest Georgiana, you came so nearly perfect from the hand of Nature that this slightest possible defect, which we hesitate whether to term a defect or a beauty, shocks me, as being the visible mark of earthly imperfection."

"Shocks you, my husband!" cried Georgiana, deeply hurt; at first reddening with momentary anger, but then bursting into tears. "Then why did you take me from my mother's side? You cannot love what shocks you!"

To explain this conversation it must be mentioned that in the center of Georgiana's left cheek there was a singular mark, deeply interwoven, as it were, with the texture and substance of her face. In the usual state of her complexion — a healthy though delicate bloom — the mark wore a tint of deeper crimson, which imperfectly defined its shape amid the surrounding rosiness. When she blushed it gradually became more indistinct, and finally vanished amid the triumphant rush of blood that bathed the whole cheek with its brilliant glow. But if any shifting motion caused her to turn pale, there was the mark again, a crimson stain upon the snow, in what Aylmer sometimes deemed an almost fearful distinctness. Its shape bore not a little similarity to the human hand, though of the smallest pygmy size. Georgiana's lovers were wont to say that some fairy at her birth hour had laid her tiny hand upon the infant's cheek, and left this impress there in token of the magic endowments that were to give her such sway over all hearts. Many a desperate swain would have risked life for the privilege of pressing his lips to the mysterious hand. It must not be concealed, however, that the impression wrought by this fairy sign manual varied exceedingly, according to the difference of temperament in the beholders. Some fastidious persons — but they were exclusively of her own sex — affirmed that the bloody hand, as they chose to call it, quite destroyed the effect of Georgiana's beauty, and rendered her countenance even hideous. But it would be as reasonable to say that one of those small blue stains which sometimes occur in the purest statuary marble would convert the Eve of Powers° to a monster. Masculine observers, if the birthmark did not heighten their admiration, contented themselves with wishing it away, that the world might possess one living specimen of ideal loveliness without the semblance of a flaw. After his marriage, — for he thought little or nothing of the matter before, — Aylmer discovered that this was the case with himself.

Eve of Powers: A statue, *Eve before the Fall,* by Hiram Powers (1805–1873), a sculptor known for his idealized portraits of feminine purity.

Had she been less beautiful,—if Envy's self could have found aught else to sneer at,—he might have felt his affection heightened by the prettiness of this mimic hand, now vaguely portrayed, now lost, now stealing forth again and glimmering to and fro with every pulse of emotion that throbbed within her heart; but seeing her otherwise so perfect, he found this one defect grow more and more intolerable with every moment of their united lives. It was the fatal flaw of humanity which Nature, in one shape or another, stamps ineffaceably on all her productions, either to imply that they are temporary and finite, or that their perfection must be wrought by toil and pain. The crimson hand expressed the ineludible gripe° in which mortality clutches the highest and purest of earthly mold, degrading them into kindred with the lowest, and even with the very brutes, like whom their visible frames return to dust. In this manner, selecting it as the symbol of his wife's liability to sin, sorrow, decay, and death, Aylmer's somber imagination was not long in rendering the birthmark a frightful object, causing him more trouble and horror than ever Georgiana's beauty, whether of soul or sense, had given him delight.

At all the seasons which should have been their happiest, he invariably and without intending it, nay, in spite of a purpose to the contrary, reverted to this one disastrous topic. Trifling as it at first appeared, it so connected itself with innumerable trains of thought and modes of feeling that it became the central point of all. With the morning twilight Aylmer opened his eyes upon his wife's face and recognized the symbol of imperfection; and when they sat together at the evening hearth his eyes wandered stealthily to her cheek, and beheld, flickering with the blaze of the wood fire, the spectral hand that wrote mortality where he would fain have worshiped. Georgiana soon learned to shudder at his gaze. It needed but a glance with the peculiar expression that his face often wore to change the roses of her cheek into a deathlike paleness, amid which the crimson hand was brought strongly out, like a bas-relief of ruby on the whitest marble.

Late one night when the lights were growing dim, so as hardly to betray the   10
stain on the poor wife's cheek, she herself, for the first time, voluntarily took up the subject.

"Do you remember, my dear Aylmer," said she, with a feeble attempt at a smile, "have you any recollection of a dream last night about this odious hand?"

"None! none whatever!" replied Aylmer, starting; but then he added, in a dry, cold tone, affected for the sake of concealing the real depth of his emotion, "I might well dream of it; for before I fell asleep it had taken a pretty firm hold of my fancy."

"And you did dream of it?" continued Georgiana hastily, for she dreaded lest a gush of tears should interrupt what she had to say. "A terrible dream! I wonder that you can forget it. Is it possible to forget this one expression?—'It is in her heart now; we must have it out!' Reflect, my husband; for by all means I would have you recall that dream."

The mind is in a sad state when Sleep, the all-involving, cannot confine her specters within the dim region of her sway, but suffers them to break forth, af-

---

gripe: Grip.

frighting this actual life with secrets that perchance belong to a deeper one. Aylmer now remembered his dream. He had fancied himself with his servant Aminadab, attempting an operation for the removal of the birthmark; but the deeper went the knife, the deeper sank the hand, until at length its tiny grasp appeared to have caught hold of Georgiana's heart; whence, however, her husband was inexorably resolved to cut or wrench it away.

15   When the dream had shaped itself perfectly in his memory, Aylmer sat in his wife's presence with a guilty feeling. Truth often finds its way to the mind close muffled in robes of sleep, and then speaks with uncompromising directness of matters in regard to which we practice an unconscious self-deception during our waking moments. Until now he had not been aware of the tyrannizing influence acquired by one idea over his mind, and of the lengths which he might find in his heart to go for the sake of giving himself peace.

"Aylmer," resumed Georgiana solemnly, "I know not what may be the cost to both of us to rid me of this fatal birthmark. Perhaps its removal may cause cureless deformity; or it may be the stain goes as deep as life itself. Again: do we know that there is a possibility, on any terms, of unclasping the firm grip of this little hand which was laid upon me before I came into the world?"

"Dearest Georgiana, I have spent much thought upon the subject," hastily interrupted Aylmer. "I am convinced of the perfect practicability of its removal."

"If there be the remotest possibility of it," continued Georgiana, "let the attempt be made at whatever risk. Danger is nothing to me; for life, while this hateful mark makes me the object of your horror and disgust,—life is a burden which I would fling down with joy. Either remove this dreadful hand, or take my wretched life! You have deep science. All the world bears witness of it. You have achieved great wonders. Cannot you remove this little, little mark, which I cover with the tips of two small fingers? Is this beyond your power, for the sake of your own peace, and to save your poor wife from madness?"

"Noblest, dearest, tenderest wife," cried Aylmer rapturously, "doubt not my power. I have already given this matter the deepest thought — thought which might almost have enlightened me to create a being less perfect than yourself. Georgiana, you have led me deeper than ever into the heart of science. I feel myself fully competent to render this dear cheek as faultless as its fellow; and then, most beloved, what will be my triumph when I shall have corrected what Nature left imperfect in her fairest work! Even Pygmalion,° when his sculptured woman assumed life, felt not greater ecstasy than mine will be."

20   "It is resolved, then," said Georgiana, faintly smiling. "And, Aylmer, spare me not, though you should find the birthmark take refuge in my heart at last."

Her husband tenderly kissed her cheek — her right cheek — not that which bore the impress of the crimson hand.

The next day Aylmer apprised his wife of a plan that he had formed whereby he might have opportunity for the intense thought and constant watchfulness

---

Pygmalion: In Greek mythology, the king of Cyprus who fell in love with a statue he had sculpted. Aphrodite, the goddess of love, brought the statue to life for him.

which the proposed operation would require; while Georgiana, likewise, would enjoy the perfect repose essential to its success. They were to seclude themselves in the extensive apartments occupied by Aylmer as a laboratory, and where, during his toilsome youth, he had made discoveries in the elemental powers of Nature that had roused the admiration of all the learned societies in Europe. Seated calmly in this laboratory, the pale philosopher had investigated the secrets of the highest cloud region and of the profoundest mines; he had satisfied himself of the causes that kindled and kept alive the fires of the volcano; and had explained the mystery of fountains, and how it is that they gush forth, some so bright and pure, and others with such rich medicinal virtues, from the dark bosom of the earth. Here, too, at an earlier period, he had studied the wonders of the human frame, and attempted to fathom the very process by which Nature assimilates all her precious influences from earth and air, and from the spiritual world, to create and foster man, her masterpiece. The latter pursuit, however, Aylmer had long laid aside in unwilling recognition of the truth — against which all seekers sooner or later stumble — that our great creative Mother, while she amuses us with apparently working in the broadest sunshine, is yet severely careful to keep her own secrets, and, in spite of her pretended openness, shows us nothing but results. She permits us, indeed, to mar, but seldom to mend, and, like a jealous patentee, on no account to make. Now, however, Aylmer resumed these half-forgotten investigations,— not, of course, with such hopes or wishes as first suggested them, but because they involved much physiological truth and lay in the path of his proposed scheme for the treatment of Georgiana.

As he led her over the threshold of the laboratory, Georgiana was cold and tremulous. Aylmer looked cheerfully into her face, with intent to reassure her, but was so startled with the intense glow of the birthmark upon the whiteness of her cheek that he could not restrain a strong convulsive shudder. His wife fainted.

"AminadabAminadab!" shouted Aylmer, stamping violently on the floor.

Forthwith there issued from an inner apartment a man of low stature, but   25
bulky frame, with shaggy hair hanging about his visage, which was grimed with the vapors of the furnace. This personage had been Aylmer's underworker during his whole scientific career, and was admirably fitted for that office by his great mechanical readiness, and the skill with which, while incapable of comprehending a single principle, he executed all the details of his master's experiments. With his vast strength, his shaggy hair, his smoky aspect, and the indescribable earthiness that encrusted him, he seemed to represent man's physical nature; while Aylmer's slender figure, and pale, intellectual face, were no less apt a type of the spiritual element.

"Throw open the door of the boudoir, Aminadab," said Aylmer, "and burn a pastille."°

"Yes, master," answered Aminadab, looking intently at the lifeless form of Georgiana; and then he muttered to himself, "If she were my wife, I'd never part with that birthmark."

---

pastille: Incense.

When Georgiana recovered consciousness she found herself breathing an atmosphere of penetrating fragrance, the gentle potency of which had recalled her from her deathlike faintness. The scene around her looked like enchantment. Aylmer had converted those smoky, dingy, somber rooms, where he had spent his brightest years in recondite pursuits, into a series of beautiful apartments not unfit to be the secluded abode of a lovely woman. The walls were hung with gorgeous curtains, which imparted the combination of grandeur and grace that no other species of adornment can achieve; and as they fell from the ceiling to the floor, their rich and ponderous folds, concealing all angles and straight lines, appeared to shut in the scene from infinite space. For aught Georgiana knew, it might be a pavilion among the clouds. And Aylmer, excluding the sunshine, which would have interfered with his chemical processes, had supplied its place with perfumed lamps, emitting flames of various hue, but all uniting in a soft, empurpled radiance. He now knelt by his wife's side, watching her earnestly, but without alarm; for he was confident in his science, and felt that he could draw a magic circle round her within which no evil might intrude.

"Where am I? Ah, I remember," said Georgiana faintly; and she placed her hand over her cheek to hide the terrible mark from her husband's eyes.

30   "Fear not, dearest!" exclaimed he. "Do not shrink from me! Believe me, Georgiana, I even rejoice in this single imperfection, since it will be such a rapture to remove it."

"Oh, spare me!" sadly replied his wife. "Pray do not look at it again. I never can forget that convulsive shudder."

In order to soothe Georgiana, and, as it were, to release her mind from the burden of actual things, Aylmer now put in practice some of the light and playful secrets which science had taught him among its profounder lore. Airy figures, absolutely bodiless ideas, and forms of unsubstantial beauty came and danced before her, imprinting their momentary footsteps on beams of light. Though she had some indistinct idea of the method of these optical phenomena, still the illusion was almost perfect enough to warrant the belief that her husband possessed sway over the spiritual world. Then again, when she felt a wish to look forth from her seclusion, immediately, as if her thoughts were answered, the procession of external existence flitted across a screen. The scenery and the figures of actual life were perfectly represented, but with that bewitching, yet indescribable difference which always makes a picture, an image, or a shadow so much more attractive than the original. When wearied of this, Aylmer bade her cast her eyes upon a vessel containing a quantity of earth. She did so, with little interest at first; but was soon startled to perceive the germ of a plant shooting upward from the soil. Then came the slender stalk; the leaves gradually unfolded themselves; and amid them was a perfect and lovely flower.

"It is magical!" cried Georgiana. "I dare not touch it."

"Nay, pluck it," answered Aylmer: "pluck it, and inhale its brief perfume while you may. The flower will wither in a few moments and leave nothing save its brown seed vessels; but thence may be perpetuated a race as ephemeral as itself."

35   But Georgiana had no sooner touched the flower than the whole plant suffered a blight, its leaves turning coal-black as if by the agency of fire.

"There was too powerful a stimulus," said Aylmer thoughtfully.

To make up for this abortive experiment, he proposed to take her portrait by a scientific process of his own invention. It was to be effected by rays of light striking upon a polished plate of metal. Georgiana assented; but, on looking at the result, was affrighted to find the features of the portrait blurred and indefinable; while the minute figure of a hand appeared where the cheek should have been. Aylmer snatched the metallic plate and threw it into a jar of corrosive acid.

Soon, however, he forgot these mortifying failures. In the intervals of study and chemical experiment he came to her flushed and exhausted, but seemed invigorated by her presence, and spoke in glowing language of the resources of his art. He gave a history of the long dynasty of the alchemists,° who spent so many ages in quest of the universal solvent by which the golden principle might be elicited from all things vile and base. Aylmer appeared to believe that, by the plainest scientific logic, it was altogether within the limits of possibility to discover this long-sought medium; "but," he added, "a philosopher who should go deep enough to acquire the power would attain too lofty a wisdom to stoop to the exercise of it." Not less singular were his opinions in regard to the elixir vitae. He more than intimated that it was at his option to concoct a liquid that should prolong life for years, perhaps interminably; but that it would produce a discord in Nature which all the world, and chiefly the quaffer of the immortal nostrum, would find cause to curse.

"Aylmer, are you in earnest?" asked Georgiana, looking at him with amazement and fear. "It is terrible to possess such power, or even to dream of possessing it."

"Oh, do not tremble, my love," said her husband. "I would not wrong either   40
you or myself by working such inharmonious effects upon our lives; but I would have you consider how trifling, in comparison, is the skill requisite to remove this little hand."

At the mention of the birthmark, Georgiana, as usual, shrank as if a red-hot iron had touched her cheek.

Again Aylmer applied himself to his labors. She could hear his voice in the distant furnace-room giving directions to Aminadab, whose harsh, uncouth, misshapen tones were audible in response, more like the grunt or growl of a brute than human speech. After hours of absence, Aylmer reappeared and proposed that she should now examine his cabinet of chemical products and natural treasures of the earth. Among the former he showed her a small vial, in which, he remarked, was contained a gentle yet most powerful fragrance, capable of impregnating all the breezes that blow across a kingdom. They were of inestimable value, the contents of that little vial; and, as he said so, he threw some of the perfume into the air and filled the room with piercing and invigorating delight.

---

alchemists: Medieval scientists who attempted to transform base metals such as iron and lead into gold and to create an elixir that would prolong life indefinitely.

"And what is this?" asked Georgiana, pointing to a small crystal globe containing a gold-colored liquid. "It is so beautiful to the eye that I could imagine it the elixir of life."

"In one sense it is," replied Aylmer; "or rather, the elixir of immortality. It is the most precious poison that ever was concocted in this world. By its aid I could apportion the lifetime of any mortal at whom you might point your finger. The strength of the dose would determine whether he were to linger out years, or drop dead in the midst of a breath. No king on his guarded throne could keep his life if I, in my private station, should deem that the welfare of millions justified me in depriving him of it."

45   "Why do you keep such a terrific drug?" inquired Georgiana in horror.

"Do not mistrust me, dearest," said her husband, smiling; "its virtuous potency is yet greater than its harmful one. But see! here is a powerful cosmetic. With a few drops of this in a vase of water, freckles may be washed away as easily as the hands are cleansed. A stronger infusion would take the blood out of the cheek, and leave the rosiest beauty a pale ghost."

"Is it with this lotion that you intend to bathe my cheek?" asked Georgiana, anxiously.

"Oh, no," hastily replied her husband; "this is merely superficial. Your case demands a remedy that shall go deeper."

In his interviews with Georgiana, Aylmer generally made minute inquiries as to her sensations and whether the confinement of the rooms and the temperature of the atmosphere agreed with her. These questions had such a particular drift that Georgiana began to conjecture that she was already subjected to certain physical influences, either breathed in with the fragrant air or taken with her food. She fancied likewise, but it might be altogether fancy, that there was a stirring up of her system — a strange, indefinite sensation creeping through her veins, and tingling, half painfully, half pleasurably, at her heart. Still, whenever she dared to look into the mirror, there she beheld herself pale as a white rose and with the crimson birthmark stamped upon her cheek. Not even Aylmer now hated it so much as she.

50   To dispel the tedium of the hours which her husband found it necessary to devote to the processes of combination and analysis, Georgiana turned over the volumes of his scientific library. In many dark old tomes she met with chapters full of romance and poetry. They were the works of the philosophers of the middle ages, such as Albertus Magnus, Cornelius Agrippa, Paracelsus, and the famous friar who created the prophetic Brazen Head.° All these antique naturalists stood in advance of their centuries, yet were imbued with some of their credulity, and therefore were believed, and perhaps imagined themselves to have acquired from the investigation of Nature a power above Nature, and from physics a sway over the spiritual world. Hardly less curious and imaginative were the early volumes of the Transactions of the Royal Society, in which the members, knowing

---

Brazen Head: Friar Roger Bacon, an English scientist and philosopher, was reputed to have created a brass head that could speak.

little of the limits of natural possibility, were continually recording wonders or proposing methods whereby wonders might be wrought.

But to Georgiana the most engrossing volume was a large folio from her husband's own hand, in which he had recorded every experiment of his scientific career, its original aim, the methods adopted for its development, and its final success or failure, with the circumstances to which either event was attributable. The book, in truth, was both the history and emblem of his ardent, ambitious, imaginative, yet practical and laborious life. He handled physical details as if there were nothing beyond them; yet spiritualized them all, and redeemed himself from materialism by his strong and eager aspiration towards the infinite. In his grasp the veriest clod of earth assumed a soul. Georgiana, as she read, reverenced Aylmer and loved him more profoundly than ever, but with a less entire dependence on his judgment than heretofore. Much as he had accomplished, she could not but observe that his most splendid successes were almost invariably failures, if compared with the ideal at which he aimed. His brightest diamonds were the merest pebbles, and felt to be so by himself, in comparison with the inestimable gems which lay hidden beyond his reach. The volume, rich with achievements that had won renown for its author, was yet as melancholy a record as ever mortal hand had penned. It was the sad confession and continual exemplification of the shortcomings of the composite man, the spirit burdened with clay and working in matter, and of the despair that assails the higher nature of finding itself so miserably thwarted by the earthly part. Perhaps every man of genius in whatever sphere might recognize the image of his own experience in Aylmer's journal.

So deeply did these reflections affect Georgiana that she laid her face upon the open volume and burst into tears. In this situation she was found by her husband.

"It is dangerous to read in a sorcerer's books," said he with a smile, though his countenance was uneasy and displeased. "Georgiana, there are pages in that volume which I can scarcely glance over and keep my senses. Take heed lest it prove as detrimental to you."

"It has made me worship you more than ever," said she.

"Ah, wait for this one success," rejoined he, "then worship me if you will. I shall deem myself hardly unworthy of it. But come, I have sought you for the luxury of your voice. Sing to me, dearest." 55

So she poured out the liquid music of her voice to quench the thirst of his spirit. He then took his leave with a boyish exuberance of gaiety, assuring her that her seclusion would endure but a little longer, and that the result was already certain. Scarcely had he departed when Georgiana felt irresistibly impelled to follow him. She had forgotten to inform Aylmer of a symptom which for two or three hours past had begun to excite her attention. It was a sensation in the fatal birthmark, not painful, but which induced a restlessness throughout her system. Hastening after her husband, she intruded for the first time into the laboratory.

The first thing that struck her eye was the furnace, that hot and feverish worker, with the intense glow of its fire, which by the quantities of soot clustered above it seemed to have been burning for ages. There was a distilling apparatus in full operation. Around the room were retorts, tubes, cylinders, crucibles, and other apparatus of chemical research. An electrical machine stood ready for immediate use. The atmosphere felt oppressively close, and was tainted with gaseous odors which had been tormented forth by the process of science. The severe and homely simplicity of the apartment, with its naked walls and brick pavement, looked strange, accustomed as Georgiana had become to the fantastic elegance of her boudoir. But what chiefly, indeed almost solely, drew her attention, was the aspect of Aylmer himself.

He was pale as death, anxious and absorbed, and hung over the furnace as if it depended upon his utmost watchfulness whether the liquid which it was distilling should be the draught of immortal happiness or misery. How different from the sanguine and joyous mien that he had assumed for Georgiana's encouragement!

"Carefully now, Aminadab; carefully, thou human machine; carefully, thou man of clay!" muttered Aylmer, more to himself than his assistant. "Now, if there be a thought too much or too little, it is all over."

60 "Ho! ho!" mumbled Aminadab. "Look, master! look!"

Aylmer raised his eyes hastily, and at first reddened, then grew paler than ever, on beholding Georgiana. He rushed towards her and seized her arm with a gripe that left the print of his fingers upon it.

"Why do you come hither? Have you no trust in your husband?" cried he impetuously. "Would you throw the blight of that fatal birthmark over my labors? It is not well done. Go, prying woman, go!"

"Nay, Aylmer," said Georgiana with the firmness of which she possessed no stinted endowment, "it is not you that have a right to complain. You mistrust your wife; you have concealed the anxiety with which you watch the development of this experiment. Think not so unworthily of me, my husband. Tell me all the risk we run, and fear not that I shall shrink; for my share in it is far less than your own."

"No, no, Georgiana!" said Aylmer impatiently; "it must not be."

65 "I submit," replied she calmly. "And, Aylmer, I shall quaff whatever draught you bring me; but it will be on the same principle that would induce me to take a dose of poison if offered by your hand."

"My noble wife," said Aylmer, deeply moved, "I knew not the height and depth of your nature until now. Nothing shall be concealed. Know, then, that this crimson hand, superficial as it seems, has clutched its grasp into your being with a strength of which I had no previous conception. I have already administered agents powerful enough to do aught except to change your entire physical system. Only one thing remains to be tried. If that fails us we are ruined."

"Why did you hesitate to tell me this?" asked she.

"Because, Georgiana," said Aylmer in a low voice, "there is danger."

"Danger? There is but one danger — that this horrible stigma shall be left upon my cheek!" cried Georgiana. "Remove it, remove it, whatever be the cost, or we shall both go mad!"

70 "Heaven knows your words are too true," said Aylmer sadly. "And now, dearest, return to your boudoir. In a little while all will be tested."

He conducted her back and took leave of her with a solemn tenderness which spoke far more than his words how much was now at stake. After his departure Georgiana became rapt in musings. She considered the character of Aylmer, and did it completer justice than at any previous moment. Her heart exulted, while it trembled, at his honorable love — so pure and lofty that it would accept nothing less than perfection nor miserably make itself contented with an earthlier nature than he had dreamed of. She felt how much more precious was such a sentiment than that meaner kind which would have borne with the imperfection for her sake, and have been guilty of treason to holy love by degrading its perfect idea to the level of the actual; and with her whole spirit she prayed that, for a single moment, she might satisfy his highest and deepest conception. Longer than one moment she well knew it could not be; for his spirit was ever on the march, ever ascending, and each instant required something that was beyond the scope of the instant before.

The sound of her husband's footsteps aroused her. He bore a crystal goblet containing a liquor colorless as water, but bright enough to be the draught of immortality. Aylmer was pale; but it seemed rather the consequence of a highly wrought state of mind and tension of spirit than of fear or doubt.

"The concoction of the draught has been perfect," said he, in answer to Georgiana's look. "Unless all my science have deceived me, it cannot fail."

"Save on your account, my dearest Aylmer," observed his wife, "I might wish to put off this birthmark of mortality by relinquishing mortality itself in preference to any other mode. Life is but a sad possession to those who have attained precisely the degree of moral advancement at which I stand. Were I weaker and blinder it might be happiness. Were I stronger, it might be endured hopefully. But, being what I find myself, methinks I am of all mortals the most fit to die."

"You are fit for heaven without tasting death!" replied her husband. "But why 75 do we speak of dying? The draught cannot fail. Behold its effect upon this plant."

On the window seat there stood a geranium diseased with yellow blotches, which had overspread all its leaves. Aylmer poured a small quantity of the liquid upon the soil in which it grew. In a little time, when the roots of the plant had taken up the moisture, the unsightly blotches began to be extinguished in a living verdure.

"There needed no proof," said Georgiana quietly. "Give me the goblet. I joyfully stake all upon your word."

"Drink, then, thou lofty creature!" exclaimed Aylmer, with fervid admiration. "There is no taint of imperfection on thy spirit. Thy sensible frame, too, shall soon be all perfect."

She quaffed the liquid and returned the goblet to his hand.

"It is grateful," said she, with a placid smile. "Methinks it is like water from a 80 heavenly fountain; for it contains I know not what of unobtrusive fragrance and deliciousness. It allays a feverish thirst that had parched me for many days. Now, dearest, let me sleep. My earthly senses are closing over my spirit like the leaves around the heart of a rose at sunset."

She spoke the last words with a gentle reluctance, as if it required almost more energy than she could command to pronounce the faint and lingering syllables. Scarcely had they loitered through her lips ere she was lost in slumber. Aylmer sat by her side, watching her aspect with the emotions proper to a man the whole value of whose existence was involved in the process now to be tested. Mingled with this mood, however, was the philosophic investigation characteristic of the man of science. Not the minutest symptom escaped him. A heightened flush of the cheek, a slight irregularity of breath, a quiver of the eyelid, a hardly perceptible tremor through the frame, — such were the details which, as the moments passed, he wrote down in his folio volume. Intense thought had set its stamp upon every previous page of that volume, but the thoughts of years were all concentrated upon the last.

While thus employed, he failed not to gaze often at the fatal hand, and not without a shudder. Yet once, by a strange and unaccountable impulse, he pressed it with his lips. His spirit recoiled, however, in the very act; and Georgiana, out of the midst of her deep sleep, moved uneasily and murmured as if in remonstrance. Again Aylmer resumed his watch. Nor was it without avail. The crimson hand, which at first had been strongly visible upon the marble paleness of Georgiana's cheek, now grew more faintly outlined. She remained not less pale than ever; but the birthmark, with every breath that came and went, lost somewhat of its former distinctness. Its presence had been awful; its departure was more awful still. Watch the stain of the rainbow fading out of the sky, and you will know how that mysterious symbol passed away.

"By Heaven! it is well-nigh gone!" said Aylmer to himself, in almost irrepressible ecstasy. "I can scarcely trace it now. Success! success! And now it is like the faintest rose color. The lightest flush of blood across her cheek would overcome it. But she is so pale!"

He drew aside the window curtain and suffered the light of natural day to fall into the room and rest upon her cheek. At the same time he heard a gross, hoarse chuckle, which he had long known as his servant Aminadab's expression of
85 delight.

"Ah, clod! ah, earthly mass!" cried Aylmer, laughing in a sort of frenzy, "you have served me well! Matter and spirit — earth and heaven — have both done their part in this! Laugh, thing of the senses! You have earned the right to laugh."

These exclamations broke Georgiana's sleep. She slowly unclosed her eyes and gazed into the mirror which her husband had arranged for that purpose. A faint smile flitted over her lips when she recognized how barely perceptible was now that crimson hand which had once blazed forth with such disastrous brilliancy as to scare away all their happiness. But then her eyes sought Aylmer's face with a trouble and anxiety that he could by no means account for.

"My poor Aylmer!" murmured she.

"Poor? Nay, richest, happiest, most favored!" exclaimed he. "My peerless bride, it is successful! You are perfect!"

"My poor Aylmer," she repeated, with a more than human tenderness, "you have aimed loftily; you have done nobly. Do not repent that with so high and pure a feeling, you have rejected the best the earth could offer. Aylmer, dearest Aylmer, I am dying!"

90 Alas! it was too true! The fatal hand had grappled with the mystery of life, and was the bond by which an angelic spirit kept itself in union with a mortal frame. As the last crimson tint of the birthmark — that sole token of human

imperfection — faded from her cheek, the parting breath of the now perfect woman passed into the atmosphere, and her soul, lingering a moment near her husband, took its heavenward flight. Then a hoarse, chuckling laugh was heard again! Thus ever does the gross fatality of earth exult in its invariable triumph over the immortal essence which, in this dim sphere of half development, demands the completeness of a higher state. Yet, had Aylmer reached a profounder wisdom, he need not thus have flung away the happiness which would have woven his mortal life of the selfsame texture with the celestial. The momentary circumstance was too strong for him; he failed to look beyond the shadowy scope of time, and, living once for all in eternity, to find the perfect future in the present.

◇ ◇ ◇

JAMES JOYCE   (1884–1941)

Eveline   (1914)

She sat at the window watching the evening invade the avenue. Her head was leaned against the window curtains and in her nostrils was the odor of dusty cretonne.° She was tired.

Few people passed. The man out of the last house passed on his way home; she heard his footsteps clacking along the concrete pavement and afterwards crunching on the cinder path before the new red houses. One time there used to be a field there in which they used to play every evening with other people's children. Then a man from Belfast° bought the field and built houses in it — not like their little brown houses but bright brick houses with shining roofs. The children of the avenue used to play together in that field — the Devines, the Waters, the Dunns, little Keogh the cripple, she and her brothers and sisters. Ernest, however, never played: he was too grown up. Her father used often to hunt them in out of the field with his blackthorn stick; but usually little Keogh used to keep *nix*° and call out when he saw her father coming. Still they seemed to have been rather happy then. Her father was not so bad then; and besides, her mother was alive. That was a long time ago; she and her brothers and sisters were all grown up; her mother was dead. Tizzie Dunn was dead, too, and the Waters had gone back to England. Everything changes. Now she was going to go away like the others, to leave her home.

Home! She looked around the room, reviewing all its familiar objects which she had dusted once a week for so many years, wondering where on earth all the dust came from. Perhaps she would never see again those familiar objects from which she had never dreamed of being divided. And yet during all those years she had never found out the name of the priest whose yellowing photograph hung on the wall above the broken harmonium beside the colored print of the promises

---

cretonne: Heavy cloth used for curtains and upholstery.

Belfast: Capital of present-day Northern Ireland. This story refers to a time before the Partition of Ireland.

keep nix: Keep watch (slang).

made to Blessed Margaret Mary Alacoque. He had been a school friend of her father. Whenever he showed the photograph to a visitor her father used to pass it with a casual word:

"He is in Melbourne now."

5   She had consented to go away, to leave her home. Was that wise? She tried to weigh each side of the question. In her home anyway she had shelter and food; she had those whom she had known all her life about her. Of course she had to work hard both in the house and at business. What would they say of her in the Stores when they found out that she had run away with a fellow? Say she was a fool, perhaps; and her place would be filled up by advertisement. Miss Gavan would be glad. She had always had an edge on her, especially whenever there were people listening.

"Miss Hill, don't you see these ladies are waiting?"

"Look lively, Miss Hill, please."

She would not cry many tears at leaving the Stores.

But in her new home, in a distant unknown country, it would not be like that. Then she would be married — she, Eveline. People would treat her with respect then. She would not be treated as her mother had been. Even now, though she was over nineteen, she sometimes felt herself in danger of her father's violence. She knew it was that that had given her the palpitations. When they were growing up he had never gone for her, like he used to go for Harry and Ernest, because she was a girl; but latterly he had begun to threaten her and say what he would do to her only for her dead mother's sake. And now she had nobody to protect her. Ernest was dead and Harry, who was in the church decorating business, was nearly always down somewhere in the country. Besides, the invariable squabble for money on Saturday nights had begun to weary her unspeakably. She always gave her entire wages — seven shillings — and Harry always sent up what he could but the trouble was to get any money from her father. He said she used to squander the money, that she had no head, that he wasn't going to give her his hard-earned money to throw about the streets, and much more, for he was usually fairly bad of a Saturday night. In the end he would give her the money and ask her had she any intention of buying Sunday dinner. Then she had to rush out as quickly as she could and do her marketing, holding her black leather purse tightly in her hand as she elbowed her way through the crowds and returning home late under her load of provisions. She had hard work to keep the house together and to see that the two young children, who had been left to her charge went to school regularly and got their meals regularly. It was hard work — a hard life —but now that she was about to leave it she did not find it a wholly undesirable life.

10   She was about to explore another life with Frank. Frank was very kind, manly, open-hearted. She was to go away with him by the night-boat to be his wife and to live with him in Buenos Aires where he had a home waiting for her. How well she remembered the first time she had seen him; he was lodging in a house on the main road where she used to visit. It seemed a few weeks ago. He was standing at the gate, his peaked cap pushed back on his head and his hair tumbled forward over a face of bronze. Then they had come to know each other. He used to meet her outside the Stores every evening and see her home. He took her to see *The Bohemian Girl* and she felt elated as she sat in an unaccustomed part of the the-

ater with him. He was awfully fond of music and sang a little. People knew that they were courting and, when he sang about the lass that loves a sailor, she always felt pleasantly confused. He used to call her Poppens out of fun. First of all it had been an excitement for her to have a fellow and then she had begun to like him. He had tales of distant countries. He had started as a deck boy at a pound a month on a ship of the Allan Line going out to Canada. He told her the names of the ships he had been on and the names of the different services. He had sailed through the Straits of Magellan° and he told her stories of the terrible Patagonians.° He had fallen on his feet in Buenos Aires, he said, and had come over to the old country just for a holiday. Of course, her father had found out the affair and had forbidden her to have anything to say to him.

"I know these sailor chaps," he said.

One day he had quarreled with Frank and after that she had to meet her lover secretly.

The evening deepened in the avenue. The white of two letters in her lap grew indistinct. One was to Harry; the other was to her father. Ernest had been her favorite but she liked Harry too. Her father was becoming old lately, she noticed; he would miss her. Sometimes he could be very nice. Not long before, when she had been laid up for a day, he had read her out a ghost story and made toast for her at the fire. Another day, when their mother was alive, they had all gone for a picnic to the Hill of Howth. She remembered her father putting on her mother's bonnet to make the children laugh.

Her time was running out but she continued to sit by the window, leaning her head against the window curtain, inhaling the odor of dusty cretonne. Down far in the avenue she could hear a street organ playing. She knew the air. Strange that it should come that very night to remind her of the promise to her mother, her promise to keep the home together as long as she could. She remembered the last night of her mother's illness; she was again in the close dark room at the other side of the hall and outside she heard a melancholy air of Italy. The organ player had been ordered to go away and given sixpence. She remembered her father strutting back into the sickroom saying:

"Damned Italians! coming over here!"   15

As she mused the pitiful vision of her mother's life laid its spell on the very quick of her being — that life of commonplace sacrifices closing in final craziness. She trembled as she heard again her mother's voice saying constantly with foolish insistence:

"Derevaun Seraun! Derevaun Seraun!"°

She stood up in a sudden impulse of terror. Escape! She must escape! Frank would save her. He would give her life, perhaps love, too. But she wanted to live. Why should she be unhappy? She had a right to happiness. Frank would take her in his arms, fold her in his arms. He would save her.

Straits of Magellan: Sea channel at the southern tip of South America.

Patagonians: People from Patagonia, a tableland region in southern Argentina and Chile.

Derevaun Seraun: "The end of pleasure is pain!" (Irish).

She stood among the swaying crowd in the station at the North Wall. He held her hand and she knew that he was speaking to her, saying something about the passage over and over again. The station was full of soldiers with brown baggages. Through the wide doors of the sheds she caught a glimpse of the black mass of the boat, lying in beside the quay° wall, with illumined portholes. She answered nothing. She felt her cheek pale and cold and, out of a maze of distress, she prayed to God to direct her, to show her what was her duty. The boat blew a long mournful whistle into the mist. If she went, tomorrow she would be on the sea with Frank, steaming toward Buenos Aires. Their passage had been booked. Could she still draw back after all he had done for her? Her distress awoke a nausea in her body and she kept moving her lips in silent, fervent prayer.

20   A bell clanged upon her heart. She felt him seize her hand:

"Come!"

All the seas of the world tumbled about her heart. He was drawing her into them: he would drown her. She gripped with both hands at the iron railing.

"Come!"

No! No! No! It was impossible. Her hands clutched the iron in frenzy. Amid the seas she sent a cry of anguish!

25   "Eveline! Evvy!"

He rushed beyond the barrier and called to her to follow. He was shouted at to go on but he still called to her. She set her white face to him, passive, like a helpless animal. Her eyes gave him no sign of love or farewell or recognition.

◇   ◇   ◇

JAMAICA KINCAID   (1949–   )

Girl   (1984)

Wash the white clothes on Monday and put them on the stone heap; wash the color clothes on Tuesday and put them on the clothesline to dry; don't walk barehead in the hot sun; cook pumpkin fritters in very hot sweet oil; soak your little clothes right after you take them off; when buying cotton to make yourself a nice blouse, be sure that it doesn't have gum on it, because that way it won't hold up well after a wash; soak salt fish overnight before you cook it; is it true that you sing benna° in Sunday School?; always eat your food in such a way that it won't turn someone else's stomach; on Sundays try to walk like a lady and not like the slut you are so bent on becoming; don't sing benna in Sunday School; you mustn't speak to wharf-rat boys, not even to give directions; don't eat fruits on the street —flies will follow you; *but I don't sing benna on Sundays at all and never in Sunday school;* this is how to sew on a button; this is how to make a buttonhole for the button you have just sewed on; this is how to hem a dress when you see the hem coming down and so to prevent yourself from looking like the slut I know

---

quay: A paved stretch of shoreline facing navigable water, used for loading and unloading ships.

benna: Calypso music.

you are so bent on becoming; this is how you iron your father's khaki shirt so that it doesn't have a crease; this is how you iron your father's khaki pants so that they don't have a crease; this is how you grow okra — far from the house, because okra tree harbors red ants; when you are growing dasheen, make sure it gets plenty of water or else it makes your throat itch when you are eating it; this is how you sweep a corner; this is how you sweep a whole house; this is how you sweep a yard; this is how you smile to someone you don't like too much; this is how you smile to someone you don't like at all; this is how you smile to someone you like completely; this is how you set a table for tea; this is how you set a table for dinner; this is how you set a table for dinner with an important guest; this is how you set a table for lunch; this is how you set a table for breakfast; this is how to behave in the presence of men who don't know you very well, and this way they won't recognize immediately the slut I have warned you against becoming; be sure to wash every day, even if it is with your own spit; don't squat down to play marbles — you are not a boy, you know; don't pick people's flowers — you might catch something; don't throw stones at blackbirds, because it might not be a blackbird at all; this is how to make a bread pudding; this is how to make doukona;° this is how to make pepper pot; this is how to make a good medicine for a cold; this is how to make a good medicine to throw away a child before it even becomes a child; this is how to catch a fish; this is how to throw back a fish you don't like, and that way something bad won't fall on you; this is how to bully a man; this is how a man bullies you; this is how to love a man, and if this doesn't work there are other ways, and if they don't work don't feel too bad about giving up; this is how to spit up in the air if you feel like it, and this is how to move quick so that it doesn't fall on you; this is how to make ends meet; always squeeze bread to make sure it's fresh; *but what if the baker won't let me feel the bread?*; you mean to say that after all you are really going to be the kind of woman who the baker won't let near the bread?

◇ ◇ ◇

ALICE MUNRO (1931–   )

Boys and Girls (1968)

My father was a fox farmer. That is, he raised silver foxes, in pens; and in the fall and early winter, when their fur was prime, he killed them and skinned them and sold their pelts to the Hudson's Bay Company or the Montreal Fur Traders. These companies supplied us with heroic calendars to hang, one on each side of the kitchen door. Against a background of cold blue sky and black pine forests and treacherous northern rivers, plumed adventurers planted the flags of England or of France; magnificent savages bent their backs to the portage.°

For several weeks before Christmas, my father worked after supper in the cellar of our house. The cellar was whitewashed, and lit by a hundred-watt bulb over

---

portage: Carrying boats or goods overland from one body of water to another or around an obstacle such as rapids.

the worktable. My brother Laird and I sat on the top step and watched. My father removed the pelt inside-out from the body of the fox, which looked surprisingly small, mean and rat-like, deprived of its arrogant weight of fur. The naked, slippery bodies were collected in a sack and buried at the dump. One time the hired man, Henry Bailey, had taken a swipe at me with this sack, saying, "Christmas present!" My mother thought that was not funny. In fact she disliked the whole pelting operation — that was what the killing, skinning, and preparation of the furs was called — and wished it did not have to take place in the house. There was the smell. After the pelt had been stretched inside-out on a long board my father scraped away delicately, removing the little clotted webs of blood vessels, the bubbles of fat; the smell of blood and animal fat, with the strong primitive odour of the fox itself, penetrated all parts of the house. I found it reassuringly seasonal, like the smell of oranges and pine needles.

Henry Bailey suffered from bronchial troubles. He would cough and cough until his narrow face turned scarlet, and his light blue, derisive eyes filled up with tears; then he took the lid off the stove, and, standing well back, shot out a great clot of phlegm — hsss — straight into the heart of the flames. We admired him for his performance and for his ability to make his stomach growl at will, and for his laughter, which was full of high whistlings and gurglings and involved the whole faulty machinery of his chest. It was sometimes hard to tell what he was laughing at, and always possible that it might be us.

After we had been sent to bed we could still smell fox and still hear Henry's laugh, but these things, reminders of the warm, safe, brightly lit downstairs world, seemed lost and diminished, floating on the stale cold air upstairs. We were afraid at night in the winter. We were not afraid of *outside* though this was the time of year when snowdrifts curled around our house like sleeping whales and the wind harassed us all night, coming up from the buried fields, the frozen swamp, with its old bugbear chorus of threats and misery. We were afraid of *inside*, the room where we slept. At this time the upstairs of our house was not finished. A brick chimney went up one wall. In the middle of the floor was a square hole, with a wooden railing around it; that was where the stairs came up. On the other side of the stairwell were the things that nobody had any use for any more — a soldiery roll of linoleum, standing on end, a wicker baby carriage, a fern basket, china jugs and basins with cracks in them, a picture of the Battle of Balaclava, very sad to look at. I had told Laird, as soon as he was old enough to understand such things, that bats and skeletons lived over there; whenever a man escaped from the county jail, twenty miles away, I imagined that he had somehow let himself in the window and was hiding behind the linoleum. But we had rules to keep us safe. When the light was on, we were safe as long as we did not step off the square of worn carpet which defined our bedroom-space; when the light was off no place was safe but the beds themselves. I had to turn out the light kneeling on the end of my bed, and stretching as far as I could to reach the cord.

5 In the dark we lay on our beds, our narrow life rafts, and fixed our eyes on the faint light coming up the stairwell, and sang songs. Laird sang "Jingle Bells," which he would sing any time, whether it was Christmas or not, and I sang "Danny Boy." I love the sound of my own voice, frail and supplicating, rising in the dark. We could make out the tall frosted shapes of the windows now, gloomy and white. When I

came to the part, *When I am dead, as dead I well may be* — a fit of shivering caused not by the cold sheets but by pleasurable emotion almost silenced me. *You'll kneel and say, an Ave there above me* — What was an Ave? Every day I forgot to find out.

Laird went straight from singing to sleep. I could hear his long, satisfied, bubbly breaths. Now for the time that remained to me, the most perfectly private and perhaps the best time of the whole day, I arranged myself tightly under the covers and went on with one of the stories I was telling myself from night to night. These stories were about myself, when I had grown a little older; they took place in a world that was recognizably mine, yet one that presented opportunities for courage, boldness and self-sacrifice, as mine never did. I rescued people from a bombed building (it discouraged me that the real war had gone on so far away from Jubilee). I shot two rabid wolves who were menacing the schoolyard (the teachers cowered terrified at my back). I rode a fine horse spiritedly down the main street of Jubilee, acknowledging the towns-people's gratitude for some yet-to-be-worked-out piece of heroism (nobody ever rode a horse there, except King Billy in the Orangemen's Day parade). There was always riding and shooting in these stories, though I had only been on a horse twice — bareback because we did not own a saddle — and the second time I had slid right around and dropped under the horse's feet; it had stepped placidly over me. I really was learning to shoot, but I could not hit anything yet, not even tin cans on fence posts.

Alive, the foxes inhabited a world my father made for them. It was surrounded by a high guard fence, like a medieval town, with a gate that was padlocked at night. Along the streets of this town were ranged large, sturdy pens. Each of them had a real door that a man could go through, a wooden ramp along the wire, for the foxes to run up and down on, and a kennel — something like a clothes chest with airholes — where they slept and stayed in winter and had their young. There were feeding and watering dishes attached to the wire in such a way that they could be emptied and cleaned from the outside. The dishes were made of old tin cans, and the ramps and kennels of odds and ends of old lumber. Everything was tidy and ingenious; my father was tirelessly inventive and his favourite book in the world was *Robinson Crusoe*. He had fitted a tin drum on a wheelbarrow, for bringing water down to the pens. This was my job in summer, when the foxes had to have water twice a day. Between nine and ten o'clock in the morning, and again after supper, I filled the drum at the pump and trundled it down through the barnyard to the pens, where I parked it, and filled my watering can and went along the streets. Laird came too, with his little cream and green gardening can, filled too full and knocking against his legs and slopping water on his canvas shoes. I had the real watering can, my father's, though I could only carry it three-quarters full.

The foxes all had names, which were printed on a tin plate and hung beside their doors. They were not named when they were born, but when they survived the first year's pelting and were added to the breeding stock. Those my father had named were called names like Prince, Bob, Wally and Betty. Those I had named were called Star or Turk, or Maureen or Diana. Laird named one Maud after a hired girl we had when he was little, one Harold after a boy at school, and one Mexico, he did not say why.

Naming them did not make pets out of them, or anything like it. Nobody but my father ever went into the pens, and he had twice had blood-poisoning from bites. When I was bringing them their water they prowled up and down on the paths they had made inside their pens, barking seldom — they saved that for nighttime, when they might get up a chorus of community frenzy — but always watching me, their eyes burning, clear gold, in their pointed, malevolent faces. They were beautiful for their delicate legs and heavy, aristocratic tails and the bright fur sprinkled on dark down their backs — which gave them their name — but especially for their faces, drawn exquisitely sharp in pure hostility, and their golden eyes.

10   Besides carrying water I helped my father when he cut the long grass, and the lamb's quarter and flowering money-musk, that grew between the pens. He cut with the scythe and I raked into piles. Then he took a pitchfork and threw fresh-cut grass all over the top of the pens, to keep the foxes cooler and shade their coats, which were browned by too much sun. My father did not talk to me unless it was about the job we were doing. In this he was quite different from my mother, who, if she was feeling cheerful, would tell me all sorts of things — the name of a dog she had had when she was a little girl, the names of boys she had gone out with later on when she was grown up, and what certain dresses of hers had looked like — she could not imagine now what had become of them. Whatever thoughts and stories my father had were private, and I was shy of him and would never ask him questions. Nevertheless I worked willingly under his eyes, and with a feeling of pride. One time a feed salesman came down into the pens to talk to him and my father said, "Like to have you meet my new hired man." I turned away and raked furiously, red in the face with pleasure.

"Could of fooled me," said the salesman. "I thought it was only a girl."

After the grass was cut, it seemed suddenly much later in the year. I walked on stubble in the earlier evening, aware of the reddening skies, the entering silences, of fall. When I wheeled the tank out of the gate and put the padlock on, it was almost dark. One night at this time I saw my mother and father standing talking on the little rise of ground we called the gangway, in front of the barn. My father had just come from the meathouse; he had his stiff bloody apron on, and a pail of cut-up meat in his hand.

It was an odd thing to see my mother down at the barn. She did not often come out of the house unless it was to do something — hang out the wash or dig potatoes in the garden. She looked out of place, with her bare lumpy legs, not touched by the sun, her apron still on and damp across the stomach from the supper dishes. Her hair was tied up in a kerchief, wisps of it falling out. She would tie her hair up like this in the morning, saying she did not have time to do it properly, and it would stay tied up all day. It was true, too; she really did not have time. These days our back porch was piled with baskets of peaches and grapes and pears, bought in town, and onions and tomatoes and cucumbers grown at home, all waiting to be made into jelly and jam and preserves, pickles and chili sauce. In the kitchen there was a fire in the stove all day, jars clinked in boiling water, sometimes a cheesecloth bag was strung on a pole between two chairs, straining blue-black grape pulp for jelly. I was given jobs to do and I would sit at the table peeling peaches that had been soaked in the hot water, or cutting up onions, my eyes smarting and streaming. As soon as I was done I ran out of the house, trying to get out of earshot before my mother thought of what she wanted me to do next. I hated the hot dark kitchen in summer, the green blinds and the flypapers, the same old oilcloth table and wavy mirror and bumpy linoleum. My mother was too tired and preoccupied to talk to me, she had no heart to tell about the Normal School Graduation Dance; sweat trickled over her face and she was always counting under her breath, pointing at jars, dumping cups of sugar. It seemed to me that work in the house was endless, dreary and peculiarly depressing; work done out of doors, and in my father's service, was ritualistically important.

I wheeled the tank up to the barn, where it was kept, and I heard my mother saying, "Wait till Laird gets a little bigger, then you'll have a real help."

What my father said I did not hear. I was pleased by the way he stood listening, politely as he would to a salesman or a stranger, but with an air of wanting to get on with his real work. I felt my mother had no business down here and I wanted him to feel the same way. What did she mean about Laird? He was no help to anybody. Where was he now? Swinging himself sick on the swing, going around in circles, or trying to catch caterpillars. He never once stayed with me till I was finished. 15

"And then I can use her more in the house," I heard my mother say. She had a dead-quiet, regretful way of talking about me that always made me uneasy. "I just get my back turned and she runs off. It's not like I had a girl in the family at all."

I went and sat on a feedbag in the corner of the barn, not wanting to appear when this conversation was going on. My mother, I felt, was not to be trusted. She was kinder than my father and more easily fooled, but you could not depend on her, and the real reasons for the things she said and did were not to be known. She loved me, and she sat up late at night making a dress of the difficult style I wanted, for me to wear when school started, but she was also my enemy. She was always plotting. She was plotting now to get me to stay in the house more, although she knew I hated it (*because* she knew I hated it) and keep me from working for my father. It seemed to me she would do this simply out of perversity, and to try her power. It did not occur to me that she could be lonely, or jealous. No grown-up could be; they were too fortunate. I sat and kicked my heels monotonously against a feedbag, raising dust, and did not come out till she was gone.

At any rate, I did not expect my father to pay any attention to what she said. Who could imagine Laird doing my work — Laird remembering the padlock and cleaning out the watering-dishes with a leaf on the end of a stick, or even wheeling the tank without it tumbling over? It showed how little my mother knew about the way things really were.

I have forgotten to say what the foxes were fed. My father's bloody apron reminded me. They were fed horsemeat. At this time most farmers still kept horses, and when a horse got too old to work, or broke a leg or got down and would not get up, as they sometimes did, the owner would call my father, and he and Henry went out to the farm in the truck. Usually they shot and butchered the horse there, paying the farmer from five to twelve dollars. If they had already too much meat on hand, they would bring the horse back alive, and keep it for a few days or weeks in our stable, until the meat was needed. After the war the farmers were buying tractors and gradually getting rid of horses altogether, so it sometimes happened that we got a good healthy horse, that there was just no use for any more. If this happened in the winter we might keep the horse in our stable till spring, for we had plenty of hay and if there was a lot of snow — and the plow did not always get our road cleared — it was convenient to be able to go to town with a horse and cutter.

20   The winter I was eleven years old we had two horses in the stable. We did not know what names they had had before, so we called them Mack and Flora. Mack was an old black workhorse, sooty and indifferent. Flora was a sorrel mare, a driver. We took them both out in the cutter. Mack was slow and easy to handle. Flora was given to fits of violent alarm, veering at cars and even at other horses, but we loved her speed and high-stepping, her general air of gallantry and abandon. On Saturdays we went down to the stable and as soon as we opened the door on its cosy, animal-smelling darkness Flora threw up her head, rolled her eyes, whinnied despairingly and pulled herself through a crisis of nerves on the spot. It was not safe to go into her stall; she would kick.

This winter also I began to hear a great deal more on the theme my mother had sounded when she had been talking in front of the barn. I no longer felt safe. It seemed that in the minds of the people around me there was a steady undercurrent of thought, not to be deflected, on this one subject. The word *girl* had formerly seemed to me innocent and unburdened, like the word *child*; now it appeared that it was no such thing. A girl was not, as I had supposed, simply what I was; it was what I had to become. It was a definition, always touched with emphasis, with reproach and disappointment. Also it was a joke on me. Once Laird and I were fighting, and for the first time ever I had to use all my strength against him; even so, he caught and pinned my arm for a moment, really hurting me. Henry saw this, and laughed, saying, "Oh, that there Laird's gonna show you, one of these days!" Laird was getting a lot bigger. But I was getting bigger too.

My grandmother came to stay with us for a few weeks and I heard other things. "Girls don't slam doors like that." "Girls keep their knees together when they sit down." And worse still, when I asked some questions, "That's none of girls' business." I continued to slam the doors and sit as awkwardly as possible, thinking that by such measures I kept myself free.

When spring came, the horses were let out in the barnyard. Mack stood against the barn wall trying to scratch his neck and haunches, but Flora trotted up and down and reared at the fences, clattering her hooves against the rails. Snow drifts dwindled quickly, revealing the hard grey and brown earth, the familiar rise and fall of the ground, plain and bare after the fantastic landscape of winter. There was a great feeling of opening-out, of release. We just wore rubbers now, over our shoes; our feet felt ridiculously light. One Saturday we went out to the stable and found all the doors open, letting in the unaccustomed sunlight and fresh air. Henry was there, just idling around looking at his collection of calendars which were tacked up behind the stalls in a part of the stable my mother had probably never seen.

"Come to say goodbye to your old friend Mack?" Henry said. "Here, you give him a taste of oats." He poured some oats into Laird's cupped hands and Laird went to feed Mack. Mack's teeth were in bad shape. He ate very slowly, patiently shifting the oats around in his mouth, trying to find a stump of a molar to grind it on. "Poor old Mack," said Henry mournfully. "When a horse's teeth's gone, he's gone. That's about the way."

"Are you going to shoot him today?" I said. Mack and Flora had been in the 25
stable so long I had almost forgotten they were going to be shot.

Henry didn't answer me. Instead he started to sing in a high, trembly,
mocking-sorrowful voice, Oh, *there's no more work, for poor Uncle Ned, he's
gone where the good darkies go.* Mack's thick, blackish tongue worked diligently
at Laird's hand. I went out before the song was ended and sat down on the
gangway.

I had never seen them shoot a horse, but I knew where it was done. Last summer Laird and I had come upon a horse's entrails before they were buried. We had
thought it was a big black snake, coiled up in the sun. That was around in the field
that ran up beside the barn. I thought that if we went inside the barn, and found
a wide crack or a knothole to look through, we would be able to see them do it. It
was not something I wanted to see; just the same, if a thing really happened, it
was better to see it, and know.

My father came down from the house, carrying the gun.

"What are you doing here?" he said.

"Nothing." 30

"Go on up and play around the house."

He sent Laird out of the stable. I said to Laird, "Do you want to see them shoot
Mack?" and without waiting for an answer led him around to the front door of the
barn, opened it carefully, and went in. "Be quiet or they'll hear us," I said. We
could hear Henry and my father talking in the stable, then the heavy, shuffling
steps of Mack being backed out of his stall.

In the loft it was cold and dark. Thin, crisscrossed beams of sunlight fell
through the cracks. The hay was low. It was a rolling country, hills and hollows,
slipping under our feet. About four feet up was a beam going around the walls. We
piled hay up in one corner and I boosted Laird up and hoisted myself. The beam
was not very wide; we crept along it with our hands flat on the barn walls. There
were plenty of knotholes, and I found one that gave me the view I wanted — a
corner of the barnyard, the gate, part of the field. Laird did not have a knothole
and began to complain.

I showed him a widened crack between two boards. "Be quiet and wait. If they
hear you you'll get us in trouble."

My father came in sight carrying the gun. Henry was leading Mack by the hal- 35
ter. He dropped it and took out his cigarette papers and tobacco; he rolled cigarettes for my father and himself. While this was going on Mack nosed around in
the old, dead grass along the fence. Then my father opened the gate and they took
Mack through. Henry led Mack away from the path to a patch of ground and they
talked together, not loud enough for us to hear. Mack again began searching for a
mouthful of fresh grass, which was not to be found. My father walked away in a
straight line, and stopped short at a distance which seemed to suit him. Henry was
walking away from Mack too, but sideways, still negligently holding on to the halter. My father raised the gun and Mack looked up as if he had noticed something
and my father shot him.

Mack did not collapse at once but swayed, lurched sideways and fell, first on
his side; then he rolled over on his back and, amazingly, kicked his legs for a few
seconds in the air. At this Henry laughed, as if Mack had done a trick for him.

Laird, who had drawn a long, groaning breath of surprise when the shot was fired, said out loud, "He's not dead." And it seemed to me it might be true. But his legs stopped, he rolled on his side again, his muscles quivered and sank. The two men walked over and looked at him in a businesslike way; they bent down and examined his forehead where the bullet had gone in, and now I saw his blood on the brown grass.

"Now they just skin him and cut him up," I said. "Let's go." My legs were a little shaky and I jumped gratefully down into the hay. "Now you've seen how they shoot a horse," I said in a congratulatory way, as if I had seen it many times before. "Let's see if any barn cat's had kittens in the hay." Laird jumped. He seemed young and obedient again. Suddenly I remembered how, when he was little, I had brought him into the barn and told him to climb the ladder to the top beam. That was in the spring, too, when the hay was low. I had done it out of a need for excitement, a desire for something to happen so that I could tell about it. He was wearing a little bulky brown and white checked coat, made down from one of mine. He went all the way up, just as I told him, and sat down on the top beam with the hay far below him on one side, and the barn floor and some old machinery on the other. Then I ran screaming to my father, "Laird's up on the top beam!" My father came, my mother came, my father went up the ladder talking very quietly and brought Laird down under his arm, at which my mother leaned against the ladder and began to cry. They said to me, "Why weren't you watching him?" but nobody ever knew the truth. Laird did not know enough to tell. But whenever I saw the brown and white checked coat hanging in the closet, or at the bottom of the rag bag, which was where it ended up, I felt a weight in my stomach, the sadness of unexorcized guilt.

I looked at Laird who did not even remember this, and I did not like the look on his thin, winter-pale face. His expression was not frightened or upset, but remote, concentrating. "Listen," I said, in an unusually bright and friendly voice, "you aren't going to tell, are you?"

"No," he said absently.

40   "Promise."

"Promise," he said. I grabbed the hand behind his back to make sure he was not crossing his fingers. Even so, he might have a nightmare; it might come out that way. I decided I had better work hard to get all thoughts of what he had seen out of his mind — which, it seemed to me, could not hold very many things at a time. I got some money I had saved and that afternoon we went into Jubilee and saw a show, with Judy Canova, at which we both laughed a great deal. After that I thought it would be all right.

Two weeks later I knew they were going to shoot Flora. I knew from the night before, when I heard my mother ask if the hay was holding out all right, and my father said, "Well, after to-morrow there'll just be the cow, and we should be able to put her out to grass in another week." So I knew it was Flora's turn in the morning.

This time I didn't think of watching it. That was something to see just one time. I had not thought about it very often since, but sometimes when I was busy, working at school, or standing in front of the mirror combing my hair and wondering if I would be pretty when I grew up, the whole scene would flash into my mind: I would see the easy, practised way my father raised the gun, and hear Henry laughing when Mack kicked his legs in the air. I did not have any great feeling of horror and opposition, such as a city child might have had; I was too used to seeing the death of animals as a necessity by which we lived. Yet I felt a little ashamed, and there was a new wariness, a sense of holding-off, in my attitude to my father and his work.

It was a fine day, and we were going around the yard picking up tree branches that had been torn off in winter storms. This was something we had been told to do, and also we wanted to use them to make a teepee. We heard Flora whinny, and then my father's voice and Henry's shouting, and we ran down to the barnyard to see what was going on.

The stable door was open. Henry had just brought Flora out, and she had broken away from him. She was running free in the barnyard, from one end to the other. We climbed up on the fence. It was exciting to see her running, whinnying, going up on her hind legs, prancing and threatening like a horse in a Western movie, an unbroken ranch horse, though she was just an old driver, an old sorrel mare. My father and Henry ran after her and tried to grab the dangling halter. They tried to work her into a corner, and they had almost succeeded when she made a run between them, wild-eyed, and disappeared around the corner of the barn. We heard the rails clatter down as she got over the fence, and Henry yelled, "She's into the field now!"

That meant she was in the long L-shaped field that ran up by the house. If she got around the center, heading towards the lane, the gate was open; the truck had been driven into the field this morning. My father shouted to me, because I was on the other side of the fence, nearest the lane, "Go shut the gate!"

I could run very fast. I ran across the garden, past the tree where our swing was hung, and jumped across a ditch into the lane. There was the open gate. She had not got out, I could not see her up on the road; she must have run to the other end of the field. The gate was heavy. I lifted it out of the gravel and carried it across the roadway. I had it half-way across when she came in sight, galloping straight towards me. There was just time to get the chain on. Laird came scrambling through the ditch to help me.

Instead of shutting the gate, I opened it as wide as I could. I did not make any decision to do this, it was just what I did. Flora never slowed down; she galloped straight past me, and Laird jumped up and down, yelling, "Shut it, shut it!" even after it was too late. My father and Henry appeared in the field a moment too late to see what I had done. They only saw Flora heading for the township road. They would think I had not got there in time.

They did not waste any time asking about it. They went back to the barn and got the gun and the knives they used, and put these in the truck; then they turned the truck around and came bouncing up the field toward us. Laird called to them, "Let me go too, let me go too!" and Henry stopped the truck and they took him in. I shut the gate after they were all gone.

I supposed Laird would tell. I wondered what would happen to me. I had never disobeyed my father before, and I could not understand why I had done it. Flora would not really get away. They would catch up with her in the truck. Or if they did not catch her this morning somebody would see her and telephone us this afternoon or tomorrow. There was no wild country here for her to run to, only farms. What was more, my father had paid for her, we needed the meat to feed the foxes, we needed the foxes to make our living. All I had done was make more work for my father who worked hard enough already. And when my father found out about it he was not going to trust me any more; he would know that I was not entirely on his side. I was on Flora's side, and that made me no use to anybody, not even to her. Just the same, I did not regret it; when she came running at me and I held the gate open, that was the only thing I could do.

I went back to the house, and my mother said, "What's all the commotion?" I told her that Flora had kicked down the fence and got away. "Your poor father," she said, "now he'll have to go chasing over the countryside. Well, there isn't any use planning dinner before one." She put up the ironing board. I wanted to tell her, but thought better of it and went upstairs and sat on my bed.

Lately I had been trying to make my part of the room fancy, spreading the bed with old lace curtains, and fixing myself a dressing-table with some leftovers of cretonne for a skirt. I planned to put up some kind of barricade between my bed and Laird's, to keep my section separate from his. In the sunlight, the lace curtains were just dusty rags. We did not sing at night any more. One night when I was singing Laird said, "You sound silly," and I went right on but the next night I did not start. There was not so much need to anyway, we were no longer afraid. We knew it was just old furniture over there, old jumble and confusion. We did not keep to the rules. I still stayed awake after Laird was asleep and told myself stories, but even in these stories something different was happening, mysterious alterations took place. A story might start off in the old way, with a spectacular danger, a fire or wild animals, and for a while I might rescue people; then things would change around, and instead, somebody would be rescuing me. It might be a boy from our class at school, or even Mr. Campbell, our teacher, who tickled girls under the arms. And at this point the story concerned itself at great length with what I looked like — how long my hair was, and what kind of dress I had on; by the time I had these details worked out the real excitement of the story was lost.

It was later than one o'clock when the truck came back. The tarpaulin was over the back, which meant there was meat in it. My mother had to heat dinner up all over again. Henry and my father had changed from their bloody overalls into ordinary working overalls in the barn, and they washed their arms and necks and faces at the sink, and splashed water on their hair and combed it. Laird lifted his arm to show off a streak of blood. "We shot old Flora," he said, "and cut her up in fifty pieces."

"Well, I don't want to hear about it," my mother said. "And don't come to my table like that."

55   My family made him go and wash the blood off.

We sat down and my father said grace and Henry pasted his chewing-gum on the end of his fork, the way he always did; when he took it off he would have us admire the pattern. We began to pass the bowls of steaming, overcooked vegetables. Laird looked across the table at me and said proudly, distinctly, "Anyway it was her fault Flora got away."

"What?" my father said.

"She could of shut the gate and she didn't. She just open' it up and Flora run out."

"Is that right?" my father said.

Everybody at the table was looking at me. I nodded, swallowing food with   60
great difficulty. To my shame, tears flooded my eyes.

My father made a curt sound of disgust. "What did you do that for?"

I did not answer. I put down my fork and waited to be sent from the table, still not looking up.

But this did not happen. For some time nobody said anything, then Laird said matter-of-factly, "She's crying."

"Never mind," my father said. He spoke with resignation, even good humour, the words which absolved and dismissed me for good. "She's only a girl," he said.

I didn't protest that, even in my heart. Maybe it was true.   65

◇ ◇ ◇

FLANNERY O'CONNOR   (1925–1964)

Good Country People   (1955)

Besides the neutral expression that she wore when she was alone, Mrs. Freeman had two others, forward and reverse, that she used for all her human dealings. Her forward expression was steady and driving like the advance of a heavy truck. Her eyes never swerved to left or right but turned as the story turned as if they followed a yellow line down the center of it. She seldom used the other expression because it was not often necessary for her to retract a statement, but when she did, her face came to a complete stop, there was an almost imperceptible movement of her black eyes, during which they seemed to be receding, and then the observer would see that Mrs. Freeman, though she might stand there as real as several grain sacks thrown on top of each other, was no longer there in spirit. As for getting anything across to her when this was the case, Mrs. Hopewell had given it up. She might talk her head off. Mrs. Freeman could never be brought to admit herself wrong on any point. She would stand there and if she could be brought to say anything, it was something like, "Well, I wouldn't of said it was and I wouldn't of said it wasn't," or letting her gaze range over the top kitchen shelf where there was an assortment of dusty bottles, she might remark, "I see you ain't ate many of them figs you put up last summer."

They carried on their most important business in the kitchen at breakfast. Every morning Mrs. Hopewell got up at seven o'clock and lit her gas heater and Joy's. Joy was her daughter, a large blonde girl who had an artificial leg. Mrs. Hopewell thought of her as a child though she was thirty-two years old and highly educated. Joy would get up while her mother was eating and lumber into the bathroom and slam the door, and before long, Mrs. Freeman would arrive at the back door. Joy would hear her mother call, "Come on in," and then they would talk a while in low voices that were indistinguishable in the bathroom. By the time Joy came in, they had usually finished the weather report and were on one or the other of Mrs. Freeman's daughters, Glynese or Carramae, Joy called them Glycerin and Caramel. Glynese, a redhead, was eighteen and had many admirers, Carramae, a blonde, was only fifteen but already married and pregnant. She could not keep anything on her stomach. Every morning Mrs. Freeman told Mrs. Hopewell how many times she had vomited since the last report.

Mrs. Hopewell liked to tell people that Glynese and Carramae were two of the finest girls she knew and that Mrs. Freeman was a *lady* and that she was never ashamed to take her anywhere or introduce her to anybody they might meet. Then she would tell how she had happened to hire the Freemans in the first place and how they were a godsend to her and how she had had them four years. The reason for her keeping them so long was that they were not trash. They were good country people. She had telephoned the man whose name they had given as a reference and he had told her that Mr. Freeman was a good farmer but that his wife was the nosiest woman ever to walk the earth. "She's got to be into everything," the man said. "If she don't get there before the dust settles, you can bet she's dead, that's all. She'll want to know all your business. I can stand him real good," he had said, "but me nor my wife neither could have stood that woman one more minute on this place." That had put Mrs. Hopewell off for a few days.

She had hired them in the end because there were no other applicants but she had made up her mind beforehand exactly how she would handle the woman. Since she was the type who had to be into everything, then, Mrs. Hopewell had decided, she would not only let her be into everything, she would *see to it* that she was into everything — she would give her the responsibility of everything, she would put her in charge. Mrs. Hopewell had no bad qualities of her own but she was able to use other people's in such a constructive way that she never felt the lack. She had hired the Freemans and she had kept them four years.

5   Nothing is perfect. This was one of Mrs. Hopewell's favorite sayings. Another was: that is life! And still another, the most important, was: well, other people have their opinions too. She would make these statements, usually at the table, in a tone of gentle insistence as if no one held them but her, and the large hulking Joy, whose constant outrage had obliterated every expression from her face, would stare just a little to the side of her, her eyes icy blue, with the look of someone who has achieved blindness by an act of will and means to keep it.

When Mrs. Hopewell said to Mrs. Freeman that life was like that, Mrs. Freeman would say, "I always said so myself." Nothing had been arrived at by anyone that had not first been arrived at by her. She was quicker than Mr. Freeman. When Mrs. Hopewell said to her after they had been on the place a while, "You know, you're the wheel behind the wheel," and winked, Mrs. Freeman had said, "I know it. I've always been quick. It's some that are quicker than others."

"Everybody is different," Mrs. Hopewell said.

"Yes, most people is," Mrs. Freeman said.

"It takes all kinds to make the world."

10   "I always said it did myself."

The girl was used to this kind of dialogue for breakfast and more of it for dinner; sometimes they had it for supper too. When they had no guest they ate in the kitchen because that was easier. Mrs. Freeman always managed to arrive at some point during the meal and to watch them finish it. She would stand in the doorway if it were summer but in the winter she would stand with one elbow on top of the refrigerator and look down on them, or she would stand by the gas heater, lifting the back of her skirt slightly. Occasionally she would stand against the wall and roll her head from side to side. At no time was she in any hurry to leave. All this was very trying on Mrs. Hopewell but she was a woman of great patience. She realized that nothing is perfect and that in the Freemans she had good country people and that if, in this day and age, you get good country people, you had better hang onto them.

She had had plenty of experience with trash. Before the Freemans she had averaged one tenant family a year. The wives of these farmers were not the kind you would want to be around you for very long. Mrs. Hopewell, who had divorced her husband long ago, needed someone to walk over the fields with her; and when Joy had to be impressed for these services, her remarks were usually so ugly and her face so glum that Mrs. Hopewell would say, "If you can't come pleasantly, I don't want you at all," to which the girl, standing square and rigid-shouldered with her neck thrust slightly forward, would reply, "If you want me, here I am — LIKE I AM."

Mrs. Hopewell excused this attitude because of the leg (which had been shot off in a hunting accident when Joy was ten). It was hard for Mrs. Hopewell to realize that her child was thirty-two now and that for more than twenty years she had had one leg. She thought of her still as a child because it tore her heart to think instead of the poor stout girl in her thirties who had never danced a step or had any *normal* good times. Her name was really Joy but as soon as she was twenty-one and away from home, she had had it legally changed. Mrs. Hopewell was certain that she had thought and thought until she had hit upon the ugliest name in any language. Then she had gone and had the beautiful name, Joy, changed without telling her mother until after she had done it. Her legal name was Hulga.

When Mrs. Hopewell thought the name Hulga, she thought of the broad blank hull of a battleship. She would not use it. She continued to call her Joy to which the girl responded but in a purely mechanical way.

Hulga had learned to tolerate Mrs. Freeman who saved her from taking walks   15
with her mother. Even Glynese and Carramae were useful when they occupied attention that might otherwise have been directed at her. At first she had thought she could not stand Mrs. Freeman for she had found that it was not possible to be rude to her. Mrs. Freeman would take on strange resentments and for days together she would be sullen but the source of her displeasure was always obscure; a direct attack, a positive leer, blatant ugliness to her face — these never touched her. And without warning one day, she began calling her Hulga.

She did not call her that in front of Mrs. Hopewell who would have been incensed but when she and the girl happened to be out of the house together, she would say something and add the name Hulga to the end of it, and the big spectacled Joy-Hulga would scowl and redden as if her privacy had been intruded upon. She considered the name her personal affair. She had arrived at it first purely on the basis of its ugly sound and then the full genius of its fitness had struck her. She had a vision of the name working like the ugly sweating Vulcan who stayed in the furnace and to whom, presumably, the goddess had to come when called. She saw it as the name of her highest creative act. One of her major triumphs was that her mother had not been able to turn her dust into Joy, but the greater one was that she had been able to turn it herself into Hulga. However, Mrs. Freeman's relish for using the name only irritated her. It was as if Mrs. Freeman's beady steel-pointed eyes had penetrated far enough behind her face to reach some secret fact. Something about her seemed to fascinate Mrs. Freeman and then one day Hulga realized that it was the artificial leg. Mrs. Freeman had a special fondness for the details of secret infections, hidden deformities, assaults upon children. Of diseases, she preferred the lingering or incurable. Hulga had heard Mrs. Hopewell give her the details of the hunting accident, how the leg had been literally blasted off, how she had never lost consciousness. Mrs. Freeman could listen to it any time as if it had happened an hour ago.

When Hulga stumped into the kitchen in the morning (she could walk without making the awful noise but she made it — Mrs. Hopewell was certain — because it was ugly-sounding), she glanced at them and did not speak. Mrs. Hopewell would be in her red kimono with her hair tied around her head in rags. She would be sitting at the table, finishing her breakfast and Mrs. Freeman would be hanging by her elbow outward from the refrigerator, looking down at the table. Hulga always put her eggs on the stove to boil and then stood over them with her arms folded, and Mrs. Hopewell would look at her — a kind of indirect gaze divided between her and Mrs. Freeman — and would think that if she would only keep herself up a little, she wouldn't be so bad looking. There was nothing wrong with her face that a pleasant expression wouldn't help. Mrs. Hopewell said that people who looked on the bright side of things would be beautiful even if they were not.

Whenever she looked at Joy this way, she could not help but feel that it would have been better if the child had not taken the Ph.D. It had certainly not brought her out any and now that she had it, there was no more excuse for her to go to school again. Mrs. Hopewell thought it was nice for girls to go to school to have a good time but Joy had "gone through." Anyhow, she would not have been strong enough to go again. The doctors had told Mrs. Hopewell that with the best of care, Joy might see forty-five. She had a weak heart. Joy had made it plain that if it had not been for this condition, she would be far from these red hills and good country people. She would be in a university lecturing to people who knew what she was talking about. And Mrs. Hopewell could very well picture her there, looking like a scarecrow and lecturing to more of the same. Here she went about all day in a six-year-old skirt and a yellow sweat shirt with a faded cowboy on a horse embossed on it. She thought this was funny; Mrs. Hopewell thought it was idiotic and showed simply that she was still a child. She was brilliant but she didn't have a grain of sense. It seemed to Mrs. Hopewell that every year she grew less like other people and more like herself — bloated, rude, and squint-eyed. And she said such strange things! To her own mother she had said — without warning, without excuse, standing up in the middle of a meal with her face purple and her 20 mouth half full — "Woman! do you ever look inside? Do you ever look inside and see what you are *not*? God!" she had cried sinking down again and staring at her plate, "Malebranche was right: we are not our own light. We are not our own light!" Mrs. Hopewell had no idea to this day what brought that on. She had only made the remark, hoping Joy would take it in, that a smile never hurt anyone.

The girl had taken the Ph.D. in philosophy and this left Mrs. Hopewell at a complete loss. You could say, "My daughter is a nurse," or "My daughter is a schoolteacher," or even, "My daughter is a chemical engineer." You could not say, "My daughter is a philosopher." That was something that had ended with the Greeks and Romans. All day Joy sat on her neck in a deep chair, reading. Sometimes she went for walks but she didn't like dogs or cats or birds or flowers or nature or nice young men. She looked at nice young men as if she could smell their stupidity.

One day Mrs. Hopewell had picked up one of the books the girl had just put down and opening it at random, she read, "Science, on the other hand, has to assert its soberness and seriousness afresh and declare that it is concerned solely with what-is. Nothing — how can it be for science anything but a horror and a phantasm? If science is right, then one thing stands firm: science wishes to know nothing of nothing. Such is after all the strictly scientific approach to Nothing. We know it by wishing to know nothing of Nothing." These words had been underlined with a blue pencil and they worked on Mrs. Hopewell like some evil incantation in gibberish. She shut the book quickly and went out of the room as if she were having a chill.

This morning when the girl came in, Mrs. Freeman was on Carramae. "She thrown up four times after supper," she said, "and was up twict in the night after three o'clock. Yesterday she didn't do nothing but ramble in the bureau drawer. All she did. Stand up there and see what she could run up on."

"She's got to eat," Mrs. Hopewell muttered, sipping her coffee, while she watched Joy's back at the stove. She was wondering what the child had said to the Bible salesman. She could not imagine what kind of a conversation she could possibly have had with him.

He was a tall gaunt hatless youth who had called yesterday to sell them a Bible. He had appeared at the door, carrying a large black suitcase that weighted him so heavily on one side that he had to brace himself against the door facing. He seemed on the point of collapse but he said in a cheerful voice, "Good morning, Mrs. Cedars!" and set the suitcase down on the mat. He was not a bad-looking young man though he had on a bright blue suit and yellow socks that were not pulled up far enough. He had prominent face bones and a streak of sticky-looking brown hair falling across his forehead.

"I'm Mrs. Hopewell," she said.

"Oh!" he said, pretending to look puzzled but with his eyes sparkling, "I saw it 25 said 'The Cedars' on the mailbox so I thought you was Mrs. Cedars!" and he burst out in a pleasant laugh. He picked up the satchel and under cover of a pant, he fell forward into her hall. It was rather as if the suitcase had moved first, jerking him after it. "Mrs. Hopewell!" he said and grabbed her hand. "I hope you are well!" and he laughed again and then all at once his face sobered completely. He paused and gave her a straight earnest look and said, "Lady I've come to speak of serious things."

"Well, come in," she muttered, none too pleased because her dinner was almost ready. He came into the parlor and sat down on the edge of a straight chair and put the suitcase between his feet and glanced around the room as if he were sizing her up by it. Her silver gleamed on the two sideboards; she decided he had never been in a room as elegant as this.

"Mrs. Hopewell," he began, using her name in a way that sounded almost intimate, "I know you believe in Chrustian service."

"Well yes," she murmured.

"I know," he said and paused, looking very wise with his head cocked on one side; "that you're a good woman. Friends have told me."

30   Mrs. Hopewell never liked to be taken for a fool. "What are you selling?" she asked.

"Bibles," the young man said and his eye raced around the room before he added, "I see you have no family Bible in your parlor, I see that is the one lack you got!"

Mrs. Hopewell could not say, "My daughter is an atheist and won't let me keep the Bible in the parlor." She said, stiffening slightly, "I keep my Bible by my bed-side." This was not the truth. It was in the attic somewhere.

"Lady," he said, "the word of God ought to be in the parlor."

"Well, I think that's a matter of taste," she began. "I think . . ."

35   "Lady," he said, "for a Chrustian, the word of God ought to be in every room in the house besides in his heart. I know you're a Chrustian because I can see it in every line of your face."

She stood up and said, "Well, young man, I don't want to buy a Bible and I smell my dinner burning."

He didn't get up. He began to twist his hands and looking down at them he said softly, "Well lady, I'll tell you the truth — not many people want to buy one nowadays and besides, I know I'm real simple. I don't know how to say a thing but to say it. I'm just a country boy." He glanced up into her unfriendly face. "People like you don't like to fool with country people like me!"

"Why!" she cried, "good country people are the salt of the earth! Besides, we all have different ways of doing, it takes all kinds to make the world go 'round. That's life!"

"You said a mouthful," he said.

40   "Why, I think there aren't enough good country people in the world!" she said, stirred. "I think that's what's wrong with it!"

His face had brightened. "I didn't inraduce myself," he said. "I'm Manley Pointer from out in the country around Willohobie, not even from a place, just from near a place."

"You wait a minute," she said. "I have to see about my dinner." She went out to the kitchen and found Joy standing near the door where she had been listening.

"Get rid of the salt of the earth," she said, "and let's eat."

Mrs. Hopewell gave her a pained look and turned the heat down under the vegetables. "I can't be rude to anybody," she murmured and went back into the parlor.

45   He had opened the suitcase and was sitting with a Bible on each knee.

"You might as well put those up," she told him. "I don't want one."

"I appreciate your honesty," he said. "You don't see any more real honest people unless you go way out in the country."

"I know," she said, "real genuine folks!" Through the crack in the door she heard a groan.

"I guess a lot of boys come telling you they're working their way through college," he said, "but I'm not going to tell you that. Somehow," he said, "I don't want to go to college. I want to devote my life to Chrustian service. See," he said, lowering his voice, "I got this heart condition. I may not live long. When you know it's something wrong with you and you may not live long, well then, lady . . ." He paused, with his mouth open, and stared at her.

He and Joy had the same condition! She knew that her eyes were filling with tears but she collected herself quickly and murmured, "Won't you stay for dinner? We'd love to have you!" and was sorry the instant she heard herself say it.

"Yes mam," he said in an abashed voice, "I would sher love to do that!"

Joy had given him one look on being introduced to him and then throughout the meal had not glanced at him again. He had addressed several remarks to her, which she had pretended not to hear. Mrs. Hopewell could not understand deliberate rudeness, although she lived with it, and she felt she had always to overflow with hospitality to make up for Joy's lack of courtesy. She urged him to talk about himself and he did. He said he was the seventh child of twelve and that his father had been crushed under a tree when he himself was eight years old. He had been crushed very badly, in fact, almost cut in two and was practically not recognizable. His mother had got along the best she could by hard working and she had always seen that her children went to Sunday School and that they read the Bible every evening. He was now nineteen years old and he had been selling Bibles for four months. In that time he had sold seventy-seven Bibles and had the promise of two more sales. He wanted to become a missionary because he thought that was the way you could do most for people. "He who losest his life shall find it," he said simply and he was so sincere, so genuine and earnest that Mrs. Hopewell would not for the world have smiled. He prevented his peas from sliding onto the table by blocking them with a piece of bread which he later cleaned his plate with. She could see Joy observing sidewise how he handled his knife and fork and she saw too that every few minutes, the boy would dart a keen appraising glance at the girl as if he were trying to attract her attention.

After dinner Joy cleared the dishes off the table and disappeared and Mrs. Hopewell was left to talk with him. He told her again about his childhood and his father's accident and about various things that had happened to him. Every five minutes or so she would stifle a yawn. He sat for two hours until finally she told him she must go because she had an appointment in town. He packed his Bibles and thanked her and prepared to leave, but in the doorway he stopped and wrung her hand and said that not on any of his trips had he met a lady as nice as her and he asked if he could come again. She had said she would always be happy to see him.

Joy had been standing in the road, apparently looking at something in the distance, when he came down the steps toward her, bent to the side with his heavy valise. He stopped where she was standing and confronted her directly. Mrs. Hopewell could not hear what he said but she trembled to think what Joy would say to him. She could see that after a minute Joy said something and that then the boy began to speak again, making an excited gesture with his free hand. After a minute Joy said something else at which the boy began to speak once more. Then to her amazement, Mrs. Hopewell saw the two of them walk off together, toward the gate. Joy had walked all the way to the gate with him and Mrs. Hopewell could not imagine what they had said to each other, and she had not yet dared to ask.

55   Mrs. Freeman was insisting upon her attention. She had moved from the refrigerator to the heater so that Mrs. Hopewell had to turn and face her in order to seem to be listening. "Glynese gone out with Harvey Hill again last night," she said. "She had this sty."

"Hill," Mrs. Hopewell said absently, "is that the one who works in the garage?"

"Nome, he's the one that goes to chiropracter school," Mrs. Freeman said. "She had this sty. Been had it two days. So she says when he brought her in the other night he says, 'Lemme get rid of that sty for you,' and she says, 'How?' and he says, 'You just lay yourself down acrost the seat of that car and I'll show you.' So she done it and he popped her neck. Kept on a-popping it several times until she made him quit. This morning." Mrs. Freeman said, "she ain't got no sty. She ain't got no traces of a sty."

"I never heard of that before," Mrs. Hopewell said.

"He ast her to marry him before the Ordinary," Mrs. Freeman went on, "and she told him she wasn't going to be married in no *office*."

60   "Well, Glynese is a fine girl," Mrs. Hopewell said. "Glynese and Carramae are both fine girls."

"Carramae said when her and Lyman was married Lyman said it sure felt sacred to him. She said he said he wouldn't take five hundred dollars for being married by a preacher."

"How much would he take?" the girl asked from the stove.

"He said he wouldn't take five hundred dollars," Mrs. Freeman repeated.

"Well we all have work to do," Mrs. Hopewell said.

65   "Lyman said it just felt more sacred to him," Mrs. Freeman said. "The doctor wants Carramae to eat prunes. Says instead of medicine. Says them cramps is coming from pressure. You know where I think it is?"

"She'll be better in a few weeks," Mrs. Hopewell said.

"In the tube," Mrs. Freeman said. "Else she wouldn't be as sick as she is."

Hulga had cracked her two eggs into a saucer and was bringing them to the table along with a cup of coffee that she had filled too full. She sat down carefully and began to eat, meaning to keep Mrs. Freeman there by questions if for any reason she showed an inclination to leave. She could perceive her mother's eye on her. The first round-about question would be about the Bible salesman and she did not wish to bring it on. "How did he pop her neck?" she asked.

Mrs. Freeman went into a description of how he had popped her neck. She said he owned a '55 Mercury but that Glynese said she would rather marry a man with only a '36 Plymouth who would be married by a preacher. The girl asked what if he had a '32 Plymouth and Mrs. Freeman said what Glynese had said was a '36 Plymouth.

70   Mrs. Hopewell said there were not many girls with Glynese's common sense. She said what she admired in those girls was their common sense. She said that reminded her that they had had a nice visitor yesterday, a young man selling Bibles. "Lord," she said, "he bored me to death but he was so sincere and genuine

I couldn't be rude to him. He was just good country people, you know," she said,
"—just the salt of the earth."

"I seen him walk up," Mrs. Freeman said, "and then later — I seen him walk
off," and Hulga could feel the slight shift in her voice, the slight insinuation, that
he had not walked off alone, had he? Her face remained expressionless but the color
rose into her neck and she seemed to swallow it down with the next spoonful of
egg. Mrs. Freeman was looking at her as if they had a secret together.

"Well, it takes all kinds of people to make the world go 'round," Mrs. Hopewell
said. "It's very good we aren't all alike."

"Some people are more alike than others," Mrs. Freeman said.

Hulga got up and stumped, with about twice the noise that was necessary, into
her room and locked the door. She was to meet the Bible salesman at ten o'clock
at the gate. She had thought about it half the night. She had started thinking of
it as a great joke and then she had begun to see profound implications in it. She
had lain in bed imagining dialogues for them that were insane on the surface but
that reached below to depths that no Bible salesman would be aware of. Their
conversation yesterday had been of this kind.

He had stopped in front of her and had simply stood there. His face was bony   75
and sweaty and bright, with a little pointed nose in the center of it, and his look
was different from what it had been at the dinner table. He was gazing at her with
open curiosity, with fascination, like a child watching a new fantastic animal at
the zoo, and he was breathing as if he had run a great distance to reach her. His
gaze seemed somehow familiar but she could not think where she had been regarded with it before. For almost a minute he didn't say anything. Then on what
seemed an insuck of breath, he whispered, "You ever ate a chicken that was two
days old?"

The girl looked at him stonily. He might have just put this question up for consideration at the meeting of a philosophical association. "Yes," she presently
replied as if she had considered it from all angles.

"It must have been mighty small!" he said triumphantly and shook all over with
little nervous giggles, getting very red in the face, and subsiding finally into his gaze
of complete admiration, while the girl's expression remained exactly the same.

"How old are you?" he asked softly.

She waited some time before she answered. Then in a flat voice she said,
"Seventeen."

His smiles came in succession like waves breaking on the surface of a little   80
lake. "I see you got a wooden leg," he said. "I think you're brave. I think you're real
sweet."

The girl stood blank and solid and silent.

"Walk to the gate with me," he said. "You're a brave sweet little thing and I
liked you the minute I seen you walk in the door."

Hulga began to move forward.

"What's your name?" he asked, smiling down on the top of her head.

"Hulga," she said.   85

"Hulga," he murmured, "Hulga. Hulga. I never heard of anybody name Hulga
before. You're shy, aren't you, Hulga?" he asked.

She nodded, watching his large red hand on the handle of the giant valise.

"I like girls that wear glasses," he said. "I think a lot. I'm not like these people that a serious thought don't ever enter their heads. It's because I may die."

"I may die too," she said suddenly and looked up at him. His eyes were very small and brown, glittering feverishly.

90   "Listen," he said, "don't you think some people was meant to meet on account of what all they got in common and all? Like they both think serious thoughts and all? He shifted the valise to his other hand so that the hand nearest her was free. He caught hold of her elbow and shook it a little. "I don't work on Saturday," he said. "I like to walk in the woods and see what Mother Nature is wearing. O'er the hills and far away. Pic-nics and things. Couldn't we go on a pic-nic tomorrow? Say yes, Hulga," he said and gave her a dying look as if he felt his insides about to drop out of him. He had even seemed to sway slightly toward her.

During the night she had imagined that she seduced him. She imagined that the two of them walked on the place until they came to the storage barn beyond the two back fields and there, she imagined, that things came to such a pass that she very easily seduced him and that then, of course, she had to reckon with his remorse. True genius can get an idea across even to an inferior mind. She imagined that she took his remorse in hand and changed it into a deeper understanding of life. She took all his shame away and turned it into something useful.

She set off for the gate at exactly ten o'clock, escaping without drawing Mrs. Hopewell's attention. She didn't take anything to eat, forgetting that food is usually taken on a pic-nic. She wore a pair of slacks and a dirty white shirt, and as an afterthought, she had put some Vapex on the collar of it since she did not own any perfume. When she reached the gate no one was there.

She looked up and down the empty highway and had the furious feeling that she had been tricked, that he had only meant to make her walk to the gate after the idea of him. Then suddenly he stood up, very tall, from behind a bush on the opposite embankment. Smiling, he lifted his hat which was new and wide-brimmed. He had not worn it yesterday and she wondered if he had bought it for the occasion. It was toast-colored with a red and white band around it and was slightly too large for him. He stepped from behind the bush still carrying the black valise. He had on the same suit and the same yellow socks sucked down in his shoes from walking. He crossed the highway and said, "I knew you'd come!"

The girl wondered acidly how he had known this. She pointed to the valise and asked, "Why did you bring your Bibles?"

95   He took her elbow, smiling down on her as if he could not stop. "You can never tell when you'll need the word of God, Hulga," he said. She had a moment in which she doubted that this was actually happening and then they began to climb the embankment. They went down into the pasture toward the woods. The boy walked lightly by her side, bouncing on his toes. The valise did not seem to be heavy today; he even swung it. They crossed half the pasture without saying anything and then, putting his hand easily on the small of her back, he asked softly, "Where does your wooden leg join on?"

She turned an ugly red and glared at him and for an instant the boy looked abashed. "I didn't mean you no harm," he said. "I only meant you're so brave and all. I guess God takes care of you."

"No," she said, looking forward and walking fast, "I don't even believe in God."

At this he stopped and whistled. "No!" he exclaimed as if he were too astonished to say anything else.

She walked on and in a second he was bouncing at her side, fanning with his hat. "That's very unusual for a girl," he remarked, watching her out of the corner of his eye. When they reached the edge of the wood, he put his hand on her back again and drew her against him without a word and kissed her heavily.

The kiss, which had more pressure than feeling behind it, produced that extra 100
surge of adrenalin in the girl that enables one to carry a packed trunk out of a burning house, but in her, the power went at once to the brain. Even before he released her, her mind, clear and detached and ironic anyway, was regarding him from a great distance, with amusement but with pity. She had never been kissed before and she was pleased to discover that it was an unexceptional experience and all a matter of the mind's control. Some people might enjoy drain water if they were told it was vodka. When the boy, looking expectant but uncertain, pushed her gently away, she turned and walked on, saying nothing as if such business, for her, were common enough.

He came along panting at her side, trying to help her when he saw a root that she might trip over. He caught and held back the long swaying blades of thorn vine until she had passed beyond them. She led the way and he came breathing heavily behind her. Then they came out on a sunlit hillside, sloping softly into another one a little smaller. Beyond, they could see the rusted top of the old barn where the extra hay was stored.

The hill was sprinkled with small pink weeds. "Then you ain't saved?" he asked suddenly, stopping.

The girl smiled. It was the first time she had smiled at him at all. "In my economy," she said, "I'm saved and you are damned but I told you I didn't believe in God."

Nothing seemed to destroy the boy's look of admiration. He gazed at her now as if the fantastic animal at the zoo had put its paw through the bars and given him a loving poke. She thought he looked as if he wanted to kiss her again and she walked on before he had the chance.

"Ain't there somewheres we can sit down sometime?" he murmured, his voice 105
softening toward the end of the sentence.

"In that barn," she said.

They made for it rapidly as if it might slide away like a train. It was a large two-story barn, cool and dark inside. The boy pointed up the ladder that led into the loft and said, "It's too bad we can't go up there."

"Why can't we?" she asked.

"Yer leg," he said reverently.

The girl gave him a contemptuous look and putting both hands on the ladder, 110
she climbed it while he stood below, apparently awestruck. She pulled herself expertly through the opening and then looked down at him and said, "Well, come on if you're coming," and he began to climb the ladder, awkwardly bringing the suitcase with him.

"We won't need the Bible," she observed.

"You never can tell," he said, panting. After he had got into the loft, he was a few seconds catching his breath. She had sat down in a pile of straw. A wide sheath of sunlight, filled with dust particles, slanted over her. She lay back against a bale, her face turned away, looking out the front opening of the barn where hay was thrown from a wagon into the loft. The two pink-speckled hillsides lay back against a dark ridge of woods. The sky was cloudless and cold blue. The boy dropped down by her side and put one arm under her and the other over her and began methodically kissing her face, making little noises like a fish. He did not remove his hat but it was pushed far enough back not to interfere. When her glasses got in his way, he took them off of her and slipped them into his pocket.

The girl at first did not return any of the kisses but presently she began to and after she had put several on his cheek, she reached his lips and remained there, kissing him again and again as if she were trying to draw all the breath out of him. His breath was clear and sweet like a child's and the kisses were sticky like a child's. He mumbled about loving her and about knowing when he first seen her that he loved her, but the mumbling was like the sleepy fretting of a child being put to sleep by his mother. Her mind, throughout this, never stopped or lost itself for a second to her feelings. "You ain't said you loved me none," he whispered finally, pulling back from her. "You got to say that."

She sat staring at him. There was nothing about her face or her round freezing-blue eyes to indicate that this had moved her; but she felt as if her heart had stopped and left her mind to pump her blood. She decided that for the first time in her life she was face to face with real innocence. This boy, with an instinct that came from beyond wisdom, had touched the truth about her. When after a minute, she said in a hoarse high voice, "All right," it was like surrendering to him completely. It was like losing her own life and finding it again, miraculously, in his.

115   Very gently he began to roll the slack leg up. The artificial limb, in a white sock and brown flat shoe, was bound in a heavy material like canvas and ended in an ugly jointure where it was attached to the stump. The boy's face and his voice were entirely reverent as he uncovered it and said, "Now show me how to take it off and on."

She took it off for him, and put it back on again and then he took it off himself, handling it as tenderly as if it were a real one. "See!" he said with a delighted child's face. "Now I can do it myself!"

"Put it back on," she said. She was thinking that she would run away with him and that every night he would take the leg off and every morning put it back on again. "Put it back on," she said.

"Not yet," he murmured, setting it on its foot out of her reach. "Leave it off for a while. You got me instead."

She gave a little cry of alarm but he pushed her down and began to kiss her again. Without the leg she felt entirely dependent on him. Her brain seemed to have stopped thinking altogether and to be about some other function that it was not very good at. Different expressions raced back and forth over her face. Every now and then the boy, his eyes like two steel spikes, would glance behind him where the leg stood. Finally she pushed him off and said, "Put it back on me now."

"Wait," he said. He leaned the other way and pulled the valise toward him and   120
opened it. It had a pale blue spotted lining and there were only two Bibles in it.
He took one of these out and opened the cover of it. It was hollow and contained
a pocket flask of whiskey, a pack of cards, and a small blue box with printing on
it. He laid these out in front of her one at a time in an evenly-spaced row, like one
presenting offerings at the shrine of a goddess. He put the blue box in her hand.
THIS PRODUCT TO BE USED ONLY FOR THE PREVENTION OF DIS-
EASE, she read, and dropped it. The boy was unscrewing the top of the flask. He
stopped and pointed, with a smile, to the deck of cards. It was not an ordinary
deck but one with an obscene picture on the back of each card. "Take a swig,"
he said, offering her the bottle first. He held it in front of her, but like one mesmerized, she did not move.

Her voice when she spoke had an almost pleading sound. "Aren't you," she
murmured, "aren't you just good country people?"

The boy cocked his head. He looked as if he were just beginning to understand
that she might be trying to insult him. "Yeah," he said, curling his lip slightly, "but
it ain't held me back none. I'm as good as you any day in the week."

"Give me my leg," she said.

He pushed it farther away with his foot. "Come on now, let's begin to have us
a good time," he said coaxingly. "We ain't got to know one another good yet."

"Give me my leg!" she screamed and tried to lunge for it but he pushed her   125
down easily.

"What's the matter with you all of a sudden?" he asked, frowning as he screwed
the top on the flask and put it quickly back inside the Bible. "You just a while ago
said you didn't believe in nothing. I thought you was some girl!"

Her face was almost purple. "You're a Christian!" she hissed. "You're a fine
Christian! You're just like them all — say one thing and do another. You're a
perfect Christian, you're . . ."

The boy's mouth was set angrily. "I hope you don't think," he said in a lofty indignant tone, "that I believe in that crap! I may sell Bibles but I know which end
is up and I wasn't born yesterday and I know where I'm going!"

"Give me my leg!" she screeched. He jumped up so quickly that she barely saw
him sweep the cards and the blue box into the Bible and throw the Bible into the
valise. She saw him grab the leg and then she saw it for an instant slanted for-
lornly across the inside of the suitcase with a Bible at either side of its opposite
ends. He slammed the lid shut and snatched up the valise and swung it down the
hole and then stepped through himself.

When all of him had passed but his head, he turned and regarded her with   130
a look that no longer had any admiration in it. "I've gotten a lot of interesting things," he said. "One time I got a woman's glass eye this way. And you needn't
to think you'll catch me because Pointer ain't really my name. I use a different name at every house I call at and don't stay nowhere long. And I'll tell you
another thing, Hulga," he said, using the name as if he didn't think much of
it, "you ain't so smart. I been believing in nothing ever since I was born!" and
then the toast-colored hat disappeared down the hole and the girl was left, sitting on the straw in the dusty sunlight. When she turned her churning face to-

ward the opening, she saw his blue figure struggling successfully over the green speckled lake.

Mrs. Hopewell and Mrs. Freeman, who were in the back pasture, digging up onions, saw him emerge a little later from the woods and head across the meadow toward the highway. "Why, that looks like that nice dull young man that tried to sell me a Bible yesterday," Mrs. Hopewell said, squinting. "He must have been selling them to the Negroes back in there. He was so simple," she said, "but I guess the world would be better off if we were all that simple."

Mrs. Freeman's gaze drove forward and just touched him before he disappeared under the hill. Then she returned her attention to the evil-smelling onion shoot she was lifting from the ground. "Some can't be that simple," she said. "I know I never could."

⋄   ⋄   ⋄

KATHERINE ANNE PORTER   (1890–1980)

The Jilting of Granny Weatherall   (1930)

She flicked her wrist neatly out of Doctor Harry's pudgy careful fingers and pulled the sheet up to her chin. The brat ought to be in knee breeches. Doctoring around the country with spectacles on his nose! "Get along now, take your schoolbooks and go. There's nothing wrong with me."

Doctor Harry spread a warm paw like a cushion on her forehead where the forked green vein danced and made her eyelids twitch. "Now, now, be a good girl, and we'll have you up in no time."

"That's no way to speak to a woman nearly eighty years old just because she's down. I'd have you respect your elders, young man."

"Well, Missy, excuse me." Doctor Harry patted her cheek. "But I've got to warn you, haven't I? You're a marvel, but you must be careful or you're going to be good and sorry."

5   "Don't tell me what I'm going to be. I'm on my feet now, morally speaking. It's Cornelia. I had to go to bed to get rid of her."

Her bones felt loose, and floated around in her skin, and Doctor Harry floated like a balloon around the foot of the bed. He floated and pulled down his waistcoat and swung his glasses on a cord. "Well, stay where you are, it certainly can't hurt you."

"Get along and doctor your sick," said Granny Weatherall. "Leave a well woman alone. I'll call for you when I want you. . . . Where were you forty years ago when I pulled through milk-leg and double pneumonia? You weren't even born. Don't let Cornelia lead you on," she shouted, because Doctor Harry appeared to float up to the ceiling and out. "I pay my own bills, and I don't throw my money away on nonsense!"

She meant to wave good-by, but it was too much trouble. Her eyes closed of themselves, it was like a dark curtain drawn around the bed. The pillow rose and floated under her, pleasant as a hammock in a light wind. She listened to the leaves rustling outside the window. No, somebody was swishing newspapers: no,

Cornelia and Doctor Harry were whispering together. She leaped broad awake, thinking they whispered in her ear.

"She was never like this, *never* like this!" "Well, what can we expect?" "Yes, eighty years old. . . ."

Well, and what if she was? She still had ears. It was like Cornelia to whisper   10
around doors. She always kept things secret in such a public way. She was always being tactful and kind. Cornelia was dutiful; that was the trouble with her. Dutiful and good: "So good and dutiful," said Granny, "that I'd like to spank her." She saw herself spanking Cornelia and making a fine job of it.

"What'd you say, Mother?"

Granny felt her face tying up in hard knots.

"Can't a body think, I'd like to know?"

"I thought you might want something."

"I do. I want a lot of things. First off, go away and don't whisper."   15

She lay and drowsed, hoping in her sleep that the children would keep out and let her rest a minute. It had been a long day. Not that she was tired. It was always pleasant to snatch a minute now and then. There was always so much to be done, let me see: tomorrow.

Tomorrow was far away and there was nothing to trouble about. Things were finished somehow when the time came; thank God there was always a little margin over for peace: then a person could spread out the plan of life and tuck in the edges orderly. It was good to have everything clean and folded away, with the hair brushes and tonic bottles sitting straight on the white embroidered linen: the day started without fuss and the pantry shelves laid out with rows of jelly glasses and brown jugs and white stone-china jars with blue whirligigs and words painted on them: coffee, tea, sugar, ginger, cinnamon, allspice: and the bronze clock with the lion on top nicely dusted off. The dust that lion could collect in twenty-four hours! The box in the attic with all those letters tied up, well, she'd have to go through that tomorrow. All those letters — George's letters and John's letters and her letters to them both — lying around for the children to find afterwards made her uneasy. Yes, that would be tomorrow's business. No use to let them know how silly she had been once.

While she was rummaging around she found death in her mind and it felt clammy and unfamiliar. She had spent so much time preparing for death there was no need for bringing it up again. Let it take care of itself now. When she was sixty she had felt very old, finished, and went around making farewell trips to see her children and grandchildren, with a secret in her mind: This is the very last of your mother, children! Then she made her will and came down with a long fever. That was all just a notion like a lot of other things, but it was lucky too, for she had once and for all got over the idea of dying for a long time. Now she couldn't be worried. She hoped she had better sense now. Her father had lived to be one hundred and two years old and had drunk a noggin of strong hot toddy on his last birthday. He told the reporters it was his daily habit, and he owed his long life to that. He had made quite a scandal and was very pleased about it. She believed she'd just plague Cornelia a little.

"Cornelia! Cornelia!" No footsteps, but a sudden hand on her cheek. "Bless you, where have you been?"

20   "Here, Mother."

"Well, Cornelia, I want a noggin of hot toddy."

"Are you cold, darling?"

"I'm chilly, Cornelia. Lying in bed stops the circulation. I must have told you that a thousand times."

Well, she could just hear Cornelia telling her husband that Mother was getting a little childish and they'd have to humor her. The thing that most annoyed her was that Cornelia thought she was deaf, dumb, and blind. Little hasty glances and tiny gestures tossed around her and over her head saying, "Don't cross her, let her have her way, she's eighty years old," and she sitting there as if she lived in a thin glass cage. Sometimes Granny almost made up her mind to pack up and move back to her own house where nobody could remind her every minute that she was old. Wait, wait, Cornelia, till your own children whisper behind your back!

25   In her day she had kept a better house and had got more work done. She wasn't too old yet for Lydia to be driving eighty miles for advice when one of the children jumped the track, and Jimmy still dropped in and talked things over: "Now, Mammy, you've a good business head, I want to know what you think of this? . . ." Old. Cornelia couldn't change the furniture around without asking. Little things, little things! They had been so sweet when they were little. Granny wished the old days were back again with the children young and everything to be done over. It had been a hard pull, but not too much for her. When she thought of all the food she had cooked, and all the clothes she had cut and sewed, and all the gardens she had made — well, the children showed it. There they were, made out of her, and they couldn't get away from that. Sometimes she wanted to see John again and point to them and say, Well, I didn't do so badly, did I? But that would have to wait. That was for tomorrow. She used to think of him as a man, but now all the children were older than their father, and he would be a child beside her if she saw him now. It seemed strange and there was something wrong in the idea. Why, he couldn't possibly recognize her. She had fenced in a hundred acres once, digging the post holes herself and clamping the wires with just a negro boy to help. That changed a woman. John would be looking for a young woman with the peaked Spanish comb in her hair and the painted fan. Digging post holes changed a woman. Riding country roads in the winter when women had their babies was another thing: sitting up nights with sick horses and sick negroes and sick children and hardly ever losing one. John, I hardly ever lost one of them! John would see that in a minute, that would be something he could understand, she wouldn't have to explain anything!

It made her feel like rolling up her sleeves and putting the whole place to rights again. No matter if Cornelia was determined to be everywhere at once, there were a great many things left undone on this place. She would start tomorrow and do them. It was good to be strong enough for everything, even if all you made melted and changed and slipped under your hands, so that by the time you finished you almost forgot what you were working for. What was it I set out to do? she asked herself intently, but she could not remember. A fog rose over the valley, she saw it marching across the creek swallowing the trees and moving up the hill like an army of ghosts. Soon it would be at the near edge of the orchard, and then it was time to go in and light the lamps. Come in, children, don't stay out in the night air.

Lighting the lamps had been beautiful. The children huddled up to her and breathed like little calves waiting at the bars in the twilight. Their eyes followed the match and watched the flame rise and settle in a blue curve, then they moved away from her. The lamp was lit, they didn't have to be scared and hang on to mother any more. Never, never, never more. God, for all my life I thank Thee. Without Thee, my God, I could never have done it. Hail, Mary, full of grace.

I want you to pick all the fruit this year and see that nothing is wasted. There's always someone who can use it. Don't let good things rot for want of using. You waste life when you waste good food. Don't let things get lost. It's bitter to lose things. Now, don't let me get to thinking, not when I am tired and taking a little nap before supper. . . .

The pillow rose about her shoulders and pressed against her heart and the memory was being squeezed out of it: oh, push down the pillow, somebody: it would smother her if she tried to hold it. Such a fresh breeze blowing and such a green day with no threats in it. But he had not come, just the same. What does a woman do when she has put on the white veil and set out the white cake for a man and he doesn't come? She tried to remember. No, I swear he never harmed me but in that. He never harmed me but in that . . . and what if he did? There was the day, the day, but a whirl of dark smoke rose and covered it, crept up and over into the bright field where everything was planted so carefully in orderly rows. That was hell, she knew hell when she saw it. For sixty years she had prayed against remembering him and against losing her soul in the deep pit of hell, and now the two things were mingled in one and the thought of him was a smoky cloud from hell that moved and crept in her head when she had just got rid of Doctor Harry and was trying to rest a minute. Wounded vanity, Ellen, said a sharp voice in the top of her mind. Don't let your wounded vanity get the upper hand of you. Plenty of girls get jilted. You were jilted, weren't you? Then stand up to it. Her eyelids wavered and let in streamers of blue-gray light like tissue paper over her eyes. She must get up and pull the shades down or she'd never sleep. She was in bed again and the shades were not down. How could that happen? Better turn over, hide from the light, sleeping in the light gave you nightmares. "Mother, how do you feel now?" and a stinging wetness on her forehead. But I don't like having my face washed in cold water!

Hapsy? George? Lydia? Jimmy? No, Cornelia, and her features were swollen   30 and full of little puddles. "They're coming, darling, they'll all be here soon." Go wash your face, child, you look funny.

Instead of obeying, Cornelia knelt down and put her head on the pillow. She seemed to be talking but there was no sound. "Well, are you tongue-tied? Whose birthday is it? Are you going to give a party?"

Cornelia's mouth moved urgently in strange shapes. "Don't do that, you bother me, daughter."

"O, no, Mother. Oh, no. . . ."

Nonsense. It was strange about children. They disputed your every word. "No what, Cornelia?"

35   "Here's Doctor Harry."

"I won't see that boy again. He just left five minutes ago."

"That was this morning, Mother. It's night now. Here's the nurse."

"This is Doctor Harry, Mrs. Weatherall. I never saw you look so young and happy!"

"Ah, I'll never be young again — but I'd be happy if they'd let me lie in peace and get rested."

40   She thought she spoke up loudly, but no one answered. A warm weight on her forehead, a warm bracelet on her wrist, and a breeze went on whispering, trying to tell her something. A shuffle of leaves in the everlasting hand of God. He blew on them and they danced and rattled. "Mother, don't mind, we're going to give you a little hypodermic." "Look here, daughter, how do ants get in this bed? I saw sugar ants yesterday." Did you send for Hapsy too?

It was Hapsy she really wanted. She had to go a long way back through a great many rooms to find Hapsy standing with a baby on her arm. She seemed to herself to be Hapsy also, and the baby on Hapsy's arm was Hapsy and himself and herself, all at once, and there was no surprise in the meeting. Then Hapsy melted from within and turned flimsy as gray gauze and the baby was a gauzy shadow, and Hapsy came up close and said, "I thought you'd never come," and looked at her very searchingly and said, "You haven't changed a bit!" They leaned forward to kiss, when Cornelia began whispering from a long way off, "Oh, is there anything you want to tell me? Is there anything I can do for you?"

Yes, she had changed her mind after sixty years and she would like to see George. I want you to find George. Find him and be sure to tell him I forgot him. I want him to know I had my husband just the same and my children and my house like any other woman. A good house too and a good husband that I loved and fine children out of him. Better than I hoped for even. Tell him I was given back everything he took away and more. Oh, no, oh, God, no, there was something else besides the house and the man and the children. Oh, surely they were not all? What was it? Something not given back. . . . Her breath crowded down under her ribs and grew into a monstrous frightening shape with cutting edges; it bored up into her head, and the agony was unbelievable: Yes, John, get the Doctor now, no more talk, my time has come.

When this one was born it should be the last. The last. It should have been born first, for it was the one she had truly wanted. Everything came in good time. Nothing left out, left over. She was strong, in three days she would be as well as ever. Better. A woman needed milk in her to have her full health.

"Mother, do you hear me?"

45   "I've been telling you —"

"Mother, Father Connolly's here."

"I went to Holy Communion last week. Tell him I'm not so sinful as all that."

"Father just wants to speak to you."

He could speak as much as he pleased. It was like him to drop in and inquire about her soul as if it were a teething baby, and then stay on for a cup of tea and a round of cards and gossip. He always had a funny story of some sort, usually about an Irishman who made his little mistakes and confessed them, and the point lay in some absurd thing he would blurtout in the confessional showing his struggles between native piety and original sin. Granny felt easy about her soul. Cornelia, where are your manners? Give Father Connolly a chair. She had her secret comfortable understanding with a few favorite saints who cleared a straight road to God for her. All as surely signed and sealed as the papers for the new Forty Acres. Forever . . . heirs and assigns forever. Since the day the wedding cake was not cut, but thrown out and wasted. The whole bottom dropped out of the world, and there she was blind and sweating with nothing under her feet and the walls falling away. His hand had caught her under the breast, she had not fallen, there was the freshly polished floor with the green rug on it, just as before. He had cursed like a sailor's parrot and said, "I'll kill him for you." Don't lay a hand on him, for my sake leave something to God. "Now, Ellen, you must believe what I tell you. . . ."

So there was nothing, nothing to worry about any more, except sometimes in   50 the night one of the children screamed in a nightmare, and they both hustled out shaking and hunting for the matches and calling, "There, wait a minute, here we are!" John, get the doctor now, Hapsy's time has come. But there was Hapsy standing by the bed in a white cap. "Cornelia, tell Hapsy to take off her cap. I can't see her plain."

Her eyes opened very wide and the room stood out like a picture she had seen somewhere. Dark colors with the shadows rising towards the ceiling in long angles. The tall black dresser gleamed with nothing on it but John's picture, enlarged from a little one, with John's eyes very black when they should have been blue. You never saw him, so how do you know how he looked? But the man insisted the copy was perfect, it was very rich and handsome. For a picture, yes, but it's not my husband. The table by the bed had a linen cover and a candle and a crucifix. The light was blue from Cornelia's silk lampshades. No sort of light at all, just frippery. You had to live forty years with kerosene lamps to appreciate honest electricity. She felt very strong and she saw Doctor Harry with a rosy nimbus around him.

"You look like a saint, Doctor Harry, and I vow that's as near as you'll ever come to it."

"She's saying something."

"I heard you, Cornelia. What's all this carrying-on?"

"Father Connolly's saying —"   55

Cornelia's voice staggered and bumped like a cart in a bad road. It rounded corners and turned back again and arrived nowhere. Granny stepped up in the cart very lightly and reached for the reins, but a man sat beside her and she knew him by his hands, driving the cart. She did not look in his face, for she knew without seeing, but looked instead down the road where the trees leaned over and bowed to each other and a thousand birds were singing a Mass. She felt like singing too, but she put her hand in the bosom of her dress and pulled out a rosary, and Father Connolly murmured Latin in a very solemn voice and tickled her feet. My God, will you stop that nonsense? I'm a married woman. What if he did run away and leave me to face the priest by myself? I found another a whole world better. I wouldn't have exchanged my husband for anybody except St. Michael himself, and you may tell him that for me with a thank you in the bargain.

Light flashed on her closed eyelids, and a deep roaring shook her. Cornelia, is that lightning? I hear thunder. There's going to be a storm. Close all the windows. Call the children in. . . . "Mother, here we are, all of us." "Is that you, Hapsy?" "Oh, no, I'm Lydia. We drove as fast as we could." Their faces drifted above her, drifted away. The rosary fell out of her hands and Lydia put it back. Jimmy tried to help, their hands fumbled together, and Granny closed two fingers around Jimmy's thumb. Beads wouldn't do, it must be something alive. She was so amazed her thoughts ran round and round. So, my dear Lord, this is my death and I wasn't even thinking about it. My children have come to see me die. But I can't, it's not time. Oh, I always hated surprises. I wanted to give Cornelia the amethyst set — Cornelia, you're to have the amethyst set, but Hapsy's to wear it when she wants, and, Doctor Harry, do shut up. Nobody sent for you. Oh, my dear Lord, do wait a minute. I meant to do something about the Forty Acres, Jimmy doesn't need it and Lydia will later on, with that worthless husband of hers. I meant to finish the altar cloth and send six bottles of wine to Sister Borgia for her dyspepsia. I want to send six bottles of wine to Sister Borgia, Father Connolly, now don't let me forget.

Cornelia's voice made short turns and tilted over and crashed. "Oh, Mother, oh, Mother, oh, Mother. . . ."

"I'm not going, Cornelia. I'm taken by surprise. I can't go."

60   You'll see Hapsy again. What about her? "I thought you'd never come." Granny made a long journey outward, looking for Hapsy. What if I don't find her? What then? Her heart sank down and down, there was no bottom to death, she couldn't come to the end of it. The blue light from Cornelia's lampshade drew into a tiny point in the center of her brain, it flickered and winked like an eye, quietly it fluttered and dwindled. Granny lay curled down within herself, amazed and watchful, staring at the point of light that was herself; her body was now only a deeper mass of shadow in an endless darkness and this darkness would curl around the light and swallow it up. God, give a sign!

For the second time there was no sign. Again no bridegroom and the priest in the house. She could not remember any other sorrow because this grief wiped them all away. Oh, no, there's nothing more cruel than this — I'll never forgive it. She stretched herself with a deep breath and blew out the light.

◇ ◇ ◇

RICHARD RUSSO   (1949–   )

Dog   (1996)

They're Nice to Have. A Dog.

—F. Scott Fitzgerald,

The Great Gatsby

Truth be told, I'm not an easy man. I can be an entertaining one, though it's been my experience that most people don't want to be entertained. They want to be comforted. And, of course, my idea of entertaining might not be yours. I'm in complete agreement with all those people who say, regarding movies, "I just want to be entertained." This populist position is much derided by my academic colleagues as simpleminded and unsophisticated, evidence of questionable analytical and critical acuity. But I agree with the premise, and I too just want to be entertained. That I am almost never entertained by what entertains *other* people who just want to be entertained doesn't make us philosophically incompatible. It just means we shouldn't go to movies together.

The kind of man I am, according to those who know me best, is exasperating. According to my parents, I was an exasperating child as well. They divorced when I was in junior high school, and they agree on little except that I was an impossible child. The story they tell of young William Henry Devereaux, Jr., and his first dog is eerily similar in its facts, its conclusions, even the style of its telling, no matter which of them is telling it. Here's the story they tell.

I was nine, and the house we were living in, which belonged to the university, was my fourth. My parents were academic nomads, my father, then and now, an academic opportunist, always in the vanguard of whatever was trendy and chic in literary criticism. This was the fifties, and for him, New Criticism was already old. In early middle age he was already a full professor with several published books, all of them "hot," the subject of intense debate at English department cocktail parties. The academic position he favored was the "distinguished visiting professor" variety, usually created for him, duration of visit a year or two at most, perhaps because it's hard to remain distinguished among people who know you. Usually his teaching responsibilities were light, a course or two a year. Otherwise, he was expected to read and think and write and publish and acknowledge in the preface of his next book the generosity of the institution that provided him the academic good life. My mother, also an English professor, was hired as part of the package deal, to teach a full load and thereby help balance the books.

The houses we lived in were elegant, old, high-ceilinged, drafty, either on or close to campus. They had hardwood floors and smoky fireplaces with fires in them only when my father held court, which he did either on Friday afternoons, our large rooms filling up with obsequious junior faculty and nervous grad students, or Saturday evenings, when my mother gave dinner parties for the chair of the department, or the dean, or a visiting poet. In all situations I was the only child, and I must have been a lonely one, because what I wanted more than anything in the world was a dog.

Predictably, my parents did not. Probably the terms of living in these university houses were specific regarding pets. By the time I was nine I'd been lobbying hard for a dog for a year or two. My father and mother were hoping I would outgrow this longing, given enough time. I could see this hope in their eyes and it steeled my resolve, intensified my desire. What did I want for Christmas? A dog. What did I want for my birthday? A dog. What did I want on my ham sandwich? A dog. It was a deeply satisfying look of pure exasperation they shared at such moments, and if I couldn't have a dog, this was the next best thing.

Life continued in this fashion until finally my mother made a mistake, a doozy of a blunder born of emotional exhaustion and despair. She, far more than my father, would have preferred a happy child. One spring day after I'd been badgering her pretty relentlessly she sat me down and said, "You know, a dog is something you earn." My father heard this, got up, and left the room, grim acknowledgment that my mother had just conceded the war. Her idea was to make the dog conditional. The conditions to be imposed would be numerous and severe, and I would be incapable of fulfilling them, so when I didn't get the dog it'd be my own fault. This was her logic, and the fact that she thought such a plan might work illustrates that some people should never be parents and that she was one of them.

I immediately put into practice a plan of my own to wear my mother down. Unlike hers, my plan was simple and flawless. Mornings I woke up talking about dogs and nights I fell asleep talking about them. When my mother and father changed the subject, I changed it back. "Speaking of dogs," I would say, a forkful of my mother's roast poised at my lips, and I'd be off again. Maybe no one *had* been speaking of dogs, but never mind, we were speaking of them now. At the library I checked out a half dozen books on dogs every two weeks and left them lying open around the house. I pointed out dogs we passed on the street, dogs on television, dogs in the magazines my mother subscribed to. I discussed the relative merits of various breeds at every meal. My father seldom listened to anything I said, but I began to see signs that the underpinnings of my mother's personality were beginning to corrode in the salt water of my tidal persistence, and when I judged that she was nigh to complete collapse, I took every penny of the allowance money I'd been saving and spent it on a dazzling, bejeweled dog collar and leash set at the overpriced pet store around the corner.

During this period when we were constantly "speaking of dogs," I was not a model boy. I was supposed to be "earning a dog," and I was constantly checking with my mother to see how I was doing, just how much of a dog I'd earned, but I doubt my behavior had changed a jot. I wasn't really a bad boy. Just a noisy, busy, constantly needy boy. Mr. In and Out, my mother called me, because I was in and out of rooms, in and out of doors, in and out of the refrigerator. "Henry," my mother would plead with me. "Light somewhere." One of the things I often needed was information, and I constantly interrupted my mother's reading and paper grading to get it. My father, partly to avoid having to answer my questions, spent most of his time in his book-lined office on campus, joining my mother and me only at mealtimes, so that we could speak of dogs as a family. Then he was gone again, blissfully unaware, I thought at the time, that my mother continued to glare homicidally, for long minutes after his departure, at the chair he'd so recently occupied. But he claimed to be close to finishing the book he was working on, and this was a powerful excuse to offer a woman with as much abstract respect for books and learning as my mother possessed.

Gradually, she came to understand that she was fighting a battle she couldn't win and that she was fighting it alone. I now know that this was part of a larger cluster of bitter marital realizations, but at the time I sniffed nothing in the air but victory. In late August, during what people refer to as "the dog days," when she made one last, weak condition, final evidence that I had earned a dog, I relented and truly tried to reform my behavior. It was literally the least I could do.

10   What my mother wanted of me was to stop slamming the screen door. The house we were living in, it must be said, was an acoustic marvel akin to the

Whispering Gallery in St. Paul's, where muted voices travel across a great open space and arrive, clear and intact, at the other side of the great dome. In our house the screen door swung shut on a tight spring, the straight wooden edge of the door encountering the doorframe like a gunshot played through a guitar amplifier set on stun, the crack transmitting perfectly, with equal force and clarity, to every room in the house, upstairs and down. That summer I was in and out that door dozens of times a day, and my mother said it was like living in a shooting gallery. It made her wish the door wasn't shooting blanks. If I could just remember not to slam the door, then she'd see about a dog. Soon.

I did better, remembering about half the time not to let the door slam. When I forgot, I came back in to apologize, sometimes forgetting then too. Still, that I was trying, together with the fact that I carried the expensive dog collar and leash with me everywhere I went, apparently moved my mother, because at the end of that first week of diminished door slamming, my father went somewhere on Saturday morning, refusing to reveal where, and so of course I knew. "What kind?" I pleaded with my mother when he was gone. But she claimed not to know. "Your father's doing this," she said, and I thought I saw a trace of misgiving in her expression.

When he returned, I saw why. He'd put it in the backseat, and when my father pulled the car in and parked along the side of the house, I saw from the kitchen window its chin resting on the back of the rear seat. I think it saw me too, but if so it did not react. Neither did it seem to notice that the car had stopped, that my father had gotten out and was holding the front seat forward. He had to reach in, take the dog by the collar, and pull.

As the animal unfolded its long legs and stepped tentatively, arthritically, out of the car, I saw that I had been both betrayed and outsmarted. In all the time we had been "speaking of dogs," what I'd been seeing in my mind's eye was puppies. Collie puppies, beagle puppies, Lab puppies, shepherd puppies, but none of that had been inked anywhere, I now realized. If not a puppy, a young dog. A rascal, full of spirit and possibility, a dog with new tricks to learn. *This* dog was barely ambulatory. It stood, head down, as if ashamed at something done long ago in its puppydom, and I thought I detected a shiver run through its frame when my father closed the car door behind it.

The animal was, I suppose, what might have been called a handsome dog. A purebred, rust-colored Irish setter, meticulously groomed, wonderfully mannered, the kind of dog you could safely bring into a house owned by the university, the sort of dog that wouldn't really violate the no pets clause, the kind of dog, I saw clearly, you'd get if you really didn't want a dog or to be bothered with a dog. It'd belonged, I later learned, to a professor emeritus of the university who'd been put into a nursing home earlier in the week, leaving the animal an orphan. It was like a painting of a dog, or a dog you'd hire to pose for a portrait, a dog you could be sure wouldn't move.

Both my father and the animal came into the kitchen reluctantly, my father 15 closing the screen door behind them with great care. I like to think that on the way home he'd suffered a misgiving, though I could tell that it was his intention to play the hand out boldly. My mother, who'd taken in my devastation at a glance, studied me for a moment and then my father.

"What?" he said.

My mother just shook her head.

My father looked at me, then back at her. A violent shiver palsied the dog's limbs. The animal seemed to want to lie down on the cool linoleum, but to have forgotten how. It offered a deep sigh that seemed to speak for all of us.

"He's a good dog," my father said, rather pointedly, to my mother. "A little high-strung, but that's the way with purebred setters. They're all nervous."

20 This was not the sort of thing my father knew. Clearly he was repeating the explanation he'd just been given when he picked up the dog.

"What's his name?" my mother said, apparently for something to say.

My father had neglected to ask. He checked the dog's collar for clues.

"Lord," my mother said. "Lord, lord."

"It's not like we can't name him ourselves," my father said, irritated now. "I think it's something we can manage, don't you?"

25 "You could name him after a passé school of literary criticism," my mother suggested.

"It's a she," I said, because it was.

It seemed to cheer my father, at least a little, that I'd allowed myself to be drawn into the conversation. "What do you say, Henry?" he wanted to know. "What'll we name him?"

This second faulty pronoun reference was too much for me. "I want to go out and play now," I said, and I bolted for the screen door before an objection could be registered. It slammed behind me, hard, its gunshot report even louder than usual. As I cleared the steps in a single leap, I thought I heard a thud back in the kitchen, a dull, muffled echo of the door, and then I heard my father say, "What the hell?" I went back up the steps, cautiously now, meaning to apologize for the door. Through the screen I could see my mother and father standing together in the middle of the kitchen, looking down at the dog, which seemed to be napping. My father nudged a haunch with the toe of his cordovan loafer.

He dug the grave in the backyard with a shovel borrowed from a neighbor. My father had soft hands and they blistered easily. I offered to help, but he just looked at me. When he was standing, midthigh, in the hole he'd dug, he shook his head one last time in disbelief. "Dead," he said. "Before we could even name him."

30 I knew better than to correct the pronoun again, so I just stood there thinking about what he'd said while he climbed out of the hole and went over to the back porch to collect the dog where it lay under an old sheet. I could tell by the careful way he tucked that sheet under the animal that he didn't want to touch anything dead, even newly dead. He lowered the dog into the hole by means of the sheet, but he had to drop it the last foot or so. When the animal thudded on the earth and lay still, my father looked over at me and shook his head. Then he picked up the shovel and leaned on it before he started filling in the hole. He seemed to be waiting for me to say something, so I said, "Red."

My father's eyes narrowed, as if I'd spoken in a foreign tongue. "What?" he said.

"We'll name her Red," I explained.

In the years after he left us, my father became even more famous. He is sometimes credited, if credit is the word, with being the Father of American Literary Theory. In addition to his many books of scholarship, he's also written a literary memoir that was short-listed for a major award and that offers insight into the personalities of several major literary figures of the twentieth century, now deceased. His photograph often graces the pages of the literary reviews. He went through a phase where he wore crewneck sweaters and gold chains beneath his tweed coat, but now he's mostly photographed in an oxford button-down shirt, tie, and jacket, in his book-lined office at the university. But to me, his son, William Henry Devereaux, Sr., is most real standing in his ruined cordovan loafers, leaning on the handle of a borrowed shovel, examining his dirty, blistered hands, and receiving my suggestion of what to name a dead dog. I suspect that digging our dog's grave was one of relatively few experiences of his life (excepting carnal ones) that did not originate on the printed page. And when I suggested we name the dead dog Red, he looked at me as if I myself had just stepped from the pages of a book he'd started to read years ago and then put down when something else caught his interest. "What?" he said, letting go of the shovel, so that its handle hit the earth between my feet. "What?"

It's not an easy time for any parent, this moment when the realization dawns that you've given birth to something that will never see things the way you do, despite the fact that it is your living legacy, that it bears your name.

◊   ◊   ◊

AMY TAN (1952–   )

Two Kinds (1989)

My mother believed you could be anything you wanted to be in America. You could open a restaurant. You could work for the government and get good retirement. You could buy a house with almost no money down. You could become rich. You could become instantly famous.

"Of course you can be prodigy, too," my mother told me when I was nine. "You can be best anything. What does Auntie Lindo know? Her daughter, she is only best tricky."

America was where all my mother's hopes lay. She had come here in 1949 after losing everything in China: her mother and father, her family home, her first husband, and two daughters, twin baby girls. But she never looked back with regret. There were so many ways for things to get better.

We didn't immediately pick the right kind of prodigy. At first my mother thought I could be a Chinese Shirley Temple. We'd watch Shirley's old movies on TV as though they were training films. My mother would poke my arm and say, *"Ni kan"*—You watch. And I would see Shirley tapping her feet, or singing a sailor song, or pursing her lips into a very round O while saying, "Oh my goodness."

5   "*Ni kan,*" said my mother as Shirley's eyes flooded with tears. "You already know how. Don't need talent for crying!"

Soon after my mother got this idea about Shirley Temple, she took me to a beauty training school in the Mission district and put me in the hands of a student who could barely hold the scissors without shaking. Instead of getting big fat curls, I emerged with an uneven mass of crinkly black fuzz. My mother dragged me off to the bathroom and tried to wet down my hair.

"You look like Negro Chinese," she lamented, as if I had done this on purpose.

The instructor of the beauty training school had to lop off these soggy clumps to make my hair even again. "Peter Pan is very popular these days," the instructor assured my mother. I now had hair the length of a boy's, with straight-across bangs that hung at a slant two inches above my eyebrows. I liked the haircut and it made me actually look forward to my future fame.

In fact, in the beginning, I was just as excited as my mother, maybe even more so. I pictured this prodigy part of me as many different images, trying each one on for size. I was a dainty ballerina girl standing by the curtains, waiting to hear the right music that would send me floating on my tiptoes. I was like the Christ child lifted out of the straw manger, crying with holy indignity. I was Cinderella stepping from her pumpkin carriage with sparkly cartoon music filling the air.

10   In all of my imaginings, I was filled with a sense that I would soon become *perfect*. My mother and father would adore me. I would be beyond reproach. I would never feel the need to sulk for anything.

But sometimes the prodigy in me became impatient. "If you don't hurry up and get me out of here, I'm disappearing for good," it warned. "And then you'll always be nothing."

Every night after dinner, my mother and I would sit at the Formica kitchen table. She would present new tests, taking her examples from stories of amazing children she had read in *Ripley's Believe It or Not,* or *Good Housekeeping, Reader's Digest,* and a dozen other magazines she kept in a pile in our bathroom. My mother got these magazines from people whose houses she cleaned. And since she cleaned many houses each week, we had a great assortment. She would look through them all, searching for stories about remarkable children.

The first night she brought out a story about a three-year-old boy who knew the capitals of all the states and even most of the European countries. A teacher was quoted as saying the little boy could also pronounce the names of the foreign cities correctly.

"What's the capital of Finland?" my mother asked me, looking at the magazine story.

15   All I knew was the capital of California, because Sacramento was the name of the street we lived on in Chinatown. "Nairobi!" I guessed, saying the most foreign word I could think of. She checked to see if that was possibly one way to pronounce "Helsinki" before showing me the answer.

The tests got harder — multiplying numbers in my head, finding the queen of hearts in a deck of cards, trying to stand on my head without using my hands, predicting the daily temperatures in Los Angeles, New York, and London.

One night I had to look at a page from the Bible for three minutes and then report everything I could remember. "Now Jehoshaphat had riches and honor in abundance and . . . that's all I remember, Ma," I said.

And after seeing my mother's disappointed face once again, something inside of me began to die. I hated the tests, the raised hopes and failed expectations. Before going to bed that night, I looked in the mirror above the bathroom sink and when I saw only my face staring back — and that it would always be this ordinary face — I began to cry. Such a sad, ugly girl! I made high-pitched noises like a crazed animal, trying to scratch out the face in the mirror.

And then I saw what seemed to be the prodigy side of me — because I had never seen that face before. I looked at my reflection, blinking so I could see more clearly. The girl staring back at me was angry, powerful. This girl and I were the same. I had new thoughts, willful thoughts, or rather thoughts filled with lots of won'ts. I won't let her change me, I promised myself. I won't be what I'm not.

So now on nights when my mother presented her tests, I performed listlessly, 20 my head propped on one arm. I pretended to be bored. And I was. I got so bored I started counting the bellows of the foghorns out on the bay while my mother drilled me in other areas. The sound was comforting and reminded me of the cow jumping over the moon. And the next day, I played a game with myself, seeing if my mother would give up on me before eight bellows. After a while I usually counted only one, maybe two bellows at most. At last she was beginning to give up hope.

Two or three months had gone by without any mention of my being a prodigy again. And then one day my mother was watching *The Ed Sullivan Show* on TV. The TV was old and the sound kept shorting out. Every time my mother got halfway up from the sofa to adjust the set, the sound would go back on and Ed would be talking. As soon as she sat down, Ed would go silent again. She got up, the TV broke into loud piano music. She sat down. Silence. Up and down, back and forth, quiet and loud. It was like a stiff embraceless dance between her and the TV set. Finally she stood by the set with her hand on the sound dial.

She seemed entranced by the music, a little frenzied piano piece with this mesmerizing quality, sort of quick passages and then teasing lilting ones before it returned to the quick playful parts.

"*Ni kan*," my mother said, calling me over with hurried hand gestures, "Look here."

I could see why my mother was fascinated by the music. It was being pounded out by a little Chinese girl, about nine years old, with a Peter Pan haircut. The girl had the sauciness of a Shirley Temple. She was proudly modest like a proper Chinese child. And she also did this fancy sweep of a curtsy, so that the fluffy skirt of her white dress cascaded slowly to the floor like the petals of a large carnation.

In spite of these warning signs, I wasn't worried. Our family had no piano and 25 we couldn't afford to buy one, let alone reams of sheet music and piano lessons. So I could be generous in my comments when my mother bad-mouthed the little girl on TV.

"Play note right, but doesn't sound good! No singing sound," complained my mother.

"What are you picking on her for?" I said carelessly. "She's pretty good. Maybe she's not the best, but she's trying hard." I knew almost immediately I would be sorry I said that.

"Just like you," she said. "Not the best. Because you not trying." She gave a little huff as she let go of the sound dial and sat down on the sofa.

The little Chinese girl sat down also to play an encore of "Anitra's Dance" by Grieg. I remember the song, because later on I had to learn how to play it.

30   Three days after watching *The Ed Sullivan Show*, my mother told me what my schedule would be for piano lessons and piano practice. She had talked to Mr. Chong, who lived on the first floor of our apartment building. Mr. Chong was a retired piano teacher and my mother had traded housecleaning services for weekly lessons and a piano for me to practice on every day, two hours a day, from four until six.

When my mother told me this, I felt as though I had been sent to hell. I whined and then kicked my foot a little when I couldn't stand it anymore.

"Why don't you like me the way I am? I'm *not* a genius! I can't play the piano. And even if I could, I wouldn't go on TV if you paid me a million dollars!" I cried.

My mother slapped me. "Who ask you be genius?" she shouted. "Only ask you be your best. For you sake. You think I want you be genius? Hnnh! What for! Who ask you!"

"So ungrateful," I heard her mutter in Chinese. "If she had as much talent as she has temper, she would be famous now."

35   Mr. Chong, whom I secretly nicknamed Old Chong, was very strange, always tapping his fingers to the silent music of an invisible orchestra. He looked ancient in my eyes. He had lost most of the hair on top of his head and he wore thick glasses and had eyes that always looked tired and sleepy. But he must have been younger than I thought, since he lived with his mother and was not yet married.

I met Old Lady Chong once and that was enough. She had this peculiar smell like a baby that had done something in its pants. And her fingers felt like a dead person's, like an old peach I once found in the back of the refrigerator; the skin just slid off the meat when I picked it up.

I soon found out why Old Chong had retired from teaching piano. He was deaf. "Like Beethoven!" he shouted to me. "We're both listening only in our head!" And he would start to conduct his frantic silent sonatas.

Our lessons went like this. He would open the book and point to different things, explaining their purpose: "Key! Treble! Bass! No sharps or flats! So this is C major! Listen now and play after me!"

And then he would play the C scale a few times, a simple chord, and then, as if inspired by an old, unreachable itch, he gradually added more notes and running trills and a pounding bass until the music was really something quite grand.

40   I would play after him, the simple scale, the simple chord, and then I just played some nonsense that sounded like a cat running up and down on top of

garbage cans. Old Chong smiled and applauded and then said, "Very good! But now you must learn to keep time!"

So that's how I discovered that Old Chong's eyes were too slow to keep up with the wrong notes I was playing. He went through the motions in half-time. To help me keep rhythm, he stood behind me, pushing down on my right shoulder for every beat. He balanced pennies on top of my wrists so I would keep them still as I slowly played scales and arpeggios. He had me curve my hand around an apple and keep that shape when playing chords. He marched stiffly to show me how to make each finger dance up and down, staccato like an obedient little soldier.

He taught me all these things, and that was how I also learned I could be lazy and get away with mistakes, lots of mistakes. If I hit the wrong notes because I hadn't practiced enough, I never corrected myself. I just kept playing in rhythm. And Old Chong kept conducting his own private reverie.

So maybe I never really gave myself a fair chance. I did pick up the basics pretty quickly, and I might have become a good pianist at that young age. But I was so determined not to try, not to be anybody different that I learned to play only the most ear-splitting preludes, the most discordant hymns.

Over the next year, I practiced like this, dutifully in my own way. And then one day I heard my mother and her friend Lindo Jong both talking in a loud bragging tone of voice so others could hear. It was after church, and I was leaning against the brick wall wearing a dress with stiff white petticoats. Auntie Lindo's daughter, Waverly, who was about my age, was standing farther down the wall about five feet away. We had grown up together and shared all the closeness of two sisters squabbling over crayons and dolls. In other words, for the most part, we hated each other. I thought she was snotty. Waverly Jong had gained a certain amount of fame as "Chinatown's Littlest Chinese Chess Champion."

"She bring home too many trophy," lamented Auntie Lindo that Sunday. "All 45 day she play chess. All day I have no time do nothing but dust off her winnings." She threw a scolding look at Waverly, who pretended not to see her.

"You lucky you don't have this problem," said Auntie Lindo with a sigh to my mother.

And my mother squared her shoulders and bragged: "Our problem worser than yours. If we ask Jing-mei wash dish, she hear nothing but music. It's like you can't stop this natural talent."

And right then, I was determined to put a stop to her foolish pride.

A few weeks later, Old Chong and my mother conspired to have me play in a talent show which would be held in the church hall. By then, my parents had saved up enough to buy me a secondhand piano, a black Wurlitzer spinet with a scarred bench. It was the showpiece of our living room.

For the talent show, I was to play a piece called "Pleading Child" from 50 Schumann's *Scenes from Childhood*. It was a simple, moody piece that sounded more difficult than it was. I was supposed to memorize the whole thing, playing the repeat parts twice to make the piece sound longer. But I dawdled over it, playing a few bars and then cheating, looking up to see what notes followed. I never really listened to what I was playing. I daydreamed about being somewhere else, about being someone else.

The part I liked to practice best was the fancy curtsy: right foot out, touch the rose on the carpet with a pointed foot, sweep to the side, left leg bends, look up and smile.

My parents invited all the couples from the Joy Luck Club° to witness my debut. Auntie Lindo and Uncle Tin were there. Waverly and her two older brothers had also come. The first two rows were filled with children both younger and older than I was. The littlest ones got to go first. They recited simple nursery rhymes, squawked out tunes on miniature violins, twirled Hula Hoops, pranced in pink ballet tutus, and when they bowed or curtsied, the audience would sigh in unison, "Awww," and then clap enthusiastically.

When my turn came, I was very confident. I remember my childish excitement. It was as if I knew, without a doubt, that the prodigy side of me really did exist. I had no fear whatsoever, no nervousness. I remember thinking to myself, This is it! This is it! I looked out over the audience, at my mother's blank face, my father's yawn, Auntie Lindo's stiff-lipped smile, Waverly's sulky expression. I had on a white dress layered with sheets of lace, and a pink bow in my Peter Pan haircut. As I sat down I envisioned people jumping to their feet and Ed Sullivan rushing up to introduce me to everyone on TV.

And I started to play. It was so beautiful. I was so caught up in how lovely I looked that at first I didn't worry how I would sound. So it was a surprise to me when I hit the first wrong note and I realized something didn't sound quite right. And then I hit another and another followed that. A chill started at the top of my head and began to trickle down. Yet I couldn't stop playing, as though my hands were bewitched. I kept thinking my fingers would adjust themselves back, like a train switching to the right track. I played this strange jumble through two repeats, the sour notes staying with me all the way to the end.

55   When I stood up, I discovered my legs were shaking. Maybe I had just been nervous and the audience, like Old Chong, had seen me go through the right motions and had not heard anything wrong at all. I swept my right foot out, went down on my knee, looked up and smiled. The room was quiet, except for Old Chong, who was beaming and shouting, "Bravo! Bravo! Well done!" But then I saw my mother's face, her stricken face. The audience clapped weakly, and as I walked back to my chair, with my whole face quivering as I tried not to cry, I heard a little boy whisper loudly to his mother, "That was awful," and the mother whispered back, "Well, she certainly tried."

And now I realized how many people were in the audience, the whole world it seemed. I was aware of eyes burning into my back. I felt the shame of my mother and father as they sat stiffly throughout the rest of the show.

Joy Luck Club: A name denoting the mother's circle of friends, all of whom were Chinese immigrants to the United States.

We could have escaped during intermission. Pride and some strange sense of honor must have anchored my parents to their chairs. And so we watched it all: the eighteen-year-old boy with a fake mustache who did a magic show and juggled flaming hoops while riding a unicycle. The breasted girl with white makeup who sang from *Madama Butterfly* and got honorable mention. And the eleven-year-old boy who won first prize playing a tricky violin song that sounded like a busy bee.

After the show, the Hsus, the Jongs, and the St. Clairs from the Joy Luck Club came up to my mother and father.

"Lots of talented kids," Auntie Lindo said vaguely, smiling broadly.

"That was somethin' else," said my father, and I wondered if he was referring 60 to me in a humorous way, or whether he even remembered what I had done.

Waverly looked at me and shrugged her shoulders. "You aren't a genius like me," she said matter-of-factly. And if I hadn't felt so bad, I would have pulled her braids and punched her stomach.

But my mother's expression was what devastated me: a quiet, blank look that said she had lost everything. I felt the same way, and it seemed as if everybody were now coming up, like gawkers at the scene of an accident, to see what parts were actually missing. When we got on the bus to go home, my father was humming the busy-bee tune and my mother was silent. I kept thinking she wanted to wait until we got home before shouting at me. But when my father unlocked the door to our apartment, my mother walked in and then went to the back, into the bedroom. No accusations. No blame. And in a way, I felt disappointed. I had been waiting for her to start shouting, so I could shout back and cry and blame her for all my misery.

I assumed my talent-show fiasco meant I never had to play the piano again. But two days later, after school, my mother came out of the kitchen and saw me watching TV.

"Four clock," she reminded me as if it were any other day. I was stunned, as though she were asking me to go through the talent-show torture again. I wedged myself more tightly in front of the TV.

"Turn off TV," she called from the kitchen five minutes later. 65

I didn't budge. And then I decided. I didn't have to do what my mother said anymore. I wasn't her slave. This wasn't China. I had listened to her before and look what happened. She was the stupid one.

She came out from the kitchen and stood in the arched entryway of the living room. "Four clock," she said once again, louder.

"I'm not going to play anymore," I said nonchalantly. "Why should I? I'm not a genius."

She walked over and stood in front of the TV. I saw her chest was heaving up and down in an angry way.

"No!" I said, and I now felt stronger, as if my true self had finally emerged. So 70 this was what had been inside me all along.

"No! I won't!" I screamed.

She yanked me by the arm, pulled me off the floor, snapped off the TV. She was frighteningly strong, half pulling, half carrying me toward the piano as I kicked the throw rugs under my feet. She lifted me up and onto the hard bench. I was sobbing by now, looking at her bitterly. Her chest was heaving even more and her mouth was open, smiling crazily as if she were pleased I was crying.

"You want me to be someone that I'm not!" I sobbed. "I'll never be the kind of daughter you want me to be!"

"Only two kinds of daughters," she shouted in Chinese. "Those who are obedient and those who follow their own mind! Only one kind of daughter can live in this house. Obedient daughter!"

75   "Then I wish I wasn't your daughter. I wish you weren't my mother," I shouted. As I said these things I got scared. It felt like worms and toads and slimy things crawling out of my chest, but it also felt good, as if this awful side of me had surfaced, at last.

"Too late change this," said my mother shrilly.

And I could sense her anger rising to its breaking point. I wanted to see it spill over. And that's when I remembered the babies she had lost in China, the ones we never talked about. "Then I wish I'd never been born!" I shouted. "I wish I were dead! Like them."

It was as if I had said the magic words. Alakazam! — and her face went blank, her mouth closed, her arms went slack, and she backed out of the room, stunned, as if she were blowing away like a small brown leaf, thin, brittle, lifeless.

It was not the only disappointment my mother felt in me. In the years that followed, I failed her so many times, each time asserting my own will, my right to fall short of expectations. I didn't get straight As. I didn't become class president. I didn't get into Stanford. I dropped out of college.

80   For unlike my mother, I did not believe I could be anything I wanted to be. I could only be me.

And for all those years, we never talked about the disaster at the recital or my terrible accusations afterward at the piano bench. All that remained unchecked, like a betrayal that was now unspeakable. So I never found a way to ask her why she had hoped for something so large that failure was inevitable.

And even worse, I never asked her what frightened me the most: Why had she given up hope?

For after our struggle at the piano, she never mentioned my playing again. The lessons stopped. The lid to the piano was closed, shutting out the dust, my misery, and her dreams.

So she surprised me. A few years ago, she offered to give me the piano, for my thirtieth birthday. I had not played in all those years. I saw the offer as a sign of forgiveness, a tremendous burden removed.

85   "Are you sure?" I asked shyly. "I mean, won't you and Dad miss it?"

"No, this your piano," she said firmly. "Always your piano. You only one can play."

"Well, I probably can't play anymore," I said. "It's been years."

"You pick up fast," said my mother, as if she knew this was certain. "You have natural talent. You could been genius if you want to."

"No I couldn't."

"You just not trying," said my mother. And she was neither angry nor sad. 90
She said it as if to announce a fact that could never be disproved. "Take it,"
she said.

But I didn't at first. It was enough that she had offered it to me. And after that,
every time I saw it in my parents' living room, standing in front of the bay
windows, it made me feel proud, as if it were a shiny trophy I had won back.

Last week I sent a tuner over to my parents' apartment and had the piano re-
conditioned, for purely sentimental reasons. My mother had died a few months
before and I had been getting things in order for my father, a little bit at a time. I
put the jewelry in special silk pouches. The sweaters she had knitted in yellow,
pink, bright orange — all the colors I hated — I put those in moth-proof boxes. I
found some old Chinese silk dresses, the kind with little slits up the sides. I rubbed
the old silk against my skin, then wrapped them in tissue and decided to take
them home with me.

After I had the piano tuned, I opened the lid and touched the keys. It sounded
even richer than I remembered. Really, it was a very good piano. Inside the bench
were the same exercise notes with handwritten scales, the same secondhand
music books with their covers held together with yellow tape.

I opened up the Schumann book to the dark little piece I had played at the
recital. It was on the left-hand side of the page, "Pleading Child." It looked more
difficult than I remembered. I played a few bars, surprised at how easily the notes
came back to me.

And for the first time, or so it seemed, I noticed the piece on the right-hand 95
side. It was called "Perfectly Contented." I tried to play this one as well. It had a
lighter melody but the same flowing rhythm and turned out to be quite easy.
"Pleading Child" was shorter but slower; "Perfectly Contented" was longer, but
faster. And after I played them both a few times, I realized they were two halves
of the same song.

◇　◇　◇

ANNE TYLER (1941–　)

Teenage Wasteland (1984)

He used to have very blond hair — almost white — cut shorter than other children's so that on his crown a little cowlick always stood up to catch the light. But
this was when he was small. As he grew older, his hair grew darker, and he wore
it longer — past his collar even. It hung in lank, taffy-colored ropes around his
face, which was still an endearing face, fine-featured, the eyes an unusual aqua
blue. But his cheeks, of course, were no longer round, and a sharp new Adam's
apple jogged in his throat when he talked.

In October, they called from the private school he attended to request a conference with his parents. Daisy went alone; her husband was at work. Clutching her purse, she sat on the principal's couch and learned that Donny was noisy, lazy, and disruptive; always fooling around with his friends, and he wouldn't respond in class.

In the past, before her children were born, Daisy had been a fourth-grade teacher. It shamed her now to sit before this principal as a parent, a delinquent parent, a parent who struck Mr. Lanham, no doubt, as unseeing or uncaring. "It isn't that we're not concerned," she said. "Both of us are. And we've done what we could, whatever we could think of. We don't let him watch TV on school nights. We don't let him talk on the phone till he's finished his homework. But he tells us he doesn't *have* any homework or he did it all in study hall. How are we to know what to believe?"

From early October through November, at Mr. Lanham's suggestion, Daisy checked Donny's assignments every day. She sat next to him as he worked, trying to be encouraging, sagging inwardly as she saw the poor quality of everything he did — the sloppy mistakes in math, the illogical leaps in his English themes, the history questions left blank if they required any research.

5   Daisy was often late starting supper, and she couldn't give as much attention to Donny's younger sister. "You'll never guess what happened at . . ." Amanda would begin, and Daisy would have to tell her, "Not now, honey."

By the time her husband, Matt, came home, she'd be snappish. She would recite the day's hardships — the fuzzy instructions in English, the botched history map, the morass of unsolvable algebra equations. Matt would look surprised and confused, and Daisy would gradually wind down. There was no way, really, to convey how exhausting all this was.

In December, the school called again. This time, they wanted Matt to come as well. She and Matt had to sit on Mr. Lanham's couch like two bad children and listen to the news: Donny had improved only slightly, raising a D in history to a C, and a C in algebra to a B-minus. What was worse, he had developed new problems. He had cut classes on at least three occasions. Smoked in the furnace room. Helped Sonny Barnett break into a freshman's locker. And last week, during athletics, he and three friends had been seen off the school grounds; when they returned, the coach had smelled beer on their breath.

Daisy and Matt sat silent, shocked. Matt rubbed his forehead with his fingertips. Imagine, Daisy thought, how they must look to Mr. Lanham: an overweight housewife in a cotton dress and a too-tall, too-thin insurance agent in a baggy, frayed suit. Failures, both of them — the kind of people who are always hurrying to catch up, missing the point of things that everyone else grasps at once. She wished she'd worn nylons instead of knee socks.

It was arranged that Donny would visit a psychologist for testing. Mr. Lanham knew just the person. He would set this boy straight, he said.

10   When they stood to leave, Daisy held her stomach in and gave Mr. Lanham a firm, responsible handshake.

Donny said the psychologist was a jackass and the tests were really dumb; but he kept all three of his appointments, and when it was time for the follow-up conference with the psychologist and both parents, Donny combed his hair and seemed unusually sober and subdued. The psychologist said Donny had no serious emotional problems. He was merely going through a difficult period in his life. He required some academic help and a better sense of self-worth. For this reason, he was suggesting a man named Calvin Beadle, a tutor with considerable psychological training.

In the car going home, Donny said he'd be damned if he'd let them drag him to some stupid fairy tutor. His father told him to watch his language in front of his mother.

That night, Daisy lay awake pondering the term "self-worth." She had always been free with her praise. She had always told Donny he had talent, was smart, was good with his hands. She had made a big to-do over every little gift he gave her. In fact, maybe she had gone too far, although, Lord knows, she had meant every word. Was that his trouble?

She remembered when Amanda was born. Donny had acted lost and bewildered. Daisy had been alert to that, of course, but still, a new baby keeps you so busy. Had she really done all she could have? She longed — she ached — for a time machine. Given one more chance, she'd do it perfectly — hug him more, praise him more, or perhaps praise him less. Oh, who can say . . .

The tutor told Donny to call him Cal. All his kids did, he said. Daisy thought   15
for a second that he meant his own children, then realized her mistake. He seemed too young, anyhow, to be a family man. He wore a heavy brown handlebar mustache. His hair was as long and stringy as Donny's, and his jeans as faded. Wire-rimmed spectacles slid down his nose. He lounged in a canvas director's chair with his fingers laced across his chest, and he casually, amiably questioned Donny, who sat upright and glaring in an armchair.

"So they're getting on your back at school," said Cal. "Making a big deal about anything you do wrong."

"Right," said Donny.

"Any idea why that would be?"

"Oh, well, you know, stuff like homework and all," Donny said.

"You don't do your homework?"   20

"Oh, well, I might do it sometimes but not just exactly like they want it." Donny sat forward and said, "It's like a prison there, you know? You've got to go to every class, you can never step off the school grounds."

"You cut classes sometimes?"

"Sometimes," Donny said, with a glance at his parents.

Cal didn't seem perturbed. "Well," he said, "I'll tell you what. Let's you and me try working together three nights a week. Think you can handle that? We'll see if we can show that school of yours a thing or two. Give it a month; then if you don't like it, we'll stop. If *I* don't like it, we'll stop. I mean, sometimes people just don't get along, right? What do you say to that?"

"Okay," Donny said. He seemed pleased.   25

"Make it seven o'clock till eight, Monday, Wednesday, and Friday," Cal told Matt and Daisy. They nodded. Cal shambled to his feet, gave them a little salute, and showed them to the door.

This was where he lived as well as worked, evidently. The interview had taken place in the dining room, which had been transformed into a kind of office. Passing the living room, Daisy winced at the rock music she had been hearing, without registering it, ever since she had entered the house. She looked in and saw a boy about Donny's age lying on a sofa with a book. Another boy and a girl were playing Ping-Pong in front of the fireplace. "You have several here together?" Daisy asked Cal.

"Oh, sometimes they stay on after their sessions, just to rap. They're a pretty sociable group, all in all. Plenty of goof-offs like young Donny here."

He cuffed Donny's shoulder playfully. Donny flushed and grinned.

30   Climbing into the car, Daisy asked Donny, "Well? What do you think?"

But Donny had returned to his old evasive self. He jerked his chin toward the garage. "Look," he said. "He's got a basketball net."

Now on Mondays, Wednesdays, and Fridays, they had supper early — the instant Matt came home. Sometimes, they had to leave before they were really finished. Amanda would still be eating her dessert. "Bye, honey. Sorry," Daisy would tell her.

Cal's first bill sent a flutter of panic through Daisy's chest, but it was worth it, of course. Just look at Donny's face when they picked him up: alight and full of interest. The principal telephoned Daisy to tell her how Donny had improved. "Of course, it hasn't shown up in his grades yet, but several of the teachers have noticed how his attitude's changed. Yes, sir, I think we're onto something here."

At home, Donny didn't act much different. He still seemed to have a low opinion of his parents. But Daisy supposed that was unavoidable — part of being fifteen. He said his parents were too "controlling"— a word that made Daisy give him a sudden look. He said they acted like wardens. On weekends, they enforced a curfew. And any time he went to a party, they always telephoned first to see if adults would be supervising. "For God's sake!" he said. "Don't you trust me?"

35   "It isn't a matter of trust, honey . . ." But there was no explaining to him.

His tutor called one afternoon. "I get the sense," he said, "that this kid's feeling . . . underestimated, you know? Like you folks expect the worst of him. I'm thinking we ought to give him more rope."

"But see, he's still so suggestible," Daisy said. "When his friends suggest some mischief — smoking or drinking or such — why, he just finds it hard not to go along with them."

"Mrs. Coble," the tutor said, "I think this kid is hurting. You know? Here's a serious, sensitive kid, telling you he'd like to take on some grown-up challenges, and you're giving him the message that he can't be trusted. Don't you understand how that hurts?"

"Oh," said Daisy.

40   "It undermines his self-esteem — don't you realize that?"

"Well, I guess you're right," said Daisy. She saw Donny suddenly from a whole new angle: his pathetically poor posture, that slouch so forlorn that his shoulders seemed about to meet his chin. . . . oh, wasn't it awful being young? She'd had a miserable adolescence herself and had always sworn no child of hers would ever be that unhappy.

They let Donny stay out later, they didn't call ahead to see if the parties were supervised, and they were careful not to grill him about his evening. The tutor had set down so many rules! They were not allowed any questions at all about any aspect of school, nor were they to speak with his teachers. If a teacher had some complaint, she should phone Cal. Only one teacher disobeyed — the history teacher, Miss Evans. She called one morning in February. "I'm a little concerned about Donny, Mrs. Coble."

"Oh, I'm sorry, Miss Evans, but Donny's tutor handles these things now . . ."

"I always deal directly with the parents. You are the parent," Miss Evans said, speaking very slowly and distinctly. "Now, here is the problem. Back when you were helping Donny with his homework, his grades rose from a D to a C, but now they've slipped back, and they're closer to an F."

"They are?"   45

"I think you should start overseeing his homework again."

"But Donny's tutor says . . ."

"It's nice that Donny has a tutor, but you should still be in charge of his homework. With you, he learned it. Then he passed his tests. With the tutor, well, it seems the tutor is more of a crutch. 'Donny,' I say, 'a quiz is coming up on Friday. Hadn't you better be listening instead of talking?' 'That's okay, Miss Evans,' he says. 'I have a tutor now.' Like a talisman! I really think you ought to take over, Mrs. Coble."

"I see," said Daisy. "Well, I'll think about that. Thank you for calling."

Hanging up, she felt a rush of anger at Donny. A talisman! For a talis-   50
man, she'd given up all luxuries, all that time with her daughter, her evenings at home!

She dialed Cal's number. He sounded muzzy. "I'm sorry if I woke you," she told him, "but Donny's history teacher just called. She says he isn't doing well."

"She should have dealt with me."

"She wants me to start supervising his homework again. His grades are slipping."

"Yes," said the tutor, "but you and I both know there's more to it than mere grades, don't we? I care about the *whole* child — his happiness, his self-esteem. The grades will come. Just give them time."

When she hung up, it was Miss Evans she was angry at. What a narrow woman!   55

It was Cal this, Cal that, Cal says this, Cal and I did that. Cal lent Donny an album by The Who. He took Donny and two other pupils to a rock concert. In March, when Donny began to talk endlessly on the phone with a girl named Miriam, Cal even let Miriam come to one of the tutoring sessions. Daisy was touched that Cal would grow so involved in Donny's life, but she was also a little hurt, because she had offered to have Miriam to dinner and Donny had refused. Now he asked them to drive her to Cal's house without a qualm.

This Miriam was an unappealing girl with blurry lipstick and masses of rough red hair. She wore a short, bulky jacket that would not have been out of place on a motorcycle. During the trip to Cal's she was silent, but coming back, she was more talkative. "What a neat guy, and what a house! All those kids hanging out, like a club. And the stereo playing rock . . . gosh, he's not like a grown-up at all! Married and divorced and everything, but you'd think he was our own age."

"Mr. Beadle was married?" Daisy asked.

"Yeah, to this really controlling lady. She didn't understand him a bit."

"No, I guess not," Daisy said.

60   Spring came, and the students who hung around at Cal's drifted out to the basketball net above the garage. Sometimes, when Daisy and Matt arrived to pick up Donny, they'd find him there with the others — spiky and excited, jittering on his toes beneath the backboard. It was staying light much longer now, and the neighboring fence cast narrow bars across the bright grass. Loud music would be spilling from Cal's windows. Once it was The Who, which Daisy recognized from the time that Donny had borrowed the album. *"Teenage Wasteland,"* ° she said aloud, identifying the song, and Matt gave a short, dry laugh. "It certainly is," he said. He'd misunderstood; he thought she was commenting on the scene spread before them. In fact, she might have been. The players looked like hoodlums, even her son. Why, one of Cal's students had recently been knifed in a tavern. One had been shipped off to boarding school in midterm; two had been withdrawn by their parents. On the other hand, Donny had mentioned someone who'd been studying with Cal for five years. "Five years!" said Daisy. "Doesn't anyone ever stop needing him?"

Donny looked at her. Lately, whatever she said about Cal was read as criticism. "You're just feeling competitive," he said. "And controlling."

She bit her lip and said no more.

In April, the principal called to tell her that Donny had been expelled. There had been a locker check, and in Donny's locker they found five cans of beer and half a pack of cigarettes. With Donny's previous record, his offense meant expulsion.

65   Daisy gripped the receiver tightly and said, "Well, where is he now?"

"We've sent him home," said Mr. Lanham. "He's packed up all his belongings, and he's coming home on foot."

Daisy wondered what she would say to him. She felt him looming closer and closer, bringing this brand-new situation that no one had prepared her to handle. What other place would take him? Could they enter him in public school? What were the rules? She stood at the living room window, waiting for him to show up. Gradually, she realized that he was taking too long. She checked the clock. She stared up the street again.

When an hour had passed, she phoned the school. Mr. Lanham's secretary answered and told her in a grave, sympathetic voice that yes, Donny Coble had

---

Teenage Wasteland: The song is actually "Baba O'Riley," from the band's *Who's Next* album.

most definitely gone home. Daisy called her husband. He was out of the office. She went back to the window and thought awhile, and then she called Donny's tutor.

"Donny's been expelled from school," she said, "and now I don't know where he's gone. I wonder if you've heard from him?"

There was a long silence. "Donny's with me, Mrs. Coble," he finally said. 70

"With you? How'd he get there?"

"He hailed a cab, and I paid the driver."

"Could I speak to him, please?"

There was another silence. "Maybe it'd be better if we had a conference," Cal said.

"I don't *want* a conference. I've been standing at the window picturing him 75 dead or kidnapped or something, and now you tell me you want a —"

"Donny is very, very upset. Understandably so," said Cal. "Believe me, Mrs. Coble, this is not what it seems. Have you asked Donny's side of the story?"

"Well, of course not, how could I? He went running off to you instead."

"Because he didn't feel he'd be listened to."

"But I haven't even —"

"Why don't you come out and talk? The three of us," said Cal, "will try to get 80 this thing in perspective."

"Well, all right," Daisy said. But she wasn't as reluctant as she sounded. Already, she felt soothed by the calm way Cal was taking this.

Cal answered the doorbell at once. He said, "Hi, there," and led her into the dining room. Donny sat slumped in a chair, chewing the knuckle of one thumb. "Hello, Donny," Daisy said. He flicked his eyes in her direction.

"Sit here, Mrs. Coble," said Cal, placing her opposite Donny. He himself remained standing, restlessly pacing. "So," he said.

Daisy stole a look at Donny. His lips were swollen, as if he'd been crying.

"You know," Cal told Daisy, "I kind of expected something like this. That's a 85 very punitive school you've got him in — you realize that. And any half-decent lawyer will tell you they've violated his civil rights. Locker checks! Where's their search warrant?"

"But if the rule is —" Daisy said.

"Well, anyhow, let him tell you his side."

She looked at Donny. He said, "It wasn't my fault. I promise."

"They said your locker was full of beer."

"It was a put-up job! See, there's this guy that doesn't like me. He put all these 90 beers in my locker and started a rumor going, so Mr. Lanham ordered a locker check."

"What was the boy's name?" Daisy asked.

"Huh?"

"Mrs. Coble, take my word, the situation is not so unusual," Cal said. "You can't imagine how vindictive kids can be sometimes."

"What was the boy's *name*," said Daisy, "so that I can ask Mr. Lanham if that's who suggested he run a locker check."

95   "You don't believe me," Donny said.

"And how'd this boy get your combination in the first place?"

"Frankly," said Cal, "I wouldn't be surprised to learn the school was in on it. Any kid that marches to a different drummer, why, they'd just love an excuse to get rid of him. The school is where I lay the blame."

"Doesn't *Donny* ever get blamed?"

"Now, Mrs. Coble, you heard what he —"

100   "Forget it," Donny told Cal. "You can see she doesn't trust me."

Daisy drew in a breath to say that of course she trusted him — a reflex. But she knew that bold-faced, wide-eyed look of Donny's. He had worn that look when he was small, denying some petty misdeed with the evidence plain as day all around him. Still, it was hard for her to accuse him outright. She temporized and said, "The only thing I'm sure of is that they've kicked you out of school, and now I don't know what we're going to do."

"We'll fight it," said Cal.

"We can't. Even you must see we can't."

"I could apply to Brantly," Donny said.

105   Cal stopped his pacing to beam down at him. "Brantly! Yes. They're really onto where a kid is coming from, at Brantly. Why, *I* could get you into Brantly. I work with a lot of their students."

Daisy had never heard of Brantly, but already she didn't like it. And she didn't like Cal's smile, which struck her now as feverish and avid — a smile of hunger.

On the fifteenth of April, they entered Donny in a public school, and they stopped his tutoring sessions. Donny fought both decisions bitterly. Cal, surprisingly enough, did not object. He admitted he'd made no headway with Donny and said it was because Donny was emotionally disturbed.

Donny went to his new school every morning, plodding off alone with his head down. He did his assignments, and he earned average grades, but he gathered no friends, joined no clubs. There was something exhausted and defeated about him.

The first week in June, during final exams, Donny vanished. He simply didn't come home one afternoon, and no one at school remembered seeing him. The police were reassuring, and for the first few days, they worked hard. They combed Donny's sad, messy room for clues; they visited Miriam and Cal. But then they started talking about the number of kids who ran away every year. Hundreds, just in this city. "He'll show up, if he wants to," they said. "If he doesn't, he won't."

110   Evidently, Donny didn't want to.

It's been three months now and still no word. Matt and Daisy still look for him in every crowd of awkward, heartbreaking teenage boys. Every time the phone rings, they imagine it might be Donny. Both parents have aged. Donny's sister seems to be staying away from home as much as possible.

At night, Daisy lies awake and goes over Donny's life. She is trying to figure out what went wrong, where they made their first mistake. Often, she finds herself blaming Cal, although she knows he didn't begin it. Then at other times she excuses him, for without him, Donny might have left earlier. Who really knows?

In the end, she can only sigh and search for a cooler spot on the pillow. As she falls asleep, she occasionally glimpses something in the corner of her vision. It's something fleet and round, a ball — a basketball. It flies up, it sinks through the hoop, descends, lands in a yard littered with last year's leaves and striped with bars of sunlight as white as bones, bleached and parched and cleanly picked.

◊   ◊   ◊

POETRY

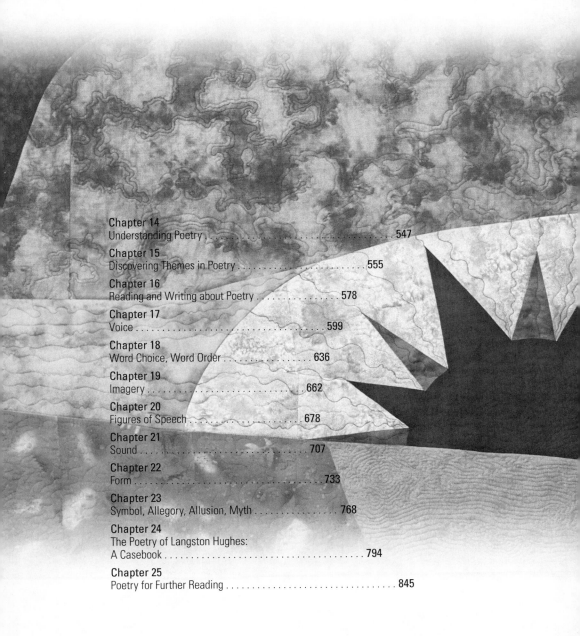

CHAPTER 14

UNDERSTANDING POETRY

MARIANNE MOORE (1887–1972)

Poetry (1921)

I, too, dislike it: there are things that are important beyond all
    this fiddle.
  Reading it, however, with a perfect contempt for it, one discovers
  in it after all, a place for the genuine.
      Hands that can grasp, eyes
        that can dilate, hair that can rise   5
           if it must, these things are important not because a

high-sounding interpretation can be put upon them but because they are
  useful. When they become so derivative as to become unintelligible,
  the same thing may be said for all of us, that we
      do not admire what   10
      we cannot understand: the bat
        holding on upside down or in quest of something to

eat, elephants pushing, a wild horse taking a roll, a tireless wolf under
  a tree, the immovable critic twitching his skin like a horse that feels
    a flea, the base-
    ball fan, the statistician —   15
      nor is it valid
        to discriminate against "business documents and

school-books";° all these phenomena are important. One must make
  a distinction
  however: when dragged into prominence by half poets, the result
    is not poetry,
    nor till the poets among us can be   20
      "literalists of

"business documents and school-books": Moore quotes the *Diaries of Tolstoy* (New York, 1917): "Where the boundary between prose and poetry lies, I shall never be able to understand. . . . Poetry is verse; prose is not verse. Or else poetry is everything with the exception of business documents and school books."

>   the imagination"°— above
>   insolence and triviality and can present
>
> for inspection, "imaginary gardens with real toads in them,"
>   shall we have
>   it. In the meantime, if you demand on the one hand,   25
>   the raw material of poetry in
>   all its rawness and
>   that which is on the other hand
>   genuine, you are interested in poetry.

NIKKI GIOVANNI (1943–   )

Poetry (1975)

poetry is motion graceful
as a fawn
gentle as a teardrop
strong like the eye
finding peace in a crowded room   5
we poets tend to think
our words are golden
though emotion speaks too
loudly to be defined
by silence   10

sometimes after midnight or just before
the dawn
we sit typewriter in hand
pulling loneliness around us
forgetting our lovers or children   15
who are sleeping
ignoring the weary wariness
of our own logic
to compose a poem

    no one understands it   20
it never says "love me" for poets are
beyond love
it never says "accept me" for poems seek not
acceptance but controversy

"literalists of the imagination": A reference (given by Moore) to W. B. Yeats's "William Blake and His Illustrations" (in *Ideas of Good and Evil,* 1903): "The limitation of his view was from the very intensity of his vision; he was a too literal realist of the imagination as others are of nature; and because he believed that the figures seen by the mind's eye, when exalted by inspiration, were 'external existences,' symbols of divine essences, he hated every grace of style that might obscure their lineaments."

it only says "i am" and therefore   25
i concede that you are too
a poem is pure energy
horizontally contained
between the mind
of the poet and the ear of the reader   30
if it does not sing discard the ear
for poetry is song
if it does not delight discard
the heart for poetry is joy
if it does not inform then close   35
off the brain for it is dead
if it cannot heed the insistent message
that life is precious

which is all we poets
wrapped in our loneliness   40
are trying to say

ARCHIBALD MACLEISH (1892–1982)

Ars Poetica° (1926)

A poem should be palpable and mute
As a globed fruit,

Dumb
As old medallions to the thumb,

Silent as the sleeve-worn stone   5
Of casement ledges where the moss has grown—

A poem should be wordless
As the flight of birds.

A poem should be motionless in time
As the moon climbs,   10

Leaving, as the moon releases
Twig by twig the night-entangled trees,

Leaving, as the moon behind the winter leaves,
Memory by memory the mind—

A poem should be motionless in time   15
As the moon climbs.

Ars Poetica: "The Art of Poetry" (Latin).

A poem should be equal to:
Not true.

For all the history of grief
An empty doorway and a maple leaf.   20

For love
The leaning grasses and two lights above the sea —

A poem should not mean
But be.

DEFINING POETRY

Throughout history and across national and cultural boundaries, poetry has held an important place. In ancient China and Japan, for example, poetry was prized above all else. One story tells of a samurai warrior who, when defeated, asked for a pen and paper. Thinking that he wanted to write a will before being executed, his captor granted his wish. Instead of writing a will, however, the warrior wrote a farewell poem that so moved his captor that he immediately released him.

To the ancient Greeks and Romans, poetry was the medium of spiritual and philosophical expression. Epics such as the *Iliad* and the *Aeneid* are written in verse, and so are dramas such as *Oedipus the King* (p. 1271) and *Antigone*. Passages of the Bible, the Koran, and the Hindu holy books are also poetry. Today, throughout the world, poetry continues to delight and to inspire. For many people, in many places, poetry is the language of the emotions, the medium of expression they use when they speak from the heart.

Despite the long-standing place of poetry in our lives, however, many people — including poets themselves — have difficulty deciding what poetry is. Is a poem "pure energy / horizontally contained / between the mind / of the poet and the ear of the reader," as Nikki Giovanni describes it? Or is a poem, as Archibald MacLeish says, "Dumb," "Silent," "wordless," and "motionless in time"? Or is it simply what Marianne Moore calls "all this fiddle"?

One way of defining poetry is to say that it uses language to condense experience into an intensely concentrated package, with each sound, each word, each image, and each line carrying great weight. But beyond this, it is difficult to pin down what makes a particular arrangement of words or lines a poem. Part of the problem is that poetry has many guises: a poem may be short or long, accessible or obscure; it may express a mood or tell a story; it may have a familiar poetic form — a sonnet, a couplet, a haiku — or follow no conventional pattern; it may or may not have a regular, identifiable meter or a rhyme scheme; it may depend heavily on elaborate imagery, figures of speech, irony, complex allusions or symbols, or repeated sounds — or it may include none of these features conventionally associated with poetry.

To further complicate the issue, different readers, different poets, different generations of readers and poets, and different cultures may have different expectations about poetry. As a result, they have different assumptions about poetry, and these different assumptions raise questions. Must poetry be written to delight or inspire, or can a poem have a political or social message — and must this message be conveyed subtly, embellished with imaginatively chosen sounds and words, or can it be explicit and straightforward? These questions, which have been debated by literary critics as well as by poets for many years, have no easy answers — perhaps no answers at all. A haiku — short, rich in imagery, adhering to a rigid formal structure — is certainly poetry, and so is a political poem like Wole Soyinka's "Telephone Conversation" (p. 6). To some Western readers, however, a haiku might seem too plain and understated to be poetic, and Soyinka's poem might seem to be a political tract masquerading as poetry. Still, most of these readers would agree that the following lines qualify as poetry.

WILLIAM SHAKESPEARE (1564–1616)

That time of year thou mayst in me behold (1609)

That time of year thou mayst in me behold
When yellow leaves, or none, or few, do hang
Upon those boughs which shake against the cold,
Bare ruined choirs, where late the sweet birds sang.
In me thou see'st the twilight of such day   5
As after sunset fadeth in the west,
Which by and by black night doth take away,
Death's second self that seals up all in rest.
In me thou see'st the glowing of such fire,
That on the ashes of his youth doth lie,   10
As the deathbed whereon it must expire,
Consumed with that which it was nourished by
    This thou perceiv'st, which makes thy love more strong,
    To love that well which thou must leave ere long.

This poem possesses many of the characteristics that Western readers associate with poetry. For instance, its lines have a regular pattern of rhyme and meter that identifies it as a **sonnet.** The poem also includes a complex network of related imagery and figures of speech that compare the lost youth of the aging speaker to the sunset and to autumn. Finally, the pair of rhyming lines at the end of the poem expresses a familiar poetic theme: the lovers' knowledge that they must eventually die makes their love stronger.

    The next poem is quite different from the preceding one, yet most readers would probably agree that it too is a poem.

LOUIS ZUKOFSKY (1904–1978)

I walk in the old street (1944)

I walk in the old street
to hear the beloved songs
afresh
this spring night.

Like the leaves — my loves wake —   5
not to be the same
or look tireless to the stars
and a ripped doorbell.

Unlike Shakespeare's sonnet, Zukofsky's poem does not have a regular metrical pattern or rhyme scheme. Its diction is more conversational than poetic, and one of its images — a "ripped doorbell" — presents a jarring contrast to the other, more conventionally "poetic" images. Nevertheless, the subject — love — is a traditional one; in fact, Zukofsky's poem echoes some of the sentiments of the Shakespeare sonnet. Finally, the poem's division into two four-line stanzas and its use of figures of speech ("Like the leaves — my loves wake —") are unmistakably poetic.

Although most readers would probably classify the two preceding works as poems, they might be less certain about the following lines.

E. E. CUMMINGS (1894–1962)

l(a (1923)

l(a

le
af
fa

ll   5

s)
one
l

iness

Unlike Shakespeare's and Zukofsky's poems, "l(a" does not seem to have any of the characteristics normally associated with poetry. It has no meter, rhyme, or imagery. It has no repeated sounds, no figures of speech. It cannot even be read aloud because its "lines" are fragments of words. In spite of its odd appearance, however, "l(a" does communicate a conventional poetic theme. Reconstructed, the words Cummings broke apart — "l (a leaf falls) one l iness" — express the loneliness and isolation of the individual, as reflected in nature. Like Shakespeare and Zukofsky, Cummings uses the image of a leaf to express his ideas about life and about human experience. At the same time, by breaking words into bits and pieces, Cummings suggests the flexibility of language and conveys the need to break out of customary ways of using words to define experience.

As the preceding discussion illustrates, defining what a poem is (and what it is not) is almost impossible. It is true that most poems, particularly those divided into stanzas, look like poems, and it is also true that poems tend to use compressed language. Beyond this, however, what makes a poem a poem is more a matter of degree than a question of whether it conforms to a strict set of rules. A poem is likely to use *more* imagery, figures of speech, rhyme, and so on than a prose piece — but, then again, it may not.

READING POETRY

Some readers say they do not like poetry because they find it obscure or intimidating. One reason some people have difficulty reading poetry is that it tends to present information in subtle (and therefore potentially confusing) ways; it does not immediately "get to the point" as journalistic articles or business letters do. One could certainly argue that by concentrating experience, poetry actually "gets to the point" in ways — and to degrees — that other kinds of writing do not. Even so, some readers see poetry as an alien form filled with obscure allusions, complex metrical schemes, and flowery diction. Others, feeling excluded from what they see as its secret language and mysterious structure, approach poetry as something that must be deciphered. Certainly, reading poetry often requires hard work and concentration. Because it is compressed, poetry often omits exposition and explanation; consequently, readers must be willing to take the time to read closely — to interpret ideas and supply missing connections. Many readers are not motivated to dig deeply for what they perceive to be uncertain rewards. But not all poems are difficult, and even those that are difficult are often well worth the effort. (For specific suggestions about how to read poetry, see Chapter 16).

RECOGNIZING KINDS OF POETRY

Most poems are either **narrative** poems, which recount a story, or **lyric** poems, which communicate a speaker's mood, feelings, or state of mind.

Narrative Poetry

Although any brief poem that tells a story, such as Edwin Arlington Robinson's "Richard Cory" (p. 907), may be considered a narrative poem, the two most familiar forms of narrative poetry are the *epic* and the *ballad.*

Epic poems recount the accomplishments of heroic figures, typically including expansive settings, superhuman feats, and gods and supernatural beings. The language of epic poems tends to be formal, even elevated, and often quite elaborate. Epics span many cultures — from the *Odyssey* (Greek) to *Beowulf* (Anglo-Saxon) to *The Epic of Gilgamesh* (Babylonian). In ancient times, epics were handed down orally; more recently, poets have written literary epics, such as John Milton's *Paradise Lost* (1667) and Nobel Prize–winning poet Derek Walcott's *Omeros* (1990), that follow many of the same conventions.

The **ballad** is another type of narrative poetry with roots in an oral tradition. Originally intended to be sung, a ballad uses repeated words and phrases, including a refrain, to advance its story. Some — but not all — ballads use the **ballad stanza.** For examples of traditional ballads in this volume, see "Bonny Barbara Allan" (p. 846) and "Western Wind" (p. 847). Dudley Randall's "Ballad of Birmingham"

(p. 628) and Gwendolyn Brooks's "The Ballad of Rudolph Reed" (p. 855) are examples of contemporary ballads.

Lyric Poetry

Like narrative poems, lyric poems take various forms.

An **elegy** is a poem in which a poet mourns the death of a specific person, as in Robert Hayden's "Homage to the Empress of the Blues" (p. 887), about the singer Bessie Smith. Other examples of this type of poem are A. E. Housman's "To an Athlete Dying Young" (p. 657) and Sherod Santos's "Spring Elegy" (p. 700).

An **ode** is a long lyric poem, formal and serious in style, tone, and subject matter. An ode typically has a fairly complex stanzaic pattern, such as the **terza rima** used by Percy Bysshe Shelley in "Ode to the West Wind" (p. 909). Another ode in this text is John Keats's "Ode on a Grecian Urn" (p. 892).

An **aubade** is a poem about morning, usually celebrating the coming of dawn. An example is Philip Larkin's "Aubade."

An **occasional poem** is written to celebrate a particular event or occasion. An example is Billy Collins's poem "The Names," read before a joint session of Congress to commomorate the first anniversary of the terrorist attacks on the World Trade Center.

A **meditation** is a lyric poem that focuses on a physical object, using this object as a vehicle for considering larger issues. Edmund Waller's "Go, lovely rose" (p. 919) is a meditation.

A **pastoral**—for example, Christopher Marlowe's "The Passionate Shepherd to His Love" (p. 589)—is a lyric poem that celebrates the simple, idyllic pleasures of country life.

A **dramatic monologue** is a poem whose speaker addresses one or more silent listeners, often revealing much more than he or she intends. Robert Browning's "My Last Duchess" (p. 605) and "Porphyria's Lover" (p. 622) and Alfred, Lord Tennyson's "Ulysses" (p. 917) are dramatic monologues.

As you read the poems in this text, you will encounter works with a wide variety of forms, styles, and themes. Some you will find appealing, amusing, uplifting, or moving; others may strike you as puzzling, intimidating, or depressing. But regardless of your critical reaction to the poems, one thing is certain: if you take the time to pay attention to the lines you are reading, and to think about them later on, you will come away from them thinking not just about the images and ideas they express but also about yourself and your world.

CHAPTER 15

DISCOVERING THEMES IN POETRY

A poem can be about anything, from the mysteries of the universe to poetry it-self. Although no subject is really inappropriate for poetic treatment, certain con-ventional subjects — love, war, nature, death, family, the folly of human desires, and the inevitability of growing old — recur frequently. A poem's **theme,** how-ever, is more than its subject.

In general terms, *theme* refers to the ideas the poet explores, the concerns the poem examines. More specifically, a poem's theme is its main point or idea. Po-ems "about nature," for instance, may praise the beauty of nature, assert the supe-riority of its simplest creatures over humans, consider its evanescence, or mourn its destruction. Similarly, poems "about death" may examine the difficulty of fac-ing one's own mortality, eulogize a friend, assert the need for the acceptance of life's cycles, cry out against death's inevitability, or explore the **carpe diem** theme ("life is brief, so let us seize the day").

In order to understand the theme of a poem, readers consider its form, its voice, its language, its images, its allusions, its sound — all of its individual elements. To-gether, these elements convey the ideas that are important in the poem. Keep in mind, however, that a poem may not communicate the same meaning to every reader. Different readers bring different backgrounds, attitudes, and experiences to a poem and therefore see different things and give weight to different ideas.

The following poem is rich enough in language and content to suggest a variety of different interpretations.

ADRIENNE RICH (1929–   )

A Woman Mourned by Daughters (1984)

Now, not a tear begun,
we sit here in your kitchen,
spent, you see, already.
You are swollen till you strain
this house and the whole sky.   5
You, whom we so often
succeeded in ignoring!
You are puffed up in death
like a corpse pulled from the sea;
we groan beneath your weight.   10

And yet you were a leaf,
a straw blown on the bed,
you had long since become
crisp as a dead insect.
What is it, if not you,   15
that settles on us now
like satins you pulled down
over our bridal heads?
What rises in our throats
like food you prodded in?   20
Nothing could be enough.
You breathe upon us now
through solid assertions
of yourself: teaspoons, goblets,
seas of carpet, a forest   25
of old plants to be watered,
an old man in an adjoining
room to be touched and fed.
And all this universe
dares us to lay a finger   30
anywhere, save exactly
as you would wish it done.

"A Woman Mourned by Daughters," a poem about the speaker's mother, explores a number of different themes: the passing of time; the relationships between mother and daughters, father and daughters, husband and wife; the power of memory. Its central theme, however, may be expressed as a **paradox**: a situation in which two opposite things seem to be true. The paradox in this poem is that in death, a person may be a stronger presence than she was in life.

Many different elements in the poem suggest this interpretation. The poem's speaker directly addresses her mother. Her voice is searching, questioning, and the poem's unpoetic diction ("You, whom we so often / succeeded in ignoring!") and metrical irregularities give it a halting, uncertain quality. The words, images, and figurative language work together to establish the central idea: alive, the mother was light as a leaf or a straw or a dead insect; dead, she seems "swollen" and "puffed up," and the daughters feel crushed by her weight. The concrete details of her life — "teaspoons, goblets, / seas of carpet, . . ." — weigh on her survivors and keep them under her spell. In her kitchen, her memory is alive; in death, she has tremendous power over her daughters.

Like most complex poems, this one supports several alternate readings. Some readers will focus on the negative language used to describe the mother; others might emphasize the images of domesticity; still others might concentrate on the role of the sisters and the almost-absent father. Any of these readings can lead to a redefinition of the poem's theme.

The following poem is also about a parent who inspires ambivalent feelings in a child.

RAYMOND CARVER (1938–1988)

Photograph of My Father in His Twenty-Second Year (1983)

October. Here in this dank, unfamiliar kitchen
I study my father's embarrassed young man's face.
Sheepish grin, he holds in one hand a string
of spiny yellow perch, in the other
a bottle of Carlsbad beer.   5

In jeans and denim shirt, he leans
against the front fender of a 1934 Ford.
He would like to pose bluff and hearty for his posterity,
wear his old hat cocked over his ear.
All his life my father wanted to be bold.   10

But the eyes give him away, and the hands
that limply offer the string of dead perch
and the bottle of beer. Father, I love you,
yet how can I say thank you, I who can't hold my liquor either,
and don't even know the places to fish?   15

Like Rich's speaker, Carver's is in a kitchen. Studying a photograph, this speaker sees through his father's façade. Instead of seeing the "bold," "bluff and hearty" young man his father wanted to be, he sees him as he was: "embarrassed" and "sheepish," with limp hands. In the last three lines of the poem, the speaker addresses his father directly, comparing his father's shortcomings and his own. This frank acknowledgment of his own vulnerability and the explicit link between father and son suggest that the poem has more to do with the speaker than with his father. Still, it is clear that the poem has something universal to say about parents and children — specifically, about the ambivalent feelings that children have for parents whose faults and failings they may have inherited.

The following poem also looks back on a parent, but here the adult speaker assumes a child's point of view.

JUDITH ORTIZ COFER (1952–   )

My Father in the Navy: A Childhood Memory (1982)

Stiff and immaculate
in the white cloth of his uniform
and a round cap on his head like a halo,
he was an apparition on leave from a shadow-world
and only flesh and blood when he rose from below   5

the waterline where he kept watch over the engines
and dials making sure the ship parted the waters
on a straight course.
Mother, brother and I kept vigil
on the nights and dawns of his arrivals,   10
watching the corner beyond the neon sign of a quasar
for the flash of white our father like an angel
heralding a new day.
His homecomings were the verses
we composed over the years making up   15
the siren's song that kept him coming back
from the bellies of iron whales
and into our nights
like the evening prayer.

Even as an adult, the speaker seems still not to know her father, whom she remembers as "Stiff and immaculate," dressed in white, "an apparition on leave from a shadow-world." She remembers him as being "like an angel," wearing his cap "like a halo." In lines 14–16, the speaker associates her father with the long-missing, long-awaited wanderer Odysseus, hero of Homer's *Odyssey*. The reference to the "siren's song" in line 16, also an allusion to the *Odyssey*, suggests the adult speaker's realization that the father is drawn back — perhaps against his will — to the family. Together, the poem's tone and imagery convey the child's view of the father as elusive and unreal — an impression the adult speaker neither confirms nor corrects. The poem seems to suggest that the speaker is still struggling to understand her father's complex role in her life; perhaps too it suggests the universal difficulty of a child's trying to understand a parent.

POEMS ABOUT PARENTS

The poems that follow share a common subject — each focuses on a parent — yet they explore a variety of themes and a variety of attitudes toward that subject. As you read, pay particular attention to the speakers' voices, which often express conventional feelings of love and admiration alongside puzzlement, frustration, and even anger.

THEODORE ROETHKE (1908–1963)

My Papa's Waltz (1948)

The whiskey on your breath
Could make a small boy dizzy;
But I hung on like death:
Such waltzing was not easy.

We romped until the pans   5
Slid from the kitchen shelf;
My mother's countenance
Could not unfrown itself.

The hand that held my wrist
Was battered on one knuckle;   10
At every step you missed
My right ear scraped a buckle.

You beat time on my head
With a palm caked hard by dirt,
Then waltzed me off to bed   15
Still clinging to your shirt.

DYLAN THOMAS (1914–1953)

Do not go gentle into that good night * (1952)

Do not go gentle into that good night,
Old age should burn and rave at close of day;
Rage, rage against the dying of the light.

Though wise men at their end know dark is right,
Because their words had forked no lightning they   5
Do not go gentle into that good night.

Good men, the last wave by, crying how bright
Their frail deeds might have danced in a green bay,
Rage, rage against the dying of the light.

Wild men who caught and sang the sun in flight,   10
And learn, too late, they grieved it on its way,
Do not go gentle into that good night.

Grave men, near death, who see with blinding sight
Blind eyes could blaze like meteors and be gay,
Rage, rage against the dying of the light.   15

And you, my father, there on the sad height,
Curse, bless, me now with your fierce tears, I pray,
Do not go gentle into that good night.
Rage, rage against the dying of the light.

* This poem was written during the last illness of the poet's father.

LUCILLE CLIFTON (1936–   )

My Mama moved among the days (1969)

My Mama moved among the days
like a dreamwalker in a field;
seemed like what she touched was hers
seemed like what touched her couldn't hold,
she got us almost through the high grass   5
then seemed like she turned around and ran
right back in
right back on in

ROBERT HAYDEN (1913–1980)

Those Winter Sundays (1962)

Sundays too my father got up early
and put his clothes on in the blueblack cold,
then with cracked hands that ached
from labor in the weekday weather made
banked fires blaze. No one ever thanked him.   5

I'd wake and hear the cold splintering, breaking.
When the rooms were warm, he'd call,
and slowly I would rise and dress,
fearing the chronic angers of that house,

Speaking indifferently to him,   10
who had driven out the cold
and polished my good shoes as well.
What did I know, what did I know
of love's austere and lonely offices?

SEAMUS HEANEY° (1939–   )

Digging (1966)

Between my finger and my thumb
The squat pen rests; snug as a gun.

Under my window, a clean rasping sound
When the spade sinks into gravelly ground:

Seamus Heaney: Heaney received the 1995 Nobel Prize in Literature.

My father, digging. I look down   5

Till his straining rump among the flowerbeds
Bends low, comes up twenty years away
Stooping in rhythm through potato drills
Where he was digging.

The coarse boot nestled on the lug, the shaft   10
Against the inside knee was levered firmly.
He rooted out tall tops, buried the bright edge deep
To scatter new potatoes that we picked
Loving their cool hardness in our hands.

By God, the old man could handle a spade.   15
Just like his old man.

My grandfather cut more turf in a day
Than any other man on Toner's bog.
Once I carried him milk in a bottle
Corked sloppily with paper. He straightened up   20
To drink it, then fell to right away

Nicking and slicing neatly, heaving sods
Over his shoulder, going down and down
For the good turf. Digging.

The cold smell of potato mould, the squelch and slap   25
Of soggy peat, the curt cuts of an edge
Through living roots awaken in my head.
But I've no spade to follow men like them.

Between my finger and my thumb
The squat pen rests.   30
I'll dig with it.

YEHUDA AMICHAI (1924–2000)

My Father (1997)

Translated from the Hebrew by Azila Talit Reisenberger.

The memory of my father is wrapped up in
white paper, like sandwiches taken for a day at work.

Just as a magician takes towers and rabbits
out of his hat, he drew love from his small body,

and the rivers of his hands   5
overflowed with good deeds.

JILL BIALOSKY (1957–   )

The Boy Beheld His Mother's Past (2001)

The ivory wedding hat came tumbling down —
how long had it been stored away, untouched
like desire repressed and bound —
and fell to the floor with less than a hush.

How long had it been stored away, untouched?   5
The boy beheld his mother's past
as dusk descended with less than a hush.
Was it possible her marriage might not last?

The boy beheld his mother's past —
Who was she? Who else did she love?   10
Was it possible her marriage might not last?
Light abandoned the skylight above
and shadowed the rug where they once danced.

Was his life governed by fate or circumstance?
The curtains trembled without a sound.   15
On the rug where they once danced
the ivory wedding hat came tumbling down.

Reading and Reacting: Poems about Parents

1. What is the child's attitude toward the parent discussed in each poem?
2. Which words and images suggest positive associations? Which help to create a negative impression?
3. How would you characterize each poem's tone? For example, is the poem sentimental, humorous, angry, resentful, or regretful?
4. What ideas about parent-child relationships are explored in each poem? What is each poem's central theme?
5. What does each poem say about the parent? What does it reveal about the child?

Related Works: "Sleepy Time Gal" (p. 46), "How to Talk to Your Mother (Notes)" (p. 100), "Two Kinds" (p. 527), "Daddy" (p. 691)

POEMS ABOUT LOVE

The conventional poetic subject of love is the focus of numerous poems. Those that follow — written as long ago as 1600 and as recently as 1996 — reflect the diverse themes that love poems have expressed over the years. As you read each poem, consider who the speaker is and whether or not he or she is speaking directly to the loved one.

CHRISTOPHER MARLOWE (1564–1593)

The Passionate Shepherd to His Love (1600)

Come live with me and be my love,
And we will all the pleasures prove
That valleys, groves, hills, and fields,
Woods, or steepy mountain yields.

And we will sit upon the rocks,   5
Seeing the shepherds feed their flocks
By shallow rivers, to whose falls
Melodious birds sing madrigals.

And I will make thee beds of roses
And a thousand fragrant posies,
A cap of flowers and a kirtle°   10
Embroidered all with leaves of myrtle;

A gown made of the finest wool
Which from our pretty lambs we pull;
Fair-linèd slippers for the cold,   15
With buckles of the purest gold;

A belt of straw and ivy buds,
With coral clasps and amber studs.
And if these pleasures may thee move,
Come live with me and be my love.   20

The shepherds' swains shall dance and sing
For thy delight each May morning.
If these delights thy mind may move,
Then live with me and be my love.

SIR WALTER RALEIGH (1552?–1618)

The Nymph's Reply to the Shepherd (1600)

If all the world and love were young,
And truth in every shepherd's tongue,
These pretty pleasures might me move
To live with thee and be thy love.

Time drives the flocks from field to fold,   5
When rivers rage and rocks grow cold;

---

kirtle: Skirt.

And Philomel° becometh dumb;
The rest complains of cares to come.

The flowers do fade, and wanton fields
To wayward winter reckoning yields: 10
A honey tongue, a heart of gall,
Is fancy's spring, but sorrow's fall.

Thy gowns, thy shoes, thy beds of roses,
Thy cap, thy kirtle, and thy posies
Soon break, soon wither, soon forgotten,   15
In folly ripe, in reason rotten.

Thy belt of straw and ivy buds,
Thy coral clasps and amber studs.
All these in me no means can move
To come to thee and be thy love.   20

But could youth last, and love still breed,
Had joys no date, nor age no need,
Then these delights my mind might move
To live with thee and be thy love.

THOMAS CAMPION (1567–1620)

There is a garden in her face (1617)

There is a garden in her face
Where roses and white lilies grow;
    A heav'nly paradise is that place
Wherein all pleasant fruits do flow.
    There cherries grow which none may buy   5
    Till "Cherry-ripe" themselves do cry.

Those cherries fairly do enclose
Of orient pearl a double row,
    Which when her lovely laughter shows,
They look like rose-buds filled with snow;   10
    Yet them nor peer nor prince can buy,
    Till "Cherry-ripe" themselves do cry.

    Her eyes like angels watch them still;
Her brows like bended bows do stand,
    Threat'ning with piercing frowns to kill   15
All that attempt, with eye or hand

Philomel: The nightingale.

Those sacred cherries to come nigh
Till "Cherry-ripe" themselves do cry.

WILLIAM SHAKESPEARE (1564–1616)

My mistress' eyes are nothing like the sun (1609)

My mistress' eyes are nothing like the sun;
Coral is far more red than her lips' red;
If snow be white, why then her breasts are dun;
If hairs be wires, black wires grow on her head.
I have seen roses damasked red and white,   5
But no such roses see I in her cheeks;
And in some perfumes is there more delight
Than in the breath that from my mistress reeks.
I love to hear her speak, yet well I know
That music hath a far more pleasing sound;   10
I grant I never saw a goddess go:
My mistress, when she walks, treads on the ground.
    And yet, by heaven, I think my love as rare
    As any she, belied with false compare.

ROBERT BROWNING (1812–1889)

Meeting at Night (1845)

The gray sea and the long black land;
And the yellow half-moon large and low;
And the startled little waves that leap
In fiery ringlets from their sleep,
As I gain the cove with pushing prow,   5
And quench its speed i' the slushy sand.

Then a mile of warm sea-scented beach;
Three fields to cross till a farm appears;
A tap at the pane, the quick sharp scratch
And blue spurt of a lighted match,   10
And a voice less loud, through its joys and fears,
Than the two hearts beating each to each!

Parting at Morning (1845)

Round the cape of a sudden came the sea,
And the sun looked over the mountain's rim:
And straight was a path of gold for him,
And the need of a world of men for me.

ELIZABETH BARRETT BROWNING (1806–1861)

How Do I Love Thee? (1850)

How do I love thee? Let me count the ways.
I love thee to the depth and breadth and height
My soul can reach, when feeling out of sight
For the ends of being and ideal grace.
I love thee to the level of every day's   5
Most quiet need, by sun and candle-light.
I love thee freely, as men strive for right.
I love thee purely, as they turn from praise.
I love thee with the passion put to use
In my old griefs, and with my childhood's faith.   10
I love thee with a love I seemed to lose
With my lost saints. I love thee with the breath,
Smiles, tears, of all my life; and, if God choose,
I shall but love thee better after death.

EDNA ST. VINCENT MILLAY (1892–1950)

What Lips My Lips Have Kissed (1923)

What lips my lips have kissed, and where, and why,
I have forgotten, and what arms have lain
Under my head till morning; but the rain
Is full of ghosts tonight, that tap and sigh
Upon the glass and listen for reply,   5
And in my heart there stirs a quiet pain
For unremembered lads that not again
Will turn to me at midnight with a cry.
Thus in the winter stands the lonely tree,
Nor knows what birds have vanished one by one,   10
Yet knows its boughs more silent than before:
I cannot say what loves have come and gone,
I only know that summer sang in me
A little while, that in me sings no more.

DOROTHY PARKER (1893–1967)

General Review of the Sex Situation (1933)

Woman wants monogamy;
Man delights in novelty.
Love is woman's moon and sun;
Man has other forms of fun.

Woman lives but in her lord;   5
Count to ten, and man is bored.
With this the gist and sum of it,
What earthly good can come of it?

SYLVIA PLATH (1932–1963)

Wreath for a Bridal (1956)

What though green leaves only witness
Such pact as is made once only; what matter
That owl voice sole 'yes', while cows utter
Low moos of approve; let sun surpliced in brightness
Stand stock still to laud these mated ones   5
Whose stark act all coming double luck joins.

Couched daylong in cloisters of stinging nettle
They lie, cut-grass assaulting each separate sense
With savor; coupled so, pure paragons of constance,
This pair seek single state from that dual battle.   10
Now speak some sacrament to parry scruple
For wedlock wrought within love's proper chapel.

Call here with flying colors all watchful birds
To people the twigged aisles; lead babel tongues
Of animals to choir: 'Look what thresh of wings   15
Wields guard of honor over these!' Starred with words
Let night bless that luck-rotted mead of clover
Where, bedded like angels, two burn one in fever.

From this holy day on, all pollen blown
Shall strew broadcast so rare a seed on wind   20
That every breath, thus teeming, set the land
Sprouting fruit, flowers, children most fair in legion
To slay spawn of dragon's teeth: speaking this promise,
Let flesh be knit, and each step hence go famous.

TED HUGHES° (1930–1998)

A Pink Wool Knitted Dress (1996)

In your pink wool knitted dress
Before anything had smudged anything
You stood at the altar. Bloomsday.

Ted Hughes: Husband of Sylvia Plath (see "Wreath for a Bridal," above).

Rain — so that a just-bought umbrella
Was the only furnishing about me   5
Newer than three years inured.
My tie — sole, drab, veteran RAF black—
Was the used-up symbol of a tie.
My cord jacket — thrice-dyed black, exhausted,
Just hanging on to itself.   10

I was a post-war, utility son-in-law!
Not quite the Frog-Prince. Maybe the Swineherd
Stealing this daughter's pedigree dreams
From under her watchtowered searchlit future.

No ceremony could conscript me   15
Out of my uniform. I wore my whole wardrobe—
Except for the odd, spare, identical item.
My wedding, like Nature, wanted to hide.
However — if we were going to be married
It had better be Westminster Abbey. Why not?   20
The Dean told us why not. That is how
I learned that I had a Parish Church.
St George of the Chimney Sweeps.
So we squeezed into marriage finally.
Your mother, brave even in this   25
US Foreign Affairs gamble,
Acted all bridesmaids and all guests,
Even — magnanimity — represented
My family
Who had heard nothing about it.   30
I had invited only their ancestors.
I had not even confided my theft of you
To a closest friend. For Best Man — my squire
To hold the meanwhile rings—
We requisitioned the sexton. Twist of the outrage: 35
He was packing children into a bus,
Taking them to the Zoo — in that downpour!
All the prison animals had to be patient
While we married.
                        You were transfigured.
                              So slender and new and naked,   40
A nodding spray of wet lilac.
You shook, you sobbed with joy, you were ocean depth
Brimming with God.
You said you saw the heavens open
And how riches, ready to drop upon us.   45
Levitated beside you, I stood subjected
To a strange tense: the spellbound future.

In that echo-gaunt, weekday chancel
I see you
Wrestling to contain your flames   50
In your pink wool knitted dress
And in your eye-pupils — great cut jewels
Jostling their tear-flames, truly like big jewels
Shaken in a dice-cup and held up to me.

Reading and Reacting: Poems about Love

1. What conventional images does each speaker use to express love?
2. Does any speaker use any images that are unexpected or shocking?
3. What ideas about love are expressed in each poem?
4. What is the tone of each poem? Is it happy? Sad? Celebratory? Regretful?
5. What does each poem reveal about the speaker? About the person to whom
the poem is addressed?

Related Works: "Living in Sin" (p. 643), "A Valediction: Forbidding Mourning"
(p. 687), "To My Dear and Loving Husband" (p. 695), "you fit into me" (p. 700),
"The Littoral Zone" (p. 258), *The Brute* (p. 1062)

POEMS ABOUT WAR

The poems that follow examine the subject of war in different nations and different historical time periods. As you read these poems, consider what thematic and
stylistic elements all (or most) of them have in common — and *why* they share
these elements.

RUPERT BROOKE (1887–1915)

The Soldier (1915)

If I should die, think only this of me;
    That there's some corner of a foreign field
That is for ever England. There shall be
    In that rich earth a richer dust concealed;
A dust whom England bore, shaped, made aware,   5
    Gave, once, her flowers to love, her ways to roam,
A body of England's breathing English air,
    Washed by the rivers, blest by suns of home.

And think, this heart, all evil shed away,
    A pulse in the eternal mind, no less   10
        Gives somewhere back the thoughts by England given;
Her sights and sounds; dreams happy as her day;
    And laughter, learnt of friends; and gentleness,
        In hearts at peace, under an English heaven.

WILFRED OWEN (1893–1918)

Anthem for Doomed Youth   (1917?)

What passing-bells for these who die as cattle?
   Only the monstrous anger of the guns.
Only the stuttering rifles' rapid rattle
Can patter out their hasty orisons.°
No mockeries now for them; no prayers nor bells,   5
   Nor any voice of mourning save the choirs,—
The shrill, demented choirs of wailing shells;
   And bugles calling for them from sad shires.

What candles may be held to speed them all?
   Not in the hands of boys, but in their eyes   10
   Shall shine the holy glimmers of good-byes.
The pallor of girls' brows shall be their pall;
Their flowers the tenderness of patient minds,
And each slow dusk a drawing-down of blinds.

WILLIAM BUTLER YEATS (1865–1939)

An Irish Airman Foresees His Death   (1919)

I know that I shall meet my fate
Somewhere among the clouds above;
Those that I fight I do not hate,
Those that I guard I do not love;
My country is Kiltartan Cross   5
My countrymen Kiltartan's poor,
No likely end could bring them loss
Or leave them happier than before.
Nor law, nor duty bade me fight,
Nor public men, nor cheering crowds,   10
A lonely impulse of delight
Drove to this tumult in the clouds;
I balanced all, brought all to mind,
The years to come seemed waste of breath,
A waste of breath the years behind   15
In balance with this life, this death.

---

orisons: Prayers.

ROBERT LOWELL (1917–1977)

For the Union Dead (1959)

"Relinquunt omnia servare rem publicam." °

The old South Boston Aquarium stands
in a Sahara of snow now. Its broken windows are boarded.
The bronze weathervane cod has lost half its scales.
The airy tanks are dry.

Once my nose crawled like a snail on the glass;   5
my hand tingled
to burst the bubbles
drifting from the noses of the cowed, compliant fish.

My hand draws back. I often sigh still
for the dark downward and vegetating kingdom   10
of the fish and reptile. One morning last March,
I pressed against the new barbed and galvanized

fence on the Boston Common. Behind their cage,
yellow dinosaur steamshovels were grunting
as they cropped up tons of mush and grass   15
to gouge their underworld garage.

Parking spaces luxuriate like civic
sandpiles in the heart of Boston.
A girdle of orange, Puritan-pumpkin colored girders
braces the tingling Statehouse,   20

shaking over the excavations, as it faces Colonel Shaw
and his bell-cheeked Negro infantry
on St. Gauden's shaking Civil War relief,
propped by a plant splint against the garage's earthquake.

Two months after marching through Boston,   25
half the regiment was dead;
at the dedication,
William James ° could almost hear the bronze Negroes breathe.

Their monument sticks like a fishbone
in the city's throat.   30
Its Colonel is as lean
as a compass-needle.

Relinquunt omnia servare rem publicam: "They gave up everything to preserve the Republic" (Latin). A monument in Boston Common bears a similar form of this quotation. Designed by Augustus Saint-Gaudens, the monument is dedicated to Colonel Robert Gould Shaw and the African American troops he commanded during a Civil War battle at Fort Wagner, South Carolina, on July 18, 1863.

William James: Harvard psychologist and philosopher (1842–1910), often called the father of modern psychology.

He has an angry wrenlike vigilance,
a greyhound's gentle tautness;
he seems to wince at pleasure,   35
and suffocate for privacy.

He is out of bounds now. He rejoices in man's lovely,
peculiar power to choose life and death—
when he leads his black soldiers to death,
he cannot bend his back.   40

On a thousand small town New England greens,
the old white churches hold their air
of sparse, sincere rebellion; frayed flags
quilt the graveyards of the Grand Army of the Republic.

The stone statues of the abstract Union Soldier   45
grow slimmer and younger each year—
wasp-waisted, they doze over muskets
and muse through their sideburns . . .

Shaw's father wanted no monument
except the ditch,   50
where his son's body was thrown
and lost with his "niggers."

The ditch is nearer.
There are no statues for the last war here;
on Boylston Street, a commercial photograph   55
shows Hiroshima boiling

over a Mosler Safe,° the "Rock of Ages"
that survived the blast. Space is nearer.
When I crouch to my television set,
the drained faces of Negro school-children rise like balloons. 60

Colonel Shaw
is riding on his bubble,
he waits
for the blessed break.

The Aquarium is gone. Everywhere,   65
giant finned cars nose forward like fish;
a savage servility
slides by on grease.

Mosler Safe: A brand of safe known for being especially strong.

DENISE LEVERTOV (1923–1997)

What Were They Like? (1966)

1) Did the people of Viet Nam
   use lanterns of stone?
2) Did they hold ceremonies
   to reverence the opening of buds?
3) Were they inclined to rippling laughter?   5
4) Did they use bone and ivory,
   jade and silver, for ornament?
5) Had they an epic poem?
6) Did they distinguish between speech and singing?

1) Sir, their light hearts turned to stone.   10
   It is not remembered whether in gardens
   stone lanterns illumined pleasant ways.
2) Perhaps they gathered once to delight in blossom,
   but after the children were killed
   there were no more buds.   15
3) Sir, laughter is bitter to the burned mouth.
4) A dream ago, perhaps. Ornament is for joy.
   All the bones were charred.
5) It is not remembered. Remember,
   most were peasants; their life   20
   was in rice and bamboo.
   When peaceful clouds were reflected in the paddies
   and the water buffalo stepped surely along terraces,
   maybe fathers told their sons old tales.
   When bombs smashed the mirrors   25
   there was time only to scream.
6) There is an echo yet, it is said,
   of their speech which was like a song.
   It is reported their singing resembled
   the flight of moths in moonlight.   30
   Who can say? It is silent now.

CARL PHILLIPS (1959–   )

On the Notion of Tenderness in Wartime (1992)

The news
that you are reading the journals of Delacroix
arrived safely,

thank you. For days
the only word here has been water: everywhere,   5

scratched into the sun-cracked bellies

of every turned-over-and-over-again stone,
I see it, but I am told
this happens — any day now,

the rains.   10
Last night I remembered our bodies
coming apart that first time,

you saying "now we're alone in the world."
Sometimes, even here,
it can still get that quiet.   15

BORIS SLUTSKY (1919–1986)

How Did They Kill My Grandmother?*

Translated by Elaine Feinstein

How did they kill my grandmother?
I'll tell you how they killed her.
One morning a tank rolled up to
a building where
the hundred and fifty Jews of our town who,   5
weightless
        from a year's starvation,
and white
        with the knowledge of death,
were gathered holding their bundles.   10
And the German polizei° were
herding the old people briskly;
and their tin mugs clanked as
the young men led them away
                        far away.   15

But my small grandmother
my seventy-year-old grandmother
began to curse and
scream at the Germans;
shouting that I was a soldier.   20
She yelled at them: My grandson
is off at the front fighting!
Don't you dare
touch me!

---

*Publication date is not available.
polizei: Police.

Listen, you   25
      can hear our guns!

Even as she went off, my grandmother
cried abuse,
      starting all over again
with her curses.   30
From every window then
Ivanovnas and Andreyevnas
Sidorovnas and Petrovnas
sobbed: You tell them, Polina
Matveyevna, keep it up!   35
They all yelled together:
      "What can we do against
this enemy, the Hun?"
Which was why the Germans chose
to kill her inside the town.   40

A bullet struck her hair
and kicked her grey plait down.
My grandmother fell to the ground.
That is how she died there.

YUSEF KOMUNYAKAA (1947–   )

Facing It (1988)

My black face fades,
hiding inside the black granite.
I said I wouldn't,
dammit: No tears.
I'm stone. I'm flesh.   5
My clouded reflection eyes me
like a bird of prey, the profile of night
slanted against morning. I turn
this way — the stone lets me go.
I turn that way — I'm inside   10
the Vietnam Veterans Memorial
again, depending on the light
to make a difference.
I go down the 58,022 names,
half-expecting to find   15
my own in letters like smoke.
I touch the name Andrew Johnson;
I see the booby trap's white flash.

Names shimmer on a woman's blouse
but when she walks away   20
the names stay on the wall.
Brushstrokes flash, a red bird's
wings cutting across my stare.
The sky. A plane in the sky.
A white vet's images floats   25
closer to me, then his pale eyes
look through mine. I'm a window.
He's lost his right arm
inside the stone. In the black mirror
a woman's trying to erase names: 30
No, she's brushing a boy's hair.

WISLAWA SZYMBORSKA (1923–   )

The End and the Beginning (1993)

After every war
someone has to clean up.
Things won't
straighten themselves up, after all.

Someone has to push the rubble   5
to the side of the road,
so the corpse-filled wagons
can pass.

Someone has to get mired
in scum and ashes,   10
sofa springs,
splintered glass,
and bloody rags.

Someone has to drag in a girder
to prop up a wall,   15
Someone has to glaze a window,
rehang a door.

Photogenic it's not,
and takes years.
All the cameras have left   20
for another war.

We'll need the bridges back,
and new railway stations.
Sleeves will go ragged
from rolling them up.   25

Someone, broom in hand,
still recalls the way it was.
Someone else listens
and nods with unsevered head.
But already there are those nearby   30
starting to mill about
who will find it dull.

From out of the bushes
sometimes someone still unearths
rusted-out arguments   35
and carries them to the garbage pile.

Those who knew
what was going on here
must make way for
those who know little.   40
And less than little.
And finally as little as nothing.

In the grass that has overgrown
causes and effects,
someone must be stretched out   45
blade of grass in his mouth
gazing at the clouds.

Reading and Reacting: Poems about War

1. What is each speaker's attitude toward war? Does the speaker seem to be focusing on a particular war or on war in general?

2. What conventional images does each poem use to express its ideas about war?

3. Do any of the poems use unusual, unexpected, or shocking images?

4. How would you describe each poem's tone? Angry? Cynical? Sad? Disillusioned? Resigned?

5. What does each poem reveal about the speaker?

Related Works: "The Man He Killed" (p. 612), "Patterns" (p. 613), "The Death of the Ball Turret Gunner" (p. 685), "Naming of Parts" (p. 905)

CHAPTER 16

READING AND WRITING ABOUT POETRY

READING POETRY

Sometimes readers approach poetry purely for pleasure. At other times, reading a poem is the first step toward writing about it. The following guidelines, designed to help you explore poetic works, focus on issues explored in chapters to come.

- Rephrase the poem in your own words. What does your paraphrase reveal about the poem's subject and central concerns? What is lost or gained in your paraphrase of the poem?
- Consider the poem's **voice.** Who is the poem's speaker? How would you characterize the poem's tone? Is the poem ironic? (See Chapter 17.)
- Study the poem's **diction,** and look up unfamiliar words in a dictionary. How does word choice affect your reaction to the poem? What do the connotations of words reveal about the poem? What level of diction is used? Is dialect used? Is word order unusual or unexpected? How does the arrangement of words contribute to your understanding of the poem? (See Chapter 18.)
- Examine the poem's **imagery.** What kind of imagery predominates? What specific images are used? Is a pattern of imagery present? How does imagery enrich the poem? (See Chapter 19.)
- Identify the poem's **figures of speech.** Does the poet use metaphor? Simile? Personification? Hyperbole? Understatement? Metonymy or synecdoche? Apostrophe? How do figures of speech affect your reading of the poem? (See Chapter 20.)
- Listen to the **sound** of the poem. Are rhythm and meter regular or irregular? How do rhythm and meter reinforce the poem's central concerns? Does the poem use alliteration? Assonance? Rhyme? How do these elements enhance the poem? (See Chapter 21.)
- Look at the poem's **form.** Is the poem written in closed or open form? Is the poem constructed as a sonnet? A sestina? A villanelle? An epigram? A haiku? Is the poem an example of concrete poetry? How does the poem's form help to communicate (or reinforce) its ideas? (See Chapter 22.)
- Consider the poem's use of **symbol, allegory, allusion,** or **myth.** Does the poem make use of symbols? Allusions? How do symbols or allusions support

its theme? Is the poem an allegory? Does the poem retell or interpret a myth? (See Chapter 23.)

- Identify the poem's **theme.** What central theme does the poem explore? What other themes are examined? How are the themes expressed? (See Chapter 15.)

Active Reading

When you approach a poem that you plan to write about, you engage in the same **active reading** strategies you use when you read a short story or a play. When you finish recording your reactions to the poem, you focus on a topic, develop ideas about that topic, decide on a thesis, prepare an outline, and then go on to draft and revise your essay.

Catherine Whittaker, a student in an introduction to literature course, was asked to write a three- to five-page essay comparing any two of the eight poems that appear in "Poems about Parents" in Chapter 15 (pp. 555–577). Her instructor told the class that the essay should reflect students' own reactions to the poems, not the opinions of literary critics. As Catherine planned and wrote her paper, she was guided by the process described in Chapter 2, "Reading and Writing about Literature."

Previewing

Catherine began her work by previewing the poems, eliminating those she considered obscure or difficult and those whose portrait of the speaker's parent did not seem sympathetic. This process helped Catherine to narrow down her choices. As she looked through "Those Winter Sundays," she was struck by words in the opening lines ("Sundays too"; "blueblack cold"). She had the same reaction to "The squat pen rests; snug as a gun" in line 2 of "Digging." In each case, the words made Catherine want to examine the poem further. She noticed too that both poems were divided into stanzas of varying lengths and that both focused on fathers. Keeping these features in mind, Catherine began a close reading of each poem.

Highlighting and Annotating

As Catherine read and reread "Those Winter Sundays" and "Digging," she recorded her comments and questions. The highlighted and annotated poems follow.

ROBERT HAYDEN (1913–1980)

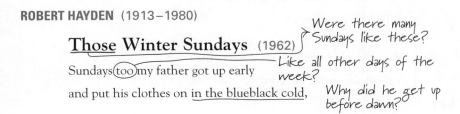

<u>Those</u> Winter Sundays (1962)

Sundays (too) my father got up early

and put his clothes on <u>in the blueblack cold,</u>

Were there many Sundays like these?

Like all other days of the week?

Why did he get up before dawn?

then with cracked hands <u>that ached</u>   } *What kind of job did*
   the father have?

<u>from labor in the weekday</u> weather made

banked fires blaze. No one ever thanked him.   5
   → *Was there a large family?*
I'd wake and hear the cold splintering, breaking.

When the rooms were warm, he'd call,

and slowly I would rise and dress,

fearing the chronic angers of that house,
   → *Were there problems in the family?*
Speaking indifferently to him,   10

who had driven out the cold
   Was there a mother
and polished my good shoes as well.   *around?*

What did I know, what did I know
   → *Offices=duties or functions*
of love's <u>austere</u> and lonely <u>offices</u>?   *assigned to someone*

Austere=without adornment
or ornamentation, simple;
harsh

SEAMUS HEANEY (1939–   )

Digging   (1966)

Between my finger and my thumb

The squat <u>pen</u> rests; <u>snug as a gun.</u> → *gun=snug?*
   → *Why a "squat" pen?*
Under my window, a clean rasping sound

When the spade sinks into gravelly ground:

My father, digging. I look down   5

Till his straining rump among the flowerbeds

Bends low, comes up <u>twenty years away</u>   *Is he thinking about*
   the past?
Stooping in rhythm through potato drills

Where he was digging.

The coarse boot nestled on the lug, the shaft   10

Against the inside knee was <u>levered firmly.</u>

Like the poets' pen?

He rooted out tall tops, buried the bright edge deep

To scatter new potatoes that (we) picked   *→ Was this a family*
task?

Loving their cool hardness in our hands.

By God, the old man could handle a spade.   15

Just like his old man.

} Two generations
could "handle a
spade." Can
the poet dig?

My grandfather cut more turf in a day

Than any other man on Toner's bog.

Once I carried him milk in a bottle

Corked sloppily with paper. He straightened up   20

To drink it, then <u>fell to right away</u> —→ *The grandfather was*
hard worker.

<u>Nicking and slicing neatly</u>, heaving sods → *Digging was an art*

Over his shoulder, going down and down

For the good turf. Digging.

The cold smell of potato mould, the squelch and slap   25

Of soggy peat, the curt cuts of an edge   *→ What does it make hi*
remember?

Through living roots <u>awaken in my head</u>.

But I've no spade to follow men like them. *What are "men like*
→ them" like?

Between my finger and my thumb

Same
as first} (The <u>squat pen</u> rests.   → *Why is this repeated?*   30
2 lines (I'll <u>dig</u> with it.
    ↳ Dig for what?

Catherine found the language of both poems appealing, and she believed her highlighting and annotating had given her some valuable insights. For example, she noticed some parallels between the two poems: both focus on the past, both portray fathers as hard workers, and neither mentions a mother.

WRITING ABOUT POETRY

Planning an Essay

Even though Catherine still had to find a specific topic for her paper, her preliminary work suggested some interesting possibilities. She was especially intrigued by the way both poems depict fathers as actively engaged in physical tasks.

Choosing a Topic

One idea Catherine thought she might want to write about was the significance of the sons' attitudes toward their fathers: although both see their fathers as hard workers, the son in "Those Winter Sundays" seems to have mixed feelings about his father's devotion to his family, whereas the son in "Digging" is more appreciative. Catherine explored this idea in two journal entries.

```
                "Those Winter Sundays"
   Why did the father get up early every morning? One could
imagine that he had a large family and little money. There
is no mention of a mother. Images are created of the utter
coldness and "chronic angers" of the house. The father not
only made fires to warm the house but also polished his
child's (or children's) shoes—maybe for church. And yet, the
child seems not to care about or appreciate the father's ef-
forts. Is he too young to say thank you, or are there other
problems in the house for which the child blames the father?
```

```
                "Digging"
   In the poem, the poet seems to be wondering what to write
about when the sounds of digging capture his attention. He
remembers the steady, artful rhythm of his father's digging
of the potatoes and how they (probably the poet and his
brothers and sisters) picked out the cool potatoes. His mem-
ories appear to be entirely appreciative of his father's and
grandfather's hard work and skill. He does, however, feel
regret that he is not like these dedicated men. Even though
he cannot use a shovel, he hopes to use his pen in order to
make his own contributions as a writer.
```

When Catherine reread her journal entries, she thought she was close to a specific topic for her paper. The more she reviewed the two poems, the more confident she felt exploring their similar views of the fathers' roles and the speakers' contrasting attitudes toward these fathers. (In fact, she had so many ideas that she did not feel she had to brainstorm to generate more material.) Before she could write a draft of her paper, however, Catherine needed to identify specific similarities and differences between the two poems.

Seeing Connections: Listing

Catherine reread the highlighted and annotated poems and then compiled the following lists.

```
                   Differences
     "Those Winter Sundays"      "Digging"
     —memories of family         —only happy memories
       problems                    are involved
```

—the child acts
 ambivalently toward
 his father

—the child admires his
 father

—atmosphere of tension

—atmosphere of happiness
 and togetherness

Similarities
—the fathers are hard workers
—the fathers appear to love their children
—similar time—impression that the events
 happened years ago
—children, now grown, appreciate their fathers'
 dedication
—children, now grown, are inspired by their
 fathers' determination

At this point, Catherine reviewed her notes carefully. As connections between the two poems came into focus, she was able to decide on a tentative thesis and on a possible order for her ideas.

Deciding on a Thesis

The more Catherine thought about the two poems, the more she focused on their similarities. She expressed a possible main idea for her paper in the following tentative thesis statement.

Although their family backgrounds are different, both
now-grown poets realize the determination and dedication
of their fathers and are consequently impassioned in
their writing.

Preparing an Outline

Catherine reviewed her notes to help her identify the specific ideas she wanted to address in her first draft. Then, she arranged those ideas in a logical order in a scratch outline.

"Those Winter Sundays"
    Poet reflects back on childhood
        —father's hard work
        —his misunderstanding and lack of appreciation
         for everything his father did
    Family setting in childhood
        —tension in the house
        —no mother mentioned in the poem
    Poet's realization of father's love and dedication

"Digging"

    Poet reminisces
        —father's skill and hard work
        —grandfather's steady heaving of sods
        —children's participation and acceptance

    Happiness of the family

    The desire for the poet to continue the tradition

Drafting an Essay

With a thesis statement and scratch outline to guide her, Catherine wrote the following first draft of her essay. Her instructor's comments appear in the margins and at the end of the paper.

first draft

A Comparison of Two Poems about Fathers

Robert Hayden's "Those Winter Sundays" and "Digging" by Seamus Heaney are poems that were inspired by fathers and composed as tributes to fathers. Although their family backgrounds are different, both now-grown (poets) realize the determination and dedication of their fathers and are consequently (impassioned) in their writing.

Careful! you're confus-ing poet and speaker.

What do you mean?

In "Those Winter Sundays," Hayden reflects back on his childhood. He remembers the many Sundays when his father got up early to start the fires to make the house warm for his children's awakening. The poet pictures his father's hands made rough by his weekday work. These same hands not only made the fires on Sunday but also polished his son's good shoes, in preparation, no doubt, for church.

Hayden also quite clearly remembers that his father was never thanked for his work. The reader imagines that the father had many children and may have been poor. There were inner tensions in the house and, quite noticeably, there is no mention of a mother.

Looking back, the poet now realizes the love and dedication with which his father took care of the

Here quotations from the poem would strengthen your discussion.

family. As a child, he never thanked his father, but now, as an adult, the poet seems to appreciate the simple kindness of his father.

In a similar sense, Seamus Heaney writes "Digging" as a tribute to his father and grandfather. He also reminisces about his father and clearly remembers the skill with which his father dug potatoes. The grandfather too is remembered, as is his technique for "heaving sods." There is an atmosphere of happiness in this poem. With the children helping the father harvest the potatoes, a sense of family togetherness is created. The reader feels that this family is a hardworking but nevertheless happy one.

add line number in parentheses.

As the poet reminisces about his childhood, he realizes that, unlike his father and grandfather, he will never be a master of digging or a person who uses physical strength to earn a living. He wishes to be like his father before him, desiring to accomplish and contribute. However, for the poet, any "digging" to be done will be by his pen, in the form of literature.

To conclude, the fathers in these poets' pasts inspire them to write. An appreciation for their fathers' dedication is achieved only after the children mature into adults. It is then that the fathers' impact on their children's lives is realized

for its true importance.

Good start! When you revise, focus on the
following:
— Edit use of "poet" and "speaker" carefully. You
  can't assume that
  these poems reflect the poets' own lives or
  attitudes toward their fathers.
— add more specific references to the poems,
  particularly quotations.
  (Don't forget to give line
  numbers.)
— Consider adding brief references to other
  poems about parents. (Check the textbook.)
— Consider rearranging your material into a point-
  by-point comparison, which will make the
  specific points of similarity and differences
  clearer.

Let's discuss this draft in a conference.

First Draft: Commentary

After submitting her first draft, Catherine met with her instructor. Together, they reviewed not only her first draft but also her annotations, journal entries, lists of similarities and differences, and scratch outline. During the conference, her instructor explained his written comments and, building on Catherine's own ideas, helped her develop a plan for revision.

Catherine's instructor agreed that the poems' similarities were worth exploring in detail. He thought, however, that her references to the poems' language and ideas needed to be much more specific and that her paper's structure — discussing "Those Winter Sundays" first and then moving on to consider "Digging" — made the specific similarities between the two poems difficult to see.

Because the class had studied other poems in which speakers try to resolve their ambivalent feelings toward their parents, Catherine's instructor also suggested that she mention these poems to provide a wider context for her ideas. Finally, he explained the difference between the perspective of the poet and that of the **speaker,** a persona the poet creates, encouraging her to edit with this difference in mind.

As she reexamined her ideas in light of her discussion with her instructor, Catherine looked again at both the annotated poems and her notes about them. She then recorded her thoughts about her progress in an additional journal entry.

> After reviewing the poems again and talking to Professor Jackson, I discovered some additional points that I want to include in my next draft. The connection between the poet's pen and the shovel is evident in "Digging," and so is the link between the cold and the tensions in the house in "Those Winter Sundays." The tone of each poem should also be discussed. Specifically, I think that the poet's choice of <u>austere</u> in "Those Winter Sundays" has significance and should be included. In my next draft, I'll expand my first draft—hopefully, without reading into the poems too much. I also need to reorganize my ideas so parallels between the two poems will be clearer.

Because this journal entry suggested a new arrangement for her ideas, Catherine prepared a new scratch outline to guide her revision.

> Reflections on their fathers
>   Both poems
>   —fathers' dedication and hard work
>
> Family similarities and differences
>   "Digging"
>   —loving and caring
>   "Those Winter Sundays"
>   —family problems (tone of the poem)

```
Lessons learned from father
    "Digging"
        —inspiration (images of pen and shovel)
        —realization of father's inner strength
    "Those Winter Sundays"
        —realization of father's inner strength
        —"austere" caring (images of cold)

Brief discussion of other poems about fathers
```

Revising and Editing an Essay

After once again reviewing all the material she had accumulated, Catherine wrote a second draft.

(second draft)

A Comparison of Two Poems about Fathers

Robert Hayden's "Those Winter Sundays" and Seamus Heaney's "Digging" are two literary pieces that are tributes to the speakers' fathers. The inspiration and admiration the speakers feel are evident in each poem. Although the nature of the two family relationships may differ, the common thread of the love of fathers for their children weaves through each poem.

Reflections on one's childhood can bring assorted memories to light. Presumably, the speakers are now adults and reminisce on their childhood with a mature sense of enlightenment not found in childhood. Both speakers describe their fathers' hard work and dedication to their families. Hayden's speaker remembers that even after working hard all week, his father would get up early on Sunday to warm the house in preparation for his children's rising. The speaker vividly portrays his father's hands, describing "cracked hands that ached / from labor in the weekday weather" (3-4). And yet, these same hands not only built the fires that drove out the cold but also polished his children's good shoes.

In a similar way, Heaney's speaker reminisces about his father's and grandfather's digging of soil and sod, elaborating on their skill and dedication to their task.

The fathers in these poems appear to be the hardest of workers, laborers who sought to support their families. Not only did they have a dedication to their work, but they also cared about and undoubtedly loved their children. Looking back, Hayden's speaker realizes that, although his childhood may not have been perfect nor his family life entirely without problems, his father loved him. Heaney's description of the potato picking makes us imagine a loving family led by a father and grandfather who worked together and included the children in both work and celebration. Heaney's speaker grows to become a man who has nothing but respect for his father and grandfather, wishing to be like them and somehow follow their greatness.

Although some similarities exist between the sons and fathers in the poems, the family life differs between the two. Perhaps it is the tone of the poems that best typifies the family atmosphere. The tone of "Digging" is wholesome, earthy, natural, and happy, emphasizing the healthy and caring nature of the poet's childhood. In reminiscing, Heaney's speaker seems to have no bad memories concerning his father or family. In contrast, the tone of Hayden's poem is very much like the coldness of the Sunday mornings. Even though the father warmed the house, the "chronic angers of that house" (9) did not leave with the cold. The speaker, as a child, seems full of resentment toward the father, no doubt blaming him for the family problems. (Curiously, it is the father and not the mother who polishes the children's good shoes. Was there no mother?) The reader senses that the father-son communication evident in Heaney's family is missing in Hayden's.

There are many other poets who have written about their fathers. Simon J. Ortiz in "My Father's Song" writes a touching tribute to his father, who taught him to respect and care for the lives of animals and to appreciate earthly wonders. In other poems, such as Theodore Roethke's "My Papa's Waltz," the fathers are depicted as imperfect, vulnerable people who try to cope with life as well as possible.

"Digging" and "Those Winter Sundays" are poems written from the inspirations of sons, admiring and appreciating their fathers. Childhood memories act not only as images of the past but also as aids for the speakers' self-realization and enlightenment. Even after childhood, the fathers' influence over their sons is evident; only now do the speakers appreciate its true importance.

Second Draft: Commentary

When she reread her second draft, Catherine thought she had accomplished some of what she had set out to do. She had, tightened her thesis statement, re-arranged her discussion, added specific details, and changed *poet* to *speaker* where necessary. However, she still was not satisfied with her analysis of the poems' language and tone (she had not, for example, considered the importance of the word *austere* or examined the significance of Heaney's equation of *spade* and *pen*). She also thought that the material in paragraph 6 about other poems, though interesting, was distracting, so she decided to try to relocate it. Finally, she planned to edit and proofread carefully as she prepared her final draft.

Whittaker 1

Catherine Whittaker

Professor Jackson

English 102

5 March 2003

Digging for Memories

Robert Hayden's "Those Winter Sundays" and Seamus Heaney's "Digging" are two literary pieces that are tributes to the speakers' fathers. Although the depiction of the families and the tones of the two poems are different, the common thread of love between fathers and children extends through the two poems, and each speaker is inspired by his father's example.

Thesis statement

Many other poets have written about children and their fathers. Simon J. Ortiz in "My Father's Song" writes a touching tribute to a father who taught the speaker to respect and care for the lives of animals and to appreciate earthly wonders. In other poems, such as Theodore Roethke's "My Papa's Waltz," fathers are depicted as imperfect, vulnerable people who try to cope with life as well as possible.

¶6 from second draft has been relocated. References to poems in Chapter 16 of this volume include complete authors' names and titles.

As all these poems reveal, reflections on childhood can bring complex memories to light, as they do for Hayden's and Heaney's speakers. Now adults, they reminisce about their childhoods with a mature sense of enlightenment not found in childhood. Both speakers describe their fathers' hard work and dedication to their families. Hayden's speaker remembers that even after working hard all week, his father would get up early on Sunday to warm

First point of similarity: Both poems focus on memory

Whittaker 2

the house in preparation for his sleeping children. The speaker vividly portrays his father's hands, describing "cracked hands that ached / from labor in the weekday weather" (lines 3-4). And yet, these same hands not only built the fires that drove out the cold but also polished his children's good shoes. In a similar way, Heaney's speaker reminisces about his father's and grandfather's digging of soil and sod, pointing out their skill and their dedication to their tasks.

> Parenthetical reference cites line numbers. (First reference to lines of poetry includes word *lines*. Subsequent references include just line numbers.)

The fathers in these poems appear to be hard workers, laborers who struggled to support their families. Not only were they dedicated to their work, but they also loved their children. Looking back, Hayden's speaker realizes that, although his childhood may not have been perfect and his family life was not entirely without problems, his father loved him. Heaney's description of the potato picking makes us imagine a loving family led by a father and grandfather who worked together and included the children in both work and celebration. Heaney's speaker grows into a man who has nothing but respect for his father and grandfather, wishing to be like them and to somehow fill their shoes.

> Second point of similarity: Both fathers are hard workers.

Although some similarities exist between the sons and fathers in the poems, the family life the two poems depict is very different. Perhaps it is the tone of the poems that best reveals the family atmosphere. The tone of "Digging" is wholesome, earthy,

Whittaker 3

natural, and happy, emphasizing the healthy and caring nature of the speaker's childhood. Heaney's
speaker seems to have no bad memories
of his father or family. In contrast, the tone of
Hayden's poem is very much like the coldness of the
Sunday mornings. Even though the father warmed the
house, the "chronic angers of that house" (9) did not
leave with the cold. The speaker, as a child, seems
to have resented his father, no doubt blaming him for
the family's problems. The reader senses that the
warm relationship between the father and the son
in Heaney's poem is absent in Hayden's.

> Focus returns to parallels between the two poems. Third point of similarity: Both speakers learn from grandfathers (discussed in two paragraphs).

   In spite of these differences, the reader cannot
go away from either poem without the impression that
both speakers learned important lessons from their
fathers. Both fathers had a great amount of inner
strength and dedication to their families. As the
years pass, Hayden's speaker has come to realize the
depth of his father's devotion to his family. He
uses the image of the "blueblack cold" (2) that was
splintered and broken by the fires lovingly prepared
by his father to suggest the father's efforts to keep
his family free from harm. The cold suggests the
tensions of the family that the father is determined
to force out of the house through his "austere and
lonely offices" (14).

   In Heaney's poem, the father and grandfather
have also had a profound impact on the young speaker.
As the memories come pouring back, the speaker's

Whittaker 3

admiration for the men who came before him forces him
to reflect on his own life and work. He realizes that
he will never have the ability (or the desire) to do
the physical labor of his relatives: "I've no spade
to follow men like them" (28). However, just as the
spade was the tool of his father and grandfather,
the pen will be the tool with which the speaker will
work. The shovel suggests the hard work, effort,
and determination of the men who came before him,
and the pen is the literary equivalent of the shovel.
Heaney's speaker has been inspired by his father and
grandfather and hopes to accomplish with a pen in the
world of literature what they accomplished with a
shovel on the land.

> Conclusion
> reinforces
> thesis.

"Digging" and "Those Winter Sundays" are poems
written from the perspective of sons who are admiring
and appreciating their fathers. Childhood memories
not only act as images of the past but also evoke the
speakers' self-realization and enlightenment. Even
after childhood, the fathers' influence over their
sons is evident; only now, however, do the speakers
appreciate its true importance.

Final Draft: Commentary

As she wrote her final draft, Catherine expanded her analysis, looking more closely at the language and tone of the two poems. To support and clarify her points, she added more direct quotations, taking care to reproduce words and punctuation marks accurately and to cite line numbers in parentheses after each quotation. (Because all the students in Catherine's class had to select poems from Chapter 15 of this anthology, their instructor did not require a works-cited page.) She also moved her discussion of other poems to paragraph 2, where it provides a smooth transition from her introduction to her discussion of Hayden and Heaney.

VOICE

What makes a poem significant? What makes it memorable? Passion and thought, emotionally charged language, fresh imagery, surprising use of metaphor . . . yes. But also, I think, the very sure sense that the moment we enter the world of the poem we are participating in another episode of the myth-journey of humankind; that a voice has taken up the tale once more. The individual experience as related or presented in the poem renews our deep, implicit faith in that greater experience. A poem remains with us to the extent that it allows us to feel that we are listening to a voice at once contemporary and ancient. This makes all the difference. —**John Haines**, *"The Hole in the Bucket"*

I have been ruminating about "personal poems" — I am inclined to agree that one turns back to less personal poems yet you surely would not remove Shakespeare's sonnets, all of Donne, much of Yeats, all of Emily Dickinson, Sappho, Millay, Wylie (or most), Wyatt from the canon, would you? The trouble is that one does not choose what one is to write about: poetry is a seizure, and not done on will. The point is I think that a "personal" poem has to go deep enough to touch the *universal:* the "I" is only a device like any other. This is not to argue — as I agree that it would be better if the muse provided more *less* personal poems. —**May Sarton**, *"Among the Visual Days"*

Someone writing a poem believes in a reader, in readers, of that poem. The "who" of that reader quivers like a jellyfish. Self-reference is always possible: that my "I" is a universal "we," that the reader is my clone. That sending letters to myself is enough for attention to be paid. That my chip of mirror contains the world.

But most often someone writing a poem believes in, depends on, a delicate, vibrating range of difference, that an "I" can become a "we" without extinguishing others, that a partly common language exists to which strangers can bring their own heartbeat, memories, images. A language that itself has learned from the heartbeat, memories, images of strangers. —**Adrienne Rich**, *What Is Found There*

EMILY DICKINSON (1830–1886)

I'm nobody! Who are you? (1891)

I'm nobody! Who are you?
Are you — Nobody — Too?
Then there's a pair of us?
Don't tell! they'd advertise — you know!

How dreary — to be — Somebody!   5
How public — like a Frog —
To tell one's name — the livelong June —
To an admiring Bog!

THE SPEAKER IN THE POEM

In fiction, the author's careful choice and arrangement of words enable readers to form an impression of the narrator and to decide whether he or she is sophisticated or unsophisticated, trustworthy or untrustworthy, innocent or experienced. Just as fiction depends on a narrator, poetry depends on a **speaker** who describes events, feelings, and ideas to readers. Finding out as much as possible about this speaker can help readers to interpret the poem. For example, the speaker in Emily Dickinson's "I'm nobody! Who are you?" seems at once shy and playful. The first stanza of the poem suggests that the speaker is a private person, perhaps with little self-esteem. As the poem continues, however, the voice becomes almost defiant. In a sense, the speaker's two voices represent two ways of relating to the world. The first voice expresses the private self — internal, isolated, and revealed through poetry; the second expresses the public self — external, self-centered, self-promoting, and inevitably superficial. Far from being defeated by shyness, the speaker claims to have chosen her status as "nobody."

One question readers might ask about "I'm nobody! Who are you?" is how close the speaker's voice is to the poet's. Readers who conclude that the poem is about the conflict between a poet's public and private selves may be tempted to see the speaker and the poet as one. But this is not necessarily the case. Like the narrator of a short story, the speaker of a poem is a **persona,** or mask, that the poet assumes. Granted, in some poems little distance exists between the poet and the speaker. Without hard evidence to support a link between speaker and poet, however, readers should not simply assume they are one and the same.

In most cases, the speaker is quite different from the poet. And even when the speaker's voice may convey the attitude of the poet either directly or indirectly. In "The Chimney Sweeper" (p. 852), for example, William Blake assumes the voice of a child to criticize the system of child labor that existed in eighteenth-century England. Even though the child speaker does not understand the conditions that cause his misery, readers sense the poet's anger as the trusting speaker describes the conditions under which he works. The poet's indignation is especially apparent in the biting irony of the last line, in which the victimized speaker innocently assures readers that if all people do their duty, "they need not fear harm."

Sometimes the poem's speaker is anonymous. In this case — as in William Carlos Williams's "Red Wheelbarrow" (p. 665), for instance — the first-person voice is absent and the speaker remains outside the poem. At other times, the speaker has a set identity — a king, a beggar, a highwayman, a sheriff, a husband, a wife, a rich man, a chimney sweep, a child, a mythical figure, an explorer, a teacher, a faithless lover, a saint, or even a flower, an animal, or a clod of earth. Whatever the case, the speaker is not the poet but rather a creation that the poet uses to convey his or her ideas. (For this reason, poems by a single poet may have very different voices. See Sylvia Plath's "Daddy" [p. 691] and "Morning Song" [p. 619], for example.)

Sometimes a poem's title tells readers that the poet is assuming a particular persona. In the following poem, for example, the title identifies the speaker as a fictional character, Gretel from the fairy tale "Hansel and Gretel."

LOUISE GLÜCK (1943–   )

Gretel in Darkness (1971)

This is the world we wanted.
All who would have seen us dead
are dead. I hear the witch's cry
break in the moonlight through a sheet
of sugar: God rewards.   5
Her tongue shrivels into gas. . . .

             Now, far from women's arms
And memory of women, in our father's hut
we sleep, are never hungry.
Why do I not forget?   10
My father bars the door, bars harm
from this house, and it is years.

No one remembers. Even you, my brother,
summer afternoons you look at me as though
you meant to leave,   15
as though it never happened.
But I killed for you. I see armed firs,
the spires of that gleaming kiln —

Nights I turn to you to hold me
but you are not there.   20
Am I alone? Spies
hiss in the stillness, Hansel
we are there still, and it is real, real,
that black forest, and the fire in earnest.

The speaker in this poem comments on her life after her encounter with the witch in the forest. Speaking to her brother, Gretel observes that they now live in the world they wanted: they live with their father in his hut, and the witch and the wicked stepmother are dead. Even so, the memory of the events in the forest haunts Gretel and makes it impossible for her to live "happily ever after." The "armed firs," the "gleaming kiln," and "the black forest" break through the "sheet of sugar" that her life has become.

By assuming the persona of Gretel, Glück is able to convey some interesting and complex ideas. On one level, Gretel represents any person who has lived through a traumatic experience. Memories of the event keep breaking through into the present, frustrating her attempts to reestablish her belief in the goodness of the world. The voice we hear is sad, alone, and frightened: "Nights I turn to you to hold me," she says, "but you are not there." Although the murder Gretel committed for her brother was justified, it seems to haunt her. "No one remembers," laments Gretel, not even her brother. At some level, she realizes that by killing the witch she has killed a part of herself, perhaps the part of women that men fear and consequently transform into witches and wicked stepmothers. The world that is left after the killing is the father's and the brother's, not hers, and she is now alone in a dark world haunted by the memories of the black forest. In this sense, Gretel — "Now, far from women's arms / And memory of women" — may be the voice of all victimized women who, because of men, act against their own best interests — and regret it.

As "Gretel in Darkness" illustrates, a title can identify a poem's speaker, but the speaker's own words can provide much more information. This is also the case in the following poem, where Spanish words help to characterize the speaker.

LEONARD ADAMÉ (1947–   )

My Grandmother Would Rock Quietly and Hum (1973)

in her house
she would rock quietly and hum
until her swelled hands
calmed

in summer   5
she wore thick stockings
sweaters
and grey braids

(when "el cheque"° came
we went to Payless   10

---

el cheque: The check.

and I laughed greedily
when given a quarter)

mornings,
sunlight barely lit
the kitchen   15
and where
there were shadows
it was not cold

she quietly rolled
flour tortillas —   20
the "papas"°
cracking in hot lard
would wake me

she had lost her teeth
and when we ate   25
she had bread
soaked in "café"°

always her eyes
were clear
and she could see   30
as I cannot yet see —
through her eyes
she gave me herself

she would sit
and talk   35
of her girlhood —
of things strange to me:
        México
        epidemics
        relatives shot   40
        her father's hopes
        of this country —
how they sank
with cement dust
to his insides   45

now
when I go
to the old house
the worn spots
by the stove   50
echo of her shuffling

---

papas: Potatoes.
café: Coffee.

and
México
still hangs in her
fading   55
calendar pictures

In this poem, the speaker is an adult recalling childhood memories of his grandmother. Spanish words — *el cheque, tortillas, papas,* and *café* — identify the speaker as Latino. His easy use of English, his comment that Mexico is strange to him, and his observation that he cannot yet see through his grandmother's eyes suggest, however, that he is not in touch with his ethnic identity. At one level, the grandmother evokes nostalgic memories of the speaker's youth. At another level, she is a living symbol of his ties with Mexico, connecting him to the ethnic culture he is trying to recover. The poem ends on an ambivalent note: even though the speaker is able to return to "the old house," the pictures of Mexico are fading, perhaps suggesting the speaker's assimilation into mainstream American culture.

Direct statements by the speaker can also help to characterize him. In the next poem, the first line of each stanza establishes the identity of the speaker — and defines his perspective.

LANGSTON HUGHES (1902–1967)

Negro (1926)

I am a Negro:
    Black as the night is black,
    Black like the depths of my Africa.

I've been a slave:
    Caesar told me to keep his door-steps clean.   5
    I brushed the boots of Washington.

I've been a worker:
    Under my hand the pyramids arose.
    I made mortar for the Woolworth Building.

I've been a singer: 10
    All the way from Africa to Georgia
    I carried my sorrow songs.
    I made ragtime.

I've been a victim:
    The Belgians cut off my hands in the Congo.   15
    They lynch me still in Mississippi.

I am a Negro:
    Black as the night is black,
    Black like the depths of my Africa.

Here the speaker, identifying himself as "a Negro," assumes each of the roles African-Americans have historically played in Western society — slave, worker, singer, and victim. By so doing, he gives voice to his ancestors who, by being forced to serve others, were deprived of their identities. By presenting not only their suffering but also their accomplishments, the speaker asserts his pride in being black. The speaker also implies that the suffering of black people has been caused by economic exploitation: Romans, Egyptians, Belgians, and Americans all used black labor to help build their societies. In this context, the speaker's implied warning is clear: except for the United States, all the societies that have exploited blacks have declined, and long after the fall of those empires, black people still endure.

In each of the preceding poems, the speaker is alone. The following poem, a **dramatic monologue,** presents a more complex situation in which the poet creates a complete dramatic scene. The speaker is developed as a character whose distinctive personality is revealed through his words as he addresses a silent listener.

ROBERT BROWNING (1812–1889)

My Last Duchess (1842)

Ferrara

That's my last Duchess painted on the wall,
Looking as if she were alive. I call
That piece a wonder, now: Frà Pandolf's° hands
Worked busily a day, and there she stands.
Will't please you sit and look at her? I said   5
"Frà Pandolf" by design, for never read
Strangers like you that pictured countenance,
The depth and passion of its earnest glance,
But to myself they turned (since none puts by
The curtain I have drawn for you, but I)   10
And seemed as they would ask me, if they durst,
How such a glance came there; so, not the first
Are you to turn and ask thus. Sir, 'twas not
Her husband's presence only, called that spot
Of joy into the Duchess' cheek: perhaps   15
Frà Pandolf chanced to say "Her mantle laps
Over my lady's wrist too much," or "Paint
Must never hope to reproduce the faint
Half-flush that dies along her throat": such stuff
Was courtesy, she thought, and cause enough   20
For calling up that spot of joy. She had

Frà Pandolf: "Brother" Pandolf, a fictive painter.

A heart — how shall I say? — too soon made glad,
Too easily impressed; she liked whate'er
She looked on, and her looks went everywhere.
Sir, 'twas all one! My favor at her breast,   25
The dropping of the daylight in the West,
The bough of cherries some officious fool
Broke in the orchard for her, the white mule
She rode with round the terrace — all and each
Would draw from her alike the approving speech,   30
Or blush, at least. She thanked men — good! but thanked
Somehow — I know not how — as if she ranked
My gift of a nine-hundred-years-old name
With anybody's gift. Who'd stoop to blame
This sort of trifling? Even had you skill   35
In speech — (which I have not) — to make your will
Quite clear to such an one, and say, "Just this
Or that in you disgusts me; here you miss,
Or there exceed the mark" — and if she let
Herself be lessoned so, nor plainly set   40
Her wits to yours, forsooth, and made excuse
—E'en then would be some stooping; and I choose
Never to stoop. Oh sir, she smiled, no doubt,
Whene'er I passed her; but who passed without
Much the same smile? This grew; I gave commands;   45
Then all smiles stopped together. There she stands
As if alive. Will't please you rise? We'll meet
The company below, then. I repeat,
The Count your master's known munificence
Is ample warrant that no just pretense   50
Of mine for dowry will be disallowed;
Though his fair daughter's self, as I avowed
At starting, is my object. Nay, we'll go
Together down, sir. Notice Neptune,° though,
Taming a sea horse, thought a rarity,   55
Which Claus of Innsbruck° cast in bronze for me!

The speaker is probably Alfonso II, duke of Ferrara, Italy, whose young wife, Lucrezia, died in 1561 after only three years of marriage. Shortly after her death, the duke began negotiations to marry again. When the poem opens, the duke is showing a portrait of his late wife to an emissary of an unnamed count who is there to arrange a marriage between the duke and the count's daughter. The duke remarks that the artist, Frà Pandolf, has caught a certain look on the duchess's face.

Neptune: In Roman mythology, the god of the sea.

Claus of Innsbruck: A fictive — or unidentified — sculptor. The count of Tyrol's capital was at Innsbrück, Austria.

This look aroused the jealousy of the duke, who thought that it should have been for him alone. According to the duke, the duchess's crime was to have a heart "too soon made glad," "Too easily impressed." Eventually the duke could stand the situation no longer; he "gave commands," and "all smiles stopped together."

Much of what readers learn about the duke's state of mind comes from what is implied by his words. As he discusses the painting, the duke unintentionally reveals himself to be obsessively possessive and jealous, referring to "my last Duchess," "My favor at her breast," and "My gift of a nine-hundred-years-old name." He keeps the portrait of his late wife well hidden behind a curtain that no one draws except him. His interest in the picture has little to do with the memory of his wife, however. In death, the duchess has become exactly what the duke always wanted her to be: a personal possession that reflects his status and good taste.

Though silent, the listener plays a subtle but important role in the poem: his presence establishes the dramatic situation that allows the character of the duke to be revealed. The purpose of the story is to communicate to the emissary exactly what the duke expects from his prospective bride and from her father. As he speaks, the duke conveys only the information that he wants the emissary to take back to his master, the count. Although the duke appears vain and superficial, he is actually extraordinarily shrewd. Throughout the poem, he turns the conversation to his own ends and gains the advantage through flattery and false modesty. Notice, for example, that he claims he has little skill in speaking when actually he is cleverly manipulating the conversation. The success of the poem lies in the poet's ability to develop the voice of this complex character, who embodies both superficial elegance and shocking cruelty.

JANICE MIRIKITANI (1942–   )

Suicide Note (1987)

. . . An Asian-American college student was reported to have jumped to her death from her dormitory window. Her body was found two days later under a deep cover of snow. Her suicide note contained an apology to her parents for having received less than a perfect four point grade average. . . .

How many notes written . . .
ink smeared like birdprints in snow.

not good enough   not pretty enough   not smart enough
dear mother and father.
I apologize   5
for disappointing you.
I've worked very hard,
                    not good enough
harder, perhaps to please you.
If only I were a son, shoulders broad   10
as the sunset threading through pine,

I would see the light in my mother's
eyes, or the golden pride reflected
in my father's dream
of my wide, male hands worthy of work   15
and comfort.
I would swagger through life
muscled and bold and assured,
drawing praises to me
like currents in the bed of wind, virile   20
with confidence.
        not good enough   not strong enough   not good enough

I apologize.
Tasks do not come easily.
Each failure, a glacier.   25
Each disapproval, a bootprint.
Each disappointment,
ice above my river.
So I have worked hard.
                not good enough   30
My sacrifice I will drop
bone by bone, perched
on the ledge of my womanhood,
fragile as wings.
                    not strong enough   35
It is snowing steadily
surely not good weather
for flying — this sparrow
sillied and dizzied by the wind
on the edge.   40
                not smart enough
I make this ledge my altar
to offer penance.
This air will not hold me,
the snow burdens my crippled wings,   45
my tears drop like bitter cloth
softly into the gutter below.
    not good enough   not strong enough   not smart enough
                Choices thin as shaved
                ice. Notes shredded   50
                drift like snow
on my broken body,
cover me like whispers
of sorries
sorries.   55
Perhaps when they find me
they will bury

my bird bones beneath
a sturdy pine
and scatter my feathers like   60
unspoken song
over this white and cold and silent
breast of earth.

Reading and Reacting

1. This poem is a suicide note that contains an apology. Why does the speaker feel she must apologize?

2. What attitude does the speaker convey toward her parents?

3. JOURNAL ENTRY Is the college student who speaks in this poem a stranger to you? Or is her voice in any way like that of students you know?

Related Works: "The Rocking-Horse Winner" (p. 349), "Teenage Wasteland" (p. 535), "The Value of Education" (p. 650), "Death Be Not Proud" (p. 869), *The Cuban Swimmer* (p. 1258)

JAMES TATE (1943–)

Nice Car, Camille (2001)

Camille drove by in her sports car with
the top down. I waved to her, but she didn't
see me, or else she just chose not to wave back.
She's an incredibly beautiful woman, but always
seems sad, sad or angry, it's hard to tell. I   5
went to school with her. We'd talk sometimes.
Her father had owned an oil company. It had been
in the family for three generations. But one of
his employees had killed him when she was six.
Then her mother married some bum and he squandered   10
most of her money gambling. Camille didn't really
make friends in school. She didn't want any. She
always managed to drive a really sexy car. She'd
always have her sunglasses on, speeding through
town as if late for an appointment. And I'd always   15
wave if I saw her. Hello, Camille. Goodbye,
Camille. That was my contribution to making her
life unforgettable.

Reading and Reacting

1. What does the poem reveal about Camille? About the speaker?

2. What does the speaker mean in lines 17–18 when he says, "That was my contribution to making her / life unforgettable"? Is he being serious or sarcastic?

3. JOURNAL ENTRY What do you think Camille and her sports car represent to the speaker?

4. CRITICAL PERSPECTIVE Poet and critic Dana Gioia, in a review of James Tate's *Selected Poems,* comments on the strengths and weaknesses of the poems in that book:

> Tate is often funny and always fun to read, even in the nihilistic poems that make up a good portion of the volume. A reader may find Tate's poetry difficult, opaque, or pointless, but no one who loves language will find him boring. Line by line, sentence by sentence, he strives to keep the reader interested and amused.

Is "Nice Car, Camile" "fun to read"? Is it "pointless," or can you find a main idea Tate is trying to communicate?

Related Works: "A Rose for Emily" (p. 91), "One day I wrote her name upon the strand" (p. 654), "Oh, my love is like a red, red rose," (p. 683), "Barbie Doll" (p. 902), "Richard Cory" (p. 907)

DORIANNE LAUX (1952–   )

The Shipfitter's Wife (1999)

I loved him most
when he came home from work,
his fingers still curled from fitting pipe,
his denim shirt ringed with sweat
and smelling of salt, the drying weeds   5
of the ocean. I'd go to where he sat
on the edge of the bed, his forehead
anointed with grease, his cracked hands
jammed between his thighs, and unlace
the steel-toed boots, stroke his ankles   10
and calves, the pads and bones of his feet.
Then I'd open his clothes and take
the whole day inside me — the ship's
gray sides, the miles of copper pipe,
the voice of the foreman clanging   15
off the hull's silver ribs. Spark of lead
kissing metal. The clamp, the winch,
the white fire of the torch, the whistle,
and the long drive home.

Reading and Reacting

1. A shipfitter does sheet-metal work and plumbing on board a ship. Why do you think the speaker says, "I loved him most / when he came home from work" (lines 1–2)?

2. What does the speaker mean in lines 12–13 when she says that she would "take the whole day" inside herself?

3. What do you think the speaker's use of the past tense signifies? Is the speaker simply remembering the past, or could the use of the past tense have some other significance?

4. JOURNAL ENTRY Is this poem about the speaker, or is it about her husband?

5. CRITICAL PERSPECTIVE In an essay entitled "Girl Writer," Dorianne Laux discusses her literary goals and influences:

> My project as a woman writer has been to write about women, to bring to light those who are invisible in their ordinariness. Models for my own writing became poets Sharon Olds and Carolyn Forché. Olds gave me permission to write passionately about domestic life, and Forché offered me the beauty of language and image as well as the power of a controlled voice. Both are women of my own generation who see the universal in the particular, heroism in the ordinary, and who are involved in the project of recording the emotional history of the world.

Do you think "The Shipfitter's Wife" conveys a sense of "heroism in the ordinary"?

Related Works: "The Story of an Hour" (p. 82), "How Do I Love Thee?" (p. 566), "What Lips My Lips Have Kissed" (p. 566), "To My Dear and Loving Husband" (p. 695)

THE TONE OF THE POEM

The **tone** of a poem conveys the speaker's attitude toward his or her subject or audience. In speech, this attitude can be conveyed easily: stressing a word in a sentence can modify or color a statement, drastically affecting the meaning of the sentence. For example, the statement "Of course, you would want to go to that restaurant" is quite straightforward, but changing the emphasis to "Of course *you* would want to go to *that* restaurant" transforms a neutral statement into a sarcastic one. For poets, however, conveying a particular tone to readers poses a challenge because readers rarely hear poets' spoken voices. Instead, poets indicate tone by using techniques such as rhyme, meter, word choice, sentence structure, figures of speech, and imagery.

The range of possible tones is wide. For example, a poem's speaker may be joyful, sad, playful, serious, comic, intimate, formal, relaxed, condescending, or ironic. In the following poem, notice how the detached tone conveys the speaker's attitude toward his subject.

ROBERT FROST (1874–1963)

Fire and Ice (1923)

Some say the world will end in fire,
Some say in ice.
From what I've tasted of desire
I hold with those who favor fire.

But if it had to perish twice,   5
I think I know enough of hate
To say that for destruction ice
Is also great
And would suffice.

Here the speaker uses word choice, rhyme, and understatement to comment on the human condition. The conciseness and the simple, regular meter and rhyme suggest an **epigram** — a short poem that makes a pointed comment in an unusually clear, and often witty, manner. This pointedness is consistent with the speaker's glib, unemotional tone, as is the last line's wry understatement that ice "would suffice." The contrast between the poem's serious message — that active hatred and indifference are equally destructive — and its informal style and offhand tone complement the speaker's detached, almost smug, posture.

Sometimes shifts in tone reveal changes in the speaker's attitude. In the next poem, changes in tone reveal a shift in the speaker's attitude toward war.

THOMAS HARDY (1840 – 1928)

The Man He Killed (1902)

"Had he and I but met
By some old ancient inn,
We should have sat us down to wet
Right many a nipperkin!°

"But ranged as infantry,   5
And staring face to face,
I shot at him as he at me,
And killed him in his place.

"I shot him dead because —
Because he was my foe,   10
Just so: my foe of course he was;
That's clear enough; although

"He thought he'd 'list,° perhaps,
Off-hand-like — just as I —
Was out of work — had sold his traps —   15
No other reason why.

---

nipperkin: A small container of liquor.
'list: Enlist.

> "Yes; quaint and curious war is!
>   You shoot a fellow down
> You'd treat if met where any bar is,
>   Or help to half-a crown."   20

The speaker in this poem is a soldier relating his wartime experiences. Quotation marks indicate that he is engaged in conversation — perhaps in a pub — and his dialect indicates that he is probably of the English working class. For him, at least at first, the object of war is simple: kill or be killed. To Hardy, this speaker represents all men who are thrust into a war without understanding its underlying social, economic, or ideological causes. In this sense, the speaker and his enemy are both victims of forces beyond their comprehension or control.

The tone of "The Man He Killed" changes as the speaker tells his story. As the poem unfolds, its sentence structure deteriorates, and this in turn helps to convey the speaker's changing attitude toward the war in which he has fought. In the first two stanzas, sentences are smooth and unbroken, establishing the speaker's matter-of-fact tone and reflecting his confidence that he has done what he had to do. In the third and fourth stanzas, broken syntax reflects the narrator's increasingly disturbed state of mind as he tells about the man he killed. The poem's singsong meter and regular rhyme scheme (*met/wet, inn/nipperkin*) suggest that the speaker is trying hard to maintain his composure; the smooth sentence structure of the last stanza and the use of a cliché ("Yes; quaint and curious war is!") show the speaker's efforts to trivialize the incident.

Sometimes a poem's tone can establish an ironic contrast between the speaker and his or her subject. The speaker's abrupt change of tone at the end of the next poem establishes such a contrast.

AMY LOWELL (1874–1925)

Patterns (1915)

I walk down the garden-paths,
And all the daffodils
Are blowing, and the bright blue squills.
I walk down the patterned garden-paths
In my stiff, brocaded gown.   5
With my powdered hair and jewelled fan,
I too am a rare
Pattern. As I wander down
The garden-paths.

My dress is richly figured,   10
And the train
Makes a pink and silver stain
On the gravel, and the thrift
Of the borders.

Just a plate of current fashion   15
Tripping by in high-heeled, ribboned shoes.
Not a softness anywhere about me,
Only whalebone° and brocade.
And I sink on a seat in the shade
Of a lime tree. For my passion   20
Wars against the stiff brocade.
The daffodils and squills
Flutter in the breeze
As they please.
And I weep;   25
For the lime-tree is in blossom
And one small flower has dropped upon my bosom.
And the plashing of waterdrops
In the marble fountain
Comes down the garden-paths.   30
The dripping never stops.
Underneath my stiffened gown
Is the softness of a woman bathing in a marble basin,
A basin in the midst of hedges grown
So thick, she cannot see her lover hiding,   35
But she guesses he is near,
And the sliding of the water
Seems the stroking of a dear
Hand upon her.
What is Summer in a fine brocaded gown!   40
I should like to see it lying in a heap upon the ground.
All the pink and silver crumpled up on the ground.

I would be the pink and silver as I ran along the paths,
And he would stumble after,
Bewildered by my laughter.   45
I should see the sun flashing from his sword-hilt and buckles
       on his shoes.
I would choose
To lead him in a maze along the patterned paths,
A bright and laughing maze for my heavy-booted lover.
Till he caught me in the shade,   50
And the buttons of his waistcoat bruised my body as he clasped me,
Aching, melting, unafraid.
With the shadows of the leaves and the sundrops,
And the plopping of the waterdrops,
All about us in the open afternoon —   55

---

whalebone: The type of bone used to stiffen corsets.

I am very like to swoon
 With the weight of this brocade,
 For the sun sifts through the shade.

Underneath the fallen blossom
In my bosom,   60
Is a letter I have hid.
It was brought to me this morning by a rider from the Duke.
Madam, we regret to inform you that Lord Hartwell
Died in action Thursday se'nnight.°
As I read it in the white, morning sunlight,   65
The letters squirmed like snakes.
"Any answer, Madam," said my footman.
"No," I told him.
"See that the messenger takes some refreshment.
No, no answer."   70
And I walked into the garden,
Up and down the patterned paths,
In my stiff, correct brocade.
The blue and yellow flowers stood up proudly in the sun,
Each one.   75
I stood upright too,
Held rigid to the pattern
By the stiffness of my gown.
Up and down I walked.
Up and down.   80

In a month he would have been my husband.
In a month, here, underneath this lime,
We would have broken the pattern;
He for me, and I for him,
He as Colonel, I as Lady,   85
On this shady seat.
He had a whim
That sunlight carried blessing.
And I answered, "It shall be as you have said."
Now he is dead.   90

In Summer and in Winter I shall walk
Up and down
The patterned garden-paths
In my stiff, brocaded gown.
The squills and daffodils   95
Will give place to pillared roses, and to asters, and to snow.

---

se'nnight: "Seven night," or a week ago Thursday.

I shall go
Up and down,
In my gown.
Gorgeously arrayed,   100
Boned and stayed.
And the softness of my body will be guarded from embrace
By each button, hook, and lace.
For the man who should loose me is dead,
Fighting with the Duke in Flanders,°   105
In a pattern called a war.
Christ! What are patterns for?

The speaker begins by describing herself walking down garden paths. She wears a stiff brocaded gown, has powdered hair, and carries a jeweled fan. By her own admission she is "a plate of current fashion." Although her tone is controlled, she is preoccupied by sensual thoughts. Beneath her "stiffened gown / Is the softness of a woman bathing in a marble basin," and the "sliding of the water" in a fountain reminds the speaker of the stroking of her lover's hand. She imagines herself shedding her brocaded gown and running with her lover along the maze of "patterned paths." The sensuality of the speaker's thoughts stands in ironic contrast to the images of stiffness and control that dominate the poem; her passion "Wars against the stiff brocade." She is also full of repressed rage. She knows that her lover has been killed, and she realizes the meaninglessness of the patterns of her life, patterns to which she has conformed, just as her lover conformed by going to war and doing what he was supposed to do. Throughout the poem, the speaker's tone reflects her barely contained anger and frustration. In the last line, when she finally lets out her rage, the poem's point about the senselessness of war becomes apparent.

ADAM ZAGAJEWSKI (1945–   )

Try to Praise the Mutilated World (2001)

Translated, from the Polish, by Clare Cavanagh

Try to praise the multilated world.
Remember June's long days,
and wild strawberries, drops of wine, the dew.
The nettles that methodically overgrow
the abandoned homesteads of exiles.   5
You must praise the mutilated world.

Flanders: A region in northwestern Europe, including part of northern France and western Belgium. Flanders was a site of fighting during World War I.

You watched the stylish yachts and ships;
one of them had a long trip ahead of it,
while salty oblivion awaited others.
You've seen the refugees heading nowhere,   10
you've heard the executioners sing joyfully.
You should praise the mutilated world.
Remember the moments when we were together
in a white room and the curtain fluttered.
Return in thought to the concert where music flared.   15
You gathered acorns in the park in autumn
and leaves eddied over the earth's scars.
Praise the mutilated world
and the gray feather a thrush lost,
and the gentle light that strays and vanishes   20
and returns.

Reading and Reacting

1. Who is the speaker? Whom is he addressing?
2. In line 1, the speaker says, "Try to praise . . ."; in line 6, he says, "You must praise . . ."; in line 12, he says, "You should praise . . ."; and in line 18, he says, "Praise . . .". What is the significance, if any, of these changes in phrasing?
3. What is the mood of the speaker? Do you think he is optimistic or pessimistic?
4. **JOURNAL ENTRY** Though written earlier, this poem was printed in the issue of *The New Yorker* that appeared immediately after the World Trade Center towers were destroyed by terrorists on September 11, 2001. Why do you think the editors chose to reprint it then?
5. **CRITICAL PERSPECTIVE** The critic and poet Adam Kirsch, writing in *The New Republic*, characterizes Adam Zagajewski as a mystical poet who looks for meaning in ordinary things and situations:

   > Like Rilke, Zagajewski is overcome at times by a powerful sense that the singular being of objects conceals some higher truth. For him, too, things are the sites of illumination.

   Kirsch goes on to say that Zagajewski writes not so much *about* moments of mystical insight, which are impossible to describe, but *around* these moments.

   > What yearns to be expressed, rather, is the experience of waiting for the sudden heightening of consciousness; waiting for it, or remembering it, or lacking it. These are situations of pathos; and the main colors in Zagajewski's palette are loss, longing, and awe, lightened from time to time with shades of wit.

   Do you think Kirsch's description of Zagajewski's poetry applies to "Try to Praise the Mutilated World"? Can you find examples in the text of "loss, longing, and awe"? Are there "shades of wit" in the poem?

Related Works: "The Fireman" (p. 369), "Hope" (p. 625) "The Second Coming" (p. 927)

WILLIAM WORDSWORTH (1770–1850)

The World Is Too Much with Us (1807)

The world is too much with us; late and soon,
Getting and spending, we lay waste our powers;
Little we see in Nature that is ours;
We have given our hearts away, a sordid boon!
This Sea that bares her bosom to the moon;   5
The winds that will be howling at all hours,
And are up-gathered now like sleeping flowers;
For this, for everything, we are out of tune;
It moves us not. Great God! I'd rather be
A Pagan suckled in a creed outworn;   10
So might I, standing on this pleasant lea,
Have glimpses that would make me less forlorn;
Have sight of Proteus° rising from the sea;
Or hear old Triton° blow his wreathèd horn.

Reading and Reacting

1. What is the speaker's attitude toward the contemporary world? How is this attitude revealed through the poem's tone?

2. This poem is a **sonnet,** a highly structured traditional form. How do the rhyme scheme and the regular meter establish the poem's tone?

3. JOURNAL ENTRY Imagine you are a modern-day environmentalist, labor organizer, or corporate executive. Write a response to the sentiments expressed in this poem.

4. CRITICAL PERSPECTIVE According to M. H. Abrams in his 1972 essay "Two Roads to Wordsworth," critics have tended to follow one of two different paths to the poet, and these approaches have yielded two different versions of the poet:

> One Wordsworth is simple, elemental, forthright, the other is complex, para-doxical, problematic; one is an affirmative poet of life, love, and joy, the other is an equivocal or self-divided poet whose affirmations are implicitly qualified . . . by a pervasive sense of morality and an ever-incipient despair of life; . . . one is the Wordsworth of light, the other the Wordsworth of [shadow], or even darkness.

Does your reading of "The World Is Too Much with Us" support one of these versions of Wordsworth over the other? Which one? Why?

Proteus: Sometimes said to be Poseidon's son, this Greek sea-god had the ability to change shapes at will and to tell the future.

Triton: The trumpeter of the sea, this sea-god is usually pictured blowing on a conch shell. Triton was the son of Poseidon, ruler of the sea.

Related Works: "The Rocking-Horse Winner" (p. 349), "Dover Beach" (p. 847), "She dwelt among the untrodden ways" (p. 924), "The Lake Isle of Innisfree" (p. 926)

SYLVIA PLATH (1932–1963)

Morning Song (1962)

Love set you going like a fat gold watch.
The midwife slapped your footsoles, and your bald cry
Took its place among the elements.

Our voices echo, magnifying your arrival. New statue.
In a drafty museum, your nakedness   5
Shadows our safety. We stand round blankly as walls.

I'm no more your mother
Than the cloud that distills a mirror to reflect its own slow
Effacement at the wind's hand.

All night your moth-breath   10
Flickers among the flat pink roses. I wake to listen:
A far sea moves in my ear.

One cry, and I stumble from bed, cow-heavy and floral
In my Victorian nightgown.
Your mouth opens clean as a cat's. The window square   15

Whitens and swallows its dull stars. And now you try
Your handful of notes;
The clear vowels rise like balloons.

Reading and Reacting

1. Who is the speaker? To whom is she speaking? What does the poem reveal about her?

2. What is the poem's subject? What attitudes about her subject do you suppose the poet expects her readers to have?

3. How is the tone of the first stanza different from that of the third? How does the tone of each stanza reflect its content?

4. **JOURNAL ENTRY** In what sense does this poem reinforce traditional ideas about motherhood? How does it undercut them?

5. **CRITICAL PERSPECTIVE** Sylvia Plath's life, which ended in suicide, was marked by emotional turbulence and instability. According to Anne Stevenson in *Bitter Fame,* her 1988 biography of Plath, in the weeks immediately preceding the composition of "Morning Song" a fit of rage over her husband's supposed infidelity caused Plath to destroy many of his books and poetic works in progress. Then, only a few days later, she suffered a miscarriage. According to Stevenson, "Morning Song" is about sleepless nights and surely reflects Plath's depression. However, in a 1991 biography, *Rough Magic*, Paul Alexander says, "Beautiful, simple, touching, 'Morning Song' was Plath's — then — definitive statement of motherhood."

Which biographer's assessment of the poem do you think makes more sense? Why?

Related Works: "The Yellow Wallpaper" (p. 161), "The Boy Beheld His Mother's Past" (p. 562), "Those Winter Sundays" (p. 560), "My Son, My Executioner" (p. 699)

ROBERT HERRICK (1591–1674)

To the Virgins, to Make Much of Time (1646)

Gather ye rosebuds while ye may,
Old Time is still a-flying;
And this same flower that smiles today,
Tomorrow will be dying.

The glorious lamp of heaven, the sun,   5
The higher he's a-getting,
The sooner will his race be run,
And nearer he's to setting.

That age is best which is the first,
When youth and blood are warmer;   10
But being spent, the worse, and worst
Times still succeed the former.

Then be not coy, but use your time,
And while ye may, go marry;
For having lost but once your prime,   15
You may forever tarry.

Reading and Reacting

1. How would you characterize the speaker? Do you think he expects his listeners to share his views? How might his expectations affect his tone?
2. This poem is developed like an argument. What is the speaker's main point? How does he support it?
3. What effect does the poem's use of rhyme have on its tone?
4. **Journal Entry** Whose side are you on — the speaker's or those he addresses?

Related Works: "Where Are You Going, Where Have You Been?" (p. 387), "Greasy Lake" (p. 441), "The Passionate Shepherd to His Love" (p. 563), "Nice Car, Camille" (p. 609), *The Brute* (p. 1062)

STEVE KOWIT (1938–)

The Grammar Lesson (1995)

A noun's a thing. A verb's the thing it does.
An adjective is what describes the noun.
In "The can of beets is filled with purple fuzz"

of and *with* are prepositions. *The's*
an article, a *can's* a noun,   5
a noun's a thing. A verb's the thing it does.

A can *can* roll — or not. What isn't was
or might be, *might* meaning not yet known.
"Our can of beets *is* filled with purple fuzz"

is present tense. While words like *our* and *us*   10
are pronouns — i.e., *it* is moldy, *they* are icky brown.
A noun's a thing; a verb's the thing it does.

Is is a helping verb. It helps because
filled isn't a full verb. *Can's* what *our* owns
in "*Our* can of beets is filled with purple fuzz."   15

See? There's almost nothing to it. Just
memorize these rules . . . or write them down!
A noun's a thing, a verb's the thing it does.
The can of beets is filled with purple fuzz.

Reading and Reacting

1. As its title indicates, this poem is a grammar lesson. It is also a **villanelle,** a traditional form that includes repeated lines. In what way do the grammar lesson and the villanelle complement each other?

2. How would you describe the tone of this poem? Do you think is it appropriate for the poem's subject?

3. **JOURNAL ENTRY** Other than a lesson in grammar, what else is being taught in this poem?

Related Works: "Gryphon" (p. 126), "ABC" (p. 646), "A Mown Lawn" (p. 727), "Jabberwocky" (p. 729), "The Waking" (p. 745)

IRONY

Just as in fiction and drama, **irony** occurs in poetry when a discrepancy exists between two levels of meaning or experience. Consider the tone of these lines by Stephen Crane:

Do not weep, maiden, for war is kind.
Because your lover threw wild hands toward the sky
And the afrightened steed ran on alone,

Do not weep.
War is kind.

How can war be "kind"? Isn't war exactly the opposite of "kind"? Surely the speaker does not intend his words to be taken literally. By making this ironic statement, the speaker actually conveys the opposite idea: war is a cruel, mindless exercise of violence.

Skillfully used, irony enables a poet to make a pointed comment about a situation or to manipulate a reader's emotions. Implicit in irony is the writer's assumption that readers will not be misled by the literal meaning of a statement. In order for irony to work, readers must recognize the disparity between what is said and what is meant, or between what a speaker thinks is occurring and what readers know to be occurring.

One kind of irony that appears in poetry is **dramatic irony,** which occurs when a speaker believes one thing and readers realize something else. In the following poem, the poet uses a deranged speaker to tell a story that is filled with irony.

ROBERT BROWNING (1812–1889)

Porphyria's Lover (1836)

The rain set early in to-night,
    The sullen wind was soon awake,
It tore the elm-tops down for spite,
    And did its worst to vex the lake:
    I listened with heart fit to break.   5
When glided in Porphyria; straight
    She shut the cold out and the storm,
And kneeled and made the cheerless grate
    Blaze up, and all the cottage warm;
    Which done, she rose, and from her form   10
Withdrew the dripping cloak and shawl,
    And laid her soiled gloves by, untied
Her hat and let the damp hair fall,
    And, last, she sat down by my side
    And called me. When no voice replied,   15
She put my arm about her waist,
    And made her smooth white shoulder bare,
And all her yellow hair displaced,
    And, stooping, made my cheek lie there,
    And spread, o'er all, her yellow hair,   20
Murmuring how she loved me — she
    Too weak, for all her heart's endeavour,
To set its struggling passion free
    From pride, and vainer ties dissever,
    And give herself to me for ever.   25

But passion sometimes would prevail,
    Nor could to-night's gay feast restrain
A sudden thought of one so pale
    For love of her, and all in vain:
So, she was come through wind and rain.   30
Be sure I looked up at her eyes
    Happy and proud; at last I knew
Porphyria worshipped me; surprise
    Made my heart swell, and still it grew
    While I debated what to do.   35
That moment she was mine, mine, fair,
    Perfectly pure and good: I found
A thing to do, and all her hair
    In one long yellow string I wound
    Three times her little throat around,   40
And strangled her. No pain felt she;
    I am quite sure she felt no pain.
As a shut bud that holds a bee,
    I warily oped her lids: again
    Laughed the blue eyes without a stain.   45
And I untightened next the tress
    About her neck; her cheek once more
Blushed bright beneath my burning kiss:
    I propped her head up as before,
    Only, this time my shoulder bore   50
Her head, which droops upon it still:
    The smiling rosy little head,
So glad it has its utmost will,
    That all it scorned at once is fled,
    And I, its love, am gained instead!   55
Porphyria's love: she guessed not how
    Her darling one wish would be heard.
And thus we sit together now,
    And all night long we have not stirred,
    And yet God has not said a word!   60

Like Browning's "My Last Duchess" (p. 605) this poem is a **dramatic monologue.**
The speaker recounts his story in a straightforward manner, seemingly unaware of
the horror of his tale. In fact, much of the effect of this poem comes from the
speaker's telling his tale of murder in a flat, unemotional tone — and from
readers' gradual realization that the speaker is mad.

    The irony of the poem, and of its title, becomes apparent as the monologue
progresses. At first, the speaker fears that Porphyria is too weak to free herself from
pride and vanity to love him. As he looks into her eyes, however, he comes to believe that she worships him. To preserve the perfection of Porphyria's love, the
speaker strangles her with her own hair. He assures his silent listener, "I am quite

sure she felt no pain." Like many of Browning's narrators, the speaker in this poem exhibits a selfish and perverse need to possess another person totally. The moment the speaker realizes that Porphyria loves him, he feels compelled to kill her and keep her his forever. According to him, she is at this point "mine, mine, fair, / Perfectly pure and good," and he believes that by murdering her, he actually fulfills "Her darling one wish"— to stay with him forever. As he attempts to justify his actions, the speaker reveals himself to be a deluded psychopathic killer.

Another kind of irony is **situational irony,** which occurs when the situation itself contradicts readers' expectations. For example, in "Porphyria's Lover" the meeting of two lovers ironically results not in joy and passion but in murder. In the next poem, the situation also creates irony.

PERCY BYSSHE SHELLEY (1792–1822)

Ozymandias° (1818)

I met a traveler from an antique land
Who said: Two vast and trunkless legs of stone
Stand in the desert. Near them, on the sand,
Half sunk, a shattered visage lies, whose frown,
And wrinkled lip, and sneer of cold command,   5
Tell that its sculptor well those passions read
Which yet survive, stamped on these lifeless things,
The hand that mocked them, and the heart that fed;
And on the pedestal these words appear:
"My name is Ozymandias, king of kings: 10
Look on my works, ye Mighty, and despair!"
Nothing beside remains. Round the decay
Of that colossal wreck, boundless and bare
The lone and level sands stretch far away.

The speaker tells a tale about a colossal statue that lies shattered in the desert. Its head lies separated from the trunk, and the face has a wrinkled lip and a "sneer of cold command." On the pedestal of the monument are words exhorting all those who pass: "Look on my works, ye Mighty, and despair!" The situational irony of the poem has its source in the contrast between the "colossal wreck" and the boastful inscription on its base. To the speaker, Ozymandias stands for the vanity of those who mistakenly think they can withstand the ravages of time.

Perhaps the most common kind of irony found in poetry is **verbal irony,** which is created when words say one thing but mean another, often exactly the opposite. When verbal irony is particularly biting, it is called **sarcasm**—for example, Stephen Crane's use of the word *kind* in his antiwar poem "War Is Kind."

Ozymandias: The Greek name for Ramses II, ruler of Egypt in the thirteenth century B.C.

In speech, verbal irony is easy to detect through the speaker's change in tone or emphasis. In writing, when these signals are absent, verbal irony becomes more difficult to convey. Poets must depend on the context of a remark or on the contrast between a word and other images in the poem to create irony.

Consider how verbal irony is communicated in the following poem.

ARIEL DORFMAN (1942–   )

Hope (1988)

Translated by Edith Grossman with the author

My son has been
missing
since May 8
of last year.

> They took him   5
> just for a few hours
> they said
> just for some routine
> questioning.

After the car left,   10
the car with no license plate,
we couldn't

find out

anything else
about him.   15
But now things have changed.
We heard from a compañero
who just got out
that five months later
they were torturing him   20
in Villa Grimaldi,
at the end of September
they were questioning him
in the red house
that belonged to the Grimaldis.   25

> They say they recognized
> his voice his screams
> they say.

Somebody tell me frankly
what times are these   30
what kind of world
what country?

What I'm asking is
how can it be
that a father's   35
joy
a mother's
joy
is knowing
that they   40
that they are still
torturing
their son?
Which means
that he was alive   45
five months later
and our greatest
hope
will be to find out
next year   50
that they're still torturing him
eight months later

and he may   might   could
still be alive.

Although it is not necessary to know the background of the poet to appreciate this poem, it does help to know that Ariel Dorfman is a native of Chile. After the assassination of Salvador Allende, Chile's elected socialist president, in September 1973, the civilian government was replaced by a military dictatorship. Civil rights were suspended, and activists, students, and members of opposition parties were arrested. Many were detained indefinitely; some simply disappeared. The irony of this poem originates in the discrepancy between what the word *hope* comes to mean in the poem and what it usually means. For most people, *hope* has positive connotations. For the speaker, however, *hope* means that his son is still being tortured eight months after his arrest. Thus, *hope* takes on a different meaning, and this irony is not lost on the speaker.

W. H. AUDEN (1907–1973)

The Unknown Citizen (1939)

(To JS/07/M/378 This Marble Monument Is Erected by the State)

He was found by the Bureau of Statistics to be
One against whom there was no official complaint,
And all the reports on his conduct agree

That, in the modern sense of an old-fashioned word, he was a saint,
For in everything he did he served the Greater Community.   5
Except for the War till the day he retired
He worked in a factory and never got fired,
But satisfied his employers, Fudge Motors Inc.
Yet he wasn't a scab or odd in his views,
For his Union reports that he paid his dues,   10
(Our report on his Union shows it was sound)
And our Social Psychology workers found
That he was popular with his mates and liked a drink.
The Press are convinced that he bought a paper every day
And that his reactions to advertisements were normal in every way.   15
Policies taken out in his name prove that he was fully insured,
And his Health-card shows he was once in hospital but left it cured.
Both Producers Research and High-Grade Living declare
He was fully sensible to the advantages of the Installment Plan
And had everything necessary to the Modern Man,   20
A phonograph, a radio, a car and a frigidaire.
Our researchers into Public Opinion are content
That he held the proper opinions for the time of year;
When there was peace, he was for peace; when there was war, he
    went.
He was married and added five children to the population,   25
Which our Eugenist° says was the right number for a parent of his
    generation,
And our teachers report that he never interfered with their
    education.
Was he free? Was he happy? The question is absurd:
Had anything been wrong, we should certainly have heard.

Reading and Reacting

1. The "unknown citizen" represents modern citizens, who, according to the poem, are programmed like machines. How does the title help to establish the tone of the poem? How does the inscription on the monument also help to establish the tone?

2. Who is the speaker? What is his attitude toward the unknown citizen? How can you tell?

3. What kinds of irony are present in the poem? Identify several examples.

4. **JOURNAL ENTRY** This poem was written in 1939. Does its message apply to contemporary society, or does the poem seem dated?

Eugenist: A person who studies eugenics, the science of human improvement through genetic manipulation.

5. CRITICAL PERSPECTIVE In 1939, the year this poem was published, Auden argued in his essay "The Public vs. The Late Mr. William Butler Yeats" that poetry can never really change anything. He reiterated this point as late as 1971 in his biographical *A Certain World:*

> By all means let a poet, if he wants to, write poems . . . that protest against this or that political evil or social injustice. But let him remember this. The only person who will benefit from them is himself; they will enhance his literary reputation among those who feel as he does. The evil or injustice, however, will remain exactly what it would have been if he had kept his mouth shut.

Do you believe that poetry — or any kind of literature — has the power to combat "evil or injustice" in the world? Do you consider "The Unknown Citizen" a political poem? How might this poem effect positive social or political change?

Related Works: "A&P" (p. 115), "The Man He Killed" (p. 612), "next to of course god america i" (p. 864), "The Satisfaction Coal Company" (p. 869), "The Love Song of J. Alfred Prufrock" (p. 871), "Please Fire Me" (p. 881), *A Doll House* (p. 975)

DUDLEY RANDALL (1914–   )

Ballad of Birmingham (1969)

(On the bombing of a church in Birmingham, Alabama, 1963)

"Mother dear, may I go downtown
Instead of out to play,
And march the streets of Birmingham
In a Freedom March today?"

"No, baby, no, you may not go,   5
For the dogs are fierce and wild,
And clubs and hoses, guns and jails
Aren't good for a little child."

"But, mother, I won't be alone.
Other children will go with me,   10
And march the streets of Birmingham
To make our country free."

"No, baby, no, you may not go,
For I fear those guns will fire.
But you may go to church instead   15
And sing in the children's choir."

She has combed and brushed her night-dark hair,
And bathed rose petal sweet,
And drawn white gloves on her small brown hands,
And white shoes on her feet.   20

The mother smiled to know her child
Was in the sacred place,
But that smile was the last smile
To come upon her face.

For when she heard the explosion,   25
Her eyes grew wet and wild.
She raced through the streets of Birmingham
Calling for her child.

She clawed through bits of glass and brick,   30
Then lifted out a shoe.
"O, here's the shoe my baby wore,
But, baby, where are you?"

Reading and Reacting

1. Who are the two speakers in the poem? How do their attitudes differ? How does the tone of the poem convey these attitudes?
2. What kinds of irony are present in the poem? Give examples of each kind you identify.
3. This poem is a **ballad,** a form of poetry traditionally written to be sung or recited. Ballads typically repeat words and phrases and have regular meter and rhyme. How do the regular rhyme, repeated words, and singsong meter affect the poem's tone?
4. **JOURNAL ENTRY** This poem was written in response to the 1963 bombing of the 16th Street Baptist Church in Birmingham, Alabama, a bombing that killed four African-American children. How does this historical background help you to understand the irony of the poem?

Related Works: "Once upon a Time" (p. 90), "Bonny Barbara Allan" (p. 846), "The Ballad of Rudolph Reed" (p. 855), "Emmett Till" (p. 875), "If We Must Die" (p. 897), *Fences* (p. 1385)

SHERMAN ALEXIE (1966 –   )

How to Write the Great American Indian Novel (1996)

All of the Indians must have tragic features: tragic noses, eyes, and
    arms.
Their hands and fingers must be tragic when they reach for tragic
    food.

The hero must be a half-breed, half white and half Indian, preferably
from a horse culture. He should often weep alone. That is mandatory.

If the hero is an Indian woman, she is beautiful. She must be slender   5
and in love with a white man. But if she loves an Indian man

then he must be a half-breed, preferably from a horse culture.
If the Indian woman loves a white man, then he has to be so white

that we can see the blue veins running through his skin like rivers.
When the Indian woman steps outof her dress, the white man gasps   10

at the endless beauty of her brown skin. She should be compared to
    nature:
brown hills, mountains, fertile valleys, dewy grass, wind, and clear
    water.

If she is compared to murky water, however, then she must have a
    secret.
Indians always have secrets, which are carefully and slowly revealed.

Yet Indian secrets can be disclosed suddenly, like a storm.   15
Indian men, of course, are storms. They should destroy the lives

of any white women who choose to love them. All white women
    love
Indian men. That is always the case. White women feign disgust

at the savage in blue jeans and T-shirt, but secretly lust after him.
White women dream about half-breed Indian men from horse
    cultures.   20

Indian men are horses, smelling wild and gamey. When the Indian
    man
unbuttons his pants, the white woman should think of topsoil.

There must be one murder, one suicide, one attempted rape.
Alcohol should be consumed. Cars must be driven at high speeds.

Indians must see visions. White people can have the same visions   25
if they are in love with Indians. If a white person loves an Indian

then the white person is Indian by proximity. White people must
    carry
an Indian deep inside themselves. Those interior Indians are
    half-breed

and obviously from horse cultures. If the interior Indian is male
then he must be a warrior, especially if he is inside a white man.   30

If the interior Indian is female, then she must be a healer, especially
    if she is inside
a white woman. Sometimes there are complications.

An Indian man can be hidden inside a white woman. An Indian
    woman
can be hidden inside a white man. In these rare instances,

everybody is a half-breed struggling to learn more about his or her
    horse culture.   35
There must be redemption, of course, and sins must be forgiven.

For this, we need children. A white child and an Indian child,
    gender
not important, should express deep affection in a childlike way.

In the Great American Indian novel, when it is finally written,
all of the white people will be Indians and all of the Indians will be
    ghosts.   40

Reading and Reacting

1. Who is the speaker of the poem? What is the speaker's attitude toward
    Native Americans? Toward the white novelists who write about them?
2. What stereotypes of Native Americans does the speaker identify? In what
    way does the speaker's tone undercut these stereotypes? How would the
    speaker prefer to see Native American characters portrayed?
3. What does the speaker mean in the last line of the poem when he says that
    when the great American Indian novel is finally written, "all of the white
    people will be Indians and all the Indians will be ghosts"?
4. JOURNAL ENTRY In what ways are the characters discussed in the poem like
    and unlike those you have seen in films?

Related Works: "This Is What It Means to Say Phoenix, Arizona" (p. 151), "Indian Boarding School: The Runaways" (p. 876), *The Cuban Swimmer* (p. 1258)

RACHEL ROSE (1970–)

What We Heard about the Japanese (2001)

We heard they would jump from buildings
at the slightest provocation: a low mark

On an exam, a lovers' spat
or an excess of shame.

We heard they were incited by shame,   5
not guilt. That they

Loved all things American.
Mistrusted anything foreign.

We heard their men liked to buy
schoolgirls' underwear   10

And their women
did not experience menopause or other

Western hysterias. We heard
they still preferred to breastfeed,

Carry handkerchiefs, ride bicycles   15
and dress their young like Victorian

Pupils. We heard that theirs
was a feminine culture. We heard

That theirs was an example of extreme
patriarchy. That rape   20

Didn't exist on these islands. We heard
their marriages were arranged, that

They didn't believe in love. We heard
they were experts in this art above all others.

That frequent earthquakes inspired insecurity   25
and lack of faith. That they had no sense of irony.

We heard even faith was an American invention.
We heard they were just like us under the skin.

Reading and Reacting

1. Who is the "we" in the repeated phrase "we heard"? What does the repetition of this phrase imply?
2. Does the speaker suggest a source (or sources) for the ideas that Americans have about the Japanese? Explain.
3. After listing the inaccurate ideas Americans have about the Japanese, the speaker ends by saying, "We heard they were just like us under the skin." What does she mean? In what way does this statement reinforce the ideas in the rest of the poem?
4. JOURNAL ENTRY What comment does this poem make about Americans? In what way does the ironic tone help the speaker make this point?

Related Works: "Two Kinds" (p. 527), "What Were They Like?" (p. 573), "Suicide Note" (p. 607), "Immigrants" (p. 761)

RACHEL ROSE (1970–)

What the Japanese Perhaps Heard (2001)

Perhaps they heard we don't understand them
very well. Perhaps this made them

Pleased. Perhaps they heard we shoot
Japanese students who ring the wrong

Bell at Hallowe'en.* That we shoot   5
at the slightest provocation: a low mark

On an exam, a lovers' spat, an excess
of guilt. Perhaps they wondered

If it was guilt we felt at the sight of that student
bleeding out among our lawn flamingos,   10

Or something recognizable to them,
something like grief. Perhaps

They heard that our culture
has its roots in desperate immigration

And lone men. Perhaps they observed   15
our skill at raising serial killers,

That we value good teeth above
good minds and have no festivals

To remember the dead. Perhaps they heard
that our grey lakes are deep enough to swallow cities,   20

That our landscape is vast wheat and loneliness.
Perhaps they ask themselves if, when grief

Wraps its wet arms around Montana, we would not prefer
the community of archipelagos

Upon which persimmons are harvested   25
and black fingers of rock uncurl their digits

In the mist. Perhaps their abacus echoes
the shape that grief takes,

One island
bleeding into the next,   30

And for us grief is an endless cornfield,
silken and ripe with poison.

Reading and Reacting

1. Is the speaker Japanese or American? How do you know? What is the speaker's attitude toward the Japanese?
2. In the title and throughout the poem, the speaker uses *perhaps*. What is the effect of this repetition? In what way does this word help the poet convey her point?

---

*Allusion to an actual incident in which a Japanese exchange student was shot by a homeowner.

3. The speaker ends by saying, "And for us grief is an endless cornfield, / silken and ripe with poison." What does she mean? According to the speaker, how is the grief of Americans different from that of the Japanese?

4. JOURNAL ENTRY "What We Heard about the Japanese" and "What the Japanese Perhaps Heard" are meant to be read together. What comment do these poems make about the relationship between Japan and the United States? Do the poems imply that cultural differences can be bridged, or do they imply the opposite?

Related Works: "The Secret Lion" (p. 54), "The True-Blue American" (p. 780)

CHECKLIST **WRITING ABOUT VOICE**

The Speaker in the Poem

✓ What do we know about the speaker?

✓ Is the speaker anonymous, or does he or she have a particular identity?

✓ How does assuming a particular persona help the poet to convey his or her ideas?

✓ Does the title give information about the speaker's identity?

✓ In what way does word choice provide information about the speaker?

✓ Does the speaker make any direct statements to readers that help establish his or her identity or character?

✓ Does the speaker address anyone? How can you tell? Does the presence of a listener seem to affect the speaker?

The Tone of the Poem

✓ What is the speaker's attitude toward his or her subject?

✓ How do word choice, rhyme, meter, sentence structure, figures of speech, and imagery help to convey the attitude of the speaker?

✓ Is the tone of the poem consistent? How do shifts in tone reflect the changing mood or attitude of the speaker?

Irony

✓ Does any dramatic irony exist in the poem?

✓ Does the poem include situational irony?

✓ Does verbal irony appear in the poem?

WRITING SUGGESTIONS: Voice

1. The poet Robert Frost once said that he wanted to write "poetry that talked." According to Frost, "whenever I write a line it is because that line has already been spoken clearly by a voice with my mind, an audible voice." Choose some poems in this chapter (or elsewhere in the book) that you consider "talking poems." Then, write an essay about how successful they are in communicating "an audible voice."

2. The theme of Herrick's poem "To the Virgins, to Make Much of Time" (p. 620) is known as **carpe diem,** or "seize the day." Read Andrew Marvell's "To His Coy Mistress" (p. 696), which has the same theme, and compare its tone with that of "To the Virgins, to Make Much of Time."

3. Read the following poem, and compare the speaker's use of the word *hope* with the way the speaker uses the word in Ariel Dorfman's "Hope" (p. 652).

EMILY DICKINSON (1830–1886)

"Hope" is the thing with feathers— (1861)

"Hope" is the thing with feathers—
That perches in the soul—
And sings the tune without the words—
And never stops — at all—

And sweetest — in the Gale — is heard —   5
And sore must be the storm—
That could abash the little Bird—
That kept so many warm—

I've heard it in the chillest land—
And on the strangest Sea—   10
Yet, never, in Extremity,
It asked a crumb — of Me.

4. Because the speaker and the poet are not the same, poems by the same author can have different voices. Compare the voices of several poems by Sylvia Plath, W. H. Auden, William Blake, or any other poet in this anthology.

CHAPTER 18

WORD CHOICE, WORD ORDER

> The poet's love of language must, if language is to reward him with unlooked-for miracles, that is, with poetry, amount to a passion. The passion for the things of the world and the passion for naming them must be in him indistinguishable. —**Denise Levertov,** *"Origins of a Poem"*

> What is known in a poem is its language, that is, the words it uses. Yet those words seem different in a poem. Even the most familiar will seem strange. In a poem, each word, being equally important, exists in absolute focus, having a weight it rarely achieves in fiction. . . . Words in a novel are subordinate to broad slices of action or characterization that push the plot forward. In a poem, they *are* the action. —**Mark Strand,** Introduction to *Best American Poems of 1991*

> I like *mountain* and *prairie* and *sky.* When I write poetry, I use such words and I also use abstract words. But it is difficult to give you a list of favorite words because words become vital — they come alive — within a certain context. A given word is extremely important and vital in one context and not very interesting in another. It depends upon what's around the word. The environment. Although some words are naturally interesting, in my opinion. Like some creatures. The fox, I think, is a creature of almost immediate interest to most people. Other words are not as immediately interesting, or are even negatively received. Like some other creatures. The lizard, for example, is a creature most people wouldn't ordinarily care about. But in its natural habitat and in its dimension of wilderness, the lizard can be seen as a beautiful thing. Its movements are very wonderful to watch. Similarly, you can take almost any word and make it interesting by the way in which you use it. —**N. Scott Momaday,** in *Ancestral Voices*

SIPHO SEPAMLA (1932–   )

Words, Words, Words*

We don't speak of tribal wars anymore
we say simple faction fights
there are no tribes around here

---

* Publication date is not available.

only nations
it makes sense you see   5
'cause from there
one moves to multinational
it makes sense you get me
'cause from there
one gets one's homeland   10
which is a reasonable idea
'cause from there
one can dabble with independence
which deserves warm applause
— the bloodless revolution   15

we are talking of words
words tossed around as if
denied location by the wind
we mean those words some spit
others grab   20
dress them up for the occasion
fling them on the lap of an audience
we are talking of those words
that stalk our lives like policemen
words no dictionary can embrace   25
words that change sooner than seasons
we mean words
that spell out our lives
words, words, words
for there's a kind of poetic licence   30
doing the rounds in these parts

Words identify and name, characterize and distinguish, compare and contrast. Words describe, limit, and embellish; words locate and measure. Without words, there cannot be a poem. Even though words may be elusive and uncertain and changeable, "tossed around as if / denied location by the wind" and "can change sooner than seasons," they still can "stalk our lives like policemen." In poetry, as in love and in politics, words matter.

Beyond the quantitative — how many words, how many letters and sylla-bles — is one much more important consideration: the *quality* of words. Which are chosen, and why? Why are certain words placed next to others? What does a word suggest in a particular context? How are the words arranged? What exactly constitutes the right word?

WORD CHOICE

In poetry, even more than in fiction or drama, words tend to become the focus — sometimes even the true subject — of a work. For this reason, the choice of one word over another can be crucial. Because poems are brief, they must compress many ideas into a few lines; poets know how much weight each individual word carries, so they choose with great care, trying to select words that imply more than they state.

A poet may choose a word because of its sound. For instance, a word may echo another word's sound, and such repetition may place emphasis on both words; it may rhyme with another word and therefore be needed to preserve the poem's rhyme scheme; or it may have a certain combination of stressed and unstressed syllables needed to maintain the poem's metrical pattern. Occasionally, a poet may even choose a word because of how it looks on the page. Most often, though, poets select words because they help to communicate their ideas.

At the same time, poets may choose words for their degree of concreteness or abstraction, specificity or generality. A *concrete* word refers to an item that is a perceivable, tangible entity —for example, a kiss or a flag. An *abstract* word refers to an intangible idea, condition, or quality, something that cannot be perceived by the senses —love or patriotism, for instance. *Specific* words refer to particular items; *general* words refer to entire classes or groups of items. As the following example illustrates, whether a word is specific or general is relative; its degree of specificity or generality depends on its relationship to other words.

> Poem → closed form poem → sonnet → seventeenth-century sonnet → Elizabethan sonnet → sonnet by Shakespeare → "My mistress' eyes are nothing like the sun"

Sometimes a poet wants a precise word, one that is both specific and concrete. At other times, a poet might prefer general or abstract language, which may allow for more subtlety — or even for intentional ambiguity.

Finally, a word may be chosen for its **connotation**— what it suggests. Every word has one or more **denotations**— what it signifies without emotional associations, judgments, or opinions. The word *family,* for example, denotes "a group of related things or people." Connotation is a more complex matter, because a single word may have many different associations. In general terms, a word may have a connotation that is positive, neutral, or negative. Thus, *family* may have a positive connotation when it describes a group of loving relatives, a neutral connotation when it describes a biological category, and an ironically negative connotation when it describes an organized crime family. Beyond this distinction, *family,* like any other word, may have a variety of emotional and social associations, suggesting loyalty, warmth, home, security, or duty. In fact, many words have somewhat different meanings in different contexts. When poets choose words, then, they must consider what a particular word may suggest to readers as well as what it denotes.

In the poem that follows, the poet chooses words for their sounds and for their relationships to other words as well as for their connotations.

WALT WHITMAN (1819–1892)

When I Heard the Learn'd Astronomer (1865)

When I heard the learn'd astronomer,
When the proofs, the figures, were ranged in columns before me,
When I was shown the charts and diagrams, to add, divide, and
    measure them,
When I sitting heard the astronomer where he lectured with much
    applause in the lecture-room,
How soon unaccountable I became tired and sick,   5
Till rising and gliding out I wander'd off by myself,
In the mystical moist night-air, and from time to time,
Look'd up in perfect silence at the stars.

This poem might be paraphrased as follows: "When I grew restless listening to an astronomy lecture, I went outside, where I found I learned more just by looking at the stars than I had learned inside." But the paraphrase is obviously neither as rich nor as complex as the poem. Through careful use of diction, Whitman establishes a dichotomy that supports the poem's central theme about the relative merits of two ways of learning.

The poem can be divided into two groups of four lines. The first four lines, unified by the repetition of "When," introduce the astronomer and his tools: "proofs," "figures," and "charts and diagrams" to be added, divided, and measured. In this section of the poem, the speaker is passive: he sits and listens ("I heard"; "I was shown"; "I sitting heard"). The repetition of "When" reinforces the dry monotony of the lecture. In the next four lines, the choice of words signals the change in the speaker's actions and reactions. The confined lecture hall is replaced by "the mystical moist night-air," and the dry lecture and the applause give way to "perfect silence"; instead of sitting passively, the speaker becomes active (he rises, glides, wanders); instead of listening, he looks. The mood of the first half of the poem is restrained: the language is concrete and physical, and the speaker is studying, receiving information from a "learn'd" authority. The rest of the poem, celebrating intuitive knowledge and feelings, is more abstract, freer. Throughout the poem, the lecture hall contrasts sharply with the natural world outside its walls.

After considering the poem as a whole, readers should not find it hard to understand why the poet selected certain words. Whitman's use of "lectured" in line 4 rather than a more neutral word like "spoke" is appropriate both because it suggests formality and distance and because it echoes "lecture-room" in the same line. The word "sick" in line 5 is striking because it connotes physical as well as emotional distress, more effectively conveying the extent of the speaker's discomfort than "bored" or "restless" would. "Rising" and "gliding" (line 6) are used rather than "standing" and "walking out" both because of the way their stressed vowel sounds echo each other (and echo "time to time" in the next line) and because of their connotation of dreaminess, which is consistent with "wander'd" (line 6) and "mystical" (line 7). The word "moist" (line 7) is chosen not only because its consonant sounds echo the *m* and *st* sounds in "mystical," but also because it establishes a contrast with the dry, airless lecture hall. Finally, line 8's "perfect silence" is a better choice than a reasonable substitute like "complete silence" or "total silence," either of which would suggest the degree of the silence but not its quality.

In the next poem, the poet also pays careful attention to word choice.

WILLIAM STAFFORD (1914–1993)

For the Grave of Daniel Boone (1957)

> The farther he went the farther home grew.
> Kentucky became another room;
> the mansion arched over the Mississippi;
> flowers were spread all over the floor.
> He traced ahead a deepening home,   5
> and better, with goldenrod:
>
> Leaving the snakeskin of place after place,
> going on — after the trees
> the grass, a bird flying after a song.
> Rifle so level, sighting so well   10
> his picture freezes down to now,
> a story-picture for children.
>
> They go over the velvet falls
> into the tapestry of his time,
> heirs to the landscape, feeling no jar: 15
> it is like evening; they are the quail
> surrounding his fire, coming in for the kill;
> their little feet move sacred sand.
>
> Children, we live in a barbwire time
> but like to follow the old hands back—   20
> the ring in the light, the knuckle, the palm,
> all the way to Daniel Boone,
> hunting our own kind of deepening home.
> From the land that was his I heft this rock.
>
> Here on his grave I put it down.   25

A number of words in "For the Grave of Daniel Boone" are noteworthy for their multiple denotations and connotations. In the first stanza, for example, "home" does not mean Boone's residence; it connotes an abstract state, a dynamic concept that grows and deepens, encompassing states and rivers while becoming paradoxically more and more elusive. In literal terms, Boone's "home" at the poem's end is a narrow, confined space: his grave. In a wider sense, his home is the United States, particularly the natural landscape he explored. Thus, the word "home" comes to have a variety of associations to readers beyond its denotative meaning, suggesting both the infinite possibilities beyond the frontier and the realities of civilization's walls and fences.

The word "snakeskin" denotes "the skin of a snake"; its most immediate connotations are smoothness and slipperiness. In this poem, however, the snakeskin signifies more, because it is Daniel Boone who is "Leaving the snakeskin of place after place." Like a snake, Boone belongs to the natural world—and, like a snake, he wanders from place to place, shedding his skin as he goes. Thus, the word "snakeskin," with its connotation of rebirth and its links to nature, passing time, and the inevitability of change, is consistent with the image of Boone as both a man of nature and a restless wanderer, "a bird flying after a song."

In the poem's third stanza, the phrases "velvet falls" and "tapestry of . . . time" seem at first to have been selected solely for their pleasing repetition of sounds ("ve_l_vet fa_ll_s"; "_t_apestry of _t_ime"). But both of these paradoxical phrases also support the poem's theme. Alive, Boone was in constant movement; he was also larger than life. Now, he has been reduced; "his picture freezes down to . . . / a story-picture for children" (lines 11–12), and he is as static and inorganic as velvet or tapestry—no longer dynamic, like "falls" and "time."

The word "barbwire" (in line 19's phrase "barbwire time") is another word whose multiple meanings enrich the poem's theme. In the simplest terms, "barbwire" denotes a metal fencing material. In light of the poem's concern with space and distance, however, "barbwire" (with its connotations of sharpness, danger, and confinement) is also the antithesis of Boone's free or peaceful wilderness, evoking images of enclosure and imprisonment and reinforcing the poem's central dichotomy between past freedom and present restriction.

The phrase "old hands" (line 20) might also have multiple meanings in the context of the poem. On one level, the hands could belong to an elderly person holding a storybook; on another level, "old hands" could refer to people with considerable life experience —like Boone, who was an "old hand" at scouting. On still another level, given the poem's concern with time, "old hands" could suggest the hands of a clock.

Through what it says literally and through what its words suggest, "For the Grave of Daniel Boone" communicates a good deal about the speaker's identification with Daniel Boone and with the nation he called home. Boone's horizons, his concept of "home," expanded as he wandered. Now, when he is frozen in time and space, a character in a child's picture book, a body in a grave, we are still "hunting our own kind of deepening home," but our horizons, like Boone's, have narrowed in this "barbwire time."

JAMES WRIGHT (1927–1980)

Autumn Begins in Martins Ferry, Ohio (1963)

In the Shreve High football stadium,
I think of Polacks nursing long beers in Tiltonsville,
And gray faces of Negroes in the blast furnace at Benwood,
And the ruptured night watchman of Wheeling Steel,
Dreaming of heroes.   5

All the proud fathers are ashamed to go home.
Their women cluck like starved pullets,
Dying for love.

Therefore,
Their sons grow suicidally beautiful   10
At the beginning of October,
And gallop terribly against each other's bodies.

Reading and Reacting

1. Evaluate Wright's decision to use each of the following words: "Polacks"
(line 2), "ruptured" (line 4), "pullets" (line 7), "suicidally" (line 10), "gallop" (line 12). Do any of these words seem unexpected, even unsettling, in
the context in which the poet uses them? Can you explain why each is used
instead of a more conventional word?

2. What thematic relationship, if any, do you see between line 5 ("Dreaming
of heroes") and line 8 ("Dying for love")? What do these lines reveal about
the people who live in Martins Ferry?

3. JOURNAL ENTRY What comment does this poem seem to be making about
small towns? About high school football?

4. CRITICAL PERSPECTIVE In her 1980 essay "James Wright: Returning to
the Heartland," Bonnie Costello discusses the poet's complex relationship
to place and its effect on "Autumn Begins in Martins Ferry, Ohio," characterizing Wright as a kind of "fugitive" or "exile" from the past his poems
reveal.

> James Wright was an elegiac poet of place. Place names echo through his
> lines as through deserted villages and wintry valleys, for Martins Ferry, Ohio;
> Fargo, North Dakota; Wheeling, West Virginia, are all dying. While he admired
> D. H. Lawrence's essay "The Spirit of Place" and tried to follow its guidelines,
> his own subject raised a special problem since it was the departure of spirit
> that he best portrayed. Wright tried repeatedly to call his spirit back, but
> his finest poems are those which catch it crossing the last hill crest or dis-
> appearing into the mist. One might argue that there is, indeed, a spirit in this
> place, one hopeless, ignorant, and long suffering, nonetheless beautiful and
> mysterious.

How does "Autumn Begins in Martins Ferry, Ohio" convey the elegiac sense
of place Costello describes?

Related Works: "To an Athlete Dying Young" (p. 657), "Ex-Basketball Player" (p. 684)

ADRIENNE RICH (1929–)

Living in Sin (1955)

She had thought the studio would keep itself,
no dust upon the furniture of love.
Half heresy, to wish the taps less vocal,
the panes relieved of grime. A plate of pears,
a piano with a Persian shawl, a cat   5
stalking the picturesque amusing mouse
had risen at his urging.
Not that at five each separate stair would writhe
under the milkman's tramp; that morning light
so coldly would delineate the scraps   10
of last night's cheese and three sepulchral bottles;
that on the kitchen shelf among the saucers
a pair of beetle-eyes would fix her own —
envoy from some black village in the mouldings . . .
Meanwhile, he, with a yawn,   15
sounded a dozen notes upon the keyboard,
declared it out of tune, shrugged at the mirror,
rubbed at his beard, went out for cigarettes;
while she, jeered by the minor demons,
pulled back the sheets and made the bed and found   20
a towel to dust the table-top,
and let the coffee-pot boil over on the stove.
By evening she was back in love again,
though not so wholly but throughout the night
she woke sometimes to feel the daylight coming   25
like a relentless milkman up the stairs.

Reading and Reacting

1. How might the poem's impact change if each of these words were deleted: "Persian" (line 5), "picturesque" (line 6), "sepulchral" (line 11), "minor" (line 19), "sometimes" (line 25)?

2. What words in the poem have strongly negative connotations? What do these words suggest about the relationship the poem describes? How does the image of the "relentless milkman" (line 26) sum up this relationship?

3. This poem, about a woman in love, uses very few words conventionally as-sociated with love poems. Instead, many of its words denote the everyday routine of housekeeping. Give examples of such words. Why do you think they are used?

4. JOURNAL ENTRY What connotations does the title have? What other phrases have similar denotative meanings? How do their connotations differ? Why do you think Rich chose the title she did?

5. CRITICAL PERSPECTIVE In "Her Cargo: Adrienne Rich and the Common Language," a 1979 essay examining the poet's work over almost thirty years, Alicia Ostriker notes that early poems by Rich, including "Living in Sin," reflect popular male poets' "resigned sense of life as a diminished thing" and only "tremble on the brink of indignation":

> They seem about to state explicitly . . . a connection between feminine subor-dination in male-dominated middle-class relationships, and emotionally lethal inarticulateness for both sexes. But the poetry . . . is minor because it is polite. It illustrates symptoms but does not probe sources. There is no disputing the ideas of the predecessors, and Adrienne Rich at this point is a cautious good poet in the sense of being a good girl, a quality noted with approval by her reviewers.

Does your reading of "Living in Sin" support Ostriker's characterization of the poem as "resigned," "polite," and "cautious"? Do you think Rich is "being a good girl"?

Related Work: "The Littoral Zone" (p. 258)

E. E. CUMMINGS (1894–1962)

in Just-° (1923)

in Just-
spring when the world is mud-
luscious the little
lame balloonman
whistles   far   and   wee   5

and eddieandbill come
running from marbles and
piracies and it's
spring

when the world is puddle-wonderful   10
the queer

---

in Just-: This poem is also known as "Chansons Innocentes I."

old balloonman whistles
far   and   wee
and bettyandisbel come dancing

from hop-scotch and jump-rope and   15
it's
spring
and
   the
       goat-footed   20

balloonMan whistles
far
and
wee

Reading and Reacting

1. In this poem, Cummings coins a number of words that he uses to modify other words. Identify these coinages. What other, more conventional, words could be used in their place? What does Cummings accomplish by using the coined words instead?

2. What do you think Cummings means by "far and wee" in lines 5, 13, and 22–24? Why do you think he arranges the three words in a different way on the page each time he uses them?

3. JOURNAL ENTRY Evaluate this poem. Do you like it? Is it memorable? Moving? Or is it just clever?

4. CRITICAL PERSPECTIVE In "Latter-Day Notes on E. E. Cummings' Language" (1955), Robert E. Maurer suggests that Cummings often coined new words in the same way that children do: for example, "by adding the normal -*er* or -*est* (*beautifuler, chiefest*), or stepping up the power of a word such as *last*, which is already superlative, and saying *lastest*," creating words such as *givingest* and *whirlingest*. In addition to "combining two or more words to form a single new one . . . to give an effect of wholeness, of one quality" (for example, *yellowgreen*), "in the simplest of his word coinages, he merely creates a new word by analogy as a child would without adding any shade of meaning other than that inherent in the prefix or suffix he utilizes, as in the words *unstrength* and *untimid*. . . ." Many early reviewers, Maurer notes, criticized such coinages because they "convey a thrill but not a precise impression," a criticism also leveled at Cummings's poetry more broadly.

Consider the coinages in "in Just-." Do you agree that many do not add "shades of meaning" or provide a "precise impression"? Or do you find that the coinages contribute to the whole in a meaningful way?

Related Works: "The Secret Lion" (p. 54), "anyone lived in a pretty how town" (p. 565), "Constantly Risking Absurdity" (p. 681), "Jabberwocky" (p. 729), "the sky was can dy" (p. 754)

ROBERT PINSKY (1940 –   )

ABC (1998)

Any body can die, evidently. Few
Go happily, irradiating joy,

Knowledge, love. Many
Need oblivion, painkillers,
Quickest respite.   5

Sweet time unafflicted,
Various world:

X = your zenith.

Reading and Reacting

1. What "rules" limit the choice of words used in this poem? What determines
the order in which they are used? Where does the poet break (or bend) the
rules he has established? Can you suggest a way for him to avoid doing so?

2. Given the constraints the poet places on himself here, how successful is he?
Is the result of his efforts a poem or just an experiment? Explain.

3. JOURNAL ENTRY This poem is tightly compressed, limited to very few words.
Rewrite it as a paragraph, adding any words you think are necessary to communicate its theme. How is your version different from the original in what
it says? In what it suggests?

4. CRITICAL PERSPECTIVE "ABC" has a very distinctive form. The poet and
critic Louise Glück has stressed the importance of form in the poetry of
Robert Pinsky:

> [I]n Pinsky's art, form does what we have come to believe only tone can do. That
> is to say, form here is not intellectual construct but rather metaphor. For the
> poems to be understood at all they must be apprehended entire, as shapes.

How does reflecting on the form, or "shape," of "ABC" help you to understand the poem?

Related Works: "I Walk in the Old Street" (p. 551), "l(a" (p. 552), "The Grammar Lesson" (p. 621), "Constantly Risking Absurdity" (p. 681)

LEVELS OF DICTION

Like other writers, poets use various levels of diction to convey their ideas.
The diction of a poem may be formal or informal or fall anywhere in between,
depending on the identity of the speaker and on the speaker's attitude toward
the reader and toward his or her subject. At one extreme, very formal poems
can be far removed in style and vocabulary from everyday speech. At the other
extreme, highly informal poems can be full of jargon, regionalisms, and slang.
Many poems, of course, use language that falls somewhere between formal and
informal diction.

Formal diction is characterized by a learned vocabulary and grammatically correct forms. In general, formal diction does not include colloquialisms, such as contractions and shortened word forms (*phone* for *telephone*). As the following poem illustrates, a speaker who uses formal diction can sound aloof and impersonal.

MARGARET ATWOOD (1939–   )

The City Planners (1966)

Cruising these residential Sunday
streets in dry August sunlight:
what offends us is
the sanities:
the houses in pedantic rows, the planted   5
sanitary trees, assert
levelness of surface like a rebuke
to the dent in our car door.
No shouting here, or
shatter of glass; nothing more abrupt   10
than the rational whine of a power mower
cutting a straight swath in the discouraged grass.

But though the driveways neatly
sidestep hysteria
by being even, the roofs all display   15
the same slant of avoidance to the hot sky,
certain things:
the smell of spilled oil a faint

sickness lingering in the garages,
a splash of paint on brick surprising as a bruise,   20
a plastic hose poised in a vicious

coil; even the too-fixed stare of the wide windows
give momentary access to
the landscape behind or under
the future cracks in the plaster   25

when the houses, capsized, will slide
obliquely into the clay seas, gradual as glaciers
that right now nobody notices.

That is where the City Planners
with the insane faces of political conspirators   30
are scattered over unsurveyed
territories, concealed from each other,
each in his own private blizzard;

guessing directions, they sketch
transitory lines rigid as wooden borders   35
on a wall in the white vanishing air

tracing the panic of suburb
order in a bland madness of snows.

Atwood's speaker is clearly concerned about the poem's central issue, but rather than use *I*, the poem uses the first-person plural (*us*) to maintain distance and to convey emotional detachment. Although phrases such as "sickness lingering in the garages" and "insane faces of political conspirators" communicate the speaker's disapproval, formal words — "pedantic," "rebuke," "display," "poised," "obliquely," "conspirators," "transitory" — help her to maintain her distance. Both the speaker herself and her attack on the misguided city planners gain credibility through her balanced, measured tone and through the use of language that is as formal and "professional" as theirs.

Informal diction is the language closest to everyday conversation. It includes colloquialisms — contractions, shortened word forms, and the like — and may also include slang, regional expressions, and even nonstandard words.

In the poem that follows, the speaker uses informal diction to highlight the contrast between James Baca, a law student speaking to the graduating class of his old high school, and the graduating seniors.

JIM SAGEL (1947–   )

Baca Grande° (1982)

> *Una vaca se topó con un ratón y le dice:*
> *"Tú—¿tan chiquito y con bigote?" Y le responde el ratón:*
> *"Y tú tan grandota —¿y sin brassiere?"°*

It was nearly a miracle
James Baca remembered anyone at all
from the old hometown gang
having been two years at Yale
    no less   5
and halfway through law school
at the University of California at Irvine
They hardly recognized him either

Baca Grande: Baca is both a phonetic spelling of the Spanish word *vaca* (cow) and the last name of one of the poem's characters. *Grande* means "large."

Una . . . brassiere?: A cow ran into a rat and said: "You — so small and with a moustache?" The rat responded: "And you — so big and without a bra?"

in his three-piece grey business suit
and surfer-swirl haircut   10
with just the menacing hint
of a tightly trimmed Zapata moustache
    for cultural balance
and relevance

He had come to deliver the keynote address   15
to the graduating class of 80
at his old alma mater
and show off his well-trained lips
which laboriously parted
    each Kennedyish "R"   20
and drilled the first person pronoun
through the microphone
like an oil bit
with the slick, elegantly honed phrases
that slid so smoothly   25
off his meticulously bleached
    tongue
He talked Big Bucks
with astronautish fervor and if he
    the former bootstrapless James A. Baca   30
could dazzle the ass
off the universe
then even you
    yes you

Joey Martinez toying with your yellow   35
    tassle
and staring dumbly into space
could emulate Mr. Baca someday
    possibly
well   40
there was of course
such a thing
as being an outrageously successful
gas station attendant too
    let us never forget   45
it doesn't really matter what you do
so long as you excel
    James said
never believing a word
of it   50
for he had already risen
    as high as they go

Wasn't nobody else
from this deprived environment
who'd ever jumped   55
        straight out of college
into the Governor's office
and maybe one day
he'd sit in that big chair
        himself   60
and when he did
he'd forget this damned town
and all the petty little people
in it
once and for all   65

That much he promised himself

"Baca Grande" uses numerous colloquialisms, including contractions; conversational placeholders, such as "no less" and "well"; shortened word forms, such as "gas"; slang terms, such as "Big Bucks"; whimsical coinages ("Kennedyish," "astronautish," "bootstrapless"); nonstandard grammatical constructions, such as "Wasn't nobody else"; and even profanity. The level of language is perfectly appropriate for the students Baca addresses — suspicious, streetwise, and unimpressed by Baca's "three-piece grey business suit" and "surfer-swirl haircut." In fact, the informal diction is a key element in the poem, expressing the gap between the slick James Baca, with "his well-trained lips / which laboriously parted / each Kennedyish 'R'" and members of his audience, with their unpretentious, forthright speech. In this sense, "Baca Grande" is as much a linguistic commentary as a social one.

MARK HALLIDAY (1949–   )

The Value of Education (2000)

I go now to the library. When I sit in the library
I am not illegally dumping bags of kitchen garbage
in the dumpster behind Clippinger Laboratory,
and a very pissed-off worker at Facilities Management
is not picking through my garbage and finding   5
several yogurt-stained and tomato-sauce-stained envelopes
with my name and address on them.
When I sit in the library,
I might doze off a little,
and what I read might not penetrate my head   10
which is mostly porridge in a bowl of bone.
However, when I sit there trying to read
I am not, you see, somewhere else being a hapless ass.

I am not leaning on the refrigerator
in the apartment of a young female colleague   15
chatting with oily pep
because I imagine she may suddenly decide to
do sex with me while her boyfriend is on a trip.
Instead I am in the library! Sitting still!
No one in town is approaching my chair   20
with a summons, or a bill, or a huge fist.
This is good. You may say,
"But this is merely a negative definition of
the value of education." Maybe so,
but would you be able to say that   25
if you hadn't been to the library?

Reading and Reacting

1. How is the speaker's life outside the library different from the life he leads inside the library?

2. Who is the speaker? What does he reveal about himself? Whom might he be addressing?

3. In lines 23–24, the speaker imagines a challenge to his comments. Do you think this criticism is valid? What do you think of the speaker's reply?

4. What phrases are repeated in this poem? Why?

5. JOURNAL ENTRY What argument is the speaker making for the benefits of the library (and for the value of education)? Is he joking, or is he serious?

Related Works: "Gryphon" (p. 126), "Teenage Wasteland" (p. 535), "When I Heard the Learn'd Astronomer" (p. 639), "Why I Went to College" (p. 748)

RICHARD WILBUR (1921–   )

For the Student Strikers (1970)

Go talk with those who are rumored to be unlike you,
And whom, it is said, you are so unlike.
Stand on the stoops of their houses and tell them why
You are out on strike.

It is not yet time for the rock, the bullet, the blunt   5
Slogan that fuddles the mind toward force.
Let the new sound in our streets be the patient sound
Of your discourse.

Doors will be shut in your faces, I do not doubt.
Yet here or there, it may be, there will start,   10
Much as the lights blink on in a block at evening,
Changes of heart.

They are your houses; the people are not unlike you;
Talk with them, then, and let it be done
Even for the grey wife of your nightmare sheriff   15
And the guardsman's son.

Reading and Reacting

1. Is this poem's diction primarily formal or informal? List the words that support your conclusion.

2. Besides its vocabulary, what elements in the poem might lead you to characterize it as formal or informal?

3. JOURNAL ENTRY This poem is an **exhortation**, a form of discourse intended to incite or encourage listeners to take action. Given the speaker's audience and subject matter, is its level of diction appropriate? Explain.

Related Works: "Try to Praise the Mutilated World" (p. 616), "The *Chicago Defender* Sends a Man to Little Rock" (p. 856)

CHARLES BUKOWSKI (1920–1994)

Dog Fight (1984)

he draws up against my rear bumper in the fast lane,
I can see his head in the rear view mirror, his eyes
are blue and he sucks upon a dead cigar.
I pull over. he passes, then slows. I don't like
this.   5
I pull back into the fast lane, engage myself upon
his rear bumper. we are as a team passing through
Compton.
I turn the radio on and light a cigarette.
he ups it 5 mph, I do likewise. we are as a team   10
entering Inglewood.
he pulls out of the fast lane and I drive past.
then I slow. when I check the rear view he is
upon my bumper again.
he has almost made me miss my turnoff at Century.   15
I hit the blinker and fire across 3 lanes of
traffic, just make the off-ramp . . .
blazing past the front of an inflammable tanker.
blue eyes comes down from behind the tanker and
we veer down the ramp in separate lanes to the signal   20
and we sit there side by side, not looking at each
other.

I am caught behind an empty school bus as he idles
behind a Mercedes.
the signal switches and he is gone. I cut to the   25
inner lane behind him, then I see that the parking
lane is open and I flash by inside of him and the
Mercedes, turn up the radio, make the green as the
Mercedes and blue eyes run the yellow into the red.
they make it as I power it and switch back ahead of   30
them in their lane in order to miss a parked vegetable
truck.
now we are running 1-2-3, not a cop in sight, we are
moving through a 1980 California July
we are driving with skillful nonchalance   35
we are moving in perfect anger
we are as a team
approaching LAX:°
1-2-3
2-3-1   40
3-2-1.

Reading and Reacting

1. "Dog Fight" describes a car race from the emotionally charged perspective
of a driver. Given this persona, comment on the appropriateness of the level
of diction of the following words: "likewise" (line 10), "upon" (line 14),
"nonchalance" (line 35), "perfect" (line 36).

2. Many of the words in the poem are **jargon**— specialized language associated
with a particular trade or profession. In this case, Bukowski uses automotive
terms and the action words and phrases that typically describe driving maneuvers. Would you characterize these words as formal, informal, or neither?
Explain.

3. What colloquialisms are present in the poem? Could noncolloquial expressions be substituted for any of them? How would such substitutions change
the poem?

4. **JOURNAL ENTRY** Look up the phrase *dog fight* in a dictionary. What meanings
are listed? Which one do you think Bukowski had in mind? Why?

5. **CRITICAL PERSPECTIVE** In a 1978 review in the *Village Voice*, critic Michael
Lally defended Bukowski's poetry:

> Despite what some criticize as prose in Bukowski's poetry, there is in much of his
> work a poetic sensibility that, though arrogantly smart-ass and self-protective as
> well as self-promotional (he's the granddaddy of "punk" sensibility for sure), is
> also sometimes poignant, emotionally revealing, uniquely "American". . . .

LAX: Los Angeles International Airport.

Is "Dog Fight" prose, or do you see in it a "poetic sensibility"? In what sense, if any, do you find it "uniquely 'American'"? Give examples from the poem to support your conclusions.

Related Works: "Chicago" (p. 751), *The Cuban Swimmer* (p. 1258)

WORD ORDER

The order in which words are arranged in a poem is as important as the choice of words. Because English sentences nearly always have a subject-verb-object sequence, with adjectives preceding the nouns they modify, a departure from this order calls attention to itself. Thus, poets can use readers' expectations about word order to their advantage. Poets often manipulate word order to place emphasis on a word. Sometimes they achieve this emphasis by using a very unconventional sequence; sometimes they simply place the word first or last in a line or place it in a stressed position in the line. Poets may also choose a particular word order to make two related — or startlingly unrelated — words fall in adjacent or parallel positions, calling attention to the similarity (or the difference) between them. In other cases, poets may manipulate syntax to preserve a poem's rhyme or meter or highlight sound correspondences that might otherwise not be noticeable. Finally, irregular syntax may be used throughout a poem to reveal a speaker's mood — for example, to give a playful quality to a poem or to suggest a speaker's disoriented state.

In the poem that follows, the placement of many words departs from conventional English syntax.

EDMUND SPENSER (1552–1599)

One day I wrote her name upon the strand (1595)

One day I wrote her name upon the strand,°
But came the waves and washed it away:
Again I wrote it with a second hand,
But came the tide and made my pains his prey.
"Vain man," said she, "that doest in vain assay,   5
A mortal thing so to immortalize,
For I myself shall like to this decay,
And eek° my name be wiped out likewise."
"Not so," quod° I, "let baser things devise,

---

strand: Beach.

eek: Also, indeed.

quod: Said.

To die in dust, but you shall live by fame: 10
My verse your virtues rare shall eternize,
And in the heavens write your glorious name.
Where whenas death shall all the world subdue,
Our love shall live, and later life renew."

"One day I wrote her name upon the strand," a sonnet, has a fixed metrical pattern and rhyme scheme. To accommodate the sonnet's rhyme and meter, Spenser makes a number of adjustments in syntax. For example, to make sure certain rhyming words fall at the ends of lines, the poet sometimes moves words out of their conventional order, as the following three comparisons illustrate.

Conventional Word Order	Inverted Sequence
"'Vain man,' she said, that doest *assay in vain*."	"'Vain man,' said she, that does *in vain assay*." ("Assay" appears at end of line 5, to rhyme with line 7's "decay.")
"My verse shall *eternize your rare virtues*."	"My verse *your virtues rare shall eternize*." ("Eternize" appears at end of line 11 to rhyme with line 9's "devise.")
"Where whenas death shall *subdue all the world*, / Our love shall live, and *later renew life*."	"Where whenas death shall *all the world subdue*, / Our love shall live, and *later life renew*." (Rhyming words "subdue" and "renew" are placed at ends of lines.)

To make sure the metrical pattern stresses certain words, the poet occasionally moves a word out of conventional order and places it in a stressed position. The following comparison illustrates this technique.

Conventional Word Order	Inverted Sequence
"But *the waves came* and washed it away."	"But *came the waves* and washed it away." (Stress in line 2 falls on "waves" rather than on "the.")

As the comparisons show, Spenser's adjustments in syntax are motivated at least in part by a desire to preserve the sonnet's rhyme and meter.

The next poem does more than simply invert words; it presents an intentionally disordered syntax.

E. E. CUMMINGS (1894–1962)

anyone lived in a pretty how town (1940)

anyone lived in a pretty how town
(with up so floating many bells down)
spring summer autumn winter
he sang his didn't he danced his did.

Women and men (both little and small)   5
cared for anyone not at all
they sowed their isn't they reaped their same
sun moon stars rain

children guessed (but only a few
and down they forgot as up they grew   10
autumn winter spring summer)
that noone loved him more by more

when by now and tree by leaf
she laughed his joy she cried his grief
bird by snow and stir by still   15
anyone's any was all to her

someones married their everyones
laughed their cryings and did their dance
(sleep wake hope and then) they
said their nevers they slept their dream   20

stars rain sun moon
(and only the snow can begin to explain
how children are apt to forget to remember
with up so floating many bells down)

one day anyone died i guess   25
(and noone stooped to kiss his face)
busy folk buried them side by side
little by little and was by was

all by all and deep by deep
and more by more they dream their sleep   30
noone and anyone earth by april
wish by spirit and if by yes.

Women and men (both dong and ding)
summer autumn winter spring
reaped their sowing and went their came   35
sun moon stars rain

At times, Cummings, like Spenser, manipulates syntax in response to the demands of rhyme and meter —for example, in line 10. But Cummings goes much further, using unconventional syntax as part of a scheme that encompasses other unusual elements of the poem, such as its unexpected departures from the musical metrical pattern (for example, in line 3 and line 8) and from the rhyme scheme (for example, in lines 3 and 4) and its use of parts of speech in unfamiliar contexts. Together, these techniques give the poem a playful quality. The refreshing disorder of the syntax (for instance, in lines 1–2, line 10, and line 24) adds to the poem's whimsical effect.

A. E. HOUSMAN (1859–1936)

To an Athlete Dying Young (1896)

The time you won your town the race
We chaired you through the market-place;
Man and boy stood cheering by,
And home we brought you shoulder-high.

Today, the road all runners come,   5
Shoulder-high we bring you home,
And set you at your threshold down,
Townsman of a stiller town.

Smart lad, to slip betimes away
From fields where glory does not stay,   10
And early though the laurel grows
It withers quicker than the rose.

Eyes the shady night has shut
Cannot see the record cut,
And silence sounds no worse than cheers   15
After earth has stopped the ears.

Now you will not swell the rout
Of lads that wore their honors out,
Runners whom renown outran
And the name died before the man.   20

So set, before its echoes fade,
The fleet foot on the sill of shade,
And hold to the low lintel up
The still-defended challenge-cup.

And round that early-laureled head   25
Will flock to gaze the strengthless dead,
And find unwithered on its curls
The garland briefer than a girl's.

Reading and Reacting

1. Where does the poem's meter or rhyme scheme require the poet to depart from conventional syntax?

2. Edit the poem so its word order is more conventional. Do your changes improve the poem?

3. JOURNAL ENTRY Who do you think the speaker is? What is his relationship to the athlete?

Related Works: "Anthem for Doomed Youth" (p. 570), "Nothing Gold Can Stay" (p. 673), "Ex-Basketball Player" (p. 684), "Spring Elegy" (p. 700)

EMILY DICKINSON (1830 – 1886)

My Life had stood — a Loaded Gun (c. 1863)

My Life had stood — a Loaded Gun —
In Corners — till a Day
The Owner passed — identified —
And carried Me away —

And now We roam in Sovereign Woods —   5
And now We hunt the Doe —
And every time I speak for Him —
The Mountains straight reply —

And do I smile, such cordial light
Upon the Valley glow —   10
It is as a Vesuvian° face
Had let its pleasure through —

And when at Night — Our good Day done —
I guard My Master's Head —
'Tis better than the Eider-Duck's°   15
Deep Pillow — to have shared —

To foe of His — I'm deadly foe —
None stir the second time —
On whom I lay a Yellow Eye —
Or an emphatic Thumb —   20

Though I than He — may longer live
He longer must — than I —
For I have but the power to kill,
Without — the power to die —

Vesuvian: The volcano Mount Vesuvius erupted in A.D. 79, destroying the city of Pompeii.

Eider-Duck's: Eider ducks produce a soft down (eiderdown) used as pillow stuffing.

Reading and Reacting

1. Identify lines in which word order departs from conventional English syntax. Can you explain in each case why the word order has been manipulated?

2. Do any words gain added emphasis by virtue of their unexpected position? Which ones? How are these words important to the poem's meaning?

3. JOURNAL ENTRY Why do you think the speaker might be comparing her life to a loaded gun?

4. CRITICAL PERSPECTIVE Writing in the *New York Times*, Elizabeth Schmidt offers this evaluation of Dickinson's poetry:

> Her formal discipline — the economy of her language and her elaborate, idiosyncratic metrical schemes — turns out to be anything but off-putting. She chose forms that readers could learn by heart, creating one of literature's great, and most unlikely, combinations of style and content. Her poems are often conceptually difficult, and yet they are also surprisingly inviting, whether they coax you to guess a riddle or carry you along to the beat of a familiar tune.

Do you find Dickinson's poetry as inviting as Schmidt does, or do you think a poem like "My Life had stood — a Loaded Gun" *is* "off-putting"?

Related Work: "I heard a Fly buzz — when I died—" (p. 866)

CHECKLIST   WRITING ABOUT WORD CHOICE AND WORD ORDER

Word Choice

✓ Which words are of key importance in the poem?

✓ What is the denotative meaning of each of these key words?

✓ Why is each word chosen instead of a synonym? (For example, is the word chosen for its sound? Its connotation? Its relationship to other words in the poem? Its contribution to the poem's metrical pattern?)

✓ What other words could be effectively used in place of words now in the poem?

✓ How would substitutions change the poem's meaning?

✓ Which key words have neutral connotations? Which have negative connotations? Which have positive connotations? Beyond its literal meaning, what does each word suggest?

✓ Are any words repeated? Why?

Levels of Diction

✓ How would you characterize the poem's level of diction? Why is this level of diction used? Is it effective?

✓ Does the poem mix different levels of diction? To what end?

✓ Does the poem use dialect? For what purpose?

Word Order

✓ Is the poem's syntax conventional, or are words arranged in unexpected order?

✓ Which phrases represent departures from conventional syntax?

✓ What is the purpose of the unusual syntax? (For example, does it preserve the poem's meter or rhyme scheme? Does it highlight particular sound correspondences? Does it place emphasis on a particular word or phrase? Does it reflect the speaker's mood?)

✓ How would the poem's impact change if conventional syntax were used?

WRITING SUGGESTIONS: Word Choice, Word Order

1. Reread the two poems by E. E. Cummings — "in Just-" (p. 675) and "anyone lived in a pretty how town" (p. 656) — in this chapter. If you like, you may also read one or two additional poems in this volume by Cummings. Do you believe Cummings chose words primarily for their sound? For their appearance on the page? What other factors might have influenced his choices?

2. Reread "For the Grave of Daniel Boone" (p. 640) alongside Delmore Schwartz's "The True-Blue American" (p. 780). What does each poem's choice of words reveal about the speaker's attitude toward his subject?

3. Analyze the choice of words and the level of diction in Margaret Atwood's "The City Planners" (p. 647), and Denise Levertov's "What Were They Like?" (p. 573). Pay particular attention to each poem's use of language to express social or political criticism.

4. **Web Activity** The following Web site contains information about Charles Bukowski:

http://www.charm.net/~ brooklyn/buk.html

The second paragraph on the Bukowski Web page includes the following observation:

> Bukowski is generally considered to be an honorary "beat writer," although he was never actually associated with Jack Kerouac, Allen Ginsberg, and the other

bona fide beat writers. His style, which exhibits a strong sense of immediacy and a refusal to embrace standard formal structure, has earned him a place in the hearts of beat generation readers.

Locate a Web site (or Web sites) that will tell you about the Beat Generation and its major literary figures — Jack Kerouac, Allen Ginsberg, and William S. Burroughs. Write an essay that identifies the "beat" characteristics of Bukowski's poem "Dog Fight" (p. 652) by drawing parallels between Bukowski's language and imagery and that of the other "beat" writers.

CHAPTER 19

IMAGERY

Images are probably the most important part of the poem. First of all, you want to tell a story, but images are what are going to shore it up and get to the heart of the matter. . . . If they're not coming, I'm not even writing a poem, it's pointless. —**Anne Sexton,** *Writers at Work,* 4th ed.

The difference between a literature that includes the image, and a literature that excludes the image (such as the newspaper or the scientific Newtonian essay) is that the first helps us to bridge the gap between ourselves and nature, and the second encourages us to remain isolated, living despairingly in the gap. Many philosophers and critics urge us to remain in the gap, and let the world of nature and the world of men fall further and further apart. We can do that; or a human being can reach out with his right hand to the natural world, and with his left hand to the world of human intelligence, and touch both at the same moment. Apparently no one but human beings can do this. —**Robert Bly,** *"What the Image Can Do"*

The poet sits before a blank piece of paper with a need to say many things in the small space of the poem. The world is huge, the poet is alone, and the poem is just a bit of language, a few scratchings of a pen surrounded by the silence of the night.

It could be that the poet wishes to tell you about his or her life. A few images of some fleeting moment when one was happy or exceptionally lucid. The secret wish of poetry is to stop time. The poet wants to retrieve a face, a mood, a cloud in the sky, a tree in the wind, and take a kind of mental photograph of that moment in which you as a reader recognize yourself. Poems are other people's snapshots in which we recognize ourselves. —**Charles Simic,** Introduction to *The Best American Poetry, 1992*

It is better to present one Image in a lifetime than to produce voluminous works. —**Ezra Pound,** *"A Retrospect"*

JANE FLANDERS (1940–)

Cloud Painter (1984)

Suggested by the life and art of John Constable°

At first, as you know, the sky is incidental —
a drape, a backdrop for trees and steeples.
Here an oak clutches a rock (already he works outdoors),
a wall buckles but does not break,
water pearls through a lock, a haywain° trembles.   5

The pleasures of landscape are endless. What we see
around us should be enough.
Horizons are typically high and far away.

Still, clouds let us drift and remember. He is, after all,
a miller's son, used to trying   10
to read the future in the sky, seeing instead
ships, horses, instruments of flight.
Is that his mother's wash flapping on the line?
His schoolbook, smudged, illegible?

In this period the sky becomes significant.   15
Cloud forms are technically correct — mares' tails,
sheep-in-the-meadow, thunderheads.
You can almost tell which scenes have been interrupted
by summer showers.

Now his young wife dies.   20
His landscapes achieve belated success.
He is invited to join the Academy. I forget
whether he accepts or not.

In any case, the literal forms give way
to something spectral, nameless. His palette shrinks   25
to gray, blue, white — the colors of charity.
Horizons sink and fade,
trees draw back till they are little more than frames,
then they too disappear.

Finally the canvas itself begins to vibrate   30
with waning light,
as if the wind could paint.
And we too, at last, stare into a space
which tells us nothing,
except that the world can vanish along with our need for it.   35

John Constable: British painter (1776–1837) noted for his landscapes.

haywain: An open horse-drawn wagon for carrying hay.

John Constable (1776–1837). *Landscape, Noon, The Haywain*. 1821. Oil on canvas, 130½ × 185½ cm. London, National Gallery.

Because the purpose of poetry — and, for that matter, of all literature — is to expand the perception of readers, poets appeal to the senses. In "Cloud Painter," Jane Flanders uses details, such as the mother's wash on the line and the smudged schoolbook, to enable readers to visualize particular scenes in John Constable's early paintings. Clouds are described so readers can picture them — "mares' tails, / sheep-in-the-meadow, thunderheads." Thus, "Cloud Painter" is not only about the work of John Constable but also about the ability of an artist — poet or painter — to call up images in the minds of an audience. To achieve this end, a poet uses **imagery,** language that evokes a physical sensation produced by one or more of the five senses — sight, hearing, taste, touch, smell.

Although the effect can be quite complex, the way images work is simple: when you read the word *red,* your memory of the various red things that you have seen determines how you picture the image. In addition, the word *red* may have emotional associations, or **connotations,** that define your response. A red sunset, for example, can have a positive connotation or a negative one, depending on whether it is associated with the end of a perfect day or with air pollution. By choosing an image carefully, poets not only create pictures in a reader's mind but also suggest a great number of imaginative associations. These associations help poets to establish the **atmosphere** or **mood** of the poem. The image of softly falling snow in "Stopping by Woods on a Snowy Evening" (p. 880), for example, creates a quiet, almost mystical mood.

Readers come to a poem with their own unique experiences, so an image in a poem does not always suggest the same thing to all readers. In "Cloud Painter," for example, the poet presents the image of an oak tree clutching a rock. Although most readers will probably see a picture that is consistent with the one the poet sees, no two images will be identical. Every reader will have his or her own distinct mental image of a tree clinging to a rock; some images will be remembered experiences, whereas others will be imaginative creations. Some readers may even be familiar enough with the work of the painter John Constable to visualize a particular tree clinging to a particular rock in one of his paintings. By conveying what the poet sees and imagines, images open readers' minds and enrich their reading with perceptions and associations different from — and possibly more original and complex than — their own.

One advantage of imagery is its extreme economy. Just a few words enable poets to evoke a range of emotions and reactions. In the following poem, just a few visual images are enough to create a picture.

WILLIAM CARLOS WILLIAMS (1883–1963)

Red Wheelbarrow (1923)

so much depends
upon

a red wheel
barrow

glazed with rain   5
water

beside the white
chickens

"Red Wheelbarrow" asks readers to pause to consider the uniqueness and mystery of everyday objects. What is immediately apparent is the poem's verbal economy. The poet does not tell readers what the barnyard smells like or what sounds the animals make. In fact, he does not even paint a detailed picture of the scene. How large is the wheelbarrow? In what condition is it? How many chickens are in the barnyard? In this poem, the answers to these questions are not important. Even without answering these questions, the poet is able to use simple imagery to create a scene on which, he says, "so much depends."

The wheelbarrow establishes a momentary connection between the poet and his world. Like a still-life painting, the red wheelbarrow beside the white chickens gives order to a world that is full of seemingly unrelated objects. By asserting the importance of the objects in the poem, the poet suggests that our ability to perceive the objects of this world gives our lives meaning and that our ability to convey our perceptions to others is central to our lives as well as to art.

Images also enable poets to present ideas that would be difficult to convey in any other way. One look at a dictionary will illustrate that concepts such as *beauty* and *mystery* are so abstract that they are difficult to define, let alone to discuss in specific terms. By choosing an image or a series of images to embody these ideas, however, poets can effectively make their feelings known, as Ezra Pound does in the brief poem that follows.

EZRA POUND (1885–1972)

In a Station of the Metro (1916)

The apparition of these faces in the crowd;
Petals on a wet, black bough.

This poem is almost impossible to paraphrase because the information it communicates is less important than the feelings associated with this information. The poem's title indicates that the first line is meant to suggest a group of people gathered in a station of the Paris subway. The scene, however, is presented not as a clear picture but as an "apparition," suggesting that it is unexpected or even dreamlike. In contrast with the image of the subway platform is the image of the people's faces as flower petals on the dark branch of a tree. Thus, the subway platform — dark, cold, wet, subterranean (associated with baseness, death, and hell) — is juxtaposed with white flowers — delicate, pale, radiant, lovely (associated with the ideal, life, and heaven). These contrasting images, presented without comment, bear the entire weight of the poem.

Although images can be strikingly visual, they can also appeal to the senses of hearing, smell, taste, and touch. The following poem uses images of sound and taste as well as visual images.

GARY SNYDER (1930–   )

Some Good Things to Be
Said for the Iron Age (1970)

A ringing tire iron
        dropped on the pavement
Whang of a saw
brusht on limbs
the taste   5
of rust

Here Snyder presents two commonplace aural images: the ringing of a tire iron and the sound of a saw. These somewhat ordinary images gain power, however, through their visual isolation in the poem. Together they produce a harsh and jarring chord that in turn creates a sense of uneasiness in the reader. This poem does more than present sensory images, though. It also conveys the speaker's interpretations of these images. The last two lines imply not only that the time in which we live (the Iron Age) is base and mundane, but also that it is declining, decaying into an age of rust. This idea is reinforced by the repeated consonant sounds in *taste* and *rust*, which encourage readers to hold the final image of the poem on their tongues. The title of the poem makes an ironic comment, suggesting that compared to the time that is approaching, the age of iron may be "good." Thus, in the mind of the poet, ordinary events gain added significance, and images that spring from everyday experience become sources of enlightenment and insight.

In short poems, such as most of those discussed above, one or two images may serve as focal points. A longer poem may introduce a cluster of related images, creating a more complex tapestry of sensory impressions — as in the following poem, where a number of related images are woven together.

SUZANNE E. BERGER (1944 –　　)

The Meal (1984)

They have washed their faces until they are pale,
their homework is beautifully complete.
They wait for the adults to lean towards each other.
The hands of the children are oval
and smooth as pine-nuts.　　　　　　　　　　　　　　5

The girls have braided and rebraided their hair,
and tied ribbons without a single mistake.
The boy has put away his coin collection.
They are waiting for the mother to straighten her lipstick,
and for the father to speak.　　　　　　　　　　　　10

They gather around the table, carefully
as constellations waiting to be named.
Their minds shift and ready, like dunes.
It is so quiet, all waiting stars and dunes.

Their forks move across their plates without scraping,　　15
they wait for the milk and the gravy
at the table with its forgotten spices.
They are waiting for a happiness to lift their eyes,
like sudden light flaring in the trees outside.

The white miles of the meal continue,　　　　　　　20
the figures still travel across a screen:
the father carving the Sunday roast,
her mouth uneven as a torn hibiscus,
their braids still gleaming in the silence.

"The Meal" presents related images that together evoke silence, order, and emptiness. It begins with the image of faces washed "until they are pale" and goes on to describe the children's oval hands as "smooth as pine-nuts." Forks move across plates "without scraping," and the table hints at the memory of "forgotten spices." Despite the poem's title, these children are emotionally starved. The attentive, well-scrubbed children sit at a table where, neither eating nor speaking, they wait for "the milk and the gravy" and for happiness that never comes. The "white miles of the meal" seem to go on forever, reinforcing the sterility and emptiness of the Sunday ritual. Suggesting an absence of sensation or feeling, a kind of paralysis, the poem's images challenge conventional assumptions about the family and its rituals.

Much visual imagery is **static,** freezing the moment and thereby giving it the timeless quality of painting or sculpture. ("The Meal" presents such a tableau, and so do "Red Wheelbarrow" and "In a Station of the Metro.") Some imagery, in contrast, is **kinetic,** conveying a sense of motion or change.

WILLIAM CARLOS WILLIAMS (1883–1963)

The Great Figure (1938)

Among the rain
and lights
I saw the figure 5
in gold
on a red   5
firetruck
moving
tense
unheeded
to gong clangs   10
siren howls
and wheels rumbling
through the dark city.

Commenting on "The Great Figure" in his autobiography, Williams explains that while walking in New York, he heard the sound of a fire engine. As he turned the corner, he saw a golden figure 5 on a red background speed by. The impression was so forceful that he immediately jotted down a poem about it. In the poem, Williams attempts to re-create the sensation the figure 5 made as it moved into his consciousness, presenting the image as if it were a picture taken by a camera with a high-speed shutter. The poet presents images in the order in which he perceived them: first the 5 and then the red fire truck howling and clanging into the darkness. Thus, "The Great Figure" uses images of sight, sound, and movement to re-create for readers the poet's experience. The American painter Charles

Demuth was fascinated by the kinetic quality of the poem. Working closely with his friend Williams, he attempted to capture the stop-action feature of the poem in a painting (see below).

A special use of imagery, called **synesthesia,** occurs when one sense is described in a way that is more appropriate for another — for instance, when a sound is described with color. When people say they are feeling *blue* or describe music as *hot,* they are using synesthesia.

Charles Henry Demuth (1883–1935). *The Figure 5 in Gold*. Oil on composition board, 36 × 29¾ in. The Metropolitan Museum of Art, The Alfred Steiglitz Collection, 1949. (49.59.1). Photograph © The Metropolitan Museum of Art.

RICHARD WILBUR (1921–   )

Sleepless at Crown Point (1973)

All night, this headland
Lunges into the rumpling
Capework of the wind.

Reading and Reacting

1. What scene is the speaker describing?
2. What is the significance of the title?
3. What are the poem's central images? How do the words "lunges" and "cape-work" help to establish these images?

Related Works: "The Story of an Hour" (p. 82), "Fog" (p. 909), "The Dance" (p. 922)

MICHAEL CHITWOOD (1978–   )

Division (2002)

Inside the shed, he'd rigged
an oil drip into the barrel stove
so that the used sludge from his trucks
burned with split hickory while he
passed the winter piecing together furniture.   5
Just a sideline, he'd say, aiming
down a board to judge it in or out of true.
"It fills in the down months and tacks
some cash on the end of the year."

In those same white weeks at school   10
I learned division. First, you made a lean-to
for the big number to go under. The little
number waited outside. You could add on
as many zeros as you wanted.
The answer appeared on the roof.   15
December and January passed into February
and a whole bedroom suite came together.
On the roof, the smoke swirled into 0s and 8s.

Reading and Reacting

1. This poem is divided into two stanzas. What is described in the first stanza? What is described in the second stanza?
2. In what way is doing carpentry like learning long division?
3. List the images that appear in the poem. How do these images reinforce the similarities between the carpenter and the boy?

4. **JOURNAL ENTRY** Other than arithmetic, to what else could the title of the poem refer?

Related Works: "Gryphon" (p. 126), "Digging" (p. 560), "The Value of Education" (p. 650)

LAM THI MY DA (1949–)

Washing Rice (2001)

My mother is washing rice in late morning
A gentle wind ruffles the shade of the palms
The yellow rice glistens in rippled water
The ripe grains and the unripe look the same
They are both the color of silk, the same color   5
But why does she keep washing, washing so long?

How many unripe grains drift away from you, Mother?
How many ripe grains stay with you and talk?
When I go out tomorrow, full of life,
Will my lesson be your hand, washing rice?   10

Reading and Reacting

1. Why is the speaker's mother washing rice? What does the washing accomplish?
2. In line 6, the speaker asks, "But why does she keep washing, washing so long?" What do you think the answer to this question might be?
3. What is the significance of the speaker's observation that the ripe and unripe grains are the same color?
4. **JOURNAL ENTRY** According to the poem, what lesson can be learned from watching the speaker's mother washing rice?

Related Works: "Those Winter Sundays" (p. 560), "To see a World in a Grain of Sand" (p. 853)

CHITRA BANERJEE DIVAKARUNI (1957–)

The Alley of Flowers (1997)

When the hot din of red trams at noon
scrapes at your nerves, and melted tar
black and viscous as lava
sticks to your stumbling shoes and coats the lining
of your throat, when directly overhead   5
the giant fist of the sun
pounds at your skull and shrivels up your eyes,

enter the alley of flowers. Here
through a ceiling of damp rushes,
light filters down like rain and old women   10
with eyes that have seen everything you can imagine
raise brass *pichkaris*
to spray ice-water onto flowers.

Mountains of flowers, white, all white,
color of innocence and female sorrow,   15
mingling their scents with the odor
of wet morning earth:
chrysanthemum, gardenia, *bel*,
the snow queen, the long-stemmed honeysuckle,
the tight buds of night-blooming jasmine twisted in garlands   20
for temple-gods and brides.
Or for the dead.

In the alley of flowers you open
your mouth to speak and find
no need for sound. On your wrist   25
the watch-hands (when did they stop) are frail
as rose-thorn. You walk slowly,
as if through water, the current cool,
pressing up against your thighs.
As if they alley has no end. Feel.   30
On your forehead, misted air like petals.
Like the sound of wings. Like
the breath of the dead, a blessing.

Reading and Reacting

1. According to the speaker, how is the alley of flowers different from the rest of the city?

2. What is the theme of the poem?

3. List the images in the poem. To what sense does each image appeal? In what way do these images reinforce the central theme of the poem?

4. JOURNAL ENTRY Flowers figure prominently in Hindu rituals for the dead. In what way does this information add to your understanding of the poem?

5. CRITICAL PERSPECTIVE Donna Seaman, writing in *Booknotes*, describes Divakaruni's poetry as "[s]trongly narrative, shimmeringly detailed, and emotionally acute," adding that it "embraces pain and beauty in its affirmation of grace."

Do you think Seaman's description applies to "The Alley of Flowers"? What instances do you see of "pain and beauty" in the poem?

Related Works: "A Clean, Well-Lighted Place" (p. 267), "Cathedral" (p. 318), "The Beginning" (p. 729), "Monet's 'Waterlilies'" (p. 757)

ROBERT FROST (1874–1963)

Nothing Gold Can Stay (1923)

Nature's first green is gold,
Her hardest hue to hold.
Her early leaf's a flower;
But only so an hour.
Then leaf subsides to leaf.   5
So Eden sank to grief.
So dawn goes down to day.
Nothing gold can stay.

Reading and Reacting

1. What central idea does this poem express?

2. What do you think the first line of the poem means? In what sense is this line ironic?

3. What is the significance of the colors green and gold in this poem? What do these colors have to do with "Eden" and "dawn"?

4. JOURNAL ENTRY How do the various images in the poem prepare readers for the last line?

5. CRITICAL PERSPECTIVE In "The Figure a Poem Means," the introduction to the first edition of his *Collected Poems* (1930), Frost laid out a theory of poetry:

> It begins in delight, it inclines to the impulse, it assumes direction with the first line laid down, it runs a course of lucky events, and ends in a clarification of life — not necessarily a great clarification . . . but a momentary stay against confusion. . . . Like a piece of ice on a hot stove the poem must ride on its own melting. . . . Read it a hundred times: it will forever keep its freshness as a metal keeps its fragrance. It can never lose its sense of a meaning that once unfolded by surprise as it went.

Explain how Frost's remarks apply to "Nothing Gold Can Stay."

Related Works: "The Secret Lion" (p. 54), "Shall I compare thee to a summer's day?" (p. 679), "God's Grandeur" (p. 888)

JEAN TOOMER (1894–1967)

Reapers (1923)

Black reapers with the sound of steel on stones
Are sharpening scythes. I see them place the hones°
In their hip-pockets as a thing that's done,

---

hones: Stones used to sharpen cutting instruments.

And start their silent swinging, one by one.
Black horses drive a mower through the weeds,   5
And there, a field rat, startled, squealing bleeds,
His belly close to ground. I see the blade,
Blood-stained, continue cutting weeds and shade.

Reading and Reacting

1. What determines the order in which the speaker arranges the images in this poem? At what point does he comment on these images?

2. The first four lines of the poem seem to suggest that the workers are content. What image contradicts this impression? How does it do so?

3. What ideas are traditionally associated with the image of the reaper? The scythe? The harvest? (You may want to consult a reference work, such as A *Dictionary of Symbols* by J. E. Cirlot.) In what way does the speaker rely on these conventional associations to help him convey his ideas? Can you appreciate the poem without understanding these associations?

4. **CRITICAL PERSPECTIVE** As Brian Joseph Benson and Mabel Mayle Dillard point out in their 1980 study *Jean Toomer,* the poet disagreed with some other artists of the Harlem Renaissance, choosing not to focus on "Negro" themes for a primarily black audience but rather to try to make his work universal in scope.

Do you think he has achieved this goal in "Reapers"?

Related Works: "A Worn Path" (p. 361), "The Solitary Reaper" (p. 924)

WILFRED OWEN (1893–1918)

Dulce et Decorum Est° (1920)

Bent double, like old beggars under sacks,
Knock-kneed, coughing like hags, we cursed through sludge,
Till on the haunting flares we turned our backs
And towards our distant rest began to trudge.
Men marched asleep. Many had lost their boots   5
But limped on, blood-shod. All went lame; all blind;
Drunk with fatigue; deaf even to the hoots
Of tired, outstripped Five-Nines° that dropped behind.

Dulce et Decorum Est: "The title and last lines are from Horace, *Odes* 3.2: "Sweet and fitting it is to die for one's country."

Five-Nines: Shells that explode on impact and release poison gas.

Gas! GAS Quick, boys! — An ecstasy of fumbling,
Fitting the clumsy helmets just in time;   10
But someone still was yelling out and stumbling
And flound'ring like a man in fire or lime . . .
Dim, through the misty panes and thick green light,
As under a green sea, I saw him drowning.
In all my dreams, before my helpless sight,   15
He plunges at me, guttering, choking, drowning.

If in some smothering dreams you too could pace
Behind the wagon that we flung him in,
And watch the white eyes writhing in his face,
His hanging face, like a devil's sick of sin;   20
If you could hear, at every jolt, the blood
Come gargling from the froth-corrupted lungs,
Obscene as cancer, bitter as the cud
Of vile, incurable sores on innocent tongues, —
My friend, you would not tell with such high zest   25
To children ardent for some desperate glory,
The old Lie: Dulce et decorum est
Pro patria mori.

Reading and Reacting

1. Who is the speaker in this poem? What is his attitude toward his subject?

2. What images are traditionally associated with soldiers? How do the images in this poem depart from these associations? Why do you think Owen selected such images?

3. To what senses (other than sight) does the poem appeal? Is any of the imagery kinetic?

4. JOURNAL ENTRY Does the knowledge that Owen died in World War I change your reaction to the poem, or are the poem's images compelling enough to eliminate the need for such biographical background?

5. CRITICAL PERSPECTIVE Like many other British poets who experienced fighting in the European trenches during World War I, Owen struggled to find a new poetic idiom to describe the horrors of this new kind of war. In his 1986 biography *Owen the Poet,* Dominic Hibberd praises the "controlled and powerful anger in 'Dulce et Decorum Est' which for some readers will be the poem's most valuable quality" and goes on to note that the "organization and clarity of the first half is replaced [beginning at line 15] by confused, choking syntax and a vocabulary of sickness and disgust, matching the nightmare which is in progress."

Give some examples to support Hibberd's statements. How do the images in the poem help establish the movement from control to confusion?

Related Works: "The Things They Carried" (p. 271), "Anthem for Doomed Youth" (p. 570), "The End and the Beginning" (p. 576)

CHECKLIST   **WRITING ABOUT IMAGERY**

✓   Do the images in the poem appeal to the sense of sight, hearing, taste, touch, or smell?

✓   Does the poem depend on a single image or on a variety of images?

✓   Does the poem depend on a cluster of related images?

✓   What details make the images memorable?

✓   What mood do the images create?

✓   Are the images static or kinetic?

✓   How do the poem's images help to convey its theme?

✓   How effective are the images? In what way do the images enhance your enjoyment of the poem?

WRITING SUGGESTIONS: Imagery

1. How are short poems such as "Some Good Things to Be Said for the Iron Age" (p. 666) and "In a Station of the Metro" (p. 666) like and unlike **haiku**?

2. After rereading "Cloud Painter" (p. 663) and "The Great Figure" (p. 668), read "Musée des Beaux Arts" (p. 787), and study the corresponding paintings (*Landscape, Noon, the Haywain* on page 664; *The Figure 5 in Gold* on page 669; and *Landscape with the Fall of Icarus*, on page 82, respectively). Then, write a paper in which you draw some conclusions about the differences between artistic and poetic images.

3. Reread "The Meal" (p. 667) and the discussion that accompanies it. Then analyze the role of imagery in the depiction of the parent/child relationships in "Washing Rice" (p. 671) and "My Papa's Waltz" (p. 558). How does each poem's imagery convey the nature of the relationship it describes?

4. Write an essay in which you discuss the color imagery in "Nothing Gold Can Stay" (p. 673) and "Reapers" (p. 673). In what way does color reinforce the themes of these poems?

5. Sometimes imagery can be used to make a comment about the society in which a scene takes place. Choose two poems in which imagery functions in this way — "For the Union Dead" (p. 571) or "The *Chicago Defender* Sends a Man to Little Rock" (p. 856), for example — and discuss how the images chosen reinforce the social statement each poem makes.

6. **WEB ACTIVITY** The following Web site contains information about Wilfred Owen:

http://www.emory.edu/ENGLISH/LostPoets/Owen2.html

On the Owen Web page, the biography includes the following statement by Owen about his decision to fight in World War I:

> I came out in order to help these boys — directly by leading them as well as an officer can; indirectly, by watching their sufferings that I may speak of them as well as a pleader can. I have done the first.

Read the biographical material, and then write an essay discussing to what degree Owen accomplished his second goal, to be a "pleader," in "Dulce et Decorum Est" (p. 674). Consider in particular his use of imagery in his descriptions of the soldiers' suffering as well as in his characterization of those who witness such suffering. In what sense does he plead for peace as well as for the men?

CHAPTER 20

FIGURES OF SPEECH

The metaphor is probably the most fertile power possessed by man. —**José Ortega y Gasset**

Poetry is made of comparisons, simple or complex, open or concealed. The richness of poetry is obtained by mixing or interweaving or juxtaposing these comparisons. The mixture is either a mechanical mixture or a chemical mixture: when the mechanical becomes chemical the explosion takes place. That is the difference between prose and poetry. In prose all comparisons are simple and uncompounded. In poetry all metaphors are mixed metaphors. —**J. Isaacs,** *The Background of Modern Poetry*

I suppose we shall never be able to distinguish absolutely and with a hard edge the image from the metaphor, any more than anyone has so distinguished prose from poetry. . . . We shall very often be able to tell, just as we can very often tell the difference between snow and rain; but there are some weathers which are either-neither, and so here there is an area where our differences will mingle. If the poet says, simply, "The red bird," we shall probably take that as an image. But as soon as we read the rest of the line —"The red bird flies across the golden floor"— there arise obscure thoughts of relationships that lead in the direction of parable: the line alone is not, strictly, a metaphor, but its resonances take it prospectively beyond a pure perception. . . . Metaphor stands somewhat as a mediating term squarely between a thing and a thought, which may be why it is so likely to compose itself about a word of sense and a word of thought, as in this example of a common Shakespearean formula: "Even to the teeth and forehead of my fault." —**Howard Nemerov,** *"On Metaphor"*

Metaphor is not to be considered, . . . as the alternative of the poet, which he may elect to use or not, since he may state the matter directly and straightforwardly if he chooses. It is frequently the only means available if he is to write at all . . . . —**Cleanth Brooks,** *"Metaphor and the Tradition"*

WILLIAM SHAKESPEARE (1564–1616)

Shall I compare thee to a summer's day? (1609)

Shall I compare thee to a summer's day?
Thou art more lovely and more temperate.
Rough winds do shake the darling buds of May,
And summer's lease hath all too short a date.
Sometime too hot the eye of heaven shines,   5
And often is his gold complexion dimmed;
And every fair from fair sometimes declines,
By chance, or nature's changing course, untrimmed.
But thy eternal summer shall not fade,
Nor lose possession of that fair thou ow'st;°   10
Nor shall death brag thou wand'rest in his shade,
When in eternal lines to time thou grow'st.
     So long as men can breathe or eyes can see,
     So long lives this, and this gives life to thee.

Although writers experiment with language in all kinds of literary works, poets in particular recognize the power of a figure of speech to take readers beyond the literal meaning of a word. For this reason, **figures of speech**—expressions that use words to achieve effects beyond the power of ordinary language — are more prominent in poetry than in other kinds of writing. For example, in the preceding sonnet, Shakespeare compares a loved one to a summer's day in order to make the point that, unlike the fleeting summer, the loved one will — within the poem — remain forever young. But this sonnet goes beyond the obvious equation (loved one = summer's day); the speaker's assertion that his loved one will live forever in his poem actually says more about his confidence in his own talent and reputation (and about the power of language) than about the loved one's beauty.

SIMILE, METAPHOR, AND PERSONIFICATION

When William Wordsworth opens a poem with "I wandered lonely as a cloud" (p. 723), he conveys a good deal more than he would if he simply said, "I wandered, lonely." By comparing himself in his loneliness to a cloud, he suggests that like the cloud he is a part of nature and that he too is drifting, passive, blown by winds, and lacking will or substance. Thus, by using a figure of speech, the poet can suggest a wide variety of feelings and associations in very few words. The phrase "I wandered lonely as a cloud" is a **simile,** a comparison between two unlike items that uses *like* or *as.* When an imaginative comparison between two unlike items does not use *like* or *as*— that is, when it says "a *is* b" rather than "a is *like* b"—it is a **metaphor.**

---

that fair thou ow'st: That beauty you possess.

Accordingly, when the speaker in Adrienne Rich's "Living in Sin" (p. 643) speaks of "daylight coming / like a relentless milkman up the stairs," she is using a strikingly original simile to suggest that daylight brings not the conventional associations of promise and awakening but rather a stale, never-ending routine that is greeted without enthusiasm. This idea is consistent with the rest of the poem, an account of an unfulfilling relationship. However, when the speaker in Audre Lorde's poem says "Rooming houses are old women" (p. 682), she uses a metaphor, equating two elements to stress their common associations with emptiness, transience, and hopelessness. At the same time, by identifying rooming houses as old women, Lorde is using **personification,** a special kind of comparison, closely related to metaphor, that gives life or human characteristics to inanimate objects or abstract ideas.

Sometimes, as in Wordsworth's "I wandered lonely as a cloud," a single brief simile or metaphor can be appreciated for what it communicates on its own. At other times, however, a simile or metaphor may be one of several related figures of speech that work together to convey a poem's meaning. The following poem, for example, presents a series of related similes. Together, they suggest the depth of the problem the poem explores in a manner that each individual simile could not do alone.

LANGSTON HUGHES (1902–1967)

Harlem (1951)

What happens to a dream deferred?

Does it dry up
like a raisin in the sun?
Or fester like a sore —
And then run?   5
Does it stink like rotten meat?
Or crust and sugar over —
like a syrupy sweet?

Maybe it just sags
like a heavy load.   10

Or does it explode?

The dream to which Hughes alludes in his 1951 poem is the dream of racial equality. It is also the American Dream — or, by extension, any important unrealized dream. His speaker offers six tentative answers to the question asked in the poem's first line, and five of the six are presented as similes. As the poem unfolds, the speaker considers different alternatives: the dream can shrivel up and die, fester, decay, crust over — or sag under the weight of the burden those who hold the dream must carry. In each case, the speaker transforms an abstract entity — a dream — into a concrete item — a raisin in the sun, a sore, rotten meat, syrupy candy, a heavy load. The final line, italicized for emphasis, gains power less from what it says than from what it leaves unsaid. Unlike the other alternatives explored in the poem, *"Or does it explode?"* is not presented as a simile. Nevertheless, because of the pattern of figurative language the poem has established, readers can supply the other, unspoken half of the comparison: ". . . like a bomb."

Sometimes a single extended simile or extended metaphor is developed throughout a poem. The next poem develops an extended simile, comparing a poet to an acrobat.

LAWRENCE FERLINGHETTI (1919–   )

Constantly Risking Absurdity (1958)

<pre>
Constantly risking absurdity
                    and death
          whenever he performs
               above the heads
                         of his audience   5
the poet like an acrobat
              climbs on rime
               to a high wire of his own making
and balancing on eyebeams
               above a sea of faces   10
          paces his way
               to the other side of day
     performing entrechats
               and sleight-of-foot tricks
and other high theatrics   15
               and all without mistaking
          any thing
               for what it may not be

     For he's the super realist
                    who must perforce perceive   20
          taut truth
               before the taking of each stance or step
in his supposed advance
               toward that still higher perch
where Beauty stands and waits   25
               with gravity
                    to start her death-defying leap

     And he
          a little charleychaplin man
               who may or may not catch   30
her fair eternal form
               spreadeagled in the empty air
     of existence
</pre>

In his extended comparison of a poet and an acrobat, Ferlinghetti characterizes the poet as a kind of all-purpose circus performer, at once swinging recklessly on a trapeze and balancing carefully on a tightrope.

What the poem suggests is that the poet, like an acrobat, works hard at his craft but manages to make it all look easy. Something of an exhibitionist, the poet is innovative and creative, taking impossible chances yet also building on traditional skills in his quest for truth and beauty. Moreover, like an acrobat, the poet is balanced "on eyebeams / above a sea of faces," for he too depends on audience reaction to help him keep his performance focused. The poet may be "the super realist," but he also has plenty of playful tricks up his sleeve: "entrechats / and sleight-of-foot tricks / and other high theatrics," including puns ("above the heads / of his audience"), unexpected rhyme ("climbs on rime"), alliteration ("taut truth"), coinages ("a little charleychaplin man"), and all the other linguistic acrobatics available to poets. (Even the arrangement of the poem's lines on the page suggests the acrobatics it describes.) Like these tricks, the poem's central simile is a whimsical one, perhaps suggesting that Ferlinghetti is poking fun at poets who take their craft too seriously. In any case, the simile helps him to illustrate the acrobatic possibilities of language in a fresh and original manner.

The following poem develops an extended metaphor, personifying rooming houses as old women.

AUDRE LORDE (1934–1992)

Rooming houses are old women (1968)

Rooming houses are old women
rocking dark windows into their whens
waiting incomplete circles
rocking
rent office to stoop to   5
community bathrooms to gas rings and
under-bed boxes of once useful garbage
city issued with a twice monthly check
and the young men next door
with their loud midnight parties   10
and fishy rings left in the bathtub
no longer arouse them
from midnight to mealtime no stops inbetween
light breaking to pass through jumbled up windows
and who was it who married the widow that Buzzie's
son messed with?   15

To Welfare and insult form the slow shuffle
from dayswork to shopping bags
heavy with leftovers
Rooming houses
are old women waiting   20
searching

through darkening windows
the end or beginning of agony
old women seen through half-ajar doors
hoping   25
they are not waiting
but being
the entrance to somewhere
unknown and desired
but not new.   30

So closely does Lorde equate rooming houses and women in this poem that at times it is difficult to tell which of the two is actually the poem's subject. Despite the poem's assertion, rooming houses are *not* old women; however, they are *comparable to* the old women who live there because their walls enclose a lifetime of disappointments as well as the physical detritus of life. Like the old women, rooming houses are in decline, rocking away their remaining years. And, like the houses they inhabit, these women's boundaries are fixed — "rent office to stoop to / community bathrooms to gas rings" — and their hopes and expectations are few. They are surrounded by other people's loud parties, but their own lives have been reduced to a "slow shuffle" to nowhere, a hopeless, frightened — and perhaps pointless — "waiting / searching." Over time, the women and the places in which they live have become one. By using an unexpected comparison between two seemingly unrelated entities, the poem illuminates both the essence of the rooming houses and the essence of their elderly occupants.

ROBERT BURNS (1759–1796)

Oh, my love is like a red, red rose   (1796)

Oh, my love is like a red, red rose
 That's newly sprung in June;
My love is like the melody
 That's sweetly played in tune.

So fair art thou, my bonny lass,   5
 So deep in love am I;
And I will love thee still, my dear,
 Till a' the seas gang° dry.

Till a' the seas gang dry, my dear,
 And the rocks melt wi' the sun;   10
And I will love thee still, my dear,
 While the sands o' life shall run.

---

gang: Go.

> And fare thee weel, my only love!
>   And fare thee weel awhile!
> And I will come again, my love   15
>   Though it were ten thousand mile.

Reading and Reacting

1. Why does the speaker compare his love to a rose? What other simile is used in the poem? For what purpose is it used?

2. Why do you suppose Burns begins his poem with similes? Would moving them to the end change the poem's impact?

3. Where does the speaker seem to exaggerate the extent of his love? Why does he exaggerate? Do you think this exaggeration weakens the effectiveness of the poem? Explain.

Related Works: "Araby" (p. 252), "My mistress' eyes are nothing like the sun" (p. 565), "How Do I Love Thee?" (p. 566), "Baca Grande" (p. 648), "To His Coy Mistress" (p. 696)

JOHN UPDIKE (1932–   )

Ex-Basketball Player (1958)

Pearl Avenue runs past the high-school lot,
Bends with the trolley tracks, and stops, cut off
Before it has a chance to go two blocks,
At Colonel McComsky Plaza. Berth's Garage
Is on the corner facing west, and there,   5
Most days, you'll find Flick Webb, who helps Berth out.

Flick stands tall among the idiot pumps—
Five on a side, the old bubble-head style,
Their rubber elbows hanging loose and low.
One's nostrils are two S's, and his eyes   10
An E and O.° And one is squat, without
A head at all — more of a football type.

Once Flick played for the high-school team, the Wizards.
He was good: in fact, the best. In '46
He bucketed three hundred ninety points,   15
A county record still. The ball loved Flick.
I saw him rack up thirty-eight or forty
In one home game. His hands were like wild birds.

ESSO: Former name of Exxon.

He never learned a trade, he just sells gas,
Checks oil, and changes flats. Once in a while,   20
As a gag, he dribbles an inner tube,
But most of us remember anyway.
His hands are fine and nervous on the lug wrench.
It makes no difference to the lug wrench, though.

Off work, he hangs around Mae's luncheonette.   25
Grease-gray and kind of coiled, he plays pinball,
Smokes those thin cigars, nurses lemon phosphates.
Flick seldom says a word to Mae, just nods
Beyond her face toward bright applauding tiers
Of Necco Wafers, Nibs, and Juju Beads.   30

Reading and Reacting

1. Explain the use of personification in the second stanza and in the poem's last two lines. What two elements make up each figure of speech? In what sense are the two elements in each pair comparable?
2. What other figures of speech can you identify in the poem? How do these figures of speech work together to communicate the poem's central theme?
3. **JOURNAL ENTRY** Who do you think this poem's speaker might be? What is his attitude toward Flick Webb? Do you think Flick himself shares this assessment? Explain.

Related Works: "Miss Brill" (p. 121), "Autumn Begins in Martins Ferry, Ohio" (p. 642), "To an Athlete Dying Young" (p. 657), "Sadie and Maud" (p. 709), *Death of a Salesman* (p. 1178)

RANDALL JARRELL (1914–1965)

The Death of the Ball Turret Gunner° (1945)

From my mother's sleep I fell into the State
And I hunched in its belly till my wet fur froze.
Six miles from earth, loosed from its dream of life,
I woke to black flak and the nightmare fighters.
When I died they washed me out of the turret with a hose.   5

Reading and Reacting

1. Who is the speaker? To what does he compare himself in the poem's first two lines? What words establish this comparison?
2. Contrast the speaker's actual identity with the one he creates for himself in lines 1–2. What elements of his actual situation do you think lead him to characterize himself as he does in these lines?

Ball turret gunner: World War II machine gunner positioned upside-down in a plexiglass sphere in the belly of a fighter plane.

3. JOURNAL ENTRY Both this poem and "Dulce et Decorum Est" (p. 674) use figures of speech to describe the horrors of war. Which poem has a greater impact on you? How does the poem's figurative language contribute to this impact?

4. CRITICAL PERSPECTIVE In a 1974 article, Frances Ferguson criticizes "The Death of the Ball Turret Gunner," arguing that the poem "thoroughly manifests the lack of a middle between the gunner's birth and his death. . . . Because the poem presents a man who seems to have lived in order to die, we forget the fiction that he must have lived." However, in a 1978 explication, Patrick J. Horner writes that the "manipulation of time reveals the stunning brevity of the gunner's waking life and the State's total disregard for that phenomenon. . . . Because of the telescoping of time, [the poem] resonates with powerful feeling."

With which critic do you agree? Do you see the "lack of a middle" as a positive or negative quality of this poem?

Related Works: "The Things They Carried" (p. 271), "An Irish Airman Foresees His Death" (p. 570), "Dulce et Decorum Est" (p. 674)

MARGE PIERCY (1934–)

The Secretary Chant (1973)

My hips are a desk.
From my ears hang
chains of paper clips.
Rubber bands form my hair.
My breasts are wells of mimeograph ink.   5
My feet bear casters.
Buzz. Click.
My head is a badly organized file.
My head is a switchboard
where crossed lines crackle.   10
Press my fingers
and in my eyes appear
credit and debit.
Zing. Tinkle.
My navel is a reject button.   15
From my mouth issue canceled reams.
Swollen, heavy, rectangular
I am about to be delivered
of a baby
Xerox machine.   20
File me under W

because I wonce
was
a woman.

Reading and Reacting

1. Examine each of the poem's figures of speech. Do they all make reasonable comparisons, or are some far-fetched or hard to visualize? Explain the relationship between the secretary and each item with which she is compared.

2. JOURNAL ENTRY Using as many metaphors and similes as you can, write a "chant" about a job you have held.

3. CRITICAL PERSPECTIVE In a review of a recent collection of Piercy's poetry, feminist critic Sandra Gilbert notes instances of "a kind of bombast" (pompous language) and remarks, "As most poets realize, political verse is almost the hardest kind to write."

In what sense can "The Secretary Chant" be seen as "political verse"? Do you think Piercy successfully achieves her political purpose, or does she undercut it with "bombast"?

Related Works: "Battle Royal" (p. 175), "Girl" (p. 492), "Women" (p. 763), "Metaphors" (p. 903)

JOHN DONNE (1572–1631)

A Valediction: Forbidding Mourning (1611)

As virtuous men pass mildly away,
   And whisper to their souls to go,
Whilst some of their sad friends do say
   The breath goes now, and some say no:

So let us melt, and make no noise,   5
   No tear-floods, nor sigh-tempests move;
'Twere profanation of our joys
   To tell the laity° our love.

Moving of th' earth brings harms and fears;
   Men reckon what it did and meant;   10
But trepidation of the spheres,
   Though greater far, is innocent.

Dull sublunary lovers' love
   (Whose soul is sense) cannot admit
Absence, because it doth remove   15
   Those things which elemented it.

---

laity: Here, "common people."

But we, by a love so much refined
    That ourselves know not what it is,
Inter-assurèd of the mind,
    Care less, eyes, lips, and hands to miss.   20

Our two souls, therefore, which are one,
    Though I must go, endure not yet
A breach, but an expansion,
    Like gold to airy thinness beat.

If they be two, they are two so   25
    As stiff twin compasses° are two:
Thy soul, the fixed foot, makes no show
    To move, but doth, if th' other do.

And though it in the center sit,
    Yet when the other far doth roam,   30
It leans and harkens after it,
    And grows erect as that comes home.

Such wilt thou be to me, who must,
    Like th' other foot, obliquely run;
Thy firmness makes my circle just,°   35
    And makes me end where I begun.

Reading and Reacting

1. Beginning with line 25, the poem develops an extended metaphor, called a **conceit,** that compares the speaker and his loved one to "twin compasses" (line 26), attached yet separate. Why is the compass an especially apt metaphor? What qualities of the compass does the poet emphasize?

2. The poem uses other figures of speech to characterize both the lovers' union and their separation. To what other events does the speaker compare his separation from his loved one? To what other elements does he compare their attachment? Do you think these comparisons are effective?

3. JOURNAL ENTRY To what other object could Donne have compared his loved one and himself? Explain the logic of the extended metaphor you suggest.

4. CRITICAL PERSPECTIVE In *John Donne and the Metaphysical Poets* (1970), Judah Stampfer writes of this poem's "thin, dry texture, its stanzas of pinched music," noting that its form "has too clipped a brevity to qualify as a song" and that its "music wobbles on a dry, measured beat." Yet, he argues, "the poem comes choked with emotional power" because "the speaker reads as a naturally reticent man, leaving his beloved in uncertainty and deep trouble." Stampfer concludes, "Easy self-expression here would be self-indulgent, if

compasses: V-shaped instruments used for drawing circles.
just: Perfect.

not reprehensible. . . . For all his careful dignity, we feel a heart is breaking here."

Do you find such emotional power in this highly intellectual poem?

Related Works: "How Do I Love Thee?" (p. 566), "To My Dear and Loving Husband" (p. 695), *A Doll House* (p. 995)

E. B. WHITE (1899–1985)

Natural History (1929)

(A Letter to Katharine, from the King Edward Hotel, Toronto)

The spider, dropping down from twig,
Unwinds a thread of her devising:
A thin, premeditated rig
To use in rising.

And all the journey down through space,   5
In cool descent, and loyal-hearted,
She builds a ladder to the place
From which she started.

Thus I, gone forth, as spiders do,
In spider's web a truth discerning,   10
Attach one silken strand to you
For my returning.

Reading and Reacting

1. In what respects does the speaker see himself as similar to a spider? Is his comparison a metaphor or a simile? What comment does the poem's title make about this comparison?

2. This is a love poem, yet it also uses language — for example, "devising" (line 2) and "rig" (line 3) — that is more technical than romantic. What other examples of such language can you identify? What does such language reveal about the comparison between the speaker and a spider?

3. JOURNAL ENTRY In line 10, the speaker says that he sees "a truth" in the spider's web. What do you think this truth is? How does it inspire the speaker?

4. CRITICAL PERSPECTIVE E. B. White is better remembered as an essayist and children's author than as a poet. In a review of *One Man's Meat*, a collection of White's essays, R. L. Duffus comments on the ways in which a good essayist resembles a poet: "Like a poet, he is both attracted and distracted by minor phenomena. While others are remaking the world he is laying out little incidental things in patterns."

Do you think the speaker in "Natural History" shows the kind of attention to small things that Duffus is describing?

Related Works: "The Swing" (p. 139), "A Valediction: Forbidding Mourning" (p. 687), "For Once, Then, Something" (p. 769), "To see a World in a Grain of Sand" (p. 853), "A Noiseless Patient Spider" (p. 920)

MARTÍN ESPADA (1957–   )

My Father as a Guitar (2000)

The cardiologist prescribed
a new medication
and lectured my father
that he had to stop working.
And my father said: *I can't.*   5
The landlord won't let me.
The heart pills are dice
in my father's hand,
gambler who needs cash
by the first of the month.   10

On the night his mother died
in faraway Puerto Rico,
my father lurched upright in bed,
heart hammering
like the fist of a man at the door   15
with an eviction notice.
Minutes later,
the telephone sputtered
with news of the dead.

Sometimes I dream   20
my father is a guitar,
with a hole in his chest
where the music throbs
between my fingers.

Reading and Reacting

1. Where does this poem use simile? Metaphor? Personification?
2. What is the speaker's attitude toward his father? In what way does the poem's central metaphor (the comparison between the speaker's father and a guitar) help the speaker express his feelings? Why do you think the poet chose to use a metaphor rather than a simile?
3. **JOURNAL ENTRY** Why do you suppose the speaker dreams that his father is a guitar? How might his dreams be related to his father's dreams about his own mother?

4. CRITICAL PERSPECTIVE "My Father as a Guitar" is taken from the collection *A Mayan Astronomer in Hell's Kitchen."* In a review of one of Espada's earlier books, Leslie Ullman discusses how the poet brings his characters to life:

> The poems in this collection tell their stories and flesh out their characters deftly, without shrillness or rhetoric, and vividly enough to invite the reader into a shared sense of loss. Espada makes vanquished individuals and curtailed family histories present by offering us their remnants, their echoes, in such a way as to make us confront the ruined whole.

Does "My Father as a Guitar" present the title character in the way Ullman describes?

Related Words: "Aguantado" (p. 448), "Do not go gentle into that good night" (p. 559), "Nothing Gold Can Stay" (p. 673), "My Son, My Executioner" (p. 699)

HYPERBOLE AND UNDERSTATEMENT

Two additional kinds of figurative language, *hyperbole* and *understatement,* also give poets opportunities to suggest meaning beyond the literal level of language.

Hyperbole is intentional exaggeration — saying more than is actually meant. In the poem "Oh, My Love Is like a Red, Red Rose" (p. 683), when the speaker says that he will love his lady until all the seas go dry, he is using hyperbole. **Understatement** is the opposite — saying less than is meant. When the speaker in the poem "Fire and Ice" (p. 611), weighing two equally grim alternatives for the end of the world, says that "for destruction ice / Is also great / And would suffice," he is using understatement. In both cases, poets rely on their readers to understand that their words are not to be taken literally.

By using hyperbole and understatement, poets enhance the impact of their poems. For example, poets can use hyperbole to convey exaggerated anger or graphic images of horror — and to ridicule and satirize as well as to inflame and shock. With understatement, poets can convey the same kind of powerful emotions subtly, without artifice or embellishment, thereby leading readers to look more closely than they would otherwise do.

The emotionally charged poem that follows uses hyperbole to convey anger and bitterness that seem almost beyond the power of words.

SYLVIA PLATH (1932–1963)

Daddy (1965)

You do not do, you do not do
Any more, black shoe
In which I have lived like a foot
For thirty years, poor and white,
Barely daring to breathe or Achoo.   5

Daddy, I have had to kill you.
You died before I had time —

Marble-heavy, a bag full of God,
Ghastly statue with one grey toe
Big as a Frisco seal   10

And a head in the freakish Atlantic
Where it pours bean green over blue
In the waters off beautiful Nauset.
I used to pray to recover you.
Ach, du.°   15

In the German tongue, in the Polish town°
Scraped flat by the roller
Of wars, wars, wars.
But the name of the town is common.
My Polack friend   20

Says there are a dozen or two.
So I never could tell where you
Put your foot, your root,
I never could talk to you.
The tongue stuck in my jaw.   25

It stuck in a barb wire snare.
Ich, ich, ich, ich,°
I could hardly speak.
I thought every German was you.
And the language obscene   30

An engine, an engine
Chuffing me off like a Jew.
A Jew to Dachau, Auschwitz, Belsen.°
I began to talk like a Jew.
I think I may well be a Jew.   35

The snows of the Tyrol, the clear beer of Vienna
Are not very pure or true.
With my gypsy ancestress and my weird luck
And my Taroc pack and my Taroc pack
I may be a bit of a Jew.   40

I have always been scared of *you,*
With your Luftwaffe,° your gobbledygoo.
And your neat moustache

Ach, du: Ah, you. (German)

Polish town: Grabôw, where Plath's father was born.

ich: "I" (German)

Dachau, Auschwitz, Belsen: Nazi concentration camps.

Luftwaffe: The German air force.

And your Aryan eye, bright blue.
Panzer°-man, panzer-man, O You—   45

Not God but a swastika
So black no sky could squeak through.
Every woman adores a Fascist,
The boot in the face, the brute
Brute heart of a brute like you.   50

You stand at the blackboard, daddy,
In the picture I have of you,
A cleft in your chin instead of your foot
But no less a devil for that, no not
Any less the black man who   55

Bit my pretty red heart in two.
I was ten when they buried you.
At twenty I tried to die
And get back, back, back to you.
I thought even the bones would do.   60

But they pulled me out of the sack,
And they stuck me together with glue.
And then I knew what to do.
I made a model of you,
A man in black with a Meinkampf° look   65

And a love of the rack and the screw.
And I said I do, I do.
So daddy, I'm finally through.
The black telephone's off at the root,
The voices just can't worm through.   70

If I've killed one man, I've killed two—
The vampire who said he was you
And drank my blood for a year,
Seven years, if you want to know.
Daddy, you can lie back now.   75

There's a stake in your fat black heart
And the villagers never liked you.
They are dancing and stamping on you.
They always *knew* it was you.
Daddy, daddy, you bastard, I'm through.   80

In her anger and frustration, the speaker sees herself as a helpless victim — a foot
entrapped in a shoe, a Jew in a concentration camp — of her father's (and, later,

---

Panzer: Protected by armor. The Panzer division was the German armored division.

Meinkampf: Mein Kampf (My Struggle) is Adolf Hitler's autobiography.

her husband's) absolute tyranny. Thus, her hated father is characterized as a "black shoe," "a bag full of God," a "Ghastly statue," and, eventually, a Nazi, a torturer, the devil, a vampire. The poem "Daddy" is widely accepted by scholars as autobiographical, and the fact that Plath's own father was actually neither a Nazi nor a sadist (nor, obviously, the devil or a vampire) makes it clear that the figures of speech in the poem are wildly exaggerated. Even so, they may convey the poet's true feelings toward her father — and, perhaps, toward the patriarchal society in which she lived.

Plath uses hyperbole to communicate these emotions to readers who she knows cannot possibly feel the way she does. Her purpose, therefore, is not only to shock but also to enlighten, to persuade, and perhaps even to empower her readers. Throughout the poem, the inflammatory language is set in ironic opposition to the childish, affectionate term "Daddy"—most strikingly in the last line's choked out "Daddy, daddy, you bastard, I'm through." The result of the exaggerated rhetoric is a poem that is vivid and shocking. And, although some might believe that Plath's almost wild exaggeration undermines the poem's impact, others would argue that the powerful language is necessary to convey the extent of the speaker's rage.

Like "Daddy," the next poem presents a situation whose emotional impact is devastating. In this case, however, the poet does not use emotional language; instead, he uses understatement, presenting the events without embellishment.

DAVID HUDDLE (1942–   )

Holes Commence Falling (1979)

The lead & zinc company
owned the mineral rights
to the whole town anyway,
and after drilling holes
for 3 or 4 years,   5
they finally found the right
place and sunk a mine shaft.
We were proud
of all that digging,
even though nobody from   10
town got hired. They
were going to dig right
under New River and hook up
with the mine at Austinville.
Then people's wells   15
started drying up just like
somebody'd shut off a faucet,
and holes commenced falling,
big chunks of people's yards

would drop 5 or 6 feet,   20
houses would shift and crack.
Now and then the company'd
pay out a little money
in damages; they got a truck
to haul water and sell it   25
to the people whose wells
had dried up, but most
everybody agreed the
situation wasn't
serious.   30

Although "Holes Commence Falling" relates a tragic sequence of events, the tone of the poem is matter-of-fact, and the language is understated. The speaker could have overdramatized the events, using inflated rhetoric to denounce big business and to predict disastrous events for the future. At the very least, he could have colored the events with realistic emotions, assigning blame to the lead and zinc company with justifiable anger. Instead, the speaker is so restrained, so nonchalant, so passive that readers must supply the missing emotions themselves — realizing, for example, that when the speaker concludes "everybody agreed the / situation wasn't / serious," he means exactly the opposite.

Throughout the poem, unpleasant events are presented without comment or emotion. As it proceeds, the poem traces the high and low points in the town's fortunes, but for every hope ("We were proud / of all that digging"), there is a disappointment ("even though nobody from / town got hired"). The lead and zinc company offers some compensation for the damage it does, but never enough. The present tense verb of the poem's title indicates that the problems the town faces — wells drying up, yards dropping, houses shifting and cracking — are regular occurrences. Eventually, readers come to see that what is not expressed, what lurks just below the surface — anger, powerlessness, resentment, hopelessness — is the poem's real subject. The speaker's laconic speech and flat tone seem to suggest an attitude of resignation, but the obvious contrast between the understated tone and the seriousness of the problem creates a sense of irony that makes the speaker's real attitude toward the lead and zinc company clear.

ANNE BRADSTREET (1612?–1672)

To My Dear and Loving Husband (1678)

If ever two were one, then surely we.
If ever man were lov'd by wife, then thee;
If ever wife was happy in a man,
Compare with me ye women if you can.
I prize thy love more than whole Mines of gold,   5
Or all the riches that the East doth hold.
My love is such that Rivers cannot quench,

Nor ought but love from thee, give recompense.
Thy love is such I can no way repay,
The heavens reward thee manifold I pray.   10
Then while we live, in love let's so persever,
That when we live no more, we may live ever.

Reading and Reacting

1. Review the claims the poem's speaker makes about her love in lines 5–8.
Are such exaggerated declarations of love necessary, or would the rest of the
poem be sufficient to convey the extent of her devotion to her husband?

2. JOURNAL ENTRY Compare this poem's declarations of love to those of John
Donne's speaker in "A Valediction: Forbidding Mourning" (p. 687). Which
speaker do you believe is more convincing? Why?

Related Works: "A Rose for Emily" (p. 91), "The Shipfitter's Wife" (p. 610),
"Bright Star! Would I Were Steadfast as Thou Art" (p. 891)

ANDREW MARVELL (1621–1678)

To His Coy Mistress (1681)

Had we but world enough and time,
This coyness, lady, were no crime.
We would sit down and think which way
To walk, and pass our long love's day.
Thou by the Indian Ganges' side   5
Should'st rubies find; I by the tide
Of Humber° would complain. I would
Love you ten years before the Flood,
And you should, if you please, refuse
Till the conversion of the Jews.   10
My vegetable love should grow
Vaster than empires, and more slow.
An hundred years should go to praise
Thine eyes, and on thy forehead gaze,
Two hundred to adore each breast,   15
But thirty thousand to the rest.
An age at least to every part,
And the last age should show your heart.
For, lady, you deserve this state,
Nor would I love at lower rate.   20
    But at my back I always hear

Humber: An estuary on the east coast of England.

Time's wingèd chariot hurrying near,
And yonder all before us lie
Deserts of vast eternity.
Thy beauty shall no more be found,   25
Nor in thy marble vault shall sound
My echoing song; then worms shall try
That long preserved virginity,
And your quaint honor turn to dust,
And into ashes all my lust.   30
The grave's a fine and private place,
But none, I think, do there embrace.
   Now therefore, while the youthful hue
Sits on thy skin like morning glew°
And while thy willing soul transpires   35
At every pore with instant fires,
Now let us sport us while we may;
And now, like amorous birds of prey,
Rather at once our time devour
Than languish in his slow-chapped° power.   40
Let us roll all our strength and all
Our sweetness up into one ball
And tear our pleasures with rough strife
Thorough the iron gates of life.
Thus, though we cannot make our sun   45
Stand still, yet we will make him run.

Reading and Reacting

1. In this poem, Marvell's speaker sets out to convince a reluctant woman to become his lover. In order to make his case more persuasive, he uses hyperbole, exaggerating time periods, sizes, spaces, and the possible fate of the woman if she refuses him. Identify as many examples of hyperbole as you can.

2. The tone of "To His Coy Mistress" is more whimsical than serious. Given this tone, what do you see as the purpose of Marvell's use of hyperbole?

3. **JOURNAL ENTRY** Using contemporary prose, paraphrase the first four lines of the poem. Then, beginning with the word *But*, compose a few new sentences, continuing the argument Marvell's speaker makes.

4. **CRITICAL PERSPECTIVE:** Critic Rosalie L. Cole, in her book *My Ecchoing Song: Andrew Marvell's Poetry of Criticism*, notes how important an awareness of death is to Marvell's poetry in general and to the poem "To His Coy Mistress" in particular:

> The speaker speaks out of a desire that may be transitory; he promises nothing beyond an experience of shared joy. This poem plucks the day, laying immense

---

glew: Dew.

slow-chapped: Slowly crushing.

stress on the day itself, a point in all time; it promises nothing beyond that except the night of endless sleep to which all mortals must go down.

Do you think Cole is correct about the emphasis Marvell places on death?

Related Works: "The Littoral Zone" (p. 258), "Where Are You Going, Where Have You Been?" (p. 387), "The Passionate Shepherd to His Love" (p. 563), "To the Virgins, to Make Much of Time" (p. 620), *The Brute* (p. 1062)

ROBERT FROST (1874–1963)

"Out, Out —" (1916)

The buzz saw snarled and rattled in the yard
And made dust and dropped stove-length sticks of wood,
Sweet-scented stuff when the breeze drew across it.
And from there those that lifted eyes could count
Five mountain ranges one behind the other   5
Under the sunset far into Vermont.
And the saw snarled and rattled, snarled and rattled,
As it ran light, or had to bear a load.
And nothing happened: day was all but done.
Call it a day, I wish they might have said   10
To please the boy by giving him the half hour
That a boy counts so much when saved from work.
His sister stood beside them in her apron
To tell them "Supper." At the word, the saw,
As if to prove saws knew what supper meant,   15
Leaped out at the boy's hand, or seemed to leap —
He must have given the hand. However it was,
Neither refused the meeting. But the hand!
The boy's first outcry was a rueful laugh,
As he swung toward them holding up the hand   20
Half in appeal, but half as if to keep
The life from spilling. Then the boy saw all —
Since he was old enough to know, big boy
Doing a man's work, though a child at heart —
He saw all spoiled. "Don't let him cut my hand off —   25
The doctor, when he comes. Don't let him, sister!"
So. But the hand was gone already.
The doctor put him in the dark of ether.
He lay and puffed his lips out with his breath.
And then — the watcher at his pulse took fright.   30
No one believed. They listened at his heart.
Little — less — nothing! — and that ended it.
No more to build on there. And they, since they
Were not the one dead, turned to their affairs.

Reading and Reacting

1. The poem's title is an **allusion** to a passage in Shakespeare's *Macbeth* (5.5.23–28) that attacks the brevity and meaninglessness of life in very emotional terms:

> "Out, out brief candle!
> Life's but a walking shadow, a poor player,
> That struts and frets his hour upon the stage
> And then is heard no more. It is a tale
> Told by an idiot, full of sound and fury,
> Signifying nothing."

   What idea do you think Frost wants to convey through the title "Out, Out —"?

2. Explain why each of the following qualifies as understatement:

   "Neither refused the meeting." (line 18)
   "He saw all spoiled." (line 25)
   "— and that ended it." (line 32)
   "No more to build on there." (line 33)

   Can you identify any other examples of understatement in the poem?

3. **JOURNAL ENTRY** Do you think the poem's impact is strengthened or weakened by its understated tone? Why?

4. **CRITICAL PERSPECTIVE** In an essay on Frost in his 1985 book *Affirming Limits*, Robert Pack focuses on the single word "So" in line 27 of "Out, Out —":

   > For a moment, his narration is reduced to the impotent word "So," and in that minimal word all his restrained grief is held. . . . That "So" is the narrator's cry of bearing witness to a story that must be what it is in a scene he cannot enter. He cannot rescue or protect the boy. . . . In the poem's sense of human help-lessness in an indifferent universe, we are all "watchers," and what we see is death without redemption, "signifying nothing." So. So? So! How shall we read that enigmatic word?

   How do you read this "enigmatic word" in the poem?

Related Works: "Happy Endings" (p. 48), "Kansas" (p. 85), "The Lottery" (p. 303), "What Were They Like?" (p. 573), "Hope" (p. 525), "The Death of the Ball Turret Gunner" (p. 685).

DONALD HALL (1928–)

My Son, My Executioner (1955)

My son, my executioner,
   I take you in my arms,
Quiet and small and just astir,
   And whom my body warms.

Sweet death, small son, our instrument   5
   Of immortality,
Your cries and hungers document
   Our bodily decay.

> We twenty-five and twenty-two,
>   Who seemed to live forever,   10
> Observe enduring life in you
>   And start to die together.

Reading and Reacting

1. Because the speaker is a young man holding his newborn son in his arms, the equation in line 1 comes as a shock. What is Hall's purpose in opening with such a startling statement?

2. In what sense is the comparison between baby and executioner a valid one? Could you argue that, given the underlying similarities between the two, Hall is *not* using hyperbole? Explain.

Related Works: "The Swing" (p. 139), "Dog" (p. 522), "Doe Season" (p. 336), "That time of year thou mayst in me behold" (p. 551), "Morning Song" (p. 619), "Sailing to Byzantium" (p. 926)

MARGARET ATWOOD (1939–)

you fit into me (1971)

> you fit into me
> like a hook into an eye
>
> a fish hook
> an open eye

Reading and Reacting

1. What positive connotations does Atwood expect readers to associate with the phrase "you fit into me"? What does the speaker seem at first to mean by "like a hook into an eye" in line 2?

2. The speaker's shift to the brutal suggestions of lines 3 and 4 is calculated to shock readers. Does the use of hyperbole here have another purpose in the context of the poem? Explain.

Related Works: "Daddy" (p. 691), *A Doll House* (p. 995)

SHEROD SANTOS (1948–)

Spring Elegy (1998)

(For Frank Vincent, my student, who died of AIDS March 17, 1997)

> All morning in class that hollow feeling of how little
> we are left to say; and then, a few hours later,
> while I was downstairs checking the afternoon mail,
> someone came in and laid out neatly on my office desk

a black-and-white photograph, a sprig of forsythia,   5
and a tenth share of his ashes in a smoked glass vial.

Reading and Reacting

1. In such a short poem on such a serious subject, why does the speaker take
the time to mention minor, unimportant details — for example, that he was
in class and that he was checking his mail?

2. What does the speaker mean in lines 1–2 by "that hollow feeling of how
little / we are left to say . . ."?

3. Why are the words "and then" in line 2 important? What do they contribute
to the poem's structure? To the poem's meaning?

4. **JOURNAL ENTRY** In what sense do the three objects placed on the speaker's
desk sum up both the student's life and his death? What do you think the
speaker's reaction to these objects is?

Related Works: "Do not go gentle into that good night" (p. 559), "To an Athlete Dying Young" (p. 657), "In Memory of Donald A. Stauffer" (p. 746), "After
great pain, a formal feeling comes —" (p. 866), "Mid-Term Break" (p. 887)

METONYMY AND SYNECDOCHE

Metonymy and synecdoche are two related figures of speech. **Metonymy** is the
substitution of the name of one thing for the name of another thing that most
readers associate with the first — for example, using *hired gun* to mean "paid assassin" or *suits* to mean "business executives." A specific kind of metonymy, called
synecdoche, is the substitution of a part for the whole (for example, using *bread*—
as in "Give us this day our daily bread"— to mean "food") or the whole for a part
(for example, saying "You can take the boy out of Brooklyn, but you can't take
Brooklyn [meaning its distinctive traits] out of the boy"). With metonymy and
synecdoche, instead of describing something by saying it is like something else (as
in simile) or by equating it with something else (as in metaphor), writers can characterize an object or concept by using a term that evokes it. The following poem
illustrates the use of synecdoche.

RICHARD LOVELACE (1618–1658)

To Lucasta Going to the Wars (1649)

Tell me not, Sweet, I am unkind
   That from the nunnery
Of thy chaste breast and quiet mind,
   To war and arms I fly.

True, a new mistress now I chase,   5
   The first foe in the field;
And with a stronger faith embrace
   A sword, a horse, a shield.

> Yet this inconstancy is such
>   As you too shall adore;   10
> I could not love thee, Dear, so much,
>   Loved I not Honor more.

Here, Lovelace's use of synecdoche allows him to condense a number of complex ideas into a very few words. In line 3, when the speaker says that he is flying from his loved one's "chaste breast and quiet mind," he is using "breast" and "mind" to stand for all his loved one's physical and intellectual attributes. In line 8, when he says that he is embracing "A sword, a horse, a shield," he is using these three items to represent the trappings of war — and, thus, to represent war itself.

THOMAS LUX (1946–   )

Henry Clay's Mouth (2000)

Senator, statesman, speaker of the House,
exceptional dancer, slim,
graceful, ugly. Proclaimed, before most, slavery
an evil, broker
of elections (burned Jackson   5
for Adams), took a pistol ball in the thigh
in a duel, delayed, by forty years,
with his compromises, the Civil War,
gambler ("I have always
paid peculiar homage to the fickle goddess"),   10
boozehound, ladies' man — which leads us
to his mouth, which was huge,
a long slash across his face,
with which he ate and prodigiously drank,
with which he modulated his melodic voice,   15
with which he liked to kiss and kiss and kiss.
He said: "Kissing is like the presidency,
it is not to be sought and not to be *declined*."
A rival, one who wanted to kiss
whom he was kissing, said: "The ample   20
dimensions of his kissing apparatus
enabled him to *rest* one side of it
while the other was on active duty."
It was written, if women had the vote,
he would have been President,   25
kissing everyone in sight,
dancing on tables ("a grand Terpsichorean
performance . . ."), kissing everyone,

sometimes two at once, kissing everyone,
the almost-President   30
of our people.

Reading and Reacting

1. What functions does Henry Clay's mouth perform? How do these functions help to define his character?

2. Is this poem an example of metonymy or synecdoche? Explain.

3. If you were to divide this poem into stanzas, where would the breaks go? Would the addition of stanza breaks make the poem more or less effective?

4. JOURNAL ENTRY On balance, is this larger-than-life portrait of Henry Clay a positive or a negative one?

Related Works: "For the Union Dead" (p. 571), "The True-Blue American" (p. 780)

APOSTROPHE

With **apostrophe,** a poem's speaker addresses an absent person or thing — for example, a historical or literary figure or even an inanimate object or an abstract concept.

In the following poem, the speaker addresses Vincent Van Gogh.

SONIA SANCHEZ (1934–   )

On Passing thru Morgantown, Pa. (1984)

i saw you
vincent van
gogh perched
on those pennsylvania
cornfields communing   5
amid secret black
bird societies. yes.
i'm sure that was
you exploding your
fantastic delirium   10
while in the
distance
red indian
hills beckoned.

Expecting her readers to be aware that Van Gogh is a Dutch postimpressionist painter known for his mental instability as well as for his art, Sanchez is able to give added meaning to a phrase such as "fantastic delirium" as well as to the poem's visual images. The speaker sees Van Gogh perched like a black bird on a fence, and at the same time she also sees what he sees. Like Van Gogh, then, the speaker sees the Pennsylvania cornfields as both a natural landscape and an "exploding" work of art.

ALLEN GINSBERG (1926–1997)

A Supermarket in California (1956)

What thoughts I have of you tonight, Walt Whitman,° for I walked
down the sidestreets under the trees with a headache self-conscious
looking at the full moon.

In my hungry fatigue, and shopping for images, I went into
the neon fruit supermarket, dreaming of your enumerations!

5   What peaches and what penumbras! Whole families shopping at
night! Aisles full of husbands! Wives in the avocados, babies in the
tomatoes!—and you, Garcia Lorca,° what were you doing down
by the watermelons?

I saw you, Walt Whitman, childless, lonely old grubber, poking
among the meats in the refrigerator and eyeing the grocery boys.°

10   I heard you asking questions of each: Who killed the pork chops?
What price bananas? Are you my Angel?

I wandered in and out of the brilliant stacks of cans following you,
and followed in my imagination by the store detective.

15   We strode down the open corridors together in our solitary fancy
tasting artichokes, possessing every frozen delicacy, and never passing
the cashier.

Where are we going, Walt Whitman? The doors close in an hour.
Which way does your beard point tonight?

20   (I touch your book° and dream of our odyssey in the supermarket
and feel absurd.)

Will we walk all night through solitary streets? The trees add shade
to shade, lights out in the houses, we'll both be lonely.

Will we stroll dreaming of the lost America of love past blue
automobiles in driveways, home to our silent cottage?

25   Ah, dear father, graybeard, lonely old courage-teacher, what
America did you have when Charon° quit poling his ferry and you

---

Walt Whitman: American poet (1819–1892) whose poems frequently praise the commonplace and often contain lengthy "enumerations."

Federico García Lorca: Spanish poet and dramatist (1899–1936).

eyeing the grocery boys: Whitman's sexual orientation is the subject of much debate. Ginsberg is suggesting here that Whitman was homosexual.

your book: Leaves of Grass.

Charon: In Greek mythology, the ferryman who transported the dead over the river Styx to Hades.

got out on a smoking bank and stood watching the boat disappear on
the black waters of Lethe?°   30

Reading and Reacting

1. In this poem, Ginsberg's speaker wanders through the aisles of a supermarket, speaking to the nineteenth-century poet Walt Whitman and asking
   Whitman a series of questions. Why do you think the speaker addresses
   Whitman? What kind of answers do you think he is looking for?
2. In paragraph 2, the speaker says he is "shopping for images." What does he
   mean? Why does he look for these images in a supermarket? Does he find
   them?
3. Is this poem about supermarkets? About Walt Whitman? About poetry?
   About love? About America? What do you see as its primary theme? Why?
4. **JOURNAL ENTRY** Does the incongruous image of the respected poet "poking /
   among the meats" (par. 4) in the supermarket strengthen the poem's impact,
   or does it undercut any serious "message" the poem might have? Explain.
5. **CRITICAL PERSPECTIVE** The critic Leslie Fiedler discusses some of the ways in
   which Ginsberg's style resembles that of Walt Whitman:

   > Everything about Ginsberg is . . . blatantly Whitmanian: his meter is resolutely
   > anti-iambic, his line groupings stubbornly anti-stanzaic, his diction aggressively
   > colloquial and American, his voice public.

   Can you identify ways in which the poem is "American" and "public"?

Related Works: "A&P" (p. 115), "Chicago" (p. 751), "Out of the Cradle Endlessly Rocking" (p. 755), "Song of Myself" (p. 920)

| CHECKLIST | **WRITING ABOUT FIGURES OF SPEECH** |

✓ Are any figures of speech present in the poem? Identify each example
of simile, metaphor, personification, hyperbole, understatement,
metonymy, synecdoche, and apostrophe.

✓ What two elements are being compared in each use of simile,
metaphor, and personification? Is the comparison logical? What
characteristics are shared by the two items being compared?

✓ Does the poet use hyperbole? Why? For example, is it used to move
or to shock readers, or is its use intended to produce a humorous or
satirical effect? Would more neutral language be more effective?

✓ Does the poet use understatement? For what purpose? Would more
emotionally charged language be more effective?

continued on next page

Lethe: In Greek mythology, the river of forgetfulness (one of five rivers in Hades).

> ✓ In metonymy and synecdoche, what item is being substituted for another? What purpose does the substitution serve?
>
> ✓ If the poem includes apostrophe, whom or what does the speaker address? What is accomplished through the use of apostrophe?
>
> ✓ How do figures of speech contribute to the impact of the poem as a whole?

WRITING SUGGESTIONS: Figures of Speech

1. Various figures of speech are often used to describe characters in literary works. Choose two or three works that focus on a single character — for example, "Miss Brill" (p. 121), "The Fireman" (p. 369), "Ex-Basketball Player" (p. 684), or "Richard Cory" (p. 907) — and explain how figures of speech are used to characterize each work's central figure. If you like, you may write about works that focus on real (rather than fictional) people — for example, "Emmett Till" (p. 875) or "Medgar Evers" (p. 858).

2. Write an essay in which you discuss the different ways poets use figures of speech to examine the nature of poetry itself. What kinds of figures of speech do poets use to describe their craft? (You might begin by reading the three poems about poetry that open Chapter 14.)

3. Write a letter replying to the speaker in a poem by Marvell, Bradstreet, Donne, or Burns that appears in this chapter. Use figures of speech to express the depth of your love and the extent of your devotion.

4. Choose three or four poems that have a common subject — for example, love, nature, war, art, or mortality — and write a paper in which you draw some general conclusions about the relative effectiveness of the poems' use of figures of speech to examine that subject. (If you like, you may focus on the poems clustered under the heads "Poems about Love," "Poems about War," and "Poems about Parents" in Chapter 15.)

5. Select a poem and a short story that treat the same subject matter, and write a paper in which you compare their use of figures of speech.

6. **WEB ACTIVITY** The following Web site contains information about Marge Piercy:

http://archer-books.com/piercy/

Read a sampling of the poems, interviews, reviews, and essays available at this site. Using the information you gather at the site, write an essay about how the figures of speech in Piercy's poetry reflect her views about society's expectations of women and about how those expectations can shape and limit women's lives.

CHAPTER 21

SOUND

A primary pleasure in poetry is . . . the pleasure of saying something over
for its own sweet sake and because it sounds just right. For myself, . . .
the thing said over will not necessarily be A Great Thought, though great
thoughts are not necessarily excluded either; it may be as near as not
to meaningless, especially if one says it without much attention to its
context. For instance, a riddling song has the refrain: Sing ninety-nine
and ninety. I can remember being charmed enough with that to say it
over and over to myself for days, without ever having a single thought
about its meaning except for a certain bemused wonder about how
different it was from singing a hundred and eighty-nine. —**Howard Nemerov,**
"Poetry and Meaning"

I've never taught a poetry writing class that has not suffered my reiteration of
Duke Ellington's line: "It don't mean a thing if it ain't got that swing." How can
you describe the feeling of reading a Roethke poem, . . . when the rhythm is
so palpable it is as if the poem could be cupped in your hands? Those poems
move great distances in meaning between sentences and yet they hold together, largely because of the sound. The same thing is operating in a song
that makes you want to get up and dance. —**Michael Ryan,** *"On the Nature
of Poetry"*

The most obvious function of the line-break is rhythmic: it can record the
slight (but meaningful) hesitations between word and word that are
characteristic of the mind's dance among perceptions but which are not
noted by grammatical punctuation. Regular punctuation is a part of
regular sentence structure, that is, of the expression of completed
thoughts; and this expression is typical of prose, even though prose is
not at all times bound by its logic. But in poems one has the opportunity
not only, as in expressive prose, to depart from the syntactic norm, but . . .
to present the dynamics of perception *along with* its arrival at full
expression. The line-break is a form of punctuation *additional* to the
punctuation that forms part of the logic of completed thoughts.
—**Denise Levertov,** *"On the Function of Line"*

WALT WHITMAN (1819–1892)

Had I the Choice*

Had I the choice to tally greatest bards,
To limn° their portraits, stately, beautiful, and emulate at will,
Homer with all his wars and warriors — Hector, Achilles, Ajax,
Or Shakespeare's woe-entangled Hamlet, Lear, Othello — Tennyson's
    fair ladies,
5   Meter or wit the best, or choice conceit to wield in perfect rhyme,
delight of singers;
These, these, O sea, all these I'd gladly barter,
Would you the undulation of one wave, its trick to me transfer,
Or breathe one breath of yours upon my verse,
And leave its odor there.

RHYTHM

Rhythm— the regular recurrence of sounds —is at the heart of all natural phenomena: the beating of a heart, the lapping of waves against the shore, the croaking of frogs on a summer's night, the whispering of wheat swaying in the wind. In fact, even mechanical phenomena, such as the movement of rush-hour traffic through a city's streets, have a kind of rhythm. Poetry, which explores these phenomena, often tries to reflect the same rhythms. Walt Whitman expresses this idea in "Had I the Choice" when he says that he would gladly trade the "perfect rhyme" of Shakespeare for the ability to reproduce "the undulation of one wave" in his verse.

Effective public speakers frequently repeat key words and phrases to create rhythm. In his speech "I Have a Dream," for example, Martin Luther King, Jr., repeats the phrase "I have a dream" to create a cadence that ties the central section of the speech together:

> I say to you today, my friends, even though we face the difficulties of today
> and tomorrow, *I still have a dream*. It is a dream deeply rooted in the Ameri-
> can dream. *I have a dream* that one day this nation will rise up and live out
> the true meaning of its creed: "We hold these truths to be self-evident, that
> all men are created equal." *I have a dream* that one day, on the red hills of
> Georgia, sons of former slaves and the sons of former slave owners will be
> able to sit down together at the table of brotherhood. *I have a dream* that
> one day even the state of Mississippi, a state sweltering with the heat of in-
> justice, sweltering with the heat of oppression, will be transformed into an oa-
> sis of freedom and justice. *I have a dream* that my four little children will one

---

*Publication date is not available.

limn: To describe, depict.

day live in a nation where they will not be judged by the color of their skin, but by the content of their character.

Poets too create rhythm by using repeated words and phrases, as Gwendolyn Brooks does in the poem that follows.

GWENDOLYN BROOKS (1917–2000)

Sadie and Maud (1945)

Maud went to college.
Sadie stayed at home.
Sadie scraped life
With a fine-tooth comb.

She didn't leave a tangle in.   5
Her comb found every strand.
Sadie was one of the livingest chits
In all the land.

Sadie bore two babies
Under her maiden name.   10
Maud and Ma and Papa
Nearly died of shame.

When Sadie said her last so-long
Her girls struck out from home.
(Sadie had left as heritage   15
Her fine-tooth comb.)

Maud, who went to college,
Is a thin brown mouse.
She is living all alone
In this old house.   20

Much of the force of this poem comes from its balanced structure and regular rhyme and meter, underscored by the repeated words "Sadie" and "Maud," which shift the focus from one subject to the other and back again ("Maud went to college / Sadie stayed home"). The poem's singsong rhythm recalls the rhymes children recite when jumping rope. This evocation of carefree childhood ironically contrasts with the adult realities that both Sadie and Maud face as they grow up: Sadie stays at home and has two children out of wedlock; Maud goes to college and ends up "a thin brown mouse." The speaker implies that the alternatives Sadie and Maud represent are both undesirable. Although Sadie "scraped life / with a fine-tooth comb," she dies young and leaves nothing to her girls but her desire to experience life. Maud, who graduated from college, shuts out life and cuts herself off from her roots.

Just as the repetition of words and phrases can create rhythm, so can the arrangement of words in a poem — and even the appearance of words on a printed page. How a poem looks is especially important in **open form** poetry (see p. 753), which dispenses with traditional patterns of versification. In the following excerpt from a poem by E. E. Cummings, for example, an unusual arrangement of words forces readers to slow down and then to speed up, creating a rhythm that emphasizes a key phrase — "The / lily":

> the moon is hiding
> in her hair.
> The
> lily
> of heaven
> full of all dreams,
> draws down.

Poetic rhythm — the repetition of stresses and pauses — is an essential element in poetry. Rhythm helps to establish a poem's mood, and, in combination with other poetic elements, it conveys the poet's emphasis and helps communicate the poem's meaning.

METER

Although rhythm can be affected by the regular repetition of words and phrases or by the arrangement of words into lines, poetic rhythm is largely created by **meter,** the recurrence of regular units of stressed and unstressed syllables. A **stress** (or accent) occurs when one syllable is emphasized more than another, unstressed, syllable: *fór • ceps, bá • sic, il • lú • sion, ma • lár • i • a.* In a poem, even one-syllable words can be stressed to create a particular effect. For example, in Elizabeth Barrett Browning's line "How do I love thee? Let me count the ways," the metrical pattern that places stress on "love" creates one meaning; stressing "I" would create another.

Scansion is the analyzing of patterns of stressed and unstressed syllables within a line. The most common method of poetic notation indicates stressed syllables with a | and unstressed syllables with a ◡. Although scanning lines gives readers the "beat" of the poem, scansion only approximates the sound of spoken language, which contains an infinite variety of stresses. By providing a graphic representation of the stressed and unstressed syllables of a poem, scansion aids understanding but is no substitute for reading the poem aloud and experimenting with various patterns of emphasis.

The basic unit of meter is a **foot** — a group of syllables with a fixed pattern of stressed and unstressed syllables. The following chart illustrates the most common types of metrical feet in English and American verse.

Foot	**Stress Pattern**	**Example**
Iamb	◡ |	They pace | in sleek | chi val | ric cer | tain ty (Adrienne Rich)

Trochee	ǀ ◡	Thou, when ǀ thou re ǀ turn'st, wilt ǀ tell me. (John Donne)
Anapest	◡ ◡ ǀ	With a hey, ǀ and a ho, ǀ and a hey ǀ nonino (William Shakespeare)
Dactyl	ǀ ◡ ◡	Constantly ǀ risking ab ǀ surdity (Lawrence Ferlinghetti)

Iambic and *anapestic* meters are called **rising meters** because they progress from unstressed to stressed syllables. *Trochaic* and *dactylic* meters are called **falling meters** because they progress from stressed to unstressed syllables.

The following types of metrical feet, less common than those listed above, are used to add emphasis or to provide variety rather than to create the dominant meter of a poem.

| Spondee | ǀ ǀ | Pomp, pride ǀ and circumstance of glorious war! (William Shakespeare) |
| Pyrrhic | ◡ ◡ | A horse! a horse! My king ǀ dom for ǀ a horse! (William Shakespeare) |

A metric line of poetry is measured by the number of feet it contains.

monometer one foot

dimeter two feet

trimeter three feet

tetrameter four feet

pentameter five feet

hexameter six feet

heptameter seven feet

octameter eight feet

The name for a metrical pattern of a line of verse identifies the name of the foot used and the number of feet the line contains. For example, the most common foot in English poetry is the **iamb,** most often occurring in lines of three or five feet.

Eight hun ǀ dred of ǀ the brave	Iambic trimeter
(William Cowper)	
O, how ǀ much more ǀ doth	Iambic pentameter
beau ǀ ty beau ǀ teous seem	
(William Shakespeare)	

Because **iambic pentameter** is so well suited to the rhythms of English speech, writers frequently use it in plays and poems. Shakespeare's plays, for example, are written in unrhymed lines of iambic pentameter called **blank verse** (see p. 736).

Many other metrical combinations are also possible; a few are illustrated here:

Like a ǀ high-born ǀ maiden	Trochaic trimeter
(Percy Bysshe Shelley)	
The As sy ǀ rian came down ǀ	Anapestic tetrameter
like the wolf ǀ on the fold	
(Lord Byron)	
Maid en most ǀ beau ti ful ǀ	Dactylic hexameter
mother most ǀ boun ti ful, ǀ la	
dy of ǀ lands, (A. C. Swinburne)	
The yel ǀ low fog ǀ that rubs ǀ its	Iambic heptameter
back ǀ upon ǀ the win ǀ	
dow-panes (T. S. Eliot)	

Scansion can be an extremely technical process, and when readers become bogged down with anapests and dactyls, they can easily forget that poetic meter is not an end in itself. Meter should be appropriate for the ideas expressed by the poem, and it should help to create a suitable tone. A light, skipping rhythm, for example, would be inappropriate for an **elegy,** and a slow, heavy rhythm would surely be out of place in an **epigram** or a limerick. The following lines of a poem by Samuel Taylor Coleridge illustrate the uses of different types of metrical feet:

> Trochee trips from long to short;
> From long to long in solemn sort
> Slow Spondee stalks; strong foot! yet ill able
> Ever to come up with Dactyl trisyllable.

Iambics march from short to long—
With a leap and a bound the swift Anapests throng;
One syllable long, with one short at each side,
Amphibrachys hastes with a stately stride—
First and last being long, middle short, Amphimacer
Strikes his thundering hoofs like a proud high-bred Racer.

A poet may use one kind of meter — iambic meter, for example — throughout a poem, but may vary line length to relieve monotony or to accommodate the demands of meaning or emphasis. In the following poem, the poet uses iambic lines of different lengths.

EMILY DICKINSON (1830–1886)

I like to see it lap the Miles— (1891)

I like to see it lap the Miles—
And lick the Valleys up—
And stop to feed itself at Tanks—
And then — prodigious step

Around a Pile of Mountains—   5
And supercilious peer
In Shanties — by the sides of Roads—
And then a Quarry pare

To fit its Ribs
And crawl between   10
Complaining all the while
In horrid — hooting stanza—
Then chase itself down Hill—

And neigh like Boanerges°—
Then — punctual as a Star   15
Stop — docile and omnipotent
At its own stable door—

This poem is a single sentence that, except for some short pauses, stretches unbroken from beginning to end. Iambic lines of varying lengths actually suggest the movements of the train that the poet describes. Lines of iambic tetrameter, such as the first, give readers a sense of the train's steady, rhythmic movement across a flat landscape, and shorter lines ("To fit its Ribs / And crawl between") suggest the train's slowing motion. Beginning with two iambic dimeter lines and progressing

---

Boanerges: A vociferous preacher and orator. Also, the name, meaning "son of thunder," Jesus gave to apostles John and James because of their fiery zeal.

to iambic trimeter lines, the third stanza increases in speed just like the train that is racing downhill "In horrid — hooting stanza —."

When a poet uses more than one type of metrical foot, any variation in a metrical pattern — the substitution of a trochee for an iamb, for instance — immediately calls attention to itself. Poets are aware of this fact and use it to their advantage. For example, in line 16 of "I like to see it lap the Miles," the poet departs from iambic meter by placing unexpected stress on the first word, *stop*. By emphasizing this word, the poet brings the flow of the poem to an abrupt halt, suggesting the jolt riders experience when a train comes to a stop. In the following segment from "The Rime of the Ancient Mariner," Samuel Taylor Coleridge also departs from his poem's dominant meter:

> The ship | was cheered, | the har | bor cleared,
> Merri | ly did | we drop
> Below | the kirk, | below | the hill,
> Below | the light | house top.

Although these lines are arranged in iambic tetrameter, the poet uses a trochee in the second line, breaking the meter in order to accommodate the natural pronunciation of "merrily" as well as to place stress on the word.

Another way of varying the meter is to introduce a pause known as a **caesura** — a Latin word meaning "a cutting" — within a line. When scanning a poem, you indicate a caesura with two parallel lines: ‖. Unless a line of poetry is extremely short, it probably will contain a caesura.

A caesura occurs after a punctuation mark or at a natural break in phrasing:

> How do I love thee? ‖ Let me count the ways.
> ELIZABETH BARRETT BROWNING

> Two loves I have ‖ of comfort and despair.
> WILLIAM SHAKESPEARE

> High on a throne of royal state, ‖ which far
> Outshone the wealth of Ormus ‖ and of Ind
> JOHN MILTON

Sometimes, more than one caesura occurs in a single line:

> 'Tis good. ‖ Go to the gate. ‖ Somebody knocks.
> WILLIAM SHAKESPEARE

Although the end of a line may mark the end of a metrical unit, it does not always coincide with the end of a sentence. Poets may choose to indicate a pause at this point, or they may continue without a break to the next line. Lines that have distinct pauses at the end — usually signaled by punctuation — are called **end-stopped lines.** Lines that do not end with strong pauses are called **run-on lines.** (Sometimes the term **enjambment** is used to describe run-on lines.) End-stopped lines can seem formal, or even forced, because their length is rigidly dictated by the poem's meter, rhythm, and rhyme scheme. In the following excerpt from John Keats's "La Belle Dame sans Merci" (p. 889), for example, rhythm, meter, and rhyme dictate the pauses that occur at the ends of the lines:

> O, what can ail thee, knight-at-arms,
>   Alone and palely loitering?
> The sedge has wither'd from the lake,
>   And no birds sing.

In contrast to end-stopped lines, run-on lines seem more natural. Because their ending points are determined by the rhythms of speech and by the meaning and emphasis the poet wishes to convey rather than by meter and rhyme, run-on lines are suited to the open form of much modern poetry. In the following lines from the 1967 poem "We Have Come Home," by the poet Lenrie Peters, run-on lines give readers the sense of spoken language:

> We have come home
> From the bloodless war
> With sunken hearts
> Our boots full of pride—
> From the true massacre of the soul
> When we have asked
> 'What does it cost
> To be loved and left alone?'

Rather than relying exclusively on end-stopped or run-on lines, poets often use a combination of the two to produce the effects they want. The following lines from "Pot Roast" by Mark Strand, for example, juxtapose end-stopped and run-on lines:

> I gaze upon the roast,
> that is sliced and laid out
> on my plate
> and over it
> I spoon the juices
> of carrot and onion.
> And for once I do not regret
> the passage of time.

ADRIENNE RICH (1929–   )

Aunt Jennifer's Tigers (1951)

Aunt Jennifer's tigers prance across a screen,
Bright topaz denizens of a world of green.
They do not fear the men beneath the tree;
They pace in sleek chivalric certainty.

Aunt Jennifer's fingers fluttering through her wool   5
Find even the ivory needle hard to pull.

The massive weight of Uncle's wedding band
Sits heavily upon Aunt Jennifer's hand.

When Aunt is dead, her terrified hands will lie
Still ringed with ordeals she was mastered by.   10
The tigers in the panel that she made
Will go on prancing, proud and unafraid.

Reading and Reacting

1. What is the dominant metrical pattern of the poem? In what way does the meter enhance the contrast the poem develops?
2. The lines in the first stanza are end-stopped, and those in the second and third stanzas combine end-stopped and run-on lines. What does the poet achieve by varying the rhythm?
3. What ideas do the caesuras in the first and fourth lines of the last stanza emphasize?
4. **JOURNAL ENTRY** What is the speaker's opinion of Aunt Jennifer's marriage? Do you think she is commenting on this particular marriage or on marriage in general?
5. **CRITICAL PERSPECTIVE** In her 1986 study of Rich's work, *The Aesthetics of Power*, Claire Keyes writes of this poem that although it is formally beautiful, almost perfect, its voice creates problems:

   [T]he tone seldom approaches intimacy, the speaker seeming fairly detached from the fate of Aunt Jennifer. . . . The dominant voice of the poem asserts the traditional theme that art outlives the person who produces it. . . . The speaker is almost callous in her disregard for Aunt's death. . . . Who cares that Aunt Jennifer dies? The speaker does not seem to; she gets caught up in those gorgeous tigers. . . . Here lies the dominant voice: Aunt is not compelling; her creation is.

   Do you agree with Keyes's interpretation of the poem?

Related Works: "Miss Brill" (p. 121), "Everyday Use" (p. 310), "Rooming houses are old women" (p. 682), "Ethics" (p. 901)

ETHERIDGE KNIGHT (1931–1991)

For Malcolm,° a Year After (1986)

Compose for Red° a proper verse;
Adhere to foot and strict iamb;
Control the burst of angry words
Or they might boil and break the dam.

Malcolm: Malcolm X (1925–1965).

Red: Malcolm X's nickname when he was a young man.

Or they might boil and overflow   5
And drench me, drown me, drive me mad.
So swear no oath, so shed no tear,
And sing no song blue Baptist sad.
Evoke no image, stir no flame,
And spin no yarn across the air.   10
Make empty anglo tea lace words—
Make them dead white and dry bone bare.

Compose a verse for Malcolm man,
And make it rime and make it prim.
The verse will die — as all men do—   15
But not the memory of him!
Death might come singing sweet like C,
Or knocking like the old folk say,
The moon and stars may pass away,
But not the anger of that day.   20

Reading and Reacting

1. Why do you think Knight chooses to write a "proper verse" in "strict iamb"? Do you think this meter is an appropriate choice for his subject?

2. What sounds and words are repeated in this poem? How does this repetition enhance the poem's rhythm?

3. Where in the poem does Knight use caesuras? Why does he use pause in each instance?

4. **JOURNAL ENTRY** How would you describe the mood of the speaker? Is the poem's meter consistent with his mood or in conflict with it? Explain.

Related Works: "Battle Royal" (p. 175), "To an Athlete Dying Young" (p. 657), "In Memory of Donald A. Stauffer" (p. 746), "Medgar Evers" (p. 858), "If We Must Die" (p. 897)

ALLITERATION AND ASSONANCE

Just as poetry depends on rhythm, it also depends on the sounds of individual words. An effect pleasing to the ear, such as "Did he who made the Lamb make thee?" from William Blake's "The Tyger" (p. 853), is called **euphony.** A jarring or discordant effect, such as "The vorpal blade went snicker-snack!" from Lewis Carroll's "Jabberwocky" (p. 729), is called **cacophony.**

One of the earliest, and perhaps the most primitive, methods of enhancing sound is **onomatopoeia,** which occurs when the sound of a word echoes its meaning, as it does in common words such as *bang, crash,* and *hiss.* Poets make broad application of this technique by using combinations of words that suggest a correspondence between sound and meaning, as Edgar Allan Poe does in these lines from his poem "The Bells:"

Yet the ear, it fully knows,
        By the twanging

> And the clanging,
> How the danger ebbs and flows;
> Yet the ear distinctly tells,
> In the jangling
> And the wrangling
> How the danger sinks and swells
> By the sinking or the swelling in the anger of the bells—
> Of the bells,—
> Of the bells, bells, bells, bells. . . .

Poe's primary objective in this poem is to re-create the sound of ringing bells. Although he succeeds, the poem (113 lines long in its entirety) is extremely tedious. A more subtle use of onomatopoetic words appears in the following passage from *An Essay on Criticism* by Alexander Pope:

> Soft is the strain when Zephyr gently blows,
> And the smooth stream in smoother numbers flows;
> But when the loud surges lash the sounding shore,
> The hoarse, rough verse should like the torrent roar:
> When Ajax strives some rock's vast weight to throw,
> The line too Labors, and the words move slow.

After earlier admonishing readers that sound must echo sense, Pope uses onomatopoetic words such as *lash* and *roar* to convey the fury of the sea, and he uses repeated consonants to echo the sounds these words suggest. Notice, for example, how the *s* and *m* sounds suggest the gently blowing Zephyr and the flowing of the smooth stream and how the series of *r* sounds echoes the torrent's roar.

Alliteration— the repetition of consonant sounds in consecutive or neighboring words, usually at the beginning of words — is another device used to enhance sound in a poem. Both Poe ("s̲inks and s̲wells") and Pope ("s̲mooth s̲tream") make use of alliteration in the preceding excerpts, and so does Alfred, Lord Tennyson in the next poem.

ALFRED, LORD TENNYSON (1809–1892)

The Eagle (1851)

> He clasps the crag with crooked hands;
> Close to the sun in lonely lands,
> Ringed with the azure world, he stands.
>
> The wrinkled sea beneath him crawls:
> He watches from his mountain walls,   5
> And like a thunderbolt he falls.

Throughout the poem, *c*, *l*, and *w* sounds occur repeatedly. The poem is drawn together by the recurrence of these sounds and, as a result, flows smoothly from beginning to end.

The following poem also uses alliteration to create special aural effects.

N. SCOTT MOMADAY (1934–   )

Comparatives (1976)

Sunlit sea,
the drift of fronds,
and banners
of bobbing boats—
the seaside   5
upon the planks,
the coil and
crescent of flesh
extending
just into death.   10

Even so,
in the distant,
inland sea,
a shadow runs,
radiant,   15
rude in the rock:
fossil fish,
fissure of bone
forever.
It is perhaps   20
the same thing,
an agony
twice perceived.

It is most like
wind on waves—   25
mere commotion,
mute and mean,
perceptible—
that is all.

Throughout the poem, Momaday uses alliteration to create a pleasing effect and to link certain words and ideas. Each stanza has its own alliterative pattern: the first stanza contains repeated *s* and *b* sounds, the second stanza contains repeated *r* and *f* sounds, and the third stanza contains repeated *w* and *m* sounds. Not only does this use of alliteration create a pleasing effect, but also it reinforces the development of the poem's theme from stanza to stanza.

 Assonance—the repetition of the same or similar vowel sounds, especially in stressed syllables—can also enrich a poem. When used solely to produce aural effects, assonance can be distracting. Consider, for example, the clumsiness of the repeated vowel sounds in Tennyson's "Many a morning on the moorland did we hear the copses ring. . . ." When used more subtly, however, assonance can enhance a poem's effectiveness.

Assonance can also unify an entire poem. In the following poem, assonance emphasizes the thematic connections among words and thus unifies the poem's ideas.

ROBERT HERRICK (1591–1674)

Delight in Disorder (1648)

A sweet disorder in the dress
Kindles in clothes a wantonness.
A lawn° about the shoulders thrown
Into a fine distractión;
An erring lace, which here and there   5
Enthralls the crimson stomacher;°
A cuff neglectful, and thereby
Ribbons to flow confusedly;
A winning wave, deserving note,
In the tempestuous petticoat;   10
A careless shoestring, in whose tie
I see a wild civility;
Do more bewitch me than when art
Is too precise in every part.

Repeated vowel sounds extend throughout this poem — for instance, "shoulders" and "thrown" in line 3; and "tie," "wild," and "precise" in lines 11, 12, and 14. Using alliteration as well as assonance, Herrick subtly links certain words — "tempestuous petticoat," for example. By connecting these words, he calls attention to the pattern of imagery that helps to convey the poem's theme.

RHYME

In addition to alliteration and assonance, poets create sound patterns with **rhyme** — the use of matching sounds in two or more words: "tight" and "might"; "born" and "horn"; "sleep" and "deep." For a rhyme to be **perfect**, final vowel and consonant sounds must be the same, as they are in each of the preceding examples. **Imperfect rhyme** (also called *near rhyme*, *slant rhyme*, *approximate rhyme*, or *consonance*) occurs when the final consonant sounds in two words are the same but vowel sounds are different — "learn / barn" or "pads / lids," for example. William Stafford uses imperfect rhyme in "Traveling through the Dark" (p. 916) when he rhymes "road" with "dead." Finally, **eye rhyme** occurs when two words look as if they should rhyme but do not — for example, "watch" and "catch."

---

lawn: A shawl made of fine fabric.

stomacher: A heavily embroidered garment worn by females over the chest and stomach.

Rhyme can also be classified according to the position of the rhyming syllables in a line of verse. The most common type of rhyme is **end rhyme,** which occurs at the end of a line:

> Tyger! Tyger! burning <u>bright</u>
> In the forests of the <u>night</u>
> > WILLIAM BLAKE, "The Tyger"

Internal rhyme occurs within a line:

> The Sun came up upon the left,
> Out of the <u>sea</u> came <u>he</u>!
> And he shone <u>bright</u> and on the <u>right</u>
> Went down into the sea.
> > SAMUEL TAYLOR COLERIDGE, "The Rime of the Ancient Mariner"

Beginning rhyme occurs at the beginning of a line:

> Red River, red river,
> <u>Slow</u> flow heat is silence
> <u>No</u> will is still as a river
> Still. Will heat move
> > T. S. ELIOT, "Virginia"

Rhyme can also be classified according to the number of corresponding syllables. **Masculine rhyme** (also called **rising rhyme**) occurs when single syllables correspond ("can" / "ran"; "descend" / "contend"). **Feminine rhyme** (also called **double rhyme** or **falling rhyme**) occurs when two syllables, a stressed one followed by an unstressed one, correspond ("ocean" / "motion"; "leaping" / "sleeping"). **Triple rhyme** occurs when three syllables correspond. Less common than the other two, triple rhyme is often used for humorous or satiric purposes, as in the following lines from the long poem *Don Juan* by Lord Byron:

> Sagest of women, even of widows, she
> > Resolved that Juan should be quite a <u>paragon</u>,
> And worthy of the noblest pedigree:
> > (His sire of Castile, his dam from <u>Aragon</u>).

In some cases — for example, when it is overused or used in unexpected places — rhyme can create unusual and even comic effects. In the following poem, humor is created by the incongruous connections established by rhymes such as "priest" / "beast" and "pajama" / "lllama."

OGDEN NASH (1902–1971)

The Lama (1931)

> The one-l lama
> He's a priest.
> The two-l llama,

He's a beast.
And I will bet   5
A silk pajama
There isn't any
Three-l lllama.

The conventional way to describe a poem's rhyme scheme is to chart rhyming sounds that appear at the ends of lines. The sound that ends the first line is designated *a*, and all subsequent lines that end in that sound are also labeled *a*. The next sound to appear at the end of a line is designated *b*, and all other lines whose last sounds rhyme with it are also designated *b*— and so on through the alphabet. The lines of the poem that follows are labeled in this manner.

RICHARD WILBUR (1921–   )

A Sketch (1975)

Into the lower right	*a*
Square of the window frame	*b*
There came	*b*
with scalloped flight	*a*
A goldfinch, lit upon	*c* 5
The dead branch of a pine,	*d*
Shining,	*d*
and then was gone,	*c*
Tossed in a double arc	*e*
Upward into the thatched	*f* 10
And cross-hatched	*f*
pine-needle dark.	*e*
Briefly, as fresh drafts stirred	*g*
The tree, he dulled and gleamed	*h*
And seemed	*h* 15
more coal than bird,	*g*
Then, dodging down, returned	*i*
In a new light, his perch	*j*
A birch —	*j*
twig, where he burned	*i* 20
In the sun's broadside ray,	*k*
Some seed pinched in his bill.	*l*
Yet still	*l*
he did not stay,	*k*
But into a leaf-choken pane,	*m* 25
Changeful as even in heaven,	*n*
Even	*n*
in Saturn's reign,	*m*

Tunneled away and hid.   *o*
And then? But I cannot well   *p*   30
Tell   *p*
   you all that he did.   *o*

It was like glancing at rough   *q*
Sketches tacked on a wall,   *r*
And all   *r*   35
   so less than enough   *q*

Of gold on beaten wing,   *s*
I could not choose that one   *t*
Be done   *t*
   as the finished thing.   *s*   40

Although the rhyme scheme of this poem (*abba, cddc,* and so on) is regular, it is hardly noticeable until it is charted. Despite its subtlety, however, the rhyme scheme is not unimportant. In fact, it reinforces the poem's meaning and binds lines into structural units, connecting the first and fourth as well as the second and third lines of each stanza. In stanza 1, "right" and "flight" draw lines 1 and 4 of the stanza together, bracketing "fame" and "came" in lines 2 and 3. The pattern begins again with the next stanza and continues through the rest of the poem. Like the elusive goldfinch the poet describes, the rhymes are difficult to follow with the eye. In this sense, the rhyme reflects the central theme of the poem: the difficulty of capturing in words a reality that, like the goldfinch, is forever shifting.

Naturally, rhyme does not have to be subtle to enrich a poem. An obvious rhyme scheme can communicate meaning by connecting ideas that are not normally linked. Notice how Alexander Pope uses this technique in the following excerpt from *An Essay on Man:*

   Honour and shame from no condition rise;
Act well your part, there all the honour lies.
Fortune in men has some small diff'rence made,
One flaunts in rags, one flutters in brocade;
The cobbler aproned, and the parson gowned,
The friar hooded, and the monarch crowned.
"What differ more (you cry) than crown and cowl?"
I'll tell you, friend; a wise man and a fool.

You'll find, if once the monarch acts the monk,
Or, cobbler-like, the parson will be drunk,
Worth makes the man, and want of it, the fellow;
The rest is all but leather or prunella.°

   Stuck o'er with titles and hung round with strings,
That thou mayest be by kings, or whores of kings.

---

prunella: Heavy cloth the color of prunes.

> Boast the pure blood of an illustrious race,
> In quiet flow from Lucrece° to Lucrece;
> But by your fathers' worth if yours you rate,
> Count me those only who were good and great.

This poem is written in **heroic couplets,** paired iambic pentameter lines with a rhyme scheme of *aa, bb, cc, dd,* and so on. In heroic couplets, greater stress falls on the second line of each pair, usually on the last word of the line. Coming at the end of the line, this word receives double emphasis: it is strengthened both because of its position in the line and because it is rhymed with the last word of the couplet's first line. In some cases, rhyme joins opposing ideas, thereby reinforcing a theme that runs through the passage: the contrast between the high and the low, the virtuous and the immoral. For example, "gowned" and "crowned" in lines 5 and 6 convey the opposite conditions of the parson and the monarch and exemplify the idea expressed in lines 3 and 4 that fortune, not virtue, determines one's station.

GERARD MANLEY HOPKINS (1844–1889)

Pied Beauty (1918)

> Glory be to God for dappled things—
>   For skies of couple-color as a brinded° cow;
>   For rose-moles all in stipple upon trout that swim;
> Fresh-firecoal chestnut-falls; finches' wings;
>   Landscape plotted and pieced —fold, fallow, and plow;   5
>   And áll trádes, their gear and tackle and trim.°
>
> All things counter, original, spare, strange;
>   Whatever is fickle, freckled (who knows how?)
>   With swift, slow; sweet, sour; adazzle, dim;
> He fathers-forth whose beauty is past change: 10
>   Praise him.

Reading and Reacting

1. Identify examples of onomatopoeia, alliteration, assonance, imperfect rhyme, and perfect rhyme. Do you think all these techniques are essential to the poem? Are any of them annoying or distracting?

2. What is the central idea of this poem? In what way do the sounds of the poem help to communicate this idea?

3. Identify examples of masculine and feminine rhyme.

Lucrece: In Roman legend, she stabbed herself after being defiled by Sextus Tarquinius.
brinded: Brindled (streaked).
trim: Equipment.

4. Journal Entry Hopkins uses both pleasing and discordant sounds in his poem. Identify uses of euphony and cacophony, and explain how these techniques affect your reactions to the poem.

Related Works: "Cathedral" (p. 318), "Women" (p. 763), "Batter My Heart, Three-Personed God" (p. 868)

W. H. AUDEN (1907–1973)

As I Walked Out One Evening (1940)

As I walked out one evening,
    Walking down Bristol Street,
The crowds upon the pavement
    Were fields of harvest wheat.

And down by the brimming river   5
    I heard a lover sing
Under an arch of the railway:
    "Love has no ending.

"I'll love you, dear, I'll love you
    Till China and Africa meet,   10
And the river jumps over the mountain
    And the salmon sing in the street,

"I'll love you till the ocean
    Is folded and hung up to dry,
And the seven stars go squawking   15
    Like geese about the sky.

"The years shall run like rabbits,
    For in my arms I hold
The Flower of the Ages,
    And the first love of the world."   20

But all the clocks in the city
    Began to whirr and chime:
"O let not Time deceive you,
    You cannot conquer Time.

"In the burrows of the Nightmare   25
    Where Justice naked is,
Time watches from the shadow
    And coughs when you would kiss.

"In headaches and in worry
    Vaguely life leaks away,   30
And Time will have his fancy
    Tomorrow or today.

"Into many a green valley
    Drifts the appalling snow;
Time breaks the threaded dances   35
    And the diver's brilliant bow.

"O plunge your hands in water,
    Plunge them in up to the wrist;
Stare, stare in the basin
    And wonder what you've missed.   40

"The glacier knocks in the cupboard,
    The desert sighs in the bed,
And the crack in the teacup opens
    A lane to the land of the dead.

"Where the beggars raffle the banknotes   45
    And the Giant is enchanting to Jack,
And the Lily-white Boy is a Roarer,
    And Jill goes down on her back.

"O look, look in the mirror,
    O look in your distress;   50
Life remains a blessing
    Although you cannot bless.

"O stand, stand at the window
    As the tears scald and start;
You shall love your crooked neighbor   55
    With your crooked heart."

It was late, late in the evening,
    The lovers they were gone;
The clocks had ceased their chiming,
    And the deep river ran on.   60

Reading and Reacting

1. Does Auden use perfect end rhyme in the second and fourth lines of every stanza? If not, why do you think he chooses not to?
2. Chart the poem's rhyme scheme. Does Auden use internal rhyme? Where does he use alliteration and assonance? In what other ways does he use sound?
3. Does Auden's use of sound reinforce the poem's content or undercut it? Explain.
4. **JOURNAL ENTRY** Could this poem be considered a love poem? How are its sentiments about love different from those conventionally expressed in poems about love?
5. **CRITICAL PERSPECTIVE** In a 1940 British review of Auden's work, T. C. Worlsey made the following comments about this poem:

    There is no technical reason why such a poem as [this] should not be popular; the metre and the rhythm are easy and helpful, and the symbols have reference to a world of experience common to every inhabitant of these islands. Here . . . the poet has gone as far as he can along the road to creating a popular poetry.

Does Auden's poem strike you as a model for "popular" poetry — that is, poetry for people who don't usually read poetry?

Related Works: "The Story of an Hour" (p. 82), "Araby" (p. 252), "Oh, my love is like a red, red rose" (p. 683), "To His Coy Mistress" (p. 696), "Not marble, nor the gilded monuments" (p. 909)

LYDIA DAVIS (1947–)

A Mown Lawn (2001)

She hated a *mown lawn*. Maybe that was because *mow* was the reverse of *wom*, the beginning of the name of what she was — a *woman*. A *mown lawn* had a sad sound to it, like a *long moan*. From her, a *mown lawn* made a *long moan*. *Lawn* had some of the letters of *man*, though the reverse of *man* would be *Nam*, a bad war. A *raw war*. *Lawn* also contained the let-   5
ters of *law*. In fact, *lawn* was a contraction of *lawman*. Certainly a *lawman* could and did *mow a lawn*. *Law and order* could be seen as starting from *lawn order*, valued by so many Americans. More *lawn* could be made using a *lawn mower*. A *lawn mower* did make *more lawn*. More *lawn* was a contraction of *more lawmen*. Did *more lawn* in America make *more law-*   10
men in America? Did *more lawn* make *more Nam*? More *mown lawn* made more *long moan*, from her. Or a *lawn mourn*. So often, she said, Americans wanted *more mown lawn*. All of America might be one *long mown lawn*. A *lawn* not *mown* grows *long*, she said: better a *long lawn*. Better a *long lawn* and a *mole*. Let the *lawman* have the *mown lawn*, she said. Or   15
the *moron*, the *lawn moron*.

Reading and Reacting

1. Identify several different types of rhyme in this poem. Then, find examples of alliteration and assonance.

2. "A Mown Lawn" does not conform to most people's idea of what a poem should look like. Do you think "A Mown Lawn" is a poem, or is it something else? Explain your answer.

3. Study the poem's italicized words and phrases. How are they related in terms of sound? What ideas do these words convey?

4. **JOURNAL ENTRY** What comment does this poem make about life in the United States?

Related Works: "Nice Car, Camille" (p. 609), "The World Is Too Much with Us" (p. 618), "The Grammar Lesson" (p. 621), "A Supermarket in California" (p. 704), "The True-Blue American" (p. 780)

ALAN SHAPIRO (1952–)

A Parting Gift (2001)

Song birds are singing from a cave of leaves
inside a tree that I imagine there
beyond the upper story window of
    the bedroom where
the lovers we no longer are   5
    are making love.

They're singing now because I say they do,
swallow and nightingale, wren, lark and thrush,
each song a different air of deepest pleasure
    all through a lush,   10
long night we'll never have again
    with one another,

a night of bird song that won't let you sleep,
a night of hearing how each tremulous thread
of melody pulls back against the urge   15
    to pull ahead,
how song weaves in and out of song
    till all songs merge

into the sheerest billowing of air
that settles and never settles over all   20
the lovers do throughout that long ago
    spectacular
lost night that's now forever my
    last gift to you.

Reading and Reacting

1. What is the rhyme scheme of this poem? At what point does Shapiro depart from this pattern? What does he gain by doing so?
2. Throughout "A Parting Gift," sounds as well as words are repeated. Find examples of each kind of repetition. What effect does this repetition create?
3. Most of this poem consists of run-on lines. Why do you think Shapiro uses this technique instead of end-stopped lines?
4. JOURNAL ENTRY What is this poem about? In what way do rhyme, repetition, and line length help Shapiro convey his ideas?

Related Works: "Parting at Morning" (p. 565), "How Do I Love Thee?" (p. 566), "The Shipfitter's Wife" (p. 610), "Spring Elegy" (p. 700), "When I Have Fears" (p. 893).

MONA VAN DUYN (1921–   )

The Beginning (2002)

The end
of passion
may refashion
a friend.

Eyes meet   5
in fear
of such dear
defeat.

The heart's core,
unbroken,   10
cringes.

The soul's door
swings open
on its hinges.

Reading and Reacting

1. This poem consists of two four-line stanzas and two three-line stanzas. What
ideas are expressed in the first two stanzas, and what ideas are expressed in
the last two stanzas? In what way does the change in stanza length help Van
Duyn express these different ideas?
2. How does the poem's rhyme scheme change from the first two stanzas to the
second two stanzas? Why do you think that Van Duyn made this change?
3. Does Van Duyn use perfect or imperfect rhyme in this poem? Explain.
4. JOURNAL ENTRY What is the significance of the poem's title? Can you think
of another title that might be more appropriate?

Related Works: "Araby" (p. 252), "Cathedral" (p. 318), "Living in Sin" (p. 643),
"Nothing Gold Can Stay" (p. 673), "What Is an Epigram?" (p. 747)

LEWIS CARROLL (1832–1898)

Jabberwocky (1871)

'Twas brillig, and the slithy toves
    Did gyre and gimble in the wabe:
All mimsy were the borogoves,
    And the mome raths outgrabe.

"Beware the Jabberwock, my son!   5
    The jaws that bite, the claws that catch!
Beware the Jubjub bird, and shun
    The frumious Bandersnatch!"

He took his vorpal sword in hand;
   Long time the manxome foe he sought —   10
So rested he by the Tumtum tree
   And stood awhile in thought.

And, as in uffish thought he stood,
   The Jabberwock, with eyes of flame,
Came whiffling through the tulgey wood,   15
   And burbled as it came!

One, two! One, two! And through and through
   The vorpal blade went snicker-snack!
He left it dead, and with its head
   He went galumphing back.   20

"And hast thou slain the Jabberwock?
   Come to my arms, my beamish boy!
O frabjous day! Callooh, Callay!"
   He chortled in his joy.

'Twas brillig, and the slithy toves   25
   Did gyre and gimble in the wabe:
All mimsy were the borogoves,
   And the mome raths outgrabe.

Reading and Reacting

1. Many words in this poem may be unfamiliar to you. Are they actual words? Use a dictionary to check before you dismiss any. Do some words seem to have meaning in the context of the poem regardless of whether they appear in the dictionary? Explain.

2. This poem contains many examples of onomatopoeia. What ideas do the various words' sounds suggest?

3. JOURNAL ENTRY Summarize the story the poem tells. In what sense is this poem a story of a young man's initiation into adulthood?

4. CRITICAL PERSPECTIVE According to Humpty Dumpty in Carroll's *Alice in Wonderland*, the nonsense words in the poem are *portmanteau words* (that is, words whose form and meaning are derived from two other distinct words — as *smog* is a portmanteau of *smoke* and *fog*). Critic Elizabeth Sewell, however, rejects this explanation: "[F]*rumious*, for instance, is not a word, and does not have two meanings packed up in it; it is a group of letters without any meaning at all. . . . [I]t looks like other words, and almost certainly more than two."

Which nonsense words in the poem seem to you to be portmanteau words, and which do not? Can you suggest possible sources for the words that are not portmanteau words?

Related Works: "A&P" (p. 115), "Gryphon" (p. 126), *The Cuban Swimmer* (p. 1258)

CHECKLIST | **WRITING ABOUT SOUND**

Rhythm and Meter

✓ Does the poem contain repeated words and phrases? If so, how do they help to create rhythm?

✓ Does the poem use one kind of meter, or does the meter vary from line to line?

✓ How does the meter contribute to the overall effect of the poem?

✓ Which lines of the poem contain caesuras? What effect do they have?

✓ Are the lines of the poem end-stopped, run-on, or a combination of the two? What effects are produced by the presence or absence of pauses at the ends of lines?

Alliteration, Assonance, and Rhyme

✓ Are there any examples of alliteration or assonance?

✓ Does the poem have a regular rhyme scheme?

✓ Does the poem use internal rhyme? Beginning rhyme?

✓ Does the poem include examples of masculine, feminine, or triple rhyme?

✓ In what ways does rhyme unify the poem?

✓ How does rhyme reinforce the poem's ideas?

WRITING SUGGESTIONS: Sound

1. William Blake's "The Tyger" appeared in a collection entitled *Songs of Experience*. Compare this poem (p. 853) to "The Lamb" (p. 852), which appeared in a collection called *Songs of Innocence*. In what way are the speakers in these two poems relatively "innocent" or "experienced"? How does sound help to convey the voice of the speakers in these two poems?

2. "Sadie and Maud" (p. 709), like "My Papa's Waltz" (p. 558), and "Daddy" (p. 691), communicates attitudes toward home and family. How does the presence or absence of rhyme in these poems help to convey the speakers' attitudes toward home and family?

3. Robert Frost once said that writing poems that have no fixed metrical pattern is like playing tennis without a net. What do you think he meant? Do you agree? After reading "Out, Out —" (p. 698), "Stopping by Woods

on a Snowy Evening" (p. 880), and "The Road Not Taken" (p. 880), write an essay in which you discuss Frost's use of meter.

4. Select two or three contemporary poems that have no end rhyme. Write an essay in which you discuss what these poets gain and lose by not using rhyme.

5. Prose writers as well as poets use techniques such as assonance and alliteration. Choose a passage of prose — from "Araby" (p. 252), "A Clean, Well-Lighted Place" (p. 267), or "Barn Burning" (p. 223), for example — and discuss its use of assonance and alliteration. Where do assonance and alliteration occur? How do these techniques help the writer create a mood?

6. WEB ACTIVITY The following Web site contains information about N. Scott Momaday:

http://www.achievement.org/autodoc/page/mom0pro-1

Read the profile on Momaday on this Web page. Note that the author states that Momaday "celebrates" western landscapes. Write an essay that provides evidence of Momaday's "celebration" of landscape in "Comparatives" (p. 719), focusing on how he uses sound to help him juxtapose images of beauty and death.

CHAPTER 22

FORM

Dryden chose the couplet because he thought it the plainest mode available, the verse "nearest prose," and he chose it in conscious reaction against the artificial stanzaic modes that had dominated English poetry during most of the sixteenth and seventeenth centuries. In short, he and his followers thought they were liberating poetry, just as Coleridge and Wordsworth liberated it a hundred years later, or Pound and Williams a hundred years after that. The history of poetry is a continual fixing and freeing of conventions. —**Hayden Carruth,** *"The Question of Poetic Form"*

Yeats said that the finished poem made a sound like the click of the lid on a perfectly made box. One-hundred-and-forty syllables, organized into a sonnet, do not necessarily make a click; the same number of syllables, dispersed in asymmetric lines of free verse, will click like a lid if the poem is good. In the sonnet and in the free verse poem, the poet improvises toward that click, and achieves his resolution in unpredictable ways. The rhymes and line lengths of the sonnet are too gross to contribute greatly to that sense of resolution. The click is our sense of lyric *form.* —**Donald Hall,** *"Goatfoot, Milktongue, Twinbird"*

No verse can be free; it must be governed by some measure, but not by the old measure. —**William Carlos Williams,** *"On Measure"*

Poetic forms — meters, rhyming patterns, the shaping of poems into symmetrical blocks of lines called couplets or stanzas — have existed since poetry was an oral activity. Such forms can easily become format, of course, where the dynamics of experience and desire are forced to fit a pattern to which they have no organic relationship. People are often taught in school to confuse closed poetic forms (or formulas) with poetry itself . . . It's a struggle not to let the form take over, lapse into format, assimilate the poetry; and that very struggle can produce a movement, a music, of its own. —**Adrienne Rich,** *"What Is Found There"*

JOHN KEATS (1795–1821)

On the Sonnet (1819)

If by dull rhymes our English must be chained,
And like Andromeda,° the sonnet sweet
Fettered, in spite of painéd loveliness,
Let us find, if we must be constrained,
Sandals more interwoven and complete   5
To fit the naked foot of Poesy:
Let us inspect the lyre, and weigh the stress
Of every chord, and see what may be gained
By ear industrious, and attention meet;
Misers of sound and syllable, no less   10
Than Midas° of his coinage, let us be
Jealous of dead leaves in the bay-wreath crown;
So, if we may not let the Muse be free,
She will be bound with garlands of her own.

BILLY COLLINS (1941–   )

Sonnet (1999)

All we need is fourteen lines, well, thirteen now,
and after this one just a dozen
to launch a little ship on love's storm chased seas,
then only ten more left like rows of beans.
How easily it goes unless you get Elizabethan   5
and insist the iambic bongos must be played
and rhymes positioned at the ends of lines,
one for every station of the cross.
But hang on here while we make the turn
into the final six where all will be resolved,   10
where longing and heartache will find an end,
where Laura will tell Petrarch to put down his pen,
take off those crazy medieval tights,
blow out the lights, and come at last to bed.

The **form** of a literary work is its structure or shape, the way its parts fit together to form a whole; **poetic form** is the design of a poem described in terms of rhyme, meter, and stanzaic pattern.

Andromeda: In Greek mythology, an Ethiopian princess chained to a rock to appease a sea monster.

Midas: A legendary king of Phrygia whose wish that everything he touched would turn to gold was granted by the god Dionysus.

Until the twentieth century, most poetry was written in **closed form** (sometimes called **fixed form**), characterized by regular patterns of meter, rhyme, line length, and stanzaic divisions. Early poems that were passed down orally — epics and ballads, for example — relied on regular form to facilitate memorization. Even after poems began to be written down, poets tended to favor regular patterns. In fact, until relatively recently, regular form was what distinguished poetry from prose. Of course, strict adherence to regular patterns sometimes produced poems that were, in John Keats's words, "chained" by "dull rhymes" and "fettered" by the rules governing a particular form. But rather than feeling "constrained" by form, many poets — like Billy Collins in the playful sonnet above — experimented with imagery, figures of speech, allusion, and other techniques, stretching closed form to its limits.

As they sought new ways in which to express themselves, poets also used forms from other cultures, adapting them to the demands of their own languages. English and American poets, for example, adopted (and still use) early French forms, such as the villanelle and the sestina, and early Italian forms, such as the Petrarchan sonnet and terza rima. The nineteenth-century American poet Henry Wadsworth Longfellow studied Icelandic epics; the twentieth-century poet Ezra Pound studied the works of French troubadours; and Pound and other twentieth-century American poets, such as Richard Wright and Carolyn Kizer, were inspired by Japanese haiku. Other American poets, such as Vachel Lindsay, Langston Hughes, and Maya Angelou, looked closer to home — to the rhythms of blues, jazz, and spirituals — for inspiration.

As time went on, more and more poets moved away from closed form to experiment with **open form** poetry (sometimes called **free verse** or *vers libre*), varying line length within a poem, dispensing with stanzaic divisions, breaking lines in unexpected places, and even abandoning any semblance of formal structure. In English, nineteenth-century poets — such as William Blake and Matthew Arnold — experimented with lines of irregular meter and length, and Walt Whitman wrote **prose poems,** open form poems whose long lines made them look like prose. (Well before this time, Asian poetry and some biblical passages had used a type of free verse.) In nineteenth-century France, Symbolist poets, such as Baudelaire, Rimbaud, Verlaine, and Mallarmé, also used free verse. In the early twentieth century, a group of American poets — including Ezra Pound, William Carlos Williams, and Amy Lowell — who were associated with a movement known as **imagism,** wrote poetry that dispensed with traditional principles of English versification, creating new rhythms and meters.

Although much contemporary English and American poetry is composed in open form, many poets also write in closed form — even in very traditional, highly structured patterns. Still, new forms, and new variations of old forms, are being created all the time. And, because contemporary poets do not necessarily feel bound by rules or restrictions about what constitutes "acceptable" poetic form, they experiment freely, trying to discover the form that best suits the poem's purpose, subject, language, and theme.

CLOSED FORM

A **closed form** (or *fixed form*) poem looks symmetrical; it has an identifiable, repeated pattern, with lines of similar length arranged in groups of two, three, four, or more. Such poems also tend to rely on regular metrical patterns and rhyme schemes.

Despite what its name suggests, closed form poetry does not have to be confining or conservative. In fact, sometimes contemporary poets experiment by using characteristics of open form poetry (such as lines of varying length) within a closed form, or by moving back and forth within a single poem from open to closed to open form. Sometimes they (like their eighteenth-century counterparts) experiment with closed form by combining different stanzaic forms (stanzas of two and three lines, for example) within a single poem.

Even when poets work within a traditional closed form, such as a *sonnet, sestina,* or *villanelle,* they can break new ground. For example, they can create a sonnet with an unexpected meter or rhyme scheme, add an extra line or even extra stanzas to a traditional sonnet form, combine two different traditional sonnet forms in a single poem, or write an abbreviated version of a sestina or villanelle. In other words, poets can use traditional forms as building blocks, combining them in innovative ways to create new patterns and new forms.

Sometimes a pattern (such as *blank verse*) simply determines the meter of a poem's individual lines. At other times, the pattern extends to the level of the *stanza,* with lines arranged into groups (*couplets, quatrains,* and so on). At still other times, as in the case of traditional closed forms like sonnets, a poetic pattern gives shape to an entire poem.

Blank Verse

Blank verse is unrhymed poetry with each line written in a set pattern of five stressed and five unstressed syllables called **iambic pentameter** (see p. 712). Many passages from Shakespeare's plays, such as the following lines from *Hamlet,* are written in blank verse:

> To sleep! perchance to dream:— ay, there's the rub;
> For in that sleep of death what dreams may come,
> When we have shuffled off this mortal coil,
> Must give us pause: there's the respect
> That makes calamity of so long life[.]

For a contemporary use of blank verse, see John Updike's "Ex-Basketball Player" (p. 684).

Stanza

A **stanza** is a group of two or more lines with the same metrical pattern — and often with a regular rhyme scheme as well — separated by blank space from other such groups of lines. The stanza in poetry is like the paragraph in prose: it groups related thoughts into units.

A two-line stanza with rhyming lines of similar length and meter is called a **couplet.** The **heroic couplet,** first used by Chaucer and especially popular throughout the eighteenth century, consists of two rhymed lines of iambic pentameter, with a weak pause after the first line and a strong pause after the second. The following example, from Alexander Pope's *An Essay on Criticism,* is a heroic couplet:

> True ease in writing comes from art, not chance,
> As those move easiest who have learned to dance.

A three-line stanza with lines of similar length and a set rhyme scheme is called a **tercet.** Percy Bysshe Shelley's "Ode to the West Wind" (p. 909) is built largely of tercets:

> O wild West Wind, thou breath of Autumn's being,
> Thou, from whose unseen presence the leaves dead
> Are driven, like ghosts from an enchanter fleeing,
>
> Yellow, and black, and pale, and hectic red,
> Pestilence-stricken multitudes: O Thou,
> Who chariotest to their dark wintry bed

Although in many tercets all three lines rhyme, "Ode to the West Wind" uses a special rhyme scheme, also used by Dante, called **terza rima.** This rhyme scheme (*aba, bcb, cdc, ded,* and so on) creates an interlocking series of stanzas: line 2's *dead* looks ahead to the rhyming words *red* and *bed,* which close lines 4 and 6, and the pattern continues throughout the poem.

A four-line stanza with lines of similar length and a set rhyme scheme is called a **quatrain.** The quatrain, the most widely used and versatile unit in English and American poetry, is used by William Wordsworth in the following excerpt from "She dwelt among the untrodden ways" (p. 924):

> A violet by a mossy stone
>   Half hidden from the eye!
> — Fair as a star, when only one
>   Is shining in the sky.

Quatrains are frequently used by contemporary poets as well — for instance, in Theodore Roethke's "My Papa's Waltz" (p. 558), Adrienne Rich's "Aunt Jennifer's Tigers" (p. 715), and William Stafford's "Traveling through the Dark" (p. 916).

One special kind of quatrain, called the **ballad stanza,** alternates lines of eight and six syllables; typically, only the second and fourth lines rhyme. The following lines from the traditional Scottish ballad "Sir Patrick Spence" illustrate the ballad stanza:

> The king sits in Dumferling toune,
>   Drinking the blude-reid wine:
> "O whar will I get guid sailor
>   To sail this schip of mine?"

Common measure, a four-line stanzaic pattern closely related to the ballad stanza, is used in hymns as well as in poetry. It differs from the ballad stanza in that its rhyme scheme is *abab* rather than *abcb.* This pattern appears in Donald Hall's poem "My Son, My Executioner" (p. 699).

Other stanzaic forms include **rhyme royal,** a seven-line stanza (*ababbcc*) set in iambic pentameter, used in Sir Thomas Wyatt's sixteenth-century poem "They Flee from Me That Sometimes Did Me Seke" as well as in Theodore Roethke's twentieth-century "I Knew a Woman"; **ottava rima,** an eight-line stanza (*abababcc*) set in iambic pentameter; and the Spenserian stanza, a nine-line form (*ababbcbcc*) whose first eight lines are set in iambic pentameter and whose last line is in iambic hexameter. The Romantic poets John Keats and Percy Bysshe Shelley were among those who used the Spenserian stanza. (See Chapter 21 for definitions and examples of various metrical patterns.)

The Sonnet

Perhaps the most familiar kind of traditional closed form poem written in English is the **sonnet,** a fourteen-line poem with a distinctive rhyme scheme and metrical pattern. The English or **Shakespearean sonnet** consists of fourteen lines divided into three quatrains and a concluding couplet, is written in iambic pentameter, and follows the rhyme scheme *abab cdcd efef gg*. The **Petrarchan sonnet,** popularized in the fourteenth century by the Italian poet Francesco Petrarch, also consists of fourteen lines of iambic pentameter, but these lines are divided into an eight-line unit called an **octave** and a six-line unit (composed of two tercets) called a **sestet.** The rhyme scheme of the octave is *abba abba*; the rhyme scheme of the sestet is *cde cde*.

The conventional structures of these sonnet forms reflect the arrangement of ideas within the poem. In the Shakespearean sonnet, the poet typically presents three "paragraphs" of related thoughts, introducing an idea in the first quatrain, developing it in the two remaining quatrains, and summing up in a succinct closing couplet. In the Petrarchan sonnet, the octave introduces a problem that is resolved in the sestet. (Many Shakespearean sonnets also have a problem-solution structure.) Some poets vary the traditional patterns somewhat to suit the poem's language or ideas. For example, they may depart from the pattern to side-step a forced rhyme or unnatural stress on a syllable, or they may shift from problem to solution in a place other than between octave and sestet.

The following poem has the form of a traditional English sonnet.

WILLIAM SHAKESPEARE (1564–1616)

When, in disgrace with Fortune and men's eyes, (1609)

When, in disgrace with Fortune and men's eyes,
I all alone beweep my outcast state,
And trouble deaf heaven with my bootless° cries,
And look upon myself and curse my fate,
Wishing me like to one more rich in hope,   5
Featured like him, like him with friends possessed,

---

bootless: Futile.

Desiring this man's art, and that man's scope,
With what I most enjoy contented least,
Yet in these thoughts myself almost despising,
Haply° I think on thee, and then my state,   10
Like to the lark at break of day arising
From sullen earth, sings hymns at heaven's gate;
     For thy sweet love rememb'red such wealth brings
     That then I scorn to change my state with kings.

This sonnet is written in iambic pentameter and has a conventional rhyme scheme: *abab* (eyes-state-cries-fate), *cdcd* (hope-possessed-scope-least), *efef* (despising-state-arising-gate), *gg* (brings-kings). In this poem, in which the speaker explains how thoughts of his loved one can rescue him from despair, each quatrain is unified by rhyme as well as by subject. In the first quatrain, the speaker presents his problem: he is down on his luck and out of favor with his peers, isolated in self-pity and cursing his fate. In the second quatrain, he develops this idea further: he is envious of others and dissatisfied with things that usually please him. In the third quatrain, the focus shifts. Although the first two quatrains develop a dependent clause ("When . . .") that introduces a problem, line 9 begins to present the resolution. In the third quatrain, the speaker explains how, in the midst of his despair and self-hatred, he thinks of his loved one, and his spirits soar. The closing couplet sums up the mood transformation the poem describes and explains its significance: when the speaker realizes the emotional riches his loved one gives him, he is no longer envious of others.

CLAUDE McKAY (1890–1948)

The White City (1922)

I will not toy with it nor bend an inch.
Deep in the secret chambers of my heart
I muse my life-long hate, and without flinch
I bear it nobly as I live my part.
My being would be a skeleton, a shell,   5
If this dark Passion that fills my every mood,
And makes my heaven in the white world's hell,
Did not forever feed me vital blood.
I see the mighty city through a mist—
The strident trains that speed the goaded mass,   10
The poles and spires and towers vapor-kissed,
The fortressed port through which the great ships pass,
The tides, the wharves, the dens I contemplate,
Are sweet like wanton loves because I hate.

Haply: Luckily.

Reading and Reacting

1. In what sense is the speaker's mood similar to that of the speaker in "When, in disgrace with fortune and men's eyes" (p. 738)? How is it different?

2. How is the speaker's description of the city in the third quatrain consistent with the emotions he expresses in lines 1–8?

3. The closing couplet of a Shakespearean sonnet traditionally sums up the sonnet's concerns. Does this happen here? Explain.

4. **JOURNAL ENTRY** What possible meanings does the phrase "the white world's hell" (line 7) have? How does it express the poem's central theme?

5. **CRITICAL PERSPECTIVE** According to Tyrone Tillery's 1992 biography of McKay, the poet chose the sonnet form because "he found [it] admirable for a moment's thought. He understood that he had a tendency to be diffuse and repetitive, and he felt that tight rhythmic and metric forms helped him check these faults." Critic Onwuchekwa Jemie, in a 1973 survey of Harlem Renaissance poets, saw a paradox in McKay's use of the "old-fashioned" sonnet form to contain "venom and rage." Noting that "[e]ach of his protest sonnets just about explodes from the page," Jemie observes that "McKay's attacks on the white world are carried out in one of that culture's most entrenched and conservative poetic forms. McKay's words deny the white world, but his form, style, language, and poetic attitude tend to affirm it." Jemie concludes, "It is the mark of his achievement that he is able to work that fragile sonnet frame into a vehicle of dynamite."

How do these observations help you to understand why McKay chose to express his ideas in a sonnet? Do you think he made the right choice?

Related Works: "Battle Royal" (p. 175), "The Man He Killed" (p. 612), "For Malcolm, a Year After" (p. 716), "We Wear the Mask" (p. 871), "If We Must Die" (p. 897)

JOHN KEATS (1795–1821)

On First Looking into Chapman's Homer° (1816)

Much have I traveled in the realms of gold,
    And many goodly states and kingdoms seen;
    Round many western islands have I been
Which bards in fealty to Apollo° hold.
Oft of one wide expanse had I been told   5
    That deep-browed Homer ruled as his demesne,°

Chapman's Homer: The translation of Homer by Elizabethan poet George Chapman.
Apollo: Greek god of light, truth, reason, male beauty; associated with music and poetry.
demesne: Realm, domain.

Yet did I never breathe its pure serene°
Till I heard Chapman speak out loud and bold.
Then felt I like some watcher of the skies
    When a new planet swims into his ken;   10
Or like stout Cortez° when with eagle eyes
    He stared at the Pacific — and all his men
Looked at each other with a wild surmise —
    Silent, upon a peak in Darien.°

Reading and Reacting

1. Is this a Petrarchan or a Shakespearean sonnet? Explain your conclusion.

2. JOURNAL ENTRY The sestet's change of focus is introduced with the word "Then" in line 9. How does the mood of the sestet differ from the mood of the octave? How does the language differ?

3. CRITICAL PERSPECTIVE Biographer Aileen Ward offers an interesting explanation to suggest the reason for the excitement Keats felt when he first encountered Chapman's Homer. Homer's epic tales of gods and heroes were known to most readers of Keats's day only in a very formal eighteenth-century translation by Alexander Pope. For instance, this is Pope's description of Ulysses escaping from a shipwreck:

      his knees no more
Perform'd their office, or his weight upheld:
His swoln heart heav'd, his bloated body swell'd:
From mouth to nose the briny torrent ran,
And lost in lassitude lay all the man,
Deprived of voice, of motion, and of breath,
The soul scarce waking in the arms of death . . .

In a rare 1616 edition of Chapman's translation, Keats discovered a very different poem:

      both knees falt'ring, both
His strong hands hanging down, and all with froth
His cheeks and nostrils flowing, voice and breath
Spent to all use, and down he sank to death.
The sea had soak'd his heart through. . . .

This, as Ward notes, was "poetry of a kind that had not been written in England for two hundred years."

Can you understand why Keats was so moved by Chapman's translation? Do you think Keats's own poem seems closer in its form and language to Pope or to Chapman?

---

serene: Air, atmosphere.
Cortez: It was Vasco de Balboa (not Hernando Cortez as Keats suggests) who first saw the Pacific Ocean, from "a peak in Darien."
Darien: Former name of the Isthmus of Panama.

Related Works: "Gryphon" (p. 126), "Araby" (p. 252), "When I Heard the Learn'd Astronomer" (p. 639)

GWENDOLYN BROOKS (1917–2000)

First Fight. Then Fiddle (1949)

First fight. Then fiddle. Ply the slipping string
With feathery sorcery; muzzle the note
With hurting love; the music that they wrote
Bewitch, bewilder. Qualify to sing
Threadwise. Devise no salt, no hempen thing   5
For the dear instrument to bear. Devote
The bow to silks and honey. Be remote
A while from malice and from murdering.
But first to arms, to armor. Carry hate
In front of you and harmony behind.   10
Be deaf to music and to beauty blind.
Win war. Rise bloody, maybe not too late
For having first to civilize a space
Wherein to play your violin with grace.

Reading and Reacting

1. What is the subject of Brooks's poem? What do you think she means by "fight" and "fiddle"?
2. What is the poem's rhyme scheme? Is it an essential element of the poem? Would the poem be equally effective if it did not include end rhyme? Why or why not?
3. Study the poem's use of capitalization and punctuation carefully. Why do you think Brooks chooses to end many of her sentences in midline? How do her choices determine how you read the poem?

Related Works: "The Soldier" (p. 569), "For the Student Strikers" (p. 651), "The White City" (p. 739), "The *Chicago Defender* Sends a Man to Little Rock" (p. 856)

The Sestina

The **sestina,** introduced in thirteenth-century France, is composed of six six-line stanzas and a three-line conclusion called an **envoi.** Although the sestina does not require end rhyme, it does require that each line end with one of six key words, which are repeated throughout the poem in a fixed order. The alternation of these six words in different positions — but always at the ends of lines — in each of the poem's six stanzas creates a rhythmic verbal pattern that unifies the poem; as the key words do in the poem that follows.

ALBERTO ALVARO RÍOS (1952–   )

Nani (1982)

Sitting at her table, she serves
the sopa de arroz° to me
instinctively, and I watch her,
the absolute mamá, and eat words
I might have had to say more   5
out of embarrassment. To speak,
now-foreign words I used to speak,
too, dribble down her mouth as she serves
me albóndigas.° No more
than a third are easy to me.   10
By the stove she does something with words
and looks at me only with her
back. I am full. I tell her
I taste the mint, and watch her speak
smiles at the stove. All my words   15
make her smile. Nani never serves
herself, she only watches me
with her skin, her hair. I ask for more.

I watch the mamá warming more
tortillas for me. I watch her   20
fingers in the flame for me.
Near her mouth, I see a wrinkle speak
of a man whose body serves
the ants like she serves me, then more words
from more wrinkles about children, words   25
about this and that, flowing more
easily from these other mouths. Each serves
as a tremendous string around her,
holding her together. They speak
nani was this and that to me   30
and I wonder just how much of me
will die with her, what were the words
I could have been, was. Her insides speak
through a hundred wrinkles, now, more
than she can bear, steel around her,   35
shouting, then, What is this thing she serves?

---

sopa de arroz: Rice soup.
albóndigas: Meatballs.

She asks me if I want more.
I own no words to stop her.
Even before I speak, she serves.

In many respects, Ríos's poem closely follows the form of the traditional sestina. For instance, it interweaves six key words — "serves," "me," "her," "words," "more," and "speak"— through six groups of six lines each, rearranging the order in which the words appear so that the first line of each group of six lines ends with the key word that closed the preceding group of lines. The poem repeats the key words in exactly the order prescribed: *abcdef, faebdc, cfdabe,* and so on. In addition, the sestina closes with a three-line envoi that includes all six of the poem's key words, three at the ends of lines and three within the lines. However, Ríos departs from the sestina form by grouping his six sets of six lines not into six separate stanzas but rather into two eighteen-line stanzas.

The sestina form suits Ríos's subject matter. The focus of the poem, on the verbal and nonverbal interaction between the poem's "me" and "her," is reinforced by each of the related words. "Nani" is a poem about communication, and the key words return to probe this theme again and again. Throughout the poem, these repeated words help to create a fluid, melodic, and tightly woven work.

ELIZABETH BISHOP (1911–1979)

Sestina (1965)

September rain falls on the house.
In the failing light, the old grandmother
sits in the kitchen with the child
beside the Little Marvel Stove,
reading the jokes from the almanac,   5
laughing and talking to hide her tears.

She thinks that her equinoctial tears
and the rain that beats on the roof of the house
were both foretold by the almanac,
but only known to a grandmother.
The iron kettle sings on the stove.   10
She cuts some bread and says to the child,

It's time for tea now; but the child
is watching the teakettle's small hard tears
dance like mad on the hot black stove,   15
the way the rain must dance on the house.
Tidying up, the old grandmother
hangs up the clever almanac

on its string. Birdlike, the almanac
hovers half open above the child,   20

hovers above the old grandmother
and her teacup full of dark brown tears.
She shivers and says she thinks the house
feels chilly, and puts more wood in the stove.

It was to be, says the Marvel Stove.   25
I know what I know, says the almanac.
With crayons the child draws a rigid house
and a winding pathway. Then the child
puts in a man with buttons like tears
and shows it proudly to the grandmother.   30

But secretly, while the grandmother
busies herself about the stove,
the little moons fall down like tears
from between the pages of the almanac
into the flower bed the child   35
has carefully placed in the front of the house.

Time to plant tears, says the almanac.
The grandmother sings to the marvellous stove
and the child draws another inscrutable house.

Reading and Reacting

1. Does the poet's adherence to a traditional form create any problems? For example, do you think the syntax is strained at any point? Explain.
2. How does this sestina use sound — meter, rhyme, alliteration, assonance, and so on? Could sound have been used more effectively? How?
3. **JOURNAL ENTRY** How are the six key words related to the poem's theme?

Related Works: "My Papa's Waltz" (p. 558), "The Meal" (p. 667), "Nani" (p. 743)

The Villanelle

The **villanelle,** first introduced in France in the Middle Ages, is a nineteen-line poem composed of five tercets and a concluding quatrain; its rhyme scheme is *aba aba aba aba aba abaa*. Two different lines are systematically repeated in the poem: line 1 appears again in lines 6, 12, and 18, and line 3 reappears as lines 9, 15, and 19. Thus, each tercet concludes with an exact (or close) duplication of either line 1 or line 3, and the final quatrain concludes by repeating both line 1 and line 3.

THEODORE ROETHKE (1908–1963)

The Waking (1953)

I wake to sleep, and take my waking slow.
I feel my fate in what I cannot fear.
I learn by going where I have to go.

We think by feeling. What is there to know?
I hear my being dance from ear to ear.   5
I wake to sleep, and take my waking slow.

Of those so close beside me, which are you?
God bless the Ground! I shall walk softly there,
And learn by going where I have to go.

Light takes the Tree; but who can tell us how?   10
The lowly worm climbs up a winding stair;
I wake to sleep, and take my waking slow.

Great Nature has another thing to do
To you and me; so take the lively air,
And, lovely, learn by going where to go.   15

This shaking keeps me steady. I should know.
What falls away is always. And is near.
I wake to sleep, and take my waking slow.
I learn by going where I have to go.

"The Waking," like all villanelles, closely intertwines threads of sounds and words. The repeated lines and the very regular rhyme and meter give the poem a monotonous, almost hypnotic, rhythm. This poem uses end rhyme and repeats entire lines. It also makes extensive use of alliteration ("I feel my fate in what I cannot fear") and internal rhyme ("I hear my being dance from ear to ear"; "I wake to sleep and take my waking slow"). The result is a tightly constructed poem of overlapping sounds and images. (For an example of another well-known villanelle, see Dylan Thomas's "Do not go gentle into that good night," p. 559.)

WILLIAM MEREDITH (1919–   )

In Memory of Donald A. Stauffer (1987)

Armed with an indiscriminate delight
His ghost left Oxford five summers ago,
Still on the sweet, obvious side of right.

How many friends and students talked all night
With this remarkable teacher? How many go   5
Still armed with his indiscriminate delight?

He liked, but often could not reach, the bright:
Young people sometimes prefer not to know
About the sweet or obvious sides of right.

But how all arrogance involves a slight   10
To knowledge, his humility would show
Them, and his indiscriminate delight

In what was true. This was why he could write
Commonplace books: his patience lingered so
Fondly on the sweet, obvious side of right.   15

What rare anthology of ghosts sits till first light
In the understanding air where he talks now,
Armed with his indiscriminate delight
There on the sweet and obvious side of right?

Reading and Reacting

1. Review the definition of *villanelle*, and explain how Meredith's poem expands the possibilities of the traditional villanelle.
2. Try to make the changes you believe are necessary to make Meredith's poem absolutely consistent with the traditional villanelle form. How does your editing change the poem?
3. **Journal Entry** What kinds of subjects do you think would be most appropriate for villanelles? Why? What subjects, if any, do you think would *not* be appropriate? Explain.

Related Works: "Do not go gentle into that good night" (p. 559), "The Grammar Lesson" (p. 621), "Spring Elegy" (p. 700), "The Waking" (p. 745)

The Epigram

Originally, an epigram was an inscription carved in stone on a monument or statue. As a literary form, an **epigram** is a very brief poem that makes a pointed, often sarcastic, comment in a surprising twist at the end. In a sense, it is a poem with a punch line. Although some epigrams rhyme, others do not. Many are only two lines long, but others are somewhat longer. What they have in common is their economy of language and their tone. One of the briefest of epigrams, written by Ogden Nash, appeared in *The New Yorker* magazine in 1931:

> The Bronx?
> No thonx.

Here, in four words, Nash manages to convey the unexpected, using rhyme and creative spelling to convey his assessment of a borough of New York City. The poem's two lines are perfectly balanced, making the contrast between the noncommittal tone of the first and the negative tone of the second quite striking.

SAMUEL TAYLOR COLERIDGE (1772–1834)

What Is an Epigram? (1802)

What is an epigram? a dwarfish whole,
Its body brevity, and wit its soul.

WILLIAM BLAKE (1757–1827)

Her Whole Life Is an Epigram (c. 1793–1811)

Her whole life is an epigram: smack, smooth & neatly penned,
Platted° quite neat to catch applause, with a sliding noose at the end.

Reading and Reacting

1. Read the two preceding epigrams, and explain the point each one makes.
2. Evaluate each poem. What qualities do you conclude make an epigram effective?

Related Works: "General Review of the Sex Situation" (p. 566), "Fire and Ice" (p. 611), "you fit into me" (p. 700)

MARTIN ESPADA (1957–)

Why I Went to College (2000)

If you don't,
my father said,
you better learn
to eat soup
through a straw,   5
'cause I'm gonna
break your jaw

Reading and Reacting

1. How is "Why I Went to College" different from Coleridge's and Blake's epigrams? How is it similar to them?
2. What function does the poem's title serve? Is it the epigram's "punch line," or does it serve another purpose?
3. What can you infer about the speaker's father from this poem? Why, for example, do you think he wants his son to go to college?
4. JOURNAL ENTRY Exactly why did the speaker go to college? Expand this short poem into a paragraph written from the speaker's point of view.

Related Works: "Baca Grande" (p. 648), "The Value of Education" (p. 650), "My Father as a Guitar" (p. 690), "'Faith' is a fine invention" (p. 865), *The Cuban Swimmer* (p. 1258)

Platted: Braided.

Haiku

Like an epigram, a haiku compresses words into a very small package. Unlike an epigram, however, a haiku focuses on an image, not an idea. A traditional Japanese form, the **haiku** is a brief unrhymed poem that presents the essence of some aspect of nature, concentrating a vivid image in three lines. Although in the strictest sense a haiku consists of seventeen syllables divided into lines of five, seven, and five syllables, respectively, not all poets conform to this rigid form.

The following poem is a translation of a classic Japanese haiku by Matsuo Basho:

> Silent and still: then
> Even sinking into the rocks,
> The cicada's screech.

Notice that this poem conforms to the haiku's three-line structure and traditional subject matter, vividly depicting a natural scene without comment or analysis.

As the next poem illustrates, haiku in English is not always consistent with the traditional haiku in form or subject matter.

RICHARD BRAUTIGAN (1935–1984)

Widow's Lament*

> It's not quite cold enough
> to go borrow some firewood
> from the neighbors.

Brautigan's haiku adheres to the traditional pattern's number of lines and syllables, and its central idea is expressed in very concentrated terms. The poem's focus, however, is not the natural world but human psychology. Moreover, without the title, the poem would be so ambiguous as to be meaningless. In this sense, the poet "cheats" the form, depending on the title's four syllables as well as on the seventeen of the poem itself to convey his ideas.

MATSUO BASHO (1644–1694)

Four Haiku*

Translated by Geoffrey Bownas and Anthony Thwaite

> Spring:
> A hill without a name
> Veiled in morning mist.

---

*Publication date is not available.

*Publication date is not available.

The beginning of autumn:
Sea and emerald paddy   5
Both the same green.

The winds of autumn
Blow: yet still green
The chestnut husks.

A flash of lightning: 10
Into the gloom
Goes the heron's cry.

Reading and Reacting

1. Haiku are admired for their extreme economy and their striking images. What are the central images in each of Basho's haiku? To what senses do these images appeal?
2. In another poem, Basho says that art begins with "The depths of the country / and a rice-planting song." What do you think he means? In what way do the preceding poems exemplify this idea?
3. Do you think the conciseness of these poems increases or decreases the impact of their images? Explain.
4. **JOURNAL ENTRY** "In a Station of the Metro" (p. 666) is Ezra Pound's version of a haiku. How successful do you think Pound was? Do you think a longer poem could have conveyed the images more effectively?

Related Works: "the sky was can dy" (p. 754), "Birches" (p. 877)

CAROLYN KIZER (1925–   )

After Basho (1984)

Tentatively, you
slip onstage this evening,
pallid, famous moon.

Reading and Reacting

1. What possible meanings might the word "After" have in the title?
2. What does the title tell readers about the writer's purpose?
3. What visual picture does the poem suggest? What mood does the poem's central image create?
4. What is the impact of "tentatively" in the first line and "famous" in the last line? How do the connotations of these words shape the image of the moon?

Related Works: "Photograph of My Father in His Twenty-Second Year" (p. 557), "Morning Song" (p. 885)

OPEN FORM

An **open form** poem (sometimes called **free verse** or *vers libre*) makes occasional use of rhyme and meter but has no easily identifiable pattern or design: no conventional stanzaic divisions, no consistent metrical pattern, no repeated rhyme scheme. Still, although open form poetry has no distinguishable pattern of meter, rhyme, or line length, it is not necessarily shapeless, untidy, or randomly ordered. All poems have form, and the form of a poem may be determined by factors such as repeated sounds, the appearance of words on the printed page, or pauses in natural speech as well as by conventional metrical patterns or rhyme schemes.

Open form poetry invites readers to participate in the creative process, to discover the relationship between form and meaning. Some modern poets believe that only open form offers them freedom to express their ideas or that the subject matter or mood of their poetry demands a relaxed, experimental approach to form. For example, when Lawrence Ferlinghetti portrays the poet as an acrobat who "climbs on rime" (p. 681), he constructs his poem in a way that is consistent with the poet/acrobat's willingness to take risks. Thus, the poem's idiosyncratic form supports its ideas about the possibilities of poetry and the poet as experimenter.

Without a predetermined pattern, however, poets must create forms that suit their needs, and they must continue to shape and reshape the look of the poem on the page as they revise its words. Thus, open form represents a challenge, a way to experiment with fresh arrangements of words and new juxtapositions of ideas.

For some poets, such as Carl Sandburg, open form provides an opportunity to create **prose poems,** poems that look like prose.

CARL SANDBURG (1878–1967)

Chicago (1914)

Hog Butcher for the World,
Tool Maker, Stacker of Wheat,
Player with Railroads and the Nation's Freight Handler;
Stormy, husky, brawling,
City of the Big Shoulders: 5

They tell me you are wicked and I believe them, for I have seen
    your painted women under the gas lamps luring the farm boys.
And they tell me you are crooked and I answer: Yes, it is true
    I have seen the gunman kill and go free to kill again.
And they tell me you are brutal and my reply is: On the faces of
    women and children I have seen the marks of wanton hunger.
And having answered so I turn once more to those who sneer at
    this my city, and I give them back the sneer and say to them:
Come and show me another city with lifted head singing so
    proud to be alive and coarse and strong and cunning.   10

Flinging magnetic curses amid the toil of piling job on job,
    here is a tall bold slugger set vivid against the little soft cities;
Fierce as a dog with tongue lapping for action, cunning as a
    savage pitted against the wilderness,
    Bareheaded,
      Shoveling,
      Wrecking,   15
      Planning,
      Building, breaking, rebuilding,
Under the smoke, dust all over his mouth, laughing with white
    teeth,
Under the terrible burden of destiny laughing as a young man
    laughs,
Laughing even as an ignorant fighter laughs who has never lost
    a battle,   20
Bragging and laughing that under his wrist is the pulse, and under
    his ribs the heart of the people,
                  Laughing!
Laughing the stormy, husky, brawling laughter of Youth,
    half-naked, sweating, proud to be Hog Butcher, Tool Maker,
    Stacker of Wheat, Player with railroads and Freight Handler
    to the Nation.

"Chicago" uses capitalization and punctuation conventionally, and it generally (though not always) divides words into lines consistent with the natural divisions of phrases and sentences. However, the poem is not divided into stanzas, and its lines vary widely in length — from a single word isolated on a line to a line crowded with words — and follow no particular metrical pattern. Instead, its form is created through its pattern of alternating sections of long and short lines; through its repeated words and phrases ("They tell me" in lines 6–8, "under" in lines 18–19, and "laughing" in lines 18–23, for example); through alliteration (for instance, "slugger set vivid against the little soft cities" in line 11); and, most of all, through the piling up of words and images into catalogs in lines 1–5, 13–17, and 22.

    In order to understand Sandburg's reasons for choosing such a form, we must consider the poem's subject matter and theme. "Chicago" celebrates the scope and power of a "Stormy, husky, brawling" city, one that is exuberant and outgoing, not sedate and civilized. Chicago the city does not follow anyone else's rules; it is, after all, "Bareheaded, / Shoveling, / Wrecking, / Planning, / Building, breaking, rebuilding," constantly active, in flux, on the move, "proud to be alive." "Fierce as a dog . . . cunning as a savage," the city is characterized as, among other things, a worker, a fighter, and a harborer of "painted women" and killers and hungry women and children. Just as Chicago itself does not conform to the rules, the poem clearly demands a departure from the orderly confines of stanzaic form and measured rhyme and meter, a kind of form better suited to "the little soft cities" than to the "tall / bold slugger" that is Chicago.

Of course, open form poetry does not have to look like Sandburg's prose poem. The following poem experiments with a different kind of open form.

LOUISE GLÜCK (1943–)

Life Is a Nice Place (1966)

Life is a nice place (They change
      the decorations
    every season; and the music,
       my dear, is just too
      marvellous, they play you   5
anything from birds to Bach. And
      every day the Host
  arranges for some clever sort
    of contest and they give
        the most   10
  fantastic prizes; I go absolutely
green. Of course, celebrities abound;
I've even seen Love waltzing around
    in amusing disguises.) to
       visit. But   15
I wouldn't want to live there.

Glück's poem includes several end rhymes ("too" / "you"; "Host" / "most"; "abound" / "around"). It also forms a recognizable pattern on the page, broadening and narrowing with some regularity. Moreover, it has a clear syntactical structure, with one main sentence interrupted by parenthetical comments, and it follows standard conventions of capitalization and punctuation. The poem clearly has a form, but its idiosyncratic stanzaic divisions and uneven patterns of rhyme and meter mark it as fresh and original.

The poem's unusual form suits both its subject and its sarcastic tone. It is divided into five sentences, but only the final sentence ends at the end of a line. Moreover, the first sentence ("Life is a nice place . . . to visit") begins in line 1 but does not conclude until the end of the poem. The long parenthetical intrusion, unusual in itself, keeps readers from seeing at first that the poem is a grim new twist on an old cliché: "Life is a nice place . . . / to visit. But / I wouldn't want to live there."

The poem's first line is ironic, because the life the speaker presents is anything but "nice": it is shallow, false, and ultimately meaningless. A cross between a stage set and a cocktail party, this "life" is a place where love is elusive ("waltzing around / in amusing disguises") and nature is artificially re-created by piped-in music and painted backdrops. Glück's unconventional form visually reinforces the empty cycles of this life. Breaks in lines are determined not by conventional phrasing or punctuation but largely by the poem's shape; the result is unusual word groups such as "every season; and the music, . . . is just too" and "fantastic prizes; I go absolutely." These odd juxtapositions suggest the random quality of the speaker's encounters and, perhaps, the unpredictability of her life.

The next poem, an extreme example of open form, looks almost as if it has spilled out of a box of words.

E. E. CUMMINGS (1894–1962)

the sky was can dy (1925)

```
the
         sky
               was
can       dy lu
minous                        5
         edible
spry
         pinks shy
lemons
greens    coo l choc          10
olate
s.

     un  der,
     a  lo
co                            15
mo
     tive    s pout
               ing
               vi
               o          20
               lets
```

Like many of Cummings's poems, this one seems ready to skip off the page. Its ir-regular line length and its unconventional capitalization, punctuation, and word divisions immediately draw readers' attention to its form. Despite these oddities, and despite the absence of orderly rhyme and meter, the poem does have its con-ventional elements. A closer examination reveals that the poem's theme — the beauty of the sky — is quite conventional; that the poem is divided, though some-what crudely, into two sections; and that the poet does use some rhyme — "spry" and "shy," for example. However, Cummings's sky is described not in traditional terms but rather as something "edible," not only in terms of color but of flavor as well. The breaks within words ("can dy lu / minous"; "coo l choc / olate / s") seem to expand each word's possibilities, visually stretching them to the limit, extending their taste and visual image over several lines and, in the case of the last two words, visually reinforcing the picture the words describe. In addition, the isolation of syllables exposes hidden rhyme, as in "lo / co / mo" and "lu" / "coo." By using open form, Cummings makes a clear statement about the capacity of a poem to move beyond the traditional boundaries set by words and lines.

WALT WHITMAN (1819–1892)

from "Out of the Cradle Endlessly Rocking" (1881)

Out of the cradle endlessly rocking,
Out of the mocking-bird's throat, the musical shuttle,
Out of the Ninth-month° midnight,
Over the sterile sands and the fields beyond, where the child
    leaving his bed wander'd alone, bareheaded, barefoot,
Down from the shower'd halo,   5
Up from the mystic play of shadows twining and twisting as if
    they were alive,
Out from the patches of briers and blackberries,
From the memories of the bird that chanted to me,
From your memories sad brother, from the fitful risings and
    fallings I heard,
From under that yellow half-moon late-risen and swollen as if
    with tears,   10
From those beginning notes of yearning and love there in the
    mist,
From the thousand responses of my heart never to cease,
From the myriad thence-arous'd words,
From the word stronger and more delicious than any,
From such as now they start the scene revisiting,   15
As a flock, twittering, rising, or overhead passing,
Borne hither, ere all eludes me, hurriedly,
A man, yet by these tears a little boy again,
Throwing myself on the sand, confronting the waves,
I, chanter of pains and joys, uniter of here and hereafter,   20
Taking all hints to use them, but swiftly leaping beyond them,
A reminiscence sing.

Ninth-month: The Quaker designation for September; in context, an allusion to the human birth cycle.

Reading and Reacting

1. This excerpt, the first twenty-two lines of a poem nearly two hundred lines long, has no regular metrical pattern or rhyme scheme. What gives it form?

2. How might you explain why the poem's lines vary in length?

3. JOURNAL ENTRY Compare this excerpt with the excerpt from Whitman's "Song of Myself" (p. 920). In what respects are the forms of the two poems similar?

4. CRITICAL PERSPECTIVE Reviewing a recent biography of Whitman, Geoffrey O'Brien writes of a paradox in Whitman's poetry:

> [N]either fiction nor verse as they then existed could provide Whitman with what he needed, so he invented out of necessity his own form, a reversion to what he conceived of as the most archaic bardic impulses, representing itself as the poetry of the future.

Can you see the form of "Out of the Cradle" as both "archaic" and "of the future"?

Related Works: "Chicago" (p. 751), "Song of Myself" (p. 920)

DIANE WAKOSKI (1937–   )

Sleep (1966)

The mole
lifting snouts—
full of strained black dirt
     —his perfect tunnel
     sculptured   5
     to fit
     the fat
     body. Sleep
fits tight
—must keep bringing out.   10
the fine grit
to keep size
for even one day.

Reading and Reacting

1. This poem's form seems to be in direct conflict with the logical divisions its syntax and punctuation suggest. For instance, the words in lines 4–9 are set between dashes, indicating a parenthetical comment, yet only lines 4–8 are visually aligned. Also, line 10 ends with a period, but lines 11–13 are clearly part of the same sentence as line 10. How can you account for such discrepancies?

2. How might the poem's discussion of the mole's constant search for the perfect-size tunnel have suggested the form of the poem?

3. JOURNAL ENTRY Why do you believe the poet placed the words "Sleep / fits tight" (lines 8–9) where she did? Could — or should — these words be relocated? If so, where could they be placed, and what changes in form or punctuation would then have to be made?

Related Works: "Red Wheelbarrow" (p. 665), "Reapers" (p. 673)

ROBERT HAYDEN (1913–   )

Monet's "Waterlilies"° (1966)

(For Bill and Sonja)

Today as the news from Selma° and Saigon°
poisons the air like fallout,
      I come again to see
the serene great picture that I love.
Here space and time exist in light   5
the eye like the eye of faith believes.
      The seen, the known
dissolve in irridescence, become
illusive flesh of light
      that was not, was, forever is.   10

O light beheld as through refracting tears.
Here is the aura of that world
      each of us has lost.
Here is the shadow of its joy.

Reading and Reacting

1. The speaker stands before Monet's *Waterlilies*, where he takes temporary refuge from the turbulent world. Why do you suppose Hayden chose not to use

---

Monet's "Waterlilies": Claude Monet (1840–1926), French impressionist painter. The poet's description of the painter's use of light in this particular painting is equally applicable to most of Monet's work.

Selma: A city in central Alabama. In 1965, peaceful demonstrations in support of voting rights for blacks were brutally broken up by the Selma police. Two civil rights supporters were killed: one, minister James Reeb, was beaten to death on a town street; the other, homemaker Viola Liuzzo, was shot by Ku Klux Klansmen as she was driving along a highway.

Saigon: The capital of the former South Vietnam, now known as Ho Chi Minh City. All news of the Vietnam War was cleared through Saigon by U.S. authorities.

the soothing rhythms and comforting shape of closed form to convey the serenity of the moment? Do you think he made the right choice?

2. Hayden indents lines 3, 7, 10, and 13. What purpose, if any, do these indentations serve?

3. Why do you think the last four lines are separated from the rest of the poem?

Related Works: "Facing It" (p. 575), "Try to Praise the Mutilated World" (p. 616), "The World Is Too Much with Us" (p. 618), "Cloud Painter" (p. 663), "Dover Beach" (p. 847), "Ethics" (p. 901)

WILLIAM CARLOS WILLIAMS (1883–1963)

Spring and All (1923)

By the road to the contagious hospital
under the surge of the blue
mottled clouds driven from the
northeast — a cold wind. Beyond, the
waste of broad, muddy fields   5
brown with dried weeds, standing and fallen

patches of standing water
the scattering of tall trees

All along the road the reddish
purplish, forked, upstanding, twiggy   10
stuff of bushes and small trees
with dead, brown leaves under them
leafless vines —

Lifeless in appearance, sluggish
dazed spring approaches —   15

They enter the new world naked,
cold, uncertain of all
save that they enter. All about them
the cold, familiar wind —

Now the grass, tomorrow   20
the stiff curl of wildcarrot leaf
One by one objects are defined —
It quickens: clarity, outline of leaf

But now the stark dignity of
entrance — Still, the profound change   25
has come upon them: rooted, they
grip down and begin to awaken

Reading and Reacting

1. What characteristics of closed form are present in "Spring and All"? What characteristics are absent?
2. What does Williams accomplish by isolating two sets of two lines each (lines 7–8; 14–15)?
3. "Spring and All" uses assonance, alliteration, and repetition. Give several examples of each technique, and explain what each adds to the poem.
4. **JOURNAL ENTRY** "Spring and All" includes only two periods. Elsewhere, where readers might expect to find end punctuation, the poet uses colons, dashes, or no punctuation at all. Why do you think the poet made these decisions about the use of punctuation?
5. **CRITICAL PERSPECTIVE** In the book *Spring and All*, in which this poem appeared, Williams claimed to be staking out a "new world" of poetry addressed "to the imagination." However, in *Lives of the Modern Poets* (1980), William H. Pritchard challenges this claim:

   > [T]o believe that Williams's talk about the Imagination, the "new world," points to some radical way in which this poem is in advance of more traditional versifiers seems to me mistaken. Consider the last five lines of a poem [Robert] Frost had written, in conventional meters, a few years before:
   >
   > > How Love burns through the Putting in the Seed
   > > On through the watching for that early birth
   > > When, just as the soil tarnishes with weed,
   > > The sturdy seedling with arched body comes
   > > Shouldering its way and shedding the earth crumbs.
   >
   > This birth is every bit as imaginative, every bit as much of a new world, as anything in ["Spring and All"].

   What do you think of Pritchard's evaluation of Williams's poem?

Related Works: "Spring Elegy" (p. 700), "Comparatives" (p. 719), "Pied Beauty" (p. 724)

CAROLYN FORCHÉ (1950–   )

The Colonel (1978)

What you have heard is true. I was in his house. His wife carried
a tray of coffee and sugar. His daughter filed her nails, his son went
out for the night. There were daily papers, pet dogs, a pistol on the
cushion beside him. The moon swung bare on its black cord over
the house. On the television was a cop show. It was in English.   5
Broken bottles were embedded in the walls around the house to
scoop the kneecaps from a man's legs or cut his hands to lace. On
the windows there were gratings like those in liquor stores. We had
dinner, rack of lamb, good wine, a gold bell was on the table for

calling the maid. The maid brought green mangoes, salt, a type of 10
bread. I was asked how I enjoyed the country. There was a brief
commercial in Spanish. His wife took everything away. There was
some talk then of how difficult it had become to govern. The parrot
said hello on the terrace. The colonel told it to shut up, and pushed
himself from the table. My friend said to me with his eyes: say 15
nothing. The colonel returned with a sack used to bring groceries
home. He spilled many human ears on the table. They were like
dried peach halves. There is no other way to say this. He took one
of them in his hands, shook it in our faces, dropped it into a water
glass. It came alive there. I am tired of fooling around he said. As 20
for the rights of anyone, tell your people they can go fuck themselves. He swept the ears to the floor with his arm and held the last
of his wine in the air. Something for your poetry, no? he said. Some
of the ears on the floor caught this scrap of his voice. Some of the
ears on the floor were pressed to the ground. 25

Reading and Reacting

1. Treating Forché's prose poem as prose rather than poetry, try dividing it into paragraphs. What determines where you make your divisions?
2. If you were to reshape "The Colonel" into a conventional-looking poem, what options might you have? Rewrite the poem so that it "looks like po- etry," and compare your revision to the original. Which version do you find more effective? Why?
3. What is the main theme of "The Colonel"? How does the form help Forché to communicate this theme?
4. **JOURNAL ENTRY** Do you think "The Colonel" is poetry or prose? Consider its subject matter and language as well as its form.
5. **CRITICAL PERSPECTIVE** Writing in the *New York Times Book Review*, critic Katha Pollitt focuses on "poetic clichés," which, she says, are "attempts to energize the poem by annexing a subject that is guaranteed to produce a knee-jerk response in the reader. This saves a lot of bother all around, and enables poet and reader to drowse together in a warm bath of mutual admi- ration for each other's capacity for deep feeling and right thinking." Among the poetic clichés she discusses is something she calls "the CNN poem, which retells in overheated free verse a prominent news story involving war, famine, torture, child abuse or murder."

   Do you think "The Colonel" is a "CNN poem," or do you see it as some- thing more than just a "poetic cliché"?

Related Works: "All about Suicide" (p. 5), "Hope" (p. 625).

PAT MORA (1942–   )

Immigrants (1986)

wrap their babies in the American flag,
feed them mashed hot dogs and apple pie,
name them Bill and Daisy,
buy them blonde dolls that blink blue
eyes or a football and tiny cleats   5
before the baby can even walk,
speak to them in thick English,
    hallo, babee, hallo.
whisper in Spanish or Polish
when the babies sleep, whisper   10
in a dark parent bed, that dark
parent fear, "Will they like
our boy, our girl, our fine american
boy, our fine american girl?"

Reading and Reacting

1. What do the immigrant parents want for their children? What "dark /
   parent fear" (lines 11–12) do they have? Do you think this fear is justified?
2. What, if anything, determines where the poet breaks the lines of this poem?
   Why, for example, is line 8 shorter than the others? Should the poet have
   broken any lines in different places?
3. Do you think there is any significance in the fact that the word *american* is
   not capitalized in the last two lines?
4. **JOURNAL ENTRY** Although this poem is not a **sonnet,** it does have fourteen
   lines. Does it resemble a sonnet in any other respects?

Related Works: "Two Kinds" (p. 527), "How to Write the Great American
Indian Novel" (p. 629), "The True-Blue American" (p. 780), *The Cuban Swimmer* (p. 1258)

CZESLAW MILOSZ (1911–   )

Christopher Robin (1998)

*In April of 1996 the international press carried the news of the death,
    at age seventy-five, of Christopher Robin Milne, immortalized
in a book by his father, A. A. Milne,* Winnie-the-Pooh, *as Christopher Robin.*

I must think suddenly of matters too difficult for a bear of little
brain. I have never asked myself what lies beyond the place
where we live, I and Rabbit, Piglet and Eeyore, with our friend
Christopher Robin. That is, we continued to live here, and

nothing changed, and I just ate my little something. Only
Christopher Robin left for a moment.   5

Owl says that immediately beyond our garden Time begins,
and that it is an awfully deep well. If you fall in it, you go
down and down, very quickly, and no one knows what happens
to you next. I was a bit worried about Christopher Robin falling
in, but he came back and then I asked him about the well.   10
"Old bear," he answered. "I was in it and I was falling and I
was changing as I fell. My legs became long, I was a big person,
I wore trousers down to the ground, I had a gray beard, then
I grew old, hunched, and I walked with a cane, and then I
died. It was probably just a dream, it was quite unreal. The   15
only real thing was you, old bear, and our shared fun. Now I
won't go anywhere, even if I'm called for an afternoon snack."

Reading and Reacting

1. Who is the poem's speaker? How do you know? How would you characterize
the speaker's voice?
2. For what purpose was this poem written? Considering this purpose, is the
speaker the logical one to tell the poem's story? Who else could tell this story?
3. Does this **prose poem** include any conventional poetic elements? Could you
argue that it is not in fact a poem? Explain.
4. **JOURNAL ENTRY** As the epigraph to the poem points out, the real Christopher
Robin Milne died in 1996. What has happened to the fictional Christopher
Robin? How do you know?
5. **CRITICAL PERSPECTIVE** In a critical review of *Road-side Dog*, the volume of
poems that includes "Christopher Robin," David S. Gross discusses the way
in which Milosz wrestles with fundamental issues in his work:

> This process of trying to arrive at an honest, dynamic sense of self as the basis
> for then making sense of the world has been for Milosz a lifelong vocation. *Road-
> side Dog* is the fruit of the ninth decade of his life, the tenth decade of this
> century, still trying to understand what it means to be human, what it has
> meant to be human in this century, clearly still seeking, and fashioning his
> meanings provisionally, on the basis of where he is at this latest point in his
> search for self-definition.

In what sense does "Christopher Robin" deal with the issue of "what it
means to be human"?

Related Works: "The Secret Lion" (p. 54), "The Fathers" (p. 790)

CONCRETE POETRY

With roots in the ancient Greek *pattern poems* and the sixteenth- and seventeenth-century *emblem poems*, contemporary **concrete poetry** uses words — and,
sometimes, different fonts and type sizes — to shape a picture on the page.

MAY SWENSON (1913–1989)

Women (1970)

Women   Or they
  should be   should be
    pedestals   little horses
      moving   those wooden
        pedestals   sweet   5
         moving   oldfashioned
      to the   painted
        motions   rocking
         of men   horses

       the gladdest things in the toyroom   10

     The   feelingly
    pegs   and then
   of their   unfeelingly
  ears   To be
  so familiar   joyfully   15
  and dear   ridden
  to the trusting   rockingly
fists   ridden until
To be chafed   the restored

egos dismount and the legs stride away   20

Immobile   willing
  sweetlipped   to be set
   sturdy   into motion
    and smiling   Women
     women   should be   25
    should always pedestals
     be waiting   to men

The form of a concrete poem is not something that emerges from the poem's words and images; it is something predetermined by the visual image the poet has decided to create. Although some concrete poems are little more than novelties, others — like the poem on page 763, above — can be original and enlightening.

The curved shape of the poem immediately reinforces its title, and the arrangement of words on the page suggests a variety of visual directions readers might follow. The two columns seem at first to suggest two alternatives: "Women should be . . ." / "Or they should be. . . ." A closer look, however, reveals that the poem's central figures of speech, such as woman as rocking horse and woman as pedestal, move back and forth between the two columns of images. This exchange of positions might suggest that the two possibilities are really just two ways of looking at one limited role. Thus, the experimental form of the poem visually challenges the apparent complacency of its words, suggesting that women, like words, need not fall into traditional roles or satisfy conventional expectations.

GEORGE HERBERT (1593–1633)

Easter Wings (1633)

Lord, who createdst man in wealth and store,
Though foolishly he lost the same,
Decaying more and more
Till he became
Most poor,
With thee
Oh, let me rise   5
As larks, harmoniously,
And sing this day thy victories;
Then shall the fall further the flight in me. 10

My tender age in sorrow did begin;
And still with sicknesses and shame
Thou didst so punish sin,
That I became
Most thin.   15
With thee
Let me combine,
And feel this day thy victory;
For if I imp my wing on thine,
Affliction shall advance the flight in me.   20

Reading and Reacting

1. In this example of an **emblem poem,** lines are arranged so that shape and subject matter reinforce each other. Explain how this is accomplished. (For example, how does line length support the poem's images and ideas?)

2. This poem has a definite rhyme scheme. How would you describe it? What relationship do you see between the rhyme scheme and the poem's visual divisions?

Related Works: "l(a" (p. 552), "A Valediction: Forbidding Mourning" (p. 687), "Thick and Thin" (p. 884)

GREG WILLIAMSON (1964–   )

XXV. Group Photo with Winter Trees (2002)

These were my neighbors. It's a big group pose:
On mist-gray skies, the stark, black branches etch
Horizon, lawn, in loose haphazard rows.

As if in tin, or as in some old sketch,
    That's The Great Bob. And that's our good Queen Paul   5
Whose lines, whose every nuance was precise,
    With Champagne Anne and Rick the dog. They're all
But faded now. I've seen the trees in ice,
    Decked out, (Liz, too, who helped me do the plumbing),
But I'll be gone when their spring blooms and scatters   10
    Even the children. And, God, they're all becoming.
Shades, as the new leaves turn to other matters.

Reading and Reacting

1. Why are alternate lines of this poem set in boldface type? Why are some lines set flush left and others set flush right?

2. What is the poem's rhyme scheme?

3. Do you see this as a single poem or as two separate interlocking poems? Explain.

4. JOURNAL ENTRY How does the form of this poem suggest the "group photo with winter trees" of the title? What is in the foreground? What is in the background?

5. CRITICAL PERSPECTIVE The poem "Group Photo with Winter Trees" is part of the sequence "Double Exposures" from Greg Williamson's second book, *Errors in the Script*. A review of the book notes that it "is obsessed with double vision," and points to "Double Exposures" as "[t]he most dramatic example" of this obsession. "Each poem in the sequence," it notes, "consists of two six-line stanzas printed (one flush left and the other flush right) so that they overlap in the middle of the page; each stanza can be read separately, and the whole set of alternating lines can also be read straight through. Some of the poems succeed better at this high-wire act than others, but in many cases the technique has striking results, and the sequence is decidedly a tour de force."

Do you feel that "Group Photo with Winter Trees" succeeds at its "high-wire act"? In other words, does the unusual approach Williamson takes help him communicate his point more effectively? What do you think his point is?

Related Works: "Photograph of My Father in His Twenty-Second Year" (p. 557), "This Is a Photograph of Me" (p. 849)

CHECKLIST   **WRITING ABOUT FORM**

✓   Is the poem written in open or closed form? On what characteristics do you base your conclusion?

continued on next page

✓   Why did the poet choose open or closed form? For example, is the poem's form consistent with its subject matter, tone, or theme? Is it determined by the conventions of the historical period in which it was written?

✓   If the poem is arranged in closed form, does the pattern apply to single lines, to groups of lines, or to the entire poem? What factors determine the breaks between groups of lines?

✓   Is the poem a sonnet? A sestina? A villanelle? An epigram? A haiku? How do the traditional form's conventions suit the poet's language and theme? Is the poem consistent with the requirements of the form at all times, or does it break any new ground?

✓   If the poem is arranged in open form, what determines the breaks at the ends of lines?

✓   Are certain words or phrases isolated on lines? Why?

✓   How do elements such as assonance, alliteration, rhyme, and repetition of words give the poem form?

✓   What use does the poet make of punctuation and capitalization? Of white space on the page?

✓   Is the poem a prose poem? How does this form support the poem's subject matter?

✓   Is the poem a concrete poem? How does the poet use the visual shape of the poem to convey meaning?

WRITING SUGGESTIONS: Form

1. Reread the definitions of **closed form** and **open form** in this chapter. Do you consider concrete poetry "open" or "closed"? Explain your position in a short essay, supporting your conclusion with specific references to the three concrete poems in this chapter.

2. Some poets — for example, Emily Dickinson and Robert Frost — write both open and closed form poems. Choose one open and one closed form poem by a single poet, and explain the poet's possible reasons for choosing each type of form. In your analysis of the two poems, defend the poet's choices if you can.

3. Do you see complex forms, such as the **villanelle** and the **sestina**, as exercises or even merely as opportunities for poets to show off their skills, or do you believe the special demands of the forms add something valuable to a poem? To help you answer this question, read "Do not go gentle into that good night" (p. 559), and analyze Dylan Thomas's use of the villanelle's structure to enhance his poem's theme. Or study Elizabeth Bishop's "Sestina"

(p. 744), and consider how her use of the sestina's form helps her to convey her ideas.

4. The following open form poem is an alternate version of May Swenson's "Women" (p. 763). Read the two versions carefully, and write an essay in which you compare them. What differences do you notice? Which do you think was written first? Why? Do the two poems make the same point? Which makes the point with less ambiguity? Which is more effective? Why?

Women Should Be Pedestals

Women should be pedestals
moving pedestals
moving to the motions of men
Or they should be little horses
those wooden sweet oldfashioned painted rocking horses   5
the gladdest things in the toyroom
The pegs of their ears so familiar and dear
to the trusting fists
To be chafed feelingly
and then unfeelingly   10
To be joyfully ridden
until the restored egos dismount and the legs stride away
Immobile sweetlipped sturdy and smiling
women should always be waiting
willing to be set into motion   15
Women should be pedestals to men

5. Look through Chapter 25, "Poetry for Further Reading," and identify one or two **prose poems.** Write an essay in which you consider why the form seems suitable for the poem or poems you have chosen. Is there a particular kind of subject matter that seems especially appropriate for a prose poem?

6. WEB ACTIVITY The following Web site contains information about William Carlos Williams:

http://www.learner.org/catalog/extras/vvspot/williams.html

William Carlos Williams is well known for his innovations in poetic form. View the video clip of "the Great Figure." (The text of this poem appears on page 903 of this book, and a painting based on the poem is reproduced on page 904. Then read the article on "the Poetry / Art Connection." Open the sections on Cubism and Dadaism. After reading several other Williams poems from the Web site, write an essay on the connection between visual images and the form of Williams's poetry.

CHAPTER 23

SYMBOL, ALLEGORY, ALLUSION, MYTH

What the reader gets from a symbol depends not only upon what the author has put into it but upon the reader's sensitivity and his consequent apprehension of what is there. The feeling of profundity that accompanies it comes from a gradual but never final penetration of the form. —**William York Tindall,** *"Excellent Dumb Discourse"*

Myth is an expression of "primitive" people. People in the process of making what we call civilization, and its purpose is to explain and support them against darkness. . . . Myth is also a counter against morality in a world in which life is "solitary, nasty, poor, brutish, and short." . . . Myths are also composed — if they are "composed" and not built by accretion, like deltas — by anonymous authors. It would never occur to us to wonder, for example, who wrote about Demeter and Persephone. Nobody wrote it. Everybody did. It doesn't matter. —**Adrián Oktenberg,** *From the Bottom Up*

A myth is not "a large controlling image." The future of mythical poetry does not depend upon reconciling poetry with an image. It depends rather upon making of poetry something it is always striving against human bias and superficiality to become. The poetical imagination when it attains any consistent fire and efficacy is always displacing the texture of the mind into the external world so that it becomes a theater of preternatural forces. A certain control and direction given the poetical emotions, and poetry, as it always has, becomes mythical. —**Richard Chase,** *"Notes on the Study of Myth"*

WILLIAM BLAKE (1757–1827)

The Sick Rose (1794)

O Rose thou art sick.
The invisible worm
That flies in the night,
In the howling storm:

Has found out thy bed   5
Of crimson joy:
And his dark secret love
Does thy life destroy.

SYMBOL

A **symbol** is an idea or image that suggests something else — but not in the simple way that a dollar sign stands for money or a flag represents a country. A symbol is an image that transcends its literal, or denotative, meaning in a complex way. For instance, if someone gives a rose to a loved one, it could simply be a sign of love. But in the poem "The Sick Rose," the rose has a range of contradictory and complementary meanings. For what does the rose stand? Beauty? Perfection? Passion? Something else? As this poem illustrates, the distinctive trait of a symbol is that its meaning cannot easily be pinned down or defined.

Such ambiguity can be frustrating, but it is precisely this characteristic of a symbol that enables it to enrich a poem by giving it additional layers of meaning. As Robert Frost has said, a symbol is a little thing that touches a larger thing. In the poem of his that follows, the central symbol does just this.

ROBERT FROST (1874 – 1963)

For Once, Then, Something (1923)

Others taunt me with having knelt at well-curbs
Always wrong to the light, so never seeing
Deeper down in the well than where the water
Gives me back in a shining surface picture
Me myself in the summer heaven, godlike,   5
Looking out of a wreath of fern and cloud puffs.
Once, when trying with chin against a well-curb,
I discerned, as I thought, beyond the picture,
Through the picture, a something white, uncertain,
Something more of the depths — and then I lost it.   10
Water came to rebuke the too clear water.
One drop fell from a fern, and lo, a ripple
Shook whatever it was lay there at bottom,
Blurred it, blotted it out. What was that whiteness?
Truth? A pebble of quartz? For once, then, something.   15

The central symbol in this poem is the "something" that the speaker thinks he discerns at the bottom of a well. Traditionally, the act of looking down a well suggests a search for truth. In this poem, the speaker says that he always seems to look down the well at the wrong angle, so that all he can see is his own reflection — the surface, not the depths. Once, the speaker tells us, he thought he saw something "beyond the picture," something "white, uncertain," but the image remained in-distinct, disappearing when a drop of water from a fern caused the water to ripple. The poem ends with the speaker questioning the significance of what he saw. Like a reader encountering a symbol, the speaker is left trying to come to terms with images that cannot be clearly perceived and suggestions that cannot be readily understood. In light of the elusive nature of truth, all the speaker can do is ask questions that have no definite answers.

Symbols that appear in poetic works can be *conventional* or *universal*. **Conventional symbols** are those recognized by people who share certain cultural and social assumptions. National flags, for example, evoke a general and agreed-upon response in most people of a particular country and, for better or for worse, American children have for years perceived the golden arches of McDonald's as a symbol of food and fun. **Universal symbols** are those likely to be recognized by people regardless of their culture. In 1890, the noted Scottish anthropologist Sir James George Frazer wrote the first version of his work *The Golden Bough*, in which he showed parallels between the rites and beliefs of early cultures and those of Christianity. Fascinated by Frazer's work, the psychologist Carl Jung sought to explain these parallels by formulating a theory of **archetypes,** which held that certain images or ideas reside in the subconscious of all people. According to Jung, archetypal, or universal, symbols include water, symbolizing rebirth; spring, symbolizing growth; and winter, symbolizing death.

Sometimes symbols that appear in poems can be obscure or highly idiosyn-cratic. William Blake is one of many poets (W. B. Yeats is another) whose works combine symbols from different cultural, theological, and philosophical sources to form complex networks of symbolic associations. To Blake, for example, the scientist Isaac Newton represents the tendency of scientists to quantify experi-ence while ignoring the beauty and mystery of nature. Readers cannot begin to understand Blake's use of Newton as a symbol until they have read a number of his more difficult poems.

Most often, however, symbols in poems are not so challenging. In the next poem, the poet introduces a cross — a symbol that has specific associations to people familiar with Christianity — and makes his own use of it.

JIM SIMMERMAN *

Child's Grave, Hale County, Alabama (1983)

Someone drove a two-by-four
through the heart of this hard land
that even in a good year
will notch a plow blade worthless,
snap the head off a shovel,   5
or bow a stubborn back.

---

*Birth date is not available.

He'd have had to steal
the wood from a local mill
or steal, by starlight, across
his landlord's farm, to worry　　　10
a fencepost out of its well
and lug it the three miles home.
He'd have had to leave his wife
asleep on a corn shuck mat,
leave his broken brogans°　　　15
by the stove, to slip outside,
quiet as sin, with the child
bundled in a burlap sack.
What a thing to have to do
on a cold night in December,　　　20
1936, alone
but for a raspy wind
and the red, rock-ridden dirt
things come down to in the end.
Whoever it was pounded　　　25
this shabby half-cross
into the ground must have toiled
all night to root it so:
five feet buried with the child
for the foot of it that shows.　　　30
And as there are no words
carved here, it's likely that
the man was illiterate,
or addled with fatigue,
or wrenched simple-minded　　　35
by the one simple fact.
Or else the unscored lumber
driven deep into the land
and the hump of busted rock
spoke too plainly of his grief:　　　40
forty years layed by and still
there are no words for this.

Even in non-Christian cultures, the cross on a grave is a readily identifiable symbol of death and rebirth. In this poem, however, the cross is not simply presented as a conventional Christian symbol; it is also associated with the tenant farmer's hard work and difficult life. In this sense, the cross also suggests the poverty that helped bring about the death of the child and the social conditions that existed during the Depression. These associations take readers through many layers of

---

brogans: Sturdy, heavy work shoes, frequently ankle high.

meaning, so that the cross may ultimately stand for the tenant farmer's whole life (the cross *he* has to bear), not just for the death of the child.

That interpretation by no means exhausts the possible symbolic significance of the cross in the poem. For example, the "shabby half-cross" might also suggest the rage and grief of the individual who made it, or it might call to mind the poor who live and die in anonymity. Certainly the poet could have assigned a fixed meaning to the cross that marks the child's grave, but he chose instead, by suggesting various ideas through a single powerful symbol, to let readers arrive at their own conclusions.

How do you know when an idea or image in a poem is a symbol? At what point do you decide that a particular object or idea goes beyond the literal level and takes on symbolic significance? When is a rose more than a rose or a cross more than a cross? Frequently you can recognize a symbol by its prominence or repetition. In "Child's Grave, Hale County, Alabama," for example, the cross is introduced in the first line of the poem, and it is the focal point of the poem; in "The Sick Rose," the importance of the rose is emphasized by the title.

It is not enough, however, to identify an image or idea that seems to suggest something else. Your decision that a particular item has some symbolic significance must be supported by the details of the poem and make sense within the context of the ideas developed in the poem. Moreover, the symbol must support the poem's ideas. In the following poem, the image of the volcano helps readers to understand the poem's central theme.

EMILY DICKINSON (1830–1886)

Volcanoes be in Sicily (1914)

Volcanoes be in Sicily
And South America
I judge from my Geography —
Volcanoes nearer here
A Lava step at any time   5
Am I inclined to climb —
A Crater I may contemplate
Vesuvius at Home.

This poem opens with a statement of fact: volcanoes are located in Sicily and South America. In lines 3 and 4, however, the speaker makes the improbable observation that volcanoes are located near where she is at the moment. Readers familiar with Dickinson know that her poems are highly autobiographical and that she lived in Amherst, Massachusetts. This information leads readers to suspect that they should not take the speaker's observation literally and that in the context of the poem volcanoes may have symbolic significance. But what do volcanoes suggest here?

On the one hand, volcanoes represent the awesome creative power of nature; on the other hand, they suggest its destructiveness. The speaker's contemplation of the crater of Vesuvius — the volcano that buried the ancient Roman city of Pompeii in A.D. 79 — is therefore filled with contradictory associations. Because Dickinson was a recluse, volcanoes — active, destructive, unpredictable, and dangerous — may be seen as symbolic of everything she fears in the outside world and, perhaps, within herself. Or volcanoes may even suggest her own creative power, which, like a volcano, is something to be feared as well as contemplated. She has a voyeur's attraction to danger and power, but she is also afraid of them. For this reason she (and her speaker) may feel safer contemplating Vesuvius at home — not experiencing exotic lands but simply reading a geography book.

LANGSTON HUGHES (1902–1967)

Island (1951)

Wave of sorrow,
Do not drown me now:

I see the island
Still ahead somehow.

I see the island   5
And its sands are fair:

Wave of sorrow,
Take me there.

Reading and Reacting

1. What makes you suspect that the island has symbolic significance in this poem? Explain your answer.

2. Is the "wave of sorrow" also a symbol?

3. **JOURNAL ENTRY** Beyond its literal meaning, what might the island in this poem suggest? Consider several possibilities.

4. **CRITICAL PERSPECTIVE** In *Langston Hughes*, a 1973 study of the poet's work, Onwuchekwa Jemie writes that "the black writer's problem is . . . how to actualize the oral tradition in written form":

   The black writer . . . has no long written tradition of his own to emulate; and for him to abandon the effort to translate into written form that oral medium which is the full reservoir of his culture would be to annihilate his identity and become a zombie, a programmed vehicle for "the message of another people."

   Do you think "Island" successfully "actualizes the oral tradition in written form"? What elements help it to qualify as "oral" poetry?

Related Works: "A Worn Path" (p. 361), "Sea Grapes" (p. 786), "Acquainted with the Night" (p. 876)

ALLEGORY

Allegory is a form of narrative that conveys a message or doctrine by using people, places, or things to stand for abstract ideas. **Allegorical figures,** each with a strict equivalent, form an **allegorical framework,** a set of ideas that conveys the allegory's message or lesson. Thus, the allegory takes place on two levels: a literal level that tells a story and a figurative level where the allegorical figures in the story stand for ideas, concepts, and other qualities. Like symbols, allegorical figures suggest other things. But unlike symbols, which have a range of possible meanings, allegorical figures can always be assigned specific meanings. (Because writers use allegory to instruct, they gain nothing by hiding its significance.) Thus, symbols open up possibilities for interpretation, whereas allegories tend to restrict possibilities.

Quite often an allegory involves a journey or an adventure, as in the case of Dante's *Divine Comedy*, which traces a journey through Hell, Purgatory, and Heaven. Within an allegory, everything can have meaning: the road on which the characters walk, the people they encounter, or a phrase that one of them repeats throughout the journey. Once you understand the allegorical framework, your main task is to see how the various elements fit within this system. Some allegorical poems can be relatively straightforward, but others can be so complicated that it takes a great deal of effort to unlock their meaning. In the following poem, a journey is central to the allegory.

CHRISTINA ROSSETTI (1830–1894)

Uphill (1861)

Does the road wind uphill all the way?
  Yes, to the very end.
Will the day's journey take the whole long day?
  From morn to night, my friend.

But is there for the night a resting-place?   5
  A roof for when the slow dark hours begin.
May not the darkness hide it from my face?
  You cannot miss that inn.

Shall I meet other wayfarers at night?
  Those who have gone before.   10
Then must I knock, or call when just in sight?
  They will not keep you standing at that door.

Shall I find comfort, travel-sore and weak?
  Of labor you shall find the sum.
Will there be beds for me and all who seek?   15
  Yea, beds for all who come.

"Uphill" uses a question-and-answer structure to describe a journey along an uphill road. Like the one described in John Bunyan's seventeenth-century allegory

The Pilgrim's Progress, this is a spiritual journey, one that suggests the challenges a person faces throughout life. The day-and-night duration of the journey stands for life and death, and the inn at the end of the road stands for the grave, the final resting place.

ADRIENNE RICH (1929–)

Diving into the Wreck (1973)

First having read the book of myths,
and loaded the camera,
and checked the edge of the knife-blade,
I put on
the body-armor of black rubber   5
the absurd flippers
the grave and awkward mask.
I am having to do this
not like Cousteau with his
assiduous team   10
aboard the sun-flooded schooner
but here alone.

There is a ladder.
The ladder is always there
hanging innocently   15
close to the side of the schooner.
We know what it is for,
we who have used it.
Otherwise
it's a piece of maritime floss   20
some sundry equipment.

I go down.
Rung after rung and still
the oxygen immerses me
the blue light   25
the clear atoms
of our human air.
I go down.
My flippers cripple me,
I crawl like an insect down the ladder   30
and there is no one
to tell me when the ocean
will begin.

First the air is blue and then
it is bluer and then green and then   35
black I am blacking out and yet

my mask is powerful
it pumps my blood with power
the sea is another story
the sea is not a question of power   40
I have to learn alone
to turn my body without force
in the deep element.

And now: it is easy to forget
what I came for   45
among so many who have always
lived here
swaying their crenellated fans
between the reefs
and besides   50
you breathe differently down here.

I came to explore the wreck.
The words are purposes.
The words are maps.
I came to see the damage that was done   55
and the treasures that prevail.
I stroke the beam of my lamp
slowly along the flank
of something more permanent
than fish or weed   60

the thing I came for:
the wreck and not the story of the wreck
the thing itself and not the myth
the drowned face always staring
toward the sun   65
the evidence of damage
worn by salt and sway into this threadbare beauty
the ribs of the disaster
curving their assertion
among the tentative haunters.   70

This is the place.
And I am here, the mermaid whose dark hair
streams black, the merman in his armored body
We circle silently
about the wreck   75
we dive into the hold.
I am she: I am he
whose drowned face sleeps with open eyes
whose breasts still bear the stress
whose silver, copper, vermeil cargo lies   80

obscurely inside barrels
half-wedged and left to rot
we are the half-destroyed instruments
that once held to a course
the water-eaten log   85
the fouled compass

We are, I am, you are
by cowardice or courage
the one who finds our way
back to this scene   90
carrying a knife, a camera
a book of myths
in which
our names do not appear.

Reading and Reacting

1. On one level, this poem is about a deep-sea diver's exploration of a wrecked
ship. What details suggest that the poet wants you to see something more?

2. Explain the allegorical figures presented in the poem. What, for example,
might the diver and the wreck represent?

3. Does the poem contain any symbols? How can you tell they are symbols and
not allegorical figures?

4. JOURNAL ENTRY In lines 62–63, the speaker says that she came for "the
wreck and not the story of the wreck / the thing itself and not the myth."
What do you think the speaker is really looking for?

5. CRITICAL PERSPECTIVE A number of critics have seen "Diving into the
Wreck" as an attempt by Rich to reimagine or reinvent the myths of Western culture. Rachel Blau DuPlessis makes this observation:

> In this poem of journey and transformation Rich is tapping the energies and
> plots of myth, while re-envisioning the content. While there is a hero, a quest,
> and a buried treasure, the hero is a woman; the quest is a critique of old myths;
> the treasure is knowledge. . . .

Why do you suppose Rich decided to "reinvent" myth?

Related Works: "Young Goodman Brown" (p. 292), "The Love Song of J. Alfred
Prufrock" (p. 871), "Lost Sister" (p. 913), *The Cuban Swimmer* (p. 1258)

ALLUSION

An **allusion** is a brief reference to a person, place, or event (fictional or actual)
that readers are expected to recognize. Like symbols and allegories, allusions
enrich a work by introducing associations from another context.

When poets use allusions, they assume that they and their readers have a common body of knowledge. If, when reading a poem, you come across a reference
with which you are not familiar, take the time to look it up in a dictionary or an

encyclopedia. As you have probably realized by now, your understanding of a poem may depend on your ability to interpret an unfamiliar reference.

Although most poets expect readers to recognize their references, some use allusions to exclude certain readers from their work. In his 1922 poem "The Waste Land," for example, T. S. Eliot alludes to historical events, ancient languages, and obscure literary works. He even includes a set of notes to accompany his poem, but they do little more than complicate an already difficult text. (As you might expect, critical response to this poem was mixed: some critics said that it was a work of genius, others that it was pretentious.)

Allusions can come from any source: history, the arts, other works of literature, the Bible, current events, or even the personal life of the poet. In the following poem, the Nigerian poet and playwright Wole Soyinka alludes to several contemporary political figures.

WOLE SOYINKA (1934–   )

Future Plans (1972)

The meeting is called
To odium: Forgers, framers
Fabricators Inter-
national. Chairman,
A dark horse, a circus nag turned blinkered sprinter   5

Mach Three
We rate him — one for the Knife
Two for 'iavelli, Three —
Breaking speed
Of the truth barrier by a swooping detention decree   10

Projects in view:
Mao Tse Tung in league
With Chiang Kai. Nkrumah
Makes a secret
Pact with Verwood, sworn by Hastings Banda.   15
Proven: Arafat
In flagrante cum
Golda Meir. Castro drunk
With Richard Nixon
Contraceptives stacked beneath the papal bunk . . .   20
                    . . . and more to come

This poem is structured like an agenda for a meeting. From the moment it announces that a meeting has been called "To odium" (a pun on "to *order*"), it is clear that the poem will be a bitter political satire. Those in attendance are "Forgers, framers / Fabricators." The second stanza contains three allusions that shed light on the character of the chairman. The first is to Mack the Knife, a petty criminal in Bertolt Brecht and Kurt Weill's *Threepenny Opera* (1933). The second is to Niccolò Machiavelli, whose book *The Prince* (1532) advocates the use of unscrupulous means to strengthen the state. The last is to the term *mach*, which denotes the speed of an airplane in relation to the speed of sound — mach one, two, three, and so on. By means of these allusions, the poem implies that the meeting's chairman has been chosen for his ability to engage in violence, to be ruthless, and to break the "truth barrier"— that is, to lie.

The rest of the poem alludes to individuals involved in global politics around the time it was written, in 1972 — specifically, the politics of developing nations. According to the speaker, instead of fighting for the rights of the oppressed, these people consolidate their own political power by collaborating with those who oppose their positions. Thus, Mao Tse-tung, the communist leader of China, is "in league / With" Chiang Kai-shek, his old Nationalist Chinese enemy; Yassir Arafat, the leader of the Palestine Liberation Organization, is linked with Golda Meir, the prime minister of Israel; Kwame Nkrumah, the first president of Ghana, conspires with Hendrick Verwoerd, the prime minister of South Africa, assassinated in 1966; and United States president Richard Nixon gets drunk with Cuba's communist leader, Fidel Castro. These allusions suggest the self-serving nature of political alliances and the extreme disorder of world politics. The ideological juxtapositions show the interchangeability of various political philosophies, none of which has the answer to the world's problems. Whether the poem is satirizing the United Nations and its agenda, criticizing the tendency of politics to make strange bedfellows, or showing how corrupt all politicians are, its allusions enable the poet to broaden his frame of reference and thus make the poem more meaningful to readers.

The next poem uses allusions to writers, as well as to a myth, to develop its theme.

WILLIAM MEREDITH (1919–   )

Dreams of Suicide   (1980)

(in sorrowful memory of Ernest Hemingway, Sylvia Plath, and John Berryman)

I

I reach for the awkward shotgun not to disarm
you, but to feel the metal horn,
furred with the downy membrane of dream.
More surely than the unicorn,
you are the mythical beast.   5

II

Or I am sniffing an oven. On all fours
I am imitating a totemic animal
but she is not my totem or the totem
of my people, this is not my magic oven.

III

If I hold you tight by the ankles,   10
still you fly upward from the iron railing.
Your father made these wings,
after he made his own, and now from beyond
he tells you *fly down,* in the voice
my own father might say *walk, boy.*   15

This poem is dedicated to the memory of three writers who committed suicide. In
each stanza, the speaker envisions in a dream the death of one of the writers. In the
first stanza, he dreams of Ernest Hemingway, who killed himself with a shotgun.
The speaker grasps the "metal horn" of Hemingway's shotgun and transforms Hemingway into a mythical beast who, like a unicorn, represents the rare, unique talent of the artist. In the second stanza, the speaker dreams of Sylvia Plath, who asphyxiated herself in a gas oven. He sees himself, like Plath, on his knees imitating
an animal sniffing an oven. In the third stanza, the speaker dreams of John Berryman, who leaped to his death. Berryman is characterized as Icarus, a mythological
figure who, along with his father Daedalus, fled Crete by building wings made of
feathers and wax. Together they flew away, but, ignoring his father's warning,
Icarus flew so close to the sun that the wax melted and he fell to his death in the
sea. Like Icarus, Berryman ignores the warning of his father and, like Daedalus, the
speaker tries to stop Berryman. In this poem, then, the speaker uses allusions to
make a point about the difficult lives of writers — and, perhaps, to convey his own
empathy for those who could not survive the struggle to reconcile art and life.

DELMORE SCHWARTZ (1913–1966)

The True-Blue American   (1959)

Jeremiah Dickson was a true-blue American,
For he was a little boy who understood America, for he felt that
    he must
Think about *everything;* because that's *all* there is to think about,
Knowing immediately the intimacy of truth and comedy,
Knowing intuitively how a sense of humor was a necessity   5
For one and for all who live in America. Thus, natively, and
Naturally when on an April Sunday in an ice cream parlor
    Jeremiah
Was requested to choose between a chocolate sundae and a
    banana split
He answered unhesitatingly, having no need to think of it
Being a true-blue American, determined to continue as he began: 10
Rejecting the either-or of Kierkegaard,° and many another
    European;

Søren Kierkegaard: Danish philosopher (1813–1855) who greatly influenced twentieth-century existentialism.
Either-Or (1841) is one of his best-known works.

Refusing to accept alternatives, refusing to believe the choice of
    between;
Rejecting selection; denying dilemma; electing absolute
    affirmation: knowing
        in his breast   15
            The infinite and the gold
            Of the endless frontier, the deathless West.
"Both: I will have them both!" declared this true-blue American
In Cambridge, Massachusetts, on an April Sunday, instructed
        By the great department stores, by the Five-and-Ten,   20
Taught by Christmas, by the circus, by the vulgarity and grandeur
        of Niagara Falls and the Grand Canyon,
Tutored by the grandeur, vulgarity, and infinite appetite gratified
        and Shining in the darkness, of the light
On Saturdays at the double bills of the moon pictures,   25
The consummation of the advertisements of the imagination
    of the light
Which is as it was — the infinite belief in infinite hope — of
    Columbus,
        Barnum, Edison, and Jeremiah Dickson.

Reading and Reacting

1. To what does the poem's title refer? Do you think this title has meaning beyond its identification of Jeremiah Dickson?

2. Read an encyclopedia article about Kierkegaard. Why do you suppose Schwartz alludes to him in line 11?

3. What do you think the significance of the name Jeremiah Dickson might be? Is it an allusion?

4. What is the significance of the allusions to places in lines 19–22 and to individuals in lines 27 and 28?

5. JOURNAL ENTRY How do you define a "true-blue" American? How do you think the poem's speaker would define this term?

6. CRITICAL PERSPECTIVE In his 1977 biography of Schwartz, James Atlas remarks on the poet's affinity with mass culture:

> Delmore's interest in the products of the popular mind, while in part motivated by a desire to ally himself with a wider public than was ordinarily available to poets, had none of the moralizing condescension [of other 1950s intellectuals]; it was a natural expression of his own affinities with all that was American, affinities derived from his early infatuation with baseball, tabloids, the movies, and whatever else he thought animated the drama of history. . . . He was genuinely democratic. . . .

Do you see "The True-Blue American" as a celebration of mass culture? If not, what do you think Schwartz's purpose might have been?

Related Works: "The Secret Lion" (p. 54), "Chin" (p. 237), "How to Write the Great American Indian Novel" (p. 629), "A Mown Lawn" (p. 727), "Chicago"

(p. 751), "next to of course god america i" (p. 864), "The United Fruit Co." (p. 898), *The Glass Menagerie* (p. 1416)

MYTH

A **myth** is a narrative that embodies — and in some cases helps to explain — the religious, philosophical, moral, and political values of a culture. Using gods and supernatural beings, myths try to make sense of occurrences in the natural world. (The term *myth* can also refer to a private belief system devised by an individual poet as well as to any fully realized fictitious setting in which a literary work takes place, such as the myths of William Faulkner's Yoknapatawpha County or Lawrence Durrell's Alexandria.) Contrary to popular usage, *myth* is not the same as *falsehood*. In the broadest sense, myths are stories — usually whole groups of stories — that can be true or partly true as well as false; regardless of their degree of accuracy, however, myths frequently express the deepest beliefs of a culture. According to this definition, then, the *Iliad* and the *Odyssey*, the Koran, and the Old and New Testaments can all be regarded as myths.

According to the mythologist Joseph Campbell, myths contain truths that link people together, whether they live today or lived 2,500 years ago. Myths attempt to explain phenomena that human beings care about regardless of when and where they live. It is not surprising, then, that myths frequently contain archetypal images that cut across cultural and racial boundaries and touch us at a very deep level. Many Greek myths illustrate this power. For example, when Orpheus descends into Hades to rescue his wife, Eurydice, he acts out the human desire to transcend death; and when Telemachus sets out in search of his father, Odysseus, he reminds readers that we all are lost children searching for parents. When Icarus ignores his father and flies too near the sun and when Pandora cannot resist looking into a box that she has been told not to open, we are reminded of the human weaknesses we all share.

When poets use myths, they are actually making allusions. They expect readers to bring to the poem the cultural, emotional, and ethical context of the myths to which they are alluding. At one time, when all educated individuals studied the Greek and Latin classics as well as the Bible, poets could be reasonably sure that readers would recognize the mythological allusions they made. Today, many readers are unable to understand the full significance of an allusion or its application within a poem. Although many of the poems in this anthology are accompanied by notes, these notes may not provide all the information you will need to understand each mythological allusion and to determine its significance within a poem. Occasionally, you may have to look elsewhere for answers, turning to dictionaries, encyclopedias, or collections of myths such as the *New Larousse Encyclopedia of Mythology* or *Bulfinch's Mythology*.

Sometimes a poet alludes to a myth in a title; sometimes references to various myths appear throughout a poem; at other times, an entire poem focuses on a single myth. In each case, as in the following poem, the use of myth helps to communicate the poem's theme.

COUNTEE CULLEN (1903–1946)

Yet Do I Marvel (1925)

I doubt not God is good, well-meaning, kind,
And did He stoop to quibble could tell why
The little buried mole continues blind,
Why flesh that mirrors Him must some day die,
Make plain the reason tortured Tantalus   5
Is baited by the fickle fruit, declare
If merely brute caprice dooms Sisyphus
To struggle up a never-ending stair.
Inscrutable His ways are, and immune
To catechism by a mind too strewn   10
With petty cares to slightly understand
What awful brain compels His awful hand.
Yet do I marvel at this curious thing:
To make a poet black, and bid him sing!

The speaker begins by affirming his belief in the benevolence of God but then questions why God engages in what appear to be capricious acts. As part of his catalog of questions, the speaker mentions Tantalus and Sisyphus, two figures from Greek mythology. Tantalus was a king who for his crimes was condemned to Hades. He was forced to stand in a pool of water up to his chin. Overhead hung a tree branch laden with fruit. When Tantalus got thirsty and tried to drink, the level of the water dropped, and when he got hungry and reached for fruit, it moved just out of reach. Thus, Tantalus was doomed to be near what he most desired but forever unable to obtain it. Sisyphus also was condemned to Hades. For his disrespect to Zeus, he was sentenced to endless toil. Every day, Sisyphus pushed a boulder up a steep hill. Every time he neared the top, the boulder rolled back down the hill, and Sisyphus had to begin again. Like Tantalus, the speaker in "Yet Do I Marvel" cannot have what he wants; like Sisyphus, he is forced to toil in vain. He wonders why a well-meaning God would "make a poet black, and bid him sing" in a racist society that does not listen to his voice. Thus, the poet's two allusions to Greek mythology enrich the poem by connecting the suffering of the speaker to a universal drama that has been acted out again and again.

LOUISE ERDRICH (1954–)

Windigo (1984)

For Angela
The Windigo is a flesh-eating, wintry demon with a man buried deep inside of it.
In some Chippewa stories, a young girl vanquishes this monster by forcing
boiling lard down its throat, thereby releasing the human at the core of ice.

You knew I was coming for you, little one,
when the kettle jumped into the fire.

Towels flapped on the hooks,
and the dog crept off, groaning,
to the deepest part of the woods.   5

In the hackles of dry brush a thin laughter started up.
Mother scolded the food warm and smooth in the pot
and called you to eat.
But I spoke in the cold trees:
New one, I have come for you, child hide and lie still.   10

The sumac pushed sour red cones through the air.
Copper burned in the raw wood.
You saw me drag toward you.
Oh touch me, I murmured, and licked the soles of your feet.
You dug your hands into my pale, melting fur.   15

I stole you off, a huge thing in my bristling armor.
Steam rolled from my wintry arms, each leaf shivered
from the bushes we passed
until they stood, naked, spread like the cleaned spines of fish.

Then your warm hands hummed over and shoveled themselves
    full   20
of the ice and the snow. I would darken and spill
all night running, until at last morning broke the cold earth
and I carried you home,
a river shaking in the sun.

Reading and Reacting

1. Because Erdrich writes for a diverse audience, she cannot reasonably expect all her readers to be familiar with the Native American myth in the poem. Does her epigraph provide enough information for those who are not?

2. Who is the speaker in the poem? How would you characterize the speaker? What advantage does Erdrich gain by assuming this persona?

3. What is the major theme of this poem? How does the myth of the Windigo express this theme?

4. JOURNAL ENTRY How is the Windigo described in the epigraph like and unlike the one portrayed in the poem?

5. CRITICAL PERSPECTIVE In her 1987 examination of various emerging American literatures, "The Bones of This Body Say, Dance," Lynda Koolish discusses Native American poetry:

> Earlier historical periods of Native American culture provide images of vision and power for many American Indian writers. Poetry, like prayers, chants, the telling of dreams, folktales, tribal lore, or oral history, is an essential part of the spiritual and aesthetic survival of American Indian people. . . . Like myth or folklore, legend or dream, poetry makes the unknowable intelligible. In Native American poetry, as in all these language art forms, access is provided to the mysterious and creative powers of the universe and thus to one's own inner power.

Does "Windigo" offer this kind of access to you? Why or why not?

Related Works: "Where Are You Going, Where Have You Been?" (p. 387), "Gretel in Darkness" (p. 601), "How to Write the Great American Indian Novel" (p. 629), "Fire and Ice" (p. 611), "Leda and the Swan" (p. 785)

WILLIAM BUTLER YEATS (1865–1939)

Leda and the Swan (1924)

A sudden blow: the great wings beating still
Above the staggering girl, her thighs caressed
By the dark webs, her nape caught in his bill,
He holds her helpless breast upon his breast.

How can those terrified vague fingers push   5
The feathered glory from her loosening thighs?
And how can body, laid in that white rush,
But feel the strange heart beating where it lies?

A shudder in the loins engenders there
The broken wall, the burning roof and tower   10
And Agamemnon dead.
                        Being so caught up,
So mastered by the brute blood of the air,
Did she put on his knowledge with his power
Before the indifferent beak could let her drop?   15

Reading and Reacting

1. Look up the myth of Leda in an encyclopedia. What event is described in this poem? What is the mythological significance of the event?
2. How is Leda portrayed? Why is the swan described as a "feathered glory" (line 6)? Why in the poem's last line is Leda dropped by his "indifferent beak"?
3. The third stanza refers to the Trojan War, which was indirectly caused by the event described in the poem. How does the allusion to the Trojan War help develop the theme of the poem?
4. **JOURNAL ENTRY** Does the poem answer the question asked in its last two lines? Explain.
5. **CRITICAL PERSPECTIVE** According to Richard Ellmann, this poem deals with "transcendence of opposites." The bird's "rape of the human, the coupling of god and woman, the moment at which one epoch ended and another began . . . in the act which included all these Yeats had the violent symbol for the transcendence of opposites which he needed."

   What opposite or contrary forces exist in the myth of Leda and the swan? Do you think the poem implies that these forces can be reconciled?

Related Works: "The Birthmark" (p. 477), "The Second Coming" (p. 927)

DEREK WALCOTT (1930–)

Sea Grapes° (1971)

That sail which leans on light,
tired of islands,
a schooner beating up the Caribbean

for home, could be Odysseus,
home-bound on the Aegean;   5
that father and husband's

longing, under gnarled sour grapes, is
like the adulterer hearing Nausicaa's name°
in every gull's outcry.

This brings nobody peace. The ancient war   10
between obsession and responsibility
will never finish and has been the same

for the sea-wanderer or the one on shore
now wriggling on his sandals to walk home,
since Troy sighed its last flame,   15

and the blind giant's boulder heaved the trough
from whose ground-swell the great hexameters come
to the conclusions of exhausted surf.

The classics can console. But not enough.

Reading and Reacting

1. Read a plot summary of the *Odyssey* in an encyclopedia. In the context of
the myth of Odysseus, what is the "ancient war / between obsession and responsibility" (lines 10–11) to which the speaker refers? Does this conflict
have a wider application in the context of the poem? Explain.

2. Consider the following lines from the poem: "and the blind giant's boulder
heaved the trough / from whose ground-swell the great hexameters come /
to the conclusions of exhausted surf" (lines 16–18). In what sense does the
blind giant's boulder create the "great hexameters"? In what way does the
trough end up as "exhausted surf"?

3. JOURNAL ENTRY This poem includes many references to Homer's *Odyssey*.
Could you have appreciated it if you had not read a plot summary of the
Odyssey?

4. CRITICAL PERSPECTIVE Asked in an interview about the final line of "Sea
Grapes," Derek Walcott made the following comments:

Sea Grapes: Small trees found on tropical sandy beaches.

Nausicaa's name: Nausicaa was a young princess who befriended the shipwrecked Odysseus.

All of us have been to the point where, in extreme agony and distress, you turn to a book, and look for parallels, and you look for a greater grief than maybe your own. . . . But the truth of human agony is that a book does not assuage a toothache. It isn't that things don't pass and heal. Perhaps the only privilege that a poet has is that, in that agony, whatever chafes and hurts, if the person survives, [he] produces something that is hopefully lasting and moral from the experience.

How do Walcott's remarks help to explain the poem's last line?

Related Works: "Sleepy Time Gal" (p. 46), "Gryphon" (p. 126), "My Father in the Navy: A Childhood Memory" (p. 557), "Gretel in Darkness" (p. 601), "Dover Beach" (p. 847)

W. H. AUDEN (1907–1973)

Musée des Beaux Arts (1940)

About suffering they were never wrong,
The Old Masters: how well they understood
Its human position; how it takes place
While someone else is eating or opening a window or just
    walking dully along
How, when the aged are reverently, passionately waiting   5
For the miraculous birth, there always must be
Children who did not specially want it to happen, skating
On a pond at the edge of the wood:
They never forgot
That even the dreadful martyrdom must run its course   10
Anyhow in a corner, some untidy spot
Where the dogs go on with their doggy life and the torturer's
    horse
Scratches its innocent behind on a tree.
In Brueghel's *Icarus*, for instance: how everything turns away
Quite leisurely from the disaster; the ploughman may   15
Have heard the splash, the forsaken cry,
But for him it was not an important failure; the sun shone
As it had to on the white legs disappearing into the green
Water; and the expensive delicate ship that must have seen
Something amazing, a boy falling out of the sky,   20
Had somewhere to get to and sailed calmly on.

Reading and Reacting

1. Reread the summary of the myth of Icarus on page 787, above. What does Auden's allusion contribute to the poem?

2. What point does the poet make by referring to the "Old Masters" (2)?

Brueghel, Pieter the Elder (1525?–1569). *Landscape with the Fall of Icarus.* MUSÉE D'ART AN-CIEN, BRUSSELS, BELGIUM. © Scala/Art Resource, N.Y.

3. JOURNAL ENTRY Look at Brueghel's painting *Landscape with the Fall of Icarus* on the following page. How does looking at it help you to understand the poem? To what specific details in the painting does the poet refer?

Related Works: "The Lottery" (p. 303), "One day I wrote her name upon the strand" (p. 654), "Shall I compare thee to a summer's day?" (p. 679), "Ethics" (p. 901), "Not Waving but Drowning" (p. 912), "The Second Coming" (p. 927)

T. S. ELIOT (1888–1965)

Journey of the Magi° (1927)

"A cold coming we had of it,
Just the worst time of the year
For a journey, and such a long journey:
The ways deep and the weather sharp,
The very dead of winter." *   5

Magi: The three wise men who ventured east to pay tribute to the infant Jesus (see Matthew 12.1–12).

*The five quoted lines are adapted from a passage in a 1622 Christmas Day sermon by Bishop Lancelot Andrewes.

And the camels galled, sore-footed, refractory,
Lying down in the melting snow.
There were times we regretted
The summer palaces on slopes, the terraces,
And the silken girls bringing sherbet.   10
Then the camel men cursing and grumbling
And running away, and wanting their liquor and women,
And the night-fires going out, and the lack of shelters,
And the cities hostile and the towns unfriendly
And the villages dirty and charging high prices: 15
A hard time we had of it.
At the end we preferred to travel all night,
Sleeping in snatches,
With the voices singing in our ears, saying
That this was all folly.   20

Then at dawn we came down to a temperate valley,
Wet, below the snow line, smelling of vegetation;
With a running stream and a water-mill beating the darkness,
And three trees° on the low sky,
And an old white horse° galloped away in the meadow.   25
Then we came to a tavern with vine-leaves over the lintel,
Six hands at an open door dicing for pieces of silver,°
And feet kicking the empty wine-skins.
But there was no information, and so we continued
And arrived at evening, not a moment too soon   30
Finding the place; it was (you may say) satisfactory.
All this was a long time ago, I remember,
And I would do it again, but set down
This set down
This: were we led all that way for   35
Birth or Death? There was a Birth, certainly,
We had evidence and no doubt. I had seen birth and death,
But had thought they were different; this Birth was
Hard and bitter agony for us, like Death, our death.
We returned to our places, these Kingdoms,   40
But no longer at ease here, in the old dispensation,
With an alien people clutching their gods.
I should be glad of another death.

---

three trees: The three crosses at Calvary (see Luke 23.32–33).

white horse: The horse ridden by the conquering Christ in Revelation 19.11–16.

dicing . . . silver: Echoes the soldiers dicing for Christ's garments, as well as his betrayal by Judas Iscariot for thirty pieces of silver (see Matthew 27.35 and 26.14–16).

Reading and Reacting

1. The speaker in the poem is one of the three wise men who came to pay tribute to the infant Jesus. In what way are his recollections unexpected? How would you have expected him to react to the birth of Jesus?

2. In what way do the mythical references in the poem allude to future events? Do you need to understand these allusions to appreciate the poem?

3. What does the speaker mean in line 41 when he says that the three wise men were "no longer at ease here, in the old dispensation"? What has changed for them? Why in line 43 does the speaker say that he would be glad for "another death"?

4. JOURNAL ENTRY In what ways is this poem similar to and different from the story of the three wise men told in the New Testament (Matthew 2.1–18)?

5. CRITICAL PERSPECTIVE In an analysis of "Journey of the Magi," poet and critic Anthony Hecht discusses the most common interpretation of the poem: "There seems to be something like a consensus of critical feeling about the tone of the conclusion of this poem, which, it is said, appears to border on despair and exhaustion of hope." Hecht, however, suspects that something more subtle is going on — namely, that Eliot is using the speaker of the poem to express his own imperfect acceptance of Christianity.

> Again, if I am right, about this, the poem might have a deeply personal meaning for Eliot himself, and might represent a kind of "confession," an acknowledgment that he had not yet perfectly embraced the fate to which he nominally adhered, that his imperfect spiritual status was, like the Magus's, that of a person whose faith was incomplete. . . .

Which of the two interpretations given above seems more plausible to you? Is the speaker of the poem wrestling with an incomplete faith, or is he experiencing "despair and exhaustion of hope"?

Related Works: "Araby" (p. 252), "A Clean, Well-Lighted Place" (p. 267), "Do not go gentle into that good night" (p. 559), "The World Is Too Much with Us" (p. 618), "On First Looking into Chapman's Homer" (p. 740), "The Love Song of J. Alfred Prufrock" (p. 871)

ELIZABETH HOLMES (1957–   )

The Fathers   (2001)

*Captain Hook and Mr. Darling
are traditionally played by the same actor.*

Something's familiar about that villain
striding the deck of the *Jolly Roger*, chest
puffed out under the fancy jabot —
a bit like, yes, like Father huffing around
before an evening out, proper shirtfront   5

outthrust by an important bay window.
Particular about his cuff links as a pirate
about lace at his wrists. Same air of dashing
yet dastardly middle age. A penchant
for issuing orders and threats, and tying   10
up uncooperative dogs or Indian princesses.

No wonder we sons and daughters laugh
when Hook sits on the hot toadstool
over Peter's chimney, when Tinker Bell
flits out of his grasp. And especially   15
at his slapstick flailing through the sea,
pursued by that confident long-jawed beast,
time ticking loud in its belly.

Reading and Reacting

1. Why do you think the poet includes a note explaining that the same actor who plays Captain Hook usually plays Mr. Darling? In what way does this note shed light on the poem?

2. Why does the speaker think it is natural for children to laugh at Captain Hook? Why does the speaker think it is especially funny to see Hook chased by the crocodile?

3. With whom does the speaker identify? Captain Hook? Peter Pan? How do you know?

4. JOURNAL ENTRY In what way could the story of Peter Pan be considered a myth? In what way is this designation inappropriate?

Related Works: "The Rocking-Horse Winner" (p. 349), "Gretel in Darkness" (p. 601), "Christopher Robin" (p. 761)

CHECKLIST **WRITING ABOUT SYMBOL, ALLEGORY, ALLUSION, AND MYTH**

Symbol

✓ Are there any symbols in the poem? What leads you to believe they are symbols?

✓ Are these symbols conventional?

✓ Are they universal or archetypal?

✓ Are any symbols obscure or highly idiosyncratic?

✓ What is the literal meaning of each symbol in the context of the poem?

✓ Beyond its literal meaning, what else could each symbol suggest?

continued on next page

✓ How does your interpretation of each symbol enhance your understanding of the poem?

Allegory

✓ Is the poem an allegory?

✓ Are there any allegorical figures within the poem? How can you tell?

✓ What do the allegorical figures signify on a literal level?

✓ What lesson does the allegory illustrate?

Allusion

✓ Are there any allusions in the poem?

✓ Do you recognize the names, places, historical events, or literary works to which the poet alludes?

✓ In what way does each allusion deepen the poem's meaning? Does any allusion interfere with your understanding or enjoyment of the poem? If so, how?

✓ Would the poem be more effective without a particular allusion?

Myth

✓ What myths or mythological figures are alluded to?

✓ How does the poem use myth to convey its meaning?

✓ How faithful is the poem to the myth? Does the poet add material to the myth? Are any details from the original myth omitted? Is any information distorted? Why?

WRITING SUGGESTIONS: Symbol, Allegory, Allusion, Myth

1. Read "Aunt Jennifer's Tigers" (p. 715) and "Diving into the Wreck" (p. 775) by Adrienne Rich. Then, write an essay in which you discuss similarities and differences in Rich's use of symbols in the two poems.

2. Many popular songs make use of allusion. Choose one or two popular songs that you know well, and analyze their use of allusion, paying particular attention to whether the allusions expand the impact and meaning of the song or create barriers to listeners' understanding.

3. What applications do the lessons of myth have for life today? Choose two or three poems from the section on myth, and consider how you can use myth to make generalizations about your own life.

4. Both Judith Ortiz Cofer's "My Father in the Navy: A Childhood Memory" (p. 557) and Derek Walcott's "Sea Grapes" (p. 786) allude to Homer's *Odyssey*. Read a summary of the *Odyssey* in an encyclopedia or other reference book, and then write an essay in which you compare the poets' treatments of Homer's tale. What specific use does each poet make of the story?

5. WEB ACTIVITY The following Web site contains information about Christina Rossetti:

http://www.victorianweb.org/authors/crosetti/themeov.html

Read "Death as Release from Pain in Christina Rossetti's Works" by Hoxie Neal Fairchild. Then write an essay applying Fairchild's thesis to Rossetti's poem "Uphill" (p. 774). Consider how Rossetti treats the theme of death in her poem and her use of sometimes ambiguous images of death. Does the poem imply that death offers rest after the "uphill" struggle of life?

CHAPTER 24

THE POETRY OF LANGSTON HUGHES: A CASEBOOK FOR READING, RESEARCH, AND WRITING

This chapter provides all the materials you will need to begin a research project about Langston Hughes. It includes fourteen poems by Langston Hughes; questions to stimulate discussion and writing; a collection of source materials; a student paper that shows how one student, Grace Alston, used the materials in this chapter in her research; and suggestions for further research on Hughes.

POEMS

Other poems by Hughes elsewhere in this anthology are "Negro" (p. 604), "Harlem" (p. 680), and "Island" (p. 773).

SOURCE MATERIALS

Each of the sources offers insights into the poems included in this Casebook. Three are Hughes's own words, one is largely biographical, one is a close reading of a particular poem, and still others discuss Hughes's use of poetic devices and his influences. All were selected to help you to understand this poet and to appreciate the themes and devices in his poetry. Other kinds of sources can also enrich your understanding of Hughes's accomplishments — for example, other poems by Hughes, biographical data about the author, and works of imaginative literature by other writers dealing with similar themes. Several interesting Web sites on Hughes are listed below.

● *The Academy of American Poets*. <http://www.poets.org>. Search for Langston Hughes in the upper left search box to go to the Langston Hughes page. A full site hosted by the Academy of American Poets, the Langston Hughes page includes poems — some read aloud — and a link to the academy's online exhibit "Poets of the Harlem Renaissance and After," which includes Hughes.

● *PAL: Langston Hughes (1902–1967)*. <http://www.csustan.edu/english/ reuben/pal/chap9/hughes.html>. This complete Web site on the life, works, and criticism of Langston Hughes even includes study questions, video, and audio recordings.

- *Langston Hughes Honored.* <http://www.usps.com/news/2002/ philatelic/sr02_004.htm>. This site, sponsored by the United States Postal Service, offers an interesting explanation of why the USPS chose to honor Hughes's centennial by putting his image on a postage stamp. The site includes a link to the government's other Black Heritage honorees from 1978–2002.
- *Langston Hughes.* <http://www.americaslibrary.gov/cgi-bin/page.cgi/ aa/hughes>. In addition to containing a biography of Hughes, this site has a time line of major United States events that took place during Hughes's lifetime.

In preparation for writing an essay on a topic of your choice, read the poems carefully. Then, consider the Reading and Reacting questions that follow them (p. 809) in light of what you have read, and use your responses to help you find a topic you can develop in a three- to six-page essay. Be sure to document any words or ideas that you borrow from your sources, and remember to enclose words that are not your own in quotation marks. (For guidelines on evaluating literary criticism, see p. 13; for guidelines on using source materials, see Chapter 37.)

A complete student paper, "Challenging the Father/Challenging the Self: Langston Hughes's 'The Negro Speaks of Rivers,'" which uses some of the sources included in this Casebook, begins on page 838.

LANGSTON HUGHES (1902–1967) was one of the best-known American writers of the twentieth century. As a member of the Harlem Renaissance in the 1920s, he helped found a mature but vital African American literature, one that was able to address issues of poverty and racism without sacrificing the complexities of the individual life. His earliest book of poetry, *The Weary Blues* (1926), established him at once as one of the most important poets of his generation, and his first novel, *Not Without Laughter*, was published in 1930. Not only did Hughes deal honestly with the daily lives and struggles of his people, but he did so in poems that owed much to African American musical forms, such as Jazz and Blues. Art and politics were inseparable for Hughes, and he was active throughout his life in the promotion of racial and economic justice.

Hughes was born in Joplin, Missouri, in 1902, and his early life was shaped by the racial and economic inequities that would become the focus of his writing and social activism. Although his father, James Hughes, had studied law, he was not allowed to take the bar exam because of his race, and eventually he left the United States to try his luck in Mexico. Hughes's mother, Carrie, refused to follow her husband, so the young Langston had little contact with his father until he was in his late teens. Hughes first became interested in literature when his mother took him to the library, and from that time on, he was a voracious reader, absorbing the works of writers from different times and cultures. While attending Central High School in Cleveland, Ohio, he began to write poetry, with Carl Sandburg as one of his chief influences. Upon leaving high school, Hughes began the travels that would make such a deep impression on his work. In 1920, he went to live with his father in

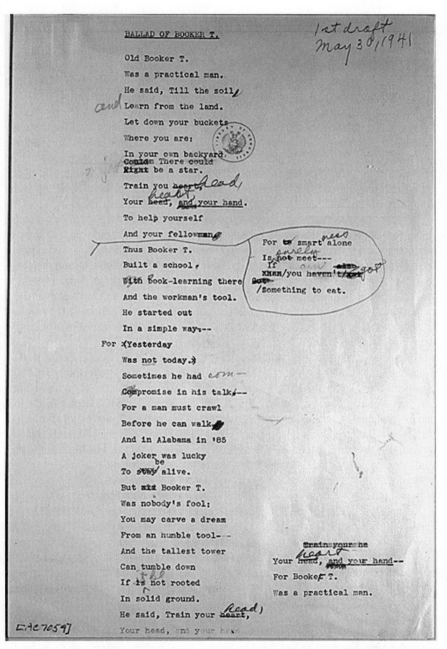

This draft of the poem "Ballad of Booker T" was hand edited by Langston Hughes in 1941.

Mexico City. On the way there, he wrote what was to become one of his best-known poems, "The Negro Speaks of Rivers." Father and son had little in common, and the trip was not successful on a personal level. At one point, Hughes even considered suicide. When he returned to the United States, he enrolled at Columbia University to study engineering, but his classes were of little interest to him, and he spent most of his time writing and absorbing the cultural life of New York's African American community.

With the publication of his first book of poetry, *The Weary Blues*, in 1926, Hughes became a visible member of the Harlem Renaissance, one of the most significant literary movements of the twentieth century. Centered in the Harlem section of New York City, the movement represented the first great flowering of African American literature and included such writers as James Weldon Johnson, Claude McKay and Countee Culleen. This period is generally considered to have ended with the publication of *God Sends Sunday*, by Arna Bontemps, in 1931.

Although he would become arguably the best-known writer of the Harlem Renaissance, Hughes's work was not universally praised by critics and peers. In fact, many of the elements that have given his work its staying power—his use of African American vernacular, his imitation of the forms of popular music, his concern for the economically disadvantaged—proved controversial at the time. There were many who felt that African American writing ought to deal primarily with uplifting stories and to do so in a manner that would be familiar to readers used to the conventions of white literature. These critics believed that Hughes's work was undercutting the advances African Americans were achieving in both literary and social life.

Hughes's response to his critics was at once understanding and straightforward. "I sympathized deeply," he later said, "with those critics and those intellectuals, and I saw clearly the need for some of the kinds of books they wanted." He went on to insist, however, that not every book by an African American could or should be about subjects that middle- or upper-class whites and blacks would find palatable: "I didn't know the upper-class Negroes well enough to write much about them. I knew only the people I had grown up with, and they weren't people whose shoes were always shined, who had been to Harvard, or who had heard of Bach. But they seemed to me good people, too."

In portraying these "good people," Hughes did not shy away from depicting the details of their often difficult lives. His subjects are often poor and frequently faced with racism. Sometimes they are in trouble with the law, and they are typically less interested in rarified topics of discussion than in paying the rent. The poor had been portrayed before in poetry: T.S. Eliot's Modernist masterwork *The Wasteland*, published in 1922, just four years before *The Weary Blues*, includes a famous and particularly unflattering exchange between two lower-class women. What distinguished Hughes's approach from Eliot's, apart from his more direct style, was his sympathy for his subjects and his intimate familiarity with their living conditions.

In writing about lower-class African Americans, people who had never "heard of Bach," Hughes devised poetic forms that imitated the cadences of Jazz and Blues, the types of music with which they were in fact familiar. Hughes found nothing wrong with Bach, but he was convinced that African Americans had their own composers and performers of genius. Nor was this simply a self-conscious attempt to find an appropriate poetic vehicle for his subject matter or to promote the art of his people: Hughes loved this music deeply, and nothing could have been more natural for him than to employ its rhythms. His later move into writing song-lyrics was a natural transition.

Always a traveler, Hughes made a fateful journey to the Soviet Union in 1932. While there, he observed aspects of the Soviet system that he felt were admirable and compared favorably with the capitalism practiced in the United States. He was especially appreciative of what he saw as the lack of racial injustice and economic inequality. He learned the Uzbek language while recuperating from an illness and began writing on a regular basis for Soviet newspapers, including *Izvestia*. He published one book devoted to impressions of the trip, *A Negro Looks at Soviet Central Asia* in 1934. Additionally, he reflected on his experiences in newspaper columns for *The Chicago Defender*.

Hughes left the Soviet Union after a little more than a year, but he did not abandon his commitment to radical social change. Back in the United States, he settled for a time in California, where he devoted himself to a number of causes although he soon had to move because of threats of violence. It would be a mistake however, to suppose that Hughes was unremittingly hostile to America. During World War II, when the United States was allied with the Soviet Union against Nazi Germany, Fascist Italy, and Imperial Japan, Hughes used his writing to support the war effort, even as he encouraged America to live up to its democratic ideals.

As part of this effort, Hughes invented a character, Jesse B. Semple, later known as Simple. Simple first appeared in newspaper columns, but these were so popular that they were later anthologized in a series of books, beginning in 1950 with *Simple Speaks His Mind*. Here Hughes uses the device of a fictional narrator talking with, and buying drinks for, his friend Semple. The popularity of the pieces derived in part from their humor and straightforward examination of racial issues and partly from Hughes's skillful use of African American vernacular. Since his first publications, Hughes had included the actual speech of the black lower class in his work, and the "Simple" books brought this strategy to a wider audience than ever before.

During the 1950s, his sympathetic comments on communism in general, and the Soviet Union in particular, caused Hughes great political difficulties. In 1953, he was called before the House Un-American Activities Committee, led by Senator Joseph McCarthy. In his testimony to the committee, Hughes denied being a communist but explained why he felt communism appealed to some African Americans. There is some debate about Hughes's actual political views during this period. Commentators who maintain that Hughes had never in fact been an extreme leftist also tend to assume that his statements to the committee were an accurate reflection of his political views at the time. Others, however, are convinced that Hughes, afraid that the writing career he had worked so hard to establish would be destroyed, was downplaying communist views he in fact still held.

Despite the disruption to his career caused by the Committee's investigation, Hughes remained an important literary and political presence for the remainder of his life. In 1961 he published *Ask Your Mama*, a work that addressed many of the racial and cultural issues that would be so important in the 1960s. He also traveled widely, often as an official representative of the United States. When Hughes died in 1967, he was completing work on his last volume of poetry, *The Panther and the Lash*, which was positively received by the critics.

Today, Hughes is remembered chiefly as a poet, but he made important contributions to virtually every imaginable genre of writing. He was an accomplished dramatist who also founded several theaters. He wrote novels, short stories, journalism, song lyrics, translations, and fiction for children. In addition to his work as a writer, Hughes edited numerous volumes and helped encourage and promote the work of younger African American writers. In the years since his death, his reputation has become even more solidly established.

Plain-spoken and highly rhythmic, his poetry continues to appeal to new readers, and to provide an example of the ways in which social commitment and literary art can be fruitfully combined.

The Negro Speaks of Rivers (1921)

I've known rivers:
I've known rivers ancient as the world and old as the flow of
   human blood in human veins.

My soul has grown deep like the rivers.

I bathed in the Euphrates° when dawns were young.
I built my hut near the Congo° and it lulled me to sleep.   5
I looked upon the Nile and raised the pyramids above it.
I heard the singing of the Mississippi when Abe Lincoln went
   down to New Orleans, and I've seen its muddy bosom turn
   all golden in the sunset.

I've known rivers:
Ancient, dusky rivers.

My soul has grown deep like the rivers.   10

The Weary Blues (1926)

Droning a drowsy syncopated tune,
Rocking back and forth to a mellow croon,
   I heard a Negro play.
Down on Lenox Avenue° the other night
By the pale dull pallor of an old gas light   5
   He did a lazy sway . . .
   He did a lazy sway . . .
To the tune o' those Weary Blues.
With his ebony hands on each ivory key
He made that poor piano moan with melody.   10
   O Blues!
Swaying to and fro on his rickety stool
He played that sad raggy tune like a musical fool.
   Sweet Blues!
Coming from a black man's soul.   15
   O Blues!
In a deep song voice with a melancholy tone

Euphrates: Major river of southwest Asia; with the Tigris, the Euphrates forms a valley sometimes referred to as the "cradle of civilization."

Congo: River in equatorial Africa, the continent's second longest.

Lenox Avenue: Street in Harlem noted for nightlife and music during the 1920s.

I heard that Negro sing, that old piano moan—
 "Ain't got nobody in all this world,
 Ain't got nobody but ma self.   20
 I's gwine to quit ma frownin'
 And put ma troubles on the shelf."
Thump, thump, thump, went his foot on the floor.
He played a few chords then he sang some more—
 "I got the Weary Blues   25
 And I can't be satisfied,
 Got the Weary Blues
 And can't be satisfied—
 I ain't happy no mo'
 And I wish that I had died."   30
And far into the night he crooned that tune.
The stars went out and so did the moon.
The singer stopped playing and went to bed
While the Weary Blues echoed through his head.
He slept like a rock or a man that's dead. 35

I, Too (1925)

I, too, sing America.

I am the darker brother.
They send me to eat in the kitchen
When company comes,
But I laugh,   5
And eat well,
And grow strong.

Tomorrow,
I'll be at the table
When company comes.   10
Nobody'll dare
Say to me,
"Eat in the kitchen,"
Then.

Besides,   15
They'll see how beautiful I am
And be ashamed—

I too, am America.

Ballad of the Landlord (1940)

Landlord, landlord,
My roof has sprung a leak.
Don't you 'member I told you about it
Way last week?

Landlord, landlord,   5
These steps is broken down.
When you come up yourself
It's a wonder you don't fall down.

Ten Bucks you say I owe you?
Ten Bucks you say is due?   10
Well, that's Ten Bucks more'n I'll pay you
Till you fix this house up new.

What? You gonna get eviction orders?
You gonna cut off my heat?
You gonna take my furniture and   15
Throw it in the street?

Um-huh! You talking high and mighty.
Talk on — till you get through.
You ain't gonna be able to say a word
If I land my fist on you.   20

Police! Police!
Come and get this man!
He's trying to ruin the government
And overturn the land!

Copper's whistle!   25
Patrol bell!
Arrest.

Precinct Station.   .
Iron cell.
Headlines in press: 30

MAN THREATENS LANDLORD
                                   ∴

TENANT HELD NO BAIL
                               ∴

JUDGE GIVES NEGRO 90 DAYS IN COUNTY JAIL

Theme for English B (1949)

The instructor said,

> *Go home and write*
> *a page tonight.*
> *And let that page come out of you—*
> *Then, it will be true.*   5

I wonder if it's that simple?
I am twenty-two, colored, born in Winston-Salem.
I went to school there, then Durham, then here

to this college on the hill above Harlem.
I am the only colored student in my class.   10
The steps from the hill lead down into Harlem,
through a park, then I cross St. Nicholas,
Eighth Avenue, Seventh, and I come to the Y,
the Harlem Branch Y, where I take the elevator
up to my room, sit down and write this page: 15

It's not easy to know what is true for you or me
at twenty-two, my age. But I guess I'm what
I feel and see and hear, Harlem, I hear you:
hear you, hear me — we two — you, me, talk on this page.
(I hear New York, too) Me — who?   20
Well, I like to eat, sleep, drink, and be in love.
I like to work, read, learn, and understand life.
I like a pipe for a Christmas present,
or records — Bessie,° bop,° or Bach.
I guess being colored doesn't make me *not* like   25
the same things other folks like who are other races.
So will my page be colored that I write?
Being me, it will not be white.
But it will be
a part of you, instructor.   30
You are white—
yet a part of me, as I am a part of you.
That's American.
Sometimes perhaps you don't want to be a part of me.
Nor do I often want to be a part of you.   35
But we are, that's true!
As I learn from you,
I guess you learn from me—
although you're older — and white—
and somewhat more free.   40

This is my page for English B.

Dream Boogie (1951)

Good morning, daddy!
Ain't you heard
The boogie-woogie° rumble

Bessie: Bessie Smith (1894–1937), blues singer.

bop: Short for "bebop," a jazz style developed in the early 1940s by Charlie Parker, Dizzy Gillespie, and others.

boogie-woogie: A popular black musical style with variants in both blues and jazz; more specifically, a vigorous piano style marked by heavy and repeated bass figures. Some commentators have also suggested that it was slang for syphilis.

Of a dream deferred?

Listen closely: 5
You'll hear their feet
Beating out and beating out a—

> *You think*
> *It's a happy beat?*

Listen to it closely: 10
Ain't you heard
something underneath
like a—

> *What did I say?*

Sure,   15
I'm happy!
Take it away!

> *Hey, pop!*
> *Re-bop!*
> *Mop!*   20

> *Y-e-a-h!*

Birmingham Sunday
(September 15, 1963)° (1967)

    Four little girls
Who went to Sunday School that day
And never came back home at all
But left instead
Their blood upon the wall   5
With spattered flesh
And bloodied Sunday dresses
Torn to shreds by dynamite
That China made aeons ago—
Did not know   10
That what China made
Before China was ever Red at all
Would redden with their blood
This Birmingham-on-Sunday wall.

    Four tiny girls   15
Who left their blood upon that wall,

September 15, 1963: On this date, only weeks after Martin Luther King, Jr.'s historic March on Washington, D.C., four young African-American girls were killed at their Sunday school in Birmingham, Alabama, by a bomb, likely in response to recent civil rights organizing in the area. The case has never been fully solved.

In little graves today await
The dynamite that might ignite
The fuse of centuries of Dragon Kings°
Whose tomorrow sings a hymn   20
The missionaries never taught Chinese
In Christian Sunday School
To implement the Golden Rule.

    Four little girls
Might be awakened someday soon   25
By songs upon the breeze
As yet unfelt among magnolia trees.

Old Walt (1954)

Old Walt Whitman
Went finding and seeking,
Finding less than sought
Seeking more than found,
Every detail minding   5
Of the seeking or the finding.

Pleasured equally
In seeking as in finding,
Each detail minding,
Old Walt went seeking   10
And finding.

Genius Child (1947)

This is a song for the genius child.
Sing it softly, for the song is wild.
Sing it softly as ever you can—
Lest the song get out of hand.

Nobody loves a genius child.   5

Can you love an eagle,
Tame or wild?

Wild or tame,
Can you love a monster
Of a frightening name?   10

Dragon Kings: In Chinese myth and lore, the dragon is a beneficent force that dispenses blessings in both the natural and the supernatural worlds. Eventually the dragon became a symbol of imperial China. The dragon has also been utilized in the mythology of white supremacist groups like the Ku Klux Klan.

Nobody loves a genius child.

Kill him— and let his soul run wild!

Park Bench (1938)

I live on a park bench,
You, Park Avenue.
Hell of a distance
Between us two.

I beg a dime for dinner—   5
You got a butler and maid.
But I'm wakin' up!
Say, ain't you afraid

That I might, just maybe,
In a year or two,   10
Move on over
To Park Avenue?

Lenox Avenue: Midnight (1926)

The rhythm of life
Is a jazz rhythm,
Honey.
The gods are laughing at us.

The broken heart of love,   5
The weary, weary heart of pain,—
    Overtones,
    Undertones,
To the rumble of street cars,
To the swish of rain.   10

Lenox Avenue,
Honey.
Midnight,
And the gods are laughing at us.

Un-American Investigators (1953)

The committee's fat,
Smug, almost secure
Co-religionists
Shiver with delight

In warm manure   5
As those investigated—
Too brave to name a name—
Have pseudonyms revealed
In Gentile game
    Of who,   10
    Born Jew,
    Is who?
Is not your name Lipshitz?
    Yes.
Did you not change it   15
For subversive purposes?
    No.
For nefarious gain?
    Not so.
Are you sure?   20
The committee shivers
With delight in
Its manure.

Dinner Guest: Me (1965)

I know I am
The Negro Problem
Being wined and dined,
Answering the usual questions
That come to white mind   5
Which seeks demurely
To probe in polite way
The why and wherewithal
Of darkness U.S.A.—
Wondering how things got this way   10
In current democratic night,
Murmuring gently
Over *fraises du bois*,
"I'm so ashamed of being white."

The lobster is delicious,   15
The wine divine,
And center of attention
At the damask table, mine.
To be a Problem on
Park Avenue at eight   20
Is not so bad.
Solutions to the Problem,
Of course, wait.

The Ballad of Booker T. (1941)

Booker T.
Was a practical man.
He said, Till the soil
And learn from the land.
Let down your bucket
Where you are.
Your fate is here
And not afar.
To help yourself
And your fellow man,
Train your head,
Your heart, and your hand.
For smartness alone's
Surely not meet —
If you haven't at the same time
Got something to eat.
Thus at Tuskegee
He built a school
With book-learning there.
And the workman's tool.
He started out
In a simple way —
For yesterday
Was not today.
Sometimes he had
Compromise in his talk-
For a man must crawl
Before he can walk —
And in Alabama in '85
A joker was lucky
To be alive.
But Booker T.
Was nobody's fool;
You may carve a dream
With an humble tool.
The tallest tower
Can tumble down
If it be not rooted
In solid ground,
So, being a far-seeing
Practical man,
He said, Train your head,
Your heart, and your hand.
Your fate is here

And not afar,
So let down your bucket
Where you are.

Reading and Reacting

1. How do historical and geographic allusions contribute to the power of "The Negro Speaks of Rivers"?

2. How does Hughes use music and musical allusions? Are the poems themselves meant to be musical?

3. Which poems are poems of protest? Does Hughes seem to place social or political goals above literary concerns?

4. Is the question of identity (especially racial identity) handled differently in "The Negro Speaks of Rivers" and "Theme for English B"? Explain.

5. How would you characterize Hughes's attitude toward America in "Theme for English B" and "I, Too"? Do you think these poems are patriotic?

6. Hughes is often celebrated for his ability to communicate complex human dilemmas in simple language and forms. Evaluate "Harlem" (p. 680) in this regard.

7. In the poem "Birmingham Sunday," why does Hughes include statements about Chinese mythology and history?

8. Is the "dream" in "Harlem" (p. 680) the same as the one in "Dream Boogie"? Do you think the poems were meant to be read side by side? Do they shed light on each other? Do they represent different approaches to a similar problem?

9. In which poems do you think the first person voice is autobiographical? In which poems is Hughes simply creating a speaker?

10. What do you think Hughes expects of readers of his poetry? Reflection? A change of heart? Action?

11. JOURNAL ENTRY Are Langston Hughes's poems relevant only to African-Americans, or do they also have relevance for other Americans — or for readers in other countries?

12. CRITICAL PERSPECTIVE In his essay "The Negro Artist and the Racial Mountain" (p. 810) Hughes states his respect for the "common people," those he admires for their lack of self-importance:

> But then there are the low-down folks, the so-called common element, and they are the majority — may the Lord be praised! The people who have their nip of gin on Saturday nights are not too important to themselves or the community, or too well fed, or too learned to watch the lazy world go round. They live on Seventh Street in Washington or State Street in Chicago, and they do not particularly care whether they are like white folks or anybody else. . . . They furnish a wealth of colorful, distinctive material for any artist because they still hold their own individuality in the face of American standardizations.

How does Hughes depict the "common people" in his poetry? What are their concerns? How have America's "standardizations" attempted to shape and change the common people, and what has been the result of those attempts?

Related Works: "Big Black Good Man" (p. 206), "Photograph of My Father in His Twenty-Second Year" (p. 557), "The Unknown Citizen" (p. 626), "Ballad of Birmingham" (p. 628), "We Real Cool" (p. 859), "Sadie and Maud" (p. 709)

LANGSTON HUGHES

from The Negro Artist and the Racial Mountain

One of the most promising of the young Negro poets said to me once, "I want to be a poet — not a Negro poet," meaning, I believe, "I want to write like a white poet": meaning subconsciously, "I would like to be a white poet," meaning behind that, "I would like to be white." And I was sorry the young man said that, for no great poet has ever been afraid of being himself. And I doubted then that, with his desire to run away spiritually from his race, this boy would ever be a great poet. But this is the mountain standing in the way of any true Negro art in America — this urge within the race toward whiteness, the desire to pour racial individuality into the mold of American standardization, and to be as little Negro and as much American as possible.

But let us look at the immediate background of this young poet. His family is of what I suppose one would call the Negro middle class: people who are by no means rich yet never uncomfortable nor hungry — smug, contented, respectable folk, members of the Baptist church. The father goes to work every morning. He is a chief steward at a large white club. The mother sometimes does fancy sewing or supervises parties for the rich families of the town. The children go to a mixed school. In the home they read white papers and magazines. And the mother often says, "Don't be like niggers" when the children are bad. A frequent phrase from the father is, "Look how well a white man does things." And so the word white comes to be unconsciously a symbol of all the virtues. It holds for the children beauty, morality, and money. The whisper of "I want to be white" runs silently through their minds. This young poet's home is, I believe, a fairly typical home of the colored middle class. One sees immediately how difficult it would be for an artist born in such a home to interest himself in interpreting the beauty of his own people. He is never taught to see that beauty. He is taught rather not to see it, or if he does, to be ashamed of it when it is not according to Caucasian patterns.

For racial culture the home of a self-styled "high-class" Negro has nothing better to offer. Instead there will perhaps be more aping of things white than in a less cultured or less wealthy home. The father is perhaps a doctor, lawyer, landowner, or politician. The mother may be a social worker, or a teacher, or she may do nothing and have a maid. Father is often dark but he has usually married the lightest woman he could find. The family attend a fashionable church where few really colored faces are to be found. And they themselves draw a color line. In the North they go to white theaters and white movies. And in the South they have at least two cars and a house "like white folks." Nordic manners, Nordic faces,

Nordic hair, Nordic art (if any), and an Episcopal heaven. A very high mountain indeed for the would-be racial artist to climb in order to discover himself and his people.

But then there are the low-down folks, the so-called common element, and they are the majority — may the Lord be praised! The people who have their nip of gin on Saturday nights are not too important to themselves or the community, or too well fed, or too learned to watch the lazy world go round. They live on Seventh Street in Washington or State Street in Chicago and they do not particularly care whether they are like white folks or anybody else. Their joy runs, bang! into ecstasy. Their religion soars to a shout. Work maybe a little today, rest a little tomorrow. Play awhile. Sing awhile. O, let's dance! These common people are not afraid of spirituals, as for a long time their more intellectual brethren were, and jazz is their child. They furnish a wealth of colorful, distinctive material for any artist because they still hold their own individuality in the face of American standardizations. And perhaps these common people will give to the world its truly great Negro artist, the one who is not afraid to be himself. Whereas the better-class Negro would tell the artist what to do, the people at least let him alone when he does appear. And they are not ashamed of him — if they know he exists at all. And they accept what beauty is their own without question.

Certainly there is, for the American Negro artist who can escape the restrictions the more advanced among his own group would put upon him, a great field of unused material ready for his art. Without going outside his race, and even among the better classes with their "white" culture and conscious American manners, but still Negro enough to be different, there is sufficient matter to furnish a black artist with a lifetime of creative work. And when he chooses to touch on the relations between Negroes and whites in this country with their innumerable overtones and undertones, surely, and especially for literature and the drama, there is an inexhaustible supply of themes at hand. To these the Negro artist can give his racial individuality, his heritage of rhythm and warmth, and his incongruous humor that so often, as in the Blues, becomes ironic laughter mixed with tears. . . .

Let the blare of Negro jazz bands and the bellowing voice of Bessie Smith singing Blues penetrate the closed ears of the colored near-intellectuals until they listen and perhaps understand. Let Paul Robeson singing Water Boy, and Rudolph Fisher writing about the streets of Harlem, and Jean Toomer holding the heart of Georgia in his hands, and Aaron Douglas drawing strange black fantasies cause the smug Negro middle class to turn from their white, respectable, ordinary books and papers to catch a glimmer of their own beauty. We younger Negro artists who create now intend to express our individual dark-skinned selves without fear or shame. If white people are pleased we are glad. If they are not, it doesn't matter. We know we are beautiful. And ugly too. The tom-tom cries and the tom-tom laughs. If colored people are pleased we are glad. If they are not, their displeasure doesn't matter either. We build our temples for tomorrow, strong as we know how, and we stand on top of the mountain, free within ourselves.

To Negro Writers

There are certain practical things American Negro writers can do through their work.

We can reveal to the Negro masses, from which we come, our potential power to transform the now ugly face of the Southland into a region of peace and plenty.

We can reveal to the white masses those Negro qualities which go beyond the mere ability to laugh and sing and dance and make music, and which are a part of the useful heritage that we place at the disposal of a future free America.

Negro writers can seek to unite blacks and whites in our country, not on the nebulous basis of an inter-racial meeting, or the shifting sands of religious brotherhood, but on the *solid* ground of the daily working-class struggle to wipe out, now and forever, all the old inequalities of the past.

Furthermore, by way of exposure, Negro writers can reveal in their novels, stories, poems, and articles:

The lovely grinning face of Philanthropy — which gives a million dollars to a Jim Crow school, but not one job to a graduate of that school; which builds a Negro hospital with second-rate equipment, then commands black patients and student-doctors to go there whether they will or no; or which, out of the kindness of its heart, erects yet another separate, segregated, shut-off, Jim Crow Y.M.C.A.

Negro writers can expose those white labor leaders who keep their unions closed against Negro workers and prevent the betterment of all workers.

We can expose, too, the sick-sweet smile of organized religion — which lies about what it doesn't know, and about what it *does* know. And the half-voodoo, half-clown, face of revivalism, dulling the mind with the clap of its empty hands.

Expose, also, the false leadership that besets the Negro people — bought and paid for leadership, owned by capital, afraid to open its mouth except in the old conciliatory way so advantageous to the exploiters.

And all the economic roots of race hatred and race fear.

And the Contentment Tradition of the O-lovely-Negroes school of American fiction, which makes an ignorant black face and a Carolina head filled with superstition, appear more desirable than a crown of gold; the jazz-band; and the O-so-gay writers who make of the Negro's poverty and misery a dusky funny paper.

And expose war. And the old My-Country-'Tis-of-Thee lie. And the colored American Legion posts strutting around talking about the privilege of dying for the nobel Red, White and Blue, when they aren't even permitted the privilege of living for it. Or voting for it in Texas. Or working for it in the diplomatic service. Or even rising, like every other good little boy, from the log cabin to the White House.

White House is right!

Dear colored American Legion, you can swing from a lynching tree, uniform and all, with pleasure — and nobody'll fight for you. Don't you know that?

Nobody even salutes you down South, dead or alive, medals or no medals, chevrons° or not, no matter how many wars you've fought in.

Let Negro writers write about the irony and pathos of the *colored* American Legion.

"*Salute, Mr. White Man!*"

"Salute, hell! . . . You're a nigger."

Or would you rather write about the moon?

Sure, the moon still shines over Harlem. Shines over Scottsboro. Shines over Birmingham, too, I reckon. Shines over Cordie Cheek's grave, down South.

Write about the moon if you want to. Go ahead. This is a free country.

But there are certain very practical things American Negro writers can do. And must do. There's a song that says, "the time ain't long." That song is right. Something has got to change in America — and change soon. We must help that change to come.

The moon's still shining as poetically as ever, but all the stars on the flag are dull. (And the stripes, too.)

We want a new and better America, where there won't be any poor, where there won't be any more Jim Crow, where there won't be any lynchings, where there won't be any munition makers, where we won't need philanthropy, nor charity, nor the New Deal, nor Home Relief.

We want an America that will be ours, a world that will be ours — we Negro workers and white workers! Black writers and white! We'll make that world!

LANGSTON HUGHES

from My Adventures as a Social Poet

Poets who write mostly about love, roses and moonlight, sunsets and snow, must lead a very quiet life. Seldom, I imagine, does their poetry get them into difficulties. Beauty and lyricism are really related to another world, to ivory towers, to your head in the clouds, feet floating off the earth.

Unfortunately, having been born poor — and also colored — in Missouri, I was stuck in the mud from the beginning. Try as I might to float off into the clouds, poverty and Jim Crow would grab me by the heels, and right back on earth I would land. A third-floor furnished room is the nearest thing I have ever had to an ivory tower.

Some of my earliest poems were social poems in that they were about people's problems — whole groups of people's problems — rather than my own personal difficulties. Sometimes, though, certain aspects of my personal problems happened to be also common to many other people. And certainly, racially speaking, my own problems of adjustment to American life were the same as those of millions of other segregated Negroes. The moon belongs to everybody, but not this American

---

chevrons: Stripes on a military uniform denoting rank.

earth of ours. That is perhaps why poems about the moon perturb no one, but poems about color and poverty do perturb many citizens. Social forces pull backwards or forwards, right or left, and social poems get caught in the pulling and hauling. Sometimes the poet himself gets pulled and hauled — even hauled off to jail.

I have never been in jail but I have been detained by the Japanese police in Tokyo and by the immigration authorities in Cuba — in custody, to put it politely — due, no doubt, to their interest in my written words. These authorities would hardly have detained me had I been a writer of the roses and moonlight school. I have never known the police of any country to show an interest in lyric poetry as such. But when poems stop talking about the moon and begin to mention poverty, trade unions, color lines, and colonies, somebody tells the police. The history of world literature has many examples of poets fleeing into exile to escape persecution, of poets in jail, even of poets killed like Placido or, more recently, Lorca in Spain.

My adventures as a social poet are mild indeed compared to the body-breaking, soul-searing experiences of poets in the recent Fascist countries or of the resistance poets of the Nazi-invaded lands during the war. For that reason, I can use so light a word as "adventure" in regard to my own skirmishes with reaction and censorship.

My adventures as a social poet began in a colored church in Atlantic City shortly after my first book, *The Weary Blues*, was published in 1926. I had been invited to come down to the shore from Lincoln University where I was a student, to give a program of my poems in the church. During the course of my program I read several of my poems in the form of the Negro folk songs, including some blues poems about hard luck and hard work. As I read I noticed a deacon approach the pulpit with a note which he placed on the rostrum beside me, but I did not stop to open the note until I had finished and had acknowledged the applause of a cordial audience. The note read, "Do not read any more blues in my pulpit." It was signed by the minister. That was my first experience with censorship.

The kind and generous woman who sponsored my writing for a few years after my college days did not come to the point quite so directly as did the minister who disliked blues. Perhaps, had it not been in the midst of the great depression of the late '20's and '30's, the kind of poems that I am afraid helped to end her patronage might not have been written. But it was impossible for me to travel from hungry Harlem to the lovely homes on Park Avenue without feeling in my soul the great gulf between the very poor and the very rich in our society. In those days, on the way to visit this kind lady I would see the homeless sleeping in subways and the hungry begging in doorways on sleet-stung winter days. It was then that I wrote a poem called "Advertisement for the Waldorf-Astoria," satirizing the slick-paper magazine advertisements of the opening of that de luxe hotel. Also I wrote:

PARK BENCH

> I live on a park bench,
> You, Park Avenue.
> Hell of a distance
> Between us two.

I beg a dime for dinner —
You got a butler and maid.
But I'm wakin' up!
Say, ain't you afraid

That I might, just maybe,
In a year or two,
Move on over
To Park Avenue?

In a little while I did not have a patron any more.

But that year I won a prize, the Harmon Gold Award for Literature, which consisted of a medal and four hundred dollars. With the four hundred dollars I went to Haiti. On the way I stopped in Cuba and I was cordially received by the writers and artists. I had written poems about the exploitation of Cuba by the sugar barons and I had translated many poems of Nicolás Guillén such as:

CANE

Negro
In the cane fields.
White man
Above the cane fields
Earth
Beneath the cane fields.
Blood
That flows from us.

This was during the days of the dictatorial Machado regime. Perhaps someone called his attention to these poems and translations because, when I came back from Haiti weeks later, I was not allowed to land in Cuba, but was detained by the immigration authorities at Santiago and put on an island until the American consul came, after three days, to get me off with the provision that I cross the country to Havana and leave Cuban soil at once.

That was my first time being put out of any place. But since that time I have been put out of or barred from quite a number of places, all because of my poetry — not the roses and moonlight poems (which I write, too) but because of poems about poverty, oppression, and segregation. Nine Negro boys in Alabama were on trial for their lives when I got back from Cuba and Haiti. The famous Scottsboro "rape" case was in full session. I visited those boys in the death house at Kilby Prison, and I wrote many poems about them. One of these poems was:

CHRIST IN ALABAMA

Christ is a Nigger,
Beaten and black —
O, bare your back.

Mary is His Mother —
Mammy of the South,
Silence your mouth.

God's His Father—
White Master above,
Grant us your love.

Most holy bastard
Of the bleeding mouth:
Nigger Christ
On the cross of the South.

Contempo, a publication of some of the students at the University of North Carolina, published the poem on its front page on the very day that I was being presented in a program of my poems at the University in Chapel Hill. That evening there were police outside the building in which I spoke, and in the air the rising tension of race that is peculiar to the South. It had been rumored that some of the local citizenry were saying that I should be run out of town, and that one of the sheriffs agreed, saying, "Sure, he ought to be run out! It's bad enough to call Christ a *bastard.* But when he calls him a *nigger,* he's gone too far!"

The next morning a third of my fee was missing when I was handed my check. One of the departments of the university jointly sponsoring my program had refused to come through with its portion of the money. Nevertheless, I remember with pleasure the courtesy and kindness of many of the students and faculty at Chapel Hill and their lack of agreement with the anti-Negro elements of the town. There I began to learn at the University of North Carolina how hard it is to be a white liberal in the South.

It was not until I had been to Russia and around the world as a writer and journalist that censorship and opposition to my poems reached the point of completely preventing me from appearing in public programs on a few occasions. It happened first in Los Angeles shortly after my return from the Soviet Union. I was to have been one of several speakers on a memorial program to be held at the colored branch Y.M.C.A. for a young Negro journalist of the community. At the behest of white higher-ups, no doubt, some reactionary Negro politicians informed the Negro Y.M.C.A. that I was a Communist. The secretary of the Negro Branch Y then informed the committee of young people in charge of the memorial that they could have their program only if I did not appear.

I have never been a Communist, but I soon learned that anyone visiting the Soviet Union and speaking with favor of it upon returning is liable to be so labeled. Indeed when Mrs. Roosevelt, Walter White, and so Christian a lady as Mrs. Bethune who has never been in Moscow, are so labeled, I should hardly be surprised! I wasn't surprised. And the young people's committee informed the Y secretary that since the Y was a public community center which they helped to support, they saw no reason why it should censor their memorial program to the extent of eliminating any speaker.

Since I had been allotted but a few moments on the program, it was my intention simply to read this short poem of mine:

Dear lovely death
That taketh all things under wing,
Never to kill,

Only to change into some other thing
This suffering flesh—
To make it either more or less
But not again the same,
Dear lovely death,
Change is thy other name.

But the Negro branch Y, egged on by the reactionary politicians (whose incomes, incidentally, were allegedly derived largely from gambling houses and other underworld activities), informed the young people's committee that the police would be at the door to prevent my entering the Y on the afternoon of the scheduled program. So when the crowd gathered, the memorial was not held that Sunday. The young people simply informed the audience of the situation and said that the memorial would be postponed until a place could be found where all the participants could be heard. The program was held elsewhere a few Sundays later. . . .

So goes the life of social poet. I am sure none of these things would ever have happened to me had I limited the subject matter of my poems to roses and moonlight. But, unfortunately, I was born poor — and colored — and almost all the prettiest roses I have seen have been in rich white people's yards — not in mine. That is why I cannot write exclusively about roses and moonlight — for sometimes in the moonlight my brothers see a fiery cross and a circle of Klansmen's hoods. Sometimes in the moonlight a dark body sways from a lynching tree — but for his funeral there are no roses.

ARNOLD RAMPERSAD

from The Origins of Poetry in Langston Hughes

In his study *The Life of the Poet: Beginning and Ending Poetic Careers* (1981) Lawrence Lipking asks three main questions, one of which concerns me here in the case of Langston Hughes: "How does an aspiring author of verses become a poet?" In the case of John Keats, for example, how did the poet arrive at "On First Looking Into Chapman's Homer" [see p. 740 in this volume], that great leap in creative ability in which Keats, sweeping from the legend of "the realms of gold" toward modern history, "catches sight not of someone else's dream but of his own reality? He stares at his future, and surmises that he may be a poet. The sense of possibility is thrilling, the moment truly awesome. Keats has discovered Keats." Or in the well-known words of Keats himself: "The Genius of Poetry must work out its own salvation in a man: It cannot be matured by law & precept, but by sensation & watchfulness in itself — That which is creative must create itself."

Can one ask a similar question about the origins of poetry in Langston Hughes, who in June 1921, at the age of nineteen, began a celebrated career when he published his own landmark poem "The Negro Speaks of Rivers" [see p. 800] in

W.E.B. Du Bois' *Crisis* magazine? Like Keats before "Chapman's Homer," Hughes had written poems before "The Negro Speaks of Rivers." Much of the poetry before "Rivers" is available for examination, since Hughes published steadily in the monthly magazine of his high school in Cleveland, Ohio. Certain aspects of this verse are noteworthy. It has nothing to do with race; it is dominated by images of the poet not as a teenager but as a little child; and, in Hughes's junior year, he published his first poem in free verse, one that showed the clear influence of Walt Whitman for the first (but not the last) time. Revealing an increase in skill, Hughes's early poetry nevertheless gives no sign of a major poetic talent in the making. At some point in his development, however, something happened to Hughes that was as mysterious and as wonderful, in its own way, as the miracle that overtook John Keats after the watchful night spent with his friend Charles Cowden Clarke and a copy of Chapman's translation. With "The Negro Speaks of Rivers" the creativity in Langston Hughes, hitherto unexpressed, suddenly created itself.

In writing thus about Hughes, are we taking him too seriously? With a few exceptions, literary critics have resisted offering even a modestly complicated theory concerning his creativity. His relentless affability and charm, his deep, open love of the black masses, his devotion to their folk forms, and his insistence on writing poetry that they could understand, all have contributed to the notion that Langston Hughes was intellectually and emotionally shallow. One wonders, then, at the source of the creative energy that drove him from 1921 to 1967 to write so many poems, novels, short stories, plays, operas, popular histories, children's books, and assorted other work. As a poet, Hughes virtually reinvented Afro-American poetry with his pioneering use of the blues and other folk forms; as Howard Mumford Jones marveled in a 1927 review, Hughes added the verse form of the blues to poetry in English (a form that continues to attract the best black poets, including Michael Harper, Sherley Anne Williams, and Raymond Patterson). One wonders, too, in his aspect as a poet, why this apparently happy, apparently shallow man defined his creativity in terms of unhappiness. "I felt bad for the next three or four years," he would write in *The Big Sea* about the period beginning more or less with the publication of "The Negro Speaks of Rivers," and "those were the years when I wrote most of my poetry. (For my best poems were all written when I felt the worst. When I was happy, I didn't write anything)."

Hughes actively promoted the image of geniality to which I have alluded. Wanting and needing to be loved, he scrubbed and polished his personality until there was no abrasive side, no jagged edge that might wound another human being. Publicly and privately, his manner belied the commonly held belief that creativity and madness are allied, that neuroses and a degree of malevolence are the fair price of art. His autobiographies, *The Big Sea* (1940) and *I Wonder As I Wander* (1956), made no enemies; to many readers, Hughes's mastery of that form consists in his ability to cross its chill deep by paddling nonchalantly on its surface. And yet in two places, no doubt deliberately, Hughes allows the reader a glimpse of inner turmoil. Both appear in the earlier book, *The Big Sea*. Both involve personal and emotional conflicts so intense that they led to physical illness. Because of their extreme rarity, as well as their strategic location in the context of his creativity, these passages deserve close scrutiny if we hope to glimpse the roots of Hughes's originality as a poet.

The first of these two illnesses took place in the summer of 1919, when Hughes (at seventeen) saw his father for the first time in a dozen years. In 1903, James Hughes had gone to Mexico, where he would become a prosperous property owner. In a lonely, impoverished, passed-around childhood in the Midwest, his son had fantasized about the man "as a kind of strong, bronze cowboy, in a big Mexican hat, going back and forth from his business in the city to his ranch in the mountains, free — in a land where there were no white folks to draw the color line, and no tenements with rent always due —just mountains and cacti: Mexico!" Elated to be invited suddenly to Mexico in 1919 at the end of his junior year in high school, Langston left the United States with high hopes for his visit.

The summer was a disaster. James Hughes proved to be an unfeeling, domineering, and materialistic man, scornful of Indians and blacks (he was himself black) and the poor in general; and contemptuous of his son's gentler pace and artistic temperament. One day, Langston could take no more: "Suddenly my stomach began to turn over and over. And I could not swallow another mouthful. Waves of heat engulfed me. My eyes burned. My body shook. I wanted more than anything on earth to hit my father, but instead I got up from the table and went back to bed. The bed went round and round and the room turned dark. Anger clotted in every vein, and my tongue tasted like dry blood." But the boy, ill for a long time, never confessed the true cause of his affliction. Having been moved to Mexico City, he declined to help his doctors: "I never told them . . . that I was sick because I hated my father." He recovered only when it was time to return to the United States.

Hughes's second major illness came eleven years later. By this time he had finished high school, returned to Mexico to live with his father for a year, attended Columbia University for one year (supported grudgingly by James Hughes), dropped out of school, and served as a messman on voyages to Africa and to Europe, where he spent several months in 1924 as a dishwasher. All the while, however, Hughes was publishing poetry in a variety of places, especially in important black journals. This activity culminated in books of verse published in 1926 (*The Weary Blues*) and 1927 (*Fine Clothes to the Jew*) that established him, with Countee Cullen, as one of two major black poets of the decade. In 1929, he graduated after three and a half years at black Lincoln University, Pennsylvania. In 1930, Hughes published his first novel, *Not Without Laughter*.

This book had been virtually dragged out of him by his patron of the preceding three years, "Godmother" (as she wished to be called), an old, white, very generous but eccentric woman who ruled Hughes with a benevolent despotism inspired by her volatile beliefs in African spirituality, folk culture, mental telepathy, and the potential of his genius. But the result of her largesse was a paradox: the more comfortable he grew, the less Hughes was inclined to create. Estranged by his apparent languor, his patron finally seized on an episode of conflict to banish him once and for all. Hughes was devastated. Surviving drafts of his letters to "Godmother" reveal him deep in self-abasement before a woman with whom he was clearly in love. Ten years later, he confessed in *The Big Sea:* "I cannot write here about that last half-hour in the big bright drawing-room high above Park Avenue . . . because when I think about it, even now, something happens in the pit of my stomach that makes me ill. That beautiful room . . . suddenly became like a trap closing in, faster and faster, the room darker and darker, until the light went out with a sudden crash in the dark, and everything became like . . . that morning in Mexico when I suddenly hated my father.

"I was violently and physically ill, with my stomach turning over and over. . . . And there was no rationalizing anything. I couldn't." For several months, according to my research (Hughes erroneously presents a far briefer time frame in *The Big Sea*), he waited in excruciating hope for a reconciliation. As in Mexico, he wasted time and money on doctors without revealing to them the source of his chronic illness (which one very ingenious Harlem physician diagnosed as a Japanese tapeworm). Rather than break his silence, Hughes even agreed to have his tonsils removed. Gradually it became clear that reconciliation was impossible. Winning a prize of four hundred dollars for his novel, Hughes fled to seclusion in hot, remote Haiti. When his money ran out some months later, he returned home, healed at last but badly scarred.

Although they occurred more than a decade apart, the two illnesses were similar. Both showed a normally placid Hughes driven into deep rage by an opponent, a rage which he was unable to ventilate because the easy expression of personal anger and indignation was anathema to him. In both cases, he developed physical symptoms of hyperventilation and, eventually, anemia. More importantly, both were triggered in a period of relatively low poetic creativity (as when he was still a juvenile poet) or outright poetic inactivity (as with his patron). In each instance, Hughes had become satisfied with this low creativity or inactivity. At both times, a certain powerful figure, first his father, then "Godmother," had opposed his right to be content. His father had opposed any poetic activity at all; "Godmother" had opposed his right to enjoy the poetical state without true poetical action, or writing. In other words, a powerful will presented itself in forceful opposition to what was, in one sense, a vacuum of expressive will on Hughes's part. (Needless to say, the *apparent* absence of will in an individual can easily be a token of the presence of a very powerful will.) The result on both occasions, which was extraordinary, was first Hughes's endurance of, then his violent rebellion against, a force of will that challenged his deepest vision of the poetic life. . . .

In his bitter struggles with his father and "Godmother," Hughes turned to the black race for direction. But one needs to remember that this appeal in itself hardly gave Hughes distinction as a poet; what made Hughes distinct was the highly original manner in which he internalized the Afro-American racial dilemma and expressed it in poems such as "When Sue Wears Red," "The Negro Speaks of Rivers," "Mother to Son," "Dream Variations," and "The Weary Blues," poems of Hughes's young manhood on which his career would rest. Of these, the most important was "The Negro Speaks of Rivers."

I've known rivers.
I've known rivers ancient as the world and old
    as the flow of human blood in human veins.

My soul has grown deep like the rivers.

I bathed in the Euphrates when dawns were young.
I built my hut near the Congo and it lulled me to sleep.
I looked upon the Nile and raised the pyramids above it.
I heard the singing of the Mississippi when Abe Lincoln went down
    to New Orleans, and I've seen its muddy bosom turn all golden
    in the sunset.

I've known rivers:
Ancient, dusky rivers.

My soul has grown deep like the rivers.

Here, the persona moves steadily from dimly starred personal memory ("I've known rivers") toward a rendezvous with modern history (Lincoln going down the Mississippi and seeing the horror of slavery that, according to legend, would make him one day free the slaves). The death wish, benign but suffusing, of its images of rivers older than human blood, of souls grown as deep as these rivers, gives way steadily to an altering, ennobling vision whose final effect gleams in the evocation of the Mississippi's "muddy bosom" turning at last "all golden in the sunset." Personal anguish has been alchemized by the poet into a gracious meditation on his race, whose despised ("muddy") culture and history, irradiated by the poet's vision, changes within the poem from mud into gold. This is a classic example of the essential process of creativity in Hughes.

The poem came to him, according to Hughes (accurately, it seems clear) about ten months after his Mexican illness, when he was riding a train from Cleveland to Mexico to rejoin his father. The time was sundown, the place the Mississippi outside St. Louis. "All day on the train I had been thinking of my father," he would write in *The Big Sea*. "Now it was just sunset and we crossed the Mississippi, slowly, over a long bridge. I looked out of the window of the Pullman at the great muddy river flowing down toward the heart of the South, and I began to think what that river, the old Mississippi, had meant to Negroes in the past — how to be sold down the river was the worst fate that could overtake a slave in bondage. Then I remembered reading how Abraham Lincoln had made a trip down the Mississippi on a raft, and how he had seen slavery at its worst, and had decided within himself that it should be removed from American life. Then I began to think of other rivers in our past — the Congo, and the Niger, and the Nile in Africa — and the thought came to me: 'I've known rivers,' and I put it down on the back of an envelope I had in my pocket, and within the space of ten or fifteen minutes, as the train gathered speed in the dusk, I had written this poem."

Here, starting with anguish over his father, Hughes discovered the compressed ritual of passivity, challenge, turmoil, and transcendence he would probably have to re-create, doubtless in variant forms, during the great poetic trysts of his life.

Even after he became a successful, published poet, the basic process remained the same, because his psychology remained largely the same even though he had become technically expert. In his second major illness, caused by his patron "Godmother," Hughes wrote poetry as he struggled for a transcendence that would be long in coming. The nature of that interim poetry is telling. When he sent some poems to a friend for a little book to be printed privately, she noticed at once that many spoke of death — "Dear lovely Death / That taketh all things under wing — / Never to kill. . . ." She called the booklet *Dear Lovely Death*. In "Afro-American Fragment," unlike in "The Negro Speaks of Rivers," Africa is seen plaintively:

> . . . Subdued and time-lost
> Are the drums — and yet
> Through some vast mist of race
> There comes this song
> I do not understand,
> This song of atavistic land,
> Of bitter yearnings lost
> Without a place —
> So long,
> So far away
> Is Africa's
> Dark face.

But when Hughes returned home, scarred but healed, after months in seclusion in Haiti, he no longer thought of loss and death. Instead, he plunged directly into the life of the black masses with a seven-month tour of the South in which he read his poetry in their churches and schools. Then he set out for the Soviet Union, where he would spend more than a year. Hughes then reached the zenith of his revolutionary ardor with poems (or verse) such as "Good Morning Revolution," "Goodbye Christ," and "Put One More 'S' in the USA."

HERMAN BEAVERS

from Dead Rocks and Sleeping Men: Aurality in the Aesthetic of Langston Hughes

In his 1940 autobiography, *The Big Sea*, Langston Hughes discusses the circumstances that led him, at the puerile age of 19, to the creation of his poem, "The Negro Speaks of Rivers" [see p. 800]. The poem came into being during a trip to Mexico, Hughes writes, "when [he] was feeling very bad."[1] Thus, he connects poetic inspiration and emotional turbulence, both of which stemmed from his attempt to understand his father's self-hatred. He relates, "All day on the train I had been thinking about my father and his strange dislike of his own people. I didn't understand it because I was a Negro, and I liked Negroes very much" (54). What is striking about the end of this passage is that one finds Hughes adopting a posture both inside and outside the race: he does not make a statement of self-love (e.g. I like myself), rather he indicates through a kind of reflexivity, that he has self-worth. In short, he is unable to articulate self-valuation, he can only construct his positionality as the mirror opposite of his father's racial feeling. But then Hughes shifts the subject and recalls that "one of the happiest jobs [he] ever had," was the time he spent working behind the soda fountain of a refreshment parlor, in "the heart of the colored neighborhood" in Cleveland. He offers this description:

> People just up from the South used to come in for ice cream and sodas and watermelon. And I never tired of *hearing* their talk, *listening* to thunderclaps of their laughter, to their troubles, to their discussions of the war and the men who had gone to Europe from the Jim Crow South, their complaints over the high rent and the long overtime hours that brought what seemed big checks, until the weekly bills were paid. (54, my emphasis)

I quote this passage at length to point to the disjointed quality Hughes's narrative assumes. In one chapter, we find the self-hatred of his father, his own admiration for the recuperative powers of newly arrived Southern blacks, and the act of composing a famous poem. The elements that form Hughes's account can be read, at least on a cursory level, as an attempt to demonstrate that his "best poems were written when [he] felt the worst" (54). This notwithstanding, what I would like to propose is that we can place the poem into an aesthetic frame that brings these three disparate elements into a more geometrical alignment.

Hughes's autobiographical account can be found in the middle of a chapter entitled, "I've Known Rivers." Having established his father as someone he neither understands nor wishes to emulate, the autobiography paints the older man as an outsider, not only geographically, but spiritually as well. That Hughes would discuss his father in relation to such an important poem, alludes to body travel of a different sort than that which he undertakes in this chapter of his autobiography. Moving further away from Cleveland, the geographical space where he encountered the individuals he describes as "the gayest and bravest people possible . . ." (54), Hughes elides the distance his father has put between himself and other blacks. He resists the impulses that lead to the latter's self-imposed exile: he is immersed in a vernacular moment and simultaneously peripheral to that moment. What differentiates the younger Hughes is that he listens to the voices of the folk and is "empowered rather than debilitated" by what he hears.[2]

In composing the poem, Hughes looks at "the great muddy river flowing down toward the heart of the South" (*The Big Sea* 55). While he suggests that it is his gaze — looking out of the train window at the Mississippi — that initiates composition, I would assert that what catalyzes his act of writing is the act of recovering the spoken word. A point emphasized, moreover, by the fact that he recounts a moment where he is listener rather than speaker.

Later in the autobiography, Hughes relates, in much less detail, the events which lead to his poem, "The Weary Blues" [see p. 800] There, he states, simply: "That winter, I wrote a poem called "The Weary Blues," about a piano-player I heard in Harlem . . ." (92). Again, Hughes's poetic composition moves forward from an aural moment where, as with "The Negro Speaks of Rivers," he is an outsider. Arnold Rampersad alludes to this when he observes:

> . . . [I]n his willingness to stand back and record, with minimal intervention as a craftsman, aspects of the drama of black religion or black music, Hughes had clearly shown already that he saw his *own art as inferior* [my emphasis] to that of either black musicians or religionists. . . . At the heart of his sense of inferiority . . . was the knowledge that he stood to a great extent *outside* the culture he worshipped.[3]

Rampersad concludes that Hughes's sense of alienation resulted from the fact that "his life had been spent away from consistent, normal involvement with the black masses whose affection and regard he craved" (64–5).

This trajectory repeats itself in "The Weary Blues." Rampersad intimates as much in his description of the poem's inception: "And then one night in March [of 1922], in a little cabaret in Harlem, he finally *wrote himself and his awkward position accurately into a poem* [my emphasis]" (65). This assessment calls our attention to an important consideration, namely, that Hughes's aural aesthetic employs the externality he felt in the African American community. That he was a writer and not a musician, preacher, or dancer meant that his artistic project was to record artistic expression, to amplify the African American vernacular speech event for the rest of the world to hear. Further, Hughes's sense that his literary representation of the folk was inferior, mere imitation, in turn means that he was positioned, as artist, as a distance from the "real source," almost as if he were a loudspeaker serving as a medium through which sound travels, rather than the source itself. In becoming comfortable with this role, Hughes traversed repeatedly the conceptual distance necessary to create authentic representations of black speech. Hence, as he achieved a greater place among the African American intellectual elite, the distance increased between him and the masses he sought to portray. Nonetheless, as his aesthetic sensibility crystallized, his conceptual movement was *toward* them.

This is evidenced by the fact that Hughes's Simple character resulted from a conversation he shared with a factory worker and his girlfriend in a Harlem bar in 1943. Intrigued as he listened to the exchange, Hughes used the qualities he discerned from the conversation to create the character, who first appeared in his column for *The Chicago Defender*.[4] Constructed as a dialogue between a narrator speaking in standard English and Jesse B. Semple (or Simple), who spoke in a more colorful, Southern idiom, the columns work out Hughes's passionate desire to honor the self-redemptive power found in the African American community. Thus, Simple became a vehicle for giving voice to the nature of his artistic project; indeed, it is he who articulates the necessity, as if it were a constant reminder to Hughes, to listen "eloquently." . . .

If we return to the moment in his autobiography where Hughes is headed to Mexico towards his father, what is clear is that he circumvents his father's hatred of blacks by reconstituting the aural joy he feels in their midst. In short, Hughes's aesthetic rests on his need to assure his readership that if his writing spoke, both to and for them, it was because he took great pains to hear them. In his multivarious roles as poet, fiction writer, autobiographer, and columnist, Langston Hughes relates to the African American community as a speaker to be sure, but here the term is dualistic: the term alludes to the act of writing as both composition and amplification. As the Rampersad biography makes very clear, Hughes never elevated books over spoken forms of eloquence and his passion for writing flowed naturally from the fact that he seized every opportunity to posit himself as a listener. *The Big Sea* begins, after all, with Hughes standing on the deck of the *S.S. Malone* (his pseudonym for the freighter, *West Hesseltine*) and throwing books into the sea (3).[5] "[B]ooks had been happening to me," he writes, "I was glad they were gone" (4). What this suggests is that Hughes never wanted to subordinate experience to literacy; books could not replace the value of improvisation. Although their disappearance from his life was temporary, one can imagine that that movement, like so many others in Hughes's life, led him towards what he so dearly loved to do: put his ear to the wind and serve as a witness for all there was to hear.

Notes

[1] Langston Hughes, *The Big Sea* (1940; New York: Hill and Wang, 1963) 54. All subsequent references to this text are from this volume.

[2] Arnold Rampersad, *The Life of Langston Hughes, Volume I: 1902–1941: I, Too, Sing America*, 2 vols. (New York: Oxford UP, 1986) 1: 64.

[3] Rampersad 64–65. My emphasis.

[4] Rampersad, *The Life of Langston Hughes, Volume II: 1941–1967: I Dream a World*, 2 vols. (New York: Oxford UP, 1988) 2: 61–62.

[5] In throwing books from Columbia into the sea, Hughes was likewise acting out the final break from his father, who had paid for him to attend. That the elder Hughes wanted Langston to "[acquire] a good business head" (*The Big Sea* 45) only drove him further towards being an artist.

STEVEN C. TRACY

from "Midnight Ruffles of Cat-Gut Lace": The Boogie Poems of Langston Hughes

The influence of the blues tradition on Langston Hughes' poetry is by now an oft-discussed and readily accepted fact, although the depth and breadth of his employment of the tradition has not often been discussed with a similar depth and breadth. A close examination of a related sequence of Hughes' blues poems offers the opportunity to explore his fusion of oral and written traditions and to examine his tremendous skills as a literary-jazz improviser. That is not to suggest that Hughes' poems are spontaneous creations. Improvisation is normally thought of as a spontaneous act, but the jazz or blues musician's improvisations are in fact bounded by several things: the musician's "vocabulary"— style, patterns, techniques, and riffs; the accepted conventions of the specific genre (even if those conventions are deliberately violated, they are, in a large sense, at work); and the boundaries of the individual piece being performed. For example, boogie-woogie pianist Pete Johnson, in his 1947 version of "Swanee River Boogie," performs the melody of the song to a boogie-woogie beat, thereafter improvising solos built around the song's chord changes, the boogie-woogie beat, and variations on the melody of the piece, combined with his arsenal of boogie-woogie riffs and performed in his inimitable style.[1] Hughes, in his 1951 collection, *Montage of a Dream Deferred*, generated a set or sequence of six "boogie" poems — "Dream Boogie" [see p. 803], "Easy Boogie," "Boogie 1 a.m.," "Lady's Boogie," "Nightmare Boogie," and "Dream Boogie: Variation"— that have in common much more than the "boogie" of the titles. The poems comprise an intricate series of interwoven "improvisations" over a set boogie-woogie rhythm, with Hughes modulating and modifying rhythm, words, imagery, moods, and themes, and constructing a complex interrelationship between music, the musical instrument, the performance, and a set of attitudes exemplified by them.

Structurally, Hughes' six boogie poems share the exciting, rushing rhythms of boogie-woogie: Hughes at work on his poems, pounding out rhythms on his typewriter keyboard. Briefly, boogie-woogie is a form of Afro-American music, normally performed on the piano, that emerged as a recognizable genre in the 1920s. As blues researcher Karl Gert zur Heide points out, "the theme of boogie is the blues, some features derive from ragtime, and the rhythmic interplay of both hands can be traced back to African roots."[2] In boogie-woogie, the improvisations executed by the pianist's right hand on the treble keys of the piano are set off against the ostinato or repeated phrases of the left hand on the bass keys. Characteristically boogie-woogie follows the twelve-bar blues chord change pattern — in the key of C, CFC GFC — employing a repeated bass pattern recognizable most often for its eight beats to the bar and performed at a medium-to-fast tempo that builds an explosive drive and swing appropriate to the dance step after which it was named. Besides identifying a dance step and a type of music, however, the term "boogie" functions in other contexts: to boogie is to raise a ruckus or act wildly or uninhibitedly; it also has sexual connotations:

> I'm gonna pull off my pants and keep on my shirt,
> I'm gonna get so low you think I'm in the dirt.
> I'm gonna pitch a boogie-woogie,
> Gonna boogie-woogie all night long.[3]

In this tune, singer Big Bill Broonzy has taken a boogie-woogie beat suitable for dancing and provided both the "wild acting" and sexual connotations that go with it. In the tradition, the word carried these connotations, and typically Hughes tried to capture the ambience of the tradition.

Hughes demonstrated his knowledge of boogie-woogie in *The First Book of Jazz*, in which he and his coauthors identified among the outstanding exponents of boogie-woogie "Pinetop" Smith, Jimmy Yancy, Meade Lux Lewis, Albert Ammons, and Pete Johnson — all important and generally recognized masters.[4] It was the spirited, exuberant, danceable, and often rhythmically complex and intricate music of perfomers like those men that provided the basis for Hughes' boogie poem rhythms and the connotations of the word and the tradition that he tried to capture in his poems.

Hughes obviously wanted us to hear the boogie rhythms in these poems: the first four poems in the boogie sequence ("Dream," "Easy," "1 a.m.," and "Lady's") are very "aural"; the words "hear" and "heard" are employed repeatedly, both in a question—

> Ain't you heard
> The boogie-woogie rumble
> Of a dream deferred?[5]

and an assertion—

> I know you've heard
> The boogie-woogie rumble
> Of a dream deferred. ("Boogie 1 a.m.")

The incessant rhythm and rumbling of boogie-woogie becomes in the poems symbolic of the dream he had delineated in his earlier poem "Dream Variations":

> To fling my arms wide
> In some place of the sun,
> To whirl and to dance
> Till the white day is done.
> Then rest at cool evening
> Beneath a tall tree
> While night comes on gently, Dark like me—
> That is my dream! ("Dream Variations")

Hughes is trying to get black people to recognize that the deferment of that dream is a large part of their lives, both by questioning and by asserting the "obvious." If they hadn't heard that boogie-woogie rumble, they could certainly hear it in the rhythms of Hughes' poems; for example, if one were to treat "Dream Boogie," the first poem of the sequence and therefore a prototype for the other poems in the sequence, as if it were a lyric to be sung to boogie-woogie music, and identify the beats and chord changes as they relate to the words, the annotation would look as follows:

> C
> 1 2 34 567 8
> Good morning, daddy!
>
> 1 2 34 5 6 7
> Ain't you heard
>
> 8   12   34   56
> The boogie-woogie rumble
>
> 7 8   12 34 56   7   8
> Of a dream deferred?
>
> F
> 1234 567
> Listen closely:
>
> 8   12 34   5 6 7 8
> You'll hear their feet

C
1 2 3 4 5 6 7 8
Beating out and beating out a —

You think
It's a happy beat?

G
1 2 3 4 5 6 7 8
Listen to it closely:

F
1 2 3 4 5 6 78
Ain't you heard

   C
1 2   3 4 5 6 7 8
Something underneath like a —

What did I say?

Sure,
I'm happy!
Take it away!

Hey pop!
Re-bop!
Mop!

Y-e-a-h! ("Dream Boogie," p. 803)

What Hughes had done is create a twelve-line, twelve-bar boogie-woogie poem, annexing an exclamatory "tag" ending like those occasionally employed in music. Here, though, Hughes has manipulated the form and rhythm: stanzas two and three are jarred by the dramatic insertion of disturbing questions that achieve their impact by rewording the line we would expect in the normal rhythm and progression of thoughts into a question. Thus, in stanza two, "Beating out and beating out a happy beat" becomes:

Beating out and beating out —

You think
It's a happy beat?

Just as Hughes shifts to the interrogative and separates those questions from their normal stanzaic group, he just as surely upsets the boogie-woogie rhythm, eventually violating even the rhyming pattern in stanza three. This is significant because stanza three draws on the first two stanzas for a repetition of important lines: "Listen closely" of stanza two becomes "Listen to it closely" (Hughes employs a common characteristic of blues lyrics, building slightly modulated lines around loose formulaic patterns) in stanza three, while "Ain't you heard" of stanza one is lifted verbatim. Stanza three, however, becomes deliberately vague — "Something underneath" — in order to force the audience to answer the subsequent question, "What did I say?" By upsetting the rhythm and asking the questions, Hughes highlights the disparity between the rumbling seriousness of the deferred dream and the superficial happiness of the beat or performance. To this masterful maneuvering of the idiom Hughes annexes the "tag" ending — in jazz and blues a four-bar section appended to the end of a tune that repeats a phrase, offers a final comment, or indicates that the performance is about to end — often for those dancing to the performance. Hughes' seven-line ending contrasts once again the happiness of the words/music performance with the underlying problem. In light of the dramatic irony with which Hughes dealt with the subject earlier, this return to the facade of carefree happiness adds psychological complexity to the poem. Hughes felt that blacks needed to recognize the reality of deferred dreams, as he has forced in stanza three, but in stanza four he emphasizes the need to retain the spirit of cultural expression and the usefulness of the elaborate role-playing that provided blacks with the opportunity for advances, while whites concentrate on the superficial happy roles that blacks played. . . .

By varying and manipulating the rhythm, words, imagery, moods, and themes of these poems, Hughes has illuminated the issue of the dream deferred from different emotional perspectives. By employing folk culture so well, he in effect gives his poems traditional authority, makes them unadulteratedly black, and establishes a continuity that makes them seem to express the ideas of the people for the people.

Notes

[1] Pete Johnson, "Swanee River Boogie," *Boogie Woogie Trio,* Storyville SLP 4006, 1976.

[2] Karl Gert zur Heide, *Deep South Piano* (London: Studio Vista, 1970), p. 11.

[3] Big Bill Broonzy, "Let's Reel and Rock," Melotone, 7-06-64, 1936, 78 R.P.M. recording.

[4] Langston Hughes, Cliff Roberts, and David Martin, *The First Book of Jazz* (New York: Franklin Watts, Inc., 1955).

[5] Langston Hughes, *Selected Poems* (New York: Vintage Books, 1974), p. 221. All further references to Hughes' poems will be followed in the text by page numbers from this work.

KAREN JACKSON FORD

from Do Right to Write Right:
Langston Hughes's Aesthetics of Simplicity

The one thing most readers of twentieth-century American poetry can say about Langston Hughes is that he has known rivers. "The Negro Speaks of Rivers" has become memorable for its lofty, oratorical tone, mythic scope, and powerful rhythmic repetitions.

> I've known rivers:
> I've known rivers ancient as the world and old as the flow of human
>   blood in human veins. (1656)

But however beautiful its cadences, the poem is remembered primarily because it is Hughes's most frequently anthologized work. The fact is, "The Negro Speaks of Rivers" is one of Hughes's most uncharacteristic poems, and yet it has defined his reputation, along with a small but constant selection of other poems included in anthologies. "A Negro Speaks of Rivers" [p. 800], "A House in Taos," "The Weary Blues" [p. 800], "Montage of a Dream Deferred," "Theme for English B" [p. 802], "Refugee in America," and "I, Too" [p. 801] — these poems invariably comprise his anthology repertoire despite the fact that none of them typifies his writing. What makes these poems atypical is exactly what makes them appealing and intelligible to the scholars who edit anthologies — their complexity. True, anthologies produced in the current market, which is hospitable to the African-American tradition and to canon reform, now include a brief selection of poems in black folk forms. But even though Hughes has fared better in anthologies than most African-American writers, only a small and predictable segment of his poetry has been preserved. A look back through the original volumes of poetry, and even through the severely redrawn *Selected Poems*, reveals a wealth of simpler poems we ought to be reading.[1]

Admittedly, an account of Hughes's poetic simplicity requires some qualification. Most obvious is the fact that he wrote poems that are not simple. "A Negro Speaks of Rivers" is oracular; "The Weary Blues" concludes enigmatically; "A House in Taos" is classically modernist in both its fragmented form and its decadent sensibility. Even more to the point, many of the poems that have been deemed simple are only ironically so. "The Black Christ," for example, is a little jingle that invokes monstrous cultural complexity. Likewise, two later books, *Ask Your Mama* (1961) and *The Panther and the Lash* (1967), contain an intricate vision of American history beneath their simple surfaces.[2] Nevertheless, the overwhelming proportion of poems in the Hughes canon consists of work in the simpler style, and even those poems that can yield complexities make use of simplicity in ways that ought not to be ignored.

The repression of the great bulk of Hughes's poems is the result of chronic critical scorn for their simplicity. Throughout his long career, but especially after his first two volumes of poetry (readers were at first willing to assume that a youthful poet might grow to be more complex), his books received their harshest reviews for a variety of "flaws" that all originate in an aesthetics of simplicity. From his first book, *The Weary Blues* (1926), to his last one, *The Panther and the Lash* (1967), the reviews invoke a litany of faults: the poems are superficial, infantile, silly, small, unpoetic, common, jejune, iterative, and, of course, simple.[3] Even his admirers reluctantly conclude that Hughes's poetics failed. Saunders Redding flatly opposes simplicity and artfulness. "While Hughes's rejection of his own growth shows an admirable loyalty to his self-commitment as the poet of the 'simple, Negro commonfolk' . . . it does a disservice to his art" (Mullen 74). James Baldwin, who recognizes the potential of simplicity as an artistic principle, faults the poems for "tak[ing] refuge . . . in a fake simplicity in order to avoid the very difficult simplicity of the experience" (Mullen 85).

Despite a lifetime of critical disappointments, then, Hughes remained loyal to the aesthetic program he had outlined in 1926 in his decisive poetic treatise, "The Negro Artist and the Racial Mountain." There he had predicted that the common people would "give to this world its truly great Negro artist, the one who is not afraid to be himself," a poet who would explore the "great field of unused [folk] material ready for his art" and recognize that this source would provide "sufficient matter to furnish a black artist with a lifetime of creative work" (692).* This is clearly a portrait of the poet Hughes would become, and he maintained his fidelity to this ideal at great cost to his literary reputation. . . .

In his column in the *Chicago Defender* on February 13, 1943, Hughes first introduced the prototype of the humorous and beloved fictional character Jesse B. Semple, nicknamed by his Harlem friends "Simple." For the next twenty-three years Hughes would continue to publish Simple stories both in the *Defender* and in several volumes of collected and edited pieces.[4] Hughes called Simple his "ace-boy," and it is surely not coincidental that the Simple stories span the years, the 1940s to the 1960s, when Langston Hughes needed a literary ace in the hole.[5] The success of the Simple stories was an important consolation of the writer's later years, when his poetry was reviewed with disappointment, his autobiography dismissed as "chit-chat," his plays refused on Broadway, and his fiction diminished in importance next to Richard Wright's *Native Son* (1940) and Ralph Ellison's *Invisible Man* (1952).[6]

It seems obvious, however, that in the long association with his ace-boy Hughes found more than popularity and financial success. In fact, his prefatory sketches of Simple attest to the character's importance, in the sheer number of times Hughes sets out to explain him and in the specific details these explanations provide.[7] All of them depict Simple as an African American Everyman, the authentic — even unmediated — voice of the community that engendered him. For instance, in "Who Is Simple?" Hughes emphasizes the authenticity of his creation: "[Simple's] first words came directly out of the mouth of a young man who lived just down the block from me" (*Best* vii). Here and elsewhere Hughes asserts a vital connection between the fictional character and the people he represents: "If there were not a lot of genial souls in Harlem as talkative as Simple, I would never have these tales to write down that are 'just like him'" (*Best* viii). The author's dedication to Simple is surely rooted in his conviction that Simple embodies and speaks for the very people to whom Hughes had committed himself back in the 1920s. But Hughes's affinity with Simple is more complete than this.

Commentators on the Simple stories have concentrated on two points: theme, "Hughes's handling of the race issue" (Mullen 20); and genre, "the generic nature of these prose sketches" (Mullen 20).[8] It is exclusively Hughes as prose artist we have acknowledged when considering these tales. However, I will argue that the Simple stories reveal a great deal about Hughes's poetic genius as well. Casting Simple as the figure of the poet illuminates Hughes's poetic program and explains his powerful affinity with his prose creation.

---

*See pages 846–47 for the quoted passage in its entirety.

Crucial in tracing Simple's significance are the "Character Notes" to the 1957 musical comedy *Simply Heavenly*, which describe Simple in terms that stress his contradictions:

> Simple is a Chaplinesque character, slight of build, awkwardly graceful, given to flights of fancy, and positive statements of opinion — stemming from a not so positive soul. He is dark with a likable smile, ordinarily dressed, except for rather flamboyant summer sports shirts. Simple tries hard to succeed, but the chips seldom fall just right. Yet he bounces like a rubber ball. He may go down, but he always bounds back up.
> (*Plays* 115)

The parallel to Charlie Chaplin, an icon of contradiction, is telling. Like Chaplin, whose physical appearance announces internal tensions (his hat is too small, his shoes too large, his vest too tight, his pants too loose), Simple is awkward yet graceful, ordinary yet flamboyant. And, again as with Chaplin, these external tensions reveal deeper ones; he is obstinate yet fanciful, decent yet flawed, and — perhaps most poignant for Hughes — optimistic despite failure.

Simple is a compelling figure for Hughes precisely because of these tensions. For these contraries — even the apparently internal ones — hang about Simple like a fool's motley. The fool's motley, of course, traditionally implies chaos; yet while his multicolored costume reflects the intricacies and contradictions around him, the fool himself may often be a perfect simpleton. This is also true of Hughes's character: though his appearance and even to some extent his character express contradiction, his fundamental nature is unequivocally simple. Obstinate, positivistic, and optimistic, Simple is able to register contradictions without finally resolving them and therefore has special significance for Hughes's poetic project. Hughes, after all, claims that "where life is simple, truth and reality are one" (*Big Sea* 311). Yet where in America is life simple for African Americans? The "where" Hughes invokes is not a place but a state of mind. The terms of his formulation — simplicity, truth, reality — are broad and vague because they are nearly synonymous to him. If one recognizes the simple facts of life, one will be able to see the truth; if one lives by the truth, one's reality will match one's ideals. Simplicity *is* truth in Hughes's vision.

Simple is the personification of such a poetics, a philosophy of composition that resorts to simplicity, not in response to singleness or triviality, but, ironically, in response to almost unspeakable contradiction. This is why he appears surrounded by complexities — his culture, his friends, even his clothing registering the confusion of the world around him. To shift the metaphor, simpleness, in both the character and the poetry, functions as a brick wall against which complexities collide. In its artless, uncomprehending refusal to incorporate contradictions, it exacerbates them. For a poet who equates simplicity with truth, cultivating a thematics and aesthetics of simplicity is essential — poetically and politically. Simplicity resists the pernicious subtleties and complexities of integrationist thought. Further, it reveals the inadequacies of such thought. But more important, it achieves these aims by reinstating the truth.

Notes

[1] Easily ninety per cent of the poems in Hughes's canon are of the sort that I am describing as simple.

[2] Jemie, Hudson, and Miller, among others, have persuasively demonstrated the intricacies of Hughes's jazz structures in these two late books.

[3] Reviews in which these epithets appear are collected in Mullen.

[4] The stories are collected in five volumes, *The Best of Simple, Simple Speaks His Mind, Simple Stakes a Claim, Simple Takes a Wife,* and *Simple's Uncle Sam.* Additionally, Hughes takes Simple to the stage with *Simply Heavenly,* a comedy about Simple's marriage.

[5] In "Who Is Simple?"—the foreword to *The Best of Simple*—Hughes concludes, "He is my ace-boy, Simple. I hope you like him, too" (viii).

[6] For a chronicle of Hughes's disappointments during these years, see Rampersad, especially chapter 8 of the second volume "In Warm Manure: 1951 to 1953." Ellison characterized *The Big Sea* as a "chit-chat" book during an interview with Rampersad in 1983 (202).

[7] Hughes wrote at least four explanations of Simple: "The Happy Journey of 'Simply Heavenly,'" "Simple and Me," "Who Is Simple?" and the "Character Notes" to *Simply Heavenly.*

[8] In his Introduction Mullen surveys the scholarship on the Simple stories; all the works he cites discuss either their racial politics or their prose structures.

Works Cited

Baldwin, James. "Sermon and Blues." Mullen 85–87.

Hudson, Theodore R. "Technical Aspects of the Poetry of Langston Hughes." *Black World* (1973): 24–45.

Hughes, Langston. *The Best of Simple.* New York: Hill, 1961.

———. *The Big Sea: An Autobiography.* New York: Knopf, 1940.

———. *Five Plays by Langston Hughes.* Bloomington: Indiana UP, 1968.

———. "The Happy Journey of 'Simply Heavenly.'" *New York Herald-Tribune* 18 Aug. 1957, sec. 4: 1+.

———. "The Negro Artist and the Racial Mountain." *The Nation* CXXII (1926): 692–94.

———. "The Negro Speaks of Rivers." *The Norton Anthology of American Literature.* Ed. Nina Baym et al. 2nd ed. New York: Norton, 1985.

———. *Selected Poems of Langston Hughes.* New York: Vintage, 1974.

———. "Simple and Me." *Phylon* 6 (1945): 349–52.

——— *Simple's Uncle Sam.* New York: Hill, 1965.

———. *Simply Heavenly. Five Plays by Langston Hughes.* Bloomington: Indiana UP, 1968.

———. "Who Is Simple?" *The Best of Simple.* New York: Hill, 1961. vii–viii.

Jemie, Onwuchekwa. *Langston Hughes: An Introduction to the Poetry.* New York: Columbia UP, 1976.

Miller, R. Baxter. *The Art and Imagination of Langston Hughes.* Lexington: UP of Kentucky, 1989.

Mullen, Edward J. *Critical Essays on Langston Hughes.* Boston: Hall, 1986.

Rampersad, Arnold. *The Life of Langston Hughes, Volume II: 1941–1967.* New York: Oxford UP, 1988.

Redding, Saunders. "Old Form, Old Rhythms, New Words." Mullen 73–74.

GEORGE B. HUTCHINSON

from Langston Hughes and the 'Other' Whitman

. . . The association of Hughes with Whitman, I suspect, is less than obvious to most readers. If Whitman is often singled out as the archetypal (white male) American poet, Hughes's experiments with black-based idioms and aesthetic principles rooted in blues, ballads, and spirituals have had an incalculable effect upon the development of a distinctive African-American poetics. Yet, like Sterling Brown after him, even in writing his "folk" poems Hughes considered himself to be following out the implications of Whitman's poetic theory (Rampersad, 1:146). At various points in his long career, Hughes put together no fewer than three separate anthologies of Whitman's poetry (one of them for children), included several Whitman poems in an anthology on *The Poetry of the Negro,* wrote a poem entitled "Old Walt" [see p. 805 in this volume] for the one hundredth anniversary of *Leaves of Grass,* and repeatedly — in lectures, newspaper columns, and introductions — encouraged black Americans to read his work. He called Whitman "America's greatest poet" and spoke of *Leaves of Grass* as the greatest expression of "the real meaning of democracy ever made on our shores." Feeling that Whitman had been ignored and, in current parlance, marginalized by the custodians of culture, Hughes indeed attempted in his own way to canonize the poet he considered "the Lincoln of our Letters" (*Chicago Defender,* July 4, 1953). . . .

One reason Whitman's poetry has resonated in the sensibilities of black American writers is that in certain of his poems he uses the condition of the slave as representative of the condition of his audience. The "you" of his songs, if it is to apply to *all* readers, must apply to slaves, those most graphically denied the right to self-determination. The poem "To You (Whoever You Are)" at times seems directly addressed to a slave:

> None has done justice to you, you have not done justice to yourself,
> None but has found you imperfect, I only find no imperfection
>   in you,
> None but would subordinate you, I only am he who will never consent
>   to subordinate you,
> I only am he who places over you no master, owner, better, God,
>   beyond what waits intrinsically in yourself. (14–17)

Arguably, Whitman here distills the specific oppression of black people in the antebellum United States into a metaphor for the hidden condition of all people — "you, whoever you are." But his slave is not just any slave — his slave is the *most* enslaved, the one rejected by all others and even by himself or herself. Eschewing pity for admiration and love, the poet projects upon his reader, as by a shamanistic charm, a spiritual freedom that will ensure self-fulfillment: "The hopples fall from your ankles, you find an unfailing sufficiency, / Old or young, male or female, rude, low, rejected by the rest, whatever you are promulges itself" (44–45). A poem such as this virtually begs for appropriation to an African American frame of reference. . . .

Hughes was the first African-American poet to sense the affinity between the inclusive "I" of Whitman (which Whitman claimed as his most important innovation — "the quite changed attitude of the ego, the one chanting or talking, towards himself and towards his fellow humanity" ("A Backward Glance," 564) and the "I" of the blues and even of the spirituals. The result of Hughes's appropriation of this triply descended "I" is amply demonstrated in one of his first published poems, "The Negro Speaks of Rivers":

> I've known rivers ancient as the world and old as the flow of human
>   blood in human veins.
>
> My soul has grown deep like the rivers.
>
> I bathed in the Euphrates when dawns were young.
> I built my hut near the Congo and it lulled me to sleep.
> I looked upon the Nile and raised the pyramids above it.
> I heard the singing of the Mississippi when Abe Lincoln went down to
>   New Orleans, and I've seen its muddy bosom turn all golden in the
>   sunset. (*Weary Blues*, 51)

Though Hughes would later, for the most part, turn away from the Whitmanesque style of free verse, the example of Whitman's break with traditional definitions of the poetic, his attempts to achieve an orally based poetics with the cadence and diction of the voice on the street, at the pond-side, or at the pulpit, provided a partial model for the young black poet looking for a way to sing his own song, which would be at the same time a song of his people.

Works Cited

Hughes, Langston. *The Weary Blues*. New York: Knopf, 1926.

———. "The Ceaseless Rings of Walt Whitman." In Perlman, et al.

Hughes, Langston, and Arna Bontemps, eds. *Poetry of the Negro, 1746–1949*. Garden City, NY: Doubleday, 1949.

Perlman, Jim, Ed Folsom, and Dan Campion, eds. *Walt Whitman: The Measure of His Song*. Minneapolis: Holy Cow! Press, 1981.

Rampersad, Arnold. *The Life of Langston Hughes*. 2 Vols. New York: Oxford, 1986.

Whitman, Walt. *Leaves of Grass: Comprehensive Reader's Edition*. Edited by Harold W. Blodgett and Sculley Bradley. New York: NYU Press, 1965.

C. D. ROGERS

Hughes's "Genius Child"

In Langston Hughes's poem "Genius Child" [see p. 805 in this volume] the content has found its structure. The perfection occurs when Hughes tames both the meaning and the structure of the lyric.

The lyricist recognizes the difficulty in handling a "genius child" that, though creative, is unruly, unloved, and incapable of being controlled. Furthermore, can one love a stereotyped "monster"— whether genius or poem? Hughes grasps the reality of the concept of genius and juxtaposes this against the reality of the poetic structure. Then he proceeds to capture the essence of genius in his structure. "Little bits of order," Robert Frost calls this creative process.

Order occurs in the structure through Hughes's play on the pronunciation of the word genius. It can be pronounced correctly two ways: with two or with three syllables. Depending on whether the word is pronounced jen-yes with two syllables or je-ne-es with three, the line contains either odd or even syllables. Odd numbers suggest genius; even numbers suggest normality and orderliness. Thus, conflict between odd and even (in both content and rhythm) moves from the title to the last line of "Genius Child." The title contains either three or four syllables, depending on pronunciation. Line 1, for example, contains either nine or ten syllables; lines 2 and 3, nine; line 4, seven. Similarly, in line 5 the pronunciation of genius determines the number of syllables in the refrain (and the orderly or irregular iambic tetrameter). Like a genius, is each line odd?

Line 6 seeks its freedom: it contains six syllables (even)— or does it? Hughes splits the line. He uses six syllables, then he breaks the phrase commonly expected to complete line 6 and places three syllables on the successive line, a total of nine syllables. He controls the next two lines the same way: six syllables for line 9 and (to complete the line) five for line 10 — odd eleven. The concept and the structure continue to vie for control. After the unruly refrain (with either eight or nine syllables) comes the final line: eight syllables, even. It neatly breaks the hypothesis of all odd syllables in lines. Thus, when the genius is brought under control, it remains true to its nature and escapes in both content and structure. The last line — "Kill him — and let his soul run wild!" with its ultimate even syllables contains also the paradoxical flight — to die, to live.

Topics for Further Research

1. As Hughes's own essays in this volume suggest, much of his life was spent actively campaigning for various causes. Research the nature of his commitments and their effect on his poetry. How did his social and political work change between 1935 and in 1955?

2. Investigate the ways in which Hughes's poetry was inspired by the accomplishments of African-American musicians. For example, how did the different musical forms of the female blues singers of the 1920s and the bebop musicians of the 1940s inspire Hughes?

3. Hughes was a primary inspiration for the artistic movement known as "negritude." Poets and writers like Nicolás Guillén, Jacques Roumain, Aimé Cesaire, and Leopold Senghor all acknowledged Hughes's influence. Find out what the "negritude" poets stood for, and write a paper in which you discuss why Hughes was so important to this movement.

4. Hughes's work was distinct from that of his two most important contemporaries, Gwendolyn Brooks and Robert Hayden, who were influenced by modernism. Using a dictionary or an encyclopedia of literary criticism, find out what modernist poetry is. Is "modernism" a useful term in discussing what distinguishes Brooks and Hayden from Hughes? Why might Hughes be skeptical about some aspects of modernism? Find a collection of the work of Brooks or Hayden, and compare some of their poems to those of Hughes.

5. Hughes was a central figure in a period of African-American artistic flowering called the Harlem Renaissance. Find out as much as you can about the Harlem Renaissance and Hughes's involvement with it. Then, write a paper in which you assess in what ways the Harlem Renaissance was important to Hughes's development as a poet.

6. Read a collection of Hughes's "Simple" Stories, newspaper columns that were later collected in book form. What is he able to do in fiction that he is unable to do in poetry? What is he able to do in poetry that he is unable to do in fiction?

Grace R. Alston

Professor Hall

African-American Literature

15 Sept. 2003

Challenging the Father/Challenging the Self:

Langston Hughes's "The Negro Speaks of Rivers"

Langston Hughes's career as a poet began with
the publication of "The Negro Speaks of Rivers" in
the June 1921 issue of <u>The Crisis</u>. Hughes wrote this
poem during a trip to Mexico to visit his father,
African-American businessman James Hughes. James
Hughes, an "unfeeling, domineering, and materialistic
man, scornful of Indians and blacks . . . and the
poor in general; and contemptuous of his son's gentler pace and artistic temperament" (Rampersad 819),
had purposefully removed himself from African-
American life in the United States. Throughout the
trip, Langston Hughes dreaded the confrontation he
knew he would have with his father about his desire
to become a writer. He was very anxious, even depressed, but as he wrote, "my best poems were all
written when I felt the worst. When I was happy, I
didn't write anything" (Rampersad 818). Hughes's relationship with his father affected him not only psychologically, but also as a writer, causing him to
adopt an ambivalent attitude toward both his subject
matter and his race.

According to Herman Beavers, Hughes's troubled
relationship with his father caused him to adopt "a
posture both inside and outside the race" (823), a

Thesis statement

Alston 2

kind of double consciousness. On the one hand,
in order to counter to his father's racial beliefs,
Hughes affirmed his blackness. On the other hand,
in an effort to maintain artistic integrity, Hughes
tried to be almost universal in his outlook (Beavers
823). Ironically, then, Hughes's desire to celebrate
blackness—with a kind of passionate objectivity—
was born out of the dysfunctional relationship he
had with his father. Not only did Hughes reject
his father's feelings about race, but he also insisted on becoming a writer even though his father
saw writing as impractical and somehow not quite
manly.

The specific form of "The Negro Speaks of
Rivers" reveals Hughes's struggle with this double consciousness. In this poem, Hughes actively
engages his father's racism, but he also develops
a voice that allows him to do more than just affirm blackness. The poem also celebrates the role
of African-Americans in the universal human
community.

Hughes understood early in life the peculiarities of this double consciousness, and he investigated ways it could be managed in poetry. As early as
high school, he believed that the role of class poet
was thrust upon him at Cleveland's Central High because he was black and supposed to have "rhythm." The
idea that his individuality was not recognized—that
he was seen in terms of racial stereotypes—caused

him great anxiety, an anxiety heightened by his father's questioning of the African-American character.
In the face of so much conflict, it is not surprising
that double consciousness became one of Hughes's poetic themes.

In "The Negro Artist and the Racial Mountain,"
Hughes argues that "white" is the standard to which
blacks have to measure up (810–11). Against this
standard, he suggests, the Negro artist has a high
mountain to climb in order to discover the self and
the community. Certainly, Hughes was able to climb
this mountain, but at what emotional cost? Some of
Hughes's best poems were written when he felt most
pessimistic about the prospects for black people; the
number of poems reflecting this pessimism suggests he
was frequently under stress. He was able, however, to
transform negative emotions into strong, accessible
poems.

Hughes's ambivalent relationship with his
father is evident in "The Negro Speaks of Rivers."
According to Arnold Rampersad, Hughes got the idea
for this poem as he glanced out of a train window
and became fascinated by the Mississippi River.
As the image of the river engulfed him, he transformed his desire to rebel against his father's disapproval into a poem (811) that Karen Jackson Ford
notes is uncharacteristic because of its strong "oratorical tone" (829). In the poem, Hughes writes
these lines:

Alston 4

I've known rivers:
I've known rivers ancient as the world and
    older than the flow of human blood in human
    veins.

My soul has grown deep like the rivers.
                                    (lines 1-3)

The words "I've known rivers" are universal—and
ironic, given the rest of the poem. The words uplift
and inspire because they remind us of shared experience. "Knowing" and "rivers" are not extraordinary;
they suggest shared feelings, and in this sharing, we
begin a process by which readers come to appreciate
blackness, the blackness Hughes's father so despised.

    The scope in "The Negro Speaks of Rivers" is
perhaps both historical and mythic. Although Hughes
depicts certain conventions of black culture in an
imaginative and symbolic way, his choice of rivers
suggests a very particular history. The Congo and
Nile illustrate the beauty of blackness and its accomplishments; they appear naturally alongside the
Euphrates and with it suggest the beginnings of civilization. In this way, Hughes makes clear to his father—and to the nation—the nobility of an African
past. Moreover, his use of the Mississippi not only
places the American river in a continuous historical
relationship with the Euphrates but also introduces
the question of slavery. Once again, Hughes is able
to perform the double task of confronting both Ameri-

Alston 5

can culture and his father. The image of defenseless
slaves being sold up and down the Mississippi River's
"muddy bosom" (7) may have reminded him of his own
defenseless position in his relationship with his father. And as the "muddy bosom" turning "golden in the
sunset" (7) suggests freedom for slaves, it may have
also meant for Hughes freedom from his father.

Repetition also contributes to the poem's effect. Because the poem promotes healing and liberation, Hughes uses words implying motion, such as
"bathed," "built," "looked," and "raised," and
"singing," emphasizing ritual and religion. The repetition of "rivers," of course, works in a slightly
different manner, but it may be the most effective
means by which Hughes communicates his feeling of
displacement. Like a kind of chant, creation of this
complex rhythm is the most striking way he rises to
his double challenge, but the success of this
"rhythm" is based in readers' collective experience,
and not on racial stereotypes.

Hughes believed that black writers had a responsibility to reveal to whites that blacks could do
more than sing, dance, laugh, and make music. He believed black writers had a role to play in racial
reconciliation (Hughes, "To Negro Writers" 812), and
his ability to affirm blackness—not just to a black
audience but to a universal one—without stereotyping
is what earns him his distinction as a poet. It is
striking that the source of his racial identity is,

at least partially, his troubled relationship with
his father. His passion for blackness increased as he
resisted his black father; at the same time, his
ability to develop a poetic persona who could speak
to the world emerged from his awareness of his own
double position.

Works Cited

Beavers, Herman. "Dead Rocks and Sleeping Men:
    Aurality in the Aesthetic of Langston Hughes."
    Kirszner and Mandell 822–23.

Ford, Karen Jackson. "Do Right to Write Right:
    Langston Hughes's Aesthetics of Simplicity."
    Kirszner and Mandell 829–33.

Hughes, Langston. "The Negro Artist and the Racial
    Mountain." Kirszner and Mandell 810–11.

---. "The Negro Speaks of Rivers." Kirszner and
    Mandell 836.

---. "To Negro Writers." Kirszner and Mandell 812–13.

Kirszner, Laurie G., and Stephen R. Mandell, eds.
    <u>Literature: Reading, Reacting, Writing</u>. 5th ed.
    Boston: Heinle: 2004.

Rampersad, Arnold. "The Origins of Poetry in Langston
    Hughes." Kirszner and Mandell 817–22.

CHAPTER 25

POETRY FOR FURTHER READING

MAYA ANGELOU (1928–   )

Africa (1975)

Thus she had lain
sugar cane sweet

deserts her hair
golden her feet
mountains her breasts   5
two Niles° her tears
Thus she has lain
Black through the years.

Over the white seas
rime white and cold   10
brigands ungentled
icicle bold
took her young daughters
sold her strong sons
churched her with Jesus   15
bled her with guns.
Thus she has lain.

Now she is rising
remember her pain
remember the losses   20
her screams loud and vain
remember her riches
her history slain
now she is striding
although she had lain.   25

Niles: The Nile River, which originates in East Africa and flows through Egypt, is the world's longest river.

ANONYMOUS

Bonny Barbara Allan

(traditional Scottish ballad)

It was in and about the Martinmas° time,
　　When the green leaves were afalling,
That Sir John Graeme, in the West Country,
　　Fell in love with Barbara Allan.

He sent his men down through the town,　　　　　　5
　　To the place where she was dwelling;
"O haste and come to my master dear,
　　Gin° ye be Barbara Allan."

O hooly,° hooly rose she up,
　　To the place where he was lying,　　　　　　10
And when she drew the curtain by:
　　"Young man, I think you're dying."

"O it's I'm sick, and very, very sick,
　　And 'tis a' for Barbara Allan."—
"O the better for me ye's never be,　　　　　　15
　　Tho your heart's blood were aspilling.

"O dinna ye mind,° young man," said she,
　　"When ye was in the tavern adrinking,
That ye made the health gae round and round,
　　And slighted Barbara Allan?"　　　　　　20

He turned his face unto the wall,
　　And death was with him dealing:
"Adieu, adieu, my dear friends all,
　　And be kind to Barbara Allan."

And slowly, slowly raise she up,　　　　　　25
　　And slowly, slowly left him,
And sighing said she could not stay,
　　Since death of life had reft him.

She had not gane a mile but twa,°
　　When she heard the dead-bell ringing,　　　　　　30

Martinmas: Saint Martin's Day, November 11.
Gin: If.
hooly: Slowly.
O dinna ye mind: Don't you remember?
twa: Two.

And every jow° that the dead-bell geid,
    It cried, "Woe to Barbara Allan!"

"O mother, mother, make my bed!
    O make it saft and narrow!
Since my love died for me today,   35
    I'll die for him tomorrow."

ANONYMOUS

Western Wind

    (English lyric)

Western wind, when wilt thou blow,
The° small rain down can rain?
Christ, if my love were in my arms,
And I in my bed again!

MATTHEW ARNOLD (1822–1888)

Dover Beach (1867)

The sea is calm tonight.
The tide is full, the moon lies fair
Upon the straits;— on the French coast the light
Gleams and is gone; the cliffs of England stand,
Glimmering and vast, out in the tranquil bay.   5
Come to the window, sweet is the night-air!
Only, from the long line of spray
Where the sea meets the moon-blanched° land,
Listen! you hear the grating roar
Of pebbles which the waves draw back, and fling,   10
At their return, up the high strand,°
Begin, and cease, and then again begin,
With tremulous cadence slow, and bring
The eternal note of sadness in.

---

jow: Stroke.
The: [So that] the.
moon-blanched: Whitened by moonlight.
strand: Beach.

Sophocles° long ago   15
Heard it on the Aegean,° and it brought
Into his mind the turbid ebb and flow
Of human misery; we
Find also in the sound a thought,
Hearing it by this distant northern sea.   20

The Sea of Faith
Was once, too, at the full, and round earth's shore
Lay like the folds of a bright girdle furled.
But now I only hear
Its melancholy, long, withdrawing roar,   25
Retreating, to the breath
Of the night-wind, down the vast edges drear
And naked shingles° of the world.

Ah, love, let us be true
To one another! for the world, which seems   30
To lie before us like a land of dreams,
So various, so beautiful, so new,
Hath really neither joy, nor love, nor light,
Nor certitude, nor peace, nor help for pain;
And we are here as on a darkling° plain   35
Swept with confused alarms of struggle and flight,
Where ignorant armies clash by night.

ELIZABETH ALEXANDER (1962–   )

Apollo (1996)

We pull off
to a road shack
in Massachusetts
to watch men walk

on the moon. We did   5
the same thing
for three two one
blast off, and now

Sophocles: Greek playwright (496–406 B.C.), author of such tragedies as *Oedipus the King* and *Antigone.*
Aegean: Sea between Greece and Turkey.
shingles: Gravel beaches.
darkling: Darkening.

we watch the same men
bounce in and out   10
of craters. I want
a Coke and a hamburger.

Because the men
are walking on the moon
which is now irrefutably   15
not green, not cheese,

not a shiny dime floating
in a cold blue,
the way I'd thought,
the road shack people don't   20

notice we are a black
family not from there,
the way it mostly goes.
This talking through

static, bouncing in space-   25
boots, tethered
to cords is much
stranger, stranger

even than we are.

MARGARET ATWOOD (1939–)

This Is a Photograph of Me (1966)

It was taken some time ago.
At first it seems to be
a smeared
print: blurred lines and grey flecks
blended with the paper;   5

then, as you scan
it, you see in the left-hand corner
a thing that is like a branch: part of a tree
(balsam or spruce) emerging
and, to the right, halfway up   10
what ought to be a gentle
slope, a small frame house.

In the background there is a lake,
and beyond that, some low hills.

(The photograph was taken   15
the day after I drowned.

I am in the lake, in the center
of the picture, just under the surface.

It is difficult to say where
precisely, or to say   20
how large or small I am:
the effect of water
on light is a distortion

but if you look long enough,
eventually   25
you will be able to see me.)

ELIZABETH BISHOP (1911–1979)

The Fish (1946)

I caught a tremendous fish
and held him beside the boat
half out of water, with my hook
fast in a corner of his mouth.
He didn't fight.   5
He hadn't fought at all.
He hung a grunting weight,
battered and venerable
and homely. Here and there
his brown skin hung in strips   10
like ancient wallpaper,
and its pattern of darker brown
was like wallpaper:
shapes like full-blown roses
stained and lost through age.   15
He was speckled with barnacles,
fine rosettes of lime,
and infested
with tiny white sea-lice,
and underneath two or three   20
rags of green weed hung down.
While his gills were breathing in
the terrible oxygen
—the frightening gills,
fresh and crisp with blood,   25
that can cut so badly—
I thought of the coarse white flesh
packed in like feathers,
the big bones and the little bonies,

the dramatic reds and blacks   30
of his shiny entrails,
and the pink swim-bladder
like a big peony.
I looked into his eyes
which were far larger than mine   35
but shallower, and yellowed,
the irises backed and packed
with tarnished tinfoil
seen through the lenses
of old scratched isinglass.   40
They shifted a little, but not
to return my stare.
—It was more like the tipping
of an object toward the light.
I admired his sullen face,   45
the mechanism of his jaw,
and then I saw
that from his lower lip
—if you could call it a lip—
grim, wet, and weaponlike,   50
hung five old pieces of fish-line,
or four and a wire leader
with the swivel still attached,
with all their five big hooks
grown firmly in his mouth.   55
A green line, frayed at the end
and crimped from the strain and snap
when it broke and he got away.
Like medals with their ribbons
frayed and wavering,   60
a five-haired beard of wisdom
trailing from his aching jaw.
I stared and stared
and victory filled up
the little rented boat,   65
from the pool of bilge
where oil had spread a rainbow
around the rusted engine
to the bailer rusted orange,
the sun-cracked thwarts,   70
the oarlocks on their strings,
the gunnels — until everything
was rainbow, rainbow, rainbow!
And I let the fish go.

WILLIAM BLAKE (1757–1827)

The Chimney Sweeper (1789)

When my mother died I was very young,
And my father sold me while yet my tongue
Could scarcely cry "'weep! 'weep! 'weep! 'weep!"
So your chimneys I sweep, and in soot I sleep.

There's little Tom Dacre, who cried when his head,   5
That curled like a lamb's back, was shaved: so I said
"Hush, Tom! never mind it, for when your head's bare
You know that the soot cannot spoil your white hair."

And so he was quiet, and that very night,
As Tom was a-sleeping, he had such a sight!   10
That thousands of sweepers, Dick, Joe, Ned, and Jack,
Were all of them locked up in coffins of black.

And by came an Angel who had a bright key,
And he opened the coffins and set them all free;
Then down a green plain leaping, laughing, they run,   15
And wash in a river, and shine in the sun.

Then naked and white, all their bags left behind,
They rise upon clouds and sport in the wind;
And the Angel told Tom, if he'd be a good boy,
He'd have God for his father, and never want joy.   20

And so Tom awoke; and we rose in the dark,
And got with our bags and our brushes to work.
Though the morning was cold, Tom was happy and warm;
So if all do their duty they need not fear harm.

WILLIAM BLAKE (1757–1827)

The Lamb (1789)

Little Lamb, who made thee?
Dost thou know who made thee?
Gave thee life & bid thee feed,
By the stream & o'er the mead;
Gave thee clothing of delight,   5
Softest clothing wooly bright;
Gave thee such a tender voice,
Making all the vales rejoice!
Little Lamb who made thee?
Dost thou know who made thee?   10

Little Lamb I'll tell thee,
Little Lamb I'll tell thee!
He is callèd by thy name,
For he calls himself a Lamb:
He is meek & he is mild,   15
He became a little child:
I a child & thou a lamb,
We are callèd by his name.
    Little Lamb God bless thee.
    Little Lamb God bless thee.   20

WILLIAM BLAKE (1757–1827)

To see a World in a Grain of Sand (1803)

To see a World in a Grain of Sand
And a Heaven in a Wild Flower,
Hold Infinity in the palm of your hand
And Eternity in an hour.

WILLIAM BLAKE (1757–1827)

The Tyger (1794)

Tyger! Tyger! burning bright
In the forests of the night,
What immortal hand or eye
Could frame thy fearful symmetry?

In what distant deeps or skies   5
Burnt the fire of thine eyes?
On what wings dare he aspire?
What the hand dare seize the fire?

And what shoulder, and what art,
Could twist the sinews of thy heart?   10
And when thy heart began to beat,
What dread hand? and what dread feet?

What the hammer? what the chain?
In what furnace was thy brain?
What the anvil? what dread grasp   15
Dare its deadly terrors clasp?

When the stars threw down their spears,
And watered heaven with their tears,

Did he smile his work to see?
Did he who made the Lamb make thee?   20

Tyger! Tyger! burning bright
In the forests of the night,
What immortal hand or eye
Dare frame thy fearful symmetry?

ANNE BRADSTREET (1612?–1672)

The Author to Her Book° (1678)

Thou ill-formed offspring of my feeble brain,
Who after birth did'st by my side remain,
Till snatched from thence by friends, less wise than true,
Who thee abroad exposed to public view;
Made thee in rags, halting, to the press to trudge,   5
Where errors were not lessened, all may judge.
At thy return my blushing was not small,
My rambling brat (in print) should mother call;
I cast thee by as one unfit for light,
Thy visage was so irksome in my sight;   10
Yet being mine own, at length affection would
Thy blemishes amend, if so I could:
I washed thy face, but more defects I saw,
And rubbing off a spot, still made a flaw.
I stretched thy joints to make thee even feet,°   15
Yet still thou run'st more hobbling than is meet;°
In better dress to trim thee was my mind,
But nought save homespun cloth in the house I find.
In this array, 'mongst vulgars° may'st thou roam;
In critics' hands beware thou dost not come;   20
And take thy way where yet thou are not known.
If for thy Father asked, say thou had'st none;
And for thy Mother, she alas is poor,
Which caused her thus to send thee out of door.

Her Book: Bradstreet addresses *The Tenth Muse,* a collection of her poetry published without her consent in 1650.
even feet: Metrical feet.
meet: Appropriate or decorous.
vulgars: Common people.

GWENDOLYN BROOKS (1917–2000)

The Ballad of Rudolph Reed (1960)

Rudolph Reed was oaken.
His wife was oaken too.
And his two girls and his good little man
Oakened as they grew.

"I am not hungry for berries.   5
I am not hungry for bread.
But hungry hungry for a house
Where at night a man in bed

"May never hear the plaster
Stir as if in pain.   10
May never hear the roaches
Falling like fat rain.

"Where never wife and children need
Go blinking through the gloom.
Where every room of many rooms   15
Will be full of room.

"Oh my home may have its east or west
Or north or south behind it.
All I know is I shall know it,
And fight for it when I find it."   20

It was in a street of bitter white
That he made his application.
For Rudolph Reed was oakener
Than others in the nation.

The agent's steep and steady stare   25
Corroded to a grin.
Why, you black old, tough old hell of a man,
Move your family in!

Nary a grin grinned Rudolph Reed,
Nary a curse cursed he,   30
But moved in his House. With his dark little wife,
And his dark little children three.

A neighbor would *look*, with a yawning eye
That squeezed into a slit.
But the Rudolph Reeds and the children three   35
Were too joyous to notice it.

For were they not firm in a home of their own
With windows everywhere

And a beautiful banistered stair
And a front yard for flowers and a back yard for grass?   40

The first night, a rock, big as two fists.
The second, a rock big as three.
But nary a curse cursed Rudolph Reed.
(Though oaken as man could be.)

The third night, a silvery ring of glass.   45
Patience ached to endure.
But he looked, and lo! small Mabel's blood
Was staining her gaze so pure.

Then up did rise our Rudolph Reed
And pressed the hand of his wife,   50
And went to the door with a thirty-four
And a beastly butcher knife.

He ran like a mad thing into the night.
And the words in his mouth were stinking.
By the time he had hurt his first white man   55
He was no longer thinking.

By the time he had hurt his fourth white man
Rudolph Reed was dead.
His neighbors gathered and kicked his corpse.
"Nigger —" his neighbors said.   60

Small Mabel whimpered all night long,
For calling herself the cause.
Her oak-eyed mother did no thing
But change the bloody gauze.

GWENDOLYN BROOKS (1917–2000)

The *Chicago Defender*° Sends a Man to Little Rock (1960)

Fall, 1957°

In Little Rock the people bear
Babes, and comb and part their hair
And watch the want ads, put repair
To roof and latch. While wheat toast burns
A woman waters multiferns.   5

Chicago Defender: A weekly newspaper for African-American readers.
Fall, 1957: When black students first entered the public high school in Little Rock, Arkansas, in 1957, the city erupted in race riots protesting desegregation.

Time upholds or overturns
The many, tight, and small concerns.

In Little Rock the people sing
Sunday hymns like anything,
Through Sunday pomp and polishing.   10

And after testament and tunes,
Some soften Sunday afternoons
With lemon tea and Lorna Doones.

I forecast
And I believe   15
Come Christmas Little Rock will cleave
To Christmas tree and trifle, weave,
From laugh and tinsel, texture fast.

In Little Rock is baseball; Barcarolle.°
That hotness in July . . . the uniformed figures raw and implacable   20
And not intellectual,
Batting the hotness or clawing the suffering dust.
The Open Air Concert, on the special twilight green. . . .
When Beethoven is brutal or whispers to lady-like air.
Blanket-sitters are solemn, as Johann troubles to lean   25
To tell them what to mean. . . .

There is love, too, in Little Rock. Soft women softly
Opening themselves in kindness,
Or, pitying one's blindness,
Awaiting one's pleasure   30
In azure
Glory with anguished rose at the root. . . .
To wash away old semi-discomfitures.
They re-teach purple and unsullen blue.
The wispy soils go. And uncertain   35
Half-havings have they clarified to sures.

In Little Rock they know
Not answering the telephone is a way of rejecting life,
That it is our business to be bothered, is our business
To cherish bores or boredom, be polite   40
To lies and love and many-faceted fuzziness.
I scratch my head, massage the hate-I-had.
I blink across my prim and pencilled pad.
The saga I was sent for is not down.
Because there is a puzzle in this town.   45
The biggest News I do not dare

Barcarolle: A Venetian gondolier's song, or a song suggesting the rhythm of rowing.

Telegraph to the Editor's chair:
"They are like people everywhere."

The angry Editor would reply
In hundred harryings of Why.   50

And true, they are hurling spittle, rock,
Garbage and fruit in Little Rock.
And I saw coiling storm a-writhe
On bright madonnas. And a scythe
Of men harassing brownish girls.   55
(The bows and barrettes in the curls
And braids declined away from joy.)

I saw a bleeding brownish boy. . . .

The lariat lynch-wish I deplored.

The loveliest lynchee was our Lord.   60

GWENDOLYN BROOKS (1917–2000)

Medgar Evers° (1964)

For Charles Evers°

The man whose height his fear improved he
arranged to fear no further. The raw
intoxicated time was time for better birth or a final death.

Old styles, old tempos, all the engagement of
the day — the sedate, the regulated fray —   5
the antique light, the Moral rose, old gusts,
tight whistlings from the past, the mothballs
in the Love at last our man forswore.

Medgar Evers annoyed confetti and assorted
brands of businessmen's eyes.   10

The shows came down: to maxims and surprise.
And palsy.

Roaring no rapt arise-ye to the dead, he
leaned across tomorrow. People said that
he was holding clean globes in his hands.   15

Medgar Evers: African-American civil rights leader who was killed by a sniper in 1963.
Charles Evers: Medgar Evers's brother.

GWENDOLYN BROOKS (1917–   )

We Real Cool (1960)

The Pool Players.
Seven at the Golden Shovel.

We real cool. We
Left School. We

Lurk late. We
Strike straight. We

Sing sin. We   5
Thin gin. We

Jazz June. We
Die soon.

GEORGE GORDON, LORD BYRON (1788–1824)

She Walks in Beauty (1815)

1

She walks in beauty, like the night
    Of cloudless climes and starry skies;
And all that's best of dark and bright
    Meet in her aspect and her eyes:
Thus mellowed to that tender light   5
    Which heaven to gaudy day denies.

2

One shade the more, one ray the less,
    Had half impaired the nameless grace
Which waves in every raven tress,
    Or softly lightens o'er her face;   10
Where thoughts serenely sweet express
    How pure, how dear their dwelling place.

3

And on that cheek, and o'er that brow,
    So soft, so calm, yet eloquent,
The smiles that win, the tints that glow,   15
    But tell of days in goodness spent,
A mind at peace with all below,
    A heart whose love is innocent!

LUCILLE CLIFTON (1936–   )

the mississippi river empties into the gulf (1999)

and the gulf enters the sea and so forth,
none of them emptying anything,
all of them carrying yesterday
forever on their white tipped backs,
all of them dragging forward tomorrow.   5
it is the great circulation
of the earth's body, like the blood
of the gods, this river in which the past
is always flowing. every water
is the same water coming round.   10
everyday someone is standing on the edge
of this river staring into time,
whispering mistakenly;
only here. only now.

SAMUEL TAYLOR COLERIDGE (1772–1834)

Kubla Khan° (1797, 1798)

Or, a Vision in a Dream. A Fragment.

In Xanadu did Kubla Khan
A stately pleasure-dome decree:
Where Alph,° the sacred river, ran
Through caverns measureless to man
Down to a sunless sea.   5
So twice five miles of fertile ground
With walls and towers were girdled round;
And there were gardens bright with sinuous rills,
Where blossomed many an incense-bearing tree;
And here were forests ancient as the hills,   10
Enfolding sunny spots of greenery.

But oh! that deep romantic chasm which slanted
Down the green hill athwart a cedarn cover!
A savage place! as holy and enchanted

Kubla Khan: Coleridge mythologizes the actual Kublai Khan, a thirteenth-century Mongol emperor, as well as the Chinese city of Xanadu.

Alph: Probably derived from the Greek river Alpheus, whose waters, according to legend, rose from the Ionian Sea in Sicily as the fountain of Arethusa.

As e'er beneath a waning moon was haunted   15
By woman wailing for her demon-lover!
And from this chasm, with ceaseless turmoil seething,
As if this earth in fast thick pants were breathing,
A mighty fountain momently was forced:
Amid whose swift half-intermitted burst   20
Huge fragments vaulted like rebounding hail,
Or chaffy grain beneath the thresher's flail:
And 'mid these dancing rocks at once and ever
It flung up momently the sacred river.
Five miles meandering with a mazy motion   25
Through wood and dale the sacred river ran,
Then reached the caverns measureless to man,
And sank in tumult to a lifeless ocean:
And 'mid this tumult Kubla heard from far
Ancestral voices prophesying war!   30

    The shadow of the dome of pleasure
    Floated midway on the waves;
    Where was heard the mingled measure
    From the fountain and the caves.
It was a miracle of rare device,   35
A sunny pleasure-dome with caves of ice!

    A damsel with a dulcimer
    In a vision once I saw:
    It was an Abyssinian maid,
    And on her dulcimer she played,   40
    Singing of Mount Abora.°
    Could I revive within me
    Her symphony and song,
    To such a deep delight 'twould win me,
That with music loud and long,   45
I would build that dome in air,
That sunny dome! those caves of ice!
And all who heard should see them there,
And all should cry, Beware! Beware!
His flashing eyes, his floating hair!   50
Weave a circle round him thrice,°
And close your eyes with holy dread,
For he on honey-dew hath fed,
And drunk the milk of Paradise.

Mount Abora: Some scholars see a reminiscence here of John Milton's *Paradise Lost* 4.280–82: "where Abassin
kings their issue guard / Mount Amara, though this by some supposed / True Paradise under the Ethiop Line."
Weave . . . thrice: A magic ritual to keep away intruding spirits.

BILLY COLLINS (1941–   )

Lines Lost among Trees (1997)

These are not the lines that came to me
while walking in the woods
with no pen
and nothing to write on anyway.

They are gone forever,   5
a handful of coins
dropped through the grate of memory,
along with the ingenious mnemonic

I devised to hold them in place—
all gone and forgotten   10
before I had returned to the clearing of lawn
in back of our quiet house

with its jars jammed with pens,
its notebooks and reams of blank paper,
its desk and soft lamp,   15
its table and the light from its windows.

So this is my elegy for them,
those six or eight exhalations,
the braided rope of the syntax,
the jazz of the timing,   20

and the little insight at the end
wagging like the short tail
of a perfectly obedient spaniel
sitting by the door.

This is my envoy to nothing   25
where I say Go, little poem—
not out into the world of strangers' eyes,
but off to some airy limbo,

home to lost epics,
unremembered names,   30
and fugitive dreams
such as the one I had last night,

which, like a fantastic city in pencil,
erased itself
in the bright morning air   35
just as I was waking up.

HART CRANE (1899–1932)

To Brooklyn Bridge (1926)

How many dawns, chill from his rippling rest
The seagull's wings shall dip and pivot him,
Shedding white rings of tumult, building high
Over the chained bay waters Liberty—

Then, with inviolate curve, forsake our eyes   5
As apparitional as sails that cross
Some page of figures to be filed away;
—Till elevators drop us from our day . . .

I think of cinemas, panoramic sleights
With multitudes bent toward some flashing scene   10
Never disclosed, but hastened to again,
Foretold to other eyes on the same screen;

And Thee, across the harbor, silver-paced
As though the sun took step of thee, yet left
Some motion ever unspent in thy stride,—   15
Implicitly thy freedom staying thee!

Out of some subway scuttle, cell or loft
A bedlamite speeds to thy parapets,
Tilting there momently, shrill shirt ballooning,
A jest falls from the speechless caravan.   20

Down Wall, from girder into street noon leaks,
A rip-tooth of the sky's acetylene;
All afternoon the cloud-flown derricks turn . . .
Thy cables breathe the North Atlantic still.

And obscure as that heaven of the Jews,   25
Thy guerdon . . . Accolade thou dost bestow
Of anonymity time cannot raise:
Vibrant reprieve and pardon thou dost show.

O harp and altar, of the fury fused,
(How could mere toil align thy choiring strings!)   30
Terrific threshold of the prophet's pledge,
Prayer of pariah, and the lover's cry,—

Again the traffic lights that skim thy swift
Unfractioned idiom, immaculate sigh of stars,
Beading thy path — condense eternity: 35
And we have seen night lifted in thine arms.

Under thy shadow by the piers I waited;
Only in darkness is thy shadow clear.

The City's fiery parcels all undone,
Already snow submerges an iron year . . .   40

O Sleepless as the river under thee,
Vaulting the sea, the prairies' dreaming sod,
Unto us lowliest sometime sweep, descend
And of the curveship lend a myth to God.

E. E. CUMMINGS (1894–1962)

Buffalo Bill's (1923)

Buffalo Bill's
defunct
       who used to
       ride a watersmooth-silver
                      stallion   5
and break onetwothreefourfive pigeonsjustlikethat
                                  Jesus
he was a handsome man
                  and what i want to know is
how do you like your blueeyed boy   10
Mister Death

E. E. CUMMINGS (1894–1962)

next to of course god america i (1926)

"next to of course god america i
love you land of the pilgrims' and so forth oh
say can you see by the dawn's early my
country 'tis of centuries come and go
and are no more what of it we should worry   5
in every language even deafanddumb
thy sons acclaim your glorious name by gorry
by jingo by gee by gosh by gum
why talk of beauty what could be more beautiful than these heroic happy dead   10

EMILY DICKINSON (1830–1886)

Success is counted sweetest (1859)

Success is counted sweetest
By those who ne'er succeed.

To comprehend a nectar°
Requires sorest need.

Not one of all the purple Host   5
Who took the Flag today
Can tell the definition
So clear of Victory

As he defeated — dying—
On whose forbidden ear   10
The distant strains of triumph
Burst agonized and clear!

"Faith" is a fine invention (1860)

"Faith" is a fine invention
When Gentlemen can *see*—
But *Microscopes* are prudent
In an Emergency.

Wild Nights — Wild Nights! (1861)

Wild Nights — Wild Nights!
Were I with thee
Wild Nights should be
Our luxury!

Futile — the Winds—   5
To a Heart in port—
Done with the Compass—
Done with the Chart!

Rowing in Eden—
Ah, the Sea!   10
Might I but moor — Tonight—
In Thee!

Nature — sometimes sears a Sapling — (1862)

Nature — sometimes sears a Sapling—
Sometimes — scalps a Tree—
Her Green People recollect it
When they do not die—

Nectar: In Greek mythology, the drink of the gods.

Fainter Leaves — to Further Seasons —   5
Dumbly testify —
We — who have the Souls —
Die oftener — Not so vitally —

After great pain, a formal feeling comes —   (1862)

After great pain, a formal feeling comes —
The Nerves sit ceremonious, like Tombs —
The stiff Heart questions was it He, that bore,
And Yesterday, or Centuries before?

The Feet, mechanical, go round —   5
Of Ground, or Air, or Ought —
A Wooden way
Regardless grown,
A Quartz contentment, like a stone —

This is the Hour of Lead —   10
Remembered, if outlived,
As Freezing persons, recollect the Snow —
First — Chill — then Stupor — then the letting go —

I heard a Fly buzz — when I died —   (1862)

I heard a Fly buzz — when I died —
The Stillness in the Room
Was like the Stillness in the Air —
Between the Heaves of Storm —

The Eyes around — had wrung them dry —   5
And Breaths were gathering firm
For that last Onset — when the King
Be witnessed — in the Room —

I willed my Keepsakes — Signed away
What portion of me be   10
Assignable — and then it was
There interposed a Fly —

With Blue — uncertain stumbling Buzz —
Between the light — and me —
And then the Windows failed — and then   15
I could not see to see —

I dwell in Possibility —   (1862)

I dwell in Possibility —
A fairer House than Prose —

More numerous of Windows—
Superior — for Doors—

Of Chambers as the Cedars—   5
Impregnable of Eye—
And for an Everlasting Roof
The Gambrels° of the Sky—

Of Visitors — the fairest—
For Occupation — This—
The spreading wide my narrow Hands
To gather Paradise—

Tell all the Truth but tell it slant — (1868)

Tell all the Truth but tell it slant—
Success in Circuit lies
Too bright for our infirm Delight
The Truth's superb surprise
As Lightning to the Children eased   5
With explanation kind
The Truth must dazzle gradually
Or every man be blind—

CHITRA BANERJEE DIVAKARUNI (1956–   )

The Brides Come to Yuba City° (1977)

The sky is hot and yellow, filled
with blue screaming birds. The train
heaved us from its belly
and vanished in shrill smoke.
Now only the tracks   5
gleam dull in the heavy air,
a ladder to eternity, each receding rung
cleaved from our husbands' ribs.
Mica-flecked, the platform dazzles, burns up
through thin *chappal* soles, lurches like   10
the ship's dark hold,
blurred month of nights, smell of vomit,

Gambrels: A gambrel roof; a ridged roof with two slopes on each side.

"The Brides Come to Yuba City": Because of immigration restrictions, the wives of many Sikhs who had emigrated from India to Yuba City, California, in the early 1900s had to remain in India until the 1940s.

a porthole like the bleached iris
of a giant unseeing eye.

Red-veiled, we lean into each other,   15
press damp palms, try
broken smiles. The man who met us at the ship
whistles a restless *Angrezi* tune
and scans the fields. Behind us,
the black wedding trunks, sharp-edged,   20
shiny, stenciled with strange men-names
our bodies do not fit into:
Mrs. Baldev Johl, Mrs. Kanwal Bains.
Inside, bright *salwar-kameezes* scented
with sandalwood. For the men,   25
kurtas and thin white gauze
to wrap their long hair.
Laddus from Jullundhur, sugar-crusted,
six kinds of lentils, a small bag
of bajra flour. Labeled in our mothers' hesitant hands,   30
packets of seeds —*methi, karela, saag*—
to burst from this new soil
like green stars.

He gives a shout, waves at the men, their slow,
uneven approach. We crease our eyes   35
through the veils' red film, cannot breathe. Thirty years
since we saw them. Or never,
like Harvinder, married last year at Hoshiarpur
to her husband's photo,
which she clutches tight to her   40
to stop the shaking. He is fifty-two,
she sixteen. Tonight —like us all—
she will open her legs to him.

The platform is endless-wide.
The men walk and walk   45
without advancing. Their lined,
wavering mouths, their eyes like drowning lights.
We cannot recognize a single face.

JOHN DONNE (1572–1631)

Batter My Heart, Three-Personed God (c. 1610)

Batter my heart, three-personed God, for You
As yet but knock, breathe, shine, and seek to mend.
That I may rise and stand, o'erthrow me, and bend
Your force to break, blow, burn, and make me new.

I, like an usurped town to another due,   5
Labor to admit You, but Oh! to no end.
Reason, Your viceroy in me, me should defend,
But is captived, and proves weak or untrue.
Yet dearly I love You, and would be lovèd fain,
But am betrothed unto Your enemy;   10
Divorce me, untie or break that knot again;
Take me to You, imprison me, for I,
Except You enthrall me, never shall be free,
Nor ever chaste, except You ravish me.

JOHN DONNE (1572–1631)

Death Be Not Proud (c. 1610)

Death be not proud, though some have callèd thee
Mighty and dreadful, for thou art not so;
For those whom thou think'st thou dost overthrow
Die not, poor death, nor yet canst thou kill me.
From rest and sleep, which but thy pictures be,   5
Much pleasure, then from thee much more must flow,
And soonest our best men with thee do go,
Rest of their bones, and soul's delivery.
Thou art slave to fate, chance, kings, and desperate men,
And dost with poison, war, and sickness dwell,   10
And poppy, or charms can make us sleep as well,
And better than thy stroke; why swell'st thou then?
One short sleep past, we wake eternally,
And death shall be no more; death, thou shalt die.

RITA DOVE (1952–   )

The Satisfaction Coal Company (1986)

1
What to do with a day.
Leaf through *Jet*. Watch T.V.
Freezing on the porch
but he goes anyhow, snow too high
for a walk, the ice treacherous.   5
Inside, the gas heater takes care of itself;
he doesn't even notice being warm.

Everyone says he looks great.
Across the street a drunk stands smiling
at something carved in a tree.   10

The new neighbor with the floating hips
scoots out to get the mail
and waves once, brightly,
storm door clipping her heel on the way in.

2

Twice a week he had taken the bus down Glendale hill   15
to the corner of Market. Slipped through
the alley by the canal and let himself in.
Started to sweep
with terrible care, like a woman
brushing shine into her hair,   20
same motion, same lullaby.
No curtains — the cop on the beat
stopped outside once in the hour
to swing his billy club and glare.

It was better on Saturdays   25
when the children came along:
he mopped while they emptied
ashtrays, clang of glass on metal
then a dry scutter. Next they counted
nailheads studding the leather cushions.   30
Thirty-four! they shouted,
that was the year and
they found it mighty amusing.

But during the week he noticed more —
lights when they gushed or dimmed   35
at the Portage Hotel, the 10:32
picking up speed past the B & O switchyard,
floorboards trembling and the explosive
kachook kachook kachook kachook
and the oiled rails ticking underneath.   40

3

They were poor then but everyone had been poor.
He hadn't minded the sweeping,
just the thought of it — like now
when people ask him what he's thinking
and he says *I'm listening.*   45

Those nights walking home alone,
the bucket of coal scraps banging his knee,
he'd hear a roaring furnace
with its dry, familiar heat. Now the nights
take care of themselves — as for the days,   50
there is the canary's sweet curdled song,
the wino smiling through his dribble.
Past the hill, past the gorge

choked with wild sumac in summer,
the corner has been upgraded.   55
Still, he'd like to go down there someday
to stand for a while, and get warm.

PAUL LAURENCE DUNBAR (1872–1906)

We Wear the Mask (1913)

We wear the mask that grins and lies,
It hides our cheeks and shades our eyes—
This debt we pay to human guile;
With torn and bleeding hearts we smile,
And mouth with myriad subtleties.   5

Why should the world be over-wise,
In counting all our tears and sighs?
Nay, let them only see us, while
    We wear the mask.

We smile, but, O great Christ, our cries   10
To thee from tortured souls arise.
We sing, but oh the clay is vile
Beneath our feet, and long the mile;
But let the world dream otherwise,
    We wear the mask!   15

T. S. ELIOT (1888–1965)

The Love Song of J. Alfred Prufrock (1917)

> *S'io credessi che mia risposta fosse*
> *A persona che mai tornasse al mondo,*
> *Questa fiamma staria senza piu scosse.*
> *Ma perciocche giammai di questo fondo*
> *Non torno vivo alcun, s'i'odo il vero,*
> *Senza tema d'infamia ti rispondo.°*

Let us go then, you and I,
When the evening is spread out against the sky
Like a patient etherized upon a table;
Let us go, through certain half-deserted streets,

The muttering retreats 5
Of restless nights in one-night cheap hotels
And sawdust restaurants with oyster-shells:
Streets that follow like a tedious argument
Of insidious intent
To lead you to an overwhelming question . . . 10
Oh, do not ask, "What is it?"
Let us go and make our visit.

In the room the women come and go
Talking of Michelangelo.

The yellow fog that rubs its back upon the window-panes, 15
The yellow smoke that rubs its muzzle on the window-panes
Licked its tongue into the corners of the evening,
Lingered upon the pools that stand in drains,
Let fall upon its back the soot that falls from chimneys,
Slipped by the terrace, made a sudden leap, 20
And seeing that it was a soft October night,
Curled once about the house, and fell asleep.

And indeed there will be time
For the yellow smoke that slides along the street,
Rubbing its back upon the window-panes; 25
There will be time, there will be time
To prepare a face to meet the faces that you meet;
There will be time to murder and create,
And time for all the works and days° of hands
That lift and drop a question on your plate; 30
Time for you and time for me,
And time yet for a hundred indecisions,
And for a hundred visions and revisions,
Before the taking of a toast and tea.

In the room the women come and go 35
Talking of Michelangelo.

And indeed there will be time
To wonder, "Do I dare?" and, "Do I dare?"
Time to turn back and descend the stair,
With a bald spot in the middle of my hair— 40
(They will say: "How his hair is growing thin!")
My morning coat, my collar mounting firmly to the chin,
My necktie rich and modest, but asserted by a simple pin—

---

works and days: Works and Days is the title of a work by the eighth-century B.C. Greek poet Hesiod that celebrates farmwork.

(They will say: "But how his arms and legs are thin!")
Do I dare   45
Disturb the universe?
In a minute there is time
For decisions and revisions which a minute will reverse.

For I have known them all already, known them all—
Have known the evenings, mornings, afternoons,   50
I have measured out my life with coffee spoons;
I know the voices dying with a dying fall°
Beneath the music from a farther room.
    So how should I presume?

And I have known the eyes already, known them all—   55
The eyes that fix you in a formulated phrase,
And when I am formulated, sprawling on a pin,
When I am pinned and wriggling on the wall,
Then how should I begin
To spit out all the butt-ends of my days and ways?   60
    And how should I presume?

And I have known the arms already, known them all—
Arms that are braceleted and white and bare
(But in the lamplight, downed with light brown hair!)
Is it perfume from a dress   65
That makes me so digress?
Arms that lie along a table, or wrap about a shawl.
    And should I then presume?
    And how should I begin?

* * *

Shall I say, I have gone at dusk through narrow streets   70
And watched the smoke that rises from the pipes
Of lonely men in shirt-sleeves, leaning out of windows? . . .

I should have been a pair of ragged claws
Scuttling across the floors of silent seas.

* * *

And the afternoon, the evening, sleeps so peacefully!   75
Smoothed by long fingers,
Asleep . . . tired . . . or it malingers,
Stretched on the floor, here beside you and me.
Should I, after tea and cakes and ices,
Have the strength to force the moment to its crisis?   80

---

dying fall: An allusion to Orsino's speech in *Twelfth Night* (1.1): "That strain again! It had a dying fall."

But though I have wept and fasted, wept and prayed,
Though I have seen my head (grown slightly bald) brought in
    upon a platter,°
I am no prophet — and here's no great matter;
I have seen the moment of my greatness flicker,
And I have seen the eternal Footman° hold my coat, and   85
    snicker,
And in short, I was afraid.

And would it have been worth it, after all,
After the cups, the marmalade, the tea,
Among the porcelain, among some talk of you and me,
Would it have been worth while,   90
To have bitten off the matter with a smile,
To have squeezed the universe into a ball
To roll it toward some overwhelming question,
To say: "I am Lazarus,° come from the dead,
Come back to tell you all, I shall tell you all"—   95
If one, settling a pillow by her head,
        Should say: "That is not what I meant at all.
        That is not it, at all."

And would it have been worth it, after all,
Would it have been worth while,   100
After the sunsets and the dooryards and the sprinkled streets,
After the novels, after the teacups, after the skirts that trail
    along the floor—
And this, and so much more?—
It is impossible to say just what I mean!
But as if a magic lantern threw the nerves in patterns on a   105
    screen:
Would it have been worth while
If one, settling a pillow or throwing off a shawl,
And turning toward the window, should say:
        "That is not it at all,
        That is not what I meant, at all."   110

* * *

No! I am not Prince Hamlet, nor was meant to be;
Am an attendant lord, one that will do
To swell a progress,° start a scene or two,

---

head . . . platter: Like John the Baptist, who was beheaded by King Herod (see Matthew 14.3–11).
eternal Footman: Perhaps death or fate.
Lazarus: A man whom Christ raised from the dead (see John 11.1–44).
a progress: Here, in the Elizabethan sense of a royal journey.

Advise the prince; no doubt, an easy tool,
Deferential, glad to be of use,   115
Politic, cautious, and meticulous;
Full of high sentence,° but a bit obtuse;
At times, indeed, almost ridiculous—
Almost, at times, the Fool.

I grow old . . . I grow old . . .   120
I shall wear the bottoms of my trousers rolled.

Shall I part my hair behind? Do I dare to eat a peach?
I shall wear white flannel trousers, and walk upon the beach.
I have heard the mermaids singing, each to each.

I do not think that they will sing to me.   125

I have seen them riding seaward on the waves
Combing the white hair of the waves blown back
When the wind blows the water white and black.

We have lingered in the chambers of the sea
By sea-girls wreathed with seaweed red and brown   130
Till human voices wake us, and we drown.

JAMES A. EMANUEL (1921–   )

Emmett Till° (1968)

I hear a whistling
Through the water.
Little Emmett
Won't be still.
He keeps floating   5
Round the darkness,
Edging through
The silent chill.
Tell me, please,
That bedtime story   10
Of the fairy
River Boy
Who swims forever,
Deep in treasures,
Necklaced in   15
A coral toy.

---

sentence: Opinions.

Emmett Till: Till, a fourteen-year-old African-American from Chicago, was visiting relatives in Mississippi in 1955 when he made what he thought was an innocent remark to a white woman. Several days later, his body was found in the river with a heavy cotton gin fan tied around his neck with barbed wire.

LOUISE ERDRICH (1954–   )

Indian Boarding School: The Runaways (1984)

Home's the place we head for in our sleep.
Boxcars stumbling north in dreams
don't wait for us. We catch them on the run.
The rails, old lacerations that we love,
shoot parallel across the face and break   5
just under Turtle Mountains.° Riding scars
you can't get lost. Home is the place they cross.

The lame guard strikes a match and makes the dark
less tolerant. We watch through cracks in boards
as the land starts rolling, rolling till it hurts   10
to be here, cold in regulation clothes.
We know the sheriff's waiting at midrun
to take us back. His car is dumb and warm.
The highway doesn't rock, it only hums
like a wing of long insults. The worn-down welts   15
of ancient punishments lead back and forth.

All runaways wear dresses, long green ones,
the color you would think shame was. We scrub
the sidewalks down because it's shameful work.
Our brushes cut the stone in watered arcs   20
and in the soak frail outlines shiver clear
a moment, things us kids pressed on the dark
face before it hardened, pale, remembering
delicate old injuries, the spines of names and leaves.

ROBERT FROST (1874–1963)

Acquainted with the Night (1928)

I have been one acquainted with the night.
I have walked out in rain — and back in rain.
I have outwalked the furthest city light.

I have looked down the saddest city lane.
I have passed by the watchman on his beat   5
And dropped my eyes, unwilling to explain.

Turtle Mountains: Erdrich is a descendant of the Turtle Mountain band of the Chippewa.

I have stood still and stopped the sound of feet
When far away an interrupted cry
Came over houses from another street,

But not to call me back or say good-by;   10
And further still at an unearthly height,
One luminary clock against the sky

Proclaimed the time was neither wrong nor right.
I have been one acquainted with the night.

ROBERT FROST (1874–1963)

Birches (1915)

When I see birches bend to left and right
Across the lines of straighter darker trees,
I like to think some boy's been swinging them.
But swinging doesn't bend them down to stay
As ice-storms do. Often you must have seen them   5
Loaded with ice a sunny winter morning
After a rain. They click upon themselves
As the breeze rises, and turn many-colored
As the stir cracks and crazes their enamel.
Soon the sun's warmth makes them shed crystal shells   10
Shattering and avalanching on the snow-crust—
Such heaps of broken glass to sweep away
You'd think the inner dome of heaven had fallen.
They are dragged to the withered bracken by the load,
And they seem not to break; though once they are bowed   15
So low for long, they never right themselves:
You may see their trunks arching in the woods
Years afterwards, trailing their leaves on the ground
Like girls on hands and knees that throw their hair
Before them over their heads to dry in the sun.   20
But I was going to say when Truth broke in
With all her matter-of-fact about the ice-storm
I should prefer to have some boy bend them
As he went out and in to fetch the cows—
Some boy too far from town to learn baseball,   25
Whose only play was what he found himself,
Summer or winter, and could play alone.
One by one he subdued his father's trees
By riding them down over and over again
Until he took the stiffness out of them,   30
And not one but hung limp, not one was left

For him to conquer. He learned all there was
To learn about not launching out too soon
And so not carrying the tree away
Clear to the ground. He always kept his poise   35
To the top branches, climbing carefully
With the same pains you use to fill a cup
Up to the brim, and even above the brim.
Then he flung outward, feet first, with a swish,
Kicking his way down through the air to the ground.   40
So was I once myself a swinger of birches.
And so I dream of going back to be.
It's when I'm weary of considerations,
And life is too much like a pathless wood
Where your face burns and tickles with the cobwebs   45
Broken across it, and one eye is weeping
From a twig's having lashed across it open.
I'd like to get away from earth awhile
And then come back to it and begin over.
May no fate willfully misunderstand me   50
And half grant what I wish and snatch me away
Not to return. Earth's the right place for love:
I don't know where it's likely to go better.
I'd like to go by climbing a birch tree,
And climb black branches up a snow-white trunk   55
Toward Heaven, till the tree could bear no more,
But dipped its top and set me down again.
That would be good both going and coming back.
One could do worse than be a swinger of birches.

ROBERT FROST (1874–1963)

Desert Places (1936)

Snow falling and night falling fast, oh, fast
In a field I looked into going past,
And the ground almost covered smooth in snow,
But a few weeds and stubble showing last.

The woods around it have it — it is theirs.   5
All animals are smothered in their lairs,
I am too absent-spirited to count;
The loneliness includes me unawares.

And lonely as it is, that loneliness
Will be more lonely ere it will be less —   10
A blanker whiteness of benighted snow
With no expression, nothing to express.

They cannot scare me with their empty spaces
Between stars — on stars where no human race is.
I have it in me so much nearer home   15
To scare myself with my own desert places.

ROBERT FROST (1874–1963)

Mending Wall (1914)

Something there is that doesn't love a wall,
That sends the frozen-ground-swell under it,
And spills the upper boulders in the sun;
And makes gaps even two can pass abreast.
The work of hunters is another thing: 5
I have come after them and made repair
Where they have left not one stone on a stone,
But they would have the rabbit out of hiding,
To please the yelping dogs. The gaps I mean,
No one has seen them made or heard them made,   10
But at spring mending-time we find them there.
I let my neighbor know beyond the hill;
And on a day we meet to walk the line
And set the wall between us once again.
We keep the wall between us as we go.   15
To each the boulders that have fallen to each.
And some are loaves and some so nearly balls
We have to use a spell to make them balance:
"Stay where you are until our backs are turned!"
We wear our fingers rough with handling them.   20
Oh, just another kind of outdoor game,
One on a side. It comes to little more:
There where it is we do not need the wall:
He is all pine and I am apple orchard.
My apple trees will never get across   25
And eat the cones under his pines, I tell him.
He only says, "Good fences make good neighbors."
Spring is the mischief in me, and I wonder
If I could put a notion in his head:
"*Why* do they make good neighbors? Isn't it   30
Where there are cows? But here there are no cows.
Before I built a wall I'd ask to know
What I was walling in or walling out,
And to whom I was like to give offense.
Something there is that doesn't love a wall,   35
That wants it down." I could say "Elves" to him,

But it's not elves exactly, and I'd rather
He said it for himself. I see him there
Bringing a stone grasped firmly by the top
In each hand, like an old-stone savage armed.   40
He moves in darkness as it seems to me,
Not of woods only and the shade of trees.
He will not go behind his father's saying,
And he likes having thought of it so well
He says again, "Good fences make good neighbors."   45

ROBERT FROST (1874–1963)

The Road Not Taken (1915)

Two roads diverged in a yellow wood,
And sorry I could not travel both
And be one traveler, long I stood
And looked down one as far as I could
To where it bent in the undergrowth;   5

Then took the other, as just as fair,
And having perhaps the better claim,
Because it was grassy and wanted wear;
Though as for that the passing there
Had worn them really about the same,   10

And both that morning equally lay
In leaves no step had trodden black.
Oh, I kept the first for another day!
Yet knowing how way leads on to way,
I doubted if I should ever come back.   15

I shall be telling this with a sigh
Somewhere ages and ages hence:
Two roads diverged in a wood, and I—
I took the one less traveled by,
And that has made all the difference.   20

ROBERT FROST (1874–1963)

Stopping by Woods on a Snowy Evening (1923)

Whose woods these are I think I know.
His house is in the village though;
He will not see me stopping here
To watch his woods fill up with snow.

My little horse must think it queer   5
To stop without a farmhouse near
Between the woods and frozen lake
The darkest evening of the year.

He gives his harness bells a shake
To ask if there is some mistake.   10
The only other sound's the sweep
Of easy wind and downy flake.

The woods are lovely, dark and deep,
But I have promises to keep,
And miles to go before I sleep,   15
And miles to go before I sleep.

DEBORAH GARRISON (1965–   )

Please Fire Me (1998)

Here comes another alpha male,
and all the other alphas
are snorting and pawing,
kicking up puffs of acrid dust

while the silly little hens   5
clatter back and forth
on quivering claws and raise
a titter about the fuss.

Here comes another alpha male—
a man's man, a dealmaker,   10
holds tanks of liquor,
charms them pantsless at lunch:

I've never been sicker.
Do I have to stare into his eyes
and sympathize? If I want my job   15
I do. Well I think I'm through

with the working world,
through with warming eggs
and being Zenlike in my detachment
from all things Ego.   20

I'd like to go
somewhere else entirely,
and I don't mean
Europe.

NIKKI GIOVANNI (1943–   )

Nikki-Rosa (1968)

childhood remembrances are always a drag
if you're Black
you always remember things like living in Woodlawn°
with no inside toilet
and if you become famous or something   5
they never talk about how happy you were to have your mother
all to yourself and
how good the water felt when you got your bath from one of those
big tubs that folk in chicago barbecue in
and somehow when you talk about home   10
it never gets across how much you
understood their feelings
as the whole family attended meetings about Hollydale
and even though you remember
your biographers never understand   15
your father's pain as he sells his stock
and another dream goes
and though you're poor it isn't poverty that
concerns you
and though they fought a lot   20
it isn't your father's drinking that makes any difference
but only that everybody is together and you
and your sister have happy birthdays and very good christmasses
and I really hope no white person ever has cause to write
        about me
because they never understand Black love is Black wealth and
        they'll   25
probably talk about my hard childhood and never understand that
all the while I was quite happy

JORIE GRAHAM (1950–   )

I Was Taught Three (1982)

names for the tree facing my window
almost within reach, elastic

with squirrels, memory banks, homes.
Castagno took itself to heart, its pods

Woodlawn: A predominantly black suburb of Cincinnati, Ohio.

like urchins clung to where they landed   5
claiming every bit of shadow

at the hem. *Chassagne,* on windier days,
nervous in taffeta gowns,

whispering, on the verge of being
anarchic, though well bred.   10

And then *chestnut,* whipped pale and clean
by all the inner reservoirs

called upon to do their even share of work.
It was not the kind of tree

got at by default — imagine that — not one   15
in which only the remaining leaf

was loyal. No, this
was all first person, and I

was the stem, holding within myself the whole
bouquet of three,   20

at once given and received: smallest roadmaps
of coincidence. What is the idea

that governs blossoming? The human tree
clothed with its nouns, or this one

just outside my window promising more firmly   25
that can be

that it will reach my sill eventually, the leaves
silent as suppressed desires, and I

a name among them.

H. D. (HILDA DOOLITTLE) (1886–1961)

Heat (1916)

O wind, rend open the heat,
cut apart the heat,
rend it to tatters.

Fruit cannot drop
through this thick air —   5
fruit cannot fall into heat
that presses up and blunts
the points of pears
and rounds the grapes.

Cut the heat—   10
plough through it,
turning it on either side
of your path.

MARILYN HACKER (1942–   )

I'm four, in itchy woolen leggings, (2000)

I'm four, in itchy woolen leggings,
the day that I can't recognize the man
down at the park entrance, waving,
as my father. He has ten
more years to live, that spring. Dapper and balding   5
he walks toward me; then I run toward him, calling
him, flustered by my flawed vision.
Underfoot, the maples' green-
winged seeds splay on mica-specked octagons.
His round face, thin nose, moustache silvered gray   10
at thirty-eight look (I think now) Hungarian.
I like his wood smell of two packs a day
as he swings me up to his shoulder
and I say, things look blurry far away
— one Saturday, two years after the war.   15

RACHEL HADAS (1948–   )

Thick and Thin (2001)

Time thickens.
Sticky, taffy-brown,
the malleable gunk of family
memories, resemblances, resentments,
anecdotes thumped and punched   5
by a succession of urgent hands
hardens and cools, but early lumps remain,
fingerprints, palmprints, even marks of teeth.
You spend a lifetime trying to smooth these out.

Time thins.   10
To the original mix nothing is added
but a steady trickle wrung from years,
a faintly salty broth, not tears, not sweat.
The solution weakens until only
a feeble fingerprint of this first scent   15

trembles half-imagined on the air.
That earliest essence — what was it again?
You spend a lifetime trying to get it back.

JOY HARJO (1951–　　)

Morning Song (2001)

The red dawn now is rearranging the earth
Thought by thought
Beauty by beauty
Each sunrise a link in the ladder
The ladder the backbone   5
Of shimmering deity
Child stirring in the web of your mother
Do not be afraid
Old man turning to walk through the door
Do not be afraid   10

THOMAS HARDY (1840–1928)

The Convergence of the Twain (1912)

(Lines on the loss of the 'Titanic')

I

In a solitude of the sea
 Deep from human vanity,
And the Pride of Life that planned her, stilly couches she.

II

 Steel chambers, late the pyres°
 Of her salamandrine fires,°   5
Cold currents thrid,° and turn to rhythmic tidal lyres.

III

 Over the mirrors meant
 To glass the opulent
The sea-worm crawls — grotesque, slimed, dumb, indifferent.

---

pyres: Funeral pyres; piles of wood on which corpses were burned in ancient rites.
salamandrine fires: An allusion to the old belief that salamanders could live in fire.
thrid: Thread (archaic verb form).

IV

Jewels in joy designed   10
To ravish the sensuous mind
Lie lightless, all their sparkles bleared and black and blind.

V

Dim moon-eyed fishes near
Gaze at the gilded gear
And query: "What does this vaingloriousness down here?" . . .   15

VI

Well: while was fashioning
This creature of cleaving wing,
The Immanent° Will that stirs and urges everything

VII

Prepared a sinister mate
For her — so gaily great —   20
A Shape of Ice, for the time far and dissociate.

VIII

And as the smart ship grew
In stature, grace, and hue,
In shadowy silent distance grew the Iceberg too.

IX

Alien they seemed to be: 25
No mortal eye could see
The intimate welding of their later history,

X

Or sign that they were bent
By paths coincident
On being anon° twin halves of one august° event,   30

XI

Till the Spinner of the Years
Said "Now!" And each one hears,
And consummation comes, and jars two hemispheres.

Immanent: Inherent, dwelling within.

anon: Soon.

august: Awe-inspiring, majestic.

ROBERT HAYDEN (1913–   )

Homage to the Empress of the Blues° (1966)

Because there was a man somewhere in a candystripe silk shirt,
gracile and dangerous as a jaguar and because a woman moaned
for him in sixty-watt gloom and mourned him Faithless Love
Twotiming Love Oh Love Oh Careless Aggravating Love,

> She came out on the stage in yards of pearls, emerging like   5
> a favorite scenic view, flashed her golden smile and sang.

Because grey laths began somewhere to show from underneath
torn hurdygurdy lithographs of dollfaced heaven;
and because there were those who feared alarming fists of snow
on the door and those who feared the riot-squad of statistics,   10

> She came out on the stage in ostrich feathers, beaded satin,
> and shone that smile on us and sang.

SEAMUS HEANEY (1939–   )

Mid-Term Break (1966)

I sat all morning in the college sick bay
Counting bells knelling classes to a close.
At two o'clock our neighbors drove me home.

In the porch I met my father crying—
He had always taken funerals in his stride—   5
And Big Jim Evans saying it was a hard blow.

The baby cooed and laughed and rocked the pram
When I came in, and I was embarrassed
By old men standing up to shake my hand

And tell me they were "sorry for my trouble,"   10
Whispers informed strangers I was the eldest,
Away at school, as my mother held my hand

In hers and coughed out angry tearless sighs.
At ten o'clock the ambulance arrived
With the corpse, stanched and bandaged by the nurses.   15

Empress of the Blues: Bessie Smith (1894–1937), American jazz singer.

Next morning I went up into the room. Snowdrops
And candles soothed the bedside; I saw him
For the first time in six weeks. Paler now,

Wearing a poppy bruise on his left temple,
He lay in the four foot box as in his cot.   20
No gaudy scars, the bumper knocked him clear.

A four foot box, a foot for every year.

VICTOR HERNÁNDEZ CRUZ (1949–   )

Anonymous (1982)

And if I lived in those olden times
With a funny name like Choicer or
Henry Howard, Earl of Surrey, what chimes!
I would spend my time in search of rhymes
Make sure the measurement termination surprise   5
In the court of kings snapping till woo sunrise
Plus always be using the words *alas* and *hath*
And not even knowing that that was my path
Just think on the Lower East Side of Manhattan
It would have been like living in satin   10
Alas! The projects hath not covered the river
Thou see-est vision to make thee quiver
Hath I been delivered to that "wildernesse"
So past
I would have been the last one in the   15
Dance to go
Taking note the minuet so slow
All admire my taste
Within thou *mambo* of much more haste.

GERARD MANLEY HOPKINS (1844–1889)

God's Grandeur (1877)

The world is charged with the grandeur of God.
    It will flame out, like shining from shook foil;
    It gathers to a greatness, like the ooze of oil
Crushed. Why do men then now not reck his rod?
Generations have trod, have trod, have trod;   5
    And all is seared with trade; bleared, smeared with toil;

And wears man's smudge and shares man's smell: the soil
Is bare now, nor can foot feel, being shod.
And for all this, nature is never spent;
    There lives the dearest freshness deep down things;   10
And though the last lights off the black West went
    Oh, morning, at the brown brink eastward, springs—
Because the Holy Ghost over the bent
    World broods with warm breast and with ah! bright wings.

DONALD JUSTICE (1925–)

School Letting Out   (2002)

(Fourth or Fifth Grade)

The afternoons of going home from school
Past the young fruit trees and the winter flowers,
The schoolyard cries fading behind you then,
And small boys running to catch up, as though
It were an honor somehow to be near—   5
And all forgiven now, even the dog
Who, straining at his tether, starts to bark,
Not from anger but some secret joy.

JOHN KEATS (1795–1821)

La Belle Dame sans Merci:
A Ballad°   (1819, 1820)

1

O what can ail thee, knight at arms,
    Alone and palely loitering?
The sedge has wither'd from the lake,
    And no birds sing.

2

O what can ail thee, knight at arms,   5
    So haggard and so woe-begone?
The squirrel's granary is full,
    And the harvest's done.

"La Belle Dame sans Merci": The title, which means "The Lovely Lady without Pity," was taken from a medieval poem by Alain Chartier.

3

I see a lily on thy brow
    With anguish moist and fever dew,   10
And on thy cheeks a fading rose
    Fast withereth too.

4

I met a lady in the meads,
    Full beautiful, a fairy's child;
Her hair was long, her foot was light,   15
    And her eyes were wild.

5

I made a garland for her head,
    And bracelets too, and fragrant zone;°
She look'd at me as she did love,
    And made sweet moan.   20

6

I set her on my pacing steed,
    And nothing else saw all day long,
For sidelong would she bend, and sing
    A fairy's song.

7

She found me roots of relish sweet,   25
    And honey wild, and manna dew,
And sure in language strange she said—
    I love thee true.

8

She took me to her elfin grot,°
    And there she wept, and sigh'd full sore,   30
And there I shut her wild wild eyes
    With kisses four.

9

And there she lullèd me asleep,
    And there I dream'd — Ah! woe betide!
The latest° dream I ever dream'd   35
    On the cold hill's side.

---

fragrant zone: Belt.
grot: Grotto.
latest: Last.

10

I saw pale kings, and princes too,
    Pale warriors, death pale were they all;
They cried — "La belle dame sans merci
      Hath thee in thrall!"   40

11

I saw their starv'd lips in the gloom°
    With horrid warning gapèd wide,
And I awoke and found me here
      On the cold hill's side.

12

And this is why I sojourn here,   45
    Alone and palely loitering,
Though the sedge is wither'd from the lake,
      And no birds sing.

JOHN KEATS (1795–1821)

Bright Star! Would I Were Steadfast as Thou Art (1819)

Bright star! would I were steadfast as thou art —
    Not in lone splendor hung aloft the night,
And watching, with eternal lids apart,
    Like nature's patient, sleepless Eremite°
The moving waters at their priest-like task   5
    Of pure ablution° round earth's human shores,
Or gazing on the new soft-fallen mask
    Of snow upon the mountains and the moors —
No — yet still steadfast, still unchangeable,
    Pillowed upon my fair love's ripening breast,   10
To feel for ever its soft fall and swell,
    Awake for ever in a sweet unrest,
Still, still to hear her tender-taken breath,
And so live ever — or else swoon to death.

gloam: Twilight.
Eremite: Hermit, religious recluse.
ablution: Washing, cleansing.

JOHN KEATS (1795–1821)

Ode on a Grecian Urn (1819)

1

Thou still unravish'd bride of quietness,
    Thou foster-child of silence and slow time,
Sylvan° historian, who canst thus express
A flowery tale more sweetly than our rhyme:
What leaf-fring'd legend haunts about thy shape   5
    Of deities or mortals, or of both,
        In Tempe° or the dales of Arcady?°
    What men or gods are these? What maidens loth?
What mad pursuit? What struggle to escape?
        What pipes and timbrels? What wild ecstasy?   10

2

Heard melodies are sweet, but those unheard
    Are sweeter; therefore, ye soft pipes, play on;
Not to the sensual ear, but, more endear'd,
    Pipe to the spirit ditties of no tone:
Fair youth, beneath the trees, thou canst not leave   15
    Thy song, nor ever can those trees be bare;
        Bold lover, never, never canst thou kiss,
Though winning near the goal — yet, do not grieve;
        She cannot fade, though thou hast not thy bliss,
    For ever wilt thou love, and she be fair!   20

3

Ah, happy, happy boughs! that cannot shed
    Your leaves, nor ever bid the spring adieu;
And, happy melodist, unwearied,
    For ever piping songs for ever new;
More happy love! more happy, happy love!   25
    For ever warm and still to be enjoy'd,
        For ever panting, and for ever young;
All breathing human passion far above,
    That leaves a heart high-sorrowful and cloy'd,
        A burning forehead, and a parching tongue.   30

Sylvan: Pertaining to woods or forests.

Tempe: A beautiful valley in Greece.

Arcady: The valleys of Arcadia, a mountainous region on the Greek peninsula. Like Tempe, they represent a rustic pastoral ideal.

4

Who are these coming to the sacrifice?
　　To what green altar, O mysterious priest,
Lead'st thou that heifer lowing at the skies,
　　And all her silken flanks with garlands drest?
What little town by river or sea shore,　　　　　　　　35
　　Or mountain-built with peaceful citadel,
　　　　Is emptied of this folk, this pious morn?
And, little town, thy streets for evermore
　　Will silent be; and not a soul to tell
　　　　Why thou art desolate, can e'er return.　　　40

5

O Attic° shape! Fair attitude! with brede°
　　Of marble men and maidens overwrought,°
With forest branches and the trodden weed;
　　Thou, silent form, dost tease us out of thought
As doth eternity: Cold Pastoral!　　　　　　　　　45
　　When old age shall this generation waste,
　　　　Thou shalt remain, in midst of other woe
Than ours, a friend to man, to whom thou say'st,
　　"Beauty is truth, truth beauty," — that is all
　　　　Ye know on earth, and all ye need to know.　　50

JOHN KEATS (1795–1821)

When I Have Fears (1818)

When I have fears that I may cease to be
　　Before my pen has gleaned my teeming brain,
Before high-piléd books, in charact'ry,°
　　Hold like rich garners the full-ripened grain;
When I behold, upon the night's starred face,　　　5
　　Huge cloudy symbols of a high romance,
And think that I may never live to trace
　　Their shadows, with the magic hand of chance;
And when I feel, fair creature of an hour,
　　That I shall never look upon thee more,　　　10

Attic: Characteristic of Athens or Athenians.

brede: Braid.

overwrought: Elaborately ornamented.

charact'ry: Print.

Never have relish in the faery power
 Of unreflecting love! — then on the shore
Of the wide world I stand alone, and think
Till Love and Fame to nothingness do sink.

ARON KEESBURY (1971–)

On the Robbery across the Street (1998)

(An eyewitness to the Brinks heist)°

I tell them, look. Sure, I was around.
The tenant from four
come down to the store
that night to see can he get a cat.

Tony or Jimmy, his name is.   5
Henry maybe. Mike? Joe?
Maybe Jimmy. Look, I don't know
but he's a nice boy anyway. Wears specs,

you know. He come down
asks me, says can I get a cat   10
upstairs? I says sure. Keep that
sandy crap out of the drains, though —

clogs them all up, you know.
Then I got to get all new pipes.
So he runs upstairs. He's all hyped   15
up like I ain't seen the cat he's got

already. Maybe two,
three weeks he's got a cat up there.
These kids. Jazzing all around, I swear,
think they can get away with murder. 20

But he's a nice boy and I tell the cops,
I say, look. I been in this store here
for thirty-seven years.
Thirty-seven years in this store.

I tell them sure. I say, look.   25
I was here, I was around
that night. I been in this town
thirty-seven years.
And I don't see nothing.

Brinks heist: A 1950 robbery of a Brink's armored car station in Boston, MA, and the subject of the 1978 movie *The Brinks Job.*

JANE KENYON (1947–1995)

A Boy Goes into the World (1990)

My brother rode off on his bike
into the summer afternoon, but
Mother called me back
from the end of the sandy drive:
"It's different for girls."   5

He'd be gone for hours, come back
with things: a cocoon, gray-brown
and papery around a stick;
a puff ball, ripe, wrinkled,
and exuding spores; owl pellets—   10
bits of undigested bone and fur;
and pieces of moss that might
have made toupees for preposterous
green men, but went instead
into a wide-necked jar for a terrarium.   15

He mounted his plunder on poster
board, gluing and naming
each piece. He has long since
forgotten those days and things, but
I at last can claim them as my own.   20

LI-YOUNG LEE (1957–   )

The Gift (1986)

To pull the metal splinter from my palm
my father recited a story in a low voice.
I watched his lovely face and not the blade.
Before the story ended, he'd removed
the iron silver I thought I'd die from.   5

I can't remember the tale,
but hear his voice still, a well
of dark water, a prayer.
And I recall his hands,
two measures of tenderness   10
he laid against my face,
the flames of discipline
he raised above my head.

Had you entered that afternoon
you would have thought you saw a man   15
planting something in a boy's palm,
a silver tear, a tiny flame.
Had you followed that boy
you would have arrived here,
where I bend over my wife's right hand.   20

Look how I shave her thumbnail down
so carefully she feels no pain.
Watch as I lift the splinter out.
I was seven when my father
took my hand like this,   25

and I did not hold that shard
between my fingers and think,
Metal that will bury me,
christen it Little Assassin,
Ore Going Deep for My Heart.   30
And I did not lift up my wound and cry,
Death visited here!
I did what a child does
when he's given something to keep.
I kissed my father.   35

PHILIP LEVINE (1928–   )

Llanto (1994)

For Ernesto Trejo

Plum, almond, cherry have come and gone,
the wisteria has vanished in
the dawn, the blackened roses rusting
along the barbed-wire fence explain

how April passed so quickly into   5
this hard wind that waited in the west.
Ahead is summer and the full sun
riding at ease above the stunned town

no longer yours. Brother, you are gone,
that which was earth gone back to earth,   10
that which was human scattered like rain
into the darkened wild eyes of herbs

that see it all, into the valley oak
that will not sing, that will not even talk.

CLAUDE McKAY (1890 – 1948)

If We Must Die (1922)

If we must die, let it not be like hogs
Hunted and penned in an inglorious spot,
While round us bark the mad and hungry dogs,
Making their mock at our accursed lot.
If we must die, O let us nobly die,   5
So that our precious blood may not be shed
In vain; then even the monsters we defy
Shall be constrained to honor us though dead!
O kinsmen! we must meet the common foe!
Though far outnumbered let us show us brave,   10
And for their thousand blows deal one deathblow!
What though before us lies the open grave?
Like men we'll face the murderous, cowardly pack,
Pressed to the wall, dying, but fighting back!

W.S. MERWIN (1927–   )

For the Anniversary of My Death (1967)

Every year without knowing it I have passed the day
When the last fires will wave to me
And the silence will set out
Tireless traveller
Like the beam of a lightless star   5

Then I will no longer
Find myself in life as in a strange garment
Surprised at the earth
And the love of one woman
And the shamelessness of men   10
As today writing after three days of rain
Hearing the wren sing and the falling cease
And bowing not knowing to what

JOHN MILTON (1608 – 1674)

When I consider how my light is spent° (1655?)

When I consider how my light is spent,
    Ere half my days in this dark world and wide,
    And that one talent° which is death to hide

---

how my light is spent: A meditation on his blindness.
one talent: See Jesus' parable of the talents in Matthew 25.14–30.

Lodged with me useless, though my soul more bent
To serve therewith my Maker, and present   5
    My true account, lest He returning chide;
    "Doth God exact day-labor, light denied?"
I fondly° ask. But Patience, to prevent
That murmur, soon replies, "God doth not need
    Either man's work or His own gifts. Who best   10
    Bear His mild yoke, they serve Him best. His state
Is kingly: thousands at His bidding speed,
And post o'er land and ocean without rest;
They also serve who only stand and wait."

PABLO NERUDA (1904–1973)

The United Fruit Co.° (1950)

Translated by Robert Bly

When the trumpet sounded, it was
all prepared on the earth,
and Jehovah parceled out the earth
to Coca-Cola, Inc., Anaconda,
Ford Motors, and other entities: 5
The Fruit Company, Inc.
reserved for itself the most succulent,
the central coast of my own land,
the delicate waist of America.
It rechristened its territories   10
as the "Banana Republics"
and over the sleeping dead,
over the restless heroes
who brought about the greatness,
the liberty and the flags,   15
it established the comic opera:
abolished the independencies,
presented crowns of Caesar,
unsheathed envy, attracted
the dictatorship of the flies,   20
Trujillo flies, Tacho flies,
Carias flies, Martinez flies,
Ubico flies,° damp flies

---

fondly: Foolishly.

United Fruit Co.: Incorporated in New Jersey in 1899 by Andrew Preston and Minor C. Keith, United Fruit became a major force in growing, transporting, and merchandising Latin American produce, especially bananas. The company is notorious for its involvement in politics and is a symbol for many people of "Yankee" imperialism and oppression.

Trujillo, Tacho, Carias, Martinez, Ubico: Political dictators.

of modest blood and marmalade,
drunken flies who zoom   25
over the ordinary graves,
circus flies, wise flies
well trained in tyranny.
Among the bloodthirsty flies
the Fruit Company lands its ships,   30
taking off the coffee and the fruit;
the treasure of our submerged
territories flows as though
on plates into the ships.

Meanwhile Indians are falling   35
into the sugared chasms
of the harbors, wrapped
for burial in the mist of the dawn:
a body rolls, a thing
that has no name, a fallen cipher,   40
a cluster of dead fruit
thrown down on the dump.

SHARON OLDS (1942–   )

The One Girl at the Boys' Party (1983)

When I take my girl to the swimming party
I set her down among the boys. They tower and
bristle, she stands there smooth and sleek,
her math scores unfolding in the air around her.
They will strip to their suits, her body hard and   5
indivisible as a prime number,
they'll plunge in the deep end, she'll subtract
her height from ten feet, divide it into
hundreds of gallons of water, the numbers
bouncing in her mind like molecules of chlorine   10
in the bright blue pool. When they climb out,
her ponytail will hang its pencil lead
down her back, her narrow silk suit
with hamburgers and french fries printed on it
will glisten in the brilliant air, and they will   15
see her sweet face, solemn and
sealed, a factor of one, and she will
see their eyes, two each,
their legs, two each, and the curves of their sexes,
one each, and in her head she'll be doing her   20
wild multiplying, as the drops
sparkle and fall to the power of a thousand from her body.

FRANK O'HARA (1926–1966)

Autobiographia Literaria (1971)

When I was a child
I played by myself in a
corner of the schoolyard
all alone.

I hated dolls and I   5
hated games, animals were
not friendly and birds
flew away.

If anyone was looking
for me I hid behind a   10
tree and cried out "I am
an orphan."

And here I am, the
center of all beauty!
writing these poems!   15
Imagine!

JUDITH ORTIZ COFER (1952–   )

Claims (1990)

Last time I saw her, Grandmother
had grown seamed as a bedouin tent.
She had claimed the right
to sleep alone, to own
her nights, to never bear   5
the weight of sex again, nor to accept
its gift of comfort, for the luxury
of stretching her bones.
She's carried eight children,
three had sunk in her belly, *náufragos*,   10
she called them, shipwrecked babies
drowned in her black waters.
Children are made in the night and
steal your days
for the rest of your life, amen. She said this   15
to each of her daughters in turn. Once she had made a pact
with man and nature and kept it. Now like the sea,
she is claiming back her territory.

LINDA PASTAN (1932–   )

Ethics (1980)

In ethics class so many years ago
our teacher asked this question every fall:
if there were a fire in a museum
which would you save, a Rembrandt painting
or an old woman who hadn't many   5
years left anyhow? Restless on hard chairs
caring little for pictures or old age
we'd opt one year for life, the next for art
and always half-heartedly. Sometimes
the woman borrowed my grandmother's face   10
leaving her usual kitchen to wander
some drafty, half imagined museum.
One year, feeling clever, I replied
why not let the woman decide herself?
Linda, the teacher would report, eschews   15
the burdens of responsibility.
This fall in a real museum I stand
before a real Rembrandt, old woman,
or nearly so, myself. The colors
within this frame are darker than autumn,   20
darker even than winter — the browns of earth,
though earth's most radiant elements burn
through the canvas. I know now that woman
and painting and season are almost one
and all beyond saving by children.   25

LUCIA MARIA PERILLO (1958–   )

Scott Wonders If His Daughter Will Understand Tragedy If He Kills Rock and Roll (1992)

"Indignation is the soul's defense against the wound of doubt" — Allan Bloom

Two bottles of wine to reach this conclusion:
now that he's sixty, one thing he regrets
is never buying an M16 while they were legal
and going into the record department at Woolworth's
or K-Mart or maybe even a whole store devoted to   5
those insidious rhythms. He imagines firing
a couple of rounds into the stacked LPs,
sending black shards everywhere. "My daughter,"
he says, "I can't count the nights I heard her

screeching along with those idiot refrains   10
... *Inna Gadda Da Vida* ... *Inna-Gadda-Da-Vida baby* ...
It was like an exorcism going on up there."
That's why her life is a shambles, he explains,
her never passing so much as English 101—
at community college, for God's sake. He teaches   15
at the university, for thirty years a course on Tragedy.
He's read *Oedipus Rex* every semester all these years
and at the end of each he's still breaking down in tears,
unable to define the nature of human suffering.
And the students, bobbing their heads in sympathy   20
... they're complete strangers, while his own daughter
is off somewhere drawing her astrological chart,
her Scorpio always rising. And tonight he realizes
that if he'd had the courage, he might have saved her.
Verdi, Bizet ... they'd probably fall by the wayside too,   25
his submachine gun unable to spare his beloved operas.
And suddenly that makes him sad, to think
of the gypsy Carmen lying dead in the shop aisles,
the final chorus of "Love is a rebellious bird ..."
welling up like blood while Don José cries: 30
Arrest me ... I killed her ... Carmen! My adored Carmen!

MARGE PIERCY (1934–   )

Barbie Doll (1973)

This girlchild was born as usual
and presented dolls that did pee-pee
and miniature GE stoves and irons
and wee lipsticks the color of cherry candy.
Then in the magic of puberty, a classmate said: 5
You have a great big nose and fat legs.

She was healthy, tested intelligent,
possessed strong arms and back,
abundant sexual drive and manual dexterity.
She went to and fro apologizing.   10
Everyone saw a fat nose on thick legs.

She was advised to play coy,
exhorted to come on hearty,
exercise, diet, smile and wheedle.
Her good nature wore out   15
like a fan belt.
So she cut off her nose and her legs
and offered them up.

In the casket displayed on satin she lay
with the undertaker's cosmetics painted on,   20
a turned-up putty nose,
dressed in a pink and white nightie.
Doesn't she look pretty? everyone said.
Consummation at last.
To every woman a happy ending.   25

ROBERT PINSKY (1940–   )

If You Could Write One Great Poem, What Would You Want It to Be About? (1996)

(Asked of four student poets at the Illinois Schools for the Deaf and Visually Impaired)

Fire: because it is quick, and can destroy.
Music: place where anger has its place.
Romantic Love — the cold or stupid ask why.
Sign: that it is a language, full of grace,

That it is visible, invisible, dark and clear,   5
That it is loud and noiseless and is contained
Inside a body and explodes in air
Out of a body to conquer from the mind.

SYLVIA PLATH (1932–1963)

Metaphors (1960)

I'm a riddle in nine syllables,
An elephant, a ponderous house,
A melon strolling on two tendrils.
O red fruit, ivory, fine timbers!
This loaf's big with its yeasty rising.   5
Money's new-minted in this fat purse.
I'm a means, a stage, a cow in calf.
I've eaten a bag of green apples,
Boarded the train there's no getting off.

SYLVIA PLATH (1932–1963)

Mirror (1963)

I am silver and exact. I have no preconceptions.
Whatever I see I swallow immediately
Just as it is, unmisted by love or dislike.

I am not cruel, only truthful—
The eye of a little god, four-cornered.   5
Most of the time I meditate on the opposite wall.
It is pink, with speckles. I have looked at it so long
I think it is a part of my heart. But it flickers.
Faces and darkness separate us over and over.

Now I am a lake. A woman bends over me,   10
Searching my reaches for what she really is.
Then she turns to those liars, the candles or the moon.
I see her back, and reflect it faithfully.
She rewards me with tears and an agitation of hands.
I am important to her. She comes and goes.   15
Each morning it is her face that replaces the darkness.
In me she has drowned a young girl, and in me an old woman
Rises toward her day after day, like a terrible fish.

EZRA POUND (1885–1972)

The River-Merchant's Wife: A Letter° (1916)

While my hair was still cut straight across my forehead
I played about the front gate, pulling flowers.
You came by on bamboo stilts, playing horse,
You walked about my seat, playing with blue plums.
And we went on living in the village of Chokan:°   5
Two small people, without dislike or suspicion.

At fourteen I married My Lord you.
I never laughed, being bashful.
Lowering my head, I looked at the wall.
Called to, a thousand times, I never looked back.   10

At fifteen I stopped scowling,
I desired my dust to be mingled with yours
Forever and forever and forever.
Why should I climb the lookout?

At sixteen you departed,   15
You went into far Ku-to-yen,° by the river of swirling eddies,
And you have been gone five months.
The monkeys make sorrowful noise overhead.

"The River-Merchant's Wife: A Letter": This is one of the many translations Pound made of Chinese poems. The poem is a free translation of Li Po's (701–762) "Two Letters from Chang-Kan."
Chokan: Chang-Kan.
Ku-to-yen: An island in the river Ch'ū-t'ang.

You dragged your feet when you went out.
By the gate now, the moss is grown, the different mosses,   20
Too deep to clear them away!
The leaves fall early this autumn, in wind.
The paired butterflies are already yellow with August
Over the grass in the West garden;
They hurt me. I grow older.   25
If you are coming down through the narrows of the river Kiang,°
Please let me know beforehand,
And I will come out to meet you
    As far as Cho-fu-sa.°

HENRY REED (1914–1986)

Naming of Parts (1946)

Today we have naming of parts. Yesterday,
We had daily cleaning. And tomorrow morning,
We shall have what to do after firing. But today,
Today we have naming of parts. Japonica°
Glistens like coral in all of the neighboring gardens,   5
    And today we have naming of parts.

This is the lower sling swivel. And this
Is the upper sling swivel, whose use you will see,
When you are given your slings. And this is the piling swivel,
Which in your case you have not got. The branches   10
Hold in the gardens their silent, eloquent gestures,
    Which in our case we have not got.

This is the safety-catch, which is always released
With an easy flick of the thumb. And please do not let me
See anyone using his finger. You can do it quite easy   15
If you have any strength in your thumb. The blossoms
Are fragile and motionless, never letting anyone see
    Any of them using their finger.

And this you can see is the bolt. The purpose of this
Is to open the breech, as you see. We can slide it   20
Rapidly backwards and forwards: we call this

Kiang: The Japanese name for the river Ch'ū-t'ang. Pound's translations are based on commentaries derived from Japanese scholars; therefore, he usually uses Japanese instead of Chinese names.

Cho-fu-sa: A beach several hundred miles upstream of Nanking.

Japonica: A shrub having waxy flowers in a variety of colors.

Easing the spring. And rapidly backwards and forwards
The early bees are assaulting and fumbling the flowers:
     They call it easing the Spring.

They call it easing the Spring: it is perfectly easy   25
If you have any strength in your thumb: like the bolt,
And the breech, and the cocking-piece, and the point of balance,
Which in our case we have not got; and the almond-blossom
Silent in all of the gardens and the bees going backwards and
          forwards,
     For today we have the naming of parts.   30

EDWIN ARLINGTON ROBINSON (1869–1935)

Miniver Cheevy (1910)

Miniver Cheevy, child of scorn,
     Grew lean while he assailed the seasons;
He wept that he was ever born,
     And he had reasons.

Miniver loved the days of old   5
     When swords were bright and steeds were prancing;
The vision of a warrior bold
     Would set him dancing.

Miniver sighed for what was not,
     And dreamed, and rested from his labors;   10
He dreamed of Thebes° and Camelot,°
And Priam's neighbors.°

Miniver mourned the ripe renown
     That made so many a name so fragrant;
He mourned Romance, now on the town,   15
     And Art, a vagrant.

Miniver loved the Medici,°
     Albeit he had never seen one;
He would have sinned incessantly
     Could he have been one.   20

Thebes: The setting of many Greek legends, including that of Oedipus.

Camelot: The legendary site of King Arthur's court.

Priam's neighbors: Priam was the last king of Troy; his "neighbors" included Helen, Aeneas, and Hector.

Medici: Rulers of Florence, Italy, from the fifteenth through the eighteenth centuries. During the Renaissance, Lorenzo de Medici was a renowned patron of the arts.

Miniver cursed the commonplace
    And eyed a khaki suit with loathing;
He missed the medieval grace
    Of iron clothing.

Miniver scorned the gold he sought,   25
    But sore annoyed was he without it;
Miniver thought, and thought, and thought,
    And thought about it.

Miniver Cheevy, born too late,
    Scratched his head and kept on thinking;   30
Miniver coughed, and called it fate,
And kept on drinking.

EDWARD ARLINGTON ROBINSON (1869–1935)

Richard Cory (1897)

Whenever Richard Cory went down town,
We people on the pavement looked at him:
He was a gentleman from sole to crown,
Clean favored, and imperially slim.

And he was always quietly arrayed,   5
And he was always human when he talked;
But still he fluttered pulses when he said,
"Good-morning," and he glittered when he walked.

And he was rich — yes, richer than a king —
And admirably schooled in every grace: 10
In fine, we thought that he was everything
To make us wish that we were in his place.

So on we worked, and waited for the light,
And went without the meat, and cursed the bread;
And Richard Cory, one calm summer night,   15
Went home and put a bullet through his head.

CARL SANDBURG (1878–1967)

Fog (1916)

The fog comes
on little cat feet.
It sits looking
over harbor and city
on silent haunches   5
and then moves on.

SONIA SANCHEZ (1934–)

right on: white america (1970)

this country might have
been a pio
   neer land
once.
    but.   there ain't   5
no mo
    indians   blowing
custer's° mind
        with a different
image of america.   10
           this country
might have
       needed shoot/
outs/ daily/
     once.   15
      but. there ain't
no mo real/ white/ allamerican
          bad/guys.
just.
  u & me.   20
     blk/ and un/armed.
this country might have
been a pion
     eer land.   once.
            and it still is.   25
check out
    the falling
gun/shells   on our blk/tomorrows.

WILLIAM SHAKESPEARE (1564–1616)

Let me not to the marriage of true minds (1609)

Let me not to the marriage of true minds
Admit impediments.° Love is not love

---

custer: General George Armstrong Custer (1839–1876) was killed by Sioux in his "last stand" at the Little Bighorn in Montana.

Admit impediments: A reference to "The Order of Solemnization of Matrimony" in the Anglican Book of Common Prayer: "I require that if either of you know any impediments why ye may not be lawfully joined together in Matrimony, ye do now confess it."

Which alters when it alteration finds,
Or bends with the remover to remove:
Oh, no! it is an ever-fixéd mark,   5
That looks on tempests and is never shaken;
It is the star to every wandering bark,
Whose worth's unknown, although his height be taken.°
Love's not Time's fool,° though rosy lips and cheeks
Within his bending sickle's compass come;
Love alters not with his brief hours and weeks,   10
But bears it out even to the edge of doom.°
    If this be error and upon me proved,
    I never writ, nor no man ever loved.

WILLIAM SHAKESPEARE (1564–1616)

Not marble, nor the gilded monuments (1609)

Not marble, nor the gilded monuments
Of princes, shall outlive this powerful rhyme;
But you shall shine more bright in these contents
Than unswept stone, besmeared with sluttish time.
When wasteful war shall statues overturn,   5
And broils root out the work of masonry,
Nor Mars° his sword nor war's quick fire shall burn
The living record of your memory.
'Gainst death and all-oblivious enmity
Shall you pace forth; your praise shall still find room   10
Even in the eyes of all posterity
That wear this world out to the ending doom.
    So, till the judgment that yourself arise,
    You live in this, and dwell in lovers' eyes.

PERCY BYSSHE SHELLEY (1792–1822)

Ode to the West Wind (1820)

I

O wild West Wind, thou breath of Autumn's being,
Thou, from whose unseen presence the leaves dead
Are driven, like ghosts from an enchanter fleeing,

Whose worth's . . . taken: Although the altitude of a star may be measured, its worth is unknowable.

Love's not Time's fool: Love is not mocked by Time.

doom: Doomsday.

Mars: The Roman god of war.

Yellow, and black, and pale, and hectic red,°
Pestilence-stricken multitudes: O Thou,   5
Who chariotest to their dark wintry bed

The winged seeds, where they lie cold and low,
Each like a corpse within its grave, until
Thine azure sister of the Spring° shall blow

Her clarion o'er the dreaming earth, and fill   10
(Driving sweet buds like flocks to feed in air)
With living hues and odours plain and hill:

Wild Spirit, which art moving everywhere;
Destroyer and Preserver; hear, O hear!

II

Thou on whose stream, mid the steep sky's commotion,   15
Loose clouds like Earth's decaying leaves are shed,
Shook from the tangled boughs of Heaven and Ocean,

Angels of rain and lightning: there are spread
On the blue surface of thine aery surge,
Like the bright hair uplifted from the head   20

Of some fierce Maenad,° even from the dim verge
Of the horizon to the zenith's height,
The locks of the approaching storm. Thou Dirge

Of the dying year, to which this closing night
Will be the dome of a vast sepulchre,   25
Vaulted with all thy congregated might

Of vapours, from whose solid atmosphere
Black rain and fire and hail will burst: O hear!

III

Thou who didst waken from his summer dreams
The blue Mediterranean, where he lay,   30
Lulled by the coil of his crystalline streams,

Beside a pumice isle in Baiae's bay,°
And saw in sleep old palaces and towers
Quivering within the wave's intenser day,

Yellow . . . hectic red: A reference to a tubercular fever that produces flushed cheeks.

azure . . . Spring: The west wind of the spring.

Maenad: A female votary who danced wildly in ceremonies for Dionysus (or Bacchus), Greek god of wine and vegetation, who according to legend died in the fall and was reborn in the spring.

Baiae's bay: A bay in the Mediterranean Sea, west of Naples. It was known for the opulent villas built by Roman emperors along its shores.

All overgrown with azure moss and flowers   35
So sweet, the sense faints picturing them! Thou
For whose path the Atlantic's level powers

Cleave themselves into chasms, while far below
The sea-blooms and the oozy woods which wear
The sapless foliage of the ocean, know   40

Thy voice, and suddenly grow grey with fear,
And tremble and despoil themselves: O hear!

IV

If I were a dead leaf thou mightest bear;
If I were a swift cloud to fly with thee;
A wave to pant beneath thy power, and share   45

The impulse of thy strength, only less free
Than thou, O Uncontrollable! If even
I were as in my boyhood, and could be

The comrade of thy wanderings over Heaven,
As then, when to outstrip thy skiey speed   50
Scarce seemed a vision; I would ne'er have striven

As thus with thee in prayer in my sore need,
Oh! lift me as a wave, a leaf, a cloud!
I fall upon the thorns of life! I bleed!

A heavy weight of hours has chained and bowed   55
One too like thee: tameless, and swift, and proud.

V

Make me thy lyre,° even as the forest is:
What if my leaves are falling like its own!
The tumult of thy mighty harmonies

Will take from both a deep, autumnal tone,   60
Sweet though in sadness. Be thou, Spirit fierce,
My spirit! Be thou me, impetuous one!

Drive my dead thoughts over the universe
Like withered leaves to quicken a new birth!
And, by the incantation of this verse,   65

Scatter, as from an unextinguished hearth
Ashes and sparks, my words among mankind!
Be through my lips to unawakened Earth

---

lyre: An Aeolian harp, a stringed instrument that produces musical sounds when exposed to the wind.

The trumpet of a prophecy! O Wind,
If Winter comes, can Spring be far behind?   70

LOUIS SIMPSON (1923–   )

A Shearling Coat (1999)

Alexander Ortiz and Arlyne Gonzales
were walking home from a movie.

A car drew up, and two men
got out. One had a gun, the other

tugged at her shearling coat.   5
"Don't hurt her," Ortiz said, "she's pregnant."

The gunman shot him twice,
in the chest and throat.

"What you do that for?" said the other.
"C' mon, c'mon, get the jacket,"   10

the gunman said, and they left,
with a shot at Gonzales.

She had thrown herself down
on top of the dying man.

And I shall be wanting to be rid   15
of this thing till the end of my days.

STEVIE SMITH (1902–1971)

Not Waving but Drowning (1957)

Nobody heard him, the dead man,
But still he lay moaning:
I was much further out than you thought
And not waving but drowning.

Poor chap, he always loved larking   5
And now he's dead
It must have been too cold for him his heart gave way,
They said.

Oh, no no no, it was too cold always
(Still the dead one lay moaning)   10
I was much too far out all my life
And not waving but drowning.

CATHY SONG (1955–   )

Lost Sister (1983)

1

In China,
even the peasants
named their first daughters
Jade—
the stone that in the far fields   5
could moisten the dry season,
could make men move mountains
for the healing green of the inner hills
glistening like slices of winter melon.

And the daughters were grateful: 10
they never left home.
To move freely was a luxury
stolen from them at birth.
Instead, they gathered patience,
learning to walk in shoes   15
the size of teacups,°
without breaking—
the arc of their movements
as dormant as the rooted willow,
as redundant as the farmyard hens.   20
But they traveled far
in surviving,
learning to stretch the family rice,
to quiet the demons,
the noisy stomachs.   25

2

There is a sister
across the ocean,
who relinquished her name,
diluting jade green
with the blue of the Pacific.   30
Rising with a tide of locusts,
she swarmed with others
to inundate another shore.
In America,

---

shoes . . . teacups: A reference to the practice of binding young girls' feet so that they remain small. This practice, which crippled women, was common in China until the communist revolution.

there are many roads   35
and women can stride along with men.

But in another wilderness,
the possibilities,
the loneliness,
can strangulate like jungle vines.   40
The meager provisions and sentiments
of once belonging—
fermented roots, Mah-Jongg° tiles and firecrackers—
set but a flimsy household
in a forest of nightless cities.   45
A giant snake rattles above,
spewing black clouds into your kitchen.
Dough-faced landlords
slip in and out of your keyholes,
making claims you don't understand,   50
tapping into your communication systems
of laundry lines and restaurant chains.

You find you need China:
your one fragile identification,
a jade link   55
handcuffed to your wrist.
You remember your mother
who walked for centuries,
footless—
and like her,   60
you have left no footprints,
but only because
there is an ocean in between,
the unremitting space of your rebellion.

GARY SOTO (1952–   )

Black Hair (1985)

At eight I was brilliant with my body.
In July, that ring of heat
We all jumped through, I sat in the bleachers
Of Romain Playground, in the lengthening
Shade that rose from our dirty feet.   5
The game before us was more than baseball.

Mah-Jongg: Or mahjong, an ancient Chinese game played with dice and tiles.

It was a figure — Hector Moreno
Quick and hard with turned muscles,
His crouch the one I assumed before an altar
Of worn baseball cards, in my room.   10
I came here because I was Mexican, a stick
Of brown light in love with those
Who could do It — the triple and hard slide,
The gloves eating balls into double plays.
What could I do with 50 pounds, my shyness,   15
My black torch of hair, about to go out?
Father was dead, his face no longer
Hanging over the table or our sleep,
And mother was the terror of mouths
Twisting hurt by butter knives.   20

In the bleachers I was brilliant with my body,
Waving players in and stomping my feet,
Growing sweaty in the presence of white shirts.
I chewed sunflower seeds. I drank water
And bit my arm through the late innings.   25
When Hector lined balls into deep
Center, in my mind I rounded the bases
With him, my face flared, my hair lifting
Beautifully, because we were coming home
To the arms of brown people.   30

WOLE SOYINKA (1934 –   )

Hamlet (1972)

He stilled his doubts, they rose to halt and lame
A resolution on the rack. Passion's flame
Was doused in fear of error, his mind's unease
Bred indulgence to the state's disease
Ghosts embowelled his earth; he clung to rails   5
In a gallery of abstractions, dissecting tales
As "told by an idiot." Passionless he set a stage
Of passion for the guilt he would engage.

Justice despaired. The turn and turn abouts
Of reason danced default to duty's counterpoint   10
Till treachery scratched the slate of primal clay
Then Metaphysics waived a thought's delay —
It took the salt in the wound, the "point
Envenom'd too" to steel the prince of doubts.

WILLIAM STAFFORD (1914–1993)

Traveling through the Dark (1962)

Traveling through the dark I found a deer
dead on the edge of the Wilson River road.
It is usually best to roll them into the canyon:
that road is narrow; to swerve might make more dead.

By glow of the tail-light I stumbled back of the car   5
and stood by the heap, a doe, a recent killing;
she had stiffened already, almost cold.
I dragged her off; she was large in the belly.

My fingers touching her side brought me the reason—
her side was warm; her fawn lay there waiting,   10
alive, still, never to be born.
Beside that mountain road I hesitated.

The car aimed ahead its lowered parking lights;
under the hood purred the steady engine.
I stood in the glare of the warm exhaust turning red;   15
around our group I could hear the wilderness listen.

I thought hard for us all — my only swerving —
then pushed her over the edge into the river.

WALLACE STEVENS (1879–1955)

The Emperor of Ice-Cream (1923)

Call the roller of big cigars,
The muscular one, and bid him whip
In kitchen cups concupiscent curds.
Let the wenches dawdle in such dress
As they are used to wear, and let the boys   5
Bring flowers in last month's newspapers.
Let be be finale of seem.
The only emperor is the emperor of ice-cream.

Take from the dresser of deal,°
Lacking the three glass knobs, that sheet   10
On which she embroidered fantails° once
And spread it so as to cover her face.

---

deal: Fir or pine wood.

fantails: According to Stevens, "the word fantails does not mean fans, but fantail pigeons."

If her horny feet protrude, they come
To show how cold she is, and dumb.
Let the lamp affix its beam.   15
The only emperor is the emperor of ice-cream.

MARK STRAND (1934–   )

Old Man Leaves Party (1998)

It was clear when I left the party
That though I was over eighty I still had
A beautiful body. The moon shone down as it will
On moments of deep introspection. The wind held its breath.
And look, somebody left a mirror leaning against a tree.   5
Making sure that I was alone, I took off my shirt.
The flowers of bear grass nodded their moonwashed heads.
I took off my pants and the magpies circled the redwoods.
Down in the valley the creaking river was flowing once more.
How strange that I should stand in the wilds alone with my body.   10
I know what you are thinking. I was like you once. But now
With so much before me, so many emerald trees, and
Weed-whitened fields, mountains and lakes, how could I not
Be only myself, this dream of flesh, from moment to moment?

ALFRED, LORD TENNYSON (1809–1892)

Ulysses° (1833)

It little profits that an idle king,
By this still hearth, among these barren crags,
Matched with an agèd wife, I mete and dole
Unequal laws unto a savage race
That hoard, and sleep, and feed, and know not me.   5
I cannot rest from travel; I will drink
Life to the lees. All times I have enjoyed
Greatly, have suffered greatly, both with those
That loved me, and alone; on shore, and when
Through scudding drifts the rainy Hyades°   10

Ulysses: A legendary Greek king of Ithaca and hero of Homer's *Odyssey,* Ulysses (or Odysseus) is noted for his daring and cunning. After his many adventures — including encounters with the Cyclops, the cannibalistic Laestrygones, and the enchantress Circe — Ulysses returned home to his faithful wife, Penelope. Tennyson portrays an older Ulysses pondering his situation.

Hyades: A group of stars whose rising was supposedly followed by rain and thus stormy seas.

Vexed the dim sea. I am become a name;
For always roaming with a hungry heart
Much have I seen and known — cities of men
And manners, climates, councils, governments,
Myself not least, but honored of them all —   15
And drunk delight of battle with my peers,
Far on the ringing plains of windy Troy.°
I am a part of all that I have met;
Yet all experience is an arch wherethrough
Gleams that untraveled world whose margin fades   20
Forever and forever when I move.
How dull it is to pause, to make an end,
To rust unburnished, not to shine in use!
As though to breathe were life! Life piled on life
Were all too little, and of one to me   25
Little remains; but every hour is saved
From that eternal silence, something more,
A bringer of new things; and vile it were
For some three suns to store and hoard myself,
And this grey spirit yearning in desire   30
To follow knowledge like a sinking star,
Beyond the utmost bound of human thought.
    This is my son, mine own Telemachus,
To whom I leave the scepter and the isle —
Well-loved of me, discerning to fulfill   35
This labor, by slow prudence to make mild
A rugged people, and through soft degrees
Subdue them to the useful and the good.
Most blameless is he, centered in the sphere
Of common duties, decent not to fail   40
In offices of tenderness, and pay
Meet adoration to my household gods,
When I am gone. He works his work, I mine.
    There lies the port; the vessel puffs her sail;
There gloom the dark, broad seas. My mariners,   45
Souls that have toiled, and wrought, and thought with me —
That ever with a frolic welcome took
The thunder and the sunshine, and opposed
Free hearts, free foreheads — you and I are old;
Old age hath yet his honor and his toil.   50
Death closes all; but something ere the end,
Some work of noble note, may yet be done,

Troy: An ancient city in Asia Minor. According to legend, Paris, king of Troy, abducted Helen, the beautiful wife of
Menelaus, king of Sparta, initiating the Trojan War, in which numerous Greek heroes, including Ulysses, fought.

Not unbecoming men that strove with Gods.
The lights begin to twinkle from the rocks;
The long day wanes; the low moon climbs; the deep   55
Moans round with many voices. Come, my friends,
'Tis not too late to seek a newer world.
Push off, and sitting well in order smite
The sounding furrows; for my purpose holds
To sail beyond the sunset, and the baths   60
Of all the western stars, until I die.
It may be that the gulfs will wash us down;
It may be we shall touch the Happy Isles,°
And see the great Achilles,° whom we knew.
Though much is taken, much abides; and though   65
We are not now that strength which in old days
Moved earth and heaven, that which we are, we are—
One equal temper of heroic hearts,
Made weak by time and fate, but strong in will
To strive, to seek, to find, and not to yield.   70

EDMUND WALLER (1606–1687)

Go, lovely rose (1645)

Go, lovely rose,
Tell her that wastes her time and me
　　That now she knows,
When I resemble her to thee,
How sweet and fair she seems to be.   5

　　Tell her that's young
And shuns to have her graces spied,
　　That hadst thou sprung
In deserts where no men abide,
Thou must have uncommended died.   10

　　Small is the worth
Of beauty from the light retired:
　　Bid her come forth,
Suffer herself to be desired,
And not blush so to be admired.   15

Happy Isles: Elysium, or Paradise, believed to be in the far western ocean.
Achilles: Greek hero of the Trojan War.

      Then die, that she
    The common fate of all things rare
        May read in thee,
    How small a part of time they share
    That are so wondrous sweet and fair.   20

On Being Brought from Africa to America (1773)

'Twas mercy brought me from my *Pagan* land,
Taught my benighted soul to understand
That there's a God, that there's a *Saviour* too:
Once I redemption neither sought nor knew.
Some view our sable race with scornful eye,   5
"Their colour is a diabolic die."
Remember, *Christians*, *Negroes*, black as *Cain*,
May be refin'd, and join th' angelic train.

A Noiseless Patient Spider (1881)

A noiseless patient spider,
I mark'd where on a little promontory it stood isolated,
Mark'd how to explore the vacant vast surrounding,
It launch'd forth filament, filament, filament, out of itself,
Ever unreeling them, ever tirelessly speeding them.   5

And you O my soul where you stand,
Surrounded, detached, in measureless oceans of space,
Ceaselessly musing, venturing, throwing, seeking the spheres to
    connect them,
Till the bridge you will need be form'd, till the ductile anchor
    hold,
Till the gossamer thread you fling catch somewhere, O my soul.   10

from Song of Myself (1855)

1

I celebrate myself, and sing myself,
And what I assume you shall assume,
For every atom belonging to me as good belongs to you.

I loafe and invite my soul,
I lean and loafe at my ease observing a spear of summer grass.   5

My tongue, every atom of my blood, form'd from this soil, this air,
Born here of parents born here from parents the same, and their
    parents the same,
I, now thirty-seven years old in perfect health begin,
Hoping to cease not till death.

Creeds and schools in abeyance,   10
Retiring back a while sufficed at what they are, but never forgotten,
I harbor for good or bad, I permit to speak at every hazard,
Nature without check with original energy.

2

Houses and rooms are full of perfumes, the shelves are crowded
    with perfumes,
I breathe the fragrance myself and know it and like it,   15
The distillation would intoxicate me also, but I shall not let it.

The atmosphere is not a perfume, it has no taste of the distillation,
    it is odorless,
It is for my mouth forever, I am in love with it,
I will go to the bank by the wood and become undisguised
    and naked,
I am mad for it to be in contact with me.   20

The smoke of my own breath,
Echoes, ripples, buzz'd whispers, love-root, silk-thread, crotch
    and vine,
My respiration and inspiration, the beating of my heart, the
    passing of blood and air through my lungs,
The sniff of green leaves and dry leaves, and of the shore and
    dark-color'd sea-rocks, and of hay in the barn,
The sound of the belch'd words of my voice loos'd to the eddies
    of the wind,   25
A few light kisses, a few embraces, a reaching around of arms,
The play of shine and shade on the trees as the supple boughs wag,
The delight alone or in the rush of the streets, or along the fields
    and hill-sides,
The feeling of health, the full-noon trill, the song of me rising
    from bed and meeting the sun.

Have you reckon'd a thousand acres much? have you reckon'd the
    earth much?   30
Have you practis'd so long to learn to read?
Have you felt so proud to get at the meaning of poems?

Stop this day and night with me and you shall possess the origin
    of all poems,

You shall possess the good of the earth and sun, (there are millions
  of suns left,)
You shall no longer take things at second or third hand, nor look
  through the eyes of the dead, nor feed on the spectres in books,   35
You shall not look through my eyes either, nor take things
  from me,
You shall listen to all sides and filter them from your self.

WILLIAM CARLOS WILLIAMS (1883–1963)

The Dance (1944)

In Breughel's° great picture, The Kermess,°
the dancers go round, they go round and
around, the squeal and the blare and the
tweedle of bagpipes, a bugle and fiddles
tipping their bellies (round as the thick-   5
sided glasses whose wash they impound)
their hips and their bellies off balance
to turn them. Kicking and rolling about
the Fair Grounds, swinging their butts, those
shanks must be sound to bear up under such   10
rollicking measures, prance as the dance
in Breughel's great picture, The Kermess.

WILLIAM WORDSWORTH (1770–1850)

Composed upon Westminster Bridge, September 3, 1802 (1807)

Earth has not anything to show more fair:
Dull would he be of soul who could pass by
A sight so touching in its majesty:
This City now doth, like a garment, wear
The beauty of the morning; silent, bare,   5
Ships, towers, domes, theatres, and temples lie
Open unto the fields, and to the sky;
All bright and glittering in the smokeless air.
Never did sun more beautifully steep
In his first splendor, valley, rock, or hill;   10

Breughel: Peter Breughel (1525–1569), a Flemish painter (also spelled Brueghel).
The Kermess: The Church Mass, Breughel's painting (1567) of peasants dancing at a church festival.

Ne'er saw I, never felt, a calm so deep!
The river glideth at his own sweet will:
Dear God! the very houses seem asleep;
And all that mighty heart is lying still!

WILLIAM WORDSWORTH (1770–1850)

I wandered lonely as a cloud (1807)

I wandered lonely as a cloud
   That floats on high o'er vales and hills,
When all at once I saw a crowd,
   A host, of golden daffodils,
Beside the lake, beneath the trees,   5
Fluttering and dancing in the breeze.

Continuous as the stars that shine
   And twinkle on the milky way,
They stretched in never-ending line
   Along the margin of a bay: 10
Ten thousand saw I at a glance,
Tossing their heads in sprightly dance.

The waves beside them danced; but they
   Out-did the sparkling waves in glee;
A poet could not but be gay,   15
   In such a jocund company;
I gazed — and gazed — but little thought
What wealth the show to me had brought:

For oft, when on my couch I lie
   In vacant or in pensive mood,   20
They flash upon that inward eye
   Which is the bliss of solitude;
And then my heart with pleasure fills,
And dances with the daffodils.

WILLIAM WORDSWORTH (1770–1850)

My heart leaps up when I behold (1807)

My heart leaps up when I behold
   A rainbow in the sky:
So was it when my life began;
So is it now I am a man;
So be it when I shall grow old,   5
   Or let me die!

The Child is father of the Man;
And I could wish my days to be
Bound each to each by natural piety.

WILLIAM WORDSWORTH (1770–1850)

She dwelt among the untrodden ways (1800)

She dwelt among the untrodden ways
   Beside the springs of Dove,°
A Maid whom there were none to praise
   And very few to love:

A violet by a mossy stone   5
   Half hidden from the eye!
—Fair as a star, when only one
   Is shining in the sky.

She lived unknown, and few could know
   When Lucy ceased to be;   10
But she is in her grave, and, oh,
   The difference to me!

WILLIAM WORDSWORTH (1770–1850)

The Solitary Reaper° (1807)

Behold her, single in the field,
Yon solitary Highland lass!
Reaping and singing by herself;
Stop here, or gently pass!
Alone she cuts and binds the grain,   5
And sings a melancholy strain;
O listen! for the vale profound
Is overflowing with the sound.

No nightingale did ever chaunt
More welcome notes to weary bands   10
Of travelers in some shady haunt
Among Arabian sands.
A voice so thrilling ne'er was heard
In springtime from the cuckoo-bird,

Dove: A river in the Lake District of England.
Reaper: A person who harvests grain.

Breaking the silence of the seas   15
Among the farthest Hebrides.°

Will no one tell me what she sings?—
Perhaps the plaintive numbers flow
For old, unhappy, far-off things,
And battles long ago.   20
Or is it some more humble lay,
Familiar matter of today?
Some natural sorrow, loss, or pain,
That has been, and may be again?

Whate'er the theme, the maiden sang   25
As if her song could have no ending;
I saw her singing at her work,
And o'er the sickle° bending—
I listened, motionless and still;
And, as I mounted up the hill,   30
The music in my heart I bore
Long after it was heard no more.

WILLIAM BUTLER YEATS (1865–1939)

Crazy Jane Talks with the Bishop (1933)

I met the Bishop on the road
And much said he and I.
"Those breasts are flat and fallen now,
Those veins must soon be dry;
Live in a heavenly mansion,   5
Not in some foul sty."

"Fair and foul are near of kin,
And fair needs foul," I cried.
"My friends are gone, but that's a truth
Nor grave nor bed denied,   10
Learned in bodily lowliness
And in the heart's pride.

"A woman can be proud and stiff
When on love intent;
But Love has pitched his mansion in   15
The place of excrement;
For nothing can be sole or whole
That has not been rent."

Hebrides: A group of islands off the west coast of Scotland.

sickle: A curved blade used for harvesting grain or cutting grass.

WILLIAM BUTLER YEATS (1865–1939)

The Lake Isle of Innisfree (1892)

I will arise and go now, and go to Innisfree,°
And a small cabin build there, of clay and wattles° made:
Nine bean-rows will I have there, a hive for the honey-bee,
And live alone in the bee-loud glade.

And I shall have some peace there, for peace comes dropping slow,   5
Dropping from the veils of the morning to where the cricket sings;
There midnight's all a glimmer, and noon a purple glow,
And evening full of the linnet's wings.

I will arise and go now, for always night and day
I hear lake water lapping with low sounds by the shore;   10
While I stand on the roadway, or on the pavements grey,
I hear it in the deep heart's core.

WILLIAM BUTLER YEATS (1865–1939)

Sailing to Byzantium (1927)

That is no country for old men. The young
In one another's arms, birds in the trees
—Those dying generations — at their song,
The salmon-falls, the mackerel-crowded seas,
Fish, flesh, or fowl, commend all summer long   5
Whatever is begotten, born, and dies.
Caught in that sensual music all neglect
Monuments of unaging intellect.

An aged man is but a paltry thing,
A tattered coat upon a stick, unless   10
Soul clap its hands and sing, and louder sing
For every tatter in its mortal dress,
Nor is there singing school but studying
Monuments of its own magnificence;
And therefore I have sailed the seas and come   15
To the holy city of Byzantium.

O sages standing in God's holy fire
As in the gold mosaic of a wall,
Come from the holy fire, perne in a gyre,
And be the singing-masters of my soul.   20
Consume my heart away; sick with desire

Innisfree: An island in Lough (Lake) Gill, County Sligo, in Ireland.
wattles: Stakes interwoven with twigs or branches, used for walls and roofing.

And fastened to a dying animal
It knows not what it is; and gather me
Into the artifice of eternity.

Once out of nature I shall never take   25
My bodily form from any natural thing,
But such a form as Grecian goldsmiths make
Of hammered gold and gold enameling
To keep a drowsy Emperor awake;
Or set upon a golden bough to sing   30
To lords and ladies of Byzantium
Of what is past, or passing, or to come.

WILLIAM BUTLER YEATS (1865–1939)

The Second Coming° (1921)

Turning and turning in the widening gyre°
The falcon cannot hear the falconer;
Things fall apart; the center cannot hold;
Mere anarchy is loosed upon the world,
The blood-dimmed tide is loosed, and everywhere   5
The ceremony of innocence is drowned;
The best lack all conviction, while the worst
Are full of passionate intensity.°

Surely some revelation is at hand;
Surely the Second Coming is at hand;   10
The Second Coming! Hardly are those words out
When a vast image out of *Spiritus Mundi*°
Troubles my sight: somewhere in sands of the desert
A shape with lion body and the head of a man,
A gaze blank and pitiless as the sun,   15
Is moving its slow thighs, while all about it
Reel shadows of the indignant desert birds.
The darkness drops again; but now I know
That twenty centuries° of stony sleep
Were vexed to nightmare by a rocking cradle,   20
And what rough beast, its hour come round at last,
Slouches towards Bethlehem to be born?

The Second Coming: The phrase usually refers to the return of Christ. Yeats theorized cycles of history, much like the turning of a wheel. Here he offers a poetic comment on his view of the dissolution of civilization at the end of one such cycle.

gyre: Spiral.

Mere . . . intensity: Lines 4–8 refer to the Russian Revolution of 1917.

Spiritus Mundi: Literally, "Spirit of the World" (Latin). Yeats believed all souls to be connected by a "Great Memory."

twenty centuries: The centuries between the birth of Christ and the twentieth century, in which Yeats was writing.

D R A M A

CHAPTER 26

UNDERSTANDING DRAMA

DRAMATIC LITERATURE

The distinctive appearance of a script, with its stage directions, character parts, and divisions into acts and scenes, identifies **drama** as a unique form of literature. A play is written to be performed in front of an audience by actors who take on the roles of the characters and who present the story through dialogue and action. (An exception is **closet drama,** which is meant to be read, not performed.) Indeed, the term *theater* comes from the Greek word *theasthai,* which means "to view" or "to see." Thus, drama is different from novels and short stories, which are meant to be read.

Dramatic works differ from other prose works in a number of other ways as well. Unlike novels and short stories, plays do not usually have narrators to tell the audience what a character is thinking or what happened in the past; the audience knows only what the characters reveal. Drama develops primarily by means of **dialogue,** the lines spoken by the characters. The plot and the action of drama unfold on the stage as the characters interact. Playwrights employ various techniques to compensate for the absence of a narrator. For example, playwrights use **monologues**—extended speeches by one character. (A monologue in which a character expresses private thoughts while alone on the stage is called a **soliloquy.**) Playwrights can also use **asides**—brief comments by an actor who addresses the audience but is not heard by the other characters — to reveal the thoughts of the speaker. Like the observations of a narrator, these dramatic techniques give the audience insight into a character's motives and attitudes. In addition, makeup, costumes, scenery, and lighting enhance a dramatic performance, as do actors' and directors' interpretations of dialogue and stage directions.

ORIGINS OF THE MODERN THEATER

The Ancient Greek Theater

The dramatic presentations of ancient Greece developed out of religious rites performed to honor gods or to mark the coming of spring. Playwrights such as Aeschylus (525–456 B.C.), Sophocles (496–406 B.C.), and Euripides (480?–406 B.C.) composed plays to be performed and judged at competitions held during the yearly Dionysian festivals. Works were chosen by a selection board and evaluated by a panel of judges. To compete in the contest, authors had to submit three

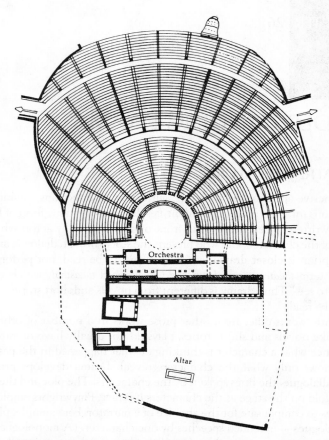

The Theater of Dionysus at Athens. From W. B. Worthen, *The Harcourt Brace Anthology of Drama,* 3rd Edition (Fort Worth: Harcourt, 2000) 16.

tragedies, which could be either based on a common theme or unrelated, and one comedy. Unfortunately, relatively few of these ancient Greek plays survive today.

The open-air semicircular ancient Greek theater, built into the side of a hill, looked much like a primitive version of a modern sports stadium. Some Greek theaters, such as the Athenian theater, could seat almost seventeen thousand spectators. Sitting in tiered seats, the audience would look down on the *orchestra,* or "dancing place," occupied by the **chorus** — originally a group of men (led by an individual called the *choragos*) who danced and chanted, then later a group of onlookers who commented on the drama. Raised a few steps above the orchestra was a platform on which the actors performed. Behind this platform was a *skene,* or building, that originally served as a resting place or dressing room. (The modern word *scene* is derived from the Greek *skene.*) Behind the skene was a line of pillars called a *colonnade,* which was covered by a roof. Actors used the skene for entrances and exits; beginning with the plays of Sophocles, painted backdrops were hung there. These backdrops, however, were most likely more decorative than realistic. Historians believe that realistic props and scenery were probably absent from the ancient Greek theater. Instead, the setting was suggested by the play's dialogue, and the audience had to imagine the specific physical details of a scene.

Two mechanical devices were used. One, a rolling cart or platform, was sometimes employed to introduce action that had occurred offstage. For example, actors frozen in position could be rolled onto the roof of the skene to illustrate an event such as the killing of Oedipus's father, which occurred before the play began. Another mechanical device, a small crane, was used to show gods ascending to or descending from heaven. Such devices enabled playwrights to dramatize the myths that were celebrated at the Dionysian festivals.

The ancient Greek theater was designed to enhance acoustics. The flat stone wall of the skene reflected the sound from the orchestra and the stage, and the curved shape of the amphitheater captured the sound, enabling the audience to hear the lines spoken by the actors. Each actor wore a stylized mask, or **persona,** to convey to the audience the personality traits of the particular character being portrayed — a king, a soldier, a wise old man, a young girl (female roles were played by men). The mouths of these masks were probably constructed so they amplified the voice and projected it into the audience. In addition, the actors wore *kothorni*, high shoes that elevated them above the stage, perhaps also helping to project their voices. Due to the excellent acoustics, audiences who see plays performed in these ancient theaters today can hear clearly without microphones or speaker systems.

Because actors wore masks and because males played the parts of women and gods as well as men, acting methods in the ancient Greek theater were probably not realistic. In their masks, high shoes, and full-length tunics (called *chiton*), actors could not hope to appear natural or to mimic the attitudes of everyday life. Instead, they probably recited their lines while standing in stylized poses, with emotions conveyed more by gesture and tone than by action. Typically, three actors had all the speaking roles. One actor — the **protagonist**— would play the central role and have the largest speaking part. Two other actors would divide the remaining lines between them. Although other characters would come on and off the stage, they would usually not have speaking roles.

Ancient Greek tragedies were typically divided into five parts. First came the *prologos*, or prologue, in which an actor gave the background or explanations that the audience needed to follow the rest of the drama. Then came the *párodos*, in which the chorus entered and commented on the events presented in the prologue. Following this were several *episodia*, or episodes, in which characters spoke to one another on the stage and developed the central conflict of the play. Alternating with episodes were *stasimon* (choral odes), in which the chorus commented on the exchanges that had taken place during the preceding episode. Frequently, the choral odes were divided into *strophes*, or stanzas, which were recited or sung as the chorus moved across the orchestra in one direction, and *antistrophes*, which were recited as it moved in the opposite direction. (Interestingly, the chorus stood between the audience and the actors, often functioning as an additional audience, expressing the political, social, and moral views of the community.)

Finally came the *exodos,* the last scene of the play, during which the conflict was resolved and the actors left the stage.

Using music, dance, and verse — as well as a variety of architectural and technical innovations — the ancient Greek theater was able to convey the traditional themes of tragedy. Thus, the theater powerfully expressed ideas that were central to the religious festivals in which they first appeared: the reverence for the cycles of life and death, the unavoidable dictates of the gods, and the inscrutable workings of fate.

The Elizabethan Theater

The Elizabethan theater, influenced by the classical traditions of Roman and Greek dramatists, traces its roots back to local religious pageants performed at medieval festivals during the twelfth and thirteenth centuries. Town guilds, organizations of craftsmen who worked in the same profession, reenacted Old and New Testament stories: the fall of man, Noah and the flood, David and Goliath, and the crucifixion of Christ, for example. Church fathers encouraged these plays because they brought the Bible to a largely illiterate audience. Sometimes these spectacles, called **mystery plays,** were presented in the market square or on the church steps, and at other times actors appeared on movable stages or wagons called *pageants,* which could be wheeled to a given location. (Some of these wagons were quite elaborate, with trapdoors and pulleys and an upper tier that simulated heaven.) As mystery plays became more popular, they were performed in series over several days, presenting an entire cycle of a holiday — the crucifixion and resurrection of Christ during Easter, for example.

Related to mystery plays are **morality plays,** which developed in the fourteenth and fifteenth centuries. Unlike mystery plays, which depict scenes from the Bible, morality plays allegorize the Christian way of life. Typically, characters representing various virtues and vices struggle or debate over the soul of man. *Everyman* (1500), the best known of these plays, dramatizes the good and bad qualities of Everyman and shows his struggle to determine what is of value to him as he journeys toward death.

By the middle of the sixteenth century, mystery and morality plays had lost ground to a new secular drama. One reason for this decline was that mystery and morality plays were associated with Catholicism and consequently discouraged by the Protestant clergy. In addition, newly discovered plays of ancient Greece and Rome introduced a dramatic tradition that supplanted the traditions of religious drama. English plays that followed the classic model were sensational and bombastic, often dealing with murder, revenge, and blood retribution. Appealing to privileged classes and commoners alike, these plays were extremely popular. (One source estimates that between 20,000 and 25,000 people attended performances each week.)

In spite of the popularity of the theater, actors and playwrights encountered a number of difficulties. First, they faced opposition from city officials who were averse to theatrical presentations because they thought that the crowds attending these performances spread disease. Puritans opposed the theater because they thought plays were immoral and sinful. Finally, some people attached to the royal court opposed the theater because they thought that the playwrights undermined the authority of Queen Elizabeth by spreading politically seditious ideas. As a result, during Elizabeth's rein, performances were placed under the strict control of the Master of Revels, a public official who had the power to censor plays (and did so with great regularity) and to grant licenses for performances. Acting companies that wanted to put on a performance had to obtain a license — possible only with the patronage of a powerful nobleman — and to perform the play in an area designated by the queen. Despite these difficulties, a number of actors and playwrights gained a measure of financial independence by joining together and forming acting companies. These companies of professional actors performed works such as Christopher Marlowe's *Tamburlaine* and Thomas Kyd's *The Spanish Tragedy* in tavern courtyards and then eventually in permanent theaters. According to scholars, the structures of the Elizabethan theater evolved from these tavern courtyards.

William Shakespeare's plays were performed in the Globe Theater (a corner of which was unearthed in December 1988). The Globe consisted of a large main stage that extended out into the open-air *yard* where the *groundlings*, or common people, stood. Spectators who paid more sat on small stools in two or three levels of galleries that extended in front of and around the stage. (The theater could probably seat almost two thousand people at a performance.) Most of the play's action occurred on the stage, which had no curtain and could be seen from three sides. Beneath the stage was a space called the *hell*, which could be reached when the floorboards were removed. This space enabled actors to "disappear" or descend into a hole or grave when the play called for such action. Above the stage was a roof called the *heavens*, which protected the actors from the weather and contained ropes and pulleys used to lower props or to create special effects.

At the rear of the stage was a narrow alcove covered by a curtain that could be open or closed. This curtain, often painted, functioned as a decorative rather than a realistic backdrop. The main function of this alcove was to enable actors to hide or disappear when the script called for them to do so. Some Elizabethan theaters contained a rear stage instead of an alcove. Because the rear stage was concealed by a curtain, props could be arranged on it ahead of time. When the action on the rear stage was finished, the curtain would be drawn and the action would continue on the front stage.

On either side of the rear stage was a door through which the actors could enter and exit the front stage. Above the rear stage was a curtained stage called the *chamber*, which functioned as a balcony or as any other setting located above the action taking place on the stage below. On either side of the chamber were casement windows, which actors could use when a play called for a conversation with someone leaning out a window or standing on a balcony. Above the chamber was the *music gallery*, a balcony that housed the musicians who provided musical interludes throughout the play (and that doubled as a stage if the play required it). The *huts*, windows located above the music gallery, could be used by characters playing lookouts or sentries. Because of the many acting sites, more than one action could take place simultaneously. For example, lookouts could stand in the towers of Hamlet's castle while Hamlet and Horatio walked the walls below.

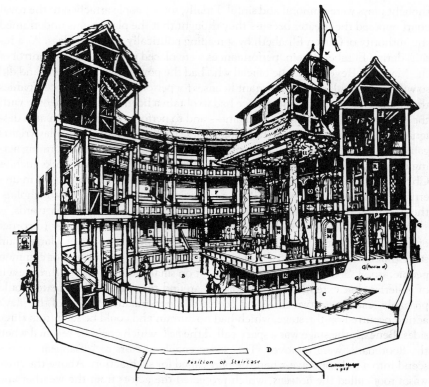

The Globe Playhouse,
1599-1613

A CONJECTURAL
RECONSTRUCTION

KEY
AA   Main entrance
B   The Yard
CC   Entrances to lowest gallery
D   Entrances to staircase and upper
        galleries
E   Corridor serving the different sections
        of the middle gallery
F   Middle gallery ('Twopenny Rooms')
G   'Gentlemen's Rooms' or 'Lords' Rooms'
H   The stage

J   The hanging being put up round the
        stage
K   The 'Hell' under the stage
L   The stage trap, leading down to the
        Hell
MM Stage doors
N   Curtained 'place behind the stage'
O   Gallery above the stage, used as re-
        quired sometimes by musicians, some-
        times by spectators, and often as part
        of the play
P   Back-stage area (the tiring-house)
Q   Tiring-house door
R   Dressing-rooms
S   Wardrobe and storage
T   The hut housing the machine for
        lowering enthroned gods, etc., to the
        stage
U   The 'Heavens'
W   Hoisting the playhouse flag

The Globe Playhouse, 1599–1613; a conjectural reconstruction. From C. Walter Hodges,
The Globe Restored: A Study of the Elizabethan Theatre. New York: Norton, 1973.

During Shakespeare's time, the theater had many limitations that challenged
the audience's imagination. Because women did not perform on the stage, young
boys — usually between the ages of ten and twelve — played all the women's
parts. In addition, there was no artificial lighting, so plays had to be performed in
daylight. Rain, wind, or clouds could disrupt a performance or ruin an image —
such as "the morn in russet mantle clad"— that the audience was asked to imagine. Finally, because few sets and props were used, the audience often had to

visualize the high walls of a castle or the trees of a forest. The plays were performed without intermission, except for musical interludes that occurred at various points. Thus, the experience of seeing one of Shakespeare's plays staged in the Elizabethan theater was different from seeing it staged today in a modern theater.

The Modern Theater

Unlike the theaters of ancient Greece and Elizabethan England, seventeenth- and eighteenth-century theaters — such as the Palais Royal, where the great French playwright Molière presented many of his plays — were covered by a roof, beautifully decorated, and illuminated by candles so that plays could be performed at night. The theater remained brightly lit even during performances, partly because there was no easy way to extinguish hundreds of candles and partly because people went to the theater as much to see each other as to see the play. A curtain opened and closed between acts. The audience of about five hundred spectators sat in a long room and viewed the play on a **picture-frame stage.** This type of stage contained the action within a **proscenium arch** that surrounded the opening through which the audience viewed the performance. Thus, the action seemed to take place in an adjoining room with one of its walls cut away. Painted scenery (some of it quite elaborate), intricately detailed costumes, and stage makeup were commonplace, and for the first time women performed female roles. In addition, a complicated series of ropes, pulleys, and cranks enabled stagehands to change scenery quickly, and sound-effects machines could give audiences the impression that they were hearing a galloping horse or a raging thunderstorm. Because the theaters were small, audiences were relatively close to the stage, so actors could use subtle movements and facial expressions to enhance their performances.

Many of the first innovations in the theater were quite basic. For example, the first stage lighting was produced by candles lining the front of the stage. This method of lighting was not only ineffective — actors were lit from below and had to step forward to be fully illuminated — but also dangerous. Costumes and even entire theaters could (and did) catch fire. Later, covered lanterns with reflectors provided more light. In the nineteenth century, a device that used an oxyhydrogen flame directed on a cylinder of lime created extremely bright illumination that could, with the aid of a lens, be concentrated into a spotlight. (It is from this method of stage lighting that we get the expression *to be in the limelight.*)

Eventually, in the twentieth century, electric lights provided a dependable and safe way of lighting the stage. Electric spotlights, footlights, and ceiling light bars made the actors clearly visible and enabled playwrights to create special effects. In Arthur Miller's *Death of a Salesman* (p. 1178), for example, lighting focuses attention on action in certain areas of the stage while leaving other areas in complete darkness.

Along with electric lighting came other innovations, such as electronic amplification. Microphones made it possible for actors to speak conversationally and to avoid using unnaturally loud "stage diction" to project their voices to the rear of the theater. Microphones placed at various points around the stage enabled actors and actresses to interact naturally and to deliver their lines audibly even without facing the audience. More recently, small wireless microphones

Thrust-Stage Theater. With seats on three sides of the stage area, the thrust stage and its background can assume many forms other than the conventional living-room interior in the illustration. Entrances can be made from the aisles, from the sides, through the stage floor, and from the back.

eliminated the unwieldy wires and the "dead spaces" left between upright or hanging microphones, allowing characters to move freely around the stage.

The true revolutions in staging came with the advent of **realism** in the middle of the nineteenth century. Until this time, scenery was painted on canvas backdrops that trembled visibly, especially when they were intersected by doors through which actors and actresses entered. With realism came settings that were accurate down to the smallest detail. (Improved lighting, which revealed the inadequacies of painted backdrops, made such realistic stage settings necessary.) Backdrops were replaced by the **box set,** three flat panels arranged to form connected walls, with the fourth wall removed so the audience had the illusion of looking into a room. The room itself was decorated with real furniture, plants, and pictures on the walls; the door of one room might connect to another completely furnished room, or a window might open to a garden filled with realistic foliage. In addition, new methods of changing scenery were employed. Elevator stages, hydraulic lifts, and moving platforms enabled directors to make complicated changes in scenery out of the audience's view.

During the late nineteenth and early twentieth centuries, however, some playwrights reacted against what they saw as the excesses of realism. They introduced **surrealistic** stage settings, in which color and scenery mirrored the uncontrolled images of dreams, and **expressionistic** stage settings, in which costumes and scenery were exaggerated and distorted to reflect the workings of a troubled, even unbalanced mind. In addition, playwrights used lighting to create areas of light, shadow, and color that reinforced the themes of the play or reflected the

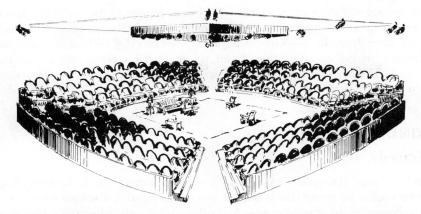

Arena Theater. The audience surrounds the stage area, which may or may not be raised. Use of scenery is limited — perhaps to a single piece of scenery standing alone in the middle of the stage.

emotions of the protagonist. Eugene O'Neill's *The Emperor Jones*, for example, used a series of expressionistic scenes to show the mental state of the terrified protagonist.

Sets in contemporary plays run the gamut from realistic to fantastic, from a detailed re-creation of a room in a production of Tennessee Williams's *The Glass Menagerie* (p. 1416) to a dreamlike set for *The Emperor Jones* and Edward Albee's *The Sandbox*. Motorized devices, such as revolving turntables, and *wagons*— scenery mounted on wheels — make possible rapid changes of scenery. The Broadway musical *Les Misérables*, for example, required scores of elaborate sets — Parisian slums, barricades, walled gardens — to be shifted as the audience watched. A gigantic barricade constructed on stage at one point in the play was later rotated to show the carnage that had taken place on both sides of a battle. Light, sound, and smoke were used to heighten the impact of the scene.

Today, as dramatists attempt to break down the barriers that separate audiences from the action they are viewing, plays are not limited to the picture-frame stage; in fact, they are performed on many different kinds of stages. Some plays take place on a **thrust stage,** which has an area that projects out into the audience. Others are performed on an **arena stage,** with the audience surrounding the actors. (This kind of performance is often called **theater in the round.**) In addition, experiments have been done with *environmental staging*, in which the stage surrounds the audience or several stages are situated at various locations throughout the audience. Plays may also be performed outdoors, in settings ranging from parks to city streets. Some playwrights even try to blur the line that divides the audience from the stage by having actors move through or sit in the audience — or even by eliminating the stage entirely. For example, *Tony 'n Tina's Wedding*, a "participatory drama" created in 1988 by the theater group Artificial Intelligence, takes place not in a theater but at a church where a wedding is performed and then at a catering hall where the wedding reception is held. Throughout the play the members of the audience function as guests, joining in the wedding celebration and mingling with the actors, who improvise freely. Recent examples of such interactive drama include *Grandma Sylvia's Funeral* and *Off the Wall,* in which audiences "attend" an art auction. Today, no single architectural form defines the theater. The modern stage is a flexible space suited to the many varieties of contemporary theatrical production.

KINDS OF DRAMA

Tragedy

In his *Poetics,* Aristotle (384–322 B.C.) sums up ancient Greek thinking about drama when he writes that a **tragedy** is a drama treating a serious subject and involving persons of significance. According to Aristotle, when the members of an audience see a tragedy, they should feel both pity (and thus closeness to the protagonist) and fear (and thus revulsion) because they recognize in themselves the potential for similar reactions. The purging of these emotions that audience members experience as they see the dramatic action unfold is called **catharsis.** For catharsis to occur, the protagonist of a tragedy must be worthy of the audience's attention and sympathy. Because of his or her exalted position, the fall of a tragic protagonist is greater than that of an average person; therefore, it arouses more pity and fear in the audience. Often the entire society suffers as a result of the actions of the protagonist. Before the action of Sophocles' *Oedipus the King* (p. 1271), for example, Oedipus has freed Thebes from the deadly grasp of the Sphinx by answering her riddle and, as a result, has been welcomed as king. But because of his sins, Oedipus is an affront to the gods and brings famine and pestilence to the city. When his fall finally comes, it is sudden and absolute.

According to Aristotle, the protagonist of a tragedy is neither all good nor all evil, but a mixture of the two. The protagonist is like the rest of us — only more exalted and possessing some weakness or flaw **(hamartia).** This tragic flaw — perhaps narrowness of vision or overwhelming pride **(hubris)** — is typically the element that creates the conditions for tragedy. Shakespeare's Romeo and Juliet, for example, are so much in love they think they can ignore the blood feud that rages between their two families. However, their naive efforts to sustain their love despite the feud lead them to their tragic deaths. Similarly, Richard III's blind ambition to gain the throne causes him to murder all those who stand in his way. His unscrupulousness sets into motion the forces that eventually cause his death.

Irony is central to tragedy. **Dramatic irony** (also called **tragic irony**) emerges from a situation in which the audience knows more about the dramatic situation than a character does. As a result, the character's words and actions may be consistent with what he or she expects but at odds with what the audience knows will happen. Thus, a character may say or do something that causes the audience to infer a meaning beyond what the character intends or realizes. The dramatic irony is clear, for example, when Oedipus announces that whoever has disobeyed the dictates of the gods will be exiled. The audience knows, although Oedipus does not, that he has just condemned himself. **Cosmic irony,** also called **irony of fate,** occurs when God, fate, or some larger, uncontrollable force seems to be intentionally deceiving characters into believing they can escape their fate. Too late, they realize that trying to avoid their destiny is futile. Years before Oedipus was born, for example, the oracle of Apollo foretold that Oedipus would kill his parents. Naturally, his parents attempted to thwart the prophecy, but ironically, their actions ensured that the prophecy would be fulfilled.

At some point in a tragedy — usually after the climax — the protagonist recognizes the reasons for his or her downfall. This recognition (and the accompanying acceptance) elevate tragic protagonists to grandeur and give their suffering meaning. Without this recognition, there would be no tragedy, just **pathos** — suffering that exists simply to satisfy the sentimental or morbid sensibilities of the audience. In spite of the death of the protagonist, then, tragedy enables the audience to see the nobility of the character and thus to experience a sense of elation. In Shakespeare's *King Lear*, for example, a king at the height of his powers decides to divide his kingdom among his three daughters. Later, he realizes that without his power, he is just a bothersome old man to his ambitious children. Only after going mad does he understand the vanity of his former existence; he dies a humbled but enlightened man.

According to Aristotle, a tragedy achieves the illusion of reality when it has *unity of action* — that is, when the play contains only those actions that lead to its tragic outcome. Later critics interpreted this constraint to mean that including subplots or mixing tragic and comic elements would destroy this unity. To the concept of unity of action, these later critics added two other requirements: *unity of place* — the requirement that the play have a single setting — and *unity of time* — the requirement that the events depicted by the play take no longer than the actual duration of the play (or, at most, a single day).

The three unities have had a long and rather uneven history. In some of his plays — *The Tempest* and *The Comedy of Errors*, for example — Shakespeare observed the unities. Most of the time, however, he had no compunctions about writing plays with subplots and frequent changes of location. He also wrote **tragicomedies,** such as *The Merchant of Venice*, which have a serious theme appropriate for tragedy but end happily, usually because of a sudden turn of events. During the eighteenth century, with its emphasis on classic form, the unities were adhered to quite strictly. In the late eighteenth and early nineteenth centuries, with the onset of romanticism and its emphasis on the natural, interest in the unities of place and time waned. Even though some modern plays (particularly one-act plays) do observe the unities — *Trifles* (p. 983), for instance, has a single setting and takes place during a period of time that corresponds to the length of the play — few modern dramatists adhere to them strictly.

Ideas about appropriate subjects for tragedy have also changed. For Aristotle, the protagonist of a tragedy had to be exceptional — a king, for example. The protagonists of Greek tragedies were usually historical or mythical figures. Shakespeare often used kings and princes as protagonists — Richard II and Hamlet, for example — but he also used people of lesser rank, as in *Romeo and Juliet* and *A Midsummer Night's Dream*. In our times, interest in the lives of monarchs has been overshadowed by involvement in the lives of ordinary people. Modern tragedies — Arthur Miller's *Death of a Salesman*, for example — are more likely to focus on a traveling salesman than on a king.

With the rise of the middle class in the nineteenth century, ideas about the nature of tragedy changed. Responding to the age's desire for sentimentality, playwrights produced **melodramas,** sensational plays that appealed mainly to the emotions. Melodramas contain many of the elements of tragedy but end happily and often rely on conventional plots and stock characters. Because the protagonists in melodramas — often totally virtuous heroines suffering at the hands of impossibly wicked villains — helplessly endure their tribulations without ever gaining insight or enlightenment, they never achieve tragic status. As a result, they remain cardboard cutouts who exist only to exploit the emotions of the audience. Melodrama survives today in many films and in television soap operas.

Realism, which arose in the late nineteenth century as a response to the artificiality of melodrama, presented serious (and sometimes tragic) themes and believable characters in the context of everyday contemporary life. Writers of realistic drama used their plays to educate their audiences about the problems of the society in which they lived. For this reason, realistic drama focuses on the commonplace and eliminates the unlikely coincidences and excessive sentimentality of melodrama. Dramatists like Henrik Ibsen scrutinize the lives of ordinary people, not larger-than-life characters. After great suffering, these characters rise above the limitations of their mediocre lives and exhibit courage or emotional strength. The insight they gain often focuses attention on a social problem — the restrictive social conventions that define the behavior of women in nineteenth-century marriages, for example. Realistic drama also features settings and props similar to those used in people's daily lives and includes dialogue that reflects the way people actually speak.

Developing alongside realism was a literary movement called **naturalism.** Like realism, naturalism rejected the unrealistic plots and sentimentality of melodrama, but unlike realism, naturalism sought to explore the depths of the human condition. Influenced by Charles Darwin's ideas about evolution and natural selection and Karl Marx's ideas about economic forces that shape people's lives, naturalism is a pessimistic philosophy that presents a world that is at worst hostile and at best indifferent to human concerns. It pictures human beings as higher-order animals who are driven by basic instincts — especially hunger, fear, and sexuality — and who are subject to economic, social, and biological forces beyond their understanding or control. For these reasons, it is well suited to tragic themes.

The nineteenth-century French writer Émile Zola did much to develop the theory of naturalism, and later so did the American writers Stephen Crane, Frank Norris, and Theodore Dreiser. Naturalism also finds its way into the work of contemporary dramatists, such as Arthur Miller. Unlike other tragic protagonists, the protagonists of naturalist works are crushed not by the gods or by fate but by poverty, animal drives, or social class. Willy Loman in *Death of a Salesman*, for example, is subject to the economic forces of a society that does not value its workers and discards those it no longer finds useful.

Comedy

A **comedy** treats themes and characters with humor and typically has a happy ending. Whereas tragedy focuses on the hidden dimensions of the tragic hero's character, comedy focuses on the public persona, the protagonist as a social being. Tragic figures are typically seen in isolation, questioning the meaning of their lives and trying to comprehend their suffering. Hamlet — draped in sable, longing for death, and self-consciously contemplating his duty — epitomizes the isolation of the tragic hero.

Unlike tragic heroes, comic figures are seen in the public arena, where people intentionally assume the masks of pretension and self-importance. The purpose of comedy is to strip away these masks and expose human beings for what they are. Whereas tragedy reveals the nobility of the human condition, comedy reveals its inherent folly, portraying human beings as selfish, hypocritical, vain, weak, irrational, and capable of self-delusion. Thus, the basic function of comedy is critical — to tell people that things are not what they seem and that appearances are not necessarily reality. In the comic world, nothing is solid or predictable, and accidents and coincidences are more important to the plot than reason. Many of Shakespeare's comedies, for example, depend on exchanged or confused identities. The wordplay and verbal nonsense of comedy add to this general confusion.

Comedies typically rely on certain familiar plot devices. Many comedies begin with a startling or unusual situation that attracts the audience's attention. In Shakespeare's *A Midsummer Night's Dream*, for example, Theseus, the duke of Athens, rules that Hermia will either marry the man her father has chosen for her or be put to death. Such an event could lead to tragedy if comedy did not intervene to save the day.

Comedy often depends on obstacles and hindrances to further its plot: the more difficult the problems the lovers face, the more satisfying their eventual triumph will be. For this reason, the plot of a comedy is usually more complex than the plot of a tragedy. Compare the rather straightforward plot of *Hamlet* (p. 1075) — a prince ordered to avenge his murdered father's death is driven mad with indecision and, after finally acting decisively, is killed himself — with the mix-ups, mistaken identities, and general confusion of *A Midsummer Night's Dream*.

Finally, comedies have happy endings. Whereas tragedy ends with death, comedy ends with an affirmation of life. Eventually, the confusion and misunderstandings reach a point where some resolution must be achieved: the difficulties of the lovers are overcome, the villains are banished, and the lovers marry — or at least express their intention to do so. In this way, the lovers establish their connection with the rest of society, and its values are affirmed.

The first comedies, written in Greece in the fifth century B.C., heavily satirized the religious and social issues of the day and were characterized by bawdy humor. In the fourth and third centuries B.C., this **Old Comedy** gave way to **New Comedy,** a comedy of romance with stock characters — lovers and untrustworthy servants, for example — and conventional settings. Lacking the bitter satire and bawdiness of Old Comedy, New Comedy depends on outrageous plots, mistaken identities, young lovers, interfering parents, and conniving servants. Ultimately, the young lovers outwit all those who stand between them and in so doing affirm the primacy of youth and love over old age and death.

Old and New Comedy represent two distinct lines of humor that extend to modern times. Old Comedy depends on **satire**—biting humor that diminishes a person, idea, or institution by ridiculing it or holding it up to scorn. Unlike most comedy, which exists simply to make people laugh, satire is social criticism, deriding hypocrisy, pretension, and vanity or condemning vice. At its best, satire appeals to the intellect, has a serious purpose, and arouses thoughtful laughter. New Comedy may also be satiric, but the satire is often tempered by elements of **farce,** comedy in which stereotypical characters engage in boisterous horseplay and slapstick humor, all the while making jokes and sexual innuendoes — as they do in Anton Chekhov's *The Brute* (p. 1062).

English comedy got its start in the sixth century A.D. in the form of farcical episodes that appeared in morality plays. During the Renaissance, comedy developed rapidly, beginning in 1533 with Nicholas Udall's *Ralph Roister Doister* and eventually evolving into Shakespeare's **romantic comedy**— such as *A Midsummer Night's Dream*, in which love is the main subject and idealized heroines and lovers endure great difficulties until the inevitable happy ending is reached.

Also during the Renaissance, particularly in the latter part of the sixteenth century, writers like Ben Jonson experimented with a different type of comedy — the **comedy of humours,** which focused on characters whose behavior was controlled by a characteristic trait, or *humour*. During the Renaissance, a person's temperament was thought to be determined by the mix of fluids, or humours, in the body. When one humour dominated, a certain type of disposition resulted. Playwrights capitalized on this belief, writing comedies in which characters are motivated by stereotypical behaviors that result from the imbalance of the humours. In comedies such as Jonson's *Volpone* and *The Alchemist*, characters such as the suspicious husband and the miser can be manipulated by others because of their predictable dispositions.

Closely related to the comedy of humours is the satiric **comedy of manners,** which developed during the sixteenth century and achieved great popularity in the nineteenth century. This form focuses on the manners and customs of society and directs its satire against characters who violate social conventions and rules of behavior. These plays tend to be memorable more for their witty dialogue than for their development of characters or setting. Oliver Goldsmith's *She Stoops to Conquer*, George Bernard Shaw's *Pygmalion*, and even some television sitcoms are examples of this type of comedy.

In the eighteenth century, a reaction against the perceived immorality of the comedy of manners led to **sentimental comedy,** which eventually achieved great popularity. This kind of comedy relies on sentimental emotion rather than on wit or humor to move an audience. It also dwells on the virtues rather than on the vices of life. The heroes of sentimental comedy are unimpeachably noble, moral, and honorable; the pure, virtuous, middle-class heroines suffer trials and tribulations calculated to move the audience to tears rather than laughter. Eventually, the distress of the hero and heroine is resolved in a sometimes contrived (but always happy) ending.

In his 1877 essay *The Idea of Comedy*, novelist and critic George Meredith suggests that comedy that appeals to the intellect should be called **high comedy.** Shakespeare's *As You Like It* and George Bernard Shaw's *Pygmalion* can be characterized as high comedy. When comedy has little or no intellectual appeal, according to Meredith, it is **low comedy.** Low comedy appears in parts of Shakespeare's *The Taming of the Shrew* and as comic relief in *Macbeth*.

The twentieth century developed its own characteristic comic forms. Most reflect the uncertainty and pessimism of a century that saw two world wars, the Holocaust, and nuclear destruction, as well as threats posed by environmental pollution and ethnic and racial conflict. Combining laughter and hints of tragedy, these modern tragicomedies feature **antiheroes,** characters who, instead of manifesting dignity and power, are ineffectual or petty. Their plight frequently elicits laughter, not pity and fear, from the audience. **Black** or **dark comedies,** for example, rely for their comedy on the morbid and the absurd. These works are usually so satiric and bitter that they threaten to slip over the edge into tragedy. The screenplay of Joseph Heller's novel *Catch-22*, which ends with a character dropping bombs on his own men, is a classic example of such comedy. **Theater of the absurd,** which includes comedies such as Samuel Beckett's *Waiting for Godot* and Tom Stoppard's *Rosencrantz and Guildenstern Are Dead*, begins with the assumption that the human condition is irrational. Typically, this type of drama does not have a discernible plot; instead, it presents a series of apparently unrelated images and illogical exchanges of dialogue meant to reinforce the idea that human beings live in a remote, confusing, and often incomprehensible universe. Absurdist dramas seem to go in circles, never progressing to a climax or achieving a resolution, reinforcing the theme of the endless and meaningless repetition that characterizes modern life.

A NOTE ON TRANSLATIONS

Many dramatic works that we read or see are translations. For example, Ibsen wrote in Norwegian, Sophocles in Greek, Molière in French, and Chekhov in Russian. Before English-speaking viewers or readers can evaluate the language of a translated play, they must understand that the language they hear or read is the translator's interpretation of what the playwright intended to communicate. Translation is interpretation, not just a search for literal equivalents; as a result, a translation is always different from the original. Moreover, different translations are different from one another. During the course of Henrik Ibsen's 1879 play *A Doll House* (p. 996), for instance, Nora, the main character, refers several times to a symbolic gesture of support she expects from her husband Torvald. In the translation in this anthology, that gesture is translated as "the miracle"; in another translation, it is translated as "the wonderful." Not only is *miracle* more consistent with idiomatic English usage, but also it is a more absolute, and therefore a more forceful, term.

The choices translators make can be very different. Compare these two versions of an exchange of dialogue from two different translations of the same Chekhov play, called *The Brute* in the translation that begins on page 1063 and *The Bear* in the alternate version.

—From *The Brute:*

SMIRNOV: You'd like me to come simpering to you in French, I suppose.
"Enchanté, madame! Merci beaucoup for not paying zee money, *madame!
Pardonnez-moi* if I 'ave disturbed you, *madame!* How *charmante* you look in
mourning, *madame!"*
MRS. POPOV: Now you're being silly, Mr. Smirnov.
SMIRNOV: *(mimicking)* "Now you're being silly, Mr. Smirnov." "You don't
know how to talk to a lady, Mr. Smirnov." Look here, Mrs. Popov. I've
known more women than you've known pussy cats. I've fought three duels
on their account. I've jilted twelve, and been jilted by nine others. Oh, yes,
Mrs. Popov, I've played the fool in my time, whispered sweet nothings,
bowed and scraped and endeavored to please. Don't tell me I don't know
what it is to love, to pine away with longing, to have the blues, to melt like
butter, to be weak as water. I was full of tender emotion. I was carried away
with passion. I squandered half my fortune on the sex. I chattered about
women's emancipation. But there's an end to everything, dear madam. . . .
(1.71–73)

—From *The Bear:*

SMIRNOV: Ach, it's astonishing! How would you like me to talk to you? In
French, perhaps? *(Lisps in anger.) Madame, je vous prie. . . . how happy I am
that you're not paying me the money. . . . Ah, pardon, I've made you uneasy!
Such lovely weather we're having today! And you look so becoming in your
mourning dress. (Bows and scrapes.)*
MRS. POPOV: That's rude and not very clever!
SMIRNOV: *(teasing)* Rude and not very clever! I don't know how to behave in
the company of ladies. Madam, in my time I've seen far more women than
you've seen sparrows. Three times I've fought duels over women; I've jilted
twelve women, nine have jilted me! Yes! There was a time when I played
the fool; I became sentimental over women, used honeyed words, fawned
on them, bowed and scraped. . . . I loved, suffered, sighed at the moon; I became limp, melted, shivered . . . I loved passionately, madly, every which
way, devil take me, I chattered away like a magpie about the emancipation
of women, ran through half my fortune as a result of my tender feelings; but
now, if you will excuse me, I'm on to your ways! I've had enough! . . .

Although both translations convey Smirnov's anger and frustration, they use different words (with different connotations), different phrasing — and even different stage directions. In *The Bear*, for instance, only one French phrase is used,
whereas *The Brute* uses several and specifies a French accent as well; other differences between the two translations include *The Bear*'s use of "teasing," "sparrows,"
and "I've had enough!" where *The Brute* uses "mimicking," "pussy cats," and "But
there's an end to everything, dear madam." (Elsewhere in the play, *The Bear* uses
profanity while *The Brute* uses more polite language.) Many words and idiomatic

expressions used in daily speech cannot be translated exactly from one language to another; as a result, the two translators make different choices to try to convey a sense of the original.

The following two short plays, August Strindberg's *The Stronger* (1890) and Jane Martin's *Beauty* (2001), move beyond the relatively fixed conventions of traditional drama. *The Stronger* blends elements of surrealism, melodrama, dark comedy, and farce to create a disturbing dramatic monologue. *Beauty*, which contains elements of fantasy and absurdist drama, makes an ironic (and humorous) comment on the way society views women. Separated by over one hundred years, both playwrights express the dreams and anxieties of the times in which they wrote.

When it first appeared, August Strindberg's *The Stronger* was considered highly experimental. In this play, Strindberg not only violates the moral prohibitions of his time by dealing explicitly with infidelity but also challenges contemporary dramatic conventions by writing a two-character play in which one character remains silent while the other speaks.

AUGUST STRINDBERG (1849–1912) was born in Stockholm, Sweden, the child of a shipping merchant and his former maid. He studied at Uppsala University but left the university without a degree. By 1872, he had moved into the artistic circles in Stockholm and had begun work as a journalist.

In 1874, Strindberg was appointed assistant librarian at the Royal Library in Stockholm. Beginning the first of several stormy marriages, he struggled over the next few years; in 1879, he declared bankruptcy. During the same period, he wrote the novel that marked his breakthrough as a writer, *The Red Room* (1879). In 1881, he left the Royal Library to devote himself to writing, and in 1883, he left Sweden to join an artists' colony near Paris. His restlessness continued, however, and he soon moved to Switzerland, later living in Denmark, Germany, and Austria before returning at last to Stockholm.

Strindberg was a prolific artist, and his work includes novels, plays, poetry, and paintings. He is considered one of the most influential dramatists in literature.

Strindberg's *The Stronger* has been called a monodrama, a dramatic monologue, and a battle of brains in one scene. *The Stronger* was the kind of experimental work being encouraged in the late nineteenth century at the Théâtre Libre in Paris, for which Strindberg wrote several plays while hoping to form his own experimental theater in Stockholm. Though written in 1889, *The Stronger* did not premiere on stage until 1907.

Cultural Context: The explicit nature of Strindberg's subject matter (*The Stronger,* for example, is about a meeting between an actress and her husband's mistress) shocked and sometimes scandalized the sensibilities of his nineteenth-century contemporaries. As a result, Strindberg had difficulty getting his plays performed in commercial theaters. For this reason, he and other playwrights became involved with the independent theater movement. By producing plays outside the control of official censors, they were able to attract an audience for their work.

AUGUST STRINDBERG

The Stronger (1889)

Translated By Elizabeth Sprigge

<u>CHARACTERS</u>
Mrs. X., *actress, married*
Miss Y., *actress, unmarried*
A Waitress

SCENE

A corner of a ladies' café [in Stockholm in the eighteen eighties].° Two small wrought-iron tables, a red plush settee and a few chairs.

Miss Y. is sitting with a half-empty bottle of beer on the table before her, reading an illustrated weekly which from time to time she exchanges for another.

Mrs. X. enters, wearing a winter hat and coat and carrying a decorative Japanese basket.

MRS. X: Why, Millie, my dear, how are you? Sitting here all alone on Christmas Eve like some poor bachelor.

Miss Y. looks up from her magazine, nods, and continues to read.

MRS. X: You know it makes me feel really sad to see you. Alone. Alone in a café and on Christmas Eve of all times. It makes me feel as sad as when once in Paris I saw a wedding party at a restaurant. The bride was reading a comic paper and the bridegroom playing billiards with the witnesses. Ah me, I said to myself, with such a beginning how will it go, and how will it end? He was playing billiards on his wedding day! And she, you were going to say, was reading a comic paper on hers. But that's not quite the same.

A waitress brings a cup of chocolate to Mrs. X. and goes out.

MRS. X: Do you know, Amelia, I really believe now you would have done better to stick to him. Don't forget I was the first who told you to forgive him. Do you remember? Then you would be married now and have a home. Think how happy you were that Christmas when you stayed with your finance's people in the country. How warmly you spoke of domestic happiness! You really quite longed to be out of the theatre. Yes, Amelia dear, home is best — next best to the stage, and as for children — but you couldn't know anything about that.

Miss Y.'s expression is disdainful. Mrs. X. sips a few spoonfuls of chocolate, then opens her basket and displays some Christmas presents.

MRS. X: Now you must see what I have bought for my little chicks. *(Takes out a doll.)* Look at this. That's for Lisa. Do you see how she can roll her eyes

---

[*In Stockholm in the eighteen eighties*] Brackets indicate translator's addition to scene.

and turn her head. Isn't she lovely? And here's a toy pistol for Maja.°
(*She loads the pistol and shoots it at Miss Y. who appears frightened.*)

MRS. X: Were you scared? Did you think I was going to shoot you? Really, I   5
didn't think you'd believe that of me. Now if *you* were to shoot *me* it
wouldn't be so surprising, for after all I did get in your way, and I know you
never forget it — although I was entirely innocent. You still think I intrigued
to get you out of the Grand Theatre, but I didn't. I didn't, however much
you think I did. Well, it's no good talking, you will believe it was me . . .
(*Takes out a pair of embroidered slippers.*) And these are for my old man, with
tulips on them that I embroidered myself. As a matter of fact I hate tulips,
but he has to have tulips on everything.

Miss Y. *looks up, irony and curiosity in her face.*

MRS. X: (*putting one hand in each slipper*) Look what small feet Bob has, hasn't
he? And you ought to see the charming way he walks — you've never seen
him in slippers, have you?

Miss Y. *laughs.*

MRS. X: Look, I'll show you. (*She makes the slippers walk across the table, and
Miss Y. laughs again.*)

MRS. X: But when he gets angry, look, he stamps his foot like this. "Those
damn girls who can never learn how to make coffee! Blast! That silly idiot
hasn't trimmed the lamp properly!" Then there's a draught under the door
and his feet get cold. "Hell, it's freezing, and the damn fools can't even keep
the stove going!" (*She rubs the sole of one slipper against the instep of the other.
Miss Y roars with laughter.*)

MRS. X: And then he comes home and has to hunt for his slippers, which
Mary has pushed under the bureau . . . Well, perhaps it's not right to make
fun of one's husband like this. He's sweet anyhow, and a good, dear
husband. You ought to have had a husband like him, Amelia. What are you
laughing at? What is it? Eh? And, you see, I know he is faithful to me. Yes, I
know it. He told me himself — what *are* you giggling at?— that while I was
on tour in Norway that horrible Frederica came and tried to seduce him.
Can you imagine anything more abominable? (*Pause.*) I'd have scratched
her eyes out if she had come around while I was at home. (*Pause.*) I'm glad
Bob told me about it himself, so I didn't just hear it from gossip. (*Pause.*)
And, as a matter of fact, Frederica wasn't the only one. I can't think why,
but all the women in the Company° seem to be crazy about my husband.
They must think his position gives him some say in who is engaged at the
Theatre. Perhaps you have run after him yourself? I don't trust you very far,
but I know he has never been attracted by you, and you always seemed to
have some sort of grudge against him, or so I felt. (*Pause. They look at one
another guardedly.*)

Maja: Pronounced "Maya."

in the Company: Translator's addition.

10   **Mrs. X:** Do come and spend Christmas Eve with us tonight, Amelia — just to show that you're not offended with us, or anyhow not with me. I don't know why, but it seems specially unpleasant not to be friends with you. Perhaps it's because I did get in your way that time . . . (*slowly*) or — I don't know — really, I don't know at all why it is.

Pause. Miss Y. gazes curiously at Mrs. X.

   Mrs. X: (*thoughtfully*) It was so strange when we were getting to know one another. Do you know, when we first met, I was frightened of you, so frightened I didn't dare let you out of my sight. I arranged all my goings and comings to be near you. I dared not be your enemy, so I became your friend. But when you came to our home, I always had an uneasy feeling, because I saw my husband didn't like you, and that irritated me — like when a dress doesn't fit. I did all I could to make him be nice to you, but it was no good — until you went and got engaged. Then you became such tremendous friends that at first it looked as if you only dared show your real feelings then — when you were safe. And then, let me see, how was it after that? I wasn't jealous — that's queer. And I remember at the christening, when you were the godmother, I told him to kiss you. He did, and you were so upset . . . As a matter of fact I didn't notice that then . . . I didn't think about it afterwards either . . . I've never thought about it — until *now!* (*Rises abruptly.*) Why don't you say something? You haven't said a word all this time. You've just let me go on talking. You have sat there with your eyes drawing all these thoughts out of me — they were there in me like silk in a cocoon — thoughts . . . Mistaken thoughts? Let me think. Why did you break off your engagement? Why did you never come to our house after that? Why don't you want to come to us tonight?

Miss Y. makes a motion, as if about to speak.

   Mrs. X: No. You don't need to say anything, for now I see it all. That was why — and why — and why. Yes. Yes, that's why it was. Yes, yes, all the pieces fit together now. That's it. I won't sit at the same table as you. (*Moves her things to the other table.*) That's why I have to embroider tulips, which I loathe, on his slippers — because you liked tulips. (*Throws the slippers on the floor.*) That's why we have to spend the summer on the lake — because you couldn't bear the seaside. That's why my son had to be called Eskil — because it was your father's name. That's why I had to wear your colours, read your books, eat the dishes you liked, drink your drinks — your chocolate, for instance. That's why — oh my God, it's terrible to think of, terrible! Everything, everything came to me from you — even your passions. Your soul bored into mine like a worm into an apple, and ate and ate and burrowed and burrowed, till nothing was left but the skin and a little black mould. I wanted to fly from you, but I couldn't. You were there like a snake, your black eyes fascinating me. When I spread my wings, they only dragged me down. I lay in the water with my feet tied together, and the harder I worked my arms, the deeper I sank — down, down, till I reached the bot-

tom, where you lay in waiting like a giant crab to catch me in your claws —
and now here I am. Oh how I hate you! I hate you, I hate you! And you just
go on sitting there, silent, calm, indifferent, not caring whether the moon
is new or full, if it's Christmas or New Year, if other people are happy or
unhappy. You don't know how to hate or to love. You just sit there without
moving — like a cat° at a mouse-hole. You can't drag your prey out, you
can't chase it, but you can out-stay it. Here you sit in your corner — you
know they call it the rat-trap after you — reading the papers to see if
anyone's ruined or wretched or been thrown out of the Company. Here you
sit sizing up your victims and weighing your chances — like a pilot his
shipwrecks for the salvage. (*Pause.*) Poor Amelia! Do you know, I couldn't be
more sorry for you. I know you are miserable, miserable like some wounded
creature, and vicious because you are wounded. I can't be angry with you. I
should like to be, but after all you are the small one — and as for your affair
with Bob, that doesn't worry me in the least. Why should it matter to me?
And if you, or somebody else taught me to drink chocolate, what's the
difference? (*Drinks a spoonful. Smugly.*) Chocolate is very wholesome
anyhow. And if I learnt from you how to dress, *tant mieux!* — that only gave
me a stronger hold over my husband, and you have lost what I gained. Yes,
to judge from various signs, I think you have now lost him. Of course, you
meant me to walk out, as you once did, and which you're now regretting.
But I won't do that, you may be sure. One shouldn't be narrow-minded, you
know. And why should nobody else want what I have? (*Pause.*) Perhaps, my
dear, taking everything into consideration, at this moment it is I who am the
stronger. You never got anything from me, you just gave away — from yourself. And now, like the thief in the night, when you woke up I had what you
had lost. Why was it then that everything you touched became worthless
and sterile? You couldn't keep a man's love — for all your tulips and your passions — but I could. You couldn't learn the art of living from your books —
but I learnt it. You bore no little Eskil, although that was your father's name.
(*Pause.*) And why is it you are silent — everywhere, always silent? Yes, I used
to think this was strength, but perhaps it was because you hadn't anything to
say, because you couldn't think of anything. (*Rises and picks up the slippers.*)
Now I am going home, taking the tulips with me — *your* tulips. You couldn't
learn from others, you couldn't bend, and so you broke like a dry stick. I did
not. Thank you, Amelia, for all your good lessons. Thank you for teaching
my husband how to love. Now I am going home — to love him.

Exit.

◇ ◇ ◇

Like *The Stronger*, Jane Martin's *Beauty* is a two-character play that contrasts
the experiences and desires of two women. Here, however, conventions of popular

---

cat: In Swedish, "stork."

culture and fairy tales are used to create a humorous play that nevertheless explores a serious contemporary theme: society's ideas about female beauty.

JANE MARTIN, a prize-winning playwright, has never made a public appearance or spoken about any of her works. In addition, she has never given an interview, and no picture of her has ever been published. As one critic wryly observed, Martin is "America's best known, unknown playwright." Martin first came to the attention of American theatrical audiences with her collection of monologues, *Talking With . . .* , a work that premiered at the 1981 Humana Festival of New American Plays at the Actors' Theatre of Louisville, Kentucky. Her other works include *Vital Signs* and *What Mama Don't Know;* her full-length plays include *Cementville;* the Pulitzer Prize–nominated *Keely and Du* (winner of the 1994 American Theatre Critics Association New Play Award); *Criminal Hearts;* and *Middle Aged White Guys.* Martin's name is widely believed to be a pseudonym. Jon Jory, artistic director of the Actors' Theatre of Louisville — and director of the premieres of all of Martin's plays — is spokesperson for the playwright and, according to some people, the playwright behind the pen name. Jory has repeatedly denied this; in an interview published on July 13, 1994, in the *Seattle Weekly,* he said that Martin "feels she could not write plays if people knew who she was, regardless of her identity or gender." In Jory's opinion, "The point in the end is the plays themseleves . . . . But if Jane's anonymity is a P. T. Barnum publicity stunt, it's one of the longest circus acts going."

Cultural Context: The story of Aladdin's magic lamp — inhabited by its powerful, wish-fulfilling genie — comes from *The Book of the Thousand Nights and a Night,* often referred to as *The Arabian Nights.* These tales probably originated with Indian, Persian, and Chinese merchants traveling the Silk Route from northern China to the Middle East and Egypt. They were written down in Arabic around A.D. 850; the first European edition appeared in 1704. Many subsequent translations have appeared, notably Richard Francis Burton's published in 1885. The *Nights* have inspired artists and writers through the centuries, from Geoffrey Chaucer to the Brontë sisters and from Charles Dickens and Robert Louis Stevenson to Salman Rushdie. In recent times, the story of Aladdin's lamp has enjoyed a renewal of interest owing to Disney's 1992 film *Aladdin.*

JANE MARTIN

Beauty (2000)

CHARACTERS
Carla
Bethany

An apartment. Minimalist set. A young woman, Carla, on the phone.

CARLA: In love with me? You're in love with me? Could you describe yourself again? Uh-huh. Uh-huh. And you spoke to me? (*A knock at the door.*) Listen, I always hate to interrupt a marriage proposal, but . . . could you possibly hold that thought? (*Puts phone down and goes to door. Bethany, the same age as Carla and a friend, is there. She carries the sort of Mideastern lamp we know of from Aladdin.*)

BETHANY: Thank God you were home. I mean, you're not going to believe this!

CARLA: Somebody on the phone. (*Goes back to it.*)

BETHANY: I mean, I just had a beach urge, so I told them at work my uncle was dying . . .

CARLA: (*motions to Bethany for quiet*) And you were the one in the leather   5
jacket with the tattoo? What was the tattoo? (*Carla again asks Bethany, who is gesturing wildly that she should hang up, to cool it.*) Look, a screaming eagle from shoulder to shoulder, maybe. There were a lot of people in the bar.

BETHANY: (*gesturing and mouthing*) I have to get back to work.

CARLA: (*on phone*) See, the thing is, I'm probably not going to marry someone I can't remember . . . particularly when I don't drink. Sorry. Sorry. Sorry. (*She hangs up.*) Madness.

BETHANY: So I ran out to the beach . . .

CARLA: This was some guy I never met who apparently offered me a beer . . .

BETHANY: . . . low tide and this . . . (*The lamp.*) . . . was just sitting there, lying   10
there . . .

CARLA: . . . and he tracks me down . . .

BETHANY: . . . on the beach, and I lift this lid thing . . .

CARLA: . . . and seriously proposes marriage.

BETHANY: . . . and a genie comes out.

CARLA: I mean, that's twice in a . . . what?   15

BETHANY: A genie comes out of this thing.

CARLA: A genie?

BETHANY: I'm not kidding, the whole Disney kind of thing, swirling smoke, and then this twenty-foot-high, see-through guy in like an Arabian outfit.

CARLA: Very funny.

BETHANY: Yes, funny, but twenty feet high! I look up and down the beach, I'm   20
alone. I don't have my pepper spray or my hand alarm. You know me, when I'm petrified I joke. I say his voice is too high for Robin Williams, and he says he's a castrati. Naturally. Who else would I meet?

CARLA: What's a castrati?

BETHANY: You know . . .

The appropriate gesture.

CARLA: Bethany, dear one, I have three modeling calls. I am meeting Ralph Lauren!

BETHANY: Okay, good. Ralph Lauren. Look, I am not kidding!

CARLA: You're not kidding what?!   25

BETHANY: There is a genie in this thingamajig.

CARLA: Uh-huh. I'll be back around eight.

BETHANY: And he offered me *wishes!*

CARLA: Is this some elaborate practical joke because it's my birthday?

30 **BETHANY:** No, happy birthday, but I'm like crazed because I'm on this deserted
      beach with a twenty-foot-high, see-through genie, so like sarcastically . . .
      you know how I need a new car . . . I said fine, gimme 25,000 dollars . . .
    CARLA: On the beach with the genie?
    BETHANY: Yeah, right, exactly, and it rains down out of the sky.
    CARLA: Oh sure.
    BETHANY: *(pulling a wad out of her purse)* Count it, those are thousands. I lost
      one in the surf.

*Carla sees the top bill. Looks at Bethany, who nods encouragement. Carla thumbs
through them.*

35 **CARLA:** These look real.
    BETHANY: Yeah.
    CARLA: And they rained down out of the sky?
    BETHANY: Yeah.
    CARLA: You've been really strange lately, are you dealing?
40 **BETHANY:** Dealing what, I've even given up chocolate.
    CARLA: Let me see the genie.
    BETHANY: Wait, wait.
    CARLA: Bethany, I don't have time to screw around. Let me see the genie or let
      me go on my appointments.
    BETHANY: Wait! So I pick up the money . . . see, there's sand on the money . . .
      and I'm like nuts so I say, you know, "Okay, look, ummm, big guy, my uncle
      is in the hospital" . . . because as you know when I said to the people at
      work my uncle was dying, I was on one level telling the truth although it
      had nothing to do with the beach, but he was in Intensive Care after the
      accident, and that's on my mind, so I say, okay, Genie, heal my uncle . . .
      which is like impossible given he was hit by two trucks, and the genie says,
      "Yes, Master" . . . like they're supposed to say, and he goes into this like kind
      of whirlwind, kicking up sand and stuff, and I'm like, "Oh my God!" and
      the air clears, and he bows, you know, and says, "It is done, Master," and I
      say, "Okay, whatever-you-are, I'm calling on my cell phone," and I get it out
      and I get this doctor who is like dumbstruck who says my uncle came to,
      walked out of Intensive Care and left the hospital! I'm not kidding, Carla.
45 **CARLA:** On your mother's grave?
    BETHANY: On my mother's grave.

They look at each other.

    CARLA: Let me see the genie.
    BETHANY: No, no, look, that's the whole thing . . . I was just, like, reacting,
      you know, responding, and that's already two wishes . . . although I'm
      really pleased about my uncle, the $25,000 thing, I could have asked for
      $10 million, and there is only one wish left.
    CARLA: So ask for $10 million.
50 **BETHANY:** I don't think so. I don't think so. I mean, I gotta focus in here.
      Do you have a sparkling water?

CARLA: No. Bethany, I'm missing Ralph Lauren now. Very possibly my one chance to go from catalogue model to the very, very big time, so, if you are joking, stop joking.

BETHANY: Not joking. See, see, the thing is, I know what I want. In my guts. Yes. Underneath my entire bitch of a life is this unspoken, ferocious, all-consuming urge . . .

CARLA: (*trying to get her to move this along*) Ferocious, all-consuming urge . . .

BETHANY: I want to be like you.

CARLA: Me?   55

BETHANY: Yes.

CARLA: Half the time you don't even like me.

BETHANY: Jealous. The ogre of jealousy.

CARLA: You're the one with the $40,000 job straight out of school. You're the one who has published short stories. I'm the one hanging on by her fingernails in modeling. The one who has creeps calling her on the phone. The one who had to have a nose job.

BETHANY: I want to be beautiful.   60

CARLA: You are beautiful.

BETHANY: Carla, I'm not beautiful.

CARLA: You have charm. You have personality. You know perfectly well you're pretty.

BETHANY: "Pretty," see, that's it. Pretty is the minor leagues of beautiful. Pretty is what people discover about you after they know you. Beautiful is what knocks them out across the room. Pretty, you get called a couple of times a year; *beautiful* is twenty-four hours a day.

CARLA: Yeah? So?   65

BETHANY: So?! We're talking *beauty* here. Don't say "So?" Beauty is the real deal. You are the center of any moment of your life. People stare. Men flock. I've seen you get offered discounts on makeup for no reason. Parents treat beautiful children better. Studies show your income goes up. You can have sex anytime you want it. Men have to know me. That takes up to a year. I'm continually horny.

CARLA: Bethany, I don't even like sex. I can't have a conversation without men coming on to me. I have no privacy. I get hassled on the street. They start pressuring me from the beginning. Half the time, it never occurs to them to start with a conversation. Smart guys like you. You've had three long-term relationships, and you're only twenty-three. I haven't had one. The good guys, the smart guys are scared to death of me. I'm surrounded by male bimbos who think a preposition is when you go to school away from home. I have no woman friends except you. I don't even want to talk about this!

BETHANY: I knew you'd say something like this. See, you're "in the club" so you can say this. It's the way beauty functions as an elite. You're trying to keep it all for yourself.

CARLA: I'm trying to tell you it's no picnic.

BETHANY: But it's what everybody wants. It's the nasty secret at large in the   70
world. It's the unspoken tidal desire in every room and on every street. It's

the unspoken, the soundless whisper . . . millions upon millions of people longing hopelessly and forever to stop being whatever they are and be beautiful, but the difference between those ardent multitudes and me is that I have a goddamn genie and one more wish!

CARLA: Well, it's not what I want. This is me, Carla. I have never read a whole book. Page six, I can't remember page four. The last thing I read was *The Complete Idiot's Guide to WordPerfect.* I leave dinner parties right after the dessert because I'm out of conversation. You know the dumb blond joke about the application where it says, "Sign here," she put Sagittarius? I've done that. Only beautiful guys approach me, and that's because they want to borrow my eye shadow. I barely exist outside a mirror! You don't want to *be me.*

BETHANY: None of you tell the truth. That's why you have no friends. We can all see you're just trying to make us feel better because we aren't in your league. This only proves to me it should be my third wish. Money can only buy things. Beauty makes you the center of the universe.

Bethany picks up the lamp.

CARLA: Don't do it. Bethany, don't wish it! I am telling you you'll regret it.

Bethany lifts the lid. There is a tremendous crash, and the lights go out. Then they flicker and come back up, revealing Bethany and Carla on the floor where they have been thrown by the explosion. We don't realize it at first, but they have exchanged places.

CARLA/BETHANY: Oh God.

75   BETHANY/CARLA: Oh God.

CARLA/BETHANY: Am I bleeding? Am I dying?

BETHANY/CARLA: I'm so dizzy. You're not bleeding.

CARLA/BETHANY: Neither are you.

BETHANY/CARLA: I feel so weird.

80   CARLA/BETHANY: Me too. I feel . . . *(Looking at her hands.)* Oh, my God, I'm wearing your jewelry. I'm wearing your nail polish.

BETHANY/CARLA: I know I'm over here, but I can see myself over there.

CARLA/BETHANY: I'm wearing your dress. I have your legs!!

BETHANY/CARLA: These aren't my shoes. I can't meet Ralph Lauren wearing these shoes!

CARLA/BETHANY: I wanted to be beautiful, but I didn't want to be you.

85   BETHANY/CARLA: Thanks a lot!!

CARLA/BETHANY: I've got to go. I want to pick someone out and get laid.

BETHANY/CARLA: You can't just walk out of here in my body!

CARLA/BETHANY: Wait a minute. Wait a minute. What's eleven eighteenths of 1,726?

BETHANY/CARLA: Why?

90   CARLA/BETHANY: I'm a public accountant. I want to know if you have my brain.

BETHANY/CARLA: One hundred thirty-two and a half.

CARLA/BETHANY: You have my brain.

BETHANY/CARLA: What shade of Rubenstein lipstick does Cindy Crawford wear with teal blue?

CARLA/BETHANY: Raging Storm.

BETHANY/CARLA: You have my brain. You poor bastard.   95

CARLA/BETHANY: I don't care. Don't you see?

BETHANY/CARLA: See what?

CARLA/BETHANY: We both have the one thing, the one and only thing everybody wants.

BETHANY/CARLA: What is that?

CARLA/BETHANY: It's better than beauty for me; it's better than brains   100
for you.

BETHANY/CARLA: What? What?!

CARLA/BETHANY: Different problems.

Blackout.

END OF PLAY

CHAPTER 27

READING AND WRITING ABOUT DRAMA

READING DRAMA

When you read a play, you will notice features it shares with works of fiction — for instance, the use of language and symbols, the interaction among characters, and the development of a theme or themes. In addition, you will notice features that distinguish it from fiction — for example, the presence of stage directions and the division into acts and scenes.

The following guidelines, designed to help you explore works of dramatic literature, focus on issues that are examined in depth in chapters to come.

- Trace the play's **plot.** What conflicts are present? Where does the rising action reach a climax? Where does the falling action begin? What techniques move the action along? (See Chapter 28.)
- Analyze the play's **characters.** Who are the central characters? What are their most distinctive traits? How do you learn about their personalities, backgrounds, appearances, and strengths and weaknesses? (See Chapter 29.)
- Examine the play's **language.** How does **dialogue** reveal characters' emotions, conflicts, opinions, and motivation? (See Chapter 29.)
- Does the play include **soliloquies** or **asides?** What do they contribute to your knowledge of the play's characters and events? (See Chapter 29.)
- How do the characters interact with one another? Do the characters change and grow in response to the play's events, or do they remain essentially unchanged? (See Chapter 29.)
- Read the play's **stage directions.** What do you learn from the descriptions of the characters, including their dress, gestures, and facial expressions? (See Chapter 29.) What information do you gain from studying the playwright's descriptions of the play's setting? Do the stage directions include information about lighting, props, music, or sound effects? (See Chapter 30.)
- Consider the play's **staging.** Where and when does the action take place? What techniques are used to convey a sense of time and place to the audience? (See Chapter 30.)

- Try to interpret the play's **themes.** What main idea does the play communicate? What additional themes are explored? (See Chapter 31.)
- Identify any symbolic elements in the play. How do such **symbols** help you to understand the play's themes? (See Chapter 31.)

Active Reading

As you read a play about which you plan to write, you follow the same process that guides you when you read any work of literature. You read actively, marking the text as you proceed. Then you go on to select a topic and generate ideas about it, decide on a thesis, prepare an outline, and write and revise several drafts.

Kimberly Allison, a student in an introduction to literature course, was given the following assignment:

> Without consulting any outside sources, write a three- to five-page essay about any play in our literature anthology. You may focus on action, character, staging, or theme, or you may consider more than one of these elements.

Previewing

Kim decided to write her paper on Susan Glaspell's play *Trifles,* which begins on page 983. She began by previewing *Trifles,* noting its brief length, its one-act structure, its list of characters, and its setting in John Wright's farmhouse. Kim noticed immediately that John Wright does not appear in the play, and his absence aroused her curiosity.

Highlighting and Annotating

As Kim read *Trifles,* she highlighted the dialogue and stage directions she thought she might want to examine closely, noted possible links among ideas, identified patterns of action and language, and jotted down questions and observations. She found herself especially interested in the female and male characters' different reactions to the objects discovered in the house and in the interaction between women and men.

The following highlighted and annotated passage illustrates some of her responses to the play:

The men laugh; the women looked abashed.   Why do the men and women react so differently?

COUNTY ATTORNEY: *(rubbing his hands over the stove)* Frank's fire didn't

do much up there, did it? Well, let's go out to the barn and get that

cleared up.

The men go outside.

Why do the men go and the women stay?

MRS. HALE: *(resentfully)* I don't know as there's anything

so strange, our takin' up our time with little things

while we're waiting for them to get the evidence

(She sits down at the big table smoothing out a block with

decision.) I don't see as it's anything to laugh about.

MRS. PETERS : *(apologetically)* Of course they've got

awful important things on their minds.

Like what?
Why does she make excuses for the men?

Pulls up a chair and joins Mrs. Hale at the table.

Kim's highlighting and annotations — most of which, like those above, focused on the play's characters — suggested some interesting possibilities for her essay.

WRITING ABOUT DRAMA
Planning an Essay

After Kim decided to write about the play's characters, she knew she had to narrow her focus. Her notes suggested that gender roles in general, and the role of the women in particular, would make an interesting topic, so she decided to explore this idea further.

Choosing a Topic

To help her decide on a direction for her paper, Kim wrote the following entry in her journal:

What is the role of the women in this play? Although the women have gone with their husbands to pick up some items for Mrs. Wright, they seem to be primarily interested in why Mrs. Wright would leave her house in such disarray. They find several objects that suggest that Mrs. Wright was lonely and that she was dominated by her husband. But these women are left on their own and seem to band together. Their guilt about not visiting Mrs. Wright also seems to connect them with the murder suspect. Mrs. Hale even begins to empathize with Mrs. Wright's loss of her bird. The women find the

details, or "trifles," of Mrs. Wright's life interesting
and learn from them the facts surrounding the murder while
the men wander aimlessly around the house and yard. The
real clue to the murder appears to be Mrs. Wright's
untended house, but the men do not seem to understand the
implications of the disorder. The women appear to have an
understanding that comes from their own experiences as
women, which the men are unable to tap into.

At this point, Kim concluded that the role of the women in *Trifles* would be the
best focus for her paper. As she went on to gather ideas to write about, she also
planned to examine the ways in which the women interacted with the men.

Finding Something to Say: Brainstorming

Kim's next step was to generate the specific ideas she would discuss in her paper.
She reread the play and her annotations, brainstorming about her topic—in particular, her ideas about men and women as she proceeded.

Sheriff Peters says there is nothing in the kitchen but
"kitchen stuff"; he thinks Mrs. Wright is a typical woman,
worried about her preserves while imprisoned for murder.
    Mrs. Hale feels animosity toward the men for laughing
about the women's interest in the quilt; she regrets not
visiting Mrs. Wright; she feels sorry for Mrs. Wright
because she had no children.
    Mr. Henderson eventually sides with the other two men,
claiming that women's worries are trifles.
    Mr. Hale mentions Mr. Wright's cheapness; he seems to
know Mr. Wright best.
    Men think women are shallow and worry only about
trifles.
    Women empathize with Mrs. Wright because they under-
stand her treatment.
    Mrs. Peters (wife of Sheriff) empathizes with
Mrs. Wright's loss of bird; notes that keeping house was
Mrs. Wright's duty.
    Mrs. Wright restricted by husband; never leaves the
house; loses control after her bird is killed.
    John Wright strips wife of her identity; controls her
every move; stops her from singing, which she enjoys; kills
canary.

When she reread her notes, the first thing Kim noticed was that the women and
men have two entirely different attitudes about women's lives and concerns: the

men think their work is much more important than that of the women, which they see as trivial; the women realize they are not much different from Mrs. Wright. Now Kim saw that in order to discuss the role of women in the play, she must first define that role in relation to the role of the men. To do so, she needed to find a logical arrangement for her ideas that would enable her to clarify the differences between the men's role and the women's.

Seeing Connections: Listing

At this point, Kim decided that listing ideas under the heads *Men* and *Women* could help her clarify the differences between men's and women's roles:

Men	Women
work outside the home	make preserves
make decisions about financial expenditures	clean house
	make quilts
think women should do just housework	raise children
	go to ladies' clubs for socializing
create and enforce law	
dictate wives' actions	must follow laws that men create
have separate identities and power	are subordinate to their husbands
actions are accepted by society	must act defiantly to break boundaries set by social role

Listing enabled Kim to confirm her idea that the men's and the women's roles are portrayed very differently in *Trifles*. In fact, both men and women seem to agree that they have different responsibilities, and both seem to understand and accept that power is unevenly distributed between the two genders.

Deciding on a Thesis

Kim's listing clarified her understanding of the limited role women have in the society portrayed in *Trifles*. This, in turn, enabled her to develop the following tentative thesis statement, which she could use to help guide her essay's first draft:

The central focus of Trifles is not on finding out who killed Mr. Wright, but on defining the limited, even sub-servient, role of women like Mrs. Wright.

Preparing an Outline

Guided by her thesis statement and the information she had collected in her notes, Kim made a scratch outline, arranging her supporting details in a logical order under appropriate headings:

<u>Mrs. Hale and Mrs. Peters had limited roles</u>
 —Subservient to husbands
 —Do domestic chores
 —Confined to kitchen
 —Identify with Minnie Wright's loneliness
<u>Minnie Wright had limited role</u>
 —Did what husband told her to do
 —Had no link with outside world
 —Couldn't sing
 —Had no friends
 —Had no identity

Drafting an Essay

Guided by her scratch outline, Kim wrote the following first draft of her essay. Before she began, she reviewed her highlighting to look for details that would illustrate and support her generalizations about the play.

first draft

The Women's Role in Trifles

Susan Glaspell's <u>Trifles</u> seems to focus on the murder of John Wright. Mr. Wright had little concern for his wife's opinions. Mr. Hale suggested that Minnie Wright was powerless against her husband, and Sheriff Henry Peters questioned whether Minnie was allowed to quilt her log cabin pattern. Perhaps, because Mr. Wright did not spend his money freely, he would have made Minnie knot the quilt because it cost less. Minnie was controlled by her husband. He forced her to perform repetitive domestic chores. The central focus of <u>Trifles</u> is not on finding out who killed Mr. Wright but on defining the limited, even subservient role of women like Mrs. Wright.

Mrs. Peters and Mrs. Hale were similar to Minnie. Mrs. Peters and Mrs. Hale also performed domestic chores and had to do what their husbands wanted them to do, and they too were confined to Mrs. Wright's kitchen. The kitchen was the focal point of the play. Mrs. Peters and Mrs. Hale remained confined to the kitchen while their husbands exercised their freedom to enter and exit the house at will. This mirrored Minnie's life because she stayed home while her husband went to work and into town. The two women discussed Minnie's isolation. Beginning to identify with Minnie's loneliness, Mrs. Peters and Mrs. Hale recognized that while they were busy in their own homes, they had, in fact, participated in isolating and confining Minnie.

Eventually, the women found that the kitchen held the clues to Mrs. Wright's loneliness and to the details of the murder. The two women discovered that Minnie's only connection to the outside world was her bird. Minnie too was a caged bird because she was kept from singing and communicating with others by her husband. And piecing together the evidence, the women came to believe that John Wright had broken the bird's neck.

At the same time, Mrs. Peters and Mrs. Hale discovered the connection between the dead canary and Minnie's situation, and they began to recognize that they had to band together in order to exert their strength against the men. They realized that Minnie's independence and identity were crushed by her husband and that their own husbands believed women's lives were trivial and unimportant. The revelation that Mrs. Peters and Mrs. Hale experienced urged them to commit an act as rebellious as the one that got Minnie in trouble: they concealed their discovery from their husbands and from the law.

Because Mrs. Hale and Mrs. Peters empathized with Minnie's condition, they suppressed the evidence they found and endured the men's insults rather than confronting their husbands. And through this, the women attempted to break through the boundaries of their social roles, just as Minnie had done before them.

First Draft: Commentary

When Kim reread her first draft, she realized that she had gone beyond the scope of her tentative thesis statement and scratch outline. She had considered not just the women's subservient role but also the actions they take to break free of this role. She decided to revise her thesis statement to reflect this new emphasis — and then to expand her paper to develop this aspect of her thesis more fully.

Kim's peer review group made the general suggestion that she develop her paper further. In addition, they thought that her paper's sentences seemed choppy — many needed to be linked with transitional words and phrases — and that her introduction was unfocused.

When Kim met with her instructor to discuss her revision plans, he encouraged her to expand her paper's focus (and thesis statement if necessary) and to use quotations and specific examples to support her ideas. He also reminded her to use the present tense in her paper — not "Mrs. Peters and Mrs. Hale *were* similar to Minnie" but "Mrs. Peters and Mrs. Hale *are* similar to Minnie." (Only events that occurred *before* the time in which the play takes place — for example, the murder itself or Minnie's girlhood experiences — should be described in past tense.)

After meeting with her instructor, Kim made a new scratch outline to guide her as she continued to revise:

Subservient role of women
—Minnie's husband didn't respect her opinion
—Didn't let her sing
—Could perform only domestic chores
Confinement of women in home
—Mrs. Hale and Mrs. Peters are confined to kitchen
—Minnie didn't belong to Ladies Aid
—Minnie was lonely at home because she had no children
—Minnie was a caged bird
Women's defiance
—Mrs. Hale and Mrs. Peters solve "mystery"
—Realize they must band together
—Take action
—Defy men's law

Revising and Editing an Essay

Before she wrote her next draft, Kim reviewed the suggestions she had recorded in meetings with classmates and with her instructor. Then, she incorporated this material, along with her own new ideas, into her second draft, which appears on pages 967–970.

second draft

Confinement and Rebellion in <u>Trifles</u>

Susan Glaspell's play <u>Trifles</u> involves the solving of a murder. Two women, Mrs. Peters and Mrs. Hale, discover that Mrs. Wright, who remains in jail throughout the play, has indeed murdered her husband. Interestingly, the women make this discovery through the examination of evidence in Mrs. Wright's kitchen, which their husbands, Sheriff Henry Peters and farmer Lewis Hale, along with the county attorney, Mr. Henderson, dismiss as women's "trifles." The focus of <u>Trifles</u>, however, is not on the murder of John Wright but on the subservient role of women, the confinement of the wife in the home, and the desperate measures women had to take to achieve autonomy.

The role of Minnie Foster (Mrs. Wright) becomes evident in the first few minutes of the play, when Mr. Hale declares, "I didn't know as what his wife wanted made much difference to John—"(984). Minnie's powerlessness is further revealed when the women discuss how Mr. Wright forced Minnie to give up the thing she loved—singing. Both of these observations suggest that Minnie's every action was controlled and stifled by her husband. She was not allowed to make decisions or be an individual; instead, she was permitted to perform only domestic chores.

Doing domestic chores was the only part of life that Minnie was allowed to exert some power over, a condition that is shared by Mrs. Peters and

Mrs. Hale, especially because these two women can be assumed to work only in the home and because their behavior as wives is also determined by their husbands.

The men are free to walk throughout the house and outside of it while the women are, not surprisingly, confined to the kitchen, just as Minnie had been confined to the house. Early in the play, Mrs. Hale refers to Minnie's isolation, saying she "kept so much to herself. She didn't even belong to the Ladies Aid" (988). Mrs. Hale goes on to mention Minnie's lack of nice clothing, which further suggests her confinement in the home: if she never left her home, she wouldn't need to look nice, and why would she want to leave home if she had no nice clothes? Minnie's isolation is further revealed when Mrs. Hale contemplates Minnie's lack of children: "Not having children makes less work—but it makes a quiet house, and Wright out to work all day, and no company when he did come in" (991). As a result, Minnie's only connection to the outside world was her bird, which becomes the symbol of Minnie's confinement because Minnie herself was a caged bird. In a sense, Mr. Wright strangled her, as he did the bird, by preventing her from talking to other people in the community. Unlike the men, Mrs. Peters and Mrs. Hale realize the connection between the dead canary and Minnie's situation as "<u>Their eyes meet</u>" and they share "<u>A look of growing comprehension, of horror</u>" (992).

The comprehension that Mrs. Peters and Mrs. Hale experience urges them to rebel by concealing their discovery from their husbands and from the law. Mrs. Peters does concede that "the law is the law" (989), but she also understands that because Mr. Wright treated his wife badly, treating her as a domestic slave and isolating her from the world, Minnie was justified in killing him. And even if Minnie had been able to communicate the abuse she suffered, the law would not take the abuse into account because the men on the jury would not be sympathetic to a woman's complaints about how her husband treated her.

The dialogue in <u>Trifles</u> reveals a huge difference in how women and men view their experiences. From the opening of the play, the gulf between the men and women emerges, and as the play progresses, the polarization of the male and female characters becomes clearer. Once the men leave the kitchen to find what they consider to be significant criminal evidence, the men and women are divided physically as well as emotionally. The men create their own community, as do the women, leading them to separate according to gender. With the women alone in the kitchen, the focus of the dialogue is on the female experience. The women discuss the preserves, the quilt, and the disarray in the kitchen, emphasizing that Mrs. Wright would not have left her home in disorder unless she had been distracted by some more pressing situation.

Women accept servitude voluntarily, making work in the home their main interest, and this role keeps them subservient. But the men further trivialize Mrs. Wright's and other women's significance when they criticize her role as homemaker. The county attorney condemns Minnie, sarcastically observing, "I shouldn't say she had the homemaking instinct" (987). Minnie attempted to keep her home clean and do her chores, but the cold exploded her preserves, and her husband dirtied the towels. What caused Minnie to neglect her chores is something of great importance: her desire for independence and freedom from the servitude she once accepted voluntarily.

What makes this play most interesting is that Mrs. Hale and Mrs. Peters come to realize that they too have volunteered to be subservient to their husbands. They even accept the fact that their husbands will trivialize their discovery about the murder, as the men earlier trivialized their discussions of Minnie's daily tasks. Therefore, the women band together and conceal the information, breaking through their subservient roles as wives. And in the end, they find their own independence and significance in society.

Second Draft: Commentary

When she read her second draft, Kim had mixed feelings. She thought it was an improvement over her first draft, primarily because she had expanded the focus of her discussion and added specific details and quotations to support her points. She also believed her essay was now clearer, with a more specific thesis statement and smoother transitions.

Even though she knew what she wanted to say, however, Kim thought her logic was somewhat difficult to follow, and she thought clearer topic sentences might correct this problem by guiding readers more smoothly through her essay. She also thought her organization, which did not follow her revised scratch outline, was somewhat confusing. (For example, she discussed the women's subservient role in two different parts of her essay — paragraphs 2 and 7.) In addition, Kim thought her third paragraph could be developed further, and she still believed her essay needed additional supporting details and quotations throughout. After rereading her notes, she wrote her final draft, which appears on the following pages.

Allison 1

Kimberly Allison

English 1013

Professor Johnson

3 Mar. 2003

Desperate Measures: Acts of Defiance in <u>Trifles</u>

    Susan Glaspell wrote her best-known play,
<u>Trifles</u>, in 1916, at a time when married women were
beginning to challenge their socially defined roles,
realizing that their identities as wives kept them in
a subordinate position in society. Because women were
demanding more autonomy, traditional institutions
such as marriage, which confined women to the home
and made them mere extensions of their husbands, were
beginning to be reexamined.

    Evidently touched by these concerns, Glaspell
chose as her play's protagonist a married woman, Minnie Foster (Mrs. Wright), who challenged society's
expectations in a very extreme way: by murdering her
husband. Minnie's defiant act has occurred before the
action begins, and during the play, two women, Mrs.
Peters and Mrs. Hale, who accompany their husbands on
an investigation of the murder scene, piece together
the details of the situation surrounding the murder.
As the events unfold, however, it becomes clear that
the focus of <u>Trifles</u> is not on who killed John Wright
but on the themes of the subordinate role of women,
the confinement of the wife in the home, and the
experiences all women share. With these themes,
Glaspell shows her audience the desperate measures
women had to take to achieve autonomy.

Allison 2

The subordinate role of women, particularly Minnie's role in her marriage, becomes evident in the first few minutes of the play, when Mr. Hale observes that the victim, John Wright, had little concern for his wife's opinions: "I didn't know as what his wife wanted made much difference to John—" (984). Here Mr. Hale suggests that Minnie was powerless against the wishes of her husband. Indeed, as these characters imply, Minnie's every act and thought were controlled by her husband, who tried to break her spirit by forcing her to perform repetitive domestic chores alone in the home. Minnie's only source of power in the household was her kitchen work, a situation that Mrs. Peters and Mrs. Hale understand because each of these women's behavior is also determined by her husband. Therefore, when Sheriff Peters makes fun of Minnie's concern about her preserves, saying, "Well, can you beat the women! Held for murder and worryin' about her preserves" (986), he is, in a sense, criticizing all three of the women for worrying about domestic matters rather than about the murder that has been committed. Indeed, the sheriff's comment suggests that he assumes women's lives are trivial, an assumption that influences the thoughts and speech of all three men.

Mrs. Peters and Mrs. Hale are similar to Minnie in another way as well: throughout the play, they are confined to the kitchen of the Wrights' house. As a result, the kitchen becomes the focal point of the play—and, ironically, the women find that the kitchen

[margin note:] Topic sentence identifies first point, paper will discuss: women's subordinate role.

[margin note:] Topic sentence introduces second point paper will discuss: women's confinement.

Allison 3

holds the clues to Mrs. Wright's loneliness and to
the details of the murder. Mrs. Peters and Mrs. Hale
remain confined to the kitchen while their husbands
enter and exit the house at will. This scenario
mirrors Minnie's daily life, as she remained in the
home while her husband went to work and into town.
The two women discuss Minnie's isolation: "Not having
children makes less work—but it makes a quiet house,
and Wright out to work all day, and no company when
he did come in" (991). Beginning to identify with
Minnie's loneliness, Mrs. Peters and Mrs. Hale recognize that, busy in their own homes, they have, in
fact, participated in isolating and confining Minnie.
Mrs. Hale declares, "Oh, I <u>wish</u> I'd come over here
once in a while! That was a crime! That was a crime!
Who's going to punish that? . . . I might have known
she needed help!" (993).

Transitional
paragraph
discusses
women's
observations
and conclusions.

Soon the two women discover that Minnie's only
connection to the outside world was her bird, the
symbol of her confinement; Minnie herself was a caged
bird who was kept from singing and communicating with
others because of her husband. And piecing together
the evidence—the disorderly kitchen, the misstitched
quilt pieces, and the dead canary—the women come to
believe that John Wright broke the bird's neck just
as he had broken Minnie's spirit. At this point,
Mrs. Peters and Mrs. Hale figure out the connection
between the dead canary and Minnie's situation. The
stage directions describe the moment when the women
become aware of the truth behind the murder: "<u>Their</u>

Allison 4

eyes meet," and the women share "A look of growing
comprehension, of horror" (992).

Through their observations and discussions in
Mrs. Wright's kitchen, Mrs. Hale and Mrs. Peters come
to understand the commonality of women's experiences.
Mrs. Hale speaks for both of them when she says, "I
know how things can be—for women. . . . We all go
through the same things—it's all just a different
kind of the same thing" (993). And once the two women
realize the experiences they share, they begin to
recognize that they must join together in order to
challenge a male-oriented society; although their experiences may seem trivial to the men, the "trifles"
of their lives are significant to them. They realize
that Minnie's independence and identity were crushed
by her husband and that their own husbands have asserted that women's lives are trivial and unimportant
as well. This realization leads them to commit an act
as defiant as the one that got Minnie into trouble:
they conceal their discovery from their husbands and
from the law.

Significantly, Mrs. Peters does acknowledge that
"the law is the law" (989), yet she still understands that because Mr. Wright treated his wife
badly, Minnie is justified in killing him. They also
realize, however, that for men the law is black and
white and that an all-male jury will not take into
account the extenuating circumstances that prompted
Minnie to kill her husband. And even if Minnie were
allowed to communicate to the all-male court the psy-

> Topic sentence
> introduces
> third point paper
> will discuss:
> commonality
> of women's
> experiences.

Allison 5

chological abuse she has suffered, the law would undoubtedly view her experience as trivial because a
woman who complained about how her husband treated
her would be seen as ungrateful.

Nevertheless, because Mrs. Hale and Mrs. Peters
empathize with Minnie's condition, they suppress the
evidence they find, enduring their husbands' conde-
scension rather than standing up to them. And through
this desperate action, the women break through the
boundaries of their social role, just as Minnie has
done. Although Minnie is imprisoned for her crime,
she has freed herself; and although Mrs. Peters and
Mrs. Hale conceal their knowledge, fearing the men
will laugh at them, these women are really challenging society and freeing themselves as well.

Conclusion places play in historical context.

In Trifles, Susan Glaspell addresses many of the
problems shared by early-twentieth-century women,
including their subordinate status and their
confinement in the home. In order to emphasize the
pervasiveness of these problems and the desperate
measures women had to take to break out of restrictive social roles, Glaspell does more than focus on
the plight of a woman who has ended her isolation and
loneliness by committing a heinous crime against society. By presenting male and female characters who
demonstrate the vast differences between male and female experience, she illustrates how men define the
roles of women and how women must challenge these
roles in search of their own significance in society
and their eventual independence.

Final Draft: Commentary

Kim made many changes in her final draft. Although her focus is much the same as it was in her previous draft, she expanded her paper considerably. Most important, she added a discussion of the commonality of women's experience in paragraph 6 and elsewhere, and this material helps to explain what motivates Mrs. Hale and Mrs. Peters to conceal evidence from their husbands.

As she expanded her essay, Kim added illustrative explanations, details, and quotations, taking care to provide accurate page numbers in parentheses after each quotation. (Because students were required to use a play from this anthology, and no outside sources, Kim's instructor did not require a works-cited page.) She also worked hard to make her topic sentences clearer, and she used information from her class notes to help her write a new introduction and conclusion that discussed the status of women at the time in which *Trifles* was written. Finally, she added a new title and revised her thesis statement to emphasize the focus of her essay on the "desperate measures" all three women are driven to in response to their subjugation and confinement.

CHAPTER 28

PLOT

We assume that, for the finest form of tragedy, the plot must be not simple but complex; and further, that it must imitate actions arousing fear and pity, since that is the distinctive function of this kind of imitation. It follows, therefore, that there are three forms of plot to be avoided. (1) A good man must not be seen passing from happiness to misery, or (2) a bad man from misery to happiness. The first situation is not fear-inspiring or piteous, but simply odious to us. The second is the most untragic that can be; it has not one of the requisites of tragedy; it does not appeal either to the human feeling in us, or to our pity, or to our fears. Nor, on the other hand, should (3) an extremely bad man be seen falling from happiness into misery. Such a story may arouse the human feeling in us, but it will not move us to either pity or fear; pity is occasioned by undeserved misfortune, and fear by that of one like ourselves; so that there will be nothing either piteous or fear-inspiring in the situation. . . .
—**Aristotle,** *Poetics,* trans. Ingram Bywater

Great character creation is a fine thing in a drama, but the sum of all its characters is the story that they enact. Aristotle puts the plot at the head of the dramatic elements; of all these he thinks plot the most difficult and the most expressive. And he is right. —**Stark Young,** *The Theatre*

How many times in my years of teaching have I stood before the blackboard guiding the abhorrent chalk carefully along a 30-degree incline to explain Freytag's triangle, that indispensable construct for mapping the ideal course of the classic novel: complications of character and situation creating a "rising action" that culminates in a climactic moment, which is followed in turn by the afterglow of denouement, the tying up of threads.

    But other roads do diverge in the . . . yellow wood, one of them representing a structure quite different, in which the climactic event . . . takes place right at the outset, and the essential action can be described as "falling." —**Sven Birkerts,** in *New York Times Book Review*

    Plot denotes the way events are arranged in a work of literature. Although the accepted conventions of drama require that the plot of a play be presented some-what differently from the plot of a short story, the same components of plot are present in both. Plot in a dramatic work, like plot in a short story, presents conflicts that are revealed, intensified, and resolved during the course of the play through the characters' actions. (See Chapter 5 for a discussion of **conflict.**)

PLOT STRUCTURE

In 1863, the German critic Gustav Freytag devised a pyramid to represent a prototype for the plot of a dramatic work. According to Freytag, a play typically begins with **exposition,** which presents characters and setting and introduces the basic situation in which the characters are involved. Then, during the **rising action,** complications develop, conflicts emerge, suspense builds, and crises occur. The rising action culminates in a **climax,** at which point the plot's tension peaks. Finally, during the **falling action,** the intensity subsides, eventually winding down to a **resolution,** or **denouement,** in which all loose ends are tied up.

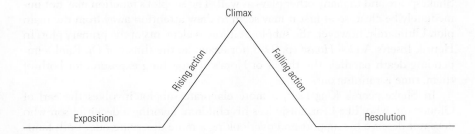

The familiar plot of a detective story follows Freytag's concept of plot: the exposition section includes the introduction of the detective and the explanation of the crime; the rising action develops as the investigation of the crime proceeds, with suspense increasing as the solution approaches; the high point of the action, the climax, comes with the revelation of the crime's solution; and the falling action presents the detective's explanation of the solution. The story concludes with a resolution typically characterized by the capture of the criminal and the restoration of order.

The action of Susan Glaspell's one-act play *Trifles* (p. 983), which in many ways resembles a detective story, might be diagrammed as follows:

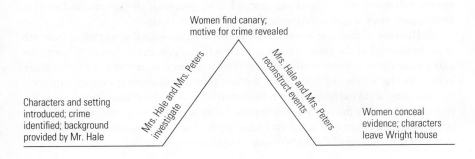

Of course, the plot of a complex dramatic work rarely conforms to the neat pattern represented by Freytag's pyramid. In fact, a play can lack exposition or resolution entirely, and the climax can occur at the beginning. Because long stretches of exposition can be dull, a playwright may arouse audience interest by moving directly into conflict. *Oedipus the King* (p. 1271), for example, begins with the conflict; so does *The Cuban Swimmer* (p. 1258). Similarly, because audiences tend to lose interest after the play's climax is reached, a playwright may choose to dispense with extended falling action. Thus, after Hamlet's death, the play ends abruptly.

Plot and Subplot

While the main plot is developing, another, parallel plot, called a **subplot**, may be developing alongside it. This structural device is common in the works of Shakespeare and in many other plays as well. The subplot's function may not immediately be clear, so at first it may seem to draw attention away from the main plot. Ultimately, however, the subplot reinforces elements of the primary plot. In Henrik Ibsen's *A Doll House* (p. 995), for example, the threat of Dr. Rank's impending death parallels the threat of Nora's approaching exposure; for both of them, time is running out.

In Shakespeare's *King Lear*, a more elaborate subplot involves the earl of Gloucester, who, like Lear, misjudges his children, favoring a deceitful son who does not deserve his support and overlooking a more deserving one. Both families suffer greatly as a result of the fathers' misplaced loyalties. Thus, the parallel plot places additional emphasis on Lear's poor judgment and magnifies the consequences of his misguided acts: both fathers, and all but one of the five children, are dead by the play's end. A subplot can also set up a contrast — as it does in *Hamlet* (p. 915), where Fortinbras acts decisively to avenge his father, an action that underscores Hamlet's hesitation and procrastination when faced with a comparable challenge.

PLOT DEVELOPMENT

In a dramatic work, plot unfolds through **action:** what characters say and do. Generally, a play does not include a narrator whose commentary ensures that events will move smoothly along. Instead, dialogue, stage directions, and staging techniques work together to move the play's action along.

Exchanges of dialogue reveal what is happening — and, sometimes, indicate what happened in the past or suggest what will happen in the future. Characters can recount past events to other characters, announce an intention to take some action in the future, or summarize events that are occurring offstage. In such cases, dialogue takes the place of formal narrative. On the printed page, stage directions efficiently move readers from one location and time period to another by specifying entrances and exits and identifying the play's structural divisions — acts and scenes — and their accompanying changes of setting.

Staging techniques also can advance a play's action. A change in lighting can shift the focus to another part of the stage — and thus to another place and time. An adjustment of **scenery** or **props**—for instance, a breakfast table, complete with morning paper, replacing a bedtime setting — can indicate that the action has moved forward in time, as can a change of costumes. In Tennessee Williams's *The Glass Menagerie* (p. 1416) various staging devices — such as words projected on a screen that preview words to be spoken by a character and visual images on screen that predict scenes to follow —help to keep the action moving. For example, a screen image of blue roses leads into a scene in which Laura tells her mother how Jim gave her the nickname "Blue Roses."

Music can also move a play's action along, predicting excitement or doom or a romantic interlude — or a particular character's entrance. Toward the end of scene 5 of *The Glass Menagerie*, for example, stage directions announce, *"The Dance-Hall Music Changes To A Tango That Has A Minor and Somewhat Ominous Tone"*; a "music legend" repeated throughout the play serves as a signature in scenes focusing on Laura.

Less often, a narrator advances the action. In Thornton Wilder's 1938 play *Our Town*, a character known as the Stage Manager functions as a narrator, not only describing the play's setting and introducing the characters to the audience but also soliciting questions from characters scattered around the audience, prompting characters, and interrupting dialogue. In *The Glass Menagerie*, the protagonist, Tom Wingfield, also serves as a narrator, summarizing what has happened and moving readers on to the next scene: "After the fiasco at Rubicam's Business College, the idea of getting a gentleman caller for Laura began to play a more important part in Mother's calculations" (scene 3).

Flashbacks

Many plays — such as *The Glass Menagerie* and Arthur Miller's *Death of a Salesman* (p. 1178)—include **flashbacks,** which depict events that occurred before the play's main action. In addition, dialogue can overcome the limitations set by the chronological action on stage by recounting events that occurred earlier. Thus, Mr. Hale in *Trifles* tells the other characters how he discovered John Wright's murder, and Nora in *A Doll House* confides her secret past to her friend Kristine. As characters on stage are brought up to date, the audience is also given necessary information —facts that are essential to an understanding of the characters' motivation. Naturally, characters must have plausible reasons for explaining past events. In *Trifles*, Mr. Hale is the only character who witnessed the events he describes, and in *A Doll House*, Kristine, formerly Nora's friend and confidante, has not seen her in years. Thus, a character's need for information provides playwrights with a convenient excuse for supplying readers with necessary background. In less realistic dramas, however, no such excuse is necessary: characters can interrupt the action to deliver long monologues or soliloquies that fill in background details — or even address the audience directly, as Tom does in *The Glass Menagerie*.

Foreshadowing

In addition to revealing past events, dialogue can **foreshadow,** or look ahead to, future action. In many cases, seemingly unimportant comments have significance that becomes clear as the play develops. For example, in act 3 of *A Doll House,* Torvald Helmer says to Kristine, "An exit should always be effective, Mrs. Linde, but that's what I can't get Nora to grasp." At the end of the play, Nora's exit is not only effective but also memorable.

Elements of staging can also suggest events to come. In *The Glass Menagerie,* the ever-present photograph of the absent father — who, Tom tells the audience in scene 1, may be seen as a symbol of "the long delayed but always expected something that we live for"—foreshadows Tom's escape. Various bits of **stage business**— gestures or movements designed to attract the audience's attention — may also foreshadow future events. In *A Doll House,* Nora's sneaking forbidden macaroons seems at first to suggest her fear of her husband, but her actions actually foreshadow her eventual defiance of his authority.

CHECKLIST **WRITING ABOUT PLOT**

✓ Summarize the play's events.

✓ What is the play's central conflict? How is it resolved? What other conflicts are present?

✓ What section of the play constitutes its rising action?

✓ Where does the play's climax occur?

✓ What crises can you identify?

✓ How is suspense created?

✓ What section of the play constitutes its falling action?

✓ Does the play contain a subplot? What is its purpose? How is it related to the main plot?

✓ Does the play include flashbacks? Does the play's dialogue contain summaries of past events or references to events in the future? How does the use of flashbacks or foreshadowing advance the play's plot?

✓ Does the play include a narrator?

✓ How does dialogue advance the play's plot?

✓ How do characters' actions advance the play's plot?

✓ How do stage directions advance the play's plot?

✓ How does staging advance the play's plot?

✓ Does the play use any other devices to advance the plot?

SUSAN GLASPELL (1882–1948) was born in Davenport, Iowa, and graduated from Drake University in 1899. First a reporter and then a freelance writer, she lived in Chicago (where she was part of the Chicago Renaissance that included poet Carl Sandburg and novelist Theodore Dreiser) and later in Greenwich Village. Her works include two plays in addition to *Trifles*, *The Verge* (1921) and *Alison's House* (1930), and several novels, including *Fidelity* (1915) and *The Morning Is near Us* (1939). With her husband, George Cram Cook, she founded the Provincetown Players, which became the staging ground for innovative plays by Eugene O'Neill, among others.

Glaspell herself wrote plays for the Provincetown Players, beginning with *Trifles*, which she created for the 1916 season although she had never previously written a drama. The play opened on August 8, 1916, with Glaspell and her husband in the cast. Glaspell said she wrote *Trifles* in one afternoon, sitting in the empty theater and looking at the bare stage: "After a time, the stage became a kitchen — a kitchen there all by itself." She remembered a murder trial she had covered in Iowa in her days as a reporter, and the story began to play itself out on the stage as she gazed. Throughout her revisions, she said, she returned to look at the stage to see whether the events she was recording came to life on it. Although Glaspell later rewrote *Trifles* in the form of a short story called "A Jury of Her Peers," the play remains her most successful and memorable work.

Cultural Context: In 1916, when *Trifles* was first produced, women were not allowed to serve on juries in most states. Even in the 1920s, only about half the states allowed women to serve on juries. Other states resisted for decades. Not until 1937, for example, did the state of New York pass a law allowing women to serve on juries.

SUSAN GLASPELL

Trifles (1916)

CHARACTERS

George Henderson, *county attorney*   **Mrs. Peters**
Henry Peters, *sheriff*   **Mrs. Hale**
Lewis Hale, *a neighboring farmer*

SCENE

The kitchen in the now abandoned farmhouse of John Wright, a gloomy kitchen, and left without having been put in order — unwashed pans under the sink, a loaf of bread outside the breadbox, a dish towel on the table — other signs of incompleted work. At the rear the outer door opens and the Sheriff comes in followed by the County Attorney and Hale. The Sheriff and Hale are men in middle life, the County Attorney is a young man; all are much bundled up and go at once to the stove. They are followed by two women — the Sheriff's wife first; she is a slight wiry woman, a thin nervous face. Mrs. Hale is larger and would ordinarily be called more comfortable looking, but she is disturbed now and looks fearfully about as she enters. The women have come in slowly, and stand close together near the door.

COUNTY ATTORNEY: *(rubbing his hands)* This feels good. Come up to the fire, ladies.

MRS. PETERS: *(after taking a step forward)* I'm not — cold.

SHERIFF: *(unbuttoning his overcoat and stepping away from the stove as if to mark the beginning of official business)* Now, Mr. Hale, before we move things about, you explain to Mr. Henderson just what you saw when you came here yesterday morning.

COUNTY ATTORNEY: By the way, has anything been moved? Are things just as you left them yesterday?

5   SHERIFF: *(looking about)* It's just the same. When it dropped below zero last night I thought I'd better send Frank out this morning to make a fire for us — no use getting pneumonia with a big case on, but I told him not to touch anything except the stove — and you know Frank.

COUNTY ATTORNEY: Somebody should have been left here yesterday.

SHERIFF: Oh — yesterday. When I had to send Frank to Morris Center for that man who went crazy — I want you to know I had my hands full yesterday. I knew you could get back from Omaha by today and as long as I went over everything here myself —

COUNTY ATTORNEY: Well, Mr. Hale, tell just what happened when you came here yesterday morning.

HALE: Harry and I had started to town with a load of potatoes. We came along the road from my place and as I got here I said, "I'm going to see if I can't get John Wright to go in with me on a party telephone." I spoke to Wright about it once before and he put me off, saying folks talked too much anyway, and all he asked was peace and quiet — I guess you know about how much he talked himself; but I thought maybe if I went to the house and talked about it before his wife, though I said to Harry that I didn't know as what his wife wanted made much difference to John —

10   COUNTY ATTORNEY: Let's talk about that later, Mr. Hale. I do want to talk about that, but tell now just what happened when you got to the house.

HALE: I didn't hear or see anything; I knocked at the door, and still it was all quiet inside. I knew they must be up, it was past eight o'clock. So I knocked again, and I thought I heard somebody say, "Come in." I wasn't sure, I'm not sure yet, but I opened the door — this door *(indicating the door by which the two women are still standing)* and there in that rocker —*(pointing to it)* sat Mrs. Wright.

They all look at the rocker.

COUNTY ATTORNEY: What — was she doing?

HALE: She was rockin' back and forth. She had her apron in her hand and was kind of — pleating it.

COUNTY ATTORNEY: And how did she —look?

15   HALE: Well, she looked queer.

COUNTY ATTORNEY: How do you mean — queer?

HALE: Well, as if she didn't know what she was going to do next. And kind of done up.

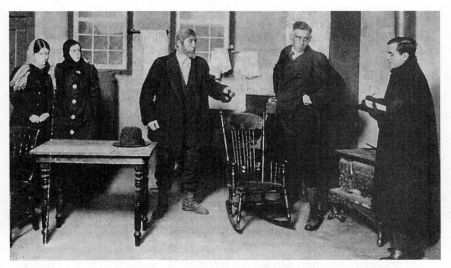

In this scene from The Provincetown Players' 1917 production of Susan Glaspell's *Trifles,* the three men discuss the crime while Mrs. Peters and Mrs. Hale look on.

COUNTY ATTORNEY: How did she seem to feel about your coming?

HALE: Why, I don't think she minded — one way or other. She didn't pay much attention. I said, "How do, Mrs. Wright, it's cold, ain't it?" And she said, "Is it?"— and went on kind of pleating at her apron. Well, I was surprised; she didn't ask me to come up to the stove, or to set down, but just sat there, not even looking at me, so I said, "I want to see John." And then she — laughed. I guess you would call it a laugh. I thought of Harry and the team outside, so I said a little sharp: "Can't I see John?" "No," she says, kind o' dull like. "Ain't he home?" says I. "Yes," says she, "he's home." "Then why can't I see him?" I asked her, out of patience. "'Cause he's dead," says she. "*Dead?*" says I. She just nodded her head, not getting a bit excited, but rockin' back and forth. "Why — where is he?" says I, not knowing what to say. She just pointed upstairs — like that. (*Himself pointing to the room above.*) I got up, with the idea of going up there. I walked from there to here — then I says, "Why, what did he die of?" "He died of a rope round his neck," says she, and just went on pleatin' at her apron. Well, I went out and called Harry. I thought I might — need help. We went upstairs and there he was lyin'—

COUNTY ATTORNEY: I think I'd rather have you go into that upstairs, where you can point it all out. Just go on now with the rest of the story. 20

HALE: Well, my first thought was to get that rope off. It looked . . . (*stops, his face twitches*) . . . but Harry, he went up to him, and he said, "No, he's dead all right, and we'd better not touch anything." So we went back down stairs. She was still sitting that same way. "Has anybody been notified?" I asked. "No," says she, unconcerned. "Who did this, Mrs. Wright?" said Harry. He said it businesslike — and she stopped pleatin' of her apron. "I don't know," she says. "You don't *know?*" says Harry. "No," says she. "Weren't you sleepin' in the bed with him?" says Harry. "Yes," says she, "but I was on the inside." "Somebody slipped a rope round his neck and strangled him and you didn't wake up?" says Harry. "I didn't wake up," she said after him. We must 'a looked as if we didn't see how that could be, for after a minute she said, "I sleep sound." Harry was going to ask her more questions but I said maybe we ought to let her tell her story first to the coroner, or the sheriff, so Harry went fast as he could to Rivers' place, where there's a telephone.

COUNTY ATTORNEY: And what did Mrs. Wright do when she knew that you had gone for the coroner?

HALE: She moved from that chair to this one over here (*pointing to a small chair in the corner*) and just sat there with her hands held together and looking down. I got a feeling that I ought to make some conversation, so I said I had come in to see if John wanted to put in a telephone, and at that she started to laugh, and then she stopped and looked at me — scared. (*The County Attorney, who has had his notebook out, makes a note.*) I dunno, maybe it wasn't scared. I wouldn't like to say it was. Soon Harry got back, and then Dr. Lloyd came, and you, Mr. Peters, and so I guess that's all I know that you don't.

COUNTY ATTORNEY: (*looking around*) I guess we'll go upstairs first — and then out to the barn and around there. (*To the Sheriff.*) You're convinced that there was nothing important here — nothing that would point to any motive.

25   SHERIFF: Nothing here but kitchen things.

The County Attorney, after again looking around the kitchen, opens the door of a cupboard closet. He gets up on a chair and looks on a shelf. Pulls his hand away, sticky.

COUNTY ATTORNEY: Here's a nice mess.

The women draw nearer.

MRS. PETERS: (*to the other woman*) Oh, her fruit; it did freeze. (*To the County Attorney.*) She worried about that when it turned so cold. She said the fire'd go out and her jars would break.

SHERIFF: Well, can you beat the women! Held for murder and worryin' about her preserves.

COUNTY ATTORNEY: I guess before we're through she may have something more serious than preserves to worry about.

30   HALE: Well, women are used to worrying over trifles.

The two women move a little closer together.

COUNTY ATTORNEY: (*with the gallantry of a young politician*) And yet, for all their worries, what would we do without the ladies? (*The women do not unbend. He goes to the sink, takes a dipperful of water from the pail and pouring it into a basin, washes his hands. Starts to wipe them on the roller towel, turns it for a cleaner place.*) Dirty towels! (*Kicks his foot against the pans under the sink.*) Not much of a housekeeper, would you say, ladies?

MRS. HALE: *(stiffly)* There's a great deal of work to be done on a farm.

COUNTY ATTORNEY: To be sure. And yet *(with a little bow to her)* I know there are some Dickson county farmhouses which do not have such roller towels.

He gives it a pull to expose its full length again.

MRS. HALE: Those towels get dirty awful quick. Men's hands aren't always as clean as they might be.

COUNTY ATTORNEY: Ah, loyal to your sex, I see. But you and Mrs. Wright   35
were neighbors. I suppose you were friends, too.

MRS. HALE: *(shaking her head)* I've not seen much of her of late years. I've not been in this house — it's more than a year.

COUNTY ATTORNEY: And why was that? You didn't like her?

MRS. HALE: I liked her all well enough. Farmers' wives have their hands full, Mr. Henderson. And then —

COUNTY ATTORNEY: Yes — ?

MRS. HALE: *(looking about)* It never seemed a very cheerful place.   40

COUNTY ATTORNEY: No — it's not cheerful. I shouldn't say she had the homemaking instinct.

MRS. HALE: Well, I don't know as Wright had, either.

COUNTY ATTORNEY: You mean that they didn't get on very well?

MRS. HALE: No, I don't mean anything. But I don't think a place'd be any cheerfuller for John Wright's being in it.

COUNTY ATTORNEY: I'd like to talk more of that a little later. I want to get   45
the lay of things upstairs now.

He goes to the left, where three steps lead to a stair door.

SHERIFF: I suppose anything Mrs. Peters does'll be all right. She was to take in some clothes for her, you know, and a few little things. We left in such a hurry yesterday.

COUNTY ATTORNEY: Yes, but I would like to see what you take, Mrs. Peters, and keep an eye out for anything that might be of use to us.

MRS. PETERS: Yes, Mr. Henderson.

The women listen to the men's steps on the stairs, then look about the kitchen.

MRS. HALE: I'd hate to have men coming into my kitchen, snooping around and criticizing.

She arranges the pans under sink which the County Attorney had shoved out of place.

MRS. PETERS: Of course it's no more than their duty.   50

MRS. HALE: Duty's all right, but I guess that deputy sheriff that came out to make the fire might have got a little of this on. *(Gives the roller towel a pull.)* Wish I'd thought of that sooner. Seems mean to talk about her for not having things slicked up when she had to come away in such a hurry.

MRS. PETERS: *(who has gone to a small table in the left rear corner of the room, and lifted one end of a towel that covers a pan)* She had bread set.

Stands still.

MRS. HALE: (*eyes fixed on a loaf of bread beside the breadbox, which is on a low shelf at the other side of the room. Moves slowly toward it.*) She was going to put this in there. (*Picks up loaf, then abruptly drops it. In a manner of returning to familiar things.*) It's a shame about her fruit. I wonder if it's all gone. (*Gets up on the chair and looks.*) I think there's some here that's all right, Mrs. Peters. Yes — here; (*holding it toward the window*) this is cherries, too. (*Looking again.*) I declare I believe that's the only one. (*Gets down, bottle in her hand. Goes to the sink and wipes it off on the outside.*) She'll feel awful bad after all her hard work in the hot weather. I remember the afternoon I put up my cherries last summer.

She puts the bottle on the big kitchen table, center of the room. With a sigh, is about to sit down in the rocking-chair. Before she is seated realizes what chair it is; with a slow look at it, steps back. The chair which she has touched rocks back and forth.

MRS. PETERS: Well, I must get those things from the front room closet. (*She goes to the door at the right, but after looking into the other room, steps back.*) You coming with me, Mrs. Hale? You could help me carry them.

They go in the other room; reappear, Mrs. Peters carrying a dress and skirt, Mrs. Hale following with a pair of shoes.

55 MRS. PETERS: My, it's cold in there.

She puts the clothes on the big table, and hurries to the stove.

MRS. HALE: (*examining her skirt*) Wright was close. I think maybe that's why she kept so much to herself. She didn't even belong to the Ladies Aid. I suppose she felt she couldn't do her part, and then you don't enjoy things when you feel shabby. She used to wear pretty clothes and be lively, when she was Minnie Foster, one of the town girls singing in the choir. But that — oh, that was thirty years ago. This all you was to take in?

MRS. PETERS: She said she wanted an apron. Funny thing to want, for there isn't much to get you dirty in jail, goodness knows. But I suppose just to make her feel more natural. She said they was in the top drawer in this cupboard. Yes, here. And then her little shawl that always hung behind the door. (*Opens stair door and looks.*) Yes, here it is.

Quickly shuts door leading upstairs.

MRS. HALE: (*abruptly moving toward her*) Mrs. Peters?
MRS. PETERS: Yes, Mrs. Hale?
60 MRS. HALE: Do you think she did it?
MRS. PETERS: (*in a frightened voice*) Oh, I don't know.
MRS. HALE: Well, I don't think she did. Asking for an apron and her little shawl. Worrying about her fruit.
MRS. PETERS: (*starts to speak, glances up, where footsteps are heard in the room above. In a low voice.*) Mr. Peters says it looks bad for her. Mr. Henderson is awful sarcastic in a speech and he'll make fun of her sayin' she didn't wake up.

MRS. HALE: Well, I guess John Wright didn't wake when they was slipping that rope under his neck.

MRS. PETERS: No, it's strange. It must have been done awful crafty and still. They say it was such a — funny way to kill a man, rigging it all up like that.   65

MRS. HALE: That's just what Mr. Hale said. There was a gun in the house. He says that's what he can't understand.

MRS. PETERS: Mr. Henderson said coming out that what was needed for the case was a motive; something to show anger, or — sudden feeling.

MRS. HALE: *(who is standing by the table)* Well, I don't see any signs of anger around here. *(She puts her hand on the dish towel which lies on the table, stands looking down at table, one half of which is clean, the other half messy.)* It's wiped to here. *(Makes a move as if to finish work, then turns and looks at loaf of bread outside the breadbox. Drops towel. In that voice of coming back to familiar things.)* Wonder how they are finding things upstairs. I hope she had it a little more red-up° up there. You know, it seems kind of *sneaking.* Locking her up in town and then coming out here and trying to get her own house to turn against her!

MRS. PETERS: But Mrs. Hale, the law is the law.

MRS. HALE: I s'pose 'tis. *(Unbuttoning her coat.)* Better loosen up your things,   70
Mrs. Peters. You won't feel them when you go out.

Mrs. Peters takes off her fur tippet, goes to hang it on hook at back of room, stands looking at the under part of the small corner table.

MRS. PETERS: She was piecing a quilt.

She brings the large sewing basket and they look at the bright pieces.

MRS. HALE: It's log cabin pattern. Pretty, isn't it? I wonder if she was goin' to quilt it or just knot it?

Footsteps have been heard coming down the stairs. The Sheriff enters followed by Hale and the County Attorney.

SHERIFF: They wonder if she was going to quilt it or just knot it!

The men laugh; the women look abashed.

COUNTY ATTORNEY: *(rubbing his hands over the stove)* Frank's fire didn't do much up there, did it? Well, let's go out to the barn and get that cleared up.

The men go outside.

MRS. HALE: *(resentfully)* I don't know as there's anything so strange, our takin'   75
up our time with little things while we're waiting for them to get the evidence. *(She sits down at the big table smoothing out a block with decision.)* I don't see as it's anything to laugh about.

---

red-up: Spruced-up (slang).

MRS. PETERS: (*apologetically*) Of course they've got awful important things on their minds.

Pulls up a chair and joins Mrs. Hale at the table.

MRS. HALE: (*examining another block*) Mrs. Peters, look at this one. Here, this is the one she was working on, and look at the sewing! All the rest of it has been so nice and even. And look at this! It's all over the place! Why, it looks as if she didn't know what she was about!

After she has said this they look at each other, then start to glance back at the door. After an instant Mrs. Hale has pulled at a knot and ripped the sewing.

MRS. PETERS: Oh, what are you doing, Mrs. Hale?

MRS. HALE: (*mildly*) Just pulling out a stitch or two that's not sewed very good. (*Threading a needle.*) Bad sewing always made me fidgety.

80 MRS. PETERS: (*nervously*) I don't think we ought to touch things.

MRS. HALE: I'll just finish up this end. (*Suddenly stopping and leaning forward.*) Mrs. Peters?

MRS. PETERS: Yes, Mrs. Hale?

MRS. HALE: What do you suppose she was so nervous about?

MRS. PETERS: Oh — I don't know. I don't know as she was nervous. I sometimes sew awful queer when I'm just tired. (*Mrs. Hale starts to say something, looks at Mrs. Peters, then goes on sewing.*) Well, I must get these things wrapped up. They may be through sooner than we think. (*Putting apron and other things together.*) I wonder where I can find a piece of paper, and string.

85 MRS. HALE: In that cupboard, maybe.

MRS. PETERS: (*looking in cupboard*) Why, here's a birdcage. (*Holds it up.*) Did she have a bird, Mrs. Hale?

MRS. HALE: Why, I don't know whether she did or not — I've not been here for so long. There was a man around last year selling canaries cheap, but I don't know as she took one; maybe she did. She used to sing real pretty herself.

MRS. PETERS: (*glancing around*) Seems funny to think of a bird here. But she must have had one, or why would she have a cage? I wonder what happened to it.

MRS. HALE: I s'pose maybe the cat got it.

90 MRS. PETERS: No, she didn't have a cat. She's got that feeling some people have about cats — being afraid of them. My cat got in her room and she was real upset and asked me to take it out.

MRS. HALE: My sister Bessie was like that. Queer, ain't it?

MRS. PETERS: (*examining the cage*) Why, look at this door. It's broke. One hinge is pulled apart.

MRS. HALE: (*looking too*) Looks as if someone must have been rough with it.

MRS. PETERS: Why, yes.

She brings the cage forward and puts it on the table.

95 MRS. HALE: I wish if they're going to find any evidence they'd be about it. I don't like this place.

MRS. PETERS: But I'm awful glad you came with me, Mrs. Hale. It would be lonesome for me sitting here alone.

MRS. HALE: It would, wouldn't it? (*Dropping her sewing.*) But I tell you what I do wish, Mrs. Peters. I wish I had come over sometimes when *she* was here. I —(*looking around the room*)— wish I had.

MRS. PETERS: But of course you were awful busy, Mrs. Hale — your house and your children.

MRS. HALE: I could've come. I stayed away because it weren't cheerful — and that's why I ought to have come. I — I've never liked this place. Maybe because it's down in a hollow and you don't see the road. I dunno what it is but it's a lonesome place and always was. I wish I had come over to see Minnie Foster sometimes. I can see now—

Shakes her head.

MRS. PETERS: Well, you mustn't reproach yourself, Mrs. Hale. Somehow we   100
just don't see how it is with other folks until — something comes up.

MRS. HALE: Not having children makes less work — but it makes a quiet house, and Wright out to work all day, and no company when he did come in. Did you know John Wright, Mrs. Peters?

MRS. PETERS: Not to know him; I've seen him in town. They say he was a good man.

MRS. HALE: Yes — good; he didn't drink, and kept his word as well as most, I guess, and paid his debts. But he was a hard man, Mrs. Peters. Just to pass the time of day with him —(*Shivers.*) Like a raw wind that gets to the bone. (*Pauses, her eye falling on the cage.*) I should think she would 'a wanted a bird. But what do you suppose went with it?

MRS. PETERS: I don't know, unless it got sick and died.

She reaches over and swings the broken door, swings it again. Both women watch it.

MRS. HALE: You weren't raised round here, were you? (*Mrs. Peters shakes her*   105
head.) You didn't know —her?

MRS. PETERS: Not till they brought her yesterday.

MRS. HALE: She — come to think of it, she was kind of like a bird herself — real sweet and pretty, but kind of timid and —fluttery. How — she — did — change. (*Silence; then as if struck by a happy thought and relieved to get back to everyday things.*) Tell you what, Mrs. Peters, why don't you take the quilt in with you? It might take up her mind.

MRS. PETERS: Why, I think that's a real nice idea, Mrs. Hale. There couldn't possibly be any objection to it, could there? Now, just what would I take? I wonder if her patches are in here — and her things.

They look in the sewing basket.

MRS. HALE: Here's some red. I expect this has got sewing things in it. (*Brings out a fancy box.*) What a pretty box. Looks like something somebody would give you. Maybe her scissors are in here. (*Opens box. Suddenly puts her hand to her nose.)* Why — *(Mrs. Peters bends nearer, then turns her face away.)* There's something wrapped up in this piece of silk.

110 MRS. PETERS: Why, this isn't her scissors.
MRS. HALE: *(lifting the silk)* Oh, Mrs. Peters — it's —

Mrs. Peters bends closer.

MRS. PETERS: It's the bird.
MRS. HALE: *(jumping up)* But, Mrs. Peters — look at it! Its neck! Look at its neck! It's all — other side *to.*
MRS. PETERS: Somebody — wrung — its — neck.

Their eyes meet. A look of growing comprehension, of horror. Steps are heard outside. Mrs. Hale slips box under quilt pieces, and sinks into her chair. Enter Sheriff and County Attorney. Mrs. Peters rises.

115 COUNTY ATTORNEY: *(as one turning from serious things to little pleasantries)* Well, ladies, have you decided whether she was going to quilt it or knot it?
MRS. PETERS: We think she was going to — knot it.
COUNTY ATTORNEY: Well, that's interesting, I'm sure. *(Seeing the birdcage.)* Has the bird flown?
MRS. HALE: *(putting more quilt pieces over the box)* We think the — cat got it.
COUNTY ATTORNEY: *(preoccupied)* Is there a cat?

Mrs. Hale glances in a quick covert way at Mrs. Peters.

120 MRS. PETERS: Well, not *now.* They're superstitious, you know. They leave.
COUNTY ATTORNEY: *(to Sheriff Peters, continuing an interrupted conversation)* No sign at all of anyone having come from the outside. Their own rope. Now let's go up again and go over it piece by piece. *(They start upstairs.)* It would have to have been someone who knew just the —

Mrs. Peters sits down. The two women sit there not looking at one another, but as if peering into something and at the same time holding back. When they talk now it is in the manner of feeling their way over strange ground, as if afraid of what they are saying, but as if they can not help saying it.

MRS. HALE: She liked the bird. She was going to bury it in that pretty box.
MRS. PETERS: *(in a whisper)* When I was a girl — my kitten — there was a boy took a hatchet, and before my eyes — and before I could get there — *(Covers her face an instant.)* If they hadn't held me back I would have — *(catches herself, looks upstairs where steps are heard, falters weakly)* — hurt him.
MRS. HALE: *(with a slow look around her)* I wonder how it would seem never to have had any children around. *(Pause.)* No, Wright wouldn't like the bird — a thing that sang. She used to sing. He killed that, too.
125 MRS. PETERS: *(moving uneasily)* We don't know who killed the bird.
MRS. HALE: I knew John Wright.
MRS. PETERS: It was an awful thing was done in this house that night, Mrs. Hale. Killing a man while he slept, slipping a rope around his neck that choked the life out of him.

MRS. HALE: His neck. Choked the life out of him.

Her hand goes out and rests on the birdcage.

MRS. PETERS: (*with rising voice*) We don't know who killed him. We don't
know.

MRS. HALE: (*her own feeling not interrupted*) If there'd been years and years of   130
nothing, then a bird to sing to you, it would be awful — still, after the bird
was still.

MRS. PETERS: (*something within her speaking*) I know what stillness is. When
we homesteaded in Dakota, and my first baby died — after he was two years
old, and me with no other then—

MRS. HALE: (*moving*) How soon do you suppose they'll be through, looking for
the evidence?

MRS. PETERS: I know what stillness is. (*Pulling herself back.*) The law has got
to punish crime, Mrs. Hale.

MRS. HALE: (*not as if answering that*) I wish you'd seen Minnie Foster when
she wore a white dress with blue ribbons and stood up there in the choir
and sang. (*A look around the room.*) Oh, I *wish* I'd come over here once in a
while! That was a crime! That was a crime! Who's going to punish that?

MRS. PETERS: (*looking upstairs*) We mustn't — take on.   135

MRS. HALE: I might have known she needed help! I know how things can
be — for women. I tell you, it's queer, Mrs. Peters. We live close together
and we live far apart. We all go through the same things — it's all just a
different kind of the same thing. (*Brushes her eyes; noticing the bottle of fruit,
reaches out for it.*) If I was you I wouldn't tell her her fruit was gone. Tell her
it *ain't.* Tell her it's all right. Take this in to prove it to her. She — she may
never know whether it was broke or not.

MRS. PETERS: (*takes the bottle, looks about for something to wrap it in; takes
petticoat from the clothes brought from the other room, very nervously begins
winding this around the bottle. In a false voice*) My, it's a good thing the men
couldn't hear us. Wouldn't they just laugh! Getting all stirred up over a
little thing like a — dead canary. As if that could have anything to do
with — with — wouldn't they *laugh!*

The men are heard coming down stairs.

MRS. HALE: (*under her breath*) Maybe they would — maybe they wouldn't.

COUNTY ATTORNEY: No, Peters, it's all perfectly clear except a reason for
doing it. But you know juries when it comes to women. If there was some
definite thing. Something to show — something to make a story about — a
thing that would connect up with this strange way of doing it—

The women's eyes meet for an instant. Enter Hale from outer door.

HALE: Well, I've got the team around. Pretty cold out there.   140

COUNTY ATTORNEY: I'm going to stay here a while by myself. (*To the Sheriff.*)
You can send Frank out for me, can't you? I want to go over everything. I'm
not satisfied that we can't do better.

SHERIFF: Do you want to see what Mrs. Peters is going to take in?

The County Attorney goes to the table, picks up the apron, laughs.

COUNTY ATTORNEY: Oh, I guess they're not very dangerous things the ladies have picked out. *(Moves a few things about, disturbing the quilt pieces which cover the box. Steps back.)* No, Mrs. Peters doesn't need supervising. For that matter, a sheriff's wife is married to the law. Ever think of it that way, Mrs. Peters?

MRS. PETERS: Not — just that way.

145   SHERIFF: *(chuckling)* Married to the law. *(Moves toward the other room.)* I just want you to come in here a minute, George. We ought to take a look at these windows.

COUNTY ATTORNEY: *(scoffingly)* Oh, windows!

SHERIFF: We'll be right out, Mr. Hale.

Hale goes outside. The Sheriff follows the County Attorney into the other room. Then Mrs. Hale rises, hands tight together, looking intensely at Mrs. Peters, whose eyes make a slow turn, finally meeting Mrs. Hale's. A moment Mrs. Hale holds her, then her own eyes point the way to where the box is concealed. Suddenly Mrs. Peters throws back quilt pieces and tries to put the box in the bag she is wearing. It is too big. She opens box, starts to take bird out, cannot touch it, goes to pieces, stands there helpless. Sound of a knob turning in the other room. Mrs. Hale snatches the box and puts it in the pocket of her big coat. Enter County Attorney and Sheriff.

COUNTY ATTORNEY: *(facetiously)* Well, Henry, at least we found out that she was not going to quilt it. She was going to — what is it you call it, ladies?

MRS. HALE: *(her hand against her pocket)* We call it — knot it, Mr. Henderson.

Reading and Reacting

1. What key events occurred before the start of the play? Why do you suppose these events are not presented in the play itself?
2. What are the "trifles" to which the title refers? How do these "trifles" advance the play's plot?
3. Glaspell's short story version of *Trifles* is called "A Jury of Her Peers." Who are Mrs. Wright's peers? What do you suppose the verdict would be if she were tried for her crime in 1916, when only men were permitted to serve on juries? If the trial were held today, do you think a jury might reach a different verdict?
4. *Trifles* is a one-act play, and all its action occurs in the Wrights' kitchen. Does this static setting slow the flow of the plot? Are there any advantages to this setting? Explain.
5. All background information about Mrs. Wright is provided by Mrs. Hale. Do you consider her to be a reliable source of information? Why or why not?
6. Mr. Hale's summary of his conversation with Mrs. Wright is the reader's only chance to hear her version of events. How might Mrs. Wright's presence change the play?

7. *Trifles* is a relatively slow-moving, "talky" play, with very little physical action. Is this a weakness of the play, or is the slow development consistent with the effect Glaspell is trying to achieve? Explain.

8. How does each of the following events advance the play's action: the men's departure from the kitchen, the discovery of the quilt pieces, the discovery of the dead bird?

9. How do the county attorney's sarcastic comments and his patronizing attitude toward Mrs. Hale and Mrs. Peters advance the play's action?

10. How do Mrs. Peters's memories of her own life advance the action?

11. What assumptions about women do the male characters make? In what ways do the female characters support or challenge these assumptions?

12. In what sense is the process of making a quilt an appropriate metaphor for the plot of *Trifles*?

13. **JOURNAL ENTRY** Do you think Mrs. Hale and Mrs. Peters do the right thing by concealing evidence?

14. **CRITICAL PERSPECTIVE** Gary A. Richardson writes in *American Drama from the Colonial Period through World War I* that in *Trifles*, Glaspell "developed a new structure for her action . . . .":

> While action in the traditional sense is minimal, Glaspell is nevertheless able to rivet attention on the two women, wed the audience to their perspective, and make a compelling case for the fairness of their actions. Existing on the margins of their society, Mrs. Peters and Mrs. Hale become emotional surrogates for the jailed Minnie Wright, effectively exonerating her action as "justifiable homicide."
>
> *Trifles* is carefully crafted to match Glaspell's subject matter — the action meanders, without a clearly delineated beginning, middle, or end . . . .

Exactly how does Glaspell "rivet attention on" Mrs. Hale and Mrs. Peters? Do you agree that the play's action "meanders, without a clearly delineated beginning, middle, and end"? If so, do you too see this "meandering" as appropriate for Glaspell's subject matter?

Related Works: "I Stand Here Ironing" (p. 187), "The Cask of Amontillado" (p. 217), "Everyday Use" (p. 310), "The Disappearance" (p. 458), "Eveline" (p. 489), "After great pain, a formal feeling comes —" (p. 866)

HENRIK IBSEN (1828–1906), Norway's foremost dramatist, was born in Skien, Norway, into a prosperous family; his father, however, lost his fortune when Ibsen was six. When Ibsen was fifteen, he was apprenticed to an apothecary away from home and was permanently estranged from his family. During his apprenticeship, he studied to enter the university and wrote plays. Although he did not pass the university entrance exam, his second play, *The Warrior's Barrow,* was produced by the Christiania Theatre in 1850. He began a life in the theater, writing plays and serving as artistic director of a theatrical company. Disillusioned by the public's lack of interest in theater, he left Norway, living in Italy and Germany with his wife and son between 1864 and 1891. By the time he returned to Norway, he was famous and revered. Ibsen's most notable plays include *Brand* (1865), *Peer Gynt*

(1867), *A Doll House* (1879), *Ghosts* (1881), *An Enemy of the People* (1882), *The Wild Duck* (1884), *Hedda Gabler* (1890), and *When We Dead Awaken* (1899).

A Doll House marks the beginning of Ibsen's successful realist period, during which he explored the ordinary lives of small-town people — in this case, what he called "a modern tragedy." Ibsen based the play on a true story, which closely paralleled the main events of the play: a wife borrows money to finance a trip for an ailing husband, repayment is demanded, she forges a check and is discovered. (In the real-life story, however, the husband demanded a divorce, and the wife had a nervous breakdown and was committed to a mental institution.) The issue in *A Doll House,* he said, is that there are "two kinds of moral law, . . . one in man and a completely different one in woman. They do not understand each other . . . ." Nora and Helmer destroy their marriage because they cannot comprehend or accept their differences. The play begins conventionally but does not fulfill the audience's expectations for a tidy resolution; as a result, it was not very successful when first performed. Nevertheless, the publication of *A Doll House* made Ibsen internationally famous.

Cultural Context: During the nineteenth century, the law treated women only a little better than it did children. Not only couldn't a woman vote, but she was also considered unable to handle her own financial affairs. A woman could not borrow money in her own name, and when she married, her finances were put in the care of her husband. Moreover, for a middle-class woman, working outside the home was out of the question. So, if a woman were to leave her husband, she was not likely to have any way of supporting herself, and she would lose custody of her children.

HENRIK IBSEN

A Doll House   (1879)

Translated By Rolf Fjelde

CHARACTERS

Torvald Helmer, *a lawyer*	**Nils Krogstad,** *a bank clerk*
Nora, *his wife*	**The Helmers' three small**
Dr. Rank	**children**
Mrs. Linde	**Anne-Marie,** *their nurse*
A Delivery Boy	**Helene,** *a maid*

The action takes place in Helmer's residence.

ACT I

A comfortable room, tastefully but not expensively furnished. A door to the right in the back wall leads to the entryway; another to the left leads to Helmer's study. Between these doors, a piano. Midway in the left-hand wall a door, and further back a window. Near the window a round table with an armchair and a small sofa. In the right-hand wall, toward the rear, a door, and nearer the foreground a porcelain stove with two armchairs and a rocking chair beside it. Between the stove and the side door, a small table.

Engravings on the walls. An étagère with china figures and other small art objects; a small bookcase with richly bound books; the floor carpeted; a fire burning in the stove. It is a winter day.

A bell rings in the entryway; shortly after we hear the door being unlocked. Nora comes into the room, humming happily to herself; she is wearing street clothes and carries an armload of packages, which she puts down on the table to the right. She has left the hall door open; and through it a Delivery Boy is seen, holding a Christmas tree and a basket, which he gives to the Maid who let them in.

Nora: Hide the tree well, Helene. The children mustn't get a glimpse of it till this evening, after it's trimmed. *(To the Delivery Boy, taking out her purse.)* How much?

Delivery Boy: Fifty, ma'am.

Nora: There's a crown. No, keep the change. *(The Boy thanks her and leaves. Nora shuts the door. She laughs softly to herself while taking off her street things. Drawing a bag of macaroons from her pocket, she eats a couple, then steals over and listens at her husband's study door.)* Yes, he's home. *(Hums again as she moves to the table right.)*

Helmer: *(from the study)* Is that my little lark twittering out there?

Nora: *(busy opening some packages)* Yes, it is.   5

Helmer: Is that my squirrel rummaging around?

Nora: Yes!

Helmer: When did my squirrel get in?

Nora: Just now. *(Putting the macaroon bag in her pocket and wiping her mouth.)* Do come in, Torvald, and see what I've bought.

Helmer: Can't be disturbed. *(After a moment he opens the door and peers in, pen*   10
in hand.) Bought, you say? All that there? Has the little spendthrift been out throwing money around again?

Nora: Oh, but Torvald, this year we really should let ourselves go a bit. It's the first Christmas we haven't had to economize.

Helmer: But you know we can't go squandering.

Nora: Oh yes, Torvald, we can squander a little now. Can't we? Just a tiny, wee bit. Now that you've got a big salary and are going to make piles and piles of money.

Helmer: Yes — starting New Year's. But then it's a full three months till the raise comes through.

Nora: Pooh! We can borrow that long.   15

Helmer: Nora! *(Goes over and playfully takes her by the ear.)* Are your scatterbrains off again? What if today I borrowed a thousand crowns, and you squandered them over Christmas week, and then on New Year's Eve a roof tile fell on my head, and I lay there—

Nora: *(putting her hand on his mouth)* Oh! Don't say such things!

Helmer: Yes, but what if it happened — then what?

Nora: If anything so awful happened, then it just wouldn't matter if I had debts or not.

Helmer: Well, but the people I'd borrowed from?   20

Nora: Them? Who cares about them! They're strangers.

HELMER: Nora, Nora, how like a woman! No, but seriously, Nora, you know
what I think about that. No debts! Never borrow! Something of freedom's
lost — and something of beauty, too — from a home that's founded on
borrowing and debt. We've made a brave stand up to now, the two of us;
and we'll go right on like that the little while we have to.

NORA: (*going toward the stove*) Yes, whatever you say, Torvald.

HELMER: (*following her*) Now, now, the little lark's wings mustn't droop.
Come on, don't be a sulky squirrel. (*Taking out his wallet.*) Nora, guess what
I have here.

25   NORA: (*turning quickly*) Money!

HELMER: There, see. (*Hands her some notes.*) Good grief, I know how costs go
up in a house at Christmastime.

NORA: Ten — twenty — thirty — forty. Oh, thank you, Torvald; I can manage
no end on this.

HELMER: You really will have to.

NORA: Oh yes, I promise I will! But come here so I can show you everything I
bought. And so cheap! Look, new clothes for Ivar here — and a sword.
Here a horse and a trumpet for Bob. And a doll and a doll's bed here for
Emmy; they're nothing much, but she'll tear them to bits in no time
anyway. And here I have dress material and handkerchiefs for the maids.
Old Anne-Marie really deserves something more.

30   HELMER: And what's in that package there?

NORA: (*with a cry*) Torvald, no! You can't see that till tonight!

HELMER: I see. But tell me now, you little prodigal, what have you thought of
for yourself?

NORA: For myself? Oh, I don't want anything at all.

HELMER: Of course you do. Tell me just what — within reason — you'd most
like to have.

35   NORA: I honestly don't know. Oh, listen, Torvald —

HELMER: Well?

NORA: (*fumbling at his coat buttons, without looking at him*) If you want to give
me something, then maybe you could — you could —

HELMER: Come on, out with it.

NORA: (*hurriedly*) You could give me money, Torvald. No more than you think
you can spare; then one of these days I'll buy something with it.

40   HELMER: But Nora —

NORA: Oh, please, Torvald darling, do that! I beg you, please. Then I could
hang the bills in pretty gilt paper on the Christmas tree. Wouldn't that
be fun?

HELMER: What are those little birds called that always fly through their
fortunes?

NORA: Oh yes, spendthrifts; I know all that. But let's do as I say, Torvald; then
I'll have time to decide what I really need most. That's very sensible, isn't it?

HELMER: (*smiling*) Yes, very — that is, if you actually hung onto the money I
give you, and you actually used it to buy yourself something. But it goes for
the house and for all sorts of foolish things, and then I only have to lay out
some more.

NORA: Oh, but Torvald— 45
HELMER: Don't deny it, my dear little Nora. (*Putting his arm around her waist.*) Spendthrifts are sweet, but they use up a frightful amount of money. It's incredible what it costs a man to feed such birds.
NORA: Oh, how can you say that! Really, I save everything I can.
HELMER: (*laughing*) Yes, that's the truth. Everything you can. But that's nothing at all.
NORA: (*humming, with a smile of quiet satisfaction*) Hm, if you only knew what expenses we larks and squirrels have, Torvald.
HELMER: You're an odd little one. Exactly the way your father was. You're 50 never at a loss for scaring up money; but the moment you have it, it runs right out through your fingers; you never know what you've done with it. Well, one takes you as you are. It's deep in your blood. Yes, these things are hereditary, Nora.
NORA: Ah, I could wish I'd inherited many of Papa's qualities.
HELMER: And I couldn't wish you anything but just what you are, my sweet little lark. But wait; it seems to me you have a very — what should I call it?— a very suspicious look today—
NORA: I do?
HELMER: You certainly do. Look me straight in the eye.
NORA: (*looking at him*) Well? 55
HELMER: (*shaking an admonitory finger*) Surely my sweet tooth hasn't been running riot in town today, has she?
NORA: No. Why do you imagine that?
HELMER: My sweet tooth really didn't make a little detour through the confectioner's?
NORA: No, I assure you, Torvald—
HELMER: Hasn't nibbled some pastry? 60
NORA: No, not at all.
HELMER: Nor even munched a macaroon or two?
NORA: No, Torvald, I assure you, really—
HELMER: There, there now. Of course I'm only joking.
NORA: (*going to the table, right*) You know I could never think of going 65
against you.
HELMER: No, I understand that; and you *have* given me your word. (*Going over to her.*) Well, you keep your little Christmas secrets to yourself, Nora darling. I expect they'll come to light this evening, when the tree is lit.
NORA: Did you remember to ask Dr. Rank?
HELMER: No. But there's no need for that; it's assumed he'll be dining with us. All the same, I'll ask him when he stops by here this morning. I've ordered some fine wine. Nora, you can't imagine how I'm looking forward to this evening.
NORA: So am I. And what fun for the children, Torvald!
HELMER: Ah, it's so gratifying to know that one's gotten a safe, secure job, and 70
with a comfortable salary. It's a great satisfaction, isn't it?
NORA: Oh, it's wonderful!

HELMER: Remember last Christmas? Three whole weeks before, you shut yourself in every evening till long after midnight, making flowers for the Christmas tree, and all the other decorations to surprise us. Ugh, that was the dullest time I've ever lived through.

NORA: It wasn't at all dull for me.

HELMER: *(smiling)* But the outcome *was* pretty sorry, Nora.

75 NORA: Oh, don't tease me with that again. How could I help it that the cat came in and tore everything to shreds.

HELMER: No, poor thing, you certainly couldn't. You wanted so much to please us all, and that's what counts. But it's just as well that the hard times are past.

NORA: Yes, it's really wonderful.

HELMER: Now I don't have to sit here alone, boring myself, and you don't have to tire your precious eyes and your fair little delicate hands —

NORA: *(clapping her hands)* No, is it really true, Torvald, I don't have to? Oh, how wonderfully lovely to hear! *(Taking his arm.)* Now I'll tell you just how I've thought we should plan things. Right after Christmas —*(The doorbell rings.)* Oh, the bell. *(Straightening the room up a bit.)* Somebody would have to come. What a bore!

80 HELMER: I'm not at home to visitors, don't forget.

MAID: *(from the hall doorway)* Ma'am, a lady to see you —

NORA: All right, let her come in.

MAID: *(to Helmer)* And the doctor's just come too.

HELMER: Did he go right to my study?

85 MAID: Yes, he did.

Helmer goes into his room. The Maid shows in Mrs. Linde, dressed in traveling clothes, and shuts the door after her.

MRS. LINDE: *(in a dispirited and somewhat hesitant voice)* Hello, Nora.

NORA: *(uncertain)* Hello—

MRS. LINDE: You don't recognize me.

NORA: No, I don't know —but wait, I think —*(Exclaiming.)* What! Kristine! Is it really you?

90 MRS. LINDE: Yes, it's me.

NORA: *Kristine!* To think I didn't recognize you. But then, how could I? *(More quietly.)* How you've changed, Kristine!

MRS. LINDE: Yes, no doubt I have. In nine — ten long years.

NORA: Is it so long since we met! Yes, it's all of that. Oh, these last eight years have been a happy time, believe me. And so now you've come in to town, too. Made the long trip in the winter. That took courage.

MRS. LINDE: I just got here by ship this morning.

95 NORA: To enjoy yourself over Christmas, of course. Oh, how lovely! Yes, enjoy ourselves, we'll do that. But take your coat off. You're not still cold? *(Helping her.)* There now, let's get cozy here by the stove. No, the easy chair there! I'll take the rocker here. *(Seizing her hands.)* Yes, now you have your old look again; it was only in that first moment. You're a bit more pale, Kristine — and maybe a bit thinner.

Mrs. Linde: And much, much older, Nora.

Nora: Yes, perhaps a bit older; a tiny, tiny bit; not much at all. (*Stopping short; suddenly serious.*) Oh, but thoughtless me, to sit here, chattering away. Sweet, good Kristine, can you forgive me?

Mrs. Linde: What do you mean, Nora?

Nora: (*softly*) Poor Kristine, you've become a widow.

Mrs. Linde: Yes, three years ago.

Nora: Oh, I knew it, of course; I read it in the papers. Oh, Kristine, you must believe me; I often thought of writing you then, but I kept postponing it, and something always interfered.

Mrs. Linde: Nora dear, I understand completely.

Nora: No, it was awful of me, Kristine. You poor thing, how much you must have gone through. And he left you nothing?

Mrs. Linde: No.

Nora: And no children?

Mrs. Linde: No.

Nora: Nothing at all, then?

Mrs. Linde: Not even a sense of loss to feed on.

Nora: (*looking incredulously at her*) But Kristine, how could that be?

Mrs. Linde: (*smiling wearily and smoothing her hair*) Oh, sometimes it happens, Nora.

Nora: So completely alone. How terribly hard that must be for you. I have three lovely children. You can't see them now; they're out with the maid. But now you must tell me everything—

Mrs. Linde: No, no, no, tell me about yourself.

Nora: No, you begin. Today I don't want to be selfish. I want to think only of you today. But there *is* something I must tell you. Did you hear of the wonderful luck we had recently?

Mrs. Linde: No, what's that?

Nora: My husband's been made manager in the bank, just think!

Mrs. Linde: Your husband? How marvelous!

Nora: Isn't it? Being a lawyer is such an uncertain living, you know, especially if one won't touch any cases that aren't clean and decent. And of course Torvald would never do that, and I'm with him completely there. Oh, we're simply delighted, believe me! He'll join the bank right after New Year's and start getting a huge salary and lots of commissions. From now on we can live quite differently—just as we want. Oh, Kristine, I feel so light and happy! Won't it be lovely to have stacks of money and not a care in the world?

Mrs. Linde: Well, anyway, it would be lovely to have enough for necessities.

Nora: No, not just for necessities, but stacks and stacks of money!

Mrs. Linde: (*smiling*) Nora, Nora, aren't you sensible yet? Back in school you were such a free spender.

Nora: (*with a quiet laugh*) Yes, that's what Torvald still says. (*Shaking her finger.*) But "Nora, Nora" isn't as silly as you all think. Really, we've been in no position for me to go squandering. We've had to work, both of us.

MRS. LINDE: You too?

NORA: Yes, at odd jobs — needlework, crocheting, embroidery, and such — (*casually*) and other things too. You remember that Torvald left the department when we were married? There was no chance of promotion in his office, and of course he needed to earn more money. But that first year he drove himself terribly. He took on all kinds of extra work that kept him going morning and night. It wore him down, and then he fell deathly ill. The doctors said it was essential for him to travel south.

MRS. LINDE: Yes, didn't you spend a whole year in Italy?

125 NORA: That's right. It wasn't easy to get away, you know. Ivar had just been born. But of course we had to go. Oh, that was a beautiful trip, and it saved Torvald's life. But it cost a frightful sum, Kristine.

MRS. LINDE: I can well imagine.

NORA: Four thousand, eight hundred crowns it cost. That's really a lot of money.

MRS. LINDE: But it's lucky you had it when you needed it.

NORA: Well, as it was, we got it from Papa.

130 MRS. LINDE: I see. It was just about the time your father died.

NORA: Yes, just about then. And, you know, I couldn't make that trip out to nurse him. I had to stay here, expecting Ivar any moment, and with my poor sick Torvald to care for. Dearest Papa, I never saw him again, Kristine. Oh, that was the worst time I've known in all my marriage.

MRS. LINDE: I know how you loved him. And then you went off to Italy?

NORA: Yes. We had the means now, and the doctors urged us. So we left a month after.

MRS. LINDE: And your husband came back completely cured?

135 NORA: Sound as a drum!

MRS. LINDE: But — the doctor?

NORA: Who?

MRS. LINDE: I thought the maid said he was a doctor, the man who came in with me.

NORA: Yes, that was Dr. Rank — but he's not making a sick call. He's our closest friend, and he stops by at least once a day. No, Torvald hasn't had a sick moment since, and the children are fit and strong, and I am, too. (*Jumping up and clapping her hands.*) Oh, dear God, Kristine, what a lovely thing to live and be happy! But how disgusting of me — I'm talking of nothing but my own affairs. (*Sits on a stool close by Kristine, arms resting across her knees.*) Oh, don't be angry with me! Tell me, is it really true that you weren't in love with your husband? Why did you marry him, then?

140 MRS. LINDE: My mother was still alive, but bedridden and helpless — and I had my two younger brothers to look after. In all conscience, I didn't think I could turn him down.

NORA: No, you were right there. But was he rich at the time?

MRS. LINDE: He was very well off, I'd say. But the business was shaky, Nora. When he died, it all fell apart, and nothing was left.

NORA: And then —?

Mrs. Linde: Yes, so I had to scrape up a living with a little shop and a little teaching and whatever else I could find. The last three years have been like one endless workday without a rest for me. Now it's over, Nora. My poor mother doesn't need me, for she's passed on. Nor the boys, either; they're working now and can take care of themselves.

Nora: How free you must feel— 145

Mrs. Linde: No — only unspeakably empty. Nothing to live for now. (*Standing up anxiously.*) That's why I couldn't take it any longer out in that desolate hole. Maybe here it'll be easier to find something to do and keep my mind occupied. If I could only be lucky enough to get a steady job, some office work—

Nora: Oh, but Kristine, that's so dreadfully tiring, and you already look so tired. It would be much better for you if you could go off to a bathing resort.

Mrs. Linde: (*going toward the window*) I have no father to give me travel money, Nora.

Nora: (*rising*) Oh, don't be angry with me.

Mrs. Linde: (*going to her*) Nora dear, don't you be angry with me. The worst 150 of my kind of situation is all the bitterness that's stored away. No one to work for, and yet you're always having to snap up your opportunities. You have to live; and so you grow selfish. When you told me the happy change in your lot, do you know I was delighted less for your sakes than for mine?

Nora: How so? Oh, I see. You think Torvald could do something for you.

Mrs. Linde: Yes, that's what I thought.

Nora: And he will, Kristine! Just leave it to me; I'll bring it up so delicately — find something attractive to humor him with. Oh, I'm so eager to help you.

Mrs. Linde: How very kind of you, Nora, to be so concerned over me — doubly kind, considering you really know so little of life's burdens yourself.

Nora: I—? I know so little—? 155

Mrs. Linde: (*smiling*) Well my heavens — a little needlework and such — Nora, you're just a child.

Nora: (*tossing her head and pacing the floor*) You don't have to act so superior.

Mrs. Linde: Oh?

Nora: You're just like the others. You all think I'm incapable of anything serious—

Mrs. Linde: Come now— 160

Nora: That I've never had to face the raw world.

Mrs. Linde: Nora dear, you've just been telling me all your troubles.

Nora: Hm! Trivial! (*Quietly.*) I haven't told you the big thing.

Mrs. Linde: Big thing? What do you mean?

Nora: You look down on me so, Kristine, but you shouldn't. You're proud that 165 you worked so long and hard for your mother.

Mrs. Linde: I don't look down on a soul. But it *is* true: I'm proud — and happy, too — to think it was given to me to make my mother's last days almost free of care.

Nora: And you're also proud thinking of what you've done for your brothers.

MRS. LINDE: I feel I've a right to be.

NORA: I agree. But listen to this, Kristine — I've also got something to be proud and happy for.

170   MRS. LINDE: I don't doubt it. But whatever do you mean?

NORA: Not so loud. What if Torvald heard! He mustn't, not for anything in the world. Nobody must know, Kristine. No one but you.

MRS. LINDE: But what is it, then?

NORA: Come here. (*Drawing her down beside her on the sofa.*) It's true — I've also got something to be proud and happy for. I'm the one who saved Torvald's life.

MRS. LINDE: Saved —? Saved how?

175   NORA: I told you about the trip to Italy. Torvald never would have lived if he hadn't gone south —

MRS. LINDE: Of course; your father gave you the means —

NORA: (*smiling*) That's what Torvald and all the rest think, but —

MRS. LINDE: But —?

NORA: Papa didn't give us a pin. I was the one who raised the money.

180   MRS. LINDE: You? That whole amount?

NORA: Four thousand, eight hundred crowns. What do you say to that?

MRS. LINDE: But Nora, how was it possible? Did you win the lottery?

NORA: (*disdainfully*) The lottery? Pooh! No art to that.

MRS. LINDE: But where did you get it from then?

185   NORA: (*humming, with a mysterious smile*) Hmm, tra-la-la-la.

MRS. LINDE: Because you couldn't have borrowed it.

NORA: No? Why not?

MRS. LINDE: A wife can't borrow without her husband's consent.

NORA: (*tossing her head*) Oh, but a wife with a little business sense, a wife who knows how to manage —

190   MRS. LINDE: Nora, I simply don't understand —

NORA: You don't have to. Whoever said I *borrowed* the money? I could have gotten it other ways. (*Throwing herself back on the sofa.*) I could have gotten it from some admirer or other. After all, a girl with my ravishing appeal —

MRS. LINDE: You lunatic.

NORA: I'll bet you're eaten up with curiosity, Kristine.

MRS. LINDE: Now listen here, Nora — you haven't done something indiscreet?

195   NORA: (*sitting up again*) Is it indiscreet to save your husband's life?

MRS. LINDE: I think it's indiscreet that without his knowledge you —

NORA: But that's the point: he mustn't know! My Lord, can't you understand? He mustn't ever know the close call he had. It was to *me* the doctors came to say his life was in danger — that nothing could save him but a stay in the south. Didn't I try strategy then! I began talking about how lovely it would be for me to travel abroad like other young wives; I begged and I cried; I told him please to remember my condition, to be kind and indulge me; and then I dropped a hint that he could easily take out a loan. But at that, Kristine, he nearly exploded. He said I was frivolous, and it was his duty as man of the house not to indulge me in whims and fancies — as I think he called them. Aha, I thought, now you'll just have to be saved — and that's when I saw my chance.

MRS. LINDE: And your father never told Torvald the money wasn't from him?

NORA: No, never. Papa died right about then. I'd considered bringing him into my secret and begging him never to tell. But he was too sick at the time — and then, sadly, it didn't matter.

MRS. LINDE: And you've never confided in your husband since?   200

NORA: For heaven's sake, no! Are you serious? He's so strict on that subject. Besides — Torvald, with all his masculine pride — how painfully humiliating for him if he ever found out he was in debt to me. That would just ruin our relationship. Our beautiful, happy home would never be the same.

MRS. LINDE: Won't you ever tell him?

NORA: (*thoughtfully, half smiling*) Yes — maybe sometime, years from now, when I'm no longer so attractive. Don't laugh! I only mean when Torvald loves me less than now, when he stops enjoying my dancing and dressing up and reciting for him. Then it might be wise to have something in reserve —(*Breaking off.*) How ridiculous! That'll never happen — Well, Kristine, what do you think of my big secret? I'm capable of something too, hm? You can imagine, of course, how this thing hangs over me. It really hasn't been easy meeting the payments on time. In the business world there's what they call quarterly interest and what they call amortization, and these are always so terribly hard to manage. I've had to skimp a little here and there, wherever I could, you know. I could hardly spare anything from my house allowance, because Torvald has to live well. I couldn't let the children go poorly dressed; whatever I got for them, I felt I had to use up completely — the darlings!

MRS. LINDE: Poor Nora, so it had to come out of your own budget, then?

NORA: Yes, of course. But I was the one most responsible, too. Every time   205
Torvald gave me money for new clothes and such, I never used more than half; always bought the simplest, cheapest outfits. It was a godsend that everything looks so well on me that Torvald never noticed. But it did weigh me down at times, Kristine. It *is* such a joy to wear fine things. You understand.

MRS. LINDE: Oh, of course.

NORA: And then I found other ways of making money. Last winter I was lucky enough to get a lot of copying to do. I locked myself in and sat writing every evening till late in the night. Ah, I was tired so often, dead tired. But still it was wonderful fun, sitting and working like that, earning money. It was almost like being a man.

MRS. LINDE: But how much have you paid off this way so far?

NORA: That's hard to say, exactly. These accounts, you know, aren't easy to figure. I only know that I've paid out all I could scrape together. Time and again I haven't known where to turn. (*Smiling.*) Then I'd sit here dreaming of a rich old gentleman who had fallen in love with me—

MRS. LINDE: What! Who is he?   210

NORA: Oh, really! And that he'd died, and when his will was opened, there in big letters it said, "All my fortune shall be paid over in cash, immediately, to that enchanting Mrs. Nora Helmer."

MRS. LINDE: But Nora dear — who *was* this gentleman?

NORA: Good grief, can't you understand? The old man never existed; that was only something I'd dream up time and again whenever I was at my wits' end for money. But it makes no difference now; the old fossil can go where he pleases for all I care; I don't need him or his will — because now I'm free. (*Jumping up.*) Oh, how lovely to think of that, Kristine! Carefree! To know you're carefree, utterly carefree; to be able to romp and play with the children, and to keep up a beautiful, charming home — everything just the way Torvald likes it! And think, spring is coming, with big blue skies. Maybe we can travel a little then. Maybe I'll see the ocean again. Oh yes, it *is* so marvelous to live and be happy!

The front doorbell rings.

MRS. LINDE: (*rising*) There's the bell. It's probably best that I go.

215   NORA: No, stay. No one's expected. It must be for Torvald.

MAID: (*from the hall doorway*) Excuse me, ma'am — there's a gentleman here to see Mr. Helmer, but I didn't know — since the doctor's with him —

NORA: Who is the gentleman?

KROGSTAD: (*from the doorway*) It's me, Mrs. Helmer.

Mrs. Linde starts and turns away toward the window.

NORA: (*stepping toward him, tense, her voice a whisper*) You? What is it? Why do you want to speak to my husband?

220   KROGSTAD: Bank business — after a fashion. I have a small job in the investment bank, and I hear now your husband is going to be our chief —

NORA: In other words, it's —

KROGSTAD: Just dry business, Mrs. Helmer. Nothing but that.

NORA: Yes, then please be good enough to step into the study. (*She nods indifferently as she sees him out by the hall door, then returns and begins stirring up the stove.*)

MRS. LINDE: Nora — who was that man?

225   NORA: That was a Mr. Krogstad — a lawyer.

MRS. LINDE: Then it really was him.

NORA: Do you know that person?

MRS. LINDE: I did once — many years ago. For a time he was a law clerk in our town.

NORA: Yes, he's been that.

230   MRS. LINDE: How he's changed.

NORA: I understand he had a very unhappy marriage.

MRS. LINDE: He's a widower now.

NORA: With a number of children. There now, it's burning. (*She closes the stove door and moves the rocker a bit to one side.*)

MRS. LINDE: They say he has a hand in all kinds of business.

NORA: Oh? That may be true: I wouldn't know. But let's not think about   235
business. It's so dull.

Dr. Rank enters from Helmer's study.

RANK: *(still in the doorway)* No, no, really — I don't want to intrude, I'd just
as soon talk a little while with your wife. *(Shuts the door, then notices
Mrs. Linde.)* Oh, beg pardon. I'm intruding here too.

NORA: No, not at all. *(Introducing him.)* Dr. Rank, Mrs. Linde.

RANK: Well now, that's a name much heard in this house. I believe I passed
the lady on the stairs as I came.

MRS. LINDE: Yes, I take the stairs very slowly. They're rather hard on me.

RANK: Uh-hm, some touch of internal weakness?   240

MRS. LINDE: More overexertion, I'd say.

RANK: Nothing else? Then you're probably here in town to rest up in a round
of parties?

MRS. LINDE: I'm here to look for work.

RANK: Is that the best cure for overexertion?

MRS. LINDE: One has to live, Doctor.   245

RANK: Yes, there's a common prejudice to that effect.

NORA: Oh, come on, Dr. Rank — you really do want to live yourself.

RANK: Yes, I really do. Wretched as I am, I'll gladly prolong my torment
indefinitely. All my patients feel like that. And it's quite the same, too,
with the morally sick. Right at this moment there's one of those moral
invalids in there with Helmer—

MRS. LINDE: *(softly)* Ah!

NORA: Who do you mean?   250

RANK: Oh, it's a lawyer, Krogstad, a type you wouldn't know. His character is
rotten to the root — but even he began chattering all-importantly about
how he had to *live*.

NORA: Oh? What did he want to talk to Torvald about?

RANK: I really don't know. I only heard something about the bank.

NORA: I didn't know that Krog — that this man Krogstad had anything to do
with the bank.

RANK: Yes, he's gotten some kind of berth down there. *(To Mrs. Linde.)*   255
I don't know if you also have, in your neck of the woods, a type of person
who scuttles about breathlessly, sniffing out hints of moral corruption,
and then maneuvers his victim into some sort of key position where
he can keep an eye on him. It's the healthy these days that are out in
the cold.

MRS. LINDE: All the same, it's the sick who most need to be taken in.

RANK: *(with a shrug)* Yes, there we have it. That's the concept that's turning
society into a sanatorium.

Nora, lost in her thoughts, breaks out into quiet laughter and claps her hands.

RANK: Why do you laugh at that? Do you have any real idea of what
society is?

NORA: What do I care about dreary old society? I was laughing at something quite different — something terribly funny. Tell me, Doctor — is everyone who works in the bank dependent now on Torvald?

260 RANK: Is that what you find so terribly funny?

NORA: (*smiling and humming*) Never mind, never mind! (*Pacing the floor.*) Yes, that's really immensely amusing: that we — that Torvald has so much power now over all those people. (*Taking the bag out of her pocket.*) Dr. Rank, a little macaroon on that?

RANK: See here, macaroons! I thought they were contraband here.

NORA: Yes, but these are some that Kristine gave me.

MRS. LINDE: What? I —?

265 NORA: Now, now, don't be afraid. You couldn't possibly know that Torvald had forbidden them. You see, he's worried they'll ruin my teeth. But hmp! Just this once! Isn't that so, Dr. Rank? Help yourself! (*Puts a macaroon in his mouth.*) And you too, Kristine. And I'll also have one, only a little one — or two, at the most. (*Walking about again.*) Now I'm really tremendously happy. Now there's just one last thing in the world that I have an enormous desire to do.

RANK: Well! And what's that?

NORA: It's something I have such a consuming desire to say so Torvald could hear.

RANK: And why can't you say it?

NORA: I don't dare. It's quite shocking.

270 MRS. LINDE: Shocking?

RANK: Well, then it isn't advisable. But in front of us you certainly can. What do you have such a desire to say so Torvald could hear?

NORA: I have such a huge desire to say — to hell and be damned!

RANK: Are you crazy?

MRS. LINDE: My goodness, Nora!

275 RANK: Go on, say it. Here he is.

NORA: (*hiding the macaroon bag*) Shh, shh, shh!

Helmer comes in from his study, hat in hand, overcoat over his arm.

NORA: (*going toward him*) Well, Torvald dear, are you through with him?

HELMER: Yes, he just left.

NORA: Let me introduce you — this is Kristine, who's arrived here in town.

280 HELMER: Kristine —? I'm sorry, but I don't know—

NORA: Mrs. Linde, Torvald dear. Mrs. Kristine Linde.

HELMER: Of course. A childhood friend of my wife's, no doubt?

MRS. LINDE: Yes, we knew each other in those days.

NORA: And just think, she made the long trip down here in order to talk with you.

285 HELMER: What's this?

MRS. LINDE: Well, not exactly—

NORA: You see, Kristine is remarkably clever in office work, and so she's terribly eager to come under a capable man's supervision and add more to what she already knows—

HELMER: Very wise, Mrs. Linde.

NORA: And then when she heard that you'd become a bank manager — the story was wired out to the papers — then she came in as fast as she could and — Really, Torvald, for my sake you can do a little something for Kristine, can't you?

HELMER: Yes, it's not at all impossible. Mrs. Linde, I suppose you're a widow?   290

MRS. LINDE: Yes.

HELMER: Any experience in office work?

MRS. LINDE: Yes, a good deal.

HELMER: Well, it's quite likely that I can make an opening for you—

NORA: (*clapping her hands*) You see, you see!   295

HELMER: You've come at a lucky moment, Mrs. Linde.

MRS. LINDE: Oh, how can I thank you?

HELMER: Not necessary. (*Putting his overcoat on.*) But today you'll have to excuse me—

RANK: Wait, I'll go with you. (*He fetches his coat from the hall and warms it at the stove.*)

NORA: Don't stay out long, dear.   300

HELMER: An hour; no more.

NORA: Are you going too, Kristine?

MRS. LINDE: (*putting on her winter garments*) Yes, I have to see about a room now.

HELMER: Then perhaps we can all walk together.

NORA: (*helping her*) What a shame we're so cramped here, but it's quite   305
impossible for us to—

MRS. LINDE: Oh, don't even think of it! Good-bye, Nora dear, and thanks for everything.

NORA: Good-bye for now. Of course you'll be back this evening. And you too, Dr. Rank. What? If you're well enough? Oh, you've got to be! Wrap up tight now.

In a ripple of small talk the company moves out into the hall; children's voices are heard outside on the steps.

NORA: There they are! There they are! (*She runs to open the door. The children come in with their nurse, Anne-Marie.*) Come in, come in! (*Bends down and kisses them.*) Oh, you darlings —! Look at them, Kristine. Aren't they lovely!

RANK: No loitering in the draft here.

HELMER: Come, Mrs. Linde — this place is unbearable now for anyone but   310
mothers.

Dr. Rank, Helmer, and Mrs. Linde go down the stairs. Anne-Marie goes into the living room with the children. Nora follows, after closing the hall door.

NORA: How fresh and strong you look. Oh, such red cheeks you have! Like apples and roses. (*The children interrupt her throughout the following.*) And it was so much fun? That's wonderful. Really? You pulled both Emmy and Bob on the sled? Imagine, all together! Yes, you're a clever boy, Ivar. Oh, let me hold her a bit, Anne-Marie. My sweet little doll baby! (*Takes the smallest from the nurse and dances with her.*) Yes, yes, Mama will dance with Bob as well. What? Did you throw snowballs? Oh, if I'd only been there! No, don't bother, Anne-Marie — I'll undress them myself. Oh yes, let me. It's such fun. Go in and rest; you look half frozen. There's hot coffee waiting for you on the stove. (*The nurse goes into the room to the left. Nora takes the children's winter things off, throwing them about, while the children talk to her all at once.*) Is that so? A big dog chased you? But it didn't bite? No, dogs never bite little, lovely doll babies. Don't peek in the packages, Ivar! What is it? Yes, wouldn't you like to know. No, no, it's an ugly something. Well? Shall we play? What shall we play? Hide-and-seek? Yes, let's play hide-and-seek. Bob must hide first. I must? Yes, let me hide first. (*Laughing and shouting, she and the children play in and out of the living room and the adjoining room to the right. At last Nora hides under the table. The children come storming in, search, but cannot find her, then hear her muffled laughter, dash over to the table, lift the cloth up and find her. Wild shouting. She creeps forward as if to scare them. More shouts. Meanwhile, a knock at the hall door; no one has noticed it. Now the door half opens, and Krogstad appears. He waits a moment; the game goes on.*)

KROGSTAD: Beg pardon, Mrs. Helmer—

NORA: (*with a strangled cry, turning and scrambling to her knees*) Oh! What do you want?

KROGSTAD: Excuse me. The outer door was ajar; it must be someone forgot to shut it—

315   NORA: (*rising*) My husband isn't home, Mr. Krogstad.

KROGSTAD: I know that.

NORA: Yes — then what do you want here?

KROGSTAD: A word with you.

NORA: With —? (*To the children, quietly.*) Go in to Anne-Marie. What? No, the strange man won't hurt Mama. When he's gone, we'll play some more. (*She leads the children into the room to the left and shuts the door after them. Then, tense and nervous.*) You want to speak to me?

320   KROGSTAD: Yes, I want to.

NORA: Today? But it's not yet the first of the month—

KROGSTAD: No, it's Christmas Eve. It's going to be up to you how merry a Christmas you have.

NORA: What is it you want? Today I absolutely can't—

KROGSTAD: We won't talk about that till later. This is something else. You do have a moment to spare, I suppose?

325   NORA: Oh yes, of course — I do, except—

KROGSTAD: Good. I was sitting over at Olsen's Restaurant when I saw your husband go down the street—

NORA: Yes?

KROGSTAD: With a lady.

NORA: Yes. So?

330   KROGSTAD: If you'll pardon my asking: wasn't that lady a Mrs. Linde?

NORA: Yes.

KROGSTAD: Just now come into town?

NORA: Yes, today.

KROGSTAD: She's a good friend of yours?

NORA: Yes, she is. But I don't see— 335

KROGSTAD: I also knew her once.

NORA: I'm aware of that.

KROGSTAD: Oh? You know all about it. I thought so. Well, then let me ask you short and sweet: is Mrs. Linde getting a job in the bank?

NORA: What makes you think you can cross-examine me, Mr. Krogstad— you, one of my husband's employees? But since you ask, you might as well know— yes, Mrs. Linde's going to be taken on at the bank. And I'm the one who spoke for her, Mr. Krogstad. Now you know.

KROGSTAD: So I guessed right. 340

NORA: (*pacing up and down*) Oh, one does have a tiny bit of influence, I should hope. Just because I am a woman, don't think it means that—When one has a subordinate position, Mr. Krogstad, one really ought to be careful about pushing somebody who—hm—

KROGSTAD: Who has influence?

NORA: That's right.

KROGSTAD: (*in a different tone*) Mrs. Helmer, would you be good enough to use your influence on my behalf?

NORA: What? What do you mean? 345

KROGSTAD: Would you please make sure that I keep my subordinate position in the bank?

NORA: What does that mean? Who's thinking of taking away your position?

KROGSTAD: Oh, don't play the innocent with me. I'm quite aware that your friend would hardly relish the chance of running into me again; and I'm also aware now whom I can thank for being turned out.

NORA: But I promise you—

KROGSTAD: Yes, yes, yes, to the point: there's still time, and I'm advising you 350 to use your influence to prevent it.

NORA: But Mr. Krogstad, I have absolutely no influence.

KROGSTAD: You haven't? I thought you were just saying—

NORA: You shouldn't take me so literally. I! How can you believe that I have any such influence over my husband?

KROGSTAD: Oh, I've known your husband from our student days. I don't think the great bank manager's more steadfast than any other married man.

NORA: You speak insolently about my husband, and I'll show you the door. 355

KROGSTAD: The lady has spirit.

NORA: I'm not afraid of you any longer. After New Year's, I'll soon be done with the whole business.

KROGSTAD: (*restraining himself*) Now listen to me, Mrs. Helmer. If necessary, I'll fight for my little job in the bank as if it were life itself.

NORA: Yes, so it seems.

KROGSTAD: It's not just a matter of income; that's the least of it. It's something 360 else—All right, out with it! Look, this is the thing. You know, just like all the others, of course, that once, a good many years ago, I did something rather rash.

NORA: I've heard rumors to that effect.

KROGSTAD: The case never got into court; but all the same, every door was closed in my face from then on. So I took up those various activities you know about. I had to grab hold somewhere; and I dare say I haven't been among the worst. But now I want to drop all that. My boys are growing up. For their sakes, I'll have to win back as much respect as possible here in town. That job in the bank was like the first rung in my ladder. And now your husband wants to kick me right back down in the mud again.

NORA: But for heaven's sake, Mr. Krogstad, it's simply not in my power to help you.

KROGSTAD: That's because you haven't the will to —but I have the means to make you.

365 NORA: You certainly won't tell my husband that I owe you money?

KROGSTAD: Hm —what if I told him that?

NORA: That would be shameful of you. *(Nearly in tears.)* This secret —my joy and my pride —that he should learn it in such a crude and disgusting way —learn it from you. You'd expose me to the most horrible unpleasantness—

KROGSTAD: Only unpleasantness?

NORA: *(vehemently)* But go on and try. It'll turn out the worse for you, because then my husband will really see what a crook you are, and then you'll *never* be able to hold your job.

370 KROGSTAD: I asked if it was just domestic unpleasantness you were afraid of.

NORA: If my husband finds out, then of course he'll pay what I owe at once, and then we'd be through with you for good.

KROGSTAD: *(a step closer)* Listen, Mrs. Helmer —you've either got a very bad memory, or else no head at all for business. I'd better put you a little more in touch with the facts.

NORA: What do you mean?

KROGSTAD: When your husband was sick, you came to me for a loan of four thousand, eight hundred crowns.

375 NORA: Where else could I go?

KROGSTAD: I promised to get you that sum—

NORA: And you got it.

KROGSTAD: I promised to get you that sum, on certain conditions. You were so involved in your husband's illness, and so eager to finance your trip, that I guess you didn't think out all the details. It might just be a good idea to remind you. I promised you the money on the strength of a note I drew up.

NORA: Yes, and that I signed.

380 KROGSTAD: Right. But at the bottom I added some lines for your father to guarantee the loan. He was supposed to sign down there.

NORA: Supposed to? He did sign.

KROGSTAD: I left the date blank. In other words, your father would have dated his signature himself. Do you remember that?

NORA: Yes, I think—

KROGSTAD: Then I gave you the note for you to mail to your father. Isn't that so?

NORA: Yes.   385

KROGSTAD: And naturally you sent it at once — because only some five, six days later you brought me the note, properly signed. And with that, the money was yours.

NORA: Well, then; I've made my payments regularly, haven't I?

KROGSTAD: More or less. But — getting back to the point — those were hard times for you then, Mrs. Helmer.

NORA: Yes, they were.

KROGSTAD: Your father was very ill, I believe.   390

NORA: He was near the end.

KROGSTAD: He died soon after?

NORA: Yes.

KROGSTAD: Tell me, Mrs. Helmer, do you happen to recall the date of your father's death? The day of the month, I mean.

NORA: Papa died the twenty-ninth of September.   395

KROGSTAD: That's quite correct; I've already looked into that. And now we come to a curious thing — (*taking out a paper*) which I simply cannot comprehend.

NORA: Curious thing? I don't know —

KROGSTAD: This is the curious thing: that your father co-signed the note for your loan three days after his death.

NORA: How — ? I don't understand.

KROGSTAD: Your father died the twenty-ninth of September. But look.   400
Here your father dated his signature October second. Isn't that curious, Mrs. Helmer? (*Nora is silent.*) Can you explain it to me? (*Nora remains silent.*) It's also remarkable that the words "October second" and the year aren't written in your father's hand, but rather in one that I think I know. Well, it's easy to understand. Your father forgot perhaps to date his signature, and then someone or other added it, a bit sloppily, before anyone knew of his death. There's nothing wrong in that. It all comes down to the signature. And there's no question about *that*, Mrs. Helmer. It really *was* your father who signed his own name here, wasn't it?

NORA: (*after a short silence, throwing her head back and looking squarely at him*) No, it wasn't. I signed Papa's name.

KROGSTAD: Wait, now — are you fully aware that this is a dangerous confession?

NORA: Why? You'll soon get your money.

KROGSTAD: Let me ask you a question — why didn't you send the paper to your father?

NORA: That was impossible. Papa was so sick. If I'd asked him for his   405
signature, I also would have had to tell him what the money was for. But I couldn't tell him, sick as he was, that my husband's life was in danger. That was just impossible.

KROGSTAD: Then it would have been better if you'd given up the trip abroad.

NORA: I couldn't possibly. The trip was to save my husband's life. I couldn't give that up.

KROGSTAD: But didn't you ever consider that this was a fraud against me?

NORA: I couldn't let myself be bothered by that. You weren't any concern of mine. I couldn't stand you, with all those cold complications you made, even though you knew how badly off my husband was.

410   KROGSTAD: Mrs. Helmer, obviously you haven't the vaguest idea of what you've involved yourself in. But I can tell you this: it was nothing more and nothing worse than I once did — and it wrecked my whole reputation.

NORA: You? Do you expect me to believe that you ever acted bravely to save your wife's life?

KROGSTAD: Laws don't inquire into motives.

NORA: Then they must be very poor laws.

KROGSTAD: Poor or not — if I introduce this paper in court, you'll be judged according to law.

415   NORA: This I refuse to believe. A daughter hasn't a right to protect her dying father from anxiety and care? A wife hasn't a right to save her husband's life? I don't know much about laws, but I'm sure that somewhere in the books these things are allowed. And you don't know anything about it — you who practice the law? You must be an awful lawyer, Mr. Krogstad.

KROGSTAD: Could be. But business — the kind of business we two mixed up in — don't you think I know about that? All right. Do what you want now. But I'm telling you *this:* if I get shoved down a second time, you're going to keep me company. (*He bows and goes out through the hall.*)

NORA: (*pensive for a moment, then tossing her head*) Oh, really! Trying to frighten me! I'm not so silly as all that. (*Begins gathering up the children's clothes, but soon stops.*) But —? No, but that's impossible! I did it out of love.

THE CHILDREN: (*in the doorway, left*) Mama, that strange man's gone out the door.

NORA: Yes, yes, I know it. But don't tell anyone about the strange man. Do you hear? Not even Papa!

420   THE CHILDREN: No, Mama. But now will you play again?

NORA: No, not now.

THE CHILDREN: Oh, but Mama, you promised.

NORA: Yes, but I can't now. Go inside; I have too much to do. Go in, go in, my sweet darlings. (*She herds them gently back in the room and shuts the door after them. Settling on the sofa, she takes up a piece of embroidery and makes some stitches, but soon stops abruptly.*) No! (*Throws the work aside, rises, goes to the hall door and calls out.*) Helene! Let me have the tree in here. (*Goes to the table, left, opens the table drawer, and stops again.*) No, but that's utterly impossible!

MAID: (*with the Christmas tree*) Where should I put it, ma'am?

425   NORA: There. The middle of the floor.

MAID: Should I bring anything else?

NORA: No, thanks. I have what I need.

The Maid, who has set the tree down, goes out.

NORA: (*absorbed in trimming the tree*) Candles here — and flowers here. That terrible creature! Talk, talk, talk! There's nothing to it at all. The tree's going to be lovely. I'll do anything to please you, Torvald. I'll sing for you, dance for you —

Helmer comes in from the hall, with a sheaf of papers under his arm.

NORA: Oh! You're back so soon?

HELMER: Yes. Has anyone been here?   430

NORA: Here? No.

HELMER: That's odd. I saw Krogstad leaving the front door.

NORA: So? Oh yes, that's true. Krogstad was here a moment.

HELMER: Nora, I can see by your face that he's been here, begging you to put in a good word for him.

NORA: Yes.   435

HELMER: And it was supposed to seem like your own idea? You were to hide it from me that he'd been here. He asked you that, too, didn't he?

NORA: Yes, Torvald, but—

HELMER: Nora, Nora, and you could fall for that? Talk with that sort of person and promise him anything? And then in the bargain, tell me an untruth.

NORA: An untruth —?

HELMER: Didn't you say that no one had been here? (*Wagging his finger.*) My   440
little songbird must never do that again. A songbird needs a clean beak to warble with. No false notes. (*Putting his arm about her waist.*) That's the way it should be, isn't it? Yes, I'm sure of it. (*Releasing her.*) And so, enough of that. (*Sitting by the stove.*) Ah, how snug and cozy it is here. (*Leafing among his papers.*)

NORA: (*busy with the tree, after a short pause*) Torvald!

HELMER: Yes.

NORA: I'm so much looking forward to the Stenborgs' costume party, day after tomorrow.

HELMER: And I can't wait to see what you'll surprise me with.

NORA: Oh, that stupid business!   445

HELMER: What?

NORA: I can't find anything that's right. Everything seems so ridiculous, so inane.

HELMER: So my little Nora's come to *that* recognition?

NORA: (*going behind his chair, her arms resting on its back*) Are you very busy, Torvald?

HELMER: Oh—   450

NORA: What papers are those?

HELMER: Bank matters.

NORA: Already?

HELMER: I've gotten full authority from the retiring management to make all necessary changes in personnel and procedure. I'll need Christmas week for that. I want to have everything in order by New Year's.

455 **NORA:** So that was the reason this poor Krogstad —

HELMER: Hm.

NORA: (*still leaning on the chair and slowly stroking the nape of his neck*) If you weren't so very busy, I would have asked you an enormous favor, Torvald.

HELMER: Let's hear. What is it?

NORA: You know, there isn't anyone who has your good taste — and I want so much to look well at the costume party. Torvald, couldn't you take over and decide what I should be and plan my costume?

460 **HELMER:** Ah, is my stubborn little creature calling for a lifeguard?

NORA: Yes, Torvald, I can't get anywhere without your help.

HELMER: All right — I'll think it over. We'll hit on something.

NORA: Oh, how sweet of you. (*Goes to the tree again. Pause.*) Aren't the red flowers pretty —? But tell me, was it really such a crime that this Krogstad committed?

HELMER: Forgery. Do you have any idea what that means?

465 **NORA:** Couldn't he have done it out of need?

HELMER: Yes, or thoughtlessness, like so many others. I'm not so heartless that I'd condemn a man categorically for just one mistake.

NORA: No, of course not, Torvald!

HELMER: Plenty of men have redeemed themselves by openly confessing their crimes and taking their punishment.

NORA: Punishment —?

470 **HELMER:** But now Krogstad didn't go that way. He got himself out by sharp practices, and that's the real cause of his moral breakdown.

NORA: Do you really think that would —?

HELMER: Just imagine how a man with that sort of guilt in him has to lie and cheat and deceive on all sides, has to wear a mask even with the nearest and dearest he has, even with his own wife and children. And with the children, Nora — that's where it's most horrible.

NORA: Why?

HELMER: Because that kind of atmosphere of lies infects the whole life of a home. Every breath the children take in is filled with the germs of something degenerate.

475 **NORA:** (*coming closer behind him*) Are you sure of that?

HELMER: Oh, I've seen it often enough as a lawyer. Almost everyone who goes bad early in life has a mother who's a chronic liar.

NORA: Why just — the mother?

HELMER: It's usually the mother's influence that's dominant, but the father's works in the same way, of course. Every lawyer is quite familiar with it. And still this Krogstad's been going home year in, year out, poisoning his own children with lies and pretense; that's why I call him morally lost. (*Reaching his hands out toward her.*) So my sweet little Nora must promise me never to plead his cause. Your hand on it. Come, come, what's this? Give me your hand. There, now. All settled. I can tell you it'd be impossible for me to work alongside of him. I literally feel physically revolted when I'm anywhere near such a person.

NORA: *(withdraws her hand and goes to the other side of the Christmas tree)* How hot it is here! And I've got so much to do.

HELMER: *(getting up and gathering his papers)* Yes, and I have to think about getting some of these read through before dinner. I'll think about your costume, too. And something to hang on the tree in gilt paper, I may even see about that. *(Putting his hand on her head.)* Oh you, my darling little songbird. *(He goes into his study and closes the door after him.)*   480

NORA: *(softly, after a silence)* Oh, really! It isn't so. It's impossible. It must be impossible.

ANNE-MARIE: *(in the doorway, left)* The children are begging so hard to come in to Mama.

NORA: No, no, no, don't let them in to me! You stay with them, Anne-Marie.

ANNE-MARIE: Of course, ma'am. *(Closes the door.)*

NORA: *(pale with terror)* Hurt my children —! Poison my home? *(A moment's pause; then she tosses her head.)* That's not true. Never. Never in all the world.   485

ACT II

Same room. Beside the piano the Christmas tree now stands stripped of ornaments, burned-down candle stubs on its ragged branches. Nora's street clothes lie on the sofa. Nora, alone in the room, moves restlessly about; at last she stops at the sofa and picks up her coat.

NORA: *(dropping the coat again)* Someone's coming! *(Goes toward the door, listens.)* No — there's no one. Of course — nobody's coming today, Christmas Day — or tomorrow, either. But maybe —*(Opens the door and looks out.)* No, nothing in the mailbox. Quite empty. *(Coming forward.)* What nonsense! He won't do anything serious. Nothing terrible could happen. It's impossible. Why, I have three small children.

Anne-Marie, with a large carton, comes in from the room to the left.

ANNE-MARIE: Well, at last I found the box with the masquerade clothes.

NORA: Thanks. Put it on the table.

ANNE-MARIE: *(does so)* But they're all pretty much of a mess.

NORA: Ahh! I'd love to rip them in a million pieces!   5

ANNE-MARIE: Oh, mercy, they can be fixed right up. Just a little patience.

NORA: Yes, I'll go get Mrs. Linde to help me.

ANNE-MARIE: Out again now? In this nasty weather? Miss Nora will catch cold — get sick.

NORA: Oh, worse things could happen — How are the children?

ANNE-MARIE: The poor mites are playing with their Christmas presents, but—   10

NORA: Do they ask for me much?

ANNE-MARIE: They're so used to having Mama around, you know.

NORA: Yes. But Anne-Marie, I *can't* be together with them as much as I was.

ANNE-MARIE: Well, small children get used to anything.

15 NORA: You think so? Do you think they'd forget their mother if she was gone
for good?

ANNE-MARIE: Oh, mercy — gone for good!

NORA: Wait, tell me, Anne-Marie — I've wondered so often — how could you
ever have the heart to give your child over to strangers?

ANNE-MARIE: But I had to, you know, to become little Nora's nurse.

NORA: Yes, but how could you *do* it?

20 ANNE-MARIE: When I could get such a good place? A girl who's poor and
who's gotten in trouble is glad enough for that. Because that slippery fish,
he didn't do a thing for me, you know.

NORA: But your daughter's surely forgotten you.

ANNE-MARIE: Oh, she certainly has not. She's written to me, both when she
was confirmed and when she was married.

NORA: (*clasping her about the neck*) You old Anne-Marie, you were a good
mother for me when I was little.

ANNE-MARIE: Poor little Nora, with no other mother but me.

25 NORA: And if the babies didn't have one, then I know that you'd —What silly
talk! (*Opening the carton.*) Go in to them. Now I'll have to — Tomorrow
you can see how lovely I'll look.

ANNE-MARIE: Oh, there won't be anyone at the party as lovely as Miss Nora.
(*She goes off into the room, left.*)

NORA: (*begins unpacking the box, but soon throws it aside*) Oh, if I dared to go
out. If only nobody would come. If only nothing would happen here while
I'm out. What craziness — nobody's coming. Just don't think. This muff —
needs a brushing. Beautiful gloves, beautiful gloves. Let it go. Let it go!
One, two, three, four, five, six —(*With a cry.*) Oh, there they are! (*Poises to
move toward the door, but remains irresolutely standing. Mrs. Linde enters from
the hall, where she has removed her street clothes.*)

NORA: Oh, it's you, Kristine. There's no one else out there? How good that
you've come.

MRS. LINDE: I hear you were up asking for me.

30 NORA: Yes, I just stopped by. There's something you really can help me with.
Let's get settled on the sofa. Look, there's going to be a costume party
tomorrow evening at the Stenborgs' right above us, and now Torvald
wants me to go as a Neapolitan peasant girl and dance the tarantella that
I learned in Capri.

MRS. LINDE: Really, are you giving a whole performance?

NORA: Torvald says yes, I should. See, here's the dress. Torvald had it made
for me down there; but now it's all so tattered that I just don't know—

MRS. LINDE: Oh, we'll fix that up in no time. It's nothing more than the
trimmings — they're a bit loose here and there. Needle and thread?
Good, now we have what we need.

NORA: Oh, how sweet of you!

35 MRS. LINDE: (*sewing*) So you'll be in disguise tomorrow, Nora. You know
what? I'll stop by then for a moment and have a look at you all dressed up.
But listen, I've absolutely forgotten to thank you for that pleasant evening
yesterday.

NORA: *(getting up and walking about)* I don't think it was as pleasant as usual
yesterday. You should have come to town a bit sooner, Kristine —Yes,
Torvald really knows how to give a home elegance and charm.

MRS. LINDE: And you do, too, if you ask me. You're not your father's daughter
for nothing. But tell me, is Dr. Rank always so down in the mouth as
yesterday?

NORA: No, that was quite an exception. But he goes around critically ill all
the time — tuberculosis of the spine, poor man. You know, his father was
a disgusting thing who kept mistresses and so on — and that's why the
son's been sickly from birth.

MRS. LINDE: *(lets her sewing fall to her lap)* But my dearest Nora, how do you
know about such things?

NORA: *(walking more jauntily)* Hmp! When you've had three children, then   40
you've had a few visits from —from women who know something of
medicine, and they tell you this and that.

MRS. LINDE: *(resumes sewing; a short pause)* Does Dr. Rank come here
every day?

NORA: Every blessed day. He's Torvald's best friend from childhood, and *my*
good friend, too. Dr. Rank almost belongs to this house.

MRS. LINDE: But tell me — is he quite sincere? I mean, doesn't he rather enjoy
flattering people?

NORA: Just the opposite. Why do you think that?

MRS. LINDE: When you introduced us yesterday, he was proclaiming that he'd   45
often heard my name in this house; but later I noticed that your husband
hadn't the slightest idea who I really was. So how could Dr. Rank —?

NORA: But it's all true, Kristine. You see, Torvald loves me beyond words, and,
as he puts it, he'd like to keep me all to himself. For a long time he'd almost
be jealous if I even mentioned any of my old friends back home. So of
course I dropped that. But with Dr. Rank I talk a lot about such things,
because he likes hearing about them.

MRS. LINDE: Now listen, Nora; in many ways you're still like a child. I'm
a good deal older than you, with a little more experience. I'll tell you
something: you ought to put an end to all this with Dr. Rank.

NORA: What should I put an end to?

MRS. LINDE: Both parts of it, I think. Yesterday you said something about
a rich admirer who'd provide you with money—

NORA: Yes, one who doesn't exist — worse luck. So?   50

MRS. LINDE: Is Dr. Rank well off?

NORA: Yes, he is.

MRS. LINDE: With no dependents?

NORA: No, no one. But—

MRS. LINDE: And he's over here every day?   55

NORA: Yes, I told you that.

MRS. LINDE: How can a man of such refinement be so grasping?

NORA: I don't follow you at all.

MRS. LINDE: Now don't try to hide it, Nora. You think I can't guess who
loaned you the forty-eight hundred crowns?

60   NORA: Are you out of your mind? How could you think such a thing! A friend
        of ours, who comes here every single day. What an intolerable situation
        that would have been!

MRS. LINDE: Then it really wasn't him.

NORA: No, absolutely not. It never even crossed my mind for a moment —
        And he had nothing to lend in those days; his inheritance came later.

MRS. LINDE: Well, I think that was a stroke of luck for you, Nora dear.

NORA: No, it never would have occurred to me to ask Dr. Rank — Still, I'm
        quite sure that if I had asked him—

65   MRS. LINDE: Which you won't, of course.

NORA: No, of course not. I can't see that I'd ever need to. But I'm quite
        positive that if I talked to Dr. Rank—

MRS. LINDE: Behind your husband's back?

NORA: I've got to clear up this other thing; *that's* also behind his back. I've *got*
        to clear it all up.

MRS. LINDE: Yes, I was saying that yesterday, but—

70   NORA: (*pacing up and down*) A man handles these problems so much better
        than a woman—

MRS. LINDE: One's husband does, yes.

NORA: Nonsense. (*Stopping.*) When you pay everything you owe, then you get
        your note back, right?

MRS. LINDE: Yes, naturally.

NORA: And can rip it into a million pieces and burn it up — that filthy scrap
        of paper!

75   MRS. LINDE: (*looking hard at her, laying her sewing aside, and rising slowly*) Nora,
        you're hiding something from me.

NORA: You can see it in my face?

MRS. LINDE: Something's happened to you since yesterday morning. Nora,
        what is it?

NORA: (*hurrying toward her*) Kristine! (*Listening.*) Shh! Torvald's home. Look,
        go in with the children a while. Torvald can't bear all this snipping and
        stitching. Let Anne-Marie help you.

MRS. LINDE: (*gathering up some of the things*) All right, but I'm not leaving here
        until we've talked this out. (*She disappears into the room, left, as Torvald
        enters from the hall.*)

80   NORA: Oh, how I've been waiting for you, Torvald dear.

HELMER: Was that the dressmaker?

NORA: No, that was Kristine. She's helping me fix up my costume. You know,
        it's going to be quite attractive.

HELMER: Yes, wasn't that a bright idea I had?

NORA: Brilliant! But then wasn't I good as well to give in to you?

85   HELMER: Good — because you give in to your husband's judgment? All right,
        you little goose, I know you didn't mean it like that. But I won't disturb you.
        You'll want to have a fitting, I suppose.

NORA: And you'll be working?

HELMER: Yes. (*Indicating a bundle of papers.*) See. I've been down to the bank.
        (*Starts toward his study.*)

NORA: Torvald.

HELMER: *(stops)* Yes.

NORA: If your little squirrel begged you, with all her heart and soul, for   90
  something —?

HELMER: What's that?

NORA: Then would you do it?

HELMER: First, naturally, I'd have to know what it was.

NORA: Your squirrel would scamper about and do tricks, if you'd only be sweet
  and give in.

HELMER: Out with it.   95

NORA: Your lark would be singing high and low in every room —

HELMER: Come on, she does that anyway.

NORA: I'd be a wood nymph and dance for you in the moonlight.

HELMER: Nora — don't tell me it's that same business from this morning?

NORA: *(coming closer)* Yes, Torvald, I beg you, please!   100

HELMER: And you actually have the nerve to drag that up again?

NORA: Yes, yes, you've got to give in to me; you *have* to let Krogstad keep his
  job in the bank.

HELMER: My dear Nora, I've slated his job for Mrs. Linde.

NORA: That's awfully kind of you. But you could just fire another clerk instead
  of Krogstad.

HELMER: This is the most incredible stubbornness! Because you go and give an   105
  impulsive promise to speak up for him, I'm expected to —

NORA: That's not the reason, Torvald. It's for your own sake. That man does
  writing for the worst papers; you said it yourself. He could do you any
  amount of harm. I'm scared to death of him —

HELMER: Ah, I understand. It's the old memories haunting you.

NORA: What do you mean by that?

HELMER: Of course, you're thinking about your father.

NORA: Yes, all right. Just remember how those nasty gossips wrote in the   110
  papers about Papa and slandered him so cruelly. I think they'd have had
  him dismissed if the department hadn't sent you up to investigate, and
  if you hadn't been so kind and open-minded toward him.

HELMER: My dear Nora, there's a notable difference between your father and
  me. Your father's official career was hardly above reproach. But mine is; and
  I hope it'll stay that way as long as I hold my position.

NORA: Oh, who can ever tell what vicious minds can invent? We could be so
  snug and happy now in our quiet, carefree home — you and I and the
  children, Torvald! That's why I'm pleading with you so—

HELMER: And just by pleading for him you make it impossible for me to keep
  him on. It's already known at the bank that I'm firing Krogstad. What if it's
  rumored around now that the new bank manager was vetoed by his wife—

NORA: Yes, what then —?

HELMER: Oh yes — as long as our little bundle of stubbornness gets her   115
  way —! I should go and make myself ridiculous in front of the whole
  office — give people the idea I can be swayed by all kinds of outside
  pressure. Oh, you can bet I'd feel the effects of that soon enough!

Besides — there's something that rules Krogstad right out at the bank
as long as I'm the manager.

NORA: What's that?

HELMER: His moral failings I could maybe overlook if I had to —

NORA: Yes, Torvald, why not?

HELMER: And I hear he's quite efficient on the job. But he was a crony of mine
back in my teens — one of those rash friendships that crop up again and
again to embarrass you later in life. Well, I might as well say it straight out:
we're on a first-name basis. And that tactless fool makes no effort at all to
hide it in front of others. Quite the contrary — he thinks that entitles him
to take a familiar air around me, and so every other second he comes
booming out with his "Yes, Torvald!" and "Sure thing, Torvald!" I tell you,
it's been excruciating for me. He's out to make my place in the bank
unbearable.

120 NORA: Torvald, you can't be serious about all this.

HELMER: Oh no? Why not?

NORA: Because these are such petty considerations.

HELMER: What are you saying? Petty? You think I'm petty!

NORA: No, just the opposite, Torvald dear. That's exactly why —

125 HELMER: Never mind. You call my motives petty; then I might as well be just
that. Petty! All right! We'll put a stop to this for good. (*Goes to the hall door
and calls.*) Helene!

NORA: What do you want?

HELMER: (*searching among his papers*) A decision. (*The Maid comes in.*) Look
here; take this letter; go out with it at once. Get hold of a messenger and
have him deliver it. Quick now. It's already addressed. Wait, here's some
money.

MAID: Yes, sir. (*She leaves with the letter.*)

HELMER: (*straightening his papers*) There, now, little Miss Willful.

130 NORA: (*breathlessly*) Torvald, what was that letter?

HELMER: Krogstad's notice.

NORA: Call it back, Torvald! There's still time. Oh, Torvald, call it back! Do
it for my sake — for your sake, for the children's sake! Do you hear, Torvald;
do it! You don't know how this can harm us.

HELMER: Too late.

NORA: Yes, too late.

135 HELMER: Nora dear, I can forgive you this panic, even though basically you're
insulting me. Yes, you are! Or isn't it an insult to think that *I* should be
afraid of a courtroom hack's revenge? But I forgive you anyway, because this
shows so beautifully how much you love me. (*Takes her in his arms.*) This is
the way it should be, my darling Nora. Whatever comes, you'll see: when it
really counts, I have strength and courage enough as a man to take on the
whole weight myself.

NORA: (*terrified*) What do you mean by that?

HELMER: The whole weight, I said.

NORA: (*resolutely*) No, never in all the world.

HELMER: Good. So we'll share it, Nora, as man and wife. That's as it should be. (*Fondling her.*) Are you happy now? There, there, there — not these frightened dove's eyes. It's nothing at all but empty fantasies — Now you should run through your tarantella and practice your tambourine. I'll go to the inner office and shut both doors, so I won't hear a thing; you can make all the noise you like. (*Turning in the doorway.*) And when Rank comes, just tell him where he can find me. (*He nods to her and goes with his papers into the study, closing the door.*)

NORA: (*standing as though rooted, dazed with fright, in a whisper*) He really could do it. He will do it. He'll do it in spite of everything. No, not that, never, never! Anything but that! Escape! A way out — (*The doorbell rings.*) Dr. Rank! Anything but that! *Anything*, whatever it is! (*Her hands pass over her face, smoothing it; she pulls herself together, goes over and opens the hall door. Dr. Rank stands outside, hanging his fur coat up. During the following scene, it begins getting dark.*) 140

NORA: Hello, Dr. Rank. I recognized your ring. But you mustn't go in to Torvald yet; I believe he's working.

RANK: And you?

NORA: For you, I always have an hour to spare — you know that. (*He has entered, and she shuts the door after him.*)

RANK: Many thanks. I'll make use of these hours while I can.

NORA: What do you mean by that? While you can? 145

RANK: Does that disturb you?

NORA: Well, it's such an odd phrase. Is anything going to happen?

RANK: What's going to happen is what I've been expecting so long — but I honestly didn't think it would come so soon.

NORA: (*gripping his arm*) What is it you've found out? Dr. Rank, you have to tell me!

RANK: (*sitting by the stove*) It's all over with me. There's nothing to be done about it. 150

NORA: (*breathing easier*) Is it you — then —?

RANK: Who else? There's no point in lying to one's self. I'm the most miserable of all my patients, Mrs. Helmer. These past few days I've been auditing my internal accounts. Bankrupt! Within a month I'll probably be laid out and rotting in the churchyard.

NORA: Oh, what a horrible thing to say.

RANK: The thing itself is horrible. But the worst of it is all the other horror before it's over. There's only one final examination left; when I'm finished with that, I'll know about when my disintegration will begin. There's something I want to say. Helmer with his sensitivity has such a sharp distaste for anything ugly. I don't want him near my sickroom.

NORA: Oh, but Dr. Rank— 155

RANK: I won't have him in there. Under no condition. I'll lock my door to him — As soon as I'm completely sure of the worst, I'll send you my calling card marked with a black cross, and you'll know then the wreck has started to come apart.

NORA: No, today you're completely unreasonable. And I wanted you so much to be in a really good humor.

RANK: With death up my sleeve? And then to suffer this way for somebody else's sins. Is there any justice in that? And in every single family, in some way or another, this inevitable retribution of nature goes on —

NORA: *(her hands pressed over her ears)* Oh, stuff! Cheer up! Please — be gay!

160   RANK: Yes, I'd just as soon laugh at it all. My poor, innocent spine, serving time for my father's gay army days.

NORA: *(by the table, left)* He was so infatuated with asparagus tips and *pâté de foie gras*, wasn't that it?

RANK: Yes — and with truffles.

NORA: Truffles, yes. And then with oysters, I suppose?

RANK: Yes, tons of oysters, naturally.

165   NORA: And then the port and champagne to go with it. It's so sad that all these delectable things have to strike at our bones.

RANK: Especially when they strike at the unhappy bones that never shared in the fun.

NORA: Ah, that's the saddest of all.

RANK: *(looks searchingly at her)* Hm.

NORA: *(after a moment)* Why did you smile?

170   RANK: No, it was you who laughed.

NORA: No, it was you who smiled, Dr. Rank!

RANK: *(getting up)* You're even a bigger tease than I'd thought.

NORA: I'm full of wild ideas today.

RANK: That's obvious.

175   NORA: *(putting both hands on his shoulders)* Dear, dear Dr. Rank, you'll never die for Torvald and me.

RANK: Oh, that loss you'll easily get over. Those who go away are soon forgotten.

NORA: *(looks fearfully at him)* You believe that?

RANK: One makes new connections, and then —

NORA: Who makes new connections?

180   RANK: Both you and Torvald will when I'm gone. I'd say you're well under way already. What was that Mrs. Linde doing here last evening?

NORA: Oh, come — you can't be jealous of poor Kristine?

RANK: Oh yes, I am. She'll be my successor here in the house. When I'm down under, that woman will probably —

NORA: Shh! Not so loud. She's right in there.

RANK: Today as well. So you see.

185   NORA: Only to sew on my dress. Good gracious, how unreasonable you are. *(Sitting on the sofa.)* Be nice now, Dr. Rank. Tomorrow you'll see how beautifully I'll dance; and you can imagine then that I'm dancing only for you — yes, and of course for Torvald, too — that's understood. *(Takes various items out of the carton.)* Dr. Rank, sit over here and I'll show you something.

RANK: *(sitting)* What's that?

NORA: Look here. Look.

RANK: Silk stockings.

NORA: Flesh-colored. Aren't they lovely? Now it's so dark here, but tomorrow — No, no, no, just look at the feet. Oh well, you might as well look at the rest.

RANK: Hm— 190

NORA: Why do you look so critical? Don't you believe they'll fit?

RANK: I've never had any chance to form an opinion on that.

NORA: (glancing at him a moment) Shame on you. (Hits him lightly on the ear with the stockings.) That's for you. (Puts them away again.)

RANK: And what other splendors am I going to see now?

NORA: Not the least bit more, because you've been naughty. (She hums a little 195 and rummages among her things.)

RANK: (after a short silence) When I sit here together with you like this, completely easy and open, then I don't know — I simply can't imagine — whatever would have become of me if I'd never come into this house.

NORA: (smiling) Yes, I really think you feel completely at ease with us.

RANK: (more quietly, staring straight ahead) And then to have to go away from it all—

NORA: Nonsense, you're not going away.

RANK: (his voice unchanged) — and not even be able to leave some poor show 200 of gratitude behind, scarcely a fleeting regret — no more than a vacant place that anyone can fill.

NORA: And if I asked you now for —? No—

RANK: For what?

NORA: For a great proof of your friendship—

RANK: Yes, yes?

NORA: No, I mean — for an exceptionally big favor— 205

RANK: Would you really, for once, make me so happy?

NORA: Oh, you haven't the vaguest idea what it is.

RANK: All right, then tell me.

NORA: No, but I can't, Dr. Rank — it's all out of reason. It's advice and help, too — and a favor—

RANK: So much the better. I can't fathom what you're hinting at. Just speak 210 out. Don't you trust me?

NORA: Of course. More than anyone else. You're my best and truest friend, I'm sure. That's why I want to talk to you. All right, then, Dr. Rank: there's something you can help me prevent. You know how deeply, how inexpressibly dearly Torvald loves me; he'd never hesitate a second to give up his life for me.

RANK: (leaning close to her) Nora — do you think he's the only one—

NORA: (with a slight start) Who —?

RANK: Who'd gladly give up his life for you.

NORA: (heavily) I see. 215

RANK: I swore to myself you should know this before I'm gone. I'll never find a better chance. Yes, Nora, now you know. And also you know now that you can trust me beyond anyone else.

NORA: *(rising, natural and calm)* Let me by.

RANK: *(making room for her, but still sitting)* Nora —

NORA: *(in the hall doorway)* Helene, bring the lamp in. *(Goes over to the stove.)* Ah, dear Dr. Rank, that was really mean of you.

220 RANK: *(getting up)* That I've loved you just as deeply as somebody else? Was *that* mean?

NORA: No, but that you came out and told me. That was quite unnecessary —

RANK: What do you mean? Have you known —?

The Maid comes in with the lamp, sets it on the table, and goes out again.

RANK: Nora — Mrs. Helmer — I'm asking you: have you known about it?

NORA: Oh, how can I tell what I know or don't know? Really, I don't know what to say — Why did you have to be so clumsy, Dr. Rank! Everything was so good.

225 RANK: Well, in any case, you now have the knowledge that my body and soul are at your command. So won't you speak out?

NORA: *(looking at him)* After that?

RANK: Please, just let me know what it is.

NORA: You can't know anything now.

RANK: I have to. You mustn't punish me like this. Give me the chance to do whatever is humanly possible for you.

230 NORA: Now there's nothing you can do for me. Besides, actually, I don't need any help. You'll see — it's only my fantasies. That's what it is. Of course! *(Sits in the rocker, looks at him, and smiles.)* What a nice one you are, Dr. Rank. Aren't you a little bit ashamed, now that the lamp is here?

RANK: No, not exactly. But perhaps I'd better go — for good?

NORA: No, you certainly can't do that. You must come here just as you always have. You know Torvald can't do without you.

RANK: Yes, but *you?*

NORA: You know how much I enjoy it when you're here.

235 RANK: That's precisely what threw me off. You're a mystery to me. So many times I've felt you'd almost rather be with me than with Helmer.

NORA: Yes — you see, there are some people that one loves most and other people that one would almost prefer being with.

RANK: Yes, there's something to that.

NORA: When I was back home, of course I loved Papa most. But I always thought it was so much fun when I could sneak down to the maids' quarters, because they never tried to improve me, and it was always so amusing, the way they talked to each other.

RANK: Aha, so it's *their* place that I've filled.

240 NORA: *(jumping up and going to him)* Oh, dear, sweet Dr. Rank, that's not what I mean at all. But you can understand that with Torvald it's just the same as with Papa —

The Maid enters from the hall.

MAID: Ma'am — please! *(She whispers to Nora and hands her a calling card.)*

NORA: *(glancing at the card)* Ah! *(Slips it into her pocket.)*

RANK: Anything wrong?

NORA: No, no, not at all. It's only some — it's my new dress —

RANK: Really? But — there's your dress. 245

NORA: Oh, that. But this is another one — I ordered it — Torvald mustn't know —

RANK: Ah, now we have the big secret.

NORA: That's right. Just go in with him — he's back in the inner study. Keep him there as long as —

RANK: Don't worry. He won't get away. *(Goes into the study.)*

NORA: *(to the Maid)* And he's standing waiting in the kitchen? 250

MAID: Yes, he came up by the back stairs.

NORA: But didn't you tell him somebody was here?

MAID: Yes, but that didn't do any good.

NORA: He won't leave?

MAID: No, he won't go till he's talked with you, ma'am. 255

NORA: Let him come in, then — but quietly. Helene, don't breathe a word about this. It's a surprise for my husband.

MAID: Yes, yes, I understand — *(Goes out.)*

NORA: This horror — it's going to happen. No, no, no, it can't happen, it mustn't. *(She goes and bolts Helmer's door. The Maid opens the hall door for Krogstad and shuts it behind him. He is dressed for travel in a fur coat, boots, and a fur cap.)*

NORA: *(going toward him)* Talk softly. My husband's home.

KROGSTAD: Well, good for him. 260

NORA: What do you want?

KROGSTAD: Some information.

NORA: Hurry up, then. What is it?

KROGSTAD: You know, of course, that I got my notice.

NORA: I couldn't prevent it, Mr. Krogstad. I fought for you to the bitter end, 265
but nothing worked.

KROGSTAD: Does your husband's love for you run so thin? He knows everything I can expose you to, and all the same he dares to —

NORA: How can you imagine he knows anything about this?

KROGSTAD: Ah, no — I can't imagine it either, now. It's not at all like my fine Torvald Helmer to have so much guts —

NORA: Mr. Krogstad, I demand respect for my husband!

KROGSTAD: Why, of course — all due respect. But since the lady's keeping it 270
so carefully hidden, may I presume to ask if you're also a bit better informed than yesterday about what you've actually done?

NORA: More than you ever could teach me.

KROGSTAD: Yes, I *am* such an awful lawyer.

NORA: What is it you want from me?

KROGSTAD: Just a glimpse of how you are, Mrs. Helmer. I've been thinking about you all day long. A cashier, a night-court scribbler, a — well, a type like me also has a little of what they call a heart, you know.

NORA: Then show it. Think of my children. 275

KROGSTAD: Did you or your husband ever think of mine? But never mind. I simply wanted to tell you that you don't need to take this thing too seriously. For the present, I'm not proceeding with any action.

NORA: Oh no, really! Well — I knew that.

KROGSTAD: Everything can be settled in a friendly spirit. It doesn't have to get around town at all; it can stay just among us three.

NORA: My husband must never know anything of this.

280   KROGSTAD: How can you manage that? Perhaps you can pay me the balance?

NORA: No, not right now.

KROGSTAD: Or you know some way of raising the money in a day or two?

NORA: No way that I'm willing to use.

KROGSTAD: Well, it wouldn't have done you any good, anyway. If you stood in front of me with a fistful of bills, you still couldn't buy your signature back.

285   NORA: Then tell me what you're going to do with it.

KROGSTAD: I'll just hold onto it — keep it on file. There's no outsider who'll even get wind of it. So if you've been thinking of taking some desperate step —

NORA: I have.

KROGSTAD: Been thinking of running away from home —

NORA: I have!

290   KROGSTAD: Or even of something worse —

NORA: How could you guess that?

KROGSTAD: You can drop those thoughts.

NORA: How could you guess I was thinking of *that*?

KROGSTAD: Most of us think about *that* at first. I thought about it too, but I discovered I hadn't the courage —

295   NORA: (*lifelessly*) I don't either.

KROGSTAD: (*relieved*) That's true, you haven't the courage? You too?

NORA: I don't have it — I don't have it.

KROGSTAD: It would be terribly stupid, anyway. After that first storm at home blows out, why, then — I have here in my pocket a letter for your husband —

NORA: Telling everything?

300   KROGSTAD: As charitably as possible.

NORA: (*quickly*) He mustn't ever get that letter. Tear it up. I'll find some way to get money.

KROGSTAD: Beg pardon, Mrs. Helmer, but I think I just told you —

NORA: Oh, I don't mean the money I owe you. Let me know how much you want from my husband, and I'll manage it.

KROGSTAD: I don't want any money from your husband.

305   NORA: What do you want, then?

KROGSTAD: I'll tell you what. I want to recoup, Mrs. Helmer; I want to get on in the world — and there's where your husband can help me. For a year and a half I've kept myself clean of anything disreputable — all that time struggling with the worst conditions; but I was satisfied, working my way up step by step. Now I've been written right off, and I'm just not in the mood to come crawling back. I tell you, I want to move on. I want to get back in the bank — in a better position. Your husband can set up a job for me —

NORA: He'll never do that!

KROGSTAD: He'll do it. I know him. He won't dare breathe a word of protest. And once I'm in there together with him, you just wait and see! Inside of a year, I'll be the manager's right-hand man. It'll be Nils Krogstad, not Torvald Helmer, who runs the bank.

NORA: You'll never see the day!

KROGSTAD: Maybe you think you can — 310

NORA: I have the courage now — for *that*.

KROGSTAD: Oh, you don't scare me. A smart, spoiled lady like you —

NORA: You'll see; you'll see!

KROGSTAD: Under the ice, maybe? Down in the freezing, coal-black water? There, till you float up in the spring, ugly, unrecognizable, with your hair falling out —

NORA: You don't frighten me. 315

KROGSTAD: Nor do you frighten me. One doesn't do these things, Mrs. Helmer. Besides, what good would it be? I'd still have him safe in my pocket.

NORA: Afterwards? When I'm no longer — ?

KROGSTAD: Are you forgetting that *I'll* be in control then over your final reputation? (*Nora stands speechless, staring at him.*) Good; now I've warned you. Don't do anything stupid. When Helmer's read my letter, I'll be waiting for his reply. And bear in mind that it's your husband himself who's forced me back to my old ways. I'll never forgive him for that. Good-bye, Mrs. Helmer. (*He goes out through the hall.*)

NORA: (*goes to the hall door, opens it a crack, and listens*) He's gone. Didn't leave the letter. Oh no, no, that's impossible too! (*Opening the door more and more.*) What's that? He's standing outside — not going downstairs. He's thinking it over? Maybe he'll — ? (*A letter falls in the mailbox; then Krogstad's footsteps are heard, dying away down a flight of stairs. Nora gives a muffled cry and runs over toward the sofa table. A short pause.*) In the mailbox. (*Slips warily over to the hall door.*) It's lying there. Torvald, Torvald — now we're lost!

MRS. LINDE: (*entering with the costume from the room, left*) There now, I can't see anything else to mend. Perhaps you'd like to try — 320

NORA: (*in a hoarse whisper*) Kristine, come here.

MRS. LINDE: (*tossing the dress on the sofa*) What's wrong? You look upset.

NORA: Come here. See that letter? *There!* Look — through the glass in the mailbox.

MRS. LINDE: Yes, yes, I see it.

NORA: That letter's from Krogstad — 325

MRS. LINDE: Nora — it's Krogstad who loaned you the money!

NORA: Yes, and now Torvald will find out everything.

MRS. LINDE: Believe me, Nora, it's best for both of you.

NORA: There's more you don't know. I forged a name.

330   MRS. LINDE: But for heaven's sake —?

NORA: I only want to tell you that, Kristine, so that you can be my witness.

MRS. LINDE: Witness? Why should I —?

NORA: If I should go out of my mind — it could easily happen—

MRS. LINDE: Nora!

335   NORA: Or anything else occurred — so I couldn't be present here—

MRS. LINDE: Nora, Nora, you aren't yourself at all!

NORA: And someone should try to take on the whole weight, all of the guilt, you follow me—

MRS. LINDE: Yes, of course, but why do you think —?

NORA: Then you're the witness that it isn't true, Kristine. I'm very much myself; my mind right now is perfectly clear; and I'm telling you: nobody else has known about this; I alone did everything. Remember that.

340   MRS. LINDE: I will. But I don't understand all this.

NORA: Oh, how could you ever understand it? It's the miracle now that's going to take place.

MRS. LINDE: The miracle?

NORA: Yes, the miracle. But it's so awful, Kristine. It mustn't take place, not for anything in the world.

MRS. LINDE: I'm going right over and talk with Krogstad.

345   NORA: Don't go near him; he'll do you some terrible harm!

MRS. LINDE: There was a time once when he'd gladly have done anything for me.

NORA: He?

MRS. LINDE: Where does he live?

NORA: Oh, how do I know? Yes. (*Searches in her pocket.*) Here's his card. But the letter, the letter —!

350   HELMER: (*from the study, knocking on the door*) Nora!

NORA: (*with a cry of fear*) Oh! What is it? What do you want?

HELMER: Now, now, don't be so frightened. We're not coming in. You locked the door — are you trying on the dress?

NORA: Yes, I'm trying it. I'll look just beautiful, Torvald.

MRS. LINDE: (*who has read the card*) He's living right around the corner.

355   NORA: Yes, but what's the use? We're lost. The letter's in the box.

MRS. LINDE: And your husband has the key?

NORA: Yes, always.

MRS. LINDE: Krogstad can ask for his letter back unread; he can find some excuse—

NORA: But it's just this time that Torvald usually—

360   MRS. LINDE: Stall him. Keep him in there. I'll be back as quick as I can. (*She hurries out through the hall entrance.*)

NORA: (*goes to Helmer's door, opens it, and peers in*) Torvald!

HELMER: (*from the inner study*) Well — does one dare set foot in one's own living room at last? Come on, Rank, now we'll get a look —(*In the doorway.*) But what's this?

NORA: What, Torvald dear?

HELMER: Rank had me expecting some grand masquerade.

RANK: (*in the doorway*) That was my impression, but I must have been   365
    wrong.

NORA: No one can admire me in my splendor — not till tomorrow.

HELMER: But Nora dear, you look so exhausted. Have you practiced too hard?

NORA: No, I haven't practiced at all yet.

HELMER: You know, it's necessary —

NORA: Oh, it's absolutely necessary, Torvald. But I can't get anywhere without   370
    your help. I've forgotten the whole thing completely.

HELMER: Ah, we'll soon take care of that.

NORA: Yes, take care of me, Torvald, please! Promise me that? Oh, I'm so
    nervous. That big party — You must give up everything this evening
    for me. No business — don't even touch your pen. Yes? Dear Torvald,
    promise?

HELMER: It's a promise. Tonight I'm totally at your service — you little
    helpless thing. Hm — but first there's one thing I want to — (*Goes toward
    the hall door.*)

NORA: What are you looking for?

HELMER: Just to see if there's any mail.   375

NORA: No, no, don't do that, Torvald!

HELMER: Now what?

NORA: Torvald, please. There isn't any.

HELMER: Let me look, though. (*Starts out. Nora, at the piano, strikes the first
    notes of the tarantella. Helmer, at the door, stops.*) Aha!

NORA: I can't dance tomorrow if I don't practice with you.   380

HELMER: (*going over to her*) Nora dear, are you really so frightened?

NORA: Yes, so terribly frightened. Let me practice right now; there's still time
    before dinner. Oh, sit down and play for me, Torvald. Direct me. Teach me,
    the way you always have.

HELMER: Gladly, if it's what you want. (*Sits at the piano.*)

NORA: (*snatches the tambourine up from the box, then a long, varicolored shawl,
    which she throws around herself, whereupon she springs forward and cries out*)
    Play for me now! Now I'll dance!

Helmer plays and Nora dances. Rank stands behind Helmer at the piano and looks on.

HELMER: (*as he plays*) Slower. Slow down.   385

NORA: Can't change it.

HELMER: Not so violent, Nora!

NORA: Has to be just like this.

HELMER: (*stopping*) No, no, that won't do at all.

NORA: (*laughing and swinging her tambourine*) Isn't that what I told you?   390

RANK: Let me play for her.

HELMER: (*getting up*) Yes, go on. I can teach her more easily then.

*Rank sits at the piano and plays; Nora dances more and more wildly. Helmer has sta-
tioned himself by the stove and repeatedly gives her directions; she seems not to hear them;
her hair loosens and falls over her shoulders; she does not notice, but goes on dancing.
Mrs. Linde enters.*

MRS. LINDE: *(standing dumbfounded at the door)* Ah —!

NORA: *(still dancing)* See what fun, Kristine!

395 HELMER: But Nora darling, you dance as if your life were at stake.

NORA: And it is.

HELMER: Rank, stop! This is pure madness. Stop it, I say!

Rank breaks off playing, and Nora halts abruptly.

HELMER: *(going over to her)* I never would have believed it. You've forgotten everything I taught you.

NORA: *(throwing away the tambourine)* You see for yourself.

400 HELMER: Well, there's certainly room for instruction here.

NORA: Yes, you see how important it is. You've got to teach me to the very last minute. Promise me that, Torvald?

HELMER: You can bet on it.

NORA: You mustn't, either today or tomorrow, think about anything else but me; you mustn't open any letters — or the mailbox—

HELMER: Ah, it's still the fear of that man—

405 NORA: Oh yes, yes, that too.

HELMER: Nora, it's written all over you — there's already a letter from him out there.

NORA: I don't know. I guess so. But you mustn't read such things now; there mustn't be anything ugly between us before it's all over.

RANK: *(quietly to Helmer)* You shouldn't deny her.

HELMER: *(putting his arm around her)* The child can have her way. But tomorrow night, after you've danced—

410 NORA: Then you'll be free.

MAID: *(in the doorway, right)* Ma'am, dinner is served.

NORA: We'll be wanting champagne, Helene.

MAID: Very good, ma'am. *(Goes out.)*

HELMER: So — a regular banquet, hm?

415 NORA: Yes, a banquet — champagne till daybreak! *(Calling out.)* And some macaroons, Helene. Heaps of them — just this once.

HELMER: *(taking her hands)* Now, now, now — no hysterics. Be my own little lark again.

NORA: Oh, I will soon enough. But go on in — and you, Dr. Rank. Kristine, help me put up my hair.

RANK: *(whispering, as they go)* There's nothing wrong — really wrong, is there?

HELMER: Oh, of course not. It's nothing more than this childish anxiety I was telling you about. *(They go out, right.)*

420 NORA: Well?

MRS. LINDE: Left town.

NORA: I could see by your face.

MRS. LINDE: He'll be home tomorrow evening. I wrote him a note.

NORA: You shouldn't have. Don't try to stop anything now. After all, it's a wonderful joy, this waiting here for the miracle.

425 MRS. LINDE: What is it you're waiting for?

NORA: Oh, you can't understand that. Go in to them: I'll be along in
a moment.

*Mrs. Linde goes into the dining room. Nora stands a short while as if composing herself;
then she looks at her watch.*

NORA: Five. Seven hours to midnight. Twenty-four hours to the midnight
after, and then the tarantella's done. Seven and twenty-four? Thirty-one
hours to live.

HELMER: *(in the doorway, right)* What's become of the little lark?

NORA: *(going toward him with open arms)* Here's your lark!

ACT III

*Same scene. The table, with chairs around it, has been moved to the center of the room.
A lamp on the table is lit. The hall door stands open. Dance music drifts down from the
floor above. Mrs. Linde sits at the table, absently paging through a book, trying to read,
but apparently unable to focus her thoughts. Once or twice she pauses, tensely listening
for a sound at the outer entrance.*

MRS. LINDE: *(glancing at her watch)* Not yet — and there's hardly any time left.
If only he's not —*(Listening again.)* Ah, there he is. *(She goes out in the hall
and cautiously opens the outer door. Quiet footsteps are heard on the stairs. She
whispers:)* Come in. Nobody's here.

KROGSTAD: *(in the doorway)* I found a note from you at home. What's back of
all this?

MRS. LINDE: I just *had* to talk to you.

KROGSTAD: Oh? And it just *had* to be here in this house?

MRS. LINDE: At my place it was impossible; my room hasn't a private   5
entrance. Come in; we're all alone. The maid's asleep, and the Helmers
are at the dance upstairs.

KROGSTAD: *(entering the room)* Well, well, the Helmers are dancing tonight?
Really?

MRS. LINDE: Yes, why not?

KROGSTAD: How true — why not?

MRS. LINDE: All right, Krogstad, let's talk.

KROGSTAD: Do we two have anything more to talk about?   10

MRS. LINDE: We have a great deal to talk about.

KROGSTAD: I wouldn't have thought so.

MRS. LINDE: No, because you've never understood me, really.

KROGSTAD: Was there anything more to understand — except what's all too
common in life? A calculating woman throws over a man the moment
a better catch comes by.

MRS. LINDE: You think I'm so thoroughly calculating? You think I broke it off   15
lightly?

KROGSTAD: Didn't you?

MRS. LINDE: Nils — is that what you really thought?

KROGSTAD: If you cared, then why did you write me the way you did?

MRS. LINDE: What else could I do? If I had to break off with you, then it was
   my job as well to root out everything you felt for me.

20 KROGSTAD: *(wringing his hands)* So that was it. And this — all this, simply
   for money!

MRS. LINDE: Don't forget I had a helpless mother and two small brothers. We
   couldn't wait for you, Nils; you had such a long road ahead of you then.

KROGSTAD: That may be; but you still hadn't the right to abandon me for
   somebody else's sake.

MRS. LINDE: Yes — I don't know. So many, many times I've asked myself if
   I did have that right.

KROGSTAD: *(more softly)* When I lost you, it was as if all the solid ground
   dissolved from under my feet. Look at me; I'm a half-drowned man now,
   hanging onto a wreck.

25 MRS. LINDE: Help may be near.

KROGSTAD: It was near — but then you came and blocked it off.

MRS. LINDE: Without my knowing it, Nils. Today for the first time I learned
   that it's you I'm replacing at the bank.

KROGSTAD: All right — I believe you. But now that you know, will you step
   aside?

MRS. LINDE: No, because that wouldn't benefit you in the slightest.

30 KROGSTAD: Not "benefit" me, hm! I'd step aside anyway.

MRS. LINDE: I've learned to be realistic. Life and hard, bitter necessity have
   taught me that.

KROGSTAD: And life's taught me never to trust fine phrases.

MRS. LINDE: Then life's taught you a very sound thing. But you do have to
   trust in actions, don't you?

KROGSTAD: What does that mean?

35 MRS. LINDE: You said you were hanging on like a half-drowned man to
   a wreck.

KROGSTAD: I've good reason to say that.

MRS. LINDE: I'm also like a half-drowned woman on a wreck. No one to suffer
   with; no one to care for.

KROGSTAD: You made your choice.

MRS. LINDE: There wasn't any choice then.

40 KROGSTAD: So — what of it?

MRS. LINDE: Nils, if only we two shipwrecked people could reach across to
   each other.

KROGSTAD: What are you saying?

MRS. LINDE: Two on one wreck are at least better off than each on
   his own.

KROGSTAD: Kristine!

45 MRS. LINDE: Why do you think I came into town?

KROGSTAD: Did you really have some thought of me?

MRS. LINDE: I have to work to go on living. All my born days, as long as I can
   remember, I've worked, and it's been my best and my only joy. But now I'm
   completely alone in the world; it frightens me to be so empty and lost. To

work for yourself — there's no joy in that. Nils, give me something — someone to work for.

KROGSTAD: I don't believe all this. It's just some hysterical feminine urge to go out and make a noble sacrifice.

MRS. LINDE: Have you ever found me to be hysterical?

KROGSTAD: Can you honestly mean this? Tell me — do you know everything   50
about my past?

MRS. LINDE: Yes.

KROGSTAD: And you know what they think I'm worth around here.

MRS. LINDE: From what you were saying before, it would seem that with me you could have been another person.

KROGSTAD: I'm positive of that.

MRS. LINDE: Couldn't it happen still?   55

KROGSTAD: Kristine — you're saying this in all seriousness? Yes, you are! I can see it in you. And do you really have the courage, then — ?

MRS. LINDE: I need to have someone to care for; and your children need a mother. We both need each other. Nils, I have faith that you're good at heart — I'll risk everything together with you.

KROGSTAD: (gripping her hands) Kristine, thank you, thank you — Now I know I can win back a place in their eyes. Yes — but I forgot —

MRS. LINDE: (listening) Shh! The tarantella. Go now! Go on!

KROGSTAD: Why? What is it?   60

MRS. LINDE: Hear the dance up there? When that's over, they'll be coming down.

KROGSTAD: Oh, then I'll go. But — it's all pointless. Of course, you don't know the move I made against the Helmers.

MRS. LINDE: Yes, Nils, I know.

KROGSTAD: And all the same, you have the courage to — ?

MRS. LINDE: I know how far despair can drive a man like you.   65

KROGSTAD: Oh, if I only could take it all back.

MRS. LINDE: You easily could — your letter's still lying in the mailbox.

KROGSTAD: Are you sure of that?

MRS. LINDE: Positive. But —

KROGSTAD: (looks at her searchingly) Is that the meaning of it, then? You'll save   70
your friend at any price. Tell me straight out. Is that it?

MRS. LINDE: Nils — anyone who's sold herself for somebody else once isn't going to do it again.

KROGSTAD: I'll demand my letter back.

MRS. LINDE: No, no.

KROGSTAD: Yes, of course. I'll stay here till Helmer comes down; I'll tell him to give me my letter again — that it only involves my dismissal — that he shouldn't read it —

MRS. LINDE: No, Nils, don't call the letter back.   75

KROGSTAD: But wasn't that exactly why you wrote me to come here?

MRS. LINDE: Yes, in that first panic. But it's been a whole day and night since then, and in that time I've seen such incredible things in this house.

Helmer's got to learn everything; this dreadful secret has to be aired; those two have to come to a full understanding; all these lies and evasions can't go on.

KROGSTAD: Well, then, if you want to chance it. But at least there's one thing I can do, and do right away —

MRS. LINDE: *(listening)* Go now, go, quick! The dance is over. We're not safe another second.

80 KROGSTAD: I'll wait for you downstairs.

MRS. LINDE: Yes, please do; take me home.

KROGSTAD: I can't believe it; I've never been so happy. *(He leaves by way of the outer door; the door between the room and the hall stays open.)*

MRS. LINDE: *(straightening up a bit and getting together her street clothes)* How different now! How different! Someone to work for, to live for — a home to build. Well, it is worth the try! Oh, if they'd only come! *(Listening.)* Ah, there they are. Bundle up. *(She picks up her hat and coat. Nora's and Helmer's voices can be heard outside; a key turns in the lock, and Helmer brings Nora into the hall almost by force. She is wearing the Italian costume with a large black shawl about her; he has on evening dress, with a black domino open over it.)*

NORA: *(struggling in the doorway)* No, no, no, not inside! I'm going up again. I don't want to leave so soon.

85 HELMER: But Nora dear —

NORA: Oh, I beg you, please, Torvald. From the bottom of my heart, *please* — only an hour more!

HELMER: Not a single minute, Nora darling. You know our agreement. Come on, in we go; you'll catch cold out here. *(In spite of her resistance, he gently draws her into the room.)*

MRS. LINDE: Good evening.

NORA: Kristine!

90 HELMER: Why, Mrs. Linde — are you here so late?

MRS. LINDE: Yes, I'm sorry, but I did want to see Nora in costume.

NORA: Have you been sitting here, waiting for me?

MRS. LINDE: Yes. I didn't come early enough; you were all upstairs; and then I thought I really couldn't leave without seeing you.

HELMER: *(removing Nora's shawl)* Yes, take a good look. She's worth looking at, I can tell you that, Mrs. Linde. Isn't she lovely?

95 MRS. LINDE: Yes, I should say —

HELMER: A dream of loveliness, isn't she? That's what everyone thought at the party, too. But she's horribly stubborn — this sweet little thing. What's to be done with her? Can you imagine, I almost had to use force to pry her away.

NORA: Oh, Torvald, you're going to regret you didn't indulge me, even for just a half hour more.

HELMER: There, you see. She danced her tarantella and got a tumultuous hand — which was well earned, although the performance may have been a bit too naturalistic — I mean it rather overstepped the proprieties of art. But never mind — what's important is, she made a success, an overwhelming success. You think I could let her stay on after that and spoil the effect? Oh no; I took my lovely little Capri girl — my capricious little Capri girl, I should say — took her under my arm; one quick tour of the ballroom, a curtsy to every side, and then — as they say in novels — the beautiful vision disappeared. An exit should always be effective, Mrs. Linde, but that's what I can't get Nora to grasp. Phew, it's hot in here. (*Flings the domino on a chair and opens the door to his room.*) Why's it dark in here? Oh yes, of course. Excuse me. (*He goes in and lights a couple of candles.*)

NORA: (*in a sharp, breathless whisper*) So?

MRS. LINDE: (*quietly*) I talked with him.   100

NORA: And —?

MRS. LINDE: Nora — you must tell your husband everything.

NORA: (*dully*) I knew it.

MRS. LINDE: You've got nothing to fear from Krogstad, but you have to speak out.

NORA: I won't tell.   105

MRS. LINDE: Then the letter will.

NORA: Thanks, Kristine. I know now what's to be done. Shh!

HELMER: (*reentering*) Well, then, Mrs. Linde — have you admired her?

MRS. LINDE: Yes, and now I'll say good night.

HELMER: Oh, come, so soon? Is this yours, this knitting?   110

MRS. LINDE: Yes, thanks. I nearly forgot it.

HELMER: Do you knit, then?

MRS. LINDE: Oh yes.

HELMER: You know what? You should embroider instead.

MRS. LINDE: Really? Why?   115

HELMER: Yes, because it's a lot prettier. See here, one holds the embroidery so, in the left hand, and then one guides the needle with the right — so — in an easy, sweeping curve — right?

MRS. LINDE: Yes, I guess that's —

HELMER: But, on the other hand, knitting — it can never be anything but ugly. Look, see here, the arms tucked in, the knitting needles going up and down — there's something Chinese about it. Ah, that was really a glorious champagne they served.

MRS. LINDE: Yes, good night, Nora, and don't be stubborn any more.

HELMER: Well put, Mrs. Linde!   120

MRS. LINDE: Good night, Mr. Helmer.

HELMER: (*accompanying her to the door*) Good night, good night. I hope you get home all right. I'd be very happy to — but you don't have far to go. Good night, good night. (*She leaves. He shuts the door after her and returns.*) There, now, at last we got her out the door. She's a deadly bore, that creature.

NORA: Aren't you pretty tired, Torvald?

HELMER: No, not a bit.

NORA: You're not sleepy?   125

HELMER: Not at all. On the contrary, I'm feeling quite exhilarated. But you? Yes, you really look tired and sleepy.

NORA: Yes, I'm very tired. Soon now I'll sleep.

HELMER: See! You see! I was right all along that we shouldn't stay longer.

NORA: Whatever you do is always right.

130 HELMER: (*kissing her brow*) Now my little lark talks sense. Say, did you notice what a time Rank was having tonight?

NORA: Oh, was he? I didn't get to speak with him.

HELMER: I scarcely did either, but it's a long time since I've seen him in such high spirits. (*Gazes at her a moment, then comes nearer her.*) Hm — it's marvelous, though, to be back home again — to be completely alone with you. Oh, you bewitchingly lovely young woman!

NORA: Torvald, don't look at me like that!

HELMER: Can't I look at my richest treasure? At all that beauty that's mine, mine alone — completely and utterly.

135 NORA: (*moving around to the other side of the table*) You mustn't talk to me that way tonight.

HELMER: (*following her*) The tarantella is still in your blood, I can see — and it makes you even more enticing. Listen. The guests are beginning to go. (*Dropping his voice.*) Nora — it'll soon be quiet through this whole house.

NORA: Yes, I hope so.

HELMER: You do, don't you, my love? Do you realize — when I'm out at a party like this with you — do you know why I talk to you so little, and keep such a distance away; just send you a stolen look now and then — you know why I do it? It's because I'm imagining then that you're my secret darling, my secret young bride-to-be, and that no one suspects there's anything between us.

NORA: Yes, yes; oh, yes, I know you're always thinking of me.

140 HELMER: And then when we leave and I place the shawl over those fine young rounded shoulders — over that wonderful curving neck — then I pretend that you're my young bride, that we're just coming from the wedding, that for the first time I'm bringing you into my house — that for the first time I'm alone with you — completely alone with you, your trembling young beauty! All this evening I've longed for nothing but you. When I saw you turn and sway in the tarantella — my blood was pounding till I couldn't stand it — that's why I brought you down here so early—

NORA: Go away, Torvald! Leave me alone. I don't want all this.

HELMER: What do you mean? Nora, you're teasing me. You will, won't you? Aren't I your husband —?

A knock at the outside door.

NORA: (*startled*) What's that?

HELMER: (*going toward the hall*) Who is it?

145 RANK: (*outside*) It's me. May I come in a moment?

HELMER: (*with quiet irritation*) Oh, what does he want now? (*Aloud.*) Hold on. (*Goes and opens the door.*) Oh, how nice that you didn't just pass us by!

RANK: I thought I heard your voice, and then I wanted so badly to have a look in. (*Lightly glancing about.*) Ah, me, these old familiar haunts. You have it snug and cozy in here, you two.

HELMER: You seemed to be having it pretty cozy upstairs, too.

RANK: Absolutely. Why shouldn't I? Why not take in everything in life? As much as you can, anyway, and as long as you can. The wine was superb —

HELMER: The champagne especially.   150

RANK: You noticed that too? It's amazing how much I could guzzle down.

NORA: Torvald also drank a lot of champagne this evening.

RANK: Oh?

NORA: Yes, and that always makes him so entertaining.

RANK: Well, why shouldn't one have a pleasant evening after a well spent day?   155

HELMER: Well spent? I'm afraid I can't claim that.

RANK: *(slapping him on the back)* But I can, you see!

NORA: Dr. Rank, you must have done some scientific research today.

RANK: Quite so.

HELMER: Come now — little Nora talking about scientific research!   160

NORA: And can I congratulate you on the results?

RANK: Indeed you may.

NORA: Then they were good?

RANK: The best possible for both doctor and patient — certainty.

NORA: *(quickly and searchingly)* Certainty?   165

RANK: Complete certainty. So don't I owe myself a gay evening afterwards?

NORA: Yes, you're right, Dr. Rank.

HELMER: I'm with you — just so long as you don't have to suffer for it in the morning.

RANK: Well, one never gets something for nothing in life.

NORA: Dr. Rank — are you very fond of masquerade parties?   170

RANK: Yes, if there's a good array of odd disguises —

NORA: Tell me, what should we two go as at the next masquerade?

HELMER: You little featherhead — already thinking of the next!

RANK: We two? I'll tell you what: you must go as Charmed Life —

HELMER: Yes, but find a costume for *that!*   175

RANK: Your wife can appear just as she looks every day.

HELMER: That was nicely put. But don't you know what you're going to be?

RANK: Yes, Helmer, I've made up my mind.

HELMER: Well?

RANK: At the next masquerade I'm going to be invisible.   180

HELMER: That's a funny idea.

RANK: They say there's a hat — black, huge — have you never heard of the hat that makes you invisible? You put it on, and then no one on earth can see you.

HELMER: *(suppressing a smile)* Ah, of course.

RANK: But I'm quite forgetting what I came for. Helmer, give me a cigar, one of the dark Havanas.

HELMER: With the greatest of pleasure. *(Holds out his case.)*   185

RANK: Thanks. *(Takes one and cuts off the tip.)*

NORA: *(striking a match)* Let me give you a light.

RANK: Thank you. *(She holds the match for him; he lights the cigar.)* And now good-bye.

In this scene Doctor Rank, Helmer, and Nora have just returned from the party; Nora is wearing her tarantella costume.

HELMER: Good-bye, good-bye, old friend.
190 NORA: Sleep well, Doctor.
RANK: Thanks for that wish.
NORA: Wish me the same.
RANK: You? All right, if you like — Sleep well. And thanks for the light. (*He nods to them both and leaves.*)
HELMER: (*his voice subdued*) He's been drinking heavily.
195 NORA: (*absently*) Could be. (*Helmer takes his keys from his pocket and goes out in the hall.*) Torvald — what are you after?
HELMER: Got to empty the mailbox; it's nearly full. There won't be room for the morning papers.
NORA: Are you working tonight?
HELMER: You know I'm not. Why — what's this? Someone's been at the lock.
NORA: At the lock —?
200 HELMER: Yes, I'm positive. What do you suppose —? I can't imagine one of the maids —? Here's a broken hairpin. Nora, it's yours —
NORA: (*quickly*) Then it must be the children —
HELMER: You'd better break them of that. Hm, hm — well, opened it after all. (*Takes the contents out and calls into the kitchen.*) Helene! Helene, would you put out the lamp in the hall. (*He returns to the room, shutting the hall door, then displays the handful of mail.*) Look how it's piled up. (*Sorting through them.*) Now what's this?
NORA: (*at the window*) The letter! Oh, Torvald, no!

HELMER: Two calling cards — from Rank.

NORA: From Dr. Rank? 205

HELMER: *(examining them)* "Dr. Rank, Consulting Physician." They were on top. He must have dropped them in as he left.

NORA: Is there anything on them?

HELMER: There's a black cross over the name. See? That's a gruesome notion. He could almost be announcing his own death.

NORA: That's just what he's doing.

HELMER: What! You've heard something? Something he's told you? 210

NORA: Yes. That when those cards came, he'd be taking his leave of us. He'll shut himself in now and die.

HELMER: Ah, my poor friend! Of course I knew he wouldn't be here much longer. But so soon — And then to hide himself away like a wounded animal.

NORA: If it has to happen, then it's best it happens in silence — don't you think so, Torvald?

HELMER: *(pacing up and down)* He'd grown right into our lives. I simply can't imagine him gone. He with his suffering and loneliness — like a dark cloud setting off our sunlit happiness. Well, maybe it's best this way. For him, at least. *(Standing still.)* And maybe for us too, Nora. Now we're thrown back on each other, completely. *(Embracing her.)* Oh you, my darling wife, how can I hold you close enough? You know what, Nora — time and again I've wished you were in some terrible danger, just so I could stake my life and soul and everything, for your sake.

NORA: *(tearing herself away, her voice firm and decisive)* Now you must read your 215 mail, Torvald.

HELMER: No, no, not tonight. I want to stay with you, dearest.

NORA: With a dying friend on your mind?

HELMER: You're right. We've both had a shock. There's ugliness between us — these thoughts of death and corruption. We'll have to get free of them first. Until then — we'll stay apart.

NORA: *(clinging about his neck)* Torvald — good night! Good night!

HELMER: *(kissing her on the cheek)* Good night, little songbird. Sleep well, 220 Nora. I'll be reading my mail now. *(He takes the letters into his room and shuts the door after him.)*

NORA: *(with bewildered glances, groping about, seizing Helmer's domino, throwing it around her, and speaking in short, hoarse, broken whispers)* Never see him again. Never, never. *(Putting her shawl over her head.)* Never see the children either — them, too. Never, never. Oh, the freezing black water! The depths — down — Oh, I wish it were over — He has it now; he's reading it — now. Oh no, no, not yet. Torvald, good-bye, you and the children —*(She starts for the hall; as she does, Helmer throws open his door and stands with an open letter in his hand.)*

HELMER: Nora!

NORA: *(screams)* Oh —!

HELMER: What is this? You know what's in this letter?

225   NORA: Yes, I know. Let me go! Let me out!

HELMER: *(holding her back)* Where are you going?

NORA: *(struggling to break loose)* You can't save me, Torvald!

HELMER: *(slumping back)* True! Then it's true what he writes? How horrible! No, no, it's impossible — it can't be true.

NORA: It *is* true. I've loved you more than all this world.

230   HELMER: Ah, none of your slippery tricks.

NORA: *(taking one step toward him)* Torvald —!

HELMER: What *is* this you've blundered into!

NORA: Just let me loose. You're not going to suffer for my sake. You're not going to take on my guilt.

HELMER: No more playacting. *(Locks the hall door.)* You stay right here and give me a reckoning. You understand what you've done? Answer! You understand?

235   NORA: *(looking squarely at him, her face hardening)* Yes. I'm beginning to understand everything now.

HELMER: *(striding about)* Oh, what an awful awakening! In all these eight years — she who was my pride and joy — a hypocrite, a liar — worse, worse — a criminal! How infinitely disgusting it all is! The shame! *(Nora says nothing and goes on looking straight at him. He stops in front of her.)* I should have suspected something of the kind. I should have known. All your father's flimsy values — Be still! All your father's flimsy values have come out in you. No religion, no morals, no sense of duty — Oh, how I'm punished for letting him off! I did it for your sake, and you repay me like this.

NORA: Yes, like this.

HELMER: Now you've wrecked all my happiness — ruined my whole future. Oh, it's awful to think of. I'm in a cheap little grafter's hands; he can do anything he wants with me, ask for anything, play with me like a puppet — and I can't breathe a word. I'll be swept down miserably into the depths on account of a featherbrained woman.

NORA: When I'm gone from this world, you'll be free.

240   HELMER: Oh, quit posing. Your father had a mess of those speeches too. What good would that ever do me if you were gone from this world, as you say? Not the slightest. He can still make the whole thing known; and if he does, I could be falsely suspected as your accomplice. They might even think that I was behind it — that I put you up to it. And all that I can thank you for — you that I've coddled the whole of our marriage. Can you see now what you've done to me?

NORA: *(icily calm)* Yes.

HELMER: It's so incredible, I just can't grasp it. But we'll have to patch up whatever we can. Take off the shawl. I said, take if off! I've got to appease him somehow or other. The thing has to be hushed up at any cost. And as for you and me, it's got to seem like everything between us is just as it was — to the outside world, that is. You'll go right on living in this house, of course. But you can't be allowed to bring up the children; I don't dare

trust you with them — Oh, to have to say this to someone I've loved so
much! Well, that's done with. From now on happiness doesn't matter; all
that matters is saving the bits and pieces, the appearance —(*The doorbell
rings. Helmer starts.*) What's that? And so late. Maybe the worst —? You
think he'd —? Hide, Nora! Say you're sick. (*Nora remains standing
motionless. Helmer goes and opens the door.*)

MAID: (*half dressed, in the hall*) A letter for Mrs. Helmer.

HELMER: I'll take it. (*Snatches the letter and shuts the door.*) Yes, it's from him.
You don't get it; I'm reading it myself.

NORA: Then read it.   245

HELMER: (*by the lamp*) I hardly dare. We may be ruined, you and I. But — I've
got to know. (*Rips open the letter, skims through a few lines, glances at an
enclosure, then cries out joyfully.*) Nora! (*Nora looks inquiringly at him.*)
Nora! Wait —better check it again —Yes, yes, it's true. I'm saved. Nora,
I'm saved!

NORA: And I?

HELMER: You too, of course. We're both saved, both of us. Look. He's sent back
your note. He says he's sorry and ashamed — that a happy development in
his life — oh, who cares what he says! Nora, we're saved! No one can hurt
you. Oh, Nora, Nora —but first, this ugliness all has to go. Let me see —
(*Takes a look at the note.*) No, I don't want to see it; I want the whole thing
to fade like a dream. (*Tears the note and both letters to pieces, throws them into
the stove and watches them burn.*) There — now there's nothing left — He
wrote that since Christmas Eve you — Oh, they must have been three
terrible days for you, Nora.

NORA: I fought a hard fight.

HELMER: And suffered pain and saw no escape but — No, we're not going to   250
dwell on anything unpleasant. We'll just be grateful and keep on repeating:
it's over now, it's over! You hear me, Nora? You don't seem to realize — it's
over. What's it mean — that frozen look? Oh, poor little Nora, I
understand. You can't believe I've forgiven you. But I have, Nora; I swear
I have. I know that what you did, you did out of love for me.

NORA: That's true.

HELMER: You loved me the way a wife ought to love her husband. It's
simply the means that you couldn't judge. But you think I love you any
the less for not knowing how to handle your affairs? No, no —just
lean on me; I'll guide you and teach you. I wouldn't be a man if this feminine helplessness didn't make you twice as attractive to me. You mustn't
mind those sharp words I said — that was all in the first confusion of
thinking my world had collapsed. I've forgiven you, Nora; I swear I've
forgiven you.

NORA: My thanks for your forgiveness. (*She goes out through the door, right.*)

HELMER: No, wait —(*Peers in.*) What are you doing in there?

NORA: (*inside*) Getting out of my costume.   255

HELMER: (*by the open door*) Yes, do that. Try to calm yourself and collect your
thoughts again, my frightened little songbird. You can rest easy now; I've
got wide wings to shelter you with. (*Walking about close by the door.*) How

snug and nice our home is, Nora. You're safe here; I'll keep you like a hunted dove I've rescued out of a hawk's claws. I'll bring peace to your poor, shuddering heart. Gradually it'll happen, Nora; you'll see. Tomorrow all this will look different to you; then everything will be as it was. I won't have to go on repeating I forgive you; you'll feel it for yourself. How can you imagine I'd ever conceivably want to disown you — or even blame you in any way? Ah, you don't know a man's heart, Nora. For a man there's something indescribably sweet and satisfying in knowing he's forgiven his wife — and forgiven her out of a full and open heart. It's as if she belongs to him in two ways now: in a sense he's given her fresh into the world again, and she's become his wife and his child as well. From now on that's what you'll be to me — you little, bewildered, helpless thing. Don't be afraid of anything, Nora; just open your heart to me, and I'll be conscience and will to you both — (*Nora enters in her regular clothes.*) What's this? Not in bed? You've changed your dress?

NORA: Yes, Torvald, I've changed my dress.

HELMER: But why now, so late?

NORA: Tonight I'm not sleeping.

260 HELMER: But Nora dear—

NORA: (*looking at her watch*) It's still not so very late. Sit down, Torvald; we have a lot to talk over. (*She sits at one side of the table.*)

HELMER: Nora — what is this? That hard expression—

NORA: Sit down. This'll take some time. I have a lot to say.

HELMER: (*sitting at the table directly opposite her*) You worry me, Nora. And I don't understand you.

265 NORA: No, that's exactly it. You don't understand me. And I've never understood you either — until tonight. No, don't interrupt. You can just listen to what I say. We're closing out accounts, Torvald.

HELMER: How do you mean that?

NORA: (*after a short pause*) Doesn't anything strike you about our sitting here like this?

HELMER: What's that?

NORA: We've been married now eight years. Doesn't it occur to you that this is the first time we two, you and I, man and wife, have ever talked seriously together?

270 HELMER: What do you mean — seriously?

NORA: In eight whole years — longer even — right from our first acquaintance, we've never exchanged a serious word on any serious thing.

HELMER: You mean I should constantly go and involve you in problems you couldn't possibly help me with?

NORA: I'm not talking of problems. I'm saying that we've never sat down seriously together and tried to get to the bottom of anything.

HELMER: But dearest, what good would that ever do you?

275 NORA: That's the point right there: you've never understood me. I've been wronged greatly, Torvald —first by Papa, and then by you.

HELMER: What! By us — the two people who've loved you more than anyone else?

NORA: *(shaking her head)* You never loved me. You've thought it fun to be in love with me, that's all.

HELMER: Nora, what a thing to say!

NORA: Yes, it's true now, Torvald. When I lived at home with Papa, he told me all his opinions, so I had the same ones too; or if they were different I hid them, since he wouldn't have cared for that. He used to call me his doll-child, and he played with me the way I played with my dolls. Then I came into your house—

HELMER: How can you speak of our marriage like that?   280

NORA: *(unperturbed)* I mean, then I went from Papa's hands into yours. You arranged everything to your own taste, and so I got the same taste as you — or I pretended to; I can't remember. I guess a little of both, first one, then the other. Now when I look back, it seems as if I'd lived here like a beggar — just from hand to mouth. I've lived by doing tricks for you, Torvald. But that's the way you wanted it. It's a great sin what you and Papa did to me. You're to blame that nothing's become of me.

HELMER: Nora, how unfair and ungrateful you are! Haven't you been happy here?

NORA: No, never. I thought so — but I never have.

HELMER: Not — not happy!

NORA: No, only lighthearted. And you've always been so kind to me. But our   285
home's been nothing but a playpen. I've been your doll-wife here, just as at home I was Papa's doll-child. And in turn the children have been my dolls. I thought it was fun when you played with me, just as they thought it fun when I played with them. That's been our marriage, Torvald.

HELMER: There's some truth in what you're saying — under all the raving exaggeration. But it'll all be different after this. Playtime's over; now for the schooling.

NORA: Whose schooling — mine or the children's?

HELMER: Both yours and the children's, dearest.

NORA: Oh, Torvald, you're not the man to teach me to be a good wife to you.

HELMER: And you can say that?   290

NORA: And I — how am I equipped to bring up children?

HELMER: Nora!

NORA: Didn't you say a moment ago that that was no job to trust me with?

HELMER: In a flare of temper! Why fasten on that?

NORA: Yes, but you were so very right. I'm not up to the job. There's another   295
job I have to do first. I have to try to educate myself. You can't help me with that. I've got to do it alone. And that's why I'm leaving you now.

HELMER: *(jumping up)* What's that?

NORA: I have to stand completely alone, if I'm ever going to discover myself and the world out there. So I can't go on living with you.

HELMER: Nora, Nora!

NORA: I want to leave right away. Kristine should put me up for the night—

HELMER: You're insane! You've no right! I forbid you!   300

NORA: From here on, there's no use forbidding me anything. I'll take with me whatever is mine. I don't want a thing from you, either now or later.

HELMER: What kind of madness is this!

NORA: Tomorrow I'm going home — I mean, home where I came from. It'll be easier up there to find something to do.

HELMER: Oh, you blind, incompetent child!

305 NORA: I must learn to be competent, Torvald.

HELMER: Abandon your home, your husband, your children! And you're not even thinking what people will say.

NORA: I can't be concerned about that. I only know how essential this is.

HELMER: Oh, it's outrageous. So you'll run out like this on your most sacred vows.

NORA: What do you think are my most sacred vows?

310 HELMER: And I have to tell you that! Aren't they your duties to your husband and children?

NORA: I have other duties equally sacred.

HELMER: That isn't true. What duties are they?

NORA: Duties to myself.

HELMER: Before all else, you're a wife and a mother.

315 NORA: I don't believe in that any more. I believe that, before all else, I'm a human being, no less than you — or anyway, I ought to try to become one. I know the majority thinks you're right, Torvald, and plenty of books agree with you, too. But I can't go on believing what the majority says, or what's written in books. I have to think over these things myself and try to understand them.

HELMER: Why can't you understand your place in your own home? On a point like that, isn't there one everlasting guide you can turn to? Where's your religion?

NORA: Oh, Torvald, I'm really not sure what religion is.

HELMER: What —?

NORA: I only know what the minister said when I was confirmed. He told me religion was this thing and that. When I get clear and away by myself, I'll go into that problem too. I'll see if what the minister said was right, or, in any case, if it's right for me.

320 HELMER: A young woman your age shouldn't talk like that. If religion can't move you, I can try to rouse your conscience. You do have some moral feeling? Or, tell me — has that gone too?

NORA: It's not easy to answer that, Torvald. I simply don't know. I'm all confused about these things. I just know I see them so differently from you. I find out, for one thing, that the law's not at all what I'd thought — but I can't get it through my head that the law is fair. A woman hasn't a right to protect her dying father or save her husband's life! I can't believe that.

HELMER: You talk like a child. You don't know anything of the world you live in.

NORA: No, I don't. But now I'll begin to learn for myself. I'll try to discover who's right, the world or I.

HELMER: Nora, you're sick; you've got a fever. I almost think you're out of your head.

NORA: I've never felt more clearheaded and sure in my life.   325
HELMER: And — clearheaded and sure — you're leaving your husband and children?
NORA: Yes.
HELMER: Then there's only one possible reason.
NORA: What?
HELMER: You no longer love me.   330
NORA: No. That's exactly it.
HELMER: Nora! You can't be serious!
NORA: Oh, this is so hard, Torvald — you've been so kind to me always. But I can't help it. I don't love you any more.
HELMER: (*struggling for composure*) Are you also clearheaded and sure about that?
NORA: Yes, completely. That's why I can't go on staying here.   335
HELMER: Can you tell me what I did to lose your love?
NORA: Yes, I can tell you. It was this evening when the miraculous thing didn't come — then I knew you weren't the man I'd imagined.
HELMER: Be more explicit; I don't follow you.
NORA: I've waited now so patiently eight long years — for, my Lord, I know miracles don't come every day. Then this crisis broke over me, and such a certainty filled me: *now* the miraculous event would occur. While Krogstad's letter was lying out there, I never for an instant dreamed that you could give in to his terms. I was so utterly sure you'd say to him: go on, tell your tale to the whole wide world. And when he'd done that —
HELMER: Yes, what then? When I'd delivered my own wife into shame and disgrace —!   340
NORA: When he'd done that, I was so utterly sure that you'd step forward, take the blame on yourself and say: I am the guilty one.
HELMER: Nora —!
NORA: You're thinking I'd never accept such a sacrifice from you? No, of course not. But what good would my protests be against you? That was the miracle I was waiting for, in terror and hope. And to stave that off, I would have taken my life.
HELMER: I'd gladly work for you day and night, Nora — and take on pain and deprivation. But there's no one who gives up honor for love.
NORA: Millions of women have done just that.   345
HELMER: Oh, you think and talk like a silly child.
NORA: Perhaps. But you neither think nor talk like the man I could join myself to. When your big fright was over — and it wasn't from any threat against me, only for what might damage you — when all the danger was past, for you it was just as if nothing had happened. I was exactly the same, your little lark, your doll, that you'd have to handle with double care now that I'd turned out so brittle and frail. (*Gets up.*) Torvald — in that instant it dawned on me that for eight years I've been living here with a stranger, and that I'd even conceived three children — oh, I can't stand the thought of it! I could tear myself to bits.

HELMER: *(heavily)* I see. There's a gulf that's opened between us — that's clear. Oh, but Nora, can't we bridge it somehow?

NORA: The way I am now, I'm no wife for you.

350 **HELMER:** I have the strength to make myself over.

NORA: Maybe — if your doll gets taken away.

HELMER: But to part! To part from you! No, Nora, no — I can't imagine it.

NORA: *(going out, right)* All the more reason why it has to be. *(She reenters with her coat and a small overnight bag, which she puts on a chair by the table.)*

HELMER: Nora, Nora, not now! Wait till tomorrow.

355 **NORA:** I can't spend the night in a strange man's room.

HELMER: But couldn't we live here like brother and sister —

NORA: You know very well how long that would last. *(Throws her shawl about her.)* Good-bye, Torvald. I won't look in on the children. I know they're in better hands than mine. The way I am now, I'm no use to them.

HELMER: But someday, Nora — someday —?

NORA: How can I tell? I haven't the least idea what'll become of me.

360 **HELMER:** But you're my wife, now and wherever you go.

NORA: Listen, Torvald — I've heard that when a wife deserts her husband's house just as I'm doing, then the law frees him from all responsibility. In any case, I'm freeing you from being responsible. Don't feel yourself bound, any more than I will. There has to be absolute freedom for us both. Here, take your ring back. Give me mine.

HELMER: That too?

NORA: That too.

HELMER: There it is.

365 **NORA:** Good. Well, now it's all over. I'm putting the keys here. The maids know all about keeping up the house — better than I do. Tomorrow, after I've left town, Kristine will stop by to pack up everything that's mine from home. I'd like those things shipped up to me.

HELMER: Over! All over! Nora, won't you ever think about me?

NORA: I'm sure I'll think of you often, and about the children and the house here.

HELMER: May I write you?

NORA: No — never. You're not to do that.

370 **HELMER:** Oh, but let me send you —

NORA: Nothing. Nothing.

HELMER: Or help you if you need it.

NORA: No. I accept nothing from strangers.

HELMER: Nora — can I never be more than a stranger to you?

375 **NORA:** *(picking up the overnight bag)* Ah, Torvald — it would take the greatest miracle of all —

HELMER: Tell me the greatest miracle!

NORA: You and I both would have to transform ourselves to the point that — Oh, Torvald, I've stopped believing in miracles.

HELMER: But I'll believe. Tell me! Transform ourselves to the point that —?

NORA: That our living together could be a true marriage. *(She goes out down the hall.)*

Helmer: (*sinks down on a chair by the door, face buried in his hands*) Nora! Nora! 380
(*Looking about and rising.*) Empty. She's gone. (*A sudden hope leaps in him.*)
The greatest miracle —?

From below, the sound of a door slamming shut.

Reading and Reacting

1. What is your attitude toward Nora at the beginning of the play? How does your attitude toward her change as the play progresses? What actions and lines of dialogue change your assessment of her?

2. List the key events that occur before the start of the play. How do we learn of each event?

3. In act 1, how do the various references to macaroons in the stage directions reinforce plot developments?

4. Explain the role of each of the following in advancing the play's action: the Christmas tree, the locked mailbox, the telegram Dr. Rank receives, Dr. Rank's calling cards.

5. In act 2, Torvald says, "Whatever comes, you'll see: when it really counts, I have strength and courage enough as a man to take on the whole weight myself." How does this statement influence Nora's subsequent actions?

6. How do the upcoming costume party and Nora's dance influence the development of the play's plot? Where does the play's climax occur?

7. Explain how the following foreshadow events that will occur later in the play: Torvald's comments about Krogstad's children (act 1); Torvald's attitude toward Nora's father (act 2); Krogstad's suggestions about suicide (act 2).

8. In addition to the play's main plot — which concerns the blackmail of Nora by Krogstad and her attempts to keep her crime secret from Torvald — the play contains several subplots. Some of them developed before the start of the play, and some unfold alongside the main plot. Identify these subplots. How do they advance the themes of survival, debt, sacrifice, and duty that run through the play?

9. Is Kristine Linde essential to the play? How might the play be different without her?

10. Is Mrs. Linde as much of a "modern woman" as Nora? Is she actually *more* of a modern woman? Explain.

11. Do you think *A Doll House* is primarily about the struggle between the needs of the individual and the needs of society, or about the conflict between women's roles in the family and in the larger society? Explain.

12. **Journal Entry** Nora makes a drastic decision at the end of the play. Do you think she overreacts? What other options does she have? What other options might she have today?

13. **Critical Perspective** Since its earliest performances, there has been much comment on the conclusion of *A Doll House*. Many viewers have found the play's ending unrealistically harsh. In fact, a famous German actress refused to play the scene as written because she insisted she would never leave her children. (Ibsen reluctantly rewrote the ending for her; in this version,

Helmer forces Nora to the doorway of the children's bedroom, and she sinks to the floor as the curtain falls.) Moreover, many critics have found it hard to accept Nora's transformation from, in Elizabeth Hardwick's words, "the girlish, charming wife to the radical, courageous heroine setting out alone" ("Ibsen's Women" in *Seduction and Betrayal*).

What is your response to the play's ending? Do you think it makes sense in light of what we have learned about Nora and her marriage? Or do you, for example, agree with Hardwick that Nora's abandonment of her children is not only implausible but also a "rather casual" gesture that "drops a stain on our admiration of Nora"?

Related Works: "The Story of an Hour" (p. 82), "The Rocking-Horse Winner" (p. 349), "The Birthmark" (p. 477), "Girl" (p. 492), "Barbie Doll" (p. 902)

WRITING SUGGESTIONS: Plot

1. Central to the plots of both *Trifles* and *A Doll House* is a woman who commits a crime. Compare and contrast the reactions of the two plays' other characters, particularly each woman's friends, to her crime.

2. In both *Trifles* and *A Doll House,* the plot depends to some extent on the fact that male characters misjudge — and perhaps underestimate — women. Write an essay in which you compare and contrast the attitudes the men in these plays hold toward women, the ways in which they reveal these attitudes, and the ways in which the women react.

3. Both of the plays in this chapter deal with troubled marriages. Suppose you were a marriage counselor and one of the couples came to you for help. What would you say to them? Write an essay in which you give the troubled couple advice for saving their marriage.

4. **WEB ACTIVITY** The following Web site contains information about Henrik Ibsen:

http://www.hf.uio.no/ibsensenteret/index_eng.html

According to this Web site from the University of Oslo, Ibsen is considered the father of modern drama. Locate a Web site that gives a thorough definition of *modernism*. Then, write an essay showing how *A Doll House* exhibits the characteristics of modernism.

CHAPTER 29

CHARACTER

Character in a play is like a blank check which a dramatist accords to the actor for him to fill in — not entirely blank, for a number of indications of individuality are already there, but to a far less definite and absolute degree than in the novel. —**Thornton Wilder,** *"Some Thoughts on Playwriting"*

A character living onstage is a union of the creative talents of the actor and the dramatist. Any argument over which of the two is more important is futile because they are completely interdependent. The actor requires the character created by the dramatist to provide the initial and vital stimulus. The dramatist requires the embodiment of the character by the actor to bring his creation to fulfillment. The result of this collaboration is the finished performance to which both the actor and the dramatist have made a unique contribution. The result can be neither Shakespeare's Macbeth nor the actor's Macbeth. It must be the actor *as* Shakespeare's Macbeth. —**Charles McGraw,** *Acting Is Believing,* 2d ed.

Shakespeare is above all writers, at least above all modern writers, the poet of nature: the poet that holds up to his readers a faithful mirror of manners and life. His characters are not modified by the customs of particular places, unpracticed by the rest of the world; by the peculiarities of studies or professions, which can operate but upon small numbers; or by the accidents of transient fashions or temporary opinions: they are the genuine progeny of common humanity, such as the world will always supply, and observation will always find. —*From the preface to Samuel Johnson's edition of Shakespeare*

A sensible playwright would write a play with three or four people. Three is best. A man and his dog is even better. —**Tom Stoppard,** quoted in the *New York Times*

In Tennessee Williams's 1945 play *The Glass Menagerie* (p. 1416), the protagonist, Tom Wingfield, functions as the play's narrator. Stepping out of his role as a character and speaking directly to the audience, he directs the play's action, music, lighting, and other elements. In addition, he summarizes characters' actions, explains their motivation, and discusses the significance of their behavior in the context of the play — commenting on his own character's actions as well. As narrator, Tom also presents useful background information about the characters.

For instance, when he introduces his coworker, Jim, he prepares the audience for Jim's entrance and helps them to understand his subsequent actions:

> In high school Jim was a hero. He had tremendous Irish good nature and vitality with the scrubbed and polished look of white chinaware. He seemed to move in a continual spotlight. . . . But Jim apparently ran into more interference after his graduation . . . . His speed had definitely slowed. Six years after he left high school he was holding a job that wasn't much better than mine. (scene 6)

Most plays, however, do not include narrators who present background. Instead, the audience learns about characters from their own words and from comments by others about them, as well as from the characters' actions and from the playwright's stage directions. Also, at a performance, the audience can see the actors' interpretations of the characters.

Characters in plays, like characters in novels and short stories, may be **round** or **flat, static** or **dynamic.** Generally speaking, major characters are likely to be round, whereas minor characters are likely to be flat. Through the language and the actions of the characters, audiences learn whether the characters are multidimensional, skimpily developed, or perhaps merely **foils,** players whose main purpose is to shed light on more important characters. Audiences also learn about the emotions, attitudes, and values that help to shape the characters — their hopes and fears, their strengths and weaknesses. In addition, by comparing characters' early words and actions with later ones, audiences learn from the play whether or not characters grow and change emotionally.

CHARACTERS' WORDS

Characters' words reveal the most about their attitudes, feelings, beliefs, and values. Sometimes information is communicated (to other characters as well as to the audience) in a **monologue**— an extended speech by one character. This device is used throughout August Strindberg's *The Stronger* (p. 947). A **soliloquy**— a monologue revealing a character's thoughts and feelings, directed at the audience and presumed not to be heard by other characters — can also convey information about a character. For example, Hamlet's well-known soliloquy that begins "To be or not to be" eloquently communicates his distraught mental state — his resentment of his mother and uncle, his confusion about what course of action to take, his suicidal thoughts. Finally, **dialogue**— an exchange of words between two characters — can reveal misunderstanding or conflict between them, or it can show their agreement, mutual support, or similar beliefs.

In Henrik Ibsen's *A Doll House* (p. 995), dialogue reveals a good deal about the characters. Nora Helmer, the spoiled young wife, broke the law and has kept her crime secret from her husband. Through her words, we learn about her motivation, her emotions, and her reactions to other characters and to her potentially dangerous situation. We learn, for instance, that she is flirtatious —"If your little squirrel begged you, with all her heart and soul . . ."— and that she is childishly unrealistic about the consequences of her actions. When her husband, Torvald, asks what she would do if he was seriously injured, leaving her in debt, she says, "If anything so awful happened, then it just wouldn't matter if I had debts or not." When Torvald presses, "Well, but the people I'd borrowed from?" she dismisses them: "Them? Who cares about them! They're strangers." As the play progresses, Nora's lack of understanding of the power of the law becomes more and more significant as she struggles with her moral and ethical dilemma.

The inability of both Nora and Torvald to confront ugly truths is also revealed through their words. When, in act 1, Nora tells Krogstad, her blackmailer, that his revealing her secret could expose her to "the most horrible unpleasantness," he responds, "Only unpleasantness?" Yet later on, in act 3, Torvald uses the same word, fastidiously dismissing the horror with, "No, we're not going to dwell on anything unpleasant."

The ease with which Torvald is able to dismiss his dying friend Dr. Rank in act 3 ("He with his suffering and loneliness — like a dark cloud setting off our sunlit happiness. Well, maybe it's best this way.") foreshadows the lack of support he will give Nora immediately thereafter. Especially revealing is his use of *I* and *my* and *me*, which convey his self-centeredness:

> Now you've wrecked all my happiness — ruined my whole future. Oh, it's awful to think of. I'm in a cheap little grafter's hands; he can do anything he wants with me, ask for anything, play with me like a puppet — and I can't breathe a word. I'll be swept down miserably into the depths on account of a featherbrained woman.

Just as Torvald's words reveal that he has not been changed by the play's events, Nora's words show that she has changed significantly. Her dialogue near the end of act 3 shows that she has become a responsible, determined woman — one who understands her situation and her options and is no longer blithely oblivious to her duties. When she says, "I've never felt more clearheaded and sure in my life," she is calm and decisive. When she says, "Our home's been nothing but a playpen. I've been your doll-wife here, just as at home I was Papa's doll-child," she reveals a new self-awareness. When she confronts her husband, she displays complete honesty — perhaps for the first time in her relationship with Torvald.

Sometimes what other characters say to or about a character can reveal more to an audience than the character's own words. For instance, in *A Doll House*, when the dying Dr. Rank says, apparently without malice, "[Torvald] Helmer with his sensitivity has such a sharp distaste for anything ugly," readers not only think ill of the man who is too "sensitive" to visit his sick friend but also question his ability to withstand situations that may be emotionally or morally "ugly" as well.

When a character is offstage for much (or even all) of the action, the audience must rely on other characters' assessments of the absent character. In Susan Glaspell's *Trifles* (p. 983), the play's focus is on an absent character, Minnie Wright, who is described solely through other characters' remarks. The evidence suggests that Mrs. Wright killed her husband, and only Mrs. Hale's and Mrs. Peters's comments about Mrs. Wright's dreary life can delineate her character and suggest a likely motive for the murder. Although we never meet

Mrs. Wright, we learn essential information from the other women: that as a young girl she liked to sing and that more recently she was so distraught about the lack of beauty in her life that even her sewing revealed her distress. Similarly, the father in *The Glass Menagerie* never appears (and therefore never speaks), but the play's other characters describe him as "A telephone man who — fell in love with long-distance!" — the absent husband and father who symbolizes abandonment and instability to Laura and Amanda and the possibility of freedom and escape to Tom.

Whether they are in the form of a monologue, a soliloquy, or dialogue, and whether they reveal information about the character who is speaking or about someone else, a character's words are always revealing. Explicitly or implicitly, they convey a character's nature, attitudes, and relationships with other characters. A character may, for instance, use learned words, foreign words, elaborate figures of speech, irony or sarcasm, regionalisms, slang, jargon, clichés, or profanity. Words can also be used to indicate tone — for example, to express irony. Any of these uses of language may communicate vital information to the audience about a character's background, attitudes, and motivation. And, of course, a character's language may change as a play progresses, and this change too may be revealing.

Formal and Informal Language

One character in a dramatic work may be very formal and aloof, using absolutely correct grammar, a learned vocabulary, and long, complex sentences; another may be informal, using conversational speech, colloquialisms, and slang. At times, two characters with different levels of language may be set in opposition for dramatic effect, as they are in Irish playwright George Bernard Shaw's play *Pygmalion* (1912), which updates the ancient Greek myth of a sculptor who creates (and falls in love with) a statue of a woman. In Shaw's version, a linguistics professor sets out to teach "proper" speech and manners to a lowly flower seller. Throughout the play, the contrasting language of Henry Higgins, the professor, and Eliza Doolittle, the flower seller, indicates their differing social standing:

LIZA: I ain't got no mother. Her that turned me out was my sixth stepmother. But I done without them. And I'm a good girl, I am.

HIGGINS: Very well, then, what on earth is all this fuss about?

A character's accent or dialect may also be significant. In comedies of manners, for instance, rustic or provincial characters, identified by their speech, were often objects of humor. In *Pygmalion*, Eliza Doolittle uses cockney dialect, the dialect spoken in the East End of London. At first, her colorful, distinctive language (complete with expressions like *Nah-ow*, *garn*, and *ah-ah-ah-ow-ow-ow-oo*) and her nonstandard grammatical constructions make her an object of ridicule; later, the transformation of her speech parallels the dramatic changes in her character.

Plain and Elaborate Style

A character's speech can be simple and straightforward or complex and convoluted; it can be plain and unadorned, or it can be embellished with elaborate **figures of speech.** The relative complexity or lack of complexity of a character's speech can have different effects on the audience. For example, a character whose language is simple and unsophisticated may seem to be unintelligent, unenlightened, gullible, or naive — especially if he or she also uses slang, dialect, or colloquial expressions. Conversely, a character's plain, down-to-earth language can convey common sense or intelligence. Plain language can also be quite emotionally powerful. Thus, Willy Loman's speech in act 2 of *Death of a Salesman* (p. 1178), about an eighty-four-year-old salesman named Dave Singleman, moves the audience with its sincerity and directness:

> Do you know? When he died — and by the way he died the death of a
> salesman, in his green velvet slippers in the smoker of the New York,
> New Haven and Hartford, going into Boston — when he died, hundreds
> of salesmen and buyers were at his funeral. Things were sad on a lotta trains
> for months after that.

Like plain speech, elaborate language may have different effects in different contexts. Sometimes, use of figures of speech can make a character seem to have depth and insight and analytical skills absent in other characters. In the following excerpt from a soliloquy from *Hamlet,* for example, complex language reveals the depth of Hamlet's anguished self-analysis:

HAMLET: O, that this too too solid flesh would melt,
 Thaw, and resolve itself into a dew!
 Or that the Everlasting had not fix'd
 His canon 'gainst self-slaughter! O God! O God!
 How weary, stale, flat, and unprofitable
 Seem to me all the uses of this world!
 Fie on't, O fie, 'tis an unweeded garden,
 That grows to seed . . . .

In those lines, Hamlet compares the world to a garden gone to seed. His use of imagery and figures of speech vividly communicates his feelings about the world and his internal struggle against the temptation to commit suicide.

Sometimes, however, elaborate language may make a character seem pompous or untrustworthy. In the following passages from Shakespeare's *King Lear,* Goneril and Regan, the deceitful daughters, use complicated verbal constructions to conceal their true feelings from their father, King Lear. Cordelia — the loyal, loving daughter — uses simple, straightforward language that suggests her sincerity and lack of artifice. Compare the three speeches:

GONERIL: Sir, I love you more than words can wield the matter;
 Dearer than eyesight, space, and liberty;
 Beyond what can be valued, rich or rare;

No less than life, with grace, health, beauty, honour;
As much as child e'er lov'd, or father found;
A love that makes breath poor, and speech unable.
Beyond all manner of so much I love you. . . .

REGAN: Sir, I am made
Of the selfsame metal that my sister is,
And prize me at her worth. In my true heart
I find she names my very deed of love;
Only she comes too short, that I profess
Myself an enemy to all other joys
Which the most precious square of sense possesses,
And find I am alone felicitate
In your dear Highness' love. . . .

CORDELIA: Unhappy that I am, I cannot heave
My heart into my mouth. I love your Majesty
According to my bond; no more no less. . . .

Cordelia's unwillingness, even when she is prodded by Lear, to exaggerate her feelings or misrepresent her love through inflated language shows the audience her honesty and nobility. The contrast between her language and that of her sisters makes their very different motives clear to the audience.

Tone

Tone reveals a character's mood or attitude. Tone can be flat or hysterical, bitter or accepting, affectionate or aloof, anxious or calm. Contrasts in tone can indicate differences in outlook or emotional state between two characters; changes in tone from one point in the play to another can suggest corresponding changes within a character. At the end of *A Doll House*, for instance, Nora is resigned to what she must do, and her language is appropriately controlled. Her husband, however, is desperate to change her mind, and his language reflects this desperation. The following exchanges from act 3 of the play illustrate their contrasting emotional states:

HELMER: But to part! To part from you! No, Nora, no — I can't imagine it.

NORA: (*going out, right*) All the more reason why it has to be.

HELMER: Over! All over! Nora, won't you ever think about me?

NORA: I'm sure I'll think of you often, and about the children and the house here.

In earlier scenes between the two characters, Nora is emotional — at times, hysterical — and her husband is considerably more controlled. As the preceding dialogue indicates, both Nora and Torvald Helmer change drastically during the course of the play.

Irony

Irony, a contradiction or discrepancy between two different levels of meaning, can reveal a great deal about character. **Verbal irony** — a contradiction between what a character says and what he or she means — is very important in drama, where the verbal interplay between characters may carry the weight of the play. For example, when Nora and Dr. Rank discuss the latest news about his health in *A Doll House,* there is deep irony in his use of the phrase "complete certainty." Although the phrase usually suggests reassuring news, here it is meant to suggest death, and both Nora and Dr. Rank understand this.

Dramatic irony depends on the audience's knowing something that a character has not yet realized, or on one character's knowing something that other characters do not know. In some cases, dramatic irony is created by an audience's awareness of historical background or events of which characters are unaware. Familiar with the story of Oedipus, for instance, the audience knows that the man who has caused all the problems in Thebes — the man Oedipus vows to find and take revenge on — is Oedipus himself. In other cases, dramatic irony emerges when the audience learns something — something the characters do not yet know or comprehend — from a play's unfolding action. The central irony in *A Doll House,* for example, is that the family's "happy home" rests on a foundation of secrets, lies, and deception. Torvald does not know about the secrets, and Nora does not understand how they have poisoned her marriage. The audience, however, quickly becomes aware of the atmosphere of deceit — and aware of how it threatens the family's happiness.

Dramatic irony may also be conveyed through dialogue. Typically, dramatic irony is revealed when a character, in conversation, delivers lines that give the audience information that other characters, offstage at the time, do not know. In *A Doll House,* the audience knows — because Nora has explained her situation to Kristine — that Nora spent the previous Christmas season hard at work, earning money to pay her secret debt. Torvald, however, remains unaware of her activities and believes her story that she was using the time to make holiday decorations, which the cat destroyed. This belief is consistent with his impression of her as an irresponsible child, yet the audience has quite a different impression of Nora. This discrepancy, one of many contradictions between the audience's view of Nora and Torvald's view of her, helps to create dramatic tension in the play.

Finally, **asides** (comments to the audience that other characters do not hear) can create dramatic irony by undercutting dialogue, providing ironic contrast between what the characters on stage know and what the audience knows. In Anton Chekhov's *The Brute* (p. 1062), for example, the audience knows that Mr. Smirnov is succumbing to Mrs. Popov's charms because he says, in an aside, "My God, what eyes she has! They're setting me on fire." Mrs. Popov, however, is not yet aware of his infatuation. The discrepancy between the audience's awareness and the character's adds to the play's humor.

CHARACTERS' ACTIONS

Through their actions, characters convey their values and attitudes to the audience. Actions also reveal aspects of a character's personality. When Laura Wingfield, a character in *The Glass Menagerie*, hides rather than face the "gentleman caller," audiences see how shy she is; when Nora in *A Doll House* plays hide-and-seek with her children, eats forbidden macaroons, and takes childish joy in Christmas, her immaturity is apparent.

Audiences also learn about characters from what they do *not* do. Thus, Nora's failure to remain in touch with her friend Kristine, who has had a hard life, reveals her selfishness, and the failure of Mrs. Peters and Mrs. Hale in *Trifles* to communicate their evidence to the sheriff indicates their support for Mrs. Wright and their understanding of what motivated her to take such drastic action.

Audiences also learn a good deal about characters by observing how they interact with other characters. In William Shakespeare's *Othello*, Iago is the embodiment of evil, and as the play's action unfolds, we discover his true nature. He reveals the secret marriage of Othello and Desdemona to her father; he schemes to arouse Othello's jealousy, making him believe Desdemona has been unfaithful with his lieutenant, Cassio; he persuades Cassio to ask Desdemona to plead his case with Othello, knowing this act will further arouse Othello's suspicions; he encourages Othello to be suspicious of Desdemona's defense of Cassio; he plants Desdemona's handkerchief in Cassio's room; and, finally, he persuades Othello to kill Desdemona and then kills his own wife, Emilia, to prevent her from exposing his role in the intrigue. As the play progresses, then, Iago's dealings with others consistently reveal him to be evil and corrupt.

STAGE DIRECTIONS

When we read a play, we also read the playwright's italicized **stage directions,** the notes that concern **staging**— the scenery, props, lighting, music, sound effects, costumes, and other elements that contribute to the way the play looks and sounds to an audience (see Chapter 30). In addition to commenting on staging, stage directions may supply physical details about the characters, suggesting their age, appearance, movements, gestures, relative positions, and facial expressions. These details may in turn convey additional information about characters: appearance may reveal social position or economic status, expressions may reveal attitudes, and so on. Stage directions may also indicate the manner in which a line of dialogue is to be delivered —haltingly, confidently, hesitantly, or loudly, for instance. The way a line is spoken may reveal a character to be excited, upset, angry, shy, or disappointed. Finally, stage directions may indicate *changes* in characters —for instance, a character whose speech is described as timid in early scenes may deliver lines emphatically and forcefully later on in the play.

Some plays' stage directions provide a good deal of detail about character; others do little more than list characters' names. Arthur Miller is one playwright who often chooses to provide detailed information about character through stage directions. In *Death of a Salesman*, for instance, Miller's stage directions at the beginning of act 1 characterize Willy Loman immediately and specifically:

> He is past sixty years of age, dressed quietly. Even as he crosses the stage to the doorway of the house, his exhaustion is apparent. He unlocks the door, comes into the kitchen, and thankfully lets his burden down, feeling the soreness of his palms. A word-sigh escapes his lips . . .

Subsequent stage directions indicate how lines are to be spoken. For example, in the play's opening lines, Willy's wife Linda calls out to him *"with some trepidation"*; Linda speaks *"very carefully, delicately,"* and Willy speaks *"with casual irritation."* These instructions to readers (and actors) are meant to suggest the strained relationship between the two characters.

George Bernard Shaw is notorious for the full character description in his stage directions. In these directions — seen by readers of the play but not heard by audiences — he communicates complex information about characters' attitudes and values, strengths and weaknesses, motivation and reactions, and relationships with other characters. In doing so, Shaw functions as a narrator, explicitly communicating his own attitudes toward various characters. (Unlike the voice of Tom Wingfield in *The Glass Menagerie*, however, the voice in Shaw's stage directions is not also the voice of a character in the play; it is the voice of the playwright.) Shaw's stage directions for *Pygmalion* initially describe Eliza Doolittle as follows:

> She is not at all an attractive person. She is perhaps eighteen, perhaps twenty, hardly older. She wears a little sailor hat of black straw that has long been exposed to the dust and soot of London and has seldom if ever been brushed. Her hair needs washing rather badly; its mousy color can hardly be natural. She wears a shoddy black coat that reaches nearly to her knees and is shaped to her waist. She has a brown skirt with a coarse apron. Her boots are much the worse for wear. She is no doubt as clean as she can afford to be; but compared to the ladies she is very dirty. Her features are no worse than theirs; but their condition leaves something to be desired; and she needs the services of a dentist.

Rather than providing an objective summary of the character's most notable physical attributes, Shaw injects subjective comments (*"seldom if ever brushed"*; *"color can hardly be natural"*; *"no doubt as clean as she can afford to be"*) that reveal his attitude toward Eliza. This initially supercilious attitude, which he shares with Professor Higgins, is tempered considerably by the end of the play, helping to make Eliza's transformation more obvious to readers than it would be if measured by her words and actions alone. By act 5, the tone of the stage directions characterizing Eliza has changed to admiration: *"Eliza enters, sunny, self-possessed, and giving a staggeringly convincing exhibition of ease of manner."*

Stage directions in *Hamlet* are not nearly as comprehensive. Characters are introduced with only the barest identifying tags: "Claudius, *King of Denmark*"; "Hamlet, *Son to the former, and nephew to the present King*"; "Gertrude, *Queen of Denmark, mother to Hamlet.*" Most stage directions do little more than chronicle the various characters' entrances and exits or specify particular physical actions: *"Enter Ghost"*; *"Spreads his arms"*; *"Ghost beckons Hamlet"*; *"He kneels"*; *"Sheathes his sword"*; *"Leaps in the grave."* Occasionally, stage directions specify a prop (*"Puts *down the skull"*); a sound effect (*"A noise within"*); or a costume (*"Enter the ghost in his night-gown"*). Such brevity is typical of Shakespeare's plays, in which characters are delineated almost solely by their words — and, not incidentally, by the way actors have interpreted the characters over the years. In fact, because Shakespeare's stage directions only suggest characters' gestures, physical reactions, movements, and facial expressions, actors have been left quite free to experiment, reading various interpretations into Shakespeare's characters.

ACTORS' INTERPRETATIONS

When we watch a play, we gain insight into a character not merely through what the character says and does or how other characters react, but also through the way an actor interprets the role. If a playwright does not specify a character's mannerisms, gestures, or movements, or does not indicate how a line is to be delivered (and sometimes even if he or she does), an actor is free to interpret the role as he or she believes it should be played. Even when a playwright *does* specify such actions, the actor has a good deal of freedom to decide which gestures or expressions will convey a particular emotion.

In "Some Thoughts on Playwriting," American dramatist Thornton Wilder argues that "the theatre is an art which reposes upon the work of many collaborators" rather than on "one governing selecting will." Citing examples from Shakespeare and Ibsen, Wilder illustrates the great degree of "intervention" that may occur in dramatic productions. For instance, Wilder observes, Shakespeare's Shylock has been portrayed by two different actors as "noble, wronged and indignant" and as "a vengeful and hysterical buffoon" — and both performances were considered legitimate interpretations. As noted earlier, the absence of detailed stage directions in Shakespeare's plays makes possible (and perhaps even encourages) such widely diverging interpretations. However, as Wilder points out, even when playing roles created by a dramatist such as Ibsen, whose stage directions are typically quite specific, actors and directors have a good deal of leeway. Thus, actress Janet McTeer, who played the part of Ibsen's Nora in the 1997 London production of *A Doll House*, saw Nora and Torvald, despite their many problems, as "the perfect couple," deeply in love and involved in a passionate marriage. "You have to make that marriage sexually credible," McTeer told the *New York Times*, "to imagine they have a wonderful time in bed, so there becomes something to lose. If you play them as already past it or no longer attracted to each other, then there is no play." This interpretation is not inconsistent with the play, but it does go beyond what Ibsen actually wrote.

Similarly, the role of Catherine in David Auburn's *Proof* has been played by several actresses — among them Mary-Louise Parker, Jennifer Jason Leigh, Anne Heche, Gwyneth Paltrow, and Lea Salonga — and each actress interpreted this complex character in a different way. As *New York Times* theater critic John Rockwell observes, "Catherine can be loopy-ethereal-sexy (Ms. Parker), earthy and even a little bitter (Ms. Leigh), or adorable-needy-fragile (Ms. Heche), and Mr. Auburn's structure and characters and ideas still work."

Irish playwright Samuel Beckett devotes a good deal of attention to indicating actors' movements and gestures and their physical reactions to one another.

In his 1952 play *Waiting for Godot*, for example, Beckett seems to choreograph every gesture, every emotion, every intention, with stage directions:

- *(he looks at them ostentatiously in turn to make it clear they are both meant)*
- *Vladimir seizes Lucky's hat. Silence of Lucky. He falls. Silence. Panting of the victors.*
- *Estragon hands him the boot. Vladimir inspects it, throws it down angrily.*
- *Estragon pulls, stumbles, falls. Long silence.*
- *He goes feverishly to and fro, halts finally at extreme left, broods.*

Clearly, Beckett provides full and obviously carefully thought-out stage directions and, in so doing, attempts to retain a good deal of control over his characters. Still, in a 1988 production of *Godot*, director Mike Nichols and comic actors Robin Williams and Steve Martin felt free to improvise, adding gestures and movements not specified or even hinted at — and most critics believed that this production managed to remain true to the tragicomic spirit of Beckett's existentialist play. In a sense, then, the playwright's words on the page are just the beginning of the character's lives.

CHECKLIST WRITING ABOUT CHARACTER

✓ Does any character serve as a narrator? If so, what information does this narrator supply about the other characters? How reliable is the narrator?

✓ Are the major characters fully developed?

✓ Do the major characters change and grow during the course of the play, or do they remain essentially unchanged?

✓ What function does each of the minor characters serve in the play?

✓ What elements reveal changes in the characters?

✓ What is revealed about the characters through their words?

✓ Do characters use foreign words, regionalisms, slang, jargon, clichés, or profanity? What does such use of language reveal about characters? About theme?

✓ Is the language formal or informal?

✓ Do characters speak in dialect? Do they have accents?

✓ Is the language elaborate or plain?

continued on next page

✓ Do different characters exhibit contrasting styles or levels of language? What is the significance of these differences?

✓ In what way does language reveal characters' emotional states?

✓ Does the tone or style of any character's language change significantly as the play progresses? What does this change reveal?

✓ Does the play include verbal irony? Dramatic irony? How is irony conveyed? What purpose does irony achieve?

✓ What is revealed about the characters through what others say about them?

✓ Is the audience encouraged to react sympathetically to the character?

✓ What is revealed about the characters through their actions?

✓ What is revealed about the characters through the playwright's stage directions?

✓ How might different actors' interpretations change an audience's understanding of the characters?

ANTON CHEKHOV (1860–1904) is an important nineteenth-century Russian playwright and short story writer. He became a doctor and, as a young adult, supported the rest of his family after his father's bankruptcy. After his early adult years in Moscow, Chekhov spent the rest of his life in the country, moving to Yalta, a resort town in Crimea, for his health (he suffered from tuberculosis). He continued to write plays, mostly for the Moscow Art Theatre, although he could not supervise their production as he would have wished. His plays include *The Seagull* (1896), *Uncle Vanya* (1898), *The Three Sisters* (1901), and *The Cherry Orchard* (1904).

 The Brute, or *The Bear* (1888), is one of a number of one-act farces Chekhov wrote just before his major plays. It is based on a French farce (*Les Jurons de Cadillac* by Pierre Breton) about a man who cannot refrain from swearing. The woman he loves offers to marry him if he can avoid swearing for one hour; he can't do it, but he fails so charmingly that she agrees to marry him anyway.

Cultural Context: When Anton Chekhov published *The Brute* in 1888, Russia was ruled by Tsar Alexander III. His father and predecessor, Alexander II, known as "Tsar Liberator" for freeing the Russian serfs in 1861, had been assassinated by a hand-thrown bomb in 1881 as he was about to sign a decree that reformers hoped would lead to the creation of a Russian national assembly. The conservative Alexander III opposed any lessening of the Tsar's autocratic power. Under his rule, publications were subject to censorship, and his censors banned *The Brute* because they considered its themes and characters coarse and improper.

ANTON CHEKHOV

The Brute

A JOKE IN ONE ACT (1888)

English Version By Eric Bentley

CHARACTERS

Mrs. Popov, *widow and landowner,*   **Gardener**
small, with dimpled cheeks   **Coachman**
Mr. Grigory S. Smirnov, *gentleman*   **Hired Men**
farmer, middle-aged
Luka, *Mrs. Popov's footman, an old man*

SCENE

The drawing room of a country house. Mrs. Popov, in deep mourning, is staring hard at a photograph. Luka is with her.

LUKA: It's not right, ma'am, you're killing yourself. The cook has gone off with the maid to pick berries. The cat's having a high old time in the yard catching birds. Every living thing is happy. But you stay moping here in the house like it was a convent, taking no pleasure in nothing. I mean it, ma'am! It must be a full year since you set foot out of doors.

MRS. POPOV: I must never set foot out of doors again, Luka. Never! I have nothing to set foot out of doors *for*. My life is done. *He* is in his grave. I have buried myself alive in this house. We are *both* in our graves.

LUKA: You're off again, ma'am. I just won't listen to you no more. Mr. Popov is dead, but what can we do about that? It's God's doing. God's will be done. You've cried over him, you've done your share of mourning, haven't you? There's a limit to everything. You can't go on weeping and wailing forever. My old lady died, for that matter, and I wept and wailed over her a whole month long. Well, that was it. I couldn't weep and wail all my life. She just wasn't worth it. *(He sighs.)* As for the neighbors, you've forgotten all about them, ma'am. You don't visit them and you don't let them visit you. You and I are like a pair of spiders — excuse the expression, ma'am — here we are in this house like a pair of spiders, we never see the light of day. And it isn't like there was no nice people around either. The whole county's swarming with 'em. There's a regiment quartered at Riblov, and the officers are so good-looking! The girls can't take their eyes off them — There's a ball at the camp every Friday — The military band plays most every day of the week — What do you say, ma'am? You're young, you're pretty, you could enjoy yourself! Ten years from now you may want to strut and show your feathers to the officers, and it'll be too late.

MRS. POPOV: *(firmly)* You must never bring this subject up again, Luka. Since Popov died, life has been an empty dream to me, you know that. *You* may think I am alive. Poor ignorant Luka! You are wrong. I am dead. I'm in my grave. Never more shall I see the light of day, never strip from my body this . . . raiment of death! Are you listening, Luka? Let his ghost learn how I love him! Yes, *I* know, and *you* know, he was often unfair to me, he was cruel to me, and he was unfaithful to me. What of it? *I* shall be faithful to *him,* that's all. I will show him how *I* can love. Hereafter, in a better world than this, he will welcome me back, the same loyal girl I always was—

5   LUKA: Instead of carrying on this way, ma'am, you should go out in the garden and take a bit of a walk, ma'am. Or why not harness Toby and take a drive? Call on a couple of the neighbours, ma'am?

MRS. POPOV: (*breaking down*) Oh, Luka!

LUKA: Yes, ma'am? What have I said, ma'am? Oh, dear!

MRS. POPOV: Toby! You said Toby! He adored that horse. When he drove me out to the Korchagins and the Vlasovs, it was always with Toby! He was a wonderful driver, do you remember, Luka? So graceful! So strong! I can see him now, pulling at those reins with all his might and main! Toby! Luka, tell them to give Toby an extra portion of oats today.

LUKA: Yes, ma'am.

A bell rings.

10   MRS. POPOV: Who is that? Tell them I'm not at home.

LUKA: Very good, ma'am. (*Exit.*)

MRS. POPOV: (*gazing again at the photograph*) You shall see, my Popov, how a wife can love and forgive. Till death do us part. Longer than that. Till death re-unite us forever! (*Suddenly a titter breaks through her tears.*) Aren't you ashamed of yourself, Popov? Here's your little wife, being good, being faithful, so faithful she's locked up here waiting for her own funeral, while you — doesn't it make you ashamed, you naughty boy? You were terrible, you know. You were unfaithful, and you made those awful scenes about it, you stormed out and left me alone for weeks—

Enter Luka.

LUKA: (*upset*) There's someone asking for you, ma'am. Says he must—

MRS. POPOV: I suppose you told him that since my husband's death I see no one?

15   LUKA: Yes, ma'am. I did, ma'am. But he wouldn't listen, ma'am. He says it's urgent.

MRS. POPOV: (*shrilly*) I see no one!!

LUKA: He won't take no for an answer, ma'am. He just curses and swears and comes in anyway. He's a perfect monster, ma'am. He's in the dining room right now.

MRS. POPOV: In the dining room, is he? I'll give him his come-uppance. Bring him in here this minute.

Exit Luka.

(*Suddenly sad again.*) Why do they do this to me? Why? Insulting my grief, intruding on my solitude? (*She sighs.*) I'm afraid I'll have to enter a convent. I will, I *must* enter a convent!

Enter Mr. Smirnov and Luka.

SMIRNOV: *(to Luka)* Dolt! Idiot! You talk too much! *(Seeing Mrs. Popov. With dignity.)* May I have the honor of introducing myself, madam? Grigory S. Smirnov, landowner and lieutenant of artillery, retired. Forgive me, madam, if I disturb your peace and quiet, but my business is both urgent and weighty.

MRS. POPOV: *(declining to offer him her hand)* What is it you wish, sir?   20

SMIRNOV: At the time of his death, your late husband — with whom I had the honor to be acquainted, ma'am — was in my debt to the tune of twelve hundred rubles. I have two notes to prove it. Tomorrow, ma'am, I must pay the interest on a bank loan. I have therefore no alternative, ma'am, but to ask you to pay me the money today.

MRS. POPOV: Twelve hundred rubles? But what did my husband owe it to you for?

SMIRNOV: He used to buy his oats from me, madam.

MRS. POPOV: *(to Luka, with a sigh)* Remember what I said, Luka: tell them to give Toby an extra portion of oats today!

Exit Luka.

My dear Mr. — what was the name again?

SMIRNOV: Smirnov, ma'am.   25

MRS. POPOV: My dear Mr. Smirnov, if Mr. Popov owed you money, you shall be paid — to the last ruble, to the last kopeck. But today — you must excuse me, Mr. — what was it?

SMIRNOV: Smirnov, ma'am.

MRS. POPOV: Today, Mr. Smirnov, I have no ready cash in the house. *(Smirnov starts to speak.)* Tomorrow, Mr. Smirnov, no, the day after tomorrow, all will be well. My steward will be back from town. I shall see that he pays what is owing. Today, no. In any case, today is exactly seven months from Mr. Popov's death. On such a day you will understand that I am in no mood to think of money.

SMIRNOV: Madam, if you don't pay up now, you can carry me out feet foremost. They'll seize my estate.

MRS. POPOV: You can have your money. *(He starts to thank her.)* Tomorrow.   30
(He again starts to speak.) That is: the day after tomorrow.

SMIRNOV: I don't need the money the day after tomorrow. I need it today.

MRS. POPOV: I'm sorry, Mr. —

SMIRNOV: *(shouting)* Smirnov!

MRS. POPOV: *(sweetly)* Yes, of course. But you can't have it today.

SMIRNOV: But I can't wait for it any longer!   35

MRS. POPOV: Be sensible, Mr. Smirnov. How can I pay you if I don't have it?

SMIRNOV: You don't have it?

MRS. POPOV: I don't have it.

SMIRNOV: Sure?

MRS. POPOV: Positive.   40

SMIRNOV: Very well. I'll make a note to that effect. *(Shrugging.)* And then they want me to keep cool. I meet the tax commissioner on the street, and he says, "Why are you always in such a bad humor, Smirnov?" Bad humor! How can I help it, in God's name? I need money, I need it desperately. Take yesterday: I leave home at the crack of dawn, I call on all my debtors. Not a one of them pays up. Footsore and weary. I creep at midnight into some little dive, and try to snatch a few winks of sleep on the floor by the vodka barrel. Then today, I come here, fifty miles from home, saying to myself, "At last, at last, I can be sure of something," and you're not in the mood! You give me a mood! Christ, how can I help getting all worked up?

MRS. POPOV: I thought I'd made it clear, Mr. Smirnov, that you'll get your money the minute my steward is back from town.

SMIRNOV: What the hell do I care about your steward? Pardon the expression, ma'am. But it was you I came to see.

MRS. POPOV: What language! What a tone to take to a lady! I refuse to hear another word. (*Quickly, exit.*)

45   SMIRNOV: Not in the mood, huh? "Exactly seven months since Popov's death," huh? How about me? (*Shouting after her.*) Is there this interest to pay, or isn't there? I'm asking you a question: is there this interest to pay, or isn't there? So your husband died, and you're not in the mood, and your steward's gone off some place, and so forth and so on, but what can *I* do about all that, huh? What do *you* think I should do? Take a running jump and shove my head through the wall? Take off in a balloon? You don't know my *other* debtors. I call on Gruzdeff. Not at home. I look for Yaroshevitch. He's hiding out. I find Kooritsin. He kicks up a row, and I have to throw him through the window. I work my way right down the list. Not a kopeck. Then I come to you, and God damn it to hell, if you'll pardon the expression, you're not in the mood! (*Quietly, as he realizes he's talking to air.*) I've spoiled them all, that's what, I've let them play me for a sucker. Well, I'll show them. I'll show this one. I'll stay right here till she pays up. Ugh! (*He shudders with rage.*) I'm in a rage! I'm in a positively towering rage! Every nerve in my body is trembling at forty to the dozen! I can't breathe, I feel ill, I think I'm going to faint, hey, you there!

Enter Luka.

LUKA: Yes, sir? Is there anything you wish, sir?

SMIRNOV: Water! Water! No, make it vodka.

Exit Luka.

Consider the logic of it. A fellow creature is desperately in need of cash, so desperately in need that he has to seriously contemplate hanging himself, and this woman, this mere chit of a girl, won't pay up, and why not? Because, forsooth, she isn't in the mood! Oh, the logic of women! Come to that, I never have liked them, I could do without the whole sex. Talk to a woman? I'd rather sit on a barrel of dynamite, the very thought gives me gooseflesh. Women! Creatures of poetry and romance! Just to see one in the distance gets me mad. My legs start twitching with rage. I feel like yelling for help.

Enter Luka, handing Smirnov a glass of water.

LUKA: Mrs. Popov is indisposed, sir. She is seeing no one.
SMIRNOV: Get out.

Exit Luka.

Indisposed, is she? Seeing no one, huh? Well, she can see me or not, but I'll be here, I'll be right here till she pays up. If you're sick for a week, I'll be here for a week. If you're sick for a year, I'll be here for a year. You won't get around *me* with your widow's weeds and your schoolgirl dimples. I know all about dimples. (*Shouting through the window.*) Semyon, let the horses out of those shafts, we're not leaving, we're staying, and tell them to give the horses some oats, yes, oats, you fool, what do you think? (*Walking away from the window.*) What a mess, what an unholy mess! I didn't sleep last night, the heat is terrific today, not a damn one of 'em has paid up, and here's this — this skirt in mourning that's not in the mood! My head aches, where's that —(*He drinks from the glass.*) Water, ugh! You there!

Enter Luka.

LUKA: Yes, sir. You wish for something, sir?   50
SMIRNOV: Where's that confounded vodka I asked for?

Exit Luka.

(*Smirnov sits and looks himself over.*) Oof! A fine figure of a man I am! Unwashed, uncombed, unshaven, straw on my vest, dust all over me. The little woman must've taken me for a highwayman. (*Yawns.*) I suppose it wouldn't be considered polite to barge into a drawing room in this state, but who cares? I'm not a visitor, I'm a creditor — most unwelcome of guests, second only to Death.

Enter Luka.

LUKA: (*handing him the vodka*) If I may say so, sir, you take too many
　　liberties, sir.
SMIRNOV: What?!
LUKA: Oh, nothing, sir, nothing.
SMIRNOV: Who in hell do you think you're talking to? Shut your mouth!   55
LUKA: (*aside*) There's an evil spirit abroad. The Devil must have sent him.
　　Oh! (*Exit Luka.*)
SMIRNOV: What a rage I'm in! I'll grind the whole world to powder. Oh, I feel
　　ill again. You there!

Enter Mrs. Popov.

MRS. POPOV: (*looking at the floor*) In the solitude of my rural retreat,
　　Mr. Smirnov, I've long since grown unaccustomed to the sound of the
　　human voice. Above all, I cannot bear shouting. I must beg you not to
　　break the silence.

SMIRNOV: Very well. Pay me my money and I'll go.

60   MRS. POPOV: I told you before, and I tell you again, Mr. Smirnov. I have no cash, you'll have to wait till the day after tomorrow. Can I express myself more plainly?

SMIRNOV: And *I* told *you* before, and *I* tell *you* again, that I need the money today, that the day after tomorrow is too late, and that if you don't pay, and pay now, I'll have to hang myself in the morning!

MRS. POPOV: But I have no cash. This is quite a puzzle.

SMIRNOV: You won't pay, huh?

MRS. POPOV: I *can't* pay, Mr. Smirnov.

65   SMIRNOV: In that case, I'm going to sit here and wait. (*Sits down.*) You'll pay up the day after tomorrow? Very good. Till the day after tomorrow, here I sit. (*Pause. He jumps up.*) Now look, do I have to pay that interest tomorrow, or don't I? Or do you think I'm joking?

MRS. POPOV: I must ask you not to raise your voice, Mr. Smirnov. This is not a stable.

SMIRNOV: Who said it was? Do I have to pay the interest tomorrow or not?

MRS. POPOV: Mr. Smirnov, do you know how to behave in the presence of a lady?

SMIRNOV: No, madam, I do not know how to behave in the presence of a lady.

70   MRS. POPOV: Just what I thought. I look at you, and I say: ugh! I hear you talk, and I say to myself: "That man doesn't know how to talk to a lady."

SMIRNOV: You'd like me to come simpering to you in French, I suppose. "*Enchanté, madame! Merci beaucoup* for not paying zee money, *madame! Pardonnez-moi* if I 'ave disturbed you, *madame!* How *charmante* you look in mourning, *madame!*"

MRS. POPOV: Now you're being silly, Mr. Smirnov.

SMIRNOV: (*mimicking*) "Now you're being silly, Mr. Smirnov." "You don't know how to talk to a lady, Mr. Smirnov." Look here, Mrs. Popov, I've known more women than you've known pussy cats. I've fought three duels on their account. I've jilted twelve, and been jilted by nine others. Oh, yes, Mrs. Popov, I've played the fool in my time, whispered sweet nothings, bowed and scraped and endeavored to please. Don't tell me I don't know what it is to love, to pine away with longing, to have the blues, to melt like butter, to be weak as water. I was full of tender emotion. I was carried away with passion. I squandered half my fortune on the sex. I chattered about women's emancipation. But there's an end to everything, dear madam. Burning eyes, dark eyelashes, ripe, red lips, dimpled cheeks, heaving bosoms, soft whisperings, the moon above; the lake below — I don't give a rap for that sort of nonsense any more, Mrs. Popov. I've found out about women. Present company excepted, they're liars. Their behavior is mere play acting; their conversation is sheer gossip. Yes, dear lady, women, young or old, are false, petty, vain, cruel, malicious, unreasonable. As for intelligence, any sparrow could give them points. Appearances, I admit, can be deceptive. In appearance, a woman may be all poetry and romance, goddess and angel, muslin and fluff. To look at her exterior is to be

transported to heaven. But I have looked at her interior, Mrs. Popov, and
what did I find there — in her very soul? A crocodile. *(He has gripped the
back of the chair so firmly that it snaps.)* And, what is more revolting, a
crocodile with an illusion, a crocodile that imagines tender sentiments are
its own special province, a crocodile that thinks itself queen of the realm
of love! Whereas, in sober fact, dear madam, if a woman can love anything
except a lapdog you can hang me by the feet on that nail. For a man, love
is suffering, love is sacrifice. A woman just swishes her train around
and tightens her grip on your nose. Now, you're a woman, aren't you,
Mrs. Popov? You must be an expert on some of this. Tell me, quite frankly,
did you ever know a woman to be — faithful, for instance? Or even sincere?
Only old hags, huh? Though some women are old hags from birth. But as
for the others? You're right: a faithful woman is a freak of nature — like a
cat with horns.

MRS. POPOV: Who *is* faithful, then? Who *have* you cast for the faithful lover?
Not man?

SMIRNOV: Right first time, Mrs. Popov: man.   75

MRS. POPOV: *(going off into a peal of bitter laughter)* Man! Man is faithful! that's
a new one! *(Fiercely.)* What right do you have to say this, Mr. Smirnov?
Men faithful? Let me tell you something. Of all the men I have ever known
my late husband Popov was the best. I loved him, and there are women
who know how to love, Mr. Smirnov. I gave him my youth, my happiness,
my life, my fortune. I worshipped the ground he trod on — and what
happened? The best of men was unfaithful to me, Mr. Smirnov. Not once
in a while. All the time. After he died, I found his desk drawer full of love
letters. While he was alive, he was always going away for the week-end. He
squandered my money. He made love to other women before my very eyes.
But, in spite of all, Mr. Smirnov, *I* was faithful. Unto death. And beyond.
I am *still* faithful, Mr. Smirnov! Buried alive in this house, I shall wear
mourning till the day I, too, am called to my eternal rest.

SMIRNOV: *(laughing scornfully)* Expect me to believe that? As if I couldn't see
through all this hocus-pocus. Buried alive! Till you're called to your eternal
rest! Till when? Till some little poet — or some little subaltern with his
first moustache — comes riding by and asks: "Can that be the house of the
mysterious Tamara who for love of her late husband has buried herself
alive, vowing to see no man?" Ha!

MRS. POPOV: *(flaring up)* How dare you? How dare you insinuate —?

SMIRNOV: You may have buried yourself alive, Mrs. Popov, but you haven't
forgotten to powder your nose.

MRS. POPOV: *(incoherent)* How dare you? How —?   80

SMIRNOV: Who's raising his voice now? Just because I call a spade a spade.
Because I shoot straight from the shoulder. Well, don't shout at me, I'm not
your steward.

MRS. POPOV: I'm not shouting, you're shouting! Oh, leave me alone!

SMIRNOV: Pay me the money, and I will.

MRS. POPOV: You'll get no money out of me!

85   SMIRNOV: Oh, so that's it!

MRS. POPOV: Not a ruble, not a kopeck. Get out! Leave me alone!

SMIRNOV: Not being your husband, I must ask you not to make scenes with
        me. *(He sits.)* I don't like scenes.

MRS. POPOV: *(choking with rage)* You're sitting down?

SMIRNOV: Correct, I'm sitting down.

90   MRS. POPOV: I asked you to leave!

SMIRNOV: Then give me the money. *(Aside.)* Oh, what a rage I'm in,
        what a rage!

MRS. POPOV: The impudence of the man! I won't talk to you a moment
        longer. Get out. *(Pause.)* Are you going?

SMIRNOV: No.

MRS. POPOV: No?!

95   SMIRNOV: No.

MRS. POPOV: On your head be it. Luka!

Enter Luka.

        Show the gentleman out, Luka.

LUKA: *(approaching)* I'm afraid, sir, I'll have to ask you, um, to leave, sir,
        now, um —

SMIRNOV: *(jumping up)* Shut your mouth, you old idiot! Who do you think
        you're talking to? I'll make mincemeat of you.

LUKA: *(clutching his heart)* Mercy on us! Holy saints above! *(He falls into an
        armchair.)* I'm taken sick! I can't breathe!!

100   MRS. POPOV: Then where's Dasha? Dasha! Dasha! Come here at once!
        (She rings.)

LUKA: They gone picking berries, ma'am, I'm alone here — Water, water, I'm
        taken sick!

MRS. POPOV: *(to Smirnov)* Get out, you!

SMIRNOV: Can't you even be polite with me, Mrs. Popov?

MRS. POPOV: *(clenching her fists and stamping her feet)* With you? You're a wild
        animal, you were never house-broken!

105   SMIRNOV: What? What did you say?

MRS. POPOV: I said you were a wild animal, you were never house-broken.

SMIRNOV: *(advancing upon her)* And what right do you have to talk to me
        like that?

MRS. POPOV: Like what?

SMIRNOV: You have insulted me, madam.

110   MRS. POPOV: What of it? Do you think I'm scared of you?

SMIRNOV: So you think you can get away with it because you're a woman.
        A creature of poetry and romance, huh? Well, it doesn't go down with me.
        I hereby challenge you to a duel.

LUKA: Mercy on us! Holy saints alive! Water!

SMIRNOV: I propose we shoot it out.

MRS. POPOV: Trying to scare me again? Just because you have big fists and
        a voice like a bull? You're a brute.

SMIRNOV: No one insults Grigory S. Smirnov with impunity! And I don't care   115
  if you *are* a female.

MRS. POPOV: (*trying to outshout him*) Brute, brute, brute!

SMIRNOV: The sexes are equal, are they? Fine: then it's just prejudice to expect
  men alone to pay for insults. I hereby challenge—

MRS. POPOV: (*screaming*) All right! You want to shoot it out? All right! Let's
  shoot it out!

SMIRNOV: And let it be here and now!

MRS. POPOV: Here and now! All right! I'll have Popov's pistols here in one   120
  minute! (*Walks away, then turns.*) Putting one of Popov's bullets through
  your silly head will be a pleasure! Au revoir. (*Exit.*)

SMIRNOV: I'll bring her down like a duck, a sitting duck. I'm not one of your
  little poets, I'm no little subaltern with his first moustache. No, sir, there's
  no weaker sex where I'm concerned!

LUKA: Sir! Master! (*He goes down on his knees.*) Take pity on a poor old man,
  and do me a favor: go away. It was bad enough before, you nearly scared me
  to death. But a duel—!

SMIRNOV: (*ignoring him*) A duel! That's equality of the sexes for you! That's
  women's emancipation! Just as a matter of principle I'll bring her down like
  a duck. But what a woman! "Putting one of Popov's bullets through your
  silly head . . ." Her cheeks were flushed, her eyes were gleaming! And, by
  God, she's accepted the challenge! I never knew a woman like this before!

LUKA: Sir! Master! Please go away! I'll always pray for you!

SMIRNOV: (*again ignoring him*) What a woman! Phew!! *She's* no sour puss, *she's*   125
  no cry baby. She's fire and brimstone. She's a human cannon ball. What a
  shame I have to kill her!

LUKA: (*weeping*) Please, kind sir, please, go away!

SMIRNOV: (*as before*) I like her, isn't that funny? With those dimples and all?
  I like her. I'm even prepared to consider letting her off that debt. And
  where's my rage? It's gone. I never knew a woman like this before.

Enter Mrs. Popov with pistols.

MRS. POPOV: (*boldly*) Pistols, Mr. Smirnov! (*Matter of fact.*) But before we
  start, you'd better show me how it's done. I'm not too familiar with these
  things. In fact I never gave a pistol a second look.

LUKA: Lord, have mercy on us, I must go hunt up the gardener and the
  coachman. Why has this catastrophe fallen upon us, O Lord? (*Exit.*)

SMIRNOV: (*examining the pistols*) Well, it's like this. There are several makes: 130
  one is the Mortimer, with capsules, especially constructed for dueling.
  What you have here are Smith and Wesson triple-action revolvers, with
  extractor, first-rate job, worth ninety rubles at the very least. You hold it
  this way. (*Aside.*) My God, what eyes she has! They're setting me on fire.

MRS. POPOV: This way?

SMIRNOV: Yes, that's right. You cock the trigger, take aim like this, head up,
  arm out like this. Then you just press with this finger here, and it's all over.
  The main thing is, keep cool, take slow aim, and don't let your arm jump.

MRS. POPOV: I see. And if it's inconvenient to do the job here, we can go out in the garden.

SMIRNOV: Very good. Of course, I should warn you: I'll be firing in the air.

135   MRS. POPOV: What? This is the end. Why?

SMIRNOV: Oh, well — because — for private reasons.

MRS. POPOV: Scared, huh? (*She laughs heartily.*) Now don't you try to get out of it, Mr. Smirnov. My blood is up. I won't be happy till I've drilled a hole through that skull of yours. Follow me. What's the matter? Scared?

SMIRNOV: That's right. I'm scared.

MRS. POPOV: Oh, come on, what's the matter with you?

140   SMIRNOV: Well, um, Mrs. Popov, I, um, I like you.

MRS. POPOV: (*laughing bitterly*) Good God! He likes me, does he? The gall of the man. (*Showing him the door.*) You may leave, Mr. Smirnov.

SMIRNOV: (*Quietly puts the gun down, takes his hat, and walks to the door. Then he stops and the pair look at each other without a word. Then, approaching gingerly.*) Listen, Mrs. Popov. Are you still mad at me? I'm in the devil of a temper myself, of course. But then, you see — what I mean is — it's this way — the fact is — (*Roaring.*) Well, is it my fault, damn it, if I like you? (*Clutches the back of a chair. It breaks.*) Christ, what fragile furniture you have here. I like you. Know what I mean? I could fall in love with you.

MRS. POPOV: I hate you. Get out!

SMIRNOV: What a woman! I never saw anything like it. Oh, I'm lost, I'm done for, I'm a mouse in a trap.

145   MRS. POPOV: Leave this house, or I shoot!

SMIRNOV: Shoot away! What bliss to die of a shot that was fired by that little velvet hand! To die gazing into those enchanting eyes. I'm out of my mind. I know: you must decide at once. Think for one second, then decide. Because if I leave now, I'll never be back. Decide! I'm a pretty decent chap. Landed gentleman, I should say. Ten thousand a year. Good stable. Throw a kopeck up in the air, and I'll put a bullet through it. Will you marry me?

MRS. POPOV: (*indignant, brandishing the gun*) We'll shoot it out! Get going! Take your pistol!

SMIRNOV: I'm out of my mind. I don't understand anything any more. (*Shouting.*) You there! That vodka!

MRS. POPOV: No excuses! No delays! We'll shoot it out!

150   SMIRNOV: I'm out of my mind. I'm falling in love. I *have* fallen in love. (*He takes her hand vigorously; she squeals.*) I love you. (*He goes down on his knees.*) I love you as I've never loved before. I jilted twelve, and was jilted by nine others. But I didn't love a one of them as I love you. I'm full of tender emotion. I'm melting like butter. I'm weak as water. I'm on my knees like a fool, and I offer you my hand. It's a shame, it's a disgrace. I haven't been in love in five years. I took a vow against it. And now, all of a sudden, to be swept off my feet, it's a scandal. I offer you my hand, dear lady. Will you or won't you? You won't? Then don't! (*He rises and walks toward the door.*)

MRS. POPOV: I didn't say anything.

SMIRNOV: *(stopping)* What?

MRS. POPOV: Oh, nothing, you can go. Well, no, just a minute. No, you can go. Go! I detest you! But, just a moment. Oh, if you knew how furious I feel! *(Throws the gun on the table.)* My fingers have gone to sleep holding that horrid thing. *(She is tearing her handkerchief to shreds.)* And what are you standing around for? Get out of here!

SMIRNOV: Goodbye.

MRS. POPOV: Go, go, go! *(Shouting.)* Where are you going? Wait a minute! No, no, it's all right, just go. I'm fighting mad. Don't come near me, don't come near me!

SMIRNOV: *(who is coming near her)* I'm pretty disgusted with myself — falling in love like a kid, going down on my knees like some moongazing whipper-snapper, the very thought gives me gooseflesh. *(Rudely.)* I love you. But it doesn't make sense. Tomorrow, I have to pay that interest, and we've already started mowing. *(He puts his arm about her waist.)* I shall never forgive myself for this.

MRS. POPOV: Take your hands off me, I hate you! Let's shoot it out!

A long kiss. Enter Luka with an axe, the Gardener with a rake, the coachman with a pitchfork, hired men with sticks.

LUKA: *(seeing the kiss)* Mercy on us! Holy saints above!

MRS. POPOV: *(dropping her eyes)* Luka, tell them in the stable that Toby is *not* to have any oats today.

Reading and Reacting

1. Are Mr. Smirnov and Mrs. Popov round or flat characters? Are they static or dynamic?
2. Which of the two characters do you think has the upper hand in their relationship?
3. Although Mrs. Popov's husband is dead, he is, in a sense, an important character in *The Brute*. What do we know about him? How does he influence the play's two main characters?
4. Why are Mrs. Popov and Mr. Smirnov distrustful of members of the opposite sex? How is this distrust revealed to the audience?
5. Do you think this play reinforces gender stereotypes or challenges them? Explain.
6. Because *The Brute* is a **farce,** Chekhov's characters frequently exaggerate for comic effect. For instance, Smirnov tells Mrs. Popov, "I've known more women than you've known pussy cats. I've fought three duels on their account. I've jilted twelve, and been jilted by nine others." Give some additional examples of such broadly exaggerated language, and explain its likely effect on the audience.
7. Give some examples of physical actions used to reinforce emotions or attitudes in *The Brute*.

8. Explain and illustrate how the characters' words reveal each of the following moods: Mrs. Popov's anger at Mr. Smirnov, Mrs. Popov's ambivalence toward her late husband, Mr. Smirnov's impatience with Mrs. Popov, Mr. Smirnov's stubbornness.

9. As the play progresses, Mrs. Popov's changing language communicates her changing attitude toward her husband. Give some examples that illustrate this change in attitude.

10. What can you infer about Mrs. Popov's relationship with Luka from the language she uses when she addresses him? From the language he uses with her? What function does Luka serve in the play?

11. At what point in the play does Mr. Smirnov's speech become more elaborate? What does his use of figures of speech suggest?

12. Where in the play does dramatic irony occur? Is verbal irony also present?

13. Identify all the asides in the play. What is their function?

14. **JOURNAL ENTRY** If you had to take a side in the dispute between Mrs. Popov and Mr. Smirnov, whose side would you be on? Why?

15. **CRITICAL PERSPECTIVE** Critic Harvey Pilcher characterizes *The Brute*, like Chekhov's other one-act "farce-vaudevilles," as a "comedy of situation":

> Although they contain an assortment of comic ingredients — parody, slapstick, misunderstandings, the absurd, the grotesque, irony, and social satire — the vaudevilles still belong to the genre of "comedy of situation." This is because . . . the emphasis for an audience is "not on mystery and surprise, but on the working-out of a known situation . . . not so much on what will happen next as to how it will happen." In the best of the comedy of situation stories, the situation itself opens the door to comedy of characterization. There is a comic psychological inevitability about the way Smirnov . . . fails to live up to his misogynistic principles and [Mrs. Popov] abandons the role of the faithful widow . . . .

In what way is the "comedy of situation" Pilcher describes similar to today's television "situation comedies" (sitcoms)?

Related Works: "Big Black Good Man" (p. 206), "The Cask of Amontillado" (p. 217), "General Review of the Sex Situation" (p. 566), "You fit into me" (p. 700), "Women" (p. 763)

WILLIAM SHAKESPEARE (1564–1616) was born in Stratford-on-Avon, England, and raised his family there, although he spent most of his adult life in London. Though relatively little is known of his daily life, he was deeply involved in all aspects of the theater: he was an actor who joined the Lord Chamberlain's Men (an acting company) in 1594; a shareholder in that company; a part owner of the Globe Theater from 1599; and, most significantly, the author of at least thirty-six plays. Most of his plays were not published during his lifetime; his friends issued the first legitimate version of his collected plays, the First Folio edition, in 1623.

It is difficult to date many of Shakespeare's plays exactly because they must be dated by records of their first performance (often hard to come by) and topical references in the text. We do know from an entry in the *Stationers' Register* that a play called the *Re-*

venge of Hamlett Prince Denmarke was presented around July 26, 1602, though Shakespeare's company probably first staged the play at the Globe Theater in 1600 or 1601. Some scholars believe the play was composed as early as 1598, though no earlier, because it was not among Shakespeare's plays listed in Francis Meres's *Palladis Tamis*, published in 1598.

Cultural Context: *Hamlet* was based on a real event that was widely known in Shakespeare's time. In 1538, the Duke of Urbino, a famous military and political leader, was found dead. Later, his barber surgeon confessed to the killing, saying that a political rival had paid him to put poison in the Duke's ears. Shakespeare was impressed enough by this notorious crime to adapt it to his own use in *Hamlet* where Hamlet's father is killed by the same unusual means.

WILLIAM SHAKESPEARE

Hamlet

Prince of Denmark* (c. 1600)

CHARACTERS

Claudius, *King of Denmark*
Hamlet, *son to the former and nephew to the present King*
Polonius, *Lord Chamberlain*
Horatio, *friend to Hamlet*
Laertes, *son to Polonius*
courtiers { **Voltimand**
Cornelius
Rosencrantz
Guildenstern
Osric
A Gentleman
A Priest
Francisco, *a soldier*
officers { **Marcellus**
Bernardo

Reynaldo, *servant to Polonius*
Players
Two Clowns, *grave-diggers*
Fortinbras, *Prince of Norway*
A Captain
English Ambassadors
Ghost of Hamlet's Father
Gertrude, *Queen of Denmark and mother of Hamlet*
Ophelia, *daughter to Polonius*
Lords, Ladies, Officers, Soldiers, Sailors Messengers, and other Attendants

ACT I
SCENE 1

Elsinore. A platform before the castle.

Francisco at his post. Enter to him Bernardo.

BERNARDO: Who's there?
FRANCISCO: Nay, answer me: stand, and unfold yourself.

---

* Note that individual lines are numbered in the following play. When a line is shared by one or more characters, it is counted as one line.

BERNARDO:	Long live the king!
FRANCISCO:	Bernardo?
5	BERNARDO:	He.
FRANCISCO:	You come most carefully upon your hour.
BERNARDO:	'Tis now struck twelve; get thee to bed, Francisco.
FRANCISCO:	For this relief much thanks: 'tis bitter cold,

FRANCISCO: For this relief much thanks: 'tis bitter cold,
        And I am sick at heart.
10   BERNARDO: Have you had quiet guard?
    FRANCISCO: Not a mouse stirring.
    BERNARDO: Well, good-night.
        If you do meet Horatio and Marcellus,
        The rivals of my watch, bid them make haste.
15   FRANCISCO: I think I hear them.— Stand, ho! Who is there?

Enter Horatio and Marcellus.

    HORATIO: Friends to this ground.
    MARCELLUS: And liegemen to the Dane.
    FRANCISCO: Give you good-night.
    MARCELLUS: O, farewell, honest soldier:
20   Who hath reliev'd you?
    FRANCISCO: Bernardo has my place.
        Give you good-night.

Exit.

    MARCELLUS: Holla! Bernardo!
    BERNARDO: Say.
25   What, is Horatio there?
    HORATIO: A piece of him.
    BERNARDO: Welcome, Horatio:— welcome, good Marcellus.
    MARCELLUS: What, has this thing appear'd again to-night?
    BERNARDO: I have seen nothing.
30   MARCELLUS: Horatio says 'tis but our fantasy,
        And will not let belief take hold of him
        Touching this dreaded sight, twice seen of us:
        Therefore I have entreated him along
        With us to watch the minutes of this night;
35   That, if again this apparition come
        He may approve our eyes and speak to it.
    HORATIO: Tush, tush, 'twill not appear.
    BERNARDO: Sit down awhile,
        And let us once again assail your ears,
40   That are so fortified against our story,
        What we two nights have seen.
    HORATIO: Well, sit we down,
        And let us hear Bernardo speak of this.
    BERNARDO: Last night of all,
45   When yon same star that's westward from the pole

Had made his course to illume that part of heaven
Where now it burns, Marcellus and myself,
The bell then beating one,—
MARCELLUS: Peace, break thee off; look where it comes again!

Enter Ghost, armed.

BERNARDO: In the same figure, like the king that's dead.   50
MARCELLUS: Thou art a scholar; speak to it, Horatio.
BERNARDO: Looks it not like the king? mark it, Horatio.
HORATIO: Most like:— it harrows me with fear and wonder.
BERNARDO: It would be spoke to.
MARCELLUS: Question it, Horatio.   55
HORATIO: What art thou, that usurp'st this time of night,
    Together with that fair and warlike form
    In which the majesty of buried Denmark
    Did sometimes march? by heaven I charge thee, speak!
MARCELLUS: It is offended.   60
BERNARDO: See, it stalks away!
HORATIO: Stay! speak, speak! I charge thee, speak!

Exit Ghost.

MARCELLUS: 'Tis gone, and will not answer.
BERNARDO: How now, Horatio! you tremble and look pale:
    Is not this something more than fantasy?   65
    What think you on't?
HORATIO: Before my God, I might not this believe
    Without the sensible and true avouch
    Of mine own eyes.
MARCELLUS: Is it not like the king?   70
HORATIO: As thou art to thyself:
    Such was the very armor he had on
    When he the ambitious Norway combated;
    So frown'd he once when, in an angry parle,°
    He smote the sledded Polacks on the ice.   75
    'Tis strange.
MARCELLUS: Thus twice before, and just at this dead hour,
    With martial stalk hath he gone by our watch.
HORATIO: In what particular thought to work I know not;
    But, in the gross and scope of my opinion,   80
    This bodes some strange eruption to our state.
MARCELLUS: Good now, sit down, and tell me, he that knows,
    Why this same strict and most observant watch
    So nightly toils the subject of the land;

---

parle: Parley, or conference.

85   And why such daily cast of brazen cannon,
        And foreign mart for implements of war;
        Why such impress of shipwrights, whose sore task
        Does not divide the Sunday from the week;
        What might be toward, that this sweaty haste
90   Doth make the night joint-laborer with the day:
        Who is't that can inform me?

HORATIO: That can I;
        At least, the whisper goes so. Our last king,
        Whose image even but now appear'd to us,
95   Was, as you know, by Fortinbras of Norway,
        Thereto prick'd on by a most emulate pride,
        Dar'd to the combat; in which our valiant Hamlet,—
        For so this side of our known world esteem'd him,—
        Did slay this Fortinbras; who, by a seal'd compact,
100   Well ratified by law and heraldry,
        Did forfeit, with his life, all those his lands.
        Which he stood seiz'd of,° to the conqueror:
        Against the which, a moiety competent°
        Was gagéd° by our king; which had return'd
105   To the inheritance of Fortinbras,
        Had he been vanquisher; as by the same cov'nant,
        And carriage of the article design'd,
        His fell to Hamlet. Now, sir, young Fortinbras,
        Of unimproved mettle hot and full,
110   Hath in the skirts of Norway, here and there,
        Shark'd up a list of landless resolutes,
        For food and diet, to some enterprise
        That hath a stomach in't: which is no other,—
        As it doth well appear unto our state,—
115   But to recover of us by strong hand,
        And terms compulsatory, those foresaid lands
        So by his father lost: and this, I take it,
        Is the main motive of our preparations,
        The source of this our watch, and the chief head
120   Of this post-haste and romage° in the land.

BERNARDO: I think it be no other, but e'en so:
        Well may it sort that this portentous figure
        Comes armed through our watch; so like the king
        That was and is the question of these wars.

---

seiz'd of: Possessed.

moiety competent: A sufficient portion of his lands.

gagéd: Engaged or pledged.

post-haste and romage: General activity.

HORATIO: A mote it is to trouble the mind's eye.   125
    In the most high and palmy state of Rome,
    A little ere the mightiest Julius fell,
    The graves stood tenantless, and the sheeted dead
    Did squeak and gibber in the Roman streets:
    As, stars with trains of fire and dews of blood,   130
    Disasters in the sun; and the moist star,
    Upon whose influence Neptune's empire stands,
    Was sick almost to doomsday with eclipse:
    And even the like precurse of fierce events,—
    As harbingers preceding still the fates,   135
    And prologue to the omen coming on,—
    Have heaven and earth together demonstrated
    Unto our climature and countrymen.—
    But, soft, behold! lo, where it comes again!

Re-enter Ghost.

    I'll cross it, though it blast me.— Stay, illusion!   140
    If thou hast any sound or use of voice,
    Speak to me:
    If there be any good thing to be done,
    That may to thee do ease, and grace to me,
    Speak to me: 145
    If thou art privy to thy country's fate,
    Which, happily,° foreknowing may avoid,
    O, speak!
    Or if thou has uphoarded in thy life
    Extorted treasure in the womb of earth,   150
    For which, they say, you spirits oft walk in death,

Cock crows.

    Speak of it:— stay, and speak! — Stop it, Marcellus.
MARCELLUS: Shall I strike at it with my partisan?°
HORATIO: Do, if it will not stand.
BERNARDO: 'Tis here!   155
HORATIO: 'Tis here!
MARCELLUS: 'Tis gone!

Exit Ghost.

    We do it wrong, being so majestical,
    To offer it the show of violence;
    For it is, as the air, invulnerable,   160
    And our vain blows malicious mockery.

---

happily: Haply, or perhaps.

partisan: Pike.

BERNARDO: It was about to speak when the cock crew.

HORATIO: And then it started like a guilty thing
Upon a fearful summons. I have heard,
165 The cock, that is the trumpet to the morn,
Doth with his lofty and shrill-sounding throat
Awake the god of day; and at his warning,
Whether in sea or fire, in earth or air,
The extravagant and erring spirit hies
170 To his confine: and of the truth herein
This present object made probation.°

MARCELLUS: It faded on the crowing of the cock.
Some say that ever 'gainst that season comes
Wherein our Saviour's birth is celebrated,
175 The bird of dawning singeth all night long:
And then, they say, no spirit can walk abroad;
The nights are wholesome; then no planets strike,
No fairy takes, nor witch hath power to charm;
So hallow'd and so gracious is the time.

180 **HORATIO:** So have I heard, and do in part believe.
But, look, the morn, in russet mantle clad,
Walks o'er the dew of yon high eastern hill:
Break we our watch up: and, by my advice,
Let us impart what we have seen to-night
185 Unto young Hamlet; for, upon my life,
This spirit, dumb to us, will speak to him:
Do you consent we shall acquaint him with it,
As needful in our loves, fitting our duty?

MARCELLUS: Let's do't, I pray; and I this morning know
190 Where we shall find him most conveniently.

Exeunt.

SCENE 2

Elsinore. A room of state in the castle.

Enter the King, Queen, Hamlet, Polonius, Laertes, Voltimand, Cornelius, Lords, and Attendants.

KING: Though yet of Hamlet our dear brother's death
The memory be green; and that it us befitted
To bear our hearts in grief, and our whole kingdom
To be contracted in one brow of woe;
5 Yet so far hath discretion fought with nature
That we with wisest sorrow think on him,
Together with remembrance of ourselves.
Therefore our sometime sister, now our queen,

---

probation: Proof.

The imperial jointress of this warlike state,
Have we, as 'twere with defeated joy,—   10
With one auspicious and one dropping eye,
With mirth and funeral, and with dirge in marriage,
In equal scale weighing delight and dole,—
Taken to wife: nor have we herein barr'd
Your better wisdoms, which have freely gone   15
With this affair along:—for all, our thanks.
Now follows that you know, young Fortinbras,
Holding a weak supposal of our worth,
Or thinking by our late dear brother's death
Our state to be disjoint and out of frame,   20
Colleagued with the dream of his advantage,
He hath not fail'd to pester us with message,
Importing the surrender of those lands
Lost by his father, with all bonds of law,
To our most valiant brother. So much for him.—   25
Now for ourself, and for this time of meeting:
Thus much the business is:— we have here writ
To Norway, uncle of young Fortinbras,—
Who, impotent and bed-rid, scarcely hears
Of this his nephew's purpose,— to suppress   30
His further gait herein; in that the levies,
The lists, and full proportions, are all made
Out of his subject:— and we here despatch
You, good Cornelius, and you, Voltimand,
For bearers of this greeting to old Norway;   35
Giving to you no further personal power
To business with the king more than the scope
Of these dilated articles allow.
Farewell; and let your haste commend your duty.

CORNELIUS and **VOLTIMAND:** In that and all things will we show our duty.   40
KING: We doubt it nothing: heartily farewell.

Exeunt Voltimand and Cornelius.

And now, Laertes, what's the news with you?
You told us of some suit; what is't, Laertes?
You cannot speak of reason to the Dane,
And lose your voice: what wouldst thou beg, Laertes,   45
That shall not be my offer, nor thy asking?
The head is not more native to the heart,
The hand more instrumental to the mouth,
Than is the throne of Denmark to thy father.
What wouldst thou have, Laertes?   50
LAERTES: Dread my lord,
Your leave and favor to return to France;
From whence though willingly I came to Denmark,

To show my duty in your coronation;
55   Yet now, I must confess, that duty done,
My thoughts and wishes bend again toward France.
And bow them to your gracious leave and pardon.
KING: Have you your father's leave? What says Polonius?
POLONIUS: He hath, my lord, wrung from me my slow leave
60   By laborsome petition; and at last
Upon his will I seal'd my hard consent:
I do beseech you, give him leave to go.
KING: Take thy fair hour, Laertes; time be thine,
And thy best graces spend it at thy will!—
65   But now, my cousin Hamlet, and my son,—
HAMLET: [*Aside*] A little more than kin, and less than kind.
KING: How is it that the clouds still hang on you?
HAMLET: Not so, my lord; I am too much i' the sun.
QUEEN: Good Hamlet, cast thy nighted color off,
70   And let thine eye look like a friend on Denmark.
Do not for ever with thy vailed° lids
Seek for thy noble father in the dust:
Thou know'st 'tis common,— all that live must die,
Passing through nature to eternity.
75 HAMLET: Ay, madam, it is common.
QUEEN: If it be,
Why seems it so particular with thee?
HAMLET: Seems, madam! nay, it is; I know not seems.
'Tis not alone my inky cloak, good mother,
80   Nor customary suits of solemn black,
Nor windy suspiration of forc'd breath,
No, nor the fruitful river in the eye,
Nor the dejected 'havior of the visage,
Together with all forms, moods, shows of grief,
85   That can denote me truly: these, indeed, seem;
For they are actions that a man might play:
But I have that within which passeth show;
These but the trappings and the suits of woe.
KING: 'Tis sweet and cómmendable in your nature, Hamlet,
90   To give these mourning duties to your father:
But, you must know, your father lost a father;
That father lost, lost his; and the survivor bound,
In filial obligation, for some term
To do obsequious sorrow: but to persever
95   In obstinate condolement is a course
Of impious stubbornness; 'tis unmanly grief:

---

vailed: Downcast.

It shows a will most incorrect to heaven;
A heart unfortified, a mind impatient;
An understanding simple and unschool'd:
For what we know must be, and is as common   100
As any the most vulgar thing to sense,°
Why should we, in our peevish opposition,
Take it to heart? Fie! 'tis a fault to heaven,
A fault against the dead, a fault to nature,
To reason most absurd; whose common theme   105
Is death of fathers, and who still° hath cried,
From the first corse till he that died to-day,
This must be so. We pray you, throw to earth
This unprevailing woe; and think of us
As of a father: for let the world take note   110
You are the most immediate to our throne;
And with no less nobility of love
Than that which dearest father bears his son
Do I impart toward you. For your intent
In going back to school in Wittenberg,   115
It is most retrograde to our desire:
And we beseech you bend you to remain
Here, in the cheer and comfort of our eye,
Our chiefest courtier, cousin, and our son.
QUEEN: Let not thy mother lose her prayers, Hamlet: 120
I pray thee, stay with us; go not to Wittenberg.
HAMLET: I shall in all my best obey you, madam.
KING: Why, 'tis a loving and a fair reply:
Be as ourself in Denmark. — Madam, come;
This gentle and unforc'd accord of Hamlet   125
Sits smiling to my heart: in grace whereof,
No jocund health that Denmark drinks to-day
But the great cannon to the clouds shall tell;
And the king's rouse° the heavens shall bruit° again,
Re-speaking earthly thunder. Come away.   130

Exeunt all but Hamlet.

HAMLET: O, that this too too solid flesh would melt,
Thaw, and resolve itself into a dew!
Or that the Everlasting had not fix'd
His canon 'gainst self-slaughter! O God! O God!

---

any . . . sense: Anything that is very commonly seen or heard.

still: Ever, or always.

rouse: Drink.

bruit: Echo.

135   How weary, stale, flat, and unprofitable
       Seem to me all the uses of this world!
       Fie on't! O fie! 'tis an unweeded garden,
       That grows to seed; things rank and gross in nature
       Possess it merely. That it should come to this!
140   But two months dead! — nay, not so much, not two:
       So excellent a king; that was, to this,
       Hyperion° to a satyr: so loving to my mother,
       That he might not beteem the winds of heaven
       Visit her face too roughly. Heaven and earth!
145   Must I remember? why, she would hang on him
       As if increase of appetite had grown
       By what it fed on: and yet, within a month, —
       Let me not think on't, — Frailty, thy name is woman! —
       A little month; or ere those shoes were old
150   With which she follow'd my poor father's body
       Like Niobe, all tears; — why she, even she, —
       O God! a beast, that wants discourse of reason,
       Would have mourn'd longer, — married with mine uncle,
       My father's brother; but no more like my father
155   Than I to Hercules: within a month;
       Ere yet the salt of most unrighteous tears
       Had left the flushing in her galled eyes,
       She married: — O, most wicked speed, to post
       With such dexterity to incestuous sheets!
160   It is not, nor it cannot come to good;
       But break, my heart, — for I must hold my tongue!

Enter Horatio, Marcellus, and Bernardo.

HORATIO: Hail to your lordship!
HAMLET: I am glad to see you well:
       Horatio, — or I do forget myself.
165   **HORATIO:** The same, my lord, and your poor servant ever.
       HAMLET: Sir, my good friend; I'll change that name with you:
       And what make you from Wittenberg, Horatio? — Marcellus?
       MARCELLUS: My good lord, —
       HAMLET: I am very glad to see you. — Good even, sir. —
170   But what, in faith, make you from Wittenberg?
       HORATIO: A truant disposition, good my lord.
       HAMLET: I would not hear your enemy say so;
       Nor shall you do mine ear that violence,
       To make it truster of your own report
175   Against yourself: I know you are no truant.

Hyperion: The Greek sun-god, the brightest and most beautiful of the gods.

But what is your affair in Elsinore?
We'll teach you to drink deep ere you depart.
HORATIO: My lord, I came to see your father's funeral.
HAMLET: I pray thee, do not mock me, fellow-student;
 I think it was to see my mother's wedding.   180
HORATIO: Indeed, my lord, it follow'd hard upon.
HAMLET: Thrift, thrift, Horatio! the funeral-bak'd meats
 Did coldly furnish forth the marriage tables.
 Would I had met my dearest foe° in heaven
 Ere I had ever seen that day, Horatio!—   185
 My father,—methinks I see my father.
HORATIO: Where, my lord?
HAMLET: In my mind's eye, Horatio.
HORATIO: I saw him once; he was a goodly° king.
HAMLET: He was a man, take him for all in all,   190
 I shall not look upon his like again.
HORATIO: My lord, I think I saw him yester-night.
HAMLET: Saw who?
HORATIO: My lord, the king your father.
HAMLET: The king my father!   195
HORATIO: Season your admiration° for awhile
 With an attent ear, till I may deliver,
 Upon the witness of these gentlemen,
 This marvel to you.
HAMLET: For God's love, let me hear.   200
HORATIO: Two nights together had these gentlemen,
 Marcellus and Bernardo, in their watch,
 In the dead vast and middle of the night,
 Been thus encounter'd. A figure like your father,
 Arm'd at all points exactly, cap-a-pe,°   205
 Appears before them, and with solemn march
 Goes slow and stately by them: thrice he walk'd
 By their oppress'd° and fear-surprised eyes,
 Within his truncheon's length; whilst they, distill'd
 Almost to jelly with the act of fear,   210
 Stand dumb, and speak not to him. This to me
 In dreadful secrecy impart they did;
 And I with them the third night kept the watch:
 Where, as they had deliver'd, both in time,

---

dearest foe: Worst enemy.

goodly: Handsome.

admiration: Astonishment.

cap-a-pe: From head to toe.

oppress'd: Overwhelmed.

215   Form of the thing, each word made true and good,
         The apparition comes: I knew your father;
         These hands are not more like.
HAMLET: But where was this?
MARCELLUS: My lord, upon the platform where we watch'd.
220 HAMLET: Did you not speak to it?
HORATIO: My lord, I did;
         But answer made it none: yet once methought
         It lifted up its head, and did address
         Itself to motion, like as it would speak:
225   But even then the morning cock crew loud,
         And at the sound it shrunk in haste away,
         And vanish'd from our sight.
HAMLET: 'Tis very strange.
HORATIO: As I do live, my honor'd lord, 'tis true;
230   And we did think it writ down in our duty
         To let you know of it.
HAMLET: Indeed, indeed, sirs, but this troubles me.
         Hold you the watch to-night?
MARCELLUS and BERNARDO: We do, my lord.
235 HAMLET: Arm'd, say you?
MARCELLUS and BERNARDO: Arm'd, my lord.
HAMLET: From top to toe?
MARCELLUS and BERNARDO: My lord, from head to foot.
HAMLET: Then saw you not his face?
240 HORATIO: O yes, my lord; he wore his beaver up.
HAMLET: What, look'd he frowningly?
HORATIO: A countenance more in sorrow than in anger.
HAMLET: Pale or red?
HORATIO: Nay, very pale.
245 HAMLET: And fix'd his eyes upon you?
HORATIO: Most constantly.
HAMLET: I would I had been there.
HORATIO: It would have much amaz'd you.
HAMLET: Very like, very like. Stay'd it long?
250 HORATIO: While one with moderate haste might tell° a hundred.
MARCELLUS and BERNARDO: Longer, longer.
HORATIO: Not when I saw't.
HAMLET: His beard was grizzled, — no?
HORATIO: It was, as I have seen it in his life,
255   A sable silver'd.
HAMLET: I will watch to-night;
         Perchance 'twill walk again.

---

tell: Count.

HORATIO: I warrant it will.
HAMLET: If it assume my noble father's person
    I'll speak to it, though hell itself should gape   260
    And bid me hold my peace. I pray you all,
    If you have hitherto conceal'd this sight,
    Let it be tenable in your silence still;
    And whatsoever else shall hap to-night,
    Give it an understanding, but no tongue: 265
    I will requite your loves. So, fare ye well:
    Upon the platform, 'twixt eleven and twelve,
    I'll visit you.
ALL: Our duty to your honor.
HAMLET: Your loves, as mine to you: farewell.   270

Exeunt Horatio, Marcellus, and Bernardo.

    My father's spirit in arms; all is not well;
    I doubt some foul play: would the night were come!
    Till then sit still, my soul: foul deeds will rise,
    Though all the earth o'erwhelm them, to men's eyes.

Exit.

                            SCENE 3

A room in Polonius' house.

Enter Laertes and Ophelia.

LAERTES: My necessaries are embark'd: farewell:
    And, sister, as the winds give benefit,
    And convoy° is assistant, do not sleep,
    But let me hear from you.
OPHELIA: Do you doubt that?   5
LAERTES: For Hamlet, and the trifling of his favor,
    Hold it a fashion and a toy in blood:
    A violet in the youth of primy nature,
    Forward, not permanent, sweet, not lasting,
    The perfume and suppliance of a minute;   10
    No more.
OPHELIA: No more but so?
LAERTES: Think it no more:
    For nature, crescent,° does not grow alone
    In thews and bulk; but as this temple° waxes,   15

---

convoy: Means of conveyance.
crescent: Growing.
temple: Body.

The inward service of the mind and soul
Grows wide withal. Perhaps he loves you now;
And now no soil nor cautel° doth besmirch
The virtue of his will: but you must fear,
His greatness weigh'd, his will is not his own;

20

For he himself is subject to his birth:
He may not, as unvalu'd persons do,
Carve for himself; for on his choice depends
The safety and the health of the whole state;
And therefore must his choice be circumscrib'd

25

Unto the voice and yielding of that body
Whereof he is the head. Then if he says he loves you,
It fits your wisdom so far to believe it
As he in his particular act and place
May give his saying deed; which is no further

30

Than the main° voice of Denmark goes withal.
Then weigh what loss your honor may sustain
If with too credent ear you list his songs,
Or lose your heart, or your chaste treasure open
To his unmaster'd importunity.

35

Fear it, Ophelia, fear it, my dear sister;
And keep within the rear of your affection,
Out of the shot and danger of desire.
The chariest maid is prodigal enough
If she unmask her beauty to the moon:

40

Virtue itself scrapes not calumnious strokes:
The canker galls the infants of the spring
Too oft before their buttons be disclos'd;
And in the morn and liquid dew of youth
Contagious blastments are most imminent.

45

Be wary, then; best safety lies in fear:
Youth to itself rebels, though none else near.

OPHELIA: I shall the effect of this good lesson keep
As watchman to my heart. But, good my brother,
Do not, as some ungracious pastors do,

50

Show me the steep and thorny way to heaven;
Whilst like a puff'd and reckless libertine,
Himself the primrose path of dalliance treads,
And recks not his own rede.°

LAERTES: O, fear me not.

55

I stay too long:—but here my father comes.

---

cautel: Deceit.

main: Strong, or mighty.

rede: Counsel.

Enter Polonius.

    A double blessing is a double grace;
    Occasion smiles upon a second leave.
POLONIUS: Yet here, Laertes! aboard, aboard, for shame!
    The wind sits in the shoulder of your sail,   60
    And you are stay'd for. There,—my blessing with you!

Laying his hand on Laertes' head.

    And these few precepts in thy memory
    See thou character.° Give thy thoughts no tongue,
    Nor any unproportion'd thought his act.
    Be thou familiar, but by no means vulgar.   65
    The friends thou hast, and their adoption tried,
    Grapple them to thy soul with hoops of steel;
    But do not dull thy palm with entertainment
    Of each new-hatch'd, unfledg'd comrade. Beware
    Of entrance to a quarrel; but, being in,   70
    Bear't that the opposéd may beware of thee.
    Give every man thine ear, but few thy voice:
    Take each man's censure,° but reserve thy judgment.
    Costly thy habit as thy purse can buy,
    But not express'd in fancy; rich, not gaudy: 75
    For the apparel oft proclaims the man;
    And they in France of the best rank and station
    Are most select and generous chief in that.
    Neither a borrower nor a lender be:
    For a loan oft loses both itself and friend;   80
    And borrowing dulls the edge of husbandry.
    This above all,— to thine own self be true;
    And it must follow, as the night the day,
    Thou canst not then be false to any man.
    Farewell: my blessing season this in thee!   85
LAERTES: Most humbly do I take my leave, my lord.
POLONIUS: The time invites you; go, your servants tend.°
LAERTES: Farewell, Ophelia; and remember well
    What I have said to you.
OPHELIA: 'Tis in my memory lock'd,   90
    And you yourself shall keep the key of it.
LAERTES: Farewell. [*Exit.*]
POLONIUS: What is't, Ophelia, he hath said to you?

---

in . . . character: Engrave in your mind.

censure: Opinion.

tend: Wait.

OPHELIA: So please you, something touching the Lord Hamlet.

95 POLONIUS: Marry, well bethought:
      'Tis told me he hath very oft of late
      Given private time to you; and you yourself
      Have of your audience been most free and bounteous:
      If it be so,— as so 'tis put on me,

100   And that in way of caution,— I must tell you,
      You do not understand yourself so clearly
      As it behoves my daughter and your honor.
      What is between you? give me up the truth.

OPHELIA: He hath, my lord, of late made many tenders
105   Of his affection to me.

POLONIUS: Affection! pooh! you speak like a green girl,
      Unsifted in such perilous circumstance.
      Do you believe his tenders,° as you call them?

OPHELIA: I do not know, my lord, what I should think.

110 POLONIUS: Marry, I'll teach you: think yourself a baby;
      That you have ta'en these tenders for true pay,
      Which are not sterling. Tender yourself more dearly;
      Or,— not to crack the wind of the poor phrase,
      Wronging it thus,— you'll tender me a fool.

115 OPHELIA: My lord, he hath impórtun'd me with love
      In honorable fashion.

POLONIUS: Ay, fashion you may call it; go to, go to.

OPHELIA: And hath given countenance to his speech, my lord,
      With almost all the holy vows of heaven.

120 POLONIUS: Ay, springes to catch woodcocks. I do know,
      When the blood burns, how prodigal the soul
      Lends the tongue vows: these blazes, daughter,
      Giving more light than heat,— extinct in both,
      Even in their promise, as it is a-making,—

125   You must not take for fire. From this time
      Be somewhat scanter of your maiden presence;
      Set your entreatments at a higher rate
      Than a command to parley. For Lord Hamlet,
      Believe so much in him, that he is young;

130   And with a larger tether may he walk
      Than may be given you: in few, Ophelia,
      Do not believe his vows; for they are brokers,°—
      Not of that die which their investments show,
      But mere implorators of unholy suits,

135   Breathing like sanctified and pious bawds,

---

tenders: Offers.

brokers: Procurers.

The better to beguile. This is for all,—
I would not, in plain terms, from this time forth,
Have you so slander any moment leisure
As to give words or talk with the Lord Hamlet.
Look to't, I charge you; come your ways.   140
OPHELIA: I shall obey, my lord.

Exeunt.

SCENE 4

The platform.

Enter Hamlet, Horatio, and Marcellus.

HAMLET: The air bites shrewdly; it is very cold.
HORATIO: It is a nipping and an eager air.
HAMLET: What hour now?
HORATIO: I think it lacks of twelve.
MARCELLUS: No, it is struck.   5
HORATIO: Indeed? I heard it not: then it draws near the season
    Wherein the spirit held his wont to walk.

A flourish of trumpets, and ordnance shot off within.

    What does this mean, my lord?
HAMLET: The king doth wake to-night, and takes his rouse,
    Keeps wassail, and the swaggering upspring° reels;   10
    And, as he drains his draughts of Rhenish down,
    The kettle-drum and trumpet thus bray out
    The triumph of his pledge.°
HORATIO: Is it a custom?
HAMLET: Ay, marry, is't: 15
    But to my mind,— though I am native here,
    And to the manner born,— it is a custom
    More honor'd in the breach than the observance.
    This heavy-headed revel east and west
    Makes us traduc'd and tax'd of other nations: 20
    They clepe us drunkards, and with swinish phrase
    Soil our addition;° and, indeed, it takes
    From our achievements, though perform'd at height,
    The pith and marrow of our attribute.
    So oft it chances in particular men   25
    That, for some vicious mole of nature in them,

---

upspring: A dance.
triumph . . . pledge: The glory of his toasts.
addition: Reputation.

As in their birth,—wherein they are not guilty,
Since nature cannot choose his origin,—
By the o'ergrowth of some complexion,
30   Oft breaking down the pales and forts of reason;
Or by some habit, that too much o'erleavens
The form of plausive° manners;—that these men,—
Carrying, I say, the stamp of one defect,
Being nature's livery or fortune's star,—
35   Their virtues else,—be they as pure as grace,
As infinite as man may undergo,—
Shall in the general censure take corruption
From that particular fault: the dram of evil
Doth all the noble substance of a doubt
40   To his own scandal.

HORATIO: Look, my lord, it comes!

Enter Ghost.

HAMLET: Angels and ministers of grace defend us!—
Be thou a spirit of health or goblin damn'd,
Bring with thee airs from heaven or blasts from hell,
45   Be thy intents wicked or charitable,
Thou com'st in such a questionable shape
That I will speak to thee: I'll call thee Hamlet,
King, father, royal Dane: O, answer me!
Let me not burst in ignorance; but tell
50   Why thy canóniz'd bones, hearsèd in death,
Have burst their cerements; why the sepulchre,
Wherein we saw thee quietly in-urn'd,
Hath op'd his ponderous and marble jaws
To cast thee up again! What may this mean,
55   That thou, dead corse, again in còmplete steel,
Revisit'st thus the glimpses of the moon,
Making night hideous and we° fools of nature
So horridly to shake our disposition
With thoughts beyond the reaches of our souls?
60   Say, why is this? wherefore? what should we do?

Ghost beckons Hamlet.

HORATIO: It beckons you to go away with it,
As if it some impartment did desire
To you alone.

---

plausive: Pleasing.

we: Us.

MARCELLUS: Look, with what courteous action
    It waves you to a more removed ground: 65
    But do not go with it.
HORATIO: No, by no means.
HAMLET: It will not speak; then will I follow it.
HORATIO: Do not, my lord.
HAMLET: Why, what should be the fear? 70
    I do not set my life at a pin's fee;
    And for my soul, what can it do to that,
    Being a thing immortal as itself?
    It waves me forth again;— I'll follow it.
HORATIO: What if it tempt you toward the flood, my lord. 75
    Or to the dreadful summit of the cliff
    That beetles o'er his base into the sea,
    And there assume some other horrible form,
    Which might deprive your sovereignty of reason,
    And draw you into madness? think of it: 80
    The very place puts toys of desperation,
    Without more motive, into every brain
    That looks so many fathoms to the sea
    And hears it roar beneath.
HAMLET: It waves me still.— 85
    Go on; I'll follow thee.
MARCELLUS: You shall not go, my lord.
HAMLET: Hold off your hands.
HORATIO: Be rul'd; you shall not go.
HAMLET: My fate cries out, 90
    And makes each petty artery in this body
    As hardy as the Némean lion's° nerve.—

Ghost beckons.

    Still am I call'd;— unhand me, gentlemen;—[*Breaking from them*]
    By heaven, I'll make a ghost of him that lets° me.
    I say, away!— Go on; I'll follow thee. 95

Exeunt Ghost and Hamlet.

HORATIO: He waxes desperate with imagination.
MARCELLUS: Let's follow; 'tis not fit thus to obey him.
HORATIO: Have after.— To what issue will this come?
MARCELLUS: Something is rotten in the state of Denmark.
HORATIO: Heaven will direct it. 100

Némean lion's: The fierce lion that Hercules was called upon to slay as one of his "twelve labors."
lets: Hinders.

MARCELLUS: Nay, let's follow him.

Exeunt.

SCENE 5

A more remote part of the platform.

Enter Ghost and Hamlet.

HAMLET: Where wilt thou lead me? speak, I'll go no further.
GHOST: Mark me.
HAMLET: I will.
GHOST: My hour is almost come,
5   When I to sulphurous and tormenting flames
       Must render up myself.
HAMLET: Alas, poor ghost!
GHOST: Pity me not, but lend thy serious hearing
       To what I shall unfold.
10 HAMLET: Speak; I am bound to hear.
GHOST: So art thou to revenge, when thou shalt hear.
HAMLET: What?
GHOST: I am thy father's spirit;
       Doom'd for a certain term to walk the night,
15   And, for the day, confin'd to waste in fires
       Till the foul crimes° done in my days of nature
       Are burnt and purg'd away. But that I am forbid
       To tell the secrets of my prison-house,
       I could a tale unfold whose lightest word
20   Would harrow up thy soul; freeze thy young blood;
       Make thy two eyes, like stars, start from their spheres;
       Thy knotted and combined locks to part,
       And each particular hair to stand on end,
       Like quills upon the fretful porcupine:
25   But this eternal blazon° must not be
       To ears of flesh and blood. — List, list, O, list! —
       If thou didst ever thy dear father love, —
HAMLET: O God!
GHOST: Revenge his foul and most unnatural murder.
30 HAMLET: Murder!
GHOST: Murder — most foul, as in the best it is;
       But this most foul, strange, and unnatural.

---

foul crimes: Sins or faults.

eternal blazon: Disclosure of information concerning the other world.

HAMLET: Haste me to know't, that I, with wings as swift
    As meditation or the thoughts of love,
    May sweep to my revenge.   35
GHOST: I find thee apt;
    And duller shouldst thou be than the fat weed
    That rots itself in ease on Lethe° wharf,
    Wouldst thou not stir in this. Now, Hamlet,
    'Tis given out that, sleeping in mine orchard,   40
    A serpent stung me; so the whole ear of Denmark
    Is by a forged process of my death
    Rankly abus'd: but know, thou noble youth,
    The serpent that did sting thy father's life
    Now wears his crown.   45
HAMLET: O my prophetic soul! mine uncle!
GHOST: Ay, that incestuous, that adulterate beast,
    With witchcraft of his wit, with traitorous gifts,—
    O wicked wit and gifts that have the power
    So to seduce! — won to his shameful lust   50
    The will of my most seeming virtuous queen:
    O Hamlet, what a falling-off was there!
    From me, whose love was of that dignity
    That it went hand in hand even with the vow
    I made to her in marriage: and to decline   55
    Upon a wretch whose natural gifts were poor
    To those of mine!
    But virtue, as it never will be mov'd,
    Though lewdness court it in a shape of heaven;
    So lust, though to a radiant angel link'd,   60
    Will sate itself in a celestial bed
    And prey on garbage.
    But, soft! methinks I scent the morning air;
    Brief let me be. — Sleeping within mine orchard,
    My custom always in the afternoon,   65
    Upon my sécure hour thy uncle stole,
    With juice of cursed hebenon° in a vial,
    And in the porches of mine ears did pour
    The leperous distilment; whose effect
    Holds such an enmity with blood of man   70
    That, swift as quicksilver, it courses through
    The natural gates and alleys of the body;

Lethe: The river of forgetfulness of the past, out of which the dead drink.

hebenon: Ebony.

And with a sudden vigor it doth posset°
And curd, like eager° droppings into milk,
75   The thin and wholesome blood: so did it mine;
And a most instant tetter bark'd about,
Most lazar-like,° with vile and loathsome crust,
All my smooth body.
Thus was I, sleeping, by a brother's hand,
80   Of life, of crown, of queen, at once despatch'd:
Cut off even in the blossoms of my sin,
Unhousel'd, unanointed, unanel'd;
No reckoning made, but sent to my account
With all my imperfections on my head:
85   O, horrible! O, horrible! most horrible!
If thou hast nature in thee, bear it not;
Let not the royal bed of Denmark be
A couch for luxury° and damned incest.
But, howsoever thou pursu'st this act,
90   Taint not thy mind, nor let thy soul contrive
Against thy mother aught: leave her to heaven,
And to those thorns that in her bosom lodge,
To prick and sting her. Fare thee well at once!
The glowworm shows the matin to be near,
95   And 'gins to pale his uneffectual fire:
Adieu, adieu! Hamlet, remember me. [*Exit.*]
HAMLET: O all you host of heaven! O earth! what else?
And shall I couple hell?— O, fie!— Hold, my heart;
And you, my sinews, grow not instant old,
100   But bear me stiffly up.— Remember thee!
Ay, thou poor ghost, while memory holds a seat
In this distracted globe. Remember thee!
Yea, from the table of my memory
I'll wipe away all trivial fond° recórds,
105   All saws of books, all forms, all pressures past,
That youth and observation copied there;
And thy commandment all alone shall live
Within the book and volume of my brain,
Unmix'd with baser matter: yes, by heaven.—
110   O most pernicious woman!
O villain, villain, smiling, damned villain!

---

posset: Coagulate.
eager: Acid.
lazar-like: Like a leper, whose skin is rough.
luxury: Lechery.
fond: Foolish.

My tables,—meet it is I set it down,
That one may smile, and smile, and be a villain;
At least, I am sure, it may be so in Denmark:

Writing.

So, uncle, there you are. Now to my word;   115
It is, *Adieu, adieu! remember me:*
I have sworn't.
HORATIO: [*Within*] My lord, my lord,—
MARCELLUS: [*Within*]   Lord Hamlet,—
HORATIO: [*Within*]   Heaven secure him!   120
MARCELLUS: [*Within*] So be it!
HORATIO: [*Within*] Illo, ho, ho, my lord!
HAMLET: Hillo, ho, ho, boy! come, bird, come.°

Enter Horatio and Marcellus.

MARCELLUS: How is't, my noble lord?
HORATIO: What news, my lord?   125
HAMLET: O, wonderful!
HORATIO: Good my lord, tell it.
HAMLET: No; you'll reveal it.
HORATIO: Not I, my lord, by heaven.
MARCELLUS: Nor I, my lord.   130
HAMLET: How say you, then; would heart of man once think it?—
    But you'll be secret?
HORATIO and MARCELLUS: Ay, by heaven, my lord.
HAMLET: There's ne'er a villain dwelling in all Denmark
    But he's an arrant knave.   135
HORATIO: There needs no ghost, my lord, come from the grave
    To tell us this.
HAMLET: Why, right; you are i' the right;
    And so, without more circumstance at all,
    I hold it fit that we shake hands and part: 140
    You, as your business and desire shall point you,—
    For every man has business and desire,
    Such as it is;— and for mine own poor part,
    Look you, I'll go pray.
HORATIO: These are but wild and whirling words, my lord.   145
HAMLET: I'm sorry they offend you, heartily;
    Yes, faith, heartily.
HORATIO: There's no offence, my lord.
HAMLET: Yes, by Saint Patrick, but there is, Horatio,
    And much offence too. Touching this vision here,—   150

Hillo . . . come: Hamlet uses the word "bird" because this is a falconer's call.

It is an honest ghost, that let me tell you:
For you desire to know what is between us,
O'ermaster't as you may. And now, good friends,
As you are friends, scholars, and soldiers,
155 Give me one poor request.

HORATIO: What is't, my lord? we will.

HAMLET: Never make known what you have seen to-night.

HORATIO and MARCELLUS: My lord, we will not.

HAMLET: Nay, but swear't.

160 HORATIO: In faith,
My lord, not I.

MARCELLUS: Nor I, my lord, in faith.

HAMLET: Upon my sword.

MARCELLUS: We have sworn, my lord, already.

165 HAMLET: Indeed, upon my sword, indeed.

GHOST: [*Beneath*] Swear.

HAMLET: Ha, ha, boy! say'st thou so? art thou there, truepenny?—
Come on,— you hear this fellow in the cellarage,—
Consent to swear.

170 HORATIO: Propose the oath, my lord.

HAMLET: Never to speak of this that you have seen,
Swear by my sword.

GHOST: [*Beneath*] Swear.

HAMLET: *Hic et ubique?*° then we'll shift our ground.—
175 Come hither, gentlemen,
And lay your hands again upon my sword:
Never to speak of this that you have heard,
Swear by my sword.

GHOST: [*Beneath*] Swear.

180 HAMLET: Well said! old mole! canst work i' the earth so fast?
A worthy pioneer!°— Once more remove, good friends.

HORATIO: O day and night, but this is wondrous strange!

HAMLET: And therefore as a stranger give it welcome.
There are more things in heaven and earth, Horatio,
185 Than are dreamt of in your philosophy.
But come;—
Here, as before, never, so help you mercy,
How strange or odd soe'er I bear myself,—
As I, perchance, hereafter shall think meet
190 To put an antic disposition on,—
That you, at such times seeing me, never shall,

Hic et ubique: "Here and everywhere" (Latin).

pioneer: A soldier who digs trenches and undermines fortresses.

With arms encumber'd° thus, or this headshake,
Or by pronouncing of some doubtful phrase,
As, *Well, well, we know;* — or, *We could, an if we would;* —
Or, *If we list to speak;* — or, *There be, an if they might;* —   195
Or such ambiguous giving out, to note
That you know aught of me: — this not to do,
So grace and mercy at your most need help you,
Swear.
GHOST: [*Beneath*] Swear.   200
HAMLET: Rest, rest, perturbed spirit! — So, gentlemen,
With all my love I do commend to you:
And what so poor a man as Hamlet is
May do, to express his love and friending to you,
God willing, shall not lack. Let us go in together;   205
And still your fingers on your lips, I pray.
The time is out of joint: — O cursed spite,
That ever I was born to set it right! —
Nay, come, let's go together.

Exeunt.

ACT II
SCENE 1

A room in Polonius' house.

Enter Polonius and Reynaldo.

POLONIUS: Give him this money and these notes, Reynaldo.
REYNALDO: I will, my lord.
POLONIUS: You shall do marvelous wisely, good Reynaldo,
Before you visit him, to make inquiry
On his behavior.   5
REYNALDO: My lord, I did intend it.
POLONIUS: Marry, well said; very well said. Look you, sir,
Inquire me first what Danskers° are in Paris;
And how, and who, what means, and where they keep,
What company, at what expense; and finding,   10
By this encompassment and drift of question,
That they do know my son, come you more nearer
Than your particular demands will touch it:
Take you, as 'twere, some distant knowledge of him;

---

encumber'd: Folded.
Danskers: Danes.

15   As thus, *I know his father and his friends,*
        And in part him; — do you mark this, Reynaldo?
    REYNALDO: Ay, very well, my lord.
    POLONIUS: *And in part him;* — *but,* you may say, *not well:*
        But if 't be he I mean, he's very wild;
20   *Addicted so and so;* and there put on him
        What forgeries you please; marry, none so rank
        As may dishonor him; take heed of that;
        But, sir, such wanton, wild, and usual slips
        As are companions noted and most known
25   To youth and liberty.
    REYNALDO: As gaming, my lord.
    POLONIUS: Ay, or drinking, fencing, swearing, quarreling,
        Drabbing:° — you may go so far.
    REYNALDO: My lord, that would dishonor him.
30 POLONIUS: Faith, no; as you may season it in the charge.
        You must not put another scandal on him,
        That he is open to incontinency;
        That's not my meaning: but breathe his faults so quaintly
        That they may seem the taints of liberty;
35   The flash and outbreak of a fiery mind;
        A savageness in unreclaimed blood,
        Of general assault.
    REYNALDO: But, my good lord,—
    POLONIUS: Wherefore should you do this?
40 REYNALDO: Ay, my lord,
        I would know that.
    POLONIUS: Marry, sir, here's my drift;
        And I believe it is a fetch of warrant:°
        You laying these slight sullies on my son.
45   As 'twere a thing a little soil'd i' the working,
        Mark you,
        Your party in converse, him you would sound,
        Having ever seen in the prenominate crimes
        The youth you breathe of guilty, be assur'd
50   He closes with you in this consequence;
        Good sir, or so; or *friend,* or *gentleman,* —
        According to the phrase or the addition°
        Of man and country.
    REYNALDO: Very good, my lord.

Drabbing: Going about with loose women.
fetch of warrant: A good device.
addition: Form of address.

POLONIUS: And then, sir, does he this,—he does,—   55
    What was I about to say?—By the mass, I was
    About to say something:—where did I leave?
REYNALDO: At *closes in the consequence,*
    At *friend or so,* and *gentleman.*
POLONIUS: At—closes in the consequence,—ay, marry;   60
    He closes with you thus:—*I know the gentleman;*
    I saw him yesterday, or t'other day,
    Or then, or then; with such, or such; and, as you say,
    There was he gaming; there o'ertook in's rouse;
    There falling out at tennis: or perchance,   65
    I saw him enter such a house of sale,—
    Videlicet, a brothel,—or so forth.—
    See you now;
    Your bait of falsehood takes this carp of truth:
    And thus do we of wisdom and of reach,   70
    With windlasses, and with assays of bias,
    By indirections find directions out:
    So, by my former lecture and advice,
    Shall you my son. You have me, have you not?
REYNALDO: My lord, I have.   75
POLONIUS: God b' wi' you; fare you well.
REYNALDO: Good my lord!
POLONIUS: Observe his inclination in yourself.
REYNALDO: I shall, my lord.
POLONIUS: And let him ply his music.   80
REYNALDO: Well, my lord.
POLONIUS: Farewell!

Exit Reynaldo.

Enter Ophelia.

    How now, Ophelia! what's the matter?
OPHELIA: Alas, my lord, I have been so affrighted.
POLONIUS: With what, i' the name of God?   85
OPHELIA: My lord, as I was sewing in my chamber,
    Lord Hamlet,—with his doublet all unbrac'd;
    No hat upon his head; his stockings foul'd,
    Ungarter'd, and down-gyved° to his ankle;
    Pale as his shirt; his knees knocking each other;   90
    And with a look so piteous in purport
    As if he had been loosed out of hell
    To speak of horrors,—he comes before me.

---

down-gyved: Dangling like chains.

POLONIUS: Mad for thy love?

95   OPHELIA: My lord, I do not know;
     But truly I do fear it.
POLONIUS: What said he?
OPHELIA: He took me by the wrist, and held me hard;
     Then goes he to the length of all his arm;
100 And with his other hand thus o'er his brow,
     He falls to such perusal of my face
     As he would draw it. Long stay'd he so;
     At last, — a little shaking of mine arm,
     And thrice his head thus waving up and down, —
105 He rais'd a sigh so piteous and profound
     That it did seem to shatter all his bulk
     And end his being; that done, he lets me go:
     And, with his head over his shoulder turn'd,
     He seem'd to find his way without his eyes;
110 For out o' doors he went without their help,
     And to the last bended their light on me.
POLONIUS: Come, go with me: I will go seek the king.
     This is the very ecstasy° of love;
     Whose violent property fordoes itself,°
115 And leads the will to desperate undertakings,
     As oft as any passion under heaven
     That does afflict our nature. I am sorry, —
     What, have you given him any hard words of late?
OPHELIA: No, my good lord; but, as you did command,
120 I did repel his letters, and denied
     His access to me.
POLONIUS: That hath made him mad.
     I am sorry that with better heed and judgment
     I had not quoted him: I fear'd he did but trifle,
125 And meant to wreck thee; but, beshrew my jealousy!
     It seems it is as proper to our age
     To cast beyond ourselves in our opinions
     As it is common for the younger sort
     To lack discretion. Come, go we to the king:
130 This must be known; which, being kept close, might move
     More grief to hide than hate to utter love.

Exeunt.

---

ecstasy: Madness.

fordoes itself: Destroys itself.

SCENE 2

A room in the castle.

Enter King, Queen, Rosencrantz, Guildenstern, and Attendants.

KING: Welcome, dear Rosencrantz and Guildenstern!
    Moreover that we much did long to see you,
    The need we have to use you did provoke
    Our hasty sending. Something have you heard
    Of Hamlet's transformation; so I call it,   5
    Since nor the exterior nor the inward man
    Resembles that it was. What it should be,
    More than his father's death, that thus hath put him
    So much from the understanding of himself,
    I cannot dream of: I entreat you both,   10
    That being of so young days brought up with him,
    And since so neighbor'd to his youth and humor,
    That you vouchsafe your rest here in our court
    Some little time: so by your companies
    To draw him on to pleasures, and to gather,   15
    So much as from occasion you may glean,
    Whether aught, to us unknown, afflicts him thus,
    That, open'd, lies within our remedy.
QUEEN: Good gentlemen, he hath much talk'd of you;
    And sure I am two men there are not living   20
    To whom he more adheres. If it will please you
    To show us so much gentry and good-will
    As to expend your time with us awhile,
    For the supply and profit of our hope,
    Your visitation shall receive such thanks   25
    As fits a king's remembrance.
ROSENCRANTZ: Both your majesties
    Might, by the sovereign power you have of us,
    Put your dread pleasures more into command
    Than to entreaty.   30
GUILDENSTERN: We both obey,
    And here give up ourselves, in the full bent,
    To lay our service freely at your feet,
    To be commanded.
KING: Thanks, Rosencrantz and gentle Guildenstern.   35
QUEEN: Thanks, Guildenstern and gentle Rosencrantz:
    And I beseech you instantly to visit
    My too-much-changed son.— Go, some of you,
    And bring these gentlemen where Hamlet is.
GUILDENSTERN: Heavens make our presence and our practices   40
    Pleasant and helpful to him!

QUEEN: Ay, amen!

Exeunt Rosencrantz, Guildenstern, and some Attendants.

Enter Polonius.

POLONIUS: The ambassadors from Norway, my good lord,
          Are joyfully return'd.
45   KING: Thou still has been the father of good news.
     POLONIUS: Have I, my lord? Assure you, my good liege,
          I hold my duty, as I hold my soul,
          Both to my God and to my gracious king:
          And I do think,— or else this brain of mine
50   Hunts not the trail of policy° so sure
          As it hath us'd to do,— that I have found
          The very cause of Hamlet's lunacy.
     KING: O, speak of that; that do I long to hear.
     POLONIUS: Give first admittance to the ambassadors;
55   My news shall be the fruit to that great feast.
     KING: Thyself do grace to them, and bring them in.

Exit Polonius.

          He tells me, my sweet queen, that he hath found
          The head and source of all your son's distemper.
     QUEEN: I doubt it is no other but the main,—
60   His father's death and our o'erhasty marriage.
     KING: Well, we shall sift him.

Re-enter Polonius, with Voltimand and Cornelius.

                              Welcome, my good friends!
          Say, Voltimand, what from our brother Norway?
     VOLTIMAND: Most fair return of greetings and desires.
65   Upon our first, he sent out to suppress
          His nephew's levies; which to him appear'd
          To be a preparation 'gainst the Polack;
          But, better look'd into, he truly found
          It was against your highness: whereat griev'd,—
70   That so his sickness, age, and impotence
          Was falsely borne in hand,— sends out arrests
          On Fortinbras; which he, in brief, obeys;
          Receives rebuke from Norway; and, in fine,
          Makes vows before his uncle never more
75   To give the assay of arms against your majesty.
          Whereon old Norway, overcome with joy,

---

trail of policy: Statecraft.

Gives him three thousand crowns in annual fee;
And his commission to employ those soldiers,
So levied as before, against the Polack:
With an entreaty, herein further shown, [*gives a paper*]   80
That it might please you to give quiet pass
Through your dominions for this enterprise,
On such regards of safety and allowance
As therein are set down.
KING: It likes us well;   85
And at our more consider'd time we'll read,
Answer, and think upon this business.
Meantime we thank you for your well-took labor:
Go to your rest; at night we'll feast together:
Most welcome home!   90

Exeunt Voltimand and Cornelius.

POLONIUS: This business is well ended.—
My liege, and madam,— to expostulate
What majesty should be, what duty is,
Why day is day, night night, and time is time,
Were nothing but to waste night, day, and time.   95
Therefore, since brevity is the soul of wit,
And tediousness the limbs and outward flourishes,
I will be brief:— your noble son is mad:
Mad call I it; for to define true madness,
What is't but to be nothing else but mad?   100
But let that go.
QUEEN: More matter with less art.
POLONIUS: Madam, I swear I use no art at all.
That he is mad, 'tis true 'tis pity;
And pity 'tis 'tis true: a foolish figure;   105
But farewell it, for I will use no art.
Mad let us grant him, then: and now remains
That we find out the cause of this effect;
Or rather say, the cause of this defect,
For this effect defective comes by cause: 110
Thus it remains, and the remainder thus.
Perpend.
I have a daughter,—have whilst she is mine,—
Who, in her duty and obedience, mark,
Hath given me this: now gather, and surmise   115

Reads

    To the celestial, and my soul's idol, the most beautified Ophelia,—
That's an ill phrase, a vile phrase,—*beautified* is a vile phrase: but you shall
hear. Thus:

Reads

> *In her excellent white bosom, these, &c.*

120   QUEEN: Came this from Hamlet to her?
       POLONIUS: Good madam, stay a while; I will be faithful.

Reads

> *Doubt thou the stars are fire;*
> *Doubt that the sun doth move;*
> *Doubt truth to be a liar;*
125 > *But never doubt I love.*

> O dear Ophelia, I am ill at these numbers, I have not art to reckon my groans: but
> that I love thee best, O most best, believe it. Adieu.
> *Thine evermore, most dear lady, whilst this machine is to him,*
>
>   Hamlet

       This, in obedience, hath my daughter show'd me:
130   And more above, hath his solicitings,
       As they fell out by time, by means, and place,
       All given to mine ear.
       KING: But how hath she
       Receiv'd his love?
135   POLONIUS: What do you think of me?
       KING: As of a man faithful and honorable.
       POLONIUS: I would fain prove so. But what might you think,
       When I had seen this hot love on the wing,—
       As I perceiv'd it, I must tell you that,
140   Before my daughter told me,— what might you,
       Or my dear majesty your queen here, think,
       If I had play'd the desk or table-book;°
       Or given my heart a winking, mute and dumb;
       Or look'd upon this love with idle sight;—
145   What might you think? No, I went round to work,
       And my young mistress thus I did bespeak:
       Lord Hamlet is a prince out of thy sphere;
       This must not be: and then I precepts gave her,
       That she should lock herself from his resort,
150   Admit no messengers, receive no tokens.
       Which done, she took the fruits of my advice;
       And he, repulsed,— a short tale to make,—
       Fell into a sadness; then into a fast;
       Thence to a watch; thence into a weakness;
155   Thence to a lightness; and, by this declension,

---

table-book: Memorandum pad.

Into the madness wherein now he raves
And all we wail for.
KING: Do you think 'tis this?
QUEEN: It may be, very likely.
POLONIUS: Hath there been such a time, — I'd fain know that, —   160
That I have positively said, 'Tis so,
When it prov'd otherwise?
KING: Not that I know.
POLONIUS: Take this from this, if this be otherwise: [*Pointing to his head and
shoulder*]
If circumstances lead me, I will find   165
Where truth is hid, though it were hid indeed
Within the center.
KING: How may we try it further?
POLONIUS: You know, sometimes he walks for hours together
Here in the lobby.   170
QUEEN: So he does, indeed.
POLONIUS: At such a time I'll loose my daughter to him:
Be you and I behind an arras° then;
Mark the encounter: if he love her not,
And be not from his reason fall'n thereon,   175
Let me be no assistant for a state,
But keep a farm and carters.
KING: We will try it.
QUEEN: But look, where sadly the poor wretch comes reading.
POLONIUS: Away, I do beseech you, both away: 180
I'll board° him presently: — O, give me leave.

Exeunt King, Queen, and Attendants.

Enter Hamlet, reading.

How does my good Lord Hamlet?
HAMLET: Well, God-a-mercy.
POLONIUS: Do you know me, my lord?
HAMLET: Excellent, excellent well; you're a fishmonger.   185
POLONIUS: Not I, my lord.
HAMLET: Then I would you were so honest a man.
POLONIUS: Honest, my lord!
HAMLET: Ay, sir; to be honest, as this world goes, is to be one man picked out
of ten thousand.   190
POLONIUS: That's very true, my lord.
HAMLET: For if the sun breed maggots in a dead dog, being a god kissing
carrion, — Have you a daughter?

---

arras: Tapestry, hung some distance away from a wall.
board: Address.

POLONIUS: I have, my lord.

195 HAMLET: Let her not walk i' the sun: conception is a blessing; but not as your
daughter may conceive: — friend, look to't.

POLONIUS: How say you by that? — [*Aside*] Still harping on my daughter: —
yet he knew me not at first; he said I was a fishmonger: he is far gone, far
gone: and truly in my youth I suffered much extremity for love; very near

200 this. I'll speak to him again. — What do you read, my lord?

HAMLET: Words, words, words.

POLONIUS: What is the matter, my lord?

HAMLET: Between who?

POLONIUS: I mean, the matter that you read, my lord.

205 HAMLET: Slanders, sir: for the satirical slave says here that old men have gray
beards; that their faces are wrinkled; their eyes purging thick amber and
plum-tree gum; and that they have a plentiful lack of wit, together with
most weak hams: all which, sir, though I most powerfully and potently
believe, yet I hold it not honesty to have it thus set down; for you yourself,

210 sir, should be old as I am, if, like a crab, you could go backward.

POLONIUS: [*Aside*] Though this be madness, yet there is method in't. — ill you
walk out of the air, my lord?

HAMLET: Into my grave?

POLONIUS: Indeed, that is out o' the air. — [*Aside*] How pregnant° sometimes

215 his replies are! a happiness that often madness hits on, which reason and
sanity could not so prosperously be delivered of. I will leave him, and suddenly contrive the means of meeting between him and my daughter. —
More honorable lord, I will most humbly take my leave of you.

HAMLET: You cannot, sir, take from me anything that I will more willingly

220 part withal, — except my life, except my life, except my life.

POLONIUS: Fare you well, my lord.

HAMLET: These tedious old fools!

Enter Rosencrantz and Guildenstern.

POLONIUS: You go to seek the Lord Hamlet; there he is.

ROSENCRANTZ: [*To Polonius*] God save you, sir!

Exit Polonius.

225 GUILDENSTERN: Mine honored lord!

ROSENCRANTZ: My most dear lord!

HAMLET: My excellent good friends! How dost thou, Guildenstern? Ah,
Rosencrantz? Good lads, how do ye both?

ROSENCRANTZ: As the indifferent children of the earth.

230 GUILDENSTERN: Happy in that we are not overhappy; on fortune's cap we are
not the very button.

HAMLET: Nor the soles of her shoe?

ROSENCRANTZ: Neither, my lord.

---

pregnant: Ready, and clever.

HAMLET: Then you live about her waist, or in the middle of her favors?
GUILDENSTERN: Faith, her privates we.   235
HAMLET: In the secret parts of fortune? O, most true; she is a strumpet.
  What's the news?
ROSENCRANTZ: None, my lord, but that the world's grown honest.
HAMLET: Then is doomsday near: but your news is not true. Let me question
  more in particular: what have you, my good friends, deserved at the hands   240
  of fortune, that she sends you to prison hither?
GUILDENSTERN: Prison, my lord!
HAMLET: Denmark's a prison.
ROSENCRANTZ: Then is the world one.
HAMLET: A goodly one; in which there are many confines, wards, and dun-   245
  geons, Denmark being one o' the worst.
ROSENCRANTZ: We think not so, my lord.
HAMLET: Why, then, 'tis none to you; for there is nothing either good or bad,
  but thinking makes it so: to me it is a prison.
ROSENCRANTZ: Why, then, your ambition makes it one; 'tis too narrow   250
  for your mind.
HAMLET: O God, I could be bounded in a nutshell, and count myself a king of
  infinite space, were it not that I have bad dreams.
GUILDENSTERN: Which dreams, indeed, are ambition; for the very substance
  of the ambitious is merely the shadow of a dream.   255
HAMLET: A dream itself is but a shadow.
ROSENCRANTZ: Truly, and I hold ambition of so airy and light a quality that it
  is but a shadow's shadow.
HAMLET: Then are our beggars bodies, and our monarchs and outstretched
  heroes the beggars' shadows. Shall we to the court? for, by my fay, I   260
  cannot reason.
ROSENCRANTZ and GUILDENSTERN: We'll wait upon you.
HAMLET: No such matter: I will not sort you with the rest of my servants, for,
  to speak to you like an honest man, I am most dreadfully attended. But, in
  the beaten way of friendship, what make you at Elsinore?   265
ROSENCRANTZ: To visit you, my lord; no other occasion.
HAMLET: Beggar that I am, I am even poor in thanks; but I thank you: and
  sure, dear friends, my thanks are too dear a halfpenny. Were you not sent
  for? Is it your own inclining? Is it a free visitation? Come, deal justly with
  me: come, come; nay, speak.   270
GUILDENSTERN: What should we say, my lord?
HAMLET: Why, anything — but to the purpose. You were sent for; and there is
  a kind of confession in your looks, which your modesties have not craft
  enough to color: I know the good king and queen have sent for you.
ROSENCRANTZ: To what end, my lord?   275
HAMLET: That you must teach me. But let me conjure you, by the rights of
  our fellowship, by the consonancy of our youth, by the obligation of our
  ever-preserved love, and by what more dear a better proposer could charge
  you withal, be even and direct with me, whether you were sent for or no?
ROSENCRANTZ: What say you? [*To Guildenstern*]   280

HAMLET: [*Aside*] Nay, then, I have an eye of you. — If you love me, hold
not off.

GUILDENSTERN: My lord, we were sent for.

HAMLET: I will tell you why; so shall my anticipation prevent your discovery,
285   and your secrecy to the king and queen moult no feather. I have of late, —
but wherefore I know not, — lost all my mirth, forgone all custom of exercises; and, indeed, it goes so heavily with my disposition that this goodly
frame, the earth, seems to me a sterile promontory; this most excellent
canopy, the air, look you, this brave o'erhanging firmament, this majestical
290   roof fretted° with golden fire, — why, it appears no other thing to me than
a foul and pestilent congregation of vapors. What a piece of work is man!
How noble in reason! how infinite in faculties! in form and moving, how
express and admirable! in action, how like an angel! in apprehension, how
like a god! the beauty of the world! the paragon of animals! And yet, to me,
295   what is this quintessence of dust? man delights not me; no, nor woman
neither, though by your smiling you seem to say so.

ROSENCRANTZ: My lord, there was no such stuff in my thoughts.

HAMLET: Why did you laugh, then, when I said, *Man delights not me?*

ROSENCRANTZ: To think, my lord, if you delight not in man, what lenten en-
300   tertainment° the players shall receive from you: we coted° them on the
way; and hither are they coming, to offer you service.

HAMLET: He that plays the king shall be welcome, — his majesty shall have
tribute of me; the adventurous knight shall use his foil and target; the lover
shall not sigh gratis; the humorous° man shall end his part in peace; the
305   clown shall make those laugh whose lungs are tickled o' the sere;° and the
lady shall say her mind freely, or the blank verse shall halt° for't. — What
players are they?

ROSENCRANTZ: Even those you were wont to take delight in, — the tragedi-
ans of the city.

310   **HAMLET:** How chances it they travel? their residence, both in reputation and
profit, was better both ways.

ROSENCRANTZ: I think their inhibition° comes by the means of the late
innovation.

HAMLET: Do they hold the same estimation they did when I was in the city?
315   Are they so followed?

ROSENCRANTZ: No, indeed, they are not.

HAMLET: How comes it? do they grow rusty?

---

roof fretted: A roof with fretwork.

lenten entertainment: Poor reception.

coted: Passed.

humorous: Eccentric.

whose lungs . . . sere: Whose lungs, for laughter, are easily tickled.

halt: Limp.

inhibition: Difficulty, preventing them from remaining in the capital.

ROSENCRANTZ: Nay, their endeavor keeps in the wonted pace; but there is, sir, an aery° of children, little eyases,° that cry out on the top of question, and are most tyrannically clapped for't: these are now the fashion; and so berattle the common stages,— so they call them,— that many wearing rapiers are afraid of goose-quills, and dare scarce come thither.   320

HAMLET: What, are they children? who maintains 'em? how are they escoted?° Will they pursue the quality° no longer than they can sing? will they not say afterwards, if they should grow themselves to common players,— as it is most like, if their means are no better,— their writers do them wrong, to make them exclaim against their own succession?   325

ROSENCRANTZ: Faith, there has been much to do on both sides; and the nation holds it no sin to tarre° them to controversy: there was for awhile no money bid for argument, unless the poet and the player went to cuffs in the question.   330

HAMLET: Is't possible?

GUILDENSTERN: O, there has been much throwing about of brains.

HAMLET: Do the boys carry it away?

ROSENCRANTZ: Ay, that they do, my lord; Hercules and his load° too.   335

HAMLET: It is not strange; for mine uncle is king of Denmark, and those that would make mouths at him while my father lived, give twenty, forty, fifty, an hundred ducats a-piece for his picture in little. 'Sblood, there is something in this more than natural, if philosophy could find it out.

Flourish of trumpets within.

GUILDENSTERN: There are the players.   340

HAMLET: Gentlemen, you are welcome to Elsinore. Your hands, come: the appurtenance of welcome is fashion and ceremony: let me comply with you in this garb; lest my extent° to the players, which, I tell you, must show fairly outward, should more appear like entertainment° than yours. You are welcome: but my uncle-father and aunt-mother are deceived.   345

GUILDENSTERN: In what, my dear lord?

HAMLET: I am but mad north-north-west: when the wind is southerly I know a hawk from a handsaw.

Enter Polonius.

---

aery: Brood of birds of prey.

little eyases: Young hawks; a reference to the boys' companies that became popular rivals of Shakespeare's company of players.

escoted: Financially supported.

quality: Profession.

to tarre: To egg them on.

his load: The globe, or the world.

extent: Show of friendliness.

entertainment: Welcome.

POLONIUS: Well be with you, gentlemen!

350   HAMLET: Hark you, Guildenstern;— and you too;— at each ear a hearer: that
great baby you see there is not yet out of his swathing-clouts.

ROSENCRANTZ: Happily he's the second time come to them; for they say an
old man is twice a child.

HAMLET: I will prophesy he comes to tell me of the players; mark it. You say
355   right, sir: o' Monday morning; 'twas so indeed.

POLONIUS: My lord, I have news to tell you.

HAMLET: My lord, I have news to tell you. When Roscius was an actor
in Rome,—

POLONIUS: The actors are come hither, my lord.

360   HAMLET: Buzz, buzz!

POLONIUS: Upon mine honor,—

HAMLET: Then came each actor on his ass,—

POLONIUS: The best actors in the world, either for tragedy, comedy, history,
pastoral, pastoral-comical, historical-pastoral, tragical-historical, tragical-
365   comical-historical-pastoral, scene individable,° or poem unlimited:°
Seneca cannot be too heavy nor Plautus too light. For the law of writ and
the liberty,° these are the only men.

HAMLET: O Jephthah, judge of Israel, what a treasure hadst thou!

POLONIUS: What a treasure had he, my lord?

370   HAMLET: Why—

> One fair daughter, and no more,
> The which he loved passing well.

POLONIUS: [*Aside*] Still on my daughter.

HAMLET: Am I not i' the right, old Jephthah?

375   POLONIUS: If you call me Jephthah, my lord, I have a daughter that I love
passing well.

HAMLET: Nay, that follows not.

POLONIUS: What follows, then, my lord?

HAMLET: Why—

380   > As by lot, God wot,
> and then, you know,
> It came to pass, as most like it was,

the first row of the pious chanson will show you more; for look where my
abridgement comes.

Enter four or five Players.

385   You are welcome, masters; welcome, all:— I am glad to see thee well:—
welcome, good friends.— O, my old friend! Thy face is valanced since I

---

scene individable: A play that observes the unities of time and place.

poem unlimited: A typical multiscene Elizabethan drama, not restricted by the unities; examples are *Hamlet, Macbeth, King Lear,* and nearly any other play by Shakespeare.

For the law . . . liberty: For the laws of the unities and for playwriting that is not so restricted.

saw thee last; comest thou to beard me in Denmark?—What, my young
lady and mistress! By'r lady, your ladyship is nearer heaven than when I saw
you last, by the altitude of a chopine.° Pray God, your voice, like a piece of
uncurrent gold, be not cracked within the ring.— Masters, you are all wel-   390
come. We'll e'en to't like French falconers, fly at anything we see: we'll
have a speech straight: come, give us a taste of your quality; come, a
passionate speech.

1ST PLAYER: What speech, my lord?

HAMLET: I heard thee speak me a speech once,—but it was never acted; or, if   395
it was, not above once; for the play, I remember, pleased not the million;
'twas caviare to the general: but it was,— as I received it, and others whose
judgments in such matters cried in the top of mine,— an excellent play,
well digested in the scenes, set down with as much modesty as cunning. I
remember, one said there were no sallets in the lines to make the matter   400
savory, nor no matter in the phrase that might indite the author of affecta-
tion; but called it an honest method, as wholesome as sweet, and by very
much more handsome than fine. One speech in it I chiefly loved: 'twas
Aeneas' tale to Dido; and thereabout of it especially where he speaks of
Priam's slaughter: if it live in your memory, begin at this line;— let me see,   405
let me see:—

> The rugged Pyrrhus, like the Hyrcanian beast,°

— it is not so:— it begins with Pyrrhus:—

> The rugged Pyrrhus,—he whose sable arms,
> Black as his purpose, did the night resemble   410
> When he lay couched in the ominous horse,—
> Hath now this dread and black complexion smear'd
> With heraldry more dismal; head to foot
> Now is he total gules; horridly trick'd
> With blood of fathers, mothers, daughters, sons,   415
> Bak'd and impasted with the parching streets,
> That lend a tyrannous and damned light
> To their vile murders: roasted in wrath and fire,
> And thus o'er-sized with coagulate gore,
> With eyes like carbuncles, the hellish Pyrrhus   420
> Old grandsire Priam seeks.—

So proceed you.

POLONIUS: 'Fore God, my lord, well spoken, with good accent and
good discretion.

1ST PLAYER: Anon he finds him   425
Striking too short at Greeks; his antique sword,

---

chopine: A wooden stilt more than a foot high used under a woman's shoe; a Venetian fashion introduced into
England.

The rugged . . .: This speech is an example of the declamatory style of drama, which Shakespeare surely must
have considered outmoded.

Rebellious to his arm, lies where it falls,
Repugnant to command: unequal match'd,
Pyrrhus at Priam drives; in rage strikes wide;
430   But with the whiff and wind of his fell sword
The unnerved father falls. Then senseless Ilium,
Seeming to feel this blow, with flaming top
Stoops to his base; and with a hideous crash
Takes prisoner Pyrrhus' ear: for, lo! his sword,
435   Which was declining on the milky head
Of reverend Priam, seem'd i' the air to stick:
So, as a painted tyrant, Pyrrhus stood;
And, like a neutral to his will and matter,
Did nothing.
440   But as we often see, against some storm,
A silence in the heavens, the rack stand still,
The blood winds speechless, and the orb below
As hush as death, anon the dreadful thunder
Doth rend the region; so, after Pyrrhus' pause,
445   A roused vengeance sets him new a-work;
And never did the Cyclops' hammers fall
On Mars his armor, forg'd for proof eterne,
With less remorse than Pyrrhus' bleeding sword
Now falls on Priam.—
450   Out, out, thou strumpet, Fortune! All you gods,
In general synod, take away her power;
Break all the spokes and fellies from her wheel,
And bowl the round knave down the hill of heaven,
As low as to the fiends!
455   **POLONIUS:** This is too long.
HAMLET: It shall to the barber's, with your beard.— Pr'ythee, say on.— He's
for a jig, or a tale of bawdry, or he sleeps:— say on; come to Hecuba.
1ST PLAYER: But who, O, who had seen the mobled queen,—
HAMLET: *The mobled queen?*
460   **POLONIUS:** That's good; *mobled queen* is good.
1ST PLAYER: Run barefoot up and down, threatening the flames
With bissom rheum; a clout upon that head
Where late the diadem stood; and, for a robe,
About her lank and all o'er-teemed loins,
465   A blanket, in the alarm of fear caught up;—
Who this had seen, with tongue in venom steep'd,
'Gainst Fortune's state would treason have pronounc'd:
But if the gods themselves did see her then,
When she saw Pyrrhus make malicious sport
470   In mincing with his sword her husband's limbs,
The instant burst of clamor that she made,—
Unless things mortal move them not at all,—

Would have made milch the burning eyes of heaven,
And passion in the gods.

POLONIUS: Look, whether he has not turn'd his color, and has tears in's   475
    eyes.— Pray you, no more.

HAMLET: 'Tis well; I'll have thee speak out the rest soon.— Good my lord,
    will you see the players well bestowed? Do you hear, let them be well used;
    for they are the abstracts and brief chronicles of the time; after your death
    you were better have a bad epitaph than their ill report while you live.   480

POLONIUS: My lord, I will use them according to their desert.

HAMLET: God's bodikin, man, better: use every man after his desert, and who
    should scape whipping? Use them after your own honor and dignity: the
    less they deserve the more merit is in your bounty. Take them in.

POLONIUS: Come, sirs.   485

HAMLET: Follow him, friends: we'll hear a play to-morrow.

Exit Polonius with all the Players but the First.

Dost thou hear me, old friend; can you play the Murder of Gonzago?

1ST PLAYER: Ay, my lord.

HAMLET: We'll ha't to-morrow night. You could, for a need, study a speech
    of some dozen or sixteen lines which I would set down and insert in't?   490
    could you not?

1ST PLAYER: Ay, my lord.

HAMLET: Very well.— Follow that lord; and look you mock him not.

Exit First Player.

—My good friends, [*to Rosencrantz and Guildenstern*] I'll leave you till night:
    you are welcome to Elsinore.   495

ROSENCRANTZ: Good my lord!

Exeunt Rosencrantz and Guildenstern.

HAMLET: Ay, so God b' wi' ye!— Now I am alone.
    O, what a rogue° and peasant slave am I!
    Is it not monstrous that this player here,
    But in a fiction, in a dream of passion,   500
    Could force his soul so to his own conceit°
    That from her working all his visage wan'd;
    Tears in his eyes, distraction in's aspéct,
    A broken voice, and his whole function suiting
    With forms to his conceit? And all for nothing!   505
    For Hecuba!
    What's Hecuba to him or he to Hecuba,
    That he should weep for her? What would he do,

rogue: Wretched creature.
conceit: Conception.

Had he the motive and the cue for passion
510   That I have? He would drown the stage with tears,
And cleave the general ear with horrid speech;
Make mad the guilty, and appal the free;
Confound the ignorant, and amaze, indeed,
The very faculties of eyes and ears.
515   Yet I,
A dull and muddy-mettled rascal, peak,
Like John-a-dreams, unpregnant of my cause,
And can say nothing; no, not for a king
Upon whose property and most dear life
520   A damn'd defeat was made. Am I a coward?
Who calls me villain? breaks my pate across?
Plucks off my beard and blows it in my face?
Tweaks me by the nose? gives me the lie i' the throat,
As deep as to the lungs? who does me this, ha?
525   'Swounds, I should take it: for it cannot be
But I am pigeon-liver'd, and lack gall
To make oppression bitter; or ere this
I should have fatted all the region kites
With this slave's offal: — bloody, bawdy villain!
530   Remorseless, treacherous, lecherous, kindless villain!
O, vengeance!
Why, what an ass am I! This is most brave,
That I, the son of a dear father murder'd,
Prompted to my revenge by heaven and hell,
535   Must, like a whore, unpack my heart with words,
And fall a-cursing like a very drab,
A scullion!
Fie upon't! foh! — About, my brain! I have heard
That guilty creatures, sitting at a play,
540   Have by the very cunning of the scene
Been struck so to the soul that presently
They have proclaim'd their malefactions;
For murder, though it have no tongue, will speak
With most miraculous organ. I'll have these players
545   Play something like the murder of my father
Before mine uncle: I'll observe his looks;
I'll tent° him to the quick: if he but blench,
I know my course. The spirit that I have seen
May be the devil: and the devil hath power
550   To assume a pleasing shape; yea, and perhaps

---

tent: Probe.

Out of my weakness and my melancholy,—
As he is very potent with such spirits,—
Abuses me to damn me: I'll have grounds
More relative than this:— the play's the thing
Wherein I'll catch the conscience of the king. [*Exit.*]   555

ACT III
SCENE 1

A room in the castle.

Enter King, Queen, Polonius, Ophelia, Rosencrantz, and Guildenstern.

KING: And can you, by no drift of circumstance,
    Get from him why he puts on this confusion,
    Grating so harshly all his days of quiet
    With turbulent and dangerous lunacy?
ROSENCRANTZ: He does confess he feels himself distracted;   5
    But from what cause he will by no means speak.
GUILDENSTERN: Nor do we find him forward to be sounded;
    But, with a crafty madness, keeps aloof
    When we would bring him on to some confession
    Of his true state.   10
QUEEN: Did he receive you well?
ROSENCRANTZ: Most like a gentleman.
GUILDENSTERN: But with much forcing of his disposition.
ROSENCRANTZ: Niggard of question; but, of our demands,
    Most free in his reply.   15
QUEEN: Did you assay him
    To any pastime?
ROSENCRANTZ: Madam, it so fell out that certain players
    We o'er-raught on the way: of these we told him;
    And there did seem in him a kind of joy   20
    To hear of it: they are about the court;
    And, as I think, they have already order
    This night to play before him.
POLONIUS: 'Tis most true:
    And he beseech'd me to entreat your majesties   25
    To hear and see the matter.
KING: With all my heart; and it doth much content me
    To hear him so inclin'd.
    Good gentlemen, give him a further edge,
    And drive his purpose on to these delights.   30
ROSENCRANTZ: We shall, my lord.

Exeunt Rosencrantz and Guildenstern.

KING: Sweet Gertrude, leave us too;
    For we have closely sent for Hamlet hither
    That he, as 'twere by accident, may here
35   Affront Ophelia:
    Her father and myself,—lawful espials,°—
    Will so bestow ourselves that, seeing, unseen,
    We may of their encounter frankly judge;
    And gather by him, as he is behav'd,
40   If't be the affliction of his love or no
    That thus he suffers for.

QUEEN: I shall obey you:—
    And for your part, Ophelia, I do wish
    That your good beauties be the happy cause
45   Of Hamlet's wildness: so shall I hope your virtues
    Will bring him to his wonted way again,
    To both your honors.

OPHELIA: Madam, I wish it may.

Exit Queen.

POLONIUS: Ophelia, walk you here.— Gracious, so please you,
50   We will bestow ourselves.—[*To Ophelia*] Read on this book;
    That show of such an exercise may color
    Your loneliness.—We are oft to blame in this,—
    'Tis too much prov'd,— that with devotion's visage
    And pious action we do sugar o'er
55   The devil himself.

KING: [*Aside*]   O, 'tis too true!
    How smart a lash that speech doth give my conscience!
    The harlot's cheek, beautied with plastering art,
    Is not more ugly to the thing that helps it
60   Than is my deed to my most painted word:
    O heavy burden!

POLONIUS: I hear him coming: let's withdraw, my lord.

Exeunt King and Polonius.

Enter Hamlet.

HAMLET: To be, or not to be,— that is the question:
    Whether 'tis nobler in the mind to suffer
65   The slings and arrows of outrageous fortune,
    Or to take arms against a sea of troubles,
    And by opposing end them?— To die,— to sleep,—
    No more; and by a sleep to say we end
    The heart-ache and the thousand natural shocks

---

espials: Spies.

That flesh is heir to, — 'tis a consummation   70
Devoutly to be wish'd. To die, — to sleep; —
To sleep! perchance to dream: — ay, there's the rub;
For in that sleep of death what dreams may come,
When we have shuffled off this mortal coil,
Must give us pause: there's the respect   75
That makes a calamity of so long life;
For who would bear the whips and scorns of time,
The oppressor's wrong, the proud man's contumely,
The pangs of déspis'd love, the law's delay,
The insolence of office, and the spurns   80
That patient merit of the unworthy takes,
When he himself might his quietus make
With a bare bodkin?° who would fardels° bear,
To grunt° and sweat under a weary life,
But that the dread of something after death, —   85
The undiscover'd country, from whose bourn°
No traveler returns, — puzzles the will,
And makes us rather bear those ills we have
Than to fly to others that we know not of?
Thus conscience does make cowards of us all;   90
And thus the native hue of resolution
Is sicklied o'er with the pale cast of thought;
And enterprises of great pith and moment,
With this regard, their currents turn awry,
And lose the name of action. — Soft you now!   95
The fair Ophelia. — Nymph, in thy orisons°
Be all my sins remember'd.

OPHELIA: Good my lord,
    How does your honor for this many a day?   100
HAMLET: I humbly thank you; well, well, well.
OPHELIA: My lord, I have remembrances of yours,
    That I have longed long to re-deliver;
    I pray you, now receive them.
HAMLET: No, not I;   105
    I never gave you aught.
OPHELIA: My honor'd lord, you know right well you did;
    And with them, words of so sweet breath compos'd
    As made the things more rich: their perfume lost,

---

bodkin: Stiletto.
fardels: Burdens.
grunt: Groan.
bourn: Boundary.
orisons: Prayers.

Take these again; for to the noble mind
110   Rich gifts wax poor when givers prove unkind.
There, my lord.

HAMLET: Ha, ha! are you honest?

OPHELIA: My lord?

HAMLET: Are you fair?

115   **OPHELIA:** What means your lordship?

HAMLET: That if you be honest and fair, your honesty should admit no
discourse to your beauty.

OPHELIA: Could beauty, my lord, have better commerce than with honesty?

HAMLET: Ay, truly; for the power of beauty will sooner transform honesty from
120   what it is to a bawd than the force of honesty can translate beauty into his
likeness: this was sometime a paradox, but now the time gives it proof. I did
love you once.

OPHELIA: Indeed, my lord, you made me believe so.

HAMLET: You should not have believed me; for virtue cannot so inoculate our
125   old stock but we shall relish of it: I loved you not.

OPHELIA: I was the more deceived.

HAMLET: Get thee to a nunnery: why wouldst thou be a breeder of sinners? I am
myself indifferent° honest; but yet I could accuse me of such things that it
were better my mother had not borne me: I am very proud, revengeful, am-
130   bitious; with more offences at my beck than I have thoughts to put them in,
imagination to give them shape, or time to act them in. What should such
fellows as I do crawling between heaven and earth? We are arrant knaves,
all; believe none of us. Go thy ways to a nunnery. Where's your father?

OPHELIA: At home, my lord.

135   **HAMLET:** Let the doors be shut upon him, that he may play the fool nowhere
but in's own house. Farewell.

OPHELIA: O, help him, you sweet heavens!

HAMLET: If thou dost marry, I'll give thee this plague for thy dowry, — be thou
as chaste as ice, as pure as snow, thou shalt not escape calumny. Get thee to
140   a nunnery, go: farewell. Or, if thou wilt needs marry, marry a fool; for wise
men know well enough what monsters you make of them. To a nunnery, go;
and quickly too. Farewell.

OPHELIA: O heavenly powers, restore him!

HAMLET: I have heard of your paintings too, well enough; God has given you
145   one face and you make yourselves another: you jig, you amble, and you lisp,
and nickname God's creatures, and make your wantonness your ignorance.
Go to, I'll no more on't; it hath made me mad. I say, we will have no more
marriages: those that are married already, all but one, shall live; the rest
shall keep as they are. To a nunnery, go. [*Exit.*]

150   **OPHELIA:** O, what a noble mind is here o'erthrown!
The courtier's, soldier's, scholar's eye, tongue, sword:
The expectancy and rose of the fair state,

---

indifferent: Tolerably.

The glass of fashion and the mould of form,
The observ'd of all observers, — quite, quite down!
And I, of ladies most deject and wretched   155
That suck'd the honey of his music vows,
Now see that noble and most sovereign reason,
Like sweet bells jangled, out of tune and harsh;
That unmatch'd form and feature of blown° youth
Blasted with ecstasy: O, woe is me,   160
To have seen what I have seen, see what I see!

Re-enter King and Polonius.

KING: Love! his affections do not that way tend;
    Nor what he spake, though it lack'd form a little,
    Was not like madness. There's something in his soul
    O'er which his melancholy sits on brood;   165
    And I do doubt° the hatch and the disclose
    Will be some danger: which for to prevent,
    I have in quick determination
    Thus set it down:— he shall with speed to England
    For the demand of our neglected tribute: 170
    Haply, the seas and countries different,
    With variable objects, shall expel
    This something-settled matter in his heart;
    Whereon his brains still beating puts him thus
    From fashion of himself. What think you on't?   175

POLONIUS: It shall do well: but yet do I believe
    The origin and commencement of his grief
    Sprung from neglected love.— How now, Ophelia!
    You need not tell us what Lord Hamlet said;
    We heard it all.— My lord, do as you please;   180
    But if you hold it fit, after the play,
    Let his queen mother all alone entreat him
    To show his grief: let her be round with him;
    And I'll be plac'd, so please you, in the ear
    Of all their conference. If she finds him not,°   185
    To England send him; or confine him where
    Your wisdom best shall think.

KING: It shall be so:
    Madness in great ones must not unwatch'd go.

Exeunt.

---

blown: Full-blown.

doubt: Fear.

finds him not: Does not find him out.

SCENE 2

A hall in the castle.

Enter Hamlet and certain Players.

HAMLET: Speak the speech, I pray you, as I pronounced it to you, trippingly on
the tongue: but if you mouth it, as many of your players do, I had as lief the
town-crier spoke my lines. Nor do not saw the air too much with your
hand, thus; but use all gently: for in the very torrent, tempest, and, as I may
5 say, the whirlwind of passion, you must acquire and beget a temperance that
may give it smoothness. O, it offends me to the soul, to hear a robustious
periwigpated fellow tear a passion to tatters, to very rags, to split the ears of
the groundlings, who, for the most part, are capable of nothing but inexplicable dumb shows and noise: I could have such a fellow whipped for
10 o'erdoing Termagant;° it out-herods Herod:° pray you, avoid it.

1ST PLAYER: I warrant your honor.

HAMLET: Be not too tame neither, but let your own discretion be your tutor;
suit the action to the word, the word to the action; with this special obser-
vance, that you o'erstep not the modesty of nature: for anything so over-
15 done is from the purpose of playing, whose end, both at the first and now,
was and is, to hold, as 'twere, the mirror up to nature; to show virtue her
own feature, scorn her own image, and the very age and body of the time
his form and pressure. Now, this overdone or come tardy off, though it
make the unskilful laugh, cannot but make the judicious grieve; the censure
20 of the which one must, in your allowance, o'erweigh a whole theater of
others. O, there be players that I have seen play,— and heard others praise,
and that highly,— not to speak it profanely, that, neither having the accent
of Christians, nor the gait of Christian, pagan, nor man, have so strutted
and bellowed that I have thought some of nature's journeymen had made
25 men, and not made them well, they imitated humanity so abominably.

1ST PLAYER: I hope we have reformed that indifferently with us, sir.

HAMLET: O, reform it altogether. And let those that play your clowns speak
no more than is set down for them: for there be of them that will themselves laugh, to set on some quantity of barren spectators to laugh too;
30 though, in the meantime, some necessary question of the play be then to be
considered: that's villainous, and shows a most pitiful ambition in the fool
that uses it. Go, make you ready.

Exeunt Players.

Enter Polonius, Rosencrantz, and Guildenstern.

How now, my lord! will the king hear this piece of work?

Termagant: A violent pagan deity, supposedly Mohammedan.

out-herods Herod: Outrants the ranting Herod, who figures in medieval drama.

POLONIUS: And the queen, too, and that presently.
HAMLET: Bid the players make haste. 35

Exit Polonius.

Will you two help to hasten them?
ROSENCRANTZ and **GUILDENSTERN:** We will, my lord. [*Exeunt.*]
HAMLET: What, ho, Horatio!

Enter Horatio.

HORATIO: Here, sweet lord, at your service.
HAMLET: Horatio, thou art e'en as just a man 40
As e'er my conversation cop'd withal.
HORATIO: O, my dear lord,—
HAMLET: Nay, do not think I flatter;
For what advancement may I hope from thee,
That no revénue hast, but thy good spirits, 45
To feed and clothe thee? Why should the poor be flatter'd?
No, let the candied tongue lick ábsurd pomp;
And crook the pregnant hinges of the knee
Where thrift may follow fawning. Dost thou hear?
Since my dear soul was mistress of her choice, 50
And could of men distinguish, her election
Hath seal'd thee for herself: for thou hast been
As one, in suffering all, that suffers nothing;
A man that Fortune's buffets and rewards
Hast ta'en with equal thanks: and bless'd are those 55
Whose blood and judgment are so well commingled
That they are not a pipe for Fortune's finger
To sound what stop she please. Give me that man
That is not passion's slave, and I will wear him
In my heart's core, ay, in my heart of heart, 60
As I do thee.— Something too much of this.—
There is a play to-night before the king;
One scene of it comes near the circumstance
Which I have told thee of my father's death:
I pr'ythee, when thou see'st that act a-foot, 65
Even with the very comment of thy soul
Observe mine uncle: if this his occulted guilt
Do not itself unkennel in one speech,
It is a damned ghost that we have seen;
And my imaginations are as foul 70
As Vulcan's stithy.° Give him heedful note:
For I mine eyes will rivet to his face;

---

stithy: Smithy.

And, after, we will both our judgments join
In censure of his seeming.

75 HORATIO: Well, my lord:
If he steal aught the whilst this play is playing,
And scape detecting, I will pay the theft.

HAMLET: They are coming to the play; I must be idle:°
Get you a place.

*Danish march. A flourish. Enter King, Queen, Polonius, Ophelia, Rosencrantz, Guild-
enstern, and others.*

80 KING: How fares our cousin Hamlet?

HAMLET: Excellent, i'faith; of the chameleon's dish: I eat the air,°
promise-crammed: you cannot feed capons so.

KING: I have nothing with this answer, Hamlet; these words are not mine.

HAMLET: No, nor mine now. [*To Polonius*] My lord, you played once i'the
85   university, you say?

POLONIUS: That did I, my lord, and was accounted a good actor.

HAMLET: And what did you enact?

POLONIUS: I did enact Julius Caesar: I was killed i' the Capitol; Brutus
killed me.

90 HAMLET: It was a brute part of him to kill so capital a calf there. — Be the
players ready.

ROSENCRANTZ: Ay, my lord; they stay upon your patience.

QUEEN: Come hither, my good Hamlet, sit by me.

HAMLET: No, good mother, here's metal more attractive.

95 POLONIUS: O, ho! do you mark that? [*To the King*]

HAMLET: Lady, shall I lie in your lap? [*Lying down at Ophelia's feet*]

OPHELIA: No, my lord.

HAMLET: I mean, my head upon your lap?

OPHELIA: Ay, my lord.

100 HAMLET: Do you think I meant country matters?

OPHELIA: I think nothing, my lord.

HAMLET: That's a fair thought to lie between maids' legs.

OPHELIA: What is, my lord?

HAMLET: Nothing.

105 OPHELIA: You are merry, my lord.

HAMLET: Who, I?

OPHELIA: Ay, my lord.

HAMLET: O, your only jig-maker. What should a man do but be merry? for,
look you, how cheerfully my mother looks, and my father died within's
110   two hours.

OPHELIA: Nay, 'tis twice two months, my lord.

---

idle: Foolish.

of the chameleon's . . . the air: Chameleons were believed to live on air.

Hamlet: So long? Nay, then, let the devil wear black, for I'll have a suit of
sables. O heavens! die two months ago, and not forgotten yet? Then there's
hope a great man's memory may outlive his life half a year: but, by'r lady, he
must build churches, then; or else shall he suffer not thinking on, with the   115
hobby-horse, whose epitaph is, *For, O, for, O, the hobby-horse is forgot.*

Trumpets sound. The dumb show enters.

*Enter a King and a Queen, very lovingly; the Queen embracing him and he her. She
kneels, and makes show of protestation unto him. He takes her up, and declines his head
upon her neck: lays him down upon a bank of flowers: she, seeing him asleep, leaves
him. Anon comes in a fellow, takes off his crown, kisses it, and pours poison in the King's
ears, and exit. The Queen returns; finds the King dead, and makes passionate action.
The Poisoner, with some two or three Mutes, comes in again, seeming to lament with
her. The dead body is carried away. The Poisoner woos the Queen with gifts: she seems
loth and unwilling awhile, but in the end accepts his love.*

Exeunt.

Ophelia: What means this, my lord?
Hamlet: Marry, this is miching mallecho;° it means mischief.
Ophelia: Belike this show imports the argument of the play.

Enter Prologue.

Hamlet: We shall know by this fellow: the players cannot keep counsel;   120
they'll tell all.
Ophelia: Will he tell us what this show meant?
Hamlet: Ay, or any show that you'll show him: be not you ashamed to show,
he'll not shame to tell you what it means.
Ophelia: You are naught, you are naught: I'll mark the play.   125
Prologue:

> For us, and for our tragedy,
> Here stooping to your clemency,
> We beg your hearing patiently.

Hamlet: Is this a prologue, or the posy° of a ring?
Ophelia: 'Tis brief, my lord.   130
Hamlet: As woman's love.

Enter a King and a Queen.

Prologue King: Full thirty times hath Phoebus' cart gone round
Neptune's salt wash and Tellus' orbed ground,°
And thirty dozen moons with borrow'd sheen

---

miching mallecho: A sneaking misdeed.
posy: Motto or inscription.
orbed ground: The globe.

135   About the world have times twelve thirties been,
        Since love our hearts, and Hymen did our hands
        Unite commutual in most sacred bands.
PROLOGUE QUEEN: So many journeys may the sun and moon
        Make us again count o'er ere love be done!
140   But, woe is me, you are so sick of late,
        So far from cheer and from your former state
        That I distrust you.° Yet, though I distrust,
        Discomfort you, my lord, it nothing must:
        For women's fear and love holds quantity,°
145   In neither aught, or in extremity.
        Now, what my love is, proof hath made you know;
        And as my love is siz'd, my fear is so:
        Where love is great, the littlest doubts are fear;
        Where little fears grow great, great love grows there.
150 **PROLOGUE KING:** Faith, I must leave thee, love, and shortly too;
        My operant powers their functions leave° to do:
        And thou shalt live in this fair world behind,
        Honor'd, belov'd; and haply one as kind
        For husband shalt thou,—
155 **PROLOGUE QUEEN:**   O, confound the rest!
        Such love must needs be treason in my breast:
        In second husband let me be accurst!
        None wed the second but who kill'd the first.
HAMLET: [*Aside*] Wormwood, wormwood.
160 **PROLOGUE QUEEN:** The instances that second marriage move
        Are base respects of thrift, but none of love:
        A second time I kill my husband, dead,
        When second husband kisses me in bed.
PROLOGUE KING: I do believe you think what now you speak;
165   But what we do determine oft we break.
        Purpose is but the slave to memory;
        Of violent birth, but poor validity;
        Which now, like fruit unripe, sticks on the tree;
        But fall unshaken when they mellow be.
170   Most necessary 'tis that we forget
        To pay ourselves what to ourselves is debt:
        What to ourselves in passion we propose,
        The passion ending, doth the purpose lose.
        The violence of either grief or joy

---

distrust you: Worry about you.

holds quantity: Correspond in degree.

leave: Cease.

Their own enactures with themselves destroy: 175
Where joy most revels grief doth most lament;
Grief joys, joy grieves, on slender accident.
This world is not for aye; nor 'tis not strange
That even our loves should with our fortunes change;
For 'tis a question left us yet to prove   180
Whether love lead fortune or else fortune love.
The great man down, you mark his favorite flies;
The poor advanc'd makes friends of enemies.
And hitherto doth love on fortune tend:
For who not needs shall never lack a friend;   185
And who in want a hollow friend doth try,
Directly seasons him his enemy.
But, orderly to end where I begun,—
Our wills and fates do so contrary run
That our devices still are overthrown;   190
Our thoughts are ours, their ends none of our own:
So think thou wilt no second husband wed;
But die thy thoughts when thy first lord is dead.
PROLOGUE QUEEN: Nor earth to me give food, nor heaven light!
   Sport and repose lock from me day and night!   195
   To desperation turn my trust and hope!
   An anchor's° cheer in prison be my scope!
   Each opposite, that blanks the face of joy,
   Meet what I would have well, and it destroy!
   Both here and hence, pursue me lasting strife,   200
   If, once a widow, ever I be wife!
HAMLET: If she should break it now! [*To Ophelia*]
PROLOGUE KING: 'Tis deeply sworn. Sweet, leave me here awhile;
   My spirits grow dull, and fain I would beguile
   The tedious day with sleep. [*Sleeps*]   205
PROLOGUE QUEEN: Sleep rock thy brain,
   And never come mischance between us twain! [*Exit.*]
HAMLET: Madam, how like you this play?
QUEEN: The lady doth protest too much, methinks.
HAMLET: O, but she'll keep her word.   210
KING: Have you heard the argument? Is there no offence in't?
HAMLET: No, no, they do but jest, poison in jest; no offence i' the world.
KING: What do you call the play?
HAMLET: The Mouse-trap. Marry, how? Tropically.° This play is the image of a
   murder done in Vienna: Gonzago is the duke's name: his wife, Baptista: you   215

---

anchor's: Anchorite's, or hermit's.

Tropically: Figuratively, or metaphorically; by means of a "trope."

shall see anon; 'tis a knavish piece of work: but what o' that? your majesty,
and we that have free souls, it touches us not: let the galled jade wince, our
withers are unwrung.

Enter Lucianus.

This is one Lucianus, nephew to the king.

220 OPHELIA: You are a good chorus, my lord.

HAMLET: I could interpret between you and your love, if I could see the pup-
pets dallying.

OPHELIA: You are keen, my lord, you are keen.

HAMLET: It would cost you a groaning to take off my edge.

225 OPHELIA: Still better, and worse.

HAMLET: So you must take your husbands.— Begin, murderer; pox, leave thy
damnable faces and begin. Come:— *The croaking raven doth bellow for*
revenge.

LUCIANUS: Thoughts black, hands apt, drugs fit, and time agreeing;

230 Confederate season, else no creature seeing;
Thou mixture rank, of midnight weeds collected,
With Hecate's ban° thrice blasted, thrice infected,
Thy natural magic and dire property
On wholesome life usurp immediately.

Pours the poison into the sleeper's ears.

235 HAMLET: He poisons him i' the garden for's estate. His name's Gonzago: the
story is extant, and writ in choice Italian: you shall see anon how the murderer gets the love of Gonzago's wife.

OPHELIA: The king rises.

HAMLET: What, frighted with false fire!

240 QUEEN: How fares my lord?

POLONIUS: Give o'er the play.

KING: Give me some light:— away!

ALL: Lights, lights, lights!

Exeunt all but Hamlet and Horatio.

HAMLET:

Why, let the stricken deer go weep,
245   The hart ungalled play;
For some must watch, while some must sleep:
So runs the world away.—

Would not this, sir, and a forest of feathers, if the rest of my fortunes turn
Turk with me, with two Provencial roses on my razed shoes, get me a
250 fellowship in a cry° of players, sir?

Hecate's ban: The spell of the goddess of witchcraft.
cry: Company.

HORATIO: Half a share.
HAMLET: A whole one, I.

> For thou dost know, O Damon dear,
>   This realm dismantled was
> Of Jove himself; and now reigns here
>   A very, very — pajock.°   255

HORATIO: You might have rhymed.
HAMLET: O good Horatio, I'll take the ghost's word for a thousand pound.
    Didst perceive?
HORATIO: Very well, my lord.   260
HAMLET: Upon the talk of the poisoning,—
HORATIO: I did very well note him.
HAMLET: Ah, ha!— Come, some music! come, the recorders!—

> For if the king like not the comedy,
> Why, then, belike,— he likes it not, perdy.   265

Come, some music!

Re-enter Rosencrantz and Guildenstern.

GUILDENSTERN: Good my lord, vouchsafe me a word with you.
HAMLET: Sir, a whole history.
GUILDENSTERN: The king, sir,—
HAMLET: Ay, sir, what of him?   270
GUILDENSTERN: Is, in his retirement, marvelous distempered.
HAMLET: With drink, sir?
GUILDENSTERN: No, my lord, rather with choler.
HAMLET: Your wisdom should show itself more richer to signify this to his
    doctor; for, for me to put him to his purgation would perhaps plunge him   275
    into far more choler.
GUILDENSTERN: Good my lord, put your discourse into some frame, and start
    not so wildly from my affair.
HAMLET: I am tame, sir:— pronounce.
GUILDENSTERN: The queen, your mother, in most great affliction of spirit,   280
    hath sent me to you.
HAMLET: You are welcome.
GUILDENSTERN: Nay, good my lord, this courtesy is not of the right breed. If it
    shall please you to make me a wholesome answer, I will do you mother's
    commandment: if not, your pardon and my return shall be the end of my   285
    business.
HAMLET: Sir, I cannot.
GUILDENSTERN: What, my lord?

---

pajock: Peacock.

HAMLET: Make you a wholesome answer; my wit's diseas'd: but, sir, such an-
290   swer as I can make, you shall command; or, rather, as you say, my mother:
          therefore no more, but to the matter: my mother, you say,—
ROSENCRANTZ: Then thus she says: your behavior hath struck her into amaze-
          ment and admiration.
HAMLET: O wonderful son, that can so astonish a mother!—But is there no
295   sequel at the heels of this mother's admiration?
ROSENCRANTZ: She desires to speak with you in her closet° ere you go to bed.
HAMLET: We shall obey, were she ten times our mother. Have you any further
          trade with us?
ROSENCRANTZ: My lord, you once did love me.
300   HAMLET: So I do still, by these pickers and stealers.°
ROSENCRANTZ: Good, my lord, what is your cause of distemper? you do,
          surely, bar the door upon your own liberty if you deny your griefs to
          your friend.
HAMLET: Sir, I lack advancement.
305   ROSENCRANTZ: How can that be, when you have the voice of the king
          himself for your succession in Denmark?
HAMLET: Ay, but *While the grass grows,*—the proverb is something musty.

Re-enter the Players, with recorders.

          O, the recorders:—let me see one.—To withdraw with you:—why do you
          go about to recover the wind of me, as if you would drive me into a toil?
310   GUILDENSTERN: O, my lord, if my duty be too bold, my love is too
          unmannerly.
HAMLET: I do not well understand that. Will you play upon this pipe?
GUILDENSTERN: My lord, I cannot.
HAMLET: I pray you.
315   GUILDENSTERN: Believe me, I cannot.
HAMLET: I do beseech you.
GUILDENSTERN: I know no touch of it, my lord.
HAMLET: 'Tis as easy as lying: govern these ventages° with your finger and
          thumb, give it breath with your mouth, and it will discourse most eloquent
320   music. Look you, these are the stops.
GUILDENSTERN: But these cannot I command to any utterance of harmony; I
          have not the skill.
HAMLET: Why, look you now, how unworthy a thing you make of me! You
          would play upon me; you would seem to know my stops; you would pluck
325   out the heart of my mystery; you would sound me from my lowest note to
          the top of my compass: and there is much music, excellent voice, in this
          little organ; yet cannot you make it speak. 'Sblood, do you think that I am

---

closet: Boudoir.

pickers and stealers: Fingers.

ventages: Holes.

easier to be played on than a pipe? Call me what instrument you will,
though you can fret me you cannot play upon me.

Enter Polonius.

   God bless you, sir!   330
POLONIUS: My lord, the queen would speak with you, and presently.
HAMLET: Do you see yonder cloud that's almost in shape of a camel?
POLONIUS: By the mass, and 'tis like a camel indeed.
HAMLET: Methinks it is like a weasel.
POLONIUS: It is backed like a weasel.   335
HAMLET: Or like a whale?
POLONIUS: Very like a whale.
HAMLET: Then will I come to my mother by and by.—They fool me to the
   top of my bent.—I will come by and by.
POLONIUS: I will say so.   340
HAMLET: By and by is easily said.

Exit Polonius.

   Leave me, friends.

Exeunt Rosencrantz, Guildenstern, Horatio, and Players.

   'Tis now the very witching time of night,
   When churchyards yawn, and hell itself breathes out
   Contagion to this world: now could I drink hot blood,   345
   And do such bitter business as the day
   Would quake to look on. Soft! now to my mother.—
   O heart, lose not thy nature; let not ever
   The soul of Nero° enter this firm bosom:
   Let me be cruel, not unnatural: 350
   I will speak daggers to her, but use none;
   My tongue and soul in this be hypocrites,—
   How in my words soever she be shent,
   To give them seals never, my soul, consent! [*Exit.*]

SCENE 3

A room in the castle.

Enter King, Rosencrantz, and Guildenstern.

KING: I like him not; nor stands it safe with us
   To let his madness range. Therefore prepare you;
   I your commission with forthwith despatch,
   And he to England shall along with you:
   The terms of our estate may not endure   5

Nero: The Roman emperor Nero killed his mother, a crime of which Hamlet does not want to be guilty.

Hazard so dangerous as doth hourly grow
Out of his lunacies.

GUILDENSTERN: We will ourselves provide:
Most holy and religious fear it is
10   To keep those many many bodies safe
That live and feed upon your majesty.

ROSENCRANTZ: The single and peculiar life is bound,
With all the strength and armor of the mind,
To keep itself from 'noyance; but much more
15   That spirit upon whose weal depend and rest
The lives of many. The cease of majesty
Dies not alone; but like a gulf doth draw
What's near it with it: it is a massy wheel,
Fix'd on the summit of the highest mount,
20   To whose huge spokes ten thousand lesser things
Are mortis'd and adjoin'd; which, when it falls,
Each small annexment, petty consequence,
Attends the boisterous ruin. Never alone
Did the king sigh, but with a general groan.

25   **KING:** Arm you, I pray you, to this speedy voyage;
For we will fetters put upon this fear,
Which now goes too free-footed.

ROSENCRANTZ and **GUILDENSTERN:** We will haste us.

Exeunt Rosencrantz and Guildenstern.

Enter Polonius.

POLONIUS: My lord, he's going to his mother's closet:
30   Behind the arras I'll convey myself
To hear the process; I'll warrant she'll tax him home:°
And, as you said, and wisely was it said,
'Tis meet that some more audience than a mother,
Since nature makes them partial, should o'erhear
35   The speech, of vantage. Fare you well, my liege:
I'll call upon you ere you go to bed,
And tell you what I know.

KING: Thanks, dear my lord.

Exit Polonius.

O, my offence is rank, it smells to heaven;
40   It hath the primal eldest curse upon't,—
A brother's murder!— Pray can I not,
Though inclination be as sharp as will:

---

tax him home: Reprove him properly.

My stronger guilt defeats my strong intent;
And, like a man to double business bound,
I stand in pause where I shall first begin,   45
And both neglect. What if this cursed hand
Were thicker than itself with brother's blood,—
Is there not rain enough in the sweet heavens
To wash it white as snow? Whereto serves mercy
But to confront the visage of offence?   50
And what's in prayer but this twofold force,—
To be forestalled ere we come to fall,
Or pardon'd being down? Then I'll look up;
My fault is past. But, O, what form of prayer
Can serve my turn? Forgive me my foul murder?—   55
That cannot be; since I am still possess'd
Of those effects for which I did the murder,—
My crown, mine own ambition, and my queen.
May one be pardon'd and retain the offence?°
In the corrupted currents of this world   60
Offence's gilded hand may shove by justice;
And oft 'tis seen the wicked prize itself
Buys out the law: but 'tis not so above;
There is no shuffling,— there the action lies
In his true nature; and we ourselves compell'd,   65
Even to the teeth and forehead of our faults,
To give in evidence. What then? what rests?°
Try what repentance can: what can it not?
Yet what can it when one can not repent?
O wretched state! O bosom black as death!   70
O limed° soul, that, struggling to be free,
Art more engag'd! Help, angels! make assay:
Bow, stubborn knees; and, heart, with strings of steel,
Be soft as sinews of the new-born babe!
All may be well. [*Retires and kneels*]   75

Enter Hamlet.

HAMLET: Now might I do it pat, now he is praying;
And now I'll do't — and so he goes to heaven;
And so am I reveng'd:— that would be scann'd:
A villain kills my father; and for that,
I, his sole son, do this same villain send   80
To heaven.

---

retain the offence: Retain the gains won by the offense.
rests: Remains.
limed: Snared.

O, this is hire and salary, not revenge.
He took my father grossly, full of bread;
With all his crimes broad blown, as flush as May;
85   And how his audit stands who knows save heaven?
But in our circumstance and course of thought
'Tis heavy with him: and am I, then, reveng'd,
To take him in the purging of his soul,
When he is fit and season'd for his passage?
90   No.
Up, sword; and know thou a more horrid hent:°
When he is drunk, asleep, or in his rage;
Or in the incestuous pleasure of his bed;
At gaming, swearing; or about some act
95   That has no relish of salvation in't;—
Then trip him, that his heels may kick at heaven;
And that his soul may be as damn'd and black
As hell, whereto it goes. My mother stays:
This physic but prolongs thy sickly days. [*Exit.*]

The King rises and advances.

100   KING: My words fly up, my thoughts remain below:
Words without thoughts never to heaven go. [*Exit.*]

SCENE 4

Another room in the castle.

Enter Queen and Polonius.

POLONIUS: He will come straight. Look you lay home to him:
Tell him his pranks have been too broad to bear with,
And that your grace hath screen'd and stood between
Much heat and him. I'll silence me e'en here.
5   Pray you, be round with him.
HAMLET: [*Within*] Mother, mother, mother!
QUEEN: I'll warrant you:
Fear me not:— withdraw, I hear him coming.

Polonius goes behind the arras.

Enter Hamlet.

HAMLET: Now, mother, what's the matter?
10   QUEEN: Hamlet, thou hast thy father much offended.
HAMLET: Mother, you have my father much offended.
QUEEN: Come, come, you answer with an idle tongue.

---

hent: Opportunity.

HAMLET: Go, go, you question with a wicked tongue.
QUEEN: Why, how now, Hamlet!
HAMLET: What's the matter now?   15
QUEEN: Have you forgot me?
HAMLET: No, by the rood, not so:
   You are the queen, your husband's brother's wife;
   And, — would it were not so! — you are my mother.
QUEEN: Nay, then, I'll set those to you that can speak.   20
HAMLET: Come, come, and sit you down; you shall not budge;
   You go not till I set you up a glass
   Where you may see the inmost part of you.
QUEEN: What wilt thou do? thou wilt not murder me?—
   Help, help, ho!   25
POLONIUS: [Behind] What, ho! help, help, help!
HAMLET: How now! a rat?
   [Draws.]
   Dead, for a ducat, dead! [Makes a pass through the arras]
POLONIUS: [Behind] O, I am slain! [Falls and dies.]
QUEEN: O me, what hast thou done?   30
HAMLET: Nay, I know not:
   Is it the king? [Draws forth Polonius]
QUEEN: O, what a rash and bloody deed is this!
HAMLET: A bloody deed! — almost as bad, good mother,
   As kill a king and marry with his brother.   35
QUEEN: As kill a king!
HAMLET: Ay, lady, 'twas my word. —
   Thou wretched, rash, intruding fool, farewell! [To Polonius]
   I took thee for thy better: take thy fortune;
   Thou find'st to be too busy is some danger.—   40
   Leave wringing of your hands: peace; sit you down,
   And let me wring your heart: for so I shall,
   If it be made of penetrable stuff;
   If damned custom have not braz'd it so
   That it is proof and bulwark against sense.   45
QUEEN: What have I done, that thou dar'st wag thy tongue
   In noise so rude against me?
HAMLET: Such an act
   That blurs the grace and blush of modesty;
   Calls virtue hypocrite; takes off the rose   50
   From the fair forehead of an innocent love,
   And sets a blister there; makes marriage-vows
   As false as dicers' oaths: O, such a deed
   As from the body of contraction plucks
   The very soul, and sweet religion makes   55
   A rhapsody of words: heaven's face doth glow;
   Yea, this solidity and compound mass,

With tristful° visage, as against the doom,
Is thought-sick at the act.

60   QUEEN: Ah me, what act,
That roars so loud, and thunders in the index?

HAMLET: Look here upon this picture and on this,—
The counterfeit presentment of two brothers.
See what grace was seated on this brow;
65   Hyperion's curls; the front of Jove himself;
An eye like Mars, to threaten and command;
A station like the herald Mercury
New-lighted on a heaven-kissing hill;
A combination and a form, indeed,
70   Where every god did seem to set his seal,
To give the world assurance of a man:
This was your husband. — Look you now, what follows:
Here is your husband, like a mildew'd ear
Blasting his wholesome brother. Have you eyes?
75   Could you on this fair mountain leave to feed,
And batten on this moor? Ha! have you eyes?
You cannot call it love; for at your age
The hey-day in the blood is tame, it's humble,
And waits upon the judgment: and what judgment
80   Would step from this to this? Sense, sure, you have,
Else could you not have motion: but sure that sense
Is apoplex'd: for madness would not err;
Nor sense to ecstasy was ne'er so thrill'd
But it reserv'd some quantity of choice
85   To serve in such a difference. What devil was't
That thus hath cozen'd you at hoodman-blind?°
Eyes without feeling, feeling without sight,
Ears without hand or eyes, smelling sans all,
Or but a sickly part of one true sense
90   Could not so mope.
O shame! where is thy blush! Rebellious hell,
If thou canst mutine in a matron's bones,
To flaming youth let virtue be as wax,
And melt in her own fire: proclaim no shame
95   When the compulsive ardor gives the charge,
Since frost itself as actively doth burn,
And reason panders° will.

---

tristful: Gloomy.

cozen'd . . . hoodman-blind: Tricked you at blindman's buff.

panders: Becomes subservient to.

QUEEN: O Hamlet, speak no more:
    Thou turn'st mine eyes into my very soul;
    And there I see such black and grained spots   100
    As will not leave their tinct.°
HAMLET: Nay, but to live
    In the rank sweat of an enseamed bed,
    Stew'd in corruption, honeying and making love
    Over the nasty sty,—   105
QUEEN: O, speak to me no more;
    These words like daggers enter in mine ears;
    No more, sweet Hamlet.
HAMLET: A murderer and a villain;
    A slave that is not twentieth part the tithe   110
    Of your precedent lord; a vice of kings;°
    A cutpurse of the empire and the rule,
    That from a shelf the precious diadem stole,
    And put it in his pocket!
QUEEN: No more.   115
HAMLET: A king of shreds and patches,—

Enter Ghost.

    Save me, and hover o'er me with your wings,
    You heavenly guards!—What would your gracious figure?
QUEEN: Alas, he's mad!
HAMLET: Do you not come your tardy son to chide,   120
    That, laps'd in time and passion, lets go by
    The important acting of your dread command?
    O, say!
GHOST: Do not forget: this visitation
    Is but to whet thy almost blunted purpose.   125
    But, look, amazement on thy mother sits:
    O, step between her and her fighting soul,—
    Conceit in weakest bodies strongest works,—
    Speak to her, Hamlet.
HAMLET: How is it with you, lady?   130
QUEEN: Alas, how is't with you,
    That you do bend your eye on vacancy,
    And with the incorporal air do hold discourse?
    Forth at your eyes your spirits wildly peep;
    And, as the sleeping soldiers in the alarm,   135
    Your bedded hair, like life in excrements,°

As will not . . . tinct: As will not yield up their color.

a vice of kings: A buffoon among kings; the character "Vice" in morality plays.

in excrements: In outgrowths or extremities.

Starts up and stands on end. O gentle son,
Upon the heat and flame of thy distemper
Sprinkle cool patience. Whereon do you look?

140   **HAMLET:** On him, on him! Look you, how pale he glares!
His form and cause conjoin'd, preaching to stones,
Would make them capable.—Do not look upon me;
Lest with this piteous action you convert
My stern effects: then what I have to do

145   Will want true color; tears perchance for blood.

  QUEEN: To whom do you speak this?
  HAMLET: Do you see nothing there?
  QUEEN: Nothing at all; yet all that is I see.
  HAMLET: Nor did you nothing hear?

150   **QUEEN:** No, nothing but ourselves.
  HAMLET: Why, look you there! look, how it steals away!
My father, in his habit as he liv'd!
Look, where he goes, even now, out at the portal!

Exit Ghost.

  QUEEN: This is the very coinage of your brain:
155   This bodiless creation ecstasy
Is very cunning in.
  HAMLET: Ecstasy!
My pulse, as yours, doth temperately keep time.
And makes as healthful music: it is not madness
160   That I have utter'd: bring me to the test,
And I the matter will re-word; which madness
Would gambol from. Mother, for love of grace,
Lay not that flattering unction to your soul,
That not your trespass, but my madness speaks:
165   It will but skin and film the ulcerous place,
Whilst rank corruption, mining all within,
Infects unseen. Confess yourself to Heaven;
Repent what's past; avoid what is to come;
And do not spread the compost on the weeds,
170   To make them ranker. Forgive me this my virtue;
For in the fatness° of these pursy times
Virtue itself of vice must pardon beg,
Yea, curb and woo for leave to do him good.

  QUEEN: O Hamlet, thou hast cleft my heart in twain.
175   **HAMLET:** O, throw away the worser part of it,
And live the purer with the other half.
Good-night: but go not to mine uncle's bed;

---

fatness: Corruption.

Assume a virtue, if you have it not.
That monster custom, who all sense doth eat,
Of habits devil, is angel yet in this,— 180
That to the use of actions fair and good
He likewise gives a frock or livery
That aptly is put on. Refrain to-night;
And that shall lend a kind of easiness
To the next abstinence: the next more easy; 185
For use almost can change the stamp of nature,
And either curb the devil, or throw him out
With wondrous potency. Once more, good-night:
And when you are desirous to be bless'd,
I'll blessing beg of you.— For this same lord [*pointing to Polonius*] 190
I do repent: but Heaven hath pleas'd it so,
To punish me with this, and this with me,
That I must be their° scourge and minister.
I will bestow him, and will answer well
The death I gave him. So, again, good-night.— 195
I must be cruel only to be kind:
Thus bad begins and worse remains behind.—
One word more, good lady.
QUEEN: What shall I do?
HAMLET: Not this, by no means, that I bid you do: 200
Let the bloat king tempt you again to bed;
Pinch wanton on your cheek; call you his mouse;
And let him, for a pair of reechy kisses,
Or paddling in your neck with his damn'd fingers,
Make you to ravel all this matter out, 205
That I essentially am not in madness,
But mad in craft. 'Twere good you let him know;
For who that's but a queen, fair, sober, wise,
Would from a paddock,° from a bat, a gib,°
Such dear concernings hide? who would do so? 210
No, in despite of sense and secrecy,
Unpeg the basket on the house's top,
Let the birds fly, and, like the famous ape,
To try conclusions, in the basket creep,
And break your own neck down. 215
QUEEN: Be thou assur'd, if words be made of breath
And breath of life, I have not life to breathe
What thou hast said to me.

---

their: Heaven's, or the heavens'.

paddock: Toad.

gib: Tomcat.

HAMLET: I must to England; you know that?
220   QUEEN: Alack,
         I had forgot: 'tis so concluded on.
      HAMLET: There's letters seal'd: and my two school-fellows,—
         Whom I will trust as I will adders fang'd,
         They bear the mandate; they must sweep my way,
225   And marshal me to knavery. Let it work;
         For 'tis the sport to have the éngineer
         Hoist with his own petard: and't shall go hard
         But I will delve one yard below their mines,
         And blow them at the moon: O, 'tis most sweet,
230   When in one line two crafts directly meet.—
         This man shall set me packing:
         I'll lug the guts into the neighbor room.—
         Mother, good-night.— Indeed, this counsellor
         Is now most still, most secret, and most grave,
235   Who was in life a foolish prating knave.
         Come, sir, to draw toward an end with you:—
         Good-night, mother.

      Exeunt severally; Hamlet dragging out Polonius.

                              ACT IV
                              SCENE 1

A room in the castle.

Enter King, Queen, Rosencrantz, and Guildenstern.

      KING: There's matter in these sighs, these prófound heaves:
         You must translate: 'tis fit we understand them.
         Where is your son?
      QUEEN: Bestow this place on us a little while. [*To Rosencrantz and
         Guildenstern, who go out*]
5   Ah, my good lord, what have I seen to-night!
      KING: What, Gertrude? How does Hamlet?
      QUEEN: Mad as the sea and wind, when both contend
         Which is the mightier: in his lawless fit,
10   Behind the arras hearing something stir,
         He whips his rapier out, and cries, A rat, a rat!
         And, in this brainish apprehension,° kills
         The unseen good old man.
      KING: O heavy deed!
         It had been so with us had we been there:

---

brainish apprehension: Mad notion.

His liberty is full of threats to all;   15
To you yourself, to us, to every one.
Alas, how shall this bloody deed be answer'd?
It will be laid to us, whose providence
Should have kept short, restrain'd, and out of haunt
This mad young man: but so much was our love,   20
We would not understand what was most fit;
But, like the owner of a foul disease,
To keep it from divulging, let it feed
Even on the pith of life. Where is he gone?
QUEEN: To draw apart the body he hath kill'd: 25
O'er whom his very madness, like some ore
Among a mineral of metals base,
Shows itself pure; he weeps for what is done.
KING: O Gertrude, come away!
The sun no sooner shall the mountains touch   30
But we will ship him hence: and this vile deed
We must, with all our majesty and skill,
Both countenance and excuse.— Ho, Guildenstern!

Enter Rosencrantz and Guildenstern.

Friends both, go join you with some further aid:
Hamlet in madness hath Polonius slain,   35
And from his mother's closet hath he dragg'd him:
Go seek him out; speak fair, and bring the body
Into the chapel. I pray you, haste in this.

Exeunt Rosencrantz and Guildenstern.

Come, Gertrude, we'll call up our wisest friends;
And let them know both what we mean to do   40
And what's untimely done: so haply slander,—
Whose whisper o'er the world's diameter,
As level as the cannon to his blank,
Transports his poison'd shot,— may amiss our name,
And hit the woundless air.— O, come away!   45
My soul is full of discord and dismay.

Exeunt.

SCENE 2

Another room in the castle.

Enter Hamlet.

HAMLET: Safely stowed.
ROSENCRANTZ and GUILDENSTERN: [*Within*] Hamlet! Lord Hamlet!
HAMLET: What noise? who calls on Hamlet?
O, here they come.

Enter Rosencrantz and Guildenstern.

5   ROSENCRANTZ: What have you done, my lord, with the dead body?
HAMLET: Compounded it with dust, whereto 'tis kin.
ROSENCRANTZ: Tell us where 'tis, that we may take it thence,
     And bear it to the chapel.
HAMLET: Do not believe it.
10   ROSENCRANTZ: Believe what?
HAMLET: That I can keep your counsel, and not mine own. Besides, to be
     demanded of a sponge! — what replication should be made by the son of
     a king?
ROSENCRANTZ: Take you me for a sponge, my lord?
15   HAMLET: Ay, sir; that soaks up the king's countenance, his rewards, his
     authorities. But such officers do the king best service in the end: he keeps
     them, like an ape, in the corner of his jaw; first mouthed, to be last
     swallowed: when he needs what you have gleaned, it is but squeezing you,
     and, sponge, you shall be dry again.
20   ROSENCRANTZ: I understand you not, my lord.
HAMLET: I am glad of it: a knavish speech sleeps in a foolish ear.
ROSENCRANTZ: My lord, you must tell us where the body is, and go with us to
     the king.
HAMLET: The body is with the king, but the king is not with the body. The
25   king is a thing,—
GUILDENSTERN: A thing, my lord!
HAMLET: Of nothing: bring me to him.
     Hide fox, and all after.

Exeunt.

SCENE 3

Another room in the castle.

Enter King, attended.

KING: I have sent to seek him, and to find the body.
     How dangerous is it that this man goes loose!
     Yet must not we put the strong law on him:
     He's lov'd of the distracted multitude,
5   Who like not in their judgment, but their eyes;
     And where 'tis so, the offender's scourge is weigh'd,
     But never the offence. To bear all smooth and even,
     This sudden sending him away must seem
     Deliberate pause: diseases desperate grown
10   By desperate appliance are reliev'd,
     Or not at all.

Enter Rosencrantz.

     How now! what hath befallen!

ROSENCRANTZ: Where the dead body is bestow'd, my lord,
    We cannot get from him.
KING: But where is he?   15
ROSENCRANTZ: Without, my lord; guarded, to know your pleasure.
KING: Bring him before us.
ROSENCRANTZ: Ho, Guildenstern! bring in my lord.

Enter Hamlet and Guildenstern.

KING: Now, Hamlet, where's Polonius?
HAMLET: At supper.   20
KING: At supper! where?
HAMLET: Not where he eats, but where he is eaten: a certain convocation of
    politic worms are e'en at him. Your worm is your only emperor for diet: we
    fat all creatures else to fat us, and we fat ourselves for maggots: your fat king
    and your lean beggar is but variable service,— two dishes, but to one table: 25
    that's the end.
KING: Alas, alas!
HAMLET: A man may fish with the worm that hath eat of a king, and eat of
    the fish that hath fed of that worm.
KING: What does thou mean by this?   30
HAMLET: Nothing but to show you how a king may go a progress through the
    guts of a beggar.
KING: Where is Polonius?
HAMLET: In heaven; send thither to see: if your messenger find him not there,
    seek him i' the other place yourself. But, indeed, if you find him not within   35
    this month, you shall nose him as you go up the stairs into the lobby.
KING: Go seek him there. [*To some Attendants*]
HAMLET: He will stay till ye come.

Exeunt Attendants.

KING: Hamlet, this deed, for thine especial safety,—
    Which we do tender, as we dearly grieve   40
    For that which thou hast done,—must send thee hence
    With fiery quickness: therefore prepare thyself;
    The bark is ready, and the wind at help,
    The associates tend, and everything is bent
    For England.   45
HAMLET: For England!
KING: Ay, Hamlet.
HAMLET: Good.
KING: So is it, if thou knew'st our purposes.
HAMLET: I see a cherub that sees them.— But, come; for England!—   50
    Farewell, dear mother.
KING: Thy loving father, Hamlet.
HAMLET: My mother: father and mother is man and wife; man and wife is one
    flesh; and so, my mother.— Come, for England! [*Exit.*]

55   KING: Follow him at foot; tempt him with speed aboard;
          Delay it not; I'll have him hence to-night:
          Away! for everything is seal'd and done
          That else leans on the affair, pray you, make haste.

Exeunt Rosencrantz and Guildenstern.

          And, England, if my love thou hold'st at aught,—
60   As my great power thereof may give thee sense,
          Since yet thy cicatrice looks raw and red
          After the Danish sword, and thy free awe
          Pays homage to us,— thou mayst not coldly set
          Our sovereign process; which imports at full,
65   By letters conjuring to that effect,
          The present death of Hamlet. Do it, England;
          For like the hectic in my blood he rages,
          And thou must cure me: till I know 'tis done,
          Howe'er my haps, my joys will ne'er begin. [*Exit.*]

SCENE 4

A plain in Denmark.

Enter Fortinbras, and Forces marching.

FORTINBRAS: Go, from me greet the Danish king:
          Tell him that, by his license, Fortinbras
          Craves the conveyance of a promis'd march
          Over his kingdom. You know the rendezvous,
5   If that his majesty would aught with us,
          We shall express our duty in his eye,
          And let him know so.
CAPTAIN: I will do't, my lord.
FORTINBRAS: Go softly on.

Exeunt Fortinbras and Forces.

Enter Hamlet, Rosencrantz, Guildenstern, &c.

10   HAMLET: Good sir, whose powers are these?
CAPTAIN: They are of Norway, sir.
HAMLET: How purpos'd, sir, I pray you?
CAPTAIN: Against some part of Poland.
HAMLET: Who commands them, sir?
15   CAPTAIN: The nephew to old Norway, Fortinbras.
HAMLET: Goes it against the main of Poland, sir,
          Or for some frontier?
CAPTAIN: Truly to speak, and with no addition,
          We go to gain a little patch of ground
20   That hath in it no profit but the name.

To pay five ducats, five, I would not farm it;
Nor will it yield to Norway or the Pole
A ranker° rate should it be sold in fee.
HAMLET: Why, then the Polack never will defend it.
CAPTAIN: Yes, it is already garrison'd.   25
HAMLET: Two thousand souls and twenty thousand ducats
    Will not debate the question of this straw:
    This is the imposthume° of much wealth and peace,
    That inward breaks, and shows no cause without
    Why the man dies.— I humbly thank you, sir.   30
CAPTAIN: God b' wi' you, sir. [Exit.]
ROSENCRANTZ: Will't please you go, my lord?
HAMLET: I'll be with you straight. Go a little before.

Exeunt all but Hamlet.

    How all occasions do inform against me,
    And spur my dull revenge! What is a man,   35
    If his chief good and market of his time
    Be but to sleep and feed? a beast, no more.
    Sure he that made us with such large discourse,°
    Looking before and after, gave us not
    That capability and godlike reason   40
    To fust° in us unus'd. Now, whether it be
    Bestial oblivion or some craven scruple
    Of thinking too precisely on the event,—
    A thought which, quarter'd, hath but one part wisdom
    And ever three parts coward,— I do not know   45
    Why yet I live to say, *This thing's to do;*
    Sith° I have cause, and will, and strength, and means
    To do't. Examples, gross as earth, exhort me:
    Witness this army, of such mass and charge,
    Led by a delicate and tender prince;   50
    Whose spirit, with divine ambition puff'd,
    Makes mouths at the invisible event;
    Exposing what is mortal and unsure
    To all that fortune, death, and danger dare,
    Even for an egg-shell. Rightly to be great   55
    Is not to stir without great argument,
    But greatly to find quarrel in a straw

---

ranker: Dearer.
imposthume: Ulcer.
discourse: Reasoning faculty.
fust: Grow musty.
Sith: Since.

When honor's at the stake. How stand I, then,
That have a father kill'd, a mother stain'd,
60 Excitements of my reason and my blood,
And let all sleep? while, to my shame, I see
The imminent death of twenty thousand men,
That, for a fantasy and trick of fame,
Go to their graves like beds; fight for a plot
65 Whereon the numbers cannot try the cause,
Which is not tomb enough and continent°
To hide the slain?— O, from this time forth,
My thoughts be bloody, or be nothing worth! [*Exit.*]

SCENE 5

Elsinore. A room in the castle.

Enter Queen and Horatio.

QUEEN: I will not speak with her.
HORATIO: She is importunate; indeed, distract:
        Her mood will needs be pitied.
QUEEN: What would she have?
5 HORATIO: She speaks much of her father; says she hears
        There's tricks i' the world; and hems, and beats her heart;
        Spurns enviously at straws; speaks things in doubt,
        That carry but half sense: her speech is nothing,
        Yet the unshapéd use of it doth move
10   The hearers to collection; they aim at it,
        And botch the words up fit to their own thoughts;
        Which, as her winks, and nods, and gestures yield them,
        Indeed would make one think there might be thought,
        Though nothing sure, yet much unhappily.
15   'Twere good she were spoken with; for she may strew
        Dangerous conjectures in ill-breeding minds.
QUEEN: Let her come in.

Exit Horatio.

        To my sick soul, as sin's true nature is,
        Each toy seems prologue to some great amiss:
20   So full of artless jealousy is guilt,
        It spills itself in fearing to be spilt.

Re-enter Horatio and Ophelia.

OPHELIA: Where is the beauteous majesty of Denmark?

---

continent: Container.

QUEEN: How now, Ophelia!
OPHELIA: [*Sings*]

> How should I your true love know
>   From another one?
> By his cockle hat and staff,
>   And his sandal shoon.

25

QUEEN: Alas, sweet lady, what imports this song?
OPHELIA: Say you? nay, pray you, mark.

Sings

> He is dead and gone, lady,
>   He is dead and gone;
> At his head a grass green turf,
>   At his heels a stone.

30

QUEEN: Nay, but, Ophelia,—
OPHELIA: Pray you, mark.

35

Sings

> White his shroud as the mountain snow,

Enter King.

QUEEN: Alas, look here, my lord.
OPHELIA: [*Sings*]

> Larded with sweet flowers;
> Which bewept to the grave did go
> With true-love showers.

40

KING: How do you, pretty lady?
OPHELIA: Well, God 'ild you!° They say the owl was a baker's daughter.
  Lord, we know what we are, but know not what we may be.
  God be at your table!
KING: Conceit upon her father.

45

OPHELIA: Pray you, let's have no words of this; but when they ask you what it
  means, say you this:

Sings.

> To-morrow is Saint Valentine's day
>   All in the morning betime,
> And I a maid at your window,
>   To be your Valentine.
> Then up he rose, and donn'd his clothes,
>   And dupp'd the chamber-door;

50

'ild you: Yield you — i.e., reward you.

> Let in the maid, that out a maid
>
> 55   Never departed more.

KING: Pretty Ophelia!

OPHELIA: Indeed, la, without an oath, I'll make an end on't;

Sings

> By Gis° and by Saint Charity,
>   Alack, and fie for shame!
> 60 Young men will do't, if they come to't;
>   By cock, they are to blame.
> Quoth she, before you tumbled me,
>   You promis'd me to wed.
> So would I ha' done, by yonder sun,
> 65   An thou hadst not come to my bed.

KING: How long hath she been thus?

OPHELIA: I hope all will be well. We must be patient: but I cannot choose but weep, to think they should lay him i' the cold ground. My brother shall know of it: and so I thank you; for your good counsel.— Come, my 70 coach!— Good-night, ladies; good-night, sweet ladies; good-night, good-night. [*Exit.*]

KING: Follow her close; give her good watch, I pray you.

Exit Horatio.

> O, this is the poison of deep grief; it springs
> All from her father's death. O Gertrude, Gertrude,
> 75 When sorrows come, they come not single spies,
> But in battalions! First, her father slain:
> Next, your son gone; and he most violent author
> Of his own just remove: the people muddied,
> Thick and unwholesome in their thoughts and whispers
> 80 For good Polonius' death; and we have done but greenly
> In hugger-mugger° to inter him: poor Ophelia
> Divided from herself and her fair judgment,
> Without the which we are pictures, or mere beasts:
> Last, and as much containing as all these,
> 85 Her brother is in secret come from France;
> Feeds on his wonder, keeps himself in clouds,
> And wants not buzzers to infect his ear
> With pestilent speeches of his father's death;
> Wherein necessity, of matter beggar'd,
> 90 Will nothing stick our person to arraign

Gis: A contraction for "by Jesus."

In hugger-mugger: In great secrecy and haste.

In ear and ear. O my dear Gertrude, this,
Like to a murdering piece,° in many places
Gives me superfluous death.

A noise within.

QUEEN: Alack, what noise is this?
KING: Where are my Switzers?° let them guard the door.   95

Enter a Gentleman.

What is the matter?
GENTLEMAN: Save yourself, my lord:
The ocean, overpeering of his list,
Eats not the flats with more impetuous haste
Than young Laertes, in a riotous head,   100
O'erbears your officers. The rabble call him lord;
And, as the world were now but to begin,
Antiquity forgot, custom not known,
The ratifiers and props of every word,
They cry, *Choose we, Laertes shall be king!*   105
Caps, hands, and tongues applaud it to the clouds,
Laertes shall be king, Laertes king!
QUEEN: How cheerfully on the false trail they cry!
O, this is counter, you false Danish dogs!
KING: The doors are broke.   110

Noise within.

Enter Laertes armed; Danes following.

LAERTES: Where is this king?— Sirs, stand you all without.
DANES: No, let's come in.
LAERTES: I pray you, give me leave.
DANES: We will, we will. [*They retire without the door.*]
LAERTES: I thank you:— keep the door.— O thou vile king,   115
Give me my father!
QUEEN: Calmly, good Laertes.
LAERTES: That drop of blood that's calm proclaims me bastard;
Cries cuckold to my father; brands the harlot
Even here, between the chaste unsmirched brow   120
Of my true mother.
KING: What is the cause, Laertes,
That thy rebellion looks so giant-like?—
Let him go, Gertrude; do not fear our person:

---

murdering piece: A cannon.

Switzers: Bodyguard of Swiss mercenaries.

125   There's such divinity doth hedge a king,
         That treason can but peep to what it would,
         Acts little of his will. — Tell me, Laertes,
         Why thou art thus incens'd. — Let him go, Gertrude:—
         Speak, man.
130   **LAERTES:** Where is my father?
     KING: Dead.
     QUEEN: But not by him.
     KING: Let him demand his fill.
     LAERTES: How came he dead? I'll not be juggled with:
135   To hell, allegiance! vows, to the blackest devil!
         Conscience and grace, to the profoundest pit!
         I dare damnation:— to this point I stand,—
         That both the worlds I give to negligence,
         Let come what comes; only I'll be reveng'd
140   Most thoroughly for my father.
     KING: Who shall stay you?
     LAERTES: My will, not all the world:
         And for my means, I'll husband them so well,
         They shall go far with little.
145   **KING:**   Good Laertes,
         If you desire to know the certainty
         Of your dear father's death, is't writ in your revenge
         That, sweepstake, you will draw both friend and foe,
         Winner or loser?
150   **LAERTES:** None but his enemies.
     KING: Will you know them, then?
     LAERTES: To his good friends thus wide I'll ope my arms;
         And, like the kind life-rendering pelican,°
         Repast them with my blood.
155   **KING:**   Why, now you speak
         Like a good child and a true gentleman.
         That I am guiltless of your father's death,
         And am most sensible in grief for it,
         It shall as level to your judgment pierce
160   As day does to your eye.
     DANES: [*Within*]   Let her come in.
     LAERTES: How now! what noise is that?

Re-enter Ophelia, fantastically dressed with straws and flowers.

         O heat, dry up my brains! tears seven times salt
         Burn out the sense and virtue of mine eyes!—
165   By heaven, thy madness shall be paid by weight

---

life-rendering pelican: The mother pelican was believed to draw blood from herself to feed her young.

Till our scale turn the beam. O rose of May!
Dear maid, kind sister, sweet Ophelia!—
O heavens! is't possible a young maid's wits
Should be as mortal as an old man's life!
Nature is fine in love; and where 'tis fine   170
It sends some precious instance of itself
After the thing it loves.

OPHELIA: [*Sings*]

> They bore him barefac'd on the bier;
>   Hey no nonny, nonny, hey nonny;
> And on his grave rain'd many a tear,—   175
>   Fare you well, my dove!

LAERTES: Hadst thou thy wits, and didst persuade revenge,
It could not move thus.

OPHELIA: You must sing, *Down-a-down, and you call him a-down-a*. O, how the
wheel becomes it! It is the false steward, that stole his master's daughter.   180

LAERTES: This nothing's more than matter.

OPHELIA: There's rosemary, that's for remembrance; pray, love, remember: and
there is pansies that's for thoughts.

LAERTES: A document in madness,— thoughts and remembrance fitted.

OPHELIA: There's fennel for you, and columbines:— there's rue for you; and   185
here's some for me:— we may call it herb-grace o' Sundays:—
O, you must wear your rue with a difference.— There's a daisy:— I would
give you some violets, but they withered all when my father died:— they
say, he made a good end,—

Sings

> For bonny sweet Robin is all my joy,—   190

LAERTES: Thoughts and affliction, passion, hell itself,
She turns to favor and to prettiness.

OPHELIA: [*Sings*]

> And will he not come again?
> And will he not come again?
>   No, no, he is dead,   195
>   Go to thy death-bed,
> He never will come again.
> His beard was as white as snow
> All flaxen was his poll:
>   He is gone, he is gone,   200
>   And we cast away moan:
> God ha' mercy on his soul!

And of all Christian souls, I pray God.— God b' wi' ye. [*Exit.*]

LAERTES: Do you see this, O God?

KING: Laertes, I must commune with your grief,   205
Or you deny me right. Go but apart,

Make choice of whom your wisest friends you will,
And they shall hear and judge 'twixt you and me:
If by direct or by collateral hand
210   They find us touch'd, we will our kingdom give,
Our crown, our life, and all that we call ours,
To you in satisfaction; but if not,
Be you content to lend your patience to us,
And we shall jointly labor with your soul
215   To give it due content.

LAERTES: Let this be so;
His means of death, his obscure burial,—
No trophy, sword, nor hatchment° o'er his bones
No noble rite nor formal ostentation,—
220   Cry to be heard, as 'twere from heaven to earth,
That I must call't in question.

KING: So you shall;
And where the offence is, let the great axe fall.
I pray you, go with me.

Exeunt.

SCENE 6

Another room in the castle.

Enter Horatio and a Servant.

HORATIO: What are they that would speak with me?
SERVANT: Sailors, sir: they say they have letters for you.
HORATIO: Let them come in.—

Exit Servant.

I do not know from what part of the world
5   I should be greeted, if not from Lord Hamlet.

Enter Sailors.

1ST SAILOR: God bless you, sir.
HORATIO: Let him bless thee too.
1ST SAILOR: He shall, sir, an't please him. There's a letter for you, sir; it comes
from the ambassador that was bound for England; if your name be Horatio,
10   as I am let to know it is.
HORATIO: [*Reads*] *Horatio, when thou shalt have overlooked this, give these fellows
some means to the king: they have letters for him. Ere we were two days old at sea,
a pirate of very warlike appointment gave us chase. Finding ourselves too slow of
sail, we put on a compelled valor; and in the grapple I boarded them; on the instant*

---

hatchment: A tablet with coat of arms.

they got clear of our ship; so I alone became their prisoner. They have dealt with 15
me like thieves of mercy: but they knew what they did; I am to do a good turn for
them. Let the king have the letters I have sent; and repair thou to me with as much
haste as thou wouldst fly death. I have words to speak in thine ear will make thee
dumb; yet are they much too light for the bore of the matter. These good fellows
will bring thee where I am. Rosencrantz and Guildenstern hold their course for 20
England: of them I have much to tell thee. Farewell. He that thou knowest thine.

Hamlet

Come, I will give you way for these your letters;
And do't the speedier, that you may direct me
To him from whom you brought them.

Exeunt.

SCENE 7

Another room in the castle.

Enter King and Laertes.

KING: Now must your conscience my acquittance seal,
  And you must put me in your heart for friend,
  Sith you have heard, and with a knowing ear,
  That he which hath your noble father slain
  Pursu'd my life. 5
LAERTES: It well appears:—but tell me
  Why you proceeded not against these feats,
  So crimeful and so capital in nature,
  As by your safety, wisdom, all things else,
  You mainly were stirr'd up. 10
KING: O, for two special reasons;
  Which may to you, perhaps, seem much unsinew'd,
  But yet to me they are strong. The queen his mother
  Lives almost by his looks; and for myself,—
  My virtue or my plague, be it either which,— 15
  She's so conjunctive to my life and soul,
  That, as the star moves not but in his sphere,
  I could not but by her. The other motive,
  Why to a public count I might not go,
  Is the great love the general gender bear him; 20
  Who, dipping all his faults in their affection,
  Would, like the spring that turneth wood to stone,
  Convert his gyves to graces; so that my arrows,
  Too slightly timber'd for so loud a wind,
  Would have reverted to my bow again, 25
  And not where I had aim'd them.
LAERTES: And so have I a noble father lost;
  A sister driven into desperate terms,—

Whose worth, if praises may go back again,
30   Stood challenger on mount of all the age
For her perfections:—but my revenge will come.
KING: Break not your sleeps for that: you must not think
That we are made of stuff so flat and dull
That we can let our beard be shook with danger,
35   And think it pastime. You shortly shall hear more:
I lov'd your father, and we love ourself;
And that, I hope, will teach you to imagine,—

Enter a Messenger.

How now! what news?
MESSENGER: Letters, my lord, from Hamlet:
40   This to your majesty; this to the queen.
KING: From Hamlet! Who brought them?
MESSENGER: Sailors, my lord, they say; I saw them not:
They were given me by Claudio,—he receiv'd them
Of him that brought them.
45 **KING:** Laertes, you shall hear them.—Leave us.

Exit Messenger.

[*Reads*] *High and mighty,—You shall know I am set naked on your kingdom.*
To-morrow shall I beg leave to see your kingly eyes: when I shall, first asking
your pardon thereunto, recount the occasions of my sudden and more strange
return.   *Hamlet*

50   What should this mean? Are all the rest come back?
Or is it some abuse,° and no such thing?
LAERTES: Know you the hand?
KING: 'Tis Hamlet's character:°—*Naked,*—
And in a postscript here, he says, *alone.*
55   Can you advise me?
LAERTES: I am lost in it, my lord. But let him come;
It warms the very sickness in my heart,
That I shall live, and tell him to his teeth,
Thus diddest thou.
60 **KING:**   If it be so, Laertes,—
As how should it be so? how otherwise?—
Will you be rul'd by me?
LAERTES: Ay, my lord:
So you will not o'errule me to a peace.
65 **KING:** To thine own peace. If he be now return'd,—
As checking at his voyage, and that he means

---

abuse: Ruse.
character: Handwriting.

No more to undertake it, — I will work him
To an exploit, now ripe in my device,
Under the which he shall not choose but fall:
And for his death no wind of blame shall breathe;   70
But even his mother shall uncharge the practice
And call it accident.

LAERTES: My lord, I will be rul'd;
The rather if you could devise it so
That I might be the organ.   75

KING: It falls right.
You have been talk'd of since your travel much,
And that in Hamlet's hearing, for a quality
Wherein they say you shine: your sum of parts
Did not together pluck such envy from him   80
As did that one; and that, in my regard,
Of the unworthiest siege.

LAERTES: What part is that, my lord?

KING: A very riband in the cap of youth,
Yet needful too; for youth no less becomes   85
The light and careless livery that it wears
Than settled age his sables and his weeds,
Importing health and graveness. — Two months since,
Here was a gentleman of Normandy, —
I've seen myself, and serv'd against, the French,   90
And they can well on horseback: but this gallant
Had witchcraft in't; he grew unto his seat;
And to such wondrous doing brought his horse,
As he had been incorps'd and demi-natur'd°
With the brave beast: so far he topp'd my thought,   95
That I, in forgery of shapes and tricks,°
Come short of what he did.

LAERTES: A Norman was't?

KING: A Norman.

LAERTES: Upon my life, Lamond.   100

KING: The very same.

LAERTES: I know him well: he is the brooch, indeed,
And gem of all the nation.

KING: He made confession of you;
And gave you such a masterly report   105
For art and exercise in your defence,
And for your rapier most especially,
That he cried out, 'twould be a sight indeed

As . . . demi-natur'd: Made as one body and formed into half man, half horse — or centaur.

in forgery . . . tricks: In imagining tricks of horsemanship.

If one could match you: the scrimers° of their nation,
110   He swore, had neither motion, guard, nor eye,
If you oppos'd them. Sir, this report of his
Did Hamlet so envenom with his envy,
That he could nothing do but wish and beg
Your sudden coming o'er, to play with him.
115   Now, out of this,—
LAERTES: What out of this, my lord?
KING: Laertes, was your father dear to you?
Or are you like the painting of a sorrow,
A face without a heart?
120   LAERTES: Why ask you this?
KING: Not that I think you did not love your father;
But that I know love is begun by time;
And that I see, in passages of proof,°
Time qualifies the spark and fire of it.
125   There lives within the very flame of love
A kind of wick or snuff that will abate it;
And nothing is at a like goodness still;
For goodness, growing to a pleurisy,°
Dies in his own too much: that we would do
130   We should do when we would; for this *would* changes,
And hath abatements and delays as many
As there are tongues, or hands, or accidents;
And then this *should* is like a spendthrift sigh
That hurts by easing. But to the quick o' the ulcer:
135   Hamlet comes back: what would you undertake
To show yourself your father's son in deed
More than in words?
LAERTES: To cut his throat i' the church.
KING: No place, indeed, should murder sanctuarize;
140   Revenge should have no bounds. But, good Laertes,
Will you do this, keep close within your chamber.
Hamlet return'd shall know you are come home:
We'll put on those shall praise your excellence,
And set a double varnish on the fame
145   The Frenchman gave you; bring you, in fine, together,
And wager on yours heads: he, being remiss,°
Most generous, and free from all contriving,
Will not peruse the foils; so that, with ease,

---

scrimers: Fencers.

passages of proof: The evidence of experience.

pleurisy: Plethora, an excess of blood.

remiss: Unguarded and free from suspicion.

Or with a little shuffling, you may choose
A sword unbated, and, in a pass of practice,   150
Requite him for your father.
LAERTES: I will do't it:
And, for that purpose, I'll anoint my sword.
I bought an unction of a mountebank,
So mortal that but dip a knife in it,   155
Where it draws blood no cataplasm so rare,°
Collected from all simples that have virtue
Under the moon, can save the thing from death
That is but scratch'd withal: I'll touch my point
With this contagion, that, if I gall him slightly,   160
It may be death.
KING: Let's further think of this;
Weigh what convenience both of time and means
May fit us to our shape: if this should fail,
And that our drift look through our bad performance,   165
'Twere better not assay'd: therefore this project
Should have a back or second, that might hold
If this should blast in proof. Soft! let me see:—
We'll make a solemn wager on your cunnings,—
I ha't: 170
When in your motion you are hot and dry,—
As make your bouts more violent to that end,—
And that he calls for drink, I'll have prepar'd him
A chalice for the nonce;° whereon but sipping,
If he by chance escape your venom'd stuck   175
Our purpose may hold there.

Enter Queen.

         How now, sweet queen!
QUEEN: One woe doth tread upon another's heel,
So fast they follow:— your sister's drown'd, Laertes.
LAERTES: Drown'd! O, where?   180
QUEEN: There is a willow grows aslant a brook,
That shows his hoar leaves in the glassy stream;
There with fantastic garlands did she come
Of crowflowers, nettles, daisies, and long purples,
That liberal shepherds give a grosser name,   185
But our cold maids do dead men's fingers call them.
There, on the pendant boughs her coronet weeds

---

no cataplasm so rare: No poultice, however remarkably efficacious.
nonce: Purpose.

Clambering to hang, an envious° sliver broke;
When down her weedy trophies and herself
190   Fell in the weeping brook. Her clothes spread wide;
And, mermaid-like, awhile they bore her up:
Which time she chanted snatches of old tunes;
As one incapable of her own distress,
Or like a creature native and indu'd
195   Unto that element: but long it could not be
Till that her garments, heavy with their drink,
Pull'd the poor wretch from her melodious lay
To muddy death.

LAERTES: Alas, then, she is drown'd?
200 QUEEN: Drown'd, drown'd.
LAERTES: Too much of water hast thou, poor Ophelia,
And therefore I forbid my tears: but yet
It is our trick; nature her custom holds,
Let shame say what it will: when these are gone,
205   The woman will be out.° — Adieu, my lord:
I have a speech of fire, that fain would blaze,
But that this folly douts it.° [*Exit.*]

KING: Let's follow, Gertrude;
How much I had to do to calm his rage!
210   Now fear I this will give it start again;
Therefore let's follow.

Exeunt.

ACT V

SCENE 1

A churchyard.

Enter two Clowns° with spades, &c.

1ST CLOWN: Is she to be buried in Christian burial that wilfully seeks her
own salvation?
2ND CLOWN: I tell thee she is; and therefore make her grave straight: the
crowner° hath sat on her, and finds it Christian burial.
5   1ST CLOWN: How can that be, unless she drowned herself in her own defence?
2ND CLOWN: Why, 'tis found so.

---

envious: Malicious.
The women . . . out: I.e., "I shall be ruthless."
douts it: Drowns it.
Clowns: Rustic fellows.
crowner: Coroner.

1ST CLOWN: It must be *se offendendo*,° it cannot be else. For here lies the
point: if I drown myself wittingly, it argues an act: and an act hath three
branches; it is to act, to do, and to perform: argal,° she drowned herself
wittingly.   10

2ND CLOWN: Nay, but hear you, goodman delver,—

1ST CLOWN: Give me leave. Here lies the water; good: here stands the man;
good: if the man go to this water and drown himself, it is, will he, nill he,
he goes,—mark you that: but if the water come to him and drown him, he
drowns not himself: argal, he that is not guilty of his own death shortens   15
not his own life.

2ND CLOWN: But is this law?

1ST CLOWN: Ay, marry, is't; crowner's quest law.

2ND CLOWN: Will you ha' the truth on't? If this had not been a gentlewoman
she should have been buried out of Christian burial.   20

1ST CLOWN: Why, there thou say'st: and the more pity that great folks should
have countenance in this world to drown or hang themselves more than
their even-Christian.°— Come, my spade. There is no ancient gentlemen
but gardeners, ditchers, and grave-makers; they hold up Adam's profession.

2ND CLOWN: Was he a gentleman?   25

1ST CLOWN: He was the first that ever bore arms.

2ND CLOWN: Why, he had none.

1ST CLOWN: What, art a heathen? How dost thou understand the Scripture?
The Scripture says, Adam digged: could he dig without arms? I'll put another question to thee: if thou answerest me not to the purpose, confess   30
thyself,°—

2ND CLOWN: Go to.

1ST CLOWN: What is he that builds stronger than either the mason, the
shipwright, or the carpenter?

2ND CLOWN: The gallows-maker; for that frame outlives a thousand tenants.   35

1ST CLOWN: I like thy wit well, in good faith: the gallows does well; but how
does it well? it does well to those that do ill: now thou dost ill to say the
gallows is built stronger than the church: argal, the gallows may do well to
thee. To't again, come.

2ND CLOWN: Who builds stronger than a mason, a shipwright, or a carpenter?   40

1ST CLOWN: Ay, tell me that, and unyoke.

2ND CLOWN: Marry, now I can tell.

1ST CLOWN: To't.

2ND CLOWN: Mass, I cannot tell.

Enter Hamlet and Horatio, at a distance.

---

se offendendo: In self-offense; he means *se defendendo,* in self-defense.

argal: He means *ergo,* therefore.

even-Christian: Fellow Christian.

confess thyself: "Confess thyself an ass," perhaps.

45 **1ST CLOWN:** Cudgel thy brains no more about it, for your dull ass will not
mend his pace with beating; and when you are asked this question next, say
a grave-maker; the houses that he makes last till doomsday. Go, get thee to
Yaughan: fetch me a stoup of liquor.

Exit Second Clown.

Digs and sings.

> In youth, when I did love, did love,
50 >   Methought it was very sweet,
> To contract, O, the time, for, ah, my behove,°
>   O, methought there was nothing meet.

HAMLET: Has this fellow no feeling of his business, that he sings at
grave-making?
55 **HORATIO:** Custom hath made it in him a property of easiness.
HAMLET: 'Tis e'en so: the hand of little employment hath the daintier sense.
1ST CLOWN: [*Sings*]

> But age, with his stealing steps,
>   Hath claw'd me in his clutch,
> And hath shipp'd me intil the land,
60 >   As if I had never been such.

Throws up a skull

HAMLET: That skull had a tongue in it, and could sing once: how the knave
joels° it to the ground, as if it were Cain's jawbone, that did the first
murder! This might be the pate of a politician, which this ass now
o'erreaches; one that would circumvent God, might it not?
65 **HORATIO:** It might, my lord.
HAMLET: Or of a courtier; which could say, *Good-morrow, sweet lord! How dost
thou, good lord?* This might be my lord such-a-one, that praised my lord
such-a-one's horse, when he meant to beg it,—might it not?
HORATIO: Ay, my lord.
70 **HAMLET:** Why, e'en so: and now my Lady Worm's; chapless,° and knocked
about the mazard° with a sexton's spade: here's fine revolution, an we had
the trick to see't. Did these bones cost no more the breeding but to play at
loggats° with 'em? Mine ache to think on't.
1ST CLOWN: [*Sings*]

> A pick-axe and a spade, a spade,
75 >   For and a shrouding sheet:

---

behove: Behoof, or advantage.

joels: Throws.

chapless: Without a lower jaw.

mazard: Head.

loggats: A game in which small pieces of wood are hurled at a stake.

> O, a pit of clay for to be made
> For such a guest is meet.

Throws up another.

HAMLET: There's another: why may not that be the skull of a lawyer? Where be his quiddits° now, his quillets,° his cases, his tenures, and his tricks? why does he suffer this rude knave now to knock him about the sconce with a dirty shovel, and will not tell him of his action of battery? Hum! This fellow might be in's time a great buyer of land, with his statutes, his recognizances, his fines, his double vouchers, his recoveries: is this the fine of his fines, and the recovery of his recoveries, to have his fine pate full of fine dirt? will his vouchers vouch him no more of his purchases, and double ones too, than the length and breadth of a pair of indentures? The very conveyances of his lands will hardly lie in this box; and must the inheritor himself have no more, ha? 80

85

HORATIO: Not a jot more, my lord.

HAMLET: Is not parchment made of sheep-skins? 90

HORATIO: Ay, my lord, and of calf-skins too.

HAMLET: They are sheep and calves which seek out assurance in that. I will speak to this fellow.—Whose grave's this, sir?

1ST CLOWN: Mine, sir.—[*Sings*]

> O, a pit of clay for to be made
> For such a guest is meet. 95

HAMLET: I think it be thine indeed; for thou liest in't.

1ST CLOWN: You lie out on't, sir, and therefore it is not yours: for my part, I do not lie in't, and yet it is mine.

HAMLET: Thou dost lie in't, to be in't, and say it is thine: 'tis for the dead, not for the quick; therefore thou liest. 100

1ST CLOWN: 'Tis a quick lie, sir: 'twill away again from me to you.

HAMLET: What man dost thou dig it for?

1ST CLOWN: For no man, sir.

HAMLET: What woman, then? 105

1ST CLOWN: For none, neither.

HAMLET: Who is to be buried in't?

1ST CLOWN: One that was a woman, sir; but, rest her soul, she's dead.

HAMLET: How absolute the knave is! we must speak by the card, or equivocation will undo us. By the Lord, Horatio, these three years I have taken note of it; the age is grown so picked° that the toe of the peasant comes so near the heel of the courtier, he galls his kibe.°— How long hast thou been a grave-maker? 110

---

quiddits: Quiddities, "whatnesses"— that is, hair-splittings.

quillets: Quibbling distinctions.

picked: Refined or educated.

galls his kibe: Rubs and irritates the chilblain sore on the courtier's heel.

1ST CLOWN: Of all the days i' the year, I came to't that day that our last King
115   Hamlet o'ercame Fortinbras.

HAMLET: How long is that since?

1ST CLOWN: Cannot you tell that? every fool can tell that: it was the very day
       that young Hamlet was born,—he that is mad, and sent into England.

HAMLET: Ay, marry, why was he sent into England?

120 1ST CLOWN: Why, because he was mad: he shall recover his wits there; or, if
       he do not, it's no great matter there.

HAMLET: Why?

1ST CLOWN: 'Twill not be seen in him there; there the men are as mad as he.

HAMLET: How came he mad?

125 1ST CLOWN: Very strangely, they say.

HAMLET: How strangely?

1ST CLOWN: Faith, e'en with losing his wits.

HAMLET: Upon what ground?

1ST CLOWN: Why, here in Denmark: I have been sexton here, man and boy,
130   thirty years.

HAMLET: How long will a man lie i' the earth ere he rot?

1ST CLOWN: Faith, if he be not rotten before he die,—as we have many
       pocky corses now-a-days, that will scarce hold the laying in,—he will last
       you some eight year or nine year: a tanner will last you nine year.

135 HAMLET: Why he more than another?

1ST CLOWN: Why, sir, his hide is so tanned with his trade that he will keep
       out water a great while; and your water is a sore decayer of your whoreson
       dead body. Here's a skull now; this skull has lain in the earth three-and-
       twenty years.

140 HAMLET: Whose was it?

1ST CLOWN: A whoreson mad fellow's it was: whose do you think it was?

HAMLET: Nay, I know not.

1ST CLOWN: A pestilence on him for a mad rogue! 'a poured a flagon of
       Rhenish on my head once. This same skull, sir, was Yorick's skull, the
145   king's jester.

HAMLET: This?

1ST CLOWN: E'en that.

HAMLET: Let me see. [*Takes the skull*]— Alas, poor Yorick!— I knew him,
       Horatio; a fellow of infinite jest, of most excellent fancy: he hath borne me
150   on his back a thousand times; and now, how abhorred in my imagination it
       is! my gorge rises at it. Here hung those lips that I have kissed I know not
       how oft. Where be your gibes now? your gambols? your songs? your flashes
       of merriment, that were wont to set the table on a roar? Not one now, to
       mock your own grinning? quite chap-fallen? Now get you to my lady's
155   chamber, and tell her, let her paint an inch thick, to this favor° she must
       come; make her laugh at that.— Pr'ythee, Horatio, tell me one thing.

---

favor: Face.

HORATIO: What's that, my lord?
HAMLET: Dost thou think Alexander looked o' this fashion i' the earth?
HORATIO: E'en so.
HAMLET: And smelt so? pah! [*Throws down the skull*]   160
HORATIO: E'en so, my lord.
HAMLET: To what base uses we may return, Horatio! Why may not
   imagination trace the noble dust of Alexander till he find it stopping
   a bung-hole?
HORATIO: 'Twere to consider too curiously to consider so.   165
HAMLET: No, faith, not a jot; but to follow him thither with modesty enough,
   and likelihood to lead it: as thus; Alexander died, Alexander was buried,
   Alexander returneth into dust; the dust is earth; of earth we make loam;
   and why of that loam whereto he was converted might they not stop
   a beer-barrel?   170

   >Imperious Caesar, dead and turn'd to clay,
   >   Might stop a hole to keep the wind away:
   >O, that that earth which kept the world in awe
   >   Should patch a wall to expel the winter's flaw!—

   But soft! but soft! aside.— Here comes the king.   175

*Enter Priests, &c., in procession; the corpse of Ophelia, Laertes and Mourners follow-
ing; King, Queen, their Trains, &c.*

   The queen, the courtiers: who is that they follow?
   And with such maimed rites? This doth betoken
   The corse they follow did with desperate hand
   Fordo its own life: 'twas of some estate.
   Couch we awhile and mark. [*Retiring with Horatio*]   180
LAERTES: What ceremony else?
HAMLET: That is Laertes,
   A very noble youth: mark.
LAERTES: What ceremony else?
1ST PRIEST: Her obsequies have been as far enlarg'd   185
   As we have warrantise: her death was doubtful,
   And, but that great command o'ersways the order,
   She should in ground unsanctified have lodg'd
   Till the last trumpet; for charitable prayers,
   Shards, flints, and pebbles, should be thrown on her,   190
   Yet here she is allowed her virgin rites,
   Her maiden strewments, and the bringing home
   Of bell and burial.
LAERTES: Must there no more be done?
1ST PRIEST: No more be done: 195
   We should profane the service of the dead
   To sing a *requiem*, and such rest to her
   As to peace-parted souls.

LAERTES: Lay her i' the earth;—
200   And from her fair and unpolluted flesh
       May violets spring! — I tell thee, churlish priest,
       A ministering angel shall my sister be
       When thou liest howling.
       HAMLET: What, the fair Ophelia!
205   QUEEN: Sweets to the sweet: farewell! [*Scattering flowers*]
       I hop'd thou shouldst have been my Hamlet's wife;
       I thought thy bride-bed to have deck'd, sweet maid,
       And not have strew'd thy grave.
       LAERTES: O, treble woe
210   Fall ten times treble on that cursed head
       Whose wicked deed thy most ingenious sense
       Depriv'd thee of! — Hold off the earth awhile,
       Till I have caught her once more in mine arms:

Leaps into the grave.

       Now pile your dust upon the quick and dead,
215   Till of this flat a mountain you have made,
       To o'er-top old Pelion° or the skyish head
       Of blue Olympus.
       HAMLET: [*Advancing*] What is he whose grief
       Bears such an emphasis? whose phrase of sorrow
220   Conjures the wandering stars, and makes them stand
       Like wonder-wounded hearers? this is I, Hamlet the
       Dane. [*Leaps into the grave*]
       LAERTES: The devil take thy soul! [*Grappling with him*]
       HAMLET: Thou pray'st not well.
225   I pr'ythee, take thy fingers from my throat;
       For, though I am not splenitive and rash,
       Yet have I in me something dangerous,
       Which let thy wiseness fear: away thy hand.
       KING: Pluck them asunder.
230   QUEEN: Hamlet! Hamlet!
       ALL: Gentlemen,—
       HORATIO: Good my lord, be quiet.

The Attendants part them, and they come out of the grave.

       HAMLET: Why, I will fight with him upon this theme
       Until my eyelids will no longer wag.
235   QUEEN: O my son, what theme?
       HAMLET: I lov'd Ophelia; forty thousand brothers
       Could not, with all their quantity of love,
       Make up my sum. — What wilt thou do for her?

Pelion: A mountain in Greece.

KING: O, he is mad, Laertes.
QUEEN: For love of God, forbear him.   240
HAMLET: 'Swounds, show me what thou'lt do:
    Woul't weep? woul't fight? woul't fast? woul't tear thyself?
    Woul't drink up eisel?° eat a crocodile?
    I'll do't.— Dost thou come here to whine?
    To outface me with leaping in her grave?   245
    Be buried quick° with her, and so will I:
    And, if thou prate of mountains, let them throw
    Millions of acres on us, till our ground,
    Singeing his pate against the burning zone,°
    Make Ossa° like a wart! Nay, an thou'lt mouth,   250
    I'll rant as well as thou.
QUEEN: This is mere madness:
    And thus awhile the fit will work on him;
    Anon, as patient as the female dove,
    When that her golden couplets are disclos'd,°   255
    His silence will sit drooping.
HAMLET: Hear you, sir;
    What is the reason that you use me thus?
    I lov'd you ever: but it is no matter;
    Let Hercules himself do what he may,   260
    The cat will mew, and dog will have his day. [*Exit.*]
KING: I pray thee, good Horatio, wait upon him.—

Exit Horatio.

    [*To Laertes*] Strengthen your patience in our last night's speech;
    We'll put the matter to the present push.—
    Good Gertrude, set some watch over your son.—   265
    This grave shall have a living monument:
    An hour of quiet shortly shall we see;
    Till then, in patience our proceeding be.

Exeunt.

SCENE 2

A hall in the castle.

Enter Hamlet and Horatio.

HAMLET: So much for this, sir: now let me see the other;
    You do remember all the circumstance?

---

eisel: Vinegar.
quick: Alive.
burning zone: The fiery zone of the celestial sphere.
Ossa: A high mountain in Greece.
When . . . are disclos'd: When the golden twins are hatched.

HORATIO: Remember it, my lord!

HAMLET: Sir, in my heart there was a kind of fighting

5   That would not let me sleep: methought I lay
         Worse than the mutines in the bilboes.° Rashly,
         And prais'd be rashness for it,—let us know,
         Our indiscretion sometimes serves us well,
         When our deep plots do fail: and that should teach us

10   There's a divinity that shapes our ends,
         Rough-hew them how we will.

HORATIO: This is most certain.

HAMLET: Up from my cabin,

         My sea-gown scarf'd about me, in the dark

15   Grop'd I to find out them: had my desire;
         Finger'd their packet; and, in fine, withdrew
         To mine own room again: making so bold,
         My fears forgetting manners, to unseal
         Their grand commission; where I found, Horatio,

20   O royal knavery! an exact command,—
         Larded with many several sorts of reasons,
         Importing Denmark's health and England's too,
         With, ho! such bugs° and goblins in my life,—
         That, on the supervise, no leisure bated,

25   No, not to stay the grinding of the axe,
         My head should be struck off.

HORATIO: Is't possible?

HAMLET: Here's the commission: read it at more leisure.

         But wilt thou hear me how I did proceed?

30   **HORATIO:**   I beseech you.

HAMLET: Being thus benetted round with villainies,—

         Ere I could make a prologue to my brains,
         They had begun the play,—I sat me down;
         Devis'd a new commission; wrote it fair:

35   I once did hold it, as our statists do,
         A baseness to write fair, and labor'd much
         How to forget that learning; but, sir, now
         It did me yeoman's service. Wilt thou know
         The effect of what I wrote?

40   **HORATIO:**   Ay, good my lord.

HAMLET: An earnest conjuration from the king,—

         As England was his faithful tributary;
         As love between them like the palm might flourish;
         As peace should still her wheaten garland wear

---

mutines . . . bilboes: Mutineers in the iron stocks on board ship.

bugs: Bugbears.

And stand a comma° 'tween their amities;   45
And many such like as's of great charge,—
That, on the view and know of these contents,
Without debatement further, more or less,
He should the bearers put to sudden death,
Not shriving-time allow'd.   50

HORATIO: How was this seal'd?

HAMLET: Why, even in that was heaven ordinant.
I had my father's signet in my purse,
Which was the model of that Danish seal:
Folded the writ up in form of the other;   55
Subscrib'd it; gav't the impression; plac'd it safely,
The changeling never known. Now, the next day
Was our sea-fight; and what to this was sequent
Thou know'st already.

HORATIO: So Guildenstern and Rosencrantz go to't.   60

HAMLET: Why, man, they did make love to this employment;
They are not near my conscience; their defeat
Does by their own insinuation° grow:
'Tis dangerous when the baser nature° comes
Between the pass and fell° incensed points   65
Of mighty opposites.

HORATIO: Why, what a king is this!

HAMLET: Does it not, think'st thee, stand me now upon,°
He that hath kill'd my king and whor'd my mother;
Popp'd in between the election and my hopes;   70
Thrown out his angle for my proper life,
And with such cozenage,°—is't not perfect conscience
To quit him with this arm? and is't not to be damn'd,
To let this canker of our nature come
In further evil?   75

HORATIO: It must be shortly known to him from England
What is the issue of the business there.

HAMLET: It will be short: the interim is mine;
And a man's life's no more than to say One.
But I am very sorry, good Horatio,   80
That to Laertes I forgot myself;

---

comma: Link.

insinuation: By their own "sticking their noses" into the business.

baser nature: Men of lower rank.

fell: Fierce.

Does . . . upon: I.e., "Don't you think it is my duty?"

cozenage: Deceit.

For by the image of my cause I see
The portraiture of his: I'll court his favors:
But, sure, the bravery° of his grief did put me
85   Into a towering passion.

HORATIO: Peace; who comes here?

Enter Osric.

OSRIC: Your lordship is right welcome back to Denmark.

HAMLET: I humbly thank you, sir.— Dost know this water-fly?

HORATIO: No, my good lord.

90   HAMLET: Thy state is the more gracious; for 'tis a vice to know him. He hath
much land, and fertile: let a beast be lord of beasts, and his crib shall stand
at the king's mess: 'tis a chough;° but, as I say, spacious in the possession
of dirt.

OSRIC: Sweet lord, if your lordship were at leisure, I should impart a thing to
95   you from his majesty.

HAMLET: I will receive it with all diligence of spirit. Put your bonnet to his
right use; 'tis for the head.

OSRIC: I thank your lordship, 'tis very hot.

HAMLET: No, believe me, 'tis very cold; the wind is northerly.

100   OSRIC: It is indifferent cold, my lord, indeed.

HAMLET: Methinks it is very sultry and hot for my complexion.

OSRIC: Exceedingly, my lord; it is very sultry,— as't were,— I cannot tell
how.— But, my lord, his majesty bade me signify to you that he has laid
a great wager on your head. Sir, this is the matter,—

105   HAMLET: I beseech you, remember,—

Hamlet moves him to put on his hat.

OSRIC: Nay, in good faith; for mine ease, in good faith. Sir, here is newly come
to court Laertes; believe me, an absolute gentleman, full of most excellent
differences, of very soft society and great showing: indeed, to speak feelingly
of him, he is the card or calendar of gentry, for you shall find in him the
110   continent of what part a gentleman would see.

HAMLET: Sir, his definement suffers no perdition in you;— though, I know, to
divide him inventorially would dizzy the arithmetic of memory, and yet but
yaw neither, in respect of his quick sail. But, in the verity of extolment,
I take him to be a soul of great article; and his infusion of such dearth° and
115   rareness as, to make true diction of him, his semblable is his mirror; and
who else would trace him, his umbrage,° nothing more.

---

bravery: Ostentation.

his crib . . . chough: He shall have his trough at the king's table: he is a chattering fool.

dearth: Rareness, or excellence.

umbrage: Shadow.

OSRIC: Your lordship speaks most infallibly of him.

HAMLET: The concernancy, sir? why do we wrap the gentleman in our more rawer breath?

OSRIC: Sir? 120

HORATIO: Is't not possible to understand in another tongue? You will do't sir, really.

HAMLET: What imports the nomination° of this gentleman?

OSRIC: Of Laertes?

HORATIO: His purse is empty already; all's golden words are spent. 125

HAMLET: Of him, sir.

OSRIC: I know, you are not ignorant,—

HAMLET: I would you did, sir; yet, in faith, if you did, it would not much approve me.°—Well, sir.

OSRIC: You are not ignorant of what excellence Laertes is,— 130

HAMLET: I dare not confess that, lest I should compare with him in excellence; but to know a man well were to know himself.

OSRIC: I mean, sir, for his weapon; but in the imputation laid on him by them, in his meed he's unfellowed.°

HAMLET: What's his weapon? 135

OSRIC: Rapier and dagger.

HAMLET: That's two of his weapons: but, well.

OSRIC: The king, sir, hath wagered with him six Barbary horses: against the which he has imponed,° as I take it, six French rapiers and poniards, with their assigns, as girdle, hangers, and so: three of the carriages, in faith, are 140 very dear to fancy, very responsive to the hilts, most delicate carriages, and of very liberal conceit.

HAMLET: What call you the carriages?

HORATIO: I knew you must be edified by the margent° ere you had done.

OSRIC: The carriages, sir, are the hangers. 145

HAMLET: The phrase would be more german to the matter if we could carry cannon by our sides: I would it might be hangers till then. But, on: six Barbary horses against six French swords, their assigns, and three liberal conceited carriages; that's the French bet against the Danish: why is this imponed, as you call it? 150

OSRIC: The king, sir, hath laid, that in a dozen passes between you and him he shall not exceed you three hits: he hath laid on twelve for nine; and it would come to immediate trial if your lordship would vouchsafe the answer.

HAMLET: How if I answer no?

---

nomination: Naming.

if you . . . approve me: If you, who are a fool, thought me not ignorant, that would not be particularly to my credit.

in . . . unfellowed: In his worth he has no equal.

imponed: Staked.

edified . . . margent: Informed by a note in the margin of your instructions.

155   OSRIC: I mean, my lord, the opposition of your person in trial.°
    HAMLET: Sir, I will walk here in the hall: if it please his majesty, it is the
        breathing time of day with me: let the foils be brought, the gentleman
        willing, and the king hold his purpose, I will win for him if I can; if not,
        I will gain nothing but my shame and the odd hits.
160   OSRIC: Shall I re-deliver you° e'en so?
    HAMLET: To this effect, sir; after what flourish your nature will.
    OSRIC: I commend my duty to your lordship.
    HAMLET: Yours, yours.

Exit Osric.

    He does well to commend it himself; there are no tongues else for's turn.
165   HORATIO: This lapwing runs away with the shell on his head.°
    HAMLET: He did comply with his dug before he sucked it.° Thus has he, —
        and many more of the same bevy, that I know the drossy age dotes on, —
        only got the tune of the time, and outward habit of encounter; a kind of
        yesty collection,° which carries them through and through the most
170   fanned and winnowed opinions; and do but blow them to their trial,
        the bubbles are out.

Enter a Lord.

    LORD: My lord, his majesty commended him to you by young Osric, who
        brings back to him that you attend him in the hall: he sends to know if
        your pleasure hold to play with Laertes, or that you will take longer time.
175   HAMLET: I am constant to my purposes; they follow the king's pleasure: if his
        fitness speaks, mine is ready; now or whensoever, provided I be so able
        as now.
    LORD: The king and queen and all are coming down.
    HAMLET: In happy time.
180   LORD: The queen desires you to use some gentle entertainment to Laertes
        before you fall to play.
    HAMLET: She well instructs me.

Exit Lord.

    HORATIO: You will lose this wager, my lord.
    HAMLET: I do not think so; since he went into France I have been in
185   continual practice: I shall win at the odds. But thou wouldst not think
        how ill all's here about my heart: but it is no matter.

---

the opposition . . . trial: The presence of your person as Laertes' opponent in the fencing contest.

re-deliver you: Carry back your answer.

This lapwing . . . head: This precocious fellow is like a lapwing that starts running when it is barely out of the shell.

He . . . sucked it: He paid compliments to his mother's breast before he sucked it.

yesty collection: Yeasty or frothy affair.

HORATIO: Nay, good my lord,—

HAMLET: It is but foolery; but it is such a kind of gain-giving° as would
perhaps trouble a woman.

HORATIO: If your mind dislike anything, obey it: I will forestall their repair   190
hither, and say you are not fit.

HAMLET: Not a whit, we defy augury: there's a special providence in the fall of
a sparrow. If it be now, 'tis not to come; if it be not to come, it will be now;
if it be not now, yet it will come: the readiness is all. Since no man has
aught of what he leaves, what is't to leave betimes?°   195

Enter King, Queen, Laertes, Lords, Osric, and Attendants with foils, &c.

KING: Come, Hamlet, come, and take this hand from me.

The King puts Laertes' hand into Hamlet's.

HAMLET: Give me your pardon, sir: I have done you wrong:
But pardon't, as you are a gentleman.
This presence knows, and you must needs have heard,
How I am punish'd with sore distraction.   200
What I have done,
That might your nature, honor, and exception
Roughly awake, I here proclaim was madness.
Was't Hamlet wrong'd Laertes? Never Hamlet:
If Hamlet from himself be ta'en away,   205
And when he's not himself does wrong Laertes,
Then Hamlet does it not, Hamlet denies it.
Who does it, then? His madness: if't be so,
Hamlet is of the faction that is wrong'd;
His madness is poor Hamlet's enemy.   210
Sir, in this audience,
Let my disclaiming from a purpos'd evil
Free me so far in your most generous thoughts
That I have shot mine arrow o'er the house
And hurt my brother.   215

LAERTES: I am satisfied in nature,
Whose motive, in this case, should stir me most
To my revenge: but in my terms of honor
I stand aloof; and will no reconcilement
Till by some elder masters of known honor   220
I have a voice and precedent of peace
To keep my name ungor'd. But till that time
I do receive your offer'd love like love,
And will not wrong it.

---

gain-giving: Misgiving.

what . . . betimes?: What does an early death matter?

225   HAMLET: I embrace it freely;
  And will this brother's wager frankly play.°—
  Give us the foils; come on.
LAERTES: Come, one for me.
HAMLET: I'll be your foil, Laertes; in mine ignorance
230   Your skill shall, like a star in the darkest night,
  Stick fiery off indeed.
LAERTES: You mock me, sir.
HAMLET: No, by this hand.
KING: Give them the foils, young Osric.
235   Cousin Hamlet,
  You know the wager?
HAMLET: Very well, my lord;
  Your grace hath laid the odds o' the weaker side.
KING: I do not fear it; I have seen you both;
240   But since he's better'd, we have therefore odds.
LAERTES: This is too heavy, let me see another.
HAMLET: This likes me well. These foils have all a length?

They prepare to play.

OSRIC: Ay, my good lord.
KING: Set me the stoups of wine upon that table,—
245   If Hamlet give the first or second hit,
  Or quit in answer of the third exchange,
  Let all the battlements their ordnance fire;
  The king shall drink to Hamlet's better breath;
  And in the cup an union° shall he throw,
250   Richer than that which four successive kings
  In Denmark's crown have worn. Give me the cups;
  And let the kettle° to the trumpet speak,
  The trumpet to the cannoneer without,
  The cannons to the heavens, the heavens to earth,
255   *Now the king drinks to Hamlet.* — Come, begin;—
  And you, the judges, bear a wary eye.
HAMLET: Come on, sir.
LAERTES: Come, my lord.

They play.

HAMLET: One.
260   LAERTES: No.
HAMLET: Judgment.

---

frankly play: Fence with a heart free from resentment.

an union: A pearl.

kettle: Kettledrum.

OSRIC: A hit, a very palpable hit.
LAERTES: Well; — again.
KING: Stay, give me a drink. — Hamlet, this pearl is thine;
    Here's to thy health. —   265

Trumpets sound, and cannon shot off within.

    Give him the cup.
HAMLET: I'll play this bout first; set it by awhile. —
    Come. — Another hit; what say you?

They play.

LAERTES: A touch, a touch, I do confess.
KING: Our son shall win.   270
QUEEN: He's fat, and scant of breath. —
    Here, Hamlet, take my napkin, rub thy brows:
    The queen carouses to thy fortune, Hamlet.
HAMLET: Good madam!
KING: Gertrude, do not drink.   275
QUEEN: I will, my lord; I pray you, pardon me.
KING: [*Aside*] It is the poison'd cup; it is too late.
HAMLET: I dare not drink yet, madam; by and by.
QUEEN: Come, let me wipe thy face.
LAERTES: My lord, I'll hit him now.   280
KING: I do not think't.
LAERTES: [*Aside*] And yet 'tis almost 'gainst my conscience.
HAMLET: Come, for the third, Laertes: you but dally;
    I pray you, pass with your best violence:
    I am afeard you make a wanton of me.   285
LAERTES: Say you so? come on.

They play.

OSRIC: Nothing, neither way.
LAERTES: Have at you now!

Laertes wounds Hamlet; then, in scuffling, they change rapiers, and Hamlet wounds Laertes.

KING: Part them; they are incens'd.
HAMLET: Nay, come, again.   290

The Queen falls.

OSRIC: Look to the queen there, ho!
HORATIO: They bleed on both sides. — How is it, my lord?
OSRIC: How is't, Laertes?
LAERTES: Why, as a woodcock to my own springe, Osric;
    I am justly kill'd with mine own treachery.   295
HAMLET: How does the queen?

KING: She swoons to see them bleed.

QUEEN: No, no, the drink, the drink,— O my dear Hamlet,—
  The drink, the drink!— I am poison'd. [*Dies.*]

300 HAMLET: O villainy!— Ho! let the door be lock'd:
  Treachery! seek it out.

Laertes falls.

LAERTES: It is here, Hamlet: Hamlet, thou art slain;
  No medicine in the world can do thee good;
  In thee there is not half an hour of life;
305 The treacherous instrument is in thy hand,
  Unbated and envenom'd: the foul practice
  Hath turn'd itself on me; lo, here I lie,
  Never to rise again: thy mother's poison'd:
  I can no more:— the king, the king's to blame.

310 HAMLET: The point envenom'd too!—
  Then venom to thy work. [*Stabs the King.*]

OSRIC and LORDS: Treason! treason!

KING: O, yet defend me, friends; I am but hurt.

HAMLET: Here, thou incestuous, murderous, damned Dane,
315 Drink off this potion.— Is thy union here?
  Follow my mother.

King dies.

LAERTES: He is justly serv'd;
  It is a poison temper'd by himself.—
  Exchange forgiveness with me, noble Hamlet:
320 Mine and my father's death come not upon thee,
  Nor thine on me! [*Dies.*]

HAMLET: Heaven make thee free of it! I follow thee.—
  I am dead, Horatio.—Wretched queen, adieu!—
  You that look pale and tremble at this chance,
325 That art but mutes or audience to this act,
  Had I but time,— as this fell sergeant, death,
  Is strict in his arrest,— O, I could tell you,—
  But let it be.— Horatio, I am dead;
  Thou liv'st; report me and my cause aright
330 To the unsatisfied.°

HORATIO: Never believe it:
  I am more an antique Roman than a Dane,—
  Here's yet some liquor left.

HAMLET: As thou'rt a man,
335 Give me the cup; let go; by heaven, I'll have't.—
  O good Horatio, what a wounded name,

---

the unsatisfied: The uninformed.

Things standing thus unknown, shall live behind me!
If thou didst ever hold me in thy heart,
Absent thee from felicity awhile,
And in this harsh world draw thy breath in pain,   340
To tell my story.—

March afar off, and shot within.

                                What warlike noise is this?
OSRIC: Young Fortinbras, with conquest come from Poland,
    To the ambassadors of England gives
    This warlike volley.   345
HAMLET: O, I die, Horatio;
    The potent poison quite o'er-crows my spirit:
    I cannot live to hear the news from England;
    But I do prophesy the election lights
    On Fortinbras: he has my dying voice;   350
    So tell him, with the occurrents, more and less,
    Which have solicited. °— The rest is silence. [*Dies.*]
HORATIO: Now cracks a noble heart.— Good-night, sweet prince,
    And flights of angels sing thee to thy rest!
    Why does the drum come hither?   355

March within. Enter Fortinbras, the English Ambassadors, and others.

FORTINBRAS: Where is this sight?
HORATIO: What is it you would see?
    If aught of woe or wonder, cease your search.
FORTINBRAS: This quarry cries on havoc.°— O proud death,
    What feast is toward in thine eternal cell,   360
    That thou so many princes at a shot
    So bloodily hast struck?
1ST AMBASSADOR: The sight is dismal;
    And our affairs from England come too late:
    The ears are senseless that should give us hearing,   365
    To tell him his commandment is fulfill'd,
    That Rosencrantz and Guildenstern are dead:
    Where should we have our thanks?
HORATIO: Not from his mouth,
    Had it the ability of life to thank you: 370
    He never gave commandment for their death.
    But since, so jump° upon this bloody question,
    You from the Polack wars, and you from England,

So tell him . . . solicited: So tell him, together with the events, more or less, that have brought on this tragic affair.

This quarry . . . havoc: This collection of dead bodies cries out havoc.

so jump: So opportunely.

375

Are here arriv'd, give order that these bodies
High on a stage be placed to the view;
And let me speak to the yet unknowing world
How these things came about: so shall you hear
Of carnal, bloody, and unnatural acts;

380

Of accidental judgments, casual slaughters;
Of deaths put on by cunning and forc'd cause;
And, in this upshot, purposes mistook
Fall'n on the inventors' heads: all this can I
Truly deliver.

FORTINBRAS: Let us haste to hear it,

385

And call the noblest to the audience.
For me, with sorrow I embrace my fortune:
I have some rights of memory in this kingdom,°
Which now to claim my vantage doth invite me.

HORATIO: Of that I shall have also cause to speak,

390

And from his mouth whose voice will draw on more:
But let this same be presently perform'd,
Even while men's minds are wild: lest more mischance
On plots and errors happen.

FORTINBRAS: Let four captains

395

Bear Hamlet like a soldier to the stage;
For he was likely, had he been put on,°
To have prov'd most royally: and, for his passage,
The soldier's music and the rites of war
Speak loudly for him.—

400

Take up the bodies.— Such a sight as this
Becomes the field, but here shows much amiss.
Go, bid the soldiers shoot.

A dead march

Exeunt, bearing off the dead bodies: after which a peal of ordnance is shot off.

Reading and Reacting

1. What are Hamlet's most notable character traits?

2. Review each of Hamlet's **soliloquies.** Judging from his own words, do you believe his assessments of his own problems are accurate? Are his assessments of other characters' behavior accurate? Point to examples from the soliloquies that reveal Hamlet's insight or lack of insight.

3. Is Hamlet a sympathetic character? Where (if anywhere) do you find yourself growing impatient with him or disagreeing with him?

I have . . . kingdom: I have some unforgotten rights to this kingdom.

put on: Tested by succession to the throne.

4. What is the emotional impact on the audience of having Hamlet behave so cruelly toward Ophelia after his "To be or not to be" soliloquy (act 3, scene 1)?

5. What do other characters' comments reveal about Hamlet's character *before* the key events in the play begin to unfold? For example, in what way has he changed since he returned to the castle and found out about his father's death?

6. Claudius is presented as the play's villain. Is he all bad, or does he have any redeeming qualities?

7. List those in the play whom you believe to be **flat characters.** Why do you characterize each individual in this way? What does each of these flat characters contribute to the play?

8. Is Fortinbras simply Hamlet's **foil,** or does he have another essential role? Explain.

9. Each of the play's major characters has one or more character flaws that influence plot development. What specific weaknesses do you see in Claudius, Gertrude, Polonius, Laertes, Ophelia, and Hamlet himself? Through what words or actions is each weakness revealed? How does each weakness contribute to the play's action?

10. Why doesn't Hamlet kill Claudius as soon as the Ghost tells him what Claudius did? Why doesn't he kill him when he has the chance in act 3? What words or actions reveal his motivation for hesitating? What are the implications of his failure to act?

11. Why does Hamlet pretend to be insane? Why does he arrange for the "play within a play" to be performed? Why does he agree to the duel with Laertes? In each case, what words or actions reveal his motivation to the audience?

12. Is the Ghost an essential character, or could the information he reveals and the reactions he arouses come from another source? Explain. (Keep in mind that the ghost is a **stock character** in Elizabethan revenge tragedies.)

13. Describe Hamlet's relationship with his mother. Do you consider this a typical mother/son relationship? Why or why not?

14. In the graveyard scene (act 5, scene 1), the gravediggers make many ironic comments. In what way do these comments shed light on the events taking place in the play?

15. **Journal Entry** Both Gertrude and Ophelia are usually seen as weak women, firmly under the influence of the men in their lives. Do you think this characterization of them as passive and dependent is accurate? Explain.

16. **Critical Perspective** In *The Meaning of Shakespeare,* (1951), Harold Goddard reads *Hamlet* as, in part, a play about war, with a grimly ironic conclusion in that "all the Elder Hamlet's conquests have been for nothing — for less than nothing. Fortinbras, his former enemy, is to inherit the kingdom! Such is the end to which the Ghost's thirst for vengeance has led." He goes on to describe the play's ending:

> The dead Hamlet is borne out "like a soldier" and the last rites over his body are to be the rites of war. The final word of the text is "shoot." The last sounds we

hear are a dead march and the reverberations of ordnance being shot off. The end crowns the whole. The sarcasm of fate could go no further. Hamlet, who aspired to nobler things, is treated at death as if he were the mere image of his father: a warrior. Shakespeare knew what he was about in making the conclusion of his play martial. Its theme has been war as well as revenge. It is the story of the Minotaur over again, of that monster who from the beginning of human strife has exacted his annual tribute of youth. No sacrifice ever offered to it was more precious than Hamlet. But he was not the last.

If ever a play seems expressly written for the twentieth century, it is *Hamlet*. It should be unnecessary to underscore its pertinence to an age in which, twice within three decades, the older generation has called on the younger generation to settle a quarrel with the making of which it had nothing to do. So taken, *Hamlet* is an allegory of our time. Imagination or violence, Shakespeare seems to say, there is no other alternative.

Can you find other evidence in the play to support the idea that one of its major themes is war? Do you agree that the play is "an allegory of our time"?

Related Works: "The Cask of Amontillado" (p. 217), "Young Goodman Brown" (p. 292), *Oedipus the King* (p. 1271), *The Glass Menagerie* (p. 1416)

ARTHUR MILLER (1915–   ) was born in New York City and graduated in 1938 from the University of Michigan, where he began to write plays. His first big success, which won the New York Drama Critics Circle Award, was *All My Sons* (1947), about a man who has knowingly manufactured faulty airplane parts. Other significant plays are *The Crucible* (1953), based on the Salem witch trials of 1692, which Miller saw as parallel to contemporary investigations by the House Un-American Activities Committee; *A View from the Bridge* (1955); and *After the Fall* (1955). He was married for a time to actress Marilyn Monroe and wrote the screenplay for her movie *The Misfits* (1961). His play *The Last Yankee* opened off-Broadway in 1993, *Broken Glass* was both published and performed in 1994, and *Mr. Peter's Connection* was published in 1998. In 2001, Miller was awarded an NEH fellowship and the John H. Finney Award for Exemplary Service to New York City.

Death of a Salesman is his most significant work, a play that quickly became an American classic. Miller has said he is very much influenced by the structure of Greek tragedy, and in his play he shows that a tragedy can also be the story of an ordinary person told in realistic terms. The play is frequently produced, and Miller continues to be involved in new productions because, as he says, with each production he learns to see the play differently. When he directed *Death of a Salesman* in China in 1983, audiences perceived it as primarily the story of the mother. In the 1983, Broadway production, Miller himself realized "at a certain point that it was far more the story of Biff, the son, than it was of Willy Loman, the salesman of the title."

Cultural Context: At the time *Death of a Salesman* was written, in 1949, the United States was experiencing the largest economic expansion in its history. Businesses were consolidating, and large, impersonal corporations were replacing the mom-and-pop stores that once dominated the American business scene. At the same time, the first

Levittown, completed in 1946, anticipated the mass movement of population from older urban neighborhoods to the suburbs. Both these trends are evident in Miller's play. In 1999, *Death of a Salesman* was revived on Broadway and won a Tony Award for Best Revival of a Play.

ARTHUR MILLER

Death of a Salesman

CERTAIN PRIVATE CONVERSATIONS IN TWO ACTS
AND A REQUIEM (1949)

CHARACTERS

Willy Loman	**The Woman**
Linda, *his wife*	**Howard Wagner**
Biff } *his sons*	**Jenny**
Happy }	**Stanley**
Uncle Ben	**Miss Forsythe**
Charley	**Letta**
Bernard	

The action takes place in Willy Loman's house and yard and in various places he visits in the New York and Boston of today.

Throughout the play, in the stage directions, left and right mean stage left and stage right.

ACT I

A melody is heard, played upon a flute. It is small and fine, telling of grass and trees and the horizon. The curtain rises.

Before us is the Salesman's house. We are aware of towering, angular shapes behind it, surrounding it on all sides. Only the blue light of the sky falls upon the house and forestage; the surrounding area shows an angry glow of orange. As more light appears, we see a solid vault of apartment houses around the small, fragile-seeming home. An air of the dream clings to the place, a dream rising out of reality. The kitchen at center seems actual enough, for there is a kitchen table with three chairs, and a refrigerator. But no other fixtures are seen. At the back of the kitchen there is a draped entrance, which leads to the livingroom. To the right of the kitchen, on a level raised two feet, is a bedroom furnished only with a brass bedstead and a straight chair. On a shelf over the bed a silver athletic trophy stands. A window opens onto the apartment house at the side.

Behind the kitchen, on a level raised six and a half feet, is the boys' bedroom, at present barely visible. Two beds are dimly seen, and at the back of the room a dormer window. (This bedroom is above the unseen livingroom.) At the left a stairway curves up to it from the kitchen.

The entire setting is wholly or, in some places, partially transparent. The roofline of the house is one-dimensional; under and over it we see the apartment buildings. Before the house lies an apron, curving beyond the forestage into the orchestra. This forward area serves as the back yard as well as the locale of all Willy's imaginings and of his city scenes. Whenever the action is in the present the actors observe the imaginary wall-lines, entering the house only through the door at the left. But in the scenes of the past these boundaries are broken, and characters enter or leave a room by stepping "through" a wall onto the forestage.

From the right, Willy Loman, the Salesman, enters, carrying two large sample cases. The flute plays on. He hears but is not aware of it. He is past sixty years of age, dressed quietly. Even as he crosses the stage to the doorway of the house, his exhaustion is apparent. He unlocks the door, comes into the kitchen, and thankfully lets his burden down, feeling the soreness of his palms. A word-sigh escapes his lips — it might be "Oh, boy, oh, boy." He closes the door, then carries his cases out into the livingroom, through the draped kitchen doorway.

Linda, his wife, has stirred in her bed at the right. She gets out and puts on a robe, listening. Most often jovial, she has developed an iron repression of her exceptions to Willy's behavior — she more than loves him, she admires him, as though his mercurial nature, his temper, his massive dreams and little cruelties, served her only as sharp reminders of the turbulent longings within him, longings which she shares but lacks the temperament to utter and follow to their end.

LINDA: *(hearing Willy outside the bedroom, calls with some trepidation)* Willy!
WILLY: It's all right. I came back.
LINDA: Why? What happened? *(Sight pause.)* Did something happen, Willy?
WILLY: No, nothing happened.
5 LINDA: You didn't smash the car, did you?
WILLY: *(with casual irritation)* I said nothing happened. Didn't you hear me?
LINDA: Don't you feel well?
WILLY: I am tired to the death. *(The flute has faded away. He sits on the bed beside her, a little numb.)* I couldn't make it. I just couldn't make it, Linda.
LINDA: *(very carefully, delicately)* Where were you all day? You look terrible.
10 WILLY: I got as far as a little above Yonkers. I stopped for a cup of coffee. Maybe it was the coffee.
LINDA: What?
WILLY: *(after a pause)* I suddenly couldn't drive any more. The car kept going onto the shoulder, y'know?
LINDA: *(helpfully)* Oh. Maybe it was the steering again. I don't think Angelo knows the Studebaker.
WILLY: No, it's me, it's me. Suddenly I realize I'm goin' sixty miles an hour and I don't remember the last five minutes. I'm — I can't seem to — keep my mind to it.
15 LINDA: Maybe it's your glasses. You never went for your new glasses.
WILLY: No, I see everything. I came back ten miles an hour. It took me nearly four hours from Yonkers.
LINDA: *(resigned)* Well, you'll just have to take a rest, Willy, you can't continue this way.
WILLY: I just got back from Florida.
LINDA: But you didn't rest your mind. Your mind is overactive, and the mind is what counts, dear.

WILLY: I'll start out in the morning. Maybe I'll feel better in the morning. (*She* 20
is taking off his shoes.) These goddam arch supports are killing me.

LINDA: Take an aspirin. Should I get you an aspirin? It'll soothe you.

WILLY: (*with wonder*) I was driving along, you understand? And I was fine.
I was even observing the scenery. You can imagine, me looking at scenery,
on the road every week of my life. But it's so beautiful up there, Linda, the
trees are so thick, and the sun is warm. I opened the windshield and just let
the warm air bathe over me. And then all of a sudden I'm goin' off the
road! I'm tellin' ya, I absolutely forgot I was driving. If I'd've gone the other
way over the white line I might've killed somebody. So I went on again —
and five minutes later I'm dreamin' again, and I nearly — (*He presses two
fingers against his eyes.*) I have such thoughts, I have such strange thoughts.

LINDA: Willy, dear. Talk to them again. There's no reason why you can't work
in New York.

WILLY: They don't need me in New York. I'm the New England man. I'm vital
in New England.

LINDA: But you're sixty years old. They can't expect you to keep traveling 25
every week.

WILLY: I'll have to send a wire to Portland. I'm supposed to see Brown and
Morrison tomorrow morning at ten o'clock to show the line. Goddammit,
I could sell them! (*He starts putting on his jacket.*)

LINDA: (*taking the jacket from him*) Why don't you go down to the place tomorrow and tell Howard you've simply got to work in New York? You're too
accommodating, dear.

WILLY: If old man Wagner was alive I'd a been in charge of New York now!
That man was a prince, he was a masterful man. But that boy of his, that
Howard, he don't appreciate. When I went north the first time, the Wagner
Company didn't know where New England was!

LINDA: Why don't you tell those things to Howard, dear?

WILLY: (*encouraged*) I will, I definitely will. Is there any cheese? 30

LINDA: I'll make you a sandwich.

WILLY: No, go to sleep. I'll take some milk. I'll be up right away. The boys in?

LINDA: They're sleeping. Happy took Biff on a date tonight.

WILLY: (*interested*) That so?

LINDA: It was so nice to see them shaving together, one behind the other, in 35
the bathroom. And going out together. You notice? The whole house smells
of shaving lotion.

WILLY: Figure it out. Work a lifetime to pay off a house. You finally own it, and
there's nobody to live in it.

LINDA: Well, dear, life is a casting off. It's always that way.

WILLY: No, no, some people — some people accomplish something. Did Biff
say anything after I went this morning?

LINDA: You shouldn't have criticized him, Willy, especially after he just got off
the train. You mustn't lose your temper with him.

WILLY: When the hell did I lose my temper? I simply asked him if he was 40
making any money. Is that a criticism?

LINDA: But, dear, how could he make any money?

WILLY: (*worried and angered*) There's such an undercurrent in him. He became a moody man. Did he apologize when I left this morning?

LINDA: He was crestfallen, Willy. You know how he admires you. I think if he finds himself, then you'll both be happier and not fight any more.

WILLY: How can he find himself on a farm? Is that a life? A farmhand? In the beginning, when he was young, I thought, well, a young man, it's good for him to tramp around, take a lot of different jobs. But it's more than ten years now and he has yet to make thirty-five dollars a week!

45 LINDA: He's finding himself, Willy.

WILLY: Not finding yourself at the age of thirty-four is a disgrace!

LINDA: Shh!

WILLY: The trouble is he's lazy, goddammit!

LINDA: Willy, please!

50 WILLY: Biff is a lazy bum!

LINDA: They're sleeping. Get something to eat. Go on down.

WILLY: Why did he come home? I would like to know what brought him home.

LINDA: I don't know. I think he's still lost, Willy. I think he's very lost.

WILLY: Biff Loman is lost. In the greatest country in the world a young man with such — personal attractiveness, gets lost. And such a hard worker. There's one thing about Biff — he's not lazy.

55 LINDA: Never.

WILLY: (*with pity and resolve*) I'll see him in the morning; I'll have a nice talk with him. I'll get him a job selling. He could be big in no time. My God! Remember how they used to follow him around in high school? When he smiled at one of them their faces lit up. When he walked down the street . . . (*He loses himself in reminiscences.*)

LINDA: (*trying to bring him out of it*) Willy, dear, I got a new kind of American-type cheese today. It's whipped.

WILLY: Why do you get American when I like Swiss?

LINDA: I just thought you'd like a change —

60 WILLY: I don't want a change! I want Swiss cheese. Why am I always being contradicted?

LINDA: (*with a covering laugh*) I thought it would be a surprise.

WILLY: Why don't you open a window in here, for God's sake?

LINDA: (*with infinite patience*) They're all open, dear.

WILLY: The way they boxed us in here. Bricks and windows, windows and bricks.

65 LINDA: We should've bought the land next door.

WILLY: The street is lined with cars. There's not a breath of fresh air in the neighborhood. The grass don't grow any more, you can't raise a carrot in the back yard. They should've had a law against apartment houses. Remember those two beautiful elm trees out there? When I and Biff hung the swing between them?

LINDA: Yeah, like being a million miles from the city.

WILLY: They should've arrested the builder for cutting those down. They massacred the neighborhood. (*Lost.*) More and more I think of those days, Linda. This time of year it was lilac and wisteria. And then the peonies would come out, and the daffodils. What fragrance in this room!

LINDA: Well, after all, people had to move somewhere.

WILLY: No, there's more people now.   70

LINDA: I don't think there's more people. I think —

WILLY: There's more people! That's what's ruining this country! Population is getting out of control. The competition is maddening! Smell the stink from that apartment house! And another on the other side . . . How can they whip cheese?

On Willy's last line, Biff and Happy raise themselves up in their beds, listening.

LINDA: Go down, try it. And be quiet.

WILLY: (*turning to Linda, guiltily*) You're not worried about me, are you, sweetheart?

BIFF: What's the matter?   75

HAPPY: Listen!

LINDA: You've got too much on the ball to worry about.

WILLY: You're my foundation and my support, Linda.

LINDA: Just try to relax, dear. You make mountains out of molehills.

WILLY: I won't fight with him any more. If he wants to go back to Texas, let   80
him go.

LINDA: He'll find his way.

WILLY: Sure. Certain men just don't get started till later in life. Like Thomas Edison, I think. Or B. F. Goodrich. One of them was deaf. (*He starts for the bedroom doorway.*) I'll put my money on Biff.

LINDA: And Willy — if it's warm Sunday we'll drive in the country. And we'll open the windshield, and take lunch.

WILLY: No, the windshields don't open on the new cars.

LINDA: But you opened it today.   85

WILLY: Me? I didn't. (*He stops.*) Now isn't that peculiar! Isn't that remarkable —
(*He breaks off in amazement and fright as the flute is heard distantly.*)

LINDA: What, darling?

WILLY: That is the most remarkable thing.

LINDA: What, dear?

WILLY: I was thinking of the Chevvy. (*Slight pause.*) Nineteen twenty-eight . . .   90
when I had that red Chevvy — (*Breaks off.*) That funny? I coulda sworn
I was driving that Chevvy today.

LINDA: Well, that's nothing. Something must've reminded you.

WILLY: Remarkable. Ts. Remember those days? The way Biff used to simonize that car? The dealer refused to believe there was eighty thousand miles on it. (*He shakes his head.*) Heh! (*To Linda.*) Close your eyes, I'll be right up.
(*He walks out of the bedroom.*)

Jo Mielziner's celebrated set for the premiere production of Arthur Miller's *Death of a Salesman,* showing the cut-away house and the downstage playing area.

HAPPY: *(to Biff)* Jesus, maybe he smashed up the car again!

LINDA: *(calling after Willy)* Be careful on the stairs, dear! The cheese is on the middle shelf! *(She turns, goes over to the bed, takes his jacket, and goes out of the bedroom.)*

Light has risen on the boys' room. Unseen, Willy is heard talking to himself, "Eighty thousand miles," and a little laugh. Biff gets out of bed, comes downstage a bit, and stands attentively. Biff is two years older than his brother Happy, well built, but in these days bears a worn air and seems less self-assured. He has succeeded less, and his dreams are stronger and less acceptable than Happy's. Happy is tall, powerfully made. Sexuality is like a visible color on him, or a scent that many women have discovered. He, like his brother, is lost, but in a different way, for he has never allowed himself to turn his face toward defeat and is thus more confused and hard-skinned, although seemingly more content.

95 **HAPPY:** *(getting out of bed)* He's going to get his license taken away if he keeps that up. I'm getting nervous about him, y'know, Biff?

BIFF: His eyes are going.

HAPPY: No, I've driven with him. He sees all right. He just doesn't keep his mind on it. I drove into the city with him last week. He stops at a green light and then it turns red and he goes. *(He laughs.)*

BIFF: Maybe he's color-blind.

HAPPY: Pop? Why he's got the finest eye for color in the business. You know that.

100 **BIFF:** *(sitting down on his bed)* I'm going to sleep.

HAPPY: You're not still sour on Dad, are you, Biff?

BIFF: He's all right, I guess.

WILLY: *(underneath them, in the livingroom)* Yes, sir, eighty thousand miles — eighty-two thousand!

BIFF: You smoking?

HAPPY: *(holding out a pack of cigarettes)* Want one? 105

BIFF: *(taking a cigarette)* I can never sleep when I smell it.

WILLY: What a simonizing job, heh!

HAPPY: *(with deep sentiment)* Funny, Biff, y'know? Us sleeping in here again? The old beds. *(He pats his bed affectionately.)* All the talk that went across those two beds, huh? Our whole lives.

BIFF: Yeah. Lotta dreams and plans.

HAPPY: *(with a deep and masculine laugh)* About five hundred women would 110 like to know what was said in this room.

They share a soft laugh.

BIFF: Remember that big Betsy something — what the hell was her name — over on Bushwick Avenue?

HAPPY: *(combing his hair)* With the collie dog!

BIFF: That's the one. I got you in there, remember?

HAPPY: Yeah, that was my first time — I think. Boy, there was a pig! *(They laugh, almost crudely.)* You taught me everything I know about women. Don't forget that.

BIFF: I bet you forgot how bashful you used to be. Especially with girls. 115

HAPPY: Oh, I still am, Biff.

BIFF: Oh, go on.

HAPPY: I just control it, that's all. I think I got less bashful and you got more so. What happened, Biff? Where's the old humor, the old confidence? *(He shakes Biff's knee. Biff gets up and moves restlessly about the room.)* What's the matter?

BIFF: Why does Dad mock me all the time?

HAPPY: He's not mocking you, he — 120

BIFF: Everything I say there's a twist of mockery on his face. I can't get near him.

HAPPY: He just wants you to make good, that's all. I wanted to talk to you about Dad for a long time, Biff. Something's — happening to him. He — talks to himself.

BIFF: I noticed that this morning. But he always mumbled.

HAPPY: But not so noticeable. It got so embarrassing I sent him to Florida. And you know something? Most of the time he's talking to you.

BIFF: What's he say about me? 125

HAPPY: I can't make it out.

BIFF: What's he say about me?

HAPPY: I think the fact that you're not settled, that you're still kind of up in the air . . .

BIFF: There's one or two other things depressing him, Happy.

HAPPY: What do you mean? 130

BIFF: Never mind. Just don't lay it all to me.

HAPPY: But I think if you just got started — I mean — is there any future for you out there?

BIFF: I tell ya, Hap, I don't know what the future is. I don't know — what I'm supposed to want.

HAPPY: What do you mean?

135 **BIFF:** Well, I spent six or seven years after high school trying to work myself up. Shipping clerk, salesman, business of one kind or another. And it's a measly manner of existence. To get on that subway on the hot mornings in summer. To devote your whole life to keeping stock, or making phone calls, or selling or buying. To suffer fifty weeks of the year for the sake of a two-week vacation, when all you really desire is to be outdoors, with your shirt off. And always to have to get ahead of the next fella. And still — that's how you build a future.

HAPPY: Well, you really enjoy it on a farm? Are you content out there?

BIFF: *(with rising agitation)* Hap, I've had twenty or thirty different kinds of jobs since I left home before the war, and it always turns out the same. I just realized it lately. In Nebraska when I herded cattle, and the Dakotas, and Arizona, and now in Texas. It's why I came home now, I guess, because I realized it. This farm I work on, it's spring there now, see? And they've got about fifteen new colts. There's nothing more inspiring or — beautiful than the sight of a mare and a new colt. And it's cool there now, see? Texas is cool now, and it's spring. And whenever spring comes to where I am, I suddenly get the feeling, my God, I'm not gettin' anywhere! What the hell am I doing, playing around with horses, twenty-eight dollars a week! I'm thirty-four years old, I oughta be makin' my future. That's when I come running home. And now, I get here, and I don't know what to do with myself. *(After a pause.)* I've always made a point of not wasting my life, and every time I come back here I know that all I've done is to waste my life.

HAPPY: You're a poet, you know that, Biff? You're a — you're an idealist!

BIFF: No, I'm mixed up very bad. Maybe I oughta get married. Maybe I oughta get stuck into something. Maybe that's my trouble. I'm like a boy. I'm not married, I'm not in business, I just — I'm like a boy. Are you content, Hap? You're a success, aren't you? Are you content?

140 **HAPPY:** Hell, no!

BIFF: Why? You're making money, aren't you?

HAPPY: *(moving about with energy, expressiveness)* All I can do now is wait for the merchandise manager to die. And suppose I get to be merchandise manager? He's a good friend of mine, and he just built a terrific estate on Long Island. And he lived there about two months and sold it, and now he's building another one. He can't enjoy it once it's finished. And I know that's just what I would do. I don't know what the hell I'm workin' for. Sometimes I sit in my apartment — all alone. And I think of the rent I'm paying. And it's crazy. But then, it's what I always wanted. My own apartment, a car, and plenty of women. And still, goddammit, I'm lonely.

BIFF: *(with enthusiasm)* Listen, why don't you come out West with me?

HAPPY: You and I, heh?

145 **BIFF:** Sure, maybe we could buy a ranch. Raise cattle, use our muscles. Men built like we are should be working out in the open.

HAPPY: *(avidly)* The Loman Brothers, heh?

BIFF: *(with vast affection)* Sure, we'd be known all over the counties!

HAPPY: *(enthralled)* That's what I dream about, Biff. Sometimes I want to just rip my clothes off in the middle of the store and outbox that goddam merchandise manager. I mean I can outbox, outrun, and outlift anybody in that store, and I have to take orders from those common, petty sons-of-bitches till I can't stand it any more.

BIFF: I'm telln' you, kid, if you were with me I'd be happy out there.

HAPPY: *(enthused)* See, Biff, everybody around me is so false that I'm constantly lowering my ideals . . .   150

BIFF: Baby, together we'd stand up for one another, we'd have someone to trust.

HAPPY: If I were around you —

BIFF: Hap, the trouble is we weren't brought up to grub for money. I don't know how to do it.

HAPPY: Neither can I!

BIFF: Then let's go!   155

HAPPY: The only thing is — what can you make out there?

BIFF: But look at your friend. Builds an estate and then hasn't the peace of mind to live in it.

HAPPY: Yeah, but when he walks into the store the waves part in front of him. That's fifty-two thousand dollars a year coming through the revolving door, and I got more in my pinky finger than he's got in his head.

BIFF: Yeah, but you just said —

HAPPY: I gotta show some of those pompous, self-important executives over   160
there that Hap Loman can make the grade. I want to walk into the store the way he walks in. Then I'll go with you, Biff. We'll be together yet, I swear. But take those two we had tonight. Now weren't they gorgeous creatures?

BIFF: Yeah, yeah, most gorgeous I've had in years.

HAPPY: I get that any time I want, Biff. Whenever I feel disgusted. The only trouble is, it gets like bowling or something. I just keep knockin' them over and it doesn't mean anything. You still run around a lot?

BIFF: Naa. I'd like to find a girl — steady, somebody with substance.

HAPPY: That's what I long for.

BIFF: Go on! You'd never come home.   165

HAPPY: I would! Somebody with character, with resistance! Like Mom, y'know? You're gonna call me a bastard when I tell you this. That girl Charlotte I was with tonight is engaged to be married in five weeks. *(He tries on his new hat.)*

BIFF: No kiddin'!

HAPPY: Sure, the guy's in line for the vice-presidency of the store. I don't know what gets into me, maybe I just have an overdeveloped sense of competition or something, but I went and ruined her, and furthermore I can't get rid of her. And he's the third executive I've done that to. Isn't that a crummy characteristic? And to top it all, I go to their weddings! *(Indignantly, but laughing.)* Like I'm not supposed to take bribes. Manufacturers offer me a hundred-dollar bill now and then to throw an order their way. You know how honest I am, but it's like this girl, see. I hate myself for it. Because I don't want the girl, and, still, I take it and — I love it!

BIFF: Let's go to sleep.

170 **HAPPY:** I guess we didn't settle anything, heh?

BIFF: I just got one idea that I think I'm going to try.

HAPPY: What's that?

BIFF: Remember Bill Oliver?

HAPPY: Sure, Oliver is very big now. You want to work for him again?

175 **BIFF:** No, but when I quit he said something to me. He put his arm on my shoulder, and he said, "Biff, if you ever need anything, come to me."

HAPPY: I remember that. That sounds good.

BIFF: I think I'll go to see him. If I could get ten thousand or even seven or eight thousand dollars I could buy a beautiful ranch.

HAPPY: I bet he'd back you. 'Cause he thought highly of you, Biff, I mean, they all do. You're well liked, Biff. That's why I say to come back here, and we both have the apartment. And I'm telln' you, Biff, any babe you want . . .

BIFF: No, with a ranch I could do the work I like and still be something. I just wonder though. I wonder if Oliver still thinks I stole that carton of basketballs.

180 **HAPPY:** Oh, he probably forgot that long ago. It's almost ten years. You're too sensitive. Anyway, he didn't really fire you.

BIFF: Well, I think he was going to. I think that's why I quit. I was never sure whether he knew or not. I know he thought the world of me, though. I was the only one he'd let lock up the place.

WILLY: (*below*) You gonna wash the engine, Biff?

HAPPY: Shh!

Biff looks at Happy, who is gazing down, listening. Willy is mumbling in the parlor.

HAPPY: You hear that?

They listen. Willy laughs warmly.

185 **BIFF:** (*growing angry*) Doesn't he know Mom can hear that?

WILLY: Don't get your sweater dirty, Biff!

A look of pain crosses Biff's face.

HAPPY: Isn't that terrible? Don't leave again, will you? You'll find a job here. You gotta stick around. I don't know what to do about him, it's getting embarrassing.

WILLY: What a simonizing job!

BIFF: Mom's hearing that!

190 **WILLY:** No kiddin', Biff, you got a date? Wonderful!

HAPPY: Go on to sleep. But talk to him in the morning, will you?

BIFF: (*reluctantly getting into bed*) With her in the house. Brother!

HAPPY: (*getting into bed*) I wish you'd have a good talk with him.

The light on their room begins to fade.

BIFF: (*to himself in bed*) That selfish, stupid . . .

195 **HAPPY:** Sh . . . Sleep, Biff.

Their light is out. Well before they have finished speaking, Willy's form is dimly seen below in the darkened kitchen. He opens the refrigerator, searches in there, and takes out a bottle of milk. The apartment houses are fading out, and the entire house and surroundings become covered with leaves. Music insinuates itself as the leaves appear.

WILLY: Just wanna be careful with those girls, Biff, that's all. Don't make any promises. No promises of any kind. Because a girl, y'know, they always believe what you tell'em, and you're very young, Biff, you're too young to be talking seriously to girls.

Light rises on the kitchen. Willy, talking, shuts the refrigerator door and comes downstage to the kitchen table. He pours milk into a glass. He is totally immersed in himself, smiling faintly.

WILLY: Too young entirely, Biff. You want to watch your schooling first. Then when you're all set, there'll be plenty of girls for a boy like you. (*He smiles broadly at a kitchen chair.*) That so? The girls pay for you? (*He laughs.*) Boy, you must really be makin' a hit.

Willy is gradually addressing — physically — a point offstage, speaking through the wall of the kitchen, and his voice has been rising in volume to that of a normal conversation.

WILLY: I been wondering why you polish the car so careful. Ha! Don't leave the hubcaps, boys. Get the chamois to the hubcaps. Happy, use newspaper on the windows, it's the easiest thing. Show him how to do it, Biff! You see, Happy? Pad it up, use it like a pad. That's it, that's it, good work. You're doin' all right, Hap. (*He pauses, then nods in approbation for a few seconds, then looks upward.*) Biff, first thing we gotta do when we get time is clip that big branch over the house. Afraid it's gonna fall in a storm and hit the roof. Tell you what. We get a rope and sling her around, and then we climb up there with a couple of saws and take her down. Soon as you finish the car, boys, I wanna see ya. I got a surprise for you, boys.

BIFF: (*offstage*) Whatta ya got, Dad?

WILLY: No, you finish first. Never leave a job till you're finished — remember   200
that. (*Looking toward the "big trees."*) Biff, up in Albany I saw a beautiful hammock. I think I'll buy it next trip, and we'll hang it right between those two elms. Wouldn't that be something? Just swingin' there under those branches. Boy, that would be . . .

Young Biff and Young Happy appear from the direction Willy was addressing. Happy carries rags and a pail of water. Biff, wearing a sweater with a block "S," carries a football.

BIFF: (*pointing in the direction of the car offstage*) How's that, Pop, professional?

WILLY: Terrific. Terrific job, boys. Good work, Biff.

HAPPY: Where's the surprise, Pop?

WILLY: In the back seat of the car.

HAPPY: Boy! (*He runs off.*)   205

BIFF: What is it, Dad? Tell me, what'd you buy?

WILLY: (*laughing, cuffs him*) Never mind, something I want you to have.

BIFF: (*turns and starts off*) What is it, Hap?

HAPPY: (*offstage*) It's a punching bag!

210 **BIFF:** Oh, Pop!
WILLY: It's got Gene Tunney's° signature on it!

Happy runs onstage with a punching bag.

BIFF: Gee, how'd you know we wanted a punching bag?
WILLY: Well, it's the finest thing for the timing.
HAPPY: *(lies down on his back and pedals with his feet)* I'm losing weight, you
   notice, Pop?
215 **WILLY:** *(to Happy)* Jumping rope is good too.
BIFF: Did you see the new football I got?
WILLY: *(examining the ball)* Where'd you get a new ball?
BIFF: The coach told me to practice my passing.
WILLY: That so? And he gave you the ball, heh?
220 **BIFF:** Well, I borrowed it from the locker room. *(He laughs confidentially.)*
WILLY: *(laughing with him at the theft)* I want you to return that.
HAPPY: I told you he wouldn't like it!
BIFF: *(angrily)* Well, I'm bringing it back!
WILLY: *(stopping the incipient argument, to Happy)* Sure, he's gotta practice with
   a regulation ball, doesn't he? *(To Biff.)* Coach'll probably congratulate you
   on your initiative!
225 **BIFF:** Oh, he keeps congratulating my initiative all the time, Pop.
WILLY: That's because he likes you. If somebody else took that ball there'd be
   an uproar. So what's the report, boys, what's the report?
BIFF: Where'd you go this time, Dad? Gee we were lonesome for you.
WILLY: *(pleased, puts an arm around each boy and they come down to the apron)*
   Lonesome, heh?
BIFF: Missed you every minute.
230 **WILLY:** Don't say? Tell you a secret, boys. Don't breathe it to a soul. Someday
   I'll have my own business, and I'll never have to leave home any more.
HAPPY: Like Uncle Charley, heh?
WILLY: Bigger than Uncle Charley! Because Charley is not — liked. He's liked,
   but he's not — well liked.
BIFF: Where'd you go this time, Dad?
WILLY: Well, I got on the road, and I went north to Providence. Met the Mayor.
235 **BIFF:** The Mayor of Providence!
WILLY: He was sitting in the hotel lobby.
BIFF: What'd he say?
WILLY: He said, "Morning!" And I said, "You've got a fine city here, Mayor."
   And then he had coffee with me. And then I went to Waterbury. Water-
   bury is a fine city. Big clock city, the famous Waterbury clock. Sold a nice
   bill there. And then Boston — Boston is the cradle of the Revolution. A
   fine city. And a couple of other towns in Mass., and on to Portland and
   Bangor and straight home!

Gene Tunney's: James Joseph ("Gene") Tunney (1897–1978)—American boxer, world heavyweight champion
from his defeat of Jack Dempsey in 1926 until his retirement in 1928.

BIFF: Gee, I'd love to go with you sometime, Dad.

WILLY: Soon as summer comes. 240

HAPPY: Promise?

WILLY: You and Hap and I, and I'll show you all the towns. America is full of beautiful towns and fine, upstanding people. And they know me, boys, they know me up and down New England. The finest people. And when I bring you fellas up, there'll be open sesame for all of us, 'cause one thing, boys: I have friends. I can park my car in any street in New England, and the cops protect it like their own. This summer, heh?

BIFF AND HAPPY: (*together*) Yeah! You bet!

WILLY: We'll take our bathing suits.

HAPPY: We'll carry your bags, Pop! 245

WILLY: Oh, won't that be something! Me comin' into the Boston store with you boys carryin' my bags. What a sensation!

Biff is prancing around, practicing passing the ball.

WILLY: You nervous, Biff, about the game?

BIFF: Not if you're gonna be there.

WILLY: What do they say about you in school, now that they made you captain?

HAPPY: There's a crowd of girls behind him everytime the classes change. 250

BIFF: (*taking Willy's hand*) This Saturday, Pop, this Saturday — just for you, I'm going to break through for a touchdown.

HAPPY: You're supposed to pass.

BIFF: I'm takin' one play for Pop. You watch me, Pop, and when I take off my helmet, that means I'm breakin' out. Then you watch me crash through that line!

WILLY: (*kisses Biff*) Oh, wait'll I tell this in Boston!

Bernard enters in knickers. He is younger than Biff, earnest and loyal, a worried boy.

BERNARD: Biff, where are you? You're supposed to study with me today. 255

WILLY: Hey, looka Bernard. What're you lookin' so anemic about, Bernard?

BERNARD: He's gotta study, Uncle Willy. He's got Regents next week.

HAPPY: (*tauntingly, spinning Bernard around*) Let's box, Bernard!

BERNARD: Biff! (*He gets away from Happy.*) Listen, Biff, I heard Mr. Birnbaum say that if you don't start studyin' math he's gonna flunk you, and you won't graduate. I heard him!

WILLY: You better study with him, Biff. Go ahead now. 260

BERNARD: I heard him!

BIFF: Oh, Pop, you didn't see my sneakers! (*He holds up a foot for Willy to look at.*)

WILLY: Hey, that's a beautiful job of printing!

BERNARD: (*wiping his glasses*) Just because he printed University of Virginia on his sneakers doesn't mean they've got to graduate him, Uncle Willy!

WILLY: (*angrily*) What're you talking about? With scholarships to three universities they're gonna flunk him? 265

BERNARD: But I heard Mr. Birnbaum say —

WILLY: Don't be a pest, Bernard! (*To his boys.*) What an anemic!

BERNARD: Okay, I'm waiting for you in my house, Biff.

Bernard goes off. The Lomans laugh.

WILLY: Bernard is not well liked, is he?

270 **BIFF:** He's liked, but he's not well liked.

HAPPY: That's right, Pop.

WILLY: That's just what I mean. Bernard can get the best marks in school, y'understand, but when he gets out in the business world, y'understand, you are going to be five times ahead of him. That's why I thank Almighty God you're both built like Adonises. Because the man who makes an appearance in the business world, the man who creates personal interest, is the man who gets ahead. Be liked and you will never want. You take me, for instance. I never have to wait in line to see a buyer. "Willy Loman is here!" That's all they have to know, and I go right through.

BIFF: Did you knock them dead, Pop?

WILLY: Knocked 'em cold in Providence, slaughtered 'em in Boston.

275 **HAPPY:** *(on his back, pedaling again)* I'm losing weight, you notice, Pop?

Linda enters, as of old, a ribbon in her hair, carrying a basket of washing.

LINDA: *(with youthful energy)* Hello, dear!

WILLY: Sweetheart!

LINDA: How'd the Chevvy run?

WILLY: Chevrolet, Linda, is the greatest car ever built. *(To the boys.)* Since when do you let your mother carry wash up the stairs?

280 **BIFF:** Grab hold there, boy!

HAPPY: Where to, Mom?

LINDA: Hang them up on the line. And you better go down to your friends, Biff. The cellar is full of boys. They don't know what to do with themselves.

BIFF: Ah, when Pop comes home they can wait!

WILLY: *(laughs appreciatively)* You better go down and tell them what to do, Biff.

285 **BIFF:** I think I'll have them sweep out the furnace room.

WILLY: Good work, Biff.

BIFF: *(goes through wall-line of kitchen to doorway at back and calls down)* Fellas! Everybody sweep out the furnace room! I'll be right down!

VOICES: All right! Okay, Biff.

BIFF: George and Sam and Frank, come out back! We're hangin' up the wash! Come on, Hap, on the double! *(He and Happy carry out the basket.)*

290 **LINDA:** The way they obey him!

WILLY: Well, that's training, the training. I'm tellin' you, I was sellin' thousands and thousands, but I had to come home.

LINDA: Oh, the whole block'll be at that game. Did you sell anything?

WILLY: I did five hundred gross in Providence and seven hundred gross in Boston.

LINDA: No! Wait a minute, I've got a pencil. *(She pulls pencil and paper out of her apron pocket.)* That makes your commission . . . Two hundred — my God! Two hundred and twelve dollars!

295 **WILLY:** Well, I didn't figure it yet, but . . .

LINDA: How much did you do?

WILLY: Well, I — I did — about a hundred and eighty gross in Providence. Well, no — it came to — roughly two hundred gross on the whole trip.

LINDA: (*without hesitation*) Two hundred gross. That's . . . (*She figures.*)

WILLY: The trouble was that three of the stores were half closed for inventory in Boston. Otherwise I woulda broke records.

LINDA: Well, it makes seventy dollars and some pennies. That's very good. 300

WILLY: What do we owe?

LINDA: Well, on the first there's sixteen dollars on the refrigerator —

WILLY: Why sixteen?

LINDA: Well, the fan belt broke, so it was a dollar eighty.

WILLY: But it's brand new. 305

LINDA: Well, the man said that's the way it is. Till they work themselves in, y'know.

They move through the wall-line into the kitchen.

WILLY: I hope we didn't get stuck on that machine.

LINDA: They got the biggest ads of any of them!

WILLY: I know, it's a fine machine. What else?

LINDA: Well, there's nine-sixty for the washing machine. And for the vacuum 310 cleaner there's three and a half due on the fifteenth. Then the roof, you got twenty-one dollars remaining.

WILLY: It don't leak, does it?

LINDA: No, they did a wonderful job. Then you owe Frank for the carburetor.

WILLY: I'm not going to pay that man! That goddam Chevrolet, they ought to prohibit the manufacture of that car!

LINDA: Well, you owe him three and a half. And odds and ends, comes to around a hundred and twenty dollars by the fifteenth.

WILLY: A hundred and twenty dollars! My God, if business don't pick up I 315 don't know what I'm gonna do!

LINDA: Well, next week you'll do better.

WILLY: Oh, I'll knock them dead next week. I'll go to Hartford. I'm very well liked in Hartford. You know, the trouble is, Linda, people don't seem to take to me.

They move onto the forestage.

LINDA: Oh, don't be foolish.

WILLY: I know it when I walk in. They seem to laugh at me.

LINDA: Why? Why would they laugh at you? Don't talk that way, Willy. 320

Willy moves to the edge of the stage. Linda goes into the kitchen and starts to darn stockings.

WILLY: I don't know the reason for it, but they just pass me by. I'm not noticed.

LINDA: But you're doing wonderful, dear. You're making seventy to a hundred dollars a week.

WILLY: But I gotta be at it ten, twelve hours a day. Other men — I don't know — they do it easier. I don't know why — I can't stop myself — I talk

too much. A man oughta come in with a few words. One thing about
Charley. He's a man of few words, and they respect him.

LINDA: You don't talk too much, you're just lively.

325 WILLY: (*smiling*) Well, I figure, what the hell, life is short, a couple of jokes.
(*To himself.*) I joke too much! (*The smile goes.*)

LINDA: Why? You're—

WILLY: I'm fat. I'm very—foolish to look at, Linda. I didn't tell you, but
Christmas time I happened to be calling on F. H. Stewarts, and a salesman
I know, as I was going in to see the buyer I heard him say something
about—walrus. And I—I cracked him right across the face. I won't take
that. I simply will not take that. But they do laugh at me. I know that.

LINDA: Darling . . .

WILLY: I gotta overcome it. I know I gotta overcome it. I'm not dressing to
advantage, maybe.

330 LINDA: Willy, darling, you're the handsomest man in the world—

WILLY: Oh, no, Linda.

LINDA: To me you are. (*Slight pause.*) The handsomest.

*From the darkness is heard the laughter of a woman. Willy doesn't turn to it, but it
continues through Linda's lines.*

LINDA: And the boys, Willy. Few men are idolized by their children the way
you are.

*Music is heard as behind a scrim, to the left of the house, The Woman, dimly seen, is
dressing.*

WILLY: (*with great feeling*) You're the best there is, Linda, you're a pal, you know
that? On the road—on the road I want to grab you sometimes and just kiss
the life outa you.

*The laughter is loud now, and he moves into a brightening area at the left, where The
Woman has come from behind the scrim and is standing, putting on her hat, looking into
a "mirror" and laughing.*

335 WILLY: 'Cause I get so lonely—especially when business is bad and there's
nobody to talk to. I get the feeling that I'll never sell anything again, that
I won't make a living for you, or a business, a business for the boys. (*He talks
through The Woman's subsiding laughter; The Woman primps at the "mirror."*)
There's so much I want to make for—

THE WOMAN: Me? You didn't make me, Willy. I picked you.

WILLY: (*pleased*) You picked me?

THE WOMAN: (*who is quite proper-looking, Willy's age*) I did. I've been sitting at
that desk watching all the salesmen go by, day in, day out. But you've got
such a sense of humor, and we do have such a good time together, don't we?

340 WILLY: Sure, sure. (*He takes her in his arms.*) Why do you have to go now?

THE WOMAN: It's two o'clock . . .

WILLY: No, come on in! (*He pulls her.*)

THE WOMAN: . . . my sisters'll be scandalized. When'll you be back?

WILLY: Oh, two weeks about. Will you come up again?

THE WOMAN: Sure thing. You do make me laugh. It's good for me. *(She
squeezes his arm, kisses him.)* And I think you're a wonderful man. 345

WILLY: You picked me, heh?

THE WOMAN: Sure. Because you're so sweet. And such a kidder.

WILLY: Well, I'll see you next time I'm in Boston.

THE WOMAN: I'll put you right through to the buyers.

WILLY: *(slapping her bottom)* Right. Well, bottoms up! 350

THE WOMAN: *(slaps him gently and laughs)* You just kill me, Willy. *(He suddenly
grabs her and kisses her roughly.)* You kill me. And thanks for the stockings.
I love a lot of stockings. Well, good night.

WILLY: Good night. And keep your pores open!

THE WOMAN: Oh, Willy!

*The Woman bursts out laughing, and Linda's laughter blends in. The Woman disappears
into the dark. Now the area at the kitchen table brightens. Linda is sitting where she was
at the kitchen table, but now is mending a pair of silk stockings.*

LINDA: You are, Willy. The handsomest man. You've got no reason to feel
that —

WILLY: *(coming out of The Woman's dimming area and going over to Linda)* I'll
make it all up to you, Linda, I'll —

LINDA: There's nothing to make up, dear. You're doing fine, better than — 355

WILLY: *(noticing her mending)* What's that?

LINDA: Just mending my stockings. They're so expensive —

WILLY: *(angrily, taking them from her)* I won't have you mending stockings in
this house! Now throw them out!

Linda puts the stockings in her pocket.

BERNARD: *(entering on the run)* Where is he? If he doesn't study!

WILLY: *(moving to the forestage, with great agitation)* You'll give him the answers! 360

BERNARD: I do, but I can't on a Regents! That's a state exam! They're liable to
arrest me!

WILLY: Where is he? I'll whip him, I'll whip him!

LINDA: And he'd better give back that football, Willy, it's not nice.

WILLY: Biff! Where is he? Why is he taking everything?

LINDA: He's too tough with the girls, Willy. All the mothers are afraid of him! 365

WILLY: I'll whip him!

BERNARD: He's driving the car without a license!

The Woman's laugh is heard.

WILLY: Shut up!

LINDA: All the mothers —

WILLY: Shut up! 370

BERNARD: *(backing quietly away and out)* Mr. Birnbaum says he's stuck up.

WILLY: Get outa here!

BERNARD: If he doesn't buckle down he'll flunk math! *(He goes off.)*

LINDA: He's right, Willy, you've gotta—

375 **WILLY:** (*exploding at her*) There's nothing the matter with him! You want him to be a worm like Bernard? He's got spirit, personality . . .

As he speaks, Linda, almost in tears, exits into the livingroom. Willy is alone in the kitchen, wilting and staring. The leaves are gone. It is night again, and the apartment houses look down from behind.

WILLY: Loaded with it. Loaded! What is he stealing? He's giving it back, isn't he? Why is he stealing? What did I tell him? I never in my life told him anything but decent things.

Happy in pajamas has come down the stairs; Willy suddenly becomes aware of Happy's presence.

HAPPY: Let's go now, come on.

WILLY: (*sitting down at the kitchen table*) Huh! Why did she have to wax the floors herself? Everytime she waxes the floors she keels over. She knows that!

HAPPY: Shh! Take it easy. What brought you back tonight?

380 **WILLY:** I got an awful scare. Nearly hit a kid in Yonkers. God! Why didn't I go to Alaska with my brother Ben that time! Ben! That man was a genius, that man was success incarnate! What a mistake! He begged me to go.

HAPPY: Well, there's no use in —

WILLY: You guys! There was a man started with the clothes on his back and ended up with diamond mines!

HAPPY: Boy, someday I'd like to know how he did it.

WILLY: What's the mystery? The man knew what he wanted and went out and got it! Walked into a jungle, and comes out, the age of twenty-one, and he's rich! The world is an oyster, but you don't crack it open on a mattress!

385 **HAPPY:** Pop, I told you I'm gonna retire you for life.

WILLY: You'll retire me for life on seventy goddam dollars a week? And your women and your car and your apartment, and you'll retire me for life! Christ's sake, I couldn't get past Yonkers today! Where are you guys, where are you? The woods are burning! I can't drive a car!

Charley has appeared in the doorway. He is a large man, slow of speech, laconic, immovable. In all he says, despite what he says, there is pity, and now, trepidation. He has a robe over his pajamas, slippers on his feet. He enters the kitchen.

CHARLEY: Everything all right?

HAPPY: Yeah, Charley, everything's . . .

WILLY: What's the matter?

390 **CHARLEY:** I heard some noise. I thought something happened. Can't we do something about the walls? You sneeze in here, and in my house hats blow off.

HAPPY: Let's go to bed, Dad. Come on.

Charley signals to Happy to go.

WILLY: You go ahead, I'm not tired at the moment.

HAPPY: *(to Willy)* Take it easy, huh? *(He exits.)*

WILLY: What're you doin' up?

CHARLEY: *(sitting down at the kitchen table opposite Willy)* Couldn't sleep good. 395
I had a heartburn.

WILLY: Well, you don't know how to eat.

CHARLEY: I eat with my mouth.

WILLY: No, you're ignorant. You gotta know about vitamins and things like
that.

CHARLEY: Come on, let's shoot. Tire you out a little.

WILLY: *(hesitantly)* All right. You got cards? 400

CHARLEY: *(taking a deck from his pocket)* Yeah, I got them. Someplace. What is
it with those vitamins?

WILLY: *(dealing)* They build up your bones. Chemistry.

CHARLEY: Yeah, but there's no bones in a heartburn.

WILLY: What are you talkin' about? Do you know the first thing about it?

CHARLEY: Don't get insulted. 405

WILLY: Don't talk about something you don't know anything about.

They are playing. Pause.

CHARLEY: What're you doin' home?

WILLY: A little trouble with the car.

CHARLEY: Oh. *(Pause.)* I'd like to take a trip to California.

WILLY: Don't say. 410

CHARLEY: You want a job?

WILLY: I got a job, I told you that. *(After a slight pause.)* What the hell are you
offering me a job for?

CHARLEY: Don't get insulted.

WILLY: Don't insult me.

CHARLEY: I don't see no sense in it. You don't have to go on this way. 415

WILLY: I got a good job. *(Slight pause.)* What do you keep comin' in here for?

CHARLEY: You want me to go?

WILLY: *(after a pause, withering)* I can't understand it. He's going back to Texas
again. What the hell is that?

CHARLEY: Let him go.

WILLY: I got nothin' to give him, Charley, I'm clean, I'm clean. 420

CHARLEY: He won't starve. None a them starve. Forget about him.

WILLY: Then what have I got to remember?

CHARLEY: You take it too hard. To hell with it. When a deposit bottle is
broken you don't get your nickel back.

WILLY: That's easy enough for you to say.

CHARLEY: That ain't easy for me to say. 425

WILLY: Did you see the ceiling I put up in the livingroom?

CHARLEY: Yeah, that's a piece of work. To put up a ceiling is a mystery to me.
How do you do it?

WILLY: What's the difference?

CHARLEY: Well, talk about it.

WILLY: You gonna put up a ceiling? 430

CHARLEY: How could I put up a ceiling?

WILLY: Then what the hell are you bothering me for?

CHARLEY: You're insulted again.

WILLY: A man who can't handle tools is not a man. You're disgusting.

435 CHARLEY: Don't call me disgusting, Willy.

Uncle Ben, carrying a valise and an umbrella, enters the forestage from around the right corner of the house. He is a stolid man, in his sixties, with a mustache and an authoritative air. He is utterly certain of his destiny, and there is an aura of far places about him. He enters exactly as Willy speaks.

WILLY: I'm getting awfully tired, Ben.

Ben's music is heard. Ben looks around at everything.

CHARLEY: Good, keep playing; you'll sleep better. Did you call me Ben?

Ben looks at his watch.

WILLY: That's funny. For a second there you reminded me of my brother Ben.

BEN: I have only a few minutes. (*He strolls, inspecting the place. Willy and Charley continue playing.*)

440 CHARLEY: You never heard from him again, heh? Since that time?

WILLY: Didn't Linda tell you? Couple of weeks ago we got a letter from his wife in Africa. He died.

CHARLEY: That so.

BEN: (*chuckling*) So this is Brooklyn, eh?

CHARLEY: Maybe you're in for some of his money.

445 WILLY: Naa, he had seven sons. There's just one opportunity I had with that man . . .

BEN: I must make a train, William. There are several properties I'm looking at in Alaska.

WILLY: Sure, sure! If I'd gone with him to Alaska that time, everything would've been totally different.

CHARLEY: Go on, you'd froze to death up there.

WILLY: What're you talking about?

450 BEN: Opportunity is tremendous in Alaska, William. Surprised you're not up there.

WILLY: Sure, tremendous.

CHARLEY: Heh?

WILLY: There was the only man I ever met who knew the answers.

CHARLEY: Who?

455 BEN: How are you all?

WILLY: (*taking a pot, smiling*) Fine, fine.

CHARLEY: Pretty sharp tonight.

BEN: Is Mother living with you?

WILLY: No, she died a long time ago.

460 CHARLEY: Who?

BEN: That's too bad. Fine specimen of a lady, Mother.

WILLY: (*to Charley*) Heh?

BEN: I'd hoped to see the old girl.

CHARLEY: Who died?

BEN: Heard anything from Father, have you? 465

WILLY: (*unnerved*) What do you mean, who died?

CHARLEY: (*taking a pot*) What're you talkin' about?

BEN: (*looking at his watch*) William, it's half-past eight!

WILLY: (*as though to dispel his confusion he angrily stops Charley's hand*) That's my build!

CHARLEY: I put the ace — 470

WILLY: If you don't know how to play the game I'm not gonna throw my money away on you!

CHARLEY: (*rising*) It was my ace, for God's sake!

WILLY: I'm through, I'm through!

BEN: When did Mother die?

WILLY: Long ago. Since the beginning you never knew how to play cards. 475

CHARLEY: (*picks up the cards and goes to the door*) All right! Next time I'll bring a deck with five aces.

WILLY: I don't play that kind of game!

CHARLEY: (*turning to him*) You should be ashamed of yourself!

WILLY: Yeah?

CHARLEY: Yeah! (*He goes out.*) 480

WILLY: (*slamming the door after him*) Ignoramus!

BEN: (*as Willy comes toward him through the wall-line of the kitchen*) So you're William.

WILLY: (*shaking Ben's hand*) Ben! I've been waiting for you so long! What's the answer? How did you do it?

BEN: Oh, there's a story in that.

Linda enters the forestage, as of old, carrying the wash basket.

LINDA: Is this Ben? 485

BEN: (*gallantly*) How do you do, my dear.

LINDA: Where've you been all these years? Willy's always wondered why you—

WILLY: (*pulling Ben away from her impatiently*) Where is Dad? Didn't you follow him? How did you get started?

BEN: Well, I don't know how much you remember.

WILLY: Well, I was just a baby, of course, only three or four years old— 490

BEN: Three years and eleven months.

WILLY: What a memory, Ben!

BEN: I have many enterprises, William, and I have never kept books.

WILLY: I remember I was sitting under the wagon in — was it Nebraska?

BEN: It was South Dakota, and I gave you a bunch of wild flowers. 495

WILLY: I remember you walking away down some open road.

BEN: (*laughing*) I was going to find Father in Alaska.

WILLY: Where is he?

BEN: At that age I had a very faulty view of geography, William. I discovered after a few days that I was heading due south, so instead of Alaska, I ended up in Africa.

500   **Linda:** Africa!

Willy: The Gold Coast!

Ben: Principally, diamond mines.

Linda: Diamond mines!

Ben: Yes, my dear. But I've only a few minutes—

505   **Willy:** No! Boys! Boys! *(Young Biff and Happy appear.)* Listen to this. This is
your Uncle Ben, a great man! Tell my boys, Ben!

Ben: Why, boys, when I was seventeen I walked into the jungle, and when I
was twenty-one I walked out. *(He laughs.)* And by God I was rich.

Willy: *(to the boys)* You see what I been talking about? The greatest things can
happen!

Ben: *(glancing at his watch)* I have an appointment in Ketchikan Tuesday week.

Willy: No, Ben! Please tell about Dad. I want my boys to hear. I want them to
know the kind of stock they spring from. All I remember is a man with a
big beard, and I was in Mamma's lap, sitting around a fire, and some kind of
high music.

510   **Ben:** His flute. He played the flute.

Willy: Sure, the flute, that's right!

New music is heard, a high, rollicking tune.

Ben: Father was a very great and a very wild-hearted man. We would start in
Boston, and he'd toss the whole family into the wagon, and then he'd drive
the team right across the country; through Ohio, and Indiana, Michigan,
Illinois, and all the Western states. And we'd stop in the towns and sell the
flutes that he'd made on the way. Great inventor, Father. With one gadget
he made more in a week than a man like you could make in a lifetime.

Willy: That's just the way I'm bringing them up, Ben — rugged, well liked,
all-around.

Ben: Yeah? *(To Biff.)* Hit that, boy —hard as you can. *(He pounds his
stomach.)*

515   **Biff:** Oh, no, sir!

Ben: *(taking boxing stance)* Come on, get to me! *(He laughs.)*

Willy: Go to it, Biff! Go ahead, show him!

Biff: Okay! *(He cocks his fist and starts in.)*

Linda: *(to Willy)* Why must he fight, dear?

520   **Ben:** *(sparring with Biff)* Good boy! Good boy!

Willy: How's that, Ben, heh?

Happy: Give him the left, Biff!

Linda: Why are you fighting?

Ben: Good boy! *(Suddenly comes in, trips Biff, and stands over him, the point of
his umbrella poised over Biff's eye.)*

525   **Linda:** Look out, Biff!

Biff: Gee!

Ben: *(patting Biff's knee)* Never fight fair with a stranger, boy. You'll never get
out of the jungle that way. *(Taking Linda's hand and bowing.)* It was an honor
and a pleasure to meet you, Linda.

Linda: *(withdrawing her hand coldly, frightened)* Have a nice — trip.

BEN: *(to Willy)* And good luck with your — what do you do?

WILLY: Selling. 530

BEN: Yes. Well . . . *(He raises his hand in farewell to all.)*

WILLY: No, Ben, I don't want you to think . . . *(He takes Ben's arm to show him.)* It's Brooklyn, I know, but we hunt too.

BEN: Really, now.

WILLY: Oh, sure, there's snakes and rabbits and — that's why I moved out here. Why, Biff can fell any one of these trees in no time! Boys! Go right over to where they're building the apartment house and get some sand. We're gonna rebuild the entire front stoop right now! Watch this, Ben!

BIFF: Yes, sir! On the double, Hap! 535

HAPPY: *(as he and Biff run off)* I lost weight, Pop, you notice?

Charley enters in knickers, even before the boys are gone.

CHARLEY: Listen, if they steal any more from that building the watchman'll put the cops on them!

LINDA: *(to Willy)* Don't let Biff . . .

Ben laughs lustily.

WILLY: You shoulda seen the lumber they brought home last week. At least a dozen six-by-tens worth all kinds of money.

CHARLEY: Listen, if that watchman — 540

WILLY: I gave them hell, understand. But I got a couple of fearless characters there.

CHARLEY: Willy, the jails are full of fearless characters.

BEN: *(clapping Willy on the back, with a laugh at Charley)* And the stock exchange, friend!

WILLY: *(joining in Ben's laughter)* Where are the rest of your pants?

CHARLEY: My wife bought them. 545

WILLY: Now all you need is a golf club and you can go upstairs and go to sleep. *(To Ben.)* Great athlete! Between him and his son Bernard they can't hammer a nail!

BERNARD: *(rushing in)* The watchman's chasing Biff!

WILLY: *(angrily)* Shut up! He's not stealing anything!

LINDA: *(alarmed, hurrying off left)* Where is he? Biff, dear! *(She exits.)*

WILLY: *(moving toward the left, away from Ben)* There's nothing wrong. What's 550 the matter with you?

BEN: Nervy boy. Good!

WILLY: *(laughing)* Oh, nerves of iron, that Biff!

CHARLEY: Don't know what it is. My New England man comes back and he's bleedin', they murdered him up there.

WILLY: It's contacts, Charley, I got important contacts!

CHARLEY: *(sarcastically)* Glad to hear it, Willy. Come in later, we'll shoot a 555 little casino. I'll take some of your Portland money. *(He laughs at Willy and exits.)*

WILLY: *(turning to Ben)* Business is bad, it's murderous. But not for me, of course.

BEN: I'll stop by on my way back to Africa.

WILLY: *(longingly)* Can't you stay a few days? You're just what I need, Ben, because I — I have a fine position here, but I — well, Dad left when I was such a baby and I never had a chance to talk to him and I still feel — kind of temporary about myself.

BEN: I'll be late for my train.

They are at opposite ends of the stage.

560   **WILLY:**   Ben, my boys — can't we talk? They'd go into the jaws of hell for me, see, but I —

BEN: William, you're being first-rate with your boys. Outstanding, manly chaps!

WILLY: *(hanging on to his words)* Oh, Ben, that's good to hear! Because sometimes I'm afraid that I'm not teaching them the right kind of — Ben, how should I teach them?

BEN: *(giving great weight to each word, and with a certain vicious audacity)* William, when I walked into the jungle, I was seventeen. When I walked out I was twenty-one. And, by God, I was rich! *(He goes off into darkness around the right corner of the house.)*

WILLY: . . . was rich! That's just the spirit I want to imbue them with! To walk into a jungle! I was right! I was right! I was right!

Ben is gone, but Willy is still speaking to him as Linda, in nightgown and robe, enters the kitchen, glances around for Willy, then goes to the door of the house, looks out and sees him. Comes down to his left. He looks at her.

565   **LINDA:**   Willy, dear? Willy?

WILLY: I was right!

LINDA: Did you have some cheese? *(He can't answer.)* It's very late, darling. Come to bed, heh?

WILLY: *(looking straight up)* Gotta break your neck to see a star in this yard.

LINDA: You coming in?

570   **WILLY:**   What ever happened to that diamond watch fob? Remember? When Ben came from Africa that time? Didn't he give me a watch fob with a diamond in it?

LINDA: You pawned it, dear. Twelve, thirteen years ago. For Biff's radio correspondence course.

WILLY: Gee, that was a beautiful thing. I'll take a walk.

LINDA: But you're in your slippers.

WILLY: *(starting to go around the house at the left)* I was right! I was! *(Half to Linda, as he goes, shaking his head.)* What a man! There was a man worth talking to. I was right!

575   **LINDA:**   *(calling after Willy)* But in your slippers, Willy!

Willy is almost gone when Biff, in his pajamas, comes down the stairs and enters the kitchen.

BIFF: What is he doing out there?

LINDA: Sh!

BIFF: God Almighty, Mom, how long has he been doing this?

LINDA: Don't, he'll hear you.

BIFF: What the hell is the matter with him?   580

LINDA: It'll pass by morning.

BIFF: Shouldn't we do anything?

LINDA: Oh, my dear, you should do a lot of things, but there's nothing to do, so go to sleep.

Happy comes down the stairs and sits on the steps.

HAPPY: I never heard him so loud, Mom.

LINDA: Well, come around more often; you'll hear him. (*She sits down at the*   585
table and mends the lining of Willy's jacket.)

BIFF: Why didn't you ever write me about this, Mom?

LINDA: How would I write to you? For over three months you had no address.

BIFF: I was on the move. But you know I thought of you all the time. You know that, don't you, pal?

LINDA: I know, dear, I know. But he likes to have a letter. Just to know that there's still a possibility for better things.

BIFF: He's not like this all the time, is he?   590

LINDA: It's when you come home he's always the worst.

BIFF: When I come home?

LINDA: When you write you're coming, he's all smiles, and talks about the future, and — he's just wonderful. And then the closer you seem to come, the more shaky he gets, and then, by the time you get here, he's arguing, and he seems angry at you. I think it's just that maybe he can't bring himself to — to open up to you. Why are you so hateful to each other? Why is that?

BIFF: (*evasively*) I'm not hateful, Mom.

LINDA: But you no sooner come in the door than you're fighting!   595

BIFF: I don't know why. I mean to change. I'm tryin', Mom, you understand?

LINDA: Are you home to stay now?

BIFF: I don't know. I want to look around, see what's doin'.

LINDA: Biff, you can't look around all your life, can you?

BIFF: I just can't take hold, Mom. I can't take hold of some kind of a life.   600

LINDA: Biff, a man is not a bird, to come and go with the springtime.

BIFF: Your hair . . . (*He touches her hair.*) Your hair got so gray.

LINDA: Oh, it's been gray since you were in high school. I just stopped dyeing it, that's all.

BIFF: Dye it again, will ya? I don't want my pal looking old. (*He smiles.*)

LINDA: You're such a boy! You think you can go away for a year and . . . You've   605
got to get it into your head now that one day you'll knock on this door and there'll be strange people here —

BIFF: What are you talking about? You're not even sixty, Mom.

LINDA: But what about your father?

BIFF: (*lamely*) Well, I meant him too.

HAPPY: He admires Pop.

LINDA: Biff, dear, if you don't have any feeling for him, then you can't have   610
any feeling for me.

BIFF: Sure I can, Mom.

LINDA: No. You can't just come to see me, because I love him. (*With a threat, but only a threat, of tears.*) He's the dearest man in the world to me, and I won't have anyone making him feel unwanted and low and blue. You've got to make up your mind now, darling, there's no leeway any more. Either he's your father and you pay him that respect, or else you're not to come here. I know he's not easy to get along with — nobody knows that better than me — but . . .

WILLY: (*from the left, with a laugh*) Hey, hey, Biffo!

BIFF: (*starting to go out after Willy*) What the hell is the matter with him? (*Happy stops him.*)

615   LINDA: Don't — don't go near him!

BIFF: Stop making excuses for him! He always, always wiped the floor with you. Never had an ounce of respect for you.

HAPPY: He's always had respect for—

BIFF: What the hell do you know about it?

HAPPY: (*surlily*) Just don't call him crazy!

620   BIFF: He's got no character — Charley wouldn't do this. Not in his own house — spewing out that vomit from his mind.

HAPPY: Charley never had to cope with what he's got to.

BIFF: People are worse off than Willy Loman. Believe me, I've seen them!

LINDA: Then make Charley your father, Biff. You can't do that, can you? I don't say he's a great man. Willy Loman never made a lot of money. His name was never in the paper. He's not the finest character that ever lived. But he's a human being, and a terrible thing is happening to him. So attention must be paid. He's not to be allowed to fall into his grave like an old dog. Attention, attention must be finally paid to such a person. You called him crazy—

BIFF: I didn't mean—

625   LINDA: No, a lot of people think he's lost his — balance. But you don't have to be very smart to know what his trouble is. The man is exhausted.

HAPPY: Sure!

LINDA: A small man can be just as exhausted as a great man. He works for a company thirty-six years this March, opens up unheard-of territories to their trademark, and now in his old age they take his salary away.

HAPPY: (*indignantly*) I didn't know that, Mom.

LINDA: You never asked, my dear! Now that you get your spending money someplace else you don't trouble your mind with him.

630   HAPPY: But I gave you money last—

LINDA: Christmas time, fifty dollars! To fix the hot water it cost ninety-seven fifty! For five weeks he's been on straight commission, like a beginner, an unknown!

BIFF: Those ungrateful bastards!

LINDA: Are they any worse than his sons? When he brought them business, when he was young, they were glad to see him. But now his old friends, the old buyers that loved him so and always found some order to hand him in a pinch — they're all dead, retired. He used to be able to make six, seven calls a day in Boston. Now he takes his valises out of the car and puts them back and takes them out again and he's exhausted. Instead of walking he talks now. He drives seven hundred miles, and when he gets there no one knows him any more, no one welcomes him. And what goes through a man's mind, driving seven hundred miles home without having earned a cent? Why shouldn't he talk to himself? Why? When he has to go to Charley and borrow fifty dollars a week and pretend to me that it's his pay? How long can that go on? How long? You see what I'm sitting here and waiting for? And you tell me he has no character? The man who never worked a day but for your benefit? When does he get the medal for that? Is this his reward — to turn around at the age of sixty-three and find his sons, who he loved better than his life, one a philandering bum —

HAPPY: Mom!

LINDA: That's all you are, my baby! (*To Biff.*) And you! What happened to the love you had for him? You were such pals! How you used to talk to him on the phone every night! How lonely he was till he could come home to you!   635

BIFF: All right, Mom. I'll live here in my room, and I'll get a job. I'll keep away from him, that's all.

LINDA: No, Biff. You can't stay here and fight all the time.

BIFF: He threw me out of this house, remember that.

LINDA: Why did he do that? I never knew why.

BIFF: Because I know he's a fake and he doesn't like anybody around who knows!   640

LINDA: Why a fake? In what way? What do you mean?

BIFF: Just don't lay it all at my feet. It's between me and him — that's all I have to say. I'll chip in from now on. He'll settle for half my pay check. He'll be all right. I'm going to bed. (*He starts for the stairs.*)

LINDA: He won't be all right.

BIFF: (*turning on the stairs, furiously*) I hate this city and I'll stay here. Now what do you want?

LINDA: He's dying, Biff.   645

Happy turns quickly to her, shocked.

BIFF: (*after a pause*) Why is he dying?

LINDA: He's been trying to kill himself.

BIFF: (*with great horror*) How?

LINDA: I live from day to day.

BIFF: What're you talking about?   650

LINDA: Remember I wrote you that he smashed up the car again? In February?

BIFF: Well?

LINDA: The insurance inspector came. He said that they have evidence. That all these accidents in the last year — weren't — weren't — accidents.

HAPPY: How can they tell that? That's a lie.

LINDA: It seems there's a woman . . . (*She takes a breath as —*)   655

BIFF: (*sharply but contained*) What woman?

LINDA: (*simultaneously*) . . . and this woman . . .

LINDA: What?

BIFF: Nothing. Go ahead.

660   LINDA: What did you say?

BIFF: Nothing. I just said what woman?

HAPPY: What about her?

LINDA: Well, it seems she was walking down the road and saw his car. She says that he wasn't driving fast at all, and that he didn't skid. She says he came to that little bridge, and then deliberately smashed into the railing, and it was only the shallowness of the water that saved him.

BIFF: Oh, no, he probably just fell asleep again.

665   LINDA: I don't think he fell asleep.

BIFF: Why not?

LINDA: Last month . . . (*With great difficulty.*) Oh, boys, it's so hard to say a thing like this! He's just a big stupid man to you, but I tell you there's more good in him than in many other people. (*She chokes, wipes her eyes.*) I was looking for a fuse. The lights blew out, and I went down the cellar. And behind the fuse box — it happened to fall out — was a length of rubber pipe — just short.

HAPPY: No kidding?

LINDA: There's a little attachment on the end of it. I knew right away. And sure enough, on the bottom of the water heater there's a new little nipple on the gas pipe.

670   HAPPY: (*angrily*) That — jerk.

BIFF: Did you have it taken off?

LINDA: I'm — I'm ashamed to. How can I mention it to him? Every day I go down and take away that little rubber pipe. But, when he comes home, I put it back where it was. How can I insult him that way? I don't know what to do. I live from day to day, boys. I tell you, I know every thought in his mind. It sounds so old-fashioned and silly, but I tell you he put his whole life into you and you've turned your backs on him. (*She is bent over in the chair, weeping, her face in her hands.*) Biff, I swear to God! Biff, his life is in your hands!

HAPPY: (*to Biff*) How do you like that damned fool!

BIFF: (*kissing her*) All right, pal, all right. It's all settled now. I've been remiss. I know that, Mom, but now I'll stay, and I swear to you, I'll apply myself. (*Kneeling in front of her, in a fever of self-reproach.*) It's just — you see, Mom, I don't fit in business. Not that I won't try. I'll try, and I'll make good.

675   HAPPY: Sure you will. The trouble with you in business was you never tried to please people.

BIFF: I know, I—

HAPPY: Like when you worked for Harrison's. Bob Harrison said you were tops, and then you go and do some damn fool thing like whistling whole songs in the elevator like a comedian.

BIFF: (*against Happy*) So what? I like to whistle sometimes.

HAPPY: You don't raise a guy to a responsible job who whistles in the elevator!

LINDA: Well, don't argue about it now.

680   HAPPY: Like when you'd go off and swim in the middle of the day instead of taking the line around.

BIFF: *(his resentment rising)* Well, don't you run off? You take off sometimes, don't you? On a nice summer day?

HAPPY: Yeah, but I cover myself!

LINDA: Boys!

HAPPY: If I'm going to take a fade the boss can call any number where I'm sup-   685
posed to be and they'll swear to him that I just left. I'll tell you something
that I hate to say, Biff, but in the business world some of them think you're
crazy.

BIFF: *(angered)* Screw the business world!

HAPPY: All right, screw it! Great, but cover yourself!

LINDA: Hap, Hap!

BIFF: I don't care what they think! They've laughed at Dad for years, and you
know why? Because we don't belong in this nut-house of a city! We should
be mixing cement on some open plain, or — or carpenters. A carpenter is
allowed to whistle!

Willy walks in from the entrance of the house, at left.

WILLY: Even your grandfather was better than a carpenter. *(Pause. They*   690
watch him.) You never grew up. Bernard does not whistle in the elevator,
I assure you.

BIFF: *(as though to laugh Willy out of it)* Yeah, but you do, Pop.

WILLY: I never in my life whistled in an elevator! And who in the business
world thinks I'm crazy?

BIFF: I didn't mean it like that, Pop. Now don't make a whole thing out of it,
will ya?

WILLY: Go back to the West! Be a carpenter, a cowboy, enjoy yourself!

LINDA: Willy, he was just saying —   695

WILLY: I heard what he said!

HAPPY: *(trying to quiet Willy)* Hey, Pop, come on now . . .

WILLY: *(continuing over Happy's line)* They laugh at me, heh? Go to Filene's, go
to the Hub, go to Slattery's, Boston. Call out the name Willy Loman and
see what happens! Big shot!

BIFF: All right, Pop.

WILLY: Big!   700

BIFF: All right!

WILLY: Why do you always insult me?

BIFF: I didn't say a word. *(To Linda.)* Did I say a word?

LINDA: He didn't say anything, Willy.

WILLY: *(going to the doorway of the livingroom)* All right, good night, good night.   705

LINDA: Willy, dear, he just decided . . .

WILLY: *(to Biff)* If you get tired hanging around tomorrow, paint the ceiling
I put up in the livingroom.

BIFF: I'm leaving early tomorrow.

HAPPY: He's going to see Bill Oliver, Pop.

WILLY: *(interestedly)* Oliver? For what?   710

BIFF: *(with reserve, but trying, trying)* He always said he'd stake me. I'd like to
go into business, so maybe I can take him up on it.

LINDA: Isn't that wonderful?

WILLY: Don't interrupt. What's wonderful about it? There's fifty men in the City of New York who'd stake him. *(To Biff.)* Sporting goods?

BIFF: I guess so. I know something about it and—

715   WILLY: He knows something about it! You know sporting goods better than Spalding, for God's sake! How much is he giving you?

BIFF: I don't know, I didn't even see him yet, but—

WILLY: Then what're you talkin' about?

BIFF: *(getting angry)* Well, all I said was I'm gonna see him, that's all!

WILLY: *(turning away)* Ah, you're counting your chickens again.

720   BIFF: *(starting left for the stairs)* Oh, Jesus, I'm going to sleep!

WILLY: *(calling after him)* Don't curse in this house!

BIFF: *(turning)* Since when did you get so clean!

HAPPY: *(trying to stop them)* Wait a . . .

WILLY: Don't use that language to me! I won't have it!

725   HAPPY: *(grabbing Biff, shouts)* Wait a minute! I got an idea. I got a feasible idea. Come here, Biff, let's talk this over now, let's talk some sense here. When I was down in Florida last time, I thought of a great idea to sell sporting goods. It just came back to me. You and I, Biff — we have a line, the Loman Line. We train a couple of weeks, and put on a couple of exhibitions, see?

WILLY: That's an idea!

HAPPY: Wait! We form two basketball teams, see? Two water-polo teams. We play each other. It's a million dollars' worth of publicity. Two brothers, see? The Loman Brothers. Displays in the Royal Palms — all the hotels. And banners over the ring and the basketball court: "Loman Brothers." Baby, we could sell sporting goods!

WILLY: That is a one-million-dollar idea.

LINDA: Marvelous!

730   BIFF: I'm in great shape as far as that's concerned.

HAPPY: And the beauty of it is, Biff, it wouldn't be like a business. We'd be out playin' ball again . . .

BIFF: *(enthused)* Yeah, that's . . .

WILLY: Million-dollar . . .

HAPPY: And you wouldn't get fed up with it, Biff. It'd be the family again. There'd be the old honor, and comradeship, and if you wanted to go off for a swim or somethin'— well, you'd do it! Without some smart cooky gettin' up ahead of you!

735   WILLY: Lick the world! You guys together could absolutely lick the civilized world.

BIFF: I'll see Oliver tomorrow. Hap, if we could work that out . . .

LINDA: Maybe things are beginning to—

WILLY: *(wildly enthused, to Linda)* Stop interrupting! *(To Biff.)* But don't wear sport jacket and slacks when you see Oliver.

BIFF: No, I'll—

740   WILLY: A business suit, and talk as little as possible, and don't crack any jokes.

BIFF: He did like me. Always liked me.

LINDA: He loved you!

WILLY: (*to Linda*) Will you stop! (*To Biff.*) Walk in very serious. You are not applying for a boy's job. Money is to pass. Be quiet, fine, and serious. Everybody likes a kidder, but nobody lends him money.

HAPPY: I'll try to get some myself, Biff. I'm sure I can.

WILLY: I can see great things for you, kids, I think your troubles are over. But remember, start big and you'll end big. Ask for fifteen. How much you gonna ask for?   745

BIFF: Gee, I don't know —

WILLY: And don't say "Gee." "Gee" is a boy's word. A man walking in for fifteen thousand dollars does not say "Gee!"

BIFF: Ten, I think, would be top though.

WILLY: Don't be so modest. You always started too low. Walk in with a big laugh. Don't look worried. Start off with a couple of your good stories to lighten things up. It's not what you say, it's how you say it — because personality always wins the day.

LINDA: Oliver always thought the highest of him —   750

WILLY: Will you let me talk?

BIFF: Don't yell at her, Pop, will ya?

WILLY: (*angrily*) I was talking, wasn't I!

BIFF: I don't like you yelling at her all the time, and I'm tellin' you, that's all.

WILLY: What're you, takin' over this house?   755

LINDA: Willy —

WILLY: (*turning on her*) Don't take his side all the time, goddammit!

BIFF: (*furiously*) Stop yelling at her!

WILLY: (*suddenly pulling on his cheek, beaten down, guilt ridden*) Give my best to Bill Oliver — he may remember me. (*He exits through the livingroom doorway.*)

LINDA: (*her voice subdued*) What'd you have to start that for? (*Biff turns away.*) You see how sweet he was as soon as you talked hopefully? (*She goes over to Biff.*) Come up and say good night to him. Don't let him go to bed that way.   760

HAPPY: Come on, Biff, let's buck him up.

LINDA: Please, dear. Just say good night. It takes so little to make him happy. Come. (*She goes through the livingroom doorway, calling upstairs from within the livingroom.*) Your pajamas are hanging in the bathroom. Willy!

HAPPY: (*looking toward where Linda went out*) What a woman! They broke the mold when they made her. You know that, Biff?

BIFF: He's off salary. My God, working on commission!

HAPPY: Well, let's face it: he's no hot-shot selling man. Except that sometimes, you have to admit, he's a sweet personality.   765

BIFF: (*deciding*) Lend me ten bucks, will ya? I want to buy some new ties.

HAPPY: I'll take you to a place I know. Beautiful stuff. Wear one of my striped shirts tomorrow.

BIFF: She got gray. Mom got awful old. Gee, I'm gonna go in to Oliver tomorrow and knock him for a —

HAPPY: Come on up. Tell that to Dad. Let's give him a whirl. Come on.

770 **BIFF:** *(steamed up)* You know, with ten thousand bucks, boy!

HAPPY: *(as they go into the livingroom)* That's the talk, Biff, that's the first time I've heard the old confidence out of you! *(From within the livingroom, fading off.)* You're gonna live with me, kid, and any babe you want you just say the word . . . *(The last lines are hardly heard. They are mounting the stairs to their parents' bedroom.)*

LINDA: *(entering her bedroom and addressing Willy, who is in the bathroom. She is straightening the bed for him)* Can you do anything about the shower? It drips.

WILLY: *(from the bathroom)* All of a sudden everything falls to pieces! Goddam plumbing, oughta be sued, those people. I hardly finished putting it in and the thing . . . *(His words rumble off.)*

LINDA: I'm just wondering if Oliver will remember him. You think he might?

775 **WILLY:** *(coming out of the bathroom in his pajamas)* Remember him? What's the matter with you, you crazy? If he'd've stayed with Oliver he'd be on top by now! Wait'll Oliver gets a look at him. You don't know the average caliber any more. The average young man today —*(he is getting into bed)*— is got a caliber of zero. Greatest thing in the world for him was to bum around.

Biff and Happy enter the bedroom. Slight pause.

WILLY: *(stops short, looking at Biff)* Glad to hear it, boy.

HAPPY: He wanted to say good night to you, sport.

WILLY: *(to Biff)* Yeah. Knock him dead, boy. What'd you want to tell me?

BIFF: Just take it easy, Pop. Good night. *(He turns to go.)*

780 **WILLY:** *(unable to resist)* And if anything falls off the desk while you're talking to him —like a package or something— don't you pick it up. They have office boys for that.

LINDA: I'll make a big breakfast —

WILLY: Will you let me finish? *(To Biff.)* Tell him you were in the business in the West. Not farm work.

BIFF: All right, Dad.

LINDA: I think everything —

785 **WILLY:** *(going right through her speech)* And don't undersell yourself. No less than fifteen thousand dollars.

BIFF: *(unable to bear him)* Okay. Good night, Mom. *(He starts moving.)*

WILLY: Because you got a greatness in you, Biff, remember that. You got all kinds a greatness . . . *(He lies back, exhausted. Biff walks out.)*

LINDA: *(calling after Biff)* Sleep well, darling!

HAPPY: I'm gonna get married, Mom. I wanted to tell you.

790 **LINDA:** Go to sleep, dear.

HAPPY: *(going)* I just wanted to tell you.

WILLY: Keep up the good work. *(Happy exits.)* God . . . remember that Ebbets Field game? The championship of the city?

LINDA: Just rest. Should I sing to you?

WILLY: Yeah. Sing to me. *(Linda hums a soft lullaby.)* When that team came out —he was the tallest, remember?

LINDA: Oh, yes. And in gold. 795

Biff enters the darkened kitchen, takes a cigarette, and leaves the house. He comes downstage into a golden pool of light. He smokes, staring at the night.

WILLY: Like a young god. Hercules — something like that. And the sun, the sun all around him. Remember how he waved to me? Right up from the field, with the representatives of three colleges standing by? And the buyers I brought, and the cheers when he came out — Loman, Loman, Loman! God Almighty, he'll be great yet. A star like that, magnificent, can never really fade away!

The light on Willy is fading. The gas heater begins to glow through the kitchen wall, near the stairs, a blue flame beneath red coils.

LINDA: *(timidly)* Willy, dear, what has he got against you?
WILLY: I'm so tired. Don't talk any more.

Biff slowly returns to the kitchen. He stops, stares toward the heater.

LINDA: Will you ask Howard to let you work in New York?
WILLY: First thing in the morning. Everything'll be all right. 800

Biff reaches behind the heater and draws out a length of rubber tubing. He is horrified and turns his head toward Willy's room, still dimly lit, from which the strains of Linda's desperate but monotonous humming rise.

WILLY: *(staring through the window into the moonlight)* Gee, look at the moon moving between the buildings!

Biff wraps the tubing around his hand and quickly goes up the stairs. Curtain.

ACT II

Music is heard, gay and bright. The curtain rises as the music fades away. Willy, in shirt sleeves, is sitting at the kitchen table, sipping coffee, his hat in his lap. Linda is filling his cup when she can.

WILLY: Wonderful coffee. Meal in itself.
LINDA: Can I make you some eggs?
WILLY: No. Take a breath.
LINDA: You look so rested, dear.
WILLY: I slept like a dead one. First time in months. Imagine, sleeping till ten 5 on a Tuesday morning. Boys left nice and early, heh?
LINDA: They were out of here by eight o'clock.
WILLY: Good work!
LINDA: It was so thrilling to see them leaving together. I can't get over the shaving lotion in this house.
WILLY: *(smiling)* Mmm —
LINDA: Biff was very changed this morning. His whole attitude seemed to be 10 hopeful. He couldn't wait to get downtown to see Oliver.

WILLY: He's heading for a change. There's no question, there simply are certain men that take longer to get — solidified. How did he dress?

LINDA: His blue suit. He's so handsome in that suit. He could be a — anything in that suit!

Willy gets up from the table. Linda holds his jacket for him.

WILLY: There's no question, no question at all. Gee, on the way home tonight I'd like to buy some seeds.

LINDA: *(laughing)* That'd be wonderful. But not enough sun gets back there. Nothing'll grow any more.

15 WILLY: You wait, kid, before it's all over we're gonna get a little place out in the country, and I'll raise some vegetables, a couple of chickens . . .

LINDA: You'll do it yet, dear.

Willy walks out of his jacket. Linda follows him.

WILLY: And they'll get married, and come for a weekend. I'd build a little guest house. 'Cause I got so many fine tools, all I'd need would be a little lumber and some peace of mind.

LINDA: *(joyfully)* I sewed the lining . . .

WILLY: I could build two guest houses, so they'd both come. Did he decide how much he's going to ask Oliver for?

20 LINDA: *(getting him into the jacket)* He didn't mention it, but I imagine ten or fifteen thousand. You going to talk to Howard today?

WILLY: Yeah. I'll put it to him straight and simple. He'll just have to take me off the road.

LINDA: And Willy, don't forget to ask for a little advance, because we've got the insurance premium. It's the grace period now.

WILLY: That's a hundred . . . ?

LINDA: A hundred and eight, sixty-eight. Because we're a little short again.

25 WILLY: Why are we short?

LINDA: Well, you had the motor job on the car . . .

WILLY: That goddam Studebaker!

LINDA: And you got one more payment on the refrigerator . . .

WILLY: But it just broke again!

30 LINDA: Well, it's old, dear.

WILLY: I told you we should've bought a well-advertised machine. Charley bought a General Electric and it's twenty years old and it's still good, that son-of-a-bitch.

LINDA: But, Willy —

WILLY: Whoever heard of a Hastings refrigerator? Once in my life I would like to own something outright before it's broken! I'm always in a race with the junkyard! I just finished paying for the car and it's on its last legs. The refrigerator consumes belts like a goddam maniac. They time those things. They time them so when you finally paid for them, they're used up.

LINDA: *(buttoning up his jacket as he unbuttons it)* All told, about two hundred dollars would carry us, dear. But that includes the last payment on the mortgage. After this payment, Willy, the house belongs to us.

WILLY: It's twenty-five years! 35

LINDA: Biff was nine years old when we bought it.

WILLY: Well, that's a great thing. To weather a twenty-five year mortgage is—

LINDA: It's an accomplishment.

WILLY: All the cement, the lumber, the reconstruction I put in this house! There ain't a crack to be found in it any more.

LINDA: Well, it served its purpose. 40

WILLY: What purpose? Some stranger'll come along, move in, and that's that. If only Biff would take this house, and raise a family . . . (*He starts to go.*) Good-by, I'm late.

LINDA: (*suddenly remembering*) Oh, I forgot! You're supposed to meet them for dinner.

WILLY: Me?

LINDA: At Frank's Chop House on Forty-eighth near Sixth Avenue.

WILLY: Is that so! How about you? 45

LINDA: No, just the three of you. They're gonna blow you to a big meal!

WILLY: Don't say! Who thought of that?

LINDA: Biff came to me this morning, Willy, and he said, "Tell Dad, we want to blow him to a big meal." Be there six o'clock. You and your two boys are going to have dinner.

WILLY: Gee whiz! That's really somethin'. I'm gonna knock Howard for a loop, kid. I'll get an advance, and I'll come home with a New York job. Goddammit, now I'm gonna do it!

LINDA: Oh, that's the spirit, Willy! 50

WILLY: I will never get behind a wheel the rest of my life!

LINDA: It's changing, Willy, I can feel it changing!

WILLY: Beyond a question. G'by, I'm late. (*He starts to go again.*)

LINDA: (*calling after him as she runs to the kitchen table for a handkerchief*) You got your glasses?

WILLY: (*feels for them, then comes back in*) Yeah, yeah, got my glasses. 55

LINDA: (*giving him the handkerchief*) And a handkerchief.

WILLY: Yeah, handkerchief.

LINDA: And your saccharine?

WILLY: Yeah, my saccharine.

LINDA: Be careful on the subway stairs. 60

She kisses him, and a silk stocking is seen hanging from her hand. Willy notices it.

WILLY: Will you stop mending stockings? At least while I'm in the house. It gets me nervous. I can't tell you. Please.

Linda hides the stocking in her hand as she follows Willy across the forestage in front of the house.

LINDA: Remember, Frank's Chop House.

WILLY: (*passing the apron*) Maybe beets would grow out there.

LINDA: (*laughing*) But you tried so many times.

WILLY: Yeah. Well, don't work hard today. (*He disappears around the right corner* 65 *of the house.*)

LINDA: Be careful!

As Willy vanishes, Linda waves to him. Suddenly the phone rings. She runs across the stage and into the kitchen and lifts it.

LINDA: Hello? Oh, Biff! I'm so glad you called, I just . . . Yes, sure, I just told him. Yes, he'll be there for dinner at six o'clock, I didn't forget. Listen, I was just dying to tell you. You know that little rubber pipe I told you about? That he connected to the gas heater? I finally decided to go down the cellar this morning and take it away and destroy it. But it's gone! Imagine? He took it away himself, it isn't there! *(She listens.)* When? Oh, then you took it. Oh — nothing, it's just that I'd hoped he'd taken it away himself. Oh, I'm not worried, darling, because this morning he left in such high spirits, it was like the old days! I'm not afraid any more. Did Mr. Oliver see you? . . . Well, you wait there then. And make a nice impression on him, darling. Just don't perspire too much before you see him. And have a nice time with Dad. He may have big news too! . . . That's right, a New York job. And be sweet to him tonight, dear. Be loving to him. Because he's only a little boat looking for a harbor. *(She is trembling with sorrow and joy.)* Oh, that's wonderful, Biff, you'll save his life. Thanks, darling. Just put your arm around him when he comes into the restaurant. Give him a smile. That's the boy . . . Good-by, dear. . . . You got your comb? . . . That's fine. Good-by, Biff dear.

In the middle of her speech, Howard Wagner, thirty-six, wheels in a small typewriter table on which is a wire-recording machine and proceeds to plug it in. This is on the left forestage. Light slowly fades on Linda as it rises on Howard. Howard is intent on threading the machine and only glances over his shoulder as Willy appears.

WILLY: Pst! Pst!

HOWARD: Hello, Willy, come in.

70   WILLY: Like to have a little talk with you, Howard.

HOWARD: Sorry to keep you waiting. I'll be with you in a minute.

WILLY: What's that, Howard?

HOWARD: Didn't you ever see one of these? Wire recorder.

WILLY: Oh. Can we talk a minute?

75   HOWARD: Records things. Just got delivery yesterday. Been driving me crazy, the most terrific machine I ever saw in my life. I was up all night with it.

WILLY: What do you do with it?

HOWARD: I bought it for dictation, but you can do anything with it. Listen to this. I had it home last night. Listen to what I picked up. The first one is my daughter. Get this. *(He flicks the switch and "Roll out the Barrel" is heard being whistled.)* Listen to that kid whistle.

WILLY: That is lifelike, isn't it?

HOWARD: Seven years old. Get that tone.

80   WILLY: Ts, ts. Like to ask a little favor if you . . .

The whistling breaks off, and the voice of Howard's Daughter is heard.

HIS DAUGHTER: "Now you, Daddy."

HOWARD: She's crazy for me! (*Again the same song is whistled.*) That's me! Ha!
    (*He winks.*)
WILLY: You're very good!

The whistling breaks off again. The machine runs silent for a moment.

HOWARD: Sh! Get this now, this is my son.   85
HIS SON: "The capital of Alabama is Montgomery; the capital of Arizona is
    Phoenix; the capital of Arkansas is Little Rock; the capital of California is
    Sacramento . . ." (*And on, and on.*)
HOWARD: (*holding up five fingers*) Five years old, Willy!
WILLY: He'll make an announcer some day!
HIS SON: (*continuing*) "The capital . . ."
HOWARD: Get that — alphabetical order! (*The machine breaks off suddenly.*)
    Wait a minute. The maid kicked the plug out.
WILLY: It certainly is a —   90
HOWARD: Sh, for God's sake!
HIS SON: "It's nine o'clock, Bulova watch time. So I have to go to sleep."
WILLY: That really is —
HOWARD: Wait a minute! The next is my wife.

They wait.

HOWARD'S VOICE: "Go on, say something." (*Pause.*) "Well, you gonna   95
    talk?"
HIS WIFE: "I can't think of anything."
HOWARD'S VOICE: "Well, talk — it's turning."
HIS WIFE: (*shyly, beaten*) "Hello." (*Silence.*) "Oh, Howard, I can't talk into
    this . . ."
HOWARD: (*snapping the machine off*) That was my wife.
WILLY: That is a wonderful machine. Can we —   100
HOWARD: I tell you, Willy, I'm gonna take my camera, and my bandsaw, and
    all my hobbies, and out they go. This is the most fascinating relaxation
    I ever found.
WILLY: I think I'll get one myself.
HOWARD: Sure, they're only a hundred and a half. You can't do without it.
    Supposing you wanna hear Jack Benny, see? But you can't be at home at
    that hour. So you tell the maid to turn the radio on when Jack Benny
    comes on, and this automatically goes on with the radio . . .
WILLY: And when you come home you . . .
HOWARD: You can come home twelve o'clock, one o'clock, any time you like,   105
    and you get yourself a Coke and sit yourself down, throw the switch, and
    there's Jack Benny's program in the middle of the night!
WILLY: I'm definitely going to get one. Because lots of time I'm on the road,
    and I think to myself, what I must be missing on the radio!
HOWARD: Don't you have a radio in the car?
WILLY: Well, yeah, but who ever thinks of turning it on?
HOWARD: Say, aren't you supposed to be in Boston?
WILLY: That's what I want to talk to you about, Howard. You got a minute?   110

He draws a chair in from the wing.

HOWARD: What happened? What're you doing here?

WILLY: Well . . .

HOWARD: You didn't crack up again, did you?

WILLY: Oh, no. No . . .

115 **HOWARD:** Geez, you had me worried there for a minute. What's the
trouble?

WILLY: Well, to tell you the truth, Howard, I've come to the decision that I'd
rather not travel any more.

HOWARD: Not travel! Well, what'll you do?

WILLY: Remember, Christmas time, when you had the party here? You said
you'd try to think of some spot for me here in town.

HOWARD: With us?

120 **WILLY:** Well, sure.

HOWARD: Oh, yeah, yeah. I remember. Well, I couldn't think of anything for
you, Willy.

WILLY: I tell ya, Howard. The kids are all grown up, y'know. I don't need much
any more. If I could take home — well, sixty-five dollars a week, I could
swing it.

HOWARD: Yeah, but Willy, see I—

WILLY: I tell ya why, Howard. Speaking frankly and between the two of us,
y'know — I'm just a little tired.

125 **HOWARD:** Oh, I could understand that, Willy. But you're a road man, Willy,
and we do a road business. We've only got a half-dozen salesmen on the
floor here.

WILLY: God knows, Howard, I never asked a favor of any man. But I was with
the firm when your father used to carry you in here in his arms.

HOWARD: I know that, Willy, but—

WILLY: Your father came to me the day you were born and asked me what I
thought of the name of Howard, may he rest in peace.

HOWARD: I appreciate that, Willy, but there just is no spot here for you. If I
had a spot I'd slam you right in, but I just don't have a single, solitary spot.

He looks for his lighter. Willy has picked it up and gives it to him. Pause.

130 **WILLY:** *(with increasing anger)* Howard, all I need to set my table is fifty dollars
a week.

HOWARD: But where am I going to put you, kid?

WILLY: Look, it isn't a question of whether I can sell merchandise, is it?

HOWARD: No, but it's a business, kid, and everybody's gotta pull his own
weight.

WILLY: *(desperately)* Just let me tell you a story, Howard—

135 **HOWARD:** 'Cause you gotta admit, business is business.

WILLY: *(angrily)* Business is definitely business, but just listen for a minute. You
don't understand this. When I was a boy — eighteen, nineteen — I was
already on the road. And there was a question in my mind as to whether
selling had a future for me. Because in those days I had a yearning to go to

Alaska. See, there were three gold strikes in one month in Alaska, and I
felt like going out. Just for the ride, you might say.

HOWARD: *(barely interested)* Don't say.

WILLY: Oh, yeah, my father lived many years in Alaska. He was an adventurous man. We've got quite a little streak of self-reliance in our family.
I thought I'd go out with my older brother and try to locate him, and
maybe settle in the North with the old man. And I was almost decided
to go, when I met a salesman in the Parker House. His name was Dave
Singleman. And he was eighty-four years old, and he'd drummed merchandise in thirty-one states. And old Dave, he'd go up to his room, y'understand, put on his green velvet slippers — I'll never forget — and pick up
his phone and call the buyers, and without ever leaving his room, at the
age of eighty-four, he made his living. And when I saw that, I realized
that selling was the greatest career a man could want. 'Cause what could
be more satisfying than to be able to go, at the age of eighty-four, into
twenty or thirty different cities, and pick up a phone, and be remembered
and loved and helped by so many different people? Do you know? when
he died — and by the way he died the death of a salesman, in his green
velvet slippers in the smoker of the New York, New Haven and Hartford,
going into Boston — when he died, hundreds of salesmen and buyers were
at his funeral. Things were sad on a lotta trains for months after that. *(He
stands up. Howard has not looked at him.)* In those days there was personality
in it, Howard. There was respect, and comradeship, and gratitude in it.
Today, it's all cut and dried, and there's no chance for bringing friendship
to bear — or personality. You see what I mean? They don't know me any
more.

HOWARD: *(moving away, to the right)* That's just the thing, Willy.

WILLY: If I had forty dollars a week — that's all I'd need. Forty dollars, Howard.   140

HOWARD: Kid, I can't take blood from a stone, I—

WILLY: *(desperation is on him now)* Howard, the year Al Smith was nominated,
your father came to me and—

HOWARD: *(starting to go off)* I've got to see some people, kid.

WILLY: *(stopping him)* I'm talking about your father! There were promises made
across this desk! You mustn't tell me you've got people to see — I put thirty-
four years into this firm, Howard, and now I can't pay my insurance! You
can't eat the orange and throw the peel away — a man is not a piece of
fruit! *(After a pause.)* Now pay attention. Your father — in 1928 I had a big
year. I averaged a hundred and seventy dollars a week in commissions.

HOWARD: *(impatiently)* Now, Willy, you never averaged—   145

WILLY: *(banging his hand on the desk)* I averaged a hundred and seventy dollars
a week in the year of 1928! And your father came to me — or rather, I was
in the office here — it was right over this desk — and he put his hand on
my shoulder—

HOWARD: *(getting up)* You'll have to excuse me, Willy, I gotta see some people.
Pull yourself together. *(Going out.)* I'll be back in a little while.

On Howard's exit, the light on his chair grows very bright and strange.

WILLY: Pull myself together! What the hell did I say to him? My God, I was yelling at him! How could I! (*Willy breaks off, staring at the light, which occupies the chair, animating it. He approaches this chair, standing across the desk from it.*) Frank, Frank, don't you remember what you told me that time? How you put your hand on my shoulder, and Frank . . . (*He leans on the desk and as he speaks the dead man's name he accidentally switches on the recorder, and instantly —*)

HOWARD'S SON: ". . . of New York is Albany. The capital of Ohio is Cincinnati, the capital of Rhode Island is . . ." (*The recitation continues.*)

150 WILLY: (*leaping away with fright, shouting*) Ha! Howard! Howard! Howard!

HOWARD: (*rushing in*) What happened?

WILLY: (*pointing at the machine, which continues nasally, childishly, with the capital cities*) Shut it off! Shut it off!

HOWARD: (*pulling the plug out*) Look, Willy . . .

WILLY: (*pressing his hands to his eyes*) I gotta get myself some coffee. I'll get some coffee . . .

Willy starts to walk out. Howard stops him.

155 HOWARD: (*rolling up the cord*) Willy, look . . .

WILLY: I'll go to Boston.

HOWARD: Willy, you can't go to Boston for us.

WILLY: Why can't I go?

HOWARD: I don't want you to represent us. I've been meaning to tell you for a long time now.

160 WILLY: Howard, are you firing me?

HOWARD: I think you need a good long rest, Willy.

WILLY: Howard—

HOWARD: And when you feel better, come back, and we'll see if we can work something out.

WILLY: But I gotta earn money, Howard. I'm in no position—

165 HOWARD: Where are your sons? Why don't your sons give you a hand?

WILLY: They're working on a very big deal.

HOWARD: This is no time for false pride, Willy. You go to your sons and tell them that you're tired. You've got two great boys, haven't you?

WILLY: Oh, no question, no question, but in the meantime . . .

HOWARD: Then that's that, heh?

170 WILLY: All right, I'll go to Boston tomorrow.

HOWARD: No, no.

WILLY: I can't throw myself on my sons. I'm not a cripple!

HOWARD: Look, kid, I'm busy this morning.

WILLY: (*grasping Howard's arm*) Howard, you've got to let me go to Boston!

175 HOWARD: (*hard, keeping himself under control*) I've got a line of people to see this morning. Sit down, take five minutes, and pull yourself together, and then go home, will ya? I need the office, Willy. (*He starts to go, turns, remembering the recorder, starts to push off the table holding the recorder.*) Oh, yeah. Whenever you can this week, stop by and drop off the samples. You'll

feel better, Willy, and then come back and we'll talk. Pull yourself together, kid, there's people outside.

Howard exits, pushing the table off left. Willy stares into space, exhausted. Now the music is heard — Ben's music — first distantly, then closer, closer. As Willy speaks, Ben enters from the right. He carries valise and umbrella.

WILLY: Oh, Ben, how did you do it? What is the answer? Did you wind up the Alaska deal already?

BEN: Doesn't take much time if you know what you're doing. Just a short business trip. Boarding ship in an hour. Wanted to say good-by.

WILLY: Ben, I've got to talk to you.

BEN: *(glancing at his watch)* Haven't the time, William.

WILLY: *(crossing the apron to Ben)* Ben, nothing's working out. I don't know   180
what to do.

BEN: Now, look here, William. I've bought timberland in Alaska and I need a man to look after things for me.

WILLY: God, timberland! Me and my boys in those grand outdoors!

BEN: You've a new continent at your doorstep, William. Get out of these cities, they're full of talk and time payments and courts of law. Screw on your fists and you can fight for a fortune up there.

WILLY: Yes, yes! Linda! Linda!

Linda enters as of old, with the wash.

LINDA: Oh, you're back?   185

BEN: I haven't much time.

WILLY: No, wait! Linda, he's got a proposition for me in Alaska.

LINDA: But you've got — *(To Ben.)* He's got a beautiful job here.

WILLY: But in Alaska, kid, I could —

LINDA: You're doing well enough, Willy!   190

BEN: *(to Linda)* Enough for what, my dear?

LINDA: *(frightened of Ben and angry at him)* Don't say those things to him! Enough to be happy right here, right now. *(To Willy, while Ben laughs.)* Why must everybody conquer the world? You're well liked, and the boys love you, and someday — *(to Ben)* — why, old man Wagner told him just the other day that if he keeps it up he'll be a member of the firm, didn't he, Willy?

WILLY: Sure, sure. I am building something with this firm, Ben, and if a man is building something he must be on the right track, mustn't he?

BEN: What are you building? Lay your hand on it. Where is it?

WILLY: *(hesitantly)* That's true, Linda, there's nothing.   195

LINDA: Why? *(To Ben.)* There's a man eighty-four years old —

WILLY: That's right, Ben, that's right. When I look at that man I say, what is there to worry about?

BEN: Bah!

WILLY: It's true, Ben. All he has to do is go into any city, pick up the phone, and he's making his living and you know why?

200   BEN: *(picking up his valise)* I've got to go.
      WILLY: *(holding Ben back)* Look at this boy!

Biff, in his high school sweater, enters carrying suitcase. Happy carries Biff's shoulder guards, gold helmet, and football pants.

WILLY: Without a penny to his name, three great universities are begging for him, and from there the sky's the limit, because it's not what you do, Ben. It's who you know and the smile on your face! It's contacts, Ben, contacts! The whole wealth of Alaska passes over the lunch table at the Commodore Hotel, and that's the wonder, the wonder of this country, that a man can end with diamonds here on the basis of being liked! *(He turns to Biff.)* And that's why when you get out on that field today it's important. Because thousands of people will be rooting for you and loving you. *(To Ben, who has again begun to leave.)* And Ben! when he walks into a business office his name will sound out like a bell and all the doors will open to him! I've seen it, Ben, I've seen it a thousand times! You can't feel it with your hand like timber, but it's there!

BEN: Good-by, William.

WILLY: Ben, am I right? Don't you think I'm right? I value your advice.

205   BEN: There's a new continent at your doorstep, William. You could walk out rich. Rich. *(He is gone.)*

WILLY: We'll do it here, Ben! You hear me? We're gonna do it here!

Young Bernard rushes in. The gay music of the boys is heard.

BERNARD: Oh, gee, I was afraid you left already!

WILLY: Why? What time is it?

BERNARD: It's half-past one!

210   WILLY: Well, come on, everybody! Ebbets Field° next stop! Where's the pennants? *(He rushes through the wall-line of the kitchen and out into the livingroom.)*

LINDA: *(to Biff)* Did you pack fresh underwear?

BIFF: *(who has been limbering up)* I want to go!

BERNARD: Biff, I'm carrying your helmet, ain't I?

HAPPY: No, I'm carrying the helmet.

215   BERNARD: Oh, Biff, you promised me.

HAPPY: I'm carrying the helmet.

BERNARD: How am I going to get in the locker room?

LINDA: Let him carry the shoulder guards. *(She puts her coat and hat on in the kitchen.)*

BERNARD: Can I, Biff? 'Cause I told everybody I'm going to be in the locker room.

220   HAPPY: In Ebbets Field it's the clubhouse.

BERNARD: I meant the clubhouse. Biff!

HAPPY: Biff!

Ebbets Field: The home park of the Brooklyn Dodgers.

BIFF: (grandly, after a slight pause) Let him carry the shoulder guards.

HAPPY: (as he gives Bernard the shoulder guards) Stay close to us now.

Willy rushes in with the pennants.

WILLY: (handing them out) Everybody wave when Biff comes out on the field.   225
(Happy and Bernard run off.) You set now, boy?

The music has died away.

BIFF: Ready to go, Pop. Every muscle is ready.

WILLY: (at the edge of the apron) You realize what this means?

BIFF: That's right, Pop.

WILLY: (feeling Biff's muscles) You're comin' home this afternoon captain of the
All-Scholastic Championship Team of the City of New York.

BIFF: I got it, Pop. And remember, pal, when I take off my helmet, that   230
touchdown is for you.

WILLY: Let's go! (He is starting out, with his arm around Biff, when Charley
enters, as of old, in knickers.) I got no room for you, Charley.

CHARLEY: Room? For what?

WILLY: In the car.

CHARLEY: You goin' for a ride? I wanted to shoot some casino.

WILLY: (furiously) Casino! (Incredulously.) Don't you realize what today is?   235

LINDA: Oh, he knows, Willy. He's just kidding you.

WILLY: That's nothing to kid about!

CHARLEY: No, Linda, what's goin' on?

LINDA: He's playing in Ebbets Field.

CHARLEY: Baseball in this weather?   240

WILLY: Don't talk to him. Come on, come on! (He is pushing them out.)

CHARLEY: Wait a minute, didn't you hear the news?

WILLY: What?

CHARLEY: Don't you listen to the radio? Ebbets Field just blew up.

WILLY: You go to hell! (Charley laughs. Pushing them out.) Come on, come on!   245
We're late.

CHARLEY: (as they go) Knock a homer, Biff, knock a homer!

WILLY: (the last to leave, turning to Charley) I don't think that was funny,
Charley. This is the greatest day of his life.

CHARLEY: Willy, when are you going to grow up?

WILLY: Yeah, heh? When this game is over, Charley, you'll be laughing out of
the other side of your face. They'll be calling him another Red Grange.°
Twenty-five thousand a year.

CHARLEY: (kidding) Is that so?   250

WILLY: Yeah, that's so.

CHARLEY: Well, then, I'm sorry, Willy. But tell me something.

WILLY: What?

Red Grange: Harold Edward ("Red") Grange (1903–1991)—American football player. A running back for the
New York Yankees football team and the Chicago Bears, Grange was elected to the Football Hall of Fame in 1963.

CHARLEY: Who is Red Grange?

255 WILLY: Put up your hands. Goddam you, put up your hands!

Charley, chuckling, shakes his head and walks away, around the left corner of the stage. Willy follows him. The music rises to a mocking frenzy.

WILLY: Who the hell do you think you are, better than everybody else? You don't know everything, you big, ignorant, stupid . . . Put up your hands!

Light rises, on the right side of the forestage, on a small table in the reception room of Charley's office. Traffic sounds are heard. Bernard, now mature, sits whistling to himself. A pair of tennis rackets and an overnight bag are on the floor beside him.

WILLY: (*offstage*) What are you walking away for? Don't walk away! If you're going to say something say it to my face! I know you laugh at me behind my back. You'll laugh out of the other side of your goddam face after this game. Touchdown! Touchdown! Eighty thousand people! Touchdown! Right between the goal posts.

Bernard is a quiet, earnest, but self-assured young man. Willy's voice is coming from right upstage now. Bernard lowers his feet off the table and listens. Jenny, his father's secretary, enters.

JENNY: (*distressed*) Say, Bernard, will you go out in the hall?

BERNARD: What is that noise? Who is it?

260 JENNY: Mr. Loman. He just got off the elevator.

BERNARD: (*getting up*) Who's he arguing with?

JENNY: Nobody. There's nobody with him. I can't deal with him any more, and your father gets all upset everytime he comes. I've got a lot of typing to do, and your father's waiting to sign it. Will you see him?

WILLY: (*entering*) Touchdown! Touch —(*He sees Jenny.*) Jenny, Jenny, good to see you. How're ya? Workin'? Or still honest?

JENNY: Fine. How've you been feeling?

265 WILLY: Not much any more, Jenny. Ha, ha! (*He is surprised to see the rackets.*)

BERNARD: Hello, Uncle Willy.

WILLY: (*almost shocked*) Bernard! Well, look who's here! (*He comes quickly, guiltily, to Bernard and warmly shakes his hand.*)

BERNARD: How are you? Good to see you.

WILLY: What are you doing here?

270 BERNARD: Oh, just stopped by to see Pop. Get off my feet till my train leaves. I'm going to Washington in a few minutes.

WILLY: Is he in?

BERNARD: Yes, he's in his office with the accountant. Sit down.

WILLY: (*sitting down*) What're you going to do in Washington?

BERNARD: Oh, just a case I've got there, Willy.

275 WILLY: That so? (*indicating the rackets*) You going to play tennis there?

BERNARD: I'm staying with a friend who's got a court.

WILLY: Don't say. His own tennis court. Must be fine people, I bet.

BERNARD: They are, very nice. Dad tells me Biff's in town.

WILLY: *(with a big smile)* Yeah, Biff's in. Working on a very big deal, Bernard.

BERNARD: What's Biff doing? 280

WILLY: Well, he's been doing very big things in the West. But he decided to establish himself here. Very big. We're having dinner. Did I hear your wife had a boy?

BERNARD: That's right. Our second.

WILLY: Two boys! What do you know!

BERNARD: What kind of a deal has Biff got?

WILLY: Well, Bill Oliver — very big sporting-goods man — he wants Biff very 285 badly. Called him in from the West. Long distance, carte blanche, special deliveries. Your friends have their own private tennis court?

BERNARD: You still with the old firm, Willy?

WILLY: *(after a pause)* I'm — I'm overjoyed to see how you made the grade, Bernard, overjoyed. It's an encouraging thing to see a young man really — really — Looks very good for Biff — very — *(He breaks off, then.)* Bernard — *(He is so full of emotion, he breaks off again.)*

BERNARD: What is it, Willy?

WILLY: *(small and alone)* What — what's the secret?

BERNARD: What secret? 290

WILLY: How — how did you? Why didn't he ever catch on?

BERNARD: I wouldn't know that, Willy.

WILLY: *(confidentially, desperately)* You were his friend, his boyhood friend. There's something I don't understand about it. His life ended after that Ebbets Field game. From the age of seventeen nothing good ever happened to him.

BERNARD: He never trained himself for anything.

WILLY: But he did, he did. After high school he took so many correspondence 295 courses. Radio mechanics; television; God knows what, and never made the slightest mark.

BERNARD: *(taking off his glasses)* Willy, do you want to talk candidly?

WILLY: *(rising, faces Bernard)* I regard you as a very brilliant man, Bernard. I value your advice.

BERNARD: Oh, the hell with the advice, Willy. I couldn't advise you. There's just one thing I've always wanted to ask you. When he was supposed to graduate, and the math teacher flunked him—

WILLY: Oh, that son-of-a-bitch ruined his life.

BERNARD: Yeah, but, Willy, all he had to do was go to summer school and 300 make up that subject.

WILLY: That's right, that's right.

BERNARD: Did you tell him not to go to summer school?

WILLY: Me? I begged him to go. I ordered him to go!

BERNARD: Then why wouldn't he go?

WILLY: Why? Why! Bernard, that question has been trailing me like a ghost 305 for the last fifteen years. He flunked th e subject, and laid down and died like a hammer hit him!

BERNARD: Take it easy, kid.

WILLY: Let me talk to you — I got nobody to talk to. Bernard, Bernard, was it my fault? Y'see? It keeps going around in my mind, maybe I did something to him. I got nothing to give him.

BERNARD: Don't take it so hard.

WILLY: Why did he lay down? What is the story there? You were his friend!

310 **BERNARD:** Willy, I remember, it was June, and our grades came out. And he'd flunked math.

WILLY: That son-of-a-bitch!

BERNARD: No, it wasn't right then. Biff just got very angry, I remember, and he was ready to enroll in summer school.

WILLY: (*surprised*) He was?

BERNARD: He wasn't beaten by it at all. But then, Willy, he disappeared from the block for almost a month. And I got the idea that he'd gone up to New England to see you. Did he have a talk with you then?

Willy stares in silence.

315 **BERNARD:** Willy?

WILLY: (*with a strong edge of resentment in his voice*) Yeah, he came to Boston. What about it?

BERNARD: Well, just that when he came back — I'll never forget this, it always mystifies me. Because I'd thought so well of Biff, even though he'd always taken advantage of me. I loved him, Willy, y'know? And he came back after that month and took his sneakers — remember those sneakers with "University of Virginia" printed on them? He was so proud of those, wore them every day. And he took them down in the cellar, and burned them up in the furnace. We had a fist fight. It lasted at least half an hour. Just the two of us, punching each other down the cellar, and crying right through it. I've often thought of how strange it was that I knew he'd given up his life. What happened in Boston, Willy?

Willy looks at him as at an intruder.

BERNARD: I just bring it up because you asked me.

WILLY: (*angrily*) Nothing. What do you mean, "What happened?" What's that got to do with anything?

320 **BERNARD:** Well, don't get sore.

WILLY: What are you trying to do, blame it on me? If a boy lays down is that my fault?

BERNARD: Now, Willy, don't get —

WILLY: Well, don't — don't talk to me that way! What does that mean, "What happened?"

Charley enters. He is in his vest, and he carries a bottle of bourbon.

CHARLEY: Hey, you're going to miss that train. (*He waves the bottle.*)

325 **BERNARD:** Yeah, I'm going. (*He takes the bottle.*) Thanks, Pop. (*He picks up his rackets and bag.*) Good-by, Willy, and don't worry about it. You know, "If at first you don't succeed . . ."

WILLY: Yes, I believe in that.

BERNARD: But sometimes, Willy, it's better for a man just to walk away.

WILLY: Walk away?

BERNARD: That's right.

WILLY: But if you can't walk away? 330

BERNARD: (*after a slight pause*) I guess that's when it's tough. (*Extending his hand.*) Good-by, Willy.

WILLY: (*shaking Bernard's hand*) Good-by, boy.

CHARLEY: (*an arm on Bernard's shoulder*) How do you like this kid? Gonna argue a case in front of the Supreme Court.

BERNARD: (*protesting*) Pop!

WILLY: (*genuinely shocked, pained, and happy*) No! The Supreme Court! 335

BERNARD: I gotta run, 'By, Dad!

CHARLEY: Knock 'em dead, Bernard!

Bernard goes off.

WILLY: (*as Charley takes out his wallet*) The Supreme Court! And he didn't even mention it!

CHARLEY: (*counting out money on the desk*) He don't have to — he's gonna do it.

WILLY: And you never told him what to do, did you? You never took any 340 interest in him.

CHARLEY: My salvation is that I never took any interest in anything. There's some money — fifty dollars. I got an accountant inside.

WILLY: Charley, look . . . (*With difficulty.*) I got my insurance to pay. If you can manage it — I need a hundred and ten dollars.

Charley doesn't reply for a moment; merely stops moving.

WILLY: I'd draw it from my bank but Linda would know, and I . . .

CHARLEY: Sit down, Willy.

WILLY: (*moving toward the chair*) I'm keeping an account of everything, 345 remember. I'll pay every penny back. (*He sits.*)

CHARLEY: Now listen to me, Willy.

WILLY: I want you to know I appreciate . . .

CHARLEY: (*sitting down on the table*) Willy, what're you doin'? What the hell is goin' on in your head?

WILLY: Why? I'm simply . . .

CHARLEY: I offered you a job. You can make fifty dollars a week. And I won't 350 send you on the road.

WILLY: I've got a job.

CHARLEY: Without pay? What kind of a job is a job without pay? (*He rises.*) Now, look, kid, enough is enough. I'm no genius but I know when I'm being insulted.

WILLY: Insulted!

CHARLEY: Why don't you want to work for me?

WILLY: What's the matter with you? I've got a job. 355

CHARLEY: Then what're you walkin' in here every week for?

WILLY: (*getting up*) Well, if you don't want me to walk in here —

CHARLEY: I am offering you a job.

WILLY: I don't want your goddam job!

360   CHARLEY: When the hell are you going to grow up?

WILLY: (*furiously*) You big ignoramus, if you say that to me again I'll rap you one! I don't care how big you are! (*He's ready to fight.*)

Pause.

CHARLEY: (*kindly, going to him*) How much do you need, Willy?

WILLY: Charley, I'm strapped. I'm strapped. I don't know what to do. I was just fired.

CHARLEY: Howard fired you?

365   WILLY: That snotnose. Imagine that? I named him. I named him Howard.

CHARLEY: Willy, when're you gonna realize that them things don't mean anything? You named him Howard, but you can't sell that. The only thing you got in this world is what you can sell. And the funny thing is that you're a salesman, and you don't know that.

WILLY: I've always tried to think otherwise, I guess. I always felt that if a man was impressive, and well liked, that nothing—

CHARLEY: Why must everybody like you? Who liked J. P. Morgan?° Was he impressive? In a Turkish bath he'd look like a butcher. But with his pockets on he was very well liked. Now listen, Willy, I know you don't like me, and nobody can say I'm in love with you, but I'll give you a job because —just for the hell of it, put it that way. Now what do you say?

WILLY: I — I just can't work for you, Charley.

370   CHARLEY: What're you, jealous of me?

WILLY: I can't work for you, that's all, don't ask me why.

CHARLEY: (*angered, takes out more bills*) You been jealous of me all your life, you damned fool! Here, pay your insurance. (*He puts the money in Willy's hand.*)

WILLY: I'm keeping strict accounts.

CHARLEY: I've got some work to do. Take care of yourself. And pay your insurance.

375   WILLY: (*moving to the right*) Funny, y'know? After all the highways, and the trains, and the appointments, and the years, you end up worth more dead than alive.

CHARLEY: Willy, nobody's worth nothin' dead. (*After a slight pause.*) Did you hear what I said?

Willy stands still, dreaming.

CHARLEY: Willy!

WILLY: Apologize to Bernard for me when you see him. I didn't mean to argue with him. He's a fine boy. They're all fine boys, and they'll end up big — all of them. Someday they'll all play tennis together. Wish me luck, Charley. He saw Bill Oliver today.

CHARLEY: Good luck.

J. P. Morgan: John Pierpont Morgan (1837–1913)—American financier.

WILLY: (*on the verge of tears*) Charley, you're the only friend I got. Isn't that a   380
remarkable thing? (*He goes out.*)

CHARLEY: Jesus!

Charley stares after him a moment and follows. All light blacks out. Suddenly raucous music is heard, and a red glow rises behind the screen at right. Stanley, a young waiter, appears, carrying a table, followed by Happy, who is carrying two chairs.

STANLEY: (*putting the table down*) That's all right, Mr. Loman, I can handle it myself. (*He turns and takes the chairs from Happy and places them at the table.*)

HAPPY: (*glancing around*) Oh, this is better.

STANLEY: Sure, in the front there you're in the middle of all kinds a noise. Whenever you got a party, Mr. Loman, you just tell me and I'll put you back here. Y'know, there's a lotta people they don't like it private, because when they go out they like to see a lotta action around them because they're sick and tired to stay in the house by theirself. But I know you, you ain't from Hackensack. You know what I mean?

HAPPY: (*sitting down*) So, how's it coming, Stanley?   385

STANLEY: Ah, it's a dog's life. I only wish during the war they'd a took me in the Army. I coulda been dead by now.

HAPPY: My brother's back, Stanley.

STANLEY: Oh, he come back, heh? From the Far West.

HAPPY: Yeah, big cattle man, my brother, so treat him right. And my father's coming too.

STANLEY: Oh, your father too!   390

HAPPY: You got a couple of nice lobsters?

STANLEY: Hundred per cent, big.

HAPPY: I want them with the claws.

STANLEY: Don't worry, I don't give you no mice. (*Happy laughs.*) How about some wine? It'll put a head on the meal.

HAPPY: No. You remember, Stanley, that recipe I brought you from overseas?   395
With the champagne in it?

STANLEY: Oh, yeah, sure. I still got it tacked up yet in the kitchen. But that'll have to cost a buck apiece anyways.

HAPPY: That's all right.

STANLEY: What'd you, hit a number or somethin'?

HAPPY: No, it's a little celebration. My brother is — I think he pulled off a big deal today. I think we're going into business together.

STANLEY: Great! That's the best for you. Because a family business, you know   400
what I mean?— that's the best.

HAPPY: That's what I think.

STANLEY: 'Cause what's the difference? Somebody steals? It's in the family. Know what I mean? (*Sotto voce.*) Like this bartender here. The boss is goin' crazy what kinda leak he's got in the cash register. You put it in but it don't come out.

HAPPY: (*raising his head*) Sh!

STANLEY: What?

HAPPY: You notice I wasn't lookin' right or left, was I?   405

STANLEY: No.

HAPPY: And my eyes are closed.

STANLEY: So what's the—

HAPPY: Strudel's comin'.

410 STANLEY: (*catching on, looks around*) Ah, no, there's no—

He breaks off as a furred, lavishly dressed Girl enters and sits at the next table. Both follow her with their eyes.

STANLEY: Geez, how'd ya know?

HAPPY: I got radar or something. (*Staring directly at her profile.*) Oooooooo . . . Stanley.

STANLEY: I think that's for you, Mr. Loman.

HAPPY: Look at that mouth. Oh, God. And the binoculars.

415 STANLEY: Geez, you got a life, Mr. Loman.

HAPPY: Wait on her.

STANLEY: (*going to The Girl's table*) Would you like a menu, ma'am?

GIRL: I'm expecting someone, but I'd like a—

HAPPY: Why don't you bring her — excuse me, miss, do you mind? I sell champagne, and I'd like you to try my brand. Bring her a champagne, Stanley.

420 GIRL: That's awfully nice of you.

HAPPY: Don't mention it. It's all company money. (*He laughs.*)

GIRL: That's a charming product to be selling, isn't it?

HAPPY: Oh, gets to be like everything else. Selling is selling, y'know.

GIRL: I suppose.

425 HAPPY: You don't happen to sell, do you?

GIRL: No, I don't sell.

HAPPY: Would you object to a compliment from a stranger? You ought to be on a magazine cover.

GIRL: (*looking at him a little archly*) I have been.

Stanley comes in with a glass of champagne.

HAPPY: What'd I say before, Stanley? You see? She's a cover girl.

430 STANLEY: Oh, I could see, I could see.

HAPPY: (*to The Girl*) What magazine?

GIRL: Oh, a lot of them. (*She takes the drink.*) Thank you.

HAPPY: You know what they say in France, don't you? "Champagne is the drink of the complexion"— Hya, Biff!

Biff has entered and sits with Happy.

BIFF: Hello, kid. Sorry I'm late.

435 HAPPY: I just got here. Uh, Miss —?

GIRL: Forsythe.

HAPPY: Miss Forsythe, this is my brother.

BIFF: Is Dad here?

HAPPY: His name is Biff. You might've heard of him. Great football player.

440 GIRL: Really? What team?

HAPPY: Are you familiar with football?

GIRL: No, I'm afraid I'm not.

HAPPY: Biff is quarterback with the New York Giants.

GIRL: Well, that is nice, isn't it? (*She drinks.*)

HAPPY: Good health.   445

GIRL: I'm happy to meet you.

HAPPY: That's my name. Hap. It's really Harold, but at West Point they called me Happy.

GIRL: (*now really impressed*) Oh, I see. How do you do? (*She turns her profile.*)

BIFF: Isn't Dad coming?

HAPPY: You want her?   450

BIFF: Oh, I could never make that.

HAPPY: I remember the time that idea would never come into your head. Where's the old confidence, Biff?

BIFF: I just saw Oliver —

HAPPY: Wait a minute. I've got to see that old confidence again. Do you want her? She's on call.

BIFF: Oh, no. (*He turns to look at The Girl.*)   455

HAPPY: I'm telling you. Watch this. (*Turning to The Girl.*) Honey? (*She turns to him.*) Are you busy?

GIRL: Well, I am . . . but I could make a phone call.

HAPPY: Do that, will you, honey? And see if you can get a friend. We'll be here for a while. Biff is one of the greatest football players in the country.

GIRL: (*standing up*) Well, I'm certainly happy to meet you.

HAPPY: Come back soon.   460

GIRL: I'll try.

HAPPY: Don't try, honey, try hard.

The Girl exits. Stanley follows, shaking his head in bewildered admiration.

HAPPY: Isn't that a shame now? A beautiful girl like that? That's why I can't get married. There's not a good woman in a thousand. New York is loaded with them, kid!

BIFF: Hap, look —

HAPPY: I told you she was on call!   465

BIFF: (*strangely unnerved*) Cut it out, will ya? I want to say something to you.

HAPPY: Did you see Oliver?

BIFF: I saw him all right. Now look, I want to tell Dad a couple of things and I want you to help me.

HAPPY: What? Is he going to back you?

BIFF: Are you crazy? You're out of your goddam head, you know that?   470

HAPPY: Why? What happened?

BIFF: (*breathlessly*) I did a terrible thing today, Hap. It's been the strangest day I ever went through. I'm all numb, I swear.

HAPPY: You mean he wouldn't see you?

BIFF: Well, I waited six hours for him, see? All day. Kept sending my name in. Even tried to date his secretary so she'd get me to him, but no soap.

475 **HAPPY:** Because you're not showin' the old confidence, Biff. He remembered you, didn't he?

BIFF: *(stopping Happy with a gesture)* Finally, about five o'clock, he comes out. Didn't remember who I was or anything. I felt like such an idiot, Hap.

HAPPY: Did you tell him my Florida idea?

BIFF: He walked away. I saw him for one minute. I got so mad I could've torn the walls down! How the hell did I ever get the idea I was a salesman there? I even believed myself that I'd been a salesman for him! And then he gave me one look and — I realized what a ridiculous lie my whole life has been! We've been talking in a dream for fifteen years. I was a shipping clerk.

HAPPY: What'd you do?

480 **BIFF:** *(with great tension and wonder)* Well, he left, see. And the secretary went out. I was all alone in the waiting-room. I don't know what came over me, Hap. The next thing I know I'm in his office — paneled walls, everything. I can't explain it. I — Hap, I took his fountain pen.

HAPPY: Geez, did he catch you?

BIFF: I ran out. I ran down all eleven flights. I ran and ran and ran.

HAPPY: That was an awful dumb — what'd you do that for?

BIFF: *(agonized)* I don't know, I just — wanted to take something, I don't know. You gotta help me, Hap. I'm gonna tell Pop.

485 **HAPPY:** You crazy? What for?

BIFF: Hap, he's got to understand that I'm not the man somebody lends that kind of money to. He thinks I've been spiting him all these years and it's eating him up.

HAPPY: That's just it. You tell him something nice.

BIFF: I can't.

HAPPY: Say you got a lunch date with Oliver tomorrow.

490 **BIFF:** So what do I do tomorrow?

HAPPY: You leave the house tomorrow and come back at night and say Oliver is thinking it over. And he thinks it over for a couple of weeks, and gradually it fades away and nobody's the worse.

BIFF: But it'll go on forever!

HAPPY: Dad is never so happy as when he's looking forward to something!

Willy enters.

HAPPY: Hello, scout!

495 **WILLY:** Gee, I haven't been here in years!

Stanley has followed Willy in and sets a chair for him. Stanley starts off but Happy stops him.

HAPPY: Stanley!

Stanley stands by, waiting for an order.

BIFF: *(going to Willy with guilt, as to an invalid)* Sit down, Pop. You want a drink?

WILLY: Sure, I don't mind.

BIFF: Let's get a load on.

500 **WILLY:** You look worried.

BIFF: N-no. (*To Stanley.*) Scotch all around. Make it doubles.

STANLEY: Doubles, right. (*He goes.*)

WILLY: You had a couple already, didn't you?

BIFF: Just a couple, yeah.

WILLY: Well, what happened, boy? (*Nodding affirmatively, with a smile.*)   505
Everything go all right?

BIFF: (*takes a breath, then reaches out and grasps Willy's hand*) Pal . . . (*He is smiling bravely, and Willy is smiling too.*) I had an experience today.

HAPPY: Terrific, Pop.

WILLY: That so? What happened?

BIFF: (*high, slightly alcoholic, above the earth*) I'm going to tell you everything from first to last. It's been a strange day. (*Silence. He looks around, composes himself as best he can, but his breath keeps breaking the rhythm of his voice.*) I had to wait quite a while for him, and—

WILLY: Oliver?   510

BIFF: Yeah, Oliver. All day, as a matter of cold fact. And a lot of — instances — facts, Pop, facts about my life came back to me. Who was it, Pop? Who ever said I was a salesman with Oliver?

WILLY: Well, you were.

BIFF: No, Dad, I was a shipping clerk.

WILLY: But you were practically—

BIFF: (*with determination*) Dad, I don't know who said it first, but I was never a   515
salesman for Bill Oliver.

WILLY: What're you talking about?

BIFF: Let's hold on to the facts tonight, Pop. We're not going to get anywhere bullin' around. I was a shipping clerk.

WILLY: (*angrily*) All right, now listen to me—

BIFF: Why don't you let me finish?

WILLY: I'm not interested in stories about the past or any crap of that kind   520
because the woods are burning, boys, you understand? There's a big blaze going on all around. I was fired today.

BIFF: (*shocked*) How could you be?

WILLY: I was fired, and I'm looking for a little good news to tell your mother, because the woman has waited and the woman has suffered. The gist of it is that I haven't got a story left in my head, Biff. So don't give me a lecture about facts and aspects. I am not interested. Now what've you got to say to me?

Stanley enters with three drinks. They wait until he leaves.

WILLY: Did you see Oliver?

BIFF: Jesus, Dad!

WILLY: You mean you didn't go up there?   525

HAPPY: Sure he went up there.

BIFF: I did. I — saw him. How could they fire you?

WILLY: (*on the edge of his chair*) What kind of a welcome did he give you?

BIFF: He won't even let you work on commission?

WILLY: I'm out! (*Driving.*) So tell me, he gave you a warm welcome?   530

HAPPY: Sure, Pop, sure!

BIFF: *(driven)* Well, it was kind of —

WILLY: I was wondering if he'd remember you. *(To Happy.)* Imagine, man doesn't see him for ten, twelve years and gives him that kind of a welcome!

HAPPY: Damn right!

535 **BIFF:** *(trying to return to the offensive)* Pop, look —

WILLY: You know why he remembered you, don't you? Because you impressed him in those days.

BIFF: Let's talk quietly and get this down to the facts, huh?

WILLY: *(as though Biff had been interrupting)* Well, what happened? It's great news, Biff. Did he take you into his office or'd you talk in the waiting-room?

BIFF: Well, he came in, see, and —

540 **WILLY:** *(with a big smile)* What'd he say? Betcha he threw his arm around you.

BIFF: Well, he kinda —

WILLY: He's a fine man. *(To Happy.)* Very hard man to see, y'know.

HAPPY: *(agreeing)* Oh, I know.

WILLY: *(to Biff)* Is that where you had the drinks?

545 **BIFF:** Yeah, he gave me a couple of — no, no!

HAPPY: *(cutting in)* He told him my Florida idea.

WILLY: Don't interrupt. *(To Biff.)* How'd he react to the Florida idea?

BIFF: Dad, will you give me a minute to explain?

WILLY: I've been waiting for you to explain since I sat down here! What happened? He took you into his office and what?

550 **BIFF:** Well — I talked. And — and he listened, see.

WILLY: Famous for the way he listens, y'know. What was his answer?

BIFF: His answer was — *(He breaks off, suddenly angry.)* Dad, you're not letting me tell you what I want to tell you!

WILLY: *(accusing, angered)* You didn't see him, did you?

BIFF: I did see him!

555 **WILLY:** What'd you insult him or something? You insulted him, didn't you?

BIFF: Listen, will you let me out of it, will you just let me out of it!

HAPPY: What the hell!

WILLY: Tell me what happened!

BIFF: *(to Happy)* I can't talk to him!

A single trumpet note jars the ear. The light of green leaves stains the house, which holds the air of night and a dream. Young Bernard enters and knocks on the door of the house.

560 **YOUNG BERNARD:** *(frantically)* Mrs. Loman, Mrs. Loman!

HAPPY: Tell him what happened!

BIFF: *(to Happy)* Shut up and leave me alone!

WILLY: No, no! You had to go and flunk math!

BIFF: What math? What're you talking about?

565 **YOUNG BERNARD:** Mrs. Loman, Mrs. Loman!

Linda appears in the house, as of old.

WILLY: *(wildly)* Math, math, math!

BIFF: Take it easy, Pop!

YOUNG BERNARD: Mrs. Loman!

WILLY: *(furiously)* If you hadn't flunked you'd've been set by now!

BIFF: Now, look, I'm gonna tell you what happened, and you're going to listen   570
to me.

YOUNG BERNARD: Mrs. Loman!

BIFF: I waited six hours —

HAPPY: What the hell are you saying?

BIFF: I kept sending in my name but he wouldn't see me. So finally he . . .
(He continues unheard as light fades low on the restaurant.)

YOUNG BERNARD: Biff flunked math!   575

LINDA: No!

YOUNG BERNARD: Birnbaum flunked him! They won't graduate him!

LINDA: But they have to. He's gotta go to the university. Where is he? Biff!
Biff!

YOUNG BERNARD: No, he left. He went to Grand Central.

LINDA: Grand — You mean he went to Boston!   580

YOUNG BERNARD: Is Uncle Willy in Boston?

LINDA: Oh, maybe Willy can talk to the teacher. Oh, the poor, poor boy!

Light on house area snaps out.

BIFF: *(at the table, now audible, holding up a gold fountain pen)* . . . so I'm washed
up with Oliver, you understand? Are you listening to me?

WILLY: *(at a loss)* Yeah, sure. If you hadn't flunked —

BIFF: Flunked what? What're you talking about?   585

WILLY: Don't blame everything on me! I didn't flunk math — you did!
What pen?

HAPPY: That was awful dumb, Biff, a pen like that is worth —

WILLY: *(seeing the pen for the first time)* You took Oliver's pen?

BIFF: *(weakening)* Dad, I just explained it to you.

WILLY: You stole Bill Oliver's fountain pen!   590

BIFF: I didn't exactly steal it! That's just what I've been explaining to you!

HAPPY: He had it in his hand and just then Oliver walked in, so he got
nervous and stuck it in his pocket!

WILLY: My God, Biff!

BIFF: I never intended to do it, Dad!

OPERATOR'S VOICE: Standish Arms, good evening!   595

WILLY: *(shouting)* I'm not in my room!

BIFF: *(frightened)* Dad, what's the matter? *(He and Happy stand up.)*

OPERATOR: Ringing Mr. Loman for you!

WILLY: I'm not there, stop it!

BIFF: *(horrified, gets down on one knee before Willy)* Dad, I'll make good, I'll   600
make good. *(Willy tries to get to his feet. Biff holds him down.)* Sit down now.

WILLY: No, you're no good, you're no good for anything.

BIFF: I am, Dad, I'll find something else, you understand? Now don't worry
about anything. *(He holds up Willy's face.)* Talk to me, Dad.

OPERATOR: Mr. Loman does not answer. Shall I page him?

WILLY: *(attempting to stand, as though to rush and silence the Operator)* No, no, no!

605 HAPPY: He'll strike something, Pop.

WILLY: No, no . . .

BIFF: *(desperately, standing over Willy)* Pop, listen! Listen to me! I'm telling you something good. Oliver talked to his partner about the Florida idea. You listening? He — he talked to his partner, and he came to me . . . I'm going to be all right, you hear? Dad, listen to me, he said it was just a question of the amount!

WILLY: Then you . . . got it?

HAPPY: He's gonna be terrific, Pop!

610 WILLY: *(trying to stand)* Then you got it, haven't you? You got it! You got it!

BIFF: *(agonized, holds Willy down)* No, no. Look, Pop. I'm supposed to have lunch with them tomorrow. I'm just telling you this so you'll know that I can still make an impression, Pop. And I'll make good somewhere, but I can't go tomorrow, see?

WILLY: Why not? You simply —

BIFF: But the pen, Pop!

WILLY: You give it to him and tell him it was an oversight!

615 HAPPY: Sure, have lunch tomorrow!

BIFF: I can't say that —

WILLY: You were doing a crossword puzzle and accidentally used his pen!

BIFF: Listen, kid, I took those balls years ago, now I walk in with his fountain pen? That clinches it, don't you see? I can't face him like that! I'll try elsewhere.

PAGE'S VOICE: Paging Mr. Loman!

620 WILLY: Don't you want to be anything?

BIFF: Pop, how can I go back?

WILLY: You don't want to be anything, is that what's behind it?

BIFF: *(now angry at Willy for not crediting his sympathy)* Don't take it that way! You think it was easy walking into that office after what I'd done to him? A team of horses couldn't have dragged me back to Bill Oliver!

WILLY: Then why'd you go?

625 BIFF: Why did I go? Why did I go? Look at you! Look at what's become of you!

Off left, The Woman laughs.

WILLY: Biff, you're going to go to that lunch tomorrow, or —

BIFF: I can't go. I've got no appointment!

HAPPY: Biff, for . . . !

WILLY: Are you spiting me?

630 BIFF: Don't take it that way! Goddammit!

WILLY: *(strikes Biff and falters away from the table)* You rotten little louse! Are you spiting me?

THE WOMAN: Someone's at the door, Willy!

BIFF: I'm no good, can't you see what I am?

HAPPY: *(separating them)* Hey, you're in a restaurant! Now cut it out, both of you! *(The Girls enter.)* Hello, girls, sit down.

The Woman laughs, off left.

MISS FORSYTHE: I guess we might as well. This is Letta. 635
THE WOMAN: Willy, are you going to wake up?
BIFF: *(ignoring Willy)* How're ya, miss, sit down. What do you drink?
MISS FORSYTHE: Letta might not be able to stay long.
LETTA: I gotta get up very early tomorrow. I got jury duty. I'm so excited! Were you fellows ever on a jury?
BIFF: No, but I been in front of them! *(The Girls laugh.)* This is my father. 640
LETTA: Isn't he cute? Sit down with us, Pop.
HAPPY: Sit him down, Biff!
BIFF: *(going to him)* Come on, slugger, drink us under the table. To hell with it! Come on, sit down, pal.

On Biff's last insistence, Willy is about to sit.

THE WOMAN: *(now urgently)* Willy, are you going to answer the door!

The Woman's call pulls Willy back. He starts right, befuddled.

BIFF: Hey, where are you going? 645
WILLY: Open the door.
BIFF: The door?
WILLY: The washroom . . . the door . . . where's the door?
BIFF: *(leading Willy to the left)* Just go straight down.

Willy moves left.

THE WOMAN: Willy, Willy, are you going to get up, get up, get up, get up? 650

Willy exits left.

LETTA: I think it's sweet you bring your daddy along.
MISS FORSYTHE: Oh, he isn't really your father!
BIFF: *(at left, turning to her resentfully)* Miss Forsythe, you've just seen a prince walk by. A fine, troubled prince. A hard-working, unappreciated prince. A pal, you understand? A good companion. Always for his boys.
LETTA: That's so sweet.
HAPPY: Well, girls, what's the program? We're wasting time. Come on, Biff. 655
Gather round. Where would you like to go?
BIFF: Why don't you do something for him?
HAPPY: Me!
BIFF: Don't you give a damn for him, Hap?
HAPPY: What're you talking about? I'm the one who—
BIFF: I sense it, you don't give a good goddam about him. *(He takes the rolled-up* 660
hose from his pocket and puts it on the table in front of Happy.) Look what
I found in the cellar, for Christ's sake. How can you bear to let it go on?
HAPPY: Me? Who goes away? Who runs off and—
BIFF: Yeah, but he doesn't mean anything to you. You could help him — I can't!
Don't you understand what I'm talking about? He's going to kill himself,
don't you know that?

HAPPY: Don't I know it! Me!

BIFF: Hap, help him! Jesus . . . help him . . . Help me, help me, I can't bear to look at his face! (*Ready to weep, he hurries out, up right.*)

665 **HAPPY:** (*starting after him*) Where are you going?

MISS FORSYTHE: What's he so mad about?

HAPPY: Come on, girls, we'll catch up with him.

MISS FORSYTHE: (*as Happy pushes her out*) Say, I don't like that temper of his!

HAPPY: He's just a little overstrung, he'll be all right!

670 **WILLY:** (*off left, as The Woman laughs*) Don't answer! Don't answer!

LETTA: Don't you want to tell your father —

HAPPY: No, that's not my father. He's just a guy. Come on, we'll catch Biff, and, honey, we're going to paint this town! Stanley, where's the check! Hey, Stanley!

They exit. Stanley looks toward left.

STANLEY: (*calling to Happy indignantly*) Mr. Loman! Mr. Loman!

Stanley picks up a chair and follows them off. Knocking is heard off left. The Woman enters, laughing. Willy follows her. She is in a black slip; he is buttoning his shirt. Raw, sensuous music accompanies their speech.

WILLY: Will you stop laughing? Will you stop?

675 **THE WOMAN:** Aren't you going to answer the door? He'll wake the whole hotel.

WILLY: I'm not expecting anybody.

THE WOMAN: Whyn't you have another drink, honey, and stop being so damn self-centered?

WILLY: I'm so lonely.

THE WOMAN: You know you ruined me, Willy? From now on, whenever you come to the office, I'll see that you go right through to the buyers. No waiting at my desk any more, Willy. You ruined me.

680 **WILLY:** That's nice of you to say that.

THE WOMAN: Gee, you are self-centered! Why so sad? You are the saddest self-centeredest soul I ever did see-saw. (*She laughs. He kisses her.*) Come on inside, drummer boy. It's silly to be dressing in the middle of the night. (*As knocking is heard.*) Aren't you going to answer the door?

WILLY: They're knocking on the wrong door.

THE WOMAN: But I felt the knocking. And he heard us talking in here. Maybe the hotel's on fire!

WILLY: (*his terror rising*) It's a mistake.

685 **THE WOMAN:** Then tell him to go away!

WILLY: There's nobody there.

THE WOMAN: It's getting on my nerves, Willy. There's somebody standing out there and it's getting on my nerves!

WILLY: (*pushing her away from him*) All right, stay in the bathroom here, and don't come out. I think there's a law in Massachusetts about it, so don't come out. It may be that new room clerk. He looked very mean. So don't come out. It's a mistake, there's no fire.

The knocking is heard again. He takes a few steps away from her, and she vanishes into the wing. The light follows him, and now he is facing Young Biff, who carries a suitcase. Biff steps toward him. The music is gone.

BIFF: Why didn't you answer?

WILLY: Biff! What are you doing in Boston?   690

BIFF: Why didn't you answer? I've been knocking for five minutes, I called you on the phone —

WILLY: I just heard you. I was in the bathroom and had the door shut. Did anything happen home?

BIFF: Dad — I let you down.

WILLY: What do you mean?

BIFF: Dad . . .   695

WILLY: Biffo, what's this about? (*Putting his arm around Biff.*) Come on, let's go downstairs and get you a malted.

BIFF: Dad, I flunked math.

WILLY: Not for the term?

BIFF: The term. I haven't got enough credits to graduate.

WILLY: You mean to say Bernard wouldn't give you the answers?   700

BIFF: He did, he tried, but I only got a sixty-one.

WILLY: And they wouldn't give you four points?

BIFF: Birnbaum refused absolutely. I begged him, Pop, but he won't give me those points. You gotta talk to him before they close the school. Because if he saw the kind of man you are, and you just talked to him in your way, I'm sure he'd come through for me. The class came right before practice, see, and I didn't go enough. Would you talk to him? He'd like you, Pop. You know the way you could talk.

WILLY: You're on. We'll drive right back.

BIFF: Oh, Dad, good work! I'm sure he'll change it for you!   705

WILLY: Go downstairs and tell the clerk I'm checkin' out. Go right down.

BIFF: Yes, Sir! See, the reason he hates me, Pop — one day he was late for class so I got up at the blackboard and imitated him. I crossed my eyes and talked with a lithp.

WILLY: (*laughing*) You did? The kids like it?

BIFF: They nearly died laughing!

WILLY: Yeah? What'd you do?   710

BIFF: The thquare root of thixthy twee is . . . (*Willy bursts out laughing; Biff joins him.*) And in the middle of it he walked in!

Willy laughs and The Woman joins in offstage.

WILLY: (*without hesitating*) Hurry downstairs and—

BIFF: Somebody in there?

WILLY: No, that was next door.

The Woman laughs offstage.

BIFF: Somebody got in your bathroom!   715

WILLY: No, it's the next room, there's a party —

THE WOMAN: *(enters, laughing. She lisps this)* Can I come in? There's
    something in the bathtub, Willy, and it's moving!

Willy looks at Biff, who is staring open-mouthed and horrified at The Woman.

WILLY: Ah — you better go back to your room. They must be finished painting
    by now. They're painting her room so I let her take a shower here. Go back,
    go back . . . *(He pushes her.)*
THE WOMAN: *(resisting)* But I've got to get dressed, Willy, I can't—
720 WILLY: Get out of here! Go back, go back . . . *(Suddenly striving for the
    ordinary.)* This is Miss Francis, Biff, she's a buyer. They're painting her
    room. Go back, Miss Francis, go back . . .
THE WOMAN: But my clothes, I can't go out naked in the hall!
WILLY: *(pushing her offstage)* Get outa here! Go back, go back!

Biff slowly sits down on his suitcase as the argument continues offstage.

THE WOMAN: Where's my stockings? You promised me stockings, Willy!
WILLY: I have no stockings here!
725 THE WOMAN: You had two boxes of size nine sheers for me, and I want them!
WILLY: Here, for God's sake, will you get outa here!
THE WOMAN: *(enters holding a box of stockings)* I just hope there's nobody in
    the hall. That's all I hope. *(To Biff.)* Are you football or baseball?
BIFF: Football.
THE WOMAN: *(angry, humiliated)* That's me too. G'night. *(She snatches her
    clothes from Willy, and walks out.)*
730 WILLY: *(after a pause)* Well, better get going. I want to get to the school first
    thing in the morning. Get my suits out of the closet. I'll get my valise. *(Biff
    doesn't move.)* What's the matter? *(Biff remains motionless, tears falling.)*
    She's a buyer. Buys for J. H. Simmons. She lives down the hall — they're
    painting. You don't imagine —*(He breaks off. After a pause.)* Now listen,
    pal, she's just a buyer. She sees merchandise in her room and they have to
    keep it looking just so . . . *(Pause. Assuming command.)* All right, get my
    suits. *(Biff doesn't move.)* Now stop crying and do as I say. I gave you an or-
    der. Biff, I gave you an order! Is that what you do when I give you an order?
    How dare you cry! *(Putting his arm around Biff.)* Now look, Biff, when you
    grow up you'll understand about these things. You mustn't — you mustn't
    overemphasize a thing like this. I'll see Birnbaum first thing in the morning.
BIFF: Never mind.
WILLY: *(getting down beside Biff)* Never mind! He's going to give you those
    points. I'll see to it.
BIFF: He wouldn't listen to you.
WILLY: He certainly will listen to me. You need those points for the U. of
    Virginia.
735 BIFF: I'm not going there.
WILLY: Heh? If I can't get him to change that mark you'll make it up in
    summer school. You've got all summer to—
BIFF: *(his weeping breaking from him)* Dad . . .

WILLY: *(infected by it)* Oh, my boy . . .

BIFF: Dad . . .

WILLY: She's nothing to me, Biff. I was lonely, I was terribly lonely. 740

BIFF: You — you gave her Mama's stockings! *(His tears break through and he rises to go.)*

WILLY: *(grabbing for Biff)* I gave you an order!

BIFF: Don't touch me, you — liar!

WILLY: Apologize for that!

BIFF: You fake! You phony little fake! You fake! *(Overcome, he turns quickly* 745 *and weeping fully goes out with his suitcase. Willy is left on the floor on his knees.)*

WILLY: I gave you an order! Biff, come back here or I'll beat you! Come back here! I'll whip you!

Stanley comes quickly in from the right and stands in front of Willy.

WILLY: *(shouts at Stanley)* I gave you an order . . .

STANLEY: Hey, let's pick it up, pick it up, Mr. Loman. *(He helps Willy to his feet.)* Your boys left with the chippies. They said they'll see you home.

A second waiter watches some distance away.

WILLY: But we were supposed to have dinner together.

Music is heard, Willy's theme.

STANLEY: Can you make it? 750

WILLY: I'll — sure, I can make it. *(Suddenly concerned about his clothes.)* Do I — I look all right?

STANLEY: Sure, you look all right. *(He flicks a speck off Willy's lapel.)*

WILLY: Here — here's a dollar.

STANLEY: Oh, your son paid me. It's all right.

WILLY: *(putting it in Stanley's hand)* No, take it. You're a good boy. 755

STANLEY: Oh, no, you don't have to . . .

WILLY: Here — here's some more, I don't need it any more. *(After a slight pause.)* Tell me — is there a seed store in the neighborhood?

STANLEY: Seeds? You mean like to plant?

As Willy turns, Stanley slips the money back into his jacket pocket.

WILLY: Yes. Carrots, peas . . .

STANLEY: Well, there's hardware stores on Sixth Avenue, but it may be too 760 late now.

WILLY: *(anxiously)* Oh, I'd better hurry. I've got to get some seeds. *(He starts off to the right.)* I've got to get some seeds, right away. Nothing's planted. I don't have a thing in the ground.

Willy hurries out as the light goes down. Stanley moves over to the right after him, watches him off. The other waiter has been staring at Willy.

STANLEY: *(to the waiter)* Well, whatta you looking at?

The waiter picks up the chairs and moves off right. Stanley takes the table and follows him. The light fades on this area. There is a long pause, the sound of the flute coming over. The light gradually rises on the kitchen, which is empty. Happy appears at the door of the house, followed by Biff. Happy is carrying a large bunch of long-stemmed roses. He enters the kitchen, looks around for Linda. Not seeing her, he turns to Biff, who is just outside the house door, and makes a gesture with his hands, indicating "Not here, I guess." He looks into the livingroom and freezes. Inside, Linda, unseen, is seated, Willy's coat on her lap. She rises ominously and quietly and moves toward Happy, who backs up into the kitchen, afraid.

HAPPY: Hey, what're you doing up? (*Linda says nothing but moves toward him implacably.*) Where's Pop? (*He keeps backing to the right, and now Linda is in full view in the doorway to the livingroom.*) Is he sleeping?

LINDA: Where were you?

765   **HAPPY:** (*trying to laugh it off*) We met two girls, Mom, very fine types. Here, we brought you some flowers. (*Offering them to her.*) Put them in your room, Ma.

She knocks them to the floor at Biff's feet. He has now come inside and closed the door behind him. She stares at Biff, silent.

HAPPY: Now what'd you do that for? Mom, I want you to have some flowers —

LINDA: (*cutting Happy off, violently to Biff*) Don't you care whether he lives or dies?

HAPPY: (*going to the stairs*) Come upstairs, Biff.

BIFF: (*with a flare of disgust, to Happy*) Go away from me! (*To Linda.*) What do you mean, lives or dies? Nobody's dying around here, pal.

770   **LINDA:** Get out of my sight! Get out of here!

BIFF: I wanna see the boss.

LINDA: You're not going near him!

BIFF: Where is he? (*He moves into the livingroom and Linda follows.*)

LINDA: (*shouting after Biff*) You invite him for dinner. He looks forward to it all day — (*Biff appears in his parents' bedroom, looks around, and exits*) — and then you desert him there. There's no stranger you'd do that to!

775   **HAPPY:** Why? He had a swell time with us. Listen, when I — (*Linda comes back into the kitchen*) — desert him I hope I don't outlive the day!

LINDA: Get out of here!

HAPPY: Now look, Mom . . .

LINDA: Did you have to go to women tonight? You and your lousy rotten whores!

Biff re-enters the kitchen.

HAPPY: Mom, all we did was follow Biff around trying to cheer him up! (*To Biff.*) Boy, what a night you gave me!

780   **LINDA:** Get out of here, both of you, and don't come back! I don't want you tormenting him any more. Go on now, get your things together! (*To Biff.*) You can sleep in his apartment. (*She starts to pick up the flowers and stops herself.*) Pick up this stuff, I'm not your maid any more. Pick it up, you bum, you!

Happy turns his back to her in refusal. Biff slowly moves over and gets down on his knees, picking up the flowers.

LINDA: You're a pair of animals! Not one, not another living soul would have had the cruelty to walk out on that man in a restaurant!

BIFF: *(not looking at her)* Is that what he said?

LINDA: He didn't have to say anything. He was so humiliated he nearly limped when he came in.

HAPPY: But, Mom he had a great time with us —

BIFF: *(cutting him off violently)* Shut up!   785

Without another word, Happy goes upstairs.

LINDA: You! You didn't even go in to see if he was all right!

BIFF: *(still on the floor in front of Linda, the flowers in his hand; with self-loathing)* No. Didn't. Didn't do a damned thing. How do you like that, heh? Left him babbling in a toilet.

LINDA: You louse. You . . .

BIFF: Now you hit it on the nose! *(He gets up, throws the flowers in the wastebasket.)* The scum of the earth, and you're looking at him!

LINDA: Get out of here!   790

BIFF: I gotta talk to the boss, Mom. Where is he?

LINDA: You're not going near him. Get out of this house!

BIFF: *(with absolute assurance, determination)* No. We're gonna have an abrupt conversation, him and me.

LINDA: You're not talking to him!

Hammering is heard from outside the house, off right. Biff turns toward the noise.

LINDA: *(suddenly pleading)* Will you please leave him alone?   795

BIFF: What's he doing out there?

LINDA: He's planting the garden!

BIFF: *(quietly)* Now? Oh, my God!

Biff moves outside, Linda following. The light dies down on them and comes up on the center of the apron as Willy walks into it. He is carrying a flashlight, a hoe and a handful of seed packets. He raps the top of the hoe sharply to fix it firmly, and then moves to the left, measuring off the distance with his foot. He holds the flashlight to look at the seed packets, reading off the instructions. He is in the blue of night.

WILLY: Carrots . . . quarter-inch apart. Rows . . . one-foot rows. *(He measures it off.)* One foot. *(He puts down a package and measures off.)* Beets. *(He puts down another package and measures again.)* Lettuce. *(He reads the package, puts it down.)* One foot — *(He breaks off as Ben appears at the right and moves slowly down to him.)* What a proposition, ts, ts. Terrific, terrific. 'Cause she's suffered, Ben, the woman has suffered. You understand me? A man can't go out the way he came in, Ben, a man has got to add up to something. You can't, you can't — *(Ben moves toward him as though to interrupt.)* You gotta consider, now. Don't answer so quick. Remember, it's a guaranteed twenty-thousand-dollar proposition. Now look, Ben, I want you to go through the ins and outs of this thing with me. I've got nobody to talk to, Ben, and the woman has suffered, you hear me?

800   BEN: *(standing still, considering)* What's the proposition?

WILLY: It's twenty thousand dollars on the barrelhead. Guaranteed, gilt-edged, you understand?

BEN: You don't want to make a fool of yourself. They might not honor the policy.

WILLY: How can they dare refuse? Didn't I work like a coolie to meet every premium on the nose? And now they don't pay off? Impossible!

BEN: It's called a cowardly thing, William.

805   WILLY: Why? Does it take more guts to stand here the rest of my life ringing up a zero?

BEN: *(yielding)* That's a point, William. *(He moves, thinking, turns.)* And twenty thousand — that *is* something one can feel with the hand, it is there.

WILLY: *(now assured, with rising power)* Oh, Ben, that's the whole beauty of it! I see it like a diamond, shining in the dark, hard and rough, that I can pick up and touch in my hand. Not like — like an appointment! This would not be another damned-fool appointment, Ben, and it changes all the aspects. Because he thinks I'm nothing, see, and so he spites me. But the funeral — *(Straightening up.)* Ben, that funeral will be massive! They'll come from Maine, Massachusetts, Vermont, New Hampshire! All the old-timers with the strange license plates — that boy will be thunder-struck, Ben, because he never realized — I am known! Rhode Island, New York, New Jersey — I am known, Ben, and he'll see it with his eyes once and for all. He'll see what I am, Ben! He's in for a shock, that boy!

BEN: *(coming down to the edge of the garden)* He'll call you a coward.

WILLY: *(suddenly fearful)* No, that would be terrible.

810   BEN: Yes. And a damned fool.

WILLY: No, no, he mustn't, I won't have that! *(He is broken and desperate.)*

BEN: He'll hate you, William.

The gay music of the boys is heard.

WILLY: Oh, Ben, how do we get back to all the great times? Used to be so full of light, and comradeship, the sleigh-riding in winter, and the ruddiness on his cheeks. And always some kind of good news coming up, always something nice coming up ahead. And never even let me carry the valises in the house, and simonizing, simonizing that little red car! Why, why can't I give him something and not have him hate me?

BEN: Let me think about it. *(He glances at his watch.)* I still have a little time. Remarkable proposition, but you've got to be sure you're not making a fool of yourself.

Ben drifts off upstage and goes out of sight. Biff comes down from the left.

815   WILLY: *(suddenly conscious of Biff, turns and looks up at him, then begins picking up the packages of seeds in confusion)* Where the hell is that seed?

(Indignantly.) You can't see nothing out here! They boxed in the whole goddam neighborhood!

BIFF: There are people all around here. Don't you realize that?

WILLY: I'm busy. Don't bother me.

BIFF: *(taking the hoe from Willy)* I'm saying good-by to you, Pop. *(Willy looks at him, silent, unable to move.)* I'm not coming back any more.

WILLY: You're not going to see Oliver tomorrow?

BIFF: I've got no appointment, Dad.   820

WILLY: He put his arm around you, and you've got no appointment?

BIFF: Pop, get this now, will you? Everytime I've left it's been a fight that sent me out of here. Today I realized something about myself and I tried to explain it to you and I — I think I'm just not smart enough to make any sense out of it for you. To hell with whose fault it is or anything like that. *(He takes Willy's arm.)* Let's just wrap it up, heh? Come on in, we'll tell Mom. *(He gently tries to pull Willy to the left.)*

WILLY: *(frozen, immobile, with guilt in his voice)* No, I don't want to see her.

BIFF: Come on! *(He pulls again, and Willy tries to pull away.)*

WILLY: *(highly nervous)* No, no, I don't want to see her.   825

BIFF: *(tries to look into Willy's face, as if to find the answer there)* Why don't you want to see her?

WILLY: *(more harshly now)* Don't bother me, will you?

BIFF: What do you mean, you don't want to see her? You don't want them calling you yellow, do you? This isn't your fault; it's me, I'm a bum. Now come inside! *(Willy strains to get away.)* Did you hear what I said to you?

Willy pulls away and quickly goes by himself into the house. Biff follows.

LINDA: *(to Willy)* Did you plant, dear?

BIFF: *(at the door, to Linda)* All right, we had it out. I'm going and I'm not   830
writing any more.

LINDA: *(going to Willy in the kitchen)* I think that's the best way, dear. 'Cause there's no use drawing it out, you'll just never get along.

Willy doesn't respond.

BIFF: People ask where I am and what I'm doing, you don't know, and you don't care. That way it'll be off your mind and you can start brightening up again. All right? That clears it, doesn't it? *(Willy is silent, and Biff goes to him.)* You gonna wish me luck, scout? *(He extends his hand.)* What do you say?

LINDA: Shake his hand, Willy.

WILLY: *(turning to her, seething with hurt)* There's no necessity to mention the pen at all, y'know.

BIFF: *(gently)* I've got no appointment, Dad.   835

WILLY: *(erupting fiercely)* He put his arm around . . .?

BIFF: Dad, you're never going to see what I am, so what's the use of arguing? If I strike oil I'll send you a check. Meantime forget I'm alive.

WILLY: *(to Linda)* Spite, see?

BIFF: Shake hands, Dad.

840   **Willy:** Not my hand.
Biff: I was hoping not to go this way.
Willy: Well, this is the way you're going. Good-by.

Biff looks at him a moment, then turns sharply and goes to the stairs.

Willy: *(stops him with)* May you rot in hell if you leave this house!
Biff: *(turning)* Exactly what is it that you want from me?
845   **Willy:** I want you to know, on the train, in the mountains, in the valleys, wherever you go, that you cut down your life for spite!
Biff: No, no.
Willy: Spite, spite, is the word of your undoing! And when you're down and out, remember what did it. When you're rotting somewhere beside the railroad tracks, remember, and don't you dare blame it on me!
Biff: I'm not blaming it on you!
Willy: I won't take the rap for this, you hear?

Happy comes down the stairs and stands on the bottom step, watching.

850   **Biff:** That's just what I'm telling you!
Willy: *(sinking into a chair at the table, with full accusation)* You're trying to put a knife in me — don't think I don't know what you're doing!
Biff: All right, phony! Then let's lay it on the line. *(He whips the rubber tube out of his pocket and puts it on the table.)*
Happy: You crazy —
Linda: Biff! *(She moves to grab the hose, but Biff holds it down with his hand.)*
855   **Biff:** Leave it there! Don't move it!
Willy: *(not looking at it)* What is that?
Biff: You know goddam well what that is.
Willy: *(caged, wanting to escape)* I never saw that.
Biff: You saw it. The mice didn't bring it into the cellar! What is this supposed to do, make a hero out of you? This supposed to make me sorry for you?
860   **Willy:** Never heard of it.
Biff: There'll be no pity for you, you hear it? No pity!
Willy: *(to Linda)* You hear the spite!
Biff: No, you're going to hear the truth — what you are and what I am!
Linda: Stop it!
865   **Willy:** Spite!
Happy: *(coming down toward Biff)* You cut it now!
Biff: *(to Happy)* The man don't know who we are! The man is gonna know! *(To Willy.)* We never told the truth for ten minutes in this house!
Happy: We always told the truth!
Biff: *(turning on him)* You big blow, are you the assistant buyer? You're one of the two assistants to the assistant, aren't you?
870   **Happy:** Well, I'm practically —
Biff: You're practically full of it! We all are! And I'm through with it. *(To Willy.)* Now hear this, Willy, this is me.
Willy: I know you!

BIFF: You know why I had no address for three months? I stole a suit in Kansas City and I was in jail. (*To Linda, who is sobbing.*) Stop crying. I'm through with it.

Linda turns away from them, her hands covering her face.

WILLY: I suppose that's my fault!

BIFF: I stole myself out of every good job since high school!⁣ 875

WILLY: And whose fault is that?

BIFF: And I never got anywhere because you blew me so full of hot air I could never stand taking orders from anybody! That's whose fault it is!

WILLY: I hear that!

LINDA: Don't, Biff!

BIFF: It's goddam time you heard that! I had to be boss big shot in two weeks, 880 and I'm through with it!

WILLY: Then hang yourself! For spite, hang yourself!

BIFF: No! Nobody's hanging himself, Willy! I ran down eleven flights with a pen in my hand today. And suddenly I stopped, you hear me? And in the middle of that office building, do you hear this? I stopped in the middle of that building and I saw — the sky. I saw the things that I love in this world. The work and the food and time to sit and smoke. And I looked at the pen and said to myself, what the hell am I grabbing this for? Why am I trying to become what I don't want to be? What am I doing in an office, making a contemptuous, begging fool of myself, when all I want is out there, waiting for me the minute I say I know who I am! Why can't I say that, Willy? (*He tries to make Willy face him, but Willy pulls away and moves to the left.*)

WILLY: (*with hatred, threateningly*) The door of your life is wide open!

BIFF: Pop! I'm a dime a dozen, and so are you!

WILLY: (*turning on him now in an uncontrolled outburst*) I am not a dime a 885 dozen! I am Willy Loman, and you are Biff Loman!

Biff starts for Willy, but is blocked by Happy. In his fury, Biff seems on the verge of attacking his father.

BIFF: I am not a leader of men, Willy, and neither are you. You were never anything but a hard-working drummer who landed in the ash can like all the rest of them! I'm one dollar an hour, Willy! I tried seven states and couldn't raise it. A buck an hour! Do you gather my meaning? I'm not bringing home any prizes any more, and you're going to stop waiting for me to bring them home!

WILLY: (*directly to Biff*) You vengeful, spiteful mutt!

Biff breaks from Happy. Willy, in fright, starts up the stairs. Biff grabs him.

BIFF: (*at the peak of his fury*) Pop, I'm nothing! I'm nothing, Pop. Can't you understand that? There's no spite in it any more. I'm just what I am, that's all.

Biff's fury has spent itself, and he breaks down, sobbing, holding on to Willy, who dumbly fumbles for Biff's face.

WILLY: (*astonished*) What're you doing? What're you doing? (*To Linda.*) Why is he crying?

890 BIFF: (*crying, broken*) Will you let me go, for Christ's sake? Will you take that phony dream and burn it before something happens? (*Struggling to contain himself, he pulls away and moves to the stairs.*) I'll go in the morning. Put him — put him to bed. (*Exhausted, Biff moves up the stairs to his room.*)

WILLY: (*after a long pause, astonished, elevated*) Isn't that remarkable? Biff — he likes me!

LINDA: He loves you, Willy!

HAPPY: (*deeply moved*) Always did, Pop.

WILLY: Oh, Biff! (*Staring wildly.*) He cried! Cried to me! (*He is choking with his love, and now cries out his promise.*) That boy — that boy is going to be magnificent!

Ben appears in the light just outside the kitchen.

895 BEN: Yes, outstanding, with twenty thousand behind him.

LINDA: (*sensing the racing of his mind, fearfully, carefully*) Now come to bed, Willy. It's all settled now.

WILLY: (*finding it difficult not to rush out of the house*) Yes, we'll sleep. Come on. Go to sleep, Hap.

BEN: And it does take a great kind of man to crack the jungle.

In accents of dread, Ben's idyllic music starts up.

HAPPY: (*his arm around Linda*) I'm getting married, Pop, don't forget it. I'm changing everything. I'm gonna run that department before the year is up. You'll see, Mom. (*He kisses her.*)

900 BEN: The jungle is dark but full of diamonds, Willy.

Willy turns, moves, listening to Ben.

LINDA: Be good. You're both good boys, just act that way, that's all.

HAPPY: 'Night, Pop. (*He goes upstairs.*)

LINDA: (*to Willy*) Come, dear.

BEN: (*with greater force*) One must go in to fetch a diamond out.

905 WILLY: (*to Linda, as he moves slowly along the edge of the kitchen, toward the door*) I just want to get settled down, Linda. Let me sit alone for a little.

LINDA: (*almost uttering her fear*) I want you upstairs.

WILLY: (*taking her in his arms*) In a few minutes, Linda. I couldn't sleep right now. Go on, you look awful tired. (*He kisses her.*)

BEN: Not like an appointment at all. A diamond is rough and hard to the touch.

WILLY: Go on now. I'll be right up.

910 LINDA: I think this is the only way, Willy.

WILLY: Sure, it's the best thing.

BEN: Best thing!

WILLY: The only way. Everything is gonna be — go on, kid, get to bed. You look so tired.

LINDA: Come right up.

WILLY: Two minutes. 915

Linda goes into the livingroom, then reappears in her bedroom. Willy moves just outside the kitchen door.

WILLY: Loves me. (*Wonderingly.*) Always loved me. Isn't that a remarkable thing? Ben, he'll worship me for it!

BEN: (*with promise*) It's dark there, but full of diamonds.

WILLY: Can you imagine that magnificence with twenty thousand dollars in his pocket?

LINDA: (*calling from her room*) Willy! Come up!

WILLY: (*calling from the kitchen*) Yes! Yes! Coming! It's very smart, you realize 920
that, don't you, sweetheart? Even Ben sees it. I gotta go, baby. 'By! By! (*Going over to Ben, almost dancing.*) Imagine? When the mail comes he'll be ahead of Bernard again!

BEN: A perfect proposition all around.

WILLY: Did you see how he cried to me? Oh, if I could kiss him, Ben!

BEN: Time, William, time!

WILLY: Oh, Ben, I always knew one way or another we were gonna make it, Biff and I!

BEN: (*looking at his watch*) The boat. We'll be late. (*He moves slowly off into the* 925
darkness.)

WILLY: (*elegiacally, turning to the house*) Now when you kick off, boy, I want a seventy-yard boot, and get right down the field under the ball, and when you hit, hit low and hit hard, because it's important, boy. (*He swings around and faces the audience.*) There's all kinds of important people in the stands, and the first thing you know . . . (*Suddenly realizing he is alone.*) Ben! Ben, where do I . . . ? (*He makes a sudden movement of search.*) Ben, how do I . . . ?

LINDA: (*calling*) Willy, you coming up?

WILLY: (*uttering a gasp of fear, whirling about as if to quiet her*) Sh! (*He turns around as if to find his way; sounds, faces, voices, seem to be swarming in upon him and he flicks at them, crying.*) Sh! Sh! (*Suddenly music, faint and high, stops him. It rises in intensity, almost to an unbearable scream. He goes up and down on his toes, and rushes off around the house.*) Shhh!

LINDA: Willy?

There is no answer. Linda waits. Biff gets up off his bed. He is still in his clothes. Happy sits up. Biff stands listening.

LINDA: (*with real fear*) Willy, answer me! Willy! 930

There is the sound of a car starting and moving away at full speed.

LINDA: No!

BIFF: (*rushing down the stairs*) Pop!

As the car speeds off, the music crashes down in a frenzy of sound, which becomes the soft pulsation of a single cello string. Biff slowly returns to his bedroom. He and Happy gravely don their jackets. Linda slowly walks out of her room. The music has developed into a dead march. The leaves of day are appearing over everything. Charley and Bernard, somberly dressed, appear and knock on the kitchen door. Biff and Happy slowly descend the stairs to the kitchen as Charley and Bernard enter. All stop a moment when Linda, in clothes of mourning, bearing a little bunch of roses, comes through the draped doorway into the kitchen. She goes to Charley and takes his arm. Now all move toward the audience, through the wall-line of the kitchen. At the limit of the apron, Linda lays down the flowers, kneels, and sits back on her heels. All stare down at the grave.

<u>REQUIEM</u>

CHARLEY: It's getting dark, Linda.

Linda doesn't react. She stares at the grave.

BIFF: How about it, Mom? Better get some rest, heh? They'll be closing the gate soon.

Linda makes no move. Pause.

HAPPY: *(deeply angered)* He had no right to do that! There was no necessity for it. We would've helped him.

CHARLEY: *(grunting)* Hmmm.

5 **BIFF:** Come along, Mom.

LINDA: Why didn't anybody come?

CHARLEY: It was a very nice funeral.

LINDA: But where are all the people he knew? Maybe they blame him.

CHARLEY: Naa. It's a rough world, Linda. They wouldn't blame him.

10 **LINDA:** I can't understand it. At this time especially. First time in thirty-five years we were just about free and clear. He only needed a little salary. He was even finished with the dentist.

CHARLEY: No man only needs a little salary.

LINDA: I can't understand it.

BIFF: There were a lot of nice days. When he'd come home from a trip; or on Sundays, making the stoop; finishing the cellar; putting on the new porch; when he built the extra bathroom; and put up the garage. You know something, Charley, there's more of him in that front stoop than in all the sales he ever made.

CHARLEY: Yeah. He was a happy man with a batch of cement.

15 **LINDA:** He was so wonderful with his hands.

BIFF: He had the wrong dreams. All, all, wrong.

HAPPY: *(almost ready to fight Biff)* Don't say that!

BIFF: He never knew who he was.

CHARLEY: *(stopping Happy's movement and reply. To Biff.)* Nobody dast blame this man. You don't understand: Willy was a salesman. And for a salesman, there is no rock bottom to the life. He don't put a bolt to a nut, he don't tell you the law or give you medicine. He's a man out there in the blue, riding on a smile and a shoeshine. And when they start not smiling back — that's an earthquake. And then you get yourself a couple of spots on your hat, and you're finished. Nobody dast blame this man. A salesman is got to dream, boy. It comes with the territory.

BIFF: Charley, the man didn't know who he was.　　　　　　　　　　　　　20

HAPPY: (*infuriated*) Don't say that!

BIFF: Why don't you come with me, Happy?

HAPPY: I'm not licked that easily. I'm staying right in this city, and I'm gonna beat this racket! (*He looks at Biff, his chin set.*) The Loman Brothers!

BIFF: I know who I am, kid.

HAPPY: All right, boy. I'm gonna show you and everybody else that Willy　　25 Loman did not die in vain. He had a good dream. It's the only dream you can have — to come out number-one man. He fought it out here, and this is where I'm gonna win it for him.

BIFF: (*with a hopeless glance at Happy, bends toward his mother*) Let's go, Mom.

LINDA: I'll be with you in a minute. Go on, Charley. (*He hesitates.*) I want to, just for a minute. I never had a chance to say good-by.

Charley moves away, followed by Happy. Biff remains a slight distance up and left of Linda. She sits there, summoning herself. The flute begins, not far away, playing behind her speech.

LINDA: Forgive me, dear. I can't cry. I don't know what it is, but I can't cry. I don't understand it. Why did you ever do that? Help me, Willy, I can't cry. It seems to me that you're just on another trip. I keep expecting you. Willy, dear, I can't cry. Why did you do it? I search and search and I search, and I can't understand it, Willy. I made the last payment on the house today. Today, dear. And there'll be nobody home. (*A sob rises in her throat.*) We're free and clear. (*Sobbing more fully, released.*) We're free. (*Biff comes slowly toward her.*) We're free . . . We're free . . .

Biff lifts her to her feet and moves out up right with her in his arms. Linda sobs quietly. Bernard and Charley come together and follow them, followed by Happy. Only the music of the flute is left on the darkening stage as over the house the hard towers of the apartment buildings rise into sharp focus, and—

The Curtain Falls

Reading and Reacting

1. With which character in the play do you most identify? Why?

2. Is Willy a likeable character? What words and actions —both Willy's and those of other characters —help you form your conclusion?

3. How does the existence of The Woman affect your overall impression of Willy? What does she reveal about his character?

4. What does Willy's attitude toward his sons indicate about his character? How is this attitude revealed?

5. Does this play have a hero? A villain? Explain.

6. In the absence of a narrator, what devices does Miller use to provide exposition —basic information about character and setting?

7. The conversation between Biff and Happy in act 1 reveals many of their differences. List some of the differences between these two characters.

8. In numerous remarks, Willy expresses his philosophy of business. Summarize some of his key ideas about the business world. How realistic do you think these ideas are? How do these ideas help to delineate his character?

9. In act 1, Linda tells Willy, "Few men are idolized by their children the way you are." Is she sincere, is she being ironic, or is she just trying to make Willy feel better?

10. How do the frequent flashbacks help to explain what motivates Willy? How else could this background information have been presented in the play? Are there advantages to using flashbacks instead of the alternative you suggest?

11. Is Linda simply a stereotype of the long-suffering wife, or is she an individualized, multidimensional character? Explain.

12. Willy Loman lives in Brooklyn, New York; his "territory" is New England. What is the significance to him of the "faraway places"—Africa, Alaska, California, Texas, and the like—mentioned in the play?

13. Explain the function of Bernard in the play.

14. The play concludes with a requiem. What is a requiem? What information about each of the major characters is supplied in this brief section? Is this information essential to your understanding or appreciation of the play, or would the play have been equally effective without the requiem? Explain.

15. JOURNAL ENTRY Do you believe Willy Loman is an innocent victim of the society in which he lives, or do you believe there are flaws in his character that make him at least partially responsible for his own misfortune? Explain.

16. CRITICAL PERSPECTIVE In his 1949 essay "Tragedy and the Common Man," Arthur Miller attempts to define modern tragedy:

> There is a misconception of tragedy with which I have been struck in review after review, and in many conversations with writers and readers alike. It is the idea that tragedy is of necessity allied to pessimism. Even the dictionary says nothing more about the word than that it means a story with a sad or unhappy ending. This impression is so firmly fixed that I almost hesitate to claim that in truth tragedy implies more optimism in its author than does comedy, and that its final result ought to be the reinforcement of the onlooker's brightest opinions of the human animal. . . .
>
> Pathos truly is the mode for the pessimist. But tragedy requires a nicer balance between what is possible and what is impossible. And it is curious, although edifying, that the plays we revere, century after century, are the tragedies. In them, and in them alone, lies the belief—optimistic, if you will, in the perfectibility of man.

Death of a Salesman, like other tragedies, is certainly "a story with a sad or unhappy ending." Do you find the play at all optimistic?

Related Works: "Do not go gentle into that good night" (p. 559), "Those Winter Sundays" (p. 560), "The Love Song of J. Alfred Prufrock" (p. 871), *Oedipus the King* (p. 1271), *Fences* (p. 1358).

WRITING SUGGESTIONS: Character

1. In *Death of a Salesman,* each character pursues his or her version of the American Dream. Choose two characters, define their idea of the American dream, and explain how each tries to make the dream a reality. In each case, consider the obstacles the character encounters, and try to account for the character's success or lack of success. If you like, you may consider other works in which the American Dream is central — for example, "Two Kinds" (p. 527), "Immigrants" (p. 761), or *Fences* (p. 1358).

2. Minor characters are often flat characters; in many cases, their sole function is to advance the plot or to highlight a particular trait in a major character. Sometimes, however, minor characters may be of more than minor importance. Choose one minor character from *Hamlet* or *Death of a Salesman* (or from a play in another chapter), and write a paper in which you discuss how the play would be different without this character.

3. Watch a film version of *Marty* or *Death of a Salesman.* Write an essay in which you evaluate the actors' interpretation of the central character.

4. **WEB ACTIVITY** The following Web site contains information about Arthur Miller:

http://www.deathofasalesman.com/rev-49-nytimes3.htm

In "Tragedy and the Common Man," Miller states, "I believe that the common man is as apt a subject for tragedy in its highest sense as kings were." He goes on to further define the tragic hero:

> I think the tragic feeling is evoked in us when we are in the presence of a character who is ready to lay down his life, if need be, to secure one thing — his sense of personal dignity. From Orestes to Hamlet, Medea to Macbeth, the underlying struggle is that of the individual attempting to gain his "rightful" position in his society.

After reading "Tragedy and the Common Man," locate a Web site that explains Aristotle's definition of tragedy. Write an essay in which you examine Willy Loman as a modern-day tragic hero, considering Aristotle's definition of tragedy as well as Miller's.

CHAPTER 30

STAGING

In reading a play rather than witnessing it on stage, we . . . have to imagine what it might look like in performance, projecting in our mind's eye an image of the setting and the props, as well as the movements, gestures, facial expressions, and vocal intonations of the characters. . . . And we — like the director, designers, and actors — must develop our understanding of the play and our idea of the play in performance primarily from a careful reading of the dialogue, as well as from whatever stage directions and other information the dramatist might provide about the characters and the setting.
—**Carl H. Klaus, Miriam Gilbert, and Braford S. Field, Jr.,** *Stages of Drama*

The playwright as playwright is in part a director. If he is truly a man of the theatre (some playwrights only suffer the theatre but do not feel they belong to it) the playwright "sees" the play on the stage as he writes. His dialogue as well as his notations of stage behavior suggest movement and part of the total physical life that the script is to acquire when it is produced. —**Harold Clurmon,** *On Directing*

Whether the director sees . . . a play as tragedy, comedy or even farce will have an immediate and very practical effect on his handling of the production: it will influence his casting, the design of the set and costumes, the tone, rhythm and pacing of the performance. And, above all, the style in which it is to be acted. —**Martin Esslin,** *An Anatomy of Drama*

The argument is sometimes advanced that the complete verisimilitude of the movies is more enjoyable than the necessarily limited illusionism of the live theater. Hollywood producers evidently believe the public in general holds such an opinion. Yet accepting conventions can be a source of pleasure for its own sake, just as children have always had fun putting on shows in the cellar by ignoring the steampipe or else turning it into the Brooklyn Bridge.
—**Thelma Altshuler and Richard Paul Jenaro,** *Responses to Drama*

Staging refers to the elements of a play's production that determine how the play looks and sounds to an audience. It encompasses the **stage settings,** or **sets**— scenery and props — as well as the costumes, lighting, sound effects, and music that bring the play to life on the stage. In short, staging is everything that goes into making a written script a play.

Most contemporary staging in the West has concentrated on re-creating the outside world. This concept of staging, which has dominated Western theatrical productions for centuries, would seem alien in many non-Western theaters. Japanese Kabuki dramas and No plays, for example, depend on staging conventions that make no attempt to mirror reality or everyday speech. Scenery and costumes are largely symbolic, and often actors wear highly stylized makeup or masks. Although some European and American playwrights have been strongly influenced by non-Western staging, the majority of plays being produced in the West still try to create the illusion of reality.

STAGE DIRECTIONS

Usually a playwright presents instructions for the staging of a play in **stage directions** — notes that comment on the scenery, the movements of the performers, the lighting, and the placement of props. (In the absence of detailed stage directions, dialogue can provide information about staging.) Sometimes these stage directions are quite simple, leaving much to the imagination of the director. Consider how little specific information about the setting of the play is provided in these stage directions from Samuel Beckett's 1952 absurdist play *Waiting for Godot*:

ACT I

A country road. A tree. Evening.

Often, however, playwrights furnish much more detailed information about staging. Consider these notes from Anton Chekhov's *The Cherry Orchard*:

ACT I

A room, which has always been called the nursery. One of the doors leads into Anya's room. Dawn, sun rises during the scene. May, the cherry trees in flower, but it is cold in the garden with the frost of the early morning. Windows closed.
  Enter Dunyasha with a candle and Lopahin with a book in his hand.

These comments indicate that the first act takes place in a room with more than one door and that several windows reveal cherry trees in bloom. They also specify that the lighting should simulate the sun rising at dawn and that certain characters should enter carrying particular props. Still, Chekhov leaves it up to those staging the play to decide on the costumes for the characters and on the furniture that will be placed around the room.

Some stage directions are even more specific. Irish playwright George Bernard Shaw's long, complex stage directions are legendary in the theater. Note the degree of detail he provides in these stage directions from his 1906 comedy *The Doctor's Dilemma*:

The consulting-room has two windows looking on Queen Anne Street. Between the two is a marble-topped console, with haunched gilt legs ending in sphinx claws. The huge pier-glass [a long narrow mirror that fits between two windows] which surmounts it is mostly disabled from reflection by elaborate painting on its surface of palms, ferns, lilies, tulips, and sunflowers. The adjoining wall contains the fireplace, with two arm-chairs before it. As we happen to face the corner we see nothing of the other two walls. On the right of the fireplace, or rather on the right of any person facing the fireplace, is the door. On the left is the writing-table at which Redpenny [a medical student] sits. It is an untidy table with a microscope, several test tubes, and a spirit lamp [an alcohol burner] standing up through its litter of papers. There is a couch in the middle of the room, at right angles to the console, and parallel to the fireplace. A chair stands between the couch and the window. Another in the corner. Another at the other end of the windowed wall. . . . The wallpaper and carpets are mostly green. . . . The house, in fact, was so well furnished in the middle of the XIXth century that it stands unaltered to this day and is still quite presentable.

Not only does Shaw describe the furniture to be placed on stage, but he also includes a good deal of detail — specifying, for example, "gilt legs ending in sphinx claws" and "test tubes and a spirit lamp" that clutter the writing table. In addition, he defines furniture placement and specifies color.

Regardless of how detailed the stage directions are, they do not eliminate the need for creative interpretations on the part of the producer, director, set designers, and actors (See "Actors' Interpretations," p. 1060). Stage directions — and, for that matter, the entire script — are the foundation on which to construct the play that the audience finally sees. Many directors see stage directions as suggestions, not requirements, and some consider them more confusing than helpful. Therefore, directors may choose to interpret a play's stage directions quite loosely — or even to ignore them entirely.

THE USES OF STAGING

Staging is a key element of drama, and details that the audience sees and hears — such as costumes, props, scenery, lighting, and music and sound effects — communicate important information about characters and their motivation as well as about the play's theme.

Costumes

Costumes not only establish the historical period in which a play is set but also provide insight into the characters who wear them. When Hamlet first appears, he is profoundly disillusioned and quite melancholy. This fact was immediately apparent to Shakespeare's audience because Hamlet is dressed in sable, which to the Elizabethans signified a melancholy nature. In Tennessee Williams's *The Glass Menagerie* (p. 1416), Laura's dress of soft violet material and her hair ribbon reflect her delicate, childlike innocence. In contrast, her mother's *"imitation velvety-looking cloth [coat] with imitation fur collar"* and her *"enormous black patent-leather pocketbook"* reveal her somewhat pathetic attempt to achieve respectability. Later in the play, awaiting the "gentleman caller," Laura's mother wears a dress that is both outdated and inappropriately youthful, suggesting both her need to relive her own past and her increasingly desperate desire to marry off her daughter.

Props

Props (short for *properties*)— pictures, furnishings, objects, and the like — can also help audiences to interpret a play's characters and themes. For example, the handkerchief in Shakespeare's *Othello* gains significance as the play progresses. It begins as an innocent object and ends as the piece of evidence that convinces Othello his wife is committing adultery. Sometimes props can have symbolic significance. During the Renaissance, flowers had symbolic meaning. In act 4 of *Hamlet*, Ophelia, who is mad, gives flowers to various characters. In a note to the play, the critic Thomas Parrott points out the symbolic significance of her gifts: to Claudius, the murderer of Hamlet's father, she gives fennel and columbines, which signify flattery and ingratitude; to the Queen, she gives rue and daisies, which symbolize sadness and unfaithfulness. Although modern audiences would not understand the significance of these flowers, many people in Shakespeare's Elizabethan audience would have been aware of their meaning.

The furnishings in a room can also reveal a lot about a play's characters and themes. Willy Loman's house in Arthur Miller's *Death of a Salesman* (p. 1178) is sparsely furnished, revealing the declining financial status of the family. The kitchen contains a table and three chairs and the bedroom only a brass bed and a straight chair. Over the bed on a shelf is Biff's silver athletic trophy, a constant reminder of his loss of status. Like Willy Loman's house, the Wingfield apartment in *The Glass Menagerie* reflects its inhabitants' modest economic circumstances. For example, the living room, which contains a sofa that opens into a bed, also serves as a bedroom for Laura. In addition, one piece of furniture highlights a central theme of the play: an old-fashioned cabinet in the living room displays a collection of transparent glass animals that, like Laura, are too fragile to be removed from their surroundings.

Scenery and Lighting

Playwrights often use scenery and lighting to create imaginative stage settings. In *Death of a Salesman*, the house is surrounded by *"towering angular shapes"* of apartment houses that emphasize the *"small, fragile-seeming home."* Arthur Miller calls for a set that is *"wholly, or in some places, transparent."* Whenever the action is in the present, the actors observe the imaginary boundaries that separate rooms or mark the exterior walls of the house. But when the characters reenact past events, they walk over the boundaries and come to the front of the stage. By lighting up and darkening different parts of the stage, Miller shifts from the present to the past and back again.

The set of *The Glass Menagerie* is also innovative, combining imaginative backdrops with subtle lighting. As the curtain rises, the audience sees the dark rear wall of the Wingfield tenement, which is flanked on both sides by alleys lined with clotheslines, garbage cans, and fire escapes. After Tom delivers his opening narrative, the rear wall becomes transparent, revealing the interior of the Wingfield apartment. To create this effect, Williams used a **scrim,** a curtain that when illuminated from the front appears solid but when illuminated from the back becomes transparent. For Williams, such "atmospheric touches" represented a new direction in theater that contrasted with the theater of "realistic conventions."

Contemporary playwrights often use sets that combine realistic and nonrealistic elements. In his 1988 Tony Award-winning play M. *Butterfly,* for example, David Henry Hwang employs not only scrims but also a large red lacquered ramp that runs from the bottom to the top of the stage. The action takes place beneath, on, and above the ramp, creating an effect not unlike that created by Shakespeare's multiple stages. At several points in the play, a character who acts as the narrator sits beneath the ramp, addressing the audience, while at the same time a character on top of the ramp acts out the narrator's words.

Music and Sound Effects

Staging involves more than visual elements such as costumes and scenery; it also involves music and sound effects. The stage directions for *Death of a Salesman,* for example, begin, "*A melody is heard, played upon a flute.*" Although not specifically identified, the music is described as "*small and fine, telling of grass and trees and the horizon.*" Interestingly, this music stands in stark contrast to the claustrophobic urban setting of the play. Music also has a major role in *The Glass Menagerie,* where a single recurring tune, like circus music, weaves in and out of the play. This musical motif gives emotional impact to certain lines and suggests the fantasy world into which Laura has retreated.

Sound effects play an important part in Henrik Ibsen's *A Doll House* (p. 995). At the very end of the play, after his wife has left him, Torvald Helmer sits alone on the stage. Notice in the following stage directions how the final sound effect cuts short Helmer's attempt at self-deluding optimism:

HELMER: (*sinks down on a chair by the door, face buried in his hands*) Nora! Nora! (*Looking about and rising.*) Empty. She's gone. (*A sudden hope leaps in him.*) The greatest miracle — ?

From below, the sound of a door slamming shut.

When you read a play, it may be difficult to appreciate the effect that staging can have on a performance. As you read, pay particular attention to the stage directions, and use your imagination to visualize the scenes the playwright describes. In addition, try to imagine the play's sights and sounds, and consider the options for staging that are suggested as characters speak to one another. Although even such careful reading cannot substitute for actually seeing a play performed, it can help you imagine the play as it might appear on the stage.

A FINAL NOTE

Because of a play's limited performance time, and because of space and financial limitations, not every action or event can be represented on stage. Frequently, incidents that would involve many actors or require elaborate scenery are only suggested. For example, a violent political riot may be suggested by a single scuffle, a full-scale wedding by the kiss between bride and groom, a gala evening at the opera by a well-dressed group in box seats, and a trip to an exotic locale by a departure scene. Other events are suggested by sounds offstage — for example, the roar of a crowd may suggest an athletic event.

CHECKLIST **WRITING ABOUT STAGING**

✓ What information about staging is contained in the stage directions of the play?

✓ What information about staging is suggested by the play's dialogue?

✓ What information about staging is left to the imagination?

✓ How might different decisions about staging change the play?

✓ Do the stage directions provide information about how characters are supposed to look or behave?

✓ What costumes are specified? In what ways do costumes give insight into the characters who wear them?

✓ What props play an important part in the play? Do these props have symbolic meaning?

✓ Is the scenery used in the play special or unusual in any way?

✓ What kind of lighting is specified by the stage directions? In what way does this lighting affect your reaction to the play?

✓ In what ways are music and sound effects used in the play? Are musical themes associated with any characters? Do music or sound effects heighten the emotional impact of certain lines?

✓ How does staging help to communicate the play's themes?

✓ What events occur offstage? Why? How are they suggested?

MILCHA SANCHEZ-SCOTT (1949 or 1950 –   ) is a Los Angeles–based writer of plays that include *Dog Lady* and *The Cuban Swimmer*, both one-act plays (1984); *Roosters*, published in *On New Ground: Contemporary Hispanic American Plays* (1987); and *Stone Wedding*, produced at the Los Angeles Theater Center (1988). Also produced by the Los Angeles Theater Center was her play *Carmen*, adapted from Georges Bizet's opera of the same title.

Sanchez-Scott, born in Bali, is the daughter of an Indonesian mother and a Colombian-Mexican father. Her early childhood was spent in Mexico, South America, and Britain, before her family moved to San Diego when she was fourteen. Since then, she has worked as an actress, as a maid, and at an employment agency.

Writing in *Time* magazine, William A. Henry observes that the visionary or halluci-
natory elements in Sanchez-Scott's plays derive from the Latin American "magic realism" tradition of Jorge Luis Borges and Gabriel García Márquez. In *Roosters,* Henry
notes that what seems "a straightforward depiction of the life of farmlands gives way
to mysterious visitations, symbolic cockfights enacted by dancers, virginal girls wearing
wings, archetypal confrontations between father and son."

In 1984, the New York production of *The Cuban Swimmer* was noteworthy for an in-
geniously designed set that realistically re-created on stage Pacific Ocean waves, a
helicopter, and a boat. According to the *New York Times,* "The audience [could] almost
feel the resisting tides and the California oil slick that are represented by a watery-blue
floor and curtain." Jeannette Mirabel, as the Cuban swimmer, made an "auspicious"
debut in the play, according to the *Times;* "In a tour de force of balletic movements, she
[kept] her arms fluttering in the imaginary waters throughout the play."

Cultural Context: Under the terms of the Cuban Migration Accords, an agreement between the United States and the Cuban government, the United States can admit up to
twenty thousand Cuban defectors each year.

MILCHA SANCHEZ-SCOTT

The Cuban Swimmer   (1984)

CHARACTERS

Margarita Suárez, *the swimmer*	**Abuela,** *her grandmother*
Eduardo Suárez, *her father, the coach*	**Voice of Mel Munson**
Simón Suárez, *her brother*	**Voice of Mary Beth White**
Aída Suárez, *her mother*	**Voice of Radio Operator**

SETTING

The Pacific Ocean between San Pedro and Catalina Island.

TIME

Summer.

Live conga drums can be used to punctuate the action of the play.

SCENE 1

*Pacific Ocean. Midday. On the horizon, in perspective, a small boat enters upstage left,
crosses to upstage right, and exits. Pause. Lower on the horizon, the same boat, in larger
perspective, enters upstage right, crosses and exits upstage left. Blackout.*

SCENE 2

*Pacific Ocean. Midday. The swimmer, Margarita Suárez, is swimming. On the boat
following behind her are her father, Eduardo Suárez, holding a megaphone, and Simón,
her brother, sitting on top of the cabin with his shirt off, punk sunglasses on, binoculars
hanging on his chest.*

EDUARDO: *(leaning forward, shouting in time to Margarita's swimming)* Uno, dos, uno, dos. Y uno, dos . . . keep your shoulders parallel to the water.

SIMÓN: I'm gonna take these glasses off and look straight into the sun.

EDUARDO: *(through megaphone)* Muy bien, muy bien . . . but punch those arms in, baby.

SIMÓN: *(looking directly at the sun through binoculars)* Come on, come on, zap me. Show me something. *(He looks behind at the shoreline and ahead at the sea.)* Stop! Stop, Papi! Stop!

Aída Suárez and Abuela, the swimmer's mother and grandmother, enter running from the back of the boat.

AÍDA and ABUELA: *Qué? Qué es?*   5

AÍDA: *Es un* shark?

EDUARDO: Eh?

ABUELA: *Que es un* shark *dicen?*

Eduardo blows whistle. Margarita looks up at the boat.

SIMÓN: No, *Papi,* no shark, no shark. We've reached the halfway mark.

ABUELA: *(looking into the water)* A dónde está?   10

AÍDA: It's not in the water.

ABUELA: Oh, no? Oh, no?

AÍDA: No! A *poco* do you think they're gonna have signs in the water to say you are halfway to Santa Catalina? No. It's done very scientific. A *ver, hijo,* explain it to your grandma.

SIMÓN: Well, you see, Abuela — *(He points behind.)* There's San Pedro. *(He points ahead.)* And there's Santa Catalina. Looks halfway to me.

Abuela shakes her head and is looking back and forth, trying to make the decision, when suddenly the sound of a helicopter is heard.

ABUELA: *(looking up)* Virgencita de la Caridad del Cobre. *Qué es eso?*   15

Sound of helicopter gets closer. Margarita looks up.

MARGARITA: *Papi, Papi!*

A small commotion on the boat, with Everybody pointing at the helicopter above. Shadows of the helicopter fall on the boat. Simón looks up at it through binoculars.

Papi — qué es? What is it?

EDUARDO: *(through megaphone)* Uh . . . uh . . . uh, *un momentico* . . . mi hija. . . . Your *papi's* got everything under control, understand? Uh . . . you just keep stroking. And stay . . . uh . . . close to the boat.

SIMÓN: Wow, Papi! We're on TV, man! Holy Christ, we're all over the fucking U.S.A.! It's Mel Munson and Mary Beth White!

AÍDA: *Por Dios!* Simón, don't swear. And put on your shirt.

Aída fluffs her hair, puts on her sunglasses and waves to the helicopter. Simón leans over the side of the boat and yells to Margarita.

20   **SIMÓN:** Yo, Margo! You're on TV, man.

EDUARDO: Leave your sister alone. Turn on the radio.

MARGARITA: *Papi! Qué está pasando?*

ABUELA: *Que es la televisión dicen? (She shakes her head.) Porque como yo no puedo ver nada sin mis espejuelos.*

Abuela rummages through the boat, looking for her glasses. Voices of Mel Munson and Mary Beth White are heard over the boat's radio.

MEL'S VOICE: As we take a closer look at the gallant crew of *La Havana* . . . and there . . . yes, there she is . . . the little Cuban swimmer from Long Beach, California, nineteen-year-old Margarita Suárez. The unknown swimmer is our Cinderella entry . . . a bundle of tenacity, battling her way through the choppy, murky waters of the cold Pacific to reach the Island of Romance . . . Santa Catalina . . . where should she be the first to arrive, two thousand dollars and a gold cup will be waiting for her.

25   **AÍDA:** Doesn't even cover our expenses.

ABUELA: *Qué dice?*

EDUARDO: Shhhh!

MARY BETH'S VOICE: This is really a family effort, Mel, and—

MEL'S VOICE: Indeed it is. Her trainer, her coach, her mentor, is her father, Eduardo Suárez. Not a swimmer himself, it says here, Mr. Suárez is head usher of the Holy Name Society and the owner-operator of Suárez Treasures of the Sea and Salvage Yard. I guess it's one of those places—

30   **MARY BETH'S VOICE:** If I might interject a fact here, Mel, assisting in this swim is Mrs. Suárez, who is a former Miss Cuba.

MEL'S VOICE: And a beautiful woman in her own right. Let's try and get a closer look.

Helicopter sound gets louder. Margarita, frightened, looks up again.

MARGARITA: *Papi!*

EDUARDO: *(through megaphone) Mi hija,* don't get nervous . . . it's the press. I'm handling it.

AÍDA: I see how you're handling it.

35   **EDUARDO:** *(through megaphone)* Do you hear? Everything is under control. Get back into your rhythm. Keep your elbows high and kick and kick and kick and kick . . .

ABUELA: *(finds her glasses and puts them on) Ay sí, es la televisión* . . . *(She points to helicopter.) Qué lindo mira* . . . *(She fluffs her hair, gives a big wave.) Aló América! Viva mi Margarita, viva todo los Cubanos en los Estados Unidos!*

AÍDA: *Ay por Dios,* Cecilia, the man didn't come all this way in his helicopter to look at you jumping up and down, making a fool of yourself.

ABUELA: I don't care. I'm proud.

AÍDA: He can't understand you anyway.

40   **ABUELA:** *Viva* . . . *(She stops.)* Simón, *comó se dice viva?*

SIMÓN: Hurray.

ABUELA: Hurray for *mi Margarita* y for all the Cubans living *en* the United
   States, *y un abrazo* . . . *Simón, abrazo* . . .

SIMÓN: A big hug.

ABUELA: *Sí,* a big hug to all my friends in Miami, Long Beach, Union City,
   except for my son Carlos, who lives in New York in sin! He lives . . .
   (*she crosses herself*) in Brooklyn with a Puerto Rican woman in sin! *No*
   decente . . .

SIMÓN: Decent.   45

ABUELA: Carlos, *no decente.* This family, *decente.*

AÍDA: Cecilia, *por Dios.*

MEL'S VOICE: Look at that enthusiasm. The whole family has turned out
   to cheer little Margarita on to victory! I hope they won't be too
   disappointed.

MARY BETH'S VOICE: She seems to be making good time, Mel.

MEL'S VOICE: Yes, it takes all kinds to make a race. And it's a testimonial   50
   to the all-encompassing fairness . . . the greatness of this, the Wrigley
   Invitational Women's Swim to Catalina, where among all the professionals
   there is still room for the amateurs . . . like these, the simple people we see
   below us on the ragtag *La Havana,* taking their long-shot chance to victory.
   Vaya con Dios!

Helicopter sound fading as family, including Margarita, watch silently. Static as Simón
turns radio off. Eduardo walks to bow of boat, looks out on the horizon.

EDUARDO: (*to himself*) Amateurs.

AÍDA: Eduardo, that person insulted us. Did you hear, Eduardo? That he called
   us a simple people in a ragtag boat? Did you hear . . . ?

ABUELA: (*clenching her fist at departing helicopter*) *Mal-Rayo los parta!*

SIMÓN: (*same gesture*) Asshole!

Aída follows Eduardo as he goes to side of boat and stares at Margarita.

AÍDA: This person comes in his helicopter to insult your wife, your family, your   55
   daughter . . .

MARGARITA: (*pops her head out of the water*) Papi?

AÍDA: Do you hear me, Eduardo? I am not simple.

ABUELA: *Sí.*

AÍDA: I am complicated.

ABUELA: *Sí, demasiada complicada.*   60

AÍDA: Me and my family are not so simple.

SIMÓN: Mom, the guy's an asshole.

ABUELA: (*shaking her fist at helicopter*) Asshole!

AÍDA: If my daughter was simple, she would not be in that water swimming.

MARGARITA: Simple? *Papi* . . . ?   65

AÍDA: *Ahora,* Eduardo, this is what I want you to do. When we get to Santa
   Catalina, I want you to call the TV station and demand an apology.

EDUARDO: *Cállete mujer! Aquí mando yo.* I will decide what is to be done.

MARGARITA: *Papi,* tell me what's going on.

EDUARDO: Do you understand what I am saying to you, Aída?

70   SIMÓN: *(leaning over side of boat, to Margarita)* Yo Margo! You know that Mel Munson guy on TV? He called you a simple amateur and said you didn't have a chance.

ABUELA: *(leaning directly behind Simón.)* Mi hija, insultó a la familia. Desgraciado!

AÍDA: *(leaning in behind Abuela)* He called us peasants! And your father is not doing anything about it. He just knows how to yell at me.

EDUARDO: *(through megaphone)* Shut up! All of you! Do you want to break her concentration? Is that what you are after? Eh?

Abuela, Aída, and Simón shrink back. Eduardo paces before them.

Swimming is rhythm and concentration. You win a race *aquí. (Pointing to his head.)* Now . . . *(to Simón)* you, take care of the boat, Aída y Mama . . . do something. Anything. Something practical.

Abuela and Aída get on knees and pray in Spanish.

Hija, give it everything, eh? . . . *por la familia. Uno . . . dos. . . .* You must win.

Simón goes into cabin. The prayers continue as lights change to indicate bright sunlight, later in the afternoon.

SCENE 3

Tableau for a couple of beats. Eduardo on bow with timer in one hand as he counts strokes per minute. Simón is in the cabin steering, wearing his sunglasses, baseball cap on backward. Abuela and Aída are at the side of the boat, heads down, hands folded, still muttering prayers in Spanish.

AÍDA and ABUELA: *(crossing themselves)* En el nombre del Padre, del Hijo y del Espíritu Santo amén.

75   EDUARDO: *(through megaphone)* You're stroking seventy-two!

SIMÓN: *(singing)* Mama's stroking, Mama's stroking seventy-two. . . .

EDUARDO: *(through megaphone)* You comfortable with it?

SIMÓN: *(singing)* Seventy-two, seventy-two, seventy-two for you.

AÍDA: *(looking at the heavens)* Ay, Eduardo, *ven acá,* we should be grateful that *Nuestro Señor* gave us such a beautiful day.

80   ABUELA: *(crosses herself)* Si, gracias a Dios.

EDUARDO: She's stroking seventy-two, with no problem. *(He throws a kiss to the sky.)* It's a beautiful day to win.

AÍDA: Qué hermoso! So clear and bright. Not a cloud in the sky. Mira! Mira! Even rainbows on the water . . . a sign from God.

SIMÓN: *(singing)* Rainbows on the water . . . you in my arms . . .

ABUELA and EDUARDO: *(Looking the wrong way.)* Dónde?

85   AÍDA: *(pointing toward Margarita)* There, dancing in front of Margarita, leading her on . . .

EDUARDO: Rainbows on . . . *Ay coño!* It's an oil slick! You . . . you . . .
(*To Simón.*) Stop the boat. (*Runs to bow, yelling.*) Margarita! Margarita!

On the next stroke, Margarita comes up all covered in black oil.

MARGARITA: *Papi! Papi . . . !*

Everybody goes to the side and stares at Margarita, who stares back. Eduardo freezes.

AÍDA: *Apúrate,* Eduardo, move . . . what's wrong with you . . . *no me oíste,* get
my daughter out of the water.

EDUARDO: (*softly*) We can't touch her. If we touch her, she's disqualified.

AÍDA: But I'm her mother.   90

EDUARDO: Not even by her own mother. Especially by her own mother. . . .
You always want the rules to be different for you, you always want to be the
exception. (*To Simón.*) And you . . . you didn't see it, eh? You were playing
again?

SIMÓN: *Papi,* I was watching . . .

AÍDA: (*interrupting*) *Pues,* do something Eduardo. You are the big coach,
the monitor.

SIMÓN: Mentor! Mentor!

EDUARDO: How can a person think around you? (*He walks off to bow, puts head*   95
in hands.)

ABUELA: (*looking over side*) *Mira como todos los* little birds are dead. (*She crosses*
herself.)

AÍDA: Their little wings are glued to their sides.

SIMÓN: Christ, this is like the La Brea tar pits.

AÍDA: They can't move their little wings.

ABUELA: *Esa niña tiene que moverse.*   100

SIMÓN: Yeah, Margo, you gotta move, man.

Abuela and Simón gesture for Margarita to move. Aída gestures for her to swim.

ABUELA: *Anda niña, muévete.*

AÍDA: Swim, *hija,* swim or the *aceite* will stick to your wings.

MARGARITA: *Papi?*

ABUELA: (*taking megaphone*) Your *papi* say "move it!"   105

Margarita with difficulty starts moving.

ABUELA, AÍDA AND SIMÓN: (*laboriously counting*) *Uno, dos . . . uno, dos . . .*
anda . . . uno, dos.

EDUARDO: (*running to take megaphone from Abuela*) *Uno, dos . . .*

Simón races into cabin and starts the engine. Abuela, Aída and Eduardo count together.

SIMÓN: (*looking ahead*) *Papi,* it's over there!

EDUARDO: Eh?

SIMÓN: (*pointing ahead and to the right*) It's getting clearer over there.   110

EDUARDO: (*through megaphone*) Now pay attention to me. Go to the
right.

Simón, Abuela, Aída and Eduardo all lean over side. They point ahead and to the right, except Abuela, who points to the left.

Family: *(shouting together) Para yá! Para yá!*

Lights go down on boat. A special light on Margarita, swimming through the oil, and on Abuela, watching her.

Abuela: *Sangre de mi sangre,* you will be another to save us. En Bolondron, where your great-grandmother Luz Suárez was born, they say one day it rained blood. All the people, they run into their houses. They cry, they pray, *pero* your great-grandmother Luz she had *cojones* like a man. She run outside. She look straight at the sky. She shake her fist. And she say to the evil one, "Mira . . . *(beating her chest) coño, Diablo, aquí estoy si me quieres.*" And she open her mouth, and she drunk the blood.

Blackout

SCENE 4

Lights up on boat. Aída and Eduardo are on deck watching Margarita swim. We hear the gentle, rhythmic lap, lap, lap of the water, then the sound of inhaling and exhaling as Margarita's breathing becomes louder. Then Margarita's heartbeat is heard, with the lapping of the water and the breathing under it. These sounds continue beneath the dialogue to the end of the scene.

Aída: *Dios mío.* Look how she moves through the water. . . .

115 **Eduardo:** You see, it's very simple. It is a matter of concentration.

Aída: The first time I put her in water she came to life, she grew before my eyes. She moved, she smiled, she loved it more than me. She didn't want my breast any longer. She wanted the water.

Eduardo: And of course, the rhythm. The rhythm takes away the pain and helps the concentration.

Pause. Aída and Eduardo watch Margarita.

Aída: Is that my child or a seal. . . .

Eduardo: Ah, a seal, the reason for that is that she's keeping her arms very close to her body. She cups her hands, and then she reaches and digs, reaches and digs.

120 **Aída:** To think that a daughter of mine . . .

Eduardo: It's the training, the hours in the water. I used to tie weights around her little wrists and ankles.

Aída: A spirit, an ocean spirit, must have entered my body when I was carrying her.

Eduardo: *(to Margarita)* Your stroke is slowing down.

Pause. We hear Margarita's heartbeat with the breathing under, faster now.

Aída: Eduardo, that night, the night on the boat . . .

125 **Eduardo:** Ah, the night on the boat again . . . the moon was . . .

AÍDA: The moon was full. We were coming to America. . . . *Qué romantico.*

Heartbeat and breathing continue.

EDUARDO: We were cold, afraid, with no money, and on top of everything, you were hysterical, yelling at me, tearing at me with your nails. (*Opens his shirt, points to the base of his neck.*) Look, I still bear the scars . . . telling me that I didn't know what I was doing . . . saying that we were going to die. . . .

AÍDA: You took me, you stole me from my home . . . you didn't give me a chance to prepare. You just said we have to go now, now! Now, you said. You didn't let me take anything. I left everything behind. . . . I left everything behind.

EDUARDO: Saying that I wasn't good enough, that your father didn't raise you so that I could drown you in the sea.

AÍDA: You didn't let me say even a good-bye. You took me, you stole me, you   130
tore me from my home.

EDUARDO: I took you so we could be married.

AÍDA: That was in Miami. But that night on the boat, Eduardo. . . . We were not married, that night on the boat.

EDUARDO: *No pasó nada!* Once and for all get it out of your head, it was cold, you hated me, and we were afraid. . . .

AÍDA: *Mentiroso!*

EDUARDO: A man can't do it when he is afraid.   135

AÍDA: Liar! You did it very well.

EDUARDO: I did?

AÍDA: *Sí.* Gentle. You were so gentle and then strong . . . my passion for you so deep. Standing next to you . . . I would ache . . . looking at your hands I would forget to breathe, you were irresistible.

EDUARDO: I was?

AÍDA: You took me into your arms, you touched my face with your fingertips   140
. . . you kissed my eyes . . . *la esquina de la boca y* . . .

EDUARDO: *Sí, sí,* and then . . .

AÍDA: I look at your face on top of mine, and I see the lights of Havana in your eyes. That's when you seduced me.

EDUARDO: Shhh, they're gonna hear you.

Lights go down. Special on Aída.

AÍDA: That was the night. A woman doesn't forget those things . . . and later that night was the dream . . . the dream of a big country with fields of fertile land and big, giant things growing. And there by a green, slimy pond I found a giant pea pod and when I opened it, it was full of little, tiny baby frogs.

Aída crosses herself as she watches Margarita. We hear louder breathing and heartbeat.

MARGARITA: Santa Teresa. Little Flower of God, pray for me. San Martín de   145
Porres, pray for me. Santa Rosa de Lima, *Virgencita de la Caridad del Cobre,* pray for me. . . . Mother pray for me.

SCENE 5

Loud howling of wind is heard, as lights change to indicate unstable weather, fog and mist. Family on deck, braced and huddled against the wind. Simón is at the helm.

AÍDA: *Ay Dios mío, qué viento.*

EDUARDO: *(through megaphone)* Don't drift out . . . that wind is pushing you out. *(To Simón.)* You! Slow down. Can't you see your sister is drifting out?

SIMÓN: It's the wind, *Papi.*

AÍDA: Baby, don't go so far. . . .

150   ABUELA: *(to heaven) Ay Gran Poder de Dios, quita este maldito viento.*

SIMÓN: Margo! Margo! Stay close to the boat.

EDUARDO: Dig in. Dig in hard. . . . Reach down from your guts and dig in.

ABUELA: *(to heaven) Ay Virgen de la Caridad del Cobre, por lo más tú quieres a pararla.*

AÍDA: *(putting her hand out, reaching for Margarita)* Baby, don't go far.

Abuela crosses herself. Action freezes. Lights get dimmer, special on Margarita. She keeps swimming, stops, starts again, stops, then, finally exhausted, stops altogether. The boat stops moving.

155   EDUARDO: What's going on here? Why are we stopping?

SIMÓN: *Papi,* she's not moving! Yo Margo!

The family all run to the side.

EDUARDO: *Hija!* . . . *Hijita!* You're tired, eh?

AÍDA: *Por supuesto* she's tired. I like to see you get in the water, waving your arms and legs from San Pedro to Santa Catalina. A person isn't a machine, a person has to rest.

SIMÓN: Yo, Mama! Cool out, it ain't fucking brain surgery.

160   EDUARDO: *(to Simón)* Shut up, you. *(Louder to Margarita.)* I guess your mother's right for once, huh? . . . I guess you had to stop, eh? . . . Give your brother, the idiot . . . a chance to catch up with you.

SIMÓN: *(clowning like Mortimer Snerd)* Dum dee dum dee dum ooops, ah shucks . . .

EDUARDO: I don't think he's Cuban.

SIMÓN: *(like Ricky Ricardo) Oye,* Lucy! I'm home! Ba ba lu!

EDUARDO: *(joins in clowning, grabbing Simón in a headlock)* What am I gonna do with this idiot, eh? I don't understand this idiot. He's not like us, Margarita. *(Laughing.)* You think if we put him into your bathing suit with a cap on his head . . . *(He laughs hysterically.)* You think anyone would know . . . huh? Do you think anyone would know? *(Laughs.)*

165   SIMÓN: *(vamping) Ay, mi amor.* Anybody looking for tits would know.

Eduardo slaps Simón across the face, knocking him down. Aída runs to Simón's aid. Abuela holds Eduardo back.

MARGARITA: *Mía culpa! Mía culpa!*

ABUELA: *Qué dices hija?*

MARGARITA: *Papi,* it's my fault, it's all my fault. . . . I'm so cold, I can't move. . . . I put my face in the water . . . and I hear them whispering . . . laughing at me. . . .

AÍDA: Who is laughing at you?

MARGARITA: The fish are all biting me . . . they hate me . . . they whisper   170
about me. She can't swim, they say. She can't glide. She has no grace. . . . Yellowtails, bonita, tuna, man-o'-war, snub-nose sharks, *los baracudas* . . . they all hate me . . . only the dolphins care . . . and sometimes I hear the whales crying . . . she is lost, she is dead. I'm so numb, I can't feel. *Papi! Papi!* Am I dead?

EDUARDO: *Vamos,* baby, punch those arms in. Come on . . . do you hear me?

MARGARITA: *Papi . . . Papi . . .* forgive me. . . .

All is silent on the boat. Eduardo drops his megaphone, his head bent down in dejection. Abuela, Aída, Simón, all leaning over the side of the boat. Simón slowly walks away.

AÍDA: *Mi hija, qué tienes?*

SIMÓN: Oh, Christ, don't make her say it. Please don't make her say it.

ABUELA: Say what? *Qué cosa?*   175

SIMÓN: She wants to quit, can't you see she's had enough?

ABUELA: *Mira, para eso. Esta niña* is turning blue.

AÍDA: *Oyeme, mi hija.* Do you want to come out of the water?

MARGARITA: *Papi?*

SIMÓN: *(to Eduardo)* She won't come out until *you* tell her.   180

AÍDA: Eduardo . . . answer your daughter.

EDUARDO: *Le dije* to concentrate . . . concentrate on your rhythm. Then the rhythm would carry her . . . ay, it's a beautiful thing, Aída. It's like yoga, like meditation, the mind over matter . . . the mind controlling the body . . . that's how the great things in the world have been done. I wish you . . . I wish my wife could understand.

MARGARITA: *Papi?*

SIMÓN: *(to Margarita)* Forget him.

AÍDA: *(imploring)* Eduardo, *por favor.*   185

EDUARDO: *(walking in circles)* Why didn't you let her concentrate? Don't you understand, the concentration, the rhythm is everything. But no, you wouldn't listen. *(Screaming to the ocean.)* Goddamn Cubans, why, God, why do you make us go everywhere with our families? *(He goes to back of boat.)*

AÍDA: *(opening her arms)* Mi hija, ven, come to Mami. *(Rocking.)* Your *mami* knows.

Abuela has taken the training bottle, puts it in a net. She and Simón lower it to Margarita.

SIMÓN: Take this. Drink it. *(As Margarita drinks, Abuela crosses herself.)*

ABUELA: *Sangre de mi sangre.*

Music comes up softly. Margarita drinks, gives the bottle back, stretches out her arms, as if on a cross. Floats on her back. She begins a graceful backstroke. Lights fade on boat as special lights come up on Margarita. She stops. Slowly turns over and starts to swim, gradually picking up speed. Suddenly as if in pain she stops, tries again, then stops in pain again. She becomes disoriented and falls to the bottom of the sea. Special on Margarita at the bottom of the sea.

190   MARGARITA: *Ya no puedo* . . . I can't. . . . A person isn't a machine . . . *es mi culpa* . . . Father forgive me . . . *Papi! Papi!* One, two. *Uno, dos. (Pause.) Papi! A dónde estás? (Pause.)* One, two, one, two. *Papi! Ay, Papi!* Where are you . . . ? Don't leave me. . . . Why don't you answer me? *(Pause. She starts to swim, slowly.) Uno, dos, uno, dos.* Dig in, dig in. *(Stops swimming.) Por favor, Papi! (Starts to swim again.)* One, two, one, two. Kick from your hip, kick from your hip. *(Stops swimming. Starts to cry.)* Oh God, please. . . . *(Pause.)* Hail Mary, full of grace . . . dig in, dig in . . . the Lord is with thee. . . . *(She swims to the rhythm of her Hail Mary.)* Hail Mary, full of grace . . . dig in, dig in . . . the Lord is with thee . . . dig in, dig in. . . . Blessed art thou among women. . . . *Mami*, it hurts. You let go of my hand. I'm lost. . . . And blessed is the fruit of thy womb, now and at the hour of our death. Amen. I don't want to die, I don't want to die.

Margarita is still swimming. Blackout. She is gone.

SCENE 6

Lights up on boat, we hear radio static. There is a heavy mist. On deck we see only black outline of Abuela with shawl over her head. We hear the voices of Eduardo, Aída, and Radio Operator.

EDUARDO'S VOICE: *La Havana!* Coming from San Pedro. Over.

RADIO OPERATOR'S VOICE: Right, DT6-6, you say you've lost a swimmer.

AÍDA'S VOICE: Our child, our only daughter . . . listen to me. Her name is Margarita Inez Suárez, she is wearing a black one-piece bathing suit cut high in the legs with a white racing stripe down the sides, a white bathing cap with goggles and her whole body covered with a . . . with a . . .

EDUARDO'S VOICE: With lanolin and paraffin.

195   AÍDA'S VOICE: *Sí . . . con lanolin and paraffin.*

More radio static. Special on Simón, on the edge of the boat.

SIMÓN: Margo! Yo Margo! *(Pause.)* Man don't do this. *(Pause.)* Come on. . . . Come on. . . . *(Pause.)* God, why does everything have to be so hard? *(Pause.)* Stupid. You know you're not supposed to die for this. Stupid. It's his dream and he can't even swim. *(Pause.)* Punch those arms in. Come home. Come home. I'm your little brother. Don't forget what Mama said. You're not supposed to leave me behind. *Vamos, Margarita*, take your little brother, hold his hand tight when you cross the street. He's so little. *(Pause.)* Oh, Christ, give us a sign. . . . I know! I know! Margo, I'll send you a message . . . like mental telepathy. I'll hold my breath, close my eyes, and I'll bring you home. *(He takes a deep breath; a few beats.)* This time I'll beep . . . I'll send out sonar signals like a dolphin. *(He imitates dolphin sounds.)*

The sound of real dolphins takes over from Simón, then fades into sound of Abuela saying the Hail Mary in Spanish, as full lights come up slowly.

SCENE 7

Eduardo coming out of cabin, sobbing, Aída holding him. Simón anxiously scanning the horizon. Abuela looking calmly ahead.

EDUARDO: *Es mi culpa, sí, es mi culpa.* (He hits his chest.)

AÍDA: *Ya, ya viejo* . . . it was my sin . . . I left my home.

EDUARDO: Forgive me, forgive me. I've lost our daughter, our sister, our granddaughter, *mi carne, mi sangre, mis ilusiones.* (To heaven.) *Dios mío,* take me . . . take me, I say . . . Goddammit, take me!

SIMÓN: I'm going in.   200

AÍDA AND EDUARDO: No!

EDUARDO: (grabbing and holding Simón, speaking to heaven) God, take me, not my children. They are my dreams, my illusions . . . and not this one, this one is my mystery . . . he has my secret dreams. In him are the parts of me I cannot see.

Eduardo embraces Simón. Radio static becomes louder.

AÍDA: I . . . I think I see her.

SIMÓN: No, it's just a seal.

ABUELA: (looking out with binoculars) Mi nietacita, dónde estás? (She feels her   205
heart.) I don't feel the knife in my heart . . . my little fish is not lost.

Radio crackles with static. As lights dim on boat, Voices of Mel and Mary Beth are heard over the radio.

MEL'S VOICE: Tragedy has marred the face of the Wrigley Invitational Women's Race to Catalina. The Cuban swimmer, little Margarita Suárez, has reportedly been lost at sea. Coast Guard and divers are looking for her as we speak. Yet in spite of this tragedy the race must go on because . . .

MARY BETH'S VOICE: (interrupting loudly) Mel!

MEL'S VOICE: (startled) What!

MARY BETH'S VOICE: Ah . . . excuse me, Mel . . . we have a winner. We've just received word from Catalina that one of the swimmers is just fifty yards from the breakers . . . it's, oh, it's . . . Margarita Suárez!

Special on family in cabin listening to radio.

MEL'S VOICE: What? I thought she died!   210

Special on Margarita, taking off bathing cap, trophy in hand, walking on the water.

MARY BETH'S VOICE: Ahh . . . unless . . . unless this is a tragic . . . No . . . there she is, Mel. Margarita Suárez! The only one in the race wearing a black bathing suit cut high in the legs with a racing stripe down the side.

Family cheering, embracing.

SIMÓN: *(screaming)* Way to go, Margo!

MEL'S VOICE: This is indeed a miracle! It's a resurrection! Margarita Suárez, with a flotilla of boats to meet her, is now walking on the waters, through the breakers . . . onto the beach, with crowds of people cheering her on. What a jubilation! This is a miracle!

Sound of crowds cheering. Lights and cheering sounds fade.

Blackout

Reading and Reacting

1. *The Cuban Swimmer* is a short play with a single setting. In what other locations could Sanchez-Scott have set the play's action? What might she have gained or lost by using these additional settings?

2. What lighting and sound effects does the play call for? In what way do these effects advance the action of the play? In what way — if any — do they help to communicate the play's theme?

3. Although most of the play is in English, the characters frequently speak Spanish. What are the advantages and disadvantages of this use of Spanish? In what way does the mixing of English and Spanish reflect one of the play's themes?

4. What function do the voices of Mel and Mary Beth serve in the play?

5. What conflicts develop among the family members as the play proceeds? In what way might these conflicts represent the problems of other immigrants to the United States?

6. In what sense is Mel's final comment "This is a miracle!" ironic?

7. Do you think this play comments on the position of women in American culture? In Cuban-American culture?

8. Could this play be seen as an **allegory?** What is the value of seeing it in this way?

9. Throughout much of the play, Margarita is swimming in full view of the audience. Devise three ways in which a director could achieve this effect on stage. Which way would you choose if you were directing the play?

10. As the headnote to the play explains, the 1984 New York production of *The Cuban Swimmer* had an extremely realistic set. Could the play be staged unrealistically, with the characters on a raised platform instead of a boat? How do you think this kind of set would affect the audience?

11. JOURNAL ENTRY Are you able to empathize with Margarita's struggle? What elements of the play make it easy or difficult for you to do so?

12. CRITICAL PERSPECTIVE In a 1998 article in the *New York Times*, theater critic Brooks Atkinson said, "Nothing is better for good actors than a stage with no scenery." How do you interpret Atkinson's comment? Do you think this remark could be applied to the staging of *The Cuban Swimmer*?

Related Works: "The Secret Lion" (p. 54), "Chin" (p. 237), "Two Kinds" (p. 527), "How to Write the Great American Indian Novel" (p. 629), "Baca Grande" (p. 648), "Harlem" (p. 680), "My Father as a Guitar" (p. 690)

SOPHOCLES (496 – 406 B.C.), along with Aeschylus and Euripides, is one of the three great Greek tragic dramatists. He lived during the great flowering and subsequent decline of fifth-century B.C. Athens — the high point of Greek civilization. Born as Greece struggled against the Persian Empire and moved to adopt democracy, he lived as an adult under Pericles during the golden age of Athens and died as it became clear that Athens would lose the Peloponnesian War. Sophocles was an active participant in the public life of Athens, serving as a collector of tribute from Athenian subjects and later as a general. He wrote at least 120 plays, only seven have survived, including three plays about Oedipus: *Oedipus the King* (c. 430 B.C.), *Oedipus at Colonus* (411? B.C.), and *Antigone* (441 B.C.).

　　Oedipus the King, or *Oedipus Rex* (sometimes called *Oedipus the Tyrant*), was performed shortly after a great plague in Athens (probably in 429 or 425 B.C.) and as Athens was falling into decline. The play opens with an account of a plague in Thebes, Oedipus's kingdom. Over the years, *Oedipus the King* has attracted impressive critical attention, from Aristotle's use of it as a model for his definition of tragedy to Freud's use of its power as evidence of the validity of the so-called Oedipus complex.

Cultural Context: Between 431 and 404 B.C., the second Peloponnesian War (which Athens lost) raged between Athens and Sparta. After a Spartan army invaded Attica in 431 B.C., the Athenians hid behind the walls of their city while the Athenian fleet began raids. Between 430 and 428 B.C., a plague wiped out at least a quarter of the Athenian population. It is during this tumultuous time that Sophocles wrote of Oedipus and his troubles.

SOPHOCLES

Oedipus the King* (c. 430 B.C.)

Translated By Thomas Gould

CHARACTERS

Oedipus,° *the King of Thebes*	**Tiresias,** *a blind seer or prophet*
Priest of Zeus, *leader of the suppliants*	**Jocasta,** *the queen of Thebes*
Creon, *Oedipus's brother-in-law*	**Messenger,** *from Corinth, once a shepherd*
Chorus, *a group of Theban elders*	**Herdsman,** *once a servant of Laius*
Choragos, *spokesman of the Chorus*	**Second Messenger,** *a servant of Oedipus*

MUTES

Suppliants, *Thebans seeking Oedipus's help*
Attendants, *for the Royal Family*
Servants, *to lead Tiresias and Oedipus*
Antigone, *daughter of Oedipus and Jocasta*
Ismene, *daughter of Oedipus and Jocasta*

---

* Note that individual lines are numbered in the following play. When a line is shared by two or more characters, it is counted as one line.

Oedipus: The name, meaning "swollen foot," refers to the mutilation of Oedipus's feet by his father, Laius, before the infant was sent to Mount Cithaeron to be put to death by exposure.

The action takes place during the day in front of the royal palace in Thebes. There are two altars (left and right) on the proscenium and several steps leading down to the orchestra. As the play opens, Thebans of various ages who have come to beg Oedipus for help are sitting on these steps and in part of the orchestra. These suppliants are holding branches of laurel or olive which have strips of wool° wrapped around them. Oedipus enters from the palace (the central door of the skene).

PROLOGUE°

OEDIPUS: My children, ancient Cadmus'° newest care,
    why have you hurried to those seats, your boughs
    wound with the emblems of the suppliant?
    The city is weighed down with fragrant smoke,
5   with hymns to the Healer° and the cries of mourners.
    I thought it wrong, my sons, to hear your words
    through emissaries, and have come out myself,
    I, Oedipus, a name that all men know.

Oedipus addresses the Priest.

    Old man — for it is fitting that you speak
10   for all — what is your mood as you entreat me,
    fear or trust? You may be confident
    that I'll do anything. How hard of heart
    if an appeal like this did not rouse my pity!
PRIEST: You, Oedipus, who hold the power here,
15   you see our several ages, we who sit
    before your altars — some not strong enough
    to take long flight, some heavy in old age,
    the priests, as I of Zeus,° and from our youths
    a chosen band. The rest sit with their windings
20   in the markets, at the twin shrines of Pallas,°
    and the prophetic embers of Ismēnos.°
    Our city, as you see yourself, is tossed
    too much, and can no longer lift its head
    above the troughs of billows red with death.
25   It dies in the fruitful flowers of the soil,

---

wool: Branches wrapped with wool are traditional symbols of prayer or supplication.

Prologue: The portion of the play containing the exposition, or explanation, of what has gone before and what is now happening.

Cadmus: Oedipus's great-great-grandfather (although Oedipus does not know this) and the founder of Thebes.

Healer: Apollo, god of prophecy, light, healing, justice, purification, and destruction.

Zeus: Father and king of the gods.

Pallas: Athena, goddess of wisdom, arts, crafts, and war.

Ismēnos: A reference to the temple of Apollo near the river Ismēnos in Thebes. Prophecies were made here by "reading" the ashes of the altar fires.

it dies in its pastured herds, and in its women's
barren pangs. And the fire-bearing god°
has swooped upon the city, hateful plague,
and he has left the house of Cadmus empty.
Black Hades° is made rich with moans and weeping. 30
Not judging you an equal of the gods,
do I and the children sit here at your hearth,
but as the first of men, in troubled times
and in encounters with divinities.
You came to Cadmus' city and unbound 35
the tax we had to pay to the harsh singer,°
did it without a helpful word from us,
with no instruction; with a god's assistance
you raised up our life, so we believe.
Again now Oedipus, our greatest power, 40
we plead with you, as suppliants, all of us,
to find us strength, whether from a god's response,
or learned in some way from another man.
I know that the experienced among men
give counsels that will prosper best of all. 45
Noblest of men, lift up our land again!
Think also of yourself; since now the land
calls you its Savior for your zeal of old,
oh let us never look back at your rule
as men helped up only to fall again! 50
Do not stumble! Put our land on firm feet!
The bird of omen was auspicious then,
when you brought that luck; be that same man again!
The power is yours; if you will rule our country,
rule over men, not in an empty land. 55
A towered city or a ship is nothing
if desolate and no man lives within.
OEDIPUS: Pitiable children, oh I know, I know
the yearnings that have brought you. Yes, I know
that you are sick. And yet, though you are sick, 60

---

fire-bearing god: Contagious fever viewed as a god.

Black Hades: Refers both to the underworld where the spirits of the dead go and to the god of the underworld.

harsh singer: The Sphinx, a monster with a woman's head, a lion's body, and wings. The "tax" from which Oedipus freed Thebes was the destruction of all the young men who failed to solve the Sphinx's riddle and were subsequently devoured. The Sphinx always asked the same riddle: "What goes on four legs in the morning, two legs at noon, and three legs in the evening, and yet is weakest when supported by the largest number of feet?" Oedipus discovered the correct answer — man, who crawls in infancy, walks in his prime, and uses a stick in old age — and thus ended the Sphinx's reign of terror. The Sphinx destroyed herself when Oedipus answered the riddle. Oedipus's reward for freeing Thebes of the Sphinx was the throne and the hand of the recently widowed Jocasta.

there is not one of you so sick as I.
For your affliction comes to each alone,
for him and no one else, but my soul mourns
for me and for you, too, and for the city.

65 You do not waken me as from a sleep,
for I have wept, bitterly and long,
tried many paths in the wanderings of thought,
and the single cure I found by careful search
I've acted on: I sent Menoeceus' son,

70 Creon, brother of my wife, to the Pythian
halls of Phoebus,° so that I might learn
what I must do or say to save this city.
Already, when I think what day this is,
I wonder anxiously what he is doing.

75 Too long, more than is right, he's been away.
But when he comes, then I shall be a traitor
if I do not do all that the god reveals.

PRIEST: Welcome words! But look, those men have signaled
that it is Creon who is now approaching!

80 OEDIPUS: Lord Apollo! May he bring Savior Luck,
a Luck as brilliant as his eyes are now!

PRIEST: His news is happy, it appears. He comes,
forehead crowned with thickly berried laurel.°

OEDIPUS: We'll know, for he is near enough to hear us.

Enter Creon along one of the parados.

85 Lord, brother in marriage, son of Menoeceus!
What is the god's pronouncement that you bring?

CREON: It's good. For even troubles, if they chance
to turn out well, I always count as lucky.

OEDIPUS: But what was the response? You seem to say

90 I'm not to fear — but not to take heart either.

CREON: If you will hear me with these men present,
I'm ready to report — or go inside.

Creon moves up the steps toward the palace.

OEDIPUS: Speak out to all! The grief that burdens me
concerns these men more than it does my life.

95 CREON: Then I shall tell you what I heard from the god.
The task Lord Phoebus sets for us is clear:
drive out pollution sheltered in our land,
and do not shelter what is incurable.

Pythian halls . . . Phoebus: The temple of Phoebus, Apollo's oracle or prophet at Delphi.
laurel: Creon is wearing a garland of laurel leaves, sacred to Apollo.

OEDIPUS: What is our trouble? How shall we cleanse ourselves?
CREON: We must banish or murder to free ourselves   100
    from a murder that blows storms through the city.
OEDIPUS: What man's bad luck does he accuse in this?
CREON: My Lord, a king named Laius ruled our land
    before you came to steer the city straight.
OEDIPUS: I know. So I was told — I never saw him.   105
CREON: Since he was murdered, you must raise your hand
    against the men who killed him with their hands.
OEDIPUS: Where are they now? And how can we ever find
    the track of ancient guilt now hard to read?
CREON: In our own land, he said. What we pursue,   110
    that can be caught; but not what we neglect.
OEDIPUS: Was Laius home, or in the countryside —
    or was he murdered in some foreign land?
CREON: He left to see a sacred rite, he said;
    He left, but never came home from his journey.   115
OEDIPUS: Did none of his party see it and report —
    someone we might profitably question?
CREON: They were all killed but one, who fled in fear,
    and he could tell us only one clear fact.
OEDIPUS: What fact? One thing could lead us on to more   120
    if we could get a small start on our hope.
CREON: He said that bandits chanced on them and killed him —
    with the force of many hands, not one alone.
OEDIPUS: How could a bandit dare so great an act —
    unless this was a plot paid off from here!   125
CREON: We thought of that, but when Laius was killed,
    we had no one to help us in our troubles.
OEDIPUS: It was your very kingship that was killed!
    What kind of trouble blocked you from a search?
CREON: The subtle-singing Sphinx asked us to turn   130
    from the obscure to what lay at our feet.
OEDIPUS: Then I shall begin again and make it plain.
    It was quite worthy of Phoebus, and worthy of you,
    to turn our thoughts back to the murdered man,
    and right that you should see me join the battle   135
    for justice to our land and to the god.
    Not on behalf of any distant kinships,
    it's for myself I will dispel this stain.
    Whoever murdered him may also wish
    to punish me — and with the selfsame hand.   140
    In helping him I also serve myself.
    Now quickly, children: up from the altar steps,
    and raise the branches of the suppliant!
    Let someone go and summon Cadmus' people:
    say I'll do anything.

Exit an Attendant along one of the parados.

145   Our luck will prosper
       if the god is with us, or we have already fallen.
     PRIEST: Rise, my children; that for which we came,
       he has himself proclaimed he will accomplish.
       May Phoebus, who announced this, also come
150   as Savior and reliever from the plague.

Exit Oedipus and Creon into the palace. The Priest and the Suppliants exit left and right along the parados. After a brief pause, the Chorus (including the Choragos) enters the orchestra from the parados.

PARADOS°
STROPHE 1°

CHORUS: Voice from Zeus,° sweetly spoken, what are you
     that have arrived from golden
     Pytho° to our shining
     Thebes? I am on the rack, terror
155   shakes my soul.
     Delian Healer,° summoned by "iē!"
     I await in holy dread what obligation, something new
     or something back once more with the revolving years,
       you'll bring about for me.
160   Oh tell me, child of golden Hope,
       deathless Response!

ANTISTROPHE 1

I appeal to you first, daughter of Zeus,
       deathless Athena,
       and to your sister who protects this land,
165   Artemis,° whose famous throne is the whole circle
       of the marketplace,
     and Phoebus, who shoots from afar: iō!
     Three-fold defenders against death, appear!
     If ever in the past, to stop blind ruin
170   sent against the city,
     you banished utterly the fires of suffering,
       come now again!

Parados: A song sung by the Chorus on first entering.

Strophe: Probably refers to the direction in which the Chorus danced while reciting specific stanzas. *Strophe* may have indicated dance steps to stage left, *antistrophe* to stage right.

Voice from Zeus: A reference to Apollo's prophecy. Zeus taught Apollo how to prophesy.

Pytho: Delphi.

Delian Healer: Apollo.

Artemis: Goddess of virginity, childbirth, and hunting.

STROPHE 2

Ah! Ah! Unnumbered are the miseries
I bear. The plague claims all
our comrades. Nor has thought found yet a spear   175
by which a man shall be protected. What our glorious
earth gives birth to does not grow. Without a birth
from cries of labor
     do the women rise.
One person after another   180
     you may see, like flying birds,
faster than indomitable fire, sped
to the shore of the god that is the sunset.°

ANTISTROPHE 2

And with their deaths unnumbered dies the city.
Her children lie unpitied on the ground,   185
spreading death, unmourned.
Meanwhile young wives, and gray-haired mothers with them,
on the shores of the altars, from this side and that,
suppliants from mournful trouble,
     cry out their grief.   190
A hymn to the Healer shines,
     the flute a mourner's voice.
Against which, golden goddess, daughter of Zeus,
     send lovely Strength.

STROPHE 3

Causing raging Ares°— who,   195
     armed now with no shield of bronze,
burns me, coming on amid loud cries—
to turn his back and run from my land,
with a fair wind behind, to the great
     hall of Amphitritē,°   200
or to the anchorage that welcomes no one,
Thrace's troubled sea!
If night lets something get away at last,
     it comes by day.
Fire-bearing god . . .   205
     you who dispense the might of lightning,
Zeus! Father! Destroy him with your thunderbolt!

Enter Oedipus from the palace.

---

god . . . sunset: Hades, god of the underworld.
Ares: God of war and destruction.
Amphitritē: The Atlantic Ocean.

ANTISTROPHE 3

Lycēan Lord!° From your looped
      bowstring, twisted gold,
210   I wish indomitable missiles might be scattered
and stand forward, our protectors; also fire-bearing
radiance of Artemis, with which
      she darts across the Lycian mountains.
I call the god whose head is bound in gold,
215   with whom this country shares its name,
Bacchus,° wine-flushed, summoned by "euoi!,"
      Maenads' comrade,
to approach ablaze
      with gleaming . . .
220   pine, opposed to that god-hated god.

EPISODE 1°

OEDIPUS: I hear your prayer. Submit to what I say
and to the labors that the plague demands
and you'll get help and a relief from evils.
I'll make the proclamation, though a stranger
225   to the report and to the deed. Alone,
had I no key, I would soon lose the track.
Since it was only later that I joined you,
to all the sons of Cadmus I say this:
whoever has clear knowledge of the man
230   who murdered Laius, son of Labdacus,
I command him to reveal it all to me —
nor fear if, to remove the charge, he must
accuse himself: his fate will not be cruel —
he will depart unstumbling into exile.
235   But if you know another, or a stranger,
to be the one whose hand is guilty, speak:
I shall reward you and remember you.
But if you keep your peace because of fear,
and shield yourself or kin from my command,
240   hear you what I shall do in that event:
I charge all in this land where I have throne
and power, shut out that man — no matter who —
both from your shelter and all spoken words,
nor in your prayers or sacrifices make

Lycēan Lord: Apollo.

Bacchus: Dionysus, god of fertility and wine.

Episode: The portion of ancient Greek plays that appears between choric songs.

him partner, nor allot him lustral° water.   245
All men shall drive him from their homes: for he
is the pollution that the god-sent Pythian
response has only now revealed to me.
In this way I ally myself in war
with the divinity and the deceased.°   250
And this curse, too, against the one who did it,
whether alone in secrecy, or with others:
may he wear out his life unblest and evil!
I pray this, too: if he is at my hearth
and in my home, and I have knowledge of him,   255
may the curse pronounced on others come to me.
All this I lay to you to execute,
for my sake, for the god's, and for this land
now ruined, barren, abandoned by the gods.
Even if no god had driven you to it,   260
you ought not to have left this stain uncleansed,
the murdered man a nobleman, a king!
You should have looked! But now, since, as it happens,
It's I who have the power that he had once,
and have his bed, and a wife who shares our seed,   265
and common bond had we had common children
(had not his hope of offspring had bad luck—
but as it happened, luck lunged at his head);
because of this, as if for my own father,
I'll fight for him, I'll leave no means untried,   270
to catch the one who did it with his hand,
for the son of Labdacus, of Polydōrus,
of Cadmus before him, and of Agēnor.°
This prayer against all those who disobey:
the gods send out no harvest from their soil,   275
nor children from their wives. Oh, let them die
victims of this plague, or of something worse.
Yet for the rest of us, people of Cadmus,
we the obedient, may Justice, our ally,
and all the gods, be always on our side!   280
CHORAGOS:° I speak because I feel the grip of your curse:
the killer is not I. Nor can I point
to him. The one who set us to this search,
Phoebus, should also name the guilty man.

---

lustral: Purifying.

the deceased: Laius.

son . . . Agēnor: Refers to Laius by citing his genealogy.

Choragos: Leader of the Chorus and principal commentator on the play's action.

285 OEDIPUS: Quite right, but to compel unwilling gods —
         no man has ever had that kind of power.
     CHORAGOS: May I suggest to you a second way?
     OEDIPUS: A second or a third — pass over nothing!
     CHORAGOS: I know of no one who sees more of what
290   Lord Phoebus sees than Lord Tiresias.
         My Lord, one might learn brilliantly from him.
     OEDIPUS: Nor is this something I have been slow to do.
         At Creon's word I sent an escort — twice now!
         I am astonished that he has not come.
295 CHORAGOS: The old account is useless. It told us nothing.
     OEDIPUS: But tell it to me. I'll scrutinize all stories.
     CHORAGOS: He is said to have been killed by travelers.
     OEDIPUS: I have heard, but the one who did it no one sees.
     CHORAGOS: If there is any fear in him at all,
300   he won't stay here once he has heard that curse.
     OEDIPUS: He won't fear words: he had no fear when he did it.

Enter Tiresias from the right, led by a Servant and two of Oedipus's Attendants.

     CHORAGOS: Look there! There is the man who will convict him!
         It's the god's prophet they are leading here,
         one gifted with the truth as no one else.
305 OEDIPUS: Tiresias, master of all omens —
         public and secret, in the sky and on the earth —
         your mind, if not your eyes, sees how the city
         lives with a plague, against which Thebes can find
         no Saviour or protector, Lord, but you.
310   For Phoebus, as the attendants surely told you,
         returned this answer to us: liberation
         from the disease would never come unless
         we learned without a doubt who murdered Laius —
         put them to death, or sent them into exile.
315   Do not begrudge us what you may learn from birds
         or any other prophet's path you know!
         Care for yourself, the city, care for me,
         care for the whole pollution of the dead!
         We're in your hands. To do all that he can
320   to help another is man's noblest labor.
     TIRESIAS: How terrible to understand and get
         no profit from the knowledge! I knew this,
         but I forgot, or I had never come.
     OEDIPUS: What's this? You've come with very little zeal.
325 TIRESIAS: Let me go home! If you will listen to me,
         You will endure your troubles better — and I mine.
     OEDIPUS: A strange request, not very kind to the land
         that cared for you — to hold back this oracle!

TIRESIAS: I see your understanding comes to you
    inopportunely. So that won't happen to me . . .   330
OEDIPUS: Oh, by the gods, if you understand about this,
    don't turn away! We're on our knees to you.
TIRESIAS: None of you understands! I'll never bring
    my grief to light — I will not speak of yours.
OEDIPUS: You know and won't declare it! Is your purpose   335
    to betray us and to destroy this land!
TIRESIAS: I will grieve neither of us. Stop this futile
    cross-examination. I'll tell you nothing!
OEDIPUS: Nothing? You vile traitor! You could provoke
    a stone to anger! You still refuse to tell?   340
    Can nothing soften you, nothing convince you?
TIRESIAS: You blamed anger in me — you haven't seen.
    The kind that lives with you, so you blame me.
OEDIPUS: Who wouldn't fill with anger, listening
    to words like yours which now disgrace this city?   345
TIRESIAS: It will come, even if my silence hides it.
OEDIPUS: If it will come, then why won't you declare it?
TIRESIAS: I'd rather say no more. Now if you wish,
    respond to that with all your fiercest anger!
OEDIPUS: Now I am angry enough to come right out   350
    with this conjecture: you, I think, helped plot
    the deed; you did it — even if your hand,
    cannot have struck the blow. If you could see,
    I should have said the deed was yours alone.
TIRESIAS: Is that right! Then I charge you to abide   355
    by the decree you have announced: from this day
    say no word to either these or me,
    for you are the vile polluter of this land!
OEDIPUS: Aren't you appalled to let a charge like that
    come bounding forth? How will you get away?   360
TIRESIAS: You cannot catch me. I have the strength of truth.
OEDIPUS: Who taught you this? Not your prophetic craft!
TIRESIAS: You did. You made me say it. I didn't want to.
OEDIPUS: Say what? Repeat it so I'll understand.
TIRESIAS: I made no sense? Or are you trying me?   365
OEDIPUS: No sense I understood. Say it again!
TIRESIAS: I say you are the murderer you seek.
OEDIPUS: Again that horror! You'll wish you hadn't said that.
TIRESIAS: Shall I say more, and raise your anger higher?
OEDIPUS: Anything you like! Your words are powerless.   370
TIRESIAS: You live, unknowing, with those nearest to you
    in the greatest shame. You do not see the evil.
OEDIPUS: You won't go on like that and never pay!
TIRESIAS: I can if there is any strength in truth.

375   OEDIPUS: In truth, but not in you! You have no strength,
      blind in your ears, your reason, and your eyes.
   TIRESIAS: Unhappy man! Those jeers you hurl at me
      before long all these men will hurl at you.
   OEDIPUS: You are the child of endless night; it's not
380   for me or anyone who sees to hurt you.
   TIRESIAS: It's not my fate to be struck down by you.
      Apollo is enough. That's his concern.
   OEDIPUS: Are these inventions Creon's or your own?
   TIRESIAS: No, your affliction is yourself, not Creon.
385   OEDIPUS: Oh success! — in wealth, kingship, artistry,
      in any life that wins much admiration —
      the envious ill will stored up for you!
      to get at my command, a gift I did not
      seek, which the city put into my hands,
390   my loyal Creon, colleague from the start,
      longs to sneak up in secret and dethrone me.
      So he's suborned this fortuneteller — schemer!
      deceitful beggar-priest! — who has good eyes
      for gains alone, though in his craft he's blind.
395   Where were your prophet's powers ever proved?
      Why, when the dog who chanted verse° was here,
      did you not speak and liberate this city?
      Her riddle wasn't for a man chancing by
      to interpret; prophetic art was needed,
400   but you had none, it seems — learned from birds
      or from a god. I came along, yes I,
      Oedipus the ignorant, and stopped her —
      by using thought, not augury from birds.
      And it is I whom you now wish to banish,
405   so you'll be close to the Creontian throne.
      You — and the plot's concocter — will drive out
      pollution to your grief: you look quite old
      or you would be the victim of that plot!
   CHORAGOS: It seems to us that this man's words were said
410   in anger, Oedipus, and yours as well.
      Insight, not angry words, is what we need,
      the best solution to the god's response.
   TIRESIAS: You are the king, and yet I am your equal
      in my right to speak. In that I too am Lord.
415   for I belong to Loxias,° not you.
      I am not Creon's man. He's nothing to me.

---

dog . . . verse: The Sphinx.
Loxias: Apollo.

Hear this, since you have thrown my blindness at me:
Your eyes can't see the evil to which you've come,
nor where you live, nor who is in your house.
Do you know your parents? Not knowing, you are   420
their enemy, in the underworld and here.
A mother's and a father's double-lashing
terrible-footed curse will soon drive you out.
Now you can see, then you will stare into darkness.
What place will not be harbor to your cry,   425
or what Cithaeron° not reverberate
when you have heard the bride-song in your palace
to which you sailed? Fair wind to evil harbor!
Nor do you see how many other woes
will level you to yourself and to your children.   430
So, at my message, and at Creon, too,
splatter muck! There will never be a man
ground into wretchedness as you will be.

OEDIPUS: Am I to listen to such things from him!
May you be damned! Get out of here at once!   435
Go! Leave my palace! Turn around and go!

Tiresias begins to move away from Oedipus.

TIRESIAS: I wouldn't have come had you not sent for me.
OEDIPUS: I did not know you'd talk stupidity,
or I wouldn't have rushed to bring you to my house.
TIRESIAS: Stupid I seem to you, yet to your parents   440
who gave you natural birth I seemed quite shrewd.
OEDIPUS: Who? Wait! Who is the one who gave me birth?
TIRESIAS: This day will give you birth,° and ruin too.
OEDIPUS: What murky, riddling things you always say!
TIRESIAS: Don't you surpass us all at finding out?   445
OEDIPUS: You sneer at what you'll find has brought me greatness.
TIRESIAS: And that's the very luck that ruined you.
OEDIPUS: I wouldn't care, just so I saved the city.
TIRESIAS: In that case I shall go. Boy, lead the way!
OEDIPUS: Yes, let him lead you off. Here, underfoot,   450
you irk me. Gone, you'll cause no further pain.
TIRESIAS: I'll go when I have said what I was sent for.
Your face won't scare me. You can't ruin me.
I say to you, the man whom you have looked for
as you pronounced your curses, your decrees   455
on the bloody death of Laius — he is here!

Cithaeron: The mountain on which Oedipus was to be exposed as an infant.
This day . . . birth: On this day, you will learn who your parents are.

A seeming stranger, he shall be shown to be
a Theban born, though he'll take no delight
in that solution. Blind, who once could see,
460   a beggar who was rich, through foreign lands
he'll go and point before him with a stick.
To his beloved children, he'll be shown
a father who is also brother; to the one
who bore him, son and husband; to his father,
465   his seed-fellow and killer. Go in
and think this out; and if you find I've lied,
say then I have no prophet's understanding!

Exit Tiresias, led by a Servant. Oedipus exits into the palace with his Attendants.

<u>STASIMON 1°</u>
STROPHE 1

CHORUS: Who is the man of whom the inspired
             rock of Delphi° said
470   he has committed the unspeakable
             with blood-stained hands?
Time for him to ply a foot
mightier than those of the horses
             of the storm in his escape;
475   upon him mounts and plunges the weaponed
son of Zeus,° with fire and thunderbolts,
and in his train the dreaded goddesses
of Death, who never miss.

ANTISTROPHE 1

The message has just blazed,
480   gleaming from the snows
of Mount Parnassus: we must track
             everywhere the unseen man.
He wanders, hidden by wild
forests, up through caves
485   and rocks, like a bull,
anxious, with an anxious foot, forlorn.
He puts away from him the mantic° words come from earth's
navel,° at its center, yet these live
forever and still hover round him.

Stasimon: Greek choral ode between episodes.
rock of Delphi: Apollo's oracle at Delphi.
son of Zeus: Apollo.
mantic: prophetic.
earth's navel: Delphi.

STROPHE 2

Terribly he troubles me,   490
  the skilled interpreter of birds!°
I can't assent, nor speak against him.
  Both paths are closed to me.
I hover on the wings of doubt,
  not seeing what is here nor what's to come.   495
What quarrel started in the house of Labdacus°
or in the house of Polybus,°
  either ever in the past
  or now, I never
heard, so that . . . with this fact for my touchstone   500
I could attack the public
  fame of Oedipus, by the side of the Labdaceans
an ally, against the dark assassination.

ANTISTROPHE 2

No, Zeus and Apollo
  understand and know things   505
mortal; but that another man
  can do more as a prophet than I can—
for that there is no certain test,
  though, skill to skill,
one man might overtake another.   510
No, never, not until
  I see the charges proved,
when someone blames him shall I nod assent.
For once, as we all saw, the winged maiden° came
against him: he was seen then to be skilled,   515
  proved, by that touchstone, dear to the people. So,
never will my mind convict him of the evil.

EPISODE 2

Enter Creon from the right door of the skene and speaks to the Chorus.

CREON: Citizens, I hear that a fearful charge
  is made against me by King Oedipus!
  I had to come. If, in this crisis,   520
  he thinks that he has suffered injury
  from anything that I have said or done,

---

interpreter of birds: Tiresias. The Chorus is troubled by his accusations.
house of Labdacus: The line of Laius.
Polybus: Oedipus's foster father.
winged maiden: The Sphinx.

I have no appetite for a long life —
bearing a blame like that! It's no slight blow
525   the punishment I'd take from what he said:
it's the ultimate hurt to be called traitor
by the city, by you, by my own people!
CHORAGOS: The thing that forced that accusation out
could have been anger, not the power of thought.
530 CREON: But who persuaded him that thoughts of mine
had led the prophet into telling lies?
CHORAGOS: I do not know the thought behind his words.
CREON: But did he look straight at you? Was his mind right
when he said that I was guilty of this charge?
535 CHORAGOS: I have no eyes to see what rulers do.
But here he comes himself out of the house.

Enter Oedipus from the palace.

OEDIPUS: What? You here? And can you really have
the face and daring to approach my house
when you're exposed as its master's murderer
540   and caught, too, as the robber of my kingship?
Did you see cowardice in me, by the gods,
or foolishness, when you began this plot?
Did you suppose that I would not detect
your stealthy moves, or that I'd not fight back?
545   It's your attempt that's folly, isn't it —
tracking without followers or connections,
kingship which is caught with wealth and numbers?
CREON: Now wait! Give me as long to answer back!
Judge me for yourself when you have heard me!
550 OEDIPUS: You're eloquent, but I'd be slow to learn
from you, now that I've seen your malice toward me.
CREON: That I deny. Hear what I have to say.
OEDIPUS: Don't you deny it! You are the traitor here!
CREON: If you consider mindless willfulness
555   a prized possession, you are not thinking sense.
OEDIPUS: If you think you can wrong a relative
and get off free, you are not thinking sense.
CREON: Perfectly just, I won't say no. And yet
what is this injury you say I did you?
560 OEDIPUS: Did you persuade me, yes or no, to send
someone to bring that solemn prophet here?
CREON: And I still hold to the advice I gave.
OEDIPUS: How many years ago did your King Laius . . .
CREON: Laius! Do what? Now I don't understand.
565 OEDIPUS: Vanish — victim of a murderous violence?
CREON: That is a long count back into the past.
OEDIPUS: Well, was this seer then practicing his art?

CREON: Yes, skilled and honored just as he is today.
OEDIPUS: Did he, back then, ever refer to me?
CREON: He did not do so in my presence ever. 570
OEDIPUS: You did inquire into the murder then.
CREON: We had to, surely, though we discovered nothing.
OEDIPUS: But the "skilled" one did not say this then? Why not?
CREON: I never talk when I am ignorant.
OEDIPUS: But you're not ignorant of your own part. 575
CREON: What do you mean? I'll tell you if I know.
OEDIPUS: Just this: if he had not conferred with you
    he'd not have told about my murdering Laius.
CREON: If he said that, you are the one who knows.
    But now it's fair that you should answer me. 580
OEDIPUS: Ask on! You won't convict me as the killer.
CREON: Well then, answer. My sister is your wife?
OEDIPUS: Now there's a statement that I can't deny.
CREON: You two have equal power in this country?
OEDIPUS: She gets from me whatever she desires. 585
CREON: And I'm a third? The three of us are equals?
OEDIPUS: That's where you're treacherous to your kinsman!
CREON: But think about this rationally, as I do.
    First look at this: do you think anyone
    prefers the anxieties of being king 590
    to untroubled sleep — if he has equal power?
    I'm not the kind of man who falls in love
    with kingship. I am content with a king's power.
    And so would any man who's wise and prudent.
    I get all things from you, with no distress; 595
    as king I would have onerous duties, too.
    How could the kingship bring me more delight
    than this untroubled power and influence?
    I'm not misguided yet to such a point
    that profitable honors aren't enough. 600
    As it is, all wish me well and all salute;
    those begging you for something have me summoned,
    for their success depends on that alone.
    Why should I lose all this to become king?
    A prudent mind is never traitorous. 605
    Treason's a thought I'm not enamored of;
    nor could I join a man who acted so.
    In proof of this, first go yourself to Pytho
    and ask if I brought back the true response.
    Then, if you find I plotted with that portent 610
    reader,° don't have me put to death by your vote

---

portent reader: Apollo's oracle or prophet.

only — I'll vote myself for my conviction.
Don't let an unsupported thought convict me!
It's not right mindlessly to take the bad
615   for good or to suppose the good are traitors.
Rejecting a relation who is loyal
is like rejecting life, our greatest love.
In time you'll know securely without stumbling,
for time alone can prove a just man just,
620   though you can know a bad man in a day.

CHORAGOS: Well said, to one who's anxious not to fall.
Swift thinkers, Lord, are never safe from stumbling.

OEDIPUS: But when a swift and secret plotter moves
against me, I must make swift counterplot.
625   If I lie quiet and await his move,
he'll have achieved his aims and I'll have missed.

CREON: You surely cannot mean you want me exiled!

OEDIPUS: Not exiled, no. Your death is what I want!

CREON: If you would first define what envy is . . .

630   OEDIPUS: Are you still stubborn? Still disobedient?

CREON: I see you cannot think!

OEDIPUS: For me I can.

CREON: You should for me as well!

OEDIPUS: But you're a traitor!

CREON: What if you're wrong?

OEDIPUS: Authority must be maintained.

CREON: Not if the ruler's evil.

OEDIPUS: Hear that, Thebes!

635   CREON: It is my city too, not yours alone!

CHORAGOS: Please don't, my Lords! Ah, just in time, I see
Jocasta there, coming from the palace.
With her help you must settle your quarrel.

Enter Jocasta from the palace.

JOCASTA: Wretched men! What has provoked this ill-
640   advised dispute? Have you no sense of shame,
with Thebes so sick, to stir up private troubles?
Now go inside! And Creon, you go home!
Don't make a general anguish out of nothing!

CREON: My sister, Oedipus your husband here
645   sees fit to do one of two hideous things:
to have me banished from the land — or killed!

OEDIPUS: That's right: I caught him, Lady, plotting harm
against my person — with a malignant science.

CREON: May my life fail, may I die cursed, if I
650   did any of the things you said I did!

JOCASTA: Believe his words, for the god's sake, Oedipus,

in deference above all to his oath
to the gods. Also for me, and for these men!

KOMMOS°

STROPHE 1

CHORUS: Consent, with will and mind,
    my king, I beg of you!   655
OEDIPUS: What do you wish me to surrender?
CHORUS: Show deference to him who was not feeble in time past
    and is now great in the power of his oath!
OEDIPUS: Do you know what you're asking?
CHORUS: Yes.
OEDIPUS: Tell me then.
CHORUS: Never to cast into dishonored guilt, with an unproved   660
    assumption, a kinsman who has bound himself by curse.
OEDIPUS: Now you must understand, when you ask this,
    you ask my death or banishment from the land.

STROPHE 2

CHORUS: No, by the god who is the foremost of all gods,
    the Sun! No! Godless,   665
        friendless, whatever death is worst of all,
    let that be my destruction, if this
        thought ever moved me!
    But my ill-fated soul
        this dying land   670
    wears out — the more if to these older troubles
    she adds new troubles from the two of you!
OEDIPUS: Then let him go, though it must mean my death,
    or else disgrace and exile from the land.
    My pity is moved by your words, not by his—   675
    he'll only have my hate, wherever he goes.
CREON: You're sullen as you yield; you'll be depressed
    when you've passed through this anger. Natures like yours
    are hardest on themselves. That's as it should be.
OEDIPUS: Then won't you go and let me be?   680
CREON: I'll go.
    Though you're unreasonable, they know I'm righteous.

Exit Creon.

ANTISTROPHE 1

CHORUS: Why are you waiting, Lady?
    Conduct him back into the palace!
JOCASTA: I will, when I have heard what chanced.

Kommos: A dirge or lament sung by the Chorus and one or more of the chief characters.

685   CHORUS: Conjectures — words alone, and nothing based on thought.
       But even an injustice can devour a man.
    JOCASTA: Did the words come from both sides?
    CHORUS: Yes.
    JOCASTA: What was said?
    CHORUS: To me it seems enough! enough! the land already troubled,
       that this should rest where it has stopped.
690   OEDIPUS: See what you've come to in your honest thought,
       in seeking to relax and blunt my heart?

ANTISTROPHE 2

    CHORUS: I have not said this only once, my Lord.
       That I had lost my sanity,
          without a path in thinking —
695   be sure this would be clear
          if I put you away
       who, when my cherished land
          wandered crazed
       with suffering, brought her back on course.
700   Now, too, be a lucky helmsman!
    JOCASTA: Please, for the god's sake, Lord, explain to me
       the reason why you have conceived this wrath?
    OEDIPUS: I honor you, not them,° and I'll explain
       to you how Creon has conspired against me.
705   JOCASTA: All right, if that will explain how the quarrel started.
    OEDIPUS: He says I am the murderer of Laius!
    JOCASTA: Did he claim knowledge or that someone told him?
    OEDIPUS: Here's what he did: he sent that vicious seer
       so he could keep his own mouth innocent.
710   JOCASTA: Ah then, absolve yourself of what he charges!
       Listen to this and you'll agree, no mortal
       is ever given skill in prophecy.
       I'll prove this quickly with one incident.
       It was foretold to Laius — I shall not say
715   by Phoebus himself, but by his ministers —
       that when his fate arrived he would be killed
       by a son who would be born to him and me.
       And yet, so it is told, foreign robbers
       murdered him, at a place where three roads meet.
720   As for the child I bore him, not three days passed
       before he yoked the ball-joints of its feet,°
       then cast it, by others' hands, on a trackless mountain.

---

them: The Chorus.

ball-joints of its feet: The ankles.

That time Apollo did not make our child
a patricide, or bring about what Laius
feared, that he be killed by his own son.   725
That's how prophetic words determined things!
Forget them. The things a god must track
he will himself painlessly reveal.
OEDIPUS: Just now, as I was listening to you, Lady,
what a profound distraction seized my mind!   730
JOCASTA: What made you turn around so anxiously?
OEDIPUS: I thought you said that Laius was attacked
and butchered at a place where three roads meet.
JOCASTA: That is the story, and it is told so still.
OEDIPUS: Where is the place where this was done to him?   735
JOCASTA: The land's called Phocis, where a two-forked road
comes in from Delphi and from Daulia.
OEDIPUS: And how much time has passed since these events?
JOCASTA: Just prior to your presentation here
as king this news was published to the city.   740
OEDIPUS: Oh, Zeus, what have you willed to do to me?
JOCASTA: Oedipus, what makes your heart so heavy?
OEDIPUS: No, tell me first of Laius' appearance,
what peak of youthful vigor he had reached.
JOCASTA: A tall man, showing his first growth of white.   745
He had a figure not unlike your own.
OEDIPUS: Alas! It seems that in my ignorance
I laid those fearful curses on myself.
JOCASTA: What is it, Lord? I flinch to see your face.
OEDIPUS: I'm dreadfully afraid the prophet sees.   750
But I'll know better with one more detail.
JOCASTA: I'm frightened too. But ask: I'll answer you.
OEDIPUS: Was his retinue small, or did he travel
with a great troop, as would befit a prince?
JOCASTA: There were just five in all, one a herald.   755
There was a carriage, too, bearing Laius.
OEDIPUS: Alas! Now I see it! But who was it,
Lady, who told you what you know about this?
JOCASTA: A servant who alone was saved unharmed.
OEDIPUS: By chance, could he be now in the palace?   760
JOCASTA: No, he is not. When he returned and saw
you had the power of the murdered Laius,
he touched my hand and begged me formally
to send him to the fields and to the pastures,
so he'd be out of sight, far from the city.   765
I did. Although a slave, he well deserved
to win this favor, and indeed far more.
OEDIPUS: Let's have him called back in immediately.

JOCASTA: That can be done, but why do you desire it?

770 OEDIPUS: I fear, Lady, I have already said
      too much. That's why I wish to see him now.

JOCASTA: Then he shall come; but it is right somehow
      that I, too, Lord, should know what troubles you.

OEDIPUS: I've gone so deep into the things I feared
775   I'll tell you everything. Who has a right
      greater than yours, while I cross through this chance?
      Polybus of Corinth was my father,
      my mother was the Dorian Meropē.
      I was first citizen, until this chance
780   attacked me — striking enough, to be sure,
      but not worth all the gravity I gave it.
      This: at a feast a man who'd drunk too much
      denied, at the wine, I was my father's son.
      I was depressed and all that day I barely
785   held it in. Next day I put the question
      to my mother and father. They were enraged
      at the man who'd let this fiction fly at me.
      I was much cheered by them. And yet it kept
      grinding into me. His words kept coming back.
790   Without my mother's or my father's knowledge
      I went to Pytho. But Phoebus sent me away
      dishonoring my demand. Instead, other
      wretched horrors he flashed forth in speech.
      He said that I would be my mother's lover,
795   show offspring to mankind they could not look at,
      and be his murderer whose seed I am.°
      When I heard this, and ever since, I gauged
      the way to Corinth by the stars alone,
      running to a place where I would never see
800   the disgrace in the oracle's words come true.
      But I soon came to the exact location
      where, as you tell of it, the king was killed.
      Lady, here is the truth. As I went on,
      when I was just approaching those three roads,
805   a herald and a man like him you spoke of
      came on, riding a carriage drawn by colts.
      Both the man out front and the old man himself°
      tried violently to force me off the road.
      The driver, when he tried to push me off,
810   I struck in anger. The old man saw this, watched

---

be . . . am: I would murder my father.
old man himself: Laius.

me approach, then leaned out and lunged down
with twin prongs° at the middle of my head!
He got more than he gave. Abruptly — struck
once by the staff in this my hand — he tumbled
out, head first, from the middle of the carriage.   815
And then I killed them all. But if there is
a kinship between Laius and this stranger,
who is more wretched than the man you see?
Who was there born more hated by the gods?
For neither citizen nor foreigner   820
may take me in his home or speak to me.
No, they must drive me off. And it is I
who have pronounced these curses on myself!
I stain the dead man's bed with these my hands,
by which he died. Is not my nature vile?   825
Unclean? — if I am banished and even
in exile I may not see my own parents,
or set foot in my homeland, or else be yoked
in marriage to my mother, and kill my father,
Polybus, who raised me and gave me birth?   830
If someone judged a cruel divinity
did this to me, would he not speak the truth?
You pure and awful gods, may I not ever
see that day, may I be swept away
from men before I see so great and so   835
calamitous a stain fixed on my person!

CHORAGOS: These things seem fearful to us, Lord, and yet,
    until you hear it from the witness, keep hope!

OEDIPUS: That is the single hope that's left to me,
    to wait for him, that herdsman — until he comes.   840

JOCASTA: When he appears, what are you eager for?

OEDIPUS: Just this: if his account agrees with yours
    then I shall have escaped this misery.

JOCASTA: But what was it that struck you in my story?

OEDIPUS: You said he spoke of robbers as the ones   845
    who killed him. Now: if he continues still
    to speak of many, then I could not have killed him.
    One man and many men just do not jibe.
    But if he says one belted man, the doubt
    is gone. The balance tips toward me. I did it.   850

JOCASTA: No! He told it as I told you. Be certain.
    He can't reject that and reverse himself.
    The city heard these things, not I alone.

---

lunged . . . prongs: Laius strikes Oedipus with a two-pronged horse goad, or whip.

But even if he swerves from what he said,
855   he'll never show that Laius' murder, Lord,
occurred just as predicted. For Loxias
expressly said my son was doomed to kill him.
The boy — poor boy — he never had a chance
to cut him down, for he was cut down first.
860   Never again, just for some oracle
will I shoot frightened glances right and left.

OEDIPUS: That's full of sense. Nonetheless, send a man
to bring that farm hand here. Will you do it?

JOCASTA: I'll send one right away. But let's go in.
865   Would I do anything against your wishes?

Exit Oedipus and Jocasta through the central door into the palace.

STASIMON 2
STROPHE 1

CHORUS: May there accompany me
the fate to keep a reverential purity in what I say,
in all I do, for which the laws have been set forth
and walk on high, born to traverse the brightest,
870   highest upper air; Olympus° only
is their father, nor was it
mortal nature
that fathered them, and never will
oblivion lull them into sleep;
875   the god in them is great and never ages.

ANTISTROPHE 1

The will to violate, seed of the tyrant,
if it has drunk mindlessly of wealth and power,
without a sense of time or true advantage,
mounts to a peak, then
880   plunges to an abrupt . . . destiny,
where the useful foot
is of no use. But the kind
of struggling that is good for the city
I ask the god never to abolish.
885   The god is my protector: never will I give that up.

STROPHE 2

But if a man proceeds disdainfully
    in deeds of hand or word
and has no fear of Justice

Olympus: Mount Olympus, home of the gods, and treated as a god itself.

or reverence for shrines of the divinities
(may a bad fate catch him   890
    for his luckless wantonness!),
if he'll not gain what he gains with justice
and deny himself what is unholy,
or if he clings, in foolishness, to the untouchable
(what man, finally, in such an action, will have strength   895
enough to fend off passion's arrows from his soul?),
if, I say, this kind of
    deed is held in honor—
why should I join the sacred dance?

ANTISTROPHE 2

No longer shall I visit and revere   900
    Earth's navel,° the untouchable,
nor visit Abae's° temple,
    or Olympia,°
if the prophecies are not matched by events
    for all the world to point to.   905
No, you who hold the power, if you are rightly called
Zeus the king of all, let this matter not escape you
and your ever-deathless rule,
for the prophecies to Laius fade . . .
and men already disregard them;   910
nor is Apollo anywhere
    glorified with honors.
Religion slips away.

<u>EPISODE 3</u>

Enter Jocasta from the palace carrying a branch wound with wool and a jar of incense. She is attended by two women.

JOCASTA: Lords of the realm, the thought has come to me
    to visit shrines of the divinities   915
with suppliant's branch in hand and fragrant smoke.
For Oedipus excites his soul too much
with alarms of all kinds. He will not judge
the present by the past, like a man of sense.
He's at the mercy of all terror-mongers.   920

Jocasta approaches the altar on the right and kneels.

Earth's navel: Delphi.
Abae's: Abae was a town in Phocis where there was another oracle of Apollo.
Olympia: Site of the oracle of Zeus.

Since I can do no good by counseling,
Apollo the Lycēan! — you are the closest —
I come a suppliant, with these my vows,
for a cleansing that will not pollute him.
925　　For when we see him shaken we are all
afraid, like people looking at their helmsman.

Enter a Messenger along one of the parados. He sees Jocasta at the altar and then addresses the Chorus.

MESSENGER: I would be pleased if you would help me, stranger.
Where is the palace of King Oedipus?
Or tell me where he is himself, if you know.
930　　Chorus: This is his house, stranger. He is within.
This is his wife and mother of his children.
MESSENGER: May she and her family find prosperity,
if, as you say, her marriage is fulfilled.
JOCASTA: You also, stranger, for you deserve as much
935　　for your gracious words. But tell me why you've come.
What do you wish? Or what have you to tell us?
MESSENGER: Good news, my Lady, both for your house and husband.
JOCASTA: What is your news? And who has sent you to us?
MESSENGER: I come from Corinth. When you have heard my news
940　　you will rejoice, I'm sure — and grieve perhaps.
JOCASTA: What is it? How can it have this double power?
MESSENGER: They will establish him their king, so say
the people of the land of Isthmia.°
JOCASTA: But is old Polybus not still in power?
945　**MESSENGER:** He's not, for death has clasped him in the tomb.
JOCASTA: What's this? Has Oedipus' father died?
MESSENGER: If I have lied then I deserve to die.
JOCASTA: Attendant! Go quickly to your master,
and tell him this.

Exit an Attendant into the palace.

Oracles of the gods!
950　　Where are you now? The man whom Oedipus
fled long ago, for fear that he should kill him —
he's been destroyed by chance and not by him!

Enter Oedipus from the palace.

OEDIPUS: Darling Jocasta, my beloved wife,
Why have you called me from the palace?
955　**JOCASTA:** First hear what this man has to say. Then see
what the god's grave oracle has come to now!

---

land of Isthmia: Corinth, Greek city-state situated on an isthmus.

OEDIPUS: Where is he from? What is this news he brings me?
JOCASTA: From Corinth. He brings news about your father:
    that Polybus is no more! that he is dead!
OEDIPUS: What's this, old man? I want to hear you say it.   960
MESSENGER: If this is what must first be clarified,
    please be assured that he is dead and gone.
OEDIPUS: By treachery or by the touch of sickness?
MESSENGER: Light pressures tip agéd frames into their sleep.
OEDIPUS: You mean the poor man died of some disease.   965
MESSENGER: And of the length of years that he had tallied.
OEDIPUS: Aha! Then why should we look to Pytho's vapors,°
    or to the birds that scream above our heads?°
    If we could really take those things for guides,
    I would have killed my father. But he's dead!   970
    He is beneath the earth, and here am I,
    who never touched a spear. Unless he died
    of longing for me and I "killed" him that way!
    No, in this case, Polybus, by dying, took
    the worthless oracle to Hades with him.   975
JOCASTA: And wasn't I telling you that just now?
OEDIPUS: You were indeed. I was misled by fear.
JOCASTA: You should not care about this anymore.
OEDIPUS: I must care. I must stay clear of my mother's bed.
JOCASTA: What's there for man to fear? The realm of chance   980
    prevails. True foresight isn't possible.
    His life is best who lives without a plan.
    This marriage with your mother — don't fear it.
    How many times have men in dreams, too, slept
    with their own mothers! Those who believe such things   985
    mean nothing endure their lives most easily.
OEDIPUS: A fine, bold speech, and you are right, perhaps,
    except that my mother is still living,
    so I must fear her, however well you argue.
JOCASTA: And yet your father's tomb is a great eye.   990
OEDIPUS: Illuminating, yes. But I still fear the living.
MESSENGER: Who is the woman who inspires this fear?
OEDIPUS: Meropē, Polybus' wife, old man.
MESSENGER: And what is there about her that alarms you?
OEDIPUS: An oracle, god-sent and fearful, stranger.   995
MESSENGER: Is it permitted that another know?
OEDIPUS: It is. Loxias once said to me
    I must have intercourse with my own mother

Pytho's vapors: Prophecies of the oracle at Delphi.

birds . . . heads: Prophecies derived from interpreting the flights of birds.

and take my father's blood with these my hands.
1000   So I have long lived far away from Corinth.
This has indeed brought much good luck, and yet,
to see one's parents' eyes is happiest.
MESSENGER: Was it for this that you have lived in exile?
OEDIPUS: So I'd not be my father's killer, sir.
1005   MESSENGER: Had I not better free you from this fear,
my Lord? That's why I came — to do you service.
OEDIPUS: Indeed, what a reward you'd get for that!
MESSENGER: Indeed, this is the main point of my trip,
to be rewarded when you get back home.
1010   OEDIPUS: I'll never rejoin the givers of my seed!°
MESSENGER: My son, clearly you don't know what you're doing.
OEDIPUS: But how is that, old man? For the gods' sake, tell me!
MESSENGER: If it's because of them you won't go home.
OEDIPUS: I fear that Phoebus will have told the truth.
1015   MESSENGER: Pollution from the ones who gave you seed?
OEDIPUS: That is the thing, old man, I always fear.
MESSENGER: Your fear is groundless. Understand that.
OEDIPUS: Groundless? Not if I was born their son.
MESSENGER: But Polybus is not related to you.
1020   OEDIPUS: Do you mean Polybus was not my father?
MESSENGER: No more than I. We're both the same to you.
OEDIPUS: Same? One who begot me and one who didn't?
MESSENGER: He didn't beget you any more than I did.
OEDIPUS: But then, why did he say I was his son?
1025   MESSENGER: He got you as a gift from my own hands.
OEDIPUS: He loved me so, though from another's hands?
MESSENGER: His former childlessness persuaded him.
OEDIPUS: But had you bought me, or begotten me?
MESSENGER: Found you. In the forest hallows of Cithaeron.
1030   OEDIPUS: What were you doing traveling in that region?
MESSENGER: I was in charge of flocks which grazed those mountains.
OEDIPUS: A wanderer who worked the flocks for hire?
MESSENGER: Ah, but that day I was your savior, son.
OEDIPUS: From what? What was my trouble when you took me?
1035   MESSENGER: The ball-joints of your feet might testify.
OEDIPUS: What's that? What makes you name that ancient trouble?
MESSENGER: Your feet were pierced and I am your rescuer.
OEDIPUS: A fearful rebuke those tokens left for me!
MESSENGER: That was the chance that names you who you are.
1040   OEDIPUS: By the gods, did my mother or my father do this?
MESSENGER: That I don't know. He might who gave you to me.

---

givers of my seed: Meaning i.e., my parents." Oedipus still thinks Meropē and Polybus are his parents.

Framed by a masked member of the Chorus and Jocasta—played here by Laurence Olivier in the landmark 1945 production of *Oedipus the King*—seems to finally recognize the "truth" that he has been seeking.

OEDIPUS: From someone else? You didn't chance on me?

MESSENGER: Another shepherd handed you to me.

OEDIPUS: Who was he? Do you know? Will you explain!

MESSENGER: They called him one of the men of — was it Laius?   1045

OEDIPUS: The one who once was king here long ago?

MESSENGER: That is the one! The man was shepherd to him.

OEDIPUS: And is he still alive so I can see him?

MESSENGER: But you who live here ought to know that best.

OEDIPUS: Does any one of you now present know   1050
about the shepherd whom this man has named?
Have you seen him in town or in the fields? Speak out!
The time has come for the discovery!

CHORAGOS: The man he speaks of, I believe, is the same
as the field hand you have already asked to see.   1055
But it's Jocasta who would know this best.

OEDIPUS: Lady, do you remember the man we just
now sent for — is that the man he speaks of?

JOCASTA: What? The man he spoke of? Pay no attention!
His words are not worth thinking about. It's nothing.   1060

OEDIPUS: With clues like this within my grasp, give up?
Fail to solve the mystery of my birth?

JOCASTA: For the love of the gods, and if you love your life,
    give up this search! My sickness is enough.

1065 OEDIPUS: Come! Though my mothers for three generations
    were in slavery, you'd not be lowborn!

JOCASTA: No, listen to me! Please! Don't do this thing!

OEDIPUS: I will not listen; I will search out the truth.

JOCASTA: My thinking is for you — it would be best.

1070 OEDIPUS: This "best" of yours is starting to annoy me.

JOCASTA: Doomed man! Never find out who you are!

OEDIPUS: Will someone go and bring that shepherd here?
    Leave her to glory in her wealthy birth!

JOCASTA: Man of misery! No other name

1075   shall I address you by, ever again.

Exit Jocasta into the palace after a long pause.

CHORAGOS: Why has your lady left, Oedipus,
    hurled by a savage grief? I am afraid
    disaster will come bursting from this silence.

OEDIPUS: Let it burst forth! However low this seed

1080   of mine may be, yet I desire to see it.
    She, perhaps — she has a woman's pride —
    is mortified by my base origins.
    But I who count myself the child of Chance,
    the giver of good, shall never know dishonor.

1085   She is my mother,° and the months my brothers
    who first marked out my lowness, then my greatness.
    I shall not prove untrue to such a nature
    by giving up the search for my own birth.

<u>STASIMON 3</u>
STROPHE

CHORUS: If I have mantic power

1090   and excellence in thought,
    by Olympus,
        you shall not, Cithaeron, at tomorrow's
    full moon,
    fail to hear us celebrate you as the countryman

1095   of Oedipus, his nurse and mother,
    or fail to be the subject of our dance,
        since you have given pleasure
    to our king.
    Phoebus, whom we summon by "iē!,"

1100   may this be pleasing to you!

She . . . mother: Chance is my mother.

ANTISTROPHE

Who was your mother, son?
which of the long-lived nymphs
after lying with Pan,°
    the mountain roaming . . . Or was it a bride
of Loxias?°   1105
For dear to him are all the upland pastures.
Or was it Mount Cyllēnē's lord,°
or the Bacchic god,°
    dweller of the mountain peaks,
who received you as a joyous find   1110
from one of the nymphs of Helicon,
the favorite sharers of his sport?

EPISODE 4

OEDIPUS: If someone like myself, who never met him,
    may calculate — elders, I think I see
    the very herdsman we've been waiting for.   1115
    His many years would fit that man's age,
    and those who bring him on, if I am right,
    are my own men. And yet, in real knowledge,
    you can outstrip me, surely: you've seen him.

Enter the old Herdsman escorted by two of Oedipus's Attendants. At first, the Herdsman will not look at Oedipus.

CHORAGOS: I know him, yes, a man of the house of Laius,   1120
    a trusty herdsman if he ever had one.
OEDIPUS: I ask you first, the stranger come from Corinth:
    is this the man you spoke of?
MESSENGER: That's he you see.
OEDIPUS: Then you, old man. First look at me! Now answer:
    did you belong to Laius' household once?   1125
HERDSMAN: I did. Not a purchased slave but raised in the palace.
OEDIPUS: How have you spent your life? What is your work?
HERDSMAN: Most of my life now I have tended sheep.
OEDIPUS: Where is the usual place you stay with them?
HERDSMAN: On Mount Cithaeron. Or in that district.   1130
OEDIPUS: Do you recall observing this man there?
HERDSMAN: Doing what? Which is the man you mean?
OEDIPUS: This man right here. Have you had dealings with him?

Pan: God of shepherds and woodlands, half man and half goat.
Loxias: Apollo.
Mount Cyllēnē's lord: Hermes, messenger of the gods.
Bacchic god: Dionysus.

HERDSMAN: I can't say right away. I don't remember.

1135   MESSENGER: No wonder, master. I'll bring clear memory
to his ignorance. I'm absolutely sure
he can recall it, the district was Cithaeron,
he with a double flock, and I, with one,
lived close to him, for three entire seasons,

1140   six months along, from spring right to Arcturus.°
Then for the winter I'd drive mine to my fold,
and he'd drive his to Laius' pen again.
Did any of the things I say take place?

HERDSMAN: You speak the truth, though it's from long ago.

1145   MESSENGER: Do you remember giving me, back then,
a boy I was to care for as my own?

HERDSMAN: What are you saying? Why do you ask me that?

MESSENGER: There, sir, is the man who was that boy!

HERDSMAN: Damn you! Shut your mouth! Keep your silence!

1150   OEDIPUS: Stop! Don't you rebuke his words.
Your words ask for rebuke far more than his.

HERDSMAN: But what have I done wrong, most royal master?

OEDIPUS: Not telling of the boy of whom he asked.

HERDSMAN: He's ignorant and blundering toward ruin.

1155   OEDIPUS: Tell it willingly — or under torture.

HERDSMAN: Oh god! Don't — I am old — don't torture me!

OEDIPUS: Here! Someone put his hands behind his back!

HERDSMAN: But why? What else would you find out, poor man?

OEDIPUS: Did you give him the child he asks about?

1160   HERDSMAN: I did. I wish that I had died that day!

OEDIPUS: You'll come to that if you don't speak the truth.

HERDSMAN: It's if I speak that I shall be destroyed.

OEDIPUS: I think this fellow struggles for delay.

HERDSMAN: No, no! I said already that I gave him.

1165   OEDIPUS: From your own home, or got from someone else?

HERDSMAN: Not from my own. I got him from another.

OEDIPUS: Which of these citizens? What sort of house?

HERDSMAN: Don't — by the gods! — don't, master, ask me more!

OEDIPUS: It means your death if I must ask again.

1170   HERDSMAN: One of the children of the house of Laius.

OEDIPUS: A slave — or born into the family?

HERDSMAN: I have come to the dreaded thing, and I shall say it.

OEDIPUS: And I to hearing it, but hear I must.

HERDSMAN: He was reported to have been — his son.

1175   Your lady in the house could tell you best.

OEDIPUS: Because she gave him to you?

Arcturus: A star that is first seen in September in the sky over Greece.

HERDSMAN: Yes, my lord.
OEDIPUS: What was her purpose?
HERDSMAN: I was to kill the boy.
OEDIPUS: The child she bore?
HERDSMAN: She dreaded prophecies.
OEDIPUS: What were they?
HERDSMAN: The word was that he'd kill his parents.
OEDIPUS: Then why did you give him up to this old man?   1180
HERDSMAN: In pity, master — so he would take him home,
  to another land. But what he did was save him
  for this supreme disaster. If you are the one
  he speaks of — know your evil birth and fate!
OEDIPUS: Ah! All of it was destined to be true!   1185
  Oh light, now may I look my last upon you,
  shown monstrous in my birth, in marriage monstrous,
  a murderer monstrous in those I killed.

Exit Oedipus, running into the palace.

STASIMON 4
STROPHE 1

CHORUS: Oh generations of mortal men,
  while you are living, I will   1190
   appraise your lives at zero!
  What man
  comes closer to seizing lasting blessedness
  than merely to seize its semblance,
  and after living in this semblance, to plunge?   1195
  With your example before us,
  with your destiny, yours,
   suffering Oedipus, no mortal
  can I judge fortunate.

ANTISTROPHE 1

For he,° outranging everybody,   1200
shot his arrow° and became the lord
  of wide prosperity and blessedness,
oh Zeus, after destroying
the virgin with the crooked talons,°
singer of oracles; and against death,   1205
in my land, he arose a tower of defense.

---

he: Oedipus.

shot his arrow: Took his chances; made a guess at the Sphinx's riddle.

virgin . . . talons: The Sphinx.

From which time you were called my king
and granted privileges supreme — in mighty
Thebes the ruling lord.

STROPHE 2

1210   But now — whose story is more sorrowful than yours?
Who is more intimate with fierce calamities,
with labors, now that your life is altered?
Alas, my Oedipus, whom all men know:
one great harbor°—
1215   one alone sufficed for you,
as son and father,
when you tumbled,° plowman° of the woman's chamber.
How, how could your paternal
furrows, wretched man,
1220   endure you silently so long.

ANTISTROPHE 2

Time, all-seeing, surprised you living an unwilled life
and sits from of old in judgment on the marriage, not a marriage,
where the begetter is the begot as well.
Ah, son of Laius . . . ,
1225   would that — oh, would that
I had never seen you!
I wail, my scream climbing beyond itself
from my whole power of voice. To say it straight:
from you I got new breath —
1230   but I also lulled my eye to sleep.°

EXODOS°

Enter the Second Messenger from the palace.

SECOND MESSENGER: You who are first among the citizens,
what deeds you are about to hear and see!
What grief you'll carry, if, true to your birth,
you still respect the house of Labdacus!
1235   Neither the Ister nor the Phasis river
could purify this house, such suffering
does it conceal, or soon must bring to light —
willed this time, not unwilled. Griefs hurt worst
which we perceive to be self-chosen ones.

---

one great harbor: Metaphorical allusion to Jocasta's body.
tumbled: Were born and had sex.
plowman: Plowing is used here as a sexual metaphor.
I . . . sleep: I failed to see the corruption you brought.
Exodos: The final scene, containing the play's resolution.

CHORAGOS: They were sufficient, the things we knew before,   1240
    to make us grieve. What can you add to those?
SECOND MESSENGER: The thing that's quickest said and quickest heard:
    our own, our royal one, Jocasta's dead.
CHORAGOS: Unhappy queen! What was responsible?
SECOND MESSENGER: Herself. The bitterest of these events   1245
    is not for you, you were not there to see,
    but yet, exactly as I can recall it,
    you'll hear what happened to that wretched lady.
    She came in anger through the outer hall,
    and then she ran straight to her marriage bed,   1250
    tearing her hair with the fingers of both hands.
    Then, slamming shut the doors when she was in,
    she called to Laius, dead so many years,
    remembering the ancient seed which caused
    his death, leaving the mother to the son   1255
    to breed again an ill-born progeny.
    She mourned the bed where she, alas, bred double —
    husband by husband, children by her child.
    From this point on I don't know how she died,
    for Oedipus then burst in with a cry,   1260
    and did not let us watch her final evil.
    Our eyes were fixed on him. Wildly he ran
    to each of us, asking for his spear
    and for his wife — no wife: where he might find
    the double mother-field, his and his children's.   1265
    He raved, and some divinity then showed him —
    for none of us did so who stood close by.
    With a dreadful shout — as if some guide were leading —
    he lunged through the double doors; he bent the hollow
    bolts from the sockets, burst into the room,   1270
    and there we saw her, hanging from above,
    entangled in some twisted hanging strands.
    He saw, was stricken, and with a wild roar
    ripped down the dangling noose. When she, poor woman,
    lay on the ground, there came a fearful sight: 1275
    he snatched the pins of worked gold from her dress,
    with which her clothes were fastened: these he raised
    and struck into the ball-joints of his eyes.°
    He shouted that they would no longer see
    the evils he had suffered or had done,   1280
    see in the dark those he should not have seen,
    and know no more those he once sought to know.
    While chanting this, not once but many times

---

ball-joints of his eyes: His eyeballs. Oedipus blinds himself in both eyes at the same time.

1285
he raised his hand and struck into his eyes.
Blood from his wounded eyes poured down his chin,
not freed in moistening drops, but all at once
a stormy rain of black blood burst like hail.
These evils, coupling them, making them one,
have broken loose upon both man and wife.

1290
The old prosperity that they had once
was true prosperity, and yet today,
mourning, ruin, death, disgrace, and every
evil you could name — not one is absent.

CHORAGOS: Has he allowed himself some peace from all this grief?

1295
SECOND MESSENGER: He shouts that someone slide the bolts and show
to all the Cadmeians the patricide,
his mother's — I can't say it, it's unholy —
so he can cast himself out of the land,
not stay and curse his house by his own curse.

1300
He lacks the strength, though, and he needs a guide,
for his is a sickness that's too great to bear.
Now you yourself will see: the bolts of the doors
are opening. You are about to see
a vision even one who hates must pity.

Enter the blinded Oedipus from the palace, led in by a household Servant.

1305
CHORAGOS: Terrifying suffering for men to see,
more terrifying than any I've ever
come upon. Oh man of pain
what madness reached you? Which god from far off,
surpassing in range his longest spring,

1310
struck hard against your god-abandoned fate?
Oh man of pain,
I cannot look upon you — though there's so much
I would ask you, so much to hear,
so much that holds my eyes —

1315
such is the shudder you produce in me.

OEDIPUS: Ah! Ah! I am a man of misery.
Where am I carried? Pity me! Where
is my voice scattered abroad on wings?
Divinity, where has your lunge transported me?

1320
CHORAGOS: To something horrible, not to be heard or seen.

<u>KOMMOS</u>
STROPHE 1

OEDIPUS: Oh, my cloud
of darkness, abominable, unspeakable as it attacks me,
not to be turned away, brought by an evil wind!
Alas!

Again alas! Both enter me at once: 1325
the sting of the prongs,° the memory of evils!
CHORUS: I do not marvel that in these afflictions
you carry double griefs and double evils.

ANTISTROPHE 1

OEDIPUS: Ah, friend,
so you at least are there, resolute servant! 1330
Still with a heart to care for me, the blind man.
Oh! Oh!
I know that you are there. I recognize
even inside my darkness, that voice of yours.
CHORUS: Doer of horror, how did you bear to quench 1335
your vision? What divinity raised your hand?

STROPHE 2

OEDIPUS: It was Apollo there, Apollo, friends,
who brought my sorrows, vile sorrows to their perfection,
these evils that were done to me.
But the one who struck them with his hand, 1340
that one was none but I, in wretchedness.
For why was I to see
when nothing I could see would bring me joy?
CHORUS: Yes, that is how it was.
OEDIPUS: What could I see, indeed, 1345
or what enjoy — what greeting
is there I could hear with pleasure, friends?
Conduct me out of the land
as quickly as you can!
Conduct me out, my friends, 1350
the man utterly ruined,
supremely cursed,
the man who is by gods
the most detested of all men!
CHORUS: Wretched in disaster and in knowledge: 1355
oh, I could wish you'd never come to know!

ANTISTROPHE 2

OEDIPUS: May he be destroyed, whoever freed the savage shackles
from my feet when I'd been sent to the wild pasture,
whoever rescued me from murder
and became my savior — 1360
a bitter gift:
if I had died then,

---

prongs: Refers both to the whip that Laius used and to the two gold pins that Oedipus used to blind himself.

I'd not have been such grief to self and kin.

CHORUS: I also would have had it so.

1365   OEDIPUS: I'd not have returned to be my father's
          murderer; I'd not be called by men
          my mother's bridegroom.
          Now I'm without a god,
               child of a polluted parent,
1370   fellow progenitor with him
               who gave me birth in misery.
          If there's an evil that
               surpasses evils, that
          has fallen to the lot of Oedipus.

1375   CHORAGOS: How can I say that you have counseled well?
          Better not to be than live a blind man.

       OEDIPUS: That this was not the best thing I could do —
          don't tell me that, or advise me any more!
          Should I descend to Hades and endure
1380   to see my father with these eyes? Or see
          my poor unhappy mother? For I have done,
          to both of these, things too great for hanging.
          Or is the sight of children to be yearned for,
          to see new shoots that sprouted as these did?
1385   Never, never with these eyes of mine!
          Nor city, nor tower, nor holy images
          of the divinities! For I, all-wretched,
          most nobly raised — as no one else in Thebes —
          deprived myself of these when I ordained
1390   that all expel the impious one — god-shown
          to be polluted, and the dead king's son!°
          Once I exposed this great stain upon me,
          could I have looked on these with steady eyes?
          No! No! And if there were a way to block
1395   the source of hearing in my ears, I'd gladly
          have locked up my pitiable body,
          so I'd be blind and deaf. Evils shut out —
          that way my mind could live in sweetness.
          Alas, Cithaeron, why did you receive me?
1400   Or when you had me, not killed me instantly?
          I'd not have had to show my birth to mankind.
          Polybus, Corinth, halls — ancestral,
          they told me — how beautiful was your ward,
          a scar that held back festering disease!
1405   Evil my nature, evil my origin.

---

l . . . son: Oedipus refers to his own curse against the murderer as well as his sins of patricide and incest.

You, three roads, and you, secret ravine,
you oak grove, narrow place of those three paths
that drank my blood° from these hands, from him
who fathered me, do you remember still
the things I did to you? When I'd come here,   1410
what I then did once more? Oh marriages! Marriages!
You gave us life and when you'd planted us
you sent the same seed up, and then revealed
fathers, brothers, sons, and kinsman's blood,
and brides, and wives, and mothers, all the most   1415
atrocious things that happen to mankind!
One should not name what never should have been.
Somewhere out there, then, quickly, by the gods,
cover me up, or murder me, or throw me
to the ocean where you will never see me more!   1420

Oedipus moves toward the Chorus and they back away from him.

Come! Don't shrink to touch this wretched man!
Believe me, do not be frightened! I alone
of all mankind can carry these afflictions.

Enter Creon from the palace with Attendants.

CHORAGOS: Tell Creon what you wish for. Just when we need him
he's here. He can act, he can advise you.   1425
He's now the land's sole guardian in your place.
OEDIPUS: Ah! Are there words that I can speak to him?
What ground for trust can I present? It's proved
that I was false to him in everything.
CREON: I have not come to mock you, Oedipus,   1430
nor to reproach you for your former falseness.
You men, if you have no respect for sons
of mortals, let your awe for the all-feeding
flames of lordy Hēlius° prevent
your showing unconcealed so great a stain,   1435
abhorred by earth and sacred rain and light.
Escort him quickly back into the house!
If blood kin only see and hear their own
afflictions, we'll have no impious defilement.
OEDIPUS: By the gods, you've freed me from one terrible fear,   1440
so nobly meeting my unworthiness:
grant me something — not for me; for you!

---

my blood: I.e., "the blood of my father, Laius."
Hēlius: The sun.

CREON: What do you want that you should beg me so?

OEDIPUS: To drive me from the land at once, to a place
1445   where there will be no man to speak to me!

CREON: I would have done just that — had I not wished
        to ask first of the god what I should do.

OEDIPUS: His answer was revealed in full — that I,
        the patricide, unholy, be destroyed.

1450 CREON: He said that, but our need is so extreme,
        it's best to have sure knowledge what must be done.

OEDIPUS: You'll ask about a wretched man like me?

CREON: Is it not time you put your trust in the god?

OEDIPUS: But I bid you as well, and shall entreat you.
1455   Give her who is within what burial
        you will — you'll give your own her proper rites;
        but me — do not condemn my fathers' land
        to have me dwelling here while I'm alive,
        but let me live on mountains — on Cithaeron
1460   famed as mine, for my mother and my father,
        while they yet lived, made it my destined tomb,
        and I'll be killed by those who wished my ruin!
        And yet I know: no sickness will destroy me,
        nothing will: I'd never have been saved
1465   when left to die unless for some dread evil.
        Then let my fate continue where it will!
        As for my children, Creon, take no pains
        for my sons — they're men and they will never lack
        the means to live, wherever they may be —
1470   but my two wretched, pitiable girls,
        who never ate but at my table, never
        were without me — everything that I
        would touch, they'd always have a share of it —
        please care for them! Above all, let me touch
1475   them with my hands and weep aloud my woes!
        Please, my Lord!
        Please, noble heart! Touching with my hands,
        I'd think I held them as when I could see.

Enter Antigone and Ismene from the palace with Attendants.

        What's this?
1480   Oh gods! Do I hear, somewhere, my two dear ones
        sobbing? Has Creon really pitied me
        and sent to me my dearest ones, my children?
        Is that it?

CREON: Yes, I prepared this for you, for I knew
1485   you'd feel this joy, as you have always done.

OEDIPUS: Good fortune, then, and, for your care, be guarded
    far better by divinity than I was!
    Where are you, children? Come to me! Come here
    to these my hands, hands of your brother, hands
    of him who gave you seed, hands that made   1490
    these once bright eyes to see now in this fashion.

Oedipus embraces his daughters.

    He, children, seeing nothing, knowing nothing,
    he fathered you where his own seed was plowed.
    I weep for you as well, though I can't see you,
    imagining your bitter life to come,   1495
    the life you will be forced by men to live.
    What gatherings of townsmen will you join,
    what festivals, without returning home
    in tears instead of watching holy rites?
    And when you've reached the time for marrying,   1500
    where, children, is the man who'll run the risk
    of taking on himself the infamy
    that will wound you as it did my parents?
    What evil is not here? Your father killed
    his father, plowed the one who gave him birth,   1505
    and from the place where he was sown, from there
    he got you, from the place he too was born.
    These are the wounds: then who will marry you?
    No man, my children. No, it's clear that you
    must wither in dry barrenness, unmarried.   1510

Oedipus addresses Creon.

    Son of Menoeceus! You are the only father
    left to them — we two who gave them seed
    are both destroyed: watch that they don't become
    poor, wanderers, unmarried — they are your kin.
    Let not my ruin be their ruin, too!   1515
    No, pity them! You see how young they are,
    bereft of everyone, except for you.
    Consent, kind heart, and touch me with your hand!

Creon grasps Oedipus's right hand.

    You, children, if you had reached an age of sense,
    I would have counseled much. Now, pray you may live   1520
    always where it's allowed, finding a life
    better than his was, who gave you seed.
CREON: Stop this now. Quiet your weeping. Move away, into the house.
OEDIPUS: Bitter words, but I obey them.
CREON: There's an end to all things.

OEDIPUS: I have first this request.

1525 CREON: Tell me. I shall judge when I will hear it.

OEDIPUS: Banish me from my homeland.

CREON: You must ask that of the god.

OEDIPUS: But I am the gods' most hated man!

CREON: Then you will soon get what you want.

OEDIPUS: Do you consent?

CREON: I never promise when, as now, I'm ignorant.

OEDIPUS: Then lead me in.

CREON: Come. But let your hold fall from your children.

OEDIPUS: Do not take them from me, ever!

1530 CREON: Do not wish to keep all of the power.
You had power, but that power did not follow you through life.

Oedipus's daughters are taken from him and led into the palace by Attendants. Oedipus is led into the palace by a Servant. Creon and the other Attendants follow. Only the Chorus remains.

CHORUS: People of Thebes, my country, see: here is that Oedipus —
he who "knew" the famous riddle, and attained the highest power,
whom all citizens admired, even envying his luck!

1535 See the billows of wild troubles which he has entered now!
Here is the truth of each man's life: we must wait, and see his end,
scrutinize his dying day, and refuse to call him happy
till he has crossed the border of his life without pain.

Exit the Chorus along each of the parados.

Reading and Reacting

1. The ancient Greeks used no scenery in their theatrical productions. In the absence of scenery, how is the setting established at the beginning of *Oedipus the King*?

2. In order not to detract from the language of *Oedipus the King*, some contemporary productions use very simple costumes. Do you agree with this decision? If so, why? If not, what kind of costumes would you use?

3. In some recent productions of *Oedipus the King*, actors wear copies of ancient Greek masks. What are the advantages and disadvantages of using such masks in a contemporary production of the play?

4. In the ancient Greek theater, the *strophe* and *antistrophe* were sung or chanted by the chorus as it danced back and forth across the stage. If you were staging the play today, would you retain the chorus or do away with it entirely? What would be gained or lost with each alternative?

5. Why does Sophocles have Oedipus blind himself offstage? What would be the effect of having Oedipus perform this act in full view of the audience?

6. In what ways does Sophocles observe the **unities** of time, place, and action described on page 941? How does Sophocles manage to present information

about what happened years before the action of the play while still maintaining the three unities?

7. The ancient Greek audience that viewed *Oedipus the King* was familiar with the plot of the play. Given this situation, how does Sophocles create suspense? What are the advantages and disadvantages of using a story that the audience already knows?

8. By the end of the play, what has Oedipus learned about himself? About the gods? About the quest for truth? Is he a tragic or a pathetic figure? (See pages 940–41 for a discussion of *tragedy* and *pathos*.)

9. Today, many directors employ *color-blind casting*— that is, they cast an actor in a role without regard to his or her race. Do you think this practice could be used in casting *Oedipus the King*? How, for example, would you react to an African American as Oedipus or to an Asian American as Creon?

10. JOURNAL ENTRY Do you think Oedipus deserves his fate? Why or why not?

11. CRITICAL PERSPECTIVE In "On Misunderstanding the *Oedipus Rex*," F. R. Dodds argues that Sophocles did not intend that Oedipus's tragedy be seen as rising from a "grave moral flaw." Neither, says Dodds, was Oedipus a "mere puppet" of the gods. Rather, "what fascinates us is the spectacle of a man freely choosing, from the highest motives, a series of actions which lead to his own ruin":

> Oedipus is great, not in virtue of a great worldly position — for his worldly position is an illusion which will vanish like a dream — but in virtue of his inner strength: strength to pursue the truth at whatever personal cost, and strength to accept and endure it when found. . . . Oedipus is great because he accepts the responsibility for *all* his acts, including those which are objectively most horrible, though subjectively innocent.

Do you agree with Dodds's arguments? Do you see Oedipus as someone who has inner strength or as a morally flawed victim of the gods?

Related Works: "Barn Burning" (p. 223), "Young Goodman Brown" (p. 292), "'Out, Out —'" (p. 698), "Ulysses" (p. 917), *Hamlet* (p. 1075).

WRITING SUGGESTIONS: Staging

1. Discuss the problems that the original staging of *Oedipus the King* poses for contemporary audiences and offer some possible solutions.

2. Discuss and analyze the staging techniques used in a play that is not in this chapter — for example, *Trifles* (p. 983) or *Wit* (p. 1320).

3. Choose a short story that appears in this anthology, and explain how you would stage it if it were a play. What props, costumes, lighting, and sound effects would you choose? What events would occur offstage? Possible subjects for this paper might include "A&P" (p. 115) or "The Story of an Hour" (p. 82).

4. Suppose you were asked to update the staging of *Oedipus the King* for a contemporary production. What scenery, props, and costumes would you use to transform the setting to create a contemporary drama?

5. WEB ACTIVITY The following Web site contains information about Sophocles and Greek Tragedy:

http://depthome.brooklyn.cuny.edu/classics/tragedy.html

On this Web site, Roger Dunkle writes, in "An Introduction to Greek Tragedy," that while many tragedies end in misery, "there are also tragedies in which a satisfactory solution of the tragic situation is attained."

Read Dunkle's article, and write an essay discussing whether there is a "satisfactory solution" in *Oedipus*. In your essay, focus on the consequences of the tragedy and how the society is affected by it.

CHAPTER 31

THEME

> Plays are like doors to me. They can be as massive and ornate as cathedrals or as small and intimate as keyholes. They can be as real as the kitchen sink or as ephemeral as dreams. When we read them in the quiet or sit in a darkened theatre space and listen we step over the threshold of the door that the playwright has opened for us. We walk into their secret garden or jungle and hopefully we are taken on an adventurous odyssey. —**Marsha Mason**, *Women Playwrights*

> [D]rama is one of the things that makes possible a solution to the problem of socializing people. In other words, we are born private, and we die private, but we live of necessity in direct relation to other people, even if we live alone. And dramatic conflict of significance always verges on and deals with the way men live together. And this is incomprehensible to Man as a private person. He is always trying to find out where he stands in his society, whether he uses those terms or not. He always wants to know whether his life has a meaning, and that meaning is always in relation to others. It is always in relation to his society, it's always in relation to his choices, to the absence of his choices, which are dominated by other people. I think that when we speak of dramatic significance we're really talking about, either openly or unknowingly, about the dilemma of living together, of living a social existence, and the conflict is endless between Man and his fellows and between his own instincts and the social necessity. —**Arthur Miller**, *The Playwrights Speak*

> I can't even count how many times I've heard the line, "Where did the idea for this play come from?" . . . Ideas emerge from plays — not the other way around. . . . I think explanation destroys [a play] and makes it less than it is. —**Sam Shepard**, Fool for Love *and Other Plays*

Like a short story or a novel, a play is open to interpretation. Readers' reactions are influenced by the language of the text, and audiences' reactions are influenced by the performance on stage. Just as in fiction, every element of a play — its title, its conflicts, its dialogue, its characters, and its staging, for instance — can shed light on its themes.

TITLES

The **title** of a play can provide insight into its themes. The ironic title of Susan Glaspell's *Trifles* (p. 983), for example, suggests that women's concern with "trifles" may get to the heart of the matter more effectively than the preoccupations of self-important men do. Wendy Wasserstein's *Tender Offer* is another title that offers clues to a theme of the play. It not only suggests the father's preoccupation with business (a company makes a *tender offer* when it wants to buy another company), but also makes the point that parents need to take the time to relate (make tender offers) to their children. Likewise, the title *Fences* (p. 1358) offers clues to a major theme of August Wilson's play, suggesting that the main character in the play, is kept from his goals by barriers that are constructed by himself as well as by society. Finally, the title of Anton Chekhov's *The Brute* (p. 1062) effectively calls attention to the play's ideas about male-female relationships. The title may refer to Smirnov, who says that he has never liked women — whom he characterizes as "creatures of poetry and romance." Or it may refer to Mrs. Popov's late husband, to whose memory she has dedicated her life despite the fact that he was repeatedly unfaithful. Either alternative reinforces the play's tongue-in-cheek characterization of men as "brutes."

CONFLICTS

The unfolding plot of a play — especially the **conflicts** that develop — can also reveal the play's themes. In Henrik Ibsen's *A Doll House* (p. 995), for example, at least three major conflicts are present: one between Nora and her husband Torvald, one between Nora and Krogstad (an old acquaintance), and one between Nora and society. Each of these conflicts sheds light on the themes of the play.

Through Nora's conflict with Torvald, Ibsen examines the constraints placed on women and men by marriage in the nineteenth century. Both Nora and Torvald are imprisoned within their respective roles: Nora must be passive and childlike, and Torvald must be proper and always in control. Nora, therefore, expects her husband to be noble and generous and, in a crisis, to sacrifice himself for her. When he fails to live up to her expectations, she is profoundly disillusioned.

Nora's conflict with Krogstad underscores Ibsen's criticisms of the class system in nineteenth-century Norway. At the beginning of the play, Nora finds it "immensely amusing: that we — that Torvald has so much power over . . . people." Krogstad, a bank clerk who is in the employ of Torvald, visits Nora in act 1 to enlist her aid in saving his job. It is clear that she sees him as her social inferior. When Krogstad questions her about a woman with whom he has seen her, she replies, "What makes you think you can cross-examine me, Mr. Krogstad — you, one of my husband's employees?" Nora does not realize that she and Krogstad are, ironically, very much alike: both occupy subordinate positions and therefore have no power to determine their own destinies.

Finally, through Nora's conflict with society, Ibsen examines an important theme of his play: the destructive nature of the forces that subjugate women. Nineteenth-century society was male dominated. A married woman could not borrow money without her husband's signature, own real estate in her own name, or enter into contracts. In addition, all her assets — including inheritances and trust funds — automatically became the property of her husband at the time of marriage. As a result of her sheltered life, Nora at the beginning of the play is completely innocent of the consequences of her actions. Most readers share Dr. Rank's confusion when he asks Nora, "Why do you laugh at that? Do you have any idea of what society is?" It is Nora's disillusionment at finding out that Torvald and the rest of society are not what she has been led to believe they are that ultimately causes her to rebel. By walking out the door at the end of the play, Nora rejects not only her husband and her children (to whom she has no legal right once she leaves), but also society and its laws.

Those three conflicts underscore many of the themes that dominate *A Doll House*. First, the conflicts show that marriage in the nineteenth century imprisons both men and women in narrow, constricting roles. They also show that middle-class Norwegian society is narrow, smug, and judgmental. (Krogstad is looked down upon for a crime years after he committed it, and Nora is looked down upon because she borrows money to save her husband's life.) Finally, the conflicts show that society does not offer individuals — especially women — the freedom to lead happy and fulfilling lives. Only when the social and economic conditions that govern society change, Ibsen suggests, can women and men live together in mutual esteem.

DIALOGUE

Dialogue can also give insight into a play's themes. Sometimes a character suggests — or even explicitly states — a theme. In act 3 of *A Doll House*, for example, Nora's friend, Mrs. Linde, comes as close as any character to expressing the central concern of the play when she says, "Helmer's got to learn everything; this dreadful secret has to be aired; those two have to come to a full understanding; all these lies can't go on." As the play goes on to demonstrate, the lies that exist both in marriage and in society are obstacles to love and happiness.

One of the main themes of Arthur Miller's *Death of a Salesman* (p. 1178) — the questionable validity of the American Dream, given the nation's social, political, and economic realities — is suggested by the play's dialogue. As his son Biff points out, Willy Loman's stubborn belief in upward mobility and material success is based more on fantasy than on fact:

WILLY: *(with hatred, threatening)* The door of your life is wide open!
BIFF: Pop! I am a dime a dozen, and so are you!
WILLY: *(turning on him now in an uncontrolled outburst)* I am not a dime a
    dozen! I am Willy Loman, and you are Biff Loman!

Biff starts for Willy, but is blocked by Happy. In his fury, Biff seems on the verge of attacking his father.

BIFF: I am not a leader of men, Willy, and neither are you. You were never anything but a hard-working drummer who landed in the ash can like all the rest of them! I'm one dollar an hour, Willy! I tried seven states and couldn't raise it. A buck an hour! Do you gather my meaning? I'm not bringing home any prizes any more, and you're going to stop waiting for me to bring them home!

Though not explicitly stating the theme of the play, this exchange strongly suggests that Biff rejects the materialistic values to which Willy clings.

CHARACTERS

Because a dramatic work focuses on a central character, or protagonist, the development of this character can shed light on a play's themes. Willy Loman in *Death of a Salesman* is developed in great detail. At the beginning of the play, he feels trapped, exhausted, and estranged from his surroundings. As Willy gradually sinks from depression into despair, the action of the play shifts from the present to the past, showing the events that shaped his life. His attitudes, beliefs, dreams, and dashed hopes reveal him to be an embodiment of the major theme of the play — that an unquestioning belief in the American dream of success and upward mobility is unrealistic and possibly destructive.

Nora in *A Doll House* changes a great deal during the course of the play. At the beginning, she is more her husband's possession than an adult capable of shaping her own destiny. Nora's status becomes apparent in the first act when Torvald gently scolds his "little spendthrift" and refers to her as his "little lark" and his "squirrel." She is reduced to childish deceptions, such as hiding her macaroons when her husband enters the room. After Krogstad accuses her of committing forgery and threatens to expose her, she expects her husband to rise to the occasion and take the blame for her. When Torvald instead accuses her of being a hypocrite, a liar, and a criminal, Nora's neat little world comes crashing down. As a result of this experience, Nora changes; no longer is she the submissive and obedient wife. Instead, she becomes confident and assertive, ultimately telling Torvald that their marriage is a sham and that she can no longer stay with him. This abrupt shift in Nora's personality gives the audience a clear understanding of the major themes of the play.

Unlike Willy and Nora, Laura in Tennessee Williams's *The Glass Menagerie* (p. 1416) is a character who changes very little during the course of the play. Laura suffers from such pathological shyness that she is unable to attend typing class, let alone talk to a potential suitor. Although the "gentleman caller" draws Laura out of her shell for a short time, she soon withdraws again. Laura's inability to change reinforces the play's theme that contemporary society, with its emphasis on progress, has no place for people like Laura who live in private worlds "of glass animals and old, worn-out phonograph records."

STAGING

Scenery and props may also convey the themes of a play. In *Death of a Salesman*, Biff's trophy, which is constantly in the audience's view, ironically underscores the futility of Willy's efforts to achieve success. Similarly, the miniature animals in *The Glass Menagerie* reflect the fragility of Laura's character and the futility of her efforts to fit into the modern world. And, in *Trifles*, the depressing farm house, the broken birdcage and the dead canary suggest Mrs. Wright's misery and the reason she murdered her husband.

Special lighting effects and music can also suggest a play's themes. Throughout *The Glass Menagerie*, for example, words and pictures are projected onto a section of the set between the front room and dining room walls. In scene 1, as Tom's mother, Amanda, tells him about her experiences with her "gentlemen callers," an image of her as a girl greeting callers appears on the screen. As Amanda continues, the words *"Où sont Les Neiges"* — "Where are the snows [of yesteryear]?" — appear on the screen. Later in the play, when Laura and her mother discuss a boy Laura knew, his picture is projected on the screen, showing him as a high school hero carrying a silver cup. In addition to the slides, Williams uses music — a recurring tune, dance music, and "Ave Maria" — to increase the emotional impact of certain scenes. Williams also uses shafts of light focused on selected areas or characters to create a dreamlike atmosphere for the play. Collectively, the slides, music, and lighting reinforce the theme that those who retreat into the past eventually become estranged from the present.

A FINAL NOTE

As you read, your values and beliefs influence your interpretation of a play's themes. For instance, your interest in feminism could lead you to focus on the submissive, almost passive, role of Willy's wife, Linda, in *Death of a Salesman*. As a result, you could conclude that the play shows how, in the post–World War II United States, women like Linda often sacrificed their own happiness for their husbands. Remember, however, that the details of a play, not just your own feelings or assumptions, must support your interpretation.

CHECKLIST **WRITING ABOUT THEME**

✓ What is the central theme of the play?

✓ What other themes can you identify?

✓ Does the title of the play suggest a theme?

✓ What conflicts exist in the play? In what way do they shed light on the themes of the play?

> ✓ Do any characters' statements express or imply a theme of the play?
>
> ✓ Do any characters change during the play? How do these changes suggest the play's themes?
>
> ✓ Do certain characters resist change? How does their failure to change suggest a theme of the play?
>
> ✓ Do scenery and props help to communicate the play's themes?
>
> ✓ Does music reinforce certain ideas in the play?
>
> ✓ Does lighting underscore the themes of the play?

MARGARET EDSON (1961–   ) was born in Washington, D.C. After earning a bachelor's degree in history at Smith College, she worked as a unit clerk in the cancer and AIDS inpatient unit of a major research hospital in Washington, D.C. In 1992, she earned an MA in English from Georgetown University; she then taught English as a Second Language and first grade in the District of Columbia public schools. In 1998, Edson moved to Atlanta, Georgia, where she now teaches kindergarten. Her first play, *Wit,* was written in 1991; after several small productions across the country, it opened on Broadway and won the Pulitzer Prize for drama in 1999 (it was later made into a movie starring Emma Thompson). Edson's other awards include a Drama League of New York Playwright Award (1993), a Los Angeles Drama Critics Circle Award (1996), a Connecticut Drama Critics Circle Award (1998), and a Berrilla Kerr Foundation Playwrights Award (1998). She was awarded a Fellowship of Southern Writers Drama Award in 1999.

Cultural Context: The work of English poet John Donne (1572–1631) has been variously received throughout the centuries. The influential eighteenth-century critic Samuel Johnson described the poetry as "metaphysical," using that term pejoratively to refer to poems in which the "most heterogeneous ideas are yoked together by violence." Donne's poems certainly do delight in violent yokings, combining passionate feeling, intellectual play, and verbal dexterity ("wit"), and relishing puns, paradoxes, and seeming outlandish conceits. For this reason, his poetry is the ideal metaphor to express the complicated, intertwined, and sometimes contradictory themes in *Wit.* Although Donne's poetry fell out of favor in the seventeenth and eighteenth centuries, it enjoyed a renaissance in the early twentieth century among poets and critics, notably T. S. Eliot.

MARGARET EDSON

Wit

CHARACTERS

Vivian Bearing, Ph.D.
50; professor of seventeenth-century poetry at the university

E. M. Ashford, D. Phil.
80; professor emerita of English literature
Mr. Bearing

Harvey Kelekian, M.D.	*Vivian's father*
50; chief of medical oncology,	**Lab Technicians**
University Hospital	**Clinical Fellows**
Jason Posner, M.D.	**Students**
28; clinical fellow, Medical Oncology Branch	**Code Team**
Susie Monahan, R.N., B.S.N.	
28; primary nurse, Cancer Inpatient Unit	

The play may be performed with a cast of nine: the four Technicians, Fellows, Students, and Code Team Members should double; Dr. Kelekian and Mr. Bearing should double.

NOTES

Most of the action, but not all, takes place in a room of the University Hospital Comprehensive Cancer Center. The stage is empty, and furniture is rolled on and off by the technicians.

Jason and Kelekian wear lab coats, but each has a different shirt and tie every time he enters. Susie wears white jeans, white sneakers, and a different blouse each entrance.

Scenes are indicated by a line rule in the script; there is no break in the action between scenes, but there might be a change in lighting. There is no intermission.

Vivian has a central-venous-access catheter over her left breast, so the IV tubing goes there, not into her arm. The IV pole, with a Port-a-Pump attached, rolls easily on wheels. Every time the IV pole reappears, it has a different configuration of bottles.

Vivian Bearing walks on the empty stage pushing her IV pole. She is fifty, tall and very thin, barefoot, and completely bald. She wears two hospital gowns — one tied in the front and one tied in the back — a baseball cap, and a hospital ID bracelet. The house lights are at half strength. Vivian looks out at the audience, sizing them up.

VIVIAN: *(In false familiarity, waving and nodding to the audience)* Hi. How are you feeling today? Great. That's just great. *(In her own professorial tone)* This is not my standard greeting, I assure you.

I tend toward something a little more formal, a little less inquisitive, such as, say, "Hello."

But it is the standard greeting here.

There is some debate as to the correct response to this salutation. Should one reply "I feel good," using "feel" as a copulative to link the subject, "I," to its subjective complement, "good"; or "I feel well," modifying with an adverb the subject's state of being?

I don't know. I am a professor of seventeenth-century poetry, specializing in the Holy Sonnets of John Donne.

So I just say, "Fine."

Of course it is not very often that I do feel fine.

I have been asked "How are you feeling today?" while I was throwing up into a plastic washbasin. I have been asked as I was emerging from a four-hour operation with a tube in every orifice, "How are you feeling today?"

I am waiting for the moment when someone asks me this question and I am dead.

I'm a little sorry I'll miss that.

It is unfortunate that this remarkable line of inquiry has come to me so late in my career. I could have exploited its feigned solicitude to great advantage: as I was distributing the final examination to the graduate course in seventeenth-century textual criticism —"Hi. How are you feeling today?"

Of course I would not be wearing this costume at the time, so the question's *ironic significance* would not be fully apparent.

As I trust it is now.

Irony is a literary device that will necessarily be deployed to great effect.

I ardently wish this were not so. I would prefer that a play about me be cast in the mythic-heroic-pastoral mode; but the facts, most notably stage-four metastatic ovarian cancer, conspire against that. *The Faerie Queene* this is not.

And I was dismayed to discover that the play would contain elements of . . . *humor.*

I have been, at best, an *unwitting* accomplice. (*She pauses.*) It is not my intention to give away the plot; but I think I die at the end.

They've given me less than two hours.

If I were poetically inclined, I might employ a threadbare metaphor — the sands of time slipping through the hourglass, the two-hour glass.

Now our sands are almost run;
More a little, and then dumb.

Shakespeare. I trust the name is familiar.

At the moment, however, I am disinclined to poetry.

I've got less than two hours. Then: curtain.

She disconnects herself from the IV pole and shoves it to a crossing Technician. The house lights go out.

VIVIAN: I'll never forget the time I found out I had cancer.

Dr. Harvey Kelekian enters at a big desk piled high with papers.

KELEKIAN: You have cancer.

VIVIAN: (*To audience*) See? Unforgettable. It was something of a shock. I had to sit down. (*She plops down.*)

5 **KELEKIAN:** Please sit down. Miss Bearing, you have advanced metastatic ovarian cancer.

VIVIAN: Go on.

KELEKIAN: You are a professor, Miss Bearing.

VIVIAN: Like yourself, Dr. Kelekian.

KELEKIAN: Well, yes. Now then. You present with a growth that, unfortunately, went undetected in stages one, two, and three. Now it is an insidious adenocarcinoma, which has spread from the primary adnexal mass —

10 **VIVIAN:** "Insidious"?

KELEKIAN: "Insidious" means undetectable at an—

VIVIAN: "Insidious" *means* treacherous.

KELEKIAN: Shall I continue?

VIVIAN: By all means.

KELEKIAN: Good. In invasive epithelial carcinoma, the most effective treatment modality is a chemotherapeutic agent. We are developing an experimental combination of drugs designed for primary-site ovarian, with a target specificity of stage three-and-beyond administration. Am I going too fast? Good. You will be hospitalized as an in-patient for treatment each cycle. You will be on complete intake-and-output measurement for three days after each treatment to monitor kidney function. After the initial eight cycles, you will have another battery of tests.

The antineoplastic will inevitably affect some healthy cells, including those lining the gastrointestinal tract from the lips to the anus, and the hair follicles. We will of course be relying on your resolve to withstand some of the more pernicious side effects.

VIVIAN: Insidious. Hmm. Curious word choice. Cancer. Cancel. 15

"By cancer nature's changing course untrimmed."
No — that's not it.
(*To Kelekian*) No.

Must read something about cancer.

Must get some books, articles. Assemble a bibliography.

Is anyone doing research on cancer?

Concentrate.

Antineoplastic. Anti: against Neo: new. Plastic. To mold. Shaping. Antineoplastic. Against new shaping.

Hair follicles. My resolve.

"Pernicious" That doesn't seem—

KELEKIAN: Miss Bearing?

VIVIAN: I beg your pardon?

KELEKIAN: Do you have any questions so far?

VIVIAN: Please, go on.

KELEKIAN: Perhaps some of these terms are new. I realize— 20

VIVIAN: No, no. Ah. You're being very thorough.

KELEKIAN: I make a point of it. And I always emphasize it with my students—

VIVIAN: So do I. "Thoroughness"— I always tell my students, but they are constitutionally averse to painstaking work.

KELEKIAN: Yours, too.

VIVIAN: Oh, it's worse every year. 25

KELEKIAN: And this is not dermatology, it's medical oncology, for Chrissake.

VIVIAN: My students read through a text once —*once!*— and think it's time for a break.

KELEKIAN: Mine are blind.

VIVIAN: Well, mine are deaf.

30 KELEKIAN: (*Resigned, but warmly*) You just have to hope . . .

VIVIAN: (*Not so sure*) I suppose.

Pause.

KELEKIAN: Where were we, Dr. Bearing?

VIVIAN: I believe I was being thoroughly diagnosed.

KELEKIAN: Right. Now. The tumor is spreading very quickly, and this treatment is very aggressive. So far, so good?

35 VIVIAN: Yes.

KELEKIAN: Better not teach next semester.

VIVIAN: (*Indignant*) Out of the question.

KELEKIAN: The first week of each cycle you'll be hospitalized for chemotherapy; the next week you may feel a little tired; the next two weeks'll be fine, relatively. This cycle will repeat eight times, as I said before.

VIVIAN: Eight months like that?

40 KELEKIAN: This treatment is the strongest thing we have to offer you. And, as research, it will make a significant contribution to our knowledge.

VIVIAN: Knowledge, yes.

KELEKIAN: (*Giving her a piece of paper*) Here is the informed-consent form. Should you agree, you sign there, at the bottom. Is there a family member you want me to explain this to?

VIVIAN: (*Signing*) That won't be necessary.

KELEKIAN: (*Taking back the paper*) Good. The important thing is for you to take the full dose of chemotherapy. There may be times when you'll wish for a lesser dose, due to the side effects. But we've got to go full-force. The experimental phase has got to have the maximum dose to be of any use. Dr. Bearing—

45 VIVIAN: Yes?

KELEKIAN: You must be very tough. Do you think you can be very tough?

VIVIAN: You needn't worry.

KELEKIAN: Good. Excellent.

Kelekian and the desk exit as Vivian stands and walks forward.

VIVIAN: (*Hesitantly*) I should have asked more questions, because I know there's going to be a test.

I have cancer, insidious cancer, with pernicious side effects — no, the *treatment* has pernicious side effects.

I have stage-four metastatic ovarian cancer. There is no stage five. Oh, and I have to be very tough. It appears to be a matter, as the saying goes, of life and death.

I know all about life and death. I am, after all, a scholar of Donne's Holy Sonnets, which explore mortality in greater depth than any other body of work in the English language.

And I know for a fact that I am tough. A demanding professor. Uncompromising. Never one to turn from a challenge. That is why I chose, while a student of the great E. M. Ashford, to study Donne.

Professor E. M. Ashford, fifty-two, enters, seated at the same desk as Kelekian was. The scene is twenty-eight years ago. Vivian suddenly turns twenty-two, eager and intimidated.

VIVIAN: Professor Ashford? 50

E.M.: Do it again.

VIVIAN: *(To audience)* It was something of a shock. I had to sit down. *(She plops down.)*

E.M.: Please sit down. Your essay on Holy Sonnet Six, Miss Bearing, is a melodrama, with a veneer of scholarship unworthy of you — to say nothing of Donne. Do it again.

VIVIAN: I, ah . . .

E.M.: You must begin with a text, Miss Bearing, not with a feeling. 55

> Death be not proud, though some have called thee
> Mighty and dreadfull, for, thou art not soe.

You have entirely missed the point of the poem, because, I must tell you, you have used an edition of the text that is inauthentically punctuated. In the Gardner edition—

VIVIAN: That edition was checked out of the library—

E.M.: Miss Bearing!

VIVIAN: Sorry.

E.M.: You take this too lightly, Miss Bearing. This is Metaphysical Poetry, not The Modern Novel. The standards of scholarship and critical reading which one would apply to any other text are simply insufficient. The effort must be total for the results to be meaningful. Do you think the punctuation of the last line of this sonnet is merely an insignificant detail?

The sonnet begins with a valiant struggle with death, calling on all the forces of intellect and drama to vanquish the enemy. But it is ultimately about overcoming the seemingly insuperable barriers separating life, death, and eternal life.

In the edition you chose, this profoundly simple meaning is sacrificed to hysterical punctuation:

> And Death —*capital D*— shall be no more —*semicolon!*
> Death —*capital D*—*comma*—thou shalt die— *exclamation point!*

If you go in for this sort of thing, I suggest you take up Shakespeare.

Gardner's edition of the Holy Sonnets returns to the Westmoreland manuscript source of 1610 — not for sentimental reasons, I assure you, but because Helen Gardner is a *scholar.* It reads:

> And death shall be no more, *comma,* Death thou shalt die.

As she recites this line, she makes a little gesture at the comma.

Nothing but a breath — a comma — separates life from life everlasting. It is very simple really. With the original punctuation restored, death is no longer something to act out on a stage, with exclamation points. It's a comma, a pause.

This way, the *uncompromising* way, one learns something from this poem, wouldn't you say? Life, death. Soul, God. Past, present. Not insuperable barriers, not semicolons, just a comma.

60   VIVIAN: Life, death . . . I see. (*Standing*) It's a metaphysical conceit. It's wit! I'll go back to the library and rewrite the paper —

E.M.: (*Standing, emphatically*) It is *not wit*, Miss Bearing. It is truth. (*Walking around the desk to her*) The paper's not the point.

VIVIAN: It isn't?

E.M.: (*Tenderly*) Vivian. You're a bright young woman. Use your intelligence. Don't go back to the library. Go out. Enjoy yourself with your friends. Hmm?

Vivian walks away. E.M. slides off.

VIVIAN: (*As she gradually returns to the hospital*) I, ah, went outside. The sun was very bright. I, ah, walked around, past the . . . There were students on the lawn, talking about nothing, laughing. The insuperable barrier between one thing and another is . . . just a comma? Simple human truth, uncompromising scholarly standards? They're *connected*? I just couldn't . . .

I went back to the library.

Anyway.

All right. Significant contribution to knowledge.

Eight cycles of chemotherapy. Give me the full dose, the full dose every time.

In a burst of activity, the hospital scene is created.

65   VIVIAN: The attention was flattering. For the first five minutes. Now I know how poems feel.

Susie Monahan, Vivian's primary nurse, gives Vivian her chart, then puts her in a wheelchair and takes her to her first appointment: chest x-ray. This and all other diagnostic tests are suggested by light and sound.

TECHNICIAN 1: Name.

VIVIAN: My name? Vivian Bearing.

TECHNICIAN 1: Huh?

70   VIVIAN: Bearing. B-E-A-R-I-N-G. Vivian. V-I-V-I-A-N.

TECHNICIAN 1: Doctor.

VIVIAN: Yes, I have a Ph.D.

TECHNICIAN 1: *Your* doctor.

VIVIAN: Oh. Dr. Harvey Kelekian.

Technician 1 positions her so that she is leaning forward and embracing the metal plate, then steps offstage.

VIVIAN: *I am a doctor of philosophy* —

75   TECHNICIAN 1: (*From offstage*) Take a deep breath, and hold it. (*Pause, with light and sound*) Okay.

VIVIAN: — a scholar of seventeenth-century poetry.

TECHNICIAN 1: (*From offstage*) Turn sideways, arms behind your head, and hold it. (*Pause*) Okay.

VIVIAN: I have made an immeasurable contribution to the discipline of English literature. (*Technician 1 returns and puts her in the wheelchair.*) I am, in short, a force.

Technician 1 rolls her to upper GI series, where Technician 2 picks up.

TECHNICIAN 2: Name.

VIVIAN: Lucy, Countess of Bedford.   80

TECHNICIAN 2: (*Checking a printout*) I don't see it here.

VIVIAN: My name is Vivian Bearing. B-E-A-R-I-N-G. Dr. Kelekian is my doctor.

TECHNICIAN 2: Okay. Lie down. (*Technician 2 positions her on a stretcher and leaves. Light and sound suggest the filming.*)

VIVIAN: After an outstanding undergraduate career, I studied with Professor E. M. Ashford for three years, during which time I learned by instruction and example what it means to be a scholar of distinction.

As her research fellow, my principal task was the alphabetizing of index cards for Ashford's monumental critical edition of Donne's *Devotions upon Emergent Occasions*.

During the procedure, another Technician takes the wheelchair away.

I am thanked in the preface: "Miss Vivian Bearing for her able assistance."

My dissertation, "Ejaculations in Seventeenth-Century Manuscript and Printed Editions of the Holy Sonnets: A Comparison," was revised for publication in the *Journal of English Texts*, a very prestigious venue for a first appearance.

TECHNICIAN 2: Where's your wheelchair?   85

VIVIAN: I do not know. I was busy just now.

TECHNICIAN 2: Well, how are you going to get out of here?

VIVIAN: Well, I do not know. Perhaps you would like me to stay.

TECHNICIAN 2: I guess I got to go find you a chair.

VIVIAN: (*Sarcastically*) Don't inconvenience yourself on my behalf. (*Technician   90
2 leaves to get a wheelchair.*)

My second article, a classic explication of Donne's sonnet "Death be not proud," was published in *Critical Discourse*.

The success of the essay prompted the University Press to solicit a volume on the twelve Holy Sonnets in the 1633 edition, which I produced in the remarkably short span of three years. My book, entitled *Made Cunningly*, remains an immense success, in paper as well as cloth.

In it, I devote one chapter to a thorough examination of each sonnet, discussing every word in extensive detail.

Technician 2 returns with a wheelchair.

TECHNICIAN 2: Here.

VIVIAN: I summarize previous critical interpretations of the text and offer my own analysis. It is exhaustive.

Technician 2 deposits her at CT scan.

Bearing. B-E-A-R-I-N-G. Kelekian.

Technician 3 has Vivian lie down on a metal stretcher. Light and sound suggest the procedure.

TECHNICIAN 3: Here. Hold still.

VIVIAN: For how long?

95 **TECHNICIAN 3:** Just a little while. *(Technician 3 leaves. Silence)*

VIVIAN: The scholarly study of poetic texts requires a capacity for scrupulously detailed examination, particularly the poetry of John Donne.

The salient characteristic of the poems is wit: "Itchy outbreaks of far-fetched wit," as Donne himself said.

To the common reader — that is to say, the undergraduate with a B-plus or better average — wit provides an invaluable exercise for sharpening the mental faculties, for stimulating the flash of comprehension that can only follow hours of exacting and seemingly pointless scrutiny.

Technician 3 puts Vivian back in the wheelchair and wheels her toward the unit. Partway, Technician 3 gives the chair a shove and Susie Monahan, Vivian's primary nurse, takes over. Susie rolls Vivian to the exam room.

To the scholar, to the mind comprehensively trained in the subtleties of seventeenth-century vocabulary, versification, and theological, historical, geographical, political, and mythological allusions, Donne's wit is . . . a way to see how good you really are.

After twenty years, I can say with confidence, no one is quite as good as I.

By now, Susie has helped Vivian sit on the exam table. Dr. Jason Posner, clinical fellow, stands in the doorway.

JASON: Ah, Susie?

SUSIE: Oh, hi.

JASON: Ready when you are.

100 **SUSIE:** Okay. Go ahead. Ms. Bearing, this is Jason Posner. He's going to do your history, ask you a bunch of questions. He's Dr. Kelekian's fellow.

Susie is busy in the room, setting up for the exam.

JASON: Hi, Professor Bearing. I'm Dr. Posner, clinical fellow in the medical oncology branch, working with Dr. Kelekian.

Professor Bearing, I, ah, I was an undergraduate at the U. I took your course in seventeenth-century poetry.

VIVIAN: You did?

JASON: Yes. I thought it was excellent.

VIVIAN: Thank you. Were you an English major?

Jason: No. Biochemistry. But you can't get into medical school unless you're 105
well-rounded. And I made a bet with myself that I could get an A in the
three hardest courses on campus.

Susie: Howdjya do, Jace?

Jason: Success.

Vivian: *(Doubtful)* Really?

Jason: A minus. It was a very tough course. *(To Susie)* I'll call you.

Susie: Okay. *(She leaves.)* 110

Jason: I'll just pull this over. *(He gets a little stool on wheels.)* Get the prox-
emics right here. There. *(Nervously)* Good. Now. I'm going to be taking
your history. It's a medical interview, and then I give you an exam.

Vivian: I believe Dr. Kelekian has already done that.

Jason: Well, I know, but Dr. Kelekian wants *me* to do it, too. Now. I'll be
taking a few notes as we go along.

Vivian: Very well.

Jason: Okay. Let's get started. How are you feeling today? 115

Vivian: Fine, thank you.

Jason: Good. How is your general health?

Vivian: Fine.

Jason: Excellent. Okay. We know you are an academic.

Vivian: Yes, we've established that. 120

Jason: So we don't need to talk about your interesting work.

Vivian: No.

The following questions and answers go extremely quickly.

Jason: How old are you?

Vivian: Fifty.

Jason: Are you married? 125

Vivian: No.

Jason: Are your parents living?

Vivian: No.

Jason: How and when did they die?

Vivian: My father, suddenly, when I was twenty, of a heart attack. My mother, 130
slowly, when I was forty-one and forty-two, of cancer. Breast cancer.

Jason: Cancer?

Vivian: Breast cancer.

Jason: I see. Any siblings?

Vivian: No.

Jason: Do you have any questions so far? 135

Vivian: Not so far.

Jason: Well, that about does it for your life history.

Vivian: Yes, that's all there is to my life history.

Jason: Now I'm going to ask you about your past medical history. Have you
ever been hospitalized?

Vivian: I had my tonsils out when I was eight. 140

Jason: Have you ever been pregnant?

VIVIAN: No.

JASON: Ever had heart murmurs? High blood pressure?

VIVIAN: No.

145   JASON: Stomach, liver, kidney problems?

VIVIAN: No.

JASON: Venereal diseases? Uterine infections?

VIVIAN: No.

JASON: Thyroid, diabetes, cancer?

150   VIVIAN: No — cancer, yes.

JASON: When?

VIVIAN: Now.

JASON: Well, not including now.

VIVIAN: In that case, no.

155   JASON: Okay. Clinical depression? Nervous breakdowns? Suicide attempts?

VIVIAN: No.

JASON: Do you smoke?

VIVIAN: No.

JASON: Ethanol?

160   VIVIAN: I'm sorry?

JASON: Alcohol.

VIVIAN: Oh. Ethanol. Yes, I drink wine.

JASON: How much? How often?

VIVIAN: A glass with dinner occasionally. And perhaps a Scotch every now and then.

165   JASON: Do you use substances?

VIVIAN: Such as.

JASON: Marijuana, cocaine, crack cocaine, PCP, ecstasy, poppers—

VIVIAN: No.

JASON: Do you drink caffeinated beverages?

170   VIVIAN: Oh, yes!

JASON: Which ones?

VIVIAN: Coffee. A few cups a day.

JASON: How many?

VIVIAN: Two . . . to six. But I really don't think that's immoderate—

175   JASON: How often do you undergo routine medical checkups?

VIVIAN: Well, not as often as I should, probably, but I've felt fine, I really have.

JASON: So the answer is?

VIVIAN: Every three to . . . five years.

JASON: What do you do for exercise?

180   VIVIAN: Pace.

JASON: Are you having sexual relations?

VIVIAN: Not at the moment.

JASON: Are you pre- or post-menopausal?—

VIVIAN: Pre.

185   JASON: When was the first day of your last period?

VIVIAN: Ah, ten days — two weeks ago.

JASON: Okay. When did you first notice your present complaint?

VIVIAN: This time, now?

JASON: Yes.

VIVIAN: Oh, about four months ago. I felt a pain in my stomach, in my abdomen, like a cramp, but not the same. 190

JASON: How did it feel?

VIVIAN: Like a cramp.

JASON: But not the same?

VIVIAN: No, duller, and stronger. I can't describe it.

JASON: What came next? 195

VIVIAN: Well, I just, I don't know, I started noticing my body, little things. I would be teaching, and feel a sharp pain.

JASON: What kind of pain?

VIVIAN: Sharp, and sudden. Then it would go away. Or I would be tired. Exhausted. I was working on a major project, the article on John Donne for *The Oxford Encyclopedia of English Literature*. It was a great honor. But I had a very strict deadline.

JASON: So you would say you were under stress?

VIVIAN: It wasn't so much more stress than usual, I just couldn't withstand it this time. I don't know. 200

JASON: So?

VIVIAN: So I went to Dr. Chin, my gynecologist, after I had turned in the article, and explained all this. She examined me, and sent me to Jefferson the internist, and he sent me to Kelekian because he thought I might have a tumor.

JASON: And that's it?

VIVIAN: Till now.

JASON: Hmmm. Well, that's very interesting. 205

Nervous pause.

Well, I guess I'll start the examination. It'll only take a few minutes. Why don't you, um, sort of lie back, and — oh — relax.

He helps her lie back on the table, raises the stirrups out of the table, raises her legs and puts them in the stirrups, and puts a paper sheet over her.

Be very relaxed. This won't hurt. Let me get this sheet. Okay. Just stay calm. Okay. Put your feet in these stirrups. Okay. Just. There. Okay? Now. Oh, I have to go get Susie. Got to have a girl here. Some crazy clinical rule. Um. I'll be right back. Don't move.

Jason leaves. Long pause. He is seen walking quickly back and forth in the hall, and calling Susie's name as he goes by.

VIVIAN: (*To herself*) I wish I had given him an A. (*Silence*)

Two times one is two.

Two times two is four.

Two times three is six.

Um.

Oh.

Death be not proud, though some have called thee
Mighty and dreadfull, for, thou art not soe,
For, those, whom thou think'st, thou dost overthrow,
Die not, poore death, nor yet canst thou kill mee . . .

JASON: *(In the hallway)* Has anybody seen Susie?

VIVIAN: *(Losing her place for a second)* Ah.

Thou'art slave to Fate, chance, kings, and desperate men,
And dost with poyson, warre, and sicknesse dwell,
And poppie,' or charmes can make us sleepe as well,
And better than thy stroake; why swell'st thou then?

JASON: *(In the hallway)* She was here just a minute ago.

210 VIVIAN:

One short sleepe past, wee wake eternally,
And death shall be no more —*comma*— Death thou shalt die.

Jason and Susie return.

JASON: Okay. Here's everything. Okay.

SUSIE: What is this? Why did you leave her—

JASON: *(To Susie)* I had to find you. Now, come on. *(To Vivian)* We're ready,
Professor Bearing. *(To himself, as he puts on exam gloves)* Get these on. Okay.
Just lift this up. Ooh. Okay. *(As much to himself as to her)* Just relax. *(He
begins the pelvic exam, with one hand on her abdomen and the other inside her,
looking blankly at the ceiling as he feels around.)* Okay. *(Silence)* Susie, isn't
that interesting, that I had Professor Bearing.

SUSIE: Yeah. I wish I had taken some literature. I don't know anything about
poetry.

215 JASON: *(Trying to be casual)* Professor Bearing was very highly regarded on
campus. It looked very good on my transcript that I had taken her course.
(Silence) They even asked me about it in my interview for med school —
(He feels the mass and does a double take.) Jesus! *(Tense silence. He is amazed
and fascinated.)*

SUSIE: What?

VIVIAN: What?

JASON: Um. *(He tries for composure.)* Yeah. I survived Bearing's course. No
problem. Heh. *(Silence)* Yeah, John Donne, those metaphysical poets, that
metaphysical wit. Hardest poetry in the English department. Like to see
them try biochemistry. *(Silence)* Okay. We're about done. Okay. That's it.
Okay, Professor Bearing. Let's take your feet out, there. *(He takes off his
gloves and throws them away.)* Okay. I gotta go. I gotta go.

*Jason quickly leaves. Vivian slowly gets up from this scene and walks stiffly away. Susie
cleans up the exam room and exits.*

VIVIAN: *(Walking downstage to audience)* That . . . was . . . hard. That . . . was . . .

Kathleen Chalfant as Vivian, and Paula Pizzi as Suzie in a New York Production of *Wit.*

One thing can be said for an eight-month course of cancer treatment: it is highly educational. I am learning to suffer.

Yes, it is mildly uncomfortable to have an electrocardiogram, but the . . . agony . . . of a proctosigmoidoscopy sweeps it from memory. Yes, it was embarrassing to have to wear a nightgown all day long — two nightgowns! — but that seemed like a positive privilege compared to watching myself go bald. Yes, having a former student give me a pelvic exam was thoroughly *degrading*— and I use the term deliberately — but I could not have imagined the depths of humiliation that—

Oh, God — (*Vivian runs across the stage to her hospital room, dives onto the bed, and throws up into a large plastic washbasin.*) Oh, God. Oh. Oh. (*She lies slumped on the bed, fastened to the IV, which now includes a small bottle with a bright orange label.*) Oh, God. It can't be. (*Silence*) Oh, God. Please. Steady. Steady. (*Silence*) Oh — Oh, no! (*She throws up again, moans, and retches in agony.*) Oh, God. What's left? I haven't eaten in two days. What's left to puke?

You may remark that my vocabulary has taken a turn for the Anglo-Saxon.

God, I'm going to barf my brains out.

(*She begins to relax.*) If I actually did barf my brains out, it would be a great loss to my discipline. Of course, not a few of my colleagues would be relieved. To say nothing of my students.

It's not that I'm controversial. Just uncompromising. Ooh — (*She lunges for the basin. Nothing*) Oh. (*Silence*) False alarm. If the word went round that Vivian Bearing had barfed her brains out . . .

Well, first my colleagues, most of whom are my former students, would scramble madly for my position. Then their consciences would flare up, so to honor *my* memory they would put together a collection of *their* essays about John Donne. The volume would begin with a warm introduction, capturing my most endearing qualities. It would be short. But sweet.

Published *and* perished.

Now, watch this, I have to ring the bell (*She presses the button on the bed*) to get someone to come and measure this emesis, and record the amount on a chart of my intake and output. This counts as output.

Susie enters.

220 SUSIE: (*Brightly*) How you doing, Ms. Bearing? You having some nausea?
VIVIAN: (*Weakly*) Uhh, yes.
SUSIE: Why don't I take that? Here.
VIVIAN: It's about 300 cc's.
SUSIE: That all?
225 VIVIAN: It was very hard work.

Susie takes the basin to the bathroom and rinses it.

SUSIE: Yup. Three hundred. Good guess. (*She marks the graph.*) Okay. Anything else I can get for you? Some Jell-O or anything?
VIVIAN: Thank you, no.
SUSIE: You okay all by yourself here?
VIVIAN: Yes.
230 SUSIE: You're not having a lot of visitors, are you?
VIVIAN: (*Correcting*) None, to be precise.
SUSIE: Yeah, I didn't think so. Is there somebody you want me to call for you?
VIVIAN: That won't be necessary.
SUSIE: Well, I'll just pop my head in every once in a while to see how you're coming along. Kelekian and the fellows should be in soon. (*She touches Vivian's arm.*) If there's anything you need, you just ring.
235 VIVIAN: (*Uncomfortable with kindness*) Thank you.
SUSIE: Okay. Just call. (*Susie disconnects the IV bottle with the orange label and takes it with her as she leaves. Vivian lies still. Silence*)

VIVIAN: In this dramatic structure you will see the most interesting aspects of my tenure as an in-patient receiving experimental chemotherapy for advanced metastatic ovarian cancer.

But as I am a *scholar* before . . . an impresario, I feel obliged to document what it is like here most of the time, between the dramatic climaxes. Between the spectacles.

In truth, it is like this:

She ceremoniously lies back and stares at the ceiling.

You cannot imagine how time . . . can be . . . so still.
It hangs. It weighs. And yet there is so little of it.
It goes so slowly, and yet it is so scarce.
If I were writing this scene, it would last a full fifteen minutes. I would lie here, and you would sit there.

She looks at the audience, daring them.

Not to worry. Brevity is the soul of wit.
But if you think eight months of cancer treatment is tedious for the *audience*, consider how it feels to play my part.
All right. All right. It is Friday morning: Grand Rounds. (*Loudly, giving a cue*) Action.

Kelekian enters, followed by Jason and four other Fellows.

KELEKIAN: Dr. Bearing.
VIVIAN: Dr. Kelekian.
KELEKIAN: Jason.

240

Jason moves to the front of the group.

JASON: Professor Bearing. How are you feeling today?
VIVIAN: Fine.
JASON: That's great. That's just great. (*He takes a sheet and carefully covers her legs and groin, then pulls up her gown to reveal her entire abdomen. He is barely audible, but his gestures are clear.*)

VIVIAN: "Grand Rounds." The term is theirs. Not "Grand" in the traditional sense of sweeping or magnificent. Not "Rounds" as in a musical canon, or a *round* of applause (though either would be refreshing at this point). Here, "Rounds" seems to signify darting *around* the main issue . . . which I suppose would be the struggle for life . . . *my* life . . . with heated discussions of side effects, other complaints, additional treatments.

Grand Rounds is not Grand Opera. But compared to lying here, it is positively *dramatic*.

Full of subservience, hierarchy,

JASON: Very late detection. Staged as a four upon admission. Hexamethophosphacil with Vinplatin to potentiate. Hex at 300 mg. per meter squared, Vin at 100. Today is cycle two, day three. Both cycles at the *full dose*. (*The Fellows are impressed.*)
The primary site is —*here* (*He puts his finger on the spot on her abdomen*), behind the left ovary. Metastases are suspected in the peritoneal cavity —here. And —here. (*He touches those spots.*)

Full lymphatic involvement. (*He moves his hands over her entire body.*)

gratuitous displays, sublimated rivalries — I feel right at home. It is just like a graduate seminar.

With one important difference: in Grand Rounds, *they* read *me* like a book. Once I did the teaching, now I am taught.

This is much easier. I just hold still and look cancerous. It requires less acting every time.

245   Excellent command of details.

At the time of first-look surgery, a significant part of the tumor was de-bulked, mostly in this area —*here.* (*He points to each organ, poking her abdomen.*) Left, right ovaries. Fallopian tubes. Uterus. All out.

Evidence of primary-site shrinkage. Shrinking in metastatic tumors has not been documented. Primary mass frankly palpable in pelvic exam, frankly, all through here —*here.* (*Some Fellows reach and press where he is pointing.*)

KELEKIAN: Excellent command of details.

VIVIAN: (*To herself*) I taught him, you know—

KELEKIAN: Okay. Problem areas with Hex and Vin. (*He addresses all the Fellows, but Jason answers first and they resent him.*)

FELLOW 1: Myelosu—

JASON: (*Interrupting*) Well, first of course is myelosuppression, a lowering of blood-cell counts. It goes without saying. With this combination of agents, nephrotoxicity will be next.

250   KELEKIAN: Go on.

JASON: The kidneys are designed to filter out impurities in the bloodstream. In trying to filter the chemotherapeutic agent out of the bloodstream, the kidneys shut down.

KELEKIAN: Intervention.

JASON: Hydration.

KELEKIAN: Monitoring.

255   JASON: Full recording of fluid intake and output, as you see here on these graphs, to monitor hydration and kidney function. Totals monitored daily by the clinical fellow, as per the protocol.

KELEKIAN: Anybody else. Side effects.

FELLOW 1: Nausea and vomiting.

KELEKIAN: Jason.

JASON: Routine.

260   FELLOW 2: Pain while urinating.

JASON: Routine. (*The Fellows are trying to catch Jason.*)

FELLOW 3: Psychological depression.

JASON: No way.

The Fellows are silent.

KELEKIAN: (*Standing by Vivian at the head of the bed*) Anything else. Other complaints with Hexamethophosphacil and Vinplatin. Come on. (*Silence. Kelekian and Vivian wait together for the correct answer.*)

FELLOW 4: Mouth sores.   265
JASON: Not yet.
FELLOW 2: (*Timidly*) Skin rash?
JASON: Nope.
KELEKIAN: (*Sharing this with Vivian*) Why do we waste our time,
    Dr. Bearing?
VIVIAN: (*Delighted*) I do not know, Dr. Kelekian.   270
KELEKIAN: (*To the Fellows*) Use your eyes, (*All Fellows look closely at* Vivian.)
    Jesus God. Hair loss.
FELLOWS: (*All protesting. Vivian and Kelekian are amused.*)
        — Come on.
        — You can see it.
        — It doesn't count.
        — No fair.
KELEKIAN: Jason.
JASON: (*Begrudgingly*) Hair loss after first cycle of treatment.
KELEKIAN: That's better. (*To Vivian*) Dr. Bearing. Full dose. Excellent. Keep   275
    pushing the fluids.

The Fellows leave. Kelekian stops Jason.

KELEKIAN: Jason.
JASON: Huh?
KELEKIAN: Clinical.
JASON: Oh, right. (*To Vivian*) Thank you, Professor Bearing. You've been very
    cooperative. (*They leave her with her stomach uncovered.*)
VIVIAN: Wasn't that . . . Grand? (*She gets up without the IV pole.*) At times, this   280
    obsessively detailed examination, this *scrutiny* seems to me to be a nefarious
    business. On the other hand, what is the alternative? Ignorance? Ignorance
    may be . . . bliss; but it is not a very noble goal.
        So I play my part.
        (*Pause*)
        I receive chemotherapy, throw up, am subjected to countless indigni-
    ties, feel better, go home. Eight cycles. Eight neat little strophes. Oh, there
    have been the usual variations, subplots, red herrings: hepatotoxicity (liver
    poison), neuropathy (nerve death).
        (*Righteously*) They are medical terms. I look them up.
        It has always been my custom to treat words with respect.
        I can recall the time — the very hour of the very day — when I knew
    words would be my life's work.

---

*A pile of six little white books appears, with Mr. Bearing, Vivian's father, seated behind
an open newspaper.*

    It was my fifth birthday.

Vivian, now a child, flops down to the books.

I liked that one best.

MR. BEARING: (*Disinterested but tolerant, never distracted from his newspaper*) Read another.

VIVIAN: I think I'll read . . . (*She takes a book from the stack and reads its spine intently*) The Tale of the Flopsy Bunnies. (*Reading the front cover*) The Tale of the Flopsy Bunnies. It has little bunnies on the front.

(*Opening to the title page*) The Tale of the Flopsy Bunnies by Beatrix Potter. (*She turns the page and begins to read.*)

It is said that the effect of eating too much lettuce is sopor — sop — or — what is that word?

MR. BEARING: Sound it out.

VIVIAN: Sop — or —fic. Sop — or —i —fic. Soporific. What does that mean?

285 **MR. BEARING:** Soporific. Causing sleep.

VIVIAN: Causing sleep.

MR. BEARING: Makes you sleepy.

VIVIAN: "Soporific" means "makes you sleepy"?

MR. BEARING: Correct.

290 **VIVIAN:** "Soporific" means "makes you sleepy." Soporific.

MR. BEARING: Now use it in a sentence. What has a soporific effect on *you*?

VIVIAN: A soporific effect on me.

MR. BEARING: What makes you sleepy?

VIVIAN: Aahh — nothing.

295 **MR. BEARING:** Correct.

VIVIAN: What about you?

MR. BEARING: What has a soporific effect on me? Let me think: boring conversation, I suppose, after dinner.

VIVIAN: Me too, boring conversation.

MR. BEARING: Carry on.

300 **VIVIAN:**

It is said that the effect of eating too much lettuce is soporific.

The little bunnies in the picture are asleep! They're sleeping! Like you said, because of *soporific*!

She stands up, and Mr. Bearing exits.

The illustration bore out the meaning of the word, just as he had explained it. At the time, it seemed like magic.

So imagine the effect that the words of John Donne first had on me: ratiocination, concatenation, coruscation, tergiversation.

Medical terms are less evocative. Still, I want to know what the doctors mean when they . . . anatomize me. And I will grant that in this particular field of endeavor they possess a more potent arsenal of terminology than I. My only defense is the acquisition of vocabulary.

Susie enters and puts her arm around Vivian's shoulders to hold her up. Vivian is shaking, feverish, and weak.

VIVIAN: *(All at once)* Fever and neutropenia.
SUSIE: When did it start?
VIVIAN: *(Having difficulty speaking)* I — I was at home — reading — and I — felt so bad. I called. Fever and neutropenia. They said to come in.
SUSIE: You did the right thing to come. Did somebody drive you?
VIVIAN: Cab. I took a taxi.   305
SUSIE: *(She grabs a wheelchair and helps Vivian sit. As Susie speaks, she takes Vivian's temperature, pulse, and respiration rate.)* Here, why don't you sit? Just sit there a minute. I'll get Jason. He's on call tonight. We'll get him to give you some meds. I'm glad I was here on nights. I'll make sure you get to bed soon, okay? It'll just be a minute. I'll get you some juice, some nice juice with lots of ice.

Susie leaves quickly. Vivian sits there, agitated, confused, and very sick. Susie returns with the juice.

VIVIAN: Lights. I left all the lights on at my house.
SUSIE: Don't you worry. It'll be all right.

Jason enters, roused from his sleep and not fully awake. He wears surgical scrubs and puts on a lab coat as he enters.

JASON: *(Without looking at Vivian)* How are you feeling, Professor Bearing?
VIVIAN: My teeth — are chattering.   310
JASON: Vitals.
SUSIE: *(Giving Vivian juice and a straw, without looking at Jason)* Temp 39.4. Pulse 120. Respiration 36. Chills and sweating.
JASON: Fever and neutropenia. It's a "shake and bake." Blood cultures and urine, stat. Admit her. Prepare for reverse isolation. Start with acetaminophen. Vitals every four hours. *(He starts to leave.)*
SUSIE: *(Following him)* Jason — I think you need to talk to Kelekian about lowering the dose for the next cycle. It's too much for her like this.
JASON: Lower the dose? No way. Full dose. She's tough. She can take it. Wake   315
me up when the counts come from the lab.

He pads off. Susie wheels Vivian to her room, and Vivian collapses on the bed. Susie connects Vivian's IV, then wets a washcloth and rubs her face and neck. Vivian remains delirious. Susie checks the IV and leaves with the wheelchair.

After a while, Kelekian appears in the doorway holding a surgical mask near his face. Jason is with him, now dressed and clean-shaven.

KELEKIAN: Good morning, Dr. Bearing. Fifth cycle. Full dose. Definite progress. Everything okay.
VIVIAN: *(Weakly)* Yes.
KELEKIAN: You're doing swell. Isolation is no problem. Couple of days. Think of it as a vacation.
VIVIAN: Oh.

Jason starts to enter, holding a mask near his face, just like Kelekian.

KELEKIAN: Jason.
320 JASON: Oh, Jesus. Okay, okay.

He returns to the doorway, where he puts on a paper gown, mask, and gloves. Kelekian leaves.

VIVIAN: *(To audience)* In isolation, I am isolated. For once I can use a term literally. The chemotherapeutic agents eradicating my cancer have also eradicated my immune system. In my present condition, every living thing is a health hazard to me . . .

Jason comes in to check the intake-and-output.

JASON: *(Complaining to himself)* I really have not got time for this . . .
VIVIAN: . . . particularly health-care professionals.
325 JASON: *(Going right to the graph on the wall)* Just to look at the I&O sheets for one minute, and it takes me half an hour to do precautions. Four, seven, eleven. Two-fifty twice. Okay. *(Remembering)* Oh, Jeez. Clinical. Professor Bearing. How are you feeling today?
VIVIAN: *(Very sick)* Fine. Just shaking sometimes from the chills.
JASON: IV will kick in anytime now. No problem. Listen, gotta go. Keep pushing the fluids.

As he exits, he takes off the gown, mask, and gloves.

VIVIAN: *(Getting up from bed with her IV pole and resuming her explanation)* I am not in isolation because I have cancer, because I have a tumor the size of a grapefruit. No. I am in isolation because I am being treated for cancer. My treatment imperils my health.

Herein lies the paradox. John Donne would revel in it. I would revel in it, if he wrote a poem about it. My students would flounder in it, because paradox is too difficult to understand. Think of it as a puzzle, I would tell them, an intellectual game.

(She is trapped.) Or, I *would have* told them. Were it a game. Which it is not.

(Escaping) If they were here, if I were lecturing: How I would *perplex* them! I could work my students into a frenzy. Every ambiguity, every shifting awareness. I could draw so much from the poems.

I could be so powerful.

———————————

Vivian stands still, as if conjuring a scene. Now at the height of her powers, she grandly disconnects herself from the IV. Technicians remove the bed and hand her a pointer.

VIVIAN: The poetry of the early seventeenth century, what has been called the metaphysical school, considers an intractable mental puzzle by exercising the outstanding human faculty of the era, namely *wit.*

The greatest wit — the greatest English poet, some would say — was John Donne. In the Holy Sonnets, Donne applied his capacious, agile wit to the larger aspects of the human experience: life, death, and God.

In his poems, metaphysical quandaries are addressed, but never resolved. Ingenuity, virtuosity, and a vigorous intellect that jousts with the most exalted concepts: these are the tools of wit.

The lights dim. A screen lowers, and the sonnet "If poysonous mineralls," from the Gardner edition, appears on it. Vivian recites.

> If poysonous mineralls, and if that tree,
> Whose fruit threw death on else immortall us,
> If lecherous goats, if serpents envious
> Cannot be damn'd; Alas; why should I bee?
> Why should intent or reason, borne in mee,
> Make sinnes, else equall, in mee, more heinous?
> And mercy being easie, 'and glorious
> To God, in his sterne wrath, why threatens hee?
> But who am I, that dare dispute with thee?
> O God, Oh! of thine onely worthy blood,
> And my teares, make a heavenly Lethean flood,
> And drowne in it my sinnes blacke memorie.
> That thou remember them, some claime as debt,
> I thinke it mercy, if thou wilt forget.

Vivian occasionally whacks the screen with a pointer for emphasis. She moves around as she lectures.

Aggressive intellect. Pious melodrama. And a final, fearful point. Donne's Holy Sonnet Five, 1609. From the Ashford edition, based on Gardner.

The speaker of the sonnet has a brilliant mind, and he plays the part convincingly; but in the end he finds God's *forgiveness* hard to believe, so he crawls under a rock to *hide*.

If arsenic and serpents are not damned, then why is he? In asking the question, the speaker turns eternal damnation into an intellectual game. Why would God choose to do what is *hard*, to condemn, rather than what is *easy*, and also *glorious*— to show mercy?

(Several scholars have disputed Ashford's third comma in line six, but none convincingly.)

But. Exception. Limitation. Contrast. The argument shifts from cleverness to melodrama, an unconvincing eruption of piety: "O" "God" "Oh!"

A typical prayer would plead "Remember me, O Lord." (This point is nicely explicated in an article by Richard Strier — a former student of mine who once sat where you do now, although I dare say he was *awake*— in the May 1989 issue of *Modern Philology*.) True believers ask to be *remembered* by God. The speaker of this sonnet asks God to forget. (*Vivian moves in front of the screen, and the projection of the poem is cast directly upon her.*) Where is the hyperactive intellect of the first section? Where is the histrionic outpouring of the second? When the speaker considers his own *sins,* and the inevitability of God's *judgment,* he can conceive of but one resolution: to *disappear.* (*Vivian moves away from the screen.*) Doctrine assures us that no sinner is denied *forgiveness,* not even one whose sins are overweening *intel-*

lect or overwrought *dramatics*. The speaker does not need to *hide* from God's *judgment*, only to accept God's *forgiveness*. It is very simple. Suspiciously simple.

We want to correct the speaker, to remind him of the assurance of salvation. But it is too late. The poetic encounter is over. We are left to our own consciences. Have we outwitted Donne? Or have we been outwitted?

Susie comes on.

330   SUSIE: Ms. Bearing?
VIVIAN: *(Continuing)* Will the po—
SUSIE: Ms. Bearing?
VIVIAN: *(Crossly)* What is it?
SUSIE: You have to go down for a test. Jason just called. They want another ultrasound. They're concerned about a bowel obstruction — Is it okay if I come in?
335   VIVIAN: No. Not now.
SUSIE: I'm sorry, but they want it now.
VIVIAN: Not right now. It's not *supposed* to be now.
SUSIE: Yes, they want to do it now. I've got the chair.
VIVIAN: It should not be now. I am in the middle of — this. I have *this* planned for now, not ultrasound. No more tests. We've covered that.
340   SUSIE: I know, I know, but they need for it to be now. It won't take long, and it isn't a bad procedure. Why don't you just come along.
VIVIAN: *I do not want to go now!*
SUSIE: Ms. Bearing.

Silence. Vivian raises the screen, walks away from the scene, hooks herself to the IV, and gets in the wheelchair. Susie wheels Vivian, and a Technician takes her.

TECHNICIAN: Name.
VIVIAN: B-E-A-R-I-N-G. Kelekian.
345   TECHNICIAN: It'll just be a minute.
VIVIAN: Time for your break.
TECHNICIAN: Yup.

The Technician leaves.

VIVIAN: *(Mordantly)* Take a break!

_____

Vivian sits weakly in the wheelchair.

VIVIAN:

> This is my playes last scene, here heavens appoint
> My pilgrimages last mile; and my race
> Idly, yet quickly runne, hath this last pace,
> My spans last inch, my minutes last point,
> And gluttonous death will instantly unjoynt
> My body, 'and soule

John Donne. 1609.

I have always particularly liked that poem. In the abstract. Now I find the image of "my minute's last point" a little too, shall we say, *pointed*.

I don't mean to complain, but I am becoming very sick. Very, very sick. Ultimately sick, as it were.

In everything I have done, I have been steadfast, resolute — some would say in the extreme. Now, as you can see, I am distinguishing myself in illness.

I have survived eight treatments of Hexamethophosphacil and Vinplatin at the *full* dose, ladies and gentlemen. I have broken the record. I have become something of a celebrity. Kelekian and Jason are simply delighted. I think they foresee celebrity status for themselves upon the appearance of the journal article they will no doubt write about me.

But I flatter myself. The article will not be about *me*, it will be about my ovaries. It will be about my peritoneal cavity, which, despite their best intentions, is now crawling with cancer.

What we have come to think of as *me* is, in fact, just the specimen jar, just the dust jacket, just the white piece of paper that bears the little black marks.

My next line is supposed to be something like this:

"It is such a *relief* to get back to my room after those infernal tests."

This is hardly true.

It would be *a relief* to be a cheerleader on her way to Daytona Beach for Spring Break.

To get back to my room after those infernal tests is just the next thing that happens.

She returns to her bed, which now has a commode next to it. She is very sick.

Oh, God. It is such a relief to get back to my goddamn room after those goddamn tests.

Jason enters.

JASON: Professor Bearing. Just want to check the I&O. Four-fifty, six, five.   350
Okay. How are you feeling today? (*He makes notations on his clipboard throughout the scene.*)
VIVIAN: Fine.
JASON: That's great. Just great.
VIVIAN: How are my fluids?
JASON: Pretty good. No kidney involvement yet. That's pretty amazing, with Hex and Vin.
VIVIAN: How will you know when the kidneys are involved?   355
JASON: Lots of in, not much out.
VIVIAN: That simple.
JASON: Oh, no way. Compromised kidney function is a highly complex reaction. I'm simplifying for you.
VIVIAN: Thank you.
JASON: We're supposed to.   360

VIVIAN: Bedside manner.

JASON: Yeah, there's a whole course on it in med school. It's required. Colossal waste of time for researchers. (*He turns to go.*)

VIVIAN: I can imagine. (*Trying to ask something important*) Jason?

JASON: Huh?

365 **VIVIAN:** (*Not sure of herself*) Ah, what . . . (*Quickly*) What were you just saying?

JASON: When?

VIVIAN: Never mind.

JASON: Professor Bearing?

VIVIAN: Yes.

370 **JASON:** Are you experiencing confusion? Short-term memory loss?

VIVIAN: No.

JASON: Sure?

VIVIAN: Yes. (*Pause*) I was just wondering: why cancer?

JASON: Why cancer?

375 **VIVIAN:** Why not open-heart surgery?

JASON: Oh yeah, why not *plumbing*. Why not run a *lube rack*, for all the surgeons know about *Homo sapiens sapiens*. No way. Cancer's the only thing I ever wanted.

VIVIAN: (*Intrigued*) Huh.

JASON: No, really. Cancer is . . . (*Searching*)

VIVIAN: (*Helping*) Awesome.

380 **JASON:** (*Pause*) Yeah. Yeah, that's right. It is. It is awesome. How does it do it? The intercellular regulatory mechanisms — especially for proliferation and differentiation — the malignant neoplasia just don't get it. You grow normal cells in tissue culture in the lab, and they replicate just enough to make a nice, confluent monolayer. They divide twenty times, or fifty times, but eventually they conk out. You grow cancer cells, and they never stop. No contact inhibition whatsoever. They just pile up, just keep replicating forever. (*Pause*) That's got a funny name. Know what it is?

VIVIAN: No. What?

JASON: Immortality in culture.

VIVIAN: Sounds like a symposium.

JASON: It's an error in judgment, in a molecular way. But *why*? Even on the protistic level the normal cell–cell interactions are so subtle they'll take your breath away. Golden-brown algae, for instance, the lowest multicellular life form on earth — they're *idiots*— and it's incredible. It's perfect. So what's up with the cancer cells? Smartest guys in the world, with the best labs, funding — they don't know what to make of it.

385 **VIVIAN:** What about you?

JASON: Me? Oh, I've got a couple of ideas, things I'm kicking around. Wait till I get a lab of my own. If I can survive this . . . *fellowship*.

VIVIAN: The part with the human beings.

JASON: Everybody's got to go through it. All the great researchers. They want us to be able to converse intelligently with the clinicians. As though *researchers* were the impediments. The clinicians are such troglodytes. So smarmy. Like we have to hold hands to discuss creatinine clearance. Just cut the crap, I say.

VIVIAN: Are you going to be sorry when I — Do you ever miss people?

JASON: Everybody asks that. Especially girls. 390

VIVIAN: What do you tell them?

JASON: I tell them yes.

VIVIAN: Are they persuaded?

JASON: Some.

VIVIAN: Some. I see. (*With great difficulty*) And what do you say when a 395 patient is . . . apprehensive . . . frightened.

JASON: Of who?

VIVIAN: I just . . . Never mind.

JASON: Professor Bearing, who is the President of the United States?

VIVIAN: I'm fine, really. It's all right.

JASON: You sure? I could order a test — 400

VIVIAN: No! No, I'm fine. Just a little tired.

JASON: Okay. Look. Gotta go. Keep pushing the fluids. Try for 2,000 a day, okay?

VIVIAN: Okay. To use your word. Okay.

Jason leaves.

VIVIAN: (*Getting out of bed, without her IV*) So. The young doctor, like the senior scholar, prefers research to humanity. At the same time the senior scholar, in her pathetic state as a simpering victim, wishes the young doctor would take more interest in personal contact.

Now I suppose we shall see, through a series of flashbacks, how the senior scholar ruthlessly denied her simpering students the touch of human kindness she now seeks.

Students appear, sitting at chairs with writing desks attached to the right arm.

VIVIAN: (*Commanding attention*) How then would you characterize (*pointing to* 405 a student) — you.

STUDENT 1: Huh?

VIVIAN: How would you characterize the animating force of this sonnet?

STUDENT 1: Huh?

VIVIAN: In this sonnet, what is the principal poetic device? I'll give you a hint. It has nothing to do with football. What propels this sonnet?

STUDENT 1: Um. 410

VIVIAN: (*Speaking to the audience*) Did I say (*tenderly*) "You are nineteen years old. You are so young. You don't know a sonnet from a steak sandwich." (*Pause*) By no means.

(*Sharply, to Student 1*) You can come to this class prepared, or you can excuse yourself from this class, this department, and this university. Do not think for a moment that I will tolerate anything in between.

(*To the audience, defensively*) I was teaching him a lesson. (*She walks away from Student 1, then turns and addresses the class.*)

So we have another instance of John Donne's agile wit at work: not so much *resolving* the issues of life and God as *reveling* in their complexity.

STUDENT 2: But why?

VIVIAN: Why what?

STUDENT 2: Why does Donne make everything so *complicated*? *(The other Students laugh in agreement.)* No, really, *why*?

415   **VIVIAN:** *(To the audience)* You know, someone asked me that every year. And it was always one of the smart ones. What could I say? *(To Student 2)* What do you think?

STUDENT 2: I think it's like he's hiding. I think he's really confused, I don't know, maybe he's scared, so he hides behind all this complicated stuff, hides behind this *wit*.

VIVIAN: *Hides* behind *wit*?

STUDENT 2: I mean, if it's really something he's sure of, he can say it more simple — simply. He doesn't have to be such a brain, or such a performer. It doesn't have to be such a big deal.

The other Students encourage him.

VIVIAN: Perhaps he is suspicious of simplicity.

420   **STUDENT 2:** Perhaps, but that's pretty stupid.

VIVIAN: *(To the audience)* That observation, despite its infelicitous phrasing, contained the seed of a perspicacious remark. Such an unlikely occurrence left me with two choices. I could draw it out, or I could allow the brain to rest after that heroic effort. If I pursued, there was the chance of great insight, or the risk of undergraduate banality. I could never predict. *(To Student 2)* Go on.

STUDENT 2: Well, if he's trying to figure out God, and the meaning of life, and big stuff like that, why does he keep running away, you know?

VIVIAN: *(To the audience, moving closer to Student 2)* So far so good, but they can think for themselves only so long before they begin to self-destruct.

STUDENT 2: Um, it's like, the more you hide, the less — no, wait — the more you are getting closer — although you don't know it — and the simple thing is there — you see what I mean?

425   **VIVIAN:** *(To the audience, looking at Student 2, as suspense collapses)* Lost it.
    (She walks away and speaks to the audience.) I distinctly remember an exchange between two students after my lecture on pronunciation and scansion. I overheard them talking on their way out of class. They were young and bright, gathering their books and laughing at the expense of seventeenth-century poetry, at *my* expense.
    (To the class) To scan the line properly, we must take advantage of the contemporary flexibility in "i-o-n" endings, as in "expansion." The quatrain stands:

> Our two souls therefore, which are one,
>   Though I must go, endure not yet
> A breach, but an ex-*pan*-see-on,
>   Like gold to airy thinness beat.

Bear this in mind in your reading. That's all for today.

The Students get up in a chaotic burst. Student 3 and Student 4 pass by Vivian on their way out.

STUDENT 3: I hope I can get used to this pronuncia-see-on.

STUDENT 4: I know. I hope I can survive this course and make it to gradua-see-on.

They laugh. Vivian glowers at them. They fall silent, embarrassed.

VIVIAN: *(To the audience)* That was a witty little exchange, I must admit. It showed the mental acuity I would praise in a poetic text. But I admired only the studied application of wit, not its spontaneous eruption.

Student 1 interrupts.

STUDENT 1: Professor Bearing? Can I talk to you for a minute?

VIVIAN: You may.   430

STUDENT 1: I need to ask for an extension on my paper. I'm really sorry, and I know your policy, but see —

VIVIAN: Don't tell me. Your grandmother died.

STUDENT 1: You knew.

VIVIAN: It was a guess.

STUDENT 1: I have to go home.   435

VIVIAN: Do what you will, but the paper is due when it is due.

As Student 1 leaves and the classroom disappears, Vivian watches. Pause.

VIVIAN: I don't know. I feel so much — what is the word? I look back, I see these scenes, and I . . .

Long silence. Vivian walks absently around the stage, trying to think of something. Finally, giving up, she trudges back to bed.

———————

VIVIAN: It was late at night, the graveyard shift. Susie was on. I could hear her in the hall.

I wanted her to come and see me. So I had to create a little emergency. Nothing dramatic.

Vivian pinches the IV tubing. The pump alarm beeps.

It worked.

Susie enters, concerned.

SUSIE: Ms. Bearing? Is that you beeping at four in the morning? *(She checks the tubing and presses buttons on the pump. The alarm stops.)* Did that wake you up? I'm sorry. It just gets occluded sometimes.

VIVIAN: I was awake.   440

SUSIE: You were? What's the trouble, sweetheart?

VIVIAN: *(To the audience, roused)* Do not think for a minute that anyone calls me "Sweetheart." But then . . . I allowed it. *(To Susie)* Oh, I don't know.

S<small>USIE</small>: You can't sleep?

V<small>IVIAN</small>: No. I just keep thinking.

445 S<small>USIE</small>: If you do that too much, you can get kind of confused.

V<small>IVIAN</small>: I know. I can't figure things out. I'm in a . . . *quandary*, having
these . . . *doubts*.

S<small>USIE</small>: What you're doing is very hard.

V<small>IVIAN</small>: Hard things are what I like best.

S<small>USIE</small>: It's not the same. It's like it's out of control, isn't it?

450 V<small>IVIAN</small>: *(Crying, in spite of herself)* I'm scared.

S<small>USIE</small>: *(Stroking her)* Oh, honey, of course you are.

V<small>IVIAN</small>: I want . . .

S<small>USIE</small>: I know. It's hard.

V<small>IVIAN</small>: I don't feel sure of myself anymore.

455 S<small>USIE</small>: And you used to feel sure.

V<small>IVIAN</small>: *(Crying)* Oh, yes, I used to feel sure.

S<small>USIE</small>: Vivian. It's all right. I know. It hurts. I know. It's all right. Do you want
a tissue? It's all right. *(Silence)* Vivian, would you like a Popsicle?

V<small>IVIAN</small>: *(Like a child)* Yes, please.

S<small>USIE</small>: I'll get it for you. I'll be right back.

460 V<small>IVIAN</small>: Thank you.

Susie leaves.

V<small>IVIAN</small>: *(Pulling herself together)* The epithelial cells in my GI tract have been
killed by the chemo. The cold Popsicle feels good, it's something I can
digest, and it helps keep me hydrated. For your information.

*Susie returns with an orange two-stick Popsicle. Vivian unwraps it and breaks it
in half.*

V<small>IVIAN</small>: Here.

S<small>USIE</small>: Sure?

V<small>IVIAN</small>: Yes.

465 S<small>USIE</small>: Thanks. *(Susie sits on the commode by the bed. Silence)* When I was a kid,
we used to get these from a truck. The man would come around and ring
his bell and we'd all run over. Then we'd sit on the curb and eat our
Popsicles.
      Pretty profound, huh?

V<small>IVIAN</small>: It sounds nice.

Silence

S<small>USIE</small>: Vivian, there's something we need to talk about, you need to think
about.

Silence

V<small>IVIAN</small>: My cancer is not being cured, is it.

S<small>USIE</small>: Huh-uh.

470 V<small>IVIAN</small>: They never expected it to be, did they.

SUSIE: Well, they thought the drugs would make the tumor get smaller, and it has gotten a lot smaller. But the problem is that it started in new places too. They've learned a lot for their research. It was the best thing they had to give you, the strongest drugs. There just isn't a good treatment for what you have yet, for advanced ovarian. I'm sorry. They should have explained this—

VIVIAN: I knew.

SUSIE: You did.

VIVIAN: I read between the lines.

SUSIE: What you have to think about is your "code status." What you want   475
them to do if your heart stops.

VIVIAN: Well.

SUSIE: You can be "full code," which means that if your heart stops, they'll call a Code Blue and the code team will come and resuscitate you and take you to Intensive Care until you stabilize again. Or you can be "Do Not Resuscitate," so if your heart stops we'll . . . well, we'll just let it. You'll be "DNR." You can think about it, but I wanted to present both choices before Kelekian and Jason talk to you.

VIVIAN: You don't agree about this?

SUSIE: Well, they like to save lives. So anything's okay, as long as life continues. It doesn't matter if you're hooked up to a million machines. Kelekian is a great researcher and everything. And the fellows, like Jason, they're really smart. It's really an honor for them to work with him. But they always . . . want to know more things.

VIVIAN: I always want to know more things. I'm a scholar. Or I was when I   480
had shoes, when I had eyebrows.

SUSIE: Well, okay then. You'll be full code. That's fine.

Silence

VIVIAN: No, don't complicate the matter.

SUSIE: It's okay. It's up to you—

VIVIAN: Let it stop.

SUSIE: Really?   485

VIVIAN: Yes.

SUSIE: So if your heart stops beating—

VIVIAN: Just let it stop.

SUSIE: Sure?

VIVIAN: Yes.   490

SUSIE: Okay. I'll get Kelekian to give the order, and then—

VIVIAN: Susie?

SUSIE: Uh-huh?

VIVIAN: You're still going to take care of me, aren't you?

SUSIE: 'Course, sweetheart. Don't you worry.   495

As Susie leaves, Vivian sits upright, full of energy and rage.

VIVIAN: That certainly was a *maudlin* display. Popsicles? "Sweetheart"? I can't believe my life has become so . . . *corny.*

But it can't be helped. I don't see any other way. We are discussing life and death, and not in the abstract, either; we are discussing *my* life and *my* death, and my brain is dulling, and poor Susie's was never very sharp to begin with, and I can't conceive of any other . . . *tone*.

(*Quickly*) Now is not the time for verbal swordplay, for unlikely flights of imagination and wildly shifting perspectives, for metaphysical conceit, for wit.

And nothing would be worse than a detailed scholarly analysis. Erudition. Interpretation. Complication.

(*Slowly*) Now is a time for simplicity. Now is a time for, dare I say it, kindness.

(*Searchingly*) I thought being extremely smart would take care of it. But I see that I have been found out. Ooohhh.

I'm scared. Oh, God. I want . . . I want . . . No. I want to hide. I just want to curl up in a little ball. (*She dives under the covers.*)

Vivian wakes in horrible pain. She is tense, agitated, fearful. Slowly she calms down and addresses the audience.

VIVIAN: (*Trying extremely hard*) I want to tell you how it feels. I want to explain it, to use *my* words. It's as if . . . I can't . . . There aren't . . . I'm like a student and this is the final exam and I don't know what to put down because I don't understand the question and I'm *running out of time*.

The time for extreme measures has come. I am in terrible pain. Susie says that I need to begin aggressive pain management if I am going to stand it.

"It": such a little word. In this case, I think "it" signifies "being alive."

I apologize in advance for what this palliative treatment modality does to the dramatic coherence of my play's last scene. It can't be helped. They have to do something. I'm in terrible pain.

Say it, Vivian. *It hurts like hell. It really does.*

Susie enters. Vivian is writhing in pain.

Oh, God. Oh, God.

SUSIE: Sshh. It's okay. Sshh. I paged Kelekian up here, and we'll get you some meds.

VIVIAN: Oh, God, it is so painful. So painful. So much pain. So much pain.

500   SUSIE: I know, I know, it's okay. Sshh. Just try and clear your mind. It's all right. We'll get you a Patient-Controlled Analgesic. It's a little pump, and you push a little button, and you decide how much medication you want. (*Importantly*) It's very simple, and it's up to you.

Kelekian storms in; Jason follows with chart.

KELEKIAN: Dr. Bearing. Susie.

SUSIE: Time for Patient-Controlled Analgesic. The pain is killing her.

KELEKIAN: Dr. Bearing, are you in pain? (*Kelekian holds out his hand for chart; Jason hands it to him. They read.*)

VIVIAN: (*Sitting up, unnoticed by the staff*) Am I in pain? I don't believe this. Yes, I'm in goddamn pain. (*Furious*) I have a fever of 101 spiking to 104. And I have bone metastases in my pelvis and both femurs. (*Screaming*) There is cancer eating away at my goddamn bones, and I did not know there could be such pain on this earth.

> (*She flops back on the bed and cries audibly to them.*) Oh, God.

KELEKIAN: (*Looking at Vivian intently*) I want a morphine drip.   505

SUSIE: What about Patient-Controlled? She could be more alert—

KELEKIAN: (*Teaching*) Ordinarily, yes. But in her case, no.

SUSIE: But—

KELEKIAN: (*To Susie*) She's earned a rest. (*To Jason*) Morphine, ten push now, then start at ten an hour. (*To Vivian*) Dr. Bearing, try to relax. We're going to help you through this, don't worry. Dr. Bearing? Excellent. (*He squeezes Vivian's shoulder. They all leave.*)

VIVIAN: (*Weakly, painfully, leaning on her IV pole, she moves to address the*   510
audience.) Hi. How are you feeling today?

Silence

> These are my last coherent lines. I'll have to leave the action to the professionals.
>
> It came so quickly, after taking so long. Not even time for a proper conclusion.

Vivian concentrates with all her might, and she attempts a grand summation, as if trying to conjure her own ending.

> And Death —*capital D*— shall be no more — semicolon.
> Death —*capital D*— thou shalt die —*ex-cla-mation point!*

She looks down at herself, looks out at the audience, and sees that the line doesn't work. She shakes her head and exhales with resignation.

> I'm sorry.

She gets back into bed as Susie injects morphine into the IV tubing. Vivian lies down and, in a final melodramatic gesture, shuts the lids of her own eyes and folds her arms over her chest.

VIVIAN: I trust this will have a soporific effect.

SUSIE: Well, I don't know about that, but it sure makes you sleepy.

This strikes Vivian as delightfully funny. She starts to giggle, then laughs out loud. Susie doesn't get it.

SUSIE: What's so funny? (*Vivian keeps laughing.*) What?

VIVIAN: Oh! It's that —"Soporific" *means* "makes you sleepy."

SUSIE: It does?   515

VIVIAN: Yes. (*Another fit of laughter*)

SUSIE: (*Giggling*) Well, that was pretty dumb—

VIVIAN: No! No, no! It was *funny!*

SUSIE: (*Starting to catch on*) Yeah, I guess so. (*Laughing*) In a dumb sort of way. (*This sets them both off laughing again*) I never would have gotten it. I'm glad you explained it.

520 VIVIAN: (*Simply*) I'm a teacher.

They laugh a little together. Slowly the morphine kicks in, and Vivian's laughs become long sighs. Finally she falls asleep. Susie checks everything out, then leaves. Long silence

---

Jason and Susie chat as they enter to insert a catheter.

JASON: Oh, yeah. She was a great scholar. Wrote tons of books, articles, was the head of everything. (*He checks the I&O sheet.*) Two hundred. Seventy-five. Five-twenty. Let's up the hydration. She won't be drinking anymore. See if we can keep her kidneys from fading. Yeah, I had a lot of respect for her, which is more than I can say for the *entire* biochemistry department.

SUSIE: What do you want? Dextrose?

JASON: Give her saline.

SUSIE: Okay.

525 JASON: She gave a hell of a lecture. No notes, not a word out of place. It was pretty impressive. A lot of students hated her, though.

SUSIE: Why?

JASON: Well, she wasn't exactly a cupcake.

SUSIE: (*Laughing, fondly*) Well, she hasn't exactly been a cupcake here, either. (*Leaning over Vivian and talking loudly and slowly in her ear*) Now, Ms. Bearing, Jason and I are here, and we're going to insert a catheter to collect your urine. It's not going to hurt, don't you worry. (*During the conversation she inserts the catheter.*)

JASON: Like she can hear you.

530 SUSIE: It's just nice to do.

JASON: Eight cycles of Hex and Vin at the full dose. Kelekian didn't think it was possible. I wish they could all get through it at full throttle. Then we could really have some data.

SUSIE: She's not what I imagined. I thought somebody who studied poetry would be sort of dreamy, you know?

JASON: Oh, not the way she did it. It felt more like boot camp than English class. This guy John Donne was incredibly intense. Like your whole brain had to be in knots before you could get it.

SUSIE: He made it hard on purpose?

535 JASON: Well, it has to do with the subject. The Holy Sonnets we worked on most, they were mostly about Salvation Anxiety. That's a term I made up in one of my papers, but I think it fits pretty well. Salvation Anxiety. You're this brilliant guy, I mean, brilliant — this guy makes Shakespeare sound like a Hallmark card. And you know you're a sinner. And there's this promise of salvation, the whole religious thing. But you just can't deal with it.

SUSIE: How come?

JASON: It just doesn't stand up to scrutiny. But you can't face life without it either. So you write these screwed-up sonnets. Everything is brilliantly convoluted. Really tricky stuff. Bouncing off the walls. Like a game, to make the puzzle so complicated.

The catheter is inserted. Susie puts things away.

SUSIE: But what happens in the end?
JASON: End of what?
SUSIE: To John Donne. Does he ever get it?   540
JASON: Get what?
SUSIE: His Salvation Anxiety. Does he ever understand?
JASON: Oh, no way. The puzzle takes over. You're not even trying to solve it anymore. Fascinating, really. Great training for lab research. Looking at things in increasing levels of complexity.
SUSIE: Until what?
JASON: What do you mean?   545
SUSIE: Where does it end? Don't you get to solve the puzzle?
JASON: Nah. When it comes right down to it, research is just trying to quantify the complications of the puzzle.
SUSIE: But you *help* people! You save lives and stuff.
JASON: Oh, yeah, I save some guy's life, and then the poor slob gets hit by a bus!
SUSIE: (*Confused*) Yeah, I guess so. I just don't think of it that way. Guess you   550
can tell I never took a class in poetry.
JASON: Listen, if there's one thing we learned in Seventeenth-Century Poetry, it's that you can forget about that sentimental stuff. *Enzyme Kinetics* was more poetic than Bearing's class. Besides, you can't think about that *meaning-of-life* garbage all the time or you'd go nuts.
SUSIE: Do you believe in it?
JASON: In what?
SUSIE: Umm. I don't know, the meaning-of-life garbage. (*She laughs a little.*)
JASON: What do they *teach* you in nursing school? (*Checking Vivian's pulse*)   555
She's out of it. Shouldn't be too long. You done here?
SUSIE: Yeah, I'll just . . . tidy up.
JASON: See ya. (*He leaves.*)
SUSIE: Bye, Jace. (*She thinks for a minute, then carefully rubs baby oil on Vivian's hands. She checks the catheter, then leaves.*)

Professor E. M. Ashford, now eighty, enters.

E.M.: Vivian? Vivian? It's Evelyn. Vivian?
VIVIAN: (*Waking, slurred*) Oh, God. (*Surprised*) Professor Ashford. Oh,   560
God.
E.M.: I'm in town visiting my great-grandson, who is celebrating his fifth birthday. I went to see you at your office, and they directed me here. (*She lays her jacket, scarf, and parcel on the bed.*) I have been walking all over town. I had forgotten how early it gets chilly here.
VIVIAN: (*Weakly*) I feel so bad.
E.M.: I know you do. I can see. (*Vivian cries.*) Oh, dear, there, there. There, there. (*Vivian cries more, letting the tears flow.*) Vivian, Vivian.

(E.M. looks toward the hall, then furtively slips off her shoes and swings up on the bed. She puts her arm around Vivian.) There, there. There, there, Vivian. *(Silence)*

It's a windy day. *(Silence)*

Don't worry, dear. *(Silence)*

Let's see. Shall I recite to you? Would you like that? I'll recite something by Donne.

VIVIAN: *(Moaning)* Nooooooo.

565   **E.M.:** Very well. *(Silence)* Hmmm. *(Silence)* Little Jeffrey is very sweet. Gets into everything.

Silence. E.M. takes a children's book out of the paper bag and begins reading. Vivian nestles in, drifting in and out of sleep.

Let's see. *The Runaway Bunny.* By Margaret Wise Brown. Pictures by Clement Hurd. Copyright 1942. First Harper Trophy Edition, 1972. Now then.

Once there was a little bunny who wanted to run away.
So he said to his mother, "I am running away."

"If you run away," said his mother, "I will run after you. For you are my little bunny."

"If you run after me," said the little bunny, "I will become a fish in a trout stream and I will swim away from you."

"If you become a fish in a trout stream," said his mother, "I will become a fisherman and I will fish for you."

(Thinking out loud) Look at that. A little allegory of the soul. No matter where it hides, God will find it. See, Vivian?

VIVIAN: *(Moaning)* Uhhhhhh.

E.M.:

"If you become a fisherman," said the little bunny, "I will be a bird and fly away from you."

"If you become a bird and fly away from me," said his mother, "I will be a tree that you come home to."

(To herself) Very clever.

"Shucks," said the little bunny, "I might just as well stay where I am and be your little bunny."

And so he did.

"Have a carrot," said the mother bunny.

(To herself) Wonderful.

Vivian is now fast asleep. E.M. slowly gets down and gathers her things. She leans over and kisses her.

It's time to go. And flights of angels sing thee to thy rest. *(She leaves.)*

Jason strides in and goes directly to the I&O sheet without looking at Vivian.

JASON: Professor Bearing. How are you feeling today? Three p.m. IV hydration totals. Two thousand in. Thirty out. Uh-oh. That's it. Kidneys gone.
    (He looks at Vivian.) Professor Bearing? Highly unresponsive. Wait a second — *(Puts his head down to her mouth and chest to listen for heartbeat and breathing)* Wait a sec — Jesus Christ! *(Yelling)* CALL A CODE!

Jason throws down the chart, dives over the bed, and lies on top of her body as he reaches for the phone and punches in the numbers.

    (To himself) Code: 4-5-7-5. *(To operator)* Code Blue, room 707. Code Blue, room 707. Dr. Posner — P-O-S-N-E-R. Hurry up!

He throws down the phone and lowers the head of the bed.

    Come on, come on, COME ON.

He begins CPR, kneeling over Vivian, alternately pounding frantically and giving mouth-to-mouth resuscitation. Over the loudspeaker in the hall, a droning voice repeats "Code Blue, room 707. Code Blue, room 707."

    One! Two! Three! Four! Five! *(He breathes in her mouth.)*

Susie, hearing the announcement, runs into the room.

SUSIE: WHAT ARE YOU DOING?
JASON: A GODDAMN CODE. GET OVER HERE!   570
SUSIE: She's DNR! *(She grabs him.)*
JASON: *(He pushes her away.)* She's Research!
SUSIE: She's NO CODE!

Susie grabs Jason and hurls him off the bed.

JASON: Ooowww! Goddamnit, Susie!
SUSIE: She's no code!   575
JASON: Aaargh!
SUSIE: Kelekian put the order in — you saw it! You were right there, Jason!
    Oh, God, the code! *(She runs to the phone. He struggles to stand.)* 4-5-7-5.

The Code Team swoops in. Everything changes. Frenzy takes over. They knock Susie out of the way with their equipment.

SUSIE: *(At the phone)* Cancel code, room 707. Sue Monahan, primary nurse.
    Cancel code. Dr. Posner is here.
JASON: *(In agony)* Oh, God.
CODE TEAM: 580
    — Get out of the way!
    — Unit staff out!
    — Get the board!
    — Over here!

They throw Vivian's body up at the waist and stick a board underneath for CPR. In a whirlwind of sterile packaging and barked commands, one team member attaches a respirator, one begins CPR, and one prepares the defibrillator. Susie and Jason try to stop them but are pushed away. The loudspeaker in the hall announces "Cancel code, room 707. Cancel code, room 707."

CODE TEAM:

  —Bicarb amp!

  —I got it! *(To Susie)* Get out!

  —One, two, three, four, five!

  —Get ready to shock! *(To Jason)* Move it!

SUSIE: *(Running to each person, yelling)* STOP! Patient is DNR!

JASON: *(At the same time, to the Code Team)* No, no! Stop doing this. STOP!

CODE TEAM:

  —Keep it going!

  —What do you get?

  —Bicarb amp!

  —No pulse!

585 **SUSIE:** She's NO CODE! Order was given — *(She dives for the chart and holds it up as she cries out)* Look! Look at this! DO NOT RESUSCITATE. KELEKIAN.

CODE TEAM: *(As they administer electric shock, Vivian's body arches and bounces back down.)*

  —Almost ready!

  —Hit her!

  —CLEAR!

  —Pulse? Pulse?

JASON: *(Howling)* I MADE A MISTAKE!

Pause. The Code Team looks at him. He collapses on the floor.

SUSIE: No code! Patient is no code.

CODE TEAM HEAD: Who the hell are you?

590 **SUSIE:** Sue Monahan, primary nurse.

CODE TEAM HEAD: Let me see the goddamn chart. CHART!

CODE TEAM: *(Slowing down)*

  —What's going on?

  —Should we stop?

  —What's it say?

SUSIE: *(Pushing them away from the bed)* Patient is no code. Get away from her!

(Susie lifts the blanket. Vivian steps out of the bed.	**CODE TEAM HEAD:** *(Reading)* Do Not Resuscitate. Kelekian. Shit.
She walks away from the scene, toward a little light.	*(The Code Team stops working.)*
595 *She is now attentive and eager, moving slowly toward the light.*	**JASON:** *(Whispering)* Oh, God.
She takes off her cap and lets it drop. She slips off her bracelet.	**CODE TEAM HEAD:** Order was put in yesterday.

She loosens the ties and the top gown slides to the floor. She lets the second gown fall.

The instant she is naked, and beautiful, reaching for the light—

Lights out.)

CODE TEAM:
—It's a doctor fuck-up.
—What is he, a resident?
—Got us up here on a DNR.
—Called a code on a no-code.

JASON: Oh, God.

(The bedside scene fades.)

Reading and Reacting

1. On the surface, *Wit* is the story of Vivian Bearing's journey from life to death. What other journey does the play describe?

2. Early in the play, Vivian is an unsympathetic character. In what sense is she unsympathetic? Does she become more likeable as the play progresses?

3. Vivian Bearing is a world-renowned authority on the work of the seventeenth-century poet John Donne. She is used to being listened to and having control. How does her situation change when she becomes a patient? How do these changes affect her bearing and her confidence?

4. One critic observed that Vivian's intellect is both her strength and her weakness. Do you agree? Explain your answer.

5. When she is told that she has cancer, Vivian replies nonchalantly, "It appears to be a matter, as the saying goes, of life and death. I know all about life and death, I am, after all, a scholar of John Donne's Holy Sonnets, which explore mortality. . . ." (p. 1321). Do you think Vivian really knows "all about life and death"? To what degree do John Donne's Holy Sonnets help her cope with her cancer and her impending death?

6. According to the critic M. H. Abrams, in the sixteenth and seventeenth centuries, *wit* referred to "the ability to develop brilliant, surprising, and paradoxical figures of speech." What does it mean today? To what aspect of *wit* does the title of the play refer?

7. At the beginning of the play, Vivian looks down on Susie, her nurse. Toward the end of play, Vivian's attitude toward Susie seems to change. What causes Vivian to change her opinion of Susie?

8. Vivian is part of a clinical trial for a new experimental drug. What is her attitude toward the researchers? What is their attitude toward her? What comment does *Wit* seem to be making about the medical establishment?

9. Vivian is suffering from ovarian cancer. In what way is this disease symbolic of the things that are missing from her life?

10. *Wit* begins with Vivian addressing the audience. As the play progresses, she takes the audience back in time and shows them what led her to become a literary scholar. What does she want to communicate to the audience? Is she successful? Is this information essential to the play? Explain.

11. Is Vivian a tragic character? Does she, like Hamlet and Oedipus, have a tragic flaw? If so, what is it? Does she learn from her suffering?

12. Jason, Vivian's doctor and former student, speaks the last line in the play. Why do you think the play ends with his comment? In what way is he like Vivian? In what way is he different from her? What has he learned by the end of the play?

13. JOURNAL ENTRY Do you think Vivian was a good teacher? What were her strengths? What were her weaknesses?

14. CRITICAL PERSPECTIVE Near the end of the play, Vivian's teacher and mentor E. M. Ashford visits Vivian and reads her a children's story. Commenting on this scene during a 2000 interview, playwright Margaret Edson makes the following point:

> The play shows, especially in the beginning, when she's explaining how great she is, even as she's being torn apart, the build-up of tools and protection and armor and skill and knowledge, and gradually, her increasing willingness to let it go, to drop off those things. So the first third of the play is her gathering things in. Then gradually she lets one thing go and then another thing go — she loses her shoes, then she loses her eyebrows, then she loses her dignity, then she loses her posture as a professor. The last thing she has to let go of is John Donne, which she does, and then she has to let go of her erudition, which she does, reluctantly. She has a lot of things weighing her down — which were of her own doing, of her own devising, and she was proud of them — but her redemption had to come through a taking off.

What does Edson mean when she says that Vivian "has a lot of things weighing her down"? Why does she have "to drop off those things" before she can be redeemed?

Related Works: "Gryphon" (p. 126), "Cathedral" (p. 318), "Do not go gentle into that good night" (p. 559), "A Valediction: Forbidding Mourning" (p. 687), "In Memory of Donald A. Stauffer" (p. 746), "After great pain, a formal feeling comes —" (p. 866), "Death Be Not Proud" (p. 869)

AUGUST WILSON (1945–) was born in Pittsburgh, Pennsylvania, and lived in the African American neighborhood known as the Hill. After leaving school at fifteen, he participated in the Black Arts movement in Pittsburgh, submitting poems to local African American publications. In 1969, Wilson and his friend Rob Penny founded the Black Horizons Theatre Company, for which Wilson produced and directed plays. Although Wilson wrote plays while living in Pittsburgh, his work began to gain recognition only after 1978, when he moved to St. Paul, Minnesota. There, in 1982, Lloyd Richards, dean of the Yale School of Drama and artistic director of the Yale Repertory Company, staged a performance of Wilson's *Ma Rainey's Black Bottom.*

Wilson's plays give powerful voice to the African American experience by exploring the historical and metaphysical roots of African American culture and by reflecting the rhythmic patterns of African American storytelling. In addition to *Ma Rainey's Black Bottom,* a Tony Award winner, Wilson's plays include *Fences* (1985), which won a Pulitzer Prize in 1987; *Joe Turner's Come and Gone* (1986); *Two Trains Running* (1989), which won Wilson his fifth New York Drama Critics Circle Award; *The Piano Lesson* (1987), which won a second Pulitzer Prize for Wilson in 1990; and *Seven Guitars* (1996).

Fences explores how the long-upheld color barrier in professional baseball affects the main character, Troy, who struggles with the pain of never realizing his dream of becoming a big-league player. Throughout the play, Troy retreats behind literal and figurative barriers that impair his relationships with his family.

Cultural Context: Jackie Robinson was the first African American to play major-league baseball. As a member of the Brooklyn Dodgers, he played his first game on April 15, 1947, against the Boston Braves. Robinson was a twenty-eight-year-old first baseman when he broke baseball's color barrier.

AUGUST WILSON

Fences (1985)

CHARACTERS

Troy Maxson	**Gabriel,** *Troy's brother*
Jim Bono, *Troy's friend*	**Cory,** *Troy and Rose's son*
Rose, *Troy's wife*	**Raynell,** *Troy's daughter*
Lyons, *Troy's oldest son by previous marriage*	

SETTING

The setting is the yard which fronts the only entrance to the Maxson household, an ancient two-story brick house set back off a small alley in a big-city neighborhood. The entrance to the house is gained by two or three steps leading to a wooden porch badly in need of paint.

A relatively recent addition to the house and running its full width, the porch lacks congruence. It is a sturdy porch with a flat roof. One or two chairs of dubious value sit at one end where the kitchen window opens onto the porch. An old-fashioned icebox stands silent guard at the opposite end.

The yard is a small dirt yard, partially fenced, except for the last scene, with a wooden sawhorse, a pile of lumber, and other fence-building equipment set off to the side. Opposite is a tree from which hangs a ball made of rags. A baseball bat leans against the tree. Two oil drums serve as garbage receptacles and sit near the house at right to complete the setting.

THE PLAY

Near the turn of the century, the destitute of Europe sprang on the city with tenacious claws and an honest and solid dream. The city devoured them. They swelled its belly until it burst into a thousand furnaces and sewing machines, a thousand butcher shops and bakers' ovens, a thousand churches and hospitals and funeral parlors and money-lenders. The city grew. It nourished itself and offered each man a partnership limited only by his talent, his guile, and his willingness and capacity for hard work. For the immigrants of Europe, a dream dared and won true.

The descendants of African slaves were offered no such welcome or participation. They came from places called the Carolinas and the Virginias, Georgia, Alabama, Mississippi, and Tennessee. They came strong, eager, searching. The city rejected them and they fled and settled along the riverbanks and under bridges in shallow, ramshackle houses made of sticks and tarpaper. They collected rags and wood. They sold the use of their muscles and their bodies. They cleaned houses and washed clothes, they shined shoes, and in quiet desperation and vengeful pride, they stole, and lived in pursuit of their own dream. That they could breathe free, finally, and stand to meet life with the force of dignity and whatever eloquence the heart could call upon.

By 1957, the hard-won victories of the European immigrants had solidified the industrial might of America. War had been confronted and won with new energies that used loyalty and patriotism as its fuel. Life was rich, full, and flourishing. The Milwaukee Braves won the World Series, and the hot winds of change that would make the sixties a turbulent, racing, dangerous, and provocative decade had not yet begun to blow full.

ACT I
SCENE 1

It is 1957. Troy and Bono enter the yard, engaged in conversation. Troy is fifty-three years old, a large man with thick, heavy hands; it is this largeness that he strives to fill out and make an accommodation with. Together with his blackness, his largeness informs his sensibilities and the choices he has made in his life.

Of the two men, Bono is obviously the follower. His commitment to their friendship of thirty-odd years is rooted in his admiration of Troy's honesty, capacity for hard work, and his strength, which Bono seeks to emulate.

It is Friday night, payday, and the one night of the week the two men engage in a ritual of talk and drink. Troy is usually the most talkative and at times he can be crude and almost vulgar, though he is capable of rising to profound heights of expression. The men carry lunch buckets and wear or carry burlap aprons and are dressed in clothes suitable to their jobs as garbage collectors.

BONO: Troy, you ought to stop that lying!

TROY: I ain't lying! The nigger had a watermelon this big. (*He indicates with his hands.*) Talking about . . . "What watermelon, Mr. Rand?" I liked to fell out! "What watermelon, Mr. Rand?" . . . And it sitting there big as life.

BONO: What did Mr. Rand say?

TROY: Ain't said nothing. Figure if the nigger too dumb to know he carrying a watermelon, he wasn't gonna get much sense out of him. Trying to hide that great big old watermelon under his coat. Afraid to let the white man see him carry it home.

5   BONO: I'm like you . . . I ain't got no time for them kind of people.

TROY: Now what he look like getting mad 'cause he see the man from the union talking to Mr. Rand?

BONO: He come to me talking about . . . "Maxson gonna get us fired." I told him to get away from me with that. He walked away from me calling you a troublemaker. What Mr. Rand say?

TROY: Ain't said nothing. He told me to go down the Commissioner's office next Friday. They called me down there to see them.

BONO: Well, as long as you got your complaint filed, they can't fire you. That's what one of them white fellows tell me.

TROY: I ain't worried about them firing me. They gonna fire me 'cause I asked a 10
question? That's all I did. I went to Mr. Rand and asked him, "Why? Why
you got the white mens driving and the colored lifting?" Told him, "what's
the matter, don't I count? You think only white fellows got sense enough to
drive a truck. That ain't no paper job! Hell, anybody can drive a truck.
How come you got all whites driving and the colored lifting?" He told me
"take it to the union." Well, hell, that's what I done! Now they wanna
come up with this pack of lies.

BONO: I told Brownie if the man come and ask him any questions . . . just tell
the truth! It ain't nothing but something they done trumped up on you
'cause you filed a complaint on them.

TROY: Brownie don't understand nothing. All I want them to do is change the
job description. Give everybody a chance to drive the truck. Brownie can't
see that. He ain't got that much sense.

BONO: How you figure he be making out with that gal be up at Taylors' all the
time . . . that Alberta gal?

TROY: Same as you and me. Getting just as much as we is. Which is to say
nothing.

BONO: It is, huh? I figure you doing a little better than me . . . and I ain't saying 15
what I'm doing.

TROY: Aw, nigger, look here . . . I know you. If you had got anywhere near that
gal, twenty minutes later you be looking to tell somebody. And the first one
you gonna tell . . . that you gonna want to brag to . . . is me.

BONO: I ain't saying that. I see where you be eyeing her.

TROY: I eye all the women. I don't miss nothing. Don't never let nobody tell
you Troy Maxson don't eye the women.

BONO: You been doing more than eyeing her. You done bought her a drink
or two.

TROY: Hell yeah, I bought her a drink! What that mean? I bought you one, 20
too. What that mean 'cause I buy her a drink? I'm just being polite.

BONO: It's all right to buy her one drink. That's what you call being polite. But
when you wanna be buying two or three . . . that's what you call eyeing her.

TROY: Look here, as long as you known me . . . you ever known me to chase
after women?

BONO: Hell yeah! Long as I done known you. You forgetting I knew you when.

TROY: Naw, I'm talking about since I been married to Rose?

BONO: Oh, not since you been married to Rose. Now, that's the truth, there. I 25
can say that.

TROY: All right then! Case closed.

BONO: I see you be walking up around Alberta's house. You supposed to be at
Taylors' and you be walking up around there.

TROY: What you watching where I'm walking for? I ain't watching after you.

BONO: I seen you walking around there more than once.

TROY: Hell, you liable to see me walking anywhere! That don't mean nothing 30
cause you see me walking around there.

BONO: Where she come from anyway? She just kinda showed up one day.

TROY: Tallahassee. You can look at her and tell she one of them Florida gals. They got some big healthy women down there. Grow them right up out the ground. Got a little bit of Indian in her. Most of them niggers down in Florida got some Indian in them.

BONO: I don't know about that Indian part. But she damn sure big and healthy. Woman wear some big stockings. Got them great big old legs and hips as wide as the Mississippi River.

TROY: Legs don't mean nothing. You don't do nothing but push them out of the way. But them hips cushion the ride!

35   **BONO:**   Troy, you ain't got no sense.

TROY: It's the truth! Like you riding on Goodyears!

Rose enters from the house. She is ten years younger than Troy, her devotion to him stems from her recognition of the possibilities of her life without him: a succession of abusive men and their babies, a life of partying and running the streets, the Church, or aloneness with its attendant pain and frustration. She recognizes Troy's spirit as a fine and illuminating one and she either ignores or forgives his faults, only some of which she recognizes. Though she doesn't drink, her presence is an integral part of the Friday night rituals. She alternates between the porch and the kitchen, where supper preparations are under way.

ROSE: What you all out here getting into?

TROY: What you worried about what we getting into for? This is men talk, woman.

ROSE: What I care what you all talking about? Bono, you gonna stay for supper?

40   **BONO:**   No, I thank you, Rose. But Lucille say she cooking up a pot of pigfeet.

TROY: Pigfeet! Hell, I'm going home with you! Might even stay the night if you got some pigfeet. You got something in there to top them pigfeet, Rose?

ROSE: I'm cooking up some chicken. I got some chicken and collard greens.°

TROY: Well, go on back in the house and let me and Bono finish what we was talking about. This is men talk. I got some talk for you later. You know what kind of talk I mean. You go on and powder it up.

ROSE: Troy Maxson, don't you start that now!

45   **TROY:**   *(puts his arm around her)* Aw, woman . . . come here. Look here, Bono . . . when I met this woman . . . I got out that place, say, "Hitch up my pony, saddle up my mare . . . there's a woman out there for me somewhere. I looked here. Looked there. Saw Rose and latched on to her." I latched on to her and told her — I'm gonna tell you the truth — I told her, "Baby, I don't wanna marry, I just wanna be your man." Rose told me . . . tell him what you told me, Rose.

ROSE: I told him if he wasn't the marrying kind, then move out the way so the marrying kind could find me.

TROY: That's what she told me. "Nigger, you in my way. You blocking the view! Move out the way so I can find me a husband." I thought it over two or three days. Come back —

---

collard greens: A leafy green vegetable.

Rose: Ain't no two or three days nothing. You was back the same night.

Troy: Come back, told her . . . "Okay, baby . . . but I'm gonna buy me a banty rooster and put him out there in the backyard . . . and when he see a stranger come, he'll flap his wings and crow . . ." Look here, Bono, I could watch the front door by myself . . . it was that back door I was worried about.

Rose: Troy, you ought not talk like that. Troy ain't doing nothing but telling a lie.   50

Troy: Only thing is . . . when we first got married . . . forget the rooster . . . we ain't had no yard!

Bono: I hear you tell it. Me and Lucille was staying down there on Logan Street. Had two rooms with the outhouse in the back. I ain't mind the outhouse none. But when that goddamn wind blow through there in the winter . . . that's what I'm talking about! To this day I wonder why in the hell I ever stayed down there for six long years. But see, I didn't know I could do no better. I thought only white folks had inside toilets and things.

Rose: There's a lot of people don't know they can do no better than they doing now. That's just something you got to learn. A lot of folks still shop at Bella's.

Troy: Ain't nothing wrong with shopping at Bella's. She got fresh food.

Rose: I ain't said nothing about if she got fresh food. I'm talking about what she charge. She charge ten cents more than the A&P.   55

Troy: The A&P ain't never done nothing for me. I spends my money where I'm treated right. I go down to Bella, say, "I need a loaf of bread, I'll pay you Friday." She give it to me. What sense that make when I got money to go and spend it somewhere else and ignore the person who done right by me? That ain't in the Bible.

Rose: We ain't talking about what's in the Bible. What sense it make to shop there when she overcharge?

Troy: You shop where you want to. I'll do my shopping where the people been good to me.

Rose: Well, I don't think it's right for her to overcharge. That's all I was saying.

Bono: Look here . . . I got to get on. Lucille going be raising all kind of hell.   60

Troy: Where you going, nigger? We ain't finished this pint. Come here, finish this pint.

Bono: Well, hell, I am . . . if you ever turn the bottle loose.

Troy: (hands him the bottle) The only thing I say about the A&P is I'm glad Cory got that job down there. Help him take care of his school clothes and things. Gabe done moved out and things getting tight around here. He got that job . . . He can start to look out for himself.

Rose: Cory done went and got recruited by a college football team.

Troy: I told that boy about that football stuff. The white man ain't gonna let   65
him get nowhere with that football. I told him when he first come to me with it. Now you come telling me he done went and got more tied up in it. He ought to go and get recruited in how to fix cars or something where he can make a living.

Rose: He ain't talking about making no living playing football. It's just something the boys in school do. They gonna send a recruiter by to talk to you.

He'll tell you he ain't talking about making no living playing football. It's a honor to be recruited.

Troy: It ain't gonna get him nowhere. Bono'll tell you that.

Bono: If he be like you in the sports . . . he's gonna be all right. Ain't but two men ever played baseball as good as you. That's Babe Ruth° and Josh Gibson.° Them's the only two men ever hit more home runs than you.

Troy: What it ever get me? Ain't got a pot to piss in or a window to throw it out of.

70   **Rose:** Times have changed since you was playing baseball, Troy. That was before the war. Times have changed a lot since then.

Troy: How in hell they done changed?

Rose: They got lots of colored boys playing ball now. Baseball and football.

Bono: You right about that, Rose. Times have changed, Troy. You just come along too early.

Troy: There ought not never have been no time called too early! Now you take that fellow . . . what's that fellow they had playing right field for the Yankees back then? You know who I'm talking about, Bono. Used to play right field for the Yankees.

75   **Rose:** Selkirk?

Troy: Selkirk! That's it! Man batting .269, understand? .269. What kind of sense that make? I was hitting .432 with thirty-seven home runs! Man batting .269 and playing right field for the Yankees! I saw Josh Gibson's daughter yesterday. She walking around with raggedy shoes on her feet. Now I bet you Selkirk's daughter ain't walking around with raggedy shoes on her feet! I bet you that!

Rose: They got a lot of colored baseball players now. Jackie Robinson° was the first. Folks had to wait for Jackie Robinson.

Troy: I done seen a hundred niggers play baseball better than Jackie Robinson. Hell, I know some teams Jackie Robinson couldn't even make! What you talking about Jackie Robinson. Jackie Robinson wasn't nobody. I'm talking about if you could play ball then they ought to have let you play. Don't care what color you were. Come telling me I come along too early. If you could play . . . then they ought to have let you play.

Troy takes a long drink from the bottle.

Rose: You gonna drink yourself to death. You don't need to be drinking like that.

80   **Troy:** Death ain't nothing. I done seen him. Done wrassled with him. You can't tell me nothing about death. Death ain't nothing but a fastball on the

---

Babe Ruth: George Herman Ruth (1895–1948), American baseball player. He played for the New York Yankees during the 1910s and '20s and is remembered for his home-run hitting and his flamboyant lifestyle.

Josh Gibson: (1911–1947), American baseball player. He played in the Negro Leagues in the 1920s, '30s, and '40s and was known as "the Negro Babe Ruth." An unwritten rule against hiring black players kept him out of the major leagues.

Jackie Robinson: John Roosevelt Robinson (1919–1972). He became the first African American to play major-league baseball when he was hired by the Brooklyn Dodgers in 1947.

outside corner. And you know what I'll do to that! Lookee here, Bono . . . am I lying? You get one of them fastballs, about waist high, over the outside corner of the plate where you can get the meat of the bat on it . . . and good god! You can kiss it goodbye. Now, am I lying?

BONO: Naw, you telling the truth there. I seen you do it.

TROY: If I'm lying . . . that 450 feet worth of lying! (*Pause.*) That's all death is to me. A fastball on the outside corner.

ROSE: I don't know why you want to get on talking about death.

TROY: Ain't nothing wrong with talking about death. That's part of life. Every-body gonna die. You gonna die, I'm gonna die. Bono's gonna die. Hell, we all gonna die.

ROSE: But you ain't got to talk about it. I don't like to talk about it.   85

TROY: You the one brought it up. Me and Bono was talking about baseball . . . you tell me I'm gonna drink myself to death. Ain't that right, Bono? You know I don't drink this but one night out of the week. That's Friday night. I'm gonna drink just enough to where I can handle it. Then I cuts it loose. I leave it alone. So don't you worry about me drinking myself to death. 'Cause I ain't worried about Death. I done seen him. I done wrestled with him.

Look here, Bono . . . I looked up one day and Death was marching straight at me. Like Soldiers on Parade! The Army of Death was marching straight at me. The middle of July, 1941. It got real cold just like it be win-ter. It seem like Death himself reached out and touched me on the shoul-der. He touch me just like I touch you. I got cold as ice and Death standing there grinning at me.

ROSE: Troy, why don't you hush that talk.

TROY: I say . . . what you want, Mr. Death? You be wanting me? You done brought your army to be getting me? I looked him dead in the eye. I wasn't fearing nothing. I was ready to tangle. Just like I'm ready to tangle now. The Bible say be ever vigilant. That's why I don't get but so drunk. I got to keep watch.

ROSE: Troy was right down there in Mercy Hospital. You remember he had pneumonia? Laying there with a fever talking plumb out of his head.

TROY: Death standing there staring at me . . . carrying that sickle in his   90
hand. Finally he say, "You want bound over for another year?" See, just like that . . . "You want bound over for another year?" I told him, "Bound over hell! Let's settle this now!"

It seem like he kinda fell back when I said that, and all the cold went out of me. I reached down and grabbed that sickle and threw it just as far as I could throw it . . . and me and him commenced to wrestling.

We wrestled for three days and three nights. I can't say where I found the strength from. Every time it seemed like he was gonna get the best of me, I'd reach way down deep inside myself and find the strength to do him one better.

ROSE: Every time Troy tell that story he find different ways to tell it. Different things to make up about it.

TROY: I ain't making up nothing. I'm telling you the facts of what happened. I wrestled with Death for three days and three nights and I'm standing here to tell you about it. *(Pause.)* All right. At the end of the third night we done weakened each other to where we can't hardly move. Death stood up, throwed on his robe . . . had him a white robe with a hood on it. He throwed on that robe and went off to look for his sickle. Say, "I'll be back." Just like that. "I'll be back." I told him, say, "Yeah, but . . . you gonna have to find me!" I wasn't no fool. I wan't going looking for him. Death ain't nothing to play with. And I know he's gonna get me. I know I got to join his army . . . his camp followers. But as long as I keep my strength and see him coming . . . as long as I keep up my vigilance . . . he's gonna have to fight to get me. I ain't going easy.

BONO: Well, look here, since you got to keep up your vigilance . . . let me have the bottle.

TROY: Aw hell, I shouldn't have told you that part. I should have left out that part.

95 **ROSE:** Troy be talking that stuff and half the time don't even know what he be talking about.

TROY: Bono know me better than that.

BONO: That's right. I know you. I know you got some Uncle Remus° in your blood. You got more stories than the devil got sinners.

TROY: Aw hell, I done seen him too! Done talked with the devil.

ROSE: Troy, don't nobody wanna be hearing all that stuff.

Lyons enters the yard from the street. Thirty-four years old, Troy's son by a previous marriage, he sports a neatly trimmed goatee, sport coat, white shirt, tieless and buttoned at the collar. Though he fancies himself a musician, he is more caught up in the rituals and "idea" of being a musician than in the actual practice of the music. He has come to borrow money from Troy, and while he knows he will be successful, he is uncertain as to what extent his lifestyle will be held up to scrutiny and ridicule.

100 **LYONS:** Hey, Pop.

TROY: What you come "Hey, Popping" me for?

LYONS: How you doing, Rose? *(He kisses her.)* Mr. Bono. How you doing?

BONO: Hey, Lyons . . . how you been?

TROY: He must have been doing all right. I ain't seen him around here last week.

105 **ROSE:** Troy, leave your boy alone. He come by to see you and you wanna start all that nonsense.

TROY: I ain't bothering Lyons. *(Offers him the bottle.)* Here . . . get you a drink. We got an understanding. I know why he come by to see me and he know I know.

LYONS: Come on, Pop . . . I just stopped by to say hi . . . see how you was doing.

Uncle Remus: The fictional narrator of *Uncle Remus: His Songs and His Sayings* (1880) and a number of sequels by Joel Chandler Harris. Uncle Remus tells tales about characters such as Brer Rabbit and the Tarbaby in exaggerated dialect, now widely considered to be a derogatory representation of African Americans.

TROY: You ain't stopped by yesterday.

ROSE: You gonna stay for supper, Lyons? I got some chicken cooking in the oven.

LYONS: No, Rose . . . thanks. I was just in the neighborhood and thought I'd   110
stop by for a minute.

TROY: You was in the neighborhood all right, nigger. You telling the truth there. You was in the neighborhood cause it's my payday.

LYONS: Well, hell, since you mentioned it . . . let me have ten dollars.

TROY: I'll be damned! I'll die and go to hell and play blackjack with the devil before I give you ten dollars.

BONO: That's what I wanna know about . . . that devil you done seen.

LYONS: What . . . Pop done seen the devil? You too much, Pops.   115

TROY: Yeah, I done seen him. Talked to him too!

ROSE: You ain't seen no devil. I done told you that man ain't had nothing to do with the devil. Anything you can't understand, you want to call it the devil.

TROY: Look here, Bono . . . I went down to see Hertzberger about some furniture. Got three rooms for two-ninety-eight. That what it say on the radio. "Three rooms . . . two-ninety-eight." Even made up a little song about it. Go down there . . . man tell me I can't get no credit. I'm working every day and can't get no credit. What to do? I got an empty house with some raggedy furniture in it. Cory ain't got no bed. He's sleeping on a pile of rags on the floor. Working every day and can't get no credit. Come back here — Rose'll tell you — madder than hell. Sit down . . . try to figure what I'm gonna do. Come a knock on the door. Ain't been living here but three days. Who know I'm here? Open the door . . . devil standing there bigger than life. White fellow . . . white fellow . . . got on good clothes and everything. Standing there with a clipboard in his hand. I ain't had to say nothing. First words come out of his mouth was . . . "I understand you need some furniture and can't get no credit." I liked to fell over. He say, "I'll give you all the credit you want, but you got to pay the interest on it." I told him, "Give me three rooms worth and charge whatever you want." Next day a truck pulled up here and two men unloaded them three rooms. Man what drove the truck give me a book. Say send ten dollars, first of every month to the address in the book and everything will be all right. Say if I miss a payment the devil was coming back and it'll be hell to pay. That was fifteen years ago. To this day . . . the first of the month I send my ten dollars, Rose'll tell you.

ROSE: Troy lying.

TROY: I ain't never seen that man since. Now you tell me who else that could   120
have been but the devil? I ain't sold my soul or nothing like that, you understand. Naw, I wouldn't have truck with the devil about nothing like that. I got my furniture and pays my ten dollars the first of the month just like clockwork.

BONO: How long you say you been paying this ten dollars a month?

TROY: Fifteen years!

BONO: Hell, ain't you finished paying for it yet? How much the man done charged you?

TROY: Ah hell, I done paid for it. I done paid for it ten times over! The fact is I'm scared to stop paying it.

125 ROSE: Troy lying. We got that furniture from Mr. Glickman. He ain't paying no ten dollars a month to nobody.

TROY: Aw hell, woman. Bono know I ain't that big a fool.

LYONS: I was just getting ready to say . . . I know where there's a bridge for sale.

TROY: Look here, I'll tell you this . . . it don't matter to me if he was the devil. It don't matter if the devil give credit. Somebody has got to give it.

ROSE: It ought to matter. You going around talking about having truck with the devil . . . God's the one you gonna have to answer to. He's the one gonna be at the Judgment.

130 LYONS: Yeah, well, look here, Pop . . . let me have that ten dollars. I'll give it back to you. Bonnie got a job working at the hospital.

TROY: What I tell you, Bono? The only time I see this nigger is when he wants something. That's the only time I see him.

LYONS: Come on, Pop, Mr. Bono don't want to hear all that. Let me have the ten dollars. I told you Bonnie working.

TROY: What that mean to me? "Bonnie working." I don't care if she working. Go ask her for the ten dollars if she working. Talking about "Bonnie working." Why ain't you working?

LYONS: Aw, Pop, you know I can't find no decent job. Where am I gonna get a job at? You know I can't get no job.

135 TROY: I told you I know some people down there. I can get you on the rubbish if you want to work. I told you that the last time you came by here asking me for something.

James Earl Jones as Troy in a 1986 production of *Fences* at the Goodman Theatre.

LYONS: Naw, Pop . . . thanks. That ain't for me. I don't wanna be carrying nobody's rubbish. I don't wanna be punching nobody's time clock.

TROY: What's the matter, you too good to carry people's rubbish? Where you think that ten dollars you talking about come from? I'm just sup- posed to haul people's rubbish and give my money to you 'cause you too lazy to work. You too lazy to work and wanna know why you ain't got what I got.

ROSE: What hospital Bonnie working at? Mercy?

LYONS: She's down at Passavant working in the laundry.

TROY: I ain't got nothing as it is. I give you that ten dollars and I got to eat   140
beans the rest of the week. Naw . . . you ain't getting no ten dollars here.

LYONS: You ain't got to be eating no beans. I don't know why you wanna say that.

TROY: I ain't got no extra money. Gabe done moved over to Miss Pearl's paying her the rent and things done got tight around here. I can't afford to be giving you every payday.

LYONS: I ain't asked you to give me nothing. I asked you to loan me ten dollars. I know you got ten dollars.

TROY: Yeah, I got it. You know why I got it? 'Cause I don't throw my money away out there in the streets. You living the fast life . . . wanna be a musi- cian . . . running around in them clubs and things . . . then, you learn to take care of yourself. You ain't gonna find me going and asking nobody for nothing. I done spent too many years without.

LYONS: You and me is two different people, Pop.   145

TROY: I done learned my mistake and learned to do what's right by it. You still trying to get something for nothing. Life don't owe you nothing. You owe it to yourself. Ask Bono. He'll tell you I'm right.

LYONS: You got your way of dealing with the world . . . I got mine. The only thing that matters to me is the music.

TROY: Yeah, I can see that! It don't matter how you gonna eat . . . where your next dollar is coming from. You telling the truth there.

LYONS: I know I got to eat. But I got to live too. I need something that gonna help me to get out of the bed in the morning. Make me feel like I belong in the world. I don't bother nobody. I just stay with the music 'cause that's the only way I can find to live in the world. Otherwise there ain't no telling what I might do. Now I don't come criticizing you and how you live. I just come by to ask you for ten dollars. I don't wanna hear all that about how I live.

TROY: Boy, your mama did a hell of a job raising you.   150

LYONS: You can't change me, Pop. I'm thirty-four years old. If you wanted to change me, you should have been there when I was growing up. I come by to see you . . . ask for ten dollars and you want to talk about how I was raised. You don't know nothing about how I was raised.

ROSE: Let the boy have ten dollars, Troy.

TROY: (to Lyons) What the hell you looking at me for? I ain't got no ten dol- lars. You know what I do with my money. (To Rose.) Give him ten dollars if you want him to have it.

ROSE: I will. Just as soon as you turn it loose.

155 TROY: (*handing Rose the money*) There it is. Seventy-six dollars and forty-two
         cents. You see this, Bono? Now, I ain't gonna get but six of that back.

ROSE: You ought to stop telling that lie. Here, Lyons. (*She hands him the money.*)

LYONS: Thanks, Rose. Look . . . I got to run . . . I'll see you later.

TROY: Wait a minute. You gonna say "thanks, Rose" and ain't gonna look to
         see where she got that ten dollars from? See how they do me, Bono?

LYONS: I know she got it from you, Pop. Thanks. I'll give it back to you.

160 TROY: There he go telling another lie. Time I see that ten dollars . . . he'll be
         owing me thirty more.

LYONS: See you, Mr. Bono.

BONO: Take care, Lyons!

LYONS: Thanks, Pop. I'll see you again.

Lyons exits the yard.

TROY: I don't know why he don't go and get him a decent job and take care of
         that woman he got.

165 BONO: He'll be all right, Troy. The boy is still young.

TROY: The *boy* is thirty-four years old.

ROSE: Let's not get off into all that.

BONO: Look here . . . I got to be going. I got to be getting on. Lucille gonna be
         waiting.

TROY: (*puts his arm around Rose*) See this woman, Bono? I love this woman. I
         love this woman so much it hurts. I love her so much . . . I done run out of
         ways of loving her. So I got to go back to basics. Don't you come by my
         house Monday morning talking about time to go to work . . . 'cause I'm still
         gonna be stroking!

170 ROSE: Troy! Stop it now!

BONO: I ain't paying him no mind, Rose. That ain't nothing but gin-talk. Go
         on, Troy. I'll see you Monday.

TROY: Don't you come by my house, nigger! I done told you what I'm gonna be
         doing.

The lights go down to black.

SCENE 2

*The lights come up on Rose hanging up clothes. She hums and sings softly to herself. It
is the following morning.*

ROSE: (*sings*)
                Jesus, be a fence all around me every day

                Jesus, I want you to protect me as I travel on my way.

                Jesus, be a fence all around me every day.

Troy enters from the house.

                Jesus, I want you to protect me

                As I travel on my way.

(*To Troy.*) 'Morning, You ready for breakfast? I can fix it soon as I finish
hanging up these clothes?

TROY: I got the coffee on. That'll be all right. I'll just drink some of that this
morning.

ROSE: That 651 hit yesterday. That's the second time this month. Miss Pearl   175
hit for a dollar . . . seem like those that need the least always get lucky. Poor
folks can't get nothing.

TROY: Them numbers don't know nobody. I don't know why you fool with
them. You and Lyons both.

ROSE: It's something to do.

TROY: You ain't doing nothing but throwing your money away.

ROSE: Troy, you know I don't play foolishly. I just play a nickel here and a
nickel there.

TROY: That's two nickels you done thrown away.   180

ROSE: Now I hit sometimes . . . that makes up for it. It always comes in handy
when I do hit. I don't hear you complaining then.

TROY: I ain't complaining now. I just say it's foolish. Trying to guess out of six
hundred ways which way the number gonna come. If I had all the money
niggers, these Negroes, throw away on numbers for one week — just one
week — I'd be a rich man.

ROSE: Well, you wishing and calling it foolish ain't gonna stop folks from playing numbers. That's one thing for sure. Besides . . . some good things come
from playing numbers. Look where Pope done bought him that restaurant
off of numbers.

TROY: I can't stand niggers like that. Man ain't had two dimes to rub together.
He walking around with his shoes all run over bumming money for
cigarettes. All right. Got lucky there and hit the numbers . . .

ROSE: Troy, I know all about it.   185

TROY: Had good sense, I'll say that for him. He ain't throwing his money away.
I seen niggers hit the numbers and go through two thousand dollars in four
days. Man bought him that restaurant down there . . . fixed it up real
nice . . . and then didn't want nobody to come in it! A Negro go in there
and can't get no kind of service. I seen a white fellow come in there and
order a bowl of stew. Pope picked all the meat out the pot for him. Man
ain't had nothing but a bowl of meat! Negro come behind him and ain't got
nothing but the potatoes and carrots. Talking about what numbers do for
people, you picked a wrong example. Ain't done nothing but make a worser
fool out of him than he was before.

ROSE: Troy, you ought to stop worrying about what happened at work yesterday.

TROY: I ain't worried. Just told me to be down there at the Commissioner's
office on Friday. Everybody think they gonna fire me. I ain't worried about
them firing me. You ain't got to worry about that. (*Pause.*) Where's Cory?
Cory in the house? (*Calls.*) Cory?

ROSE: He gone out.

TROY: Out, huh? He gone out 'cause he know I want him to help me with this   190
fence. I know how he is. That boy scared of work.

Gabriel enters. He comes halfway down the alley and, hearing Troy's voice, stops.

TROY: *(continues)* He ain't done a lick of work in his life.

ROSE: He had to go to football practice. Coach wanted them to get in a little extra practice before the season start.

TROY: I got his practice . . . running out of here before he get his chores done.

ROSE: Troy, what is wrong with you this morning? Don't nothing set right with you. Go on back in there and go to bed . . . get up on the other side.

195 TROY: Why something got to be wrong with me? I ain't said nothing wrong with me.

ROSE: You got something to say about everything. First it's the numbers . . . then it's the way the man runs his restaurant . . . then you done got on Cory. What's it gonna be next? Take a look up there and see if the weather suits you . . . or is it gonna be how you gonna put up the fence with the clothes hanging in the yard.

TROY: You hit the nail on the head then.

ROSE: I know you like I know the back of my hand. Go on in there and get you some coffee . . . see if that straighten you up. 'Cause you ain't right this morning.

Troy starts into the house and sees Gabriel. Gabriel starts singing. Troy's brother, he is seven years younger than Troy. Injured in World War II, he has a metal plate in his head. He carries an old trumpet tied around his waist and believes with every fiber of his being that he is the Archangel Gabriel.° He carries a chipped basket with an assortment of discarded fruits and vegetables he has picked up in the strip district and which he attempts to sell.

GABRIEL: *(singing)*

> Yes, ma'am, I got plums
> You ask me how I sell them
> Oh ten cents apiece
> Three for a quarter
> Come and buy now
> 'Cause I'm here today
> And tomorrow I'll be gone

Gabriel enters.

Hey, Rose!

200 ROSE: How you doing, Gabe?

GABRIEL: There's Troy . . . Hey, Troy!

TROY: Hey, Gabe.

Exit into kitchen.

Archangel Gabriel: A messenger of God.

ROSE: *(To Gabriel.)* What you got there?

GABRIEL: You know what I got, Rose. I got fruits and vegetables.

ROSE: *(looking in basket)* Where's all these plums you talking about?

GABRIEL: I ain't got no plums today, Rose. I was just singing that. Have some   205
tomorrow. Put me in a big order for plums. Have enough plums tomorrow
for St. Peter and everybody.

Troy reenters from kitchen, crosses to steps.

(To Rose.) Troy's mad at me.

TROY: I ain't mad at you. What I got to be mad at you about? You ain't done   210
nothing to me.

GABRIEL: I just moved over to Miss Pearl's to keep out from in your way. I ain't
mean no harm by it.

TROY: Who said anything about that? I ain't said anything about that.

GABRIEL: You ain't mad at me, is you?

TROY: Naw . . . I ain't mad at you, Gabe. If I was mad at you I'd tell you about it.

GABRIEL: Got me two rooms. In the basement. Got my own door too. Wanna
see my key? *(He holds up a key.)* That's my own key! Ain't nobody else got a
key like that. That's my key! My two rooms!

TROY: Well, that's good, Gabe. You got your own key . . . that's good.

ROSE: You hungry, Gabe? I was just fixing to cook Troy his breakfast.

GABRIEL: I'll take some biscuits. You got some biscuits? Did you know when I   215
was in heaven . . . every morning me and St. Peter° would sit down by the
gate and eat some big fat biscuits? Oh, yeah! We had us a good time. We'd sit
there and eat us them biscuits and then St. Peter would go off to sleep and
tell me to wake him up when it's time to open the gates for the judgment.

ROSE: Well, come on . . . I'll make up a batch of biscuits.

Rose exits into the house.

GABRIEL: Troy . . . St. Peter got your name in the book. I seen it. It say . . .
Troy Maxson. I say . . . I know him! He got the same name like what I got.
That's my brother!

TROY: How many times you gonna tell me that, Gabe?

GABRIEL: Ain't got my name in the book. Don't have to have my name. I done
died and went to heaven. He got your name though. One morning St. Peter
was looking at his book . . . marking it up for the judgment . . . and he let
me see your name. Got it in there under M. Got Rose's name . . . I ain't
seen it like I seen yours . . . but I know it's in there. He got a great big book.
Got everybody's name what was ever been born. That's what he told me.
But I seen your name. Seen it with my own eyes.

TROY: Go on in the house there. Rose going to fix you something to eat.   220

St. Peter: Disciple of Christ, believed to be the guard at the gates of heaven.

GABRIEL: Oh, I ain't hungry. I done had breakfast with Aunt Jemima. She
come by and cooked me up a whole mess of flapjacks. Remember how we
used to eat them flapjacks?

TROY: Go on in the house and get you something to eat now.

GABRIEL: I got to sell my plums. I done sold some tomatoes. Got me two quarters. Wanna see? (*He shows Troy his quarters.*) I'm gonna save them and buy
me a new horn so St. Peter can hear me when it's time to open the gates.
(*Gabriel stops suddenly. Listens.*) Hear that? That's the hellhounds. I got to
chase them out of here. Go on get out of here! Get out!

Gabriel exits singing.

> Better get ready for the Judgment
> Better get ready for the Judgment
> My Lord is coming down

Rose enters from the house.

TROY: He's gone off somewhere.

225 GABRIEL: (*offstage*)

> Better get ready for the Judgment
> Better get ready for the Judgment morning
> Better get ready for the Judgment
> My God is coming down

ROSE: He ain't eating right. Miss Pearl say she can't get him to eat nothing.

TROY: What you want me to do about it, Rose? I done did everything I can for
the man. I can't make him get well. Man got half his head blown away . . .
what you expect?

ROSE: Seem like something ought to be done to help him.

TROY: Man don't bother nobody. He just mixed up from that metal plate he
got in his head. Ain't no sense for him to go back into the hospital.

230 ROSE: Least he be eating right. They can help him take care of himself.

TROY: Don't nobody wanna be locked up, Rose. What you wanna lock him up
for? Man go over there and fight the war . . . messin' around with them Japs,
get half his head blown off . . . and they give him a lousy three thousand
dollars. And I had to swoop down on that.

ROSE: Is you fixing to go into that again?

TROY: That's the only way I got a roof over my head . . . 'cause of that metal
plate.

ROSE: Ain't no sense you blaming yourself for nothing. Gabe wasn't in no condition to manage that money. You done what was right by him. Can't nobody say you ain't done what was right by him. Look how long you took
care of him . . . till he wanted to have his own place and moved over there
with Miss Pearl.

235 TROY: That ain't what I'm saying, woman! I'm just stating the facts. If my
brother didn't have that metal plate in his head . . . I wouldn't have a pot to
piss in or a window to throw it out of. And I'm fifty-three years old. Now
see if you can understand that!

Troy gets up from the porch and starts to exit the yard.

ROSE: Where you going off to? You been running out of here every Saturday for weeks. I thought you was gonna work on this fence?

TROY: I'm gonna walk down to Taylors'. Listen to the ball game. I'll be back in a bit. I'll work on it when I get back.

He exits the yard. The lights go to black.

SCENE 3

The lights come up on the yard. It is four hours later. Rose is taking down the clothes from the line. Cory enters carrying his football equipment.

ROSE: Your daddy like to had a fit with you running out of here this morning without doing your chores.

CORY: I told you I had to go to practice.

ROSE: He say you were supposed to help him with this fence.   240

CORY: He been saying that the last four or five Saturdays, and then he don't never do nothing, but go down to Taylors'. Did you tell him about the recruiter?

ROSE: Yeah, I told him.

CORY: What he say?

ROSE: He ain't said nothing too much. You get in there and get started on your chores before he gets back. Go on and scrub down them steps before he gets back here hollering and carrying on.

CORY: I'm hungry. What you got to eat, Mama?   245

ROSE: Go on and get started on your chores. I got some meat loaf in there. Go on and make you a sandwich . . . and don't leave no mess in there.

Cory exits into the house. Rose continues to take down the clothes. Troy enters the yard and sneaks up and grabs her from behind.

Troy! Go on, now. You liked to scared me to death. What was the score of the game? Lucille had me on the phone and I couldn't keep up with it.

TROY: What I care about the game? Come here, woman. *(He tries to kiss her.)*

ROSE: I thought you went down Taylors' to listen to the game. Go on, Troy! You supposed to be putting up this fence.

TROY: *(attempting to kiss her again)* I'll put it up when I finish with what is at hand.

ROSE: Go on, Troy. I ain't studying you.   250

TROY: *(chasing after her)* I'm studying you . . . fixing to do my homework!

ROSE: Troy, you better leave me alone.

TROY: Where's Cory? That boy brought his butt home yet?

ROSE: He's in the house doing his chores.

TROY: *(calling)* Cory! Get your butt out here, boy!   255

Rose exits into the house with the laundry. Troy goes over to the pile of wood, picks up a board, and starts sawing. Cory enters from the house.

TROY: You just now coming in here from leaving this morning?

CORY: Yeah, I had to go to football practice.

TROY: Yeah, what?

CORY: Yessir.

260 **TROY:** I ain't but two seconds off you noway. The garbage sitting in there overflowing . . . you ain't done none of your chores . . . and you come in here talking about "Yeah."

CORY: I was just getting ready to do my chores now, Pop . . .

TROY: Your first chore is to help me with this fence on Saturday. Everything else come after that. Now get that saw and cut them boards.

Cory takes the saw and begins cutting the boards. Troy continues working. There is a long pause.

CORY: Hey, Pop . . . why don't you buy a TV?

TROY: What I want with a TV? What I want one of them for?

265 **CORY:** Everybody got one. Earl, Ba Bra . . . Jesse!

TROY: I ain't asked you who had one. I say what I want with one?

CORY: So you can watch it. They got lots of things on TV. Baseball games and everything. We could watch the World Series.

TROY: Yeah . . . and how much this TV cost?

CORY: I don't know. They got them on sale for around two hundred dollars.

270 **TROY:** Two hundred dollars, huh?

CORY: That ain't that much, Pop.

TROY: Naw, it's just two hundred dollars. See that roof you got over your head at night? Let me tell you something about that roof. It's been over ten years since that roof was last tarred. See now . . . the snow comes this winter and sit up there on that roof like it is . . . and it's gonna seep inside. It's just gonna be a little bit . . . ain't gonna hardly notice it. Then the next thing you know, it's gonna be leaking all over the house. Then the wood rot from all that water and you gonna need a whole new roof. Now, how much you think it cost to get that roof tarred?

CORY: I don't know.

TROY: Two hundred and sixty-four dollars . . . cash money. While you thinking about a TV, I got to be thinking about the roof . . . and whatever else go wrong here. Now if you had two hundred dollars, what would you do . . . fix the roof or buy a TV?

275 **CORY:** I'd buy a TV. Then when the roof started to leak . . . when it needed fixing . . . I'd fix it.

TROY: Where you gonna get the money from? You done spent it for a TV. You gonna sit up and watch the water run all over your brand new TV.

CORY: Aw, Pop. You got money. I know you do.

TROY: Where I got it at, huh?

CORY: You got it in the bank.

280 **TROY:** You wanna see my bankbook? You wanna see that seventy-three dollars and twenty-two cents I got sitting up in there.

CORY: You ain't got to pay for it all at one time. You can put a down payment on it and carry it on home with you.

TROY: Not me. I ain't gonna owe nobody nothing if I can help it. Miss a payment and they come and snatch it right out your house. Then what you got? Now, soon as I get two hundred dollars clear, then I'll buy a TV. Right now, as soon as I get two hundred and sixty-four dollars, I'm gonna have this roof tarred.

CORY: Aw . . . Pop!

TROY: You go on and get you two hundred and buy one if ya want it. I got better things to do with my money.

CORY: I can't get no two hundred dollars. I ain't never seen two hundred dollars. 285

TROY: I'll tell you what . . . you get you a hundred dollars and I'll put the other hundred with it.

CORY: All right, I'm gonna show you.

TROY: You gonna show me how you can cut them boards right now.

Cory begins to cut the boards. There is a long pause.

CORY: The Pirates won today. That makes five in a row.

TROY: I ain't thinking about the Pirates. Got an all-white team. Got that 290 boy . . . that Puerto Rican boy . . . Clemente.° Don't even half-play him. That boy could be something if they give him a chance. Play him one day and sit him on the bench the next.

CORY: He gets a lot of chances to play.

TROY: I'm talking about playing regular. Playing every day so you can get your timing. That's what I'm talking about.

CORY: They got some white guys on the team that don't play every day. You can't play everybody at the same time.

TROY: If they got a white fellow sitting on the bench . . . you can bet your last dollar he can't play! The colored guy got to be twice as good before he get on the team. That's why I don't want you to get all tied up in them sports. Man on the team and what it get him? They got colored on the team and don't use them. Same as not having them. All them teams the same.

CORY: The Braves got Hank Aaron° and Wes Covington.° Hank Aaron hit 295 two home runs today. That makes forty-three.

TROY: Hank Aaron ain't nobody. That what you supposed to do. That's how you supposed to play the game. Ain't nothing to it. It's just a matter of

---

Roberto Clemente: (1934–1972), Major League baseball player for the Pittsburg Pirates, known as much for his humanitarianism as his unique batting style and ability. Clemente received the Most Valuable Player Award in 1966 and died in a plane crash in 1972 while shuttling supplies to Nicaraguan earthquake victims.

Hank Aaron: Henry Aaron (1934–   ), American baseball player who broke Babe Ruth's career home run record with a lifetime total of 755 home runs. The holder of 12 other Major League records, Aaron spent his Major League career with the Braves, first in Milwaukee and later in their hometown of Atlanta.

Wes Covington: John Wesley Covington (1932–   ), American baseball player known for his ability to frustrate pitchers by wasting time at the plate. In an eleven year career, Covington played for six Major League teams, beginning with the Milwaukee Braves and retiring with the Los Angeles Dodgers in 1966.

timing . . . getting the right follow-through. Hell, I can hit forty-three home runs right now!

CORY: Not off no major-league pitching, you couldn't.

TROY: We had better pitching in the Negro leagues. I hit seven home runs off of Satchel Paige.° You can't get no better than that!

CORY: Sandy Koufax.° He's leading the league in strikeouts.

300 TROY: I ain't thinking of no Sandy Koufax.

CORY: You got Warren Spahn° and Lew Burdette.° I bet you couldn't hit no home runs off of Warren Spahn.

TROY: I'm through with it now. You go on and cut them boards. (Pause.) Your mama tell me you done got recruited by a college football team? Is that right?

CORY: Yeah. Coach Zellman say the recruiter gonna be coming by to talk to you. Get you to sign the permission papers.

TROY: I thought you supposed to be working down there at the A&P. Ain't you suppose to be working down there after school?

305 CORY: Mr. Stawicki say he gonna hold my job for me until after the football season. Say starting next week I can work weekends.

TROY: I thought we had an understanding about this football stuff? You suppose to keep up with your chores and hold that job down at the A&P. Ain't been around here all day on a Saturday. Ain't none of your chores done . . . and now you telling me you done quit your job.

CORY: I'm going to be working weekends.

TROY: You damn right you are! And ain't no need for nobody coming around here to talk to me about signing nothing.

CORY: Hey, Pop . . . you can't do that. He's coming all the way from North Carolina.

310 TROY: I don't care where he coming from. The white man ain't gonna let you get nowhere with that football noway. You go on and get your book-learning so you can work yourself up in that A&P or learn how to fix cars or build houses or something, get you a trade. That way you have something can't nobody take away from you. You go on and learn how to put your hands to some good use. Besides hauling people's garbage.

Satchel Page: Leroy Robert Paige (1906–1982), American baseball player. He played in the Negro Leagues from the 1920s until 1948, when he joined the Cleveland Indians; he reportedly pitched 55 no-hit games during his career. Joe DiMaggio called him "the best pitcher I have ever faced."

Sandy Koufax: Sanford Koufax (1935–   ), left-handed pitcher who won 129 games and lost only 47 for the Los Angeles Dodgers in the six seasons between 1961 and 1966; he won three Cy Young Awards and pitched four no-hit games, the last of which (1965) was a perfect game.

Warren Spahn: (1921–   ), left-handed pitcher who at the time of his retirement in 1966 held the National League record of 363 wins; he won 20 or more games in four consecutive seasons (1947–1950) and in several other seasons during the 1950s.

Lew Burdette: Selva Lewis Burdette (1926–   ), American baseball player who pitched and won three games for the Milwaukee Braves against the New York Yankees in the 1957 World Series; for that Series, his ERA was an amazingly low .067.

CORY: I get good grades, Pop. That's why the recruiter wants to talk with you. You got to keep up your grades to get recruited. This way I'll be going to college. I'll get a chance . . .

TROY: First you gonna get your butt down there to the A&P and get your job back.

CORY: Mr. Stawicki done already hired somebody else 'cause I told him I was playing football.

TROY: You a bigger fool than I thought . . . to let somebody take away your job so you can play some football. Where you gonna get your money to take out your girlfriend and whatnot? What kind of foolishness is that to let somebody take away your job?

CORY: I'm still gonna be working weekends.   315

TROY: Naw . . . naw. You getting your butt out of here and finding you another job.

CORY: Come on, Pop! I got to practice. I can't work after school and play football too. The team needs me. That's what Coach Zellman say . . .

TROY: I don't care what nobody else say. I'm the boss . . . you understand? I'm the boss around here. I do the only saying what counts.

CORY: Come on, Pop!

TROY: I asked you . . . did you understand?   320

CORY: Yeah . . .

TROY: What?!

CORY: Yessir.

TROY: You go on down there to that A&P and see if you can get your job back. If you can't do both . . . then you quit the football team. You've got to take the crookeds with the straights.

CORY: Yessir. (*Pause.*) Can I ask you a question?   325

TROY: What the hell you wanna ask me? Mr. Stawicki the one you got the questions for.

CORY: How come you ain't never liked me?

TROY: Liked you? Who the hell say I got to like you? What law is there say I got to like you? Wanna stand up in my face and ask a damn fool-ass question like that. Talking about liking somebody. Come here, boy, when I talk to you.

Cory comes over to where Troy is working. He stands slouched over and Troy shoves him on his shoulder.

Straighten up, goddammit! I asked you a question . . . what law is there say I got to like you?

CORY: None.

TROY: Well, all right then! Don't you eat every day? (*Pause.*) Answer me when   330
I talk to you! Don't you eat every day?

CORY: Yeah.

TROY: Nigger, as long as you in my house, you put that sir on the end of it when you talk to me!

CORY: Yes . . . sir.

TROY: You eat every day.

335   CORY: Yessir!

TROY: Got a roof over your head.

CORY: Yessir!

TROY: Got clothes on your back.

CORY: Yessir.

340   TROY: Why you think that is?

CORY: 'Cause of you.

TROY: Ah, hell I know it's 'cause of me . . . but why do you think that is?

CORY: *(hesitant)* 'Cause you like me.

TROY: Like you? I go out of here every morning . . . bust my butt . . . putting up with them crackers° every day . . . 'cause I like you? You are the biggest fool I ever saw. *(Pause.)* It's my job. It's my responsibility! You understand that? A man got to take care of his family. You live in my house . . . sleep you behind on my bedclothes . . . fill you belly up with my food . . . 'cause you my son. You my flesh and blood. Not 'cause I like you! 'Cause it's my duty to take care of you. I owe a responsibility to you! Let's get this straight right here . . . before it go along any further . . . I ain't got to like you. Mr. Rand don't give me my money come payday cause he likes me. He give me 'cause he owe me. I done give you everything I had to give you. I gave you your life! Me and your mama worked that out between us. And liking your black ass wasn't part of the bargain. Don't you try and go through life worrying about if somebody like you or not. You best be making sure they doing right by you. You understand what I'm saying, boy?

345   CORY: Yessir.

TROY: Then get the hell out of my face, and get on down to that A&P.

Rose has been standing behind the screen door for much of the scene. She enters as Cory exits.

ROSE: Why don't you let the boy go ahead and play football, Troy? Ain't no harm in that. He's just trying to be like you with the sports.

TROY: I don't want him to be like me! I want him to move as far away from my life as he can get. You the only decent thing that ever happened to me. I wish him that. But I don't wish him a thing else from my life. I decided seventeen years ago that boy wasn't getting involved in no sports. Not after what they did to me in the sports.

ROSE: Troy, why don't you admit you was too old to play in the major leagues? For once . . . why don't you admit that?

350   TROY: What do you mean too old? Don't come telling me I was too old. I just wasn't the right color. Hell, I'm fifty-three years old and can do better than Selkirk's .269 right now!

ROSE: How's was you gonna play ball when you were over forty? Sometimes I can't go no sense out of you.

---

crackers: Derogatory term for white people, generally poor southern whites.

TROY: I got good sense, woman. I got sense enough not to let my boy get hurt over playing no sports. You been mothering that boy too much. Worried about if people like him.

ROSE: Everything that boy do . . . he do for you. He wants you to say "Good job, son." That's all.

TROY: Rose, I ain't got time for that. He's alive. He's healthy. He's got to make his own way. I made mine. Ain't nobody gonna hold his hand when he get out there in that world.

ROSE: Times have changed from when you was young, Troy. People change. 355 The world's changing around you and you can't even see it.

TROY: (*slow, methodical*) Woman . . . I do the best I can do. I come in here every Friday. I carry a sack of potatoes and a bucket of lard. You all line up at the door with your hands out. I give you the lint from my pockets. I give you my sweat and my blood. I ain't got no tears. I done spent them. We go upstairs in that room at night . . . and I fall down on you and try to blast a hole into forever. I get up Monday morning . . . find my lunch on the table. I go out. Make my way. Find my strength to carry me through to the next Friday. (*Pause.*) That's all I got, Rose. That's all I got to give. I can't give nothing else.

Troy exits into the house. The lights go down to black.

SCENE 4

It is Friday. Two weeks later. Cory starts out of the house with his football equipment. The phone rings.

CORY: (*calling*) I got it! (*He answers the phone and stands in the screen door talking.*) Hello? Hey, Jesse. Naw . . . I was just getting ready to leave now.

ROSE: (*calling*) Cory!

CORY: I told you, man, them spikes° is all tore up. You can use them if you want, but they ain't no good. Earl got some spikes.

ROSE: (*calling*) Cory! 360

CORY: (*calling to Rose*) Mam? I'm talking to Jesse. (*Into phone.*) When she say that? (*Pause.*) Aw, you lying, man. I'm gonna tell her you said that.

ROSE: (*calling*) Cory, don't you go nowhere!

CORY: I got to go to the game, Ma! (*Into the phone.*) Yeah, hey, look, I'll talk to you later. Yeah, I'll meet you over Earl's house. Later. Bye, Ma.

Cory exits the house and starts out the yard.

ROSE: Cory, where you going off to? You got that stuff all pulled out and thrown all over your room.

CORY: (*in the yard*) I was looking for my spikes. Jesse wanted to borrow my 365 spikes.

---

spikes: Athletic shoes with sharp metal grips set into the soles.

ROSE: Get up there and get that cleaned up before your daddy get back in here.
CORY: I got to go to the game! I'll clean it up *when I get back.*

Cory exits.

ROSE: That's all he need to do is see that room all messed up.

Rose exits into the house. Troy and Bono enter the yard. Troy is dressed in clothes other than his work clothes.

BONO: He told him the same thing he told you. Take it to the union.
370 TROY: Brownie ain't got that much sense. Man wasn't thinking about nothing.
          He wait until I confront them on it . . . then he wanna come crying
          seniority. *(Calls.)* Hey, Rose!
BONO: I wish I could have seen Mr. Rand's face when he told you.
TROY: He couldn't get it out of his mouth! Liked to bit his tongue! When they
          called me down there to the Commissioner's office . . . he thought they was
          gonna fire me. Like everybody else.
BONO: I didn't think they was gonna fire you. I thought they was gonna put
          you on the warning paper.
TROY: Hey, Rose! *(To Bono.)* Yeah, Mr. Rand like to bit his tongue.

Troy breaks the seal on the bottle, takes a drink, and hands it to Bono.

375 BONO: I see you run right down to Taylors' and told that Alberta gal.
TROY: *(calling)* Hey, Rose! *(To Bono.)* I told everybody. Hey, Rose! I went
          down there to cash my check.
ROSE: *(entering from the house)* Hush all that hollering, man! I know you out
          here. What they say down there at the Commissioner's office?
TROY: You supposed to come when I call you, woman. Bono'll tell you that.
          (To Bono.) Don't Lucille come when you call her?
ROSE: Man, hush your mouth, I ain't no dog . . . talk about "come when you
          call me."
380 TROY: *(puts his arm around Rose)* You hear this, Bono? I had me an old dog
          used to get uppity like that. You say, "C'mere, Blue!" . . . and he just lay
          there and look at you. End up getting a stick and chasing him away trying
          to make him come.
ROSE: I ain't studying you and your dog. I remember you used to sing that old
          song.
TROY: *(he sings)*
                    Hear it ring! Hear it ring!
                    I had a dog his name was Blue.
ROSE: Don't nobody wanna hear you sing that old song.
TROY: *(sings)*
                    You know Blue was mighty true.
385 ROSE: Used to have Cory running around here singing that song.
BONO: Hell, I remember that song myself.
TROY: *(sings)*
                    You know Blue was a good old dog.
                    Blue treed a possum in a hollow log.

That was my daddy's song. My daddy made up that song.

ROSE: I don't care who made it up. Don't nobody wanna hear you sing it.

TROY: *(makes a song like calling a dog)* Come here, woman.

ROSE: You come in here carrying on, I reckon they ain't fired you. What they   390
say down there at the Commissioner's office?

TROY: Look here, Rose . . . Mr. Rand called me into his office today when I got
back from talking to them people down there . . . it come from up top . . .
he called me in and told me they was making me a driver.

ROSE: Troy, you kidding!

TROY: No I ain't. Ask Bono.

ROSE: Well, that's great, Troy. Now you don't have to hassle them people no
more.

Lyons enters from the street.

TROY: Aw hell, I wasn't looking to see you today. I thought you was in jail. Got   395
it all over the front page of the *Courier* about them raiding Sefus's place . . .
where you be hanging out with all them thugs.

LYONS: Hey, Pop . . . that ain't got nothing to do with me. I don't go down
there gambling. I go down there to sit in with the band. I ain't got nothing
to do with the gambling part. They got some good music down there.

TROY: They got some rogues . . . is what they got.

LYONS: How you been, Mr. Bono? Hi, Rose.

BONO: I see where you playing down at the Crawford Grill tonight.

ROSE: How come you ain't brought Bonnie like I told you? You should have   400
brought Bonnie with you, she ain't been over in a month of Sundays.

LYONS: I was just in the neighborhood . . . thought I'd stop by.

TROY: Here he come . . .

BONO: Your daddy got a promotion on the rubbish. He's gonna be the first colored driver. Ain't got to do nothing but sit up there and read the paper like
them white fellows.

LYONS: Hey, Pop . . . if you knew how to read you'd be all right.

BONO: Naw . . . naw . . . you mean if the nigger knew how to *drive* he'd be all   405
right. Been fighting with them people about driving and ain't even got a
license. Mr. Rand know you ain't got no driver's license?

TROY: Driving ain't nothing. All you do is point the truck where you want it
to go. Driving ain't nothing.

BONO: Do Mr. Rand know you ain't got no driver's license? That's what I'm
talking about. I ain't asked if driving was easy. I asked if Mr. Rand know you
ain't got no driver's license.

TROY: He ain't got to know. The man ain't got to know my business. Time he
find out, I have two or three driver's licenses.

LYONS: *(going into his pocket)* Say, look here, Pop . . .

TROY: I knew it was coming. Didn't I tell you, Bono? I know what kind of   410
"Look here, Pop" that was. The nigger fixing to ask me for some money. It's
Friday night. It's my payday. All them rogues down there on the avenue . . .
the ones that ain't in jail . . . and Lyons is hopping in his shoes to get down
there with them.

LYONS: See, Pop . . . if you give somebody else a chance to talk sometimes, you'd see that I was fixing to pay you back your ten dollars like I told you. Here . . . I told you I'd pay you when Bonnie got paid.

TROY: Naw . . . you go ahead and keep that ten dollars. Put it in the bank. The next time you feel like you wanna come by here and ask me for something . . . you go on down there and get that.

LYONS: Here's your ten dollars, Pop. I told you I don't want you to give me nothing. I just wanted to borrow ten dollars.

TROY: Naw . . . you go on and keep that for the next time you want to ask me.

415   **LYONS:** Come on, Pop . . . here go your ten dollars.

ROSE: Why don't you go on and let the boy pay you back, Troy?

LYONS: Here you go, Rose. If you don't take it I'm gonna have to hear about it for the next six months. (*He hands her the money.*)

ROSE: You can hand yours over here too, Troy.

TROY: You see this, Bono. You see how they do me.

420   **BONO:** Yeah, Lucille do me the same way.

Gabriel is heard singing offstage. He enters.

GABRIEL: Better get ready for the Judgment! Better get ready for . . . Hey! . . . Hey! . . . There's Troy's boy!

LYONS: How are you doing, Uncle Gabe?

GABRIEL: Lyons . . . The King of the Jungle! Rose . . . hey, Rose. Got a flower for you. (*He takes a rose from his pocket.*) Picked it myself. That's the same rose like you is!

ROSE: That's right nice of you, Gabe.

425   **LYONS:** What you been doing, Uncle Gabe?

GABRIEL: Oh, I been chasing hellhounds and waiting on the time to tell St. Peter to open the gates.

LYONS: You been chasing hellhounds, huh? Well . . . you doing the right thing, Uncle Gabe. Somebody got to chase them.

GABRIEL: Oh, yeah . . . I know it. The devil's strong. The devil ain't no pushover. Hellhounds snipping at everybody's heels. But I got my trumpet waiting on the judgment time.

LYONS: Waiting on the Battle of Armageddon, huh?

430   **GABRIEL:** Ain't gonna be too much of a battle when God get to waving that Judgment sword. But the people's gonna have a hell of a time trying to get into heaven if them gates ain't open.

LYONS: (*putting his arm around Gabriel*) You hear this, Pop. Uncle Gabe, you all right!

GABRIEL: (*laughing with Lyons*) Lyons! King of the Jungle.

ROSE: You gonna stay for supper, Gabe? Want me to fix you a plate?

GABRIEL: I'll take a sandwich, Rose. Don't want no plate. Just wanna eat with my hands. I'll take a sandwich.

435   **ROSE:** How about you, Lyons? You staying? Got some short ribs cooking.

LYONS: Naw, I won't eat nothing till after we finished playing. (*Pause.*) You ought to come down and listen to me play, Pop.

TROY: I don't like that Chinese music. All that noise.

ROSE: Go on in the house and wash up, Gabe . . . I'll fix you a sandwich.

GABRIEL: *(to Lyons, as he exits)* Troy's mad at me.

LYONS: What you mad at Uncle Gabe for, Pop?   440

ROSE: He thinks Troy's mad at him cause he moved over to Miss Pearl's.

TROY: I ain't mad at the man. He can live where he want to live at.

LYONS: What he move over there for? Miss Pearl don't like nobody.

ROSE: She don't mind him none. She treats him real nice. She just don't allow all that singing.

TROY: She don't mind that rent he be paying . . . that's what she don't mind.   445

ROSE: Troy, I ain't going through that with you no more. He's over there cause he want to have his own place. He can come and go as he please.

TROY: Hell, he could come and go as he please here. I wasn't stopping him. I ain't put no rules on him.

ROSE: It ain't the same thing, Troy. And you know it.

Gabriel comes to the door.

Now, that's the last I wanna hear about that. I don't wanna hear nothing else about Gabe and Miss Pearl. And next week . . .

GABRIEL: I'm ready for my sandwich, Rose.

ROSE: And next week . . . when that recruiter come from that school . . . I   450
want you to sign that paper and go on and let Cory play football. Then that'll be the last I have to hear about that.

TROY: *(to Rose as she exits into the house)* I ain't thinking about Cory nothing.

LYONS: What . . . Cory got recruited? What school he going to?

TROY: That boy walking around here smelling his piss . . . thinking he's grown. Thinking he's gonna do what he want, irrespective of what I say. Look here, Bono . . . I left the Commissioner's office and went down to the A&P . . . that boy ain't working down there. He lying to me. Telling me he got his job back . . . telling me he working weekends . . . telling me he working after school . . . Mr. Stawicki tell me he ain't working down there at all!

LYONS: Cory just growing up. He's just busting at the seams trying to fill out your shoes.

TROY: I don't care what he's doing. When he get to the point where he wanna   455
disobey me . . . then it's time for him to move on. Bono'll tell you that. I bet he ain't never disobeyed his daddy without paying the consequences.

BONO: I ain't never had a chance. My daddy came on through . . . but I ain't never knew him to see him . . . or what he had on his mind or where he went. Just moving on through. Searching out the New Land. That's what the old folks used to call it. See a fellow moving around from place to place . . . woman to woman . . . called it searching out the New Land. I can't say if he ever found it. I come along, didn't want no kids. Didn't know if I was gonna be in one place long enough to fix on them right as their daddy. I figured I was going searching too. As it turned out I been hooked up with Lucille near about as long as your daddy been with Rose. Going on sixteen years.

TROY: Sometimes I wish I hadn't known my daddy. He ain't cared nothing about no kids. A kid to him wasn't nothing. All he wanted was for you to learn how to walk so he could start you to working. When it come time for eating . . . he ate first. If there was anything left over, that's what you got. Man would sit down and eat two chickens and give you the wing.

LYONS: You ought to stop that, Pop. Everybody feed their kids. No matter how hard times is . . . everybody care about their kids. Make sure they have something to eat.

TROY: The only thing my daddy cared about was getting them bales of cotton in to Mr. Lubin. That's the only thing that mattered to him. Sometimes I used to wonder why he was living. Wonder why the devil hadn't come and got him. "Get them bales of cotton in to Mr. Lubin" and find out he owe him money . . .

460   LYONS: He should have just went on and left when he saw he couldn't get nowhere. That's what I would have done.

TROY: How he gonna leave with eleven kids? And where he gonna go? He ain't knew how to do nothing but farm. No, he was trapped and I think he knew it. But I'll say this for him . . . he felt a responsibility toward us. Maybe he ain't treated us the way I felt he should have . . . but without that responsibility he could have walked off and left us . . . made his own way.

BONO: A lot of them did. Back in those days what you talking about . . . they walk out their front door and just take on down one road or another and keep on walking.

LYONS: There you go? That's what I'm talking about.

BONO: Just keep on walking till you come to something else. Ain't you never heard of nobody having the walking blues? Well, that's what you call it when you just take off like that.

465   TROY: My daddy ain't had them walking blues! What you talking about? He stayed right there with his family. But he was just as evil as he could be. My mama couldn't stand him. Couldn't stand that evilness. She run off when I was about eight. She sneaked off one night after he had gone to sleep. Told me she was coming back for me. I ain't never seen her no more. All his women run off and left him. He wasn't good for nobody.

When my turn come to head out, I was fourteen and got to sniffing around Joe Canewell's daughter. Had us an old mule we called Greyboy. My daddy sent me out to do some plowing and tied up Greyboy and went to fooling around with Joe Canewell's daughter. We done found us a nice little spot, got real cozy with each other. She about thirteen and we done figured we was grown anyway . . . so we down there enjoying ourselves . . . ain't thinking about nothing. We didn't know Greyboy had got loose and wandered back to the house and my daddy was looking for me. We down there by the creek enjoying ourselves when my daddy come up on us. Surprised us. He had them leather straps off the mule and commenced to whupping me like there was no tomorrow. I jumped up, mad and embarrassed. I was scared of my daddy. When he commenced to whupping on me . . . quite naturally I run to get out of the way. (*Pause.*) Now I thought he was mad 'cause I ain't done my work. But I see where he was chasing me off so he could have that gal for himself. When I see what the matter of it was, I lost all fear of my daddy. Right there is where I become a man . . . at fourteen years of age. (*Pause.*) Now it was my turn to run him off. I picked up them same reins that he had used on me. I picked up them reins and commenced to whupping on him. The gal jumped up and run off . . . and when my daddy turned to face me, I could see why the devil had never come to get him . . . cause he was the devil himself. I don't know what happened. When I woke up, I was laying right there by the creek, and Blue . . . this old dog we had . . . was licking my face. I thought I was blind. I couldn't see nothing. Both my eyes were swollen shut. I laid there and cried. I didn't know what I was gonna do. The only thing I knew was the time had come for me to leave my daddy's house. And right there the world suddenly got big. And it was a long time before I could cut it down to where I could handle it.

Part of that cutting down was when I got to the place where I could feel him kicking in my blood and knew that the only thing that separated us was the matter of a few years.

Gabriel enters from the house with a sandwich.

LYONS: What you got there, Uncle Gabe?

GABRIEL: Got me a ham sandwich. Rose gave me a ham sandwich.

TROY: I don't know what happened to him. I done lost touch with everybody except Gabriel. But I hope he's dead. I hope he found some peace.

LYONS: That's a heavy story, Pop. I didn't know you left home when you was fourteen.

TROY: And didn't know nothing. The only part of the world I knew was the forty-two acres of Mr. Lubin's land. That's all I knew about life.   470

LYONS: Fourteen's kinda young to be out on your own. (*Phone rings.*) I don't even think I was ready to be out on my own at fourteen. I don't know what I would have done.

TROY: I got up from the creek and walked on down to Mobile.° I was through with farming. Figured I could do better in the city. So I walked the two hundred miles to Mobile.

LYONS: Wait a minute . . . you ain't walked no two hundred miles, Pop. Ain't nobody gonna walk no two hundred miles. You talking about some walking there.

BONO: That's the only way you got anywhere back in them days.

LYONS: Shhh. Damn if I wouldn't have hitched a ride with somebody!   475

TROY: Who you gonna hitch it with? They ain't got no cars and things like they got now. We talking about 1918.

ROSE: (*entering*) What you all out here getting into?

Mobile: City and seaport in southwestern Alabama.

TROY: *(to Rose)* I'm telling Lyons how good he got it. He don't know nothing about this I'm talking.

ROSE: Lyons, that was Bonnie on the phone. She say you supposed to pick her up.

480 LYONS: Yeah, okay, Rose.

TROY: I walked on down to Mobile and hitched up with some of them fellows that was heading this way. Got up here and found out . . . not only couldn't you get a job . . . you couldn't find no place to live. I thought I was in freedom. Shhh. Colored folks living down there on the riverbanks in whatever kind of shelter they could find for themselves. Right down there under the Brady Street Bridge. Living in shacks made of sticks and tarpaper. Messed around there and went from bad to worse. Started stealing. First it was food. Then I figured, hell, if I steal money I can buy me some food. Buy me some shoes too! One thing led to another. Met your mama. I was young and anxious to be a man. Met your mama and had you. What I do that for? Now I got to worry about feeding you and her. Got to steal three times as much. Went out one day looking for somebody to rob . . . that's what I was, a robber. I'll tell you the truth. I'm ashamed of it today. But it's the truth. Went to rob this fellow . . . pulled out my knife . . . and he pulled out a gun. Shot me in the chest. I felt just like somebody had taken a hot branding iron and laid it on me. When he shot me I jumped at him with my knife. They told me I killed him and they put me in the penitentiary and locked me up for fifteen years. That's where I met Bono. That's where I learned how to play baseball. Got out that place and your mama had taken you and went on to make life without me. Fifteen years was a long time for her to wait. But that fifteen years cured me of that robbing stuff. Rose'll tell you. She asked me when I met her if I had gotten all that foolishness out of my system. And I told her, "Baby, it's you and baseball all what count with me." You hear me, Bono? I meant it too. She say, "Which one comes first?" I told her, "Baby, ain't no doubt it's baseball . . . but you stick and get old with me and we'll both outlive this baseball." Am I right, Rose? And it's true.

ROSE: Man, hush your mouth. You ain't said no such thing. Talking about "Baby, you know you'll always be number one with me." That's what you was talking.

TROY: You hear that, Bono. That's why I love her.

BONO: Rose'll keep you straight. You get off the track, she'll straighten you up.

485 ROSE: Lyons, you better get on up and get Bonnie. She waiting on you.

LYONS: *(gets up to go)* Hey, Pop, why don't you come on down to the Grill and hear me play

TROY: I ain't going down there. I'm too old to be sitting around in them clubs.

BONO: You got to be good to play down at the Grill.

LYONS: Come on, Pop . . .

490 TROY: I got to get up in the morning.

LYONS: You ain't got to stay long.

TROY: Naw, I'm gonna get my supper and go on to bed.

LYONS: Well, I got to go. I'll see you again.

TROY: Don't you come around my house on my payday.

ROSE: Pick up the phone and let somebody know you coming. And bring   495
Bonnie with you. You know I'm always glad to see her.

LYONS: Yeah, I'll do that, Rose. You take care now. See you, Pop. See you,
Mr. Bono. See you, Uncle Gabe.

GABRIEL: Lyons! King of the Jungle!

Lyons exits.

TROY: Is supper ready, woman? Me and you got some business to take care of.
I'm gonna tear it up too.

ROSE: Troy, I done told you now!

TROY: (*puts his arm around Bono*) Aw hell, woman . . . this is Bono. Bono like   500
family. I done known this nigger since . . . how long I done know you?

BONO: It's been a long time.

TROY: I done know this nigger since Skippy was a pup. Me and him done been
through some times.

BONO: You sure right about that.

TROY: Hell, I done know him longer than I known you. And we still standing
shoulder to shoulder. Hey, look here, Bono . . . a man can't ask for no more
than that. (*Drinks to him.*) I love you, nigger.

BONO: Hell, I love you too . . . I got to get home see my woman. You got yours   505
in hand. I got to go get mine.

*Bono starts to exit as Cory enters the yard, dressed in his football uniform. He gives Troy
a hard, uncompromising look.*

CORY: What you do that for, Pop?

He throws his helmet down in the direction of Troy.

ROSE: What's the matter? Cory . . . what's the matter?

CORY: Papa done went up to the school and told Coach Zellman I can't play
football no more. Wouldn't even let me play the game. Told him to tell the
recruiter not to come.

ROSE: Troy . . .

TROY: What you Troying me for. Yeah, I did it. And the boy know why I did it.   510

CORY: Why you wanna do that to me? That was the one chance I had.

ROSE: Ain't nothing wrong with Cory playing football, Troy.

TROY: The boy lied to me. I told the nigger if he wanna play football . . . to
keep up his chores and hold down that job at the A&P. That was the
conditions. Stopped down there to see Mr. Stawicki . . .

CORY: I can't work after school during the football season, Pop! I tried to tell
you that Mr. Stawicki's holding my job for me. You don't never want to
listen to nobody. And then you wanna go and do this to me!

TROY: I ain't done nothing to you. You done it to yourself.   515

CORY: Just cause you didn't have a chance! You just scared I'm gonna be better
than you, that's all.

TROY: Come here.

ROSE: Troy . . .

Cory reluctantly crosses over to Troy.

TROY: All right! See. You done made a mistake.

520 **CORY:** I didn't even do nothing!

TROY: I'm gonna tell you what your mistake was. See . . . you swung at the ball and didn't hit it. That's strike one. See, you in the batter's box now. You swung and you missed. That's strike one. Don't you strike out!

Lights fade to black.

ACT II

SCENE 1

The following morning. Cory is at the tree hitting the ball with the bat. He tries to mimic Troy, but his swing is awkward, less sure. Rose enters from the house.

ROSE: Cory, I want you to help me with this cupboard.

CORY: I ain't quitting the team. I don't care what Poppa say.

ROSE: I'll talk to him when he gets back. He had to go see about your Uncle Gabe. The police done arrested him. Say he was disturbing the peace. He'll be back directly. Come on in here and help me clean out the top of this cupboard.

Cory exits into the house. Rose sees Troy and Bono coming down the alley.

Troy . . . what they say down there?

TROY: Ain't said nothing. I give them fifty dollars and they let him go. I'll talk to you about it. Where's Cory?

5 **ROSE:** He's in there helping me clean out these cupboards.

TROY: Tell him to get his butt out here.

Troy and Bono go over to the pile of wood. Bono picks up the saw and begins sawing.

TROY: *(to Bono)* All they want is the money. That makes six or seven times I done went down there and got him. See me coming they stick out their *hands.*

BONO: Yeah. I know what you mean. That's all they care about . . . that money. They don't care about what's right. *(Pause.)* Nigger, why you got to go and get some hard wood? You ain't doing nothing but building a little old fence. Get you some soft pine wood. That's all you need.

TROY: I know what I'm doing. This is outside wood. You put pine wood inside the house. Pine wood is inside wood. This here is outside wood. Now you tell me where the fence is gonna be?

10 **BONO:** You don't need this wood. You can put it up with pine wood and it'll stand as long as you gonna be here looking at it.

TROY: How you know how long I'm gonna be here, nigger? Hell, I might just live forever. Live longer than old man Horsely.

BONO: That's what Magee used to say.

TROY: Magee's a damn fool. Now you tell me who you ever heard of gonna pull their own teeth with a pair of rusty pliers.

BONO: The old folks . . . my granddaddy used to pull his teeth with pliers. They ain't had no dentists for the colored folks back then.

TROY: Get clean pliers! You understand? Clean pliers! Sterilize them! Besides 15 we ain't living back then. All Magee had to do was walk over to Doc Goldblum's.

BONO: I see where you and that Tallahassee gal . . . that Alberta . . . I see where you all done got tight.

TROY: What you mean "got tight"?

BONO: I see where you be laughing and joking with her all the time.

TROY: I laughs and jokes with all of them, Bono. You know me.

BONO: That ain't the kind of laughing and joking I'm talking about. 20

Cory enters from the house.

CORY: How you doing, Mr. Bono?

TROY: Cory? Get that saw from Bono and cut some wood. He talking about the wood's too hard to cut. Stand back there, Jim, and let that young boy show you how it's done.

BONO: He's sure welcome to it.

Cory takes the saw and begins to cut the wood.

Whew-e-e! Look at that. Big old strong boy. Look like Joe Louis.° Hell, must be getting old the way I'm watching that boy whip through that wood.

CORY: I don't see why Mama want a fence around the yard noways.

TROY: Damn if I know either. What the hell she keeping out with it? She ain't 25 got nothing nobody want.

BONO: Some people build fences to keep people out . . . and other people build fences to keep people in. Rose wants to hold on to you all. She loves you.

TROY: Hell, nigger, I don't need nobody to tell me my wife loves me. Cory . . . go on in the house and see if you can find that other saw.

CORY: Where's it at?

TROY: I said find it! Look for it till you find it!

Cory exits into the house.

What's that supposed to mean? Wanna keep us in?

BONO: Troy . . . I done known you seem like damn near my whole life. You and 30 Rose both. I done know both of you all for a long time. I remember when you met Rose. When you was hitting them baseballs out the park. A lot of them gals was after you then. You had the pick of the litter. When you picked Rose, I was happy for you. That was the first time I knew you had any sense. I said . . . My man Troy knows what he's doing . . . I'm gonna follow this nigger . . . he might take me somewhere. I been following you too. I done learned a whole heap of things about life watching you. I done

---

Joe Louis: Joseph Louis Barrow (1914–1981), American boxer known as the "Brown Bomber." In 1937, he became the youngest boxer ever to win the Heavyweight Championship, which he defended twenty-five times; he retired undefeated in 1949.

learned how to tell where the shit lies. How to tell it from the alfalfa. You done learned me a lot of things. You showed me how to not make the same mistakes . . . to take life as it comes along and keep putting one foot in front of the other. (*Pause.*) Rose a good woman, Troy.

TROY: Hell, nigger, I know she a good woman. I been married to her for eighteen years. What you got on your mind, Bono?

BONO: I just say she a good woman. Just like I say anything. I ain't got to have nothing on my mind.

TROY: You just gonna say she a good woman and leave it hanging out there like that? Why you telling me she a good woman?

BONO: She loves you, Troy. Rose loves you.

35 TROY: You saying I don't measure up. That's what you trying to say. I don't measure up 'cause I'm seeing this other gal. I know what you trying to say.

BONO: I know what Rose means to you, Troy. I'm just trying to say I don't want to see you mess up.

TROY: Yeah, I appreciate that, Bono. If you was messing around on Lucille I'd be telling you the same thing.

BONO: Well, that's all I got to say. I just say that because I love you both.

TROY: Hell, you know me . . . I wasn't out there looking for nothing. You can't find a better woman than Rose. I know that. But seems like this woman just stuck onto me where I can't shake her loose. I done wrestled with it, tried to throw her off me . . . but she just stuck on tighter. Now she's stuck on for good.

40 BONO: You's in control . . . that's what you tell me all the time. You responsible for what you do.

TROY: I ain't ducking the responsibility of it. As long as it sets right in my heart . . . then I'm okay. 'Cause that's all I listen to. It'll tell me right from wrong every time. And I ain't talking about doing Rose no bad turn. I love Rose. She done carried me a long ways and I love and respect her for that.

BONO: I know you do. That's why I don't want to see you hurt her. But what you gonna do when she find out? What you got then? If you try and juggle both of them . . . sooner or later you gonna drop one of them. That's common sense.

TROY: Yeah, I hear what you saying, Bono. I been trying to figure a way to work it out.

BONO: Work it out right, Troy. I don't want to be getting all up between you and Rose's business . . . but work it so it come out right.

45 TROY: Ah hell, I get all up between you and Lucille's business. When you gonna get that woman that refrigerator she been wanting? Don't tell me you ain't got no money now. I know who your banker is. Mellon don't need that money bad as Lucille want that refrigerator. I'll tell you that.

BONO: Tell you what I'll do . . . when you finish building this fence for Rose . . . I'll buy Lucille that refrigerator.

TROY: You done stuck your foot in your mouth now!

Troy grabs up a board and begins to saw. Bono starts to walk out the yard.

Hey, nigger . . . where you going?

BONO: I'm going home. I know you don't expect me to help you now. I'm protecting my money. I wanna see you put that fence up by yourself. That's what I want to see. You'll be here another six months without me.

TROY: Nigger, you ain't right.

BONO: When it comes to my money . . . I'm right as fireworks on the Fourth   50
of July.

TROY: All right, we gonna see now. You better get out your bankbook.

Bono exits, and Troy continues to work. Rose enters from the house.

ROSE: What they say down there? What's happening with Gabe?

TROY: I went down there and got him out. Cost me fifty dollars. Say he was disturbing the peace. Judge set up a hearing for him in three weeks. Say to show cause why he shouldn't be recommitted.

ROSE: What was he doing that cause them to arrest him?

TROY: Some kids were teasing him and he run them off home. Say he was   55
howling and carrying on. Some folks seen him and called the police. That's all it was.

ROSE: Well, what's you say? What'd you tell the judge?

TROY: Told him I'd look after him. It didn't make no sense to recommit the man. He stuck out his big greasy palm and told me to give him fifty dollars and take him on home.

ROSE: Where's he at now? Where'd he go off to?

TROY: He's gone about his business. He don't need nobody to hold his hand.

ROSE: Well, I don't know. Seem like that would be the best place for him if   60
they did put him into the hospital. I know what you're gonna say. But that's what I think would be best.

TROY: The man done had his life ruined fighting for what? And they wanna take and lock him up. Let him be free. He don't bother nobody.

ROSE: Well, everybody got their own way of looking at it I guess. Come on and get your lunch. I got a bowl of lima beans and some cornbread in the oven. Come and get something to eat. Ain't no sense you fretting over Gabe.

Rose turns to go into the house.

TROY: Rose . . . got something to tell you.

ROSE: Well, come on . . . wait till I get this food on the table.

TROY: Rose!   65

She stops and turns around.

I don't know how to say this. (*Pause.*) I can't explain it none. It just sort of grows on you till it gets out of hand. It starts out like a little bush . . . and the next thing you know it's a whole forest.

ROSE: Troy . . . what is you talking about?

TROY: I'm talking, woman, let me talk. I'm trying to find a way to tell you . . . I'm gonna be a daddy. I'm gonna be somebody's daddy.

ROSE: Troy . . . you're not telling me this? You're gonna be . . . what?

TROY: Rose . . . now . . . see . . .

70   ROSE: You telling me you gonna be somebody's daddy? You telling your *wife* this?

Gabriel enters from the street. He carries a rose in his hand.

GABRIEL: Hey, Troy! Hey, Rose!

ROSE: I have to wait eighteen years to hear something like this.

GABRIEL: Hey, Rose . . . I got a flower for you. (*He hands it to her.*) That's a rose. Same rose like you is.

ROSE: Thanks, Gabe.

75   GABRIEL: Troy, you ain't mad at me is you? Them bad mens come and put me away. You ain't mad at me is you?

TROY: Naw, Gabe, I ain't mad at you.

ROSE: Eighteen years and you wanna come with this.

GABRIEL: (*takes a quarter out of his pocket*) See what I got? Got a brand new quarter.

TROY: Rose . . . it's just . . .

80   ROSE: Ain't nothing you can say, Troy. Ain't no way of explaining that.

GABRIEL: Fellow that give me this quarter had a whole mess of them. I'm gonna keep this quarter till it stop shining.

ROSE: Gabe, go on in the house there. I got some watermelon in the Frigidaire. Go on and get you a piece.

GABRIEL: Say, Rose . . . you know I was chasing hellhounds and them bad mens come and get me and take me away. Troy helped me. He come down there and told them they better let me go before he beat them up. Yeah, he did!

ROSE: You go on and get you a piece of watermelon, Gabe. Them bad mens is gone now.

85   GABRIEL: Okay, Rose . . . gonna get me some watermelon. The kind with the stripes on it.

Gabriel exits into the house.

ROSE: Why, Troy? Why? After all these years to come dragging this in to me now. It don't make no sense at your age. I could have expected this ten or fifteen years ago, but not now.

TROY: Age ain't got nothing to do with it, Rose.

ROSE: I done tried to be everything a wife should be. Everything a wife could be. Been married eighteen years and I got to live to see the day you tell me you been seeing another woman and done fathered a child by her. And you know I ain't never wanted no half nothing in my family. My whole family is half. Everybody got different fathers and mothers . . . my two sisters and my brother. Can't hardly tell who's who. Can't never sit down and talk about Papa and Mama. It's your papa and your mama and my papa and my mama . . .

TROY: Rose . . . stop it now.

90   ROSE: I ain't never wanted that for none of my children. And now you wanna drag your behind in here and tell me something like this.

Troy: You ought to know. It's time for you to know.

Rose: Well, I don't want to know, goddamn it!

Troy: I can't just make it go away. It's done now. I can't wish the circumstance of the thing away.

Rose: And you don't want to either. Maybe you want to wish me and my boy away. Maybe that's what you want? Well, you can't wish us away. I've got eighteen years of my life invested in you. You ought to have stayed upstairs in my bed where you belong.

Troy: Rose . . . now listen to me . . . we can get a handle on this thing. We can talk this out . . . come to an understanding.   95

Rose: All of a sudden it's "we." Where was "we" at when you was down there rolling around with some godforsaken woman? "We" should have come to an understanding before you started making a damn fool of your-self. You're a day late and a dollar short when it comes to an understanding with me.

Troy: It's just . . . She gives me a different idea . . . a different understanding about myself. I can step out of this house and get away from the pressures and problems . . . be a different man. I ain't got to wonder how I'm gonna pay the bills or get the roof fixed. I can just be a part of myself that I ain't never been.

Rose: What I want to know . . . is do you plan to continue seeing her. That's all you can say to me.

Troy: I can sit up in her house and laugh. Do you understand what I'm saying. I can laugh out loud . . . and it feels good. It reaches all the way down to the bottom of my shoes. (*Pause.*) Rose, I can't give that up.

Rose: Maybe you ought to go on and stay down there with her . . . if she's a   100
better woman than me.

Troy: It ain't about nobody being a better woman or nothing. Rose, you ain't the blame. A man couldn't ask for no woman to be a better wife than you've been. I'm responsible for it. I done locked myself into a pattern trying to take care of you all that I forgot about myself.

Rose: What the hell was I there for? That was my job, not some-body else's.

Troy: Rose, I done tried all my life to live decent . . . to live a clean . . . hard . . . useful life. I tried to be a good husband to you. In every way I knew how. Maybe I come into the world backwards, I don't know. But . . . you born with two strikes on you before you come to the plate. You got to guard it closely . . . always looking for the curve ball on the inside corner. You can't afford to let none get past you. You can't afford a call strike. If you go-ing down . . . you going down swinging. Everything lined up against you. What you gonna do. I fooled them, Rose. I bunted. When I found you and Cory and a halfway decent job . . . I was safe. Couldn't nothing touch me. I wasn't gonna strike out no more. I wasn't going back to the penitentiary. I wasn't gonna lay in the streets with a bottle of wine. I was safe. I had me a family. A job. I wasn't gonna get that last strike. I was on first looking for one of them boys to knock me in. To get me home.

Rose: You should have stayed in my bed, Troy.

105   **TROY:** Then when I saw that gal . . . she firmed up my backbone. And I got to thinking that if I tried . . . I just might be able to steal second. Do you understand after eighteen years I wanted to steal second.

ROSE: You should have held me tight. You should have grabbed me and held on.

TROY: I stood on first base for eighteen years and I thought . . . well, goddamn it . . . go on for it!

ROSE: We're not talking about baseball! We're talking about you going off to lay in bed with another woman . . . and then bring it home to me. That's what we're talking about. We ain't talking about no baseball.

TROY: Rose, you're not listening to me. I'm trying the best I can to explain it to you. It's not easy for me to admit that I been standing in the same place for eighteen years.

110   **ROSE:** I been standing with you! I been right here with you, Troy. I got a life too. I gave eighteen years of my life to stand in the same spot with you. Don't you think I ever wanted other things? Don't you think I had dreams and hopes? What about my life? What about me. Don't you think it ever crossed my mind to want to know other men? That I wanted to lay up somewhere and forget about my responsibilities? That I wanted someone to make me laugh so I could feel good? You not the only one who's got wants and needs. But I held on to you, Troy. I took all my feelings, my wants and needs, my dreams . . . and I buried them inside you. I planted a seed and watched and prayed over it. I planted myself inside you and waited to bloom. And it didn't take me no eighteen years to find out the soil was hard and rocky and it wasn't never gonna bloom.

But I held on to you, Troy. I held you tighter. You was my husband. I owed you everything I had. Every part of me I could find to give you. And upstairs in that room . . . with the darkness falling in on me . . . I gave everything I had to try and erase the doubt that you wasn't the finest man in the world. And wherever you was going . . . I wanted to be there with you. 'Cause you was my husband. 'Cause that's the only way I was gonna survive as your wife. You always talking about what you give . . . and what you don't have to give. But you take too. You take . . . and don't even know nobody's giving!

Rose turns to exit into the house; Troy grabs her arm.

TROY: You say I take and don't give!

ROSE: Troy! You're hurting me!

TROY: You say I take and don't give!

ROSE: Troy . . . you're hurting my arm! Let go!

115   **TROY:** I done give you everything I got. Don't you tell that lie on me.

ROSE: Troy!

TROY: Don't you tell that lie on me!

Cory enters from the house.

CORY: Mama!

ROSE: Troy. You're hurting me.
TROY: Don't you tell me about no taking and giving.   120

Cory comes up behind Troy and grabs him. Troy, surprised, is thrown off balance just as Cory throws a glancing blow that catches him on the chest and knocks him down. Troy is stunned, as is Cory.

ROSE: Troy. Troy. No!

Troy gets to his feet and starts at Cory.

    Troy . . . no. Please! Troy!

Rose pulls on Troy to hold him back. Troy stops himself.

TROY: *(to Cory)* All right. That's strike two. You stay away from around me,
    boy. Don't you strike out. You living with a full count. Don't you strike out.

Troy exits out the yard as the lights go down.

SCENE 2

It is six months later, early afternoon. Troy enters from the house and starts to exit the yard. Rose enters from the house.

ROSE: Troy, I want to talk to you.
TROY: All of a sudden, after all this time, you want to talk to me, huh? You ain't
    wanted to talk to me for months. You ain't wanted to talk to me last night.
    You ain't wanted no part of me then. What you wanna talk to me about now?
ROSE: Tomorrow's Friday.   125
TROY: I know what day tomorrow is. You think I don't know tomorrow's Fri-
    day? My whole life I ain't done nothing but look to see Friday coming and
    you got to tell me it's Friday.
ROSE: I want to know if you're coming home.
TROY: I always come home, Rose. You know that. There ain't never been a
    night I ain't come home.
ROSE: That ain't what I mean . . . and you know it. I want to know if you're
    coming straight home after work.
TROY: I figure I'd cash my check . . . hang out at Taylors' with the boys . . .   130
    maybe play a game of checkers . . .
ROSE: Troy, I can't live like this. I won't live like this. You livin' on borrowed
    time with me. It's been going on six months now you ain't been coming
    home.
TROY: I be here every Friday. Every night of the year. That's 365 days.
ROSE: I want you to come home tomorrow after work.
TROY: Rose . . . I don't mess up my pay. You know that now. I take my pay and
    I give it to you. I don't have no money but what you give me back. I just
    want to have a little time to myself . . . a little time to enjoy life.
ROSE: What about me? When's my time to enjoy life?   135
TROY: I don't know what to tell you, Rose. I'm doing the best I can.

ROSE: You ain't been home from work but time enough to change your clothes and run out . . . and you wanna call that the best you can do?

TROY: I'm going over to the hospital to see Alberta. She went into the hospital this afternoon. Look like she might have the baby early. I won't be gone long.

ROSE: Well, you ought to know. They went over to Miss Pearl's and got Gabe today. She said you told them to go ahead and lock him up.

140   TROY: I ain't said no such thing. Whoever told you that is telling a lie. Pearl ain't doing nothing but telling a big fat lie.

ROSE: She ain't had to tell me. I read it on the papers.

TROY: I ain't told them nothing of the kind.

ROSE: I saw it right there on the papers.

TROY: What it say, huh?

145   ROSE: It said you told them to take him.

TROY: Then they screwed that up, just the way they screw up everything. I ain't worried about what they got on the paper.

ROSE: Say the government send part of his check to the hospital and the other part to you.

TROY: I ain't got nothing to do with that if that's the way it works. I ain't made up the rules about how it work.

ROSE: You did Gabe just like you did Cory. You wouldn't sign the paper for Cory . . . but you signed for Gabe. You signed that paper.

The telephone is heard ringing inside the house.

150   TROY: I told you I ain't signed nothing, woman! The only thing I signed was the release form. Hell, I can't read. I don't know what they had on that paper! I ain't signed nothing about sending Gabe away.

ROSE: I said send him to the hospital . . . you said let him be free . . . now you done went down there and signed him to the hospital for half his money. You went back on yourself, Troy. You gonna have to answer for that.

TROY: See now . . . you been over there talking to Miss Pearl. She done got mad cause she ain't getting Gabe's rent money. That's all it is. She's liable to say anything.

ROSE: Troy, I seen where you signed the paper.

TROY: You ain't seen nothing I signed. What she doing got papers on my brother anyway? Miss Pearl telling a big fat lie. And I'm gonna tell her about it too! You ain't seen nothing I signed. Say . . . you ain't seen nothing I signed.

Rose exits into the house to answer the telephone. Presently she returns.

155   ROSE: Troy . . . that was the hospital. Alberta had the baby.

TROY: What she have? What is it?

ROSE: It's a girl.

TROY: I better get on down to the hospital to see her.

ROSE: Troy . . .

TROY: Rose . . . I got to go see her now. That's only right . . . what's the   160
matter . . . the baby's all right, ain't it?

ROSE: Alberta died having the baby.

TROY: Died . . . you say she's dead? Alberta's dead?

ROSE: They said they done all they could. They couldn't do nothing for her.

TROY: The baby? How's the baby?

ROSE: They say it's healthy. I wonder who's gonna bury her.   165

TROY: She had family, Rose. She wasn't living in the world by herself.

ROSE: I know she wasn't living in the world by herself.

TROY: Next thing you gonna want to know if she had any insurance.

ROSE: Troy, you ain't got to talk like that.

TROY: That's the first thing that jumped out your mouth. "Who's gonna bury   170
her?" Like I'm fixing to take on that task for myself.

ROSE: I am your wife. Don't push me away.

TROY: I ain't pushing nobody away. Just give me some space. That's all. Just
give me some room to breathe.

Rose exits into the house. Troy walks about the yard.

TROY: (*with a quiet rage that threatens to consume him*) All right . . . Mr. Death.
See now . . . I'm gonna tell you what I'm gonna do. I'm gonna take and
build me a fence around this yard. See? I'm gonna build me a fence around
what belongs to me. And then I want you to stay on the other side. See?
You stay over there until you're ready for me. Then you come on. Bring your
army. Bring your sickle. Bring your wrestling clothes. I ain't gonna fall down
on my vigilance this time. You ain't gonna sneak up on me no more. When
you ready for me . . . when the top of your list say Troy Maxson . . . that's
when you come around here. You come up and knock on the front door.
Ain't nobody else got nothing to do with this. This is between you and me.
Man to man. You stay on the other side of the fence until you ready for me.
Then you come up and knock on the front door. Anytime you want. I'll be
ready for you.

The lights go down to black.

SCENE 3

*The lights come up on the porch. It is late evening three days later. Rose sits listening to
the ball game waiting for Troy. The final out of the game is made and Rose switches off
the radio. Troy enters the yard carrying an infant wrapped in blankets. He stands back
from the house and calls.*

*Rose enters and stands on the porch. There is a long, awkward silence, the weight
of which grows heavier with each passing second.*

TROY: Rose . . . I'm standing here with my daughter in my arms. She ain't
but a wee bittie little old thing. She don't know nothing about grownups'
business. She innocent . . . and she ain't got no mama.

175 **ROSE:** What you telling me for, Troy?

She turns and exits into the house.

TROY: Well . . . I guess we'll just sit out here on the porch.

He sits down on the porch. There is an awkward indelicateness about the way he handles the baby. His largeness engulfs and seems to swallow it. He speaks loud enough for Rose to hear.

A man's got to do what's right for him. I ain't sorry for nothing I done. It felt right in my heart. (*To the baby.*) What you smiling at? Your daddy's a big man. Got these great big old hands. But sometimes he's scared. And right now your daddy's scared 'cause we sitting out here and ain't got no home. Oh, I been homeless before. I ain't had no little baby with me. But I been homeless. You just be out on the road by your lonesome and you see one of them trains coming and you just kinda go like this . . .

He sings a lullaby.

> Please, Mr. Engineer let a man ride the line
> Please, Mr. Engineer let a man ride the line
> I ain't got no ticket please let me ride the blinds

Rose enters from the house. Troy, hearing her steps behind him, stands and faces her.

She's my daughter, Rose. My own flesh and blood. I can't deny her no more than I can deny them boys. (*Pause.*) You and them boys is my family. You and them and this child is all I got in the world. So I guess what I'm saying is . . . I'd appreciate it if you'd help me take care of her.

ROSE: Okay, Troy . . . you're right. I'll take care of your baby for you . . . 'cause . . . like you say . . . she's innocent . . . and you can't visit the sins of the father upon the child. A motherless child has got a hard time. (*She takes the baby from him.*) From right now . . . this child got a mother. But you a womanless man.

Rose turns and exits into the house with the baby. Lights go down to black.

SCENE 4

It is two months later. Lyons enters from the street. He knocks on the door and calls.

LYONS: Hey, Rose! (*Pause.*) Rose!

ROSE: (*from inside the house*) Stop that yelling. You gonna wake up Raynell. I just got her to sleep.

180 **LYONS:** I just stopped by to pay Papa this twenty dollars I owe him. Where's Papa at?

ROSE: He should be here in a minute. I'm getting ready to go down to the church. Sit down and wait on him.

LYONS: I got to go pick up Bonnie over her mother's house.

ROSE: Well, sit it down there on the table. He'll get it.

LYONS: *(enters the house and sets the money on the table)* Tell Papa I said thanks. I'll see you again.

ROSE: All right, Lyons. We'll see you. 185

Lyons starts to exit as Cory enters.

CORY: Hey, Lyons.

LYONS: What's happening, Cory? Say man, I'm sorry I missed your graduation. You know I had a gig and couldn't get away. Otherwise, I would have been there, man. So what you doing?

CORY: I'm trying to find a job.

LYONS: Yeah I know how that go, man. It's rough out there. Jobs are scarce.

CORY: Yeah, I know. 190

LYONS: Look here, I got to run. Talk to Papa . . . he know some people. He'll be able to help get you a job. Talk to him . . . see what he say.

CORY: Yeah . . . all right, Lyons.

LYONS: You take care. I'll talk to you soon. We'll find some time to talk.

Lyons exits the yard. Cory wanders over to the tree, picks up the bat, and assumes a batting stance. He studies an imaginary pitcher and swings. Dissatisfied with the result, he tries again. Troy enters. They eye each other for a beat. Cory puts the bat down and exits the yard. Troy starts into the house as Rose exits with Raynell. She is carrying a cake.

TROY: I'm coming in and everybody's going out.

ROSE: I'm taking this cake down to the church for the bake sale. Lyons was by 195
to see you. He stopped by to pay you your twenty dollars. It's laying in there on the table.

TROY: *(going into his pocket)* Well . . . here go this money.

ROSE: Put it in there on the table, Troy. I'll get it.

TROY: What time you coming back?

ROSE: Ain't no use in you studying me. It don't matter what time I come back.

TROY: I just asked you a question, woman. What's the matter . . . can't I ask 200
you a question?

ROSE: Troy, I don't want to go into it. Your dinner's in there on the stove. All you got to do is heat it up. And don't you be eating the rest of them cakes in there. I'm coming back for them. We having a bake sale at the church tomorrow.

Rose exits the yard. Troy sits down on the steps, takes a pint bottle from his pocket, opens it, and drinks. He begins to sing.

TROY:

> Hear it ring! Hear it ring!
> Had an old dog his name was Blue
> You know Blue was mighty true
> You know Blue was a good old dog
> Blue treed a possum in a hollow log
> You know from that he was a good old dog

Bono enters the yard.

BONO: Hey, Troy.

TROY: Hey, what's happening, Bono?

205   **BONO:** I just thought I'd stop by to see you.

TROY: What you stop by and see me for? You ain't stopped by in a month of Sundays. Hell, I must owe you money or something.

BONO: Since you got your promotion I can't keep up with you. Used to see you every day. Now I don't even know what route you working.

TROY: They keep switching me around. Got me out in Greentree now . . . hauling white folks' garbage.

BONO: Greentree, huh? You lucky, at least you ain't got to be lifting them barrels. Damn if they ain't getting heavier. I'm gonna put in my two years and call it quits.

210   **TROY:** I'm thinking about retiring myself.

BONO: You got it easy. You can *drive* for another five years.

TROY: It ain't the same, Bono. It ain't like working the back of the truck. Ain't got nobody to talk to . . . feel like you working by yourself. Naw, I'm thinking about retiring. How's Lucille?

BONO: She all right. Her arthritis get to acting up on her sometime. Saw Rose on my way in. She going down to the church, huh?

TROY: Yeah, she took up going down there. All them preachers looking for somebody to fatten their pockets. *(Pause.)* Got some gin here.

215   **BONO:** Naw, thanks. I just stopped by to say hello.

TROY: Hell, nigger . . . you can take a drink. I ain't never known you to say no to a drink. You ain't got to work tomorrow.

BONO: I just stopped by. I'm fixing to go over to Skinner's. We got us a domino game going over his house every Friday.

TROY: Nigger, you can't play no dominoes. I used to whup you four games out of five.

BONO: Well, that learned me. I'm getting better.

220   **TROY:** Yeah? Well, that's all right.

BONO: Look here . . . I got to be getting on. Stop by sometime, huh?

TROY: Yeah, I'll do that, Bono. Lucille told Rose you bought her a new refrigerator.

BONO: Yeah, Rose told Lucille you had finally built your fence . . . so I figured we'd call it even.

TROY: I knew you would.

225   **BONO:** Yeah . . . okay. I'll be talking to you.

TROY: Yeah, take care, Bono. Good to see you. I'm gonna stop over.

BONO: Yeah. Okay, Troy.

Bono exits. Troy drinks from the bottle.

TROY:

>   Old Blue died and I dig his grave
>   Let him down with a golden chain

Every night when I hear old Blue bark
I know Blue treed a possum in Noah's Ark.
Hear it ring! Hear it ring!

Cory enters the yard. They eye each other for a beat. Troy is sitting in the middle of the steps. Cory walks over.

CORY: I got to get by.

TROY: Say what? What's you say?   230

CORY: You in my way. I got to get by.

TROY: You got to get by where? This is my house. Bought and paid for. In full. Took me fifteen years. And if you wanna go in my house and I'm sitting on the steps . . . you say excuse me. Like your mama taught you.

CORY: Come on, Pop . . . I got to get by.

Cory starts to maneuver his way past Troy. Troy grabs his leg and shoves him back.

TROY: You just gonna walk over top of me?

CORY: I live here too!   235

TROY: (*advancing toward him*) You just gonna walk over top of me in my own house?

CORY: I ain't scared of you.

TROY: I ain't asked if you was scared of me. I asked you if you was fixing to walk over top of me in my own house? That's the question. You ain't gonna say excuse me? You just gonna walk over top of me?

CORY: If you wanna put it like that.

TROY: How else am I gonna put it?   240

CORY: I was walking by you to go into the house 'cause you sitting on the steps drunk, singing to yourself. You can put it like that.

TROY: Without saying excuse me???

Cory doesn't respond.

I asked you a question. Without saying excuse me???

CORY: I ain't got to say excuse me to you. You don't count around here no more.

TROY: Oh, I see . . . I don't count around here no more. You ain't got to say excuse me to your daddy. All of a sudden you done got so grown that your daddy don't count around here no more . . . Around here in his own house and yard that he done paid for with the sweat of his brow. You done got so grown to where you gonna take over. You gonna take over my house. Is that right? You gonna wear my pants. You gonna go in there and stretch out on my bed. You ain't got to say excuse me 'cause I don't count around here no more. Is that right?

CORY: That's right. You always talking this dumb stuff. Now, why don't you just   245
get out my way?

TROY: I guess you got someplace to sleep and something to put in your belly. You got that, huh? You got that? That's what you need. You got that, huh?

CORY: You don't know what I got. You ain't got to worry about what I got.

TROY: You right! You one hundred percent right! I done spent the last seventeen years worrying about what you got. Now it's your turn, see? I'll tell you what to do. You grown . . . we done established that. You a man. Now, let's see you act like one. Turn your behind around and walk out this yard. And when you get out there in the alley . . . you can forget about this house. See? 'Cause this is my house. You go on and be a man and get your own house. You can forget about this. 'Cause this is mine. You go on and get yours 'cause I'm through with doing for you.

CORY: You talking about what you did for me . . . what'd you ever give me?

250   TROY: Them feet and bones! That pumping heart, nigger! I give you more than anybody else is ever gonna give you.

CORY: You ain't never gave me nothing! You ain't never done nothing but hold me back. Afraid I was gonna be better than you. All you ever did was try and make me scared of you. I used to tremble every time you called my name. Every time I heard your footsteps in the house. Wondering all the time . . . what's Papa gonna say if I do this? . . . What's he gonna say if I do that? . . . What's Papa gonna say if I turn on the radio? And Mama, too . . . she tries . . . but she's scared of you.

TROY: You leave your mama out of this. She ain't got nothing to do with this.

CORY: I don't know how she stand you . . . after what you did to her.

TROY: I told you to leave your mama out of this!

He advances toward Cory.

255   CORY: What you gonna do . . . give me a whupping? You can't whup me no more. You're too old. You just an old man.

TROY: (*shoves him on his shoulder*) Nigger! That's what you are. You just another nigger on the street to me!

CORY: You crazy! You know that?

TROY: Go on now! You got the devil in you. Get on away from me!

CORY: You just a crazy old man . . . talking about I got the devil in me.

260   TROY: Yeah, I'm crazy! If you don't get on the other side of that yard . . . I'm gonna show you how crazy I am! Go on . . . get the hell out of my yard.

CORY: It ain't your yard. You took Uncle Gabe's money he got from the army to buy this house and then you put him out.

TROY: (*advances on Cory*) Get your black ass out of my yard!

Troy's advance backs Cory up against the tree. Cory grabs up the bat.

CORY: I ain't going nowhere! Come on . . . put me out! I ain't scared of you.

TROY: That's my bat!

265   CORY: Come on!

TROY: Put my bat down!

CORY: Come on, put me out.

Cory swings at Troy, who backs across the yard.

What's the matter? You so bad . . . put me out!

Troy advances toward Cory.

CORY: *(backing up)* Come on! Come on!
TROY: You're gonna have to use it! You wanna draw that bat back on me . . .
you're gonna have to use it.
CORY: Come on! . . . Come on!

270

Cory swings the bat at Troy a second time. He misses. Troy continues to advance toward him.

TROY: You're gonna have to kill me! You wanna draw that bat back on me.
You're gonna have to kill me.

Cory, backed up against the tree, can go no farther. Troy taunts him. He sticks out his head and offers him a target.

Come on! Come on!

Cory is unable to swing the bat. Troy grabs it.

TROY: Then I'll show you.

Cory and Troy struggle over the bat. The struggle is fierce and fully engaged. Troy ultimately is the stronger and takes the bat away from Cory and stands over him ready to swing. He stops himself.

Go on and get away from around my house.

Cory, stung by his defeat, picks himself up, walks slowly out of the yard and up the alley.

CORY: Tell Mama I'll be back for my things.
TROY: They'll be on the other side of that fence.

Cory exits.

TROY: I can't taste nothing. Helluljah! I can't taste nothing no more. *(Troy as-*
sumes a batting posture and begins to taunt Death, the fastball on the outside corner.) Come on! It's between you and me now! Come on! Anytime you
want! Come on! I be ready for you . . . but I ain't gonna be easy.

275

The lights go down on the scene.

SCENE 5

The time is 1965. The lights come up in the yard. It is the morning of Troy's funeral. A funeral plaque with a light hangs beside the door. There is a small garden plot off to the side. There is noise and activity in the house as Rose, Gabriel, and Bono have gathered. The door opens and Raynell, seven years old, enters dressed in a flannel nightgown. She crosses to the garden and pokes around with a stick. Rose calls from the house.

ROSE: Raynell!
RAYNELL: Mam?

ROSE: What you doing out there?
RAYNELL: Nothing.

Rose comes to the door.

280 ROSE: Girl, get in here and get dressed. What you doing?
RAYNELL: Seeing if my garden growed.
ROSE: I told you it ain't gonna grow overnight. You got to wait.
RAYNELL: It don't look like it never gonna grow. Dag!
ROSE: I told you a watched pot never boils. Get in here and get dressed.
285 RAYNELL: This ain't even no pot, Mama.
ROSE: You just have to give it a chance. It'll grow. Now you come on and do
what I told you. We got to be getting ready. This ain't no morning to be
playing around. You hear me?
RAYNELL: Yes, mam.

Rose exits into the house. Raynell continues to poke at her garden with a stick. Cory enters. He is dressed in a Marine corporal's uniform, and carries a duffel bag. His posture is that of a military man, and his speech has a clipped sternness.

CORY: *(to Raynell)* Hi. *(Pause.)* I bet your name is Raynell.
RAYNELL: Uh huh.
290 CORY: Is your mama home?

Raynell runs up on the porch and calls through the screen door.

RAYNELL: Mama . . . there's some man out here. Mama?

Rose comes to the door.

ROSE: Cory? Lord have mercy! Look here, you all!

Rose and Cory embrace in a tearful reunion as Bono and Lyons enter from the house dressed in funeral clothes.

BONO: Aw, looka here . . .
ROSE: Done got all grown up!
295 CORY: Don't cry, Mama. What you crying about?
ROSE: I'm just so glad you made it.
CORY: Hey Lyons. How you doing, Mr. Bono.

Lyons goes to embrace Cory.

LYONS: Look at you, man. Look at you. Don't he look good, Rose. Got them
Corporal stripes.
ROSE: What took you so long?
300 CORY: You know how the Marines are, Mama. They got to get all their
paperwork straight before they let you do anything.
ROSE: Well, I'm sure glad you made it. They let Lyons come. Your Uncle
Gabe's still in the hospital. They don't know if they gonna let him out or
not. I just talked to them a little while ago.
LYONS: A Corporal in the United States Marines.

BONO: Your daddy knew you had it in you. He used to tell me all the time.

LYONS: Don't he look good, Mr. Bono?

BONO: Yeah, he remind me of Troy when I first met him. (*Pause.*) Say, Rose, Lucille's down at the church with the choir. I'm gonna go down and get the pallbearers lined up. I'll be back to get you all.

ROSE: Thanks, Jim.

CORY: See you, Mr. Bono.

LYONS: (*with his arm around Raynell*) Cory . . . look at Raynell. Ain't she precious? She gonna break a whole lot of hearts.

ROSE: Raynell, come and say hello to your brother. This is your brother, Cory. You remember Cory.

RAYNELL: No, Mam.

CORY: She don't remember me, Mama.

ROSE: Well, we talk about you. She heard us talk about you. (*To Raynell.*) This is your brother, Cory. Come on and say hello.

RAYNELL: Hi.

CORY: Hi. So you're Raynell. Mama told me a lot about you.

ROSE: You all come on into the house and let me fix you some breakfast. Keep up your strength.

CORY: I ain't hungry, Mama.

LYONS: You can fix me something, Rose. I'll be in there in a minute.

ROSE: Cory, you sure you don't want nothing? I know they ain't feeding you right.

CORY: No, Mama . . . thanks. I don't feel like eating. I'll get something later.

ROSE: Raynell . . . get on upstairs and get that dress on like I told you.

Rose and Raynell exit into the house.

LYONS: So . . . I hear you thinking about getting married.

CORY: Yeah, I done found the right one, Lyons. It's about time.

LYONS: Me and Bonnie been split up about four years now. About the time Papa retired. I guess she just got tired of all them changes I was putting her through. (*Pause.*) I always knew you was gonna make something out yourself. Your head was always in the right direction. So . . . you gonna stay in . . . make it a career . . . put in your twenty years?

CORY: I don't know. I got six already, I think that's enough.

LYONS: Stick with Uncle Sam and retire early. Ain't nothing out here. I guess Rose told you what happened with me. They got me down the workhouse. I thought I was being slick cashing other people's checks.

CORY: How much time you doing?

LYONS: They give me three years. I got that beat now. I ain't got but nine more months. It ain't so bad. You learn to deal with it like anything else. You got to take the crookeds with the straights. That's what Papa used to say. He used to say that when he struck out. I seen him strike out three times in a row . . . and the next time up he hit the ball over the grandstand. Right out there in Homestead Field. He wasn't satisfied hitting in the seats . . . he want to hit it over everything! After the game he had two hundred people standing around waiting to shake his hand. You got to take the crookeds with the straights. Yeah, Papa was something else.

Cory: You still playing?

Lyons: Cory . . . you know I'm gonna do that. There's some fellows down there we got us a band . . . we gonna try and stay together when we get out . . . but yeah, I'm still playing. It still helps me to get out of bed in the morning. As long as it do that I'm gonna be right there playing and trying to make some sense out of it.

330 **Rose:** *(calling)* Lyons, I got these eggs in the pan.

Lyons: Let me go on and get these eggs, man. Get ready to go bury Papa. *(Pause.)* How you doing? You doing all right?

Cory nods. Lyons touches him on the shoulder and they share a moment of silent grief. Lyons exits into the house. Cory wanders about the yard. Raynell enters.

Raynell: Hi.

Cory: Hi.

Raynell: Did you used to sleep in my room?

335 **Cory:** Yeah . . . that used to be my room.

Raynell: That's what Papa call it. "Cory's room." It got your football in the closet.

Rose comes to the door.

Rose: Raynell, get in there and get them good shoes on.

Raynell: Mama, can't I wear these? Them other ones hurt my feet.

Rose: Well, they just gonna have to hurt your feet for a while. You ain't said they hurt your feet when you went down to the store and got them.

340 **Raynell:** They didn't hurt then. My feet done got bigger.

Rose: Don't you give me no backtalk now. You get in there and get them shoes on.

Raynell exits into the house.

Ain't too much changed. He still got that piece of rag tied to that tree. He was out here swinging that bat. I was just ready to go back in the house. He swung that bat and then he just fell over. Seem like he swung it and stood there with this grin on his face . . . and then he just fell over. They carried him on down to the hospital, but I knew there wasn't no need . . . why don't you come on in the house?

Cory: Mama . . . I got something to tell you. I don't know how to tell you this . . . but I've got to tell you . . . I'm not going to Papa's funeral.

Rose: Boy, hush your mouth. That's your daddy you talking about. I don't want hear that kind of talk this morning. I done raised you to come to this? You standing there all healthy and grown talking about you ain't going to your daddy's funeral?

Cory: Mama . . . listen . . .

345 **Rose:** I don't want to hear it, Cory. You just get that thought out of your head.

Cory: I can't drag Papa with me everywhere I go. I've got to say no to him. One time in my life I've got to say no.

ROSE: Don't nobody have to listen to nothing like that. I know you and your daddy ain't seen eye to eye, but I ain't got to listen to that kind of talk this morning. Whatever was between you and your daddy . . . the time has come to put it aside. Just take it and set it over there on the shelf and forget about it. Disrespecting your daddy ain't gonna make you a man, Cory. You got to find a way to come to that on your own. Not going to your daddy's funeral ain't gonna make you a man.

CORY: The whole time I was growing up . . . living in his house . . . Papa was like a shadow that followed you everywhere. It weighed on you and sunk into your flesh. It would wrap around you and lay there until you couldn't tell which one was you anymore. That shadow digging in your flesh. Trying to crawl in. Trying to live through you. Everywhere I looked, Troy Maxson was staring back at me . . . hiding under the bed . . . in the closet. I'm just saying I've got to find a way to get rid of that shadow, Mama.

ROSE: You just like him. You got him in you good.

CORY: Don't tell me that, Mama.   350

ROSE: You Troy Maxson all over again.

CORY: I don't want to be Troy Maxson. I want to be me.

ROSE: You can't be nobody but who you are, Cory. That shadow wasn't nothing but you growing into yourself. You either got to grow into it or cut it down to fit you. But that's all you got to make life with. That's all you got to measure yourself against that world out there. Your daddy wanted you to be everything he wasn't . . . and at the same time he tried to make you into everything he was. I don't know if he was right or wrong . . . but I do know he meant to do more good than he meant to do harm. He wasn't always right. Sometimes when he touched he bruised. And sometimes when he took me in his arms he cut.

When I first met your daddy I thought . . . Here is a man I can lay down with and make a baby. That's the first thing I thought when I seen him. I was thirty years old and had done seen my share of men. But when he walked up to me and said, "I can dance a waltz that'll make you dizzy." I thought, Rose Lee, here is a man that you can open yourself up to and be filled to bursting. Here is a man that can fill all them empty spaces you been tipping around the edges of. One of them empty spaces was being somebody's mother.

I married your daddy and settled down to cooking his supper and keeping clean sheets on the bed. When your daddy walked through the house he was so big he filled it up. That was my first mistake. Not to make him leave some room for me. For my part in the matter. But at that time I wanted that. I wanted a house that I could sing in. And that's what your daddy gave me. I didn't know to keep up his strength I had to give up little pieces of mine. I did that. I took on his life as mine and mixed up the pieces so that you couldn't hardly tell which was which anymore. It was my choice. It was my life and I didn't have to live it like that. But that's what life offered me in the way of being a woman and I took it. I grabbed hold of it with both hands.

By the time Raynell came into the house, me and your daddy had done lost touch with one another. I didn't want to make my blessing off of nobody's misfortune . . . but I took on to Raynell like she was all them babies I had wanted and never had.

The phone rings.

Like I'd been blessed to relive a part of my life. And if the Lord see fit to keep up my strength . . . I'm gonna do her just like your daddy did you . . . I'm gonna give her the best of what's in me.

RAYNELL: *(entering, still with her old shoes)* Mama . . . Reverend Tollivier on the phone.

Rose exits into the house.

355   **RAYNELL:** Hi.
CORY: Hi.
RAYNELL: You in the Army or the Marines?
CORY: Marines.
RAYNELL: Papa said it was the Army. Did you know Blue?
360   **CORY:** Blue? Who's Blue?
RAYNELL: Papa's dog what he sing about all the time.
CORY: *(singing)*

> Hear it ring! Hear it ring!
> I had a dog his name was Blue
> You know Blue was mighty true
> You know Blue was a good old dog
> Blue treed a possum in a hollow log
> You know from that he was a good old dog.
> Hear it ring! Hear it ring!

Raynell joins in singing.

CORY AND RAYNELL:

> Blue treed a possum out on a limb
> Blue looked at me and I looked at him
> Grabbed that possum and put him in a sack
> Blue stayed there till I came back
> Old Blue's feets was big and round
> Never allowed a possum to touch the ground.
> Old Blue died and I dug his grave
> I dug his grave with a silver spade
> Let him down with a golden chain
> And every night I call his name
> Go on Blue, you good dog you
> Go on Blue, you good dog you

RAYNELL:

> Blue laid down and died like a man
> Blue laid down and died . . .

BOTH: 365

> Blue laid down and died like a man
> Now he's treeing possums in the Promised Land
> I'm gonna tell you this to let you know
> Blue's gone where the good dogs go
> When I hear old Blue bark
> When I hear old Blue bark
> Blue treed a possum in Noah's Ark°
> Blue treed a possum in Noah's Ark.

Rose comes to the screen door.

ROSE: Cory, we gonna be ready to go in a minute.
CORY: (*to Raynell*) You go on in the house and change them shoes like Mama
    told you so we can go to Papa's funeral.
RAYNELL: Okay, I'll be back.

*Raynell exits into the house. Cory gets up and crosses over to the tree. Rose stands in the
screen door watching him. Gabriel enters from the alley.*

GABRIEL: (*calling*) Hey, Rose!
ROSE: Gabe?   370
GABRIEL: I'm here, Rose. Hey Rose, I'm here!

Rose enters from the house.

ROSE: Lord . . . Look here, Lyons!
LYONS: See, I told you, Rose . . . I told you they'd let him come.
CORY: How you doing, Uncle Gabe?
LYONS: How you doing, Uncle Gabe?   375
GABRIEL: Hey, Rose. It's time. It's time to tell St. Peter to open the gates. Troy,
    you ready? You ready, Troy. I'm gonna tell St. Peter to open the gates. You
    get ready now.

*Gabriel, with great fanfare, braces himself to blow. The trumpet is without a mouth-
piece. He puts the end of it into his mouth and blows with great force, like a man who
has been waiting some twenty-odd years for this single moment. No sound comes out of
the trumpet. He braces himself and blows again with the same result. A third time he
blows. There is a weight of impossible description that falls away and leaves him bare and
exposed to a frightful realization. It is a trauma that a sane and normal mind would be
unable to withstand. He begins to dance. A slow, strange dance, eerie and life-giving.
A dance of atavistic signature and ritual. Lyons attempts to embrace him. Gabriel
pushes Lyons away. He begins to howl in what is an attempt at song, or perhaps a song
turning back into itself in an attempt at speech. He finishes his dance and the gates of
heaven stand open as wide as God's closet.*

    That's the way that go!

Noah's Ark: See Genesis 6.14–20.

Reading and Reacting

1. Obviously, fences are a central metaphor of the play. To what different kinds of fences does the play's title refer?

2. In what ways are the fathers and sons in this play alike? In what ways are they different? Does the play imply that sons must inevitably follow in their fathers' footsteps?

3. What purpose does the section of the stage directions entitled "The Play" (p. 1359) serve? How does it prepare readers for the events to follow?

4. What is the significance of the fact that the play is set in 1957? Given the racial climate of the country at that time, how realistic are Cory's ambitions? How reasonable are his father's criticisms?

5. In what ways has Troy's character been shaped by his contact with the white world?

6. Is Troy a tragic hero? If so, what is his flaw?

7. Which of the play's characters, if any, do you consider to be stereotypes? What comment do you think the play makes about stereotypes?

8. In what ways does the conflict between Troy and his son reflect conflicts within the African American community? Does the play suggest any possibilities for compromise?

9. Which characters do you like? Which do you dislike? Why?

10. Do you consider the message of this play to be optimistic or pessimistic? Explain.

11. JOURNAL ENTRY How would the play be different if the characters were white? What would remain the same?

12. CRITICAL PERSPECTIVE Robert Brustein, theater critic and artistic director of Harvard's American Repertory Theater, has criticized Wilson on the ground that "his recurrent theme is the familiar American charge of victimization"; in *Fences*, he argues, "Wilson's larger purpose depends on his conviction that Troy's potential was stunted not [by] 'his own behavior' but by centuries of racist oppression."

Do you agree with Brustein's characterization of Wilson's theme? Or do you think there is another theme that Brustein misses?

Related Works: "Big Black Good Man" (p. 206), "Ex-Basketball Player" (p. 684), "Yet Do I Marvel" (p. 783), "The *Chicago Defender* Sends a Man to Little Rock" (p. 856), *Death of a Salesman* (p. 1178)

WRITING SUGGESTIONS: Theme

1. In some performances of *Wit*, lighting has been used for emphasis to great advantage. In one performance, when Vivian returned to the center of the stage to deliver her monologues, the rest of the stage was bathed in darkness, and all the hospital scenes were lit with a harsh white light. Identify several scenes in this play that could benefit from creative lighting, and explain how your lighting could help to communicate various aspects of the play's theme.

2. Write an essay in which you analyze the baseball images in *Fences*. How do the references to baseball help develop the play's themes?

3. One of the themes of *Fences* is the dream a family has for its children. Compare the development of this theme in *Fences* and in another play in this book — for example, *The Cuban Swimmer* (p. 1258) or *The Glass Menagerie* (p. 1416).

4. WEB ACTIVITY The following Web site contains information about August Wilson:

http://www.humboldt.edu/~ah/wilson/reviews/index.html

From the Web page, link to the review "Theater: Family Ties in Wilson's *Fences*," where critic Frank Rich offers the following analysis:

> The struggle between father and son over conflicting visions of black identity, aspirations and values is the play's narrative fulcrum, and a paradigm of violent divisions that would later tear apart a society. As written, the conflict is also a didactic one, reminiscent of old-fashioned plays, black and white, about disputes between first-generation American parents and their rebellious children.

Write an essay exploring the struggle between father and son in *Fences*, concentrating on how the struggle is fueled by "visions of black identity" and the conflict between all "first-generation American parents and their rebellious children."

CHAPTER 32

TENNESSEE WILLIAMS'S *THE GLASS MENAGERIE:* A CASEBOOK FOR READING, RESEARCH, AND WRITING

This chapter provides all the materials you will need to begin a research project about Tennessee Williams's *The Glass Menagerie*. It includes the 1945 play *The Glass Menagerie* by Tennessee Williams; questions to stimulate discussion and writing; a collection of source materials;* a paper that shows how one student, Heather Jenkins, used the materials in this chapter in her research; and suggestions for further research on Williams.

SOURCE MATERIALS

---

* Note that some of the articles included in this Casebook do not use the parenthetical documentation style recommended by the most recent guidelines set by the Modern Language Association and explained in Chapter 34.

- Williams, Tennessee. From *Tennessee Williams: Memoirs*. New York: Doubleday, 1975. A memoir written by the playwright. . . . . (p. 1479)
- Williams, Dakin, and Shepherd Meade. From *Tennessee Williams: An Intimate Biography*. New York: Arbor House, 1983. A memoir written by the playwright's brother and a personal friend. (p. 1482)
- Evans, Jean. "Interview 1945." *New York PM* (1945). A magazine interview with Tennessee Williams conducted during the initial New York run of *The Glass Menagerie*. . . . . (p. 1483)
- King, Thomas L. From "Irony and Distance in *The Glass Menagerie*." *Educational Theatre Journal* 25.2 (May 1973): 85–94. Excerpts from an article that discusses the importance of Tom's soliloquies. . . . . (p. 1484)
- Tischler, Nancy Marie Patterson. From *Student Companion to Tennessee Williams*. Westport, CT: Greenwood, 2000. Excerpt in which the author discusses the use of symbolism and other stylistic approaches in the work of the playwright. . . . . (p. 1487)
- Stein, Roger B. From "*The Glass Menagerie* Revisited: Catastrophe without Violence." *Western Humanities Review* 18 (Spring 1964): 141–53. Excerpt in which the author discusses religious themes in *The Glass Menagerie*. . . . . (p. 1489)
- Scanlan, Tom. From *Family, Drama, and American Dreams*. New York: Greenwood, 1978. A discussion of the portrayal of family life in *The Glass Menagerie*. . . . . (p. 1491)
- Williams Tennessee. "Portrait of a Girl in Glass." *Collected Stories*. New York: New Directions, 1985. A 1943 short story that Williams later developed into *The Glass Menagerie*. . . . . (p. 1494)

Each of these sources offers insights that can help you to understand, enjoy, and write about *The Glass Menagerie*. Some offer historical perspectives; some are biographical; others discuss literary devices or offer interpretations. All were selected to help you to understand this classic American play and appreciate its characters and themes. Other kinds of sources can also enrich your understanding of Williams's accomplishments — for example, other plays by Williams, biographical data about the author, or works of imaginative literature by other writers dealing with similar themes. In addition, the following Web sites devoted to Williams can offer insights into his work.

- *The Mississippi Writer's Page — Tennessee Williams*. <http://www.olemiss.edu/depts/english/ms-writers/dir/williams_tennessee/>. The best place to get started might be this site from the Department of English at the University of Mississippi. It contains a collection of articles on Williams detailing biographical information, a comprehensive list of published titles, various awards and honors, and a selected bibliography of additional resources. It also includes information on other Mississippi authors and on the state of Mississippi.
- *Tennessee Williams Photos*. <http://www.mtsu.edu/~crharris/Tennessee_Williams_photos.html>. This is Christopher R. Harris's

photography of Tennessee Williams, depicted in black and white in several locations of New Orleans, Louisiana.

- *Online Newshour:* Streetcar Named Desire.<http://www.pbs.org/ newshour/bb/entertainment/july-dec97/streetcar_11-11a.html>. The Public Broadcasting System put together this site, celebrating the fiftieth anniversary of *A Streetcar Named Desire*. The site includes a discussion board and London Theatre Company reviews of the play.
- *Tennessee Williams, Mississippi Writer.* <http://shs.starkville.k12.ms.us/ mswm/MSWritersAndMusicians/writers/Williams.html>. The Mississippi Writers and Musicians Project of Starkville High School created this site. It cites all of Tennessee Williams's written works and contains a Williams biography and several literary reviews, one specifically of *The Glass Menagerie*.
- *Tennessee Williams.* <http://www.gatewayno.com/culture/ TWilliams.html>. This site includes a biography of Tennessee Williams and information about the themes of sexual frustration as it appears in the author's works.
- *PAL (Perspectives in American Literature): Tennessee Williams (1911–1983).* <http://www.csustan.edu/english/reuben/pal/chap8/williams.html>. This site includes an extensive bibliography of works by and about Tennessee Williams. Scroll to the bottom for an interesting "assessment" of Williams.

In preparation for writing an essay on a topic of your choice about *The Glass Menagerie*, read the play and the accompanying source materials carefully. After doing so, explore — in your journal, in group discussions, or in brainstorming notes — the possibilities suggested by the Reading and Reacting questions on pages 1467–68. Keep in mind the ideas expressed in the critical articles, memoirs, and interviews as well as those in the play itself. Your goal is to decide on a topic you can develop in a three- to six-page essay. Remember to document any words or ideas that you borrow from the play or from other sources, enclosing your borrowed words in quotation marks. (For guidelines on evaluating literary criticism, see p. 13; for guidelines on using source materials, see Chapter 38, "Writing a Research Paper.")

A complete student paper, "Laura's Gentleman Caller," based on some of the source materials in this Casebook, begins on page 1503.

TENNESSEE WILLIAMS (1911–1983) was born Thomas Lanier Williams in Columbus, Mississippi, on March 26, 1911. His father, who came from a well-to-do and well-connected Tennessee family, was a shoe salesman who was often on the road. His mother was the daughter of a minister, and her genteel ways left her ill-equipped to handle her three rowdy children, who spent more and more time with their maternal grandfather. An Episcopalian, Williams's grandfather had a stern manner and inviolable views about right and wrong. His grandson, however, did not always abide by these rules and mocked him playfully whenever he could. When Williams was eight, his family moved to St. Louis, Missouri.

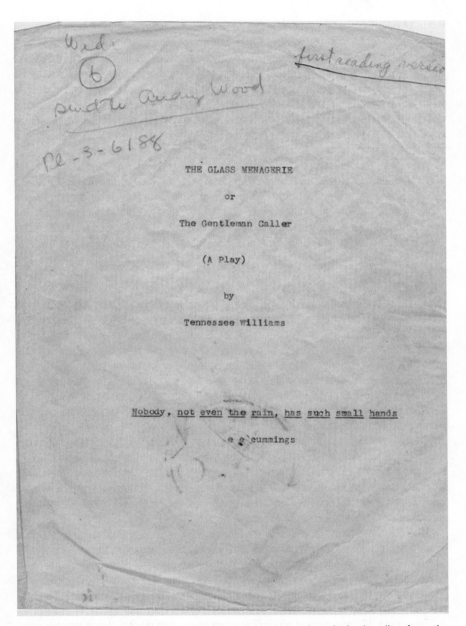

This title page, from a 1944 manuscript, includes as its epigraph the last line from the E. E. Cummings poem "somewhere i have never travelled, gladly beyond."

In Missouri, only eight years later — when he was sixteen — Williams made his first mark on the literary world by winning five dollars and placing third in a national essay contest sponsored by *Smart Set* magazine. His essay was entitled "Can a Good Wife Be a Good Sport?" After winning this award, he began to submit his writing widely. He enrolled at the University of Missouri, but he found that college did not give him enough opportunity to write, so he left and worked at his father's shoe company — and as a waiter, an elevator operator, and a theater usher — while he wrote. Hoping to learn playwriting, he eventually went back to college and graduated from the University of Iowa in 1938. A year later, he adopted his college nickname and began to publish as Tennessee Williams.

Williams's earliest staged play, *Cairo, Shanghai, Bombay,* was produced in Memphis in 1937, followed closely by *Candles to the Sun* and *The Fugitive Kind.* Williams's career rocketed, and he went on to write over fifty plays, ten works of fiction, several books of poetry, and other collections of writing, including his letters and memoirs. His most successful plays include *The Glass Menagerie* (1945), A *Streetcar Named Desire* (1947), *Cat on a Hot Tin Roof* (1955), *Night of the Iguana* (1961), and *Sweet Bird of Youth* (1959). A recently rediscovered early play, *Not about Nightingales,* was staged in New York in 1999.

The Glass Menagerie (1945), Williams's first major success, won the New York Drama Critics Circle Award, freeing Williams to write plays full-time. *The Glass Menagerie* was written partly in Provincetown, Massachusetts, the site of Susan Glaspell's theater company (Glaspell is the author of the play *Trifles,* in Chapter 31), and partly in Hollywood, where Williams was working as a screenwriter. Williams saw the play as somewhat autobiographical: he said his sister Rose had a collection of glass animals in her room in St. Louis, and he gave his own real first name to Tom, Laura's brother in the play. In the first movie version of the play, the story was altered to include a second, more promising Gentleman Caller at its conclusion, giving it a happy ending. To the end of his life, Williams strongly disliked this change.

Tennessee Williams found acclaim wherever he took his plays, from the age of thirty-four and the remarkable success of *The Glass Menagerie* until the end of his life. He received four New York Drama Critics Circle Awards, won a Pulitzer Prize for *Streetcar* in 1948, and saw both *Streetcar* and *The Glass Menagerie* made into successful Hollywood films. *Cat on a Hot Tin Roof* (for which he won his second Pulitzer), *Orpheus Descending,* and *Night of the Iguana* were also filmed.

Like *The Glass Menagerie,* Williams's other work was largely autobiographical, often drawing comparisons between his family and his characters and using the backdrops with which he was most familiar. Williams moved around a good deal — from New Orleans, to Key West, to New York City, to Provincetown. Each locale had a significant homosexual population, which suited Williams's sexual orientation well. He was a committed partner and suffered greatly when his love of many years, Frank Merlo, died of cancer in 1961.

Tennessee Williams battled alcoholism, drug abuse, and mental illness through much of his life. Along with his older sister Rose, he fought constantly against the fear that he might go insane. (At a young age, he had suffered a mental breakdown.) In the end, Williams choked to death on a bottle cap in his rooms at the Hotel Elysée in New York City.

His life and his work helped make Tennessee Williams one of America's best playwrights and one of the signature writers of the American South. His plays were bold and sometimes considered tawdry while those of his predecessors had been considered genteel and polite. Still, just as he was able to burst onto Broadway, he was able to spring on his readers a new type of drama that would forever change the way they saw the South.

TENNESSEE WILLIAMS

The Glass Menagerie (1945)

Nobody, not even the rain, has such small hands.
E. E. Cummings

CHARACTERS

Amanda Wingfield, *the mother. A little woman of great but confused vitality clinging frantically to another time and place. Her characterization must be carefully created, not copied from type. She is not paranoiac, but her life is paranoia. There is much to admire in Amanda, and as much to love and pity as there is to laugh at. Certainly she has endurance and a kind of heroism, and though her foolishness makes her unwittingly cruel at times, there is tenderness in her slight person.*

Laura Wingfield, *her daughter. Amanda, having failed to establish contact with reality, continues to live vitally in her illusions, but Laura's situation is even graver. A childhood illness has left her crippled, one leg slightly shorter than the other, and held in a brace. This defect need not be more than suggested on the stage. Stemming from this, Laura's separation increases till she is like a piece of her own glass collection, too exquisitely fragile to move from the shelf.*

Tom Wingfield, *her son. And the narrator of the play. A poet with a job in a warehouse. His nature is not remorseless, but to escape from a trap he has to act without pity.*

Jim O'Connor, *the gentleman caller. A nice, ordinary, young man.*

SCENE

An alley in St. Louis.

PART I

Preparation for a Gentleman Caller.

PART II

The Gentleman Calls.

TIME

Now and the Past.

SCENE 1

The Wingfield apartment is in the rear of the building, one of those vast hive-like conglomerations of cellular living-units that flower as warty growths in overcrowded urban centers of lower middle-class population and are symptomatic of the impulse of this largest and fundamentally enslaved section of American society to avoid fluidity and differentiation and to exist and function as one interfused mass of automatism.

The apartment faces an alley and is entered by a fire-escape, a structure whose name is a touch of accidental poetic truth, for all of these huge buildings are always burning with the slow and implacable fires of human desperation. The fire-escape is included in the set — that is, the landing of it and steps descending from it.

The scene is memory and is therefore nonrealistic. Memory takes a lot of poetic license. It omits some details; others are exaggerated, according to the emotional value of the articles it touches, for memory is seated predominantly in the heart. The interior is therefore rather dim and poetic.

At the rise of the curtain, the audience is faced with the dark, grim rear wall of the Wingfield tenement. This building, which runs parallel to the footlights, is flanked on both sides by dark, narrow alleys which run into murky canyons of tangled clotheslines, garbage cans and the sinister latticework of neighboring fire-escapes. It is up and down these side alleys that exterior entrances and exits are made, during the play. At the end of Tom's opening commentary, the dark tenement wall slowly reveals (by means of a transparency) the interior of the ground floor Wingfield apartment.

Downstage is the living room, which also serves as a sleeping room for Laura, the sofa unfolding to make her bed. Upstage, center, and divided by a wide arch or second proscenium with transparent faded portieres (or second curtain), is the dining room. In an old-fashioned what-not in the living room are seen scores of transparent glass animals. A blown-up photograph of the father hangs on the wall of the living room, facing the audience, to the left of the archway. It is the face of a very handsome young man in a doughboy's First World War cap. He is gallantly smiling, ineluctably smiling, as if to say, "I will be smiling forever."

The audience hears and sees the opening scene in the dining room through both the transparent fourth wall of the building and the transparent gauze portieres of the dining-room arch. It is during this revealing scene that the fourth wall slowly ascends, out of sight. This transparent exterior wall is not brought down again until the very end of the play, during Tom's final speech.

The narrator is an undisguised convention of the play. He takes whatever license with dramatic convention as is convenient to his purposes.

Tom enters dressed as a merchant sailor from the alley, stage left, and strolls across the front of the stage to the fire-escape. There he stops and lights a cigarette. He addresses the audience.

TOM: Yes, I have tricks in my pocket, I have things up my sleeve. But I am the opposite of a stage magician. He gives you illusion that has the appearance of truth. I give you truth in the pleasant disguise of illusion. To begin with, I turn back time. I reverse it to that quaint period, the thirties, when the huge middle class of America was matriculating in a school for the blind. Their eyes had failed them, or they had failed their eyes, and so they were having their fingers pressed forcibly down on the fiery Braille alphabet of a dissolving economy. In Spain there was revolution.° Here there was only

---

revolution: The Spanish Civil War (1936–1939).

shouting and confusion. In Spain there was Guernica.° Here there were disturbances of labor, sometimes pretty violent, in otherwise peaceful cities such as Chicago, Cleveland, Saint Louis. . . . This is the social background of the play.

Music.

The play is memory. Being a memory play, it is dimly lighted, it is sentimental, it is not realistic. In memory everything seems to happen to music. That explains the fiddle in the wings. I am the narrator of the play, and also a character in it. The other characters are my mother, Amanda, my sister, Laura, and a gentleman caller who appears in the final scenes. He is the most realistic character in the play, being an emissary from a world of reality that we were somehow set apart from. But since I have a poet's weakness for symbols, I am using this character also as a symbol; he is the long-delayed but always expected something that we live for. There is a fifth character in the play who doesn't appear except in this larger-than-life photograph over the mantel. This is our father who left us a long time ago. He was a telephone man who fell in love with long distances; he gave up his job with the telephone company and skipped the light fantastic out of town. . . . The last we heard of him was a picture post-card from Mazatlan, on the Pacific coast of Mexico, containing a message of two words — "Hello — Good-bye!" and an address. I think the rest of the play will explain itself. . . .

Amanda's voice becomes audible through the portieres.

Legend On Screen: "Où Sont Les Neiges."°

He divides the portieres and enters the upstage area.
    Amanda and Laura are seated at a drop-leaf table. Eating is indicated by gestures without food or utensils. Amanda faces the audience. Tom and Laura are seated in profile.
    The interior has lit up softly and through the scrim we see Amanda and Laura seated at the table in the upstage area.

AMANDA: *(calling)* Tom?
TOM: Yes, Mother.
AMANDA: We can't say grace until you come to the table!
TOM: Coming, Mother. *(He bows slightly and withdraws, reappearing a few   5
    moments later in his place at the table.)*
AMANDA: *(to her son)* Honey, don't *push* with your *fingers*. If you have to
    push with something, the thing to push with is a crust of bread. And

---

Guernica: A Basque town in northern Spain, bombed and practically destroyed on April 27, 1937, by German planes aiding fascist General Francisco Franco's Nationalists. The destruction is depicted in one of Pablo Picasso's most famous paintings, *Guernica* (1937).

"Où Sont Les Neiges": "Where the snows [of yesteryear]." A famous line by French poet Francois Villon (1431–1463?).

chew — chew! Animals have sections in their stomachs which enable
them to digest food without mastication, but human beings are supposed
to chew their food before they swallow it down. Eat food leisurely, son, and
really enjoy it. A well-cooked meal has lots of delicate flavors that have to
be held in the mouth for appreciation. So chew your food and give your
salivary glands a chance to function!

Tom deliberately lays his imaginary fork down and pushes his chair back from the table.

TOM: I haven't enjoyed one bite of this dinner because of your constant directions on how to eat it. It's you that makes me rush through meals with your
hawk-like attention to every bite I take. Sickening — spoils my appetite —
all this discussion of animals' secretion — salivary glands — mastication!

AMANDA: *(lightly)* Temperament like a Metropolitan star! *(He rises and crosses
downstage.)* You're not excused from the table.

TOM: I am getting a cigarette.

10   AMANDA: You smoke too much.

Laura rises.

LAURA: I'll bring in the blanc mange.

He remains standing with his cigarette by the portieres during the following.

AMANDA: *(rising)* No, sister, no, sister — you be the lady this time and I'll be
the darky.

LAURA: I'm already up.

AMANDA: Resume your seat, little sister — I want you to stay fresh and
pretty — for gentlemen callers!

15   LAURA: I'm not expecting any gentlemen callers.

AMANDA: *(crossing out to kitchenette. Airily)* Sometimes they come when they
are least expected! Why, I remember one Sunday afternoon in Blue
Mountain — *(Enters kitchenette.)*

TOM: I know what's coming!

LAURA: Yes. But let her tell it.

TOM: Again?

20   LAURA: She loves to tell it.

Amanda returns with bowl of dessert.

AMANDA: One Sunday afternoon in Blue Mountain — your mother received — *seventeen!* — gentlemen callers! Why, sometimes there weren't
chairs enough to accommodate them all. We had to send the nigger over
to bring in folding chairs from the parish house.

TOM: *(remaining at portieres)* How did you entertain those gentlemen
callers?

AMANDA: I understood the art of conversation!

TOM: I bet you could talk.

25   AMANDA: Girls in those days *knew* how to talk, I can tell you.

TOM: Yes?

Image: Amanda As A Girl On A Porch Greeting Callers.

AMANDA: They knew how to entertain their gentlemen callers. It wasn't enough for a girl to be possessed of a pretty face and a graceful figure — although I wasn't slighted in either respect. She also needed to have a nimble wit and a tongue to meet all occasions.

TOM: What did you talk about?

AMANDA: Things of importance going on in the world! Never anything coarse or common or vulgar. (*She addresses Tom as though he were seated in the vacant chair at the table though he remains by portieres. He plays this scene as though he held the book.*) My callers were gentlemen — all! Among my callers were some of the most prominent young planters of the Mississippi Delta — planters and sons of planters!

Tom motions for music and a spot of light on Amanda. Her eyes lift, her face glows, her voice becomes rich and elegiac.

Screen Legend: "Où Sont Les Neiges."

There was young Champ Laughlin who later became vice-president of the Delta Planters Bank. Hadley Stevenson who was drowned in Moon Lake and left his widow one hundred and fifty thousand in Government bonds. There were the Cutrere brothers, Wesley and Bates. Bates was one of my bright particular beaux! He got in a quarrel with that wild Wainright boy. They shot it out on the floor of Moon Lake Casino. Bates was shot through the stomach. Died in the ambulance on his way to Memphis. His widow was also well-provided for, came into eight or ten thousand acres, that's all. She married him on the rebound — never loved her — carried my picture on him the night he died! And there was that boy that every girl in the Delta had set her cap for! That beautiful, brilliant young Fitzhugh boy from Green County!

TOM: What did he leave his widow?   30

AMANDA: He never married! Gracious, you talk as though all of my old admirers had turned up their toes to the daisies!

TOM: Isn't this the first you mentioned that still survives?

AMANDA: That Fitzhugh boy went North and made a fortune — came to be known as the Wolf of Wall Street! He had the Midas touch, whatever he touched turned to gold! And I could have been Mrs. Duncan J. Fitzhugh, mind you! But — I picked your *father!*

LAURA: (*rising*) Mother, let me clear the table.

AMANDA: No dear, you go in front and study your typewriter chart. Or prac-   35
tice your shorthand a little. Stay fresh and pretty! — It's almost time for our gentlemen callers to start arriving. (*She flounces girlishly toward the kitch-enette.*) How many do you suppose we're going to entertain this afternoon?

Tom throws down the paper and jumps up with a groan.

LAURA: (*alone in the dining room*) I don't believe we're going to receive any, Mother.

AMANDA: (reappearing, airily) What? No one — not one? You must be joking! (Laura nervously echoes her laugh. She slips in a fugitive manner through the half-open portieres and draws them gently behind her. A shaft of very clear light is thrown on her face against the faded tapestry of the curtains.) (Music: "The Glass Menagerie" under faintly.) (Lightly.) Not one gentleman caller? It can't be true! There must be a flood, there must have been a tornado!

LAURA: It isn't a flood, it's not a tornado, Mother. I'm just not popular like you were in Blue Mountain. . . . (Tom utters another groan. Laura glances at him with a faint, apologetic smile. Her voice catching a little.) Mother's afraid I'm going to be an old maid.

The Scene Dims Out With "Glass Menagerie" Music.

SCENE 2

"Laura, Haven't You Ever Liked Some Boy?"

On the dark stage the screen is lighted with the image of blue roses.

Gradually Lura's figure becomes apparent and the screen goes out.

The music subsides.

Laura is seated in the delicate ivory chair at the small clawfoot table.

She wears a dress of soft violet material for a kimono — her hair tied back from her forehead with a ribbon.

She is washing and polishing her collection of glass.

Amanda appears on the fire-escape steps. At the sound of her ascent, Laura catches her breath, thrusts the bowl of ornaments away and seats herself stiffly before the diagram of the typewriter keyboard as though it held her spellbound. Something has happened to Amanda. It is written in her face as she climbs to the landing: a look that is grim and hopeless and a little absurd.

She has on one of those cheap or imitation velvety-looking cloth coats with imitation fur collar. Her hat is five or six years old, one of those dreadful cloche hats that were worn in the late twenties, and she is clasping an enormous black patent-leather pocketbook with nickel clasp and initials. This is her fulldress outfit, the one she usually wears to the D.A.R.°

Before entering she looks through the door.

She purses her lips, opens her eyes wide, rolls them upward and shakes her head.

Then she slowly lets herself in the door. Seeing her mother's expression Laura touches her lips with a nervous gesture.

LAURA: Hello, Mother, I was — (She makes a nervous gesture toward the chart on the wall. Amanda leans against the shut door and stares at Laura with a martyred look.)

AMANDA: Deception? Deception? (She slowly removes her hat and gloves, continuing the swift suffering stare. She lets the hat and gloves fall on the floor — a bit of acting.)

D.A.R.: Daughters of the American Revolution, an organization for female descendants of participants in the American Revolution, founded in 1890. That Amanda is a member says much about her concern with the past, as well as about her pride and affectations.

LAURA: *(shakily)* How was the D.A.R. meeting? *(Amanda slowly opens her purse and removes a dainty white handkerchief which she shakes out delicately and delicately touches to her lips and nostrils.)* Didn't you go to the D.A.R. meeting, Mother?

AMANDA: *(faintly, almost inaudibly)* — No. — No. *(Then more forcibly.)* I did not have the strength — to go the D.A.R. In fact, I did not have the courage! I wanted to find a hole in the ground and hide myself in it forever! *(She crosses slowly to the wall and removes the diagram of the typewriter keyboard. She holds it in front of her for a second, staring at it sweetly and sorrowfully — then bites her lips and tears it in two pieces.)*

LAURA: *(faintly)* Why did you do that, Mother? *(Amanda repeats the same procedure with the chart of the Gregg Alphabet.)* Why are you— 5

AMANDA: Why? Why? How old are you, Laura?

LAURA: Mother, you know my age.

AMANDA: I thought that you were an adult; it seems that I was mistaken. *(She crosses slowly to the sofa and sinks down and stares at Laura.)*

LAURA: Please don't stare at me, Mother.

Amanda closes her eyes and lowers her head. Count ten.

AMANDA: What are we going to do, what is going to become of us, what is the future? 10

Count ten.

LAURA: Has something happened, Mother? *(Amanda draws a long breath and takes out the handkerchief again. Dabbing process.)* Mother, has — something happened?

AMANDA: I'll be all right in a minute. I'm just bewildered — *(count five)* — by life. . . .

LAURA: Mother, I wish that you would tell me what's happened.

AMANDA: As you know, I was supposed to be inducted into my office at the D.A.R. this afternoon. *(Image: A Swarm Of Typewriters.)* But I stopped off at Rubicam's Business College to speak to your teachers about your having a cold and ask them what progress they thought you were making down there.

LAURA: Oh. . . . 15

AMANDA: I went to the typing instructor and introduced myself as your mother. She didn't know who you were. Wingfield, she said. We don't have any such student enrolled at the school! I assured her she did, that you had been going to classes since early in January. "I wonder," she said, "if you could be talking about that terribly shy little girl who dropped out of school after only a few days' attendance?" "No," I said, "Laura, my daughter, has been going to school every day for the past six weeks!" "Excuse me," she said. She took the attendance book out and there was your name, unmistakably printed, and all the dates you were absent until they decided that you had dropped out of school. I still said, "No, there must have been some mistake! There must have been some mix-up in the records!" And she said,

"No — I remember her perfectly now. Her hand shook so that she couldn't hit the right keys! The first time we gave a speed-test, she broke down completely — was sick at the stomach and almost had to be carried into the wash-room! After that morning she never showed up any more. We phoned the house but never got any answer" — while I was working at Famous and Barr, I suppose, demonstrating those — Oh! I felt so weak I could barely keep on my feet. I had to sit down while they got me a glass of water! Fifty dollars' tuition, all of our plans — my hopes and ambitions for you — just gone up the spout, just gone up the spout like that. (*Laura draws a long breath and gets awkwardly to her feet. She crosses to the Victrola and winds it up.*) What are you doing?

LAURA: Oh! (*She releases the handle and returns to her seat.*)

AMANDA: Laura, where have you been going when you've gone out pretending that you were going to business college?

LAURA: I've just been going out walking.

20   AMANDA: That's not true.

LAURA: It is. I just went walking.

AMANDA: Walking? Walking? In winter? Deliberately courting pneumonia in that light coat? Where did you walk to, Laura?

LAURA: It was the lesser of two evils, Mother. (*Image: Winter Scene In Park.*) I couldn't go back up. I — threw up — on the floor!

AMANDA: From half past seven till after five every day you mean to tell me you walked around in the park, because you wanted to make me think that you were still going to Rubicam's Business College?

25   LAURA: It wasn't as bad as it sounds. I went inside places to get warmed up.

AMANDA: Inside where?

LAURA: I went in the art museum and the bird-houses at the Zoo. I visited the penguins every day! Sometimes I did without lunch and went to the movies. Lately I've been spending most of my afternoons in the Jewel-box, that big glass house where they raise the tropical flowers.

AMANDA: You did all this to deceive me, just for the deception? (*Laura looks down.*) Why?

LAURA: Mother, when you're disappointed, you get that awful suffering look on your face, like the picture of Jesus' mother in the museum!

30   AMANDA: Hush!

LAURA: I couldn't face it.

Pause. A whisper of strings.

Legend: "The Crust Of Humility."

AMANDA: (*hopelessly fingering the huge pocketbook*) So what are we going to do the rest of our lives? Stay home and watch the parades go by? Amuse ourselves with the glass menagerie, darling? Eternally play those worn-out phonograph records your father left as a painful reminder of him? We won't have a business career — we've given that up because it gave us nervous indigestion! (*Laughs wearily.*) What is there left but dependency all our lives?

I know so well what becomes of unmarried women who aren't prepared to occupy a position. I've seen such pitiful cases in the South — barely tolerated spinsters living upon the grudging patronage of sister's husband or brother's wife! — stuck away in some little mouse-trap of a room — encouraged by one in-law to visit another — little birdlike women without any nest — eating the crust of humility all their life! Is that the future that we've mapped out for ourselves? I swear it's the only alternative I can think of! It isn't a very pleasant alternative, is it? Of course — some girls *do* marry. (*Laura twists her hands nervously.*) Haven't you ever liked some boy?

LAURA: Yes I liked one once. (*Rises.*) I came across his picture a while ago.

AMANDA: (*with some interest*) He gave you his picture?

LAURA: No, it's in the year-book.   35

AMANDA: (*disappointed*) Oh — a high-school boy.

Screen Image: Jim As A High-School Hero Bearing A Silver Cup.

LAURA: Yes. His name was Jim. (*Laura lifts the heavy annual from the clawfoot table.*) Here he is in *The Pirates of Penzance.*°

AMANDA: (*absently*) The what?

LAURA: The operetta the senior class put on. He had a wonderful voice and we sat across the aisle from each other Mondays, Wednesdays and Fridays in the Aud. Here he is with the silver cup for debating! See his grin?

AMANDA: (*absently*) He must have had a jolly disposition.   40

LAURA: He used to call me — Blue Roses.

Image: Blue Roses.

AMANDA: Why did he call you such a name as that?

LAURA: When I had that attack of pleurosis — he asked me what was the matter when I came back. I said pleurosis — he thought that I said Blue Roses! So that's what he always called me after that. Whenever he saw me, he'd holler, "Hello, Blue Roses!" I didn't care for the girl that he went out with. Emily Meisenbach. Emily was the best-dressed girl at Soldan. She never struck me, though, as being sincere . . . It says in the Personal Section — they're engaged. That's — six years ago! They must be married by now.

AMANDA: Girls that aren't cut out for business careers usually wind up married to some nice man. (*Gets up with a spark of revival.*) Sister, that's what you'll do!

Laura utters a startled, doubtful laugh. She reaches quickly for a piece of glass.

LAURA: But, Mother—   45

AMANDA: Yes? (*Crossing to photograph.*)

LAURA: (*in a tone of frightened apology*) I'm — crippled!

Image: Screen.

The Pirates of Penzance: A musical by Gilbert and Sullivan.

AMANDA: Nonsense! Laura, I've told you never, never to use that word. Why, you're not crippled, you just have a little defect — hardly noticeable, even! When people have some slight disadvantage like that, they cultivate other things to make up for it — develop charm — and vivacity — and — charm! That's all you have to do! (*She turns again to the photograph.*) One thing your father had *plenty* of — was *charm!*

Tom motions to the fiddle in the wings.

The Scene Fades Out With Music.

SCENE 3

Legend On The Screen: "After The Fiasco —"

Tom speaks from the fire-escape landing.

TOM: After the fiasco at Rubicam's Business College, the idea of getting a gentleman caller for Laura began to play a more important part in Mother's calculations. It became an obsession. Like some archetype of the universal unconscious, the image of the gentleman caller haunted our small apartment. . . . (*Image: Young Man At Door With Flowers.*) An evening at home rarely passed without some allusion to this image, this spectre, this hope. . . . Even when he wasn't mentioned, his presence hung in Mother's preoccupied look and in my sister's frightened, apologetic manner — hung like a sentence passed upon the Wingfields! Mother was a woman of action as well as words. She began to take logical steps in the planned direction. Late that winter and in the early spring — realizing that extra money would be needed to properly feather the nest and plume the bird — she conducted a vigorous campaign on the telephone, roping in subscribers to one of those magazines for matrons called *The Home-maker's Companion,* the type of journal that features the serialized sublimations of ladies of letters who think in terms of delicate cup-like breasts, slim, tapering waists, rich, creamy thighs, eyes like wood-smoke in autumn, fingers that soothe and caress like strains of music, bodies as powerful as Etruscan sculpture.

Screen Image: A Glamour Magazine Cover.

Amanda enters with phone on long extension cord. She is spotted in the dim stage.

AMANDA: Ida Scott? This is Amanda Wingfield! We *missed* you at the D.A.R. last Monday! I said to myself: She's probably suffering with that sinus condition! How is that sinus condition? Horrors! Heaven have mercy! — You're a Christian martyr, yes, that's what you are, a Christian martyr! Well, I just now happened to notice that your subscription to the *Companion's* about to expire! Yes, it expires with the next issue, honey! — just when that wonderful new serial by Bessie Mae Hopper is getting off to such an exciting start. Oh, honey, it's something that you can't miss! You remember how *Gone With the Wind* took everybody by storm? You simply couldn't go out if you hadn't read it. All everybody *talked* was Scarlett O'Hara. Well, this is a book that critics already compare to *Gone With the Wind*. It's the *Gone With the Wind* of the post–World War generation! —What?— Burning?— Oh, honey, don't let them burn, go take a look in the oven and I'll hold the wire! Heavens — I think she's hung up!

Dim Out.

Legend On Screen: "You Think I'm In Love With Continental Shoemakers?"

Before the stage is lighted, the violent voices of Tom and Amanda are heard. They are quarreling behind the portieres. In front of them stands Laura with clenched hands and panicky expression.
A clear pool of light on her figure throughout this scene.

TOM: What in Christ's name am I—
AMANDA: *(shrilly)* Don't you use that—
TOM: Supposed to do!   5
AMANDA: Expression! Not in my—
TOM: Ohhh!
AMANDA: Presence! Have you gone out of your senses?
TOM: I have, that's true, *driven* out!
AMANDA: What is the matter with you, you —big —big —IDIOT!   10
TOM: Look — I've got *no thing*, no single thing—
AMANDA: Lower your voice!
TOM: In my life here that I can call my OWN! Everything is—
AMANDA: Stop that shouting!
TOM: Yesterday you confiscated my books! You had the nerve to—   15
AMANDA: I took that horrible novel back to the library — yes! That hideous book by that insane Mr. Lawrence.° *(Tom laughs wildly.)* I cannot control the output of diseased minds or people who cater to them —*(Tom laughs still more wildly.)* BUT I WON'T ALLOW SUCH FILTH BROUGHT INTO MY HOUSE! No, no, no, no, no!
TOM: House, house! Who pays rent on it, who makes a slave of himself to—
AMANDA: *(fairly screeching)* Don't you DARE to—
TOM: No, no, *I* mustn't say things! *I've* got to just—
AMANDA: Let me tell you—   20
TOM: I don't want to hear any more! *(He tears the portieres open. The upstage area is lit with a turgid smoky red glow.)*

Amanda's hair is in metal curlers and she wears a very old bathrobe, much too large for her slight figure, a relic of the faithless Mr. Wingfield.
An upright typewriter and a wild disarray of manuscripts are on the drop-leaf table. The quarrel was probably precipitated by Amanda's interruption of his creative labor. A chair lying overthrown on the floor.
Their gesticulating shadows are cast on the ceiling by the fiery glow.

Mr. Lawrence: English novelist D.H. Lawrence (1885–1930). The reference is to his 1928 novel *Lady Chatterley's Lover,* which was banned in the United States and England because of its frank treatment of sexuality.

AMANDA: You *will* hear more, you—

TOM: No, I won't hear more, I'm going out!

AMANDA: You come right back in—

25 TOM: Out, out out! Because I'm—

AMANDA: Come back here, Tom Wingfield! I'm not through talking to you!

TOM: Oh, go—

LAURA: *(desperately)* Tom!

AMANDA: You're going to listen, and no more insolence from you! I'm at the end of my patience! *(He comes back toward her.)*

30 TOM: What do you think I'm at? Aren't I supposed to have any patience to reach the end of, Mother? I know, I know. It seems unimportant to you, what I'm *doing*— what I *want* to do —having a little *difference* between them! You don't think that—

AMANDA: I think you've been doing things that you're ashamed of. That's why you act like this. I don't believe that you go every night to the movies. Nobody goes to the movies night after night. Nobody in their right mind goes to the movies as often as you pretend to. People don't go to the movies at nearly midnight, and movies don't let out at two A.M. Come in stumbling. Muttering to yourself like a maniac! You get three hours' sleep and then go to work. Oh, I can picture the way you're doing down there. Moping, doping, because you're in no condition.

TOM: *(wildly)* No, I'm in no condition!

AMANDA: What right have you got to jeopardize your job? Jeopardize the security of us all? How do you think we'd manage if you were—

TOM: Listen! You think I'm crazy *about* the *warehouse? (He bends fiercely toward her slight figure.)* You think I'm in love with the Continental Shoemakers? You think I want to spend fifty-five *years* down there in that —*celotex interior!* with —*fluorescent —* tubes! Look! I'd rather somebody picked up a crowbar and battered out my brains — than go back mornings! I *go!* Every time you come in yelling that God damn *"Rise and Shine!" "Rise and Shine!"* I say to myself *"How lucky dead* people are!" But I get up. I *go!* For sixty-five dollars a month I give up all that I dream of doing and being *ever!* And you say self —*self's* all I ever think of. Why, listen, if self is what I thought of, Mother, I'd be where he is —GONE! *(Pointing to father's picture.)* As far as the system of transportation reaches! *(He starts past her. She grabs his arm.)* Don't grab at me, Mother!

35 AMANDA: Where are you going?

TOM: I'm going to the *movies!*

AMANDA: I don't believe that lie!

TOM: *(crouching toward her, overtowering her tiny figure. She backs away, gasping)* I'm going to opium dens! Yes, opium dens, dens of vice and criminals' hangouts, Mother. I've joined the Hogan gang, I'm a hired assassin, I carry a tommy-gun in a violin case! I run a string of cat-houses in the Valley! They call me Killer, Killer Wingfield, I'm leading a double-life, a simple, honest warehouse worker by day, by night a dynamic *czar of the underworld, Mother.* I go to gambling casinos, I spin away fortunes on the roulette table! I wear a patch over one eye and a false mustache, sometimes I put on green whiskers. On those occasions they call me —*El Diablo!* Oh, I could tell you things to make you sleepless! My enemies plan to dynamite this place. They're going to blow us all sky-high some night! I'll be glad, very happy, and so will you! You'll go up, up on a broomstick, over Blue Mountain with seventeen gentlemen callers! You ugly —babbling old —*witch.* . . . (*He goes through a series of violent, clumsy movements, seizing his overcoat, lunging to the door, pulling it fiercely open. The women watch him, aghast. His arm catches in the sleeve of the coat as he struggles to pull it on. For a moment he is pinioned by the bulky garment. With an outraged groan he tears the coat off again, splitting the shoulders of it, and hurls it across the room. It strikes against the shelf of Laura's glass collection, there is a tinkle of shattering glass. Laura cries out as if wounded.*)

Music Legend: "The Glass Menagerie."

LAURA: *My glass!* —menagerie. . . . (*She covers her face and turns away.*)

But Amanda is still stunned and stupefied by the "ugly witch" so that she barely notices this occurrence. Now she recovers her speech.

AMANDA: (*in an awful voice*) I won't speak to you — until you apologize! (*She crosses through portieres and draws them together behind her. Tom is left with Laura. Laura clings weakly to the mantel with her face averted. Tom stares at her stupidly for a moment. Then he crosses to shelf. Drops awkwardly to his knees to collect the fallen glass, glancing at Laura as if he would speak but couldn't.*)   40

"The Glass Menagerie" steals in as

The Scene Dims Out.

SCENE **4**

The interior is dark. Faint in the alley.

    A deep-voiced bell in a church is tolling the hour of five as the scene commences.

    Tom appears at the top of the alley. After each solemn boom of the bell in the tower, he shakes a little noise-maker or rattle as if to express the tiny spasm of man in contrast to the sustained power and dignity of the Almighty. This and the unsteadiness of his advance make it evident that he has been drinking.

    As he climbs the few steps to the fire-escape landing light steals up inside. Laura appears in night-dress, observing Tom's empty bed in the front room.

    Tom fishes in his pockets for the door-key, removing a motley assortment of articles in the search, including a perfect shower of movie-ticket stubs and an empty bottle. At last he finds the key, but just as he is about to insert it, it slips from his fingers. He strikes a match and crouches below the door.

TOM: (*bitterly*) One crack — and it falls through!

Laura opens the door.

LAURA: Tom! Tom, what are you doing?
TOM: Looking for a door-key.
LAURA: Where have you been all this time?

5 TOM: I have been to the movies.

LAURA: All this time at the movies?

TOM: There was a very long program. There was a Garbo picture and a Mickey Mouse and a travelogue and a newsreel and a preview of coming attractions. And there was an organ solo and a collection for the milk-fund — simultaneously — which ended up in a terrible fight between a fat lady and an usher!

LAURA: (innocently) Did you have to stay through everything?

TOM: Of course! And, oh, I forgot! There was a big stage show! The headliner on this stage show was Malvolio the Magician. He performed wonderful tricks, many of them, such as pouring water back and forth between pitchers. First it turned to wine and then it turned to beer and then it turned to whiskey. I know it was whiskey it finally turned into because he needed somebody to come up out of the audience to help him, and I came up — both shows! It was Kentucky Straight Bourbon. A very generous fellow, he gave souvenirs. (He pulls from his back pocket a shimmering rainbow-colored scarf.) He gave me this. This is his magic scarf. You can have it, Laura. You wave it over a canary cage and you get a bowl of gold-fish. You wave it over the gold-fish bowl and they fly away canaries. . . . But the wonderfullest trick of all was the coffin trick. We nailed him into a coffin and he got out of the coffin without removing one nail. (He has come inside.) There is a trick that would come in handy for me — get me out of this 2 by 4 situation! (Flops onto bed and starts removing shoes.)

10 LAURA: Tom — Shhh!

TOM: What you shushing me for?

LAURA: You'll wake up Mother.

TOM: Goody, goody! Pay 'er back for all those "Rise an' Shines." (Lies down, groaning.) You know it don't take much intelligence to get yourself into a nailed-up coffin, Laura. But who in hell ever got himself out of one without removing one nail?

As if in answer, the father's grinning photograph lights up.

Scene Dims Out.

Immediately following: The church bell is heard striking six. At the sixth stroke the alarm clock goes off in Amanda's room, and after a few moments we hear her calling: "Rise and Shine! Rise and Shine! Laura, go tell your brother to rise and shine!"

TOM: (sitting up slowly) I'll rise —but I won't shine.

The light increases.

15 AMANDA: Laura, tell your brother his coffee is ready.

Laura slips into front room.

LAURA: Tom! it's nearly seven. Don't make Mother nervous. (He stares at her stupidly. Beseechingly.) Tom, speak to Mother this morning. Make up with her, apologize, speak to her!

TOM: She won't to me. It's her that started not speaking.

LAURA: If you just say you're sorry she'll start speaking.

TOM: Her not speaking — is that such a tragedy?

LAURA: Please — please!   20

AMANDA: *(calling from kitchenette)* Laura, are you going to do what I asked you to do, or do I have to get dressed and go out myself?

LAURA: Going, going — soon as I get on my coat! *(She pulls on a shapeless felt hat with nervous, jerky movement, pleadingly glancing at Tom. Rushes awkwardly for coat. The coat is one of Amanda's inaccurately made-over, the sleeves too short for Laura.)* Butter and what else?

AMANDA: *(entering upstage)* Just butter. Tell them to charge it.

LAURA: Mother, they make such faces when I do that.

AMANDA: Sticks and stones may break my bones, but the expression on   25 Mr. Garfinkel's face won't harm us! Tell your brother his coffee is getting cold.

LAURA: *(at door)* Do what I asked you, will you, will you, Tom?

He looks sullenly away.

AMANDA: Laura, go now or just don't go at all!

LAURA: *(rushing out)* Going — going! *(A second later she cries out. Tom springs up and crosses to the door. Amanda rushes anxiously in. Tom opens the door.)*

TOM: Laura?

LAURA: I'm all right. I slipped, but I'm all right.   30

AMANDA: *(peering anxiously after her)* If anyone breaks a leg on those fire-escape steps, the landlord ought to be sued for every cent he possesses! *(She shuts door. Remembers she isn't speaking and returns to other room.)*

As Tom enters listlessly for his coffee, she turns her back to him and stands rigidly facing the window on the gloomy gray vault of the areaway. Its light on her face with its aged but childish features is cruelly sharp, satirical as a Daumier print.

Music Under: "Ave Maria."

Tom glances sheepishly but sullenly at her averted figure and slumps at the table. The coffee is scalding hot; he sips it and gasps and spits it back in the cup. At his gasp, Amanda catches her breath and half turns. Then catches herself and turns back to window.

   Tom blows on his coffee, glancing sidewise at his mother. She clears her throat. Tom clears his. He starts to rise. Sinks back down again, scratches his head, clears his throat again. Amanda coughs. Tom raises his cup in both hands to blow on it, his eyes staring over the rim of it at his mother for several moments. Then he slowly sets the cup down and awkwardly and hesitantly rises from the chair.

TOM: *(hoarsely)* Mother. I — I apologize. Mother. *(Amanda draws a quick, shuddering breath. Her face works grotesquely. She breaks into childlike tears.)* I'm sorry for what I said, for everything that I said, I didn't mean it.

AMANDA: *(sobbingly)* My devotion has made me a witch and so I make myself hateful to my children!

TOM: No, you *don't.*

35   AMANDA: I worry so much, don't sleep, it makes me nervous!

TOM: (gently) I understand that.

AMANDA: I've had to put up a solitary battle all these years. But you're my
right-hand bower! Don't fall down, don't fail!

TOM: (gently) I try, Mother.

AMANDA: (with great enthusiasm) Try and you will SUCCEED! (The notion makes
her breathless.) Why, you — you're just full of natural endowments! Both of
my children — they're unusual children! Don't you think I know it? I'm
so —proud! Happy and —feel I've — so much to be thankful for but —
Promise me one thing, son!

40   TOM: What, Mother?

AMANDA: Promise, son, you'll — never be a drunkard!

TOM: (turns to her grinning) I will never be a drunkard, Mother.

AMANDA: That's what frightened me so, that you'd be drinking! Eat a bowl of
Purina!

TOM: Just coffee, Mother.

45   AMANDA: Shredded wheat biscuit?

TOM: No. No, Mother, just coffee.

AMANDA: You can't put in a day's work on an empty stomach. You've got
ten minutes — don't gulp! Drinking too-hot liquids makes cancer of the
stomach. . . . Put cream in.

TOM: No, thank you.

AMANDA: To cool it.

50   TOM: No! No, thank you, I want it black.

AMANDA: I know, but it's not good for you. We have to do all that we can to
build ourselves up. In these trying times we live in, all that we have to cling
to is — each other. . . . That's why it's so important to — Tom, I — I sent
out your sister so I could discuss something with you. If you hadn't spoken
I would have spoken to you. (Sits down.)

TOM: (gently) What is it, Mother, that you want to discuss?

AMANDA: Laura!

Tom puts his cup down slowly.

Legend On Screen: "Laura."

Music: "The Glass Menagerie."

TOM: — Oh.— Laura . . .

55   AMANDA: (touching his sleeve) You know how Laura is. So quiet but —
still water runs deep! She notices things and I think she — broods
about them. (Tom looks up.) A few days ago I came in and she was
crying.

TOM: What about?

AMANDA: You.

TOM: Me?

AMANDA: She has an idea that you're not happy here.

60   TOM: What gave her that idea?

AMANDA: What gives her any idea? However, you do act strangely. I — I'm not criticizing, understand *that*! I know your ambitions do not lie in the warehouse, that like everybody in the whole wide world — you've had to — make sacrifices, but — Tom — Tom — life's not easy, it calls for — Spartan endurance! There's so many things in my heart that I cannot describe to you! I've never told you but I —*loved* your father. . . .

TOM: (gently) I know that, Mother.

AMANDA: And you — when I see you taking after his ways! Staying out late — and — well, you *had* been drinking the night you were in that — terrifying condition! Laura says that you hate the apartment and that you go out nights to get away from it! Is that true, Tom?

TOM: No. You say there's so much in your heart that you can't describe to me. That's true of me, too. There's so much in my heart that I can't describe to *you!* So let's respect each other's —

AMANDA: But, why —*why*, Tom — are you always so *restless?* Where do you go to, nights? 65

TOM: I — go to the movies.

AMANDA: Why do you go to the movies so much, Tom?

TOM: I go to the movies because — I like adventure. Adventure is something I don't have much of at work, so I go to the movies.

AMANDA: But, Tom, you go to the movies *entirely* too *much!*

TOM: I like a lot of adventure. 70

Amanda looks baffled, then hurt. As the familiar inquisition resumes he becomes hard and impatient again. Amanda slips back into her querulous attitude toward him.

Image On Screen: Sailing Vessel With Jolly Roger.

AMANDA: Most young men find adventure in their careers.

TOM: Then most young men are not employed in a warehouse.

AMANDA: The world is full of young men employed in warehouses and offices and factories.

TOM: Do all of them find adventure in their careers?

AMANDA: They do or they do without it! Not everybody has a craze for adventure. 75

TOM: Man is by instinct a lover, a hunter, a fighter, and none of those instincts are given much play at the warehouse!

AMANDA: Man is by instinct! Don't quote instinct to me! Instinct is something that people have got away from! It belongs to animals! Christian adults don't want it!

TOM: What do Christian adults want, then, Mother?

AMANDA: Superior things! Things of the mind and the spirit! Only animals have to satisfy instincts! Surely your aims are somewhat higher than theirs! Than monkeys — pigs —

TOM: I reckon they're not. 80

AMANDA: You're joking. However, that isn't what I wanted to discuss.

TOM: (rising) I haven't much time.

AMANDA: *(pushing his shoulders)* Sit down.

TOM: You want me to punch in red at the warehouse, Mother?

85   AMANDA: You have five minutes. I want to talk about Laura.

Legend: "Plans And Provisions."

TOM: All right! What about Laura?

AMANDA: We have to be making plans and provisions for her. She's older than
you, two years, and nothing has happened. She just drifts along doing nothing. It frightens me terribly how she just drifts along.

TOM: I guess she's the type that people call home-girls.

AMANDA: There's no such type, and if there is, it's a pity! That is unless the
home is hers, with a husband!

90   TOM: What?

AMANDA: Oh, I can see the handwriting on the wall as plain as I see the nose
in front of my face! It's terrifying! More and more you remind me of your fa-
ther! He was out all hours without explanation — Then *left! Good-bye!*
And me with the bag to hold. I saw that letter you got from the Merchant
Marine. I know what you're dreaming of. I'm not standing here blindfolded.
Very well, then. Then *do* it! But not till there's somebody to take your place.

TOM: What do you mean?

AMANDA: I mean that as soon as Laura has got somebody to take care of her,
married, a home of her own, independent — why, then you'll be free to go
wherever you please, on land, on sea, whichever way the wind blows! But
until that time you've got to look out for your sister. I don't say me because
I'm old and don't matter! I say for your sister because she's young and dependent. I put her in business college — a dismal failure! Frightened her so
it made her sick to her stomach. I took her over to the Young People's
League at the church. Another fiasco. She spoke to nobody, nobody spoke
to her. Now all she does is fool with those pieces of glass and play those
worn-out records. What kind of a life is that for a girl to lead!

TOM: What can I do about it?

95   AMANDA: Overcome selfishness! Self, self, self is all that you ever think of!
*(Tom springs up and crosses to get his coat. It is ugly and bulky. He pulls on a
cap with earmuffs.)* Where is your muffler? Put your wool muffler on! *(He
snatches it angrily from the closet and tosses it around his neck and pulls both
ends tight.)* Tom! I haven't said what I had in mind to ask you.

TOM: I'm too late to —

AMANDA: *(catching his arms — very importunately. Then shyly)* Down at the
warehouse, aren't there some — nice young men?

TOM: No!

AMANDA: There *must* be — *some* . . .

100   TOM: Mother —

Gesture.

AMANDA: Find out one that's clean-living — doesn't drink and — ask him out
for sister!

TOM: What?

AMANDA: For *sister!* To *meet!* Get *acquainted!*

TOM: *(stamping to door)* Oh, my *go-osh!*

AMANDA: Will you? *(He opens door. Imploringly.)* Will you? *(He starts down.)* 105
Will you? *Will* you, dear?

TOM: *(calling back)* YES!

Amanda closes the door hesitantly and with a troubled but faintly hopeful expression.

(Screen Image: A Glamour Magazine Cover.)

Spot Amanda at phone.

AMANDA: Ella Cartwright? This is Amanda Wingfield! How are you, honey?
How is that kidney condition? *(Count five.)* Horrors! *(Count five.)* You're a
Christian martyr, yes, honey, that's what you are, a Christian martyr! Well,
I just happened to notice in my little red book that your subscription to the
Companion has just run out! I knew that you wouldn't want to miss out on
the wonderful serial starting in this new issue. It's by Bessie Mae Hopper,
the first thing she's written since *Honeymoon for Three.* Wasn't that a
strange and interesting story? Well, this one is even lovelier, I believe.
It has a sophisticated society background. It's all about the horsey set on
Long Island!

Fade Out.

SCENE 5

(Legend On Screen: "Annunciation.") Fade with music.

*It is early dusk of a spring evening. Supper has just been finished in the Wingfield apart-
ment. Amanda and Laura in light colored dresses are removing dishes from the table, in
the upstage area, which is shadowy, their movements formalized almost as a dance or
ritual, their moving forms as pale and silent as moths.*

    *Tom, in white shirt and trousers, rises from the table and crosses toward the
fire-escape.*

AMANDA: *(as he passes her)* Son, will you do me a favor?

TOM: What?

AMANDA: Comb your hair! You look so pretty when your hair is combed!
*(Tom slouches on sofa with evening paper. Enormous caption "Franco Tri-
umphs.")* There is only one respect in which I would like you to emulate
your father.

TOM: What respect is that?

AMANDA: The care he always took of his appearance. He never allowed 5
himself to look untidy. *(He throws down the paper and crosses to fire-escape.)*
Where are you going?

TOM: I'm going out to smoke.

AMANDA: You smoke too much. A pack a day at fifteen cents a pack. How
much would that amount to in a month? Thirty times fifteen is how much,

Tom? Figure it out and you will be astounded at what you could save. Enough to give you a night-school course in accounting at Washington U! Just think what a wonderful thing that would be for you, son!

Tom is unmoved by the thought.

TOM: I'd rather smoke. (*He steps out on landing, letting the screen door slam.*)
AMANDA: (*sharply*) I know! That's the tragedy of it. . . . (*Alone, she turns to look at her husband's picture.*)

Dance Music: "All The World Is Waiting For The Sunrise!"

10   **TOM:** (*to the audience*) Across the alley from us was the Paradise Dance Hall. On evenings in spring the windows and doors were open and the music came outdoors. Sometimes the lights were turned out except for a large glass sphere that hung from the ceiling. It would turn slowly about and filter the dusk with delicate rainbow colors. Then the orchestra played a waltz or a tango, something that had a slow and sensuous rhythm. Couples would come outside, to the relative privacy of the alley. You could see them kissing behind ash-pits and telephone poles. This was the compensation for lives that passed like mine, without any change or adventure. Adventure and change were imminent in this year. They were waiting around the corner for all these kids. Suspended in the mist over Berchtesgaden,° caught in the folds of Chamberlain's umbrella°— In Spain there was Guernica! But here there was only hot swing music and liquor, dance halls, bars, and movies, and sex that hung in the gloom like a chandelier and flooded the world with brief, deceptive rainbows. . . . All the world was waiting for bombardments!

Amanda turns from the picture and comes outside.

AMANDA: (*sighing*) A fire-escape landing's a poor excuse for a porch. (*She spreads a newspaper on a step and sits down, gracefully and demurely as if she were settling into a swing on a Mississippi veranda.*) What are you looking at?
TOM: The moon.
AMANDA: Is there a moon this evening?
TOM: It's rising over Garfinkel's Delicatessen.
15   **AMANDA:** So it is! A little silver slipper of a moon. Have you made a wish on it yet?
TOM: Um-hum.
AMANDA: What did you wish for?
TOM: That's a secret.

Berchtesgaden: A resort in Germany, in the Bavarian Alps; the site of Adolf Hitler's fortified retreat, the Berghof.
Chamberlain's umbrella: (Arthur) Neville Chamberlain (1869–1940)— Conservative Party prime minister of England (1937–1940) who advocated a policy of appeasement toward Hitler. Political cartoons often showed him carrying an umbrella.

AMANDA: A secret, huh? Well, I won't tell mine either. I will be just as
mysterious as you.

TOM: I bet I can guess what yours is.   20

AMANDA: Is my head so transparent?

TOM: You're not a sphinx.

AMANDA: No, I don't have secrets. I'll tell you what I wished for on the moon.
Success and happiness for my precious children! I wish for that whenever
there's a moon, and when there isn't a moon, I wish for it, too.

TOM: I thought perhaps you wished for a gentleman caller.

AMANDA: Why do you say that?   25

TOM: Don't you remember asking me to fetch one?

AMANDA: I remember suggesting that it would be nice for your sister if you
brought home some nice young man from the warehouse. I think I've made
that suggestion more than once.

TOM: Yes, you have made it repeatedly.

AMANDA: Well?

TOM: We are going to have one.   30

AMANDA: What?

TOM: A gentleman caller!

The Annunciation Is Celebrated With Music.

Amanda rises.

Image On Screen: Caller With Bouquet.

AMANDA: You mean you have asked some nice young man to come over?

TOM: Yep. I've asked him to dinner.

AMANDA: You really did?   35

TOM: I did!

AMANDA: You did, and did he —*accept?*

TOM: He did!

AMANDA: Well, well — well, well! That's —lovely!

TOM: I thought that you would be pleased.   40

AMANDA: It's definite, then?

TOM: Very definite.

AMANDA: Soon?

TOM: Very soon.

AMANDA: For heaven's sake, stop putting on and tell me some things, will you? 45

TOM: What things do you want me to tell you?

AMANDA: Naturally I would like to know when he's *coming!*

TOM: He's coming tomorrow.

AMANDA: *Tomorrow?*

TOM: Yep. Tomorrow.   50

AMANDA: But, Tom!

TOM: Yes, Mother?

AMANDA: Tomorrow gives me no time!

TOM: Time for what?

55   AMANDA: Preparations! Why didn't you phone me at once, as soon as you
asked him, the minute that he accepted? Then, don't you see, I could have
been getting ready!

TOM: You don't have to make any fuss.

AMANDA: Oh, Tom, Tom, Tom, of course I have to make a fuss! I want things
nice, not sloppy! Not thrown together. I'll certainly have to do some fast
thinking, won't I?

TOM: I don't see why you have to think at all.

AMANDA: You just don't know. We can't have a gentleman caller in a pig-sty!
All my wedding silver has to be polished, the monogrammed table linen
ought to be laundered! The windows have to be washed and fresh curtains
put up. And how about clothes? We have to *wear* something, don't we?

60   TOM: Mother, this boy is no one to make a fuss over!

AMANDA: Do you realize he's the first young man we've introduced to your sister? It's terrible, dreadful, disgraceful that poor little sister has never received
a single gentleman caller! Tom, come inside! *(She opens the screen door.)*

TOM: What for?

AMANDA: I want to ask you some things.

TOM: If you're going to make such a fuss, I'll call it off, I'll tell him not to come.

65   AMANDA: You certainly won't do anything of the kind. Nothing offends people
worse than broken engagements. It simply means I'll have to work like a
Turk! We won't be brilliant, but we'll pass inspection. Come on inside.
(Tom follows, groaning.) Sit down.

TOM: Any particular place you would like me to sit?

AMANDA: Thank heavens I've got that new sofa! I'm also making payments
on a floor lamp I'll have sent out! And put the chintz covers on, they'll
brighten things up! Of course I'd hoped to have these walls re-papered. . . .
What is the young man's name?

TOM: His name is O'Connor.

AMANDA: That, of course, means fish — tomorrow is Friday! I'll have that
salmon loaf — with Durkee's dressing! What does he do? He works at the
warehouse?

70   TOM: Of course! How else would I—

AMANDA: Tom, he — doesn't drink?

TOM: Why do you ask me that?

AMANDA: Your father *did*!

TOM: Don't get started on that!

75   AMANDA: He *does* drink, then?

TOM: Not that I know of!

AMANDA: Make sure, be certain! The last thing I want for my daughter's a
boy who drinks!

TOM: Aren't you being a little premature? Mr. O'Connor has not yet appeared
on the scene!

AMANDA: But will tomorrow. To meet your sister, and what do I know about
his character? Nothing! Old maids are better off than wives of drunkards!

80   TOM: Oh, my God!

AMANDA: Be still!

TOM: *(leaning forward to whisper)* Lots of fellows meet girls whom they don't marry!

AMANDA: Oh, talk sensibly, Tom — and don't be sarcastic! *(She has gotten a hairbrush.)*

TOM: What are you doing?

AMANDA: I'm brushing that cow-lick down! What is this young man's position at the warehouse? 85

TOM: *(submitting grimly to the brush and the interrogation)* This young man's position is that of a shipping clerk, Mother.

AMANDA: Sounds to me like a fairly responsible job, the sort of a job *you* would be in if you just had more *get-up*. What is his salary? Have you got any idea?

TOM: I would judge it to be approximately eighty-five dollars a month.

AMANDA: Well — not princely, but —

TOM: Twenty more than I make. 90

AMANDA: Yes, how well I know! But for a family man, eighty-five dollars a month is not much more than you can just get by on. . . .

TOM: Yes, but Mr. O'Connor is not a family man.

AMANDA: He might be, mightn't he? Some time in the future?

TOM: I see. Plans and provisions.

AMANDA: You are the only young man that I know of who ignores the fact 95 that the future becomes the present, the present the past, and the past turns into everlasting regret if you don't plan for it!

TOM: I will think that over and see what I can make of it.

AMANDA: Don't be supercilious with your mother! Tell me some more about this — what do you call him?

TOM: James D. O'Connor. The D. is for Delaney.

AMANDA: Irish on *both* sides! *Gracious!* And doesn't drink?

TOM: Shall I call him up and ask him right this minute? 100

AMANDA: The only way to find out about those things is to make discreet in-quiries at the proper moment. When I was a girl in Blue Mountain and it was suspected that a young man drank, the girl whose attentions he had been receiving, if any girl *was*, would sometimes speak to the minister of his church, or rather her father would if her father was living, and sort of feel him out on the young man's character. That is the way such things are discreetly handled to keep a young woman from making a tragic mistake!

TOM: Then how did you happen to make a tragic mistake?

AMANDA: That innocent look of your father's had everyone fooled! He *smiled* — the world was *enchanted!* No girl can do worse than put herself at the mercy of a handsome appearance! I hope that Mr. O'Connor is not too good-looking.

TOM: No, he's not too good-looking. He's covered with freckles and hasn't too much of a nose.

AMANDA: He's not right-down homely, though? 105

TOM: Not right-down homely. Just medium homely, I'd say.

AMANDA: Character's what to look for in a man.

TOM: That's what I've always said, Mother.

AMANDA: You've never said anything of the kind and I suspect you would never give it a thought.

110 **TOM:** Don't be suspicious of me.

AMANDA: At least I hope he's the type that's up and coming.

TOM: I think he really goes in for self-improvement.

AMANDA: What reason have you to think so?

TOM: He goes to night school.

115 **AMANDA:** (*beaming*) Splendid! What does he do, I mean study?

TOM: Radio engineering and public speaking!

AMANDA: Then he has visions of being advanced in the world! Any young man who studies public speaking is aiming to have an executive job some day! And radio engineering? A thing for the future! Both of these facts are very illuminating. Those are the sort of things that a mother should know concerning any young man who comes to call on her daughter. Seriously or — not.

TOM: One little warning. He doesn't know about Laura. I didn't let on that we had dark ulterior motives. I just said, why don't you come have dinner with us? He said okay and that was the whole conversation.

AMANDA: I bet it was! You're eloquent as an oyster. However, he'll know about Laura when he gets here. When he sees how lovely and sweet and pretty she is, he'll thank his lucky stars he was asked to dinner.

120 **TOM:** Mother, you mustn't expect too much of Laura.

AMANDA: What do you mean?

TOM: Laura seems all those things to you and me because she's ours and we love her. We don't even notice she's crippled any more.

AMANDA: Don't say crippled! You know that I never allow that word to be used!

TOM: But face facts, Mother. She is and — that's not all—

125 **AMANDA:** What do you mean "not all"?

TOM: Laura is very different from other girls.

AMANDA: I think the difference is all to her advantage.

TOM: Not quite all — in the eyes of others — strangers — she's terribly shy and lives in a world of her own and those things make her seem a little peculiar to people outside the house.

AMANDA: Don't say peculiar.

130 **TOM:** Face the facts. She is.

The Dance-Hall Music Changes To A Tango That Has A Minor And Somewhat Ominous Tone.

AMANDA: In what way is she peculiar — may I ask?

TOM: (*gently*) She lives in a world of her own — a world of — little glass ornaments, Mother. . . . (*Gets up. Amanda remains holding brush, looking at him, troubled.*) She plays old phonograph records and — that's about all — (*He glances at himself in the mirror and crosses to door.*)

AMANDA: *(sharply)* Where are you going?

TOM: I'm going to the movies. *(Out screen door.)*

AMANDA: Not to the movies, every night to the movies! *(Follows quickly to* 135
screen door.) I don't believe you always go to the movies! *(He is gone.
Amanda looks worriedly after him for a moment. Then vitality and optimism return and she turns from the door. Crossing to portieres.)* Laura! Laura! *(Laura
answers from kitchenette.)*

LAURA: Yes, Mother.

AMANDA: Let those dishes go and come in front! *(Laura appears with dish
towel. Gaily.)* Laura, come here and make a wish on the moon!

LAURA: *(entering)* Moon —moon?

AMANDA: A little silver slipper of a moon. Look over your left shoulder,
Laura, and make a wish! *(Laura looks faintly puzzled as if called out of sleep.
Amanda seizes her shoulders and turns her at an angle by the door.)* Now!
Now, darling, *wish!*

LAURA: What shall I wish for, Mother? 140

AMANDA: *(her voice trembling and her eyes suddenly filling with tears)* Happiness!
Good Fortune!

The violin rises and the stage dims out.

SCENE 6

Image: High-School Hero.

TOM: And so the following evening I brought Jim home to dinner. I had
known Jim slightly in high school. In high school Jim was a hero. He had
tremendous Irish good nature and vitality with the scrubbed and polished
look of white chinaware. He seemed to move in a continual spotlight.
He was a star in basketball, captain of the debating club, president of the
senior class and the glee club and he sang the male lead in the annual
light operas. He was always running or bounding, never just walking. He
seemed always at the point of defeating the law of gravity. He was shooting
with such velocity through his adolescence that you would logically
expect him to arrive at nothing short of the White House by the time
he was thirty. But Jim apparently ran into more interference after his
graduation from Soldan. His speed had definitely slowed. Six years after
he left high school he was holding a job that wasn't much better than
mine.

Image: Clerk.

He was the only one at the warehouse with whom I was on friendly terms. I
was valuable to him as someone who could remember his former glory, who had
seen him win basketball games and the silver cup in debating. He knew of my secret practice of retiring to a cabinet of the washroom to work on poems when
business was slack in the warehouse. He called me Shakespeare. And while the
other boys in the warehouse regarded me with suspicious hostility, Jim took a

humorous attitude toward me. Gradually his attitude affected the others, their hostility wore off and they also began to smile at me as people smile at an oddly fashioned dog who trots across their path at some distance.

   I knew that Jim and Laura had known each other at Soldan, and I had heard Laura speak admiringly of his voice. I didn't know if Jim remembered her or not. In high school Laura had been as unobtrusive as Jim had been astonishing. If he did remember Laura, it was not as my sister, for when I asked him to dinner, he grinned and said, "You know, Shakespeare, I never thought of you as having folks!" He was about to discover that I did. . . .

Light Up Stage.

Legend On Screen: "The Accent Of A Coming Foot."

Friday evening. It is about five o'clock of a late spring evening which comes "scattering poems in the sky."
   A delicate lemony light is in the Wingfield apartment.
   Amanda has worked like a Turk in preparation for the gentleman caller. The results are astonishing. The new floor lamp with its rose-silk shade is in place, a colored paper lantern conceals the broken light fixture in the ceiling, new billowing white curtains are at the windows, chintz covers are on chairs and sofa, a pair of new sofa pillows make their initial appearance.
   Open boxes and tissue paper are scattered on the floor.
   Laura stands in the middle with lifted arms while Amanda crouches before her, adjusting the hem of the new dress, devout and ritualistic. The dress is colored and designed by memory. The arrangement of Laura's hair is changed; it is softer and more becoming. A fragile, unearthly prettiness has come out in Laura: she is like a piece of translucent glass touched by light, given a momentary radiance, not actual, not lasting.

AMANDA: *(impatiently)* Why are you trembling?
LAURA: Mother, you've made me so nervous!
AMANDA: How have I made you nervous?
5 LAURA: By all this fuss! You make it seem so important!
AMANDA: I don't understand you, Laura. You couldn't be satisfied with just sitting home, and yet whenever I try to arrange something for you, you seem to resist it. *(She gets up.)* Now take a look at yourself. No, wait! Wait just a moment — I have an idea!
LAURA: What is it now?

Amanda produces two powder puffs which she wraps in handkerchiefs and stuffs in Laura's bosom.

LAURA: Mother, what are you doing?
10 AMANDA: They call them "Gay Deceivers"!
LAURA: I won't wear them!
AMANDA: You will!
LAURA: Why should I?
AMANDA: Because, to be painfully honest, your chest is flat.
LAURA: You make it seem like we were setting a trap.

AMANDA: All pretty girls are a trap, a pretty trap, and men expect them to be.   15
   (*Legend: "A Pretty Trap."*) Now look at yourself, young lady. This is the
   prettiest you will ever be! I've got to fix myself now! You're going to be
   surprised by your mother's appearance! (*She crosses through portieres,
   humming gaily.*)

Laura moves slowly to the long mirror and stares solemnly at herself.
   *A wind blows the white curtains inward in a slow, graceful motion and with a faint,
sorrowful sighing.*

AMANDA: (*offstage*) It isn't dark enough yet. (*She turns slowly before the mirror
   with a troubled look.*)

Legend On Screen: "This Is My Sister: Celebrate Her With Strings!" Music.

AMANDA: (*laughing, off*) I'm going to show you something. I'm going to make
   a spectacular appearance!
LAURA: What is it, Mother?
AMANDA: Possess your soul in patience — you will see! Something I've
   resurrected from that old trunk! Styles haven't changed so terribly much
   after all. . . . (*She parts the portieres.*) Now just look at your mother! (*She
   wears a girlish frock of yellowed voile with a blue silk sash. She carries a bunch
   of jonquils — the legend of her youth is nearly revived. Feverishly.*) This is the
   dress in which I led the cotillion. Won the cakewalk twice at Sunset Hill,
   wore one spring to the Governor's ball in Jackson! See how I sashayed
   around the ballroom, Laura? (*She raises her skirt and does a mincing step
   around the room.*) I wore it on Sundays for my gentlemen callers! I had it on
   the day I met your father — I had malaria fever all that spring. The change
   of climate from East Tennessee to the Delta — weakened resistance — I
   had a little temperature all the time — not enough to be serious — just
   enough to make me restless and giddy! Invitations poured in — parties all
   over the Delta! — "Stay in bed," said Mother, "you have fever!" — but
   I just wouldn't. — I took quinine but kept on going, going! — Evenings,
   dances! — Afternoons, long, long rides! Picnics — lovely! — So lovely,
   that country in May. All lacy with dogwood, literally flooded with
   jonquils! — That was the spring I had the craze for jonquils. Jonquils
   became an absolute obsession. Mother said, "Honey, there's no more
   room for jonquils." And still I kept bringing in more jonquils. Whenever,
   wherever I saw them, I'd say, "Stop! Stop! I see jonquils!" I made the
   young men help me gather the jonquils! It was a joke, Amanda and her
   jonquils! Finally there were no more vases to hold them, every available
   space was filled with jonquils. No vases to hold them? All right, I'll hold
   them myself! And then I —(*She stops in front of the picture.*) (*Music*) met
   your father! Malaria fever and jonquils and then — this —boy. . . . (*She
   switches on the rose-colored lamp.*) I hope they get here before it starts to
   rain. (*She crosses upstage and places the jonquils in bowl on table.*) I gave
   your brother a little extra change so he and Mr. O'Connor could take the
   service car home.

20   LAURA: *(with altered look)* What did you say his name was?
AMANDA: O'Connor.
LAURA: What is his first name?
AMANDA: I don't remember. Oh, yes, I do. It was — Jim!

Laura sways slightly and catches hold of a chair.

Legend On Screen: "Not Jim!"

LAURA: *(faintly)* Not — Jim!
25   AMANDA: Yes, that was it, it was Jim! I've never known a Jim that wasn't nice!

Music: Ominous.

LAURA: Are you sure his name is Jim O'Connor?
AMANDA: Yes. Why?
LAURA: Is he the one that Tom used to know in high school?
AMANDA: He didn't say so. I think he just got to know him at the warehouse.
30   LAURA: There was a Jim O'Connor we both knew in high school — *(Then, with effort.)* If that is the one that Tom is bringing to dinner — you'll have to excuse me, I won't come to the table.
AMANDA: What sort of nonsense is this?
LAURA: You asked me once if I'd ever liked a boy. Don't you remember I showed you this boy's picture?
AMANDA: You mean the boy you showed me in the year book?
LAURA: Yes, that boy.
35   AMANDA: Laura, Laura, were you in love with that boy?
LAURA: I don't know, Mother. All I know is I couldn't sit at the table if it was him!
AMANDA: It won't be him! It isn't the least bit likely. But whether it is or not, you will come to the table. You will not be excused.
LAURA: I'll have to be, Mother.
AMANDA: I don't intend to humor your silliness, Laura. I've had too much from you and your brother, both! So just sit down and compose yourself till they come. Tom has forgotten his key so you'll have to let them in, when they arrive.
40   LAURA: *(panicky)* Oh, Mother — *you* answer the door!
AMANDA: *(lightly)* I'll be in the kitchen — busy!
LAURA: Oh, Mother, please answer the door, don't make me do it!
AMANDA: *(crossing into kitchenette)* I've got to fix the dressing for the salmon. Fuss, fuss — silliness! — over a gentleman caller!

Door swings shut. Laura is left alone.

Legend: "Terror!"

She utters a low moan and turns off the lamp — sits stiffly on the edge of the sofa, knotting her fingers together.

Legend On Screen: "The Opening Of A Door!"

Tom and Jim appear on the fire-escape steps and climb to landing. Hearing their approach, Laura rises with a panicky gesture. She retreats to the portieres.
   The doorbell. Laura catches her breath and touches her throat. Low drums.

AMANDA: *(calling)* Laura, sweetheart! The door!

Laura stares at it without moving.

JIM: I think we just beat the rain.   45
TOM: Uh-huh. *(He rings again, nervously. Jim whistles and fishes for a
   cigarette.)*
AMANDA: *(very, very gaily)* Laura, that is your brother and Mr. O'Connor!
   Will you let them in, darling?

Laura crosses toward kitchenette door.

LAURA: *(breathlessly)* Mother — you go to the door!

*Amanda steps out of kitchenette and stares furiously at Laura. She points imperiously
at the door.*

LAURA: Please, please!
AMANDA: *(in a fierce whisper)* What is the matter with you, you silly thing?   50
LAURA: *(desperately)* Please, you answer it, *please!*
AMANDA: I told you I wasn't going to humor you, Laura. Why have you cho-
   sen this moment to lose your mind?
LAURA: Please, please, please, you go!
AMANDA: You'll have to go to the door because I can't!
LAURA: *(despairingly)* I can't either!   55
AMANDA: Why?
LAURA: I'm *sick!*
AMANDA: I'm sick, too — of your nonsense! Why can't you and your brother
   be normal people? Fantastic whims and behavior! *(Tom gives a long ring.)*
   Preposterous goings on! Can you give me one reason — *(Calls out lyrically.)*
   COMING! JUST ONE SECOND! — why should you be afraid to open a door?
   Now you answer it, Laura!
LAURA: Oh, oh, oh . . . *(She returns through the portieres. Darts to the Victrola
   and winds it frantically and turns it on.)*
AMANDA: Laura Wingfield, you march right to that door!   60
LAURA: Yes — yes, Mother!

*A faraway, scratchy rendition of "Dardanella" softens the air and gives her strength to
move through it. She slips to the door and draws it cautiously open. Tom enters with the
caller, Jim O'Connor.*

TOM: Laura, this is Jim. Jim, this is my sister, Laura.
JIM: *(stepping inside)* I didn't know that Shakespeare had a sister!
LAURA: *(retreating stiff and trembling from the door)* How — how do you do?
JIM: *(heartily extending his hand)* Okay!   65

Laura touches it hesitantly with hers.

JIM: Your hand's *cold*, Laura!

LAURA: Yes, well — I've been playing the Victrola. . . .

JIM: Must have been playing classical music on it! You ought to play a little hot swing music to warm you up!

LAURA: Excuse me — I haven't finished playing the Victrola. . . .

She turns awkwardly and hurries into the front room. She pauses a second by the Victrola. Then catches her breath and darts through the portieres like a frightened deer.

70 JIM: *(grinning)* What was the matter?

TOM: Oh — with Laura? Laura is — terribly shy.

JIM: Shy, huh? It's unusual to meet a shy girl nowadays. I don't believe you ever mentioned you had a sister.

TOM: Well, now you know. I have one. Here is the *Post Dispatch*. You want a piece of it?

JIM: Uh-huh.

75 TOM: What piece? The comics?

JIM: Sports! *(Glances at it.)* Ole Dizzy Dean° is on his bad behavior.

TOM: *(disinterested)* Yeah? *(Lights cigarette and crosses back to fire-escape door.)*

JIM: Where are *you* going?

TOM: I'm going out on the terrace.

80 JIM: *(goes after him)* You know, Shakespeare — I'm going to sell you a bill of goods!

TOM: What goods?

JIM: A course I'm taking.

TOM: Huh?

JIM: In public speaking! You and me, we're not the warehouse type.

85 TOM: Thanks — that's good news. But what has public speaking got to do with it?

JIM: It fits you for — executive positions!

TOM: Awww.

JIM: I tell you it's done a helluva lot for me.

Image: Executive At Desk.

TOM: In what respect?

90 JIM: In every! Ask yourself what is the difference between you an' me and men in the office down front? Brains? — No! — Ability? — No! Then what? Just one little thing —

TOM: What is that one little thing?

JIM: Primarily it amounts to — social poise! Being able to square up to people and hold your own on any social level!

AMANDA: *(offstage)* Tom?

Dizzy Dean: Jay Hanna Dean (1910–1974), American baseball player who pitched for the St. Louis Cardinals (1930, 1932–1937), winning 30 games in 1934 and averaging 24 wins in his first five full seasons. From 1938 to 1941, he played for the Chicago Cubs.

TOM: Yes, Mother?

AMANDA: Is that you and Mr. O'Connor? 95

TOM: Yes, Mother.

AMANDA: Well, you just make yourselves comfortable in there.

TOM: Yes, Mother.

AMANDA: Ask Mr. O'Connor if he would like to wash his hands.

JIM: Aw — no — thank you — I took care of that at the warehouse. Tom — 100

TOM: Yes?

JIM: Mr. Mendoza was speaking to me about you.

TOM: Favorably?

JIM: What do you think?

TOM: Well— 105

JIM: You're going to be out of a job if you don't wake up.

TOM: I am waking up—

JIM: You show no signs.

TOM: The signs are interior.

Image On Screen: The Sailing Vessel With Jolly Roger Again.

TOM: I'm planning to change. (*He leans over the rail speaking with quiet exhilara-* 110
tion. The incandescent marquees and signs of the first-run movie houses light his
face from across the alley. He looks like a voyager.) I'm right at the point of
committing myself to a future that doesn't include the warehouse and
Mr. Mendoza or even a night-school course in public speaking.

JIM: What are you gassing about?

TOM: I'm tired of the movies.

JIM: Movies!

TOM: Yes, movies! Look at them — (*A wave toward the marvels of Grand Ave-*
nue.) All of those glamorous people —having adventures —hogging it all,
gobbling the whole thing up! You know what happens? People go to the
movies instead of moving! Hollywood characters are supposed to have all the
adventures for everybody in America, while everybody in America sits in a
dark room and watches them have them! Yes, until there's a war. That's
when adventure becomes available to the masses! *Everyone's* dish, not only
Gable's! Then the people in the dark room come out of the dark room to
have some adventures themselves — Goody, goody — It's our turn now, to
go to the South Sea Island — to make a safari — to be exotic, far-off — But
I'm not patient. I don't want to wait till then. I'm tired of the *movies* and
I am *about* to *move!*

JIM: (*incredulously*) Move? 115

TOM: Yes.

JIM: When?

TOM: Soon!

JIM: Where? Where?

Theme three music seems to answer the question, while Tom thinks it over. He searches
among his pockets.

120   **TOM:** I'm starting to boil inside. I know I seem dreary, but inside — well, I'm boiling! Whenever I pick up a shoe, I shudder a little thinking how short life is and what I am doing! — Whatever that means. I know it doesn't mean shoes — except as something to wear on a traveler's feet! (*Finds paper.*) Look —

JIM: What?

TOM: I'm a member.

JIM: (*reading*) The Union of Merchant Seamen.

TOM: I paid my dues this month, instead of the light bill.

125   **JIM:** You will regret it when they turn the lights off.

TOM: I won't be here.

JIM: How about your mother?

TOM: I'm like my father. The bastard son of a bastard! See how he grins? And he's been absent going on sixteen years!

JIM: You're just talking, you drip. How does your mother feel about it?

130   **TOM:** Shhh — Here comes Mother! Mother is not acquainted with my plans!

AMANDA: (*enters portieres*) Where are you all?

TOM: On the terrace, Mother.

They start inside. She advances to them. Tom is distinctly shocked at her appearance. Even Jim blinks a little. He is making his first contact with girlish Southern vivacity and in spite of the night-school course in public speaking is somewhat thrown off the beam by the unexpected outlay of social charm.

Certain responses are attempted by Jim but are swept aside by Amanda's gay laughter and chatter. Tom is embarrassed but after the first shock Jim reacts very warmly. Grins and chuckles, is altogether won over.

Image: Amanda As A Girl.

AMANDA: (*coyly smiling, shaking her girlish ringlets*) Well, well, well, so this is Mr. O'Connor. Introductions entirely unnecessary. I've heard so much about you from my boy. I finally said to him, Tom — good gracious! — why don't you bring this paragon to supper? I'd like to meet this nice young man at the warehouse! — Instead of just hearing him sing your praises so much! I don't know why my son is so stand-offish — that's not Southern behavior! Let's sit down and — I think we could stand a little more air in here! Tom, leave the door open. I felt a nice fresh breeze a moment ago. Where has it gone? Mmm, so warm already! And not quite summer, even. We're going to burn up when summer really gets started. However, we're having — we're having a very light supper. I think light things are better fo' this time of year. The same as light clothes are. Light clothes an' light food are what warm weather calls fo'. You know our blood gets so thick during th' winter — it takes a while fo' us to *adjust* ou'selves! — when the season changes . . . It's come so quick this year. I wasn't prepared. All of a sudden — heavens! Already summer! — I ran to the trunk an' pulled out this light dress — Terribly old! Historical almost! But feels so good — so good an' co-ol, y'know. . . .

Tom: Mother—

Amanda: Yes, honey?   135

Tom: How about — supper?

Amanda: Honey, you go ask Sister if supper is ready! You know that Sister is
in full charge of supper! Tell her you hungry boys are waiting for it.
(To Jim.) Have you met Laura?

Jim: She—

Amanda: Let you in? Oh, good, you've met already! It's rare for a girl as sweet
an' pretty as Laura to be domestic! But Laura is, thank heavens, not only
pretty but also very domestic. I'm not at all. I never was a bit. I never could
make a thing but angel-food cake. Well, in the South we had so many servants. Gone, gone, gone. All vestiges of gracious living! Gone completely!
I wasn't prepared for what the future brought me. All of my gentlemen
callers were sons of planters and so of course I assumed that I would be married to one and raise my family on a large piece of land with plenty of servants. But man proposes — and woman accepts the proposal! — To vary
that old, old saying a little bit — I married no planter! I married a man who
worked for the telephone company! — that gallantly smiling gentleman
over there! *(Points to the picture.)* A telephone man who — fell in love with
long-distance! — Now he travels and I don't even know where! — But what
am I going on for about my — tribulations? Tell me yours — I hope you
don't have any! Tom?

Tom: *(returning)* Yes, Mother?   140

Amanda: Is supper nearly ready?

Tom: It looks to me like supper is on the table.

Amanda: Let me look —*(She rises prettily and looks through portieres.)* Oh,
lovely — But where is Sister?

Tom: Laura is not feeling well and says that she thinks she'd better not come
to the table.

Amanda: What?— Nonsense! — Laura? Oh, Laura!   145

Laura: *(offstage, faintly)* Yes, Mother.

Amanda: You really must come to the table. We won't be seated until you
come to the table! Come in, Mr. O'Connor. You sit over there and I'll —
Laura? Laura Wingfield! You're keeping us waiting, honey! We can't say
grace until you come to the table!

*The back door is pushed weakly open and Laura comes in. She is obviously quite faint,
her lips trembling, her eyes wide and staring. She moves unsteadily toward the table.*

Legend: "Terror!"

*Outside a summer storm is coming abruptly. The white curtains billow inward at the
windows and there is a sorrowful murmur and deep blue dusk.*
   Laura suddenly stumbles — She catches at a chair with a faint moan.

Tom: Laura!

Amanda: Laura! *(There is a clap of thunder.)* *(Legend: "Ah!")* *(Despairingly.)*
Why, Laura, you are sick, darling! Tom, help your sister into the living

room, dear! Sit in the living room, Laura — rest on the sofa. Well! *(To the gentleman caller.)* Standing over the hot stove made her ill! — I told her that it was just too warm this evening, but — *(Tom comes back in. Laura is on the sofa.)* Is Laura all right now?

150   **TOM:** Yes.

AMANDA: What *is* that? Rain? A nice cool rain has come up! *(She gives the gentleman caller a frightened look.)* I think we may — have grace — now . . . *(Tom looks at her stupidly.)* Tom, honey — you say grace!

TOM: Oh . . . "For these and all thy mercies —" *(They bow their heads, Amanda stealing a nervous glance at Jim. In the living room Laura, stretched on the sofa, clenches her hand to her lips, to hold back a shuddering sob.)* God's Holy Name be praised—

The Scene Dims Out.

SCENE 7

A Souvenir.

Half an hour later. Dinner is just being finished in the upstage area which is concealed by the drawn portieres.

   As the curtain rises Laura is still huddled upon the sofa, her feet drawn under her, her head resting on a pale blue pillow, her eyes wide and mysteriously watchful. The new floor lamp with its shade of rose-colored silk gives a soft, becoming light to her face, bringing out the fragile, unearthly prettiness which usually escapes attention. There is a steady murmur of rain, but it is slackening and stops soon after the scene begins; the air outside becomes pale and luminous as the moon breaks out.

   A moment after the curtain rises, the lights in both rooms flicker and go out.

JIM: Hey, there, Mr. Light Bulb!

Amanda laughs nervously.

Legend: "Suspension Of A Public Service."

AMANDA: Where was Moses when the lights went out? Ha-ha. Do you know the answer to that one, Mr. O'Connor?

JIM: No, Ma'am, what's the answer?

AMANDA: In the dark! *(Jim laughs appreciatively.)* Everybody sit still. I'll light the candles. Isn't it lucky we have them on the table? Where's a match? Which of you gentlemen can provide a match?

5   **JIM:** Here.

AMANDA: Thank you, sir.

JIM: Not at all, Ma'am!

AMANDA: I guess the fuse has burnt out. Mr. O'Connor, can you tell a burntout fuse? I know I can't and Tom is a total loss when it comes to mechanics. *(Sound: Getting Up: Voices Recede A Little To Kitchenette.)* Oh, be careful you don't bump into something. We don't want our gentleman caller to break his neck. Now wouldn't that be a fine howdy-do?

JIM: Ha-ha! Where is the fuse-box?

AMANDA: Right here next to the stove. Can you see anything?   10

JIM: Just a minute.

AMANDA: Isn't electricity a mysterious thing? Wasn't it Benjamin Franklin who tied a key to a kite? We live in such a mysterious universe, don't we? Some people say that science clears up all the mysteries for us. In my opinion it only creates more! Have you found it yet?

JIM: No, Ma'am. All these fuses look okay to me.

AMANDA: Tom!

TOM: Yes, Mother?   15

AMANDA: That light bill I gave you several days ago. The one I told you we got the notices about?

TOM: Oh.—Yeah.

Legend: "Ha!"

AMANDA: You didn't neglect to pay it by any chance?

TOM: Why, I—

AMANDA: Didn't! I might have known it!   20

JIM: Shakespeare probably wrote a poem on that light bill, Mrs. Wingfield.

AMANDA: I might have known better than to trust him with it! There's such a high price for negligence in this world!

JIM: Maybe the poem will win a ten-dollar prize.

AMANDA: We'll just have to spend the remainder of the evening in the nineteenth century, before Mr. Edison made the Mazda lamp!

JIM: Candlelight is my favorite kind of light.   25

AMANDA: That shows you're romantic! But that's no excuse for Tom. Well, we got through dinner. Very considerate of them to let us get through dinner before they plunged us into everlasting darkness, wasn't it, Mr. O'Connor?

JIM: Ha-ha!

AMANDA: Tom, as a penalty for your carelessness you can help me with the dishes.

JIM: Let me give you a hand.

AMANDA: Indeed you will not!   30

JIM: I ought to be good for something.

AMANDA: Good for something? (*Her tone is rhapsodic.*) You? Why, Mr. O'Connor, nobody, *nobody's* given me this much entertainment in years — as you have!

JIM: Aw, now, Mrs. Wingfield!

AMANDA: I'm not exaggerating, not one bit! But Sister is all by her lonesome. You go keep her company in the parlor! I'll give you this lovely old candelabrum that used to be on the altar at the church of the Heavenly Rest. It was melted a little out of shape when the church burnt down. Lightning struck it one spring. Gypsy Jones was holding a revival at the time and he intimated that the church was destroyed because the Episcopalians gave card parties.

JIM: Ha-ha.   35

AMANDA: And how about coaxing Sister to drink a little wine? I think it
would be good for her! Can you carry both at once?

JIM: Sure. I'm Superman!

AMANDA: Now, Thomas, get into this apron!

The door of kitchenette swings closed on Amanda's gay laughter; the flickering light approaches the portieres.

Laura sits up nervously as he enters. Her speech at first is low and breathless from the almost intolerable strain of being alone with a stranger.

The Legend: "I Don't Suppose You Remember Me At All!"

In her first speeches in this scene, before Jim's warmth overcomes her paralyzing shyness, Laura's voice is thin and breathless as though she has run up a steep flight of stairs.

Jim's attitude is gently humorous. In playing this scene it should be stressed that while the incident is apparently unimportant, it is to Laura the climax of her secret life.

JIM: Hello, there, Laura.

40 LAURA: *(faintly)* Hello. *(She clears her throat.)*

JIM: How are you feeling now? Better?

LAURA: Yes. Yes, thank you.

JIM: This is for you. A little dandelion wine. *(He extends it toward her with extravagant gallantry.)*

LAURA: Thank you.

45 JIM: Drink it — but don't get drunk! *(He laughs heartily. Laura takes the glass uncertainly; laughs shyly.)* Where shall I set the candles?

LAURA: Oh — oh, anywhere . . .

JIM: How about here on the floor? Any objections?

LAURA: No.

JIM: I'll spread a newspaper under to catch the drippings. I like to sit on the floor. Mind if I do?

50 LAURA: Oh, no.

JIM: Give me a pillow?

LAURA: What?

JIM: A pillow!

LAURA: Oh . . . *(Hands him one quickly.)*

55 JIM: How about you? Don't you like to sit on the floor?

LAURA: Oh — yes.

JIM: Why don't you, then?

LAURA: I — will.

JIM: Take a pillow! *(Laura does. Sits on the other side of the candelabrum. Jim crosses his legs and smiles engagingly at her.)* I can't hardly see you sitting way over there.

60 LAURA: I can — see you.

JIM: I know, but that's not fair, I'm in the limelight. *(Laura moves her pillow closer.)* Good! Now I can see you! Comfortable?

LAURA: Yes.

JIM: So am I. Comfortable as a cow. Will you have some gum?

LAURA: No, thank you.

JIM: I think that I will indulge, with your permission. (*Musingly unwraps it and* 65
  holds it up.) Think of the fortune made by the guy that invented the first
  piece of chewing gum. Amazing, huh? The Wrigley Building is one of the
  sights of Chicago.—I saw it summer before last when I went up to the
  Century of Progress. Did you take in the Century of Progress?

LAURA: No, I didn't.

JIM: Well, it was quite a wonderful exposition. What impressed me most was
  the Hall of Science. Gives you an idea of what the future will be in
  America, even more wonderful than the present time is! (*Pause. Smiling at
  her.*) Your brother tells me you're shy. Is that right, Laura?

LAURA: I — don't know.

JIM: I judge you to be an old-fashioned type of girl. Well, I think that's a pretty
  good type to be. Hope you don't think I'm being too personal — do you?

LAURA: (*hastily, out of embarrassment*) I believe I *will* take a piece of gum, if 70
  you — don't mind. (*Clearing her throat.*) Mr. O'Connor, have you — kept up
  with your singing?

JIM: Singing? Me?

LAURA: Yes. I remember what a beautiful voice you had.

JIM: When did you hear me sing?

Voice Offstage In The Pause.

Voice (*offstage*):

> O blow, ye winds, heigh-ho,
> A-roving I will go!
> I'm off to my love
> With a boxing glove—
> Ten thousand miles away!

JIM: You say you've heard me sing?

LAURA: Oh, yes! Yes, very often . . . I — don't suppose you remember 75
  me — at all?

JIM: (*smiling doubtfully*) You know I have an idea I've seen you before. I had
  that idea soon as you opened the door. It seemed almost like I was about to
  remember your name. But the name that I started to call you — wasn't a
  name! And so I stopped myself before I said it.

LAURA: Wasn't it — Blue Roses?

JIM: (*springs up, grinning*) Blue Roses! My gosh, yes — Blue Roses! That's what
  I had on my tongue when you opened the door! Isn't it funny what tricks
  your memory plays? I didn't connect you with the high school somehow or
  other. But that's where it was; it was high school. I didn't even know you
  were Shakespeare's sister! Gosh, I'm sorry.

LAURA: I didn't expect you to. You — barely knew me!

JIM: But we did have a speaking acquaintance, huh? 80

LAURA: Yes, we — spoke to each other.

JIM: When did you recognize me?

LAURA: Oh, right away!

JIM: Soon as I came in the door?

85 LAURA: When I heard your name I thought it was probably you. I knew that Tom used to know you a little in high school. So when you came in the door —Well, then I was — sure.

JIM: Why didn't you *say* something, then?

LAURA: (*breathlessly*) I didn't know what to say, I was — too surprised!

JIM: For goodness' sakes! You know, this sure is funny!

LAURA: Yes! Yes, isn't it, though . . .

90 JIM: Didn't we have a class in something together?

LAURA: Yes, we did.

JIM: What class was that?

LAURA: It was — singing — Chorus!

JIM: Aw!

95 LAURA: I sat across the aisle from you in the Aud.

JIM: Aw.

LAURA: Mondays, Wednesdays and Fridays.

JIM: Now I remember — you always came in late.

LAURA: Yes, it was so hard for me, getting upstairs. I had that brace on my leg — it clumped so loud!

100 JIM: I never heard any clumping.

LAURA: (*wincing at the recollection*) To me it sounded like — thunder!

JIM: Well, well, well. I never even noticed.

LAURA: And everybody was seated before I came in. I had to walk in front of all those people. My seat was in the back row. I had to go clumping all the way up the aisle with everyone watching!

JIM: You shouldn't have been self-conscious.

105 LAURA: I know, but I was. It was always such a relief when the singing started.

JIM: Aw, yes, I've placed you now! I used to call you Blue Roses. How was it that I got started calling you that?

LAURA: I was out of school a little while with pleurosis. When I came back you asked me what was the matter. I said I had pleurosis — you thought I said Blue Roses. That's what you always called me after that!

JIM: I hope you didn't mind.

LAURA: Oh, no — I liked it. You see, I wasn't acquainted with many — people. . . .

110 JIM: As I remember you sort of stuck by yourself.

LAURA: I — I — never had much luck at — making friends.

JIM: I don't see why you wouldn't.

LAURA: Well, I — started out badly.

JIM: You mean being —

115 LAURA: Yes, it sort of — stood between me —

JIM: You shouldn't have let it!

LAURA: I know, but it did, and —

JIM: You were shy with people!

LAURA: I tried not to be but never could —

JIM: Overcome it? 120

LAURA: No, I — I never could!

JIM: I guess being shy is something you have to work out of kind of gradually.

LAURA: (*sorrowfully*) Yes — I guess it —

JIM: Takes time!

LAURA: Yes— 125

JIM: People are not so dreadful when you know them. That's what you have to remember! And everybody has problems, not just you, but practically everybody has got some problems. You think of yourself as having the only problems, as being the only one who is disappointed. But just look around you and you will see lots of people as disappointed as you are. For instance, I hoped when I was going to high school that I would be further along at this time, six years later, than I am now —You remember that wonderful write-up I had in *The Torch?*

LAURA: Yes! (*She rises and crosses to table.*)

JIM: It said I was bound to succeed in anything I went into! (*Laura returns with the annual.*) Holy Jeez! *The Torch!* (*He accepts it reverently. They smile across it with mutual wonder. Laura crouches beside him and they begin to turn through it. Laura's shyness is dissolving in his warmth.*)

LAURA: Here you are in *Pirates of Penzance!*

JIM: (*wistfully*) I sang the baritone lead in that operetta. 130

LAURA: (*rapidly*) So —*beautifully!*

JIM: (*protesting*) Aw—

LAURA: Yes, yes — beautifully — beautifully!

JIM: You heard me?

LAURA: All three times! 135

JIM: No!

LAURA: Yes!

JIM: All three performances?

LAURA: (*looking down*) Yes.

JIM: Why? 140

LAURA: I — wanted to ask you to — autograph my program.

JIM: Why didn't you ask me to?

LAURA: You were always surrounded by your own friends so much that I never had a chance to.

JIM: You should have just—

LAURA: Well, I — thought you might think I was— 145

JIM: Thought I might think you was — what?

LAURA: Oh—

JIM: (*with reflective relish*) I was beleaguered by females in those days.

LAURA: You were terribly popular!

JIM: Yeah— 150

LAURA: You had such a —friendly way—

JIM: I was spoiled in high school.

LAURA: Everybody —liked you!

JIM: Including you?

155   LAURA: I — yes, I — I did, too — (*She gently closes the book in her lap.*)

JIM: Well, well, well!— Give me that program, Laura. (*She hands it to him. He signs it with a flourish.*) There you are —better late than never!

LAURA: Oh, I — what a — surprise!

JIM: My signature isn't worth very much right now. But some day —maybe — it will increase in value! Being disappointed is one thing and being discouraged is something else. I am disappointed but I'm not discouraged. I'm twenty-three years old. How old are you?

LAURA: I'll be twenty-four in June.

160   JIM: That's not old age!

LAURA: No, but—

JIM: You finished high school?

LAURA: (*with difficulty*) I didn't go back.

JIM: You mean you dropped out?

165   LAURA: I made bad grades in my final examinations. (*She rises and replaces the book and the program. Her voice strained.*) How is — Emily Meisenbach getting along?

JIM: Oh, that kraut-head!

LAURA: Why do you call her that?

JIM: That's what she was.

LAURA: You're not still — going with her?

170   JIM: I never see her.

LAURA: It said in the Personal Section that you were —engaged!

JIM: I know, but I wasn't impressed by that — propaganda!

LAURA: It wasn't — the truth?

JIM: Only in Emily's optimistic opinion!

175   LAURA: Oh—

Legend: "What Have You Done Since High School?"

Jim lights a cigarette and leans indolently back on his elbows smiling at Laura with a warmth and charm which light her inwardly with altar candles. She remains by the table and turns in her hands a piece of glass to cover her tumult.

JIM: (*after several reflective puffs on a cigarette*) What have you done since high school? (*She seems not to hear him.*) Huh? (*Laura looks up.*) I said what have you done since high school, Laura?

LAURA: Nothing much.

JIM: You must have been doing something these six long years.

LAURA: Yes.

180   JIM: Well, then, such as what?

LAURA: I took a business course at business college—

JIM: How did that work out?

LAURA: Well, not very — well — I had to drop out, it gave me —indigestion—

Jim laughs gently.

JIM: What are you doing now?

LAURA: I don't do anything — much. Oh, please don't think I sit around doing   185
nothing! My glass collection takes up a good deal of my time. Glass is
something you have to take good care of.

JIM: What did you say — about glass?

LAURA: Collection I said — I have one — (*She clears her throat and turns away
again, acutely shy.*)

JIM: (*abruptly*) You know what I judge to be the trouble with you? Inferiority
complex! Know what that is? That's what they call it when someone low-
rates himself! I understand it because I had it, too. Although my case was
not so aggravated as yours seems to be. I had it until I took up public speaking, developed my voice, and learned that I had an aptitude for science.
Before that time I never thought of myself as being outstanding in any way
whatsoever! Now I've never made a regular study of it, but I have a friend
who says I can analyze people better than doctors that make a profession of
it. I don't claim that to be necessarily true, but I can sure guess a person's
psychology, Laura! (*Takes out his gum.*) Excuse me, Laura. I always take it
out when the flavor is gone. I'll use this scrap of paper to wrap it in. I know
how it is to get it stuck on a shoe. Yep — that's what I judge to be your principal trouble. A lack of confidence in yourself as a person. You don't have
the proper amount of faith in yourself. I'm basing that fact on a number of
your remarks and also on certain observations I've made. For instance that
clumping you thought was so awful in high school. You say that you even
dreaded to walk into class. You see what you did? You dropped out of school,
you gave up an education because of a clump, which as far as I know was
practically nonexistent! A little physical defect is what you have. Hardly
noticeable even! Magnified thousands of times by imagination! You know
what my strong advice to you is? Think of yourself as *superior* in some way!

LAURA: In what way would I think?

JIM: Why, man alive, Laura! Just look about you a little. What do you see? A   190
world full of common people! All of 'em born and all of 'em going to die!
Which of them has one-tenth of your good points! Or mine! Or anyone
else's, as far as that goes — Gosh! Everybody excels in some one thing.
Some in many! (*Unconsciously glances at himself in the mirror.*) All you've
got to do is discover in *what*! Take me, for instance. (*He adjusts his tie at the
mirror.*) My interest happens to lie in electro-dynamics. I'm taking a course
in radio engineering at night school, Laura, on top of a fairly responsible
job at the warehouse. I'm taking that course and studying public speaking.

LAURA: Ohhhh.

JIM: Because I believe in the future of television! (*Turning back to her.*) I wish
to be ready to go up right along with it. Therefore I'm planning to get in on
the ground floor. In fact, I've already made the right connections and all
that remains is for the industry itself to get underway! Full steam — (*His
eyes are starry.*) Knowledge— Zzzzzp! Money— Zzzzzzp! —Power! That's the
cycle democracy is built on! (*His attitude is convincingly dynamic. Laura
stares at him, even her shyness eclipsed in her absolute wonder. He suddenly
grins.*) I guess you think I think a lot of myself!

LAURA: No — o-o-o, I—

JIM: Now how about you? Isn't there something you take more interest in than anything else?

195 LAURA: Well, I do — as I said — have my — glass collection—

A peal of girlish laughter from the kitchen.

JIM: I'm not right sure I know what you're talking about. What kind of glass is it?

LAURA: Little articles of it, they're ornaments mostly! Most of them are little animals made out of glass, the tiniest little animals in the world. Mother calls them a glass menagerie! Here's an example of one, if you'd like to see it! This one is one of the oldest. It's nearly thirteen. *(He stretches out his hand.)* *(Music: "The Glass Menagerie.")* Oh, be careful — if you breathe, it breaks!

JIM: I'd better not take it. I'm pretty clumsy with things.

LAURA: Go on, I trust you with him! *(Places it in his palm.)* There now — you're holding him gently! Hold him over the light, he loves the light! You see how the light shines through him?

200 JIM: It sure does shine!

LAURA: I shouldn't be partial, but he is my favorite one.

JIM: What kind of a thing is this one supposed to be?

LAURA: Haven't you noticed the single horn on his forehead?

JIM: A unicorn, huh?

205 LAURA: Mmm-hmmm!

JIM: Unicorns, aren't they extinct in the modern world?

LAURA: I know!

JIM: Poor little fellow, he must feel sort of lonesome.

LAURA: *(smiling)* Well, if he does he doesn't complain about it. He stays on a shelf with some horses that don't have horns and all of them seem to get along nicely together.

210 JIM: How do you know?

LAURA: *(lightly)* I haven't heard any arguments among them!

JIM: *(grinning)* No arguments, huh? Well, that's a pretty good sign! Where shall I set him?

LAURA: Put him on the table. They all like a change of scenery once in a while!

JIM: *(stretching)* Well, well, well, well — Look how big my shadow is when I stretch!

215 LAURA: Oh, oh, yes — it stretches across the ceiling!

JIM: *(crossing to door)* I think it's stopped raining. *(Opens fire-escape door.)* Where does the music come from?

LAURA: From the Paradise Dance Hall across the alley.

JIM: How about cutting the rug a little, Miss Wingfield?

LAURA: Oh, I—

220 JIM: Or is your program filled up? Let me have a look at it. *(Grasps imaginary card.)* Why, every dance is taken! I'll just have to scratch some out. *(Waltz Music: "La Golondrina.")* Ahhh, a waltz! *(He executes some sweeping turns by himself, then holds his arms toward Laura.)*

LAURA: *(breathlessly)* I — can't dance!

JIM: There you go, that inferiority stuff!

LAURA: I've never danced in my life!

JIM: Come on, try!

LAURA: Oh, but I'd step on you!   225

JIM: I'm not made out of glass.

LAURA: How — how — how do we start?

JIM: Just leave it to me. You hold your arms out a little.

LAURA: Like this?

JIM: A little bit higher. Right. Now don't tighten up, that's the main thing   230
   about it — relax.

LAURA: (*laughing breathlessly*) It's hard not to.

JIM: Okay.

LAURA: I'm afraid you can't budge me.

JIM: What do you bet I can't? (*He swings her into motion.*)

LAURA: Goodness, yes, you can!   235

JIM: Let yourself go, now, Laura, just let yourself go.

LAURA: I'm—

JIM: Come on!

LAURA: Trying!

JIM: Not so stiff — Easy does it!   240

LAURA: I know but I'm—

JIM: Loosen th' backbone! There now, that's a lot better.

LAURA: Am I?

JIM: Lots, lots better! (*He moves her about the room in a clumsy waltz.*)

LAURA: Oh, my!   245

JIM: Ha-ha!

LAURA: Goodness, yes you can!

JIM: Ha-ha-ha! (*They suddenly bump into the table, Jim stops.*) What did we
   hit on?

LAURA: Table.

JIM: Did something fall off it? I think—   250

LAURA: Yes.

JIM: I hope that it wasn't the little glass horse with the horn!

LAURA: Yes.

JIM: Aw, aw, aw. Is it broken?

LAURA: Now it is just like all the other horses.   255

JIM: It's lost its—

LAURA: Horn! It doesn't matter. Maybe it's a blessing in disguise.

JIM: You'll never forgive me. I bet that that was your favorite piece of glass.

LAURA: I don't have favorites much. It's no tragedy, Freckles. Glass breaks so
   easily. No matter how careful you are. The traffic jars the shelves and things
   fall off them.

JIM: Still I'm awfully sorry that I was the cause.   260

LAURA: (*smiling*) I'll just imagine he had an operation. The horn was removed
   to make him feel less —freakish! (*They both laugh.*) Now he will feel more
   at home with the other horses, the ones that don't have horns . . .

Laura in the arms of the gentleman caller while Tom and Amanda look on in Tennessee Williams's *The Glass Menagerie* at the Williamstown Theatre Festival.

JIM: Ha-ha, that's very funny! (*Suddenly serious.*) I'm glad to see that you have a sense of humor. You know — you're — well — very different! Surprisingly different from anyone else I know! (*His voice becomes soft and hesitant with a genuine feeling.*) Do you mind me telling you that? (*Laura is abashed beyond speech.*) You make me feel sort of — I don't know how to put it! I'm usually pretty good at expressing things, but — This is something that I don't know how to say! (*Laura touches her throat and clears it — turns the broken unicorn in her hands.*) (*Even softer.*) Has anyone ever told you that you were pretty? (*Pause: Music.*) (*Laura looks up slowly, with wonder, and shakes her head.*) Well, you are! In a very different way from anyone else. And all the nicer because of the difference, too. (*His voice becomes low and husky. Laura turns away, nearly faint with the novelty of her emotions.*) I wish you were my sister. I'd teach you to have some confidence in yourself. The different people are not like other people, but being different is nothing to be ashamed of. Because other people are not such wonderful people. They're one hundred times one thousand. You're one times one! They walk all over the earth. You just stay here. They're common as — weeds, but — you — well, you're — *Blue Roses!*

Image On Screen: Blue Roses.

Music Changes.

LAURA: But blue is wrong for — roses . . .
JIM: It's right for you — You're — pretty!

LAURA: In what respect am I pretty? 265

JIM: In all respects — believe me! Your eyes — your hair — are pretty! Your hands are pretty! *(He catches hold of her hand.)* You think I'm making this up because I'm invited to dinner and have to be nice. Oh, I could do that! I could put on an act for you, Laura, and say lots of things without being very sincere. But this time I am. I'm talking to you sincerely. I happened to notice you had this inferiority complex that keeps you from feeling comfortable with people. Somebody needs to build your confidence up and make you proud instead of shy and turning away and — blushing — Somebody ought to — ought to — kiss you, Laura! *(His hand slips slowly up her arm to her shoulder.) (Music Swells Tumultuously.) (He suddenly turns her about and kisses her on the lips. When he releases her Laura sinks on the sofa with a bright, dazed look. Jim backs away and fishes in his pocket for a cigarette.) (Legend On Screen: "Souvenir.")* Stumble-john! *(He lights the cigarette, avoiding her look. There is a peal of girlish laughter from Amanda in the kitchen. Laura slowly raises and opens her hand. It still contains the little broken glass animal. She looks at it with a tender, bewildered expression.)* Stumble-john! I shouldn't have done that — That was way off the beam. You don't smoke, do you? *(She looks up, smiling, not hearing the question. He sits beside her a little gingerly. She looks at him speechlessly — waiting. He coughs decorously and moves a little farther aside as he considers the situation and senses her feelings, dimly, with perturbation. Gently.)* Would you — care for a — mint? *(She doesn't seem to hear him but her look grows brighter even.)* Peppermint — Life Saver? My pocket's a regular drug store — wherever I go . . . *(He pops a mint in his mouth. Then gulps and decides to make a clean breast of it. He speaks slowly and gingerly.)* Laura, you know, if I had a sister like you, I'd do the same thing as Tom, I'd bring out fellows — introduce her to them. The right type of boys of a type to — appreciate her. Only — well — he made a mistake about me. Maybe I've got no call to be saying this. That may not have been the idea in having me over. But what if it was? There's nothing wrong about that. The only trouble is that in my case — I'm not in a situation to do the right thing. I can't take down your number and say I'll phone. I can't call up next week and — ask for a date. I thought I had better explain the situation in case you misunderstood it and — hurt your feelings. . . . *(Pause. Slowly, very slowly, Laura's look changes, her eyes returning slowly from his to the ornament in her palm.)*

Amanda utters another gay laugh in the kitchen.

LAURA: *(faintly)* You — won't — call again?

JIM: No, Laura. I can't. *(He rises from the sofa.)* As I was just explaining, I've — got strings on me, Laura, I've — been going steady! I go out all the time with a girl named Betty. She's a home-girl like you, and Catholic, and Irish, and in a great many ways we — get along fine. I met her last summer on a moonlight boat trip up the river to Alton, on the *Majestic.* Well — right away from the start it was — love! *(Legend: Love!) (Laura sways slightly forward and grips the arm of the sofa. He fails to notice, now enrapt in his own comfortable being.)* Being in love has made a new man of me! *(Leaning stiffly forward, clutching the arm of the sofa, Laura struggles visibly with her storm. But Jim is oblivious, she is a long way off.*) The power of love is really pretty tremendous! Love is something that — changes the whole world, Laura! (*The storm abates a little and Laura leans back. He notices her again.*) It happened that Betty's aunt took sick, she got a wire and had to go to Centralia. So Tom — when he asked me to dinner — I naturally just accepted the invitation, not knowing that you — that he — that I — (*He stops awkwardly.*) Huh — I'm a stumble-john! (*He flops back on the sofa. The holy candles in the altar of Laura's face have been snuffed out! There is a look of almost infinite desolation. Jim glances at her uneasily.*) I wish that you would — say something. (*She bites her lip which was trembling and then bravely smiles. She opens her hand again on the broken glass ornament. Then she gently takes his hand and raises it level with her own. She carefully places the unicorn in the palm of his hand, then pushes his fingers closed upon it.*) What are you — doing that for? You want me to have him? — Laura? (*She nods.*) What for?

LAURA: A — souvenir . . .

She rises unsteadily and crouches beside the Victrola to wind it up.

Legend On Screen: "Things Have A Way Of Turning Out So Badly."

Or Image: "Gentleman Caller Waving Good-bye! — Gaily."

At this moment Amanda rushes brightly back in the front room. She bears a pitcher of fruit punch in an old-fashioned cut-glass pitcher and a plate of macaroons. The plate has a gold border and poppies painted on it.

270 AMANDA: Well, well, well! Isn't the air delightful after the shower? I've made you children a little liquid refreshment. (*Turns gaily to the gentleman caller.*) Jim, do you know that song about lemonade?

> "Lemonade, lemonade
> Made in the shade and stirred with a spade —
> Good enough for any old maid!"

JIM: (*uneasily*) Ha-ha! No — I never heard it.

AMANDA: Why, Laura! You look so serious!

JIM: We were having a serious conversation.

AMANDA: Good! Now you're better acquainted!

275 JIM: (*uncertainly*) Ha-ha! Yes.

AMANDA: You modern young people are much more serious-minded than my generation. I was so gay as a girl!

JIM: You haven't changed, Mrs. Wingfield.

AMANDA: Tonight I'm rejuvenated! The gaiety of the occasion, Mr. O'Connor! (*She tosses her head with a peal of laughter. Spills lemonade.*) Oooo! I'm baptizing myself!

JIM: Here — let me —

280 AMANDA: (*setting the pitcher down*) There now. I discovered we had some maraschino cherries. I dumped them in, juice and all!

JIM: You shouldn't have gone to that trouble, Mrs. Wingfield.

AMANDA: Trouble, trouble? Why it was loads of fun! Didn't you hear me cutting up in the kitchen? I bet your ears were burning! I told Tom how outdone with him I was for keeping you to himself so long a time! He should have brought you over much, much sooner! Well, now that you've found your way, I want you to be a very frequent caller! Not just occasional but all the time. Oh, we're going to have a lot of gay times together! I see them coming! Mmm, just breathe that air! So fresh, and the moon's so pretty! I'll skip back out — I know where my place is when young folks are having a — serious conversation!

JIM: Oh, don't go out, Mrs. Wingfield. The fact of the matter is I've got to be going.

AMANDA: Going, now? You're joking! Why, it's only the shank of the evening, Mr. O'Connor!

JIM: Well, you know how it is.   285

AMANDA: You mean you're a young workingman and have to keep workingmen's hours. We'll let you off early tonight. But only on the condition that next time you stay later. What's the best night for you? Isn't Saturday night the best night for you workingmen?

JIM: I have a couple of time-clocks to punch, Mrs. Wingfield. One at morning, another one at night!

AMANDA: My, but you are ambitious! You work at night, too?

JIM: No, Ma'am, not work but — Betty! (*He crosses deliberately to pick up his hat. The band at the Paradise Dance Hall goes into a tender waltz.*)

AMANDA: Betty? Betty? Who's Betty! (*There is an ominous cracking sound in*   290
the sky.*)

JIM: Oh, just a girl. The girl I go steady with! (*He smiles charmingly. The sky falls.*)

Legend: "The Sky Falls."

AMANDA: (*a long-drawn exhalation*) Ohhhh . . . Is it a serious romance Mr. O'Connor?

JIM: We're going to be married the second Sunday in June.

AMANDA: Ohhhh — how nice! Tom didn't mention that you were engaged to be married.

JIM: The cat's not out of the bag at the warehouse yet. You know how they are.   295
They call you Romeo and stuff like that. (*He stops at the oval mirror to put on his hat. He carefully shapes the brim and the crown to give a discreetly dashing effect.*) It's been a wonderful evening, Mrs. Wingfield. I guess this is what they mean by Southern hospitality.

AMANDA: It really wasn't anything at all.

JIM: I hope it don't seem like I'm rushing off. But I promised Betty I'd pick her up at the Wabash depot, an' by the time I get my jalopy down there her train'll be in. Some women are pretty upset if you keep 'em waiting.

AMANDA: Yes, I know — The tyranny of women! (*Extends her hand.*) Good-bye, Mr. O'Connor. I wish you luck — and happiness — and success! All three of them, and so does Laura! — Don't you, Laura?

Laura: Yes!

300 Jim: (*taking her hand*) Good-bye, Laura. I'm certainly going to treasure that souvenir. And don't you forget the good advice I gave you. (*Raises his voice to a cheery shout.*) So long, Shakespeare! Thanks again, ladies — Good night!

He grins and ducks jauntily out.

Still bravely grimacing, Amanda closes the door on the gentleman caller. Then she turns back to the room with a puzzled expression. She and Laura don't dare to face each other. Laura crouches beside the Victrola to wind it.

Amanda: (*faintly*) Things have a way of turning out so badly. I don't believe that I would play the Victrola. Well, well — well — Our gentleman caller was engaged to be married! Tom!

Tom: (*from back*) Yes, Mother?

Amanda: Come in here a minute. I want to tell you something awfully funny.

Tom: (*enters with macaroon and a glass of the lemonade*) Has the gentleman caller gotten away already?

305 Amanda: The gentleman caller has made an early departure. What a wonderful joke you played on us!

Tom: How do you mean?

Amanda: You didn't mention that he was engaged to be married.

Tom: Jim? Engaged?

Amanda: That's what he just informed us.

310 Tom: I'll be jiggered! I didn't know about that.

Amanda: That seems very peculiar.

Tom: What's peculiar about it?

Amanda: Didn't you call him your best friend down at the warehouse?

Tom: He is, but how did I know?

315 Amanda: It seems extremely peculiar that you wouldn't know your best friend was going to be married!

Tom: The warehouse is where I work, not where I know things about people!

Amanda: You don't know things anywhere! You live in a dream; you manufacture illusions! (*He crosses to door.*) Where are you going?

Tom: I'm going to the movies.

Amanda: That's right, now that you've had us make such fools of ourselves. The effort, the preparations, all the expense! The new floor lamp, the rug, the clothes for Laura! All for what? To entertain some other girl's fiancé! Go to the movies, go! Don't think about us, a mother deserted, an unmarried sister who's crippled and has no job! Don't let anything interfere with your selfish pleasure! Just go, go, go — to the movies!

320 Tom: All right, I will! The more you shout about my selfishness to me the quicker I'll go, and I won't go to the movies!

Amanda: Go, then! Then go to the moon — you selfish dreamer!

Tom smashes his glass on the floor. He plunges out on the fire-escape, slamming the door. Laura screams — cut by door.

Dance-hall music up. Tom goes to the rail and grips it desperately, lifting his face in the chill white moonlight penetrating the narrow abyss of the alley.

Legend On Screen: "And So Good-bye . . ."

Tom's closing speech is timed with the interior pantomime. The interior scene is played as though viewed through sound-proof glass. Amanda appears to be making a comforting speech to Laura who is huddled upon the sofa. Now that we cannot hear the mother's speech, her silliness is gone and she has dignity and tragic beauty. Laura's dark hair hides her face until at the end of the speech she lifts it to smile at her mother. Amanda's gestures are slow and graceful, almost dancelike, as she comforts the daughter. At the end of her speech she glances a moment at the father's picture — then withdraws through the portieres. At close of Tom's speech, Laura blows out the candles, ending the play.

TOM: I didn't go to the moon, I went much further — for time is the longest distance between two places — Not long after that I was fired for writing a poem on the lid of a shoe-box. I left Saint Louis. I descended the steps of this fire-escape for a last time and followed, from then on, in my father's footsteps, attempting to find in motion what was lost in space — I traveled around a great deal. The cities swept about me like dead leaves, leaves that were brightly colored but torn away from the branches. I would have stopped, but was pursued by something. It always came upon me unawares, taking me altogether by surprise. Perhaps it was a familiar bit of music. Perhaps it was only a piece of transparent glass. Perhaps I am walking along a street at night, in some strange city, before I have found companions. I pass the lighted window of a shop where perfume is sold. The window is filled with pieces of colored glass, tiny transparent bottles in delicate colors, like bits of a shattered rainbow. Then all at once my sister touches my shoulder. I turn around and look into her eyes . . . Oh, Laura, Laura, I tried to leave you behind me, but I am more faithful than I intended to be! I reach for a cigarette, I cross the street, I run into the movies or a bar, I buy a drink, I speak to the nearest stranger — anything that can blow your candles out! *(Laura bends over the candles.)* — for nowadays the world is lit by lightning! Blow out your candles, Laura — and so good-bye . . .

She blows the candles out.

The Scene Dissolves.

Reading and Reacting

1. Who is this play really about — Tom, Laura, or Amanda?

2. What is the function of the absent father in the play?

3. Besides serving as a possible suitor for Laura, what other roles does Jim play?

4. Identify references to historical events occurring at the time of the play's action. How are these events related to the play's central theme?

5. Is Tom's primary role in the play actor, character, playwright, or narrator? Explain.

6. How do the music, the lighting, and the words and pictures projected on slides — which Tennessee Williams called "extra-literary accents"— contribute to the play's action? Are they essential? (Note that at the urging of the director, Williams eliminated these "accents" when the play opened on Broadway.)

7. In his production notes, Tennessee Williams calls *The Glass Menagerie* a "memory play." What do you think he means?

8. Discuss how props help to develop the play. For example, consider the picture of the father, the Victrola, the fire escape, the telephone, the alarm clock, the high school yearbook, the unicorn, and the candles.

9. What events and dialogue foreshadow Tom's escape? Do you see this escape as inevitable? Do you see it as successful? Explain.

10. Do Amanda and Laura change as the play proceeds? What do you think will happen to them after the action of the play is over? What is the significance of Laura's blowing out the candles at the end of the play?

11. Identify several examples of religious imagery in the play—for example, the Paradise Dance Hall. What is the significance of this imagery? In what way does it relate to the major theme of the play?

12. JOURNAL ENTRY Do you think Tom's decision to leave his family is a sign of strength or of weakness?

13. CRITICAL PERSPECTIVE Literary critic Roger Boxill contrasts the short story "Portrait of a Girl in Glass" (p. 1698) and *The Glass Menagerie*. According to Boxill, "'Portrait' is a wistful memory, *Menagerie* is a moving elegy."

Do you agree with Boxill's assessment of these two works? What do you think are the major differences between the short story and the play that developed out of it?

Related Works: "A&P" (p. 115), "Barn Burning" (p. 223), "Eveline" (p. 489), "The Road Not Taken" (p. 880)

TENNESSEE WILLIAMS

Author's Production Notes
(Preface to the Published Edition)

Being a "memory play," The Glass Menagerie can be presented with unusual freedom of convention. Because of its considerably delicate or tenuous material, atmospheric touches and subtleties of direction play a particularly important part. Expressionism and all other unconventional techniques in drama have only one valid aim, and that is a closer approach to truth. When a play employs unconventional techniques, it is not, or certainly shouldn't be, trying to escape its responsibility of dealing with reality, or interpreting experience, but is actually or should be attempting to find a closer approach, a more penetrating and vivid expression of things as they are. The straight realistic play with its genuine Frigidaire and authentic ice-cubes, its characters that speak exactly as its audience speaks, corresponds to the academic landscape and has the same virtue of a photographic likeness. Everyone should know nowadays the unimportance of the photographic in art: that truth, life, or reality is an organic thing which the poetic imagination can represent or suggest, in essence, only through transformation, through changing into other forms than those which were merely present in appearance.

These remarks are not meant as a preface only to this particular play. They have to do with a conception of a new, plastic theatre which must take the place of the exhausted theater of realistic conventions if the theatre is to resume vitality as a part of our culture.

The Screen Device: There is *only one important difference between the original and acting version of the play* and that is the *omission* in the latter of the device which I tentatively included in my *original* script. This device was the use of a screen on which were projected magic-lantern slides bearing images or titles. I do not regret the omission of this device from the present Broadway production. The extraordinary power of Miss Taylor's performance° made it suitable to have the utmost simplicity in the physical production. But I think it may be interesting to some readers to see how this device was conceived. So I am putting it into the published manuscript. These images and legends, projected from behind, were cast on a section of wall between the front-room and dining-room areas, which should be indistinguishable from the rest when not in use.

The purpose of this will probably be apparent. It is to give accent to certain values in each scene. Each scene contains a particular point (or several) which is structurally the most important. In an episodic play, such as this, the basic structure or narrative line may be obscured from the audience; the effect may seem fragmentary rather than architectural. This may not be the fault of the play so much as a lack of attention in the audience. The legend or image upon the screen will strengthen the effect of what is merely allusion in the writing and allow the primary point to be made more simply and lightly than if the entire responsibility were on the spoken lines. Aside from this structural value, I think the screen will have a definite emotional appeal, less definable but just as important. An imaginative producer or director may invent many other uses for this device than those indicated in the present script. In fact the possibilities of the device seem much larger to me than the instance of this play can possibly utilize.

The Music: Another extra-literary accent in this play is provided by the use of music. A single recurring tune, "The Glass Menagerie," is used to give emotional

---

Miss Taylor's performance: In the original production, the role of Amanda Wingfield was played by the American stage actress Laurette Taylor (1884–1946).

emphasis to suitable passages. This tune is like circus music, not when you are on the grounds or in the immediate vicinity of the parade, but when you are at some distance and very likely thinking of something else. It seems under those circumstances to continue almost interminably and it weaves in and out of the preoccupied consciousness; then it is the lightest, most delicate music in the world and perhaps the saddest. It expresses the surface vivacity of life with the underlying strain of immutable and inexpressible sorrow. When you look at a piece of delicately spun glass you think of two things: how beautiful it is and how easily it can be broken. Both of those ideas should be woven into the recurring tune, which dips in and out of the play as if it were carried on a wind that changes. It serves as a thread of connection and allusion between the narrator with his separate point in time and space and the subject of his story. Between each episode it returns as reference to the emotion, nostalgia, which is the first condition of the play. It is primarily Laura's music and therefore comes out most clearly when the play focuses upon her and the lovely fragility of glass which is her image.

The Lighting: The lighting in the play is not realistic. In keeping with the atmosphere of memory, the stage is dim. Shafts of light are focused on selected areas or actors, sometimes in contradistinction to what is the apparent center. For instance, in the quarrel scene between Tom and Amanda, in which Laura has no active part, the clearest pool of light is on her figure. This is also true of the supper scene, when her silent figure on the sofa should remain the visual center. The light upon Laura should be distinct from the others, having a peculiar pristine clarity such as light used in early religious portraits of female saints or madonnas. A certain correspondence to light in religious paintings, such as El Greco's, where the figures are radiant in atmosphere that is relatively dusky, could be effectively used throughout the play. (It will also permit a more effective use of the screen.) A free, imaginative use of light can be of enormous value in giving a mobile, plastic quality to plays of a more or less static nature.

T.W.

JAMES FISHER

from "The Angels of Fructification°": Tennessee Williams, Tony Kushner, and Images of Homosexuality on the American Stage

Who, if I were to cry out, would hear me among the angelic orders?[1]
—*Rainer Maria Rilke*

Still obscured by glistening exhaltations, the angels of fructification had now begun to meet the tumescent phallus of the sun. Vastly the wheels of the earth sang Allelulia! And the seven foaming oceans bellowed Oh![2]
— *Tennessee Williams*

Fructification: The producing of fruit.

Williams was the theatre's angel of sexuality — the dramatist most responsible for forcefully introducing sexual issues, both gay and straight, to the American stage. The fruit of his labor is particularly evident in the subsequent generations of playwrights who present gay characters and situations with increasing frankness, depth, and lyricism. Such works bloom most particularly after the 1960s, and most richly in Tony Kushner's epic *Angels in America,* which has been described by critics as one of the most important American plays of the past fifty years. . . .[3]

In reflecting on the history of homosexuals in American theatre, Kushner believes that "there's a natural proclivity for gay people — who historically have often spent their lives hiding — to feel an affinity for the extended make-believe and donning of roles that is part of theater. It's reverberant with some of the central facts of our lives."[4] It is not surprising that, in a society in which homosexuals were firmly closeted before the 1960s, the illusions of the stage provided a safe haven. Williams could not be as open about his sexuality in his era as Kushner can be now, and thus had to work with overtly heterosexual situations and characters. Williams's creative achievements grow out of a guarded self-awareness and desire for self-preservation, as well as the constraints of the prevailing values of his day.

Donald Windham believes that Williams "loved being homosexual. I think he loved it more than he loved anybody, more than he loved anything except writing,"[5] and Edward A. Sklepowich seems to agree when he writes that "Williams treats homosexuality with a reverence that at times approaches chauvinism."[6] In fact, Williams was often ambivalent about homosexuality — either his own or anyone else's — in his writings. Although his sexuality was well known in the theatrical community, it is unclear when Williams first "came out" publicly. His 1970 appearance on David Frost's television program seems the earliest public declaration. When Frost asked him to comment on his sexuality, Williams replied, "I don't want to be involved in some sort of a scandal, but I've covered the waterfront."[7] He also told Frost that "everybody has some elements of homosexuality in him, even the most heterosexual of us," but a few years later he wrote, "I have never found the subject of homosexuality a satisfactory theme for a full-length play, despite the fact that it appears as frequently as it does in my short fiction. Yet never even in my short fiction does the sexual activity of a person provide the story with its true inner substance."[8] A couple of years later, in an interview in the *Village Voice,* Williams made the point with bluntness: "I've nothing to conceal. Homosexuality isn't the theme of my plays. They're about all human relationships. I've never faked it,"[9] and in 1975 he stated, "Sexuality is part of my work, of course, because sexuality is a part of my life and everyone's life. I see no essential difference between the love of two men for each other and the love of a man for a woman; no essential difference, and that's why I've examined both. . . ."[10] In his novel, *Moise and the World of Reason* (1975), Williams is franker in his depiction of homosexuality than in any of his plays. However, more important than issues of homosexuality, the characters in the novel feel the absence of love and a need for connection — constant themes in all of Williams's work. There is no question that, as a rule, Williams was writing about love and not gender. He criticized sexual promiscuity as "a distortion of the love impulse,"[11] and for him, this impulse, in whatever form, was sacred. . . .

To understand, in part, why Williams obscured homosexuality in his plays, Gore Vidal explains that Williams "had the most vicious press of almost any American writer I can think of. Fag-baiting was at its peak in the fifties when he was at his peak and it has never given up, actually."[12] Donald Spoto believes that Williams's ambivalence had to do, in part, with the fact that he wanted "to be controversial — the hard-drinking, openly homosexual writer with nothing to hide — and at the same time, a man of his own time, a Southern gentleman from a politer era who would never abandon propriety and privacy."[13] This view might indicate why Williams seemed uncomfortable with public displays of drag or campiness, which, he writes, are

> imposed upon homosexuals by our society. The obnoxious forms of it will rapidly disappear as Gay Lib begins to succeed in its serious crusade to assert, for its genuinely misunderstood and persecuted minority, a free position in society which will permit them to respect themselves, at least to the extent that, individually, they deserve respect — and I think that degree is likely to be much higher than commonly supposed.[14]

And it was in the arena of the arts, Williams believed, that the gay sensibility was most likely to first engender such respect. In his *Memoirs* he states, "There is no doubt in my mind that there is more sensibility — which is equivalent to more talent — among the 'gays' of both sexes than among the 'norms' . . .". At the same time, Williams wished to attract a broader audience than gays for his work and seems to have believed that a so-called gay play would limit his access to universal acceptance.

Williams's concern about acceptance was not without some justice. He did not have to look too far back into the preceding decades of American drama to see that the audience was, at best, uncertain about its willingness to accept homosexual characters and issues. The first American play to deal openly with homosexuality is believed to be Mae West's *The Drag*, which generated so much controversy that it closed before completing a tumultuous pre-Broadway tour in 1927. A few other curiosities appeared in the subsequent decades, most notably Lillian Hellman's *The Children's Hour* (1934), in which the question of a lesbian relationship is at the center. Of course, secondary homosexual characters appear in a few plays of the 1930s and 1940s, but they are rarely identified as such. Simon Stimson, the alcoholic choir master of Thornton Wilder's *Our Town* (1938), is a vivid example of such types, typical in that he is comparatively unimportant to the plot and that he is seen mostly as a tragi-comic victim. With the appearance of Robert Anderson's *Tea and Sympathy* (1953), in which a sensitive young man is viewed by his peers as a homosexual (even though it later becomes clear that he is not), gay issues and characters slowly come out of the shadows.

During the 1950s, other playwrights introduced gay characters and issues, but often not in their most visible work. William Inge, inspired to become a playwright by Williams's example, did not feature openly homosexual characters in any of his major plays, but in a few lesser-known one-acts he does so vividly. Inge's *The Tiny Closet* (1959), for example, features a man boarding in a rooming house where the nosy landlady has been attempting to break into a padlocked closet in his room. As soon as the man goes out, the landlady and her friend manage to break in and discover an array of elegant women's hats. The landlady's violation — and the presumption that she will cause him public disgrace — leaves the man's ultimate fate in question. Inge's blunt attack on intolerance[15] was written in the aftermath of the McCarthy era and was a forerunner of later gay plays, particularly those written after the late 1960s, which argue for greater acceptance for homosexuals.

Mid-twentieth century dramatists employed various techniques to present gay characters and situations. One device often used is "transference," the act of hiding gay viewpoints and situations behind a mask of heterosexuality. Edward Albee, often accused of using transference in the writing of such plays as *Who's Afraid of Virginia Woolf?* (1962), is a gay dramatist who also emerged in the 1950s. With the homosexual triumvirate of Williams, Inge, and Albee dominating the non-musical Broadway stage — and despite the fact that none of them had publicly acknowledged their own sexuality — *New York Times* drama critic Stanley Kauffmann "outed" them in 1966. Although he does not give their names, it is clear to whom he is referring in his article "Homosexual Drama and Its Disguises." Kauffmann implies that homosexual writers have no right to write about anything but gay characters — an attitude which would logically imply that men are unable to write about women and vice versa. Kauffmann's notion, undoubtedly all too prevalent in the mid 1960s, becomes clearer when he writes:

> Conventions and puritanisms in the Western world have forced [homosexuals] to wear masks for generations, to hate themselves, and thus to hate those who make them hate themselves. Now that they have a certain relative freedom, they vent their feelings in camouflaged form. . . . They emphasize manner and style because these elements of art, at which they are often adept, are legal tender in their transactions with the world. These elements are, or can be, esthetically divorced from such other considerations as character and idea.[16]

Albee firmly refutes the idea that he, or Williams, employs transference in his plays: "Tennessee never did that, and I can't think of any self-respecting worthwhile writer who would do that sort of thing. It's beneath contempt to suggest it, and it's beneath contempt to do it.[17] Gore Vidal's explanation of the centrality of women characters in Williams's plays seems a valid alternative to understanding his work and the reasons critics see transference in his plays. Vidal believes that for Williams, a woman was "always more interesting as she was apt to be the victim of a society."[18] Williams understood, as Strindberg did, that there are many aspects of the female in the male and vice-versa. And, also like Strindberg, Williams's pained, driven, poetic, and passionate characters are unquestionably extensions of his own persona regardless of their gender.

Notes

[1] Ranier Maria Rilke, "Duino Elegies. The Ninth Elegy," in *Selected Works. Vol. 11. Poetry,* trans. J. B. Leishman (Norfolk, Connecticut, and New York: A New Directions Book, 1960), pp. 244–245.

[2] Tennessee Williams, "The Angels of Fructification," in *In the Winter of Cities. Selected Poems of Tennessee Williams* (New York: New Directions, 1956, 1964), p. 34.

[3] Kushner's theatrical output thus far includes the plays *Yes, Yes, No, No* (1985; children's play), *Stella* (1987; adapted from a play by Goethe), *A Bright Room Called Day* (1987), *Hydriotaphia* (1987), *The Illusion* (1988; freely adapted from a play by Pierre Corneille), *Angels in America. Part One. Millenium Approaches* (1990), *Angels in America. Part Two. Perestroika* (1991), *Widows* (1991; written with Ariel Dorfman, adapted from Dorfman's novel), *Slavs* (1994), and *The Dybbuk* (1995; adapted from S. Ansky's play).

[4] Bob Blanchard, "Playwright of Pain and Hope," *Progressive Magazine.* October 1994, p. 42.

[5] Donald Windham interviewed in "Tennessee Williams. Orpheus of the American Stage," a film by Merrill Brockway broadcast on "American Masters" (PBS-TV), 1994.

[6] Edward A. Sklepowich, "In Pursuit of the Lyric Quarry: The Image of the Homosexual in Tennessee Williams' Prose Fiction," in *Tennessee Williams: A Tribute,* ed. Jac Tharpe (Jackson: University Press of Mississippi, 1977), p. 541.

[7] David Frost, *The Americans* (New York: Stein and Day, 1970), p. 40.

[8] Tennessee Williams, "Let Me Hang It All Out." *New York Times,* March 4, 1975, Section 11, p. 1.

[9] Tennessee Williams interviewed by Arthur Bell, *Village Voice,* February 24, 1972.

[10] Tennessee Williams interviewed by Robert Berkvist, *New York Times,* December 21, 1975.

[11] Tennessee Williams interviewed on "The Lively Arts" program (BBC-TV), 1976.

[12] Gore Vidal interviewed in "Tennessee Williams. Orpheus of the American Stage," a film by Merrill Brockway for "American Masters" (PBS-TV), 1994.

[13] Donald Spoto, *The Kindness of Strangers, The Life of Tennessee Williams* (Boston / Toronto: Little, Brown and Co., 1985), p. 292.

[14] Tennessee Williams, *Memoirs* (New York: Doubleday, 1975), p. 63.

[15] Inge's one-act *The Boy in the Basement* (1962) makes a similar plea for tolerance.

[16] Stanley Kauffmann, "Homosexual Drama and Its Disguises," *New York Times,* January 23, 1966, Section 2, p. 1.

[17] Edward Albee, cited in *The Playwright's Art. Conversations with Contemporary American Dramatists,* ed. Jackson R. Bryer (New Brunswick, New Jersey: Rutgers University Press, 1995), p. 21.

[18] Gore Vidal interviewed in "Tennessee Williams. Orpheus of the American Stage," a film by Merrill Brockway for "American Masters" (PBS-TV), 1994.

ERIC P. LEVY

from Through Soundproof Glass: The Prison of Self-consciousness in *The Glass Menagerie*

In his production notes introducing *The Glass Menagerie*, Tennessee Williams refers to nostalgia as "the first condition of the play." This appraisal at first seems accurate, for the drama disposes the past in a series of receding planes by which the very notion of nostalgia is progressively deepened. From the perspective of Tom, the narrator and a chief character, the past when he started "to boil inside" with the urge to leave home becomes a haunting memory from which his present struggles vainly to flee. But the confining power of that past derives from his mother's nostalgic attachment to her own more distant past and the desperate need to exploit motherhood as a means of reviving "*the legend of her youth.*"

Yet once we analyze how Amanda manipulates maternity, a factor in the play more fundamental than nostalgia will begin to emerge. This principle is self-consciousness — a term which, as we shall see, the text supplies and in its own way defines. Each character is hampered in relating to others by the need to inhabit a private world where the fundamental concern is with self-image. Some characters (Amanda and Jim) use others as mirrors to reflect the self-image with which they themselves wish to identify. Other characters (Laura and Tom) fear that through relation to others they will be reduced to mere reflections, trapped in the mirror of the other's judgment. In virtue of this preoccupation with self-image and the psychological mirrors sustaining it, the world of the play is aptly named after glass. Indeed, Laura's remark ironically becomes the motto of the play: "My glass collection takes up a good deal of time. Glass is something you have to take good care of."

Let us begin be examining Amanda's influence on Laura. Unwittingly, Amanda exploits her maternal concern about Laura's lack of marital prospects as a means of identifying with her own past when she herself was visited one Sunday afternoon in Blue Mountain by "seventeen! — gentlemen callers." In effect, she turns her daughter into a mirror in which her own flattering self-image is reflected, but to do so she must first turn herself or, more precisely, her parental judgment, into a mirror reflecting Laura's limitations. The play itself suggests this seminal image. After helping Laura dress and groom herself, Amanda instructs her to stand in front of a real mirror: "Now look at yourself, young lady. This is the prettiest you will ever be! . . . I've got to fix myself now! You're going to be surprised by your mother's appearance!" Then "*Laura moves slowly to the long mirror and stares solemnly at herself.*"

Look closely at what is happening here. Amanda slights Laura's appearance even as she praises it. Laura is told that she has reached her peak at this moment: she will never again be as attractive. But Laura's limitation only enhances Amanda's excitement about her own "spectacular appearance!" The literal mirror in which Laura beholds her own image ultimately symbolizes her mother's judgment of her. Yet the fundamental purpose of that judgment is to provide, by contrast, a flattering self-image for Amanda. Though on this occasion Amanda's judgment seems benign, it participates in a subtle pattern of comparison by which Laura is made to identify with the sense of her own "Inferiority" to her mother. Indeed, at one point she alludes explicitly to this fact: "I'm just not popular like you were in Blue Mountain." Laura is, in her own words, "crippled." But her primary handicap concerns, not the limp caused by a slight inequality in the length of her legs, but the negative self-consciousness instilled by her mother. In fact Jim, the gentleman caller, approaches this very diagnosis. When Laura recalls how in high school she "had to go clumping all the way up the aisle with everyone watching," Jim advises: "You shouldn't have been self-conscious."

The effect of Laura's self-consciousness is to make her intensely protective of her self-image and to shield it from exposure to anyone outside the home. Whenever she is forced to interact or perform in public, she becomes suddenly ill with nausea and must withdraw. The most extreme example of this syndrome is her brief attendance at Rubicam's Business College where, according to the typing instructor, Laura "broke down completely — was sick at the stomach and almost had to be carried into the wash room." She has a similar reaction after the arrival of Jim at the Wingfield home, and reclines alone on her couch while the others dine in another room. As a result of this withdrawal reflex, Laura has no life outside preoccupation with her own vulnerability.

But paradoxically, the very intensity of this preoccupation changes the meaning of the vulnerability it concerns. By focusing on the fear of humiliating exposure, Laura eventually identifies, not with the shame evoked by her self-image, but with the desperate need to avoid suffering it. In this context, the playwright's commentary on Laura gains greater profundity: "Laura's separation increases till she is like a piece of her own glass collection, too exquisitely fragile to move from the shelf." At bottom, the purpose of Laura's withdrawal *is* to heighten her "fragility;" for, through belief in the damaging effect of exposure, she exchanges a negative self-image for one more flattering. Sensitivity to shame allows Laura to identify with her worthiness, not of ridicule, but of delicate care and compassion. Yet instead of leading to "confidence," this escape from shame depends on increasing her insecurity. She is safe from exposure to shame only if she identifies with her inability to endure it. But lack of confidence is Laura's secret wish, or it protects from confronting anything more threatening in life than her own familiar anxiety. Indeed, whenever she is encouraged to go beyond this anxiety, her reflex is to pick up one of her "little glass ornaments." She does this when Amanda reminds her of the need for eventual marriage and during the conversation with Jim.

JACQUELINE O'CONNOR

from Dramatizing Dementia:
Madness in the Plays of Tennessee Williams

Many of Williams's plays take place in confined space, and the setting often suggests that the characters will face permanent confinement at the play's end. *The Glass Menagerie* is set in "one of those hive-like conglomerations of cellular living-units . . . symptomatic of the impulse of this largest and fundamentally enslaved section of American society to avoid fluidity and differentiation." Confinement figures as a major theme in this drama; Tom speaks frequently about the confinement that keeps him from fulfilling his dreams. In scene three, he berates his mother for the lack of privacy he feels in the apartment, telling her: "I've got no thing, no single thing — in my life that I can call my own!" He feels confined in his job, sarcastically wondering if Amanda thinks he wants to spend "fifty-five years down there in that —*celotex interior!* with —*fluorescent — tubes!*" When he returns from a night out, he brags to Laura about the magician who performed the coffin trick: "We nailed him into a coffin and he got out of the coffin without removing one nail." This, he claims, constitutes a "trick that would come in handy for me — get me out of this 2 × 4 situation!" Tom escapes from the oppressive apartment and the dead-end job, but does not find the freedom he expects, for he cannot forget his sister or the ties he feels to her, which bind him even in her absence.

Laura is voluntarily confined in the apartment, which, according to her mother, will lead to permanent confinement if she does not pursue a career or marriage. She will end up one of those "barely tolerated spinsters . . . stuck away in some little mouse-trap of a room." To the audience Laura's plight seems as constricted as the future her mother predicts, but if Laura's life proceeds as Lucretia's and Blanche's do, the "mouse-trap of a room" might well be in the state asylum. As Tom realizes, Laura is not just crippled: "In the eyes of others — strangers — she's terribly shy and lives in a world of her own and those things make her seem a little peculiar to people outside the house." Amanda's comment highlights Laura's social shortcomings, while Tom's remark focuses on her psychological ones: both assessments emphasize Laura's isolation.

EDWINA DAKIN WILLIAMS°

from Remember Me to Tom

I had not read *Menagerie*, knew nothing of its story except the snatches I glimpsed at rehearsals. After the curtain went up, I became lost in the magic of the words and the superb performance of its four players. You couldn't call *Laurette or Julie*° pretty but they imbued their parts with a strong spiritual quality.

This was the first of Tom's plays I had seen, . . . and I was thrilled to think he had created a play without a wasted word and one in which every moment added drama. I don't think there's been a play like it, before or since.

The audience, too, seemed spellbound throughout and particularly when Mr. Dowling° stood to one side of the stage and uttered the words, "I didn't go to the moon, I went much further — for time is the longest distance between two

---

Edwina Dakin Williams: Tennessee Williams's mother.

Laurette or Julie: In the original production, Laurette Taylor played Amanda Wingfield, and Julie Haydon played Laura.

Mr. Dowling: In the original production, Eddie Dowling played Tom Wingfield. He also was the play's director.

places. . . . Oh, Laura, Laura, I tried to leave you behind me, but I am more faithful than I intended to be! I reach for a cigarette, I cross the street, I run into the movies or a bar, I buy a drink, I speak to the nearest stranger — anything that can blow your candles out!"

At this moment, in the center of the stage behind a thin veil of a curtain, Julie bent low over the candles in her tenement home as Mr. Dowling said sadly, "—for nowadays the world is lit by lightning! Blow out your candles, Laura — and so good-bye. . . ."

And the curtain dropped slowly on the world premiere of *The Glass Menagerie*.

At first it was so quiet I thought the audience didn't like the play. A young woman behind me clapped wildly, as though to make up for the lack of applause, and I heard her remark indignantly, "These Chicago audiences make me mad! This is a beautiful play."

Then, all of a sudden, a tumultuous clapping of hands broke out. The audience had been recovering from the mood into which the play had plunged it. Gratefully I turned to the young woman, who I later found out was a student of English at the University of Chicago, and asked, "Would you like to meet the author? I'm his mother." When Tom arrived to take me backstage, I introduced the young woman, breathless with excitement, and we invited her to go behind the scenes with us.

I wanted to congratulate Laurette, who had brought down the house with her amazing performance as Amanda Wingfield, the faded, fretful, dominating mother lost in the dream world of her past, bullying her son into finding a gentleman caller for his abnormally shy sister.

I entered Laurette's dressing room, not knowing what to expect, for she was sometimes quite eccentric. She was sitting with her feet propped up on the radiator, trying to keep warm. Before I had a chance to get out a word, she greeted me.

"Well, how did you like you'seff, Miz' Williams?" she asked.

I was so shocked I didn't know what to say. It had not occurred to me as I watched Tom's play that *I* was Amanda. But I recovered quickly.

"You were magnificent," I said quietly to Laurette.

Someone mentioned to Tom the opposite receptions given *Angels*° and *Menagerie* and he explained this by saying, "You can't mix sex and religion . . but you can always write safely about mothers."

To which I say, "Ah, can you, Tom?"

Over the years both subtly and not so subtly, I have often been reminded that the character of Amanda was rooted in me, and this is not generally meant as a compliment. The critics have described Amanda in such inelegant words as "an old witch riding a broomstick," "a raddled belle of the old South, sunk deep in frustration," "the scuffed, rundown slipper that outlived the ball," "a simple, sanely insane, horrible Mother, pathetic and terribly human and terribly real" and "a bit of a scold, a bit of a snob."

Angels: Refers to Williams's play, *Battle of Angels* (written 1940, published 1945), revised as *Orpheus Descending* (1957).

Tom's own description of Amanda as stated in the play held that she was "a little woman of great but confused vitality clinging frantically to another time and place. Her characterization must be carefully created, not copied from type. She is not paranoiac, but her life is paranoia. There is much to admire in Amanda, and as much to love and pity as there is to laugh at. Certainly she has endurance and a kind of heroism, and though her foolishness makes her unwittingly cruel at times, there is tenderness in her slight person."

Tom has contradicted himself when asked if the play were based on his life. Once he told a reporter it was a "memory play," adding, "My mother and sister will never forgive me for that." Another time he said, "It was derived from years of living." Then again, he denied it was autobiographical, calling it "a dream or fantasy play. The gentleman caller is meant to be the symbol of the world and its attitude toward the unrealistic dreamers who are three characters of the play."

I think it is high time the ghost of Amanda was laid. I am *not* Amanda. I'm sure if Tom stops to think, he realizes I am not. The only resemblance I have to Amanda is that we both like jonquils.

TENNESSEE WILLIAMS

from Tennessee Williams: Memoirs

Rose was a popular girl in high school but only for a brief while. Her beauty was mainly in her expressive green-gray eyes and in her curly auburn hair. She was too narrow-shouldered and her state of anxiety when in male company inclined her to hunch them so they looked even narrower; this made her strong-featured, very Williams head seem too large for her thin, small-breasted body. She also, when she was on a date, would talk with an almost hysterical animation which few young men knew how to take.

The first real breakdown occurred shortly after I had suffered the heart attack that ended my career as a clerk-errand boy at the shoe company.

My first night back from St. Vincent's, as I mentioned, Rose came walking like a somnambulist into my tiny bedroom and said, "We must all die together."

I can assure you that the idea did not offer to me an irresistible appeal. Being now released at last from my three years as a clerk-typist at Continental, God damn it I was in no mood to consider group suicide with the family, not even at Rose's suggestion — however appropriate the suggestion may have been.

For several days Rose was demented. One afternoon she put a kitchen knife in her purse and started to leave for her psychiatrist's office with apparent intent of murder.

The knife was noticed by Mother and snatched away.

Then a day or so later this first onset of dementia praecox passed off and Rose was, at least on the surface, her usual (now very quiet) self again.

A few days later I departed for Memphis to recuperate at my grandparents' little house on Snowden Avenue near Southwestern University in Memphis.

I think it was about this time that our wise old family doctor told Mother that Rose's physical and mental health depended upon what struck Miss Edwina as a monstrous thing — an arranged, a sort of "therapeutic" marriage. Obviously old Doc Alexander had hit upon the true seat of Rose's afflictions. She was a very normal — but highly sexed — girl who was tearing herself apart mentally and physically by those repressions imposed upon her by Miss Edwina's monolithic Puritanism.

I may have inadvertently omitted a good deal of material about the unusually close relations between Rose and me. Some perceptive critic of the theatre made the observation that the true theme of my work is "incest." My sister and I had a close relationship, quite unsullied by any carnal knowledge. As a matter of fact, we were rather shy of each other, physically, there was no casual physical intimacy of the sort that one observes among the Mediterranean people in their family relations. And yet our love was, and is, the deepest in our lives and was, perhaps, very pertinent to our withdrawal from extra-familial attachments.

There were years when I was in the shoe company and summers when I was a student at the State University of Missouri when my sister and I spent nearly all our evenings together aside from those which I spent with Hazel.

What did we do those evenings, Rose and I? Well, we strolled about the business streets of University City. It was a sort of ritual with a pathos that I assure you was never caught in *Menagerie* nor in my story "Portrait of Girl in Glass," on which *Menagerie* was based.

I think it was Delmar — that long, long street which probably began near the Mississippi River in downtown St. Louis and continued through University City and on out into the country — that Rose and I strolled along in the evenings. There was a root-beer stand at which we always stopped. Rose was inordinately fond of root-beer, especially on warm summer evenings. And before and after our root-beer stop, we would window-shop. Rose's passion, as well as Blanche's, was clothes. And all along that part of Delmar that cut through University City were little shops with lighted windows at night in which were displayed dresses and accessories for women. Rose did not have much of a wardrobe and so her window-shopping on Delmar was like a hungry child's gazing through the window-fronts of restaurants. Her taste in clothes was excellent.

"How about *that* dress, Rose?"

"Oh no, that's tacky. But this one here's very nice."

The evening excursions lasted about an hour and a half, and although, as I've noted, we had a physical shyness of each other, never even touching hands except when dancing together in the Enright apartment, I'd usually follow her into her bedroom when we came home, to continue our warmly desultory chats. I felt most at home in that room, which was furnished with the white ivory bedroom set that had been acquired with the family's "furnished apartment" on Westminster Place when we first moved to St. Louis in 1918.

It was the only attractive room in the apartment — or did it seem so because it was my sister's?

I have mentioned our dancing together.

Rose taught me to dance to the almost aboriginal standing (nonhorned) Victrola that had been acquired in Mississippi and shipped to St. Louis at the time of the disastrous family move there.

As I drifted away from my sister, during this period, she drew close to our little Boston terrier Jiggs. She was constantly holding and hugging him and now and then Miss Edwina would say:

"Miss Florence, I'm afraid that you forget we have neighbors and Mrs. Ebbs upstairs sometimes complains when Cornelius° raises his voice."

Miss Florence would be likely to reply something to the effect that Mrs. Ebbs upstairs could go to hell, for all it mattered to her. . . .

The last time I was in St. Louis, for a visit at Christmas, I had my brother Dakin drive me about all the old places where we had lived in my childhood. It was a melancholy tour. Westminster Place and Forest Park Boulevard had lost all semblance of their charm in the twenties. The big old residences had been converted into sleazy rooming-houses or torn down for nondescript duplexes and small apartment buildings.

The Kramer residence was gone: in fact, all of the family, including dear Hazel, were by then dead.

This can only serve as a preamble, in this "thing," to the story of my great love for Hazel, and not at all an adequate one at that. . . .

In my adolescence in St. Louis, at the age of sixteen, several important events in my life occurred. It was in the sixteenth year that I wrote "The Vengeance of Nitocris" and received my first publication in a magazine and the magazine was *Weird Tales*. The story wasn't published till June of 1928. That same year my grandfather Dakin took me with him on a tour of Europe with a large party of Episcopalian ladies from the Mississippi Delta. . . . And, it was in my sixteenth year that my deep nervous problems approached what might well have been a crisis as shattering as that which broke my sister's mind, lastingly, when she was in her twenties.

I was at sixteen a student at University City High School in St. Louis and the family was living in a cramped apartment at 6254 Enright Avenue.

University City was not a fashionable suburb of St. Louis and our neighborhood, while a cut better than that of the Wingfields in *Menagerie*, was only a little cut better: it was an ugly region of hive-like apartment buildings, for the most part, and fire escapes and pathetic little patches of green among concrete driveways.

My younger brother, Dakin, always an indomitable enthusiast at whatever he got into, had turned our little patch of green behind the apartment on Enright into quite an astonishing little vegetable garden. If there were flowers in it, they were, alas, obscured by the profuse growth of squash, pumpkins, and other edible flora.

Cornelius: Cornelius Coffin — father of Tennessee Williams.

I would, of course, have preempted all the space with rosebushes but I doubt they would have borne roses. The impracticalities, let's say the fantastic impracticalities, of my adolescence were not at all inclined to successful ends: and I can recall no roses in all the years that I spent in St. Louis and its environs except the two living Roses in my life, my grandmother, Rose O. Dakin, and, of course, my sister, Rose Isabel.

My adolescent problems took their most violent form in a shyness of a pathological degree. Few people realize, now, that I have always been and even remain in my years as a crocodile an extremely shy creature — in my crocodile years I compensate for this shyness by the typical Williams heartiness and bluster and sometimes explosive fury of behavior. In my high school days I had no disguise, no faÁade. And it was at University City High School that I developed the habit of blushing whenever anyone looked me in the eyes, as if I harbored behind them some quite dreadful or abominable secret.

DAKIN WILLIAMS° AND SHEPHERD MEADE

from Tennessee Williams: An Intimate Biography

While they were at the Webster Groves house a minor episode occurred that Tom might have made into a one-act play. All the actors were strictly in character. Dakin remembers it well. It was a Saturday midnight in August and still very hot. Tom telephoned. He was in his old Scatterbolt jalopy out on Sappington Road, and had run out of gas. (Very much in character. Tom never did and never would remember to put either oil or gas in cars.) "What *can* we do?" cried Rose frantically. (And in character.)

"Well," said Edwina, organizing things (in character), "your father has the car — and it's Saturday, so *he* won't be home until dawn." (Cornelius in character, and Edwina in character for putting it that way.)

Edwina decided that Rose and Dakin should get a taxi, stop for a can of gas and find Tom. They followed his directions, and there he was, standing with Scatterbolt beside a closed gas station.

"Oh, where have you been, Tom?" said Rose.

Tom answered, "To the movies."

"Mother won't believe that," said Rose, who didn't believe it either, knowing that Tom always said that as a cover story when he'd been with anybody his mother didn't approve of, which was practically everybody.

And that was what happened. When they reached home, Edwina was wearing her standard look of advanced suffering, like Amanda's in *The Glass Menagerie*.

"I was at the movies, mother," Tom said.

Dakin Williams: Tennessee Williams's brother.

"I don't believe that lie!" Edwina said, in character.

"Well, you can go to hell then!" said Tom, going a bit beyond his character.

And then, Dakin remembers, "Mother's eyes shot up in their sockets toward the ceiling. She staggered backward as if struck by a physical blow. Cunningly she glanced behind her to be sure there was an overstuffed chair in the correct position, and proceeded to fall backward in a well-planned and frequently performed faint."

"Oh, my God!" gasped Rose (in character). "Tom, look what you've done! You've killed our mother!"

But Dakin wasn't worried. He had seen his mother "pull this on a monthly basis when arguing with dad over bills." He was, however, impressed by the performance, which he thought was better than usual.

If there'd only been a gentleman caller around, the whole scene might have come right out of one of Tom's plays.

JEAN EVANS

Interview 1945

I'd read four of Mr. Williams's one-act plays. All but one had been about poverty-stricken people whose situations seemed hopeless. I asked Mr. Williams if he always wrote about unhappy, trapped, hopeless people. He'd been half-reclining against a pillow on his bed, but he sat up now.

"I hadn't thought of them as being hopeless," he said. "That's not really what I was writing about. It's human valor that moves me. The one dominant theme in most of my writings, the most magnificent thing in all human nature, is valor — and endurance.

"The mother's valor is the core of *The Glass Menagerie*," he went on. "She's confused, pathetic, even stupid, but everything has *got* to be all right. She fights to make it that way in the only way she knows how."

We talked a little about his other plays and then, a trifle anxiously, he asked if I had found them without humor. I said no. There was a great deal of humor in them if he meant the wry kind that sprang out of incredibly miserable situations, the kind that made an audience want to cry while it was laughing. He nodded.

"George Jean Nathan,° in his review of *Menagerie*, said I was *deficient* in humor," Williams remarked. His manner was casual, but there was an edge of annoyance in his voice. "He said that all the humor had been embroidered into the play by Mr. Dowling." (Dowling is co-producer of the play, plays the narrator, and the son, Tom) "I'd love for somebody who knows my other work to refute him."

George Jean Nathan: American editor and drama critic (1882–1958). His review of the play appeared in the *New York Journal American* on April 9, 1945.

He paused, and then went on defensively, "Not one line of *Glass Menagerie* was changed after the final draft came back from the typist. A scene was inserted, the drunk scene. That was Mr. Dowling's idea, but entirely of my authorship. And one line by Mr. Dowling, was added. The last line, where he says to the audience, 'Here's where memory stops and your imagination begins.'" He paused. "Mr. Dowling did a great job. A magnificent job. But there was humor *contained* in the play. I had that in mind, along with the rest, when I was writing it."

Mr. Nathan had also written that the play, as originally written, was *freakish*. I wanted to know if Mr. Williams liked writing plays unconventional in form.

"If you mean unconventional in that my plays are light on plot and heavy on characterization, yes. But not in structure. *Glass Menagerie* is not at all freakish in structure.

"Have you read Saroyan's° *Get Away, Old Man?*" Williams gave a peal of gay, sudden laughter that rang through the room. "There's a play that would give Mr. Nathan pause. The curtain goes up and down, up and down, all through the play."

He said he liked Saroyan very much, "his short stories perhaps, more than his plays."

I said I'd like Saroyan better if he were able to admit there was evil under the sun. Mr. Williams smiled. "His point of view — his attitude — I suppose you could say, is childish," he said. "Saroyan's characters are all little Saroyans. He multiplies himself like rabbits. But he is himself so interesting, that he usually gets away with writing only about himself."

How did he think the human situation could be improved? I asked. He looked as though the question had startled him.

"It's a social and economic problem, of course," he said, "not something mystical. I don't think there will be any equity in American life until at least 90 percent of our population are living under different circumstances. The white collar worker, for instance. Most people consider him pretty well off. I think his situation is horrible.

"I'd like to see people getting a lot more for what they invest in the way of effort and time. It's insane for human beings to work their whole lives away at dull, stupid, routine, anesthetizing jobs for just a little more than the necessities of life. There should be time — and money — for development. For living."

THOMAS L. KING

from Irony and Distance in *The Glass Menagerie*

Tennessee Williams's *The Glass Menagerie*, though it has achieved a firmly established position in the canon of American plays, is often distorted, if not misunderstood, by readers, directors, and audiences. The distortion results from an

---

Saroyan's: William Saroyan (1908–1981), American writer of short stories, plays, novels, and memoirs.

overemphasis on the scenes involving Laura and Amanda and their plight, so that the play becomes a sentimental tract on the trapped misery of two women in St. Louis. This leads to the neglect of Tom's soliloquies — speeches that can be ignored or discounted only at great peril, since they occupy such a prominent position in the play. When not largely ignored, they are in danger of being treated as nostalgic yearnings for a former time. But they are not sentimental excursions into the past, paralleling Amanda's, for while they contain sentiment and nostalgia, they also evince a pervasive humor and irony and, indeed, form and contain the entire play. . . .

The play . . . is not Amanda's. Amanda is a striking and a powerful character, but the play is Tom's. Tom opens the play and he closes it; he also opens the second act and two further scenes in the first act — his is the first word and the last. Indeed, Amanda, Laura, and the Gentleman Caller do not appear in the play at all as separate characters. In a sense, as [reviewer], Stark Young noted, Tom is the only character in the play, for we see not the characters but Tom's memory of them — Amanda and the rest are merely aspects of Tom's consciousness. Tom's St. Louis is not an objective one, but a solipsist's created by Tom, the artist-magician, and containing Amanda, Laura, and the Gentleman Caller. Tom is the Prospero of *The Glass Menagerie*, and its world is the world of Tom's mind even more than *Death of a Salesman*'s is the world of Willy Loman's mind. The play is warped and distorted when any influence gives Amanda, Laura, or the glass menagerie any undue prominence. If Amanda looms large, she looms large in Tom's mind, not in her own right: though of course the image that finally dominates Tom's mind is that of Laura and the glass menagerie.

The full meaning of the scenes between the soliloquies lies not in themselves alone but also in the commentary provided by Tom standing outside the scenes and speaking with reasonable candor to the audience and reader. Moreover, the comment that the soliloquies makes is not a sentimental one; that is, they are not only expressions of a wistful nostalgia for the lost, doomed world of Amanda, Laura, and the glass menagerie but also contain a good deal of irony and humor which work in the opposite direction. They reveal Tom as an artist figure whose utterances show how the artist creates, using the raw material of his own life. . . .

Generally, each soliloquy oscillates between a sentimental memory of the past, which draws the narrator into it, and a wry irony which keeps him from being fully engulfed and controlled by it. This tension is found in all the soliloquies, though it is not always handled in the same way: sometimes the fond memory is predominant and sometimes the irony, but both are always present. At times, Tom seems almost deliberately to court disaster by creating for himself and the audience a memory so lovely and poignant that the pain of giving it up to return to reality is too much to bear, but return he does with mockery and a kind of wit that interrupts the witchery of memory just short of a withdrawn madness surrounded by soft music and a mind filled with "delicate rainbow colors." In short, Tom toys with the same madness in which his sister Laura is trapped but saves himself with irony. . . .

The opening soliloquy . . . reveals a number of elements that are to be important in the play: it establishes a tension between sentimental nostalgia and detached irony as well as a narrator who is to function as stage magician. The narrator disavows this, but we cannot take him at his word. He says that he is the opposite of a stage magician, but only because his truth looks like illusion rather than the other way round; he is still the magician who creates the play. He says that the play is sentimental rather than realistic, but that is a half truth, for while it contains large doses of sentiment, for the narrator at least, irony sometimes quenches the sentiment. Indeed, Irving Babbit's° phrase describing romantic irony is appropriate here: "Hot baths of sentiment . . . followed by cold douches of irony." . . .

The culmination of all the soliloquies, and of the tension between irony and nostalgia that is carefully developed in them, is in the final one. Tom's last speech contains just two touches of ironic detachment, but these are critical and are the foci on which this speech and, indeed, for Tom, the whole play turns. The speech begins with a touch of ironic humor. In the preceding scene, Amanda has told Tom to go to the moon. He begins his final speech with "I didn't go to the moon." This is a decidedly humorous line, indicating that Tom still has access to his detachment, but the audience is not laughing anymore, its detachment has been broken down. The speech then quickly moves into a tone of lyric regret:

> I didn't go to the moon, I went much further — for time is the longest distance between two places. Not long after that I was fired for writing a poem on the lid of a shoe-box. I left Saint Louis. I descended the steps of this fire-escape for a last time and followed, from then on, in my father's footsteps, attempting to find in motion what was lost in space. I traveled around a great deal. The cities swept about me like dead leaves, leaves that were brightly colored but torn away from the branches. I would have stopped, but I was pursued by something. It always came upon me unawares, taking me altogether by surprise. Perhaps it was a familiar bit of music. Perhaps it was only a piece of transparent glass. Perhaps I am walking along a street at night, in some strange city, before I have found companions. I pass the lighted window of a shop where perfume is sold. The window is filled with pieces of colored glass, tiny transparent bottles in delicate colors, like bits of a shattered rainbow. Then all at once my sister touches my shoulder. I turn around and look into her eyes. Oh, Laura, Laura, I tried to leave you behind me, but I am more faithful than I intended to be! I reach for a cigarette, I cross the street, I run into the movies or a bar, I buy a drink, I speak to the nearest stranger — anything that can blow your candles out!
>
> For nowadays the world is lit by lightning! Blow out your candles, Laura — and so good-bye.

The irony in this passage is no longer humorous. When Tom says "I didn't go to the moon," no one is laughing, and the final, ironic "and so good-bye" is not even potentially humorous. Tom seems to have been captured by the memory and the audience has almost certainly been captured, but Tom, in the end, still has his detachment. Laura's candles go out and Tom is relieved of his burden, uttering a

---

Babbit's: Irving Babbit (1865–1933), American scholar-critic and professor of French literature at Harvard.

final, flip farewell, but the audience has been more faithful than it intended to be; they are left behind, tricked by Tom who is free for the moment while they must face their grief, their cruelty, for they are the world that the Wingfields were somehow set apart from, they are the ones who shattered the rainbow.

The soliloquies, then, are of a piece: they all alternate between sentiment and irony, between mockery and nostalgic regret, and they all end with an ironic tag, which, in most cases, is potentially humorous. They show us the artist manipulating his audience, seeming to be manipulated himself to draw them in, but in the end resuming once more his detached stance. When Tom departs, the audience is left with Laura and Amanda alone before the dead, smoking candles, and Tom escapes into his artist's detachment having exorcized the pain with the creation of the play. This is the trick that Tom has in his pocket.

NANCY MARIE PATTERSON TISCHLER

from **Student Companion to Tennessee Williams**

Williams loved symbols. Having started his writing as a lyric poet, he explained that he had a "poet's weakness for symbols." This trait was undoubtedly also a result of his early saturation with the symbolism and thought of the Episcopal Church. He came to see almost every aspect of life as symbolic of some greater truth.

He had originally designed *The Glass Menagerie* as a Christmas story (Letter to Audrey Wood, 12/43), with the opening scene one of gift giving. The change in his point of attack to a family meal, though more secular, is nonetheless introduced by a demand that Tom come to the table so that they can say "grace," which incidentally, they then omit; but it is also to make his failed, secular "communion" a commentary on the painful relationship in this community of believers. Nothing should be more ordinary and comfortable than breaking bread together, yet the Wingfield children can perform no function without scrutiny and advice from the hovering mother. An echo of this scene is a second announcement of the impending blessing, this time a summons for Laura to come to the table when Jim O'Connor is their guest for dinner. Pretending that Laura has prepared the meal for their visitor, Amanda again dominates the event, making it her solo performance rather than a shared experience of hospitality. She turns the ritual of eating into a contest of wills. She has transformed a communion into a celebration of her personal sacrifices and a reinforcement of her children's obligations to her as their appropriately grateful response.

Amanda soon reveals herself as a symbol of the "devouring mother." Though apparently nurturing, she thwarts and hobbles her children, dominating not only their eating habits, but their entire lives, keeping them safely in the nest with her. Portraying herself as a martyr to their needs, she actually requires their submission to feed her own pride, crippling Laura by her outrageous expectations. If she could, she would emasculate Tom as well. As her own beauty fades, her appetite for adulation increases, making her a harpy rather than a saint. In a fit of anger, Tom calls his mother an ugly old "witch." Williams was to continue embellishing his archetypal monster-woman as he met more complex and powerful ogres throughout his career.

The central image in this play, from which the work takes its name, is Laura's glass menagerie. Williams' biographers have traced the origins of this image to a tragic young woman in Clarksdale, Mississippi (Leverich 1995, 55). Within the play, it allows us to see the childlike fixation on a private world of make-believe animals, and delicacy of this isolated girl.

This culture, frozen in time, would limit Tom's reading to proper works by polite writers and Laura's choices. In scene after scene, Williams shows Amanda as a victim of her own assumptions about how women should behave, how they should spend their lives, whom they should marry, what domestic chores they should perform, how they should dress, entertain, and talk. She is not just a peculiar old woman: she is a symbol of a dying civilization.

On an even more universal level, this story is about the effects of the industrial revolution on the American family. Although Williams emphasizes the Depression context of the narrative, we know that the pressures on Tom Wingfield extend beyond the span of the 1930s. The growth of big industries in the nineteenth and twentieth centuries had both forced families from the farms and small towns and lured them to great cities, where the personal needs of fragile folk are easily neglected. The polluted air, boring work, and separation from a caring community proved harmful to the mental and physical health of many displaced people.

The emphasis on the "hivelike" buildings of ugly colors with their fire escapes underscores the separation from nature, beauty, and human values. This is not the proper habitat for the dreamer, the poet, or the fragile cripple. Yet, all too often, it is the setting for the young man or woman in urban America. Williams, in *The Glass Menagerie*, is providing us a microcosm in which we can visualize the larger questions of the entire era.

Taking it as a symbol of Laura herself, fragile and beautiful, the author plays with the more specific figure of the unicorn. Here we see the complete development of a complex idea, hinted at in the dialogue. We know from medieval iconography that this mythical figure is identified with virgins and therefore with sexuality. Although it looks like a horse the unicorn not a horse, but is a unique (if mythical) creature. Thus, when Jim accidentally breaks off its horn, he has not transformed it into a horse: it remains a unicorn, but is now a damaged unicorn that manages to look like an ordinary horse. In some ways, this is what Amanda has done to Laura, distorted her true childish nature to make her seem like all the normal young ladies being courted by nice young gentlemen. (The "gay deceivers" are delightful symbols of Laura's underdeveloped sexuality and Amanda's pressures to appear sexy.) Laura's pained responses to her mother's cruel questions about her plans for the evening expose the anguish that this teasing causes the sensitive girl.

The mock-courtship scene between Laura and Jim contains another cluster of images. Tom, having misused the money for the electric bill, has plunged them into darkness. Amanda, always eager to adopt romantic attitudes, furnishes them with a candelabra, a relic from a church fire, and thereby returns them to the nineteenth century — the family's native habitat. Jim briefly enters into their game of playing at pre-electric life, settles on the floor, and enjoys a childlike moment of shared memories with Laura. But we soon learn that he lives fully in the "Century of Progress," which Laura is blocked from entering. Jim tries, in an act of egocentric kindness, to move her into the adult world of dancing and kissing, but Laura remains a lonely little girl who had a playmate over to visit for the evening. That scene foreshadows the final words, "For nowadays the world is lit by lightning! Blow out your candles, Laura — and so goodbye" . . . .

Other images also populate the play. Williams loved the ocean and frequently used the sea as an escape symbol. His sailors, pirates, and buccaneers are the gallant figures who sail away from the dreary land to have adventures denied to most of mankind. Certainly Americans have known this imagery from their earliest days, America itself being the grand adventure for most of our ancestors. For at least three of Williams' literary heroes° — Melville, O'Neill, and Crane — the sea voyage was also the escape into the life of literature.

Tennessee Williams' delight in earlier poets, novelists, and dramatists gives additional richness to the texture of the phrasing in *The Glass Menagerie*. For example, Tom's final portrayal of cities as leaves blown by the wind, "brightly colored, but torn away from the branches" echoes Shelley's "Ode to the West Wind."° Fortunately, such similes work effectively even if the listener fails to pick up the source of the allusion. We need not picture the famous medieval unicorn tapestry in order to delight in the unicorn reference. Nor do we need to know about D. H. Lawrence's rainbow° of sexuality in order to understand the rainbow colors at the Paradise Dance Hall. Blue Mountain is the right name for a romantic past, and Moon Lake is the ideal name for adventures in love. The words carry the message, regardless of our specific knowledge of Clarksdale's geography. Williams lets his words tell their own stories. The viewer can delight in the surface brilliance or dig deep into allusions, allowing several levels of possible resonance. . . .

ROGER B. STEIN

from The Glass Menagerie Revisited: Catastrophe without Violence

The religious overtones of *The Glass Menagerie* are even more pervasive. Though they never obscure the literal line of the story or seem self-conscious, as they do in some of the later plays, these overtones add a dimension to the play which reaches beyond individual pathos and social tragedy. Williams's stage directions

---

literary heroes: Herman Melville (1819–1891), Eugene O'Neill (1888–1953), and Stephen Crane (1871–1900).

Shelley's "Ode to the West Wind": See Chapter 27, page 1233.

D. H. Lawrence's rainbow: Lawrence's novel *The Rainbow* was published in 1915.

clearly indicate his intention. As with Hannah in *The Night of the Iguana*, he tells us that the lighting for Laura should resemble that "used in early religious portraits of female saints or madonnas." The scene where Tom tells his mother that a gentleman caller will appear Williams entitles "Annunciation." The dressing of Laura for the caller's appearance should be "devout and ritualistic." During her scene with Jim she is lit "inwardly with altar candles," and when Jim withdraws after kissing her Williams informs us that the "holy candles in the altar of Laura's face have been snuffed out. There is a look of almost infinite desolation."

Those overtones extend beyond Williams's hints to the director and become a crucial part of the fabric of dramatic action. The first scene in both the Acting Version and the Library Edition of the play opens on this note. In the former, Amanda narrates her "funny experience" of being denied a seat in the Episcopal church because she has not rented a pew. The idea of the Wingfields' exclusion from Christian ceremony is established thus at the outset, and it is underlined by the ensuing talk of digesting food, mastication, and salivary glands. In the Wingfield apartment, eating is an animal process only; it lacks ritual significance. The Library Edition opens with Amanda's call to Tom, "We can't say grace until you come to the table," and then moves on to the question of digestion. The lines are different, but their import is the same. When the gentleman caller comes, the scene is repeated, only this time it is Laura whose absence holds up "grace."

Amanda, who condemns instinct and urges Tom to think in terms of the mind and spirit, as "Christian adults" do, is often characterized in Christian terms. Her music, in the Library Edition, is "Ave Maria." As a girl she could only cook angel food cake. She urges Laura, "Possess your soul in patience," and then speaks of her dress for the dinner scene as "resurrected" from a trunk. Her constant refrain to Tom is "Rise an' Shine," and she sells subscriptions to her friends by waking them early in the morning and then sympathizing with them as "Christian martyrs." Laura is afraid to tell her mother she has left the business school because "when you're disappointed, you get that awful suffering look on your face, like the picture of Jesus' mother in the museum!"

The next picture Laura mentions is the one of Jim in the yearbook; though the context seems secular enough at this point — Jim is a high school hero — his religious function emerges later on. In the "Annunciation" scene, when Amanda learns that the gentleman caller's name is O'Connor, she says, "That, of course, means fish — tomorrow is Friday!" The remark functions not only literally, since Jim is Irish Catholic, but also figuratively, for the fish is the traditional symbol of Christ. In a very real sense both Amanda and Laura are searching for a Savior who will come to help them, to save them, to give their drab lives meaning.

Tom is unable to play this role himself. Though he appears as the angel of the Annunciation, he denies the world of belief and in a bitter speech to his mother calls himself "El Diablo." With him Christian terms appear only as imprecations: "what in Christ's name" or "that God damn Rise and Shine." When Tom returns home drunk one night, he tells Laura of a stage show he has seen which is shot through with Christian symbolism, none of which he perceives. Here the magician, Malvolio, whose name suggests bad will, dislike, or even hate, plays the role of the modern Christ. He performs the miracle of turning water into wine and then goes on to blasphemy by turning the wine into beer and then whiskey. He also produces his proper symbol, the fish, but it is goldfish, as if stained by modern materialism. Most important, perhaps, he escapes from a nailed coffin. But Tom reads the symbolism of this trick in personal terms only. When Laura tries to keep him from awakening Amanda, Tom retorts:

> Goody goody! Pay 'er back for all those "Rise an' Shine's." You know it don't take much intelligence to get yourself into a nailed-up coffin, Laura. But who in hell ever got himself out of one without removing one nail?

The illumination of the father's photograph at this point suggests one answer to this question, but the pattern of Christian imagery in the drama, especially when reinforced here by the "Rise an' Shine" refrain, should suggest to us another answer — the resurrection itself — which Tom's rejection of Christian belief prevents him from seeing.

It remains therefore for Jim to come as the Savior to this Friday night supper. The air of expectancy is great, with the ritualistic dressing of Laura, the tension, and the oppressive heat. Jim's arrival is marked by the coming of rain, but the hopes of fertility and renewal which this might suggest are soon dashed. Laura's attempt to come to the dinner table is a failure, signaled by a clap of thunder, and Tom's muttered grace, "For these and all thy mercies, God's Holy Name be praised," is bitterly ironic, mocked by what follows. The only paradise within reach is Paradise Dance Hall, with its "Waste Land" mood of slow and sensuous rhythms and couples kissing behind ashpits and telephone poles, "the compensation for lives that passed . . . without any change or adventure," as Tom remarks. The failure of electric power after dinner — previsioning the blackout of the world — leads to Amanda's joking question, "Where was Moses when the lights went off?" This suggests another savior who would lead his people from the desert into the promised land, but the answer to her question is "In the dark."

Jim's attempt to play the modern savior is an abysmal failure. In the after-dinner scene, he offers Laura the sacrament — wine and "life-savers," in this case — and a Dale Carnegie version of the Sermon on the Mount — self-help rather than divine help — but to no avail. At the end of the play Laura and Amanda are, as the joke bitterly reminds us, "in the dark," and Tom's last lines announce the final failure, the infinite desolation: "For nowadays the world is lit by lightning. Blow out your candles, Laura — and so goodbye."

TOM SCANLAN

from Family, Drama, and American Dreams

The major dilemmas of family life are imbedded in the dramatic action of Williams's plays, and the ideal that haunts his characters is family-related. Moreover, those plays which have been most successful artistically have been those mostly about the family. . . .

In the earlier plays Williams dramatized the family world in a state of collapse; in later ones family collapse is antecedent to the action. These two situations are combined in *The Glass Menagerie*, Williams's first successful play (and probably his most popular one [1]). The play is a perfect fusion of the two subjects and so is a figure for Williams's entire career. In it the family is long lost and, also, we witness its struggle before it is lost. Williams captures the poignancy of family memories in a way all his own, without sacrificing the core of dramatic conflict which makes such memories less static.

The play is a prime example of Williams's artistry in establishing the relation between his own dramatic world and the conventions of realistic domestic drama to which his audience owes great allegiance, as he well knew. The play occurs in the mind of Tom Wingfield, who drifts in and out of the action both as narrator and participant in a peculiarly appropriate way. From the moment at the beginning when the scrim of the tenement wall dissolves and we enter the Wingfields' apartment, we are reminded of the household of so many family plays. The realistic convention of the fourth wall is evoked as Tom remembers his family.

Tom's evocation is self-conscious, for as "stage manager" he has control over the setting. But Tom is also at the mercy of his memories and irresistibly must relive them. The play keeps us poised between these two styles, these two times, throughout. This is, in fact, its strongest and most subtle conflict. Like Tom, we are continually tempted into the world of a realistic family struggle, but never allowed to enter it completely. The projections and lighting keep the effect slightly stylized during the scenes, the fragmented structure blocks us from too long an absorption in the action, and the re-appearance of Tom as narrator forces us back to the present. It is Tom's final reappearance in this role, when the action of the memory play is completed, which releases the tension created between the two styles and dramatizes, in a final rush of emotion, the irretrievable loss of the family which Tom can never escape.

Tom cannot shake the memory of his family from his mind; the dissolution of time and space in the play — that is, in his consciousness —heightens the importance of what he is remembering to make it the most significant thing about his existence. What he remembers — the bulk of the play — centers around two lines of action. The first is his desire to escape from his family just as his father had done before him: "He was a telephone man who fell in love with long distances." [2] Tom, a would-be writer, is caught between a domineering mother and a stultifying warehouse job. He escapes to the porch, to the movies, to the saloon. And finally, in the end, we learn that he has followed his father out into long distances. The second line of action, the principal one, concerns his mother, Amanda, and her attempts to establish some kind of life for Tom's crippled sister, Laura. Amanda pins her hopes on getting "sister" married, after Laura fails because of painful shyness to continue in business school. A "gentleman caller" is found, Jim O'Connor, "an emissary from the world of reality," but all of Amanda's hopes are crushed as he turns out to be already engaged.

The plot is slight stuff, as Williams himself knew. [3] The effect of the play derives in part from the contrast between its two lines of action. Amanda is given over to memories of her past life of happiness as a young southern debutante in Blue Mountain, Mississippi, where on one incredible Sunday she had seventeen gentlemen callers. She imitates the manners and graciousness of those days, a faintly ludicrous parody of southern gentility, the played-out tradition of the antebellum South and its family of security. But she has spirit, too, and responds to the problems of raising two children in a St. Louis tenement during the Depression. Her practicality is what gives her dignity; as she cares for Laura we realize how much Amanda herself needs to be cared for. Her refusal to give in to her nostalgia, even while she indulges in it, enhances her character and makes us susceptible to her longing.

Tom is smothered by such a woman. He fights with her, in part, because she continually tells him what to do: how to eat; how to sleep; how to get ahead. But he fights, also, because her standards represent the conventionality of family responsibility. . . . The absent father, who still represents the memory of romantic family love to Amanda, is the possibility of romantic escape from family to Tom.[4] He loves his sister Laura, yet he will not accept the responsibility for her which Amanda demands of him. The Wingfields are only a ghost of the family of security, but even this demand to be close-knit repels the restless Tom.

Tom's love for Laura needs to be emphasized, I think, not only because it is one part of the final image of the play — the moment of revelation toward which the action tends — but because it shows Williams's interest in the special qualities of those whom the world has hurt. They are the delicate and fragile people, too sensitive to be able to withstand the crude and harsh necessities by which life drives us along. They have an extraordinary awareness of hidden, almost mystical, qualities of spiritual beauty; and this openness dooms them to be crushed or perverted by the animal vigor of the world.

Laura's specialness is seen largely in contrast with Jim, her gentleman caller. He is, by all odds, the kindest of Williams's emissaries from reality, perhaps because his faith in the American dream of self-improvement and success is so complete as to be itself a touching illusion. . . .

There will be no normal love of marriage and family for Laura nor for any of the Wingfields. Laura is too tender, too special, too fragile like her glass menagerie. It is Tom's painful sensitivity to Laura's predicament which makes him love her and which drives him from her. But he cannot escape Laura. The necessity of leaving her, and the guilt over doing so, haunt him:

> Oh, Laura, Laura, I tried to leave you behind me, but I am more faithful than I intended to be! I reach for a cigarette, I cross the street, I run into the movies or a bar, I buy a drink, I speak to the nearest stranger — anything that can blow your candles out!
>
> (*Laura bends over the candles.*)
>
> For nowadays the world is lit by lightning! Blow out your candles, Laura — and so good-bye. . . .
>
> (*She blows the candles out.*)[5]

Laura's painful encounter with the world's lightning represents all of the Wingfields. Amanda's last glance at her husband's picture reveals as much of her as does Tom's final speech of him. The family is the supreme case of love trying to struggle against the world, and the family fails. Fundamentally romantic, Williams evokes the beauty of failure, the beauty which must fail. . . .

Notes

[1] Jackson, *Broken World*, p. viii, note 1.

[2] Williams, *Menagerie*, p. 145.

[3] "A free, imaginative use of light can be of enormous value in giving a mobile, plastic quality to plays of a more or less static nature." Williams, "Production Notes," *Menagerie*, p. 134.

[4] Tischler, *Williams*, p. 97.

[5] Williams, *Menagerie*, p. 237.

TENNESSEE WILLIAMS

Portrait of a Girl in Glass

We lived in a third floor apartment on Maple Street in Saint Louis, on a block which also contained the Ever-ready Garage, a Chinese laundry, and a bookie shop disguised as a cigar store.

Mine was an anomalous character, one that appeared to be slated for radical change or disaster, for I was a poet who had a job in a warehouse. As for my sister Laura, she could be classified even less readily than I. She made no positive motion toward the world but stood at the edge of the water, so to speak, with feet that anticipated too much cold to move. She'd never have budged an inch, I'm pretty sure, if my mother who was a relatively aggressive sort of woman had not shoved her roughly forward, when Laura was twenty years old, by enrolling her as a student in a nearby business college. Out of her "magazine money" (she sold subscriptions to women's magazines), Mother had paid my sister's tuition for a term of six months. It did not work out. Laura tried to memorize the typewriter keyboard, she had a chart at home, she used to sit silently in front of it for hours, staring at it while she cleaned and polished her infinite number of little glass ornaments. She did this every evening after dinner. Mother would caution me to be very quiet. "Sister is looking at her typewriter chart!" I felt somehow that it would do her no good, and I was right. She would seem to know the positions of the keys until the weekly speed drill got underway, and then they would fly from her mind like a bunch of startled birds.

At last she couldn't bring herself to enter the school any more. She kept this failure a secret for a while. She left the house each morning as before and spent six hours walking around the park. This was in February, and all the walking outdoors regardless of weather brought on influenza. She was in bed for a couple of weeks with a curiously happy little smile on her face. Of course Mother phoned

WILLIAMS: PORTRAIT OF A GIRL IN GLASS

the business college to let them know she was ill. Whoever was talking on the other end of the line had some trouble, it seems, in remembering who Laura was, which annoyed my mother and she spoke up pretty sharply. "Laura has been attending that school of yours for two months, you certainly ought to recognize her name!" Then came the stunning disclosure. The person sharply retorted, after a moment or two, that now she *did* remember the Wingfield girl, and that she had not been at the business college *once* in about a month. Mother's voice became strident. Another person was brought to the phone to verify the statement of the first. Mother hung up and went to Laura's bedroom where she lay with a tense and frightened look in place of the faint little smile. Yes, admitted my sister, what they said was true. "I couldn't go any longer, it scared me too much, it made me sick at the stomach!"

After this fiasco, my sister stayed at home and kept in her bedroom mostly. This was a narrow room that had two windows on a dusky areaway between two wings of the building. We called this areaway Death Valley for a reason that seems worth telling. There were a great many alley cats in the neighborhood and one particularly vicious dirty white Chow who stalked them continually. In the open or on the fire escapes they could usually elude him but now and again he cleverly contrived to run some youngster among them into the cul-de-sac of this narrow areaway at the far end of which, directly beneath my sister's bedroom windows, they made the blinding discovery that what had appeared to be an avenue of escape was really a locked arena, a gloomy vault of concrete and brick with walls too high for any cat to spring, in which they must suddenly turn to spit at their death until it was hurled upon them. Hardly a week went by without a repetition of this violent drama. The areaway had grown to be hateful to Laura because she could not look out on it without recalling the screams and the snarls of killing. She kept the shades drawn down, and as Mother would not permit the use of electric current except when needed, her days were spent almost in perpetual twilight. There were three pieces of dingy ivory furniture in the room, a bed, a bureau, a chair. Over the bed was a remarkably bad religious painting, a very effeminate head of Christ with teardrops visible just below the eyes. The charm of the room was produced by my sister's collection of glass. She loved colored glass and had covered the walls with shelves of little glass articles, all of them light and delicate in color. These she washed and polished with endless care. When you entered the room there was always this soft, transparent radiance in it which came from the glass absorbing whatever faint light came through the shades on Death Valley. I have no idea how many articles there were of this delicate glass. There must have been hundreds of them. But Laura could tell you exactly. She loved each one.

She lived in a world of glass and also a world of music. The music came from a 1920 Victrola and a bunch of records that dated from about the same period, pieces such as "Whispering" or "The Love Nest" or "Dardanella." These records were souvenirs of our father, a man whom we barely remembered, whose name was spoken rarely. Before his sudden and unexplained disappearance from our lives, he had made this gift to the household, the phonograph and the records, whose music remained as a sort of apology for him. Once in a while, on payday at the warehouse, I would bring home a new record. But Laura seldom cared for these new records, maybe because they reminded her too much of the noisy tragedies in Death Valley or the speed drills at the business college. The tunes she loved were the ones she had always heard. Often she sang to herself at night in her bedroom. Her voice was thin, it usually wandered off-key. Yet it had a curious childlike sweetness. At eight o'clock in the evening I sat down to write in my own mousetrap of a room. Through the closed doors, through the walls, I would hear my sister singing to herself, a piece like "Whispering" or "I Love You" or "Sleepy Time Gal," losing the tune now and then but always preserving the minor atmosphere of the music. I think that was why I always wrote such strange and sorrowful poems in those days. Because I had in my ears the wispy sound of my sister serenading her pieces of colored glass, washing them while she sang or merely looking down at them with her vague blue eyes until the points of gem-like radiance in them gently drew the arching particles of reality from her mind and finally produced a state of hypnotic calm in which she even stopped singing or washing the glass and merely sat without motion until my mother knocked at the door and warned her against the waste of electric current.

I don't believe that my sister was actually foolish. I think the petals of her mind had simply closed through fear, and it's no telling how much they had closed upon in the way of secret wisdom. She never talked very much, not even to me, but once in a while she did pop out with something that took you by surprise.

After work at the warehouse or after I'd finished my writing in the evening, I'd drop in her room for a little visit because she had a restful and soothing effect on nerves that were worn rather thin from trying to ride two horses simultaneously in two opposite directions.

I usually found her seated in the straight-back ivory chair with a piece of glass cupped tenderly in her palm.

"What are you doing? Talking to it?" I asked.

"No," she answered gravely, "I was just looking at it."

On the bureau were two pieces of fiction which she had received as Christmas or birthday presents. One was a novel called the *Rose-Garden Husband* by someone whose name escapes me. The other was *Freckles* by Gene Stratton Porter. I never saw her reading the *Rose-Garden Husband*, but the other book was one that she actually lived with. It had probably never occurred to Laura that a book was something you read straight through and then laid aside as finished. The character Freckles, a one-armed orphan youth who worked in a lumber camp, was someone that she invited into her bedroom now and then for a friendly visit just as she did me. When I came in and found this novel open upon her lap, she would gravely remark that Freckles was having some trouble with the foreman of the lumber camp or that he had just received an injury to his spine when a tree fell on him. She frowned with genuine sorrow when she reported these misadventures of her storybook hero, possibly not recalling how successfully he came through them all, that the injury to the spine fortuitously resulted in the discovery of rich parents and that the bad-tempered foreman has a heart of gold at the end of the book. Freckles became involved in romance with a girl he called The Angel, but my sister usually stopped reading when this girl became too prominent in the story. She closed the book or turned back to the lonelier periods in the orphan's story. I only remember her making one reference to this heroine of the novel. "The Angel is nice," she said, "but seems to be kind of conceited about her looks."

Then one time at Christmas, while she was trimming the artificial tree, she picked up the Star of Bethlehem that went on the topmost branch and held it gravely toward the chandelier.

"Do stars have five points really?" she enquired.

This was the sort of thing that you didn't believe and that made you stare at Laura with sorrow and confusion.

"No," I told her, seeing she really meant it, "they're round like the earth and most of them much bigger."

She was gently surprised by this new information. She went to the window to look up at the sky which was, as usual during Saint Louis winters, completely shrouded by smoke.

"It's hard to tell," she said, and returned to the tree.

So time passed on till my sister was twenty-three. Old enough to be married, but the fact of the matter was she had never even had a date with a boy. I don't believe this seemed as awful to her as it did to Mother.

At breakfast one morning Mother said to me, "Why don't you cultivate some nice young friends? How about down at the warehouse? Aren't there some young men down there you could ask to dinner?"

This suggestion surprised me because there was seldom quite enough food on her table to satisfy three people. My mother was a terribly stringent housekeeper, God knows we were poor enough in actuality, but my mother had an almost obsessive dread of becoming even poorer. A not unreasonable fear since the man of the house was a poet who worked in a warehouse, but one which I thought played too important a part in all her calculations.

Almost immediately Mother explained herself.

"I think it might be nice," she said, "for your sister."

I brought Jim home to dinner a few nights later. Jim was a big red-haired Irishman who had the scrubbed and polished look of well-kept chinaware. His big square hands seemed to have a direct and very innocent hunger for touching his friends. He was always clapping them on your arms or shoulders and they burned through the cloth of your shirt like plates taken out of an oven. He was the best-liked man in the warehouse and oddly enough he was the only one that I was on good terms with. He found me agreeably ridiculous I think. He knew of my secret practice of retiring to a cabinet in the lavatory and working on rhyme schemes when work was slack in the warehouse, and of sneaking up on the roof now and then to smoke my cigarette with a view across the river at the undulant open country of Illinois. No doubt I was classified as screwy in Jim's mind as much as in the others', but while their attitude was suspicious and hostile when they first knew me, Jim's was warmly tolerant from the beginning. He called me Slim, and gradually his cordial acceptance drew the others around, and while he remained the only one who actually had anything to do with me, the others had now begun to smile when they saw me as people smile at an oddly fashioned dog who crosses their path at some distance.

Nevertheless it took some courage for me to invite Jim to dinner. I thought about it all week and delayed the action till Friday noon, the last possible moment, as the dinner was set for that evening.

"What are you doing tonight?" I finally asked him.

"Not a God damn thing," said Jim. "I had a date but her Aunt took sick and she's hauled her freight to Centralia!"

"Well," I said, "why don't you come over for dinner?"

"Sure!" said Jim. He grinned with astonishing brightness.

I went outside to phone the news to Mother.

Her voice that was never tired responded with an energy that made the wires crackle.

"I suppose he's Catholic?" she said.

"Yes," I told her, remembering the tiny silver cross on his freckled chest.

"Good!" she said. "I'll bake a salmon loaf!"

And so we rode home together in his jalopy.

I had a curious feeling of guilt and apprehension as I led the lamb-like Irishman up three flights of cracked marble steps to the door of Apartment F, which was not thick enough to hold inside it the odor of baking salmon.

Never having a key, I pressed the bell.

"Laura!" came Mother's voice. "That's Tom and Mr. Delaney! Let them in!"

There was a long, long pause.

"Laura?" she called again. "I'm busy in the kitchen, you answer the door!"

Then at last I heard my sister's footsteps. They went right past the door at which we were standing and into the parlor. I heard the creaking noise of the phonograph crank. Music commenced. One of the oldest records, a march of Sousa's, put on to give her the courage to let in a stranger.

The door came timidly open and there she stood in a dress from Mother's wardrobe, a black chiffon ankle-length and high-heeled slippers on which she balanced uncertainly like a tipsy crane of melancholy plumage. Her eyes stared back at us with a glass brightness and her delicate wing-like shoulders were hunched with nervousness.

"Hello!" said Jim, before I could introduce him.

He stretched out his hand. My sister touched it only for a second.

"Excuse me!" she whispered, and turned with a breathless rustle back to her bedroom door, the sanctuary beyond it briefly revealing itself with the tinkling, muted radiance of glass before the door closed rapidly but gently on her wraith-like figure.

Jim seemed to be incapable of surprise.

"Your sister?" he asked.

"Yes, that was her," I admitted. "She's terribly shy with strangers."

"She looks like you," said Jim, "except she's pretty."

Laura did not reappear till called to dinner. Her place was next to Jim at the drop-leaf table and all through the meal her figure was slightly tilted away from his. Her face was feverishly bright and one eyelid, the one on the side toward Jim, had developed a nervous wink. Three times in the course of the dinner she dropped her fork on her plate with a terrible clatter and she was continually raising the water glass to her lips for hasty little gulps. She went on doing this even after the water was gone from the glass. And her handling of the silver became more awkward and hurried all the time.

I thought of nothing to say.

To Mother belonged the conversational honors, such as they were. She asked the caller about his home and family. She was delighted to learn that his father had a business of his own, a retail shoe store somewhere in Wyoming. The news that he went to night school to study accounting was still more edifying. What was his heart set on beside the warehouse? Radio-engineering? My, my, my! It was easy to see that here was a very up-and-coming young man who was certainly going to make his place in the world!

Then she started to talk about her children. Laura, she said, was not cut out for business. She was domestic, however, and making a home was really a girl's best bet.

Jim agreed with all this and seemed not to sense the ghost of an implication. I suffered through it dumbly, trying not to see Laura trembling more and more beneath the incredible unawareness of Mother.

And bad as it was, excruciating in fact, I thought with dread of the moment when dinner was going to be over, for then the diversion of food would be taken away, we would have to go into the little steam-heated parlor. I fancied the four of us having run out of talk, even Mother's seemingly endless store of questions about Jim's home and his job all used up finally — the four of us, then, just sitting there in the parlor, listening to the hiss of the radiator and nervously clearing our throats in the kind of self-consciousness that gets to be suffocating.

But when the blancmange was finished, a miracle happened.

Mother got up to clear the dishes away. Jim gave me a clap on the shoulders and said, "Hey, Slim, let's go have a look at those old records in there!"

He sauntered carelessly into the front room and flopped down on the floor beside the Victrola. He began sorting through the collection of worn-out records and reading their titles aloud in a voice so hearty that it shot like beams of sunlight through the vapors of self-consciousness engulfing my sister and me.

He was sitting directly under the floor-lamp and all at once my sister jumped up and said to him, "Oh — you have freckles!"

Jim grinned. "Sure that's what my folks call me — Freckles!"

"Freckles?" Laura repeated. She looked toward me as if for the confirmation of some too wonderful hope. I looked away quickly, not knowing whether to feel relieved or alarmed at the turn that things were taking.

Jim had wound the Victrola and put on *Dardanella*.

He grinned at Laura.

"How about you an' me cutting the rug a little?"

"What?" said Laura breathlessly, smiling and smiling.

"Dance!" he said, drawing her into his arms.

As far as I knew she had never danced in her life. But to my everlasting wonder she slipped quite naturally into those huge arms of Jim's, and they danced round and around the small steam-heated parlor, bumping against the sofa and chairs and laughing loudly and happily together. Something opened up in my sister's face. To say it was love is not too hasty a judgment, for after all he had freckles and that was what his folks called him. Yes, he had undoubtedly assumed the identity — for all practical purposes — of the one-armed orphan youth who lived in the Limberlost, that tall and misty region to which she retreated whenever the walls of Apartment F became too close to endure.

Mother came back in with some lemonade. She stopped short as she entered the portieres.

"Good heavens! Laura? Dancing?"

Her look was absurdly grateful as well as startled.

"But isn't she stepping all over you, Mr. Delaney?"

"What if she does?" said Jim, with bearish gallantry. "I'm not made of eggs!"

"Well, well, well!" said Mother, senselessly beaming.

"She's light as a feather!" said Jim. "With a little more practice she'd dance as good as Betty!"

There was a little pause of silence.

"Betty?" said Mother.

"The girl I go out with!" said Jim.

"Oh!" said Mother.

She set the pitcher of lemonade carefully down and with her back to the caller and her eyes on me, she asked him just how often he and the lucky young lady went out together.

"Steady!" said Jim.

Mother's look, remaining on my face, turned into a glare of fury.

"Tom didn't mention that you went out with a girl!"

"Nope," said Jim. "I didn't mean to let the cat out of the bag. The boys at the warehouse'll kid me to death when Slim gives the news away."

He laughed heartily but his laughter dropped heavily and awkwardly away as even his dull senses were gradually penetrated by the unpleasant sensation the news of Betty had made.

"Are you thinking of getting married?" said Mother.

"First of next month!" he told her.

It took her several moments to pull herself together. Then she said in a dismal tone, "How nice! If Tom had only told us we could have asked you *both*!"

Jim had picked up his coat.

"Must you be going?" said Mother.

"I hope it don't seem like I'm rushing off," said Jim, "but Betty's gonna get back on the eight o'clock train an' by the time I get my jalopy down to the Wabash depot —"

"Oh, then, we mustn't keep you."

Soon as he'd left, we all sat down, looking dazed.

Laura was the first to speak.

"Wasn't he nice?" she asked. "And all those freckles!"

"Yes," said Mother. Then she turned to me.

"You didn't mention that he was engaged to be married!"

"Well, how did I know that he was engaged to be married?"

"I thought you called him your best friend down at the warehouse?"

"Yes, but I didn't know he was going to be married!"

"How peculiar!" said Mother. "How very peculiar!"

"No," said Laura gently, getting up from the sofa. "There's nothing peculiar about it."

She picked up one of the records and blew on its surface a little as if it were dusty, then set it softly back down.

"People in love," she said, "take everything for granted."

What did she mean by that? I never knew.

She slipped quietly back to her room and closed the door.

Not very long after that I lost my job at the warehouse. I was fired for writing a poem on the lid of a shoe-box. I left Saint Louis and took to moving around. The cities swept about me like dead leaves, leaves that were brightly colored but torn away from the branches. My nature changed. I grew to be firm and sufficient.

In five years' time I had nearly forgotten home. I had to forget it, I couldn't carry it with me. But once in a while, usually in a strange town before I have found companions, the shell of deliberate hardness is broken through. A door comes softly and irresistibly open. I hear the tired old music my unknown father left in the place he abandoned as faithlessly as I. I see the faint and sorrowful radiance of the glass, hundreds of little transparent pieces of it in very delicate colors. I hold my breath, for if my sister's face appears among them — the night is hers!

June 1943 (Published 1948)

Topics for Further Research

1. *The Glass Menagerie* is set in St. Louis. Find out whether natives of St. Louis consider themselves Southerners. To what extent are the characters and themes of the play regional and to what extent are they universal?

2. In the Jean Evans article "Interview 1945" (p. 1483), Williams responds to the question of his use of "plays unconventional in form." In his response, he states that his plays are "light on plot and heavy on characterization." How does such an emphasis benefit *The Glass Menagerie?* What other plays most represent this method?

3. In "Family, Drama, and American Dreams," Tom Scanlan states that Williams "consciously manipulated his subject matter and his tone, playing off the oppressiveness of the family of security against a teasing stylized realism." Do you agree? How does Williams use realism in the play? How does this affect the subject matter?

4. Williams has called himself a "moral symbolist" in the tradition of Nathaniel Hawthorne. Williams, however, has made sexuality's mystery one of his central metaphors. How has he portrayed sexuality in his plays? What is his moral message? How has his portrayal both resembled and differed from Hawthorne's in such works as *The Scarlet Letter*, "Young Goodman Brown" (p. 292), and "Rappaccini's Daughter"?

5. Williams writes about his characters' attempt to escape their reality, and most often their reality is one of loneliness. What methods do his characters use to try to escape their loneliness? Do any of his characters succeed in their attempt? When they do not succeed, what cause their failure? Are the successes and failures of Williams's lonely characters similar to or different from those of Chayefsky's *Marty*?

Jenkins 1

Heather Jenkins

English 202

Professor Spand

17 April 2003

Laura's Gentleman Caller

One of the major points of debate about Tennessee Williams's play <u>The Glass Menagerie</u> centers on the character Jim O'Connor, the "gentleman caller." Jim is an outgoing young man who approaches life lightheartedly, and his friendliness and charm make him a good suitor for Laura. But beside being Laura's suitor, what role does Jim play in the drama? Is Jim merely another character lost in the play's world of illusion, or is he something more? The answers to these questions become clear when we examine Jim's behavior and his influence on the other characters.

Thesis statement

One possible interpretation of Jim's role is that as someone who has created his own illusions, he encourages other characters to dream and fantasize. Jim's vision of the future is a grand (and unrealistic) one. He dreams of becoming part of the newly formed television industry, and throughout his appearance on stage, he rambles on about himself and his plans for the future:

First possible interpretation of gentleman caller: dreamer

> Because I believe in the future of television! <u>(Turning back to her.)</u> I wish to be ready to go up right along with it. Therefore I'm planning to get in on the ground floor. In fact, I've already made the right

Jenkins 2

connections and all that remains is
for the industry itself to get underway!
Full steam— <u>(His eyes are starry.)</u> Knowledge—Zzzzzp! <u>Money</u>—Zzzzzp!—<u>Power</u>! That's
the cycle democracy is built on! <u>(His attitude is convincingly dynamic. Laura stares
at him, even her shyness eclipsed in her
absolute wonder. He suddenly grins.)</u> I
guess you think I think a lot of myself!
(1459)

Jim's fantasies about the future play into and
reinforce Amanda's romantic fantasies. Amanda's plans
to find Laura a husband surface long before Jim enters the Wingfield house, but when Amanda learns that
Jim will attend their dinner, her dream of entertaining gentlemen callers in the Southern tradition becomes a reality. As a result, she begins to have unrealistically high expectations for Jim's visit. When
Jim charms Amanda and attempts to impress her with
his dreams of success, he unknowingly fulfills her
fantasy.

*Second possible
interpretation of
gentleman caller:
savior*

Another possible interpretation of Jim's role is
that he acts as a savior. In his article *"The Glass
Menagerie"* Revisited: Catastrophe without Violence,"
Roger B. Stein, discussing the "religious overtones"
(1489) in the play, sees Jim in exactly this way.
According to Stein, the play's action and language as
well as Williams's stage directions make it clear
that Laura's meeting with Jim can be seen in reli-

Jenkins 3

gious—specifically Christian—terms. It is obvious that Laura needs a savior, but, as Stein observes, Tom is not able to play this role, and
it "remains therefore for Jim to come as the
Savior to this Friday night supper" (1491). In the
simplest terms, Jim's role as possible savior for
Laura—and, perhaps, for her family—is suggested by
his ability to reach out to Laura and encourage her
to enjoy the pleasures of the real world: dancing and
romance.

Jim's role as Laura's savior can also be seen in
the short story "Portrait of a Girl in Glass," from
which the play evolved. In the story, Jim and Laura
begin to dance almost immediately after they are left
alone. Although their encounter in the story is less
intimate than the one in the play, Laura responds to
Jim with joy and hope. In the play, Laura's visit
with Jim evokes a similar response: she enjoys the
feeling of being valued and accepted. Therefore, when
Jim announces his departure (and his engagement),
Laura realizes what she has lost and is overwhelmed
with emotion.

Ironically, however, just as Jim offers Laura
a way to escape her world of illusions, he abandons
her, leaving her trapped in her own world. For this
reason, Jim fails as a savior. One might argue that
he consciously rejects his role as a savior. Still,
we must remember that Jim enters the play unaware of
the family's expectations; he views the visit purely

Jim's failure
in role as
savior

as an opportunity to pass the time and to meet his friend's family, not as a prelude to romance. Jim's perception of his visit is made clear in "Portrait of a Girl in Glass," where he agrees to visit the Wingfields only because he has nothing else to do:

> "What are you doing tonight?" I finally asked him.
>
> "Not a God damn thing," said Jim. "I had a date but her Aunt took sick and she's hauled her freight to Centralia!"
>
> "Well," I said, "why don't you come over for dinner?"
>
> "Sure!" said Jim. He grinned with astonishing brightness. (1498)

Third possible interpretation of gentleman caller: realist

Although both these interpretations of Jim's role offer insights into the play, neither adequately explains Jim's function. Perhaps the best explanation of Jim's role comes from the play itself, where Jim is called "an emissary from a world of reality" (1421). In this sense, his solid presence in the play emphasizes the fragility of the other characters, who live in a world of illusion and fading memories. As an emissary of reality, Jim lives in the real world and realizes the importance of striving for a better life. He attends public speaking and radio engineering classes so that he can advance beyond his low-level job at the warehouse. He scolds Tom for wanting to be a poet, an impractical goal for anyone

Jenkins 5

living during the economic depression of the 1930s. Likewise, Jim challenges Laura to cast off her feelings of deformity and difference; he does not understand why Laura has given up hope and isolated herself. The contrast between Jim and Laura emphasizes not only Laura's vulnerability but also her family's consuming and ultimately debilitating delusions.

Because Jim lives in a world of reality, he is the only character who escapes the illusions that engulf the Wingfields. Jim's connection with reality allows him to continue to search for a better life, something that none of the Wingfields will ever attain. Even though Tom escapes the confines of the apartment, he is unable to leave behind the imaginary world his mother and his sister have created. Moreover, like his father, Tom leaves not to seek reality but to escape from one dream world into another, one that is little different from the movies in which he has lost himself. As the play ends, Tom delivers a monologue about how he has been unable to leave the memory of his sister behind. And we are reminded of Jim, the happy and healthy gentleman caller, who has moved on.

Although Jim is referred to as the gentleman caller, his role in the play is much more complex. In one sense, Jim is a dreamer, detached from reality, enchanted by his own egotistical vision of how people should behave. In another sense, he is a kind of savior who reaches out to Laura, conveying the warmth

Jenkins 6

and compassion of a saint. But these two images are
overshadowed by Jim's role as an emissary from the
real world who journeys to the seductive world of
fantasy and whose presence there emphasizes the destructive power of dreams that have become delusions.
In this role, Jim is "the kindest of Williams's emissaries from reality, perhaps because his faith in the
American dream of self-improvement and success is so
complete as to be itself a touching illusion" (Scanlan 1493).

Jenkins 7

Works Cited

Kirszner, Laurie G., and Stephen R. Mandell, eds.
   Literature: Reading, Reacting, Writing.
   5th ed. Boston: Heinle, 2004.

Scanlan, Tom. From Family, Drama, and American
   Dreams. Kirszner and Mandell 1491–94.

Stein, Roger B. "The Glass Menagerie Revisited:
   Catastrophe without Violence." Kirszner and Mandell 1489–91.

Williams, Tennessee. The Glass Menagerie. Kirszner
   and Mandell 1416–67.

---. "Portrait of a Girl in Glass." Kirszner and
   Mandell 1494–1501.

WRITING ABOUT LITERATURE

CHAPTER 33

THREE SPECIAL WRITING ASSIGNMENTS

When you write a paper about literature, you have many options (some of these options are listed in Chapter 2, p. 21). Very often, however, you will be asked to respond to one of three special assignments: to write a comparison-contrast paper, to write an explication, or to write a character analysis. In the pages that follow, we offer guidelines for responding to each of these assignments as well as an annotated model student paper and a list of suggested topics for each kind of paper.

WRITING A COMPARISON-CONTRAST PAPER

When you write a comparison-contrast paper, you look first for significant similarities between your two subjects. For example, two characters may have a similar motivation or similar goals or flaws; two stories may have similar settings; two plays may have similar plots; and two poems may have parallels in their use of sound or imagery. Once you have identified the main similarities, you consider why these similarities are important and what they reveal about the characters or works.

There are two ways to arrange material in a comparison-contrast essay. When you write a **point-by-point comparison**, you discuss one point of similarity at a time, alternating between subjects. When you write a **subject-by-subject comparison**, you approach each subject separately, discussing all your points for one subject and then for the other. The outlines that follow illustrate how you could use either a point-by-point or a subject-by-subject strategy to support the same thesis statement.

THESIS STATEMENT: Both "Doe Season" and "Boys and Girls" focus on a young girl who learns that her gender limits her and comes to accept that such limitations are inevitable.

Point-by-Point Comparison

First point: In both stories, the girls are tomboys who like being with their fathers.

"Doe Season": Andy goes hunting with her father.

"Boys and Girls": The narrator does chores with her father.

Second point: In both stories, the girls struggle against expectations of others.
  "Doe Season": Mac and Charlie challenge Andy's right to hunt.
  "Boys and Girls": Narrator's mother expects her to do household chores.

Third Point: In both stories, the girls learn that they are limited by their gender.
  "Doe Season": Andy shoots the deer and runs away in horror, thinking of her mother.
  "Boys and Girls": The narrator fails to save Flora (the horse) and realizes she is "only a girl."

Subject-by-Subject Comparison

First subject: "Doe Season"
  First point: Andy is a tomboy who is excited about going hunting with her father.
  Second point: Charlie and Mac challenge her right to be there.
  Third point: Through her encounter with the deer, she learns that she is not as brave as she thought she was.

Second subject: "Boys and Girls"
  First point: Like Andy, the narrator likes being with her father and is glad not to be in the house with her mother.
  Second point: Like Andy, she is criticized by those who think she belongs at home.
  Third point: Like Andy, she learns through her encounter with an animal — in her case, the horse whose life she cannot save — that she is limited by her gender.

CHECKLIST   **WRITING A COMPARISON-CONTRAST PAPER**

✓ Have you chosen two subjects that have significant parallels?

✓ Does your thesis statement identify the two subjects you are comparing and tell why they are alike (and perhaps also acknowledge their differences)?

✓ Does your paper's structure follow either a point-by-point or a subject-by-subject pattern?

✓ Does each of your topic sentences identify the subject you are discussing and the point you are focusing on in the paragraph?

✓ Do transitional words and phrases clearly lead readers from subject to subject and from point to point?

✓ Have you followed your instructor's format and documentation guidelines?

Sample Student Paper: Comparing Two Fictional Characters

The following student paper, "The Dangerous Consequences of Societal Limbo," is a point-by-point comparison of two characters created by William Faulkner: Emily Grierson in "A Rose for Emily" and Abner (Ab) Snopes in "Barn Burning." Note that because the student author was permitted to write only about works in this anthology, his instructor did not require a works-cited page.

Quinn 1

David Quinn

Professor Warren

Literature 1120

27 March 2003

The Dangerous Consequences of Societal Limbo

Introduction   In his many works of fiction, William Faulkner explores the lives of characters who live in the closed society of the American South, a society rooted in traditional values. In the stories "Barn Burning" and "A Rose for Emily," Faulkner explores what happens when individuals lose their connection to this society and its values. Both Abner Snopes, a rebellious sharecropper, and Emily Grierson, an unmarried woman from a prominent family, are isolated

Thesis statement   from their respective communities, and both find themselves in a kind of societal limbo. Once in that limbo, they no longer feel the need to adhere to the values of their society and, as a result, are free to violate both traditional and moral rules.

Emily's isolation   Initially, Emily's isolation is not her own creation; it is thrust upon her. From childhood on, Emily is never really allowed to be part of Jefferson society; she is seen as having a "high and mighty" attitude (Faulkner, "Rose" 93). Her father stands between her and the rest of the town, refusing to allow her to date the young men who pursue her, whom he sees as somehow not good enough for her. As a result, her only close relationship is with her father, who essentially becomes her whole world. Recalling both father and daughter, the narrator depicts them as

Quinn 2

static and alone, trapped in a living portrait, "Miss
Emily a slender figure in white in the background,
her father a spraddled silhouette in the foreground,
his back to her and clutching a horsewhip" (Faulkner,
"Rose" 94), framed by the archway of the entrance to
their house. When Emily's father dies, and the townspeople insist on removing his body from her home, the
only world she knows is physically taken from her,
and she has nothing to take its place. Without her
father, without friends, without a husband, she withdraws from her community—and, thus, is free to defy
its rules with a shocking act of violence.

   While Emily's removal from society is forced
upon her, Abner Snopes voluntarily rejects his soci-   Ab's isolation
ety's values from the beginning. During the Civil
War, he does not fight alongside the Confederate
army; instead, he adopts an aggressive neutrality,
stealing from both sides for his own personal gain.
He is finally caught by the side he betrays when a
Confederate policeman shoots him in the heel as Abner
tries to escape on a stolen horse. Unable to see his
own fault in that episode, Abner uses his injury as
an excuse for a personal vendetta against society.
However, because he has a wife and three children
whom he must feed and provide for, Ab must constantly
return to the society that he turned his back on.
This conflict between his rebellious nature and his
need to work as a sharecropper makes him unstable.
Like Emily, he does not see himself as part of the

Quinn 3

community, and therefore he feels free to violate its rules.

Transitional paragraph

Once Emily and Abner are estranged from their respective communities, they no longer see themselves as bound by the society's laws and rules. This makes it possible for Abner to burn barns and for Emily to commit murder.

Emily's antisocial act

Emily's courting and capturing of Homer Barron fills the void left by her father's death; for her, the act of poisoning Homer is a perverse method of regaining control. With this act, she takes away the very life that attracted her to him, but she is able to hold on to him as a physical entity. As an exile from society, Emily can rationalize this antisocial act: in her eyes, murder is no longer considered wrong; it is merely a method of preservation, a means to an end that ensures that Homer will remain with her until her death. Once Emily has completed the gruesome task of poisoning her "husband," she further withdraws from her community, and her neighbors, the narrator included, never suspect her secret. Without suspicion from the townspeople, Emily is left alone, free to live as she chooses.

Ab's anti-social acts

Abner's impotent rage and search for vengeance push him to lash out violently at almost anyone with whom he comes in contact. His method of destruction comes in the primitive form of fire, which he uses not to kill but simply to threaten. In the two barn burnings of the story, Abner incites confrontations

Quinn 4

and then uses the burnings as a way of getting even for imagined offenses. In one incident, for example, Mr. Harris, a landowner, finds that Abner's hog ate a section of his corn crop. When Harris demands a dollar pound fee for the return of the hog, Abner sends him a threatening message: "Wood and hay kin burn" (Faulkner, "Barn" 223). Despite Harris's efforts to resolve their dispute, Abner is determined to carry out his threat. Ultimately, the barn burnings further alienate Ab from the society whose laws he is defying.

Like Ab Snopes, Emily makes her own rules and develops her own twisted concepts of justice and revenge. Although she is not directly punished by the community for her crime, Emily suffers terribly. She may possess the body of Homer Barron, but his death renders her incapable of holding onto him as a person and a husband. The result of her gradual estrangement from society—involuntary at first but eventually confirmed by her willing violent act—is complete isolation from the real world and withdrawal into an empty world of her own.

Emily's punishment

Although Ab operates from within a similar societal limbo, he is unable to escape society's punishment. Sarty Snopes, Abner's son, is a firsthand witness to his father's second barn burning. Sarty is caught in a moral dilemma, pulled between the values of his community and the selfish motives of his father. Rather than remain in the alienated condition

Ab's punishment

that his father has created for his family, Sarty re-
nounces his loyalty to Abner and turns his father in
to plantation owner Major De Spain.

Conclusion
        Despite their estrangement from society, then,
neither Emily nor Ab is ultimately able to escape its
influence. In withdrawing from their respective communities, Emily Grierson and Abner Snopes are able to
defy its traditions and break its rules, but they
also create empty lives for themselves and tragedy
for those closest to them.

Suggested Topics for Comparison-Contrast Papers

Comparing Two Poems: "The Soldier" and "Dulce et Decorum Est"; "Hope" and "'Hope' is the thing with feathers —"; "Wreath for a Bridal" and "A Pink Wool Knitted Dress" (For a model student paper that compares two poems, see "Digging for Memories," p. 594.)

Comparing Two Plays: rivalry and role reversal in *The Stronger* and *Beauty*; father/son relationships in *Fences* and *Death of a Salesman*; illness in *A Doll House* and *Wit*

Comparing a Story and a Poem: "The Rocking-Horse Winner" and "Suicide Note" (children desperate to please their parents); "A Rose for Emily" and "Porphyria's Lover" (obsessive love)

Comparing a Story and a Play: loneliness and desperation in *Trifles* and "A Rose for Emily"

Comparing Two Characters: Queenie ("A&P") and Miss Ferenczi ("Gryphon"); Vivian and Jason (*Wit*); Carla and Bethany (*Beauty*)

Comparing Two Works by a Single Author: John Updike's "A&P" and "Ex-Basketball Player"; Tennessee Williams's *The Glass Menagerie* and "Portrait of a Girl in Glass"

Comparing a Work of Literature to a Work of Art: Jane Flanders's poem "Cloud Painter" and John Constable's painting *Landscape, Noon, the Haywain*; William Carlos Williams's poem "The Great Figure" and Charles Henry Demuth's painting *The Figure 5 in Gold*; W. H. Auden's poem "Musée des Beaux Arts" and Pieter Brueghel's painting *Landscape with the Fall of Icarus*

Note: For additional possibilities for comparison-contrast papers, see the "Related Works" lists that follow many of the selections.

WRITING AN EXPLICATION

When you write an explication (of a poem, a short story, or a scene in a play), you scrutinize a work or a portion of a work, carefully examining its parts in order to get a sense of the whole. For example, you might decide to do a close reading and analysis of a story's characters, symbols, and setting; of a poem's language, rhyme scheme, meter, and form; or of a play's dialogue and staging. One way to approach a work you wish to explicate is to apply the guidelines for reading fiction (p. 52), poetry (p. 578), or drama (p. 958) in a systematic way. Another way is to use The Personal Poetry Project mark-up tool on the CD-Rom accompanying this book.

When you organize your material in an explication, you should proceed systematically from one element to another, considering each element — plot, setting, point of view, and so on — in turn. If you are analyzing several elements, you will probably choose to group the less significant elements together in a single paragraph or section of your paper and then devote several paragraphs to one particularly important element, carefully considering how symbols, for example, shed light on the work. (You might also choose to devote your entire paper to a discussion of just one element.) For each element you discuss, you will give examples from the work you are explicating, quoting words, phrases, lines, and passages that illustrate each point you are making about the work.

CHECKLIST   **WRITING AN EXPLICATION**

✓ Is the work you have chosen sufficiently rich to support an explication?

✓ Do you focus on one element of literature at a time?

✓ Do topic sentences make clear which element (or elements) you are focusing on in each paragraph?

✓ Do you use quotations from the work to illustrate your points?

✓ Does your thesis state the central point about the work that your explication supports?

✓ Have you followed your instructor's format and documentation guidelines?

Sample Student Paper: Explicating a Poem

The following student paper, "A Lingering Doubt," is an explication of Robert Frost's poem "The Road Not Taken." Note that because the student author was permitted to write only about works in this anthology, her instructor did not require a works-cited page.

Craff 1

Jeanette Craff

Professor Rosenberg

English 102

13 February 2003

A Lingering Doubt

Sometimes it is tempting to look back on a lifetime of choices and decisions and to think "What if?
What if I had made a different choice? Would my
life be better? Worse? More interesting?" In Robert
Frost's poem "The Road Not Taken," the speaker does
just this: he looks back at a time in his life when
he came to a fork in the road and chose one path over
another. He tells readers that he "took the one less
traveled by, / And that has made all the difference"
(lines 19-20). At first, this statement seems to suggest that the speaker is satisfied with the decision
he made long ago. However, many elements in the
poem—its structure, its language, and even its
title—suggest that the speaker is regretting his decision, not celebrating it.

The title of the poem, "The Road Not Taken," immediately suggests that the speaker is focusing not
on the choice he <u>did</u> make long ago but on the road
he chose <u>not</u> to take. The poem's language supports
this interpretation. Frost begins his poem with the
speaker recalling that "Two roads diverged in a yellow wood" and saying that he is sorry [he] could not
travel both" (1-2). The image Frost uses of the two
roads diverging is an obvious metaphor for the
choices a person has to make in the course of a life-

Introduction

Thesis statement

Overview of
poem's language
and theme

time. As a young man, the speaker was not aware of
any major difference between the two roads. He sees
one as "just as fair" (6) as the other and uses words
and phrases such as "equally" (11) and "really about
the same" (10). However, in the third stanza of the
poem, the older and wiser speaker, looking back on
that period of his life, says that he still might
take the other road "another day" (13). That the mature speaker still continues to examine a decision he
made earlier in life suggests that he may not be completely satisfied with that decision.

Analysis of poem's structure

A close look at the poem suggests that it is
the departures from the expected structure and meter
that make the poem's meaning clear. The poem is divided into four stanzas, each made up of five lines.
The regular meter of these four stanzas conveys a
sense of tranquillity and certainty. The regularity
of the poem's rhyme scheme (a,b,a,a,b) also contributes to the poem's natural fluidity. This
fluidity is evident, for example, in the first
stanza:

> Two roads diverged in a yellow wood,
> And sorry I could not travel both
> And be one traveler, long I stood
> And looked down one as far as I could
> To where it bent in the undergrowth;
>
> (1-5)

Here, the end rhyme of lines 1, 3, and 4 and of lines
2 and 5, as well as the even line lengths (each line

contains nine syllables) make the poem flow smoothly.

However, the poem does not maintain this fluidity. In other stanzas, lines range from eight to ten
syllables in length, and the important final stanza
breaks from the poem's sense of smoothness by ending
with a line that is an awkward departure from the
rest of the poem:

> I shall be telling this with a sigh
> Somewhere ages and ages hence:
> Two roads diverged in a wood, and I—
> I took the one less traveled by,
> And that has made all the difference.
>
> (16-20)

In this stanza, line 20 has nine syllables as lines
16 and 18 do, but unlike them, it also has an irregular meter ("And that has made all the difference"),
which forces readers to hesitate on the word "all"
before landing on "difference." This hesitation,
coupled with the hesitation signaled by the dash that
ends line 18, reveals the speaker's doubts about his
decision. When the speaker was young, he did not notice any significant difference between the two
roads, or the life choices, presented to him. Now,
looking back, he believes that there was a difference, and he may be lamenting the fact that he will
never know where life would have taken him had he
chosen differently.

Departure from expected meter is not the only
tactic Frost uses to convey a sense of hesitation and

Further analysis
of poem's
structure

Analysis of
poem's
language

Craff 4

an air of regret. Frost's choice of words also plays
an important part in helping readers understand the
poem's theme. In the first stanza, for example, the
speaker thinks back to the period of his life in
which he had to choose between two separate paths,
and he says that he was "sorry [he] could not travel
both" (2). The word "sorry" helps to establish the
tone of regret that pervades the poem.

In the second stanza, Frost begins to use words
and phrases to convey a sense of indecision and doubt
in the speaker's voice. The speaker attempts to
pacify himself by saying that the road he chose had
"perhaps the better claim" (7), but then he is quick
to say that the passage of time had worn both roads
"really about the same" (10). The words "perhaps" and
"really" suggest indecision, and Frost's choice of
these words helps to convey the doubt in the
speaker's mind.

The speaker's sense of regret deepens in the
third stanza as he continues to think back on his decision. When the speaker says, "Oh, I kept the first
for another day!" (13), the word "Oh" expresses his
regret. The exclamation point at the end of the
statement helps reinforce the finality of his decision. When the speaker continues, "Yet knowing how
way leads on to way, / I doubted if I should ever
come back" (14–15), the word "Yet" is filled with
uncertainty.

Craff 5

In the poem's final stanza, the speaker suddenly leaves his thoughts of the past and speaks in the future tense: "I shall be telling this [story] with a sigh" (16). Frost's use of the word "sigh" here is very revealing because it connotes resignation or regret. After the speaker sighs, he concludes, "Two roads diverged in a wood, and I— / I took the one less traveled by, / And that has made all the difference" (18-20). Both the dash and the repetition of the word "I" convey his lingering doubts over the decision he made long ago.

Although this doubt is evident throughout the poem, "The Road Not Taken" has frequently been interpreted as optimistic because of the speaker's final statement that the choice he made "has made all the difference" (20). However, "made all the difference" can be interpreted as neutral (or even negative) as well as positive, and so the speaker's statement at the end of the poem may actually be a statement of regret, not celebration. The "difference" mentioned in the final line has left a doubt in the speaker's mind, and, as Frost suggests in the title of his poem, the speaker is left thinking about the road he did not take and will never be able to take.

Conclusion

Suggested Topics for Explication Papers

Fiction

Focus on Form: "Kansas"; "Girl"

Focus on Language: "Battle Royal"; "How to Talk to Your Mother (Notes)"

Focus on Character: "The Fireman"; "Aguantado"

Focus on Setting: "Greasy Lake"

Focus on Point of View: "The Disappearance"; "I Stand Here Ironing"

Focus on Plot: "Happy Endings"; "Sleepy Time Gal"

Note: For two model student papers that explicate short stories, see "'The Secret Lion': Everything Changes" (p. 72) and "'A&P': A Class Act" (p. 1765).

Poetry

Focus on Voice: "Ballad of the Landlord"; "Not Waving but Drowning"; "Daddy"; "Volcanoes be in Sicily"

Focus on Word Choice: "Jabberwocky"

Focus on Imagery: "Emmett Till"; "The Lake Isle of Innisfree"; "Dover Beach"; "Ode on a Grecian Urn"

Focus on Figures of Speech: "Dulce et Decorum Est"; "Metaphors"

Focus on Sound: "Acquainted with the Night"; "La Belle Dame sans Merci"

Focus on Form: "Buffalo Bill's"; "When I consider how my light is spent"; "What Were They Like?"

Focus on Symbol, Allegory, Allusion, Myth: "The Second Coming"

Drama

Focus on Character: Dr. Rank in *A Doll House*; Ophelia in *Hamlet*

Focus on Staging: Tom's monologues in *The Glass Menagerie*; Vivian's and Jason's parallel speeches in *Wit*; the Requiem in *Death of a Salesman*

Focus on Language: Vivian's analysis of poetic texts in *Wit*; imagery and figures of speech in *The Brute*; one speech in *Hamlet*

Focus on Symbolism: The quilt in *Trifles*

WRITING A CHARACTER ANALYSIS

When you write an analysis of a character in a short story or play, you examine the character's language, behavior, background, interaction with other characters, and reaction to his or her environment. Everything you are told about a character — and everything you can reasonably infer about him or her from words, actions, or appearance — can help you to understand the character. In your analysis, you can focus on the influences that shaped the character, the character's effect on others, how the character changes during the course of the story or play, or what motivates him or her to act (or not to act).

CHECKLIST **WRITING A CHARACTER ANALYSIS**

✓ Have you chosen a character who is interesting enough to make him or her a suitable focus for your paper?

✓ Have you considered the character's words, actions, appearance, and interactions with others?

✓ Have you considered how and why the character changes — or why he or she fails to change?

✓ Have you considered how the work would be different if the character had made different choices?

✓ Have you considered how the work would be different without the character?

✓ Have you considered what motivates the character to act (or not to act)?

✓ Have you followed your instructor's format and documentation guidelines?

Sample Student Paper: Analyzing a Character in a Play

The following student paper, "Linda Loman: Breaking the Mold," analyzes a character in Arthur Miller's play *Death of a Salesman*. Note that because the student author was permitted to write only about works in this anthology, her instructor did not require a works-cited list.

Caroline Dube

Professor Nelson

English 1302

14 March 2003

Linda Loman: Breaking the Mold

In many ways, Linda Loman appears to play the part of the stereotypical dutiful and loving wife in Arthur Miller's <u>Death of a Salesman</u>. She eagerly greets her husband, ignores his shortcomings, and maintains an upbeat attitude, all while managing the bills, waxing the floors, and mending the clothes. Her kindness and infinite patience seem to establish her as a foil for Willy, with his turbulent temperament. In addition, the majority of her actions seem to be only reactions to the other characters in the play. However, a closer look at Linda reveals a more complex woman: a fully developed character with dreams, insights, and flashes of defiance.

Unlike stock characters, whose motivations seem transparent and obvious, Linda has dreams that are both complex and realistically human. The stage directions that introduce Linda describe her as sharing Willy's "turbulent longings" but lacking the temperament to pursue them (1180). It seems she has applied the wisdom she shares with Willy, that "life is a casting off," to her own cast-away dreams (1181). Linda's hopes seem more realistic than Willy's. She wants Biff to settle down, the mortgage to be paid off, and the members of her family to coexist happily. These modest aspirations are the product of

Thesis statement

Linda's hopes and dreams

Dube 2

Linda's timeworn experience. The fact that Linda is
unable to chase unrealistic goals, as Willy does,
does not make her a flat character (or even a less
interesting one); instead, her weaknesses give her
character a degree of depth and human realism.

At times, Linda takes on the role of family
peacemaker—a role we would expect her to play consistently throughout the play if she were simply a
stock character. But Linda breaks out of the obedient
wife mode on several occasions. When Willy insists
that she stop mending her stockings, Linda quietly
puts them into her pocket to resume her mending later. When Biff and Happy show they are ashamed of
their father, Linda fiercely lashes out at them in
his defense, calling Happy a "philandering bum" and
threatening to kick Biff out of the house for good
(1205). Though initially, she cannot bring herself to
remove the rubber pipe that Willy used to commit suicide, Linda says she had finally decided to destroy
the pipe when Biff removed it. She does not always
have an opportunity to follow through on her threats,
but Linda demonstrates clearly that she will not always follow orders—especially when she is protecting
Willy.

Linda seems to be the cheerful voice of the family, but beneath the surface, she is keenly aware
of the ongoing problems. She knows that Charley has
been giving money to Willy every week, but she says
nothing for fear of embarrassing Willy. She senses

Linda's actions

Linda's
awareness
of family
problems

Dube 3

Willy's suicidal tendencies and even finds physical
evidence of his plans. Linda is the first to raise
doubts about Biff's plans to ask Mr. Oliver for
money, suggesting he may not remember Biff. Above
all, Linda understands human nature and how the minds
of those around her work. She gives an honest
description of her husband and his situation:

> I don't say he's a great man. Willy
> Loman never made a lot of money. His
> name was never in the paper. He's not the
> finest character that ever lived. But he's
> a human being, and a terrible thing is hap-
> pening to him. So attention must be paid.
>
> (1204)

Linda sees past her sons' exaggerated lies and is not
afraid to criticize them for their selfish choices.
She pretends to be unaware of their shortcomings, but
her feigned obliviousness is simply another layer in
her multifaceted personality.

Linda's failure to confront family problem

  Linda appears to be the steadiest character in
the play, providing stability for the other characters, but her constant brushing aside of problems actually makes her the most responsible for the ultimate tragedy of the play. She lies to Willy in order
to soothe him, telling him he has "too much on the
ball to worry about" (1183) and is "the handsomest
man in the world" (1194). In the process, she allows
him to continue believing in the unattainable dreams
that ultimately lead him to self-destruct. She also

Dube 4

makes exceptions for her sons, suggesting Willy can simply talk to Biff's teacher to change his grade and encouraging Biff's business plans even when she knows he will not succeed. As a result, failure hits Biff hard because he has not been forced to think realistically.

    In the end, Linda goes beyond the stereotypical confines of her role as ever-supportive wife and mother. There are many layers to her character: beneath her simple goals of owning the home and living happily with her family lie years of disappointments and failed dreams. Hidden beneath her eagerness to please is her willingness to defy orders to defend her husband. And, although she seems not to notice what is going on, she is perceptive about the family's problems long before others show awareness. Her actions clearly show that she is more than a minor supporting character. Linda is deeply involved in the actions and impulses of the other characters in the play. As a fully developed character, she has complex motivations and human qualities (including faults) that set her apart from stock characters. As her son Happy notes, "They broke the mold when they made her" (1209).

Conclusion

Suggested Topics for Character Analysis Papers

Fiction

Major Characters: Olaf in "Big Black Good Man"; Lieutenant Cross in "The Things They Carried"; Dee in "Everyday Use"; the mother in "Two Kinds"

Minor Characters: the mother in "The Rocking-Horse Winner"; the husband in "The Swing"

Note: For a model student paper analyzing a major character in a short story, see "And Again She Makes the Journey: Character and Act in Eudora Welty's 'A Worn Path'" (p. 1554). For a model student paper analyzing characters' motivation, see "Desperate Measures: Acts of Defiance in *Trifles*" (p. 972).

Drama

Major Characters: Miss Y in *The Stronger*; Linda in *Death of a Salesman*; Amanda in *The Glass Menagerie*.

Minor Characters: E. M. Ashford in *Wit*; Luka in *The Brute*; Polonius in *Hamlet*; Mrs. Linde in *A Doll House*.

Note: For a model student paper analyzing a minor character in a play, see "Laura's Gentleman Caller" (p. 1503).

CHAPTER 34

WRITING A RESEARCH PAPER

When you write a paper about a literary topic, you often supplement your own interpretations with information from other sources. These sources may include works of literature as well as books and journal articles by literary critics (see p. 12). You may get this information from print sources, from electronic databases in the library, or from the Internet. You should not, however, let the task of gathering information make you forget all you have learned about writing a paper on a literary topic. Remember, your primary task is to present your ideas clearly and convincingly. For this reason, you will have a much easier time writing a literary research paper if you follow the process discussed in the pages that follow.

CHOOSING A TOPIC

Your instructor may assign a topic or may allow you to choose one. If you choose a topic, make sure your topic is narrow enough for your paper's length, the amount of time you have for writing, and the number of sources your instructor expects you to use.

Daniel Collins, a student in an introduction to literature course, was given three weeks to write a five- to seven-page research paper on one of the short stories the class had read. Daniel chose to write about Eudora Welty's "A Worn Path" because he liked the story and because the main character, Phoenix Jackson, interested him. He knew, however, that he would have to narrow his topic before he could begin. In class, Daniel's instructor had asked some provocative questions about the significance of Phoenix Jackson's journey. Daniel thought that this topic might work well because he could explore it in five pages and could complete the paper within the three-week time limit.

LOOKING FOR SOURCES

To see whether you will be able to find enough material about your topic, do a quick survey of your library's resources. Before you start, meet with a reference librarian, who can save you time by pointing you to the most useful resources.

Begin your survey by consulting your library's online central information system. Frequently, this system includes the library's catalog as well as a number of bibliographic databases, such as *Readers' Guide to Periodical Literature* and *Humanities Index*. Then, consult general reference works like encyclopedias and specialized dictionaries and browse your search engine's subject guides to get an overview of your subject.

A quick look at his library's central information system showed Daniel that his library's holdings included several books and numerous articles on Eudora Welty. He noted the titles of the most promising sources so he could find them later.

NARROWING YOUR TOPIC

As you survey the resources of your library, the titles of books and articles as well as the subject headings of the catalog should help you to narrow your topic.

Daniel found two critical articles that discussed the significance of Phoenix Jackson's journey, and he hoped they would help him to understand why Phoenix Jackson continued her journey despite all the hardships she encountered. Daniel knew that he would have to do more than just summarize his sources; he would have to make a point about the journey, one that he could support with examples from the story as well as from his research.

DOING RESEARCH

Once you have narrowed your topic, you are ready to look for the information you will need to develop your ideas. Go back to the library and check out any books you think will be useful. Then, consult reference works — indexes and bibliographies, for example — to find relevant articles. If you find articles in print form, use the copy machines in the library to photocopy them (and be sure to copy down the publication information you will need to document these sources). Also search electronic databases (either CD-ROM or online), such as *Expanded Academic ASAP*, to find relevant articles. Usually, you can download information from these databases to a diskette or print out a hard copy. Finally, browse the World Wide Web, beginning at a site such as *Voice of the Shuttle: Web Page for Humanities Research*, at <http://vos.ucsb.edu>, and following the links to other relevant sites.

Daniel was lucky enough to find everything he needed in his college library. He retrieved two articles about the Welty story, and he found two more listed in *Humanities Index*. Finally, a more careful search of his library's online central information system revealed that among the library's holdings was a videotape of "A Worn Path" that included an interview with the author.

TAKING NOTES

Once you have located your sources, you should begin to record the information you think will be useful for your paper. There is no single correct way to take notes; different writers take notes differently. Some writers store information in a computer file that they have created for this purpose; others keep their notes on 3-by-5-inch cards. Whatever system you use, be sure to record the author's full name as well as complete publication information. You will need this information later on to compile your works-cited list (see p. 1544).

When you take notes from a source, you have three options: you can *paraphrase*, *summarize*, or *quote*.

When you **paraphrase**, you put the author's ideas into your own words, keeping the order and emphasis of the original. You paraphrase when you want to make a difficult or complex discussion accessible to readers so that you can comment on it or use it to support your own points. Here is a passage from Roland Bartel's article "Life and Death in Eudora Welty's 'A Worn Path,'" followed by Daniel's paraphrase.

Original

The assumption that the grandson is dead helps explain Phoenix Jackson's stoical behavior in the doctor's office. She displays a "ceremonial stiffness" as she sits "bolt upright" staring "straight ahead, her face solemn and withdrawn into rigidity." This passiveness suggests her psychological dilemma — she cannot explain why she made the journey. Her attempt to blame the lapse of memory on her illiteracy is unconvincing. Her lack of education is hardly an excuse for forgetting her grandson, but it goes a long way toward explaining her inability to articulate her subconscious motives for her journey.

Paraphrase

As Roland Bartel points out in "Life and Death in Eudora Welty's 'A Worn Path,'" Phoenix Jackson's lack of response at the doctor's office makes sense if we assume that her grandson is dead. She sits still, without showing any emotion, and she does not answer people's questions. Although she says her forgetfulness is due to her lack of education, this excuse doesn't seem believable to Bartel, who observes that although her lack of education does not explain why she forgets about her grandson, it might account for her failure to understand why she makes the trip to the city.

When you write a **summary,** you also put an author's ideas into your own words. A summary, however, presents just the general point of a passage. For this reason, a summary is always shorter than the original. Here is Daniel's summary of the passage from Bartel's article.

Summary

As Roland Bartel points out in "Life and Death in Eudora Welty's 'A Worn Path,'" Phoenix Jackson's actions at the doctor's office make sense only if we assume that her grandson is dead and that she does not fully understand her reasons for making her trip.

When you *quote,* you reproduce a passage exactly, word for word and punctuation mark for punctuation mark, enclosing the entire passage in quotation marks. Because too many quotations can distract readers, use a quotation only when you think that the author's words will add something — memorable wording, for example — to your paper.

INTEGRATING SOURCES

To integrate a summary, paraphrase, or quotation smoothly into your paper, use a phrase that introduces your source and its author — *Bartel points out, according to Bartel, Bartel claims,* or *Bartel says,* for example. You can place this identifying phrase at various points in a sentence.

According to Roland Bartel, "The assumption that the grandson is dead helps explain Phoenix Jackson's stoical behavior in the doctor's office."

"The assumption that the grandson is dead helps explain Phoenix Jackson's stoical behavior in the doctor's office," **observes Roland Bartel in his article** "Life and Death in Eudora Welty's 'A Worn Path.'"

"The assumption that the grandson is dead," **notes the literary critic Roland Bartel,** "helps explain Phoenix Jackson's stoical behavior in the doctor's office."

Avoiding Plagiarism

Plagiarism is taking credit for ideas or words that are not your own. Sometimes plagiarism is *intentional,* but often it is *unintentional* — occurring, for example, when you paste a quoted passage from your computer file directly into your paper and forget to use quotation marks and documentation. The best way to avoid plagiarism is to keep careful notes, to distinguish between your ideas and those of your sources, and to give credit to your sources with **documentation.** For literary research, documentation consists of in-text citations and a works-cited list (see p. 1544).

In general, you document words and ideas borrowed from your sources. (This rule applies to both print and electronic sources.) Of course, there are certain items that do not need to be documented: common knowledge (information every reader will probably know), facts available from a variety of reference sources, familiar sayings and well-known quotations, and your own original research (interviews and surveys you conduct, for example).

You can avoid the possibility of plagiarism if you remember exactly what types of information require documentation.

- *Document all word-for-word quotations from a source.* Whenever you use a writer's exact words, document them. Even if you quote only a word or two within a paraphrase or summary, you must document the quoted words separately, after the final quotation marks.

- *Document ideas from a source that you put into your own words.* Be sure to document all paraphrases or summaries of a source, including an author's judgments, conclusions, and arguable assertions.
- *Document all tables, charts, graphs, or statistics from a source.* Because tables and graphs are almost always the product of someone's original research, they must be documented. (Even if you compile your own table using data from a source, you must still credit the source.)

> **NOTE:** Plagiarism can also occur when a paraphrase or summary too closely follows the wording and sentence structure of the original. Even if you do not use the exact words of the original, and even if you provide documentation, you commit plagiarism if you simply use synonyms and closely follow the sentence structure of your source. Acceptable paraphrases and summaries do more than change words; they use original phrasing and syntax to convey the source's meaning.

DRAFTING A THESIS STATEMENT

After you have taken notes, review the information you have gathered, and use it to help you draft a thesis statement. Your **thesis statement,** a single sentence that states the main idea of your paper, should make a point that you will support with a combination of your own ideas and the ideas you have drawn from your research.

After reviewing his notes, Daniel developed this thesis statement about Eudora Welty's "A Worn Path."

Thesis statement
```
   What is most important is Phoenix Jackson's character and
her act of making the journey.
```

As you draft and revise your paper, your thesis statement will probably change. Still, it gives your ideas focus and enables you to organize them into an outline.

MAKING AN OUTLINE

Once you have drafted a thesis statement, you can construct an outline from your notes. Write your thesis statement at the top of the page. Then, review your notes, and arrange them in the order in which you plan to use them. As you construct your outline, arrange these points under appropriate headings. When it is completed, your outline will show you how much support you have for each of your points, and it will be your guide when you write a draft of your paper. Your outline, which covers the body paragraphs of your essay, can be a *sentence outline*, in which each idea is expressed as a sentence, or a *topic outline*, in which each idea is expressed in a word or a short phrase.

After reviewing his notes, Daniel constructed the following topic outline. Notice that he uses roman numerals for first-level headings, capital letters for second-level headings, and arabic numerals for third-level headings. Notice too that all points in the outline are parallel.

Thesis Statement: What is most important is Phoenix Jackson's character and her act of making the journey.

```
  I. Critical interpretations of "A Worn Path"
     A. Heroic act of sacrifice
     B. Journey of life
     C. Religious pilgrimage
 II. Focus on journey
     A. Little information about Jackson and her grandson
     B. Nurse's question
     C. Jackson's reply
III. Jackson's character
     A. Interaction between Jackson's character and journey
        1. Significance of Jackson's first name
        2. Jackson as a complex character
     B. Jackson's physical problems
        1. Failing eyesight
        2. Difficulty walking
 IV. Jackson's spiritual strength
     A. Belief in God
     B. Child of nature
  V. Jackson's emotional strength
     A. Love for grandson
     B. Fearlessness and selflessness
     C. Determination
```

WRITING YOUR PAPER

Once you have constructed your outline, you can begin to draft your paper. Follow your outline as you write, using your notes as the need arises.

Your paper's **introduction** will usually be a single paragraph. In addition to identifying the work or works you are writing about and stating your thesis, the introduction to a literary research paper may present an overview of your topic, a survey of critical opinion, or necessary background information.

The **body** of your paper supports your thesis statement, with each of your paragraphs developing a single point. Support your points with examples from the literary work you are discussing or with summaries, paraphrases, and quotations from your sources. You should also include your own observations and inferences.

Your paper's **conclusion,** usually a single paragraph (but sometimes more), restates your main points and reinforces your thesis statement.

Remember, the purpose of your first draft is to get ideas down on paper so that you can react to them. You should expect to revise, possibly writing several drafts.

The final draft of Daniel Collins's paper on Eudora Welty's "A Worn Path" appears on page 1554.

DOCUMENTING SOURCES

Documentation is the acknowledgment of information from outside sources that you use in your paper. Students writing about literature use the documentation style recommended by the Modern Language Association (MLA), a professional organization of more than 25,000 teachers and students of English and other languages. This style of documentation has three parts: *parenthetical references* in the text, a *works-cited list* at the end of the paper, and *explanatory notes.**

Parenthetical References in the Text

MLA documentation style uses parenthetical references within the text to refer to an alphabetical works-cited list at the end of the paper. A parenthetical reference should contain just enough information to guide readers to the appropriate entry on your works-cited list. A typical parenthetical reference consists of the author's last name and a page number.

> Gwendolyn Brooks uses the sonnet form to create poems that have a wide social and aesthetic range (Williams 972).

If you use more than one source by the same author, include a shortened title in the parenthetical reference.

> Brooks knows not only Shakespeare, Spenser, and Milton, but also the full range of African-American poetry (Williams, "Brooks's Way" 972).

If you mention the author's name or the title of the work in your paper, only a page reference is needed.

> According to Gladys Margaret Williams in "Gwendolyn Brooks's Way with the Sonnet," Brooks combines a sensitivity to poetic forms with a depth of emotion appropriate for her subject matter (972-73).

---

* For more information, see the *MLA Handbook for Writers of Research Papers,* 6th ed. (New York: MLA, 2003). You can also consult the MLA Web site at <http://www.mla.org>.

CHECKLIST **GUIDELINES FOR PUNCTUATING PARENTHETICAL REFERENCES**

✓ *Paraphrases and summaries*

Place the parenthetical reference after the last word of the sentence and before the final punctuation:

In her works, Brooks combines the pessimism of modernist poetry with the optimism of the Harlem Renaissance (Smith 978).

✓ *Direct quotations run in with the text*

Place the parenthetical reference after the quotation marks and before the final punctuation:

According to Gary Smith, Brooks's <u>A Street in Bronzeville</u> "conveys the primacy of suffering in the lives of poor Black women" (980).

According to Gary Smith, the poems in <u>A Street in Bronzeville</u> "served notice that Brooks had learned her craft . . ." (978).

Along with Thompson, we must ask, "Why did it take so long for critics to acknowledge that Gwendolyn Brooks is an important voice in twentieth-century American poetry" (123)?

✓ *Quotations set off from the text*

Omit the quotation marks, and place the parenthetical reference one space after the final punctuation. (For guidelines for setting off long quotations, see p. 31.)

For Gary Smith, the identity of Brooks's African-American women is inextricably linked with their sense of race and poverty:

> For Brooks, unlike the Renaissance poets, the victimization of poor Black women becomes not simply a minor chord but a predominant theme of <u>A Street in Bronzeville</u>. Few, if any, of her female characters are able to free themselves from a web of poverty that threatens to strangle their lives. (980)

Sample Parenthetical References

An entire work

August Wilson's play <u>Fences</u> treats many themes frequently expressed in modern drama.

When citing an entire work, state the name of the author in your paper instead of in a parenthetical reference.

A work by two or three authors

Myths cut across boundaries and cultural spheres and reappear in strikingly similar forms from country to country (Feldman and Richardson 124).

The effect of a work of literature depends on the audience's predispositions that derive from membership in various social groups (Hovland, Janis, and Kelley 87).

A work by more than three authors

Hawthorne's short stories frequently use a combination of allegorical and symbolic methods (Guerin et al. 91).

The abbreviation *et al.* is Latin for "and others."

A work in an anthology

In his essay "Flat and Round Characters," E. M. Forster distinguishes between one-dimensional characters and those that are well developed (Stevick 223–31).

The parenthetical reference cites the anthology (edited by Stevick) that contains Forster's essay; full information about the anthology appears in the list of works cited.

A work with volume and page numbers

Critics consider <u>The Zoo Story</u> to be one of Albee's best plays (Eagleton 2:17).

An indirect source

Wagner observed that myth and history stood before him "with opposing claims" (qtd. in Winkler 10).

The abbreviation *qtd. in* ("quoted in") indicates that the quoted material was not taken from the original source.

A play with numbered lines

"Give thy thoughts no tongue," says Polonius, "Nor any unproportioned thought his act" (<u>Ham</u>. 1.3.64–65).

The parentheses contain the act, scene, and line numbers (in arabic numerals), separated by periods. When included in parenthetical references, titles of the books of the Bible and well-known literary works are often abbreviated —*Gen.* for *Genesis* and *Ado* for *Much Ado about Nothing*, for example.

A poem

"I muse my life-long hate, and without flinch / I bear it nobly as I live my part," says Claude McKay in his bitterly ironic poem "The White City" (lines 3–4).

Notice that a slash (/) is used to separate lines of poetry run in with the text. (The slash is preceded and followed by one space.) The parenthetical reference cites the lines quoted. Include the word *line* or *lines* for the first reference but just the numbers for subsequent references.

An electronic source

If you are citing a source from the Internet or from an online service to which your library subscribes, remember that these sources frequently do not contain page numbers. If the source uses paragraph, section, or screen numbers, use the abbreviation "par." "sec.," or the full word "screen."

```
    The earliest type of movie censoring came in the form of
licensing fees, and in Deer River, Minnesota, "a licensing
fee of $200 was deemed not excessive for a town of 1000"
(Ernst, par. 20).
```

If the source has no page numbers or markers of any kind, cite the entire work. (When readers get to the works-cited list, they will be able to determine the nature of the source.)

```
In her article "Limited Horizons," Lynne Cheney says that
schools do best when students read literature not for what
it tells them about the workplace, but for its insights into
the human condition.

Because of its parody of communism, the film Antz is actu-
ally an adult film masquerading as a child's tale (Clemin).
```

The List of Works Cited

Parenthetical references refer to a **works-cited list** that includes all the sources you refer to in your paper. Begin the works-cited list on a new page, continuing the page numbers of the paper. For example, if the text of the paper ends on page 6, the works-cited section will begin on page 7.

INFORMAL DOCUMENTATION

Sometimes, when you are writing a paper that includes quotations from a single source that the entire class has read, or if all your sources are from your textbook, your instructor may give you permission to use *informal documentation*. Because both the instructor and the class are familiar with the sources, you supply the authors' last names and page numbers in parentheses but do not include a works-cited list.

Center the title *Works Cited* one inch from the top of the page. Arrange entries alphabetically, according to the last name of each author. Use the first word of the title if the author is unknown (articles —*a*, *an*, and *the*— at the beginning of a title are not considered first words). To conserve space, publishers' names are abbreviated — for example, *Heinle* (for Heinle & Heinle) and *U. of California P* (for University of California Press). Double-space the entire works-cited list between and within entries. Begin typing each entry at the left margin, and indent subsequent lines five spaces (or one-half inch). Each works-cited entry has three divisions — author, title, and publishing information — separated by periods. The *MLA Handbook for Writers of Research Papers* shows a single space after all end punctuation.

Below is a directory of the sample entries that follow.

Entries for Books
1. A book by a single author
2. A book by two or three authors
3. A book by more than three authors
4. Two or more works by the same author
5. An edited book
6. A book with a volume number
7. A short story, poem, or play in a collection of the author's work
8. A short story in an anthology
9. A poem in an anthology
10. A play in an anthology
11. An article in an anthology
12. More than one selection from the same anthology
13. A translation

Entries for Articles
14. An article in a journal with continuous pagination throughout an annual volume
15. An article with separate pagination in each issue
16. An article in a magazine
17. An article in a daily newspaper
18. An article in a reference book

Entries for Other Sources
19. A film or videocassette
20. An interview
21. A lecture or an address

Entries for Electronic Sources (Internet)
22. A scholarly project or information database on the Internet
23. A document within a scholarly project or information database on the Internet
24. A personal site on the Internet
25. A book on the Internet
26. An article in a scholarly journal on the Internet
27. An article in an encyclopedia on the Internet
28. An article in a newspaper on the Internet
29. An article in a magazine on the Internet
30. A painting or photograph on the Internet
31. An e-mail
32. An online posting

Entries for Electronic Sources (Subscription Service)
33. A scholarly journal article with separate pagination in each issue from a subscription service
34. A scholarly journal article with continuous pagination throughout an annual volume from a subscription service

35. A monthly magazine article from a subscription service
36. A newspaper article from a subscription service
37. A reference book article from a subscription service
38. A dictionary definition from a subscription service
Entries for Other Electronic Sources
39. A nonperiodical publication on CD-ROM
40. A periodical publication on CD-ROM

Entries for Books

1. *A book by a single author*

```
Kingston, Maxine Hong. The Woman Warrior: Memoirs of a
     Girlhood among Ghosts. New York: Knopf, 1976.
```

2. *A book by two or three authors*

```
Feldman, Burton, and Robert D. Richardson. The Rise of
     Modern Mythology. Bloomington: Indiana UP, 1972.
```

Notice that only the *first* author's name is in reverse order.

3. *A book by more than three authors*

```
Guerin, Wilfred, et al., eds. A Handbook of Critical
     Approaches to Literature. 3rd ed. New York: Harper,
     1992.
```

Instead of using *et al.*, you may list all the authors' names in the order in which they appear on the title page.

4. *Two or more works by the same author*

```
Novoa, Juan-Bruce. Chicano Authors: Inquiry by Interview.
     Austin: U of Texas P, 1980.
---. "Themes in Rudolfo Anaya's Work." Address given at
     New Mexico State University, Las Cruces. 11 Apr.
     1987.
```

List two or more works by the same author in alphabetical order by title. Include the author's full name in the first entry; use three unspaced hyphens followed by a period to take the place of the author's name in second and subsequent entries.

5. *An edited book*

```
Oosthuizen, Ann, ed. Sometimes When It Rains: Writings by
     South African Women. New York: Pandora, 1987.
```

Notice that here the abbreviation *ed.* stands for *editor*.

6. *A book with a volume number*

When all the volumes of a multivolume work have the same title, list the number of the volume you used.

```
Eagleton, T. Allston. A History of the New York Stage.
    Vol. 2. Englewood Cliffs: Prentice, 1987.
```

When each volume of a multivolume work has a separate title, list the title of the volume you used.

```
Durant, Will, and Ariel Durant. The Age of Napoleon: A
    History of European Civilization from 1789 to 1815.
    New York: Simon, 1975.
```

The Age of Napoleon is volume 2 of *The Story of Civilization.* You need not provide information about the work as a whole.

7. *A short story, poem, or play in a collection of the author's work*
```
Gordimer, Nadine. "Once upon a Time." "Jump" and Other
    Stories. New York: Farrar, 1991. 23-30.
```

8. *A short story in an anthology*
```
Salinas, Marta. "The Scholarship Jacket." Nosotros:
    Latina Literature Today. Ed. Maria del Carmen Boza,
    Beverly Silva, and Carmen Valle. Binghamton: Bilin-
    gual, 1986. 68-70.
```

Note that here the abbreviation *Ed.* stands for *Edited by.* The inclusive page numbers follow the year of publication.

9. *A poem in an anthology*
```
Simmerman, Jim. "Child's Grave, Hale County, Alabama."
    The Pushcart Prize, X: Best of the Small Presses.
    Ed. Bill Henderson. New York: Penguin, 1986. 198-99.
```

10. *A play in an anthology*
```
Hughes, Langston. Mother and Child. Black Drama Anthol-
    ogy. Ed. Woodie King and Ron Miller. New York: NAL,
    1986. 399-406.
```

11. *An article in an anthology*
```
Forster, E. M. "Flat and Round Characters." The Theory of
    the Novel. Ed. Philip Stevick. New York: Free, 1980.
    223-31.
```

12. *More than one selection from the same anthology*
If you are using more than one selection from an anthology, cite the anthology in a separate entry. Then, list each individual selection separately, including the author and title of the selection, the anthology editor's last name, and the inclusive page numbers.

```
Baxter, Charles. "Gryphon." Kirszner and Mandell 136-47.
Kirszner, Laurie G., and Stephen R. Mandell, eds. Liter-
     ature: Reading, Reacting, Writing. 5th ed. Boston:
     Heinle, 2004.
Rich, Adrienne. "Diving into the Wreck." Kirszner and
     Mandell 1019-21.
```

13. A translation

```
Carpentier, Alejo. Reasons of State. Trans. Francis Par-
     tridge. New York: Norton, 1976.
```

Entries for Articles

Article citations include the author's name; the title of the article (in quotation marks); the name of the periodical (underlined); and the pages on which the full article appears (without the abbreviations *p.* or *pp.*).

14. An article in a journal with continuous pagination throughout an annual volume

```
LeGuin, Ursula K. "American Science Fiction and the
        Other." Science Fiction Studies 2 (1975): 208-10.
```

15. An article with separate pagination in each issue

```
Grossman, Robert. "The Grotesque in Faulkner's 'A Rose
     for Emily.'" Mosaic 20.3 (1987): 40-55.
```

Note that *20.3* signifies volume 20, issue 3.

16. An article in a magazine

```
Milosz, Czeslaw. "A Lecture." The New Yorker 22 June
     1992: 32.
"Solzhenitsyn: An Artist Becomes an Exile." Time 25 Feb.
     1974: 34+.
```

Note that *34+* indicates that the article appears on pages that are not consecutive; in this case, the article begins on page 34 and continues on page 37. An article with no listed author is entered by title on the works-cited list.

17. An article in a daily newspaper

```
Oates, Joyce Carol. "When Characters from the Page Are
     Made Flesh on the Screen." New York Times 23 Mar.
     1986, late ed.: C1+.
```

C1+ indicates that the article begins on page 1 of Section C and continues on a subsequent page.

18. *An article in a reference book*
Do not include publication information for well-known reference books.

> "Dance Theatre of Harlem." The New Encyclopaedia Britannica: Micropaedia. 15th ed. 1987.

Include publication information when citing reference books that are not well known.

> Grimstead, David. "Fuller, Margaret Sarah." Encyclopedia of American Biography. Ed. John A. Garraty. New York: Harper, 1974.

Entries for Other Sources

19. *A film or videocassette*
> "A Worn Path." By Eudora Welty. Dir. John Reid and Claudia Velasco. Perf. Cora Lee Day and Conchita Ferrell. Videocassette. Harcourt, 1994.

20. *An interview*
> Brooks, Gwendolyn. "An Interview with Gwendolyn Brooks." Triquarterly 60 (1984): 405–10.

21. *A lecture or an address*
> Novoa, Juan-Bruce. "Themes in Rudolfo Anaya's Work." Literature Colloquium. New Mexico State University. Las Cruces. 11 Apr. 1987.

Entries for Electronic Sources (Internet)

MLA style recognizes relevant publication information is not always available for electronic sources. Include in your citation whatever information you can reasonably obtain. Include both the date of the electronic publication (if available) and the date you accessed the source. In addition, include the URL (electronic address) in angle brackets. If you have to carry the URL over to the next line, divide it after a slash. If the URL is excessively long, use just the URL of the site's search page, or use the URL of the site's home page, followed by the word *path* and a colon and then the sequence of links to follow.

22. *A scholarly project or information database on the Internet*
> Philadelphia Writers Project. Ed. Miriam Kotzen Green. May 1998. Drexel U. 12 June 1999 <http://www.Drexel.edu/letrs/wwp/>.

23. A document within a scholarly project or information database on the Internet

"D-Day: June 7th, 1944." <u>The History Channel Online</u>. 1999. History Channel. 7 June 1999 <http:// historychannel.com/thisday/today/997690.html>.

24. A personal site on the Internet

Yerkes, James. <u>Chiron's Forum: John Updike Home Page</u>. 23 June 1999. 30 June 1999 <http://www.users.fast.net/ ~joyerkers/item9.html>.

25. A book on the Internet

Douglass, Frederick. <u>My Bondage and My Freedom</u>. Boston: 1855. 8 June 1999 <gopher://gopher.vt.edu: 10024/22/ 178/3>.

26. An article in a scholarly journal on the Internet

Dekoven, Marianne. "Utopias Limited: Post-Sixties and Postmodern American Fiction." <u>Modern Fiction Studies</u> 41.1 (1995): 13 pp. 17 Mar. 1999 <http://muse.jhu. edu/journals/mfs.v041/41.1dwkovwn.html>.

When you cite information from the print version of an electronic source, include the publication information for the printed source, the number of pages or paragraphs (if available), and the date of access.

27. An article in an encyclopedia on the Internet

"Hawthorne, Nathaniel." <u>Britannica Online</u>. Vers. 98.2. Apr. 1998. Encyclopedia Britannica. 16 May 1998 <http://www.eb/com/:220>.

28. An article in a newspaper on the Internet

Lohr, Steve. "Microsoft Goes to Court." <u>New York Times on the Web</u> 19 Oct. 1998. 29 Apr. 1999 <http://www. nytimes.com/web/docroot/library.cyber/week/ 1019business.html>.

29. An article in a magazine on the Internet

Weiser, Jay. "The Tyranny of Informality." <u>Time</u> 26 Feb. 1996 1 Mar. 1999 <http://www.enews.com/magazines. tnr/current/022696.3.html>.

30. A painting or photograph on the Internet

Lange, Dorothea, <u>Looking at Pictures</u>. 1936. Museum of Mod. Art, New York. 17 July 2000 <http://moma.org/ exhibitions/lookingatphotographs/lang-fr.html>.

31. *An e-mail*
> Adkins, Camille. E-mail to the author. 28 June 2001.

32. *An online posting*
> Gilford, Mary. "Dog Heroes in Children's Literature." On-
> line posting. 17 Mar. 1999. 12 Apr. 1999 <news:alt.
> animals.dogs>.

Entries for Electronic Sources (Online Subscription Service)

Online subscription services can be divided into those you subscribe to, such as America Online, and those that your college library subscribes to, such as Extended Academic ASAP, Lexis-Nexis, and ProQuest Direct.

To cite information from an online service to which you subscribe, you have two options. If the service provides a URL, follow the examples in entries 22 through 30. If the service enables you to use a keyword to access material, provide the keyword (following the date of access) at the end of the entry.

> "Kafka, Franz." Compton's Encyclopedia Online. Vers.
> 3.0.2000. America Online. 8 June 2001. Keyword:
> Compton's.

If, instead of a keyword, you follow a series of topic labels, list them (separated by semicolons) after the word *Path*.

> "Elizabeth Adams." History Resources. 11 Nov. 2001.
> America Online. 28 Apr. 2001. Path: Research; Biol-
> ogy; Women in Science; Biographies.

To cite information from an online service to which your library subscribes, include the underlined name of the database (if known), the name of the service, the library, the date of access, and the URL of the online service's home page.

> Luckenbill, Trent. "Environmental Litigation: Down the
> Endless Corridor." Environment 17 July 2001: 34-42.
> ABI/INFORM GLOBAL. ProQuest Direct. Drexel U Lib.,
> Philadelphia. 12 Oct. 2001 <http://www.umi.com/
> proquest>.

33. *A scholarly journal article with separate pagination in each issue from an online service*
> Schaefer, Richard J. "Editing Strategies in Television
> News Documentaries." Journal of Communication 47.4
> (1997): 69-89. InfoTrac OneFile Plus. Gale Group
> Databases. Augusta R. Kolwyck Lib., Chattanooga, TN.
> 2 Oct. 2002 <http://library.cstcc.cc.tn.us/
> ref3.shtml>.

34. A scholarly journal article with continuous pagination throughout an annual volume from an online service

> Hudson, Nicholas. "Samuel Johnson, Urban Culture, and the Geography of Postfire London." <u>Studies in English Literature</u> 42 (2002): 557–80. <u>MasterFILE Premier</u>. EBSCOhost. Augusta R. Kolwyck Lib., Chattanooga, TN. 2 Oct. 2002 <http://library.cstcc.cc.tn.us/ref3.shtml>.

35. A monthly magazine article from an online service

> Livermore, Beth. "Meteorites on Ice." <u>Astronomy</u> July 1993: 54–58. <u>Expanded Academic ASAP Plus</u>. Gale Group Databases. Augusta R. Kolwyck Lib., Chattanooga, TN. 2 Oct. 2002 <http://library.cstcc.cc.tn.us/ref3.shtml>.

36. A newspaper article from an online service

> Meyer, Greg. "Answering Questions about the West Nile Virus." <u>Dayton Daily News</u> 11 July 2002: Z3–Z7. <u>LexisNexis Academic</u>. Augusta R. Kolwyck Lib., Chattanooga, TN. 2 Oct. 2002 <http://library.cstcc.cc.tn.us/ref3.shtml>.

37. A reference book article from an online service

> Laird, Judith. "Geoffrey Chaucer." <u>Cyclopedia of World Authors</u>. 1997. <u>MagillOnLiterature</u>. <u>EBSCOhost</u>. Augusta R. Kolwyck Lib., Chattanooga, TN. 2 Oct. 2002 <http://library.cstcc.cc.tn.us/ref3.shtml>.

38. A dictionary definition from an online service

> "Migraine." <u>Mosby's Medical, Nursing, and Allied Health Dictionary</u>. 1998 ed. <u>Health Reference Center</u>. Gale Group Databases. Augusta R. Kolwyck Lib., Chattanooga, TN. 2 Oct. 2002 <http://library.cstcc.cc.tn.us/ref3.shtml>.

Entries for Other Electronic Sources

39. A nonperiodical publication on CD-ROM

> "Windhover." <u>The Oxford English Dictionary</u>. 2nd ed. CD-ROM. Oxford: Oxford UP, 1992.

40. A periodical publication on CD-ROM

> Zurbach, Kate. "The Linguistic Roots of Three Terms." <u>Linguistic Quarterly</u> 37 (1994): 12–47. <u>InfoTrac</u>: <u>Magazine Index Plus</u>. CD-ROM. Information Access. Jan. 1996.

WARNING: Using information from an Internet source can be risky. Contributors are not necessarily experts, and they frequently are inaccurate or misinformed. Unless you can be certain that the information you are obtaining from these sources is reliable, do not use it. You can check the reliability of an Internet source by asking your instructor or librarian for guidance.

Content Notes

Use **content notes**, indicated by a superscript (a raised number) in the text, to cite several sources at once or to provide commentary or explanations that do not fit smoothly into your paper. The full text of these notes appears on the first numbered page following the last page of the paper. (If your paper has no content notes, the works-cited page follows the last page of the paper.) Like works-cited entries, content notes are double-spaced within and between entries. However, the first line of each explanatory note is indented five spaces (or one-half inch), and subsequent lines are flush with the left-hand margin.

To Cite Several Sources

In the paper

        Surprising as it may seem, there have been many attempts to define literature.[1]

In the note

        [1] For an overview of critical opinion, see Arnold 72; Eagleton 1-2; Howe 43-44; and Abrams 232-34.

To Provide Explanations

In the paper

        In recent years, gothic novels have achieved great popularity.[3]

In the note

        [3] Gothic novels, works written in imitation of medieval romances, originally relied on supernatural occurrences. They flourished in the late eighteenth and early nineteenth centuries.

Sample Literature Papers with MLA Documentation

The two literature papers that follow, written for introduction to literature courses, use MLA documentation style. The first was written by Daniel Collins, whose writing process you followed earlier in this chapter. The second, written by Tim Westmoreland, uses electronic sources.

Daniel Collins

Professor Smith

English 201

31 January 2003

And Again She Makes the Journey: Character and
        Act in Eudora Welty's "A Worn Path"

Over the past fifty years, Eudora Welty's "A
Worn Path," the tale of an elderly black woman, Phoenix Jackson, traveling to the city to obtain medicine for her sick grandson, has been the subject of
much critical interpretation. Critics have speculated
on the meaning of the many death and rebirth symbols,
including the scarecrow, which the old woman believes
is a ghost; the buzzard who watches her travel; the
skeleton-like branches that reach out to slow her;
and her first name, Phoenix. From the study of these
symbols, various critics have concluded that "A Worn
Path" represents either a "heroic act of sacrifice,"
"a parable for the journey of life," or "a religious
pilgrimage" (Keys 354). It is certainly true, as
these interpretations imply, that during her journey Phoenix Jackson struggles through difficult ter-
rain and encounters many dangers and that despite
these obstacles she does not abandon her quest. However, what is most important in the story is neither
the symbols associated with the quest nor the quest
itself. What is most important is Phoenix Jackson'scharacter and her act of making the journey.

Eudora Welty discusses the character of Phoenix
Jackson in a videotaped interview. Here, Welty points

out that Jackson's first name refers to a mythical bird that dies and is reborn every five hundred years. She explains, however, that despite her character's symbolic name, Phoenix Jackson is a complex being with human frailties and emotions (Henley).

Phoenix Jackson has a number of physical problems that challenge her ability to perform daily tasks. Because of her age, she has failing eyesight, which distorts her perception of the objects she encounters during her journey. For instance, Phoenix mistakes a patch of thorns for "a pretty little <u>green</u> bush," (Welty 362), and she believes a scarecrow is the ghost of a man. Likewise, she has difficulty walking, so she must use a cane; at one point, she is unable to bend and tie her own shoes. Because of these physical disabilities, readers might expect her to fail in her attempt to reach town, because "the journey is long; the path, though worn, is difficult" (Keys 354). So what gives Phoenix Jackson the energy and endurance for the journey? The question can best be answered by looking at her inner qualities: although Jackson's body is weak, she has great spiritual and emotional strength.

Phoenix Jackson's spiritual strength comes from her oneness with nature and her belief in God. This oneness with nature, claims James Saunders, helps her overcome the challenges that she encounters (67). Because Phoenix Jackson is "a child of nature," her impaired vision, although it slows her journey, does

Collins 3

not stop it, because as Saunders explains, "mere human vision would not have been sufficient for the journey" (67). Instead of allowing her failing vision to restrict her actions, Phoenix Jackson relies on her spiritual connection with nature; thus, she warns various animals to "Keep out from under these feet . . ." (Welty 362). Additionally, her spiritual strength comes from her belief in God—a quality seen when she refers to God watching her steal the hunter's nickel.

Phoenix Jackson's spiritual strength is complemented by her emotional strength. Her love for her grandson compels her to endure any difficulty and to defy any personal danger. Thus, throughout her journey, she demonstrates fearlessness and selflessness. For example, when the hunter threatens her with his gun, she tells him that she has faced worse dangers. Even after stealing and accepting nickels, she remains intent upon buying a paper windmill for her grandson—and does not consider replacing her own worn shoes.

In a video interview, Eudora Welty explains how she created the paradoxical Phoenix Jackson—outwardly frail and inwardly strong. Welty tells how she noticed an "old lady" slowly making her way across a "silent horizon,"[1] driven by an overwhelming determination to reach her destination; as Welty says, "she had a purpose" (Henley). Welty created Phoenix Jackson in the image of this determined woman. In

Collins 4

order to emphasize the character's strength, Welty
had her make the journey to Natchez to get medication
for her grandson. Because the act had to be performed
repeatedly, the journey became a ritual that had to
be completed at all costs. Thus, as Welty explains in
the interview, the act of making the journey is the
most important element in the story (Henley).

In order to convey the significance of the journey, Welty focuses on the process of the journey. For
this reason, readers receive little information about
the daily life of the boy and his grandmother or
about the illness for which the boy is being treated.
Regardless of the boy's condition—or even whether he
is alive or dead—Jackson must complete her journey
(Henley). The nurse's statement—"The doctor said as
long as you came to get it [the medicine], you could
have it" (Welty 366)—reinforces the ritualistic nature of Jackson's journey, a journey that Bartel suggests is a "subconscious" act (289). Thus, Phoenix
Jackson cannot answer the nurse's questions because
she does not consciously know what compels her to
make the journey. According to Welty, the character's
silence and disorientation can also be attributed to
her relief and disillusionment upon completing the
ritualistic journey (Henley). Nevertheless, next
Saturday, Phoenix Jackson will again walk "miles and
miles, and will continue to do so, regardless of the
difficulties facing her, along the worn path that

leads through the wilderness of the Natchez Trace, cheerfully performing her labor of love" (Howard 84).

Clearly, the interaction of character (Phoenix Jackson) and act (the ritual journey in search of medication) is the most important element of Welty's story. By relying heavily on the characterization of Phoenix Jackson and by describing her difficult encounters during her ritual journey to town, Welty emphasizes how spiritual and emotional strength can overcome physical frailty and how determination and fearlessness can overcome any danger. These moral messages become clear by the time Phoenix reaches the doctor's office. The image of the elderly woman determinedly walking across the horizon, the image that prompted Welty's writing of the story, remains in the minds of the readers, and significantly, it is the final image of the videotape of "A Worn Path."

Note

[1]Unlike the written version of "A Worn Path," the video of the short story ends not at the doctor's office but with a vision similar to the one that inspired Welty to write the story—the elderly black woman silently walking along the horizon at dusk.

Collins 7

Works Cited

Bartel, Roland. "Life and Death in Eudora Welty's 'A Worn Path.'" <u>Studies in Short Fiction</u> 14 (1977): 288–90.

Henley, Beth. <u>Interview with Eudora Welty</u>. Dir. John Reid and Claudia Velasco. Videocassette. Harcourt, 1994.

Howard, Zelma Turner. <u>The Rhetoric of Eudora Welty's Short Stories</u>. Jackson: UP of Mississippi, 1973.

Keys, Marilyn. "'A Worn Path': The Way of Dispossession." <u>Studies in Short Fiction</u> 16 (1979): 354–56.

Saunders, James Robert. "'A Worn Path': The Eternal Quest of Welty's Phoenix Jackson." <u>Southern Literary Journal</u> 25.1 (Fall 1992): 62–73.

Welty, Eudora. "A Worn Path." <u>Literature: Reading, Reacting, Writing</u>. 5th ed. Ed. Laurie G. Kirszner and Stephen R Mandell. Boston: Heinle, 2004. 361–67.

"<u>A Worn Path</u>." By Eudora Welty. Dir. John Reid and Claudia Velasco. Perf. Cora Lee Day and Conchita Ferrell. Videocassette. Harcourt, 1994.

Tim Westmoreland

Professor Adkins

Literature 2101

5 April 2003

"A&P": A Class Act

John Updike's "A&P," like many of his other works, is a "profoundly American" story about social inequality and an attempt to bridge the gap between social classes (Steiner 105). The story is told by an eighteen-year-old boy who is working as a checkout clerk in an A&P in a small New England town five miles from the beach. The narrative is delivered in a slangy, colloquial voice that tells of a brief but powerful encounter with a "beautiful but inaccessible girl" from another social and economic level (Wells). Sammy, the narrator, is working his cash register on a slow Thursday afternoon when, as he says, "In walks these three girls in nothing but bathing suits" (Up- dike, "A&P" 115). Lengel, the store's manager—a Sun- day school teacher and "self appointed moral police- man"—confronts the girls, telling them that they should be decently dressed (Wells, par. 7). It is a moment of embarrassment and insight for all parties concerned, and in an apparently impulsive act, Sammy quits his job. Although the plot is simple, what is at the heart of this story is complex: a noble gesture that serves as a futile attempt to cross social and economic boundaries that are all but unbridgeable.

Westmoreland 2

Through Sammy's eyes, we see the class conflict that defines the story. The privileged young girls in bathing suits are in sharp contrast to the few customers who are shopping in the store. Sammy refers to the customers as "sheep" and describes one of them as "a witch about fifty with rouge on her cheekbones and no eyebrows" (Updike, "A&P" 115). Other customers are characterized in equally negative terms—for example, "houseslaves in pin curlers" (Updike, "A&P" 117) and "an old party in baggy gray pants" (Updike, "A&P" 118). Unlike the other customers, the leader of the three girls is described as a "queen":

> She came down a little hard on her heels,
> as if she didn't walk in her bare feet
> that much, putting down her heels and
> then letting the weight move along to
> her toes as if she was testing the floor
> with every step, putting a little delib-
> erate extra action into it. (Updike,
> "A&P" 116)

The mere fact that "Queenie" does not seem to have walked barefoot much seems to hint at a social gap between the girls and the other customers. However, it seems clear that Sammy realizes that Queenie and her friends come from farther away than just the beach. They have come to test the floors of the less well-off and do it openly, in defiance of social rules. In a sense, they are "slumming."

Queenie, whose name suggests her superior status, understands her position in social as well as
sexual terms. She has come to the A&P to purchase
"Kingfish Fancy Herring Snacks in Pure Sour Cream"
for her parents, while Sammy has to spend the summer
working. Even the choice of the exotic and expensive
herring snacks hints at their different backgrounds.
Regardless, the two act in ways that are not all that
different. Both are self-consciously trying out new
roles, with Sammy trying to rise above his station in
life and Queenie trying to move below hers. As Queenie arrives at the register, Sammy observes, "Now her
hands are empty, not a ring or a bracelet, . . . and
I wonder where the money's coming from. Still with
that prim look she lifts a folded dollar bill out of
the hollow at the center of her nubbled pink top"
(Updike, "A&P" 118). With this gesture, she not only
tests her own sexual powers but also sinks to the
level of the supermarket and its workers and customers. Despite her act, though, Sammy knows how different Queenie's world is from his:

> I slid right down her voice into her
> living room. Her father and the other
> men were standing around in ice-cream
> coats and bow ties and the women were
> in sandals picking up herring snacks
> on toothpicks off a big plate and they
> were all holding drinks the color of
> water with olives and sprigs of mint

Westmoreland 4

in them. When my parents have somebody
over they get lemonade and if it's
a real racy affair Schlitz in tall
glasses with "They'll Do It Every
Time" cartoons stencilled on. (Updike,
"A&P" 118)

As Updike says in a 1996 interview, "[Sammy] is a
blue-collar kid longing for a white-collar girl"
(Murray, e-mail).

At this point in the story, as Sammy says,
"everybody's luck begins to run out" (Updike, "A&P"
118). Lengel, the store manager (who, according to
Updike, was named after a strict boss for whom his
mother once worked), represents "the cruel and uneth-
ical" rules that govern matters of social etiquette
(Murray, Interview). In the story, he confronts the
girls, telling them that they are indecently dressed.
"'We are decent,' Queenie says suddenly, her lower
lip pushing, getting sore now that she remembers her
place, a place from which the crowd that runs the A&P
must look pretty crummy." (Updike, "A&P" 118). Suddenly, Sammy can no longer be a detached observer
and, in a gesture of defiance, he quits. The real
question here is why he quits. Updike himself says,
"I wonder to what extent his gesture of quitting has
to do with the fact that she is rich and he is poor"
(Murray, Interview).

By quitting, Sammy challenges social inequality,
but is his response heroic posturing or an action

Westmoreland 5

that expresses his long-standing frustration? In
other words, does Sammy quit because of what Updike
calls a "misunderstanding of how the world is put together" (Murray, Interview) or because he is "a boy
who's tried to reach out of his immediate environment
towards something bigger and better" (Updike, "Still
Afraid" 55)? Although Sammy's action may be simply
impulsive—Sammy even states it would be fatal not to
go through with his initial gesture—it seems likely
that he is taking a deliberate stand against what he
sees as social injustice. Unlike Queenie's act of defiance, Sammy's gesture will have long-term consequences (Oates). As Updike points out, in Sammy's
small town everyone will find out what he has done,
and he may be "known. . .as a quitter" (Murray, Interview). Sammy's understanding and acceptance of
these consequences ("'You'll feel this for the
rest of your life,' Lengel says, and I know that's
true, . . .") and of the limitations his social class
imposes upon him, constitute his initiation into
adulthood (Updike, "A&P" 119). Whether quitting is
Sammy's first step toward overcoming these limitations or a romantic gesture he will live to regret
remains to be seen.[1] As Updike says, "How blind we
are, as we awkwardly push outward into the world!"
(Updike, "Still Afraid" 57).

Although it is true that both Queenie and Sammy
attempt to cross social boundaries, the reasons for
their actions are different. Queenie's provocative

gesture is well thought out; she deliberately relinquishes her trappings, her clothes and jewelry. If
only for a few minutes, she concedes her dignity and
wealth in order to flaunt her sexuality and her
power. In contrast, Sammy chooses impulsively, in
what Updike calls a "hot flash," a "moment of manly
decisiveness," to take action and, ultimately,
gives up both his dignity and his power (Murray, <u>In-
terview</u>). He gains only a brief moment of glory before he finds himself alone in the parking lot. In
this instant, he confronts the social inequality and
the unspeakable frustration it represents. According
to Updike, Sammy cannot win, though in a "noble surrender of his position," he gains an understanding of
the weight he must bear (Murray, <u>Interview</u>).

Note

[1]In an e-mail message, Donald Murray agrees that Sammy's quitting will have implications for him that it will not have for Queenie and her friends. He goes on to say, however, that it is also possible that the young women will remain "imprisoned in their class," while Sammy may have a chance of escaping the limitations of his.

Westmoreland 8

Works Cited

Murray, Donald. E-mail to the author. 2 April 2003.

---. <u>Interview with John Updike</u>. Dir. Bruce Schwartz.
Videocassette. Harcourt, 1997.

Oates, Joyce Carol. "John Updike's American Comedies." <u>Joyce Carol Oates on John Updike</u>. 5 Apr.
1998. 28 June 1999 <http://www.usfca
.edu/fac-staff/southerr/Onupdike.html>.

Steiner, George. "Supreme Fiction: America Is in
the Details." <u>The New Yorker</u> 11 Mar. 1996. America Online. 20 Mar. 1999. Keyword: New Yorker
Magazine.

Updike, John. "A&P." <u>Literature: Reading, Reacting,
Writing</u>. 5th ed. Ed. Laurie G. Kirszner and
Stephen R. Mandell. Boston: Heinle, 2004.
115-19.

---. "Still Afraid of Being Caught." <u>New York Times</u>
8 Oct. 1995: 55+. <u>New York Times Ondisc</u>. CD-ROM.
UMI-Proquest. Jan. 1999.

Wells, Walter. "John Updike's 'A&P': A Return Visit
to Araby." <u>Studies in Short Fiction</u> 30.2 (Spring
1993): 15 pars. <u>Infotrac: Magazine Index Plus</u>.
CD-ROM. Information Access. Mar. 1999.

CHAPTER 35

USING LITERARY CRITICISM IN YOUR WRITING

As you become aware of various schools of literary criticism, you see new ways to think — and to write — about fiction, poetry, and drama. Just as you value the opinions of your peers and your professors, you also will find that the ideas of literary critics can enrich your own reactions to and evaluations of literature. Keep in mind that no single school of literary criticism offers the "right" way of approaching what you read; no single critic provides the definitive analysis of any short story, poem, or play. As you become aware of the richly varied possibilities of literary criticism, you will begin to ask new questions and discover new insights about the works you read.

FORMALISM

Formalism stresses the importance of literary form to the meaning of a work. Formalist scholars consider each work of literature in isolation. They consider biographical, historical, and social matters to be irrelevant to the real meaning of a play, short story, novel, or poem. For example, a formalist would see the relationship between Adam and Eve in *Paradise Lost* as entirely unrelated to John Milton's own marital concerns, and they would view theological themes in the same work as entirely separate from Milton's deep involvement with the Puritan religious and political cause in seventeenth-century England. Formalists also would regard Milton's intentions and readers' responses to the epic poem as irrelevant. Instead, formalists would read the text closely, paying attention to organization and structure, to verbal nuances (suggested by word choice and use of figurative language), and to multiple meanings (often created through the writer's use of paradox and irony). The formalist critic tries to reconcile the tensions and oppositions inherent in the text in order to develop a unified reading.

The formalist movement in English-language criticism began in England with I. A. Richard's *Practical Criticism* (1929). To explain and introduce his theory, Richards asked students to interpret famous poems without telling them the poets' names. This strategy encouraged close reading of the text rather than reliance on information about a poet's reputation, the details of a poet's life, or historical context. The American formalist movement, called **New Criticism,** was made popular by college instructors who realized that formalist criticism provided a useful way for students to work along with an instructor in interpreting a literary work rather than passively listening to a lecture on biographical, literary, and historical influences. The New Critical theorists Cleanth Brooks and Robert Penn Warren put together a series of textbooks (*Understanding Poetry*, *Understanding Fiction*, and *Understanding Drama*, first published in the late 1930s) that were used in colleges for years. After the 1950s, many New Critics began to reevaluate their theories and to broaden their approaches. Although few scholars currently maintain a strictly formalist approach, nearly every critical movement, including feminist, Marxist, psychoanalytic, structuralist, and deconstructionist criticism, owes a debt to the close reading techniques introduced by the formalists.

A FORMALIST READING: Kate Chopin's "The Storm"

If you were to apply formalist criticism to Chopin's "The Storm," you might begin by noting the story's three distinctive sections. What relationship do the sections bear to one another? What do we learn from the word choice, the figures of speech, and the symbols in these sections? And, most important, how do these considerations lead readers to a unified view of the story?

In the first section of "The Storm," readers meet Bobinôt and his son Bibi. The description of the approaching clouds as "sombre," "sinister," and "sullen" suggests an atmosphere of foreboding, yet the alliteration of these words also introduces a poetic tone. The conversation between father and son in the final part of this section contrasts, yet does not conflict with, the rather formal language of the introduction. Both Bobinôt and Bibi speak in Cajun dialect, suggesting their humble origins, yet their words have a rhythm that echoes the poetic notes struck in the description of the storm. As the section closes, Bobinôt, thinking of his wife, Calixta, at home, buys a can of the shrimp he knows she likes and holds the treasure "stolidly," ironically suggesting the protection he cannot offer his wife in his separation from her during the coming storm.

The long second section brings readers to the story's central action. Calixta, as she watches the rain, sees her former lover, Alcée, riding up to seek shelter. As in the first section, the language of the narrator is somewhat formal and always poetic, filled with sensuous diction and images. For instance, we see Calixta "unfasten[ing] her white sacque at the throat" and, later, Alcée envisions her lips "as red and moist as pomegranate seed." Again, paralleling the first section, the conversation of the characters is carried on in dialect, suggesting their lack of sophistication and their connection to the powerful natural forces that surround them. The lovemaking that follows, then, seems both natural and poetic. There is nothing sordid about this interlude and, as the final sections of the story suggest through their rather ordinary, matter-of-fact language, nothing has been harmed by Calixta and Alcée's yielding to passion.

In section 3, Bobinôt brings home the shrimp, symbol of his love for Calixta, and, although we recognize the tension between Bobinôt's shy, gentle approach and Alcée's passion, readers can accept the final sentence as literal rather than ironic. The "storms" (both the rain and the storm of passion) have passed, and no one has been hurt. The threat suggested in the opening sentences has been diffused; both the power and the danger evoked by the poetic diction of the first two sections have disappeared, to be replaced entirely by the rhythms of daily life and speech.

FOR FURTHER READING: Formalism

Brooks, Cleanth. *The Well Wrought Urn.* 1947.
Empson, William. *Seven Types of Ambiguity.* 1930.
Hartman, Geoffrey H. *Beyond Formalism.* 1970.
Stallman, Robert W. *Critiques and Essays in Criticism. 1920–1948.* 1949.
Wellek, René. *A History of Modern Criticism.* Vol. 6. 1986.
Wimsatt, W. K. *The Verbal Icon.* 1954.

READER-RESPONSE CRITICISM

Reader-response criticism suggests a critical view that opposes formalism, seeing the reader's interaction with the text as central to interpretation. Unlike formalists, reader-response critics do not believe that a work of literature exists as a separate, closed entity. Instead, they consider the reader's contribution to the text as essential. A poem, short story, novel, or play is not a solid piece of fabric but rather a series of threads separated by gaps that readers must fill in, drawing on their own experiences and knowledge.

As we read realistic fiction (fiction in which the world of the text closely resembles what we call reality), we may not notice that we are contributing our interpretation. As we read one sentence and then the next, we develop expectations; and, in realistic stories, these expectations are generally met. Nevertheless, nearly every reader supplies personal meanings and observations, making each reader's experience with a work unique and distinctive from every other reader's experience with the same work. For example, imagine Shakespeare's *Romeo and Juliet* as it might be read by a fourteen-year-old high school student and by her father. The young woman, whose age is the same as Juliet's, is almost certain to identify closely with the female protagonist and to "read" Lord Capulet, Juliet's father, as overbearing and rigid. The young reader's father, however, may be drawn to the poignant passage where Capulet talks with a prospective suitor, urging that he wait while Juliet has time to enjoy her youth. Capulet describes the loss of his other children and calls Juliet "the hopeful lady of my earth." Although the young woman reading this line may interpret it as yet another indication of Capulet's possessiveness, her father may see it as a sign of love and even generosity. The twenty-first-century father may "read" Capulet as a man willing to risk offending a friend in order to keep his daughter safe from the rigors of early marriage (and early childbearing). Whose interpretation is correct? Reader-response theorists would say that both readings are entirely possible and therefore equally "right."

The differing interpretations produced by different readers can be seen as simply the effect of the different personalities (and personal histories) involved in constructing meaning from the same series of clues. Not only does the reader "create" the work of literature, in large part, but the literature itself may work on the reader as he or she reads, altering the reader's experience and thus the reader's interpretation. For example, the father reading *Romeo and Juliet* may alter his sympathetic view of Capulet as he continues through the play and observes Capulet's later, angry exchanges with Juliet.

Reader-response theorists believe in the importance of *recursive reading*—that is, reading and rereading with the idea that no interpretation is carved in stone. A second or third interaction with the text may well produce a new interpretation. This changing view is particularly likely when the rereading takes place significantly later than the initial reading. For example, if the young woman just described reread *Romeo and Juliet* when she was middle-aged and herself the mother of teenage children, her reaction to Capulet would quite likely be different from her reaction when she read the work at age fourteen.

In one particular application of reader-response theory, called *reception theory*, the idea of developing readings is applied to the general reading public rather than to individual readers. Reception theory, as proposed by Hans Robert Jauss ("Literary History as a Challenge to Literary Theory," *New Literary History*, Vol. 2 [1970–71]), suggests that each new generation reads the same works of literature differently. Because each generation of readers has experienced different historical events, read different books, and been aware of different critical theories, each generation will view the same works very differently from its predecessors. Certainly a quick look at the summary of literary history in the Appendix will support this idea. (Consider, for example, the changing views toward Shakespeare from the seventeenth century to the present.)

Reader-response criticism has received serious attention since the 1960s, when Norman Holland formulated the theory in *The Dynamics of Literary Response* (1968). The German critic Wolfgang Iser (*The Implied Reader*, 1974) argued that in order to be an effective reader, one must be familiar with the conventions and "codes" of writing. This, then, is one reason for studying literature in a classroom, not to produce approved interpretations but to develop strategies and information that will make sense of a text. Stanley Fish, an American critic, goes even further, arguing that there may not be any "objective" text at all (*Is There a Text in This Class?*, 1980). Fish says that no two readers read the same book, though readers can be trained to have relatively similar responses to a text if they have had relatively similar experiences. For instance, readers who went to college and took an introduction to literature course in which they learned to respond to the various elements of literature, such as character, theme, irony, and figurative language, are likely to have similar responses to a text.

READER-RESPONSE READINGS: Kate Chopin's "The Storm"

To demonstrate possible reader-response readings, we can look at the same story previously considered from a formalist perspective. (Of course, if several formalist critics read the story, they too would each write a somewhat different interpretation.)

Written by a twenty-five-year-old man who has studied American literature

> In Kate Chopin's "The Storm," attention must be paid to the two adult male characters, Bobinôt and Alcée. Usually, in a love triangle situation, one man is portrayed more sympathetically than the other. But Chopin provides us with a dilemma. Alcée is not a cavalier seducer; he genuinely cares for Calixta. Neither is he a brooding hero. There is nothing gruff or angry about Alcée, and he returns to his family home with no apparent harm done following the passionate interlude. On the other hand, Bobinôt is not a cruel or abusive husband. We can see no clear reason for Calixta's affair except for her desire to fulfill a sexual longing for Alcée.

Written by an eighteen-year-old male student in a first-year literature course

> Bibi doesn't seem to be a very important character in the story, but we should pay attention to him as a reflection of his father. At the beginning of the story, Bibi worries about his mother and he expresses his concern to his father. Bobinôt tries to reassure his son, but he gets up and buys a treat for Calixta as much to comfort himself as to get something for her. Then Bibi sits with his father, and it seems as if he has transferred all his worries to Bobinôt. In the third section of the story, after Calixta and Alcée have had their love affair, Bibi and Bobinôt come home. They both seem like children, worried about how Calixta will react. She, of course, is nice to them because she feels so guilty. At the end of section 3, both father and son are happy and enjoying themselves. You can't help but feel great sympathy for them both because they are so loving and simple and because they have been betrayed by Calixta, who has not behaved the way a loving mother and wife should.

Written by a forty-five-year-old woman who has studied Kate Chopin's life and work

> A decade after the controversial novel *The Awakening* was published in 1899, one critic protested, "To think of Kate Chopin, who once contented herself with mild yarns about genteel Creole life . . . blowing us a hot blast like that!" (qtd. in Gilbert and Gubar 981). This literary observer was shocked, as one might expect from an early-twentieth-century reader, by Chopin's frank picture of sexual relations, and particularly of the sexual feelings of the novel's heroine. One cannot help but wonder, however, whether the scandalized reader was really widely acquainted with Chopin.
>
> Certainly he could not have read "The Storm." This short story is surprising for many reasons, but primarily because it defies the sexual mores of the late nineteenth century by showing a woman who is neither evil nor doomed enjoying, even glorying in, her sexuality. Calixta is presented as a good wife and loving mother, concerned about her husband and son who are away from home during the storm. Yet her connection to Bobinôt and Bibi does not keep her from passionately enjoying her interlude with Alcée. She goes to his arms unhesitatingly, with no false modesty or guilt (feigned or real) to hold her back. Somehow, this scenario does not seem to fit the definition of "a mild yarn about genteel Creole life."

FOR FURTHER READING: Reader-Response Criticism

Bleich, David. *Subjective Criticism*. 1978.
Fish, Stanley. *Is There a Text in This Class?* 1980.
Holland, Norman. *The Dynamics of Literary Response*. 1968.

Iser, Wolfgang. *The Implied Reader.* 1974.

————. *The Act of Reading: A Theory of Aesthetic Response.* 1978.

Rosenblatt, Louise. *The Reader, the Text, the Poem.* 1978.

Sulleiman, Susan, and Inge Crosman, eds. *The Reader in the Text.* 1980.

Tomkins, Jane P., ed. *Reader-Response Criticism.* 1980.

SOCIOLOGICAL CRITICISM

Like reader-response criticism, **sociological criticism** takes issue with formalism. Sociological theorists maintain that the literary work cannot be separated from the social context in which it was created, insisting that literature reflects society and derives its essential existence and significance from the social situations to which it responds. Sociological critics speculate about why a particular work might have been written and explore the ways in which it reacts to a specific situation.

For instance, a sociological literary scholar might note with interest that Shakespeare's history plays about Richard II, Henry IV, and Henry V deal with the consequences of uncertain royal succession and usurpation. These dramas were written during the final years of the reign of Queen Elizabeth I, a monarch who had not produced an heir and refused to designate one. Although the plays cited were set considerably before Elizabeth's time, a sociological critic might conclude that they reflect the English concern about the threat of monarchic chaos should Elizabeth die with no clear line of succession.

In the twentieth century, two strong arms of sociological criticism emerged as dominant: **feminist criticism** and **Marxist criticism.** They remain particularly forceful theories because most of their practitioners have a strong commitment to these ideologies, which they apply as they read literature. Although Feminism and Marxism share a concern with segments of society that have been underrepresented and often ignored, scholars working in these fields do not necessarily agree on what constitutes the best response to the issues highlighted by sociological critiques. Both of these views are supported by modern critical theories such as the reader-response idea of gaps in the text that must be filled in through the reader's own experience and knowledge. In addition, the techniques of New Criticism (in particular, close reading of the text), psychoanalysis, and structuralism have allowed sociological critics to focus on what had been overlooked or skewed in traditional readings and to analyze how the experience of marginal and minority groups has been represented in literature. Sociological critics have also employed poststructuralist strategies to reveal and question the assumptions made within their disciplines and to analyze the cultural contexts of their own work.

The late twentieth century has also seen the rise of a third group of theorists, who focus on the relationship between marginalization and ideology. **Postcolonialists, multiculturalists,** and **race theorists** share with other sociological critics a concern with underrepresented and ignored populations, but these schools of criticism focus on representations of ethnic and racial difference. Scholars working from a multicultural perspective seek to develop a more inclusive attitude towards literature, highlighting the contributions of authors working in non-white and non-Western traditions. Although both multiculturalist and postcolonialist critics study the social implications of interactions between members of different cultures, postcolonial criticism (like that of the influential critic Edward Said in his landmark text *Orientalism*) analyzes the effects of imperialist discourses on colonized peoples. Race theorists also examine the relationship between literary discourses and racial and ethnic identities in specific political and social contexts, as reflected in the work of bell hooks and Henry Louis Gates, Jr. The differences between these branches of criticism are sometimes difficult to articulate, however, as the scholars working in these fields often employ similar strategies of interpretation and analysis.

FEMINIST CRITICISM

Throughout the nineteenth century, women such as the Brontë sisters, George Eliot (Mary Ann Evans), Elizabeth Barrett Browning, and Christina Rossetti struggled for the right to be taken as seriously as their male counterparts. In addition, in 1929 Virginia Woolf, an experimental novelist and literary critic, published *A Room of One's Own*, which described the difficulties that women writers faced and defined a tradition of literature written by women.

Feminist criticism emerged as a defined approach to literature in the late 1960s. Modern feminist criticism began with works such as Mary Ellman's *Thinking about Women* (1968), which focuses on the negative female stereotypes in books authored by men and points out alternative feminine characteristics suggested by women authors. Another pioneering feminist work was Kate Millet's *Sexual Politics* (1969), which analyzes the societal mechanisms that perpetuate male domination of women. Since that time, feminist writings, though not unified in one theory or methodology, have appeared in ever-growing numbers. Some feminist critics have adapted psychoanalytic, Marxist, or other poststructuralist theories, and others have broken new ground. In general, feminist critics take the view that our culture — and by extension our literature — is primarily patriarchal (controlled by males).

According to feminist critics, what is at issue is not anatomical sex, but gender. As Simone de Beauvoir explained, a person is not born feminine, as our society defines it, but rather becomes so because of cultural conditioning. According to feminist critics, paternalist Western culture has defined the feminine as "other" to the male, as passive and emotional in opposition to the dominating and rational masculine.

Feminist critics claim that paternalist cultural stereotypes pervade works of literature in the **canon** — those works generally acknowledged to be the best and most significant. Feminists point out that the canon consists of works almost exclusively written by males and about male experiences. Female characters, when they do appear, are often subordinate to male characters. A female reader of these works must either identify with the male protagonist or accept a marginalized role.

One response of feminist critics is to reinterpret works in the traditional canon. As Judith Fetterley explains in *The Resisting Reader* (1978), the reader "revisions" the text, focusing on the covert sexual bias in a literary work. For example, a feminist scholar studying Shakespeare's *Macbeth* might look closely at the role played by Lady Macbeth and argue that she was not simply a cold-hearted villain but a victim of the circumstances of her time: women in her day were not permitted to follow their own ambitions but were relegated to supporting roles, living their lives through achievements of their husbands and sons.

A second focus of feminist scholars has been the redefinition of the canon. By seeking out, analyzing, and evaluating little-known works by women, feminist scholars have rediscovered women writers who were ignored or shunned by the reading public and by critics of their own times. Thus, writers such as Kate Chopin and Charlotte Perkins Gilman (see "The Yellow Wallpaper," p. 160), who wrote during the late nineteenth and early twentieth centuries, are now recognized as worthy of study and consideration.

A FEMINIST READING: Tillie Olsen's "I Stand Here Ironing"

To approach Tillie Olsen's "I Stand Here Ironing" from a feminist perspective, you might focus on the passages in which the narrator describes her relationships and encounters with men.

> Some readings of Tillie Olsen's "I Stand Here Ironing" suggest that the narrator made choices that doomed her oldest daughter to a life of confusion. If we look at the narrator's relationships with the men in her life, however, we can see that she herself is the story's primary victim.
>
> At nineteen, the narrator was a mother abandoned by her husband, who left her a note saying that he "could no longer endure . . . sharing want" (188) with his wife and infant daughter. This is the first desertion we hear about in the narrator's life, and although she agonizingly describes her painful decisions and the mistakes she made with her daughter Emily, we cannot help but recognize that she was the one who stayed and tried to make things right. Her actions contrast sharply with those of her husband, who ran away, implying that his wife and daughter were burdens too great for him to bear.
>
> The second abandonment is more subtle than the first but no less devastating. After the narrator remarried, she was again left alone to cope with a growing family when her second husband went off to war. True, this desertion was for a "noble" purpose and probably was not voluntary, but the narrator, nevertheless, had to seek one of the low-paying jobs available to women to supplement her allotment checks. She was again forced to leave her children because her husband had to serve the needs of the male-dominated military establishment.
>
> The narrator was alone at crucial points in Emily's life and had to turn away from her daughter in order to survive. Although she has been brought up in a world that teaches women to depend on men, she learns that she is ultimately alone. Although the desertions she endured were not always intentional, she had to bear the brunt of circumstances that were not her choice but were foisted on her by the patriarchal society in which she lives.

FOR FURTHER READING: Feminist Criticism

Benstock, Shari, ed. *Feminist Issues in Literary Scholarship*. 1987.
Engleton, Mary, ed. *Feminist Issues in Literary Theory: A Reader*. 1986.
Gilbert, Sandra, and Susan Gubar. *The Madwoman in the Attic*. 1979.
————. *No Man's Land*. 3 vols. 1988, 1989, 1994.
————, eds. *The Norton Anthology of Literature by Women*. 1985.
Heilbrun, Carolyn G. *Hamlet's Mother and Other Women*. 1990.
Jacobus, Mary. *Reading Woman: Essays in Feminist Criticism*. 1986.
Miller, Nancy, K., ed. *The Poetics of Gender*. 1986.
————. *Subject to Change*. 1988.
Showalter, Elaine. *A Literature of Their Own*. 1977.
————. *Sister's Choice: Tradition and Change in American Women's Writing*. 1991.

MARXIST CRITICISM

Scholars influenced by Marxist criticism base their readings of literature on the social and economic theories of Karl Marx (*Das Kapital*, 1867–94) and his colleague and coauthor Friedrich Engels (*The Communist Manifesto*, 1884). Marx and Engels believed that the dominant capitalist middle class would eventually be challenged and overthrown by the working class. In the meantime, however, middle-class capitalists would exploit the working class, who produce excess products and profits yet do not share in the benefits of their labor. Marx and Engels further regarded all parts of the society in which they lived — religious, legal, educational, governmental — as tainted by what they saw as the corrupt values of middle-class capitalists.

Marxist critics apply these views about class struggle to their readings of poetry, fiction, and drama. They tend to analyze the literary works of any historical era as products of the ideology, or network of concepts, that supports the interests of the cultural elite and suppresses those of the working class. Some Marxist critics see all Western literature as distorted by the privileged views of the elite class, but most believe that a few creative writers reject the distorted views of their society and see clearly the wrongs to which working-class people have been subjected. For example, George Lukacs, a Hungarian Marxist critic, proposed that great works of literature create their own worlds and reflect life with clarity. These great works, though not written by Marxists, can be studied for their revealing examples of class conflict and other Marxist concerns. A Marxist critic would look with favor on Charles Dickens, who in nearly every novel pointed out inequities in the political, legal, and educational establishments of his time. Readers who remember Oliver Twist's pitiful plea for "more" workhouse porridge (refused by evil Mr. Bumble, who skims money from funds intended to feed the impoverished inmates) cannot help but see fertile ground for the Marxist critic, who would certainly applaud Dickens's scathing criticism of Victorian social and economic inequality.

Marxist criticism developed in the 1920s and 1930s in Germany and the Soviet Union. Since 1960, British and American Marxism has received greatest attention, with works such as Raymond Williams's *Culture and Society, 1780–1950* (1960) and Terry Eagleton's *Criticism and Ideology* (1976).

A MARXIST READING: Tillie Olsen's "I Stand Here Ironing"

In a Marxist reading of Tillie Olsen's "I Stand Here Ironing," you might concentrate on events that demonstrate how the narrator's and Emily's fates have been directly affected by the capitalist society of the United States.

> Tillie Olsen's "I Stand Here Ironing" stands as a powerful indictment of the capitalist system. The narrator and her daughter Emily are repeatedly exploited and defeated by the pressures of the economic system in which they live.
>
> The narrator's first child, Emily, is born into the world of the 1930s depression — an economic disaster brought on by the excesses and greed of Wall Street. When the young mother is deserted by her first husband, there are no government programs in place to help her. She says it was the "pre-relief, pre-WPA world of the depression" that forced her away from her child and into "a job hashing at night" (188). Although she is willing to work, she is paid so poorly that she must finally send Emily to live with her husband's family. Raising the money to bring Emily back takes a long time; and after this separation, Emily's health, both physical and emotional, is precarious.
>
> When Emily gets the measles, we get a hard look at what the few social programs that existed during the Depression were like. The child is sent — at the urging of a government social worker — to a convalescent home. The narrator notes bitterly, "They still send children to that place. I see pictures on the society page of sleek young women planning affairs to raise money for it, or dancing at the affairs, or decorating Easter eggs or filling Christmas stockings for the children" (189). The privileged class basks in the artificial glow of their charity work for the poor, yet the newspapers never show pictures of the hospitalized children who are kept isolated from everyone they loved and forced to eat "runny eggs . . . or mush with lumps" (190). Once again the mother is separated from her daughter by a system that discriminates against the poor. Because the family cannot afford private treatment, Emily is forced to undergo treatment in a public institution that not only denies her any contact with her family but also cruelly forbids her to save the letters she receives from home. Normal family relationships are severely disrupted by an uncaring economic structure that only grudgingly offers aid to the poor.
>
> It is clear that the division between mother and daughter is created and worsened by the social conditions in which they live. Because they are poor, they are separated at crucial times and, therefore, never get to know each other fully. Thus, neither can truly understand the ordeals the other has been forced to endure.

FOR FURTHER READING: Marxist Criticism

Agger, Ben. *The Discourse of Domination*. 1992.
Bullock, Chris, and David Peck, eds. *Guide to Marxist Literary Criticism*. 1980.
Eagleton, Terry. *Marxism and Literary Criticism*. 1976.

Frow, John. *Marxism and Literary History*. 1986.
Holub, Renate, and Antonio Gramsci. *Beyond Marxism and Postmodernism*. 1992.
Jameson, Fredric. *Marxism and Form*. 1971.
Lentricchia, Frank. *Criticism and Social Change*. 1983.
Ohmann, Richard M. *Politics of Letters*. 1987.
Strelka, Joseph P., ed. *Literary Criticism and Sociology*. 1973.
Williams, Raymond. *Culture and Society, 1780–1950*. 1960.
———. *Marxism and Literature*. 1977.

NEW HISTORICISM

New Historicist critics relate a text to the historical and cultural contexts of the period in which it was created and the periods in which it was critically evaluated. These contexts are not considered simply as "background" but as integral parts of a text. According to the New Historicists, history is not objective facts; rather, like literature, history is subject to interpretation and reinterpretation depending on the power structure of a society. Louis Althusser, for example, suggests that ideology intrudes in the discourse of an era, subjecting readers to the interests of the ruling establishment. Michel Foucault reflects that the discourse of an era defines the nature of "truth" and what behaviors are acceptable, sane, or criminal. "Truth," according to Foucault, is produced by the interaction of power and the systems in which the power flows, and it changes as society changes. Mikhail Bakhtin suggests that all discourse is dialogic, containing within it many independent and sometimes conflicting voices.

Literature, in the opinion of the New Historical critics, cannot be interpreted without reference to the time and place in which it was written. Criticism likewise cannot be evaluated without reference to the time and place in which it was written. A flaw of much criticism, according to the New Historicists, is the consideration of a literary text as if it were an organic whole. Such an approach ignores the diversity of conflicting voices in a text and in the cultural context in which a text is embedded. Indeed, Stephen Greenblatt prefers the term "cultural poetics" to New Historicism because it acknowledges the integral role that literature and art play in the culture of any era. Works of art and literature, according to Greenblatt, actively foster subversive elements or voices but somehow constrain those forces in ways that defuse challenges to the dominant culture.

New Historicists also point out that readers, like texts, are influenced and shaped by the cultural context of their eras and that a thoroughly objective "reading" of a text is therefore impossible. Acknowledging that all readers to some degree "appropriate" a text, some New Historicists present their criticism of texts as "negotiations" between past and present contexts. Thus, criticism of a particular work of literature would draw from both the cultural context of the era in which the text was written and the critic's present cultural context, and the critic would acknowledge how the latter context influences interpretation of the former.

Since the early 1970s, feminist critics have adopted some New Historicist positions, focusing on male-female power conflicts. And critics interested in multicultural texts have stressed the role of the dominant white culture in suppressing or marginalizing the texts of nonwhites. Marxist critics, including Raymond Williams, have adopted the term "cultural materialism" in discussing their mode of New Historicism, which focuses on the political significance of a literary text.

A NEW HISTORICIST READING: Charlotte Perkins Gilman's "The Yellow Wallpaper"

A New Historicist scholar might write an essay about "The Yellow Wallpaper" as an illustration of the destructive effects of the patriarchal culture of the late nineteenth century on women. This reading would be vastly different from that of most nineteenth-century critics, who interpreted the story as a harrowing case study of female mental illness. Even some early-twentieth-century readings posited that the narrator's mental illness is the result of her individual psychological problems. In a New Historicist reading, however, you might focus on the social conventions of the time, which produced conflicting discourses that drove the narrator to madness.

> The female narrator of "The Yellow Wallpaper," who is writing in her private journal (which is the text of the short story), explains that her husband, a physician, has diagnosed her as having a "temporary nervous depression — a slight hysterical tendency" (161). She says she should believe such a physician "of high standing" (161) and cooperate with his treatment, which is to confine her to a room in an isolated country estate and compel her to rest and have no visitors and not to write. The "cure" is intended to reduce her nervousness, she further explains. But as the story unfolds, the narrator reveals that she suspects the treatment will not cure her because it leaves her alone with her thoughts without even her writing to occupy her mind. Her husband's "cure" forces her into a passive role and eliminates any possibility of asserting her own personality. However, she guiltily suggests that her own lack of confidence in her husband's diagnosis may be what is preventing her cure.
>
> The text of "The Yellow Wallpaper" can be divided into at least two conflicting discourses: (1) the masculine discourse of the husband, who has the authority both of a highly respected physician and of a husband, two positions reinforced by the patriarchal culture of the time; and (2) the feminine discourse of the narrator, whose hesitant personal voice contradicts the masculine voice but undermines itself because it keeps reminding her that women should obey their husbands and their physicians. A third discourse underlies the two dominant ones — that of the gothic horror tale, a popular genre of the late nineteenth century. The narrator in "The Yellow Wallpaper" is isolated against her will in a room with barred windows in an almost deserted palatial country mansion she describes as "The most beautiful place!" (162). She is at the mercy of her captor, in this case her husband. She is not sure whether she is hallucinating, and she thinks the mansion may be haunted. She does not know whom to trust, not being sure whether her husband really wants to "cure" her or to punish her for expressing her rebellion.
>
> The narrator learns to hide her awareness of the conflicting discourses. She avoids mentioning her thoughts and fears about her illness or her fancies about the house being haunted, and she hides her writing. She speaks reasonably and

in "a very quiet voice" (169). But this inability to speak freely to anyone is a kind of torture, and alone in her room with the barred windows, she takes up discourse with the wallpaper. At first she describes it as "One of those sprawling flamboyant patterns committing every artistic sin" (163). But she is fascinated by the pattern, which has been distorted by mildew and by the tearing away of some sections. The narrator begins to strip off the wallpaper to free a woman she thinks is trapped inside; and, eventually, she visualizes herself as that woman, trapped yet freed by the destruction of the wallpaper. The narrator retreats, or escapes into madness, driven there by the multiple discourses she cannot resolve.

FOR FURTHER READING: New Historicist Criticism

Brook, Thomas. *The New Historicism and Other Old Fashioned Topics*. 1991.

Coates, Christopher. "What Was the New Historicism?" *Centennial Review* 32.2 (Spring 1993): 267–80.

Geertz, Clifford. "Thick Description: Toward an Interpretive Theory of Culture." *The Interpretation of Cultures*. By Clifford Geertz. 1973.

Greenblatt, Stephen, ed. *Representing the English Renaissance*. 1988.

Levin, David. "American Historicism: Old and New." *American Literary History* 6.3 (Fall 1994): 527–38.

Rabinov, Paul, ed. *The Foucault Reader*. 1986.

Veeser, H. Aram, ed. *The New Historicism*. 1989.

PSYCHOANALYTIC CRITICISM

Psychoanalytic criticism focuses on a work of literature as an expression in fictional form of the inner workings of the human mind. The premises and procedures used in psychoanalytic criticism were developed by Sigmund Freud (1846–1939), though some critics disagree strongly with his conclusions and their therapeutic and literary applications. Feminists, for example, take issue with Freud's notion that women are inherently masochistic.

Some of the major points of Freud's theories depend on the idea that much of what is most significant to us does not take place in our conscious life. Freud believed that we are forced (mostly by the rigors of having to live in harmony with other people) to repress much of our experience and many of our desires in order to coexist peacefully with others. Some of this repressed experience Freud saw as available to us through dreams and other unconscious structures. He believed that literature could often be interpreted as the reflection of our unconscious life.

Freud was among the first psychoanalytic critics, often using techniques developed for interpreting dreams to interpret literature. Among other analyses, he wrote an insightful study of Dostoevsky's *The Brothers Karamazov* as well as brief commentaries on several of Shakespeare's plays, including *A Midsummer Night's Dream*, *Macbeth*, *King Lear*, and *Hamlet*. The study of *Hamlet* may have inspired a classic of psychoanalytic criticism: Ernest Jones's *Hamlet and Oedipus* (1949), in which Jones explains Hamlet's strange reluctance to act against his uncle Claudius as resulting from Hamlet's unresolved longings for his mother and subsequent drive to eliminate his father. Because Hamlet's own father is dead, Jones argues, Claudius becomes, in the young man's subconscious mind, a father substitute. Hamlet, then, cannot make up his mind to kill his uncle because he sees not a simple case of revenge (for Claudius's murder of his father) but rather a complex web that includes incestuous desire for his own mother (now wed to Claudius). Jones extends his analysis to include the suggestion that Shakespeare himself experienced such a conflict and reflected his own Oedipal feelings in *Hamlet*.

A French psychoanalyst, Jacques Lacan (1901–1981), combined Freudian theories with structuralist literary theories to argue that the essential alienating experience of the human psyche is the acquisition of language. Lacan believed that once you can name yourself and distinguish yourself from others, you enter the difficult social world that requires you to repress your instincts. Like Lacan, who modified and adapted psychoanalytic criticism to connect it to structuralism, many twentieth-century literary scholars, including Marxists and feminists, have found useful approaches in psychoanalytic literary theory (see, for example, Mary Jacobus's *Reading Woman: Essays in Feminist Criticism*, 1986).

PSYCHOANALYTIC TERMS

To fully appreciate psychoanalytic criticism, readers need to understand the following terms:

- *id*— The part of the mind that determines sexual drives and other unconscious compulsions that urge individuals to unthinking gratification.
- *ego*— The conscious mind that strives to deal with the demands of the id and to balance its needs with messages from the superego.
- *superego*— The part of the unconscious that seeks to repress the demands of the id and to prevent gratification of basic physical appetites. The superego is a sort of censor that represents the prohibitions of society, religion, family beliefs, and so on.
- *condensation*— A process that takes place in dreams (and in literature) when several elements from the repressed unconscious are linked together to form a new yet disguised whole.
- *symbolism*— Use of representative objects to stand for forbidden (often sexual) objects. This process takes place in dreams and in literature. For instance, a pole, knife, or gun may stand for the penis.
- *displacement*— Substitution of a socially acceptable desire for a desire that is not acceptable. This process takes place in dreams or in literature. For example, a woman who experiences sexual desires for her son may instead dream of being intimate with a neighbor who has the same first name as (or who looks like) her son.
- *Oedipus complex*— Repressed desire of a son to unite sexually with his mother and kill his father. According to Freud, all young boys go through this stage, but most resolve these conflicts before puberty.
- *projection*— Defense mechanism in which people mistakenly see in others antisocial impulses they fail to recognize in themselves.

- *subject*— The term used in Lacanian theory to designate a speaking person, or a person who has assumed a position within language. The Lacanian subject of language is split, or characterized by unresolvable tension between the conscious perception of the self (Freud's ego) and the unconscious desires that motivate behavior.

A PSYCHOANALYTIC READING: Edgar Allan Poe's "The Cask of Amontillado"

Edgar Allan Poe died in 1849, six years before Freud was born, so Poe could not possibly have known Freud's work. Nevertheless, psychoanalytic critics argue that the principles discovered by Freud and those who followed him are inherent in human nature. Therefore, they believe it is perfectly plausible to use modern psychiatric terms when analyzing a work written before their invention. If you approached Poe's "The Cask of Amontillado" from a psychoanalytic perspective, you might write the following interpretation.

Montresor, the protagonist of Poe's "The Cask of Amontillado," has long fascinated readers who have puzzled over his motives for the story's climactic action when he imprisons his rival, Fortunato, and leaves him to die. Montresor claims that Fortunato insulted him and dealt him a "thousand injuries" (217). Yet when we meet Fortunato, although he appears something of a pompous fool, none of his actions — or even his comments — seems powerful enough to motivate Montresor's thirst for revenge.

If, however, we consider a defense mechanism, first named "projection" and described by Sigmund Freud, we gain a clearer picture of Montresor. Those who employ projection are often people who experience antisocial impulses yet are not conscious of these impulses. It seems highly likely that Fortunato did not persecute Montresor; rather, Montresor himself experienced the impulse to act in a hostile manner toward Fortunato. We know, for instance, that Fortunato belongs to the exclusive Order of Masons because he gives Montresor the secret Masonic sign. Montresor's failure to recognize the sign shows that he is a mason only in the grimmest literal sense. Montresor clearly resents Fortunato's high standing and projects onto Fortunato all of his own hostility toward those who (he thinks) have more or know more than he does. Thus, he imagines that Fortunato's main business in life is to persecute and insult him.

Montresor's obsessive behavior further indicates his pathology. He plans Fortunato's punishment with the cunning one might ordinarily reserve for a major battle, cleverly figuring out a way to keep his servants from the house and to lure the ironically named Fortunato to his death. Each step of the revenge is carefully plotted. This is no sudden crime of passion but rather the diabolically planned act of a deeply disturbed mind.

If we understand Montresor's need to take all of the hatred and anger that is inside himself and to rid himself of those socially unacceptable emotions by projecting them on to someone else, then we can see how he rationalizes a crime that seems otherwise nearly unmotivated. By killing Fortunato, Montresor symbolically kills the evil in himself. It is interesting to note that the final lines of the story support this reading. Montresor observes that "For the half of a century no mortal has disturbed" the bones. In other words, the unacceptable emotions have not again been aroused. His last words, a Latin phrase from the Mass for the Dead meaning "rest in peace," suggest that only through his heinous crime has he found release from the torment of his own hatred.

FOR FURTHER READING: Psychoanalytic Criticism

Freud, Sigmund. *The Interpretation of Dreams*. 1900.

Gardner, Shirley N., ed. *The (M)other Tongue: Essays in Feminist Psychoanalytic Interpretation*. 1985.

Hartman, Geoffrey H., ed. *Psychoanalysis and the Question of the Text*. 1979.

Kris, Ernst. *Psychoanalytic Explorations in Art*. 1952.

Kristeva, Julia. *Desire in Language*. 1980.

Nelson, Benjamin, ed. *Sigmund Freud on Creativity and the Unconscious*. 1958.

Wright, Elizabeth. *Psychoanalytic Criticism: Theory in Practice*. 1984.

STRUCTURALISM

Structuralism, a literary movement with roots in linguistics and anthropology, concentrates on literature as a system of signs that have no inherent meaning except in their agreed-upon or conventional relation to one another. Structuralism is usually described by its proponents not as a new way to interpret literary works but rather as a way to understand how works of literature come to have meaning. Because structuralism developed from linguistic theory, some structuralists use linguistic approaches to literature. When they talk about literary texts, they use the terms (such as *morpheme* and *phoneme*) that linguists use as they study the nature of language. Many structuralists, however, use the linguistic model as an analogy. To understand the analogy, you need to know a bit of linguistic theory.

The French linguist Ferdinand de Saussure (*Course in General Linguistics*, 1915) suggested that the relationship between an object and the name we use to designate if is purely arbitrary. What, for example, makes "C-A-T" signify a small, furry animal with pointed ears and whiskers? Only our learned expectation makes us associate *cat* with the family feline pet. Had we grown up in France, we would make the same association with *chat*, or in Mexico with *gato*. The words we use to designate objects (linguists call these words *signs*) make sense only within the large context of our entire language system and will not be understood as meaningful by someone who does not know that language system. Further, Saussure pointed out, signs become truly useful only when we use them to designate difference. For instance, the word *cat* becomes useful when we want to differentiate a small furry animal that meows from a small furry animal that barks. Saussure was interested in how language, as a structure of conventions, worked. He asked intriguing questions about the underlying rules that allow this made-up structure of signs to work, and, as a result, his pioneering study caught the interest of scholars in many fields.

Many literary scholars saw linguistic structuralism as analogous to the study of literary works. Literary structuralism leads readers to think of poems, short stories, novels, and plays not as self-contained and individual entities that have some kind of inherent meaning but rather as part of a larger literary system. To fully appreciate and analyze the work, the reader must understand the system within which it operates. Like linguistic structuralism, literary structuralism focuses on the importance of difference. We must, for example, understand the difference between the structure of poetry and the structure of prose before we can make sense of a sentence like this:

> so much depends
> upon
> a red wheel
> barrow

WILLIAM CARLOS WILLIAMS, "Red Wheelbarrow" (p. 665)

* * *

Readers unacquainted with the conventions of poetry would find those lines meaningless and confusing, although if they knew the conventions of prose, they would readily understand this sentence:

> So much depends upon a red wheelbarrow.

The way we interpret any group of "signs," then, depends on how they are structured and on the way we understand the system that governs their structure.

Structuralists believe that literature is basically artificial because although it uses the same "signs" as everyday language, whose purpose is to give information, the purpose of literature is *not* primarily to relay data. For example, a poem like Dylan Thomas's "Do not go gentle into that good night" (p. 559) is written in the linguistic form of a series of commands, yet the poem goes much further than that. Its meaning is created not only by our understanding the lines as a series of commands but also by our recognition of the poetic form, the rhyming conventions, and the figures of speech that Thomas uses. We can only fully discuss the poem within the larger context of our literary knowledge.

Structuralism also provides the foundation for poststructuralism, a theoretical movement that informs the fields of deconstructionist and New Historicist criticism and has influenced the work of many psychoanalytic and sociological critics. Although structuralists claim that language functions by arbitrarily connecting words (signifiers) to ideas (signifieds), poststructuralists develop the implications of this claim, arguing that because the connection of a word to an idea is purely arbitrary, any operation of language is inherently unstable. Poststructuralists believe that to study a literary text is to study a continuously shifting set of meanings.

A STRUCTURALIST READING: William Faulkner's "Barn Burning"

A structuralist reading tries to bring to light some of the assumptions about language and form that we are likely to take for granted. Looking at the opening paragraph of Faulkner's "Barn Burning," from the point of view of structuralist criticism, you might first look at an interpretation that reads the passage as a stream of Sarty's thoughts. The structuralist critic might then consider the assumptions a reader would have to make to see what Faulkner has written as the thoughts of an illiterate child. Next, the structuralist might look at evidence to suggest the language in this section operates outside the system of language that would be available to Sarty and that, therefore, "Barn Burning" opens not with a simple recounting of the main character's thoughts but rather with something far more complex.

> The opening paragraph of William Faulkner's "Barn Burning" is often read as an excursion into the mind of Sarty, the story's young protagonist. When we read the passage closely, however, we note that a supposedly simple consciousness is represented in a highly complex way. For Sarty — uneducated and illiterate — the "scarlet devils" and "silver curve of fish" on the labels of food tins serve as direct signs appealing to his hunger. It is unlikely, however, that Sarty could consciously understand what he sees and express it as metaphor. We cannot, then, read this opening passage as a recounting of the thoughts that pass through Sarty's mind. Instead, these complex sentences and images offer possibilities that reach beyond the limits of Sarty's linguistic system.
>
> Because our own knowledge is wider than Sarty's, the visual images the narrator describes take on meanings for us that are unavailable to the young boy. For example, like Sarty, we know that the "scarlet devils" stand for deviled ham. Yet the devils also carry another possible connotation. They may indicate evil and thus serve to emphasize the despair and grief Sarty feels are ever present. So we are given images that flash through the mind of an illiterate young boy, apparently intended to suggest his poverty and ignorance (he cannot read the words on the labels), yet we are led to see a highly complicated set of meanings. When we encounter later in the passage Sarty's articulated thought, "*our enemy . . . ourn! mine and hisn both! . . .*," his down-to-earth dialect shows clearly the sharp distinction between the system of language the narrator uses to describe Sarty's view of the store shelves and the system of language Sarty uses to describe what he sees and feels.

FOR FURTHER READING: Structuralism

Barthes, Roland. *Critical Essays*. 1964.
Culler, Jonathan. *Structuralist Poetics*. 1975.
Greimas, A. J. *Structured Semantics: An Attempt at a Method*. Trans. McDowell, Schleifer, and Velie. 1983.
Hawkes, Terence. *Structuralism and Semiotics*. 1977.
Lentricchia, Frank. *After the New Criticism*. 1980.
Pettit, Philip. *The Concept of Structuralism: A Critical Analysis*. 1975.
Scholes, Robert. *Structuralism in Literature: An Introduction*. 1974.

DECONSTRUCTION

Deconstruction is a literary movement developed from structuralism. Deconstructionists argue that every text contains within it some ingredient undermining its purported system of meaning. In other words, the structure that seems to hold the text together is unstable because it depends on the conclusions of a particular ideology (for instance, the idea that women are inferior to men or that peasants are content with their lowly position in life), conclusions that are not really as natural or inevitable as the text may pretend. The practice of finding the point at which the text falls apart because of these internal inconsistencies is called deconstruction.

Deconstructive theorists share with formalists and structuralists a concern for the work itself rather than for biographical, historical, or ideological influences. Like formalists, deconstructionists focus on possibilities for multiple meanings within texts. However, while formalists seek to explain paradox by discovering tensions and ironies that can lead to a unified reading, deconstructionists insist on the primacy of multiple possibilities. They maintain that any given text is capable of yielding many divergent readings, all of which are equally valid yet may in some way undermine and oppose one another.

Like structuralists, deconstructionists see literary texts as part of larger systems of discourse. A key structuralist technique is identifying opposites in an attempt to show the structure of language used in a work. Having identified the opposites, the structuralist rests the case. Deconstructionists, however, go further. Jacques Derrida, a French philosopher, noticed that these oppositions do not simply reflect linguistic structures but are the linguistic response to the way people deal with their beliefs (their ideologies). For instance, if you believe strongly that democracy is the best possible form of government, you tend to lump other forms of government into the category "nondemocracies." If a government is nondemocratic, that — not its other distinguishing characteristics — would be significant to you. This typical ideological response operates in all kinds of areas of belief, even ones we are not aware of. Deconstructionists contend that texts tend to give away their ideological biases by means of this opposition.

Derrida called this distinction between "A" and "Not-A" (rather than between "A" and "B") *différance*, a word he coined to suggest a concept represented by the French verb *différer*, which has two meanings: "to be different" and "to defer." (Note that in Derrida's new term an "a" is substituted for an "e" — a distinction that can be seen in writing but not heard in speaking.) When a deconstructionist uncovers *différance* through careful examination of a text, he or she also finds an (often unwitting) ideological bias. Deconstructionists argue that the reader must transcend such ideological biases and must instead acknowledge contradictory possibilities as equally worthy of consideration. No one meaning can or should be designated as correct.

Deconstruction, then, is not really a system of criticism (and, in fact, deconstructionists resist being labeled as a school of criticism). Rather, deconstruction offers a way to take apart a literary text and thereby reveal its separate layers. Deconstructionists often focus on the metaphorical nature of language, claiming that all language is basically metaphoric because the sign we use to designate any given object or action stands apart from the object itself. In fact, deconstructionists believe that all writing is essentially literary and metaphorical because language, by its very nature, can only *stand for* what we call reality or truth; it cannot *be* reality or truth.

A major contribution of deconstructive critics lies in their playful approach to language and to literary criticism. They refuse to accept as absolute any one way of reading poetry, fiction, or drama, and they guard against what they see as the fixed conclusions and arbitrary operating assumptions of many schools of criticism.

A DECONSTRUCTIONIST READING: Flannery O'Connor's "A Good Man Is Hard to Find"

A deconstructionist reading of Flannery O'Connor's "A Good Man Is Hard to Find" might challenge the essentially religious interpretations the author offered of her own stories in essays and letters. If you were applying deconstructionist criticism to the story, you might argue that the author's reading of the story is no more valid than anyone else's, and that the story can just as legitimately be read as an investigation of the functions of irony in language.

> Flannery O'Connor explained that the grotesque and violent aspects of her stories are intended to shock the reader into recognizing the inhospitable nature of the world and thereby the universal human need for divine grace. The last sentence of "A Good Man Is Hard to Find" is spoken by The Misfit, who has just murdered a family of travelers: "It's no real pleasure in life." However, the language of O'Connor's stories is extremely ironic — that is, her narrators and characters often say one thing but mean another. So it is possible that their statements are not empirically true but are representations of a persona or elements of a story they have created using language.
>
> The Grandmother, for example, lives almost entirely in fictions — newspaper clippings, stories for the grandchildren, her belief that The Misfit is a good man. In contrast, The Misfit is more literal than the Grandmother in his perception of reality. He knows, for example, whether the car turned over once or twice. But he too is posing, at first as the tough guy who rejects religious and societal norms by saying, ". . . it's nothing for you to do but enjoy the few minutes you got left the best way you can — by killing somebody or burning down his house or doing some other meanness to him. No pleasure but meanness. . . ." Finally, he poses as the pessimist — or, according to O'Connor's reading, the Christian — who claims, "It's no real pleasure in life." The contradictions in The Misfit's language make it impossible to tell which of these façades is "real."

FOR FURTHER READING: Deconstruction

Abrams, M. H. "Rationality and the Imagination in Cultural History." *Critical Inquiry* 2 (1976): 447–64. (Abrams claims deconstructionists are parasites who depend on other critics to come up with interpretations that can be deconstructed.)

Arac, Jonathan, Wlad Godzich, and Wallace Martin, eds. *The Yale Critics: Deconstruction in America.* 1983.

Berman, Art. *From the New Criticism to Deconstruction.* 1988.

Culler, Jonathan. *On Deconstruction: Theory and Criticism after Structuralism.* 1982.

Jefferson, Ann. "Structuralism and Post-Structuralism." *Modern Literary Theory: A Comparative Introduction*. 1982.

Johnson, Barbara. *The Critical Difference: Essays in the Contemporary Rhetoric of Reading*. 1980.

Leitsch, Vincent B. *Deconstructive Theory and Practice*. 1982.

Lynn, Steven. "A Passage into Critical Theory." *College English* 52 (1990): 258–71.

Miller, J. Hillis. "The Critic as Host." *Deconstruction and Criticism*. Ed. Harold Bloom et al. 1979. (a response to Abrams's article, listed above)

Norris, Christopher. *Deconstruction: Theory and Practice*. 1982.

CHAPTER 36

WRITING ESSAY EXAMS ABOUT LITERATURE

Taking exams is a skill that you have been developing throughout your life as a student. Both short-answer and essay exams require you to study, to recall what you know, and to budget your time carefully as you write your answers. Only essay questions, however, ask you to synthesize information and to arrange ideas in a series of clear, logically connected sentences and paragraphs. For this reason, taking essay exams requires writing skills. To write an essay exam or even a paragraph-length answer, you must do more than memorize facts; you must identify and express the relationships among them. In other words, you must think critically about your subject, and you must plan, shape, draft, and revise an essay that clearly communicates your ideas to your audience.

PLANNING AN ESSAY EXAM ANSWER

Because you are under pressure during an exam and tend to write quickly, you may be tempted to skip the planning and revision stages of the writing process. But if you write in a frenzy and hand in your exam without a second glance, you are likely to produce a disorganized or even incoherent answer. With careful planning and editing, you can write an answer that demonstrates your understanding of the material.

Review Your Material

Be sure you know beforehand the scope and format of the exam. How much of your textbook and class notes will the exam cover — the entire semester's work or only the material covered since the last test? Will you have to answer every question, or will you be able to choose among alternatives? Will the exam test your ability to recall specific facts, or will it require you to demonstrate your understanding of the course material by drawing conclusions?

Exams challenge you to recall and express in writing what you already know — what you have read, what you have heard in class, what you have reviewed in your notes. Before you even begin an exam, you must study: reread your textbook and class notes, highlight key points, and perhaps outline particularly important sections of your notes. When you prepare for a short-answer exam, you may memorize facts without analyzing their relationship to one another or their relationship to a body of knowledge as a whole: the definition of romanticism, the date of Queen Victoria's death, two examples of irony, four characteristics of a villanelle. When you prepare for an essay exam, however, you must do more than remember bits of information; you also must make connections among ideas.

When you are sure you know what to expect, try to anticipate the essay questions your instructor might ask. Try out likely questions on classmates, and see whether you can do some collaborative brainstorming to outline answers to possible questions. If you have time, you might even practice answering one or two in writing.

Consider Your Audience and Purpose

The audience for any exam is the instructor who prepared it. As you read the questions, think about what your instructor has emphasized in class. Although you may certainly arrange material in a new way or use it to make an original point, keep in mind that your purpose is to demonstrate that you understand the material, not to make clever remarks or introduce irrelevant information. In addition, you should make every effort to use the vocabulary of the discipline for which you are writing and to follow the specific **conventions** for writing about literature (p. 33).

Read through the Entire Exam

Your time is usually limited when you take an exam, so plan carefully. How long should a "one-paragraph" or "essay-length" answer be? How much time should you devote to answering each question? The exam question itself may specify the time allotted for each answer, so look for that information. More often, the point value of each question or the number of questions on the exam indicates how much time to spend on each answer. If an essay question is worth 50 out of 100 points, for example, you will probably have to spend at least half of your time planning, writing, and revising your answer.

Before you begin to write, read the entire exam carefully to determine your priorities and your strategy. First, be sure that your copy of the test is complete and that you understand exactly what each question requires. If you need clarification, ask your instructor or proctor for help. Then, decide where to start. If there is more than one question on the exam, responding first to the one you feel most confident about is usually a good strategy. This approach ensures that you will not become bogged down responding to a question that baffles you and be left with too little time to write a strong answer to a question that you understand well.

Read the Question Carefully

To write an effective answer, you need to understand the question. As you read any essay question, you may find it helpful to underline key words and important terms. <u>Summarize in detail</u> the contributions of American <u>writers</u> of the <u>Harlem Renaissance,</u> <u>briefly outlining</u> the contributions of <u>artists and musicians.</u>

Then, look carefully at the question's wording. If the question calls for a comparison and contrast of *two* works of literature, a description or analysis of one work, no matter how comprehensive, will not be acceptable. If a question asks for causes *and* effects, a discussion of causes alone will be insufficient.

KEY WORDS IN EXAM QUESTIONS

- Explain
- Compare
- Contrast
- Trace
- Evaluate
- Discuss

- Clarify
- Relate
- Justify
- Analyze
- Interpret1
- Describe

- Classify
- Identify
- Illustrate
- Define
- Support
- Summarize

As its key words indicate, the following question requires a very specific kind of response. The first response to it simply *identifies* three characteristics of *one* kind of detective story and is therefore not acceptable.

Question

Identify <u>three differences</u> between the <u>hard-boiled detective story</u> and the <u>classical detective story.</u>

Unacceptable answer

The hard-boiled detective story, popularized in <u>Black Mask</u> magazine in the 1930s and 1940s, is very different from the classical detective stories of Edgar Allan Poe or Agatha Christie. The hard-boiled stories feature a down-on-his-luck detective who is constantly tempted and betrayed. His world is dark and chaotic, and the crimes he tries to solve are not out-of-the-ordinary occurrences; they are the norm. These stories have no happy endings; even when the crime is solved, the world is still corrupt.

The next answer, which *contrasts* the two kinds of detective stories, is acceptable.

Acceptable answer

The hard-boiled detective story differs from the classical detective story in its characters, its setting, and its plot. The classical detective is usually well educated and well off; he is aloof from the other characters and therefore can remain in total control of the situation. The hard-boiled detective, on the other hand, is typically a decent but down-on-his-luck man who is drawn into the chaos around him, constantly tempted and betrayed. In the orderly world of the classical detective, the crime is a temporary disruption. In the hard-boiled detective's dark and chaotic world, the crimes he tries to solve are not out-of-the-ordinary occurrences; they are the norm. In the classical detective story, order is restored at the end. Hard-boiled stories have no happy endings; even when the crime is solved, the world is still corrupt.

Brainstorm to Find Ideas

Once your understand the question, you need to find something to say. Begin by **brainstorming**, quickly listing all the relevant ideas you can remember. Then, identify the most important points on your list, and delete the others. A quick review of the exam question and your supporting ideas should lead you toward a workable thesis for your essay answer.

SHAPING AN ESSAY EXAM ANSWER

State your Thesis

Often, you can rephrase the exam question as a **thesis statement**. For example, the question "Summarize in detail the contributions of American writers of the Harlem Renaissance, briefly outlining the contributions of artists and musicians" suggests the following thesis statement:

Effective thesis statement

Writers of the Harlem Renaissance—notably Richard Wright, Gwendolyn Brooks, Zora Neale Hurston, and Langston Hughes— made significant contributions to American literature; artists and musicians of the movement also left an important legacy.

An effective thesis statement addresses all aspects of the question but highlights only relevant concerns. The following thesis statements are not effective:

Vague thesis statement

The Harlem Renaissance produced many important writers, artists, and musicians.

Incomplete thesis statement

The Harlem Renaissance's writers, such as Richard Wright, Gwendolyn Brooks, Zora Neale Hurston, and Langston Hughes, made significant contributions to American literature.

Irrelevant thesis statement
```
The writers of the Harlem Renaissance had a greater im-
pact on American literature than the writers of the Beat
generation, such as Jack Kerouac.
```

Make a Scratch Outline

Because time is limited, you should plan your answer before you write it. There-fore, once you have decided on a suitable thesis, you should make a **scratch outline** that lists the points you will use to support your thesis.

On the inside cover of your exam book, arrange your supporting points in the order in which you plan to discuss them. Once you have completed your outline, check it against the exam question to make certain it covers everything the question calls for — and *only* what the question calls for.

A scratch outline for an answer to the question "Summarize in detail the con-tributions of American writers of the Harlem Renaissance, briefly outlining the contributions of artists and musicians" might look like this:

Scratch Outline

Thesis statement
```
Writers of the Harlem Renaissance—notably Richard Wright,
Gwendolyn Brooks, Zora Neale Hurston, and Langston Hughes—
made significant contributions to American literature;
artists and musicians of the movement also left an important
legacy.
```

Supporting points
```
Writers
Wright—Uncle Tom's Children, Black Boy, Native Son
Brooks—poetry (classical forms; social issues)
Hurston—Their Eyes Were Watching God, essays,
autobiography
Hughes—poetry (ballads, blues); "Simple" stories
Artists and Musicians
Henry Tanner
Duke Ellington
```

DRAFTING AND REVISING AN ESSAY EXAM ANSWER

Referring to your outline, you can now begin to draft your answer. Don't bother crafting an elaborate or unusual **introduction;** your time is precious, and so is your reader's. A simple statement of your thesis that summarizes your answer is your best introductory strategy: this approach is efficient, and it reminds you to address the question directly.

To develop the **body** of the essay, follow your outline point by point, using specifically worded topic sentences to introduce your supporting points and clear transitions to indicate your progression from point to point (and to help your instructor see that you are answering the question in full). Such signals, along with parallel sentence structure and repeated key words, will make your essay easy to follow.

The most effective **conclusion** for an essay exam is a clear, simple restatement of the thesis or a summary of the essay's main points.

Essay answers should be complete and detailed, but they should not contain irrelevant material. Every unnecessary fact or opinion increases your chance of error, so don't repeat yourself or volunteer unrequested information, and don't express your own feelings or opinions unless such information is specifically called for. In addition, be sure to support all your general statements with specific examples.

Leave enough time to reread and revise what you have written. When you reread, try to view your answer from a fresh perspective. Is your thesis statement clearly worded? Does your essay support your thesis and answer the question? Are your facts correct, and are your ideas presented in a logical order? Review your topic sentences and transitions. Check sentence structure and word choice, spelling and punctuation. If a sentence — or even a whole paragraph — seems irrelevant, cross it out. If you suddenly remember something you want to add, you can insert a few additional words with a caret (^). Neatly insert a longer addition at the end of your answer, box it, and label it so your instructor will know where it belongs. Finally, be sure that you have written legibly and that you have not inadvertently left out any words.

Sample Student Essay Exam Answer

The essay exam answer on pages 1596–98 was written in response to the following question:

Question

Fictional characters (like real people) do not always behave as others wish or expect them to. Sometimes they rebel against these expectations and act quite differently. In a clearly written and supported essay, explain how the specific actions of any four characters in works we have read this semester defy the expectations of those around them. Then briefly consider the consequences of each character's decision to rebel.

As you read the response to the question, notice that the student writer does not include any irrelevant information. She does not, for example, provide unnecessary plot summary or discuss more than four characters; she covers only what the question asks for. Guided by the question's key words —*explain* and *briefly consider*— she explains how each character's actions are defiant and outlines the consequences of those actions.

Student Essay Exam Answer

Introduction
rephrases exam
question and
introduces four
characters to be
discussed

Thesis Statement

First character's
actions
explained

Consequences
of actions

Second
character's
actions
explained

Many characters we have read about this semester do not behave as others believe they should behave. This is apparent in the actions of Connie in "Where Are You Going, Where Have You Been?" Nora in A Doll House, Marty in Marty, and the narrator in "Boys and Girls." For each of these characters, rebellion comes with a significant sacrifice.

Connie's rebellion is somewhat typical for a teenager: she rebels against the constraints her parents put on her to be a "good girl" by being a "bad girl" (at least in their terms). The makeup and style of clothing that Connie wears when she is away from home reinforce this "bad girl" image. Her behavior—staying out late, lying about where she is going, having "trashy daydreams"—creates a problem for her parents because she is not conforming to their standards and because she is not conducting herself in a manner they consider appropriate. Her actions also put a strain on the relationship between her and her sister, who is the perfect example of a "good girl." Her determination to rebel ultimately makes her stay home from the family outing, and this in turn leaves her alone and vulnerable to Arnold's advances. Thus, her rebellious actions lead to probable violence (she goes with Arnold, who we know has frightening plans for her). The ending of the story is ambiguous. We do not know it she ever comes back; possibly, her innocent rebellion leads to her death.

Nora in A Doll House rebels only after she understands the conflict between the duty to herself to be a "real" person and the duty to her husband and children. Throughout the play, we see this conflict escalating until Nora has no choice but to act to resolve it, choosing to go against the norms of society and against how others think she should act. This behavior creates a problem for Torvald because of the image it presents to others. Torvald's greatest fear is that society will not accept him, and when Nora admits what she has done, he panics. At the end of the play, Nora chooses to be true to herself even though the person closest to her does not approve—and even though she will lose her children. She will be a stronger person because she had the courage to stand up for herself.

> Consequences of actions

Marty's rebellious act is simply his decision to call Clara even though his friends and his mother do not approve. Although Marty is an adult, he is very much still a teenager in some ways. He has not yet broken away from his mother, and he continues to seek approval from her (and from his friends). He struggles to please his mother—by going to the dance, by allowing Aunt Catherine to move in—even when her desires are in conflict with his own. Marty's action at the play's end—calling Clara—will create a problem for his mother and his friends, who fear his growing independence and fight his decision to pursue a relationship with Clara. But Marty, like Nora, chooses to be true to himself and to do what he thinks is the right thing for him, rather than what others force upon him. He risks hurting his mother, alienating his friends, and losing the only life he

> Third character's actions explained

> Consequences of actions

knows. But for Marty, the potential gains seem worth the risk.

Transitional
paragraph
Connie, Nora, and Marty all break with society; all struggle to be independent. For all three, this independence has a cost. Connie may lose her life, Nora gives up her marriage and her children, and Marty leaves behind the comforting, secure existence he has known. The narrator of "Boys and Girls," however, is a special case.

Fourth
character's
actions
explained
Although the protagonist of "Boys and Girls" is in conflict with society's expectations at the beginning of the story, the ending shows that she no longer wants to be involved in the conflict between men's roles and women's roles. While at the beginning of the story she enjoys being outside with her father, by the end she is resigned to being considered a woman. She makes one grand rebellious gesture—

Consequences
of actions
freeing Flora from captivity—but she knows it is useless, and she is resigned to her fate. At the story's end, there is no longer a conflict between what she wants and what society wants her to be. She has resolved the conflict between herself and society because now what society wants from her has become what she wants also: to be and act like a woman.

Conclusion
Although each character deals with conflict and rebellion in a different way, all four struggle within themselves when decisions they must make are in conflict with the norms and expectations of society. For all four, rebellion leads to sacrifice.

Credits

Heinle has made every effort to trace the ownership of all copyrighted material and to secure permissions from the copyright holders. In the event of any question regarding the use of any material, we will be pleased to make the necessary corrections in future printings.

Chinua Achebe, "Dead Man's Path" by Chinua Achebe. Reprinted by permission of Harold Ober Associates Inc.

Leonard Adamé, "My Grandmother Would Rock Quietly and Hum" by Leonard Adamé. Copyright © 1973 by Leonard Adamé. No portion of this text may be reprinted without written permission of the author.

Elizabeth Alexander, "Apollo" from *Body of Life* by Elizabeth Alexander. Reprinted by permission of Tia Chucha Press.

Sherman Alexie, "How to Write the Great American Indian Novel" by Sherman Alexie reprinted from *The Summer of the Black Widows*. Copyright © 1996 by Sherman Alexie. By permission of Hanging Loose Press. "This Is What It Means to Say Phoenix, Arizona" from *The Lone Ranger and Tonto Fistfight in Heaven* by Sherman Alexie. Copyright © 1993 by Sherman Alexie. Used by permission of Grove/Atlantic, Inc.

Maya Angelou, "Africa" by Maya Angelou from *Oh Pray My Wings Are Gonna Fit Me Well* by Maya Angelou, copyright © 1975 by Maya Angelou. Used by permission of Random House, Inc. "My Arkansas" from *And Still I Rise* by Maya Angelou, copyright © 1978 by Maya Angelou. Used by permission of Random House, Inc.

Margaret Atwood, "Happy Endings" from *Good Bones and Simple Murders* by Margaret Atwood. Copyright © 1983, 1992, 1994 by O.W. Toad Ltd. A Nan A. Talese Book. Used by permission of Doubleday, a division of Random House, Inc. and McClelland & Stewart Ltd., The Canadian Publishers. "This Is a Photograph of Me" by Margaret Atwood from *The Circle Game*. Copyright © 1966, 1998 by Margaret Atwood. Reprinted with the permission of House of Anansi Press, Toronto. "You Fit Into Me" by Margaret Atwood from *Power Politics*. Copyright © 1971. Reprinted with the permission of Stoddart Publishing Co. Limited, 34 Lesmill Rd., Don Mills, Ont., Canada M3B 2T6. "The City Planners" by Margaret Atwood from *The Circle Game*. Copyright © 1966. Reprinted with the permission of Stoddart Publishing Co. Limited, 34 Lesmill Rd., Don Mills, Ont., Canada M3B 2T6.

W.H. Auden, "The Unknown Citizen," copyright 1940 and renewed 1968 by W.H. Auden, "Musée des Beaux Arts," copyright 1940 and renewed 1968 by W.H. Auden, from *W.H. Auden: The Collected Poems* by W.H. Auden. Used by permission of Random House, Inc. "As I Walked Out One Evening," copyright 1940 and renewed 1968 by W.H. Auden from *W.H. Auden: The Collected Poems* by W.H. Auden. Used by permission of Random House, Inc.

Toni Cade Bambara, "The Lesson," copyright © 1972 by Toni Cade Bambara, from *Gorilla, My Love* by Toni Cade Bambara. Used by permission of Random House, Inc.

Andrea Barrett, "The Littoral Zone" from *Ship Fever and Other Stories* by Andrea Barrett. Copyright © 1996 by Andrea Barrett. Used by permission of W.W. Norton & Company, Inc.

Matsuo Basho, "Spring," "The Beginnings of Autumn," "The Winds of Autumn," and "A Flash of Lightning" by Matsuo Basho from *The Penguin Book of Japanese Verse*, translated by Geoffrey Bownas and Anthony Thwaite (Penguin Books 1964, Revised Edition 1998). Translation copyright © Geoffrey Bownas and Anthony Thwaite, 1964, 1998. Reprinted by permission of Penguin Books Limited.

Rick Bass, "The Fireman" by Rick Bass. Reprinted by permission of the author.

Charles Baxter, "Gryphon" from *Through the Safety Net* by Charles Baxter, copyright © 1985 by Charles Baxter. Used by permission of Vintage Books, a division of Random House, Inc.

Mark Halliday, "The Value of Education" by Mark Halliday from *Slate* Magazine, June 21, 2000. Reprinted by permission of United Media.

Joy Harjo, "Morning Song" from *A Map to the Next World: Poems and Tales* by Joy Harjo. Copyright © 2000 by Joy Harjo. Used by permission of W.W. Norton & Company, Inc.

Robert Hayden, "Homage to the Empress of the Blues." Copyright © 1966, 1962 by Robert Hayden, "Monet's 'Waterlilies'" and "Those Winter Sundays." Copyright © 1966 by Robert Hayden, from *Angle Of Ascent: New and Selected Poems* by Robert Hayden. Copyright © 1975, 1972, 1970, 1966 by Robert Hayden. Used by permission of Liveright Publishing Corporation.

Seamus Heaney, "Digging" and "Mid-Term Break" from *Opened Ground: Selected Poems 1966–1996* by Seamus Heaney. Copyright © 1998 by Seamus Heaney. Reprinted by permission of Farrar, Straus and Giroux, LLC.

Ernest Hemingway, "A Clean, Well-Lighted Place" reprinted with permission of Scribner, an imprint of Simon & Schuster Adult Publishing Group, from *The Short Stories of Ernest Hemingway*. Copyright 1933 by Charles Scribner's Sons. Copyright renewed 1961 by Mary Hemingway.

Victor Hernandez Cruz, "Anonymous" by Victor Hernandez Cruz. Copyright © 1982–2002 by Victor Hernandez Cruz. Reprinted by permission of the author.

Elizabeth Holmes, "The Fathers" by Elizabeth Holmes from *Seneca Review*, No. 1, Spring 2001. Copyright © 2001 Elizabeth Holmes. Reprinted by permission of the author.

David Huddle, "Holes Commence Falling" from *Paper Boy* by David Huddle. Reprinted by permission of the author.

Langston Hughes, "To Negro Writers." Copyright 1935 by Langston Hughes. "My Adventures as a Social Poet." Copyright 1947 by Langston Hughes. "The Negro Artist and the Racial Mountain." Copyright 1926 by Langston Hughes—first published in *The Nation*. Reprinted by permission of Harold Ober Associates Incorporated. "Theme for English B," "Negro," "The Negro Speaks of Rivers," "Harlem," "Island," "I, Too," "Birmingham Sunday," "Dream Boogie," and "The Weary Blues" from *The Collected Poems of Langston Hughes* by Langston Hughes, copyright © 1994 by The Estate of Langston Hughes. Used by permission of Alfred A. Knopf, a division of Random House, Inc. "Ballad of the Landlord" from *The Collected Poems of Langston Hughes* by Langston Hughes. Copyright © 1994 by The Estate of Langston Hughes. Used by permission of Alfred A. Knopf, a division of Random House, Inc. "Ballad of Booker T," "Old Walt," "Genius Child," "Lenox Avenue: Midnight," "The Un-American Investigators," "Dinner Guest: Me" and "Park Bench" from *The Collected Poems of Langston Hughes* by Langston Hughes. Copyright © 1994 by The Estate of Langston Hughes. Used by permission of Alfred A. Knopf, a division of Random House, Inc.

Ted Hughes, "A Pink Wool Knitted Dress" from *Birthday Letters* by Ted Hughes. Copyright © 1998 by Ted Hughes. Reprinted by permission of Farrar, Straus and Giroux, LLC.

George B. Hutchinson, "Langston Hughes and the 'Other' Whitman" by George B. Hutchinson from *The Continuing Presence of Walt Whitman: The Life after the Life* edited by Robert K. Martin. Reprinted by permission of the University of Iowa Press; copyright 1992.

Henrik Ibsen, *A Doll House* from *The Complete Major Prose Plays of Henrik Ibsen* by Henrik Ibsen, translated by Rolf Fjelde, copyright © 1965, 1970, 1978 by Rolf Fjelde. Used by permission of Dutton Signet, a division of Penguin Putnam Inc.

Shirley Jackson, "The Lottery" from *The Lottery* by Shirley Jackson. Copyright 1948, 1949 by Shirley Jackson. Copyright renewed © 1976, 1977 by Laurence Hyman, Barry Hyman, Mrs. Sarah Webster and Mrs. Joanne Schnurer. Reprinted by permission of Farrar, Straus and Giroux, LLC.

Randall Jarrell, "The Death of the Ball Turret Gunner" from *The Complete Poems* by Randall Jarrell. Copyright © 1969, renewed 1997 by Mary von S. Jarrell. Reprinted by permission of Farrar, Straus and Giroux, LLC.

Gish Jen, "Chin" from *Who's Irish* by Gish Jen, copyright © 1999 by Gish Jen. Used by permission of Alfred A. Knopf, a division of Random House, Inc.

James Joyce, "Araby" and "Eveline" from *Dubliners* by James Joyce, copyright 1916 by B.W. Heubsch. Definitive text Copyright © 1967 by the Estate of James Joyce. Used by permission of Viking Penguin, a division of Penguin Putnam Inc.

Photos

INDEX OF FIRST LINES OF POETRY

AUTHORS AND TITLES INDEX

INDEX OF LITERARY TERMS